中华人民共和国
海关进出口税则

十位编码·监管条件·申报说明·出口退税·政策法规·海关代征税一览表

2007中英文对照版　附光盘

中华人民共和国海关进出口税则 编委会　编

Customs Import and Export Tariff

of the People's Republic of China

Decade Coding of HS, Customs Control Conditions, Declare Explanation, Regulations, Export Drawback, Detailed Customs Duties Levied on Commission Basis

---

Compiled by the Editorial Department of the Customs Import and Export Tariff of the People's Republic of China

---

经 济 日 报 出 版 社
Economic Daily Press

图书在版编目(CIP)数据

中华人民共和国海关进出口税则. 2007/《中华人民共和国海关进出口税则》编委会编. —北京:经济日报出版社,2007.1

ISBN 978-7-80180-630-7

Ⅰ. 中…　Ⅱ. 中…　Ⅲ. 海关税则—中国—2007—汉、英　Ⅳ. F752.50

中国版本图书馆 CIP 数据核字(2006)第 158376 号

中华人民共和国海关进出口税则(2007 年中英文对照版)

作　　者:中华人民共和国进出口税则编委会
责任编辑:范静泊
责任校对:王军
出版发行:经济日报出版社
地　　址:北京宣武区白纸坊东街 2 号(邮政编码:100054)
电　　话:(发行部)010-85997935　(编辑部)010-85997326
网　　址:www.fhgt.com.cn
E-mail:jjrb58@sina.com
经　　销:全国新华书店
印　　刷:北京中科印刷有限公司印装
开　　本:850×1168mm　1/16
印　　张:86
字　　数:2600 千字
版　　次:2007 年 1 月第一版
印　　次:2007 年 1 月第一次印刷
书　　号:ISBN 978-7-80180-630-7/F.269
定　　价:260.00 元

税率适用说明

税则号列 Tariff Item.	货品名称	最惠国(%) MFN	协定(%)CT 东盟 CA	中巴 CP	中智 CC	普通 Gen	增值税率 VAT	出口退税 ED	计量单位 Unit	监管条件 SC	Article Description
0804.4000	-鳄梨	25	T3	5	20	80	13	5	千克	AB	-Avocados

一、《关税税则》正文栏目税率适用说明

1. 最惠国税率

原产于共同适用最惠国待遇条款的世界贸易组织成员的进口货物,原产于与中华人民共和国签订含有相互给予最惠国待遇条款的双边贸易协定的国家或地区的进口货物,以及原产于中华人民共和国境内的进口货物,适用最惠国税率。

2. 协定税率

原产于与中华人民共和国签订含有关税优惠条款的区域性贸易协定的国家或地区的进口货物,适用协定税率。

(1)东盟协定税率:根据《中国-东盟全面经济合作框架协议》要求适用原产于与文莱达鲁萨兰国、印度尼西亚共和国、马来西亚、缅甸联邦、菲律宾共和国、新加坡共和国、泰王国、孟加拉人民共和国、越南社会主义共和国、老挝人民民主共和国等东南亚国家联盟成员国的部分进口货物。

注:①《关税税则》正文栏目"东盟"一栏中适用原产于文莱达鲁萨兰国、印度尼西亚共和国、马来西亚、缅甸联邦、菲律宾共和国、新加坡共和国、泰王国、孟加拉人民共和国等八国部分进口货物。此栏中所列商品税目、税率八国统一执行。

②《关税税则》附件3"中国-东盟全面经济合作框架协议十国实施税率表"适用原产于与文莱达鲁萨兰国、印度尼西亚共和国、马来西亚、缅甸联邦、菲律宾共和国、新加坡共和国、泰王国、越南社会主义共和国、老挝人民民主共和国、孟加拉人民共和国等十国部分进口货物。此表所列商品税目,十国分别执行不同税率。

以上将东盟协定税目税率分成两部分,因为我国关税征收是遵循从低征收的规律,为了方便读者在查阅商品税率时进行比较,所以将东盟其中八国相同税率列在正文部分;其余十国商品税率分别执行的商品税目税率单独列成一个附件,即附件3。

(2)中巴协定税率

根据《中国-巴基斯坦自由贸易协定》要求适用原产于巴基斯坦部分进口货物。

(3)中智协定税

根据《中国-智利自由贸易协定》要求适用于原产于智利的部分进口货物。

3. 普通税率

原产于无任何贸易优惠协定的国家或地区进口货物,以及原产地不明的进口货物,适用普通税率。

4. 增值税率

海关代征的进口货物法定增值税率,栏目空白时为免征,其他分为13%和17%两种。

5. 出口退税率

国家为鼓励出口对出口商品已征收的国内税部分或全部退还给出口企业的税率,本书所列出口退税率仅供企业参考(详细税目税率请见财政部编著的《中华人民共和国进出口货物征、退(免)税对照手册及法规汇编》一书)

《关税税则》各栏英文缩写解释

最惠国(MFN):Most Favored Nation

东盟协定(CA):Association of Southeast Asian Nations

中巴协定(CP):China-Pakistan

中智协定(CC):China-Chile

普通协定(Gen):General

增值税率(VAT):Value-added tax

出口退税(ED):Export Drawback

监管条件(SC):Supervision Conditions

二、《关税税则》附件税率适用说明

1. 亚太协定税率

根据《亚太贸易协定》要求适用于原产于亚洲及太平洋经济和社会理事会发展中国家成员国的部分进口货物(见附件8)。

2. 香港、澳门更紧密经贸关系安排已完成原产地标准核准商品税率根据《内地与香港关于建立更紧密经贸关系的安排》及其补充协定和《内地与澳门关于建立更紧密经贸关系的安排》及其补充协定要求原产于香港、澳门部分进口货物(见附件7)。

3. 特惠税率

原产于与中华人民共和国签订含有特殊关税优惠条款的贸易协定的国家或地区的部分进口货物(见附件9)

(1)亚太贸易协定特惠税率:适用原产于孟加拉人民共和国和老挝人民民主共和国部分进口货物。

(2)中国-东盟自由贸易区特惠税率:适用原产于柬埔寨王国、老挝人民民主共和国、缅甸联邦部分进口货物。

(3)非洲28国特惠税率:适用原产于贝宁共和国、布隆迪共和国、佛得角共和国、中非共和国、科摩罗联盟、刚果民主共和国、吉布提共和国、赤道几内亚共和国、厄立特里亚国、埃塞俄比亚联邦民主共和国、几内亚共和国、几内亚比绍共和国、莱索托王国、利比里亚共和国、马达加斯加共和国、马里共和国、毛里塔尼亚伊斯兰共和国、莫桑克比共和国、尼日亚共和国、卢旺达共和国、塞拉利昂共和国、苏丹共和国、坦桑尼亚联合共和国、多哥共和国、乌干达共和国、赞比亚共和国、塞内加尔共和国。

(4)阿富汗等5国特惠税率:适用原产于阿富汗伊斯兰共和国、也门民主人民共和国、马尔代夫共和国、萨摩亚独立国和瓦努阿图共和国的部分进口货物。

4. 暂定税率

(1)适用于最惠国税率的进口货物有暂定税率的,应当适用暂定税率;适用协定税率、特惠税率的进口货物有暂定税率的,应当从低适用税率;适用普通税率的进口货物,不适用暂定税率。

(2)适用出口税率的出口货物有暂定税率的,应当适用暂定税率。

(3)暂定税率仅在当年有效。

5. 关税减免

特定地区、特定企业或者特定用途的进出口货物减征或者免征关税的,以及其他依法减征或者免征关税的,按照国务院的有关规定执行。

三、《关税税则》正文栏目符号说明

1. 税率栏目内标有T2的表示从量税、复合税,具体税率参见附件2。

2. "东盟"栏目内标有T3的表示执行东盟十国分别实施税率,具体税率参见附件3。

3. 税率栏目前标有*的,表示该税率为实行进口关税配额的商品的配额外税率,配额内税率参见附件4。

4. 在税号前标有*的,表示该税目的部分商品凭信息产业部出具的用于信息技术产品的证明,可按本税则附件5的税率计征税款。

Application of Tariff Rates

I. The Guideline to the Application of Tariff Rates Listed in the Columns of "Tax Code"

1. The Most Favored Nation (MFN) Tariff Rate

The MFN tariff rates shall apply to goods imported form and originating in the members of the World Trade Organization providing that the MFN treatment is trciprocal between the People's Republic of China and these members; or those countries of regions with which the People's of China has concluded bilateral agreements for reciprocal tariff preference; or the custom territory of the People's Republic of China.

2. The Agreement Tariff Rate

The agreement tariff rates shall apply to goods imported from and originating in the countries or regions which join together with the People's Republic of China into regional trade agreement for tariff preferences.

(1) ASEAN Conventional Tariff Rates: in accordance with the Framework Agreement on Comprehensive Economic Cooperation between China and ASEAN, the ASEAN Conventional Tariff Rates are applicable to part of the imported products originated from ASEAN such as Brunei Darussalam, The Republic of Indonesia, Malaysia, The Union of Myanmar, The Republic of The Philippines, The Republic of Singapore, The Kingdom of Thailand, The People's Republic of Bangladesh, The Socialist Republic of Vietnam and Lao People's Democratic Republic.

Notes: ① listed in the column "ASEAN" in the Tax Code are those applicable for part of the imported products originated from the following eight countries: Brunei Darussalam, The Republic of Indonesia, Malaysia, The Union of Myanmar, The Republic of The Philippines, the Republic of Singapore, The Kingdom of Thailand and The People's Republic of Bangladesh. The tax items and tax rates for commodities listed in this column are unified for these eight countries.

② Annex 3 of Tax Code "The Tax Rate Table for the Ten Countries Under The Framework Agreement on Comprehensive Economic Cooperation between China and ASEAN" shall be applicable to part of the imported products originated from Brunei Darussalam, The Republic of Indonesia, Malaysia, The Union of Myanmar, The Republic of The Philippines, the Republic of Singapore, The Kingdom of Thailand, The People's Republic of Bangladesh, The Socialist Republic of Vietnam and Lao People's Democratic Republic. For the tax items listed in this table, the ten countries implement different tariff rates respectively.

The ASEAN conventional tax items and tax rates are divided into two parts, as the lower tax rates always prevail in China should there are two applicable rates. In order to facilitate the readers in making comparisons when checking the tariff rates of commodities, the identical tax rates that apply to the commodities from the eight countries of ASEAN are therefore listed in the text, while the tariff items and tariff rates of the rest of the commodities for the ten countries are listed separately in the annex 3.

(2) The Conventional Tariff Rates for Pakistan

Applicable to part of imported products originated from Pakistan according to China – Pakistan Free Trade Agreement.

(3) The Conventional Tariff Rates for Chile

Applicable to part of imported products originated from Chile according to China – Chile Free Trade Agreement

3. General Tariff Rates

General tariff rates shall be applied to any imported products originated from countries or regions with which no trade preferential agreement have been reached, or imported products whose places of origin are not identified.

4. Value Added Tax Rate

The prescribed value added tax of imported products collected by the Customs is to be exempted if the column is left blank, otherwise either a 13% or 17% of tax rates shall be imposed.

5. Rate of Export Rebate Tax

The rate of which the taxes collected are rebated partially or completely to encourage export. The rate of export rebate tax are listed in this book for reference (for more detailed tax items and tax rates, please refer to The Brochure for the Imposition, Rebate (Exemption) of Import and Export Tariffs and Collection of Provisions of People's Republic of China compiled by Ministry of Finance)

The Explanations for the Abbreviations in Tax Code

(MFN): Most Favored Nation
(CA): Association of Southeast Asian Nations
(CP): China – Pakistan
(CC): China – Chile
(Gen): General
(VAT): Value – added tax
(ED): Export Drawback
(SC): Supervision Conditions

II. The Guideline for the Application of the Tax Rates in Annex of Tax Code

1. Asian – Pacific Conventional Tariff Rate

Applicable to part of imported products originated from the Developing Nations of Asia and Pacific Economic and Social Council according to Asian – Pacific Trade Agreement.

2. Hong Kong and Macao Closer Economic Partnership Arrangement has completed the approval of the criteria of the place of origin and the commodity tax rates.

Applicable to part of imported products originated from Hong Kong and Macao according to Mainland and Hong Kong Closer Economic Partnership Arrangement, Mainland and Macao Closer Economic Partnership Arrangement and its supplementary requirements.

3. The Special Preferential Tariff Rate

The special preferential tariff rates shall apply to goods imported from and originated in countries or regions that have concluded special tariff preferential agreement with the People's Republic of China.

(1) Preferential Tariff Rates of Asian – Pacific Trade Agreement: Applicable to part of imported products originated from The People's Republic of Bangladesh and Lao People's Democratic Republic.

(2) Preferential Tariff Rates for China – AESAN Free Trade Zone: Applicable to part of imported products originated from Applicable to part of imported products originated from The Kingdom of Cambodia, Lao People's Democratic Republic and The Union of Burma.

(3) Preferential Tariff Rates for 28 countries in Africa: applicable to products originated from The Republic of Benin, The Republic of Burundi, The Republic of Cape Verde, The Central African Republic, Union of Comoros, The Democratic Republic of Congo, The Republic of Djibouti, The Republic of Equatorial Guinea, The State of Eritrea, The Federal Democratic Republic of Ethiopia, The Republic of Guinea, The Republic of Guinea – Bissau, The Kingdom of Lesotho, The Republic of Liberia, The Republic of Madagascar, The Republic of Mali, The Islamic Republic of Mauritania, The Republic of Mozambique, The Republic of Nigeria, The Republic of Rwanda, The Republic of Sierra Leone, The Republic of Sudan, The United Republic of Tanzania, The Republic of Togo, The Republic of Uganda, The Republic of Zambia and The Republic of Senegal.

(4) The Preferential Tariff Rates of 5 countries: applicable to part of imported products originated from The Islamic Republic of Afghanistan, The People's Democratic Republic of Yemen, The Republic of Maldives, The Independent State of Samoa and The Republic of Vanuatu.

4. The Interim Tariff Rates

(1) The interim import tariff rates have the priority over the MFN tariff rates for application. Goods eligible for interim import tariff rates, when imported under the agreement tariff rates or special preferential tariff rates, will be levied under the lower of the two rates.

(2) The interim export tariff rates have the priority over the export tariff rates for application.

(3) Interim tariff rates are effective in one year from January 1st to December 31st.

5. Exemption and Reduction

Customs duties shall be reduced or exempted in accordance with the provisions set out in the relevant regulations by the State Council on goods imported into or exported out the designated areas, the designated enterprises, or for designated uses.

III. The Explanations for Symbols in the Column of Tax Code

1. T2 in the columns of tax rates means Specific Duty, Compound Duty. Please refer to Annex 2 for specific tax rates.

2. T3 in the Column of "ASEAN" means to implement various tax rates of ten countries of ASEAN respectively. Please refer to Annex 3 for each specific tax rates.

3. Rate marked with * ahead mena that the import goods are subject to Quota Control. In – Quota Interim import duty rates see Appendix 2.

4. Heading Nos. marked with * ahead mean that if the commodity specified in the headings are, with certificates issued by The Information Industry Ministry, imported for the purpose of manufacturing of information technological products, upon which Interim Import Duty Rates of Appendix 5 shall be levied.

编者按

从2007年1月1日起,《中华人民共和国海关进出口税则》(以下简称税则)将进行较大范围的调整,变化情况如:第一从2007年1月1日起,我国将继续按照加入世界贸易组织的关税减让承诺,调整后,2007年的关税总水平将由9.9%降低至9.8%,其中,农产品平均税率为15.2%,工业品平均税率为8.95%。;第二世界海关组织每四年至六年对HS编码进行一次调整,2007年是继2002年之后的又一次重大调整,因此2007版《税则》商品编码也相应进行了重大调整;第三从2006年4月1日起开始实施新的消费税税率税目,2007版《税则》中涉及到的相关内容也进行相应调整。

为配合海关总署出台的进出口商品申报最新规定,本《税则》添加了"进出口商品规范申报说明"附件(以下简称《申报说明》),为企业填制报关单、加工手册等报关单证提供了规范依据。《申报说明》对不同商品设置了特定的申报要素内容。报关单中的"商品名称、规格型号"栏应当按照《申报说明》中相应商品所列申报要素各项内容填写。

为方便海关等有关管理部门、从事进出口的企业、报关企业、预录入企业和其他单位及个人了解最新的进出口税则税率、进口环节代征税税率和海关监管条件,准确地将外贸单证中的英文商品名称翻译成规范的中文名称,及时办理报关手续,我们编写了《中华人民共和国海关进出口税则》(中英文对照版),(以下简称《中英文税则》)。

为便于使用本书,现将《中英文税则》说明如下:

第一部分为《关税税则》:

第1列为"税则号列",其8位数与财政部关税税则委员会所调整编制的税目税率数据完全一致,并在此基础上增加了海关申报所需的10位数编码;

第2列为"货品的中文名称";

第3列为"最惠国税率",适用原产于世贸组织成员或与我国签有互惠双边贸易协定的国家或地区进口的货物;

第4列为"协定税率",其中第一栏是"中国-东盟协定税率",适用于原产于东盟经济框架协议范围内国家部分进口货物;第2栏是中巴协定税率,适用原产于巴基斯坦部分进口的货物;第3栏是中智协定税率普通税率,适用原产于智利部分进口的货物;

第5列为"普通税率"适用原产于上述3、4列以外国家或地区进口的货物;

第6列为"增值税率",栏目空白时为免征,其他分为13%和17%两种;

第7列为"出口退税率",栏内数字表示相应退税税率;

第8列为"计量单位",为海关统计使用的法定计量单位;

第9列为"监管条件",相应的代码表示在一般贸易进口或出口时应向海关提交的监管证件代码;

第10列为"货品的英文名称"。

随后加列了进出口商品规范申报说明、进口商品暂定税率表、从量税和复合税税率表、进口商品关税配额税率表、非全税目信息技术产品税率表、中国-东盟自由贸易区相关税率表、进口商品消费税税率表、特惠税目税率表、内地与香港及澳门优惠关税安排税目税率表等以及2007年出口税则和出口商品暂定税率表。

第二部分汇集财政部、商务部、海关总署等相关部委最新颁布的有关外贸管理方面的法律、法规及管理办法,并配有准确的英文翻译。中英文对照的参考,有利于相关人员更好掌握进出口贸易管理法律、法规及管理办法。欲知更全面,更详细的中英文对照法规,请登录网址:www. fhgt. com. cn。

为方便读者在海关报关和计算关税,本书另含有报关自动化系统常用代码表及海关计税方法两部分。

由于作者水平的限制和时间仓促,本书不足之处在所难免,恳请社会各界和广大读者批评指正。其中不准确和不全面之处敬请以发布的规范性文件为准!

Editor's Note

By Jan. 1st 2007, an extensive adjustment will have been made to Import & Export Tariff Regulations of the People's Republic of China (hereafter referred to as Tariff Regulations). The following are the adjustments: firstly, by Jan. 1st in 2007, China will continue to carry on its commitment of tariff concession as a member of WTO. After the adjustment, the general tariff level will be reduced to 9.8% from 9.9%. For agricultural products, the average tariff will be 15.2% and 8.95% for industrial products. Secondly, World Customs Organization makes adjustment to HS coding every four to six years and the readjustment in 2007 will be another important one. Therefore, 2007 Tariff Regulations will make readjustment to the product coding accordingly; thirdly, as new tax rates and tax items of excise have been implemented since April 4th 2006, 2007 Tariff Regulations will make relevant adjustments in accordance.

To go with the newly issued regulations by Custom of P. R. C. on the import and export goods, Instruction on Import and Export Commodities Standard Declaration (hereafter referred to as Declaration Instruction) has been added into Tariff Regulations, providing standards for enterprises to prepare customs declaration documents. Declaration Instruction sets key declaration factors for different commodities. The columns as to the description of goods and specification of goods should be filled in according to the key factors listed in Declaration Statement.

Aiming at assisting Customs and other governing bodies, enterprises participating import and export, Customs brokers, other trading partners and persons to query up – to – date tariff rates, other rates related to import and Custom supervision conditions, translate English commodity names in trade documents into standard Chinese names and go through declaring procedures to Customs, this Press compiles this Customs Import and Export Tariff of the People's Republic of China (Chinese – English Version, referred to as Chinese – English Tariff later)

For ease of using this bood, the Chinese – English Tariff is explained as follow:

The first part is about Tariff Regulations:

Column 1 is Serial Number, the eight digits of which are in accordance with the data of tax items and rates adjusted and compiled by the Ministry of Finance Tariff Regulation committee, onto which the code of ten digits required in customs declaration is added;

Column 2 is Commodity Chinese name;

Column 3 is Most – Favored – Nation rate, applicable to the goods originally produced in the members of WTO or in countries and regions that have bilateral trade agreement with China.

Column 4 is agreement tariff rate, in which the first column is China – ASEAN agreement rate, applicable to certain import goods originated from countries involved in the Framework Agreement on Comprehensive Economic Co – operation between P. R. C. and ASEAN; the second column is China – Pakistan agreement rate, applicable to certain import goods originally produced in Pakistan; the third column is China – Chile agreement rate, applicable to certain import goods originated from Chile.

Column5 is average rate, applicable to the import goods originally produced in countries and regions other than the ones in rank 3 and 4.

Column 6 is VAT Rate, it will be exempted when this column is empty, and in other conditions the VAT rate is either 13% or 17%;

Column 7 is Export Drawback Rate, the numbers is this Column represents export drawback rates;

Column 8 is Measurement Unit which is the official measurement units applied by Customs;

Column 9 is Supervision Conditions, respective codes represent the licenses or other documents that should be submitted to Customs at import or export in general trade pattern. For specific names, please refer to List of License names and their codes attached in this bood.

Column 10 is Commodity English name.

In the following ranks, there are standard declaration instructions on imported and exported goods, Interim rates on imported and exported goods, tables of specific duty and compound duty, table of duty quota and rate on imported and exported goods, Table of Duty Rate on Specific Information Technology Products, table of China – ASEAN free trade zone related duty rate, table of excise on imported goods, table of Special Preferential Duty Rate, table of duty items and rate under mainland – Hong Kong – Macao Preferential Tariff Arrangement

The second part gathers relevant laws, rule and regulations on foreign trade management issued by Ministry of Finance, Ministry of Commerce, and Custom of P. R. C, with accurate English translation. A Chinese – English version is of great use for readers to have a good command of the laws, rules and regulations on foreign trade management.

For the convenience of reader in customs declaration and customs tax calculation, this book is enclosed with two additional parts: the table of codes commonly used in automatic declaration system and customs tax calculation method. Please log on to www.fhgt.com.cn for more detailed and complete version of lawsand regulations with both Chinese and English tran Slation Facilieies used for medical treatment, surgery, dentistry or veterinary.

Due to limits of time and the knowledge of the author, some weaknesses in this book should be inevitable. Here I am open to readers' corrections and comments with great sincerity. If there is any inaccuracy and inadequacy, the official documents prevail.

总目录

Table of Contents

7. 欲知更全面,更详细的中英文对照法规,请登录网址:www. fhgt. com. cn。
Please log on to www. fhgt. com. cn. for more detailed and complete version of laws and regulations with both Chinese and English translation Facilities used for medical treatment, surgery, dentistry or veterinary

1

中华人民共和国海关进口税则

（2007 年 1 月 1 日起实施）

Customs Import Tariff of the People's Republic of China

（Enforced from January 1，2007）

目　　录

INDEX

归类总规则

GENERAL RULES FOR THE INTERPRETATION OF THE HARMONIZED SYSTEM

货品在本税则目录上的归类，应遵循以下原则：

规则一 类、章及分章的标题，仅为查找方便而设；具有法律效力的归类，应按税目条文和有关类注或章注确定，如税目、类注或章注无其他规定，按以下规则确定。

规则二 （一）税目所列货品，应视为包括该项货品的不完整品或未制成品，只要在进口或出口时该项不完整品或未制成品具有完整品或制成品的基本特征；还应视为包括该项货品的完整品或制成品（或按本款可作为完整品或制成品归类的货品）在进口或出口时的未组装件或拆散件。

（二）税目中所列材料或物质，应视为包括该种材料或物质与其他材料或物质混合或组合的物品。税目所列某种材料或物质构成的货品，应视为包括全部或部分由该种材料或物质构成的货品。由一种以上材料或物质构成的货品，应按规则三归类。

规则三 当货品按规则二（二）或由于其他原因看起来可归入两个或两个以上税目时，应按以下规则归类：

（一）列名比较具体的税目，优先于列名一般的税目。但是，如果两个或两个以上税目都仅述及混合或组合货品所含的某部分材料或物质，或零售的成套货品中的某些货品，即使其中某个税目对该货品描述得更为全面、详细，这些货品在有关税目的列名应视为同样具体。

（二）混合物、不同材料构成或不同部件组成的组合物以及零售的成套货品，如果不能按照规则三（一）归类时，在本款可适用的条件下，应按构成货品基本特征的材料或部件归类。

Classification of goods in the Nomenclature shall be governed by the following Rules:

1. The titles of Sections, Chapters and sub-Chapters are provided for ease of reference only; for legal purposes, classification shall be determined according to the terms of the headings and any relative Section or Chapter Notes and provided such headings or Notes do not otherwise require, according to the following provisions.

2. (a) Any reference in a heading to an article shall be taken to incl9ude a reference to that article incomplete or unfinished, provided that, as presented, the incomplete or unfinished article has the essential character of the complete or finished article. It shall also be taken to include a reference to that article complete or finished (or falling to be classified as complete or finished by virtue of this Rule), presented unassembled or disassembled.

(b) Any reference in a heading to a material or substance shall be taken to include a reference to mixtures or combinations of that material or substance with other materials or substances. Any reference to goods of a given material or substance shall be taken to include a reference to goods consisting wholly or partly of such material or substance. The classification of goods consisting of more than one material or substance shall be according to the principles of Rule 3.

3. When by application of Rule 2(b) or for any other reason, goods are, *prima facie*, classifiable under two or more headings, classification shall be effected as follows:

(a) The heading which provides the most specific description shall be preferred to headings providing a more general description. However, when two or more headings each refer to part only of the materials or substances contained in mixed or composite goods or to part only of the items in a set put up for retail sale, those headings are to be regarded as equally specific in relation to those goods, even if one of them gives a more complete or precise description of the goods.

(b) Mixtures, composite goods consisting of different materials or made up of different components, and goods put up in sets for retail sale, which cannot be classified by reference to Rule 3 (a), shall be classified as they consisted of the material or component which gives them their essential character, insofar as this criterion is applicable.

（三）货品不能按照规则三（一）或（二）归类时，应按号列顺序归入其可归入的最末一个税目。

（c）When goods cannot be classified by reference to Rule 3(a) or Rule 3(b), they shall be classified under the heading which occurs last in numerical order among those which equally merit consideration.

规则四 根据上述规则无法归类的货品，应归入与其最相类似的货品的税目。

4. Goods which cannot be classified in accordance with the above Rules shall be classified under the heading appropriate to the goods to which they are most akin.

规则五 除上述规则外，本规则适用于下列货品的归类：

（一）制成特殊形状仅适用于盛装某个或某套物品并适合长期使用的照像机套、乐器盒、枪套、绘图仪器盒、项链盒及类似容器，如果与所装物品同时进口或出口，并通常与所装物品一同出售的，应与所装物品一并归类。但本款不适用于本身构成整个货品基本特征的容器。

（二）除规则五（一）规定的以外，与所装货品同时进口或出口的包装材料或包装容器，如果通常是用来包装这类货品的，应与所装货品一并归类。但明显可重复使用的包装材料和包装容器可不受本款限制。

5. In addition to the foregoing Rules, the following Rules shall apply in respect of the goods referred to therein:

(a) Camera cases, musical instrument cases, gun cases, drawing instrument cases, necklace cases and similar containers, specially shaped or fitted to contain a specific article or set of articles, suitable for long-term use and presented with the articles for which they are intended, shall be classified with such articles when of a kind normally sold therewith. This Rule does not, however, apply to containers which give the whole its essential character;

(b) Subject to the provisions of Rule 5(a) above, packing materials and packing containers presented with the goods therein shall be classified with the goods if they are of a kind normally used for packing such goods. However, this provision is not binding when such packing materials or packing containers are clearly suitable for repetitive use.

规则六 货品在某一税目项下各子目的法定归类，应按子目条文或有关的子目注释以及以上各条规则来确定，但子目的比较只能在同一数级上进行。除本税则目录条文另有规定的以外，有关的类注、章注也适用于本规则。

6. For legal purposes, the classification of goods in the subheadings of a heading shall be determined according to the terms of those subheadings and any related Subheading Notes and, *mutatis mutandis*, to the above Rules, on the understanding that only subheadings at the same level are comparable. For the purposes of this Rule the relative Section and Chapter Notes also apply, unless the context otherwise requires.

第一类
活动物;动物产品

注释:

一、本类所称的各属种动物,除条文另有规定的以外,均包括其幼仔在内。

二、除条文另有规定的以外,本目录所称干的产品,均包括经脱水、蒸发或冷冻干燥的产品。

SECTION Ⅰ
LIVE ANIMALS; ANIMAL PRODUCTS

Notes:

1. Any reference in this Section to a particular genus or species of an animal, except where the context otherwise requires, includes a reference to the young of that genus or species.
2. Except where the context otherwise requires, throughout the Nomenclature any reference to "dried" products also covers products which have been dehydrated, evaporated or freeze-dried.

第一章
活 动 物

注释:

本章包括所有活动物,但下列各项除外:

一、税目03.01、03.06或03.07的鱼、甲壳动物、软体动物及其他水生无脊椎动物;

二、税目30.02的培养微生物及其他产品;

三、税目95.08的动物。

Chapter 1
Live animals

Notes:

This Chapter covers all live animals except:

1. Fish and crustaceans, molluscs and other aquatic invertebrates, of heading No. 03.01, 03.06 or 03.07;
2. Cultures of micro-organisms and other products of heading No. 30.02; and
3. Animals of heading No. 95.08.

税则号列 Tariff Item.	货品名称	最惠国(%) MFN	协定(%) CT 东盟 CA	中巴 CP	中智 CC	普通 Gen	增值税率 VAT	出口退税 ED	计量单位 Unit	监管条件 SC	Article Description
01.01	马、驴、骡:										**Live horses, asses, mules and hinnies:**
	-改良种用:										-Pure-bred breeding
0101.1010	---马	0				0	13	5	头		---Horses
0101.1010 10	改良种用濒危野马	0				0	13	5	头	AFEB	Wild horses in imminent dangers, pure-bred breeding
0101.1010 90	其他改良种用马	0				0	13	5	头	AB	Other horses, pure-bred breeding
0101.1020	---驴	0				0	13	5	头		---Asses
0101.1020 10	改良种用的濒危野驴	0				0	13	5	头	AFEB	Wild asses in imminent dangers, pure-bred breeding
0101.1020 90	改良种用的其他驴	0				0	13	5	头	AB	Other asses, pure-bred breeding
	-其他:										-Other:
0101.9010	---马	10	0		8	30	13	5	头		---Horses
0101.9010 10	非改良种用濒危野马	10				30	13	5	头	AFEB	Wild horses, not for breeding in imminent dangers
0101.9010 90	非改良种用马	10				30	13	5	头	AB	Horses, not for breeding
0101.9090	---驴、骡	10	0		8	30	13	5	头		---Asses, mules and hinnies
0101.9090 10	非改良种用濒危野驴	10				30	13	5	头	AFEB	Wild asses, not for breeding in imminent dangers
0101.9090 90	非改良种用其他驴、骡	10				30	13	5	头	AB	Other asses mules, not for breeding
01.02	牛:										**Live bovine animals:**
0102.1000	-改良种用	0				0	13	5	头		-Pure-bred breeding
0102.1000 10	改良种用濒危野牛	0				0	13	5	头	AFEB	Wild bovine in imminent dangers, pure-bred breeding
0102.1000 90	其他改良种用牛	0				0	13	5	头	AB	Other bovine, pure-bred breeding
0102.9000	-其他	10	T3		8	30	13	5	头		-Other
0102.9000 10	非改良种用野牛	10				30	13	5	头	4xABEF	Wild bovine, not for breeding
0102.9000 90	非改良种用其他牛	10				30	13	5	头	4xAB	Other bovine, not for breeding
01.03	猪:										**Live swine:**
0103.1000	-改良种用	0					13	5	头		-Pure-bred breeding

税则号列 Tariff Item.	货 品 名 称	最惠国(%) MFN	协定(%)CT 东盟 CA	 中巴 CP	 中智 CC	普通 Gen	增值税率 VAT	出口退税 ED	计量单位 Unit	监管条件 SC	Article Description
0103.1000 10	改良种用的鹿猪、姬猪	0				0	13	5	头	AFEB	Pig-deer (*Babyrousa*)、pygmy pig (*Porcula*), pure-bred breeding
0103.1000 90	其他改良种用的猪	0				0	13	5	头	AB	Other swine, pure-bred breeding
	-其他:										-Other:
	--重量在50千克以下:										--Weighing less than 50kg:
0103.9110	---重量在10千克以下	10	T3		0	50	13	5	头		---Weighing less than 10kg
0103.9110 10	重量在10公斤以下的其他野猪(改良种用的除外)	10				50	13	5	头	4xABFE	Other wild swine, W < 10kg (other than pure-bred breeding)
0103.9110 90	重量在10公斤以下的其他猪(改良种用的除外)	10				50	13	5	头	4xAB	Other swine, W < 10kg (other than pure-bred breeding)
0103.9120	---重量在10公斤及以上,但在50千克以下	10	T3		0	50	13	5	头		---Weighing 10kg or more, but less than 50kg
0103.9120 10	10公斤≤重量<50公斤的其他野猪(改良种用的除外)	10				50	13	5	头	4xABFE	Other wild swine, 10kg ≤ W < 50kg (other than pure-bred breeding)
0103.9120 90	10公斤≤重量<50公斤的其他猪(改良种用的除外)	10				50	13	5	头	4xAB	Other swine, 10kg ≤ W < 50kg (other than pure-bred breeding)
0103.9200	--重量在50公斤及以上	10	T3		0	50	13	5	头		--Weighing 50kg or more
0103.9200 10	重量在50公斤及以上的其他野猪(改良种用的除外)	10				50	13	5	头	4xABFE	Other wild live swine, W≥50kg (other than pure-bred breeding)
0103.9200 90	重量在50公斤及以上的其他猪(改良种用的除外)	10				50	13	5	头	4xAB	Other swine, W ≥ 50kg (other than pure-bred breeding)
01.04	绵羊、山羊:										**Live sheep and goats:**
	-绵羊:										-Sheep:
0104.1010	---改良种用	0				0	13	5	头	AB	---Pure-bred breeding
0104.1090	---其他	10	0		0	50	13	5	头	AB	---Other
	-山羊:										-Goats:
0104.2010	---改良种用	0				0	13	5	头	AB	---Pure-bred breeding
0104.2090	---其他	10	T3		0	50	13	5	头	AB	---Other
01.05	家禽,即鸡、鸭、鹅、火鸡及珍珠鸡:										**Live poultry, that is to say, fowls of the species *Gallus domesticus*, ducks, geese, turkeys and guinea fowls:**
	-重量不超过185克:										-Weighing not more than 185g:
	--鸡:										--Fowls of the species *Gallus domesticus*:
0105.1110	---改良种用	0				0	13	5	只	AB	---Pure-bred breeding
0105.1190	---其他	10	T3		8	50	13	5	只	AB	---Other
	--火鸡:										--Turkeys:
0105.1210	---改良种用	0				0	13	5	只	AB	---Pure-bred breeding
0105.1290	---其他	10	T3		8	50	13	5	只	AB	---Other
	--其他:										--Other:
0105.1910	---改良种用	0				0	13	5	只	AB	---Pure-bred breeding
0105.1990	---其他	10	T3		0	50	13	5	只	AB	---Other
	-其他:										-Other:
	--鸡:										--Fowls of the species *Gallus domesticus*:
0105.9410	---改良种用	0				0	13	5	只	4xAB	---Pure-bred breeding
0105.9490	---其他	10	T3		0	50	13	5	只	4xAB	---Other
	--其他:										--Other:

税则号列 Tariff Item.	货品名称	最惠国(%) MFN	协定(%) 东盟 CA	协定(%) 中巴 CP	协定(%) 中智 CC	普通 Gen	增值税率 VAT	出口退税 ED	计量单位 Unit	监管条件 SC	Article Description
0105.9910	---改良种用	0				0	13	5	只	AB	---Pure-bred breeding
	---其他:										---Other:
0105.9991	----鸭	10	T3		0	50	13	5	只	AB	----Ducks
0105.9992	----鹅	10	T3		0	50	13	5	只	AB	----Geese
0105.9993	----珍珠鸡	10	T3		0	50	13	5	只	4xAB	----Guinea fowls
0105.9994	----火鸡	10	T3		0	50	13	5	只	AB	----Turkeys
01.06	**其他活动物:**										**Other live animals:**
	-哺乳动物:										-Mammals:
	--灵长目:										--Primates:
0106.1110	---改良种用	0				0	13	5	只/千克	AFEB	---pure-bred breeding
0106.1190	---其他	10	0		0	50	13	5	只/千克	AFEB	---Other
0106.1200	--鲸、海豚及鼠海豚(鲸目哺乳动物);海牛及儒艮(海牛目哺乳动物)	10	0		0	50	13	5	只/千克	AFEB	--Whales, dolphins and porpoises (mammals of the order Cetacea); manatees and dugongs (mammals of the order Sirenia)
	--其他:										--Other:
0106.1910	---改良种用	0				0	13	5	只/千克		---pure-bred breeding
0106.1910 10	其他改良种用濒危野生哺乳动物(包括人工驯养、繁殖的)	0				0	13	5	只/千克	ABFE	Other wild mammals in imminent dangers, primates, pure-bred breeding, including domesticated and artificially bred
0106.1910 90	其他改良种用非野生的哺乳动物	0				0	13	5	只/千克	AB	Other mammals, primates, non-wild, pure-bred breeding
0106.1920	---食用	10	0		8	50	13	5	只/千克		---For human consumption
0106.1920 10	其他食用濒危野生哺乳动物(包括人工驯养、繁殖的)	10				50	13	5	只/千克	AFEB	Other wild mammals in imminent dangers, primates, for human consumption, including domesticated and artificially bred
0106.1920 90	其他食用非野生的哺乳动物	10				50	13	5	只/千克	AB	Other mammals, primates, non-wild, for human consumption
0106.1990	---其他	10	0		8	50	13	5	只/千克		---Other
0106.1990 10	其他濒危野生哺乳动物(包括人工驯养、繁殖的)	10				50	13	5	只/千克	AFEB	Other wild mammals in imminent dangers, primates, including domesticated and artificially bred
0106.1990 90	其他非野生的哺乳动物	10				50	13	5	只/千克	AB	Other mammals, primates, non-wild
	-爬行动物(包括蛇及龟鳖):										-Reptiles (including snakes and turtles):
	---改良种用:										---pure-bred breeding:
0106.2011	----鳄鱼苗	0				0	13	5	只/千克	AFEB	----Crocodiles for cultivation
0106.2019	----其他	0				0	13	5	只/千克	FEAB	----Other
0106.2020	---食用	10	0		0	50	13	5	只/千克		---For human consumption
0106.2020 10	食用野生蛇(包括人工驯养、繁殖的)	10				50	13	5	只/千克	AFEB	Wild snakes, for human consumption, including domesticated and artificially bred
0106.2020 20	食用野生龟鳖(包括人工驯养、繁殖的)	10				50	13	5	只/千克	ABFE	Wild turtles, for human consumption, including domesticated and artificially bred
0106.2020 90	其他食用爬行动物(包括人工驯养、繁殖的)	10				50	13	5	只/千克	FEAB	Other reptiles, for human consumption, including domesticated and artificially bred
0106.2090	---其他	10	0		0	50	13	5	只/千克	FEAB	---Other

税则号列 Tariff Item.	货品名称	最惠国(%) MFN	协定(%) CT			普通 Gen	增值税率 VAT	出口退税 ED	计量单位 Unit	监管条件 SC	Article Description
			东盟 CA	中巴 CP	中智 CC						
	-鸟:										-Birds:
	--猛禽:										--Birds of prey:
0106.3110	---改良种用	0				0	13	5	只/千克	AFEB	---pure-bred breeding
0106.3190	---其他	10	0		0	50	13	5	只/千克	ABFE	---Other
	--鹦形目(包括普通鹦鹉、长尾鹦鹉、金刚鹦鹉及美冠鹦鹉):										--Psittaciformes(including parrots, parakeets, macaws and cockatoos):
0106.3210	---改良种用	0				0	13	5	只/千克		---Pure-bred breeding
0106.3210 10	改良种用虎皮鹦鹉	0				0	13	5	只/千克	AB	Budgerigar, pure-bred breeding
0106.3210 20	改良种用鸡尾鹦鹉	0				0	13	5	只/千克	AB	Cockatiel (*Nymphicus hollandicus*), pure-bred breeding
0106.3210 90	改良种用其他鹦形目的鸟(包括人工驯养、繁殖的)	0				0	13	5	只/千克	ABFE	Other birds, psittaciformes, pure-bred breeding, including domesticated and artificially bred
0106.3290	---其他	10	0		0	50	13	5	只/千克		---Other
0106.3290 10	非改良种用虎皮鹦鹉	10				50	13	5	只/千克	AB	Budgerigar, other than pure-bred breeding
0106.3290 20	非改良种用鸡尾鹦鹉	10				50	13	5	只/千克	AB	Cockatiel (*Nymphicus hollandicus*), other than pure-bred breeding
0106.3290 90	非改良种用其他鹦形目的鸟(包括人工驯养、繁殖的)	10				50	13	5	只/千克	AFEB	Other birds, psittaciformes, including domesticated and artificially bred, other than pure-bred breeding
	--其他:										--Other:
0106.3910	---改良种用	0				0	13	5	只/千克		---pure-bred breeding
0106.3910 10	其他濒危野生改良种用的鸟(包括人工驯养、繁殖的)	0				0	13	5	只/千克	ABFE	Other wild birds in imminent dangers, pure-bred breeding, including domesticated and artificially bred
0106.3910 90	其他非野生的改良种用的鸟	0				0	13	5	只/千克	AB	Other birds, non-wild, pure-bred breeding
	---食用:										---For human consumption:
0106.3921	----乳鸽	10	0		0	50	13	5	只/千克	AB	----Squabs
0106.3922	----鸵鸟	10	0		0	50	13	5	只/千克	FEAB	----Ostrich
0106.3923	----野鸭	10	0		0	50	13	5	只/千克	FEAB	----Teals
0106.3929	----其他	10	0		0	50	13	5	只/千克		----Other
0106.3929 10	其他食用濒危野生鸟(包括人工驯养、繁殖的)	10				50	13	5	只/千克	ABFE	Other wild birds in imminent dangers, for human consumption, including domesticated and artificially bred
0106.3929 90	其他食用非野生的鸟	10				50	13	5	只/千克	AB	Other birds for human consumption, non-wild
0106.3990	---其他	10	0		0	50	13	5	只/千克		---Other
0106.3990 10	其他濒危野生鸟(包括人工驯养、繁殖的)	10				50	13	5	只/千克	ABFE	Other wild bird in imminent dangers, including domesticated and artificially bred
0106.3990 90	其他非野生的鸟	10				50	13	5	只/千克	AB	Other birds non-wild
	-其他:										-Other:
	---改良种用:										---Pure-bred breeding:
0106.9011	----蛙苗	0				0	13	5	只/千克		----Tadpole and young frogs
0106.9011 10	改良种用濒危蛙苗	0				0	13	5	只/千克	ABFE	Tadpole and young frogs in imminent dangers, pure-bred breeding

税则号列 Tariff Item.	货 品 名 称	最惠国(%) MFN	协定(%)CT 东盟 CA	中巴 CP	中智 CC	普通 Gen	增值税率 VAT	出口退税 ED	计量单位 Unit	监管条件 SC	Article Description
0106.9011 90	其他改良种用蛙苗	0				0	13	5	只/千克	AB	Other tadpole and young frogs, pure-bred breeding
0106.9019	----其他	0				0	13	5	只/千克		----Other
0106.9019 10	其他改良种用濒危野生动物(包括人工驯养、繁殖的)	0				0	13	5	只/千克	ABFE	Other wild animals in imminent dangers, pure-bred breeding, including domesticated and artificially bred
0106.9019 90	其他改良种用非野生动物	0				0	13	5	只/千克	AB	Other animals, non-wild, pure-bred breeding
0106.9020	---食用	10	0	9	8	50	13	5	只/千克		---For human consumption
0106.9020 10	其他濒危野生食用动物(包括人工驯养、繁殖的)	10				50	13	5	只/千克	ABFE	Other wild animals in imminent dangers, for human consumption, including domesticated and artificially bred
0106.9020 90	其他非野生食用动物	10				50	13	5	只/千克	AB	Other animals, non-wild, for human consumption
0106.9090	---其他	10	0	9	8	50	13	5	只/千克		---Other
0106.9090 10	其他濒危野生动物(包括人工驯养、繁殖的)	10				50	13	5	只/千克	ABFE	Other wild animals in imminent dangers, including domesticated and artificially bred
0106.9090 90	其他非野生动物	10				50	13	5	只/千克	AB	Other animals, non-wild

第二章
肉及食用杂碎

Chapter 2
Meat and edible meat offal

注释：

本章不包括：

一、税目 02.01 至 02.08 或 02.10 的不适合供人食用的产品；

二、动物的肠、膀胱、胃（税目 05.04）或动物血（税目 05.11、30.02）；

三、税目 02.09 所列产品以外的动物脂肪（第十五章）。

Notes：

This Chapter does not cover：

1. Products of the kinds described in headings Nos. 02.01 to 02.08 or 02.10, unfit or unsuitable for human consumption；
2. Guts, bladders or stomachs of animals (heading No. 05.04) or animal blood (heading No. 05.11 or 30.02)；or
3. Animal fat, other than products of heading No. 02.09 (Chapter15).

税则号列 Tariff Item.	货品名称	最惠国(%) MFN	协定(%) CT			普通 Gen	增值税率 VAT	出口退税 ED	计量单位 Unit	监管条件 SC	Article Description
			东盟 CA	中巴 CP	中智 CC						
02.01	鲜、冷牛肉：										**Meat of bovine animals, fresh or chilled：**
0201.1000	-整头及半头	20	T3		12	70	13	5	千克		-Carcasses and half-carcasses
0201.1000 10	整头及半头鲜或冷藏的野牛肉	20				70	13	5	千克	4xABFE	Meat of wild bovine animals, carcasses and half-carcasses, fresh or chilled
0201.1000 90	其他整头及半头鲜或冷藏的牛肉	20				70	13	5	千克	4xAB	Other meat of bovine animals, carcasses and half-carcasses, fresh or chilled
0201.2000	-带骨肉	12	T3		9.6	70	13	5	千克		-Other cuts with bone in
0201.2000 10	鲜或冷藏的带骨野牛肉	12				70	13	5	千克	4xABFE	Meat of wild bovine animals, with bone in, fresh or chilled
0201.2000 90	其他鲜或冷藏的带骨牛肉	12				70	13	5	千克	4xAB	Other meat of bovine animals, with bone in, fresh or chilled
0201.3000	-去骨肉	12	T3		9.6	70	13	5	千克		-Boneless
0201.3000 10	鲜或冷藏的去骨野牛肉	12				70	13	5	千克	4xABFE	Meat of wild bovine animals, boneless, fresh or chilled
0201.3000 90	其他鲜或冷藏的去骨牛肉	12				70	13	5	千克	4xAB	Other meat of bovine animals, boneless, fresh or chilled
02.02	冻牛肉：										**Meat of bovine animals, frozen：**
0202.1000	-整头及半头	25	T3		15	70	13	5	千克		-Carcasses and half-carcasses
0202.1000 10	冻藏的整头及半头野牛肉	25				70	13	5	千克	4xABFE	Meat of wild bovine animals, carcasses and half-carcasses, frozen
0202.1000 90	其他冻藏的整头及半头牛肉	25				70	13	5	千克	4xAB	Other meat of bovine animals, carcasses and half-carcasses, frozen
0202.2000	-带骨肉	12	T3		9.6	70	13	5	千克		-Other cuts with bone in
0202.2000 10	冻藏的带骨野牛肉	12				70	13	5	千克	4xABFE	Meat of wild bovine animals, with bone in, frozen
0202.2000 90	其他冻藏的带骨牛肉	12				70	13	5	千克	4xAB	Other meat of bovine animals, with bone in, frozen
0202.3000	-去骨肉	12	T3		9.6	70	13		千克		-Boneless
0202.3000 10	冻藏的去骨野牛肉	12				70	13	5	千克	4xABFE	Meat of wild bovine animals, boneless, frozen
0202.3000 90	其他冻藏的去骨牛肉	12				70	13	13	千克	4xAB	Other meat of bovine animals, boneless, frozen
02.03	鲜、冷、冻猪肉：										**Meat of swine, fresh, chilled or frozen：**
	-鲜或冷的：										-Fresh or chilled：
	--整头及半头：										--Carcasses and half-carcasses：
0203.1110	---乳猪	20	T3		12	70	13	5	千克		---sucking pig

税则号列 Tariff Item.	货品名称	最惠国(%) MFN	协定(%) CT			普通 Gen	增值税率 VAT	出口退税 ED	计量单位 Unit	监管条件 SC	Article Description
			东盟 CA	中巴 CP	中智 CC						
0203.1110 10	鲜或冷藏的整头及半头野乳猪肉	20				70	13	5	千克	4xABFE	Meat of wild sucking pig, carcasses and half-carcasses, fresh or chilled
0203.1110 90	其他鲜或冷藏的整头及半头乳猪肉	20				70	13	5	千克	4xAB	Meat of sucking pig, carcasses and half-carcasses, fresh or chilled
0203.1190	---其他	20	T3		12	70	13	5	千克		---Other
0203.1190 10	其他鲜或冷藏的整头及半头野猪肉	20				70	13	5	千克	4xABFE	Other meat of wild swine, carcasses and half-carcasses, fresh or chilled
0203.1190 90	其他鲜或冷藏的整头及半头猪肉	20				70	13	5	千克	4xAB	Other meat of swine, carcasses and half-carcasses, fresh or chilled
0203.1200	--带骨的前腿、后腿及其肉块	20	T3		16	70	13	5	千克		--Hams, shoulders and cuts thereof, with bone in
0203.1200 10	鲜或冷带骨野猪前腿、后腿及肉块	20				70	13	5	千克	4xABFE	Hams, shoulders and cuts thereof, with bone in, of wild swine, fresh or chilled
0203.1200 90	鲜或冷的带骨猪前腿、后腿及其肉块	20				70	13	5	千克	4xAB	Hams, shoulders and cuts thereof, with bone in, of swine, fresh or chilled
0203.1900	--其他	20	T3		0	70	13	5	千克		--Other
0203.1900 10	其他鲜或冷藏的野猪肉	20				70	13	5	千克	4xABFE	Other meat of wild swine, fresh
0203.1900 90	其他鲜或冷藏的猪肉	20				70	13	5	千克	4xAB	Other meat of swine, fresh or chilled
	-冻的:										-Frozen:
	--整头及半头:										--Carcasses and half-carcasses:
0203.2110	---乳猪	12	T3		9.6	70	13	5	千克		---Sucking pig
0203.2110 10	冻整头及半头野乳猪肉	12				70	13	5	千克	4xABFE	Meat of wild sucking pig, carcasses and half-carcasses, frozen
0203.2110 90	冻整头及半头乳猪肉	12				70	13	5	千克	4xAB	Meat of sucking pig, carcasses and half-carcasses, frozen
0203.2190	---其他	12	T3		9.6	70	13	5	千克		---Other
0203.2190 10	其他冻整头及半头野猪肉	12				70	13	5	千克	4xABFE	Other meat of wild swine, carcasses and half-carcasses, frozen
0203.2190 90	其他冻整头及半头猪肉	12				70	13	5	千克	4xAB	Other meat of swine, carcasses and half-carcasses, frozen
0203.2200	--带骨的前腿、后腿及其肉块	12	T3		7.2	70	13	5	千克		--Hams, shoulders and cuts thereof, with bone in
0203.2200 10	冻带骨野猪前腿、后腿及肉	12				70	13	5	千克	4xABFE	Hams, shoulders and cuts thereof, with bone in, of wild swine, frozen
0203.2200 90	冻藏的带骨猪前腿、后腿及其肉块	12				70	13	5	千克	4xAB	Hams, shoulders and cuts thereof, with bone in, of wild swine, frozen
0203.2900	--其他	12	T3		7.2	70	13	5	千克		--Other
0203.2900 10	冻藏野猪其他肉	12				70	13	5	千克	4xABFE	Other meat of wild swine, frozen
0203.2900 90	其他冻藏猪肉	12				70	13	5	千克	4xAB	Other meat of swine, frozen
02.04	**鲜、冷、冻绵羊肉或山羊肉:**										**Meat of sheep or goats, fresh, chilled or frozen:**
0204.1000	-鲜或冷的整头及半头羔羊	15	0		9	70	13	5	千克	AB	-Carcasses and half-carcasses of lamb, fresh or chilled
	-其他鲜或冷的绵羊肉:										-Other meat of sheep, fresh or chilled:
0204.2100	--整头及半头	23	0		13.8	70	13	5	千克	AB	--Carcasses and half-carcasses
0204.2200	--带骨肉	15	0		9	70	13	5	千克	AB	--Other cuts with bone in
0204.2300	--去骨肉	15	0		0	70	13	5	千克	AB	--Boneless
0204.3000	-冻的整头及半头羔羊	15	0		12	70	13	5	千克	AB	-Carcasses and half-carcasses of lamb, frozen

税则号列 Tariff Item.	货 品 名 称	最惠国(%) MFN	协定(%)CT 东盟 CA	中巴 CP	中智 CC	普通 Gen	增值税率 VAT	出口退税 ED	计量单位 Unit	监管条件 SC	Article Description
	-其他冻的绵羊肉:										-Other meat of sheep, frozen:
0204.4100	--整头及半头	23	0		18.4	70	13	5	千克	AB	--Carcasses and half-carcasses
0204.4200	--带骨肉	12	0		9.6	70	13	5	千克	AB	--Other cuts with bone in
0204.4300	--去骨肉	15	0		12	70	13	13	千克	AB	--Boneless
0204.5000	-山羊肉	20	T3		12	70	13	13	千克	AB	-Meat of goats
02.05	**鲜、冷、冻马、驴、骡肉:**										**Meat of horses, asses, mules or hinnies, fresh, chilled or frozen:**
0205.0000	鲜、冷、冻马、驴、骡肉	20	0		12	70	13	5	千克		Meat of horses, asses, mules or hinnies, fresh, chilled or frozen
0205.0000 10	鲜、冷或冻的濒危野马、野驴肉	20				70	13	5	千克	ABFE	Meat of wild horses in imminent dangers, asses, fresh chilled or frozen
0205.0000 90	鲜、冷或冻的马、驴、骡肉	20				70	13	5	千克	AB	Other meat of horses, asses, mules or hinnies, fresh、chilled or frozen
02.06	**鲜、冷、冻牛、猪、绵羊、山羊、马、驴、骡的食用杂碎:**										**Edible offal of bovine animals, swine, sheep, goats, horses, asses, mules or hinnies, fresh, chilled or frozen:**
0206.1000	-鲜、冷牛杂碎	12	0		7.2	70	13	5	千克	4xAB	-Of bovine animals, fresh or chilled
	-冻牛杂碎:										-Of bovine animals, frozen:
0206.2100	--舌	12	0		9.6	70	13	5	千克	4xAB	--Tongues
0206.2200	--肝	12	0		7.2	70	13	5	千克	4xAB	--Livers
0206.2900	--其他	12	0		9.6	70	13	5	千克	4xAB	--Other
0206.3000	-鲜、冷猪杂碎	20	0		12	70	13	5	千克	4xAB	-Of swine, fresh or chilled
	-冻猪杂碎:										-Of swine, frozen:
0206.4100	--肝	20	0		0	70	13	5	千克	4xAB	--Livers
0206.4900	--其他	12	0		9.6	70	13	5	千克	4xAB	--Other
0206.8000	-其他鲜或冷杂碎	20	0		12	70	13	5	千克		-Other, fresh or chilled
0206.8000 10	鲜或冷的羊杂碎	20				70	13	5	千克	AB	Edible offal of sheep or goats, fresh or chilled
0206.8000 90	鲜或冷的马、驴、骡杂碎	20				70	13	5	千克	AB	Edible offal of horses, asses, mules or hinnies, fresh or chilled
0206.9000	-其他冻杂碎	18	0		14.4	70	13	5	千克		-Other, frozen
0206.9000 10	冻藏的羊杂碎	18				70	13	5	千克	AB	Edible offal of sheep or goats, frozen
0206.9000 90	冻藏的马、驴、骡杂碎	18				70	13	5	千克	AB	Edible offal of horses, asses, mules or hinnies, frozen
02.07	**税目01.05所列家禽的鲜、冷、冻肉及食用杂碎:**										**Meat and edible offal, of the poultry of heading No. 01.05, fresh, chilled or frozen:**
	-鸡:										-Of fowls of the species *Gallus domesticus*:
0207.1100	--整只,鲜或冷的	20	T3		12	70	13	5	千克	4x7AB	--Not cut in pieces, fresh or chilled
0207.1200	--整只,冻的	T2	T3		T2	T2	13	5	千克	4x7AB	--Not cut in pieces, frozen
	--块及杂碎,鲜或冷的:										--Cuts and offal, fresh or chilled:
	---块:										---Cuts:
0207.1311	----带骨的	20	T3		12	70	13	13	千克	4x7AB	----With bone
0207.1319	----其他	20	T3		12	70	13	13	千克	4x7AB	----Other
	---杂碎:										---offal:
0207.1321	----翼(不包括翼尖)	20	T3		12	70	13	13	千克	4x7AB	----Midjoint wing
0207.1329	----其他	20	T3		12	70	13	5	千克	7AB4x	----Other
	--块及杂碎,冻的:										--Cuts and offal, frozen:

税则号列 Tariff Item.	货 品 名 称	最惠国(%) MFN	协定(%) CT 东盟 CA	中巴 CP	中智 CC	普通 Gen	增值税率 VAT	出口退税 ED	计量单位 Unit	监管条件 SC	Article Description
	---块:										---Cuts:
0207.1411	----带骨的	T2	T3		T2	T2	13	13	千克	7AB4x	----With bone in
0207.1419	----其他	T2	T3		T2	T2	13	13	千克	7AB4x	----Other
	---杂碎:										---Offal:
0207.1421	----翼(不包括翼尖)	T2	T3		T2	T2	13	13	千克	7AB4x	----Midjoint wing
0207.1422	----鸡爪	T2	T3		T2	T2	13	13	千克	7AB4x	----Chicken claw
0207.1429	----其他	T2	T3		T2	T2	13	5	千克	7AB4x	----Other
	-火鸡:										-Of turkeys:
0207.2400	--整只,鲜或冷的	20	T3		12	70	13	5	千克	AB	--Not cut in pieces, fresh or chilled
0207.2500	--整只,冻的	20	T3		16	70	13	5	千克	AB	--Not cut in pieces, frozen
0207.2600	--块及杂碎,鲜或冷的	20	T3		12	70	13	5	千克	AB	--Cuts and offal, fresh or chilled
0207.2700	--块及杂碎,冻的	10	T3		8	70	13	5	千克	AB	--Cuts and offal, frozen
	-鸭、鹅或珍珠鸡:										-Of ducks, geese or guinea fowls:
	--整只,鲜或冷的:										--Not cut in pieces, fresh or chilled:
0207.3210	---鸭	20	T3		12	70	13	5	千克	AB	---OF ducks
0207.3220	---鹅	20	T3		12	70	13	5	千克	AB	---OF geese
0207.3230	---珍珠鸡	20	T3		12	70	13	5	千克	AB	---OF guinea fowls
	--整只,冻的:										--Not cut in pieces, frozen:
0207.3310	---鸭	20	T3		12	70	13	5	千克	AB	---Ducks
0207.3320	---鹅	20	T3		12	70	13	5	千克	AB	---Geese
0207.3330	---珍珠鸡	20	T3		12	70	13	5	千克	AB	---Guinea fowls
0207.3400	--肥肝,鲜或冷的	20	T3		12	70	13	5	千克	AB	--Fatty livers(*foie gras*), fresh or chilled
0207.3510	---鸭块及杂碎	20	T3		12	70	13	5	千克	AB	---Cuts and offal of ducks
0207.3520	---鹅块及杂碎	20	T3		12	70	13	5	千克	AB	---Cuts and offal of geese
0207.3530	---珍珠鸡块及杂碎	20	T3		12	70	13	5	千克	AB	---Cuts and offal of guinea fowls
	--其他,冻的:										--Other, frozen:
0207.3610	---鸭块及杂碎	20	T3		12	70	13	5	千克	AB	---Cuts and offal of ducks
0207.3620	---鹅块及杂碎	20	T3		12	70	13	5	千克	AB	---Cuts and offal of geese
0207.3630	---珍珠鸡块及杂碎	20	T3		12	70	13	5	千克	AB	---Cuts and offal of guinea fowls
02.08	**其他鲜、冷、冻肉及食用杂碎:**										**Other meat and edible meat offal, fresh, chilled or frozen:**
	-家兔或野兔的:										-Of rabbits or hares:
0208.1010	---鲜、冷兔肉,兔头除外	20	0		16	70	13	5	千克	AB	---Meat of rabbits, fresh or chilled, excluding head
0208.1020	---冻兔肉,兔头除外	20	0		16	70	13	5	千克	AB	---Meat of rabbits, frozen, excluding head
0208.1090	---其他	20	0		16	70	13	13	千克		---Other
0208.1090 10	鲜、冷或冻濒危野兔肉及其食用杂碎(不包括兔头)	20				70	13	13	千克	ABFE	Meat of hares in imminent dangers (cluding edible), fresh、chilled or frozen
0208.1090 90	鲜、冷或冻家兔食用杂碎	20				70	13	5	千克	AB	Edible offal of rabbits, fresh、chilled or frozen
0208.3000	-灵长目的	23	0		13.8	70	13	5	千克	ABFE	-Of primates
0208.4000	-鲸、海豚及鼠海豚(鲸目哺乳动物)的;海牛及儒艮(海牛目哺乳动物)的	23	0		13.8	70	13	5	千克	ABFE	-Of whales, dolphins and porpoises (mammals of the order Cetacea); of manatees and dugongs(mammals of the order Sirenia)
0208.5000	-爬行动物(包括蛇及龟鳖)的	23	0		13.8	70	13	5	千克	ABFE	-Of reptiles (including snakes and turtles)
	-其他:										-Other:

税则号列 Tariff Item.	货品名称	最惠国(%) MFN	协定(%)CT 东盟 CA	中巴 CP	中智 CC	普通 Gen	增值税率 VAT	出口退税 ED	计量单位 Unit	监管条件 SC	Article Description
0208.9010	---乳鸽的	20	0		16	70	13	5	千克	AB	---Squabs
0208.9090	---其他	23	0		13.8	70	13	5	千克		---Other
0208.9090 10	其他鲜、冷或冻的濒危野生动物肉	23				70	13	5	千克	ABFE	Other meat of wild animals in imminent dangers, fresh、chilled or frozen
0208.9090 90	其他鲜、冷或冻肉及食用杂碎	23				70	13	5	千克	AB	Other meat and edible offal, fresh、chilled or frozen
02.09	**未炼制或用其他方法提取的不带瘦肉的肥猪肉、猪脂肪及家禽脂肪,鲜、冷、冻、干、熏、盐腌或盐渍的:**										**Pig fat free of lean meat and poultry fat not rendered or otherwise extracted, fresh, chilled, frozen, salted, in brine, dried or smoked:**
0209.0000	未炼制或用其他方法提取的不带瘦肉的肥猪肉、猪脂肪及家禽脂肪,鲜、冷、冻、干、熏、盐腌或盐渍的	20	0		16	70	13	5	千克	AB	Pig fat free of lean meat and poultry fat not rendered or otherwise extracted, fresh, chilled, frozen, salted, in brine, dried or smoked
02.10	**肉及食用杂碎,干、熏、盐腌或盐渍的;可供食用的肉或杂碎的细粉、粗粉:**										**Meat and edible meat offal, salted, in brine, dried or smoked; edible flours and meals of meat or meat offal:**
	-猪肉:										-Meat of swine:
	--带骨的前腿、后腿及其肉块:										--Hams, shoulders and cuts thereof, with bone in:
0210.1110	---带骨的腿	25	T3		15	80	13	5	千克		---Hams and shoulders, with bone in
0210.1110 10	干、熏、盐制的带骨鹿猪、姬猪腿	25				80	13	5	千克	ABFE	Hams and shoulders of pig-deer (*Babyrousa*)、pygmy pig (*Porcula*), with bone in, salted, in brine, dried or smoked
0210.1110 90	其他干、熏、盐制的带骨猪腿	25				80	13	5	千克	AB	Other hams and shoulders of swine, with bone in, salted, in brine, dried or smoked
0210.1190	---其他	25	T3		15	80	13	5	千克		---Other
0210.1190 10	干、熏、盐制的带骨鹿猪、姬猪腿肉块	25				80	13	5	千克	ABFE	Other cuts of pig-deer (*Babyrousa*)、pygmy pig (*Porcula*), with bone in, salted, in brine, dried or smoked
0210.1190 90	其他干、熏、盐制的带骨猪腿肉	25				80	13	5	千克	AB	Other meat of hams and shoulders, with bone in, salted, in brine, dried or smoked
0210.1200	--腹肉(五花肉)	25	T3		15	80	13	5	千克		--Bellies (streaky) and cuts thereof
0210.1200 10	干、熏、盐制的鹿猪、姬猪腹肉(指五花肉)	25				80	13	5	千克	ABFE	Bellies (streaky) and cuts thereof, of pig-deer (*Babyrousa*)、pygmy pig (*Porcula*), salted, in brine, dried or smoked
0210.1200 90	其他干、熏、盐制的猪腹肉(指五花肉)	25				80	13	5	千克	AB	Other bellies (streaky) and cuts thereof of swine, salted, in brine, dried or smoked
0210.1900	--其他	25	T3		20	80	13	5	千克		--Other
0210.1900 10	干、熏、盐制的鹿猪、姬猪其他肉	25				80	13	5	千克	ABFE	Other meat of wild swine, salted, in brine, dried or smoked
0210.1900 90	其他干、熏、盐制的其他猪肉	25				80	13	5	千克	AB	Other meat of swine, salted, in brine, dried or smoked
0210.2000	-牛肉	25	0		0	80	13	5	千克		-Meat of bovine animals

税则号列 Tariff Item.	货品名称	最惠国(%) MFN	协定(%) CT 东盟 CA	中巴 CP	中智 CC	普通 Gen	增值税率 VAT	出口退税 ED	计量单位 Unit	监管条件 SC	Article Description
0210.2000 10	干、熏、盐制的濒危野牛肉	25				80	13	5	千克	ABFE	Meat of wild bovine animals in imminent dangers, salted, in brine, dried or smoked
0210.2000 90	干、熏、盐制的其他牛肉	25				80	13	5	千克	AB	Meat of bovine animals, salted, in brine, dried or smoked
	-其他,包括可供食用的肉或杂碎的细粉、粗粉:										-Other, including edible flours and meals of meat and meat offal:
0210.9100	--灵长目的	25	0		15	80	13	5	千克	ABFE	--Of primates
0210.9200	--鲸、海豚及鼠海豚(鲸目哺乳动物);海牛及儒艮(海牛目哺乳动物)的	25	0		15	80	13	5	千克	ABFE	--Of whales, dolphins and porpoises (mammals of the order Cetacea); of manatees and dugongs (mammals of the order Sirenia)
0210.9300	--爬行动物(包括蛇及龟鳖)的	25	0		15	80	13	5	千克	ABFE	--Of reptiles (including snakes and turtles)
0210.9900	--其他	25	T3		20	80	13	5	千克		--Other
0210.9900 10	干、熏、盐制其他濒危动物肉及杂碎(包括可供食用的肉或杂碎的细粉、粗粉)	25				80	13	5	千克	ABFE	Meat and edible offal of other wild animals in imminent dangers (including edible flours and meals of meat and meat offal), salted, in brine, dried or smoked
0210.9900 90	干、熏、盐制的其他肉及食用杂碎(包括可供食用的肉或杂碎的细粉、粗粉)	25				80	13	5	千克	AB	Other meat and edible offal (including edible flours and meals of meat and meat offal), salted, in brine, dried or smoked

第三章
鱼、甲壳动物，软体动物及其他水生无脊椎动物

Chapter 3
Fish and crustaceans, molluscs and other aquatic invertebrates

注释：

一、本章不包括：

（一）税目 01.06 的哺乳动物

（二）税目 01.06 的哺乳动物的肉（税目 02.08 或 02.10）

（三）因品种或鲜度不适合供人食用的死鱼（包括鱼肝及鱼卵）、死甲壳动物、死软体动物及其他死水生无脊椎动物（第五章）；不适合供人食用的鱼、甲壳动物、软体动物、其他水生无脊椎动物的粉、粒（税目 23.01）；

（四）鲟鱼子酱及用鱼卵制成的鲟鱼子酱代用品（税目 16.04）。

二、本章所称“团粒”，是指直接挤压或加入少量粘合剂制成的粒状产品。

Notes:

1. This Chapter does not cover:

(a) Mammals of heading No. 01.06;

(b) Meat of mammals of heading No. 01.06 (heading No. 02.08 or 02.10)

(c) Fish (including livers and roes thereof) or crustaceans, molluscs or other aquatic invertebrates, dead and unfit or unsuitable for human consumption by reason of either their species or their condition (Chapter 5); flours, meals or pellets of fish or of crustaceans, molluscs or other aquatic invertebrates, unfit for human consumption (heading No. 23.01); or

(d) Caviar or caviar substitutes prepared from fish eggs (heading No. 16.04).

2. In this Chapter, the term "pellets" means products which have been agglomerated either directly by compression or by the addition of a small quantity of binder.

税则号列 Tariff Item.	货品名称	最惠国(%) MFN	协定(%)CT 东盟 CA	中巴 CP	中智 CC	普通 Gen	增值税率 VAT	出口退税 ED	计量单位 Unit	监管条件 SC	Article Description
03.01	活鱼：										**Live fish:**
0301.1000	-观赏鱼	17.5	0		10.5	80	13	5	条/千克		-Ornamental fish
0301.1000 10	观赏用鲸鲨、噬人鲨、姥鲨	17.5				80	13	5	条/千克	ABFE	Ornamental whale shark (*Rhincodon*), man-eating shark (*Cacharodon*), basking shark (*Cetorhinus*)
0301.1000 20	观赏用红龙鱼	17.5				80	13	5	条/千克	ABFE	Ornamental red arowana (*Scleropages formosa*)
0301.1000 30	观赏用胭脂鱼	17.5				80	13	5	条/千克	ABFE	Ornamental mullet (*Myxocyprinus*)
0301.1000 40	观赏用海马	17.5				80	13	5	条/千克	ABFE	Ornamental sea horse (*Hippocampus*)
0301.1000 50	观赏用巨骨舌鱼	17.5				80	13	5	条/千克	ABFE	Ornamental pirarucu (*Arapaima*)
0301.1000 60	观赏用其他濒危鱼	17.5				80	13	5	条/千克	ABFE	Other ornamental fish in imminent danger
0301.1000 90	其他观赏鱼	17.5				80	13	5	条/千克	AB	Other ornamental fish
	-其他活鱼：										-Other live fish:
	--鳟鱼：										--Trout (*Salmo trutta*, *Oncorhynchus mykiss*, *Oncorhynchus clarki*, *Oncorhynchus aguabonita*, *Oncorhynchus gilae*, *Oncorhynchus apache* and *Oncorhynchus chrysogaster*):
0301.9110	---鱼苗	0				0	13	5	千克	AB	---Fry
0301.9190	---其他	10.5	0	8	6.3	40	13	5	千克	AB	---Other
	--鳗鱼：										--Eels (*Anguilla spp.*):
0301.9210	---鱼苗	0	0			0	13		千克		---Fry
0301.9210 10	花鳗鲡鱼苗	0				0	13		千克	ABE	Fry of marbled eels (*Anguilla marmorata*)
0301.9210 90	其他鳗鱼苗	0				0	13		千克	AB	Other fry eels (*Anguilla marmorata*)
0301.9290	---其他	10	0	6.7	0	40	13	5	千克		---Other
0301.9290 10	花鳗鲡	10				40	13	5	千克	ABE	Marbled eels (*Anguilla marmorata*)
0301.9290 90	其他活鳗鱼	10				40	13	5	千克	AB	Other live eels (*Anguilla marmorata*)
	--鲤鱼：										--Carp:

税则号列 Tariff Item.	货品名称	最惠国(%) MFN	协定(%) CT			普通 Gen	增值税率 VAT	出口退税 ED	计量单位 Unit	监管条件 SC	Article Description
			东盟 CA	中巴 CP	中智 CC						
0301.9310	---鱼苗	0				0	13	5	千克		---Fry
0301.9310 10	濒危鲤鱼苗	0				0	13	5	千克	ABFE	Carp fry in imminent dangers
0301.9310 90	其他鲤鱼苗	0				0	13	5	千克	AB	Other carp fry
0301.9390	---其他	10.5	0	8	6.3	40	13	5	千克		---Other
0301.9390 10	活濒危鲤鱼	10.5				40	13	5	千克	ABFE	Live carp, in imminent dangers
0301.9390 90	其他活鲤鱼	10.5				40	13	5	千克	AB	Other live carp
	--蓝鳍金枪鱼:										--Thunnus thynnus
0301.9410	---鱼苗	0				0	13	5	千克	AB	---Eels
0301.9490	---其他	10.5	0	8	8.4	40	13	5	千克	AB	---Other
	--南方蓝鳍金枪鱼:										--Thunnus maccoy:
0301.9510	---鱼苗	0				0	13	5	千克	AB	---Eels
0301.9590	---其他	10.5	0	8	8.4	40	13	5	千克	AB	---Other
	--其他:										--Other:
	---鱼苗:										---Fry:
0301.9911	----鲈鱼	0				0	13	5	千克	AB	----Of perches
0301.9912	----鲟鱼	0				0	13	5	千克	ABFE	----Of sturgeon
0301.9919	----其他	0				0	13	5	千克		----Other
0301.9919 10	其他濒危鱼苗	0				0	13	5	千克	ABFE	Other fry in imminent dangers
0301.9919 90	其他鱼苗	0				0	13	5	千克	AB	Other fry
	---其他:										---Other:
0301.9991	----罗非鱼	10.5	0		8.4	40	13	5	千克	AB	----Tilapia
0301.9992	----鲀	10.5	0	8	8.4	40	13	5	千克	AB	----Puffer fish
0301.9999	----其他	10.5	0	8	8.4	40	13	5	千克		----Other
0301.9999 10	其他濒危活鱼	10.5				40	13	5	千克	ABFE	Other live fish, in imminent dangers
0301.9999 90	其他活鱼	10.5				40	13	5	千克	AB	Other live fish
03.02	**鲜、冷鱼,但税目03.04的鱼片及其他鱼肉除外:**										**Fish, fresh or chilled, excluding fish fillets and other fish meat of heading No. 03.04:**
	-鲑鱼,但鱼肝及鱼卵除外:										-Salmonidae, excluding livers and roes
0302.1100	--鳟鱼	12	0		9.6	40	13	5	千克	AB	--Trout (*Salmo trutta*, *Oncorhynchus mykiss*, *Oncorhynchus clarki*, *Oncorhynchus aguabonita*, *Oncorhynchus gilae*, *Oncorhynchus apache* and *Oncorhynchus chrysogaster*)
0302.1210	---大西洋鲑鱼	10	0		8	40	13	5	千克	AB	---Atlantic salmon(*salmo salar*)
0302.1220	---大马哈鱼和多瑙哲罗鱼	10	0		8	40	13	5	千克	AB	---Pacific salmon (*Oncorhynchus nerka*, *Oncorhynchus gorbuscha*, *Oncorhynchus keta*, *Oncorhynchus tschawytscha*, *Oncorhynchus kisutch*, *Oncorhynchus masou* and *Oncorhynchus rhodurus*) and Danube salmon (*Hucho hucho*)
0302.1900	--其他	12	0	8	7.2	40	13	5	千克		--Other
0302.1900 10	鲜或冷川陕哲罗鲑(鱼肝及鱼卵除外)	12				40	13	5	千克	ABE	Chuan-shan taimen (*Hucho taimen*) (excluding livers and roes), fresh or chilled
0302.1900 20	鲜或冷秦岭细鳞鲑(鱼肝及鱼卵除外)	12				40	13	5	千克	ABE	Qinling lenok (*Brachymystax lenok*) (excluding livers and roes), fresh or chilled

税则号列 Tariff Item.	货品名称	最惠国(%) MFN	协定(%)CT			普通 Gen	增值税率 VAT	出口退税 ED	计量单位 Unit	监管条件 SC	Article Description
			东盟 CA	中巴 CP	中智 CC						
0302.1900 90	其他鲜或冷鲑鱼(鱼肝及鱼卵除外)	12				40	13	5	千克	AB	Other salmon, (excluding livers and roes), fresh、chilled
	-比目鱼,但鱼肝及鱼卵除外:										-Flat fish (*Pleuronectidae*, *Bothidae*, *Cynoglossidae*, *Soleidae*, *Scophthalmidae* *and Citharidae*), excluding livers and roes:
0302.2100	--庸鲽鱼	12	T3	9	7.2	40	13	5	千克	AB	--Halibut (*Reinhardtius hippoglossoides*, *Hippoglossus hippoglossus*, *Hippoglossus stenolepis*)
0302.2200	--鲽鱼	12	0	9	7.2	40	13	5	千克	AB	--Plaice (*Pleuronectes platessa*)
0302.2300	--鳎鱼	12	0	9	7.2	40	13	5	千克	AB	--Sole (*Solea spp.*)
0302.2900	--其他鲜或冷比目鱼(鱼肝及鱼卵除外)	12	T3	6	9.6	40	13	5	千克	AB	--Other
0302.3100	--长鳍金枪鱼	12	0	9	9.6	40	13	5	千克	AB	--Albacore or longfinned tunas (*Thunnus alalunga*)
0302.3200	--黄鳍金枪鱼	12	0	9	7.2	40	13	5	千克	AB	--Yellowfin tunas (*Thunnus albacares*)
0302.3300	--鲣鱼	12	0	8	7.2	40	13	5	千克	AB	--Skipjack or stripe-bellied bonito
0302.3400	--大眼金枪鱼	12	T3	8	7.2	40	13	5	千克	AB	--Bigeye tunas (*Thunnus obesus*)
0302.3500	--蓝鳍金枪鱼	12	T3		7.2	40	13	5	千克	AB	--Bluefin tunas(*Thunnus thynnus*)
0302.3600	--南金枪鱼	12	T3		7.2	40	13	5	千克	AB	--Southern bluefin tunas (*Thunnus maccoyii*)
0302.3900	--其他	12	0	8	7.2	40	13	5	千克	AB	--Other
0302.4000	-鲱鱼	12	0	8	7.2	40	13	5	千克	AB	-Herrings (*Clupea harengus*, *Clupea pallasii*), excluding livers and roes
0302.5000	-鳕鱼,但鱼肝及鱼卵除外	12	0	8	7.2	40	13	5	千克	AB	-Cod (*Gadus morhua. Gadus ogac*, *Gadus macrocephalus*), excluding livers and roes
	-其他鱼,但鱼肝及鱼卵除外:										-Other fish, excluding livers and roes:
0302.6100	--沙丁鱼、黍鲱鱼	12	0	8	7.2	40	13	5	千克	AB	--Sardines (*Sardina pilchardus*, *Sardinops spp.*) sardinella (*Sardinella spp.*), brisling or sprats (*Sprattus sprattus*)
0302.6200	--黑线鳕鱼	12	0	8	7.2	40	13	5	千克	AB	--Haddock (*Melanogrammus aeglefinus*)
0302.6300	--绿青鳕鱼	12	0	8	7.2	40	13	5	千克	AB	--Coalfish (*Pollachius virens*)
0302.6400	--鲭鱼	12	0	8	7.2	40	13	5	千克	AB	--Mackerel (*Scomber scombrus*, *Scomber australasicus*, *Scomber Japonicus*)
0302.6500	--角鲨及其他鲨鱼	12	T3	9	9.6	40	13	5	千克		--Dogfish and other sharks
0302.6500 10	鲜或冷鲸鲨、噬人鲨、姥鲨(鱼肝及鱼卵除外)	12				40	13	5	千克	ABFE	Whale shark (*Rhincodon*), man-eating shark (*Cacharodon*), basking shark (*Cetorhinus*), (excluding livers and roes), fresh or chilled
0302.6500 90	其他鲜或冷角鲨及其他鲨鱼(鱼肝及鱼卵除外)	12				40	13	5	千克	AB	Other dogfish and other sharks (excluding livers and roes), fresh、chilled
0302.6600	--鳗鱼	12	T3	8	7.2	40	13	5	千克		--Eels (*Anguilla spp.*)
0302.6600 10	鲜或冷花鳗鲡(鱼肝及鱼卵除外)	12				40	13	5	千克	ABE	Marbled eels (excluding livers and roes), fresh or chilled
0302.6600 90	其他鲜或冷鳗鱼(鱼肝及鱼卵除外)	12				40	13	5	千克	AB	Other eels (excluding livers and roes), fresh、chilled

税则号列 Tariff Item.	货 品 名 称	最惠国(%) MFN	协定(%)CT 东盟 CA	中巴 CP	中智 CC	普通 Gen	增值税率 VAT	出口退税 ED	计量单位 Unit	监管条件 SC	Article Description
0302.6700	--剑鱼	12	T3	8	9.6	40	13	5	千克	AB	--Xiphias gladius
0302.6800	--南极犬牙鱼	12	T3	8	9.6	40	13	5	千克	AB	--Dissostichus spp.
	--其他:										--Other:
0302.6910	---带鱼	12	T3	8	9.6	40	13	5	千克	AB	---Scabber fish(*Trichurius*)
0302.6920	---黄鱼	12	T3	8	9.6	40	13	5	千克	AB	---Yellow croaker (*Pseudosicaena*)
0302.6930	---鲳鱼	12	T3	8	9.6	40	13	5	千克	AB	---Butterfish (*Pamus*)
0302.6940	---罗非鱼	12	T3		9.6	40	13	5	千克	AB	---Tilapia
0302.6950	---鲀	12	T3	8	9.6	40	13	5	千克	AB	---Puffer fish
0302.6990	---其他	12	T3	8	9.6	40	13	5	千克		---Other
0302.6990 01	鲜或冷的鲈鱼(鱼肝及鱼卵除)	12				40	13		千克	AB	Perch (excluding livers and roes), fresh or chilled
0302.6990 10	其他未列名濒危鲜、冷鱼(鱼肝及鱼卵除外)	12				40	13	5	千克	ABEF	Other fish in imminent dangers (excluding livers and roes) fresh or chilled
0302.6990 90	其他鲜或冷鱼(鱼肝及鱼卵除外)	12				40	13	5	千克	AB	Other fish (excluding livers and roes), fresh or chilled
0302.7000	-鱼肝及鱼卵	12	0		7.2	50	13	5	千克		-Livers and roes
0302.7000 10	鲜或冷濒危鱼种的肝及鱼卵	12				50	13	5	千克	ABFE	Livers and roes of fish in imminent dangers, fresh or chilled
0302.7000 90	其他鲜或冷鱼肝及鱼卵	12				50	13	5	千克	AB	Other livers and roes, fresh chilled
03.03	**冻鱼,但税目03.04的鱼片及其他鱼肉除外:**										**Fish, frozen, excluding fish fillets and other fish meat of heading No. 03.04:**
	-大马哈鱼,但鱼肝及鱼卵除外:										-Pacific salmon (*Oncorhynchus nerka*, *Oncorhynchus gorbuscha*, *Oncorhynchus keta*, *Oncorhynchus tschawytscha*, *Oncorhynchus kisutch*, *Oncorhynchus masou and Oncorhynchus rhodurus*), excluding livers and roes:
0303.1100	--红大马哈鱼	10	T3	6.7	8	40	13	5	千克	AB	--Sockeye salmon (red salmon) (*Oncorhynchus nerka*)
0303.1900	--其他	10	T3	6.7	8	40	13	5	千克	AB	--Other
	-其他鲑鱼,但鱼肝及鱼卵除外:										-Other salmonidae, excluding livers and roes:
0303.2100	--鳟鱼	12	0		9.6	40	13	5	千克	AB	--Trout (*Salmo trutta*, *Oncorhynchus my kiss*, *Oncorhynchus clarki*, *Oncorhynchus aguabonita*, *Oncorhynchus gilae*, *Oncorhynchus apache and Oncorhynchus chrysogaster*).
	--大西洋鲑鱼及多瑙哲罗鱼:										--Atlantic salmon (*Salmo salar*) and Danube salmon (*Hucho hucho*):
0303.2210	---大西洋鲑鱼	10	0		8	40	13	5	千克	AB	---Atlantic salmon(*Salmo salar*)
0303.2220	---多瑙哲罗鱼	10	0		8	40	13	5	千克	AB	---Danube salmon
0303.2900	--其他	10	0	6.7	6	40	13	5	千克		--Other
0303.2900 10	冻川陕哲罗鲑(鱼肝及鱼卵除外)	10				40	13	5	千克	ABE	Chuan-shan taimen (*Hucho taimen*), (excluding livers and roes) frozen
0303.2900 20	冻秦岭细鳞鲑(鱼肝及鱼卵除外)	10				40	13	5	千克	ABE	Qinling lenok (*Brachymystax lenok*), (excluding livers and roes) frozen
0303.2900 90	其他冻鲑鱼(鱼肝及鱼卵除外)	10				40	13	5	千克	AB	Other salmon, (excluding livers and roes) frozen

税则号列 Tariff Item.	货品名称	最惠国(%) MFN	协定(%) CT 东盟 CA	中巴 CP	中智 CC	普通 Gen	增值税率 VAT	出口退税 ED	计量单位 Unit	监管条件 SC	Article Description
	-比目鱼，但鱼肝及鱼卵除外：										-Flatfish (*Pleuronectidae*, *Bothidae*, *Cynoglossidae*, *Soleidae*, *Scophthalmidae and Citharidae*), excluding livers and roes:
	--庸鲽鱼：										--Halibut (*Reinhardtius hippoglossoides*, *Hippoglossus hippoglossus*, *Hippoglossus stenolepis*):
0303.3110	---格陵兰庸鲽鱼	10	0	6.7	0	40	13	5	千克	AB	---Greenland halibut
0303.3190	---其他	10	0	6.7	0	40	13	5	千克	AB	---Other
0303.3200	--鲽鱼	12	0	8	7.2	40	13	5	千克	AB	--Plaice (*Pleuronectes platessa*)
0303.3300	--鳎鱼	12	0	8	7.2	40	13	5	千克	AB	--Sole (*Solea spp.*)
0303.3900	--其他	10	T3	8	8	40	13	5	千克	AB	--Other
	-金枪鱼、鲣鱼，但鱼肝及鱼卵除外：										-Tunas (*of the genus Thunnus*), skipjack or stripe-bellied bonito (*Euthynnus* (*Katsuwonus*) *pelamis*), excluding livers and roes:
0303.4100	--长鳍金枪鱼	12	0	9	7.2	40	13	5	千克	AB	--Albacore or longfinned tunas (*Thunnus alalunga*)
0303.4200	--黄鳍金枪鱼	12	0	9	7.2	40	13	5	千克	AB	--Yellowfin tunas (*Thunnus albacares*)
0303.4300	--鲣鱼	12	0	9	7.2	40	13	5	千克	AB	--Skipjack or stripe-bellied bonito
0303.4400	--大眼金枪鱼	12	T3		7.2	40	13	5	千克	AB	--Bigeye tunas(*Thunnus obesus*)
0303.4500	--蓝鳍金枪鱼	12	T3		7.2	40	13	5	千克	AB	--Bluefin tunas(*Thunnus thynnus*)
0303.4600	--南金枪鱼	12	T3		7.2	40	13	5	千克	AB	--Southern bluefin tunas (*Thunnus maccoyii*)
0303.4900	--其他	12	0	9	9.6	40	13	5	千克	AB	--Other
	-鲱鱼(大西洋鲱鱼、太平洋鲱鱼)及鳕鱼(大西洋鳕鱼、太平洋鳕鱼、格陵兰鳕鱼)，但鱼肝及鱼卵除外：										-Herrings (*Clupea harengus*, *Clupea pallasii*), excluding livers and roes ling (Atlantic ling, Pacific ling, Green ling)
0303.5100	--鲱鱼(大西洋鲱鱼、太平洋鲱鱼)	10	0	6.7	0	40	13	5	千克	AB	--Herrings(Clupea harengus, clupea pallosii)
0303.5200	--鳕鱼(大西洋鳕鱼、太平洋鳕鱼、格陵兰鳕鱼)	10	0	6.7	6	40	13	5	千克	AB	--Ling (Atlantic ling, Pacific ling, Green ling)
	-剑鱼和南极犬牙鱼，但鱼肝及鱼卵除外：										-Xiphias gladius and Dissostichus, excluding livers and roes:
0303.6100	--剑鱼	10	T3	5	8	40	13	5	千克	AB	--Xiphias gladius
0303.6200	--南极犬牙鱼	10	T3	5	8	40	13	5	千克	AB	--Dissostichus SPP.
	-其他鱼，但鱼肝及鱼卵除外：										-Other fish, excluding livers and roes:
0303.7100	--沙丁鱼、黍鲱鱼	12	0	8	9.6	40	13	5	千克	AB	--Sardines (*Sardina pilchardus*, *Sardinops spp.*) sardinella (*Sardinella spp.*), brisling or sprats (*Sprattus sprattus*)
0303.7200	--黑线鳕鱼	12	0	8	7.2	40	13	5	千克	AB	--Haddock (Melanogrammus aeglefinus)
0303.7300	--绿青鳕鱼	12	0	8	7.2	40	13	5	千克	AB	--Coalfish (*Pollachius virens*)
0303.7400	--鲭鱼	10	0	6.7	8	40	13	5	千克	AB	--Mackerel (*Scomber scombrus*, *Scomber australasicus*, *Scomber japonicus*)
0303.7500	--角鲨及其他鲨鱼	12	0	9	9.6	40	13	5	千克		--Dogfish and other sharks

税则号列 Tariff Item.	货品名称	最惠国(%) MFN	协定(%)CT 东盟 CA	 中巴 CP	 中智 CC	普通 Gen	增值税率 VAT	出口退税 ED	计量单位 Unit	监管条件 SC	Article Description
0303.7500 10	冻鲸鲨、噬人鲨、姥鲨(鱼肝及鱼卵除外)	12				40	13	5	千克	ABFE	Whale shark (*Rhincodon*), man-eating shark (*Cacharodon*), basking shark (*Cetorhinus*), excluding livers and roes, frozen
0303.7500 90	其他冻角鲨及其他鲨鱼(鱼肝及鱼卵除外)	12				40	13	5	千克	AB	Other dogfish and other sharks, (excluding livers and roes) frozen
0303.7600	--鳗鱼	12	0	8	9.6	40	13	5	千克		--Eels (*Anguilla spp.*)
0303.7600 10	冻花鳗鲡(鱼肝及鱼卵除外)	12				40	13	5	千克	ABE	Marbled eels (*Anguilla marmorata*), frozen
0303.7600 90	其他冻鳗鱼(鱼肝及鱼卵除外)	12				40	13	5	千克	AB	Other eels (*Anguilla spp.*) (*Anguilla marmorata*), frozen
0303.7700	--尖吻鲈鱼	12	0	8	7.2	40	13	5	千克	AB	--Sea bass (*Dicentrarchus labrax*, *Dicentrarchus punctatus*)
0303.7800	--狗鳕鱼(无须鳕鱼、长鳍鳕鱼)	12	0		9.6	40	13	5	千克	AB	--Hake (*Merluccius spp. Urophycis spp.*)
	--其他:										--Other:
0303.7910	---带鱼	10	T3	5	8	40	13	5	千克	AB	---Scabber fish (*Trichurius*)
0303.7920	---黄鱼	10	T3	5	8	40	13	5	千克	AB	---Yellow croaker (*Pseudosicaena*)
0303.7930	---鲳鱼	10	T3	5	8	40	13	5	千克	AB	---Butterfish (*Pampus*)
0303.7940	---罗非鱼	10	T3	5	8	40	13	5	千克	AB	---*Tilapia*
0303.7990	---其他	10	T3	5	8	40	13	5	千克		---Other
0303.7990 01	其他冻鲈鱼(鱼肝鱼卵除外)	10				40	13	5	千克	AB	Other perch (excluding livers and roes), chilled
0303.7990 10	其他未列名濒危冻鱼(鱼肝及鱼卵除外)	10	0			40	13	5	千克	ABFE	Other fish in imminent dangers, not elsewhere specified or included (excluding livers and roes), frozen
0303.7990 90	其他未列名冻鱼(鱼肝及鱼卵除外)	10				40	13	5	千克	AB	Other fish, not elsewhere specified or included, (excluding livers and roes), frozen
0303.8000	-鱼肝及鱼卵	10	0	9	8	50	13	5	千克		-Livers and roes
0303.8000 10	冻濒危鱼种的肝及鱼卵	10				50	13	5	千克	ABFE	Livers and roes of fish in imminent dangers, frozen
0303.8000 90	其他冻鱼肝及鱼卵	10				50	13	5	千克	AB	Other livers and roes, frozen
03.04	**鲜、冷、冻鱼片及其他鱼肉(不论是否绞碎):**										**Fish fillets and other fish meat (whether or not minced), fresh, chilled or frozen:**
	-鲜或冷的										-Fresh or chilled:
0304.1100	--剑鱼	12	T3	9	9.6	70	13	5	千克	AB	--Xiphias gladius
0304.1200	--南极犬牙鱼	12	T3	9	9.6	70	13	5	千克	AB	--Dissostichus SPP.
0304.1900	--其他	12	T3	9	9.6	70	13	5	千克		--Other
0304.1900 10	其他鲜或冷的濒危鱼片及其他鱼肉(不论是否绞碎)	12				70	13	5	千克	ABFE	Fillets and meat of fish in imminent dangers, whether or not minced, fresh or chilled
0304.1900 90	其他鲜或冷的鱼片及其他鱼肉(不论是否绞碎)	12				70	13	5	千克	AB	Fish fillets and other fish meat, whether or not minced, chilled
	-冻鱼片:										-Frozen fillets:
0304.2100	--剑鱼	10	T3		8	70	13	5	千克	AB	--Xiphias gladius
0304.2200	--南极犬牙鱼	10	T3		8	70	13	5	千克	AB	--Dissostichus SPP.
	--其他										--Other

税则号列 Tariff Item.	货品名称	最惠国(%) MFN	协定(%) CT 东盟 CA	中巴 CP	中智 CC	普通 Gen	增值税率 VAT	出口退税 ED	计量单位 Unit	监管条件 SC	Article Description
0304.2910	---罗非鱼的	10	T3		8	70	13	5	千克	AB	---Of African crucian carps (*Tilapia mossambica or Tilapia nilotica*)
	---叉尾鱼回鱼的										---Fork tail fish return to fish' s
0304.2921	----斑点叉尾鮰鱼的	10	T3		8	70	13	5	千克	AB	----Fleck Fork tail fish , return to fish's
0304.2929	----其他	10	T3		8	70	13	5	千克	AB	----Other
0304.2990	---其他鱼的	10	T3		8	70	13	5	千克		---Of other fish
0304.2990 10	冻的其他濒危鱼片(不论是否绞碎)	10				70	13	5	千克	FEAB	Fillets of other fish in imminent dangers, whether or not minced, frozen
0304.2990 90	其他冻鱼片(不论是否绞碎)	10				70	13	5	千克	AB	Other fish fillets, whether or not minced, frozen
	-其他:										-Other:
0304.9100	--剑鱼	10	T3		8	70	13	5	千克	AB	--Xiphias gladius
0304.9200	--南极犬牙鱼	10	T3		8	70	13	5	千克	AB	--Dissostichus SPP.
0304.9900	--其他:	10	T3		8	70	13	5	千克		--Other:
0304.9900 10	濒危鱼类其他冻鱼肉(不论是否绞碎)	10				70	13	5	千克	ABFE	Other meat of fish in imminent dangers, whether or not minced, chilled
0304.9900 90	其他冻鱼肉(不论是否绞碎)	10				70	13	5	千克	AB	Other fish meat, whether or not minced, frozen
03.05	**干、盐腌或盐渍的鱼;熏鱼,不论在熏制前或熏制过程中是否烹煮;适合供人食用的鱼的细粉、粗粉及团粒:**										**Fish, dried, salted or in brine; smoked fish, whether or not cooked before or during the smoking process; flours, meals and pellets of fish, fit for human consumption:**
0305.1000	-适合供人食用的鱼的细粉、粗粉及团粒	10	0		0	80	13	5	千克	AB	-Flours, meals and pellets of fish, fit for human consumption
0305.2000	-干、熏、盐腌或盐渍的鱼肝及鱼卵	10	0		8	80	13	5	千克		-Livers and roes of fish, dried, smoked, salted or in brine
0305.2000 10	干、熏、盐制的濒危鱼种肝、卵	10				80	13	5	千克	ABFE	Livers and roes of fish in imminent dangers, dried, smoked, salted or in brine
0305.2000 90	其他干、熏、盐制的鱼肝及鱼卵	10				80	13	5	千克	AB	Other Livers and roes of fish, dried, smoked, salted or in brine
0305.3000	-干、盐腌或盐渍的鱼片,但熏制的除外	10	T3	7.8	8	80	13	5	千克		-Fish fillets, dried, salted or in brine, but not smoked
0305.3000 10	干或盐制濒危鱼类的鱼片(熏制的除外)	10				80	13	5	千克	FEAB	Fish fillets of fish in imminent danger, dried, salted or in brine (not smoked)
0305.3000 90	干或盐制的其他鱼片(熏制的除外)	10				80	13	5	千克	AB	Fish fillets, dried, salted or in brine (not smoked)
	-熏鱼,包括鱼片:										-Smoked fish, including fillets:
	--大马哈鱼、大西洋鲑鱼及多瑙哲罗鱼:										--Pacific salmon (*Oncorhynchus nerka, Oncorhynchus gorbuscha, Oncorhynchus keta, Oncorhynchus tschawytscha, Oncorhynchus kisutch, Oncorhynchus masou and Oncorhynchus rhodurus*), Atlantic salmon (*Salmo salar*) and Danube salmon (*Hucho hucho*):
0305.4110	---大西洋鲑鱼	14	0		8.4	80	13	5	千克	AB	---Atlantic salmon
0305.4120	---大马哈鱼及多瑙哲罗鱼	14	0		8.4	80	13	5	千克	AB	---Pacific salmon and Danube salmon
0305.4200	--鲱鱼(大西洋鲱鱼、太平洋鲱鱼)	16	0		9.6	80	13	5	千克	AB	--Herrings (*Clupea harengus, Clupea pallasii*)

税则号列 Tariff Item.	货品名称	最惠国(%) MFN	协定(%)CT 东盟 CA	中巴 CP	中智 CC	普通 Gen	增值税率 VAT	出口退税 ED	计量单位 Unit	监管条件 SC	Article Description
0305.4900	--其他	14	0		11.2	80	13	5	千克	AB	--Other
	-干鱼,不论是否盐腌,但熏制的除外:										-Dried fish, whether or not salted but not smoked:
0305.5100	--鳕鱼	16	0		9.6	80	13	5	千克	AB	--Cod (*Gadus morhua*, *Gadus ogac*, *Gadus macrocephalus*)
	--其他:										--Other:
0305.5910	---海龙、海马	2	T3		0	20	13	5	千克	FEAB	---Pipefish and hippocampi
0305.5920	---鱼翅	15	T3		12	80	13	5	千克		---Sharks' fins
0305.5920 10	干鲸鲨、噬人鲨、姥鲨鱼翅(不论是否盐腌,但熏制的除外)	15				80	13	5	千克	FEAB	Sharks' fins of whale shark (*Rhincodon*), man-eating shark (*Cacharodon*), basking shark (*Cetorhinus*), dried, (whether or not salted but not smoked)
0305.5920 90	其他干鱼翅(不论是否盐腌,但熏制的除外)	15				80	13	5	千克	AB	Other sharks' fins, dried, (whether or not salted but not smoked)
0305.5990	---其他	16	T3		12.8	80	13	5	千克		---Other
0305.5990 10	其他濒危干鱼(不论是否盐腌,但熏制的除外)	16				80	13	5	千克	AFEB	Other fish in imminent dangers, dried (whether or not salted but not smoked)
0305.5990 90	其他干鱼(不论是否盐腌,但熏制的除外)	16				80	13	5	千克	AB	Other fish, dried (whether or not salted but not smoked)
	-盐腌及盐渍的鱼,但干或熏制的除外:										-Fish, salted but not dried nor smoked and fish in brine:
0305.6100	--鲱鱼(大西洋鲱鱼、太平洋鲱鱼)	16	0	11.1	9.6	80	13	5	千克	AB	--Herrings (*Clupea harengus*, *Clupea pallasii*)
0305.6200	--鳕鱼	16	0	12	9.6	80	13	5	千克	AB	--Cod (*Gadus morhua*, *Gadus ogac*, *Gadus Macrocephalus*)
0305.6300	--鳀鱼	16	T3	12	12.8	80	13	5	千克	AB	--Anchovies (*Engraulis spp.*)
	--其他:										--Other:
0305.6910	---带鱼	16	T3		12.8	80	13	5	千克	AB	---Scabber fish (*Trichurius*)
0305.6920	---黄鱼	16	T3		12.8	80	13	5	千克	AB	---Yellow croaker (*Pseudosicaena*)
0305.6930	---鲳鱼	16	T3		12.8	80	13	5	千克	AB	---Butterfish (*Pampus*)
0305.6940	---罗非鱼	16	T3		12.8	80	13	5	千克	AB	---*Tilapia*
0305.6990	---其他	16	T3		12.8	80	13	5	千克		---Other
0305.6990 10	盐腌及盐渍的其他濒危鱼(干或熏制的除外)	16				80	13	5	千克	ABFE	Other fish in imminent dangers, salted or in brine (not dried nor smoked)
0305.6990 90	盐腌及盐渍的其他鱼(干或熏制的除外)	16				80	13	5	千克	AB	Other fish, salted or in brine (not dried nor smoked)
03.06	**带壳或去壳的甲壳动物,活、鲜、冷、冻、干、盐腌或盐渍的;蒸过或用水煮过的带壳甲壳动物,不论是否冷、冻、干、盐腌或盐渍的;适合供人食用的甲壳动物的细粉、粗粉及团粒:**										**Crustaceans, whether in shell or not, live, fresh, chilled, frozen, dried, salted or in brine; crustaceans, in shell, cooked by steaming or by boiling in water, whether or not chilled, frozen, dried, salted or in brine; flours, meals and pellets of crustaceans, fit for human consumption:**
	-冻的:										-Frozen:
0306.1100	--龙虾	10	0		0	70	13	5	千克	AB	--Rock lobster and other sea crawfish (*Palinurus spp.*, *Panulirus spp.*, *Jasus spp.*)
0306.1200	--大螯虾	10	0	7.2	0	70	13	5	千克	AB	--Lobsters (*Homarus spp.*)

税则号列 Tariff Item.	货品名称	最惠国(%) MFN	协定(%)CT 东盟 CA	中巴 CP	中智 CC	普通 Gen	增值税率 VAT	出口退税 ED	计量单位 Unit	监管条件 SC	Article Description
	--小虾及对虾:										--Shrimps and prawns:
	---小虾:										---Shrimps:
0306.1311	----虾仁	8	T3	4	0	70	13	5	千克	AB	----Shelled
0306.1312	----北方长额虾	5	T3	2.5	0	70	13	5	千克	AB	----Northem pandalus (*Pandalus*)
0306.1319	----其他	5	T3	2.5	0	70	13	5	千克	AB	----Other
	---对虾:										---Prawns:
0306.1321	----虾仁	8	T3	4	0	70	13	5	千克	AB	----Shelled
0306.1329	----其他	5	T3	2.5	3	70	13	5	千克	AB	----Other
	--蟹:										--Crabs:
0306.1410	---梭子蟹	10	T3		8	70	13	5	千克	AB	---Swimming crab
0306.1490	---其他	10	T3		8	70	13	5	千克	AB	---Other
	--其他,包括适合供人食用的甲壳动物的细粉、粗粉及团粒:										--Other, including flours, meals and pellets of crustaceans, fit for human consumption:
	---淡水小龙虾:										---Freshwater crawfish:
0306.1911	----虾仁	16	T3		0	70	13	5	千克	aAB	----Shelled
0306.1919	----其他	16	T3		0	70	13	5	千克	aAB	----Other
0306.1990	---其他	16	T3		12.8	70	13	5	千克	AB	---Other
	-未冻的:										-Not frozen:
	--龙虾:										--Rock lobster and other sea crawfish (*Palinurus spp.*, *Panulirus spp.*, *Jasus spp.*):
0306.2110	---种苗	0				0	13	5	千克	AB	---For cultivation
0306.2190	---其他	15	0		0	70	13	5	千克	AB	---Other
	--大螯虾:										--Lobsters (*Homarus spp.*):
0306.2210	---种苗	0				0	13	5	千克	AB	---For cultivation
0306.2290	---其他	15	0		0	70	13	5	千克	AB	---Other
	--小虾及对虾:										--Shrimps and prawns:
0306.2310	---种苗	0				0	13	5	千克	AB	---For cultivation
	---其他:										---Other:
0306.2391	----鲜、冷对虾	15	T3		0	70	13	5	千克	AB	----Prawns, fresh or chilled
0306.2399	----其他	12	T3		0	70	13	5	千克		----Other
0306.2399 01	鲜、冷小虾	12				70	13	5	千克	AB	Shrimps, fresh or chilled
0306.2399 90	活、干、盐腌或超车渍的带壳或去壳对虾小虾(及蒸过用水煮过的带壳对虾,小虾,不论是否干、盐腌或盐渍)	12				70	13	5	千克	AB	Alive, dried or salted shrimps and boiled or steamed shrimpos with or without shells
	--蟹:										--Crabs:
0306.2410	---种苗	0				0	13	5	千克	AB	---For cultivation
	---其他:										---Other:
0306.2491	----中华绒螯蟹	14	T3		11.2	70	13	5	千克	AB	----Freshwater crabs, live
0306.2492	----梭子蟹	14	T3		11.2	70	13	5	千克	AB	----Swimming crab
0306.2499	----其他	14	T3		11.2	70	13	5	千克	AB	----Other
	--其他,包括适合供人食用的甲壳动物的细粉、粗粉及团粒:										--Other, including flours, meals and pellets of crustaceans, fit for human consumption:
0306.2910	---种苗	0				0	13	5	千克	AB	---For cultivation
0306.2990	---其他	14	0		11.2	70	13	5	千克	AB	---Other

税则号列 Tariff Item.	货品名称	最惠国(%) MFN	协定(%)CT 东盟 CA	 中巴 CP	 中智 CC	普通 Gen	增值税率 VAT	出口退税 ED	计量单位 Unit	监管条件 SC	Article Description
03.07	**带壳或去壳的软体动物,活、鲜、冷、冻、干、盐腌或盐渍的;不属于甲壳动物和软体动物的水生无脊椎动物,活、鲜、冷、冻、干、盐腌或盐渍的;适合供人食用的水生无脊椎动物(甲壳动物除外)的细粉、粗粉及团粒:**										**Molluscs, whether in shell or not, live, fresh, chilled, frozen, dried, salted or in brine; aquatic invertebrates other than crustaceans and molluscs, live, fresh, chilled, frozen, dried, salted or in brine; flours, meals and pellets of aquatic invertebrates other than crustaceans, fit for human consumption:**
	-牡蛎(蚝):										-Oysters:
0307.1010	---种苗	0				0	13	5	千克	AB	---For cultivation
0307.1090	---其他	14	0		11.2	70	13	5	千克	AB	---Other
	-扇贝,包括海扇:										-Scallops, including queen scallops, of the genera *Pecten*, *Chlamys or Placopecten*:
	--活、鲜或冷的:										--Live, fresh or chilled:
0307.2110	---种苗	0				0	13	5	千克		---For cultivation
0307.2110 10	大珠母贝种苗	0				0	13	5	千克	ABE	Giant pearl shell (Pinctada maxima), for cultivation
0307.2110 90	其他扇贝种苗(包括海扇种苗)	0				0	13	5	千克	AB	Other scallops, including queen scallops, for cultivation
0307.2190	---其他	14	0		11.2	70	13	5	千克		---Other
0307.2190 10	其他活、鲜冷大珠母贝	14				70	13	5	千克	ABE	Giant pearl shell (Pinctada maxima), live, live fresh or chilled
0307.2190 90	其他活、鲜、冷扇贝(包括海扇,种苗除外)	14				70	13	5	千克	AB	Other scallops (including queen scallops), chilled, excluding for cultivation
0307.2900	--其他	14	0		11.2	80	13	5	千克		--Other
0307.2900 10	其他冻、干、盐腌或盐渍的大珠母贝	14				80	13	5	千克	ABE	Other Giant pearl shell (Pinctada maxima), frozen, dried, salted or in brine
0307.2900 90	其他冻、干、盐腌或盐渍的扇贝(包括海扇)	14				80	13	5	千克	AB	Other other scallops (including queen scallops), frozen, dried, salted or in brine
	-贻贝:										-Mussels (*Mytilus spp.*, *Perna spp.*):
	--活、鲜或冷的:										--Live, fresh or chilled:
0307.3110	---种苗	0				0	13	5	千克	AB	---For cultivation
0307.3190	---其他	14	0		8.4	70	13	5	千克		---Other
0307.3190 01	鲜冷贻贝	14				70	13	5	千克	AB	Mussels, fresh or chilled
0307.3190 90	其他活贻贝	14				70	13	5	千克	AB	Other mussels, live
0307.3900	--其他	14	0	9.8	11.2	70	13	5	千克		--Other
0307.3900 01	冻贻贝	14				70	13	5	千克	AB	Mussels, frozen
0307.3900 90	其他干、盐腌或盐渍的贻贝	14				70	13	5	千克	AB	Other mussels, dried, salted or in brine
	-墨鱼及鱿鱼:										-Cuttle fish (*Sepia officinalis*, *Rossia macrosoma*, *Sepiola spp.*) and squid (*Ommastrephes spp.*, *Loligo spp.*, *Nototodarus spp.*, *Sepioteuthis spp.*):
	--活、鲜或冷的:										--Live, fresh or chilled:
0307.4110	---种苗	0				0	13	5	千克	AB	---For cultivation

税则号列 Tariff Item.	货 品 名 称	最惠国(%) MFN	协定(%) 东盟 CA	中巴 CP	CT 中智 CC	普通 Gen	增值税率 VAT	出口退税 ED	计量单位 Unit	监管条件 SC	Article Description
0307.4190	---其他	12	0		9.6	70	13	5	千克	AB	---Other
0307.4900	--其他	12	0	10	9.6	70	13	5	千克	AB	--Other
	-章鱼:										-Octopus (*Octopus spp.*):
0307.5100	--活、鲜或冷的	17	0		13.6	70	13	5	千克	AB	--Live, fresh or chilled
0307.5900	--其他	17	0		13.6	70	13	5	千克	AB	--Other
	-蜗牛及螺:										-Snails, other than sea snails:
0307.6010	---种苗	0					13	5	千克		---For cultivation
0307.6010 10	濒危蜗牛及螺种苗	0				0	13	5	千克	ABFE	Snails other than sea snails in imminent dangers, for cultivation
0307.6010 90	其他蜗牛及螺种苗	0				0	13	5	千克	AB	Other snails other than sea snails, for cultivation
0307.6090	---其他	14	0		8.4	70	13	5	千克		---Other
0307.6090 10	其他濒危蜗牛及螺	14				70	13	5	千克	ABFE	Other snails other than sea snails in imminent dangers, for cultivation
0307.6090 90	其他蜗牛及螺(活、鲜、冷、冻、干、盐腌或盐渍的)	14				70	13	5	千克	AB	Other snails other than sea snails, live, fresh, chilled, frozen, dried, salted or in brine
	-其他,包括适合供人食用的水生无脊椎动物(甲壳动物除外)的细粉、粗粉及团粒:										-Other, including flours, meals and pellets of aquatic invertebrates other than crustaceans, fit for human consumption:
	--活、鲜或冷的:										--Live, fresh or chilled:
0307.9110	---种苗	0				0	13	5	千克		---For cultivation
0307.9110 10	濒危水生无脊椎动物的种苗(不包括甲壳动物的种苗)	0				0	13	5	千克	AFEB	Aquatic invertebrates, in imminent dangers, for cultivation, excluding crustaceans for cultivation
0307.9110 90	其他水生无脊椎动物的种苗(不包括甲壳动物的种苗)	0				0	13	5	千克	AB	Other aquatic invertebrates for cultivation (excluding crustaceans for cultivation)
	---其他:										---Other:
0307.9191	----鲍鱼	14	0		11.2	80	13	5	千克	AB	----Abalone
0307.9192	----沙蚕	14	0		11.2	70	13	5	千克	AB	----Clamworm
0307.9193	----蛤	14	0		11.2	70	13	5	千克	AB	----clams
0307.9199	----其他	14	0		11.2	70	13	5	千克		----Other
0307.9199 10	其他濒危活、鲜、冷水生无脊椎动物(鲍鱼除外)	14				70	13	5	千克	ABFE	Other aquatic invertebrates in imminent dangers, live, fresh or chilled (other than abalon)
0307.9199 90	其他活、鲜水生无脊椎动物(鲍鱼除外)	14				70	13	5	千克	AB	Other aquatic invertebrates, live, fresh (other than abalon)
	--其他:										--Other:
0307.9910	---鲍鱼	10	0		8	80	13	5	千克	AB	---Abalone
0307.9920	---海参	10	0		8	80	13	5	千克	AB	---Sea cucumbers (*beches-de-mer*)
0307.9920 10	冻、干、盐腌、盐渍加拉帕戈斯海参	10				80	13	5	千克	ABFE	Galapagos sea cucumber (*beches-de-mer*), frozen, dried, salted or in brine
0307.9920 90	其他冻、干、盐腌或盐渍的海参	10				80	13	5	千克	AB	Other sea cucumbers (*beches-de-mer*), frozen, dried, salted or in brine
0307.9930	---蛤	10	0		8	70	13	5	千克	AB	---clams
0307.9990	---其他	10	0		8	70	13	5	千克		---Other

税则号列 Tariff Item.	货品名称	最惠国(%) MFN	协定(%)CT 东盟 CA	中巴 CP	中智 CC	普通 Gen	增值税率 VAT	出口退税 ED	计量单位 Unit	监管条件 SC	Article Description
0307.9990 10	其他冻干盐制濒危水生无脊椎动物(包括供人食用的水生无脊椎动物粉、团粒,甲壳动物除外)	10				70	13	5	千克	ABFE	Other aquatic invertebrates, in imminent dangers, frozen, dried, salted or in brine (including flours, meals and pellets of aquatic invertebrates, other than crustaceans, fit for human consumption)
0307.9990 90	其他冻、干、盐制水生无脊椎动物(包括供人食用的水生无脊椎动物粉、团粒,甲壳动物除外)	10				70	13	5	千克	AB	Other aquatic invertebrates, frozen, dried, salted or in brine, (including flours, meals and pellets of aquatic invertebrates, other than crustaceans, fit for human consumption)

第四章
乳品；蛋品；天然蜂蜜；其他食用动物产品

注释：

一、所称"乳"，是指全脂乳及半脱脂或全脱脂的乳。

二、税目04.05所称：

（一）"黄油"，仅指从乳中提取的天然黄油、乳清黄油及调制黄油（新鲜、加盐或酸败的，包括罐装黄油），按重量计乳脂含量在80%及以上，但不超过95%，乳的无脂固形物最大含量不超过2%，以及水的最大含量不超过16%。黄油中不含添加的乳化剂，但可含有氯化钠、食用色素、中和盐及无害乳酸菌的培养物。

（二）"乳酱"是一种油包水型可涂抹的乳状物，乳脂是该制品所含的唯一脂肪，按重量计其含量在39%及以上，但小于80%。

三、乳清经浓缩并加入乳或乳脂制成的产品，若同时具有下列三种特性，则视为乳酪归入税目04.06：

（一）按干重计乳脂含量在5%及以上的；

（二）按重量计干质成分至少为70%，但不超过85%的；

（三）已成形或可以成形的。

四、本章不包括：

（一）按重量计乳糖含量（以干燥无水乳糖计）超过95%的乳清制品（税目17.02）；

（二）白蛋白（包括按重量计干质成分的乳清蛋白含量超过80%的两种或两种以上的乳清蛋白浓缩物）（税目35.02）及球蛋白（税目35.04）。

子目注释：

一、子目0404.10所称"改性乳清"，是指由乳清成分构成的制品，即全部或部分去除乳糖、蛋白或矿物质的乳清、加入天然乳清成分的乳清及由混入天然乳清成分制成的产品。

二、子目0405.10所称"黄油"，不包括脱水黄油及印度酥油（子目0405.90）。

Chapter 4
Dairy produce; birds' eggs; natural honey; edible products of animal origin, not elsewhere specified or included

Notes:

1. The expression "milk" means full cream milk or partially or completely skimmed milk.
2. For the purposes of heading No. 04.05:

(a) The term "butter" means natural butter, whey butter or recombined butter (fresh, salted or rancid, including canned butter) derived exclusively from milk, with a milkfat content of 80% or more but not more than 95% by weight, a maximum milk solids-not-fat content of 2% by weight and a maximum water content of 16% by weight. Butter does not contain emulsifiers, but may contain sodium chloride, food colours, neutralizing salts and cultures of harmless lactic-acid-producing bacteria.

(b) The expression "dairy spreads" means a spreadable emulsion of the water-in-oil type, containing milkfat as the only fat in the product, with a milkfat content of 39% or more but less than 80% by weight.

3. Products obtained by the concentration of whey and with the addition of milk or milkfat are to be classified as cheese in heading No. 04.06. Provided that they have the three following characteristics:

(a) A milkfat content, by weight of the dry matter, of 5% or more;

(b) A dry matter content, by weight, of at least 70% but not exceeding 85%; and

(c) They are moulded or capable of being moulded.

4. This Chapter does not cover:

(a) Products obtained from whey, containing by weight more than 95% lactose, expressed as anhydrous lactose calculated on the dry matter (heading No. 17.02); or

(b) Albumins (including concentrates of two or more whey proteins, containing by weight more than 80% whey proteins, calculated on the dry matter) (heading No. 35.02) or globulins (heading No. 35.04)

Subheading Notes:

1. For the purposes of subheading No. 0404.10, the expression "modified whey" means products consisting of whey constituents, i.e., whey from which all or part of the lactose, proteins or minerals have been removed, whey to which natural whey constituents have been added and products obtained by mixing natural whey constituents.
2. For the purposes of subheading No. 0405.10 the term "butter" does not include dehydrated butter or ghee (subheading No. 0405.90).

税则号列 Tariff Item.	货品名称	最惠国(%) MFN	协定(%) CT 东盟 CA	中巴 CP	中智 CC	普通 Gen	增值税率 VAT	出口退税 ED	计量单位 Unit	监管条件 SC	Article Description
04.01	未浓缩及未加糖或其他甜物质的乳及奶油：										**Milk and cream, not concentrated nor containing added sugar or other sweetening matter:**

税则号列 Tariff Item.	货品名称	最惠国(%) MFN	协定(%) CT			普通 Gen	增值税率 VAT	出口退税 ED	计量单位 Unit	监管条件 SC	Article Description
			东盟 CA	中巴 CP	中智 CC						
0401.1000	-按重量计脂肪含量不超过1%	15	0		12	40	17	13	千克	AB	-Of a fat content, by weight, not exceeding 1%
0401.2000	-按重量计脂肪含量超过1%,但不超过6%	15	0		12	40	17	13	千克	AB	-Of a fat content, by weight, exceeding 1% but not exceeding 6%
0401.3000	-按重量计脂肪含量超过6%	15	0		12	40	17	13	千克	AB	-Of a fat content, by weight, exceeding 6%
04.02	**浓缩、加糖或其他甜物质的乳及奶油:**										**Milk and cream, concentrated or containing added sugar or other sweetening matter:**
0402.1000	-粉状、粒状或其他固体形状,按重量计脂肪含量不超过1.5%	10	0	7	8	40	17	13	千克	AB	-In powder, granules or other solid forms, of a fat content, by weight, not exceeding 1.5%
	-粉状、粒状或其他固体形状,按重量计脂肪含量超过1.5%:										-In powder, granules or other solid forms, of a fat content, by weight, exceeding 1.5%:
0402.2100	--未加糖或其他甜物质	10	0	7	8	40	17	13	千克	AB	--Not containing added sugar or other sweetening matter
0402.2900	--其他	10	0		8	40	17	13	千克	AB	--Other
	-其他:										-Other:
0402.9100	--未加糖或其他甜物质	10	0		8	90	17	13	千克	AB	--Not containing added sugar or other sweetening matter
0402.9900	--其他	10	0		8	90	17	13	千克	AB	--Other
04.03	**酪乳、结块的乳及奶油、酸乳、酸乳酒及其他发酵或酸化的乳和奶油,不论是否浓缩、加糖、加其他甜物质、加香料、加水果、加坚果或加可可:**										**Buttermilk, curdled milk and cream, yogurt, kephir and other fermented or acidified milk and cream, whether or not concentrated or containing added sugar or other sweetening matter or flavoured or containing added fruit, nuts or cocoa:**
0403.1000	-酸乳	10	0		8	90	17	13	千克	AB	-Yogurt
0403.9000	-其他	20	0		16	90	17	13	千克	AB	-Other
04.04	**乳清,不论是否浓缩、加糖或其他甜物质;其他税目未列名的含天然乳的产品,不论是否加糖或其他甜物质:**										**Whey, whether or not concentrated or containing added sugar or other sweetening matter; products consisting of natural milk constituents, whether or not containing added sugar or other sweetening matter, not elsewhere specified or included:**
0404.1000	-乳清及改性乳清,不论是否浓缩、加糖或其他甜物质	6	0		0	30	17	13	千克	AB	-Whey and modified whey, whether or not concentrated or containing added sugar or other sweetening matter
0404.9000	-其他	20	0		12	90	17	13	千克	AB	-Other
04.05	**黄油及其他从乳中提取的脂和油;乳酱:**										**Butter and other fats and oils derived from milk; dairy spreads:**
0405.1000	-黄油	10	0		8	90	17	13	千克	AB	-Butter
0405.2000	-乳酱	10	0	8.1	0	90	17	13	千克	AB	-Dairy spreads
0405.9000	-其他	10	0		0	90	17	13	千克	AB	-Other
04.06	**乳酪及凝乳:**										**Cheese and curd:**

税则号列 Tariff Item.	货品名称	最惠国(%) MFN	协定(%)CT 东盟 CA	协定(%)CT 中巴 CP	协定(%)CT 中智 CC	普通 Gen	增值税率 VAT	出口退税 ED	计量单位 Unit	监管条件 SC	Article Description
0406.1000	-鲜乳酪(未熟化或未固化的),包括乳清乳酪;凝乳	12	0		9.6	90	17	13	千克	AB	-Fresh (unripened or uncured) cheese, including whey cheese, and curd
0406.2000	-各种磨碎或粉化的乳酪	12	0		0	90	17	13	千克	AB	-Grated or powdered cheese, of all kinds
0406.3000	-经加工的乳酪,但磨碎或粉化的除外	12	0		7.2	90	17	13	千克	AB	-Processed cheese, not grated or powdered
0406.4000	-蓝纹乳酪及娄地青霉生产的带纹理的其他乳酪	15	0		9	90	17	13	千克	AB	-Blue cheese and other colored cheese produced by P. roquefortin
0406.9000	-其他乳酪	12	0		7.2	90	17	13	千克	AB	-Other cheese
04.07	**带壳禽蛋,鲜、腌制或煮过的:**										**Birds' eggs, in shell, fresh, preserved or cooked:**
0407.0010	---种用蛋	0				0	13	5	个/千克		---For hatching
0407.0010 10	种用濒危野禽蛋	0				0	13	5	个/千克	AFEB	Wild birds' eggs, for hatching, in imminent dangers
0407.0010 90	种用禽蛋	0				0	13	5	个/千克	AB	Birds' eggs, for hatching
	---其他带壳鲜蛋:										---Other, in shell, fresh:
0407.0021	----鸡蛋	20	T3		0	80	13	5	个/千克	AB	----Of hens
0407.0022	----鸭蛋	20	T3		0	80	13	5	个/千克	AB	----Of ducks
0407.0023	----鹅蛋	20	T3		0	80	13	5	个/千克	AB	----Of geese
0407.0029	----其他	20	T3		0	80	13	5	个/千克		----Other
0407.0029 10	其他带壳鲜濒危野鸟卵	20				80	13	5	个/千克	ABFE	Other wild birds' eggs in shell, fresh, in imminent dangers
0407.0029 90	其他带壳鲜禽蛋	20				80	13	5	个/千克	AB	Other birds' eggs in shell, fresh
	---其他:										---Other:
0407.0091	----咸蛋	20	T3		0	90	13	5	个/千克	AB	----Salted eggs
0407.0092	----皮蛋	20	T3		0	90	13	5	个/千克	AB	----Lime-preserved eggs
0407.0099	----其他	20	T3		0	90	13	5	个/千克		----Other
0407.0099 10	其他腌制或煮过的带壳濒危野鸟卵	20				90	13	5	个/千克	ABFE	Other wild birds' eggs, in shell, preserved or cooked, in imminent dangers
0407.0099 90	其他腌制或煮过的带壳禽蛋	20				90	13	5	个/千克	AB	Other birds' eggs, in shell, preserved or cooked
04.08	**去壳禽蛋及蛋黄,鲜、干、冻、蒸过或水煮、制成型或用其他方法保藏的,不论是否加糖或其他甜物质:**										**Birds' eggs, not in shell, and egg yolks, fresh, dried, cooked by steaming or by boiling in water, moulded, frozen or otherwise preserved, whether or not containing added sugar or other sweetening matter:**
	-蛋黄:										-Egg yolks:
0408.1100	--干的	20	T3		12	90	13	5	千克	AB	--Dried
0408.1900	--其他	20	T3		12	90	13	5	千克	AB	--Other
	-其他:										-Other:
0408.9100	--干的	20	T3		16	90	13	5	千克	AB	--Dried
0408.9900	--其他	20	T3		12	90	13	5	千克	AB	--Other
04.09	**天然蜂蜜:**										**Natural honey:**
0409.0000	天然蜂蜜	15	T3		12	80	13	5	千克	aAB	Natural honey
04.10	**其他税目未列名的食用动物产品:**										**Edible products of animal origin, not elsewhere specified or included:**
0410.0010	---燕窝	25	0		15	80	17	5	千克	AB	---Salanganes' nests
	---蜂产品										---Bee products:
0410.0041	----鲜蜂王浆	15	0		9	70	13	5	千克	aAB	----Pure royal jelley

税则号列 Tariff Item.	货 品 名 称	最惠国(%) MFN	协定(%) CT 东盟 CA	中巴 CP	中智 CC	普通 Gen	增值税率 VAT	出口退税 ED	计量单位 Unit	监管条件 SC	Article Description
0410.0042	----鲜蜂王浆粉	15	0		9	70	17	5	千克	aAB	----Pure royal jelley, in powder
0410.0043	----蜂花粉	20	0		12	70	17	5	千克	AB	----Bee pollen
0410.0049	----其他	20	0		12	70	17	5	千克	AB	----Other
0410.0090	---其他	20	0		12	70	17	5	千克		---Other
0410.0090 10	其他编号未列名濒危野生动物产品(食用)	20				70	17	5	千克	ABFE	Other edible products of wild animal origin, not elsewhere specified or included, in imminent dangers
0410.0090 90	其他编号未列名的食用动物产品	20				70	17	5	千克	AB	Other edible products of animal origin, not elsewhere specified or included

第五章 其他动物产品

Chapter 5 Products of animal origin, not elsewhere specified or included

注释:

一、本章不包括:

(一)食用产品(整个或切块的动物肠、膀胱和胃以及液态或干制的动物血除外);

(二)生皮或毛皮(第四十一章、第四十三章),但税目05.05的货品及税目05.11的生皮或毛皮的边角废料仍归入本章;

(三)马毛及废马毛以外的动物纺织原料(第十一类);

(四)供制帚、制刷用的成束、成簇的材料(税目96.03)。

二、仅按长度而未按发根和发梢整理的人发,视为未加工品,归入税目05.01。

三、本目录所称"兽牙",是指象、河马、海象、一角鲸和野猪的长牙、犀角及其他动物的牙齿。

四、本目录所称"马毛",是指马科、牛科动物的鬃毛和尾毛。

Notes:

1. This Chapter does not cover:
   (a) Edible products (other than guts, bladders and stomachs of animals, whole and pieces thereof, and animal blood, liquid or dried);
   (b) Hides or skins (including furskins) other than goods of heading No. 05.05 and parings and similar waste of raw hides or skins of heading No. 05.11 (Chapter 41 or 43)
   (c) Animal textile materials, other than horsehair and horsehair waste (Section XI); or
   (d) Prepared knots or tufts for broom or brush making (heading No. 96.03).
2. For the purposes of heading No. 05.01, the sorting of human hair by length (provided the root ends and tip ends respectively are not arranged together) shall be deemed not to constitute working.
3. Throughout the Nomenclature, elephant, hippopotamus, walrus, narwhal and wild boar tusks, rhinoceros horns and the teeth of all animals are regarded as "ivory".
4. Throughout the Nomenclature, the expression "horsehair" means hair of the manes or tails of equine or bovine animals.

税则号列 Tariff Item.	货品名称	最惠国(%) MFN	协定(%) CT 东盟 CA	中巴 CP	中智 CC	普通 Gen	增值税率 VAT	出口退税 ED	计量单位 Unit	监管条件 SC	Article Description
05.01	**未经加工的人发,不论是否洗涤;废人发:**										**Human hair, unworked, whether or not washed or scoured; waste of human hair:**
0501.0000	未经加工的人发,不论是否洗涤;废人发	15	0		9	90	17	13	千克	B9	Human hair, unworked, whether or not washed or scoured; waste of human hair
05.02	**猪鬃、猪毛;獾毛及其他制刷用兽毛;上述鬃毛的废料:**										**Pigs', hogs' or boars' bristles and hair; badger hair and other brush making hair; waste of such bristles or hair:**
	-猪鬃、猪毛及其废料:										-Pigs', hogs' or boars' bristles and hair and waste thereof:
0502.1010	---猪鬃	20	0		12	90	13	5	千克	AB	---Bristles
0502.1020	---猪毛	20	0		12	90	13	5	千克	AB	---Hair
0502.1030	---废料	20	0		12	90	13	5	千克	B9	---Waste
	-其他:										-Other:
	---獾毛及其他制刷用兽毛:										---Badger hair and other brush making hair:
0502.9011	----山羊毛	20	0		12	90	13	5	千克	AB	----Goat hair
0502.9012	----黄鼠狼尾毛	20	0		12	90	13	5	千克	AB	----Weasel tail hair
0502.9019	----其他	20	0		12	90	13	5	千克		----Other
0502.9019 10	濒危獾毛及其他制刷用濒危兽毛	20				90	13	5	千克	ABFE	Badger hair and other brush making hair of animal in imminent dangers
0502.9019 90	其他獾毛及其他制刷用兽毛	20				90	13	5	千克	AB	Other badger hair and other brush making hair
0502.9020	---废料	20	0		12	90	13	5	千克		---Waste

税则号列 Tariff Item.	货品名称	最惠国(%) MFN	协定(%) CT 东盟 CA	中巴 CP	中智 CC	普通 Gen	增值税率 VAT	出口退税 ED	计量单位 Unit	监管条件 SC	Article Description
0502.9020 10	濒危獾毛及其他制刷濒危兽毛废料	20				90	13	5	千克	9BE	Waste of badger hair and other brush making hair of animal in imminent dangers
0502.9020 90	其他獾毛及其他制刷用兽毛的废料	20				90	13	5	千克	B9	Waste of badger hair and other brush making hair
05.04	**整个或切块的动物(鱼除外)的肠、膀胱及胃,鲜、冷、冻、干、熏、盐腌或盐渍的:**										**Guts, bladders and stomachs of animals (other than fish), whole and pieces thereof, fresh, chilled, frozen, salted, in brine, dried or smoked:**
	---肠衣:										---Casings:
0504.0011	----盐渍猪肠衣(猪大肠头除外)	20	0	10	16	90	13	13	千克	AB	----Hog casings, salted
0504.0012	----盐渍绵羊肠衣	18	0	9	14.4	90	13	13	千克	AB	----Sheep casings, salted
0504.0013	----盐渍山羊肠衣	18	0	9	14.4	90	13	13	千克	AB	----Goat casings, salted
0504.0014	----盐渍猪大肠头	20	0	10	16	90	13	13	千克	AB	----Hog fat-ends, salted
0504.0019	----其他	18	0	9	14.4	90	13	13	千克	AB	----Other
	---胃:										---Gizzard:
0504.0021	----冷、冻的鸡胗	T2	0	T2	T2	T2	13	5	千克	7AB	----Cold, frozen gizzard
0504.0029	----其他	20	0	10	16	90	13	5	千克	AB	----Other
0504.0090	---其他	20	0	10	16	80	13	5	千克	AB	---Other
05.05	**带有羽毛或羽绒的鸟皮及鸟体其他部分;羽毛及不完整羽毛(不论是否修边)、羽绒,仅经洗涤、消毒或为了保藏而作过处理,但未经进一步加工;羽毛或不完整羽毛的粉末及废料:**										**Skins and other parts of birds, with their feathers or down; feathers and parts of feathers (whether or not with trimmed edges) and down, not further worked than cleaned, disinfected or treated for preservation; powder and waste of feathers or parts of feathers:**
0505.1000	-填充用羽毛;羽绒	10	0	7.5	0	100	13	5	千克		-Feathers of a kind used for stuffing; down
0505.1000 10	填充用濒危野生禽类羽毛;羽绒(仅经洗涤、消毒等处理,未进一步加工)	10				100	13	5	千克	ABFE	Feathers of wild birds in imminent dangers, of a kind used for stuffing; down, not further worked than cleaned, disinfected or treated for preservation
0505.1000 90	其他填充用羽毛;羽绒(仅经洗涤、消毒等处理,未进一步加工)	10				100	13	5	千克	AB	Feathers of other birds, of a kind used for stuffing; down, not further worked than cleaned, disinfected or treated for preservation
	-其他:										-Other:
0505.9010	---羽毛或不完整羽毛的粉末及废料	10	0		0	35	13	5	千克	AB	---Powder and waste of feathers or parts of feathers
0505.9090	---其他	10	0		0	90	13	5	千克		---Other
0505.9090 10	其他濒危野生禽类羽毛、羽绒(包括带有羽毛或羽绒的鸟皮及鸟体的其他部分)	10				90	13	5	千克	AFEB	Feathers and down of wild birds in imminent dangers (including skins and other parts of birds, with their feathers or down)
0505.9090 90	其他羽毛、羽绒(包括带有羽毛或羽绒的鸟皮及鸟体的其他部分)	10				90	13	5	千克	AB	Feathers and down of other birds (including skins and other parts of birds, with their feathers or down)

税则号列 Tariff Item.	货品名称	最惠国(%) MFN	协定(%)CT 东盟 CA	中巴 CP	中智 CC	普通 Gen	增值税率 VAT	出口退税 ED	计量单位 Unit	监管条件 SC	Article Description
05.06	**骨及角柱,未经加工或经脱脂、简单整理(但未切割成形)、酸处理或脱胶;上述产品的粉末及废料:**										**Bones and horn-cores, unworked, defatted, simply prepared (but not cut to shape), treated with acid or degelatinized; powder and waste of these products:**
0506.1000	-经酸处理的骨胶原及骨	12	0		7.2	50	17		千克	AB	-Ossein and bones treated with acid
	-其他:										-Other:
	---骨粉、骨废料:										---Powder and waste of bones:
0506.9011	----含牛羊成分的	12	0		9.6	35	17		千克		----Of bovine and sheep
0506.9011 10	含牛羊成分的骨废料(未经加工或仅经脱脂等加工的)	12				35	17		千克	ABP	Waste of bones, containing bovine composition or sheep and goats thereof, unworked, defatted, simply prepared
0506.9011 90	含牛羊成分的骨粉(未经加工或仅经脱脂等加工的)	12				35	17		千克	AB	Powder of bones, containing bovine composition or sheep and goats thereof, unworked, defatted, simply prepared
0506.9019	----其他	12	0		9.6	35	17		千克		----Other
0506.9019 10	其他骨废料(未经加工或仅经脱脂等加工的)	12				35	17		千克	ABP	Other waste of bones, unworked, defatted, simply prepared
0506.9019 90	其他骨粉(未经加工或仅经脱脂等加工的)	12				35	17		千克	AB	Other powder of bones, unworked, defatted, simply prepared
0506.9090	---其他	12	0		9.6	50	13		千克		---Other
0506.9090 11	已脱胶的虎骨(指未经加工或经脱脂等加工的)	12				50	13		千克	89	Tiger-bone (*as tigris*), degelatinized, unworked, defatted, simply prepared
0506.9090 19	未脱胶的虎骨(指未经加工或经脱脂等加工的)	12				50	13		千克	89	Tiger-bone (*as tigirs*), not degelatinized, unworked, defatted, simply prepared
0506.9090 21	已脱胶的豹骨(指未经加工或经脱脂等加工的)	12				50	13		千克	ABFE	Leopard-bone, degelatinized, unworked, defatted, simply prepared
0506.9090 29	未脱胶的豹骨(指未经加工或经脱脂等加工的)	12				50	13		千克	ABFE	Leopard-bone, not degelatinized, unworked, defatted, simply prepared
0506.9090 31	已脱胶的濒危野生动物的骨及角柱(不包括虎骨、豹骨、指未经加工或经脱脂等加工的)	12				50	13		千克	AFEB	Bones and horn-cores of wild animals in imminent dangers, degelatinized (other than tiger-bone, leopard-bone, unworked, defatted, simply prepared)
0506.9090 39	未脱胶的濒危野生动物的骨及角柱(不包括虎骨、豹骨、指未经加工或经脱脂等加工的)	12				50	13		千克	AFEB	Bones and horn-cores of wild animals in imminent dangers, not degelatinized (other than tiger-bone, leopard-bone, unworked, defatted, simply prepared)
0506.9090 91	已脱胶的其他骨及角柱(不包括虎骨、豹骨、指未经加工或经脱脂等加工的)	12				50	13		千克	AB	Bones and horn-cores of other animals, degelatinized (other than tiger-bone, leopard-bone, unworked, defatted, simply prepared)
0506.9090 99	未脱胶的其他骨及角柱(不包括虎骨、豹骨、指未经加工或经脱脂等加工的)	12				50	13		千克	AB	Bones and horn-cores of other animals, not degelatinized (other than tiger-bone, leopard-bone, unworked, defatted, simply prepared)

税则号列 Tariff Item.	货品名称	最惠国(%) MFN	协定(%)CT 东盟 CA	中巴 CP	中智 CC	普通 Gen	增值税率 VAT	出口退税 ED	计量单位 Unit	监管条件 SC	Article Description
05.07	**兽牙、龟壳、鲸须、鲸须毛、角、鹿角、蹄、甲、爪及喙,未经加工或仅简单整理但未切割成形;上述产品的粉末及废料:**										**Ivory, tortoise-shell, whalebone and whalebone hair, horns, antlers, hooves, nails, claws and beaks, unworked or simply prepared but not cut to shape; powder and waste of these products:**
0507.1000	-兽牙;兽牙粉末及废料	10	T3		0	30	13	5	千克		-Ivory; ivory powder and waste
0507.1000 10	犀牛角	10				30	13	5	千克	89	Rhinocerus horn (*cornu rhinocerotis*)
0507.1000 20	其他濒危野生兽牙、兽牙粉末及废料	10				30	13	5	千克	AFEB	Lvory and powder or waste thereof of wild animals in imminent dangers
0507.1000 90	兽牙、兽牙粉末及废料	10				30	13	5	千克	AB	Lvory and powder or waste thereof of other animals
	-其他:										-Other:
0507.9010	---羚羊角及其粉末和废料	3	T3		0	14	13	5	千克	ABFE	---Antelope horns and powder or waste thereof
0507.9020	---鹿茸及其粉末	11	T3		6.6	30	13	5	千克	ABFE	---Pilose antlers and powder thereof
0507.9090	---其他	10	T3		0	50	13	5	千克	AFEB	---Other
05.08	**珊瑚及类似品,未经加工或仅简单整理但未经进一步加工;软体动物壳、甲壳动物壳、棘皮动物壳、墨鱼骨,未经加工或仅简单整理但未切割成形;上述壳、骨的粉末及废料:**										**Coral and similar materials, unworked or simply prepared but not otherwise worked; shells of molluscs, crustaceans or echinoderms and cuttle-bone, unworked or simply prepared but not cut to shape, powder and waste thereof:**
0508.0010	---粉末及废料	12	0		9.6	35	13	5	千克		---Powder and waste
0508.0010 10	珊瑚及濒危水产品的粉末、碎料(包括介、贝、棘皮动物壳、黑鱼骨的粉末,废料)	12				35	13	5	千克	AFEB	Powder and waste of coral (including shells of molluscs, crustaceans or echinoderms and cuttle-bone)
0508.0010 90	其他水产品壳、骨的粉末及废料(包括介、贝壳、棘皮动物壳、墨鱼骨的粉末及废料)	12				35	13	5	千克	AB	Powder and waste of other aquatic products (including shells of molluscs, crustaceans or echinoderms and cuttle-bone)
0508.0090	---其他	12	0		9.6	50	13	5	千克		---Other
0508.0090 10	珊瑚及濒危水产品的壳、骨(包括介、贝、棘皮动物的壳、墨鱼骨)	12				50	13	5	千克	AFEB	Shells, bone of Coral and aquatic products in imminent dangers (including shells of molluscs, crustaceans or echinoderms and cuttle-bone)
0508.0090 90	其他水产品的壳、骨(包括介、贝、棘皮动物的壳、墨鱼骨)	12				50	13	5	千克	AB	Shells and bone of other aquatic products (including shells of molluscs, crustaceans or echinoderms and cuttle-bone)
05.10	**龙涎香、海狸香、灵猫香及麝香;斑蝥;胆汁,不论是否干制;供配制药用的腺体及其他动物产品,鲜、冷、冻或用其他方法暂时保藏的:**										**Ambergris, castoreum, civet and musk; cantharides; bile, whether or not dried; glands and other animal products used in the preparation of pharmaceutical products, fresh, chilled, frozen or otherwise provisionally preserved:**
0510.0010	---黄药	3	0		0	14	13	5	千克		---Bezoar

税则号列 Tariff Item.	货品名称	最惠国(%) MFN	协定(%)CT 东盟 CA	中巴 CP	中智 CC	普通 Gen	增值税率 VAT	出口退税 ED	计量单位 Unit	监管条件 SC	Article Description
0510.0010 10	牛黄	3				14	13	5	千克	8A	Calculus bovis
0510.0010 20	猴枣	3				14	13	5	千克	QAFEB	Calculus macaca mulatta
0510.0010 90	其他黄药(不包括牛黄)	3				14	13	5	千克	AFEB	Other bezoar (excluding calculus bovis)
0510.0020	---龙涎香、海狸香、灵猫香	7	0		0	50	13	5	千克	AFEB	---Ambergris, castoreum and civet
0510.0030	---麝香	7	T3		0	20	13		千克	8AF	---Musk
0510.0040	---斑蝥	7	T3		0	50	13	5	千克	QAB	---Cantharides
0510.0090	---其他	6	T3		0	20	13	5	千克		---Other
0510.0090 10	其他濒危野生动物胆汁及其他产品(不论是否干制;鲜、冷、冻或用其他方法暂时保藏的)	6				20	13	5	千克	AFEB	Bile and other products of other wild animals in imminent dangers (whether or not dried, fresh, chilled, frozen or otherwise provisionally preserved)
0510.0090 90	胆汁,配药用腺体及其他动物产品(不论是否干制;鲜、冷、冻或用其他方法暂时保藏的)	6				20	13	5	千克	AB	Bile, glands and other animal products used in the preparation of pharmaceutical products (whether or not dried, fresh, chilled, frozen or otherwise provisionally preserved)
05.11	**其他税目未列名的动物产品;不适合供人食用的第一章或第三章的死动物:**										**Animal products not elsewhere specified or included; dead animals of Chapter 1 or 3, unfit for human consumption:**
0511.1000	-牛的精液	0				0	13	5	千克		-Bovine semen
0511.1000 10	濒危野生牛的精液	0				0	13	5	千克	ABFE	Semen of wild bovine in imminent dangers
0511.1000 90	其他牛的精液	0				0	13	5	千克	AB	Other bovine semen
	-其他:										-Other:
	--鱼、甲壳动物、软体动物、其他水生无脊椎动物的产品;第三章的死动物										--Products of fish or crustaceans, molluscs or other aquatic invertebrates; dead animals of Chapter 3
	---鱼的:										---Fish:
0511.9111	----受精鱼卵	12	0		9.6	35	13	5	千克		----Fertilized fish eggs
0511.9111 10	濒危鱼的受精卵	12				35	13	5	千克	ABFE	Fertilized fish eggs, in imminent dangers
0511.9111 90	其他受精鱼卵	12				35	13	5	千克	AB	Other fertilized fish eggs
0511.9119	----其他	12	0		9.6	35	13	5	千克		----Other
0511.9119 10	濒危鱼的非食用产品(包括鱼肚)	12				35	13	5	千克	ABFE	Products of fish in imminent dangers (including fish maw), unfit for human consumption
0511.9119 90	其他鱼的非食用产品(包括鱼肚)	12				35	13	5	千克	AB	Other fertilized fish eggs (including fish maw)
0511.9190	---其他	12	0		9.6	35	13	5	千克		---Other
0511.9190 10	濒危水生无脊椎动物产品(包括甲壳动物,软体动物,第三章死动物)	12				35	13	5	千克	ABFE	Products of fish or crustaceans in imminent dangers, molluscs or other aquatic invertebrates; dead animals of Chapter 3
0511.9190 90	其他水生无脊椎动物产品(包括甲壳动物,软体动物,第三章死动物)	12				35	13	5	千克	AB	Other products of fish or crustaceans, molluscs or other aquatic invertebrates; dead animals of Chapter 3
	--其他:										--Other:

税则号列 Tariff Item.	货品名称	最惠国(%) MFN	协定(%)CT 东盟 CA	中巴 CP	中智 CC	普通 Gen	增值税率 VAT	出口退税 ED	计量单位 Unit	监管条件 SC	Article Description
0511.9910	---动物精液(牛的精液除外)	0				0	13	5	千克		---Animal semen, other than bovine semen
0511.9910 10	濒危野生动物精液(牛的精液除外)	0				0	13	5	千克	AFEB	Semen of wild animals in imminent dangers (other than bovine semen)
0511.9910 90	其他动物精液(牛的精液除外)	0				0	13	5	千克	AB	Semen of other animals (other than bovine semen)
0511.9920	---动物胚胎	0				0	13	5	千克		---Animal embryo
0511.9920 10	濒危野生动物胚胎	0				0	13	5	千克	AFEB	Embryo of wild animals in imminent dangers
0511.9920 90	其他动物胚胎	0				0	13	5	千克	AB	Embryo of other animals
0511.9930	---蚕种	0				0	13	5	千克	AB	---Silkworm graine
0511.9940	---马毛及废马毛,不论是否制成有或无衬垫的毛片	15	0		9	90	13	5	千克		---Horsehair and horsehair waster whether or not put up as a layer with or without supporting material
0511.9940 10	废马毛(不论是否制成有或无衬垫的毛片)	15				90	13	5	千克	9B	Horsehair waster (whether or not put up as a lalyer with or without supporting material)
0511.9940 90	其他马毛(不论是否制成有或无衬垫的毛片)	15				90	13	5	千克	AB	Other hoursehair (whether or not put up as a lalyer with or without supporting material)
0511.9990	---其他	12	0		7.2	35	13	5	千克		---Other
0511.9990 10	其他编号未列名濒危野生动物产品(包括不适合供人食用的第一章的死动物)	12				35	13	5	千克	AFEB	Products of wild animal in imminent dangers, not elsewhere specified or included; dead animals of Chapter 1 or 3, unfit for human consumption
0511.9990 90	其他编号未列名的动物产品(包括不适合供人食用的第一章的死动物)	12				35	13	5	千克	AB	Animal products not elsewhere specified or included; dead animals of Chapter 1 or 3, unfit for human consumption

第二类
植 物 产 品

SECTION Ⅱ
VEGETABLE PRODUCTS

注释：

本类所称"团粒"，是指直接挤压或加入按重量计比例不超过3%的粘合剂制成的粒状产品。

Notes:

In this Section the term "pellets" means products which have been agglomerated either directly by compression or by the addition of a binder in a proportion not exceeding 3% by weight.

第六章
活树及其他活植物；鳞茎、根及类似品；插花及装饰用簇叶

Chapter 6
Live trees and other plants; bulbs, roots and the like; cut flowers and ornamental foliage

注释：

一、除税目06.01的菊苣植物及其根以外，本章只包括通常由苗圃或花店供应为种植或装饰用的活树及其他货品（包括植物秧苗）；但不包括马铃薯、洋葱、青葱、大蒜及其他第七章的产品。

二、税目06.03、06.04的各种货品，包括全部或部分用这些货品制成的花束、花篮、花圈及类似品，不论是否有其他材料制成的附件。但这些货品不包括税目97.01的拼贴画或类似的装饰板。

Notes:

1. Subject to the second part of heading No. 06.01 this Chapter covers only live trees and goods (including seeding vegetables) of a kind commonly supplied by nursery gardeners or florists for planting or for ornamental use; nevertheless it does not include potatoes, onions, shallots, garlic or other products of Chapter 7.

2. Any reference in heading No. 06.03 or 06.04 to goods of any kind shall be construed as including a reference to bouquets, floral baskets, wreaths and similar articles made wholly or partly of goods of that kind, account not being taken of accessories of other materials. However, these headings do not include collages or similar decorative plaques of heading No. 97.01.

税则号列 Tariff Item.	货品名称	最惠国(%) MFN	协定(%)CT 东盟 CA	中巴 CP	中智 CC	普通 Gen	增值税率 VAT	出口退税 ED	计量单位 Unit	监管条件 SC	Article Description
06.01	**鳞茎、块茎、块根、球茎、根颈及根茎，休眠、生长或开花的；菊苣植物及其根，但税目12.12的根除外：**										**Bulbs, tubers, tuberous roots, corms, crowns and rhizomes, dormant, in growth or in flower; chicory plants and roots other than roots of heading No. 12.12:**
	-休眠的鳞茎、块茎、块根、球茎、根颈及根茎：										-Bulbs, tubers, tuberous roots, corms, crowns and rhizomes, dormant:
0601.1010	---番红花球茎	4	0	2	0	14	13	5	个/千克	AB	---Stigma croci corms
	---其他：										---Other:
0601.1091	----种用	0				0	13	5	个/千克		----Seed
0601.1091 10	种用休眠的兰花块茎（包括球茎、根颈及根茎）	0				0	13	5	个/千克	AFEB	Orchid tubers, dormant, seed (including corms, crowns and rhizomes)
0601.1091 91	种用休眠其他濒危植物鳞茎等（包括球茎、根颈、根茎、鳞茎、块茎，块根）	0				0	13	5	个/千克	ABFE	Bulbs, tubers, tuberous roots, dormant, seed (including corms, crowns and rhizomes) of plants in imminent dangers
0601.1091 99	种用休眠的其他鳞茎、块茎、块根（包括球茎、根颈及根茎）	0				0	13	5	个/千克	AB	Other bulbs, tubers, tuberous roots, dormant, seed (including corms, crowns and rhizomes)
0601.1099	----其他	5	0	2.5	0	40	13	5	个/千克		----Other
0601.1099 10	其他休眠的兰花块茎（包括球茎、根颈及根茎）	5				40	13	5	个/千克	AFEB	Other orchid tubers, dormant (including corms, crowns and rhizomes)

税则号列 Tariff Item.	货品名称	最惠国(%) MFN	协定(%)CT 东盟 CA	中巴 CP	中智 CC	普通 Gen	增值税率 VAT	出口退税 ED	计量单位 Unit	监管条件 SC	Article Description
0601.1099 91	其他休眠濒危植物鳞茎等(包括球茎、根颈、根茎、鳞茎、块茎、块根)	5				40	13	5	个/千克	AFEB	Other bulbs, tubers, tuberous roots, dormant, seed (including corms, crowns and rhizomes), of plants in imminent dangers
0601.1099 99	其他休眠的其他鳞茎、块茎、块根(包括球茎、根颈及根茎)	5				40	13	5	个/千克	AB	Other bulbs, tubers, tuberous roots, dormant, seed (including corms, crowns and rhizomes), dormant
0601.2000	-生长或开花的鳞茎、块茎、块根、球茎、根颈及根茎;菊苣植物及其根	15	0	7.5	12	80	13	5	个/千克		-Bulbs, tubers, tuberous roots, corms, crowns and rhizomes, in growth or in flower; chicory plants and roots
0601.2000 10	生长或开花的兰花块茎(包括球茎、根颈及根茎)	15				80	13	5	个/千克	AFEB	Orchid tubers, in growth or in flower (including corms, crowns and rhizomes)
0601.2000 20	生长或开花的仙客来鳞茎	15				80	13	5	个/千克	AFEB	Cyclamen tubers, in growth or in flower
0601.2000 91	生长或开花的其他濒危植物鳞茎等(包括球茎、根颈、根茎、鳞茎、块茎、块根、菊苣植物)	15				80	13	5	个/千克	AFEB	Other bulbs, tubers, tuberous roots, dormant, seed (including corms, crowns and rhizomes) tubers, in growth or in flower, in imminent dangers
0601.2000 99	生长或开花的其他鳞茎及菊苣植物(包括块茎、块根、球茎、根颈及根茎,编号1212根除外)	15				80	13	5	个/千克	AB	Other bulbs, tubers, tuberous roots, corms, crowns and rhizomes, in growth or in flower, chicory plants and roots, other than roots of heading No. 1212
06.02	**其他活植物(包括其根)、插枝及接穗;蘑菇菌丝:**										**Other live plants (including their roots) cuttings and slips; mushroom spawn:**
0602.1000	-无根插枝及接穗	0				0	13	5	株/千克		-Unrooted cuttings and slips
0602.1000 10	濒危植物的无根插枝及接穗	0				0	13	5	株/千克	ABFE	Unrooted cuttings and slips of plants in imminent dangers
0602.1000 90	其他无根插枝及接穗	0				0	13	5	株/千克	AB	Other unrooted cuttings and slips
	-食用水果或食用坚果的树、灌木,不论是否嫁接:										-Trees, shrubs and bushes, grafted or not, of kinds which bear edible fruit or nuts:
0602.2010	---种用苗木	0				0	13		株/千克	AB	---Seedlings
0602.2090	---其他	10	0	5	8	80	13	5	株/千克	AB	---Other
	-杜鹃,不论是否嫁接:										-Rhododendrons and azaleas, grafted or not:
0602.3010	---种用	0				0	13	5	株/千克	AB	---Seedlings
0602.3090	---其他	15	0		9	80	13	5	株/千克	AB	---Other
	-玫瑰,不论是否嫁接:										-Roses, grafted or not:
0602.4010	---种用	0				0	13	5	株/千克	AB	---Seedlings
0602.4090	---其他	15	0		9	80	13	5	株/千克	AB	---Other
	-其他:										-Other:
0602.9010	---蘑菇菌丝	0				0	13	5	千克	AB	---Mushroom spawn
	---其他:										---Other:
0602.9091	----种用苗木	0				0	13		株/千克		----Seedlings
0602.9091 10	种用兰花	0				0	13		株/千克	AFEB	Orchid, seedlings
0602.9091 91	其他濒危植物种用苗木	0				0	13		株/千克	AFEB	Other plants in imminent dangers seedlings
0602.9091 99	其他种用苗木	0				0	13		株/千克	AB	Other nursery stock, seedlings
0602.9092	----兰花	10	0		8	80	13	5	株/千克	ABFE	----Orchid

税则号列 Tariff Item.	货品名称	最惠国(%) MFN	协定(%)CT			普通 Gen	增值税率 VAT	出口退税 ED	计量单位 Unit	监管条件 SC	Article Description
			东盟 CA	中巴 CP	中智 CC						
0602.9093	----菊花	10	0		8	80	13	5	株/千克	AB	----Chrysanthemum
0602.9094	----百合	10	0		8	80	13	5	株/千克		----Lily
0602.9094 10	芦荟(种用除外)	10				80	13	5	株/千克	ABFEQ	Aloe, other than seedlings
0602.9094 90	其他百合(种用除外)	10				80	13	5	株/千克	AB	Other lily
0602.9095	----康乃馨	10	0		8	80	13	5	株/千克	AB	----Carnation
0602.9099	----其他	10	0	5	8	80	13	5	株/千克		----Other
0602.9099 10	苏铁(铁树)类	10				80	13	5	株/千克	AFEB	Sago cycas (*Cycas revoluta*)
0602.9099 20	仙人掌(包括仙人球、仙人柱、仙人指)	10				80	13	5	株/千克	AFEB	Cactus (ball cactus, column cactus, finger cactus)
0602.9099 91	其他濒危活植物(种用除外)	10				80	13	5	株/千克	AFEB	Other live plants in imminent dangers (other than seedlings)
0602.9099 99	其他活植物(种用除外)	10				80	13	5	株/千克	AB	Other live plants (other than seedlings)
06.03	**制花束或装饰用的插花及花蕾,鲜、干、染色、漂白、浸渍或用其他方法处理的:**										**Cut flowers and flower buds of a kind suitable for bouquets or for ornamental purposes, fresh, dried, dyed, bleached, impregnated or otherwise prepared:**
	-鲜的										-Fresh
0603.1100	--玫瑰	10	T3	5	8	100	13	5	千克	AB	--Roses
0603.1200	--康乃馨	10	T3	5	8	100	13	5	千克	AB	--Carnation
0603.1300	--兰花	10	T3	5	8	100	13	5	千克	ABEF	--Orchild
0603.1400	--菊花	10	T3	5	8	100	13	5	千克	AB	--Chrysanthemum
0603.1900	--其他	10	T3	5	8	100	13	5	千克		--Other
0603.1900 10	鲜的濒危植物的插花及花蕾(制花束或装饰用的)	10				100	13	5	千克	ABFE	Cut flowers and flower buds of plants in imminent damgers, of a kind suitable for bouquets or for ornamental purposes fresh
0603.1900 90	其他鲜的插花及花蕾(制花束或装饰用的)	10				100	13	5	千克	AB	Other cut flower and flower buds of a kind suitable for bouquets or for ornamental purposes, fresh
0603.9000	-其他	23	T3	11.5	0	100	17	5	千克		-Other
0603.9000 10	干或染色等加工濒危插花及花蕾(制花束或装饰用的,鲜的除外)	23				100	17	5	千克	ABFE	Cut flowers and flower buds of plants in imminent dangers, of a kind suitable for bouquets or for ornamental purposes dried, dyed, bleached, impregnated or otherwise prepared other than fresh
0603.9000 90	其他干或染色等加工的插花及花蕾(制花束或装饰用的,鲜的除外)	23				100	17	5	千克	AB	Other cut flowers and flower buds, dried, dyed, bleached, impregnated or otherwise prepared, other than fresh
06.04	**制花束或装饰用的不带花及花蕾的植物枝、叶或其他部分,草、苔藓及地衣,鲜、干、染色、漂白、浸渍或用其他方法处理的:**										**Foliage, branches and other parts of plants, without flowers or flower buds, and grasses, mosses and lichens, being goods of a kind suitable for bouquets or for ornamental purposes, fresh, dried, dyed, bleached, impregnated or otherwise prepared:**
0604.1000	-苔藓及地衣	23	0		18.4	100	13	5	千克	AB	-Mosses and lichens
	-其他:										-Other:
0604.9100	--鲜的	10	T3		8	100	13	5	千克		--Fresh

税则号列 Tariff Item.	货品名称	最惠国(%) MFN	协定(%) CT 东盟 CA	中巴 CP	中智 CC	普通 Gen	增值税率 VAT	出口退税 ED	计量单位 Unit	监管条件 SC	Article Description
0604.9100 10	鲜濒危植物枝、叶或其他部分,草(枝、叶或其他部分是指制花束或装饰用并且不带花及花蕾)	10				100	13	5	千克	ABFE	Foliage, branches and other parts of plants in imminent dangers, without flowers or flower buds, and grasses, mosses and lichens, being goods of a kind suitable for bouquets or for ornamental purposes, fresh
0604.9100 90	其他鲜植物枝、叶或其他部分,草(枝、叶或其他部分是指制花束或装饰用并且不带花及花蕾)	10				100	13	5	千克	AB	Other foliage, branches and other parts of plants fresh, bleached, impregnated or otherwise prepared
0604.9900	--其他	10	T3		0	100	17	5	千克		--Other
0604.9900 10	染色或经加工濒危枝、叶、草等(枝、叶或其他部分是指制花束或装饰用并且不带花及花蕾)	10				100	17	5	千克	ABFE	Foliage, branches and other parts of plants in imminent dangers, without flowers or flower buds, and grasses, mosses and lichens, being goods of a kind suitable for bouquets or for ornamental purposes, dried, dyed, bleached, impregnated or otherwise prepared
0604.9900 90	其他染色或加工的枝、叶、草等(枝、叶或其他部分是指制花束或装饰用并且不带花及花蕾)	10				100	17	5	千克	AB	Other foliage, branches and other parts of plants, dried, dyed, bleached, impregnated or otherwise prepared

第七章
食用蔬菜、根及块茎

Chapter 7
Edible vegetables and certain roots and tubers

注释：

一、本章不包括税目12.14的草料。

二、税目07.09、07.10、07.11及07.12所称"蔬菜"，包括食用的蘑菇、块菌、油橄榄、刺山柑、菜葫芦、南瓜、茄子、甜玉米、辣椒、茴香菜、欧芹、细叶芹、龙蒿、水芹、甜茉乔栾那。

三、税目07.12包括干制的归入税目07.01至07.11的各种蔬菜，但下列各项除外：

（一）作蔬菜用的脱荚干豆（税目07.13）；

（二）税目11.02至11.04所列形状的甜玉米；

（三）马铃薯细粉、粗粉、粉末、粉片、颗粒及团粒（税目11.05）；

（四）用税目07.13的干豆制成的细粉、粗粉及粉末（税目11.06）。

四、本章不包括辣椒干及辣椒粉（税目09.04）。

Notes:

1. This Chapter does not cover forage products of heading 12.14.
2. In headings Nos. 07.09, 07.10, 07.11 and 07.12 the word "vegetables" includes edible mushrooms, truffles, olives, capers, marrows, pumpkins, aubergines, sweet corn (*Zea mays var. saccharata*), fruits of the genus *Capsicum* or of the genus *Pimenta*, fennel, parsley, chervil, tarragon, cress and sweet marjoram (*Majorana hortensis or Origanum majorana*).
3. Heading No. 07.12 covers all dried vegetables of the kinds falling in headings Nos. 07.01 to 07.11, other than:
   (a) dried leguminous vegetables, shelled (heading No. 07.13);
   (b) sweet corn in the forms specified in headings Nos. 11.02 to 11.04;
   (c) flour, meal, powder, flakes, granules and pellets of potatoes (heading No. 11.05);
   (d) flour, meal and powder of the dried leguminous vegetables of heading No. 07.13 (heading No. 11.06).
4. However, dried or crushed or ground fruits of the genus *Capsicum* or of the genus *Pimenta* are excluded from this Chapter (heading No. 09.04).

税则号列 Tariff Item.	货品名称	最惠国(%) MFN	协定(%) CT 东盟 CA	中巴 CP	中智 CC	普通 Gen	增值税率 VAT	出口退税 ED	计量单位 Unit	监管条件 SC	Article Description
07.01	鲜或冷藏的马铃薯：										**Potatoes, fresh or chilled:**
0701.1000	-种用	13	0		0	70	13	5	千克	AB	-Seeds
0701.9000	-其他	13	T3	9	0	70	13	5	千克	AB	-Other
07.02	鲜或冷藏的番茄：										**Tomatoes, fresh or chilled:**
0702.0000	鲜或冷藏的番茄	13	T3		0	70	13	5	千克	AB	Tomatoes, fresh or chilled
07.03	鲜或冷藏的洋葱、青葱、大蒜、韭葱及其他葱属蔬菜：										**Onions, shallots, garlic, leeks and other alliaceous vegetables, fresh or chilled:**
	-洋葱及青葱：										-Onions and shallots:
0703.1010	---洋葱	13	T3	6.5	0	70	13	5	千克	AB	---Onions
0703.1020	---青葱	13	T3	6.5	0	70	13	5	千克	AB	---Shallots
	-大蒜：										-Garlic:
0703.2010	---蒜头	13	T3	0	0	70	13	5	千克	ABa	---Garlic bulbs
0703.2020	---蒜台及蒜苗（青蒜）	13	T3	0	0	70	13	5	千克	AB	---Garlic stems, garlic seedlings (shallots)
0703.2090	---其他	13	T3	0	0	70	13	5	千克	ABa	---Other
	-韭葱及其他葱属蔬菜：										-Leeks and other alliaceous vegetables:
0703.9010	---韭葱	13	T3		0	70	13	5	千克	AB	---Leeks
0703.9020	---大葱	13	T3		0	70	13	5	千克	AB	---Scallion
0703.9090	---其他	13	T3		0	70	13	5	千克	AB	---Other
07.04	鲜或冷藏的卷心菜、菜花、球茎甘蓝、羽衣甘蓝及类似的食用芥菜类蔬菜：										**Cabbages, cauliflowers, kohlrabi, kale and similar edible brassicas, fresh or chilled:**
0704.1000	-菜花及硬花甘蓝	10	T3		0	70	13	5	千克		-Cauliflowers and headed broccoli
0704.1000 01	鲜冷硬花甘蓝	10				70	13		千克	AB	Headed broccoli, fresh or chilled

税则号列 Tariff Item.	货品名称	最惠国(%) MFN	协定(%)CT 东盟 CA	中巴 CP	中智 CC	普通 Gen	增值税率 VAT	出口退税 ED	计量单位 Unit	监管条件 SC	Article Description
0704.1000 02	鲜、冷花椰菜(花椰菜也叫菜花)	10				70	13		千克	AB	Cauliflowers, fresh or chilled
0704.2000	-抱子甘蓝	13	0		0	70	13	5	千克	AB	-Brussels sprouts
0704.9010	---卷心菜	13	0		0	70	13	5	千克	AB	---Cabbage
0704.9020	---西兰花	13	0		0	70	13	5	千克	AB	---West orchid
0704.9090	---其他	13	0		0	70	13	5	千克		---Other
0704.9090 01	鲜冷其他甘蓝	13				70	13		千克	AB	Other Cabbage, fresh or chilled
0704.9090 90	鲜或冷藏的其他食用芥菜类蔬菜	13				70	13		千克	AB	Other edible brassicas, fresh or chilled
07.05	**鲜或冷藏的莴苣及菊苣:**										**Lettuce (*lactuca sativa*) and chicory (*Cichorium spp.*), fresh or chilled:**
	-莴苣:										-Lettuce:
0705.1100	--结球莴苣(包心生菜)	10	T3	0	0	70	13	5	千克	AB	--Cabbage lettuce (head lettuce)
0705.1900	--其他	10	T3	0	0	70	13	5	千克	AB	--Other
0705.2100	--维特罗夫菊苣	13	T3	0	0	70	13	5	千克	AB	--Witloof chicory (*Cichoriym intybus var. foliosum*)
0705.2900	--其他	13	T3	0	0	70	13	5	千克	AB	--Other
07.06	**鲜或冷藏的胡萝卜、萝卜、色拉甜菜根、婆罗门参、块根芹、小萝卜及类似的食用根茎:**										**Carrots, turnips, salad beetroot, salsify, celeriac, radishes and similar edible roots, fresh or chilled:**
0706.1000	-胡萝卜及萝卜	13	T3		0	70	13	5	千克		-Carrots and turnips
0706.1000 01	鲜冷胡萝卜	13				70	13		千克	AB	Carrots, fresh or chilled
0706.1000 90	鲜或冷藏的萝卜	13				70	13		千克	AB	Turnips, fresh or chilled
0706.9000	-其他	13	T3		0	70	13	5	千克	AB	-Other
07.07	**鲜或冷藏的黄瓜及小黄瓜:**										**Cucumbers and gherkins, fresh or chilled:**
0707.0000	鲜或冷藏的黄瓜及小黄瓜	13	T3	6.5	0	70	13	5	千克	AB	Cucumbers and gherkins, fresh or chilled
07.08	**鲜或冷藏的豆类蔬菜,不论是否脱荚:**										**Leguminous vegetables, shelled or unshelled, fresh or chilled:**
0708.1000	-豌豆	13	T3	0	0	70	13	5	千克	AB	-Peas (*Pisum sativum*)
0708.2000	-豇豆及菜豆	13	T3	0	0	70	13	5	千克	AB	-Beans (*Vigna spp.*, *Phaseolus spp.*)
0708.9000	-其他豆类蔬菜	13	T3	0	0	70	13	5	千克	AB	-Other leguminous vegetables
07.09	**鲜或冷藏的其他蔬菜:**										**Other vegetables, fresh or chilled:**
0709.2000	-芦笋	13	T3	0	0	70	13	5	千克	AB	-Asparagus
0709.3000	-茄子	13	T3	0	0	70	13	5	千克	AB	-Aubergines (egg-plants)
0709.4000	-芹菜,但块根芹除外	10	T3	0	0	70	13	5	千克	AB	-Celery, other than celeriac
	-蘑菇及块菌:										-Mushrooms and truffles:
0709.5100	--伞菌属蘑菇	13	T3	0	0	90	13	5	千克	AB	--Mushrooms of the genus *Agaricus*
	--其他:										--Other:
0709.5910	---松茸	13	T3	0	0	90	13	5	千克	ABE	---Sungmo
0709.5920	---香菇	13	T3	0	0	90	13	5	千克	ABa	---shiitake
0709.5930	---金针菇	13	T3	0	0	90	13	5	千克	AB	---Winter mushroom
0709.5940	---草菇	13	T3	0	0	90	13	5	千克	AB	---Paddy straw mushroom
0709.5950	---口蘑	13	T3	0	0	90	13	5	千克	AB	---Tricholoma mongolicum Imai
0709.5960	---块菌	13	0	0	0	90	13	5	千克	AB	---Truffles
0709.5990	---其他	13	T3	0	0	90	13	5	千克	AB	---Other
0709.6000	-辣椒,包括甜椒	13	T3	0	0	70	13	5	千克	AB	-Fruits of the genus *Capsicum* or of the genus *Pimenta*

税则号列 Tariff Item.	货 品 名 称	最惠国(%) MFN	协定(%)CT 东盟 CA	中巴 CP	中智 CC	普通 Gen	增值税率 VAT	出口退税 ED	计量单位 Unit	监管条件 SC	Article Description
0709.7000	-菠菜	13	T3	0	0	70	13	5	千克	AB	-Spinach, New Zealand spinach and orache spinach (garden spinach)
	-其他:										-Other:
0709.9010	---竹笋	13	T3	0	0	70	13	5	千克		---Bamboo shoots
0709.9010 10	鲜或冷藏的酸竹笋	13				70	13	5	千克	ABE	Bamboo shoots, pickled fresh or chilled
0709.9010 90	冷藏的竹笋	13				70	13	5	千克	AB	Bamboo shoots, chilled
0709.9090	---其他	13	0	0	0	70	13	5	千克		---Other
0709.9090 01	鲜、冷丝瓜	13				70	13		千克	AB	Sigualuo, fresh or chilled
0709.9090 02	鲜、冷青红菜	13				70	13		千克	AB	
0709.9090 03	鲜、冷小白菜	13				70	13		千克	AB	Bok - choy, fresh or chilled
0709.9090 04	鲜、冷苦瓜	13				70	13		千克	AB	Balsum, fresh or chilled
0709.9090 05	鲜、冷山葵	13				70	13		千克	AB	
0709.9090 10	鲜或冷藏的莼菜	13				70	13	5	千克	ABE	Water shield, fresh or chilled
0709.9090 90	鲜或冷藏的其他蔬菜	13				70	13	5	千克	AB	Other vegetables, fresh or chilled
07.10	**冷冻蔬菜(不论是否蒸煮):**										**Vegetables (uncooked or cooked by steaming or boiling in water), frozen:**
0710.1000	-马铃薯	13	T3		0	70	13	5	千克	AB	-Potatoes
	-豆类蔬菜,不论是否脱荚:										-Leguminous vegetables, shelled or unshelled:
0710.2100	--豌豆	13	T3		0	70	13	5	千克	AB	--Peas (*Pisum sativum*)
	--豇豆及菜豆:										--Beans (*Vigna spp.*, *Phaseolus spp.*):
0710.2210	---红小豆	13	T3		0	70	13	5	千克	AB	---Small red (Adzuki) beans (*Phaseolus* or *Vigna angularis*)
0710.2290	---其他	13	T3		0	70	13	5	千克	AB	---Other
0710.2900	--其他	13	T3		0	70	13	5	千克	AB	--Other
0710.3000	-菠菜	13	T3		0	70	13	5	千克	AB	-Spinach, New Zealand spinach and orache spinach (garden spinach)
0710.4000	-甜玉米	10	T3		0	70	13	5	千克	AB	-Sweet corn
	-其他蔬菜:										-Other vegetables:
0710.8010	---松茸	13	T3		0	70	13	5	千克	ABE	---Sungmo
0710.8020	---蒜苔及蒜苗(青蒜)	13	T3		0	70	13	5	千克	AB	---Garlic stems, garlic seedlings
0710.8030	---蒜头	13	T3		0	70	13	5	千克	AB	---Garlic bulbs
0710.8090	---其他	13	T3		0	70	13	5	千克		---Other
0710.8090 10	冷冻的大蒜瓣(不论是否蒸煮)	13				70	13	5	千克	AB	Garlic cloves, frozen (uncooked or cooked by steaming or boiling in water)
0710.8090 20	冷冻的香菇(不论是否蒸煮)	13				70	13	5	千克	AB	Xianggo mushroom, frozen (uncooked or cooked by steaming or boiling in water)
0710.8090 30	冷冻莼菜(不论是否蒸煮)	13				70	13	5	千克	ABE	Water shield, frozen (uncooked or cooked by steaming or boiling in water)
0710.8090 90	冷冻的未列名蔬菜(不论是否蒸煮)	13				70	13	5	千克	AB	Vegetables, frozen not elsewhere specified or included (uncooked or cooked by steaming or boiling in water)
0710.9000	-什锦蔬菜	10	T3		0	70	13	5	千克	AB	-Mixtures of vegetables

税则号列 Tariff Item.	货品名称	最惠国(%) MFN	协定(%) CT 东盟 CA	中巴 CP	中智 CC	普通 Gen	增值税率 VAT	出口退税 ED	计量单位 Unit	监管条件 SC	Article Description
07.11	**暂时保藏(例如,使用二氧化硫气体、盐水、亚硫酸水或其他防腐液)的蔬菜,但不适于直接食用的:**										**Vegetables provisionally preserved (for example, by sulphur dioxide gas, in brine, in suphur water or in other preservative solutions), but unsuitable in that state for immediate consumption:**
0711.2000	-油橄榄	13	0	0	0	70	13	5	千克	AB	-Olives
0711.4000	-黄瓜及小黄瓜	13	T3	0	0	70	13	5	千克	AB	-Cucumbers and gherkins
	-蘑菇及块菌:										-Mushrooms and truffles:
	--伞菌属蘑菇:										--Mushrooms of the genus *Agaricus*:
	---盐水的:										---In brine:
0711.5112	----白蘑菇	13	T3	0	0	90	13	5	千克	AB	----White mushroom
0711.5119	----其他	13	T3	0	0	90	13	5	千克	AB	----Other
0711.5190	---其他	13	T3	0	0	90	13	5	千克	AB	---Other
	--其他:										--Other:
	---盐水的:										---In brine:
0711.5911	----松茸	13	T3	0	0	90	13	5	千克	EAB	----Sungmo
0711.5919	----其他	13	T3	0	0	90	13	5	千克		----Other
0711.5919 10	盐水的香菇(不适于直接食用的)	13				90	13	5	千克	AB	Xianggu mushroom in brine, but unsuitable in that state for immediate consumption
0711.5919 90	盐水的其他非伞菌属蘑菇及块菌(不适于直接食用的)	13				90	13	5	千克	AB	Other mushroom except the genus *Agaricus* and truffles, in brine, but unsuitable in that state for immediate consumption
0711.5990	---其他	13	T3	0	0	90	13	5	千克		---Other
0711.5990 10	暂时保藏的香菇(用二氧化硫气体等物质处理,但不适于直接食用的)	13				90	13	5	千克	AB	Xianggu provisionally preserved, by sulphur dioxide gas, in brine, in suphur water or in other preservative solutions, but unsuitable in that state for immediate consumption
0711.5990 90	暂时保藏的蘑菇及块菌(用二氧化硫气体等物质处理,但不适于直接食用的)	13				90	13	5	千克	AB	Mushrooms of the genus *Agaricus* and truffles, by sulphur dioxide gas, in brine, in suphur water or in other preservative solutions, but unsuitable in that state for immediate consumption
	-其他蔬菜;什锦蔬菜:										-Other:
	---盐水的:										---Inbrine:
0711.9031	----竹笋	13	T3	0	0	70	13	5	千克		----Bamboo shoots
0711.9031 10	盐水酸竹笋(不适于直接食用的)	13				70	13	5	千克	ABE	Bamboo shoots, pickled, in brine, unsuitable in that state for immediate consumption
0711.9031 90	其他盐水竹笋(不适于直接食用的)	13				70	13	5	千克	AB	Other bamboo shoots, in brine, unsuitable in that state for immediate consumption
0711.9034	----大蒜	13	T3	0	0	70	13	5	千克		----Garlic
0711.9034 10	盐水简单腌制的大蒜头、大蒜瓣(无论是否去皮,但不适于直接食用)	13				70	13	5	千克	AB	Garlic bulbs or garlic cloves, in brine, but unsuitable in that state for immediate consumption, whether or not skinned

税则号列 Tariff Item.	货品名称	最惠国(%) MFN	协定(%)CT 东盟 CA	 中巴 CP	 中智 CC	普通 Gen	增值税率 VAT	出口退税 ED	计量单位 Unit	监管条件 SC	Article Description
0711.9034 90	盐水简单腌制的其他大蒜(不含蒜头、蒜瓣,无论是否去皮,但不适于直接食用)	13				70	13	5	千克	AB	Other garlic in brine (other than garlic bulbs, garlic cloves, whether or not skinned, but unsuitable in that state for immediate consumption)
0711.9039	----其他	13	0	0	0	70	13	5	千克	AB	----Other
	---其他:										---Other:
0711.9090	----其他	13	0	0	0	90	13	5	千克	AB	----Other
07.12	**干蔬菜,整个、切块、切片、破碎或制成粉状,但未经进一步加工的:**										**Dried vegetables, whole, cut, sliced, broken or in powder, but not further prepared:**
0712.2000	-洋葱	13	0		0	80	13	5	千克	AB	-Onions
	-蘑菇、木耳、银耳及块菌:										-Mushrooms, wood ears(*Auricularia spp.*), jelly fungi(*Tremella spp.*) and truffles:
0712.3100	--伞菌属蘑菇	13	0	9	0	80	13	5	千克	AB	--Mushrooms of the genus *Agaricus*
0712.3200	--木耳	13	0		0	100	13	5	千克	AB	--Wood ears(*Auricularia spp.*)
0712.3300	--银耳	13	0		0	90	13	5	千克	AB	--Jelly fungi (*Tremella spp.*)
	--其他:										--Other:
0712.3910	---香菇	13	T3	9	0	100	13	5	千克	AB	---Shiitake
0712.3920	---金针菇	13	T3	9	0	100	13	5	千克	AB	---Winter mushroom
0712.3930	---草菇	13	T3	9	0	100	13	5	千克	AB	---Paddy straw mushroom
0712.3940	---口蘑	13	T3	9	0	100	13	5	千克	AB	---Tricho lomamongolicum Imai
0712.3950	---牛肝菌	13	T3	9	0	100	13	5	千克	AB	---Boletus;Porani
0712.3990	---其他	13	T3	9	0	100	13	5	千克		---Other
0712.3990 10	干制松茸(整个、切块、切片、破碎或制成粉状,但未经进一步加工的)	13				100	13	5	千克	ABE	Dried sungmo, whole, cut, sliced, broken or in powder, but not further prepared
0712.3990 90	其他干制蘑菇及块菌(整个、切块、切片、破碎或制成粉状,但未经进一步加工的)	13				100	13	5	千克	AB	Other dried mushrooms of the genus *Agaricus* or truffles, whole, cut, sliced, broken or in powder, but not further prepared
	-其他蔬菜;什锦蔬菜:										-Other vegetables; mixtures of vegetables:
0712.9010	---笋干丝	13	0		0	80	13	5	千克		---Bamboo shoots
0712.9010 10	酸竹笋干丝	13				80	13	5	千克	ABE	Dried acid bamboo shoots
0712.9010 90	其他笋干丝	13				80	13	5	千克	AB	Other bamboo shoots
0712.9020	---紫萁(薇菜干)	13	0		0	80	13	5	千克	AB	---Osmund
0712.9030	---金针菜(黄花菜)	13	0		0	80	13	5	千克	AB	---Day lily flowers
0712.9040	---蕨菜	13	0		0	80	13	5	千克	AB	---Wild brake
0712.9050	---大蒜	13	0		0	80	17	5	千克		---Garlic
0712.9050 10	干燥或脱水的大蒜头、大蒜瓣(无论是否去皮)	13				80	17	5	千克	AB	Dried garlic bulbs or garlic cloves, whether or not skinned
0712.9050 90	干燥或脱水的其他大蒜(不含蒜头、蒜瓣,无论是否去皮)	13				80	17	5	千克	AB	Other dried garlic (other than garlic bulbs garlic cloves, whether or not skinned)
0712.9060	---甜椒	13	0		0	80	13	5	千克	AB	---Capsicum annuum Var. grossum
0712.9090	---其他	13	0		0	80	13	5	千克		---Other
0712.9090 10	干莼菜(整个、切块、切片、破碎或制成粉状,但未经进一步加工的)	13				80	13	5	千克	ABE	Dried water shield, whole, cut, sliced, broken or in powder, but not further prepared

税则号列 Tariff Item.	货 品 名 称	最惠国(%) MFN	协定(%) CT 东盟 CA	中巴 CP	中智 CC	普通 Gen	增值税率 VAT	出口退税 ED	计量单位 Unit	监管条件 SC	Article Description
0712.9090 90	干制的其他蔬菜及什锦蔬菜(整个、切块、切片破碎或制成粉状,但未经进一步加工的)	13				80	13	5	千克	AB	Other vegetable; mixtures of vegetables, whole, cut, sliced, broken or in powder, but not further prepared
07.13	**脱荚的干豆,不论是否去皮或分瓣:**										**Dried leguminous vegetables, shelled, whether or not skinned or split:**
	-豌豆:										-Peas (*Pisum sativum*):
0713.1010	---种用	0				0	13	5	千克	AB	---Seed
0713.1090	---其他	5	0		0	20	13	5	千克	AB	---Other
	-鹰嘴豆:										-Chickpeas (garbanzos):
0713.2010	---种用	0				0	13	5	千克	AB	---Seed
0713.2090	---其他	7	0		0	20	13	5	千克	AB	---Other
	-豇豆及菜豆:										-Beans (*Vigna spp.*, *Phaseolus spp.*):
	--绿豆:										--Beans of the species *Vigna mungo*(*L.*) *Hepper or Vigna radiata* (*L.*) *Wilczek*:
0713.3110	---种用	0				0	13	5	千克	AB	---Seed
0713.3190	---其他	3	T3	1.5	0	11	13	5	千克	AB	---Other
	--赤豆:										--Small red (Adzuki) beans (*Phaseolus* or *Vigna angularis*):
	---种用:										---Seed:
0713.3211	----红小豆	0				0	13	5	千克	aAB	----Smallred(Adzuri)beans
0713.3219	----其他	0				0	13	5	千克	aAB	----Other
0713.3290	---其他	3	T3		0	14	13	5	千克	aAB	---Other
	--芸豆:										--Kidney beans, including white pea beans (*Phaseolus vulgaris*):
0713.3310	---种用	0				0	13	5	千克	AB	---Seed
0713.3390	---其他	7.5	0		0	20	13	5	千克	AB	---Other
0713.3900	--其他	7	0	3.5	0	20	13	5	千克	AB	--Other
	-扁豆:										-Lentils:
0713.4010	---种用	0				0	13	5	千克	AB	---Seed
0713.4090	---其他	7	0		0	20	13	5	千克	AB	---Other
	-蚕豆:										-Broad beans (*Vicia faba var. Major*) and horse beans (*Vicia faba var. equina*, *Vicia faba var. minor*):
0713.5010	---种用	0				0	13	5	千克	AB	---Seed
0713.5090	---其他	7	0		0	20	13	5	千克	AB	---Other
	-其他:										-Other:
0713.9010	---种用	0				0	13	5	千克	AB	---Seed
0713.9090	---其他	7	0		0	20	13	5	千克	AB	---Other
07.14	**鲜、冷、冻或干的木薯、竹芋、兰科植物块茎、菊芋、甘薯及含有高淀粉或菊粉的类似根茎,不论是否切片或制成团粒;西谷茎髓:**										**Manioc, arrowroot, salep, Jerusalem artichokes, sweet potatoes and similar roots and tubers with high starch or inulin content, fresh, chilled, frozen or dried, whether or not sliced or in the form of pellets; sago pith:**
	-木薯:										-Manioc(cassava):
0714.1010	---鲜的	10	T3		0	30	13	5	千克	AB	---Fresh
0714.1020	---干的	5	T3		0	30	13	5	千克	AB	---Dried
0714.1030	---冷或冻的	10	T3		0	80	13	5	千克	AB	---Chilled or frozen

税则号列 Tariff Item.	货品名称	最惠国(%) MFN	协定(%)CT 东盟 CA	中巴 CP	中智 CC	普通 Gen	增值税率 VAT	出口退税 ED	计量单位 Unit	监管条件 SC	Article Description
	-甘薯:										-Sweet potatoes:
	---鲜的:										---Fresh:
0714.2011	----种用	0				50	13	5	千克	AB	----For Cultivatron
0714.2019	----其他	13	T3	6.5	0	50	13	5	千克	AB	----Other
0714.2020	---干的	13	T3	6.5	0	50	13	5	千克	AB	---Dried
0714.2030	---冷或冻的	13	T3	6.5	0	80	13	5	千克	AB	---Chilled or frozen
	-其他:										-Other:
0714.9010	---荸荠	13	T3	6.5	0	50	13	5	千克	AB	---Water chestnut
	---藕:										---Lotus(*Nelumbo nucifera*) rootstock:
0714.9021	----种用	0				0	13	5	千克	AB	----For cultivation
0714.9029	----其他	13	T3	6.5	0	50	13	5	千克	AB	----Other
0714.9030	---芋头	13	T3	6.5	0	50	13	5	千克	AB	---Taro
0714.9030 01	鲜、冷芋头(不论是否切片或制成团粒;芋头又称芋艿,为天南星科芋属植物。分旱芋、水芋)	13				50	13		千克	AB	Fresh, cold taro (no matter if it's sliced or made round; taros are also called yunai belong to Spath hyttum of the Araceae vegetables, classified into ground taros and river taros)
0714.9030 90	冻、干的芋头(不论是否切片或制成团粒;芋头又称芋艿,为天南星科芋属植物。分旱芋、水芋)	13				50	13		千克	AB	Frozen, dried taro (no matter if it's sliced or made round; taros are also called yunai belong to Spath hyttum of the Araceae vegetables, classified into ground taros and river taros)
0714.9090	---其他	13	T3	6.5	0	50	13	5	千克	AB	---Other
0714.9090 10	鲜、冷、冻、干的兰科植物块茎	13				50	13	5	千克	ABFE	Tubers of orchid family, fresh, chilled, frozen or dried
0714.9090 91	含高淀粉或菊粉其他濒危类似根茎(包括西谷茎髓,不论是否切片或制成团粒,鲜冷冻或干的)	13				50	13	5	千克	ABFE	Similar roots and tubers with high starch or inulin content, in imminent dangers, whether or not sliced or in the form of pellets; sago pith
0714.9090 99	含有高淀粉或菊粉的其他类似根茎(包括西谷茎髓,不论是否切片或制成团粒,鲜冷冻或干的)	13				50	13	5	千克	AB	Similar roots and tubers with high starch or inulin content, whether or not sliced or in the form of pellets; sago pith

第八章
食用水果及坚果；
柑桔属水果或甜瓜的果皮

Chapter 8
Edible fruit and nuts;
peel of citrus fruit or melons

注释：

一、本章不包括非供食用的坚果或水果。

二、冷藏的水果和坚果应按相应的鲜果税目归类。

三、本章的干果可以部分复水或为下列目的进行其他处理：

（一）为保藏或保持其稳定性（例如，经适度热处理或硫化处理、添加山梨酸或山梨酸钾）；

（二）为改进或保持其外观（例如，添加植物油或少量葡萄糖浆）。

但必须保持干果的特征。

Notes:

1. This Chapter does not cover inedible nuts or fruits.
2. Chilled fruits and nuts are to be classified in the same headings as the corresponding fresh fruits and nuts.
3. Dried fruit or dried nuts of this Chapter may be partially rehydrated, or treated for the following purposes:

(a) For additional preservation or stabilization (e. g. , by moderate heat treatment, sulphuring, the addition of sorbic acid or potassium sorbate).

(b) To improve or maintain their appearance (e. g. , by the addition of vegetable oil or small quantities of glucose syrup).

Provided that they retain the character of dried fruit or dried nuts.

税则号列 Tariff Item.	货品名称	最惠国(%) MFN	协定(%) 东盟 CA	协定(%) 中巴 CP	协定(%) CT 中智 CC	普通 Gen	增值税率 VAT	出口退税 ED	计量单位 Unit	监管条件 SC	Article Description
08.01	**鲜或干的椰子、巴西果及腰果，不论是否去壳或去皮：**										**Coconuts, Brazil nuts and cashew nuts, fresh or dried, whether or not shelled or peeled:**
	-椰子：										-Coconuts:
0801.1100	--干的	12	0	6	7.2	80	13	5	千克	AB	--Desiccated
	--其他：										--Other:
0801.1910	---种用	0				0	13	5	千克	AB	---Seedlings
0801.1990	---其他	12	0	6	7.2	80	13	5	千克		---Other
0801.1990 01	鲜椰子（不论是否去壳或去皮）	12				80	13	5	千克	AB	Coconuts, fresh (whether or not shelled or peeled)
0801.1990 90	其他椰子（不论是否去壳或去皮）	12				80	13	5	千克	AB	Other coconute, whether or not shelled or peeled
	-巴西果：										-Brazil nuts:
0801.2100	--未去壳	10	0		0	80	13	5	千克	AB	--In shell
0801.2200	--去壳	10	0		0	80	13	5	千克	AB	--Shelled
	-腰果：										-Cashew nuts:
0801.3100	--未去壳	20	T3		12	70	13	5	千克	AB	--In shell
0801.3200	--去壳	10	T3		0	70	13	5	千克	AB	--Shelled
08.02	**鲜或干的其他坚果，不论是否去壳或去皮：**										**Other nuts, fresh or dried, whether or not shelled or peeled:**
	-巴旦杏：										-Almonds:
0802.1100	--未去壳	24	0		19.2	70	13	5	千克	AB	--In shell
0802.1200	--去壳	10	0		8	70	13	5	千克	AB	--Shelled
	-榛子：										-Hazelnuts or filberts (*Corylus spp*):
0802.2100	--未去壳	25	0		20	70	13	5	千克	AB	--In shell
0802.2200	--去壳	10	0		0	70	13	5	千克	AB	--Shelled
	-核桃：										-Walnuts:
0802.3100	--未去壳	25	0		20	70	13	5	千克	AB	--In shell
0802.3200	--去壳	20	0		16	70	13	5	千克	AB	--Shelled
	-栗子：										-Chestnuts (*Castanea spp.*):
0802.4010	---板栗	25	0		20	70	13	5	千克	AB	---Chestnuts
0802.4090	---其他	25	0		20	70	13	5	千克	AB	---Other
0802.5000	-阿月浑子果（开心果）	10	0		0	70	13	5	千克	AB	-Pistachios

税则号列 Tariff Item.	货 品 名 称	最惠国(%) MFN	协定(%)CT 东盟 CA	中巴 CP	中智 CC	普通 Gen	增值税率 VAT	出口退税 ED	计量单位 Unit	监管条件 SC	Article Description
	-马卡达姆坚果(夏威夷果):										-Hawaiian nuts:
0802.6010	---种用	0				70	13	5	千克	AB	---Seed
0802.6090	---其他	24	0		14.4	70	13	5	千克	AB	---Other
	-其他:										-Other:
0802.9010	---槟榔	10	0	5	0	30	13	5	千克		---Betel nuts
0802.9010 01	鲜的槟榔(不论是否去壳或去皮)	10				30	13	5	千克	AB	Betel nuts, fresh, whether or not shelled or peeled
0802.9010 90	干的槟榔(不论是否去壳或去皮)	10				30	13	5	千克	AB	Betel nuts, dried, whether or not shelled or peeled
0802.9020	---白果	25	0		15	70	13	5	千克	ABE	---Gingko nuts
0802.9030	---松子仁	25	0		15	70	13	5	千克		---Pine-nuts, shelled
0802.9030 10	鲜或干的红松子仁	25				70	13	5	千克	ABE	Korean pine-nuts, shelled, fresh or dried
0802.9030 20	鲜或干的其他濒危松子仁	25				70	13	5	千克	ABFE	Other pine-nuts, shelled in imminent dangers, fresh or dried
0802.9030 90	鲜或干的其他松子仁	25				70	13	5	千克	AB	Other pine-nuts, shelled, fresh
0802.9090	---其他	24	0		14.4	70	13	5	千克		---Other
0802.9090 10	鲜或干的干榧子、红松子、榧子(不论是否去壳或去皮)	24				70	13	5	千克	ABE	Chinese torreya or pine-nuts, fresh or dried, whether or not shelled or peeled
0802.9090 20	鲜或干的其他濒危松子(不论是否去壳或去皮)	24				70	13	5	千克	ABEF	Pine nut ni imminent dangers, fresh or dried whether or not shelled or peeled
0802.9090 90	鲜或干的其他坚果(不论是否去壳或去皮)	24				70	13	5	千克	AB	Other nuts, fresh or dried, whether or not shelled or peeled
08.03	**鲜或干的香蕉,包括芭蕉:**										**Bananas, including plantains, fresh or dried:**
0803.0000	鲜或干的香蕉,包括芭蕉	10	0	6.9	8	40	13	5	千克	AB	Bananas, including plantains, fresh or dried
08.04	**鲜或干的椰枣、无花果、菠萝、鳄梨、番石榴、芒果及山竹果:**										**Dates, figs, pineapples, avocados, guavas, mangoes and mangosteens, fresh or dried:**
0804.1000	-椰枣	15	0	0	0	40	13	5	千克	AB	-Dates
0804.2000	-无花果	30	0	5	24	70	13	5	千克	AB	-Figs
0804.3000	-菠萝	12	0	0	7.2	80	13	5	千克		-Pineapples
0804.3000 01	鲜菠萝	12				80	13	5	千克	AB	Pineapples, fresh
0804.3000 90	干菠萝	12				80	13	5	千克	AB	Pineapples, dried
0804.4000	-鳄梨	25	T3	5	20	80	13	5	千克	AB	-Avocados
	-番石榴、芒果及山竹果:										-Guavas, mangoes and mangosteens:
0804.5010	---番石榴	15	0	0	9	80	13	5	千克		---Guavas
0804.5010 01	鲜番石榴	15				80	13	5	千克	AB	Guavas, fresh
0804.5010 90	干番石榴	15				80	13	5	千克	AB	Guavas, dried
0804.5020	---芒果	15	0	0	9	80	13	5	千克		---Mangoes
0804.5020 01	鲜芒果	15				80	13	5	千克	AB	Mangoes, fresh
0804.5020 90	干芒果	15				80	13	5	千克	AB	Mangoes, dried
0804.5030	---山竹果	15	0	0	9	80	13	5	千克	AB	---Mangosteens
08.05	**鲜或干的柑桔属水果:**										**Citrus fruit, fresh or dried:**
0805.1000	-橙	11	T3	0	8.8	100	13	5	千克	AB	-Oranges

税则号列 Tariff Item.	货 品 名 称	最惠国(%) MFN	协定(%)CT 东盟 CA	中巴 CP	中智 CC	普通 Gen	增值税率 VAT	出口退税 ED	计量单位 Unit	监管条件 SC	Article Description
	-柑桔;杂交柑桔:										-Mandarins (including tangerines and satsumas); clementines, wilkings and similar citrus hybrids:
0805.2010	---蕉柑	12	T3	0	9.6	100	13	5	千克	AB	---Chiao-Kan
0805.2020	---阔叶柑橘	12	T3	0	9.6	100	13	5	千克	AB	---Latifolia Citrus
0805.2090	---其他	12	T3	0	9.6	100	13	5	千克	AB	---Other
0805.4000	-葡萄柚,包括柚	12	T3	0	9.6	100	13	5	千克	AB	-Grapefruit(include a pomelo)
0805.4000 01	鲜葡萄柚,包括鲜柚	12				100	13	5	千克	AB	Grapefruit fresh(include a pomelo)
0805.4000 90	干葡萄柚,包括干柚	12				100	13	5	千克	AB	Grapefruit dries(includ a pomelo)
0805.5000	-柠檬及酸橙	11	T3	0	8.8	100	13	5	千克	AB	-Lemons (*Citrus limon*, *Citrus limonum*) and limes (*Citrus aurantifolia*, *Citrus latifolia*)
0805.9000	-其他	30	T3	5	18	100	13	5	千克	AB	-Other
08.06	**鲜或干的葡萄:**										**Grapes, fresh or dried:**
0806.1000	-鲜的	13	0		10.4	80	13	5	千克	AB	-Fresh
0806.2000	-干的	10	0		8	80	13	5	千克	AB	-Dried
08.07	**鲜的甜瓜(包括西瓜)及木瓜:**										**Melons (including watermelons) and papaws (papayas), fresh:**
	-甜瓜,包括西瓜:										-Melons (including watermelons):
0807.1100	--西瓜	25	T3	12.5	15	70	13	5	千克	AB	--Watermelons
	--其他:										--Other:
0807.1910	---哈蜜瓜	12	T3	6	0	70	13	5	千克	AB	---Hami melons
0807.1920	---罗马甜瓜及加勒比甜瓜	12	T3	6	9.6	70	13	5	千克	AB	---Cantaloupes and Galia melons
0807.1990	---其他	12	T3	6	9.6	70	13	5	千克	AB	---Other
0807.2000	-木瓜	25	T3		15	70	13	5	千克	AB	-Papaws(papayas)
08.08	**鲜的苹果、梨及榅桲:**										**Apples, pears and quinces, fresh:**
0808.1000	-苹果	10	0		8	100	13	5	千克	AB	-Apples
	-梨及榅桲:										-Pears and quinces:
	---梨:										---Pears:
0808.2012	----鸭梨及雪梨	12	0	10	9.6	100	13	5	千克	AB	----Ya pears, Hsueh pears
0808.2013	----香梨	12	0	10	9.6	100	13	5	千克	AB	----Xiang pears
0808.2019	----其他	10	0		8	100	13	5	千克	AB	----Other
0808.2020	---榅桲	16	0		12.8	100	13	5	千克	AB	---Quinces
08.09	**鲜的杏、樱桃、桃(包括油桃)、梅及李:**										**Apricots, cherries, peaches (including nectarines), plums and sloes, fresh:**
0809.1000	-杏	25	T3		20	70	13	5	千克	AB	-Apricots
0809.2000	-樱桃	10	T3		6	70	13	5	千克	AB	-Cherries
0809.3000	-桃,包括油桃	10	T3		6	70	13	5	千克	AB	-Peaches, including nectarines
0809.4000	-梅及李	10	T3		6	70	13	5	千克	AB	-Plums and sloes
0809.4000 01	鲜梅	10				70	13	5	千克	AB	Plums, fresh
0809.4000 90	鲜李子	10				70	13	5	千克	AB	Sloes, fresh
08.10	**其他鲜果:**										**Other fruit, fresh:**
0810.1000	-草莓	18.4	T3		14.7	80	13	5	千克	AB	-Strawberries
0810.2000	-木莓、黑莓、桑椹及罗甘莓	25	T3		20	80	13	5	千克	AB	-Raspberries, blackberries, mulberries and loganberries
0810.4000	-蔓越桔及越桔	30	0		24	80	13	5	千克	AB	-Cranberries, bilberries and other fruits of the genus *Vaccinium*
0810.5000	-猕猴桃	20	T3	16.5	16	80	13	5	千克	AB	-Kiwifruit
0810.6000	-榴莲	20	T3		12	80	13	5	千克	AB	-Durians

税则号列 Tariff Item.	货品名称	最惠国(%) MFN	协定(%) CT 东盟 CA	 中巴 CP	 中智 CC	普通 Gen	增值税率 VAT	出口退税 ED	计量单位 Unit	监管条件 SC	Article Description
	-其他:										-Other:
0810.9010	---荔枝	30	T3	20	0	80	13	5	千克	AB	---Lychee
0810.9020	---黑、白或红的醋栗(加仑子)及鹅莓	25	T3		20	80	13	5	千克	AB	---Black, white or red currants and goose berries
0810.9030	---龙眼	12	T3		0	80	13	5	千克	AB	---Logan
0810.9040	---红毛丹	20	T3		0	80	13	5	千克	AB	---Rambutan
0810.9050	---番荔枝	20	T3		0	80	13	5	千克	AB	---Sugar apple
0810.9060	---杨桃	20	T3		0	80	13	5	千克	AB	---Carambola
0810.9070	---莲雾	20	T3	16.4	0	80	13	5	千克	AB	---Wax apple
0810.9080	---火龙果	20	T3	16.4	0	80	13	5	千克	ABFE	---Dragonfruit
0810.9090	---其他	20	T3	16.4	16	80	13	5	千克		---Other
0810.9090 01	鲜枣	20				80	13	5	千克	AB	Fruit of wingfruit elaeagus (Elaeagus mollis Diels), fresh
0810.9090 02	鲜枇杷	20				80	13	5	千克	AB	Loquat, fresh
0810.9090 03	鲜柿子	20				80	13	5	千克	AB	Persimmon fresh
0810.9090 10	鲜的翅果油树果	20				80	13	5	千克	ABE	Persimmon, fresh
0810.9090 90	其他鲜果	20				80	13	5	千克	AB	Other fruit, fresh
08.11	**冷冻水果及坚果,不论是否蒸煮、加糖或其他甜物质:**										**Fruit and nuts, uncooked or cooked by steaming or boiling in water, frozen, whether or not containing added sugar or other sweetening matter:**
0811.1000	-草莓	30	T3		24	80	13	5	千克	AB	-Strawberries
0811.2000	-木莓、黑莓、桑椹、罗甘莓、黑、白或红的醋栗(加仑子)及鹅莓	30	T3		24	80	13	5	千克	AB	-Raspberries, blackberries, mulberries, loganberries, black, white or red currants and gooseberries
	-其他:										-Other:
0811.9010	---栗子,未去壳	30	T3		0	80	13	5	千克	AB	---Chestnuts, in shell
0811.9090	---其他	30	T3		24	80	13	5	千克		---Other
0811.9090 10	冷冻的白果	30				80	13	5	千克	ABE	Ginkgo, frozen
0811.9090 21	冷冻的红松子	30				80	13	5	千克	ABE	Korean pine-nuts, shelled, forzen
0811.9090 22	冷冻的其他濒危松子	30				80	13	5	千克	ABEF	Other pine-nuts, shelled in imminent dangers
0811.9090 30	冷冻的榧子	30				80	13	5	千克	ABE	Chinese torreya-nuts, frozen
0811.9090 40	冷冻的翅果油树果	30				80	13	5	千克	ABE	Fruit of wingfruit elaeagus (Elaeagus mollis Diels), frozen
0811.9090 90	其他未列名冷冻水果及坚果	30				80	13	5	千克	AB	Other fruit and nuts, frozen
08.12	**暂时保藏(例如,使用二氧化硫气体、盐水、亚硫酸水或其他防腐液)的水果及坚果,但不适于直接食用的:**										**Fruit and nuts, provisionally preserved (for example, by sulphur dioxide gas, in brine, in sulphur water or in other preservative solutions), but unsuitable in that state for immediate consumption:**
0812.1000	-樱桃	30	0		24	80	13	5	千克	AB	-Cherries
0812.9000	-其他	27.7	T3		22.2	80	13	5	千克		-Other

税则号列 Tariff Item.	货品名称	最惠国(%) MFN	协定(%)CT 东盟 CA	中巴 CP	中智 CC	普通 Gen	增值税率 VAT	出口退税 ED	计量单位 Unit	监管条件 SC	Article Description
0812.9000 10	暂时保存的白果(用二氧化硫气体,盐水等物质处理,但不适于直接食用的)	27.7				80	13	5	千克	ABE	Ginkgo, provisionally preserved (for example, by sulphur dioxide gas, in brine, in sulphur water or in other preservative solutions), but unsuitable in that state for immediate consumption
0812.9000 21	暂时保存的红松子(用二氧化硫气体,盐水等物质处理,但不适于直接食用的)	27.7				80	13	5	千克	ABE	Korean pine-nuts, shelled, provisionally preserved (for example, by sulphur dioxide gas, in brine, in sulphur water or in other preservative solutions), but unsuitable in that state for immediate consumption
0812.9000 22	暂时保存的其他濒危松子(用二氧化硫气体,盐水等物质处理,但不适于直接食用的)	27.7				80	13	5	千克	ABFE	Other pine-nuts, shelled, in imminent dangers provisionally preserved (for example, by sulphur dioxide gas, in brine, in sulphur water or in other preservative solutions), but unsuitable in that state for immediate consumption
0812.9000 30	暂时保存的榧子(用二氧化硫气体,盐水等物质处理,但不适于直接食用的)	27.7				80	13	5	千克	ABE	Chinese toreeya-nuts, shelled provisionally preserved (for example, by sulphur dioxide gas, in brine, in sulphur water or in other preservative solutions), but unsuitable in that state for immediate consumption
0812.9000 40	暂时保存的翅果油树果(用二氧化硫气体,盐水等物质处理,但不适于直接食用的)	27.7				80	13	5	千克	ABE	Fruit of wingfruit elaeagus (*Elaeagus mollis Diels*) provisionally preserved (for example, by sulphur dioxide gas, in brine, in sulphur water or in other preservative solutions), but unsuitable in that state for immediate consumption
0812.9000 90	暂时保存的其他水果及坚果(用二氧化硫气体,盐水等物质处理,但不适于直接食用的)	27.7				80	13	5	千克	AB	Other fruit and nuts, provisionally preserved (for example, by sulphur dioxide gas, in brine, in sulphur water or in other preservative solutions), but unsuitable in that state for immediate consumption
08.13	**税目08.01至08.06以外的干果;本章的什锦坚果或干果:**										**Fruit, dried, other than that of headings No. 08.01 to 08.06; mixtures of nuts or dried fruits of this Chapter:**
0813.1000	-杏	25	0		15	70	13	5	千克	AB	-Apricots
0813.2000	-梅及李	25	T3		20	70	13	5	千克	AB	-Prunes
0813.3000	-苹果	25	T3		20	70	13	5	千克	AB	-Apples
	-其他干果:										-Other fruit:
0813.4010	---龙眼干、肉	20	T3		0	70	13	5	千克	AB	---Longans and longan pulps
0813.4020	---柿饼	25	T3		0	70	13	5	千克	AB	---Persimmons
0813.4030	---红枣	25	T3		0	70	13	5	千克	AB	---Red jujubes
0813.4040	---荔枝干	25	T3		0	70	13	5	千克	AB	---Preserved litchi
0813.4090	---其他	25	T3		20	70	13	5	千克		---Other
0813.4090 10	翅果油树干果	25				70	13	5	千克	ABE	Fruit of wingfruit elaeagus (*Elaeagus mollis Diels*), dried

税则号列 Tariff Item.	货品名称	最惠国(%) MFN	协定(%) CT 东盟 CA	中巴 CP	中智 CC	普通 Gen	增值税率 VAT	出口退税 ED	计量单位 Unit	监管条件 SC	Article Description
0813.4090 90	其他干果(税号 0801 至 0806 的干果除外)	25				70	13	5	千克	AB	Other fruit, dried, other than that of headings No. 08.01 to 08.06
0813.5000	-本章的什锦坚果或干果	18	T3		10.8	70	13	5	千克	AB	-Mixtures of nuts or dried fruits of this Chapter
08.14	**柑桔属水果或甜瓜(包括西瓜)的果皮,鲜、冻、干或用盐水、亚硫酸水或其他防腐液暂时保藏的:**										**Peel of citrus fruit or melons (including watermelons), fresh, frozen, dried or provisionally preserved in brine, in sulphur water or in other preservative solutions:**
0814.0000	柑桔属水果或甜瓜(包括西瓜)的果皮,鲜、冻、干或用盐水、亚硫酸水或其他防腐液暂时保藏的	25	T3		20	70	13	5	千克	AB	Peel of citrus fruit or melons (including watermelons), fresh, frozen, dried or provisionally preserved in brine, in sulphur water or in other preservative solutions

第九章
咖啡、茶、马黛茶及调味香料

Chapter 9
Coffee, tea, mate and spices

注释：

一、税目 09.04 至 09.10 所列产品的混合物，应按下列规定归类：

(一)同一税目的两种或两种以上产品的混合物仍应归入该税目；

(二)不同税目的两种或两种以上产品的混合物应归入税目 09.10。

税目 09.04 至 09.10 的产品[或上述(一)或(二)项的混合物]如添加了其他物质，只要所得的混合物保持了原产品的基本特性，其归类应不受影响。基本特性已经改变的，则不应归入本章；构成混合调味品的，应归入税目 21.03。

二、本章不包括荜澄茄椒或税目 12.11 的其他产品。

Notes:

1. Mixtures of the products of headings Nos. 09.04 to 09.10 are to be classified as follows:

   (a) Mixtures of two or more of the products of the same heading are to be classified in that heading;

   (b) Mixtures of two or more of the products of different headings are to be classified in heading No. 09.10.

   The addition of other substances to the products of headings Nos. 09.04 to 09.10 (or to the mixtures referred to in paragraph (a) or (b) above) shall not affect their classification provided the resulting mixtures retain the essential character of the goods of those headings. Otherwise such mixtures are not classified in this Chapter; those constituting mixed condiments or mixed seasonings are classified in heading No. 21.03.

2. This Chapter does not cover Cubeb pepper (*Piper cubeba*) or other products of heading No. 12.11.

税则号列 Tariff Item.	货品名称	最惠国(%) MFN	协定(%) CT 东盟 CA	中巴 CP	中智 CC	普通 Gen	增值税率 VAT	出口退税 ED	计量单位 Unit	监管条件 SC	Article Description
09.01	**咖啡，不论是否焙炒或浸除咖啡碱；咖啡豆荚及咖啡豆皮；含咖啡的咖啡代用品：**										**Coffee, whether or not roasted or decaffeinated; coffee husks and skins; coffee substitutes containing coffee in any proportion:**
	-未焙炒的咖啡：										-Coffee, not roasted:
0901.1100	--未浸除咖啡碱	8			0	50	17	5	千克	AB	--Not decaffeinated
0901.1200	--已浸除咖啡碱	8			0	50	17	5	千克	AB	--Decaffeinated
	-已焙炒的咖啡：										-Coffee, roasted:
0901.2100	--未浸除咖啡碱	15			12	80	17	13	千克	AB	--Not decaffeinated
0901.2200	--已浸除咖啡碱	15	T3		12	80	17	13	千克	AB	--Decaffeinated
	-其他：										-Other:
0901.9010	---咖啡豆荚及咖啡豆皮	10	T3		0	30	17	5	千克	AB	---Coffee husks and skins
0901.9020	---含咖啡的咖啡代用品	30	T3		18	80	17	13	千克	AB	---Coffee substitutes containing coffee
09.02	**茶，不论是否加香料：**										**Tea, whether or not flavoured:**
	-绿茶(未发酵)，内包装每件净重不超过3千克：										-Green tea (not fermented) in immediate packings of a content not exceeding 3kg:
0902.1010	---花茶	15	T3	7.5	9	100	13	5	千克	AB	---Flavoured
0902.1090	---其他	15	T3	7.5	9	100	13	5	千克	AB	---Other
	-其他绿茶(未发酵)：										-Other green tea (not fermented):
0902.2010	---花茶	15	T3	7.5	9	100	13	5	千克	AB	---Flavoured
0902.2090	---其他	15	T3	7.5	9	100	13	5	千克	AB	---Other
	-红茶(已发酵)及半发酵茶，内包装每件净重不超过3千克：										-Black tea (fermented) and partly fermented tea, in immediate packings of a content not exceeding 3 kg:
0902.3010	---乌龙茶	15	T3	7.5	0	100	13	5	千克	AB	---Oolong tea
0902.3020	---普洱茶	15	T3	7.5	0	100	13	5	千克	AB	---Pu-er tea
0902.3090	---其他	15	T3	7.5	0	100	13	5	千克	AB	---Other
	-其他红茶(已发酵)及半发酵茶：									AB	-Other black tea (fermented) and other partly fermented tea:
0902.4010	---乌龙茶	15	T3	7.5	0	100	13	5	千克	AB	---Oolong tea

税则号列 Tariff Item.	货品名称	最惠国(%) MFN	协定(%)CT 东盟 CA	中巴 CP	中智 CC	普通 Gen	增值税率 VAT	出口退税 ED	计量单位 Unit	监管条件 SC	Article Description
0902.4020	---普洱茶	15	T3	7.5	0	100	13	5	千克	AB	---Pu-er tea
0902.4090	---其他	15	T3	7.5	0	100	13	5	千克	AB	---Other
09.03	**马黛茶：**										**Mate：**
0903.0000	马黛茶	10	8		0	100	13	13	千克	AB	Mate
09.04	**胡椒；辣椒干及辣椒粉：**										**Pepper of the genus *Piper*; dried or crushed or ground fruits of the genus *Capsicum or of the genus Pimenta*：**
	-胡椒：										-Pepper：
0904.1100	--未磨	20			12	70	13	5	千克		--Neither crushed nor ground
0904.1100 10	毕拨	20				70	13	5	千克	QAB	Piper longum
0904.1100 90	未磨胡椒（毕拨除外）	20				70	13	5	千克	AB	Pepper of the genus *Piper*, neither crushed nor ground (other than piper longum)
0904.1200	--已磨	20		10	12	70	13	13	千克	AB	--Crushed or ground
	-辣椒干及辣椒粉：										-Fruits of the genus *Capsicum* or of the genus *Pimenta*, dried or crushed or ground：
0904.2010	---辣椒干	20	T3	10	0	70	13	5	千克	AB	---Neither crushed nor ground
0904.2020	---辣椒粉	20	T3	10	0	70	13	13	千克	AB	---Crushed or ground
09.05	**香子兰豆：**										**Vanilla：**
0905.0000	香子兰豆	15	8		9	50	13	5	千克	AB	Vanilla
09.06	**肉桂及肉桂花：**										**Cinnamon and cinnamon-tree flowers：**
	-未磨：										-Neither crushed nor ground：
0906.1100	--锡兰肉桂	5			0	50	13	5	千克	AB	--Cinnamon
0906.1900	--其他	5			0	50	13	5	千克	AB	--Other
0906.2000	-已磨	15	8		9	50	13	13	千克	QAB	-Crushed or ground
09.07	**丁香（母丁香、公丁香及丁香梗）：**										**Cloves (whole fruit, cloves and stems)：**
0907.0000	丁香（母丁香、公丁香及丁香梗）	3			0	14	13	5	千克	QAB	Cloves (whole fruit, cloves and stems)
09.08	**肉豆蔻、肉豆蔻衣及豆蔻：**										**Nutmeg, mace and cardamoms：**
0908.1000	-肉豆蔻	8	5		0	30	13	5	千克	QABE	-Nutmeg
0908.2000	-肉豆蔻衣	8	5		0	30	13	5	千克	AEB	-Mace
0908.3000	-豆蔻	3			0	14	13	5	千克	QABE	-Cardamoms
09.09	**茴芹子、八角茴香、小茴香子、芫荽子、枯茗子及贲蒿子；杜松果：**										**Seeds of anise, badian, fennel, coriander, cumin or caraway; juniper berries：**
	-茴芹子或八角茴香：										-Seeds of anise or badian：
0909.1010	---八角茴香	20	12		0	90	13	5	千克	QAB	---Star aniseed
0909.1090	---其他	15	8		0	50	13	5	千克	AB	---Other
0909.2000	-芫荽子	15	8		9	50	13	5	千克	AB	-Seeds of coriander
0909.3000	-枯茗子	15	8	7.5	9	50	13	5	千克	AB	-Seeds of cumin
0909.4000	-贲蒿子	15	8		9	50	13	5	千克	AB	-Seeds of caraway
0909.5000	-小茴香子；杜松果	15	8		9	50	13	5	千克	QAB	-Seeds of fennel; juniper berries
09.10	**姜、番红花、姜黄、麝香草、月桂叶、咖喱及其他调味香料：**										**Ginger, saffron, turmeric (curcuma), thyme, bay leaves, curry and other spices：**
0910.1000	-姜	15	T3	7.5	9	50	13	5	千克	AB	-Ginger
0910.2000	-番红花	2			0	14	13	5	千克	QAB	-Saffron

税则号列 Tariff Item.	货　品　名　称	最惠国(%) MFN	协定(%)CT 东盟 CA	 中巴 CP	 中智 CC	普通 Gen	增值税率 VAT	出口退税 ED	计量单位 Unit	监管条件 SC	Article Description
0910.3000	-姜黄	15	8	7.5	9	50	13	5	千克	QAB	-Turmeric (curcuma)
	-其他调味香料：										-Other spices:
0910.9100	--本章注释一(二)所述的混合物	15	8	7.5	9	50	17	13	千克	AB	--Mixtures referred to in Note 1(b) to this Chapter
0910.9900	--其他	15	8		0	50	17	5	千克	AB	--Other

第十章 谷物

Chapter 10 Cereals

注释：

一、（一）本章各税目所列产品必须带有谷粒，不论是否成穗或带杆。

（二）本章不包括已去壳或经其他加工的谷物。但去壳、碾磨、磨光、上光、半熟或破碎的稻米仍应归入税目10.06。

二、税目10.05不包括甜玉米（第七章）。

子目注释：

所称“硬粒小麦”，是指硬粒小麦属的小麦及以该属具有相同染色体数目（28）的小麦种间杂交所得的小麦。

Notes:

1. (a) The products specified in the headings of this Chapter are to be classified in those headings only if grains are present, whether or not in the ear or on the stalk.

   (b) This Chapter does not cover grains which have been hulled or otherwise worked. However, rice, husked, milled, polished, glazed, parboiled or broken remains classified in heading No. 10.06

2. Heading No. 10.05 does not cover sweet corn (Chapter 7).

Subheading Note:

The term “durum wheat” means wheat of the *Triticum durum* species and the hybrids derived from the inter-specific crossing of *Triticum durum* which have the same number (28) of chromosomes as that species.

税则号列 Tariff Item.	货品名称	最惠国(%) MFN	协定(%)CT 东盟 CA	中巴 CP	中智 CC	普通 Gen	增值税率 VAT	出口退税 ED	计量单位 Unit	监管条件 SC	Article Description
10.01	**小麦及混合麦：**										**Wheat and maslin:**
1001.1000	-硬粒小麦	*65				*180	13	13	千克		-Durum wheat
1001.1000 01	硬粒小麦（配额内）	1				180	13	13	千克	4xABty	Durum wheat (in-quota)
1001.1000 90	硬粒小麦（配额外）	65				180	13	13	千克	4xABy	Durum wheat (out-quota)
	-其他：										-Other:
1001.9010	---种用	*65				*180	13	13	千克		---Seed
1001.9010 01	种用小麦（配额内）	1				180	13	13	千克	4xABty	Wheat, seed (in-quota)
1001.9010 90	种用小麦（配额外）	65				180	13	13	千克	4xABy	Wheat, seed (out-quota)
1001.9090	---其他	*65				*180	13	13	千克		---Other
1001.9090 01	其他小麦及混合麦（配额内）	1				180	13	13	千克	4xABty	Other wheat and maslin (in-quota)
1001.9090 90	其他小麦及混合麦（配额外）	65				180	13	13	千克	4xABy	Other wheat and maslin (out-quota)
10.02	**黑麦：**										**Rye:**
1002.0010	---种用	0				0	13	5	千克	AB	---Seed
1002.0090	---其他	3			0	8	13	5	千克	AB	---Other
10.03	**大麦：**										**Barley:**
1003.0010	---种用	0				160	13	5	千克	AB	---Seed
1003.0090	---其他	3		0	0	160	13	5	千克	AB	---Other
10.04	**燕麦：**										**Oats:**
1004.0010	---种用	0				0	13	5	千克	AB	---Seed
1004.0090	---其他	2			0	8	13	5	千克	AB	---Other
10.05	**玉米：**										**Maize (corn):**
1005.1000	-种用	*20				*180	13	13	千克		-Seed
1005.1000 01	种用玉米（配额内）	1				180	13	13	千克	4xAByt	Maize (cron) seed (in-quota)
1005.1000 90	种用玉米（配额外）	20				180	13	13	千克	4xABy	Maize (corn) seed (out-quota)
1005.9000	-其他	*65				*180	13	13	千克		-Other
1005.9000 01	其他玉米（配额内）	1				180	13	13	千克	4xAByt	Other maize (cron) (in-quota)
1005.9000 90	其他玉米（配额外）	65				180	13	13	千克	4xABy	Other maize (cron) (out-quota)
10.06	**稻谷、大米：**										**Rice:**
	-稻谷：										-Rice in husk (paddy or rough):
	---种用：										---Seed:

税则号列 Tariff Item.	货品名称	最惠国(%) MFN	协定(%) CT 东盟 CA	中巴 CP	中智 CC	普通 Gen	增值税率 VAT	出口退税 ED	计量单位 Unit	监管条件 SC	Article Description
1006.1011	----籼米	*65				*180	13	13	千克		----Long grain
1006.1011 01	种用籼米稻谷(配额内)	1				180	13	13	千克	4xAByt	Rice in husk (paddy or rough), shien rice (*long-grained nonglutinous rice*), seed (in-quota)
1006.1011 90	种用籼米稻谷(配额外)	65				180	13	13	千克	4xABy	Rice in husk (paddy or rough), shien rice (*long-grained nonglutinous rice*), seed (out-quota)
1006.1019	----其他	*65				*180	13	13	千克		----Other
1006.1019 01	其他种用稻谷(配额内)	1				180	13	13	千克	4xAByt	Other rice in husk (paddy or rough), seed (in-quota)
1006.1019 90	其他种用稻谷(配额外)	65				180	13	13	千克	4xABy	Other rice in husk (paddy or rough), seed (out-quota)
	---其他:										---Other:
1006.1091	----籼米	*65				*180	13	13	千克		----Long grain
1006.1091 01	其他籼米稻谷(配额内)	1				180	13	13	千克	4xAByt	Other rice in husk (paddy or rough), shien rice (*long-grained nonglutinous rice*) (in-quota)
1006.1091 90	其他籼米稻谷(配额外)	65				180	13	13	千克	4xABy	Other rice in husk (paddy or rough), shien rice (*long-grained nonglutinous rice*) (out-quota)
1006.1099	----其他	*65				*180	13	13	千克		----Other
1006.1099 01	其他稻谷(配额内)	1				180	13	13	千克	4xAByt	Other rice in husk (paddy or rough) (in-quota)
1006.1099 90	其他稻谷(配额外)	65				180	13	13	千克	4xABy	Other rice in husk (paddy or rough) (out-quota)
	-糙米:										-Husked (brown) rice:
1006.2010	---籼米	*65				180	13	13	千克		---Long grain
1006.2010 01	籼米糙米(配额内)	1				180	13	13	千克	4xAByt	Husked (brown) rice, shien rice (*long-grained nonglutinous rice*) (in-quota)
1006.2010 90	籼米糙米(配额外)	65				180	13	13	千克	4xABy	Husked (brown) rice, shien rice (*long-grained nonglutinous rice*) (out-quota)
1006.2090	---其他	*65				*180	13	13	千克		---Other
1006.2090 01	其他糙米(配额内)	1				180	13	13	千克	4xAByt	Other husked (brown) rice (in-quota)
1006.2090 90	其他糙米(配额外)	65				180	13	13	千克	4xABy	Other husked (brown) rice, (out-quota)
	-精米,不论是否磨光或上光:										-Semi-milled or wholly milled rice, whether or not polished or glazed:
1006.3010	---籼米	*65				*180	13	13	千克		---Long grain
1006.3010 01	籼米精米[不论是否磨光或上光(配额内)]	1				180	13	13	千克	4xAByt	Semi-milled or wholly milled rice, shien rice (*long-grained nonglutinous rice*), whether or not polished or glazed (in-quota)
1006.3010 90	籼米精米[不论是否磨光或上光(配额外)]	65				180	13	13	千克	4xABy	Semi-milled or wholly milled rice, shien rice (*long-grained nonglutinous rice*), whether or not polished or glazed (out-quota)
1006.3090	---其他	*65				*180	13	13	千克		---Other

税则号列 Tariff Item.	货品名称	最惠国(%) MFN	协定(%) CT 东盟 CA	中巴 CP	中智 CC	普通 Gen	增值税率 VAT	出口退税 ED	计量单位 Unit	监管条件 SC	Article Description
1006.3090 01	其他精米[不论是否磨光或上光(配额内)]	1				180	13	13	千克	4xAByt	Other semi-milled or wholly milled rice, whether or not polished or glazed (in-quota)
1006.3090 90	其他精米[不论是否磨光或上光(配额外)]	65				180	13	13	千克	4xABy	Other semi-milled or wholly milled rice, whether or not polished or glazed (out-quota)
	-碎米:										-Broken rice:
1006.4010	---籼米	*65				*180	13	13	千克		---Long grain
1006.4010 01	籼米碎米(配额内)	1				180	13	13	千克	4xAByt	Broken rice, shien rice (*long-grained nonglutinous rice*) (in-quota)
1006.4010 90	籼米碎米(配额外)	65				180	13	13	千克	4xABy	Broken rice, shien rice (*long-grained nonglutinous rice*) (out-quota)
1006.4090	---其他	*65				*180	13	13	千克		---Other
1006.4090 01	其他碎米(配额内)	1				180	13	13	千克	4xAByt	Other broken rice (in-quota)
1006.4090 90	其他碎米(配额外)	65				180	13	13	千克	4xABy	Other broken rice (out-quota)
10.07	**食用高粱:**										**Grain sorghum:**
1007.0010	---种用	0				0	13	5	千克	AB	---Seed
1007.0090	---其他	2			0	8	13	5	千克	AB	---Other
10.08	**荞麦、谷子及加那利草子;其他谷物:**										**Buckwheat, millet and canary seed; other cereals:**
1008.1000	-荞麦	2			0	8	13	5	千克	AB	-Buckwheat
1008.2000	-谷子	2			0	8	13	5	千克	AB	-Millet
1008.3000	-加那利草子	2			0	8	13	5	千克	AB	-Canary seed
	-其他谷物:										-Other cereals:
1008.9010	---种用	0				0	13	5	千克	AB	---Seed
1008.9090	---其他	3			0	8	13	5	千克	AB	---Other

第十一章

制粉工业产品;麦芽;淀粉;菊粉;面筋

注释:

一、本章不包括:

(一)作为咖啡代用品的焙制麦芽(税目09.01或21.01);

(二)税目19.01的经制作的细粉、粗粒、粗粉或淀粉;

(三)税目19.04的玉米片及其他产品;

(四)税目20.01、20.04或20.05的经制作或保藏的蔬菜;

(五)药品(第三十章);

(六)具有芳香料制品或化妆盥洗品性质的淀粉(第三十三章)。

二、(一)下表所列谷物碾磨产品按干制品重量计如果同时符合以下两个条件,应归入本章;但是,整粒、滚压、制片或磨碎的谷物胚芽均归入税目11.04:

1. 淀粉含量(按修订的尤艾斯旋光法测定)超过表列第(2)栏的比例;

2. 灰分含量(除去任何添加的矿物质)不超过表列第(3)栏的比例。

否则,应归入税目23.02。

(二)符合上述规定归入本章的产品,如果用表列第(4)或第(5)栏规定孔径的金属丝网筛过筛,其通过率按重量计不低于表列比例的,应归入税目11.01或11.02。

否则,应归入税目11.03或11.04。

谷　　物 (1)	淀粉含量 (2)	灰分含量 (3)	通过下列孔径筛子的比率	
			315微米 (4)	500微米 (5)
小麦及黑麦	45%	2.5%	80%	—
大　　麦	45%	3%	80%	—
燕　　麦	45%	5%	80%	—
玉米及高粱	45%	2%	—	90%
大　　米	45%	1.6%	80%	—
荞　　麦	45%	4%	80%	—

三、税目11.03所称"粗粒"及"粗粉",是指谷物经碾碎所得的下列产品:

(一)玉米产品,用2毫米孔径的金属丝网筛过筛,通过率按重量计不低于95%的;

Chapter 11

Products of the milling industry; malt; starches; inulin; wheat gluten

Notes:

1. This Chapter does not cover:

(a) Roasted malt put up as coffee substitutes (heading No. 09.01 or 21.01);

(b) Prepared flours, groats, meals or starches of heading No. 19.01;

(c) Corn flakes or other products of heading No. 19.04;

(d) Vegetables, prepared or preserved, ofheading No. 20.01, 20.04 or 20.05;

(e) Pharmaceutical products (Chapter 30); or

(f) Starches having the character of perfumery, cosmetic or toilet preparations (Chapter 33).

2. (A) Products from the milling of the cereals listed in the table below fall in this Chapter if they have, by weight on the dry product (However, germ of cereals, whole, rolled, flaked or ground, is always classified in heading No. 11.04.)

(a) a starch content (determined by the modified Ewers polarimetric method) exceeding that indicated in Column (2); and

(b) an ash content (after deduction of any added minerals) not exceeding that indicated in Column (3).

Otherwise, they fall in heading No. 23.02

(B) Products falling in this Chapter under the above provisions shall be classified in heading No. 11.01 or 11.02 if the percentage passing through a woven metal wire cloth sieve with the aperture indicated in Column (4) or (5) is not less, by weight, than that shown against the cereal concerned.

Otherwise, they fall in heading No. 11.03 or 11.04

Cereal (1)	Starch content (2)	Ash content (3)	Rate of passage through a sieve with an aperture of	
			315 micrometres (microns) (4)	500 micrometres (microns) (5)
Wheat and rye	45%	2.5%	80%	-
Barley	45%	3%	80%	-
Oats	45%	5%	80%	-
Maize(corn) and grain Sorghum	45%	2%	-	90%
Rice	45%	1.6%	80%	-
Buckwheat	45%	4%	80%	-

3. For the purposes of heading 11.03, the terms "groats" and "meal" mean products obtained by the fragmentation of cereal grains, of which:

(a) in the case of maize (corn) products, at least 95% by weight passes through a woven metal wire cloth sieve with an aperture of 2mm.

（二）其他谷物产品，用1.25毫米孔径的金属丝网筛过筛，通过率按重量计不低于95%的。

(b) in the case of other cereal products, at least 95% by weight passes through a woven metal wire cloth sieve with an aperture of 1.25mm.

税则号列 Tariff Item.	货品名称	最惠国(%) MFN	协定(%) CT 东盟 CA	中巴 CP	中智 CC	普通 Gen	增值税率 VAT	出口退税 ED	计量单位 Unit	监管条件 SC	Article Description
11.01	**小麦或混合麦的细粉：**										**Wheat or maslin flour:**
1101.0000	小麦或混合麦的细粉	*65				*130	13	13	千克		Wheat or maslin flour
1101.0000 01	小麦或混合麦的细粉（配额内）	6				130	13	13	千克	ABt	Wheat or maslin flour (in-quota)
1101.0000 90	小麦或混合麦的细粉（配额外）	65				130	13	13	千克	AB	Wheat or maslin flour (out-quota)
11.02	**其他谷物细粉，但小麦或混合麦的细粉除外：**										**Cereal flours other than of wheat or maslin:**
1102.1000	-黑麦细粉	5			0	14	13	5	千克	AB	-Rye flour
1102.2000	-玉米细粉	*40				*130	13	13	千克		-Maize (corn) flour
1102.2000 01	玉米细粉（配额内）	9				130	13	13	千克	ABt	Maize (cron) flour (in-quota)
1102.2000 90	玉米细粉（配额外）	40				130	13	13	千克	AB	Maize(corn)flour(out-quota)
	-其他：										-Other:
	---大米细粉：										---Rice flour:
1102.9011	----籼米的	*40				*130	13	13	千克		----Shien rice (long-grained nonglutinous rice)
1102.9011 01	籼米大米细粉（配额内）	9				130	13	13	千克	ABt	Shien rice (long-grained nonglutinous rice flourcin-quota)
1102.9011 90	籼米大米细粉（配额外）	40				130	13	13	千克	AB	Shien rce (long-grained noglutinousrice out-quota)
1102.9019	----其他	*40				*130	13	13	千克		----Other
1102.9019 01	其他大米细粉（配额内）	9				130	13	13	千克	ABt	Other rice flour (in-quota)
1102.9019 90	其他大米细粉（配额外）	40				130	13	13	千克	AB	Other rice flour (out-quota)
1102.9090	---其他	5			0	14	13	5	千克	AB	---Other
11.03	**谷物的粗粒、粗粉及团粒：**										**Cereal groats, meal and pellets:**
	-粗粒及粗粉：										-Groats and meal:
1103.1100	--小麦的	*65				*130	13	13	千克		--Of wheat
1103.1100 01	小麦粗粒及粗粉（配额内）	9				130	13	13	千克	ABt	Wheat groats and meal (in-quota)
1103.1100 90	小麦粗粒及粗粉（配额外）	65				130	13	13	千克	AB	Wheat groats and meal (out-quota)
1103.1300	--玉米的	*65				*130	13	13	千克		--Of maize (corn)
1103.1300 01	玉米粗粒及粗粉（配额内）	9				130	13	13	千克	ABt	Maize (cron) groats and meal (in-quota)
1103.1300 90	玉米粗粒及粗粉（配额外）	65				130	13	13	千克	AB	Maize (cron) groats and meal (out-quota)
	--其他：										--Other:
1103.1910	---燕麦的	5			0	14	13	5	千克	AB	---Of oats
	---大米的：										---Of rice:
1103.1921	----籼米的	*10				*70	13	13	千克		----Of long grain
1103.1921 01	籼米大米粗粒及粗粉（配额内）	9				70	13	13	千克	ABt	Shien rice (*long-grained nonglutinous rice*) groats and meal (in-quota)
1103.1921 90	籼米大米粗粒及粗粉（配额外）	10				70	13	13	千克	AB	Shien rice (*long-grained nonglutinous rice*) groats and meal (out-quota)
1103.1929	----其他	*10				*70	13	13	千克		----Other
1103.1929 01	其他大米粗粒及粗粉（配额内）	9				70	13	13	千克	ABt	Other rice groats and meal (in-quota)
1103.1929 90	其他大米粗粒及粗粉（配额外）	10				70	13	13	千克	AB	Other rice groats and meal (out-quota)

税则号列 Tariff Item.	货品名称	最惠国(%) MFN	协定(%)CT 东盟 CA	中巴 CP	中智 CC	普通 Gen	增值税率 VAT	出口退税 ED	计量单位 Unit	监管条件 SC	Article Description
1103.1990	---其他	5			0	14	13	5	千克	AB	---Other
	-团粒:										-Pellets:
1103.2010	---小麦的	*65				*180	13	13	千克		---Of wheat
1103.2010 01	小麦团粒(配额内)	10				180	13	13	千克	ABt	Wheat pellets (in-quota)
1103.2010 90	小麦团粒(配额外)	65				180	13	13	千克	AB	Wheat pellets (out-quota)
1103.2090	---其他	20	12		12	50	13	5	千克	AB	---Other
11.04	**经其他加工的谷物(例如,去壳、滚压、制片、制成粒状、切片或粗磨),但税目10.06的稻谷、大米除外;谷物胚芽,整粒、滚压、制片或磨碎的:**										**Cereal grains otherwise worked (for example, hulled, rolled, flaked, pearled, sliced or kibbled), except rice of heading No. 10.06; germ of cereals, whole, rolled, flaked or ground:**
	-滚压或制片的谷物:										-Rolled or flaked grains:
1104.1200	--燕麦的	20	12		16	50	17	5	千克	AB	--Of oats
	--其他:										--Of other cereals:
1104.1910	---大麦的	20	12		12	50	17	5	千克	AB	---Of barley
1104.1990	---其他	20	12		12	50	17	5	千克	AB	---Other
	-经其他加工的谷物(例如,去壳、制成粒状、切片或粗磨):										-Other worked grains (for example, hulled, pearled, sliced or kibbled):
1104.2200	--燕麦的	20	12		16	50	17	5	千克	AB	--Of oats
1104.2300	--玉米的	*65				*180	13	13	千克		--Of maize (corn)
1104.2300 01	经其他加工的玉米(配额内)	10				180	13	13	千克	4xAByt	Maize (cron) otherwise worked (in-quota)
1104.2300 90	经其他加工的玉米(配额外)	65				180	13	13	千克	4xABy	Maize (cron) otherwise worked (out-quota)
	--其他:										--Other:
1104.2910	---大麦的	65	12		39	114	13	5	千克	AB	---Of barley
1104.2990	---其他	20	12		12	50	13	5	千克	AB	---Other
1104.3000	-谷物胚芽,整粒、滚压、制片或磨碎的	20	12		12	50	17	5	千克	AB	-Germ of cereals, whole, rolled, flaked or ground
11.05	**马铃薯的细粉、粗粉、粉末、粉片、颗粒及团粒:**										**Flour, meal, powder, flakes, granules and pellets of potatoes:**
1105.1000	-细粉、粗粉及粉末	15	8		9	50	17	13	千克	AB	-Flour, meal and powder
1105.2000	-粉片、颗粒及团粒	15	8		12	50	17	13	千克	AB	-Flakes, granules and pellets
11.06	**用税目07.13的干豆或税目07.14的西谷茎髓及植物根茎、块茎制成的细粉、粗粉及粉末;用第八章的产品制成的细粉、粗粉及粉末:**										**Flour, meal and powder of the dried leguminous vegetables of heading No. 07.13, of sago or of roots or tubers of heading No. 07.14; or of the products of Chapter 8:**
1106.1000	-用税目07.13的干豆制成的	10	8		0	30	17	13	千克	AB	-Of the dried leguminous vegetables of heading No. 07.13
1106.2000	-用税目07.14的西谷茎髓及植物根茎、块茎制成的	20	T3		12	50	17	13	千克	AB	-Of sago or of roots or tubers of heading 07.14
1106.3000	-用第八章的产品制成的	20	12	10	16	80	17	13	千克	AB	-Of the products of Chapter 8
11.07	**麦芽,不论是否焙制:**										**Malt, whether or not roasted:**
1107.1000	-未焙制	10	8		8	50	17	13	千克	AB	-Not roasted
1107.2000	-已焙制	10	8		8	50	17	13	千克	AB	-Roasted
11.08	**淀粉;菊粉:**										**Starches; inulin:**
	-淀粉:										-Starches:

税则号列 Tariff Item.	货品名称	最惠国(%) MFN	协定(%)CT 东盟 CA	中巴 CP	中智 CC	普通 Gen	增值税率 VAT	出口退税 ED	计量单位 Unit	监管条件 SC	Article Description
1108.1100	--小麦淀粉	20	12		12	50	17	13	千克	AB	--Wheat starch
1108.1200	--玉米淀粉	20	T3		12	50	17	13	千克	AB	--Maize (corn) starch
1108.1300	--马铃薯淀粉	15	8		9	50	17	13	千克	AB	--Potato starch
1108.1400	--木薯淀粉	10	T3		0	50	17	13	千克	AB	--Manioc (cassava) starch
1108.1900	--其他	20	12		12	50	17	13	千克	AB	--Other starches
1108.2000	-菊粉	20	12		12	50	17	13	千克	AB	-Inulin
11.09	**面筋,不论是否干制:**										**Wheat gluten, whether or not dried:**
1109.0000	面筋,不论是否干制	18	12		10.8	80	17	13	千克	AB	Wheat gluten, whether or not dried

第十二章
含油子仁及果实;杂项子仁及果实;工业用或药用植物;稻草、秸杆及饲料

注释:

一、税目 12.07 主要包括油棕果及油棕仁、棉子、蓖麻子、芝麻、芥子、红花子、罂粟子、牛油树果。但不包括税目 08.01 或 08.02 的产品及油橄榄(第七章或第二十章)。

二、税目 12.08 不仅包括未脱脂的细粉和粗粉,而且包括部分或全部脱脂以及用其本身的油料全部或部分复脂的细粉和粗粉。但不包括税目 23.04 至 23.06 的残渣。

三、甜菜子、草子及其他草本植物种子、观赏用花的种子、蔬菜种子、林木种子、果树种子、巢菜子(蚕豆除外)、羽扇豆属植物种子,可一律视为种植用种子,归入税目 12.09。

但下列各项即使作种子用,也不归入税目12.09:

(一)豆类蔬菜或甜玉米(第七章);
(二)第九章的调味香料及其他产品;
(三)谷物(第十章);
(四)税目 12.01 至 12.07 或 12.11 的产品。

四、税目 12.11 主要包括下列植物或这些植物的某部分:
罗勒、琉璃苣、人参、海索草、甘草、薄荷、迷迭香、芸香、鼠尾草及苦艾。
但税目 12.11 不包括:
(一)第三十章的药品;
(二)第三十三章的芳香料制品及化妆盥洗品;
(三)税目 38.08 的杀虫剂、杀菌剂、除草剂、消毒剂及类似产品。

五、税目 12.12 的"海草及其他藻类"不包括:

(一)税目 21.02 的已死的单细胞微生物:
(二)税目 30.02 的培养微生物;
(三)税目 31.01 或 31.05 的肥料。

子目注释:

子目1 205.10 所称"低芥子酸油菜子",是指所获取的固定油中芥子酸含量按重量计低于 2%,以及所得的固体成分每克葡萄糖苷酸(酯)含量低于 30 微摩尔的油菜子。

Chapter 12
Oil seeds and oleaginous fruits; miscellaneous grains, seeds and fruit; industrial or medicinal plants; straw and fodder

Notes:

1. Heading No. 12.07 applies, *inter alia*, to palm nuts and kernels, cotton seeds, castor oil seeds, sesamum seeds, mustard seeds, safflower seeds, poppy seeds and shea nuts (karite nuts). It does not apply to products of heading No. 08.01 or 08.02 or to olives (Chapter 7 or Chapter 20).
2. Heading No. 12.08 applies not only to non-defatted flours and meals but also to flours and meals which have been defatted or partially defatted and wholly or partially refatted with their original oils. It does not, however, apply to residues of headings Nos. 23.04 to 23.06
3. For the purposes of heading No. 12.09, beet seeds, grass and other herbage seeds, seeds of ornamental flowers, vegetable seeds, seeds of forest trees, seeds of fruit trees, seeds of vetches (other than those of the species *Vicia faba*) or of lupines are to be regarded as "seeds of a kind used for sowing".

   Heading No. 12.09 does not, however, apply to the following even if for sowing:

   (a) Laguminous vegetables or sweet corn (Chapter 7);
   (b) Spices or other products of Chapter 9;
   (c) Cereals (Chapter 10); or
   (d) Products of headings Nos. 12.01 to 12.07 or 12.11
4. Heading No. 12.11 applies, *inter alia*, to the following plants or parts thereof:

   Basil, borage, ginseng, hyssop, liquorice, all species of mint, rosemary, rue, sage and wormwood.

   Heading No. 12.11 does not, however, apply to:

   (a) Medicaments of Chapter 30;
   (b) Perfumery, cosmetic or toilet preparations of Chapter 33; or
   (c) Insecticides, fungicides, herbicides, disinfectants or similar products of heading No. 38.08.
5. For the purposes of heading No. 12.12, the term "seaweeds and other algae" does not include:

   (a) Dead single-cell micro-organisms of heading No. 21.02;
   (b) Cultures of micro-organisms of heading No. 30.02; or
   (c) Fertilizers of heading No. 31.01 or 31.05.

Subheading Notes:

For the purposes of subheading No. 1205.10, the expression "low erucic acid rape or colza seeds" means rape or colza seeds yielding a fixed oil which has an erucic acid content of less than 2% by weight and yielding a solid component which contains less than 30 micromoles of glucosinolates per gram.

税则号列 Tariff Item.	货 品 名 称	最惠国(%) MFN	协定(%)CT 东盟 CA	中巴 CP	中智 CC	普通 Gen	增值税率 VAT	出口退税 ED	计量单位 Unit	监管条件 SC	Article Description
12.01	**大豆,不论是否破碎:**										**Soya beans, whether or not broken:**
1201.0010	---种用	0				180	13	5	千克	AB	---Seed
	---其他:										---Other:
1201.0091	----黄大豆	3		0	2.4	180	13	5	千克	AB	----Yellow soya beans
1201.0092	----黑大豆	3		0	0	180	13	5	千克	AB	----Black soya beans
1201.0093	----青大豆	3		0	0	180	13	5	千克	AB	----Green soya beans
1201.0099	----其他	3		0	0	180	13	5	千克	AB	----Other
12.02	**未焙炒或未烹煮的花生,不论是否去壳或破碎:**										**Ground-nuts, not roasted or otherwise cooked, whether or not shelled or broken:**
	-未去壳:										-In shell:
1202.1010	---种用	0				0	13	5	千克	AB	---Seed
1202.1090	---其他	15	8		9	70	13	5	千克	AB	---Other
1202.2000	-去壳,不论是否破碎	15	8		0	70	13	5	千克	AB	-Shelled, whether or not broken
12.03	**干椰子肉:**										**Copra:**
1203.0000	干椰子肉	15	T3	7.5	9	30	13	5	千克	AB	Copra
12.04	**亚麻子,不论是否破碎:**										**Linseed, whether or not broken:**
1204.0000	亚麻子,不论是否破碎	15	8		9	70	13	5	千克	AB	Linseed, whether or not broken
12.05	**油菜子,不论是否破碎:**										**Rape or colza seeds, whether or not broken:**
	-低芥子酸油菜子:										-Low erucic acid rape or colza seeds:
1205.1010	---种用	0				80	13		千克	AB	---Seed
1205.1090	---其他	9	5	0	7.2	80	13	5	千克	AB	---Other
	-其他:										-Other:
1205.9010	---种用	0				80	13		千克	AB	---Seed
1205.9090	---其他	9	5	0	7.2	80	13	5	千克	AB	---Other
12.06	**葵花子,不论是否破碎:**										**Sunflower seeds, whether or not broken:**
1206.0010	---种用	0				0	13	5	千克	AB	---Seed
1206.0090	---其他	15	8		12	70	13	5	千克	AB	---Other
12.07	**其他含油子仁及果实,不论是否破碎:**										**Other oil seeds and oleaginous fruits, whether or not broken:**
	-棉子:										-Cottonseed
1207.2010	---种用	0				0	13	5	千克	AB	---Seeds for cultivation
1207.2090	---其他	15	8		9	70	13	5	千克	AB	---Other
	-芝麻:										-Sesamum seeds:
1207.4010	---种用	0				0	13	5	千克	AB	---Seeds for cultivation
1207.4090	---其他	10	T3	9	0	70	13	5	千克	AB	---Other
	-芥子:										-Mustard seeds:
1207.5010	---种用	0				0	13	5	千克	AB	---Seeds for cultivation
1207.5090	---其他	15	8		9	70	13	5	千克	AB	---Other
	-其他:										-Other:
1207.9100	--罂粟子	20	12		12	70	13	5	千克	AB	--Poppy seeds
	--其他:										--Other:
1207.9910	---种用	0				0	13	5	千克	AB	---Seed
	---其他:										---Other:
1207.9991	----牛油树果	20	T3		16	70	13	5	千克	AB	----Shea nuts(*karite nuts*)
1207.9992	----油棕果子及油棕	10	8		0	70	13	5	千克	AB	----Palm nuts and bernels
1207.9993	----蓖麻子	15	T3		9	70	13	5	千克	AB	----Castor seeds
1207.9994	----红花子	20	12		12	70	13	5	千克	AB	----Safflower seeds

税则号列 Tariff Item.	货 品 名 称	最惠国(%) MFN	协定(%)CT 东盟 CA	中巴 CP	中智 CC	普通 Gen	增值税率 VAT	出口退税 ED	计量单位 Unit	监管条件 SC	Article Description
1207.9999	----其他	10	T3		8	70	13	5	千克	AB	----Other
12.08	**含油子仁或果实的细粉及粗粉,但芥子粉除外:**										**Flours and meals of oil seeds or oleaginous fruits, other than those of mustard:**
1208.1000	-大豆粉	9	5		0	70	17	5	千克	AB	-Of soya beans
1208.9000	-其他	15	8		9	80	17	13	千克	AB	-Other
12.09	**种植用的种子、果实及孢子:**										**Seeds, fruit and spores, of a kind used for sowing:**
1209.1000	-糖甜菜子	0				0	13	5	千克	AB	-Sugar beet seed
	-饲料植物种子:										-Seeds of forage plants:
1209.2100	--紫苜蓿子	0				0	13		千克	AB	--Lucerne (alfalfa) seed
1209.2200	--三叶草子	0				0	13		千克	AB	--Clover (*Trifolium spp.*) seed
1209.2300	--羊茅子	0				0	13		千克	AB	--Fescue seed
1209.2400	--草地早熟禾子	0				0	13		千克	AB	--Kentucky blue grass (*Poa pratensis L.*) seed
1209.2500	--黑麦草种子	0				0	13		千克	AB	--Rye grass (*Lolium multiflorum Lam.*, *Lolium perenne L.*) seed
	--其他:										--Other:
1209.2910	---甜菜籽,糖甜菜籽除外	0				0	13	5	千克	AB	---Sugar beet seed
1209.2990	---其他	0				0	13		千克	AB	---Other
1209.3000	-草本花卉植物种子	0				0	13		千克		-Seeds of herbaceous plants cultivated principally for their flowers
1209.3000 10	濒危草本花卉植物种子	0				0	13		千克	ABFE	Seeds of herbaceous plants cultivated principally for their flowers, in imminent dangers
1209.3000 90	其他草本花卉植物种子	0				0	13		千克	AB	Other seeds of herbaceous plants cultivated principally for their flowers
	-其他:										-Other:
1209.9100	--蔬菜种子	0				0	13		千克	AB	--Vegetable seeds
	--其他:										--Other:
1209.9910	---西瓜子	0				0	13		千克	AB	---Seeds of water melons
1209.9920	---甜瓜子	0				0	13		千克	AB	---Seeds of melons
1209.9990	---其他	0				0	13		千克		---Other
1209.9990 10	其他种植用濒危种子、果实及孢子	0				0	13		千克	ABFE	Other seeds, fruit and spores, of a kind used for sowing, in imminent dangers
1209.9990 90	其他种植用的种子、果实及孢子	0				0	13		千克	AB	Other seeds, fruit and spores, of a kind used for sowing
12.10	**鲜或干的啤酒花,不论是否研磨或制成团粒;蛇麻腺:**										**Hop cones, fresh or dried, whethr or not ground, powdered or in the form of pellets; lupulin:**
1210.1000	-啤酒花,未经研磨也未制成团粒	20	12		12	50	17	13	千克	AB	-Hop cones, neither ground nor powdered nor in the form of pellets
1210.2000	-啤酒花,经研磨或制成团粒;蛇麻腺	10	8		0	50	17	13	千克	AB	-Hop cones, ground, powdered or in the form of pellets; lupulin

税则号列 Tariff Item.	货品名称	最惠国(%) MFN	协定(%) CT			普通 Gen	增值税率 VAT	出口退税 ED	计量单位 Unit	监管条件 SC	Article Description
			东盟 CA	中巴 CP	中智 CC						
12.11	主要用作香料、药料、杀虫、杀菌或类似用途的植物或这些植物的某部分(包括子仁及果实),鲜或干的,不论是否切割、压碎或研磨成粉:										**Plants and parts of plants (including seeds and fruits), of a kind used primarily in perfumery, in pharmacy or for insecticidal, fungicidal or similar purposes, fresh or dried, whether or not cut, crushed or powdered:**
	-人参:										-Ginseng roots:
1211.2010	---西洋参	7.5			0	70	13	5	千克	AQBFE	---American ginseng
1211.2020	---野山参(西洋参除外)	20	12	16.4	12	90	13	5	千克	ABaFE	---Wild ginseng (other than American ginseng)
	---其他:										---Other:
1211.2091	----鲜的	20	12		12	50	13	5	千克	ABa	----Fresh
1211.2099	----其他	20	12		12	50	13	5	千克	ABQa	----Other
1211.3000	-古柯叶	9	5		0	50	13	5	千克		-Coca leaf
1211.3000 10	药用古柯叶(不论是否切割、压碎或研磨成粉)	9				50	13	5	千克	AB	Coca leaf of a kind used in pharmacy, whether or not cut, crushed or powdered
1211.3000 20	做香料用古柯叶(不论是否切割、压碎或研磨成粉)	9				50	13	5	千克	AB	Coca leaf of a kind used in perfumery, whether or not cut, crushed or powdered
1211.3000 90	杀虫杀菌用古柯叶(不论是否切割、压碎或研磨成粉)	9				50	13	5	千克	AB	Coca leaf of a kind used for insecticidal, fungicidal, whether or not cut, crushed or powdered
1211.4000	-罂粟杆	9	5		0	50	13	5	千克		-Poppy straw
1211.4000 10	药用罂粟杆(不论是否切割、压碎或研磨成粉)	9				50	13	5	千克	AB	Poppy straw of a kind used in pharmacy, whether or not cut, crushed or powdered
1211.4000 20	做香料用罂粟杆(不论是否切割、压碎或研磨成粉)	9				50	13	5	千克	AB	Poppy straw of a kind used in perfumery, whether or not cut, crushed or powdered
1211.4000 90	杀虫杀菌用罂粟杆(不论是否切割、压碎或研磨成粉)	9				50	13	5	千克	AB	Poppy straw of a kind used for insecticidal, fungicidal, whether or not cut, crushed or powdered
	-其他:										-Other:
	---主要用作药料的植物及其某部分:										---Of a kind used primarily in pharmacy:
1211.9011	----当归	6	5	3	0	30	13	5	千克	AQB	----Radix angelicae sinensis
1211.9012	----田七	6	5	3	0	20	13	5	千克	AQB	----Radix pseudoginseng
1211.9013	----党参	6	5	3	0	20	13	5	千克	AQB	----Radix codonopsitis
1211.9014	----黄连	6	5	3	0	20	13	5	千克	AQB	----Rhizoma coptidis
1211.9015	----菊花	6	5	3	0	20	13	5	千克	AQB	----Flos chrysanthemi
1211.9016	----冬虫夏草	6	5	3	0	20	13	5	千克	AQBE	----Cordyceps sinensis
1211.9017	----贝母	6	5	3	0	20	13	5	千克	AQB	----Bulbs fritillariae thunbergii
1211.9018	----川芎	6	5	3	0	20	13	5	千克	AQB	----Rhizoma ligustici
1211.9019	----半夏	6	5	3	0	20	13	5	千克	AQB	----Rhizoma pinelliae
1211.9021	----白芍	6	5	3	0	20	13	5	千克	AQB	----Radix paeoniae lactiflorae
1211.9022	----天麻	6	5	3	0	20	13	5	千克	AQBFE	----Rhizoma gastrodiae
1211.9023	----黄芪	6	5	3	0	30	13	5	千克	AQB	----Radix astragali
1211.9024	----大黄、籽黄	6	5	3	0	20	13	5	千克	AQB	----Rhubarb
1211.9025	----白术	6	5	3	0	20	13	5	千克	AQB	----Rhizoma atractylodis macrocephalae
1211.9026	----地黄	6	5	3	0	20	13	5	千克	AQB	----Radix rehmanniae
1211.9027	----槐米	6	5	3	0	20	13	5	千克	AQB	----Flos sophorae

税则号列 Tariff Item.	货品名称	最惠国(%) MFN	协定(%)CT 东盟 CA	中巴 CP	中智 CC	普通 Gen	增值税率 VAT	出口退税 ED	计量单位 Unit	监管条件 SC	Article Description
1211.9028	----杜仲	6	5	3	0	20	13	5	千克	AQB	----Cortex eucommiae
1211.9029	----茯苓	6	T3	3	0	20	13	5	千克	AQB	----Poria
1211.9031	----枸杞	6	5	3	0	30	13	5	千克	AQB	----Fructus lycii
1211.9032	----大海子	6	5	3	0	20	13	5	千克	AQB	----Bantaroi seeds
1211.9033	----沉香	3		1.5	0	20	13	5	千克	AQFEB	----Aloes wood
1211.9034	----沙参	6	5	3	0	20	13	5	千克	AQB	----Adenophora axilliflora
1211.9035	----青蒿	6	5		0	20	13		千克	AB	----Southernwood
1211.9036	----甘草	6	5		0	30	13	5	千克	AQB4xy	----Zhong Guo licorice(Glycyrrhiza uralenisis)
1211.9039	----其他	6	T3	3	0	20	13	5	千克		----Other
1211.9039 10	药料用麻黄草粉	6				20	13	5	千克	23AQB	Chinese ephedra (Ephedrasinica) powder, of a kind used primarily in pharmacy
1211.9039 20	药料用麻黄草	6				20	13	5	千克	8QA	Chinese ephedra (Ephedrasinica), of a kind used primarily in pharmacy
1211.9039 30	大麻	6				20	13	5	千克	AWB	Hemp
1211.9039 40	罂粟壳	6				20	13	5	千克	AWB	Poppy pod
1211.9039 50	鲜或干的木香(不论是否切割,压碎或研磨成粉)	6				20	13	5	千克	ABFE	Banksia rose, fresh or dried, whether or not cut, crushed or powdered
1211.9039 60	鲜或干的黄草及枫斗(石斛)(不论是否切割、压碎或研磨成粉)	6				20	13	5	千克	ABFE	Herba dendrobii (in straight form or in earring form), fresh or dried, whether or not cut, crushed or powdered
1211.9039 70	鲜或干的苁蓉(不论是否切割、压碎或研磨成粉)	6				20	13	5	千克	ABFE	Herba cistanche, fresh or dried, whether or not cut, crushed or powdered
1211.9039 80	鲜或干的红豆杉皮、枝叶等(不论是否切割、压碎或研磨成粉)	6				20	13	5	千克	ABFE	Bark, banch and leaf of English yew, fresh or dried, whether or not cut, crushed or powdered
1211.9039 91	其他主要用作药料鲜或干濒危植物(包括其某部分,不论是否切割、压碎或研磨成粉)	6				20	13	5	千克	ABFE	Other plants, of a kind used primarily in pharmacy, fresh or dried, whether or not cut, crushed or powdered
1211.9039 92	加纳籽、车前子壳粉、育亨宾皮(包括其某部分,不论是否切割,压碎或研磨成粉)	6				20	13	5	千克	AB	(whether or not cut, crushed or powdered)
1211.9039 99	其他主要用作药料的鲜或干的植物(包括其某部分,不论是否切割、压碎或研磨成粉)	6				20	13	5	千克	ABQ	Other plants, of a kind used primarily in pharmacy, fresh or dried, whether or not cut, crushed or powdered
1211.9050	---主要用作香料的植物及其某部分	8	5	4	0	50	13	5	千克		---Of a kind used primarily in perfumery
1211.9050 10	香料用麻黄草粉	8				50	13	5	千克	23AB	Chinese ephedra (Ephedrasinica) powder, of a kind used in perfumery
1211.9050 20	香料用麻黄草	8				50	13	5	千克	8A	Chinese ephedra (Ephedrasinica), of a kind used in perfumery

税则号列 Tariff Item.	货品名称	最惠国(%) MFN	协定(%) CT 东盟 CA	中巴 CP	中智 CC	普通 Gen	增值税率 VAT	出口退税 ED	计量单位 Unit	监管条件 SC	Article Description
1211.9050 91	主要用作香料的濒危植物(包括其某部分,不论是否切割、压碎或研磨成粉)	8				50	13	5	千克	ABFE	Other plants in imminent dangers, of a kind used in perfumery, whether or not cut, crushed or powdered
1211.9050 99	其他主要用作香料的植物(包括其某部分,不论是否切割、压碎或研磨成粉)	8				50	13	5	千克	AB	Other plants, of a kind used in perfumery, whether or not cut, crushed or powdered
	---其他:										---Other:
1211.9091	----鱼藤根、除虫菊	3		1.5	0	11	13	5	千克	AB	----Derris roots and pyrethrum
1211.9099	----其他	9	5	4.5	0	30	13	5	千克		----Other
1211.9099 10	其他用麻黄草粉	9				30	13	5	千克	23AB	Chinese ephedra (*Ephedra sinica*) powder
1211.9099 20	其他用麻黄草	9				30	13	5	千克	8A	Other Chinese ephedra (Ephedrasinica)
1211.9099 91	其他鲜或干杀虫、杀菌用濒危植物(不论是否切割,压碎或研磨成粉)	9				30	13	5	千克	ABFE	Other plants in imminent dangers, of a kind used for insecticidal, fungicidal, fresh or dried, whether or not cut, crushed or powdered
1211.9099 99	其他鲜或干的杀虫、杀菌用植物(不论是否切割、压碎或研磨成粉)	9				30	13	5	千克	AB	Other plants, of a kind used for insecticidal, fungicidal, fresh or dried, whether or not cut, crushed or powdered
12.12	**鲜、冷、冻或干的刺槐豆、海草及其他藻类、甜菜及甘蔗,不论是否碾磨;主要供人食用的其他税目未列名的果核、果仁及植物产品(包括未焙制的菊苣根):**										**Locust beans, seaweeds and other algae, sugar beet and sugar cane, fresh, chilled, frozen or dried, whether or not ground; fruit stones and kernels and other vegetable products (including unroasted chicory roots of the variety *Cichorium intybus sativum*) of a kind used primarily for human consumption, not elsewhere specified or included:**
	-海草及其他藻类:										-Seaweeds and other algae:
1212.2010	---海带	20	12	10	16	70	13	5	千克		---Sea tangle
1212.2010 10	鲜海带(不论是否碾磨)	20				70	13	5	千克	AB	Sea tangle, fresh, whether or not ground
1212.2010 90	冷、冻或干的海带(不论是否碾磨)	20				70	13	5	千克	AB	Sea tangle, chilled, frozen or dried, whether or not ground
1212.2020	---发菜	20	12	10	16	70	13	5	千克		---Black moss
1212.2020 10	鲜发菜(不论是否碾磨)	20				70	13	5	千克	8A	Black moss, fresh, whether or not ground
1212.2020 90	冷、冻或干的发菜(不论是否碾磨)	20				70	13	5	千克	8A	Black moss, chilled, frozen or dried, whether or not ground
	---裙带菜:										---Pinnatifida:
1212.2031	----干的	15	8	7.5	12	70	13	5	千克	AB	----Dried
1212.2032	----鲜的	15	8	7.5	12	70	13	5	千克	AB	----Fresh
1212.2039	----其他	15	8	7.5	12	70	13	5	千克	AB	----Other
	---紫菜:										---Laver:
1212.2041	----干的	15	8	7.5	12	70	13	5	千克	AB	----Dried
1212.2042	----鲜的	15	8	7.5	12	70	13	5	千克	AB	----Fresh

税则号列 Tariff Item.	货品名称	最惠国(%) MFN	协定(%) CT 东盟 CA	中巴 CP	中智 CC	普通 Gen	增值税率 VAT	出口退税 ED	计量单位 Unit	监管条件 SC	Article Description
1212.2049	----其他	15	8	7.5	12	70	13	5	千克	AB	----Other
1212.2050	---马尾藻	15	8	7.5	12	70	13	5	千克		---Sagarsso weed
1212.2050 10	鲜马尾藻(不论是否碾磨)	15				70	13	5	千克	AB	Sagarsso weed, fresh, whether or not ground
1212.2050 90	冷、冻或干的马尾藻(不论是否碾磨)	15				70	13	5	千克	AB	Sagarsso weed, chilled, frozen or dried, whether or not ground
1212.2090	---其他	15	8	7.5	12	70	13	5	千克		---Other
1212.2090 10	其他鲜的海草及其他藻类(不论是否碾磨)	15				70	13	5	千克	AB	Other seaweeds and other algae, fresh, whether or not ground
1212.2090 90	冷、冻或干的其他海草及其他藻类(不论是否碾磨)	15				70	13	5	千克	AB	Other seaweeds and other algae, chilled, frozen or dried, whether or not ground
	-其他:										-Other:
1212.9100	--甜菜	20	12		12	70	13	5	千克	AB	--Sugar beet
	--其他:										--Other:
	---杏、桃(包括油桃)、梅或李的核及核仁:										---Apricot, peach (including nectarine) or plum stones and kernels:
1212.9911	----苦杏仁	20	12		16	80	13	5	千克	QAB	----Bitter
1212.9912	----甜杏仁	20	12		16	80	13	5	千克	AB	----Sweet
1212.9919	----其他	20	12		16	80	13	5	千克	AB	----Other
1212.9920	---刺槐豆,包括刺槐豆子	20	12	10	12	70	13	5	千克	AB	---Locust beans, including locust beans seeds
	---其他:										---Other:
1212.9991	----黑瓜子	20	12		12	80	13	5	千克	AB	----Black watermelon seeds
1212.9992	----红瓜子	20	12		12	80	13	5	千克	AB	----Red watermelon seeds
1212.9993	----白瓜子	20	12		12	80	13	5	千克	AB	----Pumpkin seeds
1212.9994	----莲子	20	12		12	80	13	5	千克	AB	----Lotus seeds(*Semen Nelumbinis*)
1212.9995	----甘蔗	20	0		0	70	13	5	千克	AB	----Sugar cane
1212.9999	----其他	30	0		0	70	13	5	千克		----Other
1212.9999 10	其他供人食用濒危植物产品(包括未焙制的菊苣根,包括果核、仁等)	30				70	13	5	千克	ABFE	Other fruit stones and kernels and other vegetable products (including unroasted chicory roots of the variety *Cichorium intybus sativum*) of a kind used primarily for human consumption, in imminent dangers
1212.9999 90	其他供人食用果核、仁及植物产品(包括未焙制的菊苣根)	30				70	13	5	千克	AB	Other fruit stones and kernels and other vegetable products (including unroasted chicory roots of the variety *Cichorium intybus sativum*) of a kind used primarily for human consumption
12.13	**未经处理的谷类植物的茎、秆及谷壳,不论是否切碎、碾磨、挤压或制成团粒:**										**Cereal straw and husks, unprepared, whether or not chopped, ground, pressed or in the form of pellets:**
	未经处理的谷类植物的茎、秆及谷壳,不论是否切碎、碾磨、挤压或制成团粒:										Cereal straw and husks, unprepared, whether or not chopped, ground, pressed or in the form of pellets:
1213.0010	---未经处理的稻草的茎、秆	12	8		7.2	35	13	5	千克	AB	---Cereal straw urprepared
1213.0090	---其他	12	8		7.2	35	13	5	千克	AB	---Other

税则号列 Tariff Item.	货品名称	最惠国(%) MFN	协定(%)CT 东盟 CA	中巴 CP	中智 CC	普通 Gen	增值税率 VAT	出口退税 ED	计量单位 Unit	监管条件 SC	Article Description
12.14	**芜菁甘蓝、饲料甜菜、饲料用根、干草、紫苜蓿、三叶草、驴喜豆、饲料羽衣甘蓝、羽扇豆、巢菜及类似饲料,不论是否制成团粒:**										**Swedes, mangolds, fodder roots, hay, lucerne (alfalfa), clover, sainfoin, forage kale, lupines, vetches and similar forage products, whether or not in the form of pellets:**
1214.1000	-紫苜蓿粗粉及团粒	5			0	35	13		千克	AB	-Lucerne (alfalfa) meal and pellets
1214.9000	-其他	9	5		0	35	13		千克	AB	-Other

第十三章
虫胶;树胶、树脂及其他植物液、汁

Chapter 13
Lac; gums, resins and other vegetable saps and extracts

注释:

税目13.02主要包括甘草、除虫菊、啤酒花、芦荟的浸膏及鸦片,但不包括:

一、按重量计蔗糖含量在10%以上或制成糖食的甘草浸膏(税目17.04);

二、麦芽膏(税目19.01);

三、咖啡精、茶精、马黛茶精(税目21.01);

四、构成含酒精饮料的植物汁、液(第二十二章);

五、樟脑、甘草甜及税目29.14或29.38的其他产品;

六、罂粟杆浓缩物,按重量计生物碱含量不低于50%(税目29.39);

七、税目30.03或30.04的药品及税目30.06的血型试剂;

八、鞣料或染料的浸膏(税目32.01或32.03);

九、精油、浸膏、净油、香膏、提取的油树脂或精油的水馏液及水溶液;饮料制造业用的以芳香物质为基料的制剂(第三十三章);

十、天然橡胶、巴拉塔胶、古塔波胶、银胶菊胶、糖胶树胶或类似的天然树胶(税目40.01)。

Notes:

Heading No. 13.02 applies, *inter alia*, to liquorice extract and extract of pyrethrum, extrace of hops, extract of aloes and opium. The heading does not apply to:

(a) Liquorice extract containing more than 10% by weight of sucrose or put up as confectionery (heading No. 17.04);

(b) Malt extract (heading No. 19.01);

(c) Extracts of coffee, tea or mate (heading No. 21.01);

(d) Vegetable saps or extracts constituting alcoholic beverages (Chapter 22);

(e) Camphor, glycyrrhizin or other products of heading No. 29.14 or 29.38;

(f) Concentrates of poppy straw containing not less than 50% by weight of alkaloids (heading No. 29.39);

(g) Medicaments of heading No. 30.03 or 30.04 or bloodgrouping reagents (heading No. 30.06);

(h) Tanning or dyeing extracts (heading No. 32.01 or 32.03);

(i) Essential oils, concretes, absolutes, resinoids, extracted oleoresins, aqueous distillates or aqueous solutions of essential oils or preparations based on odoriferous substances of a kind used for the manufacture of beverages (Chapter 33); or

(j) Natural rubber, balata, gutta-percha, guayule, chicle or similar natural gums (heading No. 40.01).

本国注释:

子目1302.1100的鸦片,我国禁止进口。

National note:

Opium of Subheading No. 1302.1100 is subject to import ban.

税则号列 Tariff Item.	货品名称	最惠国(%) MFN	协定(%) 东盟 CA	中巴 CP	CT 中智 CC	普通 Gen	增值税率 VAT	出口退税 ED	计量单位 Unit	监管条件 SC	Article Description
13.01	虫胶;天然树胶、树脂、树胶脂及油树脂(例如,香树脂):										Lac; natural gums, resins, gum-resins and oleoresins (for example, balsams):
1301.2000	-阿拉伯胶	15	8	0	9	40	13	5	千克	AB	-Gum Arabic
	-其他:										-Other:
1301.9010	---胶黄耆树胶(卡喇杆胶)	15	8	0	9	40	13	5	千克	AB	---Gum tragacanth
1301.9020	---乳香、没药及血竭	3		0	0	17	13	5	千克	ABQ	---Olibanum, myrrh and dragon's blood
1301.9030	---阿魏	3		0	0	17	13	5	千克	AB	---Asafoetida
1301.9040	---松脂	15	8	0	9	45	13	5	千克		---Pine-resin
1301.9040 10	濒危松科植物的松脂	15				45	13	5	千克	ABE	Pine-resin of plants of pine family in imminent dangers
1301.9040 90	其他松脂	15				45	13	5	千克	AB	Other pine-resin
1301.9090	---其他	15	8	0	9	45	13	5	千克		---Other
1301.9090 10	龙血树脂、大戟脂、愈创树脂	15				45	13	5	千克	ABFE	Resin of daemonorops draco, resin of euphorbia, resin of lignum vitae
1301.9090 20	大麻脂	15				45	13	5	千克	ABW	Charas, churrus
1301.9090 91	其他濒危植物的天然树胶、树脂[包括天然树胶脂及其他油树脂(例如:香树脂)]	15				45	13	5	千克	ABFE	Other natural gums, resins, gum-resins and oleoresins (for example, balsams) of plants in imminent dangers

税则号列 Tariff Item.	货品名称	最惠国(%) MFN	协定(%) CT 东盟 CA	中巴 CP	中智 CC	普通 Gen	增值税率 VAT	出口退税 ED	计量单位 Unit	监管条件 SC	Article Description
1301.9090 99	其他天然树胶、树脂[包括天然树胶脂及其他油树脂(例如:香树脂)]	15				45	13	5	千克	AB	Other natural gums in imminent dangers, resins, gum-resins and oleoresins (for example, balsams)
13.02	**植物液汁及浸膏;果胶、果胶酸盐及果胶酸酯;从植物产品制得的琼脂、其他胶液及增稠剂,不论是否改性:**										**Vegetable saps and extracts; pectic substances, pectinates and pectates; agar-agar and other mucilages and thickeners, whether or not modified, derived from vegetable products:**
	-植物液汁及浸膏:										-Vegetable saps and extracts:
1302.1100	--鸦片	0				0	0	13	千克	WB9	--Opium
1302.1200	--甘草的	6	5		0	20	17	13	千克	4xABy	--Of liquorice
1302.1300	--啤酒花的	10	8`		0	80	17	13	千克	AB	--Of hops
	--其他:										--Other:
1302.1910	---生漆	20	12		16	90	17	5	千克	AB	---Crude lacquer
1302.1920	---印楝素	3			0	11	17	5	千克	AB	---Azadirachtin
1302.1930	---除虫菊的或含鱼藤酮植物根茎的(1302、1400)	3			0	11	17	13	千克	AB	---Of pyrethrum or of the roots of plants containing rotenone
1302.1990	---其他	20	12	15	16	80	17	13	千克		---Other
1302.1990 11	供制农药用麻黄浸膏粉	20				80	17	13	千克	23AB	Chinese ephedra extract powder for pestcide preparations
1302.1990 12	供制农药用麻黄浸膏	20				80	17	13	千克	23AB	Chinese ephedra extract for pestcide preparations
1302.1990 13	供制农药用的濒危植物液汁及浸膏	20				80	17	13	千克	ABFE	Vegetable saps and extracts for pestcide preparations in imminent dangers
1302.1990 19	供制农药用的其他植物液汁及浸膏	20				80	17	13	千克	AB	Other vegetable saps and extracts, for pestcide preparations
1302.1990 91	供制医药用麻黄浸膏粉	20				80	17	13	千克	Q23AB	Chinese ephedra extract powder, for medical purposes
1302.1990 92	供制医药用麻黄浸膏	20				80	17	13	千克	Q23AB	Chinese ephedra extract for medical purposes
1302.1990 93	其他麻黄浸膏粉	20				80	17	13	千克	23AB	Other chinese ephedra extract powder
1302.1990 94	其他麻黄浸膏	20				80	17	13	千克	23AB	Other chinese ephedra extract
1302.1990 95	红豆杉液汁及浸膏	20				80	17	13	千克	ABFE	Saps and extracts of English yew
1302.1990 96	黄草汁液及浸膏	20				80	17	13	千克	ABFE	Saps and extracts of herba dendroii
1302.1990 97	其他濒危植物液汁及浸膏	20				80	17	13	千克	ABFE	Saps and extracts of other vegetable, in imminent dangers
1302.1990 99	其他植物液汁及浸膏	20				80	17	13	千克	AB	Other vegetable saps and extracts
1302.2000	-果胶、果胶酸盐及果胶酸酯	20	12		12	80	17	13	千克	AB	-Pectic substances, pectinates and pectates
	-从植物产品制得的胶液及增稠剂,不论是否改性:										-Mucilages and thickeners, whether or not modified, derived from vegetable products:
1302.3100	--琼脂	10	8		8	80	17	13	千克	AB	--Agar-agar
1302.3200	--从刺槐豆、刺槐豆子或瓜尔豆制得的胶液及增稠剂,不论是否改性	15	8	0	12	80	17	13	千克	AB	--Mucilages and thickeners, whether or not modified, derived from locust beans, locust bean seeds or guar seeds
1302.3900	--其他	15	8		12	80	17	13	千克		--Other

税则号列 Tariff Item.	货品名称	最惠国(%) MFN	协定(%)CT 东盟 CA	中巴 CP	中智 CC	普通 Gen	增值税率 VAT	出口退税 ED	计量单位 Unit	监管条件 SC	Article Description
1302.3900 10	未列名濒危植物胶液及增稠剂	15				80	17	13	千克	ABFE	Mucilages and thickeners, derived from vegetable products in imminent dangers, not elsewhere specified or included
1302.3900 90	其他未列名植物胶液及增稠剂	15				80	17	13	千克	AB	Other mucilages and thickeners, derived from vegetable products, not elsewhere specified or included

第十四章 编结用植物材料；其他植物产品

Chapter 14 Vegetable plaiting materials; vegetable products not elsewhere specified or included

注释：

一本章不包括归入第十一类的下列产品：

主要供纺织用的植物材料或植物纤维，不论其加工程度如何；或经过处理使其只能作为纺织原料用的其他植物材料。

二、税目14.01主要包括竹（不论是否劈开、纵锯、切段、圆端、漂白、磨光、染色或进行不燃处理）、劈开的柳条、芦苇及类似品和藤心、藤丝、藤片。但不包括木片条（税目44.04）。

三、税目14.04不包括木丝（税目44.05）及供制帚、制刷用成束、成簇的材料（税目96.03）

Notes:

1. This Chapter does not cover the following products which are to be classified in Section XI:

Vegetable materials or fibres of vegetable materials of a kind used primarily in the manufacture of textiles, however prepared, or other vegetable materials which have undergone treatment so as to render them suitable for use only as textile materials.

2. Heading No. 14.01 applies, *inter alia*, to bamboos (whether or not split, sawn lengthwise, cut to length, rounded at the ends, bleached, rendered non-inflammable, polished or dyed), split osier, reeds and the like, to rattan cores and to drawn or split rattans. The heading does not apply to chipwood (heading No. 44.04).

3. Heading No. 14.04 does not apply to wood wool (heading No. 44.05) and apply to prepared knots or tufts for broom or brush making (heading No. 96.03).

税则号列 Tariff Item.	货品名称	最惠国(%) MFN	协定(%) CT 东盟 CA	中巴 CP	中智 CC	普通 Gen	增值税率 VAT	出口退税 ED	计量单位 Unit	监管条件 SC	Article Description
14.01	**主要作编结用的植物材料（例如，竹、藤、芦苇、灯芯草、柳条、酒椰叶，已净、漂白或染色的谷类植物的茎秆，椴树皮）：**										**Vegetable materials of a kind used primarily for plaiting (for example, bamboos, rattans, reeds, rushes, osier, raffia, cleaned, bleached or dyed cereal straw, and lime bark):**
1401.1000	-竹	10	8		0	70	13	5	千克		-Bamboos
1401.1000 10	酸竹	10				70	13	5	千克	ABE	Bamboos palm (*Raphia vinifera*)
1401.1000 90	其他竹	10				70	13	5	千克	AB	Other bamboos
1401.2000	-藤	10	8		0	35	13	5	千克		-Rattans
1401.2000 10	濒危藤	10				35	13	5	千克	ABFE	Rattans in imminent dangers
1401.2000 90	其他藤	10				35	13	5	千克	AB	Other rattans
	-其他：										-Other:
1401.9010	---谷类植物的茎秆（麦秸除外）	10	8		8	70	13	5	千克	AB	---Cereal straw (other than wheat straw)
1401.9020	---芦苇	10	8		0	70	13	5	千克	AB	---Reeds
1401.9030	---灯芯草属	10	8		0	70	13	5	千克		---Rushes
1401.9030 10	蔺草（已净、漂白或染色的）	10				70	13	5	千克	AB4xy	Juncaceae, cleaned, bleached or dyed
1401.9030 90	其他灯芯草属植物材料（已净、漂白或染色的）	10				70	13	5	千克	AB	Other vegetable materials rush (*Juncus spp.*) cleaned, bleached or dyed
1401.9090	---其他	10	8		8	70	13	5	千克	AB	---Other
14.04	**其他税目未列名的植物产品：**										**Vegetable products not elsewhere specified or included:**
1404.2000	-棉短绒	4			0	30	13	5	千克	AB	-Cotton linters
	-其他：										-Other:
1404.9010	---主要供染料、鞣料用的植物原料	5		4.3	0	45	13	5	千克	AB	---Raw regetable materids of a kind used primarily in dyeing or tanning
1404.9090	---其他：	15	8		9	70	13	5	千克	AB	---Other:

第三类

动、植物油、脂及其分解产品；精制的食用油脂；动、植物蜡

第十五章

动、植物油、脂及其分解产品；精制的食用油脂；动、植物蜡

注释：

一、本章不包括：

（一）税目 02.09 的猪脂肪及家禽脂肪；

（二）可可脂、可可油（税目 18.04）；

（三）按重量计税目 04.05 所列产品的含量超过 15%的食品（通常归入第二十一章）；

（四）税目 23.01 的油渣或税目 23.04 至 23.06 的残渣；

（五）第六类的脂肪酸、精制蜡、药品、油漆、清漆、肥皂、芳香料制品、化妆盥洗品、磺化油及其他货品；

（六）从油类提取的油膏（税目 40.02）。

二、税目 15.09 不包括用溶剂提取的橄榄油（税目 15.10）。

三、税目 15.18 不包括变性的油、脂及其分离品，这些货品应归入其相应的未变性油、脂及其分离品的税目。

四、皂料、油脚、硬脂沥青、甘油沥青及羊毛脂残渣，归入税目 15.22。

子目注释：

子目 1514.11 及 1514.19 所称"低芥子酸菜子油"，是指按重量计芥子酸含量低于 2%的固定油

SECTION Ⅲ

ANIMAL OR VEGETABLE FATS AND OILS AND THEIR CLEAVAGE PRODUCTS; PREPARED EDIBLE FATS; ANIMAL OR VEGETABLE WAXES

Chapter 15

Animal or vegetable fats and oils and their cleavage products; prepared edible fats; animal or vegetable waxes

Notes:

1. This Chapter does not cover:

(a) Pig fat or poultry fat of heading No. 02.09;

(b) Cocoa butter, fat or oil (heading No. 18.04);

(c) Edible preparations containing by weight more than 15% of the products of heading No. 04.05 (generally Chapter 21);

(d) Greaves (heading No. 23.01) or residues of headings Nos. 23.04 to 23.06;

(e) Fatty acids, prepared waxes, medicaments, paints, varnishes, soap, perfumery, cosmetic or toilet preparations, sulphonated oils or other goods of Section Ⅵ; or

(f) Factice derived from oils (heading No. 40.02).

2. Heading No. 15.09 does not apply to oils obtained from olives by solvent extraction (heading No. 15.10).

3. Heading No. 15.18 does not cover fats or oils or their fractions, merely denatured, which are to be classified in the heading appropriate to the corresponding undenatured fats and oils and their fractions.

4. Soap-stocks, oil foots and dregs, stearin pitch, glycerol pitch and wool grease residues fall in heading No. 15.22.

Subheading Note:

For the purposes of subheadings No. 1514.11 and 1514.19, the expression "low erucic acid rape or colza oil" means the fixed oil which has an erucic acid content of less than 2% by weight.

税则号列 Tariff Item.	货品名称	最惠国(%) MFN	协定(%) CT 东盟 CA	中巴 CP	中智 CC	普通 Gen	增值税率 VAT	出口退税 ED	计量单位 Unit	监管条件 SC	Article Description
15.01	**猪脂肪（包括已炼制的猪油）及家禽脂肪，但税目 02.09 及 15.03 的货品除外：**										**Pig fat (including lard) and poultry fat, other than that of heading No. 02.09 or 15.03:**
1501.0000	猪脂肪（包括已炼制的猪油）及家禽脂肪，但税目 02.09 及 15.03 的货品除外	10	8		0	35	17	13	千克	AB	Pig fat (including lard) and poultry fat, other than that of heading No. 02.09 or 15.03
15.02	**牛、羊脂肪，但税目 15.03 的货品除外：**										**Fats of bovine animals, sheep or goats, other than those of heading No. 15.03:**
1502.0010	---未炼制的牛、羊脂肪	8	5	0	0	70	17	5	千克	AB	---Rawv
1502.0090	---其他	8	5	0	0	30	17	13	千克	AB	---Other

税则号列 Tariff Item.	货品名称	最惠国(%) MFN	协定(%)CT 东盟 CA	 中巴 CP	 中智 CC	普通 Gen	增值税率 VAT	出口退税 ED	计量单位 Unit	监管条件 SC	Article Description
15.03	**猪油硬脂、液体猪油、油硬脂、食用或非食用脂油，未经乳化、混合或其他方法制作：**										**Lard stearin, lard oil, oleostearin, oleooil and tallow oil, not emulsified or mixed or otherwise prepared:**
1503.0000	猪油硬脂、液体猪油、油硬脂、食用或非食用脂油，未经乳化、混合或其他方法制作	10	8		0	30	17	13	千克	AB	Lard stearin, lard oil, oleostearin, oleooil and tallow oil, not emulsified or mixed or otherwise prepared
15.04	**鱼或海生哺乳动物的油、脂及其分离品，不论是否精制，但未经化学改性：**										**Fats and oils and their fractions, of fish or marine mammals, whether or not refined, but not chemically modified:**
1504.1000	-鱼肝油及其分离品	12	8		7.2	30	17	13	千克	AB	-Fish-liver oils and their fractions
1504.2000	-除鱼肝油以外的鱼油、脂及其分离品	12	8		9.6	50	17	13	千克	AB	-Fats and oils and their fractions, of fish, other than liver oils
1504.3000	-海生哺乳动物的油、脂及其分离品	14.4	8		8.6	50	17	13	千克		-Fats and oils and their fractions, of marine mammals
1504.3000 10	濒危哺乳动物的油、脂及其分离品(仅指海生)	14.4				50	17	13	千克	ABFE	Fats and oils and their fractions, of marine mammals in imminent dangers
1504.3000 90	其他海生哺乳动物油，脂及分离品	14.4				50	17	13	千克	AB	Other fats and oils and their fractions of marine mammals
15.05	**羊毛脂及从羊毛脂制得的脂肪物质(包括纯净的羊毛脂)：**										**Wool grease and fatty substances derived therefrom (including lanolin):**
1505.0000	羊毛脂及从羊毛脂制得的脂肪物质(包括纯净的羊毛脂)	20	12		16	70	17	13	千克	AB	Wool grease and fatty substances derived therefrom (including lanolin)
15.06	**其他动物油、脂及其分离品，不论是否精制，但未经化学改性：**										**Other animal fats and oils and their fractions, whether or not refined, but not chemically modified:**
1506.0000	其他动物油、脂及其分离品，不论是否精制，但未经化学改性	20	12		12	70	17	13	千克		Other animal fats and oils and their fractions, whether or not refined, but not chemically modified
1506.0000 10	其他濒危动物为原料制取的脂肪(包括河马、熊、野兔、海龟为原料的及海龟蛋油)	20				70	17	13	千克	ABFE	Fats of wild horses, wild bovine animals (including fats and oil of hippo, bear, hare, green turtle and green turtle egg)
1506.0000 90	其他动物油、脂及其分离品(不论是否精制，但未经化学改性)	20				70	17	13	千克	AB	Fats and oils and their fractions, of other animals, whether or not refined, but not chemically modified
15.07	**豆油及其分离品，不论是否精制，但未经化学改性：**										**Soya-bean oil and its fractions, whether or not refined, but not chemically modified:**
1507.1000	-初榨的，不论是否脱胶	9				190	13	13	千克	7AB	-Crude oil whether or not degummed
1507.9000	-其他	9				190	13	13	千克	7AB	-Other
15.08	**花生油及其分离品，不论是否精制，但未经化学改性：**										**Ground-nut oil and its fractions, whether or not refined, but not chemically modified:**
1508.1000	-初榨的	10	8			100	13	13	千克	AB	-Crude oil
1508.9000	-其他	10	8			100	13	13	千克	AB	-Other
15.09	**油橄榄油及其分离品，不论是否精制，但未经化学改性：**										**Olive oil and its fractions, whether or not refined, but not chemicamly modified:**
1509.1000	-初榨的	10	T3		8	30	13	13	千克	AB	-Virgin

税则号列 Tariff Item.	货品名称	最惠国(%) MFN	协定(%) 东盟 CA	协定(%) 中巴 CP	CT 中智 CC	普通 Gen	增值税率 VAT	出口退税 ED	计量单位 Unit	监管条件 SC	Article Description
1509.9000	-其他	10	8		8	30	17	13	千克	AB	-Other
15.10	**其他橄榄油及其分离品,不论是否精制,但未经化学改性,包括掺有税目15.09的油或分离品的混合物:**										**Other oils and their fractions, obtained solely from olives, whether or not refined, but not chemically modified, including blends of these oils or fractions with oils or fractions of heading 15.09:**
1510.0000	其他橄榄油及其分离品,不论是否精制,但未经化学改性,包括掺有税目15.09的油或分离品的混合物	10	8		8	30	17	13	千克	AB	Other oils and their fractions, obtained solely from olives, whether or not refined, but not chemically modified, including blends of these oils or fractions with oils or fractions of heading No. 15.09
15.11	**棕榈油及其分离品,不论是否精制,但未经化学改性:**										**Palm oil and its fractions, whether or not refined, but not chemically modified:**
1511.1000	-初榨的	9				60	13	13	千克	7AB	-Crude oil
	-其他:										-Other:
1511.9010	---棕榈液油(熔点19℃~24℃)	9				60	13	13	千克	7AB	---Palm liquid oil (melting point(19℃ - 24℃)
1511.9020	---棕榈硬脂(熔点44℃~56℃)	8				60	13	13	千克	AB	---Palm hard - fat (melting point 44℃ - 56℃)
1511.9090	---其他	9				60	17	13	千克	7AB	---Other
15.12	**葵花油、红花油或棉子油及其分离品,不论是否精制,但未经化学改性:**										**Sunflower-seed, safflower or cotton-seed oil and fractions thereof, whether or not refined, but not chemically modified:**
	-葵花油或红花油及其分离品:										-Sunflower-seed or safflower oil and fractions thereof:
1512.1100	--初榨的	9	5			160	13	11	千克	AB	--Crude oil
1512.1900	--其他	9	5			160	17	13	千克	AB	--Other
	-棉子油及其分离品:										-Cotton-seed oil and its fractions:
1512.2100	--初榨的,不论是否去除棉子酚	10	8			70	13	13	千克	AB	--Crude oil, whether or not gossypol has been removed
1512.2900	--其他	10	8			70	17	13	千克	AB	--Other
15.13	**椰子油、棕榈仁油或巴巴苏棕榈果油及其分离品,不论是否精制,但未经化学改性:**										**Coconut (copra), palm kernel or babassu oil and fractions thereof, whether or not refined, but not chemically modified:**
	-椰子油及其分离品:										-Coconut (copra) oil and its fractions:
1513.1100	--初榨的	9	T3	4.5	0	40	13	13	千克	AB	--Crude oil
1513.1900	--其他	9	T3	4.5	0	40	13	13	千克	AB	--Other
	-棕榈仁油或巴巴苏棕榈果油及其分离品:										-Palm kernel or babassu oil and fractions thereof:
1513.2100	--初榨的	9	T3		0	40	13	13	千克	AB	--Crude oil
1513.2900	--其他	9	T3		0	40	17	13	千克	AB	--Other
15.14	**菜子油或芥子油及其分离品,不论是否精制,但未经化学改性:**										**Rape, colza or mustard oil and fractions thereof, whether or not refined, but not chemically modified:**
	-低芥子酸菜子油及其分离品:										-Low erucic acid rape or colza oil and its fractions:

税则号列 Tariff Item.	货品名称	最惠国(%) MFN	协定(%)CT 东盟 CA	中巴 CP	中智 CC	普通 Gen	增值税率 VAT	出口退税 ED	计量单位 Unit	监管条件 SC	Article Description
1514.1100	--初榨的	9				170	13	13	千克	7AB	--Crude oil
1514.1900	--其他	9				170	13	11	千克	7AB	--Other
	-其他:										-Other:
	--初榨的:										--Crude oil:
1514.9110	---菜子油	9				170	13	13	千克	7AB	---Rape oil
1514.9190	---芥子油	9				170	13	13	千克	7AB	---Mustard oil
1514.9900	--其他	9				170	17	13	千克	7AB	--Other
15.15	**其他固定植物油、脂(包括希蒙得木油)及其分离品,不论是否精制,但未经化学改性:**										**Other fixed vegetable fats and oils (including jojoba oil) and fractions thereof, whether or not refined, but not chemically modified:**
	-亚麻子油及其分离品:										-Linseed oil and its fractions:
1515.1100	--初榨的	15	8		9	30	13	13	千克	AB	--Crude oil
1515.1900	--其他	15	8		9	30	17	13	千克	AB	--Other
	-玉米油及其分离品:										-Maize (corn) oil and its fractions:
1515.2100	--初榨的	10	8			160	13	13	千克	AB	--Crude oil
1515.2900	--其他	10	8			160	17	13	千克	AB	--Other
1515.3000	-蓖麻油及其分离品	10	8		0	70	17	13	千克	AB	-Castor oil and its fractions
1515.5000	-芝麻油及其分离品	12	8		7.2	20	13	13	千克	AB	-Sesame oil and its fractions
	-其他:										-Other:
1515.9010	---希蒙得木油及其分离品	20	12		16	70	17	13	千克	AB	---Jojoba oil and its fractions
1515.9020	---印楝油及其分离品	20	T3		16	70	17	13	千克	AB	---Neem oil and its fractions
1515.9030	---桐油及其分离品	20	12		12	70	17	13	千克	AB	---Tung oil and its fractions
1515.9090	---其他	20	T3		16	70	17	13	千克	AB	---Other
15.16	**动、植物油、脂及其分离品,全部或部分氢化、相互酯化、再酯化或反油酸化,不论是否精制,但未经进一步加工:**										**Animal or vegetable fats and oil and fractions thereof, partly or wholly hydrogenated, inter-esterified, reesterified or elaidinized, whether or not refined, but not further prepared:**
1516.1000	-动物油、脂及其分离品	5			0	70	17	13	千克	AB	-Animal fats and oils and fractions thereof
1516.2000	-植物油、脂及其分离品	25	T3		20	70	17	13	千克	AB	-Vegetable fats and oils and fractions thereof
15.17	**人造黄油;本章各种动、植物油、脂及其分离品混合制成的食用油、脂或制品,但税目15.16的食用油、脂及其分离品除外:**										**Margarine; edible mixtures or preparations of animal or vegetable fats or oils or of fractions of different fats or oils of this Chapter, other than edible fats or oils or their fractions of heading No. 15.16:**
1517.1000	-人造黄油,但不包括液态的	30	12		24	80	17	13	千克	AB	-Margarine, excluding liquid margarine
1517.9000	-其他	25	T3		0	70		11	千克		-Other
1517.9000 01	混合制成的动物质食用油脂或制品(税号1516的食用油、脂及其分离品除外)	25				70	17	11	千克	AB	Edible mixtures or preparations of animal fats or oil or of fractions (Other than edible fats or oil or their fractions of heading No. 15.16)
1517.9000 90	混合制成的植物质食用油脂或制品(税号1516的食用油、脂及其分离品除外)	25				70	13	11	千克	AB	Edible mixtures or preparations of vegetable fats or oil or of fractions (Other than edible fats or oil or their fractions of heading No. 15.16)

税则号列 Tariff Item.	货品名称	最惠国(%) MFN	协定(%) CT 东盟 CA	中巴 CP	中智 CC	普通 Gen	增值税率 VAT	出口退税 ED	计量单位 Unit	监管条件 SC	Article Description
15.18	**动、植物油、脂及其分离品，经过熟炼、氧化、脱水、硫化、吹制或在真空、惰性气体中加热聚合及用其他化学方法改性的，但税目15.16的产品除外；本章各种油、脂及其分离品混合制成的其他税目未列名的非食用油、脂或制品：**										**Animal or vegetable fats and oils and fractions thereof, boiled, oxidized, dehydrated, sulphurized, blown, polymerized by heat in vacuum or in inert gas or otherwise chemically modified, excluding those of heading No. 15.16; inedible mixtures or preparations of animal or vegetable fats or oils or of fractions of different fats or oils of this Chapter, not elsewhere specified or included:**
1518.0000	动、植物油、脂及其分离品，经过熟炼、氧化、脱水、硫化、吹制或在真空、惰性气体中加热聚合及用其他化学方法改性的，但税目15.16的产品除外；本章各种油、脂及其分离品混合制成的其他税目未列名的非食用油、脂或制品	10	8		8	70	17	13	千克	AB	Animal or vegetable fats and oils and fractions thereof, boiled, oxidized, dehydrated, sulphurized, blown, polymerized by heat in vacuum or in inert gas or otherwise chemically modified, excluding those of heading 15.16; inedible mixtures or preparations of animal or vegetable fats or oils or of fractions of different fats or oils of this Chapter, not elsewhere specified or included
15.20	**粗甘油；甘油水及甘油碱液：**										**Glycerol, crude; glycerol waters and glycerol lyes:**
1520.0000	粗甘油；甘油水及甘油碱液	20	12		12	50	17	13	千克	AB	Glycerol, crude; glycerol waters and glycerol lyes
15.21	**植物蜡(甘油三酯除外)、蜂蜡、其他虫蜡及鲸蜡，不论是否精制或着色：**										**Vegetable waxes (other than triglycerides), beeswax, other insect waxes and spermaceti, whether or not refined or coloured:**
1521.1000	-植物蜡	20	12		12	80	17	13	千克	AB	-Vegetable waxes
	-其他：										-Other
1521.9010	---蜂蜡	20	12		12	80	17	13	千克	AB	---Beeswax
1521.9090	---其他	20	12		12	80	17	13	千克		---Other
1521.9090 10	鲸蜡(不论是否精制或着色)	20				80	17	13	千克	AFEB	Spermaceti, whether or not refined or coloured
1521.9090 90	其他虫蜡(不论是否精制或着色)	20				80	17	13	千克	AB	Other insect waxs, whether or not refined or coloured
15.22	**油鞣回收脂；加工处理油脂物质及动、植物蜡所剩的残渣：**										**Degras; residues resulting from the treatment of fatty substances or animal or vegetable waxes:**
1522.0000	油鞣回收脂；加工处理油脂物质及动、植物蜡所剩的残渣	20	12		12	50	17	13	千克		Degras; residues resulting from the treatment of fatty substances or animal or vegetable waxes

第四类
食品；饮料、酒及醋；烟草、烟草及烟草代用品的制品

注释：

本类所称“团粒”，是指直接挤压或加入按重量计比例不超过3%的粘合剂制成的粒状产品。

第十六章
肉、鱼、甲壳动物，软体动物及其他水生无脊椎动物的制品

注释：

一、本章不包括用第二章、第三章及税目05.04所列方法制作或保藏的肉、食用杂碎、鱼、甲壳动物、软体动物或其他水生无脊椎动物。

二、本章的食品按重量计必须含有20%以上的香肠、肉、食用杂碎、动物血、鱼、甲壳动物、软体动物或其他水生无脊椎动物及其混合物。对于含有两种或两种以上前述产品的食品，则应按其中重量最大的产品归入第十六章的相应税目。但本条规定不适用于税目19.02的包馅食品和税目21.03及21.04的食品。

子目注释：

一、子目1602.10的“均化食品”，是指用肉、食用杂碎或动物血经精细均化制成供婴幼儿食用或营养用的零售包装食品（每件净重不超过250克）。为了调味、保藏或其他目的，均化食品中可以加入少量其他配料，还可以含有少量可见的肉粒或食用杂碎粒。归类时该子目优先于税目16.02的其他子目。

二、税目16.04或16.05项下各子目所列的是鱼及甲壳动物的俗名，它们与第三章中相同名称的鱼及甲壳动物种类范围相同。

SECTION Ⅳ
PREPARED FOODSTUFFS; BEVERAGES, SPIRITS AND VINEGAR, TOBACCO AND MANUFACTURED TOBACCO SUBSTITUTES

Note:

In this Section the term “pellets” means products which have been agglomerated either directly by compression or by the addition of a binder in a proportion not exceeding 3% by weight.

Chapter 16
Preparations of meat, of fish or of crustaceans, molluscs or other aquatic invertebrates

Notes:

1. This Chapter does not cover meat, meat offal, fish, crustaceans, molluscs or other aquatic invertebrates, prepared or preserved by the processes specified in Chapter 2 or 3 or heading No. 05.04.

2. Food preparations fall in this Chapter provided that they contain more than 20% by weight of sausage, meat, meat offal, blood, fish or crustaceans, molluscs or other aquatic invertebrates, or any combination thereof. In cases where the preparation contains two or more of the products mentioned above, it is classified in the heading of Chapter 16 corresponding to the component or components which predominate by weight. These provisions do not apply to the stuffed products of heading No. 19.02 or to the preparations of heading No. 21.03 or 21.04.

Subheading Notes:

1. For the purposes of subheading No. 1602.10, the expression “homogenized preparations” means preparations of meat, meat offal or blood, finely homogenized, put up for retail sale as infant food or for dietetic purposes, in containers of a net weight content not exceeding 250g. For the application of this definition no account is to be taken of small quantities of any ingredients which may have been added to the preparation for seasoning, preservation or other purposes. These preparations may contain a small quantity of visible pieces of meat or meat offal.

   This subheading takes precedence over all other subheadings of heading No. 16.02.

2. The fish and crustaceans specified in the subheadings of heading No. 16.04 or 16.05 under their common names only, are of the same species as those mentioned in Chapter 3 under the same name.

税则号列 Tariff Item.	货品名称	最惠国(%) MFN	协定(%)CT 东盟 CA	中巴 CP	中智 CC	普通 Gen	增值税率 VAT	出口退税 ED	计量单位 Unit	监管条件 SC	Article Description
16.01	肉、食用杂碎或动物血制成的香肠及类似产品；用香肠制成的食品： 肉、食用杂碎或动物血制成的香肠及类似产品；用香肠制成的食品：										**Sausages and similar products, of meat, meat offal or blood; food preparations based on these products:** Sausages and similar products, of meat, meat offal or blood; food preparations based on these products

税则号列 Tariff Item.	货品名称	最惠国(%) MFN	协定(%) 东盟 CA	中巴 CP	CT 中智 CC	普通 Gen	增值税率 VAT	出口退税 ED	计量单位 Unit	监管条件 SC	Article Description
1601.0010	---用天然肠衣做外包装的香肠及类似产品	15	T3		12	90	17	13	千克		---Sausages and similar products coated with natural casings
1601.0010 10	濒危野生动物肉,杂碎,血制天然肠衣香肠(含编号0208的野生动物,包括类似品)	15				90	17	13	千克	ABFE	Sausages packed with natural casing of meat. meat offal or blood of wild animals in imminent dangers (including wild animals of heading No. 0208 and similar products).
1601.0010 90	其他动物肉,杂碎及血制天然肠衣香肠(包括类似品)	15				90	17	13	千克	AB	Sausages packed with natural casing of meat meat offal or blood of other aminals,(including similar products.)
1601.0020	---其他香肠及类似产品	15	T3		12	90	17	13	千克		---Other saucases and similar products
1601.0020 10	濒危野生动物肉,杂碎,血制其他肠衣香肠(含编号0208的野生动物,包括类似品)	15				90	17	13	千克	ABFE	Sausages packed with other casing of meat,meal offal or blood of wild animals in imminent dangers (including wild animals of heading No. 0208 and similar products other)
1601.0020 90	其他动物肉,杂碎及血制其他肠衣香肠(包括类似品)	15				90	17	13	千克	AB	Sauages packed with other cosing of meat,meat offal or blood of other animcls(including simiple products)
1601.0030	---用香肠制成的食品	15			12	90	17	13	千克		---Sausage-based food products
1601.0030 10	用含濒危野生动物成分的香肠制的食品(含编号0208的野生动物)	15				90	17	13	千克	ABFE	Food prep arations based on Sauagses, containing composition of wild animals in imminent dangers including wild . animals in imminent dongers.
1601.0030 90	用含其他动物成分的香肠制的食品	15				90	17	13	千克	AB	Food preparation base on other sauages,containins composition of other animals
16.02	**其他方法制作或保藏的肉、食用杂碎或动物血:**										**Other Prepared or preserved meat, meat offal or blood:**
1602.1000	-均化食品	15	T3		9	90	17	13	千克		-Homogenized preparations
1602.1000 10	含濒危野生动物成分的均化食品(指用肉、食用杂碎或动物血经精细均化制成,零售包装)	15				90	17	13	千克	ABFE	Homogenized preparations containing compositions of wild animals in imminent dangers (prepared or preserved meat, meat offal or blood, put up for retail sale)
1602.1000 90	其他动物肉或食用杂碎的均化食品(指用肉、食用杂碎或动物血经精细均化制成,零售包装)	15				90	17	13	千克	AB	Homogenized preparations of other animals (prepared or preserved meat, meat offal or blood, put up for retail sale)
1602.2000	-动物肝	15	T3		9	90	17	13	千克	AB	-Of liver of any animal
	-税目01.05的家禽的:										-Of poultry of heading No. 01.05:
1602.3100	--火鸡的	15	8		9	90	17	13	千克	AB	--Of turkeys
	--鸡的:										--Of fowls of the species *Gallus domesticus*:
1602.3210	---罐头	15	T3		12	90	17	13	千克	AB	---In airtight containers
	---其他:										---Other:
1602.3291	----鸡胸肉	15	T3		9	90	17	13	千克	AB	----Chicken breastfilets
1602.3292	----鸡腿肉	15	T3		12	90	17	13	千克	AB	----Chicken Leg meat
1602.3299	----其他	15	T3		12	90	17	13	千克	AB	----Other
	--其他:										--Other:
1602.3910	---罐头	15	T3		9	90	17	13	千克	AB	---In airtight containers

税则号列 Tariff Item.	货品名称	最惠国(%) MFN	协定(%) CT 东盟 CA	中巴 CP	中智 CC	普通 Gen	增值税率 VAT	出口退税 ED	计量单位 Unit	监管条件 SC	Article Description
	---其他:										---Other:
1602.3991	----鸭的	15	T3		9	90	17	13	千克	AB	----Of duck
1602.3999	----其他	15	T3		9	90	17	13	千克	AB	----Other
	-猪的:										-Of swine:
1602.4100	--后腿及其肉块	15	T3		9	90	17	13	千克		--Hams and cuts thereof
1602.4100 10	制作或保藏的鹿猪、姬猪后腿及肉块	15				90	17	13	千克	ABFE	Prepared or preserved hams and cuts of pig-deer (*Babyrousa*)、pygmy pig (*Porcula*)
1602.4100 90	制作或保藏的猪后腿及其肉块	15				90	17	13	千克	AB	Prepared or preserved hams and cuts of swine
1602.4200	--前腿及其肉块	15	T3		9	90	17	13	千克		--Shoulders and cuts thereof
1602.4200 10	制作或保藏的鹿猪,姬猪前腿及其肉块	15				90	17	13	千克	ABFE	Prepared or preserved shoulders and cuts of pig-deer (*Babyrousa*)、pygmy pig (*Porcula*)
1602.4200 90	制作或保藏的猪前腿及其肉块	15				90	17	13	千克	AB	Prepared or preserved shoulders and cuts of swine
	--其他,包括混合的肉:										--Other, including mixtures:
1602.4910	---罐头	15	T3		12	90	17	13	千克		---In airtight containers
1602.4910 10	其他含鹿猪、姬猪肉及杂碎的罐头	15				90	17	13	千克	ABFE	Other meat, meat offal of pig-deer (*Babyrousa*)、pygmy pig (*Porcula*), tinned
1602.4910 90	其他猪肉及杂碎的罐头	15				90	17	13	千克	AB	Other meat, meat offal of swine, tinned
1602.4990	---其他	15	T3		12	90	17	13	千克		---Other
1602.4990 10	制作或保藏的其他鹿猪、姬猪肉、杂碎(包括血等)	15				90	17	13	千克	ABFE	Prepared or preserved meat, meat offal or blood of pig-deer (*Babyrousa*)、pygmy pig (*Porcula*)
1602.4990 90	制作或保藏的其他猪肉,杂碎,血	15				90	17	13	千克	AB	Prepared or preserved meat, meat offal or blood of swine
	-牛的:										-Of bovine animals:
1602.5010	---罐头	12	T3		9.6	90	17	13	千克		---In airtight containers
1602.5010 10	含濒危野牛肉的罐头	12				90	17	13	千克	ABFE	Meat of wild bovine animals in imminent dangers, tinned
1602.5010 90	其他牛肉及牛杂碎罐头(含野牛肉的除外)	12				90	17	13	千克	AB	Other meat, meat offal of bovine animals, tinned, other than meat of wild bovine animals
1602.5090	---其他	12	T3		9.6	90	17	13	千克		---Other
1602.5090 10	其他制作或保藏濒危野牛肉,杂碎(包括血等)	12				90	17	13	千克	ABFE	Other prepared or preserved meat, meat offal or blood of wild bovine animals in imminent dangers
1602.5090 90	其他制作或保藏的牛肉,杂碎,血	12				90	17	13	千克	AB	Other prepared or preserved meat, meat offal or blood of bovine animals
	-其他,包括动物血的食品:										-Other, including preparations of blood of any animal:
1602.9010	---罐头	15	T3		9	90	17	13	千克		---In airtight containers
1602.9010 10	其他濒危野生动物肉及杂碎罐头	15				90	17	13	千克	ABFE	Other meat, meat offal of wild animals in imminent dangers, tinned
1602.9010 90	其他肉及杂碎罐头	15				90	17	13	千克	AB	Other meat, meat offal of other animals, tinned
1602.9090	---其他	15	T3		9	90	17	13	千克		---Other

税则号列 Tariff Item.	货品名称	最惠国(%) MFN	协定(%)CT 东盟 CA	中巴 CP	中智 CC	普通 Gen	增值税率 VAT	出口退税 ED	计量单位 Unit	监管条件 SC	Article Description
1602.9090 10	制作或保藏其他濒危野生动物肉(包括杂碎、血)	15				90	17	13	千克	ABFE	Other prepared or preserved meat, meat offal or blood of wild animals
1602.9090 90	经制作或保藏的其他肉、杂碎及血	15				90	17	13	千克	AB	Other prepared or preserved meat, meat offal or blood of other animals
16.03	**肉、鱼、甲壳动物、软体动物或其他水生无脊椎动物的精及汁:**										**Extracts and juices of meat, fish or crustaceans, molluscs or other aquatic invertebrates:**
1603.0000	肉、鱼、甲壳动物、软体动物或其他水生无脊椎动物的精及汁	23	12		13.8	90	17	13	千克		Extracts and juices of meat, fish or crustaceans, molluscs or other aquatic invertebrates
1603.0000 10	含濒危野生动物及鱼类成分的肉(指编号0208及030192野生动物及鱼类)	23				90	17	13	千克	ABFE	Meat of containing compositions of wild animals and fish in imminent danger of heading No. 0208 or of subheading No. 030192
1603.0000 90	肉及水产品的精、汁(水产品指鱼、甲壳动物、软体动物或其他水生无脊椎动物)	23				90	17	13	千克	AB	Extracts and juices of meat, fish or crustaceans, molluscs or other aquatic invertebrates
16.04	**制作或保藏的鱼;鲟鱼子酱及鱼卵制的鲟鱼子酱代用品:**										**Prepared or preserved fish; caviar and caviar substitutes prepared from fish eggs:**
	-鱼,整条或切块,但未绞碎:										-Fish, whole or in pieces, but not minced:
	--鲑鱼:										--Salmon:
1604.1110	---大西洋鲑鱼	12	8		9.6	90	17	13	千克	AB	---Atlantic Salmon
1604.1190	---其他	12	8		9.6	90	17	13	千克		---Other
1604.1190 10	制作或保藏的川陕哲罗鲑鱼(整条或切块,但未绞碎)	12				90	17	13	千克	AEB	Prepared or preserved Shuan-shan taimen (*Hucho taimen*), whole or in pieces, but not minced
1604.1190 20	制作或保藏的秦岭细鳞鲑鱼(整条或切块,但未绞碎)	12				90	17	13	千克	AEB	Prepared or preserved Qinling lenok (*Brachymystax lenok*) whole or in pieces, but not minced
1604.1190 90	制作或保藏的其他鲑鱼	12				90	17	13	千克	AB	Prepared or preserved other salmon
1604.1200	--鲱鱼	12	8		7.2	90	17	13	千克	AB	--Herrings
1604.1300	--沙丁鱼、黍鲱鱼	5			4	90	17	13	千克	AB	--Sardines, sardinella and brisling or sprats
1604.1400	--金枪鱼、鲣鱼	5			4	90	17	13	千克	AB	--Tunas, skipjack and bonito (*Sarda spp.*)
1604.1500	--鲭鱼	12	8		9.6	90	17	13	千克	AB	--Mackerel
1604.1600	--鳀鱼	12	8		9.6	90	17	13	千克	AB	--Anchovies
	--其他:										--Other:
1604.1910	---河鳗鱼	12	8	9.9	9.6	90	17	13	千克		---River eel
1604.1910 10	制作或保藏的花鳗鲡(整条或切块,但未绞碎)	12				90	17	13	千克	aABE	Prepared or preserved marbled eels (*Anguilla marmorata*) whole or in pieces, but not minced
1604.1910 90	其他制作或保藏的(河)鳗鱼	12				90	17	13	千克	AB	Prepared or preserved river eel
1604.1920	---罗非鱼	12	8		9.6	90	17	13	千克	AB	---Tilapia
	---叉尾鱼回鱼										---Fork tail fish , return to fish's
1604.1931	----斑点叉尾鮰鱼	12	8	9.9	9.6	90	17	13	千克	AB	----Fleck Fork tail fish , return to fish's
1604.1939	----其他	12	8	9.9	9.6	90	17	13	千克	AB	----Other

税则号列 Tariff Item.	货 品 名 称	最惠国(%) MFN	协定(%) CT 东盟 CA	中巴 CP	中智 CC	普通 Gen	增值税率 VAT	出口退税 ED	计量单位 Unit	监管条件 SC	Article Description
1604.1990	---其他	12	8	9.9	9.6	90	17	13	千克		---Other
1604.1990 10	制作或保藏的濒危鱼类(整条或切块,但未绞碎)	12				90	17	13	千克	AFEB	Prepared or preserved fish in imminent danger, whole or in pieces, but not minced
1604.1990 90	制作或保藏的其他鱼(整条或切块,但未绞碎)	12				90	17	13	千克	AB	Prepared or preserved other fish, whole or in pieces, but not minced
	-其他制作或保藏的鱼:										-Other prepared or preserved fish:
	---罐头:										---In airtight containers:
1604.2011	----鱼翅	12	8	9.9	9.6	90	17	13	千克		----Shark's fin
1604.2011 10	鲸鲨、噬人鲨、姥鲨鱼翅罐头	12				90	17	13	千克	ABFE	Shark's fins of whale shark (Rhincodon), man – eating shark (Cacharodon), basking shark (Cetorhinus) in airtight containers
1604.2011 90	其他鱼翅罐头	12				90	17	13	千克	AB	Other shark's fins in airtight containers
1604.2019	----其他	12	8	9.9	9.6	90	17	13	千克		----Other
1604.2019 10	非整条或切块的濒危鱼罐头(鱼翅除外)	12				90	17	13	千克	ABFE	Fish in imminent dangers in airtight containers, other than whole or in pieces, other than shark's fins
1604.2019 90	非整条或切块的其他鱼罐头(鱼翅除外)	12				90	17	13	千克	AB	Other fish in airtight containers, other than shark's fins
	---其他:										---Other:
1604.2091	----鱼翅	12	8	9.9	9.6	90	17	13	千克		----Shark's fin
1604.2091 10	制作或保藏鲸鲨、噬人鲨、姥鲨鱼翅(非整条、非切块、非罐头)	12				90	17	13	千克	ABFE	Prepared or preserved shark's fins of whale shark (Rhincodon), man-eating shark (Cacharodon), basking shark (Cetorhinus), other than whole or in pieces, not in airtight containers
1604.2091 90	制作或保藏其他鱼翅(非整条、非切块、非罐头)	12				90	17	13	千克	AB	Prepared or preserved other shark's fins, other than whole or in pieces, not in airtight containers
1604.2099	----其他	12	8	9.9	9.6	90	17	13	千克		----Other
1604.2099 10	其他制作或保藏的濒危鱼(非整条、非切块、非罐头,鱼翅除外)	12				90	17	13	千克	ABFE	Prepared or preserved fish in imminent dangers, other than whole or in pieces, not in airtight containers, other than shark's fins
1604.2099 90	其他制作或保藏的鱼(非整条、非切块、非罐头,鱼翅除外)	12				90	17	13	千克	AB	Other Prepared or preserved fish other than whole or in pieces, not in airtight containers, other than shark's fins
1604.3000	-鲟鱼子酱及鲟鱼子酱代用品	12	8		7.2	90	17	13	千克	ABFE	-Caviar and caviar substitutes
16.05	**制作或保藏的甲壳动物、软体动物及其他水生无脊椎动物:**										**Crustaceans, molluscs and other aquatic invertebrates, prepared or preserved:**
1605.1000	-蟹	5			4	90	17	13	千克	AB	-Crab
1605.2000	-小虾及对虾	5			4	90	17	13	千克	AB	-Shrimps and prawns
1605.3000	-龙虾	5			0	90	17	13	千克	AB	-Lobster
	-其他甲壳动物:										-Other crustaceans:

税则号列 Tariff Item.	货 品 名 称	最惠国(%) MFN	协定(%)CT 东盟 CA	中巴 CP	中智 CC	普通 Gen	增值税率 VAT	出口退税 ED	计量单位 Unit	监管条件 SC	Article Description
	---淡水小龙虾:										---Freshwater crawfish:
1605.4011	----虾仁	5			0	90	17	13	千克	aAB	----Shelled
1605.4019	----其他	5			0	90	17	13	千克	aAB	----Other
1605.4090	---其他	5			3	90	17	13	千克	AB	---Other
	-其他:										-Other:
1605.9010	---海蜇	15	T3		12	90	17	13	千克	AB	---Jelly fish
1605.9020	---蛤	5		3.9	4	90	17	13	千克	AB	---Clams
1605.9090	---其他	5		3.9	4	90	17	13	千克		---Other
1605.9090 10	其他制作或保藏的濒危软体动物(包括其他水生无脊椎动物)	5				90	17	13	千克	ABFE	Other prepared or preserved molluscs and other a quatic invertebrates in imminent danger
1605.9090 90	其他制作或保藏的软体动物(包括其他水生无脊椎动物)	5				90	17	13	千克	AB	Other prepared or preserved molluscs and other a quatic invertebrates

第十七章
糖及糖食

Chapter 17
Sugars and sugar confectionery

注释：

本章不包括：

一、含有可可的糖食(税目 18.06)；

二、税目 29.40 的化学纯糖(蔗糖、乳糖、麦芽糖、葡萄糖及果糖除外)及其他产品；

三、第三十章的药品及其他产品。

子目注释：

子目 1701.11 及 1701.12 所称"原糖"，是指按重量计干燥状态的蔗糖含量低于旋光读数 99.5°的糖。

Note:

This Chapter does not cover:

(a) Sugar confectionery containing cocoa (heading No. 18.06);

(b) Chemically pure sugars (other than sucrose, lactose, maltose, glucose and fructose) or other products of heading No. 29.40; or

(c) Medicaments or other products of Chapter 30.

Subheading Note:

For the purposes of subheadings No. 1701.11 and 1701.12, "raw sugar" means sugar whose content of sucrose by weight, in the dry state, corresponds to a polarimeter reading of less than 99.5°.

税则号列 Tariff Item.	货品名称	最惠国(%) MFN	协定(%) CT 东盟 CA	中巴 CP	中智 CC	普通 Gen	增值税率 VAT	出口退税 ED	计量单位 Unit	监管条件 SC	Article Description
17.01	**固体甘蔗糖、甜菜糖及化学纯蔗糖：**										**Cane or beet sugar and chemically pure sucrose, in solid form:**
	-未加香料或着色剂的原糖：										-Raw sugar not containing added flavouring or colouring matter:
1701.1100	--甘蔗糖	*50				*125	17	13	千克		--Cane sugar
1701.1100 01	未加香料或着色剂的甘蔗原糖[按重量计干燥状态的糖含量低于旋光读数 99.5 度(配额内)]	15				125	17	13	千克	ABt	Raw cane sugar, not containing added flavouring or colouring matter, sugar whose content of sucrose by weight, in the dry state, corresponds to a polarimeter reading of less than 99.5°, (in-quota)
1701.1100 90	未加香料或着色剂的甘蔗原糖[按重量计干燥状态的糖含量低于旋光读数 99.5 度(配额外)]	50				125	17	13	千克	AB	Raw cane sugar, not containing added flavouring or colouring matter, sugar whose content of sucrose by weight, in the dry state, corresponds to a polarimeter reading of less than 99.5°, (out-quota)
1701.1200	--甜菜糖	*50				*125	17	13	千克		--Beet sugar
1701.1200 01	未加香料或着色剂的甜菜原糖[按重量计干燥状态的糖含量低于旋光读数 99.5 度(配额内)]	15				125	17	13	千克	ABt	Raw beet sugar, not containing added flavouring or colouring matter, sugar whose content of sucrose by weight, in the dry state, corresponds to a polarimeter reading of less than 99.5°, (in-quota)
1701.1200 90	未加香料或着色剂的甜菜原糖[按重量计干燥状态的糖含量低于旋光读数 99.5 度(配额外)]	50				125	17	13	千克	AB	Raw beet sugar, not containing added flavouring or colouring matter, sugar whose content of sucrose by weight, in the dry state, corresponds to a polarimeter reading of less than 99.5°, (out-quota)
	-其他：										-Other:
1701.9100	--加有香料或着色剂	*50				*125	17	13	千克		--Containing added flavouring or colouring matter
1701.9100 01	加有香料或着色剂的糖[指甘蔗糖、甜菜糖及化学纯蔗糖(配额内)]	15				125	17	13	千克	ABt	Cane or beet sugar and chemically pure sucrose, containing added flavouring or colouring matter (in-quota)

税则号列 Tariff Item.	货品名称	最惠国(%) MFN	协定(%) CT 东盟 CA	中巴 CP	中智 CC	普通 Gen	增值税率 VAT	出口退税 ED	计量单位 Unit	监管条件 SC	Article Description
1701.9100 90	加有香料或着色剂的糖［指甘蔗糖、甜菜糖及化学纯蔗糖(配额外)］	50				125	17	13	千克	AB	Cane or beet sugar and chemically pure sucrose, containing added flavouring or colouring matter (out-quota)
	--其他:										--Other:
1701.9910	---砂糖	*50				*125	17	13	千克		---Granulated sugar
1701.9910 10	砂糖(配额内)	15				125	17	13	千克	ABt	Granulated sugar (in-quota)
1701.9910 90	砂糖(配额外)	50				125	17	13	千克	AB	Granulated sugar (out-quota)
1701.9920	---绵白糖	*50				*125	17	13	千克		---Superfine sugar
1701.9920 01	绵白糖(配额内)	15				125	17	13	千克	BAt	Superfine sugar (in-quota)
1701.9920 90	绵白糖(配额外)	50				125	17	13	千克	BA	Superfine sugar (out-quota)
1701.9990	---其他	*50				*125	17	13	千克		---Other
1701.9990 01	其他精制糖(配额内)	15				125	17	13	千克	ABt	Other refined sugar (in-quota)
1701.9990 90	其他精制糖(配额外)	50				125	17	13	千克	AB	Other refined sugar (out-quota)
17.02	**其他固体糖,包括化学纯乳糖、麦芽糖、葡萄糖及果糖;未加香料或着色剂的糖浆;人造蜜,不论是否掺有天然蜂蜜;焦糖:**										**Other sugars, including chemically pure lactose, maltose, glucose and fructose, in solid form; sugar syrups not containing added flavouring or colouring matter; artificial honey, whether or not mixed with natural honey; caramel:**
	-乳糖及乳糖浆:										-Lactose and lactose syrup:
1702.1100	--按重量计干燥无水乳糖含量在99%及以上	10	8		0	80	17	13	千克	AB	--Containing by weight 99% or more lactose, expressed as anhydrous lactose, calculated on the dry matter
1702.1900	--其他	10	8		0	80	17	13	千克	AB	--Other
1702.2000	-槭糖及槭糖浆	30	12		18	80	17	13	千克	A	-Maple sugar and maple syrup
1702.3000	-葡萄糖及葡萄糖浆,不含果糖或按重量计干燥状态的果糖含量在20%以下	30	12		18	80	17	13	千克	BA	-Glucose and glucose syrup, not containing fructose or containing in the dry state less than 20% by weight of fructose
1702.4000	-葡萄糖及葡萄糖浆,按重量计干燥状态的果糖含量在20%及以上,但在50%以下	30	12		18	80	17	13	千克	BA	-Glucose and glucose syrup, containing in the dry state at least 20% but less than 50% by weight of fructose
1702.5000	-化学纯果糖	30	12		18	80	17	13	千克	A	-Chemically pure fructose
1702.6000	-其他果糖及果糖浆,按重量计干燥状态的果糖含量在50%以上	30	12		18	80	17	13	千克	BA	-Other fructose and fructose syrup, containing in the dry state more than 50% by weight of fructose
1702.9000	-其他,包括转化糖	30	12		24	80	17	13	千克		-Other, including invert sugar
1702.9000 10	人造蜜	30				80	17	13	千克	AB	Artificial honey
1702.9000 90	其他固体糖、焦糖(包括转化糖及按重量计干燥状态果糖含量50%的糖、糖浆)	30				80	17	13	千克	AB	Other sugars, caramel (including invert sugar, in the dry state 50% by weight of fructose)
17.03	**制糖后所剩的糖蜜:**										**Molasses resulting from the extraction or refining of sugar:**
1703.1000	-甘蔗糖蜜	8	5		0	50	17	13	千克	AP	-Cane molasses
1703.9000	-其他	8	5		0	50	17	13	千克	AP	-Other
17.04	**不含可可的糖食(包括白巧克力):**										**Sugar confectionery (including white chocolate), not containing cocoa:**
1704.1000	-口香糖,不论是否裹糖	12	T3	9.5	9.6	50	17	13	千克	AB	-Chewing gum, whether or not sugarcoated
1704.9000	-其他	10	T3	8.2	8	50	17	13	千克	AB	-Other

第十八章
可可及可可制品

Chapter 18
Cocoa and cocoa preparations

注释：

一、本章不包括税目 04.03、19.01、19.04、19.05、21.05、22.02、22.08、30.03、30.04 的制品。

二、税目 18.06 包括含有可可的糖食及注释一以外的其他含可可的食品。

Notes:

1. This Chapter does not cover the preparations of heading Nos. 04.03, 19.01, 19.04, 19.05, 21.05, 22.02, 22.08, 30.03, or 30.04.

2. Heading No. 18.06 includes sugar confectionery containing cocoa and, subject to Note 1 to this Chapter, other food preparations containing cocoa.

税则号列 Tariff Item.	货品名称	最惠国(%) MFN	协定(%)CT 东盟 CA	中巴 CP	中智 CC	普通 Gen	增值税率 VAT	出口退税 ED	计量单位 Unit	监管条件 SC	Article Description
18.01	**整颗或破碎的可可豆，生的或焙炒的：**										**Cocoa beans, whole or broken, raw or roasted:**
1801.0000	整颗或破碎的可可豆，生的或焙炒的	8	T3		0	30	17	13	千克	AB	Cocoa beans, whole or broken, raw or roasted
18.02	**可可荚、壳、皮及废料：**										**Cocoa shells, husks, skins and other cocoa waste:**
1802.0000	可可荚、壳、皮及废料	10	8		0	30	17	5	千克	AB	Cocoa shells, husks, skins and other cocoa waste
18.03	**可可膏，不论是否脱脂：**										**Cocoa paste, whether or not defatted:**
1803.1000	-未脱脂	10	T3		0	30	17	13	千克	AB	-Not defatted
1803.2000	-全脱脂或部分脱脂	10	T3		0	30	17	13	千克	AB	-Wholly or partly defatted
18.04	**可可脂、可可油：**										**Cocoa butter, fat and oil:**
1804.0000	可可脂、可可油	22	T3		13.2	70	17	13	千克		Cocoa butter, fat and oil
1804.0000 10	可可脂	22				70	17	13	千克	AB	Cocoa fat
1804.0000 90	可可油	22				70	17	13	千克	AB	Cocoa oil
18.05	**未加糖或其他甜物质的可可粉：**										**Cocoa powder, not containing added sugar or other sweetening matter:**
1805.0000	未加糖或其他甜物质的可可粉	15	T3		9	40	17	13	千克	AB	Cocoa powder, not containing added sugar or other sweetening matter
18.06	**巧克力及其他含可可的食品：**										**Chocolate and other food preparations containing cocoa:**
1806.1000	-加糖或其他甜物质的可可粉	10	T3		8	50	17	13	千克	AB	-Cocoa powder, containing added sugar or other sweetening matter
1806.2000	-其他重量超过 2 公斤的块状或条状含可可食品，或液状、膏状、粉状、粒状或其他散装形状的含可可食品，容器包装或内包装每件净重超过 2 公斤的	10	T3	7.7	8	50	17	13	千克	AB	-Other preparations in blocks, slabs or bars weighing more than 2kg or in liquid, paste, powder, granular or other bulk form in containers or immediate packings, of a content exceeding 2kg
	-其他块状或条状的含可可食品：										-Other, in blocks, slabs or bars:
1806.3100	--夹心	8	T3	6.4	0	50	17	13	千克	AB	--Filled
1806.3200	--不夹心	10	T3	7.7	8	50	17	13	千克	AB	--Not filled
1806.9000	-其他	8	T3	6.4	0	50	17	13	千克	AB	-Other

第十九章
谷物、粮食粉、淀粉或乳的制品;糕饼点心

注释:

一、本章不包括:

(一)按重量计含香肠、肉、食用杂碎、动物血、鱼、甲壳动物,软体动物、其他水生无脊椎动物及其混合物超过20%的食品(第十六章),但税目19.02的包馅食品除外;

(二)用粮食粉或淀粉制的专作动物饲料用的饼干及其他制品(税目23.09);

(三)第三十章的药品及其他产品。

二、税目19.01所称:

(一)"粗粒"是指第十一章谷物的粗粒;

(二)"细粉"及"粗粉",是指:

1. 第十一章谷物的细粉及粗粉;

2. 其他章植物的细粉、粗粉及粉末,但不包括干蔬菜、马铃薯和干豆类的细粉、粗粉及粉末(应分别归入税目07.12、11.05和11.06)。

三、税目19.04不包括按重量计全脱脂可可含量超过6%或用巧克力完全包裹的食品以及税目18.06的其他含可可食品(税目18.06)。

四、税目19.04所称"其他方法制作的",是指制作或加工程度超过第十章或第十一章各税目或注释所规定范围的。

Chapter 19
Preparations of cereals, flour, starch or milk; pastrycooks' products

Notes:

1. This Chapter does not cover:

(a) Except in the case of stuffed products of heading No. 19.02, food preparations containing more than 20% by weight of sausage, meat, meat offal, blood, fish or crustaceans, molluscs or other aquatic invertebrates, or any combination thereof (Chapter 16);

(b) Biscuits or other articles made from flour or from starch, specially prepared for use in animal feeding (heading No. 23.09); or

(c) Medicaments or other products of Chapter 30.

2. For the purposes of heading No. 19.01:

(a) The term "groats" means cereal groats of Chapter 11;

(b) The terms "flour" and "meal" mean:

(1) Cereal flour and meal of Chapter 11, and

(2) Flour, meal and powder of vegetable origin of any Chapter, other than flour, meal or powder of dried vegetables (heading No. 07.12), of potatoes (heading No. 11.05) or of dried leguminous vegetables (heading No. 11.06).

3. Heading No. 19.04 does not cover preparations containing more than 6% by weight of cocoa calculated on a totally defatted basis or coated with chocolate or use chocolate parcel food and other of heading No. 18.60 preparations containing cocoa (heading No. 18.06).

4. For the purposes of heading No. 19.04, the expression "otherwise prepared" means prepared or processed to an extent beyond that provided for in the headings of or Notes to Chapter 10 or 11.

税则号列 Tariff Item.	货品名称	最惠国(%) MFN	协定(%)CT 东盟 CA	中巴 CP	中智 CC	普通 Gen	增值税率 VAT	出口退税 ED	计量单位 Unit	监管条件 SC	Article Description
19.01	**麦精;细粉、粗粒、粗粉、淀粉或麦精制的其他税目未列名的食品,不含可可或按重量计全脱脂可可含量低于40%;税目04.01至04.04所列货品制的其他税目未列名的食品,不含可可或按重量计全脱脂可可含量低于5%:**										**Malt extract; food preparations of flour, groats, meal, starch or malt extract, not containing cocoa or containing less than 40% by weight of cocoa calculated on a totally defatted basis, not elsewhere specified or included; food preparations of goods of headings Nos. 04.01 to 04.04, not containing cocoa or containing less than 5%by weight of cocoa calculated on a totally defatted basis, not elsewhere specified or included:**
1901.1000	-供婴幼儿食用的零售包装食品	15	8		12	40	17	13	千克	AB	-Preparations for infant use, put up for retail sale
1901.2000	-供烘焙税目19.05所列面包糕饼用的调制品及面团	25	12		20	80	17	13	千克	AB	-Mixes and doughs for the preparation of bakers' wares of heading No. 19.05
1901.9000	-其他	10	8		8	80	17	13	千克	AB	-Other

税则号列 Tariff Item.	货品名称	最惠国(%) MFN	协定(%) CT 东盟 CA	中巴 CP	中智 CC	普通 Gen	增值税率 VAT	出口退税 ED	计量单位 Unit	监管条件 SC	Article Description
19.02	**面食,不论是否煮熟、包馅(肉馅或其他馅)或其他方法制作,例如,通心粉、面条、汤团、馄饨、饺子、奶油面卷;古斯古斯面食,不论是否制作:**										**Pasta, whether or not cooked or stuffed (with meat or other substances) or otherwise prepared, such as spaghetti, macaroni, noodles, lasagne, gnocchi, ravioli, cannelloni; couscous, whether or not prepared:**
	-生的面食,未包馅或未经其他方法制作:										-Uncooked pasta, not stuffed or otherwise prepared:
1902.1100	--含蛋	15	T3		12	80	17	5	千克	AB	--Containing eggs
1902.1900	--其他	15	T3		12	80	17	5	千克	AB	--Other
1902.2000	-包馅面食,不论是否烹煮或经其他方法制作	15	8		12	80	17	13	千克	AB	-Stuffed pasta, whether or not cooked or otherwise prepared
	-其他面食:										-Other pasta:
1902.3010	---米粉干	15	T3		0	80	17	13	千克	AB	---Rice vermicelli, cooked
1902.3020	---粉丝	15	T3		0	80	17	13	千克	AB	---Bean vermicelli, cooked
1902.3030	---即食或快熟面条	15	T3	13.1	0	80	17	13	千克	AB	---Instant noodle
1902.3090	---其他	15	T3	13.1	12	80	17	13	千克	AB	---Other
1902.4000	-古斯古斯面食	25	12		15	80	17	13	千克	AB	-Couscous
19.03	**珍粉及淀粉制成的珍粉代用品,片、粒、珠、粉或类似形状的:**										**Tapioca and substitutes therefor prepared from starch, in the form of flakes, grains, pearls, siftings or in similar forms:**
1903.0000	珍粉及淀粉制成的珍粉代用品,片、粒、珠、粉或类似形状的	15	8		9	80	17	13	千克	AB	Tapioca and substitutes therefor prepared from starch, in the form of flakes, grains, pearls, siftings or in similar forms
19.04	**谷物或谷物产品经膨化或烘炒制成的食品(例如,玉米片);其他税目未列名的预煮或经其他方法制作的谷粒(玉米除外),谷物片或经其他加工的谷粒(细粉、粗粒及粗粉除外):**										**Prepared foods obtained by the swelling or roasting of cereals or cereal products (for example, corn flakes); cereals (other than maize (corn)) in grain form or in the form of flakes or other worked grains (except flour, groats and meal), precooked or otherwise prepared, not elsewhere specified or included:**
1904.1000	-谷物或谷物产品经膨化或烘炒制成的食品	25	12		20	80	17	13	千克	AB	-Prepared foods obtained by the swelling or roasting of cereals or cereal products
1904.2000	-未烘炒谷物片制成的食品及未烘炒的谷物片与烘炒的谷物片或膨化的谷物混合制成的食品	30	12		18	80	17	13	千克	AB	-Prepared foods obtained from unroasted cereal flakes or from mixtures of unroasted cereal flakes and roasted cereal flakes or swelled cereals
1904.3000	-碾碎的干小麦	30	12		18	80	17	13	千克	AB	-Bulgur wheat
1904.9000	-其他	30	12		0	80	17	13	千克	AB	-Other
19.05	**面包、糕点、饼干及其他烘焙糕饼,不论是否含可可;圣餐饼、装药空囊、封缄、糯米纸及类似制品:**										**Bread, pastry, cakes, biscuits and other bakers' wares, whether or not containing cocoa; communion wafers, empty cachets of a kind suitable for pharmaceutical use, sealing wafers, rice paper and similar products:**
1905.1000	-黑麦脆面包片	20	12		12	80	17	13	千克	A	-Crispbread

税则号列 Tariff Item.	货 品 名 称	最惠国(%) MFN	协定(%)CT 东盟 CA	中巴 CP	中智 CC	普通 Gen	增值税率 VAT	出口退税 ED	计量单位 Unit	监管条件 SC	Article Description
1905.2000	-姜饼及类似品	20	12		12	80	17	13	千克	A	-Gingerbread and the like
	-甜饼干;华夫饼干及圣餐饼:										-Sweet biscuits;waffles and wafers:
1905.3100	--甜饼干	15	T3	12.4	12	80	17	13	千克	AB	--Sweet biscuits
1905.3200	--华夫饼干及圣餐饼	15	T3	12.4	12	80	17	13	千克	AB	--Waffles and wafers
1905.4000	-面包干、吐司及类似的烤面包	20	12		12	80	17	13	千克	AB	-Rusks, toasted bread and similar toasted products
1905.9000	-其他	20	T3	17.1	16	80	17	13	千克	AB	-Other

第二十章
蔬菜、水果、坚果或植物其他部分的制品

注释：

一、本章不包括：

（一）用第七章、第八章或第十一章所列方法制作或保藏的蔬菜、水果或坚果；

（二）按重量计含香肠、肉、食用杂碎、动物血、鱼、甲壳动物、软体动物、其他水生无脊椎动物及其混合物超过20%的食品（第十六章）；

（三）税目19.05的烘焙糕饼及其他制品；

（四）税目21.04的均化混合食品。

二、税目20.07及20.08不包括制成糖食的果冻、果膏、糖衣杏仁或类似品（税目17.04）及巧克力糖食（税目18.06）。

三、税目20.01、20.04及20.05仅酌情包括用本章注释一（一）以外的方法制作或保藏的第七章或税目11.05、11.06的产品（第八章产品的细粉、粗粉除外）。

四、干重量在7%及以上的番茄汁归入税目20.02。

五、税目20.07所称"烹煮的"，是指在常压或减压下，通过减少水分或其他方法增加产品粘稠度的热处理。

原注释五变更为注释六。

六、税目20.09所称"未发酵及未加酒精的水果汁"，是指按容量计酒精浓度（标准见第二十二章注释二）不超过0.5%的水果汁。

子目注释：

一、子目2005.10所称"均化蔬菜"，是指蔬菜经精细均化制成供婴幼儿食用或营养用的零售包装食品（每件净重不超过250克）。为了调味、保藏或其他目的，均化蔬菜中可以加入少量其他配料，还可以含有少量可见的蔬菜粒。归类时，子目2005.10优先于税目20.05的其他子目。

Chapter 20
Preparations of vegetables, fruit, nuts or other parts of plants

Notes:

1. This Chapter does not cover:

(a) Vegetables, fruit or nuts, prepared or preserved by the processes specified in Chapter 7, 8 or 11;

(b) Food preparations containing more than 20% by weight of sausage, meat, meat offal, blood, fish or crustaceans, molluscs or other aquatic invertebrates, or any combination thereof (Chapter 16); or

(c) Baked Cakes and other produce of heading No. 19.05.

(d) Homogenized composite food preparations of heading No. 21.04.

2. Headings No. 20.07 and 20.08 do not apply to fruit jellies, fruit pastes, sugar-coated almonds or the like in the form of sugar confectionery (heading No. 17.04) or chocolate confectionery (heading No. 18.06).

3. Headings Nos. 20.01, 20.04 and 20.05 cover, as the case may be, only those products of Chapter 7 or of heading No. 11.05 or 11.06 (other than flour, meal and powder of the products of Chapter 8) which have been prepared or preserved by processes other than those referred to in Note 1 (a).

4. Tomato juice the dry weight content of which is 7% or more is to be classified in heading No. 20.02.

5. For the purposes of heading No. 20.07, the expression "obtained by cooking" means obtained by heat treatment at atmospheric pressure or under reduced pressure to increase the viscosity of a product through reduction of water content or other means.

6. For the purposes of heading No. 20.09, the expression "juices, unfermented and not containing added spirit" means juices of an alcoholic strength by volume (see Note 2 to Chapter 22) not exceeding 0.5% vol.

Subheading Notes:

1. For the purposes of subheading No. 2005.10, the expression "homogenized vegetables" means preparations of vegetables, finely homogenized, put up for retail sale as infant food or for dietetic purposes, in containers of a net weight content not exceeding 250g. For the application of this definition no account is to be taken of small quantities of any ingredients which may have been added to the preparation for seasoning, preparation or other purposes. These preparations may contain a small quantity of visible pieces of vegetables. Subheading No. 2005.10 takes precedence over all other subheadings of heading No. 20.05.

二、子目 2007.10 所称“均化食品”，是指果实经精细均化制成供婴幼儿食用或营养用的零售包装食品(每件净重不超过 250 克)。为了调味、保藏或其他目的，均化食品中可以加入少量其他配料，还可以含有少量可见的果粒。归类时，子目 2007.10 优先于税目 20.07 的其他子目。

2. For the purposes of subheading No. 2007.10, the expression “homogenized preparations” means preparations of fruit, finely homogenized, put up for retail sale as infant food or for dietetic purposes, in containers of a net weight content not exceeding 250g. For the application of this definition no account is to be taken of small quantities of any ingredients which may have been added to the preparation for seasoning, preservation or other purposes. These preparations may contain a small quantity of visible pieces of fruit. Subheading No. 2007.10 takes precedence over all other subheadings of heading No. 20.07.

三、子目 2009.12、2009.21、2009.31、2009.41、2009.61 及 2009.71 所称“白利糖度值”，是指直接从白利糖度计读取的度数或在 20℃ 时从折射计读取的以蔗糖百分比含量计的折射率，在其他温度下读取的数值应折算为 20℃ 时的折射率。

3. For the purposes of subheadings No. 2009.12, 2009.21, 2009.31, 2009.41, 2009.61 and 2009.71, the expression “Brix value” means the direct reading of degrees Brix obtained from a Brix hydrometer of refractive index expressed in terms of percentage sucrose content obtained from a refractometer, at a temperature of 20℃ or corrected for 20℃ if the reading is made at a different temperature.

税则号列 Tariff Item.	货品名称	最惠国(%) MFN	协定(%) CT 东盟 CA	中巴 CP	中智 CC	普通 Gen	增值税率 VAT	出口退税 ED	计量单位 Unit	监管条件 SC	Article Description
20.01	**蔬菜、水果、坚果及植物的其他食用部分，用醋或醋酸制作或保藏的：**										**Vegetagbles, fruit, nuts and other edible parts of plants, prepared or preserved by vinegar or acetic acid:**
2001.1000	-黄瓜及小黄瓜	25	T3		15	70	17	5	千克	AB	-Cucumbers and gherkins
	-其他：										-Other:
2001.9010	---大蒜	25	T3		0	70	17	5	千克		---Garlic
2001.9010 10	用醋或醋酸腌制的大蒜头、大蒜瓣(无论是否加糖或去皮)	25				70	17	5	千克	AB	Garlic bulbs, garlic cloves. prepared by vinegar or acetic acid, whether or not added sugars or skinned
2001.9010 90	用醋或醋酸腌制的其他大蒜(不含蒜头、蒜瓣，无论是否加糖或去皮)	25				70	17	5	千克	AB	Other garlic prepared by vinegar or acetic acid, whether or not added sugars or skinned (other than garlic bulbs galic cloves)
2001.9090	---其他	25	T3		20	70	17	5	千克		---Other
2001.9090 10	用醋或醋酸制作或保藏的松茸	25				70	17	5	千克	ABE	Sungmo, prepared or preserved by vinegar or acetic acid
2001.9090 20	用醋或醋酸制作或保藏的酸竹笋	25				70	17	5	千克	ABE	Bamboo shoots, pickled, prepared or preserved by vinegar or acetic acid
2001.9090 30	用醋或醋酸制作或保藏的芦荟	25				70	17	5	千克	ABFE	Aloe, prepared or preserved by vinegar or acetic acid
2001.9090 40	用醋或醋酸制作或保藏仙人掌植物	25				70	17	5	千克	ABFE	Cactus, prepared or preserved by vinegar or acetic acid
2001.9090 50	用醋或醋酸制作或保藏的莼菜	25				70	17	5	千克	ABE	Water shield, prepared or preserved by vinegar or acetic acid
2001.9090 90	用醋制作的其他果、菜及食用植物(包括用醋酸制作或保藏的)	25				70	17	5	千克	AB	Vegetagble, fruit, nuts and other edible parts of plants, prepared or preserved by vinegar or acetic acid
20.02	**番茄，用醋或醋酸以外的其他方法制作或保藏的：**										**Tomatoes prepared or preserved otherwise than by vinegar or acetic acid:**
	-番茄，整个或切片：										-Tomatoes, whole or in pieces:
2002.1010	---罐头	19	T3		15.2	80	17	13	千克	AB	---In airtight containers
2002.1090	---其他	25	T3		20	70	17	13	千克	AB	---Other

税则号列 Tariff Item.	货品名称	最惠国(%) MFN	协定(%)CT 东盟 CA	中巴 CP	中智 CC	普通 Gen	增值税率 VAT	出口退税 ED	计量单位 Unit	监管条件 SC	Article Description
	-其他:										-Other:
2002.9010	---番茄酱罐头	20	T3		12	80	17	13	千克	AB	---Tomato paste, in airtight containers
2002.9090	---其他	18	T3		10.8	70	17	13	千克	AB	---Other
20.03	**蘑菇及块菌,用醋或醋酸以外的其他方法制作或保藏的:**										**Mushrooms and truffles, prepared or preserved otherwise than by vinegar or acetic acid:**
	-伞菌属蘑菇:										-Mushrooms :
	---罐头:										---In airtight containers:
2003.1011	----小白蘑菇	25	T3		20	90	17	13	千克	AB	----Small white agaric
2003.1019	----其他	25	T3		20	90	17	13	千克	AB	----Other
2003.1090	---其他	25	T3		20	90	17	13	千克	AB	---Other
2003.2000	-块菌	25	T3		15	90	17	13	千克	AB	-Truffles
	-其他:										-Other:
2003.9010	---罐头	25	12		0	90	17	13	千克		---In airtight containers
2003.9010 10	非用醋制作的香菇罐头[用醋或醋酸以外其他方法制作或保藏的(非伞菌属蘑菇)]	25				90	17	13	千克	AB	Xianggu mushroom, tinned, prepared or preserved otherwise than by vinegar or acetic acid
2003.9010 20	非用醋制作的松茸罐头(用醋或醋酸以外其他方法制作或保藏的)	25				90	17	13	千克	ABE	Sungmo, tinned, prepared or preserved otherwise than by vinegar or acetic acid
2003.9010 90	非用醋制作的其他蘑菇罐头[用醋或醋酸以外其他方法制作或保藏的(非伞菌属蘑菇)]	25				90	17	13	千克	AB	Other mushrooms, tinned, prepared or preserved otherwise than by vinegar or acetic acid
2003.9090	---其他	25	12		0	90	17	13	千克		---Other
2003.9090 10	非用醋制作的其他香菇[用醋或醋酸以外其他方法制作或保藏的(非伞菌属蘑菇)]	25				90	17	13	千克	AB	Other Xianggu mushroom, prepared or preserved otherwise than by vinegar or acetic acid
2003.9090 20	非用醋制作的其他松茸(用醋或醋酸以外其他方法制作或保藏的)	25				90	17	13	千克	ABE	Other sungmo prepared or preserved otherwise than by vinegar or acetic acid
2003.9090 90	非用醋制作的其他蘑菇[用醋或醋酸以外其他方法制作或保藏的(非伞菌属蘑菇)]	25				90	17	13	千克	AB	Other mushrooms, prepared or preserved otherwise than by vinegar or acetic acid
20.04	**其他冷冻蔬菜,用醋或醋酸以外的其他方法制作或保藏的,但税目20.06的产品除外:**										**Other vegetables prepared or preserved otherwise than by vinegar or acetic acid, other than products of heading No. 20.06:**
2004.1000	-马铃薯	13	T3		10.4	70	17	13	千克	AB	-Potatoes
2004.9000	-其他蔬菜及什锦蔬菜	25	T3		20	70	17	13	千克		-Other vegetables and mixtures of vegetables
2004.9000 10	非用醋制作的冷冻松茸	25				70	17	13	千克	ABE	Sungmo prepared or preserved otherwise than by vinegar or acetic acid, frozen
2004.9000 20	非用醋制作的冷冻酸竹笋	25				70	17	13	千克	ABE	Acid bamboo shoots prepared or preserved otherwise than by vinegar or acetic acid, frozen

税则号列 Tariff Item.	货品名称	最惠国(%) MFN	协定(%)CT 东盟 CA	中巴 CP	中智 CC	普通 Gen	增值税率 VAT	出口退税 ED	计量单位 Unit	监管条件 SC	Article Description
2004.9000 30	非用醋制作的冷冻芦荟	25				70	17	13	千克	ABFE	Aloe, prepared or preserved otherwise than by vinegar or acetic acid, frozen
2004.9000 40	非用醋制作的冷冻仙人掌植物	25				70	17	13	千克	ABFE	Cactus, prepared or preserved otherwise than by vinegar or acetic acid, frozen
2004.9000 90	非用醋制作的其他冷冻蔬菜(编号2006货品除外)	25				70	17	13	千克	AB	Other vegetables prepared or preserved otherwise than by vinegar or acetic acid, other than products of heading No. 20.06
20.05	**其他未冷冻蔬菜,用醋或醋酸以外的其他方法制作或保藏的,但税目20.06的产品除外:**										**Other vegetables prepared or preserved otherwise than by vinegar or acetic acid, not frozen, other than products of heading No. 20.06:**
2005.1000	-均化蔬菜	25	T3		15	70	17	13	千克	AB	-Homogenized vegetables
2005.2000	-马铃薯	15	T3		12	70	17	13	千克	AB	-Potatoes
2005.4000	-豌豆	25	T3		0	70	17	13	千克	AB	-Peas (*Pisum sativum*)
	-豇豆及菜豆:										-Beans (*Vigna spp.*, *Phaseolus spp.*):
	--脱荚的:										--Beans, shelled:
2005.5110	---罐头	25	T3		15	80	17	13	千克	AB	---In airtight containers
2005.5120	---赤豆馅	25	T3		0	70	17	13	千克	AB	---Small red bean paste
2005.5190	---其他	25	T3		15	70	17	13	千克	AB	---Other
	--其他:										--Other:
2005.5910	---罐头	25	T3		15	80	17	13	千克	AB	---In airtight containers
2005.5990	---其他	25	T3		15	70	17	13	千克	AB	---Other
	-芦笋:										-Asparagus:
2005.6010	---罐头	25	T3		15	80	17	13	千克	AB	---In airtight containers
2005.6090	---其他	25	T3		15	70	17	13	千克	AB	---Other
2005.7000	-油橄榄	10	T3		8	70	17	13	千克	AB	-Olives
2005.8000	-甜玉米	10	T3		0	80	17	13	千克	AB	-Sweet corn (*Zea mays var. saccharata*)
	-其他蔬菜及什锦蔬菜:										-Other vegetables and mixtures of vegetables:
	--竹笋:										--Bamboo:
2005.9110	---竹笋罐头:	25	T3		20	80	17	13	千克		---Bambooshoots,inairtight contqiners
2005.9110 10	非用醋制作的酸竹笋罐头	25				80	17		千克	ABFE	Bamboo shoots pickled in airtight containers preserved otherwise than by vinegar
2005.9110 90	非用醋制作的其他竹笋罐头	25				80	17		千克	AB	Other bamboo shoots in airtight containers preserved otherwise than by vinegar
2005.9190	---其他	25	T3		20	80	17	13	千克		---Other
2005.9190 10	非用醋制作的酸竹笋	25				70	17		千克	ABFE	Bamboo shoots pickled prepared or preserved otherwise than by vinegar
2005.9190 90	非用醋制作的其他竹笋	25				70	17		千克	AB	Other bamboo shoots prepared or preserved otherwise than by vinegar
	--其他:										--Other:
2005.9910	---清水马蹄罐头	25	T3		20	80	17	13	千克	AB	---Water chestnut, in airtight containers
2005.9920	---蚕豆罐头	25	T3		20	80	17	13	千克	AB	---Broad beans, in airtight containers
2005.9940	---榨菜	25	T3		0	70	17	13	千克	AB	---Hot pickled mustard tubers
2005.9950	---咸蕨菜	25	T3		0	70	17	13	千克	AB	---Chueh tsai (fiddle-head), salted
2005.9960	---咸藠头	25	T3		0	70	17	13	千克	AB	---Scallion, salted
	---其他:										---Other:

税则号列 Tariff Item.	货品名称	最惠国(%) MFN	协定(%) 东盟 CA	协定(%) 中巴 CP	协定(%) CT 中智 CC	普通 Gen	增值税率 VAT	出口退税 ED	计量单位 Unit	监管条件 SC	Article Description
2005.9991	----罐头	25	T3		20	70	17	13	千克	AB	----In airtight containers
2005.9999	----其他	25	T3		20	70	17	5	千克		----Other
2005.9999 10	非用醋制作的仙人掌	25				70	17	13	千克	ABFE	Cactus prepared or preserved otherwise than by vinegar or acetic acid
2005.9999 20	非用醋制作的芦荟	25				70	17	13	千克	ABFE	Aloe, prepared or preserved otherwise than by vinegar or acetic acid
2005.9999 90	非用醋制作的其他蔬菜及什锦蔬菜	25				70	17	13	千克	AB	Other vegetables and mixtures of vegetables
20.06	**糖渍蔬菜、水果、坚果、果皮及植物的其他部分(沥干、糖渍或裹糖的):**										**Vegetables, fruit, nuts, fruit-peel and other parts of plants, preserved by sugar (drained, glacé or crystallized):**
2006.0010	---蜜枣	30	T3		0	90	17	13	千克	AB	---Preserved jujubes
2006.0020	---橄榄	30	T3		24	90	17	13	千克	AB	---Preserved olives
2006.0090	---其他	30	T3		24	90	17	13	千克		---Other
2006.0090 10	糖渍制松茸	30				90	17	13	千克	ABE	Sungmo preserved by sugar
2006.0090 90	其他糖渍蔬菜,水果,坚果,果皮(包括糖渍植物的其他部分)	30				90	17	13	千克	AB	Other vegetables, fruit, nuts, fruit-peel and other parts of plants, preserved by sugar
20.07	**烹煮的果酱、果冻、柑桔酱、果泥及果膏,不论是否加糖或其他甜物质:**										**Jams, fruit jellies, marmalades, fruit or nut purée and fruit or nut pastes, being cooked preparations, whether or not containing added sugar or other sweetening matter:**
2007.1000	-均化食品	30	12		24	80	17	13	千克	AB	-Homogenized preparations
	-其他:										-Other:
2007.9100	--柑桔属水果	30	T3		0	80	17	13	千克	AB	--Citrus fruit
	--其他:										--Other:
2007.9910	---罐头	5			4	80	17	13	千克	AB	---In airtight containers
2007.9990	---其他	5			4	80	17	13	千克	AB	---Other
20.08	**用其他方法制作或保藏的其他税目未列名水果、坚果及植物的其他食用部分,不论是否加酒、加糖或其他甜物质:**										**Fruit, nuts and other edible parts of plants, otherwise prepared or preserved, whether or not containing added sugar or other sweetening matter or spirit, not elsewhere specified or included:**
	-坚果、花生及其他子仁,不论是否混合:										-Nuts, ground-nuts and other seeds, whether or not mixed together:
	--花生:										--Ground-nuts:
2008.1110	---花生米罐头	30	T3		0	90	17	13	千克	AB	---Ground-nut kernels, in airtight containers
2008.1120	---烘焙花生	30	T3		0	80	17	13	千克	AB	---Roasted ground-nuts
2008.1130	---花生酱	30	T3		0	90	17	13	千克	AB	---Ground-nut butter
2008.1190	---其他	30	T3		0	80	17	13	千克	AB	---Other
	--其他,包括什锦坚果及其他子仁:										--Other, including mixtures:
2008.1910	---核桃仁罐头	20	T3	10	16	90	17	13	千克	AB	---Walnut meats, in airtight containers
2008.1920	---其他果仁罐头	13	T3	6.5	10.4	90	17	13	千克	AB	---Other nuts, in airtight containers

税则号列 Tariff Item.	货品名称	最惠国(%) MFN	协定(%)CT 东盟 CA	中巴 CP	中智 CC	普通 Gen	增值税率 VAT	出口退税 ED	计量单位 Unit	监管条件 SC	Article Description
	---其他:										---Other:
2008.1991	----栗仁	10	T3	5	8	80	17	13	千克	AB	----Chestnut kernel
2008.1992	----芝麻	10	T3	5	8	80	17	13	千克	AB	----Sesames
2008.1999	----其他	10	T3	5	8	80	17	13	千克		----Other
2008.1999 10	其他方法制作保藏的红松子仁(用醋或醋酸以外其他方法制作或保藏的)	10				80	17	13	千克	ABE	Korean pine-nuts, shelled, prepared or preserved otherwise than by vinegar or acetic acid
2008.1999 90	未列名制作或保藏坚果及其他子仁(用醋或醋酸以外其他方法制作或保藏的)	10				80	17	13	千克	AB	Nuts and other seeds, prepared or preserved otherwise than by vinegar or acetic acid, not elsewhere specified or included
	-菠萝:										-Pineapples:
2008.2010	---罐头	15			0	90	17	13	千克	AB	---In airtight containers
2008.2090	---其他	15			0	80	17	13	千克	AB	---Other
	-柑桔属水果:										-Citrus fruit:
2008.3010	---罐头	20	T3		12	90	17	13	千克	ABa	---In airtight containers
2008.3090	---其他	20	T3		12	80	17	13	千克	AB	---Other
	-梨:										-Pears:
2008.4010	---罐头	20	T3		16	90	17	13	千克	AB	---In airtight containers
2008.4090	---其他	20	T3		16	80	17	13	千克	AB	---Other
2008.5000	-杏	20	T3		16	90	17	13	千克	AB	-Apricots
2008.6000	-樱桃	20	T3		16	90	17	13	千克	AB	-Cherries
	-桃:										-Peaches:
2008.7010	---罐头	10	T3		6	90	17	13	千克	AB	---In airtight containers
2008.7090	---其他	20	T3		16	80	17	13	千克	AB	---Other
2008.8000	-草莓	15	T3		12	90	17	13	千克	AB	-Strawberries
	-其他,包括子目2008.19以外的什锦果实:										-Other, including mixtures other than those of subheading 2008.19:
2008.9100	--棕榈芯	5			0	80	17	13	千克	AB	--Palm hearts
2008.9200	--什锦果实	10	T3		8	80	17	13	千克	AB	--Mixtures
	--其他:										--Other:
2008.9910	---荔枝罐头	20	T3		0	90	17	13	千克	AB	---Lychee can
2008.9920	---龙眼罐头	15	T3		0	80	17	13	千克	AB	---Longan can
2008.9990	---其他	15			12	80	17	13	千克		---Other
2008.9990 10	盐渍的裙带菜	15				80	17	13	千克	AB	Pinnatifida, in brine
2008.9990 90	未列名制作或保藏的水果、坚果(包括植物的其他食用部分)	15				80	17	13	千克	AB	Fruit or nuts, including other edible parts, prepared or preserved, not elsewhere specified or included
20.09	**未发酵及未加酒精的水果汁(包括酿酒葡萄汁)、蔬菜汁,不论是否加糖或其他甜物质:**										**Fruit juices (including grape must) and vegetable juices, unfermented and not containing added spirit, whether or not containing added sugar or other sweetening matter:**
	-橙汁:										-Orange juice:
2009.1100	--冷冻的	7.5	T3		0	90	17	13	千克	AB	--Frozen
2009.1200	--非冷冻的,白利糖度值不超过20	30	12		24	90	17	13	千克	AB	--Not frozen, of a Brix value not exceeding 20
2009.1900	--其他	30	T3		18	90	17	13	千克	AB	--Other
	-葡萄柚(包括柚)汁:										-Grapefruit juice (include a pomelo).

税则号列 Tariff Item.	货 品 名 称	最惠国(%) MFN	协定(%)CT			普通 Gen	增值税率 VAT	出口退税 ED	计量单位 Unit	监管条件 SC	Article Description
			东盟 CA	中巴 CP	中智 CC						
2009. 2100	--白利糖度值不超过 20 的	15	T3		9	90	17	13	千克	AB	--Of a Brix value not exceeding 20
2009. 2900	--其他	15	T3		9	90	17	13	千克	AB	--Other
	-其他未混合柑桔属水果汁：										-Juice of any other single citrus fruit：
	--白利糖度值不超过 20 的：										--Of a Brix value not exceeding 20：
2009. 3110	---柠檬汁	18	T3	16. 8	14. 4	90	17	13	千克	AB	---Lemon Juice
2009. 3190	---其他	18	T3	16. 8	14. 4	90	17	13	千克	AB	---Other
	--其他：										--Other：
2009. 3910	---柠檬汁	18	T3	16. 8	10. 8	90	17	13	千克	AB	---Lemon Juice
2009. 3990	---其他	18	T3	16. 8	10. 8	90	17	13	千克	AB	---Other
	-菠萝汁：										-Pineapple juice：
2009. 4100	--白利糖度值不超过 20 的	10			0	90	17	13	千克	AB	--Of a Brix value not exceeding 20
2009. 4900	--其他	10			0	90	17	13	千克	AB	--Other
2009. 5000	-番茄汁	30	T3		18	80	17	13	千克	AB	-Tomato juice
	-葡萄汁，包括酿酒葡萄汁：										-Grape juice(including grape must)：
2009. 6100	--白利糖度值不超过 30 的	20	T3		16	90	17	13	千克	AB	--Of a Brix value not exceeding 30
2009. 6900	--其他	20	T3		16	90	17	13	千克	AB	--Other
	-苹果汁：										-Apple juice：
2009. 7100	--白利糖度值不超过 20 的	20	T3		0	90	17	13	千克	aAB	--Of a Brix value not exceeding 20
2009. 7900	--其他	20	T3		16	90	17	13	千克	aAB	--Other
	-其他未混合的水果汁或蔬菜汁：										-Juice of any other single fruit or vegetable：
	---水果汁：										---Fruit juice：
2009. 8011	----椰子汁	10	T3	9	8	90	17	13	千克	AB	----Coconut milk
2009. 8012	----芒果汁	20	T3	17. 4	16	90	17	13	千克	AB	----Mango juice
2009. 8013	----西番莲果汁	20	T3	17. 4	16	90	17	13	千克	AB	----Passionfruit juice
2009. 8014	----番石榴果汁	20	T3	17. 4	16	90	17	13	千克	AB	----Guva juice
2009. 8019	----其他	20	T3	10	16	90	17	13	千克	AB	----Other
2009. 8020	---蔬菜汁	20	T3	10	16	80	17	13	千克	AB	---Vegetable juice
	-混合汁：										-Mixtures of juices：
2009. 9010	---水果汁	20	T3	17. 4	12	90	17	13	千克	AB	---Of fruit juices
2009. 9090	---其他	20	T3		12	80	17	13	千克	AB	---Other

第二十一章
杂 项 食 品

Chapter 21
Miscellaneous edible preparations

注释：

一、本章不包括：

（一）税目07.12的什锦蔬菜；

（二）含咖啡的焙炒咖啡代用品（税目09.01）；

（三）加香料的茶（税目09.02）；

（四）税目09.04至09.10的调味香料或其他产品；

（五）按重量计含香肠、肉、食用杂碎、动物血、鱼、甲壳动物、软体动物、其他水生无脊椎动物及其混合物超过20%的食品（第十六章），但税目21.03或21.04的产品除外；

（六）税目30.03或30.04的药用酵母及其他产品；

（七）税目35.07的酶制品。

二、上述注释一（二）所述咖啡代用品的精汁归入税目21.01。

三、税目21.04所称"均化混合食品"，是指两种或两种以上的基本配料，例如，肉、鱼、蔬菜或果实等，经精细均化制成供婴幼儿食用或营养用的零售包装食品（每件净重不超过250克）。为了调味、保藏或其他目的，可以加入少量其他配料，还可以含有少量可见的小块配料。

Notes:

1. This Chapter does not cover:

(a) Mixed vegetables of heading No. 07.12;

(b) Roasted coffee substitutes containing coffee in any proportion (heading No. 09.01);

(c) Flavoured tea (heading No. 09.02);

(d) Spices or other products of headings Nos. 09.04 to 09.10;

(e) Food preparations, other than the products described in heading No. 21.03 or 21.04, containing more than 20% by weight of sausage, meat, meat offal, blood, fish or crustaceans, molluscs or other aquatic invertebrates, or any combination thereof (Chapter 16);

(f) Yeast put up as a medicament or other products of heading No. 30.03 or 30.04; or

(g) Prepared enzymes of heading No. 35.07.

2. Extracts of the substitutes referred to in Note 1(b) above are to be classified in heading No. 21.01.

3. For the purposes of heading No. 21.04, the expression "homogenized composite food preparations" means preparations consisting of a finely homogenized mixture of two or more basic ingredients such as meat, fish, vegetables or fruit, put up for retail sale as infant food or for dietetic purposes, in containers of a net weight content not exceeding 250g. For the application of this definition, no account is to be taken of small quantities of any ingredients which may be added to the mixture for seasoning, preservation or other purposes. Such preparations may contain a small quantity of visible pieces of ingredients.

税则号列 Tariff Item.	货品名称	最惠国(%) MFN	协定(%)CT 东盟 CA	中巴 CP	中智 CC	普通 Gen	增值税率 VAT	出口退税 ED	计量单位 Unit	监管条件 SC	Article Description
21.01	**咖啡、茶、马黛茶的浓缩精汁及以其为基本成分或以咖啡、茶、马黛茶为基本成分的制品；烘焙菊苣和其他烘焙咖啡代用品及其浓缩精汁：**										**Extracts, essences and concentrates, of coffee, tea or maté and preparations with a basis of these products or with a basis of coffee, tea or maté; roasted chicory and other roasted coffee substitutes, and extracts, essences and concentrates thereof:**
	-咖啡浓缩精汁及以其为基本成分或以咖啡为基本成分的制品：										-Extracts, essences and concentrates of coffee, and preparations with a basis of these extracts, essences or concentrates or with a basis of coffee:
2101.1100	--浓缩精汁	17	T3		13.6	130	17	13	千克	AB	--Extracts, essences and concentrates
2101.1200	--以浓缩精汁或咖啡为基本成分的制品	30	T3		24	130	17	13	千克	AB	--Preparations with a basis of extracts, essences or concentrates or with a basis of coffee

税则号列 Tariff Item.	货品名称	最惠国(%) MFN	协定(%)CT 东盟 CA	中巴 CP	中智 CC	普通 Gen	增值税率 VAT	出口退税 ED	计量单位 Unit	监管条件 SC	Article Description
2101.2000	-茶、马黛茶浓缩精汁及以其为基本成分或以茶、马黛茶为基本成分的制品	32	12	16	25.6	130	17	13	千克	AB	-Extracts, essences and concentrates, of tea or maté, and preparations with a basis of these extracts, essences or concentrates or with a basis of tea or mate
2101.3000	-烘焙菊苣和其他烘焙咖啡代用品及其浓缩精汁	32	12		25.6	130	17	13	千克	AB	-Roasted chicory and other roasted coffee substitutes, and extracts, essences and concentrates thereof
21.02	**酵母(活性或非活性);已死的其他单细胞微生物(不包括税目30.02的疫苗);发酵粉:**										**Yeasts (active or inactive); other singlecell micro-organisms, dead (but not including vaccines of heading No. 30.02); prepared baking powders:**
2102.1000	-活性酵母	25	12		20	80	17	13	千克	AB	-Active yeasts
2102.2000	-非活性酵母;已死的其他单细胞微生物	25	12		20	70	13	13	千克	AB	-Inactive yeasts; other single-cell micro-organisms, dead
2102.3000	-发酵粉	25	12		15	70	17	13	千克	AB	-Prepared baking powders
21.03	**调味汁及其制品;混合调味品;芥子粉及其调制品:**										**Sauces and preparations therefor; mixed condiments and mixes seasonings; mustard flour and meal and prepared mustard:**
2103.1000	-酱油	28	12		16.8	90	17	13	千克	AB	-Soya sauce
2103.2000	-番茄沙司及其他番茄调味汁	15	8		12	90	17	13	千克	AB	-Tomato ketchup and other tomato sauces
2103.3000	-芥子粉及其调制品	15	8		9	70	17	13	千克	AB	-Mustard flour and meal and prepared mustard
	-其他:										-Other:
2103.9010	---味精	21	12	18.2	0	130	17	13	千克	AB	---Gourmet powder
2103.9020	---别特酒(Aromatic bitters),按体积计酒精含量44.2%~49.2%,按重量计含1.5%~6%的香料、各种配料以及4%~10%的糖	21	12		16.8	90	17	13	千克	AB	---Aromatic bitters, 44.2% - 49.2% of which is alcoholic strength by volume, 1.5% - 6% of which is spiles and various ingredients by weight and 4% ~ 10% of which is sugar by weight
2103.9090	---其他	21	12	18.4	16.8	90	17	13	千克	AB	---Other
21.04	**汤料及其制品;均化混合食品:**										**Soups and broths and preparations therefor; homogenized composite food preparations:**
2104.1000	-汤料及其制品	15	12		12	90	17	13	千克	AB	-Soups and broths and preparations therefor
2104.2000	-均化混合食品	32	12		25.6	90	17	13	千克	AB	-Homogenized composite food preparations
21.05	**冰淇淋及其他冰制食品,不论是否含可可:**										**Ice cream and other edible ice, whether or not containing cocoa:**
2105.0000	冰淇淋及其他冰制食品,不论是否含可可	19	12		15.2	90	17	13	千克	AB	Ice cream and other edible ice, whether or not containing cocoa
21.06	**其他税目未列名的食品:**										**Food preparations not elsewhere specified or included:**
2106.1000	-浓缩蛋白质及人造蛋白物质	10	8		8	90	17	13	千克	AB	-Protein concentrates and textured protein substances
	-其他:										-Other:
2106.9010	---制造碳酸饮料的浓缩物	35	12		28	100	17	13	千克	AB	---Beverage bases

税则号列 Tariff Item.	货品名称	最惠国(%) MFN	协定(%) 东盟 CA	中巴 CP	CT 中智 CC	普通 Gen	增值税率 VAT	出口退税 ED	计量单位 Unit	监管条件 SC	Article Description
2106.9020	---制造饮料用的复合酒精制品	20	12		16	180	17	13	千克	AB	---Compound alcoholic preparations of a kind used for the manufacture of beverages
2106.9030	---蜂王浆制剂	3			0	80	17	13	千克		---Royal jelly, put up as tonic essences
2106.9030 10	含濒危植物成分的蜂王浆制剂	3				80	17	13	千克	ABFE	Royal jelly, put up as tonic essences containing composition of plants in imminent dangers
2106.9030 90	其他蜂王浆制剂	3				80	17	13	千克	AB	Other royal jelly, put up as tonic essences
	---其他:										---Other:
2106.9091	----调味紫菜	20	12	18.4	0	90	17	13	千克	AB	----Seasoned laver
2106.9099	----其他	20	12	18.4	16	90	17	13	千克		----Other
2106.9099 10	含濒危动植物成分的其他编号未列名食品	20				90	17	13	千克	ABEF	Other food con taining composition of plant in imminenc dangers
2106.9099 90	其他编号未列名的食品	20				90	17	13	千克	AB	Other food preparations noelsewhe re specified or included

第二十二章
饮料、酒及醋

Chapter 22
Beverages, spirits and vinegar

注释：

一、本章不包括：

（一）本章的产品（税目 22.09 的货品除外）经配制后，用于烹饪而不适于作为饮料的制品（通常归入税目 21.03）；

（二）海水（税目 25.01）；

（三）蒸馏水、导电水及类似的纯净水（税目 28.53）；

（四）按重量计浓度超过 10% 的醋酸（税目 29.15）；

（五）税目 30.03 或 30.04 的药品；

（六）芳香料制品及盥洗品（第三十三章）。

二、本章及第二十章和第二十一章所称"按容量计酒精浓度"，应是温度在 20℃ 时测得的浓度。

三、税目 22.02 所称"无酒精饮料"，是指按容量计酒精浓度不超过 0.5% 的饮料。含酒精饮料应分别归入税目 22.03 至 22.06 或税目 22.08。

子目注释：

子目 2204.10 所称"汽酒"，是指温度在 20℃ 时装在密封容器中超过大气压力 3 巴及以上的酒。

Notes:

1. This Chapter does not cover:
   (a) Products of this Chapter (other than those of heading No. 22.09) prepared for culinary purposes and thereby rendered unsuitable for consumption as beverages (generally heading No. 21.03);
   (b) Sea water (heading No. 25.01);
   (c) Distilled or conductivity water or water of similar purity (heading No. 28.53);
   (d) Acetic acid of a concentration exceeding 10% by weight of acetic acid (heading No. 29.15);
   (e) Medicaments of heading No. 30.03 or 30.04; or
   (f) Perfumery or toilet preparations (Chapter 33).
2. For the purposes of this Chapter and of Chapter 20 and 21, the "alcoholic strength by volume" shall be determined at a temperature of 20℃.
3. For the purposes of heading No. 22.02, the term "non-alcoholic beverages" means beverages of an alcoholic strength by volume not exceeding 0.5% vol. Alcoholic beverages are classified in headings No. 22.03 to 22.06 or heading No. 22.08 as appropriate.

Subheading Note:

For the purposes of subheading No. 2204.10, the expression "sparkling wine" means wine which, when kept at a temperature of 20℃ in closed containers, has an excess pressure of not less than 3 bars.

税则号列 Tariff Item.	货品名称	最惠国(%) MFN	协定(%) CT 东盟 CA	中巴 CP	中智 CC	普通 Gen	增值税率 VAT	出口退税 ED	计量单位 Unit	监管条件 SC	Article Description
22.01	**未加糖或其他甜物质及未加味的水，包括天然或人造矿泉水及汽水；冰及雪：**										**Waters, including natural or artificial mineral waters and aerated waters, not containing added sugar or other sweetening matter nor flavoured; ice and snow:**
	-矿泉水及汽水：										-Mineral waters and aerated waters:
2201.1010	---矿泉水	20	12		12	90	17		升/千克	AB	---Mineral waters
2201.1020	---汽水	20	12		12	90	17	13	升/千克	AB	---Aerated waters
	-其他：										-Other:
2201.9010	---天然水	10	8		0	30	17		千升/吨	AB	---Natural waters
2201.9090	---其他	10	8		0	30	17		千升/吨		---Other
22.02	**加味、加糖或其他甜物质的水，包括矿泉水及汽水，其他无酒精饮料，但不包括税目 20.09 的水果汁或蔬菜汁：**										**Waters, including mineral waters and aera-ted waters, containing added sugar or other sweetening matter or flavoured, and other non-alcoholic beverages, not including fruit or vegetable juices of heading No. 20.09:**
2202.1000	-加味、加糖或其他甜物质的水，包括矿泉水及汽水	20	12		16	100	17	13	升/千克		-Waters, including mineral waters and aerated waters, containing added sugar or other sweetening matter or flavoured

税则号列 Tariff Item.	货品名称	最惠国(%) MFN	协定(%)CT 东盟 CA	中巴 CP	中智 CC	普通 Gen	增值税率 VAT	出口退税 ED	计量单位 Unit	监管条件 SC	Article Description
2202.1000 10	含濒危植物成分加味,加糖或其他甜物质水(包括矿泉水及汽水)	20				100	17	13	升/千克	ABEF	Waters, containing added sugar or other sweetening matter or flavoured in imminent dangers
2202.1000 90	其他加味,加糖或其他甜物质的水(包括矿泉水及汽水)	20				100	17	13	升/千克	AB	Other waters, containing added sugar or other sweetening matter or flavoured
2202.9000	-其他	35	T3	29.5	28	100	17	13	升/千克		-Other
2202.9000 11	含濒危植物成分散装无酒精饮料(不包括编号 2009 的水果汁或蔬菜汁)	35				100	17	13	升/千克	ABEF	Non-alcoholic beverages, in bulk (Other than fruit juices and vegetable juices of heading No. 2009)
2202.9000 19	其他散装无酒精饮料(不包括编号 2009 的水果汁或蔬菜汁)	35				100	17	13	升/千克	AB	Other non-alcoholic beverage, facked for retail (Other than fruit juices and vegetable juices of heading No. 2009)
2202.9000 91	含濒危植物成分其他包装无酒精饮料(不包括编号 2009 的水果汁或蔬菜汁)	35				100	17	13	升/千克	ABEF	Non-alcoholic beverases, with other packmg containing compositions of plant in imminent dansers (Other than fruit juices and resetable juices of heading No. 2009)
2202.9000 99	其他包装无酒精饮料(不包括编号 2009 的水果汁或蔬菜汁)	35				100	17	13	升/千克	AB	Non-alcoholic beverages, withother packing (other than fruit juices and vegetable juices of heading No. 2009)
22.03	**麦芽酿造的啤酒:**										**Beer made from malt:**
2203.0000	麦芽酿造的啤酒	T2				T2	17	13	升/千克	AB	Beer made from malt
22.04	**鲜葡萄酿造的酒,包括加酒精的;税目 20.09 以外的酿酒葡萄汁:**										**Wine of fresh grapes, including fortified wines; grape must other than that of heading No. 20.09:**
2204.1000	-汽酒	14	T3		11.2	180	17	13	升/千克	AB	-Sparkling wine
	-其他酒;加酒精抑制发酵的酿酒葡萄汁:										-Other wine; grape must with fermentation prevented or arrested by the addition of alcohol:
2204.2100	--装入 2 升及以下容器的	14	T3		11.2	180	17	13	升/千克	AB	--In containers holding 2 L or less
2204.2900	--其他	20	T3		16	180	17	13	升/千克	AB	--Other
2204.3000	-其他酿酒葡萄汁	30	T3		24	90	17	13	升/千克	A	-Other grape must
22.05	**味美思酒及其他加植物或香料的用鲜葡萄酿造的酒:**										**Vermouth and other wine of fresh grapes flavoured with plants or aromatic substances:**
2205.1000	-装入 2 升及以下容器的	65	T3		52	180	17	13	升/千克	AB	-In containers holding 2 L or less
2205.9000	-其他	65	T3		39	180	17	13	升/千克	AB	-Other
22.06	**其他发酵饮料(例如,苹果酒、梨酒、蜂蜜酒);其他税目未列名的发酵饮料的混合物及发酵饮料与无酒精饮料的混合物:**										**Other fermented beverages (for example, cider, perry, mead); mixtures of fermented beverages and mixtures of fermented beverages and non-alcoholic beverages, not elsewhere specified or included:**
2206.0000	其他发酵饮料(例如,苹果酒、梨酒、蜂蜜酒);其他税目未列名的发酵饮料的混合物及发酵饮料与无酒精饮料的混合物	46.8	T3		28.1	180	17	13	升/千克		Other fermented beverages (for example, cider, perry, mead); mixtures of fermented beverages and mixtures of fermented beverages and non-alcoholic beverages, not elsewhere specified or included
2206.0000 01	黄酒	46.8				180	17	13	升/千克	AB	Shaoxing wine

税则号列 Tariff Item.	货品名称	最惠国(%) MFN	协定(%) CT 东盟 CA	中巴 CP	中智 CC	普通 Gen	增值税率 VAT	出口退税 ED	计量单位 Unit	监管条件 SC	Article Description
2206.0000 09	其他发酵饮料(未列名发酵饮料混合物及发酵饮料与无酒精饮料混合物)	46.8				180	17	13	升/千克	AB	Other fermented beverages, including mixtures of fermented beverages not elsewhere specified or included and mixtures of fermented beverages and non-alcoholic beverages
22.07	**未改性乙醇,按容量计酒精浓度在80%及以上;任何浓度的改性乙醇及其他酒精:**										**Undenatured ethyl alcohol of an alcoholic strength by volume of 80% vol or higher; ethyl alcohol and other spirits, denatured, of any strength:**
2207.1000	-未改性乙醇,按容量计酒精浓度在80%及以上	40	T3	5	0	100	17		升/千克	ABG	-Undenatured ethyl alcohol of an alcoholic strength by volume of 80% vol or higher
2207.2000	-任何浓度的改性乙醇及其他酒精	30	T3	5	24	80	17		升/千克		-Ethyl alcohol and other spirits, denatured, of any strength
2207.2000 10	任何浓度的改性乙醇	30				80	17		升/千克	ABG	Ethyl alcohol, denatured of any strength
2207.2000 90	任何浓度的其他酒精	30				80	17		升/千克	ABG	Other spirits, of any strength
22.08	**未改性乙醇,按容量计酒精浓度在80%以下;蒸馏酒、利口酒及其他酒精饮料:**										**Undenatured ethyl alcohol of an alcoholic strength by volume of less than 80% vol; spirits, liqueurs and other spirituous beverages:**
2208.2000	-蒸馏葡萄酒制得的烈性酒	10			8	180	17	13	升/千克	AB	-Spirits obtained by distilling grape wine or grape marc
2208.3000	-威士忌酒	10			8	180	17	13	升/千克	AB	-Whiskies
2208.4000	-朗姆酒及蒸馏已发酵甘蔗产品制得的其他烈性酒	10			0	180	17	13	升/千克	AB	-Rum and other squirrel dew made by distilling fermenting sugarcane product
2208.5000	-杜松子酒	10			0	180	17	13	升/千克	AB	-Gin and geneva
2208.6000	-伏特加酒	10		8.8	0	180	17	13	升/千克	AB	-Vodka
2208.7000	-利口酒及柯迪尔酒	10		8.8	8	180	17	13	升/千克	AB	-Liqueurs and cordials
	-其他:										-Other:
2208.9010	---龙舌兰酒	10		8.8	0	180	17	13	升/千克	ABFE	---Tequila, Mezcal
2208.9090	---其他	10		8.8	8	180	17	13	升/千克		---Other
2208.9090 01	酒精浓度在80%以下的未改性乙醇	10				180	17	13	升/千克	AB	Undenatured ethyl alcohol of an alcoholic strength by volume of less than 80% vol
2208.9090 21	含濒危野生动植物成分的薯类蒸馏酒	10				180	17	13	升/千克	ABEF	Potato spirits containing endangered wild animals and plants
2208.9090 29	其他薯类蒸馏酒	10				180	17	13	升/千克	AB	Other spirits by distilling potatoes
2208.9090 91	含濒危野生动植物成分的其他蒸馏酒及酒精饮料	10				180	17	13	升/千克	ABEF	Spirits and spirituous beverages endangered wild animals and plants
2208.9090 99	其他蒸馏酒及酒精饮料	10				180	17	13	升/千克	AB	Other spirits and spirituous beverages
22.09	**醋及用醋酸制得的醋代用品:**										**Vinegar and substitutes for vinegar obtained from acetic acid:**
2209.0000	醋及用醋酸制得的醋代用品	20	12		16	70	17	13	升/千克	AB	Vinegar and substitutes for vinegar obtained from acetic acid

第二十三章
食品工业的残渣及废料；配制的动物饲料

注释：

税目23.09包括其他税目未列号的配制动物饲料，这些饲料是由动、植物原料加工而成的，并且已改变了原料的基本特性，但加工过程中的植物废料、植物残渣及副产品除外。

子目注释：

子目2306.41所称“低芥子酸油菜籽”，是指第十二章子目注释一所定义的油菜子。

Chapter 23
Residues and waste from the food industries; prepared animal fodder

Notes:

Heading No. 23.09 includes products of a kind used in animal feeding, not elsewhere specified or included, obtained by processing vegetable or animal materials to such an extent that they have lost the essential characteristics of the original material, other than vegetable waste, vegetable residues and by-products of such processing.

Subheading Note:

For the purposes of subheading No. 2306.41, the expression “low erucic acid rape or colza seeds” means seeds as defined in Subheading Note 1 to Chapter 12.

税则号列 Tariff Item.	货品名称	最惠国(%) MFN	协定(%) CT 东盟 CA	中巴 CP	中智 CC	普通 Gen	增值税率 VAT	出口退税 ED	计量单位 Unit	监管条件 SC	Article Description
23.01	**不适于供人食用的肉、杂碎、鱼、甲壳动物、软体动物或其他水生无脊椎动物的渣粉及团粒；油渣：**										**Flours, meals and pellets, of meat or meat offal, of fish or of crustaceans, molluscs or other aquatic invertebrates, unfit for human consumption; greaves:**
	-肉、杂碎的渣粉及团粒；油渣：										-Flours, meals and pellets, of meat or meat offal; greaves:
	---肉骨粉：										---Flours and meals, of meat bones:
2301.1011	----含牛羊成分的	2			0	11	13	13	千克	AB	----Of bovine and sheep
2301.1019	----其他	2			0	11	13	13	千克	AB	----Other
2301.1020	---油渣	5			0	50	13		千克	AB	---Greaves
2301.1090	---其他	5			0	30	13		千克	AB	---Other
	-鱼、甲壳动物、软体动物或其他水生无脊椎动物的渣粉及团粒：										-Flours, meals and pellets, of fish or of crustaceans, molluscs or other aquatic invertebrates:
2301.2010	---饲料用鱼粉	2		0	1.6	11	13		千克	AB	---Flours and meals of fish, of a kind used in animal feeding
2301.2090	---其他	5		0	4	30	13		千克	AB	---Other
23.02	**谷物或豆类植物在筛、碾或其他加工过程中所产生的糠、麸及其他残渣，不论是否制成团粒：**										**Bran, sharps and other residues, whether or not in the form of pellets, derived from the sifting, milling or other working of cereals or of leguminous plants:**
2302.1000	-玉米的	5			0	30	13		千克	AB	-Of maize (corn)
2302.3000	-小麦的	3			0	30	13		千克	AB	-Of wheat
2302.4000	-其他谷物的	5	T3		0	30	13		千克	AB	-Of other cereals
2302.5000	-豆类植物的	5			0	30	13		千克	AB	-Of leguminous plants
23.03	**制造淀粉过程中的残渣及类似的残渣，甜菜渣、甘蔗渣及制糖过程中的其他残渣，酿造及蒸馏过程中的糟粕及残渣，不论是否制成团粒：**										**Residues of starch manufacture and similar residues, beet-pulp, bagasses and other waste of sugar manufacture, brewing or distilling dregs and waste, whether or not in the form of pellets:**
2303.1000	-制造淀粉过程中的残渣及类似的残渣	5			0	30	13		千克	AB	-Residues of starch manufacture and similar residues

税则号列 Tariff Item.	货品名称	最惠国(%) MFN	协定(%) CT 东盟 CA	中巴 CP	中智 CC	普通 Gen	增值税率 VAT	出口退税 ED	计量单位 Unit	监管条件 SC	Article Description
2303.2000	-甜菜渣、甘蔗渣及制糖过程中的其他残渣	5			0	30	13	11	千克	AB	-Beet-pulp, bagasses and other waste of sugar manufacture
2303.3000	-酿造及蒸馏过程中的糟粕及残渣	5			0	30	13		千克	AB	-Brewing or distilling dregs and waste
23.04	**提炼豆油所得的油渣饼及其他固体残渣,不论是否碾磨或制成团粒:**										**Oil-cake and other solid residues, whether or not ground or in the form of pellets, resulting from the extraction of soyabean oil:**
2304.0010	---油渣饼	5		0	4	30	13	13	千克	AB	---Oil-cake
2304.0090	---其他	5		0	0	30	13	13	千克	AB	---Other
23.05	**提炼花生油所得的油渣饼及其他固体残渣,不论是否碾磨或制成团粒:**										**Oil-cake and other solid residues, whether or not ground or in the form of pellets, resulting from the extraction of groundnut oil:**
2305.0000	提炼花生油所得的油渣饼及其他固体残渣,不论是否碾磨或制成团粒	5			0	30	13		千克	AB	Oil-cake and other solid residues, whether or not ground or in the form of pellets, resulting from the extraction of groundnut oil
23.06	**税目23.04或23.05以外的提炼植物油脂所得的油渣饼及其他固体残渣,不论是否碾磨或制成团粒:**										**Oil-Cake and other solid residues, whether or not ground or in the form of pellets, resulting from the extraction of vegetable fats or oils, other than those of heading No. 23.04 or 23.05:**
2306.1000	-棉子的	5			0	30	13	11	千克	AB	-Of cotton seeds
2306.2000	-亚麻子的	5			0	30	13	11	千克	AB	-Of linseed
2306.3000	-葵花子的	5			0	30	13	11	千克	AB	-Of sunflower seeds
	-油菜子的:										-Of rape or colza seeds:
2306.4100	--低芥子酸的	5			0	30	13	11	千克	AB	--Of low erucic acid rape or colza seeds
2306.4900	--其他	5			0	30	13	11	千克	AB	--Other
2306.5000	-椰子或干椰肉的	5		2.5	0	30	13	11	千克	AB	-Of coconut or copra
2306.6000	-油棕果或油棕仁的	5			0	30	13	11	千克	AB	-Of palm nuts or kernels
2306.9000	-其他	5			0	30	13	11	千克	AB	-Other
23.07	**葡萄酒渣;粗酒石:**										**Wine lees; argol:**
2307.0000	葡萄酒渣;粗酒石	5			0	30	13		千克		Wine lees; argol
23.08	**动物饲料用的其他税目未列名的植物原料、废料、残渣及副产品,不论是否制成团粒:**										**Vegetable materials and vegetable waste, vegetable residues and by-products, whether or not in the form of pellets, of a kind used in animal feeding, not elsewhere specified or included:**
2308.0000	动物饲料用的其他税目未列名的植物原料、废料、残渣及副产品,不论是否制成团粒	5			0	35	13	5	千克	AB	Vegetable materials and vegetable waste, vegetable residues and by-products, whether or not in the form of pellets, of a kind used in animal feeding, not elsewhere specified or included
23.09	**配制的动物饲料:**										**Preparations of a kind used in animal feeding:**

税则号列 Tariff Item.	货　品　名　称	最惠国(%) MFN	协定(%) CT 东盟 CA	中巴 CP	中智 CC	普通 Gen	增值税率 VAT	出口退税 ED	计量单位 Unit	监管条件 SC	Article Description
	-零售包装的狗食或猫食：										-Dog or cat food, put up for retail sale：
2309.1010	---罐头	15	T3		12	90	13	11	千克	AB	---In airtight containers
2309.1090	---其他	15	T3		12	90	13	11	千克	AB	---Other
	-其他：										-Other：
2309.9010	---制成的饲料添加剂	5		2.5	4	14	17	13	千克	AB	---Preparations for use in making the complete feeds or supplementary feeds
2309.9090	---其他	6.5	T3	3.3	5.2	14	13	11	千克	AB	---Other

第二十四章 烟草及烟草代用品的制品

Chapter 24 Tobacco and manufactured tobacco substitutes

注释：

本章不包括药用卷烟（第三十章）。

Note:

This Chapter does not cover medicinal cigarettes (Chapter 30).

税则号列 Tariff Item.	货品名称	最惠国(%) MFN	协定(%) 东盟 CA	协定(%) 中巴 CP	协定(%) CT 中智 CC	普通 Gen	增值税率 VAT	出口退税 ED	计量单位 Unit	监管条件 SC	Article Description
24.01	**烟草；烟草废料：**										**Unmanufactured tobacco; tobacco refuse:**
	-未去梗的烟草：										-Tobacco, not stemmed/stripped:
2401.1010	---烤烟	10		9.4	8	70	17	13	千克	7AB	---Flue-cured
2401.1090	---其他	10			8	70	17	5	千克	7AB	---Other
	-部分或全部去梗的烟草：										-Tobacco, partly or wholly stemmed/stripped:
2401.2010	---烤烟	10			8	70	17	13	千克	7AB	---Flue-cured
2401.2090	---其他	10			8	70	17	13	千克	7AB	---Other
2401.3000	-烟草废料	10			8	70	17	13	千克	AB7	-Tobacco refuse
24.02	**烟草或烟草代用品制成的雪茄烟及卷烟：**										**Cigars, cheroots, cigarillos and cigarettes, of tobacco or of tobacco substitutes:**
2402.1000	-烟草制的雪茄烟	25			20	180	17		千支/千克	7B	-Cigars, cheroots and cigarillos, containing tobacco
2402.2000	-烟草制的卷烟	25			20	180	17		千支/千克	7AB	-Cigarettes containing tobacco
2402.9000	-其他	25			20	180	17		千支/千克		-Other
2402.9000 01	烟草代用品制的卷烟	25				180	17		千支/千克	7	Cigarettes containing tobacco substitutes
2402.9000 09	烟草代用品制的雪茄烟	25				180	17		千支/千克	7	Gigars, cheroots and cigarillos, containing tobacco substitutes
24.03	**其他烟草及烟草代用品的制品；“均化”或“再造”烟草；烟草精汁：**										**Other manufactured tobacco and manufactured tobacco substitutes; “homogenized” or “reconstituted” tobacco; tobacco extracts and essences:**
2403.1000	-供吸用的烟草，不论是否含有任何比例的烟草代用品	57		50	45.6	180	17	13	千克	7AB	-Smoking tobacco, whether or not containing tobacco substitutes in any proportion
	-其他：										-Other:
2403.9100	--“均化”或“再造”烟丝	57			45.6	180	17	13	千克		--“Homogenized” or “reconstituted” tobacco
2403.9100 10	再造烟草	57				180	17	13	千克	AB7	Reconstituted tobacco
2403.9100 90	均化烟草	57				180	17	13	千克	AB7	Homogenized tobacco
2403.9900	--其他	57			45.6	180	17	13	千克		--Other
2403.9900 10	烟草精汁	57				180	17	13	千克	7AB	Tobacco extracts and essences
2403.9900 90	其他烟草及烟草代用品的制品	57				180	17	13	千克	AB	Other manufactured tobacco and manufactured tobacco substitutes

第五类
矿　产　品

第二十五章
盐;硫磺;泥土及石料;
石膏料、石灰及水泥

注释:

一、除条文及注释四另有规定的以外,本章各税目只包括原产状态的矿产品,或只经过洗涤(包括用化学物质清除杂质而未改变产品结构的)、破碎、磨碎、研粉、淘洗、筛分以及用浮选、磁选和其他机械物理方法(不包括结晶法)精选过的货品,但不得经过焙烧、煅烧、混合或超过税目所列的加工范围。

本章产品可含有添加的抗尘剂,但所加剂料并不使原产品改变其一般用途而适用于某些特殊用途。

二、本章不包括:

(一)升华硫磺、沉淀硫磺及胶态硫磺(税目28.02);

(二)土色料,按重量计三氧化二铁含量在70%及以上(税目28.21);

(三)第三十章的药品及其他产品;

(四)芳香料制品及化妆盥洗品(第三十三章);

(五)长方砌石、路缘石、扁平石(税目68.01)、镶嵌石或类似石料(税目68.02)及铺屋顶、饰墙面或防潮用的板岩(税目68.03);

(六)宝石或半宝石(税目71.02或71.03);

(七)每颗重量不低于2.5克的氯化钠或氧化镁培养晶体(光学元件除外)(税目38.24);氯化钠或氧化镁制的光学元件(税目90.01);

(八)台球用粉块(税目95.04);

(九)书写或绘画用粉笔及裁缝划粉(税目96.09)。

三、既可归入税目25.17又可归入本章其他税目的产品,应归入税目25.17。

四、税目25.30主要包括:未膨胀的蛭石、珍珠岩及绿泥石;不论是否煅烧或混合的土色料;天然云母氧化铁;海泡石(不论是否磨光成块);琥珀;模制后未经进一步加工的片、条、杆或类似形状的粘聚海泡石及粘聚琥珀;黑玉;菱锶矿(不论是否煅烧),但不包括氧化锶;破碎陶器;砖或混凝土的碎块。

SECTION V
MINERAL PRODUCTS

Chapter 25
Salt; sulphur; earths and stone; plastering materials, lime and cement

Notes:

1. Except where their context or Note 4 to this Chapter otherwise requires, the headings of this Chapter cover only products which are in the crude state or which have been washed (even with chemical substances eliminating the impurities without changing the structure of the product), crushed, ground, powdered, levigated, sifted, screened, concentrated by flotation, magnetic separation or other mechanical or physical processes (except crystallization), but not products which have been roasted, calcined, obtained by mixing or subjected to processing beyond that mentioned in each heading.

   The products of this Chapter may contain an added antidusting agent, provided that such addition does not render the product particularly suitable for specific use rather than for general use.

2. This Chapter does not cover:

   (a) Sublimed sulphur, precipitated sulphur or colloidal sulphur (heading No. 28.02);

   (b) Earth colours containing 70% or more by weight of combined iron evaluated as Fe_2O_3 (heading No. 28.21);

   (c) Medicaments or other products of Chapter 30;

   (d) Perfumery, cosmetic or toilet preparations (Chapter 33);

   (e) Setts, curbstones or flagstones (heading No. 68.01); mosaic cubes or the like (heading No. 68.02); roofing, facing or damp course slates (heading No. 68.03);

   (f) Precious or semi-precious stones (heading No. 71.02 or 71.03);

   (g) Cultured crystals (other than optical elements) weighing not less than 2.5g each, of sodium chloride or of magnesium oxide, of heading No. 38.24; optical el-ements of sodium chloride or of magnesium oxide (heading No. 90.01);

   (h) Billiard chalks (heading No. 95.04); or

   (i) Writing or drawing chalks or tailors' chalks (heading No. 96.09).

3. Any products classifiable in heading No. 25.17 and any other heading of this Chapter are to be classified in heading No. 25.17.

4. Heading No. 25.30 applies, *inter alia*, to: vermiculite, perlite and chlorites, unexpanded; earth colours, whether or not calcined or mixed together; natural micaceous iron oxides; meerschaum (whether or not in polished pieces); amber; agglomerated meerschaum and agglomerated amber, in plates, rods, sticks or similar forms, not worked after moulding; jet; strontianite (whether or not calcined), other than strontium oxide; broken pieces of pottery, brick or concrete.

税则号列 Tariff Item.	货 品 名 称	最惠国(%) MFN	协定(%)CT 东盟 CA	 中巴 CP	 中智 CC	普通 Gen	增值税率 VAT	出口退税 ED	计量单位 Unit	监管条件 SC	Article Description
25.01	**盐(包括精制盐及变性盐)及纯氯化钠,不论是否为水溶液,也不论是否添加抗结块剂或松散剂;海水:**										**Salt (including table salt and denatured salt) and pure sodium chloride, whether or not in aqueous solution or containing added anticaking or free-flowing agents; sea water:**
	---盐:										---Salt:
2501.0011	----食用盐	0			0	0	17	13	千克	AB	----Edible salt
2501.0019	----其他	0			0	0	17	13	千克	AB	----Other
2501.0020	---纯氯化钠	3		0	1.8	35	17	13	千克	B	---Pure sodium chloride
2501.0030	---海水	0			0	0	17		千克		---Sea water
25.02	**未焙烧的黄铁矿:**										**Unroasted iron pyrites:**
2502.0000	未焙烧的黄铁矿	3		0	0	20	13		千克		Unroasted iron pyrite
25.03	**各种硫磺,但升华硫磺、沉淀硫磺及胶态硫磺除外:**										**Sulphur of all kinds, other than sublimed sulphur, precipitated sulphur and colloidal sulphur:**
2503.0000	各种硫磺,但升华硫磺、沉淀硫磺及胶态硫磺除外	3		0	1.8	17	13	11	千克		Sulphur of all kinds, other than sublimed sulphur, precipitated sulphur and colloidal sulphur
25.04	**天然石墨:**										**Natural graphite:**
	-粉末或粉片:										-In powder or in flakes:
2504.1010	---磷片	3		0	0	30	13		千克	aB	---In flakes
2504.1090	---其他	3		0	0	30	13		千克	aB	---Other
2504.9000	-其他	3		0	0	30	13		千克	aB	-Other
25.05	**各种天然砂,不论是否着色,但第二十六章的含金属矿砂除外:**										**Natural sands of all kinds, whether or not coloured, other than metal-bearing sands of Chapter 26:**
2505.1000	-硅砂及石英砂	3		0	1.8	40	13		千克	B	-Silica sands and quartz sands
2505.9000	-其他	3		0	0	40	13		千克		-Other
25.06	**石英(天然砂除外);石英岩,不论是否粗加修整或仅用锯或其他方法切割成矩形(包括正方形)的板、块:**										**Quartz (other than natural sands); quartzite, whether or not roughly trimmed or merely cut, by sawing or otherwise, into blocks or slabs of a rectangular (including square) shape:**
2506.1000	-石英	3		0	0	40	13		千克	B	-Quartz
2506.2000	-石英岩	3		0	0	40	13		千克		-Quartzite
25.07	**高岭土及类似土,不论是否煅烧:**										**Kaolin and other kaolinic clays, whether or not calcined:**
	高岭土及类似土,不论是否煅烧:										Kaolin and other kaolinic clays, whether or not calcined:
2507.0010	---高岭土	3		0	0	50	13		千克		---Kaolin
2507.0090	---其他	3		0	0	50	13		千克		---Other
25.08	**其他粘土(不包括税目68.06的膨胀粘土)、红柱石、蓝晶石及硅线石,不论是否煅烧;富铝红柱石;火泥及第纳斯土:**										**Other clays (not including expanded clays of heading No. 68.06), andalusite, kyanite and sillimanite, whether or not calcined; mullite; chamotte or dinas earths:**
2508.1000	-膨润土	3		0	0	50	13		千克		-Bentonite
2508.3000	-耐火粘土	3		0	0	20	13		千克	yB4x	-Fire-clay
2508.4000	-其他粘土	3		0	0	50	13		千克		-Other clays

税则号列 Tariff Item.	货品名称	最惠国(%) MFN	协定(%) CT 东盟 CA	中巴 CP	中智 CC	普通 Gen	增值税率 VAT	出口退税 ED	计量单位 Unit	监管条件 SC	Article Description
2508.5000	-红柱石、蓝晶石及硅线石	3		0	0	40	13		千克		-Andalusite, kyanite and sillimanite
2508.6000	-富铝红柱石	3		0	0	40	13		千克		-Mullite
2508.7000	-火泥及第纳斯土	3		0	0	20	13		千克		-Chamotte or dinas earths
2508.7000 10	火泥	3				20	13		千克		Chamotte
2508.7000 90	第纳斯土	3				20	13		千克		Dinas earths
25.09	**白垩：**										**Chalk:**
2509.0000	白垩	3		0	0	45	13		千克		Chalk
25.10	**天然磷酸钙、天然磷酸铝钙及磷酸盐白垩：**										**Natural calcium phosphates, natural aluminium calcium phosphates and phosphatic chalk:**
	-未碾磨：										-Unground:
2510.1010	---磷灰石	3		0	0	11	13		千克	aAB	---Apatite
2510.1090	---其他	3		0	0	20	13		千克	aA	---Other
	-已碾磨：										-Ground:
2510.2010	---磷灰石	3		0	1.8	11	13		千克	aAB	---Apatite
2510.2090	---其他	3		0	1.8	20	13		千克	aA	---Other
25.11	**天然硫酸钡(重晶石)；天然碳酸钡(毒重石)，不论是否煅烧，但税目28.16的氧化钡除外：**										**Natural barium sulphate (barytes); natural barium carbonate (witherite), whether or not calcined, other than barium oxide of heading No. 28.16:**
2511.1000	-天然硫酸钡(重晶石)	3		0	0	45	13		千克	B	-Natural barium sulphate (barytes)
2511.2000	-天然碳酸钡(毒重石)	3		0	0	45	13		千克		-Natural barium carbonate (witherite)
25.12	**硅质化石粗粉(例如各种硅藻土)及类似的硅质土，不论是否煅烧，其表观比重不超过1：**										**Siliceous fossil meals (for example, kieselguhr, tripolite and diatomite) and similar siliceous earths, whether or not calcined, of an apparent specific gravity of 1 or less:**
	硅质化石粗粉(例如各种硅藻土)及类似的硅质土，不论是否煅烧，其表观比重不超过1：										Siliceous fossil meals (for example, kieselguhr, tripolite and diatomite) and similar siliceous earths, whether or not calcined, of an apparent specific gravity of 1 or less:
2512.0010	---硅藻土	3		0	1.8	40	17		千克		---Kieselguhr
2512.0090	---其他	3		0	1.8	40	17		千克		---Other
25.13	**浮石；刚玉岩；天然刚玉砂；天然石榴石及其他天然磨料，不论是否热处理：**										**Pumice stone; emery; natural corundum, natural garnet and other natural abrasives, whether or not heat-treated:**
2513.1000	-浮石：	3		0	0	35	17		千克		-Pumice stone:
2513.2000	-刚玉岩、天然刚玉砂、天然石榴石及其他天然磨料	3		0	0	17	17		千克	B	-Emery, natural corundum, narural garnet and other natural abrasives
25.14	**板岩，不论是否粗加修整或仅用锯或其他方法切割成矩形(包括正方形)的板、块：**										**Slate, whether or not roughly trimmed or merely cut, by sawing or otherwise, into blocks or slabs of a rectangular (including square) shape:**

税则号列 Tariff Item.	货 品 名 称	最惠国(%) MFN	协定(%) CT 东盟 CA	中巴 CP	中智 CC	普通 Gen	增值税率 VAT	出口退税 ED	计量单位 Unit	监管条件 SC	Article Description
2514.0000	板岩,不论是否粗加修整或仅用锯或其他方法切割成矩形(包括正方形)的板、块	3		0	0	50	17		千克		Slate, whether or not roughly trimmed or merely cut, by sawing or otherwise, into blocks or slabs of a rectangular (including square) shape
25.15	**大理石、石灰华及其他石灰质碑用或建筑用石,表观比重为2.5及以上,蜡石,不论是否粗加修整或仅用锯或其他方法切割成矩形(包括正方形)的板、块:**										**Marble, travertine, ecaussine and other calcareous monumental or building stone of an apparent specific gravity of 2.5 or more, and alabaster, whether or not roughly trimmed or merely cut, by sawing or otherwise, into blocks or slabs of a rectangular (including square) shape:**
	-大理石及石灰华:										-Marble and travertine:
2515.1100	--原状或粗加修整	4			0	80	17	11	千克	A	--Crude or roughly trimmed Marble crude or roughly trimmed
2515.1200	--仅用锯或其他方法切割成矩形,包括正方形	4			0	80	17		千克	A	--Merely cut, by sawing or otherwise, into blocks or slabs of a rectangular (including square) shape
2515.2000	-其他石灰质碑用或建筑用石;蜡石	3			0	50	17		千克	A	-Ecaussine and other calcareous monumental or building stone; alabaster
25.16	**花岗石、斑岩、玄武岩、砂岩以及其他碑用或建筑用石,不论是否粗加修整或仅用锯或其他方法切割成矩形(包括正方形)的板、块:**										**Granite, porphyry, basalt, sandstone and other monumental or building stone, whether or not roughly trimmed or merely cut, by sawing or otherwise, into blocks or slabs of a rectangular (including square) shape:**
	-花岗岩:										-Granite:
2516.1100	--原状或粗加修整	4		2	0	50	17		千克	A	--Crude or roughly trimmed
2516.1200	--仅用锯或其他方法切割成矩形,包括正方形	4		2	0	50	17		千克	A	--Merely cut, by sawing or otherwise, into blocks or slabs of a rectangular (including square) shape
2516.2000	-砂岩	3		2.1	0	50	17		千克	A	-Sandstone
2516.2000 01	原状或粗加修整砂岩	3				50	17		千克	A	Crude or roughly trimmed
2516.2000 90	矩形(包括正方形)砂岩(用锯或其他方法切割成矩形的板块)	3				50	17		千克	A	Rectangular (including square) sandstone (cut, by sawing or otherwise, into blocks or slabs of a rectangular)
2516.9000	-其他碑用或建筑用石	3			0	50	17		千克	A	-Other monumental or building stone
25.17	**通常作混凝土粒料、铺路、铁道路基或其他路基用的卵石、砾石及碎石,圆石子及燧石,不论是否热处理;矿渣、浮渣及类似的工业残渣,不论是否混有本税目第一部分所列的材料;沥青碎石;税目25.15、25.16所列各种石料的碎粒、碎屑及粉末,不论是否热处理:**										**Pebbles, gravel, broken or crushed stone, of a kind commonly used for concrete aggregates, for road metalling or for railway or other ballast, shingle and flint, whether or not heat-treated; macadam of slag, dross or similar industrial waste, whether or not incorporating the materials cited in the first part of the heading; tarred macadam; granules, chippings and powder, of stones of heading No. 25.15 or 25.16, whether or not heat-treated:**

税则号列 Tariff Item.	货品名称	最惠国(%) MFN	协定(%) CT 东盟 CA	中巴 CP	中智 CC	普通 Gen	增值税率 VAT	出口退税 ED	计量单位 Unit	监管条件 SC	Article Description
2517.1000	-通常作混凝土粒料、铺路、铁道路基或其他路基用的卵石、砾石及碎石,圆石子及燧石,不论是否热处理	4			0	50	17		千克		-Pebbles, gravel, broken or crushed stone, of a kind commonly used for concrete aggregates, for road metalling or for railway or other ballast, shingle and flint, whether or not head-treated
2517.2000	-矿渣、浮渣及类似的工业残渣,不论是否混有子目2517.10所列的材料	3			0	50	17		千克	9	-Macadam of slag, dross or similar industrial waste, whether or not incorporating the materials cited in subheading No. 2517.10
2517.3000	-沥青碎石	3			0	50	17		千克	9	-Tarred macadam
	-税目25.15及25.16所列各种石料的碎粒、碎屑及粉末,不论是否热处理:										-Granules, chippings and powder, of stones of heading No. 25.15 or 25.16, whether or not heat-treated:
2517.4100	--大理石的	3			0	50	17		千克		--Of marble
2517.4900	--其他	3			0	50	17		千克		--Other
25.18	**白云石,不论是否煅烧或烧结、粗加修整或仅用锯或其他方法切割成矩形(包括正方形)的板、块;夯混白云石:**										**Dolomite, whether or not calcined or sintered, including dolomite roughly trimmed or merely cut, by sawing or otherwise, into blocks or slabs of a rectangular (including square) shape; dolomite ramming mix:**
2518.1000	-未煅烧或烧结的白云石	3		0	0	40	17		千克		-Dolomite, not calcined or sintered
2518.2000	-已煅烧或烧结的白云石	3		0	0	40	17		千克		-Calcined or sintered dolomite
2518.3000	-夯混白云石	3		0	0	40	17		千克		-Dolomite ramming mix
25.19	**天然碳酸镁(菱镁矿);熔凝镁氧矿;烧结镁氧矿,不论烧结前是否加入少量其他氧化物;其他氧化镁,不论是否纯净:**										**Natural magnesium carbonate (magnesite); fused magnesia; dead-burned (sintered) magnesia, whether or not containing small quantities of other oxides added before sintering; other magnesium oxide, whether or not pure:**
2519.1000	-天然碳酸镁(菱镁矿)	3		0	0	40	17		千克	y4x	-Natural magnesium carbonate (magnesite)
	-其他:										-Other:
2519.9010	---熔凝镁氧矿	3		0	0	40	17		千克	y4x	---Fused magnesia
2519.9020	---烧结镁氧矿(重烧镁)	3		0	0	40	17		千克	y4x	---Dead-burned (sintered) magnesia
2519.9030	---碱烧镁(轻烧镁)	3		0	0	40	17		千克	y4x	---Light-burned magnesia
	---其他:										---Other:
2519.9091	----化学纯氧化镁	3		0	0	35	17		千克	B	----Magnesium oxide, chemically pure
2519.9099	----其他	3		0	0	40	17		千克		----Other
2519.9099 10	其他氧化镁含量在70%以上的矿产品	3				40	17		千克	4xy	Other mineral products containing ≥ 70% by weight of magnesium oxide
2519.9099 90	其他氧化镁	3				40	17	5	千克		Other magnesium oxide
25.20	**生石膏;硬石膏;熟石膏(由煅烧的生石膏或硫酸钙构成),不论是否着色,也不论是否带有少量促凝剂或缓凝剂:**										**Gypsum; anhydrite; plasters (consisting of calcined gypsum or calcium sulphate) whether or not coloured, with or without small quantities of accelerators or retarders:**
2520.1000	-生石膏;硬石膏	5		0	0	80	17	13	千克		-Gypsum; anhydrite

税则号列 Tariff Item.	货 品 名 称	最惠国(%) MFN	协定(%)CT 东盟 CA	 中巴 CP	 中智 CC	普通 Gen	增值税率 VAT	出口退税 ED	计量单位 Unit	监管条件 SC	Article Description
	-熟石膏:										-Plasters:
2520.2010	---牙科用	5		0	4	40	17		千克		---For dental use
2520.2090	---其他	5		0	4	80	17		千克		---Other
25.21	**石灰石助熔剂;通常用于制造石灰或水泥的石灰石及其他钙质石:**										**Limestone flux; limestone and other calcareous stone, of a kind used for the manufacture of lime or cement:**
2521.0000	石灰石助熔剂;通常用于制造石灰或水泥的石灰石及其他钙质石	5		0	0	50	17		千克		Limestone flux; limestone and other calcareous stone, of a kind used for the manufacture of lime or cement
25.22	**生石灰、熟石灰及水硬石灰,但税目28.25的氧化钙及氢氧化钙除外:**										**Quicklime, slaked lime and hydraulic lime, other than calcium oxide and hydroxide of heading No. 28.25:**
2522.1000	-生石灰	5		0	4	80	17		千克		-Quicklime
2522.2000	-熟石灰	5		0	0	80	17		千克		-Slaked lime
2522.3000	-水硬石灰	5		0	0	80	17		千克		-Hydraulic lime
25.23	**硅酸盐水泥、矾土水泥、矿渣水泥、富硫酸盐水泥及类似的水凝水泥,不论是否着色,包括水泥熟料:**										**Portland cement, aluminous cement, slag cement, supersulphate cement and similar hydraulic cements, whether or not coloured or in the form of clinkers:**
2523.1000	-水泥熟料	8	T3		0	30	17	11	千克	A	-Cement clinkers
	-硅酸盐水泥:										-Portland cement:
2523.2100	--白水泥,不论是否人工着色	6	T3	4.5	0	30	17	11	千克	B	--White cement, whether or not artificially coloured
2523.2900	--其他	8	T3	6	0	30	17	11	千克	AB	--Other
2523.3000	-矾土水泥	6	T3		0	30	17	11	千克	B	-Aluminous cement
2523.9000	-其他水凝水泥	8	T3		0	30	17	11	千克	AB	-Other hydraulic cements
25.24	**石棉:**										**Asbestos:**
2524.1000	-青石棉:	5		0	0	30	13	11	千克	89	-Blue asbestcs
	-其他:										-Other:
2524.9010	---长纤维的	5		0	0	30	17	11	千克		---Of long fibre
2524.9010 10	长纤维阳起石石棉(包括长纤维铁石棉、透闪石石棉及直闪石石棉)	5				30	13	11	千克	89	Actinolite asbestas of long fibre (including Amosite asbestos、Tremolite asbestos or Anthopylite asbestos)
2524.9010 90	其他长纤维石棉	5				30	13	11	千克		Other asbestos of long fibre
2524.9090	---其他的	5		0	0	35	17	11	千克		---Others
2524.9090 10	其他阳起石石棉(包括其他铁石棉、透闪石石棉及直闪石石棉)	5				35	13	11	千克	89	Other actinolite asbestas (including other Amosa asbestos、Tremolite asbestos or Anthopylite asbestos)
2524.9090 90	其他石棉	5				35	13	11	千克		Other asbestos
25.25	**云母,包括云母片;云母废料:**										**Mica, including splittings; mica waste:**
2525.1000	-原状云母及劈开的云母片	5		0	0	30	13		千克		-Crude mica and mica rifted into sheets or splittings
2525.2000	-云母粉	5		0	0	30	13		千克		-Mica powder
2525.3000	-云母废料	5		0	0	30	13		千克		-Mica waste

税则号列 Tariff Item.	货品名称	最惠国(%) MFN	协定(%)CT			普通 Gen	增值税率 VAT	出口退税 ED	计量单位 Unit	监管条件 SC	Article Description
			东盟 CA	中巴 CP	中智 CC						
25.26	**天然冻石,不论是否粗加修整或仅用锯或其他方法切割成矩形(包括正方形)的板、块;滑石:**										**Natural steatite, whether or not roughly trimmed or merely cut, by sawing or otherwise, into blocks or slabs of a rectangular (including square) shape; talc:**
	-未破碎及未研粉:										-Not crushed, not powdered:
2526.1010	---冻石	3			0	50	13		千克		---Natural steatite
2526.1020	---滑石	3			0	50	13		千克	y4xB	---Talc
	-已破碎或已研粉:										-Crushed or powdered:
2526.2010	---冻石	3			0	50	17		千克		---Natural steatite
2526.2020	---滑石	3			0	50	17		千克	y4xB	---Talc
25.28	**天然硼酸盐及其精矿(不论是否煅烧),但不包括从天然盐水析离的硼酸盐;天然粗硼酸,含硼酸干重不超过85%:**										**Natural borates and concentrates thereof (whether or not calcined), but not including borates separated from natural brine; natural boric acid containing not more than 85% of H_3BO_3 calulated on the dry weight:**
2528.1000	-天然硼砂及其精矿(不论是否煅烧)	3		0	0	30	13		千克		-Natural sodium borates and concentrates thereof (whether or not calcined)
2528.9000	-其他	5		0	4	30	13		千克		-Other
25.29	**长石;白榴石;霞石及霞石正长岩;萤石(氟石):**										**Felspar; leucite; nepheline and nepheline syenite; fluorspar:**
2529.1000	-长石	3		0	0	50	13		千克		-Felspar
	-萤石:										-Fluorspar:
2529.2100	--按重量计氟化钙含量在97%及以下	3		0	0	50	13		千克	y4xB	--Containing by weight 97% or less of calcium fluoride
2529.2200	--按重量计氟化钙含量在97%以上	3		0	0	50	13		千克	y4xB	--Containing by weight more than 97% of calcium fluoride
2529.3000	-白榴石;霞石及霞石正长岩	5		0	0	50	13		千克		-Leucite; nepheline and nepheline syenite
25.30	**其他税目未列名的矿产品:**										**Mineral substances not elsewhere specified or included:**
	-未膨胀的蛭石、珍珠岩及绿泥石:										-Vermiculite, perlite and chlorites, unexpanded:
2530.1010	---绿泥石	5		0	0	30	13		千克		---Chlorites
2530.1020	---未膨胀的蛭石及珍珠岩	5		0	0	30	13		千克		---Vermiculite, perlite unexpanded
2530.2000	-硫镁矾矿及泻盐矿(天然硫酸镁)	3		0	0	30	13		千克		-Kieserite, epsomite (natural magnesium sulphates)
	-其他:										-Other:
2530.9010	---矿物性药材	3		0	0	30	13		千克		---Mineral medicinal substances
2530.9020	---稀土金属矿	0			0	0	13		千克	4xy	---Ores of rare earth metals
	---其他:										---Other:
2530.9091	----硅灰石	3		0	0	50	13		千克		----Wollastonite
2530.9099	----其他	3		0	0	50	13		千克		----Other
2530.9099 01	天青石	3				50	13		千克		Celestite
2530.9099 10	废镁砖	3				50	13		千克	y4x	Bricks of magnesia waste
2530.9099 20	叶腊石	3				50	13		千克		Pyrophyllite
2530.9099 90	其他矿产品	3				50	13		千克		Other mineral substances

第二十六章
矿砂、矿渣及矿灰

注释：

一、本章不包括：

（一）供铺路用的矿渣及类似的工业废渣（税目25.17）；

（二）天然碳酸镁（菱镁矿），不论是否煅烧（税目25.19）；

（三）储油罐的淤渣，主要成分为税号27.10项下的油品；

（四）第三十一章的碱性熔渣；

（五）矿物棉（税目68.06）；

（六）贵金属或包贵金属的废碎料；主要用于回收贵金属的含贵金属或贵金属化合物的其他废碎料（税目71.12）；

（七）通过熔炼所产生的铜锍、镍锍或钴锍（第十五类）。

二、税目26.01至26.17所称"矿砂"，是指冶金工业中提炼汞，税目28.44的金属以及第十四类、第十五类金属的矿物，即使这些矿物不用于冶金工业，也包括在内。但税目26.01至26.17不包括不是以冶金工业正常加工方法处理的各种矿物。

三、税目26.20只适用于：

（一）在工业上提炼金属或作为生产金属化合物基本原料的矿渣、矿灰及残渣，但焚化城市垃圾所产生的灰、渣除外（税目26.21）；

（二）含有砷的矿渣矿灰及残渣，不论其是否含有金属，用于提取或生产砷或金属及其化合物。

子目注释：

一、子目2620.21所称"含铅汽油的淤渣及含铅抗震化合物的淤渣"，是指取自含铅汽油及含铅抗震化合物（例如，四乙铅）储罐的淤渣，主要含有铅、铅化合物以及铁的氧化物。

二、含有砷、汞、铊及其混合物的矿渣矿灰及残渣，用于提取或生产砷、汞、铊及其化合物，归入子目2620.60。

Chapter 26
Ores, slag and ash

Notes:

1. This Chapter does not cover:

(a) Slag or similar industrial waste prepared as macadam (heading No. 25.17);

(b) Natural magnesium carbonate (magnesite), whether or not calcined (heading No. 25.19);

(c) Sludges from the storage tanks of petroleum oils, consisting mainly of such oils (heading No. 27.10);

(d) Basic slag of Chapter 31;

(e) Slag wool, rock wool or similar mineral wools (heading No. 68.06);

(f) Waste or scrap of precious metal or of metal clad with precious metal; other waste or scrap containing precious metal or precious metal compounds, of a kind used principally for the recovery of precious metal (heading No. 71.12); or

(g) Copper, nickel or cobalt mattes produced by any process of smelting (Section XV).

2. For the purposes of headings NOS 26.01 to 26.17, the term "ores" means minerals of mineralogical species actually used in the metallurgical industry for the extraction of mercury, of the metals of heading No. 28.44 or of the metals of Section XIV or XV, even if they are intended for non-metallurgical purposes. Headings Nos. 26.01 to 26.17 do not, however, include minerals which have been submitted to processes not normal to the metallurgical industry.

3. Heading No. 26.20 applies only to:

(a) Scoria ash and residues of a kind used in industry either for the extraction of metals or as a basis for the manufacture of chemical compounds of metals, excluding ash and residues from the incineration of municipal waste (heading No. 26.21); and

(b) Scoria ash and residues containing arsenic, whether or not containing metals, of a kind used either for the extraction of arsenic or matals or for the manufacture of their chemical compounds.

Subheading Notes:

1. For the purposes of subheading No. 2620.21, "leaded gasoline sludges and leaded anti-knock compound sludges" mean slud-ges obtained from storage tanks of leaded gasoline and leaded anti-knock compounds (for example, tetraethyl lead), and consisting essentially of lead, lead compounds and iron oxide.

2. Scoria ash and residues containing arsenic, mercury, thallium or their mixtures, of a kind used for the extraction of arsenic or those metals classified in subheading No. 2620.60.

税则号列 Tariff Item.	货品名称	最惠国(%) MFN	协定(%) 东盟 CA	协定(%) 中巴 CP	CT 中智 CC	普通 Gen	增值税率 VAT	出口退税 ED	计量单位 Unit	监管条件 SC	Article Description
26.01	铁矿砂及其精矿，包括焙烧黄铁矿：										**Iron ores and concentrates, including roasted iron pyrites:**
	-铁矿砂及其精矿，但焙烧黄铁矿除外：										-Iron ores and concentrates, other than roasted iron pyrites:

税则号列 Tariff Item.	货品名称	最惠国(%) MFN	协定(%) CT 东盟 CA	中巴 CP	中智 CC	普通 Gen	增值税率 VAT	出口退税 ED	计量单位 Unit	监管条件 SC	Article Description
	--未烧结:										--Non-agglomerated
2601.1110	---平均粒度小于0.8毫米的	0				0	13		千克	7A	---Of a granularity less than 0.8mm
2601.1120	---平均粒度不小于0.8毫米,但不大于6.3毫米的	0				0	13		千克	7A	---Of a granularity of 0.8 mm or more, but not exceeding 6.3 mm
2601.1190	---其他	0				0	13		千克	7A	---Other
2601.1200	--已烧结	0				0	13		千克	7A	--Agglomerated
2601.2000	-焙烧黄铁矿	0				0	13		千克	7A	-Roasted iron pyrites
26.02	**锰矿砂及其精矿,包括以干重计含锰量在20%及以上的锰铁矿及其精矿:**										**Manganese ores and concentrates, including ferruginous manganese ores and concentrates with a manganese content of 20% or more, calculated on the dry weight:**
2602.0000	锰矿砂及其精矿,包括以干重计含锰量在20%及以上的锰铁矿及其精矿	0				0	13		千克	AB	Manganese ores and concentrates, including ferruginous manganese ores and concentrates with a manganese content of 20% or more, calculated on the dry weight
26.03	**铜矿砂及其精矿:**										**Copper ores and concentrates:**
2603.0000	铜矿砂及其精矿	0				0			千克		Copper ores and concentrates
2603.0000 10	铜矿砂及其精矿(黄金价值部分)	0				0	0		千克	7A	Copper ores and concentrates (part of gold value)
2603.0000 90	铜矿砂及其精矿(非黄金价值部分)	0				0	13		千克	7A	Copper ores and concentrates (part of non-gold value)
26.04	**镍矿砂及其精矿:**										**Nickel ores and concentrates:**
2604.0000	镍矿砂及其精矿	0				0	13		千克		Nickel ores and concentrates
26.05	**钴矿砂及其精矿:**										**Cobalt ores and concentrates:**
2605.0000	钴矿砂及其精矿	0				0	13		千克		Cobalt ores and concentrates
26.06	**铝矿砂及其精矿:**										**Aluminium ores and concentrate:**
2606.0000	铝矿砂及其精矿	0				0	13		千克	47Bxy	Aluminium ores and concentrate
26.07	**铅矿砂及其精矿:**										**Lead ores and concentrates:**
2607.0000	铅矿砂及其精矿	0				0	13		千克	A	Lead ores and concentrates
26.08	**锌矿砂及其精矿:**										**Zinc ores and concentrates:**
2608.0000	锌矿砂及其精矿	0				0	13		千克		Zinc ores and concentrates
2608.0000 01	灰色饲料氧化锌(氧化锌ZnO含量大于80%)	0				0	13		千克	A4xy	Grey feed grade zinc oxide, containing > 80% by weight of ZnO
2608.0000 90	其他锌矿砂及其精矿	0				0	13		千克	A4xy	Other zinc ores and concentrates
26.09	**锡矿砂及其精矿:**										**Tin ores and concentrates:**
2609.0000	锡矿砂及其精矿	0				0	13		千克	B4xy	Tin ores and concentrates
26.10	**铬矿砂及其精矿:**										**Chromium ores and concentrates:**
2610.0000	铬矿砂及其精矿	0				0	13		千克	A	Chromium ores and concentrates
26.11	**钨矿砂及其精矿:**										**Tungsten ores and concentrates:**
2611.0000	钨矿砂及其精矿	0				0	13		千克	4xBy	Tungsten ores and concentrates
26.12	**铀或钍矿砂及其精矿:**										**Uranium or thorium ores and concentrates:**
2612.1000	-铀矿砂及其精矿	0				0	13		千克		-Uranium ores and concentrates
2612.2000	-钍矿砂及其精矿	0				0	13		千克	4xy	-Thorium ores and concentrates
26.13	**钼矿砂及其精矿:**										**Molybdenum ores and concentrates:**
2613.1000	-已焙烧	0				0	13		千克	4Baxy	-Roasted
2613.9000	-其他	0				0	13		千克	4Baxy	-Other
26.14	**钛矿砂及其精矿:**										**Titanium ores and concentrates:**

税则号列 Tariff Item.	货 品 名 称	最惠国(%) MFN	协定(%)CT 东盟 CA	中巴 CP	中智 CC	普通 Gen	增值税率 VAT	出口退税 ED	计量单位 Unit	监管条件 SC	Article Description
2614.0000	钛矿砂及其精矿	0				0	13		千克		Titanium ores and concentrates
26.15	**铌、钽、钒或锆矿砂及其精矿：**										**Niobium, tantalum, vanadium or zirconium ores and concentrates:**
2615.1000	-锆矿砂及其精矿	0				0	13		千克		-Zirconium ores and concentrates
	-其他：										-Other:
2615.9010	---水合钽铌原料(钽铌矿富集物)	0				0	13		千克		---(Hydrated Tantalum-/Niobium materials or enriched materials from Tantalum/Niobium ore)
2615.9090	---其他	0				0	13		千克		---Other
2615.9090 10	铌,钽精矿及其矿砂	0				0	13		千克		Tantalum and niobium concentrates
2615.9090 90	钒矿砂;钒精矿	0				0	13		千克		Vanadium ores and concentrates
26.16	**贵金属矿砂及其精矿：**										**Precious metal ores and concentrates:**
2616.1000	-银矿砂及其精矿	0				0	13		千克		-Silver ores and concentrates
2616.9000	-其他	0				0			千克		-Other
2616.9000 01	黄金矿砂	0				0	0		千克		Gold ores and concentrates
2616.9000 09	其他贵金属矿砂及其精矿	0				0	13		千克		Other precious metal ores and concentrates
26.17	**其他矿砂及其精矿：**										**Other ores and concentrates:**
	-锑矿砂及其精矿：										-Antimony ores and concentrates:
2617.1010	---生锑(锑精矿,选矿产品)	0				0	17		千克	4xy	---Crude antimony (Antimony concentrates which are mineral products)
2617.1090	---其他	0				0	13		千克	4xBy	---Other
	-其他：										-Other:
2617.9010	---朱砂(辰砂)	3			0	14	13		千克	X	---Cinnabar
2617.9090	---其他	0				0	13		千克		---Other
26.18	**冶炼钢铁所产生的粒状熔渣(熔渣砂)：**										**Granulated slag (slag sand) from the manufacture of iron or steel:**
2618.0010	---主要含锰	4			3.2	35	17		千克	A	---Containing mainly manganese
2618.0090	---其他	4			3.2	35	17		千克	A	---Other
26.19	**冶炼钢铁所产生的熔渣、浮渣(粒状熔渣除外)、氧化皮及其他废料：**										**Slag, dross (other than granulated slag), scalings and other waste from the manufacture of iron or steel:**
2619.0000	冶炼钢铁所产生的熔渣、浮渣(粒状熔渣除外)、氧化皮及其他废料	4			3.2	35	17		千克	AP	Slag, dross (other than granulated slag), scalings and other waste from the manufacture of iron or steel
26.20	**含有金属、砷及其化合物的矿渣、矿灰及残渣(冶炼钢铁所产生的灰、渣除外)：**										**Ash and residues (other than from the manufacture of iron or steel), containing arsenic, metals or their compounds:**
	-主要含锌：										-Containing mainly zinc:
2620.1100	--含硬锌	4			3.2	35	17		千克		--Hard zinc spelter
2620.1900	--其他	4			3.2	35	17		千克		--Other
	-主要含铅：										-Containing mainly lead:
2620.2100	--含铅汽油的淤渣及含铅抗震化合物的淤渣	4			0	35	17		千克	9	--Leaded gasoline sludges and leaded anti-knock compound sludges
2620.2900	--其他	4			0	35	17		千克	9	--Other
2620.3000	-主要含铜	4			3.2	35	17		千克	9	-Containing mainly copper
2620.4000	-主要含铝	4			0	35	17		千克		-Containing mainly aluminium

税则号列 Tariff Item.	货品名称	最惠国(%) MFN	协定(%) CT 东盟 CA	中巴 CP	中智 CC	普通 Gen	增值税率 VAT	出口退税 ED	计量单位 Unit	监管条件 SC	Article Description
2620.6000	-含砷、汞、铊及其混合物,用于提取或生产砷、汞、铊及其化合物	4			0	35	17		千克	9	-Containing arsenic, mercury, thallium or their mixtures, of a kind used for the extraction of arsenic or those metals or for the manufacture of their chemical compounds
	-其他:										-Other:
2620.9100	--含锑、铍、镉、铬及其混合物	4			0	35	17		千克	9	--Containing antimony, beryllium, cadmium, chromium or their mixtures
	--其他:										--Other:
2620.9910	---主要含钨	4			3.2	35	17		千克	y4x9	---Containing mainly tungsten
2620.9990	---其他	4			3.2	35	17		千克		---Other
2620.9990 10	含五氧化二钒>10%的矿渣、矿灰及残渣(冶炼钢铁所产生的除外)	4				35	17		千克	P	Ash and residues, containing V_2O_5 > 10% (other than from the manufacture of iron or steel)
2620.9990 90	含其他金属及其化合物的矿渣、矿灰及残渣(冶炼钢铁所产生灰渣的除外)	4				35	17		千克	9	Ash and residues, containing other metals or their compounds (other than from the manufacture of iron or steel)
26.21	**其他矿渣及矿灰,包括海藻灰(海草灰);焚化城市垃圾所产生的灰、渣:**										**Other slag and ash, including seaweed ash (kelp); ash and residues from the incineration of municipal waste:**
2621.1000	-焚化城市垃圾所产生的灰、渣	4			0	35	17		千克	9	-Ash and residues from the incineration of municipal waste
2621.9000	-其他	4			3.2	35	17		千克		-Other

第二十七章
矿物燃料、矿物油及其蒸馏产品;沥青物质;矿物蜡

注释:

一、本章不包括:

(一)单独的已有化学定义的有机化合物,但纯甲烷及纯丙烷应归入税目27.11;

(二)税目30.03及30.04的药品;

(三)税目33.01、33.02及38.05的不饱和烃混合物。

二、税目27.10所称"石油及从沥青矿物提取的油类",不仅包括石油、从沥青矿物提取的油及类似油,还包括那些用任何方法提取的主要含有不饱和烃混合物的油,但其非芳族成分的重量必须超过芳族成分。然而,它不包括温度在300℃时,压力转为1013毫巴后减压蒸馏出的液体合成聚烯烃以体积计小于60%的货品(第三十九章)。

三、税目27.10所称"废油",是指主要含石油及从沥青矿物提取的油类(参见本章注释二)的废油,不论其是否与水混合。它们包括:

(一)不再适于作为原产品使用的废油(例如,用过的润滑油、液压油及变压器油);

(二)石油储罐的淤渣油,主要含石油及高浓度的在生产原产品时使用的添加剂(例如,化学品);

(三)水乳浊液状或与水混合的废油,例如,浮油、清洗油罐所得的油或机械加工中已用过的切削油。

子目注释:

一、子目2701.11所称"无烟煤",是指含挥发物(以干燥、无矿物质计)不超过14%的煤。

二、子目2701.12所称"烟煤",是指含挥发物(以干燥、无矿物质计)超过14%,并且热值(以潮湿、无矿物质计)等于或大于5833大卡/公斤的煤。

三、子目2707.10、2707.20、2707.30及2707.40所称"粗苯"、"粗甲苯"、"粗二甲苯"、"萘",是分别指按重量计苯、甲苯、二甲苯、萘的含量在50%以上的产品。

Chapter 27
Mineral fuels, mineral oils and products of their distillation; bituminous substances; mineral waxes

Notes:

1. This Chapter does not cover:

(a) Separate chemically defined organic compounds, other than pure methane and propane which are to be classified in heading No. 27.11;

(b) Medicaments of heading No. 30.03 or 30.04; or

(c) Mixed unsaturated hydrocarbons of heading No. 33.01, 33.02 or 38.05

2. References in heading No. 27.10 to "petroleum oils and oils obtained from bituminous minerals" include not only petroleum oils and oils obtained from bituminous minerals but also similar oils, as well as those consisting mainly of mixed unsaturated hydrocarbons, obtained by any process, provided that the weight of the non-aromatic constituents exceeds that of the aromatic constituents. However, the references do not include liquid synthetic polyolefins of which less than 60% by volume distils at 300℃, after conversion to 1,013 millibars when a reduced-pressure distillation method is used (Chapter 39).

3. For the purposes of heading No. 27.10, "waste oils" means waste containing mainly petroleum oils and oils obtained from bituminous minerals (as described in Note 2 to this Chapter), whether or not mixed with water. These include:

(a) Such oils no longer fit for use as primary products (for example, used lubricating oils, used hydraulic oils and used transformer oils);

(b) Sludge oils from the storage tanks of petroleum oils, mainly containing such oils and a high concentration of additives (for example, chemicals) used in the manufacture of the primary products; and

(c) Such oils in the form of emulsions in water or mixtures with water, such as those resulting from oil spills, storage tank washings, or from the use of cutting oils for machining operations.

Subheading Notes:

1. For the purposes of subheading No. 2701.11, "anthracite" means coal having a volatile matter limit (on a dry, mineral-matter-free basis) not exceeding 14%.

2. For the purposes of subheading No. 2701.12, "bituminous coal" means coal having a volatile matter limit (on a dry, mineral-matter-free basis) exceeding 14% and a calorific value limit (on a moist, mineral-matter-free basis) equal to or greater than 5,833kcal/kg.

3. For the purposes of subheadings Nos. 2707.10, 2707.20, 2707.30 and 2707.40, the terms "benzole", "toluole", "xylole", "naphthalene" apply to products which contain more than 50% by weight of benzene, toluene, xylene, naphthalene, respectively.

四、子目2710.11所称“轻油及其制品”，是指210℃（美国材料试验学会D86法）。以下馏出物体积比不小于90%（包括损失部分）。

4. For the purposes of subheading No. 2710.11, “light oils and preparations” are those of which 90% or more by volume (including losses) distil at 210℃ (ASTM D 86 method).

税则号列 Tariff Item.	货品名称	最惠国(%) MFN	协定(%) CT 东盟 CA	中巴 CP	中智 CC	普通 Gen	增值税率 VAT	出口退税 ED	计量单位 Unit	监管条件 SC	Article Description
27.01	**煤;煤砖、煤球及用煤制成的类似固体燃料:**										**Coal; briquettes, ovoids and similar solid fuels manufactured from coal:**
	-煤,不论是否粉化,但未制成型:										-Coal, whether or not pulverized, but not agglomerated:
2701.1100	--无烟煤	3	T3		0	20	13		千克		--Anthracite
2701.1100 10	无烟煤(不论是否粉化,但未制成型)	3				20	13		千克	47ABxy	Anthracite, whether or not pulverized, but not agglomerated
2701.1100 90	无烟煤滤料	3				20	13		千克	7AB	Anthracite filter medium
	--烟煤:										--Bituminous coal:
2701.1210	---炼焦煤	3			0	20	13		千克	47ABxy	---Coking coal
2701.1290	---其他	6	5		0	20	13		千克	47ABxy	---Other
2701.1900	--其他煤	5		3.5	0	20	13		千克	47ABxy	--Other coal
2701.2000	-煤砖、煤球及用煤制成的类似固体燃料	5			0	50	17		千克		-Briquettes, ovoids and similar solid fuels manufactured from coal
27.02	**褐煤,不论是否制成型,但不包括黑玉:**										**Lignite, whether or not agglomerated, excluding jet:**
2702.1000	-褐煤,不论是否粉化,但未制成型	3			0	20	13		千克	4xy	-Lignite, whether or not pulverized, but not agglomerated
2702.2000	-制成型的褐煤	3			0	20	17		千克		-Agglomerated lignite
27.03	**泥煤(包括肥料用泥煤),不论是否制成型:**										**Peat (including peat litter), whether or not agglomerated:**
2703.0000	泥煤(包括肥料用泥煤),不论是否制成型	5			0	20	13		千克	AB	Peat (including peat litter), whether or not agglomerated
27.04	**煤、褐煤或泥煤制成的焦炭及半焦炭,不论是否制成型;甑炭:**										**Coke and semi-coke of coal, of lignite or of peat, whether or not agglomerated; retort carbon:**
2704.0010	---焦炭及半焦炭	5	T3	2.5	4	11	17		千克	4xBy	---Coke and semi-coke
2704.0090	---其他	5		2.5	4	11	17		千克		---Other
27.05	**煤气、水煤气、炉煤气及类似气体,但石油气及其他烃类气除外:**										**Coal gas, water gas, producer gas and similar gases, other than petroleum gases and other gaseous hydrocarbons:**
2705.0000	煤气、水煤气、炉煤气及类似气体,但石油气及其他烃类气除外	5			0	20	13		千克		Coal gas, water gas, producer gas and similar gases, other than petroleum gases and other gaseous hydrocarbons
27.06	**从煤、褐煤或泥煤蒸馏所得的焦油及其他矿物焦油,不论是否脱水或部分蒸馏,包括再造焦油:**										**Tar distilled from coal, from lignite or from peat, and other mineral tars, whether or not dehydrated or partially distilled, including reconstituted tars:**
2706.0000	从煤、褐煤或泥煤蒸馏所得的焦油及其他矿物焦油,不论是否脱水或部分蒸馏,包括再造焦油	6	5		0	30	17		千克		Tar distilled from coal, from lignite or from peat, and other mineral tars, whether or not dehydrated or partially distilled, including reconstituted tars

税则号列 Tariff Item.	货品名称	最惠国(%) MFN	协定(%) CT			普通 Gen	增值税率 VAT	出口退税 ED	计量单位 Unit	监管条件 SC	Article Description
			东盟 CA	中巴 CP	中智 CC						
27.07	**蒸馏高温煤焦油所得的油类及其他产品;芳族成分重量超过非芳族成分的类似产品:**										**Oils and other products of the distillation of high temperature coal tar; similar products in which the weight of the aromatic constituents exceeds that of the non-aromatic constituents:**
2707.1000	-粗苯	6	5		0	20	17	13	千克		-Benzole
2707.2000	-粗甲苯	6	5		0	30	17	13	千克		-Toluole
2707.3000	-粗二甲苯	6	5		0	20	17	13	千克		-Xylole
2707.4000	-萘	7	5	6	0	30	17	13	千克		-Naphthalene
2707.5000	-其他芳烃混合物,温度在250℃时蒸馏出的芳烃含量以体积计(包括损耗)在65%及以上(以美国标准试验法D86为准)	7	5		0	30	17	13	千克	B	-Other aromatic hydrocarbon mixtures of which 65% or more by volume (including losses) distils at 250℃ by the ASTM D86 method
	-其他:										-Other:
2707.9100	--杂酚油	7	5		0	30	17	13	千克		--Creosote oils
	--其他:										--Other:
2707.9910	---酚	7	5		0	30	17	13	千克		---Pnenols
2707.9990	---其他	7	5		0	30	17	13	千克		---Other
27.08	**从煤焦油或其他矿物焦油所得的沥青及沥青焦:**										**Pitch and pitch coke, obtained from coal tar or from other mineral tars:**
2708.1000	-沥青	7	5		5.6	35	17		千克		-Pitch
2708.2000	-沥青焦	6	5		0	11	17		千克		-Pitch coke
2708.2000 01	针状沥青焦	6				11	17		千克		Meedle-shaped petroleum coke
2708.2000 90	其他沥青焦	6				11	17		千克		Other Needle-shaped peeroleuncoke
27.09	**石油原油及从沥青矿物提取的原油:**										**Petroleum oils and oils obtained from bituminous minerals, crude:**
2709.0000	石油原油及从沥青矿物提取的原油	T2				T2	17		千克	4x7AByv	Petroleum oils and oils obtained from bituminous minerals, crude
27.10	**石油及从沥青矿物提取的油类,但原油除外;以上述油为基本成分(按重量计不低于70%)的其他税目未列名制品;废油:**										**Petroleum oils and oils obtained from bituminous minerals, other than crude; preparations not elsewhere specified or included, containing by weight 70% or more of petroleum oils or of oils obtained from bituminous minerals, these oils being the basic constituents of the preparations; waste oils:**
	-石油及从沥青矿物提取的油类(但原油除外);以上述油为基本成分(按重量计不低于70%)的其他税目未列名制品;但废油除外:										-Petroleum oils and oils obtained from bituminous minerals (other than crude) and preparations not elsewhere specified or included, containing by weight 70% or more of petroleum oils or of oils obtained from bituminous minerals, these oils being the basic constituents of the preparations, other than waste oils:
	--轻油及其制品:										--Light oils and preparations:
2710.1110	---车用汽油及航空汽油	5			4	14	17		千克	47ABvy	---Mortor gasoline, aviation gasoline

税则号列 Tariff Item.	货 品 名 称	最惠国(%) MFN	协定(%)CT 东盟 CA	中巴 CP	中智 CC	普通 Gen	增值税率 VAT	出口退税 ED	计量单位 Unit	监管条件 SC	Article Description
2710.1120	---石脑油	6	T3	5.4	4.8	20	17		千克	47ABvy	---Naphtha
2710.1130	---橡胶溶剂油、油漆溶剂油、抽提溶剂油	6			4.8	30	17	13	千克		---Rubber solvent, paint solvent, extractive solvent
	---其他:										---Other:
2710.1191	----壬烯	9			7.2	20	17	13	千克	A4y	----Nonene
2710.1191 01	壬烯(碳九异构体混合物含量高于90%)	9				20	17		千克	A4y	nonene
2710.1191 90	其他壬烯	9				20	17		千克	A4y	Other nonene
2710.1199	----其他	9			7.2	20	17	13	千克		----Other
2710.1199 10	异戊烯同分异构体混合物	9				20	17	13	千克	4Ay	Mixture of isomers of isoamylene
2710.1199 90	其他轻油及制品(包括按重量计含油≥70%的制品)	9				20	17	13	千克	4Ay	Other light oils and preparations containing≥70% by weight of oils
	--其他:										--Other:
	---煤油馏分:										---Kerosene distillages:
2710.1911	----航空煤油	9	T3		7.2	14	17		千克	47ABvy	----Aviation kerosene
2710.1912	----灯用煤油	9			7.2	14	17		千克	47ABvy	----Lamp-kerosene
2710.1919	----其他	6	T3		4.8	20	17	13	千克		----Other
2710.1919 10	正构烷烃(C_9-C_{13})	6				20	17	13	千克	4y	Normal paraffin hydrocarbon (C_9-C_{13})
2710.1919 90	其他煤油馏分的油及制品	6				20	17	13	千克	4	Other kerosene distillages oils and preparations
	---柴油及其他燃料油:										---Diesel oils and other fuel oils:
2710.1921	----轻柴油	6			4.8	11	17		千克	47ABvy	----Light diesel oil
2710.1922	----5-7号燃料油	6	T3		4.8	20	17		千克	BA7v	----Fuel oils No. 5 ~ No. 7
2710.1929	----其他	6	T3		4.8	20	17		千克		----Other
2710.1929 10	蜡油(350℃以下馏出物体积<20%,550℃以下馏出物体积>80%)	6				20	17		千克	BA7v	Paraffin oils (which <20% by volume distil <350℃, which >80% by volume distil <550℃)
2710.1929 20	重柴油	6				20	17		千克	B4A7yv	Heavy diesel oils
2710.1929 90	其他柴油及燃料油	6				20	17		千克	BA7v	Other diesel oils and other fuel oils
	---润滑油、润滑脂及其他重油:										---Lubricating oils, lubricating greases and other heavy oils products:
2710.1991	----润滑油	6	T3	5.4	4.8	17	17		千克	B4Ay	----Lubricating grease
2710.1992	----润滑脂	6	T3	5.4	4.8	17	17		千克	B4Ay	----Lubricating oils
2710.1993	----润滑油基础油	6	T3		4.8	17	17		千克	4y	----Basic oils for lubricating oils
2710.1994	----液体石蜡和重质液体石蜡	6	T3	5.4	4.8	20	17		千克	AB	----Liquid paraffin and heavy liquid paraffin
2710.1999	----其他	6			4.8	20	17		千克	B	----Other
	-废油:										-Waste oils:
2710.9100	--含多氯联苯(PCBs)、多氯三联苯(PCTs)或多溴联苯(PBBs)的	6	T3		0	20	17		千克	9	--Containing polychlorinated biphenyls (PCBs), polychlorinated terphenyls (PCTs) or polybrominated biphenyls (PBBs)
2710.9900	--其他	6	T3		0	20	17		千克	9	--Other
27.11	**石油气及其他烃类气:**										**Petroleum gases and other gaseous hydrocarbons:**
	-液化的:										-Liquefied:
2711.1100	--天然气	0				20	13		千克	47y	--Natural gas
2711.1200	--丙烷	5		3.5	4	20	13	11	千克		--Propane
	--丁烷:										--Butanes:

税则号列 Tariff Item.	货品名称	最惠国(%) MFN	协定(%) CT 东盟 CA	协定(%) CT 中巴 CP	协定(%) CT 中智 CC	普通 Gen	增值税率 VAT	出口退税 ED	计量单位 Unit	监管条件 SC	Article Description
2711.1310	---直接灌注香烟打火机及类似打火器用,其包装容器的容积超过300立方厘米	11	8		8.8	80	17	13	千克		---Liquid or liquefied-gas fuels in containers of a kind used for filling or refilling cigarette or similar lighters and of a capacity exceeding 300cm^3
2711.1390	---其他	5			4	20	13	11	千克		---Other
2711.1400	--乙烯、丙烯、丁烯及丁二烯	5			0	20	17	13	千克		--Ethylene, propylene, butylene and butadiene
	--其他:										--Other:
2711.1910	---直接灌注香烟打火机及类似打火器用的燃料,其包装容器的容积超过300立方厘米	10	5	7	8	80	17	13	千克		---Liquid or liquefied-gas fuels in containers of a kind used for filling or refilling cigarette or similar lighters and of a capacity exceeding 300cm^3
2711.1990	---其他	3		2.1	1.8	20	13	11	千克		---Other
	-气态的:										-In gaseous state:
2711.2100	--天然气	0				20	13		千克	7	--Natural gas
2711.2900	--其他	6	5		0	20	13		千克		--Other
27.12	**凡士林;石蜡、微晶石蜡、疏松石蜡、地蜡、褐煤蜡、泥煤蜡、其他矿物蜡及用合成或其他方法制得的类似产品,不论是否着色:**										**Petroleum jelly; paraffin wax, microcrystalline petroleum wax, slack wax, ozokerite, lignite wax, peat wax, other mineral waxes, and similar products obtained by synthesis or by other processes, whether or not coloured:**
2712.1000	-凡士林	8	5		6.4	45	17		千克		-Petroleum jelly
2712.2000	-石蜡,按重量计含油量小于0.75%	8	5		0	45	17		千克	4x	-Paraffin wax containing by weight less than 0.75% of oil
	-其他:										-Other:
2712.9010	---微晶石蜡	8	5		0	45	17	5	千克	4x	---Microcrystalline petroleum wax
2712.9090	---其他	8	5		0	45	17		千克		---Other
27.13	**石油焦、石油沥青及其他石油或从沥青矿物提取的油类的残渣:**										**Petroleum coke, petroleum bitumen and other residues of petroleum oils or of oils obtained from bituminous minerals:**
	-石油焦:										-Petroleum coke:
	--未煅烧:										--Not calcined:
2713.1110	---硫的重量百分比小于3%的	3			0	11	17		千克	B	---Containing by weight less than 3% of sulphur(s)
2713.1190	---其他	3			0	11	17		千克	B	---Other
	--已煅烧:										--Calcined:
2713.1210	---硫的重量百分比小于0.8%的	3			0	11	17		千克		---Containing by weight less than 0.8% of sulphur(s)
2713.1210 01	已煅烧针状石油焦(硫的重量百分比小于0.8%)	3				11	17		千克	B	Needle - shaped pitch coke, calcined (containing by weight less than 0.8% of sulphur(s))
2713.1210 90	其他已煅烧石油焦(硫的重量百分比小于0.8%)	3				11	17		千克	B	Other pitch coke, calcined (containing by weight less than 0.8% of sulphur (s))
2713.1290	---其他	3			0	11	17		千克	B	---Other
2713.2000	-石油沥青	8	5	5.6	0	35	17		千克		-Petroleum bitumen

税则号列 Tariff Item.	货 品 名 称	最惠国(%) MFN	协定(%)CT 东盟 CA	中巴 CP	中智 CC	普通 Gen	增值税率 VAT	出口退税 ED	计量单位 Unit	监管条件 SC	Article Description
2713.9000	-其他石油或从沥青矿物提取的油类的残渣	6	5		0	35	17		千克		-Other residues of petroleum oils or of oils obtained from bituminous minerals
27.14	**天然沥青(地沥青)、沥青页岩、油页岩及焦油砂;沥青岩:**										**Bitumen and asphalt, natural; bituminous or oil shale and tar sands; asphaltites and asphaltic rocks:**
2714.1000	-沥青页岩、油页岩及焦油砂	6	5		0	20	17		千克		-Bituminous or oil shale and tar sands
	-其他:										-Other:
2714.9010	---天然沥青(地沥青)	8	5		0	35	17		千克		---Natural bitumen and asphalt
2714.9020	---乳化沥青	0				20	17		千克		---Emulsified bitumen and asphalt
2714.9090	---其他	3			0	20	17		千克		---Other
27.15	**以天然沥青(地沥青)、石油沥青、矿物焦油或矿物焦油沥青为基本成分的沥青混合物(例如,沥青胶粘剂、稀释沥青):**										**Bituminous mixtures based on natural asphalt, on natural bitumen, on petroleum bitumen, on mineral tar or on mineral tar pitch (for example, bituminous mastics, cut-backs):**
2715.0000	以天然沥青(地沥青)、石油沥青、矿物焦油或矿物焦油沥青为基本成分的沥青混合物(例如,沥青胶粘剂、稀释沥青)	8	5		6.4	35	17		千克		Bituminous mixtures based on natural asphalt, on natural bitumen, on petroleum bitumen, on mineral tar or on mineral tar pitch (for example, bituminous mastics, cut-backs)
27.16	**电力:**										**Electrical energy:**
2716.0000	电力	0				8	17	13	千瓦时		Electrical energy

第六类

化学工业及其相关工业的产品

注释：

一、(一)凡符合税目28.44、28.45规定的货品(放射性矿砂除外),应分别归入这两个税目而不归入本目录的其他税目。

(二)除上述(一)款另有规定的以外,凡符合税目28.43、28.46、28.52规定的货品,应分别归入以上税目而不归入本类的其他税目。

二、除上述注释一另有规定的以外,凡由于按一定剂量或作为零售包装而可归入税目30.04、30.05、30.06、32.12、33.03、33.04、33.05、33.06、33.07、35.06、37.07及38.08的货品,应分别归入以上税目,而不归入本目录的其他税目。

三、由两种或两种以上单独成分配套的货品,其部分或全部成分属于本类范围以内,混合后则构成第六类或第七类的货品,应按混合后产品归入相应的税目,但其组成成分必须同时符合下列条件:

(一)其包装形式足以表明这些成分不需经过改装就可一起使用的;

(二)一起进口或出口的;

(三)这些成分的属性及相互比例足以表明是相互配用的。

SECTION Ⅵ
PRODUCTS OF THE CHEMICAL OR ALLIED INDUSTRIES

Notes:

1. (a) Goods (other than radioactive ores) answering to a description in heading No. 28.44 or 28.45 are to be classified in those headings and in no other heading of the Nomenclature.

   (b) Subject to paragraph (a) above, goods answering to a description in heading No. 28.43、28.46 or 28.52 are to be classified in those headings and in no other heading of this Seciton.

2. Subject to Note 1 above, goods classifiable in heading Nos. 30.04, 30.05, 30.06, 32.12, 33.03, 33.04, 33.05, 33.06, 33.07, 35.06, 37.07, or 38.08 by reason of being put up in measured doses or for retail sale are to be classified in those headings and in no other headings of the Nomenclature.

3. Goods put up in sets consisting of two or more separate constituents, some or all of which fall in this Section and are intended to be mixed together to obtain a product of Section Ⅵ or Ⅶ, are to be classified in the heading appropriate to that product, provided that the constituents are:

   (a) having regard to the manner in which they are put up, clearly identifiable as being intended to be used together without first being repacked;

   (b) presented together; and

   (c) identifiable, whether by their nature or by the relative proportions in which they are present, as being complementary one to another.

第二十八章

无机化学品;贵金属、稀土金属、放射性元素及其同位素的有机及无机化合物

注释:

一、除条文另有规定的以外,本章各税目只适用于:

(一)单独的化学元素及单独的已有化学定义的化合物,不论是否含有杂质;

(二)上述(一)款产品的水溶液;

(三)溶于其他溶剂的上述(一)款产品,但该产品处于溶液状态只是为了安全或运输所采取的正常必要方法,其所用溶剂并不使该产品改变其一般用途而适合于某些特殊用途;

(四)为了保存或运输需要,加入稳定剂(包括抗结块剂)的上述(一)、(二)、(三)款产品;

Chapter 28

Inorganic chemicals; organic or inorganic compounds of precious metals, of rare-earth metals of radioactive elements or of isotopes

Notes:

1. Except where the context otherwise requires, the headings of this Chapter apply only to:

   (a) Separate chemical elements and separate chemically defined compounds, whether or not containing impurities;

   (b) The products mentioned in (a) above dissolved in water;

   (c) The products mentioned in (a) above dissolved in other solvents, provided that the solution constitutes a normal and necessary method of putting up these products adopted solely for reasons of safety or for transport, and that the solvent does not render the product particularly suitable for specific use rather than for general use;

   (d) The products mentioned in (a), (b) or (c) above with an added stabilizer (including an anti-caking agent) necessary for their preservation or transport;

（五）为了便于识别或安全起见，加入抗尘剂或着色剂的上述（一）、（二）、（三）、（四）款产品，但所加剂料并不使原产品改变其一般用途而适合于某些特殊用途。

二、除以有机物质稳定的连二亚硫酸盐及次硫酸盐（税目28.31），无机碱的碳酸盐及过碳酸盐（税目28.36），无机碱的氰化物、氧氰化物及氰络合物（税目28.37），无机碱的雷酸盐、氰酸盐及硫氰酸盐（税目28.42），税目28.43至28.46及28.52的有机产品，以及碳化物（税目28.49）之外，本章仅包括下列碳化合物：

（一）碳的氧化物，氰化氢及雷酸、异氰酸、硫氰酸及其他简单或络合氰酸（税目28.11）；

（二）碳的卤氧化物（税目28.12）；

（三）二硫化碳（税目28.13）；

（四）硫代碳酸盐、硒代碳酸盐、碲代碳酸盐、硒代氰酸盐、碲代氰酸盐、四氰硫基二氨基络酸盐及其他无机碱络合氰酸盐（税目28.42）；

（五）用尿素固化的过氧化氢（税目28.47）、氧硫化碳、硫代羰基卤化物、氰、卤化氰、氨基氰及其金属衍生物（税目28.53），不论是否纯净，但氰氨化钙除外（第三十一章）。

三、除第六类注释一另有规定的以外，本章不包括：

（一）氯化钠或氧化镁（不论是否纯净）及第五类的其他产品；

（二）上述注释二所述以外的有机-无机化合物；

（三）第三十一章注释二、三、四或五所述的产品；

（四）税目32.06的用作发光剂的无机产品；税目32.07的搪瓷玻璃料及其他玻璃，呈粉、粒或粉片状的

（五）人造石墨（税目38.01）；税目38.13的灭火器的装配药及已装药的灭火弹；税目38.24的零售包装的除墨剂；税目38.24的每颗重量不少于2.5克的碱金属或碱土金属卤化物的培养晶体（光学元件除外）；

（六）宝石或半宝石（天然、合成或再造）及这些宝石、半宝石的粉末（税目71.02至71.05），第七十一章的贵金属及贵金属合金；

（七）第十五类的金属（不论是否纯净）、金属合金或金属陶瓷，包括硬质合金（与金属烧结的金属碳化物）；

(e) The products mentioned in (a), (b), (c) or (d) above with an added antidusting agent or a colouring substance added to facilitate their identification or for safety reasons, provided that the additions do not render the product particularly suitable for specific use rather than for general use.

2. In addition to dithionites and sulphoxylates, stabilized with organic substances (heading No. 28.31), carbonates and peroxocarbonates of inorganic bases (heading No. 28.36), cyanides, cyanide oxides and complex cyanides of inorganic bases (heading No. 28.37), fulminates, cyanates and thiocyanates, of inorganic bases (heading No. 28.46), organic products included in headings No. 28.43 to 28.46 and 28.52 and carbides (heading No. 28.49), only the following compounds of carbon are to the classified in this Chapter:

(a) Oxides of carbon, hydrogen cyanide and fulminic, isocyanic, thiocyanic and other simple or complex cyanogen acids (heading No. 28.11);

(b) Halide oxides of carbon (heading No. 28.12);

(c) Carbon disulphide (heading No. 28.13);

(d) Thiocarbonates, selenocarbonates, tellurocarbonates, selenocyanates, tellurocyanates, tetrathiocyanatodiamminochromates (reineckates) and other complex cyanates, of inorganic bases (heading No. 28.42);

(e) Hydrogen peroxide, solidified with urea (heading No. 28.47), carbon oxysulphide, thiocarbonyl halides, cyanogen, cyanogen halides and cyanamide and its metal derivatives (heading No. 28.53) other than calcium cyanamide, whether or not pure (Chapter 31).

3. Subject to the provisions of Note 1 to Section Ⅵ, this Chapter does not cover:

(a) Sodium chloride or magnesium oxide, whether or not pure, or other products of Section Ⅴ;

(b) Organo-inorganic compounds other than those mentioned in Note 2 above;

(c) Products mentioned in Note 2,3,4 or 5 to Chapter 31;

(d) Inorganic products of a kind used as luminophores, of heading No. 32.06; glass frit and other glass in the form of powder, granules of flakes, of heading No. 32.07;

(e) Artificial graphite (heading No. 38.01); products put up as charges for fire-extinguishers or put up in fire-extinguishing grenades, of heading No. 38.13; ink removers put up in packings for retail sale, of heading No. 38.24, cultured crystals (other than optical elements) weighing not less than 2.5g each, of the halides of the alkali or alkaline-earth metals, of heading No. 38.24;

(f) Precious or semi-precious stones (natural, synthetic or reconstructed) or dust or powder of such stones (headings Nos. 71.02 to 71.05), or precious metals or precious metal alloys of Chapter 71;

(g) The metals, whether or not pure, metal alloys or cermets, including sintered metal carbides (metal carbides sintered with a metal), of Section ⅩⅤ; or

（八）光学元件，例如用碱金属或碱土金属卤化物制成的（税目90.01）。

四、由本章第二分章的非金属酸和第四分章的金属酸所构成的已有化学定义的络酸，应归入税目28.11。

五、税目28.26至28.42只适用于金属盐、铵盐及过氧酸盐。除条文另有规定的以外，复盐及络盐应归入税目28.42。

六、税目28.44只适用于：

（一）锝（原子序数43）、钷（原子序数61）、钋（原子序数84）及原子序数大于84的所有化学元素；

（二）天然或人造放射性同位素（包括第十四类及第十五类的贵金属和贱金属的放射性同位素），不论是否混合；

（三）上述元素或同位素的无机或有机化合物，不论是否已有化学定义或是否混合；

（四）含有上述元素或同位素及其无机或有机化合物并且具有某种放射性强度超过74贝克勒尔/克（0.002微居里/克）的合金、分散体（包括金属陶瓷）、陶瓷产品及混合物；

（五）核反应堆已耗尽（已辐照）的燃料元件（释热元件）；

（六）放射性的残渣，不论是否有用。

税目28.44、28.45及本注释所称"同位素"，是指：

1. 单独的核素，但不包括自然界中以单一同位素状态存在的核素；
2. 同一元素的同位素混合物，其中一种或几种同位素已被浓缩，即人工地改变了该元素同位素的自然构成。

七、税目28.48包括按重量计含磷量超过15%的磷化铜（磷铜）。

八、经掺杂用于电子工业的化学元素（例如，硅、硒），如果拉制后未经加工或呈圆筒形、棒形，应归入本章；如果已切成圆片、薄片或类似形状，则归入税目38.18。

（h）Optical elements, for example, of the halides of the alkali or alkaline-earth metals (heading No. 90.01).

4. Chemically defined complex acids consisting of a nonmetal acid of sub-Chapter Ⅱ and a metal acid of sub-Chapter Ⅳ are to be classified in heading No. 28.11.

5. Headings Nos. 28.26 to 28.42 apply only to metal or ammonium salts or peroxysalts. Except where the context otherwise requires, double or complex salts are to be classified in heading No. 28.42.

6. Heading No. 28.44 applies only to:

(a) Technetium (atomic No. 43), promethium (atomic No. 61), polonium (atomic No. 84) and all elements with an atomic number greater than 84;

(b) Natural or artificial radioactive isotopes (including those of the precious metals or of the base metals of Sections ⅩⅣ and ⅩⅤ), whether or not mixed together;

(c) Compounds, inorganic or organic, of these elements or isotopes, whether or not chemically defined, whether or not mixed together;

(d) Alloys, dispersions (including cermets), ceramic products and mixtures containing these elements or isotopes or inorganic or organic compounds thereof and having a specific radioactivity exceeding 74 Bq/g (0.002μ Ci/g);

(e) Spent (irradiated) fuel elements (cartridges) of nuclear reactors;

(f) Radioactive residues whether or not usable.

The term "isotopes", for the purposes of this Note and of the wording of headings Nos. 28.44 and 28.45, refers to:

-individual nuclides, excluding, however, those existing in nature in the monoisotopic state;

-mixtures of isotopes of one and the same element, enriched in one or several of the said isotopes, that is, elements of which the natural isotopic composition has been artificially modified.

7. Heading No. 28.48 includes copper phosphide (phosphor copper) containing more than 15% by weight of phosphorus.

8. Chemical elements (for example, silicon and selenium) doped for use in electronics are to be classified in this Chapter, provided that they are in forms unworked as drawn, or in the form of cylinders or rods. When cut in the form of discs, wafers or similar forms, they fall in heading No. 38.18.

税则号列 Tariff Item.	货品名称	最惠国(%) MFN	协定(%)CT 东盟 CA	中巴 CP	中智 CC	普通 Gen	增值税率 VAT	出口退税 ED	计量单位 Unit	监管条件 SC	Article Description
	第一分章　化学元素										Ⅰ.-CHEMICAL ELEMENTS
28.01	氟、氯、溴及碘：										**Fluorine, chlorine, bromine and iodine:**
2801.1000	-氯	5.5	T3		4.4	80	17	13	千克		-Chlorine
2801.2000	-碘	5.5	5			30	17	13	千克	G	-Iodine
	-氟；溴：										-Fluorine; bromine:
2801.3010	---氟	5.5	5		0	30	17	13	千克		---Fluorine
2801.3020	---溴	5.5	5		0	30	17	13	千克		---Bromine
28.02	升华硫磺、沉淀硫磺；胶态硫磺：										**Sulphur, sublimed or precipitated; colloidal sulphur:**

税则号列 Tariff Item.	货品名称	最惠国(%) MFN	协定(%) CT			普通 Gen	增值税率 VAT	出口退税 ED	计量单位 Unit	监管条件 SC	Article Description
			东盟 CA	中巴 CP	中智 CC						
2802.0000	升华硫磺、沉淀硫磺;胶态硫磺	5.5	5		0	17	17	13	千克		Sulphur, sublimed or precipitated; colloidal sulphur
28.03	**碳(碳黑及其他税目未列名的其他形态的碳)**										**Carbon (carbon blacks and other forms of carbon not elsewhere specified or included):**
2803.0000	碳(碳黑及其他税目未列名的其他形态的碳)	5.5	T3	4.4	0	35	17	13	千克		Carbon (carbon blacks and other forms of carbon not elsewhere specified or included)
28.04	**氢、稀有气体及其他非金属**										**Hydrogen, rare gases and other non-metals:**
2804.1000	-氢	5.5	5		0	30	17	13	立方米/千克		-Hydrogen
	-稀有气体:										-Rare gases:
2804.2100	--氩	5.5	5		4.4	30	17	13	立方米/千克		--Argon
2804.2900	--其他	5.5	5		0	30	17	13	立方米/千克		--Other
2804.3000	-氮	5.5	5		0	30	17	13	立方米/千克		-Nitrogen
2804.4000	-氧	5.5	5		4.4	80	17	13	立方米/千克		-Oxygen
2804.5000	-硼;碲	5.5	5		0	17	17	13	千克		-Boron; tellurium
2804.5000 10	颗粒<500μm 的硼及其合金(含量≥97%,不论球形、椭球体、雾化、片状、研碎金属燃料)	5.5				17	17	13	千克	3	Boron and its alloys, granularity < 500μm (containing boron ≥ 97%, whether in the form of spheroid, ellipsoid, flakes, atomized or pulverized metallic fuel)
2804.5000 20	能量密度>40MJ/kg 的硼浆(硼溶于溶剂形成的硼浆)	5.5				17	17	13	千克	3	Boron paste, energy density >4 Mega J/kg, boron dissolved in solvent
2804.5000 90	碲及其他硼	5.5				17	17	13	千克		Tellurium and other boron
	-硅:										-Silicon:
	--按重量计含硅量不少于99.99%:										--Containing by weight not less than 99.99% of silicon:
2804.6110	---经掺杂用于电子工业的直径在7.5厘米及以上的单晶硅棒	4			0	11	17	13	千克	B	---Monocrystals doped for use in electronics, in the form of cylinders or rods, 7.5cm or more in diameter
2804.6120	---经掺杂用于电子工业的其他单晶硅棒	4			0	17	17	13	千克	B	---Other monocrystals doped for use in electronics, in the form of cylinders or rods
2804.6190	---其他	4			0	30	17	13	千克		---Other
2804.6190 01	含硅量不少于99.99%的多晶硅	4				30	17		千克	B	Polycrystalline silicon, the propotion of the silicon is more than 99.9%
2804.6190 90	其他含硅量不少于99.99%的硅	4				30	17		千克	B	Containing by weight not less than 99.99% of silicon
2804.6900	--其他	4			0	30	17		千克	B	--Other
	-磷:										-Phosphorus:
2804.7010	---黄磷(白磷)	5.5	5		0	30	17		千克	a	---Yellow phosphorus (white phosphorus)
2804.7090	---其他	5.5	5		0	30	17		千克		---Other
2804.7090 10	红磷	5.5				30	17		千克	G	Red phosphorus
2804.7090 90	其他磷	5.5				30	17		千克		Other phosphorus
2804.8000	-砷	5.5	5		0	30	17		千克	X	-Arsenic
	-硒:										-Selenium:

税则号列 Tariff Item.	货品名称	最惠国(%) MFN	协定(%) 东盟 CA	中巴 CP	CT 中智 CC	普通 Gen	增值税率 VAT	出口退税 ED	计量单位 Unit	监管条件 SC	Article Description
2804.9010	---经掺杂用于电子工业的晶体棒	4			3.2	17	17	13	千克		---Crystals doped for use in electronics, in the form of cylinders or rods
2804.9090	---其他	5.5	5		4.4	30	17	13	千克		---Other
28.05	**碱金属、碱土金属;稀土金属、钪及钇,不论是否相互混合或相互熔合;汞:**										**Alkali or alkaline-earth metals; rare-earth metals, scandium and yttrium, whether or not intermixed or interalloyed; mercury:**
	-碱金属及碱土金属:										-Alkali metals or alkaline-earth metals:
2805.1100	--钠	5.5	5		0	30	17	13	千克		--Sodium
2805.1200	--钙	5.5	5		0	30	17	13	千克		--Calcium
2805.1200 10	高纯度钙[金属杂质(除镁外)含量<1‰,硼含量小于十万分之一]	5.5				30	17	13	千克	3	Calcium, with a high purity, metallic impurity (other than Magnesium) < 1‰, containing boron < $1/10^5$
2805.1200 90	其他钙	5.5				30	17	13	千克		Other Calcium
2805.1900	--其他	5.5	5		0	30	17	13	千克		--Other
	-稀土金属、钪及钇,不论是否相互混合或相互熔合:										-Rare-earth metals, scandium and yttrium, whether or not intermixed or interalloyed:
	---稀土金属、钪及钇,未相互混合或相互熔合:										---Rare-earth metals, scandium and yttrium, not intermixed or interalloyed:
2805.3011	----钕	5.5	5		0	30	17		千克	4xy	----Neodymium
2805.3012	----镝	5.5	5		0	30	17		千克	4xy	----Dysprosium
2805.3013	----铽	5.5	5		0	30	17		千克	4xy	----Terbium
2805.3019	----其他	5.5	5		0	30	17		千克		----Other
2805.3019 11	金属镧(未相互混合或相互熔合)	5.5				30	17		千克	4xy	Metallic lanthanum, not intermixed or interalloyed
2805.3019 12	金属镨(未相互混合或相互熔合)	5.5				30	17		千克	4xy	Metallic praseodymium, not intermixed or interalloyed
2805.3019 13	金属钐(未相互混合或相互熔合)	5.5				30	17		千克	4xy	Metallic samarium, not intermixed or interalloyed
2805.3019 14	金属铕(未相互混合或相互熔合)	5.5				30	17		千克	4xy	Metallic europium, not intermixed or interalloyed
2805.3019 15	金属钪(未相互混合或相互熔合)	5.5				30	17		千克	4xy	Metallic Scandium, not intermixed or interalloyed
2805.3019 16	金属钇(未相互混合或相互熔合)	5.5				30	17		千克	4xy	Metallic Yttrium, not intermixed or interalloyed
2805.3019 21	颗粒<500μm的铈及其合金(含量≥97%,不论球形、椭球体、雾化、片状、研碎金属燃料)	5.5				30	17		千克	3	Cerium and its alloys, granularity < 500μm, containing cerium ≥ 97%, whether in the form of spheroid, ellipsoid, flakes, atomized or pulverized metallic fuel
2805.3019 29	其他金属铈(未相互混合或相互熔合)	5.5				30	17		千克	4xy	Other metalic cerium, not intermixed or interalloyed
2805.3019 90	其他稀土金属(未相互混合或相互熔合)	5.5				30	17		千克	4xy	Other rare-earth metals, not intermixed or interalloyed
	---稀土金属、钪及钇,相互混合或相互熔合:										---Rare-earth metals, scandium and yttrium, intermixed or interalloyed:
2805.3021	----电池级	5.5	5		0	30	17		千克	4xy	----Battery quality
2805.3029	----其他	5.5	5		0	30	17		千克	4xy	----Other

税则号列 Tariff Item.	货品名称	最惠国(%) MFN	协定(%) CT 东盟 CA	中巴 CP	中智 CC	普通 Gen	增值税率 VAT	出口退税 ED	计量单位 Unit	监管条件 SC	Article Description
2805.4000	-汞	5.5	5		4.4	17	17	5	千克	X	-Mercury
	第二分章 无机酸及非金属无机氧化物										Ⅱ.-INORGANIC ACIDS AND INORGANIC OXYGEN COMPOUNDS OF NON-METALS
28.06	**氯化氢(盐酸);氯磺酸:**										**Hydrogen chloride (hydrochloric acid); chorosulphuric acid:**
2806.1000	-氯化氢(盐酸)	5.5	T3		4.4	80	17	13	千克	32	-Hydrogen chloride (hydrochloric acid)
2806.2000	-氯磺酸	5.5	5		0	40	17	13	千克		-Chlorosulphuric acid
28.07	**硫酸;发烟硫酸:**										**Sulphuric acid; oleum:**
2807.0000	硫酸;发烟硫酸	5.5	5		4.4	35	17	13	千克		Sulphuric acid; oleum
2807.0000 10	硫酸	5.5				35	17	13	千克	32	Sulphuric acid
2807.0000 90	发烟硫酸	5.5				35	17	13	千克		Oleum
28.08	**硝酸;磺硝酸:**										**Nitric acid; sulphonitric acids:**
2808.0000	硝酸;磺硝酸	5.5	5		4.4	40	17	13	千克		Nitric acid; sulphonitric acids
2808.0000 10	红发烟硝酸	5.5				40	17	13	千克	3	Red fuming nitric acid
2808.0000 90	磺硝酸及其他硝酸	5.5				40	17	13	千克		Sulphonitric acids, other nitric acids
28.09	**五氧化二磷;磷酸;多磷酸,不论是否已有化学定义:**										**Diphosphorus pentaoxide; phosphoric acid; polyphosphoric acids, whether or not chemically defined:**
2809.1000	-五氧化二磷	1			0	8	17	13	千克		-Diphosphorus pentaoxide
	-磷酸及多磷酸:										-Phosphoric acid and polyphosphoric acids:
2809.2010	---磷酸及偏磷酸、焦磷酸	1			0	8	17	13	千克	B	---Phosphoric acid, metaphosphoric acid and pyrophosphoric acid
2809.2090	---其他	5.5	T3		0	35	17	13	千克		---Other
28.10	**硼的氧化物;硼酸:**										**Oxides of boron; boric acids:**
2810.0010	---硼的氧化物	5.5	5		4.4	30	17	13	千克		---Oxides of boron
2810.0020	---硼酸	5.5	5		4.4	30	17	13	千克		---Boric acids
28.11	**其他无机酸及非金属无机氧化物:**										**Other inorganic acids and other inorganic oxygen compounds of non-metals:**
	-其他无机酸:										-Other inorganic acids:
2811.1100	--氢氟酸	5.5	5		0	35	17		千克	3	--Hydrofluoric acid
	--其他:										--Other:
2811.1910	---氢氰酸	5.5	5		4.4	35	17	13	千克	23	---Hydrocyanic acid
2811.1990	---其他	5.5	5		4.4	35	17	13	千克		---Other
2811.1990 10	氢碘酸	5.5				35	17	13	千克	G	Hydroiodin acid
2811.1990 20	砷酸、焦砷酸、偏砷酸	5.5				35	17	13	千克	X	arsenic acid, diarsenous acid, metaardsenic acid
2811.1990 90	其他无机酸	5.5				35	17	13	千克		Other inorganic acids
	-其他非金属无机氧化物:										-Other inorganic oxygen compounds of non-metals:
2811.2100	--二氧化碳	5.5	5		0	30	17	13	千克		--Carbon dioxide
2811.2200	--二氧化硅	5.5	5		0	30	17	13	千克		--Silicon dioxide
2811.2900	--其他	5.5	5		4.4	30	17	13	千克		--Other
2811.2900 10	三氧化二砷、五氧化二砷[亚砷(酸)酐,砒霜,白砒,氧化亚砷,砷(酸)酐,三氧化砷]	5.5				30	17	13	千克	X	Arsenous oxide (*arsenic trioxide*) (including arsenic trioxide, arsenous anhydride, arsenic white)
2811.2900 20	四氧化二氮	5.5				30	17	13	千克	3	Dinitrogen tetroxide

税则号列 Tariff Item.	货品名称	最惠国(%) MFN	协定(%)CT 东盟 CA	中巴 CP	中智 CC	普通 Gen	增值税率 VAT	出口退税 ED	计量单位 Unit	监管条件 SC	Article Description
2811.2900 90	其他非金属无机氧化物	5.5				30	17	13	千克		Other inorganic oxygen compounds of non-metals
	第三分章　非金属卤化物及硫化物										Ⅲ. HALOGEN OR SULPHUR COMPOUNDS OF NON-METALS
28.12	**非金属卤化物及卤氧化物：**										**Halides and halide oxides of non-metals：**
	-氯化物及氯氧化物：										-Chlorides and chloride oxides：
2812.1010	---氯化亚砜	5.5	5		4.4	30	17	13	千克	23	---Sulphoxide chloride
2812.1020	---氧氯化磷（磷酰氯；三氯氧磷）	5.5	5		4.4	30	17	13	千克	23	---Phosphorus oxychloride (phosphoryl monochloride, phosphorus oxy-trichloride)
2812.1030	---碳酰二氯（光气）	5.5	5		4.4	30	17	13	千克	23	---Carbonyl dichloride (phosgene)
	---非金属氯化物：										---Other chlorides of non-metals：
2812.1041	----一氯化硫（氯化硫）	5.5	5		4.4	30	17	13	千克	23	----Sulfur monochloride
2812.1042	----二氯化硫	5.5	5		4.4	30	17	13	千克	23	----Sulfur dichloride
2812.1043	----三氯化磷	5.5	5		4.4	30	17	13	千克	23	----Phosphorus trichloride
2812.1044	----三氯化砷	5.5	5		4.4	30	17	13	千克	23	----Arsenic trichloride
2812.1045	----五氯化磷	5.5	5		4.4	30	17	13	千克	23	----Phosphorus pentachloride
2812.1049	----其他	5.5	5		4.4	30	17	13	千克		----Other
2812.1090	---其他	5.5	5		4.4	30	17	13	千克		---Other
2812.9000	-其他	5.5	5		0	30	17	13	千克		-Other
2812.9000 10	三氟化氯	5.5				30	17	13	千克	3	Chlorine trifluoride
2812.9000 20	三氟化砷，三溴化砷，三碘化砷（氟化亚砷，溴化亚砷，碘化亚砷）	5.5				30	17	13	千克	X	arsenic trifluoride, arsenic tribromide, arsenic triiodide (fluorinated arsenous, bromized arsenic, iodinated arsenous)
2812.9000 30	硫酰氟	5.5				30	17	13	千克	S	sulfuryl fluoride
2812.9000 90	其他非金属卤化物及卤氧化物	5.5				30	17	13	千克		Other halides and halide oxides of non-metals
28.13	**非金属硫化物；商品三硫化二磷：**										**Sulphides of non-metals; commercial phosphorus trisulphides：**
2813.1000	-二硫化碳	5.5	5		0	30	17	13	千克	X	-Carbon disulphide
2813.9000	-其他	5.5	5		0	30	17	13	千克		-Other
2813.9000 10	五硫化二磷	5.5				30	17	13	千克	23	Diphosphorus pentasulfide
2813.9000 90	其他非金属硫化物、三硫化二磷	5.5				30	17	13	千克		Other sulphides of non-metals; commercial phosphorus trisulphides
	第四分章　无机碱和金属氧化物、氢氧化物及过氧化物										Ⅳ. -INORGANIC BASES AND OXIDES, HYDROXIDES AND PEROXIDES OF METALS
28.14	**氨及氨水：**										**Ammonia, anhydrous or in aqueous solution：**
2814.1000	-氨	5.5	5		4.4	35	17	13	千克		-Anhydrous ammonia
2814.2000	-氨水	5.5	5		0	35	17	13	千克		-Ammonia in aqueous solution
28.15	**氢氧化钠（烧碱）；氢氧化钾（苛性钾）；过氧化钠及过氧化钾：**										**Sodium hydroxide (caustic soda); potassium hydroxide (caustic potash); peroxides or sodium or potassium：**
	-氢氧化钠（烧碱）；										-Sodium hydroxide (caustic soda)：
2815.1100	--固体	10		7	0	35	17	13	千克	G	--Solid
2815.1200	--水溶液（氢氧化钠浓溶液及液体烧碱）	8		5.6	0	35	17	13	千克	G	--In aqueous solution (soda lye or liquid soda)

税则号列 Tariff Item.	货品名称	最惠国(%) MFN	协定(%)CT 东盟 CA	中巴 CP	中智 CC	普通 Gen	增值税率 VAT	出口退税 ED	计量单位 Unit	监管条件 SC	Article Description
2815.2000	-氢氧化钾(苛性钾)	5.5	5		0	30	17	13	千克		-Potassium hydroxide (caustic potash)
2815.3000	-过氧化钠及过氧化钾	5.5	5		0	30	17	13	千克		-Peroxides of sodium or potassium
28.16	**氢氧化镁及过氧化镁;锶或钡的氧化物、氢氧化物及过氧化物:**										**Hydroxide and peroxide of magnesium; oxides, hydroxides and peroxides, of strontium or barium:**
2816.1000	-氢氧化镁及过氧化镁	5.5	5		0	30	17	13	千克		-Hydroxide and peroxide of magnesium
2816.4000	-锶或钡的氧化物、氢氧化物及过氧化物	5.5	5		0	30	17	13	千克		-Oxides, hydroxides and peroxides, of strontium or barium
28.17	**氧化锌及过氧化锌:**										**Zinc oxide; Zinc peroxide:**
2817.0010	---氧化锌	5.5	T3		0	40	17	13	千克		---Zinc oxide
2817.0090	---过氧化锌	5.5	T3		0	30	17	13	千克		---Zinc peroxide
28.18	**人造刚玉,不论是否已有化学定义;氧化铝;氢氧化铝:**										**Artificial corundum, whether or not chemically defined; aluminium oxide; aluminium hydroxide:**
2818.1000	-人造刚玉,不论是否已有化学定义	5.5	5		0	20	17		千克	B	-Artificial corundum, whether or not chemically defined
2818.2000	-氧化铝,但人造刚玉除外	8	T3		0	30	17		千克	A7	-Aluminium oxide, other than artificial corundum
2818.3000	-氢氧化铝	5.5	5		0	30	17		千克		-Aluminium hydroxide
28.19	**铬的氧化物及氢氧化物:**										**Chromium oxides and hydroxides:**
2819.1000	-三氧化铬	5.5	5		0	20	17	13	千克		-Chromium trioxide
2819.9000	-其他	5.5	5		0	30	17	13	千克		-Other
28.20	**锰的氧化物:**										**Manganese oxide:**
2820.1000	-二氧化锰	5.5	5		0	40	17	13	千克		-Manganese dioxide
2820.9000	-其他	5.5	5		0	30	17	13	千克		-Other
28.21	**铁的氧化物及氢氧化物;土色料,按重量计三氧化二铁含量在70%及以上:**										**Iron oxides and hydroxides; earth colours containing 70% or more by weight of combined iron evaluated as Fe_2O_3:**
2821.1000	-铁的氧化物及氢氧化物	5.5	5		0	30	17	13	千克		-Iron oxides and hydroxides
2821.2000	-土色料	5.5	5		0	45	17	13	千克		-Earth colours
28.22	**钴的氧化物及氢氧化物;商品氧化钴:**										**Cobalt oxides and hydroxides; commercial cobalt oxides:**
	钴的氧化物及氢氧化物;商品氧化钴:										Cobalt oxides and hydroxides; commercial cobalt oxides
2822.0010	---四氧化三钴	5.5	5		0	30	17	13	千克		---Tricobalt tetroxide
2822.0090	---其他	5.5	5		0	30	17	13	千克		---Other
28.23	**钛的氧化物:**										**Titanium oxides:**
2823.0000	钛的氧化物	5.5	T3		0	30	17	13	千克	B	Titanium oxides
28.24	**铅的氧化物;铅丹及铅橙:**										**Lead oxides; red lead and orange lead:**
2824.1000	-一氧化铅(铅黄、黄丹)	5.5	5		4.4	30	17	13	千克	X	-Lead monoxide (litharge, massicot)
	-其他:										-Other:
2824.9010	---铅丹及铅橙	5.5	5		4.4	45	17	13	千克	X	---Red lead and orange lead
2824.9090	---其他	5.5	5		0	30	17	13	千克		---Other
28.25	**肼(联氨)、胲(羟胺)及其无机盐;其他无机碱;其他金属氧化物、氢氧化物及过氧化物:**										**Hydrazine and hydroxylamine and their inorganic salts; other inorganic bases; other metal oxides, hydroxides and peroxides:**

税则号列 Tariff Item.	货品名称	最惠国(%) MFN	协定(%) 东盟 CA	中巴 CP	CT 中智 CC	普通 Gen	增值税率 VAT	出口退税 ED	计量单位 Unit	监管条件 SC	Article Description
	-肼(联氨)、胲(羟胺)及其无机盐:										-Hydrazine and hydroxylamine and their inorganic salts:
2825.1010	---水合肼	5.5	5		0	30	17	5	千克		---Hydrazine hydrate
2825.1010 10	纯度85%及以上的水合肼	5.5				30	17	5	千克	3	Hydrazine hydrate, purity >85%
2825.1010 90	纯度85%及以下的水合肼	5.5				30	17	5	千克		Hydrazine hydrate, purity≤85%
2825.1090	---其他	5.5	5		0	30	17	5	千克		---Other
	-锂的氧化物及氢氧化物:										-Lithium oxide and hydroxide:
2825.2010	---氢氧化锂	5.5	5		0	30	17	5	千克		---Lithium hydroxide
2825.2090	---其他	5.5	5		0	30	17	5	千克		---Other
	-钒的氧化物及氢氧化物:										-Vanadium oxides and hydroxides:
2825.3010	---五氧化二钒	5.5	5		0	30	17	5	千克	4xy	---Divanadium pentaoxide
2825.3090	---其他	5.5	5		0	30	17	5	千克	4xy	---Other
2825.4000	-镍的氧化物及氢氧化物	5.5	5		0	30	17	5	千克		-Nickel oxides and hydroxides
2825.5000	-铜的氧化物及氢氧化物	5.5	5		4.4	30	17	5	千克		-Copper oxides and hydroxides
2825.6000	-锗的氧化物及二氧化锆	5.5	5		0	30	17	5	千克	4xy	-Germanium oxides and zirconium dioxide
2825.7000	-钼的氧化物及氢氧化物	5.5	5		4.4	30	17	5	千克	4axy	-Molybdenum oxides and hydroxides
2825.8000	-锑的氧化物	5.5	5		0	30	17	5	千克	4xBy	-Antimony oxides
	-其他:										-Other:
	---钨的氧化物及氢氧化物:										---Tungsten oxides and hydroxides:
2825.9011	----钨酸	5.5	5		0	30	17	5	千克	4xBy	----Tungstic acid
2825.9012	----三氧化钨	5.5	5		0	30	17		千克	4xBy	----Tungstic oxide
2825.9019	----其他	5.5	5		0	30	17	5	千克		----Other
2825.9019 10	蓝色氧化钨	5.5				30	17	5	千克	4xy	Blue tungsten oxides and hydroxides
2825.9019 90	其他钨的氧化物及氢氧化物	5.5				30	17	5	千克		Other tungsten oxides and hydroxides
2825.9090	---其他	5.5	5		0	30	17	5	千克		---Other
	第五分章 无机酸盐、无机过氧酸盐及金属酸盐、金属过氧酸盐										V.-SALTS AND PEROXYSALTS, OF INORGANIC ACIDS AND METALS
28.26	**氟化物;氟硅酸盐、氟铝酸盐及其他氟络盐:**										**Fluorides; fluorosilicates, fluoroaluminates and other complex fluorine salts:**
	-氟化物:										-Fluorides:
2826.1200	--氟化铝	5.5	5		0	30	17	13	千克		--Of aluminium
	--其他:										--Other:
2826.1910	---铵的氟化物	5.5	5		0	30	17	13	千克		---Amine fluorid
2826.1910 10	氟化氢铵	5.5				30	17	13	千克	3	Ammonium hydrogen fluoride
2826.1910 90	其他铵的氟化物	5.5				30	17	13	千克		Other amine fluorid
2826.1920	---钠的氟化物	5.5	5		0	30	17	13	千克		---Fluorides of sodium
2826.1920 10	氟化钠	5.5				30	17	13	千克	3	Sodium fluoride
2826.1920 20	氟化氢铵	5.5				30	17	13	千克	3	Sodium hydrogen fluoride
2826.1920 90	其他纳的氟化物	5.5				30	17	13	千克		Other natrium fluorid
2826.1990	---其他	5.5	5		0	30	17	13	千克		---Other
2826.1990 10	氟化钾	5.5				30	17	13	千克	3	Potassium fluoride
2826.1990 20	氟化氢钾	5.5				30	17	13	千克	3	Potassium hydrogen fluoride
2826.1990 30	氟化铅,四氟化铅,氟化镉	5.5				30	17	13	千克	X	Mercuric fluoride, lead fluoride , lead tetrafluoride chromic fluoride (mercuric difluoro, ldad difluoro)

税则号列 Tariff Item.	货品名称	最惠国(%) MFN	协定(%)CT 东盟 CA	中巴 CP	中智 CC	普通 Gen	增值税率 VAT	出口退税 ED	计量单位 Unit	监管条件 SC	Article Description
2826.1990 90	其他氟化物	5.5				30	17	13	千克		Other fluorides
2826.3000	-六氟铝酸钠(人造冰晶石)	5.5	5		0	30	17	13	千克		-Sodium hexafluoroaluminate (synthetic cryolite)
2826.9000	-其他	5.5	5		0	30	17	13	千克		-Other
2826.9000 01	六氟磷酸锂	5.5				30	17	13	千克		Lithium hexa Fluorophosphate
2826.9000 10	氟钽酸钾	5.5				30	17	13	千克		Potassium tantalifluoride
2826.9000 30	氟硼酸铅,氟硼酸镉	5.5				30	17	13	千克	X	lead fluoboric acid, cadmium fluoboric acid
2826.9000 90	其他氟硅酸盐、氟铝酸盐(包括氟络盐)	5.5				30	17	13	千克		Other fluorosilicates, fluoroaluminates (Include fluorine complex salt)
28.27	**氯化物、氯氧化物及氢氧基氯化物;溴化物及溴氧化物;碘化物及碘氧化物:**										**Chlorides, chloride oxides and chloride hydroxides; bromides and bromide oxides; iodides and iodide oxides:**
	-氯化铵:										-Ammonium chloride:
2827.1010	---肥料用	4			0	11	17	11	千克	G	---For use as fertilizer
2827.1090	---其他	5.5	5		0	30	17	13	千克	G	---Other
2827.2000	-氯化钙	5.5	5		0	50	17	13	千克		-Calcium chloride
	-其他氯化物:										-Other chlorides:
2827.3100	--氯化镁	5.5	5		0	30	17	13	千克		--Of magnesium
2827.3200	--氯化铝	5.5	5		0	30	17	13	千克		--Of aluminium
2827.3500	--氯化镍	5.5	5		0	30	17	13	千克		--Of nickel
	--其他:										--Other:
2827.3910	---氯化锂	5.5	5	4.4	4.4	30	17	13	千克		---Lithium chloride
2827.3920	---氯化钡	5.5	5	4.4	4.4	30	17	13	千克		---Barium chloride
2827.3990	---其他	5.5	5	4.4	4.4	30	17		千克		---Other
	-氯氧化物及氢氧基氯化物:										-Chloride oxides and chloride hydroxides:
2827.4100	--铜的氯氧化物及氢氧基氯化物	5.5	5		4.4	30	17	13	千克		--Chloride oxides and hydroxides of copper
2827.4900	--其他	5.5	5		0	30	17		千克		--Other
	-溴化物及溴氧化物:										-Bromides and bromide oxides:
2827.5100	--溴化钠及溴化钾	5.5	5		0	30	17	13	千克		--Bromides of sodium or of potassium
2827.5900	--其他	5.5	5		0	30	17		千克		--Other
2827.6000	-碘化物及碘氧化物	5.5	5		4.4	30	17		千克		-Iodides and iodide oxides
28.28	**次氯酸盐;商品次氯酸钙;亚氯酸盐;次溴酸盐:**										**Hypochlorites; commercial calcium hypochlorite; chlorites; hypobromites:**
2828.1000	-商品次氯酸钙及其他钙的次氯酸盐	12	8	8.4	7.2	80	17	13	千克		-Commercial calcium hypochlorite and other calcium hypochlorites
2828.9000	-其他	5.5	T3		0	30	17	13	千克		-Other
28.29	**氯酸盐及高氯酸盐;溴酸盐及过溴酸盐;碘酸盐及高碘酸盐:**										**Chlorates and perchlorates; bromates and perbromates; iodates and periodates:**
	-氯酸盐:										-Chlorates:
2829.1100	--氯酸钠	12	8		7.2	30	17	13	千克		--Of sodium
	--其他:										--Other:
2829.1910	---氯酸钾(洋硝)	5.5	5		0	20	17	13	千克	9	---Potassium chlorate
2829.1990	---其他	5.5	5		0	30	17	13	千克		---Other
2829.9000	-其他	5.5	5		4.4	30	17	13	千克		-Other

税则号列 Tariff Item.	货品名称	最惠国(%) MFN	协定(%) CT 东盟 CA	中巴 CP	中智 CC	普通 Gen	增值税率 VAT	出口退税 ED	计量单位 Unit	监管条件 SC	Article Description
2829.9000 10	颗粒＜500μm 的球形高氯酸铵	5.5				30	17	13	千克	3	Ammonium perchlorate, spheroids. Granularity ＜500μm
2829.9000 90	其他高氯酸盐、溴酸盐等(包括过溴酸盐、碘酸盐及高碘酸盐)	5.5				30	17	13	千克		Other perchlorates; bromates and perbromates; iodates and periodates (Including the bromate iodote and height, iodic acid stops)
28.30	**硫化物;多硫化物,不论是否已有化学定义:**										**Sulphides; polysulphides, whether or not chemically defined:**
	-钠的硫化物:										-Sodium sulphides:
2830.1010	---硫化钠	5.5	5		4.4	40	17	13	千克	3	---Sodium sulphide
2830.1090	---其他	5.5	5		4.4	30	17	13	千克		---Other
	-其他										-Other
2830.9020	---硫化锑	5.5	5		0	45	17	13	千克	B	---Antimony sulphide
2830.9030	---硫化钴	5.5	5		0	30	17	13	千克		---Cobalt sulphide
2830.9090	---其他	5.5	5		0	30	17	13	千克		---Other
28.31	**连二亚硫酸盐及次硫酸盐:**										**Dithionites and sulphoxylates:**
	-钠的连二亚硫酸盐及次硫酸盐:										-Dithionites of sodium and sulphoxylates of sodium:
2831.1010	---钠的连二亚硫酸盐	5.5	5		0	30	17		千克		---Dithionites
2831.1020	---钠的次硫酸盐	5.5	5		0	30	17	13	千克		---Sulphoxylates
2831.9000	-其他	5.5	5		0	30	17	13	千克		-Other
28.32	**亚硫酸盐;硫代硫酸盐:**										**Sulphites; thiosulphates:**
2832.1000	-钠的亚硫酸盐	5.5	5		4.4	30	17	13	千克		-Sodium sulphites
2832.2000	-其他亚硫酸盐	5.5	5		0	30	17	13	千克		-Other sulphites
2832.3000	-硫代硫酸盐	5.5	5		0	30	17	13	千克		-Thiosulphates
28.33	**硫酸盐;矾;过硫酸盐:**										**Sulphates; alums; peroxosulphates (persulphates):**
	-钠的硫酸盐:										-Sodium sulphates:
2833.1100	--硫酸钠	5.5	5		4.4	40	17		千克	a	--Disodium sulphate
2833.1900	--其他	5.5	5		0	30	17	13	千克	a	--Other
	-其他硫酸盐:										-Other sulphates:
2833.2100	--硫酸镁	5.5	5		4.4	30	17	13	千克		--Of magnesium
2833.2200	--硫酸铝	5.5	T3		4.4	30	17	13	千克		--Of aluminium
2833.2400	--镍的硫酸盐	5.5	5		0	30	17	13	千克		--Of nickel
2833.2500	--铜的硫酸盐	5.5	5		4.4	30	17	13	千克	S	--Of copper
2833.2700	--硫酸钡	5.5	5		0	30	17	13	千克	G	--Of barium
	--其他:										--Other:
2833.2910	---硫酸亚铁	5.5	5		0	45	17	13	千克		---Ferrous sulphate
2833.2920	---铬的硫酸盐	5.5	5		0	30	17	13	千克		---Of chromium
2833.2930	---硫酸锌	5.5	5		0	30	17	13	千克		---Of zinc
2833.2990	---其他	5.5	5		0	30	17		千克		---Other
	-矾:										-Alums:
2833.3010	---钾铝矾	5.5	5		0	45	17	13	千克		---Potassium aluminum sulfate
2833.3090	---其他	5.5	5		0	30	17	13	千克		---Other
2833.4000	-过硫酸盐	5.5	5		0	30	17	13	千克		-Peroxosulphates (persulphates)
28.34	**亚硝酸盐;硝酸盐:**										**Nitrites; nitrates:**
2834.1000	-亚硝酸盐	5.5	5		0	30	17	13	千克		-Nitrites
	-硝酸盐:										-Nitrates:
	--硝酸钾:										--Of potassium:

税则号列 Tariff Item.	货品名称	最惠国(%) MFN	协定(%)CT 东盟 CA	中巴 CP	中智 CC	普通 Gen	增值税率 VAT	出口退税 ED	计量单位 Unit	监管条件 SC	Article Description
2834.2110	---肥料用	4			3.2	11	17	11	千克	7	---For use as fertilizer
2834.2190	---其他	5.5	5		4.4	30	17	13	千克		---Other
	--其他：										--Other：
2834.2910	---硝酸钴	5.5	5		0	30	17	13	千克		---Of cobalt
2834.2990	---其他	5.5	5		0	30	17	13	千克		---Other
28.35	**次磷酸盐、亚磷酸盐及磷酸盐；多磷酸盐，不论是否已有化学定义：**										**Phosphinates (hypophosphites), phosphonates (phosphites) and phosphates; polyphosphates, whether or not chemically defined:**
2835.1000	-次磷酸盐及亚磷酸盐	5.5	5		0	20	17	13	千克		-Phosphinates (hypophosphites) and phosphonates (phosphites)
	-磷酸盐：										-Phosphates：
2835.2200	--磷酸一钠及磷酸二钠	5.5	5		0	20	17	13	千克		--Of mono- or disodium
2835.2400	--钾的磷酸盐	5.5	5		0	20	17	13	千克		--Of potassium
2835.2500	--正磷酸氢钙(磷酸二钙)	5.5	5		0	20	17	13	千克		--Calcium hydrogenorthophosphate ("dicalcium phosphate")
2835.2600	--其他磷酸钙	5.5	5		0	20	17	13	千克		--Other phosphates of calcium
	--其他：										--Other：
2835.2910	---磷酸三钠	5.5	5		0	20	17	13	千克		---Of trisodium
2835.2990	---其他	5.5	5		0	20	17	13	千克	A	---Other
	-多磷酸盐：										-Polyphosphates：
2835.3100	--三磷酸钠(三聚磷酸钠)	5.5	T3		0	20	17	13	千克	a	--Sodium triphosphate (sodium tripolyphosphate)
2835.3900	--其他	5.5	T3		0	20	17	13	千克		--Other
28.36	**碳酸盐；过碳酸盐；含氨基甲酸铵的商品碳酸铵：**										**Carbonates; peroxocarbonates (percar-bonates); commercial ammonium carbonate containing ammonium carbamate:**
2836.2000	-碳酸钠(纯碱)	5.5	5		0	35	17	13	千克	ABG	-Disodium carbonate
2836.3000	-碳酸氢钠(小苏打)	5.5	5		0	45	17	13	千克	G	-Sodium hydrogencarbonate (sodium bicarbonate)
2836.4000	-钾的碳酸盐	5.5	5		0	30	17	13	千克		-Potassium carbonates
2836.5000	-碳酸钙	5.5	5		0	45	17	13	千克		-Calcium carbonate
2836.6000	-碳酸钡	5.5	5		0	40	17	13	千克		-Barium carbonate
	-其他：										-Other：
2836.9100	--锂的碳酸盐	5.5	5		4.4	30	17	13	千克		--Lithium carbonates
2836.9200	--锶的碳酸盐	5.5	5		0	30	17	13	千克		--Strontium carbonate
	--其他：										--Other：
2836.9910	---碳酸镁	5.5	5		4.4	45	17	13	千克		---Magnesium carbonate
2836.9930	---碳酸钴	5.5	5		4.4	30	17	13	千克		---Cobalt carbonate
2836.9940	---商品碳酸铵及其他铵的碳酸盐	5.5	5		0	30	17	13	千克		---Commericial ammonium carbonate and other ammonium corbonates
2836.9990	---其他	5.5	5		0	30	17	13	千克		---Other
28.37	**氰化物、氧氰化物及氰络合物：**										**Cyanides, cyanide oxides and complex cyanides:**
	-氰化物及氧氰化物：										-Cyanides and cyanide oxides：
	--氰化钠及氧氰化钠：										--Of sodium：
2837.1110	---氰化钠	5.5	5		4.4	20	17	13	千克	X23	---Sodium cyanide
2837.1120	---氧氰化钠	5.5	5	5	4.4	30	17	13	千克		---Sodium cyanide oxide

税则号列 Tariff Item.	货品名称	最惠国(%) MFN	协定(%)CT 东盟 CA	中巴 CP	中智 CC	普通 Gen	增值税率 VAT	出口退税 ED	计量单位 Unit	监管条件 SC	Article Description
	--其他:										--Other:
2837.1910	---氰化钾	5.5	5		0	20	17	13	千克	23X	---Potassium cyanide
2837.1990	---其他	5.5	5		0	30	17	13	千克		---Other
2837.1990 11	氰化锌,氰化亚铜、氰化铜(氰化高铜)	5.5				30	17	13	千克	X	Cyanide zinc ,Cuprouscyanide,Copper dicyanide (cupric cyanide)
2837.1990 12	氰化镍、氰化钙(氰化亚镍)	5.5				30	17	13	千克	X	Nickel chloride, calcium cyanide (Nickel)
2837.1990 13	氰化钡、氰化镉、氰化铅	5.5				30	17	13	千克	X	Barium cyanide ,Cadmium cyanide , lead cyanide
2837.1990 14	氰化钴[氰化钴(Ⅱ)\氰化钴(Ⅲ)]	5.5				30	17	13	千克	X	Cobalt cyanide [Cobalt cyanide (Co(CN)3) , Cobalt cyanide (Co(CN)2)]
2837.1990 90	其他氰化物及氧氰化物	5.5				30	17	13	千克		Other cyanides and cyanide oxides
2837.2000	-氰络合物	5.5	5		0	30	17	13	千克		-Complex cyanides
2837.2000 11	氰化镍钾,氰化钠铜锌(氰化钾镍,镍氰化钾,铜盐)	5.5				30	17	13	千克	X	Nickelate, Sodium copper-zinc cyanide (Nickelate,dipotassiu,cupric acetate)
2837.2000 12	氰化亚铜(三)钠,氰化亚铜(三)钾(紫铜盐,紫铜矾,氰化铜钠,氰化亚铜钾,亚铜氰化钾)	5.5				30	17	13	千克	X	Sodium Cuprous cyanide,potassium cuprous cyanide
2837.2000 90	其他氰络合物	5.5				30	17	13	千克		Other complex cyanide
28.39	**硅酸盐;商品碱金属硅酸盐:**										**Silicates; commercial alkali metal silicates:**
	-钠盐:										-Of sodium:
2839.1100	--偏硅酸钠	5.5	T3		0	40	17	13	千克		--Sodium metasilicates
2839.1900	--其他	5.5	T3		0	30	17	13	千克		--Other
2839.9000	-其他	5.5	5		0	30	17	13	千克		-Other
2839.9000 10	硅酸铅	5.5				30	17	13	千克	X	lead metasilicate
2839.9000 90	其他硅酸盐;商品碱金属硅酸盐	5.5				30	17	13	千克		other silicate,commodity alkali silicate
28.40	**硼酸盐及过硼酸盐:**										**Borates; peroxoborates (perborates):**
	-四硼酸钠(精炼硼砂):										-Disodium tetraborate (refined borax):
2840.1100	--无水四硼酸钠	5.5	5		0	20	17	13	千克		--Anhydrous
2840.1900	--其他	5.5	5		4.4	20	17	13	千克		--Other
2840.2000	-其他硼酸盐	5.5	5		0	30	17	13	千克		-Other borates
2840.3000	-过硼酸盐	5.5	5		0	30	17	13	千克		-Peroxoborates (perborates)
28.41	**金属酸盐及过金属酸盐:**										**Salts of oxometallic or peroxometallic acids:**
2841.3000	-重铬酸钠	5.5	5		0	20	17	5	千克		-Sodium dichromate
2841.5000	-其他铬酸盐及重铬酸盐;过铬酸盐	5.5	5		0	30	17	5	千克		-Other chromates and dichromates; peroxochromates
	-亚锰酸盐、锰酸盐及高锰酸盐:										-Manganites, manganates and permanganates:
2841.6100	--高锰酸钾	5.5	5		0	30	17	5	千克	23	--Potassium permanganate
2841.6900	--其他	5.5	5		0	30	17	5	千克		--Other
	-钼酸盐:										-Molybdates:
2841.7010	---钼酸铵	5.5	5		4.4	30	17	5	千克		---Ammonium molybdates
2841.7090	---其他	5.5	5		4.4	30	17	5	千克		---Other
	-钨酸盐:										-Tungstates (wolframates):
2841.8010	---仲钨酸铵	5.5	5		0	30	17		千克	4xBy	---Ammonium paratungstate
2841.8020	---钨酸钠	5.5	5		0	30	17	5	千克	4xBy	---Sodium tungstate

税则号列 Tariff Item.	货品名称	最惠国(%) MFN	协定(%) 东盟 CA	中巴 CP	CT 中智 CC	普通 Gen	增值税率 VAT	出口退税 ED	计量单位 Unit	监管条件 SC	Article Description
2841.8030	---钨酸钙	5.5	5		0	30	17	5	千克	4xy	---Calcium wolframate
2841.8040	---偏钨酸铵	5.5	5		0	30	17	5	千克	4xy	---Ammonium metatungstate
2841.8090	---其他	5.5	5		0	30	17	13	千克		---Other
2841.9000	-其他	5.5	5		0	30	17	13	千克		-Other
2841.9000 01	钴酸锂	5.5				30	17	13	千克		Lithium cobaltate
2841.9000 90	其他金属酸盐及过金属酸盐	5.5				30	17	5	千克		Other salts of oxometallic or peroxometallic acids
28.42	**其他无机酸盐及过氧酸盐(包括不论是否已有化学定义的硅铝酸盐),但迭氮化物除外:**										**Other salts of inorganic acids or peroxoacids (including aluminosilicates whether or not chemically defined), other than azides:**
2842.1000	-硅酸复盐及硅酸络盐,包括不论是否已有化学定义的硅铝酸盐	5.5	5		0	30	17	13	千克		-Double or complex silicates, including aluminosilicates whether or not chemically defined
	-其他:										-Other:
2842.9010	---雷酸盐、氰酸盐及硫氰酸盐	5.5	5		0	30	17	13	千克		---Fulminates, cyanates and thiocyanates
2842.9090	---其他	5.5	5		0	30	17	13	千克		---Other
2842.9090 13	亚砷酸钠,亚砷酸钾,亚砷酸钙(偏亚砷酸钠)	5.5				30	17	13	千克	X	Sodium Arsenice Potassium arsonate, Tricalcium diarsenite
2842.9090 14	亚砷酸锶,亚砷酸钡,亚砷酸铁	5.5				30	17	13	千克	X	Stry chnine, Barium arsenite, Arsenous acid
2842.9090 15	亚砷酸铜,亚砷酸锌,亚砷酸铅(亚砷酸氢铜)	5.5				30	17	13	千克	X	Copper arsonate, Arsenen ous acrd, lead arsenite
2842.9090 16	亚砷酸锑,砷酸铵,砷酸氢二铵	5.5				30	17	13	千克	X	Antinony Arsenite, Ammonium Arsenatec (Ammonium Arsenate)
2842.9090 17	砷酸钠,砷酸氢二钠,砷酸二氢钠(砷酸三钠)	5.5				30	17	13	千克	X	Sodium Arsenate Sodium Arsenace Dibasic, Sodium Arsenate Monobasic
2842.9090 18	砷酸钾,砷酸二氢钾,砷酸镁	5.5				30	17	13	千克	X	Potassium Dihy drogen Arsenate Magnesium Arsenate
2842.9090 19	砷酸钙,砷酸钡,砷酸铁(砷酸三钙)	5.5				30	17	13	千克	X	Calcium Arsenate Barium Arsenate Ferric Arsenate
2842.9090 21	砷酸亚铁,砷酸铜,砷酸锌	5.5				30	17	13	千克	X	Ferrous Arsenate, Cupric Arsenate zinc Arseate Lead Arsenite, Antirnony Arsenate Lead Selenicd Cadmium Selenide, cds.
2842.9090 22	砷酸铅,砷酸锑,偏砷酸钠	5.5				30	17	13	千克	X	Other sdts of oxometallic or pertallic acids.
2842.9090 23	硒化铅,硒化镉,碲化镉	5.5				30	17	13	千克	X	Lead selenide, Cadmium selenide, Cadmium telluride
2842.9090 90	其他无机酸盐及过氧酸盐(迭氮化物除外)	5.5				30	17	13	千克		Other salts of inorganic acids or peroxoacids
	第六分章 杂项产品										Ⅵ. -MISCELLANEOUS
28.43	**胶态贵金属;贵金属的无机或有机化合物,不论是否已有化学定义;贵金属汞齐:**										**Colloidal precious metals; inorganic or organic compounds of precious metals, whether or not chemically defined; amalgams of precious metals:**
2843.1000	-胶态贵金属	5.5	5		0	30	17		克		-Colloidal precious metals
	-银化合物:										-Silver compounds:
2843.2100	--硝酸银	5.5	5		0	30	17	13	克		--Silver nitrate
2843.2900	--其他	5.5	5		0	30	17	13	克		--Other

税则号列 Tariff Item.	货品名称	最惠国(%) MFN	协定(%) CT 东盟 CA	中巴 CP	中智 CC	普通 Gen	增值税率 VAT	出口退税 ED	计量单位 Unit	监管条件 SC	Article Description
2843.2900 10	氰化银,氰化银钾,亚砷酸银(银氰化钾,砷酸银)	5.5				30	17	13	克	X	Potassium silver cyanide、Trisiher arsenite
2843.2900 90	其他银化合物(不论是否已有化学定义)	5.5				30	17	13	克		Other silver compounds (whether or not chemically defined)
2843.3000	-金化合物	5.5	5		0	30	17		克		-Gold compounds
2843.3000 10	氰化金,氰化金钾(含金40%)等[包括氰化亚金(I)钾(含金68.3%),氰化亚金(Ⅲ)钾(含金57%)]	5.5				30	17		克	X	Aurum cyanide, aurous potassium cyanide including dipotassium hexacyanoaurate
2843.3000 90	其他金化合物(不论是否已有化学定义)	5.5				30	17		克	J	Other gold compounds (whether or not chemically defined)
2843.9000	-其他贵金属化合物;贵金属汞齐	5.5	5		4.4	30	17	13	克		-Other compounds; amalgams
2843.9000 10	氯化钯	5.5				30	17	13	克	G	Palladium chloride
2843.9000 20	氯化铂	5.5				30	17		克		Platinum chloride
2843.9000 30	其他铂化合物	5.5				30	17		克		Other platinum compounds
2843.9000 90	其他贵金属化合物,贵金属汞齐(不论是否已有化学定义)	5.5				30	17		克		Other precious metal compounds or precious amalgam (whether chemical definition exists or not)
28.44	**放射性化学元素及放射性同位素(包括可裂变或可转换的化学元素及同位素)及其化合物;含上述产品的混合物及残渣:**										**Radioactive chemical elements and radioactive isotopes (including the fissile or fertile chemical elements and isotopes) and their compounds; mixtures and residues containing these products:**
2844.1000	-天然铀及其化合物;含天然铀或天然铀化合物的合金、分散体(包括金属陶瓷)、陶瓷产品及混合物	5.5	5		0	30	17	13	克/百万贝可	23	-Natural uranium and its compounds; alloys, dispersions (including cermets), ceramic products and mixtures containing natural uranium or natural uranium compouds
2844.2000	-U_{235}浓缩铀及其化合物;钚及其化合物;含U_{235}浓缩铀、钚或它们的化合物的合金、分散体(包括金属陶瓷)、陶瓷产品及混合物	5.5	5		0	30	17	13	克/百万贝可	23	-Uranium enriched in U_{235} and its compounds; plutonium and its compounds; alloys dispersion (including cermets), ceramic products and mixtures containing uranium enriched in U_{235}, plutonium or compounds of these products
2844.3000	-U_{235}贫化铀及其化合物;钍及其化合物;含U_{235}贫化铀、钍或它们的化合物的合金、分散体(包括金属陶瓷)、陶瓷产品及混合物	5.5	5		0	30	17	13	克/百万贝可	23	-Uranium depleted in U_{235} and its compounds; thorium and its compounds; alloys, dispersions (including cermets), ceramic products and mixtures containing uranium depleted in U_{235}, thorium or compounds of these products
	-除子目2844.10、2844.20及2844.30以外的放射性元素、同位素及其化合物;含这些元素、同位素及其化合物的合金、分散体(包括金属陶瓷)、陶瓷产品及混合物:										-Radioactive elements and isotopes and compounds other than those of subheading No. 2844.10, 2844.20 or 2844.30; alloys, dispersions (including cermets), ceramic products and mixtures containing these elements, isotopes or compounds; radioactive residues:

税则号列 Tariff Item.	货品名称	最惠国(%) MFN	协定(%)CT 东盟 CA	中巴 CP	中智 CC	普通 Gen	增值税率 VAT	出口退税 ED	计量单位 Unit	监管条件 SC	Article Description
2844.4010	---镭及镭盐	4			0	14	17	13	克/百万贝可		---Radium and its salts
2844.4010 10	镭-226 及其化合物	4				14	17	13	克/百万贝可	23	Radium-226 and its compounds
2844.4010 90	其他镭及镭盐	4				14	17	13	克/百万贝可	2	Other radium and its salts
2844.4020	---钴及钴盐	4			0	14	17	13	克/百万贝可	2	---Cobalt and its salts
2844.4090	---其他	5.5	5		0	30	17	13	克/百万贝可		---Other
2844.4090 10	铀-233 及其化合物(包括呈金属、合金、化合物或浓缩物形态的各种材料)	5.5				30	17	13	克/百万贝可	23	Uranium-233 and its compounds (including metallic material, alloys, compounds or enriched materials)
2844.4090 90	其他放射性元素同位素及其化合物(编号 284410, 284420, 284430 以外的放射性元素、同位素)	5.5				30	17	13	克/百万贝可	2	Other radioactive elements and isotopes and compounds (radioactive elements and isotopes other than those of subheading No. 284410, 284420 or 284430)
2844.5000	-核反应堆已耗尽(已辐照)的燃料元件(释热元件)	5.5	5		0	30	17	13	克		-Spent (irradiated) fuel elements (cartridges) of nuclear reactors
28.45	**税目 28.44 以外的同位素;这些同位素的无机或有机化合物,不论是否已有化学定义:**										**Isotopes other than those of heading No. 28.44; compounds, inorganic or organic, of such isotopes, whether or not chemically defined:**
2845.1000	-重水(氧化氘)	5.5	5		0	30	17	13	克	3	-Heavy water (deuterium oxide)
2845.9000	-其他	5.5	5		0	30	17	13	克		-Other
2845.9000 10	除重水外的氘及氘化物	5.5				30	17	13	克	3	Deuterium and deuterides, other than heavy water
2845.9000 20	硼-10 同位素及其化合物、混合物(硼-10 同位素占硼总量 > 20% 的硼及其化合物、混合物)	5.5				30	17	13	克	3	Boron-10 and its compounds (boron and its compounds and mixtures with a containing of boron-10 > 20% of the total boron content)
2845.9000 30	富集锂-6 同位素及其化合物混合物[富集锂-6 同位素指锂-6 同位素富集度 > 7.5%(按原子数计)]	5.5				30	17	13	克	3	Lithium enriched in lithium-6 and its compounds and mixtures (lithium enriched in lithium-6 refers to enrichment of lithium-6 isotope > 7.5% (atomicity))
2845.9000 90	其他同位素及其他化合物(编号 2844 以外的同位素)	5.5				30	17	13	克		Other isotopes and other compounds (other than those of heading No. 28.44)
28.46	**稀土金属、钇、钪及其混合物的无机或有机化合物:**										**Compounds, inorganic or organic, of rare-earth metals, of yttrium or of scandium or of mixtures of these metals:**
	-铈的化合物:										-Ceric compounds:
2846.1010	---氧化铈	5.5	5	3.9	0	30	17		千克	4xBy	---Cerium oxide
2846.1020	---氢氧化铈	5.5	5	3.9	0	30	17		千克	4xy	---Cerium hydroxide
2846.1030	---碳酸铈	5.5	5	3.9	0	30	17		千克	4xy	---Cerium carbonate
2846.1090	---其他	5.5	5	3.9	0	30	17		千克		---Other
2846.1090 10	氰化铈	5.5				30	17		千克	4Xxy	cerium cyanide

税则号列 Tariff Item.	货品名称	最惠国(%) MFN	协定(%) CT 东盟 CA	中巴 CP	中智 CC	普通 Gen	增值税率 VAT	出口退税 ED	计量单位 Unit	监管条件 SC	Article Description
2846.1090 90	铈的其他化合物	5.5				30	17		千克	4xy	bother compounds with cerium
	-其他:										-Other:
	---氧化稀土(氧化铈除外):										---Rare-earth oxides (other than cerium oxide):
2846.9011	----氧化钇	5.5	5		0	30	17		千克	4xBy	----Yttrium oxide
2846.9012	----氧化镧	5.5	5		0	30	17		千克	4xBy	----Lanthanum oxide
2846.9013	----氧化钕	5.5	5		0	30	17		千克	4xBy	----Neodymium oxide
2846.9014	----氧化铕	5.5	5		0	30	17		千克	4xBy	----Europium oxide
2846.9015	----氧化镝	5.5	5		0	30	17		千克	4Bxy	----Dyxprosium oxide
2846.9016	--氧化铽	5.5	5		0	30	17		千克	4Bxy	--Terbium Dxide
2846.9019	----其他	5.5	5		0	30	17		千克		----Other
2846.9019 20	氧化铒	5.5				30	17		千克	4Bxy	Erbium oxide
2846.9019 30	氧化钆	5.5				30	17		千克	4Bxy	Gadolinium oxide
2846.9019 40	氧化钐	5.5				30	17		千克	4Bxy	Samarium oxide
2846.9019 50	氧化镨	5.5				30	17		千克	4Bxy	Praseodymium oxide
2846.9019 70	氧化镱	5.5				30	17		千克	4Bxy	Ytterbium oxide
2846.9019 80	氧化钪	5.5				30	17		千克	4Bxy	Scandium oxide
2846.9019 90	其他氧化稀土(氧化铈除外)	5.5				30	17		千克	4Bxy	Other rare-earth oxides (other than cerium oxide)
	---氯化稀土:										---Rare-earth chlorides:
2846.9028	----混合氯化稀土	5.5	5		0	30	17		千克	4xBy	----Mixture of rare-earth chlorides
2846.9029	----其他	5.5	5		0	30	17		千克	4xBy	----Other
2846.9030	---氟化稀土	5.5	5		0	30	17		千克	4xy	---Rare-earth fluorides
	---碳酸稀土:										---Rare-earth carbonate:
2846.9048	----混合碳酸稀土	5.5	5		0	30	17		千克	4xy	----Mixture of rare earth carbonate
2846.9049	----其他	5.5	5		0	30	17		千克	4xy	----Other
2846.9090	---其他	5.5	5		0	30	17		千克	4xy	---Other
28.47	**过氧化氢,不论是否用尿素固化:**										**Hydrogen peroxide, whether or not solidified with urea:**
2847.0000	过氧化氢,不论是否用尿素固化	5.5	5		0	30	17	13	千克		Hydrogen peroxide, whether or not solidified with urea
28.48	**磷化物,不论是否已有化学定义,但不包括磷铁:**										**Phosphides, whether or not chemically defined, excluding ferrophosphorus:**
2848.0000	磷化物(不论是否已有化学定义,但不包括磷铁)	5.5	5		4.4	20	17	13	千克		Phosphides, whether or not chemically defined, excluding ferrophophorus
2848.0000 10	磷化铝,磷化锌	5.5				20	17	13	千克	S	aluminum phosphide, zinc phosphide
2848.0000 90	其他磷化物(不论是否已有化学定义,但不包括磷铁)	5.5				20	17	13	千克		Other phosphides, whether or not chemically defined, excluding ferrophosphorus
28.49	**碳化物,不论是否已有化学定义:**										**Carbides, whether or not chemically defined:**
2849.1000	-碳化钙	5.5	T3		0	45	17		千克		-Of calcium
2849.2000	-碳化硅	5.5	5		0	30	17		千克	yB4x	-Of silicon
	-其他:										-Other:
2849.9010	---碳化硼	5.5	5		0	30	17	5	千克		---Of boron
2849.9020	---碳化钨	5.5	5		0	30	17		千克	B4xy	---Of tungsten
2849.9090	---其他	5.5	5		0	30	17	5	千克	B	---Other

税则号列 Tariff Item.	货 品 名 称	最惠国(%) MFN	协定(%)CT 东盟 CA	中巴 CP	中智 CC	普通 Gen	增值税率 VAT	出口退税 ED	计量单位 Unit	监管条件 SC	Article Description
28.50	**氢化物、氮化物、叠氮化物、硅化物及硼化物,不论是否已有化学定义,但可归入税目28.49的碳化物除外:**										**Hydrides, nitrides, azides, silicides and borides, whether or not chemically defined, other than compounds which are also carbides of heading No. 28.49:**
2850.0000	氢化物、氮化物、叠氮化物、硅化物及硼化物,不论是否已有化学定义,但可归入税目28.49的碳化物除外	5.5	5	3.9	0	30	17	13	千克		Hydrides, nitrides, azides, silicides and borides, whether or not chemically defined, other than compounds which are also carbides of heading No. 28.49
2850.0000 10	砷化氢(砷烷,砷化三氢,胂)	5.5				30	17	13	千克	X	AsH3(Arsenic hydride, Arsine AsH3 , Arsenic)
2850.0000 90	其他氢化物、氮化物、硅化物等(包括迭氮化物,硼化物,可归入编号2849的碳化物除外)	5.5				30	17	13	千克		Other hydrides, nitrides, azides, silicides and borides, other than compounds which are also carbides of heading No. 28.49
28.52	**汞的无机或有机化合物,汞齐除外:**										**Organic and inorganic compounds of mercury other than amalgams**
2852.0000	汞的有机或无机化合物,汞齐除外	5.5	5		0	30	17		千克	X	Inorganic and organic compounds of mercury, except amalgam
28.53	**其他无机化合物(包括蒸馏水、导电水及类似的纯净水);液态空气(不论是否除去稀有气体);压缩空气;汞齐,但贵金属汞齐除外:**										**Other inorganic compounds (including distilled or conductivity water and water of similar purity); liquid air (whether or not rare gases have been removed); compressed air; amalgams, other than amalgams of precious metals:**
2853.0010	---饮用蒸馏水	5.5	5		4.4	70	17		千克	AB	---Distilled water for human consumption
2853.0020	---氯化氰	5.5	5		4.4	30	17		千克	23	---Chlorocyanogen, cyanogen chloride
2853.0090	---其他	5.5	5		4.4	30	17		千克		---Other
2853.0090 10	饮用纯净水	5.5				30	17		千克	AB	Purified water for human consumption
2853.0090 20	氰,氰化碘,氰化溴等(包括铅汞齐氰气、碘化氰、溴化氰)	5.5				30	17		千克	X	Mercury Arsenide, Cyanogen, Cyanogen iodide , bromine cyanide (including Cyanogen Dicyanogen , iodine cyanide ,Bromine Cyanide)
2853.0090 30	单氰胺	5.5				30	17	13	千克	S	monocyanamide
2853.0090 90	其他无机化合物、压缩空气等[包括导电水、液态空气、汞齐等(贵金属汞齐除外)]	5.5				30	17		千克		Other inorganic compounds, compressed air, including conductivity water, liquid air, amalgams, other than amalgams of precious metals

第二十九章
有机化学品

注释：

一、除条文另有规定的以外，本章各税目只适用于：

（一）单独的已有化学定义的有机化合物，不论是否含有杂质；

（二）同一有机化合物的两种或两种以上异构体的混合物（不论是否含有杂质），但无环烃异构体的混合物（立体异构体除外），不论是否饱和，应归入第二十七章；

（三）税目29.36至29.39的产品，税目29.40的糖醚、糖缩醛、糖酯及其盐类和税目29.41的产品，不论是否已有化学定义；

（四）上述（一）、（二）、（三）款产品的水溶液；

（五）溶于其他溶剂的上述（一）、（二）、（三）款的产品，但该产品处于溶液状态只是为了安全或运输所采取的正常必要方法，其所用溶剂并不使该产品改变其一般用途而适合于某些特殊用途；

（六）为了保存或运输的需要，加入稳定剂（包括抗结块剂）的上述（一）、（二）、（三）、（四）、（五）各款产品；

（七）为了便于识别或安全起见，加入抗尘剂、着色剂或气味剂的上述（一）、（二）、（三）、（四）、（五）、（六）各款产品，但所加剂料并不使原产品改变其一般用途而适合于某些特殊用途；

（八）为生产偶氮染料而稀释至标准浓度的下列产品：重氮盐，用于重氮盐、可重氮化的胺及其盐类的偶合剂。

二、本章不包括：

（一）税目15.04的货品及税目15.20的粗甘油；

（二）乙醇（税目22.07或22.08）；

（三）甲烷及丙烷（税目27.11）；

（四）第二十八章注释二所述的碳化合物；

（五）尿素（税目31.02或31.05）；

（六）植物性或动物性着色料（税目32.03）、合成有机着色料、用作萤光增白剂或发光体的合成有机产品（税目32.04）及零售包装的染料或其他着色料（税目32.12）；

（七）酶（税目35.07）；

Chapter 29
Organic chemicals

Notes:

1. Except where the context otherwise requires, the headings of this Chapter apply only to:

(a) Separate chemically defined organic compounds, whether or not containing impurities;

(b) Mixtures of two or more isomers of the same organic compound (whether ornot containing impurities), except mixtures of acyclic hydrocarbon isomers (other than stereoisomers), whether or not saturated (Chapter 27);

(c) The products of headings Nos. 29.36 to 29.39 or the sugar ethers, sugar acetals and sugar esters, and their salts, of heading No. 29.40, or the products of heading No. 29.41, whether or not chemically defined;

(d) The products mentioned in (a), (b) or (c) above dissolved in water;

(e) The products mentioned in (a), (b) or (c) above dissolved in other slovents provided that the solution constitutes a normal and necessary method of putting up these products adopted solely for reasons of safety or for transport and that the solvent does not render the product particularly suitable for specific use rather than for general use;

(f) The products mentioned in (a), (b), (c), (d) or (e) above with an added stabilizer (including an anti-caking agent) necessary for their preservation or transport;

(g) The products mentioned in (a), (b), (c), (d), (e) or (f) above with an added anti-dusting agent or a colouring or odoriferous substance added to facilitate their identification or for safety reasons, provided that the additions do not render the product particularly suitable for specific use rather than for general use;

(h) The following products, diluted to standard strengths, for the production of azo dyes: diazonium salts, couplers used for these salts and diazotisable amines and their salts.

2. This Chapter does not cover:

(a) Goods of heading No. 15.04 or crude glycerol of heading No. 15.20;

(b) Ethyl alcohol (heading No. 22.07 or 22.08);

(c) Methane or propane (headng No. 27.11);

(d) The compounds of carbon mentioned in Note 2 to Chapter 28;

(e) Urea (heading No. 31.02 or 31.05);

(f) Colouring matter of vegetable or animal origin (heading No. 32.03), synthetic organic colouring matter, synthetic organic products of a kind used as fluorescent brightening agents or as luminophores (heading No. 32.04) or dyes or other colouring matter put up in forms or packings for retail sale (heading No. 32.12);

(g) Enzymes (heading No. 35.07);

（八）聚乙醛、六亚甲基四胺（乌洛托品）及类似物质，制成片、条或类似形状作为燃料用的，以及包装容器的容积不超过300立方厘米的直接灌注香烟打火机及类似打火器用的液体燃料或液化气体燃料（税目36.06）；

（九）灭火器的装配药及已装药的灭火弹（税目38.13）；零售包装的除墨剂（税目38.24）；

（十）光学元件，例如用酒石酸乙二胺制成的（税目90.01）。

三、可以归入本章两个或两个以上税目的货品，应归入有关税目中的最后一个税目。

四、税目29.04至29.06、29.08至29.11及29.13至29.20的卤化、磺化、硝化或亚硝化衍生物均包括复合衍生物，例如，卤磺化、卤硝化、磺硝化及卤磺硝化衍生物。

硝基及亚硝基不作为税目29.29的含氮基官能团。

税目29.11、29.12、29.14、29.18及29.22所称"含氧基"，仅限于税目29.05至29.20的各种含氧基（其特征为有机含氧基）。

五、（一）本章第一分章至第七分章的酸基有机化合物与这些分章的有机化合物构成的酯，应归入有关税号的最后一个税号；

（二）乙醇与本章第一分章至第七分章的酸基有机化合物所构成的酯，应按有关酸基化合物归类；

（三）除第六类注释一及第二十八章注释二另有规定的以外：

1. 第一分章至第十分章及税目29.42的有机化合物的无机盐，例如，含酸基、酚基或烯醇基的化合物及有机碱的无机盐，应归入相应的有机化合物的税目；
2. 第一分章至第十分章及税目29.42的有机化合物之间生成的盐，应按生成该盐的碱或酸（包括酚基或烯醇基化合物）归入本章有关税目中的最后一个税目；
3. 除第十一分章或税目29.41的产品外，配位化合物应按该化合物所有金属键（金属碳键除外）"断开"所形成的片段归入第二十九章有关税目中的最后一个税目。

（四）除乙醇外，金属醇化物应按相应的醇归类（税目29.05）。

(h) Metaldehyde, hexamethylenetetramine or similar substances, put up in forms (for example, tablets, sticks or similar forms) for use as fuels, or liquid or liquefied-gas fuels in containers of a kind used for filling or refilling cigarette or similar lighters and of a capacity not exceeding 300 cm^3 (heading No. 36.06);

(i) Products put up as charges for fire-extinguishers or put up in fire-extinguishing grenades, of heading No. 38.13; ink removers put up in packings for retail sale, of heading No. 38.24; or

(j) Optical elements , for example, of ethylenediamine tartrate (heading No. 90.01)

3. Goods which could be included in two or more of the headings of this Chapter are to be classified in that one of those headings which occurs last in numerical order.

4. In headings Nos. 29.04 to 29.06, 29.08 to 29.11 and 29.13 to 29.20, any reference to halogenated, sulphonated, nitrated or nitrosated derivatives includes a reference to compound derivatives, such as sulphohalogenated, nitrohalogenated, nitrosulphonated or nitrosulphohalogenated derivatives.

Nitro or nitroso groups are not to be taken as "nitrogen-functions" for the purpose of heading No. 29.29.

For the purposes of headings Nos. 29.11, 29.12, 29.14, 29.18 and 29.22, "oxygen-function" is to be restricted to the functions (the characteristic organic oxygen-containing groups) referred to in headings Nos. 29.05 to 29.20.

5. (a) The esters of acid-function organic compounds of sub-Chapters Ⅰ to Ⅶ with organic compounds of these sub-Chapters are to be classified with that compound which is classified in the heading which occurs last in numerical order in these sub-Chapters.

(b) Esters of ethyl alcohol with acid-function organic compounds of sub-Chapters Ⅰ to Ⅶ are to be classified in the same heading as the corresponding acid-function compounds.

(c) Subject to Note 1 to Section Ⅵ and Note 2 to Chapter 28:

(1) Inorganic salts of organic compounds such as acid, phenol or enol-function compounds or organic bases, of sub-Chapters Ⅰ to Ⅹ or heading No. 29.42, are to be classified in the heading appropriate to the organic compound; and

(2) Salts formed between organic compounds of sub-Chapters Ⅰ to Ⅹ or heading No. 29.42 are to be classified in the heading appropriate to the base or to the acid (including phenol or enol-function compounds) from which they are formed, whichever occurs last in numerical order in the Chapter;

(3) Except Chapter 11 or products of heading No. 29.41, matching chemicals shall be categorized into the last tax item of the related tax items in the Chapter 29 according to the division of metal bonds (excluding metal - carbon bond)

(d) Metal alcoholates are to be classified in the same heading as the corresponding alcohols except in the case of ethanol (heading No. 29.05).

（五）羧酸酰卤化物应按相应的酸归类。

六、税目29.30及29.31的化合物是指有机化合物，其分子中除含氢、氧或氮原子外，还含有与碳原子直接连接的其他非金属或金属原子（例如，硫、砷或铅）。

税目29.30（有机硫化合物）及税目29.31（其他有机－无机化合物）不包括某些磺化或卤化衍生物（含复合衍生物）。这些衍生物分子中除氢、氧、氮之外，只有具有磺化或卤化衍生物（或复合衍生物）性质的硫原子或卤素原子与碳原子直接连接。

七、税目29.32、29.33及29.34不包括三节环环氧化物、过氧化酮、醛或硫醛的环聚合物、多元羧酸酐、多元醇或酚与多元酸构成的环酯及多元酸酰亚胺。

本条规定只适用于由本条所列环化功能形成环内杂原子的化合物。

八、税目29.37所称：

（一）“激素”包括激素释放因子、激素刺激和释放因子、激素抑制剂以及激素抗体；

（二）“主要起激素作用的”，不仅适用于激素衍生物以及主要起激素作用的结构类似物，也适用于在本税目所列产品合成过程中主要用作中间体的激素衍生物以及结构类似物。

子目注释：

一、属于本章任一税目项下的一种（组）化合物的衍生物，如果该税目其他子目未明确将其包括在内，而且有关的子目中又无列名为“其他”的子目，则应与该种（组）化合物归入同一子目。

二、第二十九章注释三不适用于本章的子目。

(e) Halides of carboxylic acids are to be classified in the same heading as the corresponding acids.

6. The compounds of headings Nos. 29.30 and 29.31 are organic compounds the molecules of which contain, in addition to atoms of hydrogen, oxygen or nitrogen, atoms of other non-metals of or metals (such as sulphur, arsenic or lead) directly linked to carbon atoms.

Heading No. 29.30 (organo-sulphur compounds) and heading No. 29.31 (other organo-inorganic compounds) do not include sulphonated or halogenated derivatives (including compound derivatives) which, apart from hydrogen, oxygen and nitrogen, only have directly linked to carbon the atoms of sulphur or of a halogen which give them their nature of sulphonated or halogenated derivatives (or compound derivatives).

7. Headings Nos. 29.32, 29.33 and 29.34 do not include epoxides with a three-membered ring, ketone peroxides, cyclic polymers of aldehydes or of thioaldehydes, anhydrides of polybasic carboxylic acids, cyclic esters of polyhydric alcohols or phenols with polybasic acids, and imides of polybasic acids.

These provisions apply only when the ring-position hetero-atoms are those resulting solely form the cyclising function or functions here listed.

8. For the purposes of heading No. 29.37:

(a) the term “hormones” includes hormone-releasing or hor-mone-stimulating factors, hormone inhibitors and hormone antagonists (anti-hormones);

(b) the expression “used primarily as hormones” applies not only to hormone derivatives and structural analogues used primarily for their hormonal effect, but also to those derivatives and structural analogues used primarily as intermediates in the synthesis of products of this heading.

Subheading Note:

1. Within any one heading of this Chapter, derivatives of a chemical compound (or group of chemical compounds) are to be classified in the same subheading as that compound (or group of compounds) provided that they are not more specifically covered by any other subheading and that there is no residual subheading named “other” in the series of subheadings concerned.

2. The Note 3 of Chapter 29 does not apply to the sub－items of this chapter.

税则号列 Tariff Item.	货品名称	最惠国(%) MFN	协定(%) 东盟 CA	中巴 CP	CT 中智 CC	普通 Gen	增值税率 VAT	出口退税 ED	计量单位 Unit	监管条件 SC	Article Description
	第一分章 烃类及其卤化、磺化、硝化或亚硝化衍生物										Ⅰ.-HYDROCARBONS AND THEIR HALOGENATED, SULPHONATED, NITRATED OR NITROSATED DERIVATIVES
29.01	无环烃：										**Acyclic hydrocarbons:**
2901.1000	-饱和	2			0	30	17	13	千克		-Saturated
	-不饱和：										-Unsaturated:
2901.2100	--乙烯	2			0	20	17	13	千克		--Ethylene
2901.2200	--丙烯	2			0	20	17	13	千克		--Propene (propylene)
	--丁烯及其异构体：										--Butene (butylene) and isomers thereof:

税则号列 Tariff Item.	货品名称	最惠国(%) MFN	协定(%)CT 东盟 CA	中巴 CP	中智 CC	普通 Gen	增值税率 VAT	出口退税 ED	计量单位 Unit	监管条件 SC	Article Description
2901.2310	---1-丁烯	2			0	20	17	13	千克		---1 – butylene
2901.2320	--2-丁烯	2			0	20	17	13	千克		--2 – butylene
2901.2330	--2-甲基丙烯	2			0	20	17	13	千克		--2 – methyl propene
2901.2400	--1,3-丁二烯及异戊二烯	2			0	20	17	13	千克		--Buta-1, 3-diene and isoprene
	--其他:										--Other:
2901.2910	---异戊烯	2			0	30	17	13	千克		---Isopentene
2901.2920	---乙炔	2			0	45	17	13	千克		---Acetylene
2901.2990	---其他	2			0	30	17	13	千克		---Other
2901.2990 10	诱虫烯	2				30	17	13	千克	S	alkene
2901.2990 90	其他不饱和无环烃	2				30	17	13	千克		Other unsaturated acyclic hydrocarbon
29.02	**环烃:**										**Cyclic hydrocarbons:**
	-环烷烃、环烯及环萜烯:										-Cyclanes, cyclenes and cycloterpenes:
2902.1100	--环己烷	2			0	30	17	13	千克		--Cyclohexane
2902.1900	--其他	2			0	30	17	13	千克		--Other
2902.1900 11	1–甲基环丙烯	2				30	17	13	千克	S	1 – methyl cyclopropene
2902.1900 12	d–柠檬烯	2				30	17	13	千克	S	d – limonene
2902.1900 90	其他环烷烃、环烯及环萜稀	2				30	17	13	千克		Other cyclopropene, cycloalkene and terpene
2902.2000	-苯	2			0	20	17		千克		-Benzene
2902.3000	-甲苯	2			0	30	17	13	千克	23	-Toluene
	-二甲苯:										-Xylenes:
2902.4100	--邻二甲苯	2			0	20	17	13	千克		--*o*-Xylene
2902.4200	--间二甲苯	2			0	20	17	13	千克		--*m*-Xylene
2902.4300	--对二甲苯	2			0	20	17	13	千克		--*p*-Xylene
2902.4400	--混合二甲苯异构体	2			0	20	17	13	千克		--Mixed xylene isomers
2902.5000	-苯乙烯	2		1.4	0	30	17	13	千克		-Styrene
2902.6000	-乙苯	2			0	30	17	13	千克		-Ethylbenzene
2902.7000	-异丙基苯	2			0	30	17	13	千克		-Cumene
	-其他:										-Other:
2902.9010	---四氢萘	2			0	11	17	13	千克		---Tetrahydronaphthalene (tetralin)
2902.9020	---精萘	2			0	35	17	13	千克		---Naphthalene
2902.9030	---十二烷基苯	2			0	30	17	13	千克		---Dodecylbenzene
2902.9090	---其他	2			0	30	17	13	千克		---Other
2902.9090 10	联苯	2				30	17	13	千克	S	Biphenyl
2902.9090 90	其他芳香烃	2				30	17	13	千克		Other aromatic hydrocarbons
29.03	**烃的卤化衍生物:**										**Halogenated derivatives of hydrocarbons:**
	-无环烃的饱和氯化衍生物:										-Saturated chlorinated derivatives of acyclic hydrocarbons:
2903.1100	--一氯甲烷及氯乙烷	5.5	5		0	30	17	13	千克		--Chloromethane (methyl chloride) and chloroethane (ethyl chloride)
2903.1200	--二氯甲烷	8	5		0	30	17	13	千克		--Dichloromethane (methylene chloride)
2903.1200 01	纯度在99%及以上的二氯甲烷	8				30	17	13	千克	X	Dichloromethane (methylene chloride) (purity≥99%)
2903.1200 90	其他二氯甲烷	8				30	17	13	千克	X	Other dichloromethane (methylene chloride)
2903.1300	--三氯甲烷氯仿	10	5	9	0	30	17	13	千克	23X	--(Chloroform) trichloromethane
2903.1400	--四氯化碳	8	5		0	30	17	13	千克		--Carbon tetrachloride

税则号列 Tariff Item.	货 品 名 称	最惠国(%) MFN	协定(%)CT 东盟 CA	 中巴 CP	 中智 CC	普通 Gen	增值税率 VAT	出口退税 ED	计量单位 Unit	监管条件 SC	Article Description
2903.1400 10	非用于清洗剂的四氯化碳	8				30	17	13	千克	y4x9	Carbon tetrachloride, other than for cleaner preparation
2903.1400 90	用于清洗剂的四氯化碳	8				30	17	13	千克	89	Carbon tetrachloride, for cleaner preparation
2903.1500	--1,2-二氯乙烷(ISO)	5.5			0	30	17	13	千克	S	--1,2-Dichloroethane (ethylene dichloride) (ISO)
	--其他:										--Other:
2903.1910	---1,1,1-三氯乙烷(甲基氯仿)	8	5		0	30	17	13	千克		---1,1,1-Trichloroethane (methylchloro form)
2903.1910 10	1,1,1-三氯乙烷(甲基氯仿)(用于清洗剂的除外)	8				30	17	13	千克	y14x	1,1,1-Trichloroethane (methylchloro form) (other than for cleaner preparation)
2903.1910 90	1,1,1一三氯乙烷(甲基氯仿)(用于清洗剂的)	8				30	17	13	千克	18	1,1,1-Trichloroethane (methylchloro form) for cleaner preparation
2903.1990	---其他	5.5	5		0	30	17	13	千克		---Other
	-无环烃的不饱和氯化衍生物:										-Unsaturated chlorinated derivatives of acyclic hydrocarbons:
2903.2100	--氯乙烯	5.5	5	3.9	0	30	17	13	千克		--Vinyl chloride (chloroethylene)
2903.2200	--三氯乙烯	8	5		0	30	17	13	千克	X	--Trichloroethylene
2903.2300	--四氯乙烯(全氯乙烯)	5.5	5		0	30	17	13	千克	X	--Tetrachloroethylene (perchloroethylene)
	--其他:										--Other:
2903.2910	---3-氯-1-丙烯(氯丙烯)	5.5	5		0	30	17	13	千克		---3-Chloropropene
2903.2990	---其他	5.5	5		0	30	17	13	千克		---Other
2903.2990 10	1,1-二氯乙烯	5.5				30	17	13	千克	X	1,1-dichloroethylene
2903.2990 90	其他无环烃的不饱和氯化衍生物	5.5				30	17	13	千克		Other unsaturated chloride derivants without cycloalkanes
	-无环烃的氟化、溴化或碘化衍生物:										-Fluorinated, brominated or iodinated derivatives of acyclic hydrocarbons:
2903.3100	--1,2一二溴工烷(ISO)	5.5	5		0	30	17		千克	89	--Dibromoothare chyhemedib-romode
	--其他:										--Other:
2903.3910	---1,1,3,3,3-五氟-2-三氟甲基-1-丙烯(全氟异丁烯;八氟异丁烯)	5.5	5		0	30	17	13	千克	23	---1,1,3,3,3-Pentafluro-2-trifluromethyl-1-propene (Perfluorolisobutylene, isobutylene octafluoride)
2903.3990	---其他	5.5	5		0	30	17	13	千克		---Other
2903.3990 10	二溴甲烷	5.5				30	17	13	千克		Dibromomethane
2903.3990 20	溴甲烷(别名甲基溴)	5.5				30	17	13	千克	14xy	methyl bromide
2903.3990 90	其他无环烃的氟化、溴化或碘化衍生物	5.5				30	17	13	千克		Fluorinated, brominated or iodinated derivatives of acyclic hydrocarbons
	-含有两种或两种以上不同卤素的无环烃卤化衍生物:										-Halogenated derivatives of acyclic hydrocarbons containing two or more different halogens:
2903.4100	--三氯氟甲烷	5.5	5		0	30	17	13	千克	yl4x	--Trichloro fluoro methane
2903.4200	--二氯二氟甲烷	5.5	5		0	30	17	13	千克	yl4x	--Dichloro difluoro methane
2903.4300	--三氯三氟乙烷	5.5	5		0	30	17	13	千克		--Trichloro trifluoro ethanes
2903.4300 10	三氯三氟乙烷,用于清洗剂除外(CFC-113)	5.5				30	17	13	千克	y14x	Trichloro trifluoro ethanes other than for cleaner preparation (CFC-113)
2903.4300 90	三氯三氟乙烷,用于清洗剂(CFC-113)	5.5				30	17	13	千克	89	Trichloro trifluoro ethanes, for cleaner preparation (CFC-113)

税则号列 Tariff Item.	货品名称	最惠国(%) MFN	协定(%)CT			普通 Gen	增值税率 VAT	出口退税 ED	计量单位 Unit	监管条件 SC	Article Description
			东盟 CA	中巴 CP	中智 CC						
2903.4400	--二氯四氟乙烷及氯五氟乙烷	5.5	5		0	30	17	13	千克		--Dichloro tetrafluoro ethanes and chloropentafluoroethane
2903.4400 10	二氯四氟乙烷(CFC-114)	5.5				30	17	13	千克	y14x	Dichloro tetrafluoro ethanes (CFC-114)
2903.4400 90	氯五氟乙烷(CFC-115)	5.5				30	17	13	千克	y14x	Chloro pentafluoro ethane (CFC-115)
	--其他仅含氟和氯的全卤化衍生物:										--Other derivatives perhalogenated only with fluorine and chlorine:
2903.4510	---氯三氟甲烷	5.5	5		0	30	17	13	千克	y14x	---Chloro trifluoro methane
2903.4520	---五氯氟乙烷	5.5	5		0	30	17	13	千克		---Pentachloro fluoro ethane
2903.4530	---四氯二氟乙烷	5.5	5		0	30	17	13	千克		---Tetrachloro difluoro ethane
2903.4540	---七氯氟丙烷	5.5	5		0	30	17	13	千克		---Heptachloro fluoro propane
2903.4550	---六氯二氟丙烷	5.5	5		0	30	17	13	千克		---Hexachloro difluoro propane
2903.4560	---五氯三氟丙烷	5.5	5		0	30	17	13	千克		---Pentachloro trifluoro propane
2903.4570	---四氯四氟丙烷	5.5	5		0	30	17	13	千克		---Tetrachloro tetrafluoro propane
2903.4580	---三氯五氟丙烷	5.5	5		0	30	17	13	千克		---Trichloro pentafluoro propane
	---其他:										---Other:
2903.4591	----二氯六氟丙烷	5.5	5		0	30	17	13	千克		----Dichloro hexafluoro propane
2903.4592	----氯七氟丙烷	5.5	5		0	30	17	13	千克		----Chloro heptafluoro propane
2903.4599	----其他	5.5	5		0	30	17	13	千克		----Other
2903.4600	--溴氯二氟甲烷、溴三氟甲烷及二溴四氟乙烷	5.5	5		0	30	17	13	千克		--Bromochloro difluoro methane, bromotrifluoro methane and dibromote trafluoroethane
2903.4600 10	溴氯二氟甲烷(Halon-1211)	5.5				30	17	13	千克	y14x	Bromo chloro difluoro methane (Halon-1211)
2903.4600 20	溴三氟甲烷(Halon-1301)	5.5				30	17	13	千克	y14x	Bromo trifluoro methane (Halon-1301)
2903.4600 90	二溴四氟乙烷	5.5				30	17	13	千克		Dibromo tetrafluoro ethane
2903.4700	--其他全卤化衍生物	5.5	5		0	30	17	13	千克		--Other perhalogenated derivatives
	--其他:										--Other:
2903.4910	---其他仅含氟和氯的甲烷、乙烷及丙烷的卤化衍生物	5.5	5		0	30	17	13	千克		---Other methane, ethane and propane halogenated derivatives only with fluorine and chlorine
2903.4910 11	一氟二氯甲烷	5.5				30	17	13	千克	14xy	Mono fluoro dichloro methane
2903.4910 12	二氟一氯甲烷	5.5				30	17	13	千克	14xy	Difluoro monochloro methane
2903.4910 13	一氟一氯甲烷	5.5				30	17	13	千克	14xy	Monofluoro monochloro methane
2903.4910 14	一氟四氯乙烷	5.5				30	17	13	千克	14xy	Monofluoro tetrachloro ethane
2903.4910 15	二氟三氯乙烷	5.5				30	17	13	千克	14xy	Difluoro trichloro ethane
2903.4910 16	1,1,1-三氟-2,2-二氯乙烷	5.5				30	17	13	千克	14xy	1,1,1-Trifluoro-2,2-dichloro ethane
2903.4910 17	1,1,1,2-四氟-2-氯乙烷	5.5				30	17	13	千克	14xy	1,1,1,2-Tetrafluoro-2-chloroethane
2903.4910 18	一氟三氯乙烷	5.5				30	17	13	千克	14xy	Monofluoro trichloroethane
2903.4910 19	二氟二氯乙烷	5.5				30	17	13	千克	14xy	Difluoro dichloroethane
2903.4910 21	三氟一氯乙烷	5.5				30	17	13	千克	14xy	Trifluoro monochloroethane
2903.4910 22	一氟二氯乙烷	5.5				30	17	13	千克	14xy	Monofluoro dichloroethane
2903.4910 23	1-氟-1,1-二氯乙烷	5.5				30	17	13	千克	14xy	1-Fluoro-1,1-dichloro ethane
2903.4910 24	二氟一氯乙烷	5.5				30	17	13	千克	14xy	Difluoro monochloroethane
2903.4910 25	1,1-二氟-1-氯乙烷	5.5				30	17	13	千克	14xy	1,1-Difluoro-1-chloroethane
2903.4910 26	一氟一氯乙烷	5.5				30	17	13	千克	14xy	Monofluoro monochloroethane
2903.4910 27	一氟六氯丙烷	5.5				30	17	13	千克	14xy	Monofluoro hexachloropropane
2903.4910 28	二氟五氯丙烷	5.5				30	17	13	千克	14xy	Difluoro pentachloro propane
2903.4910 29	三氟四氯丙烷	5.5				30	17	13	千克	14xy	Trifluoro tetrapropane
2903.4910 31	四氟三氯丙烷	5.5				30	17	13	千克	14xy	Tetrafluoro trichloropropane
2903.4910 32	五氟二氯丙烷	5.5				30	17	13	千克	14xy	Pentafluoro dichloropropane

税则号列 Tariff Item.	货品名称	最惠国(%) MFN	协定(%) CT 东盟 CA	中巴 CP	中智 CC	普通 Gen	增值税率 VAT	出口退税 ED	计量单位 Unit	监管条件 SC	Article Description
2903. 4910 33	1,1,1,2,2-五氟-3,3-二氯丙烷	5. 5				30	17	13	千克	14xy	1,1,1,2,2-Pentafluoro-3,3-dichloropropane
2903. 4910 34	1,1,2,2,3-五氟-1,3-二氯丙烷	5. 5				30	17	13	千克	14xy	1,1,2,2,3-Pentafluoro-1,3-dichloropropane
2903. 4910 35	六氟一氯丙烷	5. 5				30	17	13	千克	14xy	Hexafluoro monochloro propane
2903. 4910 36	一氟五氯丙烷	5. 5				30	17	13	千克	14xy	Monofluoro pentachloro propane
2903. 4910 37	二氟四氯丙烷	5. 5				30	17	13	千克	14xy	Difluoro tetrachloropropane
2903. 4910 38	三氟三氯丙烷	5. 5				30	17	13	千克	14xy	Trifluoro trichloropropane
2903. 4910 39	四氟二氯丙烷	5. 5				30	17	13	千克	14xy	Tetrafluoro dichloropropane
2903. 4910 41	五氟一氯丙烷	5. 5				30	17	13	千克	14xy	Pentafluoro monochloropropane
2903. 4910 42	一氟四氯丙烷	5. 5				30	17	13	千克	14xy	Monofluoro tetrachloropropane
2903. 4910 43	二氟三氯丙烷	5. 5				30	17	13	千克	14xy	Difluoro trichloropropane
2903. 4910 44	三氟二氯丙烷	5. 5				30	17	13	千克	14xy	Trifluoro ddichloropropane
2903. 4910 45	四氟一氯丙烷	5. 5				30	17	13	千克	14xy	Tetrafluoro monochloropropane
2903. 4910 46	一氟三氯丙烷	5. 5				30	17	13	千克	14xy	Monofluoro trichloropropane
2903. 4910 47	二氟二氯丙烷	5. 5				30	17	13	千克	14xy	Difluoro dichloropropane
2903. 4910 48	三氟一氯丙烷	5. 5				30	17	13	千克	14xy	Trifluoro monochloro propane
2903. 4910 49	一氟二氯丙烷	5. 5				30	17	13	千克	14xy	Monofluoro dichloro propane
2903. 4910 51	二氟一氯丙烷	5. 5				30	17	13	千克	14xy	Difluoro monochloro propane
2903. 4910 52	一氟一氯丙烷	5. 5				30	17	13	千克	14xy	Monofluoro monochloro propane
2903. 4920	---其他仅含氟和溴的甲烷、乙烷及丙烷的卤化衍生物	5. 5	5		0	30	17	13	千克		---Other methane, ethane and propane halogenated derivatives with fluorine and bromine
2903. 4990	---其他	5. 5	5		0	30	17	13	千克		---Other
2903. 4990 10	二溴氯丙烷(1,2-二溴-3-氯丙烷)	5. 5				30	17	13	千克	89	dibromochloropropane(1,2 – dibromo – 3 – chloropropane)
2903. 4990 90	其他无环烃卤化衍生物(含二种或二种以上不同卤素)	5. 5				30	17	13	千克		Other halogenated derivatives of acyclic hydrocarbons containing two or more different halogens
	-环烷烃、环烯烃或萜烯烃的卤化衍生物:										-Halogenated derivatives of cyclanic, cyclenic or cycloterpenic hydrocarbons:
2903. 5100	--1,2,3,4,5,6-六氯环已烷	5. 5	5		0	30	17		千克		--1,2,3,4,5,6-Hexachlorocyclohexane
2903. 5100 10	林丹(ISO,INN)	5. 5				30	17		千克	S	Lindan(ISO,INN)
2903. 5100 90	1,2,3,4,5,6-六氯环已烷(六六六(ISO)、混合异构体)	5. 5				30	17		千克	X	1,2,3,4,5,6 – Hexachlorocyclohexane [666(ISO)]
2903. 5200	--艾[剂(ISO)、氯丹(ISO)及七氯(ISO)]	5. 5	5		0	30	17		千克		--Aldrin(ISO)、Camphechlor(ISO) or haptachlor(ISO)
2903. 5200 10	艾氏剂(ISO)及七氯(ISO)	5. 5				30	17		千克	89	Aldrin(ISO) or haptachlor(ISO)
2903. 5200 90	氯丹(ISO)(氯丹别名八氯化甲桥茚)	5. 5				30	17		千克	X	Chlordane(ISO)(Chlordane,pur,)
2903. 5900	--其他	5. 5	5		0	30	17		千克		--Other
2903. 5900 10	毒杀芬	5. 5				30	17		千克	89	camphechlor
2903. 5900 30	灭蚁灵	5. 5				30	17		千克	X	mirex(ESA)
2903. 5900 90	其他环烷烃或环烯烃等卤化衍生物	5. 5				30	17		千克		Halogentd derivs of cyclanic/cylenic/cycloterpenic hydrocarbns nes
	-芳烃卤化衍生物:										-Halogenated derivatives of aromatic hydro-carbons:

税则号列 Tariff Item.	货品名称	最惠国(%) MFN	协定(%)CT 东盟 CA	中巴 CP	中智 CC	普通 Gen	增值税率 VAT	出口退税 ED	计量单位 Unit	监管条件 SC	Article Description
	--氯苯、邻二氯苯及对二氯苯:										--Chlorobenzene, *o*-dichlorobenzene and *p*-dichlorobenzene:
2903.6110	---邻二氯苯	5.5	5		0	30	17	13	千克		---*o*-Dichlorobenzene
2903.6190	---其他	5.5	5		0	30	17	13	千克		---Other
2903.6190 10	1,4-二氯苯(对二氯苯)	5.5				30	17	13	千克	S	1,4- dichlorobenzene
2903.6190 90	氯苯	5.5				30	17	13	千克		chlorobenzene
2903.6200	--六氯苯(ISO)及滴滴涕(ISO,INN)[1,1,1-三氯-2,2-双对氯苯乙烷]	5.5	5		0	30	17		千克	X	--Hexachlorobenzene (ISO) and DDT (ISO,INN) [1,1,1-trichloro-2,2-bis (*p*-chlorophenyl) ethane]
	--其他:										--Other:
2903.6910	---对氯甲苯	5.5	5		0	30	17	13	千克		---*p*-Chlorotoluene
2903.6920	---3,4-二氯三氟甲苯	5.5	5		0	30	17	13	千克		---3,4-Dichlorotrifluoride toluene
2903.6990	---其他	5.5	5		0	30	17	13	千克		---Other
2903.6990 10	多氯联苯,多溴联苯	5.5				30	17	13	千克	89	Polychlorinated biphenyls (including derivatives of chlorinated diphenyls and 1,1-diphenyl chloride)
2903.6990 30	多氯三联苯(PCT)	5.5				30	17	13	千克	X	Hexabromodiphenyl, octabromodiphenyl, decabromodiphenyl
2903.6990 40	稗草烯	5.5				30	17	13	千克	S	Humulene
2903.6990 90	其他芳烃卤化衍生物	5.5				30	17	13	千克		Other halogenated derivatives of aromatic hydro-carbons
29.04	**烃的磺化、硝化或亚硝化衍生物,不论是否卤化:**										**Sulphonated, nitrated or nitrosated derivatives of hydrocarbons, whether or not halogenated:**
2904.1000	-仅含磺基的衍生物及其盐和乙酯	5.5	5		0	30	17	13	千克		-Derivatives containing only sulpho groups, their salts and ethyl esters
	-仅含硝基或亚硝基的衍生物:										-Derivatives containing only nitro or only nitroso groups:
2904.2010	---硝基苯	5.5	5		4.4	20	17	13	千克		---Nitrobenzene
2904.2020	---硝基甲苯	5.5	5		4.4	30	17	13	千克		---Nitrotoluene and nitrochlorobenzene
2904.2030	---二硝基甲苯	5.5	5		4.4	20	17	13	千克		---Dinitrotoluene and dinitrochlorobenzene
2904.2040	---三硝基甲苯(TNT)	5.5	5		4.4	40	17	13	千克		---Trinitrotoluene(TNT)
2904.2090	---其他	5.5	5		4.4	30	17	13	千克		---Other
2904.2090 10	六硝基芪	5.5				30	17	13	千克	3	Hexanitrostilbene
2904.2090 20	4-硝基联苯	5.5				30	17	13	千克	X	1,1-BiPheny,4-nitro
2904.2090 90	其他仅含硝基或亚硝基衍生物	5.5				30	17	13	千克		Other derivatives containing only nitro or only nitroso groups
	-其他:										-Other:
	---硝基氯化苯:										---Nitrochlorobenzene:
2904.9011	----邻硝基氯化苯	5.5	5		0	30	17	13	千克		----O-nitrochlorobenzene
2904.9012	----间硝基氯化苯	5.5	5		0	30	17	13	千克		----M-nitrochlorobenzene
2904.9013	----对硝基氯化苯	5.5	5		0	30	17	13	千克		----P-nitrochlorobenzene
2904.9020	---二硝基氯化苯	5.5	5		0	20	17	13	千克		---Dinitrochlorobenzene
2904.9030	---三氯硝基甲烷(氯化苦;硝基氯仿)	5.5	5		0	30	17	13	千克	23S	---Trichloronitromethane (chloropicrin, nitrochloroform)
2904.9090	---其他	5.5	5		0	30	17	11	千克		---Other
2904.9090 11	氯硝丙烷	5.5				30	17	11	千克	S	Saltpetre chlorine propane
2904.9090 12	四氯硝基苯	5.5				30	17	13	千克	S	tecnazene
2904.9090 13	五氯硝基苯	5.5				30	17	13	千克	S	Quintozene

税则号列 Tariff Item.	货品名称	最惠国(%) MFN	协定(%)CT 东盟 CA	协定(%)CT 中巴 CP	协定(%)CT 中智 CC	普通 Gen	增值税率 VAT	出口退税 ED	计量单位 Unit	监管条件 SC	Article Description
2904.9090 90	其他烃的磺化、硝化、亚硝化衍生物(不论是否卤化)	5.5				30	17	13	千克		Ther sulfonated nitrosated hydrocarbon derivants
	第二分章　醇类及其卤化、磺化、硝化或亚硝化衍生物										Ⅱ.-ALCOHOLS AND THEIR HALOGENATED, SULPHONATED, NITRATED OR NITROSATED DERIVATIVES
29.05	**无环醇及其卤化、磺化、硝化或亚硝化衍生物:**										**Acyclic alcohols and their halogenated, sulphonated, nitrated or nitrosated derivatives:**
	-饱和一元醇:										-Saturated monohydric alcohols:
2905.1100	--甲醇	5.5	5		4.4	30	17	13	千克		--Methanol (methyl alcohol)
	--正丙醇及异丙醇:										--Propan-1-ol (propyl alcohol) and propan-2-ol (isopropyl alcohol):
2905.1210	---正丙醇	5.5	5		4.4	30	17	13	千克		---Propan-1-ol (propyl alcohol)
2905.1220	---异丙醇	5.5	5		4.4	30	17	13	千克	G	---Propan-2-ol (isopropyl alcohol)
2905.1300	--正丁醇	5.5	5		0	30	17	13	千克		--Butan-1-ol (*n*-butyl alcohol)
	--其他丁醇:										--Other butanols:
2905.1410	---异丁醇	5.5	5		0	30	17	13	千克		---Iso-butyl alcohol
2905.1420	---仲丁醇	5.5	5		0	30	17	13	千克		---sec-butyl
2905.1430	---叔丁醇	5.5	5		0	30	17	13	千克		---Tert-butgl alcohol
2905.1610	---正辛醇	5.5	5		0	30	17	13	千克		---n – Octanol
2905.1690	---其它	5.5	5		0	30	17	13	千克		---Other
2905.1700	--十二醇、十六醇及十八醇	7	5		0	30	17	13	千克		--Dodecan-1-ol (lauryl alcohol), hexadecan-1-ol (cetyl alcohol) and octadecan-1-ol (stearyl alcohol)
	--其他:										--Other:
2905.1910	---3,3-二甲基丁-2-醇(频哪基醇)	5.5	5		4.4	30	17	13	千克	23	---3,3-Dimethyl-2-butanol (pinacolyl alcohol)
2905.1990	---其他	5.5	5		0	30	17	13	千克		---Other
2905.1990 10	三十烷醇	5.5				30	17	13	千克	S	melissyl alcohol
2905.1990 90	其他饱和一元醇	5.5				30	17	13	千克		Other saturated monohydric alcohols
	-不饱和一元醇:										-Unsaturated monohydric alcohols:
	--无环萜烯醇:										--Acyclic terpene alcohols:
2905.2210	---香叶醇、橙花醇(3,7-二甲基-2,6-辛二烯-1-醇)	5.5	5		0	30	17	13	千克		---Geraniol, nerol (cis-3,7-Dimethyl-2,6-octadien-1-ol)
2905.2220	---香茅醇(3,7-二甲基-6-辛烯-1-醇)	5.5	5		0	30	17	13	千克		---Citronellol (3, 7-Dimethyl-6-octen-1-ol)
2905.2230	---芳樟醇	5.5	5		0	30	17	13	千克		---Linalool
2905.2290	---其他	5.5	5		0	30	17	13	千克		---Other
2905.2900	--其他	5.5	5		0	30	17	13	千克		--Other
	-二元醇:										-Diols:
2905.3100	--1,2-乙二醇	5.5			0	30	17	13	千克		--Ethylene glycol (ethanediol)
2905.3200	--1,2 一丙二醇	5.5	5		0	30	17	13	千克		--Propylene glycol (propane-1,2-diol)
	--其他:										--Other:
2905.3910	---2,5-二甲基已二醇	4			0	11	17	13	千克		---2,5-dimethyl hexandiol
2905.3990	---其他	5.5	5		0	30	17	13	千克		---Other
2905.3990 10	驱蚊醇	5.5				30	17	13	千克	S	ethohexadiol
2905.3990 90	其他二元醇	5.5				30	17	13	千克		other diatomic alcohol

税则号列 Tariff Item.	货品名称	最惠国(%) MFN	协定(%) CT 东盟 CA	协定(%) CT 中巴 CP	协定(%) CT 中智 CC	普通 Gen	增值税率 VAT	出口退税 ED	计量单位 Unit	监管条件 SC	Article Description
	-其他多元醇:										-Other polyhydric alcohols:
2905.4100	--2-乙基-2-(羟甲基)丙烷-1,3-二醇(三羟甲基丙烷)	5.5	5		0	30	17	13	千克		--2-Ethyl-2-(hydroxymethyl) propane-1,3-diol (trimethylolpropane)
2905.4200	--季戊四醇	5.5	5		4.4	30	17	13	千克		--Pentaerythritol
2905.4300	--甘露糖醇	8	5		0	30	17	13	千克		--Mannitol
2905.4400	--山梨醇	14	8		8.4	40	17	13	千克		--D-glucitol (sorbitol)
2905.4500	--丙三醇(甘油)	14	8	11.2	8.4	50	17	13	千克		--Glycerol
2905.4900	--其他	5.5	5		0	30	17	13	千克		--Other
	-无环醇的卤化、磺化、硝化或亚硝化衍生物:										-Halogenated, sulphonated, nitrated or nitrosated derivatives of acyclic alcohols:
2905.5100	--乙氯维诺(INN)	5.5	5		0	30	17	13	千克	I	--Ethchlorvynol (INN)
2905.5900	--其他	5.5	5		0	30	17	13	千克		--Other
2905.5900 10	乙氯维诺的盐	5.5				30	17	13	千克	I	Salts of Ethchlorvynol (INN)
2905.5900 20	2-氯乙醇	5.5				30	17	13	千克	3	2-Chloroethanol
2905.5900 30	溴硝醇	5.5				30	17	13	千克	S	bromic saltpetre alcohol
2905.5900 90	其他无环醇的卤化、磺化等衍生物	5.5				30	17	13	千克		Other
29.06	**环醇及其卤化、磺化、硝化或亚硝化衍生物:**										**Cyclic alcohols and their halogenated, sulphonated, nitrated or nitrosated derivatives:**
	-环烷醇、环烯醇及环萜烯醇:										-Cyclanic, cyclenic and cycloterpenic:
2906.1100	--薄荷醇	5			0	70	17	13	千克		--Menthol
2906.1200	--环己醇、甲基环己醇及二甲基环己醇	5.5	5		0	30	17	13	千克		--Cyclohexanol, methylcyclohexanols and dimethylcyclohexanols
	--固醇及肌醇:										--Sterols and inositols:
2906.1310	---固醇	5.5	5		0	30	17	13	千克		---Sterol
2906.1320	---肌醇	5.5	5		0	30	17	13	千克		---Inositol
	--其他:										--Other:
2906.1910	---萜品醇	5.5	5		4.4	30	17	13	千克		---Terineols-
2906.1990	---其它	5.5	5		0	30	17	13	千克		---Other
2906.1990 11	阿法雄烷二醇(包括与5α-雄烷-3β,17β-二醇;倍他雄烷二醇)	5.5				30	17		千克	L	5α-androstane-3α,17α-diol,(5α-androstane-3β, 17α-diol,5α-androstane-3α,17β-diol)
2906.1990 12	雄烯二醇(异构体)(包括雄-4-烯-3α17β-二醇)	5.5				30	17		千克	L	5α-androstane-3β,17α-diol, (androst-4-ene-3α,17β-diol)
2906.1990 13	雄-5-烯-3α,17a-二醇(包括雄-5-烯-3α17β二醇)	5.5				30	17		千克	L	Androst-5-ene-3α,17β-diol, (androst-4-ene-3α,17β-diol)
2906.1990 90	其他环烷醇,环烯醇及环萜烯醇	5.5				30	17		千克		Cyclanic, cyclenic or cycloterpenic alcohols nes, and their halogenated, sulphonated, nitrated or nitrosated derivatives
2906.2100	--苄醇	5			0	30	17	13	千克		--Benzyl alcohol
2906.2900	--其他	5.5	5		0	30	17	13	千克		--Other
2906.2900 10	三氯杀螨醇、杀螨醇	5.5				30	17	13	千克	S	kelthane, chlorfenethol
2906.2900 90	其他芳香醇	5.5				30	17	13	千克		Other Aromatic

税则号列 Tariff Item.	货品名称	最惠国(%) MFN	协定(%)CT 东盟 CA	中巴 CP	中智 CC	普通 Gen	增值税率 VAT	出口退税 ED	计量单位 Unit	监管条件 SC	Article Description
	第三分章 酚、酚醇及其卤化、磺化、硝化或亚硝化衍生物										Ⅲ. -PHENOLS, PHENOL-ALCOHOLS, AND THEIR HALOGENATED, SULPHONATED, NITRATED OR NITROSATED DERIVATIVES
29.07	酚;酚醇:										**Phenols; phenol-alcohols:**
	-一元酚:										-Monophenols:
	--苯酚及其盐:										--Phenol (hydroxybenzene) and its salts:
2907.1110	---苯酚	5.5	5		0	30	17	13	千克		---Phenol
2907.1190	---其他	5.5	5		0	30	17	13	千克		---Other
	--甲酚及其盐:										--Cresol and its salts:
	---甲酚:										---Cresol:
2907.1211	----间甲酚	5.5	5		0	30	17	13	千克		----m-Cresol
2907.1212	----邻甲酚	5.5	5		0	30	17	13	千克		----o-Cresol
2907.1219	----其他	5.5	5		0	30	17	13	千克		----Other
2907.1290	---其他	5.5	5		0	30	17	13	千克		---Other
	--辛基酚、壬基酚及其异构体以及它们的盐:										--Octylphenol, nonylphenol and their isomers; salts thereof:
2907.1310	---壬基酚	5.5	5		0	30	17	13	千克		---Nonylphenol
2907.1390	---其他	5.5	5		0	30	17	13	千克		---Other
	--萘酚及其盐:										--Naphthols and their salts:
2907.1510	---2-萘酚(β-萘酚)	5.5	5		0	30	17	13	千克		---2-Naphthols (β-naphthol)
2907.1590	---其他	5.5	5		0	30	17	13	千克		---Other
	--其他:										--Other:
2907.1910	---邻仲丁基酚、邻异丙基酚	4			0	11	17	13	千克		---*o*-Sec-butyl phenol, *o*-isopropyl phenol
2907.1990	---其他	5.5	5		0	30	17	13	千克		---Other
2907.1990 11	邻苯基苯酚及其盐	5.5				30	17	13	千克	S	o – phenylphenol and its salt
2907.1990 12	邻烯丙基苯酚及盐	5.5				30	17	13	千克	S	o – allylphenol and its salt
2907.1990 90	其他一元酚	5.5				30	17	13	千克		other monohydric phenol
	-多元酚;酚醇:										-Polyphenols; phenol-alcohols:
2907.2100	--间苯二酚及其盐	5.5	5		0	30	17	13	千克		--*m*-Dihydroxybenzene (resorcinol) and its salts
	--对苯二酚及其盐:										--*p*-Dihydroxybenzene (hydroquinone) and its salts:
2907.2210	---对苯二酚	5.5	5		0	30	17	13	千克		---Hydroquinone
2907.2290	---其他	5.5	5		0	30	17	13	千克		---Other
2907.2300	--4,4'-异亚丙基联苯酚(双酚A,二苯基酚丙烷)及其盐	5.5	5		0	30	17	13	千克		--4,4'-Isopropylidenediphenol (bisphenol A, diphenylolpropane) and its salts
	--其他:										--Other:
2907.2910	---邻苯二酚	4			0	11	17	13	千克		---*o*-Dihydroxybenzene (catechol, pyrocatechol)
2907.2990	---其他	5.5	5		0	30	17	13	千克		---Other
2907.2990 10	毒菌酚	5.5				30	17	13	千克	S	hexachlorophene
2907.2990 90	其他多元酚;酚醇	5.5				30	17	13	千克		other polyhydric phenol, phenolic alcohol
29.08	酚及酚醇的卤化、磺化、硝化或亚硝化衍生物:										**Halogenated, sulphonated, nitrated or nitrosated derivatives of phenols or phenol-alcohols:**
	-仅含卤素取代基的衍生物及其盐:										-Derivatives containing only halogen substituents and their salts:

税则号列 Tariff Item.	货 品 名 称	最惠国(%) MFN	协定(%) CT 东盟 CA	中巴 CP	中智 CC	普通 Gen	增值税率 VAT	出口退税 ED	计量单位 Unit	监管条件 SC	Article Description
2908.1100	--五氯苯酚(ISO)	5.5	5		0	30	17		千克	X	--Pentachlorophenol
	--其他：										--Other：
2908.1910	---对氯苯酚	4			0	11	17	13	千克		---*p*-Chlorophenol
2908.1990	---其他	5.5	5		0	30	17	13	千克		---Other
2908.1990 21	格螨酯	5.5				30	17	13	千克	S	Anti – acarid ester
2908.1990 22	双氯酚	5.5				30	17	13	千克	S	Dichlorophen
2908.1990 23	五氯酚钠	5.5				30	17	13	千克	S	Santobrite
2908.1990 90	其他仅含卤素取代基的衍生物及盐	5.5				30	17	13	千克		Other derivatives containing only halogen substituents and their salts
	-其他：										-Other：
2908.9100	--地乐酚(ISO)及其盐	5.5	5		0	30	17	13	千克	89	dinoseb(ISO) and its salts
	--其他：										--Other
2908.9910	---对硝基酚、对硝基酚钠	5.5	5		0	30	17	13	千克		---*p*-Nitrophenol, sodium *p*-nitro-phenolate
2908.9910 10	4–硝基苯酚(对硝基苯酚)	5.5				30	17	13	千克	X	4 – Dinitrophenol
2908.9910 90	对硝基苯酚钠	5.5				30	17	13	千克	S	para – nitrobenzene phenol natrium
2908.9990	---其他	5.5	5		0	30	17		千克		---Other
2908.9990 21	芬螨酯	5.5				30	17	13	千克	S	fragrant acarus ester
2908.9990 22	消螨酚	5.5				30	17	13	千克	S	anti – acarus ester
2908.9990 23	戊硝酚	5.5				30	17	13	千克	S	dinosam
2908.9990 24	特乐酚	5.5				30	17	13	千克	S	tel hydroxybenzene
2908.9990 25	二硝酚	5.5				30	17		千克	89	Dintrophenol
2908.9990 90	其他酚及酚醇的卤化等衍生物(包括其磺化,硝化或亚硝化衍生物)	5.5				30	17	13	千克		Other halogenated derivatives of phenols and phenol-alcohols (including their sulphonated, nitrated or nitrosates derivatives)
	第四分章 醚、过氧化醇、过氧化醚、过氧化酮、三节环环氧化物、缩醛及半缩醛及其卤化、磺化、硝化或亚硝化衍生物										Ⅳ. -ETHERS, ALCOHOL PEROXIDES, ETHER PEROXIDES, KETONE PEROXIDES, EPOXIDES WITH A THREE-MEMBERED RING, ACETALS AND HEMIACETALS, AND THEIR HALOGENATED, SULPHONATED, NITRATED OR NITROSATED DERIVATIVES
29.09	**醚、醚醇、醚酚、醚醇酚、过氧化醇、过氧化醚、过氧化酮(不论是否已有化学定义)及其卤化、磺化、硝化或亚硝化衍生物：**										**Ethers, ether-alcohols, ether-phenols, ether-alcohol-phenols, alcohol peroxides, ether peroxides, ketone peroxides (whether or not chemically defined), and their halogenated, sulphonated, nitrated or nitrosated derivatives：**
	-无环醚及其卤化、磺化、硝化或亚硝化衍生物：										-Acyclic ethers and their halogenated, sulphonated, nitrated or nitrosated derivatives：
2909.1100	--乙醚	5.5	5		0	30	17		千克	23	--Diethyl ether
2909.1900	--其他	5.5	5		0	30	17	13	千克		--Other
2909.1900 11	八氯二丙醚	5.5				30	17	13	千克	S	8 – fluoriade dipropyl ether
2909.1900 12	二氯异丙醚	5.5				30	17	13	千克	S	Nemamort(DCIP)

税则号列 Tariff Item.	货品名称	最惠国(%) MFN	协定(%)CT 东盟 CA	中巴 CP	中智 CC	普通 Gen	增值税率 VAT	出口退税 ED	计量单位 Unit	监管条件 SC	Article Description
2909.1900 90	其他无环醚及其卤化等衍生物(包括其磺化、硝化或亚硝化衍生物)	5.5				30	17	13	千克		Other noncyclic aether and its halogenide derivants (including their sulphonated、nitrated or nitrosated derivatives.)
	-环烷醚、环烯醚或环萜烯醚及其卤化、磺化、硝化或亚硝化衍生物:										-Cyclanic, cyclenic or cycloterpenic ethers and their halogenated, sulphonated, nitrated or nitrosated derivatives:
	---环萜烯醚:										---Cycloterpenic ethers
2909.2081	----1,8-桉树脑	5.5	5		0	30	17		千克		----1,8-Eucalyptol
2909.2089	----其他	5.5	5		0	30	17		千克		----Other
2909.2090	---其他	5.5	5		0	30	17		千克		---Other
2909.3000	-芳香醚及其卤化、磺化、硝化或亚硝化衍生物	5.5	5		0	30	17	13	千克		-Aromatic ethers and their halogenated, sulphonated, nitrated or nitrosated derivatives
2909.3000 11	甲氧滴滴涕、除草醚	5.5				30	17	13	千克	S	Methoxychlor, nitrofen
2909.3000 12	醚菊酯、苄螨醚、三氟醚	5.5				30	17	13	千克	S	Aether chrysanthemum ester, benzyl aether, trifluorin aether
2909.3000 13	氯苯甲醚、甲氧除草醚	5.5				30	17	13	千克	S	Chloroanisole, methoxy nitrofen
2909.3000 14	三氟硝草醚、草枯醚	5.5				30	17	13	千克	S	Trifluorin saltpeter aether, mo 9 granular
2909.3000 15	氟除草醚、乙氧氟草醚	5.5				30	17	13	千克	S	Fluorin nitrofen, ethoxy fluorin nitrofen
2909.3000 90	其他芳香醚及其卤化、磺化、硝化衍生物(包括其亚硝化衍生物)	5.5				30	17	13	千克		Other aromatic aether and its halogenated, sulphurated and nitrified derivants
	-醚醇及其卤化、磺化、硝化或亚硝化衍生物:										-Ether-alcohols and their halogenated, sulphonated, nitrated or nitrosated derivatives:
2909.4100	--2,2'-氧联二乙醇(二甘醇)	5.5	5		0	30	17	13	千克		--2,2′-Oxydiethanol (diethylene glycol, digol)
2909.4300	--乙二醇或二甘醇的单丁醚	5.5	5		0	30	17	13	千克		--Monobutyl ethers of ethylene glycol or of diethylene glycol
2909.4400	--乙二醇或二丁醇的其他单烷基醚	5.5	5		0	30	17	13	千克		--Other monoalkylethers of ethylene glycol or of diethylene glycol
	--其他:										--Other:
2909.4910	---间苯氧基苄醇	4			3.2	11	17	13	千克		---*m*-Phenoxy benzalcohol
2909.4990	---其他	5.5	5		4.4	30	17	13	千克		---Other
2909.4990 01	2-正丙氧基乙醇	5.5				30	17	13	千克		2-Propoxyethanol
2909.4990 90	其他醚醇及其衍生物(包括其卤化、磺化、硝化或亚硝化衍生物)	5.5				30	17	13	千克		Other ether-alcohols and their halogenated, sulphonated, nitrated or nitrosated derivatives
2909.5000	-醚酚、醚醇酚及其卤化、磺化、硝化或亚硝化衍生物	5.5	5		0	30	17	13	千克		-Ether-phenols, ether-alcohol-phenols and their halogenated, sulphonated, nitrated or nitrosated derivatives
2909.6000	-过氧化醇、过氧化醚、过氧化酮及其卤化、磺化、硝化或亚硝化衍生物	5.5	5		4.4	30	17	13	千克		-Alcohol peroxides, ether peroxides, ketone peroxides and their halogenated, sulphonated, nitrated or nitrosated derivatives
29.10	三节环环氧化物、环氧醇、环氧酚、环氧醚及其卤化、磺化、硝化或亚硝化衍生物:										**Epoxides, epoxyalcohols, epoxyphenols and epoxyethers, with a three-membered ring, and their halogenated, sulphonated, nitrated or nitrosated derivatives:**

税则号列 Tariff Item.	货 品 名 称	最惠国(%) MFN	协定(%)CT 东盟 CA	中巴 CP	中智 CC	普通 Gen	增值税率 VAT	出口退税 ED	计量单位 Unit	监管条件 SC	Article Description
2910.1000	-环氧乙烷(氧化乙烯)	5.5	5		0	30	17	13	千克	X	-Oxirane (ethylene oxide)
2910.2000	-甲基环氧乙烷(氧化丙烯)	5.5	5		0	30	17	13	千克		-Methyloxirane (propylene oxide)
2910.3000	-1-氯-2,3-环氧丙烷(表氯醇)	5.5	5		0	30	17	13	千克		-1-Chloro-2,3-epoxypropane (epichlorohydrin)
2910.4000	-狄氏剂(ISO,INN)	5.5	5		0	30	17		千克	89	-Dieldrin(ISO,INN)
2910.9000	-其他	5.5	5		0	30	17	13	千克		-Other
2910.9000 10	异狄氏剂	5.5				30	17		千克	89	Endrine
2910.9000 20	灭草环	5.5				30	17	13	千克	S	Ratsbane annulus
2910.9000 90	三节环环氧化物、环氧醇(酚、醚)(包括其卤化、磺化、硝化或亚硝化的衍生物)	5.5				30	17	13	千克		Other epoxides, epoxyalcohols, epoxyphenols and epoxyethers, with a three-membered ring, and their halogenated, sulphonated, nitrated or nitrosated derivatives
29.11	**缩醛及半缩醛,不论是否含有其他含氧基,及其卤化、磺化、硝化或亚硝化衍生物:**										**Acetals and hemiacetals, whether or not with other oxygen function, and their halogenated, sulphonated, nitrated or nitrosated derivatives:**
2911.0000	缩醛及半缩醛,不论是否含有其他含氧基,(包括其卤化、磺化、硝化或亚硝化衍生物)	5.5	5		0	30	17	13	千克		Acetals and hemiacetals, whether or not with other oxygen function, and their halogenated, sulphonated, nitrated or nitrosated derivatives
	第五分章 醛基化合物										V.-ALDEHYDE-FUNCTION COMPOUNDS
29.12	**醛,不论是否含有其他含氧基;环聚醛;多聚甲醛:**										**Aldehydes, whether or not with other oxygen function; cyclic polymers of aldehydes; paraformaldehyde:**
	-不含其他含氧基的无环醛:										-Acyclic aldehydes without other oxygen function:
2912.1100	--甲醛	5.5	5		4.4	30	17	13	千克		--Methanal (formaldehyde)
2912.1200	--乙醛	5.5	5		0	30	17	13	千克	X	--Ethanal (acetaldehyde)
2912.1900	--其他	5.5	5		0	30	17	13	千克		--Other
2912.1900 01	乙二醛	5.5				30	17	13	千克		Glyoxal (ethanedial)
2912.1900 02	正丙醛	5.5				30	17	13	千克		Propionaldehyde
2912.1900 30	丙烯醛	5.5				30	17	13	千克	X	acraldehyde
2912.1900 90	其他无环醛(指不含其他含氧基)	5.5				30	17	13	千克		Other acyclic aldehydes without other oxygen function
	-不含其他含氧基的环醛:										-Cyclic aldehydes without other oxygen function:
2912.2100	--苯甲醛	5.5	5		0	30	17	13	千克		--Benzaldehyde
	--其他:										--Other:
2912.2910	---铃兰醛(对叔丁基r甲基-氧化肉桂醛)	5.5	5		0	30	17	13	千克		---Lilial (p-tert-butyl-a-methyl-oxocinnamaldehyde)
2912.2990	---其他	5.5	5		0	30	17	13	千克		---Other
2912.3000	-醛醇	5.5	5		0	30	17	13	千克		-Aldehyde-alcohols
	-醛醚、醛酚及含其他含氧基的醛:										-Aldehyde-ethers, aldehyde-phenols and aldehydes with other oxygen function:
2912.4100	--香草醛(3-甲氧基-4-羟基苯甲醛)	5.5	5		0	30	17	13	千克		--Vanillin (4-hydroxy-3-methoxybenzaldehyde)

税则号列 Tariff Item.	货 品 名 称	最惠国(%) MFN	协定(%)CT 东盟 CA	中巴 CP	中智 CC	普通 Gen	增值税率 VAT	出口退税 ED	计量单位 Unit	监管条件 SC	Article Description
2912.4200	--乙基香草醛(3-乙氧基-4-羟基苯甲醛)	5.5	5		0	30	17	13	千克		--Ethylvanillin (3-ethoxy-4-hydroxybenzaldehyde)
2912.4900	--其他	5.5	5		0	30	17	13	千克		--Other
2912.5000	-环聚醛	5.5	5		0	30	17	13	千克		-Cyclic polymers of aldehydes
2912.5000 10	四聚乙醛	5.5				30	17	13	千克	S	Methaldehyde
2912.5000 90	其他环聚醛	5.5				30	17	13	千克		Other cyclic polyaldehyde
2912.6000	-多聚甲醛	5.5	5		0	30	17	13	千克		-Paraformaldehyde
29.13	**税目 29.12 所列产品的卤化、磺化、硝化或亚硝化衍生物:**										**Halogenated, sulphonated, nitrated or nitrosated derivatives of products of heading No. 29.12:**
2913.0000	税目 29.12 所列产品的卤化、磺化、硝化或亚硝化衍生物	5.5	5		0	30	17	13	千克		Halogenated, sulphonated, nitrated or nitrosated derivatives of products of heading No. 29.12
2913.0000 10	三氯乙醛	5.5				30	17	13	千克	G	Richloroacetaldehyde
2913.0000 90	税号 2912 所列产品的其他衍生物(指卤化、磺化、硝化或亚硝化的衍生物)	5.5				30	17	13	千克		Halogenated, sulphonated, nitrated or nitrosated derivatives of products of heading No. 2912
	第六分章　酮基化合物及醌基化合物										Ⅵ. -KETONE-FUNCTION COMPOUNDS AND QUINONE-FUNCTION COMPOUNDS
29.14	**酮及醌,不论是否含有其他含氧基,及其卤化、磺化、硝化或亚硝化衍生物:**										**Ketones and quinones, whether or not with other oxygen function, and their halogenated, sulphonated, nitrated or nitrosated derivatives:**
	-不含其他含氧基的无环酮:										-Acyclic ketones without other oxygen function:
2914.1100	--丙酮	5.5	5		0	20	17	13	千克	23	--Acetone
2914.1200	--丁酮[甲基乙基(甲)酮]	5.5	5		4.4	30	17	13	千克	23	--Butanone (methyl ethyl ketone)
2914.1300	--4-甲基-2-戊酮(甲基异丁基(甲)酮)	5.5	5		0	30	17	13	千克		--4-Methyl-2-pentanone (isobutyl methyl ketone)
2914.1900	--其他	5.5	5		0	30	17	13	千克		--Other
2914.1900 10	频哪酮	5.5				30	17	13	千克	23	Pinacolone
2914.1900 90	其他不含其他含氧基的无环酮	5.5				30	17	13	千克		Other acyclic ketones, without other oxygen function
	-不含其他含氧基的环烷酮、环烯酮或环萜烯酮:										-Cyclanic, cyclenic or cycloterpenic ketones without other oxygen function:
2914.2100	--樟脑	5.5	5		0	40	17	13	千克	BS	--Camphor
2914.2200	--环已酮及甲基环已酮	5.5	5		0	30	17	13	千克		--Cyclohexanone and methylcyclohexanone
2914.2300	--芷香酮及甲基芷香酮	5.5	5		0	30	17	13	千克		--Ionones and methylionones
2914.2900	--其他	5.5	5		0	30	17	13	千克		--Other
	-不含其他含氧基的芳香酮:										-Aromatic ketones without other oxygen function:
2914.3100	--苯丙酮(苯基-2-丙酮)	5.5	5		0	30	17	13	千克	23	--Propiophenone (phenylpropan-2-one)
	--其他:										--Other:
2914.3910	---苯乙酮	4			0	11	17	13	千克		---Acetophenone
2914.3990	---其他	5.5	5		0	30	17	13	千克		---Other
2914.3990 11	杀鼠酮	5.5				30	17	13	千克	S	ratsbane copper
2914.3990 12	鼠完	5.5				30	17	13	千克	S	pindone

税则号列 Tariff Item.	货品名称	最惠国(%) MFN	协定(%)CT 东盟 CA	中巴 CP	中智 CC	普通 Gen	增值税率 VAT	出口退税 ED	计量单位 Unit	监管条件 SC	Article Description
2914.3990 13	敌鼠	5.5				30	17	13	千克	S	diphacinone
2914.3990 90	其他不含其他含氧基的芳香酮	5.5				30	17	13	千克		other aromatic ketone containing no oxide base
2914.4000	-酮醇及酮醛	5.5	5		0	30	17	13	千克		-Ketone-alcohols and ketone-aldehydes
2914.4000 10	敌鼠钠	5.5				30	17	13	千克	S	natrium diphacinone
2914.4000 20	3β-羟基-5α-雄烷-17-酮	5.5				30	17	13	千克	L	natrium diphacinone
2914.4000 90	其他酮醇及酮醛	5.5				30	17	13	千克		Other ketol and keto aldehyde
	-酮酚及含有其他含氧基的酮:										-Ketone-phenols and ketones with other oxygen function:
	---酮酚:										---Ketone-phenols
2914.5011	----覆盆子酮:	5.5	5		0	30	17	13	千克		----Raspberry ketone
2914.5019	----其他:	5.5	5		0	30	17	13	千克		----Other
2914.5090	---其他:	5.5	5		0	30	17	13	千克		---Other
2914.5090 11	苯草酮	5.5				30	17	13	千克	S	benzene grass ketone
2914.5090 12	甲氧虫酰肼	5.5				30	17	13	千克	S	methoxy acyl hydrazine
2914.5090 90	含其他含氧基的酮	5.5				30	17	13	千克		Other ketone with other oxygen function
	-醌:										-Quinones:
2914.6100	--蒽醌	5.5	5		0	30	17	13	千克		--Anthraquinone
2914.6900	--其他醌	5.5	5		0	30	17	13	千克		--Other
2914.7000	-卤化、磺化、硝化或亚硝化衍生物	5.5	5		0	30	17	13	千克		-Halogenated, sulphonated, nitrated or nitrosated derivatives
2914.7000 11	氯鼠酮	5.5				30	17	13	千克	S	chlorophacinone
2914.7000 12	二氯萘醌	5.5				30	17	13	千克	S	dichlorobenzene quinone
2914.7000 13	四氯对醌	5.5				30	17	13	千克	S	chloranil
2914.7000 14	六氯丙酮	5.5				30	17	13	千克	S	hexachloroacetone
2914.7000 15	氯敌鼠钠盐	5.5				30	17	13	千克	S	chloro diphacinon soduim salt
2914.7000 90	其他酮及醌的卤化、磺化衍生物(包括硝化或亚硝化衍生物)	5.5				30	17	13	千克		halogenated and sulphurated derivants of ketone and quinone
	第七分章 羧酸及其酸酐、酰卤化物、过氧化物和过氧酸以及它们的卤化、磺化、硝化或亚硝化衍生物										Ⅶ. -CARBOXYLIC ACIDS AND THEIR ANHYDRIDES, HALIDES, PEROXIDES AND PEROXYACIDS AND THEIR HALOGENATED, SULPHONATED, NITRATED OR NITROSATED DERIVATIVES
29.15	**饱和无环一元羧酸及其酸酐、酰卤化物、过氧化物和过氧酸以及它们的卤化、磺化、硝化或亚硝化衍生物:**										**Saturated acyclic monocarboxylic acids and their anhydrides, halides, peroxides and peroxyacids; their halogenated, sulphonated, nitrated or nitrosated derivatives:**
	-甲酸及其盐和酯:										-Formic acid, its salts and esters:
2915.1100	--甲酸	5.5	5		0	40	17	13	千克		--Formic acid
2915.1200	--甲酸盐	5.5	5		4.4	30	17	13	千克		--Salts of formic acid
2915.1300	--甲酸酯	5.5	5		0	30	17	13	千克		--Esters of formic acid
	-乙酸及其盐;乙酸酐:										-Acetic acid and its salts; acetic anhydride:
	--乙酸:										--Acetic acid:
2915.2110	---冰乙酸	5.5	5		0	30	17	13	千克	G	---Acetic acid, glacial

税则号列 Tariff Item.	货品名称	最惠国(%) MFN	协定(%) 东盟 CA	中巴 CP	CT 中智 CC	普通 Gen	增值税率 VAT	出口退税 ED	计量单位 Unit	监管条件 SC	Article Description
2915.2190	---其他	5.5	5		0	50	17	13	千克	G	---Other
2915.2400	--乙酸酐	5.5	5		0	50	17	13	千克	23	--Acetic anhydride
	--其他：										--Other：
2915.2910	---乙酸钠	5.5	5		0	50	17	13	千克	G	---Sodium acctatc
2915.2990	---其他	5.5	5		0	50	17	13	千克		---Other
2915.2990 11	乙酸铜	5.5				50	17	13	千克	S	blue verdigris
2915.2990 12	一氯醋酸钠	5.5				50	17	13	千克	S	monochloroacetic acid natrium
2915.2990 23	乙酸铅	5.5				50	17	13	千克	X	mercuric acetate
2915.2990 90	其他乙酸盐	5.5				50	17	13	千克		other acetate
	-乙酸酯：										-Esters of acetic acid：
2915.3100	--乙酸乙酯	5.5	5		0	30	17	13	千克	G	--Ethyl acetate
2915.3200	--乙酸乙烯酯	5.5	5		0	30	17	13	千克		--Vinyl acetate
2915.3300	--乙酸(正)丁酯	5.5	5		0	30	17	13	千克		--*n*-Butyl acetate
2915.3600	--地乐酚(ISO)乙酸酯	5.5	5		4.4	30	17	13	千克	S	--Dinoseb acetate (ISO) exters of acetic acid
2915.3900	--其他	5.5	5		0	30	17	13	千克		--Other
2915.3900 11	三氯杀虫酯	5.5				30	17	13	千克	S	acetofenate
2915.3900 13	特乐酯	5.5				30	17	13	千克	S	tel ester
2915.3900 14	灭螨醌	5.5				30	17	13	千克	S	antiacarus quinone
2915.3900 15	红铃虫性诱素	5.5				30	17	13	千克	S	pin bollworm – attractor
2915.3900 90	其他乙酸酯	5.5				30	17	13	千克		other acetate
2915.4000	-一氯代乙酸、二氯乙酸或三氯乙酸及其盐和酯	5.5	5		0	30	17	13	千克		-Mono-, di- or trichloroacetic acids, their salts and esters
	-丙酸及其盐和酯：										-Propionic acid, its salts and esters：
2915.5010	---丙酸	5.5	5		0	30	17	13	千克		---Propionic acid
2915.5090	---其他	5.5	5		0	30	17	13	千克		---Other
2915.6000	-丁酸、戊酸及其盐和酯	5.5	5		0	30	17	13	千克		-Butanoic acids, pentanoic acids, their salts and esters
	-棕榈酸、硬脂酸及其盐和酯：										-Palmitic acid, stearic acid, their salts and esters：
2915.7010	---硬脂酸	7	5		5.6	50	17	13	千克		---Stearic acid
2915.7090	---其他	5.5	5		4.4	30	17	13	千克		---Other
2915.9000	-其他	5.5	5		0	30	17	13	千克		-Other
2915.9000 11	茅草枯	5.5				30	17	13	千克	S	dalapon
2915.9000 12	抑草蓬	5.5				30	17	13	千克	S	erbon
2915.9000 13	四氟丙酸	5.5				30	17	13	千克	S	tetrafluoride propionic acid
2915.9000 20	氟乙酸钠	5.5				30	17	13	千克	89	sodium floroacetatesodium floroacetate
2915.9000 90	其他饱和无环一元羧酸及其酸酐[(酰卤、过氧)化物,过氧酸及该号(卤、硝、磺、亚硝)化衍生]	5.5				30	17	13	千克		Other saturaed acyclic monocarboxylic acids and their anhydrides, halides, peroxides and peroxyacids; their halogenated, sulphonated, nitrated or nitrosated derivatives
29.16	不饱和无环一元羧酸、环一元羧酸及其酸酐、酰卤化物、过氧化物和过氧酸以及它们的卤化、磺化、硝化或亚硝化衍生物：										**Unsaturated acyclic monocarboxylic acids, cyclic monocarboxylic acids, their anhydrides, halides, peroxides and peroxyacids; their halogenated, sulphonated, nitrated or nitrosated derivatives：**

税则号列 Tariff Item.	货品名称	最惠国(%) MFN	协定(%)CT 东盟 CA	中巴 CP	中智 CC	普通 Gen	增值税率 VAT	出口退税 ED	计量单位 Unit	监管条件 SC	Article Description
	-不饱和无环一元羧酸及其酸酐、酰卤化物、过氧化物和过氧酸以及它们的衍生物:										-Unsaturated acyclic monocarboxylic acids, their anhydrides, halides, peroxides, peroxyacids and their derivatives:
2916.1100	--丙烯酸及其盐	6.5	5		0	30	17	13	千克		--Acrylic acid and its salts
2916.1200	--丙烯酸酯	6.5	5		0	30	17	13	千克		--Esters of acrylic acid
2916.1200 01	丙烯酸甲酯	6.5				30	17	13	千克		Methyl acrylate
2916.1200 02	丙烯酸乙酯	6.5				30	17	13	千克		Ethyl acrylate
2916.1200 03	丙烯酸正丁酯	6.5				30	17	13	千克		n-butyl acrylate
2916.1200 04	丙烯酸2-乙基己酯	6.5				30	17	13	千克		2-ethylhexyl acrylate
2916.1200 90	其他丙烯酸酯	6.5				30	17	13	千克		Other esters of acrylic acid
2916.1300	--甲基丙烯酸及其盐	6.5	5		0	80	17	13	千克		--Methacrylic acid and its salts
2916.1400	--甲基丙烯酸酯	6.5	5		0	80	17	13	千克		--Esters of methacrylic acid
2916.1500	--油酸、亚油酸或亚麻酸及其盐和酯	6.5	5		0	30	17	13	千克		--Oleic, linoleic or linolenic acids, their salts and esters
2916.1900	--其他	6.5	5		0	30	17	13	千克		--Other
2916.1900 11	烯虫乙酯	6.5				30	17	13	千克	S	allyl ethyl ester
2916.1900 12	烯虫炔酯	6.5				30	17	13	千克	S	allyl alkyne ester
2916.1900 13	消螨普	6.5				30	17	13	千克	S	dinocap
2916.1900 90	其他不饱和无环一元羧酸(包括其酸酐、酰卤化物、过氧化物和过氧酸及它们的衍生物)	6.5				30	17	13	千克		Other unsaturated acyclic monocarboxylic acids, their anhydrides, halides, peroxides, peroxyacids and their derivatives
2916.2010	---二溴菊酸、DV菊酸甲酯	4			0	11	17	13	千克		---Dibromochrysanthemicacid, DV-chrysanthemimono carboxylate
	---其他										---Other
2916.2090	---环烷一元羧酸、环烯一元羧酸或环萜烯一元羧酸及其酸酐、酰卤化物、过氧化物和过氧酸以及它们的衍生物	6.5	5					13	千克		---Cyclanic, cyclenic or cycloterpenic monocarboxylic acids, their anhydrides, halides, peroxides, peroxyacids and their derivatives
2916.2090 01	二氯菊酰氯(DV菊酰氯)	6.5				30	17	13	千克		Dichlorochrysanoyl chloride (DV-chrysanoyl chloride)
2916.2090 21	苄菊酯、苯醚菊酯(包括右旋苯醚菊酯、富右旋反式苯醚菊酯)	6.5				30	17	13	千克	S	Dimethirn , Phenothrin (including d – Phenothrin, rich d transallethrin)
2916.2090 22	苄烯菊酯、氯菊酯(包括生物氯菊酯)	6.5				30	17	13	千克	S	butethrin, Permethrin (including biopermethrin)
2916.2090 23	氯烯炔菊酯、联苯菊酯	6.5				30	17	13	千克	S	chlorempenthrin ,Bifenthrin
2916.2090 24	七氟菊酯、四氟苯菊酯、五氟苯菊酯	6.5				30	17	13	千克	S	7 – fluorin chrysanthemum ester, 4 – benzene chrysanthemum ester, 5 – fluorin benzene chrysanthemum ester
2916.2090 25	戊菊酯、环螨酯	6.5				30	17	13	千克	S	5 – chrysanthemum ester, cyclic ester
2916.2090 26	四氟甲醚菊酯、烯炔菊酯(包括右旋烯炔菊酯、富右旋反式烯炔菊酯)	6.5				30	17	13	千克	S	4 – flourin methyl ether chrysanthemum ester, alkene chrysanthemum ester (including d – empenthrin、rich – d – t – phenothrin)
2916.2090 27	炔丙菊酯(包括右旋炔丙菊酯、富右旋反式炔丙菊酯)	6.5				30	17	13	千克	S	Prallethrin(including d – prallethrin、rich – d – t – prallethrin)
2916.2090 28	氯丙炔菊酯(包括右旋反式氯丙炔菊酯)	6.5				30	17	13	千克	S	chlorempenthrin (including d – tran – chlorempenthrin)

税则号列 Tariff Item.	货品名称	最惠国(%) MFN	协定(%) 东盟 CA	协定(%) 中巴 CP	CT 中智 CC	普通 Gen	增值税率 VAT	出口退税 ED	计量单位 Unit	监管条件 SC	Article Description
2916.2090 90	其他(环烷、环烯、环萜烯)一元羧酸(包括酸酐、酰卤化物、过氧化物和过氧酸及该税号的衍生物)	6.5				30	17	13	千克		Other cyclanic, cyclenic or cycloterpenic monocarboxylic acids, their anhydrides, halides, peroxides, peroxyacids and their derivatives
	-芳香一元羧酸及其酸酐、酰卤化物、过氧化物和过氧酸以及它们的衍生物:										-Aromatic monocarboxylic acids, their anhydrides, halides, peroxides, peroxyacids and their derivatives:
2916.3100	--苯甲酸及其盐和酯	6.5	5		0	30	17	13	千克		--Benzoic acid, its salts and esters
2916.3100 20	2-(乙酰氧基)苯甲酸	6.5				30	17	13	千克	S	2-(acetoxy)benzoic acid
2916.3100 90	其他苯甲酸及其盐和酯	6.5				30	17	13	千克		Other benzoic acid and salt and ester
2916.3200	--过氧化苯甲酰及苯甲酰氯	6.5	5		0	30	17	13	千克		--Benzoyl peroxide and benzoyl chloride
2916.3400	--苯乙酸及其盐	6.5	5		0	30	17	13	千克		--Phenylacetic acid and its salts
2916.3400 10	苯乙酸	6.5				30	17	13	千克	23	Phenylacetic acid
2916.3400 90	苯乙酸盐	6.5				30	17	13	千克		Salts of phenylacetic acid
2916.3500	--苯乙酸酯	6.5	5		0	30	17	13	千克		--Esters of phenylacetic acid
2916.3600	--乐杀螨	6.5	5		0	30	17	13	千克	S	--Binapacryi
	--其他:										--Other:
2916.3910	---邻甲基苯甲酸	6.5	5		0	30	17	13	千克		---*M*-Methylbenzoic acid
2916.3920	---布洛芬	6.5	5		0	30	17	13	千克		---Brufen (Ibuprofen)
2916.3990	---其他	6.5	5		0	30	17	13	千克		---Other
2916.3990 12	草芽畏、燕麦酯	6.5				30	17	13	千克	S	Weed killer, methachlorphenprop
2916.3990 13	5-硝基邻甲氧基苯酸钠	6.5				30	17	13	千克	S	5-Nitryl ortho-anisole natrium
2916.3990 14	对氯苯氧乙酸及其盐	6.5				30	17	13	千克	S	Para-chlorobenzene fluorin acetic acid and its salt
2916.3990 15	三碘苯甲酸	6.5				30	17	13	千克	S	Triiodobenzoic acid
2916.3990 16	萘乙酸	6.5				30	17	13	千克	S	Naphthylacetic acid
2916.3990 17	伐草克	6.5				30	17	13	千克	S	Chlorfenac
2916.3990 18	α-萘乙酸及其盐	6.5				30	17	13	千克	S	α-Naphthylacetic acid and its salt
2916.3990 90	其他芳香一元羧酸	6.5				30	17	13	千克		Other aromatic monobasic carboxylic acid
29.17	**多元羧酸及其酸酐、酰卤化物、过氧化物和过氧酸以及它们的卤化、磺化、硝化或亚硝化衍生物:**										**Polycarboxylic acids, their anhydrides, halides, peroxides and peroxyacids; their halogenated, sulphonated, nitrated or nitrosated derivatives:**
	-无环多元羧酸及其酸酐、酰卤化物、过氧化物和过氧酸以及它们的衍生物:										-Acyclic polycarboxylic acids, their anhydrides, halides, peroxides, peroxyacids and their derivatives:
	--草酸及其盐和酯:										--Oxalic acid, its salts and esters:
2917.1110	---草酸	6.5	5		0	40	17	13	千克		---Oxalic acid
2917.1120	---草酸钴	9	5		0	30	17	13	千克		---Cobalt oxalate
2917.1190	---其他	6.5	5		0	30	17	13	千克		---Other
2917.1200	--己二酸及其盐和酯	6.5	5		0	30	17	13	千克		--Adipic acid, its salts and esters
	--壬二酸、癸二酸及其盐和酯:										--Azelaic acid, sebacic acid, their salts and esters:
2917.1310	---癸二酸及其盐和酯	6.5	5		0	30	17	13	千克		---Sebacic acid, its salts and esters
2917.1390	---其他	6.5	5		0	30	17	13	千克		---Other
2917.1400	--马来酐	6.5	5		0	30	17	13	千克		--Maleic anhydride
2917.1900	--其他	6.5	5		0	30	17	13	千克		--Other
2917.1900 10	驱虫特	6.5				30	17	13	千克	S	Tabatrex Tabutrex
2917.1900 90	其他无环多元羧酸	6.5				30	17	13	千克		other cyclic polybasic carboxylic acid

税则号列 Tariff Item.	货品名称	最惠国(%) MFN	协定(%)CT 东盟 CA	中巴 CP	中智 CC	普通 Gen	增值税率 VAT	出口退税 ED	计量单位 Unit	监管条件 SC	Article Description
	-环烷多元羧酸、环烯多元羧酸、环萜烯多元羧酸及其酸酐、酰卤化物、过氧化物和过氧酸以及它们的衍生物:										-Cyclanic, cyclenic or cycloterpenic polycarboxylic acids, their anhydrides, halides, peroxides, peroxyacids and their derivatives:
2917.2010	---四氢苯酐	4			0	11	17	13	千克		---Tetrahydro benzoic anhydride
2917.2090	---其他	6.5	5		0	30	17	13	千克		---Other
2917.2090 10	驱蚊灵	6.5				30	17	13	千克	S	dimethyl carbate
2917.2090 90	其他(环烷、环烯、环萜烯)多元羧酸	6.5				30	17	13	千克		other (cycloparaffin, cycloalkene, cycloterpene) polybasic carboxylic acid
	-芳香多元羧酸及其酸酐、酰卤化物、过氧化物和过氧酸以及它们的衍生物:										-Aromatic polycarboxylic acids, their anhydrides, halides, peroxides, peroxyacids and their derivatives:
2917.3200	--邻苯二甲酸二辛酯	6.5	5		5.2	30	17	13	千克		--Dioctyl orthophthalates
2917.3300	--邻苯二甲酸二壬酯及邻苯二甲酸二癸酯	6.5	T3		5.2	30	17	13	千克		--Dinonyl or didecyl orthophthalates
	---其他邻苯甲酸酯										---Other Pimethyl phehalate
2917.3410	---邻苯二甲酸二丁酯	6.5	5		5.2	30	17	13	千克		--Dibutyl orthophthalates
2917.3410 10	驱蚊叮	6.5				30	17	13	千克	S	Anophelifuge
2917.3410 90	其他邻苯二甲酸二丁酯	6.5				30	17	13	千克		Other phthalic acid dibutyl ester
2917.3490	---其他	6.5	T3		5.2	30	17	13	千克		---Other
2917.3490 10	避蚊酯	6.5				30	17	13	千克	S	Mosquitocide
2917.3490 90	其他邻苯二甲酸酯	6.5				30	17	13	千克		Other phthalate
	--其他邻苯二甲酸酯:										--Other esters of orthophthalic acid:
2917.3500	--邻苯二甲酸酐	6.5	T3		5.2	30	17	13	千克	A	--Phthalic anhydride
	--对苯二甲酸及其盐:										--Terephthalic acid and its salts:
2917.3611	----精对苯二甲酸	7.6		7.1	0	30	17	13	千克	7	----Terephthalic acid
2917.3619	----其它	7.6		7.1	0	30	17	13	千克	7	----Other
2917.3690	---其他	6.5	5		0	30	17	13	千克		---Other
2917.3700	--对苯二甲酸二甲酯	6.5	5		0	30	17	13	千克		--Dimethyl terephthalate
	--其他:										--Other:
2917.3910	---间苯二甲酸	6.5	5		5.2	30	17	13	千克		---m-Phthalic acid
2917.3990	---其他	6.5	5		5.2	30	17	13	千克		---Other
2917.3990 11	酞菌酯	6.5				30	17	13	千克	S	phthaleins ester
2917.3990 12	氯酞酸甲酯	6.5				30	17	13	千克	S	fluorin phthaleins acid polymethylmethacrylate
2917.3990 13	氯酞酸	6.5				30	17	13	千克	S	chlorin phthalic acid
2917.3990 90	其他芳香多元羧酸	6.5				30	17	13	千克		other aromatic polybasic carboxylic acid
29.18	**含附加含氧基的羧酸及其酸酐、酰卤化物、过氧化物和过氧酸以及它们的卤化、磺化、硝化或亚硝化衍生物:**										**Carboxylic acids with additional oxygen function and their anhydrides, halides, peroxides and peroxyacids; their halogenated, sulphonated, nitrated or nitrosated derivatives:**
	-含醇基但不含其他含氧基的羧酸及其酸酐、酰卤化物、过氧化物和过氧酸以及它们的衍生物:										-Carboxylic acids with alcohol function but without other oxygen function, their anhydrides, halides, peroxides, peroxyacids and their derivatives:
2918.1100	--乳酸及其盐和酯	6.5	5		0	30	17	13	千克		--Lactic acid, its salts and esters
2918.1200	--酒石酸	6.5	5		5.2	35	17	13	千克		--Tartaric acid
2918.1300	--酒石酸盐及酒石酸酯	6.5	5		5.2	30	17	13	千克		--Salts and esters of tartaric acid

税则号列 Tariff Item.	货品名称	最惠国(%) MFN	协定(%) CT 东盟 CA	中巴 CP	中智 CC	普通 Gen	增值税率 VAT	出口退税 ED	计量单位 Unit	监管条件 SC	Article Description
2918.1400	--柠檬酸	6.5	T3		5.2	35	17	13	千克	aB	--Citric acid
2918.1500	--柠檬酸盐及柠檬酸酯	6.5	T3		0	30	17	13	千克	B	--Salts and esters of citric acid
2918.1600	--葡糖酸及其盐和酯	6.5	5		0	30	17	13	千克		--Gluconic acid, its salts and esters
2918.1800	--乙酯杀螨醇(ISO)	6.5	5		0	30	17	13	千克	S	--Chlorobenzilate(ISO)
	--其他:										--Other:
2918.1910	---2,2-二苯基-2-羟基乙酸(二苯羟乙酸;二苯乙醇酸)	6.5	5		0	30	17	13	千克	23	---2,2-Diphenyl-2-hydroxyacetic acid (a-hydroxydiphenylacetic acid, benzilic acid)
2918.1990	---其他	6.5	5		0	30	17		千克		---Other
2918.1990 10	二苯乙醇酸甲酯(包括其酸酐、酰卤化物、过氧化物和过氧酸及该号的衍生物)	6.5				30	17		千克	23	Methyl benzilate and their anhydrides, halides, peroxides, peroxyacids and their derivatives
2918.1990 30	γ-羟基丁酸及其盐	6.5				30	17	13	千克	I	γ-hydroxybutyric acid and its salts
2918.1990 41	丙酯杀螨醇	6.5				30	17	13	千克	S	propyl ester chlorfenethol
2918.1990 42	溴螨酯	6.5				30	17	13	千克	S	fenisobromolate
2918.1990 43	芴丁酯	6.5				30	17	13	千克	S	4 – ester fluorene
2918.1990 44	整形醇	6.5				30	17	13	千克	S	truing ester
2918.1990 90	其他含醇基但不含其他含氧基羧酸(包括其酸酐、酰卤化物、过氧化物和过氧酸及该号的衍生物)	6.5				30	17	13	千克		Other Carboxylic acids with phenol function but without other oxygen function, including their anhydrides, halides, peroxides, peroxyacids and their derivatives
	-含酚基但不含其他含氧基的羧酸及其酸酐、酰卤化物、过氧化物和过氧酸以及它们的衍生物:										-Carboxylic acids with phenol function but without other oxygen function, their anhydrides, halides, peroxides, peroxyacids and their derivatives:
	--水杨酸及其盐:										--Salicylic acid and its salts:
2918.2110	---水杨酸、水杨酸钠	6.5	5		0	20	17	13	千克		---Salicylic acid and sodium salicylate
2918.2190	---其他	6.5	5		0	30	17	13	千克		---Other
	--邻乙酰水杨酸及其盐和酯:										--*o*-Acetylsalicylic acid, its salts and esters:
2918.2210	---邻乙酰水杨酸(阿斯匹林)	6	5		0	20	17	13	千克		---Acetylsalicylic acid
2918.2290	---其他	6.5	5		0	30	17	13	千克		---Other
2918.2300	--水杨酸的其他酯及其盐	6.5	5		0	30	17	13	千克		--Other esters of salicylic acid and their salts
2918.2900	--其他	6.5	T3		5.2	30	17	13	千克		--Other
2918.3000	-含醛基或酮基但不含其他含氧基的羧酸及其酸酐、卤化物、过氧化物和过氧酸以及它们的衍生物	6.5	5		0	30	17	13	千克		-Carboxylic acids with aldehyde or ketone function but without other oxygen function, their anhydrides, halides, peroxides, peroxyacids and their derivatives
2918.3000 11	除虫菊素Ⅰ、除虫菊素Ⅱ	6.5				30	17	13	千克	S	PyrethrumⅠ, PyrethrumⅡ.
2918.3000 12	瓜叶菊素Ⅰ、瓜叶菊素Ⅱ	6.5				30	17	13	千克	S	jasmine ketone chrysanthemum element Ⅰ, jasmine ketone chrysanthemum element Ⅱ
2918.3000 13	茉酮菊素Ⅰ、茉酮菊素Ⅱ	6.5				30	17	13	千克	S	jasmine ketone chrysanthemum element Ⅰ, jasmine ketone chrysanthemum element Ⅱ
2918.3000 14	环戊烯丙菊酯	6.5				30	17	13	千克	S	cyclopentadiene 4 – chrysanthemum ester
2918.3000 15	调环酸、抗倒酯、环虫菊酯	6.5				30	17	13	千克	S	cycle – adjusting acid, anti – falling ester, cyclic chrysanthemum ester

税则号列 Tariff Item.	货品名称	最惠国(%) MFN	协定(%) 东盟 CA	中巴 CP	中智 CC	普通 Gen	增值税率 VAT	出口退税 ED	计量单位 Unit	监管条件 SC	Article Description
2918.3000 16	烯丙菊酯等(包括右旋烯丙菊酯、富右旋反式烯丙菊酯,右旋反式烯丙菊酯)	6.5				30	17	13	千克	S	Allethrin(including d – allethrin、rich – d – t – allethrin、d – t – allethrin)
2918.3000 17	Es_生物烯丙菊酯、生物烯丙菊酯等(包括S_生物烯丙菊酯)	6.5				30	17	13	千克	S	Es biological allyl chrysanthemum ester, biological allyl chrysanthemum ester, etc
2918.3000 90	其他含醛基或酮基不含其他含氧基羧酸(包括酸酐、酰卤化物、过氧化物和过氧酸及该税号的衍生物)	6.5				30	17	13	千克		other carboxylic acid containing aldehyde group or copper base but not other oxygen – containing group
	-其他:										-Other:
2918.9100	--2,4,5一三希(ISO)(2,4,5)一三氯苯氧基乙酸)及其盐和酯	6.5	5		0	30	17		千克	89	--2,4,5-trichlorophenoxy acetic acid
2918.9900	--其他	6.5	5		0	30	17	13	千克		--Other
2918.9900 21	2,4-滴、2,4-滴丙酸、2,4 滴丁酸等(包括精 2,4 滴丙酸)	6.5				30	17	13	千克	S	2,4 – d, 2,4 – D propionic acid 2,4 – DB (including 2,4 – DB – P)
2918.9900 22	2 甲 4 氯、2 甲 4 氯丙酸等(包括精 2 甲 4 氯丙酸)	6.5				30	17	13	千克	S	MCPA, Mecoprop (including mecoprop – P)
2918.9900 23	2 甲 4 氯丁酸	6.5				30	17	13	千克	S	potassium 4 chlorine butyric acid
2918.9900 24	麦草畏、杀草畏	6.5				30	17	13	千克	S	dicamba, tricamba
2918.9900 25	禾草灵、乳氟禾草灵	6.5				30	17	13	千克	S	herbicide, fluorin herbicide
2918.9900 26	氟萘禾草灵、甲羧除草醚	6.5				30	17	13	千克	S	fluorine naphthalene herbicide, 1 – carboxyl weeding aether
2918.9900 27	三氟羧草醚、乙羧氟草醚	6.5				30	17	13	千克	S	3 – fluorine carboxyl weeding aether, 2 – carboxyl fluorine weeding aether
2918.9900 28	氟乳醚、调果酸、座果酸	6.5				30	17	13	千克	S	fluorine aether, fruit – adjusting acid, fruit – growing acid
2918.9900 29	增糖酯、脱落酸、氯氟草醚乙酯	6.5				30	17	13	千克	S	sugar – enhancing ester, abscisic acid, chlorine fluorine aether ethyl ester
2918.9900 90	其他含其他附加含氧基羧酸(包括其酸酐、酰卤化物、过氧化物和过氧酸及该号的衍生物)	6.5				30	17	13	千克		Other carboxylic acids with other additional oxygen function and their anhydrides, halides, peroxides and peroxyacids; their
	第八分章 非金属无机酸酯及其盐以及它们的卤化、磺化、硝化或亚硝化衍生物										Ⅷ. -ESTERS OF INORGANIC ACIDS OF NON-METALS AND THEIR SALTS, AND THEIR HALOGENATED, SULPHONATED, NITRATED OR NITROSATED DERIVATIVES
29.19	**磷酸酯及其盐,包括乳磷酸盐,以及它们的卤化、磺化、硝化或亚硝化衍生物:**										**Phosphoric esters and their salts, including lactophosphates; their halogenated, sulphonated, nitrated or nitrosated derivatives:**
2919.1000	-三(2,3-二溴丙基)磷酸酯	6.5	5		0	30	17		千克	89	-Tri-(2,3-dibromopropyl) phosphate
2919.9000	-其他	6.5	5		0	30	17	13	千克		-Other
2919.9000 20	磷酸三丁酯	6.5				30	17	13	千克	3	Tributyl phosphate
2919.9000 31	敌敌钙,敌敌畏	6.5				30	17	13	千克	S	atgard, vapona

税则号列 Tariff Item.	货品名称	最惠国(%) MFN	协定(%)CT 东盟 CA	中巴 CP	中智 CC	普通 Gen	增值税率 VAT	出口退税 ED	计量单位 Unit	监管条件 SC	Article Description
2919.9000 32	速灭磷、二溴磷	6.5				30	17	13	千克	S	quick-killing phosphate, 2-bromine phosphate
2919.9000 33	巴毒磷、杀虫畏	6.5				30	17	13	千克	S	killing phosphate, insect killer
2919.9000 34	毒虫畏、甲基毒虫畏	6.5				30	17	13	千克	S	poisonous insect catcher, methyl poisonous insect killer
2919.9000 35	庚烯磷、特普	6.5				30	17	13	千克	S	heptylene phosphate, tepu
2919.9000 36	三乙膦酸铝、乙膦酸	6.5				30	17	13	千克	S	3 - phosphinic acid aluminum, 3 - phosphinic acid aluminum
2919.9000 37	氯瘟磷、伐草磷	6.5				30	17	13	千克	S	chloride phosphate, grass-killing phosphate
2919.9000 90	其他磷酸酯及其盐(包括乳磷酸盐)(包括它们的卤化、磺化、硝化或亚硝化衍生物)	6.5				30	17	13	千克		Other phosphoric esters and their salts, including lactophosphates; their halogenated, sulphonated, nitrated or nitrosated derivatives
29.20	**其他非金属无机酸酯(不包括卤化氢的酯)及其盐以及它们的卤化、磺化、硝化或亚硝化衍生物:**										**Esters of other inorganic acids of non-metals (excluding esters of hydrogen halides) and their salts; their halogenated, sulphonated, nitrated or nitrosated derivatives:**
	-硫代磷酸酯及其盐以及它们的卤化、磺化、硝化或亚硝化衍生物:										-Thiophosphoric esters (phosphorothioates) and their salts; their halogenated, sulphonated, nitrated or nitrosated derivatives:
2920.1100	--对硫磷(ISO)及甲基对硫磷	6.5	5		0	30	17	13	千克	S	--Para-phosphate(ISO) methyl para-phosphate(ISO)
2920.1900	--其他	6.5	5		0	30	17	13	千克	S	--Other
2920.1900 12	氯氧磷、虫螨畏	6.5				30	17	13	千克	S	chloride oxygen phosphate, insect killer
2920.1900 13	杀螟硫磷、除线磷	6.5				30	17	13	千克	S	Fenitrothion, dichlofention
2920.1900 14	异氯磷、皮蝇磷	6.5				30	17	13	千克	S	stranger chloride phosphate, fly phosphate
2920.1900 15	溴硫磷、乙基溴硫磷、硝虫硫磷	6.5				30	17	13	千克	S	bromine sulphur phosphate, ethyl bromine sulphur phosphate, saltpeter sulphur phosphate insect killer
2920.1900 16	甲基增效磷、增效磷	6.5				30	17	13	千克	S	methyl effect-enhancing phosphate, effect-enhancing phosphate
2920.1900 17	碘硫磷、苯稻瘟净	6.5				30	17	13	千克	S	iodine sulphor phosphor, benzene rice plague curer
2920.1900 18	甲基立枯磷、克菌磷	6.5				30	17	13	千克	S	methyl wither phosphate, bacteria phosphate
2920.1900 19	速杀硫磷、丰丙磷	6.5				30	17	13	千克	S	sulphur phosphor killer, harvest-promoting phosphate
2920.1900 90	其他硫代磷酸酯及其盐(包括它们的卤化、磺化、硝化或亚硝化衍生物)	6.5				30	17	13	千克		Other thiophosphoric esters (phosphorothioates) and their salts; their halogenated, sulphonated, nitrated or nitrosated derivatives
	-其他:										-Other:
	---亚磷酸酯:										---Phosphites:
2920.9011	----亚磷酸三甲酯	6.5	5		5.2	30	17	13	千克	23	----Trimethyl phosphite
2920.9012	----亚磷酸三乙酯	6.5	5		5.2	30	17	13	千克	23	----Triethyl phosphite

税则号列 Tariff Item.	货品名称	最惠国(%) MFN	协定(%) 东盟 CA	中巴 CP	CT 中智 CC	普通 Gen	增值税率 VAT	出口退税 ED	计量单位 Unit	监管条件 SC	Article Description
2920.9013	----亚磷酸二甲酯	6.5	5		5.2	30	17	13	千克	23	----Dimethyl phosphite
2920.9014	----亚磷酸二乙酯	6.5	5		5.2	30	17	13	千克	23	----Diethyl phosphite
2920.9019	----其他	6.5	5		5.2	30	17		千克		----Other
2920.9090	---其他	6.5	5		5.2	30	17	13	千克		---Other
2920.9090 11	硫丹	6.5				30	17	13	千克	S	Sulphur pill
2920.9090 12	治螟磷	6.5				30	17	13	千克	S	Snout moth's larva - killing phosphate
2920.9090 13	消螨通	6.5				30	17	13	千克	S	acarus killer
2920.9090 14	炔螨特	6.5				30	17	13	千克	S	acarus special killer
2920.9090 15	浸种磷	6.5				30	17	13	千克	S	seed - dipping phosphate
2920.9090 16	赛松	6.5				30	17	13	千克	S	saigong
2920.9090 90	其他无机酸酯(不包括卤化氢的酯)(包括其盐以及它们的卤化,磺化,硝化或亚硝化衍生物)	6.5				30	17	13	千克		Other esters of other inorganic acids of non-metals cexculding esters of hydrogen halides) and their salts; their halogenated, sulphonated, nitrated or nitrosated derivatives.
	第九分章 含氮基化合物										Ⅸ. -NITROGEN-FUNCTION COMPOUNDS
29.21	氨基化合物:										**Amine-function compounds:**
	-无环单胺及其衍生物以及它们的盐:										-Acyclic monoamines and their derivatives; salts thereof:
2921.1100	--甲胺、二甲胺或三甲胺及其盐	6.5	5		0	30	17	13	千克		--Methylamine, di- or trimethylamine and their salts
2921.1100 10	二甲胺	6.5				30	17	13	千克	23	Dimethylamine
2921.1100 20	二甲胺盐酸盐	6.5				30	17	13	千克	23	Salts of dimethylamine
2921.1100 90	甲胺、三甲胺及其盐	6.5				30	17	13	千克		Methylamine, trimethylamine and their salts
	--其他:										--Other:
2921.1910	---二正丙胺	4			0	11	17	13	千克		---Di-*n*-propylamine
2921.1920	---异丙胺	6.5	5		0	30	17	13	千克		---Isopropyl amine
2921.1930	---N,N-二(2-氯乙基)乙胺	6.5	5		0	30	17	13	千克	32	---N,N-Bis(2-chloroethyl) ethylamine
2921.1940	---N,N-二(2-氯乙基)甲胺	6.5	5		0	30	17	13	千克	32	---N,N-Bis(2-chloroethyl) methylamine
2921.1950	---三(2-氯乙基)胺	6.5	5		0	30	17	13	千克	32	---Tri-(2-chloroethyl) amine
2921.1960	---二烷(甲、乙、正丙或异丙)氨基乙基-2-氯及其质子化盐	6.5	5		0	30	17	13	千克	23	---N,N-Dialkyl (Me, Et, n-Pr or i-Pr) aminoethyl-2-chlorides and corresponking protonated salts
2921.1990	---其他	6.5	5		0	30	17	13	千克		---Other
2921.1990 11	三乙胺(单一成分,用做点火剂)	6.5				30	17	13	千克	3	Triethylamine(Single component, used for igniter)
2921.1990 19	月桂胺、一乙胺、正丁胺	6.5				30	17	13	千克		Laurylamine, ethylamine, n-butylamine
2921.1990 20	二异丙胺	6.5				30	17	13	千克	3	Diisopropylamine
2921.1990 31	2-氨基丁烷	6.5				30	17	13	千克	S	2 - amido butane
2921.1990 32	二氯丙烯胺	6.5				30	17	13	千克	S	2 - chloride propylene amine
2921.1990 33	胺鲜酯	6.5				30	17	13	千克	S	amine ester
2921.1990 90	其他无环单胺及其衍生物及其盐	6.5				30	17	13	千克		Other Acyclic monoamines and their derivatives; salts thereof
	-无环多胺及其衍生物以及它们的盐:										-Acyclic polyamines and their derivatives; salts thereof:
	--乙二胺及其盐:										--Ethylenediamine and its salts:

税则号列 Tariff Item.	货品名称	最惠国(%) MFN	协定(%)CT 东盟 CA	中巴 CP	中智 CC	普通 Gen	增值税率 VAT	出口退税 ED	计量单位 Unit	监管条件 SC	Article Description
2921.2110	---乙二胺	6.5	5		0	30	17	13	千克		---Ethylenediamine
2921.2190	---其他	6.5	5		0	30	17	13	千克		---Other
	--六亚甲基二胺及其盐:										--Hexamethylenediamine and its salts:
2921.2210	---己二酸己二胺盐(尼龙66盐)	6.5	5		0	20	17	13	千克		---Alkyl mercuric salt(Nylon-66 salt)
2921.2290	---其他	6.5	5		0	30	17	13	千克		---Other
2921.2900	--其他	6.5	5		0	30	17	13	千克		--Other
2921.2900 01	二乙烯三胺	6.5				30	17	13	千克		Diethylenetriamine
2921.2900 90	其他无环多胺及其衍生物(包括它们的盐)	6.5				30	17	13	千克		Other acyclic polyamines and their derivatives;salts thereof
2921.3000	-环烷单胺或多胺、环烯单胺或多胺、环萜烯单胺或多胺及其衍生物以及它们的盐	6.5	5		0	30	17	13	千克		-Cyclanic, cyclenic or cycloterpenic mono-or polyamines, and their derivatives; salts thereof
2921.3000 30	氨基羧酸环丙烷	6.5				30	17	13	千克	S	amido carboxylic acid cyclic butane
2921.3000 90	其他环(烷、烯、萜烯)单胺或多胺(包括其衍生物及它们的盐)	6.5				30	17	13	千克		Other cyclanic, cyclenic or cycloterpenic mono-or polyamines, and their derivatives; salts thereof
	-芳香单胺及其衍生物以及它们的盐:										-Aromatic monoamines and their derivatives; salts thereof:
	--苯胺及其盐:										--Aniline and its salts:
2921.4110	---苯胺	6.5	5		0	20	17	13	千克	X	---Aniline
2921.4190	---其他	6.5	5		0	30	17	13	千克		---Other
2921.4200	--苯胺衍生物及其盐	6.5	5		0	30	17	13	千克		--Aniline derivatives and their salts
2921.4200 11	氯硝胺	6.5				30	17	13	千克	S	allisan
2921.4200 12	敌锈钠	6.5				30	17	13	千克	S	rust natrium
2921.4200 13	苯草醚	6.5				30	17	13	千克	S	benzene grass aether
2921.4200 90	其他苯胺衍生物及其盐	6.5				30	17	13	千克		other benzene amine derivants and their salt
2921.4300	--甲苯胺及其衍生物以及它们的盐	6.5	5		0	30	17	13	千克		--Toluidines and their derivatives; salts thereof
2921.4300 10	氟乐灵原药	6.5				30	17	13	千克	S	Trifluralin (TC)
2921.4300 20	邻甲苯胺	6.5				30	17	13	千克		*o*-Tuluidine
2921.4300 31	溴鼠胺	6.5				30	17	13	千克	S	Bromethalin
2921.4300 32	乙丁氟灵	6.5				30	17	13	千克	S	Benfluralin
2921.4300 33	氯乙氟灵	6.5				30	17	13	千克	S	Fluchloraline
2921.4300 34	环丙氟灵	6.5				30	17	13	千克	S	Profluralin
2921.4300 35	乙丁烯氟灵	6.5				30	17	13	千克	S	Ethalfluralin
2921.4300 36	地乐灵	6.5				30	17	13	千克	S	Dlipropalin
2921.4300 37	氯乙灵	6.5				30	17	13	千克	S	Cohlornid
2921.4300 38	氟节胺	6.5				30	17	13	千克	S	Flumetralim
2921.4300 90	甲苯胺及其衍生物以及它们的盐	6.5				30	17	13	千克		Toluidines and their derivatives; salts thereof
2921.4400	--二苯胺及其衍生物以及它们的盐	6.5	5		0	30	17	17	千克		--Diphenylamine and its derivatives; salts thereof
2921.4500	--1-萘胺(α-萘胺)、2-萘胺(β-萘胺)及其衍生物以及它们的盐	6.5	5		0	30	17	13	千克		--1-Naphthylamine (α-naphthylamine), 2-naphthylamine (β-naphthylamine) and their derivatives; salts thereof
2921.4500 10	2-萘胺	6.5				30	17	13	千克	X	2-Naphthylamine
2921.4500 90	1-萘胺和2-萘胺的衍生物及盐(包括1-萘胺)	6.5				30	17	13	千克		1-Naphthylamine and 2-Naphthylamine and its deriratires salis there of

税则号列 Tariff Item.	货品名称	最惠国(%) MFN	协定(%)CT 东盟 CA	 中巴 CP	 中智 CC	普通 Gen	增值税率 VAT	出口退税 ED	计量单位 Unit	监管条件 SC	Article Description
2921.4600	--安非他明(INN)、苄非他明(INN)、右苯丙胺(INN)、乙非他明、芬坎法明(INN)、利非他明、左苯丙胺(INN)、美芬雷司(INN)、苯丁胺(INN)以及它们的盐	6.5	5		0	30	17	13	千克		--Amfetamine(INN), benzfetamine(INN), dexamfetamine (INN), etilamfetamine (INN), fencamfamin(INN), lefetamine (INN), levamfetamine(INN), mefenorex (INN) and phentermine (INN); salts thereof
2921.4600 11	安非他明、苄非他明、右苯丙胺(包括它们的盐)	6.5				30	17	13	千克	I	Amfetamine (INN), benzfetamine (INN), dexamfetamine (INN) (salts thereof)
2921.4600 12	乙非他明、芬坎法明、利非他明(包括它们的盐)	6.5				30	17	13	千克	I	Etilamfetamine (INN), fencamfamin (INN), lefetamine(INN) (salts thereof)
2921.4600 13	左苯丙胺、美芬雷司、芬特明(包括它们的盐)	6.5				30	17	13	千克	I	levamfetamine (INN), mefenorex (INN) and phentermine(INN) (salts thereof)
	--其他:										--Other:
2921.4910	---对异丙基苯胺	4			0	11	17	13	千克		---*p*-Isopropyl-aniline
2921.4920	---二甲基苯胺	6.5	5		0	20	17	13	千克		---Dimethylanilines
2921.4920 01	2,4、2,6-二甲基苯胺	6.5				20	17	13	千克		2,4、2,6-Dimethylanilines
2921.4920 90	其他二甲基苯胺	6.5				20	17	13	千克		Other Dimethylanilines
2921.4930	---2,6-甲基乙基苯胺	4			0	11	17	13	千克		---2,6-Methyl ethyl aniline
2921.4940	---2,6-二乙基苯胺	6.5	5		0	20	17	13	千克		---2,6-Diethylaniline
2921.4990	---其他	6.5	5		0	30	17	13	千克		---Other
2921.4990 11	异丙乐灵	6.5				30	17	13	千克	S	yibingleling
2921.4990 12	仲丁灵	6.5				30	17	13	千克	S	zhongdingling
2921.4990 13	二甲戊灵	6.5				30	17	13	千克	S	2 – lumichrome
2921.4990 20	4–氨基联苯	6.5				30	17	13	千克	X	4 – phenylaniline
2921.4990 90	其他芳香单胺及衍生物及它们的盐	6.5				30	17	13	千克		other aromatic monoamine and derivants and their salt
	-芳香多胺及其衍生物以及它们的盐:										-Aromatic polyamines and their derivatives; salts thereof:
	--邻-、间-、对-苯二胺、二氨基甲苯及其衍生物以及它们的盐:										--*o*-, *m*-, *p*-Phenylenediamine, diaminotoluenes, and their derivatives; salts thereof:
2921.5110	---邻苯二胺	4			0	11	17	13	千克		---*o*-Phenylenediamine
2921.5190	---其他	6.5	5		0	30	17	13	千克		---Other
2921.5190 11	氨氟灵	6.5				30	17	13	千克	S	ammonia fluorine
2921.5190 12	氨氟乐灵	6.5				30	17	13	千克	S	ammonia fluorine
2921.5190 20	2,4–二氨基甲苯	6.5				30	17	13	千克	X	2,4 – diaminotoluene
2921.5190 90	间–、对–苯二胺、二氨基甲苯等(包括衍生物及它们的盐)	6.5				30	17	13	千克		m – phenylene diamine, para – phenylene diamine, diaminotoluene, etc
2921.5900	--其他	6.5	5		0	30	17	13	千克		--Other
2921.5900 10	三氨基三硝基苯	6.5				30	17	13	千克	3	Triaminotrinitrobenzene
2921.5900 20	联苯胺(4,4'–二氨基联苯)	6.5				30	17	13	千克	89	benzidine(4,4'– diaminobiphenyl)
2921.5900 31	4,4'–二氨基–3,3'–二氯二苯基甲烷	6.5				30	17	13	千克	X	4,4'– diamino – 3,3 – dicophane 4
2921.5900 32	3,3'–二氯联苯胺	6.5				30	17	13	千克	X	3,3 – dichlorobenzidine
2921.5900 33	4,4'–二氨基二苯基甲烷	6.5				30	17	13	千克	X	4,4'– Methylenedianiline

税则号列 Tariff Item.	货品名称	最惠国(%) MFN	协定(%)CT 东盟 CA	中巴 CP	中智 CC	普通 Gen	增值税率 VAT	出口退税 ED	计量单位 Unit	监管条件 SC	Article Description
2921.5900 90	其他芳香多胺及衍生物及它们的盐	6.5				30	17	13	千克		Other aromatic polyamines and their derivatives; salts thereof
29.22	**含氧基氨基化合物：**										**Oxygen-function amino-compounds:**
	-氨基醇(但含有一种以上含氧基的除外)及其醚和酯，以及它们的盐：										-Amino-alcohols, other than those containing more than one kind of oxygen function, their ethers and esters; salts thereof:
2922.1100	--单乙醇胺及其盐	6.5	5		0	30	17	13	千克		--Monoethanolamine and its salts
2922.1100 01	单乙醇胺	6.5				30	17	13	千克		Monoethanolamine
2922.1100 90	单乙醇胺盐	6.5				30	17	13	千克		Monoethanolamine salts
2922.1200	--二乙醇胺及其盐	6.5	5		0	30	17	13	千克		--Diethanolamine and its salts
2922.1200 01	二乙醇胺	6.5				30	17	13	千克		Diethanolamine
2922.1200 90	二乙醇胺盐	6.5				30	17	13	千克		Salts of diethanolamine
	--三乙醇胺及其盐：										--Triethanolamine and its salts:
2922.1310	---三乙醇胺	6.5	5		0	30	17	13	千克	23	---Triethanolamine
2922.1320	---三乙醇胺盐	6.5	5		0	30	17	13	千克		---Salts of triethanolamine
2922.1320 01	芳基聚氧乙烯磷酸酯	6.5				30	17	13	千克		Aromatic polyoxyethylene phosphate
2922.1320 20	三乙醇胺盐酸盐	6.5				30	17	13	千克	23	Triethanolamine hydrochloride
2922.1320 90	其他三乙醇胺的盐	6.5				30	17	13	千克		Other
2922.1400	--右丙氧吩(INN)及其盐	6.5	5		0	30	17	13	千克	W	--Dextropropoxyphene(INN) and its salts
	--其他：										--Other:
2922.1910	---乙胺丁醇	6.5	5		0	30	17	13	千克		---Ethylamino butanol (Ethambutol)
	---二烷(甲、乙、正丙或异丙)氨基乙-2-醇及其质子化盐：										---N, N-Dialkyl-(Me, Et, n-Pr or i-Pr) aminoethane-2-ols and cornesponding protonated salts:
2922.1921	----二甲氨基乙醇及其质子化盐	6.5	5		0	30	17	13	千克		----N, N-Dimethylaminoethanol and corresponding protonated salts
2922.1922	----二乙氨基乙醇及其质子化盐	6.5	5		0	30	17	13	千克		----N, N-Diethylaminoethanol and corresponding protonated salts
2922.1922 10	2-二乙氨基乙醇(或称N,N-二乙基乙醇胺)	6.5				30	17	13	千克	3	2 – diethylaminoethanol (N, N – Diethylethanolamine)
2922.1922 90	二乙氨基乙醇的质子化盐	6.5				30	17	13	千克		N, N-Diethylaminoethanol and corresponding protonated salts
2922.1929	----其他	6.5	5		0	30	17	13	千克	23	----Other
2922.1930	---乙基二乙醇胺	6.5	5		0	30	17	13	千克	23	---Ethyldiethanolamine
2922.1940	---甲基二乙醇胺	6.5	5		0	30	17	13	千克	23	---Methyldiethanolamine
2922.1990	---其他	6.5	5		0	30	17	13	千克		---Other
2922.1990 10	增产胺	6.5				30	17	13	千克	S	growth amine
2922.1990 20	克仑特罗	6.5				30	17	13	千克	L	Clenbuterol
2922.1990 90	其他氨基醇及其醚、酯和它们的盐(但含有一种以上含氧基的除外)	6.5				30	17	13	千克		other alkamine and its aether, ester and their salt (other than those containing more than one kind of Oxygen function)
	-氨基萘酚和其他氨基酚(但含有一种以上含氧基的除外)及其醚和酯，以及它们的盐：										-Amino-naphthols and amino-phenols, other than those containing more than one kind of oxygen function, their ethers and esters; salts thereof:
2922.2100	--氨基羟基萘磺酸及其盐	6.5	5		0	30	17	13	千克		--Aminohydroxynaphthalenesulphonic acid and their salts
	--其他：										--Other

税则号列 Tariff Item.	货品名称	最惠国(%) MFN	协定(%)CT 东盟 CA	中巴 CP	中智 CC	普通 Gen	增值税率 VAT	出口退税 ED	计量单位 Unit	监管条件 SC	Article Description
2922.2910	---茴香胺、二茴香胺、氨基苯乙醚及其盐	6.5	5		0	30	17	13	千克		---Anisidine, dianisidine, phenetidine and their salts
2922.2990	---其他	6.5	5		0	30	17	13	千克		---Other
	-氨基醛、氨基酮和氨基醌,但含有一种以上含氧基的除外,以及它们的盐:										-Amino-aldehydes, amino-ketones and amino-quinones, other than those containing more than one kind of oxygen function; salts thereof:
2922.3100	--安非拉酮、美沙酮和去甲美沙酮以及它们的盐	6.5	5		0	30	17	13	千克		--Amfepramone (INN), methadone (INN) and normethadone (INN); salts thereof
2922.3100 10	安非拉酮及其盐	6.5				30	17	13	千克	I	Amfepramone(INN) and salts thereof
2922.3100 20	美沙酮、去甲美沙酮及它们的盐	6.5				30	17	13	千克	W	Methadone (INN), normethadone (INN) and salts thereof
2922.3900	--其他	6.5	5		0	30	17	13	千克		--Other
2922.3900 10	氯胺酮及其盐	6.5				30	17	13	千克	I	Ketamine and salts thereof
2922.3900 20	灭藻醌	6.5				30	17	13	千克	S	algae - killing quinone
2922.3900 90	其他氨基醛、氨基酮及其盐(包括氨基醌及其盐,但含有一种以上含氧基除外)	6.5				30	17	13	千克		Other amino-aldehydes, amino-ketones and amino-quinones, other than those containing more than one kind of oxygen function; salts thereof
	-氨基酸(但含有一种以上含氧基的除外)及其酯,以及它们的盐:										-Amino-acids, other than those containing more than one kind of oxygen function, and their esters; salts thereof:
	--赖氨酸及其酯,以及它们的盐:										--Lysine and its esters; salts thereof:
2922.4110	---赖氨酸	5			0	20	17	13	千克	AB	---Lysine
2922.4190	---其他	6	5		0	30	17	13	千克	AB	---Other
	--谷氨酸及其盐:										--Glutamic acid and its salts:
2922.4210	---谷氨酸	10	T3	8.6	0	90	17	13	千克	AB	---Glutamic acid
2922.4220	---谷氨酸钠	10	T3		0	130	17	13	千克	AB	---Sodium glutamate
2922.4290	---其他	6.5	T3		0	30	17	13	千克	AB	---Other
	--氨基酸(但含有一种以上含氧基的除外)及其酯,以及它们的盐:										--Anthranilic acid and its salts:
2922.4310	---邻氨基苯甲酸(氨茴酸)	6.5	5		0	20	17	13	千克	23	---Anthranilic acid
2922.4390	---其他	6.5	5		0	30	17	13	千克		---Other
2922.4400	--替利定(INN)及其盐	6.5	5		0	30	17	13	千克		--Tilidine(INN) and its salts
	--其他:										--Other:
2922.4910	---其他氨基酸	6.5	5		0	20	17	13	千克	AB	---Amino acids
	---其他:										---Other:
2922.4991	----普鲁卡因	6	5		0	20	17	13	千克		----Procaine
2922.4999	----其他	6.5	5		0	30	17	13	千克		----Other
2922.4999 11	草灭畏	6.5				30	17	13	千克	ABS	weed killer
2922.4999 12	灭杀威、灭除威、混灭威等(害扑威、速灭威、混杀威、残杀威、猛杀威)	6.5				30	17	13	千克	ABS	MPMC, XMC, Dimethacarb (CPMC, Metolcarb, propoxur, Promecarb)
2922.4999 13	兹克威、灭害威、除害威	6.5				30	17	13	千克	ABS	various pesticides
2922.4999 14	异丙威	6.5				30	17	13	千克	ABS	yibingwei

税则号列 Tariff Item.	货 品 名 称	最惠国(%) MFN	协定(%)CT 东盟 CA	中巴 CP	中智 CC	普通 Gen	增值税率 VAT	出口退税 ED	计量单位 Unit	监管条件 SC	Article Description
2922.4999 15	仲丁威、畜虫威、合杀威	6.5				30	17	13	千克	ABS	zhongdingwei, animal insect killer, all killer
2922.4999 16	甲萘威、地麦威、蜱虱威	6.5				30	17	13	千克	ABS	1 – naphthalene, rice pesticide, tick and louse killer
2922.4999 17	苯氧威、除线威	6.5				30	17	13	千克	ABS	benzene oxygen, chuxianwei
2922.4999 90	其他氨基酸及其酯及它们的盐(含有一种以上含氧基的除外)	6.5				30	17	13	千克	AB	other amino acid and their salt. (Other than those containing more than one kind of oxygen function)
2922.5000	-氨基醇酚、氨基酸酚及其他含氧基氨基化合物	6.5	5		0	30	17	13	千克		-Amino-alcohol-phenols, amino-acid-phenols and other amino-compounds with oxygen function
29.23	**季铵盐及季铵碱;卵磷脂及其他磷氨基类脂,不论是否已有化学定义:**										**Quaternary ammonium salts and hydroxides; lecithins and other phosphoaminolipids, whether or not chemically defined:**
2923.1000	-胆碱及其盐	6.5	5		0	30	17	13	千克		-Choline and its salts
2923.2000	-卵磷脂及其他磷氨基类脂	6.5	5		0	30	17	13	千克		-Lecithins and other phosphoaminolipids
2923.9000	-其他	6.5	5		0	30	17	13	千克		-Other
2923.9000 11	矮壮素	6.5				30	17	13	千克	S	chlorocholine chloride
2923.9000 12	菊胺酯	6.5				30	17	13	千克	S	chrysanthemine ester
2923.9000 90	其他季铵盐及季铵碱	6.5				30	17	13	千克		other quaternary ammonium salt and quaternary ammonium hydrate
29.24	**羧基酰胺基化合物;碳酸酰胺基化合物:**										**Carboxyamide-function compounds; amide-function compounds of carbonic acid:**
	-无环酰胺(包括无环氨基甲酸酯)及其衍生物以及它们的盐:										-Acyclic amides (including acyclic carbamates) and their derivatives; salts thereof:
2924.1100	--甲丙氨酯(INN)	6.5	5		0	30	17	13	千克	I	--Meprobamate(INN)
2924.1200	--氟乙酰胺(ISO)久效磷(ISO)及磷胺(ISO)	6.5	T3		5.2	30	17	13	千克		--Fluoroacetamide(ISO), monocrotophos (ISO). or dimecron(ISO)
2924.1200 10	氟乙酰胺(ISO)(氟乙酰胺别名敌蚜胺)	6.5				30	17	13	千克	89	Fluoroacetamide(ISO)()
2924.1200 90	久效磷(ISO)及磷胺(ISO)	6.5				30	17	13	千克	S	Monocrotophos(ISO), dimecron(ISO)()
	--其他(INN):										--Other:
2924.1910	---二甲基甲酰胺	6.5	T3		5.2	30	17	13	千克		---N, N-dimethylformamide
2924.1990	---其他	6.5	T3		5.2	30	17	13	千克		---Other
2924.1990 12	百治磷	6.5				30	17	13	千克	S	dicrotophos
2924.1990 13	溴乙酰胺	6.5				30	17	13	千克	S	bromoacetamide
2924.1990 14	霜霉威	6.5				30	17	13	千克	S	frost mold curer
2924.1990 15	叶枯炔	6.5				30	17	13	千克	S	withered leaf alkyne
2924.1990 16	二丙烯草胺	6.5				30	17	13	千克	S	2-propylene grass amine
2924.1990 17	解草烯	6.5				30	17	13	千克	S	Humulene
2924.1990 18	驱蚊酯	6.5				30	17	13	千克	S	Dimethyl phthalate
2924.1990 30	甲丙氨酯的盐	6.5				30	17	13	千克	I	Salts of meprobamate (INN)
2924.1990 40	丙烯酰胺	6.5				30	17	13	千克	X	acrylamide
2924.1990 90	其他无环酰胺(包括无环氨基甲酸酯)(包括其衍生物及其盐)	6.5				30	17	13	千克		Acyclic amides (including acyclic carbamates) (and their derivatives; salts thereof)

税则号列 Tariff Item.	货品名称	最惠国(%) MFN	协定(%) CT			普通 Gen	增值税率 VAT	出口退税 ED	计量单位 Unit	监管条件 SC	Article Description
			东盟 CA	中巴 CP	中智 CC						
	-环酰胺(包括环氨基甲酸酯)及其衍生物以及它们的盐:										-Cyclic amides (including cyclic carbamates) and their derivatives; salts thereof:
2924.2100	--酰脲及其衍生物以及它们的盐	6.5	5		0	30	17	13	千克		--Ureides and their derivatives; salts thereof
2924.2100 10	氟环脲	6.5				30	17	13	千克	S	fluorine carbamide
2924.2100 90	其他酰脲及其衍生物以及它们的盐	6.5				30	17	13	千克		other acyl carbamide and its derivants and their salt
2924.2300	--2-乙酰氨基苯甲酸(N-乙酰邻氨基苯甲酸)及其盐	6.5	5		0	30	17	13	千克		--2-Acetamidobenzoic acid (N-acetylanthranilic acid) and its salts
2924.2300 10	2-乙酰氨基苯甲酸;N-乙酰邻氨基苯甲酸(包括N-乙酰邻氨基苯甲酸	6.5				30	17	13	千克	23	2 – Acetamidobenzoic acid; (including N – acetylanthranilic acid)
2924.2300 90	2-乙酰氨基苯甲酸盐	6.5				30	17	13	千克		N – acetylanthranilic salts
2924.2400	--炔己蚁胺(INN)	6.5	5		0	30	17	13	千克	I	--Ethinamate(INN)
	--其他:										--Other:
2924.2910	---对乙酰氨基苯乙醚(非那西丁)	6	T3		4.8	30	17	13	千克	Q	---Phenacetin
2924.2920	---对乙酰氨基酚(扑热息痛)	6	T3		4.8	30	17	13	千克	aQ	---*p*-Acetaminophenol (paracetanol)
2924.2990	---其他	6.5	T3		5.2	30	17	13	千克		---Other
2924.2990 11	避蚊胺、灭锈胺、叶枯酞、水杨菌胺	6.5				30	17	13	千克	S	Deet, mebenil, withered leaf phthaleins, saligenin
2924.2990 12	萘草胺、新燕灵、非草隆、氯炔灵	6.5				30	17	13	千克	S	Grass naphthalene amine, benzoylprop ethyl, fenuron, chlorine alkyne
2924.2990 13	燕麦灵、苄胺灵、特草灵、特胺灵	6.5				30	17	13	千克	S	Carbyne, benzyl amine, weed killer, special amine killer
2924.2990 14	毒草胺、丁烯草胺、二氯己酰草胺	6.5				30	17	13	千克	S	Poisonous grass amine, butylene grass amine, dichloro hexanoyl grass amine
2924.2990 15	萘丙胺、牧草胺、溴丁酰草胺	6.5				30	17	13	千克	S	Naphthalene propyl amine, pasture amine, bromine 4-acyl grass amine, chloroformyl grass amine
2924.2990 16	氯甲酰草胺、麦草伏M、麦草伏	6.5				30	17	13	千克	S	Chloroformyl grass amine, rice grass killer
2924.2990 17	氯虫酰肼、异丙甲草胺、苯肽胺酸等(包括精异丙甲草胺、缬霉威)	6.5				30	17	13	千克	S	Halofenozide, metolachlor(including s – metolachlor, iprovalicarb)
2924.2990 31	苯胺灵、苯霜灵、丙草胺、敌稗等(包括丙炔草胺、草不隆、草完隆、除虫脲、除幼脲)	6.5				30	17	13	千克	S	Propham, Benalaxyl, Pretilachlor, Propanil (including neburon, norea, Hexaflumuron, dichlorbenzuron)
2924.2990 32	敌草胺、敌草隆、二甲苯草胺等(包括丁草胺、丁酰草胺、二甲草胺、氟苯脲、氟草隆)	6.5				30	17	13	千克	S	Napropamide, Diuron, xylachlor (including Butachlor, dimethachlor , teflubenzuron, Fluometuron)
2924.2990 33	庚酰草胺、环丙草胺、环酰草胺等(包括氟虫脲、氟铃脲、氟酰胺、氟蚁灵、氟幼脲)	6.5				30	17	13	千克	S	Enanthoyl, cypromid (including flufenoxuron, Hexaflumuron, Flutriafol, penfluron)
2924.2990 34	甲氯酰草胺、甲霜灵、环草隆等(包括环莠隆、甲草胺、甲氧隆、克草胺、枯草隆)	6.5				30	17	13	千克	S	Pentanochlor Metalaxyl, Siduron (including Lasso, Metoxuron, Ethachlor, Chloroxuron)

税则号列 Tariff Item.	货品名称	最惠国(%) MFN	协定(%) 东盟 CA	中巴 CP	CT 中智 CC	普通 Gen	增值税率 VAT	出口退税 ED	计量单位 Unit	监管条件 SC	Article Description
2924.2990 35	甲基杀草隆、枯莠隆、邻酰胺等(包括绿麦隆、氯苯胺灵、麦草氟甲酯、麦草氟异丙酯)	6.5				30	17	13	千克	S	Methyldymron, difenoxuron, mebenil (including chlortoluron, chlorpropham, flamprop - methyl, flamprop - isopropyl)
2924.2990 36	灭草隆、灭幼脲、炔苯酰草胺等(包括麦锈灵、棉胺宁、灭草灵、炔草隆、杀草胺)	6.5				30	17	13	千克	S	Monuron, chlorbenzuron, Propyzamide
2924.2990 37	虱螨脲、双苯酰草胺、双酰草胺等(包括杀草隆、杀铃脲、杀螺胺、莎稗磷、烯丙酰草胺)	6.5				30	17	13	千克	S	lufenuron diphenamide, carbetamide (including dimuron, triflumuron, niclosamide, anilofos, dichlormide)
2924.2990 38	甜菜安、特丁草胺、乙氧苯草胺等(包括甜菜宁、戊菌隆、酰草隆、乙草胺、乙霉威)	6.5				30	17	13	千克	S	Desmedipham, terbuchlor, ethobenzanid (including Phenmedipham, Pencycuron, Acetochlor, Polystyrene resin)
2924.2990 39	乙酰甲草胺、异丙隆、异草完隆等(包括异丙草胺、异丁草胺)	6.5				30	17	13	千克	S	Diethatyl - ethyl, isoproturon, Isonoruron (including Propisochlor, delachlor)
2924.2990 40	炔己蚁胺的盐	6.5				30	17	13	千克	I	Salts of ethinamate(INN)
2924.2990 90	其他环酰胺(包括环氨基甲酸酯)(包括其衍生物以及它们的盐	6.5				30	17	13	千克		Other cyclic amides (including cyclic carbamates) and their derivatives; salts thereof, other than isoprocarb, MIPS
29.25	**羧基酰亚胺化合物(包括糖精及其盐)及亚胺基化合物:**										**Carboxyimide-function compounds (including saccharin and its salts) and imine-function compounds:**
	-酰亚胺及其衍生物以及它们的盐:										-Imides and their derivatives; salts thereof:
2925.1100	--糖精及其盐	9	5		7.2	90	17	13	千克	a	--Saccharin and its salts
2925.1200	--格鲁米特(INN)	6.5	5		0	30	17	13	千克	I	--Glutethimide(INN)
2925.1900	--其他	6.5	5		0	30	17	13	千克		--Other
2925.1900 10	格鲁米特的盐	6.5				30	17	13	千克	I	Salts of glutethimide (INN)
2925.1900 21	腐霉利	6.5				30	17	13	千克	S	Anti-mold
2925.1900 22	菌核净、菌核利、甲菌利、乙菌利	6.5				30	17	13	千克	S	dimetachlone, vinclozolin, myclozolin, chlozolinate
2925.1900 23	氟烯草酸	6.5				30	17	13	千克	S	fluorine acyl grass acid
2925.1900 24	胺菊酯(包括右旋胺菊酯、右旋反式胺菊酯、富右旋反式胺菊酯)	6.5				30	17	13	千克	S	Tetramethrin (including d - tetramethrin, d - t - Tetramethrin, rich - d - t - tetramethrin
2925.1900 90	其他酰亚胺及其衍生物、盐	6.5				30	17	13	千克		Other Imides and their derivatives; salts thereof
	-亚胺及其衍生物以及它们的盐										-Imines and their derivatives; salts thereof
2925.2100	--杀虫脒(ISO)	6.5	5		0	30	17	5	千克	89	--Chlordimeform
2925.2900	--其他	6.5	5		0	30	17	13	千克		--Other
2925.2900 11	杀螨特、杀螨脒	6.5				30	17	13	千克	S	Aramite, Shamanmi
2925.2900 12	双甲脒、单甲脒、伐虫脒、丙烷脒	6.5				30	17	13	千克	S	Amitraz, Monocarboxaidine Formetanate, Propamidne
2925.2900 13	烯肟菌胺、烯肟菌酯、醚菌酯	6.5				30	17	13	千克	S	Enostroburin, kresoximmethy

税则号列 Tariff Item.	货品名称	最惠国(%) MFN	协定(%) 东盟 CA	协定(%) 中巴 CP	协定(%) CT 中智 CC	普通 Gen	增值税率 VAT	出口退税 ED	计量单位 Unit	监管条件 SC	Article Description
2925.2900 14	双胍辛胺、多果定、双胍辛胺乙酸盐等(包括双胍三辛烷基苯磺酸盐)	6.5				30	17	13	千克	S	Iminoc tadine, Dodine, (minocta dine triace tate cincludins Iminoctadine triscalbesilate)
2925.2900 15	禾草灭、氟草醚、增产肟	6.5				30	17	13	千克	S	Alloxydim-Sodium, Fluorfen
2925.2900 90	其他亚胺及其衍生物以及它们的盐	6.5				30	17	13	千克		Other imines and their derivatives; salts there of
29.26	**腈基化合物:**										**Nitrile-function compounds:**
2926.1000	-丙烯腈	6.5			0	30	17	13	千克	X	-Acrylonitrile
2926.2000	-1-氰基胍(双氰胺)	6.5	5		0	30	17	13	千克		-1-cyanoguanidine (dicyandiamide)
2926.3000	-芬普雷司(INN)及其盐;美沙酮中间体(4-氰基-2-二甲氨基-4,4-二苯基丁烷)	6.5	5		0	30	17	13	千克		-Fenproporex(INN) and its salts; methadone (INN) intermediate (4-cyano-2-dimethyl-amino-4,4-diphenylbutane)
2926.3000 10	美沙酮中间体(4-氰基-2-二甲氨基-4,4-二苯基丁烷)	6.5				30	17	13	千克	W	Methadone (INN) intermediate (4-cyano-2-dimethylamino-4, 4-diphenylbutane)
2926.3000 20	芬普雷司及其盐	6.5				30	17	13	千克	I	Fenproporex (INN) and salts thereof
	-其他:										-Other:
2926.9010	---对氯氰苄	4			3.2	11	17	13	千克		---*p*-Chlorobenzyl cyanide
2926.9020	---间苯二甲腈	6.5	5		5.2	30	17	13	千克		---*m*-Phthalonitrile
2926.9090	---其他	6.5	5		5.2	30	17	13	千克		---Other
2926.9090 10	甲氰菊酯、S-氰戊菊酯、氯氟氰菊酯	6.5				30	17	13	千克	S	Fenpropathrin, esfenvalerate, cyhalothrin
2926.9090 20	己二腈	6.5				30	17	13	千克		Hexanedinitrile
2926.9090 31	氯氰菊酯、氟氯氰菊酯等(包括高效氯氰菊酯、高效反式氯氰菊酯、高效氟氯氰菊酯)	6.5				30	17	13	千克	S	Cypermethrin, cynuthrin (including β – Cypermethrin, theta – Cypermethrin, β – Cyfluthrin)
2926.9090 32	杀螟腈、辛硫磷、甲基辛硫磷等(包括敌草腈、碘苯腈、辛酰碘苯腈、溴苯腈、辛酰溴苯腈)	6.5				30	17	13	千克	S	Cyanophos Pnoxim, phoxiom (including dichlobenil, Iodobenzonitrile, Ioxynil octanoate, Bromobenzonitrile, Bromoxynil octanoate)
2926.9090 33	氯辛硫磷、戊氰威、苯醚氰菊酯等(包括稻瘟酰胺、丙螨氰、右旋苯醚氰菊酯)	6.5				30	17	13	千克	S	Chlorphoxim, nitrilacarb, cyphenothrin
2926.9090 34	戊烯氰氯菊酯、溴氯氰菊酯(包括高效氯氟氰菊酯、精高效氯氟氰菊酯)	6.5				30	17	13	千克	S	Pentmethrin, cyphenothrin (including Lambda – cyhalothrin, gamma – cyhalothrin)
2926.9090 35	溴氰菊酯、四溴菊酯、氟丙菊酯	6.5				30	17	13	千克	S	Deltamethrin, Fralomerhrin, Acrinathrin
2926.9090 36	氟氯苯菊酯、氰戊菊酯、乙氰菊酯	6.5				30	17	13	千克	S	Flumethrin, Fenvalerate, Cycloprothrin
2926.9090 37	氟氰戊菊酯、溴氟菊酯、溴灭菊酯	6.5				30	17	13	千克	S	Flucythrinate, Bmthrinate, brofenvalerate
2926.9090 38	氰菌胺、百菌清、霜脲氰、溴菌腈	6.5				30	17	13	千克	S	Fenpiclonil, chlorothalonil, cymoxanil, bromothalonil
2926.9090 39	氟胺氰菊酯、氰氟草酯、苯氰菊酯(包括富右旋反式苯氰菊酯)	6.5				30	17	13	千克	S	Fluralinate cyhalofop – butyl, cyphenothrin (including rich – d – t – Cyphenothrin)

税则号列 Tariff Item.	货品名称	最惠国(%) MFN	协定(%)CT 东盟 CA	中巴 CP	中智 CC	普通 Gen	增值税率 VAT	出口退税 ED	计量单位 Unit	监管条件 SC	Article Description
2926.9090 90	其他腈基化合物	6.5				30	17	13	千克		Other Nitrile-function compounds
29.27	**重氮化合物、偶氮化合物及氧化偶氮化合物：**										**Diazo-, azo-. or azoxy-compounds:**
2927.0000	重氮化合物、偶氮化合物及氧化偶氮化合物	6.5	5		0	30	17	13	千克		Diazo-, azo-. or azoxy-compounds
2927.0000 10	敌磺钠(包括氧化偶氮化合物)	6.5				30	17	13	千克	S	Dexon(including azoxy - compounds)
2927.0000 90	其他重氮化合物、偶氮化合物等(包括氧化偶氮化合物)	6.5				30	17	13	千克		Other diazo - azo - compounds (including azoxy - compounds)
29.28	**肼(联氨)及胲(羟胺)的有机衍生物：**										**Organic derivatives of hydrazine or of hydroxylamine:**
2928.0000	肼(联氨)及胲(羟胺)的有机衍生物	6.5	5		0	20	17	13	千克		Organic derivatives of hydrazine or of hydroxylamine
2928.0000 10	偏二甲肼	6.5				20	17	13	千克	3	*unsym.* -Dimethylhydrazine
2928.0000 20	甲基肼	6.5				20	17	13	千克	3	Methylhydrazine
2928.0000 31	抑食肼、虫酰肼、丁酰肼	6.5				20	17	13	千克	S	tebufenozide daminozide
2928.0000 32	绿谷隆、溴谷隆、利谷隆、氯溴隆	6.5				20	17	13	千克	S	monolinuron metobromuron linuron monolinuron
2928.0000 33	溴酚肟、乙二肟	6.5				20	17	13	千克	S	bromofenoxim glyoxime
2928.0000 34	苯螨特	6.5				20	17	13	千克	S	benzoximate
2928.0000 35	醌肟腙	6.5				20	17	13	千克	S	benquinox
2928.0000 36	三甲苯草酮	6.5				20	17	13	千克	S	tralkoxydim
2928.0000 37	解草胺腈	6.5				20	17	13	千克	S	cyometrinil
2928.0000 90	其他肼(联氨)及胲(羟胺)的有机衍生物	6.5				20	17	13	千克		Organic derivatives of hydrazine or of hydroxylamine
29.29	**其他含氮基化合物：**										**Compounds with other nitrogen function:**
	-异氰酸酯：										-Isocyanates:
2929.1010	---2,4-和2,6-甲苯二异氰酸酯混合物(甲苯二异氰酸酯TDI)	6.5	5		0	30	17	13	千克		---Toluene diisocyanate
2929.1020	---二甲苯二异氰酸酯(TODI)	6.5	5		0	30	17	13	千克		---*o*-Xylene diisocyanate(TODI)
2929.1030	---二苯基甲烷二异氰酸酯(纯MDI)	6.5	5		0	30	17	13	千克		---Diphenylmethane diisocyanate
2929.1040	---六亚甲基二异氰酸酯	6.5	5		0	30	17	13	千克		---Hexamethylene diisocyanate
2929.1090	---其他	6.5	5		0	30	17	13	千克		---Other
	-其他：										-Other:
2929.9010	---环已基氨基磺酸钠(甜蜜素)	9	5		0	90	17	13	千克		---Sodium cyclamate
2929.9020	---二烷(甲、乙、正丙或异丙)氨基膦酰二卤	6.5	5		0	30	17	13	千克	23	---N,N-Dialkyl (Me, Et, n-Pr or i-Pr) phosphoramidic dihalides
2929.9030	---二烷(甲、乙、正丙或异丙)氨基膦酸二烷(甲、乙、正丙或异丙)酯	6.5	5		0	30	17	13	千克	23	---Dialkyl (Me, Et, n-Pr or i-Pr) N,N-dialkyl(Me, Et, n-Pr or i-Pr)-phosphoramidates
2929.9090	---其他	6.5	5		0	30	17	13	千克		---Other
2929.9090 11	胺丙畏、胺草磷、抑草磷等(包括甲基胺草磷)	6.5				30	17	13	千克	S	propetamaphos amiprophos butamifos etc. (including amiprophos - methl)
2929.9090 12	异柳磷、甲基异柳磷、丙胺氟磷等(包括乙酰甲胺磷)	6.5				30	17	13	千克	S	Isofenphos , isofenphos - methy mipafox etc. (including acephate)

税则号列 Tariff Item.	货品名称	最惠国(%) MFN	协定(%) CT 东盟 CA	中巴 CP	中智 CC	普通 Gen	增值税率 VAT	出口退税 ED	计量单位 Unit	监管条件 SC	Article Description
2929. 9090 13	八甲磷、育畜磷、甘氨硫磷等(包括甲氟磷、毒鼠磷、水胺硫磷)	6. 5				30	17	13	千克	S	Schradan, crufomate, phosglycin (including dimefox, phosazetin, etc)
2929. 9090 90	其他含氮基化合物	6. 5				30	17	13	千克		Compounds with other nitrogen function
	第十分章 有机—无机化合物、杂环化合物、核酸及其盐以及磺(酰)胺										X. - ORGANO-INORGANIC COMPOUNDS, HETEROCYCLIC COMPOUNDS, NUCLEIC ACIDS AND THEIR SALTS, AND SULPHONAMIDES
29. 30	**有机硫化合物:**										**Organo-sulphur compounds:**
2930. 2000	-硫代氨基甲酸盐(或酯)及二硫代氨基甲酸盐	6. 5	5		5. 2	30	17	13	千克		-Thiocarbamates (ester) and dithiocarbamates
2930. 2000 11	禾草丹、杀螟丹	6. 5				30	17	13	千克	S	Thiobencarb, cartap (Saturn, etc)
2930. 2000 12	威百亩、代森钠、丙森锌、福美铁等(包括福美锌、代森福美锌、安百亩)	6. 5				30	17	13	千克	S	Metam – sodium, propineb, ferbam (including ziram, polycarbamate, meta – ammonium
2930. 2000 13	燕麦敌、野麦畏、硫草敌、灭草猛	6. 5				30	17	13	千克	S	Di_allate, Triallate, ethiolate, vernolate
2930. 2000 14	苄草丹、戊草丹、坪草丹、仲草丹	6. 5				30	17	13	千克	S	Prosulfocarb, esprocarb, orbencarb, tiocarbazil
2930. 2000 15	丁草敌、克草敌、茵草敌、灭草敌等(包括环草敌)	6. 5				30	17	13	千克	S	Butylate, pebulate, EPTC, vernolate (including cycloate)
2930. 2000 16	硫菌威、菜草畏	6. 5				30	17	13	千克	S	Prothiocarb, sulfallate
2930. 2000 90	其他硫代氨基甲酸盐(或酯)(包括二硫代氨基甲酸盐)	6. 5				30	17	13	千克		Other thiocarbamates and dithiocarbamates
2930. 3000	-硫化二烃氨基硫羰、二硫化二烃氨基硫羰及四硫化二烃氨基硫羰	6. 5	5		0	30	17	13	千克		-Thiuram mono-, di or tetrasulphide
2930. 3000 10	福美双	6. 5				30	17	13	千克	S	Thiram
2930. 3000 90	其他一硫化二烃氨基硫羰等(包括二硫化二烃氨基硫羰及四硫化二烃氨基硫羰)	6. 5				30	17	13	千克		Other thiuram mono –, di or tetrasulphide
2930. 4000	-甲硫氨酸(蛋氨酸)	6. 5	5		0	30	17	13	千克	AB	-Methionine
2930. 5000	-敌菌丹(ISO)及甲胺磷	6. 5	5		5. 2	30	17	17	千克	S	--Chlordimeform
	-其他:										-Other:
2930. 9010	---双巯丙氨酸(胱氨酸)	6. 5	5		5. 2	30	17	13	千克	AB	---Cystine
2930. 9020	---二硫代碳酸酯(或盐)[黄原酸酯(或盐)]	6. 5	5		5. 2	30	17	13	千克		---Chlordimeform
2930. 9090	---其他	6. 5	5		5. 2	30	17	13	千克		---Other
2930. 9090 11	烯禾啶	6. 5				30	17	13	千克	S	Thiobencarb, sethoxydim(TC)
2930. 9090 12	乙硫醇	6. 5				30	17	13	千克		Ethanethiol (ethyl mercaptan)
2930. 9090 13	2-氯乙基氯甲基硫醚	6. 5				30	17	13	千克	32	2-chloroethyl chloromethyl sulfide
2930. 9090 14	二(2-氯乙基)硫醚(即芥子气)	6. 5				30	17	13	千克	32	Bis (2-chloroethyl) sulfide
2930. 9090 15	二(2-氯乙硫基)甲烷	6. 5				30	17	13	千克	32	Bis (2-chloroethyl sulfide) methane
2930. 9090 16	1,2-二(2-氯乙硫基)乙烷(即倍半芥气)	6. 5				30	17	13	千克	32	1,2-Bis(2-chloroethyl sulfide) ethane

税则号列 Tariff Item.	货品名称	最惠国(%) MFN	协定(%) CT 东盟 CA	中巴 CP	中智 CC	普通 Gen	增值税率 VAT	出口退税 ED	计量单位 Unit	监管条件 SC	Article Description
2930.9090 17	1,3-二(2-氯乙硫基)正丙烷	6.5				30	17	13	千克	32	1,3-Bis(2-chloroethyl sulfide) propane
2930.9090 18	1,4-二(2-氯乙硫基)正丁烷	6.5				30	17	13	千克	32	1,4-Bis(2-chloroethyl sulfide) butane
2930.9090 19	1,5-二(2-氯乙硫基)正戊烷	6.5				30	17	13	千克	32	1,5-Bis(2-chloroethyl sulfide) pentane
2930.9090 21	二(2-氯乙硫基甲基)醚	6.5				30	17	13	千克	32	Bis (2-chloroethyl sulfide methyl) ester
2930.9090 22	二(2-氯乙硫基乙基)醚(即氧芥气)	6.5				30	17	13	千克	32	Bis (2-chloroethyl sulfide ethyl) ester
2930.9090 23	胺吸膦(硫代磷酸二乙基-S-2-二乙氨基乙酯及烷基化或质子化盐)	6.5				30	17	13	千克	23	Amiton O,O-Diethyl S-2-(diethy lamino) ethyl phosphorothilolate and corresponding alkylated or protonated salts
2930.9090 24	烷基氨基乙-2-硫醇及相应质子盐	6.5				30	17	13	千克	23	N,N-dialkyl aminoethane-2-thiols and corresponding protonated salts
2930.9090 25	硫二甘醇[二(2-羟乙基)硫醚,硫代双乙醇]	6.5				30	17	13	千克	23	Thiodiglycol: Bis (2-hydroxyethyl) sulfide; thiodiethanol
2930.9090 26	烷基硫代膦酸烷S-2-二烷氨基乙酯(包括相应烷基化盐、质子化盐,烷基指甲、乙、正丙、异丙基)	6.5				30	17	13	千克	23	Alkyl alkane thiophosphate S 2 aminoethyl, including cyclo alkane-S-2-dialkane (Me, Et, n-Pr or i-Pr) aminoethyl and corresponding alkylated or protonated salts
2930.9090 27	含一磷原子与甲乙丙基结合化合物(不包括地虫磷)	6.5				30	17	13	千克	23	Chemicals, containing a phosphorus atom to which is boned one methyl, ethyl or propyl group
2930.9090 28	内吸磷	6.5				30	17	13	千克	X	Demeton
2930.9090 40	DL-羟基蛋氨酸	6.5				30	17	13	千克	AB	L – Methionin
2930.9090 51	甲基硫菌灵、硫菌灵、苯螨醚等(包括乙蒜素、敌灭生、丁酮威、丁酮砜威、棉铃威)	6.5				30	17	13	千克	S	Thiophanate_methyl, thiophanate, phenproxide. (including ethylicin, dimexano , butocarboxim. ,butoxycarboxim. alanycarb)
2930.9090 52	灭多威、涕灭威、乙硫苯威等(包括杀线威、甲硫威、多杀威、涕灭砜威、硫双威)	6.5				30	17	13	千克	S	Methomyl, aldicarb, ethiofencarb, (including oxamyl, methiocarb, EMPC (JMAF), aldoxycarb, thiodicarb)
2930.9090 53	丁醚脲、久效威、苯硫威等(包括敌螨特、2甲4氯乙硫酯)	6.5				30	17	13	千克	S	Diafenthiuron, thiofanox, fenothiocarb (including chlorfensulphide, MCPA – thioethyl)
2930.9090 54	杀虫双、杀虫单、灭虫脲等(包括避虫醇、烯虫硫酯、三氯杀螨砜、杀螨醚、杀螨酯)	6.5				30	17	13	千克	S	Disosultap, monosultap, chloromethiuron (including (octylthio) ethanol, triprene, tetradifon, chlorbenside, chlorfenson)
2930.9090 55	代森锌、代森锰、代森锰锌等(包括福美胂、福美甲胂、代森铵、代森联)	6.5				30	17	13	千克	S	Zineb, maneb, mancozeb, (including asomate ,urbacide(JMAP) , amobam, metiram)
2930.9090 56	烯草酮、磺草酮、嗪草酸甲酯等(包括苯氟磺胺、甲磺乐灵、氯硫酰草胺、脱叶磷)	6.5				30	17	13	千克	S	Clethodim, KIH 9201 – methyl, etc. (including benfotiamine, nitralin, chlorthiamide, S,S,S – tributyl phosphorotrithioate)
2930.9090 57	灭菌丹、克菌丹、杀螨硫醚等(包括氟杀螨、硫肟醚、莠不生)	6.5				30	17	13	千克	S	Folpet, captan, tetrasul (including FIuorbenside, sulfuryl fluoride, etc)
2930.9090 58	稻瘟净、异稻瘟净、稻丰散等(包括敌瘟磷)	6.5				30	17	13	千克	S	EBP(JMAF), iprobenfos, phenthoate

税则号列 Tariff Item.	货品名称	最惠国(%) MFN	协定(%)CT 东盟 CA	中巴 CP	中智 CC	普通 Gen	增值税率 VAT	出口退税 ED	计量单位 Unit	监管条件 SC	Article Description
2930.9090 59	安妥、灭鼠特、二硫氰基甲烷等(包括灭鼠肼、氟硫隆)	6.5				30	17	13	千克	S	Antu, Mthylene Bis (thiocyanate (including)
2930.9090 61	马拉硫磷、苏硫磷、赛硫磷等(包括丙虫磷、双硫磷、亚砜磷、异亚砜磷)	6.5				30	17	13	千克	S	Malathion sophamide amidithion etc (including propaphos temephos oxydemeton_methyl oxydeprofos)
2930.9090 62	丙溴磷、田乐磷、特丁硫磷等(包括硫丙磷、地虫硫膦、乙硫磷、丙硫磷、甲基乙拌磷)	6.5				30	17	13	千克	S	Profenofos、demephion 、terbufos etc (including sulprofos、fonofos、ethion、prothiofos、thiometon)
2930.9090 63	乐果、益硫磷、氧乐果等(包括甲拌磷、乙拌磷、虫螨磷、果虫磷)	6.5				30	17	13	千克	S	Dimethoate 、ethoate_methyl、omethoate etc (including phorate、disulfoton、chlorthiophos、cyanthoate)
2930.9090 64	氯胺磷、家蝇磷、灭蚜磷等(包括安硫磷、四甲磷、丁苯硫磷、苯线磷、蚜灭磷)	6.5				30	17	13	千克	S	Acethion , mecarbam, etc. (including formothion, mecarphon, fosmethilan, fenamiphos, vamidothion)
2930.9090 65	硫线磷、氯甲硫磷、杀虫磺等(包括砜吸磷、砜拌磷、异拌磷、三硫磷、芬硫磷)	6.5				30	17	13	千克	S	Cadusafos, chlormephos , bensultap (including demeton _ S _ methylsulphone, oxydisulfoton, isothioate, carbophenothion, phenkapton)
2930.9090 66	倍硫磷、甲基内吸磷、乙酯磷等(包括丰索磷、内吸磷、发硫磷、甲基乙酯磷)	6.5				30	17	13	千克	S	Fenthion, demeton _ S _ methyl, acetophos, (including fensulfothion, demeton, rothoate, methylacetophos)
2930.9090 67	灭线磷	6.5				30	17	13	千克	S	Ethoprophos
2930.9090 90	其他有机硫化合物	6.5				30	17	13	千克		Other organo-sulphur compounds
29.31	**其他有机—无机化合物:**										**Other organo-inorganic compounds:**
2931.0000	其他有机—无机化合物	6.5	5		5.2	30	17	13	千克		Other organo-inorganic compounds
2931.0000 01	六甲基环三硅氧烷(包括八甲基环四硅氧烷,十甲基环五硅氧烷,十二甲基环六硅氧烷)	6.5				30	17	13	千克		Hexamethyldisiloxane (including O – Chlorophenyl Cyclopentyl Ketone, etc)
2931.0000 11	烷基亚膦酰烷基-2-二烷氨基乙酯(包括相应烷基化盐或质子化盐)	6.5				30	17	13	千克	23	Etnoprophos (TC)
2931.0000 12	氯沙林、氯梭曼(氯沙林即甲基氯膦酸异丙酯,氯梭曼即甲基氯膦酸频那酯)	6.5				30	17	13	千克	23	Chloroethyl mercury, cyhexatin, plictran including phenylmercuric acetate, PMA
2931.0000 13	2-氯乙烯基二氯胂	6.5				30	17	13	千克	23	Dichloro-2-chlorovinyl-arsine
2931.0000 14	二(2-氯乙烯基)氯胂	6.5				30	17	13	千克	23	Bis (2-chlorovinyl) chloro-arsine
2931.0000 15	三(2-氯乙烯基)胂	6.5				30	17	13	千克	23	Tri (2-chlorovinyl)-arsine
2931.0000 16	烷基氟膦酸烷酯,10碳原子以下(烷基指甲、乙、正丙、异丙基,例如:沙林、梭曼)	6.5				30	17	13	千克	23	Alkyl (Me, Et, n-Pr or i-Pr) alkane fluorophosphate esters, <10 carboatoms, for example, sarin: methyl isopropyl fluorophosphate, soman: methyl pinacolyl fluorophosphate
2931.0000 17	二烷氨基氰膦酸烷酯10碳原子以下(烷基指甲、乙、正丙、异丙基,例如:塔崩)	6.5				30	17	13	千克	23	Dialkyl (Me, Et, n-Pr or i-Pr) cyanamide alkane phospate esters, <10 carboatoms, for example tabun, dimethylamino ethyl cyanophosphorate

税则号列 Tariff Item.	货品名称	最惠国(%) MFN	协定(%)CT 东盟 CA	中巴 CP	中智 CC	普通 Gen	增值税率 VAT	出口退税 ED	计量单位 Unit	监管条件 SC	Article Description
2931.0000 18	烷基膦酰二氟(烷基指甲、乙、正丙、异丙基,例如,DF:甲基膦酰二氟)	6.5				30	17	13	千克	23	Alkyl (Me, Et, n-Pr or i-Pr) phosphoryl difluoride, for example, DF, methyl phosphoryl difloride
2931.0000 21	四乙基铅,四甲基铅	6.5				30	17	13	千克	X	Tetraethyl lead, Tetramethyl pentare
2931.0000 22	锆试剂,二甲胂酸等(包括4-二甲氨基偶氮苯-4'-胂酸,卡可基酸,二甲基胂酸钠)	6.5				30	17	13	千克	X	Arsinic acid, etc. (including Arsinic acid, dimethyl -, etc.)
2931.0000 23	4-氨基苯胂酸钠,二氯化苯胂(对氨基苯胂酸钠,二氯苯胂,苯胂化二氯)	6.5				30	17	13	千克	X	4 - amino sodium phenyl - arsonate, Phenylarsine (enylarsine diiodide, Dichloride, phenylarsine diiodide, etc.)
2931.0000 24	蒽醌-1-胂酸,三环锡(普特丹)等(包括月桂酸三丁基锡,醋酸三丁基锡)	6.5				30	17	13	千克	X	Anthraquinone - 1 - arsonic acid, cyhexatin;(plictran) (including Tributyl (lauroyloxy) stannane, Tributyltin acetate)
2931.0000 25	硫酸三乙基锡,二丁基氧化锡等(包括氧化二丁基锡,乙酸三乙基锡,三乙基乙酸锡)	6.5				30	17	13	千克	X	Triethyltin sulphate, Dibutyltin (including oxide, Acetoxytriethyl, stannane)
2931.0000 26	四乙基锡,乙酸三甲基锡(四乙锡,醋酸三甲基锡)	6.5				30	17	13	千克	X	Tetra, Trimethyltin(Ethyltin, acetate)
2931.0000 27	毒菌锡[三苯基羟基锡(含量>20%)]	6.5				30	17	13	千克	X	Triphenyltin hydroxide [trimethyltin aceate(proportion >20%)]
2931.0000 28	乙酰亚砷酸铜,二苯(基)胺氯胂(祖母绿;翡翠绿;醋酸亚砷酸铜,吩吡嗪化氯;亚当氏气)	6.5				30	17	13	千克	X	C. I. pigment, etc. (emerald, Diphenylamine, Chloroarsine, etc.)
2931.0000 29	3-硝基-4-羟基苯胂酸(4-羟基-3-硝基苯胂酸)	6.5				30	17	13	千克	X	3-nitryl-4- carboxyl benzene arsine acid
2931.0000 35	乙基二氯胂,二苯(基)氯胂等(包括二氯化乙基胂,氯化二苯胂)	6.5				30	17	13	千克	X	Chlorodiphenylarsine, etc. (including Arsonous dichloride hlorodiphenylarsine,)
2931.0000 36	甲(基)胂酸,丙(基)胂酸,二碘化苯胂等(包括苯基二碘胂)	6.5				30	17	13	千克	X	Methyl arsine acid, propyl arsine acid, biiodine benzene arsine
2931.0000 37	苯胂酸,2-硝基苯胂酸等(包括邻硝基苯胂酸,3-硝基苯胂酸,间硝基苯胂酸等)	6.5				30	17	13	千克	X	Arsonic acid, phenyl, Arsonic acid, (2 - nitrophenyl) (including Arsonic acid, (2 - nitrophenyl), Arsonic acid, (3 - nitrophenyl), Benzenearsonic acid, o - nitro -
2931.0000 38	4-硝基苯胂酸,2-氨基苯胂酸(对硝基苯胂酸,邻氨基苯胂酸)	6.5				30	17	13	千克	X	4-nitrophenylarsonic acid, 2-amino benzene arsonic acid
2931.0000 39	3-氨基苯胂酸,4-氨基苯胂酸(间氨基苯胂酸,对氨基苯胂酸)	6.5				30	17	13	千克	X	3 - Aminophenylarsonic acid, 4 - Aminophenylarsonic acid(Aminophenylarsonic acid, Aminophenylarsonic acid)
2931.0000 41	草甘膦	6.5				30	17	13	千克	Sa	Glyphosate

税则号列 Tariff Item.	货 品 名 称	最惠国(%) MFN	协定(%)CT 东盟 CA	中巴 CP	中智 CC	普通 Gen	增值税率 VAT	出口退税 ED	计量单位 Unit	监管条件 SC	Article Description
2931.0000 42	草铵膦,草硫膦,杀木膦等(包括双丙氨膦,增甘膦及其盐)	6.5				30	17	13	千克	S	Glufosinate - ammonium, sulphosate, fosamine - ammonium (including bialaphos - sodium, glyphosine and its salt)
2931.0000 43	乙烯利,乙烯硅	6.5				30	17	13	千克	S	Ethephon, etacelasil
2931.0000 44	三丁氯苄磷	6.5				30	17	13	千克	S	Chlorphonium
2931.0000 45	敌百虫,氟硅菊酯,毒壤膦等(包括苯硫膦,溴苯膦,苯腈膦,丁酯膦)	6.5				30	17	13	千克	S	Trichlorfon , salifluofen, trichloronat (including EPN(ESA), leptophos, cyanofenphos , butonate)
2931.0000 46	三苯锡,三苯基乙酸锡等(包括三苯基氯化锡,三苯基氢氧化锡,苯丁锡,三唑锡)	6.5				30	17	13	千克	S	Fentin, fentin acetate (including fentin chloride, fentin hydroxide, fenbutatin oxide, azocyclotin)
2931.0000 90	其他有机-无机化合物	6.5				30	17	13	千克		Other organo - inorganic
29.32	**仅含有氧杂原子的杂环化合物:**										**Heterocyclic compounds with oxygen hetero-atom(s) only:**
	-结构上含有一个非稠合呋喃环(不论是否氢化)的化合物:										-Compounds containing an unfused furan ring (whether or not hydrogenated) in the structure:
2932.1100	--四氢呋喃	6	5		0	20	17	13	千克		--Tetrahydrofuran
2932.1200	--2-糠醛	6	5		0	20	17	13	千克	BS	--2-Furaldehyde (furfuraldehyde)
2932.1300	--糠醇及四氢糠醇	6	5		0	20	17	13	千克		--Furfuryl alcohol and tetrahydrofurfuryl alcohol
2932.1900	--其他	6.5	5		0	20	17	13	千克		--Other
	-内酯:										-Lactones:
2932.1900 11	喃烯菊酯,炔呋菊酯等(包括甲呋炔菊酯,溴苄呋菊酯,右旋炔呋菊酯)	6.5				20	17	13	千克	S	Japothrins, furamethrin (JMAF) (including proparthrin, bromethrin, d - furamethrin)
2932.1900 12	呋菌胺,酯菌胺,抑霉胺等(包括环菌胺,甲呋酰胺,二甲呋酰胺)	6.5				20	17	13	千克	S	Metomedan, cyprofuram vangard (including cyprodinil, fenfuram furcarbanil)
2932.1900 13	呋氧草醚,环庚草醚,呋草酮等(包括茵多酸)	6.5				20	17	13	千克	S	Furyloxyfen, cinmethylin, flurtamone etc. (including endothal)
2932.1900 14	楝素,呋霜灵,乙二醇缩糠醛等(包括呋菌隆,季酮螨酯)	6.5				20	17	13	千克	S	furalaxyl, furalane etc. (including furophanat spirodiclfen
2932.1900 15	苄呋菊酯(包括右旋苄呋菊酯,生物苄呋菊酯)	6.5				20	17	13	千克	S	Resmethrin (including d - resmethrin, bioresmethrin)
2932.1900 90	其他结构上有非稠合呋喃环化合物	6.5				20	17	13	千克		other compounds containing an unfused furaning in the structure
2932.2100	--香豆素、甲基香豆素及乙基香豆素	6.5	5		0	20	17	13	千克		--Coumarin, methylcoumarins and ethyl-coumarins
2932.2900	--其他内酯	6.5	5		0	20	17	13	千克		--Other lactones
	-其他:										-Other:
2932.2900 11	杀鼠灵,克鼠灵,敌鼠灵,溴鼠灵等(包括氯灭鼠灵,氟鼠灵,鼠得克,杀鼠醚)	6.5				20	17	13	千克	S	warfarin, coumafuryl, melitoxin brodifacoum etc. (including coumachlor flocoumafen, difenacoum, coumatetralyl)
2932.2900 12	赤霉酸	6.5				20	17	13	千克	S	Gibberellic acid
2932.2900 13	蝇毒磷,茴蒿素,溴敌隆,呋酰胺等(包括四氯苯酞,畜虫磷)	6.5				20	17	13	千克	S	Coumaphos, saneonin , bromadiolone, ofurace (including phthalide (JMAF), coumithoate)

税则号列 Tariff Item.	货品名称	最惠国(%) MFN	协定(%)CT 东盟 CA	中巴 CP	中智 CC	普通 Gen	增值税率 VAT	出口退税 ED	计量单位 Unit	监管条件 SC	Article Description
2932.2900 90	其他内酯	6.5				20	17	13	千克		Other lactones
2932.9100	--4-丙烯基-1,2-亚甲二氧基苯(异黄樟脑)	6.5	5		0	20	17	13	千克	23	--Isosafrole
2932.9200	--1-(1,3-苯并二𫫇茂-5-基)丙烷-2-酮	6.5	5		0	20	17	13	千克	23	--1-(1,3-Benzodioxol-5-yl)propan-2-one
2932.9300	--3,4-亚甲二氧基苯甲醛(胡椒醛)(别名洋茉莉醛、开芥菜精)	6.5	5		0	20	17	13	千克	23	--Piperonal
2932.9400	--4-烯丙基-1,2-亚甲二氧基苯(黄樟脑)	6.5	5		0	20	17	13	千克	23	--Safrole
2932.9500	--四氢大麻酚(所有的异构体)	6.5	5		0	20	17	13	千克	I	--Tetrahydrocannabinols(all is omers)
	--其他:										--Other:
2932.9910	---(呋喃酚)	4			0	11	17	13	千克		---Furan phenol
2932.9920	---2,2′-双甲氧羰基-4,4′-双甲氧基-5,6,5′,6′-双次甲二氧基联苯(联苯双酯)	6.5	5		0	20	17	13	千克		---Bifendate
2932.9990	---其他	6.5	5		0	20	17	13	千克		---Other
2932.9990 11	克百威	6.5				20	17	13	千克	S	Carbofuran
2932.9990 12	二氧威,恶虫威,丙硫克百威等(包括丁硫克百威,呋线威)	6.5				20	17	13	千克	S	Dioxocarb, bendiocarb, benfuracarb (including carbosulfan ,furathiocarb)
2932.9990 13	因毒磷,敌恶磷,碳氯灵	6.5				20	17	13	千克	S	Endothion, dioxathion, isobenzan
2932.9990 14	增效特,增效砜,增效醚,增效酯等(包括增效环,增效散)	6.5				20	17	13	千克	S	Bucarpolate, sufoxide, piperonyl butoxide, propylisorne
2932.9990 15	吡喃灵,吡喃隆,乙氧呋草黄等(包括呋草黄,氟草肟,解草腈,解草烷)	6.5				20	17	13	千克	S	Pyracarbolin, metobenzuron, ethofumesate (including benfuresate, fluxofenim, oxabetrinil, etc.)
2932.9990 16	避蚊酮,苯虫醚,鱼藤酮	6.5				20	17	13	千克	S	Butopyronoxyl, difenolan, rotenone
2932.9990 17	调呋酸,芸苔素内酯	6.5				20	17	13	千克	S	Dikegulac, brassinolide
2932.9990 21	紫杉醇	6.5				20	17	13	千克	QFE	Taxinol
2932.9990 22	三尖杉宁碱	6.5				20	17	13	千克	FE	Cephalomanine
2932.9990 23	十去乙酰基巴卡丁三(红豆杉提取物10-DAB)	6.5				20	17	13	千克	FE	10-deacetylbaccation Ⅲ
2932.9990 24	十去乙酰基紫杉醇(红豆杉提取物10-DAT)	6.5				20	17	13	千克	FE	10-deacetyltaxinol
2932.9990 25	巴卡丁三	6.5				20	17	13	千克	FE	Baccatin Ⅲ
2932.9990 26	7-表紫杉醇	6.5				20	17	13	千克	FE	7-epitaxinol
2932.9990 27	10-去乙酰7-表紫杉醇	6.5				20	17	13	千克	FE	10-deacetyl-7-epitaxinol
2932.9990 30	二亚甲基双氧安非他明及其盐(MDMA)	6.5				20	17	13	千克	I	Dimethylene dioxyamphetamine and its salts(MDMA)
2932.9990 40	替苯丙胺及其盐	6.5				20	17	13	千克	I	Tenamfetamine and its salts
2932.9990 60	二恶英,呋喃(多氯二苯并对二恶英,多氯二苯并呋喃)	6.5				20	17	13	千克	89	Dioxin, Furan (Poly chrorinate. dibenzo – p – dixins and Dibenzofurans)
2932.9990 70	1,4-二噁烷	6.5				20	17	13	千克	X	1,4-Diaxane

税则号列 Tariff Item.	货 品 名 称	最惠国(%) MFN	协定(%)CT 东盟 CA	中巴 CP	中智 CC	普通 Gen	增值税率 VAT	出口退税 ED	计量单位 Unit	监管条件 SC	Article Description
2932.9990 91	其他濒危植物提取的仅含氧杂原子的杂环化合物	6.5				20	17	13	千克	EF	Other heterocyclic compounds with oxygen hetero－atom only, distilled from endangered plants
2932.9990 99	其他仅含氧杂原子的杂环化合物	6.5				20	17	11,13	千克		Other heterocyclic compounds with oxygen hetero-atom(s) only
29.33	**仅含有氮杂原子的杂环化合物：**										**Heterocyclic compounds with nitrogen hetero-atom(s) only**
	-结构上含有一个非稠合吡唑环(不论是否氢化)的化合物：										-Compounds containing an unfused pyrazole ring (whether or not hydrogenated) in the structure：
2933.1100	--二甲基苯基吡唑酮(安替比林)及其衍生物	6.5	5	6	0	20	17	13	千克		--Phenazone (antipyrin) and its derivatives
	--其他：										--Other：
2933.1920	---安乃近	6	5		0	20	17	13	千克	Q	---Analgin
2933.1990	---其他	6.5	5		0	20	17	13	千克		---Other
2933.1990 11	吡硫磷,吡唑硫磷,敌蝇威等(包括异索威,吡唑威)	6.5				20	17	13	千克	S	Pyrazothion, pyraclofos, Dimetilan (includins Ethirimol, pyrolan)
2933.1990 12	氟虫腈,唑螨酯,吡螨胺等(包括吡唑醚菌酯)	6.5				20	17	13	千克	S	Fipronil, Fenpyroximate, Tebufenpyrad (including Pyraclost)
2933.1990 13	吡草醚,吡唑草胺,氟氯草胺等(包括野燕枯,苄草唑,吡唑特,吡草酮)	6.5				20	17	13	千克	S	ET－251, Metazachlor, Nipyralo fen (indnding Difenzoquat, Pyrazoxyfen, pyrazolate, Benzofenap)
2933.1990 90	其他结构上有非稠合吡唑环化合物	6.5				20	17	13	千克		Other compounds containing an unfused imidazole ringin the structure
	-结构上含有一个非稠合咪唑环(不论是否氢化)的化合物：										-Compounds containing an unfused imidazole ring (whether or not hydrogenated) in the structure：
2933.2100	--乙内酰脲及其衍生物	6.5	5		0	30	17	13	千克		--Hydantoin and its derivatives
2933.2900	--其他	6.5	5		0	20	17	13	千克		--Other
2933.2900 11	异菌脲	6.5				20	17	13	千克	S	Iprodine
2933.2900 12	抑霉唑,咪菌腈,咪菌酮,咪鲜胺等(包括克霉唑,咪鲜胺锰盐)	6.5				20	17	13	千克	S	Imazalil, Fenapanil, climbazole, prochloraz cinduding clotrimazole prochloraz－manganese chloride complex
2933.2900 13	咪草酸	6.5				20	17	13	千克	S	Imazamethabenz－methyl
2933.2900 14	果绿啶	6.5				20	17	13	千克	S	Glyodin
2933.2900 90	其他结构上有非稠合咪唑环化合物	6.5				20	17	13	千克		Other compounds containing an unfused imidazole ring in the structure
	-结构上含有一个非稠合吡啶环(不论是否氢化)的化合物：										-Compounds containing an unfused pyridine ring (whether or not hydrogenated) in the structure：
2933.3100	--吡啶及其盐	6	5		0	20	17	13	千克		--Pyridine and its salts
	--六氢吡啶(哌啶)及其盐：										--Piperidine and its salts：
2933.3210	---六氢吡啶(哌啶)	4			0	11	17	13	千克	23	---Hexahydropyridine (piperidine)
2933.3220	---六氢吡啶(哌啶)盐	6.5	5		0	20	17	13	千克		---Isoniazidum

税则号列 Tariff Item.	货 品 名 称	最惠国(%) MFN	协定(%) CT 东盟 CA	中巴 CP	中智 CC	普通 Gen	增值税率 VAT	出口退税 ED	计量单位 Unit	监管条件 SC	Article Description
2933.3300	--阿芬太尼(INN),阿尼利定(INN),苯氰米特(INN),溴西泮(INN),地芬诺新(INN),地芬诺酯(INN),地匹哌酮(INN),芬太尼(INN),凯托米酮(INN),哌醋甲酯(INN),喷他左辛(INN),哌替啶(INN),哌替啶中间体A(INN),苯环利定(INN),苯哌利定(INN),哌苯甲醇(INN),哌氰米特(INN),哌丙吡胺(INN)和三甲利定(INN)以及它们的盐	6.5	5		0	20	17	13	千克		--Alfentanil (INN), anileridine (INN), bezitramide (INN), bromazepam (INN), difenoxin (INN), diphenoxylate (INN), dipipanone (INN), fentanyl (INN), ketobemidone (INN), methylphenidate (INN), pentazocine (INN), pethidine (INN), pethidine (INN) intermediate A, phencyclidine (INN) (PCP), phenoperidine (INN), pipradrol (INN), piritramide (INN), propiram (INN) and trimeperidine (INN); salts thereof
2933.3300 11	阿芬太尼、芬太尼(以及它们的盐)	6.5				20	17	13	千克	W	Alfentanil (INN), fentanyl (INN); salts thereof
2933.3300 12	哌替啶、地芬诺酯(以及它们的盐)	6.5				20	17	13	千克	W	Pethidine (INN), diphenoxylate (INN); salts thereof
2933.3300 13	氰苯双哌酰胺、丙吡兰(以及它们的盐)	6.5				20	17	13	千克	W	Bezitramide (INN), propiram (INN); salts thereof
2933.3300 21	哌醋甲酯、喷他左辛、溴西泮(以及它们的盐)	6.5				20	17	13	千克	I	Methylphenidate (INN), pentazocine (INN), bromazepam (INN); salts thereof
2933.3300 22	苯环利定、哌苯甲醇、三甲利定(以及它们的盐)	6.5				20	17	13	千克	I	Phencyclidine (INN) (PCP), pipradrol (INN), trimeperidine (INN); salts thereof
2933.3300 31	地匹哌酮、凯托米酮、地芬诺新(以及它们的盐)	6.5				20	17	13	千克		Dipipanone (INN), ketobemidone (INN), difenoxin (INN); salts thereof
2933.3300 32	哌替啶中间体A、苯哌利定(以及它们的盐)	6.5				20	17	13	千克		Pethidine (INN), phenoperidine (INN); salts thereof
2933.3300 33	阿尼利定、苯氰米特(以及它们的盐)	6.5				20	17	13	千克		Anileridine (INN), piritramide (INN); salts thereof
	--其他:										--Other:
2933.3910	---二苯乙醇酸-3-奎宁环酯(即BZ)	6.5	5		0	20	17	13	千克	23	---Benzilic acid-3-quinuclidinate
2933.3920	---奎宁环-3-醇	6.5	5		0	20	17	13	千克	23	---Quinuclidine-3-ol
2933.3990	---其他	6.5	5		0	20	17	13	千克		---Other
2933.3990 10	甲基吡啶、氰基吡啶、吡啶硫铜锌(包括三甲基吡啶)	6.5				20	17	13	千克		Methyl pyridine, cyanopyridine, pyridine sulfur-copper-zinc
2933.3990 21	精吡氟禾草灵,毒死蜱	6.5				20	17	13	千克	S	Fluazifop – P – butyl, chlorpyrifos
2933.3990 22	百草枯,啶虫脒	6.5				20	17	13	千克	S	Paraquat, acetamiprid
2933.3990 23	精喹禾灵	6.5				20	17	13	千克	S	Quizalofop – p – ethyl
2933.3990 24	喹禾灵,氟吡禾灵,吡氟禾草灵等(包括炔禾灵,氟吡乙禾灵,氟吡胺,卤草定)	6.5				20	17	13	千克	S	Quizalofop, Heptenophos, fluazifop, (including chloroazifop – propyny, haloxyfop – methyl TOP, etc.)
2933.3990 25	高效氟吡甲禾灵,氟吡甲禾灵等(包括鼠特灵,灭鼠优,灭鼠安,氟鼠啶)	6.5				20	17	13	千克	S	Haloxyfop – P – methyl , haloxyfop—methy1 (including norbormide, pyrinuron, chlorophacinone, etc.)
2933.3990 26	甲基毒死蜱,吡虫啉等(包括吡氯氰菊酯,啶蜱脲,氟啶脲,哒幼酮,吡丙醚)	6.5				20	17	13	千克	S	Chlorpyrifos_methyl, Imidacloprid (including fenpirithrin, fluazuron, chlorfluazuron, pyriproxyfen, etc.)

税则号列 Tariff Item.	货品名称	最惠国(%) MFN	协定(%)CT 东盟 CA	中巴 CP	中智 CC	普通 Gen	增值税率 VAT	出口退税 ED	计量单位 Unit	监管条件 SC	Article Description
2933.3990 27	驱蝇啶,烯啶虫胺	6.5				20	17	13	千克	S	Dipropyl pyridine, nitenpyram
2933.3990 28	咪唑烟酸,甲咪唑烟酸,咪唑乙烟酸等(包括氨氯吡啶酸,三氯吡氧乙酸,氯氟吡氧乙酸,二氯吡啶酸)	6.5				20	17	13	千克	S	Imazapyr, imazapyrisopropylammonium, imazethapyr, imazethapyr – ammonium (including picloram, trichlopyr, fluroxypyr – methyl, fluroxypyr, clopyralid)
2933.3990 29	炔草酸,哌草磷,哌草丹,稗草丹等(包括吡氟酰草胺,氟啶草酮,氟硫草定,甲氧咪草烟,灭草烟)	6.5				20	17	13	千克	S	Clodinafop – propargyl, piperophos, dimepiperate, pyributicarb (including diflufenican, dithiopyr, etc.)
2933.3990 30	3-羟基-1-甲基哌啶	6.5				20	17	13	千克	23	3-hydroxy-1-methyl piperidine
2933.3990 40	3-奎宁环酮	6.5				20	17	13	千克	23	3-Quinuclidone
2933.3990 51	甲哌翁,抗倒胺,氯吡脲,吡啶醇	6.5				20	17	13	千克	S	Mepiquate chloride, inabenfide, forchlorfenuron, pyripropanol
2933.3990 52	啶菌噁唑,苯锈啶,啶斑肟等(包括啶菌腈)	6.5				20	17	13	千克	S	Cincluding pyridinitril, fenpropidin, pyrifenox
2933.3990 53	氟啶胺,氟啶虫酰胺,三氯甲基吡啶	6.5				20	17	13	千克	S	Fluazinam, flonicamid, plifenate
2933.3990 54	咪唑嗪,丁硫啶,氯苯吡啶,哌丙灵等	6.5				20	17	13	千克	S	Triazoxide, buthiobate, felodipine, piperlin
2933.3990 80	雷米芬太尼及其盐	6.5				20	17	13	千克	W	Ramifentanil and salts thereof
2933.3990 90	其他结构上有非稠合吡啶环化合物	6.5				20	17	13	千克		Other compounds containing an unfused pyridine ring in the structure
	-结构上含有一个喹啉或异喹啉环系(不论是否氢化)的化合物,但未经进一步稠合的:										-Compounds containing in the structure a quinoline or isoquinoline ring-system (whether or not hy-drogenated), not further fused:
2933.4100	--左非诺(INN)及其盐	6.5	5		0	20	17	13	千克	W	--Levorphanol(INN) and its salts
	--其他:										--Other:
2933.4910	---环丙氟哌酸	6.5	5	6	0	20	17	13	千克		---Ciprofloxacin
2933.4990	---其他	6.5	5		0	20	17	13	千克		---Other
2933.4990 11	喹啉铜,8-羟基喹啉,包括丙烯酸喹啉酯	6.5				20	17	13	千克	S	Oxine – copper, ethoxyquin, 8 – hydroxyqulnoline
2933.4990 12	咯喹酮,解草酯	6.5				20	17	13	千克	S	Pyroquilon, cloquitocet – mexyl
2933.4990 13	氯甲喹啉酸,二氯喹啉酸	6.5				20	17	13	千克	S	Quinmerac, quinclorac
2933.4990 90	其他含喹琳或异喹啉环系的化合物(但未进一步稠合的)	6.5				20	17	13	千克		Other compounds containingan unfuced pyridinering in the structure
	-结构上含有一个嘧啶环(不论是否氢化)或哌嗪环的化合物:										-Compounds containing a pyrimidine ring (whether or not hydrogenated) or piperazine ring in the structure:
2933.5200	--丙二酰脲(巴比土酸)及其盐	6.5	5		0	20	17	13	千克		--Malonylurea (barbituric acid) and its salts

税则号列 Tariff Item.	货品名称	最惠国(%) MFN	协定(%) CT 东盟 CA	协定(%) CT 中巴 CP	协定(%) CT 中智 CC	普通 Gen	增值税率 VAT	出口退税 ED	计量单位 Unit	监管条件 SC	Article Description
2933.5300	--阿洛巴比妥(INN),异戊巴比妥(INN),巴比妥(INN),布他比妥(INN),正丁巴比妥(INN),环己巴比妥(INN),甲苯巴比妥(INN),戊巴比妥(INN),苯巴比妥(INN),仲丁巴比妥(INN),司可巴比妥(INN),和乙烯比妥(INN)以及它们的盐	6.5	5		0	20	17	13	千克		--Allobarbital(INN), amobarbital(INN), barbital(INN), butalbital(INN), butobarbital(INN), cyclobarbital(INN), methylphenobarbital(INN), pentobarbital(INN), phenobarbital(INN), secbutabarbital(INN), secobarbital(INN) and vinylbital(INN); salts thereof
2933.5300 11	阿洛巴比妥、仲丁巴比妥(以及它们的盐)	6.5				20	17	13	千克	I	Allobarbital (INN), secbutabarbital (INN); salts thereof
2933.5300 12	乙烯比妥、布他比妥、正丁巴比妥(以及它们的盐)	6.5				20	17	13	千克	I	Vinylbital(INN), butalbital(INN), butobarbital(INN); salts thereof
2933.5300 13	环己巴比妥、甲苯巴比妥(以及它们的盐)	6.5				20	17	13	千克	I	Cyclobarbital (INN), methylphenobarbital (INN); salts thereof
2933.5300 14	司可巴比妥、异戊巴比妥(以及它们的盐)	6.5				20	17	13	千克	I	Secobarbital (INN), amobarbital (INN), salts thereof
2933.5300 15	戊巴比妥、苯巴比妥、巴比妥(以及它们的盐)	6.5				20	17	13	千克	I	Pentobarbital (INN), phenobarbital (INN), barbital (INN); salts thereof
2933.5400	--其他丙二酰脲(巴比土酸)的衍生物以及它们的盐	6.5	5		0	20	17	13	千克		--Other derivatives of malonylurea(barbituric acid); salts thereof
2933.5500	--氯普唑仑(INN),甲氯喹酮(INN),甲喹酮(INN)和齐培丙醇(INN)以及它们的盐	6.5	5		0	20	17	13	千克		--Loprazolam (INN), mecloqualone (INN), methaqualone (INN) and zipeprol (INN); salts thereof
2933.5500 11	甲氯喹酮、甲喹酮(以及它们的盐)	6.5				20	17	13	千克		Mecloqualone (INN), methaqualone (INN); salts thereof
2933.5500 12	氯普唑仑、齐培丙醇(以及它们的盐)	6.5				20	17	13	千克		Loprazolam(INN), zipeprol(INN); salts thereof
2933.5900	--其他	6.5	5	4.6	0	20	17	13	千克		--Other
2933.5900 11	嘧啶磷,甲基嘧啶磷,二嗪磷等(包括嘧啶氧磷,乙嘧硫磷)	6.5				20	17	13	千克	S	Pyrimithate, methyl pyrimithate, diazinon (including pirimioxyphos, etrimfos)
2933.5900 12	烯腺嘌呤,腺嘌呤,苄腺嘌呤等(包括苄氨基嘌呤,羟烯腺嘌呤)	6.5				20	17	13	千克	S	Oxyenadenine, adenine, 6 - benzylaminopurine (including 6 - benzolaminopurine, oxyenadenine)
2933.5900 13	嘧草醚,双草醚,除草定,环草定等(包括异草定,异丙酯草醚,嘧草硫醚,特草定,解草啶)	6.5				20	17	13	千克	S	Pyriminobac - methl, bispyribac - sodium, bromacil, lenacil (including isocil, pyrithiobac - sodium, terbacil, fenclorim
2933.5900 14	吡菌磷,嘧霉胺,嘧菌胺,嘧菌酯等(包括嘧菌环胺,嘧菌腙)	6.5				20	17	13	千克	S	Pyrazophos, pyrimethanil, cymoxanil. Azoxystrobin (including cyprodinil, ferimzone)
2933.5900 15	嘧啶威,抗蚜威,环虫腈,嘧螨醚等(包括嘧螨酯)	6.5				20	17	13	千克	S	Pyramat, Pirimicarb, CGA 183893, pyrimidifen (including fluacrypyrim)

税则号列 Tariff Item.	货品名称	最惠国(%) MFN	协定(%)CT 东盟 CA	中巴 CP	中智 CC	普通 Gen	增值税率 VAT	出口退税 ED	计量单位 Unit	监管条件 SC	Article Description
2933.5900 16	氯苯嘧啶醇,环丙嘧啶醇,呋嘧醇等(包括氟苯嘧啶醇)	6.5				20	17	13	千克	S	Fenarimol, ancymidol, flurpirimate (including nuarimol)
2933.5900 17	氟蚁腙,鼠立死	6.5				20	17	13	千克	S	Hydramethylnon, crimidine
2933.5900 18	二甲嘧酚,乙嘧酚,乙嘧酚磺酸酯	6.5				20	17	13	千克	S	Dimethirimol, ethirmol, bupirimate
2933.5900 19	嗪氨灵,咪唑喹啉酸,丙酯草醚	6.5				20	17	13	千克	S	Triforin, imazquim
2933.5900 90	其他结构上有嘧啶环等的化合物(包括其他结构上有哌嗪环的化合物,N-甲基哌嗪,哌嗪除外)	6.5				20	17	13	千克		Other compounds containing pyrimidine rings in the structure (including other compounds containing piperazine rings in the strcture, N-methyl piperazine, other than piperazine)
	-结构上含有一个非稠合三嗪环(不论是否氢化)的化合物:										-Compounds containing an unfused triazine ring (whether or not hydrogenated) in the structure:
2933.6100	--三聚氰胺(蜜胺)	6.5	5		0	20	17	13	千克		--Melamine
	--其他:										--Other:
2933.6910	---三聚氰氯	6	5		0	20	17	13	千克		---Cyanuric chloride
	---异氰脲酸氯化衍生物:										---Chloroisocyanurate:
2933.6921	----二氯异氰脲酸:	6.5	5		0	20	17	13	千克		----Dichloroisocyanurate acid
2933.6922	----三氯异氰脲酸:	6.5	5		0	20	17	13	千克		----Trichloroisocyanuric acid
2933.6929	----其他	6.5	5		0	20	17	13	千克		----Other
2933.6929 10	二氯异氰尿酸钠	6.5				20	17	13	千克		Sodium dic-hlord iso-cyanurate
2933.6929 90	其他异氰脲酸氯化衍生物	6.5				20	17	13	千克		Other chloroisocyanuric acid derivatives
2933.6990	---其他	6.5	5		0	20	17	13	千克		---Other
2933.6990 11	西玛津,莠去津,扑灭津,草达津等(包括特丁津,氰草津,环丙津,甘扑津,甘草津)	6.5				20	17	13	千克	S	Simazine, atrazine, propazine, trietazine (including terbuthylazine ,cyanazine,cyprazine,proglinazine,etc.)
2933.6990 12	西草净,扑草净,敌草净,莠灭净等(包括特丁净,异丙净,异戊乙净,氰草净,氟草净,甲氧丙净)	6.5				20	17	13	千克	S	Simetryn, prometryn, desmetryn, ametryn (including terbutryn, dipropetryn, dimethametryn, cyanatryn, SSH-108, etc.)
2933.6990 13	扑灭通,仲丁通	6.5				20	17	13	千克	S	Prometon, secbumeton
2933.6990 14	丁嗪草酮,环嗪酮,嗪草酮等(包括苯嗪草酮,乙嗪草酮)	6.5				20	17	13	千克	S	Isomethiozin, Hexazinone, Metribuzin, etc (including Metamitron ,Ethiozin)
2933.6990 15	灭蚜硫磷,灭蝇胺,吡蚜酮等(包括敌菌灵)	6.5				20	17	13	千克	S	Memazon, cyromazine, pymetrozime scincladins Asomatel ,anilazine
2933.6990 90	其他结构上含非稠合三嗪环化合物	6.5				20	17	13	千克		Other compounds cortainins an unfused triazin ring in the structur
	-内酰胺:										-Lactams:
2933.7100	--6-己内酰胺	9			0	35	17	13	千克	A	--6-Hexanolactam (epsilon-caprolactam)
2933.7200	--氯巴占(INN)和甲乙哌酮(INN)	9	5		0	15	17	13	千克	I	--Clobazam(INN) and methyprylon(INN)
2933.7900	--其他内酰胺	9	5		0	20	17	13	千克		--Other lactams
2933.7900 10	氯巴占和甲乙哌酮的盐	9				20	17	13	千克	I	Salts of clobazam(INN) and methyprylon(INN)

税则号列 Tariff Item.	货品名称	最惠国(%) MFN	协定(%)CT 东盟 CA	中巴 CP	中智 CC	普通 Gen	增值税率 VAT	出口退税 ED	计量单位 Unit	监管条件 SC	Article Description
2933.7900 20	灭菌磷	9				20	17	13	千克	S	Ditalimfos
2933.7900 90	其他内酰胺	9				20	17	13	千克		Other lactams
	-其他:										-Other:
2933.9100	--阿普唑仑(INN),卡马西泮(INN),氯氮卓(INN),氯硝西泮(INN),氯拉卓酸,地洛西泮(INN),地西泮(INN),艾司唑仑(INN),氯氟卓乙酯(INN),氟地西泮(INN),氟硝西泮(INN),氟西泮(INN),哈拉西泮(INN),劳拉西泮(INN),氯甲西泮(INN),马吲哚(INN),美达西泮(INN),咪达唑仑(INN),硝甲西泮(INN),去甲西泮(INN),奥沙西泮(INN),匹那西泮(INN),普拉西泮(INN),吡咯戊酮(INN),替马西泮(INN),四氢西泮(INN)和三唑仑(INN)以及它们的盐	6.5	5		0	20	17	13	千克		--Alprazolam(INN), camazepam(INN), chlordiazepoxide (INN), clonazepam (INN), clorazepate, delorazepam(INN), diazepam(INN), estazolam(INN), ethyl loflazepate(INN), fludiazepam(INN), flunitrazepam(INN), flurazepam(INN), halazepam (INN), lorazepam (INN), lormetazepam(INN), mazindol(INN), medazepam(INN), midazolam(INN), nimetazepam(INN), nitrazepam(INN), nordazepam(INN), oxazepam(INN), pinazepam(INN), prazepam(INN), pyrovalerone(INN), temazepam(INN), tetrazepam(INN) and triazolam(INN); salts thereof
2933.9100 11	阿普唑仑、卡马西泮、氯氮卓(以及它们的盐)	6.5				20	17	13	千克	I	Alprazolam(INN), camazepam(INN), chlordiazepoxide(INN); salts thereof
2933.9100 12	氯硝西泮、氯拉卓酸、地洛西泮(以及它们的盐)	6.5				20	17	13	千克	I	Clonazepam(INN), clorazepate, delorazepam(INN); salts thereof
2933.9100 13	地西泮、艾司唑仑、氯氟卓乙酯(以及它们的盐)	6.5				20	17	13	千克	I	Diazepam(INN), estazolam(INN), ethyl loflazepate(INN); salts thereof
2933.9100 14	氟地西泮、氟硝西泮、氟西泮(以及它们的盐)	6.5				20	17	13	千克	I	Fludiazepam(INN), flunitrazepam(INN), flurazepam(INN); salts thereof
2933.9100 15	哈拉西泮、劳拉西泮、氯甲西泮(以及它们的盐)	6.5				20	17	13	千克	I	Halazepam(INN), lorazepam(INN), lormetazepam(INN); salts thereof
2933.9100 16	马吲哚、咪达唑仑、硝西泮(以及它们的盐)	6.5				20	17	13	千克	I	Mazindol(INN), midazolam(INN), nitrazepam(INN); salts thereof
2933.9100 17	奥沙西泮、匹那西泮、普拉西泮(以及它们的盐)	6.5				20	17	13	千克	I	Nitrazepam(INN), nordazepam(INN), oxazepam(INN); salts thereof
2933.9100 18	去甲西泮、三唑仑(以及它们的盐)	6.5				20	17	13	千克	I	Nordazepam(INN), triazolam(INN); salts thereof
2933.9100 21	硝甲西泮、美达西泮(以及它们的盐)	6.5				20	17	13	千克		Nimetazepam(INN), medazepam(INN); salts thereof
2933.9100 22	吡咯戊酮、替马西泮、四氢西泮(以及它们的盐)	6.5				20	17	13	千克		Pyrovalerone(INN), temazepam(INN), tetrazepam(INN); salts thereof
2933.9900	--其他	6.5	5		5.2	20	17	13	千克		--Other
2933.9900 11	抑芽丹,三唑磷,虫线磷,喹硫磷等(包括哒嗪硫磷,亚胺硫磷,氯亚胺硫磷,保棉磷,益棉磷,威菌磷)	6.5				20	17	13	千克	S	Smaleic hydrazide, triazophos, thionazin, quinalphos (including pyridaphenthione (JMAF), phosmet, dialifos, azinphos_methyl, azinphos_ethyl, triamiphos)

税则号列 Tariff Item.	货品名称	最惠国(%) MFN	协定(%)CT 东盟 CA	中巴 CP	中智 CC	普通 Gen	增值税率 VAT	出口退税 ED	计量单位 Unit	监管条件 SC	Article Description
2933.9900 12	氯唑磷,炔咪菊酯等(包括呋喃虫酰肼,唑蚜威,不育胺,虫螨腈,抗螨唑,四螨嗪)	6.5				20	17	13	千克	S	SIsazofos, imiprothrin (including triaxamate, fenazaflor, clofentezine, etc.)
2933.9900 13	多菌灵,苯菌灵,氰菌灵,麦穗宁等(包括咪菌威,丙硫多菌灵,氟氯菌核利,哒菌酮,拌种咯,杀草强)	6.5				20	17	13	千克	S	Carbendazim, benomyl, cypendazole, fuberidazole (including debacarb, albendazole TOP, fluoromide (JMAF), pyridinitril, amitrole)
2933.9900 14	三唑酮,醚草敏,三唑醇,唑草酮等(包括四氯喹恶啉,己唑醇,腈苯唑,亚胺唑,四氟醚唑,氟环唑)	6.5				20	17	13	千克	S	Triadimefon, credazine (JMAF), triadimenol, isoxaflutole, fenbuconazole, imibenconazole, tertraconazole, BAS 480F
2933.9900 15	苄氯三唑醇,戊菌唑,粉唑醇等(包括联苯三唑醇,腈菌唑,环丙唑醇,烯唑醇,戊唑醇,氟硅唑)	6.5				20	17	13	千克	S	Diclobutrazol, penconzole, flutriafol (including bitertanol, myclobutanil, cyproconazole, diniconazole, tebuconazole, flusilazole)
2933.9900 16	环菌唑,叶菌唑,灭菌唑,种菌唑等(包括申嗪霉素,氟喹唑,哒螨灵,喹螨醚,氟草敏,氟咯草酮)	6.5				20	17	13	千克	S	SSF－109, metconazole, triticonazole, ipconazole (including phenazino－1－carboxylic acid, fluquinconazole, pyridaben, fenazaquin, norflurazon, fluorochloridone)
2933.9900 17	唑草酯,解草唑,四环唑,恶草酸等(包括喹禾糠酯,哒草特,咯草隆,禾草敌,唑草胺,敌草快,氯草敏)	6.5				20	17	13	千克	S	F8426, fenchlorazole; fenchlorazole－ethyl, tetcyclacis, peopaquizafop ect (including quizalofop－Ptefuryl, pyridate, cisanilide, molinate, cafenstrole, diquat, chloridazon)
2933.9900 18	氟胺草唑,酰胺磺隆,三氟苯唑等(包括吲哚丁酸,溴莠敏,哌壮素,吲熟酯,三唑磺,四唑酰草胺)	6.5				20	17	13	千克	S	Flupoxam, foramsulfuron, fluotrimazole (including 4－indol－3－ylbutylic acide (IBA), brompyrazon, piproctanly, piproctanly－bromide, ethychlozate (JMAF), etc.)
2933.9900 19	多效唑,烯效唑,抑芽唑,增效胺等(包括异麦赛津,叶枯净,叶锈特,吡喃草酮,吲哚乙酸)	6.5				20	17	13	千克	S	Paclobutrazol, uniconazole, triapenthenol, bifenthrin (including phenazine oxide, butrizol, tepraloxydim, indol－3－yl acetic acide (IAA), etc.)
2933.9900 30	布桂嗪,扎莱普隆,唑吡坦(以及他们的盐)	6.5				20	17	13	千克	I	Bucinnazine, zaleplon zolpidem; salts thereof
2933.9900 40	齐柏特罗	6.5				20	17	13	千克	L	zilpaterol
2933.9900 60	(环)四亚甲基四硝胺(俗名奥托金 HMX)	6.5				20	17	13	千克	3	Octogen (HMX)
2933.9900 70	(环)三亚甲基三硝基胺(俗名黑索金 RDX)	6.5				20	17	13	千克	3	hexogen (RDX)
2933.9900 90	其他仅含氮杂原子的杂环化合物	6.5				20	17	13	千克		Other heterocyclic compounds with oxygen hetero-atom(s) only
29.34	**核酸及其盐,不论是否已有化学定义;其他杂环化合物:**										**Nucleic acids and their salts, whether or not chemically defined; other heterocyclic compounds:**

税则号列 Tariff Item.	货品名称	最惠国(%) MFN	协定(%)CT 东盟 CA	中巴 CP	中智 CC	普通 Gen	增值税率 VAT	出口退税 ED	计量单位 Unit	监管条件 SC	Article Description
2934.1000	-结构上含有一个非稠合噻唑环(不论是否氢化)的化合物	6.5	5		0	20	17	13	千克		-Compounds containing an unfused thiazole ring (whether or not hydrogenated) in the structure
2934.1000 11	噻螨酮	6.5				20	17	13	千克	S	Hexythiazox
2934.1000 12	噻唑膦,噻唑硫磷	6.5				20	17	13	千克	S	SFosthiazate,colophonate
2934.1000 13	噻唑烟酸,噻唑菌胺	6.5				20	17	13	千克	S	Imazethapyr
2934.1000 14	氯噻啉,氟螨噻	6.5				20	17	13	千克	S	Imidaclothiz
2934.1000 15	噻菌灵,噻菌胺,噻丙腈	6.5				20	17	13	千克	S	Thiabendazole, Benthiaralicarb, isopropyl thiapronil
2934.1000 16	噻呋酰胺,噻虫胺	6.5				20	17	13	千克	S	Thifluzamide
2934.1000 17	辛噻酮,拌种灵	6.5				20	17	13	千克	S	Octhilinone,Amobam
2934.1000 18	稻瘟灵,解草胺	6.5				20	17	13	千克	S	Flurazole
2934.1000 90	结构上含有非稠合噻唑环的化合物(非稠合噻唑环不论是否氢化)	6.5				20	17	13	千克		Compounds containing an unfused thiazole ring (whether or not hydrogenated) in the structure
2934.2000	-结构上含有一个苯并噻唑环系(不论是否氢化)的化合物,但未经进一步稠合的	6.5	5		0	20	17	13	千克		-Compounds containing in the structure a benzothiazole ring-system (whether or not hydrogenated), not further fused
2934.2000 11	噻螨威	6.5				20	17	13	千克	S	tazimcarb
2934.2000 12	苯噻硫氰	6.5				20	17	13	千克	S	benthiozole
2934.2000 13	烯丙苯噻唑	6.5				20	17	13	千克	S	probenazole
2934.2000 14	草除灵	6.5				20	17	13	千克	S	benazolin ethyl
2934.2000 15	噻唑禾草灵	6.5				20	17	13	千克	S	fenthiaprop - ethyl
2934.2000 16	苯噻隆	6.5				20	17	13	千克	S	Benzthiazuron
2934.2000 17	甲基苯噻隆	6.5				20	17	13	千克	S	Methabenzthiazuron
2934.2000 18	苯噻酰草胺	6.5				20	17	13	千克	S	mefenacet
2934.2000 90	其他含一个苯并噻唑环系的化合物	6.5				20	17	13	千克		Compounds containing in the structure a benzothiazole ring - system (whether or not hydrogenated),not further fused
2934.3000	-结构上含有一个吩噻嗪环系(不论是否氢化)的化合物,但未经进一步稠合的	6.5	5		0	20	17	13	千克		-Compounds containing in the structure a phenothiazine ring-system (whether or not hydrogenated), not further fused
	-其他:										-Other:
2934.9100	--阿米雷司(INN),溴替唑仑(INN),氯塞西泮(INN),氯恶唑仑(INN),右吗拉胺(INN),卤恶唑仑(INN),凯他唑仑(INN),美索卡(INN),恶唑仑(INN),匹莫林(INN),苯甲曲嗪(INN),芬美曲嗪(INN)和舒芬太尼(INN)及它们的盐	6.5	5		0	20	17	13	千克		--Aminorex (INN), brotizolam (INN), clotiazepam(INN), cloxazolam(INN), dextromoramide (INN), haloxazolam (INN), ketazolam (INN), mesocarb (INN), oxazolam (INN), pemoline (INN), phendimetrazine (INN), phenmetrazine (INN) and sufentanil (INN); salts thereof
2934.9100 11	阿米雷司,溴替唑仑,氯噻西泮(以及它们的盐)	6.5				20	17	13	千克	I	Aminorex (INN), brotizolam (INN), clotiazepam(INN); salts thereof
2934.9100 12	氯恶唑仑,卤恶唑仑(以及它们的盐)	6.5				20	17	13	千克	I	Cloxazolam (INN), haloxazolam (INN); salts thereof
2934.9100 13	凯他唑仑,美索卡,恶唑仑(以及它们的盐)	6.5				20	17	13	千克	I	Ketazolam (INN), mesocarb (INN), oxazolam(INN); salts thereof

税则号列 Tariff Item.	货品名称	最惠国(%) MFN	协定(%) 东盟 CA	中巴 CP	CT 中智 CC	普通 Gen	增值税率 VAT	出口退税 ED	计量单位 Unit	监管条件 SC	Article Description
2934.9100 14	匹莫林,苯甲曲嗪,芬美曲嗪(以及它们的盐)	6.5				20	17	13	千克	I	Pemoline (INN), phendimetrazine (INN), phenmetrazine (INN); salts thereof
2934.9100 20	右吗拉胺,舒芬太尼(以及它们的盐)	6.5				20	17	13	千克	W	Dextromoramide (INN), sufentanil (INN); salts thereof
	--其他:										--Other:
2934.9910	---磺内酯及磺内酰胺	6.5	5		5.2	30	17	13	千克		---Sultones and sultams
2934.9920	---呋喃唑酮	6	5		4.8	20	17	13	千克		---Furazolidone
2934.9930	---核酸及其盐	6.5	5		5.2	35	17	13	千克		---Nucleic acids and their salts
2934.9990	---其他	6.5	5		5.2	20	17	13	千克		---Other
2934.9990 01	核苷酸类食品添加剂	6.5				20	17	13	千克		Ucleotideadditives
2934.9990 10	恶草酮	6.5				20	17	13	千克	S	Oxadiazon(TC)
2934.9990 21	恶唑磷,蔬果磷,茂硫磷,除害磷等(包括甲基吡恶磷,丁硫环磷,硫环磷,杀扑磷,伏杀硫磷,地胺磷)	6.5				20	17	13	千克	S	Isoxathion, dioxabenzofos, morphothion, (including azamethiphos, fosthietan, phosfolan, methidathion, phosalone, mephosfolan)
2934.9990 22	环线威,杀虫环,杀虫钉,多噻烷等(包括甲基硫环磷,噻恩菊酯,噻嗪酮,保松噻,恶虫酮,茚虫威)	6.5				20	17	13	千克	S	Tirpate, thiocyclam, trithialan, polythialan (including phosfolan_methyl, Kadethrin, Buprofezin, levamisole, metoxadiazone, indoxacarb)
2934.9990 23	恶唑禾草灵,毒鼠硅,噻鼠灵等(包括福拉比,噻节因,糠菌唑,精恶唑禾草灵)	6.5				20	17	13	千克	S	Fenoxaprop - ethyl, silatrane, difethialone (including dimethipin, bromuconazole, fenoxaprop - P, fenoxaprop - p - ethyl)
2934.9990 24	代森硫,代森环,福吗啉,咯菌腈等(包括稻瘟酯,烯酰吗啉,噻菌腈,土菌灵,恶霜灵,恶霉灵)	6.5				20	17	13	千克	S	Etem (BSI), milmeb (BSI), flumorph fludioxonil (including pefurazoate, dimethomoph, thicyofen, etridiazole, oxadixyl, hymexazol)
2934.9990 25	噻霉酮,噻森铜,丙环唑,乙环唑等(包括恶唑菌酮,金核霉素,呋菌唑,叶枯唑,呋醚唑,苯醚甲环唑)	6.5				20	17	13	千克	S	Thiediazole copper, Propiconazol, etaconazole, etc. (including Famoxadone, furconazole, bismerthiazol, furconazole_cis, difenoconazole)
2934.9990 26	嗪草酸,噻氟隆,丁噻隆,异恶隆等(包括噻苯隆,磺噻隆,恶唑隆,异恶草醚,噻吩草胺,二甲吩草胺)	6.5				20	17	13	千克	S	KIH 9201, thiazfluron, tebuthiuron, isoproturon (including thidiazuron, ethidimuron, dimefuron, isoxapyrifop, thenychlor, dimethachlor)
2934.9990 27	苯草灭,灭草松,灭草唑,解草嗪等(包括解草恶唑,异恶草松,恶嗪草酮,环苯草酮,丙炔氟草胺)	6.5				20	17	13	千克	S	Bentranil, bentazone, methazole (BSI), benoxacor (including furilazole, clomazone, oxaziclomefone, cloproxydim, flumioxazin)
2934.9990 28	氟噻乙草酯,丙炔恶草酮,噻草酮等(包括糖氨基嘌呤,苯螨噻,异恶酰草胺,异恶唑草酮)	6.5				20	17	13	千克	S	Fulthiacet - methyl, oxakiargyl, cycloxydim (including kinetin, triarathene, ixoxaben, isoxaflutole)
2934.9990 29	炔丙恶唑草,韩乐宁,噻唑锌等(包括噻菌茂,硅丰环)	6.5				20	17	13	千克	S	Nbspoxadiar, ethaboxam, Zinc thiazole (including Saijunmao,)

税则号列 Tariff Item.	货 品 名 称	最惠国(%) MFN	协定(%)CT 东盟 CA	中巴 CP	中智 CC	普通 Gen	增值税率 VAT	出口退税 ED	计量单位 Unit	监管条件 SC	Article Description
2934.9990 31	多抗霉素,灰瘟素	6.5				20	17	13	千克	S	polyoxin, blasticidin
2934.9990 32	三环唑,氧环唑	6.5				20	17	13	千克	S	tricyclazole , azaconazole
2934.9990 33	灭螨猛,克杀螨,螨蜱胺	6.5				20	17	13	千克	S	chinomethionate, thioquino, Tifatol
2934.9990 34	二氰蒽醌,吗菌威	6.5				20	17	13	千克	S	dithianon, carbamorph
2934.9990 35	十二环吗啉,十三吗啉	6.5				20	17	13	千克	S	dodemorph, Tridemorph
2934.9990 36	杀螺吗啉,丁苯吗啉	6.5				20	17	13	千克	S	trifenmorph, fenpropimorph
2934.9990 37	喹菌酮,肼菌酮	6.5				20	17	13	千克	S	oxolinic acid, Drazoxolon
2934.9990 38	萎锈灵,氧化萎锈灵	6.5				20	17	13	千克	S	carboxin, oxycellulose
2934.9990 39	棉隆,乙烯菌核利	6.5				20	17	13	千克	S	dazomet , vinclozolin
2934.9990 41	环酯草醚	6.5				20	17	13	千克	S	Pyriftalid
2934.9990 90	其他杂环化合物	6.5				20	17	13	千克		Other heterocyclic compounds
29.35	磺(酰)胺:										**Sulphonamides:**
2935.0010	---磺胺嘧啶	6.5	5		0	35	17	13	千克		---Sulphadiazine
2935.0020	---磺胺双甲基嘧啶	6.5	5		0	35	17	13	千克		---Sulfadimidine
2935.0030	---磺胺甲恶唑	6.5	5		0	35	17	13	千克		---Sulfamethoxazole
2935.0090	---其他	6.5	5		0	35	17	13	千克		---Other
2935.0090 11	氟唑磺隆,氟吡磺隆等(包括甲酰胺嘧磺隆,乙氧磺隆,氯磺隆,甲磺隆,苯磺隆,胺苯磺隆)	6.5				35	17	13	千克	S	Flucarbazone, flucetosulfuron (including foramsulfuron, ethoxysulfuron, chlorsulfuron, metsulfuron – methyl, tribenuron – methyl, ethametsulfuron)
2935.0090 12	醚苯磺隆,噻吩磺隆,醚磺隆等(包括氟胺磺隆,氟磺隆,甲嘧磺隆,氯嘧磺隆,氟嘧磺隆)	6.5				35	17	13	千克	S	Triasulfuron, thifensulfuron – methyl, cinosulfuron (including triflusulfuron – methyl, prosulfuron, sulfometuron – methyl, chlorimuron – ethyl, primisulfuron – methyl)
2935.0090 13	苄嘧磺隆,吡嘧磺隆,烟嘧磺隆等(包括啶嘧磺隆,砜嘧磺隆,唑嘧磺隆)	6.5				35	17	13	千克	S	Bensulfuron – methyl, pyrazosulfuron – ethyl, nicosulfuron (including flazasulfuron, rimsulfuron, imazosulfuron)
2935.0090 14	四唑嘧磺隆,唑吡嘧磺隆等(包括氯吡嘧磺隆,酰嘧磺隆,环丙嘧磺隆,甲基二磺隆)	6.5				35	17	13	千克	S	Imazosulfuron, etc. (including halosulfuron – methyl, amidosulfuron, cyclosulfamuron, mesosulfuron)
2935.0090 15	氟磺酰草胺,甲磺草胺等(包括唑嘧磺草胺,双氟磺草胺,五氟磺草胺)	6.5				35	17	13	千克	S	Mefluidide, sulfentrazone (including flumetsulam, florasulam, penoxsuam)
2935.0090 16	氟磺胺草醚,磺草灵等(包括单嘧磺酯,磺草唑胺)	6.5				35	17	13	千克	S	Fomesafen, asulam(including metosulam, etc)
2935.0090 17	磺草膦,氨磺乐灵等(包括甲基碘磺隆钠盐)	6.5				35	17	13	千克	S	LS 830556, oryzalin(including iodosulfuron methyl sodium)
2935.0090 18	磺菌胺,增糖胺等(包括甲苯氟磺胺,氟虫胺)	6.5				35	17	13	千克	S	Flusulfamide, fluoridamid(including tolyfluanid, sulfluramid)
2935.0090 19	畜蜱磷,伐灭磷,地散磷等(包括磺菌威,氰霜唑)	6.5				35	17	13	千克	S	Cythioate , famphur (ESA), bensulide (including methasulfocarb, cyazofamid)
2935.0090 90	其他磺(酰)胺	6.5				35	17	13	千克		Other sulphonamides
	第十一分章 维生素原、维生素及激素										XI. -PROVITAMINS, VITAMINS AND HORMONES

税则号列 Tariff Item.	货 品 名 称	最惠国(%) MFN	协定(%)CT 东盟 CA	中巴 CP	中智 CC	普通 Gen	增值税率 VAT	出口退税 ED	计量单位 Unit	监管条件 SC	Article Description
29.36	**天然或合成再制的维生素原和维生素(包括天然浓缩物)及其主要用作维生素的衍生物,上述产品的混合物,不论是否溶于溶剂:**										**Provitamins and vitamins, natural or reproduced by synthesis (including natural concentrates), derivatives thereof used primarily as vitamins, and intermixtures of the foregoing, whether or not in any solvent:**
	-未混合的维生素及其衍生物:										-Vitamins and their derivatives, unmixed:
2936.2100	--维生素 A 及其衍生物	4			0	20	17	13	千克		--Vitamins A and their derivatives
2936.2200	--维生素 B_1 及其衍生物	4			0	20	17	13	千克		--Vitamin B_1 and its derivatives
2936.2300	--维生素 B_2 及其衍生物	4			0	20	17	13	千克		--Vitamin B_2 and its derivatives
2936.2400	--D 或 DL-泛酸(维生素 B_3 或维生素 B_5)及其衍生物	4			0	20	17	13	千克		--D-or DL-Pantothenic acid (Vitamin B_3 or Vitamin B_5) and its derivatives
2936.2500	--维生素 B_6 及其衍生物	4			0	20	17	13	千克		--Vitamin B_6 and its derivatives
2936.2600	--维生素 B_{12} 及其衍生物	4			0	20	17	13	千克		--Vitamin B_{12} and its derivatives
2936.2700	--维生素 C 及其衍生物	4			3.2	20	17	13	千克	a	--Vitamin C and its derivatives
2936.2800	--维生素 E 及其衍生物	4			0	20	17	17	千克		--Vitamin E and its derivatives
2936.2900	--其他维生素及其衍生物	4			0	20	17	17	千克		--Other vitamins and their derivatives
2936.9000	-其他,包括天然浓缩物	4			3.2	20	17	13	千克		-Other, including natural concentrates
29.37	**天然或合成再制的激素、前列腺素、血栓烷、白细胞三烯及其衍生物和结构类似物,包括主要用作激素的改性链多肽:**										**Hormones, prostaglandins, thromboxanes and leukotrienes, natural or reproduced by synthesis; derivatives and structural analogues thereof, including chain modified polypeptides, used primarily as hormones:**
	-多肽激素、蛋白激素、糖蛋白激素及其衍生物和结构类似物:										-Polypeptide hormones, protein hormones and glycoprotein hormones, their derivatives and structural analogues:
2937.1100	--生长激素及其衍生物和结构类似物	4			0	20	17	13	千克	L	--Somatotropin, its derivatives and structural analogues
2937.1200	--胰岛素及其盐	4			0	20	17	13	千克	L	--Insulin and its salts
2937.1900	--其他	4			0	20	17	13	千克		--Other
2937.1900 11	促红细胞生成素(EPO)	4				20	17	13	千克	L	Erythropoietin,EPO
2937.1900 12	胰岛素样生长因子 1	4				20	17	13	千克	L	Chorionic Gonadotrophin
2937.1900 13	促性腺激素	4				20	17	13	千克	L	Chorionic Gonadotrophin
2937.1900 14	生长因子素	4				20	17	13	千克	L	Recombinant Human Epidermal Growth Factor
2937.1900 15	促皮质素	4				20	17	13	千克	L	Corticotrophin
2937.1900 90	其他多肽激素及衍生物和结构类似物(包括蛋白激素,糖蛋白激素及其衍生物和结构类似物)	4				20	17	13	千克	Q	Other polypeptide hormones, including protein hormones 、glycoprotein hormones , their derivatives and structural analogues
	-甾族激素及其衍生物和结构类似物:										-Steroidal hormones, their derivatives and structural analogues:
2937.2100	--可的松、氢化可的松、脱氢可的松及脱氢皮质醇	4			0	20	17	13	千克	Q	--Cortisone, hydrocortisone, prednisone (dehydrocortisone) and prednisolone (dehydrohydrocortisone)

税则号列 Tariff Item.	货品名称	最惠国(%) MFN	协定(%) 东盟 CA	中巴 CP	CT 中智 CC	普通 Gen	增值税率 VAT	出口退税 ED	计量单位 Unit	监管条件 SC	Article Description
	--皮质甾类激素的卤化衍生物:										--Halogenated derivatives of corticosteroidal hormones:
2937.2210	---地塞米松	4			0	30	17	13	千克	Q	---Dexamethasone
2937.2290	---其他	4			0	30	17	13	千克	Q	---Other
2937.2300	--雌(甾)激素和孕激素	4			0	30	17	13	千克		--Oestrogens and progestogens
2937.2300 10	折仑诺;孕三烯酮;替勃龙(包括四氢孕三烯酮)	4				30	17	13	千克	L	Zearalanol, gestrinone, tibolone(including tetrahydrogestrinone)
2937.2300 90	其他雌(甾)激素及孕激素	4				30	17	13	千克	Q	Other oestrogens and progestogens
2937.2900	--其他	4			0	30	17	13	千克		--Other
2937.2900 11	雄烯二醇;雄烯二酮(包括雄-4-烯-3β,17α-二醇;雄-5-烯-3β,17α-二醇)	4				30	17	13	千克	L	Androstenediol, androstenedione (including androst-4-ene-3β, 17α-diol, androst-5-ene-3, 17-dione)
2937.2900 12	雄-4-烯二醇;雄烯二酮异构体[包括倍他雄烷二醇异构体;雄烷二醇异构体;勃拉睾酮(双甲睾酮)]	4				30	17	13	千克	L	4-Androstenediol, androst-4-ene-3α,17α-diol(including 5α-androstane-3α, 17β-diol,5α-androstane-3β, 17α-diol, bolasterone)
2937.2900 13	勃地酮(宝丹酮),卡普睾酮[包括,1,4-雄二烯-3,17-二酮;氯司替勃(氯斯太宝)]	4				30	17	13	千克	L	Boldenone, calusterone(including deltal-androstene-3,17-dione, androstenediol, dehydroepiandrosterone(DHEA), desoxymethyltestosterone
2937.2900 14	达那唑,脱氢氯甲基睾酮[包括雄-1-烯-3,17-二酮;(△)雄烯二醇;普拉雄酮;去氧甲基睾酮]	4				30	17	13	千克	L	Danazol, dehydrochlormethyltestosterone (including epi-dihydrotestosterone, ethylestrenol, fluoxymesterone, formebolone)
2937.2900 15	双氢睾酮;屈他雄酮(羟甲雄酮)[包括表双氢睾酮;乙烯雌醇;氟甲睾酮;甲酰勃龙(醛甲宝龙)]	4				30	17	13	千克	L	4,5 alpha Dihydrotestosterone, drostanolone(including 4-hydroxytestosterone, 4-hydroxy-19-nortestosterone ,3α-hydroxy-5α-androstan-17-one3α)
2937.2900 16	呋咱甲氢龙(夫拉扎勃)(包括4-羟基睾酮;4-羟基诺龙;3α-羟基-5α-雄烷-17酮)	4				30	17	13	千克	L	Furazabol(methasterone(including 2α, 17α-dimethyl-5α-androstane-3-one-17β-ol)
2937.2900 17	美雄诺龙;美睾酮;美雄酮(包括2α,17α-二甲基-5α-雄烷-3-酮-17β-醇)	4				30	17	13	千克	L	Mestanolone, mesterolone, methandienone (including methyldienolone, norandrosterone)
2937.2900 18	甲基-1-睾酮;甲睾酮;甲基去甲睾酮(包括17α-甲基17β-羟茎雌-4,9(10)去二烯-3-酮;去甲雄酮)	4				30	17	13	千克	L	Methyl-1-testostero, methyltestosterone , methylnortestosterone (including methylnortestosterone, methyltrienolone
2937.2900 19	美替诺龙;美雄醇(包括17α-甲基-17β-羟基雌-4,9,11-三烯-3-酮)	4				30	17	13	千克	L	Methenolone, methandriol(19-去甲雄烯二醇,19-norandrostenedione, norethandrolone)
2937.2900 21	米勃龙;诺龙;诺勃酮;诺司替勃[包括19-去甲雄烯二醇;19-去甲雄烯二酮;诺乙雄龙(乙基诺龙)]	4				30	17	13	千克	L	

税则号列 Tariff Item.	货品名称	最惠国(%) MFN	协定(%) CT 东盟 CA	 中巴 CP	 中智 CC	普通 Gen	增值税率 VAT	出口退税 ED	计量单位 Unit	监管条件 SC	Article Description
2937.2900 22	19－去甲本胆烷醇酮[包括羟勃龙(氧宝龙);氧雄龙(氧甲氢龙)]	4				30	17	13	千克	L	19 – noretiocholanolone (including prostanozol)
2937.2900 23	羟甲睾酮,羟甲烯龙(包括[3,2－c]吡唑－5α－苯别胆烷－17β－4氢吡喃醇)	4				30	17	13	千克	L	Oxymesterone, oxymetholone (including prostanozol)
2937.2900 24	奎勃龙;司坦唑醇;司腾勃龙[包括1－睾酮;睾酮;群勃龙(追宝龙)]	4				30	17	13	千克	L	Quinbolone, stanozolol, Stenbolone (including 1 – Testosterone, Testosterone, trenbolone)
2937.2900 90	其他甾类,激素及其衍生物和结构类似物	4				30	17	13	千克	Q	Other somatotropin its derivatives and structural analogues
	-儿茶酚胺激素及其衍生物和结构类似物:										-Catecholamine hormones, their derivatives and structural analogues:
2937.3100	--肾上腺素	4			0	30	17	13	千克	Q	--Epinephrine
2937.3900	--其他	4			0	30	17	13	千克	Q	--Other
2937.4000	-氨基酸衍生物	4			0	30	17	13	千克	Q	-Amino-acid derivatives
2937.5000	-前列腺素、血栓烷和白细胞三烯及其衍生物和结构类似物	4			0	30	17	13	千克		-Prostaglandins, thromboxanes and leukotrienes, their derivatives and structural analogues
2937.9000	-其他	4			0	30	17	13	千克	Q	-Other
	第十二分章　天然或合成再制的苷(配糖物)、植物碱及其盐、醚、酯和其他衍生物										Ⅻ. -GLYCOSIDES AND VEGETABLE ALKALOIDS, NATURAL OR REPRODUCED BY SYNTHESIS, AND THEIR SALTS, ETHERS, ESTERS AND OTHER DERIVATIVES
29.38	**天然或合成再制的苷(配糖物)及其盐、醚、酯和其他衍生物:**										**Glycosides, natural or reproduced by synthesis, and their salts, ethers, esters and other derivatives:**
2938.1000	-芸香苷及其衍生物	6.5	5		0	20	17	13	千克	Q	-Rutoside (rutin) and its derivatives
2938.9000	-其他	6.5	5		0	20	17	13	千克		-Other
2938.9000 10	甘草酸粉	6.5				20	17	13	千克	y4x	Glycyrrhizic acid powder
2938.9000 20	甘草酸盐类	6.5				20	17	13	千克	y4x	Salts of glycyrrhizic acid
2938.9000 30	甘草次酸及其衍生物	6.5				20	17	13	千克	y4x	Glycyrrhetic acid and its derivatives
2938.9000 90	其他天然或合成再制的苷及其盐等(包括醚、酯和其他衍生物)	6.5				20	17	13	千克		Other glycosides, natural or reproduced by synthesis, and their salts, ethers, esters and other derivatives
29.39	**天然或合成再制的生物碱及其盐、醚、酯和其他衍生物:**										**Vegetable alkaloids, natural or reproduced by synthesis, and their salts, ethers, esters and other derivatives:**
	-鸦片碱及其衍生物以及它们的盐:										-Alkaloids of opium and their derivatives; salts thereof:

税则号列 Tariff Item.	货品名称	最惠国(%) MFN	协定(%) 东盟 CA	中巴 CP	CT 中智 CC	普通 Gen	增值税率 VAT	出口退税 ED	计量单位 Unit	监管条件 SC	Article Description
2939.1100	--罂粟杆浓缩物、丁丙诺啡(INN)、可待因、双氢可待因(INN)、乙基吗啡、埃托啡(INN)、海洛因、氢可酮(INN)、氢吗啡酮(INN)、吗啡、尼可吗啡(INN)、羟考酮(INN)、羟吗啡酮(INN)、福尔可定(INN)、醋氢可酮(INN)和蒂巴因,以及它们的盐	4			0	50	17	13	千克		--Concentrates of poppy straw; buprenorphine(INN), codeine, dihydrocodeine (INN), ethylmorphine, etorphine (INN), heroin, hydrocodone (INN), hydromorphone (INN), morphine, nicomorphine (INN), oxycodone (INN), oxymorphone(INN), pholcodine(INN), thebacon(INN) and thebaine; salts thereof
2939.1100 11	罂粟杆浓缩物	4				50	17	13	千克	W	Concentrates of poppy straw
2939.1100 12	可待因、双氢可待因、乙基吗啡(以及它们的盐)	4				50	17	13	千克	W	Codeine, dihydrocodeine (INN), ethylmorphine salts thereof
2939.1100 13	埃托啡、海洛因、氢可酮(以及它们的盐)	4				50	17	13	千克	W	Etorphine(INN), heroin, hydrocodone (INN); salts thereof
2939.1100 14	氢吗啡酮、吗啡、尼可吗啡(以及它们的盐)	4				50	17	13	千克	W	Hydromorphone (INN), morphine, nicomorphine(INN); salts thereof
2939.1100 15	羟考酮、羟吗啡酮、福尔可定(以及它们的盐)	4				50	17	13	千克	W	Oxycodone(INN), oxymorphone(INN), pholcodine(INN); salts thereof
2939.1100 16	醋氢可酮、蒂巴因(以及它们的盐)	4				50	17	13	千克	W	Thebacon (INN) and thebaine; salts thereof
2939.1100 20	丁丙诺啡及其盐	4				50	17	13	千克	I	Buprenorphine and salts thereof
2939.1900	--其他	4			0	50	17	13	千克		--Other
2939.1900 10	二氢埃托啡、吗啉乙基吗啡(以及它们的盐)	4				50	17	13	千克	W	Dihydroetorphine, morpholinylethyl morphine; salts thereof
2939.1900 90	其他鸦片碱及其衍生物及它们的盐	4				50	17	13	千克	Q	Other alkaloids of opium and their derivatives; salts thereof
2939.2000	-金鸡纳生物碱及其衍生物以及它们的盐	4			0	20	17	13	千克	Q	-Alkaloids of cinchona and their derivatives; salts thereof
2939.3000	-咖啡因及其盐	4			0	20	17	13	千克		-Caffeine and its salts
2939.3000 10	咖啡因	4				20	17	13	千克	I	Caffeine
2939.3000 90	咖啡因的盐	4				20	17	13	千克	Q	Salts of caffeine
	-麻黄碱类及其盐:										-Ephedrines and their salts:
2939.4100	--麻黄碱及其盐	4			0	20	17	13	千克		--Ephedrine and its salts
2939.4100 10	麻黄碱(麻黄素,盐酸麻黄碱)	4				20	17	13	千克	23Q	Ephedrine (ephedrine hydrochloride)
2939.4100 20	硫酸麻黄碱	4				20	17	13	千克	23Q	Ephedrine sulfate
2939.4100 30	消旋盐酸麻黄碱	4				20	17	13	千克	23Q	Racephedrine hydrochloride
2939.4100 40	草酸麻黄碱	4				20	17	13	千克	23Q	Ephedrine oxalate
2939.4100 90	麻黄碱盐	4				20	17	13	千克	Q	Salts of ephedrine
2939.4200	--假麻黄碱及其盐	4			0	20	17	13	千克		--Pseudoephedrine (INN) and its salts
2939.4200 10	伪麻黄碱(伪麻黄素、盐酸伪麻黄碱)	4				20	17	13	千克	23Q	Pseudoephedrine, pseudoephedrine, pseudoephedrine hydrochloride
2939.4200 20	硫酸伪麻黄碱	4				20	17	13	千克	23Q	Pseudoephedrine sulfate
2939.4200 90	假麻黄碱盐(D-2-甲胺基-1-苯基丙醇)	4				20	17	13	千克	Q	Salts of pseudoephedrine
2939.4300	--d-去甲假麻黄碱(INN)及其盐	4			0	20	17	13	千克	I	--d-Norpseudoephedrine and its salts
2939.4900	--其他	4			0	20	17	13	千克		--Other
2939.4900 10	盐酸甲基麻黄碱	4				20	17	13	千克	23Q	Mephedrine hydrochloride

税则号列 Tariff Item.	货品名称	最惠国(%) MFN	协定(%)CT 东盟 CA	中巴 CP	中智 CC	普通 Gen	增值税率 VAT	出口退税 ED	计量单位 Unit	监管条件 SC	Article Description
2939.4900 20	消旋盐酸甲基麻黄碱	4				20	17	13	千克	23Q	Racemephedrine hydrochloride
2939.4900 30	去甲麻黄碱及其盐	4				20	17	13	千克	23I	Methamphetamine and its salts
2939.4900 90	其他麻黄碱及其盐	4				20	17	13	千克	Q	Other ephedrines and their salts
	-茶碱和氨茶碱及其衍生物以及它们的盐：										-Theophylline and aminophylline (theophylline-ethylenediamine) and their derivatives; salts thereof:
2939.5100	--芬乙茶碱(INN)及其盐	4			0	20	17	13	千克	Q	--Fenetylline(INN) and its salts
2939.5900	--其他	4			0	20	17	13	千克	Q	--Other
	-麦角生物碱及其衍生物以及它们的盐：										-Alkaloids of rye ergot and their derivatives; salts thereof:
2939.6100	--麦角新碱及其盐	4			0	20	17	13	千克		--Ergometrine (INN) and its salts
2939.6100 10	麦角新碱	4				20	17	13	千克	3Q2	Ergometrine (INN)
2939.6100 90	麦角新碱盐	4				20	17	13	千克	Q	Salt of ergometrine (INN)
2939.6200	--麦角胺及其盐	4			0	20	17	13	千克		--Ergotamine (INN) and its salts
2939.6200 10	麦角胺	4				20	17	13	千克	3Q2	Ergotamine (INN)
2939.6200 90	麦角胺盐	4				20	17	13	千克	Q	Salts of ergotamine (INN)
2939.6300	--麦角酸及其盐	4			0	20	17	13	千克		--Lysergic acid and its salts
2939.6300 10	麦角酸	4				20	17	13	千克	3Q2	Lysergic acid
2939.6300 90	麦角酸盐	4				20	17	13	千克	Q	Salts of lysergic acid
2939.6900	--其他	4			0	20	17	13	千克	Q	--Other
	--可卡因、芽子碱、左甲苯丙胺、去氧麻黄碱(INN)、去氧麻黄碱外消旋体,它们的盐、酯及其他衍生物：										--Cocaine, ecgonine, levometamfetamine, metamfetamine(INN), metamfetamine racemate; salts, esters and other derivatives thereof:
2939.9110	---可卡因及其盐	4			0	20	17	13	千克	W	---Cocaine and its salts
2939.9190	---其他	4			0	20	17	13	千克		---Other
2939.9190 11	芽子碱、左甲苯丙胺(以及它们的盐、酯及其他衍生物)	4				20	17	13	千克		Ecgonine, levometamfetamine and their salts, esters and other derivatives
2939.9190 12	去氧麻黄碱(INN)(以及它们的盐、酯及其他衍生物)	4				20	17	13	千克		Metamfetamine(INN) and their salts, esters and other derivatives
2939.9190 13	去氧麻黄碱外消旋体(以及它们的盐、酯及其他衍生物)	4				20	17	13	千克		Metamfetamine racemate and their salts, esters and other derivatives
	--其他：										--Other:
2939.9910	---烟碱及其盐	4			0	20	17	13	千克	Q	---Nicotine and its salts
2939.9920	---番木鳖碱(士的年)及其盐	4			0	17	17	13	千克	Q	---Strychnine and its salts
2939.9990	---其他	4			0	20	17	13	千克	Q	---Other
	第十三分章 其他有机化合物										XIII. -OTHER ORGANIC COMPOUNDS
29.40	**化学纯糖,但蔗糖、乳糖、麦芽糖、葡萄糖及果糖除外;糖醚、糖缩醛、糖酯及其盐,但不包括税目29.37、29.38及29.39的产品：**										**Sugars, chemically pure, other than sucrose, lactose, maltose, glucose and fructose, sugar ethers, sugar acetals and sugar esters, and their salts, other than products of heading No. 29.37, 29.38 or 29.39:**

税则号列 Tariff Item.	货品名称	最惠国(%) MFN	协定(%) 东盟 CA	中巴 CP	CT 中智 CC	普通 Gen	增值税率 VAT	出口退税 ED	计量单位 Unit	监管条件 SC	Article Description
2940.0000	化学纯糖,但蔗糖、乳糖、麦芽糖、葡萄糖及果糖除外;糖醚、糖缩醛、糖酯及其盐,但不包括税目29.37、29.38及29.39的产品	6	5		0	30	17	13	千克	Q	Sugars, chemically pure, other than sucrose, lactose, maltose, glucose and fructose; sugar ethers, sugar acetals and sugar esters, and their salts, other than products of heading No. 29.37, 29.38 or 29.39
29.41	抗菌素:										**Antibiotics**:
	-青霉素和具有青霉烷酸结构的青霉素衍生物及其盐:										-Penicillins and their derivatives with a penicillanic acid structure; salts thereof:
	---氨苄青霉素及其盐:										---Ampicillin and its salts:
2941.1011	----氨苄青霉素	6	5	5	0	20	17	13	千克	Q	----Ampicillin
2941.1012	----氨苄青霉素三水酸	6	5	5	0	20	17	13	千克	Q	----Ampicillin trihydrate
2941.1019	----其他	6	5	5	0	20	17	13	千克	Q	----Other
	---其他:										---Other:
2941.1091	----羟氨苄青霉素	4			0	20	17	13	千克	Q	----Amoxycillin
2941.1092	----羟氨苄青霉素三水酸	4			0	20	17	13	千克	Q	----Amoxycillin trihydrate
2941.1093	----6氨基青霉烷酸(6APA)	4			0	20	17	13	千克		----6-Aminopenicillanic acid
2941.1094	----青霉素V	4			0	20	17	13	千克	Q	----Penicillin V
2941.1095	----磺苄青霉素	4			0	20	17	13	千克	Q	----Sulfobenzylpenicillin
2941.1096	----邻氯青霉素	4			0	20	17	13	千克	Q	----Cloxacillin
2941.1099	----其他	4			0	20	17	13	千克	Q	----Other
2941.2000	-链霉素及其衍生物以及它们的盐	4			0	20	17	13	千克	Q	-Streptomycins and their derivatives; salts thereof
	-四环素及其衍生物以及它们的盐:										-Tetracyclines and their derivatives; salts thereof:
	---四环素及其盐:										---Tetracyclines and their salts
2941.3011	----四环素	4			0	20	17	13	千克	Q	----Tetracyclines
2941.3012	----四环素盐	4			0	20	17	13	千克	Q	----Salts of tetracyclines
2941.3020	---四环素衍生物及其盐	4			0	20	17	13	千克	Q	---Tetracyclines derivatives and their salts
2941.4000	-氯霉素及其衍生物以及它们的盐	4			0	20	17	13	千克	Q	-Chloramphenicol and its derivatives; salts thereof
2941.5000	-红霉素及其衍生物以及它们的盐	4			0	20	17	13	千克	Q	-Erythromycin and its derivatives; salts thereof
	-其他:										-Other:
2941.9010	---庆大霉素及其衍生物以及它们的盐	4			3.2	20	17	13	千克	Q	---Gentamycin and its derivatives; salts thereof
2941.9020	---卡那霉素及其衍生物以及它们的盐	4			3.2	20	17	13	千克	Q	---Kanamycin and its derivatives; salts thereof
2941.9030	---利福平及其衍生物以及它们的盐	4			3.2	20	17	13	千克	Q	---Rifampicin (RFP); salts thereof
2941.9040	---林可霉素及其衍生物以及它们的盐	4			3.2	20	17	13	千克	Q	---Lincomycin and its derivatives; salts thereof
	---先锋霉素及其衍生物以及它们的盐:										---Cephamycin and its derivatives; salts thereof:
2941.9051	----7氨基头孢烷酸、7氨基脱乙酰氧基头孢烷酸	6	5	5	4.8	20	17	13	千克		----7-aminocephalosporianic acid, 7-amino-deacetoxycefanoic acid
2941.9052	----头孢氨苄及其盐	6	5	5	4.8	20	17	13	千克	Q	----Cefalexin and its salts
2941.9053	----头孢唑啉及其盐	6	5	5	4.8	20	17	13	千克	Q	----Cefazolin and its salts

税则号列 Tariff Item.	货品名称	最惠国(%) MFN	协定(%)CT			普通 Gen	增值税率 VAT	出口退税 ED	计量单位 Unit	监管条件 SC	Article Description
			东盟 CA	中巴 CP	中智 CC						
2941.9054	----头孢拉啶及其盐	6	5	5	4.8	20	17	13	千克	Q	----Cefradine and its salts
2941.9055	----头孢三嗪(头孢曲松)及其盐	6	5	5	4.8	20	17	13	千克	Q	----Ceftriaxone and its salts
2941.9056	----头孢哌酮及其盐	6	5	5	4.8	20	17	13	千克	Q	----Cefoperazone and its salts
2941.9057	----头孢噻肟及其盐	6	5	5	4.8	20	17	13	千克	Q	----Cefotaxime and its salts
2941.9058	----头孢克罗及其盐	6	5	5	4.8	20	17	13	千克	Q	----Cefaclor and its salts
2941.9059	----其他	6	5	5	4.8	20	17	13	千克	Q	----Other
2941.9060	---麦迪霉素及其衍生物以及它们的盐	6	5	4.2	4.8	20	17	13	千克	Q	---Midecamycin and its derivatives; salts thereof
2941.9070	---乙酰螺旋霉素及其衍生物以及它们的盐	4			3.2	20	17	13	千克	Q	---Acetyl-spiramycin and its derivatives; salts thereof
2941.9090	---其他	6	5	5	4.8	20	17	13	千克	Q	---Other
29.42	**其他有机化合物：**										**Other organic compounds:**
2942.0000	其他有机化合物	6.5	5		0	30	17	13	千克		Other organic compounds

第三十章 药　　品

注释：

一、本章不包括：

（一）食品及饮料（例如，营养品、糖尿病食品、强化食品、保健食品、滋补饮料及矿泉水）（第四类），但不包括供静脉摄入用的滋养品；

（二）经特殊煅烧或精细研磨的牙科用熟石膏（税目 25.20）；

（三）适合医药用的精油水馏液及水溶液（税目 33.01）；

（四）税目 33.03 至 33.07 的制品，不论是否具有治疗及预防疾病的作用；

（五）加有药料的肥皂及税目 34.01 的其他产品；

（六）以熟石膏为基本成分的牙科用制品（税目 34.07）；

（七）不作治疗及预防疾病用的血清蛋白（税目 35.02）。

二、税目 30.02 所称的“修饰免疫制品”，仅适用于单系抗体（MABs）、抗体片段、抗体及抗体片段缀合物。

三、税目 30.03 及 30.04 以及本章注释四（四）所述的非混合产品及混合产品，按下列规定处理：

（一）非混合产品：

1. 溶于水的非混合产品；
2. 第二十八章及第二十九章的所有货品；
3. 税目 13.02 的单一植物浸膏，只经标定或溶于溶剂的。

（二）混合产品：

1. 胶体溶液及悬浮液（胶态硫磺除外）；
2. 从植物性混合物加工所得的植物浸膏；
3. 蒸发天然矿质水所得的盐及浓缩物。

四、税目 30.06 仅适用于下列物品（这些物品只能归入税目 30.06 而不得归入本目录其他税目）：

（一）无菌外科肠线、类似的无菌缝合材料（包括外科或牙科用无菌可吸收缝线）及外伤创口闭合用的无菌粘合胶布；

（二）无菌昆布及无菌昆布塞条；

（三）外科及牙科用无菌吸收性止血材料；外科或牙科用无菌抗粘连阻隔材料，不论是否可吸收；

（四）用于病人的 X 光检查造影剂及其他诊断试剂，这些药剂是由单一产品配定剂量或由两种以上成分混合而成的；

Chapter 30 Pharmaceutical products

Notes:

1. This Chapter does not cover:

(a) Foods or beverages (such as dietetic, diabetic or fortified foods, food supplements, tonic beverages and mineral waters), other than nutritional preparations for intravenous administration (Section Ⅳ);

(b) Plasters specially calcined or finely ground for use in dentistry (heading No. 25.20);

(c) Aqueous distillates or aqueous solutions of essential oils, suitable for medicinal uses (heading No. 33.01);

(d) Preparations of headings Nos. 33.03 to 33.07, even if they have therapeutic or prophylactic properties;

(e) Soap or other products of heading No. 34.01 containing added medicaments;

(f) Preparations with a basis of plaster for use in dentistry (heading No. 34.07); or

(g) Blood albumin not prepared for therapeutic or prophylactic uses (heading No. 35.02).

2. For the purposes of heading No. 30.02, the expression "modified immunological products" applies only to monoclonal antibodies (MABs), antibody fragments, antibody conjugates and antibody fragment conjugates.

3. For the purposes of headings Nos. 30.03 and 30.04 and of Note 4 (d) to this Chapter, the following are to be treated:

(a) As unmixed products:

(1) Unmixed products dissolved in water;

(2) All goods of Chapter 28 or 29; and

(3) Simple vegetable extracts of heading No. 13.02, merely standardised or dissolved in any solvent;

(b) As products which have been mixed:

(1) Colloidal solutions and suspensions (other than colloidal sulphur);

(2) Vegetable extracts obtained by the treatment of mixtures of vegetable materials; and

(3) Salts and concentrates obtained by evaporating natural mineral waters.

4. Heading No. 30.06 applies only to the following, which are to be classified in that heading and in no other heading of the Nomenclature:

(a) Sterile surgical catgut, similar sterile suture materials and sterile tissue adhesives for surgical wound closure;

(b) Sterile laminaria and sterile laminaria tents;

(c) Sterile absorbable surgical or dental haemostatics;

(d) Opacifying preparations for X-ray examinations and diagnostic reagents designed to be administered to the patient, being unmixed products put up in measured doses or products consisting of two or more ingredients which have been mixed together for such uses;

（五）血型试剂；

（六）牙科粘固剂及其他牙科填料；骨骼粘固剂；

（七）急救药箱、药包；

（八）以激素、税目29.37的其他产品或杀精子剂为基本成分的化学避孕药物；

（九）专用于人类或作兽药用的凝胶制品，作为外科手术或体检时躯体部位的润滑剂，或者作为躯体和医疗器械之间的偶合剂；

（十）废药物，即那些因超过有效保存期等原因而不适于作原用途的药品。

（十一）可确定用于造口术的用具，即裁切成型的结肠造口述，回肠造口术、尿道造口术用袋及其具有粘性的片或底盘。

(e) Blood-grouping reagents;

(f) Dental cements and other dental fillings; bone reconstruction cements;

(g) First-aid boxes and kits;

(h) Chemical contraceptive preparations based on hormones, on other products of heading No. 29.37 or on spermicides;

(i) Gel preparations designed to be used in human or veterinary medicine as a lubricant for parts of the body for surgical operations or physical examinations or as a coupling agent between the body and medical instruments; and

(j) Waste pharmaceuticals, that is, pharmaceutical products which are unfit for their original intended purpose due to, for example, expiry of shelf life.

(k) Can determine the appliances that can be used for ostomy, that is, colostomy cut for pattern, ileostomy, urostomy bags and adhesive pieces.

税则号列 Tariff Item.	货品名称	最惠国(%) MFN	协定(%) CT 东盟 CA	中巴 CP	中智 CC	普通 Gen	增值税率 VAT	出口退税 ED	计量单位 Unit	监管条件 SC	Article Description
30.01	**已干燥的器官疗法用腺体及其他器官，不论是否制成粉末；器官疗法用腺体、其他器官及其分泌物的提取物；肝素及其盐；其他供治疗或预防疾病用的其他税目未列名的人体或动物制品：**										**Glands and other organs for organo-therapeutic uses, dried, whether or not powdered; extracts of glands or other organs or of their secretions for organo-therapeutic uses; heparin and its salts; other human or animal substances prepared for therapeutic or prophylactic uses, not elsewhere specified or included:**
3001.2000	-腺体、其他器官及其分泌物的提取物	3			0	30	17	13	千克		-Extracts of glands or other organs or of their secretions
3001.2000 10	其他濒危野生动物腺体，器官(包括分泌物)	3				30	17	13	千克	AQFEB	Extracts of glands or other organs or of their secretions of wild animals in imminent dangers
3001.2000 20	人类的腺体、器官及其分泌物提取物	3				30	17	13	千克	AQB	Human extracts of glands of organs or of their secretions
3001.2000 90	其他腺体、器官及其分泌物提取物	3				30	17	13	千克	AQB	Other extracts of glands of other organs or of their secretions
	-其他：										-Other:
3001.9010	---肝素及其盐	3			0	30	17	13	千克	AQB	---Heparin and its salts
3001.9090	---其他	3			0	30	17	13	千克		---Other
3001.9090 10	蛇毒制品(供治疗或预防疾病用)	3				30	17	13	千克	AQFEB	Venom preparations (for therapeutic or prophylactic uses)
3001.9090 91	其他濒危动物制品(供治疗或预防疾病用)	3				30	17	13	千克	ABFEQ	Other substances of animal in imminent dangers for therapeutic or prophylactic uses
3001.9090 99	其他未列名的人体或动物制品(供治疗或预防疾病用)	3				30	17	13	千克	ABQ	Other human or animal substances for therapeutic or prophylactic uses

税则号列 Tariff Item.	货品名称	最惠国(%) MFN	协定(%) CT 东盟 CA	中巴 CP	中智 CC	普通 Gen	增值税率 VAT	出口退税 ED	计量单位 Unit	监管条件 SC	Article Description
30.02	**人血;治病、防病或诊断用的动物血制品;抗血清、其他血份及修饰免疫制品,不论是否通过生物工艺加工制得;疫苗、毒素、培养微生物(不包括酵母)及类似产品:**										**Human blood; animal blood prepared for therapeutic, prophylactic or diagnostic uses; antisera and other blood fractions and modified immunological products, whether or not obtained by means of biotechnological processes; vaccines, toxins, cultures of micro-organisms (excluding yeasts) and similar products:**
3002.1000	-抗血清、其他血份及修饰免疫制品,不论是否通过生物工艺加工制得	3			1.8	20	17	13	千克	AB	-Antisera and other blood fractions and modified immunological products, whether or not obtained by means of biotechnological processes
3002.2000	-人用疫苗	3			1.8	20	17	13	千克	QAB	-Vaccines for human medicine
3002.3000	-兽用疫苗	3			1.8	20	17	13	千克	AB	-Vaccines for veterinary medicine
	-其他:										-Other:
3002.9010	---石房蛤毒素	3			1.8	20	17	13	千克	23Q	---Saxitoxin
3002.9020	---蓖麻毒素	3			1.8	20	17	13	千克	23Q	---Ricitoxin
3002.9030	---细菌及病毒	3			1.8	20	17	13	千克		---Bacteria and viruses
3002.9030 10	敏感物项管制细菌及病毒	3				20	17	13	千克	3AB	Bacteria and viruses
3002.9030 90	其他细菌及病毒	3				20	17	13	千克	AB	Other bacteria and viruses
3002.9040	---遗传物质和基因修饰生物体	3			1.8	20	17	13	千克		---Genetic materials and gene-modified organisms
3002.9040 10	敏感物项管制遗传物质和基因修饰生物体	3				20	17	13	千克	3AB	Heritable materials and gene - modified or ganisms
3002.9040 90	其他遗传物质和基因修饰生物体	3				20	17	13	千克	AB	Other Heritable materials and gene - modified or ganisms
3002.9090	---其他	3			1.8	20	17	13	千克		---Other
3002.9090 11	濒危动物血制品	3				20	17	13	千克	ABQFE	Blood preparations of animals in imminent dangers
3002.9090 19	其他人血制品、动物血制品	3				20	17	13	千克	ABQ	Other human or animal blood preparations
3002.9090 91	敏感物项管制毒素	3				20	17	13	千克	3AB	Other toxins of animals in imminent dangers including cultures of micro-organisms (excluding yeasts) and similar products
3002.9090 92	苏云金杆菌	3				20	17	13	千克	ABS	Bacillus thurins iensis
3002.9090 99	人血、其他毒素等[包括培养微生物(不包括酵母)及类似产品]	3				20	17	13	千克	AB	Other human blood, other toxins, including cultures of micro-organisms (excluding yeasts) and similar products
30.03	**两种或两种以上成分混合而成的治病或防病用药品(不包括税目30.02、30.05或30.06的货品),未配定剂量或制成零售包装:**										**Medicaments (excluding goods of heading No. 30.02, 30.05 or 30.06) consisting of two or more constituents which have been mixed together for therapeutic or prophylactic uses, not put up in measured doses or in forms or packings for retail sale:**
	-含有青霉素及具有青霉烷酸结构的青霉素衍生物或链霉素及其衍生物:										-Containing penicillins or derivatives thereof, with a penicillanic acid structure, or streptomycins or their derivatives:

税则号列 Tariff Item.	货 品 名 称	最惠国(%) MFN	协定(%)CT 东盟 CA	 中巴 CP	 中智 CC	普通 Gen	增值税率 VAT	出口退税 ED	计量单位 Unit	监管条件 SC	Article Description
	---青霉素:										---Containing penicillins:
3003.1011	----氨苄青霉素	6	T3	0	0	30	17	13	千克	Q	----Ampicillin
3003.1012	----羟氨苄青霉素	6	T3	0	0	30	17	13	千克	Q	----Amoxycillin
3003.1013	----青霉素 V	6	T3	0	0	30	17	13	千克	Q	----Penicillin V
3003.1019	----其他	6	T3	0	0	30	17	13	千克	Q	----Other
3003.1090	---其他	6	T3	0	0	30	17	13	千克	Q	---Other
	-含有其他抗菌素:										-Containing other antibiotics:
	---头孢菌素:										---Containing cephamycins:
3003.2011	----头孢噻肟	6	5	0	0	30	17	13	千克	Q	----Cefotaxime
3003.2012	----头孢他啶	6	5	0	0	30	17	13	千克	Q	----Ceftazidime
3003.2013	----头孢西丁	6	5	0	0	30	17	13	千克	Q	----Cefoxitin
3003.2014	----头孢替唑	6	5	0	0	30	17	13	千克	Q	----Ceftezole
3003.2015	----头孢克罗	6	5	0	0	30	17	13	千克	Q	----Cefaclor
3003.2016	----头孢呋辛	6	5	0	0	30	17	13	千克	Q	----Cefuroxime
3003.2017	----头孢三嗪(头孢曲松)	6	5	0	0	30	17	13	千克	Q	----Ceftriaxone
3003.2018	----头孢哌酮	6	5	0	0	30	17	13	千克	Q	----Cefoperazone
3003.2019	----其他	6	5	0	0	30	17	13	千克	Q	----Other
3003.2090	---其他	6	5	0	0	30	17	13	千克	Q	---Other
	-含有激素或税目 29.37 的其他产品,但不含抗菌素:										-Containing hormones or other products of heading 29.37 but not containing antibiotics:
3003.3100	--含有胰岛素	5		0	0	30	17	13	千克	Q	--Containing insulin
3003.3900	--其他	6	5	0	0	30	17	13	千克	Q	--Other
	-含有生物碱及其衍生物,但不含抗菌素及税目 29.37 的激素或其他产品:										-Containing alkaloids or derivatives thereof but not containing hormones or other products of heading 29.37 or antibiotics:
3003.4010	---含有奎宁或其盐	5		0	0	35	17	13	千克	Q	---Containing quinine or its salts
3003.4090	---其他	5		0	0	30	17	13	千克	Q	---Other
	-其他:										-Other:
3003.9010	---含有磺胺类	6	5	0	4.8	40	17	13	千克	Q	---Containing sulfa drugs
3003.9020	---含有青蒿素及其衍生物	5		0	4	30	17	13	千克	Q	---Containing artemisinins and their derivatives thereof
3003.9090	---其他	5		0	4	30	17	13	千克		---other
3003.9090 10	含紫杉醇的混合药品(未配定剂量或非零售包装,混合指含两种或两种以上成分)	5				30	17	13	千克	EFQ	Medicaments, containing taxinol, not put up in measured doses or in forms or packings for retail sale
3003.9090 20	含其他未列名濒危动植物混合药品(未配定剂量或非零售包装,混合指含两种或两种以上成分)	5				30	17	13	千克	QFE	Mixed medicaments, containing other constituents of animals in imminent dangers, not elsewhere specified or included, not put up in measured doses or in forms or packings for retail sale
3003.9090 90	含其他未列名成分混合药品(未配定剂量或非零售包装,混合指含两种或两种以上成分)	5				30	17	13	千克	Q	Mixed medicaments, containing other constituents, not elsewhere specified or included, not put up in measured doses or in forms or packings for retail sale

税则号列 Tariff Item.	货品名称	最惠国(%) MFN	协定(%) 东盟 CA	中巴 CP	CT 中智 CC	普通 Gen	增值税率 VAT	出口退税 ED	计量单位 Unit	监管条件 SC	Article Description
30.04	由混合或非混合产品构成的治病或防病用药品(不包括税目30.02、30.05或30.06的货品),已配定剂量(包括制成皮肤摄入形式的)或制成零售包装:										**Medicaments (excluding goods of heading No. 30.02, 30.05 or 30.06) consisting of mixed or unmixed products for therapeutic or prophylactic uses, put up in measured doses (including those in the form of transdermal administration systems) or in forms or packings for retail sale:**
	-含有青霉素及具有青霉烷酸结构的青霉素衍生物或链霉素及其衍生物:										-Containing penicillins or derivatives thereof, with a penicillanic acid structure, or streptomycins or their derivatives:
	---青霉素:										---Containing penicillins:
3004.1011	----氨苄青霉素制剂	6	5	0	4.8	30	17	13	千克	Q	----Ampicillin
3004.1012	----羟氨苄青霉素制剂	6	5	0	4.8	30	17	13	千克	Q	----Amoxycillin
3004.1013	----青霉素V制剂	6	5	0	4.8	30	17	13	千克	Q	----Penicillin V
3004.1019	----其他	6	5	0	4.8	30	17	13	千克	Q	----Other
3004.1090	---其他	6	5	0	4.8	30	17	13	千克	Q	---Other
	-含有其他抗菌素:										-Containing other antibiotics:
	---头孢菌素:										---Containing cephamycins:
3004.2011	----头孢噻肟制剂	6	5	0	4.8	30	17	13	千克	Q	----Cefotaxime
3004.2012	----头孢他啶制剂	6	5	0	4.8	30	17	13	千克	Q	----Ceftazidime
3004.2013	----头孢西丁制剂	6	5	0	4.8	30	17	13	千克	Q	----Cefoxitin
3004.2014	----头孢替唑制剂	6	5	0	4.8	30	17	13	千克	Q	----Ceftezole
3004.2015	----头孢克罗制剂	6	5	0	4.8	30	17	13	千克	Q	----Cefaclor
3004.2016	----头孢呋辛制剂	6	5	0	4.8	30	17	13	千克	Q	----Cefuroxime
3004.2017	----头孢三嗪(头孢曲松)制剂	6	5	0	4.8	30	17	13	千克	Q	----Ceftriaxone
3004.2018	----头孢哌酮制剂	6	5	0	4.8	30	17	13	千克	Q	----Cefoperazone
3004.2019	----其他	6	5	0	4.8	30	17	13	千克	Q	----Other
3004.2090	---其他	6	5	0	4.8	30	17	13	千克	Q	---Other
	-含有激素或税目29.37的其他产品,但不含抗菌素:										-Containing hormones or other products of heading No. 29.37 but not containing antibiotics:
3004.3100	--含有胰岛素	5		0	4	30	17	13	千克		--Containing insulin
3004.3100 10	已配剂量含胰岛素的单方制剂(包括零售包装)	5				30	17	13	千克	L	Monomer preparation whose dosage includes insulin (including retail wrapping)
3004.3100 90	已配剂量含胰岛素的其他药品(不含抗菌素,包括零售包装)	5				30	17	13	千克	Q	Other medicines with insulin (excluding antibiotic, including retail wrapping)
3004.3200	--含有皮质甾类激素及其衍生物或结构类似物	5		0	4	30	17	13	千克		--Containing corticosteroid hormones, their derivatives and structural analogues
3004.3200 11	已配剂量含雄烯二醇或雄烯二酮的单方制剂(包括其衍生物及结构类似物,包括零售包装)	5				30	17	13	千克	L	Monomer preparation whose dosage includes androstenediol or androstenedione (including TBEP and melatonine, including retail wrapping)

税则号列 Tariff Item.	货品名称	最惠国(%) MFN	协定(%) CT 东盟 CA	中巴 CP	中智 CC	普通 Gen	增值税率 VAT	出口退税 ED	计量单位 Unit	监管条件 SC	Article Description
3004.3200 12	已配剂量含甲酰勃龙(醛甲宝龙)的单方制剂(包括其衍生物及结构类似物,包括零售包装)	5				30	17	13	千克	L	Monomer preparation whose dosage includes formebolone (including TBEP and melatonine, including retail wrapping)
3004.3200 13	已配剂量含雄-4烯-3β,17a-二醇的单方制剂(包括其衍生物及结构类似物,包括零售包装)	5				30	17	13	千克	L	Monomer preparation whose dosage includes androst-4-ene-3β, 17α-diol (including TBEP and melatonine, including retail wrapping)
3004.3200 14	含雄-5-烯-3β,17a-二醇的单方制剂(包括其衍生物及结构类似物,已配剂量或制成零售包装)	5				30	17	13	千克	L	Monomer preparation whose dosage includes androst-5-ene-3β, 17α-diol
3004.3200 15	已配剂量含雄-4-烯二醇或乙烯雌醇的单方制剂(包括其衍生物及结构类似物,包括零售包装)	5				30	17	13	千克	L	Monomer preparation whose dosage includes 4-androstenediol or ethylestrenol (including TBEP and melatonine, including retail wrapping)
3004.3200 16	已配剂量含雄烯二酮异构体的单方制剂(包括其衍生物及结构类似物,包括零售包装)	5				30	17	13	千克	L	Monomer preparation whose dosage includes 4-androstenediol or ethylestrenol (including TBEP and melatonine, including retail wrapping)
3004.3200 17	已配剂量含倍他雄烷二醇异构体的单方制剂(包括其衍生物及结构类似物,包括零售包装)	5				30	17	13	千克	L	Monomer preparation whose dosage including TBEP and melatonine, including retail wrapping
3004.3200 18	已配剂量含雄烷二醇异构体的单方制剂(包括其衍生物及结构类似物,包括零售包装)	5				30	17	13	千克	L	Monomer preparation whose dosage includes 5α-androstane-3β,17α-diol (including TBEP and melatonine, including retail wrapping)
3004.3200 19	已配剂量含勃拉睾酮(双甲睾铜)的单方制剂(包括其衍生物及结构类似物,包括零售包装)	5				30	17	13	千克	L	Monomer preparation whose dosage includes bolasterone (including TBEP and melatonine, including retail wrapping)
3004.3200 21	已配剂量含勃地酮(宝丹酮)的单方制剂(包括其衍生物及结构类似物,包括零售包装)	5				30	17	13	千克	L	Monomer preparation whose dosage includes boldenone (including TBEP and melatonine, including retail wrapping)
3004.3200 22	已配剂量含1,4-雄二烯-3,17-二酮的单方制剂(包括其衍生物及结构类似物,包括零售包装)	5				30	17	13	千克	L	Monomer preparation whose dosage includes boldione (including TBEP and melatonine, including retail wrapping)
3004.3200 23	已配剂量含卡普睾铜或达那唑的单方制剂(包括其衍生物及结构类似物,包括零售包装)	5				30	17	13	千克	L	Monomer preparation whose dosage includes calusterone or danazol (including TBEP and melatonine, including retail wrapping)

税则号列 Tariff Item.	货品名称	最惠国(%) MFN	协定(%) 东盟 CA	中巴 CP	CT 中智 CC	普通 Gen	增值税率 VAT	出口退税 ED	计量单位 Unit	监管条件 SC	Article Description
3004.3200 24	已配剂量含氯司替勃(氯斯太宝)的单方制剂(包括其衍生物及结构类似物,包括零售包装)	5				30	17	13	千克	L	Monomer preparation whose dosage includes clostebol (including TBEP and melatonine, including retail wrapping)
3004.3200 25	已配剂量含脱氢氯甲基睾酮的单方制剂(包括其衍生物及结构类似物,包括零售包装)	5				30	17	13	千克	L	Monomer preparation whose dosage includes dehydrochloromethyltestosterone (including TBEP and melatonine, including retail wrapping)
3004.3200 26	已配剂量含雄-1-烯-3,17-二酮的单方制剂(包括其衍生物及结构类似物,包括零售包装)	5				30	17	13	千克	L	Monomer preparation whose dosage includes deltal - androstene - 3,17 - dione (including TBEP and melatonine, including retail wrapping)
3004.3200 27	已配剂量含(△)雄烯二醇的单方制剂(包括其衍生物及结构类似物,包括零售包装)	5				30	17	13	千克	L	Monomer preparation whose dosage includes deltal - androstenediol (including TBEP and melatonine, including retail wrapping)
3004.3200 28	已配剂量含普拉雄酮或屈他雄酮(羟甲雄酮)的单方制剂(包括其衍生物及结构类似物,包括零售包装)	5				30	17	13	千克	L	Monomer preparation whose dosage includes dehydroepiandrosterone (DHEA) or drostanolone
3004.3200 29	已配剂量含去氧甲基睾酮或双氢睾酮的单方制剂(包括其衍生物及结构类似物,包括零售包装)	5				30	17	13	千克	L	Monomer preparation whose dosage includes desoxymethyltestosterone or dihydrotestosterone (including TBEP and melatonine, including retail wrapping)
3004.3200 31	已配剂量含表双氢睾酮或氟甲睾酮的单方制剂(包括其衍生物及结构类似物,包括零售包装)	5				30	17	13	千克	L	Monomer preparation whose dosage includes epi - dihydrotestosterone or fluoxymesterone (including TBEP and melatonine, including retail wrapping)
3004.3200 32	已配剂量含呋咱甲氢龙(夫拉扎勃)的单方制剂(包括其衍生物及结构类似物,包括零售包装)	5				30	17	13	千克	L	Monomer preparation whose dosage includes furazabol (including TBEP and melatonine, including retail wrapping)
3004.3200 33	已配剂量含孕三烯酮或4-羟基睾酮的单方制剂(包括其衍生物及结构类似物,包括零售包装)	5				30	17	13	千克	L	Monomer preparation whose dosage includes gestrinone 4 - hydroxytestosterone (including TBEP and melatonine, including retail wrapping)
3004.3200 34	含3α-羟基-5α-雄烷-17-酮的单方制剂(包括其衍生物及结构类似物,已配剂量或制成零售包装)	5				30	17	13	千克	L	Monomer preparation whose dosage includes 3α - hydroxy - 5α - androstan - 17 - one (including TBEP and melatonine, including retail wrapping)
3004.3200 35	已配剂量含美睾酮或美雄酮的单方制剂(包括其衍生物及结构类似物,包括零售包装)	5				30	17	13	千克	L	Monomer preparation whose dosage includes mesterolone or methandienone (including TBEP and melatonine, including retail wrapping)

税则号列 Tariff Item.	货品名称	最惠国(%) MFN	协定(%)CT 东盟 CA	中巴 CP	中智 CC	普通 Gen	增值税率 VAT	出口退税 ED	计量单位 Unit	监管条件 SC	Article Description
3004.3200 36	含2α,17α－二甲基－5α－雄烷－3－酮－17β－醇的单方制剂(包括其衍生物及结构类似物,已配剂量或制成零售包装)	5				30	17	13	千克	L	Monomer preparation whose dosage includes methasterone(including TBEP and melatonine,including retail wrapping)
3004.3200 37	含17α－甲基－17β－羟基雄－4,9(10)一二烯－3－酮的单方制剂(包括其衍生物及结构类似物,已配剂量或制成零售包装)	5				30	17	13	千克	L	Monomer preparation whose dosage includes methyltrienolone(including TBEP and melatonine, including retail wrapping)
3004.3200 38	已配剂量含甲基－1－睾酮或甲基去甲睾酮的单方制剂(包括其衍生物及结构类似物,包括零售包装)	5				30	17	13	千克	L	Monomer preparation whose dosage includes methyl－1－testosterone or methylnortestosterone (including TBEP and melatonine,including retail wrapping)
3004.3200 39	含17a－甲基－17β－羟基雌－4,9,11－三烯－3－酮的单方制剂(包括其衍生物及结构类似物,已配剂量或制成零售包装)	5				30	17	13	千克	L	Monomer preparation whose dosage includes methyltrienolone(including TBEP and melatonine, including retail wrapping)
3004.3200 41	已配剂量含美雄诺龙或美替诺龙的单方制剂(包括其衍生物及结构类似物,包括零售包装)	5				30	17	13	千克	L	Monomer preparation whose dosage includes mestanolone or methandriol(including TBEP and melatonine,including retail wrapping)
3004.3200 42	已配剂量含美雄醇或甲睾酮或米勃龙的单方制剂(包括其衍生物及结构类似物,包括零售包装)	5				30	17	13	千克	L	Monomer preparation whose dosage includes methandriol or methyltestosterone or mibolerone(including TBEP and melatonine,including retail wrapping)
3004.3200 43	已配剂量含诺龙或诺勃酮或诺司替勃的单方制剂(包括其衍生物及结构类似物,包括零售包装)	5				30	17	13	千克	L	Monomer preparation whose dosage includes nandrolone or norboletone or norclostebol (including TBEP and melatonine,including retail wrapping)
3004.3200 44	含19－去甲雄烯二醇或19－去甲雄烯二酮的的单方制剂(包括其衍生物及结构类似物,已配剂量或制成零售包装)	5				30	17	13	千克	L	Monomer preparation whose dosage includes 19－norandrostenediol or 19－norandrostenedione(including TBEP and melatonine,including retail wrapping)
3004.3200 45	已配剂量含去甲雄酮或诺乙雄龙(乙基诺龙)的单方制剂(包括其衍生物及结构类似物,包括零售包装)	5				30	17	13	千克	L	Monomer preparation whose dosage includes 19－norandrosterone or norethandrolone(including TBEP and melatonine,including retail wrapping)
3004.3200 46	已配剂量含19－去甲本胆烷醇酮的单方制剂(包括其衍生物及结构类似物,包括零售包装)	5				30	17	13	千克	L	Monomer preparation whose dosage includes 19－noretiocholanolone (including TBEP and melatonine,including retail wrapping)

税则号列 Tariff Item.	货品名称	最惠国(%) MFN	协定(%)CT 东盟 CA	中巴 CP	中智 CC	普通 Gen	增值税率 VAT	出口退税 ED	计量单位 Unit	监管条件 SC	Article Description
3004.3200 47	含羟勃龙(氧宝龙)或氧雄龙(氧甲氢龙)的单方制剂(包括其衍生物及结构类似物,已配剂量或制成零售包装)	5				30	17	13	千克	L	Monomer preparation whose dosage includes oxabolone or oxandrolone (including TBEP and melatonine, including retail wrapping)
3004.3200 48	已配剂量含羟甲睾酮或羟甲烯龙的单方制剂(包括其衍生物及结构类似物,包括零售包装)	5				30	17	13	千克	L	Monomer preparation whose dosage includes oxymesterone or oxymetholone (including TBEP and melatonine, including retail wrapping)
3004.3200 49	含[3,2-c]吡唑-5α-苯别胆烷-17β-4氢吡喃醇的单方制剂(包括其衍生物及结构类似物,已配剂量或制成零售包装)	5				30	17	13	千克	L	Monomer preparation whose dosage includes prostanozol (including TBEP and melatonine, including retail wrapping)
3004.3200 51	含奎勃龙或替勃龙或群勃龙(追宝龙)的单方制剂(包括其衍生物及结构类似物,已配剂量或制成零售包装)	5				30	17	13	千克	L	Monomer preparation whose dosage includes quinbolone or tibolone or tibolone (including TBEP and melatonine, including retail wrapping)
3004.3200 52	已配剂量含司坦唑醇或司腾勃龙的单方制剂(包括其衍生物及结构类似物,包括零售包装)	5				30	17	13	千克	L	Monomer preparation whose dosage includes stanozolol or stenbolone (including TBEP and melatonine, including retail wrapping)
3004.3200 53	已配剂量含1-睾酮或睾酮的单方制剂(包括其衍生物及结构类似物,包括零售包装)	5				30	17	13	千克	L	Monomer preparation whose dosage includes 1-testosterone or testosterone (including TBEP and melatonine, including retail wrapping)
3004.3200 54	已配剂量含四氢孕三烯酮或折仑诺的单方制剂(包括其衍生物及结构类似物,包括零售包装)	5				30	17	13	千克	L	Monomer preparation whose dosage includes tetrahydrogestrinone or zeranol (including TBEP and melatonine, including retail wrapping)
3004.3200 90	已配剂量含其他皮质甾类激素的药品(包括其衍生物及结构类似物,不含抗菌素,包括零售包装)	5				30	17	13	千克	Q	Medicine whose dosage includes other corticosterodial hormones (including TBEP and melatonine, including retail wrapping)
	-含有生物碱及其衍生物,但不含抗菌素及税目No. 29.37的激素或其他产品:										-Containing alkaloids or derivatives thereof but not containing hormones, other products of heading No. 29.37 or antibiotics:
3004.3900	--其他	5		0	4	30	17	13	千克		--Other
3004.3900 11	已配剂量含克仑特罗的单方制剂(包括零售包装)	5				30	17	13	千克	L	Monomer preparation whose dosage includes clenbuterol (including retail wrapping)
3004.3900 12	已配剂量含4-羟基诺龙的单方制剂(包括零售包装)	5				30	17	13	千克	L	Monomer preparation whose dosage includes 4-hydroxy-19-nortestosterone (including retail wrapping)
3004.3900 21	已配剂量含促红细胞生成素(EPO)的单方制剂(包括零售包装)	5				30	17	13	千克	L	Monomer preparation whose dosage includes erythropoietin (EPO) (including retail wrapping)

税则号列 Tariff Item.	货 品 名 称	最惠国(%) MFN	协定(%)CT 东盟 CA	中巴 CP	中智 CC	普通 Gen	增值税率 VAT	出口退税 ED	计量单位 Unit	监管条件 SC	Article Description
3004.3900 22	已配剂量含生长激素的单方制剂(包括零售包装)	5				30	17	13	千克	L	Monomer preparation whose dosage includes growth hormone(hGH)(including retail wrapping)
3004.3900 23	已配剂量含胰岛素样生长因子1的单方制剂(包括零售包装)	5				30	17	13	千克	L	Monomer preparation whose dosage includes Insulin – lkie Growth Factor(IGF – 1)(including retail wrapping)
3004.3900 24	已配剂量含生长因子素的单方制剂(包括零售包装)	5				30	17	13	千克	L	Monomer preparation whose dosage includes mechano Growth Factors (MGFs)(including retail wrapping)
3004.3900 25	已配剂量含促性腺激素的单方制剂(包括零售包装)	5				30	17	13	千克	L	Monomer preparation whose dosage includes gonadotrophins (LH, hCG)(including retail wrapping)
3004.3900 26	已配剂量含促皮质素的单方制剂(包括零售包装)	5				30	17	13	千克	L	Monomer preparation whose dosage includes corticotrophins (including retail wrapping)
3004.3900 90	其他已配剂量含激素或税号2937产品的药品(不含抗菌素包括零售包装)	5				30	17	13	千克	Q	Other medicine whose dosage contains hormones or tax code 2937 (excluding bacteriophage, including retail wrapping)
3004.4010	---含有奎宁或其盐	5		0	4	35	17	13	千克	Q	---Containing quinine or its salts
3004.4090	---其他	5		0	4	30	17	13	千克		---Other
3004.4090 10	麻黄碱盐类单方制剂[指盐酸(伪)麻黄碱片、盐酸麻黄碱注射剂、硫酸麻黄碱片]	5				30	17	13	千克	23Q	Simple preparations, containing salts of ephedrine (ephedrine hydrochloride, ephedrine sulfate)
3004.4090 20	含可待因及衍生物及盐的复方制剂(已配定剂量或制成零售包装)	5				30	17	13	千克	I	Compound preparations, containing salts of condeine and derivatives thereof, put up in measured doses or in forms or packings for retail sale
3004.4090 30	含生物碱类精神药品的单方制剂(包括其衍生物,已配定剂量或制成零售包装)	5				30	17	13	千克	I	Simple preparations, containing psychoactiv, drugsl and its derivatives, put up in measured doses or in forms or packings for retail sale
3004.4090 40	含生物碱类麻醉药品的单方制剂(包括其衍生物,已配定剂量或制成零售包装)	5				30	17	13	千克	W	Simple preparations, containing anesthetic agents and its derivatives, put up in measured doses or in forms or packings for retail sale
3004.4090 90	已配剂量含有其他生物碱等的药品(不含抗菌素及编号29.37的激素或其他产品,包括零售包装)	5				30	17	13	千克	Q	Medicaments, containing other alkaloids, not containing antibiotics and hormones or other products of heading No. 29.37, put up in measured doses or in forms or packings for retail sale
3004.5000	-含有维生素或税目29.36所列产品的其他药品	6	5	0	4.8	40	17	13	千克	Q	-Other medicaments containing vitamins or other products of heading No. 29.36
	-其他:										-Other:
3004.9010	---含有磺胺类	6	5	0	4.8	40	17	13	千克	Q	---Containing sulfa drugs
3004.9020	---含有联苯双酯	4		0	3.2	30	17	13	千克	Q	---Containing biphenyl dicarbxybte
	---中式成药:										---Medicaments of Chinese type:

税则号列 Tariff Item.	货品名称	最惠国(%) MFN	协定(%)CT 东盟 CA	中巴 CP	中智 CC	普通 Gen	增值税率 VAT	出口退税 ED	计量单位 Unit	监管条件 SC	Article Description
3004.9051	----中药酒	3		0	1.8	30	17	13	千克		----Medicated liquors or wines
3004.9051 10	含濒危动植物成分的中药酒(已配定剂量或零售包装)	3				30	17	13	千克	FE	Medicated liquors or wines, containing composition of animal or plant in imminent danger, put up in measured doses or in forms or packings for retail sale
3004.9051 90	含其他成分的中药酒(已配定剂量或零售包装)	3				30	17	13	千克		Medicated liquors or wines, containing other composition, put up in measured doses or in forms or packings for retail sale
3004.9052	----片仔癀	3		0	1.8	30	17	13	千克	QFE	----Pien Tzu Huang
3004.9053	----白药	3		0	1.8	30	17	13	千克	QFE	----Bai Yao
3004.9054	----清凉油	3		0	1.8	30	17	13	千克	Q	----Essential balm
3004.9059	----其他	3		0	1.8	30	17	13	千克		----Other
3004.9059 10	含濒危动植物成分的中式成药(已配定剂量或零售包装)	3				30	17	13	千克	QFE	Medicaments of Chinese style, containing composition of animal or plant in imminent danger, put up in measured doses or in forms or packings for retail sale
3004.9059 90	含其他成分的中式成药(已配定剂量或零售包装)	3				30	17	13	千克	Q	Medicaments of Chinese style, containing other composition, put up in measured doses or in forms or packings for retail sale
3004.9060	---含有青蒿素及其衍生物	4		0	3.2	30	17	13	千克	Q	---Containing Artemisinins and their derivatives
3004.9090	---其他	4		0	3.2	30	17	13	千克		---Other
3004.9090 10	含濒危野生动植物成分的药品(已配定剂量或零售包装,不含紫杉醇)	4				30	17	13	千克	EFQ	Medicaments containing composition of animal or plant in imminent danger, not containing taxinol, put up in measured doses or in forms or packings for retail sale
3004.9090 20	含紫杉醇成分的药品(已配定剂量或制成零售包装)	4				30	17	13	千克	EFQ	Medicaments containing taxinol, put up in measured doses or in forms or packings for retail sale
3004.9090 30	其他含29章麻醉药品的单方制剂(已配定剂量或制成零售包装)	4				30	17	13	千克	W	Other simple preparations containing anesthetic agents of Chapter 29, put up in measured doses or in forms or packings for retail sale
3004.9090 40	其他含29章精神药品的单方制剂(已配定剂量或制成零售包装)	4				30	17	13	千克	I	Other simple preparations containing psychoactive drugs of Chapter 29, put up in measured doses or in forms or packings for retail sale
3004.9090 50	含右丙氧芬及其盐的复方制剂(已配定剂量或制成零售包装)	4				30	17	13	千克	I	Compound preparations containing propoxyphene and its salts, put up in measured doses or in forms or packings for retail sale

税则号列 Tariff Item.	货品名称	最惠国(%) MFN	协定(%)CT 东盟 CA	中巴 CP	中智 CC	普通 Gen	增值税率 VAT	出口退税 ED	计量单位 Unit	监管条件 SC	Article Description
3004.9090 60	复方樟脑酊(含阿片酊、樟脑、苯甲酸、八角茴香油等,包括零售包装)	4				30	17	13	千克	I	Tinctura camphorae composita, containing laudanum, camphor, benzoic acid, star anise oil, put up in measured doses or in forms or packings for retail sale
3004.9090 71	已配剂量含雄-4-烯-3α,17β-二醇的单方制剂(包括零售包装)	4				30	17	13	千克	L	Monomer preparation whose dosage includes 5α-androstane-3α,17α-diol or 5α-androstane-3β,17α-diol (including retail wrapping)
3004.9090 72	已配剂量含雄-5-烯-3α,17α-二醇的单方制剂(包括零售包装)	4				30	17	13	千克	L	Monomer preparation whose dosage includes androst-5-ene-3α,17α-diol(including retail wrapping)
3004.9090 73	已配剂量含雄-5-烯-3α,17β-二醇的单方制剂(包括零售包装)	4				30	17	13	千克	L	Monomer preparation whose dosage includes androst-5-ene-3α,17α-diol(including retail wrapping)
3004.9090 74	含阿法雄烷二醇或雄烯二醇(异构体)的单方制剂(已配剂量或制成零售包装)	4				30	17	13	千克	L	Monomer preparation whose dosage includes 5α-androstane-3α,17α-diol or 5α-androstane-3β,17α-diol (including retail wrapping)
3004.9090 75	已配剂量含倍他雄烷二醇的单方制剂(包括零售包装)	4				30	17	13	千克	L	Monomer preparation whose dosage includes 5α-androstane-3β,17β-diol(including retail wrapping)
3004.9090 76	已配剂量含5α-雄烷-3β,17β-二醇的单方制剂(包括零售包装)	4				30	17	13	千克	L	Monomer preparation whose dosage includes 5α-androstane-3β, 17β-diol
3004.9090 77	含3β-羟基-5α-雄烷-17-酮的单方制剂(已配剂量或制成零售包装)	4				30	17	13	千克	L	Monomer preparation whose dosage includes 3β-hydroxy-5α-androstan-17-one(including retail wrapping)
3004.9090 78	已配剂量含齐帕特罗的单方制剂(包括零售包装)	4				30	17	13	千克	L	Monomer preparation whose dosage includes zilpaterol(including retail wrapping)
3004.9090 90	其他已配定剂量的药品(包括零售包装)	4				30	17	13	千克	Q	Other medicaments, put up in measured doses or in forms or packings for retail sale
30.05	**软填料、纱布、绷带及类似物品(例如,敷料、橡皮膏、混罨剂),经过药物浸涂或制成零售包装供医疗、外科、牙科或兽医用:**										**Wadding, gauze, bandages and similar articles (for example, dressings, adhesive plasters, poultices), impregnated or coated with pharmaceutical substances or put up in forms or packings for retail sale for medical, surgical, dental or veterinary purposes:**
	-胶粘敷料及有胶粘涂层的其他物品:										-Adhesive dressings and other articles having an adhesive layer:
3005.1010	---橡皮膏	5		0	4	70	17	13	千克		---Adhesive plasters
3005.1090	---其他	5		0	4	35	17	13	千克		---Other
	-其他:										-Other:
3005.9010	---药棉、纱布、绷带	5		0	4	70	17	13	千克		---Absorbent cotton, gauze, bandages
3005.9090	---其他	5		0	4	35	17	13	千克		---Other
30.06	**本章注释四所规定的医药用品:**										**Pharmaceutical goods specified in Note 4 to this Chapter:**

税则号列 Tariff Item.	货品名称	最惠国(%) MFN	协定(%)CT 东盟 CA	中巴 CP	中智 CC	普通 Gen	增值税率 VAT	出口退税 ED	计量单位 Unit	监管条件 SC	Article Description
3006.1000	-无菌外科肠线、类似的无菌缝合材料(包括外科或牙科用无菌可吸收缝线)及外伤创口闭合用的无菌粘合胶布;无菌昆布及无菌昆布塞条;外科或牙科用无菌抗粘连阻隔材料,不论是否可吸收	5			0	30	17	13	千克		-Sterile surgical catgut, similar sterile suture materials and sterile tissue adhesives for surgical wound closure; sterile laminaria and sterile laminaria tents; sterile absorbable surgical or dental haemostatics
3006.2000	-血型试剂	3			1.8	20	17	13	千克		-Blood-grouping reagents
3006.3000	-X 光检查造影剂;用于病人的诊断试剂	4			0	30	17	13	千克	Q	-Opacifying preparations for X-ray examinations; diagnostic reagents designed to the patient
3006.4000	-牙科粘固剂及其他牙科填料;骨骼粘固剂	5			0	30	17	13	千克		-Dental cements and other dental fillings; bone reconstruction cements
3006.5000	-急救药箱、药包	5			0	30	17	13	千克		-First-aid boxes and kits
	-以激素,税目 29.37 的其他产品或余精子剂为基本成分的化学避孕药物										-Chemical contraceptive preparations based on hormones on other products of heading 29.37 or on spermicides:
3006.6010	-以激素为基本成分的避孕药	0				0	0		千克	Q	-Contrceptive preparations based on hormones
3006.6090	-其他	0				0	0		千克	Q	-Other
3006.7000	-专用于人类或作兽药用的凝胶制品,作为外科手术或体检时躯体部位的润滑剂,或者作为躯体和医疗器械之间的偶合剂	6.5	5		0	30	17	13	千克		-Gel preparations designed to be used in human or veterinary medicine as a lubricant for parts of the body for surgical operations or physical examinations or as a coupling agent between the body and medical instruments
	-其他:										-Other:
3006.9100	--可确定用于造口术的用具	10	T3	9.2	8	80	17	13	千克		
3006.9200	--废药物	5			0	30	17	13	千克	9	--Waste pharmaceuticals

第三十一章
肥　料

注释：

一、本章不包括：

（一）税目05.11的动物血；

（二）单独的已有化学定义的化合物（符合下列注释二（一）、三（一）、四（一）或五所规定的化合物除外）；

（三）税目38.24的每颗重量不低于2.5克的氯化钾培养晶体（光学元件除外）；氯化钾光学元件（税目90.01）。

二、税目31.02只适用于下列货品，但未制成税目31.05所述形状或包装：

（一）符合下列任何一条规定的货品：

1. 硝酸钠，不论是否纯净；
2. 硝酸铵，不论是否纯净；
3. 硫酸铵及硝酸铵的复盐，不论是否纯净；
4. 硫酸铵，不论是否纯净；
5. 硝酸钙及硝酸铵的复盐（不论是否纯净）或硝酸钙及硝酸铵的混合物；
6. 硝酸钙及硝酸镁的复盐（不论是否纯净）或硝酸钙及硝酸镁的混合物；
7. 氰氨化钙，不论是否纯净或用油处理；
8. 尿素，不论是否纯净。

（二）由上述（一）款任何货品相互混合的肥料。

（三）由氯化铵或上述（一）或（二）款任何货品与白垩、石膏或其他无肥效无机物混合而成的肥料。

（四）由上述（一）2或8项的货品或其混合物溶于水或液氨的液体肥料。

三、税目31.03只适用于下列货品，但未制成税目31.05所述形状或包装：

（一）符合下列任何一条规定的货品：

1. 碱性熔渣；
2. 税目25.10的天然磷酸盐，已焙烧或经过超出清除杂质范围的热处理；
3. 过磷酸钙（一过磷酸钙、二过磷酸钙或三过磷酸钙）；
4. 磷酸氢钙，按干燥无水产品重量计含氟量不低于0.2%。

Chapter 31
Fertilizers

Notes:

1. This Chapter does not cover:
   (a) Animal blood of heading No. 05.11;
   (b) Separate chemically defined compounds (other than those answering to the descriptions in Note 2(A), 3(A), 4(A) or 5 below); or
   (c) Cultured potassium chloride crystals (other than optical elements) weighing not less than 2.5g each, of heading No. 38.24; optical elements of potassium chloride (heading No. 90.01).

2. Heading No. 31.02 applies only to the following goods, provided that they are not put up in the forms or packages described in heading No. 31.05:
   (A) Goods which answer to one or other of the descriptions given below:
      (i) Sodium nitrate, whether or not pure;
      (ii) Ammonium nitrate, whether or not pure;
      (iii) Double salts, whether or not pure, of ammonium sulphate and ammonium nitrate;
      (iv) Ammonium sulphate, whether or not pure;
      (v) Double salts (whether or not pure) or mixtures of calcium nitrate and ammonium nitrate;
      (vi) Double salts (whether or not pure) or mixtures of calcium nitrate and magnesium nitrate;
      (vii) Calcium cyanamide, whether or not pure or treated with oil;
      (viii) Urea, whether or not pure.
   (B) Fertilizers consisting of any of the goods described in (A) above mixed together.
   (C) Fertilizers consisting of ammonium chloride or of any of the goods described in (A) or (B) above mixed with chalk, gypsum or other inorganic nonfertilizing substances.
   (D) Liquid fertilizers consisting of the goods of subparagraph (A)(ii) or (viii) above, or of mixtures of those goods, in an aqueous or ammoniacal solution.

3. Heading No. 31.03 applies only to the following goods, provided that they are not put up in the forms or packages described in heading No. 31.05:
   (A) Goods which answer to one or other of the descriptions given below:
      (i) Basic slag;
      (ii) Natural phosphates of heading No. 25.10, calcined or further heat-treated than for the removal of impurities;
      (iii) Superphosphates (single, double or triple);
      (iv) Calcium hydrogenorthophosphate containing not less than 0.2% by weight of flourine calculated on the dry anhydrous product.

(二)由上述(一)款的任何货品互相混合的肥料,不论含氟量多少。

(三)由上述(一)或(二)款的任何货品与白垩、石膏或其他无肥效无机物混合而成的肥料,不论含氟量多少。

四、税目31.04只适用于下列货品,但未制成税目31.05所述形状或包装:

(一)符合下列任何一条规定的货品:

1. 天然粗钾盐(例如,光卤石、钾盐镁矾及钾盐);

2. 氯化钾,不论是否纯净,但上述注释一(三)所述的产品除外;

3. 硫酸钾,不论是否纯净;

4. 硫酸镁钾,不论是否纯净。

(二)由上述(一)款任何货品相互混合的肥料。

五、磷酸二氢铵及磷酸氢二铵(不论是否纯净)及其相互之间的混合物应归入税目31.05。

六、税目31.05所称"其他肥料",仅适用于其基本成分至少含有氮、磷、钾中一种肥效元素的肥料用产品。

(B) Fertilizers consisting of any of the goods described in (A) above mixed together, but with no account being taken of the fluorine content limit.

(C) Fertilizers consisting of any of the goods described in (A) or (B) above, but with no account being taken of the fluorine content limit, mixed with chalk, gypsum or other inorganic non-fertilizing substances.

4. Heading No. 31.04 applies only to the following goods, provided that they are not put up in the forms or packages described in heading No. 31.05:

(A) Goods which answer to one or other of the descriptions given below:

(i) Crude natural potassium salts (for example, carnallite, kainite and sylvite);

(ii) Potassium chloride, whether or not pure, except as provided in Note 1(c) above;

(iii) Potassium sulphate, whether or not pure;

(iv) Magnesium potassium sulphate, whether or not pure.

(B) Fertilizers consisting of any of the goods described in (A) above mixed together.

5. Ammonium dihydrogenorthophosphate (monoammonium phosphate) and diammonium hydrogenorthophosphate (diammonium phosphate), whether or not pure, and intermixtures thereof, are to be classified in heading No. 31.05.

6. For the purposes of heading No. 31.05, the term "other fertilizers" applies only to products of a kind used as fertilizers and containing, as an essential constituent, at least one of the fertilizing elements nitrogen, phosphorus or potassium.

税则号列 Tariff Item.	货品名称	最惠国(%) MFN	协定(%) 东盟 CA	中巴 CP	中智 CC	普通 Gen	增值税率 VAT	出口退税 ED	计量单位 Unit	监管条件 SC	Article Description
31.01	**动物或植物肥料,不论是否相互混合或经化学处理;动植物产品经混合或化学处理制成的肥料:**										**Animal or vegetable fertilizers, whether or not mixed together or chemically treated; fertilizers produced by the mixing or chemical treatment of animal or vegetable products:**
	---未经化学处理:										---Not chemically treated:
3101.0011	----鸟粪	3			1.8	11	13	5	千克	AB	----Guano
3101.0019	----其他	6.5	5		5.2	30	13	5	千克	AB	----Other
3101.0090	---其他	4			3.2	11	13	11	千克		---Other
3101.0090 10	经化学处理的含动物源性成分(如粪、羽毛等)的动植物肥料	4				11	13	11	千克	AB	Animals or vegetable fertilizer, chemical trevtmene contaiwins composition of animols natural charaacter
3101.0090 90	经化学处理的其他动植物肥料	4				11	13	11	千克		Other vegetable fertilizere, chemical treatmene
31.02	**矿物氮肥及化学氮肥:**										**Mineral or chemical fertilizers, nitrogenous:**
3102.1000	-尿素,不论是否水溶液	*50		40		*150	13		千克		-Urea, whether or not in aqueous solution
3102.1000 01	尿素(配额内,不论是否水溶液)	4				150	13		千克	tA	Urea, whether or not in aqueous solution, in-quota
3102.1000 90	尿素(配额外,不论是否水溶液)	50				150	13		千克	A	Urea, whether or not in aqueous solution, out -quota

税则号列 Tariff Item.	货品名称	最惠国(%) MFN	协定(%)CT 东盟 CA	中巴 CP	中智 CC	普通 Gen	增值税率 VAT	出口退税 ED	计量单位 Unit	监管条件 SC	Article Description
	-硫酸铵;硫酸铵和硝酸铵的复盐及混合物:										-Ammonium sulphate; double salts and mixtures of ammonium sulphate and ammonium nitrate:
3102.2100	--硫酸铵	4			0	11	13	11	千克	7A	--Ammonium sulphate
3102.2900	--其他	4			0	11	13	11	千克	7	--Other
3102.3000	-硝酸铵,不论是否水溶液	4			3.2	11	13	11	千克	9	-Ammonium nitrate, whether or not in aqueous solution
3102.4000	-硝酸铵与碳酸钙或其他无肥效无机物的混合物	4			0	11	13	11	千克	7	-Mixtures of ammonium nitrate with calcium carbonate or other inorganic nonfertilizing substances
3102.5000	-硝酸钠	4			3.2	11	13	11	千克	7A	-Sodium nitrate
3102.6000	硝酸钙和硝酸钠的复盐及混合物	4			3.2	11	13	11	千克	7	Double salts and mixtures of calcium nitrate and ammonium nitrate
3102.8000	-尿素及硝酸铵混合物的水溶液或氨水溶液	4			0	11	13		千克	7	-Mixtures of urea and ammonium nitrate in aqueous or ammoniacal solution
	-其他,包括上述子目未列名的混合物:										-Other, including mixtures not specified in the foregoing subheadings:
3102.9010	---氰氨化钙	4			0	11	13	11	千克	7	---Calcium cyanamide
3102.9090	---其他	4			3.2	11	13	11	千克	7	---Other
31.03	**矿物磷肥及化学磷肥:**										**Mineral or chemical fertilizers, phosphatic:**
	-过磷酸钙:										-Superphosphates:
3103.1010	---重过磷酸钙	4			0	11	13	11	千克	7A	---Triple superphosphates
3103.1090	---其他	4			0	11	13	11	千克	7A	---Other
3103.9000	-其他	4			0	11	13	11	千克	7	-Other
31.04	**矿物钾肥及化学钾肥:**										**Mineral or chemical fertilizers, potassic:**
	-氯化钾:										-Potassium chloride:
3104.2010	---分析纯的	3			1.8	11	13	11	千克	7A	---Analytically pure
3104.2090	---其他	3			1.8	11	13	11	千克	7A	---Other
3104.3000	-硫酸钾	3			1.8	11	13	11	千克	7A	-Potassium sulphate
	-其他:										-Other:
3104.9010	---光卤石、钾盐及其他天然粗钾盐	3			0	11	13	11	千克	7	---Carnallite, Sylvite and other crude naturd potassium salts
3104.9090	---其他:	3			0	11	13	11	千克	7	---Other:
31.05	**含氮、磷、钾中两种或三种肥效元素的矿物肥料或化学肥料;其他肥料;制成片及类似形状或每包毛重不超过10千克的本章各项货品:**										**Mineral or chemical fertilizers containing two or three of the fertilizing elements nitrogen, phosphorus and potassium; other fertilizers; goods of this Chapter in tablets or similar forms or in packages of a gross weight not exceeding 10kg:**
3105.1000	-制成片及类似形状或每包毛重不超过10千克的本章各项货品	4			3.2	11	13	11	千克		-Goods of this Chapter in tablets or similar forms or in packages of a gross weight not exceeding 10kg
3105.1000 10	制成片状及类似形状或零售包装的硝酸铵(零售包装每包毛重不超过10公斤)	4				11	13	11	千克	9	Potassium nitrate, goods of this Chapter in tablets or similar forms or in packages of a gross weight≤10kg
3105.1000 90	制成片状及类似形状或零售包装的31章其他货品(零售包装每包毛重不超过10公斤)	4				11	13	11	千克	7	Other fertilizers of the chapter 31, goods of this Chapter in tablets or similar forms or in packages of a gross weight≤10kg

税则号列 Tariff Item.	货品名称	最惠国(%) MFN	协定(%) CT 东盟 CA	中巴 CP	中智 CC	普通 Gen	增值税率 VAT	出口退税 ED	计量单位 Unit	监管条件 SC	Article Description
3105.2000	-含氮、磷、钾三种肥效元素的矿物肥料或化学肥料	*50				*150	13	11	千克		-Mineral or chemical fertilizers containing the three fertilizing elements nitrogen, phosphorus and potassium
3105.2000 01	化学肥料或矿物肥料(配额内,含氮、磷、钾三种肥效元素)	4				150	13	11	千克	At	Mineral or chemical fertilizers containing the three fertilizing elemtnts nitrogen, phosphorus and potassium, in-quota
3105.2000 90	化学肥料或矿物肥料(配额外,含氮、磷、钾三种肥效元素)	50				150	13	11	千克	A	Mineral or chemical fertilizers containing the three fertilizing elemtnts nitrogen, phosphorus and potassium, out -quota
3105.3000	-磷酸氢二铵	*50				*150	13		千克		-Diammonium hydrogenorthophosphate (diammonium phosphate)
3105.3000 01	磷酸氢二铵(配额内)	4				150	13		千克	tA	Diammonium hydrogenorthophosphate (diammonium phosphate), in-quota
3105.3000 90	磷酸氢二铵(配额外)	50				150	13		千克	A	Diammonium hydrogenorthophosphate (diammonium phosphate), out -quota
3105.4000	-磷酸二氢铵及磷酸二氢铵与磷酸氢二铵的混合物	4			0	11	13		千克	7A	-Ammonium dihydrogenorthophosphate (monoammonium phosphate) and mixtures thereof with diammonium hydrogenorthophosphate (diammonium phosphate)
	-其他含氮、磷两种肥效元素的矿物肥料或化学肥料:										-Other mineral or chemical fertilizers containing the two fertilizing elements nitrogen and phosphorus:
3105.5100	--含有硝酸盐及磷酸盐	4			3.2	11	13	11	千克	7A	--Containing nitrates and phosphates
3105.5900	--其他	4			0	11	13	11	千克	7A	--Other
3105.6000	-含磷、钾两种肥效元素的矿物肥料或化学肥料	4			0	11	13	11	千克	7A	-Mineral or chemical fertilizers containing the two fertilizing elements phosphorus and potassium
3105.9000	-其他	4			3.2	11	13	11	千克	7A	-Other

第三十二章
鞣料浸膏及染料浸膏；鞣酸及其衍生物；染料、颜料及其他着色料；油漆及清漆；油灰及其他类似胶粘剂；墨水、油墨

注释：

一、本章不包括：

（一）单独的已有化学定义的化学元素及化合物（税目32.03及32.04的货品、税目32.06的用作发光体的无机产品、税目32.07所述形状的熔融石英或其他熔融硅石制成的玻璃及税目32.12的零售形状或零售包装的染料及其他着色料除外）；

（二）税目29.36至29.39、29.41及35.01至35.04的鞣酸盐及其他鞣酸衍生物；

（三）沥青胶粘剂（税目27.15）。

二、税目32.04包括生产偶氮染料用的稳定重氮盐与偶合物的混合物。

三、税目32.03、32.04、32.05及32.06也包括以着色料为基本成分的制品（例如，税目32.06包括以税目25.30或第二十八章的颜料，金属粉片及金属粉末为基本成分的制品）。该制品是用作原材料着色剂的拼料。但以上税目不包括分散在非水介质中呈液状或浆状的制漆用颜料，例如，税目32.12的瓷漆及税目32.07、32.08、32.09、32.10、32.12、32.13及32.15的其他制品。

四、税目32.08包括由税目39.01至39.13所列产品溶于挥发性有机溶剂的溶液（胶棉除外），但溶剂重量必须超过溶液重量的50%。

五、本章所称"着色料"，不包括作为油漆填料的产品，不论这些产品能否用于水浆涂料的着色。

六、税目32.12所称"压印箔"，只包括用以压印诸如书本封面或帽带之类的薄片，这些薄片由以下材料构成：

（一）金属粉（包括贵金属粉）或颜料经胶水、明胶及其他粘合剂凝结而成的；

（二）金属（包括贵金属）或颜料沉积于任何材料衬片上的。

Chapter 32
Tanning or dyeing extracts; tannins and their derivatives; dyes, pigments and other colouring matter; paints and varnishes; putty and other mastics; inks

Notes:

1. This Chapter does not cover:

(a) Separate chemically defined elements or compounds (except those of heading No. 32. 03 or 32. 04, inorganic products of a kind used as luminophores (heading No. 32. 06), glass obtained from fused quartz or other fused silica in the forms provided for in heading No. 32. 07, and also dyes and other colouring matter put up in forms or packings for retail sale, of heading No. 32. 12);

(b) Tannates or other tannin derivatives of products of headings Nos. 29. 36 to 29. 39, 29. 41 or 35. 01 to 35. 04;

(c) Mastics of asphalt or other bituminous mastics (heading No. 27. 15).

2. Heading No. 32. 04 includes mixtures of stabilized diazonium salts and couplers for the production of azo dyes.

3. Headings Nos. 32. 03, 32. 04, 32. 05 and 32. 06 apply also to preparations based on colouring matter (including, in the case of heading No. 32. 06, colouring pigments of heading No. 25. 30 or Chapter 28, metal flakes and metal powders), of a kind used for colouring any material or used as ingredients in the manufacture of colouring preparations. The headings do not apply, however, to pigments dispersed in non-aqueous media, in liquid or paste form, of a kind used in the manufacture of paints, including enamels (heading No. 32. 12), or to other preparations of heading No. 32. 07, 32. 08, 32. 09, 32. 10, 32. 12, 32. 13 or 32. 15.

4. Heading No. 32. 08 includes solutions (other than collodions) consisting of any of the products specified in headings Nos. 39. 01 to 39. 13 in volatile organic solvents when the weight of the solvent exceeds 50% of the weight of the solution.

5. The expression "colouring matter" in this Chapter does not include products of a kind used as extenders in oil paints, whether or not they are also suitable for colouring distempers.

6. The expression "stamping foils" in heading No. 32. 12 applies only to thin sheets of a kind used for printing, for example, book covers or hat bands, and consisting of:

(a) Metallic powder (including powder of precious metal) or pigment, agglomerated with glue, gelatin or other binder; or

(b) Metal (including precious metal) or pigment, deposited on a supporting sheet of any material.

税则号列 Tariff Item.	货品名称	最惠国(%) MFN	协定(%) CT 东盟 CA	中巴 CP	中智 CC	普通 Gen	增值税率 VAT	出口退税 ED	计量单位 Unit	监管条件 SC	Article Description
32.01	植物鞣料浸膏;鞣酸及其盐、醚、酯和其他衍生物:										**Tanning extracts of vegetable origin; tannins and their salts, ethers, esters and other derivatives:**
3201.1000	-坚木浸膏	5			0	35	17	13	千克		-Quebracho extract
3201.2000	-荆树皮浸膏	6.5	5		0	35	17	13	千克		-Wattle extract
	-其他:										-Other:
3201.9010	---其他鞣料浸膏	6.5	5		0	40	17	13	千克		---Other tanning extracts
3201.9010 10	其他濒危植物鞣料浸膏	6.5				40	17	13	千克	FE	Other tanning extracts of vegetable origin in imminent dangers
3201.9010 90	其他植物鞣料浸膏	6.5				40	17	13	千克		Other tanning extracts of vegetable origin
3201.9090	---其他	6.5	5		0	35	17	13	千克		---Other
32.02	有机合成鞣料;无机鞣料;鞣料制剂,不论是否含有天然鞣料;预鞣用酶制剂:										**Synthetic organic tanning substances; inorganic tanning substances; tanning preparations, whether or not containing natural tanning substances; enzymatic preparations for pre-tanning:**
3202.1000	-有机合成鞣料	6.5	5		0	35	17	13	千克		-Synthetic organic tanning substances
3202.9000	-其他	6.5	5		0	35	17	13	千克		-Other
32.03	动植物质着色料(包括染料浸膏,但动物炭黑除外),不论是否已有化学定义;本章注释三所述的以动植物质着色料为基本成分的制品:										**Colouring matter of vegetable or animal origin (including dyeing extracts but excluding animal black), whether or not chemically defined; preparations as specified in Note 3 to this Chapter based on colouring matter of vegetable or animal origin:**
	---植物质着色料及以其为基本成分的制品:										---Colouring matter of vegetable origin and preparations based thereon:
3203.0011	----天然靛蓝及以其为基本成分的制品	6.5	5		5.2	80	17	13	千克		----Natural indigo and preparations based thereon
3203.0019	----其他	6.5	5		5.2	45	17	13	千克		----Other
3203.0019 10	濒危植物质着色料及制品(制品是指以植物质着色料为基本成分的)	6.5				45	17	13	千克	FE	Colouring matter and preparations based thereon of vegetable origin in imminent dangers
3203.0019 90	其他植物质着色料及制品(制品是指以植物质着色料为基本成分的)	6.5				45	17	13	千克		Other colouring matter of vegetable origin
3203.0020	---动物质着色料及以其为基本成分的制品	6.5	5		5.2	50	17	13	千克		---Colouring matter of animal origin and preparations based thereon
32.04	有机合成着色料,不论是否已有化学定义;本章注释三所述的以有机合成着色料为基本成分的制品;用作荧光增白剂或发光体的有机合成产品,不论是否已有化学定义:										**Synthetic organic colouring matter, whether or not chemically defined; preparations as specified in Note 3 to this Chapter based on synthetic organic colouring matter; synthetic organic products of a kind used as fluorescent brightening agents or as luminophores, whether or not chemically defined:**

税则号列 Tariff Item.	货 品 名 称	最惠国(%) MFN	协定(%)CT 东盟 CA	 中巴 CP	 中智 CC	普通 Gen	增值税率 VAT	出口退税 ED	计量单位 Unit	监管条件 SC	Article Description
	-有机合成着色料及本章注释三所述的以有机合成着色料为基本成分的制品:										-Synthetic organic colouring matter and preparations based thereon as specified in Note 3 to this Chapter:
3204.1100	--分散染料及以其为基本成分的制品	7.1	5	0	0	35	17	5	千克		--Disperse dyes and preparations based thereon
3204.1200	--酸性染料(不论是否预金属络合)及以其为基本成分的制品;媒染染料及以其为基本成分的制品	7.1	5	0	0	35	17	13	千克		--Acid dyes, whether or not premetallized, and preparations based thereon; mordant dyes and preparations based thereon
3204.1300	--碱性染料及以其为基本成分的制品	6.5	5	0	0	35	17	13	千克		--Basic dyes and preparations based thereon
3204.1400	--直接染料及以其为基本成分的制品	6.5	5	0	0	35	17	13	千克		--Direct dyes and preparations based thereon
	--瓮染料(包括颜料用的)及以其为基本成分的制品:										--Vat dyes (including those usable in that state as pigments) and preparations based thereon:
3204.1510	---合成靛蓝(还原靛蓝)	6.5	5	0	0	35	17	13	千克		---Synthetic indigo(reductive indigo)
3204.1590	---其他	6.5	5	0	0	35	17	13	千克		---Other
3204.1600	--活性染料及以其为基本成分的制品	7.1	5	0	0	35	17	13	千克		--Reactive dyes and preparations based thereon
3204.1700	--颜料及以其为基本成分的制品	6.5	5	0	5.2	35	17	13	千克		--Pigments and preparations based thereon
	--其他,包括由子目号3204.11至3204.19中两个或多个子目所列着色料组成的混合物:										--Other, including mixtures of colouring matter of two or more of the subheadings Nos. 3204.11 to 3204.19:
	---硫化染料及以其为基本成分的制品:										---Sulphur dyes and preparations based thereon:
3204.1911	----硫化黑(硫化青)及以其为基本成分的制品	6.5	5	0	0	35	17	13	千克		----Sulphur black and preparations based thereon
3204.1919	----其他	6.5	5	0	0	35	17	13	千克		----Other
3204.1990	---其他	6.5	5	0	0	35	17	13	千克		---Other
3204.2000	-用作荧光增白剂的有机合成产品	6.5	5	0	0	40	17	13	千克		-Synthetic organic products of a kind used as flourescent brightening agents
	-其他:										-Other:
3204.9010	---生物染色剂及染料指示剂	6.5	5	0	0	20	17	13	千克		---Biological stains and dye indicators
3204.9090	---其他	6.5	5	0	0	40	17	13	千克		---Other
32.05	**色淀;本章注释三所述的以色淀为基本成分的制品:**										**Colour lakes; preparations as specified in Note 3 to this Chapter based on colour lakes:**
3205.0000	色淀;本章注释三所述的以色淀为基本成分的制品	6.5	5		0	35	17	13	千克		Colour lakes; preparations as specified in Note 3 to this Chapter based on colour lakes

税则号列 Tariff Item.	货 品 名 称	最惠国(%) MFN	协定(%) 东盟 CA	中巴 CP	CT 中智 CC	普通 Gen	增值税率 VAT	出口退税 ED	计量单位 Unit	监管条件 SC	Article Description
32.06	其他着色料;本章注释三所述的制品,但税目32.03、32.04及32.05的货品除外;用作发光体的无机产品,不论是否已有化学定义:										**Other colouring matter; preparations as specified in Note 3 to this Chapter, other than those of heading No. 32.03, 32.04 or 32.05; inorganic products of a kind used as luminophores, whether or not chemically defined:**
	-以二氧化钛为基本成分的颜料及制品:										-Pigments and preparations based on titanium dioxide:
	--以干物质计二氧化钛含量在80%及以上的:										--Containing 80% or more by weight of titanium dioxide calculated on the dry matter:
3206.1110	---钛白粉	6.5	5		0	30	17	13	千克	4Bxy	---Titanium White
3206.1190	---其他	6.5	5		0	30	17	13	千克	B	---Other
3206.1900	--其他	10	T3		0	30	17	13	千克	B	--Other
3206.2000	-以铬化合物为基本成分的颜料及制品	6.5	5		0	35	17	13	千克		-Pigments and preparations based on chromium compounds
	-其他着色料及其他制品:										-Other colouring matter and other preparations:
3206.4100	--群青及以其为基本成分的制品	6.5	5		0	35	17	13	千克		--Ultramarine and preparations based thereon
	--锌钡白及以硫化锌为基本成分的其他颜料和制品:										--Lithopone and other pigments and preparations based on zinc sulphide:
3206.4210	---锌钡白	6.5	5		0	30	17	13	千克		---Lithopone
3206.4290	---其他	6.5	5		0	30	17	13	千克		---Other
3206.4900	--其他	6.5	5	3.3	0	35	17	13	千克		--Other
3206.5000	-用作发光体的无机产品	6.5	5	5.9	0	35	17	13	千克		-Inorganic products of a kind used as luminophores
32.07	陶瓷、搪瓷及玻璃工业用的调制颜料、遮光剂、着色剂、珐琅和釉料、釉底料(泥釉)、光瓷釉以及类似产品;搪瓷玻璃料及其他玻璃,呈粉、粒或粉片状的:										**Prepared pigments, prepared opacifiers and prepared colours, vitrifiable enamels and glazes, engobes (slips), liquid lustres and similar preparations, of a kind used in the ceramic, enamelling or glass industry; glass frit and other glass, in the form of powder, granules or flakes:**
3207.1000	-调制颜料、遮光剂、着色剂及类似制品	5			4	50	17	13	千克		-Prepared pigments, prepared opacifiers, prepared colours and similar preparations
3207.2000	-珐琅和釉料、釉底料(泥釉)及类似制品	5			4	50	17	13	千克		-Vitrifiable enamels and glazes, engobes (slips) and similar preparations
3207.3000	-光瓷釉及类似制品	5			0	50	17	13	千克		-Liquid lustres and similar preparations
3207.4000	-搪瓷玻璃料及其他玻璃,呈粉、粒或粉片状的	5			4	50	17	13	千克		-Glass frit and other glass, in the form of powder, granules or flakes
32.08	以合成聚合物或化学改性天然聚合物为基本成分的油漆及清漆(包括瓷漆及大漆),分散于或溶于非水介质的;本章注释四所述的溶液:										**Paints and varnishes (including enamels and lacquers) based on synthetic polymers or chemically modified natural polymers, dispersed or dissolved in a nonaqueous medium; solutions as defined in Note 4 to this Chapter:**
3208.1000	-以聚酯为基本成分	10	T3	9	8	50	17	13	千克	A	-Based on polyesters

税则号列 Tariff Item.	货品名称	最惠国(%) MFN	协定(%) 东盟 CA	中巴 CP	中智 CC	普通 Gen	增值税率 VAT	出口退税 ED	计量单位 Unit	监管条件 SC	Article Description
	-以丙烯酸聚合物或乙烯聚合物为基本成分:										-Based on acrylic or vinyl polymers:
3208.2010	---以丙烯酸聚合物为基本成分	10	T3	9	8	50	17	13	千克		---Based on acrylic polymers
3208.2010 01	分散于成溶于非水介质的光导纤维用涂料(以丙烯酸酯类化合物为主要成分)	10				50	17	13	千克	A	Paints for optial fibers, based on acrylic polymers, dissolved in a nonaqueous medium
3208.2010 90	其他聚丙烯酸油漆、清漆等(溶于非水质的以丙烯酸聚合物为基本成分,包括瓷漆大漆)	10				50	17	13	千克	A	Other paints and varnishes (including enamels and lacquers), based on acrylic polymers, dissolved in a nonaqueous medium
3208.2020	---以乙烯聚合物为基本成分	10	5	9	8	50	17	13	千克	A	---Based on vinyl polymers
	-其他:										-Other:
3208.9010	---以聚胺酯类化合物为基本成分	10	T3	9	8	50	17	13	千克		---Based on polyurethane polymers
3208.9010 01	分散于或溶于非水介质的光导纤维用涂料(以聚胺酯丙烯酸酯类化合物为主要成分)	10				50	17	13	千克	A	Paints for optial fibers, based on polyurethane polymers, dissolved in a nonaqueous medium
3208.9010 90	其他聚胺酯油漆清漆等(溶于非水介质以聚胺酯类化合物为基本成分,含瓷漆大漆)	10				50	17	13	千克	A	Other paints and varnishes (including enamels and lacquers), based on polyurethane polymers, dissolved in a nonaqueous medium
3208.9090	---其他	10	T3	9	8	50	17	13	千克	A	---Other
32.09	**以合成聚合物或化学改性天然聚合物为基本成分的油漆及清漆(包括瓷漆及大漆),分散于或溶于水介质的:**										**Paints and varnishes (including enamels and lacquers) based on synthetic polymers or chemically modified natural polymers, dispersed or dissolved in an aqueous medium:**
3209.1000	-以丙烯酸聚合物或乙烯聚合物为基本成分	10	T3	9	8	50	17	13	千克	A	-Based on acrylic or vinyl polymers
	-其他:										-Other:
3209.9010	---以环氧树脂为基本成分	10	T3		8	50	17	13	千克	A	---Based on epoxy resin
3209.9020	---以氟树脂为基本成分	10	T3		8	50	17	13	千克	A	---Based on fluoride resin
3209.9090	---其他	10	T3		8	50	17	13	千克	A	---Other
32.10	**其他油漆及清漆(包括瓷漆、大漆及水浆涂料);加工皮革用的水性颜料:**										**Other paints and varnishes (including enamels, lacquers and distempers); prepared water pigments of a kind used for finishing leather:**
3210.0000	其他油漆及清漆(包括瓷漆、大漆及水浆涂料);加工皮革用的水性颜料	10	8	9	8	50	17	13	千克		Other paints and varnishes (including enamels, lacquers and distempers); prepared water pigments of a kind used for finishing leather
32.11	**配制的催干剂:**										**Prepared driers:**
3211.0000	配制的催干剂	10	T3		0	50	17	13	千克		Prepared driers

税则号列 Tariff Item.	货品名称	最惠国(%) MFN	协定(%) CT 东盟 CA	协定(%) CT 中巴 CP	协定(%) CT 中智 CC	普通 Gen	增值税率 VAT	出口退税 ED	计量单位 Unit	监管条件 SC	Article Description
32.12	制造油漆(含瓷漆)用的颜料(包括金属粉末或金属粉片),分散于非水介质中呈液状或浆状的;压印箔;零售形状及零售包装的染料或其他着色料:										**Pigments (including metallic powders and flakes) dispersed in non-aqueous media, in liquid or paste form, of a kind used in the manufacture of paints (including enamels); stamping foils; dyes and other colouring matter put up in forms or packings for retail sale:**
3212.1000	-压印箔	15	8		12	80	17	13	千克		-Stamping foils
3212.9000	-其他	10	T3		0	50	17	13	千克		-Other
32.13	艺术家、学生和广告美工用的颜料、调色料、文娱颜料及类似品,片状、管装、罐装、瓶装、扁盒装以及类似形状或包装的:										**Artists', students' or signboard painters' colours, modifying tints, amusement colours and the like, in tablets, tubes, jars, bottles, pans or in similar forms or packings:**
3213.1000	-成套的颜料	10	5		8	70	17	13	千克		-Colours in sets
3213.9000	-其他	10	5	9	0	70	17	13	千克		-Other
32.14	安装玻璃用油灰、接缝用油灰、树脂胶泥、嵌缝胶及其他类似胶粘剂;漆工用填料;非耐火涂面制剂,涂门面、内墙、地板、天花板等用:										**Glaziers' putty, graftig putty, resin cements, caulking compounds and other mastics; painters' fillings; non-refractory surfacing preparations for facades, indoor walls, floors, ceilings or the like:**
3214.1000	-安装玻璃用油灰、接缝用油灰、树脂胶泥、嵌缝胶及其他类似胶粘剂;漆工用填料	9	T3		7.2	70	17	13	千克		-Glaziers' putty, grafting putty, resin cements, caulking compounds and other mastics; painters' fillings
3214.9000	-其他	9	T3		7.2	70	17	13	千克		-Other
32.15	印刷油墨、书写或绘图墨水及其他墨类,不论是否固体或浓缩:										**Printing ink, writing or drawing ink and other inks, whether or not concentrated or solid:**
	-印刷油墨:										-Printing ink:
3215.1100	--黑色	6.5	5	4.6	5.2	45	17	13	千克		--Black
3215.1900	--其他	6.5	5	4.6	5.2	45	17	13	千克		--Other
	-其他:										-Other:
3215.9010	---书写墨水	6.5	5		0	70	17	13	千克		---Writing or drawing inks
3215.9090	---其他	10	8		0	70	17	13	千克		---Other

第三十三章
精油及香膏；芳香料制品及化妆盥洗品

Chapter 33
Essential oils and resinoids; perfumery, cosmetic or toilet preparations

注释：

一、本章不包括：

（一）税目13.01及13.02的天然油树脂及植物浸膏；

（二）税目34.01的肥皂及其他产品；

（三）税目38.05的脂松节油、木松节油和硫酸盐松节油及其他产品。

二、税目33.02所称"香料"仅指税目33.01所列的物质，从这些物质离析出来的香料组分以及合成芳香剂。

三、税目33.03至33.07主要包括适合作这些税目所列用途的零售包装产品，不论其是否混合（精油水馏液及水溶液除外）。

四、税目33.07所称"芳香料制品及化妆盥洗品"，主要适用于下列产品：香袋；通过燃烧散发香气的制品；香纸及用化妆品浸渍或涂布的纸；隐形眼镜片或假眼用的溶液；用香水或化妆品浸渍、涂布、包覆的絮胎、毡呢及无纺织物；动物用盥洗品。

Notes:

1. This Chapter does not cover:

(a) Natural oleoresins or vegetable extracts of heading No. 13.01 or 13.02;

(b) Soap or other products of heading No. 34.01; or

(c) Gum, wood or sulphate turpentine or other products of heading No. 38.05.

2. The expression "odoriferous substances" in heading No. 33.02 refers only to the substances of heading No. 33.01, to odoriferous constituents isolated from those substances or to synthetic aromatics.

3. Headings Nos. 33.03 to 33.07 apply, *inter alia*, to products, whether or not mixed (other than aqueous distillates and aqueous solutions of essential oils), suitable for use as goods of these headings and put up in packings of a kind sold by retail for such use.

4. The expression "perfumery, cosmetic or toilet preparations" in heading No. 33.07 applies, *inter alia*, to the following products: scented sachets; odoriferous preparations which operate by burning; perfumed papers and papers impregnated or coated with cosmetics; contact lens or artificial eye solutions; wadding, felt and nonwovens, impregnated, coated or covered with perfume or cosmetics; animal toilet preparations.

税则号列 Tariff Item.	货品名称	最惠国(%) MFN	协定(%)CT 东盟 CA	中巴 CP	中智 CC	普通 Gen	增值税率 VAT	出口退税 ED	计量单位 Unit	监管条件 SC	Article Description
33.01	**精油（无萜或含萜），包括浸膏及净油；香膏；提取的油树脂；用花香吸取法或浸渍法制成的含浓缩精油的脂肪、固定油、蜡及类似品；精油脱萜时所得的萜烯副产品；精油水馏液及水溶液：**										**Essential oils (terpeneless or not), including concretes and absolutes; resinoids; extracted oleoresins; concentrates of essential oils in fats, in fixed oils, in waxes or the like, obtained by enfleurage or maceration; terpenic byproducts of the deterpenation of essential oils; aqueous distillates and aqueous solutions of essential oils:**
	-柑桔属果实的精油：										-Essential oils of citrus fruit:
3301.1200	--橙油	20	12		12	80	17	13	千克	A	--Of orange
3301.1300	--柠檬油	20	12		12	80	17	13	千克	A	--Of lemon
	--其他：										--Other:
3301.1910	---白柠檬油（酸橙油）	20	12		12	80	17	13	千克	A	---Of lime
3301.1990	---其他	20	12		12	80	17	13	千克	A	---Other
	-非柑桔属果实的精油：										-Essential oils other than those of citrus fruit:
3301.2400	--胡椒薄荷油	20	12		0	90	17	13	千克	AB	--Of peppermint (Mentha piperita)
3301.2500	--其他薄荷油	15	8	14	9	90	17	13	千克	AB	--Of other mints
	--其他：										--Other:
3301.2910	---樟脑油	20	12		0	90	17	13	千克	ABE	---Of camphor
3301.2920	---香茅油	15	8		0	70	17	13	千克	AB	---Of citronella
3301.2930	---茴香油	20	12		0	80	17	5	千克	AB	---Of aniseed

税则号列 Tariff Item.	货品名称	最惠国(%) MFN	协定(%)CT 东盟 CA	中巴 CP	中智 CC	普通 Gen	增值税率 VAT	出口退税 ED	计量单位 Unit	监管条件 SC	Article Description
3301.2940	---桂油	20	12		0	80	17	13	千克	AB	---Of cassia
3301.2950	---山苍子油	20	12		0	80	17	13	千克	AB	---Of litsea cubeba
3301.2960	---桉叶油	20	12		0	80	17	13	千克	AB	---Of eucalyptus
	---其他:										---Other:
3301.2991	----老鹳草油(香叶油)	20	12		12	80	17	13	千克	A	----Of geranium
3301.2999	----其他:	15	8		9	80	17	13	千克		----Other:
3301.2999 10	黄樟油	15				80	17	13	千克	23A	Essential oil of sassafras
3301.2999 91	其他非柑桔属濒危植物果实的精油(包括浸膏及净油)	15				80	17	13	千克	AFE	Other essential oils other than those of citrus fruit in imminent dangers, including concretes and absolutes
3301.2999 99	其他非柑桔属果实的精油(包括浸膏及净油)	15				80	17	13	千克	A	Other essential oils other than those of citrus fruit, including concretes and absolutes
	-香膏:										-Resinoids:
3301.3010	---鸢尾凝脂	20	12		12	80	17	13	千克		---Balsam of irises
3301.3090	---其他	20	12		12	80	17	13	千克		---Other
3301.3090 10	其他濒危植物香膏	20				80	17	13	千克	FE	Other resinoids of plants in imminent dangers
3301.3090 90	其他香膏	20				80	17	13	千克		Other resinoids
	-其他:										-Other:
3301.9010	---提取的油树脂	20	12	18	12	80	17	13	千克		---Extracted oleoresins
3301.9010 10	濒危植物提取的油树脂	20				80	17	13	千克	FE	Extracted oleoresins of plants in imminent dangers
3301.9010 90	其他提取的油树脂	20				80	17	13	千克		Other extracted oleoresins
3301.9020	---柑桔属果实的精油脱萜烯副产品	20	12	18	12	80	17	13	千克		---Terpenic byproducts of the deterpenation of essential oils of citrus fruit
3301.9090	---其他	20	12	18	12	80	17	13	千克		---Other
33.02	**工业原料用的混合香料以及以一种或多种香料为基本成分的混合物(包括酒精溶液);生产饮料用的以香料为基本成分的其他制品:**										**Mixtures of odoriferous substances and mixtures (including alcoholic solutions) with a basis of one or more of these substances, of a kind used as raw materials in industry; other preparations based on odoriferous substances, of a kind used for the manufacture of beverages:**
	-食品或饮料工业用:										-Of a kind used in the food or drink industry:
3302.1010	---生产饮料用的以香料为基本成分的制品,按容量计酒精浓度不超过0.5%的	15	12	12.8	12	90	17	13	千克	AB	---Preparations based on odoriferous substances, of a kind used for the manufacture of beverages, alcoholic strength by volume not exceeding 0.5% vol.
3302.1090	---其他	15	12		12	130	17	13	千克		---Other
3302.1090 01	生产食品、饮料用混合香料及制品(含以香料为基本成分的混合物,按容量计酒精浓度>0.5%)	15				130	17	13	千克	AB	Mistures of odoriferous substances and preparations, alcoholic strength by vol, >0.5%, of a kind used in the food or drink industry
3302.1090 90	其他生产食品用混合香料及制品(含以香料为基本成分的混合物)	15				130	17	13	千克	AB	Other mistures of odoriferous substances and preparations, based on oboriferous substances, of a kind used in the food industry

税则号列 Tariff Item.	货品名称	最惠国(%) MFN	协定(%) CT			普通 Gen	增值税率 VAT	出口退税 ED	计量单位 Unit	监管条件 SC	Article Description
			东盟 CA	中巴 CP	中智 CC						
3302.9000	-其他	10			8	130	17	13	千克		-Other
33.03	**香水及花露水:**										**Perfumes and toilet waters:**
3303.0000	香水及花露水	10	T3	8.2	8	150	17	13	千克	AB	Perfumes and toilet waters
33.04	**美容品或化妆品及护肤品(药品除外),包括防晒油或晒黑油;指(趾)甲化妆品:**										**Beauty or make-up preparations and preparations for the care of the skin (other than medicaments), including sunscreen or sun tan preparations; manicure or pedicure preparations:**
3304.1000	-唇用化妆品	10	T3		8	150	17	13	千克	AB	-Lip make-up preparations
3304.2000	-眼用化妆品	10	T3		8	150	17	13	千克	AB	-Eye make-up preparations
3304.3000	-指(趾)甲化妆品	15	12		12	150	17	13	千克	AB	-Manicure or pedicure preparations
	-其他:										-Other:
3304.9100	--香粉,不论是否压紧	10	T3		8	150	17	13	千克	AB	--Powders, whether or not compressed
3304.9900	--其他	9.7			7.8	150	17	13	千克		--Other
3304.9900 10	护肤品(包括防晒油或晒黑油,但药品除外)	9.7				150	17	13	千克	AB	Preparations for the care of the skin, including sunscreen or sun tan preparations, other than medicaments
3304.9900 91	其他含濒危植物成分美容化妆品	9.7				150	17	13	千克	ABFE	Beauty or make-up preparations, containing composition of plants in imminent dangers
3304.9900 99	其他美容化妆品	9.7				150	17	13	千克	AB	Other beauty or make-up preparations
33.05	**护发品:**										**Preparations for use on the hair:**
3305.1000	-洗发剂(香波)	8.6	T3	7.2	6.9	150	17	13	千克		-Shampoos
3305.1000 10	含濒危植物成分的洗发剂	8.6				150	17	13	千克	ABFE	Shampoos containing composition of plants in imminent dangers
3305.1000 90	其他洗发剂(香波)	8.6				150	17	13	千克	AB	Other shampoos
3305.2000	-烫发剂	15	T3		9	150	17	13	千克	AB	-Preparations for permanent waving or straightening
3305.3000	-定型剂	15	T3		12	150	17	13	千克	AB	-Hair lacquers
3305.9000	-其他	10	T3	8.5	8	150	17	13	千克	AB	-Other
33.06	**口腔及牙齿清洁剂,包括假牙模膏及粉;清洁牙缝用的纱线(牙线),单独零售包装的:**										**Preparations for oral or dental hygiene, including denture fixative pastes and powders; yarn used to clean between the teeth (dental floss), in individual retail package:**
	-洁齿品:										-Dentifrices:
3306.1010	---牙膏	10	8	7	8	150	17	13	千克		---Toothpastes
3306.1010 10	含濒危植物成分牙膏	10				150	17	13	千克	FE	Toothpastes containing composition of plants in imminent dangers
3306.1010 90	其他牙膏	10				150	17	13	千克		Other toothpastes
3306.1090	---其他	10	8	7	8	150	17	13	千克		---Other
3306.2000	-清洁牙缝用的纱线(牙线)	10	5	9.2	8	70	17	13	千克		-Yarn used to clean between the teeth (dental floss)
3306.9000	-其他	10	8		8	70	17	13	千克		-Other

税则号列 Tariff Item.	货品名称	最惠国(%) MFN	协定(%)CT 东盟 CA	中巴 CP	中智 CC	普通 Gen	增值税率 VAT	出口退税 ED	计量单位 Unit	监管条件 SC	Article Description
33.07	**剃须用制剂、人体除臭剂、沐浴用制剂、脱毛剂和其他税目未列名的芳香料制品及化妆盥洗品;室内除臭剂,不论是否加香水或消毒剂:**										**Pre-shave, shaving or after-shave preparations, personal deodorants, bath preparations, depilatories and other perfumery, cosmetic or toilet preparations, not elsewhere specified or included; prepared room deodorizers, whether or not perfumed or having disinfectant properties:**
3307.1000	-剃须用制剂	10	8	7	8	150	17	13	千克		-Pre-shave, shaving or after-shave preparations
3307.2000	-人体除臭剂及止汗剂	10	8	7	8	150	17	13	千克		-Personal deodorants and antiperspirants
3307.3000	-香浴盐及其他沐浴用制剂	10	8	8.5	8	150	17	13	千克		-Perfumed bath salts and other bath preparations
	-室内散香或除臭制品,包括宗教仪式用的香:										-Preparations for perfuming or deodorizing rooms, including odoriferous preparations used during religious rites:
3307.4100	--神香及其他通过燃烧散发香气的制品	10	8		0	150	17	13	千克		--Agarbatti and other odoriferous preparations which operate by burning
3307.4900	--其他	10	8		8	150	17	13	千克		--Other
3307.9000	-其他	9	5	6.3	0	150	17	13	千克		-Other

第三十四章

肥皂、有机表面活性剂、洗涤剂、润滑剂、人造蜡、调制蜡、光洁剂、蜡烛及类似品、塑型用膏、“牙科用蜡”及牙科用熟石膏制剂

注释：

一、本章不包括：

（一）用作脱模剂的食用动植物油、脂混合物或制品（税目 15.17）；

（二）单独的已有化学定义的化合物；

（三）含肥皂或其他有机表面活性剂的洗发剂、洁齿品、剃须膏及沐浴用制剂（税目 33.05、33.06 及 33.07）。

二、税目 34.01 所称“肥皂”，只适用于水溶性肥皂。税目 34.01 的肥皂及其他产品可以含有添加料（例如，消毒剂、磨料粉、填料或药料）。含磨料粉的产品，只有条状、块状或模制形状可以归入税目 34.01。其他形状的应作为“去污粉及类似品”归入税目 34.05。

三、税目 34.02 所称“有机表面活性剂”，是指温度在 20℃ 时与水混合配成 0.5% 浓度的水溶液，并在同样温度下搁置一小时后与下列规定相符的产品：

（一）成为透明或半透明的液体或稳定的乳浊液而未离析出不溶解物质；

（二）将水的表面张力减低到每厘米 45 达因及以下。

四、税目 34.03 所称“石油及从沥青矿物提取的油类”，适用于第二十七章注释二所规定的产品。

五、税目 34.04 所称“人造蜡及调制蜡”，仅适用于：

（一）用化学方法生产的具有蜡质特性的有机产品，不论是否为水溶性的；

（二）各种蜡混合制成的产品；

（三）以一种或几种蜡为基本原料并含有油脂、树脂、矿物质或其他原料的具有蜡质特性的产品。

本税目不包括：

（一）税目 15.16、34.02 或 38.23 的产品，不论是否具有蜡质特性；

（二）税目 15.21 的未混合的动物蜡或未混合的植物蜡，不论是否精制或着色；

（三）税目 27.12 的矿物蜡或类似产品，不论是否相互混合或仅经着色；

Chapter 34

Soap, organic surface-active agents, washing preparations, lubricating preparations, artificial waxes, prepared waxes, polishing or scouring preparations, candles and similar articles, modelling pastes, “dental waxes” and dental preparations with a basis of plaster

Notes:

1. This Chapter does not cover:

(a) Edible mixtures or preparations of animal or vegetable fats or oils of a kind used as mould release preparations (heading No. 15.17);

(b) Separate chemically defined compounds; or

(c) Shampoos, dentifrices, shaving creams and foams, or bath preparations, containing soap or other organic surface-active agents (heading No. 33.05, 33.06 or 33.07).

2. For the purposes of heading No. 34.01, the expression “soap” applies only to soap soluble in water. Soap and the other products of heading No. 34.01 may contain added substances (for example, disinfectants, abrasive powders, fillers or medicaments). Products containing abrasive powders remain classified in heading No. 34.01 only if in the form of bars, cakes or moulded pieces or shapes. In other forms they are to be classified in heading No. 34.05 as “scouring powders and similar preparations”.

3. For the purposes of heading No. 34.02, “organic surface-active agents” are products which when mixed with water at a concentration of 0.5% at 20℃ and left to stand for one hour at the same temperature:

(a) give a transparent or translucent liquid or stable emulsion without separation of insoluble matter; and

(b) reduce the surface tension of water to 4.5×10^{-2} N/m (45 dyen/cm) or less

4. In heading No. 34.03 the expression “petroleum oils and oils obtained from bituminous minerals” applies to the products defined in Note 2 to Chapter 27.

5. In heading No. 34.04, subject to the exclusions provided below, the expression “artificial waxes and prepared waxes” applies only to:

(a) Chemically produced organic products of a waxy character, whether or not water-soluble;

(b) Products obtained by mixing different waxes;

(c) Products of a waxy character with a basis of one or more waxes and containing fats, resins, mineral substances or other materials.

The heading does not apply to:

(a) Products of heading No. 15.16, 34.02 or 38.23, even if having a waxy character;

(b) Unmixed animal waxes or unmixed vegetable waxes, whether or not refined or coloured, of heading No. 15.21;

(c) Mineral waxes or similar products of heading No. 27.12, whether or not intermixed or merely coloured; or

(四)混合、分散或溶解于液体溶剂的蜡(税目34.05、38.09等)。

(d) Waxes mixed with, dispersed in or dissolved in a liquid medium (headings Nos. 34.05, 38.09, etc.).

税则号列 Tariff Item.	货品名称	最惠国(%) MFN	协定(%) CT 东盟 CA	中巴 CP	中智 CC	普通 Gen	增值税率 VAT	出口退税 ED	计量单位 Unit	监管条件 SC	Article Description
34.01	**肥皂;作肥皂用的有机表面活性产品及制品,条状、块状或模制形状的,不论是否含有肥皂;洁肤用的有机表面活性产品及制品,液状或膏状并制成零售包装的,不论是否含有肥皂;用肥皂或洗涤剂浸渍、涂面或包覆的纸、絮胎、毡呢及无纺织物:**										**Soap; organic surface-active products and preparations for use as soap, in the form of bars, cakes, moulded pieces or shapes, whether or not containing soap; organic surface-active products and preparations for washing the skin, in the form of liquid or cream and put up for retail sale, whether or not containing soap; paper, wadding, felt and nonwovens, impregnated, coated or covered with soap or detergent:**
	-肥皂及有机表面活性产品及制品,条状、块状或模制形状的,以及用肥皂或洗涤剂浸渍、涂面或包覆的纸、絮胎、毡呢及无纺织物:										-Soap and organic surface-active products and preparations, in the form of bars, cakes, moulded pieces or shapes, and paper, wadding, felt and nonwovens, impregnated, coated or covered with soap or detergent:
3401.1100	--盥洗用(包括含有药物的产品)	10	T3	8.3	8	130	17	13	千克		--For toilet use (including medicated products)
	--其他:										--Other:
3401.1910	---洗衣皂	10	8		0	80	17	13	千克		---Laundry soap
3401.1990	---其他	15	T3		9	130	17	13	千克		---Other
3401.2000	-其他形状的肥皂	15	T3	12.4	12	130	17	13	千克		-Soap in other forms
3401.3000	-洁肤用的有机表面活性产品及制品,液状或膏状并制成零售包装的,不论是否含有肥皂	10	8		8	130	17	13	千克		-Organic surface-active products and preparations for washing the skin, in the form of liquid or cream and put up for retail sale, whether or not containing soap
34.02	**有机表面活性剂(肥皂除外);表面活性剂制品、洗涤剂(包括助洗剂)及清洁剂,不论是否含有肥皂,但税目34.01的产品除外:**										**Organic surface-active agents (other than soap); surface-active preparations, washing preparations (including auxiliary washing preparations) and cleaning preparations, whether or not containing soap, other than those of heading No. 34.01:**
	-有机表面活性剂,不论是否零售包装:										-Organic surface-active agents, whether or not put up for retail sale:
3402.1100	--阴离子型	6.5	5	6	5.2	30	17	13	千克		--Anionic
3402.1200	--阳离子型	6.5	5	6	0	30	17	13	千克		--Cationic
3402.1300	--非离子型	6.5	5	5.9	5.2	30	17	13	千克		--Non-ionic
3402.1900	--其他	6.5	5	6	5.2	30	17	13	千克		--Other
	-零售包装的制品:										-Preparations put up for retail sale:
3402.2010	---合成洗涤粉	10	8	8.5	8	80	17	13	千克		---Synthetic detergents in powder form
3402.2090	---其他	10	8	8.5	8	80	17	13	千克		---Other
3402.9000	-其他	9	8	7.8	7.2	80	17	13	千克		-Other
3402.9000 01	十二烷基苯磺酸钙甲醇溶液(非零售包装,十二烷基苯磺酸钙含量高于70%)	9				80	17	13	千克		Calcium dodecyl benzosulfonate methanol solution (content of calcium dodecyl benzosulfonate > 70%), not put up for retail sale

税则号列 Tariff Item.	货品名称	最惠国(%) MFN	协定(%) CT			普通 Gen	增值税率 VAT	出口退税 ED	计量单位 Unit	监管条件 SC	Article Description
			东盟 CA	中巴 CP	中智 CC						
3402.9000 90	非零售包装有机表面活性剂制品(包括洗涤剂及清洁剂,不论是否含有肥皂)	9				80	17	13	千克		Other organic surface-active agents, washing preparations and cleaning preparations, whether or not containing soap, not put up for retail sale
34.03	**润滑剂(包括以润滑剂为基本成分的切削油制剂、螺栓或螺母松开剂、防锈或防腐蚀制剂及脱模剂)及用于纺织材料、皮革、毛皮或其他材料油脂处理的制剂,但不包括以石油或从沥青矿物提取的油类为基本成分(按重量计不低于70%)的制剂:**										**Lubricating preparations (including cutting-oil preparations, bolt or nut release preparations, anti-rust or anticorrosion preparations and mould release preparations, based on lubricants) and preparations of a kind used for the oil or grease treatment of textile materials, leather, furskins or other materials, but excluding preparations containing, as basic constituents, 70% or more by weight of petroleum oils or of oils obtained from bituminous minerals:**
	-含有石油或从沥青矿物提取的油类:										-Containing petroleum oils or oils obtained from bituminous minerals:
3403.1100	--处理纺织材料、皮革、毛皮或其他材料的制剂	10	T3	9.5	0	50	17	13	千克		--Preparations for the treatment of textile materials, leather, furskins or other materials
3403.1900	--其他	10	8		8	50	17	13	千克		--Other
	-其他:										-Other:
3403.9100	--处理纺织材料、皮革、毛皮或其他材料的制剂	10	8		8	50	17	13	千克		--Preparations for the treatment of textile materials, leather, furskins or other materials
3403.9900	--其他	10	8		8	50	17	13	千克		--Other
34.04	**人造蜡及调制蜡:**										**Artificial waxes and prepared waxes:**
3404.2000	-聚氧乙烯(聚乙二醇)蜡	10	5		0	70	17	13	千克		-Of poly(oxyethylene) (polyethylene glycol)
3404.9000	-其他	10	5		0	70	17	13	千克		-Other
34.05	**鞋靴、家具、地板、车身、玻璃或金属用的光洁剂、擦洗膏、去污粉及类似制品(包括用这类制剂浸渍、涂面或包覆的纸、絮胎、毡呢、无纺织物、泡沫塑料或海绵橡胶),但不包括税目34.04的蜡:**										**Polishes and creams, for footwear, furniture, floors, coachwork, glass or metal, scouring pastes and powders and similar preparations (whether or not in the form of paper, wadding, felt, nonwovens, cellular plastics or cellular rubber, impregnated, coated or covered with such preparations), excluding waxes of heading No. 34.04:**
3405.1000	-鞋靴或皮革用的上光剂及类似制品	10	T3		8	80	17	13	千克		-Polishes, creams and similar preparations for footwear or leather
3405.2000	-保养木制家具、地板或其他木制品用的上光剂及类似制品	10	T3		8	80	17	13	千克		-Polishes, creams and similar preparations for the maintenance of wooden furniture, floors or other woodwork
3405.3000	-车身用的上光剂及类似制品,但金属用的光洁剂除外	10	8		8	80	17	13	千克		-Polishes and similar preparations for coachwork, other than metal polishes
3405.4000	-擦洗膏、去污粉及类似制品	10	5		0	80	17	13	千克		-Scouring pastes and powders and other scouring preparations

税则号列 Tariff Item.	货品名称	最惠国(%) MFN	协定(%) CT 东盟 CA	中巴 CP	中智 CC	普通 Gen	增值税率 VAT	出口退税 ED	计量单位 Unit	监管条件 SC	Article Description
3405.9000	-其他	10	T3	8.5	8	80	17	13	千克		-Other
34.06	各种蜡烛及类似品:										**Candles, tapers and the like:**
3406.0000	各种蜡烛及类似品	10	T3		8	130	17	13	千克		Candles, tapers and the like
3406.0000 10	含濒危动物成分的蜡烛及类似品	10				130	17	13	千克	EF	Candle and gimilar products made from on dangered animals
3406.0000 90	其他各种蜡烛及类似品	10				130	17	13	千克		Other candles, tapersand the like
34.07	塑型用膏,包括供儿童娱乐用的在内;通称为"牙科用蜡"或"牙科造形膏"的制品,成套、零售包装或制成片状、马蹄形、条状及类似形状的;以熟石膏(煅烧石膏或硫酸钙)为基本成分的牙科用其他制品:										**Modelling pastes, including those put up for children's amusement; preparations known as "dental wax" or as "dental impression compounds", put up in sets, in packings for retail sale or in plates, horseshoe shapes, sticks or similar forms; other preparations for use in dentistry, with a basis of plaster (of calcined gypsum or calcium sulphate):**
3407.0010	---牙科用蜡及造型膏	6.5	5		0	30	17	13	千克		---Preparations of a kind known as "dental wax" or as "dental impression compounds"
3407.0020	---以熟石膏为基本成分的牙科用其他制品	6.5	5		0	40	17	13	千克		---Other preparations for use in dentistry, with a basis of plaster
3407.0090	---其他	10	5		0	100	17	13	千克		---Other

第三十五章
蛋白类物质;改性淀粉;胶;酶

Chapter 35
Albuminoidal substances; modified starches; glues; enzymes

注释:

一、本章不包括:

(一)酵母(税目21.02);

(二)第三十章的血份(非治病、防病用的血清白蛋白除外)、药品及其他产品;

(三)预鞣用酶制剂(税目32.02);

(四)第三十四章的加酶的浸透剂、洗涤剂及其他产品;

(五)硬化蛋白(税目39.13);

(六)印刷工业用的明胶产品(第四十九章)。

二、税目35.05所称"糊精",是指淀粉的降解产品,其还原糖含量以右旋糖的干重量计不超过10%。

如果还原糖含量超过10%,应归入税目17.02。

Notes:

1. This Chapter does not cover:

(a) Yeasts (heading No. 21.02);

(b) Blood fractions (other than blood albumin not prepared for therapeutic or prophylactic uses), medicaments or other products of Chapter 30;

(c) Enzymatic preparations for pre-tanning (heading No. 32.02);

(d) Enzymatic soaking or washing preparations or other products of Chapter 34;

(e) Hardened proteins (heading No. 39.13); or

(f) Gelatin products of the printing industry (Chapter 49).

2. For the purposes of heading No. 35.05, the term "dextrins" means starch degradation products with a reducing sugar content, expressed as dextrose on the dry substance, not exceeding 10%.

Such products with a reducing sugar content exceeding 10% fall in heading No. 17.02.

税则号列 Tariff Item.	货品名称	最惠国(%) MFN	协定(%) 东盟 CA	协定(%) 中巴 CP	CT 中智 CC	普通 Gen	增值税率 VAT	出口退税 ED	计量单位 Unit	监管条件 SC	Article Description
35.01	酪蛋白、酪蛋白酸盐及其他酪蛋白衍生物;酪蛋白胶:										**Casein, caseinates and other casein derivatives; casein glues:**
3501.1000	-酪蛋白	10	T3		0	35	17	13	千克		-Casein
3501.9000	-其他	10	5		8	35	17	13	千克		-Other
35.02	白蛋白(包括按重量计干质成分的乳清蛋白含量超过80%的两种或两种以上的乳清蛋白浓缩物)、白蛋白盐及其他白蛋白衍生物:										**Albumins (including concentrates of two or more whey proteins, containing by weight more than 80% whey proteins, calculated on the dry matter), albuminates and other albumin derivatives:**
	-卵清蛋白:										-Egg albumin:
3502.1100	--干的	10	5		0	80	17	13	千克	AB	--Dried
3502.1900	--其他	10	5		0	80	17	13	千克	AB	--Other
3502.2000	-乳白蛋白,包括两种或两种以上的乳清蛋白浓缩物	10	5		0	35	17	13	千克		-Milk albumin, including concentrates of two or more whey proteins
3502.9000	-其他	10	5		8	35	17	13	千克		-Other
35.03	明胶(包括长方形、正方形明胶薄片,不论是否表面加工或着色)及其衍生物;鱼鳔胶;其他动物胶,但不包括税目35.01的酪蛋白胶:										**Gelatin (including gelatin in rectangular (including square) sheets, whether or not surface-worked or coloured) and gelatin derivatives; isinglass; other glues of animal origin, excluding casein glues of heading No. 35.01:**
3503.0010	---明胶及其衍生物	12	8		0	35	17	13	千克		---Gelatin and gelatin derivatives
3503.0010 01	明胶	12				35	17	13	千克	AB	Gelatin
3503.0010 90	明胶的衍生物(包括长方形、正方形明胶薄片不论是否表面加工或着色)	12				35	17	13	千克	AB	Gelatin derivatives; including gelatin in rectangular (including square) sheets, whether or not surface-worked or coloured
3503.0090	---其他	12	8		0	50	17	13	千克	AB	---Other

税则号列 Tariff Item.	货品名称	最惠国(%) MFN	协定(%)CT 东盟 CA	中巴 CP	中智 CC	普通 Gen	增值税率 VAT	出口退税 ED	计量单位 Unit	监管条件 SC	Article Description
35.04	**蛋白胨及其衍生物;其他税目未列名的蛋白质及其衍生物;皮粉,不论是否加入铬矾:**										**Peptones and their derivatives; other protein substances and their derivatives, not elsewhere specified or included; hide powder, whether or not chromed:**
3504.0010	---蛋白胨	3			0	11	17	13	千克		---Peptones
3504.0090	---其他	8	5		0	35	17	13	千克		---Other
35.05	**糊精及其他改性淀粉(例如,预凝化淀粉或酯化淀粉);以淀粉、糊精或其他改性淀粉为基本成分的胶:**										**Dextrins and other modified starches (for example, pregelatinized or esterified starches); glues based on starches, or on dextrins or other modified starches:**
3505.1000	-糊精及其他改性淀粉	12	8		9.6	50	17	13	千克		-Dextrins and other modified starches
3505.2000	-胶	20	12		12	50	17	13	千克		-Glues
35.06	**其他税目未列名的调制胶及其他调制粘合剂;适于作胶或粘合剂用的产品,零售包装每件净重不超过1公斤:**										**Prepared glues and other prepared adhesives, not elsewhere specified or included; products suitable for use as glues or adhesives, put up for retail sale as glues or adhesives, not exceeding a net weight of 1 kg:**
3506.1000	-适于作胶或粘合剂用的产品,零售包装每件净重不超过1千克	10	T3	9.2	8	90	17	13	千克		-Products suitable for use as glues or adhesives, put up for retail sale as glues or adhesives, not exceeding a net weight of 1kg
3506.1000 10	硅酮结构密封胶(零售包装每件净重不超过1千克)	10				90	17	13	千克	A	Structure sealing compound of silicone (put up for retail sale as glues or adhesives, not exceeding a net weight of 1kg)
3506.1000 90	其他适于作胶或粘合剂的零售产品(零售包装每件净重不超过1千克)	10				90	17	13	千克		Other-products suitable for use as glues or adhesives, put up for retail sale as glues or adhesives, not exceeding a net weight of 1kg
	-其他:										-Other:
	--以橡胶或税目39.01至39.13的聚合物为基本成分的粘合剂:										--Adhesives based on polymers of headings Nos. 39.01 to 39.13 or on rubber:
3506.9110	---以聚酰胺为基本成分的	10	8	7	8	90	17	13	千克		---Based on polyamide
3506.9120	---以环氧树脂为基本成分的	10	8	7	8	90	17	13	千克		---Based on epoxy resin
3506.9190	---其他	10	8	7	8	90	17	13	千克		---Other
3506.9190 10	非零售,硅酮结构密封胶	10				90	17	13	千克	A	Structure sealing compound of silicone, not put up for retail sale
3506.9190 90	其他橡胶或塑料为基本成分粘合剂[包括以人造树脂(环氧树脂除外)为基本成分的]	10				90	17	13	千克		Other adhesives based on polymers of headings Nos. 39.01 to 39.13 or on rubber
3506.9900	--其他	10	8	8.6	8	90	17	13	千克		--Other
35.07	**酶;其他税目未列名的酶制品:**										**Enzymes; prepared enzymes not elsewhere specified or included:**
3507.1000	-粗制凝乳酶及其浓缩物	6	5		0	30	17	13	千克		-Rennet and concentrates thereof
	-其他:										-Other:
3507.9010	---碱性蛋白酶	6	5		4.8	30	17	13	千克		---Basic proteinase
3507.9020	---碱性脂肪酶	6	5		4.8	30	17	13	千克		---Basic lipase
3507.9090	---其他	6	5		4.8	30	17	13	千克		---Other

第三十六章
炸药；烟火制品；火柴；引火合金；易燃材料制品

Chapter 36
Explosives; pyrotechnic products; matches; pyrophoric alloys; certain combustible preparations

注释：

一、本章不包括单独的已有化学定义的化合物，但下列注释二（一）、（二）所述物品除外。

二、税目36.06所称"易燃材料制品"，只适用于：

（一）聚乙醛、六甲撑四胺及类似物质，已制成片、棒或类似形状作燃料用的；以酒精为基本成分的固体或半固体燃料及类似的配制燃料；

（二）直接灌注香烟打火机及类似打火器用的液体燃料或液化气体燃料，其包装容器的容积不超过300立方厘米；

（三）树脂火炬、引火物及类似品。

Notes:

1. This Chapter does not cover separate chemically defined compounds other than those described in Note 2 (a) or (b) below.
2. The expression "articles of combustible materials" in heading No. 36.06 applies only to:
   (a) Metaldehyde, hexamethylenetetramine and similar substances, put up in forms (for example, tablets, sticks or similar forms) for use as fuels; fuels with as basis of alcohol, and similar prepared fuels, in solid or semi-solid form;
   (b) Liquid or liquefied-gas fuels in containers of a kind used for filling or refilling cigarette or similar lighters and of a capacity not exceeding 300 cm^3, and
   (c) Resin torches, firelighters and the like.

税则号列 Tariff Item.	货品名称	最惠国(%) MFN	协定(%)CT 东盟 CA	中巴 CP	中智 CC	普通 Gen	增值税率 VAT	出口退税 ED	计量单位 Unit	监管条件 SC	Article Description
36.01	**发射药：**										**Propellent powders:**
3601.0000	发射药	9	5		0	50	17	13	千克		Propellent powders
3601.0000 10	模压的胶质推进剂	9				50	17	13	千克	3	Colloidal propellant, molded
3601.0000 20	含硝化粘接剂及铝粉>5%的推进剂	9				50	17	13	千克	3	Propellant, containing cementing agent and aluminum powder >5%
3601.0000 90	其他发射药	9				50	17	13	千克		Other propellent powders
36.02	**配制炸药，但发射药除外：**										**Prepared explosives, other than propellent powders:**
3602.0010	---硝铵炸药	9	5		7.2	50	17	13	千克		---Based on ammonals nitrate
3602.0010 10	符合特定标准的硝胺炸药（硝胺类物质超过2%，或密度>1.8g/cm^3爆速>8000m/s）	9				50	17	13	千克	3	Explosives based on ammonals nitrate nitramine explosives up to definite standard (content of ammonals nitrate >2%, density >1.8g/cm^3, exploding velocity >8000m/s)
3602.0010 90	其他硝铵炸药，但发射药除外	9				50	17	13	千克		Other explosives based on ammonals nitrate, other than propellent powders
3602.0090	---其他	9	5		7.2	50	17	13	千克		---Other
3602.0090 10	符合特定标准的其他配制炸药（含六硝基芪>2%，或密度>1.8g/cm^3爆速>8000m/s）	9				50	17	13	千克	3	Other prepared explosives up to definite standard, (content of hexanitrostilbene >2%, density >1.8g/cm^3, exploding velocity >8000m/s)
3602.0090 90	其他配制炸药，但发射药除外	9				50	17	13	千克		Other prepared explosives, other than propellent powders
36.03	**安全导火索；导爆索；火帽或雷管；引爆器；电雷管：**										**Safety fuses; detonating fuses; percussion or detonating caps; igniters; electric detonators:**
3603.0000	安全导火索；导爆索；火帽或雷管；引爆器；电雷管	9	5		7.2	50	17	13	千克		Safety fuses; detonating fuses; percussion or detonating caps; igniters; electric detonators

税则号列 Tariff Item.	货品名称	最惠国(%) MFN	协定(%)CT 东盟 CA	中巴 CP	中智 CC	普通 Gen	增值税率 VAT	出口退税 ED	计量单位 Unit	监管条件 SC	Article Description
3603.0000 10	爆炸桥	9				50	17	13	千克	3	Detonating bridge
3603.0000 20	爆炸桥丝	9				50	17	13	千克	3	Detonating bridge filaments
3603.0000 30	冲击片	9				50	17	13	千克	3	Percussion cap
3603.0000 40	爆炸箔起爆器	9				50	17	13	千克	3	detonating foil igniter
3603.0000 50	使用单个或多个雷管的装置(由单一点火信号同时起爆,不包括仅使用起药的雷管)	9				50	17	13	千克	3	Devices with one or more detonating caps (detonated by one electric firing signal at the same time, other than those used detonating powder only)
3603.0000 60	炸药雷管点火装置(用于引爆上述税目3603各子目列名的爆炸配件的雷管)	9				50	17	13	千克	3	Ignitors of detonating caps (for detonating detonators assembled with articles of subheadings of heading 3603)
3603.0000 90	其他安全导火索、导爆索等引爆器件(包括火帽或雷管、引爆器、电雷管)	9				50	17	13	千克		Other safety fuses; detonating fuses; percussion or detonating caps; igniters; electric detonators
36.04	**烟花、爆竹、信号弹、降雨火箭、浓雾信号弹及其他烟火制品:**										**Fireworks, signalling flares, rain rockets, fog signals and other pyrotechnic articles:**
3604.1000	-烟花、爆竹	6	5		0	130	17	13	千克	B	-Fireworks
3604.9000	-其他	6	5		0	100	17	13	千克		-Other
36.05	**火柴,但税目36.04的烟火制品除外:**										**Matches, other than pyrotechnic articles of heading No. 36.04:**
3605.0000	火柴,但税目36.04的烟火制品除外	6	T3		4.8	100	17	13	千克		Matches, other than pyrotechnic articles of heading 36.04
36.06	**各种形状的铈铁及其他引火合金;本章注释二所述的易燃材料制品:**										**Ferro-cerium and other pyrophoric alloys in all forms; articles of combustible materials as specified in Note 2 to this Chapter:**
3606.1000	-直接灌注香烟打火机及类似打火器用的液体燃料或液化气体燃料,其包装容器的容积不超过300立方厘米	10	5		0	80	17	13	千克		-Liquid or liquefied-gas fuels in containers of a kind used for filling or refilling cigarette or similar lighters and of a capacity not exceeding 300 cm^3
	-其他:										-Other:
	---铈铁及其他引火合金:										---Ferro-cerium and other pyrophoric alloys:
3606.9011	----已切成形可直接使用	9	5		0	80	17	13	千克		----Cut to shape, for immediate use
3606.9019	----其他	9	5		0	50	17	13	千克		----Other
3606.9090	---其他	9	5		0	80	17	13	千克		---Other

第三十七章
照相及电影用品

Chapter 37
Photographic or cinematographic goods

注释：

一、本章不包括废碎料。

二、本章所称"摄影"，是指光或其他射线作用于感光面上直接或间接形成可见影像的过程。

Notes：

1. This Chapter does not cover waste or scrap.

2. In this Chapter the word "photographic" relates to the process by which visible images are formed, directly or indirectly, by the action of light or other forms of radiation on photosensitive surfaces.

税则号列 Tariff Item.	货品名称	最惠国(%) MFN	协定(%) 东盟 CA	协定(%) 中巴 CP	协定(%) 中智 CC	普通 Gen	增值税率 VAT	出口退税 ED	计量单位 Unit	监管条件 SC	Article Description
37.01	**未曝光的摄影感光硬片及平面软片，用纸、纸板及纺织物以外任何材料制成；未曝光的一次成像感光平片，不论是否分装：**										**Photographic plates and film in the flat, sensitized, unexposed, of any material other than paper, paperboard or textiles; instant print film in the flat, sensitized, unexposed, whether or not in packs:**
3701.1000	-X 光用	20			16	40	17	13	平方米		-For X-ray
3701.2000	-一次成像平片	5			0	40	17	13	千克		-Instant print film
	-其他硬片及软片，任何一边超过 255 毫米：										-Other plates and film, with any side exceeding 255 mm:
	---照相制版用：										---For preparing printing plates or cylinders:
3701.3021	----激光照排片	T2			0	T2	17	13	平方米		----Laser phototypesetting film
3701.3022	----PS 版	T2			0	T2	17	13	平方米		----Precoated sensitized plate
3701.3023	----CTP 版（计算机直接制版的热敏版材）	T2	T2		0	T2	17	13	平方米		----CTP plate
3701.3029	----其他	T2			0	T2	17	13	平方米		----Other
3701.3090	---其他	20	12		0	70	17	13	平方米		---Other
	-其他：										-Other:
3701.9100	--彩色摄影用	22	12		13.2	70	17	13	千克		--For colour photography (polychrome)
	--其他：										--Other:
3701.9920	---照相制版用	10	5		8	40	17	13	平方米		---For preparing printing plates or cylinders
3701.9920 10	超微粒干板	10				40	17	13	平方米		Ultramicron dry plate
3701.9920 90	照相制版用其他未曝光软片及硬片（非彩色摄影用，边长≤255mm；超微粒干版除外）	10				40	17	13	平方米		Other photographic plates and film in the flat sensitized for preparing printing plates or cylinders, with any side ≤255mm, other than ultramicron dry plate, other than for colour photography
3701.9990	---其他	25	12		20	70	17	13	平方米		---Other
37.02	**成卷的未曝光摄影感光胶片，用纸、纸板及纺织物以外任何材料制成；未曝光的一次成像感光卷片：**										**Photographic film in rolls, sensitized, unexposed, of any material other than paper, paperboard or textiles; instant print film in rolls, sensitized, unexposed:**
3702.1000	-X 光用	10			0	40	17	13	平方米		-For X-ray
	-无齿孔的其他胶片，宽度不超过 105 毫米：										-Other film, without perforations, of a width not exceeding 105 mm:
	--彩色摄影用										--For colour photography (polychrome)

税则号列 Tariff Item.	货品名称	最惠国(%) MFN	协定(%)CT 东盟 CA	中巴 CP	中智 CC	普通 Gen	增值税率 VAT	出口退税 ED	计量单位 Unit	监管条件 SC	Article Description
3702.3110	---次成像卷片	5			0	40	17	13	个/平方米		---Instant print film
3702.3190	---其它	T2	T2		T2	T2	17	13	个/平方米		---Other
	--其他涂卤化银乳液的:										--Other, with silver halide emulsion:
3702.3210	---一次成像卷片	5			0	40	17	13	平方米		---Instant print film
3702.3220	---照相制版用	T2	T2		0	T2	17	13	平方米		---For preparing printing plates or cylinders
3702.3290	---其他	T2	T2		T2	T2	17	13	平方米		---Other
	--其他:										--Other:
3702.3920	---照相制版用	T2	T2		0	T2	17	13	平方米		---For preparing printing plates or cylinders
3702.3990	---其他	T2	T2		T2	T2	17	13	平方米		---Other
	-无齿孔的其他胶片,宽度超过105毫米:										-Other film, without perforations, of a width exceeding 105 mm:
3702.4100	--彩色摄影用,宽度超过610毫米,长度超过200米	T2			T2	T2	17	13	平方米		--Of a width exceeding 610 mm and of a length exceeding 200 m, for colour photography (polychrome):
	--非彩色摄影用,宽度超过610毫米,长度超过200米:										--Of a width exceeding 610 mm and of a length exceeding 200 m, other than for colour photography:
	---照相制版用:										---For preparing printing plates or cylinders:
3702.4221	----印刷电路板制造用光致抗蚀干膜	T2	T2		0	T2	17	13	平方米		----Wide anticorrosive photographic plate for printed circuit processing
3702.4229	----其他	T2	T2		0	T2	17	13	平方米		----Other
	---其他:										---Other:
3702.4291	----红外或氦氖激光胶片	T2	T2		T2	T2	17	13	平方米		----Infrared or helium neon laser film
3702.4291 01	未曝光红外或氦氖激光胶片(宽长胶卷指宽度>800mm、长度>1000m)	0				0	17	13	平方米		Infrared or helium neon laser film, unexposed, of a width >800mm, of a length >1000m
3702.4291 90	其他未曝光红外或氦氖激光胶片(610mm<宽度≤800m、200m<长度<100m)	0				0	17	13	平方米		Other infrared or helium neon laser film, unexposed, 610mm< width ≤800mm, 200m< length ≤1000m
3702.4299	----其他	T2	T2		T2	T2	17	13	平方米		----Other
	--宽度超过610毫米,长度不超过200米:										--Of a width exceeding 610 mm and of a length not exceeding 200 m:
	---照相制版用:										---For preparing printing plates or cylinders:
3702.4321	----激光照排片	T2	T2		0	T2	17	13	平方米		----Laser phototypesetting film
3702.4329	----其他	T2	T2		0	T2	17	13	平方米		----Other
3702.4390	---其他	T2	T2		T2	T2	17	13	平方米		---Other
	--宽度超过105毫米,但不超过610毫米:										--Of a width exceeding 105 mm but not exceeding 610 mm:
	---照相制版用:										---For preparing printing plates or cylinders:
3702.4421	----激光照排片	T2	T2		0	T2	17	13	平方米		----Laser phototypesetting film
3702.4422	----印刷电路板制造用光致抗蚀干膜	T2	T2		0	T2	17	13	平方米		----Narrow anticorrosive photographic plate for printed circuit processing
3702.4429	----其他	T2	T2		0	T2	17	13	平方米		----Other
3702.4490	---其他	T2	T2		0	T2	17	13	平方米		---Other
	-彩色摄影用的其他胶片:										-Other film, for colour photography (polychrome):

税则号列 Tariff Item.	货品名称	最惠国(%) MFN	协定(%)CT 东盟 CA	中巴 CP	中智 CC	普通 Gen	增值税率 VAT	出口退税 ED	计量单位 Unit	监管条件 SC	Article Description
3702.5100	--宽度不超过16毫米,长度不超过14米	T2	T2		T2	T2	17	13	米/平方米		--Of a width not exceeding 16 mm and of a length not exceeding 14 m
3702.5200	--宽度不超过16毫米,长度超过14米	T2	T2		T2	T2	17	13	米/平方米		--Of a width not exceeding 16 mm and of a length exceeding 14 m
3702.5300	--幻灯片用,宽度超过16毫米,但不超过35毫米,长度不超过30米	T2	T2		T2	T2	17	13	米/平方米		--Of a width exceeding 16 mm but not exceeding 35 mm and of a length not exceeding 30 m, for slides
	--非幻灯片用,宽度超过16毫米,但不超过35毫米,长度不超过30米:										--Of a width exceeding 16 mm but not exceeding 35 mm and of a length not exceeding 30 m, other than for slides:
3702.5410	---宽度为35毫米,长度不超过2米	T2			0	T2	17	13	米/平方米		---Of a width 35 mm and of a length not exceeding 2 m
3702.5490	---其他	T2			0	T2	17	13	米/平方米		---Other
	--宽度超过16毫米,但不超过35毫米,长度超过30米:										--Of a width exceeding 16 mm but not exceeding 35 mm and of a length exceeding 30 m:
3702.5520	---电影胶片	T2			T2	T2	17	13	米/平方米		---Cinematographic film
3702.5590	---其他	T2			T2	T2	17	13	米/平方米		---Other
	--宽度超过35毫米:										--Of a width exceeding 35 mm:
3702.5620	---电影胶片	T2	T2		T2	T2	17	13	米/平方米		---Cinematographic film
3702.5690	---其他	T2	T2		T2	T2	17	13	米/平方米		---Other
	-其他:										-Other:
3702.9100	--宽度不超过16毫米	T2	T2		T2	T2	17	13	米/平方米		--Of a width not exceeding 16 mm
	--宽度超过16毫米,但不超过35毫米,长度不超过30米:										--Of a width exceeding 16 mm but not exceeding 35 mm and of a length not exceeding 30 m:
3702.9310	---宽度为35毫米,长度不超过2米	T2			T2	T2	17	13	米/平方米		---Of a width 35 mm and of a length not exceeding 2 m
3702.9390	---其他	T2			T2	T2	17	13	米/平方米		---Other
	--宽度超过16毫米,但不超过35毫米,长度超过30米:										--Of a width exceeding 16 mm but not exceeding 35 mm and of a length exceeding 30 m:
3702.9420	---电影胶片	T2			T2	T2	17	13	米/平方米		---Cinematographic film
3702.9490	---其他	T2			T2	T2	17	13	米/平方米		---Other
	--宽度超过35毫米:										--Of a width exceeding 35 mm:
3702.9520	---电影胶片	T2	T2		T2	T2	17	13	米/平方米		---Cinematographic film
3702.9590	---其他	T2	T2		T2	T2	17	13	米/平方米		---Other
37.03	**未曝光的摄影感光纸、纸板及纺织物:**										**Photographic paper, paperboard and textiles, sensitized, unexposed:**
	-成卷,宽度超过610毫米:										-In rolls of a width exceeding 610 mm:
3703.1010	---感光纸及纸板	18			14.4	100	17	13	千克		---Photographic paper and paperboard
3703.1090	---其他	18			14.4	70	17	13	千克		---Other
	-其他,彩色摄影用:										-Other, for colour photography (polychrome):
3703.2010	---感光纸及纸板	35			0	100	17	13	千克		---Photographic paper and paperboard
3703.2090	---其他	18			0	70	17	13	千克		---Other
	-其他:										-Other:
3703.9010	---感光纸及纸板	35			28	100	17	13	千克		---Photographic paper and paperboard
3703.9090	---其他	18			14.4	70	17	13	千克		---Other

税则号列 Tariff Item.	货品名称	最惠国(%) MFN	协定(%)CT 东盟 CA	中巴 CP	中智 CC	普通 Gen	增值税率 VAT	出口退税 ED	计量单位 Unit	监管条件 SC	Article Description
37.04	**已曝光未冲洗的摄影硬片、软片、纸、纸板及纺织物:**										**Photographic plates, film, paper, paperboard and textiles, exposed but not developed:**
3704.0010	---电影胶片	6.5	5		0	30	17	13	千克	Z	---Cinematographic film
3704.0090	---其他	18	12		10.8	70	17	13	千克		---Other
37.05	**已曝光已冲洗的摄影硬片及软片,但电影胶片除外:**										**Photographic plates and film, exposed and developed, other than cinematographic film:**
3705.1000	-供复制胶版用	18	12		14.4	70	17	13	千克		-For offset reproduction
	-其他										-Other
3705.9010	---教学专用幻灯片	0				0	17	13	千克		---Lantern slides, for educational use only
	---缩微胶片										---Mictofilms
3705.9021	----书籍、报刊的	0				0	17	13	千克		----For printed book and new spapers
3705.9029	----其他	4			0	14	17	13	千克		----Other
3705.9090	---其他	18	8		10.8	70	17	13	千克		---Other
37.06	**已曝光已冲洗的电影胶片,不论是否配有声道或仅有声道:**										**Cinematographic film, exposed and developed, whether or not incorporating sound track or consisting only of sound track:**
	-宽度在35毫米及以上:										-Of a width of 35 mm or more:
3706.1010	---教学专用	0				0	17	13	米	Z	---For educational use only
3706.1090	---其他	5			4	14	17	13	米	Z	---Other
	-其他:										-Other:
3706.9010	---教学专用	0				0	17	13	米	Z	---For educational use only
3706.9090	---其他	4			0	14	17	13	米	Z	---Other
37.07	**摄影用化学制剂(不包括上光漆、胶水、粘合剂及类似制剂);摄影用未混合产品;定量包装或零售包装可立即使用的:**										**Chemical preparations for photographic uses (other than varnishes, glues, adhesives and similar preparations); unmixed products for photographic uses, put up in measured portions or put up for retail sale in a form ready for use:**
3707.1000	-感光乳液	8	5		0	35	17	13	千克		-Sensitizing emulsions
3707.1000 01	不含银的感光乳液	8				35	17	13	千克		Sensitizing emulsions not containing silver
3707.1000 90	其他感光乳液	8				35	17	13	千克		Other sensitizing emulsions
	-其他:										-Other:
3707.9010	---冲洗照相胶卷及相片用	16	T3		12.8	100	17	13	千克		---For use in developing photographic film and photographs
3707.9020	---复印机用	10	T3		8	45	17	13	千克		---For use in photo-copying apparatus
3707.9090	---其他	8	T3		6.4	35	17	13	千克		---Other

第三十八章
杂项化学产品

注释：

一、本章不包括：

（一）单独的已有化学定义的元素及化合物，但下列各项除外：

1. 人造石墨（税目38.01）；
2. 制成税目38.08所述的形状或包装的杀虫剂、杀鼠剂、杀菌剂、除草剂、抗萌剂、植物生长调节剂、消毒剂及类似产品；
3. 灭火器的装配药及已装药的灭火弹（税目38.13）；
4. 下列注释二所规定的检定参照物；
5. 下列注释三（一）及三（三）所规定的产品。

（二）配制食品用的与食物或其他营养物质混合的化学品（一般归入税目21.06）；

（三）符合第二十六章注释三（一）或（二）的规定，含有金属、砷及其混合物的矿渣，矿灰及残渣（包括淤渣，但下水道淤泥除外）（税目26.20）；

（四）药品（税目30.03及30.04）；

（五）用于提取贱金属或生产贱金属化合物的废催化剂（税目26.20），主要用于回收贵金属的废催化剂（税目71.12），或某种形状（例如，精细粉末或纱网纱）的金属或金属合金催化剂（第十四类或第十五类）。

二、（一）税目38.22所称的“检定参照物”，是指附有证书的参照物，该证书标明了参照物属性的指标、确定这些指标的方法以及与每一指标相关的确定度，这些参照物适用于分析、校准和比较。

（二）除第二十八章和二十九章的产品外，检定参照物在本目录中应优先归入税目38.22。

三、税目38.24包括不归入本目录其他税目的下列货品：

（一）每颗重量不小于2.5克的氧化镁、碱金属或碱土金属卤化物制成的培养晶体（光学元件除外）；

（二）杂醇油；骨焦油；

（三）零售包装的除墨剂；

（四）零售包装的蜡纸改正液及其他改正液；

Chapter 38
Miscellaneous chemical products

Notes:

1. This Chapter does not cover:

(a) Separate chemically defined elements or compounds with the exception of the following:

(1) Artificial graphite (heading No. 38.01);

(2) Insecticides, rodenticides, fungicides, herbicides, anti-sprouting products and plant-growth regulators, disinfectants and similar products, put up as described in heading No. 38.08;

(3) Products put up as charges for fire-extinguishers or put up in fire-extinguishing grenades (heading No. 38.13);

(4) Certified reference materials specified in Note 2 below;

(5) Products specified in Note 3(a) or 3(c) below.

(b) Mixtures of chemicals with foodstuffs or other substances with nutritive value, of a kind used in the preparations of human foodstuffs (generally heading No. 21.06);

(c) Ash and residues (including sludges, other than sewage sludge), containing metals, arsenic or their mixtures and meeting the requirements of Note 3(a) or (b) to Chapter 26 (heading No. 26.20);

(d) Medicaments (heading No. 30.03 or 30.04);

(e) Spent catalysts of a kind used for the extraction of base metals or for the manufacture of chemical compounds of base metals (heading No. 26.20), spent catalysts of a kind used principally for the recovery of precious metal (heading No. 71.12) or catalysts consisting or metals of metal alloys in the form of, for example, finely divided powder or woven gauze (Section XIV or XV).

2. (a) For the purpose of heading No. 38.22, the expression "certified reference materials" means reference materials which are accompanied by a certificate which indicates the values of the certified properties, the methods used to detemine these values and the degree of certainty associated with each value and which are suitable for analytical, calibrating or referencing purposes;

(b) With the exception of the products of Chapter 28 or 29, for the classification of certified reference materials, heading No. 38.22 shall take precedence over any other heading in the Nomenclature.

3. Heading No. 38.24 includes the following goods which are not to be classified in any other heading of the Nomenclature:

(a) Cultured crystals (other than optical elements) weighing not less than 2.5 g each, of magnesium oxide or of the halides of the alkali or alkaline-earth metals;

(b) Fusel oil; Dippel's oil;

(c) Ink removers put up in packings for retail sale;

(d) Stencil correctors and other correcting fluids put up in packings for retail sale; and

(五)可熔性陶瓷测温器(例如,塞格测温锥)。

四、本目录所称"城市垃圾",是指从家庭、宾馆、餐馆、医院、商店、办公室等收集来的废物、马路和人行道的垃圾以及建筑垃圾或废墟废物。城市垃圾通常含有大量各种各样的材料,例如,塑料、橡胶、木材、纸张、纺织品、玻璃、金属、食物、破碎家具和其他已损坏或被丢弃的物品,但不包括:

(一)已从垃圾中分拣出来的单独的材料或物品,例如,塑料、橡胶、木材、纸张、纺织品、玻璃、金属及电池的废品,这些材料或物品应归入本目录中适当税目;

(二)工业废物;

(三)第三十章注释四(十)所规定的废药物;

(四)本章注释六(一)所规定的医疗废物。

五、税目38.25所称"下水道淤泥",是指城市污水处理厂产生的淤渣,包括预处理的废物、涮洗污垢和性质不稳定的淤泥。但适合作为肥料用的性质稳定的淤泥除外(第三十一章)。

六、税目38.25所称"其他废物"适用于:

(一)医疗废物,即医学研究、诊断、治疗以及其他内科、外科、牙科或兽医治疗所产生的被污染的废物,通常含有病菌和药物,需作专门处理(例如,脏的敷料、用过的手套及注射器);

(二)废有机溶剂;

(三)废的金属酸洗液、液压油、制动油及防冻液;

(四)其他化学工业及相关工业的废物。

但不包括主要含有石油及从沥青矿物提取的油类的废油(税目27.10)。

子目注释:

一、子目3808.50仅包括税目38.08的货品,含有一种或多种下列物质:艾氏剂(ISO);乐杀螨(ISO);毒杀芬(ISO);敌滴涕(ISO,INN)[1,1,1-三氯-2,2-双(4-氯苯基)乙烷];狄氏剂(ISO,INN);地乐酚(ISO)及其盐或酯;1,2-二溴乙烷(ISO);1,2-二氯乙烷(ISO);氟乙酰胺(ISO);七氯(ISO);六氯苯(ISO);1,2,3,4,5,6-六氯环乙烷[六六六(ISO)],包括林丹(ISO,INN);汞化合物;甲胺磷(ISO);久效磷(ISO);环氧乙烷(氧化乙烯);对硫磷(ISO);甲基对硫磷(ISO);五氯苯酚(ISO);磷胺(ISO);2,4,5-涕(ISO)(2,4,5-三氯苯氧基乙酸)及其盐或酯

二、子目3825.41和3825.49所称"废有机溶剂",是指主要含有有机溶剂的废物,不适合再作原产品使用,不论其是否用于回收溶剂。

(e) Ceramic firing testers, fusible (for example, Seger cones).

4. Throughout the Nomenclature, "municipal waste" means waste of a kind collected from households, hotels, restaurants, hospitals, shops, offices, etc., road and pavement sweepings, as well as construction and demolition waste. Municipal waste generally contains a large variety of materials such as plastics, rubber, wood, paper, textiles, glass, metals, food materials, broken furniture and other damaged or discarded articles. The term "municipal waste", however, does not cover:

(a) Individual materials or articles segregated from the waste, such as wastes of plastics, rubber, wood, paper, textiles, glass or metals and spent batteries which fall in their appropriate headings of the Nomenclature;

(b) Industrial waste;

(c) Waste pharmaceuticals, as defined in Note 4 (k) to Chapter 30;

(d) Clinical waste, as defined in Note 6 (a) below.

5. For the purposes of heading No. 38.25, "sewage sludge" means sludge arising from urban effluent treatment plant and includes pre-treatment waste, scourings and unstabilised sludge. Stabilised sludge when suitable for use as fertiliser is excluded (Chapter 31).

6. For the purposes of heading No. 38.25, the expression "other wastes" applies to:

(a) Clinical waste, that is, contaminated waste arising from medical research, diagnosis, treatment or other medical, surgical, dental or veterinary procedures, which often contain pathogens and pharmaceutical substances and require special disposal procedures (for example, soiled dressings, used gloves and used syringes);

(b) Waste organic solvents;

(c) Wastes of metal pickling liquors, hydraulic fluids, brake fluids and anti-freezing fluids; and

(d) Other wastes from chemical or allied industries.

The expression "other wastes" does not, however, cover wastes which contain mainly petroleum oils or oils obtained from bituminous minerals (heading No. 27.10).

Subheading Note:

1. Subheading No. 3808.50 only includes goods of tax item 38.08, including one or many of the following elements: HHDN, binapacry, camphechlor, captafol, chlordane, chlordimeform, chlorobenzilate, DDT, HEOD, dinoseb, (dinoseb acetate), 1, 2 - Ethylene di bromide, 1, 2 - Dichloroethane, floroacetamide, heptachlor, hexachlorobenzen, lindane, Mercury Compound, methamidophos, monocrotophos, Ethlene Oxide, parathion, parathion _ methyl, Pentachlorophenol and Phosphamidon.

2. For the purposes of subheading Nos. 3825.41 and 3825.49, "waste organic solvents" are wastes containing mainly organic solvents, not fit for further use as presented as primary products, whether or not intended for recovery of the solvents.

税则号列 Tariff Item.	货品名称	最惠国(%) MFN	协定(%) 东盟 CA	CT 中巴 CP	 中智 CC	普通 Gen	增值税率 VAT	出口退税 ED	计量单位 Unit	监管条件 SC	Article Description
38.01	**人造石墨;胶态或半胶态石墨;以石墨或其他碳为基本成分的糊状、块状、板状制品或半制品:**										**Artificial graphite; colloidal or semi-colloidal graphite; preparations based on graphite or other carbon in the form of pastes, blocks, plates or other semi-manufactures:**
3801.1000	-人造石墨	6.5	5		0	30	17	13	千克		-Artificial graphite
3801.1000 10	核级石墨(纯度高于百万分之五硼当量,密度大于1.50g/cm^3)	6.5				30	17	13	千克	3	Artificial graphite, nuclear purity (purity > 5/million boron equivalent, density > 1.50g/cm^3)
3801.1000 20	人造细晶粒整体石墨(20℃下的密度、拉伸断裂应变、热膨胀系数符合特殊要求)	6.5				30	17	13	千克	3	Artificial graphite, fine-crystalline bulk (density, tensile breaking strain, thermal expansion coefficient be in accordance with specific demands below 20℃)
3801.1000 90	其他人造石墨	6.5				30	17	13	千克	3	Other artificial graphite
3801.2000	-胶态或半胶态石墨	6.5	5		0	30	17	13	千克		-Colloidal or semi-colloidal graphite
3801.3000	-电极用碳糊及炉衬用的类似糊	6.5	5		0	35	17	13	千克		-Carbonaceous pastes for electrodes and similar pastes for furnace linings
3801.9000	-其他	6.5	5		0	35	17	13	千克	3	-Other
38.02	**活性碳;活性天然矿产品;动物炭黑,包括废动物炭黑:**										**Activated carbon; activated natural mineral products; animal black, including spent animal black:**
3802.1000	-活性碳	6.5	5	5.5	0	20	17	13	千克	G	-Activated carbon
3802.9000	-其他	10	T3		8	45	17	13	千克		-Other
3802.9000 10	濒危动物炭黑(包括废动物炭黑)	10				45	17	13	千克	FE	Black of animals in imminent dangers, activated natural mineral products
3802.9000 90	活性天然矿产品;其他动物炭黑(包括废动物炭黑)	10				45	17	13	千克		Activated natural mineral products; other animal black, including spent animal black
38.03	**妥尔油,不论是否精炼:**										**Tall oil whether or not refined:**
3803.0000	妥尔油,不论是否精炼	6.5	5		0	35	17	13	千克		Tall oil, whether or not refined
38.04	**木浆残余碱液,不论是否浓缩、脱糖或经化学处理,包括木素磺酸盐,但不包括税目38.03的妥尔油:**										**Residual lyes from the manufacture of wood pulp, whether or not concentrated, desugared or chemically treated, including lignin sulphonates, but excluding tall oil of heading No. 38.03:**
3804.0000	木浆残余碱液,不论是否浓缩、脱糖或经化学处理,包括木素磺酸盐,但不包括税目38.03的妥尔油	6.5	5		0	35	17	13	千克		Residual lyes from the manufacture of wood pulp, whether or not concentrated, desugared or chemically treated, including lignin sulphonates, but excluding tall oil of heading 38.03
38.05	**脂松节油、木松节油和硫酸盐松节油及其他萜烯油,用蒸馏或其他方法从针叶木制得;粗制二聚戊烯;亚硫酸盐松节油及其他粗制对异丙基苯甲烷;以α萜品醇为基本成分的松油:**										**Gum, wood or sulphate turpentine and other terpenic oils produced by the distillation or other treatment of coniferous woods; crude dipentene; sulphite turpentine and other crude paracymene; pine oil containing alpha-terpineol as the main constituent:**
3805.1000	-脂松节油、木松节油和硫酸盐松节油	6.5	5		0	50	17	13	千克		-Gum, wood or sulphate turpentine oils
	-其他:										-Other:
3805.9010	---松油	6.5	5		5.2	50	17	13	千克		---Ping oils

税则号列 Tariff Item.	货品名称	最惠国(%) MFN	协定(%) 东盟 CA	中巴 CP	CT 中智 CC	普通 Gen	增值税率 VAT	出口退税 ED	计量单位 Unit	监管条件 SC	Article Description
3805.9090	---其他	6.5	5		0	50	17	13	千克		---Other
38.06	**松香和树脂酸及其衍生物;松香精及松香油;再熔胶:**										**Rosin and resin acids, and derivatives thereof; rosin spirit and rosin oils; run gums:**
	-松香及树脂酸:										-Rosin and resin acids:
3806.1010	---松香	10	T3		0	70	17	13	千克	B	---Rosin
3806.1020	---树脂酸	10	5		0	70	17	13	千克	B	---Resin acides
	-松香盐、树脂酸盐及松香或树脂酸衍生物的盐,但松香加合物的盐除外:										-Salts of rosin, of resin acids or of derivatives of rosin or resin acids, other than salts of rosin adducts:
3806.2010	---松香盐及树脂酸盐	6.5	5		0	40	17	13	千克		---Salts of rosin, of resin acids
3806.2090	---其他	6.5	5		0	40	17	13	千克		---Other
3806.3000	-酯胶	6.5	5		0	50	17	13	千克	AB	-Ester gums
3806.9000	-其他	6.5	5		0	40	17	13	千克		-Other
3806.9000 10	歧化松香及松香衍生物	6.5				40	17	13	千克		Disproportionated rosin and its derivatives
3806.9000 90	其他松香及树脂酸衍生物(包括松香精及松香油;再熔胶)	6.5				40	17	13	千克		Other rosin and resin acids, and derivatives thereof; rosin spirit and rosin oils; run gums
38.07	**木焦油;精制木焦油;木杂酚油;粗木精;植物沥青;以松香、树脂酸或植物沥青为基本成分的啤酒桶沥青及类似制品:**										**Wood tar; wood tar oils; wood creosote; wood naphtha; vegetable pitch; brewers' pitch and similar preparations based on rosin, resin acids or on vegetable pitch:**
3807.0000	木焦油;精制木焦油;木杂酚油;粗木精;植物沥青;以松香、树脂酸或植物沥青为基本成分的啤酒桶沥青及类似制品	6.5	5		0	35	17	13	千克		Wood tar; wood tar oils; wood creosote; wood naphtha; vegetable pitch; brewers' pitch and similar preparations based on rosin, resin acids or on vegetable pitch
38.08	**杀虫剂、杀鼠剂、杀菌剂、除草剂、抗萌剂、植物生长调节剂、消毒剂及类似产品,零售形状、零售包装或制成制剂及成品(例如,经硫磺处理的带子、杀虫灯芯、蜡烛及捕蝇纸):**										**Insecticides, rodenticides, fungicides, herbicides, anti-sprouting products and plantgrowth regulators, disinfectants and similar products, put up in forms or packings for retail sale or as preparations or articles (for example, sulphur-treated bands, wicks and candles, and fly-papers):**
	-本章子目注释一所规定的货品:										-Goods in subheading note 1 to this Chapter:
3808.5010	-零售包装	9	5		7.2	35	17	13	千克		---Put up for retail sale
3808.5010 10	零售包装的含有一种38章子目注释一所列物质的货品	9				35	13	13	千克	AS	Including a kind of the substances specified of the subsatances specified in subheading note 1 to Chapter 38 ,put up for retail sale
3808.5010 90	零售包装的含多种38章子目注释一所列物质的货品	9				35	13	13	千克	AX	Including many kind of the substances specified of the subsatances specified in subheading note 1 to Chapter 38 ,put up for retail sale
3808.5090	---其他	5			4	11	17	13	千克		---Other

税则号列 Tariff Item.	货品名称	最惠国(%) MFN	协定(%)CT 东盟 CA	中巴 CP	中智 CC	普通 Gen	增值税率 VAT	出口退税 ED	计量单位 Unit	监管条件 SC	Article Description
3808.5090 10	非零售包装的含有一种38章子目注释一所列物质的货品	5				11	17	13	千克	AS	Including a kind of the substances specified of the subsatances specified in subheading note 1 to Chapter 38, put up for retail sale
3808.5090 90	非零包装的含多种38章子目注释一所列物质的货品	5				11	17	13	千克	AX	Including many kind of the substances specified of the subsatances specified in subheading note 1 to Chapter 38, put up for retail sale
	---其他:										---Other:
	--杀虫剂:										---Insecticides:
	---零售包装:										---Put up for retail sale
3808.9111	---蚊香	10	5	0	8	80	17	13	千克	AS	---Mospuito smudges
3808.9119	---其他	10	5	7	8	35	13	11	千克	AS	---Other
3808.9190	---其他	6	5	4.2	4.8	11	13	11	千克	AS	---Other
	---杀菌剂:										---Fungicides:
3808.9210	---零售包装	9	5		7.2	35	17		千克	S	---Put up for retail sale
3808.9290	---其他	6	5		4.8	11	13	11	千克		---Other
3808.9290 10	非零售包装的医用杀菌剂	6				11	17	11	千克		Medical fungicides, not put up for retail sale
3808.9290 21	经农药杀菌剂浸渍的纸质水果套袋	6				11	17	13	千克	S	Paper bags for fruit protecion, agricultural fungicides scaked
3808.9290 29	非零售包装的其他农用杀菌剂成药	6				11	13	11	千克	S	Non-agricultural fungicides, not put up for retail sale, including non-medical fungicides
3808.9290 90	非零售包装的非农用杀菌剂成药(包括非医用杀菌剂)	6				11	13	11	千克		Antiseptic medicine for non-agricultural use with non-retail wrapping (including antiseptic for non-doctoral use)
	--除草剂、抗菌剂及植物生长调节剂										--Herbicides anti – sprouting products and plantgrowth regulators
	---除草剂:										---Herbicides:
3808.9311	----零售包装	9	T3		7.2	35	13	11	千克	AS	----Put up for retail sale
3808.9319	----其他	5		4.5	4	11	13	11	千克	ASa	----Other
	---其他:										---Other:
3808.9391	----零售包装	9	T3	8.3	7.2	35	13	11	千克	S	----Put up for retail sale
3808.9399	----其他	6	T3	5.5	4.8	14	13	11	千克	S	----Other
3808.9400	--消毒剂	9	T3		7.2	35	17	13			--Disinfectapts
3808.9400 10	医用消毒剂	9				35	17	13	千克		Medical disinfectants
3808.9400 90	非医用消毒剂	9				35	13	11	千克		Non-medical disinfectants
	--其他:										--Other:
3808.9910	---零售包装	9	5		7.2	35	13	11	千克	S	---Put up for retail sale
3808.9990	---其他	9	5		7.2	14	13	11	千克	S	---Other
38.09	**纺织、造纸、制革及类似工业用的其他税目未列名的整理剂、染料加速着色或固色助剂及其他产品和制剂(例如,修整剂及媒染剂):**										**Finishing agents, dye carriers to accelerate the dyeing or fixing of dyestuffs and other products and preparations (for example, dressings and mordants), of a kind used in the textile, paper, leather or like industries, not elsewhere specified or included:**
3809.1000	-以淀粉物质为基本成分	10	T3	0	0	35	17	13	千克		-With a basis of amylaceous substances
	-其他:										-Other:
3809.9100	--纺织工业及类似工业用	6.5	5	0	0	35	17	13	千克		--Of a kind used in the textile or like industries

税则号列 Tariff Item.	货品名称	最惠国(%) MFN	协定(%) CT			普通 Gen	增值税率 VAT	出口退税 ED	计量单位 Unit	监管条件 SC	Article Description
			东盟 CA	中巴 CP	中智 CC						
3809.9200	--造纸工业及类似工业用	6.5	5	0	5.2	35	17	13	千克		--Of a kind used in the paper or like industries
3809.9300	--制革工业及类似工业用	6.5	5	0	5.2	35	17	13	千克		--Of a kind used in the leather or like industries
38.10	**金属表面酸洗剂;焊接用的焊剂及其他辅助剂;金属及其他材料制成的焊粉或焊膏;作焊条芯子或焊条涂料用的制品:**										**Pickling preparations for metal surfaces; fluxes and other auxiliary preparations for soldering, brazing or welding; soldering, brazing or welding powders and pastes consisting of metal and other materials; preparations of a kind used as cores or coatings for welding electrodes or rods:**
3810.1000	-金属表面酸洗剂;金属及其他材料制成的焊粉或焊膏	6.5	5	6	5.2	35	17	13	千克		-Pickling preparations for metal surfaces; soldering, brazing or welding powders and pastes consisting of metal and other materials
3810.9000	-其他	6.5	5		0	35	17	13	千克		-Other
38.11	**抗震剂、抗氧剂、防胶剂、粘度改良剂、防腐蚀制剂及其他配制添加剂,用于矿物油(包括汽油)或与矿物油同样用途的其他液体:**										**Anti-knock preparations, oxidation inhibitors, gum inhibitors, viscosity improvers, anti-corrosive preparations and other prepared additives, for mineral oils (including gasoline) or for other liquids used for the same purposes as mineral oils:**
	-抗震剂:										-Anti-knock preparations:
3811.1100	--以铅化合物为基本成分	6.5	5		0	35	17	13	千克		--Based on lead compounds
3811.1900	--其他	6.5	5		0	35	17	13	千克		--Other
	-润滑油添加剂:										-Additives for lubricating oils:
3811.2100	--含有石油或从沥青矿物提取的油类	6.5	5		5.2	35	17	13	千克		--Containing petroleum oils or oils obtained from bituminous minerals
3811.2900	--其他	6.5	5	5.5	0	35	17	13	千克		--Other
3811.9000	-其他	6.5	5		0	35	17	13	千克		-Other
38.12	**配制的橡胶促进剂;其他税目未列名的橡胶或塑料用复合增塑剂;橡胶或塑料用抗氧制剂及其他复合稳定剂:**										**Prepared rubber accelerators; compounds plasticizers for rubber or plastics, not elsewhere specified or included; anti-oxidizing preparations and other compound stabilizers for rubber or plastics:**
3812.1000	-配制的橡胶促进剂	6	5		0	20	17	13	千克		-Prepared rubber accelerators
3812.2000	-橡胶或塑料用复合增塑剂	6.5	5		5.2	35	17	13	千克		-Compound plasticizers for rubber or plastics
	-橡胶或塑料用抗氧制剂及其他复合稳定剂:										-Anti-oxidizing preparations and other compound stabilizers for rubber or plastics:
3812.3010	---橡胶防老剂	6	5		4.8	20	17	13	千克		---Rubber antioxidants
3812.3090	---其他	6.5	5	4.6	5.2	35	17	13	千克		---Other
38.13	**灭火器的装配药;已装药的灭火弹:**										**Preparations and charges for fire-extinguishers; charged fire-extinguishing grenades:**

税则号列 Tariff Item.	货品名称	最惠国(%) MFN	协定(%) CT			普通 Gen	增值税率 VAT	出口退税 ED	计量单位 Unit	监管条件 SC	Article Description
			东盟 CA	中巴 CP	中智 CC						
3813.0010	---灭火器的装配药	6.5	5		0	35	17	13	千克		---Preparations and charges for fire-extinguishers
3813.0020	---已装药的灭火弹	10	5		0	70	17	13	千克		---Charged fire-extinguishing grenades
38.14	**其他税目未列名的有机复合溶剂及稀释剂;除漆剂:**										**Organic composite solvents and thinners, not elsewhere specified or included; prepared paint or varnish removers:**
3814.0000	其他税目未列名的有机复合溶剂及稀释剂;除漆剂	10	T3	9	8	50	17	13	千克		Organic composite solvents and thinners, not elsewhere specified or included; prepared paint or varnish removers
38.15	**其他税目未列名的反应引发剂、反应促进剂、催化剂:**										**Reaction initiators, reaction accelerators and catalytic preparations, not elsewhere specified or included:**
	-载体催化剂:										-Supported catalysts:
3815.1100	--以镍及其化合物为活性物的	6.5	5		5.2	35	17	13	千克		--With nickel or nickel compounds as the active substance
3815.1200	--以贵金属及其化合物为活性物的	6.5	5		0	35	17	13	千克		--With precious metal or precious metal compounds as the active substance
3815.1200 10	载铂催化剂(为了从重水中回收氚或为了生产重水而专门设计或制备,用于加速氢和水之间的氢同位素交换反应)	6.5				35	17	13	千克	3	catalyzer containing platinum
3815.1200 90	其他以贵金属为活性物的载体催化剂	6.5				35	17	13	千克		Other supported catalysts with precious metal compounds as the active substance
3815.1900	--其他	6.5	5	4.6	5.2	35	17	13	千克		--Other
3815.9000	-其他	6.5	5	6	5.2	35	17	13	千克		-Other
38.16	**耐火的水泥、灰泥、混凝土及类似耐火混合制品,但税目38.01的产品除外:**										**Refractory cements, mortars, concretes and similar compositions, other than products of heading 38.01:**
3816.0000	耐火的水泥、灰泥、混凝土及类似耐火混合制品,但税目38.01的产品除外	6.5	T3		5.2	35	17	13	千克		Refractory cement, mortars, concretes and similar compositions, other than products of heading 38.01
38.17	**混合烷基苯及混合烷基萘,但税目27.07及29.02的货品除外:**										**Mixed alkylbenzenes and mixed alkylnaphthalenes, other than those of heading No. 27.07 or 29.02:**
3817.0000	混合烷基苯及混合烷基萘	6.5	5		0	35	17	13	千克		Mixed alkylbenzenes and alkylnaphthalenes
3817.0000 01	混合烷基苯(品目27.07及29.02的货品除外)	6.5				35	17	13	千克		Mixed alkylbenzenes, other than those of heading No. 27.07 or 29.02
3817.0000 90	混合烷基萘(品目27.07及29.02的货品除外)	6.5				35	17	13	千克		Mixed alkylnaphthalenes, other than those of heading No. 27.97 or 29.02
38.18	**经掺杂用于电子工业的化学元素,已切成圆片、薄片或类似形状;经掺杂用于电子工业的化合物:**										**Chemical elements doped for use in electronics, in the form of discs, wafers or similar forms; chemical compounds doped for use in electronics:**
	---直径在7.5厘米及以上的单晶硅切片:										---Monocrystalline sillicon, in the form of discs, wafers or similar form, 7.5 cm or more in diameter:

税则号列 Tariff Item.	货品名称	最惠国(%) MFN	协定(%) 东盟 CA	协定(%) 中巴 CP	CT 中智 CC	普通 Gen	增值税率 VAT	出口退税 ED	计量单位 Unit	监管条件 SC	Article Description
3818.0011	----直径在 15.24 厘米及以下的	0				11	17	13	千克		----Diameter not exceeding 15.24cm
3818.0019	----其他	0				11	17	13	千克		----Other
3818.0090	---其他	0				17	17	13	千克		---Other
38.19	**闸用液压油及其他液压传动用液体，不含石油或从沥青矿物提取的油类，或者按重量计石油或从沥青矿物提取的油类含量低于70%：**										**Hydraulic brake fluids and other prepared liquids for hydraulic transmission, not containing or containing less than 70% by weight of petroleum oils or oils obtained from bituminous minerals:**
3819.0000	闸用液压油及其他液压传动用液体，不含石油或从沥青矿物提取的油类，或者按重量计石油或从沥青矿物提取的油类含量低于70%	6.5	5		0	35	17	13	千克		Hydraulic brake fluids and other prepared liquids for hydraulic transmission, not containing or containing less than 70% by weight of petroleum oils or oils obtained from bituminous minerals
38.20	**防冻剂及解冻剂：**										**Anti-freezing preparations and prepared de-icing fluids:**
3820.0000	防冻剂及解冻剂	10	T3		0	35	17	13	千克		Anti-freezing preparations and prepared de-icing fluids
38.21	**制成的供微生物（包括病毒及类的品）或植物、人体、动物细胞生长或维持用的培养茎：**										The cultivating stalks that support the growth or maintenance of the microorganism (including virus and the like) or plants, human beings, animals and cells.
3821.0000	制成的供微生物（包括病毒及类似品）生长或维持用的培养茎	3			0	11	17	13	千克		The cultivating stalks that support the growth or maintenance of the microorganism (including virus and the like) or plants, human beings, animals and cells.
38.22	**附于衬背上的诊断或实验用试剂及不论是否附于衬背上的诊断或实验用配制试剂，但税目 30.02 及 30.06 的货品除外；检定参照物：**										**Diagnostic or laboratory reagents on a backing, prepared diagnostic or laboratory reagents whether or not on a backing, other than those of heading No. 30.02 or 30.06; certified reference materials:**
3822.0010	---附于衬背上的	4			3.2	35	17	13	千克		---On a backing
3822.0090	---其他	5			4	35	17	13	千克		---Other
38.23	**工业用单羧脂肪酸；精炼所得的酸性油；工业用脂肪醇：**										**Industrial monocarboxylic fatty acids; acid oils from refining; industrial fatty alcohols:**
	-工业用单羧脂肪酸；精炼所得的酸性油：										-Industrial monocarboxylic fatty acids; acid oils from refining:
3823.1100	--硬脂酸	16	T3		12.8	50	17	13	千克	B	--Stearic acid
3823.1200	--油酸	16	8		9.6	50	17	13	千克	B	--Oleic acid
3823.1300	--妥尔油脂肪酸	16	8		9.6	50	17	13	千克	B	--Tall oil fatty acids
3823.1900	--其他	16	8		9.6	50	17	13	千克	B	--Other
3823.7000	-工业用脂肪醇	13	8		7.8	50	17	13	千克	B	-Industrial fatty alcohols

税则号列 Tariff Item.	货品名称	最惠国 (%) MFN	协定(%)CT 东盟 CA	中巴 CP	中智 CC	普通 Gen	增值税率 VAT	出口退税 ED	计量单位 Unit	监管条件 SC	Article Description
38.24	**铸模及铸芯用粘合剂;其他税目未列名的化学工业及其相关工业的化学产品及配制品(包括由天然产品混合组成的):**										**Prepared binders for foundry moulds or cores; chemical products and preparations of the chemical or allied industries (including those consisting of mixtures of natural products), not elsewhere specified or included:**
3824.1000	-铸模及铸芯用粘合剂	6.5	5		0	35	17	13	千克		-Prepared binders for foundry moulds or cores
3824.3000	-自身混合或与金属粘合剂混合的未烧结金属碳化物	6.5	5		0	35	17	13	千克		-Non-agglomerated metal carbides mixed together or with metallic binders
3824.3000 10	混合的未烧结金属碳化物(包括自身混合或与金属粘合剂混合的)	6.5				35	17	13	千克	4xy	Non – agglomerated metal carbides, containing mixed together or with metallic binders
3824.3000 90	其他混合的未烧结金属碳化物(包括自身混合或与金属粘合剂混后的)	6.5				35	17	13	千克		Other non – agglomerated metal carbides, containing mixed together or with metallic binders
3824.4000	-水泥、灰泥及混凝土用添加剂	6.5	T3		5.2	35	17	13	千克		-Prepared additives for cements, mortars or concretes
3824.5000	-非耐火的灰泥及混凝土	6.5	5		5.2	35	17	13	千克		-Non-refractory mortars and concretes
3824.6000	-子目 2905.44 以外的山梨醇	14	8		8.4	40	17	13	千克		-Sorbitol other than that of subheading No. 2905.44
	-含有甲烷、乙烷或丙烷的全卤化衍生物的混合物:										-Compounds containing halogenation derivative of methane, ethane propane
3824.7100	--含全氯氟烃(CFC_{S})的不论是否含氢氯氟烃($HCFC_{S}$)、全氟烃(PFC_{S})或氢氟烃(HFC_{S})	6.5	5		0	35	17	13	千克		--Containing acyclic hydrocarbons perhalogenated only with fluorine and chlorine
3824.7100 11	二氯二氟甲烷和二氟乙烷的混合物(R-500)	6.5				35	17	13	千克	14xy	Mixed substance with dich loride and dilfluorine methane and. difluorine ethane
3824.7100 12	一氯二氟甲烷和二氯二氟甲烷的混合物(R-501)	6.5				35	17	13	千克	14xy	mixed substance with monochloride and dilfluorine methane and dichloride and dilfluorine methane
3824.7100 13	一氯二氟甲烷和一氯五氟乙烷的混合物(R-502)	6.5				35	17	13	千克	14xy	mixed substance with monochloride and dilfluorine methane and monochloride and 5 – fluorine ethane
3824.7100 14	三氟甲烷和一氯三氟甲烷的混合物(R-503)	6.5				35	17	13	千克	14xy	mixed substance with trifluorine methane and monochloride and 3 – fluorine methane
3824.7100 15	二氟甲烷和一氯五氟乙烷的混合物(R-504)	6.5				35	17	13	千克	14xy	mixed substance with dilfluorine methane and monochloride and 5 – fluorine ethane
3824.7100 16	二氯二氟甲烷和一氟一氯甲烷的混合物(R-505)	6.5				35	17	13	千克	14xy	mixed substance with dichloride and dilfluorine methane and monochloride and monofluorine methane
3824.7100 17	一氟一氯甲烷和二氯四氟乙烷的混合物(R-506)	6.5				35	17	13	千克	14xy	mixed substance with monochloride and monofluorine methane and dichloride and 4 – fluorine ethane

税则号列 Tariff Item.	货品名称	最惠国(%) MFN	协定(%)CT 东盟 CA	 中巴 CP	 中智 CC	普通 Gen	增值税率 VAT	出口退税 ED	计量单位 Unit	监管条件 SC	Article Description
3824.7100 18	二氯二氟甲烷和二氯四氟乙烷的混合物(R-400)	6.5				35	17	13	千克	14xy	mixed substance with dichloride and dil-fluorine methane and dichloride and 4 – fluorine ethane
3824.7100 90	其他含甲烷或丙烷的全氯氟烃(CFCS)的混合物(不论是否含甲烷、乙烷或丙烷的氢氯烃(HCFCS)全氟烃(PFCS)或氢氟烃(HFCS))	6.5				35	17	13	千克		Other mixtures containing perhalogenated derivatives of acyclic hydrocarbons . containing acyclic perhalogenated only with flourine and chlorine
3824.7200	--含溴氯二氟甲烷、溴三氟甲烷或二溴四氟乙烷的混合物	6.5	5		0	35	17	13	千克		--Containing Bromochlorodifluoromethane or Bromotetrafluoroethane
3824.7300	--含氢溴氟烃(HBFC$_S$)的	6.5	5		0	35	17	13	千克		--Containing HBFCs
3824.7400	--含氢氯氟烃(HCFC$_S$)的不论是否含全氟烃(PFC$_S$)或氢氟烃(HFC$_S$),但不含全氯氟烃(CFC$_S$)	6.5	5		0	35	17	13	千克		--Containing HCFCs but not CFCs, whether containing PFCs or HFCs or not
3824.7500	--含四氯化碳的	6.5	T3	6	5.2	35	17	13	千克		--Containing Carbon tetrachloride
3824.7600	--含1,1,1-三氯乙烷(甲基氯仿)的	6.5	T3	6	5.2	35	17	13	千克		
3824.7700	--含溴化甲烷(甲基溴)或溴氯甲烷的	6.5	5		0	35	17	13	千克		--Containing1,1,1 – Trichloroe or
3824.7800	--含全氟烃(PFC$_S$)或氢氟烃(HFC$_S$)的,但不含全氯氟烃(CFC$_S$)或氢氯氟烃(HCFC$_S$)的	6.5	T3	6	5.2	35	17	13	千克		--Containing PFCS and HFCs, but not CFCs or HCFCs
	-含环氧乙烷(氧化乙烯)、多溴联苯(PBB$_S$)、多氯联苯(PCB$_S$)、多氯三联苯(PCT$_S$)或三(2,3一二溴丙基)磷酸酯的混合物及制品:										-Compounds and its produce containing ethylene oxide, PBBs, PCTs or sulphosuccinic acid ester
3824.7900	--其他	6.5	5		0	35	17	13	千克		--Other
3824.8100	--含环氧乙烷(氧化乙烯)的	6.5	T3	6	5.2	35	17	13	千克		--Containing ethylene oxide
3824.8200	--含多氯联苯(PCB$_S$)、多氯三联苯(PCT$_S$)或多溴联苯(PBB$_S$)的	6.5	T3	6	5.2	35	17	13	千克	X	--Containing PCBS, PCTs or PBBs
3824.8300	--含三(2,3-二溴丙基)磷酸酯的	6.5	T3	6	5.2	35	17	13	千克		--Sulphosuccinic acid ester
	-其他:										-Other:
3824.9010	---杂醇油	6.5	T3	5.5	5.2	40	17	13	千克		---Fusel oil
3824.9020	---除墨剂、蜡纸改正液及类似品	9	T3	8.3	7.2	80	17	13	千克		---Ink-removers, stencil correctors and the like
3824.9030	---增炭剂	6.5	T3		5.2	35	17	13	千克		---Carburetant
3824.9090	---其他	6.5	5	6	0	35	17		千克		---Other
3824.9090 01	高钛渣(二氧化钛质量百分含量>70%的)	6.5				35	17		千克		Titania Slag (proportion of Titania >70%)

税则号列 Tariff Item.	货 品 名 称	最惠国(%) MFN	协定(%)CT 东盟 CA	中巴 CP	中智 CC	普通 Gen	增值税率 VAT	出口退税 ED	计量单位 Unit	监管条件 SC	Article Description
3824.9090 02	生产等离子显示屏用的银电极、价质、隐蔽、荧光粉浆料	6.5				35	17		千克		Silver electrode, medium, concealment, phosphor pastes
3824.9090 03	电极浆料(主要成分为银,镍或铜和有机溶剂,用于生产片式陶瓷电容器)	6.5				35	17		千克		Electrode paste (mainly containing silver and organic solvent, used for manufacturing chip ceramic capactiors)
3824.9090 04	水解物或水解料、DMC(六甲基环三硅氧烷,八甲基环四硅氧烷,十甲基环五硅氧烷,十二甲基环六硅氧烷中任何2种,3种或4种组成的混合物)	6.5				35	17		千克		Hydrolysis, DMC (compounds that made up of any of Hexamethyl cyclotrisiloxane, Octamethyl cyclotetraoxysilane, decamethyl cyclopentasiloxane and Dodecamethyl cyclohexasiloxane)
3824.9090 05	核苷酸类食品添加剂	6.5				35	17		千克		Ucleotideadditives
3824.9090 10	粗制碳化硅(其中碳化硅含量大于15%(按重量计))	6.5				35	17		千克	y4x	Silicon carbide, rough (Silicon carbide >15% by weight)
3824.9090 20	混胺(二甲胺和三乙胺混合物的水溶液)	6.5				35	13		千克	3	Mixed amine (the solution of mixture of Dimethylamine and Triethylamine)
3824.9090 90	其他编号未列名的化工产品	6.5				35	17		千克		Other chemical products and preparations of the chemical or allied industried, not elsewhere specified or included
38.25	**其他税目未列名的化学工业及其相关工业的副产品;城市垃圾;下水道淤泥;本章注释六所规定的其他废物:**										**Residual products of the chemical or allied industries, not elsewhere specified or included; municipal waste; sewage sludge; other wastes specified in Note 6 to this Chapter:**
3825.1000	-城市垃圾	6.5	5		0	35	17		千克	9	-Municipal waste
3825.2000	-下水道淤泥	6.5	5		0	35	17		千克	9	-Sewage sludge
3825.3000	-医疗废物	6.5	5		0	35	17		千克	9	-Clinical waste
	-废有机溶剂:										-Waste organic solvents:
3825.4100	--卤化物的	6.5	5		0	35	17		千克	9	--Halogenated
3825.4900	--其他	6.5	5		0	35	17		千克	9	--Other
3825.5000	-废的金属酸洗液、液压油、制动油及防冻液	6.5			0	35	17		千克	9	-Wastes of metal pickling liquors, hydraulic fluids, brake fluids and anti-freeze fluids
	-其他化学工业及相关工业的废物:										-Other wastes from chemical or allied industries:
3825.6100	--主要含有有机成分的	6.5	5		5.2	35	17		千克	9	--Mainly containing organic constituents
3825.6900	--其他	6.5	5		0	35	17		千克	9	--Other
3825.9000	-其他	6.5	5		0	35	17		千克		-Other
3825.9000 10	浓缩糖蜜发酵液	6.5				35	17		千克		Condensed fermented molasses
3825.9000 90	其他编号未列名化工副产品及废物	6.5				35	17		千克	9	Other residual products of the chemical or allied industries, not elsewhere specified or included

第七类

塑料及其制品;橡胶及其制品

注释:

一、由两种或两种以上单独成分配套的货品,其部分或全部成分属于本类范围以内,混合后则构成第六类或第七类的货品,应按混合后产品归入相应的税目,但其组成成分必须同时符合下列条件:

(一)其包装形式足以表明这些成分不需经过改装就可以一起使用的;

(二)一起进口或出口的;

(三)这些成分的属性及相互比例足以表明是相互配用的。

二、除税目39.18或39.19的货品外,印有花纹、文字、图画的塑料、橡胶及其制品,如果所印花纹、字画作为其主要用途,应归入第四十九章。

SECTION Ⅶ

PLASTICS AND ARTICLES THEREOF; RUBBER AND ARTICLES THEREOF

Notes:

1. Goods put up in sets consisting of two or more separate constituents, some or all of which fall in this Section and are intended to be mixed together to obtain a product of Section Ⅵ or Ⅶ, are to be classified in the heading appropriate to that product, provided that the constituents are:
   (a) having regard to the manner in which they are put up, clearly identifiable as being intended to be used together without first being repacked;
   (b) presented together; and
   (c) identifiable, whether by their nature or by the relative proportions in which they are present, as being complementary one to another.
2. Except for the goods of heading No. 39.18 or 39.19, plastics, rubber, and articles thereof, printed with motifs, characters or pictorial representations, which are not merely incidental to the primary use of the goods, fall in Chapter 49.

第三十九章
塑料及其制品

注释:

一、本目录所称"塑料",是指税目39.01至39.14的材料,这些材料能够在聚合时或聚合后在外力(一般是热力和压力,必要时加入溶剂或增塑剂)作用下通过模制、浇铸、挤压、滚轧或其他工序制成一定的形状,成形后除去外力,其形状仍保持不变。

本目录所称"塑料",还应包括钢纸,但不包括第十一类的纺织材料。

二、本章不包括:

(一)税目27.10或34.03的润滑剂;

(二)税目27.12或34.04的蜡;

(三)单独的已有化学定义的有机化合物(第二十九章);

(四)肝素及其盐(税目30.01);

(五)税目39.01至39.13所列的任何产品溶于挥发性有机溶剂的溶液(胶棉除外),但溶剂的重量必须超过溶液重量的50%(税目32.08);税目32.12的压印箔;

(六)有机表面活性剂或税目34.02的制剂;

Chapter 39
Plastics and articles thereof

Notes:

1. Throughout the Nomenclature the expression "plastics" means those materials of headings Nos. 39.01 to 39.14 which are or have been capable, either at the moment of polymerization or at some subsequent stage, of being formed under external influence (usually heat and pressure, if necessary with a solvent or plasticizer) by moulding, casting, extruding, rolling or other process into shapes which are retained on the removal of the external influence.
   Throughout the Nomenclature any reference to "plastics" also includes vulcanized fibre. The expression, however, does not apply to materials regarded as textile materials of Section Ⅺ.
2. This Chapter does not cover:
   (a) Lubricant of heading No. 27.10 or 34.03.
   (b) Waxes of heading No. 27.12 or 34.04;
   (c) Separate chemically defined organic compounds (Chapter 29);
   (d) Heparin or its salts (heading No. 30.01);
   (e) Solutions (other than collodions) consisting of any of the products specified in headings Nos. 39.01 to 39.13 in volatile organic solvents when the weight of the solvent exceeds 50% of the weight of the solution (heading Nos. 32.08); stamping foils of heading No. 32.12;
   (f) Organic surface-active agents or preparations of heading No. 34.02;

(七)再熔胶及酯胶(税目38.06);

(八)配制的添加剂,用于矿物油(包括汽油)或与矿物油同样用途的其他液体(税目38.11)

(九)以第三十九章的聚乙二醇、聚硅氧烷或其他聚合物为基本成分的液压用液体。

(十)附于塑料衬背上的诊断或实验用试剂(税目38.22);

(十一)第四十章规定的合成橡胶及其制品;

(十二)鞍具及挽具(税目42.01);税目42.02的衣箱、提箱、手提包及其他容器;

(十三)第四十六章的缏条、编结品及其他制品;

(十四)税目48.14的壁纸;

(十五)第十一类的货品(纺织原料及纺织制品);

(十六)第十二类的物品(例如,鞋靴、帽类、雨伞、阳伞、手杖、鞭子、马鞭及其零件);

(十七)税目71.17的仿首饰;

(十八)第十六类的物品(机器、机械器具或电气器具);

(十九)第十七类的航空器零件及车辆零件;

(二十)第九十章的物品(例如,光学元件、眼镜架及绘图仪器);

(二十一)第九十一章的物品(例如,钟壳及表壳);

(二十二)第九十二章的物品(例如,乐器及其零件);

(二十三)第九十四章的物品(例如,家具、灯具、照明装置、灯箱及活动房屋);

(二十四)第九十五章的物品(例如,玩具、游戏品及运动用品);

(二十五)第九十六章的物品(例如,刷子、钮扣、拉链、梳子、烟斗的嘴及柄、香烟嘴及类似品、保温瓶的零件及类似品、钢笔、活动铅笔)。

三、税目39.01至39.11仅适用于化学合成的下列货品:

(一)温度在300℃时,压力转为1013毫巴后减压蒸馏出的液体合成聚烯烃以体积计小于60%的货品(税目39.01及39.02);

(二)非高度聚合的苯并呋喃-茚树脂(税目39.11);

(三)平均至少有五个单体单元的其他合成聚合物;

(四)聚硅氧烷(税目39.10);

(五)甲阶酚醛树脂(税目39.09)及其他预聚物。

四、所称"共聚物",包括在整个聚合物中按重量计没有一种单体单元的含量在95%及以上的各种聚合物。

(g) Run gums or ester gums (heading No. 38.06);

(h) Additives, used for mineral oils (including gasoline) or other liquids having the same functions as mineral oils (heading No. 38.11)

(i) Hydraulic fluid that include elements such as polyethylene gly, silicone or other polymers in Chapter 39.

(j) Diagnostic or laboratory reagents on a backing of plastics (heading No. 38.22);

(k) Synthetic rubber, as defined for the purposes of Chapter 40, or articles thereof;

(l) Saddlery or harness (heading No. 42.01) or trunks, suitcases, handbags or other containers of heading No. 42.02;

(m) Plaits, wickerwork or other articles of Chapter 46;

(n) Wall coverings of heading No. 48.14;

(o) Goods of Section XI (textiles and textile articles);

(p) Articles of Section XII (for example, footwear, headgear, umbrellas, sun umbrellas, walking-sticks, whips, riding-crops or parts thereof);

(q) Imitation jewellery of heading No. 71.17;

(r) Articles of Section XIV (machines and mechanical or electrical appliances);

(s) Parts of aircraft or vehicles of Section XVII;

(t) Articles of Chapter 90 (for example, optical elements, spectacle frames, drawing instruments);

(v) Articles of Chapter 91 (for example, clock or watch cases);

(w) Articles of Chapter 92 (for example, musical instruments or parts thereof);

(t) Articles of Chapter 94 (for example, furniture, lamps and lighting fittings. illuminated signs, prefabricated buildings);

(x) Articles of Chapter 95 (for example, toys, games, sports requisites); or

(y) Articles of Chapter 96 (for example, brushes, buttons, slide fasteners, combs, mouthpieces or stems for smoking pipes, cigaretteholders or the like, parts of vacuum flasks or the like, pens, propelling pencils).

3. Headings Nos. 39.01 to 39.11 apply only to goods of a kind produced by chemical synthesis, falling in the following categories:

(a) Liquid synthetic polyolefins of which less than 60% by volume distils at 300℃, after conversion to 1,013 millibars when a reduced-pressure distillation method is used (headings Nos. 39.01 and 39.02);

(b) Resins, not highly polymerized, of the coumarone-indene type (heading No. 39.11);

(c) Other synthetic polymers with an average of at least 5 monomer units;

(d) Silicones (heading No. 39.10);

(e) Resols (heading No. 39.09) and other prepolymers.

4. The expression "copolymers" covers all polymers in which no single monomer unit contributes 95% or more by weight to the total polymer content.

在本章中，除条文另有规定以外，共聚物（包括共缩聚物、共加聚物、嵌段共聚物及接枝共聚物）及聚合物混合体应按聚合物中重量最大的那种共聚单体单元所构成的聚合物归入相应税目。在本注释中，归入同一税目的聚合物的共聚单体单元应作为一种单体单元对待。

For the purposes of this Chapter, except where the context otherwise requires, copolymers (including copolycondensates, co-polyaddition products, block copolymers and graft copolymers) and polymer blends are to be classified in the heading covering polymers of that comonomer unit which predominates by weight over every other single comonomer unit. For the purposes of this Note, constituent comonomer units of polymers falling in the same heading shall be taken together.

如果没有任何一种共聚单体单元重量为最大，共聚物或聚合物混合体应按号列顺序归入其可归入的最末一个税目。

If no single comonomer unit predominates, copolymers or polymer blends, as the case may be, are to be classified in the heading which occurs last in numerical order among those which equally merit consideration.

五、化学改性聚合物，即聚合物主链上的支链通过化学反应发生了变化的聚合物，应按未改性的聚合物的相应税目归类。本规定不适用于接枝共聚物。

5. Chemically modified polymers, that is those in which only appendages to the main polymer chain have been changed by chemical reaction, are to be classified in the heading appropriate to the unmodified polymer. This provision does not apply to graft copolymers.

六、税目 39.01 至 39.14 所称"初级形状"，只限于下列各种形状：

（一）液状及糊状，包括分散体（乳浊液及悬浮液）及溶液；

（二）不规则形状的块，团、粉（包括压型粉）、颗粒、粉片及类似的散装形状。

6. In headings Nos. 39.01 to 39.04, the expression "primary forms" applies only to the following forms:

(a) Liquids and pastes, including dispersions (emulsions and suspensions) and solutions;

(b) Blocks of irregular shape, lumps, powders (including moulding powders), granules, flakes and similar bulk forms.

七、税目 39.15 不适用于已制成初级形状的单一的热塑材料废碎料及下脚料（税目 39.01 至 39.14）。

7. Heading No. 39.15 does not apply to waste, parings and scrap of a single thermoplastic material, transformed into primary forms (headings Nos. 39.01 to 39.14).

八、税目 39.17 所称"管子"，是指通常用于输送或供给气体或液体的空心制品或半制品（例如，肋纹浇花软管、多孔管），还包括香肠用肠衣及其他扁平管。除肠衣及扁平管外，内截面如果不呈圆形、椭圆形、矩形（其长度不超过宽度的 1.5 倍）或正几何形，则不能视为管子，而应作为异型材。

8. For the purposes of heading No. 39.17, the expression "tubes, pipes and hoses" means hollow products, whether semi-manufactures or finished products, of a kind generally used for conveying, conducting or distributing gases or liquids (for example, ribbed garden hose, perforated tubes). This expression also includes sausage casings and other lay-flat tubing. However, except for the last-mentioned, those having an internal cross-section other than round, oval, rectangular (in which the length does not exceed 1.5 times the width) or in the shape of a regular polygon are not to be regarded as tubes, pipes and hoses but as profile shapes.

九、税目 39.18 所称"塑料糊墙品"，适用于墙壁或天花板装饰用的宽度不小于 45 厘米的成卷产品，这类产品是将塑料牢固地附着在除纸张以外任何材料的衬背上，并且在塑料面起纹、压花、着色、印制图案或用其他方法装饰。

9. For the purposes of heading No. 39.18, the expression "wall or ceiling coverings of plastics" applies to products in rolls, of a width not less than 45 cm, suitable for wall or ceiling decoration, consisting of plastics fixed permanently on a backing of any material other than paper, the layer of plastics (on the face side) being grained, embossed, coloured, design-printed or otherwise decorated.

十、税目 39.20 及 39.21 所称"板、片、膜、箔、扁条"，只适用于未切割或仅切割成矩形（包括正方形）（含切割后即可供使用的），但未经进一步加工的板、片、膜、箔扁条（第五十四章的物品除外）及正几何形块，不论是否经过印制或其他表面加工。

10. In headings Nos. 39.20 and 39.21, the expression "plates, sheets, film, foil and strip" applies only to plates, sheets, film, foil and strip (other than those of Chapter 54) and to blocks of regular geometric shape, whether or not printed or otherwise surface-woked, uncut or cut into rectangles (including squares) but not further worked (even if when so cut they become articles ready for use).

十一、税目 39.25 只适用于第二分章以前各税目未包括的下列物品：

（一）容积超过 300 升的囤、柜（包括化粪池）、罐、桶及类似容器；

11. Heading No. 39.25 applies only to the following articles, not being products covered by any of the earlier headings of sub-Chapter Ⅱ:

(a) Reservoirs, tanks (including septic tanks), vats and similar containers, of a capacity exceeding 300 L;

（二）用于地板、墙壁、隔墙、天花板或屋顶等方面的结构件；

（三）槽管及其附件；

（四）门、窗及其框架和门槛；

（五）阳台、栏杆、栅栏、栅门及类似品；

（六）窗板、百叶窗（包括威尼斯式百叶窗）或类似品及其零件、附件；

（七）商店、工棚、仓库等用的拼装式固定大型货架；

（八）建筑用的特色（例如，凹槽、圆顶及鸽棚式）装饰件；

（九）固定装于门窗、楼梯、墙壁或建筑物其他部位的附件及架座，例如，球形把手、拉手、挂钩、托架、毛巾架、开关板及其他护板。

(b) Structural elements used, for example, in floors, walls or partitions, ceilings or roofs;

(c) Gutters and fittings therefor;

(d) Doors, windows and their frames and thresholds for doors;

(e) Balconies, balustrades, fencing, gates and similar barriers;

(f) Shutters, blinds (including Venetian blinds) and similar articles and parts and fittings thereof;

(g) Large-scale shelving for assembly and permanent installation, for example, in shops, workshops, warehouses;

(h) Ornamental architectural features, for example, flutings, cupolas, dovecotes; and

(i) Fittings and mountings intended for permanent installation in or on doors, windows, staircases, walls or other parts of buildings, for example, knobs, handles, hooks, brackets, towel rails, switch-plates and other protective plates.

子目注释：

属于本章任一税目项下的聚合物（包括共聚物）及化学改性聚合物应按下列规则归类：

一、在同级子目中有一个“其他”子目的：

（一）子目所列聚合物名称冠有“聚（多）”的（例如，聚乙烯及聚酰胺-6,6），是指列名的该种聚合物单体单元含量在整个聚合物中按重量计必须占95%及以上。

（二）子目3901.30、3903.20、3903.30及3904.30所列的共聚物，如果该种共聚单体单元含量在整个聚合物中按重量计占95%及以上，即应归入上述子目。

（三）化学改性聚合物如未在其他子目具体列名，应归入列明为“其他”的子目内。

（四）不符合上述（一）、（二）、（三）款规定的聚合物，应按聚合物中重量最大的那种单体单元（与其他各种单一的共聚单体单元相比）所构成的聚合物归入该级其他相应子目。为此，归入同一子目的聚合物单体单元应作为一种单体单元对待。只有在同级子目中的聚合物共聚单体单元才可以进行比较。

二、子目3920.43所称“增塑剂”，包括“次级增塑剂”。

三、在同级子目中没有“其他”子目的：

（一）聚合物应按聚合物中重量最大的那种单体单元（与其他各种单一的共聚单体单元相比）所构成的聚合物归入该级相应子目。为此，归入同一子目的聚合物单体单元应作为一种单体单元对待。只有在同级子目中的聚合物共聚单体单元才可以进行比较。

Subheading Notes:

Within any one heading of this Chapter, polymers (including copolymers) and chemically modified polymers are to be classified according to the following provisions:

1. Where there is a subheading named "Other" in the same series:

(1) The designation in a subheading of a polymer by the prefix "poly" (e.g., polyethylene and polyamide-6,6) means that the constituent monomer unit or monomer units of the named polymer taken together must contribute 95% or more by weight of the total polymer content.

(2) The copolymers named in subheadings Nos. 3901.30, 3903.20, 3903.30 and 3904.30 are to be classified in those subheadings, provided that the comonomer units of the named copolymers contribute 95% or more by weight of the total polymer content.

(3) Chemically modified polymers are to be classified in the subheading named "Other", provided that the chemically modified polymers are not more specifically covered by another subheading.

(4) Polymers not meeting (1), (2) or (3) above, are to be classified in the subheading, among the remaining subheadings in the series, covering polymers of that monomer unit which predominates by weight over every other single comonomer unit. For this purpose, constituent monomer units of polymers falling in the same subheading shall be taken together. Only the constituent comonomer units of the polymers in the series of subheadings under consideration are to be compared.

2. For the purposes of subheading No. 3920.43, the term "plasticisers" includes secondary plasticisers.

3. Where there is no subheading named "Other" in the same series:

(1) Polymers are to be classified in the subheading covering polymers of that monomer unit which predominates by weight over every other single comonomer unit. For this purpose, constituent monomer units of polymers falling in the same subheading shall be taken together. Only the constituent comonomer units of the polymers in the series under consideration are to be compared.

（二）化学改性聚合物应按相应的未改性聚合物的子目归类。

聚合物混合体应按单体单元比例相等、种类相同的聚合物归入相应子目。

(2) Chemically modified polymers are to be classified in the subheading appropriate to the unmodified polymer.

Polymer blends are to be classified in the same subheading as polymers of the same monomer units in the same proportions.

税则号列 Tariff Item.	货品名称	最惠国(%) MFN	协定(%) 东盟 CA	协定(%) 中巴 CP	CT 中智 CC	普通 Gen	增值税率 VAT	出口退税 ED	计量单位 Unit	监管条件 SC	Article Description
	第一分章　初级形状										1. -PRIMARY FORMS
39.01	**初级形状的乙烯聚合物：**										**Polymers of ethylene, in primary forms:**
3901.1000	-聚乙烯，比重小于0.94	7.8		7.4	6.2	45	17	11	千克		-Polyethylene having a specific gravity of less than 0.94
3901.1000 01	初级形状比重<0.94的聚乙烯（进口CIF高于2000美元/吨）	7.8				45	17	11	千克	7A	Polyethylene, in primary forms, specifie gravity < 0.94, CIF > USD 2000/ton
3901.1000 90	初级形状比重<0.94的聚乙烯（进口到岸价格不超过2000美元/吨）	7.8				45	17	11	千克	7A	Polyethylene, in primary forms, specifie gravity < 0.94, CIF≤USD 2000/ton
3901.2000	-聚乙烯，比重在0.94及以上	7.8		7.4	6.2	45	17	11	千克		-Polyethylene having a specific gravity of 0.94 or more
3901.2000 01	初级形状比重≥0.94的聚乙烯（进口CIF价高于2000美元/吨）	7.8				45	17	11	千克	7A	Polyethylene, in primary forms, specifie gravity≥0.94, CIF > USD 2000/ton
3901.2000 90	初级形状比重≥0.94的聚乙烯（进口CIF价不超过2000美元/吨的）	7.8				45	17	11	千克	7A	Polyethylene, in primary forms, specifie gravity≥0.94, CIF≤USD 2000/ton
3901.3000	-乙烯-乙酸乙烯酯共聚物	6.5	5	6	5.2	45	17	11	千克	A	-Ethylene-vinyl acetate copolymers
	-其他：										-Other:
3901.9010	---乙烯-丙烯共聚物（乙丙橡胶）	6.5			0	45	17	11	千克	A	---Ethylene-propylene copolymers
3901.9020	---线型低密度聚乙烯	6.5			0	45	17	11	千克	7A	---Linearity low-density polyethylene
3901.9090	---其他	6.5		6.3	0	45	17	11	千克	A	---Other
39.02	**初级形状的丙烯或其他烯烃聚合物：**										**Polymers of propylene or of other olefins, in primary forms:**
3902.1000	-聚丙烯	7.6			6.1	45	17	11	千克		-Polypropylene
3902.1000 10	电工级初级形状聚丙烯树脂（灰分含量不大于30ppm）	7.6				45	17	11	千克	7A	Polypropylene resin in primary forms, electrical grade (ash content≤30ppm)
3902.1000 90	其他初级形状的聚丙烯	7.6				45	17	11	千克	7A	Other polypropylene in primary forms
3902.2000	-聚异丁烯	7.6	5		0	45	17	11	千克		-Polyisobutylene
	-丙烯共聚物：										-Propylene copolymers:
3902.3010	---乙烯-丙烯共聚物（乙丙橡胶）	7.6		7.1	6.1	45	17	11	千克		---Ethylene-propylene copolymers
3902.3090	---其他	7.6		7.1	6.1	45	17	11	千克		---Other
3902.9000	-其他	7.6			0	45	17	11	千克		-Other
3902.9000 10	端羧基聚丁二烯，CTPB（做粘接剂或燃料）	7.6				45	17	11	千克	3	Carboxyl-terminal polybutadiene, CTPB (used as adhesive or fuel)
3902.9000 20	端羟基聚丁二烯，HTPB（做粘接剂或燃料）	7.6				45	17	11	千克	3	Hydroxyl-terminal polybutadiene, HTPB (used as adhesive or fuel)
3902.9000 90	其他初级形状的烯烃聚合物	7.6				45	17	11	千克		Other polymers of olefins, in primary forms

税则号列 Tariff Item.	货品名称	最惠国(%) MFN	协定(%) CT 东盟 CA	中巴 CP	中智 CC	普通 Gen	增值税率 VAT	出口退税 ED	计量单位 Unit	监管条件 SC	Article Description
39.03	**初级形状的苯乙烯聚合物：**										**Polymers of styrene, in primary forms:**
	-聚苯乙烯：										-Polystyrene:
3903.1100	--可发性的	7.6		7.1	6.1	45	17	11	千克	7A	--Expansible
3903.1900	--其他	7.6		7.1	0	45	17	11	千克	7A	--Other
3903.2000	-苯乙烯-丙烯腈(SAN)共聚物	12	8		7.2	45	17	11	千克		-Styrene-acrylonitrile (SAN) copolymers
3903.3000	-丙烯腈-丁二烯-苯乙烯(ABS)共聚物	7.6		7.1	0	45	17	11	千克	A	-Acrylonitrile-butadiene-styrene (ABS) copolymers
3903.9000	-其他	7.6		7.1	6.1	45	17	11	千克		-Other
39.04	**初级形状的氯乙烯或其他卤化烯烃聚合物：**										**Polymers of vinyl chloride or of other halogenated olefins, in primary forms:**
3904.1000	-聚氯乙烯，未掺其他物质	7.6		7.1	6.1	45	17	11	千克		-Poly(vinyl chloride), not mixed with any other substances
3904.1000 01	聚氯乙烯纯粉(纯指未掺其他物质)	7.6				45	17	11	千克	7A	Poly (vinyl chloride), not mixed with any other substances, in powder
3904.1000 90	其他初级形状的纯聚氯乙烯(纯指未掺其他物质)	7.6				45	17	11	千克	7A	Other poly (vinyl chloride), not mixed with any other substances
	-其他聚氯乙烯：										-Other poly(vinyl chloride):
3904.2100	--未塑化	7.6			0	45	17	11	千克	7	--Non-plasticized
3904.2200	--已塑化	7.6			6.1	45	17	11	千克	7	--Plasticized
3904.3000	-氯乙烯-乙酸乙烯酯共聚物	9	T3	8.6	0	45	17	11	千克		-Vinyl chloride-vinyl acetate copolymers
3904.4000	-其他氯乙烯共聚物	12	T3	11.4	7.2	45	17	11	千克		-Other vinyl chloride copolymers
3904.5000	-偏二氯乙烯聚合物	7.6	5		0	45	17	11	千克		-Vinylidene chloride polymers
	-氟聚合物：										-Fluoro-polymers:
3904.6100	--聚四氟乙烯	10	8		0	45	17	11	千克		--Polytetrafluoroethylene
3904.6900	--其他	6.5	5		0	45	17	11	千克		--Other
3904.9000	-其他	10	5		0	45	17	11	千克		-Other
39.05	**初级形状的乙酸乙烯酯或其他乙烯酯聚合物；初级形状的其他乙烯基聚合物：**										**Polymers of vinyl acetate or of other vinyl esters, in primary forms; other vinyl polymers in primary forms:**
	-聚乙酸乙烯酯：										-Poly(vinyl acetate):
3905.1200	--水分散体	10	T3		8	45	17	11	千克		--In aqueous dispersion
3905.1900	--其他	10	5		0	45	17	11	千克		--Other
	-乙酸乙烯酯共聚物：										-Vinyl acetate copolymers:
3905.2100	--水分散体	10	T3		0	45	17	11	千克		--In aqueous dispersion
3905.2900	--其他	10	T3		0	45	17	11	千克		--Other
3905.3000	-聚乙烯醇，不论是否含有未水解的乙酸酯基	14	8		0	45	17	11	千克		-Poly(vinyl alcohol), whether or not containing unhydrolyzed acetate groups
	-其他：										-Other:
3905.9100	--共聚物	10	5		0	45	17	11	千克		--Copolymers
3905.9900	--其他	10	5		8	45	17	11	千克		--Other
39.06	**初级形状的丙烯酸聚合物：**										**Acrylic polymers in primary forms:**
3906.1000	-聚甲基丙烯酸甲酯	6.5	5	6	0	45	17		千克		-Poly(methyl methacrylate)
	-其他：										-Other:
3906.9010	---聚丙烯酰胺	6.5	5	6	5.2	45	17	13	千克		---Polyacrylamide
3906.9090	---其他	6.5	5	6	5.2	45	17	11	千克		---Other

税则号列 Tariff Item.	货品名称	最惠国(%) MFN	协定(%)CT 东盟 CA	中巴 CP	中智 CC	普通 Gen	增值税率 VAT	出口退税 ED	计量单位 Unit	监管条件 SC	Article Description
39.07	初级形状的聚缩醛、其他聚醚及环氧树脂;初级形状的聚碳酸酯、醇酸树脂、聚烯丙基酯及其他聚酯:										**Polyacetals, other polyethers and epoxide resins, in primary forms; polycarbonates, alkyd resins, polyallyl esters and other polyesters, in primary forms:**
	-聚缩醛:										-Polyacetals:
3907.1010	---聚甲醛	7.6		7.1	0	45	17	11	千克		---Polyoxymethylene(POM)
3907.1090	---其他	7.6	T3	7.1	0	45	17	11	千克		---Other
3907.2000	-其他聚醚	7.6		7.1	0	45	17	11	千克		-Other polyethers
3907.2000 01	聚四亚甲基醚二醇	7.6				45	17	11	千克		Polytetramethylene ether glycol
3907.2000 90	初级形状的其他聚醚	7.6				45	17	11	千克		Other polyethers
3907.3000	-环氧树脂	7.6		7.1	6.1	45	17	11	千克		-Epoxide resins
3907.3000 01	初级形状的环氧树脂[溴的重量百分比含量在18%及以上环氧树脂(如溶于溶剂,以纯环氧树脂折算溴百分比含量)]	7.6				45	17	11	千克		Epoxide resins, in primary forms, containing≥18% by weight of bromine
3907.3000 90	初级形状的环氧树脂(溴重量百分比含量在18%以下)	7.6				45	17	11	千克		Epoxide resins, in primary forms, containing <18% by weight of bromine
3907.4000	-聚碳酸酯	6.5	5	6.1	0	45	17	11	千克		-Polycarbonates
3907.5000	-醇酸树脂	10	8	9.5	8	45	17	11	千克		-Alkyd resins
	-聚对苯二甲酸乙二酯:										-Poly(ethylene terephthalate):
	---切片:										---In the form of slices or chips:
3907.6011	----高粘度	7.6			0	45	17	11	千克	A	----High viscosity
3907.6019	----其他	7.6			0	45	17	11	千克	A	----Other
3907.6090	---其他	6.5	5		0	45	17	11	千克	A	---Other
3907.7000	---聚乳酸	6.5	5	6.2	5.2	45	17	11	千克		Polylactic Acid
	-其他聚酯:										-Other polyesters:
3907.9100	--不饱和	7.6			6.1	45	17	11	千克		--Unsaturated
3907.9910	---聚对苯二甲酸丁二酯	6.5	5	6.2	5.2	45	17	11	千克		---
3907.9910 01	未经增强或改性的初级形状PBT树脂	6.5				45	17	11	千克		
3907.9910 90	其他聚对苯二甲丁二酯	6.5				45	17	11	千克		
3907.9990	---其它	6.5	5	6.2	5.2	45	17	11	千克		---Other
39.08	初级形状的聚酰胺:										**Polyamides in primary forms:**
	-聚酰胺-6、-11、-12、-6,6、-6,9、-6,10或-6,12:										-Polyamide-6, -11, -12, -6,6, -6,9, -6,10 or -6,12:
	---切片:										---In the form of slices or chips:
3908.1011	----聚酰胺-6,6切片	7.6			0	45	17	13	千克		----Of polyamide-6,6
3908.1019	----其他	7.6			0	45	17	11	千克		----Other
3908.1019 10	尼龙11、尼龙12切片(即聚酰胺-11;-12切片)	7.6				45	17	11	千克		Nylon 11, Nylon 12, in the form of slices or chips
3908.1019 90	聚酰胺-6切片等(包括聚酰胺-6,9;-6,10;-6,12)	7.6				45	17	11	千克		Polyamide -6,9; -6,10; -6,12, in the form of slices or chips
3908.1090	---其他	6.5	5		0	45	17	11	千克		---Other
3908.9000	-其他	10	8		0	45	17	11	千克		-Other
39.09	初级形状的氨基树脂、酚醛树脂及聚氨酯类:										**Amino-resins, phenolic resins and polyurethanes, in primary forms:**
3909.1000	-尿素树脂;硫尿树脂	6.5	5	6.1	5.2	45	17	11	千克		-Urea resins; thiourea resins

税则号列 Tariff Item.	货品名称	最惠国(%) MFN	协定(%)CT 东盟 CA	中巴 CP	中智 CC	普通 Gen	增值税率 VAT	出口退税 ED	计量单位 Unit	监管条件 SC	Article Description
3909.2000	-蜜胺树脂	6.5	5	6.1	0	45	17	11	千克		-Melamine resins
	-其他氨基树脂										-Other amino-resins
3909.3010	---聚(亚甲基苯基异氰酸酯)(聚合MDI或粗MDI)	6.5	T3	6	5.2	35	17	11	千克		---Polymethylene
3909.3090	---其它	6.5	5		5.2	45	17	11	千克		---Other
3909.4000	-酚醛树脂	6.5	5	6.1	5.2	45	17	11	千克		-Phenolic resins
3909.5000	-聚氨基甲酸酯	7.6		7.1	6.1	45	17	11	千克		-Polyurethanes
39.10	**初级形状的聚硅氧烷:**										**Silicones in primary forms:**
3910.0000	初级形状的聚硅氧烷	6.5	5	6.1	0	45	17	11	千克		Silicones in primary forms
39.11	**初级形状的石油树脂、苯并呋喃-茚树脂、多萜树脂、多硫化物、聚砜及本章注释三所规定的其他税目未列名产品:**										**Petroleum resins, coumarone-indene resins, polyterpenes, polysulphides, polysulphones and other products specified in Note 3 to this Chapter, not elsewhere specified or included, in primary forms:**
3911.1000	-石油树脂、苯并呋喃树脂、茚树脂、苯并呋喃-茚树脂及多萜树脂	6.5	5	6.1	0	45	17	11	千克		-Petroleum resins, coumarone, indene or coumarone-indene resins and poly-terpenes
3911.9000	-其他	6.5	5		0	45	17	11	千克		-Other
3911.9000 01	芳基酸与芳基胺预缩聚物	6.5				45	17	11	千克		Precondensed polymer of aromatic acid and aromatic amide
3911.9000 03	改性三羟乙基脲酸酯类预缩聚物	6.5				45	17	11	千克		Precondensed polymer of modified trihydroxy acetate
3911.9000 04	聚苯硫醚	6.5				45	17	11	千克		Polyphenyl sulfide
3911.9000 05	偏苯三酸酐和异氰酸预缩聚物	6.5				45	17	11	千克		Precondensed polymer of trimelltic anhydride and isocyanic acid
3911.9000 90	其他初级形状的多硫化物、聚砜等(等包括本章注释三所规定的其他编号未列名产品)	6.5				45	17	11	千克		Other polysulphides, polysulphones and other products specified in Note 3 to this Chapter, not elsewhere specified or included, in primary forms
39.12	**初级形状的其他税目未列名的纤维素及其化学衍生物:**										**Cellulose and its chemical derivatives, not elsewhere specified or included, in primary forms:**
	-乙酸纤维素:										-Cellulose acetates:
3912.1100	--未塑化	6.5	5		0	40	17	11	千克		--Non-plasticized
3912.1100 01	未塑化二醋酸纤维素等(包括未塑化三醋酸纤维素)	6.5				40	17	11	千克		Cellulose acetates (including cellulose triacetate) non-plasticized
3912.1100 90	初级形状的未塑化醋酸纤维素(未塑化二醋酸纤维素和未塑化三醋酸纤维素除外)	6.5				40	17	11	千克		Cellulose acetates, non-plasticized (other than and cellulose triacetate), in primary forms
3912.1200	--已塑化	6.5	5		0	40	17	11	千克		--Plasticized
3912.2000	-硝酸纤维素(包括胶棉)	6.5	5		0	45	17	11	千克		-Cellulose nitrates (including collodions)
	-纤维素醚:										-Cellulose ethers:
3912.3100	--羧甲基纤维素及其盐	6.5	5		0	45	17	11	千克		--Carboxymethylcellulose and its salts
3912.3900	--其他	6.5	5		5.2	45	17	11	千克		--Other
3912.9000	-其他	6.5	5		0	45	17	11	千克		-Other

税则号列 Tariff Item.	货品名称	最惠国(%) MFN	协定(%) 东盟 CA	中巴 CP	CT 中智 CC	普通 Gen	增值税率 VAT	出口退税 ED	计量单位 Unit	监管条件 SC	Article Description
39.13	**初级形状的其他税目未列名的天然聚合物(例如藻酸)及改性天然聚合物(例如,硬化蛋白、天然橡胶的化学衍生物):**										**Natural polymers (for example, alginic acid) and modified natural polymers (for example, hardened proteins, chemical derivatives of natural rubber), not elsewhere specified or included, in primary forms:**
3913.1000	-藻酸及其盐和酯	10	T3		8	45	17	11	千克		-Alginic acid, its salts and esters
3913.9000	-其他	6.5	5		0	50	17	11	千克		-Other
39.14	**初级形状的离子交换剂,以税目39.01至39.13的聚合物为基本成分的:**										**Ion-exchangers based on polymers of headings Nos. 39.01 to 39.13, in primary forms:**
3914.0000	初级形状的离子交换剂(以税目39.01至39.13的聚合物为基本成分的)	6.5	5		0	45	17	13	千克		Ion-exchangers based on polymers of headings Nos. 39.01 to 39.13, in primary forms
	第二分章 废碎料及下脚料;半制品;制成品										Ⅱ-WASTE, PARINGS AND SCRAP; SEMI-MANUFACTURES; ARTICLES
39.15	**塑料的废碎料及下脚料:**										**Waste, parings and scrap, of plastics:**
3915.1000	-乙烯聚合物的	7.6			6.1	50	17	11	千克	AP	-Of polymers of ethylene
3915.2000	-苯乙烯聚合物的	7.6			6.1	50	17	11	千克	AP	-Of polymers of styrene
3915.3000	-氯乙烯聚合物的	7.6			0	50	17	11	千克	AP	-Of polymers of vinyl chloride
	-其他塑料的:										-Of other plastics:
3915.9010	---聚对苯二甲酸乙二酯的	7.6			6.1	50	17	11	千克	AP	---Of polyethylene glycol terephthalate
3915.9090	---其他	7.6			6.1	50	17	11	千克	AP	---Other
39.16	**塑料制的单丝(截面直径超过1毫米)、条、杆、型材及异型材,不论是否经表面加工,但未经其他加工:**										**Monofilament of which any cross-sectional dimension exceeds 1 mm, rods, sticks and profile shapes, whether or not surface-worked but not otherwise worked, of plastics:**
3916.1000	-乙烯聚合物制	10	T3		8	45	17	11	千克		-Of polymers of ethylene
3916.2000	-氯乙烯聚合物制	10	5	7	8	45	17	11	千克		-Of polymers of vinyl chloride
	-其他塑料制:										-Of other plastics
3916.9010	---聚酰胺制	10	T3		0	45	17	11	千克		---Of polyamides
3916.9090	---其他	10	T3		0	45	17	11	千克		---Other
39.17	**塑料制的管子及其附件(例如,接头、肘管、法兰):**										**Tubes, pipes and hoses, and fittings therefor (for example, joints, elbows, flanges), of plastics:**
3917.1000	-硬化蛋白或纤维素材料制的人造肠衣(香肠用肠衣)	10	5		8	50	17	11	千克	A	-Artificial guts (sausage casings) of hardened protein or of cellulosic materials
	-硬管:										-Tubes, pipes and hoses, rigid:
3917.2100	--乙烯聚合物制	10	T3		8	45	17	11	千克		--Of polymers of ethylene
3917.2200	--丙烯聚合物制	10	5		0	45	17	11	千克		--Of polymers of propylene
3917.2300	--氯乙烯聚合物制	10	T3		8	45	17	11	千克		--Of polymers of vinyl chloride
3917.2900	--其他塑料制	10	T3		0	45	17	11	千克		--Of other plastics
	-其他管:										-Other tubes, pipes and hoses:
3917.3100	--软管,最小爆破压力为27.6兆帕斯卡	10	T3	7	8	45	17	11	千克		--Flexible tubes, pipes and hoses, having a minimum burst pressure of 27.6 MPa

税则号列 Tariff Item.	货品名称	最惠国(%) MFN	协定(%) CT 东盟 CA	中巴 CP	中智 CC	普通 Gen	增值税率 VAT	出口退税 ED	计量单位 Unit	监管条件 SC	Article Description
3917.3200	--其他未装有附件的管子,未经加强也未与其他材料合制	6.5	T3	4.6	5.2	45	17	11	千克		--Other, not reinforced or otherwise combined with other materials, without fittings
3917.3300	--其他装有附件的管子,未经加强也未与其他材料合制	6.5	T3	4.6	5.2	45	17	11	千克		--Other, not reinforced or otherwise combined with other materials, with fittings
3917.3900	--其他	7.6		5.3	6.1	45	17	11	千克		--Other
3917.4000	-管子附件	10	T3	7	8	45	17	11	千克		-Fittings
39.18	**块状或成卷的塑料铺地制品,不论是否胶粘;本章注释九所规定的塑料糊墙品:**										**Floor coverings of plastics, whether or not self-adhesive, in rolls or in the form of tiles; wall or ceiling coverings of plastics, as defined in Note 9 to this Chapter:**
	-氯乙烯聚合物制:										-Of polymers of vinyl chloride:
3918.1010	---糊墙品	10	5		8	45	17	11	千克		---Wall or ceiling coverings
3918.1090	---其他	10	5		8	45	17	11	千克		---Other
	-其他塑料制:										-Of other plastics:
3918.9010	---糊墙品	10	5		0	45	17	11	千克		---Wall or ceiling coverings
3918.9090	---其他	10	5		0	45	17	11	千克		---Other
39.19	**自粘的塑料板、片、膜、箔、带、扁条及其他扁平形状材料,不论是否成卷:**										**Self-adhesive plates, sheets, film, foil, tape, strip and other flat shapes, of plastics, whether or not in rolls:**
	-成卷,宽度不超过 20 厘米:										-In rolls of a width not exceeding 20 cm:
3919.1010	---丙烯酸树脂类为基本成分	6.5	T3		5.2	45	17	11	千克		---Based on acrylic resin
	---其他:										---Other:
3919.1091	----胶囊型反光膜	6.5	T3		5.2	45	17	11	千克		----Encapsulant reflective film
3919.1099	----其他	6.5	T3		5.2	45	17	11	千克		----Other
	-其他:										-Other:
3919.9010	---胶囊型反光膜	6.5	T3	4.6	5.2	45	17	11	千克		---Encapsulant reflective film
3919.9090	---其他	6.5	T3	4.6	5.2	45	17	11	千克		---Other
39.20	**其他非泡沫塑料的板、片、膜、箔及扁条,未用其他材料强化、层压、支撑或用类似方法合制:**										**Other plates, sheets, film, foil and strip, of plastics, non-cellular and not reinforced, laminated, supported or similarly combined with other materials:**
	-乙烯聚合物制:										-Of polymers of ethylene
3920.1010	---乙烯聚合物制电池隔膜	6.5	T3	4.6	5.2	45	13	13	千克		---Cell diaphragm of polymers of ethylene
3920.1090	---其他	6.5	T3	4.6	5.2	45			千克		---Other
3920.1090 01	乙烯-四氟乙烯膜[四氟乙烯单体含量约 50%],[比重 1.7-1.75g/cm^3(未用其他材料强化,层压,支撑或用类似方法合制)]	6.5				45	13		千克		Film of ethylene - tertafluoroethylene (monomer of tetrafluoroethylene ≈ 50%), with a weight of 1.7 - 1.75g/cm3, not reinforced, laminated, supported or similarly combined with other materials
3920.1090 10	农用非泡沫聚乙烯薄膜(未用其他材料强化、层压、支撑或用类似方法合制)	6.5				45	13		千克		Agricultural PE film, non-cellular, not reinforced, laminated, supported or similarly combined with other materials

税则号列 Tariff Item.	货品名称	最惠国(%) MFN	协定(%) CT 东盟 CA	中巴 CP	中智 CC	普通 Gen	增值税率 VAT	出口退税 ED	计量单位 Unit	监管条件 SC	Article Description
3920.1090 90	其他非泡沫乙烯聚合物板、片、膜、箔及扁条(未用其他材料强化、层压、支撑或用类似方法合制,非农用)	6.5				45	17	11	千克		Plates, sheets, film, foil and strip, of PE film, non-cellular, not reinforced, laminated, supported or similarly combined with other materials, non-agricultural
	-丙烯聚合物制:										-Of polymers of propylene
3920.2010	---丙烯聚合物制电池隔膜	6.5	T3		5.2	45	13	11	千克		---Battery separator, of polymers of propylene
3920.2090	---其他	6.5	T3		5.2	45			千克		---Other
3920.2090 10	农用非泡沫聚丙烯薄膜(未用其他材料强化、层压、支撑或用类似方法合制)	6.5				45	13		千克		Agricultural PP film, non-cellular, not reinforced, laminated, supported or similarly combined with other materials
3920.2090 90	非泡沫丙烯聚合物板、片、膜、箔及扁条(未用其他材料强化、层压、支撑或用类似方法合制,非农用)	6.5				45	17	11	千克		Plates, sheets, film, foil and strip, of PP film, non-cellular, not reinforced, laminated, supported or similarly combined with other materials, non-agricultural
3920.3000	-苯乙烯聚合物制	6.5	T3	4.6	5.2	45	17	11	千克		-Of polymers of styrene
	-氯乙烯聚合物制:										-Of polymers of vinyl chloride:
3920.4300	--按重量计增塑剂含量不小于6%	7.6		5.3	0	45	17	11	千克		--Containing by weight not less than 6% of plasticisers
3920.4300 10	农用软质聚氯乙烯薄膜(增塑剂含量≥6%,未用其他材料强化、层压、支撑)	7.6				45	17		千克		Agricultural PVC-P film, containing by weight not less than 6% of plasticisers, not reinforced, laminated, supported or similarly combined with other materials
3920.4300 90	氯乙烯聚合物板、片、膜、箔及扁条(增塑剂含量≥6%,未用其他材料强化、层压、支撑)	7.6				45	17	11	千克		Plates, sheets, film, foil and strip, of PVC film, containing by weight not less than 6% of plasticisers, not reinforced, laminated, supported or similarly combined with other materials
3920.4900	--其他	7.6	T3	5.3	6.1	45			千克		--Other
3920.4900 10	其他农用软质聚氯乙烯薄膜(非泡沫料的,未用其他材料强化、层压、支撑)	7.6				45	13		千克		Other agricultural PVC-P film, non-cellular, not reinforced, laminated, supported or similarly combined with other materials
3920.4900 90	其他氯乙烯聚合物板,片,膜,箔及扁条(非泡沫料的,未用其他材料强化、层压、支撑,非农用)	7.6				45	17	11	千克		Other plates, sheets, film, foil and strip, of PVC, non-cellular, not reinforced, laminated, supported or similarly combined with other materials, non-agricultural
	-丙烯酸聚合物制:										-Of acrylic polymers:
3920.5100	--聚甲基丙烯酸甲酯制	6.5	T3	4.6	0	45	17	11	千克		--Of poly(methyl methacrylate)
3920.5900	--其他	6.5	T3		0	45	17	11	千克		--Other
	-聚碳酸酯、醇酸树脂、聚烯丙酯或其他聚酯制:										-Of polycarbonates, alkyd resins, polyallyl esters or other polyesters:
3920.6100	--聚碳酸酯制	6.5	T3	4.6	5.2	45	17	11	千克		--Of polycarbonates
3920.6200	--聚对苯二甲酸乙二酯制	6.5	T3	4.6	0	45	17	11	千克		--Of poly(ethylene terephthalate)

税则号列 Tariff Item.	货品名称	最惠国(%) MFN	协定(%) CT 东盟 CA	中巴 CP	中智 CC	普通 Gen	增值税率 VAT	出口退税 ED	计量单位 Unit	监管条件 SC	Article Description
3920.6200 01	9≤厚≤15.9 微米聚酯薄膜(聚对苯二甲酸乙二酯制,型号 XA10AUDIO)	6.5				45	17	11	千克		PE film, thickness 9 ~ 15.9μ(PEPT, Type:XA10AUDIO)
3920.6200 02	5≤厚≤8.9 微米聚酯薄膜(聚对苯二甲酸乙二酯制,型号 XL07AUTEN)	6.5				45	17	11	千克		PE film, thickness 59 ~ 8.9μ(PEPT, Type:XL07AUTEN)
3920.6200 03	16≤厚≤29.9 微米聚酯薄膜[聚对苯二甲酸乙二酯制,型号 XB30CAB(N)]	6.5				45	17	11	千克		PE film, thickness16 ~ 29.9μ(PEPT, Type:XB30CAB(N))
3920.6200 04	50≤厚≤99.9 微米聚酯薄膜[聚对苯二甲酸乙二酯制,型号 XB30CAB(M)]	6.5				45	17	11	千克		PE film, thickness50 ~ 99.9μ(PEPT, Type:XB30CAB(M))
3920.6200 09	其他聚对苯二甲酸乙二酯板片膜等(包括箔及扁条,非泡沫料,未用其他材料强化、层压、支撑)	6.5				45	17	11	千克		Other plates, sheets, film, foil and strip, of poly(ethylene terephthalate), non-cellular, not reinforced, laminated, supported or similarly combined with other materials
3920.6300	--不饱和聚酯制	10	5		0	45	17	11	千克		--Of unsaturated polyesters
3920.6900	--其他聚酯制	10	T3	9	8	45	17	11	千克		--Of other polyesters
	-纤维素及其化学衍生物制:										-Of cellulose or its chemical derivatives:
3920.7100	--再生纤维素制	6.5	T3		0	45	17	11	千克		--Of regenerated cellulose
3920.7300	--乙酸纤维素制	6.5	T3		0	45	17	11	千克		--Of cellulose acetate
3920.7900	--其他纤维素纤维物制	10	5		0	45	17		千克		--Of other cellulose derivatives
	-其他塑料制:										-Of other plastics:
3920.9100	--聚乙烯醇缩丁醛制	6.5	T3		0	45	17	11	千克		--Of poly(vinyl butyral)
3920.9200	--聚酰胺制	10	T3		0	45	17	11	千克		--Of polyamides
3920.9300	--氨基树脂制	6.5	T3		0	45	17	11	千克		--Of amino-resins
3920.9400	--酚醛树脂制	10	T3	7	0	45	17	11	千克		--Of phenolic resins
	--其他塑料制:										--Of other plastics:
3920.9910	---聚四氟乙烯制	6.5	T3		0	45	17	11	千克		---Of polytetrafluoroethylene
3920.9990	---其他塑料制	6.5	T3		0	45	17	11	千克		---Of other plastics
39.21	**其他塑料板、片、膜、箔、扁条:**										**Other plates, sheets, film, foil and strip, of plastics:**
	-泡沫塑料的:										-Cellular:
3921.1100	--苯乙烯聚合物制	10	5	9	0	45	17	11	千克		--Of polymers of styrene
	--氯乙烯聚合物制:										--Of polymers of vinyl chloride:
3921.1210	---人造革及合成革	9	T3		7.2	70	17	11	千克/米	5	---Combined with textile fabrics
3921.1290	---其他	6.5	T3		5.2	45	17	11	千克	5	---Other
	--氨酯聚合物制:										--Of polyurethanes:
3921.1310	---人造革及合成革	9	T3	6.3	7.2	70	17	11	千克/米	5	---Combined with textile fabrics
3921.1390	---其他	6.5	T3	4.6	5.2	45	17	11	千克	5	---Other
3921.1400	--再生纤维素制	10	5		0	45	17	11	千克		--Of regenerated cellulose
	--其他塑料制:										--Of other plastics:
3921.1910	---人造革及合成革	9	5	6.3	0	45	17	11	千克/米		---Combined with textile fabrics
3921.1990	---其他	6.5	T3	4.6	0	45	17	11	千克		---Other
	-其他:										-Other:
3921.9020	---聚乙烯嵌有玻璃纤维的板,片	6.5	T3	4.6	5.2	45	17	11	千克		---Plates, sheets of polyethylene with glass fibres

税则号列 Tariff Item.	货品名称	最惠国(%) MFN	协定(%)CT 东盟 CA	中巴 CP	中智 CC	普通 Gen	增值税率 VAT	出口退税 ED	计量单位 Unit	监管条件 SC	Article Description
3921.9030	---聚异丁烯为基本成分的附有人造毛毡的板,片,卷材	6.5	T3	4.6	5.2	45	17	11	千克		---Plates, sheets, coils of polyisobutylene with man-made felt
3921.9090	---其他	6.5	T3	4.6	5.2	45	17	11	千克		---Other
3921.9090 10	敏感物项管制结构复合材料的层压板(用纤维和丝材增强而制成的各种预浸件和预成形件,其中增强材料的比拉伸强度大于 7.62×10^4 米和比模量大于 3.18×10^6 米)	6.5				45	17	11	千克	35	Laminated structural board made of composite materials under sensitive product control (various persoaked and fabricated parts reinforced by fibers and threads, therein the specific tensile strength of reinforcing materials is greater than 7.62×10^4m and specific modulus greater than 3.18×10^6m)
3921.9090 90	未列名塑料板,片,膜,箔,扁条	6.5				45	17	11	千克	5	Other plates, sheets, film, foil fiol and strip of plastic not elsewhere specified or included
39.22	**塑料浴缸、淋浴盘、洗涤槽、盥洗盆、坐浴盆、便盆、马桶座圈及盖、抽水箱及类似卫生洁具:**										**Baths, shower-baths, sinks, wash-basins, bidets, lavatory pans, seats and covers, flushing cisterns and similar sanitary ware, of plastics:**
3922.1000	-浴缸、淋浴盘、洗涤槽及盥洗盆	10	5		0	80	17	11	千克		-Baths, shower-baths, sinks and wash-basins
3922.2000	-马桶座圈及盖	10	5		8	80	17	11	千克		-Lavatory seats and covers
3922.2000 10	含濒危动物成分的塑料马桶座圈及盖	10				80	17	11	千克	EF	Lavatory seats and covers, containing compositions of wild animds in imminent dangers
3922.2000 90	其他塑料马桶座圈及盖	10				80	17	11	千克		
3922.9000	-其他	10	5		8	80	17	11	千克		-Other
39.23	**供运输或包装货物用的塑料制品;塑料制的塞子、盖子及类似品:**										**Articles for the conveyance or packing of goods, of plastics; stoppers, lids, caps and other closures, of plastics:**
3923.1000	-盒、箱(包括板条箱)及类似品	10	T3	7	8	80	17	11	千克		-Boxes, cases, crates and similar articles
	-袋及包(包括锥形的):										-Sacks and bags (including cones):
3923.2100	--乙烯聚合物制	10	T3		8	80	17	11	千克		--Of polymers of ethylene
3923.2900	--其他塑料制	10	T3		8	80	17	11	千克		--Of other plastics
3923.3000	-坛、瓶及类似品	6.5	T3		5.2	80	17	11	千克		-Carboys, bottles, flasks and similar articles
3923.4000	-卷轴、纡子、筒管及类似品	10	T3	7	0	35	17	13	千克		-Spools, cops, bobbins and similar supports
3923.5000	-塞子、盖子及类似品	10	T3		8	80	17	11	千克		-Stoppers, lids, caps and other closures
3923.9000	-其他	10	T3	7	8	80	17	11	千克		-Other
39.24	**塑料制的餐具、厨房用具、其他家庭用具及卫生或盥洗用具:**										**Tableware, kitchenware, other household articles and toilet articles, of plastics:**
3924.1000	-餐具及厨房用具	10	T3		8	80	17	11	千克	A	-Tableware and kitchenware
3924.9000	-其他	10	T3		8	80	17	11	千克		-Other
39.25	**其他税目未列名的建筑用塑料制品:**										**Builders' ware of plastics, not elsewhere specified or included:**
3925.1000	-囤、柜、罐、桶及类似容器,容积超过300升	10	5		8	80	17	11	千克		-Reservoirs, tanks, vats and similar containers, of a capacity exceeding 300L
3925.2000	-门、窗及其框架、门槛	10	5	7	8	80	17	11	千克		-Doors, windows and their frames and thresholds for doors

税则号列 Tariff Item.	货品名称	最惠国(%) MFN	协定(%) 东盟 CA	中巴 CP	CT 中智 CC	普通 Gen	增值税率 VAT	出口退税 ED	计量单位 Unit	监管条件 SC	Article Description
3925.3000	-窗板、百叶窗(包括威尼斯式百叶窗)或类似制品及其零件	10	5		0	80	17	11	千克		-Shutters, blinds (including Venetian blinds) and similar articles and parts thereof
3925.9000	-其他	10	5		8	80	17	11	千克		-Other
39.26	**其他塑料制品及税目39.01至39.14所列其他材料的制品:**										**Other articles of plastics and articles of other materials of headings Nos. 39.01 to 39.14:**
3926.1000	-办公室或学校用品	10	T3		8	80	17	11	千克		-Office or school supplies
3926.2000	-衣服及衣着附件(包括分指手套、连指手套及露指手套)	10	T3		8	90	17	11	千克		-Articles of apparel and clothing accessories (including gloves, mittens and mitts)
3926.3000	-家具、车厢或类似品的附件	10	T3		8	80	17	11	千克		-Fittings for furniture, coachwork or the like
3926.4000	-小雕塑品及其他装饰品	10	5	8.3	0	100	17	11	千克		-Statuettes and other ornamental articles
	-其他:										-Other:
3926.9010	---机器及仪器用零件	10	T3	9	8	35	17	11	千克		---Of a kind for used in machines or instruments
3926.9090	---其他	10	T3	9.2	8	80	17	11	千克		---Other
3926.9090 10	敏感物项管制结构复合材料的预成形件和制品(用纤维和丝材增强而制成的各种预浸件和预成形件,其中增强材料的比拉伸强度大于 7.62×10^4 米和比模量大于 3.18×10^6 米)	10				80	17	11	千克	3	Laminated structural board made of composite materials under sensitive product control (various persoaked and fabricated parts reinforced by fibers and threads, therein the specific tensile strength of reinforcing materials is greater than 7.62×10^4m and specific modulus greater than 3.18×10^6m)
3926.9090 90	其他塑料制品(包括编号3901至3914所列材料的制品)	10				80	17	11	千克		Other articles of plastics and articles of other materials of heading 39.01 to 39.14

第四十章
橡胶及其制品

注释：

一、除条文另有规定的以外，本目录所称"橡胶"，是指不论是否硫化或硬化的下列产品：天然橡胶、巴拉塔胶、古塔波胶、银胶菊胶、糖胶树胶及类似的天然树胶、合成橡胶、从油类中提取的油膏以及上述物品的再生品。

二、本章不包括：

（一）第十一类的货品（纺织原料及纺织制品）；

（二）第六十四章的鞋靴及其零件；

（三）第六十五章的帽类及其零件（包括游泳帽）；

（四）第十六类的硬质橡胶制的机械器具、电气器具及其零件（包括各种电气用品）；

（五）第九十章、第九十二章、第九十四章或第九十六章的物品；

（六）第九十五章的物品（运动用分指手套、连指手套、露指手套及税目 40.11 至 40.13 的制品除外）。

三、税目 40.01 至 40.03 及 40.05 所称"初级形状"，只限于下列形状：

（一）液状及糊状，包括胶乳（不论是否预硫化）及其他分散体和溶液；

（二）不规则形状的块，团、包、粉、粒、碎屑及类似的散装形状。

四、本章注释一和税目 40.02 所称"合成橡胶"，适用于：

（一）不饱和合成物质，即用硫磺硫化能使其不可逆地变为非热塑物质，这种物质能在温度 18℃至 29℃之间被拉长到其原长度的三倍而不致断裂，拉长到原长度的两倍时，在五分钟内能回复到不超过原长度的一倍半。为了进行上述试验，可以加入交联所需的硫化活化剂或促进剂；也允许含有注释五（二）2 及 3 所述的物质。但不能加入非交联所需的物质，例如，增量剂、增塑剂及填料；

（二）聚硫橡胶（TM）；

（三）与塑料接枝共聚或混合而改性的天然橡胶、解聚天然橡胶以及不饱和合成物质与饱和合成高聚物的混合物，但这些产品必须符合以上（一）款关于硫化、延伸及回复的要求。

五、（一）税目 40.01 及 40.02 不适用于任何凝结前或凝结后与下列物质相混合的橡胶或橡胶混合物：

Chapter 40
Rubber and articles thereof

Notes:

1. Except where the context otherwise requires, throughout the Nomenclature the expression "rubber" means the following products, whether or not vulcanized or hard: natural rubber, balata, gutta-percha, guayule, chicle and similar natural gums, synthetic rubber, factice derived from oils, and such substances reclaimed.

2. This Chapter does not cover:

(a) Goods of Section Ⅺ (textitls and textile articles);

(b) Footwear or parts thereof of Chapter 64;

(c) Headgear or parts thereof (including bathing caps) of Chapter 65;

(d) Mechanical or electrical appliances or parts thereof of Section ⅩⅥ (including electrical goods of all kinds), of hard rubber;

(e) Articles of Chapter 90, 92, 94 or 96; or

(f) Articles of Chapter 95 (other than sports gloves, mittens and mitts and articles of headings Nos. 40.11 to 40.13).

3. In headings Nos. 40.01 to 40.03 and 40.05, the expression "primary forms" applies only to the following forms:

(a) Liquids and pastes (including latex, whether or not pre-vulcanized, and other dispersions and solutions);

(b) Blocks of irregular shape, lumps, bales, powders, granules, crumbs and similar bulk forms.

4. In Note Ⅰ to this Chapter and in heading No. 40.02, the expression "synthetic rubber" applies to:

(a) Unsaturated synthetic substances which can be irreversibly transformed by vulcanization with sulphur into non-thermoplastic substances which, at a temperature between 18℃ and 29℃, will not break on being extended to three times their original length and will return, after being extended to twice their original length, within a period of five minutes, to a length not greater than one and a half times their original length. For the purposes of this test, substances necessary for the cross-linking, such as vulcanizing activators or accelerators, may be added; the presence of substances as provided for by Note 5(b) (ii) and (iii) is also permitted. However, the presence of any substances not necessary for the cross-linking, such as extenders, plasticizers and fillers, is not permitted;

(b) Thioplasts (TM); and

(c) Natural rubber modified by grafting or mixing with plastics, depolymerized natural rubber, mixtures of unsaturated synthetic substances with saturated synthetic high polymers provided that all the above-mentioned products comply with the requirements concerning vulcanization, elongation and recovery in (a) above.

5. (a) Headings Nos. 40.01 and 40.02 do not apply to any rubber or mixture of rubbers which has been compounded, before or after coagulation, with:

1. 硫化剂、促进剂、防焦剂或活性剂(为制造预硫胶乳所加入的除外);

2. 颜料或其他着色料,但仅为易于识别而加入的除外;

3. 增塑剂或增量剂(用油增量的橡胶中所加的矿物油除外)、填料、增强剂、有机溶剂或其他物质,但以下(二)款所述的除外;

(二)含有下列物质的橡胶或橡胶混合物,只要仍具有原料的基本特性,应归入税目40.01或40.02:

1. 乳化剂或防粘剂;

2. 少量的乳化剂分解产品;

3. 微量的下列物质:热敏剂(一般为制造热敏胶乳用)、阳离子表面活性剂(一般为制造阳性胶乳用)、抗氧剂、凝固剂、碎裂剂、抗冻剂、胶溶剂、保存剂、稳定剂、粘度控制剂或类似的特殊用途添加剂。

六、税目40.04所称"废碎料及下脚料",是指在橡胶或橡胶制品生产或加工过程中由于切割、磨损或其他原因所造成没有使用价值的废橡胶及下脚料。

七、全部用硫化橡胶制成的线,其任一截面的尺寸超过5毫米的,应作为带、杆或型材及异型材归入税目40.08。

八、税目40.10包括用橡胶浸渍、涂布、包覆或层压的织物制成的或用橡胶浸渍、涂布、包覆或套裹的纱线或绳制成的传动带、输送带。

九、税目40.01、40.02、40.03、40.05及40.08所称"板"、"片"、"带",仅指未切割或只简单切割成矩形(包括正方形)的板、片、带及正几何形块,不论是否具有成品的特征,也不论是否经过印制或其他表面加工,但未切割成其他形状或进一步加工。

税目40.08所称"杆"或"型材及异型材",仅指不论是否切割成一定长度或表面加工,但未经进一步加工的该类产品。

(i) vulcanizing agents, accelerators, retarders or activators (other than those added for the preparation of pre-vulcanized rubber latex);

(ii) pigments or other colouring matter, other than those added solely for the purpose of identification;

(iii) plasticizers or extenders (except mineral oil in the case of oil-extended rubber), fillers, reinforcing agents, organic solvents or any other substances, except those permitted under (b);

(b) The presence of the following substances in any rubber or mixture of rubbers shall not affect its classification in heading No. 40.01 or 40.02, as the case may be, provided that such rubber or mixture of rubbers retains its essential character as a raw material:

(i) emulsifiers or anti-tack agents;

(ii) small amounts of breakdown products of emulsifiers;

(iii) very small amounts of the following: heat-sensitive agents (generally for obtaining thermosensitive rubber latexes), cationic surface-active agents (generally for obtaining electro-positive rubber latexes), antioxidants, coagulants, crumbling agents, freeze-resisting agents, peptizers, preservatives, stabilizers, viscosity-control agents, or similar special-purpose additives,

6. For the purposes of heading No. 40.04, the expression "waste, parings and scrap" means rubber waste, parings and scrap from the manufacture or working of rubber and rubber goods definitely not usable as such because of cutting-up, wear or other reasons.

7. Thread wholly of vulcanized rubber, of which any cross-sectional dimension exceeds 5 mm, is to be classified as strip, rods or profile shapes, of heading No. 40.08.

8. Heading No. 40.10 includes conveyor or transmission belts or belting of textile fabric impregnated, coated, covered or laminated with rubber or made from textile yarn or cord impregnated, coated, covered or sheathed with rubber.

9. In headings Nos. 40.01, 40.02, 40.03, 40.05, and 40.08, the expressions "plates", "sheets" and "strip" apply only to plates, sheets and strip and to blocks of regular geometric shape, uncut or simply cut to rectangular (including square) shape, whether or not having the character of articles and whether or not printed or otherwise surface-worked, but not otherwise cut to shape or further worked.

In heading No. 40.08 the expressions "rods" and "profile shapes" apply only to such products, whether or not cut to length or surface-worked but not otherwise worked.

税则号列 Tariff Item.	货品名称	最惠国(%) MFN	协定(%) 东盟 CA	CT 中巴 CP	中智 CC	普通 Gen	增值税率 VAT	出口退税 ED	计量单位 Unit	监管条件 SC	Article Description
40.01	天然橡胶、巴拉塔胶、古塔波胶、银胶菊胶、糖胶树胶及类似的天然树胶,初级形状或板、片、带:										**Natural rubber, balata, gutta-percha, guayule, chicle and similar natural gums, in primary forms or in plates, sheets or strip:**

税则号列 Tariff Item.	货品名称	最惠国(%) MFN	协定(%) CT 东盟 CA	中巴 CP	中智 CC	普通 Gen	增值税率 VAT	出口退税 ED	计量单位 Unit	监管条件 SC	Article Description
4001.1000	-天然胶乳,不论是否预硫化	20			12	40	17	5	千克	A7B	-Natural rubber latex, whether or not pre-vulcanized
	-其他形状的天然橡胶:										-Natural rubber in other forms:
4001.2100	--烟胶片	20		17	12	40	17	5	千克	A7B	--Smoked sheets
4001.2200	--技术分类天然橡胶(TSNR)	20			0	40	17	5	千克	A7	--Technically specified natural rubber (TSNR)
4001.2900	--其他	20		17	12	40	17	5	千克	7	--Other
4001.3000	-巴拉塔胶、古塔波胶、银胶菊胶、糖胶树胶及类似的天然树胶	20	12		12	40	17	5	千克		-Balata, gutta-percha, guayule, chicle and similar natural gums
40.02	**合成橡胶及从油类提取的油膏,初级形状或板、片、带;税目40.01所列产品与本税目所列产品的混合物,初级形状或板、片、带:**										**Synthetic rubber and factice derived from oils, in primary forms or in plates, sheets or strip; mixtures of any products of heading No. 40.01 with any product of this heading, in primary forms or in plates, sheets or strip:**
	-丁苯橡胶(SBR);羧基丁苯橡胶(XSBR):										-Styrene-butadiene rubber (SBR); carboxylated styrene-butadiene rubber (XSBR):
	--胶乳:										--Latex:
4002.1110	---羧基丁苯橡胶	7.5	5		0	14	17	13	千克		---Carboxylated styrene-butadiene rubber (XSBR)
4002.1190	---其他	7.5	5		0	14	17	13	千克		---Other
	--其他:										--Other:
	---初级形状的:										---In primary forms:
4002.1911	----未经任何加工的丁苯橡胶	7.5	5		0	14	17	13	千克		----SBR, not worked
4002.1912	----充油丁苯橡胶	7.5	5		0	14	17	13	千克		----SBR, oil-filled
4002.1913	----热塑丁苯橡胶	7.5	5		0	14	17	13	千克		----SBR, thermo-plasticated
4002.1914	----充油热塑丁苯橡胶	7.5	5		0	14	17	13	千克		----SBR, oil-filled and thermo-plasticated
4002.1919	----其他	7.5			0	14	17	13	千克		----Other
4002.1990	---其他	7.5	5	7.1	0	35	17	13	千克		---Other
	-丁二烯橡胶(BR):										-Butadiene rubber (BR):
4002.1990 01	简单处理的丁苯橡胶,热塑或充油热塑丁苯橡胶除外(指为便于运输,对初级形状进行压缩、挤压等简单成型处理)	7.5				35	17	13	千克		Except simple treatment of styrene - butadiene rubber or styrene - butadiene - styrene block copolymer (referring to compression, extrusion in order to facilitate transportation)
4002.1990 90	其他丁苯橡胶及羧基丁苯橡胶板,片,带(4002199010项下的除外)	7.5				35	17	13	千克		Other styrene - butadiene rubber and carboxy terminated styrene rubber board, piece, strap (except those under item 4002199010)
4002.2010	---初级形状的	7.5	5		0	14	17	13	千克		---In primary forms
4002.2090	---其他	7.5	5	7	0	35	17	13	千克		---Other
	-异丁烯-异戊二烯(丁基)橡胶(IIR);卤代丁基橡胶(CIIR或BIIR):										-Isobutene-isoprene (butyl) rubber (IIR); halo-isobutene-isoprene rubber (CIIR or BIIR):
	--异丁烯-异戊二烯(丁基)橡胶(IIR):										--Isobutene-isoprene (butyl) rubber (IIR):
4002.3110	---初级形状的	6	5	5.6	0	14	17	13	千克		---In primary forms

税则号列 Tariff Item.	货 品 名 称	最惠国(%) MFN	协定(%)CT 东盟 CA	 中巴 CP	 中智 CC	普通 Gen	增值税率 VAT	出口退税 ED	计量单位 Unit	监管条件 SC	Article Description
4002.3190	---其他	7.5	5	7.1	0	35	17	13	千克		---Other
	--其他:										--Other:
4002.3910	---初级形状的	7.5	5		0	14	17	13	千克		---In pimary forms
4002.3990	---其他	7.5	5	7.1	0	35	17	13	千克		---Other
	-氯丁二烯(氯丁)橡胶(CR):										-Chloroprene (chlorobutadiene) rubber(CR):
4002.4100	--胶乳	7.5	5	7.1	0	14	17	13	千克		--Latex
	--其他:										--Other:
4002.4910	---初级形状的	7.5	5		0	14	17	13	千克		---In primary forms
4002.4990	---其他	7.5	5	7.1	0	35	17	13	千克		---Other
	-丁腈橡胶(NBR):										-Acrylonitrile-butadient rubber(NBR):
4002.5100	--胶乳	7.5	5	7.1	0	14	17	13	千克		--Latex
	--其他:										--Other:
4002.5910	---初级形状的	7.5	5		0	14	17	13	千克		---In primary forms
4002.5990	---其他	7.5	5		0	35	17	13	千克		---Other
	-异戊二烯橡胶(IR):										-Isoprene rubber (IR):
4002.6010	---初级形状的	3			0	14	17	13	千克		---In primary forms
4002.6090	---其他	5		4.5	0	35	17	13	千克		---Other
	-乙丙非共轭二烯橡胶(EPDM):										-Ethylene-propylene-non-conjugated diene rubber (EPDM):
4002.7010	---初级形状的	7.5	5		0	14	17	13	千克		---In primary forms
4002.7090	---其他	7.5	5	7.1	0	35	17	13	千克		---Other
4002.8000	-税目40.01所列产品与本税目所列产品的混合物	7.5	5		0	35	17	13	千克		-Mixtures of any product of heading 40.01 with any product of this heading
	-其他:										-Other:
4002.9100	--胶乳	7.5	5		0	14	17	13	千克		--Latex
	--其他:										--Other:
	---其他合成橡胶:										---Other synthetic rubber:
4002.9911	----初级形状的	7.5	5		0	14	17	13	千克		----In primary forms
4002.9919	----其他	7.5	5		0	35	17	13	千克		----Other
4002.9990	---其他	4			0	14	17	13	千克		---Other
40.03	**再生橡胶,初级形状或板、片、带:**										**Reclaimed rubber in primary forms or in plates, sheets or strip:**
4003.0000	再生橡胶,初级形状或板、片、带	8	5		0	30	17	13	千克		Reclaimed rubber in primary forms or in plates, sheets or strip
40.04	**橡胶(硬质橡胶的除外)的废碎料、下脚料及其粉、粒:**										**Waste, parings and scrap of rubber (other than hard rubber) and powders and granules obtained therefrom:**
4004.0000	橡胶(硬质橡胶的除外)的废碎料、下脚料及其粉、粒	8	5	7.6	0	30	17	13	千克		Waste, parings and scrap of rubber (other than hard rubber) and powders and granules obtained therefrom
4004.0000 10	废轮胎及其切块	8				30	17	13	千克	9	Waste rubber tyres and their cuts
4004.0000 90	橡胶废碎料及下脚料及其粉、粒(硬质橡胶的除外)	8				30	17	13	千克		Other waste, parings and scrap of rubber (other than hard rubber) and powders and granules obtained therefrom
40.05	**未硫化的复合橡胶,初级形状或板、片、带:**										**Compounded rubber, unvulcanized, in primary forms or in plates, sheets or strip:**
4005.1000	-与碳黑或硅石混合	8	5		0	35	17	13	千克		-Compounded with carbon black or silica

税则号列 Tariff Item.	货品名称	最惠国(%) MFN	协定(%)CT 东盟 CA	协定(%)CT 中巴 CP	协定(%)CT 中智 CC	普通 Gen	增值税率 VAT	出口退税 ED	计量单位 Unit	监管条件 SC	Article Description
4005.2000	-溶液;子目4005.10以外的分散体	8	5		0	35	17	13	千克		-Solutions; dispersions other than those of subheading 4005.10
	-其他:										-Other:
4005.9100	--板、片、带	8	5		0	35	17	13	千克		--Plates, sheets and strip
4005.9900	--其他	8	5		0	35	17	13	千克		--Other
40.06	**其他形状(例如,杆、管或型材及异型材)的未硫化橡胶及未硫化橡胶制品(例如,盘、环):**										**Other forms (for example, rods, tubes and profile shapes) and articles (for example, discs and rings), or unvulcanized rubber:**
4006.1000	-轮胎翻新用胎面补料胎条	8	5		0	35	17	13	千克		-"Camel-back" strips for retreading rubber tyres
	-其他:										-Other:
4006.9010	---其他形状的未硫化橡胶	8	5		0	35	17	13	千克		---Other forms of unvulcanized rubber
4006.9020	---未硫化橡胶制品	14	8		8.4	80	17	13	千克		---Articles of unvulcanized rubber
40.07	**硫化橡胶线及绳:**										**Vulcanized rubber thread and cord:**
4007.0000	硫化橡胶线及绳	14	8		8.4	80	17	13	千克		Vulcanized rubber thread and cord
40.08	**硫化橡胶(硬质橡胶除外)制的板、片、带、杆或型材及异型材:**										**Plates, sheets, strip, rods and profile shapes, of vulcanized rubber other than hard rubber:**
	-海绵橡胶制:										-Of cellular rubber:
4008.1100	--板、片、带	8	5		0	35	17	13	千克		--Plates, sheets and strip
4008.1900	--其他	8	5		0	35	17	13	千克		--Other
	-非海绵橡胶制:										-Of non-cellular rubber:
4008.2100	--板、片、带	8	5		0	35	17	13	千克		--Plates, sheets and strip
4008.2900	--其他	8	5		0	35	17	13	千克		--Other
40.09	**硫化橡胶(硬质橡胶除外)制的管子,不论是否装有附件(例如,接头、肘管、法兰):**										**Tubes, pipes and hoses, of vulcanized rubber other than hard rubber, with or without their fittings (for example, joints, elbows, flanges):**
	-未经加强或未与其他材料合制:										-Not reinforced or otherwise combined with other materials:
4009.1100	--未装有附件	10.5	T3		0	40	17	13	千克		--Without fittings
4009.1200	--装有附件	10	5		0	40	17	13	千克		--With fittings
	-用金属加强或只与金属合制:										-Reinforced or otherwise combined only with metal:
4009.2100	--未装有附件	10.5	T3		8.4	40	17	13	千克		--Without fittings
4009.2200	--装有附件	10	T3		0	40	17	13	千克		--With fittings
	-用纺织材料加强或只与纺织材料合制:										-Reinforced or otherwise combined only with textile materials:
4009.3100	--未装有附件	10.5	T3		8.4	40	17	13	千克		--Without fittings
4009.3200	--装有附件	10	5		0	40	17	13	千克		--With fittings
	-用其他材料加强或与其他材料合制:										-Reinforced or otherwise combined with other materials:
4009.4100	--未装有附件	10.5	T3		8.4	40	17	13	千克		--Without fittings
4009.4200	--装有附件	10	T3		8	40	17	13	千克		--With fittings
40.10	**硫化橡胶制的传动带或输送带及带料:**										**Conveyor or transmission belts or belting, of vulcanized rubber:**
	-输送带及带料:										-Conveyor belts or belting:
4010.1100	--仅用金属加强的	10	5		8	35	17	13	千克		--Reinforced only with metal

税则号列 Tariff Item.	货品名称	最惠国(%) MFN	协定(%) CT 东盟 CA	中巴 CP	中智 CC	普通 Gen	增值税率 VAT	出口退税 ED	计量单位 Unit	监管条件 SC	Article Description
4010.1200	--仅用纺织材料加强的	10	5		8	35	17	13	千克		--Reinforced only with textile materials
4010.1900	--其他	10	5		0	35	17	13	千克		--Other
	-传动带及带料：										-Transmission belts or belting:
4010.3100	--梯形截面的环形传动带(三角带),V形肋状的,外周长超过60厘米,但不超过180厘米	8	T3		0	35	17	13	千克		--Endless transmission belts of trapezoidal cross-section (V-belts), V-ribbed, of an outside circumference exceeding 60 cm but not exceeding 180 cm
4010.3200	--梯形截面的环形传动带(三角带),外周长超过60厘米,但不超过180厘米,V形肋状的除外	8	T3		0	35	17	13	千克		--Endless transmission belts of trapezoidal cross-section (V-belts), other than V-ribbed, of an outside circumference exceeding 60 cm but not exceeding 180 cm
4010.3300	--梯形截面的环形传动带(三角带),V形肋状的,外周长超过180厘米,但不超过240厘米	8	T3		0	35	17	13	千克		--Endless transmission belts of trapezoidal cross-section (V-belts), V-ribbed, of an outside circumference exceeding 180 cm but not exceeding 240 cm
4010.3400	--梯形截面的环形传动带(三角带),外周长超过180厘米,但不超过240厘米,V形肋状的除外	8	T3		0	35	17	13	千克		--Endless transmission belts of trapezoidal cross-section (V-belts), other than V-ribbed, of an outside circumference exceeding 180 cm but not exceeding 240 cm
4010.3500	--环形同步带,外周长超过60厘米,但不超过150厘米	10	T3		0	35	17	13	千克		--Endless synchronous belts, of an outside circumference exceeding 60 cm but not exceeding 150 cm
4010.3600	--环形同步带,外周长超过150厘米,但不超过198厘米	10	5		0	35	17	13	千克		--Endless synchronous belts, of an outside circumference exceeding 150 cm but not exceeding 198 cm
4010.3900	--其他	8	T3	7.6	0	35	17	13	千克		--Other
40.11	**新的充气橡胶轮胎：**										**New pneumatic tyres, of rubber:**
4011.1000	-机动小客车(包括旅行小客车及赛车)用	10	T3	9.4	8	50	17	13	条		-Of a kind used on motor cars (including station wagons and racing cars)
4011.1000 10	机动小客车用新的充气子午线轮胎(橡胶轮胎,包括旅行小客车及赛车用)	10				50	17	13	条	AB	New pneumatic tyres of rubber, of a kind used on motor cars (including station wagons and racing cars), radial-ply tyres
4011.1000 90	机动小客车用新充气非子午线轮胎(橡胶轮胎,包括旅行小客车及赛车用)	10				50	17	13	条	AB	New pneumatic tyres of rubber, of a kind used on motor cars (including station wagons and racing cars), other than radial-ply tyres
4011.2000	-客运机动车辆或货运机动车辆用	10	T3	9.4	8	50	17	13	条		-Of a kind used on buses or lorries
4011.2000 11	客或货运车用新的充气子午线轮胎(指机动车辆用橡胶轮胎,断面宽度≥30英寸)	10				50	17	13	条	AB	Radial-ply tyres, cross-section width ≥ 30 inches, of a kind used on buses or lorries
4011.2000 19	断面宽≥30英寸客或货车用新非子午线充气橡胶轮胎	10				50	17	13	条	AB	Non - meridian air charging rubber tyre for passenger cars or trucks with sectional width≥30 inch for
4011.2000 91	其他客或货车用新充气子午线轮胎(指机动车辆用橡胶轮胎)	10				50	17	13	条	AB	New pneumatic tyres of rubber, radial-ply tyres, of a kind used on buses or lorries

税则号列 Tariff Item.	货品名称	最惠国(%) MFN	协定(%) CT 东盟 CA	中巴 CP	中智 CC	普通 Gen	增值税率 VAT	出口退税 ED	计量单位 Unit	监管条件 SC	Article Description
4011.2000 99	客或货车用新的其他非子午线充气橡胶轮胎	10				50	17	13	条	AB	
4011.3000	-航空器用	1			0	11	17	13	条		-Of a kind used on aircraft
4011.4000	-摩托车用	15	T3		9	80	17	13	条	AB	-Of a kind used on motorcycles
4011.5000	-自行车用	20	T3		12	80	17	13	条	B	-Of a kind used on bicycles
	-其他,人字型胎面或类似胎面的:										-Other, having a "herring-bone" or similar tread:
4011.6100	--农业或林业车辆及机器用	17.5	T3		0	50	17	13	条		--Of a kind used on agricultural or forestry vehicles and machines
4011.6100 11	断面宽≥24英寸人字形子午线轮胎(新充气橡胶轮胎,含胎面类似人字形的,农林车辆机械用)	17.5				50	17	13	条	A	New pneumatic tyres of rubber, "herring-bone" tread, radial-ply tyres, cross-section width ≥24 inches, of a kind used on agricultural or forestry vehicles and machines
4011.6100 19	断面宽≥24英寸人字形非子午线轮胎(新充气橡胶轮胎,含胎面类似人字形的,农林车辆机械用)	17.5				50	17	13	条	A	Herringbone non – meridian air charging rubber tyre with sectional width≥24 inch
4011.6100 91	其他人字形胎面子午线轮胎(新充气橡胶轮胎,含胎面类似人字形的,农林车辆机械用)	17.5				50	17	13	条	A	New pneumatic tyres of rubber, "herring-bone" tread, radial-ply tyres, of a kind used on agricultural or forestry vehicles and machines
4011.6100 99	其他人字形胎面非子午线轮胎(新充气橡胶轮胎,含胎面类似人字形的,农林车辆机械用)	17.5				50	17	13	条	A	Other new pneumatic tyres of rubber, "herring-bone" tread, other than radial-ply tyres, of a kind used on agricultural or forestry vehicles and machines
4011.6200	--建筑业或工业搬运车辆及机器用,辋圈尺寸不超过61厘米	17.5	T3		14	50	17	13	条		--Of a kind used on construction or industrial handling vehicles and machines and having a rim size not exceeding 61cm
4011.6200 11	断面宽≥24英寸人字形子午线轮胎(建筑业、工业用,辋圈≤61cm,新充气橡胶胎,含类似人字形)	17.5				50	17	13	条	A	New pneumatic tyres of rubber, "herring-bone" tread, radial-ply tyres, cross-section width≥24 inches
4011.6200 19	断面宽≥24英寸人字形非子午线轮胎(建筑业、工业用,辋圈≤61cm,新充气橡胶胎,含类似人字形)	17.5				50	17	13	条	A	"Herring – bone" tread, other than radial – ply tyres, cross – section width≥24inches
4011.6200 91	其他人字形胎面子午线轮胎(建筑业、工业用,辋圈≤61cm,新充气橡胶胎,含类似人字形)	17.5				50	17	13	条	A	Other new pneumatic tyres of rubber, "herring-bone" tread, radial-ply tyres, of a kind used on construction or industrial, rim≤61cm
4011.6200 99	其他人字形胎面非子午线轮胎(建筑业、工业用,辋圈≤61cm,新充气橡胶胎,含类似人字形)	17.5				50	17	13	条	A	Other new pneumatic tyres of rubber, "herring-bone" tread, other than radial-ply tyres, of a kind used on construction or industrial rim≤61cm
4011.6300	--建筑业或工业搬运车辆及机器用,辋圈尺寸超过61厘米	17.5	T3		14	50	17	13	条		--Of a kind used on construction or industrial handling vehicles and machines and having a rim size exceeding 61cm

税则号列 Tariff Item.	货品名称	最惠国(%) MFN	协定(%)CT 东盟 CA	中巴 CP	中智 CC	普通 Gen	增值税率 VAT	出口退税 ED	计量单位 Unit	监管条件 SC	Article Description
4011.6300 11	断面宽≥24英寸人字形子午线轮胎(建筑业、工业用,辋圈>61cm,新充气橡胶胎,含类人字形)	17.5				50	17	13	条	A	New pneumatic tyres of rubber, "herring-bone" tread, radial-ply tyres, cross-section width ≥24 inches, of a kind used on construction or industrial, rim >61cm
4011.6300 19	断面宽≥24英寸人字形非子午线轮胎(建筑业、工业用,辋圈>61cm,新充气橡胶胎,含类人字形)	17.5				50	17	13	条	A	Herringbone non – meridian air charging rubber tyre with sectional width ≥ 24 inch
4011.6300 91	其他人字形胎面子午线轮胎(建筑业、工业用,辋圈>61cm,新充气橡胶胎,含类人字形)	17.5				50	17	13	条	A	Other new pneumatic tyres of rubber, "herring-bone" tread, radial-ply tyres, of a kind used on construction or industrial, rim >61cm
4011.6300 99	其他人字形胎面非子午线轮胎(建筑业、工业用,辋圈>61cm,新充气橡胶胎,含类似人字形)	17.5				50	17	13	条	A	Other new pneumatic tyres of rubber, "herring-bone" tread, other than radial-ply tyres, of a kind used on construction or industrial, rim >61cm
4011.6900	--其他	17.5	T3		14	50	17	13	条		--Other
4011.6900 11	断面宽≥30英寸人字形子午线轮胎(其他用途,新充气橡胶轮胎,含胎面类似人字形的)	17.5				50	17	13	条	A	New pneumatic tyres of rubber, "herring-bone" tread, radial-ply tyres, cross-section width ≥30 inches, of a kind other use
4011.6900 19	断面宽≥30英寸人字形非子午线轮胎(其他用途,新充气橡胶轮胎,含胎面类似人字形的)	17.5				50	17	13	条	A	"Herring – bone" tread, other than radial – ply tyres, cross – section width≥ 30inches
4011.6900 91	其他人字形胎面子午线轮胎(其他用途,新充气橡胶轮胎,含胎面类似人字形的)	17.5				50	17	13	条	A	Other new pneumatic tyres of rubber, "herring-bone" tread, radial-ply tyres, of a kind other use
4011.6900 99	其他人字形胎面非子午线轮胎(其他用途,新充气橡胶轮胎,含胎面类似人字形的)	17.5				50	17	13	条	A	New pneumatic tyres of rubber, "herring-bone" tread, other than radial-ply tyres, of a kind other use
	-其他:										-Other:
4011.9200	--农业或林业车辆及机器用	25	T3		15	50	17	13	条		--Of a kind used on agricultural or forestry vehicles and machines
4011.9200 11	其他断面宽度≥24英寸子午线轮胎(新充气橡胶轮胎,非人字形胎面,农林车辆机械用)	25				50	17	13	条	B	New pneumatic tyres of rubber, radial-ply tyres, other than "herring-bone" tread, of a kind used on agricultural or forestry vehicles and machines
4011.9200 19	其他断面宽≥24英寸非子午线轮胎(新充气橡胶轮胎,非人字形胎面,农林车辆机械用)	25				50	17	13	条	B	New pneumatic tyres of rubber, other than "herring-bone" tread or radial-ply tyres, cross-section width ≥24 inches, of a kind used on agricultural or forestry vehicles and machines

税则号列 Tariff Item.	货品名称	最惠国(%) MFN	协定(%) 东盟 CA	中巴 CP	中智 CC	普通 Gen	增值税率 VAT	出口退税 ED	计量单位 Unit	监管条件 SC	Article Description
4011.9200 91	其他新的充气橡胶子午线轮胎(新充气橡胶轮胎,非人字形胎面,农林车辆机械用)	25				50	17	13	条	B	New pneumatic tyres of rubber, radial-ply tyres, other than "herring-bone" tread, of a kind used on agricultural or forestry vehicles and machines
4011.9200 99	其他新的充气橡胶非子午线轮胎(新充气橡胶轮胎,非人字形胎面,农林车辆机械用)	25				50	17	13	条	B	New pneumatic tyres of rubber, other than "herring-bone" tread or radial-ply tyres, of a kind used on agricultural or forestry vehicles and machines
4011.9300	--建筑业或工业搬运车辆及机器用,辋圈尺寸不超过61厘米	25	T3		15	50	17	13	条		--Of a kind used on construction or industrial handling vehicles and machines and having a rim size not exceeding 61cm
4011.9300 11	其他断面宽度≥24英寸子午线轮胎(建筑业、工业用,辋圈≤61cm,新充气橡胶胎,非人字形胎面)	25				50	17	13	条	B	New pneumatic tyres of rubber, other than "herring-bone" tread, radial-ply tyres, cross-section width≥24 inches, rim≤61cm, of a kind used on construction or industrial
4011.9300 19	其他断面宽≥24英寸非子午线轮胎(建筑业、工业用,辋圈≤61cm,新充气橡胶胎,非人字形胎面)	25				50	17	13	条	B	New pneumatic tyres of rubber, other than "herring-bone" tread or radial-ply tyres, cross-section width≥24 inches, rim≤61cm, of a kind used on construction or industrial
4011.9300 91	其他新的充气橡胶子午线轮胎(建筑业、工业用,辋圈≤61cm,新充气橡胶胎,非人字形胎面)	25				50	17	13	条	B	New pneumatic tyres of rubber, other than "herring-bone" tread, radial-ply tyres, rim≤61cm, of a kind used on construction or industrial
4011.9300 99	其他新的充气橡胶非子午线轮胎(建筑业、工业用,辋圈≤61cm,新充气橡胶胎,非人字形胎面)	25				50	17	13	条	B	New pneumatic tyres of rubber, other than "herring-bone" tread or radial-ply tyres, rim≤61cm, of a kind used on construction or industrial
4011.9400	--建筑业或工业搬运车辆及机器用,辋圈尺寸超过61厘米	25	T3		20	50	17	13	条		--Of a kind used on construction or industrial handling vehicles and machines and having a rim size exceeding 61cm
4011.9400 11	其他断面宽度≥24英寸子午线轮胎(建筑业、工业用,辋圈>61cm,新充气橡胶胎,非人字形胎面)	25				50	17	13	条	B	New pneumatic tyres of rubber, other than "herring-bone" tread radial-ply tyres, cross-section width≥24 inches, rim>61cm, of a kind used on construction or industrial
4011.9400 19	其他断面宽≥24英寸非子午线轮胎(建筑业、工业用,辋圈>61cm,新充气橡胶胎,非人字形胎面)	25				50	17	13	条	B	New pneumatic tyres of rubber, other than "herring-bone" tread or radial-ply tyres, cross-section width≥24 inches, rim>61cm, of a kind used on construction or industrial
4011.9400 91	其他新的充气橡胶子午线轮胎(建筑业、工业用,辋圈>61cm,新充气橡胶胎,非人字形胎面)	25				50	17	13	条	B	New pneumatic tyres of rubber, other than "herring-bone" tread radial-ply tyres, rim>61cm, of a kind used on construction or industrial

税则号列 Tariff Item.	货品名称	最惠国(%) MFN	协定(%)CT 东盟 CA	中巴 CP	中智 CC	普通 Gen	增值税率 VAT	出口退税 ED	计量单位 Unit	监管条件 SC	Article Description
4011.9400 99	其他新的充气橡胶非子午线轮胎(建筑业、工业用,辋圈>61cm,新充气橡胶胎,非人字形胎面)	25				50	17	13	条	B	New pneumatic tyres of rubber, other than "herring-bone" tread or radial-ply tyres, rim > 61cm, of a kind used on construction or industrial
4011.9900	--其他	25	T3		20	50	17	13	条		--Other
4011.9900 11	其他断面宽度≥30英寸子午线轮胎(其他用途,新充气橡胶轮胎,非人字形胎面)	25				50	17	13	条	B	New pneumatic tyres of rubber, other than "herring-bone" tread, radial-ply tyres, cross-section width≥30 inches, of a kind other use
4011.9900 19	其他断面宽≥30英寸非子午线轮胎(其他用途,新充气橡胶轮胎,非人字形胎面)	25				50	17	13	条	B	New pneumatic tyres of rubber, other than "herring-bone" tread or radial-ply tyres, cross-section width≥30 inches, of a kind other use
4011.9900 91	其他新的充气橡胶子午线轮胎(其他用途,新充气橡胶轮胎,非人字形胎面)	25				50	17	13	条	B	Other new pneumatic tyres of rubber, other than "herring-bone" tread, radial-ply tyres, of a kind other use
4011.9900 99	其他新的充气橡胶非子午线轮胎(其他用途,新充气橡胶轮胎,非人字形胎面)	25				50	17	13	条	B	Other new pneumatic tyres of rubber, other than "herring-bone" tread or radial-ply tyres, of a kind other use
40.12	**翻新的或旧的充气橡胶轮胎;实心或半实心橡胶轮胎、橡胶胎面及橡胶轮胎衬带:**										**Retreaded or used pneumatic tyres of rubber; solid or cushion tyres, tyre treads and tyre flaps, of rubber:**
	-翻新轮胎:										-Retreaded tyres:
4012.1100	--机动小客车(包括旅行小客车及赛车)用	20	T3		12	50	17	13	条	A	--Of a kind used on motor cars (including station wagons and racing cars)
4012.1200	--机动大客车或货运机动车辆用	20	T3		12	50	17	13	条	A	--Of a kind used on buses or lorries
4012.1300	--航空器用	20	12		12	50	17	13	条		--Of a kind used on aircraft
4012.1900	--其他	20	T3		12	50	17	13	条		--Other
	-旧的充气轮胎:										-Used pneumatic tyres:
4012.2010	---汽车用	25	T3		15	50	17	13	条		---Of a kind used on motor cars, buses or lorries
4012.2010 10	汽车用旧的充气橡胶子午线轮胎	25				50	17	13	条	A	Used pneumatic tyres of rubber, radial-ply tyres radial-ply tyres of a kind used on vehicles
4012.2010 90	汽车用旧的充气橡胶非子午线轮胎	25				50	17	13	条	A	Used pneumatic tyres of rubber, other than radial-ply tyres, of a kind used on vehicles
4012.2090	---其他	25	T3		15	80	17	13	条		---Other
4012.2090 10	其他用途旧的充气橡胶子午线轮胎	25				80	17	13	条		Used pneumatic tyres of rubber, radial-ply tyres, of a kind other use
4012.2090 90	其他用旧的充气橡胶非子午线轮胎	25				80	17	13	条		Used pneumatic tyres of rubber, other than radial-ply tyres, of a kind other use
	-其他:										-Other:
4012.9010	---航空器用	3			0	11	17	13	千克		---Of a kind used on aircraft
4012.9020	---汽车用	22	T3		0	50	17	13	千克		---Of a kind used on motor cars, buses or lorries

税则号列 Tariff Item.	货品名称	最惠国(%) MFN	协定(%) CT 东盟 CA	中巴 CP	中智 CC	普通 Gen	增值税率 VAT	出口退税 ED	计量单位 Unit	监管条件 SC	Article Description
4012.9020 10	汽车用实心或半实心子午线轮胎	22				50	17	13	千克	A	Solid or cushion tyres, radial-ply tyres, of a kind used on vehicles
4012.9020 90	汽车用实心或半实心非子午线轮胎(还包括可互换橡胶胎面及橡胶轮胎衬带)	22				50	17	13	千克	A	Solid or cushion tyres, interchangeable tyre treads and tyre flaps, other than radial-ply tyres, of a kind used on vehicles
4012.9090	---其他	22	T3		0	50	17	13	千克		---Other
4012.9090 10	其他用实心或半实心子午线轮胎	22				50	17	13	千克		Other solid or cushion tyres, radial-ply tyres, of a kind other use
4012.9090 90	其他用实心或半实心非子午线轮胎(还包括可互换橡胶胎面及橡胶轮胎衬带)	22				50	17	13	千克		Other solid or cushion tyres, interchangeable tyre treads and tyre flaps, other than radial-ply tyres, of a kind other use
40.13	**橡胶内胎:**										**Inner tubes, of rubber:**
4013.1000	-机动小客车(包括旅行小客车及赛车)、客运机动车辆或货运机动车辆用	15	T3	13	0	50	17	13	条	A	-Of a kind used on motor cars (including station wagons and racing cars), buses or lorries
4013.2000	-自行车用	15	T3		9	80	17	13	条	B	-Of a kind used on bicycles
	-其他:										-Other:
4013.9010	---航空器用	3			0	11	17	13	条		---Of a kind used on aircraft
4013.9090	---其他	15	T3		9	50	17	13	条	B	---Other
40.14	**硫化橡胶(硬质橡胶除外)制的卫生及医疗用品(包括奶嘴),不论是否装有硬质橡胶制的附件:**										**Hygienic or pharmaceutical articles (including teats), of vulcanized rubber other than hard rubber, with or without fittings of hard rubber:**
4014.1000	-避孕套	0				0	0	0	千克	B	-Sheath contraceptives
4014.9000	-其他	17.5	8		10.5	50	17	13	千克		-Other
40.15	**硫化橡胶(硬质橡胶除外)制的衣着用品及附件(包括分指手套、连指手套及露指手套):**										**Articles of apparel and clothing accessories (including gloves, mittens and mitts), for all purposes, of vulcanized rubber other than hard rubber:**
	-手套:										-Gloves:
4015.1100	--外科用	8	5		0	30	17	13	双/千克	B	--Surgical
4015.1900	--其他	18	8		0	80	17	13	双/千克	B	--Other
	-其他:										-Other:
4015.9010	---医疗用	8	5		0	30	17	13	千克		---For medical purpose
4015.9090	---其他	15	8		9	90	17	13	千克		---Other
40.16	**硫化橡胶(硬质橡胶除外)的其他制品:**										**Other articles of vulcanized rubber other than hard rubber:**
	-海绵橡胶制:										-Of cellular rubber:
4016.1010	---机器及仪器用零件	8	T3		0	30	17	13	千克		---of a kind used in machines or instruments
4016.1090	---其他	15	T3		0	80	17	13	千克		---Other
	-其他:										-Other:
4016.9100	--铺地制品及门垫	18	T3		14.4	80	17	13	千克		--Floor coverings and mats
4016.9200	--橡皮擦	18	T3		10.8	80	17	13	千克		--Erasers
	--垫片、垫圈及其他密封垫:										--Gaskets, washers and other seals:
4016.9310	---机器及仪器用	8	5		0	30	17	13	千克		---Of a kind used in machines or instruments

税则号列 Tariff Item.	货品名称	最惠国(%) MFN	协定(%)CT 东盟 CA	中巴 CP	中智 CC	普通 Gen	增值税率 VAT	出口退税 ED	计量单位 Unit	监管条件 SC	Article Description
4016.9390	---其他	15	8		0	80	17	13	千克		---Other
4016.9400	--船舶或码头的碰垫,不论是否可充气	18	8		10.8	80	17	13	千克		--Boat or dock fenders, whether or not inflatable
4016.9500	--其他可充气制品	18	8		10.8	80	17	13	千克		--Other inflatable articles
	--其他:										--Other:
4016.9910	---机器及仪器用零件	8	T3	7.6	0	30	17	13	千克		---Of a kind used in machines or instruments
4016.9990	---其他	10	T3	9.5	8	80	17	13	千克		---Other
40.17	**各种形状的硬质橡胶(例如纯硬质胶),包括废碎料;硬质橡胶制品:**										**Hard rubber (for example, ebonite) in all forms, including waste and scrap; articles of hard rubber:**
4017.0010	---各种形状的硬质橡胶,包括废碎料	8	5		0	35	17	13	千克		---Hard rubber in all forms, including waste and scrap
4017.0020	---硬质橡胶制品	15	8		9	90	17	13	千克		---Articles of hard rubber

第八类

生皮、皮革、毛皮及其制品；鞍具及挽具；旅行用品、手提包及类似容器；动物肠线(蚕胶丝除外)制品

SECTION Ⅷ

RAW HIDES AND SKINS, LEATHER, FURSKINS AND ARTICLES THEREOF; SADDLERY AND HARNESS; TRAVEL GOODS, HANDBAGS AND SIMILAR CONTAINERS; ARTICLES OF ANIMAL GUT (OTHER THAN SILK-WORM GUT)

第四十一章

生皮(毛皮除外)及皮革

Chapter 41

Raw hides and skins (other than furskins) and leather

注释：

一、本章不包括：

(一)生皮的边角废料(税目05.11)；

(二)税目05.05或67.01的带羽毛或羽绒的整张或部分鸟皮；

(三)带毛生皮或已鞣的带毛皮张(第四十三章)；但下列动物的带毛生皮应归入第四十一章：牛(包括水牛)、马、绵羊及羔羊(不包括阿斯特拉罕、喀拉科尔、波斯羔羊或类似羔羊、印度、中国或蒙古羔羊)、山羊或小山羊(不包括也门或蒙古山羊及小山羊)、猪(包括西貒、小羚羊、瞪羚、骆驼(包括单峰骆驼)、驯鹿、麋、鹿、狍或狗。

二、(一)税目41.04至41.06不包括经逆鞣(包括预鞣)加工的皮(酌情归入税目41.01至41.03)；

(二)税目41.04至41.06所称"坯革"，包括在干燥前经复鞣、染色或加油(加脂)的皮。

三、本目录所称"再生皮革"，仅指税目41.15的皮革。

Notes:

1. This Chapter does not cover:

(a) Parings or similar waste, of raw hides or skins (heading No. 05.11);

(b) Birdskins or parts of birdskins, with their feathers or down, of heading No. 05.05 or 67.01; or

(c) Hides or skins, with the hair or wool on, raw, tanned or dressed (Chapter 43); the following are, however, to be classified in Chapter 41, namely, raw hides and skins with the hair or wool on, of bovine animals (including buffalo), of equine animals, of sheep or lambs (except Astrakhan, Broadtail, Caracul, Persian or similar lambs, Indian, Chinese, Mongolian or Tibetan lambs), of goats or kids (except Yemen, Mongolian or Tibetan goats and kids), of swine (including peccary), of chamois, of gazelle, of eamels (including dromedary) of reindeer, of elk, of deer, of roebucks or of dogs.

2. (a) Headings Nos. 41.04 to 41.06 do not cover hides and skins which have undergone a tanning (including pre-tanning) process which is reversible (headings Nos. 41.01 to 41.03, as the case may be).

(b) For the purposes of headings Nos. 41.04 to 41.06, the term "crust" includes hides and skins that have been retanned, coloured or fat-liquored (stuffed) prior to drying.

3. Throughout the Nomenclature the expression "composition leather" means only substances of the kind referred to in heading No. 41.15.

税则号列 Tariff Item.	货品名称	最惠国(%) MFN	协定(%) CT 东盟 CA	中巴 CP	中智 CC	普通 Gen	增值税率 VAT	出口退税 ED	计量单位 Unit	监管条件 SC	Article Description
41.01	**生牛皮(包括水牛皮)、生马皮(鲜的、盐腌的、干的、石灰浸渍的、浸酸的或以其他方法保藏,但未鞣制、未经羊皮纸化处理或进一步加工的),不论是否去毛或剖层:**										**Raw hides and skins of bovine (including buffalo) or equine animals (fresh, or salted, dried, limed, pickled or otherwise preserved, but not tanned, parchment-dressed or further prepared), whether or not dehaired or split:**
	-整张皮,完全干燥的每张重量不超过8公斤,干盐腌的不超过10公斤,鲜的、湿盐腌的或以其他方法保藏的不超过16公斤:										-Whole hides and skins, of a weight per skin not exceeding 8 kg when simply dried, 10 kg when dry-salted, or 16 kg when fresh, wet-salted or otherwise preserved:
	---牛皮:										---Of bovine animals:
4101.2011	----经逆鞣处理的	8	5	6	0	17	17		千克/张		----Have undergone a tanning which is reversible
4101.2011 10	规定重量逆鞣整张生濒危野牛皮(指每张简单干燥≤8kg,干盐渍≤10kg,鲜或湿盐≤16kg)	8				17	17		千克/张	ABFE	Whole raw hides and skins of wild bovine animals, in imminent dangers, have undergone a tanning which is reversible, w≤8kg when simply dried, w≤10kg when dry-salted, w≤16kg when fresh, wet-salted
4101.2011 90	规定重量逆鞣处理整张生牛皮(指每张,简单干燥≤8kg,干盐渍≤10kg,鲜或湿盐≤16kg)	8				17	17		千克/张	AB	Whole raw hides and skins of bovine animals, have undergone a tanning which is reversible, w≤8kg when simply dried, w≤10kg when dry-salted, w≤16kg when fresh, wet-salted
4101.2019	----其他	5			0	17	17		千克/张		----Other
4101.2019 10	规定重量非逆鞣整张濒危生野牛皮(指每张,简单干燥≤8kg,干盐渍≤10kg,鲜或湿盐≤16kg)	5				17	17		千克/张	ABFE	Whole raw hides and skins of wild bovine animals, in imminent dangers, not have undergone a tanning which is reversible, w ≤ 8kg when simply dried, w≤10kg when dry-salted, w≤16kg when fresh, wet-salted
4101.2019 90	规定重量非逆鞣处理整张生牛皮(指每张,简单干燥≤8kg,干盐渍≤10kg,鲜或湿盐≤16kg)	5				17	17		千克/张	AB	Whole raw hides and skins of bovine animals, not have undergone a tanning which is reversible, w ≤ 8kg when simply dried w ≤ 10kg when dry-salted w ≤ 16kg when fresh, wet-salted
4101.2020	---马皮	5			0	30	17		千克/张		---Of equine animals
4101.2020 10	规定重量整张濒危生野马皮(指每张,简单干燥≤8kg,干盐渍≤10kg,鲜或湿盐≤16kg	5				30	17		千克/张	ABFE	Whole raw hides and skins of wild equine animals, in imminent dangers, w≤8kg when simply dried, w≤10kg when dry-salted, w ≤ 16kg when fresh, wet-salted
4101.2020 90	规定重量整张生马皮(指每张,简单干燥≤8kg,干盐渍≤10kg,鲜或湿盐≤16kg)	5				30	17		千克/张	AB	Whole raw hides and skins of equine animals, w≤8kg when simply dried, w≤10kg when dry-salted, w≤16kg when fresh, wet-salted

税则号列 Tariff Item.	货品名称	最惠国(%) MFN	协定(%)CT 东盟 CA	协定(%)CT 中巴 CP	协定(%)CT 中智 CC	普通 Gen	增值税率 VAT	出口退税 ED	计量单位 Unit	监管条件 SC	Article Description
	-整张皮,重量超过16公斤:										-Whole hides and skins, of a weight exceeding 16 kg:
	---牛皮:										---Of bovine animals
4101.5011	----经逆鞣处理的	8.4	5	7	0	17	17		千克/张		----Have undergone a tanning which is reversible
4101.5011 10	重>16kg 逆鞣整张濒危生野牛皮	8.4				17	17		千克/张	ABFE	Whole raw hides and skins of wild equine animals, in imminent dangers, have undergone a tanning which is reversible, W>16kg
4101.5011 90	重>16kg 逆鞣处理整张生牛皮	8.4				17	17		千克/张	AB	Whole raw hides and skins of equine animals, have undergone a tanning which is reversible, W>16kg
4101.5019	----其他	5			0	17	17		千克/张		----Other
4101.5019 10	重>16kg 非逆鞣整张濒危生野牛皮	5				17	17		千克/张	ABFE	Whole raw hides and skins of wild equine animals, in imminent dangers, not have undergone a tanning which is reversible, W>16kg
4101.5019 90	重>16kg 非逆鞣处理整张生牛皮	5				17	17		千克/张	AB	Whole raw hides and skins of equine animals, not have undergone a tanning which is reversible, W>16kg
4101.5020	---马皮	5			0	30	17		千克/张		---Of equine animals
4101.5020 10	重>16kg 整张濒危生野马皮	5				30	17		千克/张	ABFE	Whole raw hides and skins of wild equine animals, in imminent dangers, W>16kg
4101.5020 90	重>16kg 整张生马皮	5				30	17		千克/张	AB	Whole raw hides and skins of equine animals, W>16kg
	-其他,包括整张或半张的背皮及腹皮:										-Other, including butts, bends and bollies:
	---牛皮:										---Of bovine animals
4101.9011	----经逆鞣处理的	8.4	5	7	0	17	17		千克		----Have undergone a reversible tanning process
4101.9011 10	其他逆鞣处理濒危生野牛皮(包括整张或半张的背皮及腹皮)	8.4				17	17		千克	FEAB	Other whole raw hides and skins (including butts, bends and bellies), of wild bovine animals, in imminent dangers, have undergone a tanning which is reversible
4101.9011 90	其他逆鞣处理生牛皮(包括整张或半张的背皮及腹皮)	8.4				17	17		千克	AB	Other whole raw hides and skins (including butts, bends and bellies), of bovine animals, have undergone a tanning which is reversible
4101.9019	----其他	5			0	17	17		千克		----Other
4101.9019 10	其他濒危生野牛皮(包括整张或半张的背皮及腹皮)	5				17	17		千克	FEAB	Other whole raw hides and skins (including butts, bends and bellies), of wild bovine animals, in imminent dangers
4101.9019 90	其他生牛皮(包括整张或半张的背皮及腹皮)	5				17	17		千克	AB	Other whole raw hides and skins (including butts, bends and bellies), of bovine animals
4101.9020	---马皮	5			0	30	17		千克		---of equine animals

税则号列 Tariff Item.	货品名称	最惠国(%) MFN	协定(%)CT 东盟 CA	中巴 CP	中智 CC	普通 Gen	增值税率 VAT	出口退税 ED	计量单位 Unit	监管条件 SC	Article Description
4101.9020 10	其他濒危生野马皮(包括整张或半张的背皮及腹皮)	5				30	17		千克	FEAB	Other whole raw hides and skins (including butts, bends and bellies), of wild equine animals,in imminent dangers
4101.9020 90	其他生马皮(包括整张或半张的背皮及腹皮)	5				30	17		千克	AB	Other whole raw hides and skins (including butts, bends and bellies), of equine animals
41.02	**绵羊或羔羊生皮(鲜的、盐渍的、干的、石灰浸渍的、浸酸的或经其他方法保藏,但未鞣制、未经羊皮纸化处理或进一步加工的),不论是否带毛或剖层,但本章注释一(三)所述不包括的生皮除外:**										**Raw skins of sheep or lambs (fresh, or salted, dried, limed, pickled or otherwise preseved, but not tanned, parchment-dressed or further prepared), whether or not with wool on or split, other than those excluded by Note 1 (c) to this Chapter:**
4102.1000	-带毛	7	5		5.6	30	17		千克/张	AB	-With wool on
	-不带毛:										-Without wool on:
	--浸酸的:										--Pickled:
4102.2110	---经逆鞣处理的	14	8		0	30	17		千克/张	AB	---Have undergone a reversible tanning process
4102.2190	---其他	9	5	8	0	30	17		千克/张	AB	---Other
	--其他:										--Other:
4102.2910	---经逆鞣处理的	14	8		8.4	30	17		千克/张	AB	---Have undergone a reversible tanning process
4102.2990	---其他	7	5	6	0	30	17		千克/张	AB	---Other
41.03	**其他生皮(鲜的、盐渍的、干的、石灰浸渍的、浸酸的或以其他方法保藏,但未鞣制、未经羊皮纸化处理或进一步加工的),不论是否去毛或剖层,但本章注释一(二)或(三)所述不包括的生皮除外:**										**Other raw hides and skins (fresh, or salted, dried, limed, pickled or otherwise preserved, but not tanned, parchment-dressed or further prepared), whether or not dehaired or split, other than those excluded by Note 1 (b) or 1 (c) to this Chapter:**
4103.2000	-爬行动物皮	9	5		0	30	17		千克/张	ABFE	-Of reptiles
4103.3000	-猪皮	9	T3		0	30	17		千克/张		-Of swine
4103.3000 10	生鹿猪、姬猪皮	9				30	17		千克/张	ABFE	Raw hides and skins of pig-deer (*Babyrousa*)、pygmy pig (*Porcula*)
4103.3000 90	生猪皮	9				30	17		千克/张	AB	Raw hides and skins of swine
	-其它:										-Other:
	---山羊板皮:										---Of goats:
4103.9011	----经退鞣外理的	14	8		8.4	35	17		千克/张	AB	----Have unaergone a tanning which is rever sible
4103.9019	----其它	9	5		0	35	17		千克/张	AB	----Other
4103.9021	----经退鞣外理的	14	8		8.4	30	17		千克/张	AB	----Have wciergohe a tanning which is reversible
4103.9029	----其它	9	5		0	30	17		千克/张	AB	----Other
4103.9090	---其他	9	T3		5.4	30	17		千克/张		---Other
4103.9090 10	其他濒危野生动物生皮(本章注释一(二)或(三)所述不包括的生皮除外)	9				30	17		千克/张	ABEF	Other raw hides and skins of wild animals, in imminent dangers, other than those excluded by Note 1 (b) or 1 (c) to this Chapter

税则号列 Tariff Item.	货品名称	最惠国(%) MFN	协定(%) 东盟 CA	中巴 CP	CT 中智 CC	普通 Gen	增值税率 VAT	出口退税 ED	计量单位 Unit	监管条件 SC	Article Description
4103.9090 90	其他生皮(本章注释一(二)或(三)所述不包括的生皮除外)	9				30	17		千克/张	AB	Other raw hides and skins of animals, other than those excluded by Note 1 (b) 1 (c) to this Chapter
41.04	**经鞣制的不带毛牛皮(包括水牛皮)、马皮及其坯革,不论是否剖层,但未经进一步加工:**										**Tanned or crust hides and skins of bovine (including buffalo) or equine animals, without hair on, whether or not split, but not further prepared:**
	-湿革(包括蓝湿皮):										-In the wet state (including wet-blue)
	--全粒面未剖层革;粒面剖层革:										--Full grains, unsplit; grain splits:
	---牛皮:										---of bovine animals:
4104.1111	----蓝湿的	7	5	3.5	0	17	17		千克		----Of web-blue
4104.1111 10	蓝湿濒危野牛皮(全粒面未剖或粒面剖层,经鞣制不带毛)	7				17	17		千克	ABFE	Tanned or crust hides and skins of wild bovine animals, in imminent dangers, without hair on, in the wet-blue state, full grains, unsplit or grain splits
4104.1111 90	全粒面未剖层或粒面剖层蓝湿牛皮(经鞣制不带毛)	7				17	17		千克	AB	Tanned or crust hides and skins of bovine animals, without hair on, in the wet-blue state, full grains, unsplit, grain splits
4104.1119	----其他	8	5	4	0	35	17		千克		----Other
4104.1119 10	湿濒危野牛皮(全粒面未剖层或粒面剖层,经鞣制不带毛)	8				35	17		千克	ABFE	Tanned or crust hides and skins of wild bovine animals, in imminent dangers, without hair on, wet, full grains, unsplit or grain splits
4104.1119 90	全粒面未剖层或粒面剖层湿牛皮(经鞣制不带毛)	8				35	17		千克	AB	Tanned or crust hides and skins of bovine animals, without hair on, full grains, unsplit or grain splits, in the wet state
4104.1120	---马皮	5		2.5	0	35	17		千克		---Of equine animals
4104.1120 10	湿濒危野马皮(全粒面未剖或粒面剖层,经鞣制不带毛)	5				35	17		千克	ABFE	Tanned or crust hides and skins of wild equine animals, in imminent dangers, without hair on, full grains, unsplit or grain splits, in the wet state
4104.1120 90	全粒面未剖层或粒面剖层湿马皮(经鞣制不带毛)	5				35	17		千克	AB	Tanned or crust hides and skins of equine animals, without hair on, full grains, unsplit or grain splits, in the wet state
	--其他:										--Other:
	---牛皮:										---Of bovine animals
4104.1911	----蓝湿的	7	5	3.5	0	17	17		千克		----Wet-blue
4104.1911 10	其他蓝湿濒危野牛皮(经鞣制不带毛)	7				17	17		千克	ABFE	Other tanned or crust hides and skins of wild bovine animals, in imminent dangers, without hair on, in the wet-blue state
4104.1911 90	其他蓝湿牛皮(经鞣制不带毛)	7				17	17		千克	AB	Other tanned or crust hides and skins, of bovine animals, without hair on, in the wet-blue state

税则号列 Tariff Item.	货品名称	最惠国(%) MFN	协定(%)CT 东盟 CA	中巴 CP	中智 CC	普通 Gen	增值税率 VAT	出口退税 ED	计量单位 Unit	监管条件 SC	Article Description
4104.1919	----其他	7	5	3.5	0	35	17		千克		----Other
4104.1919 10	其他湿濒危野牛皮(经鞣制不带毛)	7				35	17		千克	ABFE	Other tanned or crust hides and skins of wild bovine animals, in imminent dangers, without hair on, in the wet state
4104.1919 90	其他湿牛皮(经鞣制不带毛)	7				35	17		千克	AB	Other tanned or crust hides and skins of bovine animals, without hair on, in the wet state
4104.1920	---马皮	7	5	3.5	0	35	17		千克		---of equine animals
4104.1920 10	其他湿濒危野马皮(经鞣制不带毛)	7				35	17		千克	ABFE	Other tanned or crust hides and skins of wild equine animals, in imminent dangers, without hair on, in the wet state
4104.1920 90	其他湿马皮(经鞣制不带毛)	7				35	17		千克	AB	Other tanned or crust hides and skins of equine animals, without hair on, in the wet state
	-干革(坯革):										-In the dry state(crust):
4104.4100	--全粒面未剖层革;粒面剖层革	5		3.5	0	35	17		千克		--Full grains, unsplit; grain splits
4104.4100 10	濒危野牛马干革(全粒面未剖或粒面剖层,经鞣制不带毛)	5				35	17		千克	ABFE	Tanned or crust hides and skins of wild bovine or equine animals, in imminent dangers, without hair on, full grains, unsplit or grain splits, in the dry state (crust)
4104.4100 90	全粒面未剖层或粒面剖层干革(经鞣制不带毛)	5				35	17		千克	AB	Tanned or crust hides and skins, without hair on, full grains, unsplit; grain splits, in the dry state (crust)
	--其他:										--Other:
4104.4910	---机器带用牛、马皮革	5		3.5	0	20	17		千克		---For machinery belting
4104.4910 10	其他机器带用濒危野牛马皮革(经鞣制不带毛)	5				20	17		千克	FE	Tanned or crust hides and skins of wild bovine or equine animals, in imminent dangers, without hair on, for machinery belting
4104.4910 90	其他机器带用牛马皮革(经鞣制不带毛)	5				20	17		千克		Tanned or crust hides and skins of bovine, equine animals, without hair on, for machinery belting
4104.4990	---其他	7	5	4.9	0	35	17		千克		---Other
4104.4990 10	其他濒危野牛马皮革(经鞣制不带毛)	7				35	17		千克	ABFE	Other tanned or crust hides and skins of wild bovine or equine animals, without hair on
4104.4990 90	其他牛马皮革(经鞣制不带毛)	7				35	17		千克	AB	Other tanned or crust hides and skins of bovine, equine animals, without hair on
41.05	**经鞣制的不带毛绵羊或羔羊皮及其坯革,不论是否剖层,但未经进一步加工:**										**Tanned or crust skins of sheep or lambs, without wool on, whether or not split, but not further prepared:**
	-湿革(包括蓝湿皮):										-In the wet state(including wet-blue):
4105.1010	---蓝湿的	14	8	7	8.4	50	17		千克	AB	---Of wet-blue
4105.1090	---其他	10	5	5	0	50	17		千克	AB	---Other
4105.3000	-干革(坯革)	8	5	5.6	0	50	17		千克	AB	-In the dry state(crust)

税则号列 Tariff Item.	货 品 名 称	最惠国(%) MFN	协定(%)CT 东盟 CA	中巴 CP	中智 CC	普通 Gen	增值税率 VAT	出口退税 ED	计量单位 Unit	监管条件 SC	Article Description
41.06	**经鞣制的其他不带毛动物皮及其坯革,不论是否剖层,但未经进一步加工:**										**Tanned or crust hides and skins of other animals, without wool or hair on, whether or not split, but not further prepared:**
	-山羊或小山羊的:										-Of goats or kids:
4106.2100	--湿革(包括蓝湿皮)	14	8	12	8.4	50	17		千克	AB	--In the wet state (including wet – blue)
4106.2100 01	蓝湿山羊皮(经鞣制不带毛)	14				50	17		千克	AB	Tannde or crust hides and skins of goats in wet – blue, without hair on, in the wet state
4106.2100 90	其他山羊或小山羊湿革(经鞣制不带毛)	14				50	17		千克	AB	Other tanned or crust skins of goats or kids, in the dry state, without hari on, in the wet state
4106.2200	--干革(坯革)	14	8	9.8	8.4	50	17		千克	AB	--In the dry state(crust)
	-猪的:										-Of swine:
	--湿革(包括蓝湿皮):										--In the wet state(including wet-blue):
4106.3110	---蓝湿的	14	8		8.4	50	17		千克		---Wet-blue
4106.3110 10	蓝湿鹿猪、姬猪皮(经鞣制不带毛)	14				50	17		千克	FEAB	Tanned or crust hides and skins of pig-deer (*Babyrousa*)、pygmy pig (*Porcula*), without hair on, in the wet-blue state
4106.3110 90	其他蓝湿猪皮(经鞣制不带毛)	14				50	17		千克	AB	Other tanned or crust hides and skins of swine, without hair on, in the wet-blue state
4106.3190	---其他	14	8		8.4	50	17		千克		---Other
4106.3190 10	鹿猪、姬猪湿革(经鞣制不带毛)	14				50	17		千克	FEAB	Tanned or crust hides and skins of pig-deer (*Babyrousa*)、pygmy pig (*Porcula*), without hair on, in the wet state
4106.3190 90	其他猪湿革(经鞣制不带毛)	14				50	17		千克	AB	Other tanned or crust hides and skins of swine, without hair on, in the wet state
4106.3200	--干革(坯革)	14	8		8.4	50	17		千克		--In the dry state(crust)
4106.3200 10	鹿猪、姬猪干革(经鞣制不带毛,坯革)	14				50	17		千克	FEAB	Tanned or crust hides and skins of pig-deer (*Babyrousa*)、pygmy pig (*Porcula*), without hair on, in the dry state
4106.3200 90	其他猪干革(经鞣制不带毛,坯革)	14				50	17		千克	AB	Other tanned or crust hides and skins of swine, without hair on, in the dry state
4106.4000	-爬行动物的	14	8		8.4	50	17		千克	FE	-Of reptiles
	-其他:										-Other:
4106.9100	--湿革(包括蓝湿皮)	14	8		8.4	50	17		千克		--In the wet state(including wet-blue)
4106.9100 10	其他濒危野生动物湿革(经鞣制不带毛)	14				50	17		千克	FE	Tanned or crust hides and skins of other wild animals, in imminent dangers, without wool or hair on, in the wet state
4106.9100 90	其他动物湿革(经鞣制不带毛)	14				50	17		千克		Tanned or crust hides and skins of other animals, without wool or hair on, in the wet state
4106.9200	--干革(坯革)	14	8		0	50	17		千克		--In the dry state(crust)
4106.9200 10	濒危其他野生动物干革(经鞣制不带毛)	14				50	17		千克	FE	Tanned or crust hides and skins of other wild animals, in imminent dangers, without wool or hair on, in the dry state

税则号列 Tariff Item.	货品名称	最惠国(%) MFN	协定(%)CT 东盟 CA	中巴 CP	中智 CC	普通 Gen	增值税率 VAT	出口退税 ED	计量单位 Unit	监管条件 SC	Article Description
4106.9200 90	其他动物干革(经鞣制不带毛)	14				50	17		千克		Tanned or crust hides and skins of other animals, without wool or hair on, in the dry state
41.07	**经鞣制或半硝处理后进一步加工的牛皮革(包括水牛皮革)及马皮革,包括羊皮纸化处理的皮革,不论是否剖层,但税目41.14的皮革除外:**										**Leather further prepared after tanning or crusting, including parchment-dressed leather, of bovine (including buffalo) or equine animals, without hair on, whether or not split, other than leather of heading No. 41.14:**
	-整张的:										-Whole hides and skins:
	--全粒面未剖层革:										--Full grains, unsplit:
4107.1110	---牛皮	8	5		0	50	17	8	千克/张		---Of bovine animals
4107.1110 10	全粒面未剖层整张濒危野牛皮(经鞣制或半硝后进一步加工,羊皮纸化处理)	8				50	17	8	千克/张	FE	Leather further prepared after tanning or crusting, including parchment-dressed leather, of wild bovine animals, in imminent dangers, whole hides and skins, full grains, unsplit
4107.1110 90	全粒面未剖层整张牛皮(经鞣制或半硝后进一步加工,羊皮纸化处理)	8				50	17	8	千克/张		Leather further prepared after tanning or crusting, including parchment-dressed leather, of bovine animals, whole hides and skins, full grains, unsplit
4107.1120	---马皮	5			0	50	17		千克/张		---Of equine animals
4107.1120 10	全粒面未剖层整张濒危野马皮(经鞣制或半硝后进一步加工,羊皮纸化处理)	5				50	17		千克/张	FE	Leather further prepared after tanning or crusting, including parchment-dressed leather, of wild equine animals, in imminent dangers, whole hides and skins, full grains, unsplit
4107.1120 90	全粒面未剖层整张马皮(经鞣制或半硝后进一步加工,羊皮纸化处理)	5				50	17		千克/张		Leather further prepared after tanning or crusting, including parchment-dressed leather, of equine animals, whole hides and skins, full grains, unsplit
	--粒面剖层革:										--Grain splits:
4107.1210	---牛皮	8	5		0	50	17	8	千克/张		---Of bovine animals
4107.1210 10	粒面剖层整张濒危野牛皮(经鞣制或半硝后进一步加工,羊皮纸化处理)	8				50	17	8	千克/张	FE	Leather further prepared after tanning or crusting, including parchment-dressed leather, of wild bovine animals in imminent dangers, whole hides and skins, grain splits
4107.1210 90	粒面剖层整张牛皮(经鞣制或半硝后进一步加工,羊皮纸化处理)	8				50	17	8	千克/张		Leather further prepared after tanning or crusting, including parchment-dressed leather, of bovine animals, whole hides and skins, grain splits
4107.1220	---马皮	5			0	50	17		千克/张		---Of equine animals

税则号列 Tariff Item.	货品名称	最惠国(%) MFN	协定(%) CT 东盟 CA	中巴 CP	中智 CC	普通 Gen	增值税率 VAT	出口退税 ED	计量单位 Unit	监管条件 SC	Article Description
4107.1220 10	粒面剖层整张濒危野马皮(经鞣制或半硝后进一步加工,羊皮纸化处理)	5				50	17		千克/张	FE	Leather further prepared after tanning or crusting, including parchment-dressed leather, of wild equine animals, in imminent dangers, whole hides and skins, grain splits
4107.1220 90	粒面剖层整张马皮(经鞣制或半硝后进一步加工,羊皮纸化处理)	5				50	17		千克/张		Leather further prepared after tanning or crusting, including parchment-dressed leather, of equine animals, whole hides and skins, grain splits
	--其他:										--Other:
4107.1910	---机器带用	5			0	50	17		千克/张		---For machinery belting
4107.1910 10	其他机器带用整张濒危野牛马皮革(经鞣制或半硝后进一步加工,羊皮纸化处理)	5				50	17		千克/张	FE	Leather further prepared after tanning or crusting, including parchment-dressed leather, of wild bovine or wild equine amimals, in imminent dangers, whole hides and skins, for machinery belting
4107.1910 90	其他机器带用整张牛马皮革(经鞣制或半硝后进一步加工,羊皮纸化处理)	5				50	17		千克/张		Leather further prepared after tanning or crusting, including parchment-dressed leather, of bevine or equine animals, whole hides and skins, for machinery belting
4107.1990	---其他	7	5		0	50	17		千克/张		---Other
4107.1990 10	其他整张濒危野牛马皮革(经鞣制或半硝后进一步加工,羊皮纸化处理)	7				50	17		千克/张	ABFE	Other leather further prepared after tanning or crusting, including parchment-dressed leather of wild bovine or wild equine amimals, in imminent dangers, whole hides and skins
4107.1990 90	其他整张牛马皮革(经鞣制或半硝后进一步加工,羊皮纸化处理)	7				50	17		千克/张	AB	Other leather further prepared after tanning or crusting, including parchment – dressed leather of bovine or equine animals, whole hides and skins
	-其他,包括半张的:										-Other, including sides:
4107.9100	--全粒面未剖层	5			0	50	17		千克		--Full grains, unsplit
4107.9100 10	全粒面未剖层非整张濒危野牛马皮(经鞣制或半硝后进一步加工,羊皮纸化处理)	5				50	17		千克	ABFE	Leather further prepared after tanning or crusting, including parchment-dressed leather, in imminent dangers, other than whole hides and skins, full grains, unsplit
4107.9100 90	全粒面未剖层非整张革(经鞣制或半硝后进一步加工,羊皮纸化处理)	5				50	17		千克	AB	Leather further prepared after tanning or crusting, including parchment-dressed leather, other than whole hides and skins, full grains, unsplit
4107.9200	--粒面剖层革	5			0	50	17	8	千克		--Grain splits

税则号列 Tariff Item.	货品名称	最惠国(%) MFN	协定(%)CT			普通 Gen	增值税率 VAT	出口退税 ED	计量单位 Unit	监管条件 SC	Article Description
			东盟 CA	中巴 CP	中智 CC						
4107.9200 10	粒面剖层非整张濒危野牛马皮革(经鞣制或半硝后进一步加工,羊皮纸化处理)	5				50	17	8	千克	FE	Leather further prepared after tanning or crusting, including parchment-dressed leather, of wild bovine or wild equine animals, in imminent dangers, other than whole hides and skins, grain, splits
4107.9200 90	粒面剖层非整张革(经鞣制或半硝后进一步加工,羊皮纸化处理)	5				50	17	8	千克		Leather further prepared after tanning or crusting, including parchment-dressed leather, other than whole hides and skins, grain, splits
	--其他:										--Other:
4107.9910	---机器带用	5			0	50	17	13	千克		---For machinery belting
4107.9910 10	其他机器带用非整张濒危野牛马皮(经鞣制或半硝后进一步加工,羊皮纸化处理)	5				50	17	13	千克	FE	Leather further prepared after tanning or crusting, including parchment-dressed leather of bovine or equine animals, in imminent dangers, other than whole hides and skins, for machinery belting
4107.9910 90	其他机器带用非整张牛马皮革(经鞣制或半硝后进一步加工,羊皮纸化处理)	5				50	17	13	千克		Leather further prepared after tanning or crusting, including parchment-dressed leather, of bovine or equine animals, other than whole hides and skins, for machinery belting
4107.9990	---其他	7	5		0	50	17		千克		---Other
4107.9990 10	其他非整张濒危野牛马皮革(经鞣制或半硝后进一步加工,羊皮纸化处理)	7				50	17		千克	ABFE	Other leather further prepared after tanning or crusting, including parchment-dressed leather, of wild bovine or wild equine animals, in imminent dangers, other than whole hides and skins
4107.9990 90	其他非整张牛马皮革(经鞣制或半硝后进一步加工,羊皮纸化处理)	7				50	17		千克	AB	Other leather further prepared after tanning or crusting, (including parchment-dressed leather, of bovine or equine animals, other than whole hides and skins)
41.12	**经鞣制或半硝处理后进一步加工的不带毛的绵羊或羔羊皮革,包括羊皮纸化处理的,不论是否剖层,但税目41.14的皮革除外:**										**Leather further prepared after tanning or crusting, including parchment-dressed leather, of sheep or lamb, without wool on, whether or not split, other than leather of heading No. 41.14:**
4112.0000	经鞣制或半硝处理后进一步加工的不带毛的绵羊或羔羊皮革,包括羊皮纸化处理的,不论是否剖层,但税目41.14的皮革除外	8	5	5.6	0	50	17	8	千克	AB	Leather further prepared after tanning or crusting, including parchment-dressed leather, of sheep or lamb, without wool on, whether or not split, other than leather of heading No. 41.14

税则号列 Tariff Item.	货品名称	最惠国(%) MFN	协定(%)CT 东盟 CA	中巴 CP	中智 CC	普通 Gen	增值税率 VAT	出口退税 ED	计量单位 Unit	监管条件 SC	Article Description
41.13	**经鞣制或半硝处理后进一步加工的不带毛的其他动物皮革，包括羊皮纸化处理的，不论是否剖层，但税目41.14的皮革除外：**										**Leather further prepared after tanning or crusting, including parchment-dressed leather, of other animals, without wool or hair on, whether or not split, other than leather of heading No. 41.14:**
4113.1000	-山羊或小山羊的	14	8	9.8	8.4	50	17	8	千克	AB	-Of goats or kids
4113.2000	-猪皮的	14	8		8.4	50	17	8	千克		-Of swine
4113.2000 10	加工的鹿猪、姬猪皮革（经鞣制或半硝后进一步加工，不带毛，羊皮纸化处理）	14				50	17	8	千克	ABFE	Leather further prepared after tanning or crusting, including parchment-dressed leather, of pig-deer (*Babyrousa*)、pygmy pig (*Porcula*), without hair on
4113.2000 90	加工的猪皮革（经鞣制或半硝后进一步加工，不带毛，羊皮纸化处理）	14				50	17	8	千克	AB	Leather further prepared after tanning or crusting, including parchment-dressed leather, of swine, without hair on
4113.3000	-爬行动物皮的	14	8		8.4	50	17		千克	FE	-Of reptiles
4113.9000	-其他	14	8		8.4	50	17		千克		-Other
4113.9000 10	加工的其他濒危野生动物皮革（经鞣制或半硝后进一步加工，不带毛，羊皮纸化处理）	14				50	17		千克	FE	Leather further prepared after tanning or crusting, including parchment-dressed leather, of wild animals, in imminent dangers, without wool or hair on
4113.9000 90	加工的其他动物皮革（经鞣制或半硝后进一步加工，不带毛，羊皮纸化处理）	14				50	17		千克		Leather further prepared after tanning or crusting, including parchment-dressed leather, of other animals, without wool or hair on
41.14	**油鞣皮革（包括结合鞣制的油鞣皮革）；漆皮及层压漆皮；镀金属皮革：**										**Chamois (including combination chamois) leather; patent leather and patent laminated leather; metallised leather:**
4114.1000	-油鞣皮革（包括结合鞣制的油鞣皮革）	14	8		11.2	50	17		千克		-Chamois (including combination chamois) leather
4114.1000 10	油鞣其他濒危野生动物皮革（包括结合鞣制的油鞣皮革）	14				50	17		千克	FE	Chamois (including combination chamois) leather of wild animals in imminent dangers
4114.1000 90	油鞣其他动物皮革（包括结合鞣制的油鞣皮革；野生动物皮革除外）	14				50	17		千克		Chamois (including combination chamois) leather of other animals
4114.2000	-漆皮及层压漆皮；镀金属皮革	10	8	9	8	50	17		千克		-Patent leather and patent laminated leather; metallised leather
41.15	**以皮革或皮革纤维为基本成分的再生皮革，成块、成张或成条，不论是否成卷；皮革或再生皮革的边角废料，不适宜作皮革制品用；皮革粉末：**										**Composition leather with a basis of leather or leather fibre, in slabs, sheets or strip, whether or not in rolls; parings and other waste of leather or of composition leather, not suitable for the manufacture of leather articles; leather dust, powder and flour:**

税则号列 Tariff Item.	货 品 名 称	最惠国(%) MFN	协定(%)CT 东盟 CA	中巴 CP	中智 CC	普通 Gen	增值税率 VAT	出口退税 ED	计量单位 Unit	监管条件 SC	Article Description
4115.1000	-以皮革或皮革纤维为基本成分的再生皮革,成块、成张或成条,不论是否成卷	14	8		8.4	50	17		千克		-Composition leather with a basis of leather or leather fibre, in slabs, sheets or strip, whether or not in rolls
4115.2000	-皮革或再生皮革的边角废料,不适宜作皮革制品用;皮革粉末	14	8		8.4	50	17		千克		-Parings and other waste of leather or of composition leather, not suitable for the manufacture of leather articles; leather dust, powder and flour
4115.2000 10	皮革废渣、灰渣、淤渣及粉末	14				50	17		千克	9	Waste residue, ash, silt, powder and flour of leather or of composition leather
4115.2000 90	皮革或再生皮革边角料	14				50	17		千克		Parings and other waste of leather or of composition leather

第四十二章
皮革制品;鞍具及挽具;旅行用品、手提包及类似容器;动物肠线(蚕胶丝除外)制品

注释:

一、本章不包括:

(一)外科用无菌肠线或类似的无菌缝合材料(税目30.06);

(二)以毛皮或人造毛皮衬里或作面(仅饰边的除外)的衣服及衣着附件(分指手套、连指手套及露指手套除外)(税目43.03或43.04);

(三)网线袋及类似品(税目56.08);

(四)第六十四章的物品;

(五)第六十五章的帽类及其零件;

(六)税目66.02的鞭子、马鞭或其他物品;

(七)袖扣、手镯或其他仿首饰(税目71.17);

(八)单独进口或出口的挽具附件或装饰物,例如,马镫、马嚼子、马铃铛及类似品、带扣(一般归入第十五类);

(九)弦线、鼓面皮或类似品及其他乐器零件(税目92.09);

(十)第九十四章的物品(例如,家具、灯具及照明装置);

(十一)第九十五章的物品(例如,玩具、游戏品及运动用品);

(十二)税目96.06的钮扣、揿扣、钮扣芯或这些物品的其他零件、钮扣坯。

二、(一)除上述注释一所规定的以外,税目42.02也不包括:

1. 非供长期使用的带把手塑料薄膜袋,不论是否印制(税目39.23);

2. 编结材料制品(税目46.02)。

(二)税目42.02、42.03的制品,如果装有用贵金属、包贵金属、天然或养殖珍珠、宝石或半宝石(天然、合成或再造)制的零件,即使这些零件不是仅作为小配件或小饰物的,只要其未构成物品的基本特征,仍应归入上述税号。但如果这些零件已构成物品的基本特征,则应归入第七十一章。

三、税目42.03所称"衣服及衣着附件",主要包括分指手套、连指手套及露指手套(包括运动及防护手套)、围裙及其他防护用衣着、裤吊带、腰带、子弹带及腕带,但不包括表带(税目91.13)。

Chapter 42
Articles of leather; saddlery and harness; travel goods, handbags and similar containers; articles of animal gut (other than silk-worm gut)

Notes:

1. This Chapter does not cover:

(a) Sterile surgical catgut or similar sterile suture materials (heading No. 30.06);

(b) Articles of apparel or clothing accessories (except gloves, mittens and mitts), lined with furskin or artificial fur or to which furskin or artificial fur is attached on the outside except as mere trimming (heading No. 43.03 or 43.04);

(c) Made up articles of netting (heading No. 56.08);

(d) Articles of Chapter 64;

(e) Headgear or parts thereof of Chapter 65;

(f) Whips, riding-crops or other articles of heading No. 66.02;

(g) Cuff-links, bracelets or other imitation jewellery (heading No. 71.17);

(h) Fittings or trimmings for harness, such as stirrups, bits, horse brasses and buckles, separately presented (generally Section XV);

(i) Strings, skins for drums or the like, or other parts of musical instruments (heading No. 92.09);

(j) Articles of Chapter 94 (for example, furniture, lamps and lighting fittings);

(k) Articles of Chapter 95 (for example, toys, games, sports requisites);

(l) Buttons, press-fasteners, snap-fasteners, pres-sstuds, button moulds or other parts of these articles, button blanks, of heading No. 96.06.

2. (A) In addition to the provisions of Note 1 above, heading 42.02 does not cover:

(a) Bags made of sheeting of plastics, whether or not printed, with handles, not designed for prolonged use (heading No. 39.23);

(b) Articles of plaiting materials (heading No. 46.02).

(B) Articles of headings Nos. 42.02 and 42.03 which have parts of precious metal or metal clad with precious metal, of natural or cultured pearls, of precious or semi-precious stones (natural, synthetic or reconstructed) remain classified in those headings even if such parts constitute more than minor fittings or minor ornamentation, provided that these parts do not give the articles their essential character. If, on the other hand, the parts give the articles their essential character, the articles are to be classified in Chapter 71.

3. For the purpose of heading No. 42.03, the expression "articles of apparel and clothing accessories" applies, *inter alia*, to gloves, mittens and mitts (including those for sport or for protection), aprons and other protective clothing, braces, belts, bandoliers and wrist straps, but excluding watch straps (heading No. 91.13).

税则号列 Tariff Item.	货品名称	最惠国(%) MFN	协定(%)CT 东盟 CA	中巴 CP	中智 CC	普通 Gen	增值税率 VAT	出口退税 ED	计量单位 Unit	监管条件 SC	Article Description
42.01	**各种材料制成的鞍具及挽具(包括缰绳、挽绳、护膝垫、口套、鞍褥、马褡裢、狗外套及类似品),适合各种动物用:**										**Saddlery and harness for any animal (including traces, leads, knee pads, muzzles, saddle cloths, saddle bags, dog coats and the like), of any material:**
4201.0000	各种材料制成的鞍具及挽具(包括缰绳、挽绳、护膝垫、口套、鞍褥、马褡裢、狗外套及类似品),适合各种动物用	20	12	12	12	100	17	13	千克		Saddlery and harness for any animal (including traces, leads, knee pads, muzzles, saddle cloths, saddle bags, dog coats and the like), of any material
4201.0000 10	濒危野生动物材料制的鞍具及挽具(适合各种动物用)	20				100	17	13	千克	FE	Saddlery and harness for any animal of material of wild animals in imminent dangeRs
4201.0000 90	各种材料制成的鞍具及挽具(野生动物材料制的除外;适合各种动物)	20				100	17	13	千克		Saddlery and harness for any animal, of any material, other than the material of wild animals
42.02	**衣箱、提箱、小手袋、公文箱、公文包、书包、眼镜盒、望远镜盒、照相机套、乐器盒、枪套及类似容器;旅行包、食品或饮料保温包、化妆包、帆布包、手提包、购物袋、钱夹、钱包、地图盒、烟盒、烟袋、工具包、运动包、瓶盒、首饰盒、粉盒、刀叉餐具盒及类似容器,用皮革或再生皮革、塑料片、纺织材料、钢纸或纸板制成,或者全部或主要用上述材料或纸包覆制成:**										**Trunks, suit-cases, vanity-cases, executive-cases, brief-cases, school satchels, spectacle cases, binocular cases, camera cases, musical instrument cases, gun cases, holsters and similar containers; travelling-bags, insulated food or beverages bags, toilet bags, rucksacks, handbags, shopping-bags, wallets, purses, map-cases, cigarett-cases, tobacco-pouches, tool bags, sports bags, bottle-cases, jewellery boxes, powder-boxes, cutlery cases and similar containers, of leather or of composition leather, of sheeting of plastics, of textile materials, of vulcanized fibre or of paperboard, or wholly or mainly covered with such materials or with paper:**
	-衣箱、提箱、小手袋、公文箱、公文包、书包及类似容器:										-Trunks, suit-cases, vanity-cases, executive-cases, brief-cases, school satchels and similar containers:
	--以皮革、再生皮革或漆皮作面:										--With outer surface of leather, of composition leather or of patent leather:
4202.1110	---衣箱	15	8		9	100	17	13	个		---Trunks and suit-cases
4202.1110 10	以含濒危野生动物皮革作面的衣箱(包括再生皮革及漆皮)	15				100	17	13	个	FE	Trunks with outer surface of leather, of composition leather or of patent leather, of wild animals
4202.1110 90	以皮革,再生皮革,漆皮作面的衣箱(含野生动物皮革的除外)	15				100	17	13	个		Trunks with outer surface of leather, of composition leather or of patent leather, other than of wild animals
4202.1190	---其他	10	5		0	100	17	13	个		---Other
4202.1190 10	以濒危野生动物皮革作面的箱包(包括再生皮革及漆皮)	10				100	17	13	个	FE	Cases with outer surface of leather, of composition leather or of patent leather, of wild animals, in imminent dangers

税则号列 Tariff Item.	货品名称	最惠国(%) MFN	协定(%)CT 东盟 CA	中巴 CP	中智 CC	普通 Gen	增值税率 VAT	出口退税 ED	计量单位 Unit	监管条件 SC	Article Description
4202.1190 90	以皮革,再生皮革,漆皮作面的箱包(包括提箱、公文包、书包及类似容器,但不包括衣箱)	10				100	17	13	个		Suit-cases, vanity-cases, executive-cases, brief-cases, school satchels and similar xontainers, other than trunks, with outer surface of leather, of composition leather or of patent leather
	--以塑料或纺织材料作面:										--With outer surface of plastics or of textile materials:
4202.1210	---衣箱	20	T3	17	0	100	17	13	个		---Trunks and suit-cases
4202.1290	---其他	20	T3	17	0	100	17	13	个		---Other
4202.1900	--其他	20	12		12	100	17	13	个		--Other
	-手提包,不论是否有背带,包括无把手的:										-Handbags, whether or not with shoulder strap, including those without handle:
4202.2100	--以皮革、再生皮革或漆皮作面	10	5	6.9	8	100	17	13	个		--With outer surface of leather, of composition leather or of patent leather
4202.2100 10	以濒危野生动物皮革作面的手提包(包括再生皮革及漆皮)	10				100	17	13	个	FE	Handbags with outer surface of leather, of composition leather or of patent leather, of wild animals, in imminent dangers
4202.2100 90	以皮革,再生皮革,漆皮作面手提包(不论是否有背带,包括无把手的)	10				100	17	13	个		Handbags, whether or not with shoulder strap, including those without handle, with outer surface of leather, of composition leather or of patent leather
4202.2200	--以塑料片或纺织材料作面	10	T3	8.2	8	100	17	13	个		--With outer surface of plastic sheeting or of textile materials
4202.2900	--其他	20	12	14	12	100	17	13	个		--Other
	-通常置于口袋或手提包内的物品:										-Articles of a kind normally carried in the pocket or in the handbag:
4202.3100	--以皮革、再生皮革或漆皮作面	10	5	6.9	0	100	17	13	个/千克		--With outer surface of leather, of composition leather or of patent leather
4202.3100 10	以濒危野生动物皮革作面的钱包等(包括再生皮革及漆皮)	10				100	17	13	个/千克	FE	Articles (such as purses) of a kind normally carried in the pocket or in the handbag, with outer surface of leather, of composition leather or of patent leather of wild animals, in imminent dangers
4202.3100 90	以皮革,再生皮革作面钱包等物品(指通常置于口袋或手提包内的物品,包括以漆皮作面的)	10				100	17	13	个/千克		Articles (such as purses) of a kind normally carried in the pocket or in the handbag, with outer surface of leather, of composition leather or of patent leather
4202.3200	--以塑料片或纺织材料作面	20	T3	14	0	100	17	13	千克		--With outer surface of plastic sheeting or of textile materials
4202.3900	--其他	20	12	14	12	100	17	13	千克		--Other
	-其他:										-Other:
4202.9100	--以皮革、再生皮革或漆皮作面	10	5	8.5	0	100	17	13	个/千克		--With outer surface of leather, of composition leather or of patent leather
4202.9100 10	濒危野生动物皮革作面的其他容器(包括再生皮革及漆皮)	10				100	17	13	个/千克	FE	Other containers with outer surface of leather, of composition leather or of patent leather of wild animals in imminent dangers

税则号列 Tariff Item.	货品名称	最惠国(%) MFN	协定(%)CT 东盟 CA	中巴 CP	中智 CC	普通 Gen	增值税率 VAT	出口退税 ED	计量单位 Unit	监管条件 SC	Article Description
4202.9100 90	皮革、再生皮革、漆皮作面其他容器	10				100	17	13	个/千克		Other containers with outer surface of leather, of composition leather or of patent leather
4202.9200	--以塑料片或纺织材料作面	10	T3	8.5	8	100	17	13	个/千克		--With outer surface of plastic sheeting or of textile materials
4202.9900	--其他	20	12		12	100	17	13	千克		--Other
42.03	**皮革或再生皮革制的衣服及衣着附件:**										**Articles of apparel and clothing accessories, of leather or of composition leather:**
4203.1000	-衣服	10	5	0	8	100	17	13	件/千克		-Articles of apparel
4203.1000 10	濒危野生动物皮革制的衣服(包括再生野生动物皮革制作的)	10				100	17	13	件/千克	FEB	Articles of apparel of leather or of composition leather of wild animals in imminent dangers
4203.1000 90	皮革或再生皮革制的衣服(野生动物皮革制作的除外)	10				100	17	13	件/千克	B	Articles of apparel of leather or of composition leather, other than leather of wild animals
	-手套,包括连指或露指的:										-Gloves, mittens and mitts:
4203.2100	--专供运动用	20	12	5	12	100	17	13	双/千克		--Specially designed for use in sports
4203.2100 10	濒危野生动物皮革制的运动手套(包括再生野生动物皮革制作的)	20				100	17	13	双/千克	FE	Gloves, specially designed for use in sports, of leather or of composition leather, of wild animals in imminent dangers
4203.2100 90	皮革或再生皮革制专供运动用手套(包括连指或露指的;野生动物皮革制作的除外)	20				100	17	13	双/千克		Gloves, mittens and mitts, specially designed for use in sports, of leather or of composition leather, other than leather of wild animals
	--其他:										--Other:
4203.2910	---劳保手套	20	12	5	16	100	17	13	双/千克		---Working gloves
4203.2910 10	濒危野生动物皮革制的劳保手套(包括再生野生动物皮革制作的)	20				100	17	13	双/千克	FE	Working gloves, of leather or of composition leather, of wild animals in imminent dangers
4203.2910 90	皮革或再生皮革制的劳保手套(野生动物皮革制作的除外)	20				100	17	13	双/千克		Working gloves, of leather or of composition leather, other than leather of wild animals
4203.2990	---其他	20	12	5	16	100	17	13	双/千克		---Other
4203.2990 10	濒危野生动物皮革制的其他手套(包括再生野生动物皮革制作的)	20				100	17	13	双/千克	FE	Other gloves, mittens and mitts, of leather or of composition leather of wild animals in imminent dangers
4203.2990 90	皮革或再生皮革制的其他手套(包括连指或露指的)	20				100	17	13	双/千克		Gloves, mittens and mitts, of leather or of composition leather
	-腰带及子弹带:										-Belts and bandoliers:
4203.3010	---腰带	10	5	0	8	100	17	13	千克		---Belts
4203.3010 10	濒危野生动物皮革制的腰带(包括再生野生动物皮革制作的)	10				100	17	13	千克	FE	Belts of leather or of composition leather of wild animals in imminent dangers
4203.3010 90	其他动物皮革制的腰带(包括再生动物皮革制作的)	10				100	17	13	千克		Belts of leather or of composition leather of other animals
4203.3020	---子弹带	10	5	0	8	100	17	13	千克		---Bandoliers

税则号列 Tariff Item.	货品名称	最惠国(%) MFN	协定(%) CT 东盟 CA	 中巴 CP	 中智 CC	普通 Gen	增值税率 VAT	出口退税 ED	计量单位 Unit	监管条件 SC	Article Description
4203.3020 10	濒危野生动物皮革制的子弹带(包括再生野生动物皮革制作的)	10				100	17	13	千克	FE	Bandoliers of leather or of composition leather of wild animals in imminent dangers
4203.3020 90	其他动物皮革制的子弹带(包括再生动物皮革制作的)	10				100	17	13	千克		Bandoliers of leather or of composition leather of other animals
4203.4000	-其他衣着附件	20	12	5	12	100	17	13	千克		-Other clothing accessories
4203.4000 10	濒危野生动物皮革制的衣着附件(包括再生野生动物皮革制作的)	20				100	17	13	千克	FE	Clothing accessories of leather or of composition leather of wild animals in imminent dangers
4203.4000 90	皮革或再生皮革制的其他衣着附件	20				100	17	13	千克		Other clothing accessories, of leather or of composition leather
42.05	**皮革或再生皮革的其他制品:** 皮革或再生皮革的其他制品										**Other articles of leather or of composition leather:** Other articles of leather or of composition leather
4205.0010	---坐具套	12	8		7.2	100	17	13	千克		---Cove of seat
4205.0010 10	濒危野生动物皮革制的坐具套(包括再生野生动物皮革制作的)	12				100	17	13	千克	FE	Covering of seats, of leather or of composition leather of wild animals in imminent dangers
4205.0010 90	其他动物皮革制的坐具套(包括再生皮革制作的)	12				100	17	13	千克		Covering of seats, of leather or of composition leather of wild animals
4205.0020	---机器、机械器具或其他专门技术用途的	8	5		0	35	17	13	千克		---Of a kind used in machinery or mechanial appilances or for other technical uses
4205.0020 10	濒危野生动物皮革制工业用皮革或再生皮革制品(工业用指机器,机械器具或其他专门技术用途的)	8				35	17	13	千克	FE	Industry – use leather or composition leather of endangered wild animals (industry – use refers to machines, equipments or other special techniques)
4205.0020 90	其他工业用皮革或再生皮革制品(工业用指机器,机械器具或其他专门技术用途的)	8				35	17	13	千克		Other industry – use leather or composition leather (industry – use refers to machines, equipments or other special techniques)
4205.0090	---其他	12	8		7.2	100	17	13	千克		---Other
4205.0090 10	濒危野生动物皮革的其他制品(包括再生野生动物皮革制作的)	12				100	17	13	千克	FE	Other articles covering of seats, of leather or of composition leather of wild animals in imminent dangers
4205.0090 20	皮革或再生皮革制宠物用品	12				100	17	13	千克	AB	Products for petsmade of hide or renewed hide
4205.0090 90	皮革或再生皮革的其他制品	12				100	17	13	千克		Other articles covering of seats, of leather or of composition leather of wild animals
42.06	**肠线(蚕胶丝除外)、肠膜、膀胱或筋腱制品:**										**Articles of gut (other than silk-worm gut), of goldbeater's skin, of bladders or of tendons:**
4206.0000	肠线(蚕胶丝除外)、肠膜、膀胱或筋腱产品	20	12		12	90	17	13	千克		Articles of gut (other than silk-worm gut), of goldbeater's skin, of bladders or of tendons:

第四十三章
毛皮、人造毛皮及其制品

Chapter 43
Furskins and artificial fur; manufactures thereof

注释：

一、本目录所称“毛皮”，是指已鞣的各种动物的带毛毛皮，但不包括税目43.01的生毛皮。

二、本章不包括：

（一）带羽毛或羽绒的整张或部分鸟皮（税目05.05或67.01）；

（二）第四十一章的带毛生皮〔见该章注释一（三）〕；

（三）用皮革与毛皮或用皮革与人造毛皮制成的分指手套、连指手套及露指手套（税目42.03）；

（四）第六十四章的物品；

（五）第六十五章的帽类及其零件；

（六）第九十五章的物品（例如，玩具、游戏品及运动用品）。

三、税目43.03包括加有其他材料缝合的毛皮和毛皮部分品，以及缝合成衣服、衣服部分品、衣着附件或其他制品的毛皮和毛皮部分品。

四、以毛皮或人造毛皮衬里或作面（仅饰边的除外）的衣服及衣着附件（不包括注释二所述的货品），应分别归入税目43.03或43.04，但毛皮或人造毛皮仅作为装饰的除外。

五、本目录所称“人造毛皮”，是指以毛、发或其他纤维粘附或缝合于皮革、织物或其他材料之上而构成的仿毛皮，但不包括以机织或针织方法制得的仿毛皮（一般应归入税目58.01或60.01）。

Notes:

1. Throughout the Nomenclature references to “furskins”, other than to raw furskins of heading No. 43.01, apply to hides or skins of all animals which have been tanned or dressed with the hair or wool on.

2. This Chapter does not cover:

(a) Birdskins or parts of birdskins, with their feathers or down (heading No. 05.05 or 67.01);

(b) Raw hides or skins, with the hair or wool on, of Chapter 41 (see Note 1 (c) to that Chapter);

(c) Gloves, mittens and mitts, consisting of leather and furskin or of leather and artificial fur (heading No. 42.03);

(d) Articles of Chapter 64;

(e) Headgear or parts thereof of Chapter 65; or

(f) Articles of Chapter 95 (for example, toys, games, sports requisites).

3. Heading No. 43.03 includes furskins and parts thereof, assembled with the addition of other materials, and furskins and parts thereof, sewn together in the form of garments or parts or accessories of garments or in the form of other articles.

4. Articles of apparel and clothing accessories (except those excluded by Note 2) lined with furskin or artificial fur or to which furskin or artificial fur is attached on the outside except as mere trimming are to be classified in heading No. 43.03 or 43.04 as the case may be.

5. Throughout the Nomenclature the expression “artificial fur” means any imitation of furskin consisting of wool, hair or other fibres gummed or sewn on to leather, woven fabric or other materials, but does not include imitation furskins obtained by weaving or knitting (generally, heading No. 58.01 or 60.01).

税则号列 Tariff Item.	货品名称	最惠国(%) MFN	协定(%)CT 东盟 CA	中巴 CP	中智 CC	普通 Gen	增值税率 VAT	出口退税 ED	计量单位 Unit	监管条件 SC	Article Description
43.01	**生毛皮(包括适合加工皮货用的头、尾、爪及其他块、片),但税目41.01、41.02或41.03的生皮除外:**										**Raw furskins (including heads, tails, paws and other pieces or cuttings, suitable for furriers' use), other than raw hides and skins of heading No. 41.01, 41.02 or 41.03:**
4301.1000	-整张水貂皮,不论是否带头、尾或爪	15	8		9	100	17		千克	AB	-Of mink, whole, with or without head, tail or paws
4301.3000	-下列羔羊的整张毛皮,不论是否带头、尾或爪:阿斯特拉罕、喀拉科尔、波斯羔羊及类似羔羊、印度、中国或蒙古羔羊	20	12		12	90	17		千克	AB	-Of lamb, the following: Astrakhan, Broadtail, Caracul, Persian and similar lamb, Indian, Chinese, Mongolian or Tibetan lamb, whole, with or without head, tail or paws
4301.6000	-整张狐皮,不论是否带头、尾或爪	20	12		12	100	17		千克/张		-Of fox, whole, with or without head, tail or paws

税则号列 Tariff Item.	货品名称	最惠国(%) MFN	协定(%)CT 东盟 CA	中巴 CP	中智 CC	普通 Gen	增值税率 VAT	出口退税 ED	计量单位 Unit	监管条件 SC	Article Description
4301.6000 10	整张濒危生狐皮(不论是否带头,尾或爪)	20				100	17		千克/张	AFEB	Raw furskins of fox in imminent dangers, whole, with or without head, tail or paws
4301.6000 90	其他整张生狐皮(不论是否带头,尾或爪)	20				100	17		千克/张	AB	Other raw furskins of fox, whole, with or without head, tail or paws
	---整张兔皮,不论是否带头、尾或爪										---Of rabbit or hare, whole, with or without head, tail or paws
4301.8010	---兔皮	20	12		0	90	17		千克/张		
4301.8010 10	整张生濒危野兔皮(不论是否带头,尾或爪)	20				90	17		千克/张	AFEB	Raw furskins of hare in imminent dangers, whole, with or without head tail or paws
4301.8010 90	整张生兔皮(不论是否带头,尾或爪)	20				90	17		千克/张	AB	Raw furskins of rabbit, whole, with or without head tail or paws
4301.8090	---其他	20	12		0	90	17		千克/张		---Other
4301.8090 10	整张的其他生濒危野生动物毛皮(不论是否带头,尾或爪包括整张濒危生海豹皮)	20				90	17		千克/张	ABFE	Raw furskins of other wild animals in imminent dangers, whole, with or without head tail or paws Including endangered sealskin
4301.8090 90	整张的其他生毛皮(不论是否带头,尾或爪包括整张生海豹皮)	20				90	17		千克/张	AB	Raw furskins of other animals, whole, with or without head tail or paws Including endangered sealskin
	-适合加工皮货用的头、尾、爪及其他块、片:										-Heads, tails, paws and other pieces or cuttings, suitable for furriers' use:
4301.9010	---黄鼠狼尾	20	12		12	50	17		千克	EABF	---Weasel tails
4301.9090	---其他	20	12		12	90	17		千克		---Other
4301.9090 10	其他濒危野生动物未鞣头尾(加工皮货用,包括爪及其他块、片)	20				90	17		千克	ABFE	Heads, tails, paws and other pieces or cuttings, of wild animals in imminent dangers, suitable for furriers' use
4301.9090 90	适合加工皮货用的其他未鞣头、尾(包括爪及其他块、片)	20				90	17		千克	AB	Other heads, tails, paws and other pieces or cuttings of animals, suitable for furriers' use
43.02	**未缝制或已缝制(不加其他材料)的已鞣毛皮(包括头、尾、爪及其他块、片),但税目43.03的货品除外:**										**Tanned or dressed furskins (including heads, tails, paws and other pieces or cuttings), unassembled, or assembled (without the addition of other materials) other than those of heading No.43.03:**
	-未缝制的整张毛皮,不论是否带头、尾或爪:										-Whole skins, with or without head, tail or paws, not assembled:
4302.1100	--水貂皮	12	8		7.2	130	17	13	千克/张	B	--Of mink
	--其他:										--Other:
4302.1910	---灰鼠皮、白鼬皮、其他貂皮、狐皮、水獭皮、旱獭皮及猞猁皮	10	5		0	130	17	13	千克/张		---Of grey squirrel, ermine, other marten, fox, otter, marmot and lynx
4302.1910 10	已鞣未缝制的濒危狐皮(兰狐皮、银狐皮除外)	10				130	17	13	千克/张	BFE	Tanned or dressed furskins of fox, unassembled, other than furskins of blue fox, silver fox in imminent dangers

税则号列 Tariff Item.	货品名称	最惠国(%) MFN	协定(%)CT 东盟 CA	中巴 CP	中智 CC	普通 Gen	增值税率 VAT	出口退税 ED	计量单位 Unit	监管条件 SC	Article Description
4302.1910 20	已鞣未缝制的兰狐皮、银狐皮	10				130	17	13	千克/张	B	Tanned or dressed furskins of blue fox, silver fox, unassembled
4302.1910 90	已鞣未缝制的其他贵重濒危动物毛皮(灰鼠皮、白鼬皮、其他貂皮、水獭皮、旱獭皮、猞猁皮)	10				130	17	13	千克/张	BFE	Tanned or dressed furskins of grey squirrel, ermine, other marten, fox, otter, marmot and lynx, in imminent dangers, unassembled
4302.1920	---兔皮	10	5		0	100	17	13	千克/张		---Of rabbit or hare
4302.1920 10	已鞣未缝制的整张濒危野兔皮(不论是否带头、尾或爪)	10				100	17	13	千克/张	FE	Tanned or dressed furskins of hare, in imminent dangers, whole, with or without head tail or paws, unassembled
4302.1920 90	已鞣未缝制的整张兔皮(不论是否带头、尾或爪)	10				100	17	13	千克/张		Tanned or dressed furskins of rabbit, whole, with or without head tail or paws, unassembled
4302.1930	---下列羔羊皮:阿斯特拉罕、喀拉科尔、波斯羔羊及类似羔羊、印度、中国或蒙古羔羊	20	12		12	100	17	13	千克/张		---Of lamb, the following: Astrakhan, Broadtail, Caracul, Persian and similar lamb, Indian, Chinese, Mongolian or Tibetan lamb
4302.1990	---其他	10	5		0	100	17	13	千克/张		---Other
4302.1990 10	已鞣未缝制的其他濒危野生动物毛皮	10				100	17	13	千克/张	BFE	Tanned or dressed furskins of other wild animals in imminent dangers, unassembled
4302.1990 90	已鞣未缝制的其他毛皮	10				100	17	13	千克/张	B	Other tanned or dressed furskins of other animals, unassembled
4302.2000	-未缝制的头、尾、爪及其他块、片	20	12		12	100	17	13	千克		-Heads, tails, paws and other pieces or cuttings, not assembled
4302.2000 10	已鞣未缝制濒危野生动物头、尾、爪等(包括块、片)	20				100	17	13	千克	BFE	Tanned or dressed heads, tails, paws and other pieces or cuttings, of wild animals in imminent dangers unassembled
4302.2000 90	已鞣未缝制的头、尾、爪及其他块片	20				100	17	13	千克	B	Tanned or dressed heads, tails, paws and other pieces or cuttings of other animals, unassembled
	-已缝制的整张毛皮及其块、片:										-Whole skins and pieces or cuttings thereof, assembled:
4302.3010	---灰鼠、白鼬、貂、狐、水獭、旱獭及猞猁的整张毛皮及其块、片	20	12		12	130	17	13	千克		---Of grey squirrel, ermine, other marten, fox, otter, marmot and lynx
4302.3010 10	已鞣已缝制貂皮、狐皮及其块、片(兰狐银狐、水貂、艾虎的整张毛皮及块、片除外)	20				130	17	13	千克	BFE	Tanned or dressed whole skins and pieces or cuttings thereof, of marten, fox, other than whole skins and pieces or cuttings of blue fox, silver fox, mink, perwitsky (ferret-polecat), assembled
4302.3010 90	已鞣已缝制的贵重濒危动物毛皮及其块、片(灰鼠皮、白鼬皮、其他貂皮、水獭皮、旱獭皮、猞猁皮及块、片)	20				130	17	13	千克	BFE	Tanned or dressed whole skins and pieces or cuttings thereof, of grey squirrel, ermine, other marten, fox, otter, marmot and lynx, in imminent dangers, assembled

税则号列 Tariff Item.	货品名称	最惠国(%) MFN	协定(%)CT 东盟 CA	中巴 CP	中智 CC	普通 Gen	增值税率 VAT	出口退税 ED	计量单位 Unit	监管条件 SC	Article Description
4302.3090	---其他	20	12		12	100	17	13	千克		---Other
4302.3090 10	已鞣缝的其他整张濒危野生毛皮(包括块片)	20				100	17	13	千克	BFE	Tanned or dressed whole skins and pieces or cuttings thereof, of other wild animals, assembled
4302.3090 90	已鞣已缝制的其他整张毛皮及块片	20				100	17	13	千克	B	Tanned or dressed whole skins and pieces or cuttings thereof, of other animals, assembled
43.03	**毛皮制的衣服、衣着附件及其他物品:**										**Articles of apparel, clothing accessories and other articles of furskin:**
	-衣服及衣着附件:										-Articles of apparel and clothing accessories:
4303.1010	---毛皮衣服	23	12		18.4	150	17	13	千克/件		---Articles of appare
4303.1010 10	濒危野生动物毛皮衣服	23				150	17	13	千克/件	BEF	Articles of apparel of wild animals in imminent dangers
4303.1010 90	其他毛皮衣服	23				150	17	13	千克/件	B	Articles of apparel of other animals
4303.1020	---毛皮衣着附件	18	8		14.4	150	17	13	千克		---Clothing accessories
4303.1020 10	濒危野生动物毛皮衣着附件	18				150	17	13	千克	BEF	Clothing accessories of wild animals in imminent dangers
4303.1020 90	其他毛皮衣着附件	18				150	17	13	千克	B	Clothing accessories of other animals
4303.9000	-其他	18	8		0	150	17	13	千克		-Other
4303.9000 10	濒危野生动物毛皮制其他物品	18				150	17	13	千克	EF	Other articles of furskin of wild animals in imminent dangers
4303.9000 90	其他毛皮制其他物品	18				150	17	13	千克		Other articles of furskin: of other animals
43.04	**人造毛皮及其制品:**										**Artificial fur and articles thereof:**
4304.0010	---人造毛皮	18	8		10.8	130	17	13	千克		---Artificial fur
4304.0020	---人造毛皮制品	18	8		10.8	150	17	13	千克		---Articles of artificial fur

第九类
木及木制品;木炭;软木及软木制品;稻草、秸秆、针茅或其他编结材料制品;篮筐及柳条编结品

SECTION Ⅸ
WOOD AND ARTICLES OF WOOD; WOOD CHARCOAL; CORK AND ARTICLES OF CORK; MANUFACTURES OF STRAW, OF ESPARTO OR OF OTHER PLAITING MATERIALS; BASKETWARE AND WICKERWORK

第四十四章
木及木制品;木炭

注释:

一、本章不包括:

(一)主要作香料、药料、杀虫、杀菌或类似用途的木片、刨花、碎木、木粒或木粉(税目12.11);

(二)竹或主要作编结用的其他木质材料,未经加工、劈开,纵锯或切段(税目14.01);

(三)主要作染料或鞣料用的木片、刨花、木粒或木粉(税目14.04);

(四)活性炭(税目38.02);

(五)税目42.02的物品;

(六)第四十六章的货品;

(七)第六十四章的鞋靴及其零件;

(八)第六十六章的货品(例如,伞、手杖及其零件);

(九)税目68.08的货品;

(十)税目71.17的仿首饰;

(十一)第十六类或第十七类的货品(例如,机器零件,机器及器具的箱、罩、壳,车辆部件);

(十二)第十八类的货品(例如,钟壳、乐器及其零件);

(十三)火器的零件(税目93.05);

(十四)第九十四章的物品(例如,家具、灯具及照明器具、活动房屋);

(十五)第九十五章的物品(例如,玩具、游戏品及运动用品);

(十六)第九十六章的物品(例如,烟斗及其零件、钮扣、铅笔),但税目96.03所列物品的木身及木柄除外;

(十七)第九十七章的物品(例如艺术品)。

Chapter 44
Wood and articles of wood; wood charcoal

Notes:

1. This Chapter does not cover:

(a) Wood, in chips, in shavings, crushed, ground or powdered, of a kind used primarily in perfumery, in pharmacy, or for insecticidal, fungicidal or similar purposes (heading No. 12.11);

(b) Bamboos or other materials of a woody nature of a kind used primarily for plaiting, in the rough, whether or not split, sawn lengthwise or cut to length (heading No. 14.01);

(c) Wood, in chips, in shavings, ground or powdered, of a kind used primarily in dyeing or in tanning (heading No. 14.04);

(d) Activated charcoal (heading No. 38.02);

(e) Articles of heading No. 42.02;

(f) Goods of Chapter 46;

(g) Footwear or parts thereof of Chapter 64;

(h) Goods of Chapter 66 (for example, umbrellas and walking-sticks and parts thereof);

(i) Goods of heading No. 68.08;

(j) Imitation jewellery of heading No. 71.17;

(k) Goods of Section XVI or Section XVII (for example, machine parts, cases, covers, cabinets for machines and apparatus and wheel wrights' wares);

(l) Goods of Section XVIII (for example, clock cases and musical instruments and parts thereof);

(m) Parts of firearms (heading No. 93.05);

(n) Articles of Chapter 94 (for example, furniture, lamps and lighting fittings, prefabricated buildings);

(o) Articles of Chapter 95 (for example, toys, games, sports requisites);

(p) Articles of Chapter 96 (for example, smoking pipes and parts thereof, buttons, pencils) excluding bodies and handles, of wood, for articles of heading No. 96.03; or

(q) Articles, of Chapter 97 (for example, works of art).

二、本章所称"强化木",是指经过化学或物理方法处理(对于多层粘合木材,其处理应超出一般粘合需要),从而增加了密度或硬度并改善了机械强度、抗化学或抗电性能的木材。

三、税目44.14至44.21适用于木质碎料板或类似木质材料板、纤维板、层压板或强化木的制品。

四、税目44.10、44.11或44.12的产品,可以加工成税目44.09所述的各种形状,也可以加工成弯曲、瓦楞、多孔或其他形状(正方形或矩形除外),以及经其他任何加工,但未具有其他税目所列制品的特性。

五、税目44.17不包括装有第八十二章注释一所述材料制成的刀片、工作刃、工作面或其他工作部件的工具。

六、除上述注释一及其他条文另有规定的以外,本章税目中所称"木",也包括竹及其他木质材料。

子目注释:

子目4403.41至4403.49,4407.21至4407.29,4408.31至4408.39及4412.31至4412.99所称"热带木",是指下列木材:

帽柱木、卡雅楝、美木豆、箭毒木、沙捞越娑罗双、蟹木楝、阿林山榄、杜花楝、红铁木、重黄娑罗双、轻木、白驼峰楝木、连云港驼峰楝木、脂苏木、洋椿、腺瘤豆、深红娑罗双、虎斑楝、缅茄木、科特迪瓦榄仁、美洲破布木、吉贝(拉丁美洲产)、吉贝(非洲产)、轻黄牛木、丛花蔻、细孔绿心樟、重蚁木、甘巴豆、龙脑香、大非洲楝、尼索桐、翅苹婆、浅红娑罗双、浅黄榄仁、尼克(绿心)樟、铁线子、桃花心木、猴子果、夸雷木、曼森梧桐、银叶树(东南亚产)、湿生娑罗双、轻(重)坡垒、印茄木、斯文漆木、异翅香、毒籽山榄、非洲银叶树、纳托山榄、白梧桐、奥克榄、洞果漆、坎诺漆、爱里古夷苏木、蜡烛木、花梨、人面子木、危地马拉黄檀、亚马逊黄檀、巴西黑黄檀、巴西黄檀、良木芸香、重盾籽木、灯架木、四籽木、独蕊木、桉柱木、筒状非洲楝、类木棉、油楠、良木非洲楝、双龙瓣豆(鲍迪豆)、红椿、纤皮玉蕊、柚木、非洲楝、香脂苏木、维罗蔻、五齿(阿蒙、帕洛)娑罗双、白娑罗双、轻赛罗双、黄娑罗双。

2. In this Chapter, the expression "densified wood" means wood which has been subjected to chemical or physical treatment (being, in the case of layers bonded together, treatment in excess of that needed to ensure a good bond), and which has thereby acquired increased density or hardness together with improved mechanical strength or resistance to chemical or electrical agencies.

3. Headings Nos. 44.14 to 44.21 apply to articles of the respective descriptions of particle board or similar board, fibreboard, laminated wood or densified wood as they apply to such articles of wood.

4. Products of heading No. 44.10, 44.11 or 44,12 may be worked to form the shapes provided for in respect of the goods of heading No. 44.09, curved, corrugated, perforated, cut or formed to shapes other than square or rectangular or submitted to any other operation provided it does not give them the character of articles of other headings.

5. Heading No. 44.17 does not apply to tools in which the blade, working edge, working surface or other working part is formed by any of the materials specified in Note 1 to Chapter 82.

6. Subject to Note 1 above and except where the context otherwise requires, any reference to "wood" in a heading of this Chapter applies also to bamboos and other materials of a woody nature.

Subheading Note:

For the purposes of subheadings Nos. 4403.41 to 4403.49, 4407.21 to 4407.29, 4408.31 to 4408.39 and 4412.31 to 4412.99, the expression "tropical wood" means one of the following types of wood:

Abura, Acajou d'Afrique, Afrormosia, Ako, Alan, Andiroba, Aningré, Avodiré, Azobé, Balau, Balsa, Bossé clair, Bossé foncé, Cativo, Cedro, Dabema, Dark Red Meranti, Dibétou, Doussié, Framiré, Freijo, Fromager, Fuma, Geronggang, Ilomba, Imbuia, Ipé, Iroko, Jaboty, Jelutong, Jequitiba, Jongkong, Kapur, Kempas, Keruing, Kosipo, Kotibé, Koto, Light Red Meranti, Limba, Louro, Macaranduba, Mahogany, Makoré, Mandioqueira, Mansonia, Mengkulang, Meranti Bakau, Merawan, Merbau, Merpauh, Mersawa, Moabi, Niangon, Nyatoh, Obeche, Okoumé, Onzabili, Orey, Ovengkol, Ozigo, Padauk, Paldao, Palissandre de Guatemala, Palissandre de Para, Palissandre de Rio, Palissandre de Rose, Pau Amarelo, Pau Marfim, Pulai, Punah, Quaruba, Ramin, Sapelli, Saqui-Saqui, Sepetir, Sipo, Sucupira, Suren, Teak, Tauari, Tiama, Tola, Virola, White Lauan, White Meranti, White Seraya, Yellow Meranti.

税则号列 Tariff Item.	货品名称	最惠国(%) MFN	协定(%) 东盟 CA	协定(%) 中巴 CP	协定(%) CT 中智 CC	普通 Gen	增值税率 VAT	出口退税 ED	计量单位 Unit	监管条件 SC	Article Description
44.01	薪柴(圆木段、块、枝、成捆或类似形状);木片或木粒;锯末、木废料及碎片,不论是否粘结成圆木段、块、片或类似形状:										**Fuel wood, in logs, in billets, in twigs, in faggots or in similar forms; wood in chips or particles; sawdust and wood waste and scrap, whether or not agglomerated in logs, briquettes, pellets or similar forms:**
4401.1000	-薪柴(圆木段、块、枝、成捆或类似形状)	0				70	17		千克	AB	-Fuel wood, in logs, in billets, in twigs, in faggots or in similar forms

税则号列 Tariff Item.	货品名称	最惠国(%) MFN	协定(%)CT 东盟 CA	中巴 CP	中智 CC	普通 Gen	增值税率 VAT	出口退税 ED	计量单位 Unit	监管条件 SC	Article Description
	-木片或木粒:										-Wood in chips or particles:
4401.2100	--针叶木	0				8	17	13	千克		--Coniferous
4401.2100 10	濒危针叶木木片或木粒	0				8	17	13	千克	ABFE	Chips or particles of coniferous wood in imminent dangers
4401.2100 90	其他针叶木木片或木粒	0				8	17	13	千克	AB	Other chips or particles of coniferous wood
4401.2200	--非针叶木	0				8	17	13	千克		--Non-coniferous
4401.2200 10	濒危非针叶木木片或木粒	0				8	17	13	千克	ABFE	Chips or particles of non-coniferous wood in imminent dangers
4401.2200 90	其他非针叶木木片或木粒	0				8	17	13	千克	AB	Other chips or particles of non-coniferous wood
4401.3000	-锯末、木废料及碎片,不论是否粘结成圆木段、块、片或类似形状	0				8	17		千克	ABP	-Sawdust and wood waste and scrap, whether or not agglomerated in logs, briquettes, pellets or similar forms
44.02	**木炭(包括果壳炭及果核炭),不论是否结块:**										**Wood charcoal (including shell or nut charcoal), whether or not agglomerated:**
4402.1000	-竹的	10.5	8		6.3	70	17		千克		-Of bamboo
4402.9000	-其他	10.5	8		6.3	70	17		千克		-Other
4402.9000 10	以木材为原料直接烧制的木炭	10.5				70	17		千克	8	Wood charcoal, obtained by burning wood
4402.9000 90	其他木炭(包括果壳炭及果核炭,不论是否结块)	10.5				70	17		千克		Other wood charcoal (including shell or nut charcoal, whether or not agglomerated)
44.03	**原木,不论是否去皮、去边材或粗锯成方:**										**Wood in the rough, whether or not stripped of bark or sapwood, or roughly squared:**
4403.1000	-用油漆,着色剂,杂酚油或其他防腐剂处理	0				8	13		立方米		-Treated with paint, stains, creosote or other preservatives
4403.1000 10	油漆,着色剂等处理濒危树种原木(包括用杂酚油或其他防腐剂处理)	0				8	13		立方米	8AF	Wood in the rough in imminent dangers, treated with paint, stains, creosote or other preservatives
4403.1000 90	其他油漆,着色剂等处理的原木(包括用杂酚油或其他防腐剂处理)	0				8	13		立方米	8A	Other wood in the rough, treated with paint, stains, creosote or other preservatives
	-其他针叶木:										-Other, coniferous:
4403.2010	---红松和樟子松	0				8	13		立方米		---Korean pine and Mongolian scotch pine
4403.2010 10	其他红松原木(用油漆着色剂,杂酚油或其他防腐剂处理的除外)	0				8	13		立方米	8A	Korean pine wood in the rough, other than the wood treated with paint, stains, creosote or other preservatives
4403.2010 90	其他樟子松原木(用油漆着色剂,杂酚油或其他防腐剂处理的除外)	0				8	13		立方米	8A	Camphor pine wood in the rough, other than the wood treated with paint, stains, creosote or other preservatives
4403.2020	---白松(云杉和冷杉)	0				8	13		立方米	8A	---White pine (spruce and fir)
4403.2030	---辐射松	0				8	13		立方米	8A	---Radial pine
4403.2040	---落叶松	0				8	13		立方米	8A	---Larch (*Larix spp.*)
4403.2090	---其他	0				8	13		立方米		---Other
4403.2090 10	其他濒危针叶木原木	0				8	13		立方米	8AF	Coniferous wood in the rough in imminent dangers
4403.2090 90	其他针叶木原木	0				8	13		立方米	8A	Other coniferous wood in the rough

税则号列 Tariff Item.	货 品 名 称	最惠国(%) MFN	协定(%)CT 东盟 CA	中巴 CP	中智 CC	普通 Gen	增值税率 VAT	出口退税 ED	计量单位 Unit	监管条件 SC	Article Description
	-其他,本章子目注释一所列的热带木:										-Other, of tropical wood specified in Subheading Note 1 to this Chapter:
4403.4100	--深红色红柳安木、浅红色红柳安木及巴栲红柳安木	0				8	13		立方米	8A	--Dark Red Meranti, Light Red Meranti and Meranti Bakau
	--其他:										--Other:
4403.4910	---柚木	0				35	13		立方米	8A	---Teak
4403.4920	---奥克曼(奥克榄)	0				35	13		立方米	8A	---*Okoume*(Aucoumea klaineana)
4403.4930	---龙脑香木(克隆)	0				35	13		立方米	8A	---*Dipterocarpus spp.* Keruing
4403.4940	---山樟(香木)	0				35	13		立方米	8A	---Kapur (*Dryobalanops spp.*)
4403.4950	---印加木(波罗格)	0				35	13		立方米	8A	---*Intsia spp.* Merbau
4403.4960	---大干巴豆(门格里斯或康派斯)	0				35	13		立方米	8A	---Other Koompassia spp. Mengaris or Kempas
4403.4970	---异翅香木	0				35	13		立方米	8A	---Mersawa (*Anisopter spp.*)
4403.4990	---其他	0				8	13		立方米		---Other
4403.4990 10	其他本章子目注释热带濒危原木(用油漆,着色剂,杂酚油或其他防腐剂处理的除外)	0				8	13		立方米	8AF	Tropical wood in imminent dangers in the rough, specified in Subheading Note 1 to this Chapter, other than the wood treated with paint, stains, creosote or other preservatives
4403.4990 90	其他本章子目注释所列热带原木(用油漆,着色剂,杂酚油或其他防腐剂处理的除外)	0				8	13		立方米	8A	Tropical wood in the rough, specified in Subheading Note 1 to this Chapter, other than the wood treated with paint, stains, creosote or other preservatives
	-其他:										-Other:
4403.9100	--栎木(橡木)	0				8	13		立方米	8A	--Of oak (*Quercus spp.*)
4403.9200	--山毛榉木	0				8	13		立方米	8A	--Of beech (*Fagus spp.*)
	--其他:										--Other:
4403.9910	---楠木	0				35	13		立方米	8A	---Of nan mu(*Phoebe*)
4403.9920	---樟木	0				35	13		立方米	8A	---Of camphor wood
4403.9930	---红木	0				35	13		立方米	8AF	---Of rosewood
4403.9940	---泡桐木	0				8	13		立方米	8A	---Of Kiri (*Paulownia*)
4403.9950	---水曲柳	0				8	13		立方米	8A	---Ash
4403.9960	---北美硬阔叶木(包括樱桃木、黑胡桃木、枫木)	0				8	13		立方米	8A	---North American broadleaf hardwood (including cherry, black walnut and maple)
4403.9980	---其他未列名的温带非针叶木	0				8	13		立方米		---Other, temperate non-coniferous, not specified
4403.9980 10	其他未列名温带濒危非针叶木原木(用油漆,着色剂,杂酚油或其他防腐剂处理的除外)	0				8	13		立方米	8AF	Other temperate zone non-coniferous wood in imminent dangers, other than the wood treated with paint, stains, creosote or other preservatives, not elsewhere specified or included
4403.9980 90	其他未列名温带非针叶木原木(用油漆,着色剂,杂酚油或其他防腐剂处理的除外)	0				8	13		立方米	8A	Other temperate zone non-coniferous wood, other than the wood treated with paint, stains, creosote or other preservatives, not elsewhere specified or included
4403.9990	---其他	0				8	13		立方米		---Other

税则号列 Tariff Item.	货品名称	最惠国(%) MFN	协定(%)CT 东盟 CA	中巴 CP	中智 CC	普通 Gen	增值税率 VAT	出口退税 ED	计量单位 Unit	监管条件 SC	Article Description
4403.9990 10	其他未列名濒危非针叶原木(用油漆,着色剂,杂酚油或其他防腐剂处理的除外)	0				8	13		立方米	8AF	Other non-coniferous wood in imminent dangers in the rough, other than the wood treated with paint, stains, creosote or other preservatives, not elsewhere specified or included
4403.9990 90	其他未列名非针叶原木(用油漆,着色剂,杂酚油或其他防腐剂处理的除外)	0				8	13		立方米	8A	Other non-coniferous wood in the rough, other than the wood treated with paint, stains, creosote or other preservatives, not elsewhere specified or included
44.04	**箍木;木劈条;已削尖但未经纵锯的木桩;粗加修整但未经车圆、弯曲或其他方式加工的木棒,适合制手杖、伞柄、工具把柄及类似品;木片条及类似品:**										**Hoopwood; split poles; piles, pickets and stakes of wood, pointed but not sawn lengthwise; wooden sticks, roughly trimmed but not turned, bent or otherwise worked, suitable for the manufacture of walking-sticks, umbrellas, tool handles or the like; chipwood and the like:**
4404.1000	-针叶木的	8	5		6.4	50	17		千克		-Coniferous
4404.1000 10	濒危针叶木的箍木等及类似品(包括木劈条,棒及类似品)	8				50	17		千克	ABFE	Hoopwood; split poles; wooden sticks or the like; of coniferous wood in imminent dangers
4404.1000 90	其他针叶木的箍木等及类似品(包括木劈条,棒及类似品)	8				50	17		千克	AB	Other hoopwood; split poles; wooden sticks or the like; of coniferous wood
4404.2000	-非针叶木的	8	T3		6.4	50	17		千克		-Non-coniferous
4404.2000 10	濒危非针叶木箍木等(包括木劈条,棒及类似品)	8				50	17		千克	ABFE	Hoopwood; split poles, wooden sticks or the like, of non-coniferous wood in imminent dangers
4404.2000 90	其他非针叶木箍木等(包括木劈条,棒及类似品)	8				50	17		千克	AB	Other hoopwood; split poles, wooden sticks or the like, of non-coniferous wood
44.05	**木丝;木粉:**										**Wood wool; wood flour:**
4405.0000	木丝;木粉	8	5		6.4	40	17		千克	AB	Wood wool; wood flour
44.06	**铁道及电车道枕木:**										**Railway or tramway sleepers (cross-ties) of wood:**
4406.1000	-未浸渍	0				14	17		立方米	4ABxy	-Not impregnated
4406.9000	-其他	0				14	17		立方米		-Other
4406.9000 10	濒危木已浸渍铁道及电车道枕木	0				14	17		立方米	FE	Railway or tramway sleepers (crossties) of wood in imminent dangers, impregnated
4406.9000 90	其他已浸渍的铁道及电车道枕木	0				14	17		立方米		Other railway or tramway sleepers (crossties) of wood, impregnated
44.07	**经纵锯、纵切、刨切或旋切的木材,不论是否刨平、砂光或端部接合,厚度超过6mm:**										**Wood sawn or chipped lengthwise, sliced or peeled, whether or not planed, sanded or end-jointed, of a thickness exceeding 6 mm:**
	-针叶木:										-Coniferous:
4407.1010	---红松和樟子松	0				14	17		立方米		---Korean pine and Mongolian scotch pine

税则号列 Tariff Item.	货 品 名 称	最惠国(%) MFN	协定(%)CT 东盟 CA	中巴 CP	中智 CC	普通 Gen	增值税率 VAT	出口退税 ED	计量单位 Unit	监管条件 SC	Article Description
4407.1010 11	端部接合的红松厚板材(经纵锯、纵切、刨切或旋切的,厚度超过6mm)	0				14	17		立方米	ABE	Korean pine wood sawn or chipped lengthwise, sliced or peeled, end-jointed, thickness >6mm
4407.1010 19	端部接合的樟子松厚板材(经纵锯、纵切、刨切或旋切的,厚度超过6mm)	0				14	17		立方米	AB	Mongolian scotch pine wood sawn or chipped lengthwise, sliced or peeled, end-jointed, thickness >6mm
4407.1010 90	非端部接合的红松和樟子松厚板材(经纵锯、纵切、刨切或旋切的,厚度超过6mm)	0				14	17		立方米	4ABExy	Wood sawn or chipped lengthwise, sliced or peeled, of Korean pine and Mongolian scotch pine, not end-jointed, thickness >6mm
4407.1020	---白松(云杉和冷杉)	0				14	17		立方米		---White pine (spruce and fir)
4407.1020 10	端部接合的白松(云杉、冷杉)厚板材(经纵锯、纵切、刨切或旋切的,厚度超过6mm)	0				14	17		立方米	ABEF	Wood sawn or chipped lengthwise, sliced or peeled, of white pine (spruce and fir), end-jointed, thickness >6mm
4407.1020 90	非端部接合白松(云杉、冷杉)厚板材(经纵锯、纵切、刨切或旋切的,厚度超过6mm)	0				14	17		立方米	4ABEFxy	Wood sawn or chipped lengthwise, sliced or peeled, of white pine (spruce and fir), not end-jointed, thickness >6mm
4407.1030	---辐射松	0				14	17		立方米		---Rediata pine
4407.1030 10	端部接合的辐射松厚板材(经纵锯、纵切、刨切或旋切的,厚度超过6mm)	0				14	17		立方米	AB	Wood sawn or chipped lengthwise, sliced or peeled, of radial pine, end-jointed, thickness >6mm
4407.1030 90	非端部接合的辐射松厚板材(经纵锯、纵切、刨切或旋切的,厚度超过6mm)	0				14	17		立方米	4ABxy	Wood sawn or chipped lengthwise, sliced or peeled, of radial pine, not end-jointed, thickness >6mm
4407.1040	---花旗松	0				14	17		立方米		---Douglas fir (*Pseudotsuga menziesii*)
4407.1040 10	端部接合的花旗松厚板材(经纵锯、纵切、刨切或旋切的,厚度超过6mm)	0				14	17		立方米	AB	Wood sawn or chipped lengthwise, sliced or peeled, of douglas fir (Pseudotsuga menziesii), end-jointed, thickness >6mm
4407.1040 90	非端部接合的花旗松厚板材(经纵锯、纵切、刨切或旋切的,厚度超过6mm)	0				14	17		立方米	4ABxy	Wood sawn or chipped lengthwise, sliced or peeled, of douglas fir (Pseudotsuga menziesii) not end-jointed, thickness >6mm
4407.1090	---其他	0				14	17		立方米		---Other
4407.1090 11	端部接合其他濒危针叶木厚板材(经纵锯、纵切、刨切或旋切的,厚度超过6mm)	0				14	17		立方米	FEAB	Other coniferous wood in imminent dangers, sawn or chipped lengthwise, sliced or peeled, end-jointed, thickness >6mm
4407.1090 19	端部接合其他针叶木厚板材(经纵锯、纵切、刨切或旋切的,厚度超过6mm)	0				14	17		立方米	AB	Other coniferous wood sawn or chipped lengthwise, sliced or peeled, end-jointed, thickness >6mm
4407.1090 91	非端部接合其他濒危针叶木厚板材(经纵锯、纵切、刨切或旋切的,厚度超过6mm)	0				14	17		立方米	FEAB4xy	Other coniferous wood in imminent dangers, sawnor chipped lensthwise, sliced or peeled, not endjointed, thick ness >6mm

税则号列 Tariff Item.	货品名称	最惠国(%) MFN	协定(%)CT 东盟 CA	中巴 CP	中智 CC	普通 Gen	增值税率 VAT	出口退税 ED	计量单位 Unit	监管条件 SC	Article Description
4407.1090 99	非端部接合的其他针叶木厚板材（经纵锯、纵切、刨切或旋切的，厚度超过6mm）	0				14	17		立方米	AB4xy	Other coniferous wood sawn or chipped lensthwise, sliced or peeled, not endjointed, thickness >6mm
	-本章子目注释所列的热带木：										-Of tropical wood specified in subheading Note 1 to this chapter:
4407.2100	--美洲桃花心木	0				14	17		立方米		--Mahogany (Swietenia spp.)
4407.2100 10	端部接合的美洲桃花心木（经纵锯、纵切、刨切或旋切的，厚度超过6mm）	0				14	17		立方米	FEAB	Wood sawn or chipped lengthwise, sliced or peeled, of mashogany (swietenia spp.), endjointed, thickness >6mm
4407.2100 90	非端部接合的美洲桃花心木（经纵锯、纵切、刨切或旋切的，厚度超过6mm）	0				14	17		立方米	4ABEFxy	Wood sawn or chipped lengthwise, sliced or peeled, of mashogany (swietenia spp.), not - endjointed, thickness >6mm
4407.2200	--苏里南肉豆蔻木、巴西胡桃极美洲轻木	0				14	17		立方米		--Virola, Imbuia and Balsa
4407.2200 10	端部接合苏里南肉豆蔻木、巴西胡桃木及美洲轻木（经纵锯、纵切、刨切或旋切的厚度超过6mm）	0				14	17		立方米	AB	Virola wood sawn or chipped lengthwise sliced or peeled, brazilian walnut and American end-jointed, thickness 6mm
4407.2200 90	非端部接合苏里南肉豆蔻木、巴西胡桃木及美洲轻木（经纵锯、纵切、刨切或旋切的，厚度超过6mm）	0				14	17		立方米	4ABxy	Wood sawn or chipped lengthwise, slicec or peeled, brazilian walnut and American of virola, Mahogany (swieteniaspp), Imbuia and Balsa, not end-joined, thickness >6mm
4407.2500	--深红色红柳安木、浅红色红柳安木及巴栲红柳安木	0				14	17		立方米		--Dark Red Meranti, Light Red Meranti and Meranti Bakau
4407.2500 10	端部接合的红柳安木板材（指深红色、浅红色及巴栲红柳安木，厚度超过6mm）	0				14	17		立方米	AB	Wood sawn or chipped lengthwise, sliced or peeled, of Dark Red Meranti, Light Red Meranti and Meranti Bakau, end-jointed, thickness >6mm
4407.2500 90	非端部接合的红柳安木板材（指深红色、浅红色及巴栲红柳安木，经纵锯、纵切、刨切或施切的，厚度超过6mm）	0				14	17		立方米	y4xAB	Wood sawn or chipped lengthwise, sliced or peeled, of Dark Red Meranti, Light Red Meranti and Meranti Bakau, not end-jointed, thickness >6mm
4407.2600	--白柳安木、白色红柳安木、白色柳安木、黄色红柳安木及阿兰木	0				14	17		立方米		--White Lauan, White Meranti, White Seraya, Yellow Meranti and Alan
4407.2600 10	端部接合白柳安其他柳安木板（经纵锯、纵切、刨切或旋切的，厚度超过6mm）	0				14	17		立方米	AB	Wood sawn or chipped lengthwise, sliced or peeled, of White Lauan, White Meranti, White Seraya, Yellow Meranti and Alan, end-jointed, thickness >6mm
4407.2600 90	非端部接合白柳安其他柳安木板材（经纵锯、纵切、刨切或旋切的，厚度超过6mm）	0				14	17		立方米	y4xAB	Wood sawn or chipped lengthwise, sliced or peeled, of White Lauan, White Meranti, White Seraya, Yellow Meranti and Alan, not end-jointed, thickness >6mm

税则号列 Tariff Item.	货品名称	最惠国(%) MFN	协定(%)CT 东盟 CA	中巴 CP	中智 CC	普通 Gen	增值税率 VAT	出口退税 ED	计量单位 Unit	监管条件 SC	Article Description
4407.2700	--沙比利	0				40	17		立方米		--Sapelli
4407.2700 10	端部接合沙比利木板材(经从锯、纵切、刨切或旋切的,厚度超过6mm)	0				40	17		立方米	AB	Wood sawn or chipped lengihwise, sliced or peeled, of sapelli, end-jointed, thinkness >6mm
4407.2700 90	非端部接合的沙比利木板材(经纵锯、纵切,刨切或旋切的,厚度超过60mm)	0				40	17		立方米	4ABxy	Wood sawn or chipped lengthwise, sliced or peeled, of sapelli, not end-jointed, thinkness >6mm
4407.2800	--伊罗科木										--Iroko
4407.2800 10	端部接合的伊罗科木板材(经纵锯、纵切、刨切或旋切的,厚度超过6mm)	0				14	17		立方米	AB	Wood sawn or chipped lengthwise, sliced or peeled, of Iroko, end – jointed, thickness >6mm
4407.2800 90	非端部接合的伊罗科木板材(经纵锯、纵切、刨切或旋切的,厚度超过6mm)	0				14	17		立方米	4ABxy	Wood sawn or chipped lengthwise, sliced or peeled, of Iroko, not end – jointed, thickness >6mm
	--其他:										--Other:
4407.2910	---柚木	0				40	17		立方米		---Teak
4407.2910 10	端部接合的柚木板材(经纵锯、纵切、刨切或旋切的,厚度超过6mm)	0				40	17		立方米	AB	Wood sawn or chipped lengthwise, sliced or peeled, of teak, end-jointed, thickness >6mm
4407.2910 90	非端部接合的柚木板材(经纵锯、纵切、刨切或旋切的,厚度超过6毫米)	0				40	17		立方米	y4xAB	Wood sawn or chipped lengthwise, sliced or peeled, of teak, not end-jointed, thickness >6mm
4407.2920	---非洲桃花心木	0				40	17		立方米		---Acajou d' Afrique
4407.2920 10	端部接合的非洲桃花心木板材(经纵锯纵切刨切或旋切的,厚度超过6mm)	0				40	17		立方米	AB	Wood sawn or chipped lengthwise, sliced or peeled, of acajou d'afrique, end-jointed, thickness >6mm
4407.2920 90	非端部接合的非洲桃花心木木板(经纵锯纵切刨切或旋切的,厚度超过6mm)	0				40	17		立方米	4ABxy	Wood sawn or chipped lengthwise, sliced or peeled, of acajou d'afrique, not end-jointed, thickness >6mm
4407.2930	---波罗格(Merban)	0				40	17		立方米		---Merban
4407.2930 10	端部接合的波罗格(Merban)板材(经纵锯、纵切、刨切或旋切的,厚度超过6mm)	0				40	17		立方米	AB	Wood sawn or chipped lengthwise, sliced or peeled, of merban, end-jointed, thickness >6mm
4407.2930 90	非端部接合的波罗格(Merban)板材(经纵锯、纵切、刨切或旋切的,厚度超过6mm)	0				40	17		立方米	4ABxy	Wood sawn or chipped lengthwise, sliced or peeled, of merban, not end-jointed, thickness >6mm
4407.2990	---其他	0				14	17		立方米		---Other
4407.2990 11	端部接合拉敏木厚板材(经纵锯、纵切、刨切或旋切的,厚度超过6mm)	0				14	17		立方米	FEAB	Wood sawn or chipped lengthwise, sliced or peeled, of Ramin wood, not end-jointed, thickness >6mm
4407.2990 12	端部接合其他未列名濒危热带木厚板材(经纵锯、纵切、刨切或旋切的,厚度超过6mm)	0				14	17		立方米	FEAB	Other tropical wood in imminent dangers, not elsewhere specified or included, sawn or chipped lengthwise, sliced or peeled, end-jointed, thickness >6mm

税则号列 Tariff Item.	货品名称	最惠国(%) MFN	协定(%)CT 东盟 CA	中巴 CP	中智 CC	普通 Gen	增值税率 VAT	出口退税 ED	计量单位 Unit	监管条件 SC	Article Description
4407.2990 19	端部接合其他未列名热带木厚板材(经纵锯、纵切、刨切或旋切的,厚度超过6mm)	0				14	17		立方米	AB	Wood sawn or chipped lengthwise, sliced or peeled, of other tropical wood not elsewhere specified or included, end-jointed, thickness >6mm
4407.2990 91	非端部接合其他未列名濒危热带木板材(经纵锯、纵切、刨切或旋切的,厚度超过6mm)	0				14	17		立方米	y4xAFEB	Other tropical wood in imminent domsers, not elsewhere specified or included, sawn or chipped lengthwise, sliced or peeled, not endjointed, thickness >6mm
4407.2990 99	非端部接合其他未列名热带木板材(经纵锯、纵切、刨切或旋切的,厚度超过6mm)	0				14	17		立方米	y4xAB	Other tropical wood, not elsewhere specified or included, sawn or chipped lensthwise, shiced or peeled, not end-jointed, thickness >6mm
	--其他:										--Other:
4407.9100	--栎木(橡木)	0				14	17		立方米		--Of oak (*Quercus spp.*)
4407.9100 10	端部接合的栎木(橡木)厚板材(经纵锯、纵切、刨切或旋切的,厚度超过6mm)	0				14	17		立方米	AB	Wood sawn or chipped lengthwise, sliced or peeled, of oak (*Quercus spp.*), end-jointed, thickness >6mm
4407.9100 90	非端部接合的栎木(橡木)厚板材(经纵锯、纵切、刨切或旋切的,厚度超过6mm)	0				14	17		立方米	y4xAB	Wood sawn or chipped lengthwise, sliced or peeled, of oak (*Quercus spp.*), not end-jointed, thickness >6mm
4407.9200	--山毛榉木	0				14	17		立方米		--Of beech (*Fagus spp.*)
4407.9200 10	端部接合的山毛榉木厚板材(经纵锯、纵切、刨切或旋切的,厚度超过6mm)	0				14	17		立方米	ABE	Wood sawn or chipped lengthwise, sliced or peeled, of beech (*Fagus spp.*), end-jointed, thickness >6mm
4407.9200 90	非端部接合的山毛榉木厚板材(经纵锯、纵切、刨切或旋切的,厚度超过6mm)	0				14	17		立方米	4ABExy	Wood sawn or chipped lengthwise, sliced or peeled, of beech (*Fagus spp.*), not end-jointed, thickness >6mm
4407.9300	--枫木										--Maple
4407.9300 10	端部接合的枫木厚板材(经纵锯、纵切、刨切或旋切的,厚度超过6mm)	0				14	17		立方米	AB	Wood sawn or chipped lengthwise, sliced or peeled, of maple, endjointed, thickness >6mm
4407.9300 90	非端部接合的枫木厚板材(经纵锯、纵切、刨切或旋切的,厚度超过6mm)	0				14	17		立方米	4ABxy	Wood sawn or chipped lengthwise, sliced or peeled, of maple, not end – jointed, thickness >6mm
4407.9400	--樱桃木	0				14	17		立方米		Cherry
4407.9400 10	端部接合的樱桃木厚板材(经纵锯、纵切、刨切或旋切的,厚度超过6mm)	0				14	17		立方米	AB	Wood sawn or chipped lengthwise, sliced or peeled, of cherry, endjointed, thickness >6mm
4407.9400 90	非端部接合的樱桃木厚板材(经纵锯、纵切、刨切或旋切的,厚度超过6mm)	0				14	17		立方米	4AB xy	Wood sawn or chipped lengthwise, sliced or peeled, of cherry, not end – jointed, thickness >6mm
4407.9500	--白蜡木	0				14	17		立方米		Oleaceae
4407.9500 10	端部接合的白蜡木厚板材(经纵锯、纵切、刨切或旋切的,厚度超过6mm)	0				14	17		立方米	AB	Wood sawn or chipped lengthwise, sliced or peeled, of ash, endjointed, thickness >6mm

税则号列 Tariff Item.	货品名称	最惠国(%) MFN	协定(%) CT			普通 Gen	增值税率 VAT	出口退税 ED	计量单位 Unit	监管条件 SC	Article Description
			东盟 CA	中巴 CP	中智 CC						
4407.9500 90	非端部接合的白蜡木厚板材(经纵锯、纵切、刨切或旋切的,厚度超过6mm)	0				14	17		立方米	4ABxy	Wood sawn or chipped lengthwise, sliced or peeled, of ash, not end – jointed, thickness >6mm
	--其他:										--Other:
4407.9910	---樟木、楠木、红木	0				40	17		立方米		---Of camphor-wood, nanmu or rosewood
4407.9910 10	端部接合樟木、楠木、红木厚板材(经纵锯、纵切、刨切或旋切的,厚度超过6mm)	0				40	17		立方米	AFEB	Wood sawn or chipped lengthwise, sliced or peeled, of camphor-wood, nanmu or rosewood, end-jointed, thickness >6mm
4407.9910 90	非端部接合樟木、楠木、红木厚板材(经纵锯、纵切、刨切或旋切的,厚度超过6mm)	0				40	17		立方米	y4xAFEB	Wood sawn or chipped lengthwise, sliced or peeled, of camphor-wood, nanmu or rosewood, not end-jointed, thickness >6mm
4407.9920	---泡桐木	0				14	17	13	立方米		---Of paulownia
4407.9920 10	端部接合的泡桐木厚板材(经纵锯、纵切、刨切或旋切的,厚度超过6mm)	0				14	17	13	立方米	AB	Wood sawn or chipped lengthwise, sliced or peeled, of paulownia, end-jointed, thickness >6mm
4407.9920 90	非端部接合的泡桐木厚板材(经纵锯、纵切、刨切或旋切的,厚度超过6mm)	0				14	17	13	立方米	4ABxy	Wood sawn or chipped lengthwise, sliced or peeled, of paulownia, not end-jointed, thickness >6mm
4407.9930	---其他北美硬阔叶材(含黑胡桃木类)	0				14	17		立方米		---Other North American broadleaf hardwood(including black walnut)
4407.9930 10	端部接合的北美硬阔叶材厚板材(含黑胡桃木,纵锯纵切刨切或旋切,厚度超过6mm)	0				14	17		立方米	AB	Wood sawn or chipped lengthwise, sliced or peeled, of North American broadleaf hardwood (including, black walnut) temperate zone, end-jointed, thickness >6mm
4407.9930 90	非端部接合的北美硬阔叶材厚板材(含黑胡桃木,纵锯纵切刨切或旋切,厚度超过6mm)	0				14	17		立方米	4ABxy	Wood sawn or chipped lengthwise, sliced or peeled, of North American broadleaf hardwood (including, black walnut) temperate zone, not end-jointed, thickness >6mm
4407.9980	---其他温带非针叶材	0				14	17		立方米		---Other of temperate zone origin, non-coniferous wood
4407.9980 11	端部接合其他温带濒危非针叶板材(纵锯、纵切、刨切或旋切的,厚度超过6mm)	0				14	17		立方米	FEAB	Wood sawn or chipped lengthwise, sliced or peeled, of temperate zone non-coniferous wood in imminent dangers, end-jointed, thickness >6mm
4407.9980 19	端部接合的其他温带非针叶厚板材(纵锯、纵切、刨切或旋切的,厚度超过6mm)	0				14	17		立方米	AB	Wood sawn or chipped lengthwise, sliced or peeled, of temperate zone non-coniferous wood, end-jointed, thickness >6mm
4407.9980 91	非端部接合其他温带濒危非针叶厚板材(非端部结合,纵锯、纵切、刨切或旋切的,厚度超过6mm)	0				14	17		立方米	4ABFExy	Wood sawn or chipped lengthwise, sliced or peeled, of temperate zone non-coniferous wood in imminent dangers not end-jointed, thickness >6mm

税则号列 Tariff Item.	货品名称	最惠国(%) MFN	协定(%)CT 东盟 CA	中巴 CP	中智 CC	普通 Gen	增值税率 VAT	出口退税 ED	计量单位 Unit	监管条件 SC	Article Description
4407.9980 99	非端部接合的其他温带非针叶厚板(纵锯、纵切、刨切或旋切的,厚度超过6mm)	0				14	17		立方米	4ABxy	Wood sawn or chipped lengthwise, sliced or peeled, of temperate zone non-coniferous wood, not end-jointed, thickness >6mm
4407.9990	---其他	0				14	17		立方米		---Other
4407.9990 12	端部接合的濒危木厚板材(经纵锯、纵切、刨切或旋切的,厚度超过6mm)	0				14	17		立方米	AFEB	Wood sawn or chipped lengthwise, sliced or peeled, of wood in imminent dangers, end-jointed, thickness >6mm
4407.9990 19	端部接合的其他木厚板材(经纵锯、纵切、刨切或旋切的,厚度超过6mm)	0				14	17		立方米	AB	Other wood sawn or chipped lengthwise, sliced or peeled, end-jointed thickness >6mm
4407.9990 91	非端部接合的其他濒危木厚板材(经纵锯、纵切、刨切或旋切的,厚度超过6mm)	0				14	17		立方米	y4xAFEB	Wood sawn or chipped lengthwise, sliced or peeled, in imminent dangers, not end-jointed, thickness >6mm
4407.9990 99	非端部接合的其他木厚板材(经纵锯、纵切、刨切或旋切的,厚度超过6mm)	0				14	17		立方米	y4xAB	Other wood sawn or chipped lengthwise, sliced or peeled, in imminent dangers, not end-jointed, thickness >6mm
44.08	**饰面用单板(包括刨切积层木获得的单板)、制胶合板或类似多层板用单板以及其他经纵锯、刨切或旋切的木材,不论是否刨平、砂光、拼接或端部结合,厚度不超过6毫米:**										**Sheets for veneering (including those obtained by slicing laminated wood), for plywood or for other similar laminated wood and other wood, sawn lengthwise, sliced or peeled, whether or not planed, sanded, spliced or end-jointed, of a thickness not exceeding 6mm:**
	-针叶木:										-Coniferous:
	---饰面用单板:										---Veneer sheets:
4408.1011	----用胶合板等多层板制的	8			4.8	40	17		千克		----Of laminated wood of plywood
4408.1011 10	胶合板等多层板制濒危针叶木单板(厚度≤6mm,饰面用)	8				40	17		千克	ABFE	Veneer sheets of coniferous wood in imminent dangers, of laminated wood of plywood, thickness≤6mm
4408.1011 90	其他胶合板等多层板制针叶木单板(厚度≤6mm,饰面用)	8				40	17		千克	AB	Other veneer sheets of coniferous wood, of laminated wood of plywood, thickness≤6mm
4408.1019	----其他	4			3.2	40	17		千克		----Other
4408.1019 10	其他饰面濒危针叶木单板(厚度≤6mm)	4				40	17		千克	ABFE	Other veneer sheets of coniferous wood in imminent dangers, thickness ≤6mm
4408.1019 90	其他饰面针叶木单板(厚度≤6mm)	4				40	17		千克	AB	Other veneer sheets of coniferous wood, thickness≤6mm
4408.1020	---制胶合板用单板	4			3.2	17	17		千克		---Sheets for plywood
4408.1020 10	制胶合板用濒危针叶木单板(厚度≤6mm)	4				17	17		千克	ABFE	Sheets for plywood of coniferous wood in imminent dangers, thickness≤6mm
4408.1020 90	其他制胶合板用针叶木单板(厚度≤6mm)	4				17	17		千克	AB	Other sheets for plywood of coniferous wood, thickness≤6mm
4408.1090	---其他	4			3.2	30	17		千克		---Other

税则号列 Tariff Item.	货品名称	最惠国(%) MFN	协定(%)CT 东盟 CA	中巴 CP	中智 CC	普通 Gen	增值税率 VAT	出口退税 ED	计量单位 Unit	监管条件 SC	Article Description
4408.1090 10	其他濒危针叶木单板材(经纵锯,刨切或旋切的,厚度≤6mm)	4				30	17		千克	ABFE	Sheets for plywood of coniferous wood in imminent dangers, wood sawn or chipped lengthwise, sliced or peeled, thickness≤6mm
4408.1090 90	其他针叶木单板材(经纵锯,刨切或旋切的,厚度≤6mm)	4				30	17		千克	AB	Sheets for plywood of coniferous wood, wood sawn or chipped lengthwise, sliced or peeled, thickness≤6mm
	-本章子目注释一所列的热带木:										-Of tropical wood specified in Subheading Note 1 to this Chapter:
	--深红色红柳安木、浅红色红柳安木及巴栲红柳安木:										--Dark Red Meranti, Light Red Meranti and Meranti Bakau:
	---饰面用单板:										---Veneer sheets:
4408.3111	----用胶合板等多层板制的	10			0	40	17		千克	AB	----Of laminated wood of plywood
4408.3119	----其他	4			0	40	17		千克	AB	----Other
4408.3120	---制胶合板用单板	4			0	17	17		千克	AB	---Sheets for plywood
4408.3190	---其他	4			0	30	17		千克	AB	---Other
	--其他:										--Other:
	---饰面用单板:										---Veneer sheets:
4408.3911	----用胶合板等多层板制的	10			0	40	17		千克		----Of laminated wood of plywood
4408.3911 10	胶合板多层板制饰面桃花心木单板(厚度≤6mm)	10				40	17		千克	ABFE	Sheets for veneering, of acajou d'afrique, of laminated wood of plywood, thickness≤6mm
4408.3911 20	胶合板多层板制饰面拉敏木单板(厚度≤6mm)	10				40	17		千克	ABFE	Sheets for veneering, of Ramin wood, of laminated wood of plywood, thickness≤6mm
4408.3911 30	胶合板多层板制饰面濒危木单板(本章子目注释一所列其他热带木,厚度≤6mm)	10				40	17		千克	ABFE	Sheets for veneering, of other tropical wood in imminent dangers specified in Subheading Note 1 to this Chapter, of laminated wood of plywood, thickness ≤6mm
4408.3911 90	胶合板多层板制饰面热带木单板(本章子目注释一所列其他热带木,厚度≤6mm)	10				40	17		千克	AB	Sheets for veneering, of tropical wood specified in Subheading Note 1 to this Chapter, of laminated wood of plywood, thickness≤6mm
4408.3919	----其他	4			0	40	17		千克		----Other
4408.3919 10	其他饰面用桃花心木单板(厚度≤6mm)	4				40	17		千克	ABFE	Sheets for veneering of acajou d'afrique, thickness≤6mm
4408.3919 20	其他饰面用拉敏木单板(厚度≤6mm)	4				40	17		千克	ABFE	Sheets for venceering of Ramin wood, thickness≤6mm
4408.3919 30	其他饰面用濒危木单板(本章子目注释一所列其他热带木,厚度≤6mm)	4				40	17		千克	ABFE	Sheets for veneering of tropical wood in imminent dangers specified in Subheading Note 1 to this Chapter, thickness≤6mm
4408.3919 90	其他饰面本章子目注释热带木单板(厚度不超过6mm)	4				40	17		千克	AB	Sheets for veneering of tropical wood specified in Subheading Note 1 to this Chapter, thickness≤6mm
4408.3920	---制胶合板用单板	4			0	17	17		千克		---Sheets for plywood
4408.3920 10	其他桃花心木制的胶合板用单板(厚度≤6mm)	4				17	17		千克	ABFE	Other sheets for plywood, of acajou d'afrique of tropical wood specified in Subheading Note 1 to this Chapter, thickness≤6mm

税则号列 Tariff Item.	货品名称	最惠国(%) MFN	协定(%) CT			普通 Gen	增值税率 VAT	出口退税 ED	计量单位 Unit	监管条件 SC	Article Description
			东盟 CA	中巴 CP	中智 CC						
4408.3920 20	其他拉敏木制的胶合板用单板(厚度≤6mm)	4				17	17		千克	ABFE	Other sheets for plywood, of Ramin wood, thickness≤6mm
4408.3920 30	其他濒危木制的胶合板用单板(本章子目注释一所列其他热带木,厚度≤6mm)	4				17	17		千克	ABFE	Other Sheets for plywood, of tropical wood in imminent dangers specified in Subheading Note 1 to this Chapter, thickness≤6mm
4408.3920 90	其他列名热带木制的胶合板用单板(本章子目注释一所列其他热带木,厚度≤6mm)	4				17	17		千克	AB	Other sheets for plywood, of tropical wood specified in Subheading Note 1 to this Chapter, thickness≤6mm
4408.3990	---其他	4			0	30	17		千克		---Other
4408.3990 10	其他桃花心木制的其他单板(本章子目注释一所列其他热带木,厚度≤6mm)	4				30	17		千克	ABFE	Other sheets of acajou d'afrique, of tropical wood specified in Subheading Note 1 to this Chapter, thickness ≤6mm
4408.3990 20	其他拉敏木制的其他单板(本章子目注释一所列其他热带木,厚度≤6mm)	4				30	17		千克	ABFE	Other sheets of Ramin wood, of tropical wood specified in Subheading Note 1 to this Chapter, thickness≤6mm
4408.3990 30	其他列名濒危热带木制的其他单板(本章子目注释一所列其他热带木,厚度≤6mm)	4				30	17		千克	ABFE	Other of tropical wood of tropical wood in imminent dangers specified in Subheading Note 1 to this Chapter, thickness≤6mm
4408.3990 90	其他列名的热带木制的其他单板(本章子目注释一所列其他热带木,厚度≤6mm)	4				30	17		千克	AB	Other sheets of tropical wood specified in Subheading Note 1 to this Chapter, thickness≤6mm
	-其他:										-Other:
	---饰面用单板:										---Veneer sheets:
4408.9011	----用胶合板等多层板制的	4			3.2	40	17		千克		----Of laminated wood of plywood
4408.9011 10	胶合板多层板制饰面濒危木单板(厚度≤6mm)	4				40	17		千克	ABFE	Sheets for veneering, of wood, of laminated wood of wood in imminenr dansers, thickness≤6mm
4408.9011 90	胶合板多层板制饰面其他木单板(厚度≤6mm,针叶木、热带木除外)	4				40	17		千克	AB	Sheets for veneering of other wood, other than tropical coniferous wood, of laminated wood of plywood, thickness≤6mm
4408.9012	----温带非针叶木制	3			1.8	40	17		千克		----Other of temperate zone origin, non-coniferous wood
4408.9012 10	温带濒危非针叶木制饰面用木单板(厚度≤6mm,针叶木、热带木除外)	3				40	17		千克	ABFE	Sheets for veneering of temperate zone non-coniferous wood in imminent dangers, other than tropical coniferous wood, thickness≤6mm
4408.9012 90	其他温带非针叶木制饰面用木单板(厚度≤6mm,针叶木、热带木除外)	3				40	17		千克	AB	Sheets for veneering of temperate zone non-coniferous wood, other than tropical coniferous wood, thickness≤6mm
4408.9019	----其他	3			1.8	40	17		千克		----Other
4408.9019 11	家具饰面用濒危木单板(厚度≤6mm)	3				40	17		千克	ABFE	Sheets for veneering of wood in immenent dangers (thickness≤6mm)
4408.9019 19	其他家具饰面用单板(厚度≤6mm)	3				40	17		千克	AB	Other sheets for veneering of wood (thickness≤6mm)

税则号列 Tariff Item.	货品名称	最惠国(%) MFN	协定(%)CT 东盟 CA	中巴 CP	中智 CC	普通 Gen	增值税率 VAT	出口退税 ED	计量单位 Unit	监管条件 SC	Article Description
4408.9019 91	其他饰面用濒危木单板(厚度≤6mm)	3				40	17		千克	ABEF	Other sheets for veneering of wood in imminent dangers (thickness≤6mm)
4408.9019 99	其他饰面用单板(厚度≤6mm)	3				40	17		千克	AB	Other sheets for veneering (thickness≤6mm)
	---胶合板用单板:										---Sheets for plywood:
4408.9021	----温带非针叶木制	3			1.8	17	17		千克		----Other of temperate zone origin non-coniferous wood
4408.9021 10	温带濒危非针叶木制胶合板用单板(厚度≤6mm)	3				17	17		千克	ABFE	Sheets for plywood of temperate zone non-coniferous wood in imminent dangers, thickness≤6mm
4408.9021 90	其他温带非针叶木制胶合板用单板(厚度≤6mm)	3				17	17		千克	AB	Other sheets for plywood of temperate zone non-coniferous wood, thickness ≤6mm
4408.9029	----其他	3			1.8	17	17		千克		----Other
4408.9029 10	其他濒危木制胶合板用单板(厚度≤6mm)	3				17	17		千克	ABFE	Other sheets for plywood of Ramin wood in imminent dangers, thickness ≤6mm
4408.9029 90	其他木制胶合板用单板(厚度≤6mm)	3				17	17		千克	AB	Sheets for plywood of other wood, thickness≤6mm
	---其他:										---Other:
4408.9091	----温带非针叶木制	3			1.8	30	17		千克		----Of temperate non-coniferous wood
4408.9091 10	温带濒危非针叶木制其他单板材(经纵锯,刨切或旋切的,厚度≤6mm)	3				30	17		千克	ABFE	Sheets of temperate zone non-coniferous wood, sawn or chipped lengthwise, sliced or peeled, thickness ≤6mm
4408.9091 90	温带非针叶木制其他单板材(经纵锯,刨切或旋切的,厚度≤6mm)	3				30	17		千克	AB	Other sheets of temperate zone non-coniferous wood, sawn or chipped lengthwise, sliced or peeled, thickness ≤6mm
4408.9099	----其他	3			1.8	30	17		千克		----Other
4408.9099 10	其他濒危木制的其他单板材(经纵锯,刨切或旋切的,厚度≤6mm)	3				30	17		千克	ABEF	Other sheets of Ramin wood imminent dangers, sawn or chipped lengthwise, sliced or peeled, thickness≤6mm
4408.9099 90	其他木材,但针叶木、热带木除外(经纵锯,刨切或旋切的,厚度≤6mm)	3				30	17		千克	AB	Other wood other than coniferous, tropical wood, sawn or chipped lengthwise, sliced or peeled, thickness≤6mm
44.09	**任何一边、端或面制成连续形状(舌榫、槽榫、半槽榫、斜角、V形接头、珠榫、缘饰、刨圆及类似形状)的木材(包括未装拼的拼花地板用板条及缘板),不论是否刨平、砂光或端部结合:**										**Wood (including strips and friezes for parquet flooring, not assembled) continuously shaped (tongues, grooved, rebated, chamfered, V-jointed, beaded, moulded, rounded or the like) along any of its edges, ends or faces, whether or not planed, sanded or end-jointed:**
	-针叶木:										-Coniferous:
4409.1010	---地板条(块)	7.5	5		6	50	17		千克		---Floor board strips

税则号列 Tariff Item.	货品名称	最惠国(%) MFN	协定(%) CT 东盟 CA	中巴 CP	中智 CC	普通 Gen	增值税率 VAT	出口退税 ED	计量单位 Unit	监管条件 SC	Article Description
4409.1010 10	一边或面制成连续形状的濒危针叶木制地板条、块(包括未装拼的拼花地板用板条及缘板)	7.5				50	17		千克	ABEF	Strips (blocks) for parquet flooring of coniferous wood in imminent dangers, not assembled continuously shaped along any of its edges or faces
4409.1010 90	一边或面制成连续形状的其他针叶木地板条,块(包括未装拼的拼花地板用板条及缘板)	7.5				50	17		千克	AB	Strips (blocks) for parquet flooring of other coniferous wood, not assembled continuously shaped along any of its edges or faces
4409.1090	---其他	7.5	5		6	50	17		千克		---Other
4409.1090 10	一边或面制成连续形状濒危针叶木材	7.5				50	17		千克	ABFE	Wood of coniferous wood in imminent dangers, continuously shaped along any of its edges or faces
4409.1090 90	其他一边或面制成连续形状的针叶木材	7.5				50	17		千克	AB	Wood of coniferous, continuously shaped along any of its edges or faces
	-非针叶木:										-Non-coniferous:
	--竹的:										--Bam boo:
4409.2110	---地板条(块)	4			3.2	50	17		千克		---Strips (blocks) for parquet flooring
4409.2110 10	一边或面制成连续形状的濒危竹地板条、块(包括未装拼的拼花竹地板用板条及缘板)	4				50	17		千克	ABE	Strips (blocks) for parquet flooring of bamboo in imminent dangers, not assembled, continuously shaped along any of its edges or faces
4409.2110 90	一边或面制成连续形状的竹地板条、块(包括未装拼的拼花竹地板用板条及缘板)	4				50	17	13	千克	AB	Strips (blocks) for parquet flooring of bamboo, not assembled, continuously shaped along any of its edges or faces
4409.2190	---其他	4			3.2	50	17		千克		---Other
4409.2190 10	一边或面制成连续形状的其他濒危竹材	4				50	17		千克	ABE	Bamboo in imminent dangers, not assembled continuously shaped along any of its edges or faces
4409.2190 90	一边或面制成连续形状的其他竹材	4				50	17		千克	AB	Other bamboo in imminent dangers, not assembled continuously shaped along any of its edges or faces
	--其他:										--Other:
4409.2910	---地板条(块)	4			3.2	50	17		千克		---Strips(blocks)for parquet floorise
4409.2910 10	一边或面制成连续形状的拉敏木地板条、块(包括未装拼的拼花拉敏木地板用板条及缘板)	4				50	17		千克	ABFE	Strips (blocks) for parquet flooring of other, not assembled, continuously shaped along any of its edges or faces bamboo Ramin wood.
4409.2910 20	一边或面制成连续形状的桃花心木地板条、块(包括未装拼的桃花心木拼花地板用板条及缘板)	4				50	17		千克	ABFE	Strips (blocks) for parquet flooring of acajou d'afrique, not assembled, continuously shaped along any of its edges or faces(Including battens for unfurnished acajou block floor)
4409.2910 30	一边或面制成连续形状的其他濒危木地板条、块(包括未装拼的其他濒危木拼花地板用板条及缘板)	4				50	17		千克	ABFE	Strips (blocks) for parquet flooring of other wood in imminent dangers, not assembled, continuously shaped along any of its edges or faces (Including battens for wood in immnent dangers block floor)

税则号列 Tariff Item.	货品名称	最惠国(%) MFN	协定(%)CT 东盟 CA	中巴 CP	中智 CC	普通 Gen	增值税率 VAT	出口退税 ED	计量单位 Unit	监管条件 SC	Article Description
4409.2910 90	一边或面制成连续形状的其他非针叶木地板条、块(包括未装拼的其他非针叶木拼花地板用板条及缘板)	4				50	17		千克	AB	Strips (blocks) for parquet flooring of other non-coniferous wood, not assembled, continuously shaped along any of its edges or faces
4409.2990	---其他	4			3.2	50	17		千克		---Other non-coniferous
4409.2990 10	一边或面制成连续形状的拉敏木	4				50	17		千克	ABFE	Ramin wood, continuously sha- ped along any of its edges or faces
4409.2990 20	一边或面制成连续形状的桃花心木	4				50	17		千克	ABFE	Acajou d'afrique wood, continuously shaped along any of its edges or faces
4409.2990 30	一边或面制成连续形状的其他濒危木	4				50	17		千克	ABFE	Other Wood in imminent dangers, continuously shaped along any of its edges or faces
4409.2990 90	一边或面制成连续形状其他非针叶木材	4				50	17		千克	AB	Other non-coniferous wood, continuously sh-aped along any of its edges or faces
44.10	**木质碎料板及其他类似木质材料板(例如,华夫板),定向板及不论是否用树脂或其他有机粘合剂粘合:**										**Particle board and similar board (for example, waferboard) and oriented strand board, of wood or other ligneous materials, whether or not agglomerated with resins or other organic blinding substances:**
	-木制:										-Of mood:
4410.1100	--碎料板	4				40	17	5	千克	AB	--Particle board
4410.1200	--定向刨花板	4				40	17	5	千克	AB	--Directional flakeboard
4410.1900	--其他	4				40	17	5	千克	AB	--Other
4410.9000	-其他	7.5				40	17	5	千克	AB	-Other
44.11	**木纤维板或其他木质材料纤维板,不论是否用树脂或其他有机粘合剂粘合:**										**Fibreboard of wood or other ligneous materials, whether or not bonded with resins or other organic substances:**
	-中密度纤维板(MDF):										-Medium density fiber
	--厚度不超过5毫米:										--Thickness no more than 5mm
	---密度超过每立方厘米0.8克:										---Fibreboard of a density exceeding 0.8/cm^3:
4411.1211	----未经机械加工或盖面的	4				40	17	13	千克	AB	----Not mechanically worked or surface covered
4411.1219	----其他	7.5				40	17	13	千克	AB	----Other
4411.1220	---密度超过每立方厘米0.5克,但不超过每立方厘米0.8克:	4				40	17	13	千克	AB	---Fibreboard of a density exceeding 0.5 g/cm^3 but not exceeding 0.8 g/cm^3
	---其他:										---Other:
4411.1291	----未经机械加工或盖面的	7.5				40	17	13	千克	AB	----Not mechanically worked or surface covered
4411.1299	----其他	4				40	17	13	千克	AB	----Other
	--厚度超过5毫米但未超过9毫米:										--Thickness more than 5mm but less than 9mm
	---密度超过每立方厘米0.8克:										---Fibreboard of a density exceeding 0.8g/cm^3:

税则号列 Tariff Item.	货品名称	最惠国(%) MFN	协定(%)CT			普通 Gen	增值税率 VAT	出口退税 ED	计量单位 Unit	监管条件 SC	Article Description
			东盟 CA	中巴 CP	中智 CC						
4411.1311	----未经机械加工或盖面的	4				40	17	13	千克	AB	----Not mechanically worked or surface covered
4411.1319	----其他	7.5				40	17	13	千克	AB	----Other
4411.1320	---密度超过每立方厘米0.5克,但未超过每立方厘米0.8克	4				40	17	13	千克	AB	---Fibreboard of a density exceeding 0.5g/cm³ but not exceeding 0.8g/cm³
	---其他:										---Other:
4411.1391	----未经机械加工或盖面的	7.5				40	17	13	千克	AB	----Not mechanically worked orsufacce covered
4411.1399	----其他	4				40	17	13	千克	AB	----Other
	--厚度超过9毫米:										--Thickness more than 5mm
	---密度超过每立方厘米0.8克:										---Fibreboard of a density exceeding 0.8g/cm³:
4411.1411	----未经机械加工或盖面的	4				40	17	13	千克	AB	----Not mechanically worked or surface covered
4411.1419	----其他	7.5				40	17	13	千克	AB	----Other
4411.1420	---密度超过每立方厘米0.5克,但未超过每立方厘米0.8克	4				40	17	13	千克	AB	---Fibreboard of a density exceeding 0.5g/cm³ but not exceeding 0.8g/cm³
	---其他:										---Other:
4411.1491	----未经机械加工或盖面的	7.5				40	17		千克	AB	----Not mechanically worked or surface covered
4411.1499	----其他	4				40	17		千克	AB	----Other
	-其他:										-Other:
	--密度超过每立方厘米0.8克:										--Fibreboard of a density exceeding 0.8g/cm³:
4411.9210	---未经机械加工或盖面的	4				40	17	13	千克	AB	---Not mechanically worked or surface covered
4411.9290	---其他	7.5				40	17	13	千克	AB	---Other
4411.9300	--密度超过每立方厘米0.5克,但未超过每立方厘米0.8克	4				40	17		千克	AB	--Fibreboard of a density exceeding 0.5g/cm³ but not exceeding 0.8g/cm³
	--密度未超过每立方厘米0.5克										--Fibreboard of a density not exceeding 0.5g/cm³
4411.9410	---密度超过每立方厘米0.35克,但不超过每立方厘米0.5克	7.5				40	17	13	千克	AB	---Fibreboard of a density exceeding 0.35g/cm³ but not exceeding 0.5g/cm³
	---密度未超过每立方厘米0.35克										---Fibreboard of a density not exceeding 0.35g/cm³
4411.9421	----未经机械加工或盖面的	7.5				40	17	13	千克	AB	----Not mechanically worked orsuface covered
4411.9429	----其他	4				40	17	13	千克	AB	----Other
44.12	**胶合板、单板饰面板及类似的多层板:**										**Plywood, veneered panels and similar laminated wood:**
	-竹制的:										-Pamboo:
	---仅由薄木板制的胶合板,每层厚度不超过6毫米:										---Plywood consisting solely of sheets of wood, each ply not exceeding 6 mm thickness:

税则号列 Tariff Item.	货品名称	最惠国(%) MFN	协定(%)CT 东盟 CA	中巴 CP	中智 CC	普通 Gen	增值税率 VAT	出口退税 ED	计量单位 Unit	监管条件 SC	Article Description
4412.1011	----至少有一表层是本章子目注释所列的热带木	12			7.2	30	17	11	立方米/千克		----With at least one outer ply of tropical wood specified in Subheading Note 1 to this Chapter
4412.1011 11	至少有一表层为濒危热带木薄板制濒危竹胶合板(每层厚度≤6mm)	12				30	17	11	立方米/千克	ABFE	Plywood consisting solely of sheets of bamboo in imminent dangers, with at least one outer ply of non - coniferous tropical wood in imminent dagnres, each ply thickness≤6mm
4412.1011 19	至少有一表层为濒危热带木薄板制其他竹胶合板(每层厚度≤6mm)	12				30	17	11	立方米/千克	ABFE	Plywood consisting solely of sheets of bamboo in imminent dangers, with at least one outer ply of non - coniferous tropical wood in imminent dagnres, each ply thickness≤6mm
4412.1011 91	至少有一表层是其他热带木薄板制濒危竹胶合板(每层厚度≤6mm,热带木指本章子目注释所列木材)	12				30	17	11	立方米/千克	ABE	Plywood consisting solely of sheets of bamboo in imminent dangers, with at least one outer ply of non - coniferous other tropical wood, each ply thickness ≤6mm
4412.1011 99	至少有一表层是其他热带木薄板制其他竹胶合板(每层厚度≤6mm,热带木指本章子目注释所列木材)	12				30	17	11	立方米/千克	AB	Plywood consisting solely of sheets of bamboo in imminent dangers, with at least one outer ply of non - coniferous other tropical wood, each ply thickness ≤6mm
4412.1019	----其他	4				30	17		立方米/千克		--Other
4412.1019 11	至少有一表层为濒危非针叶木薄板胶合板(至少有一表层为温带非针叶木制,每层厚度≤6mm)	4				30	17		立方米/千克	ABFE	Plywood consisting solely of sheets of wood, with at least one outer ply of ono - coniferous wood in imminent dangers, each ply thickness≤6mm
4412.1019 19	其他至少有一表层为非针叶木薄板胶合板(至少有一表层为温带非针叶木制,每层厚度≤6mm)	4				30	17		立方米/千克	AB	Plywood consisting solely of sheets of wood, with at least one outer ply of ono - coniferous wood in imminent dangers, each ply thickness≤6mm
4412.1019 21	濒危竹地板层叠胶合而成的多层板(每层厚度≤6mm)	4				30	17		立方米/千克	ABE	Plywood with two or more plies of bamboo in imminent dangers, each ply thickness≤6mm
4412.1019 29	其他竹地板层叠胶合而成的多层板(每层厚度≤6mm)	4				30	17		立方米/千克	AB	Plywood with two or more plies of bamboo in imminent dangers, each ply thickness≤6mm
4412.1019 91	其他濒危竹胶合板(每层厚度≤6mm)	4				30	17		立方米/千克	ABE	Plywood consisting solely of sheets of bamboo in imminent dangers, each ply thickness≤6mm
4412.1019 99	其他竹胶合板(每层厚度≤6mm)	4				30	17		立方米/千克	AB	Other plywood consisting solely of sheets of other bamboo, each ply thickness≤6mm
4412.1020	---其他,至少有一表层是非针叶木	10				30	17		立方米/千克		---Other, with at least one outer ply of non-coniferous wood

税则号列 Tariff Item.	货品名称	最惠国(%) MFN	协定(%)CT 东盟 CA	中巴 CP	中智 CC	普通 Gen	增值税率 VAT	出口退税 ED	计量单位 Unit	监管条件 SC	Article Description
4412.1020 11	至少有一表层是濒危非针叶木的濒危竹制多层板(每层厚度≤6mm)	10				30	17		立方米/千克	ABFE	Plywood consisting solely of sheets of bamboo in imminent dangres, with at least one outer ply of ono - coniferous wood in imminent dangers, each ply thickness≤6mm
4412.1020 19	至少有一表层是其他非针叶木的其他濒危竹制多层板(每层厚度≤6mm)	10				30	17		立方米/千克	ABE	Plywood consisting solely of sheets of bamboo in imminent dangers, with at least one outer ply of ono - coniferous wood, each ply thickness≤6mm
4412.1020 91	至少有一表层是濒危非针叶木的其他竹制多层板(每层厚度≤6mm)	10				30	17		立方米/千克	ABFE	Plywood consisting solely of sheets of bamboo, with at least one outer ply of ono - coniferous wood, each ply thickness≤6mm
4412.1020 99	至少有一表层是其他非针叶木的其他竹制的层板(每层厚度≤6mm)	10				30	17		立方米/千克	AB	Plywood consisting solely of sheets of bamboo, with at least one outer ply of ono - coniferous wood, each ply thickness≤6mm
	---其他:										---Other:
4412.1091	----至少有一层是本章子目注释一所列的热带木	8				30	17	11	立方米/千克		----With at least one ply of tropical wood specified in Subheading Note 1 to this Chapter
4412.1091 10	至少有一层是热带木的濒危竹制多层板(热带木指本章子目注释所列木材)	8				30	17	11	立方米/千克	ABE	Plywood consisting solely of sheets of bamboo in imminent dangers, with at least one outer ply of tropical wood, each ply thickness≤6mm
4412.1091 90	至少有一层是热带木的其他竹制多层板(热带木指本章子目注释所列木材)	8				30	17	11	立方米/千克	AB	Plywood consisting solely of sheets of bamboo, with at least one outer ply of tropical wood, each ply thickness≤6mm
4412.1092	----至少含有一层木碎料板	10				30	17	13	立方米/千克		----Containing at least one layer of particle board
4412.1092 10	至少含有一层木碎料板的濒危竹制多层板	10				30	17	11	立方米/千克	ABE	Laminated wood, at least one outer ply of coniferous bamboo in imminent dangers, containing at least one layer of particle board
4412.1092 90	至少含有一层木碎料板的其他竹制多层板	10				30	17	11	立方米/千克	AB	Laminated wood, at least one outer ply of coniferous other bamboo, containing at least one layer of particle board
4412.1099	----其他	4			2.4	30	17	11	立方米/千克		----Other
4412.1099 10	其他濒危竹制多层板	4				30	17		立方米/千克	ABE	Other plywood of bamboo in immnent dangers
4412.1099 90	其他竹制多层板	4				30	17	11	立方米/千克	AB	Plywood of bamboo
	-其他仅由薄木板制的胶合板(竹制除外),每层厚度不超过6毫米										-Other ply wood consisting solely of sheets of wood (Other than bamboo), each ply thickness≤6mm
4412.3100	--至少有一层是本章子目注释所列的热带木	12			7.2	30	17	11	立方米/千克		--With at least one outer ply of tnpical wood specified in subheading Nate to this Chopter

税则号列 Tariff Item.	货品名称	最惠国(%) MFN	协定(%) CT 东盟 CA	中巴 CP	中智 CC	普通 Gen	增值税率 VAT	出口退税 ED	计量单位 Unit	监管条件 SC	Article Description
4412.3100 10	至少有一表层为桃花心木薄板制胶合板(每层厚度≤6mm)	12				30	17	11	立方米/千克	ABEF	Plywood consisting solely of sheets of wood, with at least one outer ply of Acajou d' afrique, each ply thickness≤6mm
4412.3100 20	至少有一表层为拉敏木薄板制胶合板(每层厚度≤6mm)	12				30	17	11	立方米/千克	ABEF	Plywood consisting solely of sheets of wood , with at least one outer ply of Ramin wood, each ply thickness≤6mm
4412.3100 30	一表层为濒危热带木薄板制胶合板(每层厚度≤6mm)	12				30	17	11	立方米/千克	ABEF	Plywood cinsisting solely of sheets of wood, with at least one outer ply of tropical wood specified in subheading Note to thils Chapter , each ply thickness≤6mm
4412.3100 90	至少有一表层是其他热带木制的胶合板(每层厚度≤6mm,竹制除外,热带木指本章子目注释所列木材)	12				30	17	11	立方米/千克	AB	Plywood consisting solely of sheets of wood, with at least one outer ply of tropical wood, specified in subheading Note to this Chapter, each ply thickness ≤6mm
4412.3210	---至少有一表层为温带非针叶木	4				30	17	11	立方米/千克		---With at least one outer ply of non-coniferous wood
4412.3210 10	至少有一表层为濒危温带非针叶木薄板胶合板(每层厚度≤6mm,竹制除外)	4				30	17	11	立方米/千克	ABEF	Plywood consisting solely of sheets of wood, with at least one outer ply of non-coniferous wood in imminent dangers, each ply thickness≤6mm
4412.3210 90	至少有一表层是其他温带非针叶木薄板制胶合板(每层厚度≤6mm,竹制除外)	4				30	17	11	立方米/千克	AB	Plywood consisting solely of sheets of wood, with at least one outer ply of non-conifeous wood, each ply thickness ≤6mm
4412.3290	---其他	4				30	17	11	立方米/千克		---Other
4412.3290 10	至少有一表层是濒危其他非针叶胶合板(每层厚度≤6mm,竹制除外)	4				30	17	11	立方米/千克	ABEF	Plywood consisting solely of sheets of wood, with at least one outer ply of non-conifeous wood, each ply thichness ≤6mm
4412.3290 90	至少有一表层是其他非针叶胶合板(每层厚度≤6mm,竹制除外)	4				30	17	11	立方米/千克	AB	Plywood consisting solely of sheets of wood, with one outer ply of non-coniferous wood, other than tropical wood, each ply thickness≤6mm)
4412.3900	--其他	4			3.2	30	17	11	立方米/千克		--Other
4412.3900 10	其他濒危薄板制胶合板(每层厚度≤6mm,竹制除外)	4				30	17	11	立方米/千克	ABFE	Plywood consisting solely of sheets of wood in imminent dangers, each ply thickness≤6mm
4412.3900 90	其他薄板制胶合板(每层厚度≤6mm,竹制除外)	4				30	17	11	立方米/千克	AB	Plywood consisting solely of sheets of wood, each ply thickness≤6mm
	--木块芯胶合板,侧板条芯胶合板及板条芯胶合板:										--Wood block core plywood, arthropleure and batten
4412.9410	---至少有一表层是非针叶木	10				30	17	11	立方米/千克		---With at least one outer ply of non-coniferous wood
4412.9410 10	至少有一表层是桃花心木的木块芯胶合板等,(还包括侧板条芯胶合板及板条芯胶合板)	10				30	17	11	立方米/千克	ABEF	The board veneer (including side batten veneer and batten veneer) with at least one surface layer of acajou board

税则号列 Tariff Item.	货品名称	最惠国(%) MFN	协定(%) CT 东盟 CA	中巴 CP	中智 CC	普通 Gen	增值税率 VAT	出口退税 ED	计量单位 Unit	监管条件 SC	Article Description
4412.9410 20	至少有一表层是拉敏木的木块芯胶合板等,(还包括侧板条芯胶合板及板条芯胶合板)	10				30	17	11	立方米/千克	ABFE	The board veneer (including side batten veneer and batten veneer) with at least one surface layer of Ramin board
4412.9410 30	至少有一表层是濒危热带木的木块芯胶合板等,(还包括侧板条芯胶合板及板条芯胶合板)	10				30	17	11	立方米/千克	ABFE	The board veneer (including side batten veneer and batten veneer) with at least one surface layer of tropical board
4412.9410 40	至少有一表层是濒危非针叶木的木块芯胶合板等(还包括侧板条芯胶合板及板条芯胶合板)	10				30	17	11	立方米/千克	ABFE	The board veneer (including side batten veneer and batten veneer) with at least one surface layer of tropical non – coniferous board
4412.9410 90	至少有一表层是非针叶木的木块芯胶合板等,(还包括侧板条芯胶合板及板条芯胶合板)	10				30	17	11	立方米/千克	AB	The board veneer (including side batten veneer and batten veneer) with at least one surface layer of non – coniferous board
	---其他										---Other
4412.9491	----至少有一层是本章子目注释所列的热带木	8				30	17	11	立方米/千克		----With at least one ply of tropical wood specified in subheading Note 1 to this Chapter
4412.9491 10	至少有一层是濒危热带木的针叶木面木块芯胶合板等(还包括侧板条芯胶合及板条芯胶合板,热带木指本章子目注释所列木材)	8				30	17	11	立方米/千克	ABFE	The board veneer (including side batten veneer and batten veneer,) with at least one surface layer of tropical coniferous board in immnent dangers specified in Subheading Note 1 to this Chapter
4412.9491 90	至少有一层为热带木的针叶木面木块芯胶合板等,(还包括侧板条芯胶合板及板条芯胶合板,热带木指本章子目注释所列木材)	8				30	17	11	立方米/千克	AB	The board veneer (including side batten veneer and batten veneer) with at least one surface layer of tropical coniferous board specified in Subheading Note 1 to this Chapter
4412.9492	----其他,至少含有一层木碎料板	10				30	17	11	立方米/千克		----Other, containing at least one layer of particle board
4412.9492 10	至少含有一层木碎料板的濒危针叶木面木块芯胶合板等,(还包括侧板条芯胶合板及板条芯胶合板)	10				30	17	11	立方米/千克	ABFE	The endangered conifer board veneer (including side batten veneer and batten veneer) with at least one layer of particle board
4412.9492 90	至少含有一层木碎料的板针叶木面木块芯胶合板等,(还包括侧板条芯胶合板及板条芯胶合板)	10				30	17	11	立方米/千克	AB	The conifer board veneer (including side batten veneer and batten veneer) with at least one layer of particle board
4412.9499	----其他	4			2.4	30	17	11	立方米/千克		----Other
4412.9499 10	其他濒危针叶木面木块芯胶合板等,(还包括侧板条芯胶合板及板条芯胶合板)	4				30	17	11	立方米/千克	ABFE	The board veneer (including side batten veneer and batten veneer) with at least one surface layer of tropical coniferous board in immnent dangers
4412.9499 90	其他针叶木面木块芯胶合板等,(还包括侧板条芯胶合板及板条芯胶合板)	4				30	17	11	立方米/千克	AB	The board veneer (including side batten veneer and batten veneer) with at least one surface layer of other tropical coniferous board in immnent dangers

税则号列 Tariff Item.	货品名称	最惠国(%) MFN	协定(%) CT 东盟 CA	 中巴 CP	 中智 CC	普通 Gen	增值税率 VAT	出口退税 ED	计量单位 Unit	监管条件 SC	Article Description
	--其他:										--Other:
4412.9910	---至少有一表层是非针叶木	10				30	17	11	立方米/千克		---With at least one outer ply of ono-coniferous wood
4412.9910 10	至少有一表层是桃花心木的多层板	10				30	17		立方米/千克	ABFE	Laminated wood, at least one outer ply of Acajou d'afrique
4412.9910 20	至少有一表层是拉敏木的多层板	10				30	17		立方米/千克	ABFE	Laminated wood, at least one outer ply of Ramin wood
4412.9910 30	至少有一表层是濒危热带木的多层板	10				30	17		立方米/千克	ABFE	Laminated wood, at least one outer ply of tropical wood
4412.9910 40	其他至少有一表层是濒危非针叶木的多层板	10				30	17		立方米/千克	ABFE	Laminated wood, at least one outer ply of non – coniferous wood in imminent dangers
4412.9910 90	其他至少有一表层是非针叶木的多层板	10				30	17		立方米/千克	AB	Laminated wood, at least one outer ply of non – coniferous wood
	---其他:										---Other:
4412.9991	----至少有一层是本章子目注释所列的热带木	8				30	17	11	立方米/千克		----With at least one outer ply of tropical wood specified in Suheading
4412.9991 10	其他至少有一层是濒危热带木的针叶木面多层板(热带木指本章子目注释所列木材)	8				30	17		立方米/千克	ABFE	The multilayer board with at least one surface layer of tropical board in immnent dangers specified in Subheading Note 1 to this Chapter
4412.9991 90	其他至少有一层是热带木的针叶木面多层板(热带木指本章子目注释所列木材)	8				30	17		立方米/千克	AB	The multilayer board with at least one surface layer of tropical board specified in Subheading Note 2 to this Chapter
4412.9992	----其他,至少含有一层木碎料板	10				30	17	11	立方米/千克		----With at least one ply of tropical wood specified in Subheading Note 1 to this Chapter
4412.9992 10	其他至少含有一层木碎料板的濒危针叶木面多层板	10				30	17		立方米/千克	ABFE	The endangered conifer board veneer with at least one layer of particle board
4412.9992 90	其他至少含有一层木碎料板的针叶木面多层板	10				30	17		立方米/千克	AB	The conifer board veneer with at least one layer of particle board
4412.9999	----其他	4			2.4	30	17	11	立方米/千克		----Other
4412.9999 10	其他濒危针叶木面多层板	4				30	17		立方米/千克	ABFE	The endangered conifer board veneer particle board
4412.9999 90	其他针叶木面多层板	4				30	17		立方米/千克	AB	The conifer board veneer particle board
44.13	**强化木,成块、板、条或异型的:**										**Densified wood, in blocks, plates, strips or profile shapes:**
4413.0000	强化木,成块、板、条或异型的	6	5		4.8	20	17	11	千克	AB	Densified wood, in blocks, plates, strips or profile shapes
44.14	**木制的画框、相框、镜框及类似品:**										**Wooden frames for paintings, photographs, mirrors or similar objects:**
4414.0000	木制的画框、相框、镜框及类似品	20				100	17	11	千克		Wooden frames for paintings, photographs, mirrors or similar objects
4414.0000 10	拉敏木制画框、相框、镜框及类似品	20				100	17	11	千克	ABFE	Frames for paintings, photographs, mirrors or similar objects, of Ramin wood
4414.0000 20	濒危木制画框、相框、镜框及类似品	20				100	17	11	千克	ABFE	Frames for paintings, photographs, mirrors or similar objects, of wood in imminent dangers

税则号列 Tariff Item.	货品名称	最惠国(%) MFN	协定(%)CT 东盟 CA	中巴 CP	中智 CC	普通 Gen	增值税率 VAT	出口退税 ED	计量单位 Unit	监管条件 SC	Article Description
4414.0000 90	木制的画框、相框、镜框及类似品	20				100	17	11	千克	AB	Wooden frames for paintings, photographs, mirrors or similar objects
44.15	**包装木箱、木盒、板条箱、圆桶及类似的包装容器;木制电缆卷筒;木托板、箱形托盘及其他装载用木板;木制的托盘护框:**										**Packing cases, boxes, crates, drums and similar packings, of wood; cable-drums of wood; pallets, box pallets and other load boards, of wood; pallet collars of wood.**
4415.1000	-箱、盒、板条箱、圆桶及类似的包装容器;电缆卷筒	7.5	T3		6	80	17	11	件		-Cases, boxes, crates, drums and similar packing; cable-drums
4415.1000 10	拉敏木制木箱及类似包装容器(电缆卷筒)	7.5				80	17	11	件	ABFE	Cases and similar packing; cable-drums, of Ramin wood (*gonystylus. spp.*)
4415.1000 20	濒危木制木箱及类似包装容器(电缆卷筒)	7.5				80	17	11	件	ABFE	Cases and similar packing; cable-drums, of wood in imminent dangers
4415.1000 90	木箱及类似的包装容器,电缆卷筒	7.5				80	17	11	件	AB	Cases and similar packing; cable-drums, of wood
4415.2000	-木托板、箱形托盘及其他装载用木板;木制的托盘护框	7.5				80	17	11	件		-Pallets, box pallets and other load boards; pallet collars
4415.2000 10	拉敏木托板、箱形托盘及装载木板(包括木制托板护框)	7.5				80	17	11	件	ABFE	Pallets, box pallets and other load boards; pallet collars, of Ramin wood (*gonystylus. spp.*)
4415.2000 20	濒危木托板,箱形托盘及装载木板(包括木制托板护框)	7.5				80	17	11	件	ABFE	Pallets, box pallets and other load boards; pallet collars, of wood in imminent dangers
4415.2000 90	木托板,箱形托盘及其他装载木板(包括木制托板护框)	7.5				80	17	11	件	AB	Pallets, box pallets and other load boards; pallet collars, of wood
44.16	**木制大桶、琵琶桶、盆和其他木制箍桶及其零件,包括桶板:**										**Casks, barrels, vats, tubs and other coopers' products and parts thereof, of wood, including staves:**
4416.0000	木制大桶、琵琶桶、盆和其他木制箍桶及其零件,包括桶板	16				80	17		千克		Casks, barrels, vats, tubs and other coopers' products and parts thereof, of wood, including staves
4416.0000 10	拉敏木制箍桶及其零件(含桶板)	16				80	17		千克	ABFE	Coopers' products and parts thereof (including staves), of Ramin wood (*gonystylus. spp.*)
4416.0000 20	濒危木制箍桶及其零件(含桶板)	16				80	17		千克	ABFE	Coopers' products and parts thereof (including staves), of wood in imminent dangers
4416.0000 90	各种木制箍桶及其零件(包括桶板)	16				80	17		千克	AB	Coopers' products and parts thereof (including staves), of other wood
44.17	**木制的工具、工具支架、工具柄、扫帚及刷子的身及柄;木制鞋靴楦及楦头:**										**Tools, tool bodies, tool handles, broom or brush bodies and handles, of wood; boot or shoe lasts and trees, of wood:**
4417.0000	木制的工具、工具支架、工具柄、扫帚及刷子的身及柄;木制鞋靴楦及楦头	16				80	17		千克		Tools, tool bodies, tool handles, broom or brush bodies and handles, of wood; boot or shoe lasts and trees, of wood

税则号列 Tariff Item.	货品名称	最惠国(%) MFN	协定(%) CT 东盟 CA	中巴 CP	中智 CC	普通 Gen	增值税率 VAT	出口退税 ED	计量单位 Unit	监管条件 SC	Article Description
4417.0000 10	拉敏木制工具、柄、木制鞋楦及楦头	16				80	17		千克	ABFE	Tools, tool handles, boot or shoe lasts and trees, of Ramin wood (*gonystylus. spp.*)
4417.0000 20	濒危木制工具,柄,木制鞋楦及楦头	16				80	17		千克	ABFE	Tools, tool handles, boot or shoe lasts and trees, of wood in imminent dangers
4417.0000 90	木制工具、柄、木制鞋靴楦及楦头	16				80	17		千克	AB	Tools, tool handles, boot or shoe lasts and trees of other wood
44.18	**建筑用木工制品,包括蜂窝结构木镶板、已装拼的拼花地板、木瓦及盖屋板:**										**Builders' joinery and carpentry of wood, including cellular wood panels, assembled parquet panels, shingles and shakes:**
4418.1000	-窗、法兰西式(落地)窗及其框架	4				70	17	11	千克		-Windows, French-windows and their frames
4418.1000 10	拉敏木制木窗、落地窗及其框架	4				70	17	11	千克	ABFE	Windows, French-windows and their frames of Ramin wood (*gonystylus. spp.*)
4418.1000 20	濒危木制木窗,落地窗及其框架	4				70	17	11	千克	ABFE	Windows, French-windows and their frames of wood in imminent dangers
4418.1000 90	木窗、落地窗及其框架	4				70	17	11	千克	AB	Windows, French-windows and their frames of other wood
4418.2000	-门及其框架和门槛	4			3.2	70	17	11	千克		-Doors and their frames and thresholds
4418.2000 10	拉敏木制的木门及其框架和门槛	4				70	17	11	千克	ABFE	Doors and their frames and thresholds of Ramin wood (*gonystylus. spp.*)
4418.2000 20	濒危木制的木门及其框架和门槛	4				70	17	11	千克	ABFE	Doors and their frames and thresholds of wood in imminent dangers
4418.2000 90	木门及其框架和门槛	4				70	17	11	千克	AB	Doors and their frames and thresholds of other wood
4418.4000	-水泥构件的模板	4			0	70	17	11	千克	AB	-Shuttering for concrete constructional work
4418.5000	-木瓦及盖屋板	7.5	T3		0	70	17	11	千克	AB	-Shingles and shakes
4418.6000	-柱和梁	4			3.2	70	17	13	千克		Poles and girder
4418.6000 10	濒危木制柱和梁	4				70	17		千克	FEAB	Endangered – wood – made poles and girder
4418.6000 90	其他木制柱和梁	4				70	17		千克	AB	Other wood – made poles and girder
	-已装拼的地板:										-Parquet panels of wood
4418.7100	--马赛克地板用	4			3.2	70	17	13	千克		--For mosaic
4418.7100 10	已装拼的拉敏木制马赛克地板	4				70	17		千克	ABFE	Ramin – made mosaic floor that has been furnished
4418.7100 20	已装拼的其他濒危木制马赛克地板	4				70	17		千克	ABFE	Other endangered – made mosaic floor that has been furnished
4418.7100 90	已装拼的其他木制马赛克地板	4				70	17		千克	AB	Other wood – made mosaic floor that has been furnished
4418.7200	--其他,多层的	4			3.2	70	17	13	千克		--Other multilayer's
4418.7200 10	已装拼的拉敏木制多层地板	4				70	17	13	千克	ABFE	Panels of other wood
4418.7200 20	已装拼的其他濒危木制多层地板	4				70	17	13	千克	ABFE	Other laminated wood, ply of wood in inninent dangers, assembled
4418.7200 90	已装拼的其他木制多层地板	4				70	17	13	千克	AB	Other wood – made Multilayer floor that has been furnished

税则号列 Tariff Item.	货品名称	最惠国(%) MFN	协定(%)CT 东盟 CA	中巴 CP	中智 CC	普通 Gen	增值税率 VAT	出口退税 ED	计量单位 Unit	监管条件 SC	Article Description
4418.7900	--其他	4			3.2	70	17	13	千克		--Other
4418.7900 10	已装拼的拉敏木制其他地板	4				70	17		千克	ABFE	Panels of other Ramin wood, assembled
4418.7900 20	已装拼的其他濒危木制地板	4				70	17		千克	ABFE	Panels of other wood, assembled
4418.7900 90	已装拼的木制其他地板	4				70	17		千克	AB	Panels of other wood, assembled
4418.9000	-其他	4			3.2	70	17	11	千克		-Other
4418.9000 10	拉敏木制其他建筑用木工制品(包括蜂窝结构的木镶板)	4				70	17	11	千克	FEAB	Builders' joinery and carpentry including cellular wood panels, of Ramin wood (*gonystylus. spp.*)
4418.9000 20	濒危木制其他建筑用木工制品(包括蜂窝结构的木镶板)	4				70	17	11	千克	FEAB	Builders' joinery and carpentry including cellular wood panels, of wood in imminent dangers
4418.9000 90	其他建筑用木工制品(包括蜂窝结构的木镶板)	4				70	17	11	千克	AB	Other builders' joinery and carpentry including cellular wood panels, of other wood
44.19	**木制餐具及厨房用具:**										**Tableware and kitchenware, of wood:**
	木制餐具及厨房用具:										Tableware and kitchenware, of wood:
	---一次性筷子:										---One-time chopsticks:
4419.0031	----木制	0				100	17	11	千克	aAB	----Wood
4419.0032	----竹制	0				100	17	11	千克		----Bamboo
4419.0032 10	酸竹制一次性筷子	0				100	17	11	千克	aABE	One-time chopsticks, of bamboo of bamboo paln
4419.0032 90	其他竹制一次性筷子	0				100	17	11	千克	aAB	Other one-time chopsticks, of bamboo
4419.0090	---其他	0				100	17	11	千克		---Other
4419.0090 10	拉敏木制的餐具及厨房用具	0				100	17	11	千克	FEAB	Tableware and kitchenware of Ramin wood
4419.0090 20	濒危木制的餐具及厨房用具	0				100	17	11	千克	FEAB	Tableware and kitchenware of wood in imminent dangers
4419.0090 90	其他木制餐具及厨房用具	0				100	17	11	千克	AB	Tableware and kitchenware, of other wood
44.20	**镶嵌木(包括细工镶嵌木);装珠宝或刀具用的木制盒子和小匣子及类似品;木制小雕像及其他装饰品;第九十四章以外的木制家具:**										**Wood marquetry and inlaid wood; caskets and cases for jewellery or cutlery, and similar articles, of wood; statuettes and other ornaments, of wood; wooden articles or furniture not falling in Chapter 94:**
	-木制小雕像及其他装饰品:										-Statuettes and other ornaments, of wood:
4420.1010	---木刻及竹刻	0				100	17	11	千克		---Wood or bamboo carvings
4420.1010 10	拉敏木制的木刻	0				100	17	11	千克	FEAB	Woodcut of Ramin wood
4420.1010 20	濒危木制的木刻	0				100	17	11	千克	FEAB	Woodcut of wood in imminent dangers
4420.1010 90	木刻及竹刻	0				100	17	11	千克	AB	Wood or bamboo carvings
4420.1020	---木扇	0				100	17	11	千克		---Wooden fans
4420.1020 10	拉敏木制的木扇	0				100	17	11	千克	FEAB	Wooden fans of Ramin wood
4420.1020 20	濒危木制的木扇	0				100	17	11	千克	FEAB	Wooden fans of wood in imminent dangers
4420.1020 90	木扇	0				100	17	11	千克	AB	Wooden fans
4420.1090	---其他	0				100	17	11	千克		---Other
4420.1090 10	拉敏木制其他小雕像及其他装饰品	0				100	17	11	千克	FEAB	Statuettes and other ornaments of strain-sensitive wood

税则号列 Tariff Item.	货品名称	最惠国(%) MFN	协定(%)CT 东盟 CA	中巴 CP	中智 CC	普通 Gen	增值税率 VAT	出口退税 ED	计量单位 Unit	监管条件 SC	Article Description
4420.1090 20	濒危木制其他小雕像及其他装饰品	0				100	17	11	千克	FEAB	Statuettes and other ornaments of wood in imminent dangers
4420.1090 90	其他木制小雕像及其他装饰品	0				100	17	11	千克	AB	Statuettes and other ornaments of other wood
	-其他:										-Other:
4420.9010	---镶嵌木	0				45	17	11	千克		---Wood marquetry and inlaid wood
4420.9010 10	拉敏木制的镶嵌木	0				45	17	11	千克	FEAB	Wood marquetry and inlaid wood of strain-sensitive wood
4420.9010 20	濒危木制的镶嵌木	0				45	17	11	千克	FEAB	Wood marquetry and inlaid wood of wood in imminent dangers
4420.9010 90	镶嵌木	0				45	17	11	千克	AB	Wood marquetry and inlaid wood
4420.9090	---其他	0				100	17	11	千克		---Other
4420.9090 10	拉敏木盒及类似品,非落地木家具(前者用于装珠宝或家俱;后者不包括第九十四章的家具)	0				100	17	11	千克	FEAB	Caskets and similar articles or furniture not falling, of Ramin wood (the former used for jewelry or furniture, the latter not including furniture falling in Chapter 94)
4420.9090 20	濒危木盒及类似品,非落地木家俱(前者用于装珠宝或家俱;后者不包括第九十四章的家具)	0				100	17	11	千克	FEAB	Caskets and similar articles or furniture not falling of wood in imminent dangers (the former used for jewelry or furniture, the latter not including furniture falling in Chapter 94)
4420.9090 90	木盒子及类似品;非落地式木家具(前者用于装珠宝或家俱;后者不包括第九十四章的家具)	0				100	17	11	千克	AB	Caskets and similar articles or furniture not falling, of wood (the former used for jewelry or furniture, the latter not including furniture falling in Chapter 94)
44.21	**其他木制品:**										**Other articles of wood:**
4421.1000	-衣架	0				90	17	11	千克		-Clothes hangers
4421.1000 10	拉敏木制木衣架	0				90	17	11	千克	FEAB	Clothes hangers of Ramin wood
4421.1000 20	濒危木制木衣架	0				90	17	11	千克	FEAB	Clothes hangers of wood in imminent dangers
4421.1000 90	木衣架	0				90	17	11	千克	AB	Clothes hangers of wood
	-其他:										-Other:
4421.9010	---卷轴、纡子、筒管、缝纫用线轴及类似品	0				35	17	11	千克		---Spools, cops, bobbins, sewing thread reels and the like
4421.9010 10	拉敏木纡子筒管卷轴线轴及类似品	0				35	17	11	千克	FEAB	Spools, cops, bobbins, sewing thread reels and the like, of Ramin wood
4421.9010 20	濒危木纡子筒管卷轴线轴及类似品	0				35	17	11	千克	FEAB	Spools, cops, bobbins, sewing thread reels and the like, of wood in imminent dangers
4421.9010 90	木卷轴、纡子、筒管、线轴及类似品	0				35	17	11	千克	AB	Spools, cops, bobbins, sewing thread reels and the like, of wood
	---园签、园棒、冰果棒、压舌片及类似一次性制品:										---Round toobtpick, round stick, ice fruit stick tongue-pressing plate and similar one-time
4421.9021	----木制	0				35	17	13	千克		----Of wood

税则号列 Tariff Item.	货品名称	最惠国(%) MFN	协定(%)CT 东盟 CA	中巴 CP	中智 CC	普通 Gen	增值税率 VAT	出口退税 ED	计量单位 Unit	监管条件 SC	Article Description
4421.9021 10	一次性拉敏木制圆签,圆棒,冰果棒,压舌片(包括类似的一次性制品)	0				35	17	13	千克	FEAB	Round toobtpick, round stick, ice fruit stick tongue-pressing plate and similar one-time of strain-sensitiv wood
4421.9021 20	一次性濒危木制圆签,圆棒,冰果棒,压舌片(包括类似的一次性制品)	0				35	17	13	千克	FEAB	Round toobtpick, round stick, ice fruit stick tongue-pressing plate and similar one-time of wood in imminent dangers
4421.9021 90	一次性其他木制圆签,圆棒,冰果棒,压舌片(包括类似的一次性制品)	0				35	17	13	千克	AB	Round toobtpick, round stick, ice fruit stick tongue-pressing plate and similar one-time of other wood
4421.9022	----竹制	0				35	17	13	千克		----of bamboos
4421.9022 10	一次性酸竹制圆签,圆棒,冰果棒,压舌片(包括类似的一次性制品)	0				35	17	13	千克	FEAB	(round toothpick, round stick, ice fruit stick, tongue - pressing plate and similar one - off products of bamboo palm)
4421.9022 90	一次性其他竹制圆签,圆棒,冰果棒,压舌片(包括类似的一次性制品)	0				35	17	13	千克	AB	(round toothpick, round stick, ice fruit stick, tongue - pressing plate and similar one - off products of bamboo)
4421.9090	---其他	0				90	17	11	千克		---Other
4421.9090 10	拉敏木制的未列名的木制品	0				90	17	11	千克	FEAB	Articles of Ramin wood, not elsewhere specified or included
4421.9090 20	濒危木制的未列名的木制品	0				90	17	11	千克	FEAB	Articles of wood in imminent dangers, not elsewhere specified or included
4421.9090 90	未列名的木制品	0				90	17	11	千克	AB	Articles of wood, not elsewhere specified or included

第四十五章 软木及软木制品

Chapter 45 Cork and articles of cork

注释：

本章不包括：

一、第六十四章的鞋靴及其零件；

二、第六十五章的帽类及其零件；

三、第九十五章的物品（例如，玩具、游戏品及运动用品）。

Notes:

This Chapter does not cover:

(a) Footwear or parts of footwear of Chapter 64;

(b) Headgear or parts of headgear of Chapter 65; or

(c) Articles of Chapter 95 (for example, toys, games, sports requisites).

税则号列 Tariff Item.	货品名称	最惠国(%) MFN	协定(%) CT			普通 Gen	增值税率 VAT	出口退税 ED	计量单位 Unit	监管条件 SC	Article Description
			东盟 CA	中巴 CP	中智 CC						
45.01	**未加工或简单加工的天然软木；软木废料；碎的、粒状的或粉状的软木：**										**Natural cork, raw or simply prepared; waste cork; crushed, granulated or ground cork:**
4501.1000	-未加工或简单加工的天然软木	6	5		0	17	17		千克	AB	-Natrual cork, raw or simply prepared
	-其他：										-Other:
4501.9010	---软木废料	0				17	17		千克	ABP	---Waste cork
4501.9020	---碎的料状的或粉状的软木（软木碎，软木料或软木粉）	0				17	17		千克	ABP	---Crushed granulated or ground cork (Cork wood is broken , the cork wood granule or cork wood turns to powder)
45.02	**天然软木，除去表皮或粗切成方形，或成长方块、正方块、板、片或条状（包括作塞子用的方块坯料）：**										**Natural cork, debarked or roughly squared, or in rectangular (including square) blocks, plates, sheets or strip, (including sharp-edged blanks for corks or stoppers):**
4502.0000	天然软木，除去表皮或粗切成方形，或成长方块、正方块、板、片或条状（包括作塞子用的方块坯料）	8	5		0	30	17		千克	AB	Natural cork, debarked or roughly squared, or in rectangular (including square) blocks, plates, sheets or strip, (including sharp-edged blanks for corks or stoppers)
45.03	**天然软木制品：**										**Articles of natural cork:**
4503.1000	-塞子	8	5		6.4	50	17		千克	AB	-Corks and stoppers
4503.9000	-其他	10.5	8		6.3	50	17		千克	AB	-Other
45.04	**压制软木（不论是否使用粘合剂压成）及其制品：**										**Agglomerated cork (with or without a binding substance) and articles of agglomerated cork:**
4504.1000	-块、板、片及条；任何形状的砖、瓦；实心圆柱体，包括圆片	8.4	5		0	30	17		千克	AB	-Blocks, plates, sheets and strip; tiles of any shape; solid cylinders, including discs
4504.9000	-其他	0				50	17		千克	AB	-Other

第四十六章
稻草、秸秆、针茅或其他编结材料制品；篮筐及柳条编结品

Chapter 46
Manufactures of straw, of esparto or of other plaiting materials; basketware and wickerwork

注释：

一、本章所称"编结材料"，是指其状态或形状适于编结、交织或类似加工的材料，包括稻草、秸秆、柳条、竹、藤灯芯草、芦苇、木片条、其他植物材料扁条（例如，树皮条、狭叶、酒椰叶纤维或其他从阔叶获取的条）、未纺的天然纺织纤维、塑料单丝及扁条、纸带，但不包括皮革、再生皮革、毡呢或无纺织物的扁条、人发、马毛、纺织粗纱或纱线以及第五十四章的单丝和扁条。

二、本章不包括：

（一）税目48.14的壁纸；

（二）不论是否编结而成的线、绳、索、缆（税目56.07）；

（三）第六十四章和第六十五章的鞋靴、帽类及其零件；

（四）编结而成的车辆或车身（第八十七章）；

（五）第九十四章的物品（例如，家具、灯具及照明装置）。

三、税目46.01所称"平行连结的成片编结材料、缏条或类似的编结材料产品"，是指编结材料、缏条及类似的编结材料产品平行排列连结成片的制品，其连结材料不论是否为纺制的纺织材料。

Notes:

1. In this Chapter the expression "plaiting materials" means materials in a state or form suitable for plaiting, interlacing or similar processes; it includes straw, osier or willow, bamboos, liane liane rushes, reeds, strips of wood, strips of other vegetable material (for example, strips of bark, narrow leaves and raffia or other strips obtained from broad leaves), unspun natural textile fibres, monofilament and strip and the like of plastics and strips of paper, but not strips of leather or composition leather or of felt or nonwovens, human hair, horsehair, textile rovings or yarns, or monofilament and strip and the like of Chapter 54.
2. This Chapter does not cover:
   (a) Wall coverings of heading No. 48.14;
   (b) Twine, cordage, ropes or cables, plaited or not (heading No. 56.07);
   (c) Footwear or headgear or parts thereof of Chapter 64 or 65;
   (d) Vehicles or bodies for vehicles of basketware (Chapter 87); or
   (e) Articles of Chapter 94 (for example, furniture, lamps and lighting fittings).
3. For the purposes of heading No. 46.01, the expression "plaiting materials, plaits and similar products of plaiting materials, bound together in parallel strands" means plaiting materials, plaits and similar products of plaiting materials, placed side by side and bound together, in the form of sheets, whether or not the binding materials are to spun textile materials.

税则号列 Tariff Item.	货品名称	最惠国(%) MFN	协定(%) 东盟 CA	协定(%) 中巴 CP	协定(%) 中智 CC	普通 Gen	增值税率 VAT	出口退税 ED	计量单位 Unit	监管条件 SC	Article Description
46.01	**用编结材料编成的缏条及类似产品，不论是否缝合成宽条；平行连结或编结的成片材料、缏条或类似的编结材料产品，不论是否制成品（例如，席子、席料、帘子）：**										**Plaits and similar products of plaiting materials, whether or not assembled into strips; plaiting materials, plaits and similar products of plaiting materials, bound together in parallel strands or woven, in sheet form, whether or not being finished articles (for example, mats, matting, screens):**
	-植物材料制的席子、席料及帘子：										-Mats, matting and screens of vegetable materials:
4601.2100	--竹制的	9	5		0	90	17	13	千克/张	AB	--Of bamboos
4601.2200	--藤制	9	5		0	100	17	13	千克/张	AB	--Of rattans
	--其他：										--Other
	---草制的：										---Of grass or straw
4601.2911	----灯心草属材料制的	9	5		0	90	17	13	千克/张		----Of rushes

税则号列 Tariff Item.	货品名称	最惠国(%) MFN	协定(%) 东盟 CA	中巴 CP	CT 中智 CC	普通 Gen	增值税率 VAT	出口退税 ED	计量单位 Unit	监管条件 SC	Article Description
4601.2911 11	蔺草制的提花席、双苜席、垫子(单位面积>1平方米,不论是否包边)	9				90	17	13	千克/张	AB4xy	Mats of Juncaceae, area > 1m^2, whether or not edged
4601.2911 12	蔺草制的其他席子(单位面积>1平方米,不论是否包边)	9				90	17	13	千克/张	4ABxy	Other mats, matting and screens, of Juncaceae, area > 1m2, whether or not edged
4601.2911 19	蔺草制的其他席子、席料及帘子(单位面积≤1平方米,不论是否包边)	9				90	17	13	千克/张	AB	Other mats, matting and screens, of Juncaceae, area > 1m2, whether or not edged
4601.2911 90	其他灯芯草属材料制的席子等(包括席子、席料、帘子、垫子)	9				90	17	13	千克/张	AB	Mats, matting and screens, of rush (*Juncus spp.*)
4601.2919	其他草制的席子,席料及帘子	9	5		0	90	17	13	千克/张	AB	Other mats, matting and screens of grass or straw materials
	---芦苇制的										---Of reeds:
4601.2921	----苇帘	9	5		0	90	17	13	千克/张	AB	----Screens of reeds
4601.2929	----其他	9	5		0	90	17	13	千克/张	AB	----Other
4601.2990	----其他	9	5		0	90	17	13	千克/张	AB	----Other
	-其他:										-Other:
	---竹制的:										---Of bamboo:
4601.9210	---鞭条及类似产品,不论是否缝合成宽条	9	5		0	100	17	13	千克	AB	---Plairts and similar productsof plaiting mater ids, whether or not ass embled into strips
4601.9290	---其他	9	5		0	90	17	13	千克	AB	---Other:
	---藤制的:										---Of rattans:
4601.9310	---鞭条及类似产品,不论是否缝合成宽条	9	5		0	100	17	13	千克	AB	---Plaits and similar products of plaiting materials, whether or not assembled into strips:
4601.9390	---其他	9	5		0	90	17	13	千克	AB	---Other:
	--其他植物材料制的:										--Other of rege table materials
	---稻草制的:										---Of straw:
4601.9411	----鞭条(绳)	10	5		0	90	17	13	千克	AB	----Plaits(colt)
4601.9419	----其他	10	5		0	90	17	13	千克	AB	----Other:
	---其他:										---Other:
4601.9491	----鞭条及类似产品,不论是否缝合成宽条	9	5		0	100	17	13	千克	AB	----Plaits and similar producs of plaiting materids, whether or not assembled into strips
4601.9499	----其他	9	5		0	90	17	13	千克	AB	----Other:
	--其他:										--Other:
4601.9910	---鞭条及类似产品,不论是否缝合成宽条	9	5		0	90	17	13	千克		---Plaits and similar products of plaiting materials, whether of not assembled into strips
4601.9990	---其他	9	5		0	90	17	13	千克		---Other
46.02	**用编结材料直接编成或用税目46.01所列货品制成的篮筐、柳条编结品及其他制品;丝瓜络制品:**										**Basketwork, wickerwork and other articles, made directly to shape from plaiting materials or made up from goods of heading No. 46.01; articles of loofah:**

税则号列 Tariff Item.	货品名称	最惠国(%) MFN	协定(%)CT 东盟 CA	中巴 CP	中智 CC	普通 Gen	增值税率 VAT	出口退税 ED	计量单位 Unit	监管条件 SC	Article Description
	-植物材料制:										-Of vegetable materials:
4602.1100	--竹制的	9	5		0	100	17	13	千克	AB	--Of bamboos
4602.1200	---藤制的	9	5		0	100	17	13	千克	AB	---Of rattans
	--其他:										--Other:
4602.1910	---草制的	9	5		0	100	17	13	千克	AB	---Of grass or straw
4602.1920	---玉米皮制的	9	5		0	100	17	13	千克	AB	Of maize - shuck
4602.1930	---柳条制的	9	5		0	100	17	13	千克	AB	---Of osier
4602.1990	---其他	9	5		0	100	17	13	千克	AB	---Other
4602.9000	-其他	9	5	8	0	100	17	13	千克		-Other

第十类
木浆及其他纤维状纤维素浆；回收（废碎）纸或纸板；纸、纸板及其制品

SECTION X
PULP OF WOOD OR OF OTHER FIBROUS CELLULOSIC MATERIAL; RECOVERED (WASTE AND SCRAP) PAPER OR PAPERBOARD; PAPER AND PAPERBOARD AND ARTICLES THEREOF

第四十七章
木浆及其他纤维状纤维素浆；回收（废碎）纸或纸板

Chapter 47
Pulp of wood or of other fibrous cellulosic material; recovered (waste and scrap) paper or paperboard

注释：

税目47.02所称“化学木浆，溶解级”，是指温度在20℃时浸入含18%氢氧化钠的苛性碱溶液内，一小时后，按重量计含有92%及以上的不溶级分的碱木浆或硫酸盐木浆，或者含有88%及以上的不溶级分的亚硫酸盐木浆。对于亚硫酸盐木浆，按重量计灰分含量不得超过0.15%。

Notes:

For the purposes of heading No. 47.02, the expression “chemical wood pulp, dissolving grades” means chemical wood pulp having by weight an insoluble fraction of 92% or more for soda or sulphate wood pulp of of 88% or more for sulphite wood pulp after one hour in a caustic soda solution containing 18% sodium bydroxide (NaOH) at 20℃, and for sulphite wood pulp an ash content that does not exceed 0.15% by weight.

税则号列 Tariff Item.	货品名称	最惠国(%) MFN	协定(%) 东盟 CA	协定(%) 中巴 CP	CT 中智 CC	普通 Gen	增值税率 VAT	出口退税 ED	计量单位 Unit	监管条件 SC	Article Description
47.01	**机械木浆：**										**Mechanical wood pulp:**
4701.0000	机械木浆	0				8	17		千克	A	Mechanical wood pulp
47.02	**化学木浆，溶解级：**										**Chemical wood pulp, dissolving grades:**
4702.0000	化学木浆，溶解级	0				8	17		千克	A	Chemical wood pulp, dissolving grades
47.03	**碱木浆或硫酸盐木浆，但溶解级的除外：**										**Chemical wood pulp, soda or sulphate, other than dissolving grades:**
	-未漂白：										-Unbleached:
4703.1100	--针叶木的	0				8	17		千克	A	--Coniferous
4703.1900	--非针叶木的	0				8	17		千克	A	--Non-coniferous
	-半漂白或漂白：										-Semi-bleached or bleached:
4703.2100	--针叶木的	0				8	17		千克	A	--Coniferous
4703.2900	--非针叶木的	0				8	17		千克	A	--Non-coniferous
47.04	**亚硫酸盐木浆，但溶解级的除外：**										**Chemical wood pulp, sulphite, other than dissolving grades:**
	-未漂白：										-Unbleached:
4704.1100	--针叶木的	0				8	17		千克	A	--Coniferous
4704.1900	--非针叶木的	0				8	17		千克	A	--Non-coniferous
	-半漂白或漂白：										-Semi-bleached or bleached:
4704.2100	--针叶木的	0				8	17		千克	A	--Coniferous
4704.2900	--非针叶木的	0				8	17		千克	A	--Non-coniferous
47.05	**用机械与化学联合制浆法制得的木浆：**										**Wood pulp obtained by a combination of mechanical and chemical pulping processes:**
4705.0000	用机械与化学联合制浆法制得的木浆	0				8	17		千克	A	Wood pulp obtained by a combination of mechanical and chemical pulping processes

税则号列 Tariff Item.	货 品 名 称	最惠国(%) MFN	协定(%)CT 东盟 CA	中巴 CP	中智 CC	普通 Gen	增值税率 VAT	出口退税 ED	计量单位 Unit	监管条件 SC	Article Description
47.06	**从回收(废碎)纸或纸板提取的纤维浆或其他纤维状纤维素浆:**										**Pulps of fibres derived from recovered (waste and scrap) paper or paperboard or of other fibrous cellulosic material:**
4706.1000	-棉短绒纸浆	0				8	17	13	千克	A	-Cotton linters pulp
4706.2000	-从回收(废碎)纸或纸板提取的纤维浆	0				8	17		千克		-Pulps of fibres derived from recovered (waste and scrap) paper or paperboard
4706.3000	-其他,竹浆	0				8	17		千克	A	-Other bamboo
	-其他:										-Other:
4706.9100	--机械浆	0				8	17		千克	A	--Mechanical
4706.9200	--化学浆	0				8	17		千克	A	--Chemical
4706.9300	--半化学浆	0				8	17		千克	A	--Semi-chemical
47.07	**回收(废碎)纸或纸板:**										**Recovered (waste and scrap) paper or paperboard:**
4707.1000	-未漂白的牛皮纸或纸板及瓦楞纸或纸板	0				8	17		千克	7ABP	-Unbleached kraft paper or paperboard or corrugated paper or paperboard
4707.2000	-主要由漂白化学木浆制成未经本体染色的其他纸和纸板	0				8	17		千克	7ABP	-Other paper or paperboard made mainly of bleached chemical pulp, not coloured in the mass
4707.3000	-主要由机械浆制成的纸或纸板(例如,报纸、杂志及类似印刷品)	0				8	17		千克	7ABP	-Paper or paperboard made mainly of mechanical pulp (for example, newspapers, journals and similar printed matter)
4707.9000	-其他,包括未分选的废碎品	0				8	17		千克	7ABP	-Other, including unsorted waste and scrap

第四十八章
纸及纸板;纸浆、纸或纸板制品

Chapter 48
Paper and paperboard; articles of paper pulp, of paper or of paperboard

注释:

一、除条文另有规定的以外,本章所称“纸”包括“纸板”(不考虑其厚度或每平方米重量如何)。

二、本章不包括:

(一)第三十章的物品;

(二)税目32.12的压印箔;

(三)香纸及用化妆品浸渍或涂布的纸(第三十三章);

(四)用肥皂或洗涤剂浸渍、覆盖或涂布的纸或纤维素絮纸(税号34.01)和用光洁剂、擦光膏及类似制剂浸渍、覆盖或涂布的纸或纤维素絮纸(税目34.05);

(五)税目37.01至37.04的感光纸或感光纸板;

(六)用诊断或实验用试剂浸渍的纸(税目38.22);

(七)第三十九章的用纸强化的层压塑料板,用塑料覆盖或涂布的单层纸或纸板(塑料部分占总厚度的一半以上),以及上述材料的制品,但税目48.14的壁纸除外;

(八)税目42.02的物品(例如旅行用品);

(九)第四十六章的物品(编结材料制品);

(十)纸纱线或纸纱线纺织物(第十一类);

(十一)六十四章或第六十五章的物品;

(十二)税目68.05的砂纸或税目68.14的用纸或纸板衬底的云母(但涂布云母粉的纸及纸板归入本章);

(十三)用纸或纸板衬底的金属箔(通常为第十四类或第十五类);

(十四)税目92.09的制品;

(十五)第九十五章的物品(例如,玩具、游戏品及运动用品)或第九十六章的物品(例如钮扣)。

三、除注释七另有规定的以外,税目48.01至48.05包括经研光、高度研光、釉光或类似处理、仿水印、表面施胶的纸及纸板;同时还包括用各种方法本体着色或染成斑纹的纸、纸板、纤维素絮纸及纤维素纤维网纸。除税目48.03另有规定的以外,上述税目不适用于经过其他方法加工的纸、纸板、纤维素絮纸或纤维素纤维网纸。

Notes:

1. For the purposes of this Chapter, except where the context otherwise requires, a reference to “paper” includes references to paperboard (irrespective of thickness or weight per m^2).

2. This Chapter does not cover:

(a) Articles of Chapter 30;

(b) Stamping foils of heading No. 32. 12;

(c) Perfumed papers or papers impregnated or coated with cosmetics (Chapter 33);

(d) Paper or cellulose wadding impregnated, coated or covered with soap or detergent (heading No. 34. 01), or with polishes, creams or similar preparations (heading No. 34. 05);

(e) Sensitized paper or paperboard of headings Nos. 37. 01 to 37. 04;

(f) Paper impregnated with diagnostic or laboratory reagents (heading No. 38. 22);

(g) Paper-reinforced stratified sheeting of plastics, or one layer of paper or paperboard coated or covered with a layer of plastics, the latter constituting more than half the total thickness, or articles of such materials, other than wall coverings of heading No. 48. 14 (Chapter 39);

(h) Articles of heading No. 42. 02 (for example, travel goods);

(i) Articles of Chapter 46 (manufactures of plaiting material);

(j) Paper yarn or textile articles of paper yarn (Section XI);

(k) Articles of Chapter 64 or Chapter 65;

(l) Abrasive paper or paperboard (heading No. 68. 05) or paper- or paperboard-backed mica (heading No. 68. 14) (paper and paperboard coated with mica powder are, however, to be classified in this Chapter);

(m) Metal foil backed with paper or paperboard (Sectionx XIV or Section XV);

(n) Articles of heading No. 92. 09; or

(o) Articles of Chapter 95 (for example, toys, games, sports requisites) or Chapter 96 (for example, buttons).

3. Subject to the provisions of Note 7, headings Nos. 48. 01 to 48. 05 include paper and paperboard which have been subjected to calendering, super-calendering, glazing or similar finishing, false watermarking or surface sizing, and also paper, paperboard, cellulose wadding and webs of cellulose fibres, coloured or marbled throughout the mass by any method. Except where heading 48. 03 otherwise requires, these headings do not apply to paper, paperboard, cellulose wadding or webs of cellulose fibres which have been otherwise processed.

四、本章所称"新闻纸",是指所含用机械或化学机械方法制得的木纤维不少于全部纤维重量的50%的未经涂布的报刊用纸,未施胶或微施胶,每面的粗糙度〔帕克印刷表面粗糙度(1兆帕)〕超过2.5微米,每平方米重量不小于40克,但不超过65克。

五、税目48.02所称"书写、印刷或类似用途的纸及纸板"及"未打孔的穿孔卡片纸及穿孔纸带纸",是指主要用漂白纸浆或用机械或化学—机械方法制得的纸浆制成的纸及纸板,并且符合下列任一标准:

每平方米重量不超过150克的纸或纸板:

(一)用机械或化学—机械方法制得的纤维含量在10%及以上,并且

1. 每平方米重量不超过80克;或
2. 本体着色;

(二)灰分含量在8%以上,并且

1. 每平方米重量不超过80克;或
2. 本体着色;

(三)灰分含量在3%以上,亮度在60%及以上;

(四)灰分含量在3%以上,但不超过8%,亮度低于60%,耐破指数等于或小于2.5千帕斯卡·平方米/克;

(五)灰分含量在3%及以下,亮度在60% 及以上,耐破指数等于或小于2.5千帕斯卡·平方米/克。

每平方米重量超过150克的纸或纸板:

(一)本体着色;或

(二)亮度在60%及以上,并且

1. 厚度在225微米及以下;或
2. 厚度在225微米以上,但不超过508微米,灰分含量在3%以上;

(三)亮度低于60%,厚度不超过254微米,灰分含量在8%以上。

税目48.02不包括滤纸及纸板(含茶袋纸)或毡纸及纸板。

六、本章所称"牛皮纸及纸板",是指所含用硫酸盐法或烧碱法制得的纤维不少于全部纤维重量的80% 的纸及纸板。

七、除税目条文另有规定的以外,符合税目48.01至48.11中两个或两个以上税目所规定的纸、纸板、纤维素絮纸及纤维素纤维网纸,应按号列顺序归入有关税目中的最末一个税目。

八、税目48.01及48.03至48.09仅适用于下列规格的纸、纸板、纤维素絮纸及纤维素纤维网纸:

4. In this Chapter the expression "newsprint" means uncoated paper of a kind used for the printing of newspapers, of which not less than 50% by weight of the total fibre content consists of wood fibres obtained by a mechanical or chemi-mechanical process, unsized or very lightly sized, having a surface roughness Parker Print Surf (1 MPa) on each side exceeding 2.5 micrometres (microns), weighing not less than 40 g/m^2 and not more than 65 g/m^2.

5. For the purposes of heading No. 48.02, the expressions "paper and paperboard, of a kind used for writing, printing or other graphic purposes" and "non perforated punch-cards and punch tape paper" mean paper and paperboard made mainly from bleached pulp or from pulp obtained by a mechanical or chemi-mechanical process and satisfying any of the following criteria:

For paper or paperboard weighing not more than 150g/m^2:

(a) containing 10% or more of fibres obtained by a mechanical or chemi-mechanical process, and
①weighing not more than 80 g/m^2, or
②coloured throughout the mass; or

(b) containing more than 8% ash, and
①weighing not more than 80 g/m^2, or
②coloured throughout the mass; or

(c) containing more than 3% ash and having a brightness of 60% or more; or

(d) containing more than 3% but not more than 8% ash, having a brightness less than 60%, and a burst index equal to or less than 2.5 kPa · m^2/g; or

(e) containing 3% ash or less, having a brightness of 60% or more and a burst index equal to or less than 2.5 kPa · m^2/g.

For paper or paperboard weighing more than 150 g/m^2:

(a) coloured throughout the mass; or

(b) having a brightness of 60% or more, and
①a caliper of 225 micrometres (microns) or less, or
②a caliper more than 225 micrometres (microns) but not more than 508 micrometres (microns) and an ash content more than 3%; or

(c) having a brightness of less than 60%, a caliper of 254 micrometres (microns) or less and an ash content of more than 8%.

Heading No. 48.02 does not, however, cover filter paper or paperboard (including tea-bag paper) or felt paper or paperboard.

6. In this Chapter "kraft paper and paperboard" means paper and paperhoard of which not less than 80% by weight of the total fibre content consists of fibres obtained by the chemical sulphate or soda processes.

7. Except where the terms of the headings otherwise require, paper, paperboard, cellulose wadding and webs of cellulose fibres answering to a description in two or more of the headings Nos. 48.01 to 48.11 are to be classified under that one of such headings which occurs last in numerical order in the Nomenclature.

8. Headings Nos. 48.01 and 48.03to 48.09 apply only to paper, paperboard, cellulose wadding and webs of cellulose fibres:

（一）成条或成卷，宽度超过 36 厘米；

（二）成张矩形（包括正方形），一边超过 36 厘米，另一边超过 15 厘米（以未折叠计）。

九、税目 48.14 所称“壁纸及类似品”，仅限于：

（一）适合作墙壁或天花板装饰用的成卷纸张，宽度不小于 45 厘米，但不超过 160 厘米：

1. 起纹、压花、染面、印有图案或经其他装饰的（例如起绒），不论是否用透明的防护塑料涂布或覆盖；

2. 表面饰有木粒或草粒而凹凸不平的；

3. 表面用塑料涂布或覆盖并起纹、压花、染面、印有图案或经其他装饰的；

4. 表面用不论是否平行连结或编织的编结材料覆盖的；

（二）适于装饰墙壁或天花板用的经上述加工的纸边及纸条，不论是否成卷；

（三）由几幅拼成的壁纸，成卷或成张，贴到墙上可组成印制的风景或图案。

既可作铺地制品，也可作壁纸的以纸或纸板为底的产品，应归入税目 48.23。

十、税目 48.20 不包括切成一定尺寸的活页纸张或卡片，不论是否印制、压花、打孔。

十一、税目 48.23 主要适用于提花机或类似机器用的穿孔纸或卡片，以及纸花边。

十二、除税目 48.14 及 48.21 的货品外，印有图案、文字或图画的纸、纸板、纤维素絮纸及其制品，如果所印图案、文字或图画作为其主要用途，应归入第四十九章。

子目注释：

一、子目 4804.11 及 4804.19 所称“牛皮挂面纸”，是指所含用硫酸盐法或烧碱法制得的木纤维不少于全部纤维重量的 80% 的成卷机器上光或研光纸及纸板，每平方米重量超过 115 克，并且最低缪伦耐破度符合下表所示（其他重量的耐破度可参照下表换算）：

重　　量 克/平方米	最低耐破度 千帕斯卡
115	393
125	417
637	200
824	300
961	400

(a) in strips or rolls of a width exceeding 36 cm; or

(b) in rectangular (including square) sheets with one side exceeding 36 cm and the other side exceeding 15 cm in the unfolded state.

9. For the purposes of heading No. 48.14, the expression "wallpaper and similar wall coverings" applies only to:

(a) Paper in rolls, of a width of not less than 45 cm and not more than 160 cm, suitable for wall or ceiling decoration:

①Grained, embossed, surface-coloured, designprinted or otherwise surface-decorated (e.g., with textile flock), whether or not coated or covered with transparent protective plastics;

②With an uneven surface resulting from the incorporation of particles of wood, straw, etc.;

③Coated or covered on the face side with plastics, the layer of plastics being grained, embossed, coloured, design-printed or otherwise decorated; or

④Covered on the face side with plaiting material, whether or not bound together in parallel strands or woven;

(b) Borders and friezes, of paper, treated as above, whether or not in rolls, suitable for wall or ceiling decoration;

(c) Wall coverings of paper made up of several panels, in rolls or sheets, printed so as to make up a scene, design or motif when applied to a wall.

Products on a base of paper or paperboard, suitable for use both as floor coverings and as wall coverings, are to be classified in heading No. 48.23.

10. Heading No. 48.20 does not cover loose sheets or cards, cut to size, whether or not printed, embossed or perforated.

11. Heading No. 48.23 applies, *inter alia*, to perforated paper or paperboard cards for Jacquard or similar machines and paper lace.

12. Except for the goods of heading No. 48.14 or 48.21, paper, paperboard, cellulose wadding and articles thereof, printed with motifs, characters or pictorial representations, which are not merely incidental to the primary use of the goods, fall in Chapter 49.

Subheading Notes:

1. For the purposes of subheadings Nos. 4804.11 and 4804.19. "kraftliner" means machine-finished or machine-glazed paper and paperboard, of which not less than 80% by weight of the total fibre content consists of wood fibres obtained by the chemical sulphate or soda processes, in rolls, weighing more than 115 g/m^2 and having a minimum Mullen bursting strength as indicated in the following table or the linearly interpolated or extrapolated equivalent for any other weight.

Weight g/m^2	Minimum Mullen bursting strength kPa
115	393
125	417
637	200
824	300
961	400

二、子目 4804.21 及 4804.29 所称“袋用牛皮纸”，是指所含用硫酸盐法或烧碱法制得的木纤维不少于全部纤维重量的 80% 的成卷机器上光纸，每平方米重量不小于 60 克，

但不超过 115 克，并且符合下列一种规格：

(一)缪伦耐破指数不小于 3.7 千帕斯卡·平方米/克，并且横向伸长率大于 4.5%，纵向伸长率大于 2%；

(二)至少能达到下表所示的最小撕裂度和抗张强度(其他重量的可参照下表换算)：

重　量 克/平方米	最小撕裂度 毫牛顿		最小抗张强度 千牛顿/米	
	纵　向	纵向 加横向	横　向	纵向 加横向
60	700	1510	1.9	6
70	830	1790	2.3	7.2
8.3	80	965	2070	2.8
10.6	100	1230	2635	3.7
12.3	115	1425	3060	4.4

三、子目 4805.11 所称“半化学的瓦楞纸”，是指所含用半化学制浆法制得的未漂白硬木纤维不少于全部纤维重量的 65% 的成卷纸张，并且在温度为 23℃ 和相对湿度为 50% 时，经过 30 分钟的瓦楞芯纸平压强度测定(CMT30)，抗压强度超过 1.8 牛顿/克/平方米。

四、子目 4805.12 包括主要用半化学法制得的草浆制成的成卷纸张，每平方米重量在 130 克及以上，并且在温度为 23℃ 和相对湿度为 50% 时，经过 30 分钟的瓦楞芯纸平压强度测定(CMT30)，抗压强度超过 1.4 牛顿/克/平方米。

五、子目 4805.24 及 4805.25 包括全部或主要用回收(废碎)纸及纸板制得的纸浆制成的纸及纸板。强韧箱纸板也可以有一面用染色纸或由漂白或未漂白的非再生浆制得的纸做表层。这些产品缪伦耐破指数不小于 2 千帕斯卡·平方米/克。

六、子目 4805.30 所称“亚硫酸盐包装纸”，是指所含用亚硫酸盐法制得的木纤维超过全部纤维重量的 40% 的机器研光纸，灰分含量不超过 8%，并且缪伦耐破指数不小于 1.47 千帕斯卡·平方米/克。

七、子目 4810.22 所称“轻质涂布纸”，是指双面涂布纸，其每平方米总重量不超过 72 克，每面每平方米的涂层重量不超过 15 克，原纸中所含用机械方法制得的木纤维不少于全部纤维重量的 50%。

2. For the puposes of subheadings Nos. 4804.21 and 4804.29, “sack kraft paper” means machine-finished paper, of which not less than 80% by weight of the total fibre content consists of fibres obtained by the chemical sulphate or soda processes, in rolls,

weighing not less than 60 g/m^2 but not more than 115 g/m^2 and meeting one of the following sets of specifications:

(a) Having a Mullen burst index of not less than 3.7 kPa·m^2/g and a stretch factor of more than 4.5% in the cross direction and of more than 2% in the machine direction.

(b) Having minima for tear and tensile as indicated in the following table or the linearly interpolated equivalent for any other weight:

Weight g/m^2	Minimum tear mN		Minimum tensile kN/m	
	Machine direction	Machine direction plus cross direction	Cross direction	Machine direction plus cross direction
60	700	1,510	1.9	6
70	830	1,790	2.3	7.2
8.3	80	965	2070	2.8
10.6	100	1230	2635	3.7
12.3	115	1425	3060	4.4

3. For the purposes of subheading No. 4805.11, “semi-chemical fluting paper” means paper, in rolls, of which not less than 65% by weight of the total fibre content consists of unbleached hardwood fibres obtained by a semi-chemical pulping process, and having a CMT 30 (Corrugated Medium Test with 30 minutes of conditioning) crush resistance exceeding 1.8 newtons/g/m^2 at 50% relative humidity, at 23℃.

4. Subheading No. 4805.12 covers paper, in rolls, made mainly of straw pulp obtained by a semi-chemical process, weighing 130 g/m^2 or more, and having a CMT 30 (Corrugated Medium Test with 30 minutes of conditioning) crush resistance exceeding 1.4 newtons/g/m^2 at 50% relative humidity, at 23℃.

5. Subheadings Nos. 4805.24 and 4805.25 cover paper and paperboard made wholly or mainly of pulp of recovered (waste and scrap) paper or paperboard. Testliner may also have a surface layer of dyed paper or of paper made of bleached or unbleached non-recovered pulp. These products have a Mullen burst index of not less than 2 kPa·m^2/g.

6. For the purposes of subheading No. 4805.30, “sulphite wrapping paper” means machine-glazed paper, of which more than 40% by weight of the total fibre content consists of wood fibres obtained by the chemical sulpohite process, having an ash content not exceeding 8% and having a Mullen burst index of not less than 1.47 kPa·m^2/g.

7. For the purposes of subheading No. 4810.22, “lightweight coated paper” means paper, coated on both sides, of a total weight not exceeding 72 g/m^2, with a coating weight not exceeding 15 g/m^2 per side, on a base of which not less than 50% by weight of the total fibre content consists of wood fibres obtained by a mechanical process.

税则号列 Tariff Item.	货品名称	最惠国(%) MFN	协定(%)CT 东盟 CA	中巴 CP	中智 CC	普通 Gen	增值税率 VAT	出口退税 ED	计量单位 Unit	监管条件 SC	Article Description
48.01	**成卷或成张的新闻纸:**										**Newsprint, in rolls or sheets:**
4801.0000	成卷或成张的新闻纸	5				30	17		千克	A	Newsprint, in rolls or sheets
48.02	**书写、印刷或类似用途的未经涂布的纸及纸板、未打孔的穿孔卡片纸及穿孔纸带纸,成卷或成张矩形(包括正方形),任何尺寸,但税目48.01或48.03的纸除外;手工制纸及纸板:**										**Uncoated paper and paperboard, of a kind used for writing, printing or other graphic purposes, and non perforated punchcards and punch tape paper, in rolls or rectangular (including square) sheets, of any size, other than paper of heading No. 48.01 or 48.03; hand-made paper and paperboard:**
4802.1000	-手工制纸及纸板	7.5				70	17		千克		-Hand-made paper and paperboard
	-光敏、热敏、电敏纸及纸板的原纸和原纸板:										-Paper and paperboard of a kind used as a base for photo-sensitive, heat-sensitive or electro-sensitive paper or paperboard:
4802.2010	---照相原纸	7.5				40	17		千克		---Photo paper base
4802.2090	---其他	7.5				40	17		千克		---Other
4802.4000	-壁纸原纸	7.5				40	17		千克		-Wallpaper base
	-其他纸及纸板,不含用机械或化学—机械方法制得的纤维或所含前述纤维不超过全部纤维重量的10%:										-Other paper and paperboard, not containing fibres obtained by a mechanical or chemi-mechanical process or of which not more than 10% by weight of the total fibre content consists of such fibres:
4802.5400	--每平方米重量小于40克	7.5				30	17		千克	A	--Weighing less than 40 g/m^2
4802.5500	--每平方米重量在40克及以上,但不超过150克,成卷	5				30	17		千克		--Weighing 40 g/m^2 or more but not more than 150 g/m^2, in rolls
4802.5500 10	40g<每平米重≤150g的胶版纸(成卷,机械或化学-机械法制得的纤维含量≤10%)	5				30	17		千克	A	Offset paper, in rolls, $40g/m^2 < w \leq 150g/m^2$, containing fibres ≤ 10%, obtained by a mechanical or chemi-mechanical process
4802.5500 90	40g<每平米重≤150g未涂布中厚纸(书写印刷用,成卷,含机械或化学-机械法制纤维≤10%)	5				30	17		千克	A	Paper, of a kind used for writing, printing or other graphic purposes, in rolls, $40g/m^2 < w \leq 150g/m^2$, containing fibres ≤10%, obtained by a mechanical or chemi-mechanical process
4802.5600	--每平方米重量在40克及以上,但不超过150克,一边不超过435毫米,另一边不超过297毫米(以未折叠计),成张的	5				30	17		千克		--Weighing 40 g/m^2 or more but not more than 150 g/m^2, in sheets with one side not exceeding 435 mm and the other side not exceeding 297 mm in the unfolded state
4802.5600 10	成张40g<每平米重≤150g胶版纸(长≤435mm,宽≤297mm含机械或化学-机械法制纤维≤10%)	5				30	17		千克	A	Offset paper, in sheets, length ≤ 435mm, width≤297mm, containing fibres≤10%, obtained by a mechanical or chemi-mechanical process
4802.5600 90	40g<每平米重≤150g未涂布纸,成张(书写印刷,长≤435mm,宽≤297mm含机械或半化学浆≤10%)	5				30	17		千克	A	Uncoated paper, of a kind used for writing, printing or other graphic purposes, in sheets, length ≤ 435mm, width ≤ 297mm, containing fibres ≤ 10%, obtained by a mechanical or chemi-mechanical process
4802.5700	--其他,每平方米重量在40克及以上,但不超过150克	5				30	17		千克		--Other, weighing 40 g/m^2 or more but not more than 150 g/m^2

税则号列 Tariff Item.	货品名称	最惠国(%) MFN	协定(%) 东盟 CA	协定(%) 中巴 CP	CT 中智 CC	普通 Gen	增值税率 VAT	出口退税 ED	计量单位 Unit	监管条件 SC	Article Description
4802.5700 10	其他 40g < 每平米重 ≤ 150g 的胶版纸(机械或化学-机械法制得的纤维含量≤10%)	5				30	17		千克	A	Other offset paper, $40g/m^2 < w \leq 150g/m^2$, containing fibres ≤ 10%, obtained by a mechanical or chemi-mechanical process
4802.5700 90	其他 40g < 每平米重 ≤ 150g 未涂中厚纸(书写印刷用,含机械或化学-机械法制纤维≤10%)	5				30	17		千克	A	Other uncoated paper, $40g/m^2 < w \leq 150g/m^2$, of a kind used for writing, printing or other graphic purposes, containing fibres ≤ 10%, obtained by a mechanical or chemi-mechanical process
4802.5800	--每平方米重量超过 150 克	5				30	17		千克	A	--Weighing more than 150 g/m^2
	-其他纸及纸板,所含用机械或化学—机械方法制得的纤维超过全部纤维重量的 10%:										-Other paper and paperboard, of which more than 10% by weight of the total fibre content consists of fibres obtained by a mechanical or chemi-mechanical process:
	--成卷的:										--In rolls:
4802.6110	---新闻纸	7.5				30	17		千克	A	---Newsprint
4802.6190	---其他	5				30	17		千克	A	---Other
4802.6200	--成张的,一边不超过 435 毫米,另一边不超过 297 毫米(以未折叠计)	5				30	17		千克	A	--In sheets with one side not exceeding 435 mm and the other side not exceeding 297 mm in the unfolded state
	--其他:										--Other:
4802.6910	---新闻纸	7.5				30	17		千克	A	---Newsprint
4802.6990	---其他	5				30	17		千克	A	---Other
48.03	**卫生纸、面巾纸、餐巾纸以及家庭或卫生用的类似纸、纤维素絮纸和纤维素纤维网纸,不论是否起纹、压花、打孔、染面、饰面或印花,成卷或成张的:**										**Toilet or facial tissue stock, towel or napkin stock and similar paper of a kind used for household or sanitary purposes, cellulose wadding and webs of cellulose fibres, whether or not creped, crinkled, embossed, perforated, surface-coloured, surface-decorated or printed, in rolls or sheets:**
4803.0000	卫生纸、面巾纸、餐巾纸以及家庭或卫生用的类似纸、纤维素絮纸和纤维素纤维网纸,不论是否起纹、压花、打孔、染面、饰面或印花,成卷或成张的	7.5				40	17		千克	A	Toilet or facial tissue stock, towel or napkin stock and similar paper of a kind used for household or sanitary purposes, cellulose wadding and webs of cellulose fibres, whether or not creped, crinkled, embossed, perforated, surface-coloured, surface-decorated or printed, in rolls or sheets
48.04	**成卷或成张的未经涂布的牛皮纸及纸板,但不包括税目 48.02 或 48.03 的货品:**										**Uncoated kraft paper and paperboard, in rolls or sheets, other than that of heading No.48.02 or 48.03:**
	-牛皮挂面纸:										-Kraftliner:
4804.1100	--未漂白	5				30	17		千克		--Unbleached

税则号列 Tariff Item.	货品名称	最惠国(%) MFN	协定(%)CT 东盟 CA	中巴 CP	中智 CC	普通 Gen	增值税率 VAT	出口退税 ED	计量单位 Unit	监管条件 SC	Article Description
4804.1100 10	每平米重115-360克未漂白、成卷或成张未涂布牛皮挂面纸(紧度不小于0.68g/cm³,耐破指数不小于2.6kPa·m²/g,横向环压指数不小于7.5N/m·m²/g,横向耐折度不小于60次,饱和牛皮纸除外。)	5				30	17		千克	A	Uncoated kraft paper and paperboard, in rolls or sheets, $115g/m^2 \leqslant 360g/m^2$ (not tighter than $0.68g/cm^3$, bursting index not smller than 2.6kPa·m^2/g, crossdirection fold endurance not less than 60 times, excluding saturated kraftpaper)
4804.1100 90	其他未漂白的牛皮挂面纸(成卷或成张的及未经涂布的)	5				30	17		千克	A	Other uncoated krafliner paper, unbleached, in rolls or sheets (uncoated kraft paper and paperboard, in rolls or sheets)
4804.1900	--其他	5				30	17		千克	A	--Other
	-袋用牛皮纸:										-Sack kraft paper:
4804.2100	--未漂白	5				30	17		千克		--Unbleached
4804.2900	--其他	5				30	17		千克		--Other
	-其他牛皮纸及纸板,每平方米重量不超过150克:										-Other kraft paper and paperboard weighing 150 g/m^2 or less:
4804.3100	--未漂白	2				30	17		千克		--Unbleached
4804.3100 10	每平米重115-150克未漂白、成卷或成张未涂布其他牛皮纸(紧度不小于0.68g/cm³,耐破指数不小于2.6Kpa·m²/g,横向环压指数不小于7.5N/m·m²/g,横向耐折度不小于60次,饱和牛皮纸除外)	2				30	17		千克	A	Uncoated kraft paper and paperboard, in rolls or sheets, $115g/m^2 \leqslant weight \leqslant 150g/m^2$ (not tighter than $0.68g/cm^3$, bursting index not smaller than 2.6kPa·m^2/g, cross-direction ring crush index not samller than 7.5N/m·m^2/g, cross direction fold endurance not less than 60 times, excluding saturated kraft paper)
4804.3100 90	其他未漂白的其他薄牛皮纸及纸板(薄纸指每平米重量≤150克,成卷或成张未经涂布的)	2				30	17		千克	A	Other uncoated kraft paper and paperboard, unbleached ($w \leqslant 150g/m2$, in rolls or sheets)
4804.3900	--其他	2				30	17		千克		--Other
	-其他牛皮纸及纸板,每平方米重量超过150克,但小于225克:										-Other kraft paper and paperboard weighing more than 150 g/m^2 but less than $225g/m^2$:
4804.3900 01	添加了耐磨材料三氧化二铝的成卷或成张的耐磨纸原纸(每平米重量≤150克)	2				30	17		千克	A	Added wear resistant papers made of AL_2o_3 ($\leqslant 150g/m^2$)
4804.3900 90	每平米重量≤150克的其他牛皮纸及纸板	2				30	17		千克	A	Other kraft paper and paperboard, weighing $\leqslant 150g/m^2$
4804.4100	--未漂白	2				30	17		千克		--Unbleached

税则号列 Tariff Item.	货 品 名 称	最惠国(%) MFN	协定(%)CT 东盟 CA	中巴 CP	中智 CC	普通 Gen	增值税率 VAT	出口退税 ED	计量单位 Unit	监管条件 SC	Article Description
4804.4100 10	150 克<每平米重<225 克未漂白、成卷或成张(未涂布其他牛皮纸(紧度不小于0.68g/cm^3,耐破指数不小于 2.6KPa·m^2/g 横向环压指数不小于 7.5N/m·m^2/g,横向耐折度不小于60 次,饱和牛皮纸除外)	2				30	17		千克	A	Uncoated kraft paper and paperboard, unbleached, 150g/m^2 < 225g/ m^2 in rolls or sheets(not tighter than 0.68g/cm3, bursting index not smaller than 2.6kPa · m2/g, cross - direction ring crush index not samller than 7.5N/m · m2/g, cross direction fold endurance not less than 60 times, excluding saturated kraft paper)
4804.4100 90	其他未漂白的其他中厚牛皮纸及纸板(中厚指 150 克<每平米重<225 克,成卷或成张未涂布的)	2				30	17		千克	A	Other Uncoated kraft paper and paperboard,unbleached,150g/m^2 <225g/ m^2 in rolls or sheets(150g/m2 < w <225g/m2,in rolls or sheets)
4804.4200	--本体均匀漂白,所含用化学方法制得的木纤维超过全部纤维重量的95%	5				30	17		千克	A	--Bleached uniformly throughout the mass and of which more than 95% by weight of the total fibre content consists of wood fibres obtained by a chemical process
4804.4900	--其他	2				30	17		千克	A	--Other
	-其他牛皮纸及纸板,每平方米重量在225 克及以上:										-Other kraft paper and paperboard weighing 225 g/m^2 or more:
4804.5100	--未漂白	2				30	17		千克		--Unbleached
4804.5100 10	每平米重 225-360 克未漂白、成卷或成张未涂布其他牛皮纸(紧度不小于0.68g/cm^3,耐破指数不小于 2.6Kpa·m^2/g,横向环压指数不小于 7.5N/m·m^2/g,横向耐折度不小于60 次,饱和牛皮纸除外)	2				30	17		千克	A	Uncoated kraft paper and paperboard, unbleached, 225g/m^2 < 360g/ m^2 in rolls or sheets(not tighter than 0.68g/cm3, bursting index not smaller than 2.6kPa · m2/g, cross - direction ring crush index not samller than 7.5N/m · m2/g, cross direction fold endurance not less than 60 times, excluding saturated kraft paper)
4804.5100 90	其他未漂白的其他厚牛皮纸及纸板(厚纸指每平米重量≥225 克,成卷或成张未经涂布的)	2				30	17		千克	A	Other Uncoated kraft paper and paperboard,unbleached,225g/m^2 <360g/ m^2 in rolls or sheets(w≥225g/m2,in rolls or sheets)
4804.5200	--本体均匀漂白,所含用化学方法制得的木纤维超过全部纤维重量的95%	5				30	17		千克	A	--Bleached uniformly throughout the mass and of which more than 95% by weight of the total fibre content consists of wood fibres obtained by a chemical process
4804.5900	--其他	2				30	17		千克	A	--Other
48.05	**成卷或成张的其他未经涂布的纸及纸板,加工程度不超过本章注释三所列范围:**										**Other uncoated paper and paperboard, in rolls or sheets, not further worked or processed than as specified in Note 3 to this Chapter:**
	-瓦楞原纸:										-Fluting paper:
4805.1100	--半化学的瓦楞原纸	7.5				30	17		千克	A	--Semi-chemical fluting paper
4805.1200	--草浆瓦楞原纸	7.5				30	17		千克	A	--Straw fluting paper
4805.1900	--其他	7.5				30	17		千克	A	--Other
	-强韧箱纸板(再生挂面纸板):										-Testliner(recycled liner board):

税则号列 Tariff Item.	货品名称	最惠国(%) MFN	协定(%)CT 东盟 CA	中巴 CP	中智 CC	普通 Gen	增值税率 VAT	出口退税 ED	计量单位 Unit	监管条件 SC	Article Description
4805.2400	--每平方米重量在150克及以下	7.5				30	17		千克	A	--Weighing 150 g/m^2 or less
4805.2500	--每平方米重量超过150克	7.5				30	17		千克	A	--Weighing more than 150 g/m^2
4805.3000	-亚硫酸盐包装纸	7.5				30	17		千克		-Sulphite wrapping paper
4805.4000	-滤纸及纸板	7.5				30	17		千克		-Filter paper and paperboard
4805.5000	-毡纸及纸板	7.5				30	17		千克		-Felt paper and paperboard
	-其他:										-Other:
	--每平方米重量在150克及以下:										--Weighing 150 g/m^2 or less:
4805.9110	---电解电容器纸	7.5				30	17		千克	A	---Insulating paper for electrolytic capaitor
4805.9190	---其他	7.5				30	17		千克		---Other
4805.9200	--每平方米重量在150克以上,但小于225克	7.5				30	17		千克	A	--Weighing more than 150 g/m^2 but less than 225 g/m^2
4805.9300	--每平方米重量在225克及以上	7.5				30	17		千克		--Weighing 225 g/m^2 or more
48.06	**成卷或成张的植物羊皮纸、防油纸、描图纸、半透明纸及其他高光泽透明或半透明纸:**										**Vegetable parchment, greaseproof papers, tracing papers and glassine and other glazed transparent or translucent papers, in rolls or sheets:**
4806.1000	-植物羊皮纸	7.5				40	17		千克		-Vegetable parchment
4806.2000	-防油纸	7.5				40	17		千克		-Greaseproof papers
4806.3000	-描图纸	7.5				30	17		千克		-Tracing papers
4806.4000	-高光泽透明或半透明纸	7.5				40	17		千克		-Glassine and other glazed transparent or translucent papers
48.07	**成卷或成张的复合纸及纸板(用粘合剂粘合各层纸或纸板制成),未经表面涂布或未浸渍,不论内层是否有加强材料:**										**Composite paper and paperboard (made by sticking flat layers of paper or paperboard together with an adhesive), not surface-coated or impregnated, whether or not internally reinforced, in rolls or sheets:**
4807.0000	成卷或成张的复合纸及纸板(用粘合剂粘合各层纸或纸板制成),未经表面涂布或未浸渍,不论内层是否有加强材料	7.5				40	17		千克		Composite paper and paperboard (made by sticking flat layers of paper or paperboard together with an adhesive), not surface-coated or impregnated, whether or not internally reinforced, in rolls or sheets
48.08	**成卷或成张的瓦楞纸及纸板(不论是否与平面纸胶合)、皱纸纸及纸板、压纹纸及纸板、穿孔纸及纸板,但税目48.03的纸除外:**										**Paper and paperboard, corrugated (with or without glued flat surface sheets), creped, crinkled, embossed or perforated, in rolls or sheets, other than paper of the kind described in heading No. 48.03:**
4808.1000	-瓦楞纸及纸板,不论是否穿孔	7.5				30	17		千克	A	-Corrugated paper and paperboard, whether or not perforated
4808.2000	-袋用皱纹牛皮纸,不论是否压花或穿孔	7.5				40	17		千克		-Sack kraft paper, creped or crinkled, whether or not embossed or perforated
4808.3000	-其他皱纹牛皮纸,不论是否压花或穿孔	7.5				40	17		千克		-Other kraft paper, creped or crinkled, whether or not embossed or perforated
4808.9000	-其他	7.5				40	17		千克		-Other

税则号列 Tariff Item.	货品名称	最惠国(%) MFN	协定(%)CT 东盟 CA	中巴 CP	中智 CC	普通 Gen	增值税率 VAT	出口退税 ED	计量单位 Unit	监管条件 SC	Article Description
48.09	**复写纸、自印复写纸及其他拷贝或转印纸(包括涂布或浸渍的油印蜡纸或胶印版纸),不论是否印制,成卷或成张的:**										**Carbon paper, self-copy paper and other copying or transfer papers (including coated or impregnated paper for duplicator stencils or offset plates), whether or not printed, in rolls or sheets:**
4809.2000	-自印复写纸	7.5				40	17		千克		-Self-copy paper
4809.9000	-其他	7.5				40	17		千克		-Other
48.10	**成卷或成张矩形(包括正方形)的任何尺寸的单面或双面涂布高岭土或其他无机物质(不论是否加粘合剂)的纸及纸板,但未涂布其他涂料,不论是否染面、饰面或印花:**										**Paper and paperboard, coated on one or both sides with kaolin (China clay) or other inorganic substances, with or without a binder, and with no other coating, whether or not surface-coloured, surface-decorated or printed, in rolls or rectangular (including square) sheets, of any size:**
	-书写、印刷或类似用途的纸及纸板,不含用机械或化学—机械方法制得的纤维或所含前述纤维不超过全部纤维重量的10%:										-Paper and paperboard of a kind used for writing, printing or other graphic purposes, not containing fibres obtained by a mechanical or chemi-mechanical process or of which not more than 10% by weight of the total fibre content consists of such fibres:
4810.1300	--成卷的	5				40	17		千克		--In rolls
4810.1300 01	成卷的铜版纸(所含用机械或化学-机械法制得的纤维≤10%)	5				40	17		千克	A	Art paper, containing fibres≤10% obtained by a mechanical or chemi-mechanical process, in rolls
4810.1300 90	涂无机物的其他书写/印刷或类似用途纸/纸板(成卷的,所含用机械或化学-机械法制得的纤维≤10%)	5				40	17		千克	A	Other paper and paperboard, of a kind used for writing, printing or other graphic purposes, containing fibres ≤ 10% obtained by a mechanical or chemi-mechanical process, in rolls
4810.1400	--成张的,一边不超过435毫米,另一边不超过297毫米(以未折叠计)	5				40	17		千克		--In sheets with one side not exceeding 435 mm and the other side not exceeding 297 mm in the unfolded state
4810.1400 01	成张的铜版纸(一边≤435mm,另一边≤297mm,机械或化学-机械纤维≤10%)	5				40	17		千克	A	Art paper, one side ≤ 435mm, other side≤297mm, containing fibres≤10% obtained by a mechanical or chemi-mechanical process, in sheets
4810.1400 90	涂无机物的其他成张的书写、印刷的纸及纸板(一边≤435mm,另一边≤297mm,机械或化学-机械纤维≤10%)	5				40	17		千克	A	Other paper and paperboard, of a kind used for writing, printing or other graphic purposes, one side≤435mm other side≤297mm, containing fibres ≤ 10%, obtained by a mechanical or chemi-mechanical process, in sheets
4810.1900	--其他	5				40	17		千克		--Other
4810.1900 01	其他铜版纸(所含用机械或化学-机械法制得的纤维≤10%)	5				40	17		千克	A	Other art paper, containing fibres ≤ 10%, obtained by a mechanical or chemi-mechanical process

税则号列 Tariff Item.	货品名称	最惠国(%) MFN	协定(%)CT 东盟 CA	中巴 CP	中智 CC	普通 Gen	增值税率 VAT	出口退税 ED	计量单位 Unit	监管条件 SC	Article Description
4810.1900 90	涂无机物的其他书写、印刷用途的纸及纸板(所含用机械或化学-机械法制得的纤维≤10%)	5				40	17		千克	A	Other paper and paperboard, of a kind used for writing, printing or other graphic purposes, containing fibres ≤ 10%, obtained by a mechanical or chemi-mechanical process
	-书写、印刷或类似用途的纸及纸板,所含用机械方法或化学—机械方法制得的纤维超过全部纤维重量的10%:										-Paper and paperboard of a kind used for writing, printing or other graphic purposes, of which more than 10% by weight of the total fibre content consists of fibres obtained by a mechanical or chemi-mechanical process:
4810.2200	--轻质涂布纸	5				40	17		千克	A	--Light-weight coated paper
4810.2900	--其他	5				40	17		千克	A	--Other
	-牛皮纸及纸板,但书写、印刷或类似用途的除外:										-Kraft paper and paperboard, other than that of a kind used for writing, printing or other graphic purposes:
4810.3100	--本体均匀漂白,所含用化学方法制得的木纤维超过全部纤维重量的95%,每平方米重量不超过150克	5				40	17		千克		--Bleached uniformly throughout the mass and of which more than 95% by weight of the total fibre content consists of wood fibres obtained by a chemical process, and weighing 150 g/m^2 or less
4810.3100 10	涂无机物的白板纸、白卡纸(薄纸指重量≤150克/平方米,含用化学方法制得木纤维)	5				40	17		千克	A	Kraft paper and paperboard, bleached w ≤ 150g/m^2, consists of wood fibres obtained by a chemical process
4810.3100 90	涂无机物的薄漂白牛皮纸及纸板(薄纸指重量≤150克/平方米,含用化学方法制得的木纤维)	5				40	17		千克	A	Kraft paper and paperboard, bleached, coated with inorganic substances, w ≤ 150g/m^2, consists of wood fibres obtained by a chemical process
4810.3200	--本体均匀漂白,所含用化学方法制得的木纤维超过全部纤维重量的95%,每平方米重量超过150克	5				40	17		千克		--Bleached uniformly throughout the mass and of which more than 95% by weight of the total fibre content consists of wood fibres obtained by a chemical process, and weighing more than 150g/m^2
4810.3200 10	涂无机物的白板纸、白卡纸(厚纸指重量>150克/平方米,含用化学方法制得的木纤维)	5				40	17		千克		Kraft paper and paperboard, bleached, w > 150g/m^2 consists of wood fibres obtained by a chemical process
4810.3200 90	涂无机物的厚漂白牛皮纸及纸板(厚纸指重量>150克/平方米,含用化学方法制得的木纤维)	5				40	17		千克		Kraft paper and paperboard, bleached, coated with inorganic substances, w > 150g/m^2, consists of wood fibres obtained by a chemical process
4810.3900	--其他	5				40	17		千克	A	--Other
	-其他纸及纸板:										-Other paper and paperboard:
4810.9200	--多层的	5				40	17		千克	A	--Multi-ply
4810.9900	--其他	7.5				40	17		千克	A	--Other

税则号列 Tariff Item.	货品名称	最惠国(%) MFN	协定(%)CT 东盟 CA	中巴 CP	中智 CC	普通 Gen	增值税率 VAT	出口退税 ED	计量单位 Unit	监管条件 SC	Article Description
48.11	**成卷或成张矩形(包括正方形)的任何尺寸的经涂布、浸渍、覆面、染面、饰面或印花的纸、纸板、纤维素絮纸及纤维素纤维网纸,但税目48.03、48.09或48.10的货品除外:**										**Paper, paperboard, cellulose wadding and webs of cellulose fibres, coated, impregnated, covered, surface-coloured, surface-decorated or printed, in rolls or rectangular (including square) sheets, of any size, other than goods of the kind described in heading No. 48.03, 48.09or 48.10:**
4811.1000	-焦油纸及纸板、沥青纸及纸板	7.5				40	17		千克		-Tarred, bituminised or asphalted paper and paperboard
	-胶粘纸及纸板:										-Gummed or adhesive paper and paperboard:
4811.4100	--自粘的	7.5				40	17		千克		--Self-adhesive
4811.4900	--其他	7.5				40	17		千克		--Other
	-用塑料(不包括粘合剂)涂布、浸渍或覆盖的纸及纸板:										-Paper and paperboard coated, impregnated or covered with plastics (excluding adhesives):
	--漂白的,每平方米重量超过150克:										--Bleached, weighing more than 150g/m^2:
4811.5110	---彩色相纸用双面涂塑纸	7.5				40	17		千克		---Paper coated on both sides with plastics for colour photography
4811.5190	---其他	7.5				40	17		千克		---Other
	--其他:										--Other:
4811.5910	---绝缘纸及纸板	7.5				30	17		千克		---Insulating paper and paperboard
4811.5990	---其他	7.5				40	17		千克		---Other
	-用蜡、石蜡、硬脂精、油或甘油涂布、浸渍、覆盖的纸及纸板:										-Paper and paperboard, coated, impregnated or covered with wax, paraffin wax, stearin, oil or glyecrol:
4811.6010	---绝缘纸及纸板	7.5				30	17		千克		---Insulating paper and paperboard
4811.6090	---其他	7.5				40	17		千克		---Other
4811.9000	-其他纸、纸板、纤维素絮纸及纤维素纤维网纸	7.5				40	17		千克		-Other paper, paperboard, cellulose wadding and webs of cellulose fibres
48.12	**纸浆制的滤块、滤板及滤片:**										**Filter blocks, slabs and plates, of paper pulp:**
4812.0000	纸浆制的滤块、滤板及滤片	7.5				40	17		千克		Filter blocks, slabs and plates, of paper pulp
48.13	**卷烟纸,不论是否切成一定尺寸、成小本或管状:**										**Cigarette paper, whether or not cut to size or in the form of booklets or tubes:**
4813.1000	-成小本或管状	7.5				100	17		千克	7	-In the form of booklets or tubes
4813.2000	-宽度不超过5厘米成卷的	7.5				100	17		千克	A7	-In rolls of a width not exceeding 5 cm
4813.9000	-其他	7.5				100	17		千克	A7	-Other
48.14	**壁纸及类似品;窗用透明纸:**										**Wallpaper and similar wall coverings; window transparencies of paper:**
4814.1000	-用木粒或草粒等饰面的壁纸	7.5				50	17		千克		-"Ingrain" paper
4814.2000	-用塑料涂面或盖面的壁纸及类似品,起纹、压花、着色、印刷图案或经其他装饰	7.5				50	17		千克		-Wallpaper and similar wall coverings, consisting of paper coated or covered, on the face side, with a grained, embossed, coloured, design-printed or otherwise decorated layer of plastics
4814.9000	-其他	7.5				50	17		千克		-Other

税则号列 Tariff Item.	货品名称	最惠国(%) MFN	协定(%)CT 东盟 CA	中巴 CP	中智 CC	普通 Gen	增值税率 VAT	出口退税 ED	计量单位 Unit	监管条件 SC	Article Description
48.16	**复写纸、自印复写纸及其他拷贝或转印纸(不包括税目48.09的纸),油印蜡纸或胶印版纸,不论是否盒装:**										**Carbon paper, self-copy paper and other copying or transfer papers (other than those of heading No. 48.09), duplicator stencils and offset plates, of paper, whether or not put up in boxes:**
4816.2000	-自印复写纸	7.5				70	17		千克		-Self-copy paper
	-其他:										-Other:
4816.9010	---热敏转印纸	7.5				40	17		千克		---Heat transfer paper
4816.9090	---其他	7.5				70	17		千克		---Other
48.17	**纸或纸板制的信封、封缄信片、素色明信片及通信卡片;纸或纸板制的盒子、袋子及夹子,内装各种纸制文具:**										**Envelopes, letter cards, plain postcards and correspondence cards, of paper or paperboard; boxes, pouches, wallets and writing compendiums, of paper or paperboard, containing an assortment of paper stationery:**
4817.1000	-信封	7.5				80	17	13	千克		-Envelopes
4817.2000	-封缄信片、素色明信片及通信卡片	7.5				80	17	13	千克		-Letter cards, plain postcards and correspondence cards
4817.3000	-纸或纸板制的盒子、袋子及夹子,内装各种纸制文具	7.5				80	17	13	千克		-Boxes, pouches, wallets and writing compendiums, of paper or paperboard, containing an assortment of paper stationery
48.18	**卫生纸及类似纸,家庭或卫生用纤维素絮纸及纤维素纤维网纸,成卷宽度不超过36厘米或切成一定尺寸或形状的;纸浆、纸、纤维素絮纸或纤维素纤维网纸制的手帕、面巾、台布、餐巾、尿布、止血塞、床单及类似的家庭、卫生或医院用品、衣服及衣着附件:**										**Toilet paper and similar paper, cellulose wadding or webs of cellulose fibres, of a kind used for household or sanitary purposes, in rolls of a width not exceeding 36 cm, or cut to size or shape; handkerchiefs, cleansing tissues, towels, tablecloths, serviettes, napkins for babies, tampons, bed sheets and similar household, sanitary or hospital articles, articles of apparel and clothing accessories, of paper pulp, paper, cellulose wadding or webs of cellulose fibres:**
4818.1000	-卫生纸	7.5				80	17	13	千克		-Toilet paper
4818.2000	-纸手帕及纸面巾	7.5				90	17	13	千克	A	-Handkerchiefs, cleansing or facial tissues and towels
4818.3000	-纸台布及纸餐巾	7.5				90	17	13	千克	A	-Tablecloths and serviettes
4818.4000	-纸卫生巾及止血塞、婴儿纸尿布、尿布衬里及类似的卫生用品	7.5				80	17	13	千克	A	-Sanitary towels and tampons, napkins and napkin liners for babies and similar sanitary articles
4818.5000	-衣服及衣着附件	7.5	5		0	90	17	13	千克	A	-Articles of apparel and clothing accessories
4818.9000	-其他	7.5				90	17	13	千克	A	-Other

税则号列 Tariff Item.	货品名称	最惠国(%) MFN	协定(%)CT 东盟 CA	中巴 CP	中智 CC	普通 Gen	增值税率 VAT	出口退税 ED	计量单位 Unit	监管条件 SC	Article Description
48.19	**纸、纸板、纤维素絮纸或纤维素纤维网纸制的箱、盒、匣、袋及其他包装容器;纸或纸板制的卷宗盒、信件盘及类似品,供办公室、商店及类似场所使用的:**										**Cartons, boxes, cases, bags and other packing containers, of paper, paperboard, cellulose wadding or webs of cellulose fibres; box files, letter trays and similar articles, of paper or paperboard of a kind used in offices, shops or the like:**
4819.1000	-瓦楞纸或纸板制的箱、盒、匣	5				80	17	13	千克		-Cartons, boxes and cases, of corrugated paper or paperboard
4819.2000	-非瓦楞纸或纸板制的可折叠箱、盒、匣	5				80	17	13	千克		-Folding cartons, boxes and cases, of noncorrugated paper or paperboard
4819.3000	-底宽40厘米及以上的纸袋	7.5	T3		6	80	17	13	千克		-Sacks and bags, having a base of a width of 40 cm or more
4819.4000	-其他纸袋,包括锥形袋	7.5				80	17	13	千克		-Other sacks and bags, including cones
4819.5000	-其他包装容器,包括唱片套	7.5				80	17	13	千克	A	-Other packing containers, including record sleeves
4819.6000	-办公室、商店及类似场所使用的卷宗盒、信件盘、存储盒及类似品	7.5				80	17	13	千克		-Box files, letter trays, storage boxes and similar articles, of a kind used in offices, shops or the like
48.20	**纸或纸板制的登记本、账本、笔记本、定货本、收据本、信笺本、记事本、日记本及类似品、练习本、吸墨纸本、活动封面(活页及非活页)、文件夹、卷宗皮、多联商业表格纸、页间夹有复写纸的本及其他文具用品;纸或纸板制的样品簿、粘贴簿及书籍封面:**										**Registers, account books, note books, order books, receipt books, letter pads, memorandum pads, diaries and similar articles, exercise books, blotting-pads, binders (loose-leaf or other), folders, file covers, manifold business forms, interleaved carbon sets and other articles of stationery, of paper or paperboard; albums for samples or for collections and book covers, of paper or paperboard:**
4820.1000	-登记本、账本、笔记本、订货本、收据本、信笺本、记事本、日记本及类似品	7.5				80	17	13	千克		-Registers, account books, note books, order books, receipt books, letter pads, memorandum pads, diaries and similar articles
4820.2000	-练习本	7.5				80	17	13	千克		-Exercise books
4820.3000	-活动封面(书籍封面除外)、文件夹及卷宗皮	7.5				80	17	13	千克		-Binders (other than book covers), folders and file covers
4820.4000	-多联商业表格纸、页间夹有复写纸的本	7.5	5		0	80	17	13	千克		-Manifold business forms and interleaved carbon sets
4820.5000	-样品簿及粘贴簿	7.5				80	17	13	千克		-Albums for samples or for collections
4820.9000	-其他	7.5				80	17	13	千克		-Other
48.21	**纸或纸板制的各种标签,不论是否印制:**										**Paper or paperboard labels of all kinds, whether or not printed:**
4821.1000	-印制	7.5				50	17	13	千克		-Printed
4821.9000	-其他	7.5				50	17	13	千克		-Other

税则号列 Tariff Item.	货品名称	最惠国(%) MFN	协定(%) CT 东盟 CA	中巴 CP	中智 CC	普通 Gen	增值税率 VAT	出口退税 ED	计量单位 Unit	监管条件 SC	Article Description
48.22	纸浆、纸或纸板(不论是否穿孔或硬化)制的筒管、卷轴、纡子及类似品:										**Bobbins, spools, cops and similar supports of paper pulp, paper or paperboard (whether or not perforated or hardened):**
4822.1000	-纺织纱线用	7.5				35	17	13	千克		-Of a kind used for winding textile yarn
4822.9000	-其他	7.5				70	17	13	千克		-Other
48.23	切成一定尺寸或形状的其他纸、纸板、纤维素絮纸及纤维素纤维网纸;纸浆、纸、纸板、纤维素絮纸及纤维素纤维网纸制的其他物品:										**Other paper, paperboard, cellulose wadding and webs of cellulose fibres, cut to size or shape; other articles of paper pulp, paper, paperboard, cellulose wadding or webs of cellulose fibres:**
	-成条或成卷的胶粘纸:										-Gummed or adhesive paper, in strips or rolls:
4823.2000	-滤纸及纸板	7.5				30	17	13	千克		-Filter paper and paperboard
4823.4000	-已印制的自动记录器用打印纸卷、纸张及纸盘	7.5				30	17	13	千克		-Rolls, sheets and dials, printed for self-recording apparatus
	-纸或纸板制的盘、碟、盆、杯及类似品										-Trays, dishes, plates, cups and the like, of paper or paperboard
4823.6100	--竹的将纸制的	7.5	5		6	90	17	13	千克	A	--Trays, dishes, plates, cups and the like, of paper making bamboo pulp
4823.6900	--其他	7.5	5		6	90	17	13	千克	A	--Other
4823.7000	-压制或模制纸浆制品	7.5				90	17	13	千克		-Moulded or pressed articles of paper pulp
	-其他:										-Other:
4823.9010	---以纸或纸为底制的铺地制品	7.5				90	17	13	千克		---Floor coverings ona base of paper or of paper board
4823.9020	---神纸及类似用品	7.5	5		6	180	17	13	千克		---Joss paper and the like
4823.9030	---纸扇	7.5	5		6	90	17	13	千克		---Paper fans
4823.9090	---其他	7.5				90	17	13	千克		---Other

第四十九章
书籍、报纸、印刷图画及其他印刷品;手稿、打字稿及设计图纸

注释:

一、本章不包括:

(一)透明基的照相负片或正片(第三十七章);

(二)立体地图、设计图表或地球仪、天体仪,不论是否印刷(税目90.23);

(三)第九十五章的扑克牌或其他物品;

(四)雕版画、印刷画、石印画的原本(税目97.02),税目97.04的邮票、印花税票、纪念封、首日封、邮政信笺及类似品,以及第九十七章的超过一百年的古物或其他物品。

二、第四十九章所称"印刷",也包括用胶版复印机、油印机印制,在自动数据处理设备控制下打印绘制,压印、冲印、感光复印、热敏复印或打字。

三、用纸以外材料装订成册的报纸、杂志和期刊,以及一期以上装订在同一封面里的成套报纸、杂志和期刊,应归入税目49.01,不论是否有广告材料。

四、税目49.01还包括:

(一)附有说明文字,每页编有号数以便装订成一册或几册的整集印刷复制品,例如,美术作品、绘画;

(二)随同成册书籍的图画附刊;

(三)供装订书籍或小册子用的散页、集页或书帖形式的印刷品,已构成一部作品的全部或部分。

但没有说明文字的印刷图画或图解,不论是否散页或书帖形式,应归入税目49.11。

五、除本章注释三另有规定的以外,税目49.01不包括主要作广告用的出版物(例如,小册子、散页印刷品、商业目录、同业公会出版的年鉴、旅游宣传品),这类出版物应归入税目49.11。

六、税目49.03所称"儿童图画书",是指以图画为主、文字为辅,供儿童阅览的书籍。

Chapter 49
Printed books, newspapers, pictures and other products of the printing industry; manuscripts, typescripts and plans

Notes:

1. This Chapter does not cover:

(a) Photographic negatives or positives on transparent bases (Chapter 37);

(b) Maps, plans or globes, in relief, whether or not printed (heading No. 90.23);

(c) Playing cards or other goods of Chapter 95; or

(d) Original engravings, prints or lithographs (heading No. 97.02), postage or revenue stamps, stamp-postmarks, first-day covers, postal stationery or the like of heading No. 97.04, antiques of an age exceeding one hundred years or other articles of Chapter 97.

2. For the purposes of Chapter 49, the term "printed" also means reproduced by means of a duplicating machine, produced under the control of an automatic data processing machine, embossed, photographed, photocopied, thermocopied or typewritten.

3. Newspapers, journals and periodicals which are bound otherwise than in paper, and sets of newspapers, journals or periodicals comprising more than one number under a single cover are to be classified in heading No. 49.01, whether or not containing advertising material.

4. Heading No. 49.01 also covers:

(a) A collection of printed reproductions of, for example, works of art or drawings, with a relative text, put up with numbered pages in a form suitable for binding into one or more volumes;

(b) A pictorial supplement accompanying, and subsidiary to, a bound volume; and

(c) Printed parts of books or booklets, in the form of assembled or separate sheets or signatures, constituting the whole or a part of a complete work and designed for binding.

However, printed pictures or illustrations not bearing a text, whether in the form of signatures or separate sheets, fall in heading No. 49.11.

5. Subject to Note 3 to this Chapter, heading No. 49.01 does not cover publications which are essentially devoted to advertising (for example, brochures, pamphlets, leaflets, trade catalogues, year books published by trade associations, tourist propaganda). Such publications are to be classified in heading No. 49.11.

6. For the purposes of heading No. 49.03, the expression "children's picture books" means books for children in which the pictures form the principal interest and the text is subsidiary.

税则号列 Tariff Item.	货 品 名 称	最惠国(%) MFN	协定(%) CT 东盟 CA	中巴 CP	中智 CC	普通 Gen	增值税率 VAT	出口退税 ED	计量单位 Unit	监管条件 SC	Article Description
49.01	**书籍、小册子、散页印刷品及类似印刷品,不论是否单张:**										**Printed books, brochures, leaflets and similar printed matter, whether or not in single sheets:**
4901.1000	-单张的,不论是否折叠	0				0	13	11	千克		-In single sheets, whether or not folded
	-其他:										-Other:
4901.9100	--字典或百科全书及其连续出版的分册	0				0	13	11	千克		--Dictionaries and encyclopaedias, and serial instalments thereof
4901.9900	--其他	0				0	13	11	千克		--Other
49.02	**报纸、杂志及期刊,不论有无插图或广告材料:**										**Newspapers, journals and periodicals, whether or not illustrated or containing advertising material:**
4902.1000	-每周至少出版四次	0				0	13	11	千克		-Appearing at least four times a week
4902.9000	-其他	0				0	13	11	千克		-Other
49.03	**儿童图画书、绘画或涂色书:**										**Children's picture, drawing or colouring books:**
4903.0000	儿童图画书、绘画或涂色书	0				0	13	11	千克		Children's picture, drawing or colouring books
49.04	**乐谱原稿或印本,不论是否装订或印有插图:**										**Music, printed or in manuscript, whether or not bound or illustrated:**
4904.0000	乐谱原稿或印本,不论是否装订或印有插图	0				0	13	11	千克		Music, printed or in manuscript, whether or not bound or illustrated
49.05	**各种印刷的地图、水道图及类似图表,包括地图册、挂图、地形图及地球仪、天体仪:**										**Maps and hydrographic or similar charts of all kinds, including atlases, wall maps, topographical plans and globes, printed:**
4905.1000	-地球仪、天体仪	0				0	17	11	千克		-Globes
	-其他:										-Other:
4905.9100	--成册的	0				0	17	11	千克		--In book form
4905.9900	--其他	0				0	17	11	千克		--Other
49.06	**手绘的建筑、工程、工业、商业、地形或类似用途的设计图纸原稿;手稿;用感光纸照相复印或用复写纸誊写的上述物品复制件:**										**Plans and drawings for architectural, engineering, industrial, commercial, topographical or similar purposes, being originals drawn by hand; hand-written text; photographic reproductions on sensitized paper and carbon copies of the foregoing:**
4906.0000	手绘的建筑、工程、工业、商业、地形或类似用途的设计图纸原稿;手稿;用感光纸照相复印或用复写纸誊写的上述物品复制件	0				0	17	13	千克		Plans and drawings for architectural, engineering, industrial, commercial, topographical or similar purposes, being originals drawn by hand; hand-written text; photographic reproductions on sensitized paper and carbon copies of the foregoing
49.07	**在承认或将承认其面值的国家流通或新发行并且未经使用的邮票、印花税票及类似票证;印有邮票或印花税票的纸品;钞票;空白支票;股票、债券及类似所有权凭证:**										**Unused postage, revenue or similar stamps of current or new issue in the country in which they have, or will have, a recognised face value; stamp-impressed paper; banknotes; cheque forms; stock, share or bond certificates and similar documents of title:**
4907.0010	---邮票	7.5				50	17	13	千克		---Postage
4907.0020	---钞票	0				50	17	13	千克		---Banknotes

税则号列 Tariff Item.	货品名称	最惠国(%) MFN	协定(%)CT 东盟 CA	中巴 CP	中智 CC	普通 Gen	增值税率 VAT	出口退税 ED	计量单位 Unit	监管条件 SC	Article Description
4907.0030	---证券凭证	0				50	17	13	千克		---Documents of title
4907.0090	---其他	7.5				50	17	13	千克		---Other
49.08	**转印贴花纸(移画印花法用图案纸):**										**Transfers (decalcomanias):**
4908.1000	-釉转印贴花纸(移画印花法用图案纸)	7.5				50	17	13	千克		-Transfers (decalcomanias), vitrifiable
4908.9000	-其他	7.5				50	17	13	千克		-Other
49.09	**印刷或有图画的明信片;印有个人问候、祝贺、通告的卡片,不论是否有图画、带信封或饰边:**										**rinted or illustrated postcards; printed cards bearing personal greetings, messages or announcements, whether or not illustrated, with or without envelopes or trimmings:**
4909.0010	---印刷或有图画的明信片	7.5				50	17	13	千克		---Printed or illustrated postcards
4909.0090	---其他	7.5				50	17	13	千克		---Other
49.10	**印刷的各种日历,包括日历芯:**										**Calendars of any kind, printed, including calendar blocks:**
4910.0000	印刷的各种日历,包括日历芯	7.5				50	17	13	千克		Calendars of any kind, printed, including calendar blocks
49.11	**其他印刷品,包括印刷的图片及照片:**										**Other printed matter, including printed pictures and photographs:**
	-商业广告品、商品目录及类似印刷品:										-Trade advertising material, commercial catalogues and the like:
4911.1010	---无商业价值的	0				0	17	13	千克		---No commercial value
4911.1090	---其他	7.5				50	17	13	千克		---Other
	-其他:										-Other:
4911.9100	--图片、设计图样及照片	7.5				50	17	13	千克		--Pictures, designs and photographs
4911.9900	--其他	7.5				50	17	13	千克		--Other

第十一类

纺织原料及纺织制品

注释：

一、本类不包括：

（一）制刷用的动物鬃、毛（税目 05.02）；马毛及废马毛（税目 05.11）；

（二）人发及人发制品（税目 05.01、67.03 或 67.04），但通常用于榨油机或类似机器的滤布除外（税目 59.11）；

（三）第十四章的棉短绒或其他植物材料；

（四）税目 25.24 的石棉、税目 68.12 或 68.13 的石棉制品或其他产品；

（五）税目 30.05 或 30.06 的物品

（六）税目 37.01 至 37.04 的感光布；

（七）截面尺寸超过 1 毫米的塑料单丝和表面宽度超过 5 毫米的塑料扁条及类似品（例如人造草）（第三十九章），以及上述单丝或扁条的缏条、织物、篮筐或柳条编结品（第四十六章）；

（八）第三十九章的用塑料浸渍、涂布、包覆或层压的机织物、针织物或钩编织物、毡呢或无纺织物及其制品；

（九）第四十章的用橡胶浸渍、涂布、包覆或层压的机织物、针织物或钩编织物、毡呢或无纺织物及其制品；

（十）带毛皮张（第四十一章或第四十三章）、税目 43.03 或 43.04 的毛皮制品、人造毛皮及其制品；

（十一）税目 42.01 或 42.02 的用纺织材料制成的物品；

（十二）第四十八章的产品或物品（例如纤维素絮纸）；

（十三）第六十四章的鞋靴及其零件、护腿、裹腿及类似品；

（十四）第六十五章的发网、其他帽类及其零件；

（十五）第六十七章的货品；

（十六）涂有研磨料的纺织材料（税目 68.05）以及税目 68.15 的碳纤维及其制品；

（十七）玻璃纤维及其制品，但可见底布的玻璃线刺绣品除外（第七十章）；

（十八）第九十四章的物品（例如，家具、寝具、灯具及照明装置）；

（十九）第九十五章的物品（例如，玩具、游戏品、运动用品及网具）；

（二十）第九十六章的物品（例如：刷子、旅行用成套缝纫用具、拉链及打字机色带）；

（二十一）第九十七章的物品。

SECTION XI

TEXTILES AND TEXTILE ARTICLES

Notes:

1. This Section does not cover:

(a) Animal brush making bristles or hair (heading No. 05. 02); horsehair or horsehair waste (heading No. 05. 03);

(b) Human hair or articles of human hair (heading No. 05. 01, 67. 03 or 67. 04), except straining cloth of a kind commonly used in oil presses or the like (heading No. 59. 11);

(c) Cotton linters or other vegetable materials of Chapter 14;

(d) Asbestos of heading No. 25. 24 or articles of asbestos or other products of heading No. 68. 12 or 68. 13;

(e) Articles of heading No. 30. 05 or 30. 06;

(f) Sensitized textiles of headings Nos. 37. 01 to 37. 04;

(g) Monofilament of which any cross-sectional dimension exceeds 1mm or strip or the like (for example, artificial straw) of an apparent width exceeding 5mm, of plastics (Chapter 39), or plaits or fabrics or other basketware or wickerwork of such monofilament or strip (Chapter 46);

(h) Woven, knitted or crocheted fabrics, felt or nonwovens, impregnated, coated, covered or laminated with plastics, or articles thereof, of Chapter 39;

(i) Woven, knitted or crocheted fabrics, felt or nonwovens, impregnated, coated, covered or laminated with rubber, or articles thereof, of Chapter 40;

(j) Hides or skins with their hair or wool on (Chapter 41 or 43) or artcles of furskin, artificial fur or articles thereof, of heading No. 43. 03 or 43. 04;

(k) Articles of textile materials of heading No. 42. 01 or 42. 02;

(l) Products or articles of Chapter 48 (for example, cellulose wadding);

(m) Footwear or parts of footwear, gaiters or leggings or similar articles of Chapter 64;

(n) Hair-nets or other headgear or parts thereof of Chapter 65;

(o) Goods of Chapter 67;

(p) Abrasive-coated textile material (Heading No. 68. 05) and also carbon fibres or articles of carbon fibres of heading No. 68. 15;

(q) Glass fibres or articles of glass fibres, other than embroidery with glass thread on a visible ground of fabric (Chapter 70);

(r) Articles of Chapter 94 (for example, furniture, bedding, lamps and lighting fittings);

(s) Articles of Chapter 95 (for example, toys, games, sports requisites and nets);

(t) Articles of Chapter 96 (for example, brushes, travel sets for sewing, slide fasteners and typewriter ribbons); or

(u) Articles of Chapter 97.

二、（一）可归入第五十章至第五十五章及税目58.09或59.02的由两种或两种以上纺织材料混合制成的货品，应按其中重量最大的那种纺织材料归类。

当没有一种纺织材料重量较大时，应按可归入的有关税目中最后一个税目所列的纺织材料归类。

（二）应用上述规定时：

1. 马毛粗松螺旋花线（税目51.10）和含金属纱线（税目56.05）均应作为一种单一的纺织材料，其重量应为它们在纱线中的合计重量；在机织物的归类中，金属线应作为一种纺织材料；

2. 在选择合适的税目时，应首先确定章，然后再确定该章的有关税目，至于不归入该章的其他材料可不予考虑；

3. 当归入第五十四章及第五十五章的货品与其他章的货品进行比较时，应将这两章作为一个单一的章对待；

4. 同一章或同一税目所列各种不同的纺织材料应作为单一的纺织材料对待。

（三）上述（一）、（二）两款规定亦适用于以下注释三、四、五或六所述纱线。

三、（一）本类的纱线（单纱、多股纱线或缆线）除下列（二）款另有规定的以外，凡符合以下规格的应作为“线、绳、索、缆”：

1. 丝或绢丝纱线，细度在20000分特以上；

2. 化学纤维纱线（包括第五十四章的用两根及以上单丝纺成的纱线），细度在10000分特以上；

3. 大麻或亚麻纱线：

（1）加光或上光的，细度在1429分特及以上；

（2）未加光或上光的，细度在20000分特以上；

4. 三股或三股以上的椰壳纤维纱线；

5. 其他植物纤维纱线，细度在20000分特以上；

6. 用金属线加强的纱线。

（二）下列各项不按上述（一）款规定办理：

1. 羊毛或其他动物毛纱线及纸纱线，但用金属线加强的纱线除外；

2. 第五十五章的化学纤维长丝丝束以及第五十四章的未加捻或捻度每米少于5转的复丝纱线；

3. 税目50.06的蚕胶丝及第五十四章的单丝；

2. (A) Goods classifiable in Chapters 50 to 55 or in heading No. 58.09 or 59.02 and of a mixture of two or more textile materials are to be classified as if consisting wholly of that one textile material which predominates by weight over any other single textile material.

When no one textile material predominates by weight, the goods are to be classified as if consisting wholly of that one textile material which is covesed by the heading which occurs last in numerical order among those which equally merit consideration.

(B) For the purposes of the above rule:

(a) Gimped horsehair yarn (heading No. 51.10) and metallized yarn (heading No. 56.05) are to be treated as a single textile material the weight of which is to be taken as the aggregate of the weights of its components; for the classification of woven fabrics, metal thread is to be regarded as a textile material;

(b) The choice of appropriate heading shall be effected by determining first the Chapter and then the applicable heading within that Chapter, disregarding any materials not classified in that Chapter;

(c) When both Chapters 54 and 55 are involved with any other Chapter, Chapters 54 and 55 are to be treated as a single Chapter;

(d) Where a Chapter or a heading refers to goods of different textile materials, such materials are to be treated as a single textile material.

(C) The provisions of paragraphs (A) and (B) above apply also to the yarns referred to in Notes 3, 4, 5 or 6 below.

3. (A) For the purposes of this Section, and subject to the exceptions in paragraph (B) below, yarns (single, multiple (folded) or cabled) of the following descriptions are to be treated as "twine, cordage, ropes and cables":

(a) Of silk or waste silk, measuring more than 20,000 decitex;

(b) Of man-made fibres (including yarn of two or more monofilaments of Chapter 54), measuring more than 10,000 decitex;

(c) Of true hemp or flax:

(Ⅰ) Polished or glazed, measuring 1,429 decitex or more; or

(Ⅱ) Not polished or glazed, measuring more than 20,000 decitex;

(d) Of coir, consisting of three or more plies;

(e) Of other vegetable fibres, measuring more than 20,000 decitex; or

(f) Reinforced with metal thread.

(B) Exceptions:

(a) Yarn of wool or other animal hair and paper yarn, other than yarn reinforced with metal thread;

(b) Man-made filament tow of Chapter 55 and multifilament yarn without twist or with a twist of less than 5 turns per metre of Chapter 54;

(c) Silk worm gut of heading No. 50.06, and monofilaments of Chapter 54;

4. 税目56.05的含金属纱线;但用金属线加强的纱线按上述(一)款6项规定办理;

5. 税目56.06的绳绒线、粗松螺旋花线及纵行起圈纱线。

四、(一)除下列(二)款另有规定的以外,第五十章、第五十一章、第五十二章、第五十四章和第五十五章所称"供零售用"纱线,是指以下列方式包装的纱线(单纱、股纱线或缆线):

1. 绕于纸板、线轴、纱管或类似芯子上,其重量(含线芯)符合下列规定:

(1)丝、绢丝或化学纤维长丝纱线,不超过85克;

(2)其他纱线,不超过125克。

2. 绕成团、绞或束,其重量符合下列规定:

(1)细度在3000分特以下的化学纤维长丝纱线,丝或绢丝纱线,不超过85克;

(2)细度在2000分特以下的任何其他纱线,不超过125克;

(3)其他纱线,不超过500克。

3. 绕成绞或束,每绞或每束中有若干用线分开的小绞或小束,每小绞或小束的重量相等,并且符合下列规定:

(1)丝、绢丝或化学纤维长丝纱线,不超过85克;

(2)其他纱线,不超过125克。

(二)下列各项不按上述(一)款规定办理:

1. 各种纺织材料制的单纱,但下列两种除外:

(1)未漂白的羊毛或动物细毛单纱;

(2)漂白、染色或印色的羊毛或动物细毛单纱,细度在5000分特以上。

2. 未漂白的多股纱线或缆线:

(1)丝或绢丝制的,不论何种包装;

(2)除羊毛或动物细毛外其他纺织材料制,成绞或成束的。

3. 漂白、染色或印色丝或绢丝制的多股纱线或缆线,细度在133分特及以下;

4. 任何纺织材料制的单纱、多股纱线或缆线:

(1)交叉绕成绞或束的;

(2)绕于纱芯上或以其他方式卷绕,明显用于纺织工业的(例如,绕于纱管、加捻管、纬纱管、锥形筒管或锭子上的或者绕成蚕茧状以供绣花机使用的纱线)。

五、税目52.04、54.01及55.08所称"缝纫线",是指下列多股纱线或缆线:

(一)绕于芯子(例如,线轴、纱管)上,重量(包括纱芯)不超过1000克;

(二)作为缝纫线上过浆的;

(三)终捻为反手(Z)捻的。

(d) Metallized yarn of Heading No. 56. 05; yarn reinforced with metal thread is subject to paragraph (A) (f) above; and

(e) Chenille yarn, gimped yarn and loop wale-yarn of heading 56. 06.

4. (A) For the purposes of Chapters 50, 51, 52, 54 and 55, the expression "put up for retail sale" in relation to yarn means, subject to the exceptions in paragraph (B) below, yarn (single, multiple (folded) or cabled) put up:

(a) On cards, reels, tubes or similar supports, of a weight (including support) not exceeding:

(Ⅰ) 85g in the case of silk, waste silk or man-made filament yarn; or

(Ⅱ) 125g in other cases;

(b) In balls, hanks or skeins of a weight not exceeding:

(Ⅰ) 85g in the case of man-made filament yarn of less than 3, 000 decitex, silk or silk waste;

(Ⅱ) 125g in the case of all other yarns of less than 2, 000 decitex; or

(Ⅲ) 500g in other cases;

(c) In hanks or skeins comprising several smaller hanks or skeins separated by dividing threads which render them independent one of the other, each of uniform weight not exceeding:

(Ⅰ) 85g in the case of silk, waste silk or man-made filament yarn; or

(Ⅱ) 125g in other cases.

(B) Exceptions:

(a) Single yarn of any textile material, except:

(Ⅰ) Single yarn of wool or fine animal hair, unbleached; and

(Ⅱ) Single yarn of wool or fine animal hair, bleached, dyed or printed, measuring more than 5, 000 decitex;

(b) Multiple (folded) or cabled yarn, unbleached:

(Ⅰ) Of silk or waste silk, however put up; or

(Ⅱ) Of other textile material except wool or fine animal hair, in hanks or skeins;

(c) Multiple (folded) or cabled yarn of silk or waste silk, bleached, dyed or printed, measuring 133 decitex or less; and

(d) Single, multiple (folded) or cabled yarn of any textile material:

(Ⅰ) In cross-reeled hanks or skeins; or

(Ⅱ) Put up on supports or in some other manner indicating its use in the textile industry (for example, on cops, twisting mill tubes, pirns, conical bobbins or spindles, or reeled in the form of cocoons for embroidery looms).

5. For the purposes of headings Nos. 52. 04, 54. 01 and 55. 08 the expression "sewing thread" means multiple (folded) or cabled yarn:

(a) Put up on supports (for example, reels, tubes) of a weight (including support) not exceeding 1, 000g;

(b) Dressed for use as sewing thread; and

(c) With a final "Z" twist.

六、本类所称“高强力纱”，是指断裂强度大于下列标准的纱线：

尼龙、其他聚酰胺或聚酯制的单纱—60 厘牛顿/特克斯；

尼龙、其他聚酰胺或聚酯制的多股纱线或缆线—53 厘牛顿/特克斯；

粘胶纤维制的单纱、多股纱线或缆线—27 厘牛顿/特克斯。

七、本类所称“制成的”，是指：

(一)裁剪成除正方形或长方形以外的其他形状的；

(二)呈制成状态，无需缝纫或其他进一步加工(或仅需剪断分隔联线)即可使用的(例如，某些抹布、毛巾、台布、方披巾、毯子)；

(三)已缝边或滚边，或者在任一边带有结制的流苏，但不包括为防止剪边脱纱而锁边或用其他简单方法处理的织物；

(四)裁剪成一定尺寸并经抽纱加工的；

(五)缝合、胶合或用其他方法拼合而成的(将两段或两段以上同样料子的织物首尾连接而成的匹头，以及由两层或两层以上的织物，不论中间有无胎料，层迭而成的匹头除外)；

(六)针织或钩编成一定形状，不论进口或出口时是单件还是以若干件相连成幅的。

八、对于第五十章至第六十章：

(一)第五十章至第五十五章和第六十章，以及除条文另有规定以外的第五十六章至第五十九章，不适用于上述注释七所规定的制成货品；

(二)第五十章至第五十五章及第六十章不包括第五十六章至第五十九章的货品。

九、第五十章至第五十五章的机织物包括由若干层平行纱线以锐角或直角相互层迭，在纱线交叉点用粘合剂或以热粘合法粘合而成的织物。

十、用纺织材料和橡胶线制成的弹性产品归入本类。

十一、本类所称“浸渍”，包括“浸泡”。

十二、本类所称“聚酰胺”，包括“芳族聚酰胺”。

十三、本类及本目录所称“弹性纱线”是指合成纤维纺织材料制成的长丝纱线(包括单丝变形纱线除外)。这些纱线可拉伸至原长的三倍而不断裂，并可在拉伸至原长两倍后五分钟内回复到不超过原长度一倍半。

十四、除条文另有规定的以外，各种服装即使成套包装供零售用，也应按各自税目分别归类。本注释所称“纺织服装”，是指税目 61.01 至 61.14 及税目 62.01 至 62.11 所列的各种服装。

6. For the purposes of this Section, the expression “high tenacity yarn” means yarn having a tenacity, expressed in cN/tex (centinewtons per tex), greater than the following:

Single yarn of nylon or other polyamides, or of polyesters 60 cN/tex

Multiple (folded) or cabled yarn of nylon or other polyamides, or of polyesters 53 cN/tex

Single, multiple (folded) or cabled yarn of viscose rayon 27 cN/tex

7. For the purposes of this Section, the expression “made up” means:

(a) Cut otherwise than into squares or rectangles;

(b) Produced in the finished state, ready for use (or merely needing separation by cutting dividing threads) without sewing or other working (for example, certain dusters, towels, table cloths, scarf squares, blankets);

(c) Hemmed or with rolled edges, or with a knotted fringe at any of the edges, but excluding fabrics the cut edges of which have been prevented from unravelling by whipping or by other simple means;

(d) Cut to size and having undergone a process of drawn thread work;

(e) Assembled by sewing, gumming or otherwise (other than piece goods consisting of two or more lengths of identical material joined end to end and piece goods composed of two or more textiles assembled in layers, whether or not padded);

(f) Knitted or crocheted to shape, whether presented as separate items or in the form of a number of items in the length.

8. For the purposes of Chapters 50 to 60:

(a) Chapters 50 to 55 and 60 and, except where the context otherwise requires, Chapters 56 to 59 do not apply to goods made up within the meaning of Note 7 above; and

(b) Chapters 50 to 55 and 60 do not apply to goods of Chapters 56 to 59.

9. The woven fabrics of Chapters 50 to 55 include fabrics consisting of layers of parallel textile yarns superimposed on each other at acute or right angles. These layers are bonded at the intersections of the yarns by an adhesive or by thermal bonding.

10. Elastic products consisting of textile materials combined with rubber threads are classified in this Section.

11. For the purposes of this Section, the expression “impregnated” includes “dipped”.

12. For the purposes of this Section, the expression “polyamides” includes “aramides”.

13. Throughout the section and Nomenclature “elastomeric yarn” Filament yarn, including monofilament, of synthetic textile material, other than textured yarn, which does not break on being extended to three times its original length and which returns, after being extended to twice its original length, within a period of five minutes, to a length not greater than one and a half times its original length.

14. Unless the context otherwise requires, textile garments of different headings are to be classified in their own headings even if put up in sets for retail sale. For the purposes of this Note, the expression “textile garments” means garments of headings Nos. 61.01 to 61.14 and headings Nos. 62.01 to 62.11.

子目注释：

一、本类及本目录所用有关名词解释如下：

（一）未漂白纱线

1. 带有纤维自然色泽并且未经漂染（不论是否整体染色）或印色的纱线；

2. 从回收纤维制得，色泽未定的纱线（本色纱）。

这种纱线可用无色浆料或易褪色染料（可轻易地用肥皂洗去）处理，如果是化学纤维纱线，则整体用消光剂（例如二氧化钛）进行处理。

（二）漂白纱线

1. 经漂白加工、用漂白纤维制得或经染白（除条文另有规定的以外）（不论是否整体染色）及用白浆料处理的纱线；

2. 用未漂白纤维和漂白纤维混纺制得的纱线；

3. 用未漂白纱和漂白纱纺成多股纱线或缆线。

（三）着色（染色或印色）纱线

1. 染成彩色（不论是否整体染色，但白色或易褪色除外）或印色的纱线，以及用染色或印色纤维纺制的纱线；

2. 用各色染色纤维混合纺制或用未漂白或漂白纤维与着色纤维混合制得的纱线（夹色纱或混色纱），以及用一种或几种颜色间隔印色而获得点纹印迹的纱线；

3. 用已经印色的纱条或粗纱纺制的纱线；

4. 用未漂白纱和漂白纱与着色纱纺成的多股纱线或缆线。

上述定义作相应调整后适用于第五十四章的单丝、扁条或类似产品。

（四）未漂白机织物

用未漂白纱线织成后未经漂白、染色或印花的机织物。这类织物可用无色浆料或易褪色染料处理。

（五）漂白机织物

1. 经漂白、染白或用白浆料处理（除条文另有规定的以外）的成匹机织物；

2. 用漂白纱线织成的机织物；

3. 用未漂白纱线和漂白纱线织成的机织物；

（六）染色机织物

1. 除条文另有规定的以外，染成白色以外的其他单一颜色或用白色以外的其他有色整理剂处理的成匹机织物；

2. 用单一颜色的着色纱线织成的机织物。

Subheading Notes:

1. In the Section and, where applicable, throughout the Nomenclature, the following expressions have the meanings hereby assigned to them:

(a) Unbleached yarn Yarn which:

(Ⅰ) has the natural colour of its constituent fibres and has not been bleached, dyed (whether or not in the mass) or printed; or

(Ⅱ) is of indeterminate colour ("grey yarn"), manufactured from garnetted stock.

Such yarn may have been treated with a colourless dressing or fugitive dye (which disappears after simple washing with soap) and, in the case of man-made fibres, treated in the mass with delustring agent (for example, titanium dioxide).

(b) Bleached yarn Yarn which:

(Ⅰ) has undergone a bleaching process, is made of bleached fibres or, unless the context otherwise requires, has been dyed white (whether or not in the mass) or treated with a white dressing;

(Ⅱ) consists of a mixture of unbleached and bleached fibres; or

(Ⅲ) is multiple (folded) or cabled and consists of unbleached and bleached yarns.

(c) Coloured (dyed or printed) yarn Yarn which:

(Ⅰ) is dyed (whether or not in the mass) other than white or in a fugitive colour, or printed, or made from dyed or printed fibres;

(Ⅱ) consists of a mixture of dyed fibres of different colours or of a mixture of unbleached or bleached fibres with coloured fibres (marl or mixture yarns), or is printed in one or more colours at intervals to give the impression of dots;

(Ⅲ) is obtained from slivers or rovings which have been printed; or

(Ⅳ) is multiple (folded) or cabled and consists of unbleached or bleached yarn and coloured yarn.

The above definitions also apply, *mutatis mutandis*, to monofilament and to strip or the like of Chapter 54.

(d) Unbleached woven fabric

Woven fabric made from unbleached yarn and which has not been bleached, dyed or printed. Such fabric may have treated with a colourless dressing or a fugitive dye.

(e) Bleached woven fabric Woven fabric which:

(Ⅰ) has been bleached or, unless the context otherwise requires, dyed white or treated with a white dressing, in the piece;

(Ⅱ) consists of bleached yarn; or

(Ⅲ) consists of unbleached and bleached yarn.

(f) Dyed woven fabric Woven fabric which:

(Ⅰ) is dyed a single uniform colour other than white (unless the context otherwise requires) or has been treated with a coloured finish other than white (unless the context otherwise requires), in the piece; or

(Ⅱ) consists of coloured yarn of a single uniform colour.

（七）色织机织物

除印花机织物以外的下列机织物：

1. 用各种不同颜色纱线或同一颜色不同深浅（纤维的自然色彩除外）纱线织成的机织物；
2. 用未漂白或漂白与着色纱线织成的机织物；
3. 用夹色纱线或混色纱线织成的机织物。

不论何种情况，布边或布头的纱线均可忽略不计。

（八）印花机织物

成匹印花的机织物，不论是否用各色纱线织成。

用刷子或喷枪，经转印纸转印、植绒或蜡防印花等方法印成花纹图案的机织物亦可视为印花机织物。

上述各类纱线或织物如经丝光工艺处理并不影响其归类。

上述（五）至（九）的定义在作必要修改后适用于针织或钩编织物。

（九）平纹织物

每根纬纱在并排的经纱间上下交错而过，而每根经纱也在并排的纬纱间上下交错而过的织物组织。

二、（一）含有两种或两种以上纺织材料的第五十六章至第六十三章的产品，应根据本类注释二对第五十章至第五十五章或税目58.09的此类纺织材料产品归类的规定来确定归类。

（二）运用本条规定时：

1. 应酌情考虑按归类总规则第三条来确定归类
2. 对由底布和绒面或毛圈面构成的纺织品，在归类时可不考虑底布的属性
3. 对税目58.10的刺绣品及其制品，归类时应只考虑底布的属性，但不见底布的刺绣品及其制品应根据绣线的属性确定归类。

(g) Woven fabric of yarns of different colours

Woven fabric (other than printed woven fabric) which:

(Ⅰ) consists of yarns of different colours or yarns of different shades of the same colour (other than the natural colour of the constituent fibres);

(Ⅱ) consists of unbleached or bleached yarn and coloured yarn; or

(Ⅲ) consists of marl or mixture yarns.

(In all cases, the yarn used in selvedges and piece ends is not taken into consideration.)

(h) Printed woven fabric

Woven fabric which has been printed in the piece, whether or not made from yarns of differenent colours. (The following are also regarded as printed woven fabrics: woven fabrics bearing designs made, for example, with a brush or spray gun, by means of transfer paper, by flocking or by the batik process.)

The process of mercerization does not affect the classification of yarns or fabrics within the above categories.

The definitions at (e) to (ij) above apply, *mutatis mutandis*, to knitted or crocheted fabrics.

(i) Plain weave

A fabric construction in which each yarn of the weft passes alternately over and under successive yarns of the warp and each yarn of the warp passes alternately over and under successive yarns of the weft.

2. (A) Products of Chapters 56 to 63 containing two or more textile materials are to be regarded as consisting wholly of that textile material which would be selected under Note 2 to this Section for the classification of the product of Chapters 50 to 55 or of heading No. 58.09 consisting of the same textile materials.

(B) For the application of this rule:

(a) where appropriate, only the part which determines the classification under interpretative Rule 3 shall be taken into account;

(b) in the case of textile products consisting of a ground fabric and a pile or looped surface, no account shall be taken of the ground fabric;

(c) in the case of embroidery of heading No. 58.10 and goods thereof, only the ground fabric shall be taken into account. However, embroidery without visible ground, and goods thereof, shall be classified with reference to the embroidering threads alone.

第五十章 蚕 丝

Chapter 50 Silk

税则号列 Tariff Item.	货 品 名 称	最惠国(%) MFN	协定(%) CT 东盟 CA	中巴 CP	中智 CC	普通 Gen	增值税率 VAT	出口退税 ED	计量单位 Unit	监管条件 SC	Article Description
50.01	**适于缫丝的蚕茧:**										**Silk-worm cocoons suitable for reeling:**
5001.0010	---适于缫丝的桑蚕茧	6	5		0	70	17	5	千克	4xABy	---Bombyx mori cocoons (Mulberry feeding silk-worm cocoons)
5001.0090	---其他	6	5		0	70	17	5	千克	A4xBy	---Other
50.02	**生丝(未加捻):**										**Raw silk (not thrown):**
	---桑蚕丝:										---Steam filature silk:
5002.0011	----厂丝	9	T3		0	80	17	13	千克	A4xBy	----Plant reeled (filature silk)
5002.0012	----土丝	9	T3		0	80	17	13	千克	A4xBy	----Home reeled
5002.0013	----双宫丝	9	T3		0	80	17	13	千克	A4xBy	----Doupion
5002.0019	----其他	9	T3		0	80	17	13	千克	A4xBy	----Other
5002.0020	---柞蚕丝	9	T3		0	80	17	13	千克	A4xBy	---Tussah silk
5002.0090	---其他	9	T3		0	80	17	13	千克	A4xBy	---Other
50.03	**废丝(包括不适于缫丝的蚕茧、废纱及回收纤维):**										**Silk waste (including cocoons unsuitable for reeling, yarn waste and garnetted stock):**
5003.0010	---未梳	9	5		0	70	17	13	千克	A4xBy	---Not carded or combed
5003.0090	---其他	9	5		0	70	17	13	千克	A4xBy	---Other
50.04	**丝纱线(绢纺纱线除外),非供零售用:**										**Silk yarn (other than yarn spun from silk waste) not put up for retail sale:**
5004.0000	丝纱线(绢纺纱线除外),非供零售用	6	T3		0	90	17	11	千克	B	Silk yarn (other than yarn spun from silk waste) not put up for retail sale
50.05	**绢纺纱线,非供零售用:**										**Yarn spun from silk waste, not put up for retail sale:**
5005.0010	---䌷丝纱线	6	5		0	90	17	11	千克		---Spun from noil
5005.0010 10	非供零售用䌷丝纱线(䌷丝为主,含丝及绢丝85%及以上纱线)	6				90	17	11	千克		Spun from noil silk, not put up for retail sale, containing≥85% by weight of silk or silk waste
5005.0010 90	非供零售用䌷丝纱线(䌷丝为主,含丝及绢丝85%以下纱线)	6				90	17	11	千克		Spun from noil silk, not put up for retail sale, containing < 85% by weight of silk or silk waste
5005.0090	---其他	6	5		0	90	17	11	千克		---Other
5005.0090 10	非供零售用其他绢纺纱线(含丝及绢丝85%及以上纱线)	6				90	17	11	千克	B	Other yarn spun from silk waste, not put up for retail sale, containing ≥ 85% by weight of silk or silk waste
5005.0090 20	非供零售用其他绢纺纱线(含丝及绢丝85%以下纱线)	6				90	17	11	千克	B	Other yarn spun from silk waste, not put up for retail sale, containing < 85% by weight of silk or silk waste
50.06	**丝纱线及绢纺纱线,供零售用;蚕胶丝:**										**Silk yarn and yarn spun from silk waste, put up for retail sale; silk-worm gut:**
5006.0000	丝纱线及绢纺纱线,供零售用;蚕胶丝	6	5		0	100	17	11	千克		Silk yarn and yarn spun from silk waste, put up for retail sale; silk-worm gut
5006.0000 10	零售用丝纱线,绢纺纱线;蚕胶丝(含丝及绢丝85%及以上纱线)	6				100	17	11	千克		Silk yarn and yarn spun from silk waste, put up for retail sale; silk-worm gut, containing≥85% by weight of silk or silk waste

税则号列 Tariff Item.	货品名称	最惠国(%) MFN	协定(%)CT 东盟 CA	中巴 CP	中智 CC	普通 Gen	增值税率 VAT	出口退税 ED	计量单位 Unit	监管条件 SC	Article Description
5006.0000 20	零售用丝纱线,绢纺纱线;蚕胶丝(含丝及绢丝85%以下纱线)	6				100	17	11	千克		Silk yarn and yarn spun from silk waste, put up for retail sale; silk-worm gut, containing <85% by weight of silk or silk waste
50.07	**丝或绢丝机织物:**										**Woven fabrics of silk or of silk waste:**
	-䌷丝机织物:										-Fabrics of noil silk:
5007.1010	---未漂白(包括未练白或练白)或漂白	10	5		0	130	17	11	米/千克		---Unbleached (unscoured or scoured) or bleached
5007.1010 10	未漂白或漂白的䌷丝机织物(包括未练白或练白的,含䌷丝85%及以上)	10				130	17	11	米/千克	B	Woven fabrics of noil silk, unbleached (unscoured or scoured) or bleached, containing≥85% by weight of noil silk
5007.1010 20	未漂白或漂白的䌷丝机织物(包括未练白或练白的,含䌷丝85%以下,棉或化纤限内)	10				130	17	11	米/千克	B	Woven fabrics of noil silk, unbleached (unscoured or scoured) or bleached, containing < 85% by weight of noil silk, cotton or man-made fibres within limitations
5007.1010 31	未漂白或漂白的䌷丝机织物(含未练或练白,䌷丝<85%与精梳羊毛\动物细毛混纺,羊毛限内)	10				130	17	11	米/千克	B	Woven fabrics of noil silk, unbleached (unscoured or scoured) or bleached, containing < 85% by weight of noil silk, mixed with combed wool or combed fine animal hair, wool within limitations
5007.1010 39	未漂白或漂白的䌷丝机织物(未练白或练白的,含䌷丝85%以下,与其他混纺,羊毛限内)	10				130	17	11	米/千克	B	Woven fabrics of noil silk, unbleached (unscoured or scoured) or bleached, containing < 85% by weight of noil silk, mixed with other fibres, wool within limitations
5007.1010 91	未漂白或漂白的䌷丝机织物(未练白或练白的,含䌷丝<85%与精梳羊毛或动物细毛混纺)	10				130	17	11	米/千克	B	Woven fabrics of noil silk, unbleached (unscoured or scoured) or bleached, containing < 85% by weight of noil silk, mixed with combed wool or combed fine animal hair
5007.1010 99	未漂白或漂白的䌷丝机织物(包括未练白或练白的,含䌷丝85%以下,与其他混纺)	10				130	17	11	米/千克	B	Woven fabrics of noil silk, unbleached (unscoured or scoured) or bleached, containing < 85% by weight of noil silk, mixed with other fibres
5007.1090	---其他	10	5		0	130	17	11	米/千克		---Other
5007.1090 10	其他䌷丝机织物(含䌷丝85%及以上)	10				130	17	11	米/千克	B	Other woven fabrics of noil silk, containing ≥85% by weight of noil silk
5007.1090 21	其他色织䌷丝机织物(含䌷丝85%以下,棉或化纤限内)	10				130	17	11	米/千克	B	Other woven fabrics of noil silk, containing <85% by weight of noil silk, coloured, cotton or man-made fibres within limitations
5007.1090 29	其他非色织䌷丝机织物(含䌷丝85%以下,棉或化纤限内)	10				130	17	11	米/千克	B	Other woven fabrics of noil silk, containing <85% by weight of noil silk, not coloured, cotton or man-made fibres within limitations

税则号列 Tariff Item.	货品名称	最惠国(%) MFN	协定(%) CT 东盟 CA	中巴 CP	中智 CC	普通 Gen	增值税率 VAT	出口退税 ED	计量单位 Unit	监管条件 SC	Article Description
5007.1090 31	其他䌷丝机织物(含䌷丝85%以下,与精梳羊毛或动物细毛混纺,羊毛限内)	10				130	17	11	米/千克	B	Other woven fabrics of noil silk, containing < 85% by weight of noil silk, mixed with combed wool or combed fine animal hair, wool within limitations
5007.1090 39	其他䌷丝机织物(含䌷丝85%以下,与其他混纺,羊毛限内)	10				130	17	11	米/千克	B	Other woven fabrics of noil silk, containing <85% by weight of noil silk, mixed with other fibres, wool within limitations
5007.1090 91	其他䌷丝机织物(含䌷丝85%以下,与精梳羊毛或动物细毛混纺)	10				130	17	11	米/千克	B	Other woven fabrics of noil silk, containing <85% by weight of noil silk, mixed with combed wool or combed fine animal hair
5007.1090 99	其他䌷丝机织物(含䌷丝85%以下,与其他混纺)	10				130	17	11	米/千克	B	Other woven fabrics of noil silk, containing <85% by weight of noil silk, mixed with other fibres
	-其他机织物,按重量计丝或绢丝(䌷丝除外)含量在85%及以上:										-Other woven fabrics, containing 85% or more by weight of silk or waste other than noil silk:
	---桑蚕丝机织物:										---Of Bombyx mori silk:
5007.2011	----未漂白(包括未练白或练白)或漂白	10	5	9	0	130	17	11	米/千克	B	----Unbleached (unscoured or scoured) or bleached
5007.2019	----其他	10	5	9	0	130	17	11	米/千克	B	----Other
	---柞蚕丝机织物:										---Of tussah silk:
5007.2021	----未漂白(包括未练白或练白)或漂白	10	5	9	0	130	17	11	米/千克	B	----Unbleached (unscoured or scoured) or bleached
5007.2029	----其他	10	5	9	0	130	17	11	米/千克	B	----Other
	---绢丝机织物:										---Of silk waste other than noil silk:
5007.2031	----未漂白(包括未练白或练白)或漂白	10	5	9	0	130	17	11	米/千克	B	----Unbleached (unscoured or scoured) or bleached
5007.2039	----其他	10	5	9	0	130	17	11	米/千克	B	----Other
5007.2090	---其他	10	5	9	0	130	17	11	米/千克		---Other
5007.2090 10	未漂白或漂白其他丝机织物(包括未练白或练白,按重量计丝或绢丝含量在85%及以上)	10				130	17	11	米/千克	B	Other woven fabrics of silk, unbleached (unscoured or scoured) or bleached, containing≥85% by weight of silk and silk waste
5007.2090 90	其他丝机织物(按重量计丝或绢丝含量在85%及以上)	10				130	17	11	米/千克	B	Other woven fabrics of silk, containing≥85% by weight of silk and silk waste
	-其他机织物:										-Other fabrics:
5007.9010	---未漂白(包括未练白或练白)或漂白	10	5	8.5	0	130	17	11	米/千克		---Unbleached (unscoured or scoured) or bleached
5007.9010 10	未漂白或漂白其他丝机织物(包括未练白或练白,含丝及绢丝85%及以上)	10				130	17	11	米/千克	B	Other woven fabrics of silk, unbleached (unscoured or scoured) or bleached, containing≥85% by weight of silk and spun silk
5007.9010 20	未漂白或漂白其他丝机织物(含未练白或练白,丝及绢丝<85%与其他混纺,棉或化纤限内)	10				130	17	11	米/千克	B	Other woven fabrics of silk, unbleached (unscoured or scoured) or bleached, containing <85% by weight of silk and spun silk, mixed, cotton or man-made fibres within limitations

税则号列 Tariff Item.	货品名称	最惠国(%) MFN	协定(%)CT 东盟 CA	中巴 CP	中智 CC	普通 Gen	增值税率 VAT	出口退税 ED	计量单位 Unit	监管条件 SC	Article Description
5007.9010 31	未漂白或漂白其他丝机织物(未练或练白,丝及绢丝<85%,与精梳羊毛\动物细毛混纺,羊毛限内)	10				130	17	11	米/千克	B	Other woven fabrics of silk, unbleached (unscoured or scoured) or bleached, containing <85% by weight of silk and spun silk, mixed with combed wool or combed fine animals hair, wool within limitations
5007.9010 39	未漂白或漂白其他丝机织物(未练白或练白,含丝及绢丝<85%,与其他混纺,羊毛限内)	10				130	17	11	米/千克	B	Other woven fabrics of silk, unbleached (unscoured or scoured) or bleached, containing <85% by weight of silk and spun silk, mixed, wool within limitations
5007.9010 91	未漂白或漂白其他丝机织物(未练白或练白,丝及绢丝<85%,与精梳羊毛或动物细毛混纺)	10				130	17	11	米/千克	B	Other woven fabrics of silk, unbleached (unscoured or scoured) or bleached, containing <85% by weight of silk and spun silk, mixed with combed wool or combed fine animals hair
5007.9010 99	未漂白或漂白其他丝机织物(未练白或练白,含丝及绢丝85%以下,与其他混纺)	10				130	17	11	米/千克	B	Other woven fabrics of silk, unbleached (unscoured or scoured) or bleached, containing <85% by weight of silk and spun silk, mixed with other fibres
5007.9090	---其他	10	5	8.5	0	130	17	11	米/千克		---Other
5007.9090 10	其他丝机织物(含丝及绢丝85%及以上)	10				130	17	11	米/千克	B	Other woven fabrics of silk, containing ≥85% by weight of silk and spun silk
5007.9090 21	其他色织丝机织物(含丝及绢丝85%以下,与其他混纺,棉或化学纤维限内)	10				130	17	11	米/千克	B	Other woven fabrics of silk, containing <85% by weight of silk and spun silk, coloured, mixed, cotton or man-made fibres within limitations
5007.9090 29	其他非色织丝机织物(含丝及绢丝85%以下,与其他混纺,棉或化学纤维限内)	10				130	17	11	米/千克	B	Other woven fabrics of silk, containing <85% by weight of silk and spun silk, not coloured, mixed, cotton or man-made within limitations
5007.9090 31	其他丝机织物(含丝及绢丝<85%以下,与精梳羊毛或动物细毛混纺,羊毛限内)	10				130	17	11	米/千克	B	Other woven fabrics of silk, containing <85% by weight of silk and spun silk, mixed with combed wool or combed fine animal hair, wool within limitations
5007.9090 39	其他丝机织物(含丝及绢丝85%以下,与其他混纺,羊毛限内)	10				130	17	11	米/千克	B	Other woven fabrics of silk, containing <85% by weight of silk and spun silk, mixed, wool within limitations
5007.9090 91	其他丝机织物(含丝及绢丝85%以下,与精梳羊毛或动物细毛混纺)	10				130	17	11	米/千克	B	Other woven fabrics of silk, containing <85% by weight of silk and spun silk, mixed with combed wool or combed fine animal hair
5007.9090 99	其他丝机织物(含丝及绢丝85%以下,与其他混纺)	10				130	17	11	米/千克	B	Other woven fabrics of silk, containing <85% by weight of silk and spun silk, mixed

第五十一章
羊毛、动物细毛或粗毛；马毛纱线及其机织物

Chapter 51
Wool, fine or coarse animal hair; horsehair yarn and woven fabric

注释：

本目录所称：

一、"羊毛"，是指绵羊或羔羊身上长的天然纤维；

二、"动物细毛"，是指下列动物的毛：羊驼、美洲驼、驼马、骆驼（包括单峰骆驼）、牦牛、安哥拉山羊、西藏山羊、喀什米尔山羊及类似山羊（普通山羊除外）、家兔（包括安哥拉兔）、野兔、海狸、河狸鼠或麝鼠；

三、"动物粗毛"，是指以上未提及的其他动物的毛，但不包括制刷用鬃、毛（税目05.02）以及马毛（税目05.11）。

Notes:

1. Throughout the Nomenclature:
   1. "Wool" means the natural fibre grown by sheep or lambs;
   2. "Fine animal hair" means the hair of alpaca, llama, vicuna, camel, (including dromedary) yak, Angora, Tibetan, Kashmir or similar goats (but not common goats), rabbit (including Angora rabbit), hare, beaver, nutria or muskrat;
   3. "Coarse animal hair" means the hair of animals not mentioned above, excluding brush-making hair and bristles (heading No. 05.02) and horsehair (heading No. 05.11).

税则号列 Tariff Item.	货品名称	最惠国(%) MFN	协定(%) 东盟 CA	中巴 CP	CT 中智 CC	普通 Gen	增值税率 VAT	出口退税 ED	计量单位 Unit	监管条件 SC	Article Description
51.01	未梳的羊毛：										**Wool, not carded or combed:**
	-含脂羊毛，包括剪前水洗毛：										-Greasy, including fleece-washed woo:
5101.1100	--剪羊毛	*38				*50	13	5	千克		--Shorn wool
5101.1100 01	未梳的含脂剪羊毛（配额内）	1				50	13	5	千克	tAB	Greasy shorn wool, not carded or combeb, in-quota
5101.1100 90	未梳的含脂剪羊毛（配额外）	38				50	13	5	千克	AB	Greasy shorn wool, not carded or combeb, out-quota
5101.1900	--其他	*38				*50	13	5	千克		--Other
5101.1900 01	未梳的其他含脂羊毛（配额内）	1				50	13	5	千克	tAB	Other greasy wool, not carded or combeb, in-quota
5101.1900 90	未梳的其他含脂羊毛（配额外）	38				50	13	5	千克	AB	Other greasy wool, not carded or combeb, out-quota
	-脱脂羊毛，未碳化：										-Degreased, not carbonized:
5101.2100	--剪羊毛	*38				*50	17	13	千克		--Shorn wool
5101.2100 01	未梳的脱脂剪羊毛（未碳化）（配额内）	1				50	17	13	千克	tAB	Degreased shorn wool, not carded or combeb, not carbonized, in-quota
5101.2100 90	未梳的脱脂剪羊毛（未碳化）（配额外）	38				50	17	13	千克	AB	Degreased shorn wool, not carded or combeb, not carbonized, out-quota
5101.2900	--其他	*38				*50	17	13	千克		--Other
5101.2900 01	未梳的其他脱脂羊毛（未碳化）（配额内）	1				50	17	13	千克	tAB	Other degreased wool, not carded or combeb, not carbonized, in-quota
5101.2900 90	未梳的其他脱脂羊毛（未碳化）（配额外）	38				50	17	13	千克	AB	Other degreased wool, not carded or combeb, not carbonized, out-quota
5101.3000	-碳化羊毛	*38				*50	17	13	千克		-Carbonized
5101.3000 01	未梳碳化羊毛（配额内）	1				50	17	13	千克	tAB	Carbonized wool, not carded or combeb, in-quota
5101.3000 90	未梳碳化羊毛（配额外）	38				50	17	13	千克	AB	Carbonized wool, not carded or combeb, qut-quota
51.02	未梳的动物细毛或粗毛：										**Fine or coarse animal hair, not carded or combed:**
	-细毛：										-Fine animal hair:
5102.1100	--喀什米尔山羊的	9	5		0	45	17		千克	AB	--Of Kashmir(cashmere) goats
	--其他：										--Other:
5102.1910	---兔毛	9	5		0	50	17	5	千克		---Of rabbit and hare

税则号列 Tariff Item.	货品名称	最惠国(%) MFN	协定(%) CT			普通 Gen	增值税率 VAT	出口退税 ED	计量单位 Unit	监管条件 SC	Article Description
			东盟 CA	中巴 CP	中智 CC						
5102.1910 10	未梳濒危兔毛	9				50	17	5	千克	ABFE	Fine or coarse animal hair, not carded or combed of rabbit and hare in imminent dangers
5102.1910 90	其他未梳兔毛	9				50	17	5	千克	AB	Other fine or coarse animal hair, not carded or combed of rabbit and hare
5102.1920	---其他山羊绒	9	5		0	45	17		千克	AB	---Of other goats
5102.1930	---骆驼毛、骆驼绒	9	5		0	45	17	5	千克		---Of camel
5102.1930 10	未梳濒危野生骆驼科动物毛、绒	9				45	17	5	千克	FEAB	Fine or coarse animal hair, not carded or combed of wild camel in imminent dangers
5102.1930 90	其他未梳骆驼毛、绒	9				45	17	5	千克	AB	Other fine or coarse animal hair, not carded or combed of camel
5102.1990	---其他	9	5		0	45	17	5	千克		---Other
5102.1990 10	未梳的其他濒危野生动物细毛	9				45	17	5	千克	FEAB	Fine hair of wild animals in imminent dangers, not carded or combeb
5102.1990 90	未梳的其他动物细毛	9				45	17	5	千克	AB	Fine hair of other animals, not carded or combeb
5102.2000	-粗毛	9	5		0	50	17	5	千克		-Coarse animal hair
5102.2000 10	未梳的濒危野生动物粗毛	9				50	17	5	千克	FEAB	Coarse hair of wild animals in imminent dangers, not carded or combeb
5102.2000 90	未梳的其他动物粗毛	9				50	17	5	千克	AB	Coarse hair of other animals, not carded or combeb
51.03	**羊毛或动物细毛或粗毛的废料,包括废纱线,但不包括回收纤维:**										**Waste of wool or of fine or coarse animal hair, including yarn waste but excluding garnetted stock:**
	-羊毛及动物细毛的落毛:										-Noils of wool or of fine animal hair:
5103.1010	---羊毛落毛	*38				*50	17	5	千克		---Of wool
5103.1010 01	羊毛落毛(配额内)	1				50	17	5	千克	tAB	Noils of wool, in-quota
5103.1010 90	羊毛落毛(配额外)	38				50	17	5	千克	AB	Noils of wool, out-quota
5103.1090	---其他	9	5		0	50	17	5	千克		---Other
5103.1090 10	其他濒危野生动物细毛的落毛	9				50	17	5	千克	FEAB	Other noils of fine hair of wild animal in imminent dangers
5103.1090 90	其他动物细毛的落毛	9				50	17	5	千克	AB	Other noils of fine hair of wild animal
	-羊毛或动物细毛的其他废料:										-Other waste of wool or of fine animal hair:
5103.2010	---羊毛废料	13.5	8		10.8	20	17	5	千克	AB	---Of wool
5103.2090	---其他	9	5		0	50	17	5	千克		---Other
5103.2090 10	其他濒危野生动物细毛废料(包括废纱线,不包括回收纤维)	9				50	17	5	千克	FEAB	Other waste of fine hair if wild animal in imminent dangers, including yarn waste but excluding garnetted stock
5103.2090 90	其他动物细毛废料(包括废纱线,不包括回收纤维)	9				50	17	5	千克	AB	Other waste of fine hair of other animal, including yarn waste but excluding garnetted stock
5103.3000	-动物粗毛废料	9	5		0	50	17	5	千克		-Waste of coarse animal hair
5103.3000 10	濒危野生动物粗毛废料(包括废纱线,不包括回收纤维)	9				50	17	5	千克	FEAB	Waste of coarse hair of wild animal, including yarn waste but excluding garnetted stock
5103.3000 90	其他动物粗毛废料(包括废纱线,不包括回收纤维)	9				50	17	5	千克	AB	Other waste of coarse hair of animal, including yarn waste but excluding garnetted stock

税则号列 Tariff Item.	货品名称	最惠国(%) MFN	协定(%)CT 东盟 CA	中巴 CP	中智 CC	普通 Gen	增值税率 VAT	出口退税 ED	计量单位 Unit	监管条件 SC	Article Description
51.04	羊毛或动物细毛或粗毛的回收纤维:										**Garnetted stock of wool or of fine or coarse animal hair:**
5104.0010	---羊毛的回收纤维	15	8		0	20	17	5	千克	AB	---Of wool
5104.0090	---其他	5			0	50	17	13	千克		---Other
5104.0090 10	其他濒危野生动物细毛(包括粗毛回收纤维)	5				50	17	13	千克	FEAB	Garnetted stock of fine or coarse hair of wild animal in imminent dangers
5104.0090 90	其他动物细毛或粗毛的回收纤维	5				50	17	13	千克	AB	Other of fine or coarse animal hair
51.05	已梳的羊毛及动物细毛或粗毛(包括精梳片毛):										**Wool and fine or coarse animal hair, carded or combed (including combed wool in fragments):**
5105.1000	-粗梳羊毛	*38				*50	17	13	千克		-Carded wool
5105.1000 01	粗梳羊毛(配额内)	3				50	17	13	千克	tAB	Carded wool, in-quota
5105.1000 90	粗梳羊毛(配额外)	38				50	17	13	千克	AB	Carded wool, out-quota
	-羊毛条及其他精梳羊毛:										-Wool tops and other combed wool:
5105.2100	--精梳片毛	*38				*50	17	13	千克		--Combed wool in fragments
5105.2100 01	精梳羊毛片毛(配额内)	3				50	17	13	千克	tAB	Combed wool in fragments, in-quota
5105.2100 90	精梳羊毛片毛(配额外)	38				50	17	13	千克	AB	Combed wool in fragments, out-quota
5105.2900	--其他	*38				*50	17	13	千克		--Other
5105.2900 01	羊毛条及其他精梳羊毛(配额内)	3				50	17	13	千克	tAB	Wool tops and other combed wool, in-quota
5105.2900 90	羊毛条及其他精梳羊毛(配额外)	38				50	17	13	千克	AB	Wool tops and other combed wool, out-quota
	-已梳动物细毛:										-Fine animal hair, carded or combed:
5105.3100	--喀什米尔山羊的	5			0	50	17		千克	AB	--Of Kashmir(cashmere) goats
	--其他:										--Other:
5105.3910	---兔毛	5			0	70	17	13	千克		---Of rabbit or hare
5105.3910 10	已梳濒危兔毛	5				70	17	13	千克	ABFE	Fine animal hair, carded or combed of rabbit and hare in imminent dangers
5105.3910 90	其他已梳兔毛	5				70	17	13	千克	AB	Other fine animal hair, carded or combed of rabbit and hare
	---其他山羊绒:										---Of other goats:
5105.3921	----无毛山羊绒	5			0	50	17		千克	AB	----Dehaired goats wool
5105.3929	----其他	5			0	50	17		千克	AB	----Other
5105.3990	---其他	5			0	50	17	13	千克		---Other
5105.3990 10	其他已梳野生动物细毛	5				50	17	13	千克	ABEF	Other fine hair of wild animals, carded or combed
5105.3990 90	其他已梳动物细毛	5				50	17	13	千克	AB	Other fine hair of animals, carded or combed
5105.4000	-已梳动物粗毛	5			0	50	17	13	千克		-Coarse animal hair, carded or combed
5105.4000 10	其他已梳濒危野生动物粗毛	5				50	17	13	千克	FEAB	Other coarse hair of wild animals, carded or combed
5105.4000 90	其他已梳动物粗毛	5				50	17	13	千克	AB	Other coarse hair of animals, carded or combed
51.06	**粗梳羊毛纱线,非供零售用:**										**Yarn of carded wool, not put up for retailsale:**
5106.1000	-按重量计羊毛含量在85%及以上	5			0	70	17	11	千克	A	-Containing 85% or more by weight of wool
5106.2000	-按重量计羊毛含量在85%以下	5			0	70	17	11	千克		-Containing less than 85% by weight of wool

税则号列 Tariff Item.	货品名称	最惠国(%) MFN	协定(%) CT 东盟 CA	中巴 CP	中智 CC	普通 Gen	增值税率 VAT	出口退税 ED	计量单位 Unit	监管条件 SC	Article Description
51.07	**精梳羊毛纱线,非供零售用:**										**Yarn of combed wool, not put up for retail sale:**
5107.1000	-按重量计羊毛含量在85%及以上	5		2.5	0	70	17	11	千克	A	-Containing 85% or more by weight of wool
5107.2000	-按重量计羊毛含量在85%以下	5			0	70	17	11	千克	A	-Containing less than 85% by weight of wool
51.08	**动物细毛(粗梳或精梳)纱线,非供零售用:**										**Yarn of fine animal hair (carded or combed), not put up for retailsale:**
5108.1000	-粗梳	5		4.3	0	70	17	11	千克		-Carded
5108.1000 10	非供零售用粗梳濒危动物细毛纱线	5				70	17	11	千克	FE	Yarn of fine hair of animals in imminent dangers, carded not put up for retailsale
5108.1000 90	其他非供零售用粗梳动物细毛纱线	5				70	17	11	千克		Yarn of fine hair of animal carded not put up for retailsale
5108.2000	-精梳	5			0	70	17	11	千克		-Combed
5108.2000 10	非供零售用精梳濒危动物细毛纱线	5				70	17	11	千克	FE	Yarn of fine hair of animal in imminent dangers, combed not put up for retail-sale
5108.2000 90	其他非供零售用精梳动物细毛纱线	5				70	17	11	千克		Yarn of fine hair of animal combed not put up for retailsale
51.09	**羊毛或动物细毛的纱线,供零售用:**										**Yarn of wool or of fine animal hair, put up for retail sale:**
5109.1000	-按重量计羊毛或动物细毛含量在85%及以上	6	5		0	80	17	11	千克		-Containing 85% or more by weight of wool or of fine animal hair
5109.9000	-其他	6	5		0	80	17	11	千克		-Other
51.10	**动物粗毛或马毛的纱线(包括马毛粗松螺旋花线),不论是否供零售用:**										**Yarn of coarse animal hair or of horse-hair (including gimped horsehair yarn), whether or not put up for retail sale:**
5110.0000	动物粗毛或马毛的纱线(包括马毛粗松螺旋花线),不论是否供零售用	6	5		0	70	17	11	千克		Yarn of coarse animal hair or of horsehair (including gimped horsehair yarn), wheth-er or not put up for retail sale
5110.0000 10	濒危动物粗毛的纱线(包括马毛粗松螺旋花线,不论是否供零售用)	6				70	17	11	千克	FE	Yarn of coarse animal hair (including gimped horsehair yarn), whether or not put up for retail sale, in imminent dan-gers
5110.0000 90	其他动物粗毛或马毛的纱线(包括毛马粗松螺旋花线,不论是否供零售用)	6				70	17	11	千克		Other yarn of coarse animal hair or of horsehair (including gimped horsehair yarn), whether or not put up for retail sale
51.11	**粗梳羊毛或粗梳动物细毛的机织物:**										**Woven fabrics of carded wool or of carded fine animal hair:**
	-按重量计羊毛或动物细毛含量在85%及以上:										-Containing 85% or more by weight of wool or of fine animal hair:
5111.1100	--每平方米重量不超过300克	10	8	8.5	0	130	17	11	米/千克		--Of a weight not exceeding 300 g/m^2
5111.1100 11	每平米重≤140克提花/装饰家具布(与粗梳羊毛或动物细毛混纺,含粗梳羊毛或动物细毛≥85%)	10				130	17	11	米/千克		Jacquard/decorative, w ≤ 140g/m^2, mixed with combed wool and fine animal hair, containing≥85% by weight of car-ded wool or of carded fine animal hair

税则号列 Tariff Item.	货品名称	最惠国(%) MFN	协定(%) CT 东盟 CA	中巴 CP	中智 CC	普通 Gen	增值税率 VAT	出口退税 ED	计量单位 Unit	监管条件 SC	Article Description
5111.1100 19	每平米重≤140克提花/装饰家具布(与其他混纺,含粗梳羊毛或动物细毛≥85%)	10				130	17	11	米/千克		Jacquard/decorative, $w \leq 140g/m^2$, mixed with other animal hair, containing≥85% by weight of carded wool or of carded fine animal hair
5111.1100 91	每平米重≤300克其他机织物(与粗梳羊毛或动物细毛混纺,含粗梳羊毛或动物细毛≥85%)	10				130	17	11	米/千克		Other woven fabrics, $w \leq 300g/m^2$, mixed with combed wool and fine animal hair, containing≥85% by weight of carded wool or of carded fine animal hair
5111.1100 99	每平米重≤300克其他机织物(与其他混纺,含粗梳羊毛或动物细毛≥85%)	10				130	17	11	米/千克		Other woven fabrics, $w \leq 300g/m^2$, mixed with other animal hair, containing≥85% by weight of carded wool or of carded fine animal hair
5111.1900	--其他	10	8	8.5	0	130	17	11	米/千克		--Other
5111.1900 11	每平米重>300克提花/装饰家具布(与粗梳羊毛或动物细毛混纺,羊毛或动物细毛含量≥85%)	10				130	17	11	米/千克		Jacquard/decorative, $w > 300g/m^2$, mixed with combed wool and fine animal hair, containing≥85% by weight of wool and fine animal hair
5111.1900 19	每平米重>300克提花/装饰家具布(与其他混纺,羊毛或动物细毛含量≥85%)	10				130	17	11	米/千克		Jacquard/decorative, $w > 300g/m^2$, mixed with other animal hair, containing≥85% by weight of wool and fine animal hair
5111.1900 91	每平米重>300克其他全毛机织物(与粗梳羊毛或动物细毛混纺,羊毛或动物细毛含量≥85%)	10				130	17	11	米/千克		Other woven fabrics, $w > 300g/m^2$, containing 100% by weight of combed wool or fine animal hair, mixed with combtd wool or fine animal hair, containing≥85% by weight of wool and fine animal hair
5111.1900 99	每平米重>300克其他全毛机织物(与其他混纺,羊毛或动物细毛含量≥85%)	10				130	17	11	米/千克		Other woven fabrics, $w > 300g/m^2$, containing 100% by weight of wool or fine animal hair, mixed with other animal hari, containing≥85% by weight of wool and fine animal hair
5111.2000	-其他,主要或仅与化学纤维长丝混纺	10	8		0	130	17	11	米/千克		-Other, mixed mainly or solely with man-made filaments
5111.2000 10	与化纤长丝混纺提花/装饰家具布(重量≤140克/平米或>300克/平米,羊毛或动物细毛含<85%)	10				130	17	11	米/千克		Jacquard/decorative, $w \leq 140g/m^2$, or $w > 300g/m^2$, mixed with man-made filaments, containing<85% by weight of wool and fine animal hair
5111.2000 90	与化纤长丝混纺其他粗梳毛机织物(羊毛或动物细毛含量<85%)	10				130	17	11	米/千克		Other woven fabrics of carded wool or of carded animal hair, mixed with man-made filaments, containing<85% by weight of wool and fine animal hair
5111.3000	-其他,主要或仅与化学纤维短纤混纺	10	8	8.5	0	130	17	11	米/千克		-Other, mixed mainly or solely with man-made staple fibres

税则号列 Tariff Item.	货品名称	最惠国(%) MFN	协定(%) 东盟 CA	中巴 CP	CT 中智 CC	普通 Gen	增值税率 VAT	出口退税 ED	计量单位 Unit	监管条件 SC	Article Description
5111.3000 10	与化纤短纤混纺提花/装饰家具布(重量≤140克/平米或>300克/平米,含羊毛或动物细毛<85%)	10				130	17	11	米/千克		Jacquard/decorative, w≤140g/m^2 or w >300g/m^2, mixed with man-made filaments, containing <85% by weight of wool and fine animal hair
5111.3000 90	与化纤短纤混纺其他粗梳毛机织物(羊毛或动物细毛含量<85%)	10				130	17	11	米/千克		Other woven fabrics of carded wool or of carded fine animal hair, mixed with man-made staple fibres, containing <85% by weight of wool and fine animal hair
5111.9000	-其他	10	8		0	130	17	11	米/千克		-Other
5111.9000 11	其他丝与粗梳羊毛或动物细毛混纺(丝及绢丝≥30%,含粗梳羊毛或动物细毛<85%,价值>$33/kg)	10				130	17	11	米/千克		Other woven fabrics, mixed with silk and combed wool or of fine animal hair, containing≥30% by weight of silk and silk waste, containing <85% by weight of carded wool or of carded fine animal hair, value >USD 33/K
5111.9000 19	其他丝混纺机织物(丝及绢丝≥30%,含粗梳羊毛或动物细毛<85%,价值>$33/kg)	10				130	17	11	米/千克		Other woven fabrics, mixed with silk, containing≥30% by weight of silk and silk waste, containing <85% by weight of carded wool or of fine animal hair, value >USD 33/K
5111.9000 21	其他毛混纺提花/装饰家具布(粗梳羊毛或动物细毛<85%,重量≤140克/平米或>300克/平米)	10				130	17	11	米/千克		Jacquard/decorative, mixed with wool or animals hair, w≤140g/m^2 or w >300g/m^2, containing <85% by weight of combed wool or of fine animal hair
5111.9000 29	其他毛混纺提花/装饰家具布(含粗梳羊/动物细毛<85%,重量≤140克/平米或>300克/平米)	10				130	17	11	米/千克		Other jacquard/decorative, mixed with wool or animal hair, containing <85% by weight of carded wool or of fine animal hair, w≤140g/m^2 or w >300g/m^2
5111.9000 91	其他机织物(与粗梳羊毛或动物细毛混纺,含粗梳羊毛或动物细毛<85%)	10				130	17	11	米/千克		Other woven fabrics, mixed with combed wool or fine animal hair, containing < 85% by weight of carded wool or of fine animal hair
5111.9000 99	其他机织物(与其他混纺,含粗梳羊毛或动物细毛<85%)	10				130	17	11	米/千克		Other woven fabrics, mixed, containing <85% by weight of carded wool or of fine animal hair
51.12	**精梳羊毛或精梳动物细毛的机织物:**										**Woven fabrics of combed wool or of combed fine animal hair:**
	-按重量计羊毛或动物细毛含量在85%及以上:										-Containing 85% or more by weight of wool or of fine animal hair:
5112.1100	--每平方米重量不超过200克	10	8	5		130	17	11	米/千克		--Of a weight not exceeding 200 g/m^2
5112.1100 10	重≤140克平米毛提花/装饰家具布(精梳羊毛或动物细毛含量≥85%)	10				130	17	11	米/千克		Jacquard/decorative, w ≤ 140g/m^2, containing≥85% by weight of combed wool or of fine animal hair
5112.1100 90	其他重量≤200克/平米毛制机织物(精梳羊毛或动物细毛含量≥85%)	10				130	17	11	米/千克		Other wool woven fabrics, w ≤ 200g/m^2, containing ≥ 85% by weight of combed wool or of fine animal hair

税则号列 Tariff Item.	货品名称	最惠国(%) MFN	协定(%) 东盟 CA	中巴 CP	CT 中智 CC	普通 Gen	增值税率 VAT	出口退税 ED	计量单位 Unit	监管条件 SC	Article Description
5112.1900	--其他	10	T3	5	0	130	17	11	米/千克		--Other
5112.1900 10	重>200克平米毛提花/装饰家具布(精梳羊毛或动物细毛含量≥85%)	10				130	17	11	米/千克		Jacquard/decorative, w > 200g/m², containing≥85% by weight of combed wool or of fine animal hair
5112.1900 90	重量>200克/平米其他毛制机织物(精梳羊毛或动物细毛含量≥85%)	10				130	17	11	米/千克		Other wool woven fabrics, w > 200g/m², containing ≥ 85% by weight of combed wool or of fine animal hair
5112.2000	-其他,主要或仅与化学纤维长丝混纺	10	8		0	130	17	11	米/千克		-Other, mixed mainly or solely with man-made filaments
5112.2000 10	与化纤长丝混纺毛制提花/家具布(精梳羊毛/动物细毛含量≤85%,重≤140g/平米或>300g/平米)	10				130	17	11	米/千克		Jacquard/decorative, w≤140g/m² or w >300g/m², mixed with man-made filaments, containing < 85% by weight of combed wool or of fine animal hair
5112.2000 90	与化纤长丝混纺其他毛制机织物(精梳羊毛或动物细毛含量≤85%)	10				130	17	11	米/千克		Other wool woven fabrics, mixed with man-made filaments, containing < 85% by weight of combed wool or of fine animal hair
5112.3000	-其他,主要或仅与化学纤维短纤混纺	10	8		0	130	17	11	米/千克		-Other, mixed mainly or solely with man-made staple fibres
5112.3000 10	与化纤短纤混纺毛制提花/家具布(精梳羊/动物细毛含量≤85%,重≤140g/平米或>300g/平米)	10				130	17	11	米/千克		Jacquard/decorative, mixed with man-made staple fibres, containing<85% by weight of combed wool or of fine animal hair, w≤140g/m² or w>300g/m²
5112.3000 90	与化纤短纤混纺其他毛制机织物(精梳羊毛或动物细毛含量≤85%)	10				130	17	11	米/千克		Other wool woven fabrics, mixed with man-made staple fibres, containing < 85% by weight of combed wool or of fine animal hair
5112.9000	-其他	10	8		0	130	17	11	米/千克		-Other
5112.9000 10	其他丝与毛混纺机织物(含精梳羊毛或动物细毛<85%,丝及绢丝≥30%,价值>$33/kg)	10				130	17	11	米/千克		Other woven fabrics, mixed with silk and wool or animal hair, containing < 85% by weight of combed wool or of fine animal hair, containing≥30% by weight of silk and spun silk, value>USD 33/K
5112.9000 20	其他精梳毛制提花/装饰家具布(含羊毛或动物细毛<85%,重量≤140g/平米或>300g/平米)	10				130	17	11	米/千克		Other jacquard/decorative of combed hair, containing < 85% by weight of wool or fine animal hair, w≤140g/m² or w>300g/m²
5112.9000 90	其他机织物(精梳羊毛或动物细毛<85%)	10				130	17	11	米/千克		Other woven fabrics, containing < 85% by weight of combed wool or of fine animal hair
51.13	**动物粗毛或马毛的机织物:**										**Woven fabrics of coarse animal hair or of horsehair:**
5113.0000	动物粗毛或马毛的机织物	10	8		0	130	17	11	米/千克		Woven fabrics of coarse animal hair or of horsehair

第五十二章 棉 花

Chapter 52 Cotton

子目注释：

子目 5209.42 及 5211.42 所称“粗斜纹布（劳动布）”，是指用不同颜色的纱线织成的三线或四线斜纹织物，包括破斜纹组织的织物，这种织物以经纱为面，经纱染成一种相同的颜色，纬纱未漂白或经漂白、染成灰色或比经纱稍浅的颜色。

Subheading Note:

For the purposes of subheadings Nos. 5209.42 and 5211.42, the expression “denim” means fabrics of yarns of different colours, of 3-thread or 4-thread twill, including broken twill, warp faced, the warp yarns of which are of one and the same colour and the weft yarns of which are unbleached, bleached, dyed grey or coloured a lighter shade of the colour of the warp yarns.

税则号列 Tariff Item.	货品名称	最惠国(%) MFN	协定(%) CT 东盟 CA	中巴 CP	中智 CC	普通 Gen	增值税率 VAT	出口退税 ED	计量单位 Unit	监管条件 SC	Article Description
52.01	**未梳的棉花：**										**Cotton, not carded or combed:**
5201.0000	未梳的棉花	*40				*125	13	13	千克		Cotton, not carded or combed
5201.0000 01	未梳的棉花[包括脱脂棉花（配额内）]	1				125	13	13	千克	t4xAB	Cotton, not carded or combed, including absorbent cotton, in-quota
5201.0000 08	未梳的棉花[包括脱脂棉花（关税配额外暂定）]	0				0	13	13	千克	4ABex	Cotton, not carded or combed, including absorben cotton (custom, out – guota, interim)
5201.0000 90	未梳的棉花[包括脱脂棉花（配额外）]	40				125	13	13	千克	4xAB	Cotton, not carded or combed, including absorbent cotton, out-quota
52.02	**废棉（包括废棉纱线及回收纤维）：**										**Cotton waste (including yarn waste and garnetted stock):**
5202.1000	-废棉纱线（包括废棉线）	10	T3		0	30	17	13	千克	AP	-Yarn waste (including thread waste)
	-其他：										-Other:
5202.9100	--回收纤维	10	T3		0	30	17	13	千克	AB	--Garnetted stock
5202.9900	--其他	10	8		0	30	17	11	千克	ABP	--Other
52.03	**已梳的棉花：**										**Cotton, carded or combed:**
5203.0000	已梳的棉花	*40				*125	17	13	千克		Cotton, carded or combed
5203.0000 01	已梳的棉花（配额内）	1				125	17	13	千克	t4xAB	Cotton, carded or combed, in-quota
5203.0000 90	已梳的棉花（配额外）	40				125	17	13	千克	4xAB	Cotton, carded or combed, out-quota
52.04	**棉制缝纫线，不论是否供零售用：**										**Cotton sewing thread, whether or not put up for retail sale:**
	-非供零售用：										-Not put up for retail sale:
5204.1100	--按重量计含棉量在85%及以上	5			0	40	17	13	千克	5	--Containing 85% or more by weight of cotton
5204.1900	--其他	5			0	40	17	13	千克	5	--Other
5204.2000	-供零售用	5			0	50	17	13	千克	5	-Put up for retail sale
52.05	**棉纱线（缝纫线除外），按重量计含棉量在85%及以上，非供零售用：**										**Cotton yarn (other than sewing thread), containing 85% or more by weight of cotton, not put up for retail sale:**
	-未精梳纤维纺制的单纱：										-Single yarn, of uncombed fibres:
5205.1100	--细度在714.29分特及以上（不超过14公支）	5	T3	3.5	0	40	17	11	千克	B	--Measuring 714.29 decitex or more (not exceeding 14 metric number)
5205.1200	--细度在714.29分特以下，但不细于232.56分特（超过14公支，但不超过43公支）	5	T3	3.5	0	40	17	11	千克	B	--Measuring less than 714.29 decitex but not less than 232.56 decitex (exceeding 14 metric number but not exceeding 43 metric number)

税则号列 Tariff Item.	货品名称	最惠国(%) MFN	协定(%) CT 东盟 CA	协定(%) CT 中巴 CP	协定(%) CT 中智 CC	普通 Gen	增值税率 VAT	出口退税 ED	计量单位 Unit	监管条件 SC	Article Description
5205.1300	--细度在232.56分特以下,但不细于192.31分特(超过43公支,但不超过52公支)	5		3.5	0	40	17	11	千克	B	--Measuring less than 232.56 decitex but not less than 192.31 decitex (exceeding 43 metric number but not exceeding 52 metric number)
5205.1400	--细度在192.31分特以下,但不细于125分特(超过52公支,但不超过80公支)	5	T3	3.5	0	40	17	11	千克	B	--Measuring less than 192.31 decitex but not less than 125 decitex (exceeding 52 metric number but not exceeding 80 metric number)
5205.1500	--细度在125分特以下(超过80公支)	5		3.5	0	40	17	11	千克	B	--Measuring less than 125 decitex (exceeding 80 metric number)
	-精梳纤维纺制的单纱:										-Single yarn, of combed fibres:
5205.2100	--细度在714.29分特及以上(不超过14公支)	5	T3	3.5	0	40	17	11	千克	5B	--Measuring 714.29 decitex or more (not exceeding 14 metric number)
5205.2200	--细度在714.29分特以下,但不细于232.56分特(超过14公支,但不超过43公支)	5		3.5	0	40	17	11	千克	5B	--Measuring less than 714.29 decitex but not less than 232.56 decitex (exceeding 14 metric number but not exceeding 43 metric number)
5205.2300	--细度在232.56分特以下,但不细于192.31分特(超过43公支,但不超过52公支)	5		3.5	0	40	17	11	千克	5B	--Measuring less than 232.56 decitex but not less than 192.31 decitex (exceeding 43 metric number but not exceeding 52 metric number)
5205.2400	--细度在192.31分特以下,但不细于125分特(超过52公支,但不超过80公支)	5	T3	3.5	0	40	17	11	千克	5B	--Measuring less than 192.31 decitex but not less than 125 decitex (exceeding 52 metric number but not exceeding 80 metric number)
5205.2600	--细度在125分特以下,但不细于106.38分特(超过80公支,但不超过94公支)	5			0	40	17	11	千克	5B	--Measuring less than 125 decitex but not less than 106.38 decitex (exceeding 80 metric number but not exceeding 94 metric number)
5205.2700	--细度在106.38分特以下,但不细于83.33分特(超过94公支,但不超过120公支)	5			0	40	17	11	千克	5B	--Measuring less than 106.38 decitex but not less than 83.33 decitex (exceeding 94 metric number but not exceeding 120 metric number)
5205.2800	--细度在83.33分特以下(超过120公支)	5			0	40	17	11	千克	5B	--Measuring less than 83.33 decitex (exceeding 120 metric number)
	-未精梳纤维纺制的多股纱线或缆线:										-Multiple (folded) or cabled yarn, of uncombed fibres:
5205.3100	--每根单纱细度在714.29分特及以上(每根单纱不超过14公支)	5		4.5	0	40	17	11	千克		--Measuring per single yarn 714.29 decitex or more (not exceeding 14 metric number per single yarn)
5205.3200	--每根单纱细度在714.29分特以下,但不细于232.56分特(每根单纱超过14公支,但不超过43公支)	5		3.5	0	40	17	11	千克		--Measuring per single yarn less than 714.29 decitex but not less than 232.56 decitex (exceeding 14 metric number but not exceeding 43 metric number per single yarn)

税则号列 Tariff Item.	货 品 名 称	最惠国(%) MFN	协定(%) CT			普通 Gen	增值税率 VAT	出口退税 ED	计量单位 Unit	监管条件 SC	Article Description
			东盟 CA	中巴 CP	中智 CC						
5205.3300	--每根单纱细度在232.56分特以下,但不细于192.31分特(每根单纱超过43公支,但不超过52公支)	5			0	40	17	11	千克		--Measuring per single yarn less than 232.56 decitex but not less than 192.31 decitex (exceeding 43 metric number but not exceeding 52 metric number per single yarn)
5205.3400	--每根单纱细度在192.31分特以下,但不细于125分特(每根单纱超过52公支,但不超过80公支)	5			0	40	17	11	千克		--Measuring per single yarn less than 192.31 decitex but not less than 125 decitex (exceeding 52 metric number but not exceeding 80 metric number per single yarn)
5205.3500	--每根单纱细度在125分特以下(每根单纱超过80公支)	5			0	40	17	11	千克		--Measuring per single yarn less than 125 decitex (exceeding 80 metric number per single yarn)
	-精梳纤维纺制的多股纱线或缆线:										-Multiple (folded) or cabled yarn, of combed fibres:
5205.4100	--每根单纱细度在714.29分特及以上(每根单纱不超过14公支)	5		4.5	0	40	17	11	千克	5	--Measuring per single yarn 714.29 decitex or more (not exceeding 14 metric number per single yarn)
5205.4200	--每根单纱细度在714.29分特以下,但不细于232.56分特(每根单纱超过14公支,但不超过43公支)	5		3.5	0	40	17	11	千克	5	--Measuring per single yarn less than 714.29 decitex but not less than 232.56 decitex (exceeding 14 metric number but not exceeding 43 metric number per single yarn)
5205.4300	--每根单纱细度在232.56分特以下,但不细于192.31分特(每根单纱超过43公支,但不超过52公支)	5			0	40	17	11	千克	5	--Measuring per single yarn less than 232.56 decitex but not less than 192.31 decitex (exceeding 43 metric number but not exceeding 52 metric number per single yarn)
5205.4400	--每根单纱细度在192.31分特以下,但不细于125分特(每根单纱超过52公支,但不超过80公支)	5			0	40	17	11	千克	5	--Measuring per single yarn less than 192.31 decitex but not less than 125 decitex (exceeding 52 metric number but not exceeding 80 metric number per single yarn)
5205.4600	--每根单纱细度在125分特以下,但不细于106.38分特(每根单纱超过80公支,但不超过94公支)	5		4.5	0	40	17	11	千克	5	--Measuring per single yarn less than 125 decitex but not less than 106.38 decitex (exceeding 80 metric number but not exceeding 94 metric number per single yarn)
5205.4700	--每根单纱细度在106.38分特以下,但不细于83.33分特(每根单纱超过94公支,但不超过120公支)	5		4.5	0	40	17	11	千克	5	--Measuring per single yarn less than 106.38 decitex but not less than 83.33 decitex (exceeding 94 metric number but not exceeding 120 metric number per single yarn)
5205.4800	--每根单纱细度在83.33分特以下(每根单纱超过120公支)	5		4.5	0	40	17	11	千克	5	--Measuring per single yarn less than 83.33 decitex (exceeding 120 metric number per single yarn)
52.06	**棉纱线(缝纫线除外),按重量计含棉量在85%以下,非供零售用:**										**Cotton yarn (other than sewing thread), containing less than 85% by weight of cotton, not put up for retail sale:**
	-未精梳纤维纺制的单纱:										-Single yarn, of uncombed fibres:

税则号列 Tariff Item.	货品名称	最惠国(%) MFN	协定(%)CT 东盟 CA	中巴 CP	中智 CC	普通 Gen	增值税率 VAT	出口退税 ED	计量单位 Unit	监管条件 SC	Article Description
5206.1100	--细度在714.29分特及以上(不超过14公支)	5		3.5	0	40	17	11	千克	B	--Measuring 714.29 decitex or more (not exceeding 14 metric number)
5206.1200	--细度在714.29分特以下,但不细于232.56分特(超过14公支,但不超过43公支)	5		3.5	0	40	17	11	千克	B	--Measuring less than 714.29 decitex but not less than 232.56 decitex (exceeding 14 metric number but not exceeding 43 metric number)
5206.1300	--细度在232.56分特以下,但不细于192.31分特(超过43公支,但不超过52公支)	5			0	40	17	11	千克	B	--Measuring less than 232.56 decitex but not less than 192.31 decitex (exceeding 43 metric number but not exceeding 52 metric number)
5206.1400	--细度在192.31分特以下,但不细于125分特(超过52公支,但不超过80公支)	5			0	40	17	11	千克	B	--Measuring less than 192.31 decitex but not less than 125 decitex (exceeding 52 metric number but not exceeding 80 metric number)
5206.1500	--细度在125分特以下(超过80公支)	5		3.5	0	40	17	11	千克	B	--Measuring less than 125 decitex (exceeding 80 metric number)
	-精梳纤维纺制的单纱:										-Single yarn, of combed fibres:
5206.2100	--细度在714.29分特及以上(不超过14公支)	5		4.5	0	40	17	11	千克	5B	--Measuring 714.29 decitex or more (not exceeding 14 metric number)
5206.2200	--细度在714.29分特以下,但不细于232.56分特(超过14公支,但不超过43公支)	5			0	40	17	11	千克	5B	--Measuring less than 714.29 decitex but not less than 232.56 decitex (exceeding 14 metric number but not exceeding 43 metric number)
5206.2300	--细度在232.56分特以下,但不细于192.31分特(超过43公支,但不超过52公支)	5			0	40	17	11	千克	5B	--Measuring less than 232.56 decitex but not less than 192.31 decitex (exceeding 43 metric number but not exceeding 52 metric number)
5206.2400	--细度在192.31分特以下,但不细于125分特(超过52公支,但不超过80公支)	5			0	40	17	11	千克	5B	--Measuring less than 192.31 decitex but not less than 125 decitex (exceeding 52 metric number but not exceeding 80 metric number)
5206.2500	--细度在125分特以下(超过80公支)	5			0	40	17	11	千克	5B	--Measuring less than 125 decitex (exceeding 80 metric number)
	-未精梳纤维纺制的多股纱线或缆线:										-Multiple (folded) or cabled yarn, of uncombed fibres:
5206.3100	--每根单纱细度在714.29分特及以上(每根单纱不超过14公支)	5			0	40	17	11	千克		--Measuring per single yarn 714.29 decitex or more (not exceeding 14 metric number per single yarn)
5206.3200	--每根单纱细度在714.29分特以下,但不细于232.56分特(每根单纱超过14公支,但不超过43公支)	5			0	40	17	11	千克		--Measuring per single yarn less than 714.29 decitex but not less than 232.56 decitex (exceeding 14 metric number but not exceeding 43 metric number per single yarn)
5206.3300	--每根单纱细度在232.56分特以下,但不细于192.31分特(每根单纱超过43公支,但不超过52公支)	5			0	40	17	11	千克		--Measuring per single yarn less than 232.56 decitex but not less than 192.31 decitex (exceeding 43 metric number but not exceeding 52 metric number per single yarn)

税则号列 Tariff Item.	货品名称	最惠国(%) MFN	协定(%)CT 东盟 CA	中巴 CP	中智 CC	普通 Gen	增值税率 VAT	出口退税 ED	计量单位 Unit	监管条件 SC	Article Description
5206.3400	--每根单纱细度在192.31分特以下,但不细于125分特(每根单纱超过52公支,但不超过80公支)	5			0	40	17	11	千克		--Measuring per single yarn less than 192.31 decitex but not less than 125 decitex (exceeding 52 metric number but not exceeding 80 metric number per single yarn)
5206.3500	--每根单纱细度在125分特以下(每根单纱超过80公支)	5			0	40	17	11	千克		--Measuring per single yarn less than 125 decitex (exceeding 80 metric number per single yarn)
	-精梳纤维纺制的多股纱线或缆线:										-Multiple (folded) or cabled yarn, of combed fibres:
5206.4100	--每根单纱细度在714.29分特及以上(每根单纱不超过14公支)	5			0	40	17	11	千克	5	--Measuring per single yarn 714.29 decitex or more (not exceeding 14 metric number per single yarn)
5206.4200	--每根单纱细度在714.29分特以下,但不细于232.56分特(每根单纱超过14公支,但不超过43公支)	5			0	40	17	11	千克	5	--Measuring per single yarn less than 714.29 decitex but not less than 232.56 decitex (exceeding 14 metric number but not exceeding 43 metric number per single yarn)
5206.4300	--每根单纱细度在232.56分特以下,但不细于192.31分特(每根单纱超过43公支,但不超过52公支)	5			0	40	17	11	千克	5	--Measuring per single yarn less than 232.56 decitex but not less then 192.31 decitex (exceeding 43 metric number but not exceeding 52 metric number per single yarn)
5206.4400	--每根单纱细度在192.31分特以下,但不细于125分特(每根单纱超过52公支,但不超过80公支)	5			0	40	17	11	千克	5	--Measuring per single yarn less than 192.31 decitex but not less than 125 decitex (exceeding 52 metric number but not exceeding 80 metric number per single yarn)
5206.4500	--每根单纱细度在125分特以下(每根单纱超过80公支)	5			0	40	17	11	千克	5	--Measuring per single yarn less than 125 decitex (exceeding 80 metric number per single yarn)
52.07	**棉纱线(缝纫线除外),供零售用:**										**Cotton yarn (other than sewing thread) put up for retail sale:**
5207.1000	-按重量计含棉量在85%及以上	6	5	5	0	50	17	11	千克	5	-Containing 85% or more by weight of cotton
5207.9000	-其他	6	5		0	50	17	11	千克	5	-Other
52.08	**棉机织物,按重量计含棉量在85%及以上,每平方米重量不超过200克:**										**Woven fabrics of cotton, containing 85% or more by weight of cotton, weighing not more than 200 g/m^2:**
	-未漂白:										-Unbleached:
5208.1100	--平纹机织物,每平方米重量不超过100克	10	5	0	0	70	17	11	米/千克		--Plain weave, weighing not more than 100 g/m^2
5208.1100 10	未漂白全棉平纹府绸及细平布(每平方米重量不超过100克,含棉85%及以上)	10				70	17	11	米/千克	AB5	Poplin and fine plain cloth of cotton, plain weave, w≤100g/m^2, containing ≥85% by weight of cotton, unbleached
5208.1100 20	未漂白全棉平纹机织平布(每平方米重量不超过100克,68号及以下)	10				70	17	11	米/千克	AB5	Plain cloth of cotton, plain weave, w≤100g/m^2, unbleached, ≤No.68

税则号列 Tariff Item.	货品名称	最惠国(%) MFN	协定(%)CT 东盟 CA	中巴 CP	中智 CC	普通 Gen	增值税率 VAT	出口退税 ED	计量单位 Unit	监管条件 SC	Article Description
5208.1100 30	未漂白全棉平纹奶酪布(每平方米重量不超过100克,含棉85%及以上)	10				70	17	11	米/千克	AB5	Cheese cloth, plain weave, w≤100g/m², containing≥85% by weight of cotton, unbleached
5208.1100 40	未漂白全棉平纹印染用布(每平方米重量不超过100克,43-68号)	10				70	17	11	米/千克	AB5	Cloth for printing and dying of cotton, plain weave, No. 43—No. 68, w≤100g/m², unbleached
5208.1100 50	未漂白全棉平纹巴里纱及薄细布(每平方米重量不超过100克,69号及以上)	10				70	17	11	米/千克	AB5	Voiles and fine thin cloth of cotton, plain weave, w≤100g/m², unbleached, ≥No. 69
5208.1100 60	未漂白全棉平纹机织打字布(每平方米重量不超过100克,含棉85%及以上)	10				70	17	11	米/千克	AB5	Typewriter ribbon of cotton, plain weave, w≤100g/m², containing≥85% by weight of cotton, unbleached
5208.1100 70	未漂白全棉医用纱布(每平方米重量不超过100克,含棉85%及以上)	10				70	17	11	米/千克	AB5	Medical qauze of cotton, w≤100g/m², containing≥85% by weight of cotton, unbleached
5208.1200	--平纹机织物,每平方米重量超过100克	10	T3	0	0	70	17	11	米/千克		--Plain weave, weighing more than 100 g/m²
5208.1200 10	未漂白全棉平纹府绸及细平布(100克<每平方米重量≤200克,含棉85%及以上)	10				70	17	11	米/千克	AB5	Poplin and fine plain cloth of cotton, plain weave, 100g/m²<w≤200g/m², containing≥85% by weight of cotton, unbleached
5208.1200 20	未漂白全棉平纹机织平布(100克<每平方米重量≤200克,68号及以下)	10				70	17	11	米/千克	AB5	Plain cloth of cotton plain weave, 100g/m²<w≤200g/m², ≤No. 68, unbleached
5208.1200 30	未漂白全棉平纹奶酪布(100克<每平方米重量≤200克,含棉85%及以上)	10				70	17	11	米/千克	AB5	Cheese cloth of cotton, plain weave, 100g/m²<w≤200g/m², containing≥85% by weight of cotton, unbleached
5208.1200 40	未漂白全棉平纹印染用布(100克<每平方米重量≤200克,43-68号)	10				70	17	11	米/千克	AB5	Cloth for printing and dying of cotton, plain weave, No. 43—No. 68, 100g/m²<w≤200g/m², unbleached
5208.1200 50	未漂白全棉平纹巴里纱及薄细布(100克<每平方米重量≤200克,69号及以	10				70	17	11	米/千克	AB5	Voiles and fine thin cloth of cotton, plain weave, 100g/m²<w≤200g/m², ≥No. 69, unbleached
5208.1300	--三线或四线斜纹机织物,包括双面斜纹机织物	10	5	0	0	70	17	11	米/千克	AB5	--3-thread or 4-thread twill, including cross twill
5208.1900	--其他机织物	10	T3	0	0	70	17	11	米/千克		--Other fabrics
5208.1900 10	未漂白其他全棉机织缎布(每平方米重量不超过200克,含棉85%及以上)	10				70	17	11	米/千克	AB5	Woven fabrics of cotton, satin weave, w≤200g/m², containing≥85% by weight of cotton, unbleached
5208.1900 20	未漂白其他全棉机织斜纹布(每平方米重量不超过200克,含棉85%及以上)	10				70	17	11	米/千克	AB5	Woven fabrics of cotton, twill weave, w≤200g/m², containing≥85% by weight of cotton, unbleached
5208.1900 30	未漂白其他全棉机织牛津布(每平方米重量不超过200克,含棉85%及以上)	10				70	17	11	米/千克	AB5	Woven fabrics of cotton oxford weave, w≤200g/m², containing≥85% by weight of cotton, unbleached
5208.1900 90	未漂白其他全棉机织物(每平方米重量不超过200克,含棉85%及以上)	10				70	17	11	米/千克	AB5	Other woven fabrics of cotton, w≤200g/m², containing≥85% by weight of cotton, unbleached
	-漂白:										-Bleached:

税则号列 Tariff Item.	货品名称	最惠国(%) MFN	协定(%)CT 东盟 CA	中巴 CP	中智 CC	普通 Gen	增值税率 VAT	出口退税 ED	计量单位 Unit	监管条件 SC	Article Description
5208.2100	--平纹机织物,每平方米重量不超过100克	10	5	0	0	70	17	11	米/千克		--Plain weave, weighing not more than 100 g/m^2
5208.2100 10	漂白全棉平纹府绸及细平布(每平方米重量不超过100克,含棉85%及以上)	10				70	17	11	米/千克	AB5	Poplin and fine plain cloth of cotton, w ≤ 100g/m^2, containing ≥ 85% by weight of cotton, bleached
5208.2100 20	漂白全棉平纹机织平布(每平方米重量不超过100克,68号及以下)	10				70	17	11	米/千克	AB5	Woven fabrics of cotton, plain weave, ≤ No.68, w≤100g/m^2, bleached
5208.2100 30	漂白全棉平纹奶酪布(每平方米重量不超过100克,含棉85%及以上)	10				70	17	11	米/千克	AB5	Cheese cloth of cotton, plain weave, w ≤ 100g/m^2, containing ≥ 85% by weight of cotton, bleached
5208.2100 40	漂白全棉平纹印染用布(每平方米重量不超过100克,43-68号)	10				70	17	11	米/千克	AB5	Cloth for printing and dying of cotton, plain weave, No. 43—No. 68, w ≤ 100g/m^2, bleached
5208.2100 50	漂白全棉平纹巴里纱及薄细布(每平方米重量不超过100克,69号及以上)	10				70	17	11	米/千克	AB5	Voiles and fine thin cloth of cotton, plain weave, w≤100g/m^2, containing≥85% by weight of cotton, ≥No.69, bleached
5208.2100 60	漂白全棉医用纱布(每平方米重量不超过100克,含棉85%及以上)	10				70	17	11	米/千克	AB5	Medical qauze of cotton, w≤100g/m^2, containing ≥ 85% by weight of cotton, bleached
5208.2200	--平纹机织物,每平方米重量超过100克	10	T3	0	0	70	17	11	米/千克		--Plain weave, weighing more than 100 g/m^2
5208.2200 10	漂白全棉平纹府绸及细平布(100g<每平方米重量≤200g,含棉85%及以上)	10				70	17	11	米/千克	AB5	Poplin and fine plain cloth of cotton, plain weave, 100g/m^2 < w≤200g/m^2, containing ≥ 85% by weight of cotton, bleached
5208.2200 20	漂白全棉平纹机织平布(100g<每平方米重量≤200g,68号及以下)	10				70	17	11	米/千克	AB5	Plain cloth of cotton, plain weave, 100g/m^2 < w ≤ 200g/m^2, ≤ No. 68, bleached
5208.2200 30	漂白全棉平纹奶酪布(100g<每平方米重量≤200g,含棉85%及以上)	10				70	17	11	米/千克	AB5	Cheese cloth of cotton, plain weave, 100g/m^2 < w≤200g/m^2, containing ≥ 85% by weight of cotton, bleached
5208.2200 40	漂白全棉平纹印染用布(100g<每平方米重量≤200g,43-68号)	10				70	17	11	米/千克	AB5	Cloth for printing and dying, of cotton, plain weave, No. 43—No. 68, 100g/m^2 < w≤200g/m^2, bleached
5208.2200 50	漂白全棉巴里纱及薄细布(100g<每平方米重量≤200g,69号及以上)	10				70	17	11	米/千克	AB5	Voiles and fine thin cloth of cotton, 100g/m^2 < w ≤ 200g/m^2, ≥ No. 69, bleached
5208.2300	--三线或四线斜纹机织物,包括双面斜纹机织物	12	8	0	0	70	17	11	米/千克	AB5	--3-thread or 4-thread twill, including cross twill
5208.2900	--其他机织物	10	5	0	0	70	17	11	米/千克		--Other fabrics
5208.2900 10	漂白其他全棉机织缎布(每平方米重量不超过200克,含棉85%及以上)	10				70	17	11	米/千克	AB5	Woven fabrics of cotton, satin weave, w ≤ 200g/m^2, containing ≥ 85% by weight of cotton, bleached
5208.2900 20	漂白其他全棉机织斜纹布(每平方米重量不超过200克,含棉85%及以上)	10				70	17	11	米/千克	AB5	Woven fabrics of cotton, twill weave, w ≤ 200g/m^2, containing ≥ 85% by weight of cotton, bleached

税则号列 Tariff Item.	货品名称	最惠国(%) MFN	协定(%) CT 东盟 CA	中巴 CP	中智 CC	普通 Gen	增值税率 VAT	出口退税 ED	计量单位 Unit	监管条件 SC	Article Description
5208.2900 30	漂白其他全棉机织牛津布(每平方米重量不超过200克,含棉85%及以上)	10				70	17	11	米/千克	AB5	Woven fabrics of cotton, oxford weave, w ≤ 200g/m², containing ≥ 85% by weight of cotton, bleached
5208.2900 90	漂白其他全棉机织物(每平方米重量不超过200克,含棉85%及以上)	10				70	17	11	米/千克	AB5	Other woven fabrics of cotton, w ≤ 200g/m², containing ≥ 85% by weight of cotton, bleached
	-染色:										-Dyed:
5208.3100	--平纹机织物,每平方米重量不超过100克	10	5	0	0	70	17	11	米/千克		--Plain weave, weighing not more than 100 g/m²
5208.3100 10	染色全棉手工织布(每平方米重量不超过100克,含棉85%及以上)	10				70	17	11	米/千克	AB5	Handwoven cloth, of cotton, plain weave, w ≤ 100g/m², containing ≥ 85% by weight of cotton, dyed
5208.3100 91	染色全棉平纹府绸及细平布(每平方米重量不超过100克,含棉85%及以上)	10				70	17	11	米/千克	AB5	Woven fabrics of cotton, plain weave, w ≤ 100g/m², containing ≥ 85% by weight of cotton, dyed
5208.3100 92	染色全棉平纹机织平布(每平方米重量不超过100克,68号及以下)	10				70	17	11	米/千克	AB5	Plain cloth of cotton, plain weave, w ≤ 100g/m², ≤ No. 68, dyed
5208.3100 93	染色全棉平纹奶酪布(每平方米重量不超过100克,含棉85%及以上)	10				70	17	11	米/千克	AB5	Cheese cloth of cotton, plain weave, w ≤ 100g/m², containing ≥ 85% by weight of cotton, dyed
5208.3100 94	染色全棉平纹印染用布(每平方米重量不超过100克,43-68号)	10				70	17	11	米/千克	AB5	Cloth for printing and dying, of cotton, plain weave, No. 43—No. 68, w ≤ 100g/m², dyed
5208.3100 95	染色全棉巴里纱及薄细布(每平方米重量不超过100克,69号及以上)	10				70	17	11	米/千克	AB5	Voiles and fine thin cloth of cotton, w ≤ 100g/m², ≥ No. 69, dyed
5208.3200	--平纹机织物,每平方米重量超过100克	10	T3	0	0	70	17	11	米/千克		--Plain weave, weighing more than 100 g/m²
5208.3200 10	染色全棉手工织布(100g<每平方米重量≤200g,含棉85%及以上)	10				70	17	11	米/千克	AB5	Handwoven cloth of cotton, 100g/m² < w ≤ 200g/m², containing ≥ 85% by weight of cotton, dyed
5208.3200 91	染色全棉平纹府绸及细平布(100g<每平方米重量≤200g,含棉85%及以上)	10				70	17	11	米/千克	AB5	Poplin and fine plain cloth of cotton, plain weave, 100g/m² < w ≤ 200g/m², containing ≥ 85% by weight of cotton, dyed
5208.3200 92	染色全棉平纹机织平布(100g<每平方米重量≤200g,68号及以下)	10				70	17	11	米/千克	AB5	Plain cloth of cotton, plain weave, 100g/m² < w ≤ 200g/m², ≤ No. 68, dyed
5208.3200 93	染色全棉平纹奶酪布(100g<每平方米重量≤200g,含棉85%及以上)	10				70	17	11	米/千克	AB5	Cheese cloth of cotton, plain weave, 100g/m² < w ≤ 200g/m², containing ≥ 85% by weight of cotton, dyed
5208.3200 94	染色全棉平纹印染用布(100g<每平方米重量≤200g,43-68号)	10				70	17	11	米/千克	AB5	Cloth for printing and dying of cotton plain weave, No. 43—No. 68 100g/m² < w ≤ 200g/m², dyed
5208.3200 95	染色全棉巴里纱及薄细布(100g<每平方米重量≤200g,69号及以上)	10				70	17	11	米/千克	AB5	Voiles and fine thin cloth of cotton, 100g/m² < w ≤ 200g/m², ≥ No. 69, dyed

税则号列 Tariff Item.	货品名称	最惠国(%) MFN	协定(%) 东盟 CA	中巴 CP	CT 中智 CC	普通 Gen	增值税率 VAT	出口退税 ED	计量单位 Unit	监管条件 SC	Article Description
5208.3300	--三线或四线斜纹机织物,包括双面斜纹机织物	10	T3	0	0	70	17	11	米/千克	AB5	--3-thread or 4-thread twill, including cross twill
5208.3900	--其他机织物	10	T3	0	0	70	17	11	米/千克		--Other fabrics
5208.3900 10	染色其他全棉机织缎布(每平方米重量不超过200克,含棉85%及以上)	10				70	17	11	米/千克	AB5	Woven fabrics of cotton, satin weave, w ≤ 200g/m², containing ≥ 85% by weight of cotton, dyed
5208.3900 20	染色其他全棉机织斜纹布(每平方米重量不超过200克,含棉85%及以上)	10				70	17	11	米/千克	AB5	Woven fabrics of cotton, twill weave, w ≤ 200g/m², containing ≥ 85% by weight of cotton, dyed
5208.3900 30	染色其他全棉机织牛津布(每平方米重量不超过200克,含棉85%及以上)	10				70	17	11	米/千克	AB5	Woven fabrics of cotton, oxford weave, w ≤ 200g/m², containing ≥ 85% by weight of cotton, dyed
5208.3900 90	染色其他全棉机织物(每平方米重量不超过200克,含棉85%及以上)	10				70	17	11	米/千克	AB5	Other woven fabrics of cotton, w ≤ 200g/m², containing ≥ 85% by weight of cotton, dyed
	-色织:										-Of yarns of different colours:
5208.4100	--平纹机织物,每平方米重量不超过100克	10	T3	0	0	70	17	11	米/千克		--Plain weave, weighing not more than 100 g/m²
5208.4100 10	色织的全棉手工织布(每平方米重量不超过100克,含棉85%及以上)	10				70	17	11	米/千克	AB5	Handwoven cloth of cotton, w ≤ 100g/m², containing ≥ 85% by weight of cotton, of yarns of different colours
5208.4100 90	色织的全棉平纹机织物(每平方米重量不超过100克,含棉85%及以上)	10				70	17	11	米/千克	AB5	Woven fabrics of cotton, plain weave, 100g/m² < w ≤ 200g/m², containing ≥ 85% by weight of cotton ≤ No. 68, of yarns of different colours
5208.4200	--平纹机织物,每平方米重量超过100克	10	T3	0	0	70	17	11	米/千克		--Plain weave, weighing more than 100 g/m²
5208.4200 10	色织的全棉手工织布(100g < 每平方米重量 ≤ 200g,含棉85%及以上)	10				70	17	11	米/千克	AB5	Handwoven cloth of cotton, 100g/m² < w ≤ 200g/m², containing ≥ 85% by weight of cotton, of yarns of different colours
5208.4200 90	色织的全棉平纹机织物(100克 < 每平方米重量 ≤ 200克,含棉85%及以上)	10				70	17	11	米/千克	AB5	Woven fabrics of cotton, plain weave, 100g/m² < w ≤ 200g/m², containing ≥ 85% by weight of cotton, ≤ No. 68, of yarns of different colours
5208.4300	--三线或四线斜纹机织物,包括双面斜纹机织物	10	5	0	0	70	17	11	米/千克	AB5	--3-thread or 4-thread twill, including cross twill
5208.4900	--其他机织物	10	T3	0	0	70	17	11	米/千克		--Other fabrics
5208.4900 10	色织的其他全棉提花机织物(每平方米重量不超过200克,含棉85%及以上)	10				70	17	11	米/千克	AB5	Other woven fabrics of cotton, jacquard weave, w ≤ 200g/m², containing ≥ 85% by weight of cotton, of yarns of different colours
5208.4900 90	色织的其他全棉机织物(每平方米重量不超过200克,含棉85%及以上)	10				70	17	11	米/千克	AB5	Other woven fabrics of cotton, w ≤ 200g/m², containing ≥ 85% by weight of cotton, of yarns of different colours
	-印花:										-Printed:
5208.5100	--平纹机织物,每平方米重量不超过100克	10	5	0	0	70	17	11	米/千克		--Plain weave, weighing not more than 100 g/m²

税则号列 Tariff Item.	货品名称	最惠国(%) MFN	协定(%) CT 东盟 CA	中巴 CP	中智 CC	普通 Gen	增值税率 VAT	出口退税 ED	计量单位 Unit	监管条件 SC	Article Description
5208.5100 10	印花全棉手工织布(每平方米重量不超过100g,含棉85%及以上)	10				70	17	11	米/千克	AB5	Handwoven cloth of cotton, $w\leq100g/m^2$, containing≥85% by weight of cotton, printed
5208.5100 91	印花全棉平纹府绸及细平布(每平方米重量不超过100g,含棉85%及以上)	10				70	17	11	米/千克	AB5	Poplin and fine plain cloth of cotton plain weave, $w\leq100g/m^2$, containing≥85% by weight of cotton, printed
5208.5100 92	印花全棉平纹机织平布(每平方米重量不超过100g,68号及以下)	10				70	17	11	米/千克	AB5	Plain cloth of cotton, plain weave, $w\leq100g/m^2$, ≤No. 68, printed
5208.5100 93	印花全棉平纹奶酪布(每平方米重量不超过100g,含棉85%及以上)	10				70	17	11	米/千克	AB5	Cheese cloth of cotton, plain weave, $w\leq100g/m^2$, containing ≥ 85% by weight of cotton, printed
5208.5100 94	印花全棉平纹印染用布(每平方米重量不超过100g,43-68号)	10				70	17	11	米/千克	AB5	Cloth for printing and dying of cotton, plain weave $w\leq100g/m^2$, No. 43 ~ No. 68, printed
5208.5100 95	印花全棉平纹巴里纱及薄细布(每平方米重量不超过100g,69号及以上)	10				70	17	11	米/千克	AB5	Voiles and fine thin cloth of cotton, $w\leq100g/m^2$, ≥No. 69, printed
5208.5200	--平纹机织物,每平方米重量超过100g	10	T3	0	0	70	17	11	米/千克		--Plain weave, weighing more than 100 g/m^2
5208.5200 10	印花的全棉手工织布(100g<每平方米重量≤200g,含棉85%及以上)	10				70	17	11	米/千克	AB5	Handwoven cloth of cotton, $100g/m^2 < w\leq200g/m^2$, containing ≥ 85% by weight of cotton, printed
5208.5200 91	印花的全棉平纹府绸及细平布(100g<每平方米重量≤200g,含棉85%及以上)	10				70	17	11	米/千克	AB5	Poplin and fine plain cloth of cotton, plain weave, $100g/m^2 < w\leq200g/m^2$, containing ≥ 85% by weight of cotton, printed
5208.5200 92	印花的全棉平纹机织平布(100g<每平方米重量≤200g,68号及以下)	10				70	17	11	米/千克	AB5	Plain cloth of cotton, plain weave, $100g/m^2 < w\leq200g/m^2$, ≤ No. 68 printed
5208.5200 93	印花的全棉平纹奶酪布(100g<每平方米重量≤200g,含棉85%及以上)	10				70	17	11	米/千克	AB5	Cheese cloth of cotton, plain weave, $100g/m^2 < w\leq200g/m^2$, containing≥85% by weight of cotton, printed
5208.5200 94	印花的全棉平纹印染用布(100g<每平方米重量≤200g,43-68号)	10				70	17	11	米/千克	AB5	Cloth for printing and dying of cotton, plain weave , $100g/m^2 < w\leq200g/m^2$, No. 43—No. 68, printed
5208.5200 95	印花的全棉巴里纱及薄细布(100g<每平方米重量≤200g,69号及以上)	10				70	17	11	米/千克	AB5	Voiles and fine thin cloth of cotton $100g/m^2 < w\leq200g/m^2$, ≥ No. 69, printed
	--其他机织物										--Other wores fabrics
5208.5910	---三线或四线斜纹机织物,包括双面斜纹机织物	10	5	0	0	70	17	11	米/千克	AB5	---3-thread or 4-thread twill, in cluding crosss twill
5208.5990	---其他机织物	10	5	0	0	70	17	11	米/千克		---Other
5208.5990 10	印花其他全棉机织缎布(每平方米重量不超过200g,含棉85%及以上)	10			5	70	17	11	米/千克	AB5	Woven fabrics of cotton, satin weave $w\leq200g/m^2$ containing≥85% by weight of cotton printed

税则号列 Tariff Item.	货品名称	最惠国(%) MFN	协定(%)CT 东盟 CA	中巴 CP	中智 CC	普通 Gen	增值税率 VAT	出口退税 ED	计量单位 Unit	监管条件 SC	Article Description
5208.5990 20	印花其他全棉机织斜纹布(每平方米重量不超过200g,含棉85%及以上)	10				70	17	11	米/千克	AB5	Woven fabrics of cotton, twill weave, w ≤ 200g/m^2, containing ≥ 85% by weight of cotton, printed
5208.5990 30	印花其他全棉机织牛津布(每平方米重量不超过200g,含棉85%及以上)	10				70	17	11	米/千克	AB5	Woven fabrics of cotton, oxford weave w ≤ 200g/m^2, containing ≥ 85% by weight of cotton, printed
5208.5990 90	印花其他全棉机织物(每平方米重量不超过200g,含棉85%及以上)	10				70	17	11	米/千克	AB5	Other woven fabrics of cotton, w ≤ 200g/m^2, containing≥85% by weight of cotton, printed
52.09	**棉机织物,按重量计含棉量在85%及以上,每平方米重量超过200克:**										**Woven fabrics of cotton, containing 85% or more by weight of cotton, weighing more than 200 g/m^2:**
	-未漂白:										-Unbleached:
5209.1100	--平纹机织物	10		0	0	70	17	11	米/千克		--Plain weave
5209.1100 10	未漂白全棉平纹府绸及细平布(指每平方米重超过200克,含棉85%及以上)	10				70	17	11	米/千克	AB5	Poplin and fine plain cloth of cotton, plain weave, w > 200g/m^2, containing≥ 85% by weight of cotton, unbleached
5209.1100 20	未漂白的全棉平纹机织平布(指每平方米重超过200克,含棉85%及以上)	10				70	17	11	米/千克	AB5	Plain cloth of cotton, plain weave, w > 200g/m^2, containing≥85% by weight of cotton, unbleached
5209.1100 30	未漂白的全棉平纹机织帆布(指每平方米重超过200克,含棉85%及以上)	10				70	17	11	米/千克	AB5	Canvas of cotton, plain weave, w > 200g/m^2, containing≥85% by weight of cotton, unbleached
5209.1200	--三线或四线斜纹机织物,包括双面斜纹机织物	10	T3	0	0	70	17	11	米/千克	AB5	--3-thread or 4-thread twill, including cross twill
5209.1900	--其他机织物	10	T3	0	0	70	17	11	米/千克		--Other fabrics
5209.1900 10	未漂白的其他全棉机织缎布(指每平方米重超过200克,含棉85%及以上)	10				70	17	11	米/千克	B5	Other woven fabrics of cotton, satin weave, w > 200g/m^2, containing ≥ 85% by weight of cotton, unbleached
5209.1900 20	未漂白的其他全棉机织斜纹布(指每平方米重超过200克,含棉85%及以上)	10				70	17	11	米/千克	B5	Other woven fabrics of cotton, twill weave, w > 200g/m^2, containing ≥ 85% by weight of cotton, unbleached
5209.1900 30	未漂白的其他全棉机织帆布(指每平方米重超过200克,含棉85%及以上)	10				70	17	11	米/千克	B5	Canvas of cotton, w > 200g/m^2, containing≥85% by weight of cotton, unbleached
5209.1900 90	未漂白的其他全棉机织物(指每平方米重超过200克,含棉85%及以上)	10				70	17	11	米/千克	B5	Other woven fabrics of cotton, w > 200g/m^2 containing≥85% by weight of cotton, unbleached
	-漂白:										-Bleached:
5209.2100	--平纹机织物	12	T3	0	0	70	17	11	米/千克		--Plain weave
5209.2100 10	漂白全棉平纹府绸及细平布(指每平方米重超过200克,含棉85%及以上)	12				70	17	11	米/千克	B5	Poplin and fine plain cloth of cotton, plain weave, w > 200g/m^2 containing≥ 85% by weight of cotton, bleached
5209.2100 20	漂白的全棉平纹机织平布(指每平方米重超过200克,含棉85%及以上)	12				70	17	11	米/千克	B5	Plain cloth of cotton, plain weave w > 200g/m^2 containing≥85% by weight of cotton, bleached
5209.2100 30	漂白的全棉平纹机织帆布(指每平方米重超过200克,含棉85%及以上)	12				70	17	11	米/千克	B5	Canvas of cotton, plain weave, w > 200g/m^2 containing≥85% by weight of cotton, bleached

税则号列 Tariff Item.	货品名称	最惠国(%) MFN	协定(%) CT 东盟 CA	中巴 CP	中智 CC	普通 Gen	增值税率 VAT	出口退税 ED	计量单位 Unit	监管条件 SC	Article Description
5209.2200	--三线或四线斜纹机织物,包括双面斜纹机织物	12	8	0	0	70	17	11	米/千克	B5	--3-thread or 4-thread twill, including cross twill
5209.2900	--其他机织物	12	T3	0	0	70	17	11	米/千克		--Other fabrics
5209.2900 10	漂白的其他全棉机织缎布(指每平方米重超过200克,含棉85%及以上)	12				70	17	11	米/千克	B5	Other woven fabrics of cotton, satin weave, w > 200g/m², containing ≥ 85% by weight of cotton, bleached
5209.2900 20	漂白的其他全棉机织斜纹布(指每平方米重超过200克,含棉85%及以上)	12				70	17	11	米/千克	B5	Other woven fabrics of cotton, twill weave, w > 200g/m², containing ≥ 85% by weight of cotton, bleached
5209.2900 30	漂白的其他全棉机织帆布(指每平方米重超过200克,含棉85%及以上)	12				70	17	11	米/千克	B5	Other canvas of cotton, w > 200g/m², containing ≥ 85% by weight of cotton, bleached
5209.2900 90	漂白的其他全棉机织物(指每平方米重超过200克,含棉85%及以上)	12				70	17	11	米/千克	B5	Other woven fabrics of cotton, w > 200g/m², containing≥85% by weight of cotton, bleached
	-染色:										-Dyed:
5209.3100	--平纹机织物	10	T3	0	0	70	17	11	米/千克		--Plain weave
5209.3100 10	染色全棉手工织布(指每平方米重超过200克,含棉85%及以上)	10				70	17	11	米/千克	AB5	Handwoven cloth of cotton w > 200g/m², containing≥85% by weight of cotton, dyed
5209.3100 91	染色全棉平纹府绸及细平布(指每平方米重超过200克,含棉85%及以上)	10				70	17	11	米/千克	AB5	Poplin and fine plain cloth of cotton, plain weave, w > 200g/m², containing≥ 85% by weight of cotton, dyed
5209.3100 92	染色的全棉平纹机织平布(指每平方米重超过200克,含棉85%及以上)	10				70	17	11	米/千克	AB5	Plain cloth of cotton, plain weave, w > 200g/m², containing≥85% by weight of cotton, dyed
5209.3100 93	染色的全棉平纹机织帆布(指每平方米重超过200克,含棉85%及以上)	10				70	17	11	米/千克	AB5	Canvas of cotton, plain weave, w > 200g/m², containing≥85% by weight of cotton, dyed
5209.3200	--三线或四线斜纹机织物,包括双面斜纹机织物	10	T3	0	0	70	17	11	米/千克	AB5	--3-thread or 4-thread twill, including cross twill
5209.3900	--其他机织物	10	T3	0	0	70	17	11	米/千克		--Other fabrics
5209.3900 10	染色的其他全棉机织缎布(指每平方米重超过200克,含棉85%及以上)	10				70	17	11	米/千克	AB5	Other woven fabrics of cotton, satin weave w > 200g/m², containing≥85% by weight of cotton, dyed
5209.3900 20	染色的其他全棉机织斜纹布(指每平方米重超过200克,含棉85%及以上)	10				70	17	11	米/千克	AB5	Other woven fabrics of cotton, twill weave, w > 200g/m², containing ≥ 85% by weight of cotton, dyed
5209.3900 30	染色的其他全棉机织帆布(指每平方米重超过200克,含棉85%及以上)	10				70	17	11	米/千克	AB5	Other canvas of cotton, w > 200g/m², containing ≥ 85% by weight of cotton, dyed
5209.3900 90	染色的其他全棉机织物(指每平方米重超过200克,含棉85%及以上)	10				70	17	11	米/千克	AB5	Other woven fabrics of cotton, w > 200g/m² containing≥85% by weight of cotton, dyed
	-色织:										-Of yarns of different colours:
5209.4100	--平纹机织物	10	T3	0	0	70	17	11	米/千克		--Plain weave
5209.4100 10	色织的全棉手工织布(指每平方米重超过200克,含棉85%及以上)	10				70	17	11	米/千克	AB5	Handwoven cloth of cotton, w > 200g/m² containing≥85% by weight of cotton, of yarns of different colours

税则号列 Tariff Item.	货品名称	最惠国(%) MFN	协定(%)CT 东盟 CA	中巴 CP	中智 CC	普通 Gen	增值税率 VAT	出口退税 ED	计量单位 Unit	监管条件 SC	Article Description
5209.4100 90	色织的全棉平纹机织物(指每平方米重超过200克,含棉85%及以上)	10				70	17	11	米/千克	AB5	Woven fabrics of cotton, plain weave, w >200g/m^2, containing≥85% by weight of cotton, of yarns of different colours
5209.4200	--粗斜纹布(劳动布)	10	T3	0	0	70	17	11	米/千克		--Denim
5209.4200 10	色织全棉蓝粗斜纹布(劳动布)(指每平方米重超过200克,含棉85%及以上)	10				70	17	11	米/千克	AB5	Blue denim of cotton, w > 200g/m^2, containing≥85% by weight of cotton, of yarns of different colours
5209.4200 90	色织其他全棉粗斜纹布(劳动布)(指每平方米重超过200克,含棉85%及以上)	10				70	17	11	米/千克	AB5	Denim of cotton, w>200g/m^2, containing ≥ 85% by weight of cotton, of yarns of different colours
5209.4300	--三线或四线斜纹机织物,包括双面斜纹机织物	10	5	0	0	70	17	11	米/千克	AB5	--Other fabrics of 3-thread or 4-thread twill, including cross twill
5209.4900	--其他机织物	10	T3	0	0	70	17	11	米/千克		--Other fabrics
5209.4900 10	色织的其他全棉提花机织物(指每平米重超过200克,含棉85%及以上)	10				70	17	11	米/千克	AB5	Other woven fabrics of cotton, jacquad weave, w>200g/m^2 containing≥85% by weight of cotton, of yarns of different colours
5209.4900 90	色织的其他全棉机织物(指每平米重超过200克,含棉85%及以上)	10				70	17	11	米/千克	AB5	Other woven fabrics of cotton, w>200g/m^2, containing≥85% by weight of cotton, of yarns of different colours
	-印花:										-Printed:
5209.5100	--平纹机织物	10	8	0	0	70	17	11	米/千克		--Plain weave
5209.5100 10	印花全棉手工织布(指每平方米重超过200克,含棉85%及以上)	10				70	17	11	米/千克	AB5	Handwoven cloth of cotton, w > 200g/m^2, containing≥85% by weight of cotton, printed
5209.5100 91	印花全棉平纹府绸及细平布(指每平方米重超过200克,含棉85%及以上)	10				70	17	11	米/千克	AB5	Poplin and fine plain cloth of cotton, plain weave, w>200g/m^2, containing≥85% by weight of cotton, printed
5209.5100 92	印花全棉平纹机织平布(指每平方米重超过200克,含棉85%及以上)	10				70	17	11	米/千克	AB5	Plain cloth of cotton, plain weave, w > 200g/m^2, containing≥85% by weight of cotton, printed
5209.5100 93	印花全棉平纹机织帆布(指每平方米重超过200克,含棉85%及以上)	10				70	17	11	米/千克	AB5	Canvas of cotton, plain weave, w > 200g/m^2, containing≥85% by weight of cotton, printed
5209.5200	--三线或四线斜纹机织物,包括双面斜纹机织物	10	5	0	0	70	17	11	米/千克	AB5	--3-thread or 4-thread twill, including cross twill
5209.5900	--其他机织物	10	5	0	0	70	17	11	米/千克		--Other fabrics
5209.5900 10	印花的其他全棉机织缎布(指每平方米重超过200克,含棉85%及以上)	10				70	17	11	米/千克	AB5	Other woven fabrics of cotton, satin weave w>200g/m^2, containing≥85% by weight of cotton, printed
5209.5900 20	印花的其他全棉机织斜纹布(指每平方米重超过200克,含棉85%及以上)	10				70	17	11	米/千克	AB5	Other woven fabrics of cotton, twill weave, w > 200g/m^2, containing ≥ 85% by weight of cotton, printed
5209.5900 30	印花的其他全棉机织帆布(指每平方米重超过200克,含棉85%及以上)	10				70	17	11	米/千克	AB5	Other canvas of cotton, w>200g/m^2, containing ≥ 85% by weight of cotton, printed
5209.5900 90	印花的其他全棉机织物(指每平方米重超过200克,含棉85%及以上)	10				70	17	11	米/千克	AB5	Other woven fabrics of cotton, w > 200g/m^2, containing≥85% by weight of cotton, printed

税则号列 Tariff Item.	货品名称	最惠国(%) MFN	协定(%) CT 东盟 CA	中巴 CP	中智 CC	普通 Gen	增值税率 VAT	出口退税 ED	计量单位 Unit	监管条件 SC	Article Description
52.10	**棉机织物,按重量计含棉量在85%以下,主要或仅与化学纤维混纺,每平方米重量不超过200克:**										**Woven fabrics of cotton, containing less than 85% by weight of cotton, mixed mainly or solely with man-made fibres, weighing not more than 200 g/m^2:**
	-未漂白:										-Unbleached:
5210.1100	--平纹机织物	12	T3	0	0	90	17	11	米/千克		--Plain weave
5210.1100 11	未漂白与聚酯短纤混纺的棉制府绸(指每平米重≤200克,含棉85%以下,含平细布)	12				90	17	11	米/千克	B5	Poplin and fine plain cloth of cotton, plain weave, mixed with polyester staple fibres w≤200g/m^2, containing <85% by weight of cotton, unbleached
5210.1100 12	未漂白与聚酯短纤混纺棉机织平布(指每平米重≤200克,≤68号,含棉85%以下)	12				90	17	11	米/千克	B5	Plain cloth of cotton plain weave, mixed with polyester staple fibres, w≤200g/m^2 containing <85% by weight of cotton, unbleached
5210.1100 13	未漂白与聚酯短纤混纺棉奶酪布(指每平米重≤200克,含棉85%以下)	12				90	17	11	米/千克	B5	Cheese cloth of cotton, plain weave, mixed with polyester staple fibres w≤200g/m^2 containing <85% by weight of cotton, unbleached
5210.1100 14	未漂白与聚酯短纤混纺棉印染布(指每平米重≤200克,43-68号,含棉85%以下)	12				90	17	11	米/千克	B5	For printing and dying of cotton, plain weave, mixed with polyester staple fibres w≤200g/m^2 containing <85% by weight of cotton, unbleached
5210.1100 15	未漂白与聚酯短纤混纺棉巴里纱(指每平米重≤200克,≥69号,含棉85%以下,含薄细布)	12				90	17	11	米/千克	B5	Voiles and fine thin cloth of cotton, plain weave, mixed with polyester staple fibres, w≤200g/m^2, containing <85% by weight of cotton, unbleached
5210.1100 91	未漂白与其他化纤混纺棉府绸(指每平米重≤200克,含棉85%以下,含细平布)	12				90	17	11	米/千克	B5	Poplin amd fine plain cloth of cotton, plain weave, mixed with other man-made fibres w≤200g/m^2, containing <85% by weight of cotton, unbleached
5210.1100 92	未漂白与其他化纤混纺棉机织平布(指每平米重≤200克,≤68号,含棉85%以下)	12				90	17	11	米/千克	B5	Plain cloth of cotton, plain weave, mixed with other man-made fibres w≤200g/m^2, containing <85% by weight of cotton, unbleached
5210.1100 93	未漂白与其他化纤混纺棉奶酪布(指每平米重≤200克,含棉85%以下)	12				90	17	11	米/千克	B5	Cheese cloth of cotton, plain weave, mixed with other man-made fibres w≤200g/m^2, containing <85% by weight of cotton, unbleached
5210.1100 94	未漂白与其他化纤混纺棉印染用布(指每平米重≤200克,43-68号,含棉85%以下)	12				90	17	11	米/千克	B5	Cloth for printing and dying of cotton, plain weave, mixed with other man-made fibres w≤200g/m^2, containing <85% by weight of cotton, unbleached
5210.1100 95	未漂白与其他化纤混纺棉巴里纱(指每平米重≤200克,≥69号,含棉85%以下,含薄细布)	12				90	17	11	米/千克	B5	Voiles and fine thin cloth of cotton, mixed with man - made fibres w≤200g/m3, containing <85% by weight of cotton, ≥No.69, unbleached
	--其他机织物:										--Other fabrics:
5210.1910	---三线或四线斜纹机织物,包括双面斜纹机织物	12	T3	0	0	90	17	11	米/千克		---3-thread or 4-thread twill, incl-uding cross twill

税则号列 Tariff Item.	货品名称	最惠国(%) MFN	协定(%)CT 东盟 CA	中巴 CP	中智 CC	普通 Gen	增值税率 VAT	出口退税 ED	计量单位 Unit	监管条件 SC	Article Description
5210.1910 10	未漂白与聚酯短纤混纺3/4线或双面棉斜纹布(指每平米重≤200克,含棉85%以下)	12				90	17	11	米/千克	B5	Woren fabl-rics of cot-ton, fwill weave, mixed with pdyester staple fibres (3 or 4-thread), w ≤ 200g/m^2, containing < 85% by weight of cotton, un-bleached
5210.1910 90	未漂白与其他化纤混纺3/4线或双面棉斜纹布(指每平米重≤200克,含棉85%以下)	12				90	17	11	米/千克	B5	Woren fab-rics of cotton, twill weave, mixed with other man-made fibres (3 or 4-thread w ≤ 200g/m^2, containing < of cotton, unbleached)
5210.1990	---其他	12	T3	0	0	90	17	11	米/千克	B5	---Other
5210.1990 11	其他未漂白与聚酯短纤混纺的缎布(每平米重≤200克,含棉85%以下)	12				90	17	11	米/千克	B5	Other woren fabrics of cotton, satin weave, mixed with polyester staple fibres, w ≤ 200g/m^2, containing < 85% by weight of cotton, unbleached
5210.1990 12	其他未漂白与聚酯短纤混纺斜纹布(每平米重≤200克,含棉85%以下)	12				90	17	11	米/千克	B5	Other woven fabrics of cotton, twill weave, mixed with polyester staple fibres, w≤200g/m^2 containing <85% by weight of cotton, unbleached
5210.1990 13	其他未漂白与聚酯短纤混纺牛津布(每平米重≤200克,含棉85%以下)	12				90	17	11	米/千克	B5	Other woven fabrics of cotton, ox ford weave, mixed with polyester staple fibres, w ≤ 200g/m^2, containing < 85% by weight of cotton, unbleached
5210.1990 19	其他未漂白与聚酯短纤混纺棉布(每平米重≤200克,含棉85%以下)	12				90	17	11	米/千克	B5	Other woven fabrics of cotton, mixed with polyester staple fibres, w ≤ 200g/m^2, containing < 85% by weight of cotton unbleached
5210.1990 91	其他未漂白与其他化纤混纺缎布(每平米重≤200克,含棉85%以下)	12				90	17	11	米/千克	B5	Other woven of cotton, stain weave, mixed with other man-made fibres, w ≤ 200g/m^2, containing < 85% by weight of cotton, unbleached
5210.1990 92	其他未漂白与其他化纤混纺斜纹布(每平米重≤200克,含棉85%以下)	12				90	17	11	米/千克	B5	Other woven fabrics of cotton, twill weave, mixed with other man-made fibres w ≤ 200 g/m^2, containing < 85% by weight of cotton, unbleached
5210.1990 93	其他未漂白与其他化纤混纺牛津布(每平米重≤200克,含棉85%以下)	12				90	17	11	米/千克	B5	Other woven fabrics of cotton, oxford weave, mixed with otbres man-made fibres, w ≤ 200g/m^2, by weight of cotton, unbleached
5210.1990 99	其他未漂白与其他化纤混纺棉布(每平米重≤200克,含棉85%以下)	12				90	17	11	米/千克	B5	Other woven fabrics of cotton, mixed with oher man-made fibres. w ≤ 200g/m^2, containing < 85% by weight of cotton, unbleached
	-漂白:										-Bleached:
5210.2100	--平纹机织物	14	8	0	0	90	17	11	米/千克		--Plain weave
5210.2100 11	漂白与聚酯短纤混纺棉府绸(每平米重≤200克,含棉85%以下,含细平布)	14				90	17	11	米/千克	B5	Poplin and fine plain cloth of cotton, plain weave, mixed with polyester staple fibres w ≤ 200g/m^2 containing < 85% by weight of cotton, bleached
5210.2100 12	漂白与聚酯短纤混纺棉机织平布(每平米重≤200克,68号及以下,含棉85%以下)	14				90	17	11	米/千克	B5	Plain cloth of cotton, plain weave, mixed with polyester staple fibres w ≤ 200g/m^2, containing < 85% by weight of cotton bleached, ≤No. 68

税则号列 Tariff Item.	货 品 名 称	最惠国(%) MFN	协定(%)CT 东盟 CA	中巴 CP	中智 CC	普通 Gen	增值税率 VAT	出口退税 ED	计量单位 Unit	监管条件 SC	Article Description
5210.2100 13	漂白与聚酯短纤混纺棉奶酪布(每平米重≤200克,含棉85%以下)	14				90	17	11	米/千克	B5	Cheese cloth of cotton, plain weave, mixed with polyester staple fibres w≤200g/m^2, containing <85% by weight of cotton, bleached
5210.2100 14	漂白与聚酯短纤混纺棉印染布(每平米重≤200克,43-68号,含棉85%以下)	14				90	17	11	米/千克	B5	Cloth for printing and dying of cotton, mixed with polyester staple fibres, w≤200g/m^2 containing <85% by weight of cotton, No.43-48, bleached
5210.2100 15	漂白与聚酯短纤混纺棉巴里纱(每平米重≤200克,69号及以上,含棉85%以下,含薄细布)	14				90	17	11	米/千克	B5	Poplin and fine thin cloth of cotton, plain weave, mixed with polyester staple fibres w≤200g/m^2, containing <85% by weight of cotton, ≥No.69, bleached
5210.2100 21	漂白与化纤长丝混纺棉府绸(每平米重≤200克,含棉85%以下,含细平布)	14				90	17	11	米/千克	B5	Poplin and fine plain cloth of cotton, plain weave, mixed with man-made filaments w≤200g/m^2, containing <85% by weight of cotton bleached
5210.2100 22	漂白与化纤长丝混纺棉机织平布(每平米重≤200克,68号及以下,含棉85%以下)	14				90	17	11	米/千克	B5	Plain cloth of cotton, plain weave, mixed with man-made filaments w≤200g/m^2, containing <85% by weight of cotton, ≤No.68, bleached
5210.2100 23	漂白与化纤长丝混纺棉奶酪布(每平米重≤200克,含棉85%以下)	14				90	17	11	米/千克	B5	Cheese cloth of cotton, plain weave, mixed with man-made filaments, w≤200g/m^2, containing <85% by weight of cotton, bleached
5210.2100 24	漂白与化纤长丝混纺棉印染布(每平米重≤200克,43-68号,含棉85%以下)	14				90	17	11	米/千克	B5	Cloth for printing and dying of cotton, plain weave, mixed with man-made filaments, w≤200g/m^2, containing <85% by weight of cotton, No.43-68, bleached
5210.2100 25	漂白与化纤长丝混纺棉巴里纱(每平米重≤200克,69号及以上,含棉85%以下,含薄细布)	14				90	17	11	米/千克	B5	Voiles and fine thin cloth of cotton, plain weave, mixed with man-made filaments w≤200g/m^2, containing <85% by weight of cotton, ≥No.69, bleached
5210.2100 91	漂白与其他化纤混纺棉府绸(每平米重≤200克,含棉85%以下,含细平布)	14				90	17	11	米/千克	B5	Poplin and fine plain cloth of cotton, plain weave, mixed with other man-mad fibres w≤200g/m^2, containing <85% by weight of cotton, bleached
5210.2100 92	漂白与其他化纤混纺棉机织平布(每平米重≤200克,68号及以下,含棉85%以下)	14				90	17	11	米/千克	B5	Plain cloth of cotton, plain weave, mixed with other man-made fibres w≤200g/m^2, containing <85% by weight of cotton, ≤No.68, bleached
5210.2100 93	漂白与其他化纤混纺棉奶酪布(每平米重≤200克,含棉85%以下)	14				90	17	11	米/千克	B5	Cheese cloth of cotton, plain weave, mixed with other man-made fibres w≤200g/m^2, containing <85% by weight of cotton, bleached

税则号列 Tariff Item.	货品名称	最惠国(%) MFN	协定(%) 东盟 CA	中巴 CP	CT 中智 CC	普通 Gen	增值税率 VAT	出口退税 ED	计量单位 Unit	监管条件 SC	Article Description
5210.2100 94	漂白与其他化纤混纺棉印染布(每平米重≤200克,43－68号,含棉85%以下)	14				90	17	11	米/千克	B5	Cloth for printing and dying of cotton, plain weave, mixed with other man-made fibres w≤200g/m^2, containing < 85% by weight of cotton, No. 43－68, bleached
5210.2100 95	漂白与其他化纤混纺棉巴里纱(每平米重≤200克,69号及以上,含棉85%以下,含薄细布)	14				90	17	11	米/千克	B5	Voiles and fine thin cloth of cotton, plain weave, mixed with other man-made fibres w ≤ 200g/m^2, containing < 85% by weight of cotton, ≥No.69, bleached
	--其他机织物:										--Other fabrics:
5210.2910	---三线四线斜纹机织物,包括双面斜纹机织物	14	8	0	0	90	17	11	米/千克		---3--thread or 4--thread twill, including cross twill
5210.2910 10	漂白与聚酯短纤混纺3/4线或双面棉斜纹布(每平米重≤200克,含棉85%以下)	14				90	17	11	米/千克	B5	Woven fabrics of cotton, twill weave, 3 or 4-thread twill, including cross twill
5210.2910 20	漂白与化纤长丝混纺3/4线或双面棉斜纹布(每平米重≤200克,含棉85%以下)	14				90	17	11	米/千克	B5	Wove fabrics of cotton, twill weav e, 3 or 4-thread, mixed with man-made filaments w≤200g/m^2, containing < 85% by weight of cotton, bleached
5210.2910 90	漂白与其他化纤混纺3/4线或双面棉斜纹布(每平米重≤200克,含棉85%以下)	14				90	17	11	米/千克	B5	3 － thread or 4 － thread twill, including cross twill, mixed with man － made fibres w ≤ 200g/m2, containing < 85% by weight of cotton
5210.2990	---其他	14	T3	0	0	90	17	11	米/千克		---Other
5210.2990 11	其他漂白与聚酯短纤混纺缎布(每平米重≤200克,含棉85%以下)	14				90	17	11	米/千克	B5	Other woven fabrics, satin weave, mixed with polyester staple fibres, w≤200g/m^2, containing < 85% by weight of cotton, bleached
5210.2990 12	其他漂白与聚酯短纤混纺斜纹布(每平米重≤200克,含棉85%以下)	14				90	17	11	米/千克	B5	Other woven fabrics, twill weave, mixed with polyester staple fibres, w≤200g/m^2, containing < 85% by weight of cotton, bleached
5210.2990 13	其他漂白与聚酯短纤混纺牛津布(每平米重≤200克,含棉85%以下)	14				90	17	11	米/千克	B5	Other woven fabrics, oxford weave, mixed with polyester staple fibres, w≤200g/m^2, containing < 85% by weight of cotton, bleached
5210.2990 19	其他漂白与聚酯短纤混纺棉布(每平米重≤200克,含棉85%以下)	14				90	17	11	米/千克	B5	Other woven fabrics, mixed with polyester staple fibres, w≤200g/m^2, containing < 85% by weight of cotton, bleached
5210.2990 21	其他漂白与化纤长丝混纺缎布(每平米重≤200克,含棉85%以下)	14				90	17	11	米/千克	B5	Other woven fabrics, satin weave, mixed with man-made filaments, w≤200g/m^2, containing < 85% by weight of cotton, bleached
5210.2990 22	其他漂白与化纤长丝混纺斜纹布(每平米重≤200克,含棉85%以下)	14				90	17	11	米/千克	B5	Other woven fabrics, twill weave, mixed with man-made filaments, w≤200g/m^2, containing < 85% by weight of cotton, bleached

税则号列 Tariff Item.	货品名称	最惠国(%) MFN	协定(%) CT 东盟 CA	中巴 CP	中智 CC	普通 Gen	增值税率 VAT	出口退税 ED	计量单位 Unit	监管条件 SC	Article Description
5210.2990 23	其他漂白与化纤长丝混纺牛津布(每平米重≤200克,含棉85%以下)	14				90	17	11	米/千克	B5	Other woven fabrics, oxford weave, mixed with man-made filaments, w≤200g/m^2, containing <85% by weight of cotton, bleached
5210.2990 29	其他漂白与化纤长丝混纺棉布(每平米重≤200克,含棉85%以下)	14				90	17	11	米/千克	B5	Other woven fabrics, mixed with man-made filaments, w≤200g/m^2, containing < 85% by weight of cotton, bleached
5210.2990 91	其他漂白与其他化纤混纺缎布(每平米重≤200克,含棉85%以下)	14				90	17	11	米/千克	B5	Other woven fabrics, satin weave, mixed with other man-made fibres, w≤200g/m^2, containing <85% by weight of cotton, bleached
5210.2990 92	其他漂白与其他化纤混纺斜纹布(每平米重≤200克,含棉85%以下)	14				90	17	11	米/千克	B5	Other woven fabrics, twill weave, mixed with other man-made fibres, w≤200g/m^2, containing <85% by weight of cotton, bleached
5210.2990 93	其他漂白与其他化纤混纺牛津布(每平米重≤200克,含棉85%以下)	14				90	17	11	米/千克	B5	Other woven fabrics, oxford weave, mixed with other man-made fibres, w≤200g/m^2, containing <85% by weight of cotton, bleached
5210.2990 99	其他漂白与其他化纤混纺棉布(每平米重≤200克,含棉85%以下)	14				90	17	11	米/千克	B5	Other woven fabrics of cotton, mixed with other man-made fibres, w≤200g/m^2, containing <85% by weight of cotton, bleached
	-染色:										-Dyed:
5210.3100	--平纹机织物	10	T3	0	0	90	17	11	米/千克		--Plain weave
5210.3100 11	染色与聚酯短纤混纺棉府绸(每平米重≤200克,含棉85%以下,含细平布)	10				90	17	11	米/千克	B5	Poplin and fine plain cloth of cotton, plain weave, mixed with polyester staple fibres w≤200g/m^2, containing <85% by weight of cotton, dyed
5210.3100 12	染色与聚酯短纤混纺棉机织平布(每平米重≤200克,68号及以下,含棉85%以下)	10				90	17	11	米/千克	B5	Plain cloth of cotton, plain weave, mixed with polyester staple fibres, w≤200g/m^2 containing <85% by weight of cotton, ≤No. 68, dyed
5210.3100 13	染色与聚酯短纤混纺棉奶酪布(每平米重≤200克,含棉85%以下)	10				90	17	11	米/千克	B5	Cheese cloth of cotton, plain weave, mixed with polyester staple fibres, w≤200g/m^2, containing <85% by weight of cotton, dyed
5210.3100 14	染色与聚酯短纤混纺棉印染布(每平米重≤200克,43-68号,含棉85%以下)	10				90	17	11	米/千克	B5	Cloth for printing and dying of cotton, plain weave, mixed with polyester staple fibres w≤200g/m^2, containing <85% by weight of cotton, No. 43-68, dyed
5210.3100 15	染色与聚酯短纤混纺棉巴里纱(每平米重≤200克,69号及以上,含棉85%以下,含薄细布)	10				90	17	11	米/千克	B5	Voiles and fine thin cloth of cotton, plain weave, mixed with polyester staple fibres w≤200g/m^2, containing <85% by weight of cotton, ≥No. 69, dyed
5210.3100 21	染色与化纤长丝混纺棉府绸(每平米重≤200克,含棉85%以下,含细平布)	10				90	17	11	米/千克	B5	Poplin and fine plain cloth of cotton, plain weave, mixed with man-made filaments, w≤200g/m^2 containing <85% by weight of cotton, dyed

税则号列 Tariff Item.	货品名称	最惠国(%) MFN	协定(%) 东盟 CA	中巴 CP	CT 中智 CC	普通 Gen	增值税率 VAT	出口退税 ED	计量单位 Unit	监管条件 SC	Article Description
5210.3100 22	染色与化纤长丝混纺棉机织平布(每平米重≤200克,含棉85%以下)	10				90	17	11	米/千克	B5	Plain cloth of cotton, plain weave, mixed with man-made filaments, w≤200g/m^2, containing < 85% by weight of cotton, dyed
5210.3100 23	染色与化纤长丝混纺棉奶酪布(每平米重≤200克,含棉85%以下)	10				90	17	11	米/千克	B5	Cheese cloth of cotton, plain weave , mixed with man-made filaments, w≤200g/m^2, containing < 85% by weight of cotton, dyed
5210.3100 24	染色与化纤长丝混纺棉印染布(每平米重≤200克,43-68号,含棉85%以下)	10				90	17	11	米/千克	B5	Cloth for printing and dying of cotton, plain weave, mixed with man-made filaments, w≤200g/m^2, containing < 85% by weight of cotton, No. 43-68, dyed
5210.3100 25	染色与化纤长丝混纺棉巴里纱(每平米重≤200克,69号及以上,含棉85%以下,含薄细布)	10				90	17	11	米/千克	B5	Voiles and fine thin cloth of cotton, plain weave, mixed with man-made filaments, w≤200g/m^2, containing < 85% by weight of cotton, ≥ No. 69, dyed
5210.3100 91	染色与其他化纤混纺棉府绸(每平米重≤200克,含棉85%以下,含细平布)	10				90	17	11	米/千克	B5	Poplin and fine plain cloth of cotton, plain weave, mixed with other man-made fibres, w≤200g/m^2, containing < 85% by weight of cotton, dyed
5210.3100 92	染色与其他化纤混纺棉机织平布(每平米重≤200克,68号及以下,含棉85%以下)	10				90	17	11	米/千克	B5	Plain cloth of cotton, plain weave, mixed with other man-made fibres, w≤200g/m^2, containing < 85% by weight of cotton, ≤No. 68, dyed
5210.3100 93	染色与其他化纤混纺棉奶酪布(每平米重≤200克,含棉85%以下)	10				90	17	11	米/千克	B5	Cheese cloth of cotton, plain weave, mixed with other man-made fibres, w≤200g/m^2, containing < 85% by weight of cotton, dyed
5210.3100 94	染色与其他化纤混纺棉印染布(每平米重≤200克,43-68号,含棉85%以下)	10				90	17	11	米/千克	B5	Cloth for printing and dying of cotton, plain weave, mixed with other man-made fibres, w≤200g/m^2, containing < 85% by weight of cotton, No. 43-68, dyed
5210.3100 95	染色与其他化纤混纺棉巴里纱(每平米重≤200克,69号及以上,含棉85%以下,含薄细布)	10				90	17	11	米/千克	B5	Voiles and fine thin cloth of cotton, plain weave, mixed with other man-made fibres w ≤ 200g/m^2, containing < 85% by weight of cotton, ≥No. 69, dyed
5210.3200	--三线或四线斜纹机织物,包括双面斜纹机织物	10	T3	0	0	90	17	11	米/千克		--3-thread or 4-thread twill, including cross twill, including double twil
5210.3200 10	染色与聚酯短纤混纺的3/4线斜纹棉布(每平米重不超过200克,含棉85%以下,含双面斜纹布)	10				90	17	11	米/千克	B5	Woven fabrics of cotton, twill weave, 3 or 4-thread, including cross twill, mixed with polyester staple fibres, w≤200g/m^2 containing < 85% by weight of cotton

税则号列 Tariff Item.	货品名称	最惠国(%) MFN	协定(%)CT 东盟 CA	中巴 CP	中智 CC	普通 Gen	增值税率 VAT	出口退税 ED	计量单位 Unit	监管条件 SC	Article Description
5210.3200 20	染色与化纤长丝混纺的3/4线斜纹棉布(每平米重不超过200克,含棉85%以下,含双面斜纹布)	10				90	17	11	米/千克	B5	Woven fabrics of cotton, twill weave, 3 or 4-thread, including cross twill, mixed with man-made filaments, w≤200g/m^2, containing <85% by weight of cotton
5210.3200 90	染色与其他化纤混纺的3/4线斜纹棉布(每平米重不超过200克,含棉85%以下,含双面斜纹布)	10				90	17	11	米/千克	B5	Woven fabrics of cotton, twill weave, 3 or 4-thread, including cross twill, mixed with other man-made fibres, w≤200g/m^2, containing <85% by weight of cotton
5210.3900	--其他机织物	10	T3	0	0	90	17	11	米/千克		--Other fabrics
5210.3900 11	其他染色与聚酯短纤混纺缎布(每平米重≤200克,含棉85%以下)	10				90	17	11	米/千克	B5	Other woven fabrics of cotton, satin weave, mixed with polyester staple fibres, w≤200g/m^2, containing <85% by weight of cotton, dyed
5210.3900 12	其他染色与聚酯短纤混纺斜纹布(每平米重≤200克,含棉85%以下)	10				90	17	11	米/千克	B5	Other woven fabrics of cotton, twill weave, mixed with polyester staple fibres, w≤200g/m^2, containing <85% by weight of cotton, dyed
5210.3900 13	其他染色与聚酯短纤混纺牛津布(每平米重≤200克,含棉85%以下)	10				90	17	11	米/千克	B5	Other woven fabrics of cotton, oxford weave, mixed with polyester staple fibres, w≤200g/m^2, containing <85% by weight of cotton, dyed
5210.3900 19	其他染色与聚酯短纤混纺棉布(每平米重≤200克,含棉85%以下)	10				90	17	11	米/千克	B5	Other woven fabrics of cotton, mixed with polyester staple fibres, w≤200g/m^2, containing <85% by weight of cotton, dyed
5210.3900 21	其他染色与化纤长丝混纺缎布(每平方米重≤200克,含棉85%以下)	10				90	17	11	米/千克	B5	Other woven fabrics of cotton, satin weave, mixed with man-made filaments, w ≤ 200g/m^2, containing < 85% by weight of cotton, dyed
5210.3900 22	其他染色与化纤长丝混纺斜纹布(每平米重≤200克,含棉85%以下)	10				90	17	11	米/千克	B5	Other woven fabrics of cotton, twill weave, mixed with man-made filaments, w ≤ 200g/m^2, containing < 85% by weight of cotton, dyed
5210.3900 23	其他染色与化纤长丝混纺牛津布(每平米重≤200克,含棉85%以下)	10				90	17	11	米/千克	B5	Other woven fabrics of cotton, oxford weave, mixed with man-made filaments, w ≤ 200g/m^2, containing < 85% by weight of cotton, dyed
5210.3900 29	其他染色与化纤长丝混纺棉布(每平米重≤200克,含棉85%以下)	10				90	17	11	米/千克	B5	Other woven fabrics of cotton mixed with man-made filaments, w ≤ 200g/m^2, containing <85% by weight of cotton, dyed
5210.3900 91	其他染色与其他化纤混纺缎布(每平米重≤200克,含棉85%以下)	10				90	17	11	米/千克	B5	Other woven fabrics of cotton, satin weave, mixed with other man-made fibres, w≤200g/m^2, containing <85% by weight of cotton, dyed

税则号列 Tariff Item.	货品名称	最惠国(%) MFN	协定(%)CT 东盟 CA	中巴 CP	中智 CC	普通 Gen	增值税率 VAT	出口退税 ED	计量单位 Unit	监管条件 SC	Article Description
5210.3900 92	其他染色与其他化纤混纺斜纹布(每平米重≤200克,含棉85%以下)	10				90	17	11	米/千克	B5	Other woven fabrics of cotton, twill weave, mixed with other man-made fibres, w≤200g/m^2, containing <85% by weight of cotton, dyed
5210.3900 93	其他染色与其他化纤混纺牛津布(每平米重≤200克,含棉85%以下)	10				90	17	11	米/千克	B5	Other woven fabrics of cotton, oxford weave, mixed with other man-made fibres, w≤200g/m^2, containing <85% by weight of cotton, dyed
5210.3900 99	其他染色与其他化纤混纺棉布(每平米重≤200克,含棉85%以下)	10				90	17	11	米/千克	B5	Other woven fabrics of cotton, mixed with other man-made fibres, w≤200g/m^2, containing < 85% by weight of cotton, dyed
	-色织:										-Of yarns of different colours:
5210.4100	--平纹机织物	10	T3	0	0	90	17	11	米/千克		--Plain weave
5210.4100 10	色织与聚酯短纤混纺棉平纹布(每平米重≤200克,含棉85%以下)	10				90	17	11	米/千克	B5	Plain cloth of cotton, plain weave, mixed with polyester staple fibres, w≤200g/m^2, containing <85% by weight of cotton, of yarns of different colours
5210.4100 20	色织与化纤长丝混纺棉平纹布(每平米重≤200克,含棉85%以下)	10				90	17	11	米/千克	B5	Plain cloth of cotton, plain weave, mixed with man-made filaments, w≤200g/m^2, containing <85% by weight of cotton, of yarns of different colours
5210.4100 90	色织与其他化纤混纺棉平纹布(每平米重≤200克,含棉85%以下)	10				90	17	11	米/千克	B5	Plain cloth of cotton, plain weave, mixed with other man-made fibres, w≤200g/m^2, containing <85% by weight of cotton, of yarns of different colours
	--其他机织物:										
5210.4910	---三线或四线斜纹机织物,包括双面斜纹机织物	10	T3	0	0	90	17	11	米/千克		---3-thread or 4-thread twill, including cross twill, including double twil
5210.4910 10	色织与聚酯短纤混纺3/4斜纹棉布(每平米重≤200克,含棉85%以下,含双面斜纹布)	10				90	17	11	米/千克	B5	Woven fabrics of cotton, twill weave(3 or 4-thread , cross twill), mixed with polyester staple fibres, w≤200g/m^2, containing <85% by weight of cotton, of yarns of different colours
5210.4910 20	色织与化纤长丝混纺3/4斜纹棉布(每平米重≤200克,含棉85%以下,含双面斜纹布)	10				90	17	11	米/千克	B5	Woven fabrics of cotton, twill weave(including 3 or 4-thread , cross twill), mixed with other man-made fibres, w≤200g/m^2, containing <85% by weight of cotton, of yarns of different colours
5210.4910 90	色织其他化纤混纺3/4斜纹棉布(每平米重≤200克,含棉85%以下,含双面斜纹布)	10				90	17	11	米/千克	B5	Woven fabrics of cotton, twill weave(including 3 or 4-thread , cross twill), mixed with other man-made fibres, w≤200g/m^2, containing <85% by weight of cotton, of yarns of different colours
5210.4990	---其他	10	T3	0	0	90	17	11	米/千克		---Other

税则号列 Tariff Item.	货 品 名 称	最惠国(%) MFN	协定(%)CT 东盟 CA	 中巴 CP	 中智 CC	普通 Gen	增值税率 VAT	出口退税 ED	计量单位 Unit	监管条件 SC	Article Description
5210.4990 11	色织与聚酯短纤混纺提花布(每平米重不超过200克,含棉85%以下)	10				90	17	11	米/千克	B5	Other woven fabrics of cotton, jacquard weave, mixed with polyester staple fibres w≤200g/m^2, containing < 85% by weight of cotton, of yarns of different colours
5210.4990 19	色织与聚酯短纤混纺其他棉布(每平方米重量不超过200克,含棉85%以下)	10				90	17	11	米/千克	B5	Other woven fabrics of cotton, mixed with polyester staple fibres, w ≤ 200g/m^2, containing < 85% by weight of cotton, of yarns of different colours
5210.4990 21	色织与化纤长丝混纺提花布(每平米重不超过200克,含棉85%以下)	10				90	17	11	米/千克	B5	Other woven fabrics of cotton jacquard weave, mixed with man-made filaments, w ≤200g/m^2, containing < 85% by weight of cotton, of yarns of different colours
5210.4990 29	色织与化纤长丝混纺其他棉布(每平米重不超过200克,含棉85%以下)	10				90	17	11	米/千克	B5	Other woven fabrics of cotton, mixed with man-made filaments, w ≤ 200g/m^2, containing < 85% by weight of cotton, of yarns of different colours
5210.4990 91	色织与其他化纤混纺提花布(每平米重不超过200克,含棉85%以下)	10				90	17	11	米/千克	B5	Other woven fabrics of cotton, jacquard weave, mixed with other man-made fibres, w ≤ 200g/m^2, containing < 85% by weight of cotton, of yarns of different colours
5210.4990 99	色织与其他化纤混纺其他棉布(每平米重不超过200克,含棉85%以下)	10				90	17	11	米/千克	B5	Other woven fabrics of cotton, mixed with other man-made fibres, w≤200g/m^2, containing < 85% by weight of cotton, of yarns of different colours
	--印花:										-Printed:
5210.5100	--平纹机织物	10	5	0	0	90	17	11	米/千克		--Plain weave
5210.5100 11	印花与聚酯短纤混纺的棉府绸(每平米重≤200克,含棉85%以下,含细平布)	10				90	17	11	米/千克	B5	Poplin and fine plain cloth of cotton, mixed with polyester staple fibres, w≤200g/m^2, containing < 85% by weight of cotton printed
5210.5100 12	印花与聚酯短纤混纺棉机织平布(每平米重≤200克,68号及以下,含棉85%以下)	10				90	17	11	米/千克	B5	Plain cloth of cotton, mixed with polyester staple fibres, w≤200g/m^2, containing < 85% by weight of cotton, ≤ No. 68, printed
5210.5100 13	印花与聚酯短纤混纺的棉奶酪布(每平米重≤200克,含棉85%以下)	10				90	17	11	米/千克	B5	Cheese cloth of cotton, mixed with polyester staple fibres w≤200g/m^2, containing < 85% by weight of cotton, printed
5210.5100 14	印花与聚酯短纤混纺棉印染布(每平米重≤200克,43–68号及以下,含棉85%以下)	10				90	17	11	米/千克	B5	Cloth for printing and dying of cotton, mixed with polyester staple fibres, w≤200g/m^2, containing < 85% by weight of cotton No. 43 – 68, printed
5210.5100 15	印花与聚酯短纤混纺棉巴里纱(每平米重≤200克,69号及以上,含棉85%以下,含薄细布)	10				90	17	11	米/千克	B5	Voiles and fine thin cloth of cotton, mixed with polyester staple fibres, w≤200g/m^2, containing < 85% by weight of cotton≥No. 69, printed

税则号列 Tariff Item.	货品名称	最惠国(%) MFN	协定(%)CT 东盟 CA	中巴 CP	中智 CC	普通 Gen	增值税率 VAT	出口退税 ED	计量单位 Unit	监管条件 SC	Article Description
5210.5100 21	印花与化纤长丝混纺的棉府绸(每平米重≤200克,含棉85%以下,含细平布)	10				90	17	11	米/千克	B5	Poplin and fine plain cloth of cotton, mixed with man-made filaments, w≤200g/m^2, containing<85% by weight of cotton, printed
5210.5100 22	印花与化纤长丝混纺棉机织平布(每平米重≤200克,68号及以下,含棉85%以下)	10				90	17	11	米/千克	B5	Plain cloth of cotton, mixed with man-made filaments, w≤200g/m^2, containing<85% by weight of cotton, ≤No. 68, printed
5210.5100 23	印花与化纤长丝混纺棉奶酪布(每平米重≤200克,含棉85%以下)	10				90	17	11	米/千克	B5	Cheese cloth of cotton, mixed with man-made filaments w≤200g/m^2, containing < 85% by weight of cotton, printed
5210.5100 24	印花与化纤长丝混纺棉印染布(每平米重≤200克,43-68号,含棉85%以下)	10				90	17	11	米/千克	B5	Cloth for printing and dying of cotton, mixed with man-made filaments, w≤200g/m^2, containing<85% by weight of cotton, No. 43-68, printed
5210.5100 25	印花与化纤长丝混纺棉巴里纱(每平米重≤200克,69号及以上,含棉85%以下,含薄细布)	10				90	17	11	米/千克	B5	Voiles, including ine thin cloth of cotton, mixed with man-made filaments, w≤200g/m^2, containing < 85% by weight of cotton≥No. 69, printed
5210.5100 91	印花与其他化纤混纺的棉府绸(每平米重≤200克,含棉85%以下,含细平布)	10				90	17	11	米/千克	B5	Poplin and fine plain cloth of cotton, mixed with other man-made fibres, w≤200g/m^2, containing<85% by weight of cotton, printed
5210.5100 92	印花与其他化纤混纺棉机织平布(每平米重≤200克,68号及以下,含棉85%以下)	10				90	17	11	米/千克	B5	Plain cloth of cotton, plain weave, mixed with other man-made fibres, w≤200g/m^2, containing<85% by weight of cotton, ≤No. 68, printed
5210.5100 93	印花与其他化纤混纺的棉奶酪布(每平米重≤200克,含棉85%以下)	10				90	17	11	米/千克	B5	Cheese cloth of cotton, mixed with other man-made fibres, w≤200g/m^2, containing < 85% by weight of cotton, printed
5210.5100 94	印花与其他化纤混纺棉印染布(每平米重≤200克,43-68号及以下,含棉85%以下)	10				90	17	11	米/千克	B5	Cloth for printing and dying of cotton, mixed with other man-made fibres, w≤200g/m^2, containing<85% by weight of cotton, No. 43-68, printed
5210.5100 95	印花与其他化纤混纺棉巴里纱(每平米重≤200克,65号及以上,含棉85%以下,含薄细布)	10				90	17	11	米/千克	B5	Voiles and ine thin cloth of cotton, mixed with other man-made fibres, w≤200g/m^2, containing<85% by weight of cotton, ≥No. 65, printed
	--其他机织物:										--Other fabrics:
5210.5910	---三线或四线斜纹机织物,包括双面斜纹机物	10	5	0	0	90	17	11	米/千克		---3-thread or 4-thread twill, including cross twill
5210.5910 10	印花与聚酯短纤混纺3/4线斜纹棉布(每平米重不超过200克,含棉85%以下,含双面斜纹布)	10				90	17	11	米/千克	B5	Woven fabrics of cotton, twill weave (3 or 4-thread, cross twill), mixed with polyester staple fibres, w≤200g/m^2, containing < 85% by weight of cotton, printed

税则号列 Tariff Item.	货品名称	最惠国(%) MFN	协定(%)CT 东盟 CA	中巴 CP	中智 CC	普通 Gen	增值税率 VAT	出口退税 ED	计量单位 Unit	监管条件 SC	Article Description
5210.5910 20	印花化纤长丝混纺3/4线斜纹棉布(每平米重不超过200克,含棉85%以下,含双面斜纹布)	10				90	17	11	米/千克	B5	Woven fabrics of cotton, twill weave(3 or 4-thread, cross twill), mixed with man-made filaments w≤200g/m^2, containing <85% by weight of cotton, printed
5210.5910 90	印花其他化纤混纺3/4线斜纹棉布(每平米重不超过200克,含棉85%以下,含双面斜纹布)	10				90	17	11	米/千克	5B	Woven fabrics of cotton, twill weave(3 or 4-thread, cross twill), mixed with other man-made fibres, w≤200g/m^2, containing < 85% by weight of cotton printed
5210.5990	---其他	10	5	0	0	90	17	11	米/千克		---Other
5210.5990 11	其他印花与聚酯短纤混纺缎布(每平米重不超过200克,含棉85%以下)	10				90	17	11	米/千克	5B	Other woven fabrics of cotton, satin weave, mixed with polyester staple fibres, w≤200g/m^2, containing < 85% by weight of cotton, printed
5210.5990 12	其他印花与聚酯短纤混纺斜纹布(每平米重不超过200克,含棉85%以下)	10				90	17	11	米/千克	5B	Other woven fabrics of cotton, twill weave, mixed with polyester staple fibres, w≤200g/m^2, containing < 85% by weight of cotton, printed
5210.5990 13	其他印花与聚酯短纤混纺牛津布(每平米重不超过200克,含棉85%以下)	10				90	17	11	米/千克	5B	Other woven fabrics of cotton, mixed with man-made filaments, w≤200g/m^2, containing <85% by weight of cotton, printed
5210.5990 19	其他印花与聚酯短纤混纺棉布(每平米重不超过200克,含棉85%以下)	10				90	17	11	米/千克	5B	Other woven fabrics of cotton, mixed withpolyester staple fibres, w≤200g/m^2, containing <85% by weight of cotton, printed
5210.5990 21	其他印花与化纤长丝混纺缎布(每平米重不超过200克,含棉85%以下)	10				90	17	11	米/千克	5B	Other woven fabrics of cotton, satin weave, mixed with man-made filaments, w≤200g/m^2, containing < 85% by weight of cotton, printed
5210.5990 22	其他印花与化纤长丝混纺斜纹布(每平米重不超过200克,含棉85%以下)	10				90	17	11	米/千克	5B	Other woven fabrics of cotton, twill weave, mixed with man-made filaments, w≤200g/m^2, containing < 85% by weight of cotton, printed
5210.5990 23	其他印花与化纤长丝混纺牛津布(每平米重不超过200克,含棉85%以下)	10				90	17	11	米/千克	5B	Other woven fabrics of cotton, oxford weave, mixed with man-made fila-ments, w≤200g/m^2, containing <85% by weight of cotton, printed
5210.5990 29	其他印花与化纤长丝混纺棉布(每平米重不超过200克,含85%以下)	10				90	17	11	米/千克	5B	Other woven fabrics of cotton, mixed with man-made filaments, w≤200g/m^2, containing <85% by weight of cotton, printed
5210.5990 91	其他印花与其他化纤混纺缎布(每平米重不超过200克,含棉85%以下)	10				90	17	11	米/千克	5B	Other woven fabrics of cotton, satin weave, mixed with other man-made fibres, wb200g/m^3, containing <85% by weight of cotton, printed

税则号列 Tariff Item.	货品名称	最惠国(%) MFN	协定(%)CT 东盟 CA	中巴 CP	中智 CC	普通 Gen	增值税率 VAT	出口退税 ED	计量单位 Unit	监管条件 SC	Article Description
5210.5990 92	其他印花与其他化纤混纺斜纹布(每平米重不超过200克,含棉85%以下)	10				90	17	11	米/千克	5B	Other woven fabrics of cotton, twill weave, mixed with other man-made fibres, w ≤ 200g/m^2, containing < 85% by weight of cotton, printed
5210.5990 93	其他印花与其他化纤混纺牛津布(每平米重不超过200克,含棉85%以下)	10				90	17	11	米/千克	5B	Other woven fabrics of cotton, oxford weave, mixed with other man-made fibres, wb200g/m^2, containing < 85% by weight of cotton, printed
5210.5990 99	其他印花与其他化纤混纺棉布(每平米重不超过200克,含棉85%以下)	10				90	17	11	米/千克	5B	Other woven fabrics of cotton, mixed with other man-made fibrews, w≤200g/m^2, containing < 85% by weight of cotton, printed
52.11	**棉机织物,按重量计含棉量在85%以下,主要或仅与化学纤维混纺,每平方米重量超过200克:**										**Woven fabrics of cotton, containing less than 85% by weight of cotton, mixed mainly or solely with man-made fibres, weighing more than 200 g/m^2:**
	-未漂白:										-Unbleached:
5211.1100	--平纹机织物	12	T3	0	0	90	17	11	米/千克		--Plain weave
5211.1100 11	未漂白与聚酯短纤混纺棉府绸(每平方米重 > 200克,含棉85%以下,含细平布)	12				90	17	11	米/千克	5B	Poplin and fine plain cloth of cotton, mixed with polyester staple fibres, w > 200g/m^2, containing < 85% by weight of cotton, unbleached
5211.1100 12	未漂白与聚酯短纤混纺棉机织平布(每平方米重 > 200克,含棉85%以下)	12				90	17	11	米/千克	5B	Plain cloth of cotton, mixed with polyester staple fibres, w > 200g/m^2, containing < 85% by weight of cotton, unbleached
5211.1100 19	未漂白与聚酯短纤混纺棉平纹帆布(每平方米重 > 200克,含棉85%以下)	12				90	17	11	米/千克	5B	Canvas of cotton, mixed with polyester staple fibres, plain weave, w > 200g/m^2, containing < 85% by weight of cotton, unbleached
5211.1100 91	未漂白与其他化纤混纺棉府绸(每平方米重 > 200克,含棉85%以下,含细平布)	12				90	17	11	米/千克	5B	Poplin and fine plain cloth of cotton, mixed with other man-made fibres, w > 200g/m^2, containing < 85% by weight of cotton, unbleached
5211.1100 92	未漂白与其他化纤混纺棉机织平布(每平方米重 > 200克,含棉85%以下)	12				90	17	11	米/千克	5B	Plain cloth of cotton, mixed with other man-made fibres, w > 200g/m^2, containing < 85% by weight of cotton, unbleached
5211.1100 99	未漂白与其他化纤混纺棉平纹帆布(每平方米重 > 200克,含棉85%以下)	12				90	17	11	米/千克	5B	Canvas of cotton, mixed with other man-made fibres, plain weave, w > 200g/m^2, containing < 85% by weight of cotton unbleached
5211.1200	--三线或四线斜纹机织物,包括双面斜纹机织物	12	T3	0	0	90	17	11	米/千克		--3-thread or 4-thread twill, including cross twill, including double twil
5211.1200 10	未漂白聚酯短纤混纺斜纹棉布(每平米重 > 200克,含棉85%以下,3/4线斜纹布,双面斜纹布)	12				90	17	11	米/千克	5B	Woven fabrics of cotton, twill weave (3-or 4-thread), mixed with polyester staple fibres, w > 200g/m^2, containing < 85% by weight of cotton, unbleached

税则号列 Tariff Item.	货品名称	最惠国(%) MFN	协定(%)CT 东盟 CA	中巴 CP	中智 CC	普通 Gen	增值税率 VAT	出口退税 ED	计量单位 Unit	监管条件 SC	Article Description
5211.1200 90	未漂白其他化纤混纺斜纹棉布(每平米重>200克,含棉85%以下,3/4线斜纹布,双面斜纹布)	12				90	17	11	米/千克	5B	Woven fabrics of cotton, twill weave (3-or 4-thread), mixed with other man-made fibres, w>200g/m², containing<85% by weight of cotton, unbleached
5211.1900	--其他机织物	12	T3	0	0	90	17	11	米/千克		--Other fabrics
5211.1900 11	未漂白与聚酯短纤混纺其他棉缎布(每平米重>200克,含棉85%以下)	12				90	17	11	米/千克	5	Other woven fabrics of cotton, satin weave, mixed with polyester staple fibres, w>200g/m², containing<85% by weight of cotton, unbleached
5211.1900 12	未漂白与聚酯短纤混纺其他棉斜纹布(每平米重>200克,含棉85%以下)	12				90	17	11	米/千克	5	Other woven fabrics of cotton, twill weave, mixed with polyester staple fibres, w>200g/m², containing<85% by weight of cotton, unbleached
5211.1900 13	未漂白与聚酯短纤混纺其他棉帆布(每平米重>200克,含棉85%以下)	12				90	17	11	米/千克	5	Other canvas of cotton, mixed with polyester staple fibres, w>200g/m², containing<85% by weight of cotton, unbleached
5211.1900 19	未漂白与聚酯短纤混纺其他棉布(每平米重>200克,含棉85%以下)	12				90	17	11	米/千克	5	Other woven fabrics of cotton, mixed with polyester staple fibres, w>200g/m², containing<85% by weight of cotton, unbleached
5211.1900 91	未漂白与其他化纤混纺其他棉缎布(每平米重>200克,含棉85%以下)	12				90	17	11	米/千克	5	Other woven fabrics of cotton, satin weave, mixed with other man-made fibres, w>200g/m², containing<85% by weight of cotton, unbleached
5211.1900 92	未漂白与其他化纤混纺其他棉斜纹布(每平米重>200克,含棉85%以下)	12				90	17	11	米/千克	5	Other woven fabrics of cotton, twill weave, mixed with other man-made fibres, w>200g/m², containing<85% by weight of cotton, unbleached
5211.1900 93	未漂白与其他化纤混纺其他棉帆布(每平米重>200克,含棉85%以下)	12				90	17	11	米/千克	5	Other canvas of cotton, mixed with other man-made fibres, w>200g/m², containing<85% by weight of cotton, unbleached
5211.1900 99	未漂白与其他化纤混纺其他棉布(每平米重>200克,含棉85%以下)	12				90	17	11	米/千克	5	Other woven fabrics of cotton, mixed with other man-made fibres, w>200g/m², containing<85% by weight of cotton, unbleached
5211.2000	-漂白	14	8	0	0	90	17	11	米/千克	5B	-Bleached
	-染色:										-Dyed:
5211.3100	--平纹机织物	10	8	0	0	90	17	11	米/千克		--Plain weave
5211.3100 11	染色与聚酯短纤混纺棉府绸(每平米重>200克,含棉85%以下,含细平布)	10				90	17	11	米/千克	5B	Poplin and fine plain cloth of cotton, mixed with polyester staple fibres, w>200g/m², containing<85% by weight of cotton, dyed
5211.3100 12	染色与聚酯短纤混纺机织平布(每平米重>200克,含棉85%以下)	10				90	17	11	米/千克	5B	Plain cloth of cotton, mixed with polyester staple fibres, w>200g/m², containing<85% by weight of cotton, dyed

税则号列 Tariff Item.	货品名称	最惠国(%) MFN	协定(%) CT 东盟 CA	中巴 CP	中智 CC	普通 Gen	增值税率 VAT	出口退税 ED	计量单位 Unit	监管条件 SC	Article Description
5211.3100 13	染色与聚酯短纤混纺平纹帆布(每平米重>200克,含棉85%以下)	10				90	17	11	米/千克	5B	Canvas of cotton, plain weave, mixed with polyester staple fibres, w>200g/m^2, containing<85% by weight of cotton, dyed
5211.3100 21	染色与化纤长丝混纺棉府绸(每平米重>200克,含棉85%以下,含细平布)	10				90	17	11	米/千克	5B	Poplin and fine plain cloth of cotton, mixed with man-made filaments, w>200g/m^2, containing<85% by weight of cotton, dyed
5211.3100 22	染色与化纤长丝混纺机织平布(每平米重>200克,含棉85%以下)	10				90	17	11	米/千克	5B	Plain cloth of cotton, mixed with man-made filaments, w>200g/m^2, containing<85% by weight of cotton, dyed
5211.3100 23	染色与化纤长丝混纺平纹帆布(每平米重>200克,含棉85%以下)	10				90	17	11	米/千克	5B	Canvas of cotton, mixed with man-made filaments, w>200g/m^2, containing<85% by weight of cotton, dyed
5211.3100 91	染色与其他化纤混纺棉府绸(每平米重>200克,含棉85%以下,含细平布)	10				90	17	11	米/千克	5B	Poplin and fine plain cloth of cotton, mixed with other man-made fibres, w>200g/m^2, containing<85% by weight of cotton, dyed
5211.3100 92	染色与其他化纤混纺机织平布(每平米重>200克,含棉85%以下)	10				90	17	11	米/千克	5B	Plain cloth of cotton, mixed with other man-made fibres, w>200g/m^2, containing < 85% by weight of cotton, dyed
5211.3100 93	染色与其他化纤混纺平纹帆布(每平米重>200克,含棉85%以下)	10				90	17	11	米/千克	5B	Canvas of cotton, plain weave, mixed with other man-made fibres, w>200g/m^2, containing<85% by weight of cotton, dyed
5211.3200	--三线或四线斜纹机织物,包括双面斜纹机织物	10	T3	0	0	90	17	11	米/千克		--3-thread or 4-thread twill, including cross twill,including double twil
5211.3200 10	染色聚酯短纤混纺3/4线斜纹棉布(每平米重>200克,含棉85%以下,含双面斜纹布)	10				90	17	11	米/千克	5B	Woven fabrics of cotton, twill weave (3 or 4-thread, cross twill), mixed with polyester staple fibres, w>200g/m^2, containing<85% by weight of cotton, dyed
5211.3200 20	染色化纤长丝混纺3/4线斜纹棉布(每平米重>200克,含棉85%以下,含双面斜纹布)	10				90	17	11	米/千克	5B	Woven fabrics of cotton, twill weave (3 or 4-thread, cross twill), mixed with man-made filaments, w>200g/m^2, containing<85% by weight of cotton, dyed
5211.3200 90	染色其他化纤混纺3/4线斜纹棉布(每平米重>200克,含棉85%以下,含双面斜纹布)	10				90	17	11	米/千克	5B	Woven fabrics of cotton, twill weave (3 or 4-thread, cross twill), mixed with other man-made fibres, w>200g/m^2, containing<85% by weight of cotton, dyed
5211.3900	--其他机织物	10	8	0	0	90	17	11	米/千克		--Other fabrics
5211.3900 11	染色与聚酯短纤混纺的棉缎布(每平米重>200克,含棉85%以下)	10				90	17	11	米/千克	5B	Woven fabrics of cotton, satin weave, mixed with polyester staple fibres, w>200g/m^2, containing<85% by weight of cotton, dyed
5211.3900 12	染色与聚酯短纤混纺的棉斜纹布(每平米重>200克,含棉85%以下)	10				90	17	11	米/千克	5B	Woven fabrics of cotton, twill weave, mixed with polyester staple fibres, w>200g/m^2, containing<85% by weight of cotton, dyed

税则号列 Tariff Item.	货品名称	最惠国(%) MFN	协定(%) CT 东盟 CA	中巴 CP	中智 CC	普通 Gen	增值税率 VAT	出口退税 ED	计量单位 Unit	监管条件 SC	Article Description
5211.3900 13	染色与聚酯短纤混纺的棉帆布(每平米重>200克,含棉85%以下)	10				90	17	11	米/千克	5B	Canvas of cotton, mixed with polyester staple fibres, w>200g/m^2, containing <85% by weight of cotton, dyed
5211.3900 19	染色与聚酯短纤混纺其他棉布(每平米重>200克,含棉85%以下)	10				90	17	11	米/千克	5B	Other woven fabrics of cotton, mixed with polyester staple fibres, w>200g/m^2, containing<85% by weight of cotton, dyed
5211.3900 21	染色与化纤长丝混纺的棉缎布(每平米重>200克,含棉85%以下)	10				90	17	11	米/千克	5B	Woven fabrics of cotton, satin weave, mixed with man-made filaments, w>200g/m^2, containing<85% by weight of cotton, dyed
5211.3900 22	染色与化纤长丝混纺的棉斜纹布(每平米重>200克,含棉85%以下)	10				90	17	11	米/千克	5B	Woven fabrics of cotton, twill weave, mixed with man-made filaments, w>200g/m^2, containing<85% by weight of cotton, dyed
5211.3900 23	染色与化纤长丝混纺的棉帆布(每平米重>200克,含棉85%以下)	10				90	17	11	米/千克	5B	Canvas of cotton, mixed with man-made filaments, w>200g/m^2, containing<85% by weight of cotton, dyed
5211.3900 29	染色与化纤长丝混纺的其他棉布(每平米重>200克,含棉85%以下)	10				90	17	11	米/千克	5B	Woven fabrics of cotton, mixed with man-made filaments, w>200g/m^2, containing <85% by weight of cotton, dyed
5211.3900 91	染色与其他化纤混纺的棉缎布(每平米重>200克,含棉85%以下)	10				90	17	11	米/千克	5B	Woven fabrics of cotton, satin weave, mixed with other man-made fibres, w>200g/m^2, containing<85% by weight of cotton, dyed
5211.3900 92	染色与其他化纤混纺的棉斜纹布(每平米重>200克,含棉85%以下)	10				90	17	11	米/千克	5B	Woven fabrics of cotton, twill weave, mixed with other man-made fibres w>200g/m^2, containing<85% by weight of cotton, dyed
5211.3900 93	染色与其他化纤混纺的棉帆布(每平米重>200克,含棉85%以下)	10				90	17	11	米/千克	5B	Canvas of cotton, mixed with other man-made fibres, w>200g/m^2, containing<85% by weight of cotton, dyed
5211.3900 99	染色与其他化纤混纺其他棉布(每平米重>200克,含棉85%以下)	10				90	17	11	米/千克	5B	Other woven fabrics of cotton, mixed with other man-made fibres, w>200g/m^2, con-taining <85% by weight of cotton, dyed
	-色织:										-Of yarns of different colours:
5211.4100	--平纹机织物	10	5	0	0	90	17	11	米/千克		--Plain weave
5211.4100 10	色织与聚酯短纤混纺平纹棉布(每平米重超过200克,含棉85%以下)	10				90	17	11	米/千克	5B	Woven fabrics of cotton, plain weave mixed with polyester staple fibres, w>200g/m^2, containing<85% by weight of cotton, of yarns of different colours
5211.4100 20	色织与化纤长丝混纺平纹棉布(每平米重超过200克,含棉85%以下)	10				90	17	11	米/千克	5B	Woven fabrics of cotton, plain weave mixed with man-made filaments, w>200g/m^2, containing<85% by weight of cotton, of yarns of different colours

税则号列 Tariff Item.	货品名称	最惠国(%) MFN	协定(%) CT 东盟 CA	中巴 CP	中智 CC	普通 Gen	增值税率 VAT	出口退税 ED	计量单位 Unit	监管条件 SC	Article Description
5211.4100 90	色织与其他化纤混纺平纹棉布(每平米重超过200克,含棉85%以下)	10				90	17	11	米/千克	5B	Woven fabrics of cotton, plain weave mixed with other man-made fibres, w > 200g/m², containing < 85% by weight of cotton, of yarns of different colours
5211.4200	--粗斜纹布(劳动布)	10	T3	0	0	90	17	11	米/千克		--Denim
5211.4200 10	色织与化纤混纺蓝色粗斜纹棉布(每平米重超过200克,含棉85%以下)	10				90	17	11	米/千克	5	Blue denim of cotton, mixed with other man-made fibres, w > 200g/m², containing < 85% by weight of cotton, of yarns of different colours
5211.4200 90	色织与化纤混纺非蓝色粗斜纹棉布(每平米重超过200克,含棉85%以下)	10				90	17	11	米/千克	5	Denim of cotton, other than blue, w > 200g/m² containing < 85% by weight of cotton, of yarns of different colours
5211.4300	--三线或四线斜纹机织物,包括双面斜纹机织物	10	5	0	0	90	17	11	米/千克		--Other fabrics of 3-thread or 4-thread twill, including cross twill, including double twil
5211.4300 10	色织与聚酯短纤混纺3/4线斜纹棉布(每平米重超过200克,含棉85%以下,含双面斜纹布)	10				90	17	11	米/千克	5	Woven fabrics of cotton, twill weave (3 or 4-thread, cross twill), mixed with polyester staple fibres, w > 200g/m², containing < 85% by weight of cotton, of yarns of different colours
5211.4300 20	色织与化纤长丝混纺3/4线斜纹棉布(每平米重超过200克,含棉85%以下,含双面斜纹布)	10				90	17	11	米/千克	5	Woven fabrics of cotton, twill weave (3 or 4-thread, cross twill), mixed with man-made filaments, w > 200g/m², containing < 85% by weight of cotton, of yarns of different colours
5211.4300 90	色织与其他化纤混纺3/4线斜纹棉布(每平米重超过200克,含棉85%以下,含双面斜纹布)	10				90	17	11	米/千克	5	Woven fabrics of cotton twill weave (3 or 4-thread, cross twill), mixed with other man-made fibres, w > 200g/m², containing < 85% by weight of cotton, 3 or 4-thread, cross twill, of yarns of different colours
5211.4900	--其他机织物	10	T3	0	0	90	17	11	米/千克		--Other fabrics
5211.4900 11	色织与聚酯短纤混纺的提花布(每平米重超过200克,含棉85%以下)	10				90	17	11	米/千克	5B	Woven fabrics, jacquard weave, mixed with polyester staple fibres, w > 200g/m², containing < 85% by weight of cotton, of yarns of different colours
5211.4900 19	色织与聚酯短纤混纺其他棉布(每平米重超过200克,含棉85%以下)	10				90	17	11	米/千克	5B	Other woven fabrics of cotton mixed with polyester staple fibres, w > 200g/m², containing < 85% by weight of cotton, of yarns of different colours
5211.4900 21	色织与化纤长丝混纺的提花布(每平米重超过200克,含棉85%以下)	10				90	17	11	米/千克	5B	Woven fabrics, jacquard weave, mixed with man-made filaments, w > 200g/m², containing < 85% by weight of cotton, of yarns of different colours
5211.4900 29	色织与化纤长丝混纺其他棉布(每平米重超过200克,含棉85%以下)	10				90	17	11	米/千克	5B	Other woven fabrics of cotton, mixed with man-made filaments, w > 200g/m², containing < 85% by weight of cotton, of yarns of different colours

税则号列 Tariff Item.	货品名称	最惠国(%) MFN	协定(%) 东盟 CA	协定(%) 中巴 CP	CT 中智 CC	普通 Gen	增值税率 VAT	出口退税 ED	计量单位 Unit	监管条件 SC	Article Description
5211.4900 91	色织与其他化纤混纺的提花布(每平米重超过200克,含棉85%以下)	10				90	17	11	米/千克	5B	Woven fabrics, jacquard weave, mixed with other man-made fibres, w > 200g/m^2, containing < 85% by weight of cotton, of yarns of different colours
5211.4900 99	色织与其他化纤混纺其他棉布(每平米重超过200克,含棉85%以下)	10				90	17	11	米/千克	5B	Other woven fabrics of cotton, mixed with other man-made fibres, w > 200g/m^2, containing < 85% by weight of cotton, of yarns of different colours
	-印花:										-Printed:
5211.5100	--平纹机织物	10	5	0	0	90	17	11	米/千克		--Plain weave
5211.5100 11	印花与聚酯短纤混纺棉府绸(每平米重超过200克,含棉85%以下,含细平布)	10				90	17	11	米/千克	5B	Poplin and fine plain cloth of cotton, mixed with polyester staple fibres w > 200g/m^2, containing < 85% by weight of cotton, printed
5211.5100 12	印花与聚酯短纤混纺的机织平布(每平米重超过200克,含棉85%以下)	10				90	17	11	米/千克	5B	Plain cloth, mixed with polyester staple fibres, w > 200g/m^2 containing < 85% by weight of cotton, printed
5211.5100 13	印花与聚酯短纤混纺的平纹帆布(每平米重超过200克,含棉85%以下)	10				90	17	11	米/千克	5B	Canvas, plain weave, mixed with polyester staple fibres w > 200g/m^2, containing < 85% by weight of cotton, printed
5211.5100 21	印花与化纤长丝混纺棉府绸(每平米重超过200克,含棉85%以下,含细平布)	10				90	17	11	米/千克	5B	Poplin and fine plain cloth of cotton, mixed with man-made filaments, w > 200g/m^2, containing < 85% by weight of cotton, printed
5211.5100 22	印花与化纤长丝混纺机织平布(每平米重超过200克,含棉85%以下)	10				90	17	11	米/千克	5B	Plain cloth, mixed with man-made filaments, w > 200g/m^2, containing < 85% by weight of cotton, printed
5211.5100 23	印花与化纤长丝混纺平纹帆布(每平米重超过200克,含棉85%以下)	10				90	17	11	米/千克	5B	Canvas, plain weave, mixed with man-made filaments, w > 200g/m^2, containing < 85% by weight of cotton, printed
5211.5100 91	印花与其他化纤混纺棉府绸(每平米重超过200克,含棉85%以下,含细平布)	10				90	17	11	米/千克	5B	Poplin and fine plain cloth of cotton, mixed with man-made filaments w > 200g/m^2, containing < 85% by weight of cotton, printed
5211.5100 92	印花与其他化纤混纺的机织平布(每平米重超过200克,含棉85%以下)	10				90	17	11	米/千克	5B	Plain cloth, mixed with man-made filaments w > 200g/m^2, containing < 85% by weight of cotton, printed
5211.5100 93	印花与其他化纤混纺的平纹帆布(每平米重超过200克,含棉85%以下)	10				90	17	11	米/千克	5B	Canvas, plain weave, mixed with man-made filaments w > 200g/m^2, containing < 85% by weight of cotton, printed
5211.5200	--三线或四线斜纹机织物,包括双面斜纹机织物	10	5	0	0	90	17	11	米/千克		--3-thread or 4-thread twill, including cross twill, including double twil
5211.5200 10	印花与聚酯短纤混纺3/4线斜纹棉布(每平米重超过200克,含棉85%以下,含双面斜纹布)	10				90	17	11	米/千克	5	Woven fabrics of cotton, twill weave (3 or 4-thread, cross twill), mixed with polyester staple fibres, w > 200g/m^2, containing < 85% by weight of cotton, printed
5211.5200 20	印花与化纤长丝混纺3/4线斜纹棉布(每平米重超过200克,含棉85%以下,含双面斜纹布)	10				90	17	11	米/千克	5	Woven fabrics of cotton, twill weave (3 or 4-thread, cross twill), mixed with man-made filaments, w > 200g/m^2, containing < 85% by weight of cotton, printed

税则号列 Tariff Item.	货品名称	最惠国(%) MFN	协定(%) CT 东盟 CA	中巴 CP	中智 CC	普通 Gen	增值税率 VAT	出口退税 ED	计量单位 Unit	监管条件 SC	Article Description
5211.5200 90	印花其他化纤混纺3/4线斜纹棉布(每平米重超过200克,含棉85%以下,含双面斜纹布)	10				90	17	11	米/千克	5	Woven fabrics of cotton, twill weave (3 or 4-thread, cross twill), mixed with other man-made fibres, w >200g/m^2, containing <85% by weight of cotton, printed
5211.5900	--其他机织物	10	5	0	0	90	17	11	米/千克		--Other fabrics
5211.5900 11	印花与聚酯短纤混纺棉缎布(每平米重超过200克,含棉85%以下)	10				90	17	11	米/千克	5	Other woven fabrics of cotton, satin weave, mixed with polyester staple fibres w > 200g/m^2, containing < 85% by weight of cotton, printed
5211.5900 12	印花与聚酯短纤混纺斜纹棉布(每平米重超过200克,含棉85%以下)	10				90	17	11	米/千克	5	Other woven fabrics of cotton, twill weave, mixed with polyester staple fibres, w > 200g/m^2, containing < 85% by weight of cotton, printed
5211.5900 13	印花与聚酯短纤混纺棉帆布(每平米重超过200克,含棉85%以下)	10				90	17	11	米/千克	5	Other canvas of cotton, mixed with polyester staple fibres, w >200g/m^2, containing <85% by weight of cotton, printed
5211.5900 19	印花与聚酯短纤混纺其他棉布(每平米重超过200克,含棉85%以下)	10				90	17	11	米/千克	5	Other woven fabrics of cotton, mixed with polyester staple fibres, w > 200g/m^2, containing <85% by weight of cotton, printed
5211.5900 21	印花与化纤长丝混纺棉缎布(每平米重超过200克,含棉85%以下)	10				90	17	11	米/千克	5	Other woven fabrics of cotton, satin weave, mixed with man-made filaments, w > 200g/m^2, containing < 85% by weight of cotton, printed
5211.5900 22	印花与化纤长丝混纺斜纹棉布(每平米重超过200克,含棉85%以下)	10				90	17	11	米/千克	5	Other woven fabrics of cotton, twill weave, mixed with man-made filaments, w > 200g/m^2, containing < 85% by weight of cotton, printed
5211.5900 23	印花与化纤长丝混纺棉帆布(每平米重超过200克,含棉85%以下)	10				90	17	11	米/千克	5	Other canvas of cotton, mixed with man-made filaments, w >200g/m^2, containing <85% by weight of cotton, printed
5211.5900 29	印花与化纤长丝混纺其他棉布(每平米重超过200克,含棉85%以下)	10				90	17	11	米/千克	5	Other woven fabrics of cotton, mixed with man-made filaments, w >200g/m^2, containing < 85% by weight of cotton, printed
5211.5900 91	印花与其他化纤混纺棉缎布(每平米重超过200克,含棉85%以下)	10				90	17	11	米/千克	5	Other woven fabrics of cotton, satin weave, mixed with other man-made fibres, w > 200g/m^2, containing < 85% by weight of cotton, printed
5211.5900 92	印花与其他化纤混纺斜纹棉布(每平米重超过200克,含棉85%以下)	10				90	17	11	米/千克	5	Other woven fabrics of cotton, twill weave, mixed with other man-made fibres w > 200g/m^2, containing < 85% by weight of cotton, printed
5211.5900 93	印花与其他化纤混纺棉帆布(每平米重超过200克,含棉85%以下)	10				90	17	11	米/千克	5	Other canvas of cotton, mixed with other man-made fibres, w >200g/m^2, containing <85% by weight of cotton printed

税则号列 Tariff Item.	货品名称	最惠国(%) MFN	协定(%) CT 东盟 CA	中巴 CP	中智 CC	普通 Gen	增值税率 VAT	出口退税 ED	计量单位 Unit	监管条件 SC	Article Description
5211.5900 99	印花与其他化纤混纺其他棉布(每平米重超过200克,含棉85%以下)	10				90	17	11	米/千克	5	Other woven fabrics of cotton, mixed with other man-made fibres, w > 200g/m^2, containing < 85% by weight of cotton, printed
52.12	**其他棉机织物:**										**Other woven fabrics of cotton:**
	-每平方米重量不超过200克:										-Weighing not more than 200 g/m^2:
5212.1100	--未漂白	12	T3	0	0	80	17	11	米/千克		--Unbleached
5212.1100 11	未漂白的其他混纺棉布(每平米重≤200克,与36%及以上精梳羊毛或动物细毛混纺)	12				80	17	11	米/千克	5B	Other woven fabrics of cotton, mixed, containing≥36% by weight of combed wool or fine animal hair, w ≤ 200g/m^2, unbleached
5212.1100 19	未漂白的其他混纺棉布(每平米重≤200克,与36%及以下精梳羊毛或动物细毛混纺)	12				80	17	11	米/千克	5B	Other woven fabrics of cotton, mixed, containing < 36% by weight of combed wool or fine animal hair, w≤200g/m^2, unbleached
5212.1100 21	未漂白的其他混纺棉布(每平米重≤200克,与36%及以上其他羊毛或动物细毛混纺)	12				80	17	11	米/千克	5B	Other woven fabrics of cotton, mixed, containing≥36% by weight other wool or fine animal hair, w≤200g/m^2, unbleached
5212.1100 29	未漂白的其他混纺棉布(每平米重≤200克,与其他羊毛或动物细毛混纺)	12				80	17	11	米/千克	5B	Other woven fabrics of cotton, mixed with other wool or fine animal hair, w ≤200g/m^2, unbleached
5212.1100 30	未漂白的其他混纺府绸及细平布(每平米重≤200克,与化纤、羊毛/动物细毛以外其他纤维混纺)	12				80	17	11	米/千克	5B	Other poplin and fine plain cloth, mixed with other fibres, other than man-made fibres, wool or fine animals hair, w≤200g/m^2, unbleached
5212.1100 40	未漂白的其他混纺棉机织平布(每平米重≤200克,与化纤、羊毛/动物细毛以外其他纤维混纺)	12				80	17	11	米/千克	5B	Other plain cloth of cotton, mixed with other fibres other than man-made fibres, wool or fine animals hair, w ≤ 200g/m^2, unbleached
5212.1100 50	未漂白的其他混纺棉印染布(每平米重≤200克,与化纤、羊毛/动物细毛以外其他纤维混纺)	12				80	17	11	米/千克	5B	Other cloth for printing and dying of cotton, mixed with other fibres other than man-made fibres, wool or fine animals hair, w≤200g/m^2, unbleached
5212.1100 60	未漂白其他混纺棉奶酪布,薄细布,巴里纱(每平米重≤200克,与化纤、羊毛/动物细毛以外其他纤维混纺)	12				80	17	11	米/千克	5B	Other cheese cloth and fine thin cloth of cotton, mixed with other fibres other than man-made fibres, wool or fine animals hair w≤200g/m^2, unbleached
5212.1100 70	未漂白的其他混纺棉缎布(每平米重≤200克,与化纤、羊毛/动物细毛以外其他纤维混纺)	12				80	17	11	米/千克	5B	Other woven fabrics of cotton, satin weave, mixed with other fibres, other than man-made fibres, wool or fine animals hair, w≤200g/m^2, unbleached
5212.1100 81	未漂白的其他混纺斜纹棉布(每平米重≤200克,与化纤、羊毛/动物细毛以外其他纤维混纺)	12				80	17	11	米/千克	5B	Other woven fabrics of cotton, twill weave, mixed with other fibres, other than man-made fibres, wool or fine animals hair, w≤200g/m^2, unbleached

税则号列 Tariff Item.	货品名称	最惠国(%) MFN	协定(%)CT 东盟 CA	中巴 CP	中智 CC	普通 Gen	增值税率 VAT	出口退税 ED	计量单位 Unit	监管条件 SC	Article Description
5212.1100 89	未漂白的其他混纺棉牛津布(每平米重≤200克,与化纤、羊毛/动物细毛以外其他纤维混纺)	12				80	17	13	米/千克	5B	Other woven fabrics of cotton, oxford weave, mixed with other fibres, other than man-made fibres, wool or fine animals hair, $w \leqslant 200g/m^2$, unbleached
5212.1100 90	未漂白的其他混纺棉布(每平米重≤200克,与化纤、羊毛/细毛以外其他纤维混纺)	12				80	17	11	米/千克	5B	Other woven fabrics of cotton, mixed with other fibres other than man-made fibres, wool or fine animals hair, $w \leqslant 200g/m^2$, unbleached
5212.1200	--漂白	14	8	0	0	80	17	11	米/千克		--Bleached
5212.1200 11	漂白的其他混纺棉布(每平米重≤200克,与36%及以上精梳羊毛或动物细毛混纺)	14				80	17	11	米/千克	5B	Other woven fabrics of cotton, $w \leqslant 200g/m^2$, mixed, containing≥36% by weight of combed wool or fine animal hair, bleached
5212.1200 19	漂白的其他混纺棉布(每平米重≤200克,与36%以下精梳羊毛或动物细毛混纺)	14				80	17	11	米/千克	5B	Other woven fabrics of cotton, $w \leqslant 200g/m^2$, mixed, containing≤36% by weight of combed wool or fine animal hair, bleached
5212.1200 21	漂白的其他混纺棉布(每平米重≤200克,与36%及以上其他羊毛或动物细毛混纺)	14				80	17	11	米/千克	5B	Other woven fabrics of cotton, $w \leqslant 200g/m^2$, mixed, containing≥36% by weight of wool or fine animal hair, bleached
5212.1200 29	漂白的其他混纺棉布(每平米重≤200克,与36%以下其他羊毛或动物细毛混纺)	14				80	17	11	米/千克	5B	Other woven fabrics of cotton, $w \leqslant 200g/m^2$, mixed, containing≤36% by weight of wool or fine animal hair, bleached
5212.1200 30	漂白的其他混纺府绸及平细布(每平米重≤200克,与除化纤/羊毛/动物细毛其他纤维混纺)	14				80	17	11	米/千克	5B	Poplin and fine plain cloth, mixed with other fibres other than man-made fibres, $w \leqslant 200g/m^2$, bleached
5212.1200 40	漂白的其他混纺棉机织平布(每平米重≤200克,与除化纤/羊毛/动物细毛其他纤维混纺)	14				80	17	11	米/千克	5B	Plain cloth, mixed with other fibres other than man-made fibres, wool or fine animal hair, $w \leqslant 200g/m^2$, bleached
5212.1200 50	漂白的其他混纺棉印染布(每平米重≤200克,与除化纤/羊毛/动物细毛其他纤维混纺)	14				80	17	11	米/千克	5B	Cloth for printing and dying, mixed with other fibres other than man-made fibres, wool or fine animal hair, $w \leqslant 200g/m^2$, bleached
5212.1200 60	漂白其他混纺棉奶酪布/薄细布/纱(每平米重≤200克,与除化纤/羊毛/动物细毛其他纤维混纺)	14				80	17	11	米/千克	5B	Cheese cloth/fine thin cloth/yarn, mixed with other fibres other than man-made fibres, wool or fine animal hair, $w \leqslant 200g/m^2$, bleached
5212.1200 71	漂白的其他混纺棉缎布(每平米重≤200克,与除化纤/羊毛/动物细毛其他纤维混纺)	14				80	17	11	米/千克	5B	Woven fabrics of cotton, satin weave, mixed with other fibres other than man-made fibres, wool or fine animal hair, $w \leqslant 200g/m^2$, bleached
5212.1200 72	漂白的其他混纺斜纹棉布(每平米重≤200克,与除化纤/羊毛/动物细毛其他纤维混纺)	14				80	17	11	米/千克	5B	Woven fabrics of cotton, twill weave, mixed with other fibres other than man-made fibres, wool or fine animal hair, $w \leqslant 200g/m^2$, bleached

税则号列 Tariff Item.	货品名称	最惠国(%) MFN	协定(%) CT 东盟 CA	中巴 CP	中智 CC	普通 Gen	增值税率 VAT	出口退税 ED	计量单位 Unit	监管条件 SC	Article Description
5212.1200 79	漂白的其他混纺棉牛津布(每平米重≤200克,与除化纤/羊毛/动物细毛其他纤维混纺)	14				80	17	11	米/千克	5B	Woven fabrics of cotton, oxford weave, mixed, with other fibres other than man-made fibres, wool or fine animal hair, w≤200g/m^2, bleached
5212.1200 90	漂白的其他混纺棉机织物(每平米重≤200克,与除化纤/羊毛/动物细毛其他纤维混纺)	14				80	17	11	米/千克	5B	Other woven fabrics of cotton, mixed with other fibres other than man-made fibres, wool or fine animal hair, w≤200g/m^2, bleached
5212.1300	--染色	10	5	0	0	80	17	11	米/千克		--Dyed
5212.1300 11	染色其他混纺棉布(每平米重≤200克,与36%及以上精梳羊毛/动物细毛混纺)	10				80	17	11	米/千克	5B	Other woven fabrics of cotton, w≤200g/m^2, mixed, containing≥36% by weight of combed wool or fine animal hair, dyed
5212.1300 19	染色其他混纺棉布(每平米重≤200克,与36%及以下精梳羊毛/动物细毛混纺)	10				80	17	11	米/千克	5B	Other woven fabrics of cotton, w≤200g/m^2, mixed, containing≤36% by weight, of combed wool or fine animal hair, dyed
5212.1300 21	染色其他混纺棉布(每平米重≤200克,与36%及以上其他羊毛/动物细毛混纺)	10				80	17	11	米/千克	5B	Other woven fabrics of cotton, w≤200g/m^2, mixed, containing≥36% by weight of wool or fine animal hair, dyed
5212.1300 29	染色其他混纺棉布(每平米重≤200克,与36%及以下其他羊毛/动物细毛混纺)	10				80	17	11	米/千克	5B	Other woven fabrics of cotton, w≤200g/m^2, mixed, containing≤36% by weight of wool or fine animal hair, dyed
5212.1300 30	染色其他混纺府绸及平细布(每平米重≤200克,与化纤以外其他纤维混纺)	10				80	17	11	米/千克	5B	Poplin and fine plain cloth, mixed with other fibres other than man-made fibres, w≤200g/m^2, dyed
5212.1300 40	染色其他混纺棉机织平布(每平米重≤200克,与化纤以外其他纤维混纺)	10				80	17	11	米/千克	5B	Plain cloth, mixed with other fibres other than man-made fibres, w≤200g/m^2, dyed
5212.1300 50	染色其他混纺棉印染布(每平米重≤200克,与化纤以外其他纤维混纺)	10				80	17	11	米/千克	5B	Cloth for printing and dying, mixed with other fibres other than man-made fibres, w≤200g/m^2, dyed
5212.1300 60	染色其他混纺奶酪布,薄细布,巴里纱(每平米重≤200克,与化纤以外其他纤维混纺)	10				80	17	11	米/千克	5B	Cheese cloth, voiles and fine thin cloth, mixed with other fibres other than man-made fibres, w≤200g/m^2, dyed
5212.1300 71	染色其他混纺棉缎布(每平米重≤200克,与化纤以外其他纤维混纺)	10				80	17	11	米/千克	5B	Other woven fabrics of cotton, satin weave, mixed with other fibres other than man-made fibres, w≤200g/m^2, dyed
5212.1300 72	染色其他混纺斜纹棉布(每平米重≤200克,与化纤以外其他纤维混纺)	10				80	17	11	米/千克	5B	Other woven fabrics of cotton, twill weave, mixed with other fibres other than man-made fibres, w≤200g/m^2, dyed
5212.1300 79	染色其他混纺棉牛津布(每平米重≤200克,与化纤以外其他纤维混纺)	10				80	17	11	米/千克	5B	Other woven fabrics of cotton, oxford weave, mixed with other fibres other than man-made fibres, w≤200g/m^2, dyed
5212.1300 90	染色其他混纺棉布(每平米重≤200克,与化纤以外其他纤维混纺)	10				80	17	11	米/千克	5B	Other woven fabrics of cotton, mixed with other fibres other than man-made fibres, w≤200g/m^2, dyed
5212.1400	--色织	10	5	0	0	80	17	11	米/千克		--Of yarns of different colours

税则号列 Tariff Item.	货品名称	最惠国(%) MFN	协定(%)CT 东盟 CA	中巴 CP	中智 CC	普通 Gen	增值税率 VAT	出口退税 ED	计量单位 Unit	监管条件 SC	Article Description
5212.1400 11	色织其他混纺棉布(每平米重≤200克,与36%及以上精梳羊毛/动物细毛混纺)	10				80	17	11	米/千克	5B	Other woven fabrics of cotton, w≤200g/m^2, mixed, containing≥36% by weight of combed wool or fine animal hair, of yarns of different colours
5212.1400 19	色织其他混纺棉布(每平米重≤200克,与36%及以下精梳羊毛/动物细毛混纺)	10				80	17	11	米/千克	5B	Other woven fabrics of cotton, w≤200g/m^2 mixed, containing≤36% by weight of combed wool or fine animal hair, of yarns of different colours
5212.1400 21	色织其他混纺棉布(每平米重≤200克,与36%及以上其他羊毛/动物细毛混纺)	10				80	17	11	米/千克	5B	Other woven fabrics of cotton, w≤200g/m^2, mixed, containing≥36% by weight of wool or fine animal hair, of yarns of different colours
5212.1400 29	色织其他混纺棉布(每平米重≤200克,与36%及以下其他羊毛/动物细毛混纺)	10				80	17	11	米/千克	5B	Other woven fabrics of cotton, mixed, containing≤36% by weight of wool or fine animal hair, w≤200g/m^2, of yarns of different colours
5212.1400 30	色织其他混纺棉提花布(每平米重≤200克,与化纤以外其他纤维混纺)	10				80	17	11	米/千克	5B	Other woven fabrics of cotton, jacquard weave, mixed with other fibres other than man-made fibres, w≤200g/m^2, of yarns of different colours
5212.1400 90	色织其他混纺棉布(每平米重≤200克,与化纤以外其他纤维混纺)	10				80	17	11	米/千克	5B	Other woven fabrics of cotton, mixed with other fibres other than man-made fibres w≤200g/m^2 of yarns of different colours
5212.1500	--印花	10	5	0	0	80	17	11	米/千克		--Printed
5212.1500 11	印花其他混纺棉布(每平米重≤200克,与36%及以上精梳羊毛/动物细毛混纺)	10				80	17	11	米/千克	5B	Other woven fabrics of cotton, mixed, containing≥36% by weight of combed wool or fine animal hair, w≤200g/m^2, printed
5212.1500 19	印花其他混纺棉布(每平米重≤200克,与36%及以下精梳羊毛/动物细毛混纺)	10				80	17	11	米/千克	5B	Other woven fabrics of cotton, mixed, containing≤36% by weight of combed wool or fine animal hair, w≤200g/m^2, printed
5212.1500 21	印花其他混纺棉布(每平米重≤200克,与36%及以上其他羊毛/动物细毛混纺)	10				80	17	11	米/千克	5B	Other woven fabrics of cotton, mixed, containing≥36% by weight of wool or fine animal hair, w≤200g/m^2, printed
5212.1500 29	印花其他混纺棉布(每平米重≤200克,与36%及以下其他羊毛/动物细毛混纺)	10				80	17	11	米/千克	5B	Other woven fabrics of cotton, mixed, containing≤36% by weight of wool or fine animal hair, w≤200g/m^2, printed
5212.1500 30	印花其他混纺府绸及平细布(每平米重≤200克,与化纤/羊毛/细毛以外其他纤维混纺)	10				80	17	11	米/千克	5B	Poplin and fine plain cloth, mixed with other fibres other than man-made fibres, wool or fine animals hair, w≤200g/m^2, printed
5212.1500 40	印花其他混纺棉机织平布(每平米重≤200克,与化纤/羊毛/细毛以外其他纤维混纺)	10				80	17	11	米/千克	5B	Plain cloth, mixed with other fibres other than man-made fibres, wool or fine animals hair, w≤200g/m^2, printed
5212.1500 50	印花其他混纺棉印染布(每平米重≤200克,与化纤/羊毛/细毛以外其他纤维混纺)	10				80	17	11	米/千克	5B	Cloth for printing and dying of cotton, mixed with other fibres other than man-made fibres, wool or fine animals hair, w≤200g/m^2, printed

税则号列 Tariff Item.	货品名称	最惠国(%) MFN	协定(%)CT 东盟 CA	中巴 CP	中智 CC	普通 Gen	增值税率 VAT	出口退税 ED	计量单位 Unit	监管条件 SC	Article Description
5212.1500 60	印花其他混纺棉奶酪布,薄细布,巴里纱(每平米重≤200克,与化纤/羊毛/细毛以外其他纤维混纺)	10				80	17	11	米/千克	5B	Cheese cloth, voiles and fine thin cloth, mixed with other fibres other than man-made fibres, wool or fine animals hair, w≤200g/m², printed
5212.1500 71	印花其他混纺棉缎布(每平米重≤200克,与化纤/羊毛/细毛以外其他纤维混纺)	10				80	17	11	米/千克	5B	Other woven fabrics of cotton, satin weave, mixed with other fibres other than man-made fibres, wool or fine animals hair, w≤200g/m², printed
5212.1500 72	印花其他混纺斜纹棉布(每平米重≤200克,与化纤/羊毛/细毛以外其他纤维混纺)	10				80	17	11	米/千克	5B	Other woven fabrics of cotton, twill weave, mixed with other fibres other than man-made fibres, wool or fine animals hair, w≤200g/m², printed
5212.1500 79	印花其他混纺棉牛津布(每平米重≤200克,与化纤/羊毛/细毛以外其他纤维混纺)	10				80	17	11	米/千克	5B	Other woven fabrics of cotton, oxford weave, mixed with other fibres other than man-made fibres, wool or fine animals hair, w≤200g/m², printed
5212.1500 90	印花其他混纺棉布(每平米重≤200克,与化纤/羊毛/细毛以外其他纤维混纺)	10				80	17	11	米/千克	5B	Other woven fabrics of cotton mixed with other fibres other than man-made fibres, wool or fine animals hair w≤200g/m², printed
	-每平方米重量超过200克:										-Weighing more than 200 g/m²:
5212.2100	--未漂白	12	8	0	0	80	17	11	米/千克		--Unbleached
5212.2100 11	未漂白其他混纺棉布(每平米重>200克,与36%及以上精梳羊毛/动物细毛混纺)	12				80	17	11	米/千克	5	Other woven fabrics of cotton, mixed, containing≥36% by weight of combed wool or fine animal hair, w>200g/m², unbleached
5212.2100 19	未漂白其他混纺棉布(每平米重>200克,与36%及以下精梳羊毛/动物细毛混纺)	12				80	17	11	米/千克	5	Other woven fabrics of cotton, mixed, containing≤36% by weight of combed wool or fine animal hair, w>200g/m², unbleached
5212.2100 21	未漂白其他混纺棉布(每平米重>200克,与36%及以上其他羊毛/动物细毛混纺)	12				80	17	11	米/千克	5	Other woven fabrics of cotton, mixed, containing≥36% by weight of wool or fine animal hair, w>200g/m², unbleached
5212.2100 29	未漂白其他混纺棉布(每平米重>200克,与36%及以下其他羊毛/动物细毛混纺)	12				80	17	11	米/千克	5	Other woven fabrics of cotton, mixed, containing≤36% by weight of wool or fine animal hair, w>200g/m², unbleached
5212.2100 30	未漂白其他混纺府绸及平细布(每平米重>200克,与化纤以外其他纤维混纺)	12				80	17	11	米/千克	5	Poplin and fine plain cloth, mixed with other fibres other than man-made fibres, w>200g/m², unbleached
5212.2100 40	未漂白其他混纺棉机织平布(每平米重>200克,与化纤以外其他纤维混纺)	12				80	17	11	米/千克	5	Plain cloth of cotton, mixed with other fibres other than man-made fibres, w>200g/m², unbleached
5212.2100 50	未漂白其他混纺棉帆布(每平米重>200克,与化纤以外其他纤维混纺)	12				80	17	11	米/千克	5	Canvas of cotton, mixed with other fibres other than man-made fibres, w>200g/m², unbleached

税则号列 Tariff Item.	货品名称	最惠国(%) MFN	协定(%) 东盟 CA	中巴 CP	CT 中智 CC	普通 Gen	增值税率 VAT	出口退税 ED	计量单位 Unit	监管条件 SC	Article Description
5212.2100 60	未漂白其他混纺棉缎布(每平米重>200克,与化纤以外其他纤维混纺)	12				80	17	11	米/千克	5	Other woven fabrics of cotton, satin weave, mixed with other fibres other than man-made fibres, w > 200g/m^2, unbleached
5212.2100 70	未漂白其他混纺斜纹棉布(每平米重>200克,与化纤以外其他纤维混纺)	12				80	17	11	米/千克	5	Other woven fabrics of cotton, twill weave, mixed with other fibres other than man-made fibres, w>200g/m^2, unbleached
5212.2100 90	未漂白其他混纺棉布(每平米重>200克,与化纤以外其他纤维混纺)	12				80	17	11	米/千克	5	Other woven fabrics of cotton, mixed with other fibres other than man-made fibres, w>200g/m^2, unbleached
5212.2200	--漂白	14	8	0	0	80	17	11	米/千克		--Bleached
5212.2200 11	漂白的其他混纺棉布(每平米重>200克,与36%及以上精梳羊毛/动物细毛混纺)	14				80	17	11	米/千克	5	Other woven fabrics of cotton, mixed, containing≥36% by weight of combed wool or fine animal hair, w > 200g/m^2, bleached
5212.2200 19	漂白的其他混纺棉布(每平米重>200克,与36%及以下精梳羊毛/动物细毛混纺)	14				80	17	11	米/千克	5	Other woven fabrics of cotton, mixed, containing≤36% by weight of combed wool or fine animal hair, w>200g/m^2, bleached
5212.2200 21	漂白的其他混纺棉布(每平米重>200克,与36%及以上其他羊毛/动物细毛混纺)	14				80	17	11	米/千克	5	Other woven fabrics of cotton, mixed, containing≥36% by weight of wool or fine animal hair, w>200g/m^2, bleached
5212.2200 29	漂白的其他混纺棉布(每平米重>200克,与36%及以下其他羊毛/动物细毛混纺)	14				80	17	11	米/千克	5	Other woven fabrics of cotton, mixed, containing≤36% by weight of wool or fine animal hair, w>200g/m^2, bleached
5212.2200 30	漂白的其他混纺府绸及细平布(每平米重>200克,与化纤/羊毛/细毛以外其他纤维混纺)	14				80	17	11	米/千克	5	Poplin and fine plain cloth, mixed with other fibres other than man-made fibres, wool or fine animals hair, w > 200g/m^2, bleached
5212.2200 40	漂白的其他混纺棉机织平布(每平米重>200克,与化纤/羊毛/细毛以外其他纤维混纺)	14				80	17	11	米/千克	5	Plain cloth of cotton, mixed with other fibres other than man-made fibres, wool or fine animals hair, w > 200g/m^2, bleached
5212.2200 50	漂白的其他混纺棉帆布(每平米重>200克,与化纤/羊毛/细毛以外其他纤维混纺)	14				80	17	11	米/千克	5	Canvas of cotton, mixed with other fibres other than man-made fibres, wool or fine animals hair, w > 200g/m^2, bleached
5212.2200 60	漂白的其他混纺棉缎布(每平米重>200克,与化纤/羊毛/细毛以外其他纤维混纺)	14				80	17	11	米/千克	5	Woven fabrics of cotton, satin weave, mixed with other fibres other than man-made fibres, wool or fine animals hair, w>200g/m^2, bleached
5212.2200 70	漂白的其他混纺棉斜纹布(每平米重>200克,与化纤/羊毛/细毛以外其他纤维混纺)	14				80	17	11	米/千克	5	Woven fabrics of cotton, twill weave, mixed with other fibres other than man-made fibres, wool or fine animals hair, w>200g/m^2, bleached

税则号列 Tariff Item.	货品名称	最惠国(%) MFN	协定(%)CT 东盟 CA	中巴 CP	中智 CC	普通 Gen	增值税率 VAT	出口退税 ED	计量单位 Unit	监管条件 SC	Article Description
5212.2200 90	漂白的其他混纺棉布(每平米重>200克,与化纤/羊毛/细毛以外其他纤维混纺)	14				80	17	11	米/千克	5	Woven fabrics of cotton, mixed with other fibres other than man-made fibres, wool or fine animals hair, w > 200g/m², bleached
5212.2300	--染色	10	5	0	0	80	17	11	米/千克		--Dyed
5212.2300 11	染色的其他混纺棉布(每平米重>200克,与36%及以上精梳羊毛/细毛混纺)	10				80	17	11	米/千克	5	Other woven fabrics of cotton, mixed, containing≥36% by weight of combed wool or fine animal hair, w>200g/m², dyed
5212.2300 19	染色的其他混纺棉布(每平米重>200克,与36%及以下精梳羊毛/细毛混纺)	10				80	17	11	米/千克	5	Other woven fabrics of cotton, mixed, containing≤36% by weight of combed wool or fine animal hair, w>200g/m², dyed
5212.2300 21	染色的其他混纺棉布(每平米重>200克,与36%及以上其他羊毛/细毛混纺)	10				80	17	11	米/千克	5	Other woven fabrics of cotton, mixed, containing≥36% by weight of wool or fine animal hair, w>200g/m², dyed
5212.2300 29	染色的其他混纺棉布(每平米重>200克,与36%及以下其他羊毛/细毛混纺)	10				80	17	11	米/千克	5	Other woven fabrics of cotton, mixed, containing≤36% by weight of wool or fine animal hair, w>200g/m², dyed
5212.2300 30	染色的其他混纺府绸及细平布(每平米重>200克,与化纤/羊毛/细毛以外其他纤维混纺)	10				80	17	11	米/千克	5	Poplin and fine plain cloth, mixed with other fibres other than man-made fibres, wool or fine animals hair, w > 200g/m², dyed
5212.2300 40	染色的其他混纺棉机织平布(每平米重>200克,与化纤/羊毛/细毛以外其他纤维混纺)	10				80	17	11	米/千克	5	Plain cloth of cotton, mixed with other fibres other than man-made fibres, wool or fine animals hair, w > 200g/m², dyed
5212.2300 50	染色的其他混纺棉帆布(每平米重>200克,与化纤/羊毛/细毛以外其他纤维混纺)	10				80	17	11	米/千克	5	Canvas of cotton, mixed with other fibres other than man-made fibres, wool or fine animals hair, w > 200g/m², dyed
5212.2300 60	染色的其他混纺棉缎布(每平米重>200克,与化纤/羊毛/细毛以外其他纤维混纺)	10				80	17	11	米/千克	5	Other woven fabrics of cotton, satin weave, mixed with other fibres other than man-made fibres, wool or fine animals hair, w>200g/m², dyed
5212.2300 70	染色的其他混纺棉斜纹布(每平米重>200克,与化纤/羊毛/细毛以外其他纤维混纺)	10				80	17	11	米/千克	5	Other woven fabrics of cotton, twill weave, mixed with other fibres other than man-made fibres, wool or fine animals hair, w>200g/m², dyed
5212.2300 90	染色的其他混纺棉布(每平米重>200克,与化纤/羊毛/细毛以外其他纤维混纺)	10				80	17	11	米/千克	5	Other woven fabrics of cotton, mixed with other fibres other than man-made fibres, wool or fine animals hair, w > 200g/m², dyed
5212.2400	--色织	10	5	0	0	80	17	11	米/千克		--Of yarns of different colours

税则号列 Tariff Item.	货品名称	最惠国(%) MFN	协定(%)CT 东盟 CA	中巴 CP	中智 CC	普通 Gen	增值税率 VAT	出口退税 ED	计量单位 Unit	监管条件 SC	Article Description
5212.2400 11	色织的其他混纺棉布(每平米重>200克,与36%及以上精梳羊毛/细毛混纺)	10				80	17	11	米/千克	5	Other woven fabrics of cotton, mixed, containing≥36% by weight of combed wool or fine animal hair, w>200g/m², of yarns of different colours
5212.2400 19	色织的其他混纺棉布(每平米重>200克,与36%及以下精梳羊毛/细毛混纺)	10				80	17	11	米/千克	5	Other woven fabrics of cotton, mixed, containing≤36% by weight of combed wool or fine animal hair, w>200g/m², of yarns of different colours
5212.2400 21	色织的其他混纺棉布(每平米重>200克,与36%及以上其他羊毛/细毛混纺)	10				80	17	11	米/千克	5	Other woven fabrics of cotton, mixed, containing≥36% by weight of wool or fine animal hair, w > 200g/m², of yarns of different colours
5212.2400 29	色织的其他混纺棉布(每平米重>200克,与36%及以下其他羊毛/细毛混纺)	10				80	17	11	米/千克	5	Other woven fabrics of cotton, mixed, containing≤36% by weight of wool or fine animal hair, w > 200g/m², of yarns of different colours
5212.2400 30	色织的其他混纺蓝色粗斜纹布(每平米重>200克,与化纤/羊毛/细毛以外其他纤维混纺)	10				80	17	11	米/千克	5	Other blue denim of cotton, mixed with other fibres other than man-made fibres, wool or fine animals hair, w > 200g/m², of yarns of different colours
5212.2400 40	色织的其他混纺提花布(每平米重>200克,与化纤/羊毛/细毛以外其他纤维混纺)	10				80	17	11	米/千克	5	Other woven fabrics of cotton, jacquard weave, mixed with other fibres other than man-made fibres, wool or fine animals hair, w > 200g/m², of yarns of different colours
5212.2400 90	色织的其他混纺棉布(每平米重>200克,与化纤/羊毛/细毛以外其他纤维混纺)	10				80	17	11	米/千克	5	Other woven fabrics of cotton, mixed with other fibres other than man-made fibres, wool or fine animals hair, w > 200g/m², of yarns of different colours
5212.2500	--印花	10	5	0	0	80	17	11	米/千克		--Printed
5212.2500 11	印花的其他混纺棉布(每平米重>200克,与36%及以上精梳羊毛/细毛混纺)	10				80	17	11	米/千克	5	Other woven fabrics of cotton, mixed, containing≥36% by weight of combed wool or fine animal hair, w>200g/m², printed
5212.2500 19	印花的其他混纺棉布(每平米重>200克,与36%及以下精梳羊毛/细毛混纺)	10				80	17	11	米/千克	5	Other woven fabrics of cotton, mixed, containing≤36% by weight of combed wool or fine animal hair, w>200g/m², printed
5212.2500 21	印花的其他混纺棉布(每平米重>200克,与36%及以上其他羊毛/细毛混纺)	10				80	17	11	米/千克	5	Other woven fabrics of cotton, mixed, containing≥36% by weight of wool or fine animal hair, w>200g/m², printed
5212.2500 29	印花的其他混纺棉布(每平米重>200克,与36%及以下其他羊毛/细毛混纺)	10				80	17	11	米/千克	5	Other woven fabrics of cotton, mixed, containing≤36% by weight of wool or fine animal hair, w>200g/m², printed
5212.2500 30	印花的其他混纺府绸及细平布(每平米重>200克,与化纤/羊毛/细毛以外其他纤维混纺)	10				80	17	11	米/千克	5	Poplin and fine plain cloth, mixed with other fibres other than man-made fibres, wool or fine animals hair, w > 200g/m², printed

税则号列 Tariff Item.	货品名称	最惠国(%) MFN	协定(%) CT 东盟 CA	中巴 CP	中智 CC	普通 Gen	增值税率 VAT	出口退税 ED	计量单位 Unit	监管条件 SC	Article Description
5212.2500 40	印花的其他混纺棉机织平布(每平米重>200克,与化纤/羊毛/细毛以外其他纤维混纺)	10				80	17	11	米/千克	5	Plain cloth of cotton, mixed with other fibres other than man-made fibres, wool or fine animals hair, w > 200g/m^2, printed
5212.2500 50	印花的其他混纺棉帆布(每平米重>200克,与化纤/羊毛/细毛以外其他纤维混纺)	10				80	17	11	米/千克	5	Canvas of cotton, mixed with other fibres other than man-made fibres, wool or fine animals hair, w > 200g/m^2, printed
5212.2500 60	印花的其他混纺棉缎布(每平米重>200克,与化纤/羊毛/细毛以外其他纤维混纺)	10				80	17	11	米/千克	5	Other woven fabrics of cotton, satin weave, mixed with other fibres other than man-made fibres, wool or fine animals hair, w>200g/m^2, printed
5212.2500 70	印花的其他混纺棉斜纹布(每平米重>200克,与化纤/羊毛/细毛以外其他纤维混纺)	10				80	17	11	米/千克	5	Other woven fabrics of cotton, twill weave, mixed with other fibres other than man-made fibres, wool or fine animals hair, w>200g/m^2, printed
5212.2500 90	印花的其他混纺棉布(每平米重>200克,与化纤/羊毛/细毛以外其他纤维混纺)	10				80	17	11	米/千克	5	Other woven fabrics of cotton other, mixed with other fibres other than man-made fibres, wool or fine animals hair, w>200g/m^2, printed

第五十三章
其他植物纺织纤维； 纸纱线及其机织物

Chapter 53
Other vegetable textile fibres; paper yarn and woven fabrics of paper yarn

税则号列 Tariff Item.	货品名称	最惠国(%) MFN	协定(%) CT			普通 Gen	增值税率 VAT	出口退税 ED	计量单位 Unit	监管条件 SC	Article Description
			东盟 CA	中巴 CP	中智 CC						
53.01	**亚麻，生的或经加工但未纺制的；亚麻短纤及废麻（包括废麻纱线及回收纤维）：**										**Flax, raw or processed but not spun; flax tow and waste (including yarn waste and garnetted stock):**
5301.1000	-生的或经沤制的亚麻	6	5		0	30	17	5	千克	AB	-Flax, raw or retted
	-破开、打成、栉梳或经其他加工但未纺制的亚麻：										-Flax, broken, scutched, hackled or otherwise processed, but not spun:
5301.2100	--破开的或打成的	6	5		0	30	17	5	千克	AB	--Broken or scutched
5301.2900	--其他	6	5		0	30	17	5	千克	AB	--Other
5301.3000	-亚麻短纤及废麻	6	5		0	30	17	5	千克	AB	-Flax tow and waste
53.02	**大麻，生的或经加工但未纺制的；大麻短纤及废麻（包括废麻纱线及回收纤维）：**										**True hemp (*Cannabis sativa L*), raw or processed but not spun; tow and waste of true hemp (including yarn waste and garnetted stock):**
5302.1000	-生的或经沤制的大麻	6	5		0	30	17	5	千克	AB	-True hemp, raw or retted
5302.9000	-其他	6	5		0	30	17	5	千克	AB	-Other
53.03	**黄麻及其他纺织用韧皮纤维（不包括亚麻、大麻及苎麻），生的或经加工但未纺制的；上述纤维的短纤及废麻（包括废纱线及回收纤维）：**										**Jute and other textile bast fibres (excluding flax, true hemp and ramie), raw or processed but not spun; tow and waste of these fibres (including yarn waste and garnetted stock):**
5303.1000	-生的或经沤制的黄麻及其他纺织用韧皮纤维	5	T3		0	20	13	5	千克	AB	-Jute and other textile bast fibres, raw or retted
5303.9000	-其他	5	T3		0	30	17	5	千克	AB	-Other
53.05	**椰壳纤维、蕉麻（马尼拉麻）、苎麻及其他税目未列名的纺织用植物纤维，生的或经加工但未纺制的；上述纤维的短纤、落麻及废料（包括废纱线及回收纤维）：**										**Coconut, abaca (Manila hemp or *Musatextilis Nee*), ramie and other vegetable textile fibres, not elsewhere specified or included, raw or processed but not spun; tow, noils and waste of these fibres (including yarn waste and garnetted stock):**
	---苎麻：										---Ramie:
5305.0011	--生的	5			0	30	17	5	千克	AB	--Raw
5305.0012	----经加工但未纺制的	5			0	30	17	5	千克	AB	----Processed but not spun
5305.0013	----短纤、落麻及废料	5			0	30	17	5	千克	AB	----Tow、noils and waste of these
5305.0019	----其他	5			0	20	17	5	千克	AB	----Other
5305.0020	---蕉麻	3			0	20	17	5	千克	AB	----Of abaca
	---其他										---Other
5305.0091	----西沙尔麻及其他纺织用龙舌兰类纤维	5			0	30	17	5	千克	AB	----Sisal and other textile fibres of the genus Asave
5305.0092	----椰壳纤维	5	T3	4	0	30	17	5	千克	AB	----Of coconut(coir)
5305.0099	----其他	5			0	30	17	5	千克	AB	----Other
53.06	**亚麻纱线：**										**Flax yarn:**
5306.1000	-单纱	6	5		0	50	17	11	千克	5B	-Single
5306.2000	-多股纱线或缆线	10	5		0	50	17	11	千克	5B	-Multiple (folded) or cabled

税则号列 Tariff Item.	货品名称	最惠国(%) MFN	协定(%)CT 东盟 CA	中巴 CP	中智 CC	普通 Gen	增值税率 VAT	出口退税 ED	计量单位 Unit	监管条件 SC	Article Description
53.07	**黄麻纱线或税目 53.03 的其他纺织用韧皮纤维纱线:**										**Yarn of jute or of other textile bast fibres of heading No. 53.03:**
5307.1000	-单纱	6	5		0	35	17	11	千克		-Single
5307.2000	-多股纱线或缆线	6	5		0	35	17	11	千克		-Multiple (folded) or cabled
53.08	**其他植物纺织纤维纱线;纸纱线:**										**Yarn of other vegetable textile fibres; paper yarn:**
5308.1000	-椰壳纤维纱线	6	5		0	45	17	11	千克		-Coir yarn
5308.2000	-大麻纱线	6	5		0	45	17	11	千克		-True hemp yarn
	-其他:										-Other:
	---苎麻纱线:										---Ramie yarn:
5308.9011	----按重量计苎麻含量在85%及以上的未漂白或漂白纱线	6	5		0	50	17	11	千克	5B	----Containing 85% or more by weight of ramie, unbleached or bleached yarn
5308.9012	----按重量计苎麻含量在85%及以上的色纱线	6	5		0	50	17	11	千克	5B	----Containing 85% or more by weight of ramie, coloured yarn
5308.9013	----按重量计苎麻含量在85%以下的未漂白或漂白纱线	6	5		0	50	17	11	千克	5B	----Containing less than 85% by weight of ramie, unbleached or bleached yarn
5308.9014	----按重量计苎麻含量在85%以下的色纱线	6	5		0	50	17	11	千克	5B	----Containing less than 85% by weight of coloured yarn
	---其他:										---Other:
5308.9091	----纸纱线	6	5		0	70	17	11	千克		----Paper yarn
5308.9099	----其他	6	5		0	45	17	11	千克		----Other
53.09	**亚麻机织物:**										**Woven fabrics of flax:**
	-按重量计亚麻含量在85%及以上:										-Containing 85% or more by weight of flax:
	--未漂白或漂白:										--Unbleached or bleached:
5309.1110	---未漂白	10	5	0	0	80	17	11	米/千克	B	---Unbleached
5309.1120	---漂白	10	5	0	0	80	17	11	米/千克	B	---Bleached
5309.1900	--其他	10	5	0	0	80	17	11	米/千克	B	--Other
	-按重量计亚麻含量在85%以下:										-Containing less than 85% by weight of flax:
	--未漂白或漂白:										--Unbleached or bleached:
5309.2110	---未漂白	10	5	0	0	80	17	11	米/千克		---Unbleached
5309.2110 11	未漂白与精梳毛混纺的亚麻机织物(亚麻含量在85%以下,含17%以上羊毛或动物细毛)	10				80	17	11	米/千克	B	Woven fabrics of flax, mixed, containing≥17% by weight of combed wool or fine animal hair, containing < 85% by weight of flax, unbleached
5309.2110 19	未漂白的其他混纺亚麻机织物(亚麻含量在85%以下,含17%以上羊毛或动物细毛)	10				80	17	11	米/千克	B	Woven fabrics of flax, mixed, containing≥17% by weight of wool or fine animal hair, containing < 85% by weight of flax, unbleached
5309.2110 21	未漂白的混纺亚麻府绸及细平布(亚麻含量在85%以下,与棉及化纤混纺,棉限内)	10				80	17	11	米/千克	B	Poplin and fine plain cloth, mixed with cotton and man-made fibres, containing < 85% by weight of flax, unbleached, cotton within limitations
5309.2110 22	未漂白的混纺亚麻机织平布(亚麻含量在85%以下,与棉及化纤混纺,棉限内)	10				80	17	11	米/千克	B	Plain cloth, mixed with cotton and man-made fibres, containing < 85% by weight of flax, unbleached, cotton within limitations

税则号列 Tariff Item.	货品名称	最惠国(%) MFN	协定(%) CT 东盟 CA	中巴 CP	中智 CC	普通 Gen	增值税率 VAT	出口退税 ED	计量单位 Unit	监管条件 SC	Article Description
5309.2110 23	未漂白的混纺亚麻机织印染用布(亚麻含量在85%以下,与棉及化纤混纺,棉限内)	10				80	17	11	米/千克	B	Woven fabrics of flax for printing and dying, mixed with cotton and man-made fibres, containing < 85% by weight of flax, unbleached, cotton within limitations
5309.2110 24	未漂白的混纺亚麻其他机织物(亚麻含量在85%以下,与棉及化纤混纺,棉限内)	10				80	17	11	米/千克	B	Other woven fabrics of flax mixed with cotton and man-made fibres, containing <85% by weight of flax, unbleached, cotton within limitations
5309.2110 25	未漂白的混纺亚麻府绸及细平布(亚麻含量在85%以下,与棉及化纤混纺,化纤限内)	10				80	17	11	米/千克	B	Poplin and fine plain cloth, mixed with cotton and man-made fibres, containing < 85% by weight of flax, unbleached, man-made fibres within limitations
5309.2110 26	未漂白的混纺亚麻机织平布(亚麻含量在85%以下,与棉及化纤混纺,化纤限内)	10				80	17	11	米/千克	B	Plain cloth, mixed with cotton and man-made fibres, containing < 85% by weight of flax, unbleached, man-made fibres within limitations
5309.2110 27	未漂白的混纺亚麻机织印染用布(亚麻含量在85%以下,与棉及化纤混纺,化纤限内)	10				80	17	11	米/千克	B	Woven fabrics of flax for printing and dying, mixed with cotton and man-made fibres, containing < 85% by weight of flax, unbleached, man-made fibres within limitations
5309.2110 28	未漂白的混纺亚麻其他机织物(亚麻含量在85%以下,与棉及化纤混纺,化纤限内)	10				80	17	11	米/千克	B	Other woven fabrics of flax, mixed with cotton and man-made fibres, containing < 85% by weight of flax, unbleached, man-made fibres within limitations
5309.2110 29	未漂白的混纺亚麻其他机织物(亚麻含量在85%以下,与棉及化纤混纺)	10				80	17	11	米/千克	B	Other woven fabrics of flax, mixed with cotton and man-made fibres, containing < 85% by weight of flax, unbleached
5309.2110 91	未漂白的混纺亚麻其他机织物(亚麻含量<85%,主要或仅与精梳羊毛或动物细毛混纺)	10				80	17	11	米/千克	B	Other woven fabrics of flax, mixed mainly or solely with combed wool or fine animal hair, containing < 85% by weight of flax, unbleached
5309.2110 99	未漂白的混纺亚麻其他机织物(亚麻含量在85%以下)	10				80	17	11	米/千克	B	Other woven fabrics of flax, mixed, containing < 85% by weight of flax, unbleached
5309.2120	---漂白	10	5	0	0	80	17	11	米/千克		---Bleached
5309.2120 11	漂白与精梳毛混纺的亚麻机织物(亚麻含量在85%以下,含17%以上羊毛或动物细毛)	10				80	17	11	米/千克	B	Woven fabrics of flax, mixed, containing≥17% by weight of combed wool or fine animal hair, containing < 85% by weight of flax, bleached
5309.2120 19	漂白的其他混纺亚麻机织物(亚麻含量在85%以下,含17%以上羊毛或动物细毛)	10				80	17	11	米/千克	B	Other woven fabrics of flax, mixed, containing≥17% by weight of wool or fine animal hair, containing < 85% by weight of flax, bleached

税则号列 Tariff Item.	货品名称	最惠国(%) MFN	协定(%) 东盟 CA	中巴 CP	CT 中智 CC	普通 Gen	增值税率 VAT	出口退税 ED	计量单位 Unit	监管条件 SC	Article Description
5309.2120 21	漂白的混纺亚麻府绸及细平布(亚麻含量在85%以下,与棉及化纤混纺,棉限内)	10				80	17	11	米/千克	B	Poplin and fine plain cloth, mixed with cotton and man-made fibres, containing < 85% by weight of flax, bleached, cotton within limitations
5309.2120 22	漂白的混纺亚麻机织平布(亚麻含量在85%以下,与棉及化纤混纺,棉限内)	10				80	17	11	米/千克	B	Plain cloth, mixed with cotton and man-made fibres, containing < 85% by weight of flax, bleached, cotton within limitations
5309.2120 23	漂白的混纺亚麻机织印染用布(亚麻含量在85%以下,与棉及化纤混纺,棉限内)	10				80	17	11	米/千克	B	Woven fabrics of flax for printing and dying, mixed with cotton and man-made fibres, containing < 85% by weight of flax, bleached, cotton within limitations
5309.2120 24	漂白的混纺亚麻其他机织物(亚麻含量在85%以下,与棉及化纤混纺,棉限内)	10				80	17	11	米/千克	B	Other woven fabrics of flax, mixed with cotton and man-made fibres, containing < 85% by weight of flax, bleached, cotton within limitations
5309.2120 25	漂白的混纺亚麻府绸及细平布(亚麻含量在85%以下,与棉及化纤混纺,化纤限内)	10				80	17	11	米/千克	B	Poplin and fine plain cloth, mixed with cotton and man-made fibres, containing < 85% by weight of flax, bleached, man-made fibres within limitations
5309.2120 26	漂白的混纺亚麻机织平布(亚麻含量在85%以下,与棉及化纤混纺,化纤限内)	10				80	17	11	米/千克	B	Plain cloth, mixed with cotton and man-made fibres, containing < 85% by weight of flax, bleached, man-made fibres within limitations
5309.2120 27	漂白的混纺亚麻机织印染用布(亚麻含量在85%以下,与棉及化纤混纺,化纤限内)	10				80	17	11	米/千克	B	Woven fabrics of flax for printing and dying, mixed with cotton and man-made fibres, containing < 85% by weight of flax, blea-ched, man-made fibres within limitations
5309.2120 28	漂白的混纺亚麻其他机织物(亚麻含量在85%以下,与棉及化纤混纺,化纤限内)	10				80	17	11	米/千克	B	Other woven fabrics of flax, mixed with cotton and man-made fibres, containing < 85% by weight of flax, bleached, man-made fibres within limitations
5309.2120 29	漂白的混纺亚麻其他机织物(亚麻含量在85%以下,与棉及化纤混纺)	10				80	17	11	米/千克	B	Other woven fabrics of flax, mixed with cotton and man-made fibres, containing < 85% by weight of flax, bleached
5309.2120 91	漂白的混纺亚麻其他机织物(亚麻含量<85%,主要或仅与精梳羊毛或动物细毛混纺)	10				80	17	11	米/千克	B	Other woven fabrics of flax, mixed mainly or solely with combed wool or fine animal hair, containing <85% by weight of flax, bleached
5309.2120 99	漂白的混纺亚麻其他机织物(亚麻含量在85%以下)	10				80	17	11	米/千克	B	Other woven fabrics of flax, containing <85% by weight of flax, bleached
5309.2900	--其他	10	5	0	0	80	17	11	米/千克		--Other

税则号列 Tariff Item.	货 品 名 称	最惠国(%) MFN	协定(%)CT 东盟 CA	中巴 CP	中智 CC	普通 Gen	增值税率 VAT	出口退税 ED	计量单位 Unit	监管条件 SC	Article Description
5309.2900 11	其他与精梳毛混纺的亚麻机织物(亚麻含量在85%以下,含17%以上羊毛或动物细毛)	10				80	17	11	米/千克	B	Other woven fabrics of flax, mixed, containing≥17% by weight of combed wool or fine animal hair, containing < 85% by weight of flax
5309.2900 19	其他混纺亚麻机织物(亚麻含量在85%以下,含17%以上羊毛或动物细毛)	10				80	17	11	米/千克	B	Other woven fabrics of flax, mixed, containing≥17% by weight of wool or fine animal hair, containing < 85% by weight of flax
5309.2900 21	其他混纺亚麻府绸及细平布(亚麻含量在85%以下,与棉及化纤混纺,棉限内)	10				80	17	11	米/千克	B	Other poplin and fine plain cloth of flax, mixed with cotton and man-made fibres, containing < 85% by weight of flax, cotton within limitations
5309.2900 22	其他混纺亚麻机织平布(亚麻含量在85%以下,与棉及化纤混纺,棉限内)	10				80	17	11	米/千克	B	Other plain cloth of falx, mixed with cotton and man-made fibres, containing < 85% by weight of flax, cotton within limitations
5309.2900 23	其他混纺亚麻机织印染用布(亚麻含量在85%以下,与棉及化纤混纺,棉限内)	10				80	17	11	米/千克	B	Other woven fabrics of flax for printing and dying, mixed with cotton and man-made fibres, containing < 85% by weight of flax, cotton within limitations
5309.2900 24	其他混纺亚麻其他机织物(亚麻含量在85%以下,与棉及化纤混纺,棉限内)	10				80	17	11	米/千克	B	Other woven fabrics of flax, mixed with cotton and man-made fibres, containing < 85% by weight of flax, cotton within limitations
5309.2900 25	其他混纺亚麻府绸及细平布(亚麻含量在85%以下,与棉及化纤混纺,化纤限内)	10				80	17	11	米/千克	B	Poplin and fine plain cloth of flax, mixed with cotton and man-made fibres, containing < 85% by weight of flax, man-made fibres within limitations
5309.2900 26	其他混纺亚麻机织平布(亚麻含量在85%以下,与棉及化纤混纺,化纤限内)	10				80	17	11	米/千克	B	Plain cloth of flax, mixed with cotton and man-made fibres, containing < 85% by weight of flax, man-made fibres within limitations
5309.2900 27	其他混纺亚麻机织印染用布(亚麻含量在85%以下,与棉及化纤混纺,化纤限内)	10				80	17	11	米/千克	B	Other woven fabrics of flax for printing and dying, mixed with cotton and man-made fibres, containing < 85% by weight of flax, man-made fibres within limitations
5309.2900 28	其他混纺亚麻其他机织物(亚麻含量在85%以下,与棉及化纤混纺,化纤限内)	10				80	17	11	米/千克	B	Other woven fabrics of flax, mixed with cotton and man-made fibres, containing < 85% by weight of flax, man-made fibres within limitations
5309.2900 29	其他混纺亚麻其他机织物(亚麻含量在85%以下,与棉及化纤混纺)	10				80	17	11	米/千克	B	Other woven fabrics of flax, mixed with cotton and man-made fibres, containing < 85% by weight of flax
5309.2900 91	其他混纺亚麻其他机织物(亚麻含量<85%,主要或仅与精梳羊毛或动物细毛混纺)	10				80	17	11	米/千克	B	Other woven fabrics of flax, mixed mainly or solely with combed wool or fine animal hair, containing < 85% by weight of flax

税则号列 Tariff Item.	货品名称	最惠国(%) MFN	协定(%)CT 东盟 CA	中巴 CP	中智 CC	普通 Gen	增值税率 VAT	出口退税 ED	计量单位 Unit	监管条件 SC	Article Description
5309.2900 99	其他混纺亚麻机织物(亚麻含量在85%以下)	10				80	17	11	米/千克	B	Other woven fabrics of flax, mixed, containing < 85% by weight of flax
53.10	**黄麻或税目53.03的其他纺织用韧皮纤维机织物:**										**Woven fabrics of jute or of other textilebast fibres of heading 53.03:**
5310.1000	-未漂白	10	5		0	40	17	11	米/千克		-Unbleached
5310.1000 11	未漂白黄麻或其他韧皮纤维机织物(宽度不超过150厘米,与精梳羊毛或动物细毛混纺)	10				40	17	11	米/千克	AB	Woven fabrics of jute or of other textilebast fibres, width ≤ 150cm, mixed with combed wool or fine animal hair, unbleached
5310.1000 19	未漂白黄麻或其他韧皮纤维机织物(宽度不超过150厘米,与其他纤维混纺)	10				40	17	11	米/千克	AB	Woven fabrics of jute or of other textilebast fibres, width ≤150cm, mixed with other fibres, unbleached
5310.1000 91	未漂白黄麻或其他韧皮纤维机织物(宽度超过150厘米,与精梳羊毛或动物细毛混纺)	10				40	17	11	米/千克	AB	Woven fabrics of jute or of other textilebast fibres, width > 150cm, mixed with combed wool or fine animal hair, unbleached
5310.1000 99	未漂白黄麻或其他韧皮纤维机织物(宽度超过150厘米,与其他纤维混纺)	10				40	17	11	米/千克	AB	Woven fabrics of jute or of other textilebast fibres, width > 150cm, mixed with other fibres, unbleached
5310.9000	-其他	10	5		0	40	17	11	米/千克		-Other
5310.9000 11	其他黄麻机织物,宽度≤150厘米(含5303其他纺织用韧皮纤维布与精梳羊毛或动物细毛混纺)	10				40	17	11	米/千克		Other woven fabrics of jute or of other textilebast fibres of heading 53.03, width≤150cm, mixed with combed wool or fine animal hair
5310.9000 19	其他黄麻机织物,宽度≤150厘米(含税号5303的其他纺织用韧皮纤维布,与其他纤维混纺)	10				40	17	11	米/千克		Other woven fabrics of jute or of other textilebast fibres of heading 53.03, width≤150cm, mixed with other fibres
5310.9000 91	其他黄麻机织物,宽度>150厘米(含5303其他纺织用韧皮纤维布与精梳羊毛或动物细毛混纺)	10				40	17	11	米/千克		Other woven fabrics of jute or of other textilebast fibres of heading 53.03, width > 150cm, mixed with combed wool or fine animal hair
5310.9000 99	其他黄麻机织物,宽度>150厘米(含税号5303的其他纺织用韧皮纤维布,与其他纤维混纺)	10				40	17	11	米/千克		Other woven fabrics of jute or of other textilebast fibres of heading 53.03, width > 150cm, mixed with other fibres
53.11	**其他纺织用植物纤维机织物;纸纱线机织物:**										**Woven fabrics of other vegetable textile fibres; woven fabrics of paper yarn:**
	---苎麻机织物:										---Woven fabrics of ramie:
5311.0012	----按重量计苎麻含量在85%及以上的未漂白机织物	10	5		0	80	17	11	米/千克		----Containing 85% or more by weight of ramie, unbleached woven fabrics
5311.0012 11	未漂白与精梳毛混纺的苎麻机织物(苎麻含量在85%及以上,含17%以上羊毛或动物细毛)	10				80	17	11	米/千克	B	Woven fabrics of ramie, mixed, containing ≥ 17% by weight of combed wool or fine animal hair, containing ≥ 85% by weight of ramie, unbleached

税则号列 Tariff Item.	货品名称	最惠国(%) MFN	协定(%) CT 东盟 CA	中巴 CP	中智 CC	普通 Gen	增值税率 VAT	出口退税 ED	计量单位 Unit	监管条件 SC	Article Description
5311.0012 19	未漂白苎麻机织物(苎麻含量在85%及以上,含17%以上羊毛或动物细毛)	10				80	17	11	米/千克	B	Woven fabrics of ramie, mixed, containing≥17% by weight of wool or fine animal hair, containing ≥ 85% by weight of ramie, unbleached
5311.0012 21	未漂白的苎麻府绸及细平布(苎麻含量在85%及以上,与棉及化纤混纺,棉限内)	10				80	17	11	米/千克	B	Poplin and fine plain cloth of ramie, mixed with cotton and man-made fibres, containing≥85% by weight of ramie, unbleached, cotton within limitations
5311.0012 22	未漂白的苎麻机织平布(苎麻含量在85%及以上,与棉及化纤混纺,棉限内)	10				80	17	11	米/千克	B	Plain cloth of ramie, mixed with cotton and man-made fibres, containing ≥ 85% by weight of ramie, unbleached, cotton within limitations
5311.0012 23	未漂白的苎麻机织印染用布(苎麻含量在85%及以上,与棉及化纤混纺,棉限内)	10				80	17	11	米/千克	B	Woven fabrics of ramie for printing and dying, mixed with cotton and man-made fibres, containing ≥ 85% by weight of ramie, unbleached, cotton within limitations
5311.0012 29	未漂白的苎麻其他机织物(苎麻含量在85%及以上,与棉及化纤混纺,棉限内)	10				80	17	11	米/千克	B	Other woven fabrics of ramie, mixed with cotton and man-made fibres, containing≥85% by weight of ramie, unbleached, cotton within limitations
5311.0012 31	未漂白的苎麻府绸及细平布(苎麻含量在85%及以上,与棉及化纤混纺,化纤限内)	10				80	17	11	米/千克	B	Poplin and fine plain cloth of ramie, mixed with cotton and man-made fibres, containing≥85% by weight of ramie unbleached, man-made fibres within limitations
5311.0012 32	未漂白的苎麻机织平布(苎麻含量在85%及以上,与棉及化纤混纺,化纤限内)	10				80	17	11	米/千克	B	Plain cloth of ramie, mixed with cotton and man-made fibres, containing ≥ 85% by weight of ramie, unbleached, man-made fibres within limitations
5311.0012 33	未漂百苎麻机织印染用布(苎麻含量在85%及以上,与棉及化纤混纺,化纤限内)	10				80	17	11	米/千克	B	Woven fabrics of ramie for printing and dying, mixed with cotton and man-made fibres, containing ≥ 85% by weight of ramie unbleached, man-made fibres within limitations
5311.0012 39	未漂白的苎麻其他机织物(苎麻含量在85%及以上,与棉及化纤混纺,化纤限内)	10				80	17	11	米/千克	B	Other woven fabrics of ramie, mixed with cotton and man-made fibres, containing≥85% by weight of ramie, unbleached, man-made fibres within limitations
5311.0012 40	未漂白的苎麻其他机织物(苎麻含量在85%及以上,与棉及化纤混纺)	10				80	17	11	米/千克	B	Other woven fabrics of ramie, mixed with cotton and man-made fibres, containing≥85% by weight of ramie, unbleached

税则号列 Tariff Item.	货品名称	最惠国(%) MFN	协定(%)CT 东盟 CA	中巴 CP	中智 CC	普通 Gen	增值税率 VAT	出口退税 ED	计量单位 Unit	监管条件 SC	Article Description
5311.0012 91	未漂白的苎麻其他机织物(苎麻含量在85%及以上,主要/仅与精梳羊毛/细毛混纺)	10				80	17	11	米/千克	B	Other woven fabrics of ramie, mixed mainly or solely with combed wool or fine animal hair, containing≥85% by weight of ramie, unbleached
5311.0012 99	未漂白的苎麻其他机织物(苎麻含量在85%及以上)	10				80	17	11	米/千克	B	Other woven fabrics of ramie, containing≥85% by weight of ramie, unbleached
5311.0013	----按重量计苎麻含量在85%及以上的其他机织物	12	8		0	80	17	11	米/千克		----Containing 85% or more by weight of ramie, other woven fabrics
5311.0013 11	与精梳毛混纺的苎麻其他机织物(苎麻含量≥85%,含17%以上羊毛或动物细毛)	12				80	17	11	米/千克	B	Other woven fabrics of ramie, mixed, containing ≥ 17% by weight of combed wool or fine animal hair, containing≥85% by weight of ramie
5311.0013 19	苎麻其他机织物(苎麻含量≥85%,羊毛/细毛>17%)	12				80	17	11	米/千克	B	Other woven fabrics of ramie, mixed, containing<17% by weight of wool or fine animal hair, containing≥85% by weight of ramie
5311.0013 21	苎麻府绸及细平布(苎麻含量≥85%,与棉及化纤混纺,棉限内)	12				80	17	11	米/千克	B	Poplin and fine plain cloth of ramie, mixed with cotton and man-made fibres, containing≥85% by weight of ramie, cotton within limitations
5311.0013 22	苎麻机织平布(苎麻含量≥85%,与棉及化纤混纺,棉限内)	12				80	17	11	米/千克	B	Plain cloth of ramie, mixed with cotton and man-made fibres, containing≥85% by weight of ramie, cotton within limitations
5311.0013 23	苎麻机织印染布(苎麻含量≥85%,与棉及化纤混纺,棉限内)	12				80	17	11	米/千克	B	Woven fabrics of ramie for printing and dying, mixed with cotton and man-made fibres, containing≥85% by weight of ramie, cotton within limitations
5311.0013 29	苎麻其他机织物(苎麻含量≥85%,与棉及化纤混纺,棉限内)	12				80	17	11	米/千克	B	Woven fabrics of ramie, mixed with cotton and man-made fibres, containing≥85% by weight of ramie, cotton within limitations
5311.0013 31	苎麻府绸及细平布(苎麻含量≥85%,与棉及化纤混纺,化纤限内)	12				80	17	11	米/千克	B	Poplin and fine plain cloth of ramie, mixed with cotton and man-made fibres, containing≥85% by weight of ramie, man-made fibres within limitations
5311.0013 32	苎麻机织平布(苎麻含量≥85%,与棉及化纤混纺,化纤限内)	12				80	17	11	米/千克	B	Plain cloth of ramie, mixed with cotton and man-made fibres, containing≥85% by weight of ramie, man-made fibres within limitations
5311.0013 33	苎麻机织印染布(苎麻含量≥85%,与棉及化纤混纺,化纤限内)	12				80	17	11	米/千克	B	Woven fabrics of ramie for printing and dying, mixed with cotton and man-made fibres, containing≥85% by weight of ramie, man-made fibres within limitations

税则号列 Tariff Item.	货品名称	最惠国(%) MFN	协定(%)CT 东盟 CA	中巴 CP	中智 CC	普通 Gen	增值税率 VAT	出口退税 ED	计量单位 Unit	监管条件 SC	Article Description
5311.0013 39	苎麻其他机织物(苎麻含量≥85%,与棉及化纤混纺,化纤限内)	12				80	17	11	米/千克	B	Other woven fabrics of ramie mixed with cotton and man-made fibres, containing ≥85% by weight of ramie, man-made fibres within limitations
5311.0013 40	苎麻其他机织物(苎麻含量≥85%,与棉及化纤混纺)	12				80	17	11	米/千克	B	Other woven fabrics of ramie mixed, with cotton and man-made fibres, containing≥85% by weight of ramie
5311.0013 91	苎麻其他机织物(苎麻含量≥85%,主要/仅与精梳羊毛/细毛混纺)	12				80	17	11	米/千克	B	Other woven fabrics of ramie, mixed mainly or solely with combed wool or fine animal hair, containing ≥ 85% by weight of ramie
5311.0013 99	苎麻其他机织物(苎麻含量≥85%)	12				80	17	11	米/千克	B	Other woven fabrics of ramie, containing≥85% by weight of ramie
5311.0014	----按重量计苎麻含量在85%以下的未漂白机织物	10	5		0	80	17	11	米/千克		----Containing less than 85% by weight of ramie, unbleached woven fabrics
5311.0014 11	未漂白与精梳羊毛混纺苎麻机织物(苎麻含量<85%,含17%以上羊毛/细毛)	10				80	17	11	米/千克	B	Other woven fabrics of ramie, containing<85% by weight of ramie containing≥17% by weight of wool or fine animal hair, unbleached
5311.0014 19	未漂白苎麻机织物(苎麻含量<85%,含17%以上羊毛/细毛)	10				80	17	11	米/千克	B	Other woven fabrics of ramie, containing≥17% by weight of wool or fine animal hair, containing < 85% by weight of ramie, unbleached
5311.0014 21	未漂白的苎麻府绸及细平布(苎麻含量在85%以下,与棉及化纤混纺,棉限内)	10				80	17	11	米/千克	B	Poplin and fine plain cloth of ramie, mixed with cotton and man-made fibres, containing<85% by weight of ramie, unbleached, cotton within limitations
5311.0014 22	未漂白的苎麻机织平布(苎麻含量在85%以下,与棉及化纤混纺,棉限内)	10				80	17	11	米/千克	B	Plain cloth of ramie, mixed with cotton and man-made fibres, containing < 85% by weight of ramie, unbleached, cotton within limitations
5311.0014 23	未漂白的苎麻机织印染用布(苎麻含量在85%以下,与棉及化纤混纺,棉限内)	10				80	17	11	米/千克	B	Woven fabrics of ramie for printing and dying, mixed with cotton and man-made fibres, containing < 85% by weight of ramie, unbleached, cotton within limitations
5311.0014 29	未漂白的苎麻其他机织物(苎麻含量在85%以下,与棉及化纤混纺,棉限内)	10				80	17	11	米/千克	B	Other woven fabrics of ramie, mixed with cotton and man-made fibres, containing<85% by weight of ramie, unbleached, cotton within limitations
5311.0014 31	未漂白的苎麻府绸及细平布(苎麻含量在85%以下,与棉及化纤混纺,化纤限内)	10				80	17	11	米/千克	B	Poplin and fine plain cloth of ramie, mixed with cotton and man-made fibres, containing<85% by weight of ramie, unbleached, man-made fibres within limitations
5311.0014 32	未漂白的苎麻机织平布(苎麻含量在85%以下,与棉及化纤混纺,化纤限内)	10				80	17	11	米/千克	B	Plain cloth of ramie, mixed with cotton and man-made fibres, containing<85% by weight of ramie, unbleached, man-made fibres within limitations

税则号列 Tariff Item.	货品名称	最惠国(%) MFN	协定(%)CT 东盟 CA	中巴 CP	中智 CC	普通 Gen	增值税率 VAT	出口退税 ED	计量单位 Unit	监管条件 SC	Article Description
5311.0014 33	未漂白的苎麻机织印染用布(苎麻含量在85%以下,与棉及化纤混纺,化纤限内)	10				80	17	11	米/千克	B	Woven fabrics of ramie for printing and dying, mixed with cotton and man-made fibres, containing < 85% by weight of ramie, unbleached, man-made fibres within limitations
5311.0014 39	未漂白的苎麻其他机织物(苎麻含量在85%以下,与棉及化纤混纺,化纤限内)	10				80	17	11	米/千克	B	Other woven fabrics of ramie, mixed with cotton and man-made fibres, containing < 85% by weight of ramie, unbleached, man-made fibres within limitations
5311.0014 40	未漂白的苎麻其他机织物(苎麻含量在85%以下,与棉及化纤混纺)	10				80	17	11	米/千克	B	Other woven fabrics of ramie, mixed with cotton and man-made fibres, containing < 85% by weight of ramie, unbleached
5311.0014 91	未漂白的苎麻其他机织物(苎麻含量<85%,主要或仅与精梳羊毛或动物细毛混纺)	10				80	17	11	米/千克	B	Other woven fabrics of ramie, mixed mainly or solely with combed wool or fine animal hair, containing < 85% by weight of ramie, unbleached
5311.0014 99	未漂白的苎麻其他机织物(苎麻含量在85%以下)	10				80	17	11	米/千克	B	Other woven fabrics of ramie, containing < 85% by weight of ramie, unbleached
5311.0015	----按重量计苎麻含量在85%以下的其他机织物	12	8		0	80	17	11	米/千克		----Containing less than 85% by weight of ramie, other woven fabrics
5311.0015 11	其他苎麻机织物,含量<85%(毛重>17%,主要或仅与精梳羊毛或动物细毛混纺)	12				80	17	11	米/千克	B	Other woven fabrics of ramie, mixed mainly or solely with combed wool or of fine animal hair, containing < 85% by weight of ramie, containing > 17% by weight of combed wool or fine animal hair
5311.0015 19	其他苎麻机织物(苎麻含量在85%以下,含17%以上羊毛或动物细毛)	12				80	17	11	米/千克	B	Other woven fabrics of ramie, mixed, containing > 17% by weight of wool or fine animal hair, containing < 85% by weight of ramie
5311.0015 21	苎麻府绸及细平布(苎麻含量在85%以下,与棉及化纤混纺,棉限内)	12				80	17	11	米/千克	B	Poplin and fine plain cloth of ramie, mixed with cotton and man-made fibres, containing < 85% by weight of ramie, cotton within limitations
5311.0015 22	苎麻机织平布(苎麻含量在85%以下,与棉及化纤混纺,棉限内)	12				80	17	11	米/千克	B	Plain cloth of ramie, mixed with cotton and man-made fibres, containing < 85% by weight of ramie, cotton within limitations
5311.0015 23	苎麻机织印染用布(苎麻含量在85%以下,与棉及化纤混纺,棉限内)	12				80	17	11	米/千克	B	Woven fabrics of ramie for printing and dying, mixed with cotton and man-made fibres, containing < 85% by weight of ramie, cotton within limitations

税则号列 Tariff Item.	货 品 名 称	最惠国 (%) MFN	协定(%)CT 东盟 CA	中巴 CP	中智 CC	普通 Gen	增值税率 VAT	出口退税 ED	计量单位 Unit	监管条件 SC	Article Description
5311.0015 29	其他苎麻机织物(苎麻含量在85%以下,与棉及化纤混纺,棉限内)	12				80	17	11	米/千克	B	Other woven fabrics of ramie, mixed with cotton and man-made fibres, containing <85% by weight of ramie, cotton within limitations
5311.0015 31	苎麻府绸及细平布(苎麻含量在85%以下,与棉及化纤混纺,化纤限内)	12				80	17	11	米/千克	B	Poplin and fine plain cloth of ramie, mixed with cotton and man-made fibres, containing < 85% by weight of ramie, man-made fibres within limitations
5311.0015 32	苎麻机织平布(苎麻含量在85%以下,与棉及化纤混纺,化纤限内)	12				80	17	11	米/千克	B	Plain cloth of ramie, mixed with cotton and man-made fibres, containing < 85% by weight of ramie, man-made fibres within limitations
5311.0015 33	苎麻机织印染用布(苎麻含量在85%以下,与棉及化纤混纺,化纤限内)	12				80	17	11	米/千克	B	Woven fabrics of ramie for printing and dying, mixed with cotton and man-made fibres, containing < 85% by weight of ramie, man-made fibres within limitations
5311.0015 39	其他苎麻机织物(苎麻含量在85%以下,与棉及化纤混纺,化纤限内)	12				80	17	11	米/千克	B	Other woven fabrics of ramie, mixed with cotton and man-made fibres, containing<85% by weight of ramie, man-made fibres within limitations
5311.0015 40	其他苎麻机织物(苎麻含量在85%以下,与棉及化纤混纺)	12				80	17	11	米/千克	B	Other woven fabrics of ramie, mixed with cotton and man-made fibres, containing<85% by weight of ramie
5311.0015 91	其他苎麻机织物(苎麻<85%,主要或仅与精梳羊毛或动物细毛混纺)	12				80	17	11	米/千克	B	Other woven fabrics of ramie, mixed mainly or solely with combed wool or fine animal hair, containing < 85% by weight of ramie
5311.0015 99	其他苎麻机织物(指按重量计苎麻含量在85%以下)	12				80	17	11	米/千克	B	Other woven fabrics of ramie, containing<85% by weight of ramie
5311.0020	---纸纱线机织物	10	5		0	90	17	11	米/千克		---Woven fabrics of paper yarn
5311.0020 10	纸纱线机织物(主要或仅与精梳羊毛或动物细毛混纺)	10				90	17	11	米/千克	B	Woven fabrics of paper yarn, mixed mainly or solely with combed wool or combed fine animal hair
5311.0020 90	纸纱线机织物	10				90	17	11	米/千克	B	Woven fabrics of paper yarn
5311.0090	---其他	10	5	9.3	0	50	17	11	米/千克		---Other
5311.0090 11	其他纺织用植物纤维机织物(毛含量>17%,主要或仅与精梳羊毛或动物细毛混纺)	10				50	17	11	米/千克	B	Other woven fabrics of other vegetable textile fibres, mixed maily or solely with combed wool or of combed fine animal hair, containing > 17% by weight of combed wool or of combed fine animal hair
5311.0090 19	其他纺织用植物纤维机织物(含17%以上羊毛或动物细毛)	10				50	17	11	米/千克	B	Other woven fabrics of other vegetable textile fibres, containing > 17% by weight of wool or fine animal hair
5311.0090 21	其他纺织用植物纤维府绸及细平布(与棉及化纤混纺,棉限内)	10				50	17	11	米/千克	B	Poplin and fine plain cloth of other vegetable textile fibres, mixed with cotton and man-made fibres, cotton within limitations

税则号列 Tariff Item.	货 品 名 称	最惠国(%) MFN	协定(%) CT 东盟 CA	中巴 CP	中智 CC	普通 Gen	增值税率 VAT	出口退税 ED	计量单位 Unit	监管条件 SC	Article Description
5311.0090 22	其他纺织用植物纤维机织平布(与棉及化纤混纺,棉限内)	10				50	17	11	米/千克	B	Plain cloth of other vegetable textile fibres, mixed with cotton and man-made fibres, cotton within limitations
5311.0090 23	其他纺织用植物纤维机织印染用布(与棉及化纤混纺,棉限内)	10				50	17	11	米/千克	B	Woven fabrics of other vegetable textile fibres for printing and dying, mixed with cotton and man-made fibres, cotton within limitations
5311.0090 29	其他纺织用植物纤维机织物(与棉及化纤混纺,棉限内)	10				50	17	11	米/千克	B	Other woven fabrics of other vegetable textile fibres, mixed with cotton and man-made fibres, cotton within limitations
5311.0090 31	其他纺织用植物纤维府绸及细平布(与棉及化纤混纺,化纤限内)	10				50	17	11	米/千克	B	Poplin and fine plain cloth of other vegetable textile fibres, mixed with cotton and man-made fibres, man-made fibres within limitations
5311.0090 32	其他纺织用植物纤维机织平布(与棉及化纤混纺,化纤限内)	10				50	17	11	米/千克	B	Plain cloth of other vegetable textile fibres, mixed with cotton and man-made fibres, man-made fibres within limitations
5311.0090 33	其他纺织用植物纤维机织印染用布(与棉及化纤混纺,化纤限内)	10				50	17	11	米/千克	B	Other woven fabrics of other vegetable textile fibres for printing and dying, mixed with cotton and man-made fibres, man-made fibres within limitations
5311.0090 39	其他纺织用植物纤维其他机织物(与棉及化纤混纺,化纤限内)	10				50	17	11	米/千克	B	Other woven fabrics of other vegetable textile fibres, mixed with cotton and man-made fibres, man-made fibres within limitations
5311.0090 40	其他纺织用植物纤维其他机织物(与棉及化纤混纺)	10				50	17	11	米/千克	B	Other woven fabrics of other vegetable textile fibres, mixed with cotton and man-made fibres
5311.0090 91	其他纺织用植物纤维其他机织物(主要或仅与精梳羊毛或动物细毛混纺)	10				50	17	11	米/千克	B	Other woven fabrics of other vegetable textile fibres, mixed mainly or solely with combed wool or fine animal hair
5311.0090 99	其他纺织用植物纤维其他机织物	10				50	17	11	米/千克	B	Other woven fabrics of other vegetable textile fibres

第五十四章
化学纤维长丝

Chapter 54
Man-made filaments

注释：

一、本目录所称“化学纤维”，是指通过下列任一方法加工制得的有机聚合物的短纤或长丝：

（一）将有机单体物质加以聚合而制成聚合物，例如，聚酰胺、聚酯、聚烯烃、聚氨基甲酸酯；或通过上述加工将聚合物经化学改性制得（例如，聚乙酸乙烯酯水解制得的聚乙烯醇）；

（二）将天然有机聚合物（例如，纤维素）溶解或化学处理制成聚合物，例如，铜铵纤维或粘胶纤维；或将天然有机聚合物（例如，纤维素、酪蛋白及其他蛋白质、或藻酸）经化学改性制成取合物，例如，醋酸纤维素纤维或藻酸盐纤维。

对于化学纤维，所称“合成”，是指（一）款所述的纤维；所称“人造”，是指（二）款所述的纤维。税目 54.04 或 54.05 的扁条及类似品不视作化学纤维。对于纺织材料，所称“化学纤维”“合成纤维”及“人造纤维”，其含义应与上述解释相同。

二、税目 54.02 及 54.03 不适用于第五十五章的合成纤维或人造纤维的长丝丝束。

Notes:

1. “Chemical fiber” mentioned in this catalog refers to organic polymer finecool or cooltouch processed through any of the following methods:

(a) Polymers polymerized from the organic elements, such as polyamide, polyester, polyolefine; or the polymers made through chemical processing (for example, poly vinyl alcohol that obtained from hydrolyze polyvinyl acetate), or

(b) Polymers made from dissolution or chemical processing of natural organic polymers (such as fibrin), for example, viscose, cuprammouium rayon; or processed from natural organic polymers (such as fibrin, casein, and other protein or alginate), such as Cellulose diacetate or alginate fiber.

The term “synthesized” chemical fiber refers to the fiber mentioned in the item (I), the term "manmade" refers to the fiber mentioned in the item (II). The flat bar under heading No. 54.04 or 54.05 or the similar products shall not be counted as chemical fiber. The term “chemical fibre” “synthetic fabric” and “artificial fibre”, its meaning should be same as the above interpretation.

2. Headings Nos. 54.02 and 54.03 do not apply to synthetic or artificial filament tow of Chapter 55.

税则号列 Tariff Item.	货品名称	最惠国(%) MFN	协定(%)CT 东盟 CA	中巴 CP	中智 CC	普通 Gen	增值税率 VAT	出口退税 ED	计量单位 Unit	监管条件 SC	Article Description
54.01	**化学纤维长丝纺制的缝纫线，不论是否供零售用：**										**Sewing thread of man-made filaments, whether or not put up for retail sale:**
	-合成纤维长丝纺制：										-Of synthetic filaments:
5401.1010	---非供零售用	5			0	70	17	11	千克	5	---Not put up for retail sale
5401.1020	---供零售用	5			0	90	17	11	千克	5	---Put up for retail sale
	-人造纤维长丝纺制：										-Of artificial filaments:
5401.2010	---非供零售用	5			0	35	17	11	千克	5	---Not put up for retail sale
5401.2020	---供零售用	5			0	90	17	11	千克	5	---Put up for retail sale
54.02	**合成纤维长丝纱线（缝纫线除外），非供零售用，包括细度在 67 分特以下的合成纤维单丝：**										**Synthetic filament yarn (other than sewing thread), not put up for retail sale, including synthetic monofilament of less than 67 decitex:**
	-尼龙或其他聚酰胺纺制的高强力纱：										-High tenacity yarn of nylon or other polyamides:
5402.1100	--芳香族聚酰胺纺制	5		0	0	70	17	11	千克	A	---Of aramides
	--其他：										--Other:
5402.1910	---聚酰胺-6（尼龙-6）纺制的	5		0	0	70	17	11	千克	A	---Of nylon-6
5402.1920	---聚酰胺-6,6（尼龙-6,6）纺制的	5		0	0	70	17	11	千克	A	---Of nylon-6,6
5402.1990	---其他	5		0	0	70	17	11	千克	A	---Other
5402.2000	-聚酯高强力纱	5		0	0	70	17	11	千克		-High tenacity yarn of polyesters

税则号列 Tariff Item.	货品名称	最惠国(%) MFN	协定(%) CT 东盟 CA	中巴 CP	中智 CC	普通 Gen	增值税率 VAT	出口退税 ED	计量单位 Unit	监管条件 SC	Article Description
5402.2000 10	非零售聚酯高强力纱(单丝/未捻或捻度<5转/米复丝单纱)	5				70	17	11	千克	A	High tenacity yarn of polyesters, single yarn, untwisted or twist < 5 turns/m multiple (folded), not put up for retail sale
5402.2000 20	非零售聚酯高强力纱(捻度≥5转/米复丝单纱)	5				70	17	11	千克	A	Hightenacity yarn of polyesters single yarn, twist ≥5 turns/m multiple (folded), not put up for retail sale
5402.2000 90	非零售聚酯高强力多股纱	5				70	17	11	千克	A	Hightenacity yarn of polyesters, multiple (folded), not put up for retail sale
	-变形纱线:										-Textured yarn:
	--尼龙或其他聚酰胺纺制,每根单纱细度不超过50特:										--Of nylon or other polyamides, measuring per single yarn not more than 50 tex:
	---弹力丝:										---Elastic filament:
5402.3111	----聚酰胺-6(尼龙-6)纺制的	5		0	0	80	17	11	千克	A	----Of nylon-6
5402.3112	----聚酰胺-6,6(尼龙-6,6)纺制的	5		0	0	80	17	11	千克	A	----Of nylon-6,6
5402.3113	----芳香族聚酰胺纺制的	5		0	0	80	17	11	千克	A	----Of aramides
5402.3119	----其他	5		0	0	80	17	11	千克	A	----Other
5402.3190	---其他	5		0	0	70	17	11	千克	A	---Other
	--尼龙或其他聚酰胺纺制,每根单纱细度超过50特:										--Of nylon or other polyamides, measuring per single yarn more than 50tex:
	---弹力丝:										---Elastic filament:
5402.3211	----聚酰胺-6(尼龙-6)纺制的	5		0	0	80	17	11	千克		----Of nylon-6
5402.3212	----聚酰胺-6,6(尼龙-6,6)纺制的	5		0	0	80	17	11	千克		----Of nylon-6,6
5402.3213	----芳香族聚酰胺纺制的	5		0	0	80	17	11	千克		----Of aramides
5402.3219	----其他	5		0	0	80	17	11	千克		----Other
5402.3290	---其他	5		0	0	70	17	11	千克		---Other
	--聚酯纺制:										--Of polyesters:
5402.3310	---弹力丝	5		0	0	90	17	11	千克	A	---Elastic filament
5402.3390	---其他	5		0	0	70	17	11	千克	A	---Other
5402.3400	--聚丙烯纺制	5		0	0	70	17	11	千克		--Of polypropy lene
5402.3900	--其他	5		0	0	70	17	11	千克		--Other
	-其他单纱,未加捻或捻度每米不超过50转:										-Other yarn, single, untwisted or with a twist not exceeding 50 turns per metre:
	--弹性纱线:										--Elasticity yarn
5402.4410	---氨纶纱线	5		0	0	70	17	11	千克		---Of paly urethane
5402.4490	--其他	5		0	0	70	17	11	千克	A	---Other
	--其他,在龙或其他聚酰胺纱线										---Other, of nylon or other polyarnidts
5402.4510	---聚酰胺-6(尼龙-6)纺制的	5		0	0	70	17	11	千克		---Of nylon-6
5402.4520	---聚酰胺-6,6(尼龙-6,6)纺制的	5		0	0	70	17	11	千克		---Of nylon-6,6
5402.4530	---芳香族聚酰胺纺制的	5		0	0	70	17	11	千克		---Of aramides
5402.4590	---其他	5		0	0	70	17	11	千克		---Other
5402.4600	--其他,部分定向聚酯纱线	5		0	0	70	17	11	千克	A	--Other, of polyesters, partially oriented
5402.4700	--其他,聚酯纱线	5		0	0	70	17	11	千克	A	--Other, of polyesters, other
	--其他										--Other:
5402.4800	--其他,聚丙烯纱线	5		0	0	70	17	11	千克		--Other, Of polypropylene
5402.4900	--其他	5		0	0	70	17	11	千克		--Other

税则号列 Tariff Item.	货品名称	最惠国(%) MFN	协定(%)CT 东盟 CA	中巴 CP	中智 CC	普通 Gen	增值税率 VAT	出口退税 ED	计量单位 Unit	监管条件 SC	Article Description
5402.4900 01	非弹性氨纶单纱(非供零售用,未加捻或捻度每米不超过50转)	5				70	17	11	千克		Single yarn of polyurethane, untwisted or twist < 5 turns/m multiple (folded), not put up for retail sale
5402.4900 90	其他合成纤维长丝单纱(非供零售用,未加捻或捻度每米不超过50转)	5				70	17	11	千克		Other single yarn of synthetic filaments untwisted or twist < 50 turns/m multiple(folded), not put up for retail sale
	-其他单纱,捻度每米超过50转:										-Other yarn, single, with a twist exceeding 50 turns per metre:
	--尼龙或其他聚酰胺纱线:										--Of nylon or other polyamides:
5402.5110	---聚酰胺-6(尼龙-6)纺制的	5		0	0	70	17	11	千克		---Of nylon-6
5402.5120	---聚酰胺-6,6(尼龙-6,6)纺制的	5		0	0	70	17	11	千克		---Of nylon-6,6
5402.5130	---芳香族聚酰胺纺制的	5		0	0	70	17	11	千克		---Of aramides
5402.5190	---其他	5		0	0	70	17	11	千克		---Other
5402.5200	--聚酯纱线	5		0	0	70	17	11	千克		--Of polyesters
	--其他:										--Other:
5402.5910	---聚丙烯纱线	5		0	0	70	17	11	千克		---Of polypropylene
5402.5990	---其他	5		0	0	70	17	11	千克		---Other
	-其他纱线(多股纱线或缆线):										-Other yarn, multiple (folded) or cabled:
	--尼龙或其他聚酰胺纺制:										--Of nylon or other polyamides:
5402.6110	---聚酰胺-6(尼龙-6)纺制的	5		0	0	70	17	11	千克		---Of nylon-6
5402.6120	---聚酰胺-6,6(尼龙-6,6)纺制的	5		0	0	70	17	11	千克		---Of nylon-6,6
5402.6130	---芳香族聚酰胺纺制的	5		0	0	70	17	11	千克		---Of aramides
5402.6190	---其他	5		0	0	70	17	11	千克		---Other
5402.6200	--聚酯纺制	5		0	0	70	17	11	千克		--Of polyesters
	--其他:										--Other:
5402.6910	---聚丙烯纱线	5		0	0	70	17	11	千克		---Of polypropylene
5402.6920	---氨纶纱线	5		0	0	70	17	11	千克		---Of polyurethane
5402.6990	---其他	5		0	0	70	17	11	千克		---Other
54.03	**人造纤维长丝纱线(缝纫线除外),非供零售用,包括细度在67分特以下的人造纤维单丝:**										**Artificial filament yarn (other than sewing thread), not put up for retail sale, including artificial monofilament of less than 67 decitex:**
5403.1000	-粘胶纤维纺制的高强力纱	5			0	35	17	11	千克		-High tenacity yarn of viscose rayon
5403.1000 10	非零售粘胶纤维高强力纱(单丝/未捻或捻度每米5转以下的复丝单纱,非供零售用)	5				35	17	11	千克		High tenacity yarn of viscose rayon, single yarn, untwisted or twist < 5 turns/m, multiple (folded), not put up for retail sale
5403.1000 20	非零售粘胶纤维高强力纱(捻度5转/米及以上的复丝单纱)	5				35	17	11	千克		High tenacity yarn of viscose rayon, single yarn, twist > 5 turns/m, multiple (folded), not put up for retail sale
5403.1000 90	非零售粘胶纤维高强力多股纱	5				35	17	11	千克		High tenacity yarn of viscose rayon, multiple (folded), not put up for retail sale
	-其他单纱:										-Other yarn, single:
5403.3100	--粘胶纤维纺制,未加捻或捻度每米不超过120转	5			0	35	17	11	千克		--Of viscose rayon, untwisted or with a twist not exceeding 120 turns per metre

税则号列 Tariff Item.	货品名称	最惠国(%) MFN	协定(%)CT 东盟 CA	中巴 CP	中智 CC	普通 Gen	增值税率 VAT	出口退税 ED	计量单位 Unit	监管条件 SC	Article Description
5403.3100 10	非零售粘胶纤维单纱(单丝/未捻或捻度每米5转以下的复丝单纱,非供零售用,包括变形纱线)	5				35	17	11	千克		Single yarn of viscose rayon, untwisted or twist < 5 turns/m multiple (folded), not put up for retail sale including Deformation yarn
5403.3100 90	非零售其他粘胶纤维单纱(捻度每米5转及以上不超过120转的复丝单纱)包括变形纱线	5				35	17	11	千克		Single yarn of viscose rayon, 120 turns/m ≥ twist ≥ 5 turns/m multiple (folded), not put up for retail sale including Deformation yarn
5403.3200	--粘胶纤维纺制,捻度每米超过120转	5			0	35	17	11	千克		--Of viscose rayon, with a twist exceeding 120 turns per metre
5403.3200 10	非零售加捻的纯粘胶纤维单纱(加捻捻度每米超过120转不超过250转包括变形纱线)	5				35	17	11	千克		Single yarn of viscose rayon, 120 turns/m < twist ≤250 turns/m, not put up for retail sale including Deformation yarn
5403.3200 90	其他非零售加捻粘胶单纱(加捻捻度每米超过250转,包括变形纱线)	5				35	17	11	千克		Single yarn of viscose rayon, twist > 250 turns/m, containing ≥ 85% by weight of viscose rayon, not put up for retail sale including Deformation yarn
	--醋酸纤维纺制:										--Of cellulose acetate:
5403.3310	---二醋酸纤维纺制	5			0	40	17	11	千克		---Of cellulose diacetate
5403.3310 10	非零售二醋酸纤维单纱(单丝/未捻或捻度每米5转以下的复丝单纱,包括变形纱线)	5				40	17	11	千克	A	Single yarn of cellulose diacetate, untwisted or twist < 5 turns/m multiple (folded), not put up for retail sale including Deformation yarn
5403.3310 20	非零售二醋酸纤维单纱(捻度5转/米及以上不超过250转,包括变形纱线)	5				40	17	11	千克	A	Single yarn of cellulose diacetate, 5 turns/m≤twist≤250 turns/m, not put up for retail sale including Deformation yarn
5403.3310 90	非零售二醋酸纤维单纱(捻度超过250转/米)	5				40	17	11	千克	A	Single yarn of cellulose diacetate, twist >250 turns/m, not put up for retail sale
5403.3390	---其他	5			0	35	17	11	千克		---Other
5403.3390 10	非零售其他醋酸纤维单纱(单丝/未捻或捻度每米5转以下的复丝单纱,非供零售用,包括变形纱线)	5				35	17	11	千克		Other single yarn of cellulose acetate, untwisted or twist < 5 turns/m multiple (folded), not put up for retail sale including Deformation yarn
5403.3390 20	非零售其他醋酸纤维单纱(捻度5转/米及以上不超过250转/米,包括变形纱线)	5				35	17	11	千克		Other single yarn of cellulose acetate, 5 turns/m ≤ twist ≤ 250 turns/m, not put up for retail sale including Deformation yarn
5403.3390 90	非零售其他醋酸纤维单纱(捻度超过250转/米,包括变形纱线)	5				35	17	11	千克		Other single yarn of cellulose acetate, twist > 250 turns/m, not put up for retail sale including Deformation yarn
5403.3900	--其他	5			0	35	17	11	千克		--Other
5403.3900 10	非零售其他人纤长丝单纱(单丝/未捻或捻度每米5转以下的复丝单纱,非供零售用,包括变形纱线)	5				35	17	11	千克		Other single yarn of artificial filaments, untwisted or twist < 5 turns/m multiple (folded), not put up for retail sale including Deformation yarn

税则号列 Tariff Item.	货 品 名 称	最惠国(%) MFN	协定(%)CT 东盟 CA	中巴 CP	中智 CC	普通 Gen	增值税率 VAT	出口退税 ED	计量单位 Unit	监管条件 SC	Article Description
5403.3900 90	非零售其他人纤长丝单纱(捻度5转/米及以上,包括变形纱线)	5				35	17	11	千克		Other single yarn of artificial filaments, twist≥5 turns/m, not put up for retail sale including Deformation yarn
	-其他纱线(多股纱线或缆线):										-Other yarn, multiple (folded) or cabled:
5403.4100	--粘胶纤维纺制	5			0	35	17	11	千克		--Of viscose rayon
5403.4200	--醋酸纤维纺制	5			0	35	17	11	千克		--Of cellulose acetate
5403.4900	--其他	5			0	35	17	11	千克		--Other
54.04	**截面尺寸不超过1毫米,细度在67分特及以上的合成纤维单丝;表观宽度不超过5毫米的合成纤维纺织材料制扁条及类似品(例如人造草):**										**Synthetic monofilament of 67 decitex or more and of which no cross-sectional dimension exceeds 1 mm; strip and the like (for example, artificial straw) of synthetic textile materials of an apparent width not exceeing 5 mm:**
	-单丝										-Monofilament
5404.1100	--弹性单丝	5			0	80	17	11	千克		--Elasticity monnfilament
5404.1100 10	细度≥67分特的涤纶纤维弹性单丝(截面尺寸不超过1mm,细度<67分特的合纤单丝归入编号5402)	5				80	17	11	千克		Monofilament of polyester, ≥67 decitex, cross-sectional dimension≤1mm, but <67 decitex, should be classified under 5402)
5404.1100 90	细度≥67分特的其他合成纤维单丝(截面尺寸不超过1mm,细度<67分特的合纤单丝归入编号5402)	5				80	17	11	千克		Other synthetic monofilament, ≥ 67 decitex, (of which no cross-sectional dimension exceed 1mm, but <67 decitex, should be classified under 5402)
5404.1200	--其他,聚丙烯单丝	5			0	80	17	11	千克		--Other, of poly propy lene
5404.1900	--其他	5			0	80	17	11	千克		--Other
5404.1900 10	细度≥67分特的涤纶纤维单丝(截面尺寸不超过1mm,细度<67分特的合纤单丝归入编号5402)	5				80	17	11	千克		Monofilament of polyester≥67 decitex, cross - sectional dimension≤1mm, but <67 decitex, should be classified under 5402
5404.1900 90	细度≥67分特的其他合成纤维单丝(截面尺寸不超过1mm,细度<67分特的合纤单丝归入编号5402)	5				80	17	11	千克		Other synthetic monofilament, ≥67 decitex, (of which no cross - sectional dimension exceed 1mm, but < 67 decitex, should be classified under 5402)
5404.9000	-其他	5			0	80	17	11	千克		-Other
54.05	**截面尺寸不超过1毫米,细度在67分特及以上的人造纤维单丝;表观宽度不超过5毫米的人造纤维纺织材料制扁条及类似品(例如人造草):**										**Artificial monofilament of 67 decitex or more and of which no cross-sectional dimension exceeds 1 mm; strip and the like (for example, artificial straw) of artificial textile materials of an apparent width not exceeding 5 mm:**
5405.0000	截面尺寸不超过1毫米,细度在67分特及以上的人造纤维单丝;表观宽度不超过5毫米的人造纤维纺织材料制扁条及类似品(例如人造草)	5			0	80	17	11	千克		Artificial monofilament of 67 decitex or more and of which no cross-sectional dimension exceeds 1 mm; strip and the like (for example, artificial straw) of artificial textile materials of an apparent width not exceeding 5 mm
54.06	**化学纤维长丝纱线(缝纫线除外),供零售用:**										**Man-made filament yarn (other than sewing thread), put up for retail sale:**

税则号列 Tariff Item.	货品名称	最惠国(%) MFN	协定(%) 东盟 CA	中巴 CP	CT 中智 CC	普通 Gen	增值税率 VAT	出口退税 ED	计量单位 Unit	监管条件 SC	Article Description
5406.0010	---合成纤维长丝纱线	5			0	90	17	11	千克	5	---Synt het icfilament yarn
5406.0020	---人造纤维长丝纱线	5			0	90	17	11	千克	5	---Artificial filament yarn
54.07	**合成纤维长丝纱线的机织物,包括税目54.04所列材料的机织物:**										**Woven fabrics of synthetic filament yarn, including woven fabrics obtained from materials of heading 54.04:**
	-尼龙或其他聚酰胺高强力纱、聚酯高强力纱纺制的机织物:										-Woven fabrics obtained from high tenacity yarn of nylon or other polyamides or of polyesters:
5407.1010	---尼龙或其他聚酰胺高强力纱制	10	T3	0	0	130	17	11	米/千克	5A	---Of nylon or other polyamides
5407.1020	---聚酯高强力纱制	10	T3	0	0	130	17	11	米/千克		---Of polyesters
5407.1020 10	聚酯高强力纱纺制机织物(重量≤170克/平米)	10				130	17	11	米/千克	5A	Woven fabrics of high tenacity yarn of polyesters, weight≤170g/m^2
5407.1020 90	聚酯高强力纱纺制机织物(重量>170克/平米)	10				130	17	11	米/千克	5A	Woven fabrics of high tenacity yarn of polyesters, weight>170g/m^2
5407.2000	-扁条及类似品的机织物	10	T3	0	0	130	17	11	米/千克		-Woven fabrics obtained from strip or the like
5407.2000 10	聚乙烯聚丙烯扁条或类似机织物(宽度3米以下)	10				130	17	11	米/千克	5A	Woven fabrics of strip or the like, of polyethylene or of polypropylene, width <3m
5407.2000 90	其他合成纤维扁条及类似品机织物	10				130	17	11	米/千克	5A	Other woven fabrics of strip or the like of synthetic fibre
5407.3000	-第十一类注释九所列的机织物	10	T3	0	0	130	17	11	米/千克		-Fabrics specified in Note 9 to Section XI
5407.3000 10	平行纱线相互层迭并粘合织物(第十一类注释九所列的机织物,含塑料>60%)	10				130	17	11	米/千克		Woven fabrics consisting of layers of parallel textile yarn superimposed on each other, the layers are bounded at the intersections of the yarns, specified in Note 9 to Section, containing >60% by weight of plastics
5407.3000 20	平行纱线相互层迭并粘合织物(第十一类注释九所列的机织物,含塑料≤60%)	10				130	17	11	米/千克	5	Woven fabrics consisting of layers of parallel textile yarn superimposed on each other, the layers are bounded at the intersections of the yarns, specified in Note 9 to Section, containing≤60% by weight of plastics
	-其他机织物,按重量计尼龙或其他聚酰胺长丝含量在85%及以上:										-Other woven fabrics, containing 85% or more by weight of filaments of nylon or other polyamides:
5407.4100	--未漂白或漂白	10	8	0	0	130	17	11	米/千克		--Unbleached or bleached
5407.4100 10	未漂白或漂白的打字机带用机织物(尼龙或其他聚酰胺长丝含量≥85%)	10				130	17	11	米/千克		Woven fabrics for typewriter ribbon, containing≥85% by weight of filaments of nylon or of other polyamides, unbleached or bleached
5407.4100 20	未漂白纯尼龙机织物(含尼龙量≥85%)	10				130	17	11	米/千克		Woven fabrics of nylon, containing ≥ 85% by weight of filaments of nylon, unbleached
5407.4100 90	未漂白的或漂白的其他机织物(其他聚酰胺长丝含量≥85%)	10				130	17	11	米/千克	5	Other woven fabrics, containing≥85% by weight of nylon-6 filaments, unbleached or bleached

税则号列 Tariff Item.	货品名称	最惠国(%) MFN	协定(%)CT 东盟 CA	中巴 CP	中智 CC	普通 Gen	增值税率 VAT	出口退税 ED	计量单位 Unit	监管条件 SC	Article Description
5407.4200	--染色	10	T3	0	0	130	17	11	米/千克	5	--Dyed
5407.4300	--色织	10	8	0	0	130	17	11	米/千克	5	--Of yarns of different colours
5407.4400	--印花	10	8	0	0	130	17	11	米/千克	5	--Printed
	-其他机织物,按重量计聚酯变形长丝含量在85%及以上:										-Other woven fabrics, containing 85% or more by weight of textured polyester filaments:
5407.5100	--未漂白或漂白	10	8	0	0	130	17	11	米/千克		--Unbleached or bleached
5407.5100 10	未漂白或漂白纯聚酯变形长丝布(聚酯变形长丝含量≥85%,重量≤170克/平米)	10				130	17	11	米/千克	5	Woven fabrics, containing ≥ 85% by weight of textured polyester filaments, weight≤170g/m² unbleached or bleached
5407.5100 20	未漂白或漂白纯聚酯变形长丝机织物(聚酯变形长丝含量≥85%,重量大于170克/平米)	10				130	17	11	米/千克	5	Woven fabrics, containing ≥ 85% by weight of textured polyester filaments, weight >170g/m², unbleached or bleached
5407.5200	--染色	10	T3	0	0	130	17	11	米/千克		--Dyed
5407.5200 10	染色的聚酯变形长丝布,含量≥85(宽<77厘米,每厘米经纱密70-142根,纬密32-71根)	10				130	17	11	米/千克	5	Woven fabrics, containing ≥ 85% by weight of textured polyester filaments, of width <77cm, warp yarn 70—142/cm, weft yarn 32—71/cm, dyed
5407.5200 91	染色的其他聚酯变形长丝机织物(聚酯变形长丝含量≥85%,重量≤170克/平米)	10				130	17	11	米/千克	5	Other woven fabrics, containing≥85% by weight of textured polyester filaments, weight≤170g/m², dyed
5407.5200 92	染色的其他聚酯变形长丝机织物(聚酯变形长丝含量≥85%,重量>170克/平米)	10				130	17	11	米/千克	5	Other woven fabrics, containing≥85% by weight of textured polyester filaments, weight >170g/m², dyed
5407.5300	--色织	10	8	0	0	130	17	11	米/千克		--Of yarns of different colours
5407.5300 10	色织的聚酯变形长丝布,含量≥85(宽<77厘米,每厘米经纱密70-142根,纬密32-71根)	10				130	17	11	米/千克	5	Woven fabrics, containing ≥ 85% by weight of textured polyester filaments, width < 77cm, warp yarn 70—142/cm, weft yarn 32—71/cm, of different colours
5407.5300 91	色织的聚酯变形长丝机织物(聚酯变形长丝含量≥85%,重量≤170克/平米)	10				130	17	11	米/千克	5	Woven fabrics, containing ≥ 85% by weight of textured polyester filaments, weight≤170g/m², of different colours
5407.5300 92	色织的聚酯变形长丝机织物(聚酯变形长丝含量≥85%重量>170克/平米)	10				130	17	11	米/千克	5	Woven fabrics, containing ≥ 85% by weight of textured polyester filaments, weight >170g/m², of different colours
5407.5400	--印花	10	8	0	0	130	17	11	米/千克		--Printed
5407.5400 10	印花的聚酯变形长丝机织物(聚酯变形长丝含量≥85%,重量≤170克/平米)	10				130	17	11	米/千克	5	Woven fabrics, containing ≥ 85% by weight of textured polyester filaments, weight ≤170g/m², printed
5407.5400 20	印花的聚酯变形长丝机织物(聚酯变形长丝含量≥85%,重量>170克/平米)	10				130	17	11	米/千克	5	Woven fabrics, containing ≥ 85% by weight of textured polyester filaments, weight >170g/m², printed
	-其他机织物,按重量计聚酯长丝含量在85%及以上:										-Other woven fabrics, containing 85% or more by weight of polyester filaments:
5407.6100	--按重量计聚酯非变形长丝含量在85%及以上	10	8	0	0	130	17	11	米/千克		--Containing 85% or more by weight of non-textured polyester filaments

税则号列 Tariff Item.	货品名称	最惠国(%) MFN	协定(%)CT 东盟 CA	中巴 CP	中智 CC	普通 Gen	增值税率 VAT	出口退税 ED	计量单位 Unit	监管条件 SC	Article Description
5407.6100 11	染色聚酯非变形长丝布,含量≥85(宽<77厘米,每厘米经纱密70－142根,纬密32－71根)	10				130	17	11	米/千克	5	Woven fabrics, containing ≥85% by weight of non-textured polyester filaments, dyed, width <77cm, warp yarn 70－142/cm, weft yarn 32－71/cm
5407.6100 12	色织聚酯非变形长丝布,含量≥85(宽<77厘米,每厘米经纱密70－142根,纬密32－71根)	10				130	17	11	米/千克	5	Woven fabrics, containing ≥85% by weight of non-textured polyester filaments, of yarns of different colours, width <77cm warp yarn 70－142/cm, weft yarn 31－71/cm
5407.6100 20	全聚酯其他非变形长丝机织物(单纱含27根丝,细75－80分特,捻度900转及以上)	10				130	17	11	米/千克	5	Woven fabrics of non-textured polyester filaments, a single yarn twisted with 27 threads, 75－80 decitex, twist >900turns/m
5407.6100 31	未漂或漂聚酯非变形长丝机织物(聚酯非变形长丝含量≥85%,重量>170克/平米)	10				130	17	11	米/千克	5	Woven fabrics, containing ≥85% by weight of non-textured polyester filaments, weight >170g/m^2, unbleached or bleached
5407.6100 32	未漂或漂聚酯非变形长丝机织物(聚酯非变形长丝含量≥85%,重量≤170克/平米)	10				130	17	11	米/千克	5	Woven fabrics, containing ≥85% by weight of non-textured polyester filaments, weight ≤170g/m^2, unbleached or bleached
5407.6100 41	染色其他聚酯非变形长丝布(聚酯非变形长丝含量≥85%,重量>170克/平米)	10				130	17	11	米/千克	5	Other woven fabrics, containing≥85% by weight of non-textured polyester filaments of weight >170g/m^2, dyed
5407.6100 42	染色其他纯聚酯非变形长丝布(聚酯非变形长丝含量≥85%,重量≤170克/平米)	10				130	17	11	米/千克	5	Other woven fabrics, containing≥85% by weight of non-textured polyester filaments, weight≤170g/m^2, dyed
5407.6100 51	色织其他聚酯非变形长丝布(聚酯非变形长丝含量≥85%,重量>170克/平米)	10				130	17	11	米/千克	5	Other woven fabrics, containing≥85% by weight of non-textured polyester filaments, weight > 170g/m^2, of different collours
5407.6100 52	色织其他聚酯非变形长丝布(聚酯非变形长丝含量≥85%,重量≤170克/平米)	10				130	17	11	米/千克	5	Other woven fabrics, containing≥85% by weight of non-textured polyester filaments of weight≤170g/m^2, of different collours
5407.6100 61	印花其他聚酯非变形长丝布(聚酯非变形长丝含量≥85%,重量>170克/平米)	10				130	17	11	米/千克	5	Other woven fabrics, containing≥85% by weight of non-textured polyester filaments, weight >170g/m^2, printed
5407.6100 62	印花其他聚酯非变形长丝布(聚酯非变形长丝含量≥85%,重量≤170克/平米)	10				130	17	11	米/千克	5	Other woven fabrics, containing≥85% by weight of non-textured polyester filaments, weight≤170g/m^2, printed
5407.6900	--其他	10	8	0	0	130	17	11	米/千克		--Other
5407.6900 11	未漂或漂其他聚酯长丝布(聚酯长丝含量≥85%,重量>170克/平米)	10				130	17	11	米/千克	5	Other woven fabrics, containing≥85% by weight of polyester filaments, weight >170g/m^2, unbleached or bleached
5407.6900 12	未漂或漂其他聚酯长丝布(聚酯长丝含量≥85%,重量≤170克/平米)	10				130	17	11	米/千克	5	Other woven fabrics, containing≥85% by weight of polyester filaments, weight ≤170g/m^2, unbleached or bleached

税则号列 Tariff Item.	货品名称	最惠国(%) MFN	协定(%)CT 东盟 CA	中巴 CP	中智 CC	普通 Gen	增值税率 VAT	出口退税 ED	计量单位 Unit	监管条件 SC	Article Description
5407.6900 21	染色其他聚酯长丝布(聚酯长丝含量≥85%,重量>170克/平米)	10				130	17	11	米/千克	5	Other woven fabrics, containing≥85% by weight of polyester filaments, weight >170g/m^2, dyed
5407.6900 22	染色其他聚酯长丝布(聚酯长丝含量≥85%,重量≤170克/平米)	10				130	17	11	米/千克	5	Other woven fabrics, containing≥85% by weight of polyester filaments, weight ≤170g/m^2, dyed
5407.6900 31	色织其他聚酯长丝布,含量≥85%(每厘米经纱密70-142根,纬密32-71根)	10				130	17	11	米/千克	5	Other woven fabrics, containing≥85% by weight of polyester filaments, warp yarn 70-142/cm, weft yarn 32-71/cm, of different collours
5407.6900 32	色织其他聚酯长丝布(聚酯长丝含量≥85%,重量>170克/平米)	10				130	17	11	米/千克	5	Other woven fabrics, containing≥85% by weight of polyester filaments, of weight>170g/m^2, of different collours
5407.6900 33	色织其他聚酯长丝布(聚酯长丝含量≥85%,重量≤170克/平米)	10				130	17	11	米/千克	5	Other woven fabrics, containing≥85% by weight of polyester filaments, of weight≤170g/m^2, of different collours
5407.6900 41	印花其他聚酯长丝布(聚酯长丝含量≥85%,重量>170克/平米)	10				130	17	11	米/千克	5	Other woven fabrics, containing≥85% by weight of polyester filaments, of weight>170g/m^2, printed
5407.6900 42	印花其他聚酯长丝布(聚酯长丝含量≥85%,重量≤170克/平米)	10				130	17	11	米/千克	5	Other woven fabrics, containing≥85% by weight of polyester filaments, of weight ≤ 170g/m^2, printed
	-其他机织物,按重量计其他合成纤维长丝含量在85%及以上:										-Other woven fabrics, containing 85% or more by weight of synthetic filaments:
5407.7100	--未漂白或漂白	10	T3	0	0	130	17	11	米/千克	5	--Unbleached or bleached
5407.7200	--染色	10	T3	0	0	130	17	11	米/千克	5	--Dyed
5407.7300	--色织	10	8	0	0	130	17	11	米/千克	5	--Of yarns of different colours
5407.7400	--印花	10	8	0	0	130	17	11	米/千克	5	--Printed
	-其他机织物,按重量计其他合成纤维长丝含量在85%以下,主要或仅与棉混纺:										-Other woven fabrics, containing less than 85% by weight of synthetic filaments, mixed mainly or solely with cotton:
5407.8100	--未漂白或漂白	10	8	0	0	130	17	11	米/千克		--Unbleached or bleached
5407.8100 10	未漂或漂白与棉混纺府绸及细平布(其他合成纤维长丝含量在85%以下)	10				130	17	11	米/千克	B	Poplin and fine plain cloth, mixed with cotton, containing < 85% by weight of synthetic filaments, unbleached or bleached
5407.8100 20	未漂或漂白的与棉混纺平布(其他合成纤维长丝含量在85%以下)	10				130	17	11	米/千克	B	Plain cloth, mixed with cotton, containing<85% by weight of synthetic filaments, unbleached or bleached
5407.8100 30	未漂或漂白的与棉混纺印染用布(混纺合纤布指按重量计其他合成纤维长丝含量在85%以下)	10				130	17	11	米/千克	B	Woven fabrics for printing and dying, mixed with cotton, containing < 85% by weight of synthetic filaments , unbleached or bleached
5407.8100 40	未漂或漂白与棉混纺缎纹或斜纹布(混纺合纤布指按重量计其他合成纤维长丝含量在85%以下)	10				130	17	11	米/千克	B	Woven fabrics satin weave, mixed with cotton, containing<85% by weight of synthetic filaments, unbleached or bleached

税则号列 Tariff Item.	货品名称	最惠国(%) MFN	协定(%) CT 东盟 CA	中巴 CP	中智 CC	普通 Gen	增值税率 VAT	出口退税 ED	计量单位 Unit	监管条件 SC	Article Description
5407.8100 90	未漂或漂白与棉混纺其他合纤布(混纺合纤布指按重量计其他合成纤维长丝含量在85%以下)	10				130	17	11	米/千克	B	Other woven fabrics, mixed with cotton containing <85% by weight of synthetic filaments, unbleached or bleached
5407.8200	--染色	10	8	0	0	130	17	11	米/千克		--Dyed
5407.8200 10	染色的与棉混纺府绸及细平布(混纺合纤布指按重量计其他合成纤维长丝含量在85%以下)	10				130	17	11	米/千克	B	Poplin and fine plain cloth, mixed with cotton, containing <85% by weight of synthetic filaments, dyed
5407.8200 20	染色的与棉混纺平布(混纺合纤布指按重量计其他合成纤维长丝含量在85%以下)	10				130	17	11	米/千克	B	Plain cloth, mixed with cotton, containing <85% by weight of synthetic filaments, dyed
5407.8200 30	染色的与棉混纺印染用布(混纺合纤布指按重量计其他合成纤维长丝含量在85%以下)	10				130	17	11	米/千克	B	Woven fabrics for printing and dying mixed with cotton, containing < 85% by weight of synthetic filaments, dyed
5407.8200 40	染色的与棉混纺缎纹或斜纹布(混纺合纤布指按重量计其他合成纤维长丝含量在85%以下)	10				130	17	11	米/千克	B	Woven fabrics satin weave or twill weave, mixed with cotton, containing < 85% by weight of synthetic filaments, dyed
5407.8200 90	染色的与棉混纺其他合成纤维布(混纺合纤布指按重量计其他合成纤维长丝含量在85%以下)	10				130	17	11	米/千克	B	Other woven fabrics, mixed with cotton, containing < 85% by weight of synthetic filaments, dyed
5407.8300	--色织	10	8	0	0	130	17	11	米/千克		--Of yarns of different colours
5407.8300 10	色织的与棉混纺府绸及细平布(混纺合纤布指按重量计其他合成纤维长丝含量在85%以下)	10				130	17	11	米/千克		Poplin and fine plain cloth, mixed with cotton, containing <85% by weight of synthetic filaments, of different colours
5407.8300 20	色织的与棉混纺平布(混纺合纤布指按重量计其他合成纤维长丝含量在85%以下)	10				130	17	11	米/千克		Plain cloth, mixed with cotton, containing <85% by weight of synthetic filaments, of different colours
5407.8300 30	色织的与棉混纺印染用布(混纺合纤布指按重量计其他合成纤维长丝含量在85%以下)	10				130	17	11	米/千克		Woven fabrics for printing and dying, mixed with cotton, containing < 85% by weight of synthetic filaments, of different colours
5407.8300 40	色织的与棉混纺缎纹或斜纹布(混纺合纤布指按重量计其他合成纤维长丝含量在85%以下)	10				130	17	11	米/千克		Woven fabrics satin weave or twill weave, mixed with cotton, containing < 85% by weight of synthetic filaments, of different colours
5407.8300 90	色织的与棉混纺其他合成纤维布(混纺合纤布指按重量计其他合成纤维长丝含量在85%以下)	10				130	17	11	米/千克		Other woven fabrics, mixed with cotton, containing < 85% by weight of synthetic filaments, of different colours
5407.8400	--印花	10	8	0	0	130	17	11	米/千克		--Printed

税则号列 Tariff Item.	货品名称	最惠国(%) MFN	协定(%)CT 东盟 CA	中巴 CP	中智 CC	普通 Gen	增值税率 VAT	出口退税 ED	计量单位 Unit	监管条件 SC	Article Description
5407.8400 10	印花的与棉混纺府绸及细平布(混纺合纤布指按重量计其他合成纤维长丝含量在85%以下)	10				130	17	11	米/千克	B	Poplin and fine plain cloth, mixed with cotton, containing < 85% by weight of synthetic filaments, printed
5407.8400 20	印花的与棉混纺平布(混纺合纤布指按重量计其他合成纤维长丝含量在85%以下)	10				130	17	11	米/千克	B	Plain cloth, mixed with cotton, containing < 85% by weight of synthetic filaments, printed
5407.8400 30	印花的与棉混纺印染用布(混纺合纤布指按重量计其他合成纤维长丝含量在85%以下)	10				130	17	11	米/千克	B	Woven fabrics for printing and dying, mixed with cotton, containing < 85% by weight of synthetic filaments, printed
5407.8400 40	印花的与棉混纺缎纹或斜纹布(混纺合纤布指按重量计其他合成纤维长丝含量在85%以下)	10				130	17	11	米/千克	B	Woven fabrics satin weave or twill weave, mixed with cotton, containing < 85% by weight of synthetic filaments, printed
5407.8400 90	印花的与棉混纺其他合成纤维布(混纺合纤布指按重量计其他合成纤维长丝含量在85%以下)	10				130	17	11	米/千克	B	Other woven fabrics, mixed with cotton, containing < 85% by weight of synthetic filaments, printed
	-其他机织物:										-Other woven fabrics:
5407.9100	--未漂白或漂白	10	8	0	0	130	17	11	米/千克		--Unbleached or bleached
5407.9100 11	未漂或漂白的其他混纺合成纤维布(与精梳羊毛或动物细毛≥36%混纺,合纤<85%)	10				130	17	11	米/千克		Other woven fabrics, mixed, containing ≥36% by weight of combed wool or fine animal hair, containing < 85% by weight of synthetic fibres, unbleached or bleached
5407.9100 19	未漂或漂白的其他混纺合成纤维布(合纤含量在85%以下,与其他羊毛或动物细毛36%及以上混纺)	10				130	17	11	米/千克		Other woven fabrics, mixed, containing ≥36% by weight of wool or fine animal hair, containing < 85% by weight of synthetic fibres, unbleached or bleached
5407.9100 21	未漂或漂白的其他混纺合成纤维布(与精梳羊毛或动物细毛<36%混纺,合纤<85%)	10				130	17	11	米/千克		Other woven fabrics, mixed, containing < 36% by weight of combed wool or fine animal hair, containing < 85% by weight of synthetic filaments, unbleached or bleached
5407.9100 29	未漂或漂白的其他混纺合成纤维布(与其他羊毛或动物细毛<36%混纺,合纤<85%)	10				130	17	11	米/千克		Other woven fabrics, mixed, containing < 36% by weight of other wool or fine animal hair, containing < 85% by weight of synthetic fibres, unbleached or bleached
5407.9100 30	未漂或漂白的其他混纺合成纤维布(与人造纤维长丝混纺,合纤含量<85%)	10				130	17	11	米/千克	5	Other woven fabrics, other, mixed with artificial filaments, containing < 85% by weight of synthetic fibres, unbleached or bleached
5407.9100 91	未漂或漂其他混纺府绸及细平布(合成纤维长丝含量在85%以下,与其他纤维混纺)	10				130	17	11	米/千克		Poplin and fine plain cloth, mixed with other fibres, containing < 85% by weight of synthetic filaments, unbleached or bleached

税则号列 Tariff Item.	货品名称	最惠国(%) MFN	协定(%) CT 东盟 CA	中巴 CP	中智 CC	普通 Gen	增值税率 VAT	出口退税 ED	计量单位 Unit	监管条件 SC	Article Description
5407.9100 92	未漂或漂白的其他混纺平布(合成纤维长丝含量在85%以下,与其他纤维混纺)	10				130	17	11	米/千克		Plain cloth, mixed with other fibres, containing <85% by weight of synthetic filaments, unbleached or bleached
5407.9100 93	未漂或漂白的其他混纺印染用布(合成纤维长丝含量在85%以下,与其他纤维混纺)	10				130	17	11	米/千克		Other woven fabrics for printing and dying, mixed with other fibres, containing < 85% by weight of synthetic filaments, unbleached or bleached
5407.9100 94	未漂或漂其他混纺缎纹或斜纹布(合成纤维长丝含量在85%以下,与其他纤维混纺)	10				130	17	11	米/千克		Other woven fabrics satin weave or twill weave, mixed with other fibres, containing <85% by weight of synthetic filaments, unbleached or bleached
5407.9100 99	未漂或漂白的其他混纺合成纤维布(合成纤维长丝含量在85%以下,与其他纤维混纺)	10				130	17	11	米/千克		Other woven fabrics, mixed with other fibres, containing < 85% by weight of synthetic filaments, unbleached or bleached
5407.9200	--染色	10	T3	0	0	130	17	11	米/千克		--Dyed
5407.9200 11	染色的其他混纺合成纤维布(与精梳羊毛或动物细毛≥36%混纺,合纤<85%)	10				130	17	11	米/千克		Other woven fabrics, mixed, containing ≥36% by weight of combed wool or fine animal hair, containing < 85% by weight, of synthetic fibres, dyed
5407.9200 19	染色的其他混纺合成纤维布(与其他羊毛或动物细毛≥36%混纺,合纤<85%)	10				130	17	11	米/千克		Other woven fabrics, mixed, containing ≥36% by weight of wool or fine animal hair, containing < 85% by weight of synthetic fibres, dyed
5407.9200 21	染色的其他混纺合成纤维布(与精梳羊毛或动物细毛<36%混纺,合纤<85%)	10				130	17	11	米/千克		Other woven fabrics, mixed, containing < 36% by weight of combed wool or fine animal hair, containing < 85% by weight, of synthetic fibres, dyed
5407.9200 29	染色的其他混纺合成纤维布(与其他羊毛或动物细毛<36%混纺,合纤<85%)	10				130	17	11	米/千克		Other woven fabrics, mixed, containing <36% by weight of wool or fine animal hair, containing < 85% by weight, of synthetic fibres, dyed
5407.9200 30	染色的其他混纺合成纤维布(与人造纤维长丝或含金属纱线混纺,合纤含量在85%以下)	10				130	17	11	米/千克	5	Other woven fabrics, mixed with artificial filaments or metallized yarn, containing <85% by weight of synthetic fibres, dyed
5407.9200 91	染色的其他混纺府绸及细平布(合成纤维长丝含量在85%以下,与其他纤维混纺)	10				130	17	11	米/千克		Poplin and fine plain cloth, mixed with other fibres, containing < 85% by weight of synthetic filaments, dyed
5407.9200 92	染色的其他混纺平布(合成纤维长丝含量在85%以下,与其他纤维混纺)	10				130	17	11	米/千克		Plain cloth, mixed with other fibres, containing <85% by weight of synthetic filaments, dyed
5407.9200 93	染色的其他混纺印染用布(合成纤维长丝含量在85%以下,与其他纤维混纺)	10				130	17	11	米/千克		Other woven fabrics for printing and dying, mixed with other fibres, containing < 85% by weight of synthetic filaments, dyed

税则号列 Tariff Item.	货品名称	最惠国(%) MFN	协定(%)CT 东盟 CA	中巴 CP	中智 CC	普通 Gen	增值税率 VAT	出口退税 ED	计量单位 Unit	监管条件 SC	Article Description
5407.9200 94	染色的其他混纺缎纹或斜纹布(合成纤维长丝含量在85%以下,与其他纤维混纺)	10				130	17	11	米/千克		Other woven fabrics satin weave or twill weave, mixed with other fibres, containing <85% by weight, of synthetic filaments, dyed
5407.9200 99	染色的其他混纺合成纤维布(合成纤维长丝含量在85%以下,与其他纤维混纺)	10				130	17	11	米/千克		Other woven fabrics, mixed with other fibres, containing < 85% by weight of synthetic filaments, dyed
5407.9300	--色织	10	8	0	0	130	17	11	米/千克		--Of yarns of different colours
5407.9300 11	色织的其他混纺合成纤维布(与精梳羊毛或动物细毛≥36%混纺,合纤<85%)	10				130	17	11	米/千克		Other woven fabrics, mixed, containing ≥36% by weight of combed wool or fine animal hair, containing <85% by weight of synthetic fibres, of different colours
5407.9300 19	色织的其他混纺合成纤维布(与其他羊毛或动物细毛≥36%混纺,合纤<85%)	10				130	17	11	米/千克		Other woven fabrics, mixed, containing ≥36% by weight of wool or fine animal hair, containing < 85% by weight of synthetic fibres, of different colours
5407.9300 21	色织的其他混纺合成纤维布(与精梳羊毛或动物细毛<36%混纺,合纤<85%)	10				130	17	11	米/千克		Other woven fabrics, mixed containing < 36% by weight of combed wool or fine animal hair, containing <85% by weight of synthetic fibres, of different colours
5407.9300 29	色织的其他混纺合成纤维布(与其他羊毛或动物细毛<36%混纺,合纤<85%)	10				130	17	11	米/千克		Other woven fabrics, mixed, containing <36% by weight of wool or fine animal hair, containing < 85% by weight of synthetic fibres, of different colours
5407.9300 30	色织其他混纺合纤布,合纤<85%(含化纤长丝≥85%,每厘米经密70-142根,纬密32-71根)	10				130	17	11	米/千克	5	Other woven fabrics, mixed, containing ≥85% by weight of synthetic fibres, warp yarn 70—142/cm, weft yarn 32—71/cm, of different colours
5407.9300 40	色织的其他混纺合成纤维布(与人造纤维长丝或含金属纱线混纺,合纤长丝含量<85%)	10				130	17	11	米/千克	5	Other woven fabrics, mixed with artificial filaments or metallized yarn, containing < 85% by weight of synthetic filaments, of different colours
5407.9300 91	色织的其他混纺府绸及细平布(合成纤维长丝含量在85%以下,与其他纤维混纺)	10				130	17	11	米/千克		Poplin and fine plain cloth, mixed with other fibres, containing < 85% by weight of synthetic filaments, of different colours
5407.9300 92	色织的其他混纺平布(合成纤维长丝含量在85%以下,与其他纤维混纺)	10				130	17	11	米/千克		Plain cloth, mixed with other fibres, containing <85% by weight of synthetic filaments, of different colours
5407.9300 93	色织的其他混纺印染用布(合成纤维长丝含量在85%以下,与其他纤维混纺)	10				130	17	11	米/千克		Other woven fabrics for printing and dying, mixed with other fibres, containing < 85% by weight of synthetic filaments, of different colours
5407.9300 94	色织的其他混纺缎纹或斜纹布(合成纤维长丝含量在85%以下,与其他纤维混纺)	10				130	17	11	米/千克		Other woven fabrics, satin weave or twill weave, mixed with other fibres, containing <85% by weight of synthetic filaments, of different colours

税则号列 Tariff Item.	货品名称	最惠国(%) MFN	协定(%)CT 东盟 CA	中巴 CP	中智 CC	普通 Gen	增值税率 VAT	出口退税 ED	计量单位 Unit	监管条件 SC	Article Description
5407.9300 99	色织的其他混纺合成纤维布(合成纤维长丝含量在85%以下,与其他纤维混纺)	10				130	17	11	米/千克		Other woven fabrics, mixed with other fibres, containing < 85% by weight of synthetic filaments, of different colours
5407.9400	--印花	10	8	0	0	130	17	11	米/千克		--Printed
5407.9400 11	印花的其他混纺合成纤维布(与精梳羊毛或动物细毛≥36%混纺,合纤<85%)	10				130	17	11	米/千克	B	Other woven fabrics, mixed, containing ≥36% by weight of combed wool or fine animal hair, containing < 85% by weight of synthetic fibres, printed
5407.9400 19	印花的其他混纺合成纤维布(与其他羊毛或动物细毛≥36%混纺,合纤<85%)	10				130	17	11	米/千克	B	Other woven fabrics, mixed, containing ≥36% by weight of wool or fine animal hair, containing < 85% by weight, of synthetic fibres, printed
5407.9400 21	印花的其他混纺合成纤维布(与精梳羊毛或动物细毛<36%混纺,合纤<85%)	10				130	17	11	米/千克	B	Other woven fabrics, mixed, containing < 36% by weight of combed wool or fine animal hair, containing < 85% by weight, of synthetic fibres, printed
5407.9400 29	印花的其他混纺合成纤维布(与其他羊毛或动物细毛<36%混纺,合纤<85%)	10				130	17	11	米/千克	B	Other woven fabrics, mixed, containing <36% by weight of wool or fine animal hair, containing < 85% by weight, of synthetic fibres, printed
5407.9400 30	印花的其他混纺合成纤维布(与人造纤维长丝或含金属纱线混纺,合纤含量<85%)	10				130	17	11	米/千克	5B	Other woven fabrics, mixed with artificial filaments or metallized yarn, containing <85% by weight of synthetic fibres, printed
5407.9400 91	印花的其他混纺府绸及细平布(合成纤维长丝含量在85%以下,与其他纤维混纺)	10				130	17	11	米/千克	B	Poplin and fine plain cloth, mixed with other fibres, containing < 85% by weight of synthetic filaments, printed
5407.9400 92	印花的其他混纺平布(合成纤维长丝含量在85%以下,与其他纤维混纺)	10				130	17	11	米/千克	B	Plain cloth, mixed with other fibres, containing < 85% by weight, of synthetic filaments, printed
5407.9400 93	印花的其他混纺印染用布(合成纤维长丝含量在85%以下,与其他纤维混纺)	10				130	17	11	米/千克	B	Other woven fabrics for printing and dying, mixed with other fibres, containing < 85% by weight of synthetic filaments, printed
5407.9400 94	印花的其他混纺缎纹或斜纹布(合成纤维长丝含量在85%以下,与其他纤维混纺)	10				130	17	11	米/千克	B	Other woven fabrics satin weave or twill weave, mixed with other fibres, containing <85% by weight of synthetic filaments, printed
5407.9400 99	印花的其他混纺合成纤维布(合成纤维长丝含量在85%以下,与其他纤维混纺)	10				130	17	11	米/千克	B	Other woven fabrics, mixed with other fibres, containing < 85% by weight of synthetic filaments, printed
54.08	**人造纤维长丝纱线的机织物,包括税目54.05所列材料的机织物:**										**Woven fabrics of artificial filament yarn, including woven fabrics obtained from materials of heading 54.05:**
5408.1000	-粘胶纤维高强力纱的机织物	10	T3	0	0	130	17	11	米/千克	B	-Woven fabrics obtained from high tenacity yarn of viscose rayon
	-其他机织物,按重量计人造纤维长丝、扁条或类似品含量在85%及以上:										-Other woven fabrics, containing 85% or more by weight of artificial filament or strip or the like:

税则号列 Tariff Item.	货 品 名 称	最惠国(%) MFN	协定(%)CT 东盟 CA	中巴 CP	中智 CC	普通 Gen	增值税率 VAT	出口退税 ED	计量单位 Unit	监管条件 SC	Article Description
	--未漂白或漂白:										--Unbleached or bleached:
5408.2110	---粘胶纤维制	12	8	0	0	130	17	11	米/千克	B	---Of yarns of viscose rayon
5408.2120	---醋纤纤维制	12	8	0	0	130	17	11	米/千克	B	---Of yarns of cellulose acetate
5408.2190	---其他	12	8	0	0	130	17	11	米/千克	B	---Other
	--染色:										--Dyed:
5408.2210	---粘胶纤维制	10	8	0	0	130	17	11	米/千克	B	---Of yarns of viscose rayon
5408.2220	---醋纤纤维制	10	8	0	0	130	17	11	米/千克	B	---Of yarns of cellulose acetate
5408.2290	---其他	10	8	0	0	130	17	11	米/千克	B	---Other
	--色织:										--Of yarns of different colours:
5408.2310	---粘胶纤维制	10	8	0	0	130	17	11	米/千克	B	---Of yarns of viscose rayon
5408.2320	---醋纤纤维制	10	8	0	0	130	17	11	米/千克	B	---Of yarns of cellulose acetate
5408.2390	---其他	10	8	0	0	130	17	11	米/千克	B	---Other
	--印花:										--Printed:
5408.2410	---粘胶纤维制	10	8	0	0	130	17	11	米/千克	B	---Of yarns of viscose rayon
5408.2420	---醋纤纤维制	10	8	0	0	130	17	11	米/千克	B	---Of yarns of cellulose acetate
5408.2490	---其他	10	8	0	0	130	17	11	米/千克	B	---Other
	-其他机织物:										-Other woven fabrics:
5408.3100	--未漂白或漂白	10	8	0	0	130	17	11	米/千克		--Unbleached or bleached
5408.3100 11	未漂白或漂白人纤长丝机织物(与精梳羊毛或动物细毛≥36%混纺,人纤<85%)	10				130	17	11	米/千克	B	Woven fabrics of artificial filaments, mixed, containing≥36% by weight of combed wool or fine animal hair, containing<85% by weight of artificial fibres, unbleached or bleached
5408.3100 19	未漂白或漂白人纤长丝机织物(与其他羊毛或动物细毛≥36%混纺,人纤<85%)	10				130	17	11	米/千克	B	Woven fabrics of artificial filaments, mixed, containing≥36% by weight of wool or fine animal hair, containing<85% by weight of artificial fibres, unbleached or bleached
5408.3100 21	未漂白或漂白人纤长丝机织物(与精梳羊毛或动物细毛<36%混纺,人纤<85%)	10				130	17	11	米/千克	B	Woven fabrics of artificial filaments, mixed, containing<36% by weight of combed wool or fine animal hair, containing<85% by weight of artificial fibres, unbleached or bleached
5408.3100 29	未漂白或漂白人纤长丝机织物(与其他羊毛或动物细毛<36%混纺,人纤<85%)	10				130	17	11	米/千克	B	Woven fabrics of artificial filaments, mixed, containing<36% by weight of wool or fine animal hair, containing<85% by weight of artificial fibres, unbleached or bleached
5408.3100 30	未漂白或漂白人纤长丝机织物(与人纤长丝混纺,人纤长丝含量在85%以下)	10				130	17	11	米/千克	B	Woven fabrics, mixed with artificial filament, containing<85% by weight of artificial filaments, unbleached or bleached
5408.3100 91	未漂白或漂白人纤长丝府绸及细平布(混纺布指按重量计人纤长丝,扁条或类似品含量在85%以下)	10				130	17	11	米/千克	B	Poplin and fine plain cloth, mixed, containing<85% by weight of filament or strip or the like of artificial fibres, unbleached or bleached
5408.3100 92	未漂白或漂白人纤长丝平布(混纺布指按重量计人纤长丝,扁条或类似品含量在85%以下)	10				130	17	11	米/千克	B	Plain cloth, mixed, containing<85% by weight of filament or strip or the like of artificial fibres, unbleached or bleached

税则号列 Tariff Item.	货品名称	最惠国(%) MFN	协定(%) CT 东盟 CA	中巴 CP	中智 CC	普通 Gen	增值税率 VAT	出口退税 ED	计量单位 Unit	监管条件 SC	Article Description
5408.3100 93	未漂白或漂白人纤长丝印染用布(混纺布指按重量计人纤长丝,扁条或类似品含量在85%以下)	10				130	17	11	米/千克	B	Woven fabrics for printing and dying, mixed, containing < 85% by weight of filament or strip or the like of artificial fibres, unbleached or bleached
5408.3100 94	未漂或漂白人纤长丝缎纹或斜纹布(混纺布指按重量计人纤长丝,扁条或类似品含量在85%以下)	10				130	17	11	米/千克	B	Woven fabrics satin weave or twill weave, mixed, containing < 85% by weight of filament or strip or the like of artificial fibres, unbleached or bleached
5408.3100 99	未漂白或漂白人纤长丝其他混纺布(混纺布指按重量计人纤长丝,扁条或类似品含量在85%以下)	10				130	17	11	米/千克	B	Other woven fabrics, mixed, containing <85% by weight of filament or strip or the like of artificial fibres, unbleached or bleached
5408.3200	--染色	10	8	0	0	130	17	11	米/千克		--Dyed
5408.3200 11	染色的人纤长丝机织物(与精梳羊毛或动物细毛≥36%混纺,人纤<85%)	10				130	17	11	米/千克	B	Woven fabrics, mixed, containing ≥ 36% by weight of combed wool or fine animal hair, containing < 85% by weight of artificial fibres, dyed
5408.3200 19	染色的人纤长丝机织物(与其他羊毛或动物细毛≥36%混纺,人纤<85%)	10				130	17	11	米/千克	B	Woven fabrics, mixed, containing ≥ 36% by weight of wool or fine animal hair, containing <85% by weight of artificial fibres, dyed
5408.3200 21	染色的人纤长丝机织物(与精梳羊毛或动物细毛<36%混纺,人纤<85%)	10				130	17	11	米/千克	B	Woven fabrics, mixed, containing < 36% by weight of combed wool or fine animal hair, containing < 85% by weight of artificial fibres, dyed
5408.3200 29	染色的人纤长丝机织物(与其他羊毛或动物细毛<36%混纺,人纤<85%)	10				130	17	11	米/千克	B	Woven fabrics, mixed, containing < 36% by weight of wool or fine animal hair, containing <85% by weight of artificial fibres, dyed
5408.3200 30	染色的人纤长丝机织物(含丝及绢丝30%及以上,每公斤价值超过$33,人纤<85%)	10				130	17	11	米/千克	B	Woven fabrics, containing ≥ 30% by weight of silk and spun silk, value > $33/kg, containing < 85% by weight of artificial fibres, dyed
5408.3200 40	染色的人纤长丝机织物(与合纤长丝混纺,人纤长丝,扁条或类似品含量在85%以下)	10				130	17	11	米/千克	B	Woven fabrics, mixed with synthetic filament, containing < 85% by weight of artificial fibres, dyed
5408.3200 91	染色的人纤长丝府绸或细平布(混纺布指按重量计人纤长丝,扁条或类似品含量在85%以下)	10				130	17	11	米/千克	B	Poplin and fine plain cloth, mixed, containing <85% by weight of filament or strip or the like of artificial fibres, dyed
5408.3200 92	染色的人纤长丝平布(混纺布指按重量计人纤长丝,扁条或类似品含量在85%以下)	10				130	17	11	米/千克	B	Plain cloth, mixed, containing < 85% by weight of filament or strip or the like of artificial fibres, dyed
5408.3200 93	染色的人纤长丝印染用布(混纺布指按重量计人纤长丝,扁条或类似品含量在85%以下)	10				130	17	11	米/千克	B	Woven fabrics for printing and dying, mixed, containing < 85% by weight of filament or strip or the like of artificial fibres, dyed

税则号列 Tariff Item.	货品名称	最惠国(%) MFN	协定(%)CT 东盟 CA	中巴 CP	中智 CC	普通 Gen	增值税率 VAT	出口退税 ED	计量单位 Unit	监管条件 SC	Article Description
5408.3200 94	染色的人纤长丝缎纹或斜纹布(混纺布指按重量计人纤长丝,扁条或类似品含量在85%以下)	10				130	17	11	米/千克	B	Woven fabrics, satin weave or twill weave, mixed, containing < 85% by weight of filament or strip or the like of artificial fibres, dyed
5408.3200 99	染色的人纤长丝其他机织物(混纺布指按重量计人纤长丝,扁条或类似品含量在85%以下)	10				130	17	11	米/千克	B	Other woven fabrics, mixed, containing <85% by weight of filament or strip or the like of artificial fibres, dyed
5408.3300	--色织	10	8	0	0	130	17	11	米/千克		--Of yarns of different colours
5408.3300 11	色织的人纤长丝机织物(与精梳羊毛或动物细毛≥36%混纺,人纤<85%)	10				130	17	11	米/千克	B	Woven fabrics of artificial filaments, mixed, containing≥36% by weight of combed wool or fine animal hair, containing<85% by weight of artificial fibres, of different colours
5408.3300 19	色织的人纤长丝机织物(与其他羊毛或动物细毛≥36%混纺,人纤<85%)	10				130	17	11	米/千克	B	Woven fabrics of artificial filaments, mixed, containing≥36% by weight of wool or fine animal hair, containing < 85% by weight of artificial fibres, of different colours
5408.3300 21	色织的人纤长丝机织物(与精梳羊毛或动物细毛<36%混纺,人纤<85%)	10				130	17	11	米/千克	B	Woven fabrics of artificial filaments, mixed, containing < 36% by weight of combed wool or fine animal hair, containing<85% by weight of artificial fibres, of different colours
5408.3300 29	色织的人纤长丝机织物(与其他羊毛或动物细毛<36%混纺,人纤<85%)	10				130	17	11	米/千克	B	Woven fabrics of artificial filaments, mixed, containing < 36% by weight of wool or fine animal hair, containing < 85% by weight of artificial fibres, of different colours
5408.3300 30	色织的人纤长丝机织物,人纤<85%(含化纤长丝≥85%,每厘米经密70-142根,纬密32-71根)	10				130	17	11	米/千克	B	Woven fabrics, containing ≥ 85% by weight of chemical filaments, containing < 85% by weight of artificial fibres, warp yarn70-142/cm, weft yarn 32-71/cm
5408.3300 40	色织的人纤长丝机织物(含丝及绢丝30%及以上,每公斤价值超过$33,人纤<85%)	10				130	17	11	米/千克	B	Woven fabrics, containing ≥ 30% by weight of silk and spun silk, value > $33/kg, containing < 85% by weight of filament or strip or the like of artificial fibres, of different colours
5408.3300 50	色织的人纤长丝机织物(与合纤长丝混纺,人纤长丝,扁条或类似品含量在85%以下)	10				130	17	11	米/千克	B	Woven fabrics, mixed with synthetic filament, containing < 85% by weight of filament or strip or the like of artificial fibres, of different colours
5408.3300 91	色织的人纤长丝府绸或细平布(混纺布指按重量计人纤长丝,扁条或类似品含量在85%以下)	10				130	17	11	米/千克	B	Poplin and fine plain cloth, containing <85% by weight of artificial filament or strip or the like, of different colours

税则号列 Tariff Item.	货品名称	最惠国(%) MFN	协定(%) CT 东盟 CA	中巴 CP	中智 CC	普通 Gen	增值税率 VAT	出口退税 ED	计量单位 Unit	监管条件 SC	Article Description
5408.3300 92	色织的人纤长丝平布(混纺布指按重量计人纤长丝,扁条或类似品含量在85%以下)	10				130	17	11	米/千克	B	Plain cloth, containing < 85% by weight of artificial filament or strip or the like, of different colours
5408.3300 93	色织的人纤长丝印染用布(混纺布指按重量计人纤长丝,扁条或类似品含量在85%以下)	10				130	17	11	米/千克	B	Woven fabrics artificial for printing and dying, containing < 85% by weight of artificial filament or strip or the like, of different colours
5408.3300 94	色织的人纤长丝缎纹或斜纹布(混纺布指按重量计人纤长丝,扁条或类似品含量在85%以下)	10				130	17	11	米/千克	B	Woven fabrics satin weave or twill weave, containing < 85% by weight of artificial filament or strip or the like, of different colours
5408.3300 99	色织的人纤长丝其他机织物(混纺布指按重量计人纤长丝,扁条或类似品含量在85%以下)	10				130	17	11	米/千克	B	Other woven fabrics of artificial filaments, containing < 85% by weight of artificial filament or strip or the like, of different colours
5408.3400	--印花	10	8	0	0	130	17	11	米/千克		--Printed
5408.3400 11	印花的人纤长丝机织物(与精梳羊毛或动物细毛≥36%混纺,人纤<85%)	10				130	17	11	米/千克	B	Woven fabrics of artificial filaments, mixed, containing ≥36% by weight of combed wool or fine animal hair, containing < 85% by weight of artificial fibres, printed
5408.3400 19	印花的人纤长丝机织物(与其他羊毛或动物细毛≥36%混纺,人纤<85%)	10				130	17	11	米/千克	B	Woven fabrics of artificial filaments, mixed, containing ≥ 36% by weight wool or fine animal hair, containing < 85% by weight of artificial fibres, printed
5408.3400 21	印花的人纤长丝机织物(与精梳羊毛或动物细毛<36%混纺,人纤<85%)	10				130	17	11	米/千克	B	Woven fabrics of artificial filaments, mixed, containing < 36% by weight of combed wool or fine animal hair, containing < 85% by weight of artificial fibres, printed
5408.3400 29	印花的人纤长丝机织物(与其他羊毛或动物细毛<36%混纺,人纤<85%)	10				130	17	11	米/千克	B	Woven fabrics of artificial filaments, mixed, containing < 36% by weight of wool or fine animal hair, containing < 85% by weight of artificial fibres, printed
5408.3400 30	印花的人纤长丝机织物(含丝及绢丝30%及以上,每公斤超过 $33,人纤<85%)	10				130	17	11	米/千克	B	Woven fabrics of artificial filaments, containing≥30% by weight of silk and spun silk, value > $33/kg, containing < 85% by weight of artificial fibres, printed
5408.3400 40	印花的人纤长丝机织物(与合纤长丝混纺,人纤长丝,扁条或类似品含量在85%以下)	10				130	17	11	米/千克	B	Woven fabrics, mixed with synthetic filament, containing < 85% by weight of filaments or strip or the like of artificial fibres, printed
5408.3400 91	印花的人纤长丝府绸或细平布(混纺布指按重量计人纤长丝,扁条或类似品含量在85%以下)	10				130	17	11	米/千克	B	Poplin and fine plain cloth, mixed, containing < 85% by weight of artificial filaments or strip or the like of artificial fibres, printed

税则号列 Tariff Item.	货品名称	最惠国(%) MFN	协定(%)CT 东盟 CA	中巴 CP	中智 CC	普通 Gen	增值税率 VAT	出口退税 ED	计量单位 Unit	监管条件 SC	Article Description
5408.3400 92	印花的人纤长丝平布(混纺布指按重量计人纤长丝,扁条或类似品含量在85%以下)	10				130	17	11	米/千克	B	Plain cloth, mixed, containing <85% by weight of filaments or strip or the like of artificial fibres, printed
5408.3400 93	印花的人纤长丝印染用布(混纺布指按重量计人纤长丝,扁条或类似品含量在85%以下)	10				130	17	11	米/千克	B	Woven fabrics for printing and dying, mixed, containing <85% by weight of filaments or strip or the like of artificial fibres, printed
5408.3400 94	印花的人纤长丝缎纹或斜纹布(混纺布指按重量计人纤长丝,扁条或类似品含量在85%以下)	10				130	17	11	米/千克	B	Woven fabrics, satin weave or twill weave, mixed, containing < 85% by weight of filaments or strip or the like of artificial fibres, printed
5408.3400 99	印花的人纤长丝其他机织物(混纺布指按重量计人纤长丝,扁条或类似品含量在85%以下)	10				130	17	11	米/千克	B	Other woven fabrics, containing <85% by weight of artificial filaments or strip or the like of artificial fibres, printed

第五十五章
化学纤维短纤

Chapter 55
Man-made staple fibres

注释：

税目55.01和55.02仅适用于每根与丝束长度相等的平行化学纤维长丝丝束。前述丝束应同时符合下列规格：

一、丝束长度超过2米；

二、捻度每米少于5转；

三、每根长丝细度在67分特以下；

四、合成纤维长丝丝束，须经拉伸处理，即本身不能被拉伸至超过本身长度的一倍；

五、丝束总细度大于20000分特。

丝束长度不超过2米的归入税目55.03或55.04。

Notes：

Headings Nos. 55.01 and 55.02 apply only to man-made filament tow, consisting of parallel filaments of a uniform length equal to the length of the tow, meeting the following specifications：

1. Length of tow exceeding 2 m；
2. Twist less than 5 turns per metre；
3. Measuring per filament less than 67 decitex；
4. Synthetic filament tow only：the tow must be drawn, that is to say, be incapable of being stretched by more than 100% of its length；
5. Total measurement of tow more than 20,000 decitex.

Tow of a length not exceeding 2 m is to be classified in heading No. 55.03 or 55.04.

税则号列 Tariff Item.	货品名称	最惠国(%) MFN	协定(%)CT 东盟 CA	中巴 CP	中智 CC	普通 Gen	增值税率 VAT	出口退税 ED	计量单位 Unit	监管条件 SC	Article Description
55.01	**合成纤维长丝丝束：**										**Synthetic filament tow：**
5501.1000	-尼龙或其他聚酰胺制	5		0	0	70	17	11	千克	A	-Of nylon or other polyamides
5501.2000	-聚酯制	5		0	0	70	17	11	千克	A	-Of polyesters
5501.3000	-聚丙烯腈或变性聚丙烯腈制	5		0	0	35	17	11	千克	A	-Acrylicor modacrylic
5501.4000	-聚丙烯制	5		0	0	70	17	11	千克	A	-Of polypropylene
5501.9000	-其他	5		0	0	70	17	11	千克	A	-Other
55.02	**人造纤维长丝丝束：**										**Artificial filament tow**
5502.0010	---二醋酸纤维丝束	3		2.1	0	40	17	11	千克	7A	---Cellulose diacetate filament tow
5502.0090	---其他	5		3.5	0	35	17	11	千克	A	---Other
55.03	**合成纤维短纤，未梳或未经其他纺前加工：**										**Synthetic staple fibres, not carded, combed or otherwise processed for spinning：**
	-尼龙或其他聚酰胺制：										-Of nylon or other polyamides
5503.1100	--芳香族聚酰胺纺制	5		0	0	70	17	11	千克	A	--Of aramides
5503.1900	--其他	5		0	0	70	17	11	千克	A	--Other
5503.2000	-聚酯制	5		0	0	70	17	11	千克	A	-Of polyesters
5503.3000	-聚丙烯腈或变性聚丙烯腈制	5		0	0	35	17	11	千克	A	-Acrylic or modacrylic
5503.4000	-聚丙烯制	5		0	0	70	17	11	千克	A	-Of polypropylene
5503.9000	-其他	5		0	0	70	17	11	千克	A	-Other
55.04	**人造纤维短纤，未梳或未经其他纺前加工：**										**Artificial staple fibres, not carded, combed or otherwise processed for spinning：**
5504.1000	-粘胶纤维制	5		0	0	35	17	11	千克	A	-Of viscose rayon
5504.9000	-其他	5		0	0	35	17	11	千克	A	-Other
55.05	**化学纤维废料（包括落棉、废纱及回收纤维）：**										**Waste (including noils, yarn waste and garnetted stock) of man-made fibres：**
5505.1000	-合成纤维的	5		0	0	70	17	11	千克	AP	-Of synthetic fibres
5505.2000	-人造纤维的	5		0	0	70	17	11	千克	AP	-Of artificial fibres
55.06	**合成纤维短纤，已梳或经其他纺前加工：**										**Synthetic staple fibres, carded, combed or otherwise processed for spinning：**
5506.1000	-尼龙或其他聚酰胺制	5			0	70	17	11	千克	A	-Of nylon or other polyamides

税则号列 Tariff Item.	货品名称	最惠国(%) MFN	协定(%) CT 东盟 CA	中巴 CP	中智 CC	普通 Gen	增值税率 VAT	出口退税 ED	计量单位 Unit	监管条件 SC	Article Description
5506.2000	-聚酯制	5	_	4.5	0	70	17	11	千克	A	-Of polyesters
5506.3000	-聚丙烯腈或变性聚丙烯腈制	5		4.5	0	35	17	11	千克	A	-Acrylic or modacrylic
5506.9000	-其他	5			0	70	17	11	千克	A	-Other
55.07	**人造纤维短纤,已梳或经其他纺前加工:**										**Artificial staple fibres, carded, combed or otherwise processed for spinning:**
5507.0000	人造纤维短纤,已梳或经其他纺前加工	5			0	35	17	11	千克	A	Artificial staple fibres, carded, combed or otherwise processed for spinning
55.08	**化学纤维短纤纺制的缝纫线,不论是否供零售用:**										**Sewing thread of man-made staple fibres, whether or not put up for retail sale:**
5508.1000	-合成纤维短纤纺制	5		4.5	0	90	17	11	千克		-Of synthetic staple fibres
5508.1000 11	非零售用聚丙烯晴短纤缝纫线	5				90	17	11	千克	5	Sewing thread of acrylic staple fibres, not put up for retail sale
5508.1000 19	非零售用其他合纤短纤缝纫线	5				90	17	11	千克	5	Sewing thread of synthetic staple fibres, not put up for retail sale
5508.1000 90	零售用合成纤维短纤缝纫线	5				90	17	11	千克	5	Sewing thread of synthetic staple fibres, put up for retail sale
5508.2000	-人造纤维短纤纺制	5			0	70	17	11	千克		-Of artificial staple fibres
5508.2000 10	非零售用人造纤维短纤缝纫线	5				70	17	11	千克	5	Sewing thread of artificial staple fibres, not put up for retail sale
5508.2000 90	零售用人造纤维短纤缝纫线	5				70	17	11	千克	5	Sewing thread of artificial staple fibres, put up for retail sale
55.09	**合成纤维短纤纺制的纱线(缝纫线除外),非供零售用:**										**Yarn (other than sewing thread) of synthetic staple fibres, not put up for retail sale:**
	-按重量计尼龙或其他聚酰胺短纤含量在85%及以上:										-Containing 85% or more by weight of staple fibres of nylon or other polyamides:
5509.1100	--单纱	5		0	0	90	17	11	千克		--Single yarn
5509.1200	--多股纱线或缆线	5		0	0	90	17	11	千克	A	--Multiple (folded) or cabled yarn
	-按重量计聚酯短纤含量在85%及以上:										-Containing 85% or more by weight of polyester staple fibres:
5509.2100	--单纱	5		0	0	90	17	11	千克		--Single yarn
5509.2200	--多股纱线或缆线	5		0	0	90	17	11	千克		--Multiple (folded) or cabled yarn
5509.2200 10	非零售聚酯短纤多股纱线或缆线(终捻为Z捻,聚酯短纤含量在85%及以上,缝纫线除外)	5				90	17	11	千克	5	Multiple (folded) or cabled yarn, with a final "Z" twist, containing≥85% by weight of polyester staple fibres, not put up for retail sale, other than sewing thread
5509.2200 90	非零售其他聚酯短纤多股纱线缆线(聚酯短纤含量在85%及以上,缝纫线除外)	5				90	17	11	千克		Other multiple (folded) or cabled yarn, containing ≥ 85% by weight of polyester staple fibres, not put up for retail sale, other than sewing thread
	-按重量计聚丙烯腈或变性聚丙烯腈短纤含量在85%及以上:										-Containing 85% or more by weight of acrylic or modacrylic staple fibres:
5509.3100	--单纱	5		0	0	90	17	11	千克		--Single yarn
5509.3200	--多股纱线或缆线	5		0	0	90	17	11	千克		--Multiple (folded) or cabled yarn

税则号列 Tariff Item.	货品名称	最惠国(%) MFN	协定(%) CT			普通 Gen	增值税率 VAT	出口退税 ED	计量单位 Unit	监管条件 SC	Article Description
			东盟 CA	中巴 CP	中智 CC						
	-其他纱线,按重量计合成纤维短纤含量在85%及以上:										-Other yarn, containing 85% or more by weight of synthetic staple fibres:
5509.4100	--单纱	5		0	0	90	17	11	千克		--Single yarn
5509.4200	--多股纱线或缆线	5		0	0	90	17	11	千克		--Multiple (folded) or cabled yarn
	-其他聚酯短纤纺制的纱线:										-Other yarn, of polyester staple fibres:
5509.5100	--主要或仅与人造纤维短纤混纺	5		0	0	90	17	11	千克		--Mixed mainly or solely with artificial staple fibres
5509.5200	--主要或仅与羊毛或动物细毛混纺	5		0	0	90	17	11	千克		--Mixed mainly or solely with wool or fine animal hair
5509.5300	--主要或仅与棉混纺	5		0	0	90	17	11	千克	B	--Mixed maninly or solely with cotton
5509.5900	--其他	5		0	0	90	17	11	千克		--Other
	-其他聚丙烯腈或变性聚丙烯腈短纤纺制的纱线:										-Other yarn, of acrylic or modacrylic staple fibres:
5509.6100	--主要或仅与羊毛或动物细毛混纺	5		0	0	90	17	11	千克		--Mixed mainly or solely with wool or fine animal hair
5509.6200	--主要或仅与棉混纺	5		0	0	90	17	11	千克		--Mixed mainly or solely with cotton
5509.6900	--其他	5		0	0	90	17	11	千克		--Other
	-其他纱线:										-Other yarn:
5509.9100	--主要或仅与羊毛或动物细毛混纺	5		0	0	90	17	11	千克		--Mixed mainly or solely with wool or fine animal hair
5509.9200	--主要或仅与棉混纺	5		0	0	90	17	11	千克		--Mixed mainly or solely with cotton
5509.9900	--其他	5		0	0	90	17	11	千克		--Other
55.10	**人造纤维短纤纺制的纱线(缝纫线除外),非供零售用:**										**Yarn (other than sewing thread) of artificial staple fibres, not put up for retail sale:**
	-按重量计人造纤维短纤含量在85%及以上:										-Containing 85% or more by weight of artificial staple fibres:
5510.1100	--单纱	5		4.5	0	70	17	11	千克		--Single yarn
5510.1200	--多股纱线或缆线	5			0	70	17	11	千克		--Multiple (folded) or cabled yarn
5510.2000	-其他纱线,主要或仅与羊毛或动物细毛混纺	5			0	70	17	11	千克		-Other yarn, mixed mainly or solely with wool or fine animal hair
5510.3000	-其他纱线,主要或仅与棉混纺	5		3.5	0	70	17	11	千克		-Other yarn, mixed mainly or solely with cotton
5510.9000	-其他	5		4.5	0	70	17	11	千克		-Other yarn
55.11	**化学纤维短纤纺制的纱线(缝纫线除外),供零售用:**										**Yarn (other than sewing thread) of man-made staple fibres, put up for retail sale:**
5511.1000	-按重量计合成纤维短纤含量在85%及以上	5			0	90	17	11	千克	5	-Of synthetic staple fibres, containing 85% or more by weight of such fibres
5511.2000	-按重量计合成纤维短纤含量在85%以下	5			0	90	17	11	千克	5B	-Of synthetic staple fibres, containing less than 85% by weight of such fibres
5511.3000	-人造纤维短纤纺制	5			0	90	17	11	千克	5	-Of artificial staple fibres
55.12	**合成纤维短纤纺制的机织物,按重量计合成纤维短纤含量在85%及以上:**										**Woven fabrics of synthetic staple fibres, containing 85% or more by weight of synthetic staple fibres:**
	-按重量计聚酯短纤含量在85%及以上:										-Containing 85% or more by weight of polyester staple fibres:
5512.1100	--未漂白或漂白	18	12	5	0	130	17	11	米/千克		--Unbleached or bleached

税则号列 Tariff Item.	货品名称	最惠国(%) MFN	协定(%)CT 东盟 CA	中巴 CP	中智 CC	普通 Gen	增值税率 VAT	出口退税 ED	计量单位 Unit	监管条件 SC	Article Description
5512.1100 10	未漂或漂白聚酯短纤机织府绸(聚脂短纤含量在85%及以上,包括细平布)	18				130	17	11	米/千克		Poplin and fine plain cloth, containing ≥85% by weight of polyester staple fibres, unbleached or bleached
5512.1100 20	未漂或漂白聚酯短纤机织平布(聚脂短纤含量在85%及以上)	18				130	17	11	米/千克		Plain cloth, containing ≥ 85% by weight of polyester staple fibres, unbleached or bleached
5512.1100 30	未漂或漂白聚酯短纤印染用布(纯聚酯布指按重量计聚脂短纤含量在85%及以上)	18				130	17	11	米/千克		Woven fabrics for printing and dying, containing≥85% by weight of polyester staple fibres, unbleached or bleached
5512.1100 40	未漂或漂白聚酯短纤平纹奶酪布(聚脂短纤含量在85%及以上,含薄细布,巴里纱)	18				130	17	11	米/千克		Cheese cloth, plain weave, including fine thin cloth, voiles, containing ≥ 85% by weight of polyester staple fibres, unbleached or bleached
5512.1100 50	未漂或漂白聚酯短纤机织帆布(纯聚酯布指按重量计聚脂短纤含量在85%及以上)	18				130	17	11	米/千克		Canvas, containing≥85% by weight of polyester staple fibres, unbleached or bleached
5512.1100 60	未漂或漂聚酯短纤其他斜纹机织物(聚脂短纤含量在85%及以上,含缎纹)	18				130	17	11	米/千克		Woven fabrics, twill weave, satin weave, containing≥85% by weight of polyester staple fibres, unbleached or bleached
5512.1100 70	未漂或漂白聚酯短纤牛津布(纯聚酯布指按重量计聚脂短纤含量在85%及以上)	18				130	17	11	米/千克		Woven fabrics, oxford weave, containing≥85% by weight of polyester staple fibres, unbleached or bleached
5512.1100 90	未漂或漂白聚酯短纤其他机织物(纯聚酯布指按重量计聚脂短纤含量在85%及以上)	18				130	17	11	米/千克		Other woven fabrics, containing≥85% by weight of polyester staple fibres, unbleached or bleached
5512.1900	--其他	10	T3	0	0	130	17	11	米/千克		--Other
5512.1900 10	聚酯短纤色织机织物(聚脂短纤含量在85%及以上,蓝粗斜纹布及提花织物除外)	10				130	17	11	米/千克		Woven fabrics, other than blue denim and jacquard weave, containing≥85% by weight of polyester staple fibres, of different collours
5512.1900 20	聚酯短纤蓝粗斜纹布(纯聚酯布指按重量计聚脂短纤含量在85%及以上)	10				130	17	11	米/千克		Blue denim, containing ≥ 85% by weight of polyester staple fibres
5512.1900 31	聚酯短纤其他机织府绸或细平布(纯聚酯布指按重量计聚脂短纤含量在85%及以上)	10				130	17	11	米/千克		Other poplin and fine plain cloth, containing ≥ 85% by weight of polyester staple fibres
5512.1900 32	聚酯短纤其他机织平布(纯聚酯布指按重量计聚脂短纤含量在85%及以上)	10				130	17	11	米/千克		Other plain cloth, containing≥85% by weight of polyester staple fibres
5512.1900 33	聚酯短纤其他机织印染用布(纯聚酯布指按重量计聚脂短纤含量在85%及以上)	10				130	17	11	米/千克		Other woven fabrics for printing and dying, containing ≥ 85% by weight of polyester staple fibres

税则号列 Tariff Item.	货品名称	最惠国(%) MFN	协定(%) 东盟 CA	中巴 CP	CT 中智 CC	普通 Gen	增值税率 VAT	出口退税 ED	计量单位 Unit	监管条件 SC	Article Description
5512.1900 34	聚酯短纤其他平纹奶酪布等(聚脂短纤含量在85%及以上,含薄细布,巴里纱)	10				130	17	11	米/千克		Other cheese cloth, including voiles and fine thin cloth, containing≥85% by weight of polyester staple fibres
5512.1900 35	聚酯短纤其他机织帆布(纯聚酯布指按重量计聚脂短纤含量在85%及以上)	10				130	17	11	米/千克		Other canvas, containing ≥ 85% by weight of polyester staple fibres
5512.1900 36	聚酯短纤其他缎纹或斜纹机织物(纯聚酯布指按重量计聚脂短纤含量在85%及以上)	10				130	17	11	米/千克		Other woven fabrics, satin weave or twill weave, containing ≥ 85% by weight of polyester staple fibres
5512.1900 37	聚酯短纤其他牛津布(纯聚酯布指按重量计聚脂短纤含量在85%及以上)	10				130	17	11	米/千克		Other woven fabrics, oxford weave, containing≥85% by weight of polyester staple fibres
5512.1900 90	聚脂短纤其他机织物(纯聚酯布指按重量计聚脂短纤含量在85%及以上)	10				130	17	11	米/千克		Other woven fabrics, containing≥85% by weight of polyester staple fibres
	-按重量计聚丙烯腈或变性聚丙烯腈短纤含量在85%及以上:										-Containing 85% or more by weight of acrylic or modacrylic staple fibres:
5512.2100	--未漂白或漂白	13	12	0	0	130	17	11	米/千克		--Unbleached or bleached
5512.2100 10	未漂或漂腈纶短纤机织府绸细平布(纯腈纶布指按重量计腈纶短纤含量在85%及以上)	13				130	17	11	米/千克		Poplin and fine plain cloth, containing ≥85% by weight of acrylic or modacrylic staple fibres, unbleached or bleached
5512.2100 20	未漂或漂白腈纶短纤机织平布(纯腈纶布指按重量计腈纶短纤含量在85%及以上)	13				130	17	11	米/千克		Plain cloth, containing ≥ 85% by weight of acrylic or modacrylic staple fibres, unbleached or bleached
5512.2100 30	未漂或漂白腈纶短纤机织印染用布(纯腈纶布指按重量计腈纶短纤含量在85%及以上)	13				130	17	11	米/千克		Woven fabrics for printing and dying, containing≥85% by weight of acrylic or modacrylic staple fibres, unbleached or bleached
5512.2100 40	未漂或漂白腈纶短纤平纹奶酪布等(腈纶短纤含量在85%及以上,含薄细布,巴里纱)	13				130	17	11	米/千克		Cheese cloth, including voiles and fine thin cloth, containing≥85% by weight of acrylic or modacrylic staple fibres, unbleached or bleached
5512.2100 50	未漂或漂白腈纶短纤机织帆布(纯腈纶布指按重量计腈纶短纤含量在85%及以上)	13				130	17	11	米/千克		Canvas, containing≥85% by weight of acrylic or modacrylic staple fibres, unbleached or bleached
5512.2100 60	未漂或漂腈纶短纤其他斜纹机织物(腈纶短纤含量在85%及以上,含缎纹机织物)	13				130	17	11	米/千克		Woven fabrics, twill weave, satin weave, containing≥85% by weight of acrylic or modacrylic staple fibres, unbleached or bleached
5512.2100 70	未漂或漂白腈纶短纤牛津布(纯腈纶布指按重量计腈纶短纤含量在85%及以上)	13				130	17	11	米/千克		Woven fabrics, oxford weave, containing ≥ 85% by weight of acrylic or modacrylic staple fibres, unbleached or bleached

税则号列 Tariff Item.	货品名称	最惠国(%) MFN	协定(%)CT 东盟 CA	中巴 CP	中智 CC	普通 Gen	增值税率 VAT	出口退税 ED	计量单位 Unit	监管条件 SC	Article Description
5512.2100 90	未漂或漂白腈纶短纤其他机织物(纯腈纶布指按重量计腈纶短纤含量在85%及以上)	13				130	17	11	米/千克		Other woven fabrics, containing≥85% by weight of acrylic or modacrylic staple fibres, unbleached or bleached
5512.2900	--其他	10	8	0	0	130	17	11	米/千克		--Other
5512.2900 10	腈纶短纤色织机织物(腈纶短纤含量在85%及以上,蓝粗斜纹布及提花织物除外)	10				130	17	11	米/千克		Woven fabrics other than blue denim and jacquard weave, containing≥85% by weight of acrylic or modacrylic staple fibres, of different collours
5512.2900 20	腈纶短纤蓝粗斜纹布(纯腈纶布指按重量计腈纶短纤含量在85%及以上)	10				130	17	11	米/千克		Blue denim, containing ≥ 85% by weight of acrylic or modacrylic staple fibres
5512.2900 31	腈纶短纤其他机织府绸或细平布(纯腈纶布指按重量计腈纶短纤含量在85%及以上)	10				130	17	11	米/千克		Poplin and fine plain cloth, containing ≥85% by weight of acrylic or modacrylic staple fibres
5512.2900 32	腈纶短纤其他机织平布(纯腈纶布指按重量计腈纶短纤含量在85%及以上)	10				130	17	11	米/千克		Plain cloth, containing ≥ 85% by weight of acrylic or modacrylic staple fibres
5512.2900 33	腈纶短纤其他机织印染用布(纯腈纶布指按重量计腈纶短纤含量在85%及以上)	10				130	17	11	米/千克		Woven fabrics for printing and dying, containing≥85% by weight of acrylic or modacrylic staple fibres
5512.2900 34	腈纶短纤其他平纹奶酪布等(腈纶短纤含量在85%及以上,含薄细布,巴里纱)	10				130	17	11	米/千克		Cheese cloth, plain weave, including voiles and fine thin cloth, containing≥85% by weight of acrylic or modacrylic staple fibres
5512.2900 35	腈纶短纤其他机织帆布(纯腈纶布指按重量计腈纶短纤含量在85%及以上)	10				130	17	11	米/千克		Canvas, containing≥85% by weight of acrylic or modacrylic staple fibres
5512.2900 36	晴纶短纤其他缎纹或斜纹机织物(纯腈纶布指按重量计腈纶短纤含量在85%及以上)	10				130	17	11	米/千克		Woven fabrics, satin weave or twill weave, containing≥85% by weight of acrylic or modacrylic staple fibres
5512.2900 37	腈纶短纤其他牛津布(纯腈纶布指按重量计腈纶短纤含量在85%及以上)	10				130	17	11	米/千克		Woven fabrics, oxford weave, containing ≥ 85% by weight of acrylic or modacrylic staple fibres
5512.2900 90	腈纶短纤其他机织物(纯腈纶布指按重量计腈纶短纤含量在85%及以上)	10				130	17	11	米/千克		Other woven fabrics, containing≥85% by weight of acrylic or modacrylic staple fibres
	-其他:										-Other:
5512.9100	--未漂白或漂白	18	12	5	0	130	17	11	米/千克		--Unbleached or bleached
5512.9100 10	未漂或漂白其他合纤短纤机织府绸(其他合纤短纤含量在85%及以上,含细平布)	18				130	17	11	米/千克		Poplin, including fine plain cloth, containing ≥ 85% by weight of synthetic staple fibres, unbleached or bleached
5512.9100 20	未漂或漂白其他合纤短纤机织平布(其他纯合纤布指按重量计其他合纤短纤含量在85%及以上)	18				130	17	11	米/千克		Plain cloth, containing ≥ 85% by weight of synthetic staple fibres, unbleached or bleached

税则号列 Tariff Item.	货品名称	最惠国(%) MFN	协定(%) CT 东盟 CA	中巴 CP	中智 CC	普通 Gen	增值税率 VAT	出口退税 ED	计量单位 Unit	监管条件 SC	Article Description
5512.9100 30	未漂或漂白其他合纤短纤印染用布(其他纯合纤布指按重量计其他合纤短纤含量在85%及以上)	18				130	17	11	米/千克		Woven fabrics for printing and dying, containing≥85% by weight of synthetic staple fibres, unbleached or bleached
5512.9100 40	未漂白或漂白其他合纤短纤平纹奶酪布(其他合纤短纤含量在85%及以上,含薄细布,巴里纱)	18				130	17	11	米/千克		Cheese cloth, including voiles and fine thin cloth, containing≥85% by weight of synthetic staple fibres, unbleached or bleached
5512.9100 50	未漂白或漂白其他合纤短纤机织帆布(其他纯合纤布指按重量计其他合纤短纤含量在85%及以上)	18				130	17	11	米/千克		Canvas, containing≥85% by weight of synthetic staple fibres, unbleached or bleached
5512.9100 60	未漂白或漂白其他合纤短纤斜纹机织物(其他合纤短纤含量在85%及以上,含缎纹机织物)	18				130	17	11	米/千克		Woven fabrics, twill weave, satin weave, containing≥85% by weight of synthetic staple fibres, unbleached or bleached
5512.9100 70	未漂白或漂白其他合纤短纤牛津布(其他纯合纤布指按重量计其他合纤短纤含量在85%及以上)	18				130	17	11	米/千克		Woven fabrics, oxford weave, containing≥85% by weight of synthetic staple fibres, unbleached or bleached
5512.9100 90	未漂白或漂白其他合纤短纤其他机织物(其他纯合纤布指按重量计其他合纤短纤含量在85%及以上)	18				130	17	11	米/千克		Other woven fabrics, containing≥85% by weight of synthetic staple fibres, unbleached or bleached
5512.9900	--其他	10	T3	0	0	130	17	11	米/千克		--Other
5512.9900 10	其他合纤短纤色织机织物(其他合纤短纤含量≥85%,蓝粗斜纹布及提花织物除外)	10				130	17	11	米/千克		Other woven fabrics, other than blue denim and jacquard weave, containing ≥85% by weight of synthetic staple fibres, of different collours
5512.9900 20	其他合纤短纤蓝粗斜纹布(其他纯合纤布指按重量计其他合纤短纤含量在85%及以上)	10				130	17	11	米/千克		Other blue denim, containing ≥ 85% by weight of synthetic staple fibres
5512.9900 31	其他合纤短纤机织府绸或细平布(其他纯合纤布指按重量计其他合纤短纤含量在85%及以上)	10				130	17	11	米/千克		Other poplin and fine plain cloth, containing ≥ 85% by weight of synthetic staple fibres
5512.9900 32	其他合纤短纤其他机织平布(其他纯合纤布指按重量计其他合纤短纤含量在85%及以上)	10				130	17	11	米/千克		Other plain cloth, containing≥85% by weight of synthetic staple fibres
5512.9900 33	其他合纤短纤其他机织印染用布(其他纯合纤布指按重量计其他合纤短纤含量在85%及以上)	10				130	17	11	米/千克		Other woven fabrics for printing and dying, containing ≥ 85% by weight of synthetic staple fibres
5512.9900 34	其他合纤短纤平纹奶酪布等(其他合纤短纤85%及以上,含薄细布,巴里纱)	10				130	17	11	米/千克		Other cheese cloth, including voiles and fine thin cloth, containing ≥85% by weight of synthetic staple fibres

税则号列 Tariff Item.	货品名称	最惠国(%) MFN	协定(%) 东盟 CA	中巴 CP	CT 中智 CC	普通 Gen	增值税率 VAT	出口退税 ED	计量单位 Unit	监管条件 SC	Article Description
5512.9900 35	其他合纤短纤其他机织帆布(其他纯合纤布指按重量计其他合纤短纤含量在85%及以上)	10				130	17	11	米/千克		Other canvas, containing ≥ 85% by weight of synthetic staple fibres
5512.9900 36	其他合纤短纤缎纹或斜纹机织物(其他纯合纤布指按重量计其他合纤短纤含量在85%及以上)	10				130	17	11	米/千克		Other woven fabrics, satin weave or twill weave, containing ≥ 85% by weight of synthetic staple fibres
5512.9900 39	其他合纤短纤其他牛津布(其他纯合纤布指按重量计其他合纤短纤含量在85%及以上)	10				130	17	11	米/千克		Other woven fabrics, oxford weave, containing≥85% by weight of synthetic staple fibres
5512.9900 90	其他合纤短纤其他机织物(其他纯合纤布指按重量计其他合纤短纤含量在85%及以上)	10				130	17	11	米/千克		Other woven fabrics, containing≥85% by weight of synthetic staple fibres
55.13	**合成纤维短纤纺制的机织物,按重量计合成纤维短纤含量在85%以下,主要或仅与棉混纺,每平方米重量不超过170克:**										**Woven fabrics of synthetic staple fibres, containing less than 85% by weight of such fibres, mixed mainly or solely with cotton, of a weight not exceeding 170 g/m^2:**
	-未漂白或漂白:										-Unbleached or bleached:
	--聚酯短纤纺制的平纹机织物:										--Of polyester staple fibres, plain weave:
5513.1110	---未漂白	16	T3	5	0	130	17	11	米/千克		---Unbleached
5513.1110 10	与棉混纺未漂白聚酯短纤平纹府绸(聚酯短纤85%以下,每平方米重量≤170克,含细平布)	16				130	17	11	米/千克	A	Poplin, including fine plain cloth, mixed with cotton, containing < 85% by weight of polyester staple fibres, weight≤170g/m^2, unbleached
5513.1110 20	与棉混纺未漂白聚酯短纤机织平布(混纺为含聚酯短纤85%以下,轻质指每平方米重量≤170克)	16				130	17	11	米/千克	A	Plain cloth, mixed with cotton, containing < 85% by weight of polyester staple fibres, weight ≤ 170g/m^2, unbleached
5513.1110 30	与棉混纺未漂白聚酯短纤平纹印染用布(混纺为含聚酯短纤85%以下,轻质指每平方米重量≤170克)	16				130	17	11	米/千克	A	Woven fabrics for printing and dying, plain weave, mixed with cotton, containing < 85% by weight of polyester staple fibres, weight ≤ 170g/m^2, unbleached
5513.1110 40	与棉混纺未漂白聚酯短纤平纹奶酪布(聚酯短纤<85%,轻质指每平方米重量≤170克,含薄细布、巴里纱)	16				130	17	11	米/千克	A	Cheese cloth, plain weave, including voiles and fine thin cloth, mixed with cotton, containing < 85% by weight of polyester staple fibres, weight≤170g/m^2, unbleached
5513.1120	---漂白	15	T3	0	0	130	17	11	米/千克		---Bleached
5513.1120 10	与棉混纺漂白聚酯短纤平纹府绸(聚酯短纤85%以下,每平方米重量≤170克,含细平布)	15				130	17	11	米/千克	A	Poplin, plain weave, including fine plain cloth, mixed with cotton, containing < 85% by weight of polyester staple fibres, weight≤170g/m^2, bleached

税则号列 Tariff Item.	货品名称	最惠国(%) MFN	协定(%)CT 东盟 CA	中巴 CP	中智 CC	普通 Gen	增值税率 VAT	出口退税 ED	计量单位 Unit	监管条件 SC	Article Description
5513.1120 20	与棉混纺漂白聚酯短纤机织平布(混纺为含聚酯短纤85%以下,轻质指每平方米重量≤170克)	15				130	17	11	米/千克	A	Plain cloth, mixed with cotton, containing <85% by weight of polyester staple fibres, weight ≤ 170g/m^2, bleached
5513.1120 30	与棉混纺漂白聚酯平纹印染用布(混纺为含聚酯短纤85%以下,轻质指每平方米重量≤170克)	15				130	17	11	米/千克	A	Woven fabrics for printing and dying, plain weave, mixed with cotton, containing < 85% by weight of polyester staple fibres, weight≤170g/m^2, bleached
5513.1120 40	与棉混纺漂白聚酯短纤平纹奶酪布等(聚酯短纤<85%,每平方米重量≤170克,含薄细布、巴里纱)	15				130	17	11	米/千克	A	Cheese cloth, plain weave, including voiles and fine thin cloth, mixed with cotton, containing <85% by weight of polyester staple fibres, weight≤170g/m^2, bleached
	--聚酯短纤纺制的三线或四线斜纹机织物,包括双面斜纹机织物:										--3-thread or 4-thread twill, including cross twill, of polyester staple fibres:
5513.1210	---未漂白	16	T3	5	0	130	17	11	米/千克	B	---Unbleached
5513.1220	---漂白	18	T3	5	0	130	17	11	米/千克		---Bleached
	--其他聚酯短纤纺制的机织物:										--Other woven fabrics of polyester staple fibres:
5513.1310	---未漂白	16	T3	5	0	130	17	11	米/千克		---Unbleached
5513.1310 10	与棉混纺未漂聚酯短纤斜纹机织物(聚酯短纤<85%,轻质指每平方米重量≤170克,含缎纹布)	16				130	17	11	米/千克		Woven fabrics, twill weave, satin weave, mixed with cotton, containing <85% by weight of polyester staple fibres, weight≤170g/m^2, unbleached
5513.1310 20	与棉混纺未漂白聚酯短纤牛津布(混纺为含聚酯短纤85%以下,轻质指每平方米重量≤170克)	16				130	17	11	米/千克		Woven fabrics, oxford weave, mixed with cotton, containing < 85% by weight of polyester staple fibres, weight≤170g/m^2, unbleached
5513.1310 90	与棉混纺未漂聚酯短纤其他机织物(混纺为含聚酯短纤85%以下,轻质指每平方米重量≤170克)	16				130	17	11	米/千克		Other woven fabrics, mixed with cotton containing <85% by weight of polyester staple fibres, weight ≤ 170g/m^2, unbleached
5513.1320	---漂白	18	T3	5	0	130	17	11	米/千克		---Bleached
5513.1320 10	与棉混纺漂白聚酯短纤斜纹机织物(含聚酯短纤85%以下,轻质指每平方米重量≤170克,含缎纹)	18				130	17	11	米/千克		Woven fabrics, twill weave, satin weave, mixed with cotton, containing <85% by weight of polyester staple fibres, weight≤170g/m^2, bleached
5513.1320 20	与棉混纺漂白聚酯短纤牛津布(混纺为含聚酯短纤85%以下,轻质指每平方米重量≤170克)	18				130	17	11	米/千克		Woven fabrics, oxford weave, mixed with cotton, containing < 85% by weight of polyester staple fibres, weight≤170g/m^2, bleached
5513.1320 90	与棉混纺漂白聚酯短纤其他机织物(混纺为含聚酯短纤85%以下,轻质指每平方米重量≤170克)	18				130	17	11	米/千克		Other woven fabrics, mixed with cotton, containing < 85% by weight of polyester staple fibres, weight≤170g/m^2, bleached
5513.1900	--其他机织物	18	T3	5	0	130	17	11	米/千克		--Other woven fabrics

税则号列 Tariff Item.	货品名称	最惠国(%) MFN	协定(%)CT 东盟 CA	中巴 CP	中智 CC	普通 Gen	增值税率 VAT	出口退税 ED	计量单位 Unit	监管条件 SC	Article Description
5513.1900 10	棉混纺未漂或漂白其他合纤短纤布(其他合短纤<85%,每平方米重≤170克,专指府绸或细平布)	18				130	17	11	米/千克		Poplin and fine plain cloth, mixed with cotton, containing <85% by weight of synthetic staple fibres, weight≤170g/m², unbleached or bleached
5513.1900 20	棉混纺未漂或漂白其他合纤短纤布(其他合短纤<85%,每平方米重量≤170克,专指机织平布)	18				130	17	11	米/千克		Plain cloth, mixed with cotton, containing <85% by weight of synthetic staple fibres, weight ≤ 170g/m², unbleached or bleached
5513.1900 30	棉混纺未漂或漂白其他合纤短纤布(其他合短纤<85%,每平方米重≤170克,专指平纹印染用布)	18				130	17	11	米/千克		Other woven fabrics, for printing and dying, mixed with cotton, containing <85% by weight of synthetic staple fibres, weight≤170g/m², unbleached or bleached
5513.1900 40	棉混纺未漂或漂白其他合纤短纤布(合短纤<85%,每平方米重≤170克,指奶酪布、薄细布、巴里纱)	18				130	17	11	米/千克		Cheese cloth, voiles and fine thin cloth, mixed with cotton, containing <85% by weight of synthetic staple fibres, weight≤170g/m², unbleached or bleached
5513.1900 50	棉混纺未漂或漂白其他合纤短纤布(其他合短纤<85%,每平米重≤170克,专指缎纹或斜纹布)	18				130	17	11	米/千克		Other woven fabrics, satin weave, twill weave, mixed with cotton, containing <85% by weight of synthetic staple fibres, weight≤170g/m², unbleached or bleached
5513.1900 60	棉混纺未漂或漂白其他合纤短纤布(其他合短纤<85%,每平方米重量≤170克,专指牛津布)	18				130	17	11	米/千克		Other woven fabrics, oxford weave, mixed with cotton, containing <85% by weight of synthetic staple fibres, weight ≤ 170g/m², unbleached or bleached
5513.1900 90	棉混纺未漂或漂白其他合纤短纤布(其他合短纤<85%,每平方米重≤170克,特指其他机织物)	18				130	17	11	米/千克		Other woven fabrics, mixed with cotton, containing <85% by weight of synthetic staple fibres, weight≤170g/m², unbleached or bleached
	-染色:										-Dyed:
5513.2100	--聚酯短纤纺制的平纹机织物	10	T3	0	0	130	17	11	米/千克		--Of polyester staple fibres, plain weave
5513.2100 10	与棉混纺染色聚酯短纤平纹府绸(聚酯短纤85%以下,每平方米重量≤170克,含细平布)	10				130	17	11	米/千克		Poplin, plain weave, including fine plain cloth, mixed with cotton containing <85% by weight of polyester staple fibres, weight≤170g/m², dyed
5513.2100 20	与棉混纺染色聚酯短纤机织平布(混纺为含聚酯短纤85%以下,轻质指每平方米重量≤170克)	10				130	17	11	米/千克		Plain cloth, mixed with cotton, containing <85% by weight of polyester staple fibres, weight≤170g/m², dyed
5513.2100 30	与棉混染色聚酯短纤平纹印染用布(混纺为含聚酯短纤85%以下,轻质指每平方米重量≤170克)	10				130	17	11	米/千克		Woven fabrics for printing and dying, mixed with cotton, containing <85% by weight of polyester staple fibres, weight≤170g/m², dyed

税则号列 Tariff Item.	货品名称	最惠国(%) MFN	协定(%)CT 东盟 CA	中巴 CP	中智 CC	普通 Gen	增值税率 VAT	出口退税 ED	计量单位 Unit	监管条件 SC	Article Description
5513.2100 40	与棉混染色聚酯短纤平纹奶酪布等(聚酯短纤 85%以下,每平方米重≤170克,含薄细布、巴里纱)	10				130	17	11	米/千克		Cheese cloth, plain weave, including voiles and fine thin cloth, mixed with cotton, containing < 85% by weight of polyester staple fibres, weight ≤ 170g/m², dyed
	----其他聚酯短纤纺制的机织物:										----Other woven fabrics of polyester staple fibres:
5513.2310	---聚酯短纤纺制的三线或四线斜纹机织物,包括双面斜纹机织物	10	T3	0	0	130	17	11	米/千克		---3-thread or 4-thread twill, including cross twill, of polyester staple fibres
5513.2390	---其他	10	T3	0	0	130	17	11	米/千克		---Other
5513.2900	--其他机织物	10	T3	0	0	130	17	11	米/千克		--Other woven fabrics
5513.2900 10	与棉混纺染色其他合纤府绸(其他合短纤 <85%,每平方米重量≤170 克,含细平布)	10				130	17	11	米/千克		Poplin, including fine plain cloth, mixed with cotton, containing < 85% by weight of synthetic staple fibres, weight≤170g/m², dyed
5513.2900 20	与棉混纺染色其他合纤短纤平布(混纺为含其他合短纤 <85%,轻质指每平方米重量≤170 克)	10				130	17	11	米/千克		Plain cloth, mixed with cotton, containing < 85% by weight of synthetic staple fibres, weight≤170g/m², dyed
5513.2900 30	与棉混纺染色其他合纤短纤平纹布(印染用,其他合短纤 <85%,指每平方米重量≤170 克)	10				130	17	11	米/千克		Plain weave for printing and dying, mixed with cotton, containing < 85% by weight of synthetic staple fibres, weight≤170g/m², dyed
5513.2900 40	与棉混染色其他合纤短纤平纹布(合短纤 <85%,每平方米重≤170 克/平米,指奶酪布、薄细布、巴里纱)	10				130	17	11	米/千克		Cheese cloth, voiles and fine thin cloth, mixed with cotton, containing < 85% by weight of synthetic staple fibres, weight≤170g/m², dyed
5513.2900 50	与棉混纺染色其他合纤短纤斜纹布(其他合短纤 <85%,每平方米重量≤170 克,含缎纹布)	10				130	17	11	米/千克		Woven fabrics, twill weave, including satin weave, mixed with cotton, containing < 85% by weight of synthetic staple fibres weight≤170g/m², dyed
5513.2900 60	与棉混纺染色其他合纤短纤牛津布(混纺为含其他合短纤 <85%,轻质指每平方米重量≤170 克)	10				130	17	11	米/千克		Woven fabrics, oxford weave, mixed with cotton, containing < 85% by weight of synthetic staple fibres weight ≤170g/m², dyed
5513.2900 90	与棉混纺染色其他合纤短纤其他布(混纺为含其他合短纤 <85%,轻质指每平方米重量≤170 克)	10				130	17	11	米/千克		Other woven fabric, mixed with cotton, containing < 85% by weight of synthetic staple fibres weight≤170g/m², dyed
	-色织:										-Of yarns of different colours:
5513.3100	--聚酯短纤纺制的平纹机织物	10	8	0	0	130	17	11	米/千克		--Of polyester staple fibres, plain weave
	--其他机织物										--Other woven fabrice
5513.3910	---聚酯短纤纺制的三线或四线斜 纹机织物,包括双面斜纹机织物	10	8	0	0	130	17	11	米/千克		---3-thread or 4-threda twill, including cross twill, of polyester staple fibres

税则号列 Tariff Item.	货品名称	最惠国(%) MFN	协定(%)CT 东盟 CA	中巴 CP	中智 CC	普通 Gen	增值税率 VAT	出口退税 ED	计量单位 Unit	监管条件 SC	Article Description
5513.3920	--其他聚酯短纤纺制的机织物	10	8	0	0	130	17	11	米/千克		--Other woven fabrics of polyester staple fibres
5513.3990	---其他	10	8	0	0	130	17	11	米/千克		---Other
	-印花:										-Printed:
5513.4100	--聚酯短纤纺制的平纹机织物	10	T3	0	0	130	17	11	米/千克		--Of polyester staple fibres, plain weave
5513.4100 10	与棉混纺印花聚酯短纤平纹府绸(聚酯短纤85%以下,每平方米重量≤170克,含细平布)	10				130	17	11	米/千克		Poplin, plain weave, including fine plain cloth, mixed with cotton, containing <85% by weight of polyester staple fibres, weight≤170g/m^2, printed
5513.4100 20	与棉混纺印花聚酯短纤机织平布(混纺为含聚酯短纤85%以下,轻质指每平方米重量≤170克)	10				130	17	11	米/千克		Plain cloth, mixed with cotton containing <85% by weight of polyester staple fibres, weight≤170g/m^2, printed
5513.4100 30	与棉混印花聚酯短纤平纹印染用布(混纺为含聚酯短纤85%以下,轻质指每平方米重量≤170克)	10				130	17	11	米/千克		Woven fabrics for printing and dying, mixed with cotton, containing < 85% by weight of polyester staple fibres, weight≤170g/m^2, printed
5513.4100 40	与棉混印花聚酯短纤平纹奶酪布等(聚酯短纤<85%,每平米重≤170克,含薄细布、巴里纱)	10				130	17	11	米/千克		Cheese cloth, including voiles and fine thin cloth, mixed with cotton, containing <85% by weight of polyester staple fibres, weight≤170g/m^2, printed
	--其他机织物:										--Other woven fabrics:
5513.4910	--聚酯短纤纺制的三线或四线斜纹机织物,包括双面斜纹机织物	10	8	0	0	130	17	11	米/千克		--3-thread or 4-thread twill including cross twill, of polyeste staple fibres
5513.4920	--其他聚酯短纤纺制的机织物	10	8	0	0	130	17	11	米/千克		--Other woven fabrics of polyester staple fibres
5513.4990	---其他	10	8	0	0	130	17	11	米/千克		---Other
55.14	**合成纤维短纤纺制的机织物,按重量计合成纤维短纤含量在85%以下,主要或仅与棉混纺,每平方米重量超过170克:**										**Woven fabrics of synthetic staple fibres, containing less than 85% by weight of such fibres, mixed mainly or solely with cotton, of a weight exceeding 170 g/m^2:**
	-未漂白或漂白:										-Unbleached or bleached:
	--聚酯短纤纺制的平纹机织物:										--Of polyester staple fibres, plain weave:
5514.1110	---未漂白	16	T3	5	0	130	17	11	米/千克		---Unbleached
5514.1110 10	与棉混纺未漂白聚酯短纤平纹府绸(聚酯短纤85%以下,每平方米重量>170克,含细平布)	16				130	17	11	米/千克		Poplin, including fine plain cloth, mixed with cotton, containing < 85% by weight of polyester staple fibres, weight>170g/m^2, unbleached
5514.1110 20	与棉混纺未漂白聚酯短纤机织平布(混纺为含聚酯短纤85%以下,重质指每平方米重量>170克)	16				130	17	11	米/千克		Plain cloth, mixed with cotton, containing<85% by weight of polyester staple fibres, weight > 170g/m^2, unbleached
5514.1110 30	与棉混纺未漂白聚酯短纤平纹帆布(混纺为含聚酯短纤85%以下,重质指每平方米重量>170克)	16				130	17	11	米/千克		Canvas, plain weave, mixed with cotton, containing < 85% by weight of polyester staple fibres, weight>170g/m^2, unbleached
5514.1120	---漂白	18	T3	5	0	130	17	11	米/千克		---Bleached

税则号列 Tariff Item.	货品名称	最惠国(%) MFN	协定(%) CT 东盟 CA	中巴 CP	中智 CC	普通 Gen	增值税率 VAT	出口退税 ED	计量单位 Unit	监管条件 SC	Article Description
5514.1120 10	与棉混纺漂白聚酯短纤平纹府绸(聚酯短纤85%以下,每平方米重量>170克,含细平布)	18				130	17	11	米/千克		Poplin, including fine plain cloth, mixed with cotton, containing < 85% by weight of polyester staple fibres, weight > 170g/m², bleached
5514.1120 20	与棉混纺漂白聚酯短纤机织平布(混纺为含聚酯短纤85%以下,重质指每平方米重量>170克)	18				130	17	11	米/千克		Plain cloth, mixed with cotton, containing < 85% by weight of polyester staple fibres, weight > 170g/m², bleached
5514.1120 30	与棉混纺漂白聚脂短纤平纹帆布(混纺为含聚酯短纤85%以下,重质指每平方米重量>170克)	18				130	17	11	米/千克		Canvas, mixed with cotton, containing < 85% by weight of polyester staple fibres, weight > 170g/m², bleached
	--聚酯短纤纺制的三线或四线斜纹机织物,包括双面斜纹机织物:										--3-thread or 4-thread twill, including cross twill, of polyester staple fibres:
5514.1210	---未漂白	16	T3	5	0	130	17	11	米/千克		---Unbleached
5514.1220	---漂白	18	T3	5	0	130	17	11	米/千克		---Bleached
	--其他机织物:										--Other woven fabrics:
	---聚酯短纤纺制的机织物:										---Other woven fabrics of polyester staple fibres:
5514.1911	----未漂白	16	T3	5	0	130	17	11	米/千克		----Unbleached
5514.1912	----漂白	18	T3	5	0	130	17	11	米/千克		----Bleached
5514.1990	---其他机织物	16	T3	5	0	130	17	11	米/千克		---Other woven fabrics
	-染色:										-Dyed:
5514.2100	--聚酯短纤纺制的平纹机织物	10	T3	0	0	130	17	11	米/千克		--Of polyester staple fibres, plain weave
5514.2100 10	与棉混纺染色聚酯短纤平纹府绸(含细平布,聚酯短纤85%以下,重质指每平方米重量>170克)	10				130	17	11	米/千克		Poplin, plain weave, including fine plain cloth, mixed with cotton, containing < 85% by weight of polyester staple fibres, weight > 170g/m², dyed
5514.2100 20	与棉混纺染色聚酯短纤机织平布(混纺为含聚酯短纤85%以下,重质指每平方米重量>170克)	10				130	17	11	米/千克		Plain cloth, plain weave, mixed with cotton, containing < 85% by weight of polyester staple fibres, weight > 170g/m², dyed
5514.2100 30	与棉混纺染色聚脂短纤平纹帆布(混纺为含聚酯短纤85%以下,重质指每平方米重量>170克)	10				130	17	11	米/千克		Canvas, mixed with cotton, containing < 85% by weight of polyester staple fibres, weight > 170g/m², dyed
5514.2200	--聚酯短纤纺制的三线或四线斜纹机织物,包括双面斜纹机织物	10	T3	0	0	130	17	11	米/千克		--3-thread or 4-thread twill, including cross twill, of polyester staple fibres
5514.2300	--其他聚酯短纤纺制的机织物	10	T3	0	0	130	17	11	米/千克		--Other woven fabrics of polyester staple fibres
5514.2300 10	与棉混纺染色聚酯短纤其他斜纹布(聚酯短纤85%以下,每平方米重量>170克,含缎纹布)	10				130	17	11	米/千克		Woven fabrics, twill weave, including satin weave, mixed with cotton, containing < 85% by weight of polyester staple fibres, weight > 170g/m², dyed

税则号列 Tariff Item.	货品名称	最惠国(%) MFN	协定(%)CT 东盟 CA	中巴 CP	中智 CC	普通 Gen	增值税率 VAT	出口退税 ED	计量单位 Unit	监管条件 SC	Article Description
5514.2300 20	与棉混纺染色聚酯短纤其他帆布(混纺为含聚酯短纤85%以下,重质指每平方米重量>170克)	10				130	17	11	米/千克		Other canvas, mixed with cotton, containing < 85% by weight of polyester staple fibres, weight > 170g/m², dyed
5514.2300 90	与棉混纺染色聚酯短纤其他机织物(混纺为含聚酯短纤85%以下,重质指每平方米重量>170克)	10				130	17	11	米/千克		Other woven fabrics, mixed with cotton, containing < 85% by weight of polyester staple fibres, weight > 170g/m², dyed
5514.2900	--其他机织物	10	8	0	0	130	17	11	米/千克		--Other woven fabrics
5514.2900 10	与棉混纺染色其他合纤短纤府绸(含细平布,其他合短纤<85%,重质指每平方米重量>170克)	10				130	17	11	米/千克		Poplin, including fine plain cloth, mixed with cotton, containing < 85% by weight of synthetic staple fibres, weight > 170g/m², dyed
5514.2900 20	与棉混纺染色其他合纤短纤平布(混纺为含其他合短纤<85%,重质指每平方米重量>170克)	10				130	17	11	米/千克		Plain cloth, mixed with cotton, containing < 85% by weight of synthetic staple fibres, weight > 170g/m², dyed
5514.2900 30	与棉混纺染色其他合纤短纤帆布(混纺为含其他合短纤<85%,重质指每平方米重量>170克)	10				130	17	11	米/千克		Other canvas, mixed with cotton, containing < 85% by weight of synthetic staple fibres, weight > 170g/m², dyed
5514.2900 40	与棉混纺染色其他合纤短纤斜纹布(含缎纹布,其他合短纤<85%,重质指每平方米重量>170克)	10				130	17	11	米/千克		Other woven fabrics twill weave, including satin weave, mixed with cotton, containing < 85% by weight of synthetic staple fibres, weight > 170g/m², dyed
5514.2900 90	与棉混纺染色其他合纤短纤其他布(混纺为含其他合短纤<85%,重质指每平方米重量>170克)	10				130	17	11	米/千克		Other woven fabrics, mixed with cotton, containing < 85% by weight of synthetic staple fibres, weight > 170g/m², dyed
	-色织:										-Of yarns of different colours:
5514.3010	--聚酯短纤纺制的平纹机织物	10	8	0	0	130	17	11	米/千克		--Of polyester staple fibres, plain weave
5514.3020	---聚酸短纤纺制的三线或四线斜纹机织物,包括双面斜纹机织物	10	T3	0	0	130	17	11	米/千克		---3-thread or 4-thread tiwll, including cross twill, of polyester staple fibres
5514.3030	---其他聚酯短纤纺制的机织物	10	T3	0	0	130	17	11	米/千克		---Other weave of polyester staple fibres
5514.3090	---其他机纺物	10	T3	0	0	130	17	11	米/千克		---Other weave
	-印花:										-Printed:
5514.4100	--聚酯短纤纺制的平纹机织物	10	8	0	0	130	17	11	米/千克		--Of polyester staple fibres, plain weave
5514.4100 10	与棉混纺印花聚酯短纤平纹府绸(聚酯短纤85%以下,每平方米重量>170克,含细平布)	10				130	17	11	米/千克		Poplin, including fine plain cloth, mixed with cotton, containing < 85% by weight of polyester staple fibres, weight > 170g/m², printed
5514.4100 20	与棉混纺印花聚酯短纤机织平布(混纺为含聚酯短纤85%以下,重质指每平方米重量>170克)	10				130	17	11	米/千克		Plain cloth, mixed with cotton, containing < 85% by weight of polyester staple fibres, weight > 170g/m², printed

税则号列 Tariff Item.	货品名称	最惠国(%) MFN	协定(%) 东盟 CA	协定(%) 中巴 CP	协定(%) CT 中智 CC	普通 Gen	增值税率 VAT	出口退税 ED	计量单位 Unit	监管条件 SC	Article Description
5514.4100 30	与棉混纺印花聚酯短纤平纹帆布(混纺为含聚酯短纤 85% 以下,重质指每平方米重量 >170 克)	10				130	17	11	米/千克		Canvas, mixed with cotton, containing <85% by weight of polyester staple fibres, weight >170g/m², printed
5514.4200	--聚酯短纤纺制的三线或四线斜纹机织物,包括双面斜纹机织物	10	8	0	0	130	17	11	米/千克		--3-thread or 4-thread twill, including cross twill, of polyester staple fibres
5514.4300	--其他聚酯短纤纺制的机织物	10	8	0	0	130	17	11	米/千克		--Other woven fabrics of polyester staple fibres
5514.4300 10	与棉混纺印花聚酯短纤其他斜纹布(含缎纹布,聚酯短纤 85% 以下,重质指每平方米重量 >170 克)	10				130	17	11	米/千克		Other woven fabrics, twill weave, including satin weave, mixed with cotton, containing <85% by weight of polyester staple fibres, weight >170g/m², printed
5514.4300 20	与棉混纺印花聚酯短纤其他帆布(混纺为含聚酯短纤 85% 以下,重质指每平方米重量 >170 克)	10				130	17	11	米/千克		Other canvas, mixed with cotton, containing < 85% by weight of polyester staple fibres, weight > 170g/m², printed
5514.4300 90	与棉混纺印花聚酯短纤其他机织物(混纺为含聚酯短纤 85% 以下,重质指每平方米重量 >170 克)	10				130	17	11	米/千克		Other woven fabrics, mixed with cotton, containing < 85% by weight of polyester staple fibres, weight > 170g/m², printed
5514.4900	--其他机织物	10	8	0	0	130	17	11	米/千克		--Other woven fabrics
5514.4900 10	与棉混纺印花其他合纤短纤府绸(含细平布,其他合短纤 <85%,重质指每平方米重量 >170 克)	10				130	17	11	米/千克		Other poplin, including fine plain cloth, mixed with cotton, containing <85% by weight of synthetic staple fibres, weight >170g/m², printed
5514.4900 20	与棉混纺印花其他合纤短纤平布(混纺为含其他合短纤 <85%,重质指每平方米重量 >170 克)	10				130	17	11	米/千克		Other plain cloth, mixed with cotton, containing <85% by weight of synthetic staple fibres weight >170g/m², printed
5514.4900 30	与棉混纺印花其他合纤短纤帆布(混纺为含其他合短纤 <85%,重质指每平方米重量 >170 克)	10				130	17	11	米/千克		Canvas, mixed with cotton, containing <85% by weight of synthetic staple fibres, weight >170g/m², printed
5514.4900 40	与棉混纺印花其他合纤短纤斜纹布(含缎纹布,其他合短纤 <85%,重质指每平方米重量 >170 克)	10				130	17	11	米/千克		Woven fabrics twill weave, including satin weave, mixed with cotton, containing <85% by weight of synthetic staple fibres, weight >170g/m², printed
5514.4900 90	与棉混纺印花其他合纤短纤其他布(混纺为含其他合短纤 <85%,重质指每平方米重量 >170 克)	10				130	17	11	米/千克		Other woven fabrics, mixed with cotton, containing < 85% by weight of synthetic staple fibres weight > 170g/m², printed
55.15	**合成纤维短纤纺制的其他机织物:**										**Other woven fabrics of synthetic staple fibres:**
	-聚酯短纤纺制:										-Of polyester staple fibres:
5515.1100	--主要或仅与粘胶纤维短纤混纺	10	T3	0	0	130	17	11	米/千克		--Mixed mainly or solely with viscose rayon staple fibres

税则号列 Tariff Item.	货品名称	最惠国(%) MFN	协定(%)CT 东盟 CA	中巴 CP	中智 CC	普通 Gen	增值税率 VAT	出口退税 ED	计量单位 Unit	监管条件 SC	Article Description
5515.1100 11	聚酯短纤蓝粗斜纹布(与粘胶纤维短纤混纺,聚酯短纤含量在85%以下)	10				130	17	11	米/千克		Blue denim, mixed with viscose rayon staple fibres, containing < 85% by weight of polyester staple fibres
5515.1100 19	聚酯短纤其他色织布(短纤含量在85%以下,提花织物除外,与粘胶纤维短纤混纺)	10				130	17	11	米/千克		Woven fabrics, other than jacquard weave, mixed with viscose rayon staple fibres, containing < 85% by weight of polyester staple fibres, of yarns of different colours
5515.1100 21	未漂或漂白聚脂短纤府绸或细平布(聚酯短纤含量在85%以下,主要或仅与粘胶纤维短纤混纺)	10				130	17	11	米/千克		Poplin and fine plain cloth, containing < 85% by weight of polyester staple fibres, mixed mainly or solely with viscose rayon staple fibres, unbleached or bleached
5515.1100 22	未漂或漂白聚脂短纤其他机织平布(聚酯短纤含量在85%以下,主要或仅与粘胶纤维短纤混纺)	10				130	17	11	米/千克		Plain cloth, containing < 85% by weight of polyester staple fibres, mixed mainly or solely with viscose rayon staple fibres, unbleached or bleached
5515.1100 23	未漂或漂白聚脂短纤其他印染用布(聚酯短纤含量在85%以下,主要或仅与粘胶纤维短纤混纺)	10				130	17	11	米/千克		Woven fabrics for printing and dying containing < 85% by weight of polyester staple fibres, mixed mainly or solely with viscose rayon staple fibres, unbleached or bleached
5515.1100 24	未漂或漂白聚脂短纤奶酪布等(短纤含量<85%,含薄细布、巴里纱,与粘胶纤维短纤混纺)	10				130	17	11	米/千克		Cheese cloth, including voiles and fine thin cloth, containing < 85% by weight of polyester staple fibres, mixed with viscose rayon staple fibres, unbleached or bleached
5515.1100 25	未漂或漂白聚脂短纤机织帆布(聚酯短纤含量在85%以下,主要或仅与粘胶纤维短纤混纺)	10				130	17	11	米/千克		Canvas, containing < 85% by weight of polyester staple fibres, mixed mainly or solely with viscose rayon staple fibres, unbleached or bleached
5515.1100 26	未漂或漂白聚脂短纤缎纹或斜纹布(聚酯短纤含量在85%以下,主要或仅与粘胶纤维短纤混纺)	10				130	17	11	米/千克		Other woven fabrics, satin weave or twill weave, unbleached or bleached containing < 85% by weight of polyester staple fibres, mixed mainly or solely with viscose rayon staple fibres
5515.1100 27	未漂或漂白聚脂短纤牛津布(聚酯短纤含量在85%以下,主要或仅与粘胶纤维短纤混纺)	10				130	17	11	米/千克		Other woven fabrics, oxford weave, containing < 85% by weight of polyester staple fibres, mixed mainly or solely with viscose rayon staple fibres, unbleached or bleached
5515.1100 29	未漂或漂白聚脂短纤其他机织物(聚酯短纤含量在85%以下,主要或仅与粘胶纤维短纤混纺)	10				130	17	11	米/千克		Other woven fabrics, containing < 85% by weight of polyester staple fibres, mixed mainly or solely with viscose rayon staple fibres, unbleached or bleached
5515.1100 31	其他聚酯短纤府绸或细平布(聚酯短纤含量在85%以下,主要或仅与粘胶纤维短纤混纺)	10				130	17	11	米/千克		Other poplin and fine plain cloth, containing < 85% by weight of polyester staple fibres, mixed mainly or solely with viscose rayon staple fibres

税则号列 Tariff Item.	货品名称	最惠国(%) MFN	协定(%) CT 东盟 CA	中巴 CP	中智 CC	普通 Gen	增值税率 VAT	出口退税 ED	计量单位 Unit	监管条件 SC	Article Description
5515.1100 32	其他聚酯短纤机织平布(聚酯短纤含量在85%以下,主要或仅与粘胶纤维短纤混纺)	10				130	17	11	米/千克		Other plain cloth, containing <85% by weight of polyester staple fibres, mixed mainly or solely with viscose rayon staple fibres
5515.1100 33	其他聚酯短纤机织印染用布(聚酯短纤含量在85%以下,主要或仅与粘胶纤维短纤混纺)	10				130	17	11	米/千克		Other woven fabrics for printing and dying, containing < 85% by weight of polyester staple fibres, mixed mainly or solely with viscose rayon staple fibres
5515.1100 34	其他聚脂短纤奶酪布等(短纤含量<85%,含薄细布、巴里纱,与粘胶纤维短纤混纺)	10				130	17	11	米/千克		Other cheese cloth, including voiles and fine thin cloth, containing < 85% by weight of polyester staple fibres, mixed mainly or solely with viscose rayon staple fibres
5515.1100 35	其他聚酯短纤机织帆布(聚酯短纤含量在85%以下,主要或仅与粘胶纤维短纤混纺)	10				130	17	11	米/千克		Other canvas, containing < 85% by weight of polyester staple fibres, mixed mainly or solely with viscose rayon staple fibres
5515.1100 36	其他聚酯短纤缎纹或斜纹机织物(聚酯短纤含量在85%以下,主要或仅与粘胶纤维短纤混纺)	10				130	17	11	米/千克		Other woven fabrics, twill weave or satin weave, containing <85% by weight of polyester staple fibres, mixed mainly or solely with viscose rayon staple fibres
5515.1100 37	其他聚酯短纤牛津布(聚酯短纤含量在85%以下,主要或仅与粘胶纤维短纤混纺)	10				130	17	11	米/千克		Other woven fabrics oxford weave, containing < 85% by weight of polyester staple fibres, mixed mainly or solely with viscose rayon staple fibres
5515.1100 39	其他聚酯短纤其他机织物(聚酯短纤含量在85%以下,主要或仅与粘胶纤维短纤混纺)	10				130	17	11	米/千克		Other woven fabrics, containing <85% by weight of polyester staple fibres, mixed mainly or solely with viscose rayon staple fibres
5515.1200	--主要或仅与化学纤维长丝混纺	10	T3	0	0	130	17	11	米/千克		--Mixed mainly or solely with man-made filaments
5515.1200 11	未漂或漂聚酯短纤府绸或细平布(聚酯短纤含量在85%以下,与化纤长丝混纺)	10				130	17	11	米/千克		Poplin and fine plain cloth, containing <85% by weight of polyester staple fibres, mixed mainly or solely with man-made filaments, unbleached or bleached
5515.1200 12	未漂或漂白聚酯短纤平布(聚酯短纤含量在85%以下,与化纤长丝混纺)	10				130	17	11	米/千克		Plain cloth, containing < 85% by weight of polyester staple fibres, mixed mainly or solely with man-made filaments, unbleached or bleached
5515.1200 13	未漂或漂白聚酯短纤印染用布(聚酯短纤含量在85%以下,与化纤长丝混纺)	10				130	17	11	米/千克		Woven fabrics for printing and dying, containing <85% by weight of polyester staple fibres, mixed mainly or solely with man-made filaments, unbleached or bleahed
5515.1200 14	未漂或漂白聚酯短纤缎纹或斜纹布(聚酯短纤含量在85%以下,与化纤长丝混纺)	10				130	17	11	米/千克		Woven fabrics, satin weave or twill weave, containing <85% by weight of polyester staple fibres, mixed mainly or solely with man-made filaments, unbleached or bleached

税则号列 Tariff Item.	货品名称	最惠国(%) MFN	协定(%)CT 东盟 CA	中巴 CP	中智 CC	普通 Gen	增值税率 VAT	出口退税 ED	计量单位 Unit	监管条件 SC	Article Description
5515.1200 19	未漂或漂白聚酯短纤其他机织物(聚酯短纤含量在85%以下,与化纤长丝混纺)	10				130	17	11	米/千克		Woven fabrics containing < 85% by weight of polyester staple fibres, mixed mainly or solely with man-made filaments, unbleached or bleached
5515.1200 21	其他聚酯短纤府绸或细平布(聚酯短纤含量在85%以下,与化纤长丝混纺)	10				130	17	11	米/千克		Other poplin and fine plain cloth, containing < 85% by weight of polyester staple fibres, mixed mainly or solely with man-made filaments
5515.1200 22	其他聚酯短纤平布(聚酯短纤含量在85%以下,与化纤长丝混纺)	10				130	17	11	米/千克		Other plain cloth, containing < 85% by weight of polyester staple fibres, mixed mainly or solely with man-made filaments
5515.1200 23	其他聚酯短纤印染用布(聚酯短纤含量在85%以下,与化纤长丝混纺)	10				130	17	11	米/千克		Other woven fabrics for printing and dying, containing < 85% by weight of polyester staple fibres, mixed mainly or solely with man-made filaments
5515.1200 24	其他聚酯短纤缎纹或斜纹机织物(聚酯短纤含量在85%以下,与化纤长丝混纺)	10				130	17	11	米/千克		Other woven fabrics, satin weave or twill weave, containing < 85% by weight of polyester staple fibres, mixed mainly or solely with man-made filaments, containing < 85% by weight of polyester staple fibres
5515.1200 29	其他聚酯短纤其他机织物(聚酯短纤含量在85%以下,与化纤长丝混纺)	10				130	17	11	米/千克		Other woven fabrics, containing < 85% by weight of polyester staple fibres, mixed mainly or solely with man-made filaments
5515.1300	--主要或仅与羊毛或动物细毛混纺	10	T3	0	0	130	17	11	米/千克		--Mixed mainly or solely with wool or fine animal hair
5515.1300 11	未漂或漂聚酯短纤与精梳毛混纺布(含羊毛或动物细毛36%及以上,聚酯短纤含量在85%以下)	10				130	17	11	米/千克		Woven fabrics, mixed, containing ≥36% by weight of combed wool or fine animal hair, containing < 85% by weight of polyester staple fibres, unbleached or bleached
5515.1300 12	未漂或漂聚酯短纤与粗梳毛混纺布(含羊毛或动物细毛36%及以上,聚酯短纤含量在85%以下)	10				130	17	11	米/千克		Woven fabrics, mixed, containing ≥ 36% by weight carded wool or of fine animal hair, containing < 85% by weight of polyester staple fibres, unbleached or bleached
5515.1300 13	未漂或漂聚酯短纤与精梳毛混纺布(含羊毛或动物细毛36%以下,聚酯短纤含量在85%以下)	10				130	17	11	米/千克		Woven fabrics, mixed, containing < 36% by weight of combed wool or fine animal hair, containing < 85% by weight of polyester staple fibres, unbleached or bleached
5515.1300 19	未漂或漂聚酯短纤与粗梳毛混纺布(含羊毛或动物细毛 < 36%,聚酯短纤含量在85%以下)	10				130	17	11	米/千克		Woven fabrics, mixed, containing < 36% by weight of carded wool or of fine animal hair, containing < 85% by weight of polyester staple fibres, unbleached or bleached
5515.1300 21	其他聚酯短纤与精梳毛混纺机织物(含羊毛或动物细毛36%及以上,聚酯短纤含量在85%以下)	10				130	17	11	米/千克		Other woven fabrics, mixed, containing ≥ 36% by weight of combed wool or fine animal hair, containing < 85% by weight of polyester staple fibres

税则号列 Tariff Item.	货品名称	最惠国(%) MFN	协定(%) CT 东盟 CA	中巴 CP	中智 CC	普通 Gen	增值税率 VAT	出口退税 ED	计量单位 Unit	监管条件 SC	Article Description
5515.1300 22	其他聚酯短纤与粗梳毛混纺机织物(含羊毛或动物细毛36%及以上,聚酯短纤含量在85%以下)	10				130	17	11	米/千克		Other woven fabrics, mixed, containing ≥36% by weight carded wool or fine animal hair, containing < 85% by weight of polyester staple fibres
5515.1300 23	其他聚酯短纤与精梳毛混纺机织物(含羊毛或动物细毛<36%,聚酯短纤含量在85%以下)	10				130	17	11	米/千克		Other woven fabrics, mixed, containing <36% by weight of combed wool or fine animal hair, containing <85% by weight of polyester staple fibres
5515.1300 29	其他聚酯短纤与粗梳毛混纺机织物(含羊毛或动物细毛<36%,聚酯短纤含量在85%以下)	10				130	17	11	米/千克		Other woven fabrics, mixed, containing <36% by weight of carded wool or fine animal hair, containing < 85% by weight of polyester staple fibres
5515.1900	--其他	10	T3	0	0	130	17	11	米/千克		--Other
5515.1900 11	聚脂短纤与其他纤维混蓝粗斜纹布(混纺为以聚酯短纤为主,但聚酯短纤含量在85%以下)	10				130	17	11	米/千克		Blue denim, twill weave, mixed with other fibres, mixed mainly with polyester staple fibers, containing <85% by weight of polyester staple fibres
5515.1900 19	聚脂短纤其他色织机织物(聚脂短纤<85%,提花织物除外,与其他纤维混纺)	10				130	17	11	米/千克		Woven fabrics, other than jacquard weave, mixed with other fibres, containing <85% by weight of polyester staple fibres
5515.1900 21	未漂或漂白聚脂短纤其他府绸(聚酯短纤含量在85%以下,与其他纤维混纺,含细平布)	10				130	17	11	米/千克		Poplin and fine plain cloth, mixed with other fibres, containing < 85% by weight of polyester staple fibres, unbleached or bleached
5515.1900 22	未漂或漂白聚脂短纤其他机织平布(聚酯短纤含量在85%以下,与其他纤维混纺)	10				130	17	11	米/千克		Plain cloth, containing < 85% by weight of polyester staple fibres, mixed with other fibres, unbleached or bleached
5515.1900 23	未漂或漂白聚脂短纤其他机织印染(聚酯短纤含量在85%以下,与其他纤维混纺)	10				130	17	11	米/千克		Woven fabrics for printing and dying, containing <85% by weight of polyester staple fibres, mixed with other fibres, unbleached or bleached
5515.1900 24	未漂或漂白聚脂短纤奶酪布等(短纤含量<85%,与其他纤维混纺,含薄细布、巴里纱)	10				130	17	11	米/千克		Cheese cloth, voiles and fine thin cloth, containing < 85% by weight of polyester staple fibres, mixed with other fibres, unbleached or bleached
5515.1900 25	未漂或漂白聚脂短纤机织帆布(聚酯短纤含量在85%以下,与其他纤维混纺)	10				130	17	11	米/千克		Canvas, containing <85% by weight of polyester staple fibres, mixed with other fibres, unbleached or bleached
5515.1900 26	未漂或漂白聚脂短纤缎纹或斜纹布(聚酯短纤含量在85%以下,与其他纤维混纺)	10				130	17	11	米/千克		Other woven fabrics, satin weave or twill weave, containing < 85% by weight of polyester staple fibres, mixed with other fibres, unbleached or bleached
5515.1900 27	未漂或漂白聚脂短纤牛津布(聚酯短纤含量在85%以下,与其他纤维混纺)	10				130	17	11	米/千克		Other woven fabrics, oxford weave, containing <85% by weight of polyester staple fibres, mixed with other fibres, unbleached or bleached

税则号列 Tariff Item.	货品名称	最惠国(%) MFN	协定(%) CT 东盟 CA	中巴 CP	中智 CC	普通 Gen	增值税率 VAT	出口退税 ED	计量单位 Unit	监管条件 SC	Article Description
5515.1900 29	未漂或漂白聚脂短纤其他机织物(聚酯短纤含量在85%以下,与其他纤维混纺)	10				130	17	11	米/千克		Other woven fabrics, containing <85% by weight of polyester staple fibres, mixed with other fibres, unbleached or bleached
5515.1900 31	其他聚脂短纤府绸或细平布(聚酯短纤含量在85%以下,与其他纤维混纺)	10				130	17	11	米/千克		Other poplin and fine plain cloth, containing < 85% by weight of polyester staple fibres, mixed with other fibres
5515.1900 32	其他聚脂短纤机织平布(聚酯短纤含量在85%以下,与其他纤维混纺)	10				130	17	11	米/千克		Other plain cloth, containing <85% by weight of polyester staple fibres, mixed with other fibres
5515.1900 33	其他聚脂短纤机织印染用布(聚酯短纤含量在85%以下,与其他纤维混纺)	10				130	17	11	米/千克		Other woven fabrics for printing and dying, containing < 85% by weight of polyester staple fibres, mixed with other fibres
5515.1900 34	其他聚脂短纤奶酪布等(短纤含量<85%,与其他纤维混纺,含薄细布、巴里纱)	10				130	17	11	米/千克		Other cheese cloth, voiles and fine thin cloth, containing < 85% by weight of polyester staple fibres, mixed with other fibres
5515.1900 35	其他聚脂短纤机织帆布(聚酯短纤含量在85%以下,与其他纤维混纺)	10				130	17	11	米/千克		Other canvas, containing < 85% by weight of polyester staple fibres, mixed with other fibres
5515.1900 36	其他聚脂短纤缎纹或斜纹机织物(聚酯短纤含量在85%以下,与其他纤维混纺)	10				130	17	11	米/千克		Other woven fabrics, satin weave or twill weave, containing < 85% by weight of polyester staple fibres, mixed with other fibres
5515.1900 37	其他聚脂短纤牛津布(聚酯短纤含量在85%以下,与其他纤维混纺)	10				130	17	11	米/千克		Other woven fabrics, oxford weave, containing <85% by weight of polyester staple fibres, mixed with other fibres
5515.1900 39	其他聚脂短纤其他机织物(聚酯短纤含量在85%以下,与其他纤维混纺)	10				130	17	11	米/千克		Other woven fabrics, containing <85% by weight of polyester staple fibres, mixed with other fibres
	-聚丙烯腈或变性聚丙烯腈短纤纺制:										-Of acrylic or modacrylic staple fibres:
5515.2100	--主要或仅与化学纤维长丝混纺	10	8	0	0	130	17	11	米/千克		--Mixed mainly or solely with man-made filaments
5515.2100 11	未漂或漂白腈纶短纤府绸或细平布(腈短纤含量在85%以下,主要或仅与化纤长丝混纺)	10				130	17	11	米/千克		Poplin and fine plain cloth, unbleached or bleached, containing < 85% by weight of acrylic or modacrylic staple fibres, mixed mainly or solely with man-made filaments
5515.2100 12	未漂或漂白腈纶短纤平布(腈短纤含量在85%以下,主要或仅与化纤长丝混纺)	10				130	17	11	米/千克		Plain cloth, unbleached or bleached, containing < 85% by weight of acrylic or modacrylic staple fibres, mixed mainly or solely with man-made filaments

税则号列 Tariff Item.	货品名称	最惠国(%) MFN	协定(%)东盟 CA	中巴 CP	中智 CC	普通 Gen	增值税率 VAT	出口退税 ED	计量单位 Unit	监管条件 SC	Article Description
5515.2100 13	未漂或漂白腈纶短纤印染用布(腈短纤含量在85%以下,主要或仅与化纤长丝混纺)	10				130	17	11	米/千克		Woven fabrics for printing and dying, unbleached or bleached, containing < 85% by weight of acrylic or modacrylic staple fibres, mixed mainly or solely with manmade filaments
5515.2100 14	未漂或漂白腈纶短纤缎纹或斜纹布(腈短纤含量在85%以下,主要或仅与化纤长丝混纺)	10				130	17	11	米/千克		Woven fabrics, satin weave or twill weave, unbleached or bleached, containing < 85% by weight of acrylic or modacrylic staple fibres, mixed mainly or solely with man-made filaments
5515.2100 19	未漂或漂白腈纶短纤其他机织物(腈短纤含量在85%以下,主要或仅与化纤长丝混纺)	10				130	17	11	米/千克		Other woven fabrics unbleached or bleached, containing < 85% by weight of acrylic staple fibres, mixed mainly or solely with man-made filaments
5515.2100 21	其他腈纶短纤混纺府绸或细平布(腈短纤含量在85%以下,主要或仅与化纤长丝混纺)	10				130	17	11	米/千克		Other poplin and fine plain cloth, containing < 85% by weight of acrylic staple fibres, mixed mainly or solely with man-made filaments
5515.2100 22	其他腈纶短纤平布(腈短纤含量在85%以下,主要或仅与化纤长丝混纺)	10				130	17	11	米/千克		Other plain cloth, containing < 85% by weight of acrylic staple fibres, mixed mainly or solely with man-made filaments
5515.2100 23	其他腈纶短纤印染用布(腈短纤含量在85%以下,主要或仅与化纤长丝混纺)	10				130	17	11	米/千克		Other woven fabrics for printing and dying, containing < 85% by weight of acrylic staple fibres, mixed mainly or solely with man-made filaments
5515.2100 24	其他腈纶短纤混纺缎纹或斜纹布(腈短纤含量在85%以下,主要或仅与化纤长丝混纺)	10				130	17	11	米/千克		Other woven fabrics, satin weave or twill weave, containing < 85% by weight of acrylic staple fibres, mixed mainly or solely with manmade filaments
5515.2100 29	其他腈纶短纤混纺其他机织物(腈短纤含量在85%以下,主要或仅与化纤长丝混纺)	10				130	17	11	米/千克		Other woven fabrics, containing < 85% by weight of acrylic staple fibres, mixed mainly or solely with man-made filaments
5515.2200	--主要或仅与羊毛或动物细毛混纺	12	8	0	0	130	17	11	米/千克		--Mixed mainly or solely with wool or fine animal hair
5515.2200 11	未漂或漂腈纶短纤与精梳毛混纺布(腈短纤含量<85%,含羊毛或动物细毛36%及以上)	12				130	17	11	米/千克		Woven fabrics, mixed, containing ≥ 36% by weight of combed wool or fine animal hair, containing < 85% by weight of acrylic staple fibres, unbleached or bleached
5515.2200 12	未漂或漂腈纶短纤与粗梳毛混纺布(腈短纤含量<85%,含羊毛或动物细毛36%及以上)	12				130	17	11	米/千克		Woven fabrics, mixed, containing ≥ 36% by weight carded wool or fine animal hair, containing < 85% by weight of acrylic staple fibres, unbleached or bleached

税则号列 Tariff Item.	货 品 名 称	最惠国 (%) MFN	协定(%)CT 东盟 CA	 中巴 CP	 中智 CC	普通 Gen	增值 税率 VAT	出口 退税 ED	计量 单位 Unit	监管 条件 SC	Article Description
5515.2200 13	未漂或漂腈纶短纤与精梳毛混纺布(腈短纤含量<85%,含羊毛或动物细毛<36%)	12				130	17	11	米/千克		Woven fabrics, mixed, containing <36% by weight of combed wool or fine animal hair, containing < 85% by weight of acrylic staple fibres, unbleached or bleached
5515.2200 19	未漂或漂腈纶短纤与粗梳毛混纺布(腈短纤含量<85%,含羊毛或动物细毛<36%)	12				130	17	11	米/千克		Woven fabrics, mixed, containing <36% by weight of carded wool or fine animal hair, containing < 85% by weight of acrylic staple fibres, unbleached or bleached
5515.2200 21	其他腈纶短纤与精梳毛混纺机织物(腈短纤含量<85%,含羊毛或动物细毛36%及以上)	12				130	17	11	米/千克		Other woven fabrics, mixed, containing ≥36% by weight of combed wool or fine animal hair, containing <85% by weight of acrylic staple fibres
5515.2200 22	其他腈纶短纤与粗梳毛混纺机织物(腈短纤含量<85%,含羊毛或动物细毛36%及以上)	12				130	17	11	米/千克		Other woven fabrics, mixed, containing ≥36% by weight carded wool or of fine animal hair, containing < 85% by weight of acrylic staple fibres
5515.2200 23	其他腈纶短纤与精梳毛混纺机织物(腈短纤含量<85%,含羊毛或动物细毛<36%)	12				130	17	11	米/千克		Other woven fabrics, mixed, containing <36% by weight of combed wool or fine animal hair, containing <85% by weight of acrylic staple fibres
5515.2200 29	其他腈纶短纤与粗梳毛混纺机织物(腈短纤含量<85%,含羊毛或动物细毛<36%)	12				130	17	11	米/千克		Other woven fabrics, mixed, containing <36% by weight of carded wool or fine animal hair, containing < 85% by weight of acrylic staple fibres
5515.2900	--其他	10	T3	0	0	130	17	11	米/千克		--Other
5515.2900 11	晴纶短纤与其他纤维混蓝粗斜纹布(混纺为以聚丙烯腈短纤为主,腈短纤含量在85%以下)	10				130	17	11	米/千克		Blue denim, twill weave, mixed, mainly with acrylic staple fibers containing <85% by weight of acrylic staple fibres
5515.2900 19	其他腈纶短纤色织机织布(腈短纤含量<85%,提花织物除外,与其他纤维混纺)	10				130	17	11	米/千克		Other woven fabrics, mixed, other than jacquard weave, containing <85% by weight of acrylic staple fibres, of different collours
5515.2900 21	其他未漂或漂白腈纶短纤府绸(腈短纤含量在85%以下,与其他纤维混纺,含细平布)	10				130	17	11	米/千克		Other poplin and fine plain cloth, containing<85% by weight of acrylic staple fibres, mixed with other fibres, unbleached or bleached
5515.2900 22	其他未漂或漂白腈纶短纤平布(腈短纤含量在85%以下,与其他纤维混纺)	10				130	17	11	米/千克		Other plain cloth, containing<85% by weight of acrylic staple fibres, mixed with other fibres, unbleached or bleached
5515.2900 23	其他未漂或漂白腈纶短纤印染用布(腈短纤含量在85%以下,与其他纤维混纺)	10				130	17	11	米/千克		Other woven fabrics for printing and dying, containing<85% by weight of acrylic staple fibres, mixed with other fibres, unbleached or bleached

税则号列 Tariff Item.	货品名称	最惠国(%) MFN	协定(%) CT 东盟 CA	中巴 CP	中智 CC	普通 Gen	增值税率 VAT	出口退税 ED	计量单位 Unit	监管条件 SC	Article Description
5515.2900 24	其他未漂或漂白腈纶短纤奶酪布等(腈短纤含量<85%,与其他纤维混纺,含薄细布、巴里纱)	10				130	17	11	米/千克		Other cheese cloth, voiles and fine thin cloth, containing <85% by weight of acrylic staple fibres, mixed with other fibres, unbleached or bleached
5515.2900 25	其他未漂或漂白腈纶短纤机织帆布(腈短纤含量在85%以下,与其他纤维混纺)	10				130	17	11	米/千克		Other canvas, containing < 85% by weight of acrylic staple fibres, mixed with other fibres, unbleached or blea-ched
5515.2900 26	其他未漂或漂白腈纶短纤缎纹布(含斜纹机织物,腈短纤含量<85%,与其他纤维混纺)	10				130	17	11	米/千克		Other woven fabrics, satin weave or twill weave, containing <85% by weight of acrylic staple fibres, mixed with other fibres, unbleached or bleached
5515.2900 27	其他未漂或漂白腈纶短纤牛津布(腈短纤含量在85%以下,与其他纤维混纺)	10				130	17	11	米/千克		Other woven fabrics, oxford weave, containing < 85% by weight of acrylic staple fibres, mixed with other fibres, unbleached or bleached
5515.2900 29	其他未漂或漂腈纶短纤其他机织物(腈短纤含量在85%以下,与其他纤维混纺)	10				130	17	11	米/千克		Other woven fabrics, containing <85% by weight of acrylic staple fibres, mixed with other fibres, unbleached or bleached
5515.2900 31	其他腈纶短纤府绸或细平布(腈短纤含量在85%以下,与其他纤维混纺)	10				130	17	11	米/千克		Other poplin and fine plain cloth, containing <85% by weight of acrylic staple fibres, mixed with other fibres
5515.2900 32	其他腈纶短纤机织平布(腈短纤含量在85%以下,与其他纤维混纺)	10				130	17	11	米/千克		Other plain cloth, containing <85% by weight of acrylic staple fibres, mixed with other fibres
5515.2900 33	其他腈纶短纤机织印染用布(腈短纤含量在85%以下,与其他纤维混纺)	10				130	17	11	米/千克		Other woven fabrics for printing and dying, containing <85% by weight of acrylic staple fibres, mixed with other fibres
5515.2900 34	其他腈纶短纤奶酪布等(腈短纤含量<85%,与其他纤维混纺,含薄细布、巴里纱)	10				130	17	11	米/千克		Other cheese cloth, voiles and fine thin cloth, containing <85% by weight of acrylic staple fibres, mixed with other fibres
5515.2900 35	其他腈纶短纤机织帆布(腈短纤含量在85%以下,与其他纤维混纺)	10				130	17	11	米/千克		Other canvas, containing < 85% by weight of acrylic staple fibres, mixed with other fibres
5515.2900 36	其他腈纶短纤与其他纤维混牛津布(腈短纤含量在85%以下,与其他纤维混纺)	10				130	17	11	米/千克		Other woven fabrics, oxford weave, containing < 85% by weight of acrylic staple fibres, mixed with other fibres
5515.2900 37	其他腈纶短纤缎纹或斜纹机织物(腈短纤含量在85%以下,与其他纤维混纺)	10				130	17	11	米/千克		Other woven fabrics, satin weave or twill weave, containing < 85% by weight of acrylic staple fibres, mixed with other fibres
5515.2900 39	其他腈纶短纤与其他纤维混机织物(混纺为以聚丙烯腈短纤为主,腈短纤含量在85%以下)	10				130	17	11	米/千克		Other woven fabrics, containing <85% by weight of acrylic staple fibres, mixed with other fibres

税则号列 Tariff Item.	货品名称	最惠国(%) MFN	协定(%) CT 东盟 CA	中巴 CP	中智 CC	普通 Gen	增值税率 VAT	出口退税 ED	计量单位 Unit	监管条件 SC	Article Description
	-其他机织物:										-Other woven fabrics:
5515.9100	--主要或仅与化学纤维长丝混纺	10	8	0	0	130	17	11	米/千克		--Mixed mainly or solely with man-made filaments
5515.9100 11	未漂或漂白其他合纤短府绸(与化纤长丝混纺,合成纤维短纤含量<85%,含细平布)	10				130	17	11	米/千克		Poplin and fine plain cloth, containing <85% by weight of synthetic staple fibres, mixed mainly or solely with man-made filaments
5515.9100 12	未漂或漂白其他合纤短纤平布(与化纤长丝混纺,合成纤维短纤含量在85%以下)	10				130	17	11	米/千克		Plain cloth, containing < 85% by weight of synthetic staple fibres, mixed mainly or solely with man-made filaments, unbleached or bleached
5515.9100 13	未漂或漂其他合纤短纤混印染用布(与化纤长丝混纺,合成纤维短纤含量在85%以下)	10				130	17	11	米/千克		Other woven fabrics for printing and dying, containing < 85% by weight of synthetic staple fibres, mixed mainly or solely with man-made filaments, unbleached or bleached
5515.9100 14	未漂或漂其他合纤短纤缎纹布等(与化纤长丝混纺,合成纤维短纤含量<85%,含斜纹机织物)	10				130	17	11	米/千克		Other woven fabrics, satin weave, twill weave, containing <85% by weight of synthetic staple fibres, mixed mainly or solely with man-made filaments, unbleached or bleached
5515.9100 19	未漂或漂其他合纤短纤其他机织物(与化纤长丝混纺,合成纤维短纤含量在85%以下)	10				130	17	11	米/千克		Other woven fabrics, containing <85% by weight of synthetic staple fibres, mixed mainly or solely with man-made filaments, unbleached or bleached
5515.9100 21	其他合纤短纤府绸或细平布(与化纤长丝混纺,合成纤维短纤含量在85%以下)	10				130	17	11	米/千克		Other poplin and fine plain cloth, containing < 85% by weight of synthetic staple fibres, mixed mainly or solely with man-made filaments
5515.9100 22	其他合纤短纤平布(与化纤长丝混纺,合成纤维短纤含量在85%以下)	10				130	17	11	米/千克		Other plain cloth, containing <85% by weight of synthetic staple fibres, mixed mainly or solely with man-made filaments
5515.9100 23	其他合纤短纤印染用布(与化纤长丝混纺,合成纤维短纤含量在85%以下)	10				130	17	11	米/千克		Other woven fabrics for printing and dying, containing < 85% by weight of synthetic staple fibres, mixed mainly or solely with man-made filaments
5515.9100 24	其他合纤短纤缎纹或斜纹机织物(与化纤长丝混纺,合成纤维短纤含量在85%以下)	10				130	17	11	米/千克		Other woven fabrics, satin weave or twill weave, containing < 85% by weight of synthetic staple fibres, mixed mainly or solely with man-made filaments
5515.9100 29	其他合纤短纤其他机织物(与化纤长丝混纺,合成纤维短纤含量在85%以下)	10				130	17	11	米/千克		Other woven fabrics, containing <85% by weight of synthetic staple fibres, mixed mainly or solely with man-made filaments
5515.9900	--其他	10	8	0	0	130	17	11	米/千克		--Other
5515.9900 11	其他合纤短纤蓝粗斜纹布(合成纤维短纤含量在85%以下,与其他纤维混纺)	10				130	17	11	米/千克		Other blue denim, twill weave, containing <85% by weight of synthetic staple fibres, mixed with other fibres

税则号列 Tariff Item.	货品名称	最惠国(%) MFN	协定(%) CT			普通 Gen	增值税率 VAT	出口退税 ED	计量单位 Unit	监管条件 SC	Article Description
			东盟 CA	中巴 CP	中智 CC						
5515.9900 19	其他合纤短纤其他色织机织物(合成纤维短纤含量<85%,与其他纤维混纺,提花织物除外)	10				130	17	11	米/千克		Other woven fabrics, of yarns of different colours, other than jacquard weave, containing <85% by weight of synthetic staple fibres, mixed with other fibres
5515.9900 21	未漂或漂白其他合纤短纤府绸(合成纤维短纤含量在85%以下,与其他纤维混纺,含细平布)	10				130	17	11	米/千克		Other poplin and fine plain cloth, containing <85% by weight of synthetic staple fibres, unbleached or bleached, mixed with other fibres
5515.9900 22	未漂或漂白其他合纤短纤其他平布(合成纤维短纤含量在85%以下,与其他纤维混纺)	10				130	17	11	米/千克		Other plain cloth, containing <85% by weight of synthetic staple fibres, unbleached or bleached, mixed with other fibres
5515.9900 23	未漂或漂白其他合纤短纤印染用布(合成纤维短纤含量在85%以下,与其他纤维混纺)	10				130	17	11	米/千克		Other woven fabrics for printing and dying, containing < 85% by weight of synthetic staple fibres, unbleached or bleached, mixed with other fibres
5515.9900 24	未漂或漂白其他合纤短纤奶酪布等(合纤短纤含量<85%,与其他纤维混纺,含薄细布、巴里纱)	10				130	17	11	米/千克		Other cheese cloth, voiles and fine thin cloth, containing < 85% by weight of synthetic staple fibres, unbleached or bleached, mixed with other fibres
5515.9900 25	未漂或漂白其他合纤短纤帆布(合成纤维短纤含量在85%以下,与其他纤维混纺)	10				130	17	11	米/千克		Other canvas, containing < 85% by weight of synthetic staple fibres, unbleached or bleached, mixed with other fibres
5515.9900 26	未漂或漂其他合纤短纤混纺缎纹布(合成纤维短纤含量<85%,与其他纤维混纺,含斜纹机织物)	10				130	17	11	米/千克		Other woven fabrics, satin weave or twill weave, containing < 85% by weight of synthetic staple fibres, unbleached or bleached, mixed with other fibres
5515.9900 27	未漂或漂白其他合纤短纤牛津布(合成纤维短纤含量在85%以下,与其他纤维混纺)	10				130	17	11	米/千克		Other woven fabrics, oxford weave, containing <85% by weight of synthetic staple fibres, unbleached or bleached, mixed with other fibres
5515.9900 29	未漂或漂其他合纤短纤其他机织物(合成纤维短纤含量在85%以下,与其他纤维混纺)	10				130	17	11	米/千克		Other woven fabrics, containing <85% by weight of synthetic staple fibres, unbleached or bleached, mixed with other fibres
5515.9900 31	其他合纤短纤府绸或细平布(合成纤维短纤含量在85%以下,与其他纤维混纺)	10				130	17	11	米/千克		Other poplin and fine plain cloth, containing < 85% by weight of synthetic staple fibres, mixed with other fibres
5515.9900 32	其他合纤短纤其他机织平布(合成纤维短纤含量在85%以下,与其他纤维混纺)	10				130	17	11	米/千克		Other plain cloth, containing <85% by weight of synthetic staple fibres, mixed with other fibres
5515.9900 33	其他合纤短纤机织印染用布(合成纤维短纤含量在85%以下,与其他纤维混纺)	10				130	17	11	米/千克		Other woven fabrics for printing and dying, containing < 85% by weight of synthetic staple fibres, mixed with other fibres

税则号列 Tariff Item.	货品名称	最惠国(%) MFN	协定(%)CT 东盟 CA	中巴 CP	中智 CC	普通 Gen	增值税率 VAT	出口退税 ED	计量单位 Unit	监管条件 SC	Article Description
5515.9900 34	其他合纤短纤奶酪布等(合纤短纤含量<85%,与其他纤维混纺,含薄细布、巴里纱)	10				130	17	11	米/千克		Other cheese cloth, voiles and fine thin cloth, containing < 85% by weight of synthetic staple fibres, mixed with other fibres
5515.9900 35	其他合纤短纤机织帆布(合成纤维短纤含量在85%以下,与其他纤维混纺)	10				130	17	11	米/千克		Other canvas, containing < 85% by weight of synthetic staple fibres, mixed with other fibres
5515.9900 36	其他合纤短纤缎纹或斜纹机织物(合成纤维短纤含量在85%以下,与其他纤维混纺)	10				130	17	11	米/千克		Other woven fabrics, satin weave or twill weave, containing < 85% by weight of synthetic staple fibres, mixed with other fibres
5515.9900 37	其他合纤短纤其他纤维混牛津布(合成纤维短纤含量在85%以下,与其他纤维混纺)	10				130	17	11	米/千克		Other woven fabrics, oxford weave, containing < 85% by weight of synthetic staple fibres, mixed with other fibres
5515.9900 39	其他合纤短纤其他机织物(合成纤维短纤含量在85%以下,与其他纤维混纺)	10				130	17	11	米/千克		Other woven fabrics, containing < 85% by weight of synthetic staple fibres, mixed with other fibres
55.16	**人造纤维短纤纺制的机织物:**										**Woven fabrics of artificial staple fibres:**
	-按重量计人造纤维短纤含量在85%及以上:										-Containing 85% or more by weight of artificial staple fibres:
5516.1100	--未漂白或漂白	12	8	0	0	130	17	11	米/千克		--Unbleached or bleached
5516.1200	--染色	10	8	0	0	130	17	11	米/千克		--Dyed
5516.1300	--色织	10	8	0	0	130	17	11	米/千克		--Of yarns of different colours
5516.1400	--印花	10	8	0	0	130	17	11	米/千克		--Printed
	-按重量计人造纤维短纤含量在85%以下,主要或仅与化学纤维长丝混纺:										-Containing less than 85% by weight of artificial staple fibres, mixed mainly or solely with man-made filaments:
5516.2100	--未漂白或漂白	12	8	0	0	130	17	11	米/千克		--Unbleached or bleached
5516.2100 10	未漂或漂白人纤短纤府绸或细平布(人造纤维短纤含量在85%以下,与化纤长丝混纺)	12				130	17	11	米/千克		Poplin and fine plain cloth, containing <85% by weight of artificial staple fibres, mixed mainly or solely with man-made filaments, unbleached or blea-ched
5516.2100 20	未漂或漂白人纤短纤平布(人造纤维短纤含量在85%以下,与化纤长丝混纺)	12				130	17	11	米/千克		Plain cloth, containing < 85% by weight of artificial staple fibres, mixed mainly or solely with man-made filaments, unbleached or bleached
5516.2100 30	未漂或漂白人纤短纤印染用布(人造纤维短纤含量在85%以下,与化纤长丝混纺)	12				130	17	11	米/千克		Woven fabrics for printing and dying, containing <85% by weight of artificial staple fibres, mixed mainly or solely with man-made filaments, unbleached or bleached

税则号列 Tariff Item.	货品名称	最惠国(%) MFN	协定(%)CT 东盟 CA	中巴 CP	中智 CC	普通 Gen	增值税率 VAT	出口退税 ED	计量单位 Unit	监管条件 SC	Article Description
5516. 2100 40	未漂或漂白人纤短纤缎纹或斜纹布(人造纤维短纤含量在85%以下,与化纤长丝混纺)	12				130	17	11	米/千克		Satin weave or twill weave, containing <85% by weight of artificial staple fibres, mixed mainly or solely with man-made filaments, unbleached or blea-ched
5516. 2100 90	未漂或漂白人纤短纤其他机织物(人造纤维短纤含量在85%以下,与化纤长丝混纺)	12				130	17	11	米/千克		Other woven fabrics, containing <85% by weight of artificial staple fibres, mixed mainly or solely with man-made filaments, unbleached or bleached
5516. 2200	--染色	10	8	0	0	130	17	11	米/千克		--Dyed
5516. 2200 10	染色人纤短纤府绸或细平布(人造纤维短纤含量在85%以下,与化纤长丝混纺)	10				130	17	11	米/千克		Poplin and fine plain cloth, containing <85% by weight of artificial staple fibres, mixed mainly or solely with man-made filaments, dyed
5516. 2200 20	染色人纤短纤平布(人造纤维短纤含量在85%以下,与化纤长丝混纺)	10				130	17	11	米/千克		Plain cloth, containing < 85% by weight of artificial staple fibres, mixed mainly or solely with man-made filaments, dyed
5516. 2200 30	染色人纤短纤印染用布(人造纤维短纤含量在85%以下,与化纤长丝混纺)	10				130	17	11	米/千克		Woven fabrics for printing and dying, containing <85% by weight of artificial staple fibres, mixed mainly or solely with man-made filaments, dyed
5516. 2200 40	染色人纤短纤缎纹或斜纹机织物(人造纤维短纤含量在85%以下,与化纤长丝混纺)	10				130	17	11	米/千克		Woven fabrics satin weave or twill weave, containing <85% by weight of artificial staple fibres, mixed mainly or solely with man-made filaments, dyed
5516. 2200 90	染色人纤短纤其他机织物(人造纤维短纤含量在85%以下,与化纤长丝混纺)	10				130	17	11	米/千克		Other woven fabrics, containing <85% by weight of artificial staple fibres, mixed mainly or solely with man-made filaments, dyed
5516. 2300	--色织	10	8	0	0	130	17	11	米/千克		--Of yarns of different colours
5516. 2300 10	色织人纤短纤府绸和细平布(人造纤维短纤含量在85%以下,与化纤长丝混纺)	10				130	17	11	米/千克		Poplin and fine plain cloth, containing <85% by weight of artificial staple fibres, mixed mainly or solely with man-made filaments, of different collours
5516. 2300 20	色织人纤短纤平布(人造纤维短纤含量在85%以下,与化纤长丝混纺)	10				130	17	11	米/千克		Plain cloth, containing < 85% by weight of artificial staple fibres, mixed mainly or solely with man-made filaments, of different collours
5516. 2300 30	色织人纤短纤印染用布(人造纤维短纤含量在85%以下,与化纤长丝混纺)	10				130	17	11	米/千克		Woven fabrics for printing and dying, containing <85% by weight of artificial staple fibres, mixed mainly or solely with man-made filaments, of different collours
5516. 2300 40	色织人纤短纤缎纹或斜纹机织物(人造纤维短纤含量在85%以下,与化纤长丝混纺)	10				130	17	11	米/千克		Woven fabrics, satin weave or twill weave, containing <85% by weight of artificial staple fibres, mixed mainly or solely with man-made filaments, of different collours

税则号列 Tariff Item.	货品名称	最惠国(%) MFN	协定(%)CT 东盟 CA	中巴 CP	中智 CC	普通 Gen	增值税率 VAT	出口退税 ED	计量单位 Unit	监管条件 SC	Article Description
5516.2300 90	色织人纤短纤其他机织物(人造纤维短纤含量在85%以下,与化纤长丝混纺)	10				130	17	11	米/千克		Other woven fabrics, containing < 85% by weight of artificial staple fibres, mixed mainly or solely with man-made filaments, of different collours
5516.2400	--印花	10	8	0	0	130	17	11	米/千克		--Printed
5516.2400 10	印花人纤府绸或细平布(人造纤维短纤含量在85%以下,与化纤长丝混纺)	10				130	17	11	米/千克		Poplin and fine plain cloth, containing < 85% by weight of artificial staple fibres, mixed mainly or solely with man-made filaments, printed
5516.2400 20	印花人纤短纤平布(人造纤维短纤含量在85%以下,与化纤长丝混纺)	10				130	17	11	米/千克		Plain cloth, containing < 85% by weight of artificial staple fibres, mixed mainly or solely with man-made filaments, printed
5516.2400 30	印花人纤短纤印染用布(人造纤维短纤含量在85%以下,与化纤长丝混纺)	10				130	17	11	米/千克		Woven fabrics for printing and dying, containing < 85% by weight of artificial staple fibres, mixed mainly or solely with man-made filaments, printed
5516.2400 40	印花人纤短纤缎纹或斜纹机织物(人造纤维短纤含量在85%以下,与化纤长丝混纺)	10				130	17	11	米/千克		Woven fabrics, satin weave or twill weave, containing < 85% by weight of artificial staple fibres, mixed mainly or solely with man-made filaments, printed
5516.2400 90	印花人纤短纤其他布(人造纤维短纤含量在85%以下,与化纤长丝混纺)	10				130	17	11	米/千克		Other woven fabrics, containing < 85% by weight of artificial staple fibres, mixed mainly or solely with man-made filaments, printed
	-按重量计人造纤维短纤含量在85%以下,主要或仅与羊毛或动物细毛混纺:										-Containing less than 85% by weight of artificial staple fibres, mixed mainly or solely with wool or fine animal hair:
5516.3100	--未漂白或漂白	12	8	0	0	130	17	11	米/千克		--Unbleached or bleached
5516.3100 11	未漂白或漂白人纤短纤与精梳毛混纺布(人造纤维短纤含量<85%,羊毛或动物细毛36%及以上)	12				130	17	11	米/千克		Woven fabrics, mixed, containing ≥ 36% by weight of combed wool or fine animal hair, containing < 85% by weight of artificial staple fibres, unbleached or bleached
5516.3100 19	未漂白或漂白人纤短纤与粗梳毛混纺布(人造纤维短纤含量<85%,羊毛或动物细毛36%及以上)	12				130	17	11	米/千克		Woven fabrics, mixed, containing ≥ 36% by weight of carded wool or fine animal hair, containing < 85% by weight of artificial staple fibres, unbleached or bleached
5516.3100 21	未漂白或漂白人纤短纤与精梳毛混纺布(人造纤维短纤含量<85%,羊毛或动物细毛<36%)	12				130	17	11	米/千克		Woven fabrics, mixed, containing < 36% by weight of combed wool or fine animal hair, containing < 85% by weight of artificial staple fibres, unbleached or bleached
5516.3100 29	未漂或漂白人纤短纤与粗梳毛混纺布(人造纤维短纤含量<85%,羊毛或动物细毛<36%)	12				130	17	11	米/千克		Woven fabrics, mixed, containing < 36% by weight of carded wool or fine animal hair, containing < 85% by weight of artificial staple fibres, unbleached or bleached
5516.3200	--染色	10	8	0	0	130	17	11	米/千克		--Dyed

税则号列 Tariff Item.	货品名称	最惠国(%) MFN	协定(%) CT 东盟 CA	中巴 CP	中智 CC	普通 Gen	增值税率 VAT	出口退税 ED	计量单位 Unit	监管条件 SC	Article Description
5516.3200 11	染色人纤短纤与精梳毛混纺机织物(人造纤维短纤含量<85%,羊毛或动物细毛36%及以上)	10				130	17	11	米/千克		Woven fabrics, mixed, containing ≥ 36% by weight of combed wool or fine animal hair, containing < 85% by weight of artificial staple fibres, dyed
5516.3200 19	染色人纤短纤与粗梳毛混纺机织物(人造纤维短纤含量<85%,羊毛或动物细毛36%及以上)	10				130	17	11	米/千克		Woven fabrics, mixed, containing ≥ 36% by weight carded of wool or fine animal hair, containing < 85% by weight of artificial staple fibres, dyed
5516.3200 21	染色人纤短纤与精梳毛混纺机织物(人造纤维短纤含量<85%,羊毛或动物细毛<36%)	10				130	17	11	米/千克		Woven fabrics, mixed, containing < 36% by weight of combed wool or fine animal hair, containing < 85% by weight of artificial staple fibres, dyed
5516.3200 29	染色人纤短纤与粗梳毛混纺机织物(人造纤维短纤含量<85%,羊毛或动物细毛<36%)	10				130	17	11	米/千克		Woven fabrics, mixed, containing < 36% by weight of carded wool or fine animal hair, containing < 85% by weight of artificial staple fibres, dyed
5516.3300	--色织	10	8	0	0	130	17	11	米/千克		--Of yarns of different colours
5516.3300 11	色织人纤短纤与精梳毛混纺机织物(人造纤维短纤含量<85%,羊毛或动物细毛36%及以上)	10				130	17	11	米/千克		Woven fabrics, mixed, containing ≥ 36% by weight of combed wool or of combed fine animal hair, containing < 85% by weight of artificial staple fibres, of different collours
5516.3300 19	色织人纤短纤与粗梳毛混纺机织物(人造纤维短纤含量<85%,羊毛或动物细毛36%及以上)	10				130	17	11	米/千克		Woven fabrics, mixed, containing ≥ 36% by weight of carded wool or fine animal hair, containing < 85% by weight of artificial staple fibres, of different collours
5516.3300 21	色织人纤短纤与精梳毛混纺机织物(人造纤维短纤含量<85%,羊毛或动物细毛<36%)	10				130	17	11	米/千克		Woven fabrics, mixed, containing < 36% by weight of combed wool or of combed fine animal hair, containing < 85% by weight of artificial staple fibres, of different collours
5516.3300 29	色织人纤短纤与粗梳毛混纺机织物(人造纤维短纤含量<85%,羊毛或动物细毛<36%)	10				130	17	11	米/千克		Woven fabrics, mixed, containing < 36% by weight of carded wool or fine animal hair, containing < 85% by weight of artificial staple fibres, of different collours
5516.3400	--印花	10	8	0	0	130	17	11	米/千克		--Printed
5516.3400 11	印花人纤短纤与精梳毛混纺机织物(人造纤维短纤含量<85%,羊毛或动物细毛36%及以上)	10				130	17	11	米/千克		Woven fabrics, mixed, containing ≥ 36% by weight of combed wool or of combed fine animal hair, containing < 85% by weight of artificial staple fibres, printed
5516.3400 19	印花人纤短纤与粗梳毛混纺机织物(人造纤维短纤含量<85%,羊毛或动物细毛36%及以上)	10				130	17	11	米/千克		Woven fabrics, mixed, containing ≥ 36% by weight of carded wool or fine animal hair, containing < 85% by weight of artificial staple fibres, printed

税则号列 Tariff Item.	货品名称	最惠国(%) MFN	协定(%) CT 东盟 CA	中巴 CP	中智 CC	普通 Gen	增值税率 VAT	出口退税 ED	计量单位 Unit	监管条件 SC	Article Description
5516.3400 21	印花人纤短纤与精梳毛混纺机织物（人造纤维短纤含量<85%，羊毛或动物细毛<36%）	10				130	17	11	米/千克		Woven fabrics, mixed, containing < 36% by weight of combed wool or of combed fine animal hair, containing < 85% by weight of artificial staple fibres, printed
5516.3400 29	印花人纤短纤与粗梳毛混纺机织物（人造纤维短纤含量<85%，羊毛或动物细毛<36%）	10				130	17	11	米/千克		Woven fabrics, mixed, containing < 36% by weight of carded wool or fine animal hair, containing < 85% by weight of artificial staple fibres, printed
	-按重量计人造纤维短纤含量在85%以下，主要或仅与棉混纺：										-Containing less than 85% by weight of artificial staple fibres, mixed mainly or solely with cotton:
5516.4100	--未漂白或漂白	12	8	0	0	130	17	11	米/千克		--Unbleached or bleached
5516.4100 10	未漂白或漂白人纤短纤府绸或细平布（人造纤维短纤含量在85%以下，与棉混纺）	12				130	17	11	米/千克		Poplin and fine plain cloth, mixed with cotton, containing < 85% by weight of artificial staple fibres, unbleached or bleached
5516.4100 20	未漂白或漂白人纤短纤与棉混纺平布（混纺为以人纤短纤为主，但人造纤维短纤含量在85%以下）	12				130	17	11	米/千克		Plain cloth, mixed with cotton, mixed maihly with artificial staple fibers, containing < 85% by weight of artificial staple fibres, unbleached or bleached
5516.4100 30	与棉混未漂白或漂白人纤短纤印染用布（混纺为以人纤短纤为主，但人造纤维短纤含量在85%以下）	12				130	17	11	米/千克		Woven fabrics for printing and dying, mixed with cotton, containing < 85% by weight of artificial staple fibres, unbleached or bleached
5516.4100 40	未漂白或漂白人纤短纤与棉混奶酪布等（人造纤维短纤含量在85%以下，含薄细布、巴里纱）	12				130	17	11	米/千克		Cheese cloth, voiles and fine thin cloth, mixed with cotton, containing < 85% by weight of artificial staple fibres, unbleached or bleached
5516.4100 50	与棉混未漂白或漂白人纤短纤机织帆布（混纺为以人纤短纤为主，但人造纤维短纤含量在85%以下）	12				130	17	11	米/千克		Canvas, mixed with cotton, containing < 85% by weight of artificial staple fibres, unbleached or bleached
5516.4100 60	与棉混未漂白或漂白人纤短纤缎纹布等（含斜纹布，人造纤维短纤含量在85%以下）	12				130	17	11	米/千克		Woven fabrics, satin weave or twill weave, mixed with cotton, containing < 85% by weight of artificial staple fibres, unbleached or bleached
5516.4100 70	与棉混未漂白或漂白人纤短纤牛津布（混纺为以人纤短纤为主，但人造纤维短纤含量在85%以下）	12				130	17	11	米/千克		Woyen fabrics, oxford weave, mixed with cotton, containing < 85% by weight of artificial staple fibres, unbleached or bleached
5516.4100 90	与棉混未漂或漂人纤短纤其他布（混纺为以人纤短纤为主，但人造纤维短纤含量在85%以下）	12				130	17	11	米/千克		Other woven fabrics, mixed with cotton, containing < 85% by weight of artificial staple fibres, unbleached or bleached
5516.4200	--染色	12	8	0	0	130	17	11	米/千克		--Dyed
5516.4200 10	与棉混染色人纤短纤府绸或细平布（混纺为以人纤短纤为主，但人造纤维短纤含量在85%以下）	12				130	17	11	米/千克		Poplin and fine plain cloth, mixed with cotton, containing < 85% by weight of artificial staple fibres, dyed

税则号列 Tariff Item.	货品名称	最惠国(%) MFN	协定(%) CT 东盟 CA	中巴 CP	中智 CC	普通 Gen	增值税率 VAT	出口退税 ED	计量单位 Unit	监管条件 SC	Article Description
5516.4200 20	与棉混染色人纤短纤平布(混纺为以人纤短纤为主,但人造纤维短纤含量在85%以下)	12				130	17	11	米/千克		Plain cloth, mixed with cotton, containing <85% by weight of artificial staple fibres, dyed
5516.4200 30	与棉混染色人纤短纤印染用布(混纺为以人纤短纤为主,但人造纤维短纤含量在85%以下)	12				130	17	11	米/千克		Woven fabrics for printing and dying, mixed with cotton, containing < 85% by weight of artificial staple fibres, dyed
5516.4200 40	与棉混染色人纤短纤奶酪布等(含薄细布,巴里纱,人造纤维短纤含量在85%以下)	12				130	17	11	米/千克		Cheese cloth, voiles and fine thin cloth, mixed with cotton, containing < 85% by weight of artificial staple fibres, dyed
5516.4200 50	与棉混染色人纤短纤机织帆布(混纺为以人纤短纤为主,但人造纤维短纤含量在85%以下)	12				130	17	11	米/千克		Canvas, mixed with cotton, containing <85% by weight of artificial staple fibres, dyed
5516.4200 60	与棉混染色人纤短纤缎纹或斜纹布(混纺为以人纤短纤为主,但人造纤维短纤含量在85%以下)	12				130	17	11	米/千克		Woven fabrics, satin weave or twill weave, mixed with cotton, containing < 85% by weight of artificial staple fibres, dyed
5516.4200 70	与棉混染色人纤短纤牛津布(混纺为以人纤短纤为主,但人造纤维短纤含量在85%以下)	12				130	17	11	米/千克		Woven fabrics, oxford weave, mixed with cotton, containing < 85% by weight of artificial staple fibres, dyed
5516.4200 90	与棉混纺染色人纤短纤其他机织物(混纺为以人纤短纤为主,但人造纤维短纤含量在85%以下)	12				130	17	11	米/千克		Woven fabrics, mixed with cotton, containing < 85% by weight of artificial staple fibres, dyed
5516.4300	--色织	10	8	0	0	130	17	11	米/千克		--Of yarns of different colours
5516.4300 10	与棉混人纤短纤色织兰色粗斜纹布(混纺为以人纤短纤为主,但人造纤维短纤含量在85%以下)	10				130	17	11	米/千克		Blue denim, twill weave, mixed with cotton, containing <85% by weight of artificial staple fibres, of different colours
5516.4300 20	与棉混纺人纤短纤色织提花机织物(混纺为以人纤短纤为主,但人造纤维短纤含量在85%以下)	10				130	17	11	米/千克		Woven fabrics, jacquard weave, mixed with cotton, containing < 85% by weight of artificial staple fibres, of different colours
5516.4300 90	与棉混纺人纤短纤其他色织机织物(混纺为以人纤短纤为主,但人造纤维短纤含量在85%以下)	10				130	17	11	米/千克		Woven fabrics, mixed with cotton, containing < 85% by weight of artificial staple fibres, of different colours
5516.4400	--印花	10	8	0	0	130	17	11	米/千克		--Printed
5516.4400 10	与棉混印花人纤短纤府绸或细平布(混纺为以人纤短纤为主,但人造纤维短纤含量在85%以下)	10				130	17	11	米/千克		Poplin and fine plain cloth, mixed with cotton, containing <85% by weight of artificial staple fibres, printed
5516.4400 20	与棉混印花人纤短纤平布(混纺为以人纤短纤为主,但人造纤维短纤含量在85%以下)	10				130	17	11	米/千克		Plain cloth, mixed with cotton, containing <85% by weight of artificial staple fibres, printed

税则号列 Tariff Item.	货品名称	最惠国(%) MFN	协定(%)CT			普通 Gen	增值税率 VAT	出口退税 ED	计量单位 Unit	监管条件 SC	Article Description
			东盟 CA	中巴 CP	中智 CC						
5516.4400 30	与棉混印花人纤短纤印染用布(混纺为以人纤短纤为主,但人造纤维短纤含量在85%以下)	10				130	17	11	米/千克		Woven fabrics for printing and dying, mixed with cotton, containing <85% by weight of artificial staple fibres, printed
5516.4400 40	与棉混纺印花人纤短纤奶酪布等(含薄细布、巴里纱、人造纤维短纤含量在85%以下)	10				130	17	11	米/千克		Cheese cloth, voiles and fine thin cloth, mixed with cotton, containing <85% by weight of artificial staple fibres, printed
5516.4400 50	与棉混纺印花人纤短纤机织帆布(混纺为以人纤短纤为主,但人造纤维短纤含量在85%以下)	10				130	17	11	米/千克		Canvas, mixed with cotton, containing <85% by weight of artificial staple fibres, printed
5516.4400 60	印花人纤短纤缎纹或斜纹机织物(与棉混纺,人造纤维短纤含量在85%以下)	10				130	17	11	米/千克		Woven fabrics, satin weave or twill weave, mixed with cotton, containing <85% by weight of artificial staple fibres, printed
5516.4400 70	与棉混纺印花人纤短纤牛津布(混纺为以人纤短纤为主,但人造纤维短纤含量在85%以下)	10				130	17	11	米/千克		Woven fabrics, oxford weave, mixed with cotton, containing < 85% by weight of artificial staple fibres, printed
5516.4400 90	与棉混纺印花人纤短纤其他机织物(混纺为以人纤短纤为主,但人造纤维短纤含量在85%以下)	10				130	17	11	米/千克		Other woven fabrics, mixed with cotton, containing <85% by weight of artificial staple fibres, printed
	-其他:										-Other:
5516.9100	--未漂白或漂白	12	8	0	0	130	17	11	米/千克		--Unbleached or bleached
5516.9100 10	未漂或漂白人纤短纤府绸或细平布(与其他纤维混纺,人造纤维短纤含量在85%以下)	12				130	17	11	米/千克		Poplin and fine plain cloth, mixed with other fibres, containing < 85% by weight of artificial staple fibres, unbleached or bleached
5516.9100 20	未漂或漂白人纤短纤机织平布(与其他纤维混纺,人造纤维短纤含量在85%以下)	12				130	17	11	米/千克		Plain cloth, mixed with other fibres, containing <85% by weight of artificial staple fibres, unbleached or bleached
5516.9100 30	未漂或漂白人纤短纤印染用布(与其他纤维混纺,人造纤维短纤含量在85%以下)	12				130	17	11	米/千克		Woven fabrics for printing and dying, mixed with other fibres, containing < 85% by weight of artificial staple fibres, unbleached or bleached
5516.9100 40	未漂或漂白人纤短纤奶酪布等(与其他纤维混纺,人纤短纤含量<85%,含薄细布,巴里纱	12				130	17	11	米/千克		Cheese cloth, voiles and fine thin cloth, mixed with other fibres, containing <85% by weight of artificial staple fibres, unbleached or bleached
5516.9100 50	未漂或漂白人纤短纤机织帆布(与其他纤维混纺,人造纤维短纤含量在85%以下)	12				130	17	11	米/千克		Canvas, mixed with other fibres, containing < 85% by weight of artificial staple fibres, unbleached or bleached

税则号列 Tariff Item.	货品名称	最惠国(%) MFN	协定(%) 东盟 CA	中巴 CP	CT 中智 CC	普通 Gen	增值税率 VAT	出口退税 ED	计量单位 Unit	监管条件 SC	Article Description
5516.9100 60	未漂或漂白人纤短纤缎纹或斜纹布(与其他纤维混纺,人造纤维短纤含量在85%以下)	12				130	17	11	米/千克		Woven fabrics, satin weave or twill weave, mixed with other fibres, containing <85% by weight of artificial staple fibres, unbleached or bleached
5516.9100 70	未漂或漂白人纤短纤牛津布(与其他纤维混纺,人造纤维短纤含量在85%以下)	12				130	17	11	米/千克		Woven fabrics, oxford weave, mixed with other fibres, containing <85% by weight of artificial staple fibres, unbleached or bleached
5516.9100 90	未漂或漂白人纤短纤其他机织物(与其他纤维混纺,人造纤维短纤含量在85%以下)	12				130	17	11	米/千克		Other woven fabrics, mixed with other fibres, containing <85% by weight of artificial staple fibres, unbleached or bleached
5516.9200	--染色	10	8	0	0	130	17	11	米/千克		--Dyed
5516.9200 10	染色人纤短纤府绸或细平布(与其他纤维混纺,人造纤维短纤含量在85%以下)	10				130	17	11	米/千克		Poplin and fine plain cloth, mixed with other fibres, containing <85% by weight of artificial staple fibres, dyed
5516.9200 20	染色人纤短纤机织平布(与其他纤维混纺,人造纤维短纤含量在85%以下)	10				130	17	11	米/千克		Plain cloth, mixed with other fibres, containing <85% by weight of artificial staple fibres, dyed
5516.9200 30	染色人纤短纤印染用布(与其他纤维混纺,人造纤维短纤含量在85%以下)	10				130	17	11	米/千克		Woven fabrics for printing and dying, mixed with other fibres, containing <85% by weight of artificial staple fibres, dyed
5516.9200 40	染色人纤短纤奶酪布等(与其他纤维混纺,人纤短纤含量<85%,含薄细布、巴里纱)	10				130	17	11	米/千克		Cheese cloth, voiles and fine thin cloth, mixed with other fibres, containing <85% by weight of artificial staple fibres, dyed
5516.9200 50	染色人纤短纤机织帆布(与其他纤维混纺,人造纤维短纤含量在85%以下)	10				130	17	11	米/千克		Canvas, mixed with other fibres, containing <85% by weight of artificial staple fibres, dyed
5516.9200 60	染色人纤短纤缎纹或斜纹机织物(与其他纤维混纺,人造纤维短纤含量在85%以下)	10				130	17	11	米/千克		Woven fabrics, satin weave or twill weave, mixed with other fibres, containing <85% by weight of artificial staple fibres, dyed
5516.9200 70	染色人纤短纤牛津布(与其他纤维混纺,人造纤维短纤含量在85%以下)	10				130	17	11	米/千克		Woven fabrics, oxford weave, mixed with other fibres, containing <85% by weight of artificial staple fibres, dyed
5516.9200 90	染色人纤短纤其他机织物(与其他纤维混纺,人造纤维短纤含量在85%以下)	10				130	17	11	米/千克		Other woven fabrics, mixed with other fibres, containing <85% by weight of artificial staple fibres, dyed
5516.9300	--色织	10	8	0	0	130	17	11	米/千克		--Of yarns of different colours
5516.9300 10	人纤短纤色织蓝粗斜纹布(与其他纤维混纺,人造纤维短纤含量在85%以下)	10				130	17	11	米/千克		Blue denim, twill weave, mixed with other fibres, containing <85% by weight of artificial staple fibres, of different collours

税则号列 Tariff Item.	货品名称	最惠国(%) MFN	协定(%) CT 东盟 CA	中巴 CP	中智 CC	普通 Gen	增值税率 VAT	出口退税 ED	计量单位 Unit	监管条件 SC	Article Description
5516.9300 20	色织人纤短纤提花机织物(与其他纤维混纺,人造纤维短纤含量在85%以下)	10				130	17	11	米/千克		Woven fabrics, jacquard weave, mixed with other fibres, containing <85% by weight of artificial staple fibres, of different collours
5516.9300 90	色织人纤短纤其他机织物(与其他纤维混纺,人造纤维短纤含量在85%以下)	10				130	17	11	米/千克		Other woven fabrics, mixed with other fibres, containing <85% by weight of artificial staple fibres, of different colours
5516.9400	--印花	10	8	0	0	130	17	11	米/千克		--Printed
5516.9400 10	印花人造纤维短纤府绸或细平布(与其他纤维混纺,按重量计人造纤维短纤含量在85%以下)	10				130	17	11	米/千克		Poplin and fine plain cloth, mixed with other fibres, containing < 85% by weight of artificial staple fibres, printed
5516.9400 20	印花人造纤维短纤机织平布(与其他纤维混纺,按重量计人造纤维短纤含量在85%以下)	10				130	17	11	米/千克		Plain cloth, mixed with other fibres, containing <85% by weight of artificial staple fibres, printed
5516.9400 30	印花人造纤维短纤印染用布(与其他纤维混纺,按重量计人造纤维短纤含量在85%以下)	10				130	17	11	米/千克		Woven fabrics for printing and dying, mixed with other fibres, containing < 85% by weight of artificial staple fibres, printed
5516.9400 40	印花人造纤维短纤奶酪布等(含薄细布、巴里纱,与其他纤维混纺,含人纤短纤<85%)	10				130	17	11	米/千克		Cheese cloth, voiles and fine thin cloth, mixed with other fibres, containing <85% by weight of artificial staple fibres, printed
5516.9400 50	印花人造纤维短纤机织帆布(与其他纤维混纺,按重量计人造纤维短纤含量在85%以下)	10				130	17	11	米/千克		Canvas, mixed with other fibres, containing < 85% by weight of artificial staple fibres, printed
5516.9400 60	印花人纤短纤缎纹或斜纹机织物(与其他纤维混纺,按重量计人造纤维短纤含量在85%以下)	10				130	17	11	米/千克		Woven fabrics, satin weave or twill weave, mixed with other fibres, containing <85% by weight of artificial staple fibres, printed
5516.9400 70	印花人造纤维短纤牛津布(与其他纤维混纺,按重量计人造纤维短纤含量在85%以下)	10				130	17	11	米/千克		Woven fabrics, oxford weave, mixed with other fibres, containing <85% by weight of artificial staple fibres, printed
5516.9400 90	印花人造纤维短纤其他机织物(与其他纤维混纺,按重量计人造纤维短纤含量在85%以下)	10				130	17	11	米/千克		Other woven fabrics, mixed with other fibres, containing <85% by weight of artificial staple fibres, printed

第五十六章
絮胎、毡呢及无纺织物；特种纱线；线、绳、索、缆及其制品

注释：

一、本章不包括：

(一)用各种物质或制剂(例如，第三十三章的香水或化妆品、税目34.01的肥皂或洗涤剂、税目34.05的光洁剂及类似制剂、税目38.09的织物柔软剂)浸渍、涂布、包覆的絮胎、毡呢或无纺织物，其中的纺织材料仅作为承载介质；

(二)税目58.11的纺织产品；

(三)以毡呢或无纺织物为底的砂布及类似品(税目68.05)；

(四)以毡呢或无纺织物为底的粘聚或复制云母(税目68.14)；

(五)以毡呢或无纺织物为底的金属箔(通常为第十四类或第十五类)。

二、所称"毡呢"，包括针刺机制毡呢以及纤维本身通过缝编工序增强了抱合力的纺织纤维网状织物。

三、税目56.02及56.03分别包括用各种性质(紧密结构或泡沫状)的塑料或橡胶浸渍、涂布、包覆或层压的毡呢及无纺织物。

税目56.03还包括用塑料或橡胶作粘合材料的无纺织物。

但税目56.02及56.03不包括：

(一)用塑料或橡胶浸渍、涂布、包覆或层压，按重量计纺织材料含量在50%及以下的毡呢或者完全嵌入塑料或橡胶之内的毡呢(第三十九章或第四十章)；

(二)完全嵌入塑料或橡胶之内的无纺织物，以及用肉眼可辨别出两面都用塑料或橡胶涂布、包覆的无纺织物，涂布或包覆所引起的颜色变化可不予考虑(第三十九章或第四十章)；

(三)与毡呢或无纺织物混制的泡沫塑料或海绵橡胶板、片或扁条，纺织材料仅在其中起增强作用(第三十九章或第四十章)。

四、税目56.04不包括用肉眼无法辨别出是否经过浸渍、涂布或包覆的纺织纱线或税目54.04或54.05的扁条及类似品(通常归入第五十章至第五十五章)；运用本条规定，可不考虑浸渍、涂布或包覆所引起的颜色变化。

Chapter 56
Wadding, felt and nonwovens; special yarns; twine, cordage, ropes and cables and articles thereof

Notes:

1. This Chapter does not cover:

(a) Wadding, felt or nonwovens, impregnated, coated or covered with substances or preparations (for example, pefumes or cosmetics of Chapter 33, soaps or detergents of heading No. 34.01, polishes, creams or similar preparations of heading No. 34.05, fabric softeners of heading No. 38.09) where the textile material is present merely as a carrying medium;

(b) Textile products of heading No. 58.11;

(c) Natural or artificial abrasive powder or grain, on a backing of felt or nonwovens (heading No. 68.05);

(d) Agglomerated or reconstituted mica, on a backing of felt or nonwovens (heading No. 68.14); or

(e) Metal foil on a backing of felt or nonwovens (Usually section XIV or XV).

2. The term "felt" includes needleloom felt and fabrics consisting of a web of textile fibres the cohesion of which has been enhanced by a stitch-bonding process using fibres from the web itself.

3. Headings Nos. 56.02 and 56.03 cover respectively felt and nonwovens, impregnated, coated, covered or laminated with plastics or rubber whatever the nature of these materials (compact or cellular). Heading No. 56.03 also includes nonwovens in which plastics or rubber forms the bonding substance.

Headings Nos. 56.02 and 56.03 do not, however, cover:

(a) Felt impregnated, coated, covered or laminated with plastics or rubber, containing 50% or less by weight of textile material or felt completely embedded in plastics or rubber (Chapter 39 or 40);

(b) Nonwovens, either completely embedded in plastics or rubber, or entirely coated or covered on both sides with such materials, provided that such coating or covering can be seen with the naked eye with no account being taken of any resulting change of colour (Chapter 39 or 40); or

(c) Plates, sheets or strips of cellular plastics or cellular rubber combined with felt or nonwovens, where the textile material is present merely for reinforcing purposes (Chapter 39 or 40).

4. Heading No. 56.04 does not cover textile yarn, or strip or the like of heading No. 54.04 or 54.05, in which the impregnation, coating or covering cannot be seen with the naked eye (usually Chapters 50 to 55); for the purpose of this provision, no account should be taken of any resulting change of colour.

税则号列 Tariff Item.	货品名称	最惠国(%) MFN	协定(%)CT 东盟 CA	中巴 CP	中智 CC	普通 Gen	增值税率 VAT	出口退税 ED	计量单位 Unit	监管条件 SC	Article Description
56.01	**纺织材料絮胎及其制品；长度不超过5毫米的纺织纤维(纤维屑)、纤维粉末及球结：**										**Wadding of textile materials and articles thereof; textile fibres, not exceeding 5 mm in length (flock), textile dust and mill neps:**
5601.1000	-絮胎制的卫生巾及止血塞、婴儿尿布或尿布垫及类似卫生用品	10	5		0	80	17	11	千克		-Sanitary towels and tampons, napkins and napkin liners for babies and similar sanitary articles, of wadding
5601.1000 10	棉絮胎制卫生巾、止血塞等(包括婴儿尿布或尿布垫及类似卫生用品)	10				80	17	11	千克		Sanitary towels and tampons, napkins and napkin liners for babies and similar sanitary articles, of wadding, of cotton
5601.1000 90	絮胎制卫生巾、止血塞等(包括婴儿尿布或尿布垫及类似卫生用品)	10				80	17	11	千克		Sanitary towels and tampons, napkins and napkin liners for babies and similar sanitary articles, of wadding, of other textile materials
	-絮胎；其他絮胎制品：										-Wadding; other articles of wadding:
5601.2100	--棉制	10	T3		0	50	17	11	千克		--Of cotton
5601.2100 10	棉制的成匹絮胎	10				50	17	11	千克		Wadding of cotton, in the piece
5601.2100 90	其他棉制的絮胎及絮胎制品	10				50	17	11	千克		Other wadding and articles of wadding of cotton
	--化学纤维制：										--Of man-made fibres:
5601.2210	---卷烟滤嘴	12	8		0	100	17	11	千克	7	---Cigarette filter tips
5601.2290	---其他	12	8		0	100	17	11	千克		---Other
5601.2290 10	化学纤维制的成匹絮胎	12				100	17	11	千克		Wadding of man-made fibres in the piece
5601.2290 90	化学纤维制的其他絮胎及絮胎制品	12				100	17	11	千克		Other wadding and articles of wadding of man-made fibres
5601.2900	--其他	10	8		0	90	17	11	千克		--Other
5601.2900 10	羊毛或动物细毛制絮胎及制品	10				90	17	11	千克		Wadding and articles of wadding of wool or fine animal hair
5601.2900 90	其他纺织材料制絮胎及制品	10				90	17	11	千克		Wadding and articles of wadding of other textile materials
5601.3000	-纤维屑、纤维粉末及球结	10	8		0	100	17	11	千克		-Textile flock and dust and mill neps
5601.3000 10	由两种或以上有机聚合物纺制的纤维(横截面为皮芯结构或并列结构或海岛结构,长度不超过5mm)	10				100	17	11	千克		Textile fibres of two or more organic polymers (skin/core, side-by-side or island-in-the-sea type cross-section, length≤5mm)
5601.3000 90	纺织纤维屑,纤维粉末及球结(纺织纤维长度不超过5mm)	10				100	17	11	千克		Textile flock and dust and mill neps, length≤5mm
56.02	**毡呢,不论是否浸渍、涂布、包覆或层压：**										**Felt, whether or not impregnated, coated, covered or laminated:**
5602.1000	-针刺机制毡呢及纤维缝编织物	10	T3		0	100	17	11	千克		-Needleloom felt and stitch-bonded fibre fabrics
5602.1000 10	毛制针刺机制毡呢及纤维缝编织(不论是否浸渍,涂布,包覆或层压)	10				100	17	11	千克		Needleloom felt and stitch-bonded fibre fabrics, of wool or other animal hair
5602.1000 90	其他纺织料制针刺机制毡呢等(含缝编织物,不论是否浸渍、涂布、包覆或层压)	10				100	17	11	千克		Needleloom felt and stitch-bonded fibre fabrics, of other textile materials

税则号列 Tariff Item.	货品名称	最惠国(%) MFN	协定(%) 东盟 CA	中巴 CP	CT 中智 CC	普通 Gen	增值税率 VAT	出口退税 ED	计量单位 Unit	监管条件 SC	Article Description
	-其他毡呢,未浸渍、涂布、包覆或层压:										-Other felt, not impregnated, coated, covered or laminated:
5602.2100	--羊毛或动物细毛制	10	8		0	100	17	11	千克		--Of wool or fine animal hair
5602.2900	--其他纺织材料制	10	8		0	100	17	11	千克		--Of other textile materials
5602.9000	-其他	10	8		0	100	17	11	千克		-Other
5602.9000 10	其他纺织材料制其他毡呢(层压)	10				100	17	11	千克		Other felt, of other textile materials, laminated
5602.9000 91	化学纤维制其他毡呢(浸渍、涂布、包覆)	10				100	17	11	千克		Other felt, of man-made fibres impregnated, coated, covered
5602.9000 99	其他纺织材料制其他毡呢(浸渍、涂布、包覆)	10				100	17	11	千克		Other felt, impregnated, coated, covered
56.03	**无纺织物,不论是否浸渍、涂布、包覆或层压:**										**Nonwovens, whether or not impregnated, coated, covered or laminated:**
	-化学纤维长丝制:										-Of man-made filaments:
	--每平方米重量不超过25克:										--Weighing not more than 25 g/m²
5603.1110	---经浸渍、涂布、包覆或层压	10	T3	0	0	70	17	11	千克		---Impregnated, coated, covered or laminated
5603.1190	---其他	10	8	0	0	130	17	11	千克		---Other
	--每平方米重量超过25克,但不超过70克:										--Weighing more than 25 g/m² but not more than 70 g/m²:
5603.1210	---经浸渍、涂布、包覆或层压	10	T3	0	0	70	17	11	千克		---Impregnated, coated, covered or laminated
5603.1290	---其他	10	8	0	0	130	17	11	千克		---Other
	--每平方米重量超过70克,但不超过150克:										--Weighing more than 70 g/m² but not more than 150 g/m²:
5603.1310	---经浸渍、涂布、包覆或层压	10	8	0	0	70	17	11	千克		---Impregnated, coated, covered or laminated
5603.1390	---其他	10	8	0	0	130	17	11	千克		---Other
	--每平方米重量超过150克:										--Weighing more than 150 g/m²:
5603.1410	---经浸渍、涂布、包覆或层压	10	8	0	0	70	17	11	千克		---Impregnated, coated, covered or laminated
5603.1490	---其他	10	8	0	0	130	17	11	千克		---Other
	-其他:										-Other:
	--每平方米重量不超过25克:										--Weighing not more than 25 g/m²:
5603.9110	---经浸渍、涂布、包覆或层压	10	8	0	0	70	17	11	千克		---Impregnated, coated, covered or laminated
5603.9190	---其他	10	8	0	0	85	17	11	千克		---Other
	--每平方米重量超过25克,但不超过70克:										--Weighing more than 25 g/m² but not more than 70 g/m²:
5603.9210	---经浸渍、涂布、包覆或层压	10	T3	0	0	70	17	11	千克		---Impregnated, coated, covered or laminated
5603.9290	---其他	10	T3	0	0	85	17	11	千克		---Other
	--每平方米重量超过70克,但不超过150克:										--Weighing more than 70 g/m² but not more than 150 g/m²:
5603.9310	---经浸渍、涂布、包覆或层压	10	T3	0	0	70	17	11	千克		---Impregnated, coated, covered or laminated
5603.9390	---其他	10	T3	0	0	85	17	11	千克		---Other
	--每平方米重量超过150克:										--Weighing more than 150 g/m²:
5603.9410	---经浸渍、涂布、包覆或层压	10	T3	0	0	70	17	11	千克		---Impregnated, coated, covered or laminated

税则号列 Tariff Item.	货品名称	最惠国(%) MFN	协定(%)CT 东盟 CA	中巴 CP	中智 CC	普通 Gen	增值税率 VAT	出口退税 ED	计量单位 Unit	监管条件 SC	Article Description
5603.9410 11	毛制铺地品衬底用物纺织物(浸渍、涂布、包覆或压层,每平米重>150克)	10				70	17	11	千克		Nonwovens floor coverings, on a backing of wool or animal hair impregnated, coated, covered or laminated, w >150g/m^2
5603.9410 19	其他材料制铺地品衬底用无纺织物(浸渍、涂布、包覆或压层,每平米重>150克)	10				70	17	11	千克		Nonwovens floor coverings, on a backing of other materials impregnated, coated, covered or laminated, w > 150g/m^2
5603.9410 90	其他材料制无纺织物(浸渍、涂布、包覆或压层,每平米重>150克)	10				70	17	11	千克		Nonwovens of other materials impregnated, coated, covered or laminated, w >150g/m^2
5603.9490	---其他	10	T3	0	0	85	17	11	千克		---Other
5603.9490 11	毛制铺地品衬底用无纺织物(每平米重>150克)	10				85	17	11	千克		Nonwovens floor coverings, on a backing of wool or animal hair, w > 150g/m^2
5603.9490 19	其他材料制铺地品衬底用无纺织物(每平米重>150克)	10				85	17	11	千克		Nonwovens floor coverings, on a backing of other materials, w >150g/m^2
5603.9490 90	其他材料制无纺织物(每平方米重量超过150克)	10				85	17	11	千克		Nonwovens of other materials, w > 150g/m^2
56.04	**用纺织材料包覆的橡胶线及绳;用橡胶或塑料浸渍、涂布、包覆或套裹的纺织纱线及税目54.04或54.05的扁条及类似品:**										**Rubber thread and cord, textile covered; textile yarn, and strip and the like of heading No. 54.04 or 54.05, impregnated, coated, covered or sheathed with rubber or plastics:**
5604.1000	-用纺织材料包覆的橡胶线及绳	5	T3	0	0	80	17	11	千克		-Rubber thread and cord, textile covered
5604.9000	-其他	5		0	0	80	17	11	千克		-Other
5604.9000 10	棉制纱线(用橡胶或塑料浸渍、涂布、包覆、套裹)	5				80	17	11	千克		Cotton yarn, impregnated, coated, covered or sheathed, with rubber or plastics
5604.9000 20	品目5404的合成纤维单丝、扁条(用橡胶或塑料浸渍、涂布、包覆、套裹)	5				80	17	11	千克		Synthetic monofilament or strip of heading 5404, impregnated or coated covered or sheathed, with rubber or plastics
5604.9000 30	品目5404的人造纤维单丝、扁条(用橡胶或塑料浸渍、涂布、包覆、套裹)	5				80	17	11	千克		Artificial monofilament or strip of heading 5404, impregnated, coated, covered or sheathed, with rubber or plastics
5604.9000 90	其他纺织纱线(用橡胶或塑料浸渍、涂布、包覆、套裹)	5				80	17	11	千克		Other textile yarn, impregnated, coated, covered or sheathed, with rubber or plastics
56.05	**含金属纱线,不论是否螺旋花线,由纺织纱线或税目54.04或54.05的扁条及类似品与金属线、扁条或粉末混合制得或用金属包覆制得:**										**Metallized yarn, whether or not gimped, being textile yarn, or strip or the like of heading No. 54.04 or 54.05, combined with metal in the form of thread, strip or powder or covered with metal:**

税则号列 Tariff Item.	货品名称	最惠国(%) MFN	协定(%) CT 东盟 CA	中巴 CP	中智 CC	普通 Gen	增值税率 VAT	出口退税 ED	计量单位 Unit	监管条件 SC	Article Description
5605.0000	含金属纱线,不论是否螺旋花线,由纺织纱线或税目54.04或54.05的扁条及类似品与金属线、扁条或粉末混合制得或用金属包覆制得	5			0	70	17	11	千克		Metallzied yarn, whether or not gimped, being textile yarn, or strip or the like of heading 54.04 or 54.05, combined with metal in the form of thread, strip or powder or covered with metal
5605.0000 10	金属涂层或层压化纤长丝等(扁条及类似品,非螺旋,未加捻或捻度每米低于5转)	5				70	17	11	千克		Man-made filament fibres, coated or laminated with metal (strip or the like, not gimped, not twisted or twist <5turns/m)
5605.0000 90	其他含金属纱线,可含螺旋花边(与金属线、扁条或粉末混合制的或用金属包覆制)	5				70	17	11	千克		Other metallized yarn, gimped, combined with metal in the form of thread, strip or powder or covered with metal
56.06	**粗松螺旋花线,税目54.04或54.05的扁条及类似品制的螺旋花线(税目56.05的货品及马毛粗松螺旋花线除外);绳绒线(包括植绒绳绒线);纵行起圈纱线:**										**Gimped yarn, and strip and the like of heading No. 54.04 or 54.05, gimped (other than those of heading No. 56, 05 and gimped horsehair yarn); chenille yarn (including flock chenille yarn); loop wale -yarn:**
5606.0000	粗松螺旋花线,税目54.04或54.05的扁条及类似品制的螺旋花线(税目56.05的货品及马毛粗松螺旋花线除外);绳绒线(包括植绒绳绒线);纵行起圈纱线	5			0	70	17	11	千克		Gimped yarn, and strip and the like of heading No. 54.04 or 54.05, gimped (other than those of heading No. 56,05 and gimped horsehair yarn); chenille yarn (including flock chenille yarn); loopwale-yarn
56.07	**线、绳、索、缆,不论是否编织或编结而成,也不论是否用橡胶或塑料浸渍、涂布、包覆或套裹:**										**Twine, cordage, ropes and cables, whether or not plaited or braided and whether or not impregnated, coated, covered or sheathed with rubber or plastics:**
	-西沙尔麻或其他纺织用龙舌兰类纤维纺制:										-Of sisal or other textile fibres of the genus Agave:
5607.2100	--包扎用绳	5			0	50	17	11	千克		--Binder or baler twine
5607.2100 10	剑麻或其他龙舌兰纤维制包扎用绳(农机用,可编织或编结,可用橡胶或塑料浸涂包覆套裹)	5				50	17	11	千克		Binder or baler twine of sisal or other textile fibres of the genus agave for agricultural machinery, plaited or braided, impregnated or coated covered or sheathed with rubber or plastics
5607.2100 90	剑麻或龙舌兰纤维制其他包扎用绳(农机用,可编织或编结,可用橡胶或塑料浸涂包覆套裹)	5				50	17	11	千克		Other binder or baler twine of sisal or other textile fibres of the genus agave for other use, plaited or braided, impregnated or coated covered or sheathed with rubber or plastics
5607.2900	--其他	5			0	50	17	11	千克		--Other
	-聚乙烯或聚丙烯纺制:										-Of polyethylene or polypropylene:
5607.4100	--包扎用绳	5			0	100	17	11	千克		--Binder or baler twine

税则号列 Tariff Item.	货品名称	最惠国(%) MFN	协定(%) 东盟 CA	中巴 CP	CT 中智 CC	普通 Gen	增值税率 VAT	出口退税 ED	计量单位 Unit	监管条件 SC	Article Description
5607.4100 10	宽的非裂膜扁条聚乙烯包扎用绳(可编织或编结,可用橡胶或塑料浸渍涂布,包覆,套裹)	5				100	17	11	千克		Binder or baler twine of polyethylene, wide strip of non-split film fibre, plaited or braided, impregnated or coated covered or sheathed, with rubber or plastics
5607.4100 90	其他聚乙烯或聚丙烯制包扎用绳(可编织或编结,可用橡胶或塑料浸渍涂布,包覆,套裹)	5				100	17	11	千克		Other binder or baler twine of polyethylene or polypropylene, plaited or braided impregnated or coated covered or sheathed with rubber or plastics
5607.4900	--其他	5			0	100	17	11	千克		--Other
5607.4900 10	宽非裂膜扁条聚乙烯其他线绳索缆(可编织或编结,用橡胶或塑料浸,涂,包,套,含聚丙烯制)	5				100	17	11	千克		Other twine, cordage, ropes and cables, of polyethylene or polypropylene, wide strip of non-split film fibre, plaited or braided, impregnated or coated covered or sheathed, with rubber or plastics
5607.4900 20	其他聚乙烯或聚丙烯制线绳索缆(未经编织或编结,可用橡胶或塑料浸渍涂布,包覆,套裹)	5				100	17	11	千克		Other twine, cordage, ropes and cables of polyethylene or polypropylene, not plaited or braided, impregnated or coated covered or sheathed, with rubber or plastics
5607.4900 90	其他聚乙烯或聚丙烯制线绳索缆(已编织或编结,可用橡胶或塑料浸渍涂布,包覆,套裹)	5				100	17	11	千克		Other twine, cordage, ropes and cables of polyethylene or polypropylene, plaited or braided, impregnated or coated covered or sheathed, with rubber or plastics
5607.5000	-其他合成纤维纺制	5			0	100	17	11	千克		-Of other synthetic fibres
5607.5000 10	其他合纤制未编织或编织线绳索缆(可用橡胶或塑料浸渍涂布,包覆,套裹)	5				100	17	11	千克		Twine, cordage, ropes and cables of other synthetic fibres, not plaited or braided, impregnated or coated covered or sheathed with rubber or plastics
5607.5000 90	其他合纤制已编织或编织线绳索缆(可用橡胶或塑料浸渍涂布,包覆,套裹)	5				100	17	11	千克		Twine, cordage, ropes and cables of other synthetic fibres, plaited or braided, impregnated or coated covered or sheathed, with rubber or plastics
	-其他:										-Other:
5607.9010	---蕉麻(马尼拉麻)或其他硬质(叶)纤维纺制	5			0	50	17	11	千克		---Of abaca (Manila hemp or *Musa textilis Nee*) or other hard (leaf) fibres
5607.9090	---其他	5	T3		0	100	17	11	千克		---Other
5607.9090 10	大麻制线,绳,索,缆(可编织或编结,可用橡胶或塑料浸渍涂布,包覆,套裹)	5				100	17	11	千克		Twine, cordage, ropes and cables of hemp, plaited or braided, impregnated or coated covered or sheathed, with rubber or plastics
5607.9090 90	其他纺织材料制线,绳,索,缆(可编织或编结,可用橡胶或塑料浸渍涂布、包覆、套裹)	5				100	17	11	千克		Twine, cordage, ropes and cables of other textile materials, plaited or braided, impregnated or coated covered or sheathed, with rubber or plastics

税则号列 Tariff Item.	货品名称	最惠国(%) MFN	协定(%) CT			普通 Gen	增值税率 VAT	出口退税 ED	计量单位 Unit	监管条件 SC	Article Description
			东盟 CA	中巴 CP	中智 CC						
56.08	**线、绳或索结制的网料；纺织材料制成的渔网及其他网：**										**Knotted netting of twine, cordage or rope; made up fishing nets and other made up nets, of textile materials：**
	-化学纤维材料制：										-Of man-made textile materials：
5608.1100	--制成的渔网	10	5		0	50	17	11	千克		--Made up fishing nets
5608.1100 10	化纤材料制成手撒线拉的渔网	10				50	17	11	千克		Casting made up fishing nets of man-made textile materials
5608.1100 90	化纤材料制成其他渔网	10				50	17	11	千克	5	Other made up fishing nets of man-made textile materials
5608.1900	--其他	12	8		0	100	17	11	千克		--Other
5608.1900 10	化纤材料制用拉线收口的诱饵包（罗网及篓状网除外）	12				100	17	11	千克		Bait bag with a drawstring, other than toils or basket-shaped nets, of man-made textile materials
5608.1900 90	化纤材料制成的网料和其他网（包括化纤线、绳、索结制的网料，罗网及篓状网除外）	12				100	17	11	千克	5	Other knotted netting of twine, cordage or rope; made up fishing nets and other made up nets, of textile materials of man-made textile materials, other than toils or basket-shaped nets
5608.9000	-其他	10	5		0	100	17	11	千克		-Other
5608.9000 11	毛、棉制的渔网	10				100	17	11	千克		Made up fishing nets of wool of animal or of cotton
5608.9000 19	其他纺织纤维制的渔网	10				100	17	11	千克		Made up fishing nets of other textile materials
5608.9000 91	棉制的其他网及网料（吊床，罗网及篓状网除外）	10				100	17	11	千克	5	Made up fishing nets of cotton, other than nammock, toils or basket-shaped nets
5608.9000 92	毛制的其他网及网料（包括棉制的网式吊床，罗网及篓状网除外）	10				100	17	11	千克		Made up nets and knotted netting of wool or animal hair, including nammock of cotton, other than toils or basket-shaped nets
5608.9000 99	其他纺织纤维制成的其他网及网料（罗网及篓状网除外）	10				100	17	11	千克		Other made up nets and knotted netting of other textile materials, other than toils or basket-shaped nets
56.09	**用纱线、税目54.04或54.05的扁条及类似品或线、绳、索、缆制成的其他税目未列名物品：**										**Articles of yarn, strip or the like of heading No. 54.04 or 54.05, twine, cordage, rope or cables, not elsewhere specified or included：**
5609.0000	用纱线、税目54.04或54.05的扁条及类似品或线、绳、索、缆制成的其他税目未列名物品	10	5		0	100	17	11	千克		Articles of yarn, strip or the like of heading No. 54.04 or 54.05, twine, cordage, rope or cables, not elsewhere specified or included

第五十七章
地毯及纺织材料的其他铺地制品

Chapter 57
Carpets and other textile floor coverings

注释：

一、本章所称"地毯及纺织材料的其他铺地制品"，是指使用时以纺织材料作面的铺地制品，也包括具有纺织材料铺地制品特征但作其他用途的物品。

二、本章不包括铺地制品衬垫。

Notes:

1. For the purposes of this Chapter, the term "carpets and other textile-floor coverings" means floor coverings in which textile materials serve as the exposed surface of the article when in use and includes articles having the characteristics of textile floor coverings but intended for use for other purposes.

2. This Chapter does not cover floor covering underlays.

税则号列 Tariff Item.	货品名称	最惠国(%) MFN	协定(%)CT 东盟 CA	中巴 CP	中智 CC	普通 Gen	增值税率 VAT	出口退税 ED	计量单位 Unit	监管条件 SC	Article Description
57.01	**结织栽绒地毯及纺织材料的其他结织栽绒铺地制品，不论是否制成的：**										**Carpets and other textile floor coverings, knotted, whether or not made up:**
5701.1000	-羊毛或动物细毛制	14	8		0	130	17	13	平方米		-Of wool or fine animal hair
	-其他纺织材料制：										-Of other textile materials:
5701.9010	---化学纤维制	16	8		0	130	17	13	平方米		---Of man-made textile materials
5701.9020	---丝制	14	8		0	100	17	13	平方米		---Of silk
5701.9090	---其他	14	8		0	100	17	13	平方米		---Other
57.02	**机织地毯及纺织材料的其他机织铺地制品，未簇绒或未植绒，不论是否制成的，包括"开来姆"、"苏麦克"、"卡拉马尼"及类似的手织地毯：**										**Carpets and other textile floor coverings, woven, not tufted or flocked, whether or not made up, including "Kelem", "Schumacks", "Karamanie" and similar hand-woven rugs:**
5702.1000	-"开来姆"、"苏麦克"、"卡拉马尼"及类似的手织地毯	14	8	0	0	130	17	13	平方米		-"Kelem", "Schumacks", "Karamanie" and similar hand-woven rugs
5702.2000	-椰壳纤维制的铺地制品	14	8	0	0	100	17	13	平方米		-Floor coverings of coconut fibres (coir)
	-其他起绒结构的铺地制品，未制成的：										-Other, of pile construction, not made up:
5702.3100	--羊毛或动物细毛制	10	8	0	0	130	17	13	平方米		--Of wool or fine animal hair
5702.3200	--化学纤维制	16	8	5	0	130	17	13	平方米		--Of man-made textile materials
5702.3900	--其他纺织材料制	14	8	0	0	100	17	13	平方米		--Of other textile materials
	-其他起绒结构的铺地制品，制成的：										-Other, of pile construction, made up:
5702.4100	--羊毛或动物细毛制	10	8	0	0	130	17	13	平方米		--Of wool or fine animal hair
5702.4200	--化学纤维制	10	8	0	0	130	17	13	平方米		--Of man-made textile materials
5702.4900	--其他纺织材料制	14	8	0	0	100	17	13	平方米		--Of other textile materials
	-其他非起绒结构的铺地制品，未制成的：										-Other, not of pile construction, not made up:
5702.5010	---羊毛或动物细毛制	14	8	0	0	130	17	13	平方米		---Of wool or fime animal hair
5702.5020	---化学纤维制	16	8	5	0	130	17	13	平方米		---Of man made textile materials
5702.5090	---其他纺织材料制	14	8	0	0	100	17	13	平方米		---Of other textrle materials
	-其他非起绒结构的铺地制品，制成的：										-Other, not of pile construction, made up:
5702.9100	--羊毛或动物细毛制	14	8	0	0	130	17	13	平方米		--Of wool or fine animal hair
5702.9200	--化学纤维制	16	8	5	0	130	17	13	平方米		--Of man-made textile materials
5702.9900	--其他纺织材料制	14	8	0	0	100	17	13	平方米		--Of other textile materials

税则号列 Tariff Item.	货品名称	最惠国(%) MFN	协定(%) 东盟 CA	中巴 CP	CT 中智 CC	普通 Gen	增值税率 VAT	出口退税 ED	计量单位 Unit	监管条件 SC	Article Description
57.03	**簇绒地毯及纺织材料的其他簇绒铺地制品,不论是否制成的:**										**Carpets and other textile floor coverings, tufted, whether or not made up:**
5703.1000	-羊毛或动物细毛制	14	T3		0	130	17	13	平方米		-Of wool or fine animal hair
5703.2000	-尼龙或其他聚酰胺制	10	8		0	130	17	13	平方米		-Of nylon or other polyamides
5703.3000	-其他化学纤维制	10	8		0	130	17	13	平方米		-Of other man-made textile materials
5703.9000	-其他纺织材料制	14	T3		0	100	17	13	平方米		-Of other textile materials
57.04	**毡呢地毯及纺织材料的其他毡呢铺地制品,未簇绒或未植绒,不论是否制成的:**										**Carpets and other textile floor coverings, of felt, not tufted or flocked, whether or not made up:**
5704.1000	-最大表面面积不超过0.3平方米	14	8		0	130	17	13	平方米		-Tiles, having a maximum surface area of 0.3 m^2
5704.9000	-其他	10	8		0	130	17	13	平方米		-Other
57.05	**其他地毯及纺织材料的其他铺地制品,不论是否制成的:**										**Other carpets and other textile floor coverings, whether or not made up:**
5705.0010	---羊毛或动物细毛制	14	T3		0	130	17	13	平方米		---Of wool or fine animal hair
5705.0020	---化学纤维制	10	T3		0	130	17	13	平方米		---Of man-made textile materials
5705.0090	---其他纺织材料制	14	T3		0	100	17	13	平方米		---Other

第五十八章
特种机织物;簇绒织物;花边;装饰毯;装饰带;刺绣品

注释:

一、本章不适用于经浸渍、涂布、包覆或层压的第五十九章注释一所述的纺织物或第五十九章的其他货品。

二、税目58.01也包括因未将浮纱割断而使表面无竖绒的纬起绒织物。

三、税目58.03所称“纱罗”,是指经线全部或部分由地经纱和绞经纱构成的织物,其中绞经纱绕地经纱半圈、一圈或几圈而形成圈状,纬纱从圈中穿过。

四、税目58.04不适用于税目56.08的线、绳、索结制的网状织物。

五、税目58.06所称“狭幅机织物”,是指:

(一)幅宽不超过30厘米的机织物,不论是否织成或从宽幅料剪成,但两侧必须有织成的、胶粘的或用其他方法制成的布边;

(二)压平宽度不超过30厘米的圆筒机织物;

(三)折边的斜裁滚条布,其未折边时的宽度不超过30厘米。

流苏状的狭幅机织物归入税目58.08。

六、税目58.10所称“刺绣品”,除了一般纺织材料绣线绣制的刺绣品外,还包括在可见底布上用金属线或玻璃线刺绣的刺绣品,也包括用珠片、饰珠或纺织材料或其他材料制的装饰用花纹图案所缝绣的贴花织物。但不包括手工针绣嵌花装饰毯(税目58.05)。

七、除税目58.09的产品外,本章还包括金属线制的用于衣着、装饰及类似用途的物品。

Chapter 58
Special woven fabrics; tufted textile fabrics; lace; tapestries; trimmings; embroidery

Notes:

1. This Chapter does not apply to textile fabrics referred to in Note 1 to Chapter 59, impregnated, coated, covered or laminated, or to other goods of Chapter 59.
2. Heading No. 58.01 also includes woven weft pile fabrics which have not yet had the floats cut, at which stage they have no pile standing up.
3. For the purpose of heading No. 58.03, "gauze" means a fabric with a warp composed wholly or in part of standing or ground threads and crossing or doup threads which cross the standing or ground threads making a half turn, a complete turn or more to form loops through which weft threads pass.
4. Heading No. 58.04 does not apply to knotted net fabrics of twine, cordage or rope, of heading No. 56.08.
5. For the purposes of heading No. 58.06, the expression "narrow woven fabrics" means:
   (a) Woven fabrics of a width not exceeding 30 cm, whether woven as such or cut from wider pieces, provided with selvedges (woven, gummed or otherwise made) on both edges;
   (b) Tubular woven fabrics of a flattened width not exceeding 30 cm; and
   (c) Bias binding with folded edges, of a width when unfolded not exceeding 30 cm.

   Narrow woven fabrics with woven fringes are to be classified in heading No. 58.08.
6. In heading No. 58.10, the expression "embroidery" means, *inter alia*, embroidery with metal or glass thread on a visible ground of textile fabric, and sewn appliquè work of sequins, beads or ornamental motifs of textile or other materials. The heading does not apply to needlework tapestry (heading No. 58.05).
7. In addition to the products of heading No. 58.09, this Chapter also includes articles made of metal thread and of a kind used in apparel, as furnishing fabrics or for similar purposes.

税则号列 Tariff Item.	货品名称	最惠国(%) MFN	协定(%)CT 东盟 CA	中巴 CP	中智 CC	普通 Gen	增值税率 VAT	出口退税 ED	计量单位 Unit	监管条件 SC	Article Description
58.01	起绒机织物及绳绒织物,但税目58.02或58.06的织物除外:										Woven pile fabrics and chenille fabrics, other than fabrics of heading No. 58.02 or 58.06:
5801.1000	-羊毛或动物细毛制	10	8	0	0	130	17	13	米/千克		-Of wool or fine animal hair
	-棉制:										-Of cotton:
5801.2100	--不割绒的纬起绒织物	12	T3	0	0	70	17	13	米/千克		--Uncut weft pile fabrics
5801.2100 10	未漂白不割绒的棉制纬起绒织物(品目5802或5806的织物除外)	12				70	17	13	米/千克		Woven weft pile fabrics of cotton, uncut, other than fabrics of heading No. 58.02 or 58.06, unbleached

税则号列 Tariff Item.	货品名称	最惠国(%) MFN	协定(%) 东盟 CA	中巴 CP	CT 中智 CC	普通 Gen	增值税率 VAT	出口退税 ED	计量单位 Unit	监管条件 SC	Article Description
5801.2100 90	其他不割绒的棉制纬起绒织物(品目5802或5806的织物除外)	12				70	17	13	米/千克		Other woven weft pile fabrics of cotton, uncut, other than fabrics of heading No. 58.02 or 58.06, unbleached
5801.2200	--割绒的灯芯绒	10	5	0	0	70	17	13	米/千克		--Cut corduroy
5801.2300	--其他纬起绒织物	10	5	0	0	70	17	13	米/千克		--Other weft pile fabrics
5801.2300 10	未漂白其他棉制纬起绒织物(品目5802或5806的织物除外)	10				70	17	13	米/千克		Other woven weft pile fabrics of cotton, other than fabrics of heading No. 58.02 or 58.06, unbleached
5801.2300 90	其他棉制纬起绒织物(品目5802或5806的织物除外)	10				70	17	13	米/千克		Other woven weft pile fabrics of cotton, other than fabrics of heading No. 58.02 or 58.06
5801.2400	--不割绒的经起绒织物(棱纹绸)	10	5	0	0	70	17	13	米/千克		--Warp pile fabrics, èpinglè (uncut)
5801.2400 10	未漂白棉制不割绒经起绒织物(棱纹绸,品目5802或5806的织物除外)	10				70	17	13	米/千克		Woven warp pile fabrics, èpinglè, of cotton, uncut, other than fabrics of heading No. 58.02 or 58.06
5801.2400 90	其他不割绒的棉制经起绒织物(棱纹绸,品目5802或5806的织物除外)	10				70	17	13	米/千克		Other woven warp pile fabrics, èpinglè, of cotton, uncut, other than fabrics of heading No. 58.02 or 58.06
5801.2500	--割绒的经起绒织物	10	5	0	0	70	17	13	米/千克		--Warp pile fabrics, cut
5801.2500 10	未漂白棉制割绒的经起绒织物(品目5802或5806的织物除外)	10				70	17	13	米/千克		Woven warp pile fabrics, èpinglè, of cotton cut, other than fabrics of heading No. 58.02 or 58.06, unbleached
5801.2500 90	其他割绒的棉制经起绒织物(品目5802或5806的织物除外)	10				70	17	13	米/千克		Other woven warp pile fabrics, èpinglè, of cotton cut, other than fabrics of heading No. 58.02 or 58.06
5801.2600	--绳绒织物	10	5	0	0	70	17	13	米/千克		--Chenille fabrics
5801.2600 10	未漂白棉制绳绒织物(品目5802或5806的织物除外)	10				70	17	13	米/千克		Woven chenille fabrics of cotton, other than fabrics of heading No. 58.02 or 58.06, unbleached
5801.2600 90	其他棉制绳绒织物(品目5802或5806的织物除外)	10				70	17	13	米/千克		Other woven chenille fabrics of cotton, other than fabrics of heading No. 58.02 or 58.06
	-化学纤维制:										-Of man-made fibres:
5801.3100	--不割绒的纬起绒织物	10	8	0	0	130	17	13	米/千克		--Uncut weft pile fabrics
5801.3200	--割绒的灯芯绒	10	8	0	0	130	17	13	米/千克		--Cut corduroy
5801.3300	--其他纬起绒织物	10	T3	0	0	130	17	13	米/千克		--Other weft pile fabrics
5801.3400	--不割绒的经起绒织物(棱纹绸)	10	8	0	0	130	17	13	米/千克		--Warp pile fabrics, èpinglè (uncut)
5801.3500	--割绒的经起绒织物	10	8	0	0	130	17	13	米/千克		--Warp pile fabrics, cut
5801.3600	--绳绒织物	10	8	0	0	130	17	13	米/千克		--Chenille fabrics
	-其他纺织材料制:										-Of other textile materials:
5801.9010	---丝及绢丝制	10	8	0	0	130	17	13	米/千克		---Of silk or silk waste
5801.9090	---其他	10	8	0	0	80	17	13	米/千克		---Other
5801.9090 10	亚麻和苎麻起绒机织物及绳绒织物(品目5802或5806的织物除外)	10				80	17	13	米/千克		Woven chenille fabrics and pile fabrics, of flax and ramie, other than fabrics of heading No. 58.02 or 58.06

税则号列 Tariff Item.	货品名称	最惠国(%) MFN	协定(%)CT 东盟 CA	中巴 CP	中智 CC	普通 Gen	增值税率 VAT	出口退税 ED	计量单位 Unit	监管条件 SC	Article Description
5801.9090 90	其他材料制起绒机织物及绳绒织物(品目 5802 或 5806 的织物除外)	10				80	17	13	米/千克		Woven chenille fabrics and pile fabrics, of other materials, other than fabrics of heading No. 58.02 or 58.06
58.02	**毛巾织物及类似的毛圈机织物,但税目 58.06 的狭幅织物除外;簇绒织物,但税目 57.03 的产品除外:**										**Terry towelling and similar woven terry fabrics, other than narrow fabrics of heading No. 58.06; tufted textile fabrics, other than products of heading No. 57.03:**
	-棉制毛巾织物及类似毛圈机织物:										-Terry towelling and similar woven terry fabrics, of cotton:
5802.1100	--未漂白	12	T3	0	0	70	17	13	米/千克	a	--Unbleached
5802.1900	--其他	10	5	0	0	70	17	13	米/千克	a	--Other
	-其他纺织材料制的毛巾织物及类似的毛圈机织物:										-Terry towelling and similar woven terry fabrics, of other textile materials:
5802.2010	---丝及绢丝制	12	8	0	0	130	17	13	米/千克		---Of silk or silk waste
5802.2010 10	丝及绢丝毛巾织物及类似毛圈织物(品目 5806 的狭幅织物除外,含丝 85% 及以上)	12				130	17	13	米/千克		Terry towelling and similar woven terry fabrics of silk or silk waste, other than narrow fabrics of heading No. 58.06 containing≥85% by weight
5802.2010 90	丝及绢丝毛巾织物及类似毛圈织物(品目 5806 的狭幅织物除外,含丝 85% 以下)	12				130	17	13	米/千克		Terry towelling and similar woven terry fabrics of silk or silk waste, other than narrow fabrics of heading No. 58.06 containing <85% by weight
5802.2020	---羊毛或动物细毛制	12	8	0	0	130	17	13	米/千克		---Of wool or fine animal hair
5802.2030	---化学纤维制	14	8	0	0	130	17	13	米/千克		---Of man-made fibres
5802.2090	---其他	12	8	0	0	80	17	13	米/千克		---Other
	-簇绒织物:										-Tufted textile fabrics:
5802.3010	---丝及绢丝制	10	8	0	0	130	17	13	米/千克		---Of silk or silk waste
5802.3010 10	丝及绢丝制簇绒织物(品目 5703 的产品除外,含丝 85% 及以上)	10				130	17	13	米/千克		Woven tufted textile fabrics of silk or silk waste, other than products of heading No. 57.03, containing≥85% by weight of silk or silk waste
5802.3010 90	其他丝及绢丝制簇绒织物(品目 5703 的产品除外,含丝 85% 以下)	10				130	17	13	米/千克		Other woven tufted textile fabrics of silk or silk waste, other than products of heading No. 57.03, containing < 85% by weight of silk or silk waste
5802.3020	---羊毛或动物细毛制	10	8	0	0	130	17	13	米/千克		---Of wool or fine animal hair
5802.3030	---棉或麻制	10	5	0	0	70	17	13	米/千克		---Of cotton or bast fibres
5802.3030 10	麻制簇绒织物(品目 5703 的产品除外)	10				70	17	13	米/千克		Woven tufted textile fabrics of bast fibres, other than products of heading No. 57.03
5802.3030 90	棉制簇绒织物(品目 5703 的产品除外)	10				70	17	13	米/千克		Woven tufted textile fabrics of cotton, other than products of heading No. 57.03
5802.3040	---化学纤维制	10	8	0	0	130	17	13	米/千克		---Of man-made fibres
5802.3090	---其他纺织材料制	10	8	0	0	80	17	13	米/千克		---Of other textile materials
58.03	**纱罗,但税目 58.06 的狭幅织物除外:**										**Gauze, other than narrow fabrics of heading No. 58.06:**
	纱罗,但税目 58.06 的狭幅织物除外:										Gauze, other than narrow fabrics of heading 58.06:

税则号列 Tariff Item.	货品名称	最惠国(%) MFN	协定(%)CT 东盟 CA	中巴 CP	中智 CC	普通 Gen	增值税率 VAT	出口退税 ED	计量单位 Unit	监管条件 SC	Article Description
	纱罗，但税目58.06的狭幅织物除外：										Gauze, other than narrow fabrics of heading No. 58.06:
5803.0010	---棉制	10	5		0	70	17	13	米/千克		---Of cotton
5803.0020	---丝及绢丝制	10	8		0	130	17	13	米/千克		---Of silk or silk waste
5803.0030	---化学纤维制	12	8		0	130	17	13	米/千克		---Of man-made fibres
5803.0090	---其他纺织材料制	10	8		0	80	17	13	米/千克		---Other of textile materials
58.04	**网眼薄纱及其他网眼织物，但不包括机织物、针织物或钩编织物；成卷、成条或成小块图案的花边，但税号60.02的织物除外：**										**Tulles and other net fabrics, not including woven, knitted or crocheted fabrics; lace in the piece, in strips or in motifs, other than fabrics of headings Nos. 60.02 to 60.06:**
	-网眼薄纱及其他网眼织物：										-Tulles and other net fabrics:
5804.1010	---丝及绢丝制	10	T3	7	0	130	17	13	千克		---Of silk or silk waste
5804.1010 10	丝及绢丝网眼薄纱及其他网眼织物(含丝85%及以上，不包括机织物，针织物或钩编织物)	10				130	17	13	千克		Tulles and other net fabrics, other than woven, knitted or crocheted fabrics, containing≥85% by weight of silk or silk waste
5804.1010 90	丝及绢丝网眼薄纱及其他网眼织物(含丝85%以下，不包括机织物，针织物或钩编织物)	10				130	17	13	千克		Tulles and other net fabrics, other than woven, knitted or crocheted fabrics, containing<85% by weight of silk or silk waste
5804.1020	---棉制	10	5	7	0	70	17	13	千克	5	---Of cotton
5804.1030	---化学纤维制	12	T3	8.4	0	130	17	13	千克	5	---Of man-made fibres
5804.1090	---其他纺织材料制	10	T3	7	0	90	17	13	千克		---Of other textile materials
	-机制花边：										-Mechanically made lace:
5804.2100	--化学纤维制	10	T3		0	130	17	13	千克	5	--Of man-made fibres
	--其他纺织材料制：										--Of other textile materials:
5804.2910	---丝及绢丝制	10	T3		0	130	17	13	千克		---Of silk or silk waste
5804.2910 10	丝及绢丝含量85%及以上机制花边(成卷成条或成小块图案的，但品目6002的织物除外)	10				130	17	13	千克		Mechanically made lace, in the piece, in strips or in motifs, other than fabrics of headings Nos. 60.02 to 60.06, containing≥85% by weight of silk or silk waste
5804.2910 90	丝及绢丝含量85%以下机制花边(成卷成条或成小块图案的，但品目6002的织物除外)	10				130	17	13	千克		Mechanically made lace, in the piece, in strips or in motifs, other than fabrics of headings Nos. 60.02 to 60.06, containing < 85% by weight of silk or silk waste
5804.2920	---棉制	10	T3		0	70	17	13	千克	5	---Of cotton
5804.2990	---其他	10	T3		0	90	17	13	千克		---Other
5804.3000	-手工制花边	10	T3		0	100	17	13	千克		-Hand-made lace
5804.3000 11	丝含量达85%及以上制手工制花边(成卷成条或成小块图案的，但品目6002的织物除外)	10				100	17	13	千克		Hand-made lace, in the piece, in strips or in motifs, other than fabrics of headings Nos. 60.02 to 60.06, containing≥85% by weight of silk or silk waste
5804.3000 19	丝含量达85%以下制手工制花边(成卷成条或成小块图案的，但品目6002的织物除外)	10				100	17	13	千克		Hand-made lace, in the piece, in strips or in motifs, other than fabrics of headings Nos. 60.02 to 60.06, containing < 85% by weight of silk or silk waste

税则号列 Tariff Item.	货品名称	最惠国(%) MFN	协定(%) CT 东盟 CA	中巴 CP	中智 CC	普通 Gen	增值税率 VAT	出口退税 ED	计量单位 Unit	监管条件 SC	Article Description
5804. 3000 20	棉或化纤制手工制花边(成卷成条或成小块图案的,但品目6002的织物除外)	10				100	17	13	千克	5	Hand-made lace, of cotton or of man-made fibres, in the piece, in strips or in motifs, other than fabrics of headings Nos. 60. 02 to 60. 06
5804. 3000 90	其他纺织材料制手工制其他花边(成卷成条或成小块图案的,但品目6002的织物除外)	10				100	17	13	千克		Other hand-made lace of other textile materials, in the piece, in strips or in motifs, other than fabrics of headings Nos. 60. 02 to 60. 06
58. 05	**“哥白林”、“弗朗德”、“奥步生”、“波威”及类似式样的手织装饰毯,以及手工针绣嵌花装饰毯(例如,小针脚或十字绣),不论是否制成的:**										**Hand-woven tapestries of the type Gobelins, Flanders, Aubusson, Beauvais and the like, and needle-worked tapestries (for example, petit point, cross stitch), whether or not made up:**
5805. 0010	---手工针绣嵌花装饰毯	12	8		0	130	17	13	平方米/千克		---Needle-worked tapestries
5805. 0010 10	毛非民间工艺针绣嵌花其他装饰毯(不论是否制成的)	12				130	17	13	平方米/千克		Needle-worked tapestries of wool or fine animal hair, non-craftsmanship, whether or not made up
5805. 0010 20	棉制手工针绣嵌花其他装饰毯(不论是否制成的)	12				130	17	13	平方米/千克		Needle-worked tapestries of cotton, whether or not made up
5805. 0010 30	化纤制手工针绣嵌花其他装饰毯(不论是否制成的)	12				130	17	13	平方米/千克		Needle-worked tapestries of man-made fibres, whether or not made up
5805. 0010 90	其他纺织料制手工针绣嵌花装饰毯(不论是否制成的)	12				130	17	13	平方米/千克		Needle-worked tapestries of other textile materials, whether or not made up
5805. 0090	---其他	12	8		0	130	17	13	平方米/千克		---Other
5805. 0090 10	毛制非民间工艺的手织装饰毯(包括“哥白林”,“弗朗德”,“奥步生”,“波威”及类似式样的)	12				130	17	13	平方米/千克		Hand-woven tapestries of the type Gobelins, Flanders, Aubusson, Beauvais and the like, of wool or fine animal hair, non-craftsmanship
5805. 0090 20	棉制“哥白林”等手织装饰毯(包括“弗朗德”,“奥步生”,“波威”及类似式样的手织装饰毯)	12				130	17	13	平方米/千克		Hand-woven tapestries of the type Gobelins, Flanders, Aubusson, Beauvais and the like, of cotton
5805. 0090 30	化纤制“哥白林”等手织装饰毯(包括“弗朗德”,“奥步生”,“波威”及类似式样的手织装饰毯)	12				130	17	13	平方米/千克		Hand-woven tapestries of the type Gobelins, Flanders, Aubusson, Beauvais and the like, of man-made fibres
5805. 0090 90	其他纺料制“哥白林”等手织装饰毯(包括“弗朗德”,“奥步生”,“波威”及类似式样的手织装饰毯)	12				130	17	13	平方米/千克		Hand-woven tapestries of the type Gobelins, Flanders, Aubusson, Beauvais and the like, of other textile materials
58. 06	**狭幅机织物,但税目58.07的货品除外;用粘合剂粘合制成的有经纱而无纬纱的狭幅织物(包扎匹头用带):**										**Narrow woven fabrics, other than goods of heading No. 58. 07; narrow fabrics consisting of warp without weft assembled by means of an adhesive (bolducs):**
	-起绒机织物(包括毛巾织物及类似的毛圈织物)及绳绒织物:										-Woven pile fabrics (including terry towelling and similar terry fabris) and chenille fabrics:
5806. 1010	---棉或麻制	10	5		0	70	17	13	千克		---Of cotton or bast fibres

税则号列 Tariff Item.	货品名称	最惠国(%) MFN	协定(%) CT 东盟 CA	中巴 CP	中智 CC	普通 Gen	增值税率 VAT	出口退税 ED	计量单位 Unit	监管条件 SC	Article Description
5806.1010 10	棉制狭幅起绒机织物及绳绒织物(包括狭幅毛巾织物及类似毛圈织物,品目5807的货品除外)	10				70	17	13	千克	5	Narrow woven pile fabrics and chenille fabrics of cotton (including terry towelling and similar terry fabris), other than goods of heading No. 58.07
5806.1010 90	麻制狭幅起绒机织物及绳绒织物(包括狭幅毛巾织物及类似毛圈织物,品目5807的货品除外)	10				70	17	13	千克		Narrow woven pile fabrics and chenille fabrics of bast fibres (including terry towelling and similar terry fabris), other than goods of heading No. 58.07
5806.1090	---其他纺织材料制	10	T3	9.1	0	80	17	13	千克		---Of other textile materials
5806.1090 10	含丝≥85%狭幅起绒及绳绒等织物(包括狭幅毛巾织物及类似毛圈织物,品目5807的货品除外)	10				80	17	13	千克		Narrow woven pile fabrics and chenille fabrics (including terry towelling and similar terry fabris), other than goods of heading No. 58.07, containing ≥85% by weight of silk or silk waste
5806.1090 20	毛制狭幅起绒织物及绳绒织物(包括狭幅毛巾织物及类似毛圈织物,品目5807的货品除外)	10				80	17	13	千克		Narrow woven pile fabrics and chenille fabrics of wool or fine animal hair (including terry towelling and similar terry fabris), other than goods of heading No. 58.07
5806.1090 30	化纤制狭幅起绒织物及绳绒织物(包括狭幅毛巾织物及类似毛圈织物,品目5807的货品除外)	10				80	17	13	千克	5	Narrow woven pile fabrics and chenille fabrics of man-made fibres (including terry towelling and similar terry fabris), other than goods of heading No. 58.07
5806.1090 90	其他材料狭幅起绒织物及绳绒织物(包括狭幅毛巾织物及类似毛圈织物,品目5807的货品除外)	10				80	17	13	千克		Narrow woven pile fabrics and chenille fabrics of other textile materials (including terry towelling and similar terry fabris), other than goods of heading No. 58.07
5806.2000	-按重量计弹性纱线或橡胶线含量在5%及以上的其他机织物	10	T3		0	100	17	13	千克	5	-Other woven fabrics, containing by weight 5% or more of elastomeric yarn or rubber thread
	-其他机织物:										-Other woven fabrics:
5806.3100	--棉制	10	T3		0	70	17	13	千克	5	--Of cotton
5806.3200	--化学纤维制	10	T3	7	0	130	17	13	千克		--Of man-made fibres
5806.3200 10	化纤制用于打字机色带狭幅机织物(品目5807的货品除外)	10				130	17	13	千克		Narrow woven fabrics, typewriter ribbon, of man-made fibres, other than goods of heading No. 58.07
5806.3200 90	化纤制其他狭幅机织物(品目5807的货品除外)	10				130	17	13	千克	5	Other narrow woven fabrics of man-made fibres, other than goods of heading No. 58.07
	--其他纺织材料制:										--Of other textile materials:
5806.3910	---丝及绢丝制	10	8		0	130	17	13	千克		---Of silk or silk waste
5806.3920	---羊毛或动物细毛制	10	8		0	130	17	13	千克		---Of wool or fine animal hair
5806.3990	---其他	10	8		0	80	17	13	千克		---Other
5806.3990 10	含金属纱线制其他狭幅机织物(品目5807的货品除外)	10				80	17	13	千克	5	Other narrow woven fabrics, other than goods of heading No. 58.07, of metallized yarn

税则号列 Tariff Item.	货品名称	最惠国(%) MFN	协定(%)CT 东盟 CA	中巴 CP	中智 CC	普通 Gen	增值税率 VAT	出口退税 ED	计量单位 Unit	监管条件 SC	Article Description
5806.3990 90	其他材料制其他狭幅机织物(品目5807的货品除外)	10				80	17	13	千克		Other narrow woven fabrics, other than goods of heading No. 58.07, of other textile materials
	-用粘合剂粘合制成的有经纱而无纬纱的织物(包扎匹头用带):										-Fabrics consisting of warp without weft assembled by means of an adhesive (bolducs):
5806.4010	---棉或麻制	10	5		0	70	17	13	千克		---Of cotton or bast fibres
5806.4090	---其他纺织材料制	10	8		0	80	17	13	千克		---Of other textile materials
58.07	**非绣制的纺织材料制标签、徽章及类似品,成匹、成条或裁成一定形状或尺寸:**										**Labels, badges and similar articles of textile materials, in the piece, in strips or cut to shape or size, not embroidered:**
5807.1000	-机织	10	T3	8.5	0	100	17	13	千克		-Woven
5807.1000 10	棉制机织非绣制标签(成匹,成条或裁成一定形状或尺寸)	10				100	17	13	千克		Woven labels in the piece, in strips or cut to shape or size, not embroidered, of cotton
5807.1000 20	化纤制机织非绣制标签(成匹、成条或裁成一定形状或尺寸)	10				100	17	13	千克		Woven labels in the piece, in strips or cut to shape or size, not embroidered, of man-made fibres
5807.1000 90	其他纺织材料制机织非绣制标签等(包括徽章及类似品,成匹、成条或裁成一定形状或尺寸)	10				100	17	13	千克		Woven labels, badges and similar articles in the piece, in strips or cut to shape or size, not embroidered, of other textile materials
5807.9000	-其他	10	8		0	100	17	13	千克		-Other
5807.9000 10	棉制非绣制的标签(成匹、成条或裁成一定形状或尺寸)	10				100	17	13	千克		Labels in the piece, in strips or cut to shape or size, not embroidered, of cotton
5807.9000 20	化纤制非绣制的标签(成匹、成条或裁成一定形状或尺寸)	10				100	17	13	千克		Labels in the piece, in strips or cut to shape or size, not embroidered, of man-made fibres
5807.9000 90	其他纺织材料制非绣制的标签等(包括徽章及类似品,成匹、成条或裁成一定形状或尺寸)	10				100	17	13	千克		Labels, badges and similar articles in the piece, in strips or cut to shape or size, not embroidered, of other textile materials
58.08	**成匹的编带;非绣制的成匹装饰带,但针织或钩编的除外;流苏、绒球及类似品:**										**Braids in the piece; ornamental trimmings in the piece, without embroidery, other than knitted or crocheted; tassels, pompons and similar articles:**
5808.1000	-成匹的编带	10	8		0	100	17	13	千克		-Braids in the piece
5808.1000 10	棉或化纤制成匹的编带	10				100	17	13	千克	5	Braids in the piece, of cotton or of man-made fibres
5808.1000 20	蕉麻或苎麻制成匹的编带(适合制造或装饰帽类用)	10				100	17	13	千克		Braids in the piece, of abaca or ramie (suitable for manufacturing or decoration of head gear)
5808.1000 90	其他纺织材料制成匹的编带	10				100	17	13	千克		Braids in the piece, of other textile materials
5808.9000	-其他	10	T3		0	100	17	13	千克		-Other

税则号列 Tariff Item.	货品名称	最惠国(%) MFN	协定(%)CT 东盟 CA	中巴 CP	中智 CC	普通 Gen	增值税率 VAT	出口退税 ED	计量单位 Unit	监管条件 SC	Article Description
5808.9000 10	棉或化纤制非绣制成匹装饰带(针织或钩编的除外)	10				100	17	13	千克	5	Ornamental trimmings in the piece, of cotton or of man-made fibres, other than knitted or crocheted
5808.9000 90	其他非绣制成匹装饰带,流苏等(含绒球及类似品,针织或钩编的除外)	10				100	17	13	千克		Other ornamental trimmings in the piece, tassels, pompons and similar articles without embroidery, other than knitted or crocheted
58.09	**其他税目未列名的金属线机织物及税目56.05所列含金属纱线的机织物,用于衣着、装饰及类似用途:**										**Woven fabrics of metal thread and woven fabrics of metallized yarn of heading No. 56.05, of a kind used in apparel, as furnishing fabrics or for similar purposes, not elsewhere specified or included:**
5809.0010	---与棉混制	10	8		0	90	17	13	米/千克	5	---Combined with cotton
5809.0020	---与化学纤维混制	10	8		0	130	17	13	米/千克	5	---Combined with man-made fibres
5809.0090	---其他	10	8		0	100	17	13	米/千克	5	---Other
58.10	**成匹、成条或成小块图案的刺绣品:**										**Embroidery in the piece, in strips or in motifs:**
5810.1000	-不见底布的刺绣品	10	8		0	130	17	13	千克	5	-Embroidery without visible ground
	-其他刺绣品:										-Other embroidery:
5810.9100	--棉制	10	8		0	130	17	13	千克		--Of cotton
5810.9200	--化学纤维制	10	8		0	130	17	13	千克		--Of man-made fibres
5810.9200 10	化学纤维制见底布刺绣标签(成匹,成条或成小块图案)	10				130	17	13	千克		Embroidered labels, without visible ground, in the piece, in strips or in motifs, of man-made fibres
5810.9200 90	其他化学纤维制见底布刺绣品(成匹,成条或成小块图案)	10				130	17	13	千克		Other embroidery visible ground, in the piece, in strips or in motifs, of man-made fibres
5810.9900	--其他纺织材料制	10	8		0	130	17	13	千克		--Of other textile materials
5810.9900 10	羊毛或动物细毛制见底布刺绣品(成匹,成条或成小块图案)	10				130	17	13	千克		Embroidery visible ground, in the piece, in strips or in motifs, of wool or fine animal hair
5810.9900 90	其他纺织材料制见底布刺绣品(成匹,成条或成小块图案)	10				130	17	13	千克		Embroidery visible ground, in the piece, in strips or in motifs, of other textile materials
58.11	**用一层或几层纺织材料与胎料经绗缝或其他方法组合制成的被褥状纺织品,但税目58.10的刺绣品除外:**										**Quilted textile products in the piece, composed of one or more layers of textile materials assembled with padding by stitching or otherwise, other than embroidery of heading No. 58.10:**
5811.0010	---丝及绢丝制	10	T3	0	0	130	17	13	千克		---Of silk or silk waste
5811.0020	---羊毛或动物细毛制	10	T3	0	0	130	17	13	千克		---Of wool or fine animal hair
5811.0030	---棉制	10	5	0	0	80	17	13	千克		---Of cotton

税则号列 Tariff Item.	货品名称	最惠国(%) MFN	协定(%) CT 东盟 CA	中巴 CP	中智 CC	普通 Gen	增值税率 VAT	出口退税 ED	计量单位 Unit	监管条件 SC	Article Description
5811.0030 10	未漂或漂白棉制被褥状纺织品(经绗缝等法用一或几层织物与胎料组合不含5810刺绣品)	10				80	17	13	千克	5	Quilted textile products in the piece, composed of one or more layers of textile materials assembled with padding by stitching or otherwise, other than embroidery of heading No. 58.10, of cotton, unbleached or bleached
5811.0030 90	其他棉制被褥状纺织品(经绗缝等法用一或几层织物与胎料组合不含5810刺绣品)	10				80	17	13	千克	5	Quilted textile products in the piece, composed of one or more layers of textile materials assembled with padding by stitching or otherwise, other than embroidery of heading No. 58.10, of cotton
5811.0040	---化学纤维制	12	T3	0	0	130	17	13	千克	5	---Of man-made fibres
5811.0090	---其他纺织材料制	10	T3	0	0	90	17	13	千克		---Of other textile materials

第五十九章
浸渍、涂布、包覆或层压的纺织物;工业用纺织制品

注释:

一、除条文另有规定的以外,本章所称“纺织物”,仅适用于第五十章至第五十五章、税目58.03及58.06的机织物、税目58.08的成匹编带和装饰带及税目60.02至60.06的针织物或钩编织物。

二、税目59.03适用于:

(一)用塑料浸渍、涂布、包覆或层压的纺织物,不论每平方米重量多少以及塑料的性质如何(紧密结构或泡沫状的),但下列各项除外:

1. 用肉眼无法辨别出是否经过浸渍、涂布、包覆或层压的织物(通常归入第五十章至第五十五章、第五十八章或第六十章);但由于浸渍、涂布、包覆或层压所引起的颜色变化可不予考虑;

2. 温度在15℃至30℃时,用手工将其绕于直径7毫米的圆柱体上会发生断裂的产品(通常归入第三十九章);

3. 纺织物完全嵌入塑料内或在其两面均用塑料完全包覆或涂布,而这种包覆或涂布用肉眼是能够辨别出的产品(但由于包覆或涂布所引起的颜色变化可不予考虑)(第三十九章);

4. 用塑料部分涂布或包覆并由此而形成图案的织物(通常归入第五十章至第五十五章、第五十八章或第六十章);

5. 与纺织物混制而其中纺织物仅起增强作用的泡沫塑料板、片或带(第三十九章);

6. 税目58.11的纺织品;

(二)由税目56.04的用塑料浸渍、涂布、包覆或套裹的纱线、扁条或类似品制成的织物。

三、税目59.05所称“糊墙织物”,是指以纺织材料作面,固定在一衬背上或在背面进行处理(浸渍或涂布以便于裱糊),适于装饰墙壁或天花板,且宽度不小于45厘米的成卷产品。

但本税目不适用于以纺织纤维屑或粉末直接粘于纸上(税目48.14)或布底上(通常归入税目59.07)的糊墙物品。

四、税目59.06所称“用橡胶处理的纺织物”是指:

(一)用橡胶浸渍、涂布、包覆或层压的纺织物:

Chapter 59
Impregnated, coated, covered or laminated textile fabrics; textile articles of a kind suitable for industrial use

Notes:

1. Except where the context otherwise requires, for the purposes of this Chapter the expression “textile fabrics” applies only to the woven fabrics of Chapters 50 to 55 and headings Nos. 58.03 and 58.06, the braids and ornamental trimmings in the piece of heading Nos. 58.08 and the knitted or crocheted fabrics of headings Nos. 60.02 to 60.06.

2. Heading No. 59.03 applies to:

(a) Textile fabrics, impregnated, coated, covered or laminated with plastics, whatever the weight per square metre and whatever the nature of the plastic material (compact or cellular), other than:

(1) Fabrics in which the impregnation, coating, or covering cannot be seen with the naked eye (usually Chapters 50 to 55, 58 or 60); for the purpose of this provision, no account should be taken of any resulting change of colour;

(2) Products which cannot, without fracturing, be bent manually around a cylinder of a diameter of 7 mm, at a temperature between 15℃ and 30℃ (usually Chapter 39);

(3) Products in which the textile fabric is either completely embedded in plastics or entirely coated or covered on both sides with such material, provided that such coating or covering can be seen with the naked eye with no account being taken of any resulting change of colour (Chapter 39);

(4) Fabrics partially coated or partially covered with plastics and bearing designs resulting from these treatments (usually Chapters 50 to 55, 58 or 60);

(5) Plates, sheets or strip of cellular plastics, combined with textile fabric, where the textile fabric is present merely for reinforcing purposes (Chapter 39); or

(6) Textile products of heading No. 58.11;

(b) Fabrics made from yarn, strip or the like, impregnated, coated, covered or sheathed with plastics, of heading No. 56.04.

3. For the purposes of heading No. 59.05, the expression “textile wall coverings” applies to products in rolls, of a width of not less than 45 cm, suitable for wall or ceiling decoration, consisting of a textile surface which has been fixed on a backing or has been treated on the back (impregnated or coated to permit pasting).

This heading does not, however, apply to wall coverings consisting of textile flock or dust fixed directly on backing of paper (heading No. 48.14) or on a textile backing (generally heading No. 59.07).

4. For the purposes of heading No. 59.06, the expression “rubberized textile fabrics” means:

(a) Textile fabrics impregnated, coated, covered or laminated with rubber,

1. 每平方米重量不超过1 500克;

2. 每平方米重量超过1 500克,按重量计纺织材料含量在50%以上;

(二)由税目56.04的用橡胶浸渍、涂布、包覆或套裹的纱线、扁条或类似品制成的织物;

(三)平行纺织纱线经橡胶粘合的织物,不论每平方米重量多少。

但本税目不包括与纺织物混制而其中纺织物仅起增强作用的海绵橡胶板、片或带(第四十章),也不包括税目58.11的纺织品。

五、税目59.07不适用于:

(一)用肉眼无法辨别出是否经过浸渍、涂布或包覆的织物(通常归入第五十章至第五十五章、第五十八章或第六十章),但由于浸渍、涂布或包覆所引起的颜色变化可不予考虑;

(二)绘有图画的织物(作为舞台、摄影布景或类似品的已绘制的画布除外);

(三)用短绒、粉末、软木粉或类似品部分覆面并由此而形成图案的织物,但仿绒织物仍归入本税目;

(四)以淀粉或类似物质为基本成分的普通浆料上浆整理的织物;

(五)以纺织物为底的木饰面板(税目44.08);

(六)以纺织物为底的砂布及类似品(税目68.05);

(七)以纺织物为底的粘聚或复制云母片(税目68.14);

(八)以纺织物为底的金属箔(通常为第十四类)。

六、税目59.10不适用于:

(一)厚度小于3毫米的纺织材料制传动带或输送带;

(二)用橡胶浸渍、涂布、包覆或层压的织物制成的或用橡胶浸渍、涂布、包覆或套裹的纱线或绳制成的传动带及运输带(税目40.10)。

七、税目59.11适用于下列不能归入第十一类其他税目的货品:

(一)下列成匹的、裁成一定长度或仅裁成矩形(包括正方形)的纺织产品(具有税目59.08至59.10所列产品特征的产品除外):

1. 用橡胶、皮革或其他材料涂布、包覆或层压的作针布用的纺织物、毡呢及毡呢衬里机织物,以及其他专门技术用途的类似织物,包括用橡胶浸渍的用于包覆纺锤(织轴)的狭幅丝绒织物。

(Ⅰ) Weighing not more than 1,500 g/m^2; or

(Ⅱ) Weighing more than 1,500 g/m^2 and containing more than 50% by weight of textile material;

(b) Fabrics made from yarn, strip or the like, impregnated, coated, covered or sheathed with rubber, of heading No. 56.04; and

(c) Fabrics composed of parallel textile yarns agglomerated with rubber, irrespective of their weight per square metre.

This heading does not, however, apply to plates, sheets or strip of cellular rubber, combined with textile fabric, where the textile fabric is present merely for reinforcing purposes (Chapter 40), or textile products of heading No. 58.11.

5. Heading No. 59.07 does not apply to:

(a) Fabrics in which the impregnation, coating or covering cannot be seen with the naked eye (usually Chapters 50 to 55, 58 or 60); for the purpose of this provision, no account should be taken of any resulting change of colour;

(b) Fabrics painted with designs (other than painted canvas being theatrical scenery, studio back-cloths or the like);

(c) Fabrics partially covered with flock, dust, powdered cork or the like and bearing designs resulting from these treatments; however, imitation pile fabrics remain classified in this heading;

(d) Fabrics finished with normal dressings having a basis of amylaceous or similar substances;

(e) Wood veneered on a backing of textile fabrics (heading No. 44.08);

(f) Natural or artificial abrasive powder or grain, on a backing of textile fabrics (heading No. 68.05);

(g) Agglomerated or reconstituted mica, on a backing of fextile fabrics (heading No. 68.14); or

(h) Metal foil on a backing of textile fabrics (Usually section XIV or section XV).

6. Heading No. 59.10 does not apply to:

(a) Transmission or conveyor belting, of textile material, of a thickness of less than 3 mm; or

(b) Transmission or conveyor belts or belting of textile fabric impregnated, coated, covered or laminated with rubber or made from textile yarn or cord impregnated, coated, covered or sheathed with rubber (heading No. 40.10).

7. Heading No. 59.11 applies to the following goods, which do not fall in any other heading of Section XI:

(a) Textile products in the piece, cut to length or simply cut to rectangular (including square) shape (other than those having the character of the products of headings Nos. 59.08 to 59.10), the following only:

(Ⅰ) Textile fabrics, felt and felt-lined woven fabrics, coated, covered or laminated with rubber, leather or other material, of a kind used for card clothing, and similar fabrics of a kind used for other technical purposes, including narrow fabrics made of velvet impregnated with rubber, for covering weaving spindles (weaving beams);

2. 筛布；

3. 用于榨油机器或类似机器的纺织材料制或人发制滤布；

4. 用多股经纱或纬纱平织而成的纺织物，不论是否毡化、浸渍或涂布，通常用于机械或其他专门技术用途；

5. 专门技术用途的增强纺织物；

6. 工业上作填塞或润滑材料的线绳、编带及类似品，不论是否涂布、浸渍或用金属加强。

（二）专门技术用途的纺织制品（税目 59.08 至 59.10 的货品除外），例如，造纸机器或类似机器（如制浆机或制石棉水泥的机器）用的环状或装有联接装置的纺织物或毡呢、密封垫、垫圈、抛光盘及其他机器零件。

（Ⅱ）Bolting cloth；

（Ⅲ）Straining cloth of a kind used in oil presses or the like, of textile material or of human hair；

（Ⅳ）Flat woven textile fabrics with multiple warp or weft, whether or not felted, impregnated or coated, of a kind used in machinery or for other technical purposes；

（Ⅴ）Textile fabrics reinforced with metal, of a kind used for technical purposes；

（Ⅵ）Cords, braids and the like, whether or not coated, impregnated or reinforced with metal, of a kind used in industry as packing or lubricating materials；

（b）Textile articles（other than those of headings Nos. 59.08 to 59.10）of a kind used for technical purposes, for example, textile fabrics and felts, endless or fitted with linking devicse, of a kind used in paper-making or similar machines（for example, for pulp or asbestos-cement）, gaskets, washers, polishing discs and other machinery parts.

税则号列 Tariff Item.	货品名称	最惠国（%）MFN	协定（%）CT 东盟 CA	中巴 CP	中智 CC	普通 Gen	增值税率 VAT	出口退税 ED	计量单位 Unit	监管条件 SC	Article Description
59.01	**用胶或淀粉物质涂布的纺织物，作书籍封面及类似用途的；描图布；制成的油画布；作帽里的硬衬布及类似硬挺纺织物：**										**Textile fabrics coated with gum or amylaceous substances, of a kind used for the outer covers of books or the like; tracing cloth; prepared painting canvas; buckram and similar stiffened textile fabrics of a kind used for hat foundations:**
	-用胶或淀粉物质涂布的纺织物，作书籍封面及类似用途的：										-Textile fabrics coated with gum or amylaceous substances, of a kind used for the outer covers of books or the like:
5901.1010	---棉或麻制	10	T3		0	80	17	11	千克		---Of cotton or bast fibres
5901.1010 10	胶或淀粉涂布的棉纺织物（作书籍封面棉织物重≥50%经漂染印花）	10				80	17	11	千克	5	Textile fabrics coated with gum or amylaceous substances, of a kind used for the outer covers of books or the like, containing≥50% by weight of cotton, bleached, dyed, printed
5901.1010 90	胶或淀粉涂布的麻及其他棉纺织（作书籍封面及类似用途的）	10				80	17	11	千克	5	Textile fabrics coated with gum or amylaceous substances, of a kind used for the outer covers of books or the like, of bast fibres and other cotton
5901.1020	---化学纤维制	10	8		0	130	17	11	千克		---Of man-made fibres
5901.1020 10	胶或淀粉涂布的涤棉短纤混纺织品（书籍封面及类似用途聚酯短纤棉混纺漂染织物>50%）	10				130	17	11	千克	5	Textile fabrics coated with gum or amylaceous substances, of a kind used for the outer covers of books or the like, containing≥50% by weight of polyester staple fibres and cotton, bleached, dyed
5901.1020 90	胶或淀粉涂布的其他化纤纺织物（作书籍封面及类似用途的）	10				130	17	11	千克	5	Other man-made textile fabrics coated with gum or amylaceous substances, of a kind used for the outer covers of books or the like, of other textile fabrics
5901.1090	---其他	10	8		0	100	17	11	千克		---Other

税则号列 Tariff Item.	货 品 名 称	最惠国(%) MFN	协定(%)CT			普通 Gen	增值税率 VAT	出口退税 ED	计量单位 Unit	监管条件 SC	Article Description
			东盟 CA	中巴 CP	中智 CC						
5901.1090 10	用胶或淀粉涂布的精梳毛纺织物(书籍封面及类似用途精梳羊毛或动物细毛织物≥50%)	10				100	17	11	千克	5	Woollen textile fabrics coated with gum or amylaceous substances, of a kind used for the outer covers of books or the like, containing≥50% by weight of combed wool or fine animal hair
5901.1090 90	用胶或淀粉涂布的其他纺织物(作书籍封面及类似用途的)	10				100	17	11	千克	5	Other textile fabrics coated with gum or amylaceous substances, of a kind used for the outer covers of books or the like, of other textile fabrics
	-其他:										-Other:
5901.9010	---制成的油画布	10	5		0	50	17	11	千克		---Prepared painting canvas
5901.9010 10	精梳毛织物制油画布(精梳羊毛或动物细毛织物重≥50%)	10				50	17	11	千克	5	Prepared painting canvas, containing ≥50% by weight of combed wool or fine animal hair
5901.9010 20	棉制油画布(棉织物重≥50%经漂白染色印花等加工)	10				50	17	11	千克	5	Prepared painting canvas, containing ≥ 50% by weight, of cotton, bleached, dyed or printed
5901.9010 30	聚酯短纤与棉混纺织物制油画(织物重≥50%经漂白染色印花等加工)	10				50	17	11	千克	5	Prepared painting canvas, containing ≥50% by weight of polyester staple fibres and cotton
5901.9010 90	其他纺织物制成的油画布	10				50	17	11	千克	5	Prepared painting canvas of other textile fabrics
	---其他:										---Other:
5901.9091	----棉或麻制	10	T3		0	80	17	11	千克		----Of cotton or bast fibres
5901.9091 10	棉制描图布,帽里硬衬布等(包括类似硬挺纺织物,棉织物≥50%经漂染印花)	10				80	17	11	千克	5	Tracing cloth, buckram and similar stiffened textile fabrics, of a kind used for hat foundations, of cotton, containing≥50% by weight of cotton, bleached dyed printed
5901.9091 90	麻及其他棉制描图布,帽里硬衬布(包括类似硬挺纺织物)	10				80	17	11	千克	5	Tracing cloth, buckram and similar stiffened textile fabrics, of a kind used for hat foundations, of bast fibres and other cotton
5901.9092	----化学纤维制	10	5		0	130	17	11	千克		----Of man-made fibres
5901.9092 10	聚酯短纤与棉混纺织物制描图布(含帽里硬衬类似硬挺纺织物,织物≥50%经漂染印)	10				130	17	11	千克	5	Tracing cloth, buckram and similar stiffened textile fabrics, of a kind used for hat foundations, mixed, containing≥50% by weight of polyester staple fibres and cotton, bleached, dyed, printed
5901.9092 90	其他化纤制描图布,帽里硬衬布等(包括类似硬挺纺织物)	10				130	17	11	千克	5	Tracing cloth, buckram and similar stiffened textile fabrics, of a kind used for hat foundations, of other man-made fibres
5901.9099	----其他	10	5		0	100	17	11	千克		----Other
5901.9099 10	精梳毛纺织物制描图布,帽里硬衬(包括类似硬挺纺织物精梳羊毛或动物细毛织物≥50%)	10				100	17	11	千克	5	Tracing cloth, buckram and similar stiffened textile fabrics, of a kind used for hat foundations, containing ≥50% by weight of combed wool or combed fine animals hair

税则号列 Tariff Item.	货品名称	最惠国(%) MFN	协定(%)CT 东盟 CA	中巴 CP	中智 CC	普通 Gen	增值税率 VAT	出口退税 ED	计量单位 Unit	监管条件 SC	Article Description
5901.9099 90	其他纺织物制描图布,帽里硬衬布(包括类似硬挺纺织物)	10				100	17	11	千克	5	Tracing cloth, buckram and similar stiffened textile fabrics, of a kind used for hat foundations, of other textile fabrics
59.02	**尼龙或其他聚酰胺,聚酯或粘胶纤维高强力纱制的帘子布:**										**Tyre cord fabric of high tenacity yarn of nylon or other polyamides, polyesters or viscose rayon:**
5902.1000	-尼龙或其他聚酰胺制	10	T3	9	0	40	17	11	千克	5	-Of nylon or other polyamides
5902.2000	-聚酯制	10	8	9	0	40	17	11	千克	5	-Of polyesters
5902.9000	-其他	10	5		0	40	17	11	千克	5	-Other
59.03	**用塑料浸渍、涂布、包覆或层压的纺织物,但税目59.02的货品除外:**										**Textile fabrics impregnated, coated, covered or laminated with plastics, other than those of heading 59.02:**
	-用聚氯乙烯浸渍、涂布、包覆或层压的:										-With poly(vinyl chloride):
5903.1010	---绝缘布或带	10	5	8.5	0	40	17	11	千克		---Insulating cloth or tape
5903.1010 10	若干平行化纤纱线粘合绝缘布或带(聚氯乙烯浸渍涂布包覆或层压,塑料占60%及以下)	10				40	17	11	千克	5	Insulating cloth or tape of mon-made fibres, impregnated, coated, covered or laminated with poly (vinyl chloride), of fabrics consisting of layers of parallel textile yarns, bonded, containing≤60% by weight of plastics
5903.1010 20	聚氯乙烯浸渍涤棉混纺绝缘布或带(聚氯乙烯涂包漂染聚酯短纤棉混纺,塑或胶<50%)	10				40	17	11	千克	5	Insulating cloth or tape of mixed with polyester staple fibres and cotton, impregnated, coated, covered or laminated with poly (vinyl chloride), containing < 50% by weight of plastics or glue
5903.1010 30	聚氯乙烯浸渍其他化纤绝缘布或带(用聚氯乙烯涂布包覆或层压,塑或胶≤70%)	10				40	17	11	千克	5	Insulating cloth or tape of man-made fibres, impregnated, coated, covered or laminated with poly (vinyl chloride), containing≤70% by weight of plastics or glue
5903.1010 90	用聚氯乙烯浸渍的其他绝缘布或带(包括用聚氯乙烯涂布,包覆或层压的)	10				40	17	11	千克		Other insulating cloth or tape, impregnated, coated, covered or laminated with poly (vinyl chloride)
5903.1020	---人造革	10	T3	8.5	0	70	17	11	米/千克		---Imitation leather
5903.1020 10	若干层平行纱线粘合的化纤人造革(用聚氯乙烯浸渍,涂布,包覆,层压,塑料占60%及以下)	10				70	17	11	千克/米	5	Imitation leather of man-made fibres, impregnated, coated, covered or laminated with poly (vinyl chloride) of fabrics consisting of layers of parallel textile yarns, bonded, containing ≤ 60% by weight of plastics
5903.1020 20	用聚氯乙烯浸渍的涤棉织物人造革(聚氯乙烯涂布漂印染聚酯短纤棉混纺,塑或胶<50%)	10				70	17	11	千克/米	5	Imitation leather of mixed with polyester staple fibres and cotton, impregnated, coated, covered or laminated with poly (vinyl chloride), containing < 50% by weight of plastics or glue

税则号列 Tariff Item.	货 品 名 称	最惠国(%) MFN	协定(%) CT 东盟 CA	中巴 CP	中智 CC	普通 Gen	增值税率 VAT	出口退税 ED	计量单位 Unit	监管条件 SC	Article Description
5903.1020 30	用聚氯乙烯浸渍的其他化纤人造革(包括用聚氯乙烯涂布包覆或层压,塑或胶≤70%)	10				70	17	11	千克/米	5	Imitation leather of man-made fibres, impregnated, coated, covered or laminated with poly (vinyl chloride), containing ≤70% by weight of plastics or glue
5903.1020 40	用聚氯乙烯浸渍的棉织物人造革(聚氯乙烯涂布,包覆或层压漂.染,印花织物不小于50%)	10				70	17	11	千克/米		Imitation leather of cotton, impregnated, coated, covered or laminated with poly (vinyl chloride), containing ≥50% by weight of cotton, bleached, dyed or printed
5903.1020 90	用聚氯乙烯浸渍的其他人造革(包括用聚氯乙烯涂布,包覆或层压的)	10				70	17	11	千克/米		Other imitation leather, impregnated, coated, covered or laminated with poly (vinyl chloride)
5903.1090	---其他	10	T3	8.5	0	90	17	11	千克		---Other
5903.1090 10	若干层平行纱线粘合化纤其他织物(聚氯乙烯浸渍涂布包覆层压,塑料占60%及以下)	10				90	17	11	千克	5	Other textile fabrics of man-made fibres, impregnated, coated, covered or laminated with poly (vinyl chloride), of fabrics consisting of layers of parallel textile yarns, bonded, containing≤60% by weight of plastics
5903.1090 21	聚氯乙烯浸渍的其他涤棉混纺织物(聚氯乙烯涂布漂印染聚酯短纤棉混纺,塑或胶<50%)	10				90	17	11	千克	5	Other textile fabrics of mixed with polyester staple fibres and cotton, impregnated, coated, covered or laminated with poly (vinyl chloride), containing <50% by weight of plastics or glue
5903.1090 29	聚氯乙烯浸渍的其他化纤织物(包括用聚氯乙烯涂布包覆层压的,塑或胶≤70%)	10				90	17	11	千克	5	Other textile fabrics of man-made fibres, impregnated, coated, covered or laminated with poly (vinyl chloride), containing ≤70% by weight of plastics or glue
5903.1090 30	聚氯乙烯浸渍的棉织物(聚氯乙烯涂布包覆层压,漂染印花织物≥50%)	10				90	17	11	千克		Other textile fabrics of cotton, impregnated, coated, covered or laminated with poly (vinyl chloride), containing ≥50% by weight of fabrics of cotton, bleached, dyed or printed
5903.1090 40	用聚氯乙烯浸渍的精梳毛织物(聚氯乙烯涂布包覆或层压,精梳羊毛或动物细毛≥50%)	10				90	17	11	千克		Other woollen textile fabrics, impregnated, coated, covered or laminated with poly (vinyl chloride), containing ≥50% by weight of combed wool or fine animal hair
5903.1090 90	聚氯乙烯浸渍的其他纺织物(包括用聚氯乙烯涂布,包覆或层压的)	10				90	17	11	千克		Other textile fabrics, impregnated, coated, covered or laminated with poly (vinyl chloride)
	-用聚氨基甲酸酯浸渍、涂布、包覆或层压的:										-With polyurethane:
5903.2010	---绝缘布或带	10	5	8.5	0	40	17	11	千克		---Insulating cloth or tape

税则号列 Tariff Item.	货品名称	最惠国(%) MFN	协定(%) CT 东盟 CA	中巴 CP	中智 CC	普通 Gen	增值税率 VAT	出口退税 ED	计量单位 Unit	监管条件 SC	Article Description
5903. 2010 10	若干平行纱线粘合化纤绝缘布或带(聚氨基甲酸酯浸渍涂布、包覆或层压,塑料占60%及以下)	10				40	17	11	千克	5	Insulating cloth or tape of man-made fibres, impregnated, coated, covered or laminated with polyurethane of fabrics consisting of layers of parallel textile yarns, bonded, containing ≤ 60% by weight of plastics
5903. 2010 20	聚氨基甲酸酯浸渍涤棉绝缘布或带(聚氨基甲酸酯浸涂漂染聚酯短纤棉混纺,塑或胶<50%)	10				40	17	11	千克	5	Insulating cloth or tape of mixed with polyester staple fibres and cotton, impregnated, coated, covered or laminated with polyurethane, containing < 50% by weight of plastics or glue
5903. 2010 30	聚氨基甲酸酯浸渍其他化纤绝缘布(包括用聚氨基甲酸酯涂布,包覆层压,塑或胶≤70%)	10				40	17	11	千克	5	Other insulating cloth or tape of man-made fibres, impregnated, coated, covered or laminated with polyurethane containing≤70% by weight of plastics or glue
5903. 2010 90	聚氨基甲酸酯浸渍其他绝缘布或带(包括用聚氨基甲酸酯涂布,包覆或层压的)	10				40	17	11	千克		Other insulating cloth or tape, impregnated, coated, covered or laminated with polyurethane
5903. 2020	---人造革	10	8	8.5	0	70	17	11	千克/米		---Imitation leather
5903. 2020 10	若干层平行纱线粘合化纤人造革(聚氨基甲酸酯浸渍涂布,包覆层压,塑料≤60%)	10				70	17	11	千克/米	5	Imitation leather of man-made fibres, impregnated, coated, covered or laminated with polyurethane, of fabrics consisting of layers of parallel textile yarns, bonded, containing ≤ 60% by weight of plastics
5903. 2020 20	用聚氨基甲酸酯浸渍的涤棉人造革(聚氨基甲酸酯涂布漂染聚酯短纤棉混纺,塑或胶<50%)	10				70	17	11	千克/米	5	Imitation leather of mixed with polyester staple fibres and cotton, impregnated, coated, covered or laminated with polyurethane, containing < 50% by weight of plastics or glue
5903. 2020 30	聚氨基甲酸酯浸渍其他化纤人造革(包括用聚氨基甲酸酯涂布,包覆层压,塑或胶≤70%)	10				70	17	11	千克/米	5	Imitation leather of man-made fibres, impregnated, coated, covered or laminated with polyurethane, other, containing ≤ 70% by weight of plastics or glue
5903. 2020 40	聚氨基甲酸酯浸渍的棉织物人造革(聚氨基甲酸酯涂布,包覆层压,漂染印织物≥50%)	10				70	17	11	千克/米		Imitation leather of cotton, impregnated, coated, covered or laminated with polyurethane, containing ≥ 50% by weight of fabrics of cotton, bleached dyed or printed
5903. 2020 90	用聚氨基甲酸酯浸渍的其他人造革(包括用聚氨基甲酸酯涂布,包覆或层压的)	10				70	17	11	千克/米		Other imitation leather, impregnated, coated, covered or laminated with polyurethane
5903. 2090	---其他	10	8	8.5	0	90	17	11	千克		---Other

税则号列 Tariff Item.	货品名称	最惠国(%) MFN	协定(%) 东盟 CA	 中巴 CP	CT 中智 CC	普通 Gen	增值税率 VAT	出口退税 ED	计量单位 Unit	监管条件 SC	Article Description
5903.2090 10	若干层平行纱线粘合化纤其他织物(聚氨基甲酸酯浸渍涂布,包覆层压,塑料≤60%)	10				90	17	11	千克	5	Other textile fabrics of man-made fibres, impregnated, coated, covered or laminated with polyurethane, of fabrics consisting of layers of parallel textile yarns, bonded, containing ≤ 60% by weight of plastics
5903.2090 21	聚氨基甲酸酯浸渍其他涤棉织物(聚氨基甲酸酯涂布漂染聚酯短纤棉混纺,塑或胶<50%)	10				90	17	11	千克	5	Other textile fabrics of mixed with polyester staple fibres and cotton, impregnated, coated, covered or laminated with polyurethane, containing < 50% by weight of plastics or glue
5903.2090 29	聚氨基甲酸酯浸渍其他化纤织物(含聚氨基甲酸酯涂布,包覆或层压,塑或胶≤70%)	10				90	17	11	千克	5	Other textile fabrics of man-made fibres, impregnated, coated, covered or laminated with polyurethane, containing ≤ 70% by weight of plastics or glue
5903.2090 30	用聚氨基甲酸酯浸渍的棉织物(聚氨基甲酸酯涂布,包覆,层压,漂染印织物≥50%)	10				90	17	11	千克		Other textile fabrics of cotton, impregnated, coated, covered or laminated with polyurethane, containing ≥ 50% by weight of fabrics of cotton, bleached dyed printed
5903.2090 41	用聚氨基甲酸酯浸渍的精梳毛织物(聚氨基甲酸酯涂布包覆层压,精梳羊毛或动物细毛≥50%)	10				90	17	11	千克		Other woollen textile fabrics, impregnated, coated, covered or laminated with polyurethane, containing ≥ 50% by weight of combed wool or fine animal hair
5903.2090 49	用聚氨基甲酸酯浸渍的其他毛织物(聚氨基甲酸酯涂布包覆或层压的,精梳毛织物除外)	10				90	17	11	千克		Other woollen textile fabrics, impregnated, coated, covered or laminated with polyurethane, other than woven fabrics, of combed wool or fine animal hair
5903.2090 90	用聚氨基甲酸酯浸渍的其他纺织物(包括用聚氨基甲酸酯涂布,包覆或层压的)	10				90	17	11	千克		Other textile fabrics, impregnated, coated, covered or laminated with polyurethane
	-其他:										-Other:
5903.9010	---绝缘布或带	10	5	8.5	0	40	17	11	千克		---Insulating cloth or tape
5903.9010 10	若干平行化纤纱线粘合绝缘布或带(其他塑料浸渍涂布,包覆或层压,塑料重≤60%)	10				40	17	11	千克	5	Insulating cloth or tape, impregnated, coated, covered or laminated with plastics, of fabrics consisting of layers of parallel textile yarns, bonded, containing ≤ 60% by weight of plastics
5903.9010 20	其他塑料浸渍涤棉混纺绝缘布或带(塑料浸涂包的漂染聚酯短纤棉混纺,塑料橡胶<50%)	10				40	17	11	千克	5	Insulating cloth or tape of mixed with polyester staple fibres and cotton, impregnated, coated, covered or laminated with plastics, containing < 50% by weight of plastics or glue
5903.9010 30	其他塑料浸渍其他化纤绝缘布或带(包括用其他塑料涂布,包覆或层压,塑料或橡胶≤70%)	10				40	17	11	千克	5	Insulating cloth or tape, impregnated, coated, covered or laminated with plastics, other, containing ≤ 70% by weight of plastics or glue

税则号列 Tariff Item.	货品名称	最惠国(%) MFN	协定(%)CT 东盟 CA	中巴 CP	中智 CC	普通 Gen	增值税率 VAT	出口退税 ED	计量单位 Unit	监管条件 SC	Article Description
5903.9010 90	用其他塑料浸渍的其他绝缘布或带(包括用其他塑料涂布,包覆或层压的)	10				40	17	11	千克		Other insulating cloth or tape, impregnated, coated, covered or laminated with plastics
5903.9020	---人造革	10	T3	8.5	0	70	17	11	千克/米		---Imitation leather
5903.9020 10	由若干层平行纱线粘合化纤人造革(用其他塑料涂布,包覆或层压,塑料重≤60%)	10				70	17	11	千克/米	5	Imitation leather of man-made fibres, impregnated, coated, covered or laminated, with plastics of fabrics consisting of layers of parallel textile yarns, bonded, containing≤60% by weight of plastics
5903.9020 20	用其他塑料浸渍的涤棉织物人造革(其他塑料涂包的漂染印聚酯短纤棉混纺,塑料或橡胶<50%)	10				70	17	11	千克/米	5	Imitation leather of mixed with polyester staple fibres and cotton, impregnated, coated, covered or laminated with plastics, containing < 50% by weight plastics or glue
5903.9020 30	用其他塑料浸渍的其他化纤人造革(包括用其他塑料涂,包,覆的,塑料或橡胶≤70%)	10				70	17	11	千克/米	5	Imitation leather of man-made fibres, impregnated, coated, covered or laminated with other plastics, containing≤70% by weight of plastics or glue
5903.9020 40	用其他塑料浸渍的棉织物人造革(用其他塑料涂,包,覆或层压,漂染印花织物≥50%)	10				70	17	11	千克/米		Imitation leather of cotton, impregnated, coated, covered or laminated with plastics, containing≥50% by weight of fabrics of cotton, bleached, dyed or printed
5903.9020 90	用其他塑料浸渍的其他人造革(包括用其他塑料涂布,包覆或层压的)	10				70	17	11	千克/米		Mmitation leather, impregnated, coated, covered or laminated with plastics
5903.9090	---其他	10	T3	8.5	0	90	17	11	千克		---Other
5903.9090 10	若干层化纤平行纱线粘合其他织物(用其他塑料浸渍涂布包覆或层压.塑料重≤60%)	10				90	17	11	千克	5	Other textile fabrics, impregnated, coated, covered or laminated with plastics, of fabrics consisting of layers of parallel textile yarns, bonded, containing≤60% by weight of plastics
5903.9090 21	其他塑料浸渍的其他涤棉混纺织物(其他塑料涂布的漂印染聚酯短纤棉混纺,塑料或橡胶<50%	10				90	17	11	千克	5	Other textile fabrics of mixed with polyester staple fibres and cotton, impregnated, coated, covered or laminated with plastics, containing < 50% by weight of plastics or glue
5903.9090 29	用其他塑料浸渍的其他化纤织物(包括用其他塑料涂布包覆或层压的.塑料或橡胶≤70%)	10				90	17	11	千克	5	Other textile fabrics of man-made fibres, impregnated, coated, covered or laminated with plastics, containing≤70% by weight of plastics or glue
5903.9090 30	用其他塑料浸渍的棉织物(用其他塑料涂布包覆或层压的,漂染印花织物≥50%)	10				90	17	11	千克		Other textile fabrics, of cotton, impregnated, coated, covered or laminated with plastics, containing≥50% by weight of fabrics of cotton, bleached, dyed or printed

税则号列 Tariff Item.	货品名称	最惠国(%) MFN	协定(%) 东盟 CA	中巴 CP	CT 中智 CC	普通 Gen	增值税率 VAT	出口退税 ED	计量单位 Unit	监管条件 SC	Article Description
5903.9090 41	用其他塑料浸渍的精梳毛织物(用其他塑料涂布包覆或层压的,精梳羊毛动物细毛≥50%)	10				90	17	11	千克		Other woollen textile fabrics, impregnated, coated, covered or laminated with plastics, containing ≥ 50% by weight of combed wool or fine animal hair
5903.9090 49	用其他塑料浸渍的其他毛织物(用其他塑料涂布包覆或层压的.精梳毛织物除外)	10				90	17	11	千克		Other woollen textile fabrics, impregnated, coated, covered or laminated with plastics, other than woven fabric, combed wool or fine animal hair
5903.9090 90	用其他塑料浸渍的其他纺织物(包括用其他塑料涂布,包覆或层压的)	10				90	17	11	千克		Other textile fabrics, impregnated, coated, covered or laminated with plastics
59.04	**列诺伦(亚麻油地毡),不论是否剪切成形;以织物为底布经涂布或覆面的铺地制品,不论是否剪切成形:**										**Linoleum, whether or not cut to shape; floor coverings consisting of a coating or covering applied on a textile backing, whether or not cut to shape:**
5904.1000	-列诺伦(亚麻油地毡)	14	T3		0	90	17	11	平方米		-Linoleum
5904.9000	-其他	14	8		0	90	17	11	平方米		-Other
59.05	**糊墙织物:**										**Textile wall coverings:**
5905.0000	糊墙织物	10	8		0	80	17	11	平方米		Textile wall coverings
5905.0000 11	以纸衬背的合成短纤制糊墙织物	10				80	17	11	平方米		Textile wall coverings of synthetic staple fibres, fixed on backing of paper
5905.0000 19	以纸衬背的人造短纤制糊墙织物	10				80	17	11	平方米		Textile wall coverings of artificial staple fibres, fixed on backing of paper
5905.0000 20	平行纱线固定的糊墙织物(固定在任何其他衬背上的)	10				80	17	11	平方米	5	Textile wall coverings of fabrics consisting of layers of parallel textile yarns, fixed on backing other than paper
5905.0000 31	其他合成短纤制糊墙织物	10				80	17	11	平方米	5	Other textile wall coverings, of synthetic fibres
5905.0000 39	其他人造短纤制糊墙织物	10				80	17	11	平方米	5	Other textile wall coverings, of artificial fibres
5905.0000 90	其他纺织糊墙织物	10				80	17	11	平方米	5	Other textile wall coverings
59.06	**用橡胶处理的纺织物,但税目59.02的货品除外:**										**Rubberized textile fabrics, other than those of heading No. 59.02:**
	-宽度不超过20厘米的胶粘带:										-Adhesive tape of a width not exceeding 20 cm:
5906.1010	---绝缘带	10	5		0	40	17	11	千克		---Insulating tape
5906.1090	---其他	10	8		0	100	17	11	千克		---Other
	-其他:										-Other:
5906.9100	--针织或钩编的	10	8		0	130	17	11	千克		--Knitted or crocheted
5906.9100 10	橡胶处理的针织或钩编化纤纺织物(按重量计塑料或橡胶不超过70%,宽>20cm)	10				130	17	11	千克	5	Rubberized textile fabries, knitted or crocheted, width >20cm, containing ≤ 70% by weight of plastics or rubber
5906.9100 90	橡胶处理的针织或钩编其他纺织物(宽>20cm)	10				130	17	11	千克		Other rubberized textile fabrics, knitted or crocheted, width >20cm
	--其他:										--Other:
5906.9910	---绝缘布或带	10	5		0	40	17	11	千克		---Insulating cloth or tape

税则号列 Tariff Item.	货品名称	最惠国(%) MFN	协定(%) CT 东盟 CA	 中巴 CP	 中智 CC	普通 Gen	增值税率 VAT	出口退税 ED	计量单位 Unit	监管条件 SC	Article Description
5906.9910 10	用橡胶处理的精梳毛纺绝缘布或带(非针织或钩编、精梳羊毛或动物细毛≥50%宽>20cm)	10				40	17	11	千克		Rubberized woollen insulating cloth or tape, containing ≥50% by weight of combed wool or fine animal hair, width >20cm, other than knitted or crocheted
5906.9910 20	用橡胶处理的棉织物绝缘布或带(非针织或钩编,漂染印花棉织物≥50%宽>20cm)	10				40	17	11	千克		Rubberized insulating cloth or tape of cotton, containing≥50% by weight of cotton, bleached, dyed or printed, width > 20cm, other than knitted or crocheted
5906.9910 31	橡胶处理聚酯短纤棉混纺绝缘布带(非针织或钩编.漂染印花混纺布≥50%宽>20cm)	10				40	17	11	千克	5	Rubberized insulating cloth or tape, mixed, containing≥50% by weight of polyester staple fibres and cotton, width > 20cm, other than knitted or crocheted
5906.9910 39	用橡胶处理的其他化纤绝缘布或带(非针织或钩编,宽>20cm,塑料或橡胶≤70%)	10				40	17	11	千克	5	Rubberized insulating cloth or tape of other man-made fibres,containing≤70% by weight of plastics or glue, width > 20cm, other than knitted or crocheted
5906.9910 90	橡胶处理宽>20cm其他绝缘布或带(非针织或钩编的,宽>20cm)	10				40	17	11	千克		Other rubberized insulating cloth or tape, width >20cm, other than knitted or crocheted
5906.9990	---其他	10	8		0	100	17	11	千克		---Other
5906.9990 10	用橡胶处理的精梳毛纺织物(精梳羊毛或动物细毛≥50%,非针织或钩编的.宽>20cm)	10				100	17	11	千克		Rubberized woollen textile fabries, containing≥50% by weight of combed wool or fine animal hair, width > 20cm, other than knitted or crocheted
5906.9990 20	用橡胶处理的其他棉纺织物(非针织或钩编,宽>20cm,漂染印花棉织物≥50%)	10				100	17	11	千克		Rubberized textile fabries of cotton, containing≥50% by weight of cotton, bleached, dyed or printed, width > 20cm, other than knitted or crocheted
5906.9990 31	用橡胶处理的聚酯短纤棉混纺织物(非针织或钩编.宽>20cm.漂染印花聚酯混纺布≥50%)	10				100	17	11	千克	5	Rubberized textile fabrics mixed, containing ≥ 50% by weight of polyester staple fibres and cotton, bleached, dyed or printed, width > 20cm, other than knitted or crocheted
5906.9990 39	用橡胶处理的其他化纤纺织物(非针织或钩编.宽>20cm.塑料或橡胶≤70%)	10				100	17	11	千克	5	Rubberized textile fabries of other man-made fibres, containing ≤ 70% by weight of plastics or glue, width > 20cm, other than knitted or crocheted
5906.9990 90	用橡胶处理的其他纺织物(非针织或钩编.宽>20cm)	10				100	17	11	千克		Other rubberized textile fabries, width >20cm, other than knitted or crocheted
59.07	**用其他材料浸渍、涂布或包覆的纺织物;作舞台、摄影布景或类似用途的已绘制画布:**										**Textile fabrics otherwise impregnated, coated or covered; painted canvas being theatrical scenery, studio backcloths or the like:**
5907.0010	---绝缘布或带	10	5	8.5	0	40	17	11	千克		---Insulating cloth or tape

税则号列 Tariff Item.	货品名称	最惠国(%) MFN	协定(%)CT 东盟 CA	中巴 CP	中智 CC	普通 Gen	增值税率 VAT	出口退税 ED	计量单位 Unit	监管条件 SC	Article Description
5907.0010 10	其他材料浸涂植物纤维绝缘布或带(用橡胶,塑料,浆料以外材料浸渍涂布或包覆,棉除外)	10				40	17	11	千克		Insulating cloth or tape of vegetable fibres (other than cotton), impregnated, coated or covered with materials other than rubber, plastic, gum or amylaceous substances
5907.0010 20	其他材料浸涂的棉制绝缘布或带(用橡胶,塑料,浆料以外材料浸涂或包覆,漂染棉织物≥50%)	10				40	17	11	千克	5	Insulating cloth or tape of cotton, containing≥50% by weight of fabrics of cotton, bleached, dyed or printed, impregnated, coated or covered with materials other than rubber, plastic, gum or amylaceous substances
5907.0010 30	其他材料浸涂涤短纤棉混纺绝缘布(橡胶,塑料,浆料以外材料浸涂或包覆,漂染涤棉织物≥50%)	10				40	17	11	千克	5	Insulating cloth or tape, mixed, containing≥50% by weight of fabrics of polyester staple fibres and cotton, bleached, dyed or printed, impregnated, coated or covered with materials other than rubber, plastic, gum or amylaceous substances
5907.0010 90	其他材料浸涂其他纺织绝缘布或带(用橡胶,塑料,浆料以外材料浸渍,涂布或包覆)	10				40	17	11	千克	5	Insulating cloth or tape, impregnated, coated or covered with materials other than rubber, plastic, gum or amylaceous substances
5907.0020	---已绘制画布	10	5	8.5	0	50	17	11	千克		---Painted canvas
5907.0020 10	其他材料浸涂植物纤维已绘制画布(用橡胶,塑料,浆料以外材料浸渍,涂布或包覆,棉除外)	10				50	17	11	千克		Painted canvas of vegetable fibres (other than cotton), impregnated, coated or covered impregnated, coated or covered with materials other than rubber, plastic, gum or amylaceous substances
5907.0020 20	其他材料浸涂精梳毛已绘制画布(橡、塑、浆料以外材料浸涂或包覆,精梳羊/动物细毛≥50%)	10				50	17	11	千克	5	Painted woollen canvas, containing ≥ 50% by weight of combed wool or combed fine animal hair, impregnated, coated or covered with materials other than rubber, plastic, gum or amylaceous substances
5907.0020 30	用其他材料浸涂的棉制已绘制画布(橡塑,浆料以外材料浸涂或包覆,漂,染棉织物≥50%)	10				50	17	11	千克	5	Painted canvas of cotton, containing≥ 50% by weight of fabrics of cotton, bleached, dyed or printed, impregnated, coated or covered with materials other than rubber, plastic, gum or amylaceous substances
5907.0020 40	其他材料浸涂涤短纤棉混已绘画布(橡,塑,浆料以外材料浸涂或包覆,漂,染涤短棉织物≥50%)	10				50	17	11	千克	5	Painted canvas mixed, containing ≥ 50% by weight of fabrics of polyester staple fibres and cotton, bleached, dyed or printed, impregnated, coated or covered with materials other than rubber, plastic, gum or amylaceous substances

税则号列 Tariff Item.	货品名称	最惠国(%) MFN	协定(%)CT 东盟 CA	 中巴 CP	 中智 CC	普通 Gen	增值税率 VAT	出口退税 ED	计量单位 Unit	监管条件 SC	Article Description
5907.0020 90	其他材料浸涂其他织物已绘制画布(用橡胶,塑料,浆料以外材料浸渍,涂布或包覆)	10				50	17	11	千克	5	Painted canvas, impregnated, coated or covered with materials other than rubber, plastic, gum or amylaceous substances
5907.0090	---其他	10	8	8.5	0	100	17	11	千克		---Other
5907.0090 10	用其他材料浸涂的植物纤维纺织物(用橡胶,塑料,浆料以外材料浸渍,涂布或包覆,棉除外)	10				100	17	11	千克		Textile fabrics of vegetable fibres (other than cotton) impregnated, coated or covered with materials other than rubber, plastic, gum or amylaceous substances
5907.0090 20	用其他材料浸涂的精梳毛纺织物(橡,塑,浆料以外材料浸涂或包覆,精梳羊/动物细毛≥50%)	10				100	17	11	千克	5	Woollen textile fabrics, containing ≥ 50% by weight of combed wool or combed fine animal hair impregnated, coated or covered with materials other than rubber, plastic, gum or amylaceous substances
5907.0090 30	用其他材料浸涂的棉制纺织物(橡,塑,浆料以外材料浸涂或包覆,漂,染棉织物≥50%)	10				100	17	11	千克	5	Textile fabrics of cotton, containing ≥ 50% by weight of fabrics of cotton, bleached, dyed or printed, impregnated, coated or covered with materials other than rubber, plastic, gum or amylaceous substances
5907.0090 40	用其他材料浸涂的涤短纤棉混纺织物(橡胶,塑料,浆料以外材料浸涂或包覆,漂、染涤棉织物≥50%)	10				100	17	11	千克	5	Textile fabrics, mixed, containing ≥ 50% by weight of fabrics of polyester staple fibres and cotton impregnated, coated or covered with materials other than rubber, plastic, gum or amylaceous substances
5907.0090 90	用其他材料浸涂的其他纺织物(用橡胶,塑料,浆料以外材料浸渍,涂布或包覆)	10				100	17	11	千克	5	Other textile fabrics, impregnated, coated or covered with materials other than rubber, plastic, gum or amylaceous substances
59.08	**用纺织材料机织、编结或针织而成的灯芯、炉芯、打火机芯、烛芯或类似品;煤气灯纱筒及纱罩,不论是否浸渍:**										**Textile wicks, woven, plaited or knitted, for lamps, stoves, lighters, candles or the like; incandescent gas mantles and tubular knitted gas mantle fabric therefor, whether or not impregnated:**
5908.0000	用纺织材料机织、编结或针织而成的灯芯、炉芯、打火机芯、烛芯或类似品;煤气灯纱筒及纱罩,不论是否浸渍	10	5		0	70	17	11	千克		Textile wicks, woven, plaited or knitted, for lamps, stoves, lighters, candles or the like; incandescent gas mantles and tubular knitted gas mantle fabric therefor, whether or not impregnated
59.09	**纺织材料制的水龙软管及类似的管子,不论有无其他材料作衬里、护套或附件:**										**Textile hosepiping and similar textile tubing, with or without lining, armour or accessories of other materials:**

税则号列 Tariff Item.	货品名称	最惠国(%) MFN	协定(%)CT 东盟 CA	中巴 CP	中智 CC	普通 Gen	增值税率 VAT	出口退税 ED	计量单位 Unit	监管条件 SC	Article Description
5909.0000	纺织材料制的水龙软管及类似的管子,不论有无其他材料作衬里、护套或附件	8	5		0	35	17	11	千克		Textile hosepiping and similar textile tubing, with or without lining, armour or accessories of other materials
59.10	**纺织材料制的传动带或输送带及带料,不论是否用塑料浸渍、涂布、包覆或压层,也不论是否用金属或其他材料加强:**										**Transmission or conveyor belts or belting, of textile material, whether or not impregnated, coated, covered or laminated with plastics, or reinforced with metal or other material:**
5910.0000	纺织材料制的传动带或输送带及带料,不论是否用塑料浸渍、涂布、包覆或压层,也不论是否用金属或其他材料加强	8	5		0	35	17	11	千克		Transmission or conveyor belts or belting, of textile material, whether or not impregnated, coated, covered or laminated with plastics, or reinforced with metal or other material
59.11	**本章注释七所规定的作专门技术用途的纺织产品及制品:**										**Textile products and articles, for technical uses, specified in Note 7 to this Chapter:**
	-用橡胶、皮革或其他材料涂布、包覆或层压的作针布用的纺织物、毡呢及毡呢衬里机织物,以及作专门技术用途的类似织物,包括用橡胶浸渍的、用于包覆纺缍(织轴)的狭幅丝绒织物:										-Textile fabrics, felt and felt-lined woven fabrics, coated, covered or laminated with rubber, leather or other material, of a kind used for card clothing, and similar fabrics of a kind used for other technical purposes, including narrow fabrics made of velvet impregnated with rubber, for covering weaving spindles (weaving beams):
5911.1010	---用橡胶浸渍的、用于包覆纺缍(织轴)的狭幅丝绒织物	8	5	7.2	0	75	17	11	千克		---Narrow pile fabrics made of velvet impregnated with rubber, for covering weaving spindles (weaving beams)
5911.1090	---其他	8	5		0	35	17	11	千克		---Other
5911.2000	-筛布,不论是否制成的	8	5		0	35	17	11	千克		-Bolting cloth, whether or not made up
5911.2000 10	丝制筛布(不论是否制成的)	8				35	17	11	千克		Bolting cloth of silk, whether or not made up
5911.2000 90	其他纺织材料制筛布(不论是否制成的,刻版筛网印布除外)	8				35	17	11	千克	5	Bolting cloth of other textile materials, whether or not made up, other than stencil screen
	-环状或装有联接装置的纺织物及毡呢,用于造纸机器或类似机器(例如,制浆机或制石棉水泥的机器):										-Textile fabrics and felts, endless or fitted with linking devices, of a kind used in paper-making or similar machines (for example, for pulp or asbestos-cement):
5911.3100	--每平方米重量在650克以下	8	5		0	35	17	11	千克		--Weighing less than 650 g/m^2
5911.3200	--每平方米重量在650克及以上	8	5		0	35	17	11	千克		--Weighing 650 g/m^2 or more
5911.4000	-用于榨油机器或类似机器的滤布,包括人发制滤布	8	5		0	35	17	11	千克		-Straining cloth of a kind used in oil presses or the like, including that of human hair
5911.9000	-其他	8	5		0	35	17	11	千克		-Other

第六十章
针织物及钩编织物

Chapter 60
Knitted or crocheted fabrics

注释：

一、本章不包括：

（一）税目 58.04 的钩编花边；

（二）税目 58.07 的针织或钩编的标签、徽章及类似品；

（三）第五十九章的经浸渍、涂布、包覆或层压的针织物及钩编织物。但经浸渍、涂布、包覆或层压的起绒针织物及起绒钩编织物仍归入税目 60.01。

二、本章还包括用金属线制的用于衣着、装饰或类似用途的织物。

三、本目录所称"针织物"，包括由纺织纱线用链式针法构成的缝编织物。

Notes:

1. This Chapter does not cover:
(a) Crochet lace of heading No. 58.04;
(b) Labels, badges or similar articles, knitted or crocheted, of heading No. 58.07; or
(c) Knitted or crocheted fabrics, impregnated, coated, covered or laminated, of Chapter 59. However, knitted or crocheted pile fabrics, impregnated, coated, covered or laminated, remain classified in heading No. 60.01.
2. This Chapter also includes fabrics made of metal thread and of a kind used in apparel, as furnishing fabrics or for similar purposes.
3. Throughout the Nomenclature any reference to "knitted" goods includes a reference to stitch-bonded goods in which the chain stitches are formed of textile yarn.

税则号列 Tariff Item.	货品名称	最惠国(%) MFN	协定(%) CT 东盟 CA	中巴 CP	中智 CC	普通 Gen	增值税率 VAT	出口退税 ED	计量单位 Unit	监管条件 SC	Article Description
60.01	**针织或钩编的起绒织物，包括"长毛绒"织物及毛圈织物：**										**Pile fabrics, including "long pile" fabrics and terry fabrics, knitted or crocheted:**
6001.1000	-"长毛绒"织物	10	T3	0	0	130	17	11	米/千克		-"Long pile" fabrics
6001.1000 10	毛制针织或钩编的长毛绒织物(羊毛及动物细毛制)	10				130	17	11	米/千克		"Long pile" fabrics, knitted or crocheted, of wool and fine animal hair
6001.1000 20	棉制针织或钩编的长毛绒织物	10				130	17	11	米/千克		"Long pile" fabrics, knitted or crocheted, of cotton
6001.1000 30	化纤制针织或钩编的长毛绒织物	10				130	17	11	米/千克		"Long pile" fabrics, knitted or crocheted, of man-made fibres
6001.1000 90	其他纺织材料制针织或钩编长毛绒织物	10				130	17	11	米/千克		Other "long pile" fabrics, knitted or crocheted, of other textile materials
	-毛圈绒头织物：										-Looped pile fabrics:
6001.2100	--棉制	10	5	0	0	70	17	11	米/千克		--Of cotton
6001.2200	--化学纤维制	10	T3	0	0	130	17	11	米/千克		--Of man-made fibres
6001.2900	--其他纺织材料制	12	T3	0	0	130	17	11	米/千克		--Of other textile materials
6001.2900 10	毛制针织或钩编毛圈绒头织物(羊毛及动物细毛制)	12				130	17	11	米/千克		Looped pile fabrics, knitted or crocheted, of wool and fine animal hair
6001.2900 90	其他材料制针织或钩编毛圈绒头布	12				130	17	11	米/千克		Other looped pile fabrics, knitted or crocheted, of other textile materials
	-其他：										-Other:
6001.9100	--棉制	10	5	0	0	70	17	11	米/千克		--Of cotton
6001.9200	--化学纤维制	10	T3	0	0	130	17	11	米/千克		--Of man-made fibres
6001.9900	--其他纺织材料制	12	T3	0	0	130	17	11	米/千克		--Of other textile materials
6001.9900 10	丝制针织或钩编其他起绒织物(按重量计含丝及绢丝85%及以上)	12				130	17	11	米/千克		Other pile fabrics, knitted or crocheted containing≥85% by weight of silk or silk waste
6001.9900 20	毛制针织或钩编其他起绒织物(羊毛及动物细毛制)	12				130	17	11	米/千克		Other pile fabrics, knitted or crocheted, of wool and fine animal hair
6001.9900 90	其他纺织材料制针织或钩编起绒织物	12				130	17	11	米/千克		Other pile fabrics, knitted or crocheted, of other textile materials

税则号列 Tariff Item.	货品名称	最惠国(%) MFN	协定(%)CT 东盟 CA	中巴 CP	中智 CC	普通 Gen	增值税率 VAT	出口退税 ED	计量单位 Unit	监管条件 SC	Article Description
60.02	**宽度不超过30厘米,按重量计弹性纱线或橡胶线含量在5%及以上的针织物或钩编织物,但税目60.01的货品除外:**										**Knitted or crocheted fabrics of a width not exceeding 30 cm, containing by weight 5% or more of elastomeric yarn or rubber thread, other than those of heading No. 60.01:**
	-按重量计弹性纱线含量在5%及以上,但不含橡胶线:										-Containing by weight 5% or more of elastomeric yarn but not containing rubber thread:
6002.4010	---棉制	10	5	0	0	70	17	11	米/千克	5	---Of cotton
6002.4020	---丝及绢丝制	10	8	0	0	130	17	11	米/千克		---Of silk or silk waste
6002.4030	---合成纤维制	10	8	0	0	130	17	11	米/千克	5	---Of synthetic fibres
6002.4040	---人造纤维制	10	8	0	0	130	17	11	米/千克	5	---Of artificial fibres
6002.4090	---其他	10	8	0	0	130	17	11	米/千克	5	---Other
	-其他:										-Other:
6002.9010	---棉制	10	T3	0	0	70	17	11	米/千克	5	---Of cotton
6002.9020	---丝及绢丝制	10	8	0	0	130	17	11	米/千克		---Of silk or silk waste
6002.9030	---合成纤维制	10	T3	0	0	130	17	11	米/千克	5	---Of syntheeic fibres
6002.9040	---人造纤维制	10	8	0	0	130	17	11	米/千克	5	---Of artificial fibres
6002.9090	---其他	10	8	0	0	130	17	11	米/千克	5	---Other
60.03	**宽度不超过30厘米的针织或钩编织物,但税目60.01或60.02的货品除外:**										**Knitted or crocheted fabrics of a width not exceeding 30 cm, other than those of heading No. 60.01 or 60.02:**
6003.1000	-羊毛或动物细毛制	10	8	0	0	130	17	11	米/千克	5	-Of wool or fine animal hair
6003.2000	-棉制	10	5	0	0	70	17	11	米/千克	5	-Of cotton
6003.2000 10	棉制宽≤30cm经编织物(按重量计弹性纱线或橡胶线含量<50%)	10				70	17	11	米/千克	5	The width of cotton≤30cm, knitted work or basketwork (elastic yarn or rubber yarn <5% in weight)
6003.2000 90	棉制≤30cm非经编针织或钩编织物(按重量计弹性纱线或橡胶线含量<50%)	10				70	17	11	米/千克	5	Not warp knit or crochete fabrics of a width not exceeding 30cm ,comtaining by weight <5% of elastomeric yarn or rubber thread , of cotton
6003.3000	-合成纤维制	10	8	0	0	130	17	11	米/千克		-Of synthetic fibres
6003.3000 10	合纤制宽小于等于30厘米经编织物(按重量计弹性纱线或橡胶线含量<50%)	10				130	17	11	米/千克	5	The width of Synthetic fiber ≤ 30cm, knitting work or basketwork (elastic yarn or rubber yarn <5% in weight)
6003.3000 90	合纤制宽小于等于30厘米非经编针织或钩编织物(按重量计弹性纱线或橡胶线含量<50%)	10				130	17	11	米/千克	5	The width of Synthetic fiber≤30cm, not knitting work or basketwork (elastic yarn or rubber yarn <5% in weight)
6003.4000	-人造纤维制	10	8	0	0	130	17	11	米/千克		-Of artificial fibres
6003.4000 10	人纤制宽小于等于30厘米经编织物(按重量计弹性纱线或橡胶线含量<50%)	10				130	17	11	米/千克	5	Warp knit fabrics of a width not exceeding 30cm ,comtaining by weight <5% of elastomeric yarn or rubber thread , of artificial fibres
6003.4000 90	人纤制宽小于等于30厘米非经编织物(按重量计弹性纱线或橡胶线含量<50%)	10				130	17	11	米/千克	5	Not warp knit fabrics of a width not exceeding 30cm ,comtaining by weight <5% of elastomeric yarn or rubber thread, of artificial fibres
6003.9000	-其他	10	8	0	0	130	17	11	米/千克	5	-Other

税则号列 Tariff Item.	货品名称	最惠国(%) MFN	协定(%)CT 东盟 CA	协定(%)CT 中巴 CP	协定(%)CT 中智 CC	普通 Gen	增值税率 VAT	出口退税 ED	计量单位 Unit	监管条件 SC	Article Description
60.04	**宽度超过30厘米,按重量计弹性纱线或橡胶线含量在5%及以上的针织物或钩编织物,但税目60.01的货品除外:**										**Knitted or crocheted fabrics of a width exceeding 30 cm, containing by weight 5% or more of elastomeric yarn or rubber thread, other than those of heading No. 60.01:**
	-按重量计弹性纱线含量在5%及以上,但不含橡胶线										-Containing by weight 5% or more of elastomeric yarn but not containing rubber thread:
6004.1010	---棉制	10	T3	0	0	70	17	11	米/千克	5	---Of cotton
6004.1020	---丝及绢丝制	10	8	0	0	130	17	11	米/千克		---Of silk or silk waste
6004.1030	---合成纤维制	10	8	0	0	130	17	11	米/千克	5	---Of synthetic fibres
6004.1040	---人造纤维制	10	8	0	0	130	17	11	米/千克	5	---Of artificial fibres
6004.1090	---其他	10	8	0	0	130	17	11	米/千克	5	---Other
	-其他:										-Other:
6004.9010	---棉制	10	5	0	0	70	17	11	米/千克	5	---Of cotton
6004.9020	---丝及绢丝制	10	8	0	0	130	17	11	米/千克		---Of silk or silk waste
6004.9030	---合成纤维制	10	8	0	0	130	17	11	米/千克	5	---Of synthetic fibres
6004.9040	---人造纤维制	10	8	0	0	130	17	11	米/千克	5	---Of artificial fibres
6004.9090	---其他	10	8	0	0	130	17	11	米/千克	5	---Other
60.05	**经编织物(包括由花边针织机织成的),但税目60.01至60.04的货品除外:**										**Warp knit fabrics (including those made on galloon knitting machines), other than those of headings Nos. 60.01 to 60.04:**
	-棉制:										-Of cotton:
6005.2100	--未漂白或漂白	10	5	0	0	70	17	11	米/千克	5	--Unbleached or bleached
6005.2200	--染色	10	5	0	0	70	17	11	米/千克	5	--Dyed
6005.2300	--色织	10	5	0	0	70	17	11	米/千克	5	--Of yarns of different colours
6005.2400	--印花	10	5	0	0	70	17	11	米/千克	5	--Printed
	-合成纤维制:										-Of synthetic fibres:
6005.3100	--未漂白或漂白	10	T3	0	0	130	17	11	米/千克		--Unbleached or bleached
6005.3100 10	漂白或未漂白合成纤维制经编透孔织物(包括由花边针织机织成的经编织物)	10				130	17	11	米/千克	5	Knitted openwork made by Bleached or unbleached synthetic fiber (including basketwork made by lace warp knitting machine)
6005.3100 90	漂白或未漂白合成纤维制经编非透孔织物(包括由花边针织机织成的经编织物)	10				130	17	11	米/千克	5	Knitted not openwork made by Bleached or unbleached synthetic fiber (including basketwork made by lace warp knitting machine)
6005.3200	--染色	10	T3	0	0	130	17	11	米/千克		--Dyed
6005.3200 10	染色合成纤维制经编透孔织物(包括由花边针织机织成的经编织物)	10				130	17	11	米/千克	5	Knitted openwork made by Dyed synthetic fiber (including basketwork made by lace warp knitting machine)
6005.3200 90	染色合成纤维制经编非透孔织物(包括由花边针织机织成的经编织物)	10				130	17	11	米/千克	5	Knitted not openwork made by Dyed synthetic fiber (including basketwork made by lace warp knitting machine)
6005.3300	--色织	10	T3	0	0	130	17	11	米/千克		--Of yarns of different colours

税则号列 Tariff Item.	货品名称	最惠国(%) MFN	协定(%)CT 东盟 CA	中巴 CP	中智 CC	普通 Gen	增值税率 VAT	出口退税 ED	计量单位 Unit	监管条件 SC	Article Description
6005.3300 10	色织合成纤维制经编透孔织物(包括由花边针织成的经编织物)	10				130	17	11	米/千克	5	Knitted openwork made by colored synthetic fiber (including basketwork made by lace warp knitting machine)
6005.3300 90	色织合成纤维制经编非透孔织物(包括由花边针织成的经编织物)	10				130	17	11	米/千克	5	Knitted not openwork made by colored synthetic fiber (including basketwork made by lace warp knitting machine)
6005.3400	--印花	10	T3	0	0	130	17	11	米/千克		--Printed
	-人造纤维制:										-Of artificial fibres:
6005.3400 10	印花合成纤维制经编透孔织物(包括由花边针织成的经编织物)	10				130	17	11	米/千克	5	Knitted openwork made by printing synthetic fiber (including basketwork made by lace warp knitting machine)
6005.3400 90	印花合成纤维制经编非透孔织物(包括由花边针织成的经编织物)	10				130	17	11	米/千克	5	Knitted not openwork made by printing synthetic fiber (including basketwork made by lace warp knitting machine)
6005.4100	--未漂白或漂白	10	8	0	0	130	17	11	米/千克		--Unbleached or bleached
6005.4100 10	漂白或未漂白人造纤维制经编透孔织物(包括由花边针织成的经编织物)	10				130	17	11	米/千克	5	Knitted openwork made by Bleached or unbleached man - made fiber (including basketwork made by lace warp knitting machine)
6005.4100 90	漂白或未漂白人造纤维制经编非透孔织物(包括由花边针织成的经编织物)	10				130	17	11	米/千克	5	Knitted not openwork made by Bleached or unbleached man - made fiber (including basketwork made by lace warp knitting machine)
6005.4200	--染色	10	8	0	0	130	17	11	米/千克		--Dyed
6005.4200 10	染色人造纤维制经编透孔(包括由花边针织成的经编织物)	10				130	17	11	米/千克	5	Knitted openwork made by Dyed man - made fiber (including basketwork made by lace warp knitting machine)
6005.4200 90	染色人造纤维制经编非透孔(包括由花边针织成的经编织物)	10				130	17	11	米/千克	5	Knitted not openwork made by Dyed man - made fiber (including basketwork made by lace warp knitting machine)
6005.4300	--色织	10	8	0	0	130	17	11	米/千克		--Of yarns of different colours
6005.4300 10	色织人造纤维制经编透孔织物(包括由花边针织成的经编织物)	10				130	17	11	米/千克	5	Knitted openwork made by colored man - made fiber (including basketwork made by lace warp knitting machine)
6005.4300 90	色织人造纤维制经编非透孔织物(包括由花边针织成的经编织物)	10				130	17	11	米/千克	5	Knitted not openwork made by colored man - made fiber (including basketwork made by lace warp knitting machine)
6005.4400	--印花	10	8	0	0	130	17	11	米/千克		--Printed
	-其他:										-Other:
6005.4400 10	印花人造纤维制经编透孔织物(包括由花边针织成的经编织物)	10				130	17	11	米/千克	5	Knitted openwork made by printing man - made fiber (including basketwork made by lace warp knitting machine)
6005.4400 90	印花人造纤维制经编非透孔织物(包括由花边针织成的经编织物)	10				130	17	11	米/千克	5	Knitted not openwork made by printing man - made fiber (including basketwork made by lace warp knitting machine)
6005.9010	---羊毛或动物细毛制	12	8	0	0	130	17	11	米/千克		---Of wool or fine animal hair
6005.9090	---其他	12	8	0	0	130	17	11	米/千克		---Other
60.06	**其他针织或钩编织物:**										**Other knitted or crocheted fabrics:**
6006.1000	-羊毛或动物细毛制	12	8	0	0	130	17	11	米/千克		-Of wool or fine animal hair

税则号列 Tariff Item.	货品名称	最惠国(%) MFN	协定(%) CT 东盟 CA	中巴 CP	中智 CC	普通 Gen	增值税率 VAT	出口退税 ED	计量单位 Unit	监管条件 SC	Article Description
	-棉制:										-Of cotton:
6006.2100	--未漂白或漂白	10	5	0	0	70	17	11	米/千克	5	--Unbleached or bleached
6006.2200	--染色	10	T3	0	0	70	17	11	米/千克	5	--Dyed
6006.2300	--色织	10	T3	0	0	70	17	11	米/千克	5	--Of yarns of different colours
6006.2400	--印花	10	5	0	0	70	17	11	米/千克	5	--Printed
	-合成纤维制:										-Of synthetic fibres:
6006.3100	--未漂白或漂白	10	T3	0	0	130	17	11	米/千克	5	--Unbleached or bleached
6006.3200	--染色	10	T3	0	0	130	17	11	米/千克	5	--Dyed
6006.3300	--色织	10	T3	0	0	130	17	11	米/千克	5	--Of yarns of different colours
6006.3400	--印花	10	8	0	0	130	17	11	米/千克	5	--Printed
	-人造纤维制:										-Of artificial fibres:
6006.4100	--未漂白或漂白	10	8	0	0	130	17	11	米/千克	5	--Unbleached or bleached
6006.4200	--染色	10	8	0	0	130	17	11	米/千克	5	--Dyed
6006.4300	--色织	10	8	0	0	130	17	11	米/千克	5	--Of yarns of different colours
6006.4400	--印花	10	8	0	0	130	17	11	米/千克	5	--Printed
6006.9000	-其他	12	8	0	0	130	17	11	米/千克		-Other
6006.9000 10	丝及绢丝制其他针织或钩编织物(按重量计含丝及绢丝85%及以上)	12				130	17	11	米/千克		Other knitted or crocheted fabrics of silk or silk waste, containing ≥ 85% by weight of silk or silk waste
6006.9000 90	其他纺织材料制其他针织或钩编织物	12				130	17	11	米/千克		Other knitted or crocheted fabrics of other textile materials

第六十一章
针织或钩编的服装及衣着附件

注释：

一、本章仅适用于制成的针织品或钩编织品。

二、本章不包括：

（一）税目62.12的货品；

（二）税目63.09的旧衣着或其他旧物品；

（三）矫形器具、外科手术带、疝气带及类似品（税目90.21）。

三、税目61.03及61.04所称：

（一）“西服套装”，是指面料用相同的织物制成的两件套或三件套的下列成套服装：

一件人体上半身穿着的外套或短上衣，除袖子外，其面料数为四片或四片以上；也可附带一件西服背心，这件背心的前片面料应与套装其他各件的面料相同，后片面料则应与外套或短上衣的衬里料相同；以及一件人体下半身穿着的服装，即不带背带或护胸的长裤、马裤、短裤（游泳裤除外）、裙子或裙裤。

西服套装各件面料质地、颜色及构成必须相同，其款式也必须相同，尺寸大小还须相互般配，但可以用不同织物滚边（缝口上缝入长条织物）。

如果数件人体下半身穿着的服装同时进口或出口（例如，两条长裤、长裤与短裤、裙 子或裙裤与长裤），构成西服套装下装的应是一条长裤，而对于女式西服套装，则应是一条裙子或裙裤，其他服装应分别归类。

所称“西服套装”，包括不论是否完全符合上述条件的下列配套服装：

1. 常礼服，由一件后襟下垂并下端开圆弧形叉的素色短上衣和一条条纹长裤组成；

2. 晚礼服（燕尾服），一般用黑色织物制成，上衣前襟较短且不闭合，背后有燕尾；

3. 无燕尾套装夜礼服，其中上衣款式与普通上衣相似（可以更为显露衬衣前胸），但有光滑丝质或仿丝质的翻领。

（二）“便服套装”，是指面料相同并作零售包装的下列成套服装（西服套装及税目61.07、61.08或61.09的物品除外）：

Chapter 61
Articles of apparel and clothing accessories, knitted or crocheted6

Notes:

1. This Chapter applies only to made up knitted or crocheted articles.

2. This Chapter does not cover:

(a) Goods of heading No. 62. 12;

(b) Worn clothing or other worn articles of heading No. 63. 09; or

(c) Orthopaedic appliances, surgical belts, trusses or the like (heaing No. 90. 21).

3. For the purposes of headings Nos. 61. 03 and 61. 04:

(a) The term “suit” means a set of garments composed of two or three pieces made up, in respect of their outer surface, in identical fabric and comprising:

-One suit coat or jacket the outer shell of which, exclusive of sleeves, consists of four or more panels, designed to cover the upper part of the body, possibly with a tailored waistcoat in addition whose front panel is made from the same fabric as the outer shell of the other components of the set and whose rear panel is made from the same fabric as the lining of the suit coat or jacket, andone garment designed to cover the lower part of the body and consisting of trousers, breeches or shorts (other than swimwear), a skirt or a divided skirt, having neither braces nor bibs.

All of the components of a suit must be of the identical fabric construction, style, colour and composition; they must also be of corresponding or compatible size. However, these components may have bindings of different fabric (the narrow fabric stitched to finish raw edges).

If several separate components to cover the lower part of the body are presented together (for example, trousers and shorts, or a skirt or divided skirt and trousers), the constituent lower part shall be one pair of trousers, or, in the case of women's or girls' suits, the skirt or divided skirt, the other garments being considered separately.

The term “suit” includes the following sets of garments, whether or not they fulfill all the above conditions:

-morning dress, comprising a plain jacket (cutaway) with rounded tails hanging well down at the back and striped trousers;

-evening dress (tailcoat), generally made of black fabric, the jacket of which is relatively short at the front, does not close and has narrow skirts cut in at the hips and hanging down behind;

-dinner jacket suits, in which the jacket is similar in style to an ordinary jacket (though perhaps revealing more of the shirt front), but has shiny silk or imitation silk lapels.

(b) The term “ensemble” means a set of garments (other than suits and articles of heading No. 61. 07, 61. 08 or 61. 09), composed of several pieces made up in identical fabric, put up for retail sale, and comprising:

一件人体上半身穿着的服装，但套衫及背心除外，因为套衫可在两件套服装中作为内衣，背心也可作为内衣；以及一件或两件不同的人体下半身穿着的服装，即长裤、护胸背带工装裤、马裤、短裤(游泳裤除外)、裙子或裙裤。

便服套装各件面料质地、款式、颜色及构成必须相同；尺寸大小也须相互般配。所称“便服套装”，不包括税目61.12的运动服及滑雪服。

四、税目61.05及61.06不包括在腰围以下有口袋的服装、带有罗纹腰带及以其他方式收紧下摆的服装或其织物至少在10厘米×10厘米的面积内沿各方向的直线长度上平均每厘米少于10针的服装。税目61.05不包括无袖服装。

五、税目61.09不包括带有束带、罗纹腰带或其他方式收紧下摆的服装。

六、对于税目61.11：

(一)所称“婴儿服装及衣着附件”，是指用于身高不超过86厘米幼儿的服装；也包括婴儿尿布；

(二)既可归入税目61.11，也可归入本章其他税目的物品，应归入税目61.11。

七、税目61.12所称“滑雪服”，是指从整个外观和织物质地来看，主要在滑雪(速度滑雪或高山滑雪)时穿着的下列服装或成套服装：

(一)“滑雪连身服”，即上下身连在一起的单件服装；除袖子和领子外，滑雪连身服可有口袋或脚带；或

(二)“滑雪套装”，即由两件或三件构成一套并作零售包装的下列服装：

一件用一条拉链扣合的带风帽的厚夹克、防风衣、防风短上衣或类似的服装，可以附带一件背心；以及一条不论是否过腰的长裤、一条马裤或一条护胸背带工装裤。

“滑雪套装”也可由一件类似以上(一)款所述的连身服和一件可套在连身服外面的有胎料背心组成。

“滑雪套装”各件颜色可以不同，但面料质地、款式及构成必须相同；尺寸大小也须相互般配。

八、既可归入税目61.13，也可归入本章其他税目的服装，除税目61.11所列的仍归入该税目外，其余的应一律归入税目61.13。

-One garment designed to cover the upper part of the body, with the exception of pullovers which may form a second upper garment in the sole context of twin sets, and of waistcoats which may also form a second upper garment, andOne or two different garments, designed to cover the lower part of the body and consisting of trousers, bib and brace overalls, breeches, shorts (other than swimwear), a skirt or a divided skirt.

All of the components of an ensemble must be of the same fabric construction, style, colour and composition; they also must be of corresponding or compatible size. The term "ensemble" does not apply to track suits or ski suits, of heading No. 61. 12.

4. Headings Nos. 61. 05 and 61. 06 do not cover garments with pockets below the waist, with a ribbed waistband or other means of tightening at the bottom of the garment, or garments having an average of less than 10 stitches per linear centimetre in each direction counted on an area measuring at least 10cm × 10cm. Heading No. 61. 05 does not cover sleeveless garments.

5. Heading No. 61. 09 does not cover garments with a drawstring, a ribbed waistband or other means of tightening at the bottom of the garment.

6. For the purposes of heading No. 61. 11:

(a) The expression "babies' garments and clothing accessories" means articles for young children of a body height not exceeding 86cm; it also covers babies' napkins;

(b) Articles which are, *prima facie*, classifiable both in heading No. 61. 11 and in other headings of this Chapter are to be classified in heading No. 61. 11.

7. For the purposes of heading No. 61. 12, "ski suits" means garments or sets of garments which, by their general appearance and texture, are identifiable as intended to be worn principally for skiing (cross-country or alpine). They consist either of:

(a) a "ski overall", that is, a one-piece garment designed to cover the upper and the lower parts of the body; in addition to sleeves and a collar the ski overall may have pockets or footstraps; or

(b) a "ski ensemble", that is, a set of garments composed of two or three pieces, put up for retail sale and comprising:

-one garment such as an anorak, wind-cheater, windjacket or similar article, closed by a slide fastener (zipper), possibly with a waistcoat in addition, and-one pair of trousers whether or not extending above waist-level, one pair of breeches or one bib and brace overall.

The "ski ensemble" may also consist of an overall similar to the one mentioned in paragraph (a) above and a type of padded, sleeveless jacket worn over the overall.

All the components of a "ski ensemble" must be made up in a fabric of the same texture, style and composition whether or not of the same colour; they also must be of corresponding or compatible size.

8. Garments which are, *prima facie*, classifiable both in heading No. 61. 13 and in other headings of this Chapter, excluding heading No. 61. 11, are to be classified in heading No. 61. 13.

九、本章的服装，凡门襟为左压右的，应视为男式；右压左的，应视为女式。但本规定不适用于其式样已明显为男式或女式的服装。无法区别是男式还是女式的服装，应按女式服装归入有关税目。

9. Garments of this Chapter desinged for left over right closure at the front shall be regarded as men's or boys' garments, and those designed for right over left closure at the front as women's or girls' garments. These provisions do not apply where the cut of the garment clearly indicates that it is designed for one or other of the sexes. Garments which cannot be identified as either men's or boys' garments or as women's or girls' garments are to be classified in the headings covering women's or girls' garments.

十、本章物品可用金属线制成。

10. Articles of this Chapter may be made of metal thread.

税则号列 Tariff Item.	货品名称	最惠国(%) MFN	协定(%) CT 东盟 CA	中巴 CP	中智 CC	普通 Gen	增值税率 VAT	出口退税 ED	计量单位 Unit	监管条件 SC	Article Description
61.01	**针织或钩编的男式大衣、短大衣、斗篷、短斗篷、带风帽的防寒短上衣(包括滑雪短上衣)、防风衣、防风短上衣及类似品，但税目61.03的货品除外：**										**Men's or boys' overcoats, car-coats, capes, cloaks, anoraks (including ski-jackets), wind-cheaters, wind-jackets and similar articles, knitted or crocheted, other than those of heading No. 61.03:**
6101.2000	-棉制	17.5	8	14	0	90	17	13	件/千克		-Of cotton
6101.2000 10	棉制针织或钩编男式大衣(包括短大衣、斗篷短斗篷及类似品，雨衣除外)	17.5				90	17	13	件/千克		Men's or boys' overcoats, car-coats, capes, cloak and similar articles, other than raincoats, knitted or crocheted, of cotton
6101.2000 21	棉制针织或钩编手工制男式防风衣(包括防寒短上衣、防风短上衣及类似品)	17.5				90	17	13	件/千克		Men's or boys' wind-cheaters, anoraks, wind-jackets and similar articles, hand-worked, knitted or crocheted, of cotton
6101.2000 29	棉制针织或钩编男式防风衣(包括防寒短上衣、防风短上衣及类似品)	17.5				90	17	13	件/千克	5	Men's or boys' wind-cheaters, anoraks, wind-jackets and similar articles, knitted or crocheted, of cotton
6101.2000 30	棉制针织或钩编男式雨衣	17.5				90	17	13	件/千克		Men's or boys' raincoats, knitted or crocheted, of cotton
6101.3000	-化学纤维制	17.5	12	12.3	0	130	17	13	件/千克		-Of man-made fibres
6101.3000 11	化纤制针织或钩编男式大衣等(含毛≥23%包括短上衣斗篷短斗篷及类似品，雨衣除外)	17.5				130	17	13	件/千克		Men's or boys' overcoats, car-coats, capes, cloak and similar articles, other than raincoats, containing ≥ 23% by weight of wool or fine animal hair, knitted or crocheted, of man-made fibres
6101.3000 19	其他化纤制针织或钩编男式大衣等(包括短大衣，斗篷，短斗篷及类似品，雨衣除外)	17.5				130	17	13	件/千克		Other men's or boys' overcoats, car-coats, capes, cloak and similar articles, other than raincoats, knitted or crocheted, of man-made fibres
6101.3000 21	化纤制针织或钩编手工男式防风衣(含毛≥23%包括防寒短上衣、防风短上衣及类似品)	17.5				130	17	13	件/千克		Men's or boys' wind-cheaters, anoraks, wind-jackets and similar articles, hand-worked, containing≥23% by weight of wool or fine animal hair, knitted or crocheted, of man-made fibres
6101.3000 22	化纤制针织或钩编男式防风衣(含毛≥23%包括防寒短上衣、防风短上衣及类似品)	17.5				130	17	13	件/千克	5	Men's or boys' wind-cheaters, anoraks, wind-jackets and similar articles, containing≥23% by weight of wool or fine animal hair, knitted or crocheted, of man-made fibres

税则号列 Tariff Item.	货品名称	最惠国(%) MFN	协定(%) CT 东盟 CA	中巴 CP	中智 CC	普通 Gen	增值税率 VAT	出口退税 ED	计量单位 Unit	监管条件 SC	Article Description
6101.3000 23	其他化纤针织钩编手工男式防风衣(包括防寒短上衣、防风短上衣及类似品)	17.5				130	17	13	件/千克		Men's or boys' wind-cheaters, anoraks, wind-jackets and similar articles, hand-worked, knitted or crocheted, of man-made fibres
6101.3000 29	其他化纤制其他男式防风衣(包括防寒短上衣、防风短上衣及类似品)	17.5				130	17	13	件/千克	5	Other men's or boys' wind-cheaters, anoraks, wind-jackets and similar articles, knitted or crocheted, of man-made fibres
6101.3000 31	化纤制针织或钩编男式雨衣(按重量计含羊毛或动物细毛≥23%)	17.5				130	17	13	件/千克		Men's or boys' raincoats, containing ≥23% by weight of wool or fine animal hair, knitted or crocheted, of man-made fibres
6101.3000 39	化纤制针织或钩编男式雨衣	17.5				130	17	13	件/千克		Other men's or boys' raincoats, knitted or crocheted, of man-made fibres
	-其他纺织材料制:										-Of other textile materials:
6101.9010	---羊毛或动物细毛制	25	12	18	0	130	17	13	件/千克		---Of wool or fine animal hair
6101.9010 10	毛制针织或钩编非手工制男式防风衣(包括防寒短上衣,防风短上衣及类似品)	25				130	17	13	件/千克	5	Men's or boys' wind-cheaters, anoraks, wind-jackets and similar articles, not hand-worked, knitted or crocheted, of wool or fine animal hair
6101.9010 90	毛制针织或钩编其他男大衣、斗篷、防风衣等(包括防寒短上衣,防风短上衣、短大衣,短斗篷及类似品)	25				130	17	13	件/千克		Men's or boys' overcoats, capes, wind-cheaters, anoraks, wind-jackets, car-coats, cloak and similar articles, knitted or crocheted, of wool or fine animal hair
6101.9090	---其他纺织材料制	17.5	12	12.3	0	130	17	13	件/千克		---Of other textile materials
61.02	**针织或钩编的女式大衣、短大衣、斗篷、短斗篷、带风帽的防寒短上衣(包括滑雪短上衣)、防风衣、防风短上衣及类似品,但税目61.04的货品除外:**										**Women's or girls' overcoats, car-coats, capes, cloaks, anoraks (including ski-jackets), wind-cheaters, wind-jackets and similar articles, knitted or crocheted, other than those of heading No. 61.04:**
6102.1000	-羊毛或动物细毛制	25	12	18	0	130	17	13	件/千克		-Of wool or fine animal hair
6102.1000 10	毛制针织或钩编女式大衣等(包括短大衣、斗篷短斗篷及类似品,雨衣除外)	25				130	17	13	件/千克		Women's or girls' overcoats, car-coats, capes, cloak and similar articles, other than raincoats, knitted or crocheted, of wool or fine animal hair
6102.1000 21	毛制针织或钩编手工制女式防风衣(包括防寒短上衣,防风短上衣及类似品)	25				130	17	13	件/千克		Women's or girls' wind-cheaters, anoraks, wind-jackets and similar articles, hand-worked, knitted or crocheted, of wool or fine animal hair
6102.1000 29	毛制针织或钩编女式防风衣(包括防寒短上衣,防风短上衣及类似品)	25				130	17	13	件/千克	5	Other women's or girls' wind-cheaters, anoraks, wind-jackets and similar articles, knitted or crocheted, of wool or fine animal hair
6102.1000 30	毛制针织或钩编女式雨衣	25				130	17	13	件/千克		Women's or girls' raincoats, knitted or crocheted, of wool or fine animal hair
6102.2000	-棉制	17.5	8	14	0	90	17	13	件/千克		-Of cotton

税则号列 Tariff Item.	货品名称	最惠国(%) MFN	协定(%) 东盟 CA	中巴 CP	CT 中智 CC	普通 Gen	增值税率 VAT	出口退税 ED	计量单位 Unit	监管条件 SC	Article Description
6102.2000 10	棉制针织或钩编女式大衣(包括短大衣、斗篷短斗篷及类似品,雨衣除外)	17.5				90	17	13	件/千克		Women's or girls' overcoats, car-coats, capes, cloak and similar articles, other than raincoats, knitted or crocheted, of cotton
6102.2000 21	棉制针织或钩编手工女式防风衣(包括防风短上衣,防寒短上衣及类似品)	17.5				90	17	13	件/千克		Women's or girls' wind-cheaters, anoraks, wind-jackets and similar articles, hand-worked, knitted or crocheted, of cotton
6102.2000 29	棉制针织或钩编女式防风衣(包括防风短上衣,防寒短上衣及类似品)	17.5				90	17	13	件/千克	5	Other women's or girls' wind-cheaters, anoraks, wind-jackets and similar articles, knitted or crocheted, of cotton
6102.2000 30	棉制针织或钩编女式雨衣	17.5				90	17	13	件/千克		Women's or girls' raincoats, knitted or crocheted, of cotton
6102.3000	-化学纤维制	17.5	12	12.3	0	130	17	13	件/千克		-Of man-made fibres
6102.3000 11	化纤制针织或钩编女式大衣等(含毛≥23%,含短大衣、斗篷短斗篷及类似品,雨衣除外)	17.5				130	17	13	件/千克		Women's or girls' overcoats, car-coats, capes, cloak and similar articles, other than raincoats, containing ≥ 23% by weight of wool or fine animal hair, knitted or crocheted, of man-made fibres
6102.3000 19	其他化纤制针织或钩编女式大衣(含短大衣、斗篷短斗篷及类似品,雨衣除外)	17.5				130	17	13	件/千克		Other women's or girls' overcoats, car-coats, capes, cloak and similar articles, other than raincoats, knitted or crocheted, of man-made fibres
6102.3000 21	化纤制针织或钩编手工女式防风衣(含毛≥23%,包括防寒短上衣,防风短上衣及类似品)	17.5				130	17	13	件/千克		Women's or girls' wind-cheaters, anoraks, wind-jackets and similar articles, hand-worked, containing ≥ 23% by weight of wool or fine animal hair, knitted or crocheted, of man-made fibres
6102.3000 22	化纤制针织或钩编女式防风衣(含毛≥23%,包括防寒短上衣,防风短上衣及类似品)	17.5				130	17	13	件/千克	5	Women's or girls' wind-cheaters, anoraks, wind-jackets and similar articles, containing≥23% by weight of wool or fine animal hair, knitted or crocheted, of man-made fibres
6102.3000 23	其他化纤制针织钩编手工女防风衣(包括防寒短上衣,防风短上衣及类似品)	17.5				130	17	13	件/千克		Women's or girls' wind-cheaters, anoraks, wind-jackets and similar articles, hand-worked, knitted or crocheted, of man-made fibres
6102.3000 29	其他化纤制针织钩编其他女防风衣(包括防寒短上衣,防风短上衣及类似品)	17.5				130	17	13	件/千克	5	Other women's or girls' wind-cheaters, anoraks, wind-jackets and similar articles, knitted or crocheted, of man-made fibres
6102.3000 31	化纤制针织或钩编女式雨衣(按重量计羊毛及动物细毛≥23%)	17.5				130	17	13	件/千克		Women's or girls' raincoats, containing ≥23% by weight of wool or fine animal hair, knitted or crocheted, of man-made fibres
6102.3000 39	化纤制针织或钩编女式雨衣	17.5				130	17	13	件/千克		Women's or girls' raincoats, knitted or crocheted, of man-made fibres
6102.9000	-其他纺织材料制	20	12	13.8	0	130	17	13	件/千克		-Of other textile materials

税则号列 Tariff Item.	货品名称	最惠国(%) MFN	协定(%)CT 东盟 CA	中巴 CP	中智 CC	普通 Gen	增值税率 VAT	出口退税 ED	计量单位 Unit	监管条件 SC	Article Description
6102.9000 11	丝及绢丝制针织或钩编女式大衣等(含丝≥70%包括短大衣、斗篷,短斗篷及类似品,雨衣除外)	20				130	17	13	件/千克		Women's or girls' overcoats, car-coats, capes, cloak and similar articles, other than raincoats, containing ≥ 70% by weight of silk or silk waste, knitted or crocheted
6102.9000 14	丝及绢丝制针织或钩编女式防风衣(含丝≥70%,包括防寒短上衣,防风短上衣及类似品)	20				130	17	13	件/千克		Women's or girls' wind-cheaters, anoraks, wind-jackets and similar articles, containing ≥ 70% by weight of silk or silk waste, knitted or crocheted
6102.9000 15	丝及绢丝制针织或钩编女式雨衣(含丝≥70%)	20				130	17	13	件/千克		Women's or girls' raincoats, containing ≥70% by weight of silk or silk waste, knitted or crocheted
6102.9000 21	其他纺织材料制针织或钩编女大衣(包括短大衣.斗篷短斗篷及类似品,雨衣除外,棉限内)	20				130	17	13	件/千克		Women's or girls' overcoats, car-coats, capes, cloak and similar articles, other than raincoats, knitted or crocheted, of other textile materials, cotton within limitations
6102.9000 22	其他纺织材料制针织或钩编女大衣(包括短大衣.斗篷短斗篷及类似品,雨衣除外,羊毛限内)	20				130	17	13	件/千克		Women's or girls' overcoats, car-coats, capes, cloak and similar articles, other than raincoats, knitted or crocheted, of other textile materials, wool within limitations
6102.9000 23	其他纺织材料制针织或钩编女大衣(包括短大衣.斗篷,短斗篷及类似品,雨衣除外,化纤限内)	20				130	17	13	件/千克		Women's or girls' overcoats, car-coats, capes, cloak and similar articles, other than raincoats, knitted or crocheted, of other textile materials, man-made fibres within limitations
6102.9000 29	其他纺织材料制针织或钩编女大衣(包括短大衣.斗篷短斗篷及类似品,雨衣除外)	20				130	17	13	件/千克		Women's or girls' overcoats, car-coats, capes, cloak and similar articles, other than raincoats, knitted or crocheted, of other textile materials
6102.9000 31	其他纺织料针织或钩编女式防风衣(包括防寒短上衣.防风短上衣及类似品,棉限内)	20				130	17	13	件/千克		Women's or girls' wind-cheaters, anoraks, wind-jackets and similar articles, knitted or crocheted, of other textile materials, cotton within limitations
6102.9000 32	其他纺织料针织或钩编女式防风衣(包括防寒短上衣.防风短上衣及类似品,羊毛限内)	20				130	17	13	件/千克		Women's or girls' wind-cheaters, anoraks, wind-jackets and similar articles, knitted or crocheted, of other textile materials, wool within limitations
6102.9000 33	其他纺织料针织或钩编女式防风衣(包括防寒短上衣.防风短上衣及类似品,化纤限内)	20				130	17	13	件/千克		Women's or girls' wind-cheaters, anoraks, wind-jackets and similar articles, knitted or crocheted, of other textile materials, man-made fibres within limitations
6102.9000 39	其他纺织料针织或钩编女式防风衣(包括防寒短上衣.防风短上衣及类似品)	20				130	17	13	件/千克		Other women's or girls' wind-cheaters, anoraks, wind-jackets and similar articles, knitted or crocheted, of other textile materials

税则号列 Tariff Item.	货品名称	最惠国(%) MFN	协定(%) 东盟 CA	 中巴 CP	CT 中智 CC	普通 Gen	增值税率 VAT	出口退税 ED	计量单位 Unit	监管条件 SC	Article Description
6102.9000 41	其他纺织材料制针织或钩编女式雨衣(棉限内)	20				130	17	13	件/千克		Women's or girls' raincoats, knitted or crocheted, of other textile materials, cotton within limitations
6102.9000 42	其他纺织材料制针织或钩编女式雨衣(羊毛限内)	20				130	17	13	件/千克		Women's or girls' raincoats, knitted or crocheted, of other textile materials, wool within limitations
6102.9000 43	其他纺织材料制针织或钩编女式雨衣(化纤限内)	20				130	17	13	件/千克		Women's or girls' raincoats, knitted or crocheted, of other textile materials, man-made fibres within limitations
6102.9000 49	其他纺织材料制针织或钩编女式雨衣	20				130	17	13	件/千克		Other women's or girls' raincoats, knitted or crocheted, of other textile materials
61.03	**针织或钩编的男式西服套装、便服套装、上衣、长裤、护胸背带工装裤、马裤及短裤(游泳裤除外):**										**Men's or boys' suits, ensembles, jackets, blazers, trousers, bib and brace overalls, breeches and shorts (other than swimwear), knitted or crocheted:**
	-西服套装:										-Suits:
6103.1010	---羊毛或动物细毛制	25	12	18	0	130	17	13	套/千克	5	---Of wool or fine animal hair
6103.1020	---合成纤维制	25	12	18	0	130	17	13	套/千克		---Of synthetic fibres
6103.1020 10	合成纤维制针织或钩编男西服套装(含羊毛或动物细毛23%及以上)	25				130	17	13	套/千克	5	Men's or boys' suits, knitted or crocheted, of synthetic fibres containing≥23% by weight of wool or fine animal hair
6103.1020 90	其他合成纤制针织或钩编男式西服套装	25				130	17	13	套/千克		Men's or boys' suits, knitted or crocheted, of synthetic fibres
6103.1090	---其他纺织材料制	17.5	T3	12.3	0	130	17	13	套/千克		---Of other textile materials
6103.1090 11	人造纤维针织或钩编男式西服套装(含羊毛或动物细毛23%及以上)	17.5				130	17	13	套/千克	5	Men's or boys' suits, knitted or crocheted, of artificial fibres, containing ≥ 23% by weight of wool or fine animal hair
6103.1090 19	其他人纤针织或钩编男式西服套装	17.5				130	17	13	套/千克		Men's or boys' suits, knitted or crocheted, of other artificial fibres
6103.1090 20	棉制针织或钩编男式西服套装	17.5				130	17	13	套/千克	5	Men's or boys' suits, knitted or crocheted, of cotton
6103.1090 30	丝及绢丝制针织或钩编男西服套装	17.5				130	17	13	套/千克		Men's or boys' suits, knitted or crocheted, of silk and silk waste
6103.1090 41	其他纺材制针织或钩编男西服套装(棉限内)	17.5				130	17	13	套/千克	5	Men's or boys' suits, knitted or crocheted, of other textile materials, cotton within limitations
6103.1090 42	其他纺材制针织或钩编男西服套装(羊毛限内)	17.5				130	17	13	套/千克	5	Men's or boys' suits, knitted or crocheted, of other textile materials, wool within limitations
6103.1090 43	其他纺材制针织或钩编男西服套装(化纤限内)	17.5				130	17	13	套/千克		Men's or boys' suits, knitted or crocheted, of other textile materials, man-made fibres within limitations
6103.1090 49	其他纺材制针织或钩编男西服套装	17.5				130	17	13	套/千克		Men's or boys' suits, knitted or crocheted, of other textile materials
	-便服套装:										-Ensembles:
6103.2200	--棉制	20	12	14.8	0	90	17	13	套/千克	5	--Of cotton
6103.2300	--合成纤维制	25	12	18	0	130	17	13	套/千克		--Of synthetic fibres

税则号列 Tariff Item.	货 品 名 称	最惠国(%) MFN	协定(%) CT 东盟 CA	中巴 CP	中智 CC	普通 Gen	增值税率 VAT	出口退税 ED	计量单位 Unit	监管条件 SC	Article Description
6103.2300 10	合成纤维制针织或钩编男便服套装(含羊毛或动物细毛23%及以上)	25				130	17	13	套/千克	5	Men's or boys' ensembles of synthetic fibres, knitted or crocheted, containing ≥23% by weight of wool or fine animal hair
6103.2300 91	其他合纤针织或钩编含毛衫或针织衬衫或裤子的男便服套装	25				130	17	13	套/千克	5	Men's or boys'ensembles, knitted or crocheted, of synthetic fibres, including hair shirt or Knitted shirt or trousers
6103.2300 99	其他合纤制针织或钩编其他男便服套装	25				130	17	13	套/千克		Men's or boys' ensembles, knitted or crocheted, of synthetic fibres
	--其他纺织材料制:										--Of other textile materials
6103.2910	---羊毛或动物细毛制	25	12	18	0	130	17	13	套/千克	5	---Of wool or fine animal hair
6103.2990	---其他	25	12	18	0	130	17	13	套/千克		---Other
6103.2990 10	丝或绢丝制针织或钩编男便服套装(含丝或绢丝70%及以上)	25				130	17	13	套/千克		Men's or boys' ensembles, knitted or crocheted containing ≥70% by weight of silk and silk waste
6103.2990 20	人造纤维制针织或钩编男便服套装	25				130	17	13	套/千克	5	Men's or boys' ensembles, knitted or crocheted, of artificial fibres
6103.2990 31	其他纺织料针织或钩编男便服套装(上装为毛衫,棉限内)	25				130	17	13	套/千克	5	Men's or boys' ensembles, knitted or crocheted, of other textile materials, the upper garment is a sweater, cotton within limitations
6103.2990 32	其他纺织料针织或钩编男便服套装(上装为毛衫,羊毛限内)	25				130	17	13	套/千克		Men's or boys' ensembles, knitted or crocheted, of other textile materials, the upper garment is a sweater, wool within limitations
6103.2990 33	其他纺织料针织或钩编男便服套装(上装为毛衫,化纤限内)	25				130	17	13	套/千克	5	Men's or boys' ensembles, knitted or crocheted, of other textile materials, the upper garment is a sweater, man-made fibres within limitations
6103.2990 34	其他纺织料针织或钩编男便服套装(上装为毛衫)	25				130	17	13	套/千克		Men's or boys' ensembles, knitted or crocheted, of other textile materials, the upper garment is a sweater
6103.2990 35	其他纺织料针织或钩编男便服套装	25				130	17	13	套/千克	5	Men's or boys' ensembles, knitted or crocheted, of other textile materials
	-上衣:										-Jackets and blazers:
6103.3100	--羊毛或动物细毛制	16	12	11.7	0	130	17	13	件/千克		--Of wool or fine animal hair
6103.3200	--棉制	16	T3	12	0	90	17	13	件/千克		--Of cotton
6103.3300	--合成纤维制	19	12	13.6	0	130	17	13	件/千克		--Of synthetic fibres
6103.3300 10	合成纤维制针织或钩编男式上衣(含羊毛或动物细毛23%及以上)	19				130	17	13	件/千克		Men's or boys' jackets and blazers, knitted or crocheted, of synthetic fibres, containing ≥23% by weight of wool or fine animal hair
6103.3300 90	其他合纤制针织或钩编男式上衣	19				130	17	13	件/千克		Other men's or boys' jackets and blazers, knitted or crocheted, of synthetic fibres
6103.3900	--其他纺织材料制	16	12	11.7	0	130	17	13	件/千克		--Of other textile materials
6103.3900 10	人造纤维制针织或钩编男式上衣	16				130	17	13	件/千克		Men's or boys' jackets and blazers, knitted or crocheted, of artificial fibres

税则号列 Tariff Item.	货品名称	最惠国(%) MFN	协定(%) CT 东盟 CA	中巴 CP	中智 CC	普通 Gen	增值税率 VAT	出口退税 ED	计量单位 Unit	监管条件 SC	Article Description
6103.3900 20	丝制针织或钩编男式上衣(含丝及绢丝70%及以上)	16				130	17	13	件/千克		Men's or boys' jackets and blazers, knitted or crocheted, containing≥70% by weight of silk or silk waste
6103.3900 31	其他纺织料制针织或钩编男式上衣(棉限内)	16				130	17	13	件/千克		Men's or boys' jackets and blazers, knitted or crocheted, of other textile materials, cotton within limitations
6103.3900 32	其他纺织料制针织或钩编男式上衣(羊毛限内)	16				130	17	13	件/千克		Men's or boys' jackets and blazers, knitted or crocheted, of other textile materials, wool within limitations
6103.3900 33	其他纺织料制针织或钩编男式上衣(化纤限内)	16				130	17	13	件/千克		Men's or boys' jackets and blazers, knitted or crocheted, of other textile materials, man-made fibres within limitations
6103.3900 39	其他纺织料制针织或钩编男式上衣	16				130	17	13	件/千克		Men's or boys' jackets and blazers, knitted or crocheted, of other textile materials
	-长裤、护胸背带工装裤、马裤及短裤:										-Trousers, bib and brace overalls, breeches and shorts:
6103.4100	--羊毛或动物细毛制	16	12	11.7	0	130	17	13	件/千克		--Of wool or fine animal hair
6103.4100 10	毛制针织或钩编护胸背带男工装裤(羊毛或动物细毛制)	16				130	17	13	件/千克		Bib and brace overalls, knitted or crocheted, of wool or fine animal hair
6103.4100 20	毛制针织或钩编男长裤(羊毛或动物细毛制,包括8-18号男童长裤)	16				130	17	13	件/千克	5	Men's trousers or boys' trousers No. 8—No. 18, knitted or crocheted, of wool or fine animal hair
6103.4100 90	毛制针织或钩编其他男裤(羊毛或动物细毛制,包括马裤、短裤及其他长裤)	16				130	17	13	件/千克	5	Other men's trousers or boys' trousers, knitted or crocheted, of wool or fine animal hair
6103.4200	--棉制	16	T3	13.6	0	90	17	13	件/千克		--Of cotton
6103.4200 11	棉制针织或钩编护胸背带男工装裤(保暖)	16				90	17	13	件/千克		Men's or boys' bib and brace overalls, thermal, knitted or crocheted, of cotton
6103.4200 12	棉针织钩编男童非保暖背带工装裤(2-7号男童护胸背带工装裤)	16				90	17	13	件/千克		Boys' bib and brace overalls, thermal, No. 2—No. 7, knitted or crocheted, of cotton
6103.4200 19	棉针织钩编男式非保暖背带工装裤(护胸背带工装裤,2-7号男童的除外)	16				90	17	13	件/千克		Men's or boys' bib and brace overalls, other than boys' No. 2—No. 7, knitted or crocheted, of cotton
6103.4200 21	棉制针织或钩编男童游戏套装长裤(指男童8-18号)	16				90	17	13	件/千克		Boys' playsuit trousers No. 8—No. 18, knitted or crocheted, of cotton
6103.4200 29	棉针织或钩编其他男童游戏套装裤(包括长裤、马裤、短裤)	16				90	17	13	件/千克		Other boys' playsuit, including trousers, breeches and shorts, knitted or crocheted, of cotton
6103.4200 30	棉制针织或钩编男长裤(包括8-18号男童长裤)	16				90	17	13	件/千克	5	Men's trousers or boys' trousers No. 8—No. 18, knitted or crocheted, of cotton
6103.4200 90	棉制针织或钩编其他男裤等(包括马裤、短裤及其他长裤)	16				90	17	13	件/千克	5	Other men's or boys' trousers, breeches and shorts, knitted or crocheted, of cotton
6103.4300	--合成纤维制	17.5	T3	12.3	0	130	17	13	件/千克		--Of synthetic fibres

税则号列 Tariff Item.	货品名称	最惠国(%) MFN	协定(%) 东盟 CA	中巴 CP	CT 中智 CC	普通 Gen	增值税率 VAT	出口退税 ED	计量单位 Unit	监管条件 SC	Article Description
6103.4300 10	合纤针织或钩编护胸背带男工装裤(含羊毛或动物细毛23%及以上)	17.5				130	17	13	件/千克		Men's or boys' bib and brace overalls, containing≥23% by weight of wool or fine animal hair, knitted or crocheted, of synthetic fibres
6103.4300 21	合成纤维制针织或钩编男长裤(含羊毛或动物细毛23%及以上,包括8-18号男童长裤)	17.5				130	17	13	件/千克	5	Men's trousers or boys' trousers No. 8—No. 18, containing≥23% by weight of wool or fine animal hair, knitted or crocheted, of synthetic fibres
6103.4300 29	合成纤维制针织或钩编其他男裤(含毛23%及以上,包括马裤、短裤及其他长裤)	17.5				130	17	13	件/千克	5	Other men's or boys' trousers, breeches and shorts, containing≥23% by weight of wool or fine animal hair, knitted or crocheted, of synthetic fibres
6103.4300 91	其他合纤制护胸背带男工装裤(针织或钩编)	17.5				130	17	13	件/千克		Other men's or boys' bib and brace overalls, knitted or crocheted, of synthetic fibres
6103.4300 92	其他合纤制男童游戏套装长裤(针织或钩编,指男童8-18号)	17.5				130	17	13	件/千克		Other boys' playsuit trousers No. 8—No. 18, knitted or crocheted, of synthetic fibres
6103.4300 93	其他合纤制男童游戏套装长裤(针织或钩编,包括马裤短裤及其他长裤)	17.5				130	17	13	件/千克		Other boys' playsuit trousers, including breeches, shorts and other trousers, knitted or crocheted, of synthetic fibres
6103.4300 94	其他合纤制针织或钩编男长裤(包括8-18号男童长裤)	17.5				130	17	13	件/千克	5	Other men's trousers, or boys' trousers No. 8—No. 18, knitted or crocheted, of synthetic fibres
6103.4300 99	其他合纤制针织或钩编其他男裤(包括马裤、短裤及其他长裤)	17.5				130	17	13	件/千克	5	Other men's or boys' trousers, breeches and shorts, knitted or crocheted, of synthetic fibres
6103.4900	--其他纺织材料制	16	T3	11.7	0	130	17	13	件/千克		--Of other textile materials
6103.4900 11	丝制男式护胸背带工装裤(针织或钩编,丝及绢丝含量在70%及以上)	16				130	17	13	件/千克		Men's or boys' bib and brace overalls, containing≥70% by weight of silk or silk waste, knitted or crocheted
6103.4900 12	丝制针织或钩编男成人长裤.马裤(含8-18号男童长裤及马裤,丝及绢丝含量在70%以上)	16				130	17	13	件/千克		Men's trousers and breeches and boys' No. 8—No. 17, containing≥70% by weight of silk or silk waste, knitted or crocheted
6103.4900 13	丝制针织或钩编其他男童长裤马裤(丝及绢丝含量在70%及以上)	16				130	17	13	件/千克		Boys' trousers and breeches, containing≥70% by weight of silk or silk waste, knitted or crocheted
6103.4900 14	丝制针织或钩编其他男式短裤(丝及绢丝含量在70%及以上)	16				130	17	13	件/千克		Other men's or boys' shorts, containing≥70% by weight of silk or silk waste, knitted or crocheted
6103.4900 21	人造纤维制男式护胸背带工装裤(针织或钩编)	16				130	17	13	件/千克		Men's or boys' bib and brace overalls of artificial fibres, knitted or crocheted
6103.4900 22	人纤制针织或钩编男人长裤.马裤(含8-18号男童长裤及马裤,含毛23%及以上)	16				130	17	13	件/千克	5	Men's trousers breeches and boys' No. 8—No. 18 of artificial fibres, containing≥23% by weight of wool or fine animal hair, knitted or crocheted

税则号列 Tariff Item.	货 品 名 称	最惠国(%) MFN	协定(%) CT 东盟 CA	中巴 CP	中智 CC	普通 Gen	增值税率 VAT	出口退税 ED	计量单位 Unit	监管条件 SC	Article Description
6103.4900 23	人纤制针织钩编其他男童长裤马裤(含毛23%及以上)	16				130	17	13	件/千克	5	Other boys' trousers breeches of artificial fibres, containing≥23% by weight of wool or fine animal hair, knitted or crocheted
6103.4900 24	人纤制针织或钩编男式短裤(含毛23%及以上)	16				130	17	13	件/千克	5	Men's or boys' shorts of artificial fibres, containing≥23% by weight of wool or fine animal hair, knitted or crocheted
6103.4900 25	其他人纤制针织或钩编男长裤马裤(含8-18号男童长裤及马裤)	16				130	17	13	件/千克	5	Other men's trousers, breeches, and boys' No. 8—No. 18, of artificial fibres, knitted or crocheted
6103.4900 26	其他人纤制针织钩编其他男童长裤(包括马裤)	16				130	17	13	件/千克	5	Other boys' trousers and breeches, of artificial fibres, knitted or crocheted
6103.4900 27	其他人纤制针织或钩编其他男短裤	16				130	17	13	件/千克	5	Other men's or boys' shorts of artificial fibres, knitted or crocheted
6103.4900 31	其他纺材制男式护胸背带工装裤(针织或钩编,棉限内)	16				130	17	13	件/千克		Men's or boys' bib and brace overalls, cotton within limitations, knitted or crocheted, of other textile materials
6103.4900 32	其他纺材制男式护胸背带工装裤(针织或钩编,羊毛限内)	16				130	17	13	件/千克		Men's or boys' bib and brace overalls, wool within limitations, knitted or crocheted, of other textile materials
6103.4900 33	其他纺材制男式护胸背带工装裤(针织或钩编,化纤限内)	16				130	17	13	件/千克		Men's or boys' bib and brace overalls, man-made fibres within limitations, knitted or crocheted, of other textile materials
6103.4900 39	其他纺材制男式护胸背带工装裤(针织或钩编)	16				130	17	13	件/千克		Other men's or boys' bib and brace overalls, knitted or crocheted, of other textile materials
6103.4900 41	其他纺材制针织或钩编男长裤马裤(包括8-18号男童长裤.马裤,棉限内)	16				130	17	13	件/千克	5	Men's trousers, breeches and boys' No. 8 ~ No. 18, knitted or crocheted, of other textile materials, cotton within limitations
6103.4900 42	其他纺材制针织或钩编男长裤马裤(包括8-18号男童长裤.马裤,羊毛限内)	16				130	17	13	件/千克	5	Men's trousers, breeches and boys' No. 8 ~ No. 18, knitted or crocheted, of other textile materials, wool within limitations
6103.4900 43	其他纺材制针织或钩编男长裤马裤(包括8-18号男童长裤.马裤,化纤限内)	16				130	17	13	件/千克	5	Men's trousers, breeches and boys' No. 8 ~ No. 18, knitted or crocheted, of other textile materials, man-made fibres within limitations
6103.4900 49	其他纺材制针织或钩编男长裤马裤(包括8-18号男童长裤.马裤)	16				130	17	13	件/千克	5	Men's trousers and breeches, including boys' No. 8 ~ No. 18, knitted or crocheted, of other textile materials
6103.4900 51	其他纺织材料制其他男童长裤马裤(针织或钩编,棉限内)	16				130	17	13	件/千克	5	Other boys' trousers and breeches, cotton within limitations, knitted or crocheted, of other textile materials
6103.4900 52	其他纺织材料制其他男童长裤马裤(针织或钩编,羊毛限内)	16				130	17	13	件/千克	5	Other boys' trousers and breeches, wool within limitations, knitted or crocheted, of other textile materials

税则号列 Tariff Item.	货品名称	最惠国(%) MFN	协定(%)CT 东盟 CA	中巴 CP	中智 CC	普通 Gen	增值税率 VAT	出口退税 ED	计量单位 Unit	监管条件 SC	Article Description
6103.4900 53	其他纺织材料制其他男童长裤马裤(针织或钩编,化纤限内)	16				130	17	13	件/千克	5	Other boys' trousers and breeches, man-made fibres within limitations, knitted or crocheted, of other textile materials
6103.4900 59	其他纺织材料制其他男童长裤马裤(针织或钩编)	16				130	17	13	件/千克	5	Other boys' trousers and breeches, knitted or crocheted, of other textile materials
6103.4900 61	其他纺材制针织或钩编男式短裤(棉限内)	16				130	17	13	件/千克	5	Other men's or boys' shorts, knitted or crocheted, of other textile materials, cotton within limitations
6103.4900 62	其他纺材制针织或钩编男式短裤(羊毛限内)	16				130	17	13	件/千克	5	Other men's or boys' shorts, knitted or crocheted, of other textile materials, wool within limitations
6103.4900 63	其他纺材制针织或钩编男式短裤(化纤限内)	16				130	17	13	件/千克	5	Other men's or boys' shorts, knitted or crocheted, of other textile materials, man-made fibres within limitations
6103.4900 69	其他纺材制针织或钩编男式短裤	16				130	17	13	件/千克	5	Other men's or boys' shorts, knitted or crocheted, of other textile materials
61.04	**针织或钩编的女式西服套装、便服套装、上衣、连衣裙、裙子、裙裤、长裤、护胸背带工装裤、马裤及短裤(游泳服除外):**										**Women's or girls' suits, ensembles, jackets, blazers, dresses, skirts, divided skirts, trousers, bib and brace overalls, breeches and shorts (other than swimwear), knitted or crocheted:**
	-西服套装:										-Suits:
6104.1300	--合成纤维制	25	T3	18	0	130	17	13	套/千克		--Of synthetic fibres
6104.1300 10	合成纤维制针织或钩编女西服套装(含羊毛或动物细毛23%及以上)	25				130	17	13	套/千克		Women's or girls' suits, knitted or crocheted containing ≥23% by weight of wool or fine animal hair, of synthetic fibres
6104.1300 90	其他合成纤维制针织或钩编女西服套装	25				130	17	13	套/千克		Women's or girls' suits, knitted or crocheted, of synthetic fibres
	--其他纺织材料制:										--Of other textile materials
6104.1910	---羊毛或动物细毛制	17.5	12	12.3	0	130	17	13	套/千克		---Of wool or fine animal hair
6104.1920	---棉制	17.5	T3	14	0	90	17	13	套/千克		---Of cottn
6104.1920 10	含裤子的棉针织或钩编女西服套装	17.5				90	17	13	套/千克	5	Women's or girl's suits, knitted or crocheted, of cotton, including trousers
6104.1920 90	不含裤子的棉针织或钩编女西服套装	17.5				90	17	13	套/千克		Women's or girl's suits, knitted or crocheted, of cotton, excluding trousers
6104.1990	---其他	17.5	T3	12.3	0	130	17	13	套/千克		---Other
6104.1990 10	含裤子的其他纺材制针织或钩编女西服套装(棉限内)	17.5				130	17	13	套/千克	5	Other women's or girls' suits, knitted or crocheted, of other textile materials, cotton within limitations, including trousers
6104.1990 90	其他纺织材料制针织或钩编女式西服套装(除合成纤维、羊毛或动物细毛、棉以外的其他纺织材料)	17.5				130	17	13	套/千克		Women's or girls' suits, knitted or crocheted, of other textile matrials, other than synthetic fibres, wool or fine animal hair, cotton materials
	-便服套装:										-Ensembles:

税则号列 Tariff Item.	货品名称	最惠国(%) MFN	协定(%) 东盟 CA	中巴 CP	CT 中智 CC	普通 Gen	增值税率 VAT	出口退税 ED	计量单位 Unit	监管条件 SC	Article Description
6104.2200	--棉制	17.5	8	14	0	90	17	13	套/千克		--Of cotton
6104.2200 10	含针织衬衫或毛衫或裤子棉制针织或钩编女便服套装	17.5				90	17	13	套/千克	5	Women's or girls' suits, knitted or crocheted, of cotton , including knitted shirt or hair shirt or trousers
6104.2200 90	其他棉针织或钩编女便服套装	17.5				90	17	13	套/千克		Other women ' s or girls ' ensembles, knitted or crocheted, of cotton
6104.2300	--合成纤维制	25	12	18	0	130	17	13	套/千克		--Of synthetic fibres
6104.2300 10	合纤制针织或钩编女便服套装(含羊毛23%及以上)	25				130	17	13	套/千克		Women's or girls' ensembles, knitted or crocheted, containing≥23% by weight of wool, of synthetic fibres
6104.2300 91	含针织衬衫或毛衫或裤子的其他合纤针织或钩编女便服套装(含毛23%以下)	25				130	17	13	套/千克	5	Women's or girls' suits, knitted or crocheted, of other synthetic fibres , including knitted shirt or hair shirt or trousers, containing < 23% by weight of hair
6104.2300 99	其他合纤制针织或钩编其他女便服套装(含毛23%以下)	25				130	17	13	套/千克		Other women's or girls' suits, knitted or crocheted, of synthetic fibres , containing < 23% by weight of hair
	--其他纺织材料制:										--Of other textile materials
6104.2910	---羊毛或动物细毛制	17.5	12	12.3	0	130	17	13	套/千克		---Of wool or fine animal hair
6104.2990	---其他	15	12	10.4	0	130	17	13	套/千克		---Of other
6104.2990 21	含针织衬衫或毛衫或裤子的人纤制其他女便服套装(针织或编织)	15				130	17	13	套/千克	5	Other women's or girls' suits, knitted or crocheted, of artificial fibres , including knitted shirt or hair shirt or trousers
6104.2990 29	人纤制其他女便服套装(针织或编织)	15				130	17	13	套/千克		Women ' s or girls ' ensembles, of wool or fine animal hair
6104.2990 31	含针织衬衫或毛衫或裤子的其他纺材针织或钩编女便服套装(棉限内)	15				130	17	13	套/千克	5	Women's or girls' suits, knitted or crocheted, of other textile materials , including knitted shirt or hair shirt or trousers, cotton within limitations
6104.2990 32	其他纺材针织或钩编女式便服套装(羊毛限内)	15				130	17	13	套/千克		Women ' s or girls ' ensembles, knitted or crocheted, of other textile materials, wool within limitations
6104.2990 33	含针织衬衫或毛衫或裤子的其他纺材针织或钩编女便服套装(化纤限内)	15				130	17	13	套/千克	5	Women's or girls' suits, knitted or crocheted, of other textile materials , including knitted shirt or hair shirt or trousers, man – made fibres within limitations
6104.2990 34	含裤子的其他纺材针织或钩编女式便服套装	15				130	17	13	套/千克	5	Women ' s or girls ' ensembles, knitted or crocheted, of other textile materials, including trousers
6104.2990 39	其他纺织材料针织或钩编其他女式便服套装	15				130	17	13	套/千克		Other women's or girls' ensembles, knitted or crocheted of synthetic fibres
	-上衣:										-Jackets and blazers:
6104.3100	--羊毛或动物细毛制	16	12	11.7	0	130	17	13	件/千克		--Of wool or fine animal hair
6104.3100 10	毛制钩编女式上衣	16				130	17	13	件/千克		Women's or girls' jackets and blazers of wool or fine animal hair, crocheted

税则号列 Tariff Item.	货品名称	最惠国(%) MFN	协定(%) CT 东盟 CA	中巴 CP	中智 CC	普通 Gen	增值税率 VAT	出口退税 ED	计量单位 Unit	监管条件 SC	Article Description
6104. 3100 90	毛制针织女式上衣	16				130	17	13	件/千克		Women's or girls' jackets and blazers of wool or fine animal hair, knitted
6104. 3200	--棉制	16	T3	13.6	0	90	17	13	件/千克		--Of cotton
6104. 3200 10	棉制钩编女式上衣	16				90	17	13	件/千克		Women's or girls' jackets and blazers of cotton, crocheted
6104. 3200 90	棉制针织女式上衣	16				90	17	13	件/千克		Women's or girls' jackets and blazers of cotton, knitted
6104. 3300	--合成纤维制	19	T3	13.6	0	130	17	13	件/千克		--Of synthetic fibres
6104. 3300 11	合成纤维制钩编女上衣(含羊毛或动物细毛23%及以上)	19				130	17	13	件/千克		Women's or girls' jackets and blazers of synthetic fibres, crocheted, containing ≥23% by weight of wool or fine animal hair
6104. 3300 19	其他合成纤维制钩编女上衣	19				130	17	13	件/千克		Other women's or girls' jackets and blazers of synthetic fibres, crocheted
6104. 3300 91	合成纤维制针织女上衣(含羊毛或动物细毛23%及以上)	19				130	17	13	件/千克		Women's or girls' jackets and blazers of synthetic fibres, knitted, containing ≥ 23% by weight of wool or fine animal hair
6104. 3300 99	其他合成纤维制针织女上衣	19				130	17	13	件/千克		Other women's or girls' jackets and blazers of synthetic fibres, knitted
6104. 3900	--其他纺织材料制	16	12	11.7	0	130	17	13	件/千克		--Of other textile materials
6104. 3900 11	丝及绢丝制钩编女上衣(含丝70%及以上)	16				130	17	13	件/千克		Women's or girls' jackets and blazers, crocheted, containing≥70% by weight of silk or silk waste
6104. 3900 19	丝及绢丝制针织女上衣(含丝70%及以上)	16				130	17	13	件/千克		Women's or girls' jackets and blazers, knitted, containing≥70% by weight of silk or silk waste
6104. 3900 21	人造纤维制钩编女上衣	16				130	17	13	件/千克		Women's or girls' jackets and blazers, crocheted, of artificial fibres
6104. 3900 29	人造纤维制针织女上衣	16				130	17	13	件/千克		Women's or girls' jackets and blazers, knitted, of artificial fibres
6104. 3900 31	其他纺织材料制钩编女上衣(棉限内)	16				130	17	13	件/千克		Women's or girls' jackets and blazers, crocheted, cotton within limitations
6104. 3900 32	其他纺织材料制钩编女上衣(羊毛限内)	16				130	17	13	件/千克		Women's or girls' jackets and blazers, crocheted, wool within limitations
6104. 3900 33	其他纺织材料制钩编女上衣(化纤限内)	16				130	17	13	件/千克		Women's or girls' jackets and blazers, crocheted, man-made fibres within limitations
6104. 3900 39	其他纺织材料制钩编女上衣	16				130	17	13	件/千克		Women's or girls' jackets and blazers, crocheted, of other textile materials
6104. 3900 41	其他纺织材料制针织女上衣(棉限内)	16				130	17	13	件/千克		Women's or girls' jackets and blazers, knitted, of other textile materials, cotton within limitations
6104. 3900 42	其他纺织材料制针织女上衣(羊毛限内)	16				130	17	13	件/千克		Women's or girls' jackets and blazers, knitted, of other textile materials, wool within limitations
6104. 3900 43	其他纺织材料制针织女上衣(化纤限内)	16				130	17	13	件/千克		Women's or girls' jackets and blazers, knitted, of other textile materials, man-made fibres within limitations

税则号列 Tariff Item.	货品名称	最惠国(%) MFN	协定(%)CT 东盟 CA	中巴 CP	中智 CC	普通 Gen	增值税率 VAT	出口退税 ED	计量单位 Unit	监管条件 SC	Article Description
6104. 3900 49	其他纺织材料制针织女上衣	16				130	17	13	件/千克		Women's or girls' jackets and blazers, knitted, of other textile materials
	-连衣裙:										-Dresses:
6104. 4100	--羊毛或动物细毛制	16	12	11. 7	0	130	17	13	件/千克	5	--Of wool or fine animal hair
6104. 4200	--棉制	16	T3	13. 6	0	90	17	13	件/千克	5	--Of cotton
6104. 4300	--合成纤维制	17. 5	T3	12. 3	0	130	17	13	件/千克		--Of synthetic fibres
6104. 4300 10	合成纤维制针织或钩编连衣裙(含羊毛或动物细毛23%及以上)	17. 5				130	17	13	件/千克	5	Dresses, knitted or crocheted, containing≥23% by weight of wool or fine animal hair, of synthetic fibres
6104. 4300 90	其他合纤制针织或钩编连衣裙	17. 5				130	17	13	件/千克	5	Other dresses knitted or crocheted of synthetic fibres
6104. 4400	--人造纤维制	16	12	11. 7	0	130	17	13	件/千克		--Of artificial fibres
6104. 4400 10	人纤制针织或钩编连衣裙(含羊毛或动物细毛23%及以上)	16				130	17	13	件/千克	5	Dresses, knitted or crocheted, containing≥23% by weight of wool or fine animal hair, of artificial fibres
6104. 4400 90	其他人纤制针织或钩编连衣裙	16				130	17	13	件/千克	5	Other dresses, knitted or crocheted of artificial fibres
6104. 4900	--其他纺织材料制	16	12	11. 7	0	130	17	13	件/千克		--Of other textile materials
6104. 4900 10	丝及绢丝制针织或钩编连衣裙(含丝70%及以上)	16				130	17	13	件/千克		Dresses, knitted or crocheted, containing≥70% by weight of silk or silk waste
6104. 4900 91	其他纺织材料制针织或钩编连衣裙(棉限内)	16				130	17	13	件/千克		Dresses, knitted or crocheted, cotton within limitations, of other textile materials
6104. 4900 92	其他纺织材料制针织或钩编连衣裙(羊毛限内)	16				130	17	13	件/千克		Dresses, knitted or crocheted, wool within limitations, of other textile materials
6104. 4900 93	其他纺织材料制针织或钩编连衣裙(化纤限内)	16				130	17	13	件/千克		Dresses, knitted or crocheted, man-made fibres within limitations, of other textile materials
6104. 4900 99	其他纺织材料制针织或钩编连衣裙	16				130	17	13	件/千克		Dresses, knitted or crocheted, of other textile materials
	-裙子及裙裤:										-Skirts and divided skirts:
6104. 5100	--羊毛或动物细毛制	14	8	10. 8	0	130	17	13	件/千克		--Of wool or fine animal hair
6104. 5200	--棉制	14	T3	10. 3	0	90	17	13	件/千克		--Of cotton
6104. 5300	--合成纤维制	16	T3	11. 7	0	130	17	13	件/千克		--Of synthetic fibres
6104. 5300 10	合纤制针织或钩编裙子及裙裤(含羊毛或动物细毛23%及以上)	16				130	17	13	件/千克		Skirts and divided skirts, knitted or crocheted, containing≥23% by weight of wool or fine animal hair
6104. 5300 90	其他合纤制针织或钩编裙子及裙裤	16				130	17	13	件/千克		Other skirts and divided skirts, knitted or crocheted, of synthetic fibres
6104. 5900	--其他纺织材料制	14		10. 8	0	130	17	13	件/千克		--Of other textile materials
6104. 5900 10	丝及绢丝制针织或钩编裙子及裙裤(含丝70%及以上)	14	T3			130	17	13	件/千克		Skirts and divided skirts, knitted or crocheted, containing≥70% by weight of silk or silk waste
6104. 5900 21	人纤制针织或钩编裙子及裙裤(含羊毛或动物23%及以上)	14				130	17	13	件/千克		Skirts and divided skirts, knitted or crocheted, of artificial fibres, containing≥23% by weight of wool or animal hair

税则号列 Tariff Item.	货品名称	最惠国(%) MFN	协定(%)CT 东盟 CA	中巴 CP	中智 CC	普通 Gen	增值税率 VAT	出口退税 ED	计量单位 Unit	监管条件 SC	Article Description
6104.5900 29	其他人纤制针织或钩编裙子及裙裤	14				130	17	13	件/千克		Skirts and divided skirts, knitted or crocheted other, of artificial fibres
6104.5900 91	其他纺材制针织或钩编裙子及裙裤(棉限内)	14				130	17	13	件/千克		Skirts and divided skirts, knitted or crocheted, of other textile materials, cotton within limitations
6104.5900 92	其他纺材制针织或钩编裙子及裙裤(羊毛限内)	14				130	17	13	件/千克		Skirts and divided skirts, knitted or crocheted, of other textile materials, wool within limitations
6104.5900 93	其他纺材制针织或钩编裙子及裙裤(化纤限内)	14				130	17	13	件/千克		Skirts and divided skirts, knitted or crocheted, of other textile materials, man-made fibres within limitations
6104.5900 99	其他纺材制针织或钩编裙子及裙裤	14				130	17	13	件/千克		Skirts and divided skirts, knitted or crocheted, of other textile materials
	-长裤、护胸背带工装裤、马裤及短裤:										-Trousers, bib and brace overalls, breeches and shorts:
6104.6100	--羊毛或动物细毛制	16	12	11.7	0	130	17	13	条/千克		--Of wool or fine animal hair
6104.6100 10	毛制针织或钩编女护胸背带工装裤	16				130	17	13	条/千克		Women's or girl's bib and brace overalls, knitted or crocheted, of wool or fine animal hair
6104.6100 20	毛制针织或钩编女长裤、马裤(包括女童7-16号)	16				130	17	13	条/千克		Women's trousers, breeches and girls' No. 7 ~ No. 16, knitted or crocheted, of wool or fine animal hair
6104.6100 90	毛制针织或钩编其他女裤(包括短裤及其他女童裤)	16				130	17	13	条/千克		Other women's trousers, including shorts and other girls' trousers, knitted or crocheted, of wool or fine animal hair
6104.6200	--棉制	16	T3	13.6	0	90	17	13	条/千克		--Of cotton
6104.6200 10	棉制针织或钩编护胸背带女工装裤(保暖护胸背带工装裤)	16				90	17	13	条/千克		Women's or girls' bib and brace overalls, thermal, knitted or crocheted, of cotton
6104.6200 20	棉针织或钩编非保暖女成人工装裤(护胸背带工装裤)	16				90	17	13	条/千克		Women's bib and brace overalls, non-thermal, knitted or crocheted, of cotton
6104.6200 30	棉制针织或钩编女童游戏套装长裤(指女童7-16号,包括马裤)	16				90	17	13	条/千克		Girls' playsuit trousers No. 7 ~ No. 16, including breeches, knitted or crocheted, of cotton
6104.6200 40	棉针织或钩编其他女童游戏套装裤(包括马裤、短裤、非保暖护胸背带工装裤及其他长裤)	16				90	17	13	条/千克		Other girls' playsuit, including breeches, shorts, bib and brace overalls and other trousers, knitted or crocheted, of cotton
6104.6200 50	棉制针织或钩编女长裤、马裤(包括女童7-16号)	16				90	17	13	条/千克	5	Women' trousers, breeches and girls' No. 7 ~ No. 16, knitted or crocheted, of cotton
6104.6200 90	棉制针织或钩编其他女裤(包括短裤及其他女童裤)	16				90	17	13	条/千克	5	Other women's, shorts and girls' trousers, knitted or crocheted, of cotton
6104.6300	--合成纤维制	17.5	T3	12.3	0	130	17	13	条/千克		--Of synthetic fibres

税则号列 Tariff Item.	货品名称	最惠国(%) MFN	协定(%) CT 东盟 CA	中巴 CP	中智 CC	普通 Gen	增值税率 VAT	出口退税 ED	计量单位 Unit	监管条件 SC	Article Description
6104.6300 10	合成纤维制护胸背带女工装裤(针织或钩编,包括女童护胸背带工装裤)	17.5				130	17	13	条/千克		Women's or girls' bib and brace overalls, knitted or crocheted, of synthetic fibres
6104.6300 21	合成纤维制针织或钩编女长裤(含毛或动物细毛23%及以上,包括女童7-16号)	17.5				130	17	13	条/千克		Women's trousers and girls' No.7 - No.16, containing≥23% by weight of wool or fine animal hair, knitted or crocheted, of synthetic fibres
6104.6300 29	合成纤维制针织或钩编其他女裤(含毛或动物细毛23%及以上,包括长裤、短裤)	17.5				130	17	13	条/千克		Other women's or girls' trousers and shorts, containing≥23% by weight of wool or fine animal hair, knitted or crocheted, of synthetic fibres
6104.6300 91	其他合纤制女童游戏套装长裤马裤(针织或钩编,指女童7-16号)	17.5				130	17	13	条/千克		Girls' playsuit trousers or breeches No.7 ~ No.16, knitted or crocheted, of synthetic fibres
6104.6300 92	其他合成纤维制女童游戏套装裤(针织或钩编,包括短裤及其他长裤)	17.5				130	17	13	条/千克		Other girls' playsuit, shorts and other trousers, knitted or crocheted, of synthetic fibres
6104.6300 99	其他合成纤维制针织或钩编女裤(包括长裤、马裤、短裤)	17.5				130	17	13	条/千克	5	Other women's or girls' trousers, breeches, shorts, knitted or crocheted, of synthetic fibres
6104.6900	--其他纺织材料制	16	T3	12	0	130	17	13	条/千克		--Of other textile materials
6104.6900 11	丝及绢丝制针织或钩编女工装裤(含丝70%及以上)	16				130	17	13	条/千克		Women's or girls' bib and brace overalls, containing ≥ 70% by weight of silk or silk waste, knitted or crocheted
6104.6900 12	丝及绢丝制针织或钩编女长裤马裤(含丝70%及以上,包括女童7-16号)	16				130	17	13	条/千克		Women's trousers, breeches and girls' No.7 ~ No.16, containing≥70% by weight of silk or silk waste, knitted or crocheted
6104.6900 13	丝及绢丝制针织或钩编女短裤(含丝70%及以上,包括女童7-16号)	16				130	17	13	条/千克		Women's shorts, including girls' No.7 ~ No.16, knitted or crocheted, containing≥70% by weight of silk or silk waste
6104.6900 19	丝及绢丝制针织或钩编其他女长裤(含丝70%及以上)	16				130	17	13	条/千克		Other women's or girls' trousers, containing≥70% by weight of silk or silk waste, knitted or crocheted
6104.6900 21	人造纤维制护胸背带女工装裤(针织或钩编)	16				130	17	13	条/千克		Women's or girls' bib and brace overalls, of artificial fibres, knitted or crocheted
6104.6900 22	人造纤维制针织或钩编女长裤马裤(含毛或动物细毛23%及以上,包括女童7-16号)	16				130	17	13	条/千克		Women's trousers, breeches and girls' No.7 ~ No.16, of artificial fibres, containing≥23% by weight of wool or fine animal hair, knitted or crocheted
6104.6900 23	人造纤维制针织或钩编其他女裤(含毛或动物细毛23%及以上,包括长裤、短裤)	16				130	17	13	条/千克		Other women's or girls' trousers, shorts of artificial fibres, containing≥23% by weight of wool or fine animal hair, knitted or crocheted
6104.6900 24	其他人造纤维制女长裤(针织或钩编,包括女童7-16号)	16				130	17	13	条/千克	5	Women's trousers and girls' No.7 ~ No.16 of artificial fibres, knitted or crocheted

税则号列 Tariff Item.	货品名称	最惠国(%) MFN	协定(%)CT 东盟 CA	协定(%)CT 中巴 CP	协定(%)CT 中智 CC	普通 Gen	增值税率 VAT	出口退税 ED	计量单位 Unit	监管条件 SC	Article Description
6104.6900 29	其他人纤制针织或钩编其他女裤(包括长裤、马裤)	16				130	17	13	条/千克	5	Other women's or girls' trousers, breeches, knitted or crocheted, of artificial fibres
6104.6900 31	其他纺材制针织或钩编女工装裤(棉限内)	16				130	17	13	条/千克		Women's or girls' bib and brace overalls, cotton within limitations, of other textile materials
6104.6900 32	其他纺材制针织或钩编女工装裤(羊毛限内)	16				130	17	13	条/千克		Women's or girls' bib and brace overalls, wool within limitations, knitted or crocheted, of other textile materials
6104.6900 33	其他纺材制针织或钩编女工装裤(化纤限内)	16				130	17	13	条/千克		Women's or girls' bib and brace overalls, man-made fibres within limitations, knitted or crocheted, of other textile materials
6104.6900 39	其他纺材制针织或钩编女工装裤	16				130	17	13	条/千克		Women's or girls' bib and brace overalls, knitted or crocheted, of other textile materials
6104.6900 41	其他纺织材料制针织或钩编女长裤(棉限内,包括女童7-16号,包括马裤)	16				130	17	13	条/千克	5	Women's trousers and breeches girls' No. 7 ~ No. 16, cotton within limitations, knitted or crocheted, of other textile materials
6104.6900 42	其他纺织材料制针织或钩编女长裤(羊毛限内,包括女童7-16号,包括马裤)	16				130	17	13	条/千克		Women's trousers breeches and girls' No. 7 ~ No. 16, wool within limitations, knitted or crocheted, of other textile materials
6104.6900 43	其他纺织材料制针织或钩编女长裤(化纤限内,包括女童7-16号,包括马裤)	16				130	17	13	条/千克	5	Women's trousers breeches, girls' No. 7 ~ No. 16, man-made fibres within limitations, knitted or crocheted, of other textile materials
6104.6900 49	其他纺织材料制针织或钩编女长裤(包括女童7-16号,包括马裤)	16				130	17	13	条/千克	5	Women's trousers breeches, including girls' No. 7 ~ No. 16, knitted or crocheted of other textile materials
6104.6900 51	其他纺织材料针织钩编其他女长裤(棉限内)	16				130	17	13	条/千克	5	Other women's or girls' trousers, of other textile materials, cotton within limitations
6104.6900 52	其他纺织材料针织钩编其他女长裤(羊毛限内)	16				130	17	13	条/千克		Other women's or girls' trousers, knitted or crocheted, of other textile materials, wool within limitations
6104.6900 53	其他纺织材料针织钩编其他女长裤(化纤限内)	16				130	17	13	条/千克	5	Other women's or girls' trousers, knitted or crocheted, of other textile materials, man-made fibres within limitations
6104.6900 59	其他纺织材料针织钩编其他女长裤	16				130	17	13	条/千克	5	Other women's or girls' trousers, knitted or crocheted, of other textile materials
6104.6900 61	其他纺织材料制针织或钩编女短裤(棉限内)	16				130	17	13	条/千克	5	Other women's or girls' shorts, knitted or crocheted, of other textile materials, cotton within limitations
6104.6900 62	其他纺织材料制针织或钩编女短裤(羊毛限内)	16				130	17	13	条/千克		Other women's or girls' shorts, knitted or crocheted, of other textile materials, wool within limitations

税则号列 Tariff Item.	货品名称	最惠国(%) MFN	协定(%) CT 东盟 CA	中巴 CP	中智 CC	普通 Gen	增值税率 VAT	出口退税 ED	计量单位 Unit	监管条件 SC	Article Description
6104.6900 63	其他纺织材料制针织或钩编女短裤(化纤限内)	16				130	17	13	条/千克	5	Other women's or girls' shorts, knitted or crocheted of other textile materials, man-made fibres within limitations
6104.6900 69	其他纺织材料制针织或钩编女短裤	16				130	17	13	条/千克	5	Other women's or girls' shorts, knitted or crocheted, of other textile materials
61.05	**针织或钩编的男衬衫:**										**Men's or boys' shirts, knitted or crocheted:**
6105.1000	-棉制	16	T3	13.6	0	90	17	13	件/千克		-Of cotton
6105.1000 11	棉制针织或钩编男童游戏套装衬衫(不带缝制领,指男童8-18号)	16				90	17	13	件/千克	5	Boys' playsuit shirts No.8 ~ No.18, having neither made-to-order collar, knitted or crocheted, of cotton
6105.1000 19	棉制其他男童游戏套装衬衫(针织或钩编)	16				90	17	13	件/千克	5	Other boys' playsuit shirts, knitted or crocheted, of cotton
6105.1000 91	其他棉制针织或钩编男衬衫(不带缝制领,包括男童8-18号)	16				90	17	13	件/千克	5	Other men's shirts having neither made-to-order collar, including boys' No.8 ~ No.18, knitted or crocheted, of cotton
6105.1000 99	其他棉制针织或钩编其他男衬衫	16				90	17	13	件/千克	5	Other men's or boys' shirts, knitted or crocheted, of cotton
6105.2000	-化学纤维制	17.5	T3	12.3	0	130	17	13	件/千克		-Of man-made fibres
6105.2000 11	化纤制针织或钩编男衬衫(含羊毛23%及以上,不带缝制领,包括男童8-18号)	17.5				130	17	13	件/千克	5	Men's shirts, containing ≥ 23% by weight of wool or fine animal hair, having neither made-to-order collar, including boys' No.8 ~ No.18, knitted or crocheted, of man-made fibres
6105.2000 19	化纤制针织或钩编其他男衬衫(含羊毛23%及以上)	17.5				130	17	13	件/千克	5	Other men's or boys' shirts, containing ≥23% by weight of wool or fine animal hair, knitted or crocheted, of man-made fibres
6105.2000 21	化纤针织或钩编男童游戏套装衬衫(不带缝制领,指男童8-18号)	17.5				130	17	13	件/千克	5	Boys' playsuit shirts No.8 ~ No.18, having neither made-to-order collar, knitted or crocheted, of man-made fibres
6105.2000 29	化纤制其他男童游戏套装衬衫(针织或钩编)	17.5				130	17	13	件/千克	5	Other boys' playsuit shirts, knitted or crocheted, of man-made fibres
6105.2000 91	其他化纤制针织或钩编男衬衫(不带缝制领,包括男童8-18号)	17.5				130	17	13	件/千克	5	Other men's shirts having neither made-to-order collar, including boys' No.8 ~ No.18, knitted or crocheted, of man-made fibres
6105.2000 99	其他化纤制针织或钩编其他男衬衫	17.5				130	17	13	件/千克	5	Other men's or boys' shirts, knitted or crocheted, of man-made fibres
6105.9000	-其他纺织材料制	16	T3	11.7	0	130	17	13	件/千克		-Of other textile materials
6105.9000 11	丝及绢丝制针织或钩编男衬衫(含丝70%及以上,不带特制领,包括男童8-18号)	16				130	17	13	件/千克		Men's shirts containing≥70% by weight of silk or silk waste, having neither made-to-order collar, including boys' No.8 ~ No.18, knitted or crocheted
6105.9000 19	丝及绢丝制针织或钩编其他男衬衫(含丝70%及以上)	16				130	17	13	件/千克		Other men's or boys' shirts containing≥70% by weight of silk or silk waste, knitted or crocheted

税则号列 Tariff Item.	货品名称	最惠国(%) MFN	协定(%) CT 东盟 CA	 中巴 CP	 中智 CC	普通 Gen	增值税率 VAT	出口退税 ED	计量单位 Unit	监管条件 SC	Article Description
6105.9000 21	羊毛或动物细毛制男衬衫(针织或钩编,不带缝制领,包括男童8-18号)	16				130	17	13	件/千克	5	Men's shirts of wool or fine animal hair, having neither made-to-order collar, including boys' No. 8 ~ No. 18, knitted or crocheted
6105.9000 29	羊毛或动物细毛制其他男衬衫(针织或钩编)	16				130	17	13	件/千克	5	Other men's or boys' shirts of wool or fine animal hair, knitted or crocheted, of other textile materials
6105.9000 31	其他纺织材料制针织或钩编男衬衫(棉限内,不带特制领,包括男童8-18号)	16				130	17	13	件/千克	5	Other men's shirts, having neither made-to-order collar, including boys' No. 8 ~ No. 18, knitted or crocheted of other textile materials, cotton within limitations
6105.9000 32	其他纺织材料制针织或钩编男衬衫(羊毛限内,不带特制领,包括男童8-18号)	16				130	17	13	件/千克		Men's shirts, having neither made-to-order collar, including boys' No. 8 ~ No. 18, knitted or crocheted of other textile materials, wool within limitations
6105.9000 33	其他纺织材料制针织或钩编男衬衫(化纤限内,不带特制领,包括男童8-18号)	16				130	17	13	件/千克	5	Men's shirts, having neither made-to-order collar, including boys' No. 8 ~ No. 18, knitted or crocheted, of other textile materials, man-made fibres within limitations
6105.9000 39	其他纺织材料制针织或钩编男衬衫(不带特制领,包括男童8-18号)	16				130	17	13	件/千克		Men's or boys' shirts, having neither made-to-order collar, including boys' No. 8 ~ No. 18, knitted or crocheted, of other textile materials
6105.9000 41	其他纺织材料制针织或钩编男衬衫(棉限内)	16				130	17	13	件/千克	5	Men's or boys' shirts, knitted or crocheted, of other textile materials, cotton within limitations
6105.9000 42	其他纺织材料制针织或钩编男衬衫(羊毛限内)	16				130	17	13	件/千克		Men's or boys' shirts, knitted or crocheted, of other textile materials, wool within limitations
6105.9000 43	其他纺织材料制针织或钩编男衬衫(化纤限内)	16				130	17	13	件/千克	5	Men's or boys' shirts, knitted or crocheted, of other textile materials, man-made fibres within limitations
6105.9000 49	其他纺织材料制针织或钩编其他男衬衫	16				130	17	13	件/千克		Other men's or boys' shirts, knitted or crocheted, of other textile materials
61.06	**针织或钩编的女衬衫:**										**Women's or girls' blouses, shirts and shirt-blouses, knitted or crocheted:**
6106.1000	-棉制	16	T3	13.6	0	90	17	13	件/千克		-Of cotton
6106.1000 10	棉制针织或钩编女童游戏套装衬衫	16				90	17	13	件/千克	5	Girls'playsuit shirts, knittedor crocheted, knitted or crocheted, of cotton
6106.1000 90	棉制针织或钩编其他女衬衫	16				90	17	13	件/千克	5	Other women's or girls' shirts, knitted or crocheted, of cotton
6106.2000	-化学纤维制	17.5	T3	12.3	0	130	17	13	件/千克		-Of man-made fibres
6106.2000 10	化纤制针织或钩编女衬衫(含羊毛23%及以上)	17.5				130	17	13	件/千克	5	Women's or girls' shirts, knitted or crocheted, containing ≥23% by weight of wool or fine animal hair, of man-made fibres

税则号列 Tariff Item.	货品名称	最惠国(%) MFN	协定(%) 东盟 CA	中巴 CP	CT 中智 CC	普通 Gen	增值税率 VAT	出口退税 ED	计量单位 Unit	监管条件 SC	Article Description
6106.2000 20	其他化纤制女童游戏套装衬衫(针织或钩编)	17.5				130	17	13	件/千克	5	Girls' playsuit shirts knitted or crocheted, of man-made fibres
6106.2000 90	其他化纤针织或钩编未列名女衬衫(针织或钩编)	17.5				130	17	13	件/千克	5	Other women's or girls' shirts, knitted or crocheted, not elsewhere specified or included, of man-made fibres
6106.9000	-其他纺织材料制	16	T3	11.7	0	130	17	13	件/千克		-Of other textile materials
6106.9000 10	丝及绢丝制针织或钩编女衬衫(含丝70%及以上)	16				130	17	13	件/千克		Women's or girls' shirts, knitted or crocheted, containing ≥70% by weight of silk or silk waste
6106.9000 20	羊毛或动物细毛针织或钩编女衬衫	16				130	17	13	件/千克	5	Women's or girls' shirts, knitted or crocheted, of wool or fine animal hair
6106.9000 31	其他纺织材料制针织或钩编女衬衫(棉限内)	16				130	17	13	件/千克	5	Women's or girls' shirts, knitted or crocheted, of other textile materials, cotton within limitations
6106.9000 32	其他纺织材料制针织或钩编女衬衫(羊毛限内)	16				130	17	13	件/千克		Women's or girls' shirts, knitted or crocheted, of other textile materials, wool within limitations
6106.9000 33	其他纺织材料制针织或钩编女衬衫(化纤限内)	16				130	17	13	件/千克	5	Women's or girls' shirts, knitted or crocheted, of other textile materials, man-made fibres within limitations
6106.9000 39	其他纺织材料制针织或钩编女衬衫	16				130	17	13	件/千克		Women's or girls' shirts, knitted or crocheted, of other textile materials
61.07	**针织或钩编的男式内裤、三角裤、长睡衣、睡衣裤、浴衣、晨衣及类似品:**										**Men's or boys' underpants, briefs, nightshirts, pyjamas, bathrobes, dressing gowns and similar articles, knitted or crocheted:**
	-内裤及三角裤:										-Underpants and briefs:
6107.1100	--棉制	14	T3		0	90	17	13	件/千克	5	--Of cotton
6107.1200	--化学纤维制	16	T3	10.9	0	130	17	13	件/千克	5	--Of man-made fibres
	--其他纺织材料制:										--Of other textile materials:
6107.1910	---丝及绢丝制	14	T3	9.3	0	130	17	13	件/千克		---Of silk or silk waste
6107.1910 10	丝及绢丝制男内裤及三角裤(含丝70%及以上,针织或钩编)	14				130	17	13	件/千克		Men's or boys' underpants and briefs, knitted or crocheted, containing ≥ 70% by weight of silk or silk waste
6107.1910 90	其他丝及绢丝制男内裤及三角裤(含丝70%以下,针织或钩编)	14				130	17	13	件/千克		Men's or boys' underpants and briefs, knitted or crocheted, other, containing <70% by weight of silk or silk waste
6107.1990	---其他	14	T3	9.3	0	130	17	13	件/千克		---Other
6107.1990 10	羊毛或动物细毛制男内裤及三角裤(针织或钩编)	14				130	17	13	件/千克		Men's or boys' underpants and briefs, knitted or crocheted, of wool or fine animal hair
6107.1990 90	其他纺织材料制男内裤及三角裤(针织或钩编)	14				130	17	13	件/千克		Men's or boys' underpants and briefs, knitted or crocheted, of other textile fibres
	-长睡衣及睡衣裤:										-Nightshirts and pyjamas:
6107.2100	--棉制	14	T3		0	90	17	13	件/千克		--Of cotton
6107.2200	--化学纤维制	16	8	10.9	0	130	17	13	件/千克		--Of man-made fibres
	--其他纺织材料制:										--Of other textile materials:
6107.2910	---丝及绢丝制	14	8	9.3	0	130	17	13	件/千克		---Of silk or silk waste

税则号列 Tariff Item.	货品名称	最惠国(%) MFN	协定(%) 东盟 CA	中巴 CP	CT 中智 CC	普通 Gen	增值税率 VAT	出口退税 ED	计量单位 Unit	监管条件 SC	Article Description
6107.2910 10	丝及绢丝制针织或钩编男睡衣裤(含丝70%及以上,包括长睡衣)	14				130	17	13	件/千克		Men's or boys' nightshirts, pyjamas, knitted or crocheted, containing ≥ 70% by weight of silk or silk waste
6107.2910 90	其他丝及绢丝制针织或钩编男睡衣(含丝70%以下,包括长睡衣)	14				130	17	13	件/千克		Men's or boys' nightshirts, pyjamas, knitted or crocheted, containing < 70% by weight of silk or silk waste
6107.2990	---其他	14	T3	9.3	0	130	17	13	件/千克		---Other
6107.2990 10	羊/动物细毛针织或钩编男睡衣裤(包括长睡衣)	14				130	17	13	件/千克		Men's or boys' nightshirts, pyjamas, knitted or crocheted, of wool or fine animal hair
6107.2990 90	其他纺材制针织或钩编男睡衣裤(包括长睡衣)	14				130	17	13	件/千克		Other men's or boys' nightshirts, pyjamas, knitted or crocheted, of other textile materials
	-其他:										-Other:
6107.9100	--棉制	14	T3		0	90	17	13	件/千克		--Of cotton
6107.9100 10	棉制针织或钩编其他睡衣裤	14				90	17	13	件/千克		Other men's or boys' pyjamas, knitted or crocheted, of cotton
6107.9100 90	棉制针织或钩编男浴衣、晨衣等(包括类似品)	14				90	17	13	件/千克		Men's or boys' bathrobes, dressing gowns and similar articles, knitted or crocheted, of cotton
	--其他纺织材料制:										--Of other textile materials
6107.9910	---化学纤维制	16	T3	10.9	0	130	17	13	件/千克		---Of man-made fibres
6107.9990	---其他	14	8	9.3	0	130	17	13	件/千克		---Of other
61.08	**针织或钩编的女式长衬裙、衬裙、三角裤、短衬裤、睡衣、睡衣裤、浴衣、晨衣及类似品:**										**Women's or girls' slips, petticoats, briefs, panties, nightdresses, pyjamas, nègligès, bathrobes, dressing gowns and similar articles, knitted or crocheted:**
	-长衬裙及衬裙:										-Slips and petticoats:
6108.1100	--化学纤维制	16	8	10.9	0	130	17	13	件/千克	5	--Of man-made fibres
	--其他纺织材料制:										--Of other textile materials:
6108.1910	---棉制	14	8		0	90	17	13	件/千克	5	---Of cotton
6108.1920	---丝及绢丝制	14	8		0	130	17	13	件/千克		---Of silk or silk waste
6108.1920 10	丝及绢丝制女式长衬裙及衬裙(针织或钩编,含丝70%及以上)	14				130	17	13	件/千克		Women's or girls' slips and petticoats, containing≥70% by weight of silk or silk waste, knitted or crocheted
6108.1920 90	其他丝及绢丝制女式长衬裙及衬裙(针织或钩编,含丝70%以下)	14				130	17	13	件/千克		Women's or girls' slips and petticoats, other, containing < 70% by weight of silk or silk waste, knitted or crocheted
6108.1990	---其他	14	8	9.3	0	130	17	13	件/千克		---Other
	-三角裤及短衬裤:										-Briefs and panties:
6108.2100	--棉制	14	T3		0	90	17	13	件/千克	5	--Of cotton
6108.2200	--化学纤维制	16	T3	10.9	0	130	17	13	件/千克		--Of man-made fibres
6108.2200 10	化纤制一次性女三角裤及短衬裤(针织或钩编)	16				130	17	13	件/千克		Women's or girls' briefs and panties, knitted or crocheted, throw away, of man-made fibres
6108.2200 90	化纤制其他女三角裤及短衬裤(针织或钩编)	16				130	17	13	件/千克	5	Other women's or girls' briefs and panties, knitted or crocheted, of man-made fibres

税则号列 Tariff Item.	货品名称	最惠国(%) MFN	协定(%)CT 东盟 CA	中巴 CP	中智 CC	普通 Gen	增值税率 VAT	出口退税 ED	计量单位 Unit	监管条件 SC	Article Description
	--其他纺织材料制:										--Of other textile materials:
6108.2910	---丝及绢丝制	14	T3	9.3	0	130	17	13	件/千克		---Of silk or silk waste
6108.2910 10	丝及绢丝制女三角裤及短衬裤(针织或钩编,含丝70%及以上)	14				130	17	13	件/千克		Women's or girls' briefs and panties, knitted or crocheted containing ≥70% by weight of silk or silk waste
6108.2910 90	其他丝及绢丝制女三角裤及短衬裤(针织或钩编,含丝70%以下)	14				130	17	13	件/千克		Other women's or girls' briefs and panties, knitted or crocheted, containing < 70% by weight of silk or silk waste
6108.2990	---其他	14	T3	9.3	0	130	17	13	件/千克		---Other
6108.2990 10	羊毛制针织钩编女三角裤及短衬裤(针织或钩编)	14				130	17	13	件/千克		Women's or girls' briefs and panties, knitted or crocheted, of wool
6108.2990 90	其他纺织材料制女三角裤及短衬裤(针织或钩编)	14				130	17	13	件/千克		Women's or girls' briefs and panties, knitted or crocheted, of other textile materials
	-睡衣及睡衣裤:										-Nightdresses and pyjamas:
6108.3100	--棉制	14	T3		0	90	17	13	件/千克		--Of cotton
6108.3200	--化学纤维制	16	T3	10.9	0	130	17	13	件/千克		--Of man-made fibres
	--其他纺织材料制:										--Of other textile materials:
6108.3910	---丝及绢丝制	14	T3	9.3	0	130	17	13	件/千克		---Of silk or silk waste
6108.3910 10	丝及绢丝制女睡衣及睡衣裤(针织或钩编,含丝70%及以上)	14				130	17	13	件/千克		Women's or girls' nightshirts and pyjamas, knitted or crocheted, containing ≥70% by weight of silk or silk waste
6108.3910 90	其他丝及绢丝制女睡衣及睡衣裤(针织或钩编,含丝70%以下)	14				130	17	13	件/千克		Other women's or girls' nightshirts and pyjamas, knitted or crocheted containing < 70% by weight of silk or silk waste
6108.3990	---其他	14	T3	9.3	0	130	17	13	件/千克		---Other
6108.3990 10	羊毛或动物细毛制女睡衣及睡衣裤(针织或钩编)	14				130	17	13	件/千克		Women's or girls' nightshirts and pyjamas, knitted or crocheted, of wool or fine animal hair
6108.3990 90	其他纺织材料制女睡衣及睡衣裤(针织或钩编)	14				130	17	13	件/千克		Women's or girls' nightshirts and pyjamas, knitted or crocheted of other textile materials
	-其他:										-Other:
6108.9100	--棉制	14	T3		0	90	17	13	件/千克		--Of cotton
6108.9100 10	棉制针织或钩编女内裤,内衣	14				90	17	13	件/千克	5	Women's or girls' briefs, panties and underwear, knitted or crocheted, of cotton
6108.9100 90	其他棉制针织或钩编女浴衣、晨衣等(包括类似品)	14				90	17	13	件/千克		Women's or girls' bathrobes, dressing gowns and similar articles, knitted or crocheted, of cotton
6108.9200	--化学纤维制	16	T3	10.9	0	130	17	13	件/千克		--Of man-made fibres
6108.9200 10	化纤制针织或钩编女内裤,内衣	16				130	17	13	件/千克	5	Women's or girls' briefs, panties and underwear, of man-made fibres
6108.9200 90	其他化纤针织或钩编女浴衣、晨衣等(包括类似品)	16				130	17	13	件/千克		Women's or girls' bathrobes, dressing gowns and similar articles, knitted or crocheted, of man-made fibres
6108.9900	--其他纺织材料制	14	8	9.3	0	130	17	13	件/千克		--Of other textile materials

税则号列 Tariff Item.	货品名称	最惠国(%) MFN	协定(%)CT 东盟 CA	中巴 CP	中智 CC	普通 Gen	增值税率 VAT	出口退税 ED	计量单位 Unit	监管条件 SC	Article Description
6108.9900 10	丝及绢丝制女浴衣、晨衣等(针织或钩编,包括类似品,含丝70%及以上)	14				130	17	13	件/千克		Women's or girls' bathrobes, dressing gowns and similar articles, containing ≥70% by weight of silk or silk waste, knitted or crocheted
6108.9900 20	羊毛或动物细毛制女浴衣、晨衣等(针织或钩编,包括类似品)	14				130	17	13	件/千克		Women's or girls' bathrobes, dressing gowns and similar articles, of wool or fine animal hair, knitted or crocheted
6108.9900 90	其他纺织材料制女浴衣、晨衣等(针织或钩编,包括类似品)	14				130	17	13	件/千克		Women's or girls' bathrobes, dressing gowns and similar articles, of other textile materials, knitted or crocheted
61.09	**针织或钩编的T恤衫、汗衫及其他背心:**										**T-shirts, singlets and other vests, knitted or crocheted:**
6109.1000	-棉制	14	T3	9.4	0	90	17	13	件/千克		-Of cotton
6109.1000 10	棉制针织或钩编T恤衫、汗衫等(内衣式,包括其他背心)	14				90	17	13	件/千克	5	T-shirts, singlets, underwear style, including other vests, of cotton, knitted or crocheted
6109.1000 21	其他棉制针织或钩编男式T恤衫(内衣除外)	14				90	17	13	件/千克	5	Other men's or boys' T-shirts, other than underwear, of cotton, knitted or crocheted
6109.1000 22	其他棉制针织或钩编女式T恤衫(内衣除外)	14				90	17	13	件/千克	5	Other women's or girls T-shirts other than underwear, of cotton, knitted or crocheted
6109.1000 91	其他棉制男式汗衫及其他背心(针织或钩编,内衣除外,包括男童8-18号)	14				90	17	13	件/千克	5	Other men's singlets and other vests, including boys' No. 8 ~ No. 18, other than underwear, of cotton, knitted or crocheted
6109.1000 92	其他棉制男式汗衫及其他背心(针织或钩编,内衣除外)	14				90	17	13	件/千克	5	Other men's or boys' singlets and other vests, other than underwear, of cotton, knitted or crocheted
6109.1000 99	其他棉制女式汗衫及其他背心(针织或钩编,内衣除外)	14				90	17	13	件/千克	5	Other women's or girls singlets and other vests, other than underwear, of cotton, knitted or crocheted
	-其他纺织材料制:										-Of other textile materials:
6109.9010	---丝及绢丝制	14	T3	9.3	0	130	17	13	件/千克		---Of silk or silk waste
6109.9010 11	丝及绢丝针织钩编T恤衫汗衫背心(内衣式,含丝≥70%)	14				130	17	13	件/千克		T-shirts, singlets and other vests, underwear, containing ≥70% by weight of silk or silk waste, knitted or crocheted
6109.9010 19	其他丝及绢丝针织钩编T恤衫背心(包括汗衫,内衣式,含丝70%以下)	14				130	17	13	件/千克		Other T-shirts, singlets and other vests, underwear, containing < 70% by weight of silk or silk waste, knitted or crocheted
6109.9010 21	丝及绢丝针织钩编汗衫背心(内衣除外,含丝≥70%,含男童8-18,女童7-16号)	14				130	17	13	件/千克		Singlets, vests, including boys' No. 8 ~ No. 18, girls' No. 7 ~ No. 16, other than underwear, containing ≥70% by weight of silk or silk waste, knitted or crocheted
6109.9010 29	其他丝及绢丝针织钩编汗衫背心(内衣除外,含丝<70%,男童8-18,女童7-16号)	14				130	17	13	件/千克		Other singlets, vests, including boys' No. 8 ~ No. 18, girls' No. 7 ~ No. 16, other than underwear, containing <70% by weight of silk or silk waste, knitted or crocheted

税则号列 Tariff Item.	货 品 名 称	最惠国(%) MFN	协定(%)CT 东盟 CA	中巴 CP	中智 CC	普通 Gen	增值税率 VAT	出口退税 ED	计量单位 Unit	监管条件 SC	Article Description
6109.9010 91	其他丝及绢丝针织钩编T恤衫汗衫(含丝≥70%,包括其他背心)	14				130	17	13	件/千克		Other T-shirts, singlets and other vests, including other vests, containing≥70% by weight of silk or silk waste, knitted or crocheted
6109.9010 99	其他丝及绢丝针织钩编T恤衫汗衫(含丝<70%,包括其他背心)	14				130	17	13	件/千克		Other of other textile materials, including other vests, containing<70% by weight of silk or silk waste, knitted or crocheted
6109.9090	---其他	14	T3	9.3	0	130	17	13	件/千克		---Other
6109.9090 11	毛制针织或钩编T恤衫、汗衫等(内衣式,长袖衫)	14				130	17	13	件/千克	5	T-shirts, singlets and other vests, underwear style, long sleeve, of wool or fine animal hair, knitted or crocheted
6109.9090 12	毛制针织或钩编男式T恤衫、汗衫(内衣式,长袖衫除外)	14				130	17	13	件/千克	5	Men's or boys' T-shirts, singlets, underwear style, other than long sleeve, of wool or fine animal hair, knitted or crocheted
6109.9090 13	毛制针织或钩编女式T恤衫、汗衫(内衣式,长袖衫除外)	14				130	17	13	件/千克	5	Women's or grils' T-shirts, singlets, underwear style, other than long sleeve, of wool or fine animal hair, knitted or crocheted
6109.9090 21	毛制针织或钩编男式其他T恤衫(内衣除外)	14				130	17	13	件/千克	5	Men's or boys' T-shirts, other than underwear, of wool or fine animal hair, knitted or crocheted
6109.9090 22	毛制针织或钩编女式其他T恤衫(内衣除外)	14				130	17	13	件/千克	5	Women's or girls' T-shirts, other than underwear, of wool or fine animal hair, knitted or crocheted
6109.9090 31	毛制男式汗衫及其他背心(针织或钩编,内衣除外,含男童8-18号)	14				130	17	13	件/千克	5	Men's singlets, vests, and boys' No. 8 ~ No. 18, other than underwear, knitted or crocheted, of wool or fine animal hair
6109.9090 32	其他毛制男式汗衫及其他背心(针织或钩编,内衣除外)	14				130	17	13	件/千克	5	Men's or boys' singlets, vests, other than underwear, of wool or fine animal hair, knitted or crocheted
6109.9090 33	其他毛制女式汗衫及其他背心(针织或钩编,内衣除外)	14				130	17	13	件/千克	5	Women's or girls singlets vests, other than underwear, of wool or fine animal hair, knitted or crocheted
6109.9090 41	化纤制针织或钩编保暖式内衣	14				130	17	13	件/千克	5	Thermal underwear, of man-made fibres, knitted or crocheted
6109.9090 42	化纤制针织或钩编其他男内衣	14				130	17	13	件/千克	5	Men's or boys' underwear, of man-made fibres, knitted or crocheted
6109.9090 43	化纤制针织或钩编其他女内衣	14				130	17	13	件/千克	5	Women's or girls' underwear, of man-made fibres, knitted or crocheted
6109.9090 51	化纤制针织或钩编男式T恤衫(内衣除外)	14				130	17	13	件/千克	5	Men's or boys' T-shirts, of man-made fibres, other than underwear, knitted or crocheted
6109.9090 52	化纤制针织或钩编女式T恤衫(内衣除外)	14				130	17	13	件/千克	5	Women's or girls' T-shirts, of man-made fibres, other than underwear, knitted or crocheted

税则号列 Tariff Item.	货品名称	最惠国(%) MFN	协定(%)CT 东盟 CA	中巴 CP	中智 CC	普通 Gen	增值税率 VAT	出口退税 ED	计量单位 Unit	监管条件 SC	Article Description
6109.9090 61	化纤针织钩编男汗衫及其他背心(内衣除外,包括男童8-18号)	14				130	17	13	件/千克	5	Men's singlets, vests, including boys' No. 8 ~ No. 18, of man-made fibres, other than underwear, knitted or crocheted
6109.9090 62	其他化纤制男式汗衫及其他背心(针织或钩编,内衣除外)	14				130	17	13	件/千克	5	Men's or boys' singlets, vests, other than underwear, of man-made fibres, knitted or crocheted
6109.9090 63	其他化纤制女式汗衫及其他背心(针织或钩编,内衣除外)	14				130	17	13	件/千克	5	Women's or girls' singlets, vests, other than underwear, of man-made fibres, knitted or crocheted
6109.9090 91	其他纺织材料制T恤衫.汗衫等(针织或钩编,内衣式,包括其他背心)	14				130	17	13	件/千克		Other T-shirts, singlets and other vests underwear style, of other textile materials, knitted or crocheted
6109.9090 92	其他纺材针织钩编汗衫及其他背心(内衣除外,包括男童8-18号,女童7-16号)	14				130	17	13	件/千克		Other singlets, and other vests, other than underwear, of other textile materials, including boys' No. 8 ~ No. 18 or girls' No. 7 ~ No. 16, knitted or crocheted
6109.9090 93	其他纺材制针织钩编T恤衫汗衫(内衣除外,包括其他背心)	14				130	17	13	件/千克		Other T-shirts, singlets and other vests, other than underwear, of other textile materials, knitted or crocheted
61.10	**针织或钩编的套头衫、开襟衫、背心及类似品:**										**Jerseys, pullovers, cardigans, waistcoats and similar articles, knitted or crocheted:**
	-羊毛或动物细毛制:										-Of wool or fine animal hair:
6110.1100	--羊毛制	14	T3	0	0	130	17	13	件/千克		--Of wool
6110.1100 11	羊毛制手工针织或钩编起绒外穿背心	14				130	17	13	件/千克	B	Waistcoats, piled, hand-worked, knitted or crocheted, of wool
6110.1100 19	羊毛制针织或钩编起绒外穿背心	14				130	17	13	件/千克	5B	Waistcoats, piled, knitted or crocheted, of wool
6110.1100 21	羊毛制手工制起绒男毛衫(针织或钩编)	14				130	17	13	件/千克	B	Men's or boys' sweater, piled, hand-worked, knitted or crocheted, of wool
6110.1100 29	羊毛针织制或钩编起绒男毛衫	14				130	17	13	件/千克	5B	Men's or boys' sweater, piled, knitted or crocheted, of wool
6110.1100 31	羊毛制手工制起绒女毛衫(针织或钩编)	14				130	17	13	件/千克	B	Women's or girls' sweater, hand-worked, piled, knitted or crocheted, of wool
6110.1100 39	羊毛制针织或钩编起绒女毛衫	14				130	17	13	件/千克	5B	Women's or girls' sweater, piled, knitted or crocheted, of wool
6110.1100 41	羊毛手工制起绒套头衫等(包括开襟衫、背心及类似品,针织或钩编)	14				130	17	13	件/千克	B	Pullovers, cardigans, waistcoats and similar articles, knitted or crocheted, of wool, hand-worked, piled
6110.1100 49	羊毛针织或钩编起绒套头衫等(包括开襟衫背心及类似品)	14				130	17	13	件/千克	5B	Pullovers, cardigans, waistcoats and similar articles, knitted or crocheted, of wool, piled
6110.1100 51	羊毛手工制非起绒外穿背心(针织或钩编)	14				130	17	13	件/千克	B	Waistcoats, hand-worked, not piled, knitted or crocheted, of wool

税则号列 Tariff Item.	货 品 名 称	最惠国(%) MFN	协定(%) CT 东盟 CA	中巴 CP	中智 CC	普通 Gen	增值税率 VAT	出口退税 ED	计量单位 Unit	监管条件 SC	Article Description
6110.1100 59	羊毛针织或钩编非起绒外穿背心	14				130	17	13	件/千克	5B	Waistcoats, not piled, knitted or crocheted, of wool
6110.1100 61	其他羊毛手工制非起绒男毛衫(针织或钩编)	14				130	17	13	件/千克	B	Other men's or boys' sweater, hand-worked, not piled, knitted or crocheted, of wool
6110.1100 69	其他羊毛针织或钩编非起绒男毛衫	14				130	17	13	件/千克	5B	Other men's or boys' sweater, not piled, knitted or crocheted of wool
6110.1100 71	其他羊毛制手工制非起绒女毛衫(针织或钩编)	14				130	17	13	件/千克	B	Other women's or girls' sweater, hand-worked, not piled, knitted or crocheted, of wool
6110.1100 79	其他羊毛针织或钩编非起绒女毛衫	14				130	17	13	件/千克	5B	Other women's or girls' sweater, not piled, knitted or crocheted, of wool
6110.1100 91	其他羊毛制手工制非起绒套头衫等(针织或钩编,包括开襟衫、背心及类似品)	14				130	17	13	件/千克	B	Pullovers, cardigans, waistcoats and similar articles, knitted or crocheted, of wool other, hand-worked, not piled
6110.1100 99	其他羊毛制非起绒套头衫等(针织或钩编,包括开襟衫、背心及类似品)	14				130	17	13	件/千克	5B	Pullovers, cardigans, waistcoats and similar articles, knitted or crocheted, of wool other, not piled
6110.1200	--喀什米尔山羊细毛制	14	8	0	0	130	17	13	件/千克		--Of Kashmir(cashmere) goats
6110.1200 11	喀什米尔山羊细毛手工起绒男套头衫(针织或钩编,包括开襟衫、外穿背心及类似品)	14				130	17	13	件/千克	B	Men's or boys' pullovers, cardigans, waistcoats and similar articles, of fine hair of Kashmir (cashmere) goats, knitted or crocheted, piled, hand-worked
6110.1200 19	喀什米尔山羊细毛制起绒男套头衫(针织或钩编,包括开襟衫、外穿背心及类似品)	14				130	17	13	件/千克	5B	Men's or boys' pullovers, cardigans, waistcoats and similar articles of fine hair of Kashmir (cashmere) goats, knitted or crocheted, piled
6110.1200 21	喀什米尔山羊细毛手工起绒女套头衫(针织或钩编,包括开襟衫、外穿背心及类似品)	14				130	17	13	件/千克	B	Women's or girls' pullovers, cardigans, waistcoats and similar articles, of fine hair of Kashmir (cashmere) goats, knitted or crocheted, piled, hand-worked
6110.1200 29	喀什米尔山羊细毛制起绒女套头衫(针织或钩编,包括开襟衫、外穿背心及类似品)	14				130	17	13	件/千克	5B	Women's or girls' pullovers, cardigans, waistcoats and similar articles, of fine hair of Kashmir (cashmere) goats, knitted or crocheted, piled
6110.1200 31	喀什米尔山羊细毛手工非起绒男套头衫(针织或钩编,包括开襟衫、外穿背心及类似品)	14				130	17	13	件/千克	B	Men's or boys' pullovers, cardigans, waistcoats and similar articles, of fine hair of Kashmir (cashmere) goats, knitted or crocheted, not piled, hand-worked
6110.1200 39	喀什米尔山羊细毛非起绒男套头衫(针织或钩编,包括开襟衫、外穿背心及类似品)	14				130	17	13	件/千克	5B	Men's or boys' pullovers, cardigans, waistcoats and similar articles, of fine hair of Kashmir (cashmere) goats, knitted or crocheted, not piled

税则号列 Tariff Item.	货 品 名 称	最惠国(%) MFN	协定(%) CT 东盟 CA	中巴 CP	中智 CC	普通 Gen	增值税率 VAT	出口退税 ED	计量单位 Unit	监管条件 SC	Article Description
6110.1200 41	喀什米尔山羊细毛手工非起绒女套头衫(针织或钩编,包括开襟衫、外穿背心及类似品)	14				130	17	13	件/千克	B	Women's or girls' pullovers, cardigans, waistcoats and similar articles, of fine hair of Kashmir (cashmere) goats, knitted or crocheted, not piled, hand-worked
6110.1200 49	喀什米尔山羊细毛非起绒女套头衫(针织或钩编,包括开襟衫、外穿背心及类似品)	14				130	17	13	件/千克	5B	Women's or girls' pullovers, cardigans, waistcoats and similar articles, of fine hair of Kashmir (cashmere) goats, knitted or crocheted, not piled
	--其他:										--Other:
6110.1910	---其他山羊细毛制	14	8	0	0	130	17	13	件/千克		---Of other goats
6110.1910 11	其他山羊细毛手工起绒男套头衫(针织或钩编,包括开襟衫、背心及类似品)	14				130	17	13	件/千克	B	Other men's or boys' pullovers, cardigans, waistcoats and similar articles, of fine hair or wool of goats other than kashmir goats, knitted or crocheted, piled, hand-worked
6110.1910 19	其他山羊细毛制起绒男套头衫(针织或钩编,包括开襟衫、背心及类似品)	14				130	17	13	件/千克	5B	Other men's or boys' pullovers, cardigans, waistcoats and similar articles, of fine hair or wool of goats other than kashmir goats, knitted or crocheted, piled
6110.1910 21	其他山羊细毛手工起绒女套头衫(针织或钩编,包括开襟衫、背心及类似品)	14				130	17	13	件/千克	B	Other women's or girls' pullovers, cardigans, waistcoats and similar articles, of fine hair or wool of goats other than kashmir goats, knitted or crocheted, piled, hand-worked
6110.1910 29	其他山羊细毛制起绒女套头衫(针织或钩编,包括开襟衫、背心及类似品)	14				130	17	13	件/千克	5B	Other women's or girls' pullovers, cardigans, waistcoats and similar articles, of fine hair or wool of goats other than kashmir goats, knitted or crocheted, piled
6110.1910 31	其他山羊细毛手工非起绒男套头衫(针织或钩编,包括开襟衫、背心及类似品)	14				130	17	13	件/千克	B	Other men's or boys' pullovers, cardigans, waistcoats and similar articles, of fine hair or wool of goats other than kashmir goats, knitted or crocheted, not piled hand-worked
6110.1910 39	其他山羊细毛非起绒男套头衫(针织或钩编,包括开襟衫、背心及类似品)	14				130	17	13	件/千克	5B	Other men's or boys' pullovers, cardigans, waistcoats and similar articles, of fine hair or wool of goats other than kashmir goats, knitted or crocheted, not piled
6110.1910 41	其他山羊细毛手工非起绒女套头衫(针织或钩编,包括开襟衫、背心及类似品)	14				130	17	13	件/千克	B	Other women's or girls' pullovers, cardigans, waistcoats and similar articles of fine hair or wool of goats other than kashmir goats, knitted or crocheted, not piled, hand-worked

税则号列 Tariff Item.	货品名称	最惠国(%) MFN	协定(%) CT 东盟 CA	中巴 CP	中智 CC	普通 Gen	增值税率 VAT	出口退税 ED	计量单位 Unit	监管条件 SC	Article Description
6110.1910 49	其他山羊细毛非起绒女套头衫(针织或钩编,包括开襟衫、背心及类似品)	14				130	17	13	件/千克	5B	Other women's or girls' pullovers, cardigans, waistcoats and similar articles, of fine hair or wool of goats other than kashmir goats, knitted or crocheted, not piled
6110.1920	---兔毛制	14	8	0	0	130	17	13	件/千克		---Of rabbit and hare
6110.1920 11	兔毛制手工针织或钩编起绒马甲	14				130	17	13	件/千克		Waistcoats, piled, hand-worked, knitted or crocheted, of rabbit' or hare' fine hair
6110.1920 19	兔毛制针织或钩编起绒马甲	14				130	17	13	件/千克	5	Waistcoats, piled, knitted or crocheted, of rabbit' or hare' fine hair
6110.1920 21	兔毛制手工针织或钩编起绒男毛衫	14				130	17	13	件/千克		Men's or boys' sweater, piled, hand-worked, knitted or crocheted, of rabbit' or hare' fine hair
6110.1920 29	兔毛制针织或钩编起绒男毛衫	14				130	17	13	件/千克	5	Men's or boys' sweater, piled, knitted or crocheted, of rabbit' or hare' fine hair
6110.1920 31	兔毛制手工针织或钩编起绒女毛衫	14				130	17	13	件/千克		Women's or girls' sweater, piled, hand-worked, knitted or crocheted, of rabbit' or hare' fine hair
6110.1920 39	兔毛制针织或钩编起绒女毛衫	14				130	17	13	件/千克	5	Women's or girls' sweater, piled, knitted or crocheted, of rabbit' or hare' fine hair
6110.1920 41	其他兔毛制手工制起绒套头衫等(针织或钩编,包括开襟衫、背心及类似品)	14				130	17	13	件/千克		Pullovers, cardigans, waistcoats and similar articles, knitted or crocheted, piled, of rabbit' or hare' fine hair, hand-worked
6110.1920 49	其他兔毛制起绒套头衫等(针织或钩编,包括开襟衫、背心及类似品)	14				130	17	13	件/千克	5	Pullovers, cardigans, waistcoats and similar articles, knitted or crocheted, piled, of rabbit' or hare' fine hair
6110.1920 51	兔毛制手工制非起绒马甲(针织或钩编)	14				130	17	13	件/千克		Waistcoats, hand-worked, not piled, knitted or crocheted, of rabbit' or hare' fine hair
6110.1920 59	兔毛制针织或钩编非起绒马甲	14				130	17	13	件/千克	5	Waistcoats, not piled, knitted or crocheted, of rabbit' or hare' fine hair
6110.1920 61	兔毛手工制非起绒男毛衫(针织或钩编)	14				130	17	13	件/千克		Men's or boys' sweater, hand-worked, not piled, knitted or crocheted, of rabbit' or hare' fine hair
6110.1920 69	兔毛针织或钩编非起绒男毛衫	14				130	17	13	件/千克	5	Men's or boys' sweater, not piled, knitted or crocheted, of rabbit' or hare' fine hair
6110.1920 71	兔毛制手工制非起绒女毛衫(针织或钩编)	14				130	17	13	件/千克		Women's or girls' sweater, hand-worked, not piled, knitted or crocheted, of rabbit' or hare' fine hair
6110.1920 79	兔毛制针织或钩编非起绒女毛衫	14				130	17	13	件/千克	5	Women's or girls' sweater, not piled, knitted or crocheted, of rabbit' or hare' fine hair

税则号列 Tariff Item.	货品名称	最惠国(%) MFN	协定(%) CT 东盟 CA	中巴 CP	中智 CC	普通 Gen	增值税率 VAT	出口退税 ED	计量单位 Unit	监管条件 SC	Article Description
6110.1920 91	其他兔毛制手工制非起绒套头衫等(针织或钩编,包括开襟衫、背心及类似品)	14				130	17	13	件/千克		Other pullovers, cardigans, waistcoats and similar articles, knitted or crocheted, not piled, of rabbit' or hare' fine hair hand-worked
6110.1920 99	其他兔毛制非起绒套头衫等(针织或钩编,包括开襟衫、背心及类似品)	14				130	17	13	件/千克	5	Other pullovers, cardigans, waistcoats and similar articles, knitted or crocheted, not piled, of rabbit' or hare' fine hair
6110.1990	---其他	14	8	0	0	130	17	13	件/千克		---Other
6110.1990 11	其他动物细毛制手工起绒马甲(针织或钩编)	14				130	17	13	件/千克		Waistcoats, piled, hand-worked, of other fine animal hair, knitted or crocheted
6110.1990 19	其他动物细毛制起绒马甲(针织或钩编)	14				130	17	13	件/千克	5	Waistcoats, piled, of other fine animal hair, knitted or crocheted
6110.1990 21	其他动物细毛手工起绒男毛衫(针织或钩编)	14				130	17	13	件/千克		Men's or boys' sweater, piled, hand-worked, of other fine animal hair, knitted or crocheted
6110.1990 29	其他动物细毛制起绒男毛衫(针织或钩编)	14				130	17	13	件/千克	5	Men's or boys' sweater, piled, of other fine animal hair, knitted or crocheted
6110.1990 31	其他动物细毛手工起绒女毛衫(针织或钩编)	14				130	17	13	件/千克		Women's or girls' sweater, piled, hand-worked, of other fine animal hair, knitted or crocheted
6110.1990 39	其他动物细毛制起绒女毛衫(针织或钩编)	14				130	17	13	件/千克	5	Women's or girls' sweater, piled, of other fine animal hair, knitted or crocheted
6110.1990 41	其他动物细毛手工起绒套头衫(针织或钩编,包括开襟衫、背心及类似品)	14				130	17	13	件/千克		Pullovers, cardigans, waistcoats and similar articles, knitted or crocheted, piled, of other fine animal hair, hand-worked
6110.1990 49	其他动物细毛制起绒套头衫(针织或钩编,包括开襟衫、背心及类似品)	14				130	17	13	件/千克	5	Pullovers, cardigans, waistcoats and similar articles, knitted or crocheted, piled, of other fine animal hair
6110.1990 51	其他动物细毛制手工非起绒马甲(针织或钩编)	14				130	17	13	件/千克		Waistcoats, hand-worked, not piled, knitted or crocheted, of other fine animal hair
6110.1990 59	其他动物细毛制非起绒马甲(针织或钩编)	14				130	17	13	件/千克	5	Waistcoats, hand-worked, knitted or crocheted, not piled, of other fine animal hair
6110.1990 61	其他动物细毛手工非起绒男毛衫(针织或钩编)	14				130	17	13	件/千克		Men's or boys' sweater, hand-worked, not piled, knitted or crocheted, of other fine animal hair
6110.1990 69	其他动物细毛非起绒男毛衫(针织或钩编)	14				130	17	13	件/千克	5	Men's or boys' sweater, knitted or crocheted, not piled, of other fine animal hair
6110.1990 71	其他动物细毛手工非起绒女毛衫(针织或钩编)	14				130	17	13	件/千克		Women's or girls' sweater, not piled, hand-worked, knitted or crocheted, of other fine animal hair

税则号列 Tariff Item.	货品名称	最惠国(%) MFN	协定(%)CT 东盟 CA	中巴 CP	中智 CC	普通 Gen	增值税率 VAT	出口退税 ED	计量单位 Unit	监管条件 SC	Article Description
6110.1990 79	其他动物细毛非起绒女毛衫(针织或钩编)	14				130	17	13	件/千克	5	Women's or girls' sweater, not piled, knitted or crocheted, of other fine animal hair
6110.1990 91	其他动物细毛手工非起绒套头衫(针织或钩编,包括开襟衫、背心及类似品)	14				130	17	13	件/千克		Pullovers, cardigans, waistcoats and similar articles, knitted or crocheted, not piled, of other fine animal hair, hand-worked
6110.1990 99	其他动物细毛非起绒套头衫(针织或钩编,包括开襟衫、背心及类似品)	14				130	17	13	件/千克	5	Pullovers, cardigans, waistcoats and similar articles, knitted or crocheted, not piled, of other fine animal hair
6110.2000	-棉制	14	T3	0	0	90	17	13	件/千克		-Of cotton
6110.2000 11	棉制儿童游戏套装紧身衫及套头衫(针织起绒,轻薄细针翻领、开领、高领,含亚麻36%以下)	14				90	17	13	件/千克	5	Boys' or girls' playsuit, jerseys, pullovers, tricolette turn-down collar, open-necked collar, high-necked collar, containing <36% by weight of flax, of cotton knitted, piled
6110.2000 12	棉制其他起绒儿童游戏套头衫等(针织钩编,包括开襟衫、背心及类似品,含亚麻36%以下)	14				90	17	13	件/千克	5	Other boys' or girls' playsuit, pullovers, cardigans, waistcoats and similar articles, containing < 36% by weight of flax, of cotton, knitted or crocheted
6110.2000 20	棉制针织或钩编起绒马甲(毛衫、背心除外)	14				90	17	13	件/千克	5	Waistcoats, piled, other than sweater, of cotton, knitted or crocheted
6110.2000 31	棉制针织起绒紧身及套头毛衫(轻薄细针翻领、开领、高领)	14				90	17	13	件/千克	5	Jerseys or pullovers, piled, tricolette turn-down collar, open-necked collar, high-necked collar, of cotton, knitted
6110.2000 32	棉制针织起绒男紧身衫及套头衫(轻薄细针翻领/开领/高领,但平床机生产、直接针织成形除外)	14				90	17	13	件/千克	5	Men's or boys' jerseys, pullovers, piled, tricolette turn-down collar, open-necked collar, high-necked collar, of cotton, knitted
6110.2000 33	棉制针织起绒女紧身衫及套头衫(轻薄细针翻领/开领/高领,但平床机生产、直接针织成形除外)	14				90	17	13	件/千克	5	Women's or girls' jerseys, pullovers, piled, tricolette turn-down collar, open-necked collar, high-necked collar, of cotton knitted
6110.2000 41	棉制针织或钩编起绒其他毛衫	14				90	17	13	件/千克	5	Other sweater, piled, of cotton, knitted or crocheted
6110.2000 42	棉制针织或钩编起绒男套头衫等(包括开襟衫、背心及类似品,但平床机生产、直接针织成形除外)	14				90	17	13	件/千克	5	Men's or boys' pullovers, cardigans, waistcoats and similar articles, piled, of cotton, knitted or crocheted
6110.2000 43	棉制针织或钩编起绒女套头衫等(包括开襟衫、背心及类似品,但平床机生产、直接针织成形除外)	14				90	17	13	件/千克	5	Women's or girls' pullovers, cardigans, waistcoats and similar articles, piled, of cotton, knitted or crocheted
6110.2000 51	其他棉儿童游戏套装紧身及套头衫(针织、非起绒、轻薄细针翻领、开领、高领)	14				90	17	13	件/千克	5	Other boys' or girls' playsuit, jerseys, pullovers, tricolette turn-down collar, open-necked collar, high-necked collar, not piled, of cotton, knitted

税则号列 Tariff Item.	货品名称	最惠国(%) MFN	协定(%) CT			普通 Gen	增值税率 VAT	出口退税 ED	计量单位 Unit	监管条件 SC	Article Description
			东盟 CA	中巴 CP	中智 CC						
6110.2000 52	其他棉儿童游戏套装套头衫等(针织或钩编、非起绒、包括开襟衫、背心及类似品)	14				90	17	13	件/千克	5	Other boys' or girls' playsuit pullovers, cardigans, waistcoats and similar articles, of cotton, knitted or crocheted not piled
6110.2000 60	其他棉制针织或钩编非起绒马甲(毛衫、背心除外)	14				90	17	13	件/千克	5	Other waistcoats, other than sweater, not piled, of cotton, knitted or crocheted
6110.2000 71	棉制针织非起绒男紧身及套头衫等(轻薄细针翻领、开领、高领)	14				90	17	13	件/千克	5	Men's or boys' jerseys, pullovers, tricolette turn-down collar, open-necked collar, high-necked collar, knitted, not piled, of cotton, knitted
6110.2000 72	棉制非起绒男紧身衫及套头衫(轻薄细针翻领/开领/高领,但平床机生产、直接针织成形除外)	14				90	17	13	件/千克	5	Men's or boys' jerseys, pullovers, tricolette turn-down collar, open-necked collar, high-necked collar, not piled, of cotton
6110.2000 73	棉制针织非起绒女紧身衫及套头衫(轻薄细针翻领/开领/高领,但平床机生产、直接针织成形除外)	14				90	17	13	件/千克	5	Women's or girls' jerseys, pullovers, tricolette turn-down collar, open-necked collar, high-necked collar, knitted, not piled, of cotton, knitted
6110.2000 91	其他棉制针织或钩编非起绒毛衫	14				90	17	13	件/千克	5	Other sweater, not piled, of cotton, knitted or crocheted
6110.2000 92	其他针织钩编棉制非起绒男套头衫等(包括开襟衫、背心及类似品,但平床机生产、直接针织成形除外)	14				90	17	13	件/千克	5	Other men's or boys' pullovers, cardigans, waistcoats and similar articles, not piled, of cotton, knitted or crocheted
6110.2000 93	棉制针织或钩编女套头衫等(包括开襟衫、背心及类似品,,但平床机生产、直接针织成形除外)	14				90	17	13	件/千克	5	Women's or girls' pullovers, cardigans, waistcoats and similar articles, not piled, of cotton, knitted or crocheted
6110.2000 99	其他棉制针织钩编套头衫等(包括开襟衫、背心及类似品)	14				90	17	13	件/千克	5	Other pullovers, cardigans, waistcoats and similar articles, not piled, of cotton, knitted or crocheted
6110.3000	-化学纤维制	16	8	5	0	130	17	13	件/千克		-Of man-made fibres
6110.3000 11	化纤儿童游戏套装紧身衫及套头衫(针织起绒轻薄细针翻领开领高领毛<23%丝<30%)	16				130	17	13	件/千克	5	Boys' or girls' playsuit, jerseys, pullovers, tricolette turn-down collar, open-necked collar, high-necked collar, containing <23% by weight of wool or fine animal hair, containing < 30% by weight of silk or silk waste, of man-made fibres, knitted, piled
6110.3000 12	化纤起绒儿童游戏套装及套头衫等(针织或钩编包括开襟衫,背心及类似品含毛<23%含丝<30%)	16				130	17	13	件/千克	5	Boys' or girls' playsuit, jerseys, pullovers, tricolette turn-down collar, open-necked collar, high-necked collar, containing <23% by weight of wool or fine animal hair, containing < 30% by weight of silk or silk waste, of man-made fibres knitted, piled

税则号列 Tariff Item.	货品名称	最惠国(%) MFN	协定(%)CT 东盟 CA	中巴 CP	中智 CC	普通 Gen	增值税率 VAT	出口退税 ED	计量单位 Unit	监管条件 SC	Article Description
6110.3000 21	化纤制针织或钩编起绒马甲(含羊毛或动物细毛23%及以上)	16				130	17	13	件/千克	5	Waistcoats, piled, containing≥23% by weight of wool or fine animal hair, of man-made fibres, knitted or crocheted
6110.3000 22	化纤制针织起绒男紧身及套头毛衫(含羊毛/动物细毛23%及以上,轻薄细针翻领开领高领)	16				130	17	13	件/千克	5	Men's or boys' jerseys, pullovers, piled, knitted, containing≥23% by weight of wool or fine animal hair, tricolette turn-down collar, open-necked collar, high-necked collar, of man-made fibres
6110.3000 23	化纤制针织或钩编起绒男毛衫(含羊毛/动物细毛23%及以上)	16				130	17	13	件/千克	5	Men's or boys' sweater, piled, containing≥23% by weight of wool or fine animal hair, of man-made fibres, knitted or crocheted
6110.3000 24	化纤制针织起绒女紧身及套头毛衫	16				130	17	13	件/千克	5	Women's or girls' jerseys, pullovers, piled, knitted, of man-made fibres
6110.3000 25	化纤制针织或钩编起绒女毛衫(含羊毛/动物细毛23%及以上)	16				130	17	13	件/千克	5	Women's or girls' sweater, piled, containing≥23% by weight of wool or fine animal hair, of man-made fibres, knitted or crocheted
6110.3000 26	其他化纤针织起绒套头衫(含羊毛或动物细毛≥23%,轻薄细针翻领、开领、高领)	16				130	17	13	件/千克	5	Other pullovers, piled, knitted, containing≥23% by weight of wool or fine animal hair, of man-made fibres, tricolette turn-down collar, open-necked collar, high-necked collar
6110.3000 29	其他化纤针织或钩编起绒开襟衫等(含羊毛或动物细毛≥23%,包括背心及类似品)	16				130	17	13	件/千克	5	Other cardigans, waistcoats and similar articles, piled, containing ≥ 23% by weight of wool or fine animal hair, of man-made fibres, knitted or crocheted
6110.3000 31	其他化纤制针织或钩编起绒马甲	16				130	17	13	件/千克	5	Other waistcoats, piled, of man-made fibres, knitted or crocheted
6110.3000 32	化纤针织或起绒男紧身及套头毛衫(轻薄细针翻领、开领、高领)	16				130	17	13	件/千克	5	Men's or boys' jerseys, pullovers, knitted or piled, tricolette turn-down collar, open-necked collar, high-necked collar, of man-made fibres
6110.3000 33	其他化纤制针织或钩编起绒男毛衫	16				130	17	13	件/千克	5	Other men's or boys' sweater, of man-made fibres, knitted or crocheted
6110.3000 34	化纤制针织起绒女紧身及套头毛衫(轻薄细针,翻领、开领、高领)	16				130	17	13	件/千克	5	Women's or girls' jerseys, pullovers, piled, knitted, tricolette turn-down collar, open-necked collar, high-necked collar, of man-made fibres
6110.3000 35	其他化纤制针织或钩编起绒女毛衫	16				130	17	13	件/千克	5	Other women's or girls' sweater, piled, of man-made fibr6es, knitted or crocheted
6110.3000 36	其他化纤针织起绒男套头衫(轻薄细针翻领/开领/高领,但平床机生产、直接针织成形除外)	16				130	17	13	件/千克	5	Other men's or boys' pullovers, piled, tricolette turn-down collar, open-necked collar, high-necked collar, of man-made fibres, knitted or crocheted

税则号列 Tariff Item.	货 品 名 称	最惠国 (%) MFN	协定(%)CT 东盟 CA	 中巴 CP	 中智 CC	普通 Gen	增值 税率 VAT	出口 退税 ED	计量 单位 Unit	监管 条件 SC	Article Description
6110. 3000 37	其他化纤针织钩编起绒男开襟衫等(包括背心及类似品,但平床机生产、直接针织成形除外)	16				130	17	13	件/千克	5	Other men's or boys' cardigans, piled, including waistcoats and similar articles, of man-made fibres, knitted or crocheted
6110. 3000 38	其他化纤起绒针织女套头衫(轻薄细针翻领/开领/高领,但平床机生产、直接针织成形除外)	16				130	17	13	件/千克	5	Other women's or girls' pullovers, piled, tricolette turn-down collar, open-necked collar, high-necked collar, of man-made fibres, knitted
6110. 3000 39	其他化纤制针织或钩编女开襟衫等(起绒,包括背心及类似品,但平床机生产、直接针织成形除外)	16				130	17	13	件/千克	5	Other women's or girls' cardigans, including waistcoats and similar articles, piled, of man-made fibres, knitted or crocheted
6110. 3000 41	化纤其他儿童游戏套装紧身及套头衫(针织非起绒,轻薄细针翻领、开领、高领)	16				130	17	13	件/千克	5	Other boys' or girls' playsuit, jerseys, pullovers, knitted, tricolette turn-down collar, open-necked collar, high-necked collar, not piled, of man-made fibres, knitted
6110. 3000 42	化纤制其他儿童游戏套装套头衫等(针制或钩编,非起绒,包括开襟衫、背心及类似品)	16				130	17	13	件/千克	5	Other boys' or girls' playsuit, including cardigans, waistcoats and similar articles, not piled, of man-made fibres, knitted or crocheted
6110. 3000 51	其他化纤制针织或钩编非起绒马甲(含羊毛或动物细毛23%及以上)	16				130	17	13	件/千克	5	Other waistcoats, containing ≥23% by weight of wool or fine animal hair, not piled, of man-made fibres, knitted or crocheted
6110. 3000 52	化纤针织非起绒男紧身及套头毛衫(含羊毛/动物细毛23%及以上,轻薄细针翻领、开领、高领)	16				130	17	13	件/千克	5	Men's or boys' jerseys, pullovers, containing≥23% by weight of wool or fine animal hair, tricolette turn-down collar, open-necked collar, high-necked collar, not piled, of man-made fibres, knitted
6110. 3000 53	化纤制针织或钩编非起绒男毛衫(含羊毛/动物细毛23%及以上)	16				130	17	13	件/千克	5	Men's or boys' sweater, containing ≥23% by weight of wool or fine animal hair, not piled, of man-made fibres, knitted or crocheted
6110. 3000 54	化纤针织非起绒女紧身及套头毛衫(含羊毛/动物细毛23%及以上,轻薄细针翻领、开领、高领)	16				130	17	13	件/千克	5	Women's or girls' jerseys, pullovers, containing≥23% by weight of wool or fine animal hair, tricolette turn-down collar, open-necked collar, high-necked collar, not piled, of man-made fibres, knitted
6110. 3000 57	化纤制针织钩编非起绒女毛衫(含羊毛/动物细毛23%及以上)	16				130	17	13	件/千克	5	Women's or girls' sweater, containing≥23% by weight of wool or fine animal hair, not piled, of man-made fibres, knitted or crocheted
6110. 3000 58	其他化纤针非起绒套头衫(含毛≥23%非起绒,轻薄细针翻领、开领、高领)	16				130	17	13	件/千克	5	Other pullovers, containing ≥23% by weight of wool or fine animal hair, tricolette turn-down collar, open-necked collar, high-necked collar, not piled, of man-made fibres, knitted

税则号列 Tariff Item.	货品名称	最惠国(%) MFN	协定(%)CT 东盟 CA	中巴 CP	中智 CC	普通 Gen	增值税率 VAT	出口退税 ED	计量单位 Unit	监管条件 SC	Article Description
6110.3000 59	其他化纤针织或钩编开襟衫等(含羊毛或动物细毛≥23%,非起线,包括背心及类似品)	16				130	17	13	件/千克	5	Other cardingans, including waistcoats and similar articles, containing ≥23% by weight of wool or fine animal hair, not piled, of man-made fibres, knitted or crocheted
6110.3000 91	其他化纤针织男紧身及套头毛衫(非起绒,轻薄细针翻领、开领、高领)	16				130	17	13	件/千克	5	Other men's or boys' jerseys, pullovers, tricolette turn-down collar, open-necked collar, high-necked collar, not piled, of man-made fibres, knitted
6110.3000 92	其他化纤针织或钩编非起绒男毛衫	16				130	17	13	件/千克	5	Other men's or boys' sweater, not piled, of man-made fibres, knitted or crocheted
6110.3000 93	化纤针织非起绒女紧身及套头毛衫(轻薄细针翻领、开领、高领)	16				130	17	13	件/千克	5	Other women's or girls' jerseys, pullovers, tricolette turn-down collar, open-necked collar, high-necked collar, not piled, of man-made fibres, knitted
6110.3000 94	其他化纤针织或钩编非起绒女毛衫	16				130	17	13	件/千克	5	Other women's or girls' sweater, not piled, of man-made fibres, knitted or crocheted
6110.3000 95	其他化纤针织非起绒男套头衫(轻薄细针翻领/开领/高领,但平床机生产、直接针织成形除外)	16				130	17	13	件/千克	5	Other men's or boys' pullovers, tricolette turn-down collar, open-necked collar, high-necked collar, not piled, of man-made fibres, knitted
6110.3000 96	其他化纤针织或钩编男开襟衫等(非起绒,包括外穿背心及类似品,但平床机生产、直接针织成形除外)	16				130	17	13	件/千克	5	Other men's or boys' cardigans, waistcoats and similar articles, not piled, of man-made fibres, knitted or crocheted
6110.3000 97	其他化纤制针织非起绒女套头衫(轻薄细针翻领/开领/高领,但平床机生产、直接针织成形除外)	16				130	17	13	件/千克	5	Other women's or girls' pullovers, tricolette turn-down collar, open-necked collar, high-necked collar, not piled of man-made fibres knitted
6110.3000 98	其他化纤制针织或钩编女开襟衫等(包括外穿背心及类似品,但平床机生产、直接针织成形除外)	16				130	17	13	件/千克	5	Other women's or girls' cardigans, waistcoats and similar articles of man-made fibres knitted or crocheted
6110.3000 99	其他化纤制针织钩编套头衫等(包括开襟衫,背心及类似品)	16				130	17	13	件/千克	5	Other pullovers, of man-made fibres, knitted or crocheted, including cardingams, waistcoats and similar articles
	-其他纺织材料制:										-Of other textile materials:
6110.9010	---丝及绢丝制	14	8	0	0	130	17	13	件/千克		---Of silk or silk waste
6110.9010 11	丝及绢丝制针织或钩编起绒毛衫等(含丝≥70%含开衫、马甲)	14				130	17	13	件/千克		Sweater, including cardigans, waistcoats, piled, containing ≥ 70% by weight of silk or silk waste, knitted or crocheted
6110.9010 19	丝及绢丝制针织或钩编起绒毛衫等(含丝<70%含开衫、马甲)	14				130	17	13	件/千克		Sweater, including cardigans, waistcoats, piled, knitted or crocheted, containing<70% by weight of silk or silk waste

税则号列 Tariff Item.	货品名称	最惠国(%) MFN	协定(%)CT 东盟 CA	中巴 CP	中智 CC	普通 Gen	增值税率 VAT	出口退税 ED	计量单位 Unit	监管条件 SC	Article Description
6110.9010 91	其他丝及绢丝针织或钩编毛衫等(非起绒,含丝≥70%含开衫、马甲)	14				130	17	13	件/千克		Other sweater, including cardigans, waistcoats, containing≥70% by weight of silk or silk waste, not piled, knitted or crocheted
6110.9010 99	其他丝及绢丝针织或钩编毛衫等(非起绒,含丝<70%含开衫、马甲)	14				130	17	13	件/千克		Other sweater, including cardigans, wais-tcoats, not piled, knitted or crocheted, containing<70% by weight of silk or silk waste
6110.9090	---其他	14	8	0	0	130	17	13	件/千克		---Other
6110.9090 11	其他纺织材料针织或钩编起绒马甲(棉限内,毛衫背心除外)	14				130	17	13	件/千克		Waistcoats, piled, other than sweater or sleeveless, knitted or crocheted, of other textile materials, cotton within limitations
6110.9090 12	其他纺织材料针织或钩编起绒马甲(羊毛限内,毛衫背心除外)	14				130	17	13	件/千克		Waistcoats, piled, other than sweater or sleeveless, knitted or crocheted, of other textile materials, wool within limitations
6110.9090 13	其他纺织材料针织或钩编起绒马甲(化纤限内,毛衫背心除外)	14				130	17	13	件/千克		Waistcoats, piled, other than sweater or sleeveless sweater, knitted or crocheted, of other textile materials, man-made fibres within limitations
6110.9090 19	其他纺织材料起绒针织或钩编马甲(毛衫背心除外)	14				130	17	13	件/千克		Waistcoats, piled, other than sweater or sleeveless sweater, knitted or crocheted, of other textile materials
6110.9090 21	其他纺织材料制针织或钩编非起绒马甲(棉限内,毛衫背心除外)	14				130	17	13	件/千克		Waistcoats, not piled, other than sweater or sleeveless sweater, knitted or crocheted, of other textile materials, cotton within limitations
6110.9090 22	其他纺织材料制针织或钩编非起绒马甲(羊毛限内,毛衫背心除外)	14				130	17	13	件/千克		Waistcoats, not piled, other than sweater or sleeveless sweater, knitted or crocheted, of other textile materials, wool within limitations
6110.9090 23	其他纺织材料制针织或钩编非起绒马甲(化纤限内,毛衫、背心除外)	14				130	17	13	件/千克		Waistcoats, not piled, other than sweater or sleeveless sweater, knitted or crocheted, of other textile materials, man-made fibres within limitations
6110.9090 29	其他纺织材料制针织或钩编马甲(非起绒,毛衫、背心除外)	14				130	17	13	件/千克		Waistcoats, not piled, other than sweater or sleeveless sweater, knitted or crocheted, of other textile materials
6110.9090 31	其他纺织材料制针织或钩编起绒毛衫(棉限内)	14				130	17	13	件/千克	5	Sweater, piled, knitted or crocheted, of other textile materials, cotton within limitations
6110.9090 33	其他纺织材料制针织或钩编起绒男毛衫(羊毛限内)	14				130	17	13	件/千克		Men's or boys' sweater, piled, knitted or crocheted, of other textile materials, wool within limitations
6110.9090 34	其他纺织材料制针织或钩编起绒女毛衫(羊毛限内)	14				130	17	13	件/千克		Women's or girls' sweater, piled, knitted or crocheted, of other textile materials, wool within limitations

税则号列 Tariff Item.	货品名称	最惠国(%) MFN	协定(%) CT 东盟 CA	中巴 CP	中智 CC	普通 Gen	增值税率 VAT	出口退税 ED	计量单位 Unit	监管条件 SC	Article Description
6110.9090 35	其他纺织材料制针织或钩编起绒男毛衫(化纤限内)	14				130	17	13	件/千克	5	Men's or boys' sweater, knitted or crocheted, of other textile materials, man-made fibres within limitations
6110.9090 36	其他纺织材料制针织或钩编起绒女毛衫(化纤限内)	14				130	17	13	件/千克	5	Women's or girls' sweater, piled, knitted or crocheted, of other textile materials, man-made fibres within limitations
6110.9090 39	其他纺织材料制针织或钩编毛衫(起绒)	14				130	17	13	件/千克		Other sweater, piled, knitted or crocheted, of other textile materials
6110.9090 41	其他纺材针织钩编起绒男套头衫等(棉限内,包括开襟衫、马甲及类似品,但平床机生产、直接针织成形除外)	14				130	17	13	件/千克	5	Men's or boys' pullovers, cardigans, waistcoats and similar articles, piled, knitted or crocheted, of other textile materials, cotton within limitations
6110.9090 42	其他纺织材料针织钩编起绒女套头衫等(棉限内,包括开襟衫、马甲及类似品,但平床机生产、直接针织成形除外)	14				130	17	13	件/千克	5	Women's or girls' pullovers, cardigans, waistcoats and similar articles, piled, knitted or crocheted, of other textile materials, cotton within limitations
6110.9090 43	其他纺织材料针织或钩编起绒套头衫等(羊毛限内,包括开襟衫、马甲及类似品)	14				130	17	13	件/千克		Pullovers, cardigans, waistcoats and similar articles, piled, knitted or crocheted, of other textile materials, wool within limitations
6110.9090 45	其他纺织材料针织钩编起绒男套头衫等(化纤限内,包括开襟衫、马甲及类似品,但平床机生产、直接针织成形除外)	14				130	17	13	件/千克	5	Men's or boys' pullovers, cardigans, waistcoats and similar articles, piled, knitted or crocheted, of other textile materials, man-made fibres within limitations
6110.9090 46	其他纺织材料针织钩编起绒女套头衫等(化纤限内,包括开襟衫、马甲及类似品,但平床机生产、直接针织成形除外)	14				130	17	13	件/千克	5	Women's or girls' pullovers, cardigans, waistcoats and similar articles, piled, knitted or crocheted, of other textile materials, man-made fibres within limitations
6110.9090 49	其他纺织材料针织或钩编套头衫等(起绒,包括开襟衫、马甲及类似品)	14				130	17	13	件/千克		Pullovers, cardigans, waistcoats and similar articles, piled, knitted or crocheted, of other textile materials
6110.9090 51	其他纺织材料针织或钩编非起绒毛衫(棉限内)	14				130	17	13	件/千克	5	Sweater, not piled, knitted or crocheted, of other textile materials, cotton within limitations
6110.9090 53	其他纺织材料针织或钩编非起绒男毛衫(羊毛限内)	14				130	17	13	件/千克		Men's or boys' sweater, not piled, knitted or crocheted, of other textile materials, wool within limitations
6110.9090 54	其他纺织材料针织或钩编非起绒女毛衫(羊毛限内)	14				130	17	13	件/千克		Women's or girls' sweater, not piled, knitted or crocheted, of other textile materials, wool within limitations

税则号列 Tariff Item.	货 品 名 称	最惠国(%) MFN	协定(%) CT 东盟 CA	中巴 CP	中智 CC	普通 Gen	增值税率 VAT	出口退税 ED	计量单位 Unit	监管条件 SC	Article Description
6110.9090 57	其他纺织材料针织或钩编非起绒男毛衫(化纤限内)	14				130	17	13	件/千克	5	Men's or boys' sweater, not piled, knitted or crocheted, of other textile materials, man-made fibres within limitations
6110.9090 58	其他纺织材料针织或钩编非起绒女毛衫(化纤限内)	14				130	17	13	件/千克	5	Women's or girls' sweater, not piled, knitted or crocheted, of other textile materials, man-made fibres within limitations
6110.9090 59	其他纺织材料针织或钩编毛衫(非起绒)	14				130	17	13	件/千克		Sweater, not piled, knitted or crocheted, of other textile materials
6110.9090 61	其他纺织材料针织钩编非起绒男套衫等(包括开襟衫、背心及类似品,但平床机生产、直接针织成形除外)	14				130	17	13	件/千克	5	Men's or boys' pullovers, cardigans, waistcoats and similar articles, not piled, knitted or crocheted, of other textile materials, cotton within limitations
6110.9090 62	其他纺织材料针织钩编非起绒女套衫等(包括开襟衫、背心及类似品,但平床机生产、直接针织成形除外)	14				130	17	13	件/千克	5	Women's or girls' pullovers, cardigans, waistcoats and similar articles, not piled, knitted or crocheted, of other textile materials, cotton within limitations
6110.9090 63	其他纺织材料针织钩编非起绒套头衫等(羊毛限内,包括开襟衫、背心及类似品)	14				130	17	13	件/千克		Other pullovers, cardigans, waistcoats and similar articles, not piled, knitted or crocheted of other textile materials, wool within limitations
6110.9090 65	其他纺织材料针织钩编非起绒男套衫等(化纤限内,包括开襟衫、背心及类似品,但平床机生产、直接针织成形除外)	14				130	17	13	件/千克	5	Men's or boys' pullovers, cardigans, waistcoats and similar articles, not piled, knitted or crocheted, of other textile materials, man-made fibres within limitations
6110.9090 66	其他纺织材料针织钩编非起绒女套衫等(化纤限内,包括开襟衫、背心及类似品,但平床机生产、直接针织成形除外)	14				130	17	13	件/千克	5	Women's or girls' pullovers, cardigans, waistcoats and similar articles, not piled, knitted or crocheted, of other textile materials, man-made fibres within limitations
6110.9090 69	其他纺织材料针织或钩编套头衫等(非起绒,包括开襟衫、背心及类似品)	14				130	17	13	件/千克		Other pullovers, cardigans, waistcoats and similar articles, not piled, knitted or crocheted, of other textile materials
6110.9090 90	其他纺织材料针织或钩编套头衫等(包括开襟衫、背心及类似品)	14				130	17	13	件/千克		Other pullovers, cardisans, waistcoats and similar articles, knities or crocheied ,of other textile materials
61.11	**针织或钩编的婴儿服装及衣着附件:**										**Babies' garments and clothing accessories, knitted or crocheted:**
6111.2000	-棉制	14	T3		0	90	17	13	千克		-Of cotton
6111.2000 10	棉制针织或钩编婴儿袜	14				90	17	13	千克	5	Babies' hosiery of cotton, knitted or crocheted
6111.2000 20	棉制婴儿分指、连指、露指手套(针制或钩编)	14				90	17	13	千克		Babies' gloves, mittens and mitts of cotton, knitted or crocheted

税则号列 Tariff Item.	货品名称	最惠国(%) MFN	协定(%) CT			普通 Gen	增值税率 VAT	出口退税 ED	计量单位 Unit	监管条件 SC	Article Description
			东盟 CA	中巴 CP	中智 CC						
6111.2000 40	棉制针织婴儿外衣、雨衣、滑雪装(针制或钩编,包括夹克类似品)	14				90	17	13	千克		Babies' coat, raincoat, ski suit, including jacked and similar articles, of cotton, knitted or crocheted
6111.2000 50	棉制针织钩编婴儿其他服装	14				90	17	13	千克		Other babies' garments of cotton, knitted or crocheted
6111.2000 90	棉制针织钩编婴儿衣着附件	14				90	17	13	千克		Babies' clothing accessories of cotton, knitted or crocheted
6111.3000	-合成纤维制	16	T3	10.9	0	130	17	13	千克		-Of synthetic fibres
6111.3000 10	合成纤维制针织或钩编婴儿袜	16				130	17	13	千克	5	Babies' hosiery of synthetic fibres, knitted or crocheted
6111.3000 20	合成纤维婴儿分指连指及露指手套(针制或钩编)	16				130	17	13	千克		Babies' gloves, mittens and mitts of synthetic fibres, knitted or crocheted
6111.3000 40	合成纤维婴儿外衣、雨衣、滑雪装(针制或钩编,包括夹克类似服装)	16				130	17	13	千克		Babies' coat, raincoat, ski suit, jacked and similar articles, of synthetic fibres, knitted or crocheted
6111.3000 50	合成纤维针织或钩编婴儿其他服装(包括衣着附件)	16				130	17	13	千克		Other babies' garments of synthetic fibres, knitted or crocheted
6111.3000 90	合成纤维针织或钩编婴儿衣着附件	16				130	17	13	千克		Babies' clothing accessories of synthetic fibres, knitted or crocheted
	-其他纺织材料制:										-Of other textile materials
6111.9010	---羊毛或动物细毛制	14	8	9.3	0	130	17	13	千克		---Of wool or fine animal hair
6111.9090	---其他	14	T3	9.3	0	130	17	13	千克		---Other
6111.9090 10	人造纤维针织或钩编婴儿袜	14				130	17	13	千克	5	Babies'hosiery of artificial fibres, knitted or crocheted
6111.9090 90	其他纺织材料制婴儿服装及衣着附件(针织或钩编)	14				130	17		千克		Babies' garments and clothing accessories, of other textile materials, knitted or crocheted
61.12	**针织或钩编的运动服、滑雪服及游泳服:**										**Track suits, ski suits and swimwear, knitted or crocheted:**
	-运动服:										-Track suits:
6112.1100	--棉制	16	8	13.6	0	90	17	13	套/千克		--Of cotton
6112.1100 11	棉制针织或钩编男式运动套装	16				90	17	13	套/千克	5	Men's or boys' track suits of cotton, knitted or crocheted
6112.1100 19	棉制针织或钩编女式运动套装	16				90	17	13	套/千克	5	Women's or girls' track suits of cotton, knitted or crocheted
6112.1200	--合成纤维制	17.5	12	12.3	0	130	17	13	套/千克		--Of synthetic fibres
6112.1200 21	合成纤维制针织或钩编男式运动服	17.5				130	17	13	套/千克	5	Men's or boys' track suits of synthetic fibres, knitted or crocheted
6112.1200 29	合成纤维制针织或钩编女式运动套装	17.5				130	17	13	套/千克	5	Women's or girls' track suits of synthetic fibres, knitted or crocheted
6112.1900	--其他纺织材料制	16	12	11.7	0	130	17	13	套/千克		--Of other textile materials
6112.1900 31	人造纤维制针织或钩编男式运动服	16				130	17	13	套/千克	5	Men's or boys' track suits of artificial fibres, knitted or crocheted
6112.1900 39	人造纤维制针织或钩编女运动套装	16				130	17	13	套/千克	5	Women's or girls' track suits of artificial fibres, knitted or crocheted
6112.1900 41	羊毛制男式运动套装(针织或钩编,含丝70%以下)	16				130	17	13	套/千克	5	Men's or boys' track suits of wool, knitted or crocheted, containing < 70% by weight of silk

税则号列 Tariff Item.	货品名称	最惠国(%) MFN	协定(%) CT 东盟 CA	中巴 CP	中智 CC	普通 Gen	增值税率 VAT	出口退税 ED	计量单位 Unit	监管条件 SC	Article Description
6112.1900 49	羊毛制女式运动套装(针织或钩编,含丝70%以下)	16				130	17	13	套/千克	5	Women's or girls' track suits of wool, knitted or crocheted, containing <70% by weight of silk
6112.1900 51	动物细毛制男式运动套装(针织或钩编,含丝70%以下)	16				130	17	13	套/千克	5	Men's or boys' track suits of other fine animal hair, knitted or crocheted, containing <70% by weight of silk
6112.1900 59	动物细毛制女式运动套装(针织或钩编,含丝70%以下)	16				130	17	13	套/千克	5	Women's or girls' track suits of other fine animal hair, knitted or crocheted, containing <70% by weight of silk
6112.1900 61	其他纺织材料制男式运动套装(针织或钩编,含丝70%以下)	16				130	17	13	套/千克	5	Men's or boys' track suits of other textile materials, knitted or crocheted, containing <70% by weight of silk
6112.1900 69	其他纺织材料制女式运动套装(针织或钩编,含丝70%以下)	16				130	17	13	套/千克	5	Women's or girls' track suits of other textile materials, knitted or crocheted, containing <70% by weight of silk
6112.1900 90	其他纺织材料制运动套装(针织或钩编,含丝70%以上)	16				130	17	13	套/千克		Track suits of other textile materials, knitted or crocheted, containing <70% by weight of silk
	-滑雪服:										-Ski suits:
6112.2010	---棉制	16	8	13.6	0	90	17	13	套/千克		---Of cotton
6112.2090	---其他	19	12	13.6	0	130	17	13	套/千克		---Other
6112.2090 10	羊毛或动物细毛针织钩编滑雪套装	19				130	17	13	套/千克		Ski suits of wool or fine animal hair, knitted or crocheted
6112.2090 21	化学纤维制针织钩编男式滑雪套装	19				130	17	13	套/千克	5	Men's or boys' ski suits of man-made fibres, knitted or crocheted
6112.2090 29	化学纤维制针织钩编女式滑雪套装	19				130	17	13	套/千克	5	Women's or girls' ski suits of man-made fibres, knitted or crocheted
6112.2090 90	其他纺织材料针织钩编滑雪套装	19				130	17	13	套/千克		Ski suits of other textile materials, knitted or crocheted
	-男式游泳服:										-Men's or boys' swimwear:
6112.3100	--合成纤维制	17.5	T3	12.3	0	130	17	13	件/千克	5	--Of synthetic fibres
6112.3900	--其他纺织材料制	16	T3	11.7	0	130	17	13	件/千克		--Of other textile materials
6112.3900 10	棉制针织或钩编男式游泳服	16				130	17	13	件/千克	5	Men's or boys' swimwear of cotton, knitted or crocheted
6112.3900 40	其他材料制针织钩编男式游泳服	16				130	17	13	件/千克		Men's or boys' swimwear of other textile materials, knitted or crocheted
6112.3900 90	其他材料制针织钩编男式游泳服(含丝及绢丝70%及以上)	16				130	17	13	件/千克		Men's or boys' swimwear, knitted or crocheted, containing≥70% by weight of silk or silk waste
	-女式游泳服:										-Women's or girls' swimwear:
6112.4100	--合成纤维制	17.5	T3	12.3	0	130	17	13	件/千克	5	--Of synthetic fibres
6112.4900	--其他纺织材料制	16	12	11.7	0	130	17	13	件/千克		--Of other textile materials
6112.4900 10	棉制针织或钩编女游泳服	16				130	17	13	件/千克	5	Women's or girls' swimwear of cotton, knitted or crocheted
6112.4900 40	其他纺织材料制针织钩编女游泳服	16				130	17	13	件/千克		Women's or girls' swimwear of other textile materials, knitted or crocheted
6112.4900 90	其他纺织材料制针织或钩编女泳服(含丝及绢丝70%及以上)	16				130	17	13	件/千克		Women's or girls' swimwear, knitted or crocheted, containing≥70% by weight of silk or silk waste

税则号列 Tariff Item.	货品名称	最惠国(%) MFN	协定(%) CT 东盟 CA	中巴 CP	中智 CC	普通 Gen	增值税率 VAT	出口退税 ED	计量单位 Unit	监管条件 SC	Article Description
61.13	**用税目59.03、59.06或59.07的针织物或钩编织物制成的服装：**										**Garments, made up of knitted or crocheted fabrics of heading No. 59.03, 59.06 or 59.07:**
6113.0000	用税目59.03、59.06或59.07的针织物或钩编织物制成的服装	16	12	11.7	0	130	17	13	件/千克		Garments, made up of knitted or crocheted fabrics of heading No. 59.03, 59.06 or 59.07
6113.0000 11	用橡胶处理的服装(针织或钩编,织物外表面由橡胶完全覆盖)	16				130	17	13	件/千克		Garments, made up of knitted or crocheted fabrics of heading No. 59.06
6113.0000 13	用塑料处理的毛、棉及化纤制服装(针织或钩编毛指羊动物细毛织物外表面由塑料完全覆盖)	16				130	17	13	件/千克		Garments of artificial fibres, of wool or fine animal hair, of man-made fibres, made up of knitted or crocheted fabrics of heading No. 59.03
6113.0000 19	用塑料处理的其他纺织材料制服装(针织或钩编,织物外表面由塑料完全覆盖)	16				130	17	13	件/千克		Garments of other textile materials, made up of knitted or crocheted fabrics of heading No. 59.03
6113.0000 21	其他橡胶处理的棉制针织钩编男上衣	16				130	17	13	件/千克		Men's or boys' jacket and blazers of cotton, made up of knitted or crocheted fabrics of heading No. 59.06
6113.0000 22	其他塑料等处理的棉制针织男上衣(包括钩编,包括用其他材料处理的)	16				130	17	13	件/千克		Men's or boys' jacket and blazers of cotton, made up of knitted or crocheted fabrics of heading No. 59.03 or 59.07
6113.0000 23	其他橡胶处理的棉针织钩编女上衣	16				130	17	13	件/千克		Women's or girls' jacket and blazers of cotton, made up of knitted or crocheted fabrics of heading No. 59.06
6113.0000 28	其他塑料等处理的棉针织女上衣(包括钩编,包括用其他材料处理的)	16				130	17	13	件/千克		Women's or girls' jacket and blazers of cotton, made up of knitted or crocheted fabrics of heading No. 59.03 or 59.07
6113.0000 31	其他橡胶处理的纺织材料制男上衣(针织或钩编,)	16				130	17	13	件/千克		Men's or boys' jacket and blazers of other textile materials, made up of knitted or crocheted fabrics of heading No. 59.06
6113.0000 32	其他塑料等处理的毛制男上衣(针织或钩编,羊毛或动物细毛制,包括用其他材料处理的)	16				130	17	13	件/千克		Men's or boys' jacket and blazers of wool or fine animal hair, made up of knitted or crocheted fabrics of heading No. 59.03 or 59.07
6113.0000 33	其他塑料等处理的毛、化纤男上衣(针织或钩编,包括用其他材料处理的)	16				130	17	13	件/千克		Men's or boys' jacket and blazers of wool or fine animal hair, of man-made fibres, made up of knitted or crocheted fabrics of heading No. 59.03 or 59.07
6113.0000 34	其他塑料等处理的纺织材料制男上衣(针织或钩编,包括用其他材料处理的)	16				130	17	13	件/千克		Men's or boys' jacket and blazers of other textile materials, made up of knitted or crocheted fabrics of heading No. 59.03 or 59.07
6113.0000 35	其他橡胶处理的纺织材料制女上衣(针织或钩编)	16				130	17	13	件/千克		Women's or girls' jacket and blazers of other textile materials, made up of knitted or crocheted fabrics of heading No. 59.06

税则号列 Tariff Item.	货品名称	最惠国(%) MFN	协定(%) 东盟 CA	中巴 CP	CT 中智 CC	普通 Gen	增值税率 VAT	出口退税 ED	计量单位 Unit	监管条件 SC	Article Description
6113.0000 36	其他塑料等处理的毛制女上衣(针织或钩编,羊毛或动物细毛制,包括用其他材料处理的)	16				130	17	13	件/千克		Women's or girls' jacket and blazers of wool or fine animal hair, made up of knitted or crocheted fabrics of heading No. 59.03 or 59.07
6113.0000 37	其他塑料等处理的化纤制女上衣(针织或钩编,包括用其他材料处理的)	16				130	17	13	件/千克		Women's or girls' jacket and blazers of man-made fibres, made up of knitted or crocheted fabrics of heading No. 59.03 or 59.07
6113.0000 38	其他塑料等处理的纺织料制女上衣(针织或钩编,包括用其他材料处理的)	16				130	17	13	件/千克		Women's or girls' jacket and blazers of other textile materials, made up of knitted or crocheted fabrics of heading No. 59.03 or 59.07
6113.0000 41	其他橡胶等处理的棉制男式长短裤(针织或钩编)	16				130	17	13	件/千克	5	Men's or boys' trousers and shorts of cotton, made up of knitted or crocheted fabrics of heading No. 59.06
6113.0000 42	其他塑料等处理的棉制男式长短裤(针织或钩编,包括用其他材料处理的)	16				130	17	13	件/千克	5	Men's or boys' trousers and shorts of cotton, made up of knitted or crocheted fabrics of heading No. 59.03 or 59.07
6113.0000 43	其他橡胶等处理的棉制女式长短裤(针织或钩编)	16				130	17	13	件/千克	5	Women's or girls' trousers and shorts of cotton, made up of knitted or crocheted fabrics of heading No. 59.06
6113.0000 44	其他塑料等处理的棉制女式长短裤(针织或钩编,包括用其他材料处理的)	16				130	17	13	件/千克	5	Women's or girls' trousers and shorts of cotton, made up of knitted or crocheted fabrics of heading No. 59.03 or 59.07
6113.0000 51	其他橡胶处理纺织材料制男长短裤(针织或钩编)	16				130	17	13	件/千克	5	Men's or boys' trousers and shorts of other textile materials, made up of knitted or crocheted fabrics of heading No. 59.06
6113.0000 53	其他塑料等处理的毛化纤制男裤(针织或钩编长短裤包括用其他材料处理的)	16				130	17	13	件/千克	5	Men's or boys' trousers and shorts of wool or fine animal hair or of man-made fibres, made up of knitted or crocheted fabrics of heading No. 59.03 or 59.07
6113.0000 54	其他塑料等处理纺织材料男长短裤(针织或钩编长短裤包括用其他材料处理的)	16				130	17	13	件/千克	5	Men's or boys' trousers and shorts of other textile materials, made up of knitted or crocheted fabrics of heading No. 59.03 or 59.07
6113.0000 57	其他橡胶处理纺织材料制女长短裤(针织或钩编)	16				130	17	13	件/千克	5	Women's or girls' trousers and shorts of other textile materials, made up of knitted or crocheted fabrics of heading No. 59.06
6113.0000 58	其他塑料等处理的毛、化纤制女裤(针织或钩编长短裤包括用其他材料处理)	16				130	17	13	件/千克	5	Women's or girls' trousers and shorts of wool or fine animal hair or of man-made fibres, made up of knitted or crocheted fabrics of heading No. 59.03 or 59.07
6113.0000 59	其他塑料等处理纺织材料制女长短裤(针织或钩编,包括用其他材料处理)	16				130	17	13	件/千克	5	Women's or girls' trousers and shorts of other textile materials, made up of knitted or crocheted fabrics of heading No. 59.03 or 59.07

税则号列 Tariff Item.	货 品 名 称	最惠国(%) MFN	协定(%) CT 东盟 CA	 中巴 CP	 中智 CC	普通 Gen	增值税率 VAT	出口退税 ED	计量单位 Unit	监管条件 SC	Article Description
6113.0000 91	其他橡胶处理棉针织或钩编服装	16				130	17	13	件/千克		Other garments of cotton, made up of knitted or crocheted fabrics of heading No. 59.06
6113.0000 92	其他塑料处理棉针织或钩编服装(包括用其他材料处理的)	16				130	17	13	件/千克		Other garments of cotton, made up of knitted or crocheted fabrics of heading No. 59.03 or 59.07
6113.0000 93	其他橡胶处理纺织材料针织服装(包括钩编服装)	16				130	17	13	件/千克		Other garments of other textile materials, made up of knitted or crocheted fabrics of heading No. 59.06
6113.0000 94	其他塑料等处理毛、化纤制针织服装(包括钩编服装,包括用其他材料处理的)	16				130	17	13	件/千克		Other garments of wool or fine animal hair or of man-made fibres, made up of knitted or crocheted fabrics of heading No. 59.03 or 59.07
6113.0000 98	其他塑料等处理纺织材料针织服装(包括钩编服装,包括用其他材料处理的)	16				130	17	13	件/千克		Other garments of other textile materials, made up of knitted or crocheted fabrics of heading No. 59.03 or 59.07
61.14	**针织或钩编的其他服装:**										**Other garments, knitted or crocheted:**
6114.2000	-棉制	16	T3		0	90	17	13	件/千克		-Of cotton
6114.2000 11	棉制针织或钩编儿童非保暖连身裤	16				90	17	13	件/千克		Boys' or girls' overall, not thermal, knitted or crocheted, of cotton
6114.2000 19	棉制针织或钩编其他连身裤	16				90	17	13	件/千克		Other overall, knitted or crocheted, of cotton
6114.2000 21	棉制针织或钩编男成人及男童 TOPS(指 8 - 18 号男童 TOPS)	16				90	17	13	件/千克	5	Men's TOPS or boys' TOPS No. 8 ~ No. 18, knitted or crocheted, of cotton
6114.2000 22	棉制针织或钩编其他男童 TOPS	16				90	17	13	件/千克	5	Other boys' TOPS, knitted or crocheted, of cotton
6114.2000 29	棉制针织或钩编女式 TOPS	16				90	17	13	件/千克	5	Women's or girls' TOPS, knitted or crocheted, of cotton
6114.2000 30	棉制针织或钩编其他运动服	16				90	17	13	件/千克		Other sports suits, knitted or crocheted, of cotton
6114.2000 40	棉制针织或钩编夏服、水洗服(包括女成人女童及男童)	16				90	17	13	件/千克		Women's or girls' and boys' summer wear, wash wear, knitted or crocheted, of cotton
6114.2000 90	棉制针织或钩编其他服装	16				90	17	13	件/千克		Other garments, knitted or crocheted, of cotton
6114.3000	-化学纤维制	17.5	12		0	130	17	13	件/千克		-Of man-made fibres
6114.3000 11	化纤制针织或钩编连身衣(含羊/动物细毛 23% 及以上)	17.5				130	17	13	件/千克		Overall, containing≥23% by weight of wool or fine animal hair, knitted or crocheted, of man-made fibres
6114.3000 12	化纤制针织或钩编紧身服及衬衫(含羊/动物细毛 23% 及以上,包括无袖罩衫)	17.5				130	17	13	件/千克		Jerseys and shirts, including cloaks, containing≥23% by weight of wool or fine animal hair, knitted or crocheted, of man-made fibres
6114.3000 13	化纤制针织或钩编其他连身衣	17.5				130	17	13	件/千克		Other overall, knitted or crocheted, of man-made fibres
6114.3000 19	化纤制针织或钩编紧身服及衬衫(包括无袖罩衫)	17.5				130	17	13	件/千克		Jerseys and shirts, including cloaks, knitted or crocheted, of man-made fibres

税则号列 Tariff Item.	货品名称	最惠国(%) MFN	协定(%) CT 东盟 CA	中巴 CP	中智 CC	普通 Gen	增值税率 VAT	出口退税 ED	计量单位 Unit	监管条件 SC	Article Description
6114.3000 21	化纤针织或钩编男成人及男TOPS(指8-18号男童TOPS)	17.5				130	17	13	件/千克	5	Men's TOPS or boys' TOPS No. 8 ~ No. 18, knitted or crocheted, of man-made fibres
6114.3000 22	化纤针织或钩编其他男童TOPS	17.5				130	17	13	件/千克	5	Other boys' TOPS, knitted or crocheted, of man-made fibres
6114.3000 29	化纤针织或钩编女式TOPS	17.5				130	17	13	件/千克	5	Women's or girls' TOPS, knitted or crocheted, of man-made fibres
6114.3000 30	化纤针织或钩编其他运动服	17.5				130	17	13	件/千克		Other sports suits, knitted or crocheted, of man-made fibres
6114.3000 40	化纤针织或钩编夏服、水洗服(包括女成人、女童及男童)	17.5				130	17	13	件/千克		Women's or girls' and boys' summer wear, wash wear, knitted or crocheted, of man-made fibres
6114.3000 90	化纤针织或钩编其他服装	17.5				130	17	13	件/千克		Other garments, knitted or crocheted, of man-made fibres
	-其他纺织材料制:	16				130	17	13	件/千克		-Of other textile materials
6114.9010	---羊毛或动物细毛制	16	8		0	130	17	13	件/千克		---Of wool or fine animal hair
6114.9090	---其他	16	T3		0	130	17	13	件/千克		---Other
61.15	**针织或钩编的连裤袜、紧身裤袜、长统袜、短袜及其他袜类,包括用以治疗静脉曲张的长统袜和无外绱鞋底的鞋类:**										**Panty hose, tights, stockings, socks and other hosiery, including stockings for varicose veins and footwear without applied soles, knitted or crocheted:**
6115.1000	-渐紧压袜类(例如,用以治疗静脉曲张的长统袜)	16	T3	9.3	0	130	17	13	双/千克		-Tight socks (e. g. for treatment of varicose vein)
	-其他连裤袜及紧身裤袜:										-Other panty hose and tights:
6115.2100	--每根单丝细度在67分特以下的合成纤维制	16	T3	14.4	0	130	17	13	双/千克		--Of synthetic fibres, measuring per single yarn less than 67 decitex
6115.2200	--每根单丝细度在67分特及以上的合成纤维制	16	T3	10.9	0	130	17	13	双/千克		--Of synthetic fibres, measuring per single yarn 67 decitex or more
	--其他纺织材料制:										--Of other textile materials:
6115.2910	---棉制	14	8		0	90	17	13	双/千克		---Of cotton
6115.2990	---其他	14	8	9.3	0	130	17	13	双/千克		---Other
6115.3000	-其他女式长统袜及中统袜,每根单丝细度在67分特以下	14	T3	9.3	0	130	17	13	双/千克		-Other women's full-length or knee-length hosiery, measuring per single yarn less than 67 decitex
6115.3000 21	合成纤维制针织或钩编女长统袜(单丝细度在67分特以下)	14				130	17	13	双/千克	5	Women's or girls' full-length hosiery of synthetic fibres, measuring per single yarn <67 decitex, knitted or crocheted
6115.3000 29	合成纤维制针织或钩编女中统袜(单丝细度在67分特以下)	14				130	17	13	双/千克	5	Women's or girls' knee-length hosiery of synthetic fibres, measuring per single yarn <67 decitex, knitted or crocheted
6115.3000 90	其他材料制女统袜(单丝细度在67分特以下)	14				130	17	13	双/千克		Women's or girls' full-length or knee-length hosiery, of other textile materials measuring per single yarn <67 decitex
	-其他:										-Other:
6115.9400	--羊毛或动物细毛制	14	8		0	130	17	13	双/千克	5	--Of wool or fine animal hair
6115.9500	--棉制	14	8		0	90	17	13	双/千克		--Of cotton

税则号列 Tariff Item.	货品名称	最惠国(%) MFN	协定(%)CT 东盟 CA	中巴 CP	中智 CC	普通 Gen	增值税率 VAT	出口退税 ED	计量单位 Unit	监管条件 SC	Article Description
6115.9500 11	棉制针织或钩编矫正袜(外科用带压缩刻度)	14				90	17	13	双/千克		Orthopedic stockings, with surgical restriction scale, of cotton, knitted or crocheted
6115.9500 19	棉制针织或钩编短袜及其他袜类	14				90	17	13	双/千克	5	Socks and other hosiery of cotton, knitted or crocheted
6115.9600	--合成纤维制	16	8	10.9	0	130	17	13	双/千克		--Of synthetic fibres
6115.9600 11	合成纤维制针织或钩编矫正袜(外科用带压缩刻度)	16				130	17	13	双/千克		Orthopedic stockings, with surgical restriction scale
6115.9600 12	合成纤维制女长统袜(针织或钩编含羊毛或动物细毛23%及以上)	16				130	17	13	双/千克	5	Women's or girls' full-length hosiery of synthetic fibres, containing ≥23% by weight of wool or fine animal hair, knitted or crocheted
6115.9600 13	合成纤维制短袜及其他袜类(针织或钩编含羊毛或动物细毛23%及以上)	16				130	17	13	双/千克	5	Socks and other hosiery of synthetic fibres, containing ≥23% by weight of wool or fine animal hair, knitted or crocheted
6115.9600 14	其他合成纤维制女长统袜(针织或钩编)	16				130	17	13	双/千克	5	Women's or girls' full-length hosiery of synthetic fibres, knitted or crocheted
6115.9600 19	其他合成纤维制短袜及其他袜类(针织或钩编)	16				130	17	13	双/千克	5	Socks and other hosiery of synthetic fibres, knitted or crocheted
6115.9900	--其他纺织材料制	14	T3	9.3	0	130	17	13	双/千克		--Of other textile materials
6115.9900 11	人造纤维制短袜及其他袜类(针织或钩编含羊毛或动物细毛23%及以上)	14				130	17	13	双/千克	5	Socks or other hosiery of artificial fibres, containing ≥23% by weight of wool or fine animal hair, knitted or crocheted
6115.9900 19	其他人造纤维制短袜及其他袜类(针织或钩编)	14				130	17	13	双/千克	5	Socks or other hosiery of artificial fibres, knitted or crocheted
6115.9900 91	其他纺织材料制短袜及其他袜类(针织或钩编,含丝70%及以上)	14				130	17	13	双/千克		Socks or other hosiery of other textile materials, containing ≥70% by weight of silk, knitted or crocheted
6115.9900 99	其他纺织材料制短袜及其他袜类(针织或钩编,含丝70%及以下)	14				130	17	13	双/千克		Socks or other hosiery of other textile materials, containing <70% by weight of silk, knitted or crocheted
61.16	**针织或钩编的分指手套、连指手套及露指手套:**										**Gloves, mittens and mitts, knitted or crocheted:**
6116.1000	-用塑料或橡胶浸渍、涂布或包覆的	14	8		0	130	17	13	双/千克		-Gloves impregnated, coated or covered with plastics or rubber
6116.1000 10	塑料或橡胶浸渍的运动手套	14				130	17	13	双/千克		Sports gloves impregnated, coated or covered with plastics or rubber
6116.1000 91	塑料或橡胶浸渍的非运动手套(含塑料或橡胶超过50%及以上)	14				130	17	13	双/千克		Nonsports gloves impregnated, coated or covered with plastics or rubber, containing≥50% by weight of plastics or rubber
6116.1000 92	塑料或橡胶浸渍的非运动手套(含塑料或橡胶不超过50%,棉限内)	14				130	17	13	双/千克		Nonsports gloves impregnated, coated or covered with plastics or rubber, containing <50% by weight of plastics or rubber, cotton within limitations

税则号列 Tariff Item.	货品名称	最惠国(%) MFN	协定(%) 东盟 CA	中巴 CP	CT 中智 CC	普通 Gen	增值税率 VAT	出口退税 ED	计量单位 Unit	监管条件 SC	Article Description
6116.1000 93	塑料或橡胶浸渍的非运动手套(含塑料或橡胶不超过50%,毛限内)	14				130	17	13	双/千克		Nonsports gloves impregnated, coated or covered with plastics or rubber, containing < 50% by weight of plastics or rubber, wool within limitations
6116.1000 94	塑料或橡胶浸渍的其他非运动手套(含塑料或橡胶不超过50%,化纤限内)	14				130	17	13	双/千克		Nonsports gloves impregnated, coated or covered with plastics or rubber, containing < 50% by weight of plastics or rubber, man-made fibres within limitations
6116.1000 99	塑料或橡胶浸渍的其他非运动手套(含塑料或橡胶不超过50%)	14				130	17	13	双/千克		Other nonsports gloves impregnated, coated or covered with plastics or rubber, containing < 50% by weight of plastics or rubber
	-其他:										-Other:
6116.9100	--羊毛或动物细毛制	14	8		0	130	17	13	双/千克		--Of wool or fine animal hair
6116.9200	--棉制	14	8		0	90	17	13	双/千克		--Of cotton
6116.9300	--合成纤维制	16	8	10.9	0	130	17	13	双/千克		--Of synthetic fibres
6116.9300 10	合成纤维制其他针织或钩编手套(含羊毛或动物细毛23%及以上)	16				130	17	13	双/千克		Mittens and mitts, containing ≥23% by weight of wool or fine animal hair, knitted or crocheted, of synthetic fibres
6116.9300 90	合成纤维制其他针织或钩编手套(含羊毛或动物细毛23%以下)	16				130	17	13	双/千克		Mittens and mitts, containing < 23% by weight of wool or fine animal hair, knitted or crocheted, of synthetic fibres
6116.9900	--其他纺织材料制	14	T3	9.3	0	130	17	13	双/千克		--Of other textile materials
6116.9900 11	人造纤维制其他针织或钩编手套(运动手套)	14				130	17	13	双/千克		Sports gloves, mittens and mitts, of artificial fibres, knitted or crocheted
6116.9900 19	人造纤维制其他针织或钩编手套(非运动手套)	14				130	17	13	双/千克		Nonsports gloves, mittens and mitts, of artificial fibres, knitted or crocheted
6116.9900 20	丝或绢丝制其他针织或钩编手套(含丝70%及以上)	14				130	17	13	双/千克		Gloves, mittens and mitts of silk or silk waste, containing ≥ 70% by weight of silk, knitted or crocheted
6116.9900 91	其他纺织材料制其他针织或钩编手套(棉限内)	14				130	17	13	双/千克		Gloves, mittens and mitts of other textile materials, knitted or crocheted, cotton within limitations
6116.9900 92	其他纺织材料制其他针织或钩编手套(毛限内)	14				130	17	13	双/千克		Gloves, mittens and mitts of other textile materials, knitted or crocheted, wool within limitations
6116.9900 93	其他纺织材料制其他针织或钩编手套(化纤限内)	14				130	17	13	双/千克		Gloves, mittens and mitts of other textile materials, knitted or crocheted, man-made fibres within limitations
6116.9900 99	未列名纺织材料制其他针织或钩编手套	14				130	17	13	双/千克		Other gloves, mittens and mitts of other textile materials, knitted or crocheted, not elsewhere specified or included
61.17	**其他制成的针织或钩编的衣着附件;服装或衣着附件的针织或钩编的零件:**										**Other made up clothing accessories, knitted or crocheted; knitted or crocheted parts of garments or of clothing accessories:**
6117.1000	-披巾、头巾、围巾、披纱、面纱及类似品	14	8	0	0	130	17	13	条/千克		-Shawls, scarves, mufflers, mantillas, veils and the like

税则号列 Tariff Item.	货 品 名 称	最惠国(%) MFN	协定(%) 东盟 CA	中巴 CP	CT 中智 CC	普通 Gen	增值税率 VAT	出口退税 ED	计量单位 Unit	监管条件 SC	Article Description
6117.1000 10	羊毛或动物细毛制针织或钩编披巾(含头巾、围巾、披纱、面纱及类似品)	14				130	17	13	条/千克		Shawls, scarves, mufflers, mantillas, veils and the like, of wool or fine animal hair
6117.1000 21	化学纤维制针织或钩编披巾、头巾(含围巾、披纱、面纱及类似品,羊毛或动物细毛≥23%)	14				130	17	13	条/千克		Shawls, scarves, mufflers, mantillas, veils and the like, of man-made fibres, containing≥23% by weight of wool or fine animal hair
6117.1000 29	其他化学纤维制披巾(含围巾、披纱、面纱及类似品,羊毛或动物细毛<23%)	14				130	17	13	条/千克		Shawls, scarves, mufflers, mantillas, veils and the like, of man-made fibres, containing≥70% by weight of wool or fine animal hair
6117.1000 30	棉制针织披巾(含围巾、披纱、面纱及类似品)	14				130	17	13	条/千克		Shawls, scarves, mufflers, mantillas, veils and the like, of cotton, knitted
6117.1000 91	其他纺织材料制针织披巾(含围巾、披纱、面纱及类似品,含丝70%及以上)	14				130	17	13	条/千克		Shawls, scarves, mufflers, mantillas, veils and the like, of other textile materials, knitted, containing ≥ 70% by weight of silk
6117.1000 99	其他纺织材料制针织披巾(含围巾、披纱、面纱及类似品,含丝70%以下)	14				130	17	13	条/千克		Shawls, scarves, mufflers, mantillas, veils and the like, of other textile materials, knitted, containing < 70% by weight of silk
	-其他附件:										--Other accessories
6117.8010	---领带及领结	14	8	0	0	130	17	13	条/千克		-Ties, bow ties and cravats
6117.8090	---其他附件	14	8	0	0	130	17	13	千克		---Other accessories
6117.9000	-零件	14	T3	0	0	130	17	13	千克		-Parts
6117.9000 10	保暖型衬里(针织或钩编)	14				130	17	13	千克		Thermal lining, knitted or crocheted
6117.9000 21	毛制针织毛衫的零件(针织或钩编,羊毛或动物细毛)	14				130	17	13	千克		Parts of sweaters of wool or fine animal hair, knitted or crocheted
6117.9000 22	毛制针织衬衫的零件(针织或钩编,羊毛或动物细毛)	14				130	17	13	千克		Parts of shirts of wool or fine animal hair, knitted or crocheted
6117.9000 23	毛制针织上衣的零件(针织或钩编,羊毛或动物细毛)	14				130	17	13	千克		Parts of jackets or blazers of wool or fine animal hair, knitted or crocheted
6117.9000 24	毛制针织长裤、马裤、短裤的零件(针织或钩编,羊毛或动物细毛)	14				130	17	13	千克		Parts of trousers, breeches, shorts, of wool or fine animal hair, knitted or crocheted
6117.9000 29	毛制其他未列名针织服装零件(针织或钩编,羊毛或动物细毛)	14				130	17	13	千克		Other part of garments of wool or fine animal hair, not elsewhere specified or included, knitted or crocheted
6117.9000 31	棉制针织毛衫的零件(针织或钩编)	14				130	17	13	千克	5	Parts of sweaters of cotton, knitted or crocheted
6117.9000 32	棉制针织衬衫的零件(针织或钩编)	14				130	17	13	千克	5	Parts of shirts of cotton, knitted or crocheted
6117.9000 33	棉制针织上衣的零件(针织或钩编)	14				130	17	13	千克		Parts of jackets or blazers of cotton, knitted or crocheted
6117.9000 34	棉制针织长裤、马裤、短裤的零件(针织或钩编)	14				130	17	13	千克	5	Parts of trousers, breeches, shorts, of cotton, knitted or crocheted
6117.9000 39	棉制其他未列名针织服装零件(针织或钩编)	14				130	17	13	千克		Other parts, of cotton, not elsewhere specified or included, knitted or crocheted

税则号列 Tariff Item.	货品名称	最惠国(%) MFN	协定(%)CT 东盟 CA	中巴 CP	中智 CC	普通 Gen	增值税率 VAT	出口退税 ED	计量单位 Unit	监管条件 SC	Article Description
6117.9000 41	化纤制针织毛衫的零件(针织或钩编)	14				130	17	13	千克	5	Parts of sweaters of man-made fibres, knitted or crocheted
6117.9000 42	化纤制针织衬衫的零件(针织或钩编)	14				130	17	13	千克	5	Parts of shirts of man-made fibres, knitted or crocheted
6117.9000 43	化纤制针织上衣的零件(针织或钩编)	14				130	17	13	千克		Parts of jackets or blazers of man-made fibres, knitted or crocheted
6117.9000 44	化纤制针织长裤、马裤、短裤零件(针织或钩编)	14				130	17	13	千克	5	Parts of trousers, breeches, shorts, of man-made fibres, knitted or crocheted
6117.9000 49	化纤制其他未列名针织服装零件(针织或钩编)	14				130	17	13	千克		Other parts of garments of man-made fibres not elsewhere specified or included, knitted or crocheted
6117.9000 91	其他材料制衣着零件(针织或钩编,含丝70%及以上)	14				130	17	13	千克		Parts of garments of other textile materials, containing≥70% by weight of silk, knitted or crocheted
6117.9000 92	其他材料制针织毛衫的零件(针织或钩编)	14				130	17	13	千克		Parts of sweaters of other textile materials, knitted or crocheted
6117.9000 93	其他材料制针织衬衫的零件(针织或钩编)	14				130	17	13	千克		Parts of shirts of other textile materials, knitted or crocheted
6117.9000 94	其他材料制针织上衣的零件(针织或钩编)	14				130	17	13	千克		Parts of jackets or blazers of other textile materials, knitted or crocheted
6117.9000 95	其他材料制长裤、马裤、短裤零件(针织或钩编)	14				130	17	13	千克	5	Parts of trousers, breeches, shorts of other textile materials, knitted or crocheted
6117.9000 99	其他材料制未列名针织服装零件(针织或钩编)	14				130	17	13	千克		Other parts of garments of other textile materials not elsewhere specified or included, knitted or crocheted

第六十二章
非针织或非钩编的服装及衣着附件

注释：

一、本章仅适用于除絮胎以外任何纺织物的制成品，但不适用于针织品或钩编织品（税目62.12的除外）。

二、本章不包括：

（一）税目63.09的旧衣着或其他旧物品；

（二）矫形器具、外科手术带、疝气带及类似品（税目90.21）。

三、税目62.03及62.04所称：

（一）"西服套装"，是指面料用相同的织物制成的两件套或三件套的下列成套服装：

一件人体上半身穿着的外套或短上衣，除袖子外，其面料为四片或四片以上；也可附带一件西服背心，这件背心的前片面料应与套装其他各件的面料相同，后片料则应与外套或短上衣的衬里料相同；以及一件人体下半身穿着的服装，即不带背带或护胸的长裤、马裤、短裤（游泳裤除外）、裙子或裙裤。

西服套装各件面料质地、颜色及构成必须相同，其款式也必须相同，尺寸大小还须相互般配，但可以用不同织物滚边（缝口上缝入长条织物）。

如果数件人体下半身穿着的服装同时进口或出口（例如，两条长裤、长裤与短裤、裙子或裙裤与长裤），构成西服套装下装的应是一条长裤，而对于女式西服套装，则应是一条裙子或裙裤，其他服装应分别归类。

所称"西服套装"，包括不论是否完全符合上述条件的下列配套服装：

1. 常礼服，由一件后襟下垂并下端开圆弧形叉的素色短上衣和一条条纹长裤组成；

2. 晚礼服（燕尾服），一般用黑色织物制成，上衣前襟较短且不闭合，背后有燕尾；

3. 无燕尾套装夜礼服，其中上衣款式与普通上衣相似（可以更为显露衬衣前胸），但有光滑丝质或仿丝质的翻领。

（二）"便服套装"，是指面料相同并作零售包装的下列成套服装（西服套装及税目62.07或62.08的物品除外）：

Chapter 62
Articles of apparel and clothing accessories, not knitted or crocheted

Notes:

1. This Chapter applies only to made up articles of any textile fabric other than wadding, excluding knitted or crocheted articles (other than those of heading No. 62. 12).

2. This Chapter does not cover:

(a) Worn clothing or other worn articles of heading No. 63. 09; or

(b) Orthopaedic appliances, surgical belts, trusses or the like (heading No. 90. 21).

3. For the purposes of headings Nos. 62. 03 and 62. 04:

(a) The term "suit" means a set of garments composed of two or three pieces made up in identical fabric and comprising:

-One suit coat or jacket the outer shell of which, exclusive of sleeves, consists of four or more panels, designed to cover the upper part of the body, possibly with a tailored waistcoat in addition whose front panel is made from the same fabric as the outer shell of the other components of the set and whose rear panel is made from the same fabric as the lining of the suit coat or jacket, andOne garment designed to cover the lower part of the body and consisting of trousers, breeches or shorts (other than swimwear), a skirt or a divided skirt, having neither braces nor bibs.

All of the components of a suit must be of the identical fabric construction, style, colour and composition; they must also be of corresponding or compatible size. However, these components may have bindings of different fabric (the narrow fabric stitched to finish raw edges).

If several separate components to cover the lower part of the body are presented together (for example, trousers and shorts, or a skirt or divided skirt and trousers), the constituent lower part shall be the trousers, or, in the case of women's or girls' suits, the skirt or divided skirt, the other garments being considered separately.

The term "suit" includes the following sets of garments, whether or not they fulfil all the above conditions:

-morning dress, comprising a plain jacket (cutaway) with rounded tails hanging well down at the back and striped trousers;

-evening dress (tailcoat), generally made of black cloth, the jacket of which is relatively short at the front, does not close and has narrow skirts cut in at the hips and hanging down behind;

-dinner jacket suits, in which the jacket is similar in style to an ordinary jacket (though perhaps revealing more of the shirt front), but has shiny silk or imitation silk lapels.

(b) The term "ensemble" means a set of garments (other than suits and articles of heading No. 62. 07 or 62. 08) composed of several pieces made up in identical fabric, put up for retail sale, and comprising:

一件人体上半身穿着的服装，但背心除外，因为背心可作为内衣；以及一件或两件不同的人体下半身穿着的服装，即长裤、护胸背带工装裤、马裤、短裤(游泳裤除外)、裙子或裙裤。

便服套装各件面料质地、款式、颜色及构成必须相同；尺寸大小也须相互般配。所称“便服套装”不包括税目62.11的运动服及滑雪服。

四、对于税目62.09：

(一)所称“婴儿服装及衣着附件”，是指用于身高不超过86厘米幼儿的服装；也包括婴儿尿布；

(二)既可归入税目62.09，也可归入本章其他税目的物品，应归入税目62.09；

五、既可归入税目62.10，也可归入本章其他税目的服装，除税目62.09所列的仍归入该税目外，其余的应一律归入税目62.10。

六、税目62.11所称“滑雪服”，是指从整个外观和织物质地来看，主要在滑雪(速度滑雪和高山滑雪)时穿着的下列服装或成套服装：

(一)“滑雪连身服”，即上下身连在一起的单件服装；除袖子和领子外，滑雪连身服可有口袋或脚带；或

(二)“滑雪套装”，即由两件或三件构成一套并作零售包装的下列服装：

一件用一条拉链扣合的带风帽的厚夹克、防风衣、防风短上衣或类似的服装，可以附带一件背心；以及一条不论是否过腰的长裤、一条马裤或一条护胸背带工装裤。

“滑雪套装”也可由一件类似以上(一)款所述的类似连身服和一件可套在连身服外面的有胎料背心组成。

“滑雪套装”各件颜色可以不同，但面料质地、款式及构成必须相同；尺寸大小也须相互般配。

七、正方形或近似正方形的围巾及围巾式样的物品，如果每边均不超过60厘米，应作为手帕归类(税目62.13)。任何一边超过60厘米的手帕，应归入税目62.14。

-one garment designed to cover the upper part of the body, with the exception of waistcoats which may also form a second upper garment, andone or two different garments, designed to cover the lower part of the body and consisting of trousers, bib and brace overalls, breeches, shorts (other than swimwear), a skirt or a divided skirt.

All of the components of an ensemble must be of the same fabric construction, style, colour and composition; they also must be of corresponding or compatible size. The term "ensemble" does not apply to track suits or ski suits, of heading No. 62.11.

4. For the purposes of heading No. 62.09:

(a) The expression "babies' garments and clothing accessories" means articles for young children of a body height not exceeding 86cm; it also covers babies' napkins;

(b) Articles which are, *prima facie*, classifiable both in heading 62.09 and in other headings of this Chapter are to be classified in heading No. 62.09.

5. Garments which are, *prima facie*, classifiable both in heading No. 62.10 and in other headings of this Chapter, excluding heading No. 62.09, are to be classified in heading No. 62.10.

6. For the purposes of heading No. 62.11, "ski suits" means garments or sets of garments which, by their general appearance and texture, are identifiable as intended to be worn principally for skiing (cross-country or alpine).

They consist either of:

(a) a "ski overall", that is, a one-piece garment designed to cover the upper and the lower parts of the body; in addition to sleeves and a collar the ski overall may have pockets or footstraps; or

(b) a "ski ensemble", that is, a set of garments composed of two or three pieces, put up for retail sale and comprising:

-one garment such as an anorak, wind-cheater, wind-jacket or similar article, closed by a slide fastener (zipper), possibly with a waistcoat in addition, and one pair of trousers whether or not extending above waist-level, one pair of breeches or one bib and brace overall.

The "ski ensemble" may also consist of an overall similar to the one mentioned in paragraph (a) above and a type of padded, sleeveless jacket worn over the overall.

All the components of a "ski ensemble" must be made up in a fabric of the same texture, style and composition whether or not of the same colour; they also must be of corresponding or compatible size.

7. Scarves and articles of the scarf type, square or approximately square, of which no side exceeds 60cm, are to be classified as handkerchiefs (heading No. 62.13). Handkerchiefs of which any side exceeds 60cm are to be classified in heading No. 62.14.

八、本章的服装，凡门襟为左压右的，应视为男式；右压左的，应视为女式。但本规定不适用于其式样已明显为男式或女式的服装。无法区别是男式还是女式的服装，应按女式服装归入有关税目。

8. Garments of this Chapter designed for left over right closure at the front shall be regarded as men's or boys' garments, and those designed for right over left closure at the front as women's or girls' garments. these provisions do not aplly where the cut of the garment clearly indicates that it is designed for other of sexes. Garments which cannot be identified as either men's or boys' garments or as women's or girls' garments are to be classified in the headings concerning women's or girls' garments.

九、本章物品可用金属线制成。

9. Articles of this Chapter may be made of metal thread.

税则号列 Tariff Item.	货品名称	最惠国(%) MFN	协定(%) CT 东盟 CA	中巴 CP	中智 CC	普通 Gen	增值税率 VAT	出口退税 ED	计量单位 Unit	监管条件 SC	Article Description
62.01	**男式大衣、短大衣、斗篷、短斗篷、带风帽的防寒短上衣(包括滑雪短上衣)、防风衣、防风短上衣及类似品，但税目62.03的货品除外：**										**Men's or boys' overcoats, car-coats, capes, cloaks, anoraks (including ski-jackets), wind-cheaters, wind-jackets and similar articles, other than those of heading No. 62.03:**
	-大衣、雨衣、短大衣、斗篷、短斗篷及类似品：										-Overcoats, raincoats, car-coats, capes, cloaks and similar articles:
6201.1100	--羊毛或动物细毛制	16	12	11.7	0	130	17	13	件/千克		--Of wool or fine animal hair
6201.1100 10	毛制男式雨衣(羊毛或动物细毛制)	16				130	17	13	件/千克	B	Men's or boys' raincoats, of wool or fine animal hair
6201.1100 90	毛制男式大衣，斗篷及类似品(含短大衣、短斗篷，羊毛或动物细毛制)	16				130	17	13	件/千克	B	Men's or boys' overcoats, car-coats, capes, cloak and similar articles, of wool or fine animal hair
	--棉制：										--Of cotton:
6201.1210	---羽绒服	16	8		0	90	17	13	件/千克	B	---Padded with feathers or down
6201.1290	---其他	16	8		0	90	17	13	件/千克		---Other
6201.1290 10	棉制男式雨衣	16				90	17	13	件/千克		Men's or boys' raincoats of cotton
6201.1290 20	棉制男式连风帽派克大衣等(含带风帽的防寒短上衣、防风衣、防风短上衣及类似品)	16				90	17	13	件/千克		Men's or boys' hooded parka, anoraks, wind-cheaters, wind-jackets and similar articles, of cotton
6201.1290 90	棉制男式大衣、斗篷及类似品(包括短大衣、短斗篷)	16				90	17	13	件/千克		Men's or boys' overcoats, car-coats, capes, cloaks and similar articles, of cotton
	--化学纤维制：										--Of man-made fibres:
6201.1310	---羽绒服	17.5	12	12.3	0	130	17	13	件/千克	B	---Padded with feathers or down
6201.1390	---其他	17.5	12	12.3	0	130	17	13	件/千克		---Other
6201.1390 10	化纤制男式雨衣	17.5				130	17	13	件/千克		Men's or boys' raincoats, of man-made fibres
6201.1390 20	化纤制男式连风帽派克大衣等(羊/动物细毛≥36%，带风帽防寒短上衣/防风衣等)	17.5				130	17	13	件/千克		Men's or boys' hooded parka, anoraks, wind-cheaters wind-jackts and similar articles, containing ≥36% by weight of wool or fine animal hair, of man-made fibres
6201.1390 30	化纤制男大衣、斗篷及类似品(包括短大衣、短斗篷，含羊毛或动物细毛36%及以上)	17.5				130	17	13	件/千克		Men's or boys' overcoats, car-coats, capes, cloak and similar articles, containing ≥36% by weight of wool or fine animal hair, of man-made fibres

税则号列 Tariff Item.	货品名称	最惠国(%) MFN	协定(%)CT 东盟 CA	 中巴 CP	 中智 CC	普通 Gen	增值税率 VAT	出口退税 ED	计量单位 Unit	监管条件 SC	Article Description
6201.1390 40	化纤制男式连风帽派克大衣等(羊/动物细毛<36%,带风帽防寒短上衣/防风衣等)	17.5				130	17	13	件/千克		Men's or boys' hooded parka, anoraks, wind-jackets and similar articles, containing < 36% by weight of wool or fine animal hair, of man-made fibres
6201.1390 90	化纤制男大衣、斗篷及类似品(包括短大衣、短斗篷,含羊毛或动物细毛36%以下)	17.5				130	17	13	件/千克		Men's or boys' overcoats, car-coats, capes, cloak and similar articles, containing < 36% by weight of wool or fine animal hair, of man-made fibres
6201.1900	--其他纺织材料制	16	12	11.7	0	100	17	13	件/千克		--Of other textile materials
6201.1900 10	其他材料制男雨衣	16				100	17	13	件/千克		Men's or boys' raincoats, of other textile materials
6201.1900 21	其他材料制男大衣、斗篷及类似品(含短大衣、斗篷、短斗篷,含丝70%及以上)	16				100	17	13	件/千克		Men's or boys' overcoats, car-coats, capes, cloak and similar articles, containing≥70% by weight of silk, of other textile materials
6201.1900 29	其他材料制男大衣、斗篷及类似品(含短大衣、斗篷、短斗篷,含丝<70%)	16				100	17	13	件/千克		Men's or boys' overcoats, car-coats, capes, cloak and similar articles, containing<70% by weight of silk, of other textile materials
6201.1900 30	其他材料制男大衣等,羊毛限内(含短大衣、斗篷、短斗篷)	16				100	17	13	件/千克		Men's or boys' overcoats, car-coats, capes, cloak and similar articles, of other textile materials, wool within limitations
6201.1900 40	其他材料制男大衣等,棉限内(含短大衣、斗篷、短斗篷)	16				100	17	13	件/千克		Men's or boys' overcoats, car-coats, capes, cloak and similar articles, of other textile materials, cotton within limitations
6201.1900 50	其他材料制男大衣等,化纤限内(含短大衣、斗篷、短斗篷)	16				100	17	13	件/千克		Men's or boys' overcoats, car-coats, capes, cloak and similar articles, of other textile materials, man-made fibres within limitations
6201.1900 90	其他材料制男大衣等(含短大衣、斗篷、短斗篷)	16				100	17	13	件/千克		Men's or boys' overcoats, car-coats, capes, cloak and similar articles, of other textile materials
	-其他:										-Other:
6201.9100	--羊毛或动物细毛制	16	12	11.7	0	130	17	13	件/千克		--Of wool or fine animal hair
6201.9100 10	毛制男式有填料无袖上衣(羊毛或动物细毛制)	16				130	17	13	件/千克		Men's or boys' cloaks, padded, of wool or fine animal hair
6201.9100 20	毛制男式带防寒衬里防风衣(羊毛或动物细毛制,含防风短上衣)	16				130	17	13	件/千克		Men's or boys' wind-cheaters, wind-jackets, with thermal lining, of wool or fine animal hair
6201.9100 30	毛制男式带风帽、有填料短上衣(羊毛或动物细毛制,含防风上衣,衬衫式样,特制领)	16				130	17	13	件/千克		Men's or boys' anoraks, wind-jackets, shirt style, padded, of wool or fine animal hair
6201.9100 90	毛制男式其他防寒上衣(羊毛或动物细毛制)	16				130	17	13	件/千克		Other men's or boys' anoraks, of wool or fine animal hair
	--棉制:										--Of cotton:
6201.9210	---羽绒服	16	T3		0	90	17	13	件/千克	B	---Padded with feathers or down

税则号列 Tariff Item.	货品名称	最惠国(%) MFN	协定(%) CT 东盟 CA	协定(%) CT 中巴 CP	协定(%) CT 中智 CC	普通 Gen	增值税率 VAT	出口退税 ED	计量单位 Unit	监管条件 SC	Article Description
6201.9290	---其他	16	T3		0	90	17	13	件/千克		---Other
6201.9290 10	棉制男式有填料无袖上衣(不带可连接袖子配件)	16				90	17	13	件/千克		Men's or boys' cloaks, padded, of cotton (not with fasteners of detachable sleeves)
6201.9290 20	棉制男式带防寒衬里防风衣(含防风短上衣)	16				90	17	13	件/千克		Men's or boys' wind-cheaters, wind-jackets, with thermal lining, of cotton
6201.9290 30	棉制男式带风帽、有填料上衣(包括防风上衣,衬衫式样,特制领)	16				90	17	13	件/千克		Men's or boys' anoraks, wind-jackets, shirt style, having made-to-order collar, padded, with hood
6201.9290 90	棉制男式其他防寒上衣(包括滑雪短上衣、防风短上衣及类似品)	16				90	17	13	件/千克		Other men's or boys' anoraks, ski-jackets, wind-cheaters, wind-jackets and similar articles, of cotton
	--化学纤维制:										--Of man-made fibres:
6201.9310	---羽绒服	17.5	T3	12.3	0	130	17	13	件/千克	B	---Padded with feathers or down
6201.9390	---其他	17.5	T3	12.3	0	130	17	13	件/千克		---Other
6201.9390 10	化纤制男式有填料无袖上衣(不带可连接袖子配件)	17.5				130	17	13	件/千克		Men's or boys' cloaks, padded, of man-made fibres
6201.9390 20	化纤制男式带风帽防寒短上衣(羊毛或动物细毛36%及以上)	17.5				130	17	13	件/千克		Men's or boys'anoraks, containing ≥ 36% by weight of wool or fine animal hair, of man-made fibres
6201.9390 30	化纤制男式带防寒衬里防风衣(含防风短上衣)	17.5				130	17	13	件/千克		Men's or boys' wind-cheaters, wind-jackets with thermal lining, of man-made fibres
6201.9390 40	化纤制男式带风帽、有填料上衣(包括防风上衣,衬衫式样,特制领)	17.5				130	17	13	件/千克		Men's or boys' anoraks, wind-jackets, shirt style, having made-to-order collar, padded, of man-made fibres
6201.9390 90	化纤制其他防寒上衣(包括带风帽防寒短上衣、防风短上衣及其他类似品)	17.5				130	17	13	件/千克		Other men's or boys' anoraks, wind-cheaters, wind-jackets and similar articles, of man-made fibres
6201.9900	--其他纺织材料制	16	T3	11.7	0	100	17	13	件/千克		--Of other textile materials
6201.9900 11	丝制男式带防寒衬里短上衣(含丝70%及以上．含防风上衣、防风短上衣)	16				100	17	13	件/千克		Men's or boys' wind-cheaters, wind-jackets, with thermal lining, containing ≥70% by weight of silk
6201.9900 12	丝制男式带特制领有填料短上衣(含丝70%及以上,含防风上衣,衬衫式样,带风帽)	16				100	17	13	件/千克		Men's or boys' wind-cheaters, wind-jackets, padded, containing ≥70% by weight of silk, having made-to-order collar, shirt style, with hood
6201.9900 19	丝制其他防寒上衣(含丝70%及以上)	16				100	17	13	件/千克		Other men's or boys' anoraks, containing ≥70% by weight of silk
6201.9900 21	丝制男式带防寒衬里短上衣(含丝70%以下,含防风上衣、防风短上衣)	16				100	17	13	件/千克		Men's or boys' wind-cheaters, wind-jackets, containing < 70% by weight of silk, with thermal lining
6201.9900 22	丝制男式带特制领有填料短上衣(含丝70%以下,含防风上衣,衬衫式样,带风帽)	16				100	17	13	件/千克		Men's or boys' wind-cheaters, anoraks, wind-jackets, padded, containing < 70% by weight of silk, shirt style, with hood
6201.9900 29	丝制其他防寒上衣(含丝70%以下)	16				100	17	13	件/千克		Other men's or boys' anoraks, containing < 70% by weight of silk

税则号列 Tariff Item.	货品名称	最惠国(%) MFN	协定(%) 东盟 CA	中巴 CP	CT 中智 CC	普通 Gen	增值税率 VAT	出口退税 ED	计量单位 Unit	监管条件 SC	Article Description
6201.9900 31	其他材料制男式带风帽防寒短上衣(棉限内,带防寒衬里)	16				100	17	13	件/千克		Men's or boys' anoraks, with thermal lining, of other textile materials, cotton within limitations
6201.9900 32	其他材料制男式带风帽防寒短上衣(羊毛限内,带防寒衬里)	16				100	17	13	件/千克		Men's or boys' anoraks, with thermal lining, of other textile materials, wool within limitations
6201.9900 33	其他材料制男式带风帽防寒短上衣(化纤限内,带防寒衬里)	16				100	17	13	件/千克		Men's or boys' anoraks, with thermal lining, of other textile materials, man-made fibres within limitations
6201.9900 39	其他材料制男式带风帽防寒短上衣(其他纺织材料制,带防寒衬里)	16				100	17	13	件/千克		Men's or boys' anoraks, with thermal lining, of other textile materials
6201.9900 41	其他材料制男式带风帽短上衣(棉限内,带特制领,有填料,衬衫式样)	16				100	17	13	件/千克		Men's or boys' anoraks, padded, having made-to-order collar, shirt style, of other textile materials, cotton within limitations
6201.9900 42	其他材料制男式带风帽短上衣(羊毛限内,带特制领,有填料,衬衫式样)	16				100	17	13	件/千克		Men's or boys' anoraks, padded, having made-to-order collar, shirt style, of other textile materials, wool within limitations
6201.9900 43	其他材料制男式带风帽短上衣(化纤限内,带特制领,有填料,衬衫式样)	16				100	17	13	件/千克		Men's or boys' anoraks, padded, having made-to-order collar, shirt style, of other textile materials, man-made fibres within limitations
6201.9900 49	其他材料制男式带风帽短上衣(其他材料制,带特制领,有填料,衬衫式样)	16				100	17	13	件/千克		Men's or boys' anoraks, padded, having made-to-order collar, shirt style, of other textile materials
6201.9900 91	其他材料制男式防寒短上衣(棉限内,含防风衣、防风短上衣类似品)	16				100	17	13	件/千克		Men's or boys' wind-cheaters, wind-jackets and similar articles, of other textile materials, cotton within limitations
6201.9900 92	其他材料制男式防寒短上衣(羊毛限内,含防风衣、防风短上衣类似品)	16				100	17	13	件/千克		Men's or boys' wind-cheaters, wind-jackets and similar articles, of other textile materials, wool within limitations
6201.9900 93	其他材料制男式防寒短上衣(化纤限内,含防风衣、防风短上衣类似品)	16				100	17	13	件/千克		Men's or boys' wind-cheaters, wind-jackets and similar articles, of other textile materials, man-made fibres within limitations
6201.9900 99	其他材料制男式其他防寒短上衣(含防风衣、防风短上衣类似品)	16				100	17	13	件/千克		Other men's or boys' anoraks, wind-cheaters, wind-jackets and similar articles, of other textile materials
62.02	**女式大衣、短大衣、斗篷、短斗篷、带风帽的防寒短上衣(包括滑雪短上衣)、防风衣、防风短上衣及类似品,但税目62.04的货品除外:**										**Women's or girls' overcoats, car-coats, capes, cloaks, anoraks (including ski-jackets), wind-cheaters, wind-jackets and similar articles, other than those of heading No. 62.04:**
	-大衣、雨衣、短大衣、斗篷、短斗篷及类似品:										-Overcoats, raincoats, car-coats, capes, cloaks and similar articles:
6202.1100	--羊毛或动物细毛制	16	12	11.7	0	130	17	13	件/千克		--Of wool or fine animal hair

税则号列 Tariff Item.	货品名称	最惠国(%) MFN	协定(%)CT 东盟 CA	中巴 CP	中智 CC	普通 Gen	增值税率 VAT	出口退税 ED	计量单位 Unit	监管条件 SC	Article Description
6202.1100 10	毛制女式雨衣(羊毛或动物细毛制)	16				130	17	13	件/千克	B	Women's or girls' raincoats, of wool or fine animal hair
6202.1100 90	毛制女式大衣、斗篷及类似品等(包括短大衣、短斗篷,羊毛或动物细毛制)	16				130	17	13	件/千克	B	Women's or girls' overcoats, car-coats, capes, cloak and similar articles, of wool or fine animal hair
	--棉制:										--Of cotton:
6202.1210	---羽绒服	16	8		0	90	17	13	件/千克	B	---Padded with feathers or down
6202.1290	---其他	16	8		0	90	17	13	件/千克		---Other
6202.1290 10	棉制女式雨衣	16				90	17	13	件/千克		Women's or girls' raincoats, of cotton
6202.1290 20	棉制女式连风帽派克大衣等(含带风帽的防寒短上衣、防风衣、防风短上衣及类似品)	16				90	17	13	件/千克		Women's or girls' hooded parka, wind-cheaters, wind-jackets and similar articles, of cotton
6202.1290 90	棉制女式大衣、斗篷及类似品(包括短大衣、短斗篷)	16				90	17	13	件/千克		Women's or girls' overcoats, car-coats, capes, cloak and similar articles, of cotton
	--化学纤维制:										--Of man-made fibres:
6202.1310	---羽绒服	19	12	13.6	0	130	17	13	件/千克	B	---Padded with feathers or down
6202.1390	---其他	19	12	13.6	0	130	17	13	件/千克		---Other
6202.1390 10	化纤制女雨衣(含羊/动物细毛<36%,含带风帽防寒上衣、防风衣及类似品)	19				130	17	13	件/千克		Women's or girls' raincoats, anoraks, wind-cheaters, wind-jackets, containing<36% by weight of wool or fine animal hair, of man-made fibres
6202.1390 20	化纤制女式连风帽派克大衣(含短大衣、短斗篷,含羊毛或动物细毛36%及以上)	19				130	17	13	件/千克		Women's or girls' hooded parka, wind-cheaters, wind-jackets and similar articles, containing≥36% by weight of wool or fine animal hair, of man-made fibres
6202.1390 30	化纤制女大衣、斗篷及类似品(含短大衣、短斗篷,含羊毛或动物细毛36%及以上)	19				130	17	13	件/千克		Women's or girls' overcoats, car-coats, capes, cloak and similar articles, containing≥36% by weight of wool or fine animal hair, of man-made fibres
6202.1390 40	化纤制女式连风帽派克大衣(含羊/动物细毛<36%,含带风帽防寒上衣、防风衣及类似品)	19				130	17	13	件/千克		Women's or girls' hooded parka, wind-cheaters, wind-jackets and similar articles, containing<36% by weight of wool or fine animal hair, of man-made fibres
6202.1390 90	化纤制女大衣、斗篷及类似品(含短大衣、短斗篷,含羊毛或动物细毛36%以下)	19				130	17	13	件/千克		Women's or girls' overcoats, car-coats, capes, cloak and similar articles, containing < 36% by weight of wool or fine animal hair, of man-made fibres
6202.1900	--其他纺织材料制	16	12	11.7	0	100	17	13	件/千克		--Of other textile materials
6202.1900 10	其他材料制女雨衣	16				100	17	13	件/千克		Women's or girls' raincoats of other textile materials
6202.1900 21	其他材料制女大衣、斗篷及类似品(含短大衣、短斗篷,含丝70%及以上)	16				100	17	13	件/千克		Women's or girls' overcoats, car-coats, capes, cloak and similar articles, containing≥70% by weight of silk, of other textile materials

税则号列 Tariff Item.	货品名称	最惠国(%) MFN	协定(%) 东盟 CA	中巴 CP	CT 中智 CC	普通 Gen	增值税率 VAT	出口退税 ED	计量单位 Unit	监管条件 SC	Article Description
6202.1900 29	其他材料制女大衣、斗篷及类似品(含短大衣、短斗篷,含丝70%及以下)	16				100	17	13	件/千克		Women's or girls' overcoats, car-coats, capes, cloak and similar articles, containing < 70% by weight of silk, of other textile materials
6202.1900 30	其他材料制女大衣等,羊毛限内(含短大衣、斗篷、短斗篷)	16				100	17	13	件/千克		Women's or girls' overcoats, car-coats, capes, cloak and similar articles, of other textile materials, wool within limitations
6202.1900 40	其他材料制女大衣等,棉限内(含短大衣、斗篷、短斗篷)	16				100	17	13	件/千克		Women's or girls' overcoats, car-coats, capes, cloak and similar articles, of other textile materials, cotton within limitations
6202.1900 50	其他材料制女大衣等,化纤限内(含短大衣、斗篷、短斗篷)	16				100	17	13	件/千克		Women's or girls' overcoats, car-coats, capes, cloak and similar articles, of other textile materials, man-made fibres within limitations
6202.1900 90	其他材料制女大衣(含短大衣、斗篷、短斗篷)	16				100	17	13	件/千克		Women's or girls' overcoats, car-coats, capes, clock, of other textile materials
	-其他:										-Other:
6202.9100	--羊毛或动物细毛制	16	12	11.7	0	130	17	13	件/千克		--Of wool or fine animal hair
6202.9100 10	毛制女式有填料无袖上衣(羊毛或动物细毛制)	16				130	17	13	件/千克		Women's or girls' cloaks, padded, of wool or fine animal hair
6202.9100 20	毛制女式带防寒衬里的短上衣(羊毛或动物细毛制,含防风衣、防风短上衣)	16				130	17	13	件/千克		Women's or girls' wind-cheaters, wind-jackets, with thermal lining, of wool or fine animal hair
6202.9100 90	毛制女式其他防寒上衣(羊毛或动物细毛制)	16				130	17	13	件/千克		Other women's or girls' anoraks, of wool or fine animal hair
	--棉制:										--Of cotton:
6202.9210	---羽绒服	16	8		0	90	17	13	件/千克	B	---Padded with feathers or down
6202.9290	---其他	16	8		0	90	17	13	件/千克		---Other
6202.9290 10	棉制女式有填料无袖上衣(不带可连接袖子配件)	16				90	17	13	件/千克		Women's or girls' cloaks, padded, of cotton (not with fasteners of detachable sleeves)
6202.9290 20	棉制女式带防寒衬里的短上衣(含防风衣、防风短上衣)	16				90	17	13	件/千克		Women's or girls' wind-cheaters, wind-jackets, with thermal lining, of cotton
6202.9290 90	棉制女式其他防寒上衣	16				90	17	13	件/千克		Other women's or girls' anoraks of cotton
	--化学纤维制:										--Of man-made fibres:
6202.9310	---羽绒服	17.5	12	12.3	0	130	17	13	件/千克	B	---Padded with feathers or down
6202.9390	---其他	17.5	12	12.3	0	130	17	13	件/千克		---Other
6202.9390 10	化纤制女式有填料无袖上衣(不带可连接袖子配件)	17.5				130	17	13	件/千克		Women's or girls' cloaks, padded, of man-made fibres
6202.9390 20	化纤制女式带风帽防寒短上衣(含羊毛或动物细毛36%及以上)	17.5				130	17	13	件/千克		Women's or girls' anoraks, containing ≥36% by weight of wool or fine animal hair, of man-made fibres
6202.9390 30	化纤制女式带防寒衬里的短上衣(含防风衣、防风短上衣)	17.5				130	17	13	件/千克		Women's or girls' wind-cheaters, wind-jackets, with thermal lining, of man-made fibres

税则号列 Tariff Item.	货品名称	最惠国(%) MFN	协定(%)CT 东盟 CA	中巴 CP	中智 CC	普通 Gen	增值税率 VAT	出口退税 ED	计量单位 Unit	监管条件 SC	Article Description
6202.9390 90	化纤制女式其他防寒上衣	17.5				130	17	13	件/千克		Other women's or girls' anoraks of man-made fibres
6202.9900	--其他纺织材料制	16	12	11.7	0	100	17	13	件/千克		--Of other textile materials
6202.9900 11	丝制女式带防寒衬里的短上衣(含丝70%及以上,含防风衣、防风短上衣)	16				100	17	13	件/千克		Women's or girls' wind-cheaters, wind-jackets, with thermal lining, containing ≥70% by weight of silk
6202.9900 19	丝制女式其他防寒上衣(含丝70%及以上)	16				100	17	13	件/千克		Other women's or girls' anoraks of silk, containing≥70% by weight of silk
6202.9900 21	丝制女式带防寒衬里的短上衣(含丝70%以下,含防风衣、防风短上衣)	16				100	17	13	件/千克		Women's or girls' wind-cheaters, wind-jackets, with thermal lining, containing <70% by weight of silk
6202.9900 29	丝制女式其他防寒上衣(含丝70%以下)	16				100	17	13	件/千克		Other women's or girls' anoraks of silk, containing<70% by weight of silk
6202.9900 31	其他材料制女式带风帽防寒短上衣(棉限内,带防寒衬里)	16				100	17	13	件/千克		Women's or girls' anoraks, with thermal lining, of other textile materials, cotton within limitations
6202.9900 32	其他材料制女式带风帽防寒短上衣(羊毛限内,带防寒衬里)	16				100	17	13	件/千克		Women's or girls' anoraks, wind-jackets, with thermal lining, of other textile materials, wool within limitations
6202.9900 33	其他材料制女式带风帽防寒短上衣(化纤限内,带防寒衬里)	16				100	17	13	件/千克		Women's or girls' anoraks, wind-jackets, with thermal lining, of other textile materials, man-made fibres within limitations
6202.9900 39	其他材料制女式带风帽防寒短上衣(其他纺织材料制,带防寒衬里)	16				100	17	13	件/千克		Women's or girls' anoraks, with thermal lining, of other textile materials
6202.9900 91	其他材料制女式防寒短上衣等(棉限内,含防风衣、防风短上衣及类似品)	16				100	17	13	件/千克		Women's or girls' wind-cheaters, wind-jackets and similar articles, of other textile materials, cotton within limitations
6202.9900 92	其他材料制女式防寒短上衣等(羊毛限内,含防风衣、防风短上衣及类似品)	16				100	17	13	件/千克		Women's or girls' wind-cheaters, wind-jackets and similar articles, of other textile materials, wool within limitations
6202.9900 93	其他材料制女式防寒短上衣等(化纤限内,含防风衣、防风短上衣及类似品)	16				100	17	13	件/千克		Women's or girls' wind-cheaters, wind-jackets and similar articles, of other textile materials, man-made fibres within limitations
6202.9900 99	其他材料制女式其他防寒短上衣等(含防风衣、防风短上衣及类似品)	16				100	17	13	件/千克		Other women's or girls' anoraks, wind-cheaters, wind-jackets and similar articles, of other textile materials
62.03	**男式西服套装、便服套装、上衣、长裤、护胸背带工装裤、马裤及短裤(游泳裤除外):**										**Men's or boys' suits, ensembles, jackets, blazers, trousers, bib and brace overalls, breeches and shorts (other than swim wear):**
	-西服套装:										-Suits:
6203.1100	--羊毛或动物细毛制	17.5	12	12.3	0	130	17	13	套/千克	5B	--Of wool or fine animal hair
6203.1200	--合成纤维制	17.5	12	12.3	0	130	17	13	套/千克		--Of synthetic fibres

税则号列 Tariff Item.	货品名称	最惠国(%) MFN	协定(%) 东盟 CA	协定(%) 中巴 CP	CT 中智 CC	普通 Gen	增值税率 VAT	出口退税 ED	计量单位 Unit	监管条件 SC	Article Description
6203.1200 10	合成纤维制男式西服套装(含羊毛或动物细毛36%及以上)	17.5				130	17	13	套/千克	5	Men's or boys' suits, containing≥36% by weight of wool or fine animal hair, of synthetic fibres
6203.1200 90	其他合纤制男式西服套装	17.5				130	17	13	套/千克		Other men's or boys' suits of synthetic fibres
	--其他纺织材料制:										--Of other textile materials:
6203.1910	---丝及绢丝制	17.5	12	12.3	0	100	17	13	套/千克		---Of silk or silk waste
6203.1910 10	丝及绢丝制男式西服套装(含丝70%及以上)	17.5				100	17	13	套/千克		Men's or boys' suits, containing≥70% by weight of silk
6203.1910 90	其他丝及绢丝制男式西服套装(含丝70%以下)	17.5				100	17	13	套/千克		Other men's or boys' suits, containing <70% by weight of silk
6203.1990	---其他	17.5	12	12.3	0	100	17	13	套/千克		---Other
6203.1990 10	棉制男式西服套装	17.5				100	17	13	套/千克	5	Men's or boys' suits of cotton
6203.1990 21	人造纤维制男式西服套装(含羊毛或动物细毛36%及以上)	17.5				100	17	13	套/千克	5	Men's or boys' suits of artificial fibres, containing≥36% by weight of wool or fine animal hair, of artificial fibres
6203.1990 29	其他人造纤维制男式西服套装	17.5				100	17	13	套/千克		Men's or boys' suits of other artificial fibres
6203.1990 91	其他材料制男式西服套装(棉限内)	17.5				100	17	13	套/千克	5	Men's or boys' suits of other textile materials, cotton within limitations
6203.1990 92	其他材料制男式西服套装(毛限内)	17.5				100	17	13	套/千克	5	Men's or boys' suits of other textile materials, wool within limitations
6203.1990 93	其他材料制男式西服套装(化纤限内)	17.5				100	17	13	套/千克		Men's or boys' suits of other textile materials, man-made fibres within limitations
6203.1990 99	其他材料制其他男式西服套装	17.5	T3			100	17	13	套/千克		Men's or boys' suits of other textile materials
	-便服套装:										-Ensembles:
6203.2200	--棉制	17.5	T3		0	90	17	13	套/千克		--Of cotton
6203.2200 10	棉制男式便服套装(工业及职业用)	17.5				90	17	13	套/千克	5B	Men's or boys' ensembles of cotton, industrial and career apparel
6203.2200 90	其他棉制男式便服套装	17.5				90	17	13	套/千克	5B	Other men's or boys' ensembles of cotton
6203.2300	--合成纤维制	17.5	12	12.3	0	130	17	13	套/千克		--Of synthetic fibres
6203.2300 11	合成纤维制其他男式便服套装(含羊毛或动物细毛≥36%,工业及职业用)	17.5				130	17	13	套/千克	5B	Other men's or boys' ensembles, containing≥36% by weight of wool or fine animal hair industrial and career apparel, of synthetic fibres
6203.2300 19	合成纤维制其他男式便服套装(含羊毛或动物细毛≥36%)	17.5				130	17	13	套/千克	5B	Other men's or boys' ensembles, containing≥36% by weight of wool or fine animal hair, of synthetic fibres
6203.2300 91	其他合成纤维制其他男式便服套装(工业及职业用)	17.5				130	17	13	套/千克	5B	Other men's or boys' ensembles, industrial and career apparel, of synthetic fibres
6203.2300 99	其他合成纤维制其他男式便服套装	17.5				130	17	13	套/千克	5B	Other men's or boys' ensembles of synthetic fibres
	--其他纺织材料制:										--Of other textile materials:
6203.2910	---丝及绢丝制	17.5	T3	12.3	0	130	17	13	套/千克		---Of silk or silk waste

税则号列 Tariff Item.	货品名称	最惠国(%) MFN	协定(%) 东盟 CA	中巴 CP	CT 中智 CC	普通 Gen	增值税率 VAT	出口退税 ED	计量单位 Unit	监管条件 SC	Article Description
6203.2910 10	丝制男式便服套装(含丝70%及以上)	17.5				130	17	13	套/千克	B	Men's or boys' ensembles, containing ≥70% by weight of silk
6203.2910 90	丝制其他男式便服套装(含丝70%以下)	17.5				130	17	13	套/千克	5B	Other men's or boys' ensembles, containing <70% by weight of silk
6203.2920	---羊毛或动物细毛制男式便服套装	17.5	12	12.3	0	130	17	13	套/千克	5	---Of wool or fine animal hair
6203.2990	---其他	17.5	T3	12.3	0	100	17	13	套/千克		---Other
6203.2990 11	人造纤维制其他男式便服套装(工业及职业用)	17.5				100	17	13	套/千克	5	Other men's or boys' ensembles of artificial fibres, industrial and career apparel
6203.2990 19	人造纤维制其他男式便服套装	17.5				100	17	13	套/千克	5	Other men's or boys' ensembles of artificial fibres
6203.2990 90	其他材料制其他男式便服套装	17.5				100	17	13	套/千克		Other men's or boys' ensembles of other textile materials
	-上衣:										-Jackets and blazers:
6203.3100	--羊毛或动物细毛制	16	T3	11.7	0	130	17	13	件/千克		--Of wool or fine animal hair
6203.3100 10	毛制男式西服式上衣(羊毛或动物细毛制)	16				130	17	13	件/千克	B	Men's or boys' suit jackets and blazers, of wool or fine animal hair
6203.3100 90	毛制男式其他上衣(羊毛或动物细毛制)	16				130	17	13	件/千克	B	Other men's or boys' jackets and blazers, of wool or fine animal hair
6203.3200	--棉制	16	T3	14.4	0	90	17	13	件/千克		--Of cotton
6203.3200 10	棉制工业及职业用男式上衣	16				90	17	13	件/千克	B	Men's or boys' jackets and blazers of cotton, industrial and career apparel
6203.3200 90	棉制其他男式上衣	16				90	17	13	件/千克	B	Men's or boys' jackets and blazers of cotton
6203.3300	--合成纤维制	17.5	12	12.3	0	130	17	13	件/千克		--Of synthetic fibres
6203.3300 11	合成纤维制男式西服式上衣(含羊毛或动物细毛36%及以上,工业及职业用)	17.5				130	17	13	件/千克	B	Men's or boys' suit jacket, containing ≥36% by weight of wool or fine animal hair, industrial and career apparel, of synthetic fibres
6203.3300 19	合成纤维制男式西服式上衣(含羊毛或动物细毛36%及以上)	17.5				130	17	13	件/千克	B	Men's or boys' suit jacket, containing ≥36% by weight of wool or fine animal hair, of synthetic fibres
6203.3300 21	合成纤维制男式其他上衣(含羊毛或动物细毛36%及以上,工业及职业用)	17.5				130	17	13	件/千克	B	Other men's or boys' jackets and blazers of synthetic fibres, containing ≥36% by weight of wool or fine animal hair, industrial and career apparel
6203.3300 29	合成纤维制男式其他上衣(含羊毛或动物细毛36%及以上)	17.5				130	17	13	件/千克	B	Other men's or boys' jackets and blazers of synthetic fibres, containing ≥36% by weight of wool or fine animal hair
6203.3300 91	其他合成纤维制男式上衣(工业及职业用)	17.5				130	17	13	件/千克	B	Other men's or boys' jackets and blazers of synthetic fibres, industrial and career apparel
6203.3300 99	其他合成纤维制男式上衣	17.5				130	17	13	件/千克	B	Other men's or boys' jackets and blazers of synthetic fibres
	--其他纺织材料制:										--Of other textile materials:
6203.3910	---丝及绢丝制	16	T3	11.7	0	130	17	13	件/千克		---Of silk or silk waste

税则号列 Tariff Item.	货品名称	最惠国(%) MFN	协定(%)CT 东盟 CA	中巴 CP	中智 CC	普通 Gen	增值税率 VAT	出口退税 ED	计量单位 Unit	监管条件 SC	Article Description
6203.3910 10	丝制男式上衣(含丝70%及以上)	16				130	17	13	件/千克	B	Men's or boys' jackets and blazers of silk, containing ≥70% by weight of silk
6203.3910 90	丝制男式上衣(含丝70%以下)	16				130	17	13	件/千克	B	Men's or boys' jackets and blazers of silk, containing < 70% by weight of silk
6203.3990	---其他	16	T3	11.7	0	100	17	13	件/千克		---Other
6203.3990 11	人造纤维制男式西服式上衣(含羊毛或动物细毛36%及以上,工业及职业用)	16				100	17	13	件/千克	B	Men's or boys' suit jacket, of artificial fibres, industrial and career apparel, containing≥36% by weight of wool or fine animal hair
6203.3990 19	人造纤维制男式西服式上衣(含羊毛或动物细毛36%及以上)	16				100	17	13	件/千克	B	Men's or boys' suit jacket, of artificial fibres, containing ≥36% by weight of wool or fine animal hair
6203.3990 21	人造纤维制男式其他上衣(含羊毛或动物细毛36%及以上,工业及职业用)	16				100	17	13	件/千克	B	Other men's or boys' jackets and blazers of artificial fibres, containing≥36% by weight of wool or fine animal hair, industrial and career apparel
6203.3990 29	人造纤维制男式其他上衣(含羊毛或动物细毛36%及以上)	16				100	17	13	件/千克	B	Other men's or boys' jackets and blazers of artificial fibres, containing≥36% by weight of wool or fine animal hair
6203.3990 31	其他人造纤维制男式上衣(工业及职业用)	16				100	17	13	件/千克	B	Men's or boys' jackets and blazers of artificial fibres, industrial and career apparel
6203.3990 39	其他人造纤维制男式上衣	16				100	17	13	件/千克	B	Men's or boys' jackets and blazers of artificial fibres
6203.3990 91	其他材料制男式上衣(棉限内)	16				100	17	13	件/千克	B	Other men's or boys' jackets and blazers of other textile materials cotton, within limitations
6203.3990 92	其他材料制男式上衣(毛限内)	16				100	17	13	件/千克	B	Other men's or boys' jackets and blazers of other textile materials, wool within limitations
6203.3990 93	其他材料制男式上衣(化纤限内)	16				100	17	13	件/千克	B	Other men's or boys' jackets and blazers of other textile materials, man-made fibres within limitations
6203.3990 99	其他材料制男式上衣	16				100	17	13	件/千克	B	Other men's or boys' jackets and blazers of other textile materials
	-长裤、护胸背带工装裤、马裤及短裤:										-Trousers, bib and brace overalls, breeches and shorts:
6203.4100	--羊毛或动物细毛制	16	12	11.7	0	130	17	13	条/千克		--Of wool or fine animal hair
6203.4100 11	毛制男式护胸背带工装裤(羊毛或动物细毛制,带防寒衬里)	16				130	17	13	条/千克	B	Men's or boys' bib and brace overalls, with thermal lining, of wool or fine animal hair
6203.4100 19	毛制男式护胸背带工装裤(羊毛或动物细毛制)	16				130	17	13	条/千克	B	Men's or boys' bib and brace overalls, of wool or fine animal hair
6203.4100 21	毛制男式长裤、马裤(羊毛或动物细毛制,带防寒衬里)	16				130	17	13	条/千克	5B	Men's or boys' trousers, breeches, with thermal lining, of wool or fine animal hair

税则号列 Tariff Item.	货品名称	最惠国(%) MFN	协定(%) 东盟 CA	中巴 CP	CT 中智 CC	普通 Gen	增值税率 VAT	出口退税 ED	计量单位 Unit	监管条件 SC	Article Description
6203.4100 22	毛制男式长裤、马裤(羊毛或动物细毛制,含8-18号男童)	16				130	17	13	条/千克	5B	Men's trousers, breeches, including boys' No. 8 ~ No. 18, of wool or fine animal hair
6203.4100 29	毛制其他男童长裤、马裤(羊毛或动物细毛制)	16				130	17	13	条/千克	5B	Other boys' trousers, breeches, of wool or fine animal hair
6203.4100 90	毛制男式短裤(羊毛或动物细毛制)	16				130	17	13	条/千克	5B	Men's or boys' shorts, of wool or fine animal hair
	--棉制:										--Of cotton:
6203.4210	---阿拉伯裤	16	T3	12.9	0	90	17	13	条/千克		---Arabian trousers
6203.4210 10	棉制男式阿拉伯裤(羽绒和水禽毛≥15%且含绒率≥35%,或含羽绒≥10%)	16				90	17	13	条/千克	5B	Men's or boys' Arabian trousers of cotton, containing ≥ 15% by weight of down or feathers and water fowl, down content rate ≥ 35%, or containing ≥ 10% by weight of down or feathers
6203.4210 90	棉制男式阿拉伯裤	16				90	17	13	条/千克	5B	Men's or boys' Arabian trousers of cotton
6203.4290	---其他	16	T3	12.9	0	90	17	13	条/千克		---Other
6203.4290 11	工、职业用棉男护胸背带工装裤(羽绒和水禽毛≥15%且含绒率≥35%,或含羽绒≥10%)	16				90	17	13	条/千克	B	Men's or boys' bib and brace overalls, industrial and career apparel, containing ≥ 15% by weight of down or feathers and water fowl, down content rate ≥ 35%, or containing ≥ 10% by weight of down or feathers, of cotton
6203.4290 12	棉制男式护胸背带工装裤(羽绒和水禽毛≥15%且含绒率≥35%,或含羽绒≥10%)	16				90	17	13	条/千克	B	Men's or boys' bib and brace overalls, containing≥15% by weight of down or feathers and water fowl, down content rate ≥ 35%, or containing ≥ 10% by weight of down or feathers, of cotton
6203.4290 13	棉制其他男成人护胸背带工装裤(带防寒衬里,工业及职业用)	16				90	17	13	条/千克	B	Other men's bib and brace overalls, with thermal lining, of cotton, industrial and career apparel
6203.4290 14	棉制其他男成人护胸背带工装裤(带防寒衬里)	16				90	17	13	条/千克	B	Other men's bib and brace overalls, with thermal lining, of cotton, industrial and career apparel
6203.4290 15	棉制其他男童护胸背带工装裤(带防寒衬里)	16				90	17	13	条/千克	B	Other boys' bib and brace overalls, with thermal lining, of cotton
6203.4290 16	棉制其他男成人护胸背带工装裤(工业及职业用)	16				90	17	13	条/千克	B	Other men's bib and brace overalls, of cotton, industrial and career apparel
6203.4290 17	棉制其他男成人护胸背带工装裤	16				90	17	13	条/千克	B	Other men's bib and brace overalls of cotton
6203.4290 19	棉制其他男童护胸背带工装裤	16				90	17	13	条/千克	B	Other boys' bib and brace overalls of cotton
6203.4290 21	工、职业用棉男长裤、马裤(羽绒和水禽毛≥15%且含绒率≥35%,或含羽绒≥10%)	16				90	17	13	条/千克	B	Men's or boys' trousers, breeches, containing≥15% by weight of down or feathers and water fowl, down content rats≥35%, industrial and career apparel, or containing≥10% by weight of down or feathers of cotton

税则号列 Tariff Item.	货品名称	最惠国(%) MFN	协定(%) CT 东盟 CA	中巴 CP	中智 CC	普通 Gen	增值税率 VAT	出口退税 ED	计量单位 Unit	监管条件 SC	Article Description
6203.4290 29	棉制男式长裤、马裤(羽绒和水禽毛≥15%且含绒率≥35%,或含羽绒≥10%)	16				90	17	13	条/千克	5B	Men's or boys' trousers, breeches, containing≥15% by weight of down or feathers and water fowl, down content rate≥35%, or containing≥10% by weight of down or feathers, of cotton
6203.4290 30	棉制男式长裤、马裤(游戏装,带防寒衬里)	16				90	17	13	条/千克	5B	Men's or boys' trousers, breeches, playsuit, with thermal lining, of cotton
6203.4290 41	棉制男式长裤、马裤(游戏装,不带防寒衬里,含8-18号男童)	16				90	17	13	条/千克	5B	Men's or boys' trousers, breeches, playsuit, including boys' No. 8 ~ No. 18, of cotton, playsuit, without thermal lining
6203.4290 49	棉制其他男童长裤、马裤(游戏装,不带防寒衬里)	16				90	17	13	条/千克	5B	Other boys' trousers, breeches, of cotton, playsuit, without thermal lining
6203.4290 51	棉制男式长裤、马裤(非游戏装,带防寒衬里,工业及职业用)	16				90	17	13	条/千克	5B	Men's or boys' trousers, breeches, of cotton, with thermal lining, industrial and career apparel (other than playsuit)
6203.4290 59	棉制男式长裤、马裤(非游戏装,带防寒衬里)	16				90	17	13	条/千克	5B	Men's or boys' trousers, breeches, of cotton, with thermal lining, other than playsuit
6203.4290 61	棉制男成人长裤、马裤(非游戏装,不带防寒衬里,工业及职业用)	16				90	17	13	条/千克	5B	Men's trousers, breeches, of cotton, industrial and career apparel, other than playsuit, without thermal lining
6203.4290 62	棉制男式长裤、马裤(非游戏装,不带防寒衬里含8-18号男童)	16				90	17	13	条/千克	5B	Men's trousers, breeches, including boys' No. 8 ~ No. 18, of cotton, other than playsuit, without thermal lining
6203.4290 69	棉制其他男童长裤、马裤(非游戏装,不带防寒衬里)	16				90	17	13	条/千克	5B	Other boys' trousers, breeches, of cotton, other than playsuit, without thermal lining
6203.4290 91	棉制男式短裤(羽绒和水禽毛≥15%且含绒率≥35%,或含羽绒≥10%)	16				90	17	13	条/千克	5B	Men's or boys' shorts of cotton, containing ≥ 15% by weight of down or feathers and water fowl, down content rate≥35%, or containing ≥ 10% by weight of down or feathers
6203.4290 92	棉制其他男式短裤(游戏装)	16				90	17	13	条/千克	5B	Other men's or boys' shorts of cotton, playsuit
6203.4290 99	棉制其他男式短裤(非游戏装)	16				90	17	13	条/千克	5B	Other men's or boys' shorts of cotton, other than playsuit
	--合成纤维制:										--Of synthetic fibres:
6203.4310	---阿拉伯裤	17.5	T3	13.1	0	130	17	13	条/千克		---Arabian trousers
6203.4310 10	合成纤维制男式阿拉伯裤(羽绒和水禽毛≥15%且含绒率≥35%,或含羽绒≥10%)	17.5				130	17	13	条/千克	5B	Men's or boys' Arabian trousers of synthetic fibres, containing ≥ 15% by weight of down or feathers and water fowl, down content rate ≥ 35%, or containing≥10% by weight of down or feathers
6203.4310 90	合成纤维制男式阿拉伯裤	17.5				130	17	13	条/千克	5B	Men's or boys' Arabian trousers of synthetic fibres

税则号列 Tariff Item.	货品名称	最惠国(%) MFN	协定(%) 东盟 CA	中巴 CP	CT 中智 CC	普通 Gen	增值税率 VAT	出口退税 ED	计量单位 Unit	监管条件 SC	Article Description
6203.4390	---其他	17.5	T3	13.1	0	130	17	13	条/千克		---Other
6203.4390 11	工、职业用合纤制男护胸背带工裤(羽绒和水禽毛≥15%且含绒率≥35%,或含羽绒≥10%)	17.5				130	17	13	条/千克	B	Men's or boys' bib and brace overalls, industrial and career apparel, containing ≥ 15% by weight of down or feathers and water fowl, down content rate ≥ 35%, or containing ≥ 10% by weight of down or feathers, of synthetic fibres
6203.4390 12	合纤制男式护胸背带工裤(羽绒和水禽毛≥15%且含绒率≥35%,或含羽绒≥10%)	17.5				130	17	13	条/千克	B	Men's or boys' bib and brace overalls, containing ≥ 15% by weight of down or feathers and water fowl, down content rate ≥ 35%, or containing ≥ 10% by weight of down or feathers, of synthetic fibres
6203.4390 13	其他合纤制男成人护胸背带工装裤(带防寒衬里,工业及职业用)	17.5				130	17	13	条/千克	B	Other men's bib and brace overalls, with thermal lining, industrial and career apparel, of synthetic fibres
6203.4390 14	其他合纤制男成人护胸背带工装裤(带防寒衬里)	17.5				130	17	13	条/千克	B	Other men's bib and brace overalls, with thermal lining, of synthetic fibres
6203.4390 15	其他合纤制男童护胸背带工装裤(带防寒衬里)	17.5				130	17	13	条/千克	B	Other boys' bib and brace overalls, with thermal lining of synthetic fibres
6203.4390 16	其他合纤制男成人护胸背带工装裤(工业及职业用)	17.5				130	17	13	条/千克	B	Other men's bib and brace overalls, industrial and career apparel, of synthetic fibres
6203.4390 17	其他成纤制男成人护胸背带工装裤	17.5				130	17	13	条/千克	B	Other men's bib and brace overalls of synthetic fibres
6203.4390 19	其他合纤制男童护胸背带工装裤	17.5				130	17	13	条/千克	B	Other boys' bib and brace overalls of synthetic fibres
6203.4390 21	工、职业用合纤男长裤、马裤(羽绒和水禽毛≥15%且含绒率≥35%,或含羽绒≥10%)	17.5				130	17	13	条/千克	B	Men's or boys' trousers, breeches, containing ≥ 15% by weight of down or feathers and water fowl, down content rate ≥ 35% or containing ≥ 10% by weight of down or feathers, of synthetic fibres
6203.4390 29	合纤制男式长裤、马裤(羽绒和水禽毛≥15%且含绒率≥35%,或含羽绒≥10%)	17.5				130	17	13	条/千克	5B	Men's or boys' trousers, breeches, containing ≥ 15% by weight of down or feathers and water fowl, down content rate ≥ 35% or containing ≥ 10% by weight of down or feathers, of synthetic fibres
6203.4390 31	其他合纤制男式长裤、马裤(带防寒衬里,含羊毛或动物细毛36%及以上,工/职业用)	17.5				130	17	13	条/千克	5B	Men's or boys' trousers, breeches, containing ≥ 36% by weight of wool or fine animal hair, with thermal lining, industrial and career apparel, of synthetic fibres

税则号列 Tariff Item.	货品名称	最惠国(%) MFN	协定(%)CT 东盟 CA	中巴 CP	中智 CC	普通 Gen	增值税率 VAT	出口退税 ED	计量单位 Unit	监管条件 SC	Article Description
6203.4390 39	其他合纤制男式长裤、马裤(带防寒衬里,含羊毛或动物细毛36%及以上)	17.5				130	17	13	条/千克	5B	Men's or boys' trousers, breeches, containing≥36% by weight of wool or fine animal hair, with thermal lining, of synthetic fibres
6203.4390 41	其他合纤制男成人长裤、马裤(不带防寒衬里,含羊/动物细毛36%及以上,工/职业用)	17.5				130	17	13	条/千克	5B	Men's trousers, breeches, containing ≥36% by weight of wool or fine animal hair, industrial and career apparel, without thermal lining, of synthetic fibres
6203.4390 42	其他合纤制男式长裤、马裤(不带防寒衬里,含羊/动物细毛36%及以上,指8-18号男童)	17.5				130	17	13	条/千克	5B	Men's trousers, breeches, including boys' No. 8 ~ No. 18, containing ≥ 36% by weight of wool or fine animal hair, without thermal lining, of synthetic fibres
6203.4390 49	其他合纤制男童长裤、马裤(不带防寒衬里,含羊/动物细毛36%及以上)	17.5				130	17	13	条/千克	5B	Boys' trousers, breeches, containing≥36% by weight of wool or fine animal hair, without thermal lining, of synthetic fibres
6203.4390 50	其他合纤制男式长裤、马裤(带防寒衬里,游戏装)	17.5				130	17	13	条/千克	5B	Other men's or boys' trousers, breeches, with thermal lining, playsuit, of synthetic fibres
6203.4390 61	其他合纤制男式长裤、马裤(不带防寒衬里,游戏装,含8-18号男童)	17.5				130	17	13	条/千克	5B	Other men's trousers, breeches, of synthetic fibres, without thermal lining, including boys' No. 8 ~ No. 18, playsuit
6203.4390 69	其他合纤制其他男童长裤、马裤(不带防寒衬里,游戏装)	17.5				130	17	13	条/千克	5B	Other boys' trousers, breeches, playsuit, of synthetic fibres, without thermal lining
6203.4390 71	其他合纤制男式长裤、马裤(带防寒衬里,非游戏装和滑雪裤,工业及职业用)	17.5				130	17	13	条/千克	5B	Other men's or boys' trousers, breeches, with thermal lining, industrial and career apparel, other than playsuit, of synthetic fibres
6203.4390 79	其他合纤制男式长裤、马裤(带防寒衬里,非游戏装和滑雪裤)	17.5				130	17	13	条/千克	5B	Other men's or boys' trousers, breeches, with thermal lining, other than playsuit, of synthetic fibres
6203.4390 81	其他合纤制男成人长裤、马裤(不带防寒衬里,非游戏装和滑雪裤,工业及职业用)	17.5				130	17	13	条/千克	5B	Other men's trousers, breeches, industrial and career apparel, of synthetic fibres, other than playsuit, without thermal lining
6203.4390 82	其他合纤制男童长裤、马裤(不带防寒衬里,非游戏装和滑雪裤,指8-18号男童)	17.5				130	17	13	条/千克	5B	Other men's trousers, breeches, including boys' No. 8 ~ No. 18, of synthetic fibres, other than playsuit, without thermal lining
6203.4390 89	其他合成纤维制其他男童长裤、马裤(不带防寒衬里,非游戏装和滑雪裤)	17.5				130	17	13	条/千克	5B	Other boys' trousers, breeches of synthetic fibres, other than playsuit, without thermal lining

税则号列 Tariff Item.	货品名称	最惠国(%) MFN	协定(%) CT 东盟 CA	中巴 CP	中智 CC	普通 Gen	增值税率 VAT	出口退税 ED	计量单位 Unit	监管条件 SC	Article Description
6203.4390 91	合纤制男式短裤(羽绒和水禽毛≥15%且含绒率≥35%,或含羽绒≥10%)	17.5				130	17	13	条/千克	5B	Men's or boys' shorts, containing ≥15% by weight of down or feathers and water fowl, down content rate ≥35% or containing≥10% by weight of down or feathers
6203.4390 92	其他合纤制男式短裤(游戏装)	17.5				130	17	13	条/千克	5B	Men's or boys' shorts, playsuit, of synthetic fibres
6203.4390 93	其他合纤制男式短裤(非游戏装)	17.5				130	17	13	条/千克	5B	Other men's or boys' shorts, other than playsuit, of synthetic fibres
6203.4390 99	其他合纤制男裤	17.5				130	17	13	条/千克	5B	Other men's or boys' trousers of synthetic fibres
	--其他纺织材料制:										--Of other textile materials:
6203.4910	---阿拉伯裤	16	T3	11.7	0	100	17	13	条/千克		---Arabian trousers
6203.4910 10	人造纤维制男式阿拉伯裤(羽绒和水禽毛≥15%且含绒率≥35%,或含羽绒≥10%)	16				100	17	13	条/千克	5B	Men's or boys' Arabian trousers of artificial fibres, containing ≥ 15% by weight of down or feathers and water fowl, down content rate≥35% or containing ≥ 10% by weight of down or feathers
6203.4910 20	人纤制男式阿拉伯裤	16				100	17	13	条/千克	5B	Men's or boys' Arabian trousers of artificial fibres
6203.4910 30	其他材料制男式阿拉伯裤(羽绒和水禽毛≥15%且含绒率≥35%,或含羽绒≥10%)	16				100	17	13	条/千克	B	Men's or boys' Arabian trousers of other textile materials, containing≥15% by weight of down or feathers and water fowl, down content rate≥35% or containing ≥ 10% by weight of down or feathers
6203.4910 90	其他材料制男式阿拉伯裤	16				100	17	13	条/千克	5B	Men's or boys' Arabian trousers of other textile materials
6203.4990	---其他	16	T3	11.7	0	100	17	13	条/千克		---Other
6203.4990 11	人纤制男成人护胸背带工装裤(带防寒衬里)	16				100	17	13	条/千克	B	Men's bib and brace overalls, with thermal lining, of artificial fibres
6203.4990 12	人纤制男童护胸背带工装裤(带防寒衬里)	16				100	17	13	条/千克	B	Boys' bib and brace overalls, with thermal lining, of artificial fibres
6203.4990 13	人纤制男成人护胸背带工装裤	16				100	17	13	条/千克	B	Men's bib and brace overalls, of artificial fibres
6203.4990 19	人纤制男童护胸背带工装裤	16				100	17	13	条/千克	B	Boys' bib and brace overalls, of artificial fibres
6203.4990 21	人纤制男式长裤、马裤(带防寒衬里,含羊毛或动物细毛36%及以上)	16				100	17	13	条/千克	5B	Men's or boys' trousers, breeches, with thermal lining, containing≥36% by weight of wool or fine animal hair, of artificial fibres
6203.4990 22	人纤制其他男式长裤、马裤(不带防寒衬里,含羊毛或动物细毛36%及以上)	16				100	17	13	条/千克	5B	Men's or boys' trousers, breeches, containing≥36% by weight of wool or fine animal hair, of artificial fibres, without thermal lining
6203.4990 23	人纤制男式长裤、马裤(带防寒衬里,游戏装)	16				100	17	13	条/千克	5B	Men's or boys' trousers, breeches, with thermal lining, playsuit, of artificial fibres

税则号列 Tariff Item.	货品名称	最惠国(%) MFN	协定(%)CT 东盟 CA	中巴 CP	中智 CC	普通 Gen	增值税率 VAT	出口退税 ED	计量单位 Unit	监管条件 SC	Article Description
6203.4990 24	人纤制其他男式长裤、马裤(不带防寒衬里,游戏装)	16				100	17	13	条/千克	5B	Men's or boys' trousers, breeches, playsuit, of artificial fibres, without thermal lining
6203.4990 25	人纤制男式长裤、马裤(带防寒衬里,非游戏装)	16				100	17	13	条/千克	5B	Men's or boys' trousers, breeches, with thermal lining, of artificial fibres, other than playsuits
6203.4990 26	人纤制其他男式长裤、马裤(不带防寒衬里,非游戏装)	16				100	17	13	条/千克	5B	Men's or boys' trousers, breeches, of artificial fibres, without thermal lining, other than playsuits
6203.4990 27	人纤制男式短裤(含羊毛或动物细毛36%及以上)	16				100	17	13	条/千克	5B	Men's or boys' shorts of artificial fibres, containing ≥36% by weight of wool or fine animal hair
6203.4990 28	人纤制男式短裤(游戏装)	16				100	17	13	条/千克	5B	Men's or boys' shorts, playsuit, of artificial fibres
6203.4990 29	人纤制男式短裤(非游戏装)	16				100	17	13	条/千克	5B	Men's or boys' shorts of artificial fibres, other than playsuit
6203.4990 31	丝制男式护胸背带工装裤(含丝70%及以上)	16				100	17	13	条/千克	B	Men's or boys' bib and brace overalls, containing≥70% by weight of silk
6203.4990 32	丝制男式长裤、马裤(含丝70%及以上,带防寒衬里)	16				100	17	13	条/千克	B	Men's or boys' trousers, breeches, containing ≥ 70% by weight of silk, with thermal lining
6203.4990 33	丝制男式长裤、马裤(含丝70%及以上,不带防寒衬里)	16				100	17	13	条/千克	B	Men's or boys' trousers, breeches, containing ≥ 70% by weight of silk, without thermal lining
6203.4990 34	丝制男式短裤(含丝70%及以上)	16				100	17	13	条/千克	B	Men's or boys' shorts, containing ≥ 70% by weight of silk
6203.4990 35	丝制男式护胸背带工装裤(含丝70%以下,带防寒衬里)	16				100	17	13	条/千克	B	Men's or boys' bib and brace overalls, containing < 70% by weight of silk, with thermal lining
6203.4990 36	丝制男式护胸背带工装裤(含丝70%以下,不带防寒衬里)	16				100	17	13	条/千克	5B	Men's or boys' bib and brace overalls, containing < 70% by weight of silk, without thermal lining
6203.4990 37	丝制男式长裤、马裤(含丝70%以下,带防寒衬里)	16				100	17	13	条/千克	5B	Men's or boys' trousers, breeches, containing < 70% by weight of silk, with thermal lining
6203.4990 38	丝制男式长裤、马裤(含丝70%以下,不带防寒衬里)	16				100	17	13	条/千克	B	Men's or boys' trousers, breeches, containing < 70% by weight of silk, without thermal lining
6203.4990 39	丝制男式短裤(含丝70%以下)	16				100	17	13	条/千克	5B	Men's or boys' shorts, containing < 70% by weight of silk
6203.4990 41	其他材料制男式长裤、马裤(棉限内,带防寒衬里)	16				100	17	13	条/千克	5B	Men's or boys' trousers, breeches, cotton within limitations, with thermal lining, of other textile materials
6203.4990 42	其他材料制男式长裤、马裤(棉限内,不带防寒衬里)	16				100	17	13	条/千克	5B	Men's or boys' trousers, breeches, cotton within limitations, of other textile materials without thermal lining
6203.4990 49	其他材料制男式短裤(棉限内)	16				100	17	13	条/千克	5B	Men's or boys' shorts, cotton within limitations, of other textile materials

税则号列 Tariff Item.	货品名称	最惠国(%) MFN	协定(%)CT 东盟 CA	 中巴 CP	 中智 CC	普通 Gen	增值税率 VAT	出口退税 ED	计量单位 Unit	监管条件 SC	Article Description
6203.4990 51	其他材料制男式长裤、马裤(毛限内,带防寒衬里)	16				100	17	13	条/千克	5B	Men's or boys' trousers, breeches, wool within limitations, with thermal lining, of other textile materials
6203.4990 52	其他材料制男式长裤、马裤(毛限内,不带防寒衬里)	16				100	17	13	条/千克	5B	Men's or boys' trousers, breeches, wool within limitations, of other textile materials, without thermal lining
6203.4990 59	其他材料制男式短裤(毛限内)	16				100	17	13	条/千克	5B	Men's or boys' shorts of other textile materials, wool within limitations
6203.4990 61	其他材料制男式长裤、马裤(化纤限内,带防寒衬里)	16				100	17	13	条/千克	5B	Men's or boys' trousers, breeches, with thermal lining, of other textile materials, man-made fibres within limitations
6203.4990 62	其他材料制男式长裤、马裤(化纤限内,不带防寒衬里)	16				100	17	13	条/千克	5B	Men's or boys' trousers, breeches without thermal lining, of other textile materials, man-made fibres within limitations
6203.4990 69	其他材料制男式短裤(化纤限内)	16				100	17	13	条/千克	5B	Men's or boys' shorts, of other textile materials, man-made fibres within limitations
6203.4990 91	其他材料制男式护胸背带工装裤(带防寒衬里)	16				100	17	13	条/千克	B	Men's or boys' bib and brace overalls, with thermal lining, of other textile materials
6203.4990 92	其他材料制男式护胸背带工装裤(不带防寒衬里)	16				100	17	13	条/千克	B	Men's or boys' bib and brace overalls, of other textile materials, without thermal lining
6203.4990 93	其他材料制男式长裤、马裤(带防寒衬里)	16				100	17	13	条/千克	5B	Men's or boys' trousers, breeches, with thermal lining, of other textile materials
6203.4990 94	其他材料制男式长裤、马裤(不带防寒衬里)	16				100	17	13	条/千克	5B	Men's or boys' trousers, breeches of other textile materials, without thermal lining
6203.4990 99	其他材料制男式短裤	16				100	17	13	条/千克	5B	Men's or boys' shorts of other textile materials
62.04	女式西服套装、便服套装、上衣、连衣裙、裙子、裙裤、长裤、护胸背带工装裤、马裤及短裤(游泳服除外):										**Women's or girls' suits, ensembles, jackets, blazers, dresses, skirts, divided skirts, trousers, bib and brace overalls, breeches and shorts (other than swimwear):**
	-西服套装:										-Suits:
6204.1100	--羊毛或动物细毛制	17.5	12	12.3	0	130	17	13	套/千克	B	--Of wool or fine animal hair
6204.1200	--棉制	17.5	T3		0	90	17	13	套/千克		--Of cotton
6204.1200 10	含裤子的棉制女式西服套装	17.5				90	17	13	套/千克	5	Women's or girls' suits, including trousers, of cotton
6204.1200 90	不含裤子的棉制女式西服套装	17.5				90	17	13	套/千克		Women's or girls' suits, not including trousers, of cotton
6204.1300	--合成纤维制	17.5	T3	12.3	0	130	17	13	套/千克		--Of synthetic fibres
6204.1300 10	合纤制女式西服套装(含羊毛或动物细毛36%及以上)	17.5				130	17	13	套/千克		Women's or girls' suits, containing ≥ 36% by weight of wool or fine animal hair, of synthetic fibres

税则号列 Tariff Item.	货品名称	最惠国(%) MFN	协定(%) CT 东盟 CA	中巴 CP	中智 CC	普通 Gen	增值税率 VAT	出口退税 ED	计量单位 Unit	监管条件 SC	Article Description
6204.1300 90	其他合纤制女式西服套装	17.5				130	17	13	套/千克		Other women's or girls' suits of synthetic fibres
	--其他纺织材料制:										--Of other textile materials:
6204.1910	---丝及绢丝制	17.5	12	12.3	0	100	17	13	套/千克		---Of silk or silk waste
6204.1910 10	丝及绢丝制女式西服套装(含丝70%及以上)	17.5				100	17	13	套/千克		Women's or girls' suits of silk and silk waste, containing ≥70% by weight of silk or silk waste
6204.1910 90	其他丝及绢丝制女式西服套装(含丝70%以下)	17.5				100	17	13	套/千克		Women's or girls' suits of silk and silk waste containing <70% by weight of silk
6204.1990	---其他	17.5	12	12.3	0	100	17	13	套/千克		---Other
6204.1990 11	人造纤维制女式西服套装(含羊毛或动物细毛36%及以上)	17.5				100	17	13	套/千克		Women's or girls' suits of artificial fibres, containing ≥36% by weight of wool or fine animal hair
6204.1990 19	其他人造纤维制女式西服套装	17.5				100	17	13	套/千克		Women's or girls' suits of artificial fibres
6204.1990 91	含裤子的其他材料制女式西服套装(棉限内)	17.5				100	17	13	套/千克	5	Women's or girls' suits of other textile materials, cotton within limitations
6204.1990 92	其他材料制女式西服套装(毛限内)	17.5				100	17	13	套/千克		Women's or girls' suits of other textile materials, wool within limitations
6204.1990 93	其他材料制女式西服套装(化纤限内)	17.5				100	17	13	套/千克		Women's or girls' suits of other textile materials, man-made fibres within limitations
6204.1990 99	其他材料制其他女式西服套装	17.5				100	17	13	套/千克		Women's or girls' suits of other textile materials
	-便服套装:										-Ensembles:
6204.2100	--羊毛或动物细毛制	17.5	12	12.3	0	130	17	13	套/千克		--Of wool or fine animal hair
6204.2200	--棉制	17.5	8		0	90	17	13	套/千克		--Of cotton
6204.2200 11	含裤子的棉制女式便服套装(工业及职业用)	17.5				90	17	13	套/千克	5B	Women's or girls' ensembles of cotton, industrial and career apparel
6204.2200 19	不含裤子的棉制女式便服套装(工业及职业用)	17.5				90	17	13	套/千克	B	Women's or girls' ensembles of cotton
6204.2200 91	含裤子的棉制非工业及职业用女式便服套装	17.5				90	17	13	套/千克	5B	Women's or girls' ensembles of cotton, including trousers ,non - industrial or career apparel
6204.2200 99	不含裤子的棉制非工业及职业用女式便服套装	17.5				90	17	13	套/千克	B	Women's or girls' ensembles of cotton, not including trousers ,non - industrial or career apparel
6204.2300	--合成纤维制	20	12	13.8	0	130	17	13	套/千克		--Of synthetic fibres
6204.2300 11	工、职业用合纤制女式便服套装(含羊毛或动物细毛≥36%)	20				130	17	13	套/千克	B	Women's or girls' ensembles of synthetic fibres, industrial and career apparel, containing≥36% by weight of wool or fine animal hair
6204.2300 19	合成纤维制其他女式便服套装(含羊毛或动物细毛≥36%)	20				130	17	13	套/千克	B	Women's or girls' ensembles of synthetic fibres, containing ≥36% by weight of wool or fine animal hair
6204.2300 91	其他合成纤维制含裤子的女式便服套装	20				130	17	13	套/千克	5B	Women's or girls' ensembles of synthetic fibres, industrial and career apparel

税则号列 Tariff Item.	货品名称	最惠国(%) MFN	协定(%) CT 东盟 CA	 中巴 CP	 中智 CC	普通 Gen	增值税率 VAT	出口退税 ED	计量单位 Unit	监管条件 SC	Article Description
6204. 2300 99	其他合成纤维制其他女式便服套装	20				130	17	13	套/千克	B	Women's or girls' ensembles of synthetic fibres
	--其他纺织材料制:										--Of other textile materials:
6204. 2910	---丝及绢丝制	20	12	13. 8	0	130	17	13	套/千克		---Of silk or silk waste
6204. 2910 10	丝制女式便服套装(含丝及绢丝≥70%)	20				130	17	13	套/千克	B	Women's or girls' ensembles, containing≥70% by weight of silk or silk waste
6204. 2910 90	丝制其他女式便服套装(含丝及绢丝<70%)	20				130	17	13	套/千克	5B	Women's or girls' ensembles, containing<70% by weight of silk or silk waste
6204. 2990	---其他	14	12	9. 9	0	100	17	13	套/千克		---Other
6204. 2990 11	含裤子的人纤制女便服套装	14				100	17	13	套/千克	5	Women's or girls' ensembles of artificial fibres, industrial and career apparel
6204. 2990 19	不含裤子的人纤制女便服套装	14				100	17	13	套/千克		Women's or girls' ensembles of artificial fibres
6204. 2990 21	含裤子其他材料制女式便服套装(棉限内)	14				100	17	13	套/千克	5	Women's or girls' ensembles of other textile materials, cotton within limitations
6204. 2990 29	不含裤子的其他材料制女式便服套装(棉限内)	14				100	17	13	套/千克		Women's or girls' ensembles of other textile materials, wool within limitations
6204. 2990 30	其他材料制女式便服套装(毛限内)	14				100	17	13	套/千克		Women's or girls' ensembles of other textile materials, man-made fibres within limitations
6204. 2990 41	含裤子的其他材料制女式便服套装(化纤限内)	14				100	17	13	套/千克	5	Women's or girls' ensembles of other textile materials
6204. 2990 49	不含裤子的其他材料制女式便服套装(化纤限内)	14				100	17	13	套/千克		Women' s or girls' ensembles, including trousers, of other textile material, man – made fibres within limitations
6204. 2990 91	含裤子的其他材料制女式便服套装	14				100	17	13	套/千克	5	Women's or girls' ensembles, including trousers, of other textile material
6204. 2990 99	不含裤子的其他材料制女式便服套装	14				100	17	13	套/千克		Women's and girl's ,ensembles of other textile materials,excluding trousers
	-上衣:										-Jackets and blazers:
6204. 3100	--羊毛或动物细毛制	16	12	11. 7	0	130	17	13	件/千克	B	--Of wool or fine animal hair
6204. 3200	--棉制	16	T3		0	90	17	13	件/千克		--Of cotton
6204. 3200 10	棉制女式上衣(工业及职业用)	16				90	17	13	件/千克	B	Women's or girls' jackets and blazers of cotton, industrial and career apparel
6204. 3200 90	棉制其他女式上衣	16				90	17	13	件/千克	B	Women's or girls' jackets and blazers of cotton
6204. 3300	--合成纤维制	17. 5	T3	12. 3	0	130	17	13	件/千克		--Of synthetic fibres
6204. 3300 10	合成纤维制女式上衣(含羊毛或动物细毛36%及以上,工业及职业用)	17. 5				130	17	13	件/千克	B	Women's or girls' jackets and blazers of synthetic fibres, containing≥36% by weight of wool or fine animal hair, industrial and career apparel

税则号列 Tariff Item.	货 品 名 称	最惠国(%) MFN	协定(%)CT 东盟 CA	中巴 CP	中智 CC	普通 Gen	增值税率 VAT	出口退税 ED	计量单位 Unit	监管条件 SC	Article Description
6204.3300 20	合成纤维制其他女式上衣(含羊毛或动物细毛36%及以上)	17.5				130	17	13	件/千克	B	Women's or girls' jackets and blazers of synthetic fibres, containing ≥36% by weight of wool or fine animal hair
6204.3300 30	合成纤维制女式上衣(工业及职业用)	17.5				130	17	13	件/千克	B	Women's or girls' jackets and blazers of synthetic fibres, industrial and career apparel
6204.3300 90	合成纤维制其他女式上衣	17.5				130	17	13	件/千克	B	Other women's or girls' jackets and blazers of synthetic fibres
	--其他纺织材料制:										--Of other textile materials:
6204.3910	---丝及绢丝制	16	12	11.7	0	130	17	13	件/千克		---Of silk or silk waste
6204.3910 10	丝制女式上衣(含丝及绢丝70%及以上)	16				130	17	13	件/千克	B	Women's or girls' jackets and blazers of silk, containing ≥70% by weight of silk or silk waste
6204.3910 90	丝制其他女式上衣(含丝及绢丝70%以下)	16				130	17	13	件/千克	B	Women's or girls' jackets and blazers of silk, containing < 70% by weight of silk or silk waste
6204.3990	---其他	16	12	11.7	0	100	17	13	件/千克		---Other
6204.3990 11	人纤制女式上衣(含羊毛或动物细毛≥36%,工业及职业用)	16				100	17	13	件/千克	B	Women's or girls' jackets and blazers of artificial fibres, containing ≥36% by weight of wool or fine animal hair, industrial and career apparel
6204.3990 12	人纤制其他女式上衣(含羊毛或动物细毛≥36%)	16				100	17	13	件/千克	B	Women's or girls' jackets and blazers of artificial fibres, containing ≥36% by weight of wool or fine animal hair
6204.3990 13	人纤制女式上衣(工业及职业用)	16				100	17	13	件/千克	B	Women's or girls' jackets and blazers of artificial fibres, industrial and career apparel
6204.3990 19	人纤制其他女式上衣	16				100	17	13	件/千克	B	Women's or girls' jackets and blazers, of artificial fibres
6204.3990 91	其他材料制女式上衣(棉限内)	16				100	17	13	件/千克	B	Women's or girls' jackets and blazers of other textile materials, cotton within limitations
6204.3990 92	其他材料制女式上衣(毛限内)	16				100	17	13	件/千克	B	Women's or girls' jackets and blazers of other textile materials, wool within limitations
6204.3990 93	其他材料制女式上衣(化纤限内)	16				100	17	13	件/千克	B	Women's or girls' jackets and blazers of other textile materials, man-made fibres within limitations
6204.3990 99	其他材料制女式上衣	16				100	17	13	件/千克	B	Women's or girls' jackets and blazers of other textile materials
	-连衣裙:										-Dresses:
6204.4100	--羊毛或动物细毛制	16	12	11.7	0	130	17	13	件/千克	5B	--Of wool or fine animal hair
6204.4200	--棉制	16	T3		0	90	17	13	件/千克	5B	--Of cotton
6204.4300	--合成纤维制	17.5	T3	12.3	0	130	17	13	件/千克		--Of synthetic fibres
6204.4300 10	合成纤维制女式连衣裙(含羊毛或动物细毛≥36%)	17.5				130	17	13	件/千克	5B	Women's or girls' dresses of synthetic fibres, containing ≥36% by weight of wool or fine animal hair
6204.4300 90	合成纤维制其他女式连衣裙	17.5				130	17	13	件/千克	5B	Other women's or girls' dresses of synthetic fibres

税则号列 Tariff Item.	货品名称	最惠国(%) MFN	协定(%) 东盟 CA	中巴 CP	CT 中智 CC	普通 Gen	增值税率 VAT	出口退税 ED	计量单位 Unit	监管条件 SC	Article Description
6204.4400	--人造纤维制	16	12	11.7	0	130	17	13	件/千克		--Of artificial fibres
6204.4400 10	人造纤维制女式连衣裙(含羊毛或动物细毛≥36%)	16				130	17	13	件/千克	5	Women's or girls' dresses of artificial fibres, containing ≥36% by weight of wool or fine animal hair
6204.4400 90	人造纤维制其他女式连衣裙	16				130	17	13	件/千克	5	Other women's or girls' dresses of artificial fibres
	--其他纺织材料制:										--Of other textile materials:
6204.4910	---丝及绢丝制	16	T3	11.7	0	130	17	13	件/千克		---Of silk or silk waste
6204.4910 10	丝制女式连衣裙(含丝及绢丝70%及以上)	16				130	17	13	件/千克	B	Women's or girls' dresses of silk, containing≥70% by weight of silk or silk waste
6204.4910 90	丝制其他女式连衣裙(含丝及绢丝70%以下)	16				130	17	13	件/千克	B	Other women's or girls' dresses of silk, containing <70% by weight of silk or silk waste
6204.4990	---其他	16	T3	11.7	0	100	17	13	件/千克		---Other
6204.4990 91	其他材料制女式连衣裙(棉限内)	16				100	17	13	件/千克		Women's or girls' dresses of other textile materials, cotton within limitations
6204.4990 92	其他材料制女式连衣裙(毛限内)	16				100	17	13	件/千克		Women's or girls' dresses of other textile materials, wool within limitations
6204.4990 93	其他材料制女式连衣裙(化纤限内)	16				100	17	13	件/千克		Women's or girls' dresses of other textile materials, man-made fibres within limitations
6204.4990 99	其他材料制其他女式连衣裙	16				100	17	13	件/千克		Women's or girls' dresses of other textile materials
	-裙子及裙裤:										-Skirts and divided skirts:
6204.5100	--羊毛或动物细毛制	14	8	9.3	0	130	17	13	件/千克	B	--Of wool or fine animal hair
6204.5200	--棉制	14	T3		0	90	17	13	件/千克	B	--Of cotton
6204.5300	--合成纤维制	16	T3	11.7	0	130	17	13	件/千克		--Of synthetic fibres
6204.5300 10	合成纤维制女式裙子及裙裤(含羊毛或动物细毛≥36%)	16				130	17	13	件/千克	B	Women's or girls' skirts and divided skirts, of synthetic fibres, containing≥36% by weight of wool or fine animal hair
6204.5300 90	合成纤维制其他女式裙子及裙裤	16				130	17	13	件/千克	B	Women's or girls' skirts and divided skirts, of synthetic fibres
	--其他纺织材料制:										--Of other textile materials
6204.5910	---丝及绢丝制	14	8	9.3	0	130	17	13	件/千克		---Of silk or silk waste
6204.5910 10	丝制女式裙子及裙裤(含丝70%及以上)	14				130	17	13	件/千克	B	Women's or girls' skirts and divided skirts, containing≥70% by weight of silk
6204.5910 90	其他丝制女式裙子及裙裤(含丝70%以下)	14				130	17	13	件/千克	B	Women's or girls' skirts and divided skirts, containing <70% by weight of silk
6204.5990	---其他	14	8	9.3	0	100	17	13	件/千克		---Other
6204.5990 11	人造纤维制女式裙子及裙裤(含羊毛或动物细毛36%及以上)	14				100	17	13	件/千克		Women's or girls' skirts and divided skirts, of artificial fibres, containing≥36% by weight of wool or fine animal hair
6204.5990 19	人造纤维制其他女式裙子及裙裤	14				100	17	13	件/千克		Women's or girls' skirts and divided skirts, of artificial fibres

税则号列 Tariff Item.	货品名称	最惠国(%) MFN	协定(%) CT 东盟 CA	中巴 CP	中智 CC	普通 Gen	增值税率 VAT	出口退税 ED	计量单位 Unit	监管条件 SC	Article Description
6204.5990 91	其他材料制女式裙子及裙裤(棉限内)	14				100	17	13	件/千克		Women's or girls' skirts and divided skirts of other textile materials, cotton within limitations
6204.5990 92	其他材料制女式裙子及裙裤(毛限内)	14				100	17	13	件/千克		Women's or girls' skirts and divided skirts of other textile materials, wool within limitations
6204.5990 93	其他材料制女式裙子及裙裤(化纤限内)	14				100	17	13	件/千克		Women's or girls' skirts and divided skirts of other textile materials, man-made fibres within limitations
6204.5990 99	其他材料制其他女式裙子及裙裤	14				100	17	13	件/千克		Women's or girls' skirts and divided skirts of other textile materials
	-长裤、护胸背带工装裤、马裤及短裤:										-Trousers, bib and brace overalls, breeches and shorts:
6204.6100	--羊毛或动物细毛制	16	12	11.7	0	130	17	13	条/千克		--Of wool or fine animal hair
6204.6100 10	毛制女式护胸背带工装裤及短裤(带防寒衬里)	16				130	17	13	条/千克	B	Women's or girls' bib and brace overalls, with thermal lining, of wool or fine animal hair
6204.6100 90	毛制女式长裤、马裤	16				130	17	13	条/千克	5B	Women's or girls' trousers, breeches, of wool or fine animal hair
6204.6200	--棉制	16	T3	14.4	0	90	17	13	条/千克		--Of cotton
6204.6200 10	棉制女式护胸背带工装裤	16				90	17	13	条/千克	B	Women's or girls' bib and brace overalls of cotton
6204.6200 21	棉制女式长裤、马裤(羽绒和水禽毛≥15%且含绒率≥35%,或含羽绒≥10%)	16				90	17	13	条/千克	5B	Women's or girls' trousers, breeches of cotton, containing ≥15% by weight of down or feathers and water fowl, down content rate ≥ 35% or containing ≥ 10% by weight of down or feathers
6204.6200 22	棉制女式长裤、马裤(游戏装)	16				90	17	13	条/千克	5B	Women's trousers, breeches, of cotton (playsuit)
6204.6200 29	其他棉制女式长裤、马裤	16				90	17	13	条/千克	5B	Women's or girls' trousers, breeches of cotton
6204.6200 91	棉制女式短裤(羽绒和水禽毛≥15%且含绒率≥35%,或含羽绒≥10%)	16				90	17	13	条/千克	B	Women's or girls' shorts of cotton, containing ≥ 15% by weight of down or feathers and water fowl, down content rate ≥ 35% or containing ≥ 10% by weight of down or feathers
6204.6200 92	棉制女式短裤(游戏装)	16				90	17	13	条/千克	B	Girls' shorts of cotton(playsuit)
6204.6200 99	其他棉制女式短裤	16				90	17	13	条/千克	5B	Other women's shorts of cotton, including girls' No. 7 ~ No. 16
6204.6300	--合成纤维制	17.5	T3	12.3	0	130	17	13	条/千克		--Of synthetic fibres
6204.6300 10	合纤制女式护胸背带工装裤	17.5				130	17	13	条/千克	B	Women's or girls' bib and brace overalls
6204.6300 21	合纤女式长裤、马裤(羽绒和水禽毛≥15%且含绒率≥35%,或含羽绒≥10%)	17.5				130	17	13	条/千克	5B	Women's or girls' trousers, breeches, containing≥15% by weight of down or feathers and water fowl, down content rate ≥ 35% or containing ≥ 10% by weight of down or feathers, of synthetic fibres

税则号列 Tariff Item.	货 品 名 称	最惠国 (%) MFN	协定(%) CT			普通 Gen	增值税率 VAT	出口退税 ED	计量单位 Unit	监管条件 SC	Article Description
			东盟 CA	中巴 CP	中智 CC						
6204.6300 22	合纤制其他女式长裤、马裤(含羊毛或动物细毛36%及以上)	17.5				130	17	13	条/千克	5B	Women's or girls' trousers, breeches, containing≥36% by weight of wool or fine animal hair, of synthetic fibres
6204.6300 23	合纤制女式长裤、马裤(游戏装)	17.5				130	17	13	条/千克	5B	Women's or girl's trousers, breeches, of synthetic ibres(playsuit)
6204.6300 24	合纤制女式长裤、马裤(滑雪裤除外)	17.5				130	17	13	条/千克	5B	Women's or girl's trousers, breeches, of synthetic ibres(other than ski pants)
6204.6300 29	合纤制女式其他长裤、马裤	17.5				130	17	13	条/千克	5B	Other women's or girls' trousers, breeches, of synthetic fibres
6204.6300 91	合纤制女式短裤(羽绒和水禽毛≥15%且含绒率≥35%,或含羽绒≥10%)	17.5				130	17	13	条/千克	B	Women's or girls' shorts, containing≥15% by weight of down or feathers and water fowl, down content rate≥35% or containing≥10% by weight of down or feathers, of synthetic fibres
6204.6300 92	合纤制女式短裤(游戏装)	17.5				130	17	13	条/千克	B	Other wonen's shorts of synthetic fibres
6204.6300 99	其他合纤制女短裤	17.5				130	17	13	条/千克	5B	Other women's or girls' trousers short, of synthefic fibres
6204.6900	--其他纺织材料制	16	T3	12	0	100	17	13	条/千克		--Of other textile materials
6204.6900 11	人纤制女式护胸背带工装裤	16				100	17	13	条/千克	B	Women's bib and brace overalls of artificial fibres
6204.6900 12	人纤制女式长裤、马裤(含羊毛或动物细毛36%及以上)	16				100	17	13	条/千克	5B	Women's trousers, breeches of artificial fibres(containing≥36% by weight of wool or fine animal hair)
6204.6900 13	人纤制女式短裤(含羊毛或动物细毛36%及以上)	16				100	17	13	条/千克	B	Wonmen's trousers, shorts, of artificial fibres(containing≥36% by weight of wool or fine animal hair)
6204.6900 14	人纤制女式长裤、马裤(游戏装)	16				100	17	13	条/千克	5B	Women's or girls' trousers, breeches, shorts, of artificial fibres, playsuit
6204.6900 15	人纤制女式短裤(游戏装)	16				100	17	13	条/千克	B	Wonmen's trousers, shorts, of artificial fibres(playsuit)
6204.6900 16	人纤制女式其他长裤、马裤	16				100	17	13	条/千克	5B	Other wonmen's trousers, breeches of artificial fibres
6204.6900 17	人纤制女式其他短裤	16				100	17	13	条/千克	5B	Women's or girl's other tuousers, short, of artificial fibres
6204.6900 21	丝制女式护胸背带工装裤	16				100	17	13	条/千克	B	Women's or girls' bib and brace overalls, of silk
6204.6900 25	丝制女式其他长裤、马裤、短裤(含丝70%及以上)	16				100	17	13	条/千克	B	Women's or girls' Other trousers, breeches, shorts, of silk, containing≥70% by weight of silk
6204.6900 26	丝制女式长裤、马裤、短裤(含丝70%及以下的游戏装)	16				100	17	13	条/千克	B	Women's or girls' trousers、breeches、shorts, of silk, containing ≤ 70% by weight of silk (playsuit)
6204.6900 29	丝制女式其他长裤、马裤、短裤(含丝70%以下)	16				100	17	13	条/千克	5B	Women's or girls' other trousers, breeches, shorts, of silk, containing < 70% by weight of silk
6204.6900 91	其他材料制女式护胸背带工装裤	16				100	17	13	条/千克	B	Women's or girls' bib and brace overalls of other textile materials

税则号列 Tariff Item.	货品名称	最惠国(%) MFN	协定(%) CT 东盟 CA	中巴 CP	中智 CC	普通 Gen	增值税率 VAT	出口退税 ED	计量单位 Unit	监管条件 SC	Article Description
6204.6900 92	其他材料制女式长裤、马裤、短裤(游戏装)	16				100	17	13	条/千克	B	Women's or girls' trousers, breeches, shorts, playsuit of other textile materials
6204.6900 93	其他材料制女式长裤、马裤、短裤(棉限内)	16				100	17	13	条/千克	5B	Women's or girls' trousers, breeches, shorts, cotton within limitations, of other textile materials
6204.6900 94	其他材料制女式长裤、马裤、短裤(羊毛限内)	16				100	17	13	条/千克	B	Trousers, breeches, shorts, wool within limitations
6204.6900 95	其他材料制女式长裤、马裤、短裤(化纤限内)	16				100	17	13	条/千克	5B	Wonmen ' s trousers, breeches, shorts, man - made fibres, of man - made fibres
6204.6900 99	其他材料制其他女式长、马、短裤	16				100	17	13	条/千克	5B	Women's or girls' other trousers, breeches, shorts, of other textile materials
62.05	**男衬衫:**										**Men's or boys' shirts:**
6205.2000	-棉制	16	T3	8	0	90	17	13	件/千克		-Of cotton
6205.2000 10	不带特制领的棉制男成人衬衫(含男童8-18号衬衫)	16				90	17	13	件/千克	5B	Men's shirts and boys' No. 8 ~ No. 18, having neither made-to-order collar, of cotton
6205.2000 91	其他棉制男童游戏套装衬衫(不包括长衬衫)	16				90	17	13	件/千克	B	Boy's shirts, playsuit, other than long shirts, of cotton
6205.2000 99	其他棉制男式衬衫	16				90	17	13	件/千克	5B	Other men's or boys' shirts, of cotton
6205.3000	-化学纤维制	16	T3	11.7	0	130	17	13	件/千克		-Of man-made fibres
6205.3000 11	不带特制领的化学纤维制男式衬衫(含羊毛或动物细毛36%及以上,含男童8-18号衬衫)	16				130	17	13	件/千克	B	Men's or boys' shirts, having neither made-to-order collar, containing ≥36% by weight of wool or fine animal hair, including boys' No. 8 ~ No. 18, of man-made fibres
6205.3000 19	不带特制领的化纤制其他男童衬衫(含羊毛或动物细毛36%及以上)	16				130	17	13	件/千克	B	Boys' shirts, having neither made-to-order collar, containing ≥36% by weight of wool or fine animal hair, of man-made fibres
6205.3000 91	化学纤维制其他男成人及男童衬衫(不带特制领,男童衬衫指8-18号)	16				130	17	13	件/千克	5B	Men's or boys' shirts having neither made-to-order collar, including boys' No. 8 ~ No. 18, of man-made fibres
6205.3000 92	化学纤维制其他男童游戏套装衬衫	16				130	17	13	件/千克	B	Other boy's shirts of playsuit, of man-made fibres
6205.3000 99	化纤制其他男成人衬衫	16				130	17	13	件/千克	5B	Other men's shirts of man-made fibres
	-其他纺织材料制:										-Of other textile materials
6205.9010	---丝及绢丝制	16	T3	11.7	0	130	17	13	件/千克		---Of silk or silk waste
6205.9010 11	不带特制领的丝制非针织男式衬衫(含丝70%及以上,含男童8-18号衬衫)	16				130	17	13	件/千克	B	Men's or boys' shirts of silk, having neither made-to-ordercollar, not knitted, containing ≥ 70% by weight of silk, including boys' No. 8 ~ No. 18
6205.9010 19	丝制非针织其他男式衬衫(含丝70%及以上)	16				130	17	13	件/千克	B	Men's or boys' shirts of silk, not knitted, containing ≥ 70% by weight of silk

税则号列 Tariff Item.	货品名称	最惠国(%) MFN	协定(%) 东盟 CA	中巴 CP	CT 中智 CC	普通 Gen	增值税率 VAT	出口退税 ED	计量单位 Unit	监管条件 SC	Article Description
6205.9010 21	丝制其他非针织男式衬衫(棉限内,不带特制领的,含男童8-18号衬衫)	16				130	17	13	件/千克	5B	Men's or boys' shirts of silk, not knitted, having neither made-to-order collar, including boys' No. 8 ~ No. 18, cotton within limitations
6205.9010 29	丝制其他非针织其他男式衬衫(棉限内)	16				130	17	13	件/千克	5B	Men's or boys' shirts of silk, not knitted, cotton within limitations
6205.9010 31	丝制其他非针织男式衬衫(羊毛限内,不带特制领的,含男童8-18号衬衫)	16				130	17	13	件/千克	B	Men's or boys' shirts of silk, not knitted, having neither made-to-order collar, including boys' No. 8 ~ No. 18, wool within limitations
6205.9010 39	丝制其他非针织其他男式衬衫(羊毛限内)	16				130	17	13	件/千克	B	Men's or boys' shirts of silk, not knitted , wool within limitations
6205.9010 41	丝制非针织男式衬衫(化纤限内,不带特制领的,含男童8-18号衬衫)	16				130	17	13	件/千克	5B	Men's or boys' shirts of silk, not knitted, having neither made-to-order collar, including boys' No. 8 ~ No. 18, man-made fibres within limitations
6205.9010 49	丝制其他非针织其他男式衬衫(化纤限内)	16				130	17	13	件/千克	5B	Men's or boys' shirts of silk, not knitted , man-made fibres within limitations
6205.9010 91	未列名丝制非针织男式衬衫(含丝70%以下,不带特制领的,含男童8-18号衬衫)	16				130	17	13	件/千克	B	Men's or boys' shirts of silk, not knitted, containing < 70% by weight of silk, having neither made-to-order collar, including boys' No. 8 ~ No. 18, not elsewhere specified or included
6205.9010 99	未列名丝制非针织其他男式衬衫(含丝70%以下)	16				130	17	13	件/千克	B	Other men's or boys' shirts of silk, not knitted, containing < 70% by weight of silk, not elsewhere specified or included
6205.9020	---羊毛或动物细毛制	16	12	11.7	0	100	17	13	件/千克	B	---Of wool or fine animal hair
6205.9090	---其他	16	T3	11.7	0	100	17	13	件/千克		---Other
6205.9090 11	其他纺织材料制男式衬衫(棉限内,不带特制领的,含男童8-18号衬衫)	16				100	17	13	件/千克	5B	Men's or boys' shirts of other textile materials, having neither made-to-order collar, including boys' No. 8 ~ No. 18, cotton within limitations
6205.9090 19	其他纺织材料制其他男式衬衫(棉纤限内)	16				100	17	13	件/千克	5B	Men's or boys' shirts of other textile materials, cotton or man-made fibres within limitations
6205.9090 21	其他纺织材料制男式衬衫(羊毛限内,不带特制领的,含男童8-18号衬衫)	16				100	17	13	件/千克	B	Men's or boys' shirts of other textile materials, having neither made-to-order collar, including boys' No. 8 ~ No. 18, wool within limitations
6205.9090 29	其他纺织材料制其他男式衬衫(羊毛化纤限内)	16				100	17	13	件/千克	B	Men's or boys' shirts of other textile materials, wool or man-made fibres within limitations
6205.9090 31	其他纺织材料制男式衬衫(化纤限内,不带制特领的,含男童8-18号衬衫)	16				100	17	13	件/千克	5B	Men's or boys' shirts of other textile materials, having neither made-to-order collar, including boys' No. 8 ~ No. 18, man-made fibres within limitations

税则号列 Tariff Item.	货品名称	最惠国(%) MFN	协定(%)CT 东盟 CA	中巴 CP	中智 CC	普通 Gen	增值税率 VAT	出口退税 ED	计量单位 Unit	监管条件 SC	Article Description
6205.9090 39	其他纺织材料制其他男式衬衫(化纤限内)	16				100	17	13	件/千克	5B	Men's or boys' shirts of other textile materials, man-made fibres within limitations
6205.9090 91	未列名纺织材料制男式衬衫(不带特制领的,含男童8-18号衬衫)	16				100	17	13	件/千克	B	Men's or boys' shirts of other textile materials, having neither made-to-order collar, including boys' No. 8 ~ No. 18, not elsewhere specified or included
6205.9090 99	未列名纺织材料制其他男式衬衫	16				100	17	13	件/千克	B	Other men's or boys' shirts of other textile materials, not elsewhere specified or included
62.06	女衬衫:										**Women's or girls' blouses, shirts and shirt-blouses:**
6206.1000	-丝及绢丝制	16	12	11.7	0	130	17	13	件/千克		-Of silk or silk waste
6206.1000 11	丝及绢丝制女式衬衫(棉限内,成人及7-16号女童衬衫)	16				130	17	13	件/千克	B	Women's or girls' shirts of silk or silk waste, cotton within limitations, including girls' No. 7 ~ No. 16
6206.1000 19	丝及绢丝制其他女童衬衫(棉限内)	16				130	17	13	件/千克	B	Other girls' shirts, cotton within limitations
6206.1000 21	丝及绢丝制女式衬衫(羊毛限内,成人及7-16号女童衬衫)	16				130	17	13	件/千克	B	Women's or girls' shirts of silk or silk waste, wool within limitations, including girls' No. 7 ~ No. 16
6206.1000 29	丝及绢丝制其他女童衬衫(羊毛限内)	16				130	17	13	件/千克	B	Other girls' shirts of silk and silk waste, wool within limitations
6206.1000 31	丝及绢丝制女式衬衫(化纤限内,成人及7-16号女童衬衫)	16				130	17	13	件/千克	B	Women's or girls' shirts of silk and silk waste, including girls' No. 7 ~ No. 16, man-made fibres within limitations
6206.1000 39	丝及绢丝制其他女童衬衫(化纤限内)	16				130	17	13	件/千克	B	Other girls' shirts of silk and silk waste, man-made fibres within limitations
6206.1000 41	丝制女成人及7-16号女童衬衫(含丝70%及以上)	16				130	17	13	件/千克	B	Women's shirts of silk, containing ≥70% by weight of silk, including girls' No. 7 ~ No. 16
6206.1000 49	其他丝及绢丝制女童衬衫(含丝70%及以上)	16				130	17	13	件/千克	B	Other girls' shirts of silk and silk waste, containing≥70% by weight of silk
6206.1000 91	丝制女成人及7-16号女童衬衫(含丝70%以下)	16				130	17	13	件/千克	B	Women's shirts of silk, containing <70% by weight of silk, including girls' No. 7 ~ No. 16
6206.1000 99	其他丝及绢丝制女童衬衫(含丝70%以下)	16				130	17	13	件/千克	B	Other girls' shirts of silk and silk waste, containing <70% by weight of silk
6206.2000	-羊毛或动物细毛制	16	12	11.7	0	130	17	13	件/千克		-Of wool or fine animal hair
6206.2000 10	毛制女成人及7-16号女童衬衫	16				130	17	13	件/千克	5B	Women's shirts and girls, No. 7 ~ No. 16, of wool or fine animal hair
6206.2000 90	其他羊毛或动物细毛制女童衬衫	16				130	17	13	件/千克	5B	Other girls' shirts of wool or fine animal hair
6206.3000	-棉制	16	T3	13.6	0	90	17	13	件/千克		-Of cotton
6206.3000 10	棉制女成人及7-16号女童衬衫	16				90	17	13	件/千克	5B	Women's shirts and girls' No. 7 ~ No. 16 of cotton
6206.3000 20	棉制女童游戏套装衫(含游戏套装衬衫)	16				90	17	13	件/千克	5B	Girls' playsuit and shirt of playsuit of cotton
6206.3000 90	其他棉制女式衬衫	16				90	17	13	件/千克	5B	Other women's or girls' shirts of cotton

税则号列 Tariff Item.	货品名称	最惠国(%) MFN	协定(%) CT 东盟 CA	协定(%) CT 中巴 CP	协定(%) CT 中智 CC	普通 Gen	增值税率 VAT	出口退税 ED	计量单位 Unit	监管条件 SC	Article Description
6206. 4000	-化学纤维制	17. 5	T3	12. 3	0	130	17	13	件/千克		-Of man-made fibres
6206. 4000 11	化学纤维制女成人及女童衬衫(含羊毛或动物细毛36%及以上,成人及7－16号女童衬衫)	17. 5				130	17	13	件/千克	5B	Women's shirts and girls' No. 7 ~ No. 16, containing≥36% by weight of wool or fine animal hair, of man-made fibres
6206. 4000 19	化学纤维制女成人及女童衬衫(含羊毛或动物细毛36%及以上)	17. 5				130	17	13	件/千克	5B	Other women's or girls' shirts, containing≥36% by weight of wool or fine animal hair, of man-made fibres
6206. 4000 20	化纤制女成人及7－16号女童衬衫	17. 5				130	17	13	件/千克	5B	Women's shirts and girls' No. 7 ~ No. 16, of man-made fibres
6206. 4000 30	化学纤维制女童游戏套装衫	17. 5				130	17	13	件/千克	5B	Girls' shirts, playsuit, of man-made fibres
6206. 4000 90	其他化学纤维制女式衬衫	17. 5				130	17	13	件/千克	5B	Other women's or girls' shirts of man-made fibres
6206. 9000	-其他纺织材料制	16	T3	11. 7	0	100	17	13	件/千克		-Of other textile materials
6206. 9000 10	其他纺织材料制女式衬衫(棉限内)	16				100	17	13	件/千克	B	Women's or girls' shirts of other textile materials cotton within limitations
6206. 9000 20	其他纺织材料制女式衬衫(羊毛限内)	16				100	17	13	件/千克	B	Women's or girls' shirts of other textile materials, wool within limitations
6206. 9000 30	其他纺织材料制女式衬衫(化纤限内)	16				100	17	13	件/千克	B	Women's or girls' shirts of other textile materials, man-made fibres within limitations
6206. 9000 91	其他纺织材料制女成人及女童衬衫(女童指7－16号)	16				100	17	13	件/千克	B	Women's shirts and girls' No. 7 ~ No. 16, of other textile materials
6206. 9000 99	其他纺织材料制女成人及女童衬衫	16				100	17	13	件/千克	B	Other women's or girls' shirts of other textile materials
62. 07	**男式背心及其他内衣、内裤、三角裤、长睡衣、睡衣裤、浴衣、晨衣及类似品:**										**Men's or boys' singlets and other vests, underpants, briefs, nightshirts, pyjamas, bathrobes, dressing gowns and similar articles:**
	-内裤及三角裤:										-Underpants and briefs:
6207. 1100	--棉制	14	T3	10. 3	0	90	17	13	件/千克	5	--Of cotton
	--其他纺织材料制:										--Of other textile materials:
6207. 1910	---丝及绢丝制	14	T3		0	130	17	13	件/千克		---Of silk or silk waste
6207. 1910 10	含丝70%及以上男式内裤及三角裤	14				130	17	13	件/千克		Men's or boys' underpants and briefs, containing≥70% by weight of silk
6207. 1910 90	含丝70%以下男式内裤及三角裤	14				130	17	13	件/千克		Men's or boys' underpants and briefs, containing <70% by weight of silk
6207. 1920	---化学纤维制	16	T3		0	130	17	13	件/千克	5	---Of man-made fibres
6207. 1990	---其他	14	T3		0	100	17	13	件/千克		---Other
6207. 1990 10	毛制男式内裤及三角裤	14				100	17	13	件/千克		Men's or boys' underpants and briefs of wool or fine animal hair
6207. 1990 90	其他材料制男式内裤及三角裤	14				100	17	13	件/千克		Men's or boys' underpants and briefs of other textile materials
	-长睡衣及睡衣裤:										-Nightshirts and pyjamas:
6207. 2100	--棉制	14	T3		0	90	17	13	件/千克		--Of cotton
6207. 2200	--化学纤维制	16	T3		0	130	17	13	件/千克	B	--Of man-made fibres
	--其他纺织材料制:										--Of other textile materials:
6207. 2910	---丝及绢丝制	14	T3		0	130	17	13	件/千克		---Of silk or silk waste

税则号列 Tariff Item.	货品名称	最惠国(%) MFN	协定(%) CT 东盟 CA	中巴 CP	中智 CC	普通 Gen	增值税率 VAT	出口退税 ED	计量单位 Unit	监管条件 SC	Article Description
6207.2910 11	含丝70%及以上男式长睡衣/睡衣裤(含8-18号男童长睡衣/睡衣裤)	14				130	17	13	件/千克	B	Men's nightshirts and pyjamas containing≥70% by weight of silk, including boys' No. 8 ~ No. 18
6207.2910 19	含丝70%以下男式长睡衣/睡衣裤(含8-18号男童长睡衣/睡衣裤)	14				130	17	13	件/千克	B	Men's or boys' nightshirts and pyjamas, containing < 70% by weight of silk, including boys' No. 8 ~ No. 18
6207.2910 91	其他含丝≥70%男童长睡衣/睡衣裤	14				130	17	13	件/千克	B	Other boys' nightshirts and pyjamas, containing≥70% by weight of silk
6207.2910 99	其他含丝<70%男童长睡衣/睡衣裤	14				130	17	13	件/千克	B	Other boys' nightshirts and pyjamas, containing<70% by weight of silk
6207.2990	---其他	14	T3		0	100	17	13	件/千克		---Other
6207.2990 10	毛制男式长睡衣及睡衣裤	14				100	17	13	件/千克		Men's or boys' nightshirts and pyjamas, of wool or fine animal hair
6207.2990 91	其他材料制男式长睡衣及睡衣裤(含8-18号男童长睡衣及睡衣裤)	14				100	17	13	件/千克		Men's or boys' nightshirts and pyjamas, of other textile materials, including boys' No. 8 ~ No. 18
6207.2990 99	其他材料制男童长睡衣及睡衣裤	14				100	17	13	件/千克		Boys' nightshirts and pyjamas of other textile materials
	-其他:										-Other:
6207.9100	--棉制	14	8		0	90	17	13	件/千克		--Of cotton
6207.9100 11	棉制男式内衣式背心	14				90	17	13	件/千克	5B	Men's or boys' singlets, vest style, of cotton
6207.9100 12	棉制男式非内衣式背心(男成人及8-18号男童背心)	14				90	17	13	件/千克	5B	Men's and boys' No. 8 ~ No. 18 singlets, of cotton, non-vest style
6207.9100 19	棉制其他男童非内衣式背心	14				90	17	13	件/千克	5B	Other boy's singlets of cotton, non-vests style
6207.9100 91	棉制男式浴衣、晨衣及类似品	14				90	17	13	件/千克	B	Men's or boys' bathrobes, dressing gowns and similar articles of cotton
6207.9100 92	棉制男式睡衣、睡裤(男成人及8-18号男童背心)	14				90	17	13	件/千克	B	Men's or boys' nightshirts and pyjamas, men's and boy's No. 8 ~ No. 18 singlets, of cotton
6207.9100 99	棉制男式其他内衣(男成人及8-18号男童背心)	14				90	17	13	件/千克	5B	Other men's or boys' vests, men's and boys' No. 8 ~ No. 18 singlets, of cotton
	--其他纺织材料制:										--Of other textile materials:
6207.9910	---丝及绢丝制	14	8	12.6	0	130	17	13	件/千克		---Of silk or silk waste
6207.9910 11	丝制男式内衣式背心(含丝70%及以上)	14				130	17	13	件/千克	B	Men's or boys' singlets of silk, vest style, containing ≥ 70% by weight of silk
6207.9910 19	丝制其他男式内衣式背心	14				130	17	13	件/千克	B	Other men's or boys' singlets of sil, vest style
6207.9910 21	丝制男式非内衣式背心(含丝70%及以上)	14				130	17	13	件/千克	B	Men's or boys' singlets of silk, non-vest style, containing≥70% by weight of silk
6207.9910 29	丝制其他男式非内衣式背心	14				130	17	13	件/千克	B	Other men's or boys' singlets of silk, non-vests style
6207.9910 91	丝制男睡衣,浴衣,晨衣及类似品(含丝70%及以上)	14				130	17	13	件/千克	B	Men's or boys' bathrobes, dressing gowns and similar articles, containing ≥70% by weight of silk

税则号列 Tariff Item.	货 品 名 称	最惠国(%) MFN	协定(%) CT 东盟 CA	协定(%) CT 中巴 CP	协定(%) CT 中智 CC	普通 Gen	增值税率 VAT	出口退税 ED	计量单位 Unit	监管条件 SC	Article Description
6207.9910 99	丝制其他男睡衣,浴衣,晨衣(含类似品)	14				130	17	13	件/千克	B	Other men's or boys' pyjamas, bathrobes, dressing gowns and similar articles, of silk
6207.9920	---化学纤维制	16	8		0	130	17	13	件/千克		---Of man-made fibres
6207.9920 11	化学纤维制男式内衣式背心	16				130	17	13	件/千克	5B	Men's or boys' singlets, vest style, of man-made fibres
6207.9920 12	化学纤维制男式非内衣式背心(男成人及8-18号男童背心)	16				130	17	13	件/千克	5B	Men's or boys' singlets, non-vests style, men's and boys' No. 8 ~ No. 18 singlets, of man-made fibres
6207.9920 19	化学纤维制其他男式非内衣式背心	16				130	17	13	件/千克	5B	Other men's or boys' singlets, non-vests style, of man-made fibres
6207.9920 21	化纤制男式浴衣、晨衣(含羊毛或动物细毛36%及以上,含类似品)	16				130	17	13	件/千克	B	Men's or boys' bathrobes, dressing gowns and similar articles, containing ≥36% by weight of wool or fine animal hair, of man-made fibres
6207.9920 29	其他化纤制男浴衣、晨衣(含类似品)	16				130	17	13	件/千克	B	Other men's or boys' bathrobes, dressing gowns and similar articles, of man-made fibres
6207.9920 91	化纤制男睡衣、睡裤(含类似品)	16				130	17	13	件/千克	B	Men's or boys' nightshirts, pyjamas and similar articles, of man-made fibres
6207.9920 99	化纤制男式其他内衣(含类似品)	16				130	17	13	件/千克	B	Other men's or boys' vest and similar articles of man-made fibres
6207.9990	---其他	14	8	12.6	0	100	17	13	件/千克		---Other
6207.9990 11	毛制男式内衣式背心	14				100	17	13	件/千克		Men's or boys' singlets, vests style, of wool or fine animal hair
6207.9990 12	毛制男式非内衣式背心(男成人及8-18号男童背心)	14				100	17	13	件/千克		Men's or boys' singlets, non-vests style, (men's and boys' No. 8 ~ No. 18), of wool or fine animal hair
6207.9990 13	毛制其他男式非内衣式背心	14				100	17	13	件/千克		Other men's or boys' singlets, non-vests style, of wool or fine animal hair
6207.9990 19	毛制男睡衣,浴衣,晨衣及类似品	14				100	17	13	件/千克		Men's or boys' bathrobes, dressing gowns and similar articles, of wool or fine animal hair
6207.9990 91	其他材料制男式内衣式背心	14				100	17	13	件/千克		Men's or boys' singlets, vests style, of other textile materials
6207.9990 92	其他材料制男式非内衣式背心	14				100	17	13	件/千克		Men's or boys' singlets, non-vests style, of other textile materials
6207.9990 99	其他材料制男睡衣、浴衣、晨衣(含类似品)	14				100	17	13	件/千克		Other men's or boys' bathrobes, dressing gowns and similar articles, of other textile materials
62.08	**女式背心及其他内衣、长衬裙、衬裙、三角裤、短衬裤、睡衣、睡衣裤、浴衣、晨衣及类似品:**										**Women's or girls' singlets and other vests, slips, petticoats, briefs, panties, night-dresses, pyjamas, nègligès, bathrobes, dressing gowns and similar articles:**
	-长衬裙及衬裙:										-Slips and petticoats:
6208.1100	--化学纤维制	16	8		0	130	17	13	件/千克	5	--Of man-made fibres
	--其他纺织材料制:										--Of other textile materials:
6208.1910	---丝及绢丝制	14	T3		0	130	17	13	件/千克		---Of silk or silk waste

税则号列 Tariff Item.	货品名称	最惠国(%) MFN	协定(%)CT 东盟 CA	中巴 CP	中智 CC	普通 Gen	增值税率 VAT	出口退税 ED	计量单位 Unit	监管条件 SC	Article Description
6208.1910 11	丝制女式长衬裙及衬裙(含7-16号女童长衬裙及衬裙,含丝70%及以上)	14				130	17	13	件/千克		Women's or girls' slips and petticoats of silk, including girls' No. 7 ~ No. 16, containing≥70% by weight of silk
6208.1910 19	丝制其他女式长衬裙及衬裙(含7-16号女童长衬裙及衬裙,含丝70%以下)	14				130	17	13	件/千克		Other women's or girls' slips and petticoats of silk, including girls' No. 7 ~ No. 16, containing<70% by weight of silk
6208.1910 91	丝制女童长衬裙及衬裙(含丝70%及以上)	14				130	17	13	件/千克		Girls' slips and petticoats of silk, containing≥70% by weight of silk
6208.1910 99	丝制其他女童长衬裙及衬裙(含丝70%以下)	14				130	17	13	件/千克		Girls' slips and petticoats of silk, containing<70% by weight of silk
6208.1920	---棉制	14	T3		0	90	17	13	件/千克	5	---Of cotton
6208.1990	---其他	14	T3		0	100	17	13	件/千克		---Other
6208.1990 10	毛制女式长衬裙及衬裙	14				100	17	13	件/千克		Women's or girls' slips and petticoats of wool or fine animal hair
6208.1990 90	其他材料制女式长衬裙及衬裙	14				100	17	13	件/千克		Women's or girls' slips and petticoats of other textile materials
	-睡衣及睡衣裤:										-Nightdresses and pyjamas:
6208.2100	--棉制	14	T3	10.3	0	90	17	13	件/千克		--Of cotton
6208.2200	--化学纤维制	16	T3		0	130	17	13	件/千克	B	--Of man-made fibres
	--其他纺织材料制:										--Of other textile materials:
6208.2910	---丝及绢丝制	14	8		0	130	17	13	件/千克		---Of silk or silk waste
6208.2910 10	丝及绢丝≥70%女式睡衣及睡衣裤	14				130	17	13	件/千克	B	Women's or girls' nightdresses and pyjamas, containing≥70% by weight of silk or silk waste
6208.2910 90	丝及绢丝<70%女式睡衣及睡衣裤	14				130	17	13	件/千克	B	Women's or girls' nightdresses and pyjamas, containing<70% by weight of silk or silk waste
6208.2990	---其他	14	8		0	100	17	13	件/千克		---Other
6208.2990 10	毛制女式睡衣及睡衣裤	14				100	17	13	件/千克		Women's or girls' nightdresses and pyjamas, of wool or fine animal hair
6208.2990 90	其他材料制女式睡衣及睡衣裤	14				100	17	13	件/千克		Women's or girls' nightdresses and pyjamas of other textile materials
	-其他:										-Other:
6208.9100	--棉制	14	T3		0	90	17	13	件/千克		--Of cotton
6208.9100 10	棉制女式内衣式背心、三角裤等(包括短衬裤)	14				90	17	13	件/千克	5B	Women's or girls' singlets, briefs, pantics, vest style, of cotton
6208.9100 21	棉制女式非内衣式背心(女成人及7-16号女童背心)	14				90	17	13	件/千克	5B	Women's or girls' singlets, non-vest style, (women's and girls No. 7 ~ No. 16) of cotton
6208.9100 29	棉制其他女式非内衣式背心	14				90	17	13	件/千克	5B	Other women's or girls' singlets, non-vest style, of cotton
6208.9100 90	棉制女式浴衣、晨衣及类似品	14				90	17	13	件/千克	B	Women's or girls' bathrobes, dressing gowns and similar articles, of cotton
6208.9200	--化学纤维制	16	T3	15	0	130	17	13	件/千克		--Of man-made fibres
6208.9200 10	化纤制女式内衣式背心、三角裤(含短衬裤)	16				130	17	13	件/千克	5B	Women's or girls' singlets, vest style, briefs, pantics, of man-made fibres

税则号列 Tariff Item.	货品名称	最惠国(%) MFN	协定(%) CT 东盟 CA	中巴 CP	中智 CC	普通 Gen	增值税率 VAT	出口退税 ED	计量单位 Unit	监管条件 SC	Article Description
6208.9200 21	化纤制女式非内衣式背心(女成人及7-16号女童背心)	16				130	17	13	件/千克	5B	Women's or girls' singlets, non-vest style (women's and girls No. 7 ~ No. 16), of man-made fibres
6208.9200 29	化纤制其他女式非内衣式背心	16				130	17	13	件/千克	5B	Other women's or girls' singlets, non-vest style, of man-made fibres
6208.9200 90	化纤制女式浴衣、晨衣及类似品	16				130	17	13	件/千克	B	Women's or girls' bathrobes, dressing gowns and similar articles, of man-made fibres
	--其他纺织材料制:										--Of other textile materials:
6208.9910	---丝及绢丝制	14	8	12.6	0	130	17	13	件/千克		---Of silk or silk waste
6208.9910 11	丝制女内衣式背心、三角裤等(含丝及绢丝≥70%,包括短衬裤)	14				130	17	13	件/千克	B	Women's or girls' singlets, briefs, pantics, vest style, containing≥70% by weight of silk or silk waste
6208.9910 19	丝制女内衣式背心、三角裤等(含丝及绢丝<70%,包括短衬裤)	14				130	17	13	件/千克	B	Women's or girls' singlets, briefs, pantics, of silk, vest style, containing <70% by weight of silk or silk waste
6208.9910 21	丝制女式非内衣式背心(含丝及绢丝70%及以上)	14				130	17	13	件/千克	B	Women's or girls' singlets of silk, non-vest style, containing≥70% by weight of silk or silk waste
6208.9910 29	丝制女式非内衣式背心(含丝70%以下)	14				130	17	13	件/千克	B	Women's or girls' singlets of silk, non-vest style, containing<70% by weight of silk
6208.9910 91	丝制女式浴衣、晨衣及类似品(含丝及绢丝70%以上)	14				130	17	13	件/千克	B	Women's or girls' bathrobes, dressing gowns and similar articles of silk, containing≥70% by weight of silk or silk waste
6208.9910 99	丝制女式浴衣、晨衣及类似品(含丝及绢丝70%及以下)	14				130	17	13	件/千克	B	Women's or girls' bathrobes, dressing gowns and similar articles, of silk, containing<70% by weight of silk or silk waste
6208.9990	---其他	14	8	12.6	0	100	17	13	件/千克		---Other
6208.9990 11	毛制女式内衣式背心、三角裤毛等(包括短衬裤)	14				100	17	13	件/千克		Women's or girls' singlets, briefs, pantics, vest style, of wool or fine animal hair
6208.9990 12	毛制女式非内衣式背心(女成人及7-16号女童背心)	14				100	17	13	件/千克		Women's and girls' No. 7 - No. 16 singlets, non-vest style, of wool or fine animal hair
6208.9990 13	毛制其他女式非内衣式背心	14				100	17	13	件/千克		Other women's or girls' singlets, non-vest style, of wool or fine animal hair
6208.9990 19	毛制女式浴衣、晨衣及类似品	14				100	17	13	件/千克		Women's or girls' bathrobes, dressing gowns and similar articles, of wool or fine animal hair
6208.9990 91	其他材料制女式内衣式背心等(含三角裤、短衬裤)	14				100	17	13	件/千克		Women's or girls' singlets, vest style, briefs, pantics, of other textile materials
6208.9990 92	其他材料制女式非内衣式背心	14				100	17	13	件/千克		Women's or girls' singlets, non-vest style, of other textile materials
6208.9990 99	其他材料制女式浴衣、晨衣(含类似品)	14				100	17	13	件/千克		Women's or girls' bathrobes, dressing gowns and similar articles, of other textile materials

税则号列 Tariff Item.	货品名称	最惠国(%) MFN	协定(%) CT 东盟 CA	中巴 CP	中智 CC	普通 Gen	增值税率 VAT	出口退税 ED	计量单位 Unit	监管条件 SC	Article Description
62.09	**婴儿服装及衣着附件:**										**Babies' garments and clothing accessories:**
	-棉制:										-Of cotton:
6209.2010	---尿布	14	T3		0	80	17	13	千克		---Babies' napkins(diapers)
6209.2090	---其他	14	T3		0	90	17	13	千克		---Other
6209.2090 10	棉制婴儿手套、袜子(含分指、连指及露指手套、长袜、短袜及其他袜)	14				90	17	13	千克		Babies' gloves, mittens, mitts, stockings, socks and similar hosiery, of cotton
6209.2090 20	棉制婴儿外衣、雨衣、滑雪装(包括夹克类似服装)	14				90	17	13	千克		Babies' coats, raincoats, ski-suits jackets and similar articles, of cotton
6209.2090 30	棉制婴儿其他服装(含裤子、衬衫、裙子、睡衣、内衣等)	14				90	17	13	千克		Babies' other garments of cotton, including trousers, shirt, skirt, night clothes, underwear
6209.2090 90	棉制婴儿衣着附件	14				90	17	13	千克		Babies' clothing accessories of cotton
6209.3000	-合成纤维制	16	T3		0	130	17	13	千克		-Of synthetic fibres
6209.3000 10	合成纤维制婴儿手套、袜子(含分指、连指及露指手套,长袜、短袜及其他袜)	16				130	17	13	千克		Babies' gloves, mittens, mitts, stockings, socks and similar hosiery, of synthetic fibres
6209.3000 20	合成纤维婴儿外衣、雨衣、滑雪装(包括夹克类似服装)	16				130	17	13	千克		Babies' coats, raincoats, ski-suits, jackets and similar articles, of synthetic fibres
6209.3000 30	合成纤维制婴儿其他服装(含裤子、衬衫、裙子、睡衣、内衣等)	16				130	17	13	千克		Babies' other garments, including trousers, shirt, skirt, night clothes, underwear, of synthetic fibres
6209.3000 90	合成纤维制婴儿衣着附件	16				130	17	13	千克		Babies' clothing accessories, of synthetic fibres
	-其他纺织材料制:										-Of other textile materials
6209.9010	---羊毛或动物细毛制	14	8		0	130	17	13	千克		---Of wool or fine animal hair
6209.9090	---其他纺织材料制	14	8		0	100	17	13	千克		---Of other texeile materials
62.10	**用税目56.02、56.03、59.03、59.06或59.07的织物制成的服装:**										**Garments, made up of fabrics of heading No. 56.02, 56.03, 59.03, 59.06 or 59.07:**
	-用税目56.02或56.03的织物制成的服装:										-Garments, made up of fabrics of heading No. 56.02 or 56.03:
6210.1010	---羊毛或动物细毛制	16	12	11.7	0	130	17	13	件/千克		---Garments, made up of wool or fine animal hair
6210.1010 10	毛制纸衬背或覆盖的无纺布服装(羊毛或动物细毛制,包括毡呢或无纺织物制服装)	16				130	17	13	件/千克		Of nonwovens or felt, paper backed or covered, of wool or fine animal hair
6210.1010 20	毛制一次性或医疗用无纺织物服装(羊毛或动物细毛制)	16				130	17	13	件/千克		Garments, made up of nonwovens, throw away or for medical use, of wool or fine animal hair
6210.1010 90	毛制其他毡呢或无纺织物服装(羊毛或动物细毛制)	16				130	17	13	件/千克		Garments, made up of felt or nonwovens, of wool or fine animal hair
6210.1020	---棉或麻制	16	8		0	90	17	13	件/千克		---Of cotton or bast fibres
6210.1020 10	棉或麻制纸衬或覆盖的无纺布服装(包括毡呢或无纺织物制服装)	16				90	17	13	件/千克		Garments, made up of felt or nonwovens, paper backed or covered, of cotton or bast fibres

税则号列 Tariff Item.	货品名称	最惠国(%) MFN	协定(%)CT 东盟 CA	 中巴 CP	 中智 CC	普通 Gen	增值税率 VAT	出口退税 ED	计量单位 Unit	监管条件 SC	Article Description
6210.1020 20	棉或麻一次性或医用无纺织物服装	16				90	17	13	件/千克		Garments, made up of nonwovens, throw-away or for medical, of cotton or bast fibres
6210.1020 90	棉或麻制其他毡呢或无纺织物服装	16				90	17	13	件/千克		Other garments, made up of felt or nonwovens, of cotton or bast fibres
6210.1030	---化学纤维制	17.5	12	12.3	0	130	17	13	件/千克		---Of man-made fibres
6210.1030 10	化纤制纸衬背或覆盖的无纺布服装(包括毡呢或无纺织物制服装)	17.5				130	17	13	件/千克		Garments, made up of felt or nonwovens, paper backed or covered, of man-made fibres
6210.1030 20	化纤制一次性或医用无纺织物服装	17.5				130	17	13	件/千克		Garments, made up of nonwovens, throw-away or for medical, of man-made fibres
6210.1030 90	化纤制其他毡呢或无纺织物服装	17.5				130	17	13	件/千克		Other garments, made up of felt or nonwovens, of man-made fibres
6210.1090	---其他纺织材料制	16	8		0	100	17	13	件/千克		---Of other textile materials
6210.1090 10	其他纺织材料制纸衬背的无纺服装(包括纸覆盖的毡呢或无纺织物制服装)	16				100	17	13	件/千克		Garments, made up of felt or nonwovens, paper backed or covered, of other textile materials
6210.1090 20	其他材料制一次性或医用无纺服装	16				100	17	13	件/千克		Garments, made up of nonwovens, throw-away or for medical, of other textile materials
6210.1090 90	其他纺织材料制其他无纺织物服装(包括毡呢制服装)	16				100	17	13	件/千克		Other garments, made up of felt or nonwovens, of other textile materials
6210.2000	-子目6201.11至6201.19所列类型的其他服装	16	12	11.7	0	100	17	13	件/千克		-Other garments, of the type described in subheadings Nos. 6201.11 to 6201.19
6210.2000 11	用塑料或橡胶处理化纤制男外装(织物外表面由塑料或橡胶完全覆盖的大衣、雨衣、斗篷等)	16				100	17	13	件/千克		Men's or boys' outer garments in subheadings Nos. 6201.11 to 6201.19, of man-made fibres, outer surface of fabrics completely covered with plastics or rubber
6210.2000 19	其他用塑料或橡胶处理化纤制男外装(含用其他材料处理的织物制大衣、雨衣、斗篷等)	16				100	17	13	件/千克		Other men's or boys' outer garments in subheadings Nos. 6201.11 to 6201.19, of man-made fibres, treated by plastics or rubber or other material
6210.2000 21	用塑料或橡胶处理的羊毛制男外装(织物外表面由塑料或橡胶完全覆盖的大衣、雨衣、斗篷等)	16				100	17	13	件/千克		Men's or boys' outer garments in subheadings Nos. 6201.11 to 6201.19 of wool, outer surface of fabrics completely covered with plastics or rubber
6210.2000 29	用塑料或橡胶处理的羊毛制男外装(含用其他材料处理的织物制大衣、雨衣、斗篷等)	16				100	17	13	件/千克		Other men's or boys' outer garments in subheadings Nos. 6201.11 to 6201.19 of wool, treated by plastics or rubber or other materials
6210.2000 31	用塑料或橡胶处理的棉制男外装(织物外表面由塑料或橡胶完全覆盖的大衣、雨衣、斗篷等)	16				100	17	13	件/千克		Men's or boys' outer garments in subheadings Nos. 6201.11 to 6201.19 of cotton, only outer surface of fabrics completely covered with plastics or rubber

税则号列 Tariff Item.	货品名称	最惠国(%) MFN	协定(%) CT 东盟 CA	中巴 CP	中智 CC	普通 Gen	增值税率 VAT	出口退税 ED	计量单位 Unit	监管条件 SC	Article Description
6210.2000 39	其他用塑料或橡胶等处理棉制男外装(含用其他材料处理的织物制大衣、雨衣、斗篷等)	16				100	17	13	件/千克		Other men's or boys' outer garments in subheadings Nos. 6201.11 to 6201.19 of cotton, treated by plastic or rubber or other materials
6210.2000 40	用塑料或橡胶处理的其他纺材男外装(织物外表面由塑料或橡胶完全覆盖的大衣、雨衣、斗篷等)	16				100	17	13	件/千克		Men's or boys' outer garments in subheadings Nos. 6201.11 to 6201.19 of other textile materials, outer surface of fabrics completely covered with plastics or rubber
6210.2000 91	用塑料或橡胶等处理的亚麻制男外装(含用其他材料处理的织物制大衣、雨衣、斗篷等)	16				100	17	13	件/千克		Men's or boys' outer garments in subheadings Nos. 6201.11 to 6201.19 of flax, treated by plastic or rubber or other materials
6210.2000 99	用塑料等处理的其他纺材制男外装(含用橡胶及其他材料处理的织物制大衣、雨衣、斗篷等)	16				100	17	13	件/千克		Other men's or boys' outer garments in subheadings Nos. 6201.11 to 6201.19 of other textile materials, treated by plastic or rubber or other materials
6210.3000	-子目6202.11至6202.19所列类型的其他服装	16	12	11.7	0	100	17	13	件/千克		-Other garments, of the type described in subheadings Nos. 6202.11 to 6202.19
6210.3000 11	用塑料或橡胶处理化纤制女外装(织物外表面由塑料或橡胶完全覆盖的大衣、雨衣、斗篷等)	16				100	17	13	件/千克		Women's or girls' outer garments in subheadings Nos. 6202.11 to 6202.19 of man-made fibres, outer surface of fabrics completely covered with plastics or rubber
6210.3000 19	其他用塑料或橡胶处理化纤制女外装(含用其他材料处理的织物制大衣、雨衣、斗篷等)	16				100	17	13	件/千克		Other women's or girls' outer garments in subheadings Nos. 6202.11 to 6202.19 of man-made fibres, treated by plastic or rubber or other materials
6210.3000 21	用塑料或橡胶处理的羊毛制女外装(织物外表面由塑料或橡胶完全覆盖的大衣、雨衣、斗篷等)	16				100	17	13	件/千克		Women's or girls' outer garments in subheadings Nos. 6202.11 to 6202.19 of wool, outer surface of fabrics completely covered with plastics or rubber
6210.3000 29	用塑料或橡胶处理的羊毛制女外装(含用其他材料处理的织物制大衣、雨衣、斗篷等)	16				100	17	13	件/千克		Other women's or girls' outer garments in subheadings Nos. 6202.11 to 6202.19, of wool, treated by plastic or rubber or other materials
6210.3000 31	用塑料或橡胶处理的棉制女外装(织物外表面由塑料或橡胶完全覆盖的大衣、雨衣、斗篷等)	16				100	17	13	件/千克		Women's or girls' outer garments in subheadings Nos. 6202.11 to 6202.19 of cotton, outer surface of fabrics completely covered with plastics or rubber
6210.3000 39	其他用塑料或橡胶等处理棉制女外装(含用其他材料处理的织物制大衣、雨衣、斗篷等)	16				100	17	13	件/千克		Other women's or girls' outer garments in subheadings Nos. 6202.11 to 6202.19 of cotton, treated by plastic or rubber or other materials
6210.3000 40	用塑料或橡胶处理的其他纺材女外装(织物外表面由塑料或橡胶完全覆盖的大衣、雨衣、斗篷等)	16				100	17	13	件/千克		Women's or girls' outer garments in subheadings Nos. 6202.11 to 6202.19 of other textile materials, only outer surface of fabrics completely covered with plastics or rubber

税则号列 Tariff Item.	货品名称	最惠国(%) MFN	协定(%) CT 东盟 CA	中巴 CP	中智 CC	普通 Gen	增值税率 VAT	出口退税 ED	计量单位 Unit	监管条件 SC	Article Description
6210.3000 91	用塑料或橡胶等处理的亚麻制女外装(含用其他材料处理的织物制大衣、雨衣、斗篷等)	16				100	17	13	件/千克		Women's or girls' outer garments in subheadings Nos. 6202. 11 to 6202. 19 of flax, treated by plastic or rubber or other materials
6210.3000 99	用塑料等处理的其他纺材制女外装(含用橡胶及其他材料处理的织物制大衣、雨衣、斗篷等)	16				100	17	13	件/千克		Other women's or girls' outer garments in subheadings Nos. 6202. 11 to 6202. 19 of other textile materials, treated by plastic or rubber or other materials
6210.4000	-其他男式服装	16	12	11.7	0	100	17	13	件/千克		-Other men's or boys' garments
6210.4000 11	用塑料或橡胶处理化纤制其他男式服装(织物外表面由塑料或橡胶完全覆盖)	16				100	17	13	件/千克		Men's or boys' outer garments of man-made fibre, outer surface of fabrics completely covered with plastic or rubber
6210.4000 12	用塑料等处理的化纤制男防风衣(含用橡胶及其他材料处理织物制带风帽防寒短上衣、风衣)	16				100	17	13	件/千克		Men's or boys' wind-cheaters, anoraks, wind-jackets, of man-made fibres, treated by plastic or rubber or other materials
6210.4000 13	用塑料等处理的化纤制男式长、短裤(滑雪裤除外)	16				100	17	13	件/千克	5	Men's or boys' trousers and shorts of man-made fibres, treated by plastic or rubber
6210.4000 19	用塑料等处理的化纤制其他男式服装(含用橡胶及其他材料处理的织物)	16				100	17	13	件/千克		Other men's or boys' garments, of man-made fibres, treated by plastic or rubber or other materials
6210.4000 21	用塑料或橡胶处理的毛制其他男外装(织物外表面由塑料或橡胶完全覆盖,羊毛或动物细毛制)	16				100	17	13	件/千克		Other men's or boys' garments, of wool or fine animal hair, outer surface of fabrics completely covered with plastic or rubber
6210.4000 22	用塑料等处理的毛制男式防风衣(含用橡胶及其他材料处理织物制带风帽防寒短上衣、风衣)	16				100	17	13	件/千克		Men's or boys' wind-cheaters, anoraks, wind-jackets, of wool or fine animal hair, treated by plastic or rubber or other materials
6210.4000 23	用塑料等处理的毛制男式长、短裤(含用橡胶及其他材料处理的毛制男式长、短裤)	16				100	17	13	件/千克	5	Men's or boys' trousers and shorts, of wool or fine animal hair, treated by rubber and their material
6210.4000 29	用塑料等处理的其他男式服装(用橡胶及其他材料处理的织物)	16				100	17	13	件/千克		Other men's or boys' garments, treated by plastic or rubber
6210.4000 31	用塑料或橡胶处理的棉制其他男外装(织物外表面由塑料或橡胶完全覆盖)	16				100	17	13	件/千克		Men's or boys' quter garments of cotton, outer surface of fabrics completely covered with plastic or rubber
6210.4000 32	用塑料等处理的棉制男式防风衣(含用橡胶及其他材料处理织物制带风帽防寒短上衣、风衣)	16				100	17	13	件/千克		Men's or boys' wind-cheaters, anoraks, wind-jackets and similar articles of cotton, treated by plastic or rubber
6210.4000 33	用塑料等处理的棉制男式长、短裤(含用橡胶及其他材料处理的棉制男式长、短裤)	16				100	17	13	件/千克	5	Men's or boys' trousers and shorts of cotton, treated by plastic or rubber

税则号列 Tariff Item.	货品名称	最惠国(%) MFN	协定(%) CT 东盟 CA	中巴 CP	中智 CC	普通 Gen	增值税率 VAT	出口退税 ED	计量单位 Unit	监管条件 SC	Article Description
6210.4000 39	用塑料等处理的棉制其他男式服装(含用橡胶及其他材料处理的织物)	16				100	17	13	件/千克		Other men's or boys' garments of cotton, treated by plastic or rubber
6210.4000 40	用塑料或橡胶处理其他纺材其他男装(塑料或橡胶处理其他纺材其他男装)	16				100	17	13	件/千克		Other men's or boys' garments of other textile materials, treated by plastic or rubber
6210.4000 91	用塑料等处理的丝制其他男式服装(含用橡胶及其他材料处理的织物,含丝及绢丝70%及以上)	16				100	17	13	件/千克		Other men's or boys' garments of silk, treated by plastic or rubber or other materials, containing ≥70% by weight of silk or silk waste
6210.4000 92	用塑料等处理其他纺材制男防风衣(含用橡胶及其他材料处理织物制带风帽防寒短上衣、风衣)	16				100	17	13	件/千克		Men's or boys' wind-cheaters, anoraks, wind-jackets, of other textile materials, treated by plastic or rubber or other materials
6210.4000 93	用塑料等处理其他纺材制男长、短裤(含用橡胶及其他材料处理的其他纺材制男长、短裤)	16				100	17	13	件/千克	5	Men's or boys' trousers and shorts, of other textile materials, treated by plastic or rubber or other materials
6210.4000 99	用塑料等处理的其他纺材制男服装(含用橡胶及其他材料处理的织物)	16				100	17	13	件/千克		Other men's or boys' garments, of other textile materials, treated by plastic or rubber
6210.5000	-其他女式服装	16	12	11.7	0	100	17	13	件/千克		-Other women's or girls' garments
6210.5000 11	用塑料或橡胶处理化纤制其他女装(织物外表面由塑料或橡胶完全覆盖)	16				100	17	13	件/千克		Women's or girls' garments of man-made fibres, outer surface of fabrics completely covered with plastic or rubber
6210.5000 12	用塑料等处理的化纤制女防风衣(含用橡胶及其他材料处理织物制带风帽防寒短上衣、风衣)	16				100	17	13	件/千克		Women's or girls' garments wind-cheaters, anoraks, wind-jackets, of man-made fibres, treated by plastic or rubber or other materials
6210.5000 13	用塑料等处理的化纤制女式长、短裤(滑雪裤除外)	16				100	17	13	件/千克	5	Women's or girls' garments trousers and shorts, of man-made fibres, treated by plastic or rubber
6210.5000 19	用塑料等处理的化纤制其他女服装(含用橡胶及其他材料处理的织物)	16				100	17	13	件/千克		Other women's or girls' garments, of man-made fibres, treated by plastic or rubber or other materials
6210.5000 21	用塑料或橡胶处理的毛制其他女外装(织物外表面由塑料或橡胶完全覆盖,羊毛或动物细毛制)	16				100	17	13	件/千克		Other women's or girls' garments, of wool or fine animal hair, outer surface of fabrics completely covered with plastic or rubber
6210.5000 22	用塑料等处理的毛制女式防风衣(含用橡胶及其他材料处理织物制带风帽防寒短上衣、风衣)	16				100	17	13	件/千克		Women's or girls' wind-cheaters, anoraks, wind-jackets, of wool or fine animal hair, treated by plastic or rubber or other materials
6210.5000 23	用塑料等处理的毛制女式长、短裤(含用橡胶及其他材料处理的毛制女式长、短裤)	16				100	17	13	件/千克	5	Women's or girls' trousers and shorts, of wool or fine animal hair, treated by plastic or rubber or other materials

税则号列 Tariff Item.	货品名称	最惠国(%) MFN	协定(%)CT 东盟 CA	中巴 CP	中智 CC	普通 Gen	增值税率 VAT	出口退税 ED	计量单位 Unit	监管条件 SC	Article Description
6210.5000 29	用塑料等处理的毛制其他女式服装(含用橡胶及其他材料处理的织物)	16				100	17	13	件/千克		Other women's or girls' garments, of wool or fine animal hair, treated by plastic or rubber
6210.5000 31	用塑料或橡胶处理的棉制其他女外装(织物外表面由塑料或橡胶完全覆盖)	16				100	17	13	件/千克		Other women's or girls' garments, of cotton, outer surface of fabrics completely covered with plastic or rubber
6210.5000 32	用塑料等处理的棉制女式防风衣(含用橡胶及其他材料处理织物制带风帽防寒短上衣、风衣)	16				100	17	13	件/千克		Women's or girls' wind-cheaters, anoraks, wind-jackets, of cotton, treated by plastic or rubber or other materials
6210.5000 33	用塑料等处理的棉制女式长、短裤(含用橡胶及其他材料处理的棉制女式长、短裤)	16				100	17	13	件/千克	5	Women's or girls' trousers and shorts of cotton, treated by plastic or rubber or other materials
6210.5000 39	用塑料等处理的棉制其他女式服装(含用橡胶及其他材料处理的棉制其他女式服装)	16				100	17	13	件/千克		Other women's or girls' garments of cotton, treated by plastic or rubber or other materials
6210.5000 40	用塑料或橡胶处理其他纺材其他女装(织物外表面由塑料或橡胶完全覆盖)	16				100	17	13	件/千克		Other women's or girls' garments of other textile materials, outer surface of fabrics completely covered with plastic or rubber
6210.5000 91	用塑料等处理的丝制其他女式服装(含用橡胶及其他材料处理的织物,含丝及绢丝70%及以上)	16				100	17	13	件/千克		Other women's or girls' garments of silk, treated by plastic or rubber, containing ≥70% by weight of silk or silk waste
6210.5000 92	用塑料等处理其他纺材制女防风衣(含用橡胶及其他材料处理织物制带风帽防寒短上衣、风衣)	16				100	17	13	件/千克		Women's or girls' wind-cheaters, anoraks, wind-jackets, of other textile materials, treated by plastic or rubber or other materials
6210.5000 93	用塑料等处理其他纺材制女长、短裤(含用橡胶及其他材料处理织物制带风帽防寒短上衣、风衣)	16				100	17	13	件/千克	5	Women's or girls' trousers and shorts, of other textile materials, treated by plastic or rubber or other materials
6210.5000 99	用塑料等处理的其他纺材制女服装(含用橡胶及其他材料处理的其他纺材制女服装)	16				100	17	13	件/千克		Other women's or girls' garments, of other textile materials, treated by plastic or rubber or other materials
62.11	**运动服、滑雪服及游泳服;其他服装:**										**Track suits, ski suits and swimwear; other garments:**
	-游泳服:										-Swimwear:
6211.1100	--男式	16	T3	11.7	0	130	17	13	件/千克		--Men's or boys'
6211.1100 10	羊毛或动物细毛制男式游泳服	16				130	17	13	件/千克		Men's or boys' swimwear of wool or fine animal hair
6211.1100 20	棉制男式游泳服	16				130	17	13	件/千克	5	Men's or boys' swimwear of cotton
6211.1100 30	化学纤维制男式游泳服(包括各种材料的织物制游泳服)	16				130	17	13	件/千克	5	Men's or boys' swimwear of man-made fibres

税则号列 Tariff Item.	货品名称	最惠国(%) MFN	协定(%) CT 东盟 CA	中巴 CP	中智 CC	普通 Gen	增值税率 VAT	出口退税 ED	计量单位 Unit	监管条件 SC	Article Description
6211.1100 41	丝制男式游泳服(含丝70%及以上)	16				130	17	13	件/千克		Men's or boys' swimwear of silk, containing≥70% by weight of silk
6211.1100 49	丝制男式游泳服(含丝70%以下)	16				130	17	13	件/千克		Men's or boys' swimwear of silk, containing<70% by weight of silk
6211.1100 90	其他纺织材料制男式游泳服	16				130	17	13	件/千克		Other men's or boys' swimwear of other textile materials
6211.1200	--女式	16	12	11.7	0	130	17	13	件/千克		--Women's or girls'
6211.1200 10	羊毛或动物细毛制女式游泳服	16				130	17	13	件/千克		Women's or girls' swimwear of wool or fine animal hair
6211.1200 20	棉制女式游泳服	16				130	17	13	件/千克	5	Women's or girls' swimwear of cotton
6211.1200 30	化学纤维制女式游泳服	16				130	17	13	件/千克	5	Women's or girls' swimwear of man-made fibres
6211.1200 41	丝制女式游泳服(含丝70%及以上)	16				130	17	13	件/千克		Women's or girls' swimwear of silk, containing≥70% by weight of silk
6211.1200 49	丝制女式游泳服(含丝70%以下)	16				130	17	13	件/千克		Women's or girls' swimwear of silk, containing<70% by weight of silk
6211.1200 90	其他纺织材料制女式游泳服	16				130	17	13	件/千克		Women's or girls' swimwear of other textile materials
	-滑雪服:										-Ski suits:
6211.2010	---棉制	16	8		0	90	17	13	套/千克	5	---Of cotton
6211.2090	---其他纺织材料制	19	12	13.6	0	130	17	13	套/千克		---Of other textile materials
6211.2090 11	含滑雪男裤的羊毛制滑雪套装	19				130	17	13	套/千克	5	Ski suits of wool, including men's or boys' ski trousers
6211.2090 19	不含滑雪男裤的羊毛制滑雪套装	19				130	17	13	套/千克		Ski suits of wool, not including men's or boys' ski trousers
6211.2090 21	含滑雪短裤或不防水滑雪裤的化纤制滑雪套装	19				130	17	13	套/千克	5	Ski suits of man-made(including ski or no water-proof trousers)
6211.2090 29	化纤制其他滑雪套装	19				130	17	13	套/千克		Other ski suits of man-made fibres
6211.2090 90	其他纺织材料制滑雪套装	19				130	17	13	套/千克	5	Ski suits of other textile materials
	-其他男式服装:										-Other garments, men's or boys':
	--棉制:										--Of cotton:
6211.3210	---阿拉伯袍	16	T3		0	90	17	13	件/千克		---Arabian robes
6211.3220	---运动服	16	T3		0	90	17	13	件/千克		--- Track suits
6211.3220 11	棉制男式运动套装(面和衬里的面料相同的运动套装)	16				90	17	13	件/千克	5	Men's or boys' track suits, outside and underside being of same fabrics, of cotton
6211.3220 19	棉制其他男式运动套装	16				90	17	13	件/千克	5	Other men's or boys'track suits of cotton
6211.3290	---其他	16	T3		0	90	17	13	件/千克		---Other
6211.3290 21	棉制男式连衣服及类似品	16				90	17	13	件/千克		Men's or boys' overall and similar articles, of cotton
6211.3290 29	棉制男式连衣裤及类似品	16				90	17	13	件/千克		Men's or boys' union suit and similar articles, of cotton
6211.3290 30	棉制男式水洗服,夏服,游戏装	16				90	17	13	件/千克		Men's or boys' summer wear, wash wear, playsuit, of cotton
6211.3290 40	棉制男式工业及职业衣着	16				90	17	13	件/千克		Men's or boys' garments of cotton, industrial and career apparel

税则号列 Tariff Item.	货品名称	最惠国(%) MFN	协定(%) CT 东盟 CA	中巴 CP	中智 CC	普通 Gen	增值税率 VAT	出口退税 ED	计量单位 Unit	监管条件 SC	Article Description
6211.3290 51	棉制男式 TOPS(男成人及 8-18 号男童 TOPS)	16				90	17	13	件/千克		Men's TOPS and boys' TOPS No. 8 ~ No. 18, of cotton
6211.3290 59	棉制其他男式 TOPS	16				90	17	13	件/千克		Other men's or boys' TOPS, of cotton
6211.3290 60	棉制男式风雪套装及类似服装	16				90	17	13	件/千克		Men's or boys' ski suits and similar articles, of cotton
6211.3290 91	棉制男衬(品目 6205 的衬衫除外)	16				90	17	13	件/千克	5	Men's or boys´shirt ,other than heading No. 6205
6211.3290 99	棉制男式其他服装(含马甲,上衣)	16				90	17	13	件/千克		Other men's or boys' garments, including vests, coats, of cotton
	--化学纤维制:										--Of man-made fibres:
6211.3310	---阿拉伯袍	17.5	12	12.3	0	130	17	13	件/千克		---Arabian robes
6211.3320	---运动服	18	12	12.3	0	130	17	13	件/千克		---Track suits
6211.3320 11	化纤制男式运动套装(面和衬里的面料相同的运动套装)	18				130	17	13	件/千克	5	Men's or boys' track suits, outside and underside being of same fabrics, of man-made fibres
6211.3320 19	化纤制其他男式运动套装	18				130	17	13	件/千克	5	Other men's or boys'track suits of man-made fibres
6211.3390	---其他	17.5	12	12.3	0	130	17	13	件/千克		---Other
6211.3390 21	化纤制男式连衣服及类似品	17.5				130	17	13	件/千克		Men's or boys' overall and similar articles, of man-made fibres
6211.3390 29	化纤制男式连衣裤及类似品	17.5				130	17	13	件/千克		Men's or boys' overall and similar articles, of man-made fibres
6211.3390 30	化纤制男式水洗服,夏服,游戏装(含类似服)	17.5				130	17	13	件/千克		Men's or boys' summer wear, wash wear, playsuit and similar articles, of man-made fibres
6211.3390 91	化纤制男式工业及职业衣着	17.5				130	17	13	件/千克		Men's or boys' garments of man-made fibres, industrial and career apparel
6211.3390 92	化纤制男式 TOPS(男成人及 8-18 号男童 TOPS)	17.5				130	17	13	件/千克		Men's TOPS and boys' TOPS No. 8 ~ No. 18, of man-made fibres
6211.3390 93	化纤制其他男式 TOPS	17.5				130	17	13	件/千克		Other men's or boys' TOPS, of man-made fibres
6211.3390 94	化纤制男式风雪套装及类似服装	17.5				130	17	13	件/千克		Men's or boys' ski suits and similar articles, of man-made fibres
6211.3390 95	化纤制男衬衫(品目 6205 的衬衫除外)	17.5				130	17	13	件/千克	5	Men's or boys' shirt of man-made fibres (other than the shirt of subheading No. 6205)
6211.3390 99	化纤制男式其他服装(含马甲、上衣)	17.5				130	17	13	件/千克		Other men's or boys' garments, including vests, coats, of man-made fibres
	--其他纺织材料制:										--Of other textile materials:
6211.3910	---丝及绢丝制	16	12	11.7	0	130	17	13	件/千克		---Of silk or silk waste
6211.3910 11	丝及绢丝制男运动服(含丝 70% 及以上)	16				130	17	13	件/千克		Men's or boys' track suits of silk, containing≥70% by weight of silk
6211.3910 19	丝及绢丝制男运动服(含丝 70% 以下)	16				130	17	13	件/千克	5	Men's or boys' track suits of silk, containing <70% by weight of silk
6211.3910 21	丝或绢丝制男连衣裤及类似品(含丝 70% 及以上)	16				130	17	13	件/千克		Men's or boys' overall and similar articles, of silk or silk waste, containing ≥70% by weight of silk

税则号列 Tariff Item.	货品名称	最惠国(%) MFN	协定(%)CT 东盟 CA	中巴 CP	中智 CC	普通 Gen	增值税率 VAT	出口退税 ED	计量单位 Unit	监管条件 SC	Article Description
6211.3910 29	丝或绢丝制男连衣裤及类似品(含丝70%以下)	16				130	17	13	件/千克		Men's or boys' overall and similar articles, containing < 70% by weight of silk
6211.3910 91	丝或绢丝制男式TOPS(含丝70%及以上)	16				130	17	13	件/千克		Men's or boys' TOPS of silk or silk waste, containing ≥70% by weight of silk
6211.3910 92	丝或绢丝制男式TOPS(含丝70%以下)	16				130	17	13	件/千克		Men's or boys' TOPS of silk or silk waste, containing < 70% by weight of silk
6211.3910 93	丝或绢丝制男式风雪套装(含类似服装,含丝70%及以上)	16				130	17	13	件/千克		Men's or boys' ski suits and similar articles, of silk or silk waste, containing ≥70% by weight of silk
6211.3910 94	丝或绢丝制男式风雪套装(含类似服装,含丝70%以下)	16				130	17	13	件/千克		Men's or boys'ski suits and similar articles, of silk or silk waste, containing <70% by weight of silk
6211.3910 95	丝或绢丝制男式其他服装(含衬衫、马甲、上衣,含丝70%及以上)	16				130	17	13	件/千克		Men's or boys'other shirts, vests, coats, of silk or silk waste, containing ≥70% by weight of silk
6211.3910 99	丝或绢丝制男式其他服装(含衬衫、马甲、上衣,含丝70%以下)	16				130	17	13	件/千克		Other men's or boys', vests, coats, of silk or silk waste, containing < 70% by weight of silk
6211.3920	---羊毛或动物细毛制	16	12	11.7	0	130	17	13	件/千克		--Of wool or fine animal hair
6211.3920 10	毛制男式运动套装	16				130	17	13	件/千克	5	Men's or boys' track suits of wool or fine animal hair
6211.3920 90	毛制男式其他服装	16				130	17	13	件/千克		Other men's or boys' shirts, of wool or fine animal hair
6211.3990	---其他	16	12	11.7	0	100	17	13	件/千克		---Other
6211.3990 10	其他纺织材料制男式运动套装	16				100	17	13	件/千克	5	Men's or boys' track suits of other textile materials
6211.3990 20	其他纺织材料制男连衣裤(含类似品)	16				100	17	13	件/千克		Men's or boys' overall and similar articles of other textile materials
6211.3990 91	其他纺织材料制男式水洗服、夏服(含游戏装等类似服装)	16				100	17	13	件/千克		Men's or boys' summer wear, wash wear, including playsuit and similar articles, of other textile materials
6211.3990 92	其他纺织材料制男式TOPS	16				100	17	13	件/千克		Men's or boys' pullovers, of other textile materials
6211.3990 93	其他纺织材料制男式风雪套装(含类似服装)	16				100	17	13	件/千克		Men's or boys' ski suits and similar articles of other textile materials
6211.3990 99	其他纺织材料制男式其他服装(含衬衫、马甲、上衣)	16				100	17	13	件/千克		Other men's or boys' shirts, vests, coats, of other textile materials
	-其他女式服装:										-Other garments, women's or girls':
6211.4100	--羊毛或动物细毛制	16	12	11.7	0	130	17	13	件/千克		--Of wool or fine animal hair
6211.4100 10	毛制女式运动套装	16				130	17	13	件/千克		Women's or girls' track suits of wool or fine animal hair
6211.4100 20	毛制女式连衣裤	16				130	17	13	件/千克		Women's or girls' overall of wool or fine animal hair
6211.4100 31	毛制女式TOPS(女成人及7-16号女童TOPS)	16				130	17	13	件/千克		Women's TOPS and girls's TOPS No. 7 ~ No. 16, of wool or fine animal hair

税则号列 Tariff Item.	货品名称	最惠国(%) MFN	协定(%) CT 东盟 CA	中巴 CP	中智 CC	普通 Gen	增值税率 VAT	出口退税 ED	计量单位 Unit	监管条件 SC	Article Description
6211.4100 39	毛制其他女童 TOP	16				130	17	13	件/千克		Other girls' TOPS, of wool or fine animal hair
6211.4100 40	毛制女式风雪套装及类似服装	16				130	17	13	件/千克		Women's or girls' ski suits and similar articles, of wool or fine animal hair
6211.4100 90	毛制女式其他服装(含衬衫、马甲、上衣、无袖罩衫)	16				130	17	13	件/千克		Other women's or girls', shirts, vests, coats, cloaks, of wool or fine animal hair
	--棉制:										--Of cotton:
6211.4210	---运动服	16	8		0	90	17	13	件/千克		--- Track suits
6211.4210 10	棉制女式运动套装(面和衬里的面料相同的运动套装)	16				90	17	13	件/千克	5	Women's or girls' track suits, outside and underside being of same fabrics, of cotton
6211.4210 90	棉制其他女式运动套装	16				90	17	13	件/千克	5	Other Women's or girls' track suits of cotton
6211.4290	---其他	16	8		0	90	17	13	件/千克		---Other
	--化学纤维制:										--Of man-made fibres:
6211.4310	---运动服	17.5	12	12.3	0	130	17	13	件/千克		---Track suits
6211.4310 10	化纤制女式运动套装(面和衬里的面料相同的运动套装)	17.5				130	17	13	件/千克	5	Women's or girls' track suits, outside and underside being of same fabrics, of man - made fibres
6211.4310 90	化纤制其他女式运动套装	17.5				90	17	13	件/千克	5	Other Women's or girls' track suits of man - made fibres
6211.4390	---其他	17.5	12	12.3	0	90	17	13	件/千克		---Other
	--其他纺织材料制:										--Of other textile materials:
6211.4910	---丝及绢丝制	16	T3	11.7	0	130	17	13	件/千克		---Of silk or silk waste
6211.4910 11	丝或绢丝制女式运动套装(含丝 70% 及以上)	16				130	17	13	件/千克		Women's or girls' track suits, of silk or silk waste, containing ≥ 70% by weight of silk
6211.4910 19	丝或绢丝制女式运动套装(含丝 70% 以下)	16				130	17	13	件/千克		Women's or girls' track suits, of silk or silk waste, containing < 70% by weight of silk
6211.4910 21	丝或绢丝制女连衣裤及类似品(含丝 70% 及以上)	16				130	17	13	件/千克		Women's or girls' overall and similar articles, of silk or silk waste, containing≥70% by weight of silk
6211.4910 29	丝或绢丝制女连衣裤及类似品(含丝 70% 以下)	16				130	17	13	件/千克		Women's or girls' overall and similar articles, of silk or silk waste, containing<70% by weight of silk
6211.4910 31	丝或绢丝制女式 TOPS(含丝 70% 及以上)	16				130	17	13	件/千克		Women's or girls' TOPS, of silk or silk waste, containing≥70% by weight of silk
6211.4910 39	丝或绢丝制女式 TOPS(含丝 70% 以下)	16				130	17	13	件/千克		Women's or girls' TOPS, of silk or silk waste, containing<70% by weight of silk
6211.4910 41	丝或绢丝制女式风雪套装(含类似服装,含丝 70% 及以上)	16				130	17	13	件/千克		Women's or girls' ski suits and similar articles, of silk or silk waste, containing≥70% by weight of silk

税则号列 Tariff Item.	货品名称	最惠国(%) MFN	协定(%) CT 东盟 CA	中巴 CP	中智 CC	普通 Gen	增值税率 VAT	出口退税 ED	计量单位 Unit	监管条件 SC	Article Description
6211.4910 49	丝或绢丝制女式风雪套装(含类似服装,含丝70%以下)	16				130	17	13	件/千克		Women's or girls' ski suits and similar articles, of silk or silk waste, containing < 70% by weight of silk
6211.4910 51	丝及绢丝制女式其他服装(含衬衫、马甲、上衣、无袖罩衫,含丝70%及以上)	16				130	17	13	件/千克		Other women's or girls' garments, including shirts vests coat, cloaks, of silk or silk waste, containing ≥70% by weight of silk
6211.4910 59	丝及绢丝制女式其他服装(含衬衫、马甲、上衣、无袖罩衫,含丝70%以下)	16				130	17	13	件/千克		Other women's or girls' garments, including shirts vests coats, cloaks, of silk or silk waste, containing < 70% by weight of silk
6211.4910 91	丝及绢丝制女式其他服装(含丝70%及以上)	16				130	17	13	件/千克		Other women's or girls' garments, of silk or silk waste, containing ≥70% by weight of silk
6211.4910 99	丝及绢丝制女式其他服装(含丝70%以下)	16				130	17	13	件/千克		Other women's or girls' garments, of silk or silk waste, containing < 70% by weight of silk
6211.4990	---其他	16	T3	11.7	0	100	17	13	件/千克		---Other
6211.4990 10	其他纺织材料制女式运动套装	16				100	17	13	件/千克	5	Other women's or girls' track suits, of other textile materials
6211.4990 20	其他纺织材料制女连衣裤(含类似品)	16				100	17	13	件/千克		Other women's or girls' overall and similar articles, of other textile materials
6211.4990 30	其他纺织材料制女式其他服装(含游戏装,类似服装)	16				100	17	13	件/千克		Other women's or girls' garments, including playsuit and similar articles, of other textile materials
6211.4990 40	其他纺织材料制女式TOPS	16				100	17	13	件/千克		Women's or girls' TOPS, of other textile materials
6211.4990 50	其他纺织材料制女式风雪套装(含类似服装)	16				100	17	13	件/千克		Women's or girls' ski suits and similar articles, of other textile materials
6211.4990 90	其他纺织材料制女式其他服装(含衬衫、马甲、上衣、无袖罩衫)	16				100	17	13	件/千克		Other women's or girls' garments including shirts, vests, coats, cloaks, of other textile materials
62.12	**胸罩、束腰带、紧身胸衣、吊裤带、吊袜带、束袜带和类似品及其零件,不论是否针织或钩编的:**										**Brassières, girdles, corsets, braces, suspenders, garters and similar articles and parts thereof, whether or not knitted or crocheted:**
	-胸罩:										-Brassières:
6212.1010	---化学纤维制	16	T3	14.4	0	130	17	13	件/千克	5	---Of man-made fibres
6212.1090	---其他纺织材料制	14	8	12.6	0	100	17	13	件/千克		---Of other textile materials
6212.1090 10	毛制其他胸罩(不论是否针织或钩编)	14				100	17	13	件/千克	5	Brassières, whether or not knitted or crocheted, of wool or fine animal hair
6212.1090 20	棉制其他胸罩(不论是否针织或钩编)	14				100	17	13	件/千克	5	Brassières, whether or not knitted or crocheted, of cotton
6212.1090 31	丝制胸罩(不论是否针织或钩编,含丝70%及以上)	14				100	17	13	件/千克		Brassières of silk, whether or not knitted or crocheted, containing≥70% by weight of silk

税则号列 Tariff Item.	货品名称	最惠国(%) MFN	协定(%) 东盟 CA	中巴 CP	中智 CC	普通 Gen	增值税率 VAT	出口退税 ED	计量单位 Unit	监管条件 SC	Article Description
6212.1090 39	丝制其他胸罩(不论是否针织或钩编,含丝70%以下)	14				100	17	13	件/千克		Brassières of silk, whether or not knitted or crocheted, containing <70% by weight of silk
6212.1090 90	其他纺织材料制其他胸罩(不论是否针织或钩编)	14				100	17	13	件/千克	5	Brassières, whether or not knitted or crocheted, of other textile materials
	-束腰带及腹带:										-Girdles and panty-girdles:
6212.2010	---化学纤维制	16	T3		0	130	17	13	件/千克	5	---Of man-made fibres
6212.2090	---其他纺织材料制	14	T3		0	100	17	13	件/千克		---Of other textile materials
6212.2090 10	毛制束胸带及腹带(不论是否针织或钩编)	14				100	17	13	件/千克		Girdles and panty-girdles, whether or not knitted or crocheted, of wool or fine animal hair
6212.2090 20	棉制束腰带及腹带(不论是否针织或钩编)	14				100	17	13	件/千克	5	Girdles and panty-girdles of silk, whether or not knitted or crocheted, of cotton
6212.2090 31	丝制束腰带及腹带(不论是否针织或钩编,含丝70%及以上)	14				100	17	13	件/千克		Girdles and panty-girdles of silk, whether or not knitted or crocheted, containing≥70% by weight of silk
6212.2090 39	丝制束腰带及腹带(不论是否针织或钩编,含丝70%以下)	14				100	17	13	件/千克		Girdles and panty-girdles of silk, whether or not knitted or crocheted, containing <70% by weight of silk
6212.2090 90	其他材料制束胸带及腹带(不论是否针织或钩编)	14				100	17	13	件/千克		Girdles and panty-girdles, whether or not knitted or crocheted, of other textile materials
	-束腰胸衣:										-Corselettes:
6212.3010	---化学纤维制	16	8		0	130	17	13	件/千克	5	---Of man-made fibres
6212.3090	---其他纺织材料制	14	8		0	100	17	13	件/千克		---Of other textile materials
6212.3090 10	毛制紧身胸衣(不论是否针织或钩编)	14				100	17	13	件/千克		Croselettes, whether or not knitted or crocheted, of wool or fine animal hair
6212.3090 20	棉制紧身胸衣(不论是否针织或钩编)	14				100	17	13	件/千克	5	Croselettes, whether or not knitted or crocheted, of cotton
6212.3090 31	丝制紧身胸衣(不论是否针织或钩编,含丝70%及以上)	14				100	17	13	件/千克		Croselettes of silk, whether or not knitted or crocheted, containing ≥ 70% by weight of silk
6212.3090 39	丝制其他紧身胸衣(不论是否针织或钩编,含丝70%以下)	14				100	17	13	件/千克		Croselettes of silk, whether or not knitted or crocheted, containing < 70% by weight of silk
6212.3090 90	其他材料制紧身胸衣(不论是否针织或钩编)	14				100	17	13	件/千克		Croselettes of other textile materials, whether or not knitted or crocheted
	-其他:										-Other:
6212.9010	---化学纤维制	16	8	14.4	0	130	17	13	件/千克		---Of man-made fibres
6212.9090	---其他纺织材料制	14	8	12.6	0	100	17	13	件/千克		---Of other textile materials
6212.9090 10	毛制吊裤带、吊袜带、束袜带等(不论是否针织或钩编,含羊毛与橡胶/塑料制的)	14				100	17	13	件/千克		Braces, suspenders, garters and similar articles, of wool and plastics/rubber, whether or not knitted or crocheted
6212.9090 20	棉制吊裤带、吊袜带、束袜带等(不论是否针织或钩编,含棉与橡胶/塑料制的)	14				100	17	13	件/千克		Braces, suspenders, garters and similar articles, of cotton and plastics/rubber, whether or not knitted or crocheted

税则号列 Tariff Item.	货品名称	最惠国(%) MFN	协定(%)CT 东盟 CA	中巴 CP	中智 CC	普通 Gen	增值税率 VAT	出口退税 ED	计量单位 Unit	监管条件 SC	Article Description
6212.9090 31	丝制吊裤带、吊袜带、束袜带等(不论是否针织或钩编,含丝70%及以上)	14				100	17	13	件/千克		Braces, suspenders, garters and similar articles, of silk, containing≥70% by weight of silk, whether or not knitted or crocheted
6212.9090 39	丝制吊裤带、吊袜带、束袜带等(不论是否针织或钩编,含丝70%以下)	14				100	17	13	件/千克		Braces, suspenders, garters and similar articles, of silk, containing<70% by weight of silk, whether or not knitted or crocheted
6212.9090 90	其他材料制吊裤带、吊袜带等(不论是否针织或钩编、包括束袜带和类似品及其零件)	14				100	17	13	件/千克		Braces, suspenders, garters and similar articles and parts thereof, of other textile materials, whether or not knitted or crocheted
62.13	**手帕:**										**Handkerchiefs:**
	-棉制:										-Of cotton:
6213.2010	---刺绣的	14	8		0	90	17	13	条/千克		---Embroidered
6213.2090	---其他	14	8		0	90	17	13	条/千克		---Other
	-其他纺织材料制:										-Of other textile materials:
6213.9020	---刺绣的	14	8		0	100	17	13	条/千克		---Embroidered
6213.9090	---其他	14	8		0	100	17	13	条/千克		---Other
6213.9090 10	化纤制其他手帕	14				100	17	13	条/千克		Other handkerchiefs of man-made fibres
6213.9090 20	麻制其他手帕	14				100	17	13	条/千克		Other handkerchiefs of flax
6213.9090 90	其他材料制手帕	14				100	17	13	条/千克		Handkerchiefs of other textile materials
62.14	**披巾、领巾、围巾、披纱、面纱及类似品:**										**Shawls, scarves, mufflers, mantillas, veils and the like:**
6214.1000	-丝及绢丝制	14	8		0	130	17	13	条/千克		-Of silk or silk waste
6214.1000 10	含丝70%及以上制披巾、头巾、围巾(包括披纱、面纱等及类似品)	14				130	17	13	条/千克		Shawls, scarves, mufflers, mantillas, veils and the like, containing≥70% by weight of silk
6214.1000 90	含丝70%以下制披巾、头巾、围巾(包括披纱、面纱等及类似品)	14				130	17	13	条/千克		Shawls, scarves, mufflers, mantillas, veils and the like, containing<70% by weight of silk
6214.2000	-羊毛或动物细毛制	14	8		0	130	17	13	条/千克		-Of wool or fine animal hair
6214.3000	-合成纤维制	16	8		0	130	17	13	条/千克		-Of synthetic fibres
6214.4000	-人造纤维制	14	8		0	130	17	13	条/千克		-Of artificial fibres
6214.9000	-其他纺织材料制	14	8		0	100	17	13	条/千克		-Of other textile materials
6214.9000 10	棉制披巾、头巾及类似品(包括围巾、披纱、面纱)	14				100	17	13	条/千克		Shawls, scarves, mufflers, mantillas, veils and the like, of cotton
6214.9000 90	其他材料制披巾、头巾及类似品(包括围巾、披纱、面纱及类似品)	14				100	17	13	条/千克		Shawls, scarves, mufflers, mantillas, veils and the like, of other textile materials
62.15	**领带及领结:**										**Ties, bow ties and cravats:**
6215.1000	-丝及绢丝制	14	8		0	130	17	13	条/千克		-Of silk or silk waste
6215.1000 11	丝及绢丝制领带及领结(非丝纺织材料含量50%及以上)	14				130	17	13	条/千克		Ties, bow ties and cravats of silk and silk waste, containing≥50% by weight of non-silk textile fabrics

税则号列 Tariff Item.	货品名称	最惠国(%) MFN	协定(%)CT 东盟 CA	中巴 CP	中智 CC	普通 Gen	增值税率 VAT	出口退税 ED	计量单位 Unit	监管条件 SC	Article Description
6215.1000 19	丝及绢丝制领带及领结(非丝纺织材料含量50%以下,外层织物含丝70%及以上)	14				130	17	13	条/千克		Ties, bow ties and cravats of silk and silk waste, containing < 50% by weight of non-silk textile fabrics, out fabrics containing≥70% by weight of silk
6215.1000 90	其他丝及绢丝制领带及领结(非丝纺织材料含量50%以下)	14				130	17	13	条/千克		Other ties, bow ties and cravats of silk and silk waste, containing < 50% by weight of non-silk textile fabrics
6215.2000	-化学纤维制	16	8	14.4	0	130	17	13	条/千克		-Of man-made fibres
6215.9000	-其他纺织材料制	14	8		0	100	17	13	条/千克		-Of other textile materials
6215.9000 10	毛制领带及领结	14				100	17	13	条/千克		Ties, bow ties and cravats, of wool or fine animal hair
6215.9000 20	棉制领带及领结	14				100	17	13	条/千克		Ties, bow ties and cravats, of cotton
6215.9000 90	其他材料制领带及领结	14				100	17	13	条/千克		Ties, bow ties and cravats, of other textile materials
62.16	**分指手套、连指手套及露指手套:**										**Gloves, mittens and mitts:**
6216.0000	分指手套、连指手套及露指手套	14	8		0	100	17	13	双/千克		Gloves, mittens and mitts
6216.0000 11	非针织物裁剪缝制成的运动手套(已浸渍塑料、橡胶,但含量不超过50%;棉限内;并四指)	14				100	17	13	双/千克		Sports mittens, not-knitted, making-up, impregnated, rubber or plastics content ≤50%(W), cotton within limitations
6216.0000 12	非针织物裁剪缝制成的非运动手套(已浸渍塑料、橡胶,但含量不超过50%;棉限内;并四指)	14				100	17	13	双/千克		Other mittens, not-knitted, making-up, impregnated, rubber or plastics content ≤50%(W), cotton within limitations, other than sport mittens
6216.0000 13	非针织物裁剪缝制成的运动手套(已浸渍塑料、橡胶,但含量不超过50%;化纤限内;并四指)	14				100	17	13	双/千克		Sports mittens, not-knitted, making-up impregnated, rubber or plastics content ≤50%(W), man-made fibres within limitations
6216.0000 14	非针织物裁剪缝制成的非运动手套(已浸渍塑料、橡胶,但含量不超过50%;化纤限内;并四指)	14				100	17	13	双/千克		Other mittens, not-knitted making-up, impregnated, rubber or plastics content ≤50%(W), man-made fibres within limitations
6216.0000 15	其他非针织物裁剪缝成的运动手套(已浸渍塑料、橡胶,但含量不超过50%;并四指)	14				100	17	13	双/千克		Other sports mittens, not-knitted, making-up, impregnated, rubber or plastics content≤50%(W)
6216.0000 19	其他非针织物制成的非运动手套(已浸渍塑料、橡胶,但含量不超过50%;并四指)	14				100	17	13	双/千克		Other mittens, not-knitted making-up, impre-gnated, rubber or plastics content ≤50%(W), other than sports mittens
6216.0000 21	其他浸渍塑料橡胶非针织运动手套(含棉、化学纤维及其他纺织纤维50%及以上;棉限内)	14				100	17	13	双/千克		Other gloves, mittens not-knitted, impregnated with rubber or plastics, cotton, man-made fibres or other textile fibres content≥50%(W), cotton within limitations, other than sports

税则号列 Tariff Item.	货品名称	最惠国(%) MFN	协定(%) 东盟 CA	中巴 CP	CT 中智 CC	普通 Gen	增值税率 VAT	出口退税 ED	计量单位 Unit	监管条件 SC	Article Description
6216.0000 22	其他浸渍塑/胶非针织非运动手套(含棉、化学纤维及其他纺织纤维50%及以上;棉限内)	14				100	17	13	双/千克		Other gloves, mittens, not-knitted, impregnated with rubber or plastics, cotton, man-made fibres or other textile fibres content≥50%(W), cotton within limitations
6216.0000 23	其他浸渍塑料橡胶非针织运动手套(含棉、化学纤维及其他纺织纤维50%及以上,化纤限内)	14				100	17	13	双/千克		Other gloves, mittens sports, not-knitted, impregnated with rubber or plastics, cotton, man-made fibres or other textile fibres content≥50%(W), man-made fibres within limitations
6216.0000 24	其他浸渍塑/胶非针织非运动手套(含棉、化学纤维及其他纺织纤维50%及以上;化纤限内)	14				100	17	13	双/千克		Other gloves, mittens, not-knitted, impregnated with rubber or plastics, cotton, man-made fibres or other textile fibres content≥50%(W), man-made fibres within limitations, other than sports
6216.0000 25	未列名浸渍塑/胶非针织运动手套(含棉、化学纤维及其他纺织纤维50%及以上)	14				100	17	13	双/千克		Other gloves, mittens sports, not-knitted, impregnated, rubber or plastics, cotton, man-made fibres or other textile fibres content≥50%(W)
6216.0000 29	未列名浸渍塑/胶非针织非运动手套(含棉、化学纤维及其他纺织纤维50%及以上)	14				100	17	13	双/千克		Other gloves, not-knitted, impregnated with rubber or plastics, cotton, man-made fibres or other textile fibres content ≥50%(W), not elsewhere specified or included, other than sports
6216.0000 31	棉非针织物制的运动手套(非浸渍塑料、橡胶;含并四指、分四指)	14				100	17	13	双/千克		Other sports gloves, mittens, not-knitted, of cotton, not impregnated with rubber or plastics
6216.0000 39	棉非针织物制的非运动手套(非浸渍塑料、橡胶;含并四指、分四指)	14				100	17	13	双/千克		Other gloves, mittens, not-knitted, of cotton, not impregnated with rubber or plastics, other than sports
6216.0000 41	化纤制非针织物制的运动手套(非浸渍塑料、橡胶;含并/分四指;含羊毛或动物细毛≥36%)	14				100	17	13	双/千克		Other sports gloves, mittens, not-knitted, of man-made fibres, containing ≥ 36% by weight of wool or fine animal hair, not impregnated with rubber or plastics
6216.0000 42	化纤制非针织物制的非运动手套(非浸渍塑料、橡胶,含并/分四指;含羊毛或动物细毛≥36%)	14				100	17	13	双/千克		Other gloves, mittens, not-knitted, of man-made fibres, containing ≥ 36% by weight of wool or fine animal hair, not impregnated with rubber or plastics, other than sports
6216.0000 43	其他化纤制非针织运动手套(非浸渍塑料、橡胶的;含并四指、分四指)	14				100	17	13	双/千克		Other sports gloves, mittens, not-knitted, of man-made fibres, not impregnated with rubber or plastics
6216.0000 49	其他化纤制非针织非运动手套(非浸渍塑料、橡胶的;含并四指、分四指)	14				100	17	13	双/千克		Other gloves, mittens, not-knitted, of man-made fibres, not impregnated with rubber or plastics other than sports
6216.0000 51	毛制非针织运动手套(非浸渍塑料、橡胶的,含并四指、分四指)	14				100	17	13	双/千克		Other sports gloves, mittens, not-knitted, of wool or fine animal hair, not impregnated with rubber or plastics

税则号列 Tariff Item.	货品名称	最惠国(%) MFN	协定(%)CT 东盟 CA	中巴 CP	中智 CC	普通 Gen	增值税率 VAT	出口退税 ED	计量单位 Unit	监管条件 SC	Article Description
6216.0000 59	毛制非针织非运动手套(非浸渍塑料、橡胶的;含并四指、分四指)	14				100	17	13	双/千克		Other gloves, mittens, not-knitted, of wool or fine animal hair, not impregnated with rubber or plastics, other than sports
6216.0000 91	其他纺织材料制非针织运动手套(非浸渍塑料、橡胶的;含分指手套、连指手套及露指手套)	14				100	17	13	双/千克		Other sports gloves, mittens and mitts, not-knitted, of other textile materials, not impregnated with rubber or plastics
6216.0000 99	其他纺织材料制非针织非运动手套(非浸渍塑料、橡胶的;含分指手套、连指手套及露指手套)	14				100	17	13	双/千克		Other gloves, mittens and mitts, not-knitted, of other textile materials, not impregnated with rubber or plastics, other than sports
62.17	**其他制成的衣着附件;服装或衣着附件的零件,但税目62.12的货品除外:**										**Other made up clothing accessories; parts of garments or of clothing accessories, other than those of heading 62.12:**
	-附件:										-Accessories:
6217.1010	---袜子及袜套	14	T3	12.2	0	130	17	13	双/千克		---Stocking, socks and sockettes
6217.1020	---和服腰带	14	T3	12.2	0	100	17	13	条/千克		---Kimono belts
6217.1090	---其他	14	T3	12.2	0	100	17	13	千克		---Other
6217.1090 10	毛制服装或衣着附件(指非针织非钩编)	14				100	17	13	千克		Garments or clothing accessories of wool or fine animal hair, not knitted or crocheted
6217.1090 20	棉制服装或衣着附件(指非针织非钩编)	14				100	17	13	千克		Garments or clothing accessories of cotton, not knitted or crocheted
6217.1090 30	化纤制服装或衣着附件(指非针织非钩编)	14				100	17	13	千克		Garments or clothing accessories of man-made fibres, not knitted or crocheted
6217.1090 41	丝制服装或衣着附件(指非针织非钩编,含丝70%及以上)	14				100	17	13	千克		Garments or clothing accessories of silk, not knitted or crocheted, containing≥70% by weight of silk
6217.1090 49	丝制服装或衣着附件(指非针织非钩编,含丝70%以下)	14				100	17	13	千克		Garments or clothing accessories of silk, not knitted or crocheted, containing <70% by weight of silk
6217.1090 90	其他服装或衣着附件(指非针织非钩编)	14				100	17	13	千克		Other garments or clothing accessories other, not knitted or crocheted
6217.9000	-零件	14	T3	12.6	0	100	17	13	千克		-Parts
6217.9000 11	羊毛或动物细毛制保暖型衬里	14				100	17	13	千克		Thermal lining of wool or fine animal hair
6217.9000 12	毛制非针织或非钩编衬衫的零件	14				100	17	13	千克		Parts of shirts, not knitted or crocheted, of wool or fine animal hair
6217.9000 13	毛制非针织或非钩编上衣的零件	14				100	17	13	千克		Parts of jackets and blazers, not knitted or crocheted, of wool or fine animal hair
6217.9000 14	毛制长裤及马裤的零件(指非针织非钩编)	14				100	17	13	千克		Parts of trousers or breeches, not knitted or crocheted, of wool or fine animal hair
6217.9000 19	其他毛制服装或衣着零件(指非针织非钩编)	14				100	17	13	千克		Other parts of other garments, not knitted or crocheted, of wool or fine animal hair
6217.9000 21	棉制保暖型衬里	14				100	17	13	千克		Thermal lining of cotton

税则号列 Tariff Item.	货品名称	最惠国(%) MFN	协定(%)CT			普通 Gen	增值税率 VAT	出口退税 ED	计量单位 Unit	监管条件 SC	Article Description
			东盟 CA	中巴 CP	中智 CC						
6217.9000 22	棉制非针织非钩编衬衫的零件	14				100	17	13	千克		Parts of shirts, not knitted or crocheted, of cotton
6217.9000 23	棉制非针织非钩编上衣的零件	14				100	17	13	千克		Parts of jackets and blazers, not knitted or crocheted, of cotton
6217.9000 24	棉制长裤及马裤的零件(指非针织非钩编)	14				100	17	13	千克	5	Parts of trousers or breeches, not knitted or crocheted, of cotton
6217.9000 29	棉制服装或衣着零件(指非针织非钩编)	14				100	17	13	千克		Other parts of garments, not knitted or crocheted, of cotton
6217.9000 31	化纤制保暖型衬里	14				100	17	13	千克		Thermal lining, of man-made fibres
6217.9000 32	化纤制非针织非钩编衬衫的零件	14				100	17	13	千克		Parts of shirts, not knitted or crocheted, of man-made fibres
6217.9000 33	化纤制非针织非钩编上衣的零件	14				100	17	13	千克		Parts of jackets and blazers, not knitted or crocheted, of man-made fibres
6217.9000 34	化纤制长裤及马裤的零件(指非针织非钩编)	14				100	17	13	千克	5	Parts of trousers or breeches, not knitted or crocheted, of man-made fibres
6217.9000 39	化纤制服装或衣着零件(指非针织非钩编)	14				100	17	13	千克		Other parts of garments, not knitted or crocheted, of man-made fibres
6217.9000 41	丝制保暖型衬里	14				100	17	13	千克		Thermal lining of silk, not knitted or crocheted
6217.9000 42	丝制服装或衣着零件(指非针织非钩编,含丝70%及以上)	14				100	17	13	千克		Parts of garments of silk, containing ≥ 70% by weight of silk, not knitted or crocheted
6217.9000 49	丝制服装或衣着零件(指非针织非钩编,含丝70%以下)	14				100	17	13	千克		Parts of garments of silk, containing < 70% by weight of silk, not knitted or crocheted
6217.9000 91	其他材料制保暖型衬里	14				100	17	13	千克		Thermal lining of other textile materials
6217.9000 92	其他材料制衬衫零件(非针织非钩编)	14				100	17	13	千克		Parts of shirts of other textile materials, not knitted or crocheted
6217.9000 93	其他材料制上衣零件(指非针织非钩编)	14				100	17	13	千克		Parts of jackets and blazers, of other textile materials, not knitted or crocheted
6217.9000 94	其他材料制长裤及马裤的零件(指非针织非钩编)	14				100	17	13	千克	5	Parts of trousers or breeches, of other textile materials, not knitted or crocheted
6217.9000 99	其他材料制服装或衣着附件(指非针织或非钩编,含各种附件的零件)	14				100	17	13	千克		Garments or clothing accessories, parts of clothing accessories, of other textile materials, not knitted or crocheted

第六十三章
其他纺织制成品;成套物品;旧衣着及旧纺织品;碎织物

注释:

一、第一分章仅适用于各种纺织物制成的物品。

二、第一分章不包括:

(一)第五十六章至第六十二章的货品;

(二)税目63.09的旧衣着或其他旧物品。

三、税目63.09仅适用于下列货品:

(一)纺织材料制品:

1. 衣着和衣着附件及其零件;
2. 毯子及旅行毯;
3. 床上、餐桌、盥洗及厨房用的织物制品;
4. 装饰用织物制品,但税目57.01至57.05的地毯及税目58.05的装饰毯除外。

(二)用石棉以外其他任何材料制成的鞋帽类。

上述物品只有同时符合下列两个条件才能归入本税目:

1. 必须明显看得出穿用过;
2. 必须以散装、捆装、袋装或类似的大包装形式进口或出口。

Chapter 63
Other made up textile articles; sets; worn clothing and worn textile articles; rags

Notes:

1. Sub-Chapter 1 applies only to made up articles, of any textile fabric.
2. Sub-Chapter 1 does not cover:
   (a) Goods of Chapters 56 to 62; or
   (b) Worn clothing or other worn articles of heading No. 63.09.
3. Heading No. 63.09 applies only to the following goods:
   (a) Articles of textile materials:
   (Ⅰ) Clothing and clothing accessories, and parts thereof;
   (Ⅱ) Blankets and travelling rugs;
   (Ⅲ) Bed linen, table linen, toilet linen and kitchen linen;
   (Ⅳ) Furnishing articles, other than carpets of headings Nos. 57.01 to 57.05 and tapestries of heading No. 58.05;
   (b) Footwear and headgear of any material other than asbestos.

   In order to be classified in this heading, the articles mentioned above must comply with both of the following requirements:
   (Ⅰ) they must show signs of appreciable wear, and
   (Ⅱ) they must be presented in bulk or in bales, sacks or similar packings.

税则号列 Tariff Item.	货品名称	最惠国(%) MFN	协定(%)CT 东盟 CA	中巴 CP	中智 CC	普通 Gen	增值税率 VAT	出口退税 ED	计量单位 Unit	监管条件 SC	Article Description
	第一分章 其他纺织制成品										Ⅰ. -OTHER MADE UP TEXTILE ARTICLES
63.01	**毯子及旅行毯:**										**Blankets and travelling rugs:**
6301.1000	-电暖毯	16	8		0	100	17	11	条		-Electric blankets
	-羊毛或动物细毛制的										- Of wool or of fine animal hair
6301.2000	毯子(电暖毯除外)及旅行毯	16	8		0	130	17	11	条/千克		-Blankets (other than electric blankets) and travelling rugs,
6301.2000 10	毛制毯子及旅行毯(羊毛或动物细毛制,非电暖的,长度不超过3米)	16				130	17	11	条/千克	B	Blankets (other than electric blankets) and travelling rugs, of wool or of fine animal hair, length≤3m
6301.2000 20	其他毛制毯子及旅行毯(羊毛或动物细毛制,非电暖的,长度超过3米)	16				130	17	11	条/千克	B	Other blankets (other than electric blankets) and travelling rugs, of wool or of fine animal hair, length > 3m
6301.3000	-棉制的毯子(电暖毯除外)及旅行毯	16	T3		0	90	17	11	条/千克		-Blankets (other than electric blankets) and travelling rugs, of cotton
6301.4000	-合成纤维制的毯子(电暖毯除外)及旅行毯	17.5	T3		0	130	17	11	条/千克	B	-Blankets (other than electric blankets) and travelling rugs, of synthetic fibres
6301.9000	-其他毯子及旅行毯	16	T3		0	90	17	11	条/千克		-Other blankets and travelling rugs
6301.9000 10	人造纤维制的毯子及旅行毯(非电暖的)	16				90	17	11	条/千克	B	Blankets (other than electric blankets) and travelling rugs of artificial fibres
6301.9000 20	丝制毯子及旅行毯(非电暖的,含丝及绢丝85%及以上)	16				90	17	11	条/千克	B	Blankets (other than electric blankets) and travelling rugs of silk, containing≥85% (W) of silk or silk waste
6301.9000 90	其他纺织材料制毯子及旅行毯(非电暖的)	16				90	17	11	条/千克	B	Other blankets (other than electric blankets) and travelling rugs, of other textile materials

税则号列 Tariff Item.	货品名称	最惠国(%) MFN	协定(%) 东盟 CA	中巴 CP	CT 中智 CC	普通 Gen	增值税率 VAT	出口退税 ED	计量单位 Unit	监管条件 SC	Article Description
63.02	**床上、餐桌、盥洗及厨房用的织物制品：**										**Bed linen, table linen, toilet linen and kitchen linen:**
	-针织或钩编的床上用织物制品：										-Bed linen, knitted or crocheted:
6302.1010	---棉制	14	T3	0	0	90	17	11	条/千克		---Of cotton
6302.1090	---其他纺织材料制	14	T3	0	0	130	17	11	条/千克		---Other
	-其他印花的床上用织物制品：										-Other bed linen, printed:
	--棉制：										--Of cotton:
6302.2110	---床单	14	T3	0	0	90	17	11	条/千克	5	---Bed sheets
6302.2190	---其他	14	T3	0	0	90	17	11	条/千克		---Other
6302.2190 10	棉制印花枕套	14				90	17	11	条/千克	5	Pillowcases, of cotton, printed
6302.2190 20	棉制印花枕罩	14				90	17	11	条/千克	5	Pillow protectors, of cotton, printed
6302.2190 90	其他棉制印花床上用织物制品	14				90	17	11	条/千克	5	Other bed linen, of cotton, printed
	--化学纤维制：										--Of man-made fibres:
6302.2210	---床单	16	T3	5	0	130	17	11	条/千克	5	---Bed sheets
6302.2290	---其他	16	T3	5	0	130	17	11	条/千克		---Other
6302.2290 10	化纤制印花枕套	16				130	17	11	条/千克	5	Pillowcases of man-made fibres, printed
6302.2290 20	化纤无纺织物制印花床用织物制品	16				130	17	11	条/千克		Bed linen of nonwoven of man-made fibres, printed
6302.2290 90	其他化纤制印花床上用织物制品	16				130	17	11	条/千克	5	Other bed linen of man-made fibres, printed
	--其他纺织材料制：										--Of other textile materials:
6302.2910	---丝及绢丝制	14	T3	0	0	130	17	11	条/千克		---Of silk or silk waste
6302.2910 10	丝及绢丝制印花床上用织物制品(含丝85%及以上)	14				130	17	11	条/千克		Bed linen of silk, containing ≥85% by weight of silk or silk waster, printed
6302.2910 90	丝及绢丝制印花床上用织物制品(含丝85%以下)	14				130	17	11	条/千克		Bed linen of silk, containing <85% by weight of silk or silk waster, printed
6302.2920	---麻制	14	T3	0	0	90	17	11	条/千克		---Of bast fibres
6302.2920 10	亚麻或苎麻制印花床上用织物制品	14				90	17	11	条/千克		Bed linen of flax or ramie, printed
6302.2920 90	其他麻制印花床上用织物制品	14				90	17	11	条/千克		Bed linen of other bast fibres, printed
6302.2990	---其他	14	T3	0	0	100	17	11	条/千克	5	---Other
	-其他床上用织物制品：										-Other bed linen:
	--棉制：										--Of cotton:
6302.3110	---刺绣的	14	T3	0	0	90	17	11	条/千克	5	---Embroidered
	---其他：										---Other:
6302.3191	----床单	14	T3	0	0	90	17	11	条/千克	5	----Bed sheets
6302.3192	----毛巾被	14	T3	0	0	90	17	11	条/千克	5a	----Towelling coverlets
6302.3199	----其他	14	T3	0	0	90	17	11	条/千克		----Other
6302.3199 10	棉制其他枕套	14				90	17	11	条/千克	5	Other pillowcases of cotton
6302.3199 20	其他棉与亚麻混纺床上用织物制品	14				90	17	11	条/千克	5	Other bed linen of blended fabrics of cotton and flax
6302.3199 30	棉制其他枕罩	14				90	17	11	条/千克	5	Pillow protectors of cotton

税则号列 Tariff Item.	货品名称	最惠国(%) MFN	协定(%)CT 东盟 CA	中巴 CP	中智 CC	普通 Gen	增值税率 VAT	出口退税 ED	计量单位 Unit	监管条件 SC	Article Description
6302.3199 90	棉制其他床上用织物制品	14				90	17	11	条/千克	5	Other bed linen of cotton
	--化学纤维制:										--Of man-made fibres:
6302.3210	---刺绣的	16	T3	5	0	130	17	11	条/千克	5	---Embroidered
6302.3290	---其他	16	T3	5	0	130	17	11	条/千克		---Other
6302.3290 10	化纤制其他床单	16				130	17	11	条/千克	5	Bed sheets of man-made fibres
6302.3290 20	化纤制其他枕套	16				130	17	11	条/千克	5	Other pillowcases, of man-made fibres
6302.3290 30	其他化纤无纺织物制床上织物制品	16				130	17	11	条/千克		Other bed linen of nonwoven fabrics, of man-made fibres
6302.3290 90	化纤制其他床上用织物制品	16				130	17	11	条/千克	5	Other bed linen, of man-made fibres
	--其他纺织材料制:										--Of other textile materials:
6302.3910	---丝及绢丝制	14	T3	0	0	130	17	11	条/千克		---Of silk or silk waste
6302.3910 10	丝及绢丝制其他床上用织物制品(含丝85%及以上)	14				130	17	11	条/千克		Other bed linen of silk and silk waste, containing silk ≥85%
6302.3910 90	丝及绢丝制其他床上用织物制品(含丝85%以下)	14				130	17	11	条/千克		Other bed linen of silk and silk waste, containing silk <85%
	---麻制:										---Of bast fibres:
6302.3921	----刺绣的	14	T3	0	0	90	17	11	条/千克		----Embroidered
6302.3921 10	亚麻或苎麻制其他床上用织物制品(刺绣的)	14				90	17	11	条/千克		Other bed linen of flax or ramie, embroidered
6302.3921 90	其他麻制其他床上用织物制品(刺绣的)	14				90	17	11	条/千克		Other bed linen of other bast fibres, embroidered
6302.3929	----其他	14	T3	0	0	90	17	11	条/千克		----Other
6302.3929 10	亚麻或苎麻制其他床上用织物制品	14				90	17	11	条/千克		Other bed linen of flax or ramie
6302.3929 90	其他麻制其他床上用织物制品	14				90	17	11	条/千克		Other bed linen of other bast fibres
	---其他:										---Other:
6302.3991	----刺绣的	14	T3	0	0	100	17	11	条/千克		----Embroidered
6302.3991 10	毛制刺绣床上用织物制品	14				100	17	11	条/千克	5	Other bed linen of wool or fine animal hair, embroidered
6302.3991 90	其他材料制刺绣床上用织物制品	14				100	17	11	条/千克		Other bed linen of other textile materials, embroidered
6302.3999	----其他	14	T3	0	0	100	17	11	条/千克		----Other
6302.3999 10	毛制刺绣床上用织物制品	14				100	17	11	条/千克	5	Other bed linen of wool or fine animal hair, embroidered
6302.3999 90	其他材料制其他床上用织物制品	14				100	17	11	条/千克		Other bed linen of other textile materials
	-针织或钩编的餐桌用织物制品:										-Table linen, knitted or crocheted:
6302.4010	---手工制	14	T3	0	0	100	17	11	件/千克		---Hand-worked
6302.4010 10	手工棉制餐桌用织物制品(指针织或钩编类的)	14				100	17	11	件/千克	B	Table linen of cotton, hand-worked
6302.4010 20	手工植物纺织纤维制餐桌用制品(指针织或钩编类的)	14				100	17	11	件/千克	B	Table linen of other vegetable textile fibres, hand-worked, knitted or crocheted
6302.4010 90	手工其他纺织材料制餐桌用制品(指针织或钩编类的)	14				100	17	11	件/千克	B	Other table linen of other textile materials, hand-worked, knitted or crocheted

税则号列 Tariff Item.	货 品 名 称	最惠国(%) MFN	协定(%)CT			普通 Gen	增值税率 VAT	出口退税 ED	计量单位 Unit	监管条件 SC	Article Description
			东盟 CA	中巴 CP	中智 CC						
6302.4090	---其他	14	T3	0	0	100	17	11	件/千克		---Other
6302.4090 10	棉制餐桌用织物制品(针织或钩编的,非手工)	14				100	17	11	件/千克		Table linen, of cotton, knitted or crocheted, other than hand-worked
6302.4090 20	植物纺织纤维制的餐桌用织物制品(针织或钩编的,非手工)	14				100	17	11	件/千克		Table linen, of other vegetable textile fibres, knitted or crocheted, other than hand-worked
6302.4090 90	其他纺织材料制餐桌用织物制品(针织或钩编的,非手工)	14				100	17	11	件/千克		Table linen, of other textile materials, knitted or crocheted, other than hand-worked
	-其他餐桌用织物制品:										-Other table linen:
	--棉制:										--Of cotton:
6302.5110	---刺绣的	14	T3	0	0	90	17	11	件/千克	5B	---Embroidered
6302.5190	---其他	14	T3	0	0	90	17	11	件/千克	5	---Other
	--化学纤维制:										--Of man-made fibres:
6302.5310	---刺绣的	14	T3	0	0	130	17	11	件/千克	5B	---Embroidered
6302.5390	---其他	16	T3	5	0	130	17	11	件/千克		---Other
6302.5390 10	化纤无纺织物制餐桌用织物制品	16				130	17	11	件/千克		Table linen of nonwoven fabrics of man-made fibres
6302.5390 90	化纤制其他餐桌用织物制品	16				130	17	11	件/千克	5	Other table linen of man-made fibres
	--其他纺织材料制:										--Of other textile materials:
	---亚麻制:										---Of flax:
6302.5911	----刺绣的	14	8	0	0	90	17	11	件/千克	B	----Embroidered
6302.5919	----其他	14	8	0	0	90	17	11	件/千克		----Other
6302.5990	---其他	14	T3	0	0	100	17	11	件/千克		---Other
6302.5990 10	羊毛或动物细毛制餐桌用织物制品	14				100	17	11	件/千克	5B	Table linen of wool or other fine animal hair
6302.5990 90	其他纺织材料制餐桌用织物制品	14				100	17	11	件/千克	B	Table linen of wool or other textile materials
	--盥洗及厨房用棉制毛巾织物或类似的毛圈织物的制品:										--Toilet linen and kitchen linen, of terry towelling or similar terry fabrics, of cotton:
6302.6010	---浴巾	14	T3	0	0	90	17	11	条/千克		---Bath towels
6302.6010 10	棉制针织或钩编毛巾织物浴巾(含类似毛圈织物的制品)	14				90	17	11	条/千克	5a	Bath towels, of terry towelling or similar terry fabrics, of cotton, knitted or crocheted
6302.6010 90	棉制非针织或非钩编毛巾织物浴巾(含类似毛圈织物的制品)	14				90	17	11	条/千克	5a	Bath towels, of terry towelling or similar terry fabrics, of cotton, not knitted or crocheted
6302.6090	---其他	14	T3	0	0	90	17	11	条/千克		---Other
6302.6090 11	棉制针织或钩编毛巾织物茶巾(包括类似毛圈织物的制品)	14				90	17	11	条/千克	a	Tea cloth, knitted or crocheted, of terry towelling or similar terry fabrics, of cotton
6302.6090 19	棉制非针织或非钩编毛巾织物茶巾(包括类似毛圈织物的制品)	14				90	17	11	条/千克	a	Tea cloth, not knitted or crocheted, of terry towelling or similar terry fabrics, of cotton
6302.6090 91	棉制其他盥洗及厨房用毛巾制品(包括类似毛圈织物的制品,针织或钩编)	14				90	17	11	条/千克	5a	Other toilet linen and kitchen linen, of terry towelling or similar terry fabrics, of cotton, knitted or crocheted

税则号列 Tariff Item.	货品名称	最惠国(%) MFN	协定(%)CT 东盟 CA	 中巴 CP	 中智 CC	普通 Gen	增值税率 VAT	出口退税 ED	计量单位 Unit	监管条件 SC	Article Description
6302.6090 99	棉制其他盥洗及厨房用毛巾制品(含类似毛圈织物的制品,非针织或非钩编)	14				90	17	11	条/千克	5a	Other toilet linen and kitchen linen, of terry towelling or similar terry fabrics, of cotton, not knitted or crocheted
	-其他:										-Other:
6302.9100	--棉制	14	T3	0	0	90	17	11	条/千克		--Of cotton
6302.9100 10	棉制茶巾(毛巾织物或类似毛圈织物的除外)	14				90	17	11	条/千克	5	Tea cloth of cotton, other than of terry towelling or similar terry fabrics
6302.9100 20	棉制毛巾(毛巾织物或类似毛圈织物的除外)	14				90	17	11	条/千克	5	Towels of cotton, other than of terry towelling or similar terry fabrics
6302.9100 90	棉制其他盥洗及厨房织物制品(毛巾织物或类似毛圈织物的除外)	14				90	17	11	条/千克	5	Other toilet linen and kitchen linen of cotton, other than of terry towelling or similar terry fabrics
6302.9300	--化学纤维制	16	T3	5	0	130	17	11	条/千克		--Of man-made fibres
6302.9300 10	化纤无纺织物制盥洗及厨房制品(毛巾织物或类似毛圈织物的除外)	16				130	17	11	条/千克		Toilet linen and kitchen linen of nonwoven fabrics of man-made fibres, other than of terry towelling or similar terry fabrics
6302.9300 90	化纤制其他盥洗及厨房织物制品(毛巾织物或类似毛圈织物的除外)	16				130	17	11	条/千克	5	Other toilet linen and kitchen linen of man-made fibres, other than of terry towelling or similar terry fabrics
	--其他纺织材料制:										--Of other textile materials:
6302.9910	---亚麻制	14	8	0	0	90	17	11	条/千克		---Of flax
6302.9990	---其他	14	T3	0	0	100	17	11	条/千克		---Other
6302.9990 10	毛制盥洗及厨房用织物制品(毛巾织物或类似毛圈织物的除外)	14				100	17	11	条/千克	5	Other toilet linen and kitchen linen, of wool or other fine animal hair
6302.9990 90	其他材料制其他盥洗及厨房织物(毛巾织物或类似毛圈织物的除外)	14				100	17	11	条/千克		Other toilet linen and kitchen linen of other textile materials, other than of terry towelling or similar terry fabrics
63.03	**窗帘(包括帷帘)及帐幔;帘帷或床帷:**										**Curtains (including drapes) and interior blinds; curtain or bed valances:**
	-针织或钩编的:										-Knitted or crocheted:
	--合成纤维制:										--Of synthetic fibres:
6303.1210	---针织的	16	T3	5	0	130	17	11	件/千克		---Knitted
6303.1210 10	合纤制针织百叶窗、卷窗和窗幔	16				130	17	11	件/千克	5	Curtains(inclucling drapes drapes) and interior or blinds; curtain or bed valances, of crocheted, of synthetic fibres
6303.1210 90	其他合纤制针织窗帘等(包括帷帘,帐幔,帘帷及床帷)	16				130	17	11	件/千克		Curtains, of knitted, of synthetic fibres (including drapes, interior blinds, curtain and bed valances)
6303.1220	---钩编的	16	T3	5	0	130	17	11	件/千克		---Crocheted
6303.1220 10	合纤制钩编百叶窗,卷帘和窗幔	16				130	17	11	件/千克	5	Curtains (including drapes) and interior blinds; curtain or bed valances of crocheted, of synthetic fibres
6303.1220 90	其他合纤制钩编的窗帘等(包括帷帘,帐幔,帘帷及床帷)	16				130	17	11	件/千克		Other curtains of crocheted, of synthetic fibres etc (including drapes, interor blinds, curtain and bed valances)
	--其他纺织材料制:										--Of other textile materials:
	---棉制:										---Of cotton:

税则号列 Tariff Item.	货品名称	最惠国(%) MFN	协定(%) 东盟 CA	中巴 CP	CT 中智 CC	普通 Gen	增值税率 VAT	出口退税 ED	计量单位 Unit	监管条件 SC	Article Description
6303.1931	----针织的	14	T3	0	0	90	17	11	件/千克		----Knitted
6303.1932	----钩织的	14	T3	0	0	90	17	11	件/千克		----Crocheted
	---其他：										---Other:
6303.1991	----针织的	14	8	0	0	130	17	11	件/千克		----Knitted
6303.1992	----钩编的	14	8	0	0	130	17	11	件/千克		----Crocheted
	-其他：										-Other:
6303.9100	--棉制	14	8	0	0	90	17	11	件/千克		--Of cotton
6303.9100 10	棉制非针织网眼窗帘(包括帷帘、帐幔、帘帷及床帷)	14				90	17	11	件/千克		Curtains (including drapes) and interior blinds; curtain or bed valances, of cotton, nets, not knitted
6303.9100 90	棉制非针织非钩编窗帘(包括帷帘、帐幔、帘帷及床帷)	14				90	17	11	件/千克		Curtains (including drapes) and interior blinds; curtain or bed valances, of cotton, nets, not knitted or crocheted
6303.9200	--合成纤维制	16	T3	5	0	130	17	11	件/千克		--Of synthetic fibres
6303.9200 10	合纤百叶窗、卷帘和窗幔(非针织非钩编)	16				130	17	11	件/千克	5	Curtains (including drapes) and interior blinds; curtain or bed valances, of nonwoven fabrics of synthetic fibres
6303.9200 90	其他合纤制非针织非钩编窗帘等(包括帷帘、帐幔、帘帷及床帷)	16				130	17	11	件/千克		Curtains (including drapes) and interior blinds; curtain or bed valances, of synthetic fibres, not knitted or crocheted
6303.9900	--其他纺织材料制	14	T3	0	0	100	17	11	件/千克		--Of other textile materials
6303.9900 10	毛制非针织非钩编窗帘(包括帷帘、帐幔、帘帷及床帷)	14				100	17	11	件/千克		Curtains (including drapes) and interior blinds; curtain or bed valances, not knitted or crocheted, of wool or fine animal hair
6303.9900 20	人造纤维制非针织非钩编窗帘(包括帷帘、帐幔、帘帷及床帷)	14				100	17	11	件/千克		Curtains (including drapes) and interior blinds; curtain or bed valances, not knitted or crocheted, of artificial fibres
6303.9900 31	丝制非针织非钩编窗帘(包括帷帘、帐幔、帘帷及床帷,含丝85%及以上)	14				100	17	11	件/千克		Curtains (including drapes) and interior blinds; curtain or bed valances, not knitted or crocheted, containing silk ≥85%
6303.9900 39	丝制非针织非钩编窗帘(含帷帘、帐幔、帘帷及床帷,含丝85%以下)	14				100	17	11	件/千克		Curtains (including drapes) and interior blinds; curtain or bed valances, not knitted or crocheted, containing silk <85%
6303.9900 40	其他纺织材料无纺织物制窗帘(包括帷帘、帐幔、帘帷及床帷)	14				100	17	11	件/千克		Curtains (including drapes) and interior blinds; curtain or bed valances, of nonwoven fabrics of other textile materials
6303.9900 50	亚麻或苎麻制非针织非钩编窗帘(包括帷帘、帐幔、帘帷及床帷)	14				100	17	11	件/千克		Curtains (including drapes) and interior blinds; curtain or bed valances, not knitted or crocheted, of flax or ramie
6303.9900 60	其他纺织材料制非针织网眼窗帘(包括帷帘、帐幔、帘帷及床帷)	14				100	17	11	件/千克		Curtains (including drapes) and interior blinds; curtain or bed valances, not knitted, nets, of other textile materials

税则号列 Tariff Item.	货品名称	最惠国(%) MFN	协定(%)CT 东盟 CA	中巴 CP	中智 CC	普通 Gen	增值税率 VAT	出口退税 ED	计量单位 Unit	监管条件 SC	Article Description
6303.9900 90	其他纺织材料制非针织非钩编窗帘(包括帷帘、帐幔、帘帷及床帷)	14				100	17	11	件/千克		Curtains (including drapes) and interior blinds; curtain or bed valances, not knitted or crocheted, of other textile materials
63.04	**其他装饰用织物制品,但税目94.04的货品除外:**										**Other furnishing articles, excluding those of heading No. 94.04:**
	-床罩:										-Bedspreads:
	--针织或钩编的:										--Knitted or crocheted:
	---针织的:										---Knitted:
6304.1121	----手工制	14	T3		0	100	17	11	件/千克		----Hand-worked
6304.1121 10	棉制手工针织床罩	14				100	17	11	件/千克		Bedspreads, knitted, hand-worked, of cotton
6304.1121 20	化纤制手工针织床罩	14				100	17	11	件/千克		Bedspreads, knitted, hand-worked, of man-made fibres
6304.1121 90	其他纺织材料制手工针织床罩	14				100	17	11	件/千克		Bedspreads, knitted, hand-worked, of other textile materials
6304.1129	----其他	14	T3		0	100	17	11	件/千克		----Other
6304.1129 10	棉制非手工针织床罩	14				100	17	11	件/千克		Bedspreads, knitted, other than hand-worked, of cotton
6304.1129 20	化纤制非手工针织床罩	14				100	17	11	件/千克		Bedspreads, knitted, other than hand-worked, of man-made fibres
6304.1129 90	其他纺织材料制非手工针织床罩	14				100	17	11	件/千克		Bedspreads, knitted, other than hand-worked, of other textile materials
	---钩编的:										---Crocheted:
6304.1131	----手工制	14	T3		0	100	17	11	件/千克		----Hand-worked
6304.1131 10	棉制手工钩编床罩	14				100	17	11	件/千克		Bedspreads, crocheted, hand-worked, of cotton
6304.1131 20	化纤制手工钩编床罩	14				100	17	11	件/千克		Bedspreads, crocheted, hand-worked, of man-made fibres
6304.1131 90	其他纺织材料制手工钩编床罩	14				100	17	11	件/千克		Bedspreads, crocheted, hand-worked, of other textile materials
6304.1139	----其他	14	T3		0	100	17	11	件/千克		----Other
6304.1139 10	棉制非手工钩编床罩	14				100	17	11	件/千克		Bedspreads, crocheted, other than hand-worked, of cotton
6304.1139 20	化纤制非手工钩编床罩	14				100	17	11	件/千克		Bedspreads, crocheted, other than hand-worked, of man-made fibres
6304.1139 90	其他纺织材料制非手工钩编床罩	14				100	17	11	件/千克		Bedspreads, crocheted, other than hand-worked, of other textile materials
	--其他:										--Other:
6304.1910	---丝及绢丝制	14	T3		0	130	17	11	件/千克		---Of silk or silk waste
6304.1910 10	丝及绢丝制非针织非钩编床罩(含丝85%及以上)	14				130	17	11	件/千克		Bedspreads of silk or silk waste, containing silk≥85%
6304.1910 90	丝及绢丝制非针织非钩编床罩(含丝85%以下)	14				130	17	11	件/千克		Bedspreads of silk or silk waste, containing silk <85%
	---棉或麻制:										---Of cotton or bast fibres:
6304.1921	----刺绣的	14	T3		0	90	17	11	件/千克		----Embroidered
6304.1921 10	亚麻或苎麻制刺绣床罩(指非针织非钩编)	14				90	17	11	件/千克		Bedspreads, embroidered, not knitted or crocheted, of flax ramie

税则号列 Tariff Item.	货品名称	最惠国(%) MFN	协定(%) 东盟 CA	中巴 CP	CT 中智 CC	普通 Gen	增值税率 VAT	出口退税 ED	计量单位 Unit	监管条件 SC	Article Description
6304.1921 20	其他麻制非针织非钩编刺绣床罩	14				90	17	11	件/千克		Bedspreads, embroidered, not knitted or crocheted, of other bast fibres
6304.1921 90	棉制非针织非钩编刺绣床罩	14				90	17	11	件/千克		Bedspreads, embroidered, not knitted or crocheted, of cotton
6304.1929	----其他	14	T3		0	90	17	11	件/千克		----Other
6304.1929 10	亚麻或苎麻制非针织非钩编床罩	14				90	17	11	件/千克		Bedspreads, not knitted or crocheted, of flax or ramie
6304.1929 91	其他麻制其他非针织非钩编床罩	14				90	17	11	件/千克		Bedspreads, not knitted or crocheted, of other bast fibres
6304.1929 99	棉制其他非针织非钩编床罩	14				90	17	11	件/千克		Bedspreads, not knitted or crocheted, of cotton
	---化学纤维制:										---Of man-made fibres:
6304.1931	----刺绣的	16	T3		0	130	17	11	件/千克		----Embroidered
6304.1939	----其他	16	T3		0	130	17	11	件/千克		----Other
	---其他纺织材料制:										---Of other textile materials:
6304.1991	----刺绣的	14	T3		0	100	17	11	件/千克		----Embroidered
6304.1991 10	毛制非针织非钩编刺绣床罩(羊毛或动物细毛制)	14				100	17	11	件/千克		Bedspreads, not knitted or crocheted, embroidered, of wool or fine animal hair
6304.1991 90	其他纺织材料制非针织刺绣床罩(含非钩编的)	14				100	17	11	件/千克		Bedspreads, not knitted or crocheted, embroidered, of other textile materials
6304.1999	----其他	14	T3		0	100	17	11	件/千克		----Other
6304.1999 10	毛制其他非针织非钩编床罩(羊毛或动物细毛制)	14				100	17	11	件/千克		Bedspreads, not knitted or crocheted, embroidered, of wool or fine animal hair
6304.1999 90	其他材料制非针织非钩编其他床罩	14				100	17	11	件/千克		Bedspreads, not knitted or crocheted, embroidered, of other textile materials
	-其他:										-Other:
	--针织或钩编的:										--Knitted or crocheted:
	---针织的:										---Knitted:
6304.9121	----手工制	14	T3		0	100	17	11	千克		----Hand-worked
6304.9121 10	棉制手工针织的其他装饰制品	14				100	17	11	千克		Other furnishing articles, knitted hand-worked, of cotton
6304.9121 20	毛制手工针织的其他装饰制品(羊毛或动物细毛制)	14				100	17	11	千克		Other furnishing articles, knitted, hand-worked, of wool or fine animal hair
6304.9121 31	丝制手工针织的其他装饰制品(含丝85%及以上)	14				100	17	11	千克		Other furnishing articles, knitted, hand-worked, containing silk ≥85%
6304.9121 39	丝制手工针织的其他装饰制品(含丝85%以下)	14				100	17	11	千克		Other furnishing articles, knitted, hand-worked, containing silk >85%
6304.9121 40	化纤制手工针织的其他装饰制品	14				100	17	11	千克		Other furnishing articles, knitted, hand-worked, of man-made fibres
6304.9121 90	其他纺织材料制手工针织其他装饰制品	14				100	17	11	千克		Other furnishing articles, knitted, hand-worked, of other textile materials
6304.9129	----其他	14	T3		0	100	17	11	千克		----Other
6304.9129 10	棉制非手工针织的其他装饰制品	14				100	17	11	千克		Other furnishing articles, knitted, not hand-worked, of cotton

税则号列 Tariff Item.	货品名称	最惠国(%) MFN	协定(%)CT 东盟 CA	协定(%)CT 中巴 CP	协定(%)CT 中智 CC	普通 Gen	增值税率 VAT	出口退税 ED	计量单位 Unit	监管条件 SC	Article Description
6304.9129 20	毛制非手工针织的其他装饰制品(羊毛或动物细毛制)	14				100	17	11	千克		Other furnishing articles, knitted, not hand-worked, of wool or fine animal hair
6304.9129 31	丝制非手工针织的其他装饰制品(含丝85%及以上)	14				100	17	11	千克		Other furnishing articles, knitted, not hand-worked, containing silk≥85%
6304.9129 39	丝制非手工针织的其他装饰制品(含丝85%以下)	14				100	17	11	千克		Other furnishing articles, knitted, not hand-worked, containing silk <85%
6304.9129 40	化纤制非手工针织其他装饰制品	14				100	17	11	千克		Other furnishing articles, knitted, not hand-worked, of man-made fibres
6304.9129 90	其他纺织材料制非手工针织其他装饰品	14				100	17	11	千克		Other furnishing articles, knitted, not hand-worked, of other textile materials
	---钩编的:										---Crocheted:
6304.9131	----手工制	14	T3		0	100	17	11	千克		----Hand-worked
6304.9131 10	棉制手工钩编的其他装饰制品	14				100	17	11	千克		Other furnishing articles, crocheted, hand-worked, of cotton
6304.9131 20	毛制手工钩编的其他装饰制品(羊毛或动物细毛制)	14				100	17	11	千克		Other furnishing articles, crocheted, hand-worked, of wool or fine animal hair
6304.9131 31	丝制手工钩编的其他装饰制品(含丝85%及以上)	14				100	17	11	千克		Other furnishing articles of silk, crocheted, hand-worked, containing silk ≥85%
6304.9131 39	丝制手工钩编的其他装饰制品(含丝85%以下)	14				100	17	11	千克		Other furnishing articles of silk, crocheted, hand-worked, containing silk <85%
6304.9131 40	化纤制手工钩编的其他装饰制品	14				100	17	11	千克		Other furnishing articles, crocheted, hand-worked, of man-made fibres
6304.9131 90	其他制手工钩编的其他装饰制品	14				100	17	11	千克		Other furnishing articles, crocheted, hand-worked, of other textile materials
6304.9139	----其他	14	T3		0	100	17	11	千克		----Other
6304.9139 10	棉制非手工钩编的其他装饰制品	14				100	17	11	千克		Other furnishing articles, crocheted, not hand-worked, of cotton
6304.9139 20	毛制非手工钩编的其他装饰制品(羊毛或动物细毛制)	14				100	17	11	千克		Other furnishing articles, crocheted, not hand-worked, of wool or fine animal hair
6304.9139 31	丝制非手工钩编的其他装饰制品(含丝85%及以上)	14				100	17	11	千克		Other furnishing articles of silk, crocheted, not hand-worked, containing silk≥85%
6304.9139 39	丝制非手工钩编的其他装饰制品(含丝85%以下)	14				100	17	11	千克		Other furnishing articles of silk, crocheted, not hand-worked, containing silk <85%
6304.9139 40	化纤制非手工钩编其他装饰制品	14				100	17	11	千克		Other furnishing articles, crocheted, not hand-worked, of man-made fibres
6304.9139 90	其他纺织材料制非手工钩编其他装饰品	14				100	17	11	千克		Other furnishing articles, crocheted, not hand-worked, of other textile materials
	--非针织或非钩编的,棉制:										--Not knitted or crocheted, of cotton:
6304.9210	---刺绣的	14	8		0	90	17	11	千克	B	---Embroidered
6304.9290	---其他	14	8		0	90	17	11	千克		---Other

税则号列 Tariff Item.	货品名称	最惠国(%) MFN	协定(%) CT 东盟 CA	中巴 CP	中智 CC	普通 Gen	增值税率 VAT	出口退税 ED	计量单位 Unit	监管条件 SC	Article Description
	--非针织或非钩编的,合成纤维制:										--Not knitted or crocheted, of synthetic fibres:
6304.9310	---刺绣的	16	T3		0	130	17	11	千克	B	---Embroidered
6304.9390	---其他	16	T3		0	130	17	11	千克		---Other
	--非针织或非钩编的,其他纺织材料制:										--Not knitted or crocheted, of other textile materials:
6304.9910	---丝及绢丝制	14	T3		0	130	17	11	千克		---Of silk or silk waste
6304.9910 10	丝制非针织非钩编的装饰制品(含绢丝制品,含丝85%及以上)	14				130	17	11	千克	B	Other furnishing articles of silk, not knitted or crocheted, containing silk or silk waste≥85%
6304.9910 90	丝制非针织非钩编的装饰制品(含绢丝制品,含丝85%以下)	14				130	17	11	千克	B	Other furnishing articles of silk, not knitted or crocheted, containing silk or silk waste <85%
	---麻制:										---Of bast fibres:
6304.9921	----刺绣的	14	T3		0	90	17	11	千克		----Embroidered
6304.9921 10	亚麻或苎麻非针织其他刺绣装饰品(含非钩编制品)	14				90	17	11	千克	B	Other furnishing articles, not knitted or crocheted, embroidered, of flax or ramie
6304.9921 90	其他麻制非针织其他刺绣装饰品(包括非钩编的)	14				90	17	11	千克	B	Other furnishing articles, not knitted or crocheted, embroidered, of other bast fibres
6304.9929	----其他	14	T3		0	90	17	11	千克		----Other
6304.9929 10	亚麻或苎麻制其他非针织的装饰品(含非钩编制品)	14				90	17	11	千克		Other furnishing articles, not knitted or crocheted, of flax or ramie
6304.9929 90	其他麻制其他非针织的装饰制品(含非钩编制品)	14				90	17	11	千克		Other furnishing articles not knitted or crocheted, of other bast fibres
6304.9990	---其他	14	T3		0	100	17	11	千克		---Other
6304.9990 10	毛制非针织非钩编装饰制品(羊毛或动物细毛制)	14				100	17	11	千克	B	Other furnishing articles, not knitted or crocheted, of wool or fine animal hair
6304.9990 20	人造纤维制非针织非钩编装饰品	14				100	17	11	千克	B	Other furnishing articles, not knitted or crocheted, of man-made fibres
6304.9990 90	其他材料制非针织非钩编装饰品	14				100	17	11	千克	B	Other furnishing articles, not knitted or crocheted, of other textile materials
63.05	**货物包装用袋:**										**Sacks and bags, of a kind used for the packing of goods:**
6305.1000	-黄麻或税目53.03的其他韧皮纺织纤维制	10	5		0	40	17	11	条/千克		-Of jute or of other textile bast fibres of heading No. 53.03
6305.1000 10	黄麻制旧的货物包装袋(含品目5303的其他韧皮纤维制)	10				40	17	11	条/千克		Sacks and bags, of a kind used for the packing of goods, of jute or of other textile bast fibres of heading No. 53.03, used
6305.1000 90	黄麻制其他货物包装袋(含品目5303的其他韧皮纤维制)	10				40	17	11	条/千克		Other sacks and bags, of a kind used for the packing of goods, of jute or of other textile bast fibres of heading No. 53.03
6305.2000	-棉制	16	8		0	90	17	11	条/千克		-Of cotton
	-化学纤维材料制:										-Of man-made textile materials:
6305.3200	--散装货物储运软袋	16	8		0	100	17	11	条/千克		--Flexible intermediate bulk containers

税则号列 Tariff Item.	货品名称	最惠国(%) MFN	协定(%)CT 东盟 CA	中巴 CP	中智 CC	普通 Gen	增值税率 VAT	出口退税 ED	计量单位 Unit	监管条件 SC	Article Description
6305.3200 11	聚乙烯或聚丙烯制软袋(针织或钩编的,用扁条及类似材料制成,散装货物周转用)	16				100	17	11	条/千克		Sacks and bags, of a kind used for the packing of goods, flexible intermediate bulk containers of PE or PP strip or the like, knitted or crocheted
6305.3200 19	聚乙烯或聚丙烯制软袋(非针织或钩编的,扁条及类似材料制成,散装货物周转用)	16				100	17	11	条/千克		Sacks and bags, of a kind used for the packing of goods, flexible intermediate bulk containers of PE or PP strip or the like, not knited or crocheted
6305.3200 90	化纤制的散装货物周转软袋	16				100	17	11	条/千克		Sacks and bags, of a kind used for the packing of goods, flexible intermediate bulk containers, of man-made fibres
6305.3300	--其他,聚乙烯、聚丙烯扁条或类似材料制	16	T3	13.6	0	100	17	11	条/千克		--Other, of polyethylene or polypropylene strip or the like
6305.3300 10	聚乙烯或聚丙烯制其他货物包装袋(针织或钩编的,用扁条及类似材料制成)	16				100	17	11	条/千克		Sacks and bags, of a kind used for the packing of goods, of PE or PP strip or the like, knitted or crocheted
6305.3300 90	聚乙烯或聚丙烯制其他货物包装袋(非针织或钩编的,用扁条及类似材料制成)	16				100	17	11	条/千克		Sacks and bags, of a kind used for the packing of goods, of PE or PP strip or the like, not knitted or crocheted
6305.3900	--其他	16	T3		0	100	17	11	条/千克		--Other
6305.9000	-其他纺织材料制	14	T3		0	90	17	11	条/千克		-Of other textile materials
6305.9000 11	亚麻制旧货物包装袋(针织或钩编的)	14				90	17	11	条/千克		Sacks and bags, of a kind used for the packing of goods, of flax, knitted or crocheted, used
6305.9000 19	其他亚麻制旧货物包装袋	14				90	17	11	条/千克		Sacks and bags, of a kind used for the packing of goods of flax, not knitted or crocheted, used
6305.9000 90	其他纺织材料制其他货物包装袋	14				90	17	11	条/千克		Other sacks and bags, of a kind used for the packing of goods, of other textile materials
63.06	**油苫布、天篷及遮阳篷;帐篷;风帆;野营用品:**										**Tarpaulins, awnings and sunblinds; tents; sails for boats, sailboards or landcraft; camping goods:**
	-油苫布、天篷及遮阳篷:										-Tarpaulins, awnings and sunblinds:
6306.1200	--合成纤维制	16	8	5	0	130	17	11	件/千克		--Of synthetic fibres
	--其他纺织材料制:										--Of other textile materials:
6306.1910	---麻制	14	8	0	0	80	17	11	件/千克		---Of bast fibres
6306.1920	---棉制	14	8	0	0	80	17	11	件/千克		Cotton
6306.1990	---其他	14	8	0	0	100	17	11	件/千克		---Other
6306.1990 10	人造纤维制油苫布、天篷及遮阳篷	14				100	17	11	件/千克		Tarpaulins, awnings and sunblinds, of man-made fibres
6306.1990 90	其他材料制油苫布、天篷及遮阳篷	14				100	17	11	件/千克		Tarpaulins, awnings and sunblinds, of other textile materials
	-帐篷:										-Tents:
6306.2200	--合成纤维制	16	8	5	0	130	17	11	件/千克		--Of synthetic fibres
6306.2200 10	合纤制移动帐篷、天篷及遮阳篷	16				130	17	11	件/千克	a	Moveable, tents, awnings and sunblinds, of synthetic fibres
6306.2200 90	合纤制帐篷	16				130	17	11	件/千克	a	Other tents of synthetic fibres

税则号列 Tariff Item.	货品名称	最惠国(%) MFN	协定(%)CT 东盟 CA	中巴 CP	中智 CC	普通 Gen	增值税率 VAT	出口退税 ED	计量单位 Unit	监管条件 SC	Article Description
	--其他纺织材料制:										--Of other textile materials
6306.2910	---棉制	14	8	0	0	80	17	11	件/千克	a	---Cotton
6306.2990	---其他	14	8	0	0	100	17	11	件/千克	a	---Other
	-风帆:										-Sails:
6306.3010	---合成纤维制	16	8	5	0	130	17	11	件/千克		---Of synthetic fibres
6306.3090	---其他纺织材料制	14	8	0	0	100	17	11	件/千克		---Of other textile materials
	-充气褥垫:										-Pneumatic mattresses:
6306.4010	--棉制	14	8	0	0	80	17	11	件/千克		--Of cotton
6306.4020	---化学纤维制	16	8	5	0	130	17	11	件/千克		---Of man-made fibres
6306.4090	---其他	14	8	0	0	100	17	11	件/千克		---Other
	-其他:										-Other:
6306.9100	--棉制	14	8	0	0	80	17	11	件/千克		--Of cotton
	--其他纺织材料制:										--Of other textile materials:
6306.9910	---麻制	14	8	0	0	80	17	11	件/千克		---Of bast fibres
6306.9920	---化学纤维制	16	8	5	0	130	17	11	件/千克		---Of man-made fibres
6306.9990	---其他	14	8	0	0	100	17	11	件/千克		---Other
63.07	**其他制成品,包括服装裁剪样:**										**Other made up articles, including dress patterns:**
6307.1000	-擦地布、擦碗布、抹布及类似擦拭用布	14	8	11.9	0	130	17	11	件/千克		-Floor-cloths, dish-cloths, dusters and similar cleaning cloths
6307.1000 11	棉制抹布、拖布及擦光布	14				130	17	11	件/千克		Floor-cloths, dish-cloths, dusters and similar cleaning cloths, of cotton
6307.1000 19	其他纺织材料抹布、拖布及擦光布	14				130	17	11	件/千克		Floor-cloths, dish-cloths, dusters and similar cleaning cloths, of other textile materials
6307.1000 21	棉制汽车修理厂加油站等工厂用巾	14				130	17	11	件/千克		Floor-cloths, dish-cloths, dusters and similar cleaning cloths, of cotton, for garages or filling-station
6307.1000 29	其他纺织材料制汽车修理厂等工厂用巾	14				130	17	11	件/千克		Floor-cloths, dish-cloths, dusters and similar cleaning cloths, of other textile materials, for garages
6307.1000 30	棉毛圈织物制酒吧用布[(46-57)厘米×(38-43)厘米]	14				130	17	11	件/千克		Terry fabrics of cotton, for bar [(46~57)cm×(38~43)cm]
6307.1000 41	棉制擦碗布	14				130	17	11	件/千克		Dish-cloths of cotton
6307.1000 49	其他纺织材料制擦碗布	14				130	17	11	件/千克		Dish-cloths of other textile materials
6307.1000 90	其他擦拭用布等(含抹布及类似擦拭用布)	14				130	17	11	件/千克		Other floor-cloths, dish-cloths, dusters and similar cleaning cloths
6307.2000	-救生衣及安全带	14	8		0	70	17	11	件/千克		-Life-jackets and life-belts
6307.9000	-其他	14	T3		0	100	17	11	千克		-Other
6307.9000 11	棉制标签、服饰辫线及流苏(含紧身胸衣、鞋及类似品的系带)	14				100	17	11	千克		Label, chain-off thread and fringes, including laces of corsets, shoelaces and similar articles, of cotton
6307.9000 19	其他制标签、服饰辫线及流苏(含紧身胸衣、鞋及类似品的系带)	14				100	17	11	千克		Label, chain-off thread and fringes, including laces of corsets, shoelaces and similar articles, of other textile materials
6307.9000 20	棉制起绒或簇绒织物制毛巾	14				100	17	11	千克	5	Towel, pile fabrics, tufted, of cotton
6307.9000 30	棉制枕壳	14				100	17	11	千克		Outershell of pillow, of cotton

税则号列 Tariff Item.	货品名称	最惠国(%) MFN	协定(%)CT			普通 Gen	增值税率 VAT	出口退税 ED	计量单位 Unit	监管条件 SC	Article Description
			东盟 CA	中巴 CP	中智 CC						
6307.9000 40	棉制被壳、羽绒被壳、盖被壳(含类似品,含棉85%以下)	14				100	17	11	千克		Outershell of down quilt or comforter, of cotton, containing cotton <85%
6307.9000 51	棉制手术用巾及其他毛巾	14				100	17	11	千克		Towel for operation and other towel, of cotton
6307.9000 59	化学纤维制未列名毛巾	14				100	17	11	千克		Towel of man-made fibres, not elsewhere specified or included
6307.9000 61	以棉作面的冷藏包	14				100	17	11	千克		Cotton facing refrigerating bag
6307.9000 62	以化纤纺织材料做面的冷藏包	14				100	17	11	千克		Man-made textile materials facing refrigerating bag
6307.9000 69	其他纺织材料做面的冷藏包	14				100	17	11	千克		Other textile materials facing refrigerating bag
6307.9000 90	纺织材料制未列名制品	14				100	17	11	千克		Other made up articles, not elsewhere specified or included, of other textile materials
	第二分章 成套物品										Ⅱ. -SETS
63.08	**由机织物及纱线构成的零售包装成套物品,不论是否带附件,用以制作小地毯、装饰毯、绣花台布、餐巾或类似的纺织物品:**										**Sets consisting of woven fabric and yarn, whether or not with accessories, for making up into rugs, tapestries, embroidered table cloths or serviettes, or similar textile articles, put up in packings for retail sale:**
6308.0000	由机织物及纱线构成的零售包装成套物品,不论是否带附件,用以制作小地毯、装饰毯、绣花台布、餐巾或类似的纺织物品	14	T3		0	130	17	11	千克		Sets consisting of woven fabric and yarn, whether or not with accessories, for making up into rugs, tapestries, embroidered table cloths or serviettes, or similar textile articles, put up in packings for retail sale
6308.0000 10	机织物及纱线制零售包装成套物品(内含羊毛纱的)	14				130	17	11	千克		Sets consisting of woven fabric and yarn, containing wool yarn, put up in packings for retail sale
6308.0000 20	机织物及纱线制零售包装成套物品(由普通棉机织物及棉衍缝被褥织物与纱线构成的)	14				130	17	11	千克	5	Sets consisting of woven fabric, guilted textile products by stitching and yarn, of cotton, put up in packings for retail sale
6308.0000 30	机织物及纱线制零售包装成套物品(由合成纤维普通机织物及衍缝被褥织物与纱线构成)	14				130	17	11	千克		Sets consisting of woven fabric, guilted textile products by stitching and yarn, of synthetic fibres, put up in packings for retail sale
6308.0000 90	其他机织物及纱线构成的成套物品(零售包装的)	14				130	17	11	千克		Other sets consisting of woven fabric and yarn, put up in packing for retail sale
	第三分章 旧衣着及旧纺织品;碎织物										Ⅲ. -WORN CLOTHING AND WORN TEXTILE ARTICLES; RAGS
63.09	**旧衣物:**										**Worn clothing and other worn articles:**
6309.0000	旧衣物	14	12		0	130	17		千克	9	Worn clothing and other worn articles
63.10	**纺织材料的新的或旧的碎织物及废线、绳、索、缆及其制品:**										**Used or new rags, scrap twine, cordage, rope and cables and worn out articles of twine, cordage, rope or cables, of textile materials:**
6310.1000	-经分拣的	14	T3		0	50	17	11	千克		-Sorted

税则号列 Tariff Item.	货品名称	最惠国(%) MFN	协定(%) CT 东盟 CA	中巴 CP	中智 CC	普通 Gen	增值税率 VAT	出口退税 ED	计量单位 Unit	监管条件 SC	Article Description
6310.1000 10	新的或未使用过的纺织材料制经分拣的碎织物等(新的或未使用过的,包括废线,绳,索,缆及其制品)	14				50	17	11	千克	AP	Not used or new rags, scrap twine, cordage, rope and cables and worn out articles of twine, cordage, rope or cables, of textile materials, sorted
6310.1000 90	其他纺织材料制经分拣的碎织物等(包括废线,绳,索,缆及其制品)	14				50	17	11	千克		Other rags, scrap twine, cordage, rope and cables and worn out articles of twine, cordage, rope or cables, of textile materials, sorted
6310.9000	-其他	14	T3		0	50	17	11	千克		-Other
6310.9000 10	新的或未使用过的纺织材料制其他碎织物等(新的或未使用过的,包括废线,绳,索,缆及其制品)	14				50	17	11	千克	AP	Not used or new rags, scrap twine, cordage, rope and cables and worn out articles of twine, cordage, rope or cables, of textile materials
6310.9000 90	其他纺织材料制碎织物等(包括废线,绳,索,缆及其制品)	14				50	17	11	千克		Other rags, scrap twine, cordage, rope and cables and worn out articles of twine, cordage, rope or cables, of textile materials

第十二类
鞋、帽、伞、杖、鞭及其零件；已加工的羽毛及其制品；人造花；人发制品

第六十四章
鞋靴、护腿和类似品及其零件

注释：

一、本章不包括：

（一）易损材料（例如，纸、塑料薄膜）制的无外绱鞋底的一次性鞋靴罩或套，这些制品应按其构成材料归类；

（二）纺织材料制的鞋靴，没有用粘、缝或其他方法将外底固定或安装在鞋面上的（第十一类）；

（三）税目 63.09 的旧鞋靴；

（四）石棉制品（税目 68.12）；

（五）矫形鞋靴或其他矫形器具及其零件（税目 90.21）；

（六）玩具鞋及装有冰刀或轮子的滑冰鞋；护胫或类似的运动防护服装（第九十五章）

二、税目 64.06 所称"零件"，不包括鞋钉、护鞋铁掌、鞋眼、鞋钩、鞋扣、饰物、编带、鞋带、绒球或其他装饰物（应分别归入相应税目）及税目 96.06 的钮扣或其他货品。

三、本章所称：

（一）"橡胶"及"塑料"，包括能用肉眼辨出其外表有一层橡胶或塑料的机织物或其他纺织产品，运用本款时橡胶或塑料仅引起颜色变化的不计在内。

（二）"皮革"，是指税目 41.07 及 41.12 至 41.14 的货品。

四、除本章注释三另有规定的以外：

（一）鞋面的材料应以占表面面积最大的那种材料为准，计算表面面积可不考虑附件及加固件，例如，护踝、裹边、饰物、扣子、拉襻、鞋眼或类似附属件。

（二）外底的主要材料应以与地面接触最广的那种材料为准，计算接触面时可不考虑鞋底钉、铁掌或类似附属件；

SECTION XII
FOOTWEAR, HEADGEAR, UMBRELLAS, SUN UMBRELLAS, WALKING-STICKS, SEAT-STICKS, WHIPS, RIDING-CROPS AND PARTS THEREOF; PREPARED FEATHERS AND ARTICLES MADE THEREWITH; ARTIFICIAL FLOWERS; ARTICLES OF HUMAN HAIR

Chapter 64
Footwear, gaiters and the like; parts of such articles

Notes:

1. This Chapter does not cover:

(a) Disposable foot or shoe coverings of flimsy material (for example, paper, sheeting of plastics) without applied soles. These products are classified according to their constituent material;

(b) Footwear of textile material, without an outer sole glued, sewn or otherwise affixed or applied to the upper (Section XI);

(c) Worn footwear of heading No. 63.09;

(d) Articles of asbestos (heading No. 68.12);

(e) Orthopaedic footwear or other orthopaedic appliances, or parts thereof (heading No. 90.21) or;

(f) Toy footwear or skating boots with ice or roller skates attached; shin-guards or similar protective sportswear (Chapter 95).

2. For the purposes of heading No. 64.06, the term "parts" does not include pegs, protectors, eyelets, hooks, buckles, ornaments, braid, laces, pompons or other trimmings (which are to be classified in their appropriate headings) or buttons or other goods of heading No. 96.06.

3. For the purposes of this Chapter:

(a) the terms "rubber" and "plastics" include woven fabrics or other textile products with an external layer of rubber or plastics being visible to the naked eye; for the purpose of this provision, no account should be taken of any resulting change of colour; and

(b) the term "leather" refers to the goods of headings Nos. 41.07 and 41.12 to 41.14.

4. Subject to Note 3 to this Chapter:

(a) the material of the upper shall be taken to be the constituent material having the greatest external surface area, no account being taken of accessories or reinforcements such as ankle patches, edging, ornamentation, buckles, tabs, eyelet stays or similar attachments;

(b) the constituent material of the outer sole shall be taken to be the material having the greatest surface area in contact with the ground, no account being taken of accessories or reinforcements such as spikes, bars, nails, protectors or similar attachments.

子目注释：

子目 6402.12、6402.19、6403.12、6403.19 及 6404.11 所称“运动鞋靴”，仅适用于：

一、带有或可装鞋底钉、止滑柱、夹钳、马蹄掌或类似品的体育专用鞋靴。

二、滑冰靴，滑雪靴及越野滑雪用鞋靴、滑雪板靴、角力靴、拳击靴及赛车鞋。

Subheading Notes:

For the purposes of subheadings Nos. 6402.12, 6402.19, 6403.12, 6403.19 and 6404.11, the expression “sports footwear” applies only to:

(1) footwear which is designed for a sporting activity and has, or has provsion for the attachment of, spikes, sprigs, stops, clips, bars or the like;

(2) skating boots, ski-boots and cross-country ski footwear, snowboard boots, wrestling boots, boxing boots and cycling shoes.

税则号列 Tariff Item.	货品名称	最惠国(%) MFN	协定(%) CT 东盟 CA	中巴 CP	中智 CC	普通 Gen	增值税率 VAT	出口退税 ED	计量单位 Unit	监管条件 SC	Article Description
64.01	**橡胶或塑料制外底及鞋面的防水鞋靴，其鞋面不是用缝、铆、钉、旋、塞或类似方法固定在鞋底上的：**										**Waterproof footwear with outer soles and uppers of rubber or of plastics, the uppers of which are neither fixed to the sole nor assembled by stitching, riveting, nailing, screwing, plugging or similar processes:**
6401.1000	-装有金属防护鞋头的鞋靴	24	T3	12	0	100	17	13	双	B	-Footwear incorporating a protective metal toe-cap
	-其他鞋靴：										-Other footwear:
6401.9200	--中、短统靴(过踝但未到膝)	24	T3	12	0	100	17	13	双	B	--Covering the ankle but not covering the knee
6401.9900	--其他	24	T3	12	0	100	17	13	双	B	--Other
64.02	**橡胶或塑料制外底及鞋面的其他鞋靴：**										**Other footwear with outer soles and uppers of rubber or plastics:**
	-运动鞋靴：										-Sports footwear:
6402.1200	--滑雪靴、越野滑雪鞋靴及滑雪板靴	10	5	5	0	100	17	13	双		--Ski-boots, cross-country ski footwear and snowboard boots
6402.1200 10	含濒危动物毛皮橡胶、塑料底及面滑雪靴(包括越野滑雪鞋靴及滑雪板靴)	10				100	17	13	双	BEF	Inverted skiing boot with rubber、plastic sole and hair of endanger animals cinchldins cross-counory skiing boots and boots for skin
6402.1200 90	其他橡胶、塑料底及面滑雪靴(包括越野滑雪鞋靴及滑雪板靴)	10				100	17	13	双	B	Other ski-boots cross-country ski footwear and snoroboard boots, with outer soles and upper of rubber or plastics
6402.1900	--其他	24	T3	12	0	100	17	13	双	B	--Other
6402.1900 10	含濒危动物毛皮其他运动鞋靴(橡胶、塑料制底及面)	24				100	17	13	双	BEF	Other sports shoes and boots containing endangered animal hair and hide (rubbor and plastic shoes and inverced)
6402.1900 90	橡胶、塑料制底及面的其他运动鞋靴	24				100	17	13	双	B	Other sport footwear, with outer soles and uppers of rubber or plastics (rubber and plastic shoes and inverted)
6402.2000	-用栓塞方法将鞋面条带装配在鞋底上的鞋	24	T3	12	0	100	17	13	双	B	-Footwear with upper straps or thongs assembled to the sole by means of plugs
	-其他鞋靴：										-Other footwear:
6402.9100	--短统靴(过踝)	24	T3	12	0	100	17	13	双	B	--Covering the ankle
6402.9900	--其他	24	T3	12	0	100	17	13	双	B	--Other
64.03	**橡胶、塑料、皮革或再生皮革制外底，皮革制鞋面的鞋靴：**										**Footwear with outer soles of rubber, plastics, leather or composition leather and upers of leather:**
	-运动鞋靴：										-Sports footwear:

税则号列 Tariff Item.	货 品 名 称	最惠国(%) MFN	协定(%)CT 东盟 CA	中巴 CP	中智 CC	普通 Gen	增值税率 VAT	出口退税 ED	计量单位 Unit	监管条件 SC	Article Description
6403.1200	--滑雪靴、越野滑雪鞋靴及滑雪板靴	24	T3		0	100	17	13	双		--Ski-boots, cross-country ski footwear and snowboard boots
6403.1200 10	野生动物皮革制鞋面的滑雪靴	24				100	17	13	双	FEB	Ski-boots, with uppers of leather of wild animals
6403.1200 90	其他皮革制鞋面的滑雪靴(包括橡胶、塑料、皮革制外底和越野滑雪鞋靴及板靴)	24				100	17	13	双	B	Ski-boots, cross-country sik footwear and snowboard boots, with outer soles of rubber, plastics, leather or composition leather and upers of leather
6403.1900	--其他	15	T3		0	100	17	13	双		--Other
6403.1900 10	野生动物皮革制鞋面其他运动鞋靴	15				100	17	13	双	FEB	Other sports footwear with uppers of leather of wild animals
6403.1900 90	皮革制鞋面的其他运动鞋靴(橡胶、塑料、皮革或再生皮革制外底)	15				100	17	13	双	B	Other sports footwear with outer soles of rubber, plastics, leather or composition leather and upers of leather
6403.2000	-皮革制外底,由交叉于脚背并绕大脚趾的皮革条带构成鞋面的鞋	24	T3		0	100	17	13	双		-Footwear with outer soles of leather, and uppers which consist of leather straps across the instep and around the big toe
6403.2000 10	野生动物皮革条带为鞋面的皮底鞋	24				100	17	13	双	BFE	Footwear with outer soles of leather and with uppers of leather straps of wild animals
6403.2000 90	其他皮革条带为鞋面的皮底鞋(皮革条带交叉于脚背并绕大脚趾的)	24				100	17	13	双	B	Footwear with outer soles of leather and with uppers which consist of leather straps across the instep and around the big toe
6403.4000	-装有金属防护鞋头的其他鞋靴	24	T3		0	100	17	13	双		-Other footwear, incorporating a protective metal toe-cap
6403.4000 10	其他含野生动物皮革面鞋靴(装有金属护鞋头的)	24				100	17	13	双	FEB	Other footwear, incorporating a protective metal toe-cap with uppers of leather of wild animals
6403.4000 90	装有金属护鞋头的其他皮革面鞋靴(橡胶、塑料、皮革或再生皮革制外底)	24				100	17	13	双	B	Other footwear, incorporating a protective metal toe-cap, with outer soles of rubber, plastics, leather or composition leather and upers of leather
	-皮革制外底的其他鞋靴:										-Other footwear with outer soles of leather:
6403.5100	--短统靴(过踝)	10	5		0	100	17	13	双		--Covering the ankle
6403.5100 10	野生动物皮革制外底皮革面短统靴(指过踝短统靴)	10				100	17	13	双	FEB	Other footwear, with outer soles of leather and upers of leather, covering the ankle, with uppers of leather, of wild animals
6403.5100 90	皮革制外底的皮革面短统靴(过踝)(运动用靴除外)	10				100	17	13	双	B	Other footwear with outer soles of leather and upers of leather covering the ankle, other than sports footwear, other than sports footwear
6403.5900	--其他	10	5		0	100	17	13	双		--Other
6403.5900 10	野生动物皮革制外底皮革面其他鞋(包括靴,运动用鞋靴除外)	10				100	17	13	双	FEB	Other other footwear with outer soles of leather and upers of leather, of wild animals, other than sports footwear

税则号列 Tariff Item.	货品名称	最惠国(%) MFN	协定(%)CT 东盟 CA	 中巴 CP	 中智 CC	普通 Gen	增值税率 VAT	出口退税 ED	计量单位 Unit	监管条件 SC	Article Description
6403.5900 90	皮革制外底的皮革面其他鞋靴(运动用鞋靴除外)	10				100	17	13	双	B	Other footwear with outer soles of leather and upers of leather of other animals, other than sports footwear
	-其他鞋靴:										-Other footwear:
6403.9100	--短统靴(过踝):	10	T3		0	100	17	13	双		--Covering the ankle
6403.9100 10	其他野生动物皮革制面的短统靴(橡胶、塑料、皮革或再生皮革制外底,运动用靴除外)	10				100	17	13	双	FEB	Footwear covering the ankle with outer soles of rubber, plastics, leather or composition leather and upers of leather, of wild animals, other than sports footwear
6403.9100 90	其他皮革制面的短统靴(过踝)(橡胶、塑料、皮革或再生皮革制外底,运动用靴除外)	10				100	17	13	双	B	Footwear covering the ankle with outer soles of rubber, plastics, leather or composition leather and upers of leather, of other animals, other than sports footwear
6403.9900	--其他	10	T3	8.5	0	100	17	13	双		--Other
6403.9900 10	野生动物皮革制面的其他鞋靴(橡胶、塑料、皮革或再生皮革制外底,运动用鞋靴除外)	10				100	17	13	双	FEB	Other footwear with outer soles of rubber, plastics, leather or composition leather and upers of leather of wild animals, other than sports footwear
6403.9900 90	其他皮革制面的其他鞋靴(橡胶、塑料、皮革或再生皮革制外底,运动用鞋靴除外)	10				100	17	13	双	B	Other footwear with outer soles of rubber, plastics, leather or composition leather and upers of leather of other animals, other than sports footwear
64.04	**橡胶、塑料、皮革或再生皮革制外底,用纺织材料制鞋面的鞋靴:**										**Footwear with outer soles of rubber, plastics, leather or composition leather and uppers of textile materials:**
	-橡胶或塑料制外底的鞋靴:										-Footwear with outer soles of rubber or plastics:
6404.1100	--运动鞋靴;网球鞋、篮球鞋、体操鞋、训练鞋及类似鞋	24	T3	12	0	100	17	13	双	B	--Sports footwear, tennis shoes, basketball shoes, gym shoes, training shoes and the like
6404.1900	--其他	24	T3	12	0	100	17	13	双	B	--Other
6404.2000	-皮革或再生皮革制外底的鞋靴	24	T3	12	0	100	17	13	双	B	-Footwear with outer soles of leather or composition leather
64.05	**其他鞋靴:**										**Other footwear:**
6405.1000	-皮革或再生皮革制鞋面的	24	T3	12	0	100	17	13	双		-With uppers of leather or composition leather
6405.1000 10	野生动物皮革制面的其他鞋靴(包括野生动物再生皮革制面的其他鞋靴)	24				100	17	13	双	FEB	Other footwear with uppers of leather or composition leather of wild animals
6405.1000 90	皮革或再生皮革制面的其他鞋靴(外底用胶、塑、皮革或复制皮革以外的材料制成)	24				100	17	13	双	B	Other footwear with uppers of leather or composition leather (with outer soles of materials other than rubber, plastics, leather or composition leather)
6405.2000	-纺织材料制鞋面的	22	T3	11	0	100	17	13	双		-With uppers of textile materials

税则号列 Tariff Item.	货品名称	最惠国(%) MFN	协定(%)CT 东盟 CA	中巴 CP	中智 CC	普通 Gen	增值税率 VAT	出口退税 ED	计量单位 Unit	监管条件 SC	Article Description
6405.2000 10	羊毛毡呢制内底及鞋面的鞋靴(外底用胶、塑、皮革或复制皮革以外材料制成)	22				100	17	13	双	B	Footwear with in soles and uppers of wool felt (with outer soles of materials other than rubber, plastics, leather or composition leather)
6405.2000 90	纺织材料制面的其他鞋靴(外底用胶、塑、皮革或复制皮革以外材料制成)	22				100	17	13	双	B	Other footwear with uppers of textile materials (with outer soles of materials other than rubber, plastics, leather or composition leather)
6405.9000	-其他	15	T3	10.5	0	100	17	13	双		-Other
64.06	**鞋靴零件(包括鞋面,不论是否带有除外底以外的其他鞋底);活动式鞋内底、跟垫及类似品;护腿、裹腿和类似品及其零件:**										**Parts of footwear (including uppers whether or not attached to soles other than outer soles); removable in-soles, heel cushions and similar articles; gaiters, leggings and similar articles, and parts thereof:**
6406.1000	-鞋面及其零件,但硬衬除外	15	8	13.2	0	90	17	13	千克		-Uppers and parts thereof, other than stiffeners
6406.1000 10	含野生动物皮的鞋面及其零件	15				90	17	13	千克	FE	Uppers and parts thereof, consist of leather of wild animals
6406.1000 90	其他鞋面及其零件(不包括硬衬及毡呢制品)	15				90	17	13	千克		Other uppers and parts thereof, other than stiffeners and articles of felt
6406.2000	-橡胶或塑料制的外底及鞋跟	15	T3		0	90	17	13	千克		-Outer soles and heels, of rubber or plastics
	-其他:										-Other:
6406.9100	--木制	15	8	10.5	0	90	17	13	千克		--Of wood
6406.9900	--其他材料制	15	8	10.5	0	90	17	13	千克		--Of other materials

第六十五章
帽类及其零件

Chapter 65
Headgear and parts thereof

注释：

一、本章不包括：

（一）税目63.09的旧帽类；

（二）石棉制帽类（税目68.12）；

（三）第九十五章的玩偶帽、其他玩具帽或狂欢节用品。

二、税目65.02不包括缝制的帽坯，但仅将条带缝成螺旋形的除外。

Notes:

1. This Chapter does not cover:

(a) Worn headgear of heading No. 63.09;

(b) Asbestos headgear (Heading No. 68.12) or;

(c) Dolls' hats, other toy hats or carnival articles of Chapter 95.

2. Heading No. 65.02 does not cover hat-shapes made by sewing, other than those obtained simply by sewing strips in spirals.

税则号列 Tariff Item.	货品名称	最惠国(%) MFN	协定(%) CT 东盟 CA	中巴 CP	中智 CC	普通 Gen	增值税率 VAT	出口退税 ED	计量单位 Unit	监管条件 SC	Article Description
65.01	**毡呢制的帽坯、帽身及帽兜，未楦制成形，也未加帽边；毡呢制的圆帽片及制帽用的毡呢筒（包括裁开的毡呢筒）：**										**Hat-forms, hat bodies and hoods of felt, neither blocked to shape nor with made brims; plateaux and manchons (including slit manchons), of felt:**
6501.0000	毡呢制的帽坯、帽身及帽兜，未楦制成形，也未加帽边；毡呢制的圆帽片及制帽用的毡呢筒（包括裁开的毡呢筒）	22	12		0	100	17	13	千克		Hat-forms, hat bodies and hoods of felt, neither blocked to shape nor with made brims; plateaux and manchons (including slit manchons), of felt
65.02	**编结的帽坯或用任何材料的条带拼制而成的帽坯，未楦制成形，也未加帽边、衬里或装饰物：**										**Hat-shapes, plaited or made by assembling strips of any material, neither blocked to shape, nor with made brims, nor lined, nor trimmed:**
6502.0000	编结的帽坯或用任何材料的条带拼制成而的帽坯，未楦制成形，也未加帽边、衬里或装饰物	20	12		0	100	17	13	千克		Hat-shapes, plaited or made by assembling strips of any material, neither blocked to shape, nor with made brims, nor lined, nor trimmed
65.04	**编结帽或用任何材料的条带拼制而成的帽类，不论有无衬里或装饰物：**										**Hats and other headgear, plaited or made by assembling strips of any material, whether or not lined or trimmed:**
6504.0000	编结帽或用任何材料的条带拼制而成的帽类，不论有无衬里或装饰物	20	12		0	130	17	13	个/千克		Hats and other headgear, plaited or made by assembling strips of any material, whether or not lined or trimmed
65.05	**针织或钩编的帽类，用成匹的花边、毡呢或其他纺织物（条带除外）制成的帽类，不论有无衬里或装饰物；任何材料制的发网，不论有无衬里或装饰物：**										**Hats and other headgear, knitted or crocheted, or made up from lace, felt or other textile fabric, in the piece (but not in strips), whether or not lined or trimmed; hair-nets of any material, whether or not lined or trimmed:**
6505.1000	-发网	10	5		0	130	17	13	个/千克		-Hair-nets
	-其他：										-Other:
6505.9010	---钩编的帽类	20	12	19	16	130	17	13	个/千克		---Hats and other headgear, knitted or crocheted

税则号列 Tariff Item.	货品名称	最惠国(%) MFN	协定(%)CT 东盟 CA	中巴 CP	中智 CC	普通 Gen	增值税率 VAT	出口退税 ED	计量单位 Unit	监管条件 SC	Article Description
6505.9020	用税目65.01的帽身、帽兜或圆帽片制成的毡呢帽类,不论有无衬里或装饰物	22	12		0	130	17	13	个/千克		Felt hats and other felt headgear, made from the hat bodies, hoods or plateaux of heading No. 65.01, whether or not lined or trimmed
6505.9090	---其他	20	12	19	16	130	17	13	个/千克		---Other
65.06	**其他帽类,不论有无衬里或装饰物:**										**Other headgear, whether or not lined or trimmed:**
6506.1000	-安全帽	10	5		0	100	17	13	个		-Safety headgear
6506.1000 10	防护面罩(带有能够滤除生物因子滤器的面罩)	10				100	17	13	个	3	Protecting cover (with veil and colander that can screen biological elements)
6506.1000 90	其他安全帽(不论有无衬里或饰物)	10				100	17	13	个		Safety caps whether or not lined or trimmed
	-其他:										-Other:
6506.9100	--橡胶或塑料制	10	5		8	100	17	13	个/千克		--Of rubber or of plastics
	-其他材料制:										-Of other materials:
6506.9910	---皮革制	10	5		8	130	17	13	个/千克		---Of leather
6506.9910 10	野生动物皮革制帽类	10				130	17	13	个/千克	FEB	Other headgear, of leather of wild animals
6506.9910 90	其他皮革制帽类	10				130	17	13	个/千克	B	Other headgear, of leather of other animals
6506.9920	---毛皮制	10	5		0	130	17	13	个/千克		---Of furskin
6506.9920 10	野生动物毛皮制帽类(无论有无衬里或饰物)	10				130	17	13	个/千克	FEB	Other headgear, of furskin of wild animals
6506.9920 90	其他毛皮制的帽类(无论有无衬里或饰物)	10				130	17	13	个/千克	B	Other headgear, of furskin of other animals
6506.9990	---其他	24	12		19.2	100	17	13	个/千克		---Other
65.07	**帽圈、帽衬、帽套、帽帮、帽骨架、帽舌及帽颏带:**										**Head-bands, linings, covers, hat foundations, hat frames, peaks and chinstraps, for headgear:**
6507.0000	帽圈、帽衬、帽套、帽帮、帽骨架、帽舌及帽颏带	24	12		0	100	17	13	千克		Head-bands, linings, covers, hat foundations, hat frames, peaks and chinstraps, for headgear
6507.0000 10	含野生动物成分的帽类附件(指帽圈、衬、套、帮、骨架、舌及颏带)	24				100	17	13	千克	FE	Head-bands, linings, covers, hat foundations, hat frames, peaks and chinstraps, for headgear, containing materials of wild animals
6507.0000 90	其他帽类附件(指帽圈、衬、套、帮、骨架、舌及颏带)	24				100	17	13	千克		Other head-bands, linings, covers, hat foundations, hat frames, peaks and chinstraps, for headgear

第六十六章
雨伞、阳伞、手杖、鞭子、马鞭及其零件

Chapter 66
Umbrellas, sun umbrellas, walking-sticks, seat-sticks, whips, riding-crops and parts thereof

注释：

一、本章不包括：

（一）丈量用杖及类似品（税目 90.17）；

（二）火器手杖、刀剑手杖、灌铅手杖及类似品（第九十三章）；

（三）第九十五章的货品（例如，玩具雨伞、玩具阳伞）。

二、税目 66.03 不包括纺织材料制的零件、附件及装饰品或者任何材料制的罩套、流苏、鞭梢、伞套及类似品。此类货品即使与税目 66.01 或 66.02 的物品一同进口或出口，只要未装配在一起，则不应视为上述税目所列物品的组成零件，而应分别归入各有关税目。

Notes:

1. This Chapter does not cover:

(a) Measure walking-sticks or the like (heading No. 90.17);

(b) Firearm-sticks, sword-sticks, loaded walking-sticks or the like (Chapter 93) or;

(c) Goods of Chapter 95 (for example, toy umbrellas, toy sun umbrellas).

2. Heading No. 66.03 does not cover parts, trimmings or accessories of textile material, or covers, tassels, thongs, umbrella cases or the like, of any material. Such goods presented with, but not fitted to, articles of heading No. 66.01 or 66.02 are to be classified separately and not to be treated as forming part of those articles.

税则号列 Tariff Item.	货品名称	最惠国(%) MFN	协定(%) CT 东盟 CA	中巴 CP	中智 CC	普通 Gen	增值税率 VAT	出口退税 ED	计量单位 Unit	监管条件 SC	Article Description
66.01	**雨伞及阳伞(包括手杖伞、庭园用伞及类似伞):**										**Umbrellas and sun umbrellas (including walking-stick umbrellas, garden umbrellas and similar umbrellas):**
6601.1000	-庭园用伞及类似伞	14	8		0	130	17	13	把		-Garden or similar umbrellas
	-其他:										-Other:
6601.9100	--折叠伞	10	5		0	130	17	13	把		--Having a telescopic shaft
6601.9900	--其他	10	5		0	130	17	13	把		--Other
66.02	**手杖、带座手杖、鞭子、马鞭及类似品:**										**Walking-sticks, seat-sticks, whips, riding-crops and the like:**
6602.0000	手杖、带座手杖、鞭子、马鞭及类似品	10	5		0	130	17	13	把		Walking-sticks, seat-sticks, whips, riding-crops and the like
6602.0000 11	含野生动物成分的手杖、带座手杖(包括马鞭、鞭子及类似品)	10				130	17	13	把	AFEB	Walking-sticks, seat-sticks, whips, riding-crops and the like, containing materials of wild animals
6602.0000 19	动植物材料制手杖、鞭子及类似品(包括带座手杖)	10				130	17	13	把	AB	Walking-sticks, seat-sticks, whips, riding-crops and the like, of vegetable materials or animal materials
6602.0000 90	其他手杖、带座手杖、鞭子及类似品	10				130	17	13	把		Other walking-sticks, seat-sticks, whips, riding-crops and the like
66.03	**税目 66.01 或 66.02 所列物品的零件及装饰品:**										**Parts, trimmings and accessories of articles of heading No. 66.01 or 66.02:**
6603.2000	-伞骨,包括装在伞柄上的伞骨	14	8		0	130	17	13	千克		-Umbrella frames, including frames mounted on shafts (sticks)
6603.9000	-其他	14	8		0	130	17	13	千克		-Other
6603.9000 10	含野生动物成分的伞、手杖(包括鞭子的其他零件及饰品)	14				130	17	13	千克	AFEB	Parts, trimmings and accessories of articles of heading No. 6601 or 6602, containing materials of wild animals
6603.9000 90	伞、手杖及鞭子的其他零件及饰品(罩套、流苏、鞭梢及纺织材料制品除外)	14				130	17	13	千克	AB	Other parts, trimmings and accessories of articles of heading No. 6601 or 6602, other than covers, tassels, thongs and other articles of textile material

第六十七章
已加工羽毛、羽绒及其制品；人造花；人发制品

注释：

一、本章不包括：

（一）人发制滤布（税目 59.11）；

（二）花边、刺绣品或其他纺织物制成的花卉图案（第十一类）；

（三）鞋靴（第六十四章）；

（四）帽类及发网（第六十五章）；

（五）玩具、运动用品或狂欢节用品（第九十五章）；

（六）羽毛掸帚、粉扑及人发制的筛子（第九十六章）。

二、税目 67.01 不包括：

（一）羽毛或羽绒仅在其中作为填充料的物品（例如税目 94.04 的寝具）；

（二）羽毛或羽绒仅作为饰物或填充料的衣服或衣着附件；

（三）税目 67.02 的人造花、叶及其部分品，以及它们的制成品。

三、税目 67.02 不包括：

（一）玻璃制品（第七十章）；

（二）用陶器、石料、金属、木料或其他材料经模铸、锻造、雕刻、冲压或用其他方法整件制成形的人造花、叶或果实；用捆扎、胶粘及类似方法以外的其他方法将部分品组合而成的上述制品。

Chapter 67
Prepared feathers and down and articles made of feathers or of down; artificial flowers; articles of human hair

Notes:

1. This Chapter does not cover:

(a) Straining cloth of human hair (heading No. 59.11);

(b) Floral motifs of lace, of embroidery or other textile fabric (Section XI);

(c) Footwear (Chapter 64);

(d) Headgear or hair-nets (Chapter 65);

(e) Toys, sports requisites or carnival articles (Chapter 95); or

(f) Feather dusters, powder-puffs or hair sieves (Chapter 96).

2. Heading No. 67.01 does not cover:

(a) Articles in which feathers or down constitute only filling or padding (for example, bedding of heading No. 94.04);

(b) Articles of apparel or clothing accessories in which feathers or down constitute no more than mere trimming or padding; or

(c) Artificial flowers or foliage or parts thereof or made up articles of heading No. 67.02.

3. Heading No. 67.02 does not cover:

(a) Articles of glass (Chapter 70); or

(b) Artificial flowers, foliage or fruit of pottery, stone, metal, wood or other materials, obtained in one piece by moulding, forging, carving, stamping or other process, or consisting of parts assembled otherwise than by binding, glueing, fitting into one another or similar methods.

税则号列 Tariff Item.	货品名称	最惠国(%) MFN	协定(%) CT 东盟 CA	中巴 CP	中智 CC	普通 Gen	增值税率 VAT	出口退税 ED	计量单位 Unit	监管条件 SC	Article Description
67.01	**带羽毛或羽绒的鸟皮及鸟体其他部分、羽毛、部分羽毛、羽绒及其制品（税目 05.05 的货品和经加工的羽管及羽轴除外）：**										**Skins and other parts of birds with their feathers or down, feathers, parts of feathers, down and articles thereof (other than goods of heading 05.05 and worked quills and scapes):**
6701.0000	带羽毛或羽绒的鸟皮及鸟体其他部分、羽毛、部分羽毛、羽绒及其制品（税目 05.05 的货品和经加工的羽管及羽轴除外）	20	12		0	130	17	13	千克		Skins and other parts of birds with their feathers or down, feathers, parts of feathers, down and articles thereof (other than goods of heading No. 05.05 and worked quills and scapes)
6701.0000 10	已加工野禽羽毛、羽绒及其制品	20				130	17	13	千克	AFEB	Skins and other parts of birds with their feathers or down, feathers, parts of feathers, down and articles thereof, of wild birds
6701.0000 90	其他已加工羽毛、羽绒及其制品（税号 0505 的货品及经加工的羽管及羽轴除外）	20				130	17	13	千克	AB	Other skins and other parts of birds with their feathers or down, feathers, parts of feathers, down and articles thereof (other than goods of heading No. 0505 and worked quills and scapes)

税则号列 Tariff Item.	货品名称	最惠国(%) MFN	协定(%) 东盟 CA	CT 中巴 CP	中智 CC	普通 Gen	增值税率 VAT	出口退税 ED	计量单位 Unit	监管条件 SC	Article Description
67.02	**人造花、叶、果实及其零件；用人造花、叶或果实制成的物品：**										**Artificial flowers, foliage and fruit and parts thereof; articles made of artificial flowers, foliage or fruit:**
6702.1000	-塑料制	20	12		0	130	17	13	千克		-Of plastics
	-其他材料制：										-Of other materials:
6702.9010	---羽毛制	20	12		0	130	17	13	千克		---Of feathers or down
6702.9010 10	野禽羽毛制花、叶、果实及其制品	20				130	17	13	千克	AFEB	Flowers, foliage and fruit and articles thereof, of feathers or down of wild birds
6702.9010 90	其他羽毛制花、叶、果实及其制品(包括花、叶、果实的零件)	20				130	17	13	千克	AB	Flowers, foliage and fruit and parts thereof; articles made of artificial flowers, foliage or fruit, of other feathers or down
6702.9020	---丝及绢丝制	24	12		0	130	17	13	千克		---Of silk or silk waste
6702.9030	---化学纤维制	24	12		0	130	17	13	千克		---Of man-made fibres
6702.9090	---其他	20	12		0	130	17	13	千克		---Other
67.03	**经梳理、稀疏、脱色或其他方法加工的人发；作假发及类似品用的羊毛、其他动物毛或其他纺织材料：**										**Human hair, dressed, thinned, bleached or otherwise worked; wool or other animal hair or other textile materials, prepared for use in making wigs or the like:**
6703.0000	经梳理、稀疏、脱色或其他方法加工的人发；作假发及类似品用的羊毛、其他动物毛或其他纺织材料	20	12	18	0	100	17	13	千克		Human hair, dressed, thinned, bleached or otherwise worked; wool or other animal hair or other textile materials, prepared for use in making wigs or the like
67.04	**人发、动物毛或纺织材料制的假发、假胡须、假眉毛、假睫毛及类似品；其他税目未列名的人发制品：**										**Wigs, false beards, eyebrows and eyelashes, switches and the like, of human or animal hair or of textile materials; articles of human hair not elsewhere specified or included:**
	-合纤纺织材料制：										-Of synthetic textile materials:
6704.1100	--整头假发	25	12		0	130	17	13	千克		--Complete wigs
6704.1900	--其他	25	12		0	130	17	13	千克		--Other
6704.2000	-人发制	15	8		0	130	17	13	千克		-Of human hair
6704.9000	-其他材料制	25	12		0	130	17	13	千克		-Of other materials

第十三类
石料、石膏、水泥、石棉、云母及类似材料的制品;陶瓷产品;玻璃及其制品

第六十八章
石料、石膏、水泥、石棉、云母及类似材料的制品

注释:

一、本章不包括:

(一)第二十五章的货品;

(二)税目48.10或48.11的经涂布、浸渍或覆盖的纸及纸板(例如,用云母粉或石墨涂布的纸及纸板、沥青纸及纸板);

(三)第五十六章或第五十九章的经涂布、浸渍或包覆的纺织物(例如,用云母粉、沥青涂布或包覆的织物);

(四)第七十一章的物品;

(五)第八十二章的工具及其零件;

(六)税目84.42的印刷用石板;

(七)绝缘子(税目85.46)或绝缘材料制的零件(税目85.47);

(八)牙科用磨锉(税目90.18);

(九)第九十一章的物品(例如,钟及钟壳);

(十)第九十四章的物品(例如,家具、灯具及照明装置、活动房屋);

(十一)第九十五章的物品(例如,玩具、游戏品及运动用品);

(十二)用第九十六章注释二(二)所述材料制成的税目96.02的物品或税目96.06的物品(例如钮扣)、税目96.09的物品(例如石笔)或税目96.10的物品(例如绘画石板);

(十三)第九十七章的物品(例如艺术品)。

二、税目68.02所称"已加工的碑石或建筑用石",不仅适用于已加工的税目25.15、25.16的各种石料,也适用于所有经类似加工的其他天然石料(例如,石英岩、燧石、白云石及冻石),但不适用于板岩。

SECTION XIII
ARTICLES OF STONE, PLASTER, CEMENT, ASBESTOS, MICA OR SIMILAR MATERIALS; CERAMIC PRODUCTS; GLASS AND GLASSWARE

Chapter 68
Articles of stone, plaster, cement, asbestos, mica or similar materials

Notes:

1. This Chapter does not cover:

(a) Goods of Chapter 25;

(b) Coated, impregnated or covered paper and paperboard of heading No. 48.10 or 48.11 (for example, paper and paperboard coated with mica powder or graphite, bituminized or asphalted paper and paperboard);

(c) Coated, impregnated or covered textile fabric of Chapter 56 or 59 (for example, fabric coated or covered with mica powder, bituminized or asphalted fabric);

(d) Articles of Chapter 71;

(e) Tools or parts of tools, of Chapter 82;

(f) Lithographic stones of heading No. 84.42;

(g) Electrical insulators (heading No. 85.46) or fittings of insulating material of heading No. 85.47;

(h) Dental burrs (heading No. 90.18);

(i) Articles of Chapter 91 (for example, clocks and clock cases);

(j) Articles of Chapter 94 (for example, furniture, lamps and lighting fittings, prefabricated buildings);

(k) Articles of Chapter 95 (for example, toys, games and sports requisites);

(l) Articles of heading No. 96.02, if made of materials specified in Note 2 (b) to Chapter 96, or of heading No. 96.06 (for example, buttons), No. 96.09 (for example, slate pencils) or No. 96.10 (for example, drawing slates);

(m) Articles of Chapter 97 (for example, works of art).

2. In heading No. 68.02, the expression "worked monumental or building stone" applies not only to the varieties of stone referred to in heading No. 25.15 or 25.16, but also to all other natural stone (for example, quartzite, flint, dolomite and steatite) similarly worked; it does not, however, apply to slate.

税则号列 Tariff Item.	货品名称	最惠国(%) MFN	协定(%)CT 东盟 CA	中巴 CP	中智 CC	普通 Gen	增值税率 VAT	出口退税 ED	计量单位 Unit	监管条件 SC	Article Description
68.01	**天然石料(不包括板岩)制的长方砌石、路缘石、扁平石:**										**Setts, curbstones and flagstones, of natural stone (except slate):**
6801.0000	天然石料(不包括板岩)制的长方砌石、路缘石、扁平石	12	8		7.2	70	17		千克	A	Setts, curbstones and flagstones, of natural stone (except slate)

税则号列 Tariff Item.	货 品 名 称	最惠国(%) MFN	协定(%) 东盟 CA	中巴 CP	CT 中智 CC	普通 Gen	增值税率 VAT	出口退税 ED	计量单位 Unit	监管条件 SC	Article Description
68.02	**已加工的碑石或建筑用石(不包括板岩)及其制品,但税目68.01的货品除外;天然石料(包括板岩)制的镶嵌石(马赛克)及类似品,不论是否有衬背;天然石料(包括板岩)制的人工染色石粒、石片及石粉:**										**Worked monumental or building stone (except slate) and articles thereof, other than goods of heading No. 68.01; mosaic cubes and the like, of natural stone (including slate), whether or not on a backing; artificially coloured granules, chippings and powder, of natural stone (including slate):**
	-砖、瓦、方块及类似品,不论是否为矩形(包括正方形),其最大表面积以可置入边长小于7厘米的方格为限;人工染色的石粒、石片及石粉:										-Tiles, cubes and similar articles, whether or not rectangular (including square), the largest surface area of which is capable of being enclosed in a square the side of which is less than 7cm; artificially coloured granules, chippings and powder:
6802.1010	---大理石	24	T3	5	14.4	90	17		千克	A	---Marble
6802.1090	---其他	20	T3	5	12	90	17		千克	A	---Other
	-简单切削或锯开并具有一个平面的其他碑石或建筑用石及其制品:										-Other monumental or building stone and articles thereof, simply cut or sawn, with a flat or even surface:
	--大理石、石灰华及蜡石:										--Marble, travertine and alabaster:
6802.2110	---大理石	10	5	0	0	90	17		千克	A	---Marble
6802.2120	---石灰华	24	T3	5	0	90	17	13	千克	A	---Travertine
6802.2190	---其他	24	T3	5	0	90	17		千克	A	---Other
6802.2300	--花岗岩	10	5	0	0	90	17		千克	A	--Granite
	--其他石:										--Other stone:
6802.2910	---其他石灰石	24	T3	5	14.4	90	17		千克	A	---Other calcareous stone
6802.2990	---其他	15	T3	0	9	90	17		千克	A	-Other
	-其他:										-Other:
	--大理石、石灰华及蜡石:										--Marble, travertine and alabaster:
6802.9110	---石刻	24	T3	5	0	90	17	13	千克	A	---Carvings
6802.9190	---其他	10	5	0	0	90	17	13	千克	A	---Other
	--其他石灰石:										--Other calcareous stone:
6802.9210	---石刻	24	T3	5	14.4	90	17	13	千克	A	---Carvings
6802.9290	---其他	10	5	0	0	90	17	13	千克	A	---Other
	--花岗岩:										--Granite:
6802.9310	---石刻	24	T3	5	0	90	17	13	千克	A	---Carvings
6802.9390	---其他	10	5	0	0	90	17	13	千克	A	---Other
	--其他石:										--Other stone:
6802.9910	---石刻	24	T3	5	19.2	90	17	13	千克	A	---Carvings
6802.9990	---其他	24	T3	5	19.2	90	17	13	千克	A	---Other
68.03	**已加工的板岩及板岩或粘聚板岩的制品:**										**Worked slate and articles of slate or of agglomerated slate:**
	已加工的板岩及板岩或粘聚板岩的制品:										Worked slate and articles of slate or of agglomerated slate:
6803.0010	---板岩制	20	12		0	80	17	13	千克		---Of slate
6803.0090	---其他	20	12		0	80	17	13	千克		---Other

税则号列 Tariff Item.	货品名称	最惠国(%) MFN	协定(%) CT 东盟 CA	中巴 CP	中智 CC	普通 Gen	增值税率 VAT	出口退税 ED	计量单位 Unit	监管条件 SC	Article Description
68.04	**未装支架的石磨、石碾、砂轮和类似品及其零件,用于研磨、磨刃、抛光、整形或切割,以及手用磨石、抛光石及其零件,用天然石料、粘聚的天然磨料、人造磨料或陶瓷制成,不论是否装有由其他材料制成的零件:**										**Millstones, grindstones, grinding wheels and the like, without frameworks, for grinding, sharpening, polishing, trueing or cutting, hand sharpening or polishing stones, and parts thereof, of natural stone, of agglomerated natural or artificial abrasives, or of ceramics, with or without parts of other materials:**
6804.1000	-碾磨或磨浆用石磨、石碾	8	5		0	40	17	13	千克		-Millstones and grindstones for milling, grinding or pulping
	-其他石磨、石碾、砂轮及类似品:										-Other millstones, grindstones, grinding wheels and the like:
6804.2100	--粘聚合成或天然金刚石制	8	5		0	17	17	13	千克	B	--Of agglomerated synthetic or natural diamond
	--其他粘聚磨料制或陶瓷制:										--Of other agglomerated abrasives or of ceramics:
6804.2210	---砂轮	8	5		0	17	17	13	千克	B	---Grinding wheels
6804.2290	---其他	8	5		0	40	17	13	千克		---Other
	--天然石料制:										--Of natural stone:
6804.2310	---砂轮	8	5		0	17	17	13	千克	B	---Grinding wheels
6804.2390	---其他	8	5		0	40	17	13	千克		---Other
	-手用磨石及抛光石:										-Hand sharpening or polishing stones:
6804.3010	---琢磨油石	8	5	6.4	0	17	17	13	千克	B	---Oilstones
6804.3090	---其他	8	5	6.4	0	40	17	13	千克	B	---Other
68.05	**砂布、砂纸及以其他材料为底的类似品,不论是否裁切、缝合或用其他方法加工成形:**										**Natural or artificial abrasive powder or grain, on a base of textile material, of paper, of paperboard or of other materials, whether or not cut to shape or sewn or otherwise made up:**
6805.1000	-砂布	8	5		6.4	40	17	13	千克	B	-On a base of woven textile fabric only
6805.2000	-砂纸	8	5		6.4	40	17	13	千克	B	-On a base of paper or paperboard only
6805.3000	-其他	8	5		0	40	17	13	千克	B	-On a base of other materials
68.06	**矿渣棉、岩石棉及类似的矿质棉;页状蛭石、膨胀粘土、泡沫矿渣及类似的膨胀矿物材料;具有隔热、隔音或吸音性能的矿物材料的混合物及制品,但税目68.11、68.12或第六十九章的货品除外:**										**Slag wool, rock wool and similar mineral wools; exfoliated vermiculite, expanded clays, foamed slag and similar expanded mineral materials; mixtures and articles of heat-insulating, sound-insulating or sound-absorbing mineral materials, other than those of heading No. 68.11 or 68.12 or of Chapter 69:**
6806.1000	-矿渣棉、岩石棉及类似的矿质棉(包括其相互混合物),块状、成片或成卷	10.5	8		6.3	40	17	13	千克		-Slag wool, rock wool and similar mineral wools (including intermixtures thereof), in bulk ,sheets or rolls
6806.1000 01	矿物纤维,渣球含量小于5%	10.5				40	17	13	千克		Mineral fiber content of dres ball shaller 5%
6806.1000 90	矿渣棉,岩石棉及类似矿质棉(包括相互混合物,块状、成片或成卷)	10.5				40	17	13	千克		Mineral dres cotton , rock cotton and similar mineral coteon

税则号列 Tariff Item.	货品名称	最惠国(%) MFN	协定(%)CT 东盟 CA	中巴 CP	中智 CC	普通 Gen	增值税率 VAT	出口退税 ED	计量单位 Unit	监管条件 SC	Article Description
6806.2000	-页状蛭石、膨胀粘土、泡沫矿渣及类似的膨胀矿物材料(包括其相互混合物)	10.5	8		6.3	40	17		千克		-Exfoliated vermiculite, expanded clays, foamed slag and similar expanded mineral materials (including intermixtures thereof)
6806.9000	-其他	10	5		0	50	17		千克		-Other
68.07	**沥青或类似原料(例如,石油沥青或煤焦油沥青)的制品:**										**Articles of asphalt or of similar material (for example, petroleum bitumen or coal tar pitch):**
6807.1000	-成卷	12	8		7.2	50	17		千克		-In rolls
6807.1000 01	聚酯—铜复合胎基改性沥青根阻防水卷材	12				50	17		千克		
6807.1000 90	成卷的沥青或类似原料的制品(如:石油沥青或煤焦油沥青)	12				50	17		千克		Articles of asphalt or of similar material in rolls (for example, petroleum bitumen or coal tar pitch)
6807.9000	-其他	12	8	9.6	7.2	50	17		千克		-Other
68.08	**镶板、平板、瓦、砖及类似品,用水泥、石膏及其他矿物粘合材料粘合植物纤维、稻草、刨花、木片屑、木粉、锯末或木废料制成:**										**Panels, boards, tiles, blocks and similar articles of vegetable fibre, of straw or of shavings, chips, particles, sawdust or other waste, of wood, agglomerated with cement, plaster or other mineral binders:**
6808.0000	镶板、平板、瓦、砖及类似品,用水泥、石膏及其他矿物粘合材料粘合植物纤维、稻草、刨花、木片屑、木粉、锯末或木废料制成	10.5	8		6.3	40	17	13	千克		Panels, boards, tiles, blocks and similar articles of vegetable fibre, of straw or of shavings, chips, particles, sawdust or other waste, of wood, agglomerated with cement, plaster or other mineral binders
68.09	**石膏制品及以石膏为基本成分的混合材料制品:**										**Articles of plaster or of compositions based on plaster:**
	-未经装饰的板、片、砖、瓦及类似品:										-Boards, sheets, panels, tiles and similar articles, not ornamented:
6809.1100	--仅用纸、纸板贴面或加强的	28	12		22.4	100	17	13	千克		--Faced or reinforced with paper or paper-board only
6809.1900	--其他	25	12		15	100	17	13	千克		--Other
6809.9000	-其他制品	25	12		15	100	17	13	千克		-Other articles
68.10	**水泥、混凝土或人造石制品,不论是否加强:**										**Articles of cement, of concrete or of artificial stone, whether or not reinforced:**
	-砖、瓦、扁平石及类似品:										-Tiles, flagstones, bricks and similar articles:
6810.1100	--建筑用砖及石砌块	10.5	8	8.4	6.3	40	17	13	千克		--Building blocks and bricks
	--其他:										--Other:
6810.1910	---人造石制	10.5	8	8.4	8.4	70	17	13	千克		---Of artificial stone
6810.1990	---其他	10.5	8	8.4	8.4	70	17	13	千克		---Other
	-其他制品:										-Other articles:
	--建筑或土木工程用的预制结构件:										--Prefabricated structural components for building or civil engineering:

税则号列 Tariff Item.	货品名称	最惠国(%) MFN	协定(%)CT 东盟 CA	中巴 CP	中智 CC	普通 Gen	增值税率 VAT	出口退税 ED	计量单位 Unit	监管条件 SC	Article Description
6810.9110	---钢筋混凝土和预应力混凝土管、杆、板、桩等	10.5	8		6.3	40	17	13	千克		---Reinforced concrete and prestressed concrete tubes, pipes, rods, plates, piles and similar articles
6810.9190	---其他	10.5	8		6.3	40	17	13	千克		---Other
	--其他:										--Other:
6810.9910	---铁道用水泥枕	8	5		0	14	17	13	千克		---Railway sleepers of cement
6810.9990	---其他	10.5	8		6.3	70	17	13	千克		---Other
68.11	**石棉水泥、纤维素水泥或类似材料的制品:**										**Articles of asbestos-cement, of cellulose fibre-cement or the like:**
	---含石棉的:										---Containing aspestos:
6811.4010	---瓦楞板	5			0	40	17	13	千克		---Corrugated sheets
6811.4020	---其他片、板、砖、瓦及类似制品	10.5	8		8.4	40	17	13	千克		---Other sheets, panels, tiles and similar articles
6811.4030	---管子及管子附件	8	5		0	40	17	13	千克		---Tubes, pipes and tube or pipe fittings
6811.4090	---其他制品	8.4	5		0	40	17	13	千克		---Other articles
	-不含石棉的:										-Not corrugated sheecs:
6811.8100	--瓦愣板	5			0	40	17	13	千克		--Corrugated sheecs
6811.8200	--其他片、板、砖、互交类似制品	10.5	8		8.4	40	17	13	千克		--Other sheecs, pomels, thes and similar articles
6811.8300	--管子反管子附伸	8	5		0	40	17	13	千克		--Tubes, pipes and tube or pipe fittings
6811.8900	--其他制品	8.4	5		0	40	17	13	千克		--Other articles
68.12	**已加工的石棉纤维;以石棉为基本成分或以石棉和碳酸镁为基本成分的混合物;上述混合物或石棉的制品(例如,纱线、机织物、服装、帽类、鞋靴、衬垫),不论是否加强,但税目68.11或68.13的货品除外:**										**Fabricated asbestos fibres; mixtures with a basis of asbestos or with a basis of asbestos and magnesium carbonate; articles of such mixtures or of asbestos (for example, thread, woven fabric, clothing, headgear, footwear, gaskets), whether or not reinforced, other than goods of heading No. 68.11 or 68.13:**
6812.8000	-青石棉的	10.5	8		6.3	40	17	13	千克		
	-其他:										-Other:
6812.9100	--服装、衣着附件、帽类及鞋靴	10.5	8		6.3	40	17	13	千克		--Clothing, clothing accessories, footwear and headgear
6812.9200	--纸、麻丝板及毡子	10.5	8		6.3	40	17	13	千克		--Paper, millboard and felt
6812.9300	--成片或成卷的压缩石棉纤维接合材料	10.5	8		6.3	40	17	13	千克		--Compressed asbestos fibre jointing, in sheets or rolls
6812.9900	--其他	10	5		0	40	17	13	千克		--Other
68.13	**以石棉、其他矿物质或纤维素为基本成分的未装配摩擦材料及其制品(例如,片、卷、带、盘、圈、垫及扇形),适于作制动器、离合器及类似品,不论是否与织物或其他材料结合而成:**										**Friction material and articles thereof (for example, sheets, rolls, strips, segments, discs, washers, pads), not mounted, for brakes, for clutches or the like, with a basis of asbestos, of other mineral substances or of cellulose, whether or not combined with textile or other materials:**
	-含石棉的:										-Containing aspestos:
6813.2010	--闸衬、闸垫	10	5		8	40	17	13	千克		--Brake linings and pads

税则号列 Tariff Item.	货品名称	最惠国(%) MFN	协定(%)CT 东盟 CA	中巴 CP	中智 CC	普通 Gen	增值税率 VAT	出口退税 ED	计量单位 Unit	监管条件 SC	Article Description
6813.2090	---其他	12	8		9.6	40	17	13	千克		---Other
	-不含石棉的:										-Not containing aspestos:
6813.8100	--闸衬、闸垫	10	5		8	40	17	13	千克		--Brake linings and pads
6813.8900	--其他	12	8		9.6	40	17	13	千克		--Other
68.14	**已加工的云母及其制品,包括粘聚或复制的云母,不论是否附于纸、纸板或其他材料上:**										**Worked mica and articles of mica, including agglomerated or reconstituted mica, whether or not on a support of paper, paperboard or other meterials:**
6814.1000	-粘聚或复制云母制的板、片、带,不论是否附于其他材料上	10.5	8		6.3	35	17	13	千克		-Plates, sheets and strips of agglomerated or reconstituted mica, whether or not on a support
6814.9000	-其他	10.5	8		6.3	35	17	13	千克		-Other
68.15	**其他税目未列名的石制品及其他矿物制品(包括碳纤维及其制品和泥煤制品):**										**Articles of stone or of other mineral substances (including carbon fibres, articles of carbon fibres and articles of peat), not elsewhere specified or included:**
6815.1000	-非电器用的石墨或其他碳精制品	15	8		9	70	17		千克	3	-Non-electrical articles of graphite or other carbon
6815.2000	-泥煤制品	15	8		9	70	17		千克		-Articles of peat
	-其他制品:										-Other articles:
6815.9100	--含有菱镁矿、白云石或铬铁矿的	15	8		9	70	17		千克		--Containing magnesite, dolomite or chromite
	--其他:										--Other:
6815.9910	---碳纤维及其制品	17.5	8		14	70	17	13	千克		---Carbon fibers and articles of carbon fibres
6815.9910 21	碳含量>90%特种碳纤维纱线(比模量≥12.3×10^6m,比极限抗拉温度≥0.3×10^6m)	17.5				70	17	13	千克	3	Yarn of carbon fiberes, cantaining >90% by weight of carbon (specific modums≥12.3×10^6m, specific extreme tensile temperature≥0.3×10^6m)
6815.9910 29	碳含量≤90%特种碳纤维纱线(比模量≥12.3×10^6m,比极限抗拉强度≥0.3×10^6m)	17.5				70	17	13	千克	3	Yarn of carbon fiberes, cantaining ≤90% by weight of carbon (specific modums≥12.3×10^6m, specific extreme tensile temperature≥0.3×10^6m)
6815.9910 91	其他碳含量>90% 碳纤维纱线	17.5				70	17	13	千克		Other Yarn of carbon fiberes, cantaining ≤90% by weight of carbon
6815.9910 99	其他碳纤维及其制品	17.5				70	17	13	千克		Other carbon fibres, articles of carbon fibres
6815.9990	---其他	17.5	8		14	70	17	13	千克		---Other

第六十九章 陶 瓷 产 品

Chapter 69 Ceramic products

注释：

一、本章仅适用于成形后经过烧制的陶瓷产品。税目69.04至69.14仅适用于不能归入税目69.01至69.03的产品。

二、本章不包括：

（一）税目28.44的产品；

（二）税目68.04的物品；

（三）第七十一章的物品（例如，仿首饰）；

（四）税目81.13的金属陶瓷；

（五）第八十二章的物品；

（六）绝缘子（税目85.46）或绝缘材料制的零件（税目85.47）；

（七）假牙（税目90.21）；

（八）第九十一章的物品（例如，钟及钟壳）；

（九）第九十四章的物品（例如，家具、灯具及照明装置、活动房屋）；

（十）第九十五章的物品（例如，玩具、游戏品及运动用品）；

（十一）税目96.06的物品（例如，钮扣）或税目96.14的物品（例如，烟斗）；

（十二）第九十七章的物品（例如，艺术品）。

Notes:

1. This Chapter applies only to ceramic products which have been fired after shaping. Headings Nos. 69.04 to 69.14 apply only to such products other than those classifiable in headings Nos. 69.01 to 69.03.

2. This Chapter does not cover:

(a) Products of heading No. 28.44;

(b) Articles of heading No. 68.04;

(c) Articles of Chapter 71 (for example, imitation jewellery);

(d) Cermets of heading No. 81.13;

(e) Articles of Chapter 82;

(f) Electrical insulators (heading No. 85.46) or fittings of insulating material of heading No. 85.47;

(g) Artificial teeth (heading No. 90.21);

(h) Articles of Chapter 91 (for example, clocks and clock cases);

(i) Articles of Chapter 94 (for example, furniture, lamps and lighting fittings, prefabricated buildings);

(j) Articles of Chapter 95 (for example, toys, games and sports requisites);

(k) Articles of heading No. 96.06 (for example, buttons) or of heading No. 96.14 (for example, smoking pipes); or

(l) Articles of Chapter 97 (for example, works of art).

税则号列 Tariff Item.	货品名称	最惠国(%) MFN	协定(%) CT 东盟 CA	中巴 CP	中智 CC	普通 Gen	增值税率 VAT	出口退税 ED	计量单位 Unit	监管条件 SC	Article Description
	第一分章 硅化石粉或类似硅土及耐火材料制品										Ⅰ.-GOODS OF SILICEOUS FOSSIL MEALS OR OF SIMILAR SILICEOUS EARTHS, AND REFRACTORY GOODS
69.01	**硅质化石粉(例如各种硅藻土)或类似硅土制的砖、块、瓦及其他陶瓷制品：**										**Bricks, blocks, tiles and other ceramic goods of siliceous fossil meals (for example, kieselguhr, tripolite or diatomite) or of similar siliceous earths:**
6901.0000	硅质化石粉(例如各种硅藻土)或类似硅土制的砖、块、瓦及其他陶瓷制品	8	5	6.4	0	50	17		千克		Bricks, blocks, tiles and other ceramic goods of siliceous fossil meals (for example, kieselguhr, tripolite or diatomite) or of similar siliceous earths
69.02	**耐火砖、块、瓦及类似耐火陶瓷建材制品，但硅质化石粉及类似硅土制的除外：**										**Refractory bricks, blocks, tiles and similar refractory ceramic constructional goods, other than those of siliceous fossil meals or similar siliceous earths:**
6902.1000	-单独或同时含有按重量计超过50%的镁、钙或铬(分别以氧化镁、氧化钙及三氧化二铬的含量计)	8	T3		6.4	30	17		千克		-Containing by weight, singly or together, more than 50% of the elements Mg, Ca or Cr, expressed as MgO, CaO or Cr_2O_3

税则号列 Tariff Item.	货品名称	最惠国(%) MFN	协定(%)CT 东盟 CA	中巴 CP	中智 CC	普通 Gen	增值税率 VAT	出口退税 ED	计量单位 Unit	监管条件 SC	Article Description
6902.2000	-含有按重量计超过50%的三氧化二铝、二氧化硅或其混合物或化合物	8	T3		6.4	30	17	13	千克		-Containing by weight more than 50% of alumina (Al_2O_3), of silica (SiO_2) or of a mixture or compound of these products
6902.9000	-其他	8	T3		0	30	17		千克		-Other
69.03	**其他耐火陶瓷制品(例如,甑、坩埚、马弗罩、喷管、栓塞、支架、烤钵、管子、护套及棒条),但硅质化石粉及类似硅土制的除外:**										**Other refractory ceramic goods (for example, retorts, crucibles, muffles, nozzles, plugs, supports, cupels, tubes, pipes, sheaths and rods), other than those of siliceous fossil meals or of similar siliceous earths:**
6903.1000	-含有按重量计超过50%的石墨、其他碳或其混合物	8	5		0	20	17		千克		-Containing by weight more than 50% of graphite or other carbon or of a mixture of these products
6903.2000	-含有按重量计超过50%的三氧化二铝或三氧化二铝和二氧化硅的混合物或化合物	8	5		6.4	20	17		千克		-Containing by weight more than 50% of alumina (AL_2O_3) or of a mixture or compound of alumina and of silica (SiO_2)
6903.9000	-其他	8	T3		6.4	20	17	13	千克		-Other
	第二分章 其他陶瓷产品										Ⅱ. -OTHER CERAMIC PRODUCTS
69.04	**陶瓷制建筑用砖、铺地砖、支撑或填充用砖及类似品:**										**Ceramic building bricks, flooring blocks, support or filler tiles and the like:**
6904.1000	-建筑用砖	15	T3		9	90	17	8	千块/千克	B	-Building bricks
6904.9000	-其他	24.5	T3		14.7	90	17	8	千克	B	-Other
69.05	**屋顶瓦、烟囱罩、通风帽、烟囱衬壁、建筑装饰物及其他建筑用陶瓷制品:**										**Roofing tiles, chimney-pots, cowls, chimney liners, architectural ornaments and other ceramic constructional goods:**
6905.1000	-屋顶瓦	24.5	T3		14.7	90	17	8	千克	B	-Roofing tiles
6905.9000	-其他	24.5	T3		14.7	90	17	8	千克	B	-Other
69.06	**陶瓷套管、导管、槽管及管子附件:**										**Ceramic pipes, conduits, guttering and pipe fittings:**
6906.0000	陶瓷套管、导管、槽管及管子附件	15	8		9	90	17	8	千克		Ceramic pipes, conduits, guttering and pipe fittings
69.07	**未上釉的陶瓷贴面砖、铺面砖,包括炉面砖及墙面砖;未上釉的陶瓷镶嵌砖(马赛克)及类似品,不论是否有衬背:**										**Unglazed ceramic flags and paving, hearth or wall tiles; unglazed ceramic mosaic cubes and the like, whether or not on a backing:**
6907.1000	-砖、瓦、块及类似品,不论是否矩形,其最大表面积以可置入边长小于7厘米的方格为限	24.5	T3		14.7	90	17	8	平方米/千克		-Tiles, cubes and similar articles, whether or not rectangular, the largest surface area of which is capable of being enclosed in a square the side of which is less than 7cm
6907.1000 10	瓷砖、陶瓷等产品,未打磨上釉陶瓷(表面最宽 <7cm)	24.5				90	17	8	平方米/千克	B	Unglazed ceramic flags and paving, hearth or wall tiles, side of square <7cm

税则号列 Tariff Item.	货品名称	最惠国(%) MFN	协定(%) 东盟 CA	协定(%) 中巴 CP	CT 中智 CC	普通 Gen	增值税率 VAT	出口退税 ED	计量单位 Unit	监管条件 SC	Article Description
6907.1000 90	未上釉的小陶瓷砖、瓦、块及类似品(小指最大表面积可置入边长 < 7cm 的方格为限)	24.5				90	17	8	平方米/千克	B	Unglazed tiles, cubes and similar articles, the largest surface area of which is capable of being enclosed in a square the side of which is less than 7cm
6907.9000	-其他	12	T3		0	90	17	8	平方米/千克	B	-Other
69.08	**上釉的陶瓷贴面砖、铺面砖,包括炉面砖及墙面砖;上釉的陶瓷镶嵌砖(马赛克)及类似品,不论是否有衬背:**										**Glazed ceramic flags and paving, hearth or wall tiles; glazed ceramic mosaic cubes and the like, whether or not on a backing:**
6908.1000	-砖、瓦、块及类似品,不论是否矩形,其最大表面积以可置入边长小于 7 厘米的方格为限	12		10.4	7.2	100	17	8	平方米/千克	B	-Tiles, cubes and similar articles, whether or not rectangular, the largest surface area of which is capable of being enclosed in a square the side of which is less than 7cm
6908.9000	-其他	12			0	100	17	13	平方米/千克	B	-Other
69.09	**实验室、化学或其他专门技术用途的陶瓷器;农业用陶瓷槽、缸及类似容器;通常供运输及盛装货物用的陶瓷罐、坛及类似品:**										**Ceramic wares for laboratory, chemical or other technical uses; ceramic troughs, tubs and similar receptacles of a kind used in agriculture; ceramic pots, jars and similar articles of a kind used for the conveyance or packing of goods:**
	-实验室、化学或其他专门技术用途的陶瓷器:										-Ceramic wares for laboratory, chemical or other technical uses:
6909.1100	--瓷制	8	5		0	30	17	8	千克		--Of porcelain or china
6909.1200	--莫氏硬度为 9 或以上的物品	8	5		0	30	17	8	千克		--Articles having a hardness equivalent to 9 or more on the Mohs scale
6909.1900	--其他	8	5		6.4	30	17	8	千克		--Other
6909.9000	-其他	21	12		12.6	90	17	8	千克		-Other
69.10	**陶瓷洗涤槽、脸盆、脸盆座、浴缸、坐浴盆、抽水马桶、水箱、小便池及类似的固定卫生设备:**										**Ceramic sinks, wash basins, wash basin pedestals, baths, bidets, water closet pans, flushing cisterns, urinals and similar sanitary fixtures:**
6910.1000	-瓷制	10		9	0	100	17	8	件	B	-Of porcelain or china
6910.9000	-其他	10			8	100	17	8	件		-Other
69.11	**瓷餐具、厨房器具及其他家用或盥洗用瓷器:**										**Tableware, kitchenware, other household articles and toilet articles, of porcelain or china:**
	-餐具及厨房器具:										-Tableware and kitchenware:
6911.1010	---餐具	12	T3	10	9.6	100	17	8	千克	AB	---Tableware
6911.1020	---厨房器具	15	T3	12.5	12	100	17	8	千克	AB	---Kitchenware
6911.9000	-其他	24.5	T3	20	14.7	100	17	8	千克	B	-Other
69.12	**陶餐具、厨房器具及其他家用或盥洗用陶器:**										**Ceramic tableware, kitchenware, other household articles and toilet articles, other than of procelain or china:**
6912.0010	---餐具	15	T3		12	100	17	8	千克	AB	---Tableware
6912.0090	---其他	15	T3		12	100	17	8	千克	AB	---Other
69.13	**塑像及其他装饰用陶瓷制品:**										**Statuettes and other ornamental ceramic articles:**

税则号列 Tariff Item.	货品名称	最惠国(%) MFN	协定(%)CT 东盟 CA	中巴 CP	中智 CC	普通 Gen	增值税率 VAT	出口退税 ED	计量单位 Unit	监管条件 SC	Article Description
6913.1000	-瓷制	15	T3		9	100	17	8	千克	B	-Of porcelain or china
6913.9000	-其他	15	T3		12	100	17	8	千克	B	-Other
69.14	**其他陶瓷制品:**										**Other ceramic articles:**
6914.1000	-瓷制	24.5	T3		14.7	100	17	8	千克		-Of porcelain or china
6914.9000	-其他	10	T3		0	100	17	8	千克		-Other

第七十章
玻璃及其制品

注释：

一、本章不包括：

（一）税目 32.07 的货品（例如，珐琅和釉料、搪瓷玻璃料及其他玻璃粉、粒或粉片）；

（二）第七十一章的物品（例如，仿首饰）；

（三）税目 85.44 的光缆、税目 85.46 的绝缘子或税目 85.47 所列绝缘材料制的零件；

（四）光导纤维、经光学加工的光学元件、注射用针管、假眼、温度计、气压计、液体比重计或第九十章的其他物品；

（五）有永久固定电光源的灯具及照明装置、灯箱标志或名牌和类似品及其零件（税目 94.05）；

（六）玩具、游戏品、运动用品、圣诞树装饰品及第九十五章的其他物品（供玩偶或第九十五章其他物品用的无机械装置的玻璃假眼除外）；

（七）钮扣、保温瓶、香水喷雾器和类似的喷雾器及第九十六章的其他物品。

二、对于税目 70.03、70.04 及 70.05：

（一）玻璃在退火前的各种处理都不视为“已加工”；

（二）玻璃切割成一定形状并不影响其作为板片归类；

（三）所称“吸收、反射或非反射层”，是指极薄的金属或化合物（例如金属氧化物）镀层，该镀层可以吸收红外线等光线或可以提高玻璃的反射性能，同时仍然使玻璃具有一定程度的透明性或半透明性；或者该镀层可以防止光线在玻璃表面的反射。

三、税目 70.06 所述产品，不论是否具有制成品的特性仍归入该税目。

四、税目 70.19 所称“玻璃棉”，是指：

（一）按重量计二氧化硅的含量在 60% 及以上的矿质棉；

（二）按重量计二氧化硅的含量在 60% 以下，但碱性氧化物（氧化钾或氧化钠）的含量在 5% 以上或氧化硼的含量在 2% 以上的矿质棉。

不符合上述规定的矿质棉归入税目 68.06。

五、本目录所称“玻璃”，包括熔融石英及其他熔融硅石。

子目注释：

子目 7013.22、7013.33 及 7013.41 及 7013.91 所称“铅晶质玻璃”，仅指按重量计氧化铅含量不低于 24% 的玻璃。

Chapter 70
Glass and glassware

Notes:

1. This Chapter does not cover:

(a) Goods of heading No. 32.07 (for example, vitrifiable enamels and glazes, glass frit, other glass in the form of powder, granules or flakes);

(b) Articles of Chapter 71 (for example, imitation jewellery);

(c) Optical fibre cables (heading No. 85.44), electrical insulators (heading 85.46) or fitting of insulating material of heading No. 85.47;

(d) Optical fibres, optically worked optical elements, hypodermic syringes, artificial eyes, thermometers, barometers, hydrometers or other articles of Chapter 90;

(e) Lamps or lighting fittings, illuminated signs, illuminated nameplates or the like, having a permanently fixed light source, or parts thereof of heading No. 94.05;

(f) Toys, games, sports requisites, Christmas tree ornaments or other articles of Chapter 95 (excluding glass eyes without mechanisms for dolls or for other articles of Chapter 95); or

(g) Buttons, fitted vacuum flasks, scent or similar sprays or other articles of Chapter 96.

2. For the purposes of headings Nos. 70.03, 70.04 and 70.05:

(a) glass is not regarded as "worked" by reason of any process it has undergone before annealing;

(b) cutting to shape does not affect the classification of glass in sheets;

(c) the expression "absorbent, reflecting or non-reflecting layer" means a microscopically thin coating of metal or of a chemical compound (for example, metal oxide) which absorbs, for example, infra-red light or improves the reflecting qualities of the glass while still allowing it to retain a degree of transparency or translucency; or which prevents light from being reflected on the surface of the glass.

3. The products referred to in heading No. 70.06 remain classified in that heading whether or not they have the character of articles.

4. For the purposes of heading No. 70.19, the expression "glass wool" means:

(a) Mineral wools with a silica (SiO_2) content not less than 60% by weight;

(b) Mineral wools with a silica (SiO_2) content less than 60% but with an alkaline oxide (K_2O or Na_2O) content exceeding 5% by weight or a boric oxide (B_2O_3) content exceeding 2% by weight.

Mineral wools which do not comply with the above specifications fall in heading No. 68.06.

5. Throughout the Nomenclature, the expression "glass" includes fused quartz and other fused silica

Subheading Note:

For the purposes of subheadings Nos. 7013.22, 7013.33, 7013,41 and 7013.91, the expression "lead crystal" means only glass having a minimum lead monoxide (PbO) content by weight of 24%.

税则号列 Tariff Item.	货品名称	最惠国(%) MFN	协定(%)CT 东盟 CA	中巴 CP	中智 CC	普通 Gen	增值税率 VAT	出口退税 ED	计量单位 Unit	监管条件 SC	Article Description
70.01	**碎玻璃及废玻璃;玻璃块料:**										**Cullet and other waste and scrap of glass; glass in the mass:**
7001.0000	碎玻璃及废玻璃;玻璃块料	12	8		7.2	50	17	11	千克		Cullet and other waste and scrap of glass; glass in the mass
70.02	**未加工的玻璃球、棒及管(税目70.18的微型玻璃球除外):**										**Glass in balls (other than microspheres of heading No. 70.18), rods or tubes, unworked:**
7002.1000	-玻璃球	12	8		7.2	50	17	11	千克		-Balls
	-玻璃棒:										-Rods:
7002.2010	---光导纤维预制棒	6	5		0	50	17	11	千克		---Preformed bars for drawing optical fibre
7002.2090	---其他	12	8		7.2	50	17	11	千克		---Other
	-玻璃管:										-Tubes:
	--熔融石英或其他熔融硅石制:										--Of fused quartz or other fused silica:
7002.3110	---光导纤维用波导级石英玻璃管	5			0	17	17	11	千克		---Waveguide quartz tubes for optical fibres use
7002.3190	---其他	14	8		8.4	50	17	11	千克		---Other
7002.3200	--温度在0℃至300℃时线膨胀系数不超过5×10^{-6}/开尔文的其他玻璃制	12	8		7.2	50	17	11	千克		--Of other glass having a linear coefficient of expansion not exceeding 5×10^{-6} per Kelvin within a temperature range of 0℃ to 300℃
7002.3900	--其他	12	8		7.2	50	17	11	千克		--Other
7002.3900 01	光通信用微光组建的玻璃毛细管定位管(外径小于3mm)	12				50	17	11	千克		Glass capillaries of micro-optical assemblies used in optical communications (external diameter <3mm)
7002.3900 90	未列名、未加工的玻璃管	12				50	17	11	千克		Other glass tubes, not elsewhere specified or included, unworked
70.03	**铸制或轧制玻璃板、片或型材及异型材,不论是否有吸收、反射或非反射层,但未经其他加工:**										**Cast glass and rolled glass, in sheets or profiles, whether or not having an absorbent, reflecting or non-reflecting layer, but not otherwise worked:**
	-非夹丝玻璃板、片:										-Non-wired sheets:
7003.1200	--整块着色、不透明、镶色或具有吸收、反射或非反射层的	15	T3		9	50	17	11	平方米		--Coloured throughout the mass (body tinted), opacified, flashed or having an absorbent, or non-reflecting reflecting layer, but not otherwise worked
7003.1900	--其他	17.5	T3		10.5	50	17	11	平方米		--Other
7003.2000	-夹丝玻璃板、片	15	T3		9	50	17	11	平方米		-Wired sheets
7003.3000	-型材及异型材	15	T3		9	50	17	11	平方米/千克		-Profiles
70.04	**拉制或吹制玻璃板、片,不论是否有吸收、反射或非反射层,但未经其他加工:**										**Drawn glass and blown glass, in sheets, whether or not having an absorbent, reflecting or non-reflecting layer, but not otherwise worked:**
7004.2000	-整块着色、不透明、镶色或具有吸收、反射或非反射层的	17.5	T3		10.5	50	17	11	平方米		-Glass, coloured throughout the mass (body tinted), opacified, flashed or having an absorbent, reflecting or non-reflecting layer
7004.9000	-其他玻璃	17.5	T3		10.5	50	17	11	平方米		-Other glass

税则号列 Tariff Item.	货品名称	最惠国(%) MFN	协定(%)CT 东盟 CA	中巴 CP	中智 CC	普通 Gen	增值税率 VAT	出口退税 ED	计量单位 Unit	监管条件 SC	Article Description
7004.9000 01	光学平板玻璃,厚度0.7mm,(未着色,透明及不具吸收层的,未经其他加工)	17.5				50	17	13	平方米		Optic plane glass, thickness below 0.7mm (not coloured , transparent and not having an absorbent ,not otherwise worked)
7004.9000 90	拉、吹制的其他玻璃板、片(未着色,透明及不具吸收层的,未经其他加工)	17.5				50	17	11	平方米		Drawn glass and blown glass , glass , in sheets (not coloured , transparent and not having an absorbent ,not otherwise worked)
70.05	**浮法玻璃板、片及表面研磨或抛光玻璃板、片,不论是否有吸收、反射或非反射层,但未经其他加工:**										**Float glass and surface ground or polished glass, in sheets, whether or not having an absorbent, reflecting or non-reflecting layer, but not otherwise worked:**
7005.1000	-具有吸收、反射或非反射层的非夹丝玻璃	15	T3		9	50	17	11	平方米		-Non-wired glass, having an absorbent, reflecting or non-reflecting layer
	-其他非夹丝玻璃:										-Other non-wired glass:
7005.2100	--整块着色、不透明、镶色或仅表面研磨的	15	T3		12	50	17	11	平方米		--Coloured throughout the mass (body tinted), opacified, flashed or merely surface ground
7005.2900	--其他	15	T3		12	50	17	11	平方米		--Other
7005.2900 01	浮珐玻璃(气泡、杂质的大小≤30微米)	15				50	17	11	平方米		Flwat glass (the size of bubble、impurity ≤30 micron
7005.2900 90	其他非夹丝浮珐玻璃板、片	15				50	17	11	平方米		Other float non－wired glass,in sheets
7005.3000	-夹丝玻璃	17.5	T3		10.5	50	17	11	平方米		-Wired glass
70.06	**经弯曲、磨边、镂刻、钻孔、涂珐琅或其他加工的税目70.03、70.04或70.05的玻璃,但未用其他材料镶框或装配:**										**Glass of heading No. 70.03, 70.04 or 70.05, bent, edge-worked, engraved, drilled, enamelled or otherwise worked, but not framed or fitted with other materials:**
7006.0000	经弯曲、磨边、镂刻、钻孔、涂珐琅或其他加工的税目70.03、70.04或70.05的玻璃,但未用其他材料镶框或装配	15	8		9	50	17	11	千克		Glass of heading No. 70.03, 70.04 or 70.05, bent, edge-worked, engraved, drilled, enamelled or otherwise worked, but not framed or fitted with other materials
70.07	**钢化或层压玻璃制的安全玻璃:**										**Safety glass, consisting of toughened (tempered) or laminated glass:**
	-钢化安全玻璃:										-Toughened (tempered) safety glass:
	--规格及形状适于安装在车辆、航空器、航天器及船舶上:										--Of size and shape suitable for incorporation in vehicles, aircraft, spacecraft or vessels:
7007.1110	---航空器、航天器及船舶用	2			0	11	17	13	千克		---For aircraft, spacecraft or vessels
7007.1110 01	空载重量≥25吨飞机的挡风玻璃	2				11	17	13	千克		Toughened (tempered) safety glass, of size and shape suitable for incorporation in aircraft W≥25 ton
7007.1110 90	航空航天器及船舶用钢化安全玻璃(其他规格及形状适于安装在航空航天器及船上的)	2				11	17	13	千克		Toughened (tempered) safety glass, of size and shape suitable for incorporation in spacecraft or vessels
7007.1190	---其他	10	5		0	50	17	13	千克	A	---Other
7007.1900	--其他	14	8		11.2	50	17	13	平方米/千克		--Other

税则号列 Tariff Item.	货品名称	最惠国(%) MFN	协定(%) CT 东盟 CA	中巴 CP	中智 CC	普通 Gen	增值税率 VAT	出口退税 ED	计量单位 Unit	监管条件 SC	Article Description
7007.1900 01	低铁钢化太阳能电池组件封装专用玻璃(指最大含铁量 0.02% Fe_2O_3,厚度为 2.5mm - 3.5mm 的玻璃)	14				50	17	13	平方米/千克		Low-ferrous toughened safety glass, specified for sealing of solar cell assemblies, (maximum ferrous content: 0.02% Fe_2O_3, thickness: 2.5mm - 3.5mm)
7007.1900 90	其他钢化安全玻璃	14				50	17	13	平方米/千克		Other toughened (tempered) safety glass
	-层压安全玻璃:										-Laminated safety glass:
	--规格及形状适于安装在车辆、航空器、航天器及船舶上:										--Of size and shape suitable for incorporation in vehicles, aircraft, spacecraft or vessels:
7007.2110	---航空器、航天器及船舶用	2			0	11	17	13	千克		---for aircraft, spacecraft or vessels
7007.2190	---其他	20	T3		16	50	17	13	千克	A	---Other
7007.2900	--其他	14	8		11.2	50	17	13	平方米/千克		--Other
70.08	**多层隔温、隔音玻璃组件:**										**Multiple-walled insulating units of glass:**
	多层隔温、隔音玻璃组件:										Multiple-walled insulating units of glass:
7008.0010	---中空或真空隔温、隔音玻璃	14	8		8.4	50	17	13	千克		---Sealed or vacuum insulating glass
7008.0090	---其他	14	8		8.4	50	17	13	千克		---Other
70.09	**玻璃镜(包括后视镜),不论是否镶框:**										**Glass mirrors, whether or not framed, including rear-view mirrors:**
7009.1000	-车辆后视镜	10	T3		8	100	17	13	千克		-Rear-view mirrors for vehicles
	-其他:										-Other:
7009.9100	--未镶框	21	T3		16.8	70	17	13	千克		--Unframed
7009.9200	--已镶框	12	T3	10.8	9.6	100	17	13	千克		--Framed
70.10	**玻璃制的坛、瓶、缸、罐、安瓿及其他容器,用于运输或盛装货物;玻璃制保藏罐;玻璃塞、盖及类似的封口器:**										**Carboys, bottles, flasks, jars, pots, phials, ampoules and other containers, of glass, of a kind used for the conveyance or packing of goods; preserving jars of glass; stoppers, lids and other closures, of glass:**
7010.1000	-安瓿	14	8		11.2	50	17	13	千克		-Ampoules
7010.2000	-塞、盖及类似的封口器	14	8		8.4	50	17	13	千克		-Stoppers, lids and other closures
	-其他:										-Other:
7010.9010	---超过1升	14	8		11.2	50	17	13	千克		---Exceeding 1L
7010.9020	---超过0.33升,但不超过1升	14	8		11.2	50	17	13	千克		---Exceeding 0.33L but not exceeding 1L
7010.9030	---超过0.15升,但不超过0.33升	14	8		11.2	50	17	13	千克		---Exceeding 0.15L but not exceeding 0.33L
7010.9090	---不超过0.15升	14	8		11.2	50	17	13	千克		---Not exceeding 0.15L
70.11	**制灯泡、阴极射线管及类似品用的未封口玻璃外壳(包括玻璃泡及管)及其玻璃零件,但未装有配件:**										**Glass envelopes (including bulbs and tubes), open, and glass parts thereof, without fittings, for electric lamps, cathode-ray tubes or the like:**
7011.1000	-电灯用	21	12		12.6	80	17	13	千克		-For electric lighting
	-阴极射线管用:										-For cathode-ray tubes:
7011.2010	---显示管玻壳及其零件	10	T3	7	0	35	17	13	千克	6	---Glass envelopes for kinescope and glass parts thereof
7011.2090	---其他	10	T3	7	0	35	17	13	千克		---Other

税则号列 Tariff Item.	货品名称	最惠国(%) MFN	协定(%)CT 东盟 CA	协定(%)CT 中巴 CP	协定(%)CT 中智 CC	普通 Gen	增值税率 VAT	出口退税 ED	计量单位 Unit	监管条件 SC	Article Description
7011.2090 01	显示管玻壳及其零件(包括零件,但未装有配件)	10				35	17	13	千克	6	Glass envelopes (including parts thereof, without fittings) for CRT display
7011.2090 90	其他阴极射线管用的未封口玻壳(包括零件,但未装有配件)	10				35	17	13	千克	6	Glass envelopes (including parts thereof, without fittings), open, for cathode-ray tubes
	-其他:										-Other:
7011.9010	---电子管用(阴极射线管用的除外)	8	5		0	35	17	13	千克		---For electronic tubes and valves (other than cathode-ray tubes)
	-阴极射线管用										-For cathode-ray tubes
7011.9090	---其他	21	12		12.6	80	17	13	千克		---Other
70.13	**玻璃器,供餐桌、厨房、盥洗室、办公室、室内装饰或类似用途(税目70.10或70.18的货品除外):**										**Glassware of a kind used for table, kitchen, toilet, office, indoor decoration or similar purposes (other than that of heading No.70.10 or 70.18):**
7013.1000	-玻璃陶瓷制	24.5	12		14.7	100	17	13	千克		-Of glass-ceramics
	-高脚杯,但玻璃陶瓷制的除外:										-other than of glass-ceramics:
7013.2200	--铅晶质玻璃制	24.5	12		14.7	100	17	13	千克		--Of lead crystal
7013.2800	--其他	8			0	100	17	13	千克	A	--Other
	-其他杯子,但玻璃陶瓷制的除外:										-other than of glass-ceramics:
7013.3300	--铅晶质玻璃制	24.5	12		14.7	100	17	13	千克		--Of lead crystal
7013.3700	--其他	8			0	100	17	13	千克	A	--Other
	-餐桌或厨房用玻璃器皿(不包括杯子),但玻璃陶瓷别的除外:										-Class ware of a kind used for table (other than drinkings glasses) or kitchem purposes other than of glass-ceramics
7013.4100	--铅晶质玻璃剂	24.5	12		14.7	100	17	13	千克	A	--Of lead crystal
7013.4200	--温度在0℃至300℃时线膨胀系数不超过5×10^{-6}/开尔文的其他玻璃剂	10	8		0	100	17	13	千克	A	--Of glasc having a linear coefficient of expansion not exceeding 5×10^{-6} per-kelvin within a temperature range of 0℃ to 300℃
7013.4900	--其他	10	T3		0	100	17	13	千克	A	--Other
	-其他玻璃器:										-Other glassware:
7013.9100	--铅晶质玻璃制	10	8		0	100	17	13	千克		--Of lead crystal
7013.9900	--其他	10	8		8	100	17	13	千克		--Other
70.14	**未经光学加工的信号玻璃器及玻璃制光学元件(税目70.15的货品除外):**										**Signalling glassware and optical elements of glass (other than those of heading No. 70.15), not optically worked:**
7014.0010	---光学仪器用光学元件毛坯	10	8		0	40	17	13	千克		---Blanks of optical elements, for optical instruments
7014.0090	---其他	17.5	8		10.5	80	17	13	千克		---Other
7014.0090 01	滤波玻璃(带有抗红外和防反辐射薄膜的)	17.5				80	17		千克		Light-filtering glass
7014.0090 90	其他未经光学加工的信号玻璃器(包括玻璃制光学元件,编号70.15的物品除外)	17.5				80	17	13	千克		Other signaling glassware and optical elements of glass(Including glass optical elements, except article with Serial No. 7015)

税则号列 Tariff Item.	货品名称	最惠国(%) MFN	协定(%) 东盟 CA	CT 中巴 CP	中智 CC	普通 Gen	增值税率 VAT	出口退税 ED	计量单位 Unit	监管条件 SC	Article Description
70.15	钟表玻璃及类似玻璃、视力矫正或非视力矫正眼镜用玻璃,呈弧面、弯曲、凹形或类似形状但未经光学加工的;制造上述玻璃用的凹面圆形及扇形玻璃:										**Clock or watch glasses and similar glasses, glasses for non-corrective or corrective spectacles, curved, bent, hollowed or the like, not optically worked; hollow glass spheres and their segments, for the manufacture of such glasses:**
	-视力矫正眼镜用玻璃:										-Glasses for corrective spectacles:
7015.1010	---变色镜片坯件	21	12		12.6	80	17	13	千克		---Blanks for photochromic spectacles
7015.1090	---其他	17.5	8		10.5	70	17	13	千克		---Other
	-其他:										-Other:
7015.9010	---钟表玻璃	17.5	8		10.5	70	17	13	千克		---Clock and watch glasses
7015.9020	---平光变色镜片坯件	18	8		10.8	80	17	13	千克		---Blanks for plane photochromic spectacles
7015.9090	---其他	12	8		7.2	80	17	13	千克		---Other
70.16	建筑用压制或模制的铺面用玻璃块、砖、片、瓦及其他制品,不论是否夹丝;供镶嵌或类似装饰用的玻璃马赛克及其他小件玻璃品,不论是否有衬背;花饰铅条窗玻璃及类似品;多孔或泡沫玻璃块、板、片及类似品:										**Paving blocks, slabs, bricks, squares, tiles and other articles of pressed or moulded glass, whether or not wired, of a kind used for building or construction purposes; glass cubes and other glass smallwares, whether or not on a backing, for mosaics or similar decorative purposes; leaded lights and the like; multicellular or foam glass in blocks, panels, plates, shells or similar forms:**
7016.1000	-供镶嵌或类似装饰用的玻璃马赛克及其他小件玻璃品,不论是否有衬背	22	12		13.2	100	17	13	千克		-Glass cubes and other glass smallwares, whether or not on a backing, for mosaics or similar decorative purposes
	-其他:										-Other:
7016.9010	---花饰铅条窗玻璃及类似品	24	T3		14.4	90	17	13	千克		---Leaded lights and the like
7016.9090	---其他	18	T3		10.8	90	17	13	千克		---Other
70.17	实验室、卫生及配药用的玻璃器,不论有无刻度或标量:										**Laboratory, hygienic or pharmaceutical glassware, whether or not graduated or calibrated:**
7017.1000	-熔融石英或其他熔融硅石制	0				30	17	13	千克		-Of fused quartz or other fused silica
7017.2000	-温度在0℃至300℃时线膨胀系数不超过5×10^{-6}/开尔文的其他玻璃制	8	5		0	30	17	13	千克		-Of other glass having a linear coefficient of expansion not exceeding 5×10^{-6} per Kelvin within a temperature range of 0℃ to 300℃
7017.9000	-其他	8	5		0	30	17	13	千克		-Other

税则号列 Tariff Item.	货品名称	最惠国(%) MFN	协定(%)CT 东盟 CA	中巴 CP	中智 CC	普通 Gen	增值税率 VAT	出口退税 ED	计量单位 Unit	监管条件 SC	Article Description
70.18	**玻璃珠、仿珍珠、仿宝石或仿半宝石和类似小件玻璃品及其制品，但仿首饰除外；玻璃假眼，但医用假眼除外；灯工方法制作的玻璃塑像及其他玻璃装饰品，但仿首饰除外；直径不超过1毫米的微型玻璃球：**										**Glass beads, imitation pearls, imitation precious or semi-precious stones and similar glass smallwares, and articles thereof other than imitation jewellery; glass eyes other than prosthetic articles; statuettes and other ornaments of lampworked glass, other than imitation jewellery; glass microspheres not exceeding 1mm in diameter:**
7018.1000	-玻璃珠、仿珍珠、仿宝石或仿半宝石及类似小件玻璃品	10	T3		0	100	17	13	千克		-Glass beads, imitation pearls, imitation precious or semi-precious stones and similar glass smallwares
7018.2000	-直径不超过1毫米的微型玻璃球	20	12		12	100	17	13	千克		-Glass microspheres not exceeding 1mm in diameter
7018.9000	-其他	20	12		12	100	17	13	千克		-Other
70.19	**玻璃纤维(包括玻璃棉)及其制品(例如，玻璃纤维纱线及其织物)：**										**Glass fibres (including glass wool) and articles thereof (for example, yarn, woven fabrics):**
	-梳条、粗纱、纱线及短切纤维：										-Slivers, rovings, yarn and chopped strands:
7019.1100	--长度不超过50毫米的短切纤维	12	8		7.2	50	17	13	千克		--Chopped strands, of a length of not more than 50mm
7019.1200	--粗纱	12	8		0	50	17	13	千克		--Rovings
7019.1200 10	复合结构用的玻璃纤维粗纱(比模量≥12.3×10^6m，比极限抗拉强度≥0.3×10^6m)	12				50	17	13	千克	3	Rovings of glass fiber, for compound structures (specific modulus ≥12.3×10^6m, specific ultimate tensile strength ≥0.3×10^6m)
7019.1200 90	玻璃纤维粗纱	12				50	17	13	千克		Glass fibres rovings
7019.1900	--其他	10	5		0	50	17	13	千克		--Other
7019.1900 11	间苯二酚甲醛胶浸渍的玻璃纤维纱(用于生产非导电玻璃纤维长丝粗纱机织轮胎帘子布的)	10				50	17	13	千克		Glass yarn impregnated with resorcylaldehyde (for woven tyre cord fabrics of nonconductive fiberglass roving)
7019.1900 12	玻璃纤维或纤丝材料(其"比模量"为3.18×10^6米或更大和"比抗拉强度"为7.62×10^4米或更大的玻璃纤维或纤丝材料)	10				50	17	13	千克	3	Yarn pf glass fiber , for compound structures (specific modulus ≥3.18×106 m , or specific ultimate tensile strength≥7.62×106 m)
7019.1900 19	其他玻璃纱线(包括长度超过50mm的短切纤维)	10				50	17	13	千克		Other yarn of glass (including chopped fibers which length exceeding 50mm)
7019.1900 90	其他玻璃纤维(含长度超过50mm的短切纤维)	10				50	17	13	千克		Other glass fibres and articles thereof (including chopped fibers which length >50mm)
	-薄片(巴厘纱)、纤维网、席、垫、板及类似无纺产品：										-Thin sheets (voiles), webs, mats, mattresses, boards and similar nonwoven products:
7019.3100	--席	5			0	40	17	13	千克		--Mats
7019.3200	--薄片(巴厘纱)	14	8		8.4	40	17	13	千克		--Thin sheets (voiles)
7019.3900	--其他	10.5	8		8.4	40	17	13	千克		--Other

税则号列 Tariff Item.	货品名称	最惠国(%) MFN	协定(%)CT 东盟 CA	中巴 CP	中智 CC	普通 Gen	增值税率 VAT	出口退税 ED	计量单位 Unit	监管条件 SC	Article Description
7019.4000	-粗纱机织物	12	8		7.2	40	17	13	千克	5	-Woven fabrics of rovings
	-其他机织物:										-Other woven fabrics:
7019.5100	--宽度不超过30厘米的	12	8		7.2	40	17	13	千克	5	--Of a width not exceeding 30cm
7019.5200	--宽度超过30厘米的长丝平纹织物,每平方米重量不超过250克,单根纱线细度不超过136特克斯	12	8		7.2	40	17	13	千克	5	--Of a width exceeding 30cm, plain weave, weighing less than 250g/m^2, of filaments measuring per single yarn not more than 136 tex
7019.5200 01	平米重≤180g覆铜箔板用玻璃纤维长丝平纹布(宽度超过30cm,单根纱线细度不超过136特)	12				40	17	13	千克	5	Glass fiberes plain weave for sticing - on copper foil (width exceeding 30cm, of filaments measuring per single yarn not more than 136 tex)
7019.5200 90	其他平米重≤250g玻璃长丝平纹布(宽度超过30cm,单根纱线细度不超过136特)	12				40	17	13	千克	5	Other class fiberes plain weave (width exceeding 30cm, of filaments measuring per single yarn not more than 136 tex)
7019.5900	--其他	12	8	8.4	7.2	40	17	13	千克	5	--Other
7019.9000	-其他	7	5		5.6	40	17	13	千克		-Other
70.20	**其他玻璃制品:**										**Other articles of glass:**
	---工业用:										---For technical use:
7020.0011	----导电玻璃	10.5	8		8.4	40	17	13	千克		----Conductivity glass
7020.0012	----绝缘子用玻璃伞盘	10.5	8	9.5	8.4	40	17	13	千克		----Glass umbrella for insulator
*7020.0019	----其他	10.5	8	8.9	8.4	40	17	13	千克		----Other
7020.0019 01	半导体晶片生产用石英反应管及夹持器(用于插入熔化和氧化炉内)	0				40	17	13	千克	s	Quartz reactor tubes and holders for production of semiconductor wafers (for inserting in melting and oxidizing furnace)
7020.0019 02	等离子模块生产用高应变点玻璃(应变点在550℃及以上)	10.5				40	17	13	千克		high strain - point glass for producing plasma module (strain point at 5500C or more)
7020.0019 90	其他工业用玻璃制品	10.5				40	17	13	千克		Other galss articles for other technical use
	---其他:										---Other:
7020.0091	----保温瓶或其他保温容器用的玻璃胆	21	12		12.6	100	17	13	个/千克	A	----Glass inners for vacuum flasksor for other vacuum vessels
7020.0099	----其他	15	8	12.8	12	100	17	13	千克		----Other
7020.0099 01	石英玻璃,平整度小于等于1微米	15				100	17	13	千克		Quartz glass, Levelling degree ≤1 μm
7020.0099 90	其他非工业用玻璃制品	15				100	17	13	千克		Other glass articles not for other technical use

第十四类
天然或养殖珍珠、宝石或半宝石、贵金属、包贵金属及其制品;仿首饰;硬币

第七十一章
天然或养殖珍珠、宝石或半宝石、贵金属、包贵金属及其制品;仿首饰;硬币

注释:

一、除第六类注释一(一)及下列各款另有规定的以外,凡制品的全部或部分由下列物品构成,均应归入本章:

(一)天然或养殖珍珠、宝石或半宝石(天然、合成或再造);

(二)贵金属或包贵金属。

二、(一)税目71.13、71.14及71.15不包括带有贵金属或包贵金属制的小零件或小装饰品(例如,交织字母、套、圈、套环)的制品,上述注释一(二)也不适用于这类制品;

(二)税目71.16不包括含有贵金属或包贵金属(仅作为小零件或小装饰品的除外)的制品。

三、本章不包括:

(一)贵金属汞齐及胶态贵金属(税目28.43);

(二)第三十章的外科用无菌缝合材料、牙科填料或其他货品;

(三)第三十二章的货品(例如光瓷釉);

(四)载体催化剂(税目38.15);

(五)第四十二章注释二(二)所述的税目42.02或42.03的物品;

(六)税目43.03或43.04的物品;

(七)第十一类的货品(纺织原料及纺织制品);

(八)第六十四章或第六十五章的鞋靴、帽类及其他物品;

(九)第六十六章的伞、手杖及其他物品;

SECTION XIV
NATURAL OR CULTURED PEARLS, PRECIOUS OR SEMI-PRECIOUS STONES, PRECIOUS METALS, METALS CLAD WITH PRECIOUS METAL, AND ARTICLES THEREOF; IMITATION JEWELLERY; COIN

Chapter 71
Natural or cultured pearls, precious or semi-precious stones, precious metals, metals clad with precious metal, and articles thereof; imitation jewellery; coin

Notes:

1. Subject to Note 1 (a) to Section Ⅵ and except as provided below, all articles consisting wholly or partly:

(a) Of natural or cultured pearls or of precious or semi-precious stones (natural, synthetic or reconstructed), or

(b) Of precious metal or of metal clad with precious metal, are to be classified in this Chapter.

2. (a) Headings Nos. 71.13, 71.14 and 71.15 do not cover articles in which precious metal or metal clad with precious metal is present as minor constituents only, such as minor fittings or minor ornamentation (for example, monograms, ferrules and rims), and paragraph (b) of the foregoing Note does not apply to such articles;

(b) Heading No. 71.16 does not cover articles containing precious metal or metal clad with precious metal (other than as minor constituents).

3. This Chapter does not cover:

(a) Amalgams of precious metal, or colloidal precious metal (heading No. 28.43);

(b) Sterile surgical suture materials, dental fillings or other goods of Chapter 30;

(c) Goods of Chapter 32 (for example, lustres);

(d) Supported catalysts (heading No. 38.15);

(e) Articles of heading No. 42.02 or 42.03 referred to in Note 2 (B) to Chapter 42;

(f) Articles of heading No. 43.03 or 43.04;

(g) Goods of Section XI (textiles and textile articles);

(h) Footwear, headgear or other articles of Chapter 64 or 65;

(i) Umbrellas, walking-sticks or other articles of Chapter 66;

(十)税目68.04或68.05及第八十二章含有宝石或半宝石(天然或合成)粉末的研磨材料制品;第八十二章装有宝石或半宝石(天然、合成或再造)工作部件的器具;第十六类的机器、机械器具、电气设备及其零件。然而,完全以宝石或半宝石(天然、合成或再造)制成的物品及其零件,除未安装的唱针用已加工蓝宝石或钻石外(税目85.22),其余仍应归入本章;

(十一)第九十章、第九十一章或第九十二章的物品(科学仪器、钟表及乐器);

(十二)武器及其零件(第九十三章);

(十三)第九十五章注释二所述物品;

(十四)根据第九十六章注释四应归入该章的物品;

(十五)雕塑品原件(税目97.03)、收藏品(税目97.05)或超过一百年的古物(税目97.06)、但天然或养殖珍珠、宝石及半宝石除外。

四、(一)所称"贵金属",是指银、金及铂。

(二)所称"铂",是指铂、铱、锇、钯、铑及钌。

(三)所称"宝石或半宝石",不包括第九十六章注释二(二)所述任何物质。

五、含有贵金属的合金(包括烧结及化合的),只要其中任何一种贵金属的含量达到合金重量的2%,即应视为本章的贵金属合金。贵金属合金应按下列规则归类:

(一)按重量计含铂量在2%及以上的合金,应视为铂合金;

(二)按重量计含金量在2%及以上,但不含铂或按重量计含铂量在2%以下的合金,应视为金合金;

(三)按重量计含银量在2%及以上的其他合金,应视为银合金。

六、除条文另有规定的以外,本目录所称贵金属应包括上述注释五所规定的贵金属合金,但不包括包贵金属或表面镀以贵金属的贱金属及非金属。

七、本目录所称"包贵金属",是指以贱金属为底料,在其一面或多面用焊接、熔接、热轧或类似机械方法覆盖一层贵金属的材料。除条文另有规定的以外,也包括镶嵌贵金属的贱金属。

(j) Abrasive goods of heading 68.04 or 68.05 or Chapter 82, containing dust or powder of precious or semi-precious stones (natural or synthetic); articles of Chapter 82 with a working part of precious or semi-precious stones (natural, synthetic or reconsturcted); machinery, mechanical appliances or electrical goods, or parts thereof, of Section XVI. However, articles and parts thereof, wholly of precious or semi-precious stones (natural, synthetic or reconstructed) remain classified in this Chapter, except unmounted worked sapphires and diamonds for styli (heading No. 85.22);

(k) Articles of Chapter 90, 91 or 92 (scientific instruments, clocks and watches, musical instruments);

(l) Arms or parts thereof (Chapter 93);

(m) Articles covered by Note 2 to Chapter 95;

(n) Articles classified in Chapter 96 by virtue of Note 4 to that Chapter;

(o) Original sculptures or statuary (heading No. 97.03), collectors' pieces (heading No. 97.05) or antiques of an age exceeding one hundred years (heading No. 97.06), other than natural or cultured pearls or precious or semi-precious stones.

4. (a) The expression "precious metal" means silver, gold and platinum.

(b) The expression "platinum" means platinum, iridium, osmium, palladium, rhodium and ruthenium.

(c) The expression "precious or semi-precious stones" does not include any of the substances specified in Note 2 (b) to Chapter 96.

5. For the purposes of this Chapter, any alloy (including a sintered mixture and an inter-metallic compound) containing precious metal is to be treated as an alloy of precious metal if any one precious metal constitutes as much as 2%, by weight, of the alloy. Alloys of precious metal are to be classified according to the following rules:

(a) An alloy containing 2% or more, by weight, of platinum is to be treated as an alloy of platinum;

(b) An alloy containing 2% or more, by weight, of gold but no platinum, or less than 2%, by weight, of platinum, is to be treated as an alloy of gold;

(c) Other alloys containing 2% or more, by weight, of silver are to be treated as alloys of silver.

6. Except where the context otherwise requires, any reference in the Nomenclature to precious metal or to any particular precious metal includes a reference to alloys treated as alloys of precious metal or of the particular metal in accordance with the rules in Note 5 above, but not to metal clad with precious metal or to base metal or nonmetals plated with precious metal.

7. Throughout the Nomenclature the expression "metal clad with precious metal" means material made with a base of metal upon one or more surfaces of which there is affixed by soldering, brazing, welding, hot-rolling or similar mechanical means a covering of precious metal. Except where the context otherwise requires, the expression also covers base metal inlaid with precious metal.

八、除第六类注释一(一)另有规定的以外,凡符合税目71.12规定的货品,应归入该税目而不归入本目录的其他税目。

九、税目71.13所称“首饰”,是指:

(一)个人用小饰物(例如,戒指、手镯、项圈、饰针、耳环 表链、表链饰物、垂饰、领带别针、袖扣、饰扣、宗教性或其他勋章及徽章)

(二)通常放置在衣袋、手提包或佩戴在身上的个人用品(例如,烟盒、鼻烟盒、口香丸或药丸盒、粉盒、链袋或念珠)。这些物品可以和下列物品组合成镶嵌下列物品:例如,天然或养殖珍珠、宝石或半宝石、合成或再造的宝石或半宝石、玳瑁壳、珍珠母、兽牙、天然或再生琥泊、黑玉或珊瑚

十、税目71.14所称“金银器”,包括装饰品、餐具、梳妆用具、吸烟用具及类似的家庭、办公室或宗教用的其他物品。

十一、税目71.17所称“仿首饰”,是指不含天然或养殖珍珠、宝石或半宝石(天然、合成或再造)及贵金属或包贵金属(仅作为镀层或小零件、小装饰品的除外)的上述注释九(一)所述的首饰(不包括税目96.06的钮扣及其他物品或税目96.15的梳子、发夹及类似品)。

8. Subject to Note 1 (a) to Section Ⅵ, goods answering to a description in heading No. 71. 12 are to be classified in that heading and in no other heading of the Nomenclature.

9. For the purposes of heading No. 71. 13, the expression “articles of jewellery” means:

(a) Any small objects of personal adornment (gem-set or not) (for example, rings, bracelets, necklaces, brooches, ear-rings, watch-chains, fobs, pendants, tie-pins, cuff-links, dress-studs, religious or other medals and insignia); and

(b) Personal use often placed in the clothing or handbags (for example, cigarette cases, snuff boxes, pomanders or pillboxes, puff boxes, bracelet bags or prayer beads). These articles can be fit together with the following article: natural or cultured pearl, teeth, natural or remade amber, jet or coral.

10. For the purposes of heading No. 71. 14, the expression “articles of goldsmiths' or silversmiths' wares” includes such articles as ornaments, tableware, toilet-ware, smokers' requisites and other articles of household, office or religious use.

11. For the purposes of heading No. 71. 17, the expression “imitation jewellery” means articles of jewellery within the meaning of paragraph (a) of Note 9 above (but not including buttons or other articles of heading 96. 06, or dress-combs, hair-slides or the like, or hairpins, of heading No. 96. 15), not incorporating natural or cultured pearls, precious or semi-precious stones (natural anthetic, or reconstructed) nor (except as plating or as minor constituents) precious metal or metal clad with precious metal.

子目注释:

一、子目7106.10、7108.11、7110.11、7110.21、7110.31及7110.41所称“粉末”,是指按重量计90%及以上可从网眼孔径为0.5毫米的筛子通过的产品;

二、子目7110.11及7110.19所称“铂”,可不受本章注释四(二)的规定约束,不包括铱、锇、钯、铑及钌;

三、对于税目71.10项下的子目所列合金的归类,按其所含铂、钯、铑、铱、锇或钌中重量最大的一种金属归类。

Subheading Notes:

1. For the purposes of subheadings Nos. 7106. 10, 7108. 11, 7110. 11, 7110. 21, 7110. 31 and 7110. 41, the expressions “powder” and “in powder form” mean products of which 90% or more by weight passes through a sieve having a mesh aperture of 0. 5mm.

2. Notwithstanding the provisions of Chapter Note 4 (b), for the purposes of subheadings Nos. 7110. 11 and 7110. 19, the expression “platinum” does not include iridium, osmium, palladium, rhodium or ruthenium.

3. For the classification of alloys in the subheadings of heading No. 71. 10, each alloy is to be classified with that metal, platinum, palladium, rhodium, iridium, osmium or ruthenium which predominates by weight over each other of these metals.

税则号列 Tariff Item.	货品名称	最惠国(%) MFN	协定(%)CT			普通 Gen	增值税率 VAT	出口退税 ED	计量单位 Unit	监管条件 SC	Article Description
			东盟 CA	中巴 CP	中智 CC						
	第一分章　天然或养殖珍珠、宝石或半宝石										Ⅰ. -NATURAL OR CULTURED PEARLS AND PRECIOUS OR SEMI-PRECIOUS STONES
71.01	**天然或养殖珍珠，不论是否加工或分级，但未成串或镶嵌；天然或养殖珍珠，为便于运输而暂穿成串：**										**Pearls, natural or cultured, whether or not worked or graded but not strung, mounted or set; ungraded pearls, natural or cultured, temporarily strung for convenience of transport:**
	-天然珍珠：										-Natural pearls:
	---未分级：										---Ungraded:
7101.1011	----黑珍珠	21	12		12.6	100	17	13	克	AB	----Tahitian pearls
7101.1019	----其他	21	12		12.6	100	17	13	克	AB	----Other
	---其他：										---Other:
7101.1091	----黑珍珠	21	12		12.6	130	17	13	克	AB	----Tahitan pearls
7101.1099	----其他	21	12		12.6	130	17	13	克	AB	----Other
	-养殖珍珠：										-Cultured pearls:
	--未加工：										--Unworked:
7101.2110	---未分级	21	12		12.6	100	17	5	千克	AB	---Ungraded
7101.2190	---其他	21	12		12.6	130	17	5	千克	AB	---Other
	--已加工：										--Worked:
7101.2210	---未分级	21	12		12.6	100	17	13	千克		---Ungraded
7101.2290	---其他	21	12		12.6	130	17	13	千克		---Other
71.02	**钻石，不论是否加工，但未镶嵌：**										**Diamonds, whether or not worked, but not mounted or set:**
7102.1000	-未分级	3			0	14	17	11	克拉	D	-Unsorted
	-工业用：										-Industrial:
7102.2100	--未加工或经简单锯开、劈开或粗磨	0				14	17	13	克拉	D	--Unworked or simply sawn, cleaved or bruted
7102.2900	--其他	0				14	17	13	克拉		--Other
	-非工业用：										-Non-industrial:
7102.3100	--未加工或经简单锯开、劈开或粗磨	3			0	14	17	13	克拉	D	--Unworked or simply sawn, cleaved or bruted
7102.3900	--其他	8	5	0	0	35	17	13	克拉		--Other
71.03	**宝石（钻石除外）或半宝石，不论是否加工或分级，但未成串或镶嵌；未分级的宝石（钻石除外）或半宝石，为便于运输而暂穿成串：**										**Precious stones (other than diamonds) and semi-precious stones, whether or not worked or graded but not strung, mounted or set; ungraded precious stones (other than diamonds) and semi-precious stones, temporarily strung for covenience of transport:**
7103.1000	-未加工或经简单锯开或粗制成形	3		2.8	1.8	14	17	13	千克		-Unworked or simply sawn or roughly shaped
	-经其他加工：										-Otherwise worked:
7103.9100	--红宝石、蓝宝石、绿宝石	8	5	4	0	35	17	13	克拉		--Rubies, sapphires and emeralds
	--其他：										--Other:
7103.9910	---翡翠	8	5	4	0	35	17	13	克拉		---Jadeite
7103.9990	---其他	8	5	4	0	35	17	13	克拉		---Other

税则号列 Tariff Item.	货品名称	最惠国(%) MFN	协定(%) CT 东盟 CA	中巴 CP	中智 CC	普通 Gen	增值税率 VAT	出口退税 ED	计量单位 Unit	监管条件 SC	Article Description
71.04	**合成或再造的宝石或半宝石,不论是否加工或分级,但未成串或镶嵌的;未分级的合成或再造的宝石或半宝石,为便于运输而暂穿成串:**										**Synthetic or reconstructed precious or semi-precious stones, whether or not worked or graded but not strung, mounted or set; ungraded synthetic or reconstructed precious or semi-precious stones, temporarily strung for convenience of transport:**
7104.1000	-压电石英	6	5		0	14	17	13	克		-Piezo-electric quartz
	-其他,未加工或经简单锯开或粗制成形:										-Other, unworked or simply sawn or roughly shaped:
7104.2010	---钻石	0				14	17	11	克		---Diamonds
7104.2090	---其他	0				14	17	11	千克		---Other
	-其他:										-Other:
	---工业用:										---For technical use:
7104.9011	----钻石	6	5		0	14	17	13	克		----Diamonds
7104.9019	----其他	6	5		0	14	17	13	克		----Other
7104.9019 01	蓝宝石衬底,由人造刚玉加工而成,厚度<0.5mm	6				14	17	13	千克		Underlay with sapphirel made of man-made corundum with thickness <0.5mm
7104.9019 90	其他工业用合成或再造宝石半宝石(包括宝石或半宝石)	6				14	17	13	千克		Other synthetic or reconstructed precious or semi – precious stones for technical use (including precious or semi – precious stones)
	---其他:										---Other:
7104.9091	----钻石	8	5		0	35	17	13	克		----Diamonds
7104.9099	----其他	8	5		0	35	17	13	千克		---Other
71.05	**天然或合成的宝石或半宝石的粉末:**										**Dust and powder of natural or synthetic precious or semi-precious stones:**
	-钻石的:										-Of diamonds:
7105.1010	---天然的	0				17	17	13	克拉		---Natural
7105.1020	---人工合成的	0				17	17	13	克拉		---Synthetic
7105.9000	-其他	0				17	17	13	克		-Other
	第二分章 贵金属及包贵金属										Ⅱ.-PRECIOUS METALS AND METALS CLAD WITH PRECIOUS METAL
71.06	**银(包括镀金、镀铂的银),未锻造、半制成或粉末状:**										**Silver (including silver plated with gold or platinum), unwrought or in semi-manufactured forms, or in powder form:**
	-银粉:										-Powder:
	---非片状粉末:										---Not Flake:
7106.1011	----平均粒径小于3微米	0				0	17	13	克	4xy	----Average diameter less than 3 micron
7106.1019	----其他	0				0	17	13	克	4xy	----Other
	---片状粉末:										---Flake 3 micron 10 micron
7106.1021	----平均粒径小于10微米	0				0	17	13	克	4xy	----Average diameter less than 10 micron
7106.1029	----其他	0				0	17	13	克	4xy	----Other
	-其他:										-Other:
	--未锻造:										--Unwrought:
7106.9110	---纯度达99.99%及以上	0				0	17	13	克	4xy	---of a purity of 99.99 perent or more
7106.9190	---其他	0				0	17	13	克	4xy	---Other

税则号列 Tariff Item.	货品名称	最惠国(%) MFN	协定(%)CT 东盟 CA	中巴 CP	中智 CC	普通 Gen	增值税率 VAT	出口退税 ED	计量单位 Unit	监管条件 SC	Article Description
	--半制成:										--Semi-manufactured:
7106.9210	---纯度达99.99%及以上	0				50	17	13	克	4xy	---of a purity of 99.99 percent or more
7106.9290	---其他	0				50	17	13	克	4xy	---Other
71.07	**以贱金属为底的包银材料:**										**Base metals clad with silver, not further worked than semi-manufactured:**
7107.0000	以贱金属为底的包银材料	10.5	8		6.3	50	17	13	千克		Base metals clad with silver, not further worked than semi-manufactured
71.08	**金(包括镀铂的金),未锻造、半制成或粉末状:**										**Gold (including gold plated with platinum) unwrought or in semi-manufactured forms, or in powder form:**
	-非货币用:										-Non-monetary:
7108.1100	--金粉	0				0	0		克	J	--Powder
7108.1200	--其他未锻造形状	0				0	0		克	J	--Other unwrought forms
7108.1300	--其他半制成形状	0				50	0		克	J	--Other semi-manufactured forms
7108.2000	-货币用	0				0	0		克	J	-Monetary
71.09	**以贱金属或银为底的包金材料:**										**Base metals or silver, clad with gold, not further worked than semi-manufactured:**
7109.0000	以贱金属或银为底的包金材料	10.5	8		6.3	50	17	13	克		Base metals or silver, clad with gold, not further worked than semi-manufactured
71.10	**铂,未锻造、半制成或粉末状:**										**Platinum, unwrought or in semi-manufactured forms, or in powder form:**
	-铂:										-Platinum:
7110.1100	--未锻造或粉末状	0				10	17		克	8x	--Unwrought or in powder form
	--其他:										--Other:
7110.1910	---板、片	0				0	0		克	8x	---Plates and sheets
7110.1990	---其他	3			0	11	0		克	4xy	---Other
	-钯:										-Palladium:
7110.2100	--未锻造或粉末状	0				10	17		克	4xy	--Unwrought or in powder form
	--其他:										--Other:
7110.2910	---板、片	0				0	17		克	4xy	---Plates and sheets
7110.2990	---其他	3			0	11	17		克	4xy	---Other
	-铑:										-Rhodium:
7110.3100	--未锻造或粉末状	0				0	17		克	4xy	--Unwrought or in powder form
	--其他:										--Other:
7110.3910	---板、片	0				0	17		克	4xy	---Plates and sheets
7110.3990	---其他	3			0	11	17		克	4xy	---Other
	-铱、锇及钌:										-Iridium, osmium and ruthenium:
7110.4100	--未锻造或粉末状	0				0	17		克	4xy	--Unwrought or in powder form
	--其他:										--Other:
7110.4910	---板、片	0				0	17		克	4xy	---Plates and sheets
7110.4990	---其他	3			0	11	17		克	4xy	---Other
71.11	**以贱金属、银或金为底的包铂材料:**										**Base metals, silver or gold, clad with platinum, not further worked than semi-manufactured:**
7111.0000	以贱金属、银或金为底的包铂材料	3			0	11	17	13	克		Base metals, silver or gold, clad with platinum, not further worked than semi-manufactured

税则号列 Tariff Item.	货品名称	最惠国(%) MFN	协定(%)CT 东盟 CA	中巴 CP	中智 CC	普通 Gen	增值税率 VAT	出口退税 ED	计量单位 Unit	监管条件 SC	Article Description
71.12	**贵金属或包贵金属的废碎料;含有贵金属或贵金属化合物的其他废碎料,主要用于回收贵金属:**										**Waste and scrap of precious metal or of metal clad with precious metal; other waste and scrap containing precious metal or precious metal compounds, of a kind used principally for the recovery of precious metal:**
	-含有贵金属或贵金属化合物的灰:										-Ash containing precious metal or precious metal compounds:
7112.3010	---含有银或银化合物的	8	5		0	50	17	13	克	9	---With silver or silver compounds
7112.3090	---其他	6	5		0	50	17		克	9	---Other
	-其他:										-Other:
	--金及包金的废碎料,但含有其他贵金属的除外:										--Of gold, including metal clad with gold but excluding sweepings containing other precious metals:
7112.9110	---金及包金的废碎料	0				0	17		克		---Of gold, or sold compounds
7112.9120	---含有金或金化合物的废碎料	6	5		0	35	17		克		---Waste and scrap with gold or gold compounds
	--铂及包铂的废碎料,但含有其他贵金属的除外:										--Of platinum, including metal clad with platinum but excluding sweepings containing other precious metals:
7112.9210	---铂及包铂的废碎料	0				0	17		克	4xy	---Of platinum
7112.9220	---含有铂或铂化合物的废碎料	6	5		4.8	35	17		克	4xy	---Wastes and scrap with platinum
	--其他:										--Other:
7112.9910	---含有银或银化合物的废碎料	8	5		6.4	35	17	13	克		---Waste and scrap with silver or silver compounds
7112.9920	---含有其他贵金属或贵金属化合物的废碎料	6	5		4.8	35	17		克		---Waste and scrap with other precious moutals
7112.9990	---其他	0				50	17		克		---Other
	第三分章 珠宝首饰、金银器及其他制品										Ⅲ. -JEWELLERY, GOLDSMITHS' AND SILVERSMITHS' WARES AND OTHER ARTICLES
71.13	**贵金属或包贵金属制的首饰及其零件:**										**Articles of jewellery and parts thereof, of precious metal or of metal clad with precious metal:**
	-贵金属制,不论是否包、镀贵金属:										-Of precious metal whether or not plated or clad with precious metal:
	--银制,不论是否包、镀其他贵金属:										--Of silver, whether or not plated or clad with other precious metal:
7113.1110	---镶嵌钻石的	20	T3	16.5	16	130	17	13	克		---Diomond mounted or set
7113.1190	---其他	20	T3	16.5	16	130	17	13	克		---Other
7113.1190 10	镶嵌濒危物种制品的银首饰及零件(不论是否包、镀其他贵金属)	20				130	17	13	克	FE	Silver jewellery and parts thereof, inlaid with articles of species in imminent dangers, whether or not plated or clad with other precious metal
7113.1190 90	其他银首饰及其零件(不论是否包、镀其他贵金属)	20				130	17	13	克		Other silver jewellery and parts thereof, whether or not plated or clad with other precious metal

税则号列 Tariff Item.	货品名称	最惠国(%) MFN	协定(%) CT 东盟 CA	中巴 CP	中智 CC	普通 Gen	增值税率 VAT	出口退税 ED	计量单位 Unit	监管条件 SC	Article Description
	--其他贵金属制,不论是否包、镀贵金属:										--Of other precious metal, whether or not plated or clad with predious metal:
	---黄金制:										---Of gold:
7113.1911	----镶嵌钻石的	20	12	14	16	130	17		克	J	----Diomond mounted
7113.1919	----其他	20	12	16	16	130	17		克		----Other
7113.1919 10	镶嵌濒危物种制品的金首饰及零件(不论是否包、镀其他贵金属)	20				130	17		克	FEJ	Gold jewellery and parts thereof, inlaid with articles of species in imminent dangers, whether or not plated or clad with other precious metal
7113.1919 90	其他黄金制首饰及其零件(不论是否包、镀其他贵金属)	20				130	17		克	J	Other gold jewellery and parts thereof, whether or not plated or clad with other precious metal
	---其他:										---Other:
7113.1991	----镶嵌钻石的	35	12	28	28	130	17		克		----Diomond mounted or set
7113.1999	----其他	35	12	28	28	130	17		克		----Other
7113.1999 10	镶嵌濒危物种制品其他贵金属首饰(不论是否包、镀其他贵金属)	35				130	17		克	FE	Jewellery and parts thereof, of precious metal, inlaid with articles of species in imminent dangers, whether or not plated or clad with other precious metal
7113.1999 90	其他贵金属制首饰及其零件(不论是否包、镀其他贵金属)	35				130	17		克		Other jewellery and parts thereof of precious metal, whether or not plated or clad with other precious metal
	-以贱金属为底的包贵金属制:										-Of base metal clad with precious metal:
7113.2010	---镶嵌钻石的	35	12	30	21	130	17	13	克		---Diamond mounted or set
7113.2090	---其他	35	12	30	21	130	17	13	克		---Other
7113.2090 10	镶嵌濒危物种制品以贱金属为底的包贵金属制首饰(包括零件)	35				130	17	13	克	FE	Jewellery and parts thereof, of base metal, inlaid with articles of species in imminent dangers, whether or not plated or clad with other precious metal
7113.2090 90	其他以贱金属为底的包贵金属制首饰(包括零件)	35				130	17	13	克		Other jewellery and parts thereof, of base metal clad with precious metal, whether or not plated or clad with other precious metal
71.14	**贵金属或包贵金属制的金银器及其零件:**										**Articles of goldsmiths' or silversmiths' wares and parts thereof, of precious metal or of metal clad with precious metal:**
	-贵金属制,不论是否包、镀贵金属:										-Of precious metal whether or not plated or clad with precious metal:
7114.1100	--银制,不论是否包、镀其他贵金属	35	12		21	100	17	13	克		--Of silver, whether or not plated or clad with other precious metal
7114.1100 10	镶嵌濒危物种制品的银器及零件(不论是否包,镀贵金属)	35				100	17	13	克	FE	Silversmiths' wares and parts thereof, inlaid with articles of species in imminent dangers, whether or not plated or clad with other precious metal

税则号列 Tariff Item.	货品名称	最惠国(%) MFN	协定(%) CT			普通 Gen	增值税率 VAT	出口退税 ED	计量单位 Unit	监管条件 SC	Article Description
			东盟 CA	中巴 CP	中智 CC						
7114.1100 90	其他银器及零件(不论是否包、镀贵金属)	35				100	17		克		Other silversmiths' wares and parts thereof, whether or not plated or clad with other precious metal
7114.1900	--其他贵金属制,不论是否包、镀贵金属	35	12		21	100	17		克		--Of other precious metal, whether or not plated or clad with precious metal
7114.1900 10	镶嵌濒危物种制品的金银器及零件(不论是否包,镀贵金属)	35				100	17		克	FE	Goldsmiths' or silversmiths' wares and parts thereof, inlaid with articles of species in imminent dangers, whether or not plated or clad with other precious metal
7114.1900 90	其他贵金属制金银器及零件(不论是否包,镀贵金属)	35				100	17		克		Other goldsmiths' or silversmiths' wares and parts thereof, of precious metal, whether or not plated or clad with other precious metal
7114.2000	-以贱金属为底的包贵金属制	35	12		21	100	17		克		-Of base metal clad with precious metal
7114.2000 10	以贱金属为底的包贵金属制金银器(镶嵌濒危物种制品,包括零件)	35				100	17		克	FE	Goldsmiths' or silversmiths' wares and parts thereof, inlaid with articles of species in imminent dangers, of base metal cald with precious metal
7114.2000 90	其他贱金属为底包贵金属制金银器(包括零件)	35				100	17		克		Other goldsmiths' or silversmiths' wares and parts thereof, of base metal cald with precious metal
71.15	**贵金属或包贵金属的其他制品:**										**Other articles of precious metal or of metal clad with precious metal:**
7115.1000	-金属丝布或格栅形状的铂催化剂	3			0	11	17	13	克		-Catalysts in the form of wire cloth or grill, of platinum
	-其他:										-Other:
7115.9010	---工业或实验室用	3			0	11	17	13	克		---For technical or laboratory use
7115.9010 10	银制工业、实验室用制品	3				11	17	13	克		Articles of silver for industrial or laboratory use
7115.9010 20	金制工业、实验室用制品	3				11	17	13	克	J	Articles of gold for industrial or laboratory use
7115.9010 90	其他工业、实验室用贵或包贵金制品	3				11	17	13	克		Articles of precious metal or of metal clad with precious metal for industrial or laboratory use
7115.9090	---其他	35	12		21	100	17	13	克		---Other
71.16	**用天然或养殖珍珠、宝石或半宝石(天然、合成或再造)制成的物品:**										**Articles of natural or cultured pearls, precious or semi-precious stones (natural, synthetic or reconstructed):**
7116.1000	-天然或养殖珍珠制	35	12		21	130	17	13	千克		-Of natural or cultured pearls
7116.2000	-宝石或半宝石(天然、合成或再造)制	35	12		28	130	17	13	千克		-Of precious or semi-precious stones (natural, synthetic or reconstructed)
71.17	**仿首饰:**										**Imitation jewellery:**
	-贱金属制,不论是否镀贵金属:										-Of base metal, whether or not plated with precious metal:
7117.1100	--袖扣、饰扣	35	12		21	130	17	13	千克		--Cuff-links and studs

税则号列 Tariff Item.	货 品 名 称	最惠国(%) MFN	协定(%)CT 东盟 CA	 中巴 CP	 中智 CC	普通 Gen	增值税率 VAT	出口退税 ED	计量单位 Unit	监管条件 SC	Article Description
7117.1900	--其他	17	T3	15.3	13.6	130	17	13	千克		--Other
7117.9000	-其他	35	T3	30	28	130	17	13	千克		-Other
71.18	硬币：										**Coin**:
7118.1000	-非法定货币的硬币(金币除外)	0				0	17	13	千克		-Coin (other than gold coin), not being legal tender
7118.9000	-其他	0				0	17		克		-Other

第十五类
贱金属及其制品

注释：

一、本类不包括：

（一）以金属粉末为基本成分的调制油漆、油墨或其他产品（税目32.07至32.10、32.12、32.13或32.15）；

（二）铈铁或其他引火合金（税目36.06）；

（三）税目65.06或65.07的帽类及其零件；

（四）税目66.03的伞骨及其他物品；

（五）第七十一章的货品（例如，贵金属合金、以贱金属为底的包贵金属、仿首饰）；

（六）第十六类的物品（机器、机械器具及电气设备）；

（七）已装配的铁路或电车轨道（税目86.08）或第十七类的其他物品（车辆、船舶、航空器）；

（八）第十八类的仪器及器具，包括钟表发条；

（九）做弹药用的铅弹（税目93.06）或第十九类的其他物品（武器、弹药）；

（十）第九十四章的物品（例如，家具、弹簧床垫、灯具及照明装置、发光标志、活动房屋）；

（十一）第九十五章的物品（例如，玩具、游戏品及运动用品）；

（十二）手用筛子、钮扣、钢笔、铅笔套、钢笔尖或第九十六章的其他物品（杂项制品）

（十三）第九十七章的物品（例如，艺术品）。

二、本目录所称“通用零件”，是指：

（一）税目73.07、73.12、73.15、73.17或73.18的物品及其他贱金属制的类似品；

（二）贱金属制的弹簧及弹簧片，但钟表发条（税目91.14）除外；

（三）税目83.01、83.02、83.08、83.10的物品及税目83.06的贱金属制的框架及镜子。

第七十三章至第七十六章（税目73.15除外）及第七十八章至第八十二章所列货品的零件，不包括上述的通用零件。

除上段及第八十三章注释一另有规定的以外，第七十二章至第七十六章及第七十八章至第八十一章不包括第八十二章、第八十三章的物品。

SECTION XV
BASE METALS AND ARTICLES OF BASE METAL

Notes:

1. This Section does not cover:

(a) Prepared paints, inks or other products with a basis of metallic flakes or powder (headings Nos. 32.07 to 32.10, 32.12, 32.13 or 32.15);

(b) Ferro-cerium or other pyrophoric alloys (heading No. 36.06);

(c) Headgear or parts thereof of heading No. 65.06 or 65.07;

(d) Umbrella frames or other articles of heading No. 66.03;

(e) Goods of Chapter 71 (for example, precious metal alloys, base metal clad with precious metal, imitation jewellery);

(f) Articles of Section XVI (machinery, mechanical appliances and electrical goods);

(g) Assembled railway or tramway track (heading No. 86.08) or other articles of Section XVII (vehicles, ships and boats, aircraft);

(h) Instruments or apparatus of Section XVIII, including clock or watch springs;

(i) Lead shot prepared for anmmunition (heading No. 93.06) or other articles of Section XIX (arms and ammunition);

(j) Articles of Chapter 94 (for example, furniture, mattress supports, lamps and lighting fittings, illuminated signs, prefabricated buildings);

(k) Articles of Chapter 95 (for example, toys, games, sports requisites);

(L) Hand sieves, buttons, pens, pencil-holders, pen nibs or other articles of Chapter 96 (miscellaneous manufactured articles); or

(m) Articles of Chapter 97 (for example, works of art).

2. Throughout the Nomenclature, the expression "parts of general use" means:

(a) Articles of heading No. 73.07, 73.12, 73.15, 73.17 or 73.18 and similar articles of other base metal;

(b) Springs and leaves for springs, of base metal, other than clock or watch springs (heading No. 91.14); and

(c) Articles of headings Nos. 83.01, 83.02, 83.08, 83.10 and frames and mirrors, of base metal, of heading No. 83.06.

In Chapters 73 to 76 and 78 to 82 (but not in heading No. 73.15) references to parts of goods do not include references to parts of general use as defined above.

Subject to the preceding paragraph and to Note 1 to Chapter 83, the articles of Chapter 82 or 83 are excluded from Chapters 72 to 76 and 78 to 81.

三、本目录所称"贱金属"是指:铁及钢、铜、镍、铝、铅、锌、锡、钨、钼、钽、镁、钴、铋、镉、钛、锆、锑、锰、铍、铬、锗、钒、镓、铪、铟、铌(钶)、铼及铊。

四、本目录所称"金属陶瓷",是指金属与陶瓷成分以极细微粒不均匀结合而成的产品。"金属陶瓷"包括硬质合金(金属碳化物与金属烧结而成)。

五、合金的归类规则(第七十二章、第七十四章所规定的铁合金及母合金除外):

(一)贱金属的合金按其所含重量最大的金属归类;

(二)由本类的贱金属和非本类的元素构成的合金,如果所含贱金属的总重量等于或超过所含其他元素的总重量,应作为本类贱金属合金归类;

(三)本类所称"合金",包括金属粉末的烧结混合物、熔化而得的不均匀紧密混合物(金属陶瓷除外)及金属间化合物。

六、除条文另有规定的以外,本目录所称的贱金属包括贱金属合金,这类合金应按上述注释五的规则进行归类。

七、复合材料制品的归类规则:

除各税目另有规定的以外,贱金属制品(包括根据"归类总规则"作为贱金属制品的混合材料制品)如果含有两种或两种以上贱金属的,按其所含重量最大的贱金属的制品归类。为此:

(一)钢、铁或不同种类的钢铁,均视为一种金属;

(二)按照注释五的规定作为某一种金属归类的合金,应视为一种金属;

(三)税目81.13的金属陶瓷,应视为一种贱金属。

八、本类所用有关名词解释如下:

(一)废碎料

在金属生产或机械加工中产生的废料及碎屑以及因破裂、切断、磨损及其他原因而明显不能作为原物使用的金属货品。

(二)粉末

按重量计90%及以上可从网眼孔径为1毫米的筛子通过的产品。

3. Throughout the Nomenclature, the expression "base metals" means: iron and steel, copper, nickel, aluminium, lead, zinc, tin, tungsten (wolfram), molybdenum, tantalum, magnesium, cobalt, bismuth, cadmium, titanium, zirconium, antimony, manganese, beryllium, chromium, germanium, vanadium, gallium, hafnium, indium, niobium (columbium), rhenium and thallium.

4. Throughout the Nomenclature, the term "cermets" means products containing a microscopic heterogeneous combination of a metallic component and a ceramic component. The term "cermets" includes sintered metal carbides (metal carbides sintered with a metal).

5. Classification of alloys (other than ferro-alloys and master alloys as defined in Chapters 72 and 74):

(a) An alloy of base metals is to be classified as an alloy of the metal which predominates by weight over each of the other metals;

(b) An alloy composed of base metals of this Section and of elements not falling within this Section is to be treated as an alloy of base metals of this Section if the total weight of such metals equals or exceeds the total weight of the other elements present;

(c) In this Section the term "alloys" includes sintered mixtures of metal powders, heterogeneous intimate mixtures obtained by melting (other than cermets) and intermetallic compounds.

6. Unless the context otherwise requires, any reference in the Nomenclature to base metal includes a reference to alloys which, by virtue of Note 5 above, are to be classified as alloys of that metal.

7. Classification of composite articles:

Except where the headings otherwise require, articles of base metal (including articles of mixed materials treated as articles of base metal under the Interpretative Rules) containing two or more base metals are to be treated as articles of the base metal predominating by weight over each of the other metals. For this purpose:

(a) Iron and steel, or different kinds of iron or steel, are regarded as one and the same metal;

(b) An alloy is regarded as being entirely composed of that metal as an alloy of which, by virtue of Note 5, it is classified; and

(c) A cermet of heading No. 81.13 is regarded as a single base metal.

8. In this Section, the following expressions have the meanings hereby assigned to them:

(a) Waste and scrap

Metal waste and scrap from the manufacture of mechanical working of metals, and metal goods definitely not usable as such because of breakage, cutting-up, wear or other reasons.

(b) Powders

Products of which 90% or more by weight passes through a sieve having a mesh aperture of 1mm.

第七十二章
钢　　铁

注释：

一、本章所述有关名词解释如下(本条注释(四)、(五)、(六)适用于本目录其他各章)：

(一)生铁

无实用可锻性的铁碳合金,按重量计含碳量在2%以上并可含有一种或几种下列含量范围的其他元素：

铬不超过10%；

锰不超过6%；

磷不超过3%；

硅不超过8%；

其他元素合计不超过10%。

(二)镜铁

按重量计含锰量在6%以上,但不超过30%的铁碳合金,其他方面符合上述(一)款所列标准。

(三)铁合金

锭、块、团或类似初级形状、连续铸造而形成的各种形状及颗粒、粉末状的合金,不论是否烧结,通常用于其他合金生产过程中的添加剂或在黑色金属冶炼中作除氧剂、脱硫剂及类似用途,一般无实用可锻性,按重量计铁元素含量在4%及以上并含有下列一种或几种元素：

铬超过10%；

锰超过30%；

磷超过3%；

硅超过8%；

除碳以外的其他元素,合计超过10%,但最高含铜量不得超过10%。

(四)钢

除税目72.03以外的黑色金属材料(某些铸造而成的种类除外),具有实用可锻性,按重量计含碳量在2%及以下,但铬钢可具有较高的含碳量。

(五)不锈钢

按重量计含碳量在1.2%及以下,含铬量在10.5%及以上的合金钢,不论是否含有其他元素。

(六)其他合金钢

不符合以上不锈钢定义的钢,含有一种或几种按重量计符合下列含量比例的元素：

Chapter 72
Iron and steel

Notes:

1. In this Chapter and, in the case of Notes (d), (e) and (f) throughout the Nomenclature, the following expressions have the meanings hereby assigned to them:

(a) Pig iron

Iron-carbon alloys not usefully malleable, containing more than 2% by weight of carbon and which may contain by weight one or more other elements within the following limits:

-not more than 10% of chromium

-not more than 6% of manganese

-not more than 3% of phosphorus

-not more than 8% of silicon

-a total of not more than 10% of other elements.

(b) Spiegeleisen

Iron-carbon alloys containing by weight more than 6% but not more than 30% of manganese and otherwise conforming to the specification at (a) above.

(c) Ferro-alloys

Alloys in pigs, blocks, lumps or similar primary forms, in forms obtained by continuous casting and also in granular or powder forms, whether or not agglomerated, commonly used as an additive in the manufacture of other alloys or as de-oxidants, de-sulphurizing agents or for similar uses in ferrous metal-lurgy and generally not usefully malleable, containing by weight 4% or more of the element iron and one or more of the following:

-more than 10% of chromium

-more than 30% of manganese

-more than 3% of phosphorus

-more than 8% of silicon

-a total of more than 10% of other elements, excluding carbon, subject to a maximum content of 10% in the case of copper.

(d) Steel

Ferrous materials other than those of heading 72.03 which (with the exception of certain types produced in the form of castings) are usefully malleable and which contain by weight 2% or less of carbon. However, chromium steels may contain higher proportions of carbon.

(e) Stainless steel

Alloy steels containing, by weight, 1.2% or less of carbon and 10.5% or more of chromium, with or without other elements.

(f) Other alloy steel

Steels not complying with the definition of stainless steel and containing by weight one or more of the following elements in the proportion shown:

铝0.3%及以上；

硼0.0008%及以上；

铬0.3%及以上；

钴0.3%及以上；

铜0.4%及以上；

铅0.4%及以上；

锰1.65%及以上；

钼0.08%及以上；

镍0.3%及以上；

铌0.06%及以上；

硅0.6%及以上；

钛0.05%及以上；

钨0.3%及以上；

钒0.1%及以上；

锆0.05%及以上；

其他元素（硫、磷、碳及氮除外）单项含量在0.1%及以上。

（七）供再熔的碎料钢铁锭

粗铸成形无缩孔或冒口的锭块产品，表面有明显瑕疵，化学成分不同于生铁、镜铁及铁合金。

（八）颗粒

按重量计不到90%可从网眼孔径为1毫米的筛子通过，而90%及以上可从网眼孔径为5毫米的筛子通过的产品。

（九）半制成品

连续铸造的实心产品，不论是否初步热轧；其他实心产品，除经初步热轧或锻造粗制成形以外未经进一步加工，包括角材、型材及异型材的坯件。

本类产品不包括成卷的产品。

（十）平板轧材

截面为矩形（正方形除外）并且不符合以上第（九）款所述定义的下列形状实心轧制产品：

1. 层叠的卷材；
2. 平直形状，其厚度如果在4.75毫米以下，则宽度至少是厚度的十倍；其厚度如果在4.75毫米及以上，其宽度应超过150毫米，并且至少应为厚度的两倍。

平板轧材包括直接轧制而成并有凸起式样（例如，凹槽、肋条形、格槽、珠粒、菱形）的产品以及穿孔、抛光或制成瓦楞形的产品，但不具有其他税目所列制品或产品的特征。

各种规格的平板轧材（矩形或正方形除外），但不具有其他税目所列制品或产品的特征，都应作为宽度为600毫米及以上的产品归类。

-0.3% or more of aluminium

-0.0008% or more of boron

-0.3% or more of chromium

-0.3% or more of cobalt

-0.4% or more of copper

-0.4% or more of lead

-1.65% or more of manganese

-0.08% or more of molybdenum

-0.3% or more of nickel

-0.06% or more of niobium

-0.6% or more of silicon

-0.05% or more of titanium

-0.3% or more of tungsten (wolfram)

-0.1% or more of vanadium

-0.05% or more of zirconium

-0.1% or more of other elements (except sulphur, phosphorus, carbon and nitrogen), taken separately.

(g) Remelting scrap ingots of iron or steel

Products roughly cast in the form of ingots without feeder-heads or hot tops, or of pigs, having obvious surface faults and not complying with the chemical composition of pig iron, spiegeleisen or ferro-alloys.

(h) Granules

Products of which less than 90% by weight passes through a sieve with a mesh aperture of 1mm and of which 90% or more by weight passes through a sieve with a mesh aperture of 5mm.

(i) Semi-finished products

Continuous cast products of solid section, whether or not subjected to primary hot-rolling; and

Other products of solid section, which have not been further worked than subjected to primary hot-rolling or roughly shaped by forging, including blanks for angles, shapes or sections.

These products are not presented in coils.

(j) Flat-rolled products

Rolled products of solid rectangular (other than square) cross-section, which do not conform to the definition at (ij) above in the form of:

-coils of successively superimposed layers; or

-straight lenghths, which if of a thickness less than 4.75mm are of a width measuring at least ten times the thickness or if of a thickness of 4.75mm or more are of a width which exceeds 150mm and measures at least twice the thickness.

Flat-rolled products include those with patterns in relief derived directly from rolling (for example, grooves, ribs, chequers, tears, buttons, lozenges) and those which have been perforated, corrugated or polished, provided that they do not thereby assume the character of articles or products of other headings.

Flat-rolled products of a shape other than rectangular or square, of any size, are to be classified as products of a width of 600mm or more, provided that they do not assume the character of articles or products of other headings.

（十一）不规则盘绕的热轧条、杆

经热轧不规则盘绕的实心产品，其截面为圆形、扇形、椭圆形、矩形（包括正方形）、三角形及其他外凸多边形（包括“扁圆形”及“变形矩形”，即相对两边为弧拱形，另外两边为等长平行直线形）。这类产品可带有在轧制过程中产生的凹痕、凸缘、槽沟或其他变形（钢筋）。

（十二）其他条、杆

不符合上述（九）、（十）、（十一）款或“丝”定义的实心产品，其全长截面均为圆形、扇形、椭圆形、矩形（包括正方形）三角形或其他外凸多边形（包括“扁圆形”及“变形矩形”，即相对两边为弧拱形，另两边为等长平行直线形）。这些产品可以：

1. 带有在轧制过程中产生的凹痕、凸缘、槽沟或其他变形（钢筋）；

2. 轧制后扭曲的。

（十三）角材、型材及异型材

不符合上述（九）、（十）、（十一）、（十二）款或“丝”定义，但其全长截面均为同样形状的实心产品。

第七十二章不包括税目73.01或73.02的产品。

（十四）丝

不符合平板轧材定义但全长截面均为同样形状的盘卷冷成形实心产品。

（十五）空心钻钢

适合钻探用的各种截面的空心条、杆，其最大外形尺寸超过15毫米但不超过52毫米，最大内孔尺寸不超过最大外形尺寸的二分之一。不符合本定义的钢铁空心条、杆应归入税目73.04。

二、用一种黑色金属包覆不同种类的黑色金属，应按其中重量最大的材料归类。

三、用电解沉积法、压铸法或烧结法所得的钢铁产品，应按其形状、成分及外观归入本章类似热轧产品的相应税目。

子目注释：

一、本章所用有关名词解释如下：

（一）合金生铁

按重量计含有一种或几种下列比例的元素的生铁：

(k) Bars and rods, hot-rolled, in irregularly wound coils

Hot-rolled products in irregularly wound coils, which have a solid cross-section in the shape of circles, segments of circles, ovals, rectangles (including squares), triangles or other convex polygons (including "flattened circles" and modified rectangles of which two opposite sides are convex arcs, the other two sides being straight, of equal length and paralled). These products may have indentations, ribs, grooves or other deformations produced during the rolling process (reinforcing bars and rods).

(L) Other bars and rods

Products which do not conform to any of the definitions at (ij), (k) or (l) above or to the definition of wire, which have a uniform solid cross-section along their whole length in the shape of circles, segments of circles, ovals, rectangles (including squares), triangles or other convex polygons (including "flattened circles" and "modified rectangles", of which two opposite sides are convex arcs, the other two sides being straight, of equal length and parallel). These products may:

-have indentations, ribs, grooves or other deformations produced during the rolling process (reinforcing bars and rods);

-be twisted after rolling.

(m) Angles, shapes and sections

Products having a uniform solid cross-section along their whole length which do not conform to any of the definitions at (ij), (k), (l) or (m) above or to the definition of wire.

Chapter 72 does not include products of heading No. 73.01 or 73.02.

(n) Wire

Cold-formed products in coils, of any uniform solid cross-section along their whole length, which do not conform to the definition of flat-rolled products.

(o) Hollow drill bars and rods

Hollow bars and rods of any cross-section, suitable for drills, of which the greatest external dimension of the cross-section exceeds 15mm but does not exceed 52mm, and of which the greatest internal dimension does not exceed one half of the greatest external dimension. Hollow bars and rods of iron or steel not conforming to this definition are to be classified in heading No. 73.04.

2. Ferrous metals clad with another ferrous metal are to be classified as products of the ferrous metal predominating by weight.

3. Iron or steel products obtained by electrolytic deposition, by pressure casting or by sintering are to be classified, according to their form, their composition and their appearance, in the headings of this Chapter appropriate to similar hot-rolled products.

Subheading Notes:

1. In this Chapter the following expressions have the meanings hereby assigned to them:

(a) Alloy pig iron

Pig iron containing, by weight, one or more of the following elements in the specified proportions:

铬0.2%以上;	-more than 0.2% of chromium
铜0.3%以上;	-more than 0.3% of copper
镍0.3%以上;	-more than 0.3% of nickel
0.1%以上的任何下列元素:	-more than 0.1% of any of the following elements:
铝、钼、钛、钨、钒。	aluminium, molybdenum, titanium, tungsten (wolfram), vanadium.
(二)非合金易切削钢	(b) Non-alloy free-cutting steel
按重量计含有一种或几种下列比例的元素的非合金钢:	Non-alloy steel containing, by weight, one or more of the following elements in the specified proportions:
硫0.08%及以上;	-0.08% or more of sulphur
铅0.1%及以上;	-0.1% or more of lead
硒0.05%以上;	-more than 0.05% of selenium
碲0.01%以上;	-more than 0.01% of tellurium
铋0.05%以上。	-more than 0.05% of bismuth.
(三)硅电钢	(c) Silicon-electrical steel
按重量计含硅量至少为0.6%但不超过6%,含碳量不超过0.08%的合金钢。这类钢还可含有按重量计不超过1%的铝,但所含其他元素的比例并不使其具有其他合金钢的特性。	Alloy steels containing by weight at least 0.6% but not more than 6% of silicon and not more than 0.08% of carbon. They may also contain by weight not more than 1% of aluminium but no other element in a proportion that would give the steel the characteristics of another alloy steel.
(四)高速钢	(d) High speed steel
不论是否含有其他元素,但至少含有按重量计合计含量在7%及以上的钼、钨、钒中两种元素的合金钢,按重量计其含碳量在0.6%及以上,含铬量在3%~6%。	Alloy steels containing, with or without other elements, at least two of the three elements molybdenum, tungsten and vanadium with a combined content by weight of 7% or more, 0.6% or more of carbon and 3% to 6% of chromium.
(五)硅锰钢	(e) Silico-manganese steel
按重量计同时含有下列元素的合金钢:	Alloy steels containing by weight:
碳不超过0.7%;	-not more than 0.7% of carbon,
锰0.5%及以上,但不超过1.9%;	-0.5% or more but not more than 1.9% of manganese, and
硅0.6%及以上,但不超过2.3%;	-0.6% or more but not more than 2.3% of silicon, but no other element in a proportion that would give the steel the characteristics of another alloy steel.
所含其他元素的比例并不使其具有其他合金钢的特性。	
二、税目72.02项下的子目所列铁合金,应按照下列规则归类:	2. For the classification of ferro-alloys in the subheadings of heading 72.02 the following rule should be observed: A ferro-alloy is considered as binary and classified under the relevant subheading (if it exists) if only one of the alloy elements exceeds the minimum percentage laid down in Chapter Note 1 (c); by analogy, it is considered respectively as ternary or quaternary if two or three alloy elements exceed the minimum percentage.
对于只有一种元素超出本章注释一(三)规定的最低百分比的铁合金,应作为二元合金归入相应的子目。以此类推,如果有两种或三种合金元素超出了最低百分比的,则可分别作为三元或四元合金。	
在运用本规定时,本章注释一(三)所述的未列名的"其他元素",按重量计单项含量必须超过10%。	For the application of this rule the unspecified "other elements" referred to in Chapter Note 1 (c) must each exceed 10% by weight.

税则号列 Tariff Item.	货品名称	最惠国(%) MFN	协定(%) 东盟 CA	中巴 CP	CT 中智 CC	普通 Gen	增值税率 VAT	出口退税 ED	计量单位 Unit	监管条件 SC	Article Description
	第一分章 原料;粒状及粉状产品										I.-PRIMARY MATERIALS; PRODUCTS IN GRANULAR OR POWDER FORM
72.01	生铁及镜铁,锭、块或其他初级形状:										**Pig iron and spiegeleisen in pigs, blocks or other primary forms:**

税则号列 Tariff Item.	货品名称	最惠国(%) MFN	协定(%)CT 东盟 CA	中巴 CP	中智 CC	普通 Gen	增值税率 VAT	出口退税 ED	计量单位 Unit	监管条件 SC	Article Description
7201.1000	-非合金生铁,按重量计含磷量在0.5%及以下	1			0	8	17		千克	AB	-Non-alloy pig iron containing by weight 0.5% or less of phosphorus
7201.2000	-非合金生铁,按重量计含磷量在0.5%以上	1			0	8	17		千克	AB	-Non-alloy pig iron containing by weight more than 0.5% of phosphorus
7201.5000	-合金生铁;镜铁	1			0	8	17		千克		-Alloy pig iron; spiegeleisen
7201.5000 10	合金生铁	1				8	17		千克	AB	Alloy pig iron
7201.5000 90	镜铁	1				8	17		千克	AB	Spiegeleisen
72.02	**铁合金:**										**Ferro-alloys:**
	-锰铁:										-Ferro-manganese:
7202.1100	--按重量计含碳量在2%以上	2			0	11	17		千克	4Bxy	--Containing by weight more than 2% of carbon
7202.1900	--其他	2			0	11	17		千克	4Bxy	--Other
	-硅铁:										-Ferro-silicon:
7202.2100	--按重量计含硅量在55%以上	2			0	11	17		千克	B	--Containing by weight more than 55% of silicon
7202.2900	--其他	2			0	11	17		千克	B	--Other
7202.3000	-硅锰铁	2			0	11	17		千克	4aBxy	-Ferro-silico-manganese
	-铬铁:										-Ferro-chromium:
7202.4100	--按重量计含碳量在4%以上	2			0	8	17		千克	4Bxy	--Containing by weight more than 4% of carbon
7202.4900	--其他	2			0	8	17		千克	4Bxy	--Other
7202.5000	-硅铬铁	2			0	11	17		千克	4Bxy	-Ferro-silico-chromium
7202.6000	-镍铁	2			0	11	17		千克	4xy	-Ferro-nickel
7202.7000	-钼铁	2			0	11	17		千克	4Baxy	-Ferro-molybdenum
	-钨铁及硅钨铁:										-Ferro-tungsten and ferro-silico-tungsten:
7202.8010	---钨铁	2			0	11	17		千克	4Bxy	---Ferro-tungsten
7202.8020	---硅钨铁	2			0	11	17		千克	4xy	---Ferro-silico-tungsten
	-其他:										-Other:
7202.9100	--钛铁及硅钛铁	2			0	11	17		千克	4xy	--Ferro-titanium and ferro-silico-titanium
	--钒铁:										--Ferro-vanadium:
7202.9210	---按重量计含钒量在75%及以上	9	5		0	30	17		千克	4Bxy	---Containing≥75% by weight of vanadium
7202.9290	---其他	9	5		0	30	17		千克	4Bxy	---Other
7202.9300	--铌铁	2			0	11	17		千克		--Ferro-niobium
7202.9300 10	铁钽铌合金(钽含量<10%)	2				11	17		千克	4xy	Ferro-tantalum-niobium alloy, containing<10% by weight of tantalum
7202.9300 90	其他铌铁	2				11	17		千克	4xy	Other ferro-niobium
7202.9900	--其他	2			0	11	17		千克	4Bxy	--Other
72.03	**直接从铁矿还原所得的铁产品及其他海绵铁产品,块、团、团粒及类似形状;按重量计纯度在99.94%及以上的铁,块、团、团粒及类似形状:**										**Ferrous products obtained by direct reduction of iron ore and other spongy ferrous products, in lumps, pellets or similar forms; iron having a minimum purity by weight of 99.94%, in lumps, pellets or similar forms:**
7203.1000	-直接从铁矿还原所得的铁产品	2			0	8	17		千克		-Ferrous products obtained by direct reduction of iron ore
7203.1000 01	热压铁块	2				8	17		千克		Ferrous products obtained by direct reduction of iron ore, in lumps, hot pressed

税则号列 Tariff Item.	货品名称	最惠国(%) MFN	协定(%)CT 东盟 CA	中巴 CP	中智 CC	普通 Gen	增值税率 VAT	出口退税 ED	计量单位 Unit	监管条件 SC	Article Description
7203.1000 90	直接从铁矿还原的铁产品(铁团、铁粒及类似形状)	2				8	17		千克		Other ferrous products obtained by direct reduction of iron ore in lumps, pellets or similar forms
7203.9000	-其他	2			0	8	17		千克		-Other
72.04	**钢铁废碎料;供再熔的碎料钢铁锭:**										**Ferrous waste and scrap; remelting scrap ingots of iron steel:**
7204.1000	-铸铁废碎料	2			0	8	17		千克	7AP	-Waste and scrap of cast iron
	-合金钢废碎料:										-Waste and scrap of alloy steel:
7204.2100	--不锈钢废碎料	0				8	17		千克	7AP	--Of stainless steel
7204.2900	--其他	0				8	17		千克	7AP	--Other
7204.3000	-镀锡钢铁废碎料	2			0	8	17		千克	7AP	-Waste and scrap of tinned iron or steel
	-其他废碎料:										-Other waste and scrap:
7204.4100	--车、刨、铣、磨、锯、锉、剪、冲加工过程中产生的废料,不论是否成捆	2			0	8	17		千克	7AP	--Turnings, shavings, chips, milling waste, sawdust, filings, trimmings and stampings, whether or not in bundles
7204.4900	--其他	0				8	17		千克		--Other
7204.4900 10	废汽车压件	0				8	17		千克	PA	Pressed scrap bails of used cars
7204.4900 20	以回收钢铁为主的废五金电器	0				8	17		千克	AP	Waste hardware and electric appliance mainly for recoverying steel and iron
7204.4900 90	未列名钢铁废碎料	0				8	17		千克	7AP	Other ferrous waste and scrap, not elsewhere specifiled or included
7204.5000	-供再熔的碎料钢铁锭	0				8	17		千克	7AP	-Remelting scrap ingots
72.05	**生铁、镜铁及钢铁的颗粒和粉末:**										**Granules and powders, of pig iron, spiegeleisen, iron or steel:**
7205.1000	-颗粒	2			0	30	17		千克		-Granules
	-粉末:										-Powders:
7205.2100	--合金钢的	2			0	17	17		千克		--Of alloy steel
7205.2900	--其他	2			0	17	17		千克		--Other
	第二分章 铁及非合金钢										Ⅱ.-IRON AND NON-ALLOY STEEL
72.06	**铁及非合金钢,锭状或其他初级形状(税目72.03的铁除外):**										**Iron and non-alloy steel in ingots or other primary forms (excluding iron of heading 72.03):**
7206.1000	-锭状	2			0	11	17		千克	AB	-Ingots
7206.9000	-其他	2			0	11	17		千克		-Other
72.07	**铁及非合金钢的半制成品:**										**Semi-finished products of iron or non-alloy steel:**
	-按重量计含碳量在0.25%以下:										-Containing by weight less than 0.25% of carbon:
7207.1100	--矩形(包括正方形)截面,宽度小于厚度的两倍	2			0	11	17		千克	AB7	--Of rectangular (including square) cross-section, the width measuring less than twice the thickness
7207.1200	--其他矩形(正方形除外)截面的	2			0	11	17		千克	AB7	--Other, of rectangular (other than square) cross-section
7207.1900	--其他	2			0	11	17		千克	AB7	--Other
7207.2000	-按重量计含碳量在0.25%及以上	2			0	11	17		千克	AB7	-Containing by weight 0.25% or more of carbon

税则号列 Tariff Item.	货品名称	最惠国(%) MFN	协定(%)CT 东盟 CA	中巴 CP	中智 CC	普通 Gen	增值税率 VAT	出口退税 ED	计量单位 Unit	监管条件 SC	Article Description
72.08	**宽度在600毫米及以上的铁或非合金钢平板轧材,经热轧,但未经包覆、镀层或涂层:**										**Flat-rolled products of iron or non-alloy steel, of a width of 600mm or more, hot-rolled, not clad, plated or coated:**
7208.1000	-除热轧外未经进一步加工的卷材,已轧压花纹	5			0	14	17	8	千克	A7	-In coils, not further worked than hot-rolled, with patterns in relief
	-其他经酸洗的卷材,除热轧外未经进一步加工:										-Other, in coils, not further worked than hot-rolled, pickled:
7208.2500	--厚度在4.75毫米及以上	5			0	14	17	8	千克	A7	--Of a thickness of 4.75mm or more
	--厚度在3毫米及以上,但小于4.75毫米:										--Of a thickness of 3mm or more but less than 4.75mm:
7208.2610	---屈服强度大于355牛顿/平方毫米	5			0	14	17	8	千克	A7	---of a yield strength exceeding 355N/mm^2
7208.2690	---其他	5			0	14	17	8	千克	A7	---Other
	--厚度小于3毫米:										--Of a thickness of less than 3mm:
7208.2710	---厚度小于1.5毫米	5			0	14	17	8	千克	A7	---Of a thickness of less than 1.5mm
7208.2790	---其他	5			0	14	17	11	千克	A7	---Other
	-其他卷材,除热轧外未经进一步加工:										-Other, in coils, not further worked than hot-rolled:
7208.3600	--厚度超过10毫米	6	T3		0	14	17	11	千克	A7	--Of a thickness exceeding 10mm
7208.3700	--厚度在4.75毫米及以上,但不超过10毫米	5			0	14	17	11	千克	A7	--Of a thickness of 4.75mm or more but not exceeding 10mm
	--厚度在3毫米及以上,但小于4.75毫米:										--Of a thickness of 3mm or more but less than 4.75mm:
7208.3810	---屈服强度大于355牛顿/平方毫米	5			0	14	17	8	千克	A7	---Of a yield strength exceeding 355N/mm^2
7208.3890	---其他	5			0	14	17	11	千克	A7	---Other
	--厚度小于3毫米:										--Of a thickness of less than 3mm:
7208.3910	---厚度小于1.5毫米	3			0	14	17	8	千克	A7	---Of a thickness of less than 1.5mm
7208.3990	---其他	3			0	14	17	11	千克	A7	---Other
7208.4000	-已轧压花纹的非卷材,除热轧外未经进一步加工	6	T3		0	17	17	8	千克	A7	-Not in coils, not further worked than hot-rolled, with patterns in relief
	-其他非卷材,除热轧外未经进一步加工:										-Other, not in coils, not further worked than hot-rolled:
	--厚度超过10毫米:										--Of a thickness exceeding 10mm:
7208.5110	---厚度超过50毫米	6	T3		4.8	17	17	11	千克	A7	---Thickness > 50mm
7208.5120	---厚度在20毫米以上,但不超过50毫米	6	T3		4.8	17	17	8	千克	A7	---Of a thickness exceeding 20mm but not exceeding 50mm
7208.5190	---其他	6	T3		4.8	17	17	11	千克	A7	---Other
7208.5200	--厚度在4.75毫米及以上,但不超过10毫米	6	T3		0	17	17	8	千克	A7	--Of a thickness of 4.75mm or more but not exceeding 10mm
	--厚度在3毫米及以上,但小于4.75毫米:										--Of a thickness of 3mm or more but less than 4.75mm:
7208.5310	---屈服强度大于355牛顿/平方毫米	6	T3	5.1	0	17	17	8	千克	A7	---Of a yield strength exceeding 355N/mm^2
7208.5390	---其他	6	T3	5.1	0	17	17	8	千克	A7	---Other
	--厚度小于3毫米:										--Of a thickness of less than 3mm:
7208.5410	---厚度小于1.5毫米	6	T3	5.1	0	17	17	8	千克	A7	---Of a thickness of less than1.5mm:
7208.5490	---其他	6	T3	5.1	0	17	17	8	千克	A7	---Other

税则号列 Tariff Item.	货品名称	最惠国(%) MFN	协定(%)CT 东盟 CA	中巴 CP	中智 CC	普通 Gen	增值税率 VAT	出口退税 ED	计量单位 Unit	监管条件 SC	Article Description
7208.9000	-其他	6	T3		0	17	17	11	千克	A7	-Other
72.09	**宽度在600毫米及以上的铁或非合金钢平板轧材，经冷轧，但未经包覆、镀层或涂层：**										**Flat-rolled products of iron or non-alloy steel, of a width of 600mm or more, cold-rolled (cold-reduced), not clad, plated or coated:**
	-卷材，除冷轧外未经进一步加工：										-In coils, not further worked than cold-rolled (cold-reduced):
	--厚度在3毫米及以上：										--Of a thickness of 3mm or more
7209.1510	---屈服强度大于355牛顿/平方毫米	6	T3		0	17	17	8	千克	A7	---Of a yield strength exceeding 355N/mm^2
7209.1590	---其他	6	T3		0	17	17	8	千克	A7	---Other
	--厚度超过1毫米，但小于3毫米：										--Of a thickness exceeding 1mm but less than 3mm:
7209.1610	---屈服强度大于275牛顿/平方毫米	6	T3	4.2	4.8	17	17	8	千克	A7	---Of a yield strength exceeding 275N/mm^2
7209.1690	---其他	6	T3	4.2	4.8	17	17	11	千克	A7	---Other
	--厚度在0.5毫米及以上，但不超过1毫米：										--Of a thickness of 0.5mm or more but not exceeding 1mm:
7209.1710	---屈服强度大于275牛顿/平方毫米	3		2.1	1.8	17	17	8	千克	A7	---Of a yield otrength exceeding 275N/mm^2
7209.1790	---其他	3		2.1	1.8	17	17	11	千克	A7	---Other
	--厚度小于0.5毫米：										--Of a thickness of less than 0.5mm:
7209.1810	---厚度小于0.3毫米	6	T3	4.2	4.8	17	17	8	千克	A7	---Of a thickness less than 0.3mm
7209.1890	---其他	6	T3	4.2	4.8	17	17	8	千克	A7	---Other
	-非卷材，除冷轧外未经进一步加工：										-Not in coils, not further worked than cold-rolled (cold-reduced):
7209.2500	--厚度在3毫米及以上	6	T3		0	17	17	8	千克	A7	--Of a thickness of 3mm or more
7209.2600	--厚度超过1毫米，但小于3毫米	6	T3		0	17	17	8	千克	A7	--Of a thickness exceeding 1mm but less than 3mm
7209.2700	--厚度在0.5毫米及以上，但不超过1毫米	6	T3	4.2	0	17	17	8	千克	A7	--Of a thickness of 0.5mm or more but not exceeding 1mm
7209.2800	--厚度小于0.5毫米	6	T3		0	17	17	8	千克	A7	--Of a thickness of less than 0.5mm
7209.9000	-其他	6	T3	4.2	0	17	17	8	千克	A7	-Other
72.10	**宽度在600毫米及以上的铁或非合金钢平板轧材，经包覆、镀层或涂层：**										**Flat-rolled products of iron or non-alloy steel, of a width of 600mm or more, clad, plated or coated:**
	-镀或涂锡的：										-Plated or coated with tin:
7210.1100	--厚度在0.5毫米及以上	10	T3		0	20	17	8	千克	A7	--Of a thickness of 0.5mm or more
7210.1200	--厚度小于0.5毫米	5			4	20	17	11	千克	A7	--Of a thickness of less than 0.5mm
7210.2000	-镀或涂铅的，包括镀铅锡钢板	4			0	20	17	8	千克	7	-Plated or coated with lead, including terneplate
7210.3000	-电镀锌的	8	T3		0	20	17	8	千克	A7	-Electrolytically plated or coated with zinc
	-用其他方法镀或涂锌的：										-Otherwise plated or coated with zinc:
7210.4100	--瓦楞形	8	T3		0	20	17	8	千克	A7	--Corrugated
7210.4900	--其他	4			0	20	17	8	千克	A7	--Other
7210.5000	-镀或涂氧化铬或铬及氧化铬的	8	T3		0	20	17	8	千克	7	-Plated or coated with chromium oxides or with chromium and chromium oxides
	-镀或涂铝的：										-Plated or coated with aluminium:

税则号列 Tariff Item.	货 品 名 称	最惠国(%) MFN	协定(%)CT 东盟 CA	中巴 CP	中智 CC	普通 Gen	增值税率 VAT	出口退税 ED	计量单位 Unit	监管条件 SC	Article Description
7210.6100	--镀或涂铝锌合金的	8	T3		6.4	20	17	8	千克	7	--Plated or coated with aluminium-zinc alloys
7210.6900	--其他	8	T3		0	20	17	8	千克	7	--Other
7210.7000	-涂漆或涂塑的	4			3.2	20	17	8	千克	7	-Painted, varnished or coated with plastics
7210.9000	-其他	8	T3		0	20	17	8	千克	7	-Other
72.11	**宽度小于600毫米的铁或非合金钢平板轧材,但未经包覆、镀层或涂层:**										**Flat-rolled products of iron or non-alloy steel, of a width of less than 600mm, not clad, plated or coated:**
	-除热轧外未经进一步加工:										-Not further worked than hot-rolled:
7211.1300	--经四面轧制或在闭合匣内轧制的非卷材,宽度超过150毫米,厚度不小于4毫米,未轧压花纹	6	T3		0	30	17	8	千克	A7	--Rolled on four faces or in a closed box pass, of a width exceeding 150mm and a thickness of not less than 4mm, not in coils and without patterns in relief
7211.1400	--其他,厚度在4.75毫米及以上	6	T3		0	30	17	8	千克	A7	--Other, of a thickness of 4.75mm or more
7211.1900	--其他	6	T3		0	30	17	8	千克	A7	--Other
	-除冷轧外未经进一步加工:										-Not further worked than cold-rolled (cold-reduced):
7211.2300	--按重量计含碳量低于0.25%	6	T3		0	30	17	11	千克	A7	--Containing by weight less than 0.25% of carbon
7211.2900	--其他	6	T3		0	30	17	8	千克	A7	--Other
7211.9000	-其他	6	T3		4.8	30	17	8	千克	A7	-Other
72.12	**宽度小于600毫米的铁或非合金钢平板轧材,经包覆、镀层或涂层:**										**Flat-rolled products of iron or non-alloy steel, of a width of less than 600mm, clad, plated or coated:**
7212.1000	-镀或涂锡的	5			0	20	17	8	千克	A7	-Plated or coated with tin
7212.2000	-电镀锌的	8	T3		0	20	17	8	千克	A7	-Electrolytically plated or coated with zinc
7212.3000	-用其他方法镀或涂锌的	8	T3		6.4	20	17	8	千克	A7	-Otherwise plated or coated with zinc
7212.4000	-涂漆或涂塑的	4			3.2	20	17	8	千克	7	-Painted, varnished or coated with plastics
7212.5000	-镀或涂其他材料的	8	T3		0	20	17	8	千克	7	-Otherwise plated or coated
7212.6000	-经包覆的	8	T3		0	20	17	8	千克	7	-Clad
72.13	**不规则盘卷的铁及非合金钢的热轧条、杆:**										**Bars and rods, hot-rolled, in irregularly wound coils, of iron or non-alloy steel:**
7213.1000	-带有轧制过程中产生的凹痕、凸缘、槽沟及其他变形的	3			1.8	20	17	8	千克	AB7	-Containing indentations, ribs, grooves or other deformations produced during the rolling process
7213.2000	-其他,易切削钢制	3			0	20	17	8	千克	AB7	-Other, of free-cutting steel
	-其他:										-Other:
7213.9100	--直径小于14毫米圆形截面的	5		4.3	4	20	17	8	千克	AB7	--Of circular cross-section measuring less than 14mm in diameter
7213.9900	--其他	5			0	20	17	8	千克	AB7	--Other
72.14	**铁或非合金钢的其他条、杆,除锻造、热轧、热拉拔或热挤压外未经进一步加工,包括轧制后扭曲的:**										**Other bars and rods of iron or non-alloy steel, not further worked than forged, hot-rolled, hot-drawn or hot-extruded, but including those twisted after rolling:**
7214.1000	-锻造的	7	T3		5.6	10	17	8	千克	AB7	-Forged

税则号列 Tariff Item.	货品名称	最惠国(%) MFN	协定(%)CT			普通 Gen	增值税率 VAT	出口退税 ED	计量单位 Unit	监管条件 SC	Article Description
			东盟 CA	中巴 CP	中智 CC						
7214.2000	-带有轧制过程中产生的凹痕、凸缘、槽沟或其他变形以及轧制后扭曲的	3		0	1.8	20	17	8	千克	AB7	-Containing indentations, ribs, grooves or other deformations produced during the rolling process or twisted after rolling
7214.3000	-其他,易切削钢制	7	T3		0	20	17	8	千克	AB7	-Other, of free-cutting steel
	-其他:										-Other:
7214.9100	--矩形(正方形除外)截面的	3			1.8	20	17	8	千克	AB7	--Of rectangular cross section (other than square)
7214.9900	--其他	3			1.8	20	17	8	千克	AB7	--Other
72.15	**铁及非合金钢的其他条、杆:**										**Other bars and rods of iron or non-alloy steel:**
7215.1000	-易切削钢制,除冷成形或冷加工外未经进一步加工	7	T3		0	20	17	8	千克	A7	-Of free-cutting steel, not further worked than cold-formed or cold-finished
7215.5000	-其他,除冷成形或冷加工外未经进一步加工	7	5		0	20	17	8	千克	A7	-Other, not further worked than cold-formed or cold-finished
7215.9000	-其他	3			0	20	17	8	千克	A7	-Other
72.16	**铁或非合金钢的角材、型材及异型材:**										**Angles, shapes and sections of iron or non-alloy steel:**
	-槽钢、工字钢及H型钢,除热轧、热拉拔或热挤压外未经进一步加工,截面高度低于80毫米:										-U, I or H sections, not further worked than hot-rolled, hot-drawn or extruded, of a height of less than 80mm:
7216.1010	---H型钢	3			0	14	17	8	千克	AB7	---H sections
7216.1020	---工字钢	3			0	14	17	11	千克	AB7	---I sections
7216.1090	---其他	3			0	14	17	8	千克	AB7	---Other
	-角钢及丁字钢,除热轧、热拉拔或热挤压外未经进一步加工,截面高度低于80毫米:										-L or T sections, not further worked than hot-rolled, hot-drawn or extruded, of a height of less than 80mm:
7216.2100	--角钢	6	T3		4.8	17	17	8	千克	AB7	--L sections
7216.2200	--丁字钢	6	5		0	14	17	8	千克	AB7	--T sections
	-槽钢、工字钢及H型钢,除热轧、热拉拔或热挤压外未经进一步加工,截面高度在80毫米及以上:										-U, I or H sections, not further worked than hot-rolled, hot-drawn or extruded of a height of 80mm or more:
7216.3100	--槽钢	6	T3		4.8	14	17	8	千克	AB7	--U sections
	--工字钢:										--I sections:
7216.3210	---截面高度在200毫米以上	6	T3		0	14	17	11	千克	AB7	---Of a height exceeding 200mm
7216.3290	---其他	6	T3		0	14	17	8	千克	AB7	---Other
	--H型钢:										--H sections:
	---截面高度在200毫米以上:										---Of a height exceeding 200mm:
7216.3311	----截面高度在800毫米以上	6	T3		0	14	17	11	千克	AB7	----Of a height exceeding 800mm
7216.3319	----其他	6	T3		0	14	17	8	千克	AB7	----Other
7216.3390	---其他	6	T3		0	14	17	8	千克	AB7	---Other
	-角钢及丁字钢,除热轧、热拉拔或热挤压外未经进一步加工,截面高度在80毫米及以上:										-L or T sections, not further worked than hot-rolled, hot-drawn or extruded, of a height of 80mm or more:
7216.4010	---角钢	3			0	17	17	8	千克	AB7	---L sections
7216.4020	---丁字钢	3			0	14	17	8	千克	AB7	---T sections

税则号列 Tariff Item.	货品名称	最惠国(%) MFN	协定(%)CT 东盟 CA	中巴 CP	中智 CC	普通 Gen	增值税率 VAT	出口退税 ED	计量单位 Unit	监管条件 SC	Article Description
	-其他角材、型材及异型材，除热轧、热拉拔或热挤压外未经进一步加工：										-Other angles, shapes and sections, not further worked than hot-rolled, hot-drawn or extruded:
7216.5010	---乙字钢	6	5		0	14	17	8	千克	AB7	---Z sections
7216.5090	---其他	3			0	20	17	8	千克	AB7	---Other
	-角材、型材及异型材，除冷成形或冷加工外未经进一步加工：										-Angles, shapes and sections, not further worked than cold-formed or cold-finished:
7216.6100	--平板轧材制的	3			1.8	20	17	8	千克	AB7	--Obtained from flat-rolled products
7216.6900	--其他	3			1.8	20	17	8	千克	AB7	--Other
	-其他：										-Other:
7216.9100	--平板轧材经冷成形或冷加工制的	3			0	20	17	8	千克	AB7	--Cold-formed or cold-finished from flat-rolled products
7216.9900	--其他	3			0	20	17	8	千克	AB7	--Other
72.17	**铁丝或非合金钢丝：**										**Wire of iron or non-alloy steel:**
7217.1000	-未经镀或涂层，不论是否抛光	8	T3		6.4	40	17	11	千克	B7	-Not plated or coated, whether or not polished
7217.2000	-镀或涂锌的	8	T3		6.4	40	17	8	千克	B7	-Plated or coated with zinc
7217.3000	-镀或涂其他贱金属的	8	T3	6.4	6.4	40	17	8	千克	B7	-Plated or coated with other base metals
7217.9000	-其他	8	T3		0	40	17	8	千克	B7	-Other
	第三分章　不锈钢										Ⅲ. -STAINLESS STEEL
72.18	**不锈钢，锭状或其他初级形状；不锈钢半制成品：**										**Stainless steel in ingots or other primary forms; semi-finished products of stainless steel:**
7218.1000	-锭状及其他初级形状	2			0	11	17	8	千克	7	-Ingots and other primary forms
	-其他：										-Other:
7218.9100	--矩形(正方形除外)截面的	2			0	11	17	8	千克	7	--Of rectangular (other than square) cross-section
7218.9900	--其他	2			0	11	17	8	千克	7	--Other
72.19	**不锈钢平板轧材，宽度在600毫米及以上：**										**Flat-rolled products of stainless steel, of a width of 600mm or more:**
	-除热轧外未经进一步加工的卷材：										-Not further worked than hot-rolled, in coils:
7219.1100	--厚度超过10毫米	4			0	14	17	8	千克	A7	--Of a thickness exceeding 10mm
7219.1200	--厚度在4.75毫米及以上，但不超过10毫米	4			0	14	17	8	千克	A7	--Of a thickness of 4.75mm or more but not exceeding 10mm
	--厚度在3毫米及以上，但小于4.75毫米：										--Of a thickness of 3mm or more but less than 4.75mm:
	---未经酸洗的：										---Not acid pickled:
7219.1311	----按重量计含镍量在7%以下铬锰系不锈钢	4			0	14	17	11	千克	A7	----Containing by weight less than7% of nickel of Ferro-chromium-manganese steel
7219.1319	----其他	4			0	14	17	11	千克	A7	----Other
	---经酸洗的：										---Acid pickled:
7219.1321	----按重量计含镍量在7%以下铬锰系不锈钢	4			0	14	17	11	千克	A7	----Containing by weight less than 7% of nickel of Ferro-chromiam-manganese steel
7219.1329	----其他	4			0	14	17	8	千克	A7	----Other
	--厚度小于3毫米：										--Of a thickness of less than 3mm:
	---未经酸洗的：										---Not acid pickled:

税则号列 Tariff Item.	货品名称	最惠国(%) MFN	协定(%)CT 东盟 CA	协定(%)CT 中巴 CP	协定(%)CT 中智 CC	普通 Gen	增值税率 VAT	出口退税 ED	计量单位 Unit	监管条件 SC	Article Description
7219.1411	----按重量计含镍量在7%以下铬锰系不锈钢	4			0	14	17	11	千克	A7	----Containing by weight less than 7% of nickel of Ferro-chromiam-marganese steel
7219.1419	----其他	4			0	14	17	11	千克	A7	----Other
	---经酸洗的：										---Acid Pickled：
7219.1421	----按重量计含镍量在7%以下铬锰系不锈钢	4			0	14	17	11	千克	A7	----Containing by weight less than 7% of nickel of ferro chromiam-manganese steel
7219.1429	----其他	4			0	14	17	8	千克	A7	----Other
	-除热轧外未经进一步加工的非卷材：										-Not further worked than hot-rolled, not in coils：
7219.2100	--厚度超过10毫米	10	8	9.3	0	40	17	8	千克	A7	--Of a thickness exceeding 10mm
7219.2200	--厚度在4.75毫米及以上，但不超过10毫米	10	8	9.3	8	40	17	8	千克	A7	--Of a thickness of 4.75mm or more but not exceeding 10mm
7219.2300	--厚度在3毫米及以上，但小于4.75毫米	10	8	9.3	0	40	17	8	千克	A7	--Of a thickness of 3mm or more but less than 4.75mm
	--厚度小于3毫米：										--Of a thickness of less than 3mm：
7219.2410	---厚度超过1毫米但小于3毫米	10	8	9.3	0	40	17	8	千克	A7	---Of a thickness exceeding 1mm, but less than 3mm
7219.2420	---厚度在0.5毫米及以上，但不超过1毫米	10	8	9.3	0	40	17	8	千克	A7	---Of a thickness of 0.5mm or more but not exceeding 1mm
7219.2430	---厚度小于0.5毫米	10	8	9.3	0	40	17	8	千克	A7	---Of a thickness of less than 0.5mm
	-除冷轧外未经进一步加工：										-Not further worked than cold-rolled (cold-reduced)：
7219.3100	--厚度在4.75毫米及以上	10	T3		8	40	17	8	千克	A7	--Of a thickness of 4.75mm or more
7219.3200	--厚度在3毫米及以上，但小于4.75毫米	10	T3		8	40	17	8	千克	A7	--Of a thickness of 3mm or more but less than 4.75mm
7219.3300	--厚度超过1毫米，但小于3毫米	10	T3		8	40	17	11	千克	A7	--Of a thickness exceeding 1mm but less than 3mm
7219.3400	--厚度在0.5毫米及以上，但不超过1毫米	10	T3		8	40	17	11	千克	A7	--Of a thickness of 0.5mm or more but not exceeding 1mm
7219.3500	--厚度小于0.5毫米	10	T3		8	40	17	8	千克	A7	--Of a thickness of less than 0.5mm
7219.9000	-其他	10	T3		0	40	17	8	千克	A7	-Other
72.20	**不锈钢平板轧材，宽度小于600毫米：**										**Flat-rolled products stainless steel, of a width of less than 600mm：**
	-除热轧外未经进一步加工：										-Not further worked than hot-rolled：
7220.1100	--厚度在4.75毫米及以上	10	8		0	20	17	8	千克	A7	--Of a thickness of 4.75mm or more
7220.1200	--厚度小于4.75毫米	10	8		0	20	17	8	千克	A7	--Of a thickness of less than 4.75mm
	-除冷轧外未经进一步加工：										-Not further worked than cold-rolled (cold-reduced)：
7220.2010	---宽度小于300毫米	10	T3		0	20	17	8	千克	A7	---Of a width of less than 300mm
7220.2090	---其他	10	T3		0	20	17	8	千克	A7	---Other
7220.9000	-其他	10	T3		0	20	17	8	千克	A7	-Other
72.21	**不规则盘卷的不锈钢热轧条、杆：**										**Bars and rods, hot-rolled, in irregularly wound coils, of stainless steel：**
7221.0000	不规则盘卷的不锈钢热轧条、杆	10	T3	8	0	20	17	8	千克	A7	Bars and rods, hot-rolled, in irregularly wound coils, of stainless steel

税则号列 Tariff Item.	货品名称	最惠国(%) MFN	协定(%) CT 东盟 CA	中巴 CP	中智 CC	普通 Gen	增值税率 VAT	出口退税 ED	计量单位 Unit	监管条件 SC	Article Description
72.22	**不锈钢其他条、杆;不锈钢角材、型材及异型材:**										**Other bars and rods of stainless steel; angles, shapes and sections of stainless steel:**
	-条、杆,除热轧、热拉拔或热挤压外未经进一步加工:										-Bars and rods, not further worked than hot-rolled, hot-drawn or extruded:
7222.1100	--圆形截面的	10	T3	9	0	40	17	8	千克	A7	--Of circular cross-section
7222.1900	--其他	10	8	9	0	40	17	8	千克	A7	--Other
7222.2000	-条、杆,除冷成形或冷加工外未经进一步加工	10	T3		0	40	17	8	千克	7	-Bars and rods, not further worked than cold-formed or cold-finished
7222.3000	-其他条、杆	10	8	8.9	6	40	17	8	千克	7	-Other bars and rods
7222.4000	-角材、型材及异型材	10	T3		0	17	17	8	千克	A7	-Angles, shapes and sections
72.23	**不锈钢丝:**										**Wire of stainless steel:**
7223.0000	不锈钢丝	10	T3		8	20	17	8	千克	7	Wire of stainless steel
	第四分章 其他合金钢;合金钢或非合金钢制的空心钻钢										Ⅳ. -OTHER ALLOY STEEL; HOLLOW DRILL BARS AND RODS, OF ALLOY OR NON-ALLOY STEEL
72.24	**其他合金钢,锭状或其他初级形状;其他合金钢制的半制成品:**										**Other alloy steel in ingots or other primary forms; semi-finished products of other alloy steel:**
7224.1000	-锭状及其他初级形状	2			0	11	17		千克	7	-Ingots and other primary forms
	-其他:										-Other:
7224.9010	---单件重量在10吨及以上的粗铸锻件坯	2			0	11	17		千克	7	---Raw casting forging stocks, individual piece weight of 10T or more
7224.9090	---其他	2			0	11	17		千克	7	---Other
72.25	**其他合金钢平板轧材,宽度在600毫米及以上:**										**Flat-rolled products of other alloy steel, of a width of 600mm or more:**
	-硅电钢制:										-Of silicon-electrical steel:
7225.1100	--取向性硅电钢	3		2.1	0	20	17	8	千克	A7	--Grain-oriented
7225.1900	--其他	6	5		0	20	17	8	千克	A7	--Other
7225.3000	-其他卷材,除热轧外未经进一步加工	3			0	14	17	8	千克	A7	-Other, not further worked than hot-rolled, in coils
7225.4000	-其他非卷材,除热轧外未经进一步加工	3			1.8	17	17	8	千克	A7	-Other, not further worked than hot-rolled, not in coils
7225.5000	-其他,除冷轧外未经进一步加工	3			1.8	17	17	8	千克	A7	-Other, not further worked than cold-rolled (cold-reduced)
	-其他:										-Other:
7225.9100	--电镀或涂锌的	7	5		0	17	17	8	千克	A7	--Electrolytically plated or coated with zinc
7225.9200	--用其他方法镀或涂锌的	7	5		0	17	17	8	千克	A7	--Otherwise plated or coated with zinc
	--其他:										--Other:
7225.9910	---高速钢制	3			0	17	17	8	千克	A7	---Of high speed steel
7225.9990	---高速钢制	7	5		0	17	17	8	千克	A7	---Other
72.26	**其他合金钢平板轧材,宽度小于600毫米:**										**Flat-rolled products of other alloy steel, of a width of less than 600mm:**
	-硅电钢制:										-Of silicon-electrical steel:
7226.1100	--取向性硅电钢	3			0	20	17	8	千克	A7	--Grain-oriented
7226.1900	--其他	3			0	20	17	11	千克	A7	--Other
7226.2000	-高速钢制	3			0	20	17	8	千克	A7	-Of high speed steel
	-其他:										-Other:
7226.9100	--除热轧外未经进一步加工	3			0	20	17	8	千克	A7	--Not further worked than hot-rolled
7226.9200	--除冷轧外未经进一步加工	3			0	20	17	8	千克	A7	--Not further worked than cold-rolled (cold-reduced)

税则号列 Tariff Item.	货品名称	最惠国(%) MFN	协定(%)CT			普通 Gen	增值税率 VAT	出口退税 ED	计量单位 Unit	监管条件 SC	Article Description
			东盟 CA	中巴 CP	中智 CC						
	--其他:										--Other:
7226.9910	---电镀或涂锌的	7	5		0	20	17	8	千克	A7	---Electrolytically plated or coated with zinc
7226.9920	---用其他方法镀或涂锌的	7	5		0	20	17	8	千克	A7	---Otherwise plated or coated with zinc
7226.9990	---其他	7	5		0	20	17	8	千克		---Other
7226.9990 01	铁镍合金带材(生产集成电路框架用)[(宽度<600mm)]	7				20	17	8	千克	A7	Other flat-rolled products of other alloy steel, Fe-Ni alloys strip, width <600mm (production of the frame for electronic integrated circuits)
7226.9900 90	其他合金板材(宽度<600mm)	7				20	17	8	千克	A7	Other flat-rolled products of other alloy steel, width <600mm
72.27	**不规则盘卷的其他合金钢热轧条、杆:**										**Bars and rods, hot-rolled, in irregularly wound coils, of other alloy steel:**
7227.1000	-高速钢制	3			0	20	17	8	千克	A7	-Of high speed steel
7227.2000	-硅锰钢制	6	5		0	20	17	8	千克	A7	-Of silico-manganese steel
7227.9000	-其他	3			0	20	17	8	千克	A7	-Other
72.28	**其他合金钢条、杆;其他合金钢角材、型材及异型材;合金钢或非合金钢制的空心钻钢:**										**Other bars and rods of other alloy steel; angles, shapes and sections, of other alloy steel; hollow drill bars and rods, of alloy or non-alloy steel:**
7228.1000	-高速钢条、杆	3			0	20	17	8	千克	A7	-Bars and rods, of high speed steel
7228.2000	-硅锰钢条、杆	6	5		0	20	17	8	千克	A7	-Bars and rods, of silico-manganese steel
7228.3000	-其他条、杆,除热轧、热拉拔或热挤压外未经进一步加工	3			0	20	17	8	千克	A7	-Other bars and rods, not further worked than hot-crolled, hot-drawn or extruded
7228.4000	-其他条、杆,除锻造外未经进一步加工	3			0	20	17	8	千克	A7	-Other bars and rods, not further worked than forged
7228.5000	-其他条、杆,除冷成形或冷加工外未经进一步加工	3			0	20	17	8	千克	A7	-Other bars and rods, not further worked than cold-formed of cold-finished
7228.6000	-其他条、杆	3			0	20	17	8	千克	A7	-Other bars and rods
	-角材、型材及异型材:										-Angles, shapes and sections:
7228.7010	---履带板型钢	6	5		4.8	17	17	8	千克	A7	---Shapes of crawler tread
7228.7090	---其他	6	5		4.8	17	17	8	千克	A7	---Other
7228.8000	-空心钻钢	7	5		5.6	35	17	8	千克	A7	-Hollow drill bars and rods
72.29	**其他合金钢丝:**										**Wire of other alloy steel:**
7229.2000	-硅锰钢丝	7	5		0	20	17	8	千克	7	-Of silico-manganese steel
	-其他:										-Other:
7229.9010	---高速钢丝	3			0	20	17	8	千克	7	---Of high speed steel
7229.9090	---其他	7	5		5.6	20	17	8	千克	7	---Other

第七十三章
钢铁制品

Chapter 73
Articles of iron or steel

注释：

一、本章所称"铸铁"，适用于经铸造而得的产品，按重量计其铁元素含量超过其他元素单项含量并与第七十二章注释一(四)所述的钢的化学成分不同。

二、本章所称"丝"，是指热或冷成形的任何截面形状的产品，但其截面尺寸均不超过16毫米。

Notes:

1. In this Chapter the expression "cast iron" applies to products obtained by casting in which iron predominates by weight over each of the other elements and which do not comply with the chemical composition of steel as defined in Note 1 (d) to Chapter 72.

2. In this Chapter the word "wire" means hot or cold-formed products of any cross-sectional shape, of which no cross-sectional dimension exceeds 16mm.

税则号列 Tariff Item.	货品名称	最惠国(%) MFN	协定(%) 东盟 CA	中巴 CP	CT 中智 CC	普通 Gen	增值税率 VAT	出口退税 ED	计量单位 Unit	监管条件 SC	Article Description
73.01	**钢铁板桩，不论是否钻孔、打眼或组装；焊接的钢铁角材、型材及异型材：**										**Sheet piling of iron or steel, whether or not drilled, punched or made from assembled elements; welded angles, shapes and sections, of iron or steel:**
7301.1000	-钢铁板桩	7	T3	6.3	0	20	17	13	千克	7	-Sheet piling
7301.2000	-角材、型材及异型材	7	5		0	30	17	13	千克	7	-Angles, shapes and sections
73.02	**铁道及电车道铺轨用钢铁材料(钢轨、护轨、齿轨、道岔尖轨、辙叉、尖轨拉杆及其他叉道段体、轨枕、鱼尾板、轨座、轨座楔、钢轨垫板、钢轨夹、底板、固定板及其他专门用于连接或加固路轨的材料)：**										**Railway or tramway track construction material of iron or steel, the following: rails, check-rails and rack rails, switch blades, crossing frogs, point rods and other crossing pieces, sleepers (cross-ties), fish-plates, chairs, chair wedges, sole plates (base plates), rail clips, bedplates, ties and other material specialized for jointing or fixing rails:**
7302.1000	-钢轨	6	5		0	14	17	13	千克	7AB	-Rails
7302.3000	-道岔尖轨、辙叉、尖轨拉杆及其他叉道段体	8	5		0	17	17	13	千克	7AB	-Switch blades, crossing frogs, point rods and other crossing pieces
7302.4000	-鱼尾板及钢轨垫板	7	5		0	17	17	13	千克	7AB	-Fish-plates and sole plates
	-其他：										-Other:
7302.9010	---轨枕	6	5	5.1	0	14	17	13	千克	7AB	---Sleepers(cross-ties)
7302.9090	---其他	7	5	6	0	17	17	13	千克	7AB	---Other
73.03	**铸铁管及空心异型材：**										**Tubes, pipes and hollow profiles, of cast iron:**
7303.0010	---内径在500毫米及以上的圆形截面管	4			0	40	17	13	千克	7	---Tubes and pipes of circular cross-section, of the internal diameter of 500mm or more
7303.0090	---其他	4			0	40	17	13	千克	7	---Other
73.04	**无缝钢铁管及空心异型材(铸铁的除外)：**										**Tubes, pipes and hollow profiles, seamless, of iron (other than cast iron) or steel:**
	-石油或天然气管道管：										-Line pipe of a kind used for oil or gas pipelines:
	--不锈钢制：										
7304.1110	---外径大于等于215.9毫米，但不超过406.4毫米	5			0	17	17	13	千克	7AB	---Having an outside diameter 215.9mm or more but not exceeding 406.4mm
7304.1120	---外径超过114.3毫米，但小于215.9毫米	5			0	17	17	13	千克	7AB	---Having an out sidediameter exceeding 114.3mm but less than 215.9mm

税则号列 Tariff Item.	货品名称	最惠国(%) MFN	协定(%)CT 东盟 CA	中巴 CP	中智 CC	普通 Gen	增值税率 VAT	出口退税 ED	计量单位 Unit	监管条件 SC	Article Description
7304.1130	---外径不超过114.3毫米	5			0	17	17	13	千克	7AB	---Having an outside diameter not exceeding 114.3mm
7304.1190	---其他	5			0	17	17	13	千克	7AB	---Other
	--其他:										--Other:
7304.1910	---外径大于等于215.9毫米,但不超过406.4毫米	5			0	17	17	13	千克	7AB	---Having an outside diameter 215.9mm or more but not exceeding 406.4mm
7304.1920	---外径超过114.3毫米,但小于215.9毫米	5			0	17	17	13	千克	7AB	---Having an outside diameter exceeding 114.3mm but less than 215.9mm
7304.1930	---外径不超过114.3毫米	5			0	17	17	13	千克	7AB	---Having an outside diameter not exceeding 114.3mm
7304.1990	---其他	5			0	17	17	13	千克	7AB	---Other
	-钻探石油及天然气用的套管、导管及钻管:										-Casing, tubing and drill pipe, of a kind used in drilling for oil or gas: Drill pipe:
	--不锈钢钻管:										
7304.2210	---外径不超过168.3毫米	4			3.2	17	17	13	千克	7AB	---Having an outside diameter not exceeding168.3mm
7304.2290	---其他	4			3.2	17	17	13	千克	7AB	---Other
	--其他钻管:										--Other drill pipe:
7304.2310	---外径不超过168.3毫米	4			3.2	17	17	13	千克	7AB	---External diameter≤168.3mm
7304.2390	---其他	4			3.2	17	17	13	千克	7AB	---Other
7304.2400	--其他不锈钢管	4		2	0	17	17	13	千克	7AB	
7304.2900	--其他	4		2	0	17	17	13	千克	7AB	--Other
	-铁或非合金钢的其他圆形截面管:										-Other, of circular cross-section, of iron or non-alloy steel:
	--冷拔或冷轧的:										--Cold-drawn or cold-rolled (cold-reduced):
7304.3110	---锅炉管	4			3.2	17	17	13	千克	7AB	---Boiler tubes and pipes
7304.3120	---地质钻管、套管	8	5		6.4	17	17	13	千克	7AB	---Geological casing and drill pipes
7304.3190	---其他	4			3.2	17	17	13	千克	AB7	---Other
	--其他:										--Other:
7304.3910	---锅炉管	4			0	17	17	13	千克	7AB	---Boiler tubes and pipes
7304.3920	---地质钻管、套管:	5			0	17	17	13	千克	7AB	---Geological casing and drill pipes
7304.3990	---其他	4			0	17	17	13	千克	AB7	---Other
	-不锈钢的其他圆形截面管:										-Other, of circular cross-section, of stainless steel:
	--冷拔或冷轧的:										--Cold-drawn or cold-rolled (cold-reduced):
7304.4110	---锅炉管	10	8		0	17	17	13	千克	7AB	---Boiler tubes and pipes
7304.4190	---其他	10	8		0	40	17	13	千克	AB7	---Other
	--其他:										--Other:
7304.4910	---锅炉管	10	8		0	17	17	13	千克	7AB	---Boiler tubes and pipes
7304.4990	---其他	10	T3		0	40	17	13	千克	AB7	---Other
	-其他合金钢的其他圆形截面管:										-Other, of circular cross-section, of other alloy steel:
	--冷拔或冷轧的:										--Cold-drawn or cold-rolled (cold-reduced):
7304.5110	---锅炉管	4			0	17	17	13	千克	7AB	---Boiler tubes and pipes
7304.5120	---地质钻管、套管	4			0	17	17	13	千克	7AB	---Geological casing and drill pipes
7304.5190	---其他	4			0	17	17	13	千克	7AB	---Other
	--其他:										--Other:

税则号列 Tariff Item.	货品名称	最惠国(%) MFN	协定(%)CT 东盟 CA	中巴 CP	中智 CC	普通 Gen	增值税率 VAT	出口退税 ED	计量单位 Unit	监管条件 SC	Article Description
7304.5910	---锅炉管	4			3.2	17	17	13	千克	7AB	---Boiler tubes and pipes
7304.5920	---地质钻管、套管	4			3.2	17	17	13	千克	7AB	---Geological casing and drill pipes
7304.5990	---其他	4			3.2	17	17	13	千克	7AB	---Other
7304.9000	-其他	4			0	17	17	13	千克	AB7	-Other
73.05	**其他圆形截面钢铁管(例如,焊、铆及用类似方法接合的管),外径超过406.4毫米:**										**Other tubes and pipes (for example, welded, riveted or similarly closed), having circular cross-sections, the external diameter of which exceeds 406.4mm, of iron or steel:**
	-石油或天然气管道管:										-Line pipe of a kind used for oil or gas pipelines:
7305.1100	--纵向埋弧焊接的	7	T3		5.6	17	17	13	千克	7AB	--Longitudinally submerged arc welded
7305.1200	--其他纵向焊接的	3			0	17	17	13	千克	7AB	--Other, longitudinally welded
7305.1900	--其他	7	T3		0	17	17	13	千克	7AB	--Other
7305.2000	-钻探石油或天然气用套管	7	T3		0	17	17	13	千克	7AB	-Casing of a kind used in drilling for oil or gas
	-其他焊接的:										-Other, welded:
7305.3100	--纵向焊接的	6	T3		4.8	30	17	13	千克	AB7	--Longitudinally welded
7305.3900	--其他	6	T3		4.8	30	17	13	千克	AB7	--Other
7305.9000	-其他	6	T3		0	30	17	13	千克	AB7	-Other
73.06	**其他钢铁管及空心异型材(例如,辊缝、焊、铆及类似方法接合的):**										**Other tubes, pipes and hollow profiles (for example, open seam or welded, riveted or similarly closed), of iron or steel:**
	-石油及天然气管道管:										-Line pipe of a kind used for oil or gas pipelines:
7306.1100	--不锈钢焊缝管	7	T3		0	17	17	13	千克	7AB	--Welded of stainless steel
7306.1900	--其他	7	T3		0	17	17	13	千克	7AB	--Other
	-钻探石油及天然气用的套管及导管:										-Casing and tubing of a kind used in drilling for oil or gas:
7306.2100	--不锈钢焊缝管	3			0	17	17	13	千克	7AB	--Welded of stainless steel
7306.2900	--其他	3			0	17	17	13	千克	7AB	--Other
7306.3000	-铁或非合金钢的其他圆形截面焊缝管	3			1.8	30	17	13	千克	7B	-Other, welded, of circular cross-section, of iron or non-alloy steel
7306.4000	-不锈钢的其他圆形截面焊缝管	6	T3		0	30	17	13	千克	7	-Other, welded, of circular cross-section, of stainless steel
7306.5000	-其他合金钢的圆形截面焊缝管	3			1.8	30	17	13	千克	7	-Other, welded, of circular cross-section, of other alloy steel
	-非圆形截面的其他焊缝管:										-Other, welded, of non-circular cross-section:
7306.6100	--矩形式正方形截面的	3			1.8	30	17	13	千克	7	
7306.6900	--其他非圆形截面的	3			1.8	30	17	13	千克	7	--Other of non-circularcross section
7306.9000	-其他	6	T3		4.8	30	17	13	千克		-Other
7306.9000 10	多壁式管道(直接与化学品接触表面由特殊耐腐蚀材料制成)	6				30	17	13	千克	37AB	Multiple - wall channel (produced by special erosion - proof materials)
7306.9000 90	未列名其他钢铁管及空心异型材	6				30	17	13	千克	AB7	Other tubes, pipes and hollow profiles, not elsewhere specified or included
73.07	**钢铁管子附件(例如,接头、肘管、管套):**										**Tube or pipe fittings (for example, couplings, elbows, sleeves), of iron or steel:**

税则号列 Tariff Item.	货品名称	最惠国(%) MFN	协定(%)CT 东盟 CA	 中巴 CP	 中智 CC	普通 Gen	增值税率 VAT	出口退税 ED	计量单位 Unit	监管条件 SC	Article Description
	-铸件:										-Cast fittings:
7307.1100	--无可锻性铸铁制	5			0	20	17	13	千克		--Of non-malleable cast iron
7307.1900	--其他	8	5		6.4	20	17	13	千克		--Other
	-其他,不锈钢制:										-Other, of stainless steel:
7307.2100	--法兰	8.4	5	6.7	0	20	17	13	千克	B	--Flanges
7307.2200	--螺纹肘管、弯管及管套	8.4	5		0	20	17	13	千克		--Threaded elbows, bends and sleeves
7307.2300	--对焊件	8.4	5		0	20	17	13	千克		--Butt welding fittings
7307.2900	--其他	8.4	5		6.7	20	17	13	千克	B	--Other
	-其他:										-Other:
7307.9100	--法兰	7	5		0	20	17	13	千克	B	--Flanges
7307.9200	--螺纹肘管、弯管及管套	4			0	20	17	13	千克		--Threaded elbows, bends and sleeves
7307.9300	--对焊件	7	5		0	20	17	13	千克		--Butt welding fittings
7307.9900	--其他	4			3.2	20	17	13	千克		--Other
73.08	**钢铁结构体(税目94.06的活动房屋除外)及其部件(例如,桥梁及桥梁体段、闸门、塔楼、格构杆、屋顶、屋顶框架、门窗及其框架、门槛、百叶窗、栏杆、支柱及立柱);上述结构体用的已加工钢铁板、杆、角材、型材、异型材、管子及类似品:**										**Structures (excluding prefabricated buildings of heading No.94.06) and parts of structures (for example, bridges and bridge-sections, lock-gates, towers, lattice masts, roofs, roofing frameworks, doors and windows and their frames and thresholds for doors, shutters, balustrades, pillars and columns), of iron or steel; plates, rods, angles, shapes, sections, tubes and the like, prepared for use in structures, of iron or steel:**
7308.1000	-桥梁及桥梁体段	8	5	0	6.4	30	17	13	千克		-Bridges and bridge-sections
7308.2000	-塔楼及格构杆	8.4	5	0	6.7	30	17	13	千克		-Towers and lattice masts
7308.3000	-门窗及其框架、门槛	10	T3	0	0	50	17	13	千克		-Doors, windows and their frames and thresholds for doors
7308.4000	-脚手架、模板或坑道支撑用的支柱及类似设备	8.4	5	0	6.7	30	17	13	千克		-Equipment for scaffolding, shuttering, propping or pit-propping
7308.9000	-其他	4		0	3.2	30	17	13	千克		-Other
73.09	**盛装物料用的钢铁囤、柜、罐、桶及类似容器(装压缩气体或液化气体的除外),容积超过300升,不论是否衬里或隔热,但无机械或热力装置:**										**Reservoirs, tanks, vats and similar containers for any material (other than compressed or liquefied gas), of iron or steel, of a capacity exceeding 300 L, whether or not lined or heat-insulated, but not fitted with mechanical or thermal equipment:**
7309.0000	盛装物料用的钢铁囤、柜、罐、桶及类似容器(装压缩气体或液化气体的除外),容积超过300升,不论是否衬里或隔热,但无机械或热力装置	10.5	8		8.4	35	17	13	千克		Reservoirs, tanks, vats and similar containers for any material (other than compressed or liquefied gas), of iron or steel, of a capacity exceeding 300 l, whether or not lined or heat-insulated, but not fitted with mechanical or thermal equipment

税则号列 Tariff Item.	货品名称	最惠国(%) MFN	协定(%) CT 东盟 CA	中巴 CP	中智 CC	普通 Gen	增值税率 VAT	出口退税 ED	计量单位 Unit	监管条件 SC	Article Description
73.10	**盛装物料用的钢铁柜、桶、罐、听、盒及类似容器(装压缩气体或液化气体的除外),容积不超过300升,不论是否衬里或隔热,但无机械或热力装置:**										**Tanks, casks, drums, cans, boxes and similar containers, for any material (other than compressed or liquefied gas), of iron or steel, of a capacity not exceeding 300 l, whether or not lined or heat-insulated, but not fitted with mechanical or thermal equipment:**
7310.1000	-容积在50升及以上	10.5	8		8.4	40	17	13	千克		-Of a capacity of 50 l or more
	-容积在50升以下:										-Of a capacity of less than 50 l:
7310.1000 10	总容积大于100升不超过300升的容器(与所处理或盛放的仪学品接触表面由特殊耐腐蚀材料制成)	10.5				40	17	13	千克	3	Containers ,100L < capacity≤300L
7310.1000 90	其他容积50升－300升钢铁制盛物容器(容积≥50升,≤300升的钢铁柜、桶、罐、听及类似容器)	10.5				40	17	13	千克		Tanks, casks, drums, cans, boxes and similar containers, 50L ≤ capacity ≤ 300L, of iron or steel
7310.2100	--焊边或卷边接合的罐	17.5	8		14	70	17	13	千克		--Cans which are to be closed by soldering or crimping
7310.2900	--其他	17.5	8		14	70	17	13	千克	A	--Other
73.11	**装压缩气体或液化气体用的钢铁容器:**										**Containers for compressed or liquefied gas, of iron or steel:**
7311.0010	---零售包装用	17.5	8		14	70	17	13	千克	6AB	---For retail packing
7311.0090	---其他	8	5		6.4	17	17	13	千克	6AB	---Other
73.12	**非绝缘的钢铁绞股线、绳、缆、编带、吊索及类似品:**										**Stranded wire, ropes, cables, plaited bands, slings and the like, of iron or steel, not electrically insulated:**
7312.1000	-绞股线、绳、缆	4			3.2	20	17	13	千克	7AB	-Stranded wire, ropes and cables
7312.9000	-其他	4			0	20	17	13	千克		-Other
73.13	**带刺钢铁丝;围篱用的钢铁绞带或单股扁丝(不论是否带刺)及松绞的双股丝:**										**Barbed wire of iron or steel; twisted hoop or single flat wire, barbed or not, and loosely twisted double wire, of a kind used for fencing, of iron or steel:**
7313.0000	带刺钢铁丝;围篱用的钢铁绞带或单股扁丝(不论是否带刺)及松绞的双股丝	7	5	6.3	5.6	70	17	13	千克		Barbed wire of iron or steel; twisted hoop or single flat wire, barbed or not, and loosely twisted double wire, of a kind used for fencing, of iron or steel
73.14	**钢铁丝制的布(包括环形带)、网、篱、格栅;网眼钢铁板:**										**Cloth (including endless bands), grill, netting and fencing, of iron or steel wire; expanded metal of iron or steel:**
	-机织品:										-Woven cloth:
7314.1200	--不锈钢制的机器用环形带	12	8		7.2	20	17	13	千克		--Endless bands for machinery, of stainless steel
7314.1400	--不锈钢制的其他机织品:	12	8		7.2	20	17	13	千克		--Other woven cloth, of stainless steel:
7314.1900	--其他	7	5		0	20	17	13	千克		--Other

税则号列 Tariff Item.	货品名称	最惠国(%) MFN	协定(%)CT 东盟 CA	中巴 CP	中智 CC	普通 Gen	增值税率 VAT	出口退税 ED	计量单位 Unit	监管条件 SC	Article Description
7314.2000	-交点焊接的网、篱及格栅，其丝的最大截面尺寸在3毫米及以上，网眼尺寸在100平方厘米及以上	7	5		0	20	17	13	千克		-Grill, netting and fencing, welded at the intersection, of wire with a maximum cross-sectional dimension of 3mm or more and having a mesh size of 100cm^2 or more
	-其他交点焊接的网、篱及格栅：										-Other grill, netting and fencing, welded at the intersection:
7314.3100	--镀或涂锌的	7	5		0	70	17	13	千克		--Plated or coated with zinc
7314.3900	--其他	7	5		0	70	17	13	千克		--Other
	-其他网、篱及格栅：										-Other grill, netting and fencing:
7314.4100	--镀或涂锌的	8	5	6	6.4	20	17	13	千克		--Plated or coated with zinc
7314.4200	--涂塑的	8	5		0	20	17	13	千克		--Coated whith plastics
7314.4900	--其他	8	5		6.4	20	17	13	千克		--Other
7314.5000	-网眼钢铁板	8	5		0	70	17	13	千克		-Expanded metal
73.15	**钢铁链及其零件：**										**Chain and parts thereof, of iron or steel:**
	-铰接链及其零件：										-Articulated link chain and parts thereof:
	--滚子链：										--Roller chain:
7315.1110	---自行车用	12	T3		0	80	17	13	千克	B	---For bicycles
7315.1120	---摩托车用	12	T3		0	80	17	13	千克		---For motorcycles
7315.1190	---其他	12	T3		0	80	17	13	千克	B	---Other
7315.1200	--其他链	12	8		7.2	80	17	13	千克		--Other chain
7315.1900	--零件	12	T3		7.2	80	17	13	千克		--Parts
7315.2000	-防滑链	12	8		7.2	80	17	13	千克	B	-Skid chain
	-其他链：										-Other chain:
7315.8100	--日字环节链	12	8		7.2	80	17	13	千克		--Stud-link
7315.8200	--其他焊接链	12	8		7.2	80	17	13	千克		--Other, welded link
7315.8900	--其他	12	T3		9.6	80	17	13	千克		--Other
7315.9000	-其他零件	10	5		0	80	17	13	千克		-Other parts
73.16	**钢铁锚、多爪锚及其零件：**										**Anchors, grapnels and parts thereof, of iron or steel:**
7316.0000	钢铁锚、多爪锚及其零件	10	5		0	40	17	13	千克		Anchors, grapnels and parts thereof, of iron or steel
73.17	**钢铁制的钉、平头钉、图钉、波纹钉、U形钉(税目83.05的货品除外)及类似品，不论钉头是否用其他材料制成，但不包括铜头钉：**										**Nails, tacks, drawing pins, corrugated nails, staples (other than those of heading 83.05) and similar articles, of iron or steel, whether or not with heads of other material, but excluding such articles with heads of copper:**
7317.0000	钢铁制的钉、平头钉、图钉、波纹钉、U形钉(税目83.05的货品除外)及类似品，不论钉头是否用其他材料制成，但不包括铜头钉	10	5		8	80	17	13	千克		Nails, tacks, drawing pins, corrugated nails, staples (other than those of heading 83.05) and similar articles, of iron or steel, whether or not with heads of other material, but excluding such articles with heads of copper
73.18	**钢铁制的螺钉、螺栓、螺母、方头螺钉、钩头螺钉、铆钉、销、开尾销、垫圈(包括弹簧垫圈)及类似品：**										**Screws, bolts, nuts, coach screws, screw hooks, rivets, cotters, cotter-pins, washers (including spring washers) and similar articles, of iron of steel:**
	-螺纹制品：										-Threaded articles:

税则号列 Tariff Item.	货 品 名 称	最惠国(%) MFN	协定(%)CT 东盟 CA	中巴 CP	中智 CC	普通 Gen	增值税率 VAT	出口退税 ED	计量单位 Unit	监管条件 SC	Article Description
7318.1100	--方头螺钉	10	5		8	80	17	13	千克	B	--Coach screws
7318.1200	--其他木螺钉	10	5		8	80	17	13	千克	B	--Other wood screws
7318.1300	--钩头螺钉及环头螺钉	10	5		0	80	17	13	千克	B	--Screw hooks and screw rings
7318.1400	--自攻螺钉	10	T3		8	80	17	13	千克	B	--Self-tapping screws
7318.1500	--其他螺钉及螺栓，不论是否带有螺母或垫圈	8	T3	4	6.4	80	17	13	千克	B	--Other screws and bolts, whether or not with their nuts or washers
7318.1600	--螺母	8	T3		6.4	80	17	13	千克	B	--Nuts
7318.1900	--其他	5			0	80	17	13	千克		--Other
	-无螺纹制品：										-Non-threaded articles:
7318.2100	--弹簧垫圈及其他防松垫圈	10	T3		0	80	17	13	千克	B	--Spring washers and other lock washers
7318.2200	--其他垫圈	10	T3		0	80	17	13	千克	B	--Other washers
7318.2300	--铆钉	10	T3		0	80	17	13	千克		--Rivets
7318.2400	--销及开尾销	10	T3		0	80	17	13	千克		--Cotters and cotter-pins
7318.2900	--其他	10	T3		8	80	17	13	千克		--Other
73.19	**钢铁制的手工缝针、编织针、引针、钩针、刺绣穿孔锥及类似制品；其他税目未列名的钢铁制安全别针及其他别针：**										**Sewing needles, knitting needles, bodkins, crochet hooks, embroidery stilettos and similar articles, for use in the hand, of iron or steel; safety pins and other pins of iron or steel, not elsewhere specified or included:**
7319.2000	-安全别针	10	5		0	90	17	13	千克		-Safety pins
7319.3000	-其他别针	10	5		0	90	17	13	千克		-Other pins
7319.9000	-其他	10	5		0	80	17	13	千克		-Other
73.20	**钢铁制弹簧及弹簧片：**										**Springs and leaves for springs, of iron or steel:**
	-片簧及簧片：										-Leaf-springs and leaves thereof:
7320.1010	---铁道车辆用	6	T3		0	14	17	13	千克		---For railway locomotives and rolling-stock
7320.1020	---汽车用	10	5		0	14	17	13	千克		---For motor vehicles
7320.1090	---其他	10	T3		0	50	17	13	千克		---Other
	-螺旋弹簧：										-Helical springs:
7320.2010	---铁道车辆用	6	T3		4.8	14	17	13	千克		---For railway locomotives and rolling-stock
7320.2090	---其他	10	T3	8.5	8	50	17	13	千克		---Other
	-其他：										-Other:
7320.9010	---铁道车辆用	6	T3		0	14	17	13	千克		---For railway locomotives and rolling-stock
7320.9090	---其他	12	T3		7.2	50	17	13	千克		---Other
73.21	**非电热的钢铁制家用炉、灶（包括附有集中供暖用的热水锅的炉）、烤肉架、烤炉、煤气灶、加热板和类似非电热的家用器具及其零件：**										**Stoves, ranges, grates, cookers (including those with subsidiary boilers for central heating), barbecues, braziers, gas-rings, plate warmers and similar non-electric domestic appliances, and parts thereof, of iron or steel:**
	-炊事器具及加热板：										-Cooking appliances and plate warmers:
7321.1100	--使用气体燃料或可使用气体燃料及其他燃料的	15	8		12	80	17	13	个	6	--For gas fuel or for both gas and other fuels
	--使用液体燃料的：										--For liquid fuel:
7321.1210	---煤油炉	21	12		12.6	80	17	13	个		---Kerosene cooking stoves

税则号列 Tariff Item.	货品名称	最惠国(%) MFN	协定(%) CT 东盟 CA	 中巴 CP	 中智 CC	普通 Gen	增值税率 VAT	出口退税 ED	计量单位 Unit	监管条件 SC	Article Description
7321.1290	---其他	21	12		12.6	80	17	13	个		---Other
7321.1900	--其他,包括器具使用固体燃料的	21	12		12.6	80	17	13	个		--Other nincluding of appliances for solid fuel
	-其他器具:										-Other appliances:
7321.8100	--使用气体燃料或可使用气体燃料及其他燃料的	23	12	13.8	0	80	17	13	个	6	--For gas fuel or for both gas and other fuels
7321.8200	--使用液体燃料的	21	12		16.8	80	17	13	个		--For liquid fuel
7321.8900	--其他,包括器具使用固体燃料的	21	12		16.8	80	17	13	个		--For solid fuel
7321.9000	-零件	12	T3	9.6	9.6	80	17	13	千克		-Parts
73.22	**非电热的钢铁制集中供暖用散热器及其零件;非电热的钢铁制空气加热器、暖气分布器(包括可分布新鲜空气或调节空气的)及其零件,装有电动风扇或鼓风机:**										**Radiators for central heating, not electrically heated, and parts thereof, of iron or steel; air heaters and hot air distributors (including distributors which can also distribute fresh or conditioned air), not electrically heated, incorporating a motor-dirven fan or blower, and parts thereof, of iron or steel:**
	-散热器及其零件:										-Radiators and parts thereof:
7322.1100	--铸铁制	21	12		12.6	80	17	13	千克		--Of cast iron
7322.1900	--其他	21	12		12.6	80	17	13	千克		--Other
7322.9000	-其他	20	12		16	80	17	13	千克		-Other
73.23	**餐桌、厨房或其他家用钢铁器具及其零件;钢铁丝绒;钢铁制擦锅器、洗刷擦光用的块垫、手套及类似品:**										**Table, kitchen or other household articles and parts thereof, of iron or steel; iron or steel wool; pot scourers and scouring or polishing pads, gloves and the like, of iron or steel:**
7323.1000	-钢铁丝绒;擦锅器及洗刷擦光用的块垫、手套及类似品	14	8		11.2	80	17	13	千克	A	-Iron or steel wool; pot scourers and scouring or polishing pads, gloves and the like
	-其他:										-Other:
7323.9100	--铸铁制,未搪瓷	20	12		12	80	17	13	千克	A	--Of cast iron, not enamelled
7323.9200	--铸铁制,已搪瓷	20	12		12	100	17	13	千克	AB	--Of cast iron, enamelled
7323.9300	--不锈钢制	12	T3	8.4	9.6	80	17	13	千克	AB	--Of stainless steel
	--钢铁(铸铁除外)制,已搪瓷:										--Of iron (other than cast iron) or steel, enamelled:
7323.9410	---面盆	20	12		16	100	17	13	千克	AB	---Basin
7323.9420	---烧锅	20	12		16	100	17	13	千克	AB	---Casserole
7323.9430	---烧烤炉	20	12		16	100	17	13	千克	AB	---Barbecue
7323.9490	---其他	20	12		16	100	17	13	千克	AB	---Other
7323.9900	--其他	20	12		16	80	17	13	千克	A	--Other
73.24	**钢铁制卫生器具及其零件:**										**Sanitary ware and parts thereof, of iron or steel:**
7324.1000	-不锈钢制洗涤槽及脸盆	18	T3		0	80	17	13	千克		-Sinks and wash basins, of stainless steel
	-浴缸:										-Baths:
7324.2100	--铸铁制,不论是否搪瓷	10	T3		8	100	17	13	千克		--Of cast iron, whether or not enamelled
7324.2900	--其他	30	T3		18	100	17	13	千克		--Other
7324.9000	-其他,包括零件	25	12		20	100	17	13	千克		-Other, including parts

税则号列 Tariff Item.	货 品 名 称	最惠国(%) MFN	协定(%)CT 东盟 CA	 中巴 CP	 中智 CC	普通 Gen	增值税率 VAT	出口退税 ED	计量单位 Unit	监管条件 SC	Article Description
73.25	**其他钢铁铸造制品:**										**Other cast articles of iron or steel:**
	-无可锻性铸铁制:										-Of non-malleable cast iron:
7325.1010	---工业用	7	5		0	40	17	13	千克		---For technical use
7325.1090	---其他	20	12		12	90	17	13	千克		---Other
	-其他:										-Other:
7325.9100	--研磨机用的研磨球及类似品	10.5	8		8.4	40	17	13	千克		--Grinding balls and similar articles for mills
	--其他:										--Other:
7325.9910	---工业用	10.5	8	8.9	8.4	40	17	13	千克		---For technical use
7325.9990	---其他	20	12	12	16	90	17	13	千克		---Other
73.26	**其他钢铁制品:**										**Other articles of iron or steel:**
	-经锻造或冲压,但未经进一步加工:										-Forged or stamped, but not further worked:
7326.1100	--研磨机用的研磨球及类似品	10.5	8		8.4	40	17	13	千克		--Grinding balls and similar articles for mills
	--其他:										--Other:
7326.1910	---工业用	10.5	8		8.4	40	17	13	千克		---For technical use
7326.1990	---其他	20	12		16	90	17	13	千克		---Other
	-钢铁丝制品:										-Articles of iron or steel wire:
7326.2010	---工业用	10	5	5	0	40	17	13	千克		---For technical use
7326.2090	---其他	18	8	12.6	0	90	17	13	千克		---Other
	-其他:										-Other:
7326.9010	---工业用	10.5	8	8.9	8.4	40	17	13	千克		---For technical use
7326.9090	---其他	8		6.8	6.4	90	17	13	千克		---Other

第七十四章
铜及其制品

Chapter 74
Copper and articles thereof

注释：

本章所用有关名词解释如下：

一、精炼铜

按重量计含铜量至少为 99.85% 的金属；或按重量计含铜量至少为 97.5%，但其他各种元素的含量不超过下表中规定的限量的金属：

其他元素表

元	素	所含重量百分比
Ag	银	0.25
As	砷	0.5
Cd	镉	1.3
Cr	铬	1.4
Mg	镁	0.8
Pb	铅	1.5
S	硫	0.7
Sn	锡	0.8
Te	碲	0.8
Zn	锌	1
Zr	锆	0.3
其他元素*，每种		0.3

*其他元素，例如，铝、铍、钴、铁、锰、镍、硅。

二、铜合金

除未精炼铜以外的金属物质，按重量计含铜量大于其他元素单项含量，但：

1. 按重量计至少有一种其他元素的含量超过上表中规定的限量；
2. 按重量计其他元素的总含量超过 2.5%。

三、铜母合金

含有其他元素，但按重量计含铜量超过 10% 的合金，该合金无实用可锻性，通常用作生产其他合金的添加剂或用作冶炼有色金属的脱氧剂、脱硫剂及类似用途。但按重量计含磷量超过 15% 的磷化铜归入税目 28.48。

Notes:

In this Chapter the following expressions have the meanings hereby assigned to them:

1. Refined copper

Metal containing at least 99.85% by weight of copper; or metal containing at least 97.5% by weight of copper, provided that the content by weight of any other element does not exceed the limit specified in the following table:

TABLE - Other elements

Element		Limiting content % by weight
Ag	Silver	0.25
As	Arsenic	0.5
Cd	Cadmium	1.3
Cr	Chromium	1.4
Mg	Magnesium	0.8
Pb	Lead	1.5
S	Sulphur	0.7
Sn	Tin	0.8
Te	Tellurium	0.8
Zn	Zinc	1
Zr	Zirconium	0.3
Other elements*, each		0.3

* Other elements are, for example, Al, Be, Co, Fe, Mn, Ni, Si.

2. Copper alloys

Metallic substances other than unrefined copper in which copper predominates by weight over each of the other elements, provided that:

(a) the content by weight of at least one of the other elements is greater than the limit specified in the foregoing table; or

(b) the total content by weight of such other elements exceeds 2.5%.

3. Master alloys

Alloys containing with other elements more than 10% by weight of copper, not usefully malleable and commonly used as an additive in the manufacture of other alloys or as de-oxidants, de-sulphurizing agents or for similar uses in the metallurgy of non-ferrous metals. However, copper phosphide (phosphor copper) containing more than 15% by weight of phosphorus falls in heading No. 28.48.

四、条、杆

轧、挤、拔或锻制的实心产品，非成卷的，其全长截面均为圆形、椭圆形、矩形（包括正方形）、等边三角形或规则外凸多边形（包括相对两边为弧拱形，另外两边为等长平行直线的“扁圆形”及“变形矩形”）。对于矩形（包括正方形）、三角形或多边形截面的产品，其全长边角可经磨圆。矩形（包括“变形矩形”）截面的产品，其厚度应大于宽度的十分之一。所述条、杆也包括同样形状及尺寸的铸造或烧结产品。该产品在铸造或烧结后再经加工（简单剪修或去氧化皮的除外），但不具有其他税目所列制品或产品的特征。

线锭及坯段，已具锥形尾端或经其他简单加工以便送入机器制成盘条或管子等的，仍应作为未锻轧铜归入税目74.03。

4. Bars and rods

Rolled, extruded, drawn or forged products, not in coils, which have a uniform solid cross-section along their whole length in the shape of circles, ovals, rectangles (including squares), equilateral triangles or regular convex polygons (including "flattened circles" and "modified rectangles", of which two opposite sides are convex arcs, the other two sides being straight, of equal length and parallel). Products, with a rectangular (including square), triangular or polygonal cross-section may have corners rounded along their whole length. The thickness of such products which have a rectangular (including "modified rectangular") cross-section exceeds one-tenth of the width. The expression also covers cast or sintered products, of the same forms and dimensions, which have been subsequently worked after production (otherwise than by simple trimming or de-scaling), provided that they have not thereby assumed the character of articles or products of other headings.

Wire-bars and billets with their ends tapered or otherwise worked simply to facilitate their entry into machines for converting them into, for example, drawing stock (wire-rod) or tubes, are however to be taken to be unwrought copper of heading No. 74.03.

五、型材及异型材

轧、挤、拔、锻制的产品或其他成型产品，不论是否成卷，其全长截面相同，但与条、杆、丝、板、片、带、箔、管的定义不相符合。同时也包括同样形状的铸造或烧结产品。该产品在铸造或烧结后再经加工（简单剪修或去氧化皮的除外），但不具有其他税目所列制品或产品的特征。

5. Profiles

Rolled, extruded, drawn, forged or formed pruducts, coiled or not, of a uniform cross-section along their whole length, which do not conform to any of the definitions of bars, rods, wire, plates, sheets, strip, foil, tubes or pipes. The expression also covers cast or sintered products, of the same forms, which have been subsequently worked after production (otherwise than by simple trimming or de-scaling), provided that they have not thereby assumed the character of articles or products of other headings.

六、丝

盘卷的轧、挤或拔制实心产品，其全长截面均为圆形、椭圆形、矩形（包括正方形）、等边三角形或规则外凸多边形（包括相对两边为弧拱形，另外两边为等长平行直线的“扁圆形”及“变形矩形”）。对于矩形（包括正方形）、三角形或多边形截面的产品，其全长边角可经磨圆。矩形（包括“变形矩形”）截面的产品，其厚度应大于宽度的十分之一。

6. Wire

Rolled, extruded or drawn products, in coils, which have a uniform solid cross-section along their whole length in the shape of circles, ovals, rectangles (including squares), equilateral triangles or regular convex polygons (including "flattened circles" and "modified rectangles", of which two opposite sides are convex arcs, the other two sides being straight, of equal length and parallel). Products with a rectangular (including square), triangular or polygonal cross-section may have corners rounded along their whole length. The thickness of such products which have a rectangular (including "modified rectangular") cross-section exceeds one-tenth of the width.

In the case of heading No. 74.14, however, the term "wire" applies only to products, whether or not in coils, of any cross-sectional shape, of which no cross-sectional dimension exceeds 6mm.

七、板、片、带、箔

成卷或非成卷的平面产品（税目74.03的未锻轧产品除外），截面均为厚度相同的实心矩形（不包括正方形），不论边角是否磨圆（包括相对两边为弧拱形，另外两边为等长平行直线的“变形矩形”），并且符合以下规格：

1. 矩形（包括正方形）的，厚度不超过宽度的十分之一；
2. 矩形或正方形以外形状的，任何尺寸，但不具有其他税目所列制品或产品的特征。

税目74.09及74.10还适用于具有花样（例如，凹槽、肋条形、格槽、珠粒及菱形）的板、片、带、箔以及穿孔、抛光、涂层或制成瓦楞形的这类产品，但不具有其他税目所列制品或产品的特征。

八、管

全长截面及管壁厚度相同并只有一个闭合空间的空心产品，成卷或非成卷的，其截面为圆形、椭圆形、矩形（包括正方形）、等边三角形或规则外凸多边形。对于截面为矩形（包括正方形）、等边三角形或规则外凸多边形的产品，不论全长边角是否磨圆，只要其内外截面为同一圆心并为同样形状及同一轴向，也可视为管子。上述截面的管子可经抛光、涂层、弯曲、攻丝、钻孔、缩腰、胀口、成锥形或装法兰、颈圈或套环。

子目注释：

本章所用有关名词解释如下：

一、铜锌合金（黄铜）

铜与锌的合金，不论是否含有其他元素。含有其他元素时：

按重量计含锌量应大于其他各种元素的单项含量；

按重量计含镍量应低于5%［参见铜镍锌合金（德银）］；

按重量计含锡量应低于3%［参见铜锡合金（青铜）］。

二、铜锡合金（青铜）

铜与锡的合金，不论是否含有其他元素。含有其他元素时，按重量计含锡量应大于其他各种元素的单项含量。当按重量计含锡量在3%及以上时，锌的含量可大于锡的含量，但必须小于10%。

7. Plates, sheets, strip and foil

Flat-surfaced products (other than the unwrought products of heading No. 74.03), coiled or not, of soild rectangular (other than square) cross-section with or without rounded corners (including " modified rectangles" of which two opposite sides are convex arcs, the other two sides being straight, of equal length and parallel) of a uniform thickness, which are:

-of rectanglular (including square) shape with a thickness not exceeding one-tenth of the width,

-of a shape other than rectangular or square, of any size, provided that they do not assume the character of articles or products of other headings.

Headings Nos. 74.09 and 74.10 apply, *inter alia*, to plates, sheets, strip and foil with patterns (for example, grooves, ribs, chequers, tears, buttons, lozenges) and to such products which have been perforated, corrugated, polished or coated, provided that they do not thereby assume the character of articles or products of other headings.

8. Tubes and pipes

Hollow products, coiled or not, which have a uniform cross-section with only one enclosed void along their whole length in the shape of circles, ovals, rectangles (including squares), equilateral triangles or regularconvex polygons, and which have a uniform wall thickness. Products with a rectangular (including square), equilateral triangular or regular convex polygonal cross-section, which may have corners rounded along their whole length, are also to be taken to be tubes and pipes provided the inner and outer cross-sections are concentric and have the same form and orientation. Tubes and pipes of the foregoing cross-sections may be polished, coated, bent, threaded, drilled, waisted, expanded, cone-shaped or fitted with flanges, collars or rings.

Subheading Note:

In this Chapter the following expressions have the meanings hereby assigned to them:

1. Copper-zinc base alloys (brasses)

Alloys of copper and zinc, with or without other elements. When other elments are present:

-zinc predominates by weight over each of such other elements;

-any nickel content by weight is less than 5% (see copper-nickel-zinc alloys (nickel silvers)); and

-any tin content by weight is less than 3% (see copper-tin alloys (bronzes)).

2. Copper-tin base alloys (bronzes)

Alloys of copper and tin, with or without other elements. When other elements are present, tin predominates by weight over each of such other elements, except that when the tin content is 3% or more the zinc content by weight may exceed that of tin but must be less than 10%.

三、铜镍锌合金(德银)

铜、镍、锌的合金,不论是否含有其他元素,按重量计含镍量在5%及以上[参见铜锌合金(黄铜)]。

四、铜镍合金

铜与镍的合金,不论是否含有其他元素,但按重量计含锌量不得大于1%。含有其他元素时,按重量计含镍量应大于其他各种元素的单项含量。

3. Copper-nickel-zinc base alloys (nickel silvers)

Alloys of copper, nickel and zinc, with or without other elements. The nickel content is 5% or more by weight (see copper-zinc alloys (brasses)).

4. Copper-nickel base alloys

Alloys of copper and nickel, with or without other elements but in any case containing by weight not more than 1% of zinc. When other elements are present, nickel predominates by weight over each of such other elements.

税则号列 Tariff Item.	货品名称	最惠国(%) MFN	协定(%) CT 东盟 CA	中巴 CP	中智 CC	普通 Gen	增值税率 VAT	出口退税 ED	计量单位 Unit	监管条件 SC	Article Description
74.01	**铜锍;沉积铜(泥铜):**										**Copper mattes; cement copper (precipitated copper):**
7401.0000	铜锍;沉积铜(泥铜)	2			0	11	17		千克	AP	Copper mattes cement copper (precipitated copped)
74.02	**未精炼铜;电解精炼用的铜阳极:**										**Unrefined copper; copper anodes for electrolytic refining:**
7402.0000	未精炼铜;电解精炼用的铜阳极	2			0	11	17		千克	A7	Unrefined copper; copper anodes for electrolytic refining
74.03	**未锻轧的精炼铜及铜合金:**										**Refined copper and copper alloys, unwrought:**
	-精炼铜:										-Refined copper:
7403.1100	--阴极及阴极型材	2			0	11	17		千克	AB7	--Cathodes and sections of cathodes
7403.1200	--线锭	2			0	11	17		千克	A7	--Wire-bars
7403.1300	--坯段	2			0	11	17		千克	A7	--Billets
7403.1900	--其他	2			0	11	17		千克	AB7	--Other
	-铜合金:										-Copper alloys:
7403.2100	--铜锌合金(黄铜)	1			0	14	17		千克	7	--Copper-zinc base alloys (brass)
7403.2200	--铜锡合金(青铜)	1			0	17	17		千克	7	--Copper-tin base alloys (bronze)
7403.2900	--其他铜合金(税目74.05的铜母合金除外)	1			0	17	17		千克	7	--Other copper alloys (other than master alloys of heading No. 74.05)
74.04	**铜废碎料:**										**Copper waste and scrap:**
7404.0000	铜废碎料	1.5			0	11	17		千克		Copper waste and scrap
7404.0000 10	以回收铜为主的废电机等(包括废电机、电线、电缆、五金电器)	1.5				11	17		千克	7AP	Waste electric machines, waste wires, cables, mainly for recoverying copper
7404.0000 90	其他铜废碎料	1.5				11	17		千克	7AP	Other copper waste and scrap
74.05	**铜母合金:**										**Master alloys of copper:**
7405.0000	铜母合金	4			3.2	17	17		千克		Master alloys of copper
74.06	**铜粉及片状粉末:**										**Copper powders and flakes:**
	-非片状粉末:										-Powders of non-lamellar structure:
7406.1010	---精炼铜制	3			1.8	14	17		千克	7	---Of refined copper
7406.1020	---铜镍合金(白铜)或铜镍锌合金(德银)制	6	5		4.8	40	17		千克	7	---Of copper-nickel base alloys (cupro-nickel) or copper-nickel-zinc base alloys (nickel silver)
7406.1030	---铜锌合金(黄铜)制	6	5		4.8	30	17		千克		---Of copper-zinc base alloys (brass)
7406.1040	---铜锡合金(青铜)制	6	5		4.8	30	17		千克		---Of copper-tin base alloys (bronze)
7406.1090	---其他铜合金制	6	5		4.8	30	17		千克	7	---Other
	-片状粉末:										-Powders of lamellar structure; flakes:
7406.2010	---精炼铜制	4			3.2	14	17		千克	7	---Of refined copper

税则号列 Tariff Item.	货 品 名 称	最惠国(%) MFN	协定(%) 东盟 CA	中巴 CP	CT 中智 CC	普通 Gen	增值税率 VAT	出口退税 ED	计量单位 Unit	监管条件 SC	Article Description
7406. 2020	---铜镍合金(白铜)或铜镍锌合金(德银)制	6	5		4. 8	40	17		千克	7	---Of copper-nickel base alloys (cu-pronick el) or copper-nickel-zinc base alloys (nickel silver)
7406. 2090	---其他铜合金制	6	5		4. 8	30	17		千克	7	---Other
74. 07	**铜条、杆、型材及异型材:**										**Copper bars, rods and profiles:**
7407. 1000	-精炼铜制	4			3. 2	14	17	5	千克	7	-Of refined copper
	-铜合金制:										-Of copper alloys:
7407. 2100	--铜锌合金(黄铜)	7	5		5. 6	20	17	5	千克	7	--Of copper-zinc base alloys (brass)
7407. 2900	--其他	7	5		0	20	17	5	千克	7	--Other
74. 08	**铜丝:**										**Copper wire:**
	-精炼铜制:										-Of refined copper:
7408. 1100	--最大截面尺寸超过6毫米	4		2. 8	3. 2	14	17	5	千克	7	--Of which the maximum cross-sectional dimension exceeds 6mm
7408. 1900	--其他	4		3. 4	3. 2	14	17	5	千克	7	--Other
	-铜合金制:										-Of copper alloys:
7408. 2100	--铜锌合金(黄铜)	7	5		5. 6	20	17	5	千克	7	--Of copper-zinc base alloys (brass)
7408. 2200	--铜镍合金(白铜)或铜镍锌合金(德银)	8	5		0	40	17	5	千克	7	--Of copper-nickel base alloys (cupro-nickel) or copper-nickel-zinc base alloys (nickel silver)
7408. 2900	--其他	7	5		0	20	17	5	千克	7	--Other
74. 09	**铜板、片及带,厚度超过0. 15毫米:**										**Copper plates, sheets and strip, of a thickness exceeding 0. 15mm:**
	-精炼铜制:										-Of refined copper:
7409. 1100	--盘卷的	4			3. 2	14	17	8	千克	A7	--In coils
7409. 1900	--其他	4			3. 2	14	17	8	千克	A7	--Other
	-铜锌合金(黄铜)制:										-Of copper-zinc base alloys (brass):
7409. 2100	--盘卷的	7	5		5. 6	20	17	8	千克	A7	--In coils
7409. 2900	--其他	7	5		5. 6	20	17	8	千克	7	--Other
	-铜锡合金(青铜)制:										-Of copper-tin base alloys (bronze):
7409. 3100	--盘卷的	7	5		0	20	17	8	千克	7	--In coils
7409. 3900	--其他	7	5		0	20	17	8	千克	7	--Other
7409. 4000	-铜镍合金(白铜)或铜镍锌合金(德银)制	7	5		5. 6	40	17	8	千克	7	-Of copper-nickel base alloys (cupro-nickel) or copper-nickel-zinc base alloys (nickel silver)
7409. 9000	-其他铜合金制	7	5		0	20	17	8	千克	7	-Of other copper alloys
74. 10	**铜箔(不论是否印花或用纸、纸板、塑料或类似材料衬背),厚度(衬背除外)不超过0. 15毫米:**										**Copper foil (whether or not printed or backed with paper, paperboard, plastics or similar backing materials) of a thickness (excluding any backing) not exceeding 0. 15mm:**
	-无衬背:										-Not backed:
7410. 1100	--精炼铜制	4		2. 8	3. 2	14	17	5	千克		--Of refined copper
7410. 1100 01	覆铜板及印刷线路板用铜箔(厚度≤0. 15mm)	4				14	17	5	千克	7	Copper foil for copper-clad board and printed circuit board, thickness ≤ 0. 15mm
7410. 1100 90	其他无衬背的精炼铜箔(厚度≤0. 15mm)	4				14	17	5	千克	7	Other copper foil of refined copper, not backed, thickness (excluding any backing) ≤0. 15mm
	--铜合金制:										--Of copper alloys:

税则号列 Tariff Item.	货品名称	最惠国(%) MFN	协定(%) CT 东盟 CA	中巴 CP	中智 CC	普通 Gen	增值税率 VAT	出口退税 ED	计量单位 Unit	监管条件 SC	Article Description
7410.1210	---铜镍合金(白铜)或铜镍锌合金(德银)	7	5		0	40	17	5	千克	7	---Of copper-nickel base alloys (cupro-nickel) or copper-nickel-zinc base alloys (nickel silver)
7410.1290	---其他	7	5		0	20	17	5	千克	7	---Other
	-有衬背:										-Backed:
7410.2100	--精炼铜制	4		3.4	0	14	17	5	千克	7	--Of refined copper
	--铜合金制:										--Of copper alloys:
7410.2210	---铜镍合金(白铜)或铜镍锌合金(德银)	7	5		0	40	17	5	千克	7	---Of copper-nickel base alloys (cupro-nickel) or copper-nickel-zinc base alloys (nickel silver)
7410.2290	---其他	7	5		0	20	17	5	千克	7	---Other
74.11	**铜管:**										**Copper tubes and pipes:**
	-精炼铜制:										-Of refined copper:
	---外径不超过25毫米的:										---External diameter≤25mm
7411.1011	----带有螺纹或翅片的	4		2.8	3.2	14	17	5	千克	A7	----
7411.1019	----其他	4		2.8	3.2	14	17	5	千克	A7	----Other
7411.1090	---其他	4		2.8	3.2	14	17	5	千克	A7	---Other
7411.2110	---盘卷的	7	5		5.6	20	17	5	千克	7	---in coils
7411.2190	---其他	7	5		5.6	20	17	5	千克	7	---Other
	-铜合金制:										-Of copper alloys:
7411.2200	--铜镍合金(白铜)或铜镍锌合金(德银)	7	5		0	40	17	5	千克	7	--Of copper-nickel base alloys (cupro-nickel) or copper-nickel-zinc base alloys (nickel silver)
7411.2900	--其他	7	5		0	20	17	5	千克	7	--Other
74.12	**铜制管子附件(例如,接头、肘管、管套):**										**Copper tube or pipe fittings (for example, couplings, elbows, sleeves):**
7412.1000	-精炼铜制	4			0	14	17	5	千克		-Of refined copper
	-铜合金制:										-Of copper alloys:
7412.2010	---铜镍合金(白铜)或铜镍锌合金(德银)	7	5	6	5.6	40	17	5	千克		---Of copper-nickel base alloys (cupro-nickel) or copper-nickel-zinc base alloys (nickel silver)
7412.2090	---其他	7	5	6	5.6	20	17	5	千克		---Other
74.13	**非绝缘的铜丝绞股线、缆、编带及类似品:**										**Stranded wire, cables, plaited bands and the like, of copper, not electrically insulated:**
7413.0000	非绝缘的铜丝绞股线、缆、编带及类似品	5			4	14	17	5	千克	AB	Stranded wire, cables, plaited bands and the like, of copper, not electrically insulated
74.15	**铜制或钢铁制带铜头的钉、平头钉、图钉、U形钉(税目83.05的货品除外)及类似品;铜制螺钉、螺栓、螺母、钩头螺钉、铆钉、销、开尾销、垫圈(包括弹簧垫圈)及类似品:**										**Nails, tacks, drawing pins, staples (other than those of heading No.83.05) and similar articles, of copper or of iron or steel with heads of copper; screws, bolts, nuts, screw hooks, rivets, cotters, cotter-pins, washers (including spring washers) and similar articles, of copper:**
7415.1000	-钉、平头钉、图钉、U形钉及类似品	8	5		0	80	17	5	千克		-Nails and tacks, drawing pins, staples and similar articles
	-其他无螺纹制品:										-Other articles, not threaded:

税则号列 Tariff Item.	货品名称	最惠国(%) MFN	协定(%)CT 东盟 CA	中巴 CP	中智 CC	普通 Gen	增值税率 VAT	出口退税 ED	计量单位 Unit	监管条件 SC	Article Description
7415.2100	--垫圈(包括弹簧垫圈)	10	T3		0	80	17	5	千克		--Washers (including spring washers)
7415.2900	--其他	10	T3		0	80	17	5	千克		--Other
	-其他螺纹制品:										-Other threaded articles:
	--螺钉;螺栓及螺母:										--Screws; bolts and nuts:
7415.3310	---木螺钉	8	5		6.4	80	17	5	千克		---Screws for wood
7415.3390	---其他	8	5		6.4	80	17	5	千克		---Other
7415.3900	--其他	10	5		0	80	17	5	千克		--Other
74.18	**餐桌、厨房或其他家用铜制器具及其零件;铜制刷锅器、洗刷擦光用的块垫、手套及类似品;铜制卫生器具及其零件:**										**Table, kitchen or other household articles and parts thereof, of copper; pot scourers and scouring or polishing pads, gloves and the like, of copper; sanitary ware and parts thereof, of copper:**
	-餐桌、厨房或其他家用器具及其零件;擦锅器及洗刷擦光用的块垫、手套及类似品:										-Table, kitchen or other household articles and parts thereof; pot scourers and scouring or polishing pads, gloves and the like:
7418.1100	--刷锅器及洗刷、擦光用的块垫、手套及类似品	18	8		14.4	80	17	5	千克	A	--Pot scourers and scouring or polishing pads, gloves and the like
	--其他:										--Other:
7418.1910	---非电热的铜制家用烹饪或供暖器具及其零件	20	12		16	80	17	5	千克	A	---Cooking or heating apparatus of a kind used for domestic purposes, non-electric, and parts thereof, of copper
7418.1990	---其他:	18	8		10.8	80	17	5	千克	A	---Other
7418.2000	-卫生器具及其零件	18	8		10.8	80	17	5	千克		-Sanitary ware and parts thereof
74.19	**其他铜制品:**										**Other articles of copper:**
7419.1000	-链条及其零件	14	8		8.4	80	17	5	千克		-Chain and parts thereof
	-其他:										-Other:
	--铸造、模压、冲压或锻造,但未经进一步加工的:										--Cast, moulded, stamped or forged, but not further worked:
7419.9110	---工业用	10	8		0	40	17	5	千克		---For technical use
7419.9190	---其他	20	12		12	80	17	5	千克		---Other
	--其他:										--Other:
7419.9920	---铜弹簧	10	5		0	40	17	5	千克		---Copper springs
7419.9930	---铜丝制的布(包括环形带)	7	5		0	20	17	5	千克		---Clot cincluding endless bands, expanded metal of copper.
7419.9940	---铜丝制的网,格栅、网眼铜板	8	5		0	20	17	5	千克		---Grill、netting、of copper wire expanded metal of copper
7419.9950	---非电热的铜制家用供暖器具及其零件	20	12		16	80	17	5	千克		---Cooking or heating copparatus of a kind used for dimestic purposes, non-electric, and pares there of, of copper
	---其他										---Other
7419.9991	----工业用	10	8	8.5	8	40	17	5	千克		----For technical use
7419.9999	----其他	20	12	17	16	80	17	5	千克		----Other

第七十五章
镍及其制品

注释：

本章所用有关名词解释如下：

一、条、杆

轧、挤、拔或锻制的实心产品，非成卷的，其全长截面均为圆形、椭圆形、矩形（包括正方形）、等边三角形或规则外凸多边形（包括相对两边为弧拱形，另外两边为等长平行直线的"扁圆形"及"变形矩形"）。对于矩形（包括正方形）、三角形或多边形截面的产品，其全长边角可经磨圆。矩形（包括"变形矩形"）截面的产品，其厚度应大于宽度的十分之一。所述条、杆也包括同样形状及尺寸的铸造或烧结产品。该产品在铸造或烧结后再经加工（简单剪修或去氧化皮的除外），但不具有其他税目所列制品或产品的特征。

二、型材及异型材

轧、挤、拔、锻制的产品或其他成型产品，不论是否成卷，其全长截面相同，但与条、杆、丝、板、片、带、箔、管的定义不相符合。同时也包括同样形状的铸造或烧结产品。该产品在铸造或烧结后再经加工（简单剪修或去氧化皮的除外），但不具有其他税目所列制品或产品的特征。

三、丝

盘卷的轧、挤或拔制实心产品，其全长截面均为圆形、椭圆形、矩形（包括正方形）、等边三角形或规则外凸多边形（包括相对两边为弧拱形，另外两边为等长平行直线的"扁圆形"及"变形矩形"）。对于矩形（包括正方形）、三角形或多边形截面的产品，其全长边角可经磨圆。矩形（包括"变形矩形"）截面的产品，其厚度应大于宽度的十分之一。

四、板、片、带、箔

成卷或非成卷的平面产品（税目75.02的未锻轧产品除外），截面均为厚度相同的实心矩形（不包括正方形），不论边角是否磨圆（包括相对两边为弧拱形，另外两边为等长平行直线的"变形矩形"），并且符合以下规格：

1. 矩形（包括正方形）的，厚度不超过宽度的十分之一；

Chapter 75
Nickel and articles thereof

Notes:

In this Chapter the following expressions have the meanings hereby assigned to them:

1. Bars and rods

Rolled, extruded, drawn or forged products, not in coils, which have a uniform soild cross-section along their whole length in the shape of circles, ovals, rectangles (including squares), equilateral triangles or regular convex polygons (including "flattened circles" and "modified rectangles", of which two opposite sides are convex arcs, the other two sides being straight, of equal length and parallel). Products with a rectangular (including square), triangular or polygonal cross-section may have corners rounded along their whole length. The thickness of such products which have a rectangular (including "modified rectangular") cross-section exceeds one-tenth of the width. The expression also covers cast or sintered products, of the same forms and dimensions, which have been subsequently worked after production (otherwise than by simple trimming or de-scaling), provided that they have not thereby assumed the character of articles or products of other headings.

2. Profiles

Rolled, extruded, drawn, forged or formed products, coiled or not, of a uniform cross-section along their whole length, which do not conform to any of the definitions of bars, rods, wire, plates, sheets, strip, foil, tubes or pipes. The expression also covers cast or sintered products, of the same forms, which have been subsequently worked after production (otherwise than by simple trimming or de-scaling), provided that they have not thereby assumed the character of articles or products of other headings.

3. Wire

Rolled, extruded or drawn products, in coils, which have a uniform soild cross-section along their whole length in the shape of circles, ovals, rectangles (in cluding squares), equilateral triangles or regular convex polygons (including "flattened circles" and "modified rectangles", of which two opposite sides are convex arcs, the other two sides being straight, of equal length and parallel). Products with a rectangular (including square), triangular or polygonal cross-section may have corners rounded along their whole length. The thickness of such products which have a rectangular (including "modified rectangular") cross-section exceeds one-tenth of the width.

4. Plates, sheets, strip and foil

Flat-surfaced products (other than the unwrought products of heading 75.02), coiled or not, of soild rectangular (other than square) cross-section with or without rounded corners (including "modified rectangles" of which two opposite sides are convex arcs, the other two sides being straight, of equal length and parallel) of a uniform thickness, which are:

-of rectanglular (including square) shape with a thickness not exceeding one-tenth of the width,

2. 矩形或正方形以外形状的，任何尺寸，但不具有其他税目所列制品或产品的特征。

税目 75.06 还适用于具有花样（例如，凹槽、肋条形、格槽、珠粒及菱形）的板、片、带、箔以及穿孔、抛光、涂层或制成瓦楞形的这类产品，但不具有其他税目所列制品或产品的特征。

五、管

全长截面及管壁厚度相同并只有一个闭合空间的空心产品，成卷或非成卷的，其截面为圆形、椭圆形、矩形（包括正方形）、等边三角形或规则外凸多边形。对于截面为矩形（包括正方形）、等边三角形或规则外凸多边形的产品，不论全长边角是否磨圆，只要其内外截面为同一圆心并为同样形状及同一轴向，也可视为管子。上述截面的管子可经抛光、涂层、弯曲、攻丝、钻孔、缩腰、胀口、成锥形或装法兰、颈圈或套环。

-of a shape other than rectangular or square, of any size, provided that they do not assume the character of articles or products of other headings.

Heading 75.06 applies, *inter alia*, to plates, sheets, strip and foil with patterns (for example, grooves, ribs, chequers, tears, buttons, lozenges) and to such products which have been perforated, corrugated, polished or coated, provided that they do not thereby assume the character of articles or products of other headings.

5. Tubes and pipes

Hollow products, coiled or not, which have a uniform cross-section with only one enclosed void along their whole length in the shape of circles, ovals, rectangles (including squares), equilateral triangles of regular convex polygons, and which have a uniform wall thickness. Products with a rectangular (including square), equilateral triangular, or regular convex polygonal cross-section, which may have corners rounded along their whole length, are also to be considered as tubes and pipes provided the inner and outer cross-sections are concentric and have the same form and orientation. Tubes and pipes of the foregoing crosssections may be polished, coated, bent, threaded, drilled, waisted, expanded, cone-shaped or fitted with flanges, collars or rings.

子目注释：

一、本章所用有关名词解释如下：

（一）非合金镍

按重量计镍及钴的含量至少为 99% 的金属，但：

1. 按重量计含钴量不超过 1.5%；
2. 按重量计其他各种元素的含量不超过下表中规定的限量：

其他元素表

元　　素		所含重量百分比
Fe	铁	0.5
O	氧	0.4
其他元素，每种		0.3

（二）镍合金

按重量计含镍量大于其他元素单项含量的金属物质，但：

1. 按重量计含钴量超过 1.5%；
2. 按重量计至少有一种其他元素的含量超过上表中规定的限量；
3. 除镍及钴以外，按重量计其他元素的总含量超过 1%。

二、子目 7508.10 所称“丝”，不受本章注释三的限制，仅适用于截面尺寸不超过 6 毫米的任何截面形状的产品，不论是否盘卷。

Subheading Notes:

1. In this Chapter the following expressions have the meanings hereby assigned to them:

(a) Nickel, not alloyed

Metal containing by weight at least 99% of nickel plus cobalt, provided that:

(Ⅰ) the cobalt by weight does not exceed 1.5%, and

(Ⅱ) the content by weight of any other element does not exceed the limit specified in the following table:

TABLE - Other elements

Element		Limiting content % by weight
Fe	Iron	0.5
O	Oxygen	0.4
Other elements, each		0.3

(b) Nickel alloys

Metallic substances in which nickel predominates by weight over each of the other elements provided that:

(Ⅰ) the content by weight of cobalt exceeds 1.5%,

(Ⅱ) the content by weight of at least one of the other elements is greater than the limit specified in the foregoing table, or

(Ⅲ) the total content by weight of elements other than nickel plus cobalt exceeds 1%.

2. Notwithstanding the provisions of Chapter Note 1 (c), for the purposes of subheading No. 7508.10 the term "wire" applies only to products, whether or not in coils, of any cross-sectional shape, of which no cross-sectional dimension exceeds 6mm.

税则号列 Tariff Item.	货品名称	最惠国(%) MFN	协定(%) CT 东盟 CA	中巴 CP	中智 CC	普通 Gen	增值税率 VAT	出口退税 ED	计量单位 Unit	监管条件 SC	Article Description
75.01	**镍锍、氧化镍烧结物及镍冶炼的其他中间产品：**										**Nickel mattes, nickel oxide sinters and other intermediate products of nickel metal-lurgy:**
7501.1000	-镍锍	3			0	11	17		千克	4xy	-Nickel mattes
	-氧化镍烧结物及镍冶炼的其他中间产品：										-Nickel oxide sinters and other intermediate products of nickel metallurgy:
7501.2010	---镍湿法冶炼中间品	3			0	11	17	13	千克	4xy	---Nickel intermediate products obtained by hydrometalluigical processing-
7501.2090	---其他	3			0	11	17		千克	4xy	---Other
75.02	**未锻轧镍：**										**Unwrought nickel:**
7502.1000	-非合金镍	3			0	11	17		千克	4xy	-Nickel, not alloyed
7502.2000	-镍合金	3			0	11	17		千克	4xy	-Nickel, alloys
75.03	**镍废碎料：**										**Nickel waste and scrap:**
7503.0000	镍废碎料	1.5			0	11	17		千克	4APxy	Nickel waste and scrap
75.04	**镍粉及片状粉末：**										**Nickel powders and flakes:**
7504.0010	---非合金镍粉及片状粉末	4			0	17	17		千克	3	---Nickel powders and flakes, not alloyed
7504.0020	---合金镍粉及片状粉末	4			0	17	17		千克		---Nickel powders and flakes, alloys
75.05	**镍条、杆、型材及异型材或丝：**										**Nickel bars, rods, profiles and wire:**
	-条、杆、型材及异型材：										-Bars, rods and profiles:
7505.1100	--非合金镍制	6	5		0	14	17	5	千克		--Of nickel, not alloyed
7505.1200	--镍合金制	6	5		0	14	17	5	千克		--Of nickel alloys
	-丝：										-Wire:
7505.2100	--非合金镍制	6	5		0	17	17	5	千克		--Of nickel, not alloyed
7505.2200	--镍合金制	6	5		0	17	17	5	千克		--Of nickel alloys
75.06	**镍板、片、带、箔：**										**Nickel plates, sheets, strip and foil:**
7506.1000	-非合金镍制	6	5		0	14	17	5	千克		-Of nickel, not alloyed
7506.2000	-镍合金制	6	5		0	14	17	5	千克		-Of nickel alloys
75.07	**镍管及管子附件（例如，接头、肘管、管套）：**										**Nickel tubes, pipes and tube or pipe fittings (for example, couplings, elbows, sleeves):**
	-镍管：										-Tubes and pipes:
7507.1100	--非合金镍制	6	5		0	17	17	13	千克		--Of nickel, not alloyed
7507.1200	--镍合金制	6	5		0	17	17	13	千克		--Of nickel alloys
7507.2000	-管子附件	6	5		0	17	17	13	千克		-Tube or pipe fittings
75.08	**其他镍制品：**										**Other articles of nickel:**
	-镍丝布、网及格栅：										-Cloth, grill and netting, of nickel wire:
7508.1010	---镍丝布	6	5		0	20	17	13	千克		---Wire cloth
7508.1080	---其他工业用镍制品	6	5		0	40	17	13	千克		---Other articles of nickel, for technical use
7508.1090	---其他	6	5		0	70	17	13	千克		---Other
	-其他：										-Other:
7508.9010	---电镀用镍阳极	4			0	14	17		千克		---Electroplating anodes
7508.9080	---其他工业用镍制品	6	5		0	40	17	13	千克		---Other articles of nickel, for technical use
7508.9090	---其他	6	5		0	70	17	13	千克		---Other

第七十六章
铝及其制品

注释：

本章所用有关名词解释如下：

一、条、杆

轧、挤、拔或锻制的实心产品，非成卷的，其全长截面均为圆形、椭圆形、矩形（包括正方形）、等边三角形或规则外凸多边形（包括相对两边为弧拱形，另外两边为等长平行直线的“扁圆形”及“变形矩形”）。对于矩形（包括正方形）、三角形或多边形截面的产品，其全长边角可经磨圆。矩形（包括“变形矩形”）截面的产品其厚度应大于宽度的十分之一。所述条、杆也包括同样形状及尺寸的铸造或烧结产品。该产品在铸造或烧结后再经加工（简单剪修或去氧化皮的除外），但不具有其他税目所列制品或产品的特征。

二、型材及异型材

轧、挤、拔、锻制的产品或其他成型产品，不论是否成卷，其全长截面相同，但与条、杆、丝、板、片、带、箔、管的定义不相符合。同时也包括同样形状的铸造或烧结产品。该产品在铸造或烧结后再经加工（简单剪修或去氧化皮的除外），但不具有其他税目所列制品或产品的特征。

三、丝

盘卷的轧、挤或拔制实心产品，其全长截面均为圆形、椭圆形、矩形（包括正方形）等边三角形或规则外凸多边形（包括相对两边为弧拱形，另外两边为等长平行直线的“扁圆形”及“变形矩形”）。对于矩形（包括正方形）、三角形或多边形截面的产品，其全长边角可经磨圆。矩形（包括“变形矩形”）截面的产品，其厚度应大于宽度的十分之一。

四、板、片、带、箔

成卷或非成卷的平面产品（税目76.01的未锻轧产品除外），截面均为厚度相同的实心矩形（不包括正方形），不论边角是否磨圆（包括相对两边为弧拱形，另外两边为等长平行直线的“变形矩形”），并且符合以下规格：

1. 矩形（包括正方形）的，厚度不超过宽度的十分之一；

Chapter 76
Aluminium and articles thereof

Notes:

In this Chapter the following expressions have the meanings hereby assigned to them:

1. Bars and rods

Rolled, extruded, drawn or forged products, not in coils, which have a uniform solid cross-section along their whole length in the shape of circles, ovals, rectangles (including squares), equilateral triangles or regular convex polygons (including “flattened circles” and “modified rectangles”, of which two opposite sides are convex arcs, the other two sides being straight, of equal length and parallel). Products with a rectangular (including square), triangular or polygonal cross-section may have corners rounded along their whole length. The thickness of such products which have a rectangular (including “modified rectangular”) cross-section exceeds one-tenth of the width. The expression also covers cast or sintered products, of the same forms and dimensions, which have been subsequently worked after production (otherwise than by simple trimming or de-scaling), provided that they have not thereby assumed the character of articles or products of other headings.

2. Profiles

Rolled, extruded, drawn, forged or formed products, coiled or not, of a uniform cross-section along their whole length, which do not conform to any of the definitions of bars, rods, wire, plates, sheets, strip, foil, tubes or pipes. The expression also covers cast or sintered products, of the same forms, which have been subsequently worked after production (otherwise than by simple trimming or de-scaling), provided that they have not thereby assumed the character of articles or products of other headings.

3. Wire

Rolled, extruded or drawn products, in coils, which have a uniform soild cross-section along their whole length in the shape of circles, ovals, rectangles (including squares), equilateral triangles or regular convex polygons (including “flattened circles” and “modified rectangles”, of which two opposite sides are convex arcs, the other two sides being straight, of equal length and parallel). Products with a rectangular (including square), triangular or polygonal cross-section may have corners rounded along their whole length. The thickness of such products which have a rectangular (including “modified rectangular”) cross-section exceeds one-tenth of the width.

4. Plates, sheets, strip and foil

Flat-surfaced products (other than the unwrought products of heading No. 76.01), coiled or not, of solid rectangular (other than square) cross-section with or without rounded corners (including “ modified rectangles” of which two opposite sides are convex arcs, the other two sides being straight, of equal length and parallel) of a uniform thickness, which are:

-of rectanglular (including square) shape with a thickness not exceeding one-tenth of the width,

2. 矩形或正方形以外形状的，任何尺寸，但不具有其他税目所列制品或产品的特征。

税目76.06和76.07还适用于具有花样（例如，凹槽、肋条形、格槽、珠粒及菱形）的板、片、带、箔以及穿孔、抛光、涂层或制成瓦楞形的这类产品，但不具有其他税目所列制品或产品的特征。

五、管

全长截面及管壁厚度相同并只有一个闭合空间的空心产品，成卷或非成卷的，其截面为圆形、椭圆形、矩形（包括正方形）、等边三角形或规则外凸多边形。对于截面为矩形（包括正方形）、等边三角形或规则外凸多边形的产品，不论全长边角是否磨圆，只要其内外截面为同一圆心并为同样形状及同一轴向，也可视为管子。上述截面的管子可经抛光、涂层、弯曲、攻丝、钻孔、缩腰、胀口、成锥形或装法兰、颈圈或套环。

-of a shape other than rectangular or square, of any size, provided that they do not assume the character of articles or products of other headings.

Headings Nos. 76.06 and 76.07 apply, *inter alia*, to plates, sheets, strip and foil with patterns (for example, grooves, ribs, chequers, tears, buttons, lozenges) and to such products which have been perforated, corrugated, polished or coated, provided that they do not thereby assume the character of articles or products of other headings.

5. Tubes and pipes

Hollow products, coiled or not, which have a uniform cross-section with only one enclosed void along their whole length in the shape of circles, ovals, rectangles (including squares), equilateral triangles or regular convex polygons, and which have a uniform wall thickness. Products with a rectangular (including square), equilateral triangular or regular convex polygonal cross-section, which may have corners rounded along their whole length, are also to be considered as tubes and pipes provided the inner and outer cross-sections are concentric and have the same form and orientation. Tubes and pipes of the foregoing cross-sections may be polished, coated, bent, threaded, drilled, waisted, expanded, cone-shaped or fitted with flanges, collars or rings.

子目注释：

一、本章所用有关名词解释如下：

（一）非合金铝

按重量计含铝量至少为99%的金属，但其他各种元素的含量不超过下表中规定的限量：

其他元素表

元　　素	所含重量百分比
Fe + Si（铁 + 硅）	1
其他元素(1)，每种	0.1(2)
①其他元素，例如，铬、铜、镁、锰、镍、锌。 ②含铜成分可大于0.1%，但不得大于0.2%，且铬和锰的含量均不得超过0.05%。	

（二）铝合金

按重量计含铝量大于其他元素单项含量的金属物质，但：

1. 按重量计至少有一种其他元素或铁加硅的含量大于上表中规定的限量；

2. 按重量计其他元素的总含量超过1%。

二、子目7616.91所称“丝”，不受本章注释三的限制，仅适用于截面尺寸不超过6毫米的任何截面形状产品，不论是否盘卷。

Subheading Notes:

1. In this Chapter the following expressions have the meanings hereby assigned to them:

(a) Aluminium, not alloyed

Metal containing by weight at least 99% of aluminium, provided that the content by weight of any other element does not exceed the limit specified in the following table:

TABLE - Other elements

Element	Limiting content % by weight
Fe + Si (iron plus silicon)	1
Other elements (1), each	0.1(2)
(1) Other elements are, for example, Cr, Cu, Mg, Mn, Ni, Zn. (2) Copper is permitted in a proportion greater than 0.1% but not more than 0.2%, provided that neither the chromium nor manganese content exceeds 0.05%.	

(b) Aluminium alloys

Metallic substances in which aluminium predominates by weight over each of the other elements, provided that:

(Ⅰ) the content by weight of at least one of the other elements or of iron plus silicon taken together is greater than the limit specified in the foregoing table; or

(Ⅱ) the total content by weight of such other elements exceeds 1%.

2. Notwithstanding the provisions of Chapter Note 1 (c), for the purposes of subheading No. 7616.91 the term "wire" applies only to products, whether or not in coils, of any cross-sectional shape, of which no cross-sectional dimension exceeds 6mm.

税则号列 Tariff Item.	货品名称	最惠国(%) MFN	协定(%) CT 东盟 CA	中巴 CP	中智 CC	普通 Gen	增值税率 VAT	出口退税 ED	计量单位 Unit	监管条件 SC	Article Description
76.01	**未锻轧铝：**										**Unwrought aluminium:**
	-非合金铝：										-Aluminium, not alloyed:
7601.1010	---按重量计含铝量在99.95%及以上	5			0	14	17		千克	AB7	---Containing by weight 99.95% or more of aluminium
7601.1090	---其他	5			0	14	17		千克	AB7	---Other
7601.2000	-铝合金	7	5	6	0	14	17		千克	7A	-Aluminium alloys
76.02	**铝废碎料：**										**Aluminium waste and scrap:**
7602.0000	铝废碎料	1.5			0	14	17		千克		Aluminium waste and scrap
7602.0000 10	以回收铝为主的废电线等(包括废电线、电缆、五金电器)	1.5				14	17		千克	7AP	Aluminium waste wires, cables, hardware and electric appliance, mainly for recoverying aluminium
7602.0000 90	铝废碎料	1.5				14	17		千克	7AP	Aluminium waste and scrap
76.03	**铝粉及片状粉末：**										**Aluminium powders and flakes:**
7603.1000	-非片状粉末	6	5		4.8	30	17		千克		-Powders of non-lamellar structure
7603.1000 10	颗粒 < 500μm 的微细球形铝粉(颗粒均匀，铝含量≥97%)	6				30	17		千克	37	Microspherical aluminum powder, granularity < 500μm, containing ≥97% by weight of aluminium
7603.1000 90	其他非片状铝粉	6				30	17		千克	7	Other powders of non-lamellar structure, of aluminium
7603.2000	-片状粉末	7	5		0	30	17		千克	7	-Powders of lamellar structure; flakes
76.04	**铝条、杆、型材及异型材：**										**Aluminium bars, rods and profiles:**
7604.1000	-非合金铝制	5			4	30	17	11	千克	7	-Of aluminium, not alloyed
	-铝合金制：										-Of aluminium alloys:
7604.2100	--空心异型材	5			0	30	17	11	千克	A7	--Hollow profiles
7604.2900	--其他	5		3.5	0	30	17	11	千克		--Other
7604.2900 10	柱形实心体铝合金[在293K(20摄氏度)时的极限抗拉强度能达到460兆帕(0.46×10^9牛顿/平方米)或更大]	5				30	17	11	千克	37A	Column solid aluminum alloy (tensile strength reaches at least 460 mega - P (1.46×10^9 Newton /Square Meters) at 293K (20 degree centigrade)
7604.2900 90	其他铝合金制条、杆、其他型材(包括异型材)	5				30	17	11	千克	A7	Other bars, rods and profiles, of aluminium alloys
76.05	**铝丝：**										**Aluminium wire:**
	-非合金铝制：										-Of aluminium, not alloyed:
7605.1100	--最大截面尺寸超过7毫米	8	5		6.4	17	17	8	千克	7	--Of which the maximum cross-sectional dimension exceeding 7mm
7605.1900	--其他	8	5	6.8	0	17	17	8	千克	7	--Other
	-铝合金制：										-Of aluminium alloys:
7605.2100	--最大截面尺寸超过7毫米	8	5		0	17	17	8	千克	7	--Of which the maximum cross-sectional dimension exceeding 7mm
7605.2900	--其他	8	5		0	17	17	8	千克	7	--Other
76.06	**铝板、片及带，厚度超过0.2毫米：**										**Aluminium plates, sheets and strip, of a thickness exceeding 0.2mm:**
	-矩形(包括正方形)：										-Rectangular (including square):
	--非合金铝制：										--Of aluminium, not alloyed:
7606.1120	---厚度在0.30毫米及以上，但不超过0.36毫米	6	5	4.2	0	50	17	11	千克	7A	---Of a thickness of 0.30mm or more but not exceeding 0.36mm
7606.1190	---其他	6	5	4.2	0	30	17	11	千克	A7	---Other

税则号列 Tariff Item.	货品名称	最惠国(%) MFN	协定(%) CT 东盟 CA	中巴 CP	中智 CC	普通 Gen	增值税率 VAT	出口退税 ED	计量单位 Unit	监管条件 SC	Article Description
	--铝合金制：										--Of aluminium alloys：
7606.1220	---厚度小于0.28毫米	6	5	4.2	0	30	17	11	千克	7A	---Of a thickness less than 0.28mm
7606.1230	---厚度在0.28毫米及以上，但不超过0.35毫米	6	5	4.2	0	30	17	11	千克	7A	---Of a thickness of 0.28mm or more but not exceeding 0.35mm
7606.1240	---厚度超过0.35毫米	6	5	4.2	0	50	17	11	千克	7A	---Of a thickness exceeding 0.35mm
	-其他：										-Other：
7606.9100	--非合金铝制	6	5		0	30	17	11	千克	7	--Of aluminium, not alloyed
7606.9200	--铝合金制	10	8		0	30	17	11	千克	A7	--Of aluminium alloys
76.07	**铝箔(不论是否印花或用纸、纸板、塑料或类似材料衬背)，厚度(衬背除外)不超过0.2毫米：**										**Aluminium foil (whether or not printed or backed with paper, paperboard, plastics or similar backing materials) of a thickness (excluding any backing) not exceeding 0.2mm：**
	-无衬背：										-Not backed：
	--轧制后未经进一步加工的：										--Rolled but not further worked：
7607.1110	---厚度不超过0.007毫米	6	5	5.7	4.8	35	17	13	千克	A7	---Of a thickness not exceeding 0.007mm
7607.1190	---其他	6	5	5.7	4.8	35	17	13	千克	A7	---Other
7607.1900	--其他	6	5	5.1	4.8	35	17	13	千克	A7	--Other
7607.2000	-有衬背	6	5		4.8	35	17	13	千克	A7	-Backed
76.08	**铝管：**										**Aluminium tubes and pipes：**
7608.1000	-非合金铝制	8	5		6.4	30	17	13	千克	7	-Of aluminium, not alloyed
7608.2000	-铝合金制	8	5		6.4	30	17	13	千克		-Of aluminium alloys
7608.2000 10	管状铝合金[在293K(20摄氏度)时的极限抗拉强度能达到460兆帕(0.46×10^9牛顿/平方米)或更大]	8				30	17	13	千克	37A	The tensile strength of tube aluminum alloy can reach at least 460 mega - Pa (1.46×10^9Newton /Square Meters) at 293K (20 degree centigrade)
7608.2000 90	其他合金铝管	8				30	17	13	千克	7A	Other aluminium tubes and pipes, alloys
76.09	**铝制管子附件(例如，接头、肘管、管套)：**										**Aluminium tube or pipe fittings (for example, couplings, elbows, sleeves)：**
7609.0000	铝制管子附件(例如，接头、肘管、管套)	8	5		0	35	17	13	千克		Aluminium tube or pipe fittings (for example, couplings, elbows, sleeves)
76.10	**铝制结构体(税目94.06的活动房屋除外)及其部件(例如，桥梁及桥梁体段、塔、格构杆、屋顶、屋顶框架、门窗及其框架、门槛、栏杆、支柱及立柱)；上述结构体用的已加工铝板、杆、型材、异型材、管子及类似品：**										**Aluminium structures (excluding prefabricated buildings of heading 94.06) and parts of structures (for example, bridges and bridge-sections, towers, lattice masts, roofs, roofing frameworks, doors and windows and their frames and thresholds for doors, balustrades, pillars and columns); aluminium plates, rods, profiles, tubes and the like, prepared for use in structures：**
7610.1000	-门窗及其框架、门槛	25	12		0	80	17	13	千克		-Doors, windows and their frames and thresholds for doors
7610.9000	-其他	6	T3		4.8	50	17	13	千克		-Other

税则号列 Tariff Item.	货品名称	最惠国(%) MFN	协定(%) CT 东盟 CA	中巴 CP	中智 CC	普通 Gen	增值税率 VAT	出口退税 ED	计量单位 Unit	监管条件 SC	Article Description
76.11	**盛装物料用的铝制囤、柜、罐、桶及类似容器(装压缩气体或液化气体的除外),容积超过300升,不论是否衬里或隔热,但无机械或热力装置:**										**Aluminium reservoirs, tanks, vats and similar containers, for any material (other than compressed or liquefied gas), of a capacity exceeding 300L, whether or not lined or heat-insulated, but not fitted with mechanical or thermal equipment:**
7611.0000	盛装物料用的铝制囤、柜、罐、桶及类似容器(装压缩气体或液化气体的除外),容积超过300升,不论是否衬里或隔热,但无机械或热力装置	12	8		7.2	35	17	13	千克		Aluminium reservoirs, tanks, vats and similar containers, for any material (other than compressed or liquefied gas), of a capacity exceeding 300 l, whether or not lined or heat-insulated, but not fitted with mechanical or thermal equipment
76.12	**盛装物料用的铝制桶、罐、听、盒及类似容器,包括软管容器及硬管容器(装压缩气体或液化气体的除外),容积不超过300升,不论是否衬里或隔热,但无机械或热力装置:**										**Aluminium casks, drums, cans, boxes and similar containers (including rigid or collapsible tubular containers), for any material (other than compressed or liquefied gas), of a capacity not exceeding 300 l, whether or not lined or heat-insulated, but not fitted with mechanical or thermal equipment:**
7612.1000	-软管容器	12	8		9.6	50	17	13	千克		-Collapsible tubular containers
	-其他:										-Other:
7612.9010	---易拉罐及罐体	30	12		24	100	17	13	千克	A	---Tear tab ends and bodies thereof
7612.9090	---其他	12	8		9.6	70	17	13	千克		---Other
76.13	**装压缩气体或液化气体用的铝制容器:**										**Aluminium containers for compressed or liquefied gas:**
7613.0010	---零售包装用	12	8		7.2	70	17	13	千克		---For retail packing
7613.0090	---其他	6	5		0	17	17	13	千克	6	---Other
76.14	**非绝缘的铝制绞股线、缆、编带及类似品:**										**Stranded wire, cables, plaited bands and the like, of aluminium, not electrically insulated:**
7614.1000	-带钢芯的	6	5		0	20	17	13	千克	AB	-With steel core
7614.9000	-其他	6	5		0	20	17	13	千克	A	-Other
76.15	**餐桌、厨房或其他家用铝制器具及其零件;铝制擦锅器、洗刷擦光用的块垫、手套及类似品;铝制卫生器具及其零件:**										**Table, kitchen or other household articles and parts thereof, of aluminium; pot scourers and scouring or polishing pads, gloves and the like, of aluminium; sanitary ware and parts thereof, of aluminium:**
	-餐桌、厨房或其他家用器具及其零件;擦锅器及洗刷擦光用的块垫、手套及类似品:										-Table, kitchen or other household articles and parts thereof; pot scourers and scouring or polishing pads, gloves and the like:
7615.1100	--擦锅器、洗刷、擦光用的块垫、手套及类似品	18	8		10.8	90	17	13	千克	A	--Pot scourers and scouring or polishing pads, gloves and the like
7615.1900	--其他	15	8		12	90	17	13	千克	A	--Other
7615.2000	-卫生器具及其零件	18	8		14.4	90	17	13	千克		-Sanitary ware and parts thereof

税则号列 Tariff Item.	货品名称	最惠国(%) MFN	协定(%) CT 东盟 CA	中巴 CP	中智 CC	普通 Gen	增值税率 VAT	出口退税 ED	计量单位 Unit	监管条件 SC	Article Description
76.16	**其他铝制品:**										**Other articles of aluminium:**
7616.1000	-钉、平头钉、U形钉(税目83.05的货品除外)、螺钉、螺栓、螺母、钩头螺钉、铆钉、销、开尾销、垫圈及类似品	10	8	8.5	0	40	17	13	千克		-Nails, tacks, staples (other than those of heading 83.05), screws, bolts, nuts, screw hooks, rivets, cotters, cotter-pins, washers and similar articles
	-其他:										-Other:
7616.9100	--铝丝制的布、网、篱及格栅	10	8		0	40	17	13	千克		--Cloth, grill, netting and fencing, of aluminium wire
	--其他:										--Other:
7616.9910	---工业用	10	8	8.5	8	40	17	13	千克		---For technical use
7616.9990	---其他	15	8	12.8	12	80	17	13	千克		---Other

第七十八章
铅及其制品

注释：

本章所用有关名词解释如下：

一、条、杆

轧、挤、拔或锻制的实心产品，非成卷的，其全长截面均为圆形、椭圆形、矩形（包括正方形）、等边三角形或规则外凸多边形（包括相对两边为弧拱形，另外两边为等长平行直线的“扁圆形”及“变形矩形”）。对于矩形（包括正方形）、三角形或多边形截面的产品，其全长边角可经磨圆。矩形（包括“变形矩形”）截面的产品，其厚度应大于宽度的十分之一。所述条、杆也包括同样形状及尺寸的铸造或烧结产品。该产品在铸造或烧结后再结加工（简单剪修或去氧化皮的除外），但不具有其他税目所列制品或产品的特征。

二、型材及异型材

轧、挤、拔、锻制的产品或其他成型产品，不论是否成卷，其全长截面相同，但与条、杆、丝、板、片、带、箔、管的定义不相符合。同时也包括同样形状的铸造或烧结产品。该产品在铸造或烧结后再结加工（简单剪修或去氧化皮的除外），但不具有其他税目所列制品或产品的特征。

三、丝

盘卷的轧、挤或拔制实心产品，其全长截面均为圆形、椭圆形、矩形（包括正方形）、等边三角形或规则外凸多边形（包括相对两边为弧拱形，另外两边为等长平行直线的“扁圆形”及“变形矩形”）。对于矩形（包括正方形）、三角形或多边形截面的产品，其全长边角可经磨圆。矩形（包括“变形矩形”）截面的产品，其厚度应大于宽度的十分之一。

四、板、片、带、箔

成卷或非成卷的平面产品（税目78.01的未锻轧产品除外），截面均为厚度相同的实心矩形（不包括正方形），不论边角是否磨圆（包括相对两边为弧拱形，另外两边为等长平行直线的“变形矩形”），并且符合以下规格：

Chapter 78
Lead and articles thereof

Notes:

In this Chapter the following expressions have the meanings hereby assigned to them:

1. Bars and rods

Rolled, extruded, drawn or forged products, not in coils, which have a uniform solid cross-section along their whole length in the shape of circles, ovals, rectangles (including squares), equilateral triangles or regular convex polygons (including "flattened circles" and "modified rectangles", of which two opposite sides are convex arcs, the other two sides being straight, of equal length and parallel). Products with a rectangular (including square), triangular or polygonal cross-section may have corners rounded along their whole length. The thickness of such products which have a rectangular (including "modified rectangular") cross-section exceeds one-tenth of the width. The expression also covers cast or sintered products, of the same forms and dimensions, which have been subsequently worked after production (otherwise than by simple trimming or de-scaling), provided that they have not thereby assumed the character of articles or products of other headings.

2. Profiles

Rolled, extruded, drawn, forged or formed products, coiled or not, of a uniform cross-section along their whole length, which do not conform to any of the definitions of bars, rods, wire, plates, sheets, strip, foil, tubes or pipes. The expression also covers cast or sintered products, of the same forms, which have been subsequently worked after production (otherwise than by simple trimming or de-scaling), provided that they have not thereby assumed the character of articles or products of other headings.

3. Wire

Rolled, extruded or drawn products, in coils, which have a uniform solid cross-section along their whole length in the shape of circles, ovals, rectangles (including squares), equilateral triangles or regular convex polygons (including "flattened circles" and "modified rectangles", of which two opposite sides are convex arcs, the other two sides being straight, of equal length and parallel). Products with a rectangular (including square), triangular or polygonal cross-section may have corners rounded along their whole length. The thickness of such products which have a rectangular (including "modified rectangular") cross-section exceeds one-tenth of the width.

4. Plates, sheets, strip and foil

Flat-surfaced products (other than the unwrought products of heading No. 78.01), coiled or not, of solid rectangular (other than square) cross-section with or without rounded corners (including "modified rectangles" of which two opposite sides are convex arcs, the other two sides being straight, of equal length and parallel) of a uniform thickness, which are:

1. 矩形(包括正方形)的,厚度不超过宽度的十分之一,
2. 矩形或正方形以外形状的,任何尺寸,但不具有其他税目所列制品或产品的特征。

税目78.04还适用于具有花样(例如,凹槽、肋条形、格槽、珠粒及菱形)的板、片、带、箔以及穿孔、抛光、涂层或制成瓦楞形的这类产品,但不具有其他税目所列制品或产品的特征。

五、管

全长截面及管壁厚度相同并只有一个闭合空间的实心产品,成卷或非成卷的,其截面为圆形、椭圆形、矩形(包括正方形)、等边三角形或规则外凸多边形。对于截面为矩形(包括正方形)、等边三角形或规则外凸多边形的产品,不论全长边角是否磨圆,只要其内外截面为同一圆心并为同样形状及同一轴向,也可视为管子。上述截面的管子可经抛光、涂层、弯曲、攻丝、钻孔、缩腰、胀口、成锥形或装法兰、颈圈或套环。

-of rectangular (including square) shape with a thickness not exceeding one-tenth of the width,

-of a shape other than rectangular or square, of any size, proviede that they do not assume the character of articles or products of other headings.

Heading No. 78.04 applies, *inter alia*, to plates, sheets, strip and foil with patterns (for example, grooves, ribs, chequers, tears, buttons, lozenges) and to such products which have been perforated, corrugated, polished or coated, provided that they do not thereby assume the character of articles or products of other headings.

5. Tubes and pipes

Hollow products, coiled or not, which have a uniform cross-section with only one enclosed void along their whole langth in the shape of circles, ovals, rectangles (including squares), equilateral triangles or regular convex polygons, and which have a uniform wall thickness. Products with a rectangular (including square), equilateral triangular or regular convex polygonal cross-section, which may have corners rounded along their whole length, are also to be considered as tubes and pipes provided the inner and outer cross-sections are concentric and have the same form and orientation. Tubes and pipes of the foregoing cross-sections may be polished, coated, bent, threaded, drilled, waisted, expanded, cone-shaped or fitted with flanges, collars or rings.

子目注释:

本章所称"精炼铅",是指:

按重量计含铅量至少为99.9%的金属,但其他各种元素的含量不超过下表中规定的限量:

其他元素表

元素		所含重量百分比
Ag	银	0.02
As	砷	0.005
Bi	铋	0.05
Ca	钙	0.002
Cd	镉	0.002
Cu	铜	0.08
Fe	铁	0.002
S	硫	0.002
Sb	锑	0.005
Sn	锡	0.005
Zn	锌	0.002
其他(例如碲),每种		0.001

Subheading Note:

In this Chapter the expression "refined lead" means:

Metal containing by weight at least 99.9% of lead, provided that the content by weight of any other element does not exceed the limit specified in the following table:

TABLE — Other elements

Element		Limiting centen% by weight
Ag	Silver	0.02
As	Arsenic	0.005
Bi	Bismuth	0.05
Ca	Calcium	0.002
Cd	Cadmium	0.002
Cu	Copper	0.08
Fe	Iron	0.002
S	Sulphur	0.002
Sb	Antimony	0.005
Sn	Tin	0.005
Zn	Zinc	0.002
Other(for example Te), each		0.001

税则号列 Tariff Item.	货 品 名 称	最惠国 (%) MFN	协定(%)CT 东盟 CA	中巴 CP	中智 CC	普通 Gen	增值 税率 VAT	出口 退税 ED	计量 单位 Unit	监管 条件 SC	Article Description
78.01	**未锻轧铅:**										**Unwrought lead:**
7801.1000	-精炼铅	3			0	20	17		千克		-Refined lead
	-其他:										-Other:
7801.9100	--按重量计所含其他元素是以锑为主的	3			1.8	20	17		千克		--Containing by weight antimony as the principal other elenent
7801.9900	--其他	3			0	20	17		千克		--Other
78.02	**铅废碎料:**										**Lead waste and scrap:**
7802.0000	铅废碎料	1.5			0	10	17		千克		Lead waste and scrap
78.04	**铅板、片、带、箔;铅粉及片状粉末:**										**Lead plates sheets, strip and foil; lead powders and flakes:**
	-板、片、带、箔:										-Plates, sheets, strip and foil:
7804.1100	--片、带及厚度(衬背除外)不超过0.2毫米的箔	6	5		0	30	17	8	千克		--Sheets, strip and foil of a thickness (excluding any backing) not exceeding 0.2mm
7804.1900	--其他	6	5		0	30	17	8	千克		--Other
7804.2000	-粉末及片状粉末	6	5		0	35	17		千克		-Powders and flakes
78.06	**其他铅制品:**										**Other articles of lead:**
7806.0010	---铅条、杆、型材及异型材或丝	6	5		0	30	17	13	千克		---Lead bars, rods, profiles and wire
7806.0090	---其他	6	5		0	40	17	13	千克		---Other

第七十九章 锌及其制品

Chapter 79 Zinc and articles thereof

注释：

本章所用名词解释如下：

一、条、杆

轧、挤、拔或锻制的实心产品，非成卷的，其全长截面均为圆形、椭圆形、矩形（包括正方形）、等边三角形或规则外凸多边形（包括相对两边为弧拱形，另外两边为等长平行直线的"扁圆形"及"变形矩形"）。对于矩形（包括正方形）、三角形或多边形截面的产品，其全长边角可经磨圆。矩形（包括"变形矩形"）截面的产品，其厚度应大于宽度的十分之一。所述条、杆也包括同样形状及尺寸的铸造或烧结产品。该产品在铸造烧结后再经加工（简单剪修或去氧化皮的除外），但不具有其他税目所列制品或产品的特征。

二、型材及异型材

轧、挤 拔、锻制的产品或其他成型产品，不论是否成卷，其全长截面相同，但与条、杆、丝、板、片、带、箔、管的定义不相符合。同时也包括同样形状的铸造或烧结产品。该产品在铸造或烧结后再经加工（简单剪修或去氧化皮的除外），但不具有其他税目所列制品或产品的特征。

三、丝

盘卷的轧、挤或拔制实心产品，其全长截面均为圆形、椭圆形、矩形（包括正方形）、等边三角形或规则外凸多边形（包括相对两边为弧拱形，另外两边为等长平行直线的"扁圆形"及"变形矩形"）。对于矩形（包括正方形）、三角形或多边形截面的产品，其全长边角可经磨圆。矩形（包括"变形矩形"）截面的产品，其厚度应大于宽度的十分之一。

Notes:

In this Chapter the following expressions have the meanings hereby assigned to them:

1. Bars and rods

   Rolled, extruded, drawn or forged products, not in coils, which have a uniform solid cross-section along their whole length in the shape of circles, ovals, rectangle (including squares), equilateral triangles or regular convex polygons (including "flattened circles" and "modified rectangles", of which two opposite sides are convex arcs, the other two sides being straight, of equal length and parallel). Products with a rectangular (including square), triangular or polygonal cross-section may have corners rounded along their whole length. The thickness of such products which have a rectangular (including "modified rectangular") cross-section exceeds one-tenth of the width. The expression also covers cast or sintered products, of the same forms and dimensions, which have been subsequently worked after production (otherwise than by simple trimming or de-scaling), provided that they have not thereby assumed the character of articles or products of other headings.

2. Profiles

   Rolled, extruded, drawn, forged or formed products, coiled or not, of a uniform cross-section along their whole length, which do not conform to any of the definitions of bars, rods, wire, plates, sheets, strip, foil, tubes or pipes. The expression also covers cast or sintered products, of the same forms, which have been subsequently worked after production (otherwise than by simple trimming or de-scaling), provided that they have not thereby assumed the character of articles or products of other headings.

3. Wire

   Rolled, extruded or drawn products, in coils, which have a uniform solid cross-section along their whole length in the shape of circles, ovals, rectangles (including squares), equilateral triangles or regular convex polygons (including "flattened circles" and "modified rectangles", of which two opposite sides are convex arcs, the other two sides being straight, of equal length and parallel). Products with a rectangular (including square), triangular or polygonal cross-section may have corners rounded along their whole length. The thickness of such products which have a rectangular (including "modified rectangular") cross-section exceeds one-tenth of the width

四、板、片、带、箔

成卷或非成卷的平面产品(税目79.01的未锻轧产品除外),截面均为厚度相同的实心矩形(不包括正方形),不论边角是否磨圆(包括相对两边为弧拱形,另外两边为等长平行直线的"变形矩形"),并且符合以下规格:

1. 矩形(包括正方形)的,厚度不超过宽度的十分之一;
2. 矩形或正方形以外形状的,任何尺寸,但不具有其他税目所列制品或产品的特征。

税目79.05还适用于具有花样(例如,凹槽、肋条形、格槽、珠粒及菱形)的板、片、带、箔以及穿孔、抛光、涂层或制成瓦楞形的这类产品,但不具有其他税目所列制品或产品的特征。

五、管

全长截面及管壁厚度相同并只有一个闭合空间的空心产品,成卷或非成卷的,其截面为圆形、椭圆形、矩形(包括正方形)、等边三角形或规则外凸多边形。对于截面为矩形(包括正方形)、等边三角形或规则外凸多边形的产品,不论全长边角是否磨圆,只要其内外截面为同一圆心并为同样形状及同一轴向,也可视为管子。上述截面的管子可经抛光、涂层、弯曲、攻丝、钻孔、缩腰、胀口、成锥形或装法兰、颈圈或套环。

4. Plates, sheets, strip and foil

Flat-surfaced products (other than the unwrought products of heading No. 79.01), coiled or not, of solid rectangular (other than square) cross-section with or without rounded corners (including "modified rectangles" of which two opposite sides are convex arcs, the other two sides being straight, of equal length and parallel) of a uniform thickness, which are:

-of rectangular (including square) shape with a thickness not exceeding one-tenth of the width,

-of a shape other than rectangular or square, of any size, provided that they do not assume the character of articles or products of other headings.

Heading No. 79.05 applies, *inter alia*, to plates, sheets strip and foil with patterns (for example, grooves, ribs chequers, tears, buttons, lozenges) and to such products which have been perforated, corrugated, polished or coated, provided that they do not thereby assume the character of articles or products of other headings.

5. Tubes and pipes

Hollow products, coiled or not, which have a uniform cross-section with only one enclosed void along their whole length in the shape of circles, ovals, rectangles (including squares), equilateral triangles or regular convex polygons, and which have a uniform wall thickness. Products with a rectangular (including square), equilateral triangular or regular convex polygonal cross-section, which may have corners rounded along their whole length, are also to be considered as tubes and pipes provided the inner and outer cross-sections are concentric and have the same form and orientation. Tubes and pipes of the foregoing cross-sections may be polished, coated, bent, threaded, drilled, waisted, expanded, cone-shaped or fitted with flanges, collars or rings.

子目注释:

本章所用有关名词解释如下:

一、非合金锌

按重量计含锌量至少为97.5%的金属。

二、锌合金

按重量计含锌量大于其他元素单项含量的金属物质,但按重量计其他元素的总含量超过2.5%。

三、锌末

冷凝锌雾所得的锌末。该产品由球形微粒组成,比锌粉更为精细,按重量计至少80%的微粒可以通过孔径为63微米的筛子,而且必须含有按重量计至少为85%的金属锌。

Subheading Note:

In this Chapter the following expressions have the meanings hereby assigned to them:

1. Zinc, not alloyed

Metal containing by weight at least 97.5% of zinc.

2. Zinc alloys

Metallic substances in which zinc predominates by weight over each of the other elements, provided that the total content by weight of such other elements exceeds 2.5%.

3. Zinc dust

Dust obtained by condensation of zinc vapour, consisting of spherical particles which are finer than zinc powders. At least 80% by weight of the particles pass through a sieve with 63 micrometres (microns) mesh. It must contain at least 85% by weight of metallic zinc.

税则号列 Tariff Item.	货品名称	最惠国(%) MFN	协定(%)CT 东盟 CA	中巴 CP	中智 CC	普通 Gen	增值税率 VAT	出口退税 ED	计量单位 Unit	监管条件 SC	Article Description
79.01	**未锻轧锌:**										**Unwrought zinc:**
	-非合金锌:										-Zinc, not alloyed:
	--按重量计含锌量在99.99%及以上:										--Containing by weight 99.99% or more of zinc:
7901.1110	---按重量计含锌量在99.995%及以上	3			0	20	17	5	千克	AB4xy	---containing by weight 99.995% or more of zinc
7901.1190	---其他	3			0	20	17		千克	AB4xy	---Other
7901.1200	--按重量计含锌量低于99.99%	3			0	20	17		千克	B4xy	--Containing by weight less than 99.99% of zinc
7901.2000	-锌合金	3			0	20	17		千克	B4xy	-Zinc alloys
79.02	**锌废碎料:**										**Zinc waste and scrap:**
7902.0000	锌废碎料	1.5			0	20	17		千克	AP	Zinc waste and scrap
79.03	**锌末、锌粉及片状粉末:**										**Zinc dust, powders and flakes:**
7903.1000	-锌末	6	5		0	20	17		千克		-Zinc dust
7903.9000	-其他	6	5		0	20	17		千克		-Other
7903.9000 10	颗粒<500μm的锌及其合金(含量≥97%,不论球形、椭球体、雾化、片状、研碎金属燃料)	6				20	17		千克	3	Zinc and its alloys, granularity <500μm (containing zinc≥97%, whether spheroid, ellipsoid, atomized, flake formed, ground metallic fuels)
7903.9000 90	其他锌粉及片状粉末	6				20	17		千克		Other zine powders and flakes
79.04	**锌条、杆、型材及异型材或丝:**										**Zinc bars, rods, profiles and wire:**
7904.0000	锌条、杆、型材及异型材或丝	6	5		0	30	17	8	千克		Zinc bars, rods, profiles and wire
79.05	**锌板、片、带、箔:**										**Zinc plates, sheets, strip and foil:**
7905.0000	锌板、片、带、箔	6	5		4.8	30	17	8	千克		Zinc plates, sheets, strip and foil
79.07	**其他锌制品:**										**Other articles of zinc:**
7907.0020	---锌制管子附件(例如,接头、肘管、管套)	6	5		0	30	17	13	千克		---Zinc tube or pipe fittings (for example, couplings, elbows, sleeves)
7907.0030	---电池壳体坯料(锌饼)	6	5		0	40	17	13	千克		---Cellpacking blanks (zinc biscuits)
7907.0090	---其他	6	5		0	40	17	13	千克		---Other

第八十章
锡及其制品

注释：

本章所用有关名词解释如下：

一、条、杆

轧、挤、拔或锻制的实心产品，非成卷的，其全长截面均为圆形、椭圆形、矩形（包括正方形）、等边三角形或规则外凸多边形（包括相对两边为弧拱形，另外两边为等长平行直线的“扁圆形”及“变形矩形”）。对于矩形（包括正方形）、三角形或多边形截面的产品，其全长边角可经磨圆。矩形（包括“变形矩形”）截面的产品，其厚度应大于宽度的十分之一。所述条、杆也包括同样形状及尺寸的铸造或烧结产品。该产品在造铸或烧结后再经加工（简单剪修或去氧化皮的除外），但不具有其他税目所列制品或产品的特征。

二、型材及异型材

轧、挤、拔、锻制的产品或其他成型产品，不论是否成卷，其全长截面相同，但与条、杆、丝、板、片、带、箔、管的定义不相符合。同时也包括同样形状的铸造或烧结产品。该产品在铸造或烧结后再经加工（简单剪修或去氧化皮的除外），但不具有其他税目所列制品或产品的特征。

三、丝

盘卷的轧、挤或拔制实心产品，其全长截面均为圆形、椭圆形、矩形（包括正方形）、等边三角形或规则外凸多边形（包括相对两边为弧拱形，另外两边为等长平行直线的“扁圆形”及“变形矩形”）。对于矩形（包括正方形）、三角形或多边形截面的产品，其全长边角可经磨圆。矩形（包括“变形矩形”）截面的产品，其厚度应大于宽度的十分之一。

Chapter 80
Tin and articles thereof

Notes:

In this Chapter the following expressions have the meanings hereby assigned to them:

1. Bars and rods

Rolled, extruded, drawn or forged products, not in coils, which have a uniform solid cross-section along their whole length in the shape of circles, ovals, rectangles (including squares), equilateral triangles or regular convex polygons (including "flattened circles" and "modified rectangles", of which two opposite sides are convex arcs, the other two sides being straight, of equal length and parallel). Products with a rectangular (including square), triangular or polygonal cross-section may have corners rounded along their whole length. The thickness of such products which have a rectangular (including "modified rectangular") cross-section exceeds one-tenth of the width. The expression also covers cast or sintered products, of the same forms and dimensions, which have been subsequently worked after production (otherwise than by simple trimming or de-scaling), provided that they have not thereby assumed the character of articles or products of other headings.

2. Profiles

Rolled, extruded, drawn, forged or formed products, coiled or not, of a uniform cross-section along their whole length, which do not conform to any of the definitions of bars, rods, wire, plates, sheets, strip, foil, tubes or pipes. The expression also covers cast or sintered products, of the same forms, which have been subsequently worked after production (otherwise than by simple trimming or de-scaling), provided that they have not thereby assumed the character of articles or products of other headings.

(c) Wire

Rolled, extruded or drawn products, in coils, which have a uniform solid cross-section along their whole length in the shape of circles, ovals, rectangles (including squares), equilateral triangles or regular convex polygons (including "flattened circles" and "modified rectangles", of which two opposite sides are convex arcs, the other two sides being straight, of equal length and parallel). Products with a rectangular (including square), triangular or polygonal cross-section may have corners rounded along their whole length. The thickness of such products which have a rectangular (including "modified rectangular") cross-section exceeds one-tenth of the width.

四、板、片、带、箔

成卷或非成卷的平面产品(税目 80.01 的未锻轧产品除外),截面均为厚度相同的实心矩形(不包括正方形),不论边角是否磨圆(包括相对两边为弧拱形,另外两边为等长平行直线的"变形矩形"),并且符合以下规格:

1. 矩形(包括正方形)的,厚度不超过宽度的十分之一;
2. 矩形或正方形以外形状的,任何尺寸,但不具有其他税目所列制品或产品的特征。

五、管

全长截面及管壁厚度相同并只有一个闭合空间的实心产品,成卷或非成卷的,其截面为圆形、椭圆形、矩形(包括正方形)、等边三角形或规则外凸多边形。对于截面为矩形(包括正方形)、等边三角形或规则外凸多边形的产品,不论全长边角是否磨圆,只要其内外截面为同一圆心并为同样形状及同一轴向,也可视为管子。上述截面的管子可经抛光、涂层、弯曲、攻丝、钻孔、缩腰、胀口、成锥形或装法兰、颈圈或套环。

4. Plates, sheets, strip and foil

Flat-surfaced products (other than the unwrought products of heading No. 80.01), coiled or not, of solid rectangular (other than square) cross-section with or without rounded corners (including "modified rectangles" of which two opposite sides are convex arcs, the other two sides being straight, of equal length and parallel) of a uniform thickness, which are:

-of rectangular (including square) shape with a thickness not exceeding one-tenth of the width,

-of a shape other than rectangular or square, of any size, proviede that they do not assume the character of articles or products of other headings.

5. Tubes and pipes

Hollow products, coiled or not, which have a uniform cross-section with only one enclosed void along their whole length in the shape of circles, ovals, rectangles (including squares), equilateral triangles or regular convex polygons, and which have a uniform wall thickness. Products with a rectangular (including square), equilateral triangular or regular convex polygonal cross-section, which may have corners rounded along their whole length, are also to be considered as tubes and pipes provided the inner and outer cross-sections are concentric and have the same form and orientation. Tubes and pipes of the foregoing cross-sections may be polished, coated, bent, threaded, drilled, waisted, expanded, cone-shaped or fitted with flanges, collars or rings.

子目注释:

本章所用有关名词解释如下:

一、非合金锡

按重量计含锡量至少为 99% 的金属,但含铋量或含铜量不超过下表中规定的限量:

其他元素表

元　　素		所含重量百分比
Bi	铋	0.1
Cu	铜	0.4

二、锡合金

按重量计含锡量大于其他元素单项含量的金属物质,但:

(一)按重量计其他元素的总含量超过 1%;或

(二)按重量计含铋量或含铜量应等于或大于上表中规定的限量。

Subheading Note:

In this Chapter the following expressions have the meanings hereby assigned to them:

1. Tin, not alloyed.

Metal containing by weight at least 99% of tin, provided that the content by weight of any bismuth or copper is less than the limit specified in the following table:

TABLE — Other elements

Element		Limiting content % by weight
Bi	Bismuth	0.1
Cu	Copper	0.4

2. Tin alloys

Metallic substances in which tin predominates by weight over each of the other elements, provided that:

(a) the total content by weight of such other elements exceeds 1%; or

(b) the content by weight of either bismuth or copper is equal to or greater than the limit specified in the foregoing table.

税则号列 Tariff Item.	货 品 名 称	最惠国(%) MFN	协定(%) CT 东盟 CA	 中巴 CP	 中智 CC	普通 Gen	增值税率 VAT	出口退税 ED	计量单位 Unit	监管条件 SC	Article Description
80.01	**未锻轧锡:**										**Unwrought tin:**
8001.1000	-非合金锡	3			0	20	17		千克	B4xy	-Tin, not alloyed
	-锡合金:										-Tin alloys:
8001.2010	---锡基巴毕脱合金	3			0	20	17		千克	4xy	---Babbitt metal
8001.2020	---焊锡	3			0	30	17		千克	B4xy	---solder
8001.2090	---其他	3			0	30	17		千克	4xy	---Other
80.02	**锡废碎料:**										**Tin waste and scrap:**
8002.0000	锡废碎料	1.5			0	30	17		千克	AP	Tin waste and scrap
80.03	**锡条、杆、型材及异型材或丝:**										**Tin bars, rods, profiles and wire:**
8003.0000	锡条、杆、型材及异型材或丝	8	5		0	40	17	5	千克	4xBy	Tin bars, rods, profiles and wire
80.07	**其他锡制品:**										**Other articles of tin:**
8007.0020	---锡板、片及带,厚度超过0.2毫米	8	5		0	40	17	13	千克	4xy	---Tin plates, sheets and strip, of a thickness exceeding 0.2mm
8007.0030	---锡箔(不论是否印花或用纸、纸板、塑料或类似材料衬背),厚度(衬背除外)不超过0.2毫米;锡粉及片状粉末	8	5		0	40	17	13	千克		---Tin foil (whether or not printed of or backed with paper, paperboard, plastics or similar backing materials), of a thickness (excluding and backing) ont exceeding0.2mm; tin powders and flakes
8007.0040	---锡管及管子附件(例如,接头、肘管、管套)	8	5		0	45	17	5	千克	4xy	---Tin tubes, pipes and tube or pipe fittings (for example, couplings, elbows, sleeves)
8007.0090	---其他	8	5		0	80	17	5	千克		---Other

第八十一章
其他贱金属、金属陶瓷及其制品

Chapter 81
Other base metals; cermets; artiles thereof

子目注释：

第七十四章注释中有关“条、杆”、“型材及异型材”、“丝”及“板、片、带、箔”的规定也适用于本章。

Subheading Note:

Note 1 to Chapter 74, defining “bars and rods”, “profiles”, “wire” and “plates, sheets, strip and foil” applies, *mutatis mutandis*, to this Chapter.

税则号列 Tariff Item.	货品名称	最惠国(%) MFN	协定(%)CT 东盟 CA	中巴 CP	中智 CC	普通 Gen	增值税率 VAT	出口退税 ED	计量单位 Unit	监管条件 SC	Article Description
81.01	**钨及其制品，包括废碎料：**										**Tungsten (wolfram) and articles thereof, including waste and scrap:**
8101.1000	-粉末	6	5		0	20	17		千克		-Powders
8101.1000 10	颗粒＜500μm 的钨及其合金(含量≥97%，不论球形、椭球体、雾化、片状、研碎金属燃料)	6				20	17		千克	3B	Tungesten and tungsten alloys, granularity < 500? m, (containing tungsten ≥ 97%, whether in the form of spheroid, elipsoid, flakes, atomized or pulverized metallic fuel)
8101.1000 90	其他钨粉末	6				20	17		千克	4xBy	Other tungsten powders
	-其他：										-Other:
8101.9400	--未锻轧钨，包括简单烧结而成的条、杆	3			0	20	17		千克	4xy	--Unwrought tungsten, including bars and rods obtained simply by sintering
8101.9600	--丝	8	5		0	20	17	13	千克		--Wire
8101.9700	--废碎料	3			0	20	17		千克	4APxy	--Waste and scrap
	--其他：										--Other:
8101.9910	---条、杆，但简单烧结而成的除外；型材及异型材、板、片、带、箔	5			0	30	17	13	千克		---Bars and rods, other than those obtained simply by sintering, profiles, plates, sheets, strip and foil
8101.9990	---其他	8	5		0	70	17	13	千克		---Other
81.02	**钼及其制品，包括废碎料：**										**Molybdenum and articles thereof, including waste and scrap:**
8102.1000	-粉末	6	5		0	20	17		千克	4xy	-Powders
	-其他：										-Other:
8102.9400	--未锻轧钼，包括简单烧结而成的条、杆	3			0	20	17		千克	4xy	--Unwrought molybdenum, including bars and rods obtained simply by sintering
8102.9500	--条、杆，但简单烧结而成的除外；型材及异型材、板、片、带、箔	8	5		0	30	17	13	千克		--Bars and rods, other than those obtained simply by sintering, profiles, plates, sheets, strip and foil
8102.9600	--丝	8	5		0	20	17	13	千克		--Wire
8102.9700	--废碎料	3			0	20	17		千克	4xy	--Waste and scrap
8102.9900	--其他	8	5		0	70	17	13	千克	4xy	--Other
81.03	**钽及其制品，包括废碎料：**										**Tantalum and articles thereof, including waste and scrap:**
8103.2011	----机装密度小于 2.29/cm^3 的	6	5		0	14	17		千克	A4xy	
8103.2019	----其他	6	5		0	14	17		千克	A4xy	----Other
8103.2090	---其他	6	5		0	14	17		千克	A4xy	---Other
8103.3000	-废碎料	6	5		0	14	17		千克	4APxy	-Waste and scrap
8103.9000	-其他	8	5		0	30	17	13	千克		-Other
8103.9000 10	钽坩埚(容积在 50 毫升至 2 升之间、钽纯度≥98%)	8				30	17	13	千克	3	Cubage is between 50 milliliter and 2 litre, tantaium≥98%

税则号列 Tariff Item.	货品名称	最惠国(%) MFN	协定(%) 东盟 CA	中巴 CP	CT 中智 CC	普通 Gen	增值税率 VAT	出口退税 ED	计量单位 Unit	监管条件 SC	Article Description
8103.9000 90	其他锻轧钽及其制品	8				30	17	13	千克	4xy	Other wrought tantalum and articles thereog
81.04	**镁及其制品,包括废碎料:**										**Magnesium and articles thereof, including waste and scrap:**
	-未锻轧镁:										-Unwrought magnesium:
8104.1100	--按重量计含镁量至少为99.8%	6	5	4.2	0	20	17		千克		--Containing at least 99.8% by weight of magnesium
8104.1900	--其他	6	5		0	20	17		千克		--Other
8104.2000	-废碎料	1.5			0	20	17		千克	AP	-Waste and scrap
8104.3000	-锉屑、车屑及颗粒,已按规格分级的;粉末	8	5		0	30	17		千克		-Raspings, turnings and granules, graded according to size; powders
8104.3000 10	颗粒<500μm的镁及其合金(含量≥97%,不论球形、椭球体、雾化、片状、研碎金属燃料)	8				30	17		千克	3	Magnesium and magnesium alloys, granularity <500μm (containing magnesium≥97%, whether spheroid, ellipsoid, atomized, flake formed, ground metallic fuels)
8104.3000 90	其他已分级的镁锉屑,车屑,颗粒;粉末	8				30	17		千克		Othcr magnesium raspings, turnings and granules, graded according to size
	-其他:										-Other:
8104.9010	---锻轧镁	8	5		0	30	17	13	千克		---Wrought magnesium
8104.9020	---镁制品	8.4	5		0	70	17	13	千克		---Magnesium articles
8104.9020 10	镁金属基复合材料(包括各种结构件和制品、各种预成形件,其中增强材料的比拉伸强度大于7.62×10⁴m和比摸量大于3.18×10⁶m)	8.4				70	17	13	千克	3B	Masnesium composite materials (including all sorts of structural parts and compound products, tensile strength reinforced materials >7.62×10⁴m)
8104.9020 90	其他镁制品	8.4				70	17	13	千克	B	
81.05	**钴锍及其他冶炼钴时所得的中间产品;钴及其制品,包括废碎料:**										**Cobalt mattes and other intermediate products of cobalt matallurgy; cobalt and articles thereof, including waste and scrap:**
	-钴锍及其他冶炼钴时所得的中间产品;未锻轧钴;粉末:										-Cobalt mattes and other intermediate products of cobalt metallurgy; unwrought cobalt; powders:
8105.2010	---钴湿法冶炼中间品	4			0	14	17		千克	4xy	---Intermediate products os cobalt wetprocessing metallurgy
8105.2090	---其他	4			0	14	17		千克		---Other
8105.2090 01	钴锍及其他冶炼钴时所得中间产品	4				14	17		千克	4xy	Mid-product smelted with cobalt and sulfur and others
8105.2090 10	钴≥99.5%的超细钴粉(费氏粒度0.8-1.5μm,松装密度0.4-0.8g/立方厘米	4				14	17		千克		Supper-fine cobalt powders, containing ≥by weight of cobalt (Fischer granularinty 0.8-1.5μm. bulk package density 0.4-0.89/cm²)
8105.2090 90	其他钴锍、未煅轧钴、粉末	4				14	17		千克	4xy	Other cobalt mattes and wburonght cobalt; powders
8105.3000	-废碎料	4			0	14	17		千克	4xy	-Waste and scrap
8105.9000	-其他	8	5		6.4	30	17	13	千克	4xy	-Other

税则号列 Tariff Item.	货品名称	最惠国(%) MFN	协定(%)CT 东盟 CA	中巴 CP	中智 CC	普通 Gen	增值税率 VAT	出口退税 ED	计量单位 Unit	监管条件 SC	Article Description
81.06	**铋及其制品,包括废碎料:**										**Bismuth and articles thereof, including waste and scrap:**
8106.0010	---未锻轧铋;废碎料;粉末	3			0	20	17		千克		---Unwroght bismuth; waste and scrap; powders
8106.0010 10	高纯度未锻轧的铋及其废料、粉末(纯度≥99.99%,含银量低于十万分之一)	3				20	17		千克	3	Highly-pure unforged and unroued his muth and its waste and powder (purity =99%)
8106.0010 90	其他未锻轧铋、废碎料、粉末	3				20	17		千克	4xy	Other unurought hismuth and its waste and pounder
8106.0090	---其他	8	5		0	30	17	13	千克		---Other
8106.0090 10	高纯度铋及铋制品(纯度≥99.99%,含银量低于十万分之一)	8				30	17	13	千克	3	Highly-pure unforged bismuth and aricles thereof(purity ≥99.99% containins less than 10000 silver)
8106.0090 90	其他铋及铋制品	8				30	17	13	千克	4xy	Other Bismuth and articles thereof
81.07	**镉及其制品,包括废碎料:**										**Cadmium and articles thereof, including waste and scrap:**
8107.2000	-未锻轧镉;粉末	3			0	14	17		千克		-Unwrought cadmium; powders
8107.3000	-废碎料	3			0	14	17		千克		-Waste and scrap
8107.9000	-其他	8	5		0	30	17	13	千克		-Other
81.08	**钛及其制品,包括废碎料:**										**Titanium and articles thereof, including waste and scrap:**
	-未锻轧钛;粉末:										-Unwrought titanium; powders:
8108.2010	---海绵钛	3			0	14	17		千克	4xy	---Titanium sponge
8108.2090	---其他	3			0	14	17		千克		---Other
8108.2090 10	颗粒<500μm的钛及其合金(含量≥97%,不论球形、椭球体、雾化、片状、研碎金属燃料)	3				14	17		千克	3	Titanium and alloys, granularity < 500μm (containing titanium ≥97%, whether spheroid, ellipsoid, atomized, flake formed, ground metallic fuels)
8108.2090 90	其他未锻轧钛;粉末	3				14	17		千克	4xy	Other unwrought titanium; powders
8108.3000	-废碎料	3			0	14	17		千克	4APxy	-Waste and scrap
	-其他:										-Other:
8108.9010	---条、杆、型材及异型材	8	5		0	30	17	13	千克		---Bars, rods, shapes and sections
8108.9010 10	钛合金,实心圆柱体,包括锻件(20℃下极限抗拉强度≥900兆帕,外径超过75mm)	8				30	17	13	千克	3	Titanium alloys, solid cylindrical, including castings (ultimate tensile strength≥900MPa at 20℃, outer diameter>75mm)
8108.9010 20	钛金属基复合材料的条、杆,型材及异型材(其中增强材料的比拉伸强度大于7.62×10^4米和比模量大于3.18×10^7米)	8				30	17	13	千克	3	Bars, rods, shaps and sections made of composite material with titanium metal (the degree of streangth of intensity waterial bigger than 7.62×10^4m, and specific modulus bigger than 3.18×10^7m)
8108.9010 90	其他钛条、杆、型材及异型材	8				30	17	13	千克		Other bars, rods, shapes and sections
8108.9020	---丝	8	5		0	30	17	13	千克		---Wire
	---板、片、带、箔:										---Plates, sheets, strap, foil:
8108.9031	----厚度不超过0.8毫米	8	5		0	30	17	13	千克		----Of a thickness not more than 0.8mm
8108.9032	----厚度超过0.8毫米	8	5		0	30	17	13	千克		----Of a thickness more than 0.8mm

税则号列 Tariff Item.	货 品 名 称	最惠国(%) MFN	协定(%) 东盟 CA	中巴 CP	CT 中智 CC	普通 Gen	增值税率 VAT	出口退税 ED	计量单位 Unit	监管条件 SC	Article Description
8108.9032 10	钛金属基复合材料的板片、带、箔(其中增强材料的比拉伸强度大于7.62×10⁴米,和比模量大于3.18×10⁷米,厚度大于0.8毫米)	8				30	17	13	千克	3	Plates. sheets, strip and foil made of conyosite material with titanium metal (the degree of strength of intensity material bigger than 3.18×10⁴mm, thickness bigger than 0.8mm)
8108.9032 90	其他厚度>0.8毫米的钛板、片、带、箔	8				30	17	13	千克		Other plates, sheets, strap. foil of bismuth thickness more than 0.8mm
8108.9040	---管	8	5		0	30	17	13	千克		---Tubes or pipes
8108.9040 10	钛合金管(20℃下极限抗拉强度≥900Mpa,外径>75mm)	8				30	17	13	千克	3	Tubes or pipes of titanium (ultimate tensile strength ≥ 900MPa at 20℃, outer diameter >75mm)
8108.9040 90	其他钛管	8				30	17	13	千克		Other titanium tubes or pipes
8108.9090	---其他	8	5		0	30	17	13	千克		---Other
81.09	**锆及其制品,包括废碎料:**										**Zirconium and articles thereof, including waste and scrap:**
8109.2000	-未锻轧锆;粉末	3			0	20	17		千克		-Unwrought zirconium; powders
8109.2000 10	颗粒<500μm的锆及其合金(含量≥97%,不论球形、椭球体、雾化、片状、研碎金属燃料)	3				20	17		千克	3	Zirconium and alloys, granularity <500μm (containing zirconium ≥97%, whether spheroid, ellipsoid, atomized, flake formed, ground metallic fuels)
8109.2000 90	其他未锻轧锆;粉末	3				20	17		千克	4xy	Other unwrought zirconium; powders
8109.3000	-废碎料	3			0	20	17		千克	4xy	-Waste and scrap
8109.9000	-其他	8	5		0	30	17	13	千克		-Other
8109.9000 10	锆管(铪与锆重量比低于1:500的锆金属和合金的管或组件)	8				30	17	13	千克	3	Tubes or pipes of zirconium and its alloys (ratio of hafnium and zirconium <1:500 by weight)
8109.9000 90	其他锻轧锆及锆制品	8				30	17	13	千克	4xy	Other wrought zirconium and articles thereof
81.10	**锑及其制品,包括废碎料:**										**Antimony and articles thereof, including waste and scrap:**
	-未锻轧锑;粉末:										-Unwrought antimony; powders:
8110.1010	---未锻轧锑	3			0	30	17		千克	4xBy	---Unwrought antimony
8110.1020	---粉末	3			0	30	17		千克	4xBy	---Powders
8110.2000	-废碎料	3			0	30	17	5	千克	4xBy	-Antimony waste and scrap
8110.9000	-其他	8	5		0	40	17	5	千克	4xy	-Other
81.11	**锰及其制品,包括废碎料:**										**Manganese and articles thereof, including waste and scrap:**
8111.0010	---未锻轧锰;废碎料;粉末	3			0	20	17		千克	4Bxy	---Unwrought manganese; waste and scrap; powders
8111.0090	---其他	8	5		0	30	17	13	千克	4xy	---Other
81.12	**铍、铬、锗、钒、镓、铪、铟、铼、铌、铊及其制品,包括废碎料:**										**Beryllium, chromium, germanium, vanadium, gallium, hafnium, indium, niobium (columbium), rhenium and thallium, and articles of these metals, including waste and scrap:**
	-铍:										-Beryllium:
8112.1200	--未锻轧铍;粉末	3			0	30	17		千克	4xy	--Unwrought; powders

税则号列 Tariff Item.	货 品 名 称	最惠国(%) MFN	协定(%)CT 东盟 CA	中巴 CP	中智 CC	普通 Gen	增值税率 VAT	出口退税 ED	计量单位 Unit	监管条件 SC	Article Description
8112. 1300	--废碎料	3			0	30	17		千克	4xy	--Waste and scrap
8112. 1900	--其他	8	5		0	30	17	13	千克	4xy	--Other
	-铬：										-Chromium：
8112. 2100	--未锻轧铬；粉末	3			0	20	17		千克	4Bxy	--Unwrought；powders
8112. 2200	--废碎料	3			0	20	17		千克	4Bxy	--Waste and scrap
8112. 2900	--其他	3			0	20	17	13	千克	4Bxy	--Other
	-铊：										-Thallium：
8112. 5100	--未锻轧铊；粉末	3			0	20	17		千克		--Unwrought；powders
8112. 5200	--废碎料	3			0	20	17		千克		--Waste and scrap
8112. 5900	--其他	8	5		0	30	17	13	千克		--Other
	-其他：										-Other：
	--未锻轧的；废碎料；粉末：										--Unwrought；waste and scrap；powders：
8112. 9210	---锗	3			0	20	17		千克	4xy	---Germanium
8112. 9220	---钒	3			0	20	17		千克		---Vanadium
8112. 9220 01	未锻轧钒氮合金	3				20	17		千克	4xy	Unwrought vanadium-nitrogen alloys
8112. 9220 90	未锻轧的钒；钒废碎料；钒粉末	3				20	17		千克	4xy	Unwrought vanadium and waste and scrap；Powders
8112. 9230	---铟	3			0	20	17		千克	4xy	---Indium
8112. 9240	---铌	3			0	20	17		千克	4xy	---Niobium
8112. 9290	---其他	3			0	20	17		千克		---Other
8112. 9290 10	未锻轧的铪，铪合金；废碎料；粉末	3				20	17		千克	3	Unwrough hafnium，hafnium alloy and waster and scrap，powders there of
8112. 9290 90	未锻轧的镓、铼、废碎料；粉末	3				20	17		千克	4xy	Other unwrough gallium，rhcnium，waste and scrap；powders
	--其他：										--Other：
8112. 9910	---锗	3			0	20	17	13	千克	4xy	---Germanium
8112. 9920	---钒	3			0	20	17	13	千克		---Vanadiurn
8112. 9920 01	其他钒氮合金	3				20	17	13	千克	4xy	Other vanadium – nitrogen alloys
8112. 9920 90	其他钒及其制品	3				20	17	13	千克	4xy	Other vanadium and articles thereof
8112. 9930	---铟	8	3		6. 4	20	17	13	千克	4xy	---Indium
8112. 9940	---铌	8	3		6. 4	20	17	13	千克	4xy	---Niobium
8112. 9990	---其他	8	5		6. 4	30	17	13	千克		---Other
8112. 9990 10	锻轧的铪及其制品	8				30	17		千克	3	Wough hafnium，and articles
8112. 9990 90	锻轧的镓、铼及其制品	8				30	17		千克	4xy	Other wrough sallium，rhcnium and arttdes therof
81. 13	**金属陶瓷及其制品，包括废碎料：**										**Cermets and articles thereof，including waste and scrap：**
8113. 0000	金属陶瓷及其制品（包括废碎料）	8. 4	5		0	30	17		千克		Cermets and articles thereof，including waste and scrap

第八十二章
贱金属工具、器具、利口器、餐匙、餐叉及其零件

Chapter 82
Tools, implements, cutlery, spoons and forks, parts thereof of base metal

注释：

一、除喷灯、轻便锻炉、带支架的砂轮、修指甲和修脚用器具及税目 82.09 的货品外，本章仅包括带有用下列材料制成的刀片、工作刃、工作面或其他工作部件的物品：

(一)贱金属；

(二)硬质合金或金属陶瓷；

(三)装于贱金属、硬质合金或金属陶瓷底座上的宝石或半宝石(天然、合成或再造)；

(四)附于贱金属底座上的磨料，当附上磨料后，所具有的切齿、沟、槽或类似结构仍保持其特性及功能。

二、本章所列物品的贱金属零件，应与该制品归入同一税目，但具体列名的零件及手工工具的工具夹具(税目 84.66)除外。第十五类注释二所述的通用零件，均不归入本章。电动剃须刀及电动毛发推剪的刀头、刀片应归入税目 85.10。

三、由税目 82.11 的一把或多把刀具与税目 82.15 至少数量相同的物品构成的成套货品应归入税目 82.15。

Notes:

1. Apart from blow lamps, portable forges, grinding wheels with frameworks, manicure or pedicure sets, and goods of heading No. 82.09, this Chapter covers only articles with a blade, working No. edge, working surface or other working part of :
   (a) Base metal;
   (b) Metal carbides or cermets;
   (c) Precious or semi-precious stones (natural, synthetic or reconstructed) on a support of base metal, metal carbide or cermet; or
   (d) Abrasive materials on a support of base metal, provided that the articles have cutting teeth, flutes, grooves, or the like, of base metal, which retain their identity and function after the application of the abrasive.
2. Parts of base metal of the articles of this Chapter are to be classified with the articles of which they are parts, except parts separately specified as such and tool-holders for hand tools (heading No. 84.66). However, parts of general use as defined in Note 2 to Section XV are in all cases excluded from this Chapter. Heads, blades and cutting plates for electric shavers or electric hair clippers are to be classified in heading No. 85.10.
3. Sets consisting of one or more knives of heading No. 82.11 and at least an equal number of articles of heading No. 82.15 are to be classified in heading No. 82.15.

税则号列 Tariff Item.	货品名称	最惠国(%) MFN	协定(%)CT 东盟 CA	中巴 CP	中智 CC	普通 Gen	增值税率 VAT	出口退税 ED	计量单位 Unit	监管条件 SC	Article Description
82.01	锹、铲、镐、锄、叉及耙；斧子、钩刀及类似砍伐工具；各种修枝用剪刀；镰刀、秣刀、树篱剪、伐木楔子及其他农业、园艺或林业用手工工具：										**Hand tools, the following: spades, shovels, mattocks, picks, hoes, forks and rakes; axes, bill hooks and similar hewing tools; secateurs and prundrs of any kind; scythes, hay knives, hedge shears, timber wedges and other tools of a kind used in agriculture, horticulture or forestry:**
8201.1000	-锹及铲	8	5		0	50	13	11	千克/把		-Spades and shovels
8201.1000 10	含植物性材料的锹及铲	8				50	13	11	千克/把	AB	Spades and shovels with parts of vegetable materials
8201.1000 90	其他锹及铲	8				50	13	11	千克/把		Other spades and shovels
8201.2000	-叉	8	5		0	50	13	11	千克/把		-Forks
8201.2000 10	含植物性材料的农用叉	8				50	13	11	千克/把	AB	Forks with parts of vegetable materials, of a kind used in agriculture
8201.2000 90	其他农用叉	8				50	13	11	千克/把		Other forks, of a kind used in agriculture
8201.3000	-镐、锄及耙	8	5		0	50	13	11	千克/把		-Mattocks, picks, hoes and rakes
8201.3000 10	含植物性材料的镐、锄、耙	8				50	13	11	千克/把	AB	Mattocks, picks, hoes and rakes with parts of vegetable materials

税则号列 Tariff Item.	货 品 名 称	最惠国(%) MFN	协定(%)CT 东盟 CA	 中巴 CP	 中智 CC	普通 Gen	增值税率 VAT	出口退税 ED	计量单位 Unit	监管条件 SC	Article Description
8201.3000 90	其他镐、锄、耙	8				50	13	11	千克/把		Other mattocks, picks, hoes and rakes
8201.4000	-斧子、钩刀及类似砍伐工具	8	5		0	50	13	11	千克/把		-Axes, bill hooks and similar hewing tools
8201.4000 10	含植物性材料的砍伐工具(包括斧子、钩刀及类似砍伐工具)	8				50	13	11	千克/把	AB	Axes, bill hooks and similar hewing tools with parts of vegetable materials
8201.4000 90	其他斧子、钩刀及类似砍伐工具	8				50	13	11	千克/把		Other axes, bill hooks and similar hewing tools
8201.5000	-修枝剪及类似的单手操作剪刀(包括家禽剪)	8	5		0	50	13	11	千克/把		-Secateurs and similar one-handed pruners and shears (including poultry shears)
8201.5000 10	含植物性材料的单手操作农用剪(包括家禽剪)	8				50	13	11	千克/把	AB	Secateurs and similar one-handed pruners and shears (including poultry shears), with parts of vegetable materials of a kind used in agriculture
8201.5000 90	其他修枝剪等单手操作农用剪(包括家禽剪)	8				50	13	11	千克/把		Other secateurs and similar one-handed pruners and shears (including poultry shears), of a kind used in agriculture
8201.6000	-树篱剪、双手修枝剪及类似的双手操作剪刀	8	5		0	50	13	11	千克/把		-Hedge shears, two-handed pruning shears and similar two-handed shears
8201.6000 10	含植物性材料的双手操作农用剪	8				50	13	11	千克/把	AB	Hedge shears, two-handed pruning shears and similar two-handed shears, with parts of vegetable materials, of a kind used in agriculture
8201.6000 90	其他修枝等双手操作农用剪	8				50	13	11	千克/把		Other hedge shears, two-handed pruning shears and similar two-handed shears, of a kind used in agriculture
8201.9000	-用于农业、园艺或林业的其他手工工具	8	5		0	50	13	13	千克/把		-Other hand tools of a kind used in agriculture, horticulture or forestry
8201.9000 10	含植物性材料的农林用手工工具	8				50	13	11	千克/把	AB	Hand tools of a kind used in agriculture, horticulture or forestry, with parts of vegetable materials
8201.9000 90	其他农业、园艺、林业用手工工具	8				50	13	11	千克/把		Other hand tools of a kind used in agriculture, horticulture or forestry
82.02	**手工锯;各种锯的锯片(包括切条、切槽或无齿锯片):**										**Hand saws; blades for saws of all kinds (including slitting, slotting or toothless saw blades):**
8202.1000	-手工锯	8.4	5		0	50	17	13	千克/把		-Hand saws
8202.2000	-带锯片	8	5		0	20	17	13	千克/条		-Band saw blades
	-圆锯片(包括切条或切槽锯片):										-Circular saw blades (including slitting or slotting saw blades):
8202.3100	--带有钢制工作部件	8	5		0	20	17	13	千克/片		--With working part of steel
8202.3900	--其他,包括部件	8	5		0	20	17	13	千克/片		--Other, including parts
8202.4000	-链锯片	8	5		0	20	17	13	千克/条		-Chain saw blades
	-其他锯片:										-Other saw blades:
	--直锯片,加工金属用:										--Straight saw blades, for working metal:
8202.9110	---机械锯用	8	5	7	0	20	17	13	千克/片		---For sawing machines
8202.9190	---其他	8	5		0	50	17	13	千克/片		---Other
	--其他:										--Other:
8202.9910	---机械锯用	8.4	5		0	20	17	13	千克/片		---For sawing machines

税则号列 Tariff Item.	货品名称	最惠国(%) MFN	协定(%)CT 东盟 CA	 中巴 CP	 中智 CC	普通 Gen	增值税率 VAT	出口退税 ED	计量单位 Unit	监管条件 SC	Article Description
8202.9990	---其他	10.5	8		6.3	50	17	13	千克/片		---Other
82.03	**钢锉、木锉、钳子(包括剪钳)、镊子、白铁剪、切管器、螺栓切头器、打孔冲子及类似手工工具:**										**Files, rasps, pliers (including cutting pliers), pincers, tweezers, metal cutting shears, pipe-cutters, bolt croppers, perforating punches and similar hand tools:**
8203.1000	-钢锉、木锉及类似工具	10.5	8		6.3	50	17	13	千克/把		-Files, rasps and similar tools
8203.2000	-钳子(包括剪钳)、镊子及类似工具	10.5	T3		0	50	17	13	千克/把	B	-Pliers (including cutting pliers), pincers, tweezers and similar tools
8203.3000	-白铁剪及类似工具	10.5	8		6.3	50	17	13	千克/把		-Metal cutting shears and similar tools
8203.4000	-切管器、螺栓切头器、打孔冲子及类似工具	10.5	8		6.3	50	17	13	千克/把		-Pipe-cutters, bolt croppers, perforating punches and similar tools
82.04	**手动扳手及扳钳(包括转矩扳手,但不包括丝锥扳手);可互换的扳手套筒,不论是否带手柄:**										**Hand-operated spanners and wrenches (including torque meter wrenches but not including tap wrenches); interchangeable spanner sockets, with or without handles:**
	-手动扳手及扳钳:										-Hand-operated spanners and wrenches:
8204.1100	--固定的	10.5	8		0	50	17	13	千克/把	B	--Non-adjustable
8204.1200	--可调的	10	5		0	50	17	13	千克/把	B	--Adjustable
8204.2000	-可互换的扳手套筒,不论是否带手柄	10	5		0	50	17	13	千克/套	B	-Interchangeable spanner sockets, with or without handles
82.05	**其他税目未列名的手工工具(包括玻璃刀);喷灯;台钳、夹钳及类似品,但作为机床附件或零件的除外;砧;轻便锻炉;带支架的手摇或脚踏砂轮:**										**Hand tools (including glaziers' diamonds), not elsewhere specified or included; blow lamps; vices, clamps and the like, other than accessories for and parts of, machine tools; anvils; portable forges; hand or pedal operated grinding wheels with frame works:**
8205.1000	-钻孔或攻丝工具	10	5		0	50	17	13	千克/个		-Drilling, threading or tapping tools
8205.2000	-锤子	10	5		0	50	17	13	千克/个		-Hammers and sledge hammers
8205.3000	-木工用刨子、凿子及类似切削工具	10.5	8		6.3	50	17	13	千克/个		-Planes, chisels, gouges and similar cutting tools for working wood
8205.4000	-螺丝刀	10.5	8		6.3	50	17	13	千克/个		-Screwdrivers
	-其他手工工具(包括玻璃刀):										-Other hand tools (including glaziers' diamonds):
8205.5100	--家用工具	10.5	8		8.4	50	17	13	千克/个		--Household tools
8205.5900	--其他	10	5	8.5	0	50	17	13	千克/个		--Other
8205.6000	-喷灯	10	5		0	50	17	13	千克/个		-Blow lamps
8205.7000	-台钳、夹钳及类似品	10.5	8		6.3	50	17	13	千克/个	B	-Vices, clamps and the like
8205.8000	-砧、轻便锻炉;带支架的手摇或脚踏砂轮	10.5	8		6.3	50	17	13	千克		-Anvils; portable forges; hand or pedal operated grindding wheels with frameworks
8205.9000	-由上述两个或多个子目所列物品组成的成套货品	10.5	8		6.3	50	17	13	千克		-Sets of articles of two or more of the foregoing subheadings
82.06	**由税目82.02至82.05中两个或多个税目所列工具组成的零售包装成套货品:**										**Tools of two or more of the headings Nos. 82.02 to 82.05, put up in sets for retail sale:**

税则号列 Tariff Item.	货 品 名 称	最惠国(%) MFN	协定(%)CT 东盟 CA	中巴 CP	中智 CC	普通 Gen	增值税率 VAT	出口退税 ED	计量单位 Unit	监管条件 SC	Article Description
8206.0000	由税目82.02至82.05中两个或多个税目所列工具组成的零售包装成套货品	10.5	8		8.4	50	17	13	千克		Tools of two or more of the headings Nos. 82.02 to 82.05, put up in sets for retail sale
82.07	**手工工具(不论是否有动力装置)及机床(例如,锻压、冲压、攻丝、钻孔、镗孔、铰孔及铣削、车削或上螺丝用的机器)的可互换工具,包括金属拉拔或挤压用模以及凿岩或钻探工具:**										**Interchangeable tools for hand tools, whether or not power-operated, or for machine-tools (for example, for pressing, stamping, punching, tapping, threading, drilling, boring, broaching, milling, turning or screw driving), including dies for drawing or extruding metal, and rock drilling or earth boring tools:**
	-凿岩或钻探工具:										-Rock drilling or earth boring tools:
8207.1300	--带有金属陶瓷制的工作部件	8	5		6.4	20	17	13	千克	B	--With working part of cermets
	--其他,包括部件:										--Other, including parts:
8207.1910	---带有天然或合成金钢石、立方氮化硼制的工作部件	8	5		6.4	20	17	13	千克	B	---With working part of natural or synthetic diamonds or cubic boron nitride
8207.1990	---其他	8	5		6.4	20	17	13	千克	B	---Other
	-金属拉拔或挤压用模:										-Dies for drawing or extruding metal:
8207.2010	---带有天然或合成金刚石、立方氮化硼制的工作部件	8	5		0	20	17	13	千克/套		---With working part of natural or synthetic diamonds or cubic boron nitride
8207.2090	---其他	8	5		0	20	17	13	千克/套		---Other
8207.3000	-锻压或冲压工具	8	5	6.8	6.4	20	17	13	千克		-Tools for pressing, stamping or punching
8207.4000	-攻丝工具	8	5		0	20	17	13	千克/件		-Tools for tapping or threading
	-钻孔工具,但凿岩及钻探用的除外:										-Tools for drilling, other than for rock drilling:
8207.5010	---带有天然或合成金刚石、立方氮化硼制的工作部件	8	5		6.4	20	17	13	千克/件	B	---With working part of natural or synthetic diamonds or cubic boron nitride
8207.5090	---其他	8	5		6.4	20	17	13	千克/件	B	---Other
	-镗孔或铰孔工具:										-Tools for boring or broaching:
8207.6010	---带有天然或合成金刚石、立方氮化硼制的工作部件	8	5		0	20	17	13	千克/件		---With working part of natural or synthetic diamonds or cubic boron nitride
8207.6090	---其他	8	5		0	20	17	13	千克/件		---Other
8207.7000	-铣削工具	8	5		6.4	20	17	13	千克/件	B	-Tools for milling
8207.8000	-车削工具	8	5	6.8	0	20	17	13	千克/件	B	-Tools for turning
	-其他可互换工具:										-Other interchangeable tools:
8207.9010	---带有天然或合成金刚石、立方氮化硼制的工作部件	8	5	6.8	0	20	17	13	千克/件		---With working part of natural or synthetic diamonds or cubic boron nitride
8207.9090	---其他	8	5	6.8	0	20	17	13	千克/件		---Other
82.08	**机器或机械器具的刀及刀片:**										**Knives and cutting blades, for machines or for mechanical appliances:**
8208.1000	-金属加工用	8	5		0	20	17	13	千克		-For metal working
8208.2000	-木器材加工用	8	5		0	20	17	13	千克		-For wood working
8208.3000	-厨房器具或食品工业机器用	8	5		0	20	17	13	千克	A	-For kitchen appliances or for machines used by the food industry
8208.4000	-农业、园艺或林业机器用	8	5		0	20	13	11	千克		-For agricultural, horticultural or forestry machines
8208.9000	-其他	8	5	7.2	0	20	17	13	千克		-Other

税则号列 Tariff Item.	货品名称	最惠国(%) MFN	协定(%)CT 东盟 CA	中巴 CP	中智 CC	普通 Gen	增值税率 VAT	出口退税 ED	计量单位 Unit	监管条件 SC	Article Description
82.09	**未装配的工具用金属陶瓷板、杆、刀头及类似品：**										**Plates, sticks, tips and the like for tools, unmounted, of cermets:**
8209.0000	未装配的工具用金属陶瓷板、杆、刀头及类似品	8	5	7.2	0	20	17	13	千克		Plates, sticks, tips and the like for tools, unmounted, of cermets
82.10	**用于加工或调制食品或饮料的手动机械器具，重量不超过10公斤：**										**Hand-operated mechanical appliances, weighing 10 kg or less, used in the preparation, conditioning or serving of food or drink:**
8210.0000	用于加工或调制食品或饮料的手动机械器具，重量不超过10公斤	18	8	16.2	14.4	80	17	13	千克	A	Hand-operated mechanical appliances, weighing 10 kg or less, used in the preparation, conditioning or serving of food or drink
82.11	**有刃口的刀及其刀片，不论是否有锯齿（包括整枝刀），但税目82.08的刀除外：**										**Knives with cutting blades, serrated or not (including pruning knives), other than knives of heading No. 82.08, and blades therefor:**
8211.1000	-成套货品	18	8	5	10.8	80	17	13	套		-Sets of assorted articles
	-其他：										-Other:
8211.9100	--刃面固定的餐刀	18	8	5	10.8	80	17	13	把	A	--Table knives having fixed blades
8211.9200	--刃面固定的其他刀	12	8	0	7.2	80	17	13	把		--Other knives having fixed blades
8211.9300	--可换刃面的刀	18	8	5	10.8	80	17	13	把		--Knives having other than fixed blades
8211.9400	--刀片	14	8	0	8.4	80	17	13	千克		--Blades
8211.9500	--贱金属制的刀柄	12	8	0	7.2	80	17	13	千克		--Handles of base metal
82.12	**剃刀及其刀片（包括未分开的刀片条）：**										**Razors and razor blades (including razor blade blanks in strips):**
8212.1000	-剃刀	12	8	0	0	80	17	13	把		-Razors
8212.2000	-安全刀片，包括未分开的刀片条	14	8	0	11.2	80	17	13	片		-Safety razor blades, including razor blade blanks in strips
8212.9000	-其他零件	12	8	0	7.2	80	17	13	千克		-Other parts
82.13	**剪刀、裁缝剪刀及类似品、剪刀片：**										**Scissors, tailors' shears and similar shears, and blades therefor:**
8213.0000	剪刀、裁缝剪刀及类似品、剪刀片	12	8	0	7.2	80	17	13	千克		Scissors, tailors' shears and similar shears, and blades therefor
82.14	**其他利口器（例如，理发推剪、屠刀、砍骨刀、切肉刀、切菜刀、裁纸刀）；修指甲及修脚用具（包括指甲锉）：**										**Other articles of cutlery (for example, hair clippers, butchers' or kitchen cleavers, choppers and mincing knives, paper knives); manicure or pedicure sets and instruments (including nail files):**
8214.1000	-裁纸刀、开信刀、改错刀、铅笔刀及其刀片	12	8	10.8	7.2	80	17	13	千克		-Paper knives, letter openers, erasing knives, pencil sharpeners and blades therefor
8214.2000	-修指甲及修脚用具（包括指甲锉）	18	8	16.2	14.4	90	17	13	千克		-Manicure or pedicure sets and instruments (including nail files)
8214.9000	-其他	18	8		10.8	80	17	13	千克		-Other
8214.9000 10	切菜刀等厨房用利口器	18				80	17	13	千克	A	Kitchen cleavers, choppers mincing knives and other articles of cutlery
8214.9000 90	理发推子等其他利口器	18				80	17	13	千克		Hair clippers and other articles of cutlery

税则号列 Tariff Item.	货 品 名 称	最惠国(%) MFN	协定(%)CT 东盟 CA	中巴 CP	中智 CC	普通 Gen	增值税率 VAT	出口退税 ED	计量单位 Unit	监管条件 SC	Article Description
82.15	**餐匙、餐叉、长柄勺、漏勺、糕点夹、鱼刀、黄油刀、糖块夹及类似的厨房或餐桌用具:**										**Spoons, forks, ladles, skimmers, cakeservers, fish-knives, butter-knives, sugar tongs and similar kitchen or tableware:**
8215.1000	-成套货品,至少其中一件物品是镀贵金属的	18	8	5	14.4	80	17	13	千克	A	-Sets of assorted articles containing at least one article plated with precious metal
8215.2000	-其他成套货品	18	8	5	10.8	80	17	13	千克	A	-Other sets of assorted articles
	-其他:										-Other:
8215.9100	--镀贵金属的	18	8	5	10.8	80	17	13	千克	A	--Plated with precious metal
8215.9900	--其他	18	8	5	14.4	80	17	13	千克	A	--Other

第八十三章
贱金属杂项制品

Chapter 83
Miscellaneous articles of base metal

注释：

一、在本章，贱金属零件应与制品一同归类。但税目73.12、73.15、73.17、73.18及73.20的钢铁制品或其他贱金属(第七十四章至第七十六章及第七十八章至第八十一章)制的类似物品不应视为本章制品的零件。

二、税目83.02所称"脚轮"，是指直径(对于有胎的，连胎计算在内，下同)不超过75毫米的或直径虽超过75毫米，但所装轮或胎的宽度必须小于30毫米的脚轮。

Notes:

1. For the purposes of this Chapter, parts of base metal are to be classified with their parent artcles. However, articles of iron or steel of heading Nos. 73.12, 73.15, 73.17, 73.18 or 73.20, or similar articles of other base metal (Chapters 74 to 76 and 78 to 81) are not to be taken as parts of articles of this Chapter.

2. For the purposes of heading No. 83.02, the word "castors" means those having a diameter (including, where appropriate, tyres) not exceeding 75mm, or those having a diameter (including, where appropriate, tyres) exceeding 75mm provided that the width of the wheel or tyre fitted thereto is less than 30mm.

税则号列 Tariff Item.	货品名称	最惠国(%) MFN	协定(%) 东盟 CA	协定(%) 中巴 CP	协定(%) 中智 CC	普通 Gen	增值税率 VAT	出口退税 ED	计量单位 Unit	监管条件 SC	Article Description
83.01	**贱金属制的锁(钥匙锁、数码锁及电动锁)；贱金属制带锁的扣环及扣环框架；上述锁的贱金属制钥匙：**										**Padlocks and locks (key, combination or electrically operated), of base metal; clasps and frames with clasps, incorporating locks, of base metal; keys for any of the foregoing articles, of base metal:**
8301.1000	-挂锁	14	T3		8.4	80	17	13	千克/把	B	-Padlocks
	-机动车用锁：										-Locks of a kind used for motor vehicles:
8301.2010	---中央控制门锁	10			0	80	17	13	千克/套		---Central controlled door lock
8301.2090	---其他	10			0	80	17	13	千克/套		---Other
8301.3000	-家具用锁	14	T3		8.4	80	17	13	千克/个	B	-Locks of a kind used for furniture
8301.4000	-其他锁	14	T3		11.2	80	17	13	千克/个	B	-Other locks
8301.5000	-带锁的扣环及扣环框架	14	8		8.4	80	17	13	千克		-Clasps and frames with clasps, incorporating locks
8301.6000	-零件	12	T3		7.2	80	17	13	千克		-Parts
8301.7000	-钥匙	10	5		0	80	17	13	千克		-Keys presented separately
83.02	**用于家具、门窗、楼梯、百叶窗、车厢、鞍具、衣箱、盒子及类似品的贱金属附件及架座；贱金属制帽架、帽钩、托架及类似品；用贱金属做支架的小脚轮；贱金属制的自动闭门器：**										**Base metal mountings, fittings and similar articles suitable for furniture, doors, staircases, windows, blinds, coachwork, saddlery, trunks, chests, caskets or the like; base metal hat-racks, hat-pegs, brackets and similar fixtures; castors with mountings of base metal; automatic door closers of base metal:**
8302.1000	-铰链(折叶)	10	5		8	80	17	13	千克		-Hinges
8302.2000	-小脚轮	12	8		9.6	80	17	13	千克		-Castors
8302.3000	-机动车辆用的其他附件及架座	10	5		0	80	17	13	千克		-Other mountings, fittings and similar articles suitable for motor vehicles
	-其他附件及架座：										-Other mountings, fittings and similar articles:
8302.4100	--建筑用	14	8		0	80	17	13	千克		--Suitable for buildings
8302.4200	--其他，家具用	12	8		9.6	80	17	13	千克		--Other, suitable for furniture

税则号列 Tariff Item.	货品名称	最惠国(%) MFN	协定(%) CT			普通 Gen	增值税率 VAT	出口退税 ED	计量单位 Unit	监管条件 SC	Article Description
			东盟 CA	中巴 CP	中智 CC						
8302.4900	--其他	12	8		0	80	17	13	千克		--Other
8302.5000	-帽架、帽钩、托架及类似品	14	8		11.2	80	17	13	千克		-Hat-racks, hat-pegs, brackets and similar fixtures
8302.6000	-自动闭门器	12	8		7.2	80	17	13	千克/个		-Automatic door closers
83.03	**装甲或加强的贱金属制保险箱、保险柜及保险库的门和带锁保险储存橱、钱箱、契约箱及类似品:**										**Armoured or reinforced safes, strong-boxes and doors and safe deposit lockers for strong-rooms, cash or deed boxes and the like, of base metal:**
8303.0000	装甲或加强的贱金属制保险箱、保险柜及保险库的门和带锁保险储存橱、钱箱、契约箱及类似品	14	8		11.2	50	17	13	千克		Armoured or reinforced safes, strong-boxes and doors and safe deposit lockers for strong-rooms, cash or deed boxes and the like, of base metal
83.04	**贱金属制的档案柜、卡片索引柜、文件盘、文件篮、笔盘、公章架及类似的办公用具,但税目94.03的办公室家具除外:**										**Filing cabinets, card-index cabinets, paper trays, paper rests, pen trays, office-stamp stands and similar office or desk equipment, of base metal, other than office furniture of heading No. 94.03:**
8304.0000	贱金属制的档案柜、卡片索引柜、文件盘、文件篮、笔盘、公章架及类似的办公用具,但税目94.03的办公室家具除外	10.5	8		6.3	80	17	13	千克		Filing cabinets, card-index cabinets, paper trays, paper rests, pen trays, office-stamp stands and similar office or desk equipment, of base metal, other than office furniture of heading No. 94.03
83.05	**活页夹、卷宗夹的贱金属附件,贱金属制的信夹、信角、文件夹、索引标签及类似的办公用品;贱金属制的成条钉书钉(例如,供办公室、室内装饰或包装用):**										**Fittings for loose-leaf binders or files, letter clips, letter corners, paper clips, indexing tags and similar office articles, of base metal; staples in strips (for example, for offices, upholstery, packaging), of base metal:**
8305.1000	-活页夹或卷宗夹的附件	10.5	8		8.4	80	17	13	千克		-Fittings for loose-leaf binders of files
8305.2000	-成条钉书钉	10.5	8		6.3	80	17	13	千克		-Staples in strips
8305.9000	-其他,包括零件	10.5	8		6.3	80	17	13	千克		-Other, including parts
83.06	**非电动的贱金属铃、钟、锣及类似品;贱金属雕塑像及其他装饰品;贱金属相框或画框及类似框架;贱金属镜子:**										**Bells, gongs and the like, non-electric, of base metal; statuettes and other ornaments, of base metal; photograph, picture or similar frames, of base metal; mirrors of base metal:**
8306.1000	-铃、钟、锣及类似品	8	5		0	80	17	13	千克		-Bells, gongs and the like
	-雕塑像及其他装饰品:										-Statuettes and other ornaments:
8306.2100	--镀贵金属的	8	5		0	100	17	13	千克		--Plated with precious metal
	-其他:										-Other:
8306.2910	---景泰蓝的	8	5		6.4	100	17	13	千克		---Cloisonne
8306.2990	---其他	8	T3		6.4	100	17	13	千克		---Other
8306.3000	-相框、画框及类似框架;镜子	8	5		0	100	17	13	千克		-Photograph, picture or similar frames; mirrors
83.07	**贱金属软管,不论是否有附件:**										**Flexible tubing of base metal, with or without fittings:**
8307.1000	-钢铁制	8.4	5		0	35	17	13	千克		-Of iron or steel
8307.9000	-其他贱金属制	8.4	5		0	35	17	13	千克		-Of other base metal

税则号列 Tariff Item.	货品名称	最惠国(%) MFN	协定(%) CT 东盟 CA	中巴 CP	中智 CC	普通 Gen	增值税率 VAT	出口退税 ED	计量单位 Unit	监管条件 SC	Article Description
83.08	**贱金属制的扣、钩、环、眼及类似品，用于衣着、鞋靴、天篷、提包、旅行用品或其他制品；贱金属制的管形铆钉及开口铆钉；贱金属制的珠子及亮晶片：**										**Clasps, frames with clasps, buckles, buckle-clasps, hooks, eyes, eyelets and the like, of base metal, of a kind used for clothing, footwear, awnings, handbags, travel goods or other made up articles; tubular or bifurcated rivets, of base metal; beads and spangles, of base metal:**
8308.1000	-钩、环及眼	10.5	8		6.3	80	17	13	千克		-Hooks, eyes and eyelets
8308.2000	-管形铆钉及开口铆钉	10.5	8		6.3	80	17	13	千克		-Tubular or bifurcated rivets
8308.9000	-其他，包括零件	10.5	8		6.3	80	17	13	千克		-Other, including parts
83.09	**贱金属制的塞子、盖子（包括冠形瓶塞、螺口盖及倒水塞）、瓶帽、螺口塞、塞子帽、封志及其他包装用附件：**										**Stoppers, caps and lids (including crown corks, screw caps and pouring stoppers), capsules for bottles, threaded bungs, bung covers, seals and other packing accessories, of base metal:**
8309.1000	-冠形瓶塞	18	8		10.8	90	17	13	千克		-Crown corks
8309.9000	-其他	12	8		9.6	80	17	13	千克		-Other
83.10	**贱金属制的标志牌、铭牌、地名牌及类似品、号码、字母及类似标志，但税目94.05的货品除外：**										**Sign-plates, name-plates, address-plates and similar plates, numbers, letters and other symbols, of base metal, excluding those of heading No. 94.05:**
8310.0000	贱金属制的标志牌、铭牌、地名牌及类似品、号码、字母及类似标志，但税目94.05的货品除外	18	8		10.8	80	17	13	千克		Sign-plates, name-plates, address-plates and similar plates, numbers, letters and other symbols, of base metal, excluding those of heading No. 94.05
83.11	**贱金属或硬质合金制的丝、条、管、板、电极及类似品，以焊剂涂面或以焊剂为芯，用于焊接或沉积金属、硬质合金；贱金属粉粘聚而成的丝或条，供金属喷镀用：**										**Wire, rods, tubes, plates, electrodes and similar products, of base metal or of metal carbides, coated or cored with flux material, of a kind used for soldering, brazing, welding or deposition of metal or of metal carbides; wire and rods, of agglomerated base metal powder, used for metal spraying:**
8311.1000	-以焊剂涂面的贱金属制电极，电弧焊用	8	5		6.4	30	17	13	千克		-Coated electrodes of base metal, for electric arc-welding
8311.2000	-以焊剂为芯的贱金属制焊丝，电弧焊用	8	5		0	30	17	13	千克		-Cored wire of base metal, for electric arc-welding
8311.3000	-以焊剂涂面或以焊剂为芯的贱金属条或丝，钎焊或气焊用	8	5		6.4	30	17	13	千克		-Coated rods and cored wire, of base metal, for soldering, brazing or welding by flame
8311.9000	-其他	8	5	5.6	6.4	30	17	13	千克		-Other

第十六类
机器、机械器具、电气设备及其零件；录音机及放声机、电视图像、声音的录制和重放设备及其零件、附件

注释：

一、本类不包括：

（一）第三十九章的塑料或税目40.10的硫化橡胶制的传动带、输送带；除硬质橡胶以外的硫化橡胶制的机器、机械器具、电气器具或其他专门技术用途的物品（税目40.16）；

（二）机器、机械器具或其他专门技术用途的皮革、再生皮革（税目42.05）或毛皮（税目43.03）的制品；

（三）各种材料（例如，第三十九章、第四十章、第四十四章、第四十八章及第十五类的材料）制的筒管、卷轴、纡子、锥形筒管、芯子、线轴及类似品；

（四）提花机及类似机器用的穿孔卡片（例如，归入第三十九章、第四十八章或第十五类的）；

（五）纺织材料制的传动带、输送带及带料（税目59.10）或专门技术用途的其他纺织材料制品（税目59.11）；

（六）税目71.02至71.04的宝石或半宝石（天然、合成或再造）或税目71.16的完全以宝石或半宝石制成的物品，但已加工未装配的唱针用蓝宝石和钻石除外（税目85.22）；

（七）第十五类注释二所规定的贱金属制通用零件（第十五类）及塑料制的类似品（第三十九章）；

（八）钻管（税目73.04）；

（九）金属丝、带制的环形带（第十五类）；

（十）第八十二章或第八十三章的物品；

（十一）第十七类的物品；

（十二）第九十章的物品；

（十三）第九十一章的钟、表及其他物品；

（十四）税目82.07的可互换工具及作为机器零件的刷子（税目96.03）；类似的可互换工具应按其构成工作部件的材料归类（例如，归入第四十章、第四十二章、第四十三章、第四十五章、第五十九章或税目68.04、69.09）；

SECTION XVI
MACHINERY AND MECHANICAL APPLIANCES; ELECTRICAL EQUIPMENT; PARTS THEREOF; SOUND RECORDERS AND REPRODUCERS, TELEVISION IMAGE AND SOUND RECORDERS AND REPRODUCERS, AND PARTS AND ACCESSORIES OF SUCH ARTICLES

Notes:

1. This Section does not cover:

(a) Transmission or conveyor belts or belting, of plastics of Chapter 39, or of vulcanized rubber (heading No. 40. 10); or other articles of a kind used in machinery or mechanical or electrical appliances or for other technical uses, of vulcanized rubber other than hard rubber (headingNo. 40. 16);

(b) Articles of leather or of composition leather (headingNo. 42. 05) or of furskin (headingNo. 43. 03), of a kind used in machinery or mechanical appliances or for other technical uses;

(c) Bobbins, spools, cops, cones, cores, reels or similar supports of any material (for example, Chapter 39, 40, 44 or 48 or Section XV);

(d) Perforated cards for Jacquard or similar machines (for example, Chapter 39 or 48 Section XV);

(e) Transmission or conveyor belts or belting of textile material (headingNo. 59. 10) or other articles of textile material for technical uses (headingNo. 59. 11);

(f) Precious or semi-precious stones (natural, synthetic or reconstructed) of headingsNos. 71. 02 to 71. 04, or articles wholly of such stones of heading 71. 16, except unmounted worked sapphires and diamonds for styli (headingNo. 85. 22);

(g) Parts of general use, as defined in Note 2 to Section XV, of base metal (Section XV), or similar goods of plastics (Chapter 39);

(h) Drill pipe (headingNo. 73. 04);

(i) Endless belts of metal wire or strip (Section XV);

(j) Articles of Chapter 82 or 83;

(k) Articles of Section XVII;

(l) Articles of Chapter 90;

(m) Clocks, watches or other articles of Chapter 91;

(n) Interchangeable tools of headingNo. 82. 07 or brushes of a kind used as parts of machines (heading 96. 03), similar interchangable tools are to be classified according to the material of working parts (for example, Chapter 40, 42, 43, 45, 59 or heading 68. 04, 69. 09);

（十五）第九十五章的物品。

（十六）打字机色带或类似色带，不论是否装轴或装盒（按其材料属性归类；如已上油或经其他方法处理能着色的，应归入税目96.12）。

二、除本类注释一、第八十四章注释一及第八十五章注释一另有规定的以外，机器零件（不属于税目84.84、85.44、85.45、85.46或85.47所列物品的零件）应按下列规定归类：

（一）凡在第八十四章、第八十五章的税目（税目84.09、84.31、84.48、84.66、84.73、84.87、85.03、85.22、85.29、85.38、85.48除外）列名的货品，均应归入该两章的相应税目；

（二）专用于或主要用于某一种机器或同一税目的多种机器（包括税目84.79或85.43的机器）的零件，应与该种机器一并归类，或酌情归入税目84.09、84.31、84.48、84.66、84.73、85.03、85.22、85.29、85.38。但能同时主要用于税目85.17和85.25至85.28所列机器的零件，应归入税目85.17；

（三）所有其他零件应酌情归入税目84.09、84.31、84.48、84.66、84.73、85.03、85.22、85.29或85.38，如不能归入上述税目，则应归入税目84.87或85.48。

三、由两部及两部以上机器装配在一起形成的组合式机器，或具有两种及两种以上互补或交替功能的机器，除条文另有规定的以外，应按具有主要功能的机器归类。

四、由不同独立部件（不论是否分开或由管道、传动装置、电缆或其他装置连接）组成的机器（包括机组），如果组合后明显具有一种第八十四章或第八十五章某个税号所列功能，则全部机器应按其功能归入有关税目。

五、上述各注释所称"机器"，是指第八十四章或第八十五章各税目所列的各种机器、设备、装置及器具。

第八十四章
核反应堆、锅炉、机器、机械器具及其零件

注释：

一、本章不包括：

（一）第六十八章的石磨、石碾及其他物品；

（二）陶瓷材料制的机器或器具（例如，泵）及供任何材料制的机器或器具用的陶瓷零件（第六十九章）；

(o) Articles of Chapter 95; or

(p) Typewriter or similar ribbons, whether or not on spools or in cartridges (classified according to their constituent material, or in heading 96.12 if inked or otherwise prepared for giving impressions).

2. Subject to Note 1 to this Section, Note 1 to Chapter 84 and Note 1 to Chapter 85, parts of machines (not being parts of the articles of headingNos. 84.84, 85.44, 85.45, 85.46 or 85.47) are to be classified according to the following rules:

(a) Parts which are goods included in any of the headings of Chapter 84 or 85 (other than headingsNos. 84.09, 84.31, 84.48, 84.66, 84.73, 84.87, 85.03, 85.22, 85.29, 85.38, and 85.48) are in all cases to be classified in their respective headings;

(b) Other parts, if suitable for use solely or principally with a particular kind of machine, or with a number of machines of the same heading (including machines of headingNos. 84.79 or 85.43) are to be classified with the machines of that kind or in headingNos. 84.09, 84.31, 84.48, 84.66, 84.73, 85.03, 85.22, 85.29 or 85.38 as appropriate. However, parts which are equally suitable for use principally with the goods of headingsNos. 85.17 and 85.25 to 85.28 are to be classified in headingNo. 85.17;

(c) All other parts are to be classified in headingNos. 84.09, 84.31, 84.48, 84.66, 84.73, 85.03, 85.22, 85.29 or 85.38 as appropriate or, failing that, in headingNo. 84.87 or 85.48.

3. Unless the context otherwise requires, composite machines consisting of two or more machines fitted together to form a whole and other machines adapted for the purpose of performing two or more complementary or alternative functions are to be classified as if consisting only of that component or as being that machine which performs the principal function.

4. Where a machine (including a combination of machines) consists of individual components (whether separate or interconnected by piping, by transmission devices, by electric cables or by other devices) intended to contribute together to a clearly defined function covered by one of the headings in Chapter 84 or Chapter 85, then the whole falls to be classified in the heading appropriate to that function.

5. For the purposes of these Notes, the expression "machine" means any machine, machinery, plant, equipment, apparatus or appliance cited in the headings of Chapter 84 or 85.

Chapter 84
Nuclear reactors, boilers, machinery and mechanical appliances; parts thereof

Notes:

1. This Chapter does not cover:

(a) Millstones, grindstones or other articles of Chapter 68;

(b) Machinery or appliances (for example, pumps) of ceramic material and ceramic parts of machinery or appliances of any material (Chapter 69);

（三）实验室用玻璃器（税目70.17）；玻璃制的机器、器具或其他专门技术用途的物品及其零件（税目70.19或70.20）；

（四）税目73.21或73.22的物品或其他贱金属制的类似物品（第七十四章至第七十六章或第七十八章至第八十一章）；

（五）税目85.08的真空吸尘器。

（六）税目85.09的家用电动器具；或税目85.25的数字照相机；

（七）非机动的手工操作地板清扫器（税目96.03）。

二、除第十六类注释三及本章注释九另有规定的以外，如果某种机器或器具既符合税目84.01至84.24或税目84.46中一个或几个税目的规定，又符合税目84.25至84.80中一个或几个税目的规定，则应酌情归入税目84.01至84.24或税目84.86中的相应税目，而不归入税目84.25至84.80中的有关税目。

但税目84.19不包括：

（一）催芽装置、孵卵器或育雏器（税目84.36）；

（二）谷物调湿机（税目84.37）；

（三）萃取糖汁的浸提装置（税目84.38）；

（四）纱线、织物及纺织制品的热处理机器（税目84.51）；

（五）温度变化（即使必不可少）仅作为辅助功能的机器设备。

税目84.22不包括：

（一）缝合袋子或类似品用的缝纫机（税目84.52）；

（二）税目84.72的办公室用机器。

税目84.24不包括：

喷墨印刷（打印）机器（税目84.43）。

三、如果用于加工各种材料的某种机床既符合税目84.56的规定，又符合税目84.57、84.58、84.59、84.60、84.61、84.64或84.65的规定，则应归入税目84.56。

四、税目84.57仅适用于可以完成下列不同形式机器操作的金属加工机床，但车床（包括车削中心）除外：

（一）按照机械加工程序从刀具库中自动更换刀具（加工中心）；

（二）同时或顺序地自动使用不同的动力头对固定不动的工件进行加工（单工位组合机床）；

（三）自动将工件送向不同的动力头（多工位组合机床）。

五、（一）税目84.71所称"自动数据处理设备"，是指：具有如下功能的机器：

(c) Laboratory glassware (headingNo. 70. 17); machinery, appliances or other articles for technical uses or parts thereof, of glass (headingNos. 70. 19 or 70. 20);

(d) Articles of headingNos. 73. 21 or 73. 22 or similar articles of other base metals (ChaptersNos. 74 to 76 or 78 to 81);

(e) Vacuum cleaners of heading No. 85. 08

(f) Electro-mechanical domestic appliances of headingNo. 85. 09; or digital cameras of headingNo. 85. 25; or

(g) Hand-operated mechanical floor sweepers, not motorized (heading 96. 03).

2. Subject to the operation of Note 3 and Note 9 to Section XVI and IX, a machine or appliance which answers to a description in one or more of the headingsNos. 84. 01 to 84. 24 and 84. 46 and at the same time to a description in one or other of the headingsNos. 84. 25 to 84. 80 is to be classified under the appropriate heading of the former group and not the latter.

HeadingNo. 84. 19 does not, however, cover:

(a) Germination plant, incubators or brooders (headingNo. 84. 36);

(b) Grain dampening machines (headingNo. 84. 37);

(c) Diffusing apparatus for sugar juice extraction (headingNo. 84. 38);

(d) Machinery for the heat-treatment of textile yarns, fabrics or made up textile articles (headingNoj. 84. 51); or

(e) Machinery or plant, designed for mechanical operation, in which a change of temperature, even if necessary, is subsidiary.

HeadingNo. 84. 22 does not cover:

(a) Sewing machines for closing bags or similar containers (headingNo. 84. 52); or

(b) Office machinery of headingNo. 84. 72.

HeadingNo. 84. 24 does not cover:

Ink-jet printing machines (headingNo. 84. 43).

3. A machine-tool for working any material which answers to a description in headingNo. 84. 56 and at the same time to a description in headingNos. 84. 57, 84. 58, 84. 59, 84. 60, 84. 61, 84. 64 or 84. 65 is to be classified in headingNo. 84. 56.

4. HeadingNo. 84. 57 applies only to machine-tools for working metal other than lathes (including turning centres), which can carry out different types of machining operations either:

(a) by automatic tool change from a magazine or the like in conformity with a machining programme (machining centres),

(b) by the automatic use, simultaneously or sequentially, of different unit heads working on a fixed position workpiece (unit construction machines, single station), or

(c) by the automatic transfer of the workpiece to different unit heads (multi-station transfer machines).

5. (A) For the purposes of headingNo. 84. 71, the expression "automatic data processing machines" are have the as follow functional machine:

1. 存储处理程序和执行程序直接需要的起码的数据；

(a) Storing the processing program or programs and at least the data immediately necessary for the execution of the program;

2. 按照用户的要求随意编辑程序；

(b) being freely programmed in accordance with the requirements of the user;

3. 按照用户指令进行算术计算；以及

(c) performing arthmetical computations specified by the user; and,

4. 在运行过程中，可不需人为干预而通过逻辑判断，执行一个处理程序，这个处理程序可改变计算机指令的执行。

(d) executing, without human intervention, a processing program which requires them to modify their execution, by logical decision during the processing run;

(二) 自动数据处理设备可以是一套由若干单独部件所组成的系统。

(B) Automatic data processing machines may be in the form of systems consisting of a variable number of separate units.

(三) 除本条注释(四及五)另有规定以外，一个部件如果符合下列所有规定，即可视为自动数据处理系统的一部分：

(C) Separately presented units of an automatic data processing machine are to be classified in headingNo. 84. 71.

1. 专用于或主要用于自功数据处理系统；

(a) It is of a kind solehy or praincipally used in an automatic doea processing system;

2. 可以直接或通过一个或几个其他部件同中央处理器相联接；

(b) It is connectable to the central processing unit either directly or through one or more other units;

3. 能够以本系统所使用的方式(代码或信号)接收或传送数据。自动数据处理设备的部件如果单独报验，应归入税目84.71 但是，键盘、X－Y 坐标输入装罩及盘(片)或存储部件，只要符合上述注释(三)2 及(三)3 所列的规定，应一律作为税目 84.71 的部件归类；

(c) Able to receive or transmit data through our system (code or message). The elements and parts of automatic data processing facilities examined separately shall be classified into heading No. 84. 71. However, keyboards, the input cover of X – Y coordinate and disks (chips) or storage parts, as long as conforming to the stipulations in the Note (III) afore, shall all be classified into heading No. 84. 71 ;

(四) 税目 84.71 不包括单独报检的下述设备，即使它们符合上述注释五(三)的所有规定：

(D) Printers, keyboards, X-Y co-ordinate input devices and disk storage units which satisfy the conditions of paragraphs (B) (b) and (B) (c) above, are in all cases to be classified as units of headingNo. 84. 71.

1. 打印机、复印机、传真机，不论是否组合成；

(a) Printers, photocopiers, fax machines, no matter whether how they are assembled,

2. 发送或接收声音、图像或其他数据的设备，包括无线或有线网络(例如，局域网或广域网)通信设备；

(b) Facilities that transmit or receive voice, pictures or other data, including wireless or wired network (such as, LAN or Wide Area Network)

3. 扬声器及传声器(麦克风)；

(c) Speaker and microphone

4. 电视摄像机、数字照相机及视频摄录一体机；

(d) Television camera, digital cemera and DV CAM

5. 监视器及投影机，未装有电视接收的装冒。

(e) Monitor and projector, without TV receivers

(五) 装有自动数据处理设备或与自动数据处理设备连接使用，但却从事数据处理以外的某项专门功能的机器，应按其功能归入相应的税目，对于无法按功能归类的，应归入未列名税目。

(E) Machines performing a specific function other than data processing and incorporating or working in conjunction with an automatic data processing machine are to be classified in the headings appropriate to their respective functions or, failing that, in residual headings.

六、税目 84.82 还包括最大直径及最小直径与标称直径相差均不超过 1% 或 0.05 毫米(以相差数值较小的为准)的抛光钢珠，其他钢珠归入税目 73.26。

6. HeadingNo. 84. 82 applies, *inter alia*, to polished steel balls, the maximum and minimum diameters of which do not differ from the nominal diameter by more than 1% or by more than 0. 05mm, whichever is less. Other steel balls are to be classified in headingNo. 73. 26.

七、具有一种以上用途的机器在归类时，其主要用途可作为唯一的用途对待。除本章注释二、第十六类注释三另有规定的以外，凡任何税目都未列明其主要用途的机器，以及没有哪一种用途是主要用途的机器，均应归入税目 84.79。税目 84.79 还包括将金属丝、纺织纱线或其他各种材料以及它们的混合材料制成绳、缆的机器(例如，捻股机、绞扭机、制缆机)。

八、税目 84.70 所称"袖珍式"，仅适用于外形尺寸不超过 170 毫米×100 毫米×45 毫米的机器。

九、(一)第八十五章注释八(一)及八(二)同样适用于本注释及税目 84.86 中所称"半导体器件"及"集成电路"。但是，本条注释及税目 84.86 所称"半导体器件"，也包括光敏半导体器件及发光二极管。

(二)本条注释及税目 84.86 所称"平板显示器的制造"，包括将各层基片制造平板，但不包括玻璃的制造或将印刷电路板或其他电子元件装配在平板上。所称"平板显示"不包括阴极射线管技术。

(三)税目 84.86 也包括下列机器及装置，其专用或主要用于：

1. 制造或修补掩膜版及刻线；
2. 组装半导体器件或集成电路；及
3. 升降、搬运、装卸单晶柱、圆片、半导体器件、集成电路及平板显示器。

(四)除十六类注释一及第八十四章注释一另有规定的以外，符合税目 84.86 规定的机器及装置，应归入该税目而不归入本目录的其他税目。

子目注释：

一、子目 8471.49 所称"系统"，是指各部件符合第八十四章注释五(三)所列条件，并且至少由一个中央处理部件、一个输入部件(例如，键盘或扫描器)和一个输出部件(例如，视频显示器或打印机)组成的自动数据处理设备。

二、子目 8482.40 仅包括滚柱直径相同，最大不超过 5 毫米，且长度至少是直径三倍的圆滚柱轴承，滚柱的两端可以磨圆。

7. A machine which is used for more than one purpose is, for the purposes of classification, to be treated as if its principal purpose were its sole purpose. Subject to Note 2 to this Chapter and Note 3 to Section XVI, a machine, the principal purpose of which is not described in any heading or for which no one purpose is the principal purpose, unless the context otherwise requires, is to be classified in headingNo. 84.79. HeadingNo. 84.79 also covers machines for making rope or cable (for example, stranding, twisting or cabling machines) from metal wire, textile yarn or any other material or from a combination of such materials.

8. For the purposes of headingNo. 84.70, the term "pocket-size" applies only to machines the dimensions of which do not exceed 170mm×100mm×45mm.

9 (1) Notes VIII(I) and VIII(II) of Chapter 85 also apply to this note and "semiconductor parts" and "integrated circuit" as mentioned in heading No. 84.86. However, the "semiconductor parts" in this note and heading No. 84.8 include photosensitive semiconductor parts and LBD.

(2) The "the production of flat panel monitor" as mentioned in this note and heading No. 84.86 includes producing flat panel using various levels of chips, but excludes production of glasses or assembling of the print circuit board or other electronic parts on the flat panel. The "flat panel display" does not include CRT technique.

(3) Heading No. 84.86 includes the following machines and equipments. They are especially or mainly used for:

a. producing or repairing reticles
b. Assemble semiconductor parts or integrated circuit, and
c. ascend or descend, transport, move, load and unload the single crystal column, wafer, semiconductor parts, integrated circuits and flat panel monitor.

(4) Except otherwise prescribed as in Note (I) of Item 16 and Note (I) of Chapter 84, all the machines and equipments that comply to the stipulations of heading No. 84.86 shall be categorized into this tax item but not other items of this catalog.

Subheading Notes:

1. For the purposes of subheadingNo. 8471.49, the term "systems" means automatic data processing machines whose units satisfy the conditions laid down in Note 5 (B) to Chapter 84 and which comprise at least a central processing unit, one input unit (e.g., a keyboard or a scanner), and one output unit (e.g., a visual display unit or a printer).

2. SubheadingNo. 8482.40 applies only to bearings with cylindrical rollers of a uniform diameter not exceeding 5mm and having a length which is at least three times the diameter. The ends of the rollers may be rounded.

税则号列 Tariff Item.	货品名称	最惠国(%) MFN	协定(%)CT 东盟 CA	中巴 CP	中智 CC	普通 Gen	增值税率 VAT	出口退税 ED	计量单位 Unit	监管条件 SC	Article Description
84.01	**核反应堆;核反应堆的未辐照燃料元件(释热元件);同位素分离机器及装置:**										**Nuclear reactors; fuel elements (cartridges), non-irradiated, for nuclear reactors; machinery and apparatus for isotopic separation:**
8401.1000	-核反应堆	2			0	8	17	13	千克	3	-Nuclear reactors
8401.2000	-同位素分离机器、装置及其零件	1			0	8	17	13	千克	3	-Machinery and apparatus for isotopic separation, and parts thereof
	-未辐照燃料元件(释热元件):										-Fuel elements (cartridges), non-irradiated:
8401.3010	---未辐照燃料元件	2			0	8	17	13	千克		---Fuel elements, non-irrdadiated
8401.3090	---未辐照燃料元件的零件	1			0	8	17	13	千克		---Parts for fuel elements non-irradiated
	-核反应堆零件:										-Parts of nuclear reactors:
8401.4010	---未辐照相关组件	1			0	8	17	13	千克		---Non-irradiated Associated Assembly
8401.4020	---堆内构件	1			0	8	17	13	千克	3	---Reactor internals
8401.4090	---其他	1			0	8	17	13	千克		---Other
8401.4090 10	核反应堆压力容器(包括其顶板)(专门设计或制造来用于容纳核反应堆的堆芯)	1				8	17	13	千克	3	Pressure containers (including end plate), specially designed and manufactured for reactor core
8401.4090 20	核反应堆控制棒和设备(专用于核反应堆裂变控制棒、支承结构或悬吊结构等)	1				8	17	13	千克	3	Control rods and reactivity control devices of nuclear reactors (fission control rod and support and suspension structures thereof, specified for nuclear reactors)
8401.4090 30	核反应堆压力管(专用于容纳核燃料元件和一次冷却剂的,压力>5.1MPa)	1				8	17	13	千克	3	Pressure tubes of nuclear reactors (specified for holding fuel elements or primary coolants, pressure>5.1MPa)
8401.4090 90	其他核反应堆零件	1				8	17	13	千克		Other parts of nuclear reactors
84.02	**蒸汽锅炉(能产生低压水蒸汽的集中供暖用的热水锅炉除外);过热水锅炉:**										**Steam or other vapour generating boilers (other than central heating hot water boilers capable also of producting low pressure steam); super-heated water boilers:**
	-蒸汽锅炉:										-Steam or other vapour generating boilers:
	--蒸发量超过45吨/时的水管锅炉:										--Watertube boilers with a steam production exceeding 45t per hour:
8402.1110	---蒸发量在900吨/时及以上的发电用锅炉	3		2.5	1.8	11	17	17	台/千克	6AB	---Boilers for generating electricity with a steam production 900t or more per hour
8402.1190	---其他	14	8	13.3	11.2	35	17	17	台/千克	6OAB	---Other
8402.1200	--蒸发量不超过45吨/时的水管锅炉	5		3.9	0	35	17	17	台/千克		--Watertube boilers with a steam production not exceeding 45t per hour
8402.1200 10	纸浆厂废料锅炉(蒸发≤45吨/时蒸汽水管锅炉)	5				35	17	17	台/千克	6OAB	Waster boilers for pulp plant
8402.1200 90	其他蒸发量未超45吨/时水管锅炉	5				35	17	17	台/千克	6OAB	Other watertube boilers, steam production≤45t/h

税则号列 Tariff Item.	货品名称	最惠国(%) MFN	协定(%)CT 东盟 CA	中巴 CP	中智 CC	普通 Gen	增值税率 VAT	出口退税 ED	计量单位 Unit	监管条件 SC	Article Description
8402.1900	--其他蒸汽锅炉，包括混合式锅炉	5			0	35	17	17	台/千克	6OAB	--Other vapour generating boilers, including hybrid boilers
8402.2000	-过热水锅炉	16	8		9.6	35	17	17	台/千克	6OAB	-Super-heated water boilers
8402.9000	-零件	2			0	11	17	17	千克		-Parts
84.03	**集中供暖用的热水锅炉，但税目84.02的货品除外：**										**Central heating boilers other than those of headingNo. 84.02:**
8403.1010	---家用型	10	5	9.5	0	80	17	13	台	6OAB	---Household type
8403.1090	---其他	10	5	9.5	0	80	17	13	台	6OAB	---Other
8403.9000	-零件	6	5		0	80	17	13	千克		-Parts
84.04	**税目84.02或84.03所列锅炉的辅助设备(例如，节热器、过热器、除灰器、气体回收器)；水蒸汽或其他蒸汽动力装置的冷凝器：**										**Auxiliary plant for use with boilers of headingNo. 84.02 or 84.03 (for example, economizers, super-heaters, soot removers, gas recoverers); condensers for steam or other vapour power units:**
	-税目84.02或84.03所列锅炉的辅助设备：										-Auxiliary plant for use with boilers of headingNo. 84.02 or 84.03:
8404.1010	---税目84.02所列锅炉的辅助设备	7	5	3.5	0	35	17	17	千克	6OBA	---For use with boilers of headingNo. 84.02
8404.1020	---税目84.03所列锅炉的辅助设备	10	5	5	0	80	17	13	千克	6BA	---For use with boilers of headingNo. 84.03
8404.2000	-水蒸汽或其他蒸汽动力装置的冷凝器	14	8		8.4	35	17	17	千克	6OBA	-Condensers for steam or other vapour power units
	-零件：										-Parts:
8404.9010	---子目8404.1020所列设备的零件	10	5	0	0	80	17	13	千克		---Of the auxiliary plant of subheadingNo. 8404.1020
8404.9090	---其他	7	5	0	0	35	17	13	千克		---Other
84.05	**煤气发生器，不论有无净化器；乙炔发生器及类似的水解气体发生器，不论有无净化器：**										**Producer gas or water gas generators, with or without their purifiers; acetylene gas generators and similar water process gas generators, with or without their purifiers:**
8405.1000	-煤气发生器，不论有无净化器；乙炔发生器及类似的水解气体发生器，不论有无净化器	14	8		11.2	30	17	17	千克	BA	-Producer gas or water gas generators, with or without their purifiers; acetylene gas generators and similar water process gas generators, with or without their purifiers
8405.9000	-零件	8	5		0	30	17	17	千克		-Parts
84.06	**汽轮机：**										**Steam turbines and other vapour turbines:**
8406.1000	-船舶动力用汽轮机	5			0	35	17	17	台/千瓦		-Turbines for marine propulsion
	-其他汽轮机：										-Other turbines:
	--输出功率超过40兆瓦的：										--Of an output exceeding 40 MW:
8406.8110	---输出功率不超过100兆瓦的	5			0	35	17	17	台/千瓦	O	---Of an output not exceeding 100 MW
8406.8120	---输出功率超过100兆瓦，但不超过350兆瓦的	5			0	35	17	17	台/千瓦	O	---Of an output exceeding 100 MW but not exceeding 350 MW
8406.8130	---输出功率超过350兆瓦的	6	5		0	11	17	17	台/千瓦	O	---Of an output exceeding 350 MW
8406.8200	--输出功率不超过40兆瓦的	5			0	35	17	17	台/千瓦	O	--Of an output not exceeding 40 MW
8406.9000	-零件	2			0	11	17	13	千克		-Parts

税则号列 Tariff Item.	货品名称	最惠国(%) MFN	协定(%)CT 东盟 CA	中巴 CP	中智 CC	普通 Gen	增值税率 VAT	出口退税 ED	计量单位 Unit	监管条件 SC	Article Description
84.07	**点燃往复式或旋转式活塞内燃发动机:**										**Spark-ignition reciprocating or rotary internal combustion piston engines:**
	-航空器发动机:										-Aircraft engines:
8407.1010	---输出功率不超过298千瓦	2			0	11	17	17	台/千瓦	6	---Of an output not exceeding 298kW
8407.1020	---输出功率超过298千瓦	2			0	11	17	13	台/千瓦	6	---Of an output exceeding 298kW
	-船舶发动机:										-Marine propulsion engines:
8407.2100	--舷外发动机	8	T3		0	35	17	13	台/千瓦	6	--Outboard motors
8407.2900	--其他	8	5		0	20	17	13	台/千瓦	6	--Other
	-用于第八十七章所列车辆的往复式活塞发动机:										-Reciprocating piston engines of a kind used for the propulsion of vehicles of Chapter 87:
8407.3100	--气缸容量(排气量)不超过50毫升	10	5		0	35	17	13	台/千瓦	y4xAB6	--Of a cylinder capacity not exceeding 50cc
8407.3200	--气缸容量(排气量)超过50毫升,但不超过250毫升	10	5		0	35	17	13	台/千瓦	y4xAB6	--Of a cylinder capacity exceeding 50cc but not exceeding 250cc
8407.3300	--气缸容量(排气量)超过250毫升,但不超过1000毫升	10			6	70	17	13	台/千瓦	ABO6	--Of a cylinder capacity exceeding 250cc but not exceeding 1000cc
	--气缸容量(排气量)超过1000毫升:										--Of a cylinder capacity exceeding 1000cc:
8407.3410	---气缸容量(排气量)超过1000毫升,但不超过3000毫升	10		7	0	70	17	17	台/千瓦	AB6O	---Of a cylinder capacity exceeding 1000cc but not exceeding 3000cc
8407.3420	---气缸容量(排气量)超过3000毫升	10		7	0	35	17	17	台/千瓦		---Of a cylinder capacity exceeding 3000cc
8407.3420 10	排气量≥5.9升的天然气发动机(第87章所列车辆用的点燃往复式活塞发动机)	10				35	17	17	台/千瓦	AB6O	Spark-ignition reciprocating piston engines of a kind used the propulsion of vehicles of chapter 87, natrual gas engine, cylinder capacity≥5900cc
8407.3420 90	其他超3000cc车用往复式活塞引擎(第87章所列车辆用的点燃往复式活塞发动机)	10				35	17	17	台/千瓦	AB6O	Spark-ignition reciprocating piston engines of a kind used the propulsion of vehicles of chapter 87, cylinder capacity > 3000cc
	-其他发动机:										-Other engines:
8407.9010	---沼气发动机	12	8		0	35	17	13	台/千瓦	6	---Biogas engines
8407.9090	---其他	18	8		0	35	17	17	台/千瓦		---Other
8407.9090 01	转速 < 3600r/min 汽油发动机(发动机用)	18				35	17	17	台/千瓦	O6	Petrol engines, rotational speed < 3600 r/min
8407.9090 02	转速 < 4650r/min 汽油发动机(税号8426-8430所列工程机械用)	18				35	17	17	台/千瓦	O6	Petrol engines, rotational speed < 4650 r/min, of a kind used the engineering machinery of headingNo. 8426 - 8430
8407.9090 90	其他往复或旋转式活塞内燃引擎(非第87章所列车辆用其他点燃往复式或旋转式活塞发动机)	18				35	17	17	台/千瓦	O6	Other spark-ignition reciprocating or rotary internal combustion piston engines, not for vehicles falling in Chapter 87
84.08	**压燃式活塞内燃发动机(柴油或半柴油发动机):**										**Compression-ignition internal combustion piston engines (diesel or semi-diesel engines):**
8408.1000	-船舶发动机	5		2.5	4	11	17	17	台/千瓦	BO6	-Marine propulsion engines
	-用于第八十七章所列车辆的发动机:										-Engines of a kind used for the propulsion of vehicles of Chapter 87:

税则号列 Tariff Item.	货品名称	最惠国(%) MFN	协定(%)CT 东盟 CA	中巴 CP	中智 CC	普通 Gen	增值税率 VAT	出口退税 ED	计量单位 Unit	监管条件 SC	Article Description
8408.2010	---输出功率在132.39千瓦(180马力)及以上	9		6.3	7.2	14		17	台/千瓦		---Of an output of 132.39kw (180h.p.) or more
8408.2010 01	输出功率在441千瓦及以上的柴油机动机(600马力)	9				14	13	17	台/千瓦	OB6	Diesel engines of a kind used the propulsion of tractors of heading 87.01, output≥132.39kw
8408.2010 10	功率≥132.39kw拖拉机用柴油机	9				14	13	17	台/千瓦	OB6	Diesel engines of a kind used the propulsion of tractors of heading 87.01, output≥132.39kw
8408.2010 90	功率≥132.39kw其他用柴油机[指87章车辆用压燃式活塞内燃发动机(132.39kw=180马力)]	9				14	17	17	台/千瓦	OB6	Compression-ignition internal combustion piston engines of a kind used the propulsion of vehicles of chapter 87, output≥132.39kw
8408.2090	---其他	25		17.5	20	35		17	台/千瓦		---Other
8408.2090 01	额定功率<100kw柴油发动机(轿车用)	25				35	17	17	台/千瓦	aOB6	Diesel engines of motor cars, rated power<100kw
8408.2090 10	功率<132.39kw拖拉机用柴油机	25				35	13	11	台/千瓦	aOB6	Diesel engines of a kind used the propulsion of tractors of chapter 87, output<132.39kw
8408.2090 90	功率<132.39kw其他用柴油机(指第87章车辆用压燃式活塞内燃发动机)	25				35	17	17	台/千瓦	aOB6	Compression-ignition internal combustion piston engines of a kind used the propulsion of vehicles of chapter 87, output<132.39kw, diesel engine
	-其他发动机:										-Other engines:
8408.9010	---机车发动机	6	T3	5.4	4.8	11	17	17	台/千瓦	BO6	---Locomotive engines
	---其他:										---Other:
8408.9091	----输出功率不超过14千瓦	5		4.5	4	35		11	台/千瓦		----Of an output not exceeding 14kw
8408.9091 11	功率≤14kw农业用单缸柴油机[非87章车辆用压燃式活塞内燃发动机(14kw=19.05马力)]	5				35	13	11	台/千瓦	aB6	Single-cylinder diesel engines for agricultural use, output ≤ 14kw (19.05H.P.), other than compression-ignition internal combustion piston engines of a kind used the propulsion of vehicles of chapter 87
8408.9091 19	功率≤14kw农业用柴油发动机[非87章车辆用压燃式活塞内燃发动机(14kw=19.05马力)]	5				35	13	11	台/千瓦	aB6	Other diesel engines for agricultural use, output≤14kw (19.05H.P.), other than compression-ignition internal combustion piston engines of a kind used the propulsion of vehicles of chapter 87
8408.9091 91	功率≤14kw其他用单缸柴油机[非87章车辆用压燃式活塞内燃发动机(14kw=19.05马力)]	5				35	17	11	台/千瓦	aB6	Single-cylinder diesel engines, for other use, output≤14kw (19.05H.P.), other than compression-ignition internal combustion piston engines of a kind used the propulsion of vehicles of chapter 87

税则号列 Tariff Item.	货品名称	最惠国(%) MFN	协定(%)CT 东盟 CA	协定(%)CT 中巴 CP	协定(%)CT 中智 CC	普通 Gen	增值税率 VAT	出口退税 ED	计量单位 Unit	监管条件 SC	Article Description
8408.9091 99	功率≤14kw 其他用柴油发动机[非 87 章车辆用压燃式活塞内燃发动机(14kw=19.05 马力)]	5				35	17	11	台/千瓦	aB6	Other diesel engines of a kind used the other purpose, output ≤ 14kw (19.05H.P.), other than compression-ignition internal combustion piston engines of a kind used the propulsion of vehicles of chapter 87
8408.9092	----输出功率超过 14 千瓦,但小于 132.39 千瓦(180 马力)	8.4	5	7.6	6.7	35		11	台/千瓦		----Of an output exceeding 14kw but not exceeding 132.39kw(180H.P.)
8408.9092 10	转速<4650r/min 柴油发动机(税号 8426－8430 所列工程机械用)	8.4				35	17	17	台/千瓦	aOB6	Diesel engine, rotational speed < 4650 r/min, of a kind used the engineering machinery of heading 8426 to 8430)
8408.9092 20	14kw<功率<132.39kw 的农业用柴油机[非 87 章车辆用压燃式活塞内燃发动机(1kw=1.36 马力)]	8.4				35	13	17	台/千瓦	aB6	Diesel engine of a kind used the agricutural purpose, 14kw < output < 132.39kw, not for vehicles falling in Chapter 87 (1kw=1.36H.P.)
8408.9092 90	14kw<功率<132.39kw 的其他用柴油机[非 87 章车辆用压燃式活塞内燃发动机(1kw=1.36 马力)]	8.4				35	17	17	台/千瓦	aOB6	Diesel engine of a kind used the other purpose, 14kw < output < 132.39kw, not for vehicles falling in Chapter 87 (1kw=1.36H.P.)
8408.9093	----输出功率在 132.39 千瓦(180 马力)及以上	5		4.5	4	14		17	台/千瓦		----Of an output of 132.39kw (180H.P.) or more
8408.9093 10	功率≥132.39kw 的农业用柴油机[非 87 章用压燃式活塞内燃发动机(132.39kw=180 马力)]	5				14	13	17	台/千瓦	B6	Diesel engine of a kind used the agricutural purpose, output ≥ 132.39kw (180H.P.), not for vehicles falling in Chapter 87
8408.9093 90	功率≥132.39kw 其他用柴油发动机[非 87 章用压燃式活塞内燃发动机(132.39kW=180 马力)]	5				14	17	17	台/千瓦	OB6	Diesel engine for other use, output≥132.39kw, not for vehicles falling in Chapter 87
84.09	**专用于或主要用于税目 84.07 或 84.08 所列发动机的零件:**										**Parts suitable for use solely or principally with the engines of headingNo. 84.07 or 84.08:**
8409.1000	-航空器发动机用	2			0	11	17	13	千克		-For aircraft engines
	-其他:										-Other:
	--专用于或主要用于点燃式活塞内燃发动机的:										--Suitable for use solely or principally with spark-ignition internal combustion piston engines:
8409.9110	---船舶发动机用	6	T3	4.2	0	17	17	13	千克		---For marine propulsion engines
	---其他:										---Other:
8409.9191	----电控燃油喷射装置	5		3.5	0	35	17	17	千克/套	O	----Electric fuel injection devices
8409.9199	----其他	5		3.5	0	35	17	17	千克		----Other
8409.9199 20	废气再循环(EGR)装置(专用或主要用于内燃发动机)	5				35	17	17	千克	a	Exhaust gas recycling device (EGR)

税则号列 Tariff Item.	货品名称	最惠国(%) MFN	协定(%) 东盟 CA	协定(%) 中巴 CP	CT 中智 CC	普通 Gen	增值税率 VAT	出口退税 ED	计量单位 Unit	监管条件 SC	Article Description
8409.9199 30	连杆(专用或主要用于内燃发动机)	5				35	17	17	千克	a	Links (connecting rods)
8409.9199 40	喷嘴(专用或主要用于内燃发动机)	5				35	17	17	千克	a	Jets (nozzles)
8409.9199 50	气门摇臂(专用或主要用于内燃发动机)	5				35	17	17	千克	a	Rocker arms (valve rockers)
8409.9199 90	其他点燃式活塞内燃发动机用零件	5				35	17	17	千克	a	Other parts suitable for use solely or principally with spark-ignition internal combustion piston engines
	--其他:										--Other:
8409.9910	---船舶发动机用	5		4.5	4	11	17	13	千克		---For marine propulsion engines
8409.9920	---机车发动机用	2		1.5	0	11	17	13	千克	a	---For locomotive engines
	---其他:										---Other:
8409.9991	----输出功率在132.39千瓦(180马力)及以上的发动机用	2		1.5	0	11	17	17	千克		----For engines with an output of 132.39kW (180H.P.) or more
8409.9999	----其他	8.4	T3	8	6.7	35	17	17	千克		----Other
8409.9999 01	电控柴油喷射装置(指编号8408所列的其他发动机用)	8.4				35	17	17	千克	Oa	Electric fuel injection devices, suitable for the engines of heading 8408
8409.9999 90	其他发动机的专用零件(指编号8407或8408所列的其他发动机用)	8.4				35	17	17	千克	a	Other parts suitable for solely with the engines, not elsewhere specified or included
84.10	**水轮机、水轮及其调节器:**										**Hydraulic turbines, water wheels, and regulators therefor:**
	-水轮机及水轮:										-Hydraulic turbines and water wheels:
8410.1100	--功率不超过1000千瓦	10	5		0	35	17	17	台		--Of a power not exceeding 1000kW
8410.1200	--功率超过1000千瓦,但不超过10000千瓦	10	8		0	35	17	17	台		--Of a power exceeding 1000kW but not exceeding 10000kW
	--功率超过10000千瓦:										--Of a power exceeding 10000kW:
8410.1310	---功率超过30000千瓦的冲击式水轮机及水轮	10	8		0	35	17	17	台		---Impulse hydraulic turbines and water wheels of a power >30000 kW
8410.1320	---功率超过35000千瓦的贯流式水轮机及水轮	10	8		0	35	17	17	台		---Radial hydraulic turbines and water wheels of a power >35000 kW
8410.1330	---功率超过200000千瓦的水泵水轮机及水轮	10	5		0	35	17	17	台		---Pumping hydraulic turbines and water wheels of a power >200000kW
8410.1390	---其他	10	5		0	35	17	17	台		---Other
	-零件,包括调节器:										-Parts, including regulators:
8410.9010	---调节器	6	5		0	35	17	17	千克/套	O	---Regulators
8410.9090	---其他	6	5		0	35	17	17	千克	O	---Other
84.11	**涡轮喷气发动机,涡轮螺桨发动机及其他燃气轮机:**										**Turbo-jets, turbo-propellers and other gas turbines:**
	-涡轮喷气发动机:										-Turbo-jets:
	--推力不超过25千牛顿:										--Of a thrust not exceeding 25kN:
8411.1110	---涡轮风扇发动机	1			0	11	17	17	台	3	---Turbofan engines
8411.1190	---其他	1			0	11	17	17	台		---Other
	--推力超过25千牛顿:										--Of a thrust exceeding 25kN:
8411.1210	---涡轮风扇发动机	1		0	0	11	17	17	台	3	---Turbofan engines
8411.1290	---其他	1		0.5	0	11	17	17	台		---Other

税则号列 Tariff Item.	货品名称	最惠国(%) MFN	协定(%) 东盟 CA	中巴 CP	CT 中智 CC	普通 Gen	增值税率 VAT	出口退税 ED	计量单位 Unit	监管条件 SC	Article Description
8411.1290 10	小型燃烧率高轻型涡轮喷气发动机(推力大于或等于90千牛顿的涡轮喷气发动机)	1				11	17	17	台	3	Turbojet engine with a smaller volume, a lighter weight, and a higher combustion rate, thrust≥90KN
8411.1290 90	其他涡轮喷气发动机(推力超过25KN)	1				11	17	17	台		Other turbo-jets, thrust >25KN
	-涡轮螺桨发动机:										-Turbo-propellers:
8411.2100	--功率不超过1100千瓦	2			0	11	17	17	台/千瓦		--Of a power not exceeding 1100kW
	--功率超过1100千瓦:										--Of a power exceeding 1100kW:
8411.2210	---功率超过1100千瓦,但不超过2238千瓦	2			0	11	17	17	台/千瓦		---Of a power exceeding 1100kW but not exceeding 2238kW
8411.2220	---功率超过2238千瓦,但不超过3730千瓦	2			0	11	17	17	台/千瓦		---Of a power exceeding 2238kW but not exceeding 3730kW
8411.2230	---功率超过3730千瓦	2			0	11	17	17	台/千瓦		---Of a power exceeding 3730kW
	-其他燃气轮机:										-Other gas turbines:
8411.8100	--功率不超过5000千瓦	15	8		12	35	17	17	台/千瓦		--Of a power not exceeding 5000kW
8411.8200	--功率超过5000千瓦	3			0	35	17	17	台/千瓦	O	--Of a power exceeding 5000kW
	-零件:										-Parts:
8411.9100	--涡轮喷气发动机或涡轮螺桨发动机用	1			0	11	17	17	千克		--Of turbo-jets or turbo-propellers
	--其他:										--Other:
8411.9910	---涡轮轴发动机用	5			4	35	17	17	千克		---Of turboshaft engines
8411.9910 01	涡轮轴航空发动机	5				35	17	17	千克		Parts of turbo - aircraft engines
8411.9910 90	其他涡轮轴发动机用零件	5				35	17	17	千克		Other part of turbo engines
8411.9990	---其他	5			4	35	17	17	千克		---Other
84.12	**其他发动机及动力装置:**										**Other engines and motors:**
	-喷气发动机,但涡轮喷气发动机除外:										-Jet engines other than turbo-jets:
8412.1010	---航空器及航天器用	3			0	11	17	17	台		---For aircraft or spacecraft
8412.1010 10	冲压喷气发动机	3				11	17	17	台	3	Ramjet engines
8412.1010 20	脉冲喷气发动机	3				11	17	17	台	3	Pulsejet engines
8412.1010 30	组合循环发动机	3				11	17	17	台	3	
8412.1010 90	其他航空、航天器用喷气发动机(涡轮喷气发动机除外)	3				11	17	17	台		Other jet engines other than turbo-jets, for aircraft or spacecraft
8412.1090	---其他	10	5		0	35	17	17	台		---Other
	-液压动力装置:										-Hydraulic power engines and motors:
8412.2100	--直线作用(液压缸)的	12	8		9.6	35	17	17	台		--Linear acting (cylinders)
	--其他:										--Other:
8412.2910	---液压马达	10	T3		8	35	17	17	台	O	---Hydraulic motors
8412.2990	---其他	14	8		11.2	35	17	17	台	O	---Other
	-气压动力装置:										-Pneumatic power engines and motors:
8412.3100	--直线作用(气压缸)的	14	8	13.3	8.4	35	17	17	台		--Linear acting (cylinders)
8412.3100 01	三坐标测量机用气缸	14				35	17	17	台		Gas vat for COMERO
8412.3100 90	其他直线作用的气压动力装置(气压缸)	14				35	17	17	台		Other pneumatic power engines and motors of linear acting (cylinders)
8412.3900	--其他	14	8		8.4	35	17	17	台	O	--Other
8412.8000	-其他	10	5		0	35	17	17	台		-Other

税则号列 Tariff Item.	货品名称	最惠国(%) MFN	协定(%) CT 东盟 CA	中巴 CP	中智 CC	普通 Gen	增值税率 VAT	出口退税 ED	计量单位 Unit	监管条件 SC	Article Description
8412.8000 10	液体火箭发动机(推力大于或等于 90 千牛顿可贮存推进剂的)	10				35	17	17	台	3	Liquid fuel rocket engine (of a thrust≥90kN, capable of storing propellant)
8412.8000 20	固体火箭发动机(总冲大于或等于 1100 千牛顿秒的)	10				35	17	17	台	3	Solid fuel rocket engine (of a total thrust ≥1100kN)
8412.8000 90	其他发动机及动力装置	10				35	17	17	台		Other engines and motors
	-零件:										-Parts:
8412.9010	---子目 8412.1010 所列机器的零件	2			0	11	17	17	千克		---For machines of subheadingNo. 8412.1010
8412.9010 10	燃烧调节装置(冲压或脉冲喷气发动机的)	2				11	17	17	千克	3	Combustion control devices for ramjet engine or pulsejet engine
8412.9010 20	火箭发动机的壳体	2				11	17	13	千克	3	Combustion control devices for ramjet engine or pulsejet engine
8412.9010 90	航空、航天器用喷气发动机的零件(涡轮喷气发动机的零件及 8412901010 除外)	2				11	17	17	千克		Parts of jet engines for aircraft or spacecraft, (other than parts of turbojets engines and parts of subheadingNo. 84129010.10)
8412.9090	---其他	8	5		0	35	17	17	千克		---Other
8412.9090 01	风力发电设备用桨叶	8				35	17	17	千克		Propeller leaf for wind - power generating device
8412.9090 90	其他发动机及动力装置的零件	8				35	17	17	千克		Components for other generator and dynamical device
84.13	**液体泵,不论是否装有计量装置;液体提升机:**										**Pumps for liquids, whether or not fitted with a measuring device; liquid elevators:**
	-装有或可装计量装置的泵:										-Pumps fitted or designed to be fitted with a measuring device:
8413.1100	--分装燃料或润滑油的泵,用于加油站或车库	10	8		0	30	17	13	台	O	--Pumps for dispensing fuel or lubricants, of the type used in filling-stations or in garages
8413.1900	--其他	10	8		0	30	17	13	台	O	--Other
8413.2000	-手泵,但子目 8413.11 或 8413.19 的货品除外	10	8		0	30	17	13	台		-Hand pumps, other than those of subheadingNo. 8413.11 or 8413.19
	-活塞式内燃发动机用的燃油泵、润滑油泵或冷却剂泵:										-Fuel, lubricating or cooling medium pumps for internal combustion piston engines:
	---燃油泵:										---Fuel pumps
8413.3021	----输出功率在 132.39 千瓦(180 马力)及以上的发动机用燃油泵	3		2.5	1.8	30	17	13	台	O	----Fuel pumps for engines of an output of 132.39kW (180hp) or more
8413.3029	----其他	3			1.8	30	17	13	台	O	----Other
8413.3030	---润滑油泵	3			1.8	30	17	13	台	O	---Lubricating pumps
8413.3090	---其他	3		2.5	1.8	30	17	13	台	O	---Other
8413.4000	-混凝土泵	8	5		6.4	30	17	13	台	O	-Concrete pumps
	-其他往复式排液泵:										-Other reciprocating positive displacement pumps:
8413.5010	---气动式	10	8		0	40		11	台		---Pneumatic
8413.5010 10	农业用气动往复式排液泵	10				40	13	11	台		Reciprocating positive displacement pumps, pneumatic, for agricutural use

税则号列 Tariff Item.	货品名称	最惠国(%) MFN	协定(%) CT 东盟 CA	协定(%) CT 中巴 CP	协定(%) CT 中智 CC	普通 Gen	增值税率 VAT	出口退税 ED	计量单位 Unit	监管条件 SC	Article Description
8413.5010 20	气动式耐腐蚀波纹或隔膜泵(流量大于0.6m³/h,接触表面由特殊耐腐蚀材料制成)	10				40	13	11	台	3O	Pneumatic erosion-resisting bellows diaphragm pump (flow capacity > 0.6m³/h, with a contact-surface of special erosion-resisting material)
8413.5010 90	其他非农业用气动往复式排液泵	10				40	17	13	台	O	Reciprocating positive displacement pumps, pneumatic, not for agricutural use
8413.5020	---电动式	10	8		0	40		11	台		---Electric
8413.5020 10	农业用电动往复式排液泵	10				40	13	11	台		Reciprocating positive displacement pumps, electric, for agricutural use
8413.5020 20	电动式耐腐蚀波纹或隔膜泵(流量大于0.6m³/h,接触表面由特殊耐腐蚀材料制成)	10				40	13	11	台	3O	Electric erosion-resisting bellows diaphragm pump (flow capacity > 0.6m³/h with a contact-surface of special erosion-resisting material)
8413.5020 30	往复式排液多重密封泵(敏感物项管制)	10				40	13	11	台	3O	Reciprocating positive displacement pumps, electric, not for argricutural use
8413.5020 90	其他非农业用电动往复式排液泵	10				40	17	11	台	O	Reciprocating positive displacement pumps, electric, not for argricutural use
8413.5030	---液压式	10	8		8	40		11	台		---Hydraulic
8413.5030 10	农业用液压往复式排液泵	10				40	13	11	台		Reciprocating positive displacement pumps, hydraulic, for agricutural use
8413.5030 20	液压式耐腐蚀波纹或隔膜泵(流量大于0.6m³/h,接触表面由特殊耐腐蚀材料制成)	10				40	13	11	台	3O	Hydraulic erosion-resisting bellows diaphragm pump, (flow capacity > 0.6m³/h with a contact-surface of special erosion-resisting material)
8413.5030 90	其他非农业用液压往复式排液泵	10				40	17	13	台	O	Reciprocating positive displacement pumps, hydraulic, not for argricutural use
8413.5090	---其他	10	8		8	40		11	台		---Other
8413.5090 10	其他农用往复式排液泵	10				40	13	11	台		Other reciprocating positive displacement pumps for agricutural use
8413.5090 20	其他耐腐蚀波纹或隔膜泵(流量大于0.6m³/h,接触表面由特殊耐腐蚀材料制成)	10				40	13	11	台	3O	Other erosion-resisting bellows diaphragm pump, (flow capacity > 0.6m³/h with a contact-surface of special erosion-resisting material)
8413.5090 90	其他非农用往复式排液泵	10				40	17	13	台	O	Other reciprocating positive displacement pumps, not for agricutural use
	-其他回转式排液泵:										-Other rotary positive displacement pumps:
8413.6010	---电动潜油泵及潜水电泵	10	8		0	40		11	台		---Electric submersible oil pumps and electric submersible pumps
8413.6010 10	农业用电动潜油泵及潜水电泵	10				40	13	11	台		Electric submersible oil pumps and electric submersible pumps for agricutural use
8413.6010 90	其他用电动潜油泵及潜水电泵	10				40	17	13	台	O	Electric submersible oil pumps and electric submersible pumps, not for argricutural use
8413.6090	---其他	10	8		0	40		11	台		---Other
8413.6090 10	农业用其他回转式排液泵	10				40	13	11	台		Rotary positive displacement pumps for agricutural use
8413.6090 20	回转式多重密封泵(敏感物项管制)	10				40	13	11	台	3O	Rotary positive displacement pumps for agricutural use

税则号列 Tariff Item.	货品名称	最惠国(%) MFN	协定(%) 东盟 CA	中巴 CP	CT 中智 CC	普通 Gen	增值税率 VAT	出口退税 ED	计量单位 Unit	监管条件 SC	Article Description
8413.6090 90	其他回转式排液泵	10				40	17	13	台	0	Other rotary positive displacement pumps
	-其他离心泵：										-Other centrifugal pumps:
8413.7010	---转速在10000转/分及以上	8	T3	7.6	0	40		11	台		---Rotational speed no less than 10000r/min
8413.7010 10	农业用其他离心泵(转速在10000转/分及以上)	8				40	13	11	台		Other centrifugal pumps for agricutural use, rotational speed≥10000r/min
8413.7010 20	液体推进剂用泵(转速≥10000转/分,出口压力≥7000千帕的)	8				40	13	11	台	3O	Liquid propellant pumps, rotational speed ≥ 10000r/min, exit press ≥ 7000KPa
8413.7010 30	离心泵多重密封泵(敏感物项管制)	8				40	13	11	台	3O	centrifugal pump multiple sealing pump
8413.7010 90	其他非农用离心泵(转速在10000转/分及以上)	8				40	17	13	台	0	Other centrifugal pumps, rotational speed ≥ 10000r/min, not for argricutural use
8413.7090	---其他	8	T3	7.6	0	40		11	台		---Other
8413.7090 10	农业用其他离心泵(转速在10000转/分以下)	8				40	13	11	台		Other centrifugal pumps, rotational speed<10000r/min, for agricutural use
8413.7090 20	一次冷却剂泵(全密封驱动泵,有惯性质量系统的泵,及鉴定为NC-1泵等)	8				40	13	11	台	3O	Primary coolant pumps (complete sealed driving pumps, pumps with inert mass system, approved NC-1pumps)
8413.7090 30	转速小于10000转/分的离心式屏蔽泵(流量大于 $0.6m^3/h$,接触表面由特殊耐腐蚀材料制成)	8				40	13	11	台	3O	Centrifugal pumps, shielded, rotational speed < 10000r/min (flow capacity > $0.6m^3/h$ with a contact-surface of special erosion-resisting material)
8413.7090 40	转速小于10000转/分的离心式磁力泵(流量大于 $0.6m^3/h$,接触表面由特殊耐腐蚀材料制成)	8				40	13	11	台	3O	Centrifugal pumps, magnetic, rotational speed < 10000r/min (flow capacity > $0.6m^3/h$ with a contact-surface of special erosion-resisting material)
8413.7090 50	液体推进剂用泵(8000转/分<转速<10000转/分,出口压力≥7000KPa的)	8				40	13	11	台	3O	Liquid propellant pumps, 8000r/min < rotational speed < 10000r/min, exit press≥7000KPa
8413.7090 60	其他离心泵多重密封泵(敏感物项管制)	8				40	17	11	台	3O	other centrifugal pump - multiple sealing pump
8413.7090 90	其他非农用离心泵(转速在10000转/分以下)	8				40	17	13	台	0	Other centrifugal pumps, not for argricutural use, rotational speed<10000r/min
	-其他泵;液体提升机：										-Other pumps; liquid elevators:
8413.8100	--泵	8	T3	4	0	40		11	台		--Pumps
8413.8100 10	农业用其他液体泵	8				40	13	11	台		Other liquid pump, for agricutural use
8413.8100 20	生产重水用多级泵(专门为利用氨-氢交换法生产重水而设计或制造的多级泵)	8				40	17	11	台	3	Multiple-staged pumps specified for heavy water (specially designed or manufactured for heavy water production with ammonia-hydrogen exchange)
8413.8100 90	其他非农用液体泵	8				40	17	13	台	0	Other liquid pump, not for argricutural use
8413.8200	--液体提升机	8	5		0	30	17	13	台		--Liquid elevators
	-零件：										-Parts:
8413.9100	--泵用	5		2.5	0	30	17	13	千克		--Of pumps
8413.9200	--液体提升机用	6	5		0	30	17	13	千克		--Of liquid elevators

税则号列 Tariff Item.	货品名称	最惠国(%) MFN	协定(%) 东盟 CA	中巴 CP	CT 中智 CC	普通 Gen	增值税率 VAT	出口退税 ED	计量单位 Unit	监管条件 SC	Article Description
84.14	**空气泵或真空泵、空气及其他气体压缩机、风机、风扇；装有风扇的通风罩或循环气罩，不论是否装有过滤器：**										**Air or vacuum pumps, air or other gas compressors and fans; ventilating or recycling hoods incorporating a fan, whether or not fitted with filters:**
8414.1000	-真空泵	8	5		0	30	17	13	台		-Vacuum pumps
8414.1000 10	耐腐蚀真空泵（流量大于 $5m^3/h$，接触表面由特殊耐腐蚀材料制成）	8				30	17	13	台	3O	Erosion-resisting vacuum pumps (flow capacity $>5m^3/h$, with a contact-surface of special erosion-resisting material)
8414.1000 20	真空泵（抽气口≥38cm，速度≥15kl/s，产生 $<10^{-4}$ 托极限真空度）	8				30	17	13	台	3O	Vacuum pumps, (inlet ≥ 38cm, speed ≥ 15kl/s, vacuum extremity $< 10^{-4}$ torr)
8414.1000 30	能在含 UF_6 气氛中使用的真空泵（用铝、镍或含镍高于60%的合金制成或为衬里的）	8				30	17	13	台	3	Vacuum pumps, suitable to be used in UF_6 atmosphere (made of or lined with aluminum, nickel or alloys containing more than 60% nickel)
8414.1000 40	专门设计或制造的抽气能力 $\geq 5m^3/min$ 的真空泵（专用于同位素气体扩散浓缩）	8				30	17	13	台	3O	Vacuum pump whose specially designed or produced air-exhausting capacity $\geq 5m^3/min$ (especially used for the diffusion and concentration of isotope gas)
8414.1000 50	能在含 UF_6 气氛中使用的真空泵（耐 UF_6 腐蚀的，也可用氟碳密封和特殊工作流体）	8				30	17	13	台	3O	Vacuum pumps, suitable to be used in UF_6 atmosphere (can be sealed with fluorine-carbon or can be used with other special working fluid)
8414.1000 90	其他真空泵	8				30	17	13	台	O	Other vacuum pumps
8414.2000	-手动或脚踏式空气泵	8	T3		0	30	17	13	台		-Hand-or foot-operated pumps
	-用于制冷设备的压缩机：										-Compressors of a kind used in refrigerating equipment:
	---电动机驱动的压缩机：										---Driven by a motor:
8414.3011	----冷藏箱或冷冻箱用，电动机额定功率不超过0.4千瓦	8		5.9	6.4	80	17	13	台	A	----For refrigerators or freezers, of a motor power not exceeding 0.4kW
8414.3012	----冷藏箱或冷冻箱用，电动机额定功率超过0.4千瓦，但不超过5千瓦	10	T3	8.5	8	80	17	13	台	A	----For refrigerators or freezers, of a motor power exceeding 0.4kW but not exceeding 5kW
8414.3013	----空气调节器用，电动机额定功率超过0.4千瓦，但不超过5千瓦	10	T3	8.5	8	80	17	13	台	A	----For air conditioning machines, of a motor power exceeding 0.4kW but not exceeding 5kW
8414.3014	----空气调节器用，电动机额定功率超过5千瓦	10	T3	8.5	8	80	17	13	台	AB	----For air conditioning machines, of a motor power exceeding 5kW
8414.3015	----冷冻或冷藏设备用，电动机额定功率超过5千瓦	10	5	9.2	8	30	17	13	台	AB	----For refrigerators or freezers, of a motor power not exceeding 5kW
8414.3019	----其他	10	T3	9	8	30	17	13	台	A	----Other
8414.3090	---非电动机驱动的压缩机	9	T3	8.1	7.2	80	17	13	台		---Driven by a non-motor
8414.3090 10	汽车空调压缩机	9				80	17	13	台		Compressors driven by a non-motor for motor vehicles
8414.3090 90	非电机驱动其他制冷设备用压缩机	9				80	17	13	台		Compressors driven by a non-motor, of a kind used in other refrigerating equipment

税则号列 Tariff Item.	货品名称	最惠国(%) MFN	协定(%)CT			普通 Gen	增值税率 VAT	出口退税 ED	计量单位 Unit	监管条件 SC	Article Description
			东盟 CA	中巴 CP	中智 CC						
8414.4000	-装在拖车底盘上的空气压缩机	8	5		6.4	30	17	13	台		-Air compressors mounted on a wheeled chassis for towing
	-风机、风扇:										-Fans:
	--台扇、落地扇、壁扇、换气扇或吊扇,包括风机,本身装有一个输出功率不超过125瓦的电动机:										--Table, floor, wall, window, ceiling or roof fans, with a self-contained electric motor of an output not exceeding 125W:
8414.5110	---吊扇	20	T3		12	130	17	13	台	AB4x	---Ceiling or roof fans
8414.5120	---换气扇	20	T3		12	130	17	13	台	AB4x	---Window fans
8414.5130	---具有旋转导风轮的风扇	12	T3		7.2	130	17	13	台	4xB	---Repeating front louver fan
	---其他:										---Other:
8414.5191	----台扇	10	5		0	130	17	13	台	AB4x	----Table fans
8414.5192	----落地扇	10	5		0	130	17	13	台	AB4x	----Floor fans
8414.5193	----壁扇	10	5		0	130	17	13	台	AB4x	----Wall fans
8414.5199	----其他	10	T3		0	130	17	13	台	4xB	----Other
	--其他:										--Other:
8414.5910	---吊扇	8	T3	7.2	6.4	30	17	13	台	AB4x	---Ceiling or roof fans
8414.5920	---换气扇	8	T3	7.2	6.4	30	17	13	台	AB4x	---Window fans
8414.5930	---离心通风机	10	T3	9.5	8	30	17	13	台	O	---Centrifugal ventilation fans
8414.5990	---其他	8	T3	7.2	6.4	30	17	13	台		---Other
8414.5990 10	罗茨式鼓风机	8				30	17	13	台	OAB	Roots blower
8414.5990 20	吸气 > $1m^3$/min 的耐 UF_6 腐蚀的鼓风机(轴向离心式或正排量鼓风机,压力比在2:1和6:1之间)	8				30	17	13	台	3ABO	Blower, suitable to be used in UF_6 atmosphere, draft ≥ $1m^3$/min (axial centrifugal fans or positive-discharge fans, pressure ratio between 2:1 ~ 6:1)
8414.5990 30	吸气 ≥ $2m^3$/min 的耐 UF_6 腐蚀鼓风机(轴向离心式或正排量鼓风机,压力比在1.2:1和6:1之间)	8				30	17	13	台	3ABO	Blower, suitable to be used in UF_6 atmosphere, draft ≥ $2m^3$/min (axial centrifugal fans or positive-discharge fans, pressure ratio between 2:1 and 6:1)
8414.5990 40	吸气 ≥ $56m^3$/s 的鼓风机(用于循环硫化氢气体的单级、低压头离心式鼓风机)	8				30	17	13	台	3ABO	Blower, extraction capability ≥ $56m^3$/s (suitable for hydrogen sulfide circulation, single-stage, low-head centrifuge fans)
8414.5990 50	电子产品散热用轴流换气扇	8				130	17	13	台	AB	Axial fans for heat elimination of electronic produxts
8414.5990 91	其他台扇、落地扇、壁扇(电动机输出功率超过125瓦的)	8				30	17	13	台	AB4x	Other table, floor, wall fans, with a electric motor, output > 125W
8414.5990 99	其他风机、风扇	8				30	17	13	台	AB	Other fans with a electric motor
	-罩的平面最大边长不超过120厘米的通风罩或循环气罩:										-Hoods having a maximum horizontal side not exceeding 120cm:
8414.6010	---抽油烟机	10	5		0	130	17	13	台		---Range hoods
	-其他:										-Other:
8414.6090	---其他	10	T3		0	130	17	13	台		---Other

税则号列 Tariff Item.	货品名称	最惠国(%) MFN	协定(%) CT 东盟 CA	中巴 CP	中智 CC	普通 Gen	增值税率 VAT	出口退税 ED	计量单位 Unit	监管条件 SC	Article Description
8414.6090 11	生物安全柜(符合世界卫生组织规定的生物安全水平三级标准,罩的最大边长≤120厘米)	10				130	17	13	台	3B	Biological safety cabinet (conform to the biological safety criterion of level - III as stipulated by WHO, the longest sides covered ≤120 cm)
8414.6090 12	活动(柔软的)隔离装置;手套箱(具有与三级生物安全柜类似标准,罩的最大边长≤120厘米)	10				130	17	13	台	3B	Active (soft) isolating device, glove boxes (up to standards similar to biological safety criterion of level - III, the longest sides covered ≤120 cm)
8414.6090 13	层流罩(柜)(垂直流密闭通风柜,具有三级生物安全柜类似标准,罩的最大边长≤120厘米)	10				130	17	13	台	3B	Other Laminar Flow Hoods (vertical closed ventilation hoods, up to standards similar to biological safety criterion of level - III, the longest sides covered ≤120 cm)
8414.6090 14	吸收塔(敏感物项管制,罩的最大边长≤120厘米)	10				130	17	13	台	3B	Absorbing column (subject to regulation of sensitive items, the longest sides covered ≤120 cm)
8414.6090 15	带有风扇的高效空气粒子过滤单元的封闭洁净设备(高效空气粒子过滤单元(HEPA),罩的最大边长≤120厘米)	10				130	17	13	台	3B	Closed cleaning facilities with fans (HEPA), the longest sides covered ≤ 120cm)
8414.6090 90	其他≤120厘米的通风罩或循环气罩(指罩的平面最大长边不超过120厘米,装有风扇的)	10				130	17	13	台		Other hoods having a maximum horizontal side not exceeding 120cm
8414.8010	---燃气轮机用的自由活塞式发生器	8	5	5.6	6.4	50	17	13	台		---Free piston generators for gas turbines
8414.8020	---二氧化碳压缩机	7	5	4.9	5.6	30	17	13	台		---CO_2 compressors
8414.8030	---发动机用增压器	7	5	4.9	0	30	17	13	台		---Supercharger for engines
8414.8030 01	轿车用增压器(最大增压压力不低于1.7Bar)	7				30	17	13	台	O	Car supercharger (the maximum increases pressure ≥1.7Bar
8414.8030 90	其他发动机用增压器	7				30	17	13	台	O	Other engine supercharger
8414.8090	---其他	7	5	4.9	0	30	17	17	台		---Other
8414.8090 10	吸气>$1m^3$/min的耐UF_6腐蚀压缩机(轴向离心式或正排量压缩机,压力比在2:1和6:1之间)	7				30	17	17	台	3O	Compressors, suitable to be used in UF_6 atmosphere, draft > $1m^3$/min (axial centrifugal fans or positive-discharge fans, pressure ratio between 2:1 and 6:1)
8414.8090 20	MLIS用UF_6/载气压缩机(能在UF_6环境中长期操作UF_6/载气混合气压缩机)	7				30	17	17	台	3O	UF_6/carrier gas compressors for MLIS, suitable to be used in UF_6 atmosphere (UF_6/carrier gas compressors for MLIS, suitable to be used in UF_6 atmosphere)
8414.8090 30	吸气≥$56m^3$/s的压缩机(用于循环硫化氢气体的单级、低压头离心式压缩机)	7				30	17	17	台	3O	Compressors for hydrogen sulfide circulation, draft≥$56m^3$/s (suitable for hydrogen sulfide circulation,, single-stage, low-head centrifuge fans)

税则号列 Tariff Item.	货品名称	最惠国(%) MFN	协定(%)CT 东盟 CA	中巴 CP	中智 CC	普通 Gen	增值税率 VAT	出口退税 ED	计量单位 Unit	监管条件 SC	Article Description
8414.8090 40	吸气≥$2m^3$/min的耐UF_6腐蚀压缩机(轴向离心式或正排量压缩机,压力比在1.2:1和6:1之间)	7				30	17	17	台	30	Compressor, suitable to be used in UF_6 atmosphere, draft ≥ $2m^3$/min (axial centrifugal fans or positive-discharge fans, pressure ratio between 2:1 and 6:1)
8414.8090 51	其他生物安全柜(符合世界卫生组织规定的生物安全水平三级标准)	7				30	17	17	台	3B	Other biological safety cabinet (conform to the biological safety criterion of level-Ⅲ as stipulated by WHO)
8414.8090 52	其他活动(柔软的)隔离装置与其他手套箱(具有与三级生物安全柜类似标准)	7				30	17	17	台	3B	Other active (soft) isolating device and other glove boxes (up to standard similar to biological safety cabinet of level Ⅲ)
8414.8090 53	其他层流罩(柜)(垂直流密闭通风柜,具有与三级生物安全柜类似标准)	7				30	17	17	台	3B	Other Laminar Flow Hoods (vertical closed ventilation hoods, up to standards similar to biological safety criterion of level-Ⅲ)
8414.8090 54	其他吸收塔(敏感物项管制)	7				30	17	17	台	3B	Absorbing column (subject to regulation of sensitive items)
8414.8090 55	其他带有风扇的高效空气粒子过滤单元的封闭洁净设备[高效空气粒子过滤单元(HEPA)]	7				30	17	17	台	3B	Other closed cleaning facilities with fans (HEPA)
8414.8090 90	其他空气泵、气体压缩机及通风罩(通风罩指装有风扇的通风罩或循环气罩,平面边长>120cm)	7				30	17	17	台	0	Other air pumps, air or other gas compressors; ventilating or recycling hoods incorporating fan, having a maximum horizontal side>120cm
	-零件:										-Parts:
	---子目8414.3011至8414.3014及8414.3090所列机器的零件:										---Of the machines of subheadingsNos. 8414.3011 to 8414.3014 and 8414.3090:
8414.9011	----压缩机进、排气阀片	8	T3	7.2	6.4	80	17	13	千克		----In take valve leaf or discharge valve leaf
8414.9019	----其他	8	T3	7.2	6.4	80	17	13	千克		----Other
8414.9020	---子目8414.5110至8414.5199及8414.6000所列机器的零件	12	T3	11.4	9.6	130	17	13	千克		---Of the machines of subheadingsNos. 8414.5110 to 8414.5199 or 8414.6000
8414.9090	---其他	7	T3	6.5	5.6	30	17	13	千克		---Other
8414.9090 10	分子泵[内部有加工或挤压的螺纹槽和加工腔的泵体(尺寸特殊)]	7				30	17	13	千克	3	Molecule pumps[pump with processed or pressed thread sroove and processed cavity inside (special size)]
8414.9090 90	编号8414其他未列名零件	7				30	17	13	千克		Parts of machines of subheadingsNo. 8414, not eleswhere specified or included
84.15	**空气调节器,装有电扇及调温、调湿装置,包括不能单独调湿的空调器:**										**Air conditioning machines, comprising a motor-driven fan and elements for changing the temperature and humidity, including those machines in which the humidity cannot be separately regulated:**

税则号列 Tariff Item.	货品名称	最惠国(%) MFN	协定(%) 东盟 CA	中巴 CP	CT 中智 CC	普通 Gen	增值税率 VAT	出口退税 ED	计量单位 Unit	监管条件 SC	Article Description
	-窗式或壁式，独立的或分体的：										-Window or wall types, self-contained or "split-system":
8415.1010	---独立式	15	T3	13.5	9	130	17	13	台	aAB	---Self-contained
	---分体式：										---Split-system:
8415.1021	----制冷量不超过4000大卡/时	15	T3	13.5	9	130	17	13	台	aAB	----Of a refrigerating effect not exceeding 4000 Cal per hour
8415.1022	----制冷量超过4000大卡/时	15	T3	13.5	9	90	17	13	台	aAB	----Of a refrigerating effect exceeding 4000 Cal per hour
8415.2000	-机动车辆上供人使用的	20			16	110	17	13	台	A	-Of a kind used for persons, in motor vehicles
	-其他：										-Other:
	--装有制冷装置及一个冷热循环换向阀的（可逆式热泵）：										--Incorporating a refrigerating unit and a valve for reversal of the cooling/heat cycle (reversible heat pumps):
8415.8110	---制冷量不超过4000大卡/时	15	T3		0	130	17	13	台	aA	---Of a refrigerating effect not exceeding 4000 Cal per hour
8415.8120	---制冷量超过4000大卡/时	20	T3		0	90	17	13	台	AB	---Of a refrigerating effect exceeding 4000 Cal per hour
	--其他，装有制冷装置的：										--Other, incorporating a refrigerating unit:
8415.8210	---制冷量不超过4000大卡/时	15	T3		0	130	17	13	台	aA	---Of a refrigerating effect not exceeding 4000 Cal per hour
8415.8220	---制冷量超过4000大卡/时	20	T3		0	90	17	13	台	AB	---Of a refrigerating effect exceeding 4000 Cal per hour
8415.8300	--未装有制冷装置的	10	T3		0	90	17	13	台	aA	--Not incorporating a refrigerating unit
	-零件：										-Parts:
8415.9010	---子目8415.1010、8415.1021、8415.8110及8415.8210所列设备的零件	10	8	8	0	130	17	13	千克		---Of the machines of subheadingNo. 8415.1010, 8415.1021, 8415.8110 or 8415.8210
8415.9090	---其他	10	8	8	0	90	17	13	千克		---Other
84.16	**使用液体燃料、粉状固体燃料或气体燃料的炉用燃烧器；机械加煤机，包括其机械炉篦、机械出灰器及类似装置：**										**Furnace burners for liquid fuel, for pulverzied solid fuel or for gas; mechanical stokers, including their mechanical grates, mechanical ash dischargers and similar appliances:**
8416.1000	-使用液体燃料的炉用燃烧器	10	8	9.5	8	35	17	13	千克	6O	-Furnace burners for liquid fuel
	-其他炉用燃烧器，包括复式燃烧器：										-Other furnace burners, including combination burners:
	---气体的：										---For gas:
8416.2011	----使用天然气的	10.5	8		6.3	35	17	13	千克	6O	----Of using naturalgas
8416.2019	----其他	10.5	8		6.3	35	17	13	千克		----Other
8416.2019 01	溴化锂空调用燃烧机	10.5				35	17	13	千克	6O	Lithium bromide burner for air - conditioning
8416.2019 90	使用其他气的炉用燃烧器（包括复式燃烧器）	10.5				35	17	13	千克	6O	Stove - use burners that use other gas (including compound burners)
8416.2090	---其他	10.5	8		6.3	35	17	13	千克	6O	---Other
8416.3000	-机械加煤机，包括其机械炉篦、机械出灰器及类似装置	8.4	5		0	35	17	13	千克	6O	-Mechanical stokers, including their mechanical grates, mechanical ash dischargers and similar appliances
8416.9000	-零件	6	5		0	35	17	13	千克		-Parts

税则号列 Tariff Item.	货 品 名 称	最惠国(%) MFN	协定(%)CT 东盟 CA	 中巴 CP	 中智 CC	普通 Gen	增值税率 VAT	出口退税 ED	计量单位 Unit	监管条件 SC	Article Description
84.17	**非电热的工业或实验室用炉及烘箱,包括焚烧炉:**										**Industrial or laboratory furnaces and ovens, including incinerators, non-electric:**
8417.1000	-矿砂、黄铁矿或金属的焙烧、熔化或其他热处理用炉及烘箱	10	T3		0	35	17	13	台	6OA	-Furnaces and ovens for the roasting, melting or other heat-treatment of ores, pyrites or of metals
8417.2000	-面包房用烤炉及烘箱,包括做饼干用的	10	5		0	35	17	13	台	A	-Bakery ovens, including biscuit ovens
	-其他:										-Other:
8417.8010	---炼焦炉	10	5		0	35	17	13	台	6A	---Coke ovens
8417.8020	---放射性废物焚烧炉	5			0	35	17	13	台	6A	---Burn furnaces for radioactive waste
8417.8030	---水泥回转窑	10	8		0	35	17	13	台	AO	---Cement rotary kilns
8417.8040	---石灰石分解炉	10	5		0	35	17	13	台	A	---Limestone decomposition furnace
8417.8090	---其他	10	T3		0	35	17	13	台		---Other
8417.8090 10	平均温度>1000℃的耐腐蚀焚烧炉(为销毁管制化学品或化学弹药用)	10				35	17	13	台	36AO	Erosion-resisting incinerators, temperature>1000℃ (for incinerating controlled chemicals or chemical ammunitions)
8417.8090 90	其他非电热的工业用炉及烘箱(包括实验室用炉、烘箱和焚烧炉)	10				35	17	13	台	6OA	Other industrial or laboratory furnaces and ovens, including incinerators, non-electric
	-零件:										-Parts:
8417.9010	---海绵铁回转窑用	7	5		0	35	17	13	千克		---For sponge iron rotary kiln
8417.9020	---炼焦炉用	7	5		0	35	17	13	千克		---For coke ovens
8417.9090	---其他	7	5		0	35	17	13	千克		---Other
84.18	**电气或非电气的冷藏箱、冷冻箱及其他制冷设备;热泵,但税目84.15的空气调节器除外:**										**Refrigerators, freezers and other refrigerating or freezing equipment, electric or other; heat pumps other than air conditioning machines of headingNo. 84.15:**
	-冷藏-冷冻组合机,各自装有单独外门的:										-Combined refrigerator-freezers, fitted with separate external doors:
8418.1010	---容积超过500升	10	T3		8	100	17	13	台		---Of a capacity exceeding 500 L
8418.1020	---容积超过200升,但不超过500升	15	T3		12	130	17	13	台	AB	---Of a capacity exceeding 200 L, not exceeding 500 L
8418.1030	---容积不超过200升	15	T3		12	130	17	13	台	AB	---Of a capacity not exceeding 200 L
	-家用型冷藏箱:										-Refrigerators, household type:
	--压缩式:										--Compression-type:
8418.2110	---容积超过150升	10	T3		8	130	17	13	台	AB	---Of a capacity exceeding 150 L
8418.2120	---容积超过50升,但不超过150升	10	T3	9	8	130	17	13	台	AB	---Of a capacity exceeding 50 L, not exceeding 150 L
8418.2130	---容积不超过50升	10	T3	9	8	130	17	13	台	AB	---Of a capacity not exceeding 50 L
	--其他:										--Other:
8418.2910	---半导体制冷式	30	T3		18	130	17	13	台	AB	---semi-conduct freezer
8418.2920	---电气吸收式	15	T3		9	130	17	13	台	A	---Absorption-type, electrical
8418.2990	---其他	30	T3		18	130	17	13	台	AB	---Other
	-柜式冷冻箱,容积不超过800升:										-Freezers of the chest type, not exceeding 800 l capacity:
8418.3010	---制冷温度在-40℃及以下	9	5		0	50	17	13	台	BA	---Of a refrigerating temperature of -40℃ or lower

税则号列 Tariff Item.	货品名称	最惠国(%) MFN	协定(%) 东盟 CA	中巴 CP	CT 中智 CC	普通 Gen	增值税率 VAT	出口退税 ED	计量单位 Unit	监管条件 SC	Article Description
	---制冷温度在-40℃以上：										---Of a refrigerating temperature higher than -40℃：
8418.3021	----容积超过500升	23	T3		0	100	17	13	台		----Of a capacity exceeding 500 L
8418.3029	----其他	30	T3		0	130	17	13	台	BA	----Other
	-立式冷冻箱，容积不超过900升：										-Freezers of the upright type, not exceeding 900 L capacity：
8418.4010	---制冷温度在-40℃及以下	9	5		0	50	17	13	台	BA	---Of a refrigerating temperature of -40℃ or lower
	---制冷温度在-40℃以上：										---Of a refrigerating temperature higher than -40℃：
8418.4021	----容积超过500升	15	T3		0	100	17	13	台		----Of a capacity exceeding 500 L
8418.4029	----其他	30	T3		0	130	17	13	台	BA	----Other
8418.5000	-装有冷藏或冷冻装置的其他设备(柜、箱、展示台、陈列箱及类似品)用于存储及展示	10	T3		8	100	17	13	台	A	-refrigerating or freezing chests, (cabinets, display counters, show-cases and similar) refrigerating or freezing furniture
	-其他制冷设备；热泵：										-Other refrigerating or freezing equipment; heat pumps：
	--热泵，税目84.15的空气调节器除外：										--Heat pumps,
8418.6120	---压缩式	10	8	7	0	90	17	13	台		---Compressed
8418.6120 10	压缩式制冷机组的热泵(介质为氢，氦的可冷却到≤23且排热>150W)	10				90	17	13	台	3	Compressed hot pump for refrigerating (medium being hydrogen or helium, and can be cooled to temperature lower than 23K, and remove heat larger than 150W)
8418.6120 90	其他压缩式热泵，税目8415的空气调节器除外	10				90	17	13	台		Other compressed hot pump, except air conditioning of tax items 8415
8418.6190	---其他	15	8	7	12	130	17	13	台		---Other
8418.6920	---制冷机组；	10	8	7	0	90	17	13	千克/台		---Refigerating units
8418.6920 10	其他压缩式制冷设备(介质为氯或氢；可冷却到≤23K且排热>150W)	10				90	17	13	千克/台	3	Other compressed refrigerating facilities (medium being hydrogen or helium, and can be cooled to temperature lower than 23K, and remove heat larger than 150W)
8418.6920 90	其他制冷机组	10				90	17	13	千克/台		Other refrigerating units
8418.6990	---其他；	10	8	7	0	130	17	13	千克/台		---Other
8418.6990 10	带制冷装置的发酵罐(不发散气溶胶，且容积大于20升)	10				130	17	13	千克/台	3	Fermentors with cooling device (not diverging aerosol, capacity >20L)
8418.6990 90	其他制冷设备	10				130	17	13	千克/台		nits whose condensers are not heat exchangers
	-零件										-Parts
8418.9100	--冷藏或冷冻设备专用的特制家具	18	8	17.1	10.8	130	17	13	千克		--Furniture designed to receive refrigerating or freezing equipment
	--其他：										--Other：
8418.9910	---制冷机组及热泵用	10	8		8	90	17	13	千克		---Of refrigerating units and heat pumps
	---其他：										---Other：
8418.9991	----制冷温度在-40℃及以下的冷冻设备用	9.5	5		7.6	50	17	13	千克		----Of freezing equipment of a refrigerating temperature of -40℃ or lower

税则号列 Tariff Item.	货品名称	最惠国(%) MFN	协定(%)CT 东盟 CA	中巴 CP	中智 CC	普通 Gen	增值税率 VAT	出口退税 ED	计量单位 Unit	监管条件 SC	Article Description
8418.9992	----制冷温度在-40℃以上,但容积超过500升的冷藏或冷冻设备用	10	5		8	100	17	13	千克		----Of refrigerating or freezing equipment of a refrigerating temperature higher than -40℃ and a capacity exceeding 500 L
8418.9999	----其他	10	8		8	130	17	13	千克		----Other
8418.9999 10	耐腐蚀冷凝器(20平方米>换热面积>0.15平方米)	10				130	17	13	千克	3	Erosion-resisting condensers ($20m^2$ > area of heat-exchange > $0.15m^2$)
8418.9999 90	编号8418其他制冷设备用零件	10				130	17	13	千克		Parts of other refrigerating or freezing equipment of headingNo. 8418
84.19	**利用温度变化处理材料的机器、装置及类似的实验室设备,例如,加热、烹煮、烘炒、蒸馏、精馏、消毒、灭菌、汽蒸、干燥、蒸发、气化、冷凝、冷却的机器设备,不论是否电热的(不包括税目85.14的炉,烘箱及其他设备),但家用的除外;非电热的快速热水器或贮备式热水器:**										**Machinery, plant or laboratory equipment, whether or not electrically heated (excluding furnaces, ovens and other equipment of headingNo. 85.14), for the treatment of materials by a process involving a change of temperature such as heating, cooking, roasting, distilling, rectifying, sterilizing, pasteurizing, steaming, drying, evaporating, vaporizing, condensing or cooling, other than machinery or plant of a kind used for domestic purposes; instantaneous or storage water heaters, non-electric:**
	-非电热的快速热水器或贮备式热水器:										-Instantaneous or storage water heaters, non-electric:
8419.1100	--燃气快速热水器	35	12		28	100	17	13	台		--Instantaneous gas water heaters
8419.1900	--其他	35	12		21	100	17	17	台		--Other
8419.2000	-医用或实验室用消毒器具	4			3.2	30	17	13	台	A	-Medical, surgical or laboratory sterilizers
	-干燥器:										-Dryers:
8419.3100	--农产品干燥用	8	5		0	30	13	11	台	A	--For agricultural products
8419.3200	--木材、纸浆、纸或纸板干燥用	9	5		7.2	30	17	13	台	A	--For wood, paper pulp, paper or paperboard
	--其他:										--Other:
8419.3910	---微空气流动陶瓷坯件干燥器	9	5	4.5	7.2	30	17	13	台	A	---Breeze pottery blanks dryers
8419.3990	---其他	9	5	4.5	7.2	30	17	13	台		---Other
8419.3990 10	冻干设备(10≤24小时凝冰量≤1000千克,并可蒸汽消毒)	9				30	17	13	台	3A	Freezer-dryers (10kg/24h ≤ volume of icing ≤ 1000kg/24h, capable of be sterilized by steam)
8419.3990 90	其他用途的干燥器	9				30	17	13	台	A	Other dryers for other use
	-蒸馏或精馏设备:										-Distilling or rectifying plant:
8419.4010	---提净塔	10	8		0	30	17	13	台	A	---Stripping towers
8419.4020	---精馏塔	10	8		0	30	17	13	台	A	---Rectifying towers
8419.4090	---其他	10	8		0	30	17	13	台		---Other
8419.4090 10	氢-低温蒸馏塔(温度≤-238℃,压力为0.5-5兆帕,内径≥1米等条件)	10				30	17	13	台	3AO	Hydrogen-low temperature distilling towers (temperature ≤ -238℃, pressure = 0.5MPa ~ 5MPa, inside diameter ≥ 1m)
8419.4090 20	耐腐蚀蒸馏塔(内径大于0.1米,接触表面由特殊耐腐蚀材料制成)	10				30	17	13	台	3AO	Erosion-resisting distilling towers (inside diameter > 0.1m, with a contact-surface of special erosion-resisting material)

税则号列 Tariff Item.	货品名称	最惠国(%) MFN	协定(%)CT 东盟 CA	中巴 CP	中智 CC	普通 Gen	增值税率 VAT	出口退税 ED	计量单位 Unit	监管条件 SC	Article Description
8419.4090 90	其他蒸馏或精馏设备	10				30	17	13	台	AO	Other distilling or rectifying plant
8419.5000	-热交换装置	10	8	9.5	8	30	17	13	台		-Heat exchange units
8419.5000 10	热交换器(专用于核反应堆的一次冷却剂回路的)	10				30	17	13	台	3ABO	Heat exchanger specified for primary coolant circuit of reactor
8419.5000 20	蒸汽发生器(专用于核反应堆内生成的热量输送到进水以产生蒸汽的)	10				30	17	13	台	3AB	Steam producers for reactors (specified for conduct heat produced in reactor into water to generate steam)
8419.5000 30	冷却 UF_6 的热交换器(在压差为100kPa下渗透压力变化率小于10Pa/h)	10				30	17	13	台	3AB	Heat exchangers for cooling UF_6 (rate of change of osmotic pressure < 10Pa/h under 100kPa differential pressure)
8419.5000 40	冷却气体用热交换器(用耐 UF_6 腐蚀材料制成或加以保护的)	10				30	17	13	台	3ABO	Heat exchangers for cooling gases (made of or protected with UF_6-resistant materials)
8419.5000 50	耐腐蚀热交换器(0.15平方米<换热面积<20平方米)	10				30	17	13	台	3ABO	Erosion-resisting heat exchangers ($20m^2$ > area of heat-exchange > $0.15m^2$)
8419.5000 90	其他热交换装置	10				30	17	13	台	OAB	Other heat exchange unite
	-液化空气或其他气体的机器:										-Machinery for liquefying air or other gases:
	---制氧机:										---Oxygen producers:
8419.6011	----制氧量在15000立方米/小时及以上	12	8		7.2	30	17	17	台	A	----Oxygen preparation volume no less than $15000m^3/h$
8419.6019	----其他	13	8		7.8	30	17	17	台	A	----Other
8419.6090	---其他	10	8		0	30	17	13	台		---Other
8419.6090 10	液化器(将来自级联的 UF_6 气体压缩并冷凝成液态 UF_6)	10				30	17	13	台	3AO	UF_6 liquefier (to compress and condense gaseous UF_6 from cascade into liquefied UF_6)
8419.6090 90	其他液化空气或其他气体用的机器	10				30	17	13	台	AO	Other machinery for liquefying air or other gases
	-其他机器设备:										-Other machinery, plant and equipment:
8419.8100	--加工热饮料或烹调、加热食品用	10	T3		8	30	17	13	台	A	--For making hot drinks or for cooking or heating food
	--其他:										--Other:
8419.8910	---加氢反应器	0				30	17	13	台	A	---Hydroformer vessels
8419.8990	---其他	0				30	17	13	台		---Other
8419.8990 10	带加热装置的发酵罐(不发散气溶胶,且容积大于20升)	0				30	17	13	台	3AO	Fermentor with heating devices, not diverging aerosol, volume > 20L
8419.8990 21	凝华器(或冷阱)(从扩散级联中取出 UF_6 并可再蒸发转移)	0				30	17	13	台	3AO	Coasulating machines under low temperature
8419.8990 22	低温制冷设备(能承受-120℃或更低的温度)	0				30	17	13	台	3A	Low-temperature refrigeration facilities (bearing -120℃ or evem lower temperature
8419.8990 23	UF_6 冷阱(能承受-20℃或更低的温度)	0				30	17	13	台	3AO	UF_6 cold trop (bearing-120℃ or even lower tem perature)

税则号列 Tariff Item.	货品名称	最惠国(%) MFN	协定(%)CT 东盟 CA	中巴 CP	中智 CC	普通 Gen	增值税率 VAT	出口退税 ED	计量单位 Unit	监管条件 SC	Article Description
8419.8990 90	其他利用温度变化处理材料的机器(包括类似的实验室设备)	0				30	17	13	台	AO	Other machinery for the treatment of materials by a process involving a change of temperature, including laboratory equipment
	-零件:										-Parts:
8419.9010	---热水器用	0				100	17	17	千克		---Of water heaters
*8419.9090	---其他	4			3.2	30	17	13	千克		---Other
84.20	**研光机或其他滚压机器及其滚筒,但加工金属或玻璃用的除外:**										**Calendering or other rolling machines, other than for metals or glass, and cylinders therefor:**
8420.1000	-研光机或其他滚压机器	8.4	5		6.72	30	17	13	台		-Calendering or other rolling machines
	-零件:										-Parts:
8420.9100	--滚筒	8	5		0	30	17	13	个/千克		--Cylinders
8420.9900	--其他	8	5		0	30	17	13	千克		--Other
84.21	**离心机,包括离心干燥机;液体或气体的过滤、净化机器及装置:**										**Centrifuges, including centrifugal dryers; filtering or purifying machinery and apparatus, for liquids or gases:**
	-离心机,包括离心干燥机:										-Centrifuges, including centrifugal dryers:
8421.1100	--奶油分离器	8.4	5		0	30	17	13	台	A	--Cream separators
	--干衣机:										--Clothes-dryers:
8421.1210	---干衣量不超过10千克	17.5	8		14	70	17	13	台		---Of a dry linen capacity not exceeding 10kg
8421.1290	---其他	8	5		6.4	30	17	13	台		---Other
	--其他:										--Other:
8421.1910	---脱水机	10	5		8	30	17	13	台		---Dewaterers
8421.1920	---固液分离机	10	T3		8	30	17	13	台		---Solid-liquor separators
*8421.1990	---其他	10	T3		8	30	17	13	台		---Other
8421.1990 20	液-液离心接触器(为化学交换过程的铀浓缩而专门设计或制造的)	10				30	17	13	台	3	Liquid-liquid centrifuge contactors for uranium concentration (specially designed or manufactured for uranium concentration in chemical exchange process)
8421.1990 30	离心分离器,包括倾析器(不发散气溶胶、可对致病性微生物进行连续分离的)	10				30	17	13	台	3	Centrifuge separator for disease microorganism (including decanters) (not diverging aerosol, capable of continuously separating disease microorganism)
8421.1990 90	其他离心机及离心干燥机	10				30	17	13	台		Other centrifuges and centrifugal dryers
	-液体的过滤、净化机器及装置:										-Filtering or purifying machinery and apparatus for liquids:
	--过滤或净化水用:										--For filtering or purifying water:
8421.2110	---家用型	25	12	17.5	20	63	17	13	台	AB	---Of the household type
8421.2190	---其他	5		3.5	4	50	17	13	台	B	---Other
8421.2200	--过滤或净化饮料(水除外)用	12	8		7.2	40	17	13	台	AB	--For filtering or purifying beverages other than water
8421.2300	--内燃发动机的滤油器	10	T3		8	40	17	13	个	B	--Oil or petrol-filters for internal combustion engines
	--其他:										--Other:

税则号列 Tariff Item.	货品名称	最惠国(%) MFN	协定(%) CT 东盟 CA	协定(%) CT 中巴 CP	协定(%) CT 中智 CC	普通 Gen	增值税率 VAT	出口退税 ED	计量单位 Unit	监管条件 SC	Article Description
8421.2910	---压滤机	5		3.5	4	40	17	13	个	BO	---Press filters
8421.2990	---其他	5		3.5	4	40	17	13			---Other
8421.2990 40	液体截流过滤设备(可连续分离致病性微生物、毒素和细胞培养物)	5				40	17	13	台	3	Liquid filters for continuously separating disease microorganism, toxins or cell cultures
8421.2990 90	其他液体的过滤、净化机器及装置	5				40	17	13	个	B	Other filtering or purifying machinery and apparatus for liquids
	-气体的过滤、净化机器及装置:										-Filtering or purifying machinery and apparatus for gases:
8421.3100	--内燃发动机的进气过滤器	10	5		8	40	17	13	个	B	--Intake air filters for internal combustion engines
	--其他:										--Other:
8421.3910	---家用型	15	8	10.5	12	100	17	13	个	B	---Of the household type
	---工业用除尘器:										---Dust collectors for industry uses:
8421.3921	----静电除尘器	5		3.5	4	40	17	13	个	B	----Electrostatic
8421.3922	----袋式除尘器	5		3.5	4	40	17	13	个	B	----Baghoused
8421.3923	----旋风式除尘器	5		3.5	4	40	17	13	个	B	----Cyclone
8421.3929	----其他	5		3.5	4	40	17	13	个	B	----Other
8421.3990	---其他	5		3.5	4	40	17	13	个	B	---Other
	-零件:										-Parts:
	--离心机用,包括离心干燥机用:										--Of centrifuges, including centrifugal dryers:
8421.9110	---干衣量不超过10千克的干衣机用	0				70	17	13	千克		---Of clothes-dryers of a dry linen capacity not exceeding 10kg
8421.9190	---其他	0				30	17	13	千克		---Other
8421.9190 11	离心机壳/收集器(容纳气体离心机的转筒组件的耐 UF_6 部件	0				30	17	13	千克	3	Centrifuge cover/collector (accommodate parts able to endure UF_6)
8421.9190 12	收集器(由内径不同的同心管组成用于供取 UF_6 气体的管件)	0				30	17	13	千克	3	Collector (parts of tube used for providing air of UF_6, made up of concentric tubes with different radiuses)
8421.9190 13	气体扩散膜(由耐 UF_6 材料制成的多细孔过滤薄膜)	0				30	17		千克	3	air diffusing film (multiple stoma filtration membrane made up of materials that are able to endure UF_6)
8421.9190 14	扩散室(含一个进气管两个出气管的容纳气体扩散膜的密闭式容器)	0				30	17	13	千克	3	expansive room (a closed spectacle that accommodate other diffusion films, with one inlet pipe and two outlet pipes)
8421.9190 90	其他离心机用零件	0				30	17	13	千克		Other parts of centrifuge cover
	--其他:										--Other:
8421.9910	---家用型过滤、净化装置用	10	T3	9	8	100	17	13	千克		---Of household-type filtering or purifying machines
8421.9990	---其他	5		4.5	4	40	17	13	千克		---Other

税则号列 Tariff Item.	货品名称	最惠国(%) MFN	协定(%)CT 东盟 CA	中巴 CP	中智 CC	普通 Gen	增值税率 VAT	出口退税 ED	计量单位 Unit	监管条件 SC	Article Description
84.22	**洗碟机;瓶子及其他容器的洗涤或干燥机器;瓶、罐、箱、袋或其他容器装填、封口、密封、贴标签的机器;瓶、罐、管、筒或类似容器的包封机器;其他包装或打包机器(包括热缩包装机器);饮料充气机:**										**Dish washing machines; machinery for cleaning or drying bottles or other containers; machinery for filling, closing, sealing or labelling bottles, cans, boxes, bags or other containers; machinery for capsuling bottles, jars, tubes and similar containers other packing or wrapping machinery (including heat-shrink wrapping machinery); machinery for aerating beverages**
	-洗碟机:										-Dish washing machines:
8422.1100	--家用型	10	5		0	90	17	13	台	B	--Of the household type
8422.1900	--其他	14	8		8.4	90	17	13	台		--Other
8422.2000	-瓶子或其他容器的洗涤或干燥机器	10	T3		8	35	17	13	台	B	-Machinery for cleaning or drying bottles or other containers
	-瓶、罐、箱、袋或其他容器的装填、封口、密封、贴标签的机器;瓶、罐、管、筒或类似容器的包封机器;饮料充气机:										-Machinery for filling, closing, sealing, or labelling bottles, cans, boxes, bags or other containers; machinery for capsuling bottles, jars, tubes and similar containers; machinery for aerating beverages:
8422.3010	---饮料及液体食品灌装设备	12	8	8.4	9.6	45	17	13	台	OA	---Bottling or canning machinery for beverages or liquid food
	---水泥包装机:										---Machinery for packing cement:
8422.3021	----全自动灌包机	12	8	8.4	9.6	45	17	13	台		----Automatic filling and sacking machines
8422.3029	----其他	12	8	8.4	9.6	45	17	13	台		----Other
8422.3030	---其他包装机	10	8	7	8	35	17	13	台	OA	---Other packing machines
8422.3090	---其他	10	T3	7	8	35	17	13	台		---Other
8422.3090 10	充装设备(敏感物项管制)	10				35	17	13	台	3A	filling equipment
8422.3090 90	饮料充气机及其他包封机	10				35	17	13	台	A	(Machinery for aerating beverages and other machinery)
8422.4000	-其他包装或打包机器(包括热缩包装机器)	10	8	9.5	8	35	17	13	台		-Other packing or wrapping machinery (including heat-shrink wrapping machinery)
	-零件:										-Parts:
8422.9010	---洗碟机用	10.5	8		8.4	90	17	13	千克		---Of dish washing machines
8422.9020	---饮料及液体食品灌装设备用	8.5	5		6.8	45	17	13	千克	A	---Of bottling or canning machinery for beverages or liquid food
8422.9090	---其他	8.5	5		6.8	35	17	13	千克		---Other
84.23	**衡器(感量为50毫克或更精密的天平除外),包括计数或检验用的衡器;衡器用的各种砝码、秤砣:**										**Weighing machinery (excluding balances of a sensitivity of 50 mg or better), including weight operated counting or checking machines; weighing machine weights of all kinds:**
8423.1000	-体重计,包括婴儿秤;家用秤	10.5	8		6.3	80	17	13	台		-Personal weighing machines, including baby scales; household scales

税则号列 Tariff Item.	货品名称	最惠国(%) MFN	协定(%)CT 东盟 CA	中巴 CP	中智 CC	普通 Gen	增值税率 VAT	出口退税 ED	计量单位 Unit	监管条件 SC	Article Description
	-输送带上连续称货的秤:										-Scales for continuous weighing of goods on conveyors:
8423.2010	---电子皮带秤	10	5		0	80	17	13	台		---Electronic belt weighing machines
8423.2090	---其他	10	5		0	80	17	13	台		---Other
	-恒定秤、物料定量装袋或装容器用的秤,包括库秤:										-Constant weight scales and scales for discharging a predetermined weight of material into a bag or container, including hopper scales:
8423.3010	---定量包装秤	10.5	8		6.3	80	17	13	台		---Rationed packing scales
8423.3020	---定量分选秤	10.5	8		6.3	80	17	13	台		---Rationed sorting scales
8423.3030	---配料秤	10.5	8		6.3	80	17	13	台		---Proporating scales
8423.3090	---其他	10.5	8		6.3	80	17	13	台		---Other
	-其他衡器:										-Other weighing machinery:
	--最大称量不超过30千克:										--Having a maximum weighing capacity not exceeding 30kg:
8423.8110	---计价秤	10.5	8		6.3	80	17	13	台	A	---Account balances
8423.8120	---弹簧秤	10.5	8		6.3	80	17	13	台		---Spring balances
8423.8190	---其他	10.5	8		6.3	80	17	13	台		---Other
	--最大称量超过30千克,但不超过5000千克:										--Having a maximum weighing capacity exceeding 30kg but not exceeding 5000kg:
8423.8210	---地中衡	10.5	8		6.3	80	17	13	台		---Weighbridges
8423.8290	---其他	10.5	8		6.3	80	17	13	台		---Other
	--其他:										--Other:
8423.8910	---地中衡	10	5		8	80	17	13	台		---Weighbridges
8423.8920	---轨道衡	10	5		8	80	17	13	台		---Track scales
8423.8930	---吊秤	10	5		8	80	17	13	台		---Hanging scales
8423.8990	---其他	10	5		8	80	17	13	台		---Other
8423.9000	-衡器用的各种砝码、秤砣;衡器的零件	10	T3		0	80	17	13	千克		-Weighing machine weights of all kinds; parts of weighing machinery
84.24	**液体或粉末的喷射、散布或喷雾的机械器具(不论是否手工操作);灭火器,不论是否装药;喷枪及类似器具;喷汽机、喷砂机及类似的喷射机器:**										**Mechanical appliances (whether or not hand-operated) for projecting, dispersing or spraying liquids or powders; fire extinguishers, whether or not charged; spray guns and similar appliances; steam or sand blasting machines and similar jet projecting machines:**
8424.1000	-灭火器,不论是否装药	8.4	5		0	70	17	13	个	A	-Fire extinguishers, whether or not charged
8424.2000	-喷枪及类似器具	8.4	5	8	0	40	17	13	个		-Spray guns and similar appliances
8424.3000	-喷汽机、喷砂机及类似的喷射机器	8.4	5		0	40	17	13	台		-Steam or sand blasting machines and similar jet projecting machines
	-其他器具:										-Other appliances:
8424.8100	--农业或园艺用	8	5	7.6	6.4	30	13	11	台		--Agricultural or horticultural
	--其他:										--Other:
8424.8910	---家用型	0				80	17	13	台	B	---Of the household type
	---其他:										---Other:

税则号列 Tariff Item.	货品名称	最惠国(%) MFN	协定(%)CT 东盟 CA	中巴 CP	中智 CC	普通 Gen	增值税率 VAT	出口退税 ED	计量单位 Unit	监管条件 SC	Article Description
8424.8991	----船用洗舱机	0				30	17	13	台		----Marine cabinet washer
8424.8999	----其他	0				30	17	13	台		----Other
8424.8999 10	分离喷嘴(由狭缝状、曲率半径极小的弯曲通道组成,内有分离楔尖)	0				30	17	13	台	3	separating nozzle
8424.8999 90	其他用途的喷射、喷雾机械器具	0				30	17	13	台		(Mechanical appliances for projecting, dispersing or spraying for other use)
	-零件:										-Parts:
8424.9010	---子目8424.1000所列器具的零件	0				70	17	13	千克		---Of the apparatus of subheading No. 8424.1000
8424.9020	---子目8424.8910所列器具的零件	0				80	17	13	千克		---Of the apparatus of subheading No. 8424.8910
8424.9090	---其他	0				30	17	13	千克		---Other
84.25	**滑车及提升机,但倒卸式提升机除外;卷扬机及绞盘;千斤顶:**										**Pulley tackle and hoists other than skip hoists; winches and capstans; jacks:**
	-滑车及提升机,但倒卸式提升机及提升车辆用的提升机除外:										-Pulley tackle and hoists other than skip hoists or hoists of a kind used for raising vehicles:
8425.1100	--电动的	6	5		0	30	17	17	台	B	--Powered by electric motor
8425.1900	--其他	5			4	30	17	17	台	B	--Other
	-卷扬机;绞盘:										-winches; capstans
	--电动的										--Powered by electric motor
8425.3110	---矿井口卷扬装置;专为井下使用设计的卷扬机:	10	5		0	30	17	17	台		---Pit-head winding gear; winches specially designed for use underground:
8425.3190	---其他	5			4	30	17	17	台		---Other
	---矿井卷扬机:										---Mine winches:
	--其他:										--Other:
8425.3910	---矿井口卷扬装置;专为井下使用设计的卷扬机:	10	5		0	30	17	17	台		---Pit-head winding gear; winches specially designed for use underground:
8425.3990	---其他	5			4	30	17	17	台		---Other
	-千斤顶;提升车辆用的提升机:										-Jacks; hoists of a kind used for raising vehicles:
8425.4100	--车库中使用的固定千斤顶系统	3		2.5	0	30	17	17	台	B	--Built-in jacking systems of a type used in garages
	--其他液压千斤顶及提升机:										--Other jacks and hoists, hydraulic:
8425.4210	---液压千斤顶	3			1.8	30	17	17	台	B	---Hydraulic jacks
8425.4290	---其他	5			4	30	17	17	台		---Other
	--其他:										--Other:
8425.4910	---其他千斤顶	5			4	30	17	17	台	B	---Other jacks
8425.4990	---其他	10	5		8	30	17	17	台		---Other
84.26	**船用桅杆式起重机;起重机,包括缆式起重机;移动式吊运架、跨运车及装有起重机的工作车:**										**Ships derricks; cranes, including cable cranes; mobile lifting frames, straddle carriers and works trucks fitted with a crane:**

税则号列 Tariff Item.	货品名称	最惠国(%) MFN	协定(%)CT 东盟 CA	 中巴 CP	 中智 CC	普通 Gen	增值税率 VAT	出口退税 ED	计量单位 Unit	监管条件 SC	Article Description
	-高架移动式起重机、桁架桥式起重机、龙门起重机、桥式起重机、移动式吊运架及跨运车:										-Overhead travelling cranes, transporter cranes, gantry cranes, bridge cranes, mobile lifting frames and straddle carriers:
	--固定支架的高架移动式起重机:										--Overhead travelling cranes on fixed support:
8426.1120	---通用桥式起重机	8	T3		6.4	30	17	17	台		---Bridge cranes, all-purpose
8426.1190	---其他	8	T3		6.4	30	17	17	台		---Other:
8426.1200	--带胶轮的移动式吊运架及跨运车	6	5		0	30	17	17	台		--Mobile lifting frames on tyres and straddle carriers
	--其他:										--Other:
8426.1910	---装船机	5		2.5	0	30	17	17	台		---Ship loading cranes
	---卸船机:										---Ship unloading cranes:
8426.1921	----抓斗式	5		3.5	0	30	17	17	台		----Grab ship unloading cranes
8426.1929	----其他	5		3.5	0	30	17	17	台	O	----Other
8426.1930	---龙门式起重机	10	5	7	0	30	17	17	台	O	---Gantry cranes
	---装卸桥:										---Loading and unlcading bridges:
8426.1941	----门式装卸桥	10	5	7	0	30	17	17	台		----Frame loading and unloading bridges
8426.1942	----集装箱装卸桥	10	5	7	0	30	17	17	台	O	----Container loading and unloading bridges
8426.1943	----其他动臂式装卸桥	10	5	7	0	30	17	17	台		----Derrick loading and unloading bridges
8426.1949	----其他	10	5	7	0	30	17	17	台		----Other
8426.1990	---其他	10	T3	7	0	30	17	17	台		---Other
8426.2000	-塔式起重机	10	5		0	30	17	17	台	O	-Tower cranes
8426.3000	-门座式起重机及座式旋臂起重机	6	5		0	30	17	17	台	O	-Portal or pedestal jib cranes
	-其他自推进机械:										-Other machinery, self-propelled:
	--带胶轮的:										--On tyres:
8426.4110	---轮胎式起重机	5			4	30	17	17	台	OB	---Wheel-mounted cranes
8426.4190	---其他	5			4	30	17	17	台	OB	---Other
	--其他:										--Other:
8426.4910	---履带式起重机	8	5		6.4	30	17	17	台	O	---Crawler cranes
8426.4990	---其他	13	8		10.4	30	17	17	台		---Other
	-其他机械:										-Other machinery:
8426.9100	--供装于公路车辆的	10	5		0	30	17	17	台	B	--Designed for mounting on road vehicles
8426.9900	--其他	6	5		4.8	30	17	17	台		--Other
84.27	**叉车;其他装有升降或搬运装置的工作车:**										**Fork-lift trucks; other works trucks fitted with lifting or handling equipment:**
	-电动机推进的机动车:										-Self-propelled trucks powered by an electric motor:
8427.1010	---有轨巷道堆垛机	9	5		7.2	30	17	17	台	OAB	---Track alleyway stackers
8427.1020	---无轨巷道堆垛机	9	5		7.2	30	17	17	台	AB	---Trackless alleyway stackers
8427.1090	---其他	9	5		7.2	30	17	17	台	OAB	---Other
	-其他机动车:										-Other self-propelled trucks:
8427.2010	---集装箱叉车	9	5	8.6	0	30	17	17	台	BA	---Fork-lift trucks cranes
8427.2090	---其他	9	5	8.6	0	30	17	17	台	BA	---Other
8427.9000	-其他车	9	5		0	30	17	17	台	BA	-Other trucks

税则号列 Tariff Item.	货品名称	最惠国(%) MFN	协定(%)CT 东盟 CA	中巴 CP	中智 CC	普通 Gen	增值税率 VAT	出口退税 ED	计量单位 Unit	监管条件 SC	Article Description
84.28	**其他升降、搬运、装卸机械(例如,升降机、自动梯、输送机、缆车):**										**Other lifting, handling, loading or unloading machinery (for example, lifts, escalators, conveyors, teleferics):**
	-升降机及倒卸式起重机:										-Lifts and skip hoists:
8428.1010	---载客电梯	8		5.6	0	30	17	17	台	OA	---Designed for the transport of persons
8428.1090	---其他	6	T3	4.2	0	30	17	17	台	OA	---Other
8428.2000	-气压升降机及输送机	5			4	30	17	17	台		-Pneumatic elevators and conveyors
	-其他用于连续运送货物或材料的升降机及输送机:										-Other continuous-action elevators and conveyors, for goods or materials:
8428.3100	--地下专用的	5			0	30	17	17	台		--Specially designed for underground use
8428.3200	--其他,斗式	5			0	30	17	17	台		--Other, bucket type
8428.3300	--其他,带式	5		4.3	4	30	17	17	台	O	--Other, belt type
	--其他:										--Other:
8428.3910	---链式	5		3.5	4	30	17	17	台	O	---Chain type
8428.3920	---辊式	5		3.5	4	30	17	17	台	O	---Roller type
8428.3990	---其他	5		3.5	4	30	17	17	台		---Other
8428.4000	-自动梯及自动人行道	5			0	30	17	17	台	OA	-Escalators and moving walkways
	-缆车、座式升降机、滑雪拉索、索道用牵引装置:										-Teleferics, chair-lifts, ski-draglines; traction mechanisms for funiculars:
8428.6010	---货运架空索道	8	5		0	30	17	17	台		---Cargo aerial cableways
	---客运架空索道:										---Passanger aerial cableways:
8428.6021	----单线循环式	8	5		0	30	17	17	台		----Monocable endless
8428.6029	----其他	8	5		0	30	17	17	台		----Other
8428.6090	---其他	8	5		0	30	17	17	台		---Other
	-其他机械										-Other machinery
8428.9010	---矿车推动机、铁道机车或货车的转车台、货车倾卸装置及类似的铁道货车搬运装置	10	5		0	30	17	17	台		---Mine wagon pushers, locmotive or wagon traversers, wagon tippers and similar railway wagon handling equipment
8428.9090	---其他	5			4	30	17	17	台		---Other
8428.9090 10	放化分离作业和热室用遥控机械手(能贯穿0.6米以上热室壁或壁厚为0.6米以上热室顶)	5				30	17	17	台	3	Remote manipulators for radioactive chemical separating operation and hot cell (capable of penetrating wall of hot cell thickness >0.6m or top of hot cell thickness ≥0.6m)
8428.9090 20	核反应堆燃料装卸机(用于在核反应堆中插入或取出燃料的操作设备)	5				30	17	17	台	3	nuclear reactor fuel loader and unloader (operational appliances used for putting inor taking out the fuels in nuclear reactor)
8428.9090 90	其他升降、搬运、装卸机械	5				30	17	17	台		Other lifting, handing, loading or unloading machinery
84.29	**机动推土机、侧铲推土机、筑路机、平地机、铲运机、机械铲、挖掘机、机铲装载机、捣固机械及压路机:**										**Self-propelled bulldozers, angledozers, graders, levellers, scrapers, mechanical shovels, excavators, shovel loaders, tamping machines and road rollers:**

税则号列 Tariff Item.	货品名称	最惠国(%) MFN	协定(%) CT 东盟 CA	中巴 CP	中智 CC	普通 Gen	增值税率 VAT	出口退税 ED	计量单位 Unit	监管条件 SC	Article Description
	-推土机及侧铲推土机:										-Bulldozers and angledozers:
	--履带式:										--Track laying:
8429.1110	---发动机输出功率超过235.36千瓦(320马力)的	7	T3		5.6	17	17	17	台	OA	---With an engine of an output exceeding 235.36kW (320hp)
8429.1190	---其他	7	T3		5.6	30	17	17	台	AO	---Other
	--其他:										--Other:
8429.1910	---发动机输出功率超过235.36千瓦(320马力)的	7	T3		0	17	17	17	台	A	---With an engine of an output exceeding 235.36kW (320hp)
8429.1990	---其他	7	T3		0	30	17	17	台	A	---Other
	-筑路机及平地机:										-Graders and levellers:
8429.2010	---发动机输出功率超过235.36千瓦(320马力)的	5			4	17	17	17	台	A	---With an engine of an output exceeding 235.36kW (320hp)
8429.2090	---其他	5			4	30	17	17	台	OA	---Other:
	-铲运机:										-Scrapers:
8429.3010	---斗容量超过10立方米的	3			0	17	17	17	台	A	---Having a capacity of shovel exceeding $10m^3$
8429.3090	---其他	5			0	30	17	17	台	A	---Other
	-捣固机械及压路机:										-Tamping machines and road rollers:
	---机动压路机:										---Self-propelled road rollers:
8429.4011	----机重18吨及以上的振动压路机	7	T3		5.6	20	17	17	台	OA	----Vibration type, of a deadweight of 18t or more
8429.4019	----其他	8	T3		6.4	40	17	17	台	OA	----Other
8429.4090	---其他	6	T3		4.8	30	17	17	台	OA	---Other
	-机械铲、挖掘机及机铲装载机:										-Mechanical shovels, excavators and shovel loaders:
8429.5100	--前铲装载机	5			4	30	17	17	台	A	--Front-end shovel loaders
	--上部结构可旋转360度的机械:										--Machinery with a 360° revolving superstructure:
	---挖掘机:										---Excavators:
8429.5211	----轮胎式	8	5	7.2	6.4	30	17	17	台	OA	----Tyre-mounted
8429.5212	----履带式	8	5		6.4	30	17	17	台	OA	----Track-mounted
8429.5219	----其他	8	5	7.2	6.4	30	17	17	台	OA	----Other
8429.5290	---其他	8	5	7.2	6.4	30	17	17	台	OA	---Other
8429.5900	--其他	8	T3		6.4	30	17	17	台	OA	--Other
84.30	泥土、矿物或矿石的运送、平整、铲运、挖掘、捣固、压实、开采或钻探机械;打桩机及拔桩机;扫雪机及吹雪机:										**Other moving, grading, levelling, scraping, excavating, tamping, compacting, extracting or boring machinery, for earth, minerals or ores; pile-drivers and pile-extractors; snow-ploughs and snow-blowers:**
8430.1000	-打桩机及拔桩机	10	5		0	30	17	17	台		-Pile-drivers and pile-extranctors
8430.2000	-扫雪机及吹雪机	10	5		0	30	17	17	台		-Snow-ploughs and snow-blowers
	-截煤机、凿岩机及隧道掘进机:										-Coal or rock cutters and tunnelling machinery:
8430.3100	--自推进的	10	T3		8	30	17	17	台	O	--Self-propelle
8430.3900	--其他	6	T3		0	30	17	17	台		--Other
	-其他钻探或凿井机械:										-Other boring or sinking machinery:
	--自推进的:										--Self-propelled:
	---石油及天然气钻探机:										---Oil and natural gas drilling machinery:

税则号列 Tariff Item.	货品名称	最惠国(%) MFN	协定(%)CT			普通 Gen	增值税率 VAT	出口退税 ED	计量单位 Unit	监管条件 SC	Article Description
			东盟 CA	中巴 CP	中智 CC						
8430.4111	----钻探深度在6000米及以上的	5			4	11	17	17	台		----Of drilling depth of 6000m or more
8430.4119	----其他	5			4	17	17	17	台		----Other
	---其他钻探机:										---Other drilling machinery:
8430.4121	----钻探深度在6000米及以上的	5			4	11	17	17	台		----Of drilling depth of 6000m or more
8430.4122	----钻探深度在6000米以下的履带式自推进钻机	5			4	17	17	17	台		----Crawler boring machinery of drilling depth <6000 m
8430.4129	----钻探深度在6000米以下的其他钻探机	5			4	17	17	17	台		----Other boring machinery of drilling depth <6000 m
8430.4190	---其他	5			4	30	17	17	台		---Other
8430.4900	--其他	5			4	30	17	17	台		--Other
	-其他自推进机械:										-Other machinery, self-propelled:
8430.5010	---其他采油机械	3			1.8	17	17	17	台		---For oil production
8430.5020	---矿用电铲	7	T3		5.6	30	17	17	台		---Mining power shovels
	---采矿钻机:										---Mining drills:
8430.5031	----牙轮直径380毫米及以上	5			4	30	17	17	台		----Gear wheel diameter more than 380mm
8430.5039	----其他	5			4	30	17	17	台		----Other
8430.5090	---其他	5			4	30	17	17	台		---Other
	-其他非自推进机械:										-Other machinery, not self-propelled:
8430.6100	--捣固或压实机械	6	T3		0	30	17	17	台		--Tamping or compacting machinery
	--其他:										--Other:
	---工程钻机:										---Engineering drills:
8430.6911	----钻筒直径在3米及以上	6	T3		0	30	17	17	台		----Boring casing diameter more than 3m
8430.6919	----其他	6	T3		0	30	17	17	台		----Other
8430.6920	---铲运机	6	T3		0	30	17	17	台		---Serapers
8430.6990	---其他	6	T3		0	30	17	17	台		---Other
84.31	**专用于或主要用于税目84.25至84.30所列机械的零件:**										**Parts suitable for use solely or principally with the machinery of headings No. 84.25 to 84.30:**
8431.1000	-税目84.25所列机械的零件	3			0	30	17	13	千克		-Of machinery of heading 84.25
8431.2000	-税目84.27所列机械的零件	6	5	5.4	0	30	17	13	千克		-Of machinery of heading 84.27
	-税目84.28所列机械的零件:										-Of machinery of heading 84.28:
8431.3100	--升降机、倒卸式起重机或自动梯的零件	3			0	30	17	13	千克		--Of lifts, skip hoists or escalators
8431.3900	--其他	5		2.5	4	30	17	13	千克		--Other
	-税目84.26、84.29、或84.30所列机械的零件:										-Of machinery of headingNo. 84.26, 84.29 or 84.30:
8431.4100	--戽斗、铲斗、抓斗、及夹斗	6	T3	5.4	4.8	17	17	13	个/千克	0	--Buckets, shovels, grabs and grips
8431.4200	--推土机或侧铲推土机用铲	6	T3		0	17	17	13	个/千克		--Bulldozer or angledozer blades
	--子目8430.41或8430.49所列钻探或凿井机械的零件:										--Parts of boring or sinking machinery of subheading 8430.41 or 8430.49:
8431.4310	---石油或天然气钻探机用	4		2.8	3.2	11	17	13	千克		---Of oil and natural gas drilling machinery
8431.4320	---其他钻探机用	4		2.8	3.2	11	17	13	千克		---Of other drilling machinery
8431.4390	---其他	5		3.5	4	17	17	13	千克		---Of sinking machinery
	--其他:										--Other:
8431.4910	---矿用电铲用	5		4.5	4	17	17	13	千克		---For mining power shovels
8431.4990	---其他	5		4.5	4	17	17	13	千克	0	---Other

税则号列 Tariff Item.	货品名称	最惠国(%) MFN	协定(%) CT 东盟 CA	中巴 CP	中智 CC	普通 Gen	增值税率 VAT	出口退税 ED	计量单位 Unit	监管条件 SC	Article Description
84.32	**农业、园艺及林业用整地或耕作机械;草坪及运动场地滚压机:**										**Agricultural, horticultural or forestry machinery for soil preparation or cultivation; lawn or sports-ground rollers:**
8432.1000	-犁	5			0	30	13	11	台		-Ploughs
	-耙、松土机、中耕机、除草机及耕耘机:										-Harrows, scarifiers, cultivators, weeders and hoes:
8432.2100	--圆盘耙	5			0	30	13	11	台		--Disc harrows
8432.2900	--其他	4			0	30	13	11	台		--Other
8432.3000	-播种机、种植机及移植机	4		3.5	0	30	13	11	台		-Seeders, planters and transplanters
8432.4000	-施肥机	4			0	30	13	11	台		-Manure spreaders and fertilizer distributors
	-其他机械:										-Other machinery:
8432.8010	---草坪及运动场地滚压机	7	5		0	40	17	13	台		---Lawn or sports-ground rollers
8432.8090	---其他	4			0	30	13	11	台		---Other
8432.9000	-零件	4			3.2	17	17	13	千克		-Parts
84.33	**收割机、脱粒机,包括草料打包机;割草机;蛋类、水果或其他农产品的清洁、分选、分级机器,但税目84.37的机器除外:**										**Harvesting or threshing machinery, including straw or fodder balers; grass or hay mowers; machines for cleaning, sorting or grading eggs, fruit or other agricultural produce, other than machinery of heading No. 84.37:**
	-草坪、公园或运动场地用的割草机:										-Mowers for lawns, parks or sports grounds:
8433.1100	--机动的,切割装置在同一水平面上旋转的	6	5		0	30	13	13	台		--Powered, with the cutting device rotating in a horizontal plane
8433.1900	--其他	6	5		0	30	17	13	台		--Other
8433.2000	-其他割草机,包括牵引装置用的刀具杆	4			0	30	13	11	台		-Other mowers, including cutter bars for tractor mounting
8433.3000	-其他干草切割、翻晒机器	5			0	30	13	11	台		-Other haymaking machinery
8433.4000	-草料打包机,包括收集打包机	5			0	30	13	11	台		-Straw or fodder balers, including pick-up balers
	-其他收割机;脱粒机:										-Other harvesting machinery; threshing machinery:
8433.5100	--联合收割机	8	5	7.6	0	17	13	11	台		--Combine harvester-threshers
8433.5100 01	功率≥160马力的联合收割机	8				17	13	11	台		Combine harvester-threshers, power ≥ 160Hp
8433.5100 90	功率<160马力的联合收割机	8				17	13	11	台		Combine harvester-threshers, power < 160Hp
8433.5200	--其他脱粒机	8	5		0	30	13	11	台		--Other threshing machinery
8433.5300	--根茎或块茎收获机	8	5		0	30	13	11	台		--Root or tuber harvesting machines
	--其他:										--Other:
8433.5910	---甘蔗收获机	8	5		6.4	30	13	11	台		---Sugarcane harvesters
8433.5920	---棉花采摘机	8	5		6.4	30	13	11	台		---Cotton machine
8433.5990	---其他	8	5		6.4	30	13	11	台		---Other
8433.5990 01	自走式青储饲料收获机	8				30	13	11	台		Mobile silage harvester (including cotton harvesters)

税则号列 Tariff Item.	货品名称	最惠国(%) MFN	协定(%)CT 东盟 CA	 中巴 CP	 中智 CC	普通 Gen	增值税率 VAT	出口退税 ED	计量单位 Unit	监管条件 SC	Article Description
8433.5990 90	其他收割机及脱粒机	8				30	13	11	台		Other harvesting or threshing machinery
8433.6000	-蛋类、水果或其他农产品的清洁、分选、分级机器	5			4	30	13	11	台		-Machines for cleaning, sorting or grading eggs, fruit or other agricultural produce
	-零件:										-Parts:
8433.9010	---联合收割机用	5			0	11	17	13	千克		---Of combine harvester-thrashers
8433.9090	---其他	3			0	17	17	13	千克		---Other
84.34	**挤奶机及乳品加工机器:**										**Milking machines and dairy machinery:**
8434.1000	-挤奶机	10	5		0	20	13	11	台		-Milking machines
8434.2000	-乳品加工机器	6	5		4.8	30	17	13	台	A	-Dairy machinery
8434.9000	-零件	5			4	17	17	13	千克	A	-Parts
84.35	**制酒、制果汁或制类似饮料用的压榨机、轧碎机及类似机器:**										**Presses, crushers and similar machinery used in the manufacture of wine, cider, fruit juices or similar beverages:**
8435.1000	-机器	10	5		8	30	17	13	台	A	-Machinery
8435.9000	-零件	6	5		0	30	17	13	千克	A	-Parts
84.36	**农业、园艺、林业、家禽饲养业或养蜂业用的其他机器,包括装有机械或热力装置的催芽设备;家禽孵卵器及育雏器:**										**Other agricultural, horticultural, forestry, poultry-keeping or bee-keeping machinery, including germination plant fitted with mechanical or thermal equipment; poultry incubators and brooders:**
8436.1000	-动物饲料配制机	7	T3		0	30	13	11	台		-Machinery for preparing animal feeding stuffs
	-家禽饲养用的机器;家禽孵卵器及育雏器:										-Poultry-keeping machinery; poultry incubators and brooders:
8436.2100	--家禽孵卵器及育雏器	5			0	30	13	11	台		--Poultry incubators and brooders
8436.2900	--其他	10	5		8	30	13	11	台		--Other
8436.8000	-其他机器	10	5		0	30	13	11	台		-Other machinery
	-零件:										-Parts:
8436.9100	--家禽饲养用机器的零件或家禽孵卵器及育雏器的零件	6	5		0	17	17	13	千克		--Of poultry-keeping machinery or poultry incubators and brooders
8436.9900	--其他	6	5		0	17	17	13	千克		--Other
84.37	**种子、谷物或干豆的清洁、分选或分级机器;谷物磨粉业加工机器或谷物、干豆加工机器,但农业用机器除外:**										**Machines for cleaning, sorting or grading seed, grain or dried leguminous vegetables; machinery used in the milling industry or for the working of cereals or dried leguminous vegetables, other than farm-type machinery:**
8437.1000	-种子、谷物或干豆的清洁、分选或分级机器	10	5		0	30	13	11	台		-Machines for cleaning, sorting or grading seed, grain or dried leguminous vegetables
8437.8000	-其他机器	10	5	8.5	0	30	17	11	台	A	-Other machinery
8437.9000	-零件	6	5		0	30	17	13	千克		-Parts

税则号列 Tariff Item.	货品名称	最惠国(%) MFN	协定(%) 东盟 CA	协定(%) 中巴 CP	协定(%) 中智 CC	普通 Gen	增值税率 VAT	出口退税 ED	计量单位 Unit	监管条件 SC	Article Description
84.38	**本章其他税目未列名的食品、饮料工业用的生产或加工机器,但提取、加工动物油脂或植物固定油脂的机器除外:**										**Machinery, not specified or included else-where in this Chapter, for the industrial preparation or manufacture of food or drink, other than machinery for the extraction or preparation of animal or fixed vegetable fats or oils:**
8438.1000	-糕点加工机器及生产通心粉、面条或类似产品的机器	7	5		5.6	30	17	13	台		-Bakery machinery and machinery for the manufacture of macaroni, spaghetti or similar products
8438.1000 10	糕点生产线	7				30	17	13	台	A	Bakery production lines
8438.1000 90	通心粉,面条的生产加工机器(包括类似产品的加工机)	7				30	17	13	台	A	Machinery for the manufacture of macaroni, spaghetti or similar products
8438.2000	-生产糖果、可可粉、巧克力的机器	8	5		6.4	30	17	13	台	A	-Machinery for the manufacture of confectionery, cocoa or chocolate
8438.3000	-制糖机器	10	5		0	30	17	13	台	A	-Machinery for sugar manufacture
8438.4000	-酿酒机器	7	5		0	30	17	13	台	A	-Brewery machinery
8438.5000	-肉类或家禽加工机器	7	5		5.6	30	17	13	台	A	-Machinery for the preparation of meat or poultry
8438.6000	-水果、坚果或蔬菜加工机器	10	T3		8	30	17	13	台	A	-Machinery for the preparation of fruits, nuts or vegetables
8438.8000	-其他机器	8.5	5	8.1	6.8	30	17	13	台	A	-Other machinery
8438.9000	-零件	5			4	30	17	13	千克	A	-Parts
84.39	**纤维素纸浆、纸及纸板的制造或整理机器:**										**Machinery for making pulp of fibrous cellulosic material or for making or finishing paper or paperboard:**
8439.1000	-制造纤维素纸浆的机器	8.4	5		6.72	30	17	13	台	O	-Machinery for making pulp of fibrous cellulosic material
8439.2000	-纸或纸板的抄造机器	8.4	5		0	30	17	13	台	O	-Machinery for making paper or paper board
8439.3000	-纸或纸板的整理机器	8.4	5		0	30	17	13	台	O	-Machinery for finishing paper or paper board
	-零件:										-Parts:
8439.9100	--制造纤维素纸浆的机器用	6	5		4.8	30	17	13	千克		--Of machinery for making pulp of fibrous cellulosic material
8439.9900	--其他	6	5	3	4.8	30	17	13	千克		--Other
84.40	**书本装订机器,包括锁线订书机:**										**Book-binding machinery, including book-sewing machines:**
	-机器:										-Machinery:
8440.1010	---锁线装订机	10	5		0	35	17	13	台		---Sewing bookbinders
8440.1020	---胶订机	12	8		7.2	35	17	13	台		---Glueing bookbinders
8440.1090	---其他	12	8		7.2	35	17	13	台		---Other
8440.9000	-零件	8	5		0	35	17	13	千克		-Parts
84.41	**其他制造纸浆制品、纸制品或纸板制品的机器,包括各种切纸机:**										**Other machinery for making up paper pulp, paper or paperboard, including cutting machines of all kinds:**
8441.1000	-切纸机	12	8		9.6	50	17	13	台		-Cutting machines

税则号列 Tariff Item.	货品名称	最惠国(%) MFN	协定(%)CT			普通 Gen	增值税率 VAT	出口退税 ED	计量单位 Unit	监管条件 SC	Article Description
			东盟 CA	中巴 CP	中智 CC						
8441.2000	-制造包、袋或信封的机器	12	8	11.4	9.6	30	17	13	台		-Machines for making bags, sacks or envelopes
	-制造箱、盒、管、桶或类似容器的机器,但模制成型机器除外:										-Machines for making cartons, boxes, cases, tubes, drums or similar containers, other than by moulding:
8441.3010	---制造纸塑铝复合罐的生产设备	13.5	8	12.8	10.8	30	17	13	台		---Machines for paper, plastic and aluminium composite can manufacture
8441.3090	---其他	13.5	8	12.8	10.8	30	17	13	台		---Other
8441.4000	-纸浆、纸或纸板制品模制成型机器	12	8		7.2	30	17	13	台	O	-Machines for moulding articles in paper pulp, paper or paperboard
	-其他机器:										-Other machinery:
8441.8010	---制造纸塑铝软包装的生产设备	12	8	11.4	9.6	30	17	13	台		---Machines for paper plastic and aluminium flexible packaging manufacture
8441.8090	---其他	12	8	11.4	9.6	30	17	13	台	O	---Other
	-零件:										-Parts:
8441.9010	---切纸机用	8	5		6.4	50	17	13	千克		---Of cutting machines
8441.9090	---其他	8.4	5		6.7	30	17	13	千克		---Other
84.42	**铸字、排字或制版用的机器、器具及设备(税目84.56至84.65的机床除外);活字、印刷用版、片、滚筒及其他部件;制成供印刷用(例如,刨平、压纹或抛光)的板、片、滚筒及石板:**										**Machinery, apparatus and equipment (other than the machine-tools of headingsNOS. 84.56 to 84.65), for type-founding or type-setting, for preparing or making printing blocks, plates, cylinders or other printing components; printing type, blocks, plates, cylinders and other printing components; blocks, plates, cylinders and lithographic stones, prepared for printing purposes (for example, planed, grained or polished):**
	-机器、器具及设备:										-Machinery, apparatus and equipment:
8442.3010	---铸字机	9	5		0	35	17	13	台		---Type casters
	---制版机器、器具及设备										---Other machinery, apparatus and equipment for typesetting
8442.3021	----计算机直接制版机器(CTP)	9	5		0	35	17	13	台		----(Computerized plate – making machine)
8442.3029	----其他制版机器、器具及设备	9	5		0	35	17	13	台		----(Other machinery, apparatrus and epuipment for typesetting)
8442.3090	---其他	9	5		0	35	17	13	台		---Other
8442.4000	-上述机器、器具及设备的零件	7	5		0	20	17	13	千克		-Parts of the foregoing machinery, apparatus or equipment
8442.4000 01	计算机直接制版机器用零件	7				20	17	13	千克		Components for computer – composing machines
8442.4000 90	其他铸字、排字、制版机器的零件	7				20	17	13	千克		Other components of typecasting, typesetting and composing machines
8442.5000	-印刷用版、滚筒及其他印刷部件;制成供印刷用(例如,刨平、压纹或抛光)的板、滚筒及石板	7	5		0	35	17	13	千克		-Printing type, blocks, plates, cylinders and other printing components; blocks, plates, cylinders and lithographic stones, prepared for printing purposes (for example, planed, grained or polished)

税则号列 Tariff Item.	货 品 名 称	最惠国(%) MFN	协定(%)CT 东盟 CA	中巴 CP	中智 CC	普通 Gen	增值税率 VAT	出口退税 ED	计量单位 Unit	监管条件 SC	Article Description
84.43	**用于税目84.42的印刷用版(片)、滚筒及其他印刷部件进行印刷的机器;其他打印机、复印机及传真机,不论是否组合式;上述机器的零件及附件:**										**Printing machinery used for printing by means of the printing type, blocks, plates, cylinders and other printing components of headingNo. 84. 42; ink-jet printing machines, other than those of headingNo. 84. 71; machines for uses ancillary to printing:**
	-用税目84.42的印刷用版(片)、滚筒及其他印刷部件进行印刷的机器:										- Printing machinery used for printing by means of the printing type, blocks, plates, cylinders and other printing components of heading 84. 42:
8443. 1100	--卷取进料式	10	5	7	8	35	17	13	台	0	--Reel fed
8443. 1200	--办公室用片取进料式(展开片尺寸一边不超过22cm,另一边不起过36cm)	12	8		7. 2	35	17	13	台		--Sheet fed, office type (sheet size not exceeding 22×36cm)
	--其他胶印机:										--Other lffset printing machinery:
8443. 1310	---平张纸进料式	10	5	7	8	35	17	13	台	0	---Sheet fed
8443. 1390	---其他	10	5	7	8	35	17	13	台	0	---Other
8443. 1400	--卷取进料式凸版印刷机,但不包括苯胺印刷机	12	8		7. 2	35	17	13	台		--Letterpress printing machinery, excluding flexographic printing
8443. 1500	--除卷取进料式以外的凸版印刷机,但不包括笨胺印刷机	12	8		9. 6	35	17	13	台		-Other than letterpress prineing machinery, excluding flexographic printing
8443. 1600	--苯胺印刷机	10	5		8	35	17	13	台		--Flexographic printing machinery
8443. 1700	--凹版印刷机	18	8	16. 2	10. 8	35	17	13	台		--Gravure printing machinery
	--其他:										--Other:
	---网式印刷机:										---Screen printing machinery:
8443. 1921	----圆网印刷机	10	5	9	0	35	17	13	台		----Cylinder screen press
8443. 1921 01	纺织用圆网印花机	10				35	17	13	台	0	Printing machines cylinder screen press, for textile
8443. 1921 90	其他圆网印刷机(用税目84.42项下商品进行印刷的机器)	10				35	17	13	台	0	Other printing machines cylinder screen press
8443. 1922	----平网印刷机	10	5	9	0	35	17	13	台		----Platen screen press
8443. 1922 01	纺织用平网印花机	10				35	17	13	台	0	Printing machines platen screen press, for textile
8443. 1922 10	用于光盘生产的盘面印刷机(用税目84.42项下商品进行印刷的机器)	10				35	17	13	台	60	Printing machines platen screen press, surface printer for CD production
8443. 1922 90	其他平网印刷机(用税目84.42项下商品进行印刷的机器)	10				35	17	13	台	0	Other printing machines platen screen press
8443. 1929	----其他	10	8	9	0	35	17	13	台	0	----Other
8443. 1980	---其他	8	5	7. 2	0	35	17	13	台	0	---Other
	-其他打印机、复印机及传真机,不论是否组合式:										-Other printers, photocopiers, fax machines, no matter whether how they are assembled:

税则号列 Tariff Item.	货品名称	最惠国(%) MFN	协定(%)CT 东盟 CA	中巴 CP	中智 CC	普通 Gen	增值税率 VAT	出口退税 ED	计量单位 Unit	监管条件 SC	Article Description
	--具有打印、复印或传真中两种及以上功能的机器，可与自动数据处理设备功网络连接：										--Machines with two or more functions of printing, photocopying or faxing, and can be commected to automatic data processing facilities or internet
8443.3110	---静电感光式	10	8		8	70	17	13	台	AB	---Photo-electrostatic
8443.3190	---其他	0				17	17	13	台	AB	---Other
	--其他，可与自动数据处理设备或网络连接：										--Other, can be connected to automatic data processing facilities or internet
	---专用于税目8471所列设备的打印机：										---Printers specially used for facilities listed with tax items 8471
8443.3211	----针式打印机	0				14	17	13	台	A	----Stylus printer
8443.3212	----激光打印机	0				14	17	13	台	A	----laser printer
8443.3213	----喷墨打印机	0				14	17	13	台	A	----Ink-jet-printer
8443.3219	----其他	0				14	17	13	台	A	----Other
	---数字式印刷设备：										---Digital printing facilitise:
8443.3221	----喷墨印刷机	8			0	30	17	13	台		----Ink-jet imprinter
8443.3221 01	幅宽>60cm的喷墨印刷设备(可与自动数据处理设备或网络连接)	8				30	17		台		Inkjet printers with breadth > 60cm (can be connected to automatic data processing facilities or internet)
8443.3221 90	其他数字式喷墨印刷机(可与自动数据处理设备或网络连接)	8				30	17		台		Other digital inkjet printers (can be connected to automatic data processing facilities or internet)
8443.3222	----静电照相印刷机(激光印刷机)	8	5	7.2	0	35	17	13	台		----Electrostatic photograph imprinter (laser imprinter)
8443.3222 01	幅宽>60cm的静电照相印刷设备(激光印刷机)(可与自动数据处理设备或网络连接)	8				35	17		台		Electrostatic printing equipments (laser printers) with breadth > 60cm ((can be connected to automatic data processing facilities or internet)
8443.3222 90	其他数字式静电照相印刷机(激光印刷机)(可与自动数据处理设备或网络连接)	8				35	17		台		Other digital electrostatic photograph printers (laser printers) (can be connected to automatic data processing facilities or internet)
8443.3229	----其他	8	5	7.2	0	30	17	13	台		----Other
8443.3290	---其他	0				17	17	13	台		---Other
8443.3290 10	传真机(可与自动数据处理设备或网络连接)	0				17	17		台	ABO	Fax machines (can be connected to automatic data processing facilities or internet)
8443.3290 90	其他印刷(打印机)，复印机和电传打字机(可与自动数据处理设备或网络连接)	0				17	17		台	AB	Other printing machines, photocopier and teleprinters (can be connected to automatic data processing facilities or internet)
	--其他：										--Other:
	---静电感光复印设备：										---Photo-Electrostatic photo copy device:
8443.3911	----将原件直接复印的(直接法)	0				70	17	13	台		----Directly photocopy the original copy (direct)
8443.3912	----将原件通过中间体转印的(间接法)	10	T3		8	70	17	13	台		----Photocopy through intermedia-te (indirect)

税则号列 Tariff Item.	货品名称	最惠国(%) MFN	协定(%) CT 东盟 CA	中巴 CP	中智 CC	普通 Gen	增值税率 VAT	出口退税 ED	计量单位 Unit	监管条件 SC	Article Description
	---其他感光复印设备:										---Other photo-electrostatic photocopy device
8443.3921	----带有光学系统的	0				70	17	13	台		----Carry optics system
8443.3922	----接触式的	20	12		12	70	17	13	台		----Contact
8443.3923	----热敏复印设备	20	12		12	70	17	13	台		----Thermo-copying apparatus
8443.3924	----热升华复印设备	20	12		12	70	17	13	台		----Thermal copying apparatus
	---数字式印刷设备										---Digital printing device
8443.3931	----喷墨印刷机	8			0	30	17	13	台		----Inkjet imprinter
8443.3932	----静电照相印刷机(激光印刷机)	8	5	7.2	0	35	17	13	台		----Electrostatic photograph imprinter (Laser imprinter)
8443.3939	---其他	8	5	7.2	0	30	17	13	台		---Other
8443.3990	---其他	0				30	17	13	台		---Other
	-零件及附件:										-Components and accessories
	--用税目84.42的印刷版、滚筒及其他印刷部伯进行印刷的机器零件及附件:										--The machinery components and accessories that use the printing components of tax item 84.42 to print
8443.9110	---印刷用辅助机器	12	8	9.6	9.6	35	17	13	千克	O	---Auxiliary machines for printing
8443.9190	---其他	6	5		0	20	17	13	千克		---Other
8443.9190 01	胶印机用墨量遥控装置(包括墨色控制装置,墨量调节装置,墨斗体等组成部分)	6				20	17		千克	O	The ink - controls for offset printing machine (including ink - color controls, the ink - quantity controls, etc)
8443.9190 90	其他用税目84.42项下商品进行印刷的机器零件与附件	6				20	17		千克		Other machine components and attachments that are used for printing goods under tax item 84.42.
	--其他:										--Other
8443.9910	---数字设备用辅助机器	12	8	9.6	9.6	35	17	13	千克	O	---Auxiliary machines for digital printins device
8443.9920	---数字印刷设备的零件	6	5	5	0	20	17	13	千克		---Components of digital printing eqyipment
8443.9990	---其他	0				35	17	13	千克		---Other
84.44	**化学纺织纤维挤压、拉伸、变形或切割机器:**										**Machines for extruding, drawing, texturing or cutting man-made textile materials:**
8444.0010	---合成纤维长丝纺丝机	10	5	7	0	30	17	13	台	O	---Synthetic filaments spinning jets
8444.0020	---合成纤维短丝纺丝机	10	5	7	0	30	17	13	台	O	---Synthetic staple fibres spinning jets
8444.0030	---人造纤维纺丝机	10	5	7	0	30	17	13	台	O	---Artificial fibres spinning jets
8444.0040	---化学纤维变形机	10	5	7	0	30	17	13	台	O	---Man-made fibres crimping machinery
8444.0050	---化学纤维切断机	10	5	7	0	30	17	13	台		---Man-made filaments cutting machinery
8444.0090	---其他	10	5	7	0	30	17	13	台	O	---Other
84.45	**纺织纤维的预处理机器;纺纱机、并线机、加捻机及其他生产纺织纱线的机器;摇纱机、络纱机(包括卷纬机)及处理税目84.46或84.47所列机器用的纺织纱线的机器:**										**Machines for preparing textile fibres; spinning, doubling or twisting machines and other machinery for producing textile yarns; textile reeling or winding (including weft-winding) machines and machines for preparing textile yarns for use on the machines of headingNo. 84.46 or 84.47:**

税则号列 Tariff Item.	货品名称	最惠国(%) MFN	协定(%)CT 东盟 CA	中巴 CP	中智 CC	普通 Gen	增值税率 VAT	出口退税 ED	计量单位 Unit	监管条件 SC	Article Description
	-纺织纤维的预处理机器:										-Machines for preparing textile fibres:
	--梳理机:										--Carding machines:
	---棉纤维型:										---For cotton type fibres:
8445.1111	----清梳联合机	10	5	9	0	30	17	13	台	ABO	----Blowing-carding-Machinery
8445.1112	----自动抓棉机	10	5	9	0	30	17	13	台	ABO	----Bale Pucker
8445.1113	----梳棉机	10	5	9	0	30	17	13	台	ABO	----Card or carding Machine
8445.1119	----其他	10	5	9	0	30	17	13	台	ABO	----Other
8445.1120	---毛纤维型	10	5	9	0	30	17	13	台	ABO	---For wool type fibres
8445.1190	---其他	10	5	9	0	30	17	13	台	AB	---Other
	--精梳机:										--Combing Machines:
8445.1210	---棉精梳机	10	5		0	30	17	13	台	ABO	---Cotton Comber
8445.1220	---毛精梳机	10	5		0	30	17	13	台	ABO	---Worsted Comber
8445.1290	---其他	10	5		0	30	17	13	台	ABO	---Other
	--拉伸机或粗纱机:										--Drawing or roving machines:
8445.1310	---拉伸机	10	5		0	30	17	13	台	AB	---Drawing machines
	---粗纱机:										---Roving machines:
8445.1321	----棉纺精纱机	10	5		0	30	17	13	台	OAB	----Cotton Roving Frames
8445.1322	----毛纺精纱机	10	5		0	30	17	13	台	OAB	----Worsted Roving Machines
8445.1329	----其他	10	5		0	30	17	13	台	OAB	----Other
8445.1900	--其他	10	5	9	8	30	17	13	台	AB	--Other
	-纺纱机:										-Textile spinning machines:
	---自由端纺纱机										---Open-end spinner
8445.2031	----转杯纺纱机	10	5	9	0	30	17	13	台	ABO	----Rotor spinning machines
8445.2032	----喷气纺纱机	10	5		0	30	17	13	台	AB	----Jet spinner
8445.2039	----其他	10	5		0	30	17	13	台	AB	----Other
	---环锭细纱机:										---Ring spining frames:
8445.2041	----棉细纱机	10.5	8	9.5	0	40	17	13	台	ABO	----Cotton Ring Spinning Frame
8445.2042	----毛细纱机	10	5		0	40	17	13	台	AB	----Worsted Ring Spinning Frame
8445.2049	----其他	10	5		0	40	17	13	台	AB	----Other
8445.2090	---其他	10	5	9	0	30	17	13	台	OA	---Other
8445.3000	-并线机或加捻机	10	5	9	0	30	17	13	台	OAB	-Textile doubling or twisting machines
	-络纱机(包括卷纬机)或摇纱机:										-Textile winding (including weft-winding) or reeling machines:
8445.4010	---自动络筒机	10	5	9	8	30	17	13	台	ABO	---Automatic bobbin winders
8445.4090	---其他	10	5	9	8	30	17	13	台	AB	---Other
	-其他:										-Other:
8445.9010	---整经机	10	5	9	8	30	17	13	台	ABO	---Warping machines
8445.9020	---浆纱机	10	5	9	8	30	17	13	台	OAB	---Sizing machines
8445.9090	---其他	10	5	9	8	30	17	13	台	OAB	---Other
84.46	织机:										**Weaving machines(looms):**
8446.1000	-所织织物宽度不超过30厘米的织机	8	5	7.2	0	30	17	13	台	A	-For weaving fabrics of a width not exceeding 30cm
	-所织织物宽度超过30厘米的梭织机:										-For weaving fabrics of width exceeding 30cm, shuttle type:
	--动力织机:										--Power looms:
8446.2110	---地毯织机	12	8	10.8	9.6	35	17	13	台	A	---For making carpets or rugs

税则号列 Tariff Item.	货品名称	最惠国(%) MFN	协定(%) CT 东盟 CA	中巴 CP	中智 CC	普通 Gen	增值税率 VAT	出口退税 ED	计量单位 Unit	监管条件 SC	Article Description
8446.2190	---其他	10	8	9	8	30	17	13	台	AB	---Other
8446.2900	--其他	10	5		8	30	17	13	台	A	--Other
	-所织织物宽度超过30厘米的无梭织机：										-For weaving fabrics of a width exceeding 30cm, shuttleless type:
8446.3020	---剑杆织机	8	5	6.8	6.4	30	17	13	台	AO	---Rapier looms
8446.3030	---片梭织机	8	5	5.6	6.4	30	17	13	台	AO	---Carrier looms
8446.3040	---喷水织机	8	5	6.8	6.4	30	17	13	台	OA	---Water jet looms
8446.3050	---喷气织机	8	5	6.8	6.4	30	17	13	台	OA	---Air jet looms
8446.3090	---其他	8	5	6.8	6.4	30	17	13	台	OA	---Other
84.47	**针织机、缝编机及制粗松螺旋花线、网眼薄纱、花边、刺绣品、装饰带、编织带或网的机器及簇绒机：**										**Knitting machines, stitch-bonding machines and machines for making gimped yarn, tulle lace, embroidery, trimmings, braid or net and machines for tufting:**
	-圆型针织机：										-Circular knitting machines:
8447.1100	--圆筒直径不超过165毫米	8	5	7	0	30	17	13	台	OAB	--With cylinder diameter not exceeding 165mm
8447.1200	--圆筒直径超过165毫米	8	5		0	30	17	13	台	OAB	--With cylinder diameter exceeding 165mm
	-平型针织机；缝编机：										-Flat knitting machines; stitch-bonding machines:
8447.2010	---经编机	8	5	6.8	0	30	17	13	台	OA	---Warp knitting machines
8447.2020	---其他平型针织机	8	5	6.8	0	30	17	13	台	OAB	---Other flat knitting machines
8447.2030	---缝编机	8	5	6.8	0	30	17	13	台	A	---Stitch-bonding machines
	-其他：										-Other:
	---簇绒机：										---Tufting machines:
8447.9011	----地毯织机	7	5	4.9	0	35	17	13	台	A	----For making carpets or rugs
8447.9019	----其他	8	5	5.6	0	30	17	13	台	A	----Other
8447.9020	---绣花机	8	5	6.8	0	30	17	13	台	A	---Embroidery machines
8447.9090	---其他	10	5	5	0	30	17	13	台	A	---Other
84.48	**税目84.44、84.45、84.46或84.47所列机器的辅助机器（例如，多臂机、提花机、自停装置及换梭装置）；专用于或主要用于税目84.44、84.45、84.46或84.47所列机器的零件、附件（例如，锭子、锭壳、钢丝针布、梳、喷丝头、梭子、综丝、综框、针织机用针）：**										**Auxiliary machinery for use with machines of headingNos. 84.44, 84.45, 84.46 or 84.47 (for example, dobbies, Jacquards, automatic stop motions, shuttle changing mechanisms); parts and accessories suitable for use solely or principally with the machines of this heading or of headingNos. 84.44, 84.45, 84.46 or 84.47 (for example, spindles and spindle flyers, card clothing, combs, extruding nipples, shuttles, healds and heald-frames, hosiery needles):**
	-税目84.44、84.45、84.46或84.47所列机器的辅助机器：										-Auxiliary machinery for machines of headingNo. 84.44, 84.45, 84.46 or 84.47:
8448.1100	--多臂机或提花机及其所用的卡片缩小、复制、穿孔或汇编机器	8	5		0	20	17	13	千克		--Dobbies and Jacquards; card reducing, copying, punching or assembling machines for use there with

税则号列 Tariff Item.	货品名称	最惠国(%) MFN	协定(%)CT 东盟 CA	协定(%)CT 中巴 CP	协定(%)CT 中智 CC	普通 Gen	增值税率 VAT	出口退税 ED	计量单位 Unit	监管条件 SC	Article Description
8448.1100 01	多臂机或提花机(转速指标500转/分以上)	8				20	17	13	千克	O	Dobbies and Jacquards (index of revolution speed >500r/min)
8448.1100 90	多臂机或提花机所用卡片缩小、复制、穿孔或汇编机器(包括其所用的卡片缩小、复制、穿孔或汇编机器)	8				20	17	13	千克	O	Other dobbies and Jacquards (including card reducing, copying, punching or assembling machines for use there with)
8448.1900	--其他	8	5		0	20	17	13	千克		--Other
	-税目84.44所列机器及其辅助机器的零件、附件:										-Parts and accessories of machines of heading 84.44 or of their auxiliary machinery:
8448.2020	---喷丝头或喷丝板	6	5		0	14	17	13	个/千克		---Extruding nipples or spinnerets
8448.2090	---其他	6	5		0	17	17	13	千克		---Other
	-税目84.45所列机器及其辅助机器的零件、附件:										-Parts and accessories of machines of headingNo. 84.45 or of their auxiliary machinery:
8448.3100	--钢丝针布	6	5		0	17	17	13	千克		--Card clothing
8448.3200	--纺织纤维预处理机器的零件、附件,但钢丝针布除外	6	5		0	17	17	13	千克		--Of machines for preparing textile fibres, other than card clothing
8448.3200 01	精梳机钳板、顶梳装置(精梳机锡林部件,精梳机车头凸轮传动,行星齿轮部件)	6				17	17	13	千克		Nippers, topcombs cylinders, head cams, epicyclic gear of combers (cykinder parts of combing machines)
8448.3200 02	精梳联合机梳理装置(精梳联合机给棉装置)	6				17	17	13	千克		Combing devices, drawing devices, of lapping and combing combines
8448.3200 03	精梳联合机盖板清洁装置	6				17	17	13	千克		Flat cleaning devices of lapping and combing combines
8448.3200 90	其他纺织纤维预处理机器的零件、附件(钢丝针布除外)	6				17	17	13	千克		Parts and accessories of machines of heading 8445 or of their auxiliary machinery, other than card clothing
	--锭子、锭壳、纺丝环、钢丝圈:										--Spindles, spindle flyers, spinning rings and ring travellers:
8448.3310	---络筒锭	6	5		0	17	17	13	个/千克		---Winding spindle
8448.3390	---其他	6	5		0	17	17	13	千克		---Other
	--其他:										--Other:
8448.3910	---气流杯	6	5		0	14	17	13	个/千克		---Open-end rotors
8448.3920	---电子清纱器	6	5		0	17	17	13	个/千克		---Electronic yarn clearers
8448.3930	---空气捻接器	6	5		0	17	17	13	个/千克		---Air twisting devices
8448.3940	---环锭细纱机紧密纺装置	6	5		0	17	17	13	个/千克		
8448.3990	---其他	6	5		0	17	17	13	千克		---Other
	-织机及其辅助机器的零件、附件:										-Parts and accessories of weaving machines (looms) or of their auxiliary machinery:
8448.4200	--织机用筘、综丝及综框	6	5		0	50	17	13	千克		--Reeds for looms, healds and heald-frames
	--其他:										--Other:
8448.4910	---接、投梭箱	6	5		0	17	17	13	个/千克		---Catching and throwing shuttle boxes
8448.4920	---引纬、送经装置	6	5		0	17	17	13	个/千克		---Weft insertion and let-off motions
8448.4930	---梭子	6	5		0	50	17	13	个/千克		---Shuttles

税则号列 Tariff Item.	货品名称	最惠国(%) MFN	协定(%)CT 东盟 CA	中巴 CP	中智 CC	普通 Gen	增值税率 VAT	出口退税 ED	计量单位 Unit	监管条件 SC	Article Description
8448.4990	---其他	6	5		0	17	17	13	千克		---Other
8448.4990 01	自动寻纬、补纬装置、打纬装置	6				17	17	13	千克		Automatic searching weft for the gripper looms, automatic mending weft for the air-jet looms
8448.4990 90	织机及其辅助机器用其他零、附件	6				17	17	13	千克		Other parts and accessories of weaving machines (looms) or of their auxiliary machinery
	-税目84.47所列机器及其辅助机器的零件、附件:										-Parts and accessories of machines of heading 84.47 or of their auxiliary machinery:
	--沉降片、织针及其他成圈机件:										--Sinkers, needles and other articles used in forming stitches:
8448.5120	---针织机用28号以下的弹簧针、钩针及复合针	6	5		0	50	17	13	千克		---Barbered needles, crotchet hooks and complex needles for knitting machines, smaler than gauge No. 28
8448.5190	---其他	6	5		0	17	17	13	千克		---Other
8448.5900	--其他	6	5		0	17	17	13	千克		--Other
84.49	**成匹、成形的毡呢或无纺织物制造或整理机器,包括制毡呢帽机器;帽模:**										**Machinery for the manufacture or finishing of felt or nonwovens in the piece or in shapes, including machinery for making felt hats; blocks for making hats:**
8449.0000	成匹、成形的毡呢或无纺织物制造或整理机器,包括制毡呢帽机器;帽模	8	5		0	30	17	13	千克		Machinery for the manufacture or finishing of felt or nonwovens in the piece or in shapes, including machinery for making felt hats; blocks for making hats
84.50	**家用型或洗衣房用洗衣机,包括洗涤干燥两用机:**										**Household or laundry-type washing machines, including machines which both wash and dry:**
	-干衣量不超过10千克的洗衣机:										-Machines, each of a dry linen capacity not exceeding 10kg:
	--全自动的:										--Fully-automatic machines:
8450.1110	---波轮式	10	T3	8.7	8	130	17	13	台	AB	---Of the continuously rotating impeller
8450.1120	---滚筒式	10	T3	8.7	8	130	17	13	台	AB	---Of the drum type
8450.1190	---其他	10	T3	8.7	8	130	17	13	台	AB	---Other
8450.1200	--其他机器,装有离心甩干机	30	T3	24.9	18	130	17	13	台	AB	--Other machines, with built-in centrifugal drier
8450.1900	--其他	30	T3		18	130	17	13	台	AB	--Other
8450.2000	-干衣量超过10千克的洗衣机	10	5		6	80	17	13	台		-Machines, each of a dry linen capacity exceeding 10kg
	-零件:										-Parts:
8450.9010	---干衣量不超过10千克的洗衣机用	5		4.2	0	130	17	13	千克		---Of the machines of subheadings Nos. 8450.1100 to 8450.1900
8450.9090	---其他	16	T3	14.4	9.6	80	17	13	千克		---Other

税则号列 Tariff Item.	货品名称	最惠国(%) MFN	协定(%)CT 东盟 CA	中巴 CP	中智 CC	普通 Gen	增值税率 VAT	出口退税 ED	计量单位 Unit	监管条件 SC	Article Description
84.51	**纱线、织物及纺织制品的洗涤、清洁、绞拧、干燥、熨烫、挤压、(包括熔压)、漂白、染色、上浆、整理、涂布或浸渍机器(税目84.50的机器除外);列诺伦(亚麻油地毡)及类似铺地制品的布基或其他底布的浆料涂布机器;纺织物的卷绕、退绕、折叠、剪切或剪齿边机器:**										**Machinery (other than machines of headingNo.84.50) for washing, cleaning, wringing, drying, ironing, pressing (including fusing presses), bleaching, dyeing, dressing, finishing, coating or impregnating textile yarns, fabrics or made up textile articles and machines for applying the paste to the base fabric or other support used in the manufacture of floor coverings such as linoleum; machines for reeling, unreeling, folding, cutting or pinking textile fabrics:**
8451.1000	-干洗机	21	12	16	12.6	80	17	13	台		-Dry-cleaning machines
	-干燥机:										-Drying machines:
8451.2100	--干衣量不超过10千克	15	T3	13.5	12	80	17	13	台		--Each of a dry linen capacity not exceeding 10kg
8451.2900	--其他	8	5	7.2	0	30	17	13	台		--Other
8451.3000	-熨烫机及挤压机(包括熔压机)	8	T3	7.2	0	30	17	13	台		-Ironing machines and presses (including fusing presses)
8451.4000	-洗涤、漂白或染色机器	8.4	5	7	0	20	17	13	台	O	-Washing, bleaching or dyeing machines
8451.5000	-纺织物的卷绕、退绕、折叠、剪切或剪齿边机器	8	5	7.2	6.4	20	17	13	台	O	-Machines for reeling, unreeling, folding, cutting or pinking textile fabrics
8451.8000	-其他机器	12	8	10.8	9.6	30	17	13	台		-Other machinery
8451.8000 01	服装定型焙烘炉;服装液氨整理机;预缩机;罐蒸	12				30	17	13	台	O	Garment setting cabinet dryer
8451.8000 02	剪绒,洗缩联合机;剪毛联合机;涂层机;柔软整理机	12				30	17	13	台	O	Pile shearing and shrinking combine, potting steamer, sheepshearing combination machine, coating machine, supple finishing machine
8451.8000 03	定型机;精练机;丝光机;磨毛机	12				30	17	13	台	O	Boarding machine; refining machine; mercerizing range; napping grinder
8451.8000 04	织物轧光机	12				30	17	13	台	O	Pile shearing and shrinking combine
8451.8000 90	编号8451未列名的其他机器	12				30	17	13	台		Other machinery of headingNo. 8451, not elsewhere specified or included
8451.9000	-零件	8	5	7.2	0	20	17	13	千克		-Parts
84.52	**缝纫机,但税目84.40的锁线订书机除外;缝纫机专用的特制家具、底座及罩盖;缝纫机针:**										**Sewing machines, other than book-sewing machines of headingNo. 84.40; furniture, bases and covers specially designed for sewing machines; sewing machine needles:**
	-家用型缝纫机:										-Sewing machines of household type:
8452.1010	---多功能型	21	T3	17	16.8	80	17	13	台	aB	---Multifuncitonal
8452.1090	---其他	21	T3	17	16.8	80	17	13	台	aB	---Other
	-其他缝纫机:										-Other sewing machines:
	--自动的:										--Automatic units:
8452.2110	---平缝机	12	8	10.7	9.6	40	17	13	台	a	---Flatseam
8452.2190	---其他	12	8	10.7	9.6	40	17	13	台	a	---Other
8452.2900	--其他	12	8	10.8	9.6	40	17	13	台	a	--Other
8452.3000	-缝纫机针	14	8	12.6	8.4	100	17	13	千克		-Sewing machine needles

税则号列 Tariff Item.	货品名称	最惠国(%) MFN	协定(%)CT 东盟 CA	中巴 CP	中智 CC	普通 Gen	增值税率 VAT	出口退税 ED	计量单位 Unit	监管条件 SC	Article Description
8452.4000	-缝纫机专用的特制家具、底座和罩盖及其零件	14	8		8.4	100	17	13	千克		-Furniture, bases and covers for sewing machines and parts thereof
	-缝纫机的其他零件:										-Other parts of sewing machines:
	---家用型缝纫机用:										---Of sewing machines of the household type:
8452.9011	----旋梭	14	8	9.8	11.2	80	17	13	千克		----Rotating shuttles
8452.9019	----其他	14	8	9.8	11.2	80	17	13	千克		----Other
	---其他:										---Other:
8452.9091	----旋梭	14	8	9.8	11.2	80	17	13	千克		----Rotating shuttles
8452.9099	----其他	14	8	9.8	11.2	80	17	13	千克		----Other
84.53	**生皮、皮革的处理、鞣制或加工机器,鞋靴、毛皮及其他皮革制品的制作或修理机器,但缝纫机除外:**										**Machinery for preparing, tanning or working hides, skins or leather or for making or repairing footwear or other articles of hides, skins or leather, other than sewing machines:**
8453.1000	-生皮、皮革的处理、鞣制或加工机器	8.4	5	8	6.7	30	17	13	台		-Machinery for preparing, tanning or working hides, skins or leather
8453.2000	-鞋靴制作或修理机器	8.4	5	8	0	30	17	13	台		-Machinery for making or repairing footwear
8453.8000	-其他机器	8.4	5		0	30	17	13	台		-Other machinery
8453.9000	-零件	8	5		0	30	17	13	千克		-Parts
84.54	**金属冶炼及铸造用的转炉、浇包、锭模及铸造机:**										**Converters, ladles, ingot moulds and casting machines, of a kind used in metallurgy or in metal foundries:**
8454.1000	-转炉	8.4	5		0	35	17	17	台		-Converters
	-锭模及浇包:										-Ingot moulds and ladles:
8454.2010	---炉外精炼设备	8.4	5		0	35	17	17	台		---Fining equipments, outside of converters
8454.2010 10	VOD炉(真空脱气炉)	8.4				35	17	17	台	O	Vacuum deoxidation oven
8454.2010 90	其他炉外精炼设备	8.4				35	17	17	台	O	Other fining equipments, outside of converters
8454.2090	---其他	8.4	5		0	35	17	17	台		---Other
	-铸造机:										-Casting machines:
8454.3010	---冷室压铸机	12	8	11.4	7.2	35	17	17	台	O	---Cold chamber die-casting machines
	---钢坯连铸机:										---Ingot continuous casting machines:
8454.3021	----方坯连铸机	10	5	9.5	0	35	17	17	台		----Ingot block
8454.3022	----板坯连铸机	12	8	11.4	7.2	35	17	17	台	O	----Ingot slab
8454.3029	----其他	12	8	11.4	7.2	35	17	17	台	O	----Other
8454.3090	---其他	12	8	11.4	7.2	35	17	17	台		---Other
	-零件:										-Parts:
8454.9010	---炉外精炼设备用	8	5		6.4	20	17	17	千克		---For the fining equipments outside of converters
	---钢坯连铸机用:										---For ingot continuous casting machines:
8454.9021	----结晶器	8	5		6.4	20	17	17	千克		----Crystallizers
8454.9022	----振动装置	8	5		6.4	20	17	17	千克		----Vibrating devices
8454.9029	----其他	8	5		6.4	20	17	17	千克		----Other
8454.9090	---其他	8	5		6.4	20	17	17	千克		---Other
84.55	**金属轧机及其轧辊:**										**Metal-rolling mills and rolls therefor:**
	-轧管机:										-Tube mills:
8455.1010	---热轧管机	12	8	8.4	7.2	35	17	17	台		---Tube mills, for hot-rolled

税则号列 Tariff Item.	货品名称	最惠国(%) MFN	协定(%)CT 东盟 CA	中巴 CP	中智 CC	普通 Gen	增值税率 VAT	出口退税 ED	计量单位 Unit	监管条件 SC	Article Description
8455.1020	---冷轧管机	12	8	8.4	7.2	35	17	17	台	O	---Tube mills for cold-rolled
8455.1030	---定减径轧管机	12	8	8.4	7.2	35	17	17	台	O	---Fixed and reduced tube mills
8455.1090	---其他	12	8	8.4	7.2	35	17	17	台	O	---Other
	-其他轧机:										-Other rolling mills:
	--热轧机或冷热联合轧机:										--Hot or combination hot and cold:
8455.2110	---板材热轧机	15	8	10.5	12	35	17	17	台	O	---Sheet mills, hot-rolled
8455.2120	---型钢轧机	15	8	10.5	12	35	17	17	台	O	---Rolled-steel section mills 5
8455.2130	---线材轧机	15	8	10.5	12	35	17	17	台	O	---Wire mills
8455.2190	---其他	15	8	10.5	12	35	17	17	台	O	---Other
	--冷轧机:										--Cold:
8455.2210	---板材冷轧机	10	5		0	35	17	17	台	O	---Sheet mills
8455.2290	---其他	15	8		9	35	17	17	台		---Other
8455.2290 10	铝箔粗轧机	15				35	17	17	台		Aluminium foil roughing mill
8455.2290 90	其他金属冷轧机	15				35	17	17	台		Other cold rolling mills of metal
8455.3000	-轧机用轧辊	8.4	5		0	20	17	17	个		-Rolls for rolling mills
8455.9000	-其他零件	8	5	4	0	20	17	17	千克		-Other parts
84.56	**用激光、其他光、光子束、超声波、放电、电化学法、电子束、离子束或等离子弧处理各种材料的加工机床:**										**Machine-tools for working any material by removal of material, by laser or other light or photon beam, ultrasonic, electro-discharge, electro-chemical, electron beam, ionic-beam or plasma arc processes:**
8456.1000	-用激光、其他光或光子束处理的	0				30	17	17	台		-Operated by laser or other light or photon beam processes
8456.1000 10	辐照元件激光切割机[切割燃料包壳以使辐照核材料能溶解,(含遥控设备)]	0				30	17	17	台	3AO	laser cutter for radiating component
8456.1000 90	其他用激光或其他光或光子束处理的机床	0				30	17	17	台	AO	Other machine - tools for working any material, operated by laser
8456.2000	-用超声波处理的	10	8		0	30	17	17	台	AB	-Operated by ultrasonic processes
	-用放电处理的:										-Operated by electro-discharge processes:
8456.3010	---数控的	9.7	5		0	30	17	17	台		---Numerically controlled
8456.3010 10	数控放电加工机床(2轴或多轴成形控制的无线型放电加工机床)	9.7				30	17	17	台	3ABO	Machine - tools, operated by electro - discharge processes, numerically controlled
8456.3010 90	其他数控的放电处理加工机床	9.7				30	17	17	台	ABO	Other Machine - tools, operated by electro - discharge processes, numerically controlled
8456.3090	---其他	10	8		0	30	17	17	台		---Other
8456.3090 10	非数控放电加工机床(2轴或多轴成形控制的无线型放电加工机床)	10				30	17	17	台	3AB	Machine - tools, operated by electro - discharge processes, not numerically controlled
8456.3090 90	其他非数控的放电处理加工机床	10				30	17	17	台	AB	Other Machine - tools, operated by electro - discharge processes, not numerically controlled
	-其他:										-Other:
8456.9010	---等离子切割机	0				30	17	17	台	AO	---Cutting machines of plasma arc
8456.9090	---其他	0				30	17	17	台	AO	---Other

税则号列 Tariff Item.	货品名称	最惠国(%) MFN	协定(%)CT 东盟 CA	中巴 CP	中智 CC	普通 Gen	增值税率 VAT	出口退税 ED	计量单位 Unit	监管条件 SC	Article Description
84.57	**加工金属的加工中心、单工位组合机床及多工位组合机床:**										**Machining centres, unit construction machines (single station) and multi-station transfer machines, for working metal:**
	-加工中心:										-Machining centres:
8457.1010	---立式	9.7	5	6.8	0	20	17	17	台	AO	---Vertical
8457.1020	---卧式	9.7	5	8.8	0	20	17	17	台	AO	---Horizontal
8457.1030	---龙门式	9.7	5	6.8	0	20	17	17	台	AO	---Plano
8457.1090	---其他	9.7	5	6.8	0	20	17	17	台	AO	---Other
8457.2000	-单工位组合机床	8	5		0	20	17	17	台	OA	-Unit construction machines (single station)
8457.3000	-多工位组合机床	5			4	20	17	17	台	OAB	-Multi-station transfer machines
84.58	**切削金属的车床(包括车削中心):**										**Lathes (including turning centres) for removing metal:**
	-卧式车床:										-Horizontal lathes:
8458.1100	--数控的	9.7	5		0	20	17	17	台	AO	--Numerically controlled
8458.1900	--其他	12	8		7.2	50	17	17	台	AB	--Other
	-其他车床:										-Other lathes:
8458.9100	--数控的	5			0	20	17	17	台	ABO	--Numerically controlled
8458.9900	--其他	12	8		7.2	50	17	17	台	AB	--Other
84.59	**切削金属的钻床、镗床、铣床、攻丝机床(包括直线移动式动力头钻床),但税目84.58的车床(包括车削中心)除外:**										**Machine-tools (including way-type unit head machines) for drilling, boring, milling, threading or tapping by removing metal, other than lathes (including turning centres) of headingNo. 84.58:**
8459.1000	-直线移动式动力头钻床	15	8		9	50	17	17	台	AB	-Way-type unit head machines
	-其他钻床:										-Other drilling machines:
8459.2100	--数控的	9.7	5		0	20	17	17	台	ABO	--Numerically controlled
8459.2900	--其他	15	8		9	50	17	17	台	AB	--Other
	-其他镗铣机床:										-Other boring-milling machines:
8459.3100	--数控的	9.7	5		0	20	17	17	台	OAB	--Numerically controlled
8459.3900	--其他	10	5		0	50	17	17	台	AB	--Other
	-其他镗床:										-Other boring machines:
8459.4010	---数控的	9.7	5		0	20	17	17	台	OAB	---Numerically controlled
8459.4090	---其他	15	8		9	50	17	17	台	AB	---Other
	-升降台式铣床:										-Milling machines, knee-type:
8459.5100	--数控的	9.7	5		0	20	17	17	台	OAB	--Numerically controlled
8459.5900	--其他	15	8		9	50	17	17	台	AB	--Other
	-其他铣床:										-Other milling machines:
	--数控的:										--Numerically controlled:
8459.6110	---龙门铣床	5			0	20	17	17	台	OAB	---Planomilling machines
8459.6190	---其他	5			0	20	17	17	台	OAB	---Other
	--其他:										--Other:
8459.6910	---龙门铣床	12	8	10	7.2	50	17	17	台	AB	---Planomilling machines
8459.6990	---其他	12	8	11	7.2	50	17	17	台	AB	---Other
8459.7000	-其他攻丝机床	12	8		7.2	50	17	17	台	AB	-Other threading or tapping machines

税则号列 Tariff Item.	货品名称	最惠国(%) MFN	协定(%)CT 东盟 CA	中巴 CP	中智 CC	普通 Gen	增值税率 VAT	出口退税 ED	计量单位 Unit	监管条件 SC	Article Description
84.60	**用磨石、磨料或抛光材料对金属或金属陶瓷进行去毛刺、刃磨、磨削、珩磨、研磨、抛光或其他精加工的机床，但税目84.61的切齿机、齿轮磨床或齿轮精加工机床除外：**										**Machine-tools for deburring, sharpening, grinding, honing, lapping, polishing or otherwise finishing metal or cermets by means of grinding stones, abrasives or polishing products, other than gear cutting, gear grinding or gear finishing machines of headingNo. 84.61:**
	-平面磨床，在任一座标的定位精度至少是0.01毫米：										-Flat-surface grinding machines, in which the positioning in any one axis can be set up to an accuracy of at least 0.01mm:
8460.1100	--数控的	9.7	5		0	20	17	17	台	OAB	--Numerically controlled
8460.1900	--其他	15	8		9	50	17	17	台	B	--Other
	-其他磨床，在任一座标的定位精度至少是0.01毫米：										-Other grinding machines, in which the positioning in any one axis can be set up to an accuracy of at least 0.01mm:
	--数控的：										--Numerically controlled:
8460.2110	---外圆磨床	9.7	5		0	20	17	17	台	OAB	---Cylindrical grinding machines
8460.2120	---内圆磨床	9.7	5		0	20	17	17	台	OAB	---Internal grinding machines
8460.2190	---其他	9.7	5		0	20	17	17	台	OAB	---Other
	--其他：										--Other:
8460.2910	---外圆磨床	15	8		9	50	17	17	台	OAB	---Cylindrical grinding machines
8460.2920	---内圆磨床	15	8		9	50	17	17	台	OAB	---Internal grinding machines
8460.2930	---轧辊磨床	13	8		7.8	50	17	17	台		---Grinding machines of roll
8460.2990	---其他	13	8		7.8	50	17	17	台	AB	---Other
	-刃磨(工具或刀具)机床：										-Sharpening (tool or cutter grinding) machines:
8460.3100	--数控的	9.7	5		0	20	17	17	台	AB	--Numerically controlled
8460.3900	--其他	15	8		9	50	17	17	台	AB	--Other
	-珩磨或研磨机床：										-Honing or lapping machines:
8460.4010	---珩磨	13	8		7.8	50	17	17	台	AB	---Honing
8460.4020	---研磨	13	8		7.8	50	17	17	台	AB	---Lapping
	-其他：										-Other:
8460.9010	---砂轮机	15	8		12	50	17	17	台	B	---Grinding wheel machines
8460.9020	---抛光机床	15	8		12	50	17	17	台	A	---Polishing machines
8460.9090	---其他	15	8		12	50	17	17	台	A	---Other
84.61	**切削金属或金属陶瓷的刨床、牛头刨床、插床、拉床、切齿机、齿轮磨床或齿轮精加工机床、锯床、切断机及其他税目未列名的切削机床：**										**Machine-tools for planing, shaping, slotting, broaching, gear cutting, gear grinding or gear finishing, sawing, cutting-off and other machine-tools working by removing metal or cermets, not elsewhere specified or included:**
	-牛头刨床或插床：										-Shaping or slotting machines:
8461.2010	---牛头刨床	15	8		9	50	17	17	台	B	---Shaping machines
8461.2020	---插床	15	8		9	50	17	17	台	B	---Slotting machines
8461.3000	-拉床	12	8		7.2	50	17	17	台	B	-Broaching machines
	-切齿机、齿轮磨床或齿轮精加工机床：										-Gear cutting, gear grinding or gear finishing machines:

税则号列 Tariff Item.	货品名称	最惠国(%) MFN	协定(%)CT 东盟 CA	中巴 CP	中智 CC	普通 Gen	增值税率 VAT	出口退税 ED	计量单位 Unit	监管条件 SC	Article Description
8461.4010	---数控的	9.7	5		0	20	17	17	台	OA	---Numerically controlled
8461.4090	---其他	15	8		9	50	17	17	台	A	---Other
8461.5000	-锯床或切断机	12	8		7.2	50	17	17	台		-Sawing or cutting-off machines
8461.5000 10	辐照元件刀具切割机[切割燃料包壳以使辐照核材料能溶解(含遥控设备)]	12				50	17	17	台	3B	Mechanic cutter for radineins component [incise the fuel sheathing soas to make the irradiation nuclear materials solvable (including the remote device)]
8461.5000 90	其他锯床或切断机	12				50	17	17	台	B	Other sawins machine or cnccer
	-其他:										-Other:
	---刨床:										---Planing machines:
8461.9011	----龙门刨床	15	8		9	50	17	17	台	B	----Double-column (open-side) planing machines
8461.9019	----其他	15	8		9	50	17	17	台	B	----Other
8461.9090	---其他	12	8		7.2	50	17	17	台	B	---Other
84.62	加工金属的锻造(包括模锻)或冲压机床;加工金属的弯曲、折叠、矫直、矫平、剪切、冲孔或开槽机床;其他加工金属或硬质合金的压力机:										**Machine-tools (including presses) for working metal by forging, hammering or die-stamping; machine-tools (including presses) for working metal by bending, folding, straightening, flattening, shearing, punching or notching; presses for working metal or metal carbides, not specified above:**
	-锻造(包括模锻)或冲压机床及锻锤:										-Forging or die-stamping machines (including presses) and hammers:
8462.1010	---数控的	9.7	5	6.8	7.8	20	17	17	台	BO	---Numerically controlled
8462.1090	---其他	12	8	8.4	9.6	50	17	17	台	BO	---Other
	-弯曲、折叠、矫直或矫平机床:										-Bending, folding, straightening or flattening machines (including presses):
	--数控的:										--Numerically controlled:
*8462.2110	---矫直机	9.7	5		0	20	17	17	台	B	---Straightening machines
8462.2190	---其他	9.7	5		0	20	17	17	台	OB	---Other
	--其他:										--Other:
*8462.2910	---矫直机	10	5		8	50	17	17	台	B	---Straightening machines
8462.2990	---其他	10	8		8	50	17	17	台	OB	---Other
	-剪切机床,但冲剪两用机除外:										-Shearing machines (including presses), other than combined punching and shearing machines:
	--数控的:										--Numerically controlled:
8462.3110	---板带纵剪机	7	5		0	20	17	17	台	OB	---Shearing lengthwise
8462.3120	---板带横剪机	7	5		0	20	17	17	台	OB	---Shearing transverse
8462.3190	---其他	7	5		0	20	17	17	台	OB	---Other
	--其他:										--Other:
8462.3910	---板带纵剪机	10	5	9.5	0	50	17	17	台	B	---Shearing lengthwise
8462.3920	---板带横剪机	10	5	9.5	0	50	17	17	台	B	---Shearing transverse
8462.3990	---其他	10	5	9.5	0	50	17	17	台	B	---Other
	-冲孔或开槽机床,包括冲剪两用机:										-Punching or notching machines (including presses), including combined punching and shearing machines:
	--数控的:										--Numerically controlled:

税则号列 Tariff Item.	货品名称	最惠国(%) MFN	协定(%) 东盟 CA	中巴 CP	CT 中智 CC	普通 Gen	增值税率 VAT	出口退税 ED	计量单位 Unit	监管条件 SC	Article Description
	---冲床:										---Punch press
8462.4111	----自动模式数控步冲压力机	9.7	5		0	20	17	17	台	B	----CNC automatic tool change punch press
8462.4119	----其他	9.7	5		0	20	17	17	台	BO	----Other
8462.4190	---其他	9.7	5		0	20	17	17	台	B	---Other
8462.4900	--其他	10	8		0	50	17	17	台	B	--Other
	-其他:										-Other:
	--液压压力机:										--Hydraulic presses:
8462.9110	---金属型材挤压机	10	5	9.2	8	50	17	17	台	OB	---Metal section squeezing machine
8462.9190	---其他	10	8	9.2	8	50	17	17	台	B	---Other
	--其他:										--Other:
8462.9910	---机械压力机	10	8	9.5	8	50	17	17	台	BO	---Mechanical presses
8462.9990	---其他	10	8	9.5	8	50	17	17	台	B	---Other
84.63	**金属或金属陶瓷的其他非切削加工机床:**										**Other machine-tools for working metal or cermets, without removing material:**
	-杆、管、型材、异型材、丝及类似品的拉拔机:										-Draw-benches for bars, tubes, profiles, wire or the like:
	---冷拔管机:										---Cold-drawing tube benches:
8463.1011	----300 吨及以下	10	5		0	50	17	13	台		----With 300t or less
8463.1019	----其他	10	8		0	50	17	13	台		----Other
8463.1020	---拔丝机	10	5		0	50	17	13	台		---Wiredrawing machines
8463.1090	---其他	10	5		0	50	17	13	台		---Other
8463.2000	-螺纹滚轧机	15	8		9	50	17	13	台		-Thread rolling machines
8463.3000	-金属丝加工机	10	5		0	50	17	13	台		-Machines for working wire
8463.9000	-其他	10	5		8	50	17	13	台		-Other
8463.9000 10	滚压成形机床(数控,装3个以上压辊)	10				50	17	13	台	3	Roll forming machines, numerically controlled, with three or more rolls
8463.9000 20	具有滚压功能的旋压成形机床(数控,装3个以上压辊)	10				50	17	13	台	3	Spin forming machines with roll forming function, numerically controlled, with three or more rolls
8463.9000 90	其他非切削加工机床(是指加工金属或金属陶瓷的)	10				50	17	13	台		Other machine-tools for working metal or cermets, without removing material
84.64	**石料、陶瓷、混凝土、石棉水泥或类似矿物材料的加工机床、玻璃冷加工机床:**										**Machine-tools for working stone, ceramics, concrete, asbestos-cement or like mineral materials or for cold working glass:**
	-锯床:										-Sawing machines:
8464.1010	---圆盘锯	0				30	17	13	台		---Of disk saw
8464.1020	---钢丝锯	0				30	17	13	台		---Of scroll saw
8464.1090	---其他	0				30	17	13	台		---Other
	-研磨或抛光机床:										-Grinding or polishing machines:
8464.2010	---玻璃研磨或抛光机床	0				30	17	13	台		---Machines for grinding or polishing glass or glassware
8464.2090	---其他	0				30	17	13	台		---Other
	-其他:										-Other:
	---玻璃的其他冷加工机床:										---Other machines for cold-working glass or glassware:
8464.9011	----切割机	0				30	17	13	台		----Cutting-off machines
8464.9012	----刻花机	0				30	17	13	台		----Carving machines

税则号列 Tariff Item.	货品名称	最惠国(%) MFN	协定(%)CT 东盟 CA	中巴 CP	中智 CC	普通 Gen	增值税率 VAT	出口退税 ED	计量单位 Unit	监管条件 SC	Article Description
8464.9019	----其他	0				30	17	13	台		----Other
8464.9090	---其他	0				30	17	13	台		---Other
84.65	**木材、软木、骨、硬质橡胶、硬质塑料或类似硬质材料的加工机床(包括用打钉或打U形钉、胶粘或其他方法组合前述材料的机器):**										**Machine-tools (including machines for nailing, stapling, glueing or otherwise assembling) for working wood, cork, bone, hard rubber, hard plastics or similar hard materials:**
8465.1000	-不需更换工具即可进行不同机械加工的机器	10	8		8	30	17	13	台	B	-Machines which can carry out different types of machining operations without tool change between such operations
	-其他:										-Other:
8465.9100	--锯床	10	5		8	30	17	13	台	B	--Sawing machines
8465.9200	--刨、铣或切削成形机器	10	8		0	30	17	13	台	B	--Planing, milling or moulding (by cutting) machines
8465.9300	--研磨、砂磨或抛光机器	10	5		0	30	17	13	台	B	--Grinding, sanding or polishing machines
8465.9400	--弯曲或装配机器	10	8		0	30	17	13	台	B	--Bending or assembling machines
8465.9500	--钻孔或凿榫机器	10	8		0	30	17	13	台	B	--Drilling or mortising machines
8465.9600	--剖开、切片或刮削机器	10	8		0	30	17	13	台	B	--Splitting, slicing or paring machines
8465.9900	--其他	10	8		8	30	17	13	台	B	--Other
84.66	**专用于或主要用于税目84.56至84.65所列机器的零件、附件,包括工件或工具的夹具、自启板牙切头、分度头及其他专用于机床的附件;各种手提工具的工具夹具:**										**Parts and accessories suitable for use solely or principally with the machines of headingsNos. 84.56 to 84.65, including work or tool holders, self-opening dieheads, dividing heads and other special attachments for machine-tools; tool holders for any type of tool for working in the hand:**
8466.1000	-工具夹具及自启板牙切头	7	5		0	17	17	13	千克		-Tool holders and self-opening dieheads
8466.2000	-工件夹具	7	5	4.9	0	17	17	13	千克	B	-Work holders
8466.3000	-分度头及其他专用于机床的附件	7	5		0	17	17	13	千克	B	-Dividing heads and other special attachments for machine-tools
	-其他:										-Other:
8466.9100	--税目84.64所列机器用	0				17	17	13	千克		--For machines of headingNo. 84.64
8466.9200	--税目84.65所列机器用	6	5		0	17	17	13	千克		--For machines of headingNo. 84.65
8466.9300	--税目84.56至84.61所列机器用	0				17	17	13	千克		--For machines of headingsNo. 84.56 to 84.61
8466.9400	--税目84.62或84.63所列机器用	6	5		4.8	17	17	13	千克		--For machines of headingNo. 84.62 or 84.63
8466.9400 10	滚压成形机床用芯轴(转筒成形用的芯轴,内径在75毫米至400毫米之间)	6				17	17	13	千克	3	Spindles of roll forming machines (spindles for forming of revolving drum, inside diameter 75mm ~ 400mm)
8466.9400 20	有滚压功能的旋压成形机用芯轴(转筒成形用的芯轴,内径在75毫米至400毫米之间)	6				17	17	13	千克	3	Spindles of spin forming machines with roll forming function (spindles for forming of revolving drum, inside diameter 75mm ~ 400mm)
8466.9400 90	编号8462-63机器用其他零件、附件	6				17	17	13	千克		Other parts and accessories suitable for machines of headingNo. 8462 or 8463

税则号列 Tariff Item.	货品名称	最惠国(%) MFN	协定(%) CT 东盟 CA	中巴 CP	中智 CC	普通 Gen	增值税率 VAT	出口退税 ED	计量单位 Unit	监管条件 SC	Article Description
84.67	**手提式风动或液压工具及本身装有电动或非电动动力装置的手提式工具:**										**Tools for working in the hand, pneumatic hydraulic or with self-contained electric or non-electric motor:**
	-风动的:										-Pneumatlic:
8467.1100	--旋转式(包括旋转冲击式的)	8	5		0	30	17	17	台		--Rotary type (including combined rotary-percussion)
8467.1900	--其他	8	5		0	30	17	17	台		--Other
	-本身装有电动动力装置的:										-With self-contained electric motor:
8467.2100	--各种钻	10	T3	9	8	30	17	17	台	BA	--Drills of all kinds
	--锯:										--Saws:
8467.2210	---链锯	10	5	9	8	30	17	17	台	BA	---Chain saws
8467.2290	---其他	10	T3	9	8	30	17	17	台	BA	---Other
	--其他:										--Other tools:
8467.2910	---砂磨工具(包括磨光机、砂光机、砂轮机等)	10	T3	8	8	30	17	17	台	BA	---Grinding tools (including burnisher, belt-sander, wheel-sander)
8467.2920	---电刨	10	5	8	8	30	17	17	台	BA	---Planings
8467.2990	---其他	10	T3	8	8	30	17	17	台	A	---Other
	-其他工具:										-Other tools:
8467.8100	--链锯	8	5		0	30	17	17	台		--Chain saws
8467.8900	--其他	8	5		0	30	17	17	台		--Other
	-零件:										-Parts:
	--链锯用:										--Of chain saws
8467.9110	---电动的	6	5	4.8	0	30	17	13	千克		---With self-contained electric motor
8467.9190	---其他	6	5		0	30	17	13	千克		---Other
8467.9200	--风动工具用	6	5		0	30	17	13	千克		--Of pneumatic tools
	--其他:										--Other:
8467.9910	---电动工具用	10	T3	9	0	30	17	13	千克		---With self-contained elecric motor
8467.9990	---其他	6	5		0	30	17	13	千克		---Other
84.68	**焊接机器及装置,不论是否兼有切割功能,但税目85.15的货品除外;气体加温表面回火机器及装置:**										**Machinery and apparatus for soldering, brazing or welding, whether or not capable of cutting, other than those of headingNo. 85.15; gas-operated surface tempering machines and appliances:**
8468.1000	-手提喷焊器	12	8		7.2	30	17	13	台		-Hand-held blow pipes
8468.2000	-其他气体焊接或表面回火机器及装置	12	8		7.2	30	17	13	台		-Other gas-operated machinery and apparatus
8468.2000 10	氩弧自动焊接机[将端塞焊接于燃料细棒(或棒)的自动焊接机]	12				30	17	13	台	3	Argon are automatic welding machine [the automatic welder machine that joint the end plug with the fuel thin-stick (or stick)]
8468.2000 90	其他气体焊接或表面回火机器及装置	12				30	17	13	台		Other gas - operated machinery and apparatus
8468.8000	--其他机器及装置	12	8		7.2	30	17	13	台		--Other machinery and apparatus
8468.9000	-零件	7	5		0	30	17	13	千克		-Parts
84.69	**打字机,但税目84.43的打印机除外;文字处理机:**										**Typewriters other than printers of headingNo. 84.71; word-processing machines:**

税则号列 Tariff Item.	货品名称	最惠国(%) MFN	协定(%) CT 东盟 CA	中巴 CP	中智 CC	普通 Gen	增值税率 VAT	出口退税 ED	计量单位 Unit	监管条件 SC	Article Description
	---自动打字机及文字处理机:										---Automatic typewriters and word-processing machines:
8469.0011	----文字处理机	0				40	17	13	台		----Word-processing machines
8469.0012	----自动打字机	12	8		7.2	40	17	13	台		----Automatic typewriters
8469.0020	---其他电动打字机	12	8	10.8	7.2	40	17	13	台		----Other typewriters, electric
8469.0030	---其他非电动打字机	12	8		7.2	40	17	17	台		---Other typewriters, non-electric
84.70	**计算机器及具有计算功能的袖珍式数据记录、重现及显示机器;装有计算装置的会计计算机、邮资盖戳机、售票机及类似机器;现金出纳机:**										**Calculating machines and pocket-size data recording, reproducing and displaying machines with calculating functions; accounting machines, postage-franking machines, ticket-issuing machines and similar machines, incorporating a calculating device; cash registers:**
8470.1000	-不需外接电源的电子计算器及具有计算功能的袖珍式数据记录、重现及显示机器	0				80	17	13	台		-Electronic calculators capable of operation without an external source of electric power and pocket-size data recording, reproducing and displaying machines with calculating functions
	-其他电子计算器:										-Other electronic calculating machines:
8470.2100	--装有打印装置的	0				80	17	13	台		--Incorporating a printing device
8470.2900	--其他	0				80	17	13	台		--Other
8470.3000	-其他计算机器	0				40	17	13	台		-Other calculating machines
	-现金出纳机:										-Cash registers:
8470.5010	---销售点终端出纳机	0				40	17	13	台		---Terminal registers for market
8470.5090	---其他	0				40	17	13	台		---Other
8470.9000	-其他	0				40	17	13	台		-Other
84.71	**自动数据处理设备及其部件;其他税目未列名的磁性或光学阅读机、将数据以代码形式转录到数据记录媒体的机器及处理这些数据的机器:**										**Automatic data processing machines and units thereof; magnetic or optical readers, machines for transcribing data onto data media in coded form and machines for processing such data, not elsewhere specified or included:**
8471.3000	-重量不超过10千克的便携数字式自动数据处理设备,至少由一个中央处理部件、一个键盘及一个显示器组成	0				70	17	17	台	A	-Portable digital automatic data processing machines, weighing not more than 10kg, consisting of at least a central processing unit, a keyboard and a display
	-其他自动数据处理设备:										-Other digital automatic data processing machines:
	--同一机壳内至少有一个中央处理部件及一个输入和输出部件,不论是否组合式:										--Comprising in the same housing at least a central processing unit and an input and output unit, whether or not combined:
8471.4110	---巨型机、大型机及中型机	0				14	17	13	台	O3	---Supermachine mainframe mini-computers
8471.4120	---小型机	0				14	17	13	台	O3	---Mini-computers
8471.4140	---微型机	0				70	17	17	台	A	---Microprocessings
8471.4190	---其他	0				70	17	17	台	O	---Other

税则号列 Tariff Item.	货品名称	最惠国(%) MFN	协定(%) CT 东盟 CA	中巴 CP	中智 CC	普通 Gen	增值税率 VAT	出口退税 ED	计量单位 Unit	监管条件 SC	Article Description
	--其他,以系统形式报检的:										--Other, presented in the form of systems:
8471.4910	---巨型机、大型机及中型机	0				29	17	13	台	O3	---Supermachine mainframe mini-computers
8471.4920	---小型机	0				29	17	13	台	O3	---Mini-computers
8471.4940	---微型机	0				70	17	17	台		---Microprocessings
	---其他:										---Other:
8471.4991	----分散型工业过程控制设备	0				70	17	13	台	O	----Processing machines for the distributed control system
8471.4999	----其他	0				70	17	13	台		----Other
	-子目 8471.41 及 8471.49 所列以外的处理部件,不论是否在同一机壳内有一个或两个下列部件:存储部件、输入部件、输出部件:										-Digital processing units other than those of subheadingNo. 8471.41 or 8471.49, whether or not containing in the same housing one or two of the following types of unit: storage units, input units, output units:
8471.5010	---巨型机、大型机及中型机的	0				14	17	13	台	3	---Supermachine mainframe mini-computers
8471.5020	---小型机的	0				14	17	13	台	O3	---Mini-computers
8471.5040	---微型机的	0				70	17	17	台		---Microprocessings
8471.5090	---其他	0				70	17	13	台		---Other
	-输入或输出部件,不论是否在同一机壳内有存储部件:										-Input or output units, whether or not containing storage units in the same housing:
8471.6040	---巨型机、大型机、中型机及小型机用终端	0				14	17	13	台		---Terminating machines for the huge computers, mainframes and mini-computers
8471.6050	---扫描仪	0				14	17	13	台		---Scanner
8471.6060	---数字化仪	0				14	17	13	台		---Digitizer
	---键盘、鼠标器:										---Keyboards, mouses:
8471.6071	----键盘	0				40	17	13	个		----Keyboards
8471.6072	----鼠标器	0				40	17	13	个		----mouses
8471.6090	---其他	0				14	17	13	台		---Other
	-存储部件:										-Storage units:
8471.7010	---硬盘驱动器	0				14	17	17	台		---Rigid disk drivers
8471.7020	---软盘驱动器	0				14	17	13	台		---Floppy disk drivers
8471.7030	---光盘驱动器	0				14	17	13	台		---CD drivers
8471.7030 10	具有刻录功能的光盘驱动器(自动数据处理设备的光盘驱动器)	0				14	17	13	台	O	CD-R drivers of automatic data processing machines
8471.7030 90	其他光盘驱动器(自动数据处理设备的光盘驱动器)	0				14	17	13	台	O	Other CD drivers of automatic data processing machines
8471.7090	---其他	0				14	17	17	台		---Other
8471.8000	-自动数据处理设备的其他部件:	0				40	17	17	台		-Other units of automatic data processing machines:
8471.9000	-其他	0				40	17	13	台		-Other

税则号列 Tariff Item.	货品名称	最惠国(%) MFN	协定(%)CT 东盟 CA	 中巴 CP	 中智 CC	普通 Gen	增值税率 VAT	出口退税 ED	计量单位 Unit	监管条件 SC	Article Description
8471.9000 10	专用于复制的光盘刻录机(也称光盘复读机)	0				40	17	13	台	O	CD burners specified for CD duplication
8471.9000 90	未列名的磁性或光学阅读器(包括将数据以代码形式转录的机器及处理这些数据的机器)	0				40	17	13	台	O	Magnetic or optical readers, not elsewhere specified or included, including machines for transcribing data onto data media in coded form and machines for processing such data
84.72	**其他办公室用机器(例如,胶版复印机、油印机、地址印写机、自动付钞机、硬币分类、计数及包装机、削铅笔机、打洞机或订书机):**										**Other office machines (for example, hectograph or stencil duplicating machines, addressing machines, automatic banknote dispensers, coin-sorting machines, coin-counting or wrapping machines, pencil-sharpening machines, perforating or stapling machines):**
8472.1000	-胶版复印机、油印机	14	8		8.4	40	17	13	台		-Duplicating machines
	-信件分类或折叠机或信件装封机、信件开封或闭封机、粘贴或盖销邮票机:										-Machines for sorting or folding mail or for inserting mail in envelopes or bands, machines for opening, closing or sealing mail and machines for affixing or cancelling postage stamps:
8472.3010	---邮政信件分拣及封装设备	10	5		0	40	17	13	台		---Machines for sorting or banding mail
8472.3090	---其他	14	8		8.4	40	17	13	台		---Other
	-其他:										-Other:
8472.9010	---自动柜员机	0				40	17	13	台		---Automated teller
	---装订用机器:										---Stapling machines:
8472.9021	----打洞机	0				40	17	13	台		----Perforator
8472.9022	----订书机	0				40	17	13	台		----Stapler
8472.9029	----其他	0				40	17	13	台		----Other
8472.9030	---碎纸机	0				40	17	13	台		---Paper shrudders
8472.9040	---地址写机及地址铭牌压印机(84720001)	14	8		8.4	40	17	13	台		---Addressing machines and ddress plate embossing machines
8472.9090	---其他	0				40	17	13	台		---Other
84.73	**专用于或主要用于税目84.69至84.72所列机器的零件、附件(罩套、提箱及类似品除外):**										**Parts and accessories (other than covers, carrying cases and the like) suitable for use solely or principally with machines of headingsNo. 84.69 to 84.72:**
8473.1000	-税目84.69所列机器的零件、附件	8	5		0	35	17	13	千克		-Parts and accessories of the machines of headingNo. 84.69
	-税目84.70所列机器的零件、附件:										-Parts and accessories of the machines of headingNo. 84.70:
8473.2100	--子目8470.10、8470.21或8470.29所列电子计算器的零件、附件	0				50	17	13	千克		--Of the electronic calculating machines of subheadingNos. 8470.10, 8470.21 or 8470.29
8473.2900	--其他	0				35	17	13	千克		--Other
	-税目84.71所列机器的零件、附件:										-Parts and accessories of the machines of headingNo. 84.71:

税则号列 Tariff Item.	货品名称	最惠国(%) MFN	协定(%)CT 东盟 CA	中巴 CP	中智 CC	普通 Gen	增值税率 VAT	出口退税 ED	计量单位 Unit	监管条件 SC	Article Description
8473.3010	---子目8471.4110、8471.4120、8471.4910、8471.4920、8471.5010、8471.5020、8471.6090、8471.7010、8471.7020、8471.7030及8471.7090所列机器及装置的零件、附件	0				14	17	17	千克		---Of the machines of subheadingNo. 8471.1000, 8471.4110, 8471.4120, 8471.4910, 8471.4920, 8471.5010, 8471.5020, 8471.6090, 8471.7010, 8471.7020, 8471.7030 or 8471.7090
8473.3090	---其他	0				40	17	17	千克		---Other
	-税目84.72所列机器的零件、附件:										-Parts and accessories of the machines of headingNo. 84.72:
8473.4010	---自动柜员机用出钞器	10.5	8		6.3	35	17	13	千克		---Banknote dispenser of automated teller
8473.4090	---其他	10.5	8		6.3	35	17	13	千克		---Other
8473.4090 01	钞票清分机零附件	10.5				35	17	13	千克		Parts and accessories of banknote checking and dispencing machine
8473.4090 90	其他办公室用机器零附件	10.5				35	17	13	千克		Other parts and accessories of office machines
8473.5000	-同样适用于税目84.69至84.72中两个或两个以上税目所列机器的零件、附件	0				35	17	13	千克		-Parts and accessories equally suitable for use with machines of two or more of the headingsNo. 84.69 to 84.72
84.74	**泥土、石料、矿石或其他固体(包括粉状、浆状)矿物质的分类、筛选、分离、洗涤、破碎、磨粉、混合或搅拌机器;固体矿物燃料、陶瓷坯泥、未硬化水泥、石膏材料或其他粉状、浆状矿产品的粘聚或成形机器;铸造用砂模的成形机器:**										**Machinery for sorting, screening, separating, washing, crushing, grinding, mixing or kneading earth, stone, ores or other mineral substances, in solid (including powder or paste) form; machinery for agglomerating, shaping or moulding solid mineral fuels, ceramic paste, unhardened cements, plastering materials or other mineral products in powder or paste form; machines for forming foundry moulds of sand:**
8474.1000	-分类、筛选、分离或洗涤机器	5			4	30	17	13	台		-Sorting, screening, separating or washing machines
	-破碎或磨粉机器:										-Crushing or grinding machines:
8474.2010	---齿辊式	5			4	30	17	13	台	O	---Toothing roller type
8474.2020	---球磨式	5			4	30	17	13	台	O	---Em-Peters
8474.2090	---其他	5			4	30	17	13	台	O	---Other
	-混合或搅拌机器:										-Mixing or kneading machines:
8474.3100	--混凝土或砂浆混合机器	7	5		0	30	17	17	台	O	--Concrete or mortar mixers
8474.3200	--矿物与沥青的混合机器	7	5		5.6	30	17	17	台	O	--Machines for mixing mineral substances with bitumen
8474.3900	--其他	5			4	30	17	17	台	O	--Other
	-其他机器:										-Other machinery:
8474.8010	---辊压成型机	5		4.5	4	30	17	17	台		---Rolling forming machines
8474.8020	---模压成型机	5		4.5	4	30	17	17	台		---Molud pressing machines
8474.8090	---其他	5		4.5	4	30	17	17	台		---Other
8474.8090 10	纸面角线石膏板搅拌成型机	5				30	17	17	台		Paper faced diagonally reinforced plaster board agitating and formating machine

税则号列 Tariff Item.	货 品 名 称	最惠国(%) MFN	协定(%)CT 东盟 CA	中巴 CP	中智 CC	普通 Gen	增值税率 VAT	出口退税 ED	计量单位 Unit	监管条件 SC	Article Description
8474.8090 90	编号8474未列名的其他机器(如矿产品的粘聚或成型机器及铸造用砂模的成型机器)	5				30	17	17	台		Other machines, not elsewhere specified or included of headingNo. 8474 (for example, machinery for agglomerating, shaping or moulding or machines for forming foundry moulds of sand)
8474.9000	-零件	5			4	30	17	13	千克	·	-Parts
84.75	**白炽灯泡、灯管、放电灯管、电子管、闪光灯泡及类似品的封装机器;玻璃或玻璃制品的制造或热加工机器:**										**Machines for assembling electric or electronic lamps, tubes or valves or flash-bulbs, in glass envelopes; machines for manufacturing or hot working glass or glassware:**
8475.1000	-白炽灯泡、灯管、放电灯管、电子管、闪光灯泡及类似品的封装机器	8	5		6.4	30	17	13	台	O	-Machines for assembling electric or electronic lamps, tubes or valves or flash-bulbs, in glass envelopes
	-玻璃或玻璃制品的制造或热加工机器:										-Machines for manufacturing or hot working glass or glassware:
8475.2100	--制造光导纤维及其预制棒的机器	10	8		0	30	17	13	台		--Machines for making optical fibres and preforms thereof
	--其他:										--Other:
	---玻璃的热加工设备:										---Equipments for hot working glass or glasswares:
8475.2911	----连续式玻璃热弯炉	10	5		0	30	17	13	台		----Continuous hot bending furnaces
8475.2912	----玻璃纤维拉丝机(光纤拉丝机除外)	10	5		0	30	17	13	台		----Fiber glass winder(excluding opticae fiber winder)
8475.2919	----其他	10	T3		0	30	17	13	台		----Other
8475.2990	---其他	10	5		0	30	17	13	台		---Other
8475.9000	-零件	8	5		6.4	30	17	13	千克		-Parts
84.76	**自动售货机(例如,出售邮票、香烟、食品或饮料的机器),包括钱币兑换机:**										**Automatic goods-vending machines (for example, postage stamp, cigarette, food or beverage machines), including money-changing machines:**
	-饮料自动销售机:										-Automatic beverage-vending machines:
8476.2100	--装有加热或制冷装置的	14	8		11.2	50	17	13	台	A	--Incorporating heating or refrigerating devices
8476.2900	--其他	15	8		9	50	17	13	台	A	--Other
	-其他机器:										-Other machines:
8476.8100	--装有加热或制冷装置的	14	8		8.4	50	17	13	台		--Incorporating heating or refrigerating devices
8476.8900	--其他	15	8		12	50	17	13	台		--Other
8476.9000	-零件	10	5		0	50	17	13	千克		-Parts
84.77	**本章其他税目未列名的橡胶或塑料及其产品的加工机器:**										**Machinery for working rubber or plastics or for the manufacture of products from these materials, not specified or included elsewhere in this Chapter:**
	-注射机:										-Injection-moulding machines:
8477.1010	---注塑机	0				45	17	13	台		---For working plastics
8477.1010 10	用于光盘生产的精密注塑机(加工塑料的)	0				45	17	13	台	60	Precision injection-moulders for CD production for working plastics

税则号列 Tariff Item.	货品名称	最惠国(%) MFN	协定(%) 东盟 CA	协定(%) 中巴 CP	CT 中智 CC	普通 Gen	增值税率 VAT	出口退税 ED	计量单位 Unit	监管条件 SC	Article Description
8477.1010 90	其他注塑机	0				45	17	13	台	O	Other machinery for working plastics
8477.1090	---其他	0				30	17	13	台		---Other
	-挤出机:										-Extruders:
8477.2010	---塑料造粒机	5		4.5	0	30	17	13	台		---Plastic pelletizers
8477.2090	---其他	5		4.5	0	30	17	13	台	O	---Other
8477.3000	-吹塑机	5			4	30	17	13	台		-Blow moulding machines
	-真空模塑机器及其他热成型机器:										-Vacuum moulding machines and other thermoforming machines:
8477.4010	---塑料中空成型机	5		4.5	0	30	17	13	台	O	---Plastics brideg-die-forming machines
8477.4020	---塑料压延成型机	5		4.5	0	30	17	13	台	O	---Plastics calender-forming machines
8477.4090	---其他	5		4.5	0	30	17	13	台		---Other
	-其他模塑或成型机器:										-Other machinery for moulding or otherwise forming:
8477.5100	--用于充气轮胎模塑或翻新的机器及内胎模塑或用其他方法成型的机器	5			4	30	17	13	台		--For moulding or retreading pneumatic tyres or for moulding or otherwise forming inner tubes
8477.5900	--其他	5		3.5	0	30	17	13	台	O	--Other
8477.8000	-其他机器	5		4.5	0	30	17	13	台	O	-Other machinery
8477.9000	-零件	0				30	17	13	千克		-Parts
84.78	**本章其他税目未列名的烟草加工及制作机器:**										**Machinery for preparing or making up tobacco, not specified or included elsewhere in this Chapter:**
8478.1000	-机器	5		2.5	0	30	17	13	台	O	-Machinery
8478.9000	-零件	10	5		0	30	17	13	千克	O	-Parts
84.79	**本章其他税目未列名的具有独立功能的机器及机械器具:**										**Machines and mechanical appliances having individual functions, not specified or included elsewhere in this Chapter:**
	-公共工程用机器:										-Machinery for public works, building or the like:
	---摊铺机:										---Spreading machines:
8479.1021	----沥青混凝土摊铺机	8	5	5.6	6.4	30	17	17	台	O	----Machines for spreading bituminous concrete
8479.1022	----稳定土摊铺机	8	5	5.6	6.4	30	17	17	台		----Stabilizer spreading machines
8479.1029	----其他	8	5	5.6	6.4	30	17	17	台	O	----Other
8479.1090	---其他	8	5	5.6	6.4	30	17	17	台		---Other
8479.2000	-提取、加工动物油脂或植物固定油脂的机器	10	8		8	30	17	13	台	A	-Machinery for the extraction or preparation of animal or fixed vegetable fats or oils
8479.3000	-木碎料板或木纤维板的挤压机及其他木材或软木处理机	10	5		0	30	17	13	台		-Presses for the manufacture of particle board or fibre building board or wood or other ligneous materials and other machinery for treating wood or cork
8479.4000	-绳或缆的制造机器	7	5		0	30	17	13	台		-Rope or cable-making machines
	-未列名工业机器人:										-Industrial robots, not elsewhere specified or included:
8479.5010	---多功能工业机器人	0				20	17	13	台		---Industrial robots for multiple uses
8479.5090	---其他	0				30	17	13	台		---Other

税则号列 Tariff Item.	货品名称	最惠国(%) MFN	协定(%) CT 东盟 CA	中巴 CP	中智 CC	普通 Gen	增值税率 VAT	出口退税 ED	计量单位 Unit	监管条件 SC	Article Description
8479.5090 10	机器人，末端操纵装置[能处理高能炸药或能抗大于5×10⁴戈瑞(硅)辐射的]	0				30	17	13	台	3	Terminal manipulators (capable of handling high-energy explosives or resisting radiance > 5×10^4 Gy (Si))
8479.5090 90	其他工业机器人(多功能工业机器人除外)	0				30	17	13	台		Other industrial robots other than industrial robots for multiple uses
8479.6000	-蒸发式空气冷却器	10	5	9	0	30	17	13	台	AB	-Evaporative air coolers
	-其他机器及机械器具：										-Other machines and mechanical appliances:
	--处理金属的机械，包括线圈绕线机：										--For treating metal, including electric wire coil-winders:
8479.8110	---绕线机	9.5	5	9	7.6	30	17	13	台		---Filament winding machines
8479.8190	---其他	9.5	5	9	7.6	30	17	13	台		---Other
8479.8200	--混合、搅拌、轧碎、研磨、筛选、均化或乳化机器	7	5	4.9	0	30	17	13	台		--Mixing, kneading, crushing, grinding, screening, sifting, homogenizing, emulsifying or stirring machines
8479.8200 10	敏感物项管制搅拌器(耐腐蚀热交换器、搅拌器用，带搅拌的发酵罐)	7				30	17	13	台	3O	Beaters subject to regulations of sensitive item (Rotproof heat exchanger and ferment jar for use of beater)
8479.8200 90	其他混合、搅拌、轧碎、研磨机器(包括筛选、均化、乳化机器)	7				30	17	13	台	O	Other mixing, kneading, crushing, grinding, screening, sifting, homogenizing, emulsifying or stirring machines
	--其他：										--Other:
8479.8910	---船舶用舵机及陀螺稳定器	0				14	17	13	台		---Steering and rudder equipment or gyroscopic stabilizers for ships
8479.8920	---空气增湿器及减湿器	0				70	17	13	台		---Air humidifiers or dehumidifiers
8479.8940	---邮政用包裹、印刷品分拣设备	0				30	17	13	台	AB	---Bundle and printed matter sorting machines used in post offices
8479.8950	---放射性废物压实机	0				30	17	13	台		---Presses for radioactive waste material
	---在印刷电路电路板上装配元器件的机器：										---Machines for assemblying elements on printed circuit boards:
8479.8961	----自动插件机	0				30	17	13	台	OAB	----Automatic plug-in machines
8479.8962	----自动贴片机	0				30	17	13	台	OAB	----Automatic coreslice adhering machines
8479.8969	----其他	0				30	17	13	台	AB	----Other
8479.8990	---其他	0				30	17	13	台		---Other
8479.8990 10	用于光盘生产的金属母盘生产设备(具有独立功能的)	0				30	17	13	台	6ABO	Metal master production equipment for CD production, having individual functions
8479.8990 20	用于光盘生产的粘合机(具有独立功能的)	0				30	17	13	台	6ABO	Assembly bonders for CD production, having individual functions
8479.8990 30	用于光盘生产的真空金属溅镀机(具有独立功能的)	0				30	17	13	台	6ABO	Vacuum metal-splashers for CD production, having individual functions
8479.8990 40	保护胶涂覆机及染料层旋涂机(光盘生产用，具有独立功能的)	0				30	17	13	台	6ABO	Protective covering coaters and color layer rotating coaters, having individual functions
8479.8990 50	敏感物项管制机器及机械器具	0				30	17	13	台	3AB	Accelerometer boresighting benches

税则号列 Tariff Item.	货品名称	最惠国(%) MFN	协定(%) CT 东盟 CA	中巴 CP	中智 CC	普通 Gen	增值税率 VAT	出口退税 ED	计量单位 Unit	监管条件 SC	Article Description
8479.8990 60	绕线机(能卷绕直径在75mm至400mm、长度为600mm或更长的)	0				30	17	13	台	3AB	Wire winders (capable of winding wire diameter 75mm ~ 400mm, length ≥ 600mm)
8479.8990 90	本章其他未列名机器及机械器具(具有独立功能的)	0				30	17	13	台	AB	Machines and mechanical appliances having individual functions, not specified or included elsewhere in this Chapter
	-零件:										-Parts:
8479.9010	---船舶用舵机及陀螺稳定器用	0				14	17	13	千克		---Of the machines of subheadingNo. 8479.8910
8479.9020	---空气增湿器及减湿器用	0				70	17	13	千克		---Of the machines of subheadingNo. 8479.8920
8479.9090	---其他	0				20	17	13	千克		---Other
8479.9090 10	绕线机的精密芯轴(专用于编号84798990.60绕线机的精密芯轴)	0				20	17	13	千克	3	Precision core axle of oil winding machine
8479.9090 90	编号8479所列机器的其他零件	0				20	17	13	千克		Other parts of machiners of heading-No. 8479
84.80	**金属铸造用型箱;型模底板;阳模;金属用型模(锭模除外)、硬质合金、玻璃、矿物材料、橡胶或塑料用型模:**										**Moulding boxes for metal foundry; mould bases; moulding patterns; moulds for metal (other than ingot moulds), metal carbides, glass, mineral materials, rubber or plastics:**
8480.1000	-金属铸造用型箱	10	5		0	20	17	13	千克		-Moulding boxes for metal foundry
8480.2000	-型模底板	8	5		0	20	17	13	千克		-Mould bases
8480.3000	-阳模	10	8		0	20	17	13	千克		-Moulding patterns
	-金属、硬质合金用型模:										-Moulds for metal or metal carbides:
8480.4100	--注模或压模	8	5	5.6	0	20	17	13	千克		--Injection or compression types
8480.4100 10	汽车及家用电器的注模或压模	8				20	17	13	千克	O	Injection or compression types for cars and household appliances
8480.4100 90	金属、硬质合金用注模或压模	8				20	17	13	千克	O	Injection or compression types for metal or metal carbides
8480.4900	--其他	8	5	5.6	0	20	17	13	千克		--Other
8480.5000	-玻璃用型模	8.4	5		0	20	17	13	套/千克		-Moulds for glass
8480.6000	-矿物材料用型模	8.4	5		6.7	20	17	13	套/千克		-Moulds for mineral materials
	-塑料或橡胶用型模:										-Moulds for rubber or plastics:
8480.7100	--注模或压模	0				20	17	13	套/千克		--Injection or compression types
8480.7100 10	用于光盘生产的专用模具	0				20	17	13	套/千克	6O	Specific moulds for CD production
8480.7100 90	其他塑料或橡胶用注模或压模	0				20	17	13	套/千克	O	Other injection or compression types for rubber or plastics
8480.7900	--其他	5		3.5	0	20	17	13	套/千克		--Other
8480.7900 10	农用双壁波纹管生产线用其他模具	5				20	17	13	套/千克		Farm machinery double-wall sylphon bellows production line
8480.7900 90	塑料或橡胶用其他型模	5				20	17	13	套/千克		Other moulds for rubber or plastics
84.81	**用于管道、锅炉、罐、桶或类似品的龙头、旋塞、阀门及类似装置,包括减压阀及恒温控制阀:**										**Taps, cocks, valves and similar appliances for pipes, boiler shells, tanks, vats or the like, including pressure-reducing valves and thermostatically controlled valves:**
8481.1000	-减压阀	5			4	30	17	13	套/千克	B	-Pressure-reducing valves

税则号列 Tariff Item.	货品名称	最惠国(%) MFN	协定(%) CT 东盟 CA	中巴 CP	中智 CC	普通 Gen	增值税率 VAT	出口退税 ED	计量单位 Unit	监管条件 SC	Article Description
	-油压或气压传动阀:										-Valves for oleohydraulic or pneumatic transmissions:
8481.2010	---油压的	5			4	30	17	13	套/千克	B	---For oleohydraulic transmissions
8481.2020	---气压的	5			4	30	17	13	套/千克	B	---For pneumatic transmissions
8481.3000	-止回阀	5			4	30	17	13	套/千克	B	-Check (nonreturn) valves
8481.4000	-安全阀或溢流阀	5			4	30	17	13	套/千克	B	-Safety or relief valves
	-其他器具:										-Other appliances:
8481.8010	---其他阀门	7	5	4.9	5.6	30	17	13	套/千克		---Other valves
8481.8010 10	敏感物项管制阀门	7				30	17	13	套/千克	3B	Erosion-resisting multiple sealing valves with leak detection hole, contacting surface made of special material
8481.8010 90	其他阀门(用于管道、锅炉、罐、桶或类似品的)	7				30	17	13	套/千克	B	Other valves for pipes, boiler shells, tanks, vats or the like
8481.8090	---其他	5			4	50	17	13	套/千克		---Other
	-零件:										-Parts:
8481.9010	---阀门用	8	5		6.4	30	17	13	千克		---Of valves
8481.9090	---其他	8	5		6.4	50	17	13	千克		---Other
84.82	**滚动轴承:**										**Ball or roller bearings:**
8482.1000	-滚珠轴承	8	5	7.6	6.4	20	17	13	套	aB	-Ball bearings
8482.2000	-锥形滚子轴承,包括锥形滚子组件	8	5		0	20	17	13	套	aB	-Tapered roller bearings, including cone and tapered roller assemblies
8482.3000	-鼓形滚子轴承	8	5		0	20	17	13	套	aB	-Spherical roller bearings
8482.4000	-滚针轴承	8	5		0	20	17	13	套	aB	-Needle roller bearings
8482.5000	-其他圆柱形滚子轴承	8	5		0	20	17	13	套	aB	-Other cylindrical roller bearings
8482.8000	-其他,包括球、柱混合轴承	8	5	5.6	6.4	20	17	13	套	aB	-Other, including combined ball/roller bearings
	-零件:										-Parts:
8482.9100	--滚珠、滚针及滚柱	8	5		0	20	17	13	千克		--Balls, needles and rollers
8482.9900	--其他	6	5		0	20	17	13	千克		--Other
84.83	**传动轴(包括凸轮轴及曲柄轴)及曲柄;轴承座及滑动轴承;齿轮及齿轮传动装置;滚珠或滚子螺杆传动装置;齿轮箱及其他变速装置,包括扭矩变换器;飞轮及滑轮,包括滑轮组;离合器及联轴器(包括万向节):**										**Transmission shafts (including cam shafts and crank shafts) and cranks; bearing housings and plain shaft bearings; gears and gearing ball or roller screws; gear boxes and other speed changers, including torque converters; flywheels and pulleys, including pulley blocks; clutches and shaft couplings (including universal joints):**
	-传动轴(包括凸轮轴及曲柄轴)及曲柄:										-Transmission shafts (including cam shafts and crank shafts) and cranks:
8483.1010	---船舶用传动轴	6	T3	5.1	4.8	14	17	13	个		---Transmission shafts for ships
8483.1090	---其他	6	T3	5.4	4.8	30	17	13	个		---Other
8483.2000	-装有滚珠或滚子轴承的轴承座	6	5		0	30	17	13	个	a	-Bearing housings, incorporating ball or roller bearings
8483.3000	-未装有滚珠或滚子轴承的轴承座;滑动轴承	6	T3		4.8	30	17	13	个		-Bearing housings, not incorporating ball or roller bearings; plain shaft bearings

税则号列 Tariff Item.	货品名称	最惠国(%) MFN	协定(%)CT			普通 Gen	增值税率 VAT	出口退税 ED	计量单位 Unit	监管条件 SC	Article Description
			东盟 CA	中巴 CP	中智 CC						
8483.3000 10	磁悬浮轴承(轴承组合件,由悬浮在充满阻尼介质的环形磁铁组成)	6				30	17	13	个	3	Magnetic suspendins bearing (assembly of bearing, compased of circular manet of supending in filled with damping medi-un)
8483.3000 20	轴承/阻尼器(安装在阻尼器上的具有枢轴/盖的轴承)	6				30	17	13	个	3	Bearing Damper (the damper set up on having pivot)
8483.3000 90	其他未装有滚珠或滚子轴承的轴承座;其他滑动轴承	6				30	17	13	个		Other bearing housing not incorporalins ball or rouer bearings; plain shaft bea-rins
	-齿轮及齿轮传动装置,但单独进口或出口的带齿的轮、链轮及其他传动元件除外;滚珠或滚子螺杆传动装置;齿轮箱及其他变速装置,包括扭矩变换器:										-Gears and gearing, other than toothed wheels, chain sprockets and other trans-mission elements presented separately; ball or roller screws; gear boxes and other speed changers, including torque converters:
8483.4010	---滚子螺杆传动装置	8	T3	5.6	6.4	30	17	13	个		---Roller Screws
8483.4020	---行星齿轮减速器	8	T3	5.6	6.4	30	17	13	个		---Planet decelerators
8483.4020 01	磨煤机用行星齿轮减速器(由螺旋伞齿轮加行星齿轮二级立式减速机构组成,转盘外圆直径为1300mm至2400mm)	8				30	17	13	个		the planetary gear decelerator for coal grinding machine (the external diame-ter of turnplate is 1300mm - 2400mm)
8483.4020 90	其他行星齿轮减速器	8				30	17	13	个		Other planet decelerators
8483.4090	---其他	8	T3	5.6	6.4	30	17	13	个		---Other
8483.4090 01	风力发电设备用变速箱	8				30	17	13	个		Transmission case for the wind - power generating facilities
8483.4090 90	其他传动装置及变速装置(指齿轮及齿轮传动装置,齿轮箱和扭矩变换器)	8				30	17	13	个		
8483.5000	-飞轮及滑轮,包括滑轮组	8	5		0	30	17	13	个		-Flywheels and pulleys, including pulley blocks
8483.6000	-离合器及联轴器(包括万向节)	8	5		0	30	17	13	个		-Clutches and shaft couplings (including universal joints)
8483.9000	-单独报验的带齿的轮、链轮及其他传动元件;零件	8	5		6.4	30	17	13	千克		-Toothed wheels, chain sprockets and other transmission elements presented separately; parts
84.84	**密封垫或类似接合衬垫,用金属片与其他材料制成或用双层或多层金属片制成;成套或各种不同材料的密封垫或类似接合衬垫,装于袋、套或类似包装内;机械密封件:**										**Gaskets and similar joints of metal sheeting combined with other material or of two or more layers of metal; sets or assortments of gaskets and similar joints, dissimilar in composition, put up in pouches, envelopes or similar packings mechanical seals:**
8484.1000	-密封垫或类似接合衬垫,用金属片与其他材料制成或用双层或多层金属片制成	8	5		0	30	17	13	千克		-Gaskets and similar joints of metal sheeting combined with other material or of two or more layers of metal
8484.2000	-机械密封件	8	5		0	30	17	13	千克		-Mechanical seals

税则号列 Tariff Item.	货品名称	最惠国(%) MFN	协定(%) CT 东盟 CA	中巴 CP	中智 CC	普通 Gen	增值税率 VAT	出口退税 ED	计量单位 Unit	监管条件 SC	Article Description
8484.2000 10	耐 UF_6 腐蚀的转动轴封(专门设计的真空密封装置,缓冲气体泄漏率 1000cm³/min)	8				30	17	13	千克	3	UF_6 resisting rotatory axleseals (specially designed vacuum seal, rate of leakage of buffer gas 1000cm³/min)
8484.2000 20	转动轴封(专门设计的带有密封式进气口和出气口的转动轴封)	8				30	17	13	千克	3	Rotatory axleseals (specially designed, with sealed inlet and outlet)
8484.2000 30	MLIS 用转动轴封(专门设计的带密封进气口和出气口的转动轴封)	8				30	17	13	千克	3	Rotatory axleseals for MLIS (specially designed, with sealed inlet and outlet)
8484.2000 90	其他机械密封件	8				30	17	13	千克		Other mechanical seals
8484.9000	-其他	8	5		0	30	17	13	千克		-Other
84.86	**专用于或主要用于制造半导体单晶柱或晶圆、半导体器件、集成电路或平板显示器的机器及装置;本章注释九(三)规定的机器及装置,零件及附件:**										**Especially or primarily for producing single crystal column or crystal circle、semiconductor devices、the machine and device of integrated circuit or plate display, that in note Ⅳ(Ⅲ) to this chapter requirment, parts or a ccessories:**
	-制造单晶柱或晶圆用的机器及装置:										-Machines and device for producing single crystal column or crystal circle
8486.1010	---利用温度变化处理单晶硅的机器及装置	0				30	17	13	台	0	---Machines and device that deal with Single crystal silicon according to changes of temperatures
8486.1020	---研磨设备	0				30	17	13	台	0	---Grinding equipment
8486.1030	---切割设备	0				30	17	13	台	0	---Incising equipment
8486.1040	---化学机械抛光设备(CMP)	0				30	17	13	台	0	---Chemical - apparatus polishing equipment
8486.1090	---其他	0				30	17	13	台	0	---other
	-制造半导体器件或集成电路用的机器及装置:										-Machines and device for producing semiconductor devices or integrated circuit:
8486.2010	---氧化扩散退火及其他热处理设备	0				30	17	13	台	0	---Diffusion, oxidatation, anneal and other heat - treatment facilities
	---薄膜沉积设备										---Pellicle deposition device
8486.2021	---化学气相沉积装置	0				30	17	13	台	0	---Chemical vapor deposition device
8486.2022	---物理气相学积装置(PVD)	0				30	17	13	台	0	---Physical Vapor Deposition device
8486.2029	----其他	0				30	17	13	台	0	----Other
	---将电处图投影或绘制到感光半导体材料上的装置:										---Use interlin kage or connecting line for inductance of chemical compound semiconductor materials:
8486.2031	----分步重复光刻机(步进光刻机)	0				100	17	13	台	0	----Lithograph
8486.2039	----其他	0				100	17	13	台	0	----Other
	---刻蚀及剥离设备										---Etching and striping equipment
8486.2041	----等离子干法刻蚀机	0				30	17	13	台	0	
8486.2049	---其他	0				30	17	13	台	0	----Other
8486.2050	---离子注入机	0				11	17	13	台	0	---Ion Implantation Machine
8486.2090	---其他	0				30	17	13	台	0	---Other
	-制造平板显示器用的机器及装置:										-Machines and appliances used to produce flat panel monitor

税则号列 Tariff Item.	货品名称	最惠国(%) MFN	协定(%)CT 东盟 CA	 中巴 CP	 中智 CC	普通 Gen	增值税率 VAT	出口退税 ED	计量单位 Unit	监管条件 SC	Article Description
8486.3010	---扩散氧化、退火及其他热处理设备	0				30	17	13	台	0	---Diffusinon, oxidatation, anneal and other heat-treatment facili ties
	---薄膜沉积设备:										---Pellicle deposition device
8486.3021	----化学气相沉积设备(CVD)	0				30	17	13	台	0	---- Chemical vapor deposition device
8486.3022	----物理气相沉积设备(PVD)	0				30	17	13	台	0	----Physical Vapor Deposition device (PVD)
8486.3029	----其他	0				30	17	13	台	0	----Other
	---将电路图投影或绘制到感光半导体材料上的装置:										---Equipments that project the circuit diagram on photo - sensitive semiconductor materials
8486.3031	----分布重复光刻机	0				100	17	13	台	0	----Lithograph
8486.3039	----其他	0				100	17	13	台	0	---Other
	---湿法蚀刻显影、剥离、清洗装置:										---Strip - cleaning device for wet - etching developing
8486.3041	----超声波清洗装置	10	8		0	30	17	13	台	0	----Ultrasonic cleaning device
8486.3049	----其他	0				30	17	13	台	0	----Other
8486.3090	---其他	0				30	17	13	台	0	---Other
	-本章注释九(三)规定的机器及装置:										-The machines and device stipulated in Note IV (III) of this chapter
8486.4010	---主要用于或专用于制作和修复掩膜版(mask)或投影掩膜版(retub)的装置	0				30	17	13	台	0	---Device mainly or specially used for producing and recovering mask and reticle
	---主要用于或专有于装配与封装半导体器件或集成电器的设备:										---Equipments mainly or specially used for assembling or sealing semicon ductor components or integrated circuits
8486.4021	----塑封机	5		4.5	0	30	17	13	台	0	----Plastic sealing machine
8486.4022	----引线键合装置	8	5	7.6	0	30	17	13	台	0	----Wire bonder facilities
8486.4029	----其他	0				17	17	13	台	0	----Other
	---主要用于或专用于升降、装卸、搬运单晶柱、晶圈、半导体器件、集成电路或平板显示器的装置										---Facilities mainly or specially used to assend and dessend, load and unload, more the single crystal colum, crystal circle semiconductor components, integrated circuit or flat panel monitor
8486.4031	----集成电器工厂专用的自动搬运机器人	0				20	17	13	台	0	----the automatic transportation specially used by integrated circuit factories Robot
8486.4039	----其他	5		3.5	4	30	17	13	台	0	----Other
	-零件及附件										
8486.9010	---升降搬运、装卸机器用(自动搬运设备用除外)	5		2.5	4	30	17	13	千克		---Ascend and descend, transport, load and unload (except automatic transportation facilities)
8486.9020	---引线键合装置用	6	5	5.7	0	30	17	13	千克		---Wire bonder facilities
8486.9090	---其他	0				17	17	13	千克		---Other

税则号列 Tariff Item.	货品名称	最惠国(%) MFN	协定(%) CT 东盟 CA	中巴 CP	中智 CC	普通 Gen	增值税率 VAT	出口退税 ED	计量单位 Unit	监管条件 SC	Article Description
84.87	**本章其他税目未列名的机器零件,不具有电气接插件、绝缘体,线圈、触点,或其他电气器材特征的:**										**The machinery components listed in other tax items of this chapter, with no electric characteristics, such as electric socket, insulator, loop touch-point**
8487.1000	-船用推进器及桨叶	6	5		0	14	17	13	千克		-Thruster of ships, and propeller leaf
8487.9000	-其他	8	5		6.4	30	17	13	千克		-Other

第八十五章
电机、电气设备及其零件；声音的录制和重放设备及其零件、附件

注释：

一、本章不包括：

（一）电暖的毯子、褥子、足套及类似品，电暖的衣服、靴、鞋、耳套或其他供人穿戴的电暖物品；

（二）税目70.11的玻璃制品；

（三）税目84.86的机器及装置；

（四）用于医疗、外科、牙科或兽医的真空设备（第九十章）

（五）第九十四章的电热家具。

二、税目85.01至85.04不适用于税目85.11、85.12、85.40、85.41或85.42的货品，但金属槽汞弧整流器仍归入税目85.04。

三、税目85.09仅包括通常供家用的下列电动器具：

（一）任何重量的地板打蜡机、食品研磨机及食品搅拌器、水果或蔬菜的榨汁器；

（二）重量不超过20千克的其他机器。

但该税目不适用于风机、风扇或装有风扇的通风罩及循环气罩（不论是否装有过滤器）（税目84.14）、离心干衣机（税目84.21）、洗碟机（税目84.22）、家用洗衣机（税目84.50）、滚筒式或其他形式的熨烫机器（税目84.20或84.51）、缝纫机（税目84.52）、电剪子（税目84.67）或电热器具（税目85.16）。

四、税目85.23所称：

（一）"固态、非易决性存储器件"（例如，"闪存卡"或"电子闪存卡"，是指带有接口的存储器件，共在同一壳体内包含一块或多块闪存（FLASHE^2PROM），以集成电路的形式装配在一块印刷电路板上。它们可以包括一个集成电路形式的控制器及分立无源元件，例如，电容器及电阻器；

（二）所称"智能卡"是指装有一块或多块集成电路微处理器、随机存取存储器（RAM）或只读存储器（ROM）芯片的卡。这些卡可带有触点、磁条或嵌入式天线，但不包含任何其他有源或无源电路元件。

Chapter 85
Electrical machinery and equipment and parts thereof; sound recorders and reproducers, television image and sound recorders and reproducers, and parts and accessories of such articles

Notes:

1. This Chapter does not cover:

(a) Electrically warmed blankets, bed pads, foot-muffs or the like; electrically warmed clothing, footwear or ear pads or other electrically warmed articles worn on or about the person;

(b) The glass - made products of heading No. 70.11.

(c) The machines and equipments of heading No. 84.86.

(d)

(e) Electrically heated furniture of Chapter 94.

2. HeadingsNo. 85.01 to 85.04 do not apply to goods described in headingNo. 85.11, 85.12, 85.40, 85.41 or 85.42. However, metal tank mercury arc rectifiers remain classified in headingNo. 85.04.

3. HeadingNo. 85.09 covers only the following electro-mechanical machines of the kind commonly used for domestic purposes:

(a) Vacuum cleaners, including dry and wet vacuum cleaners, floor polishers, food grinders and mixers, and fruit or vegetable juice extractors, of any weight;

(b) Other machines provided the weight of such machines does not exceed 20 kg.

The heading does not, however, apply to fans or ventilating or recycling hoods incorporating a fan, whether or not fitted with filters (headingNo. 84.14), centrifugal clothes-dryers (headingNo. 84.21), dish washing machines (headingNo. 84.22), household washing machines (headingNo. 84.50), roller or other ironing machines (headingNo. 84.20 or 84.51), sewing machines (headingNo. 84.52), electric scissors (headingNo. 84.67) or to electrothermic appliances (headingNo. 85.16).

4. Tax item 85.23 mentions,

(a) "Solid - state nonvolatile storage" (for example, "flash disk card" or "electronic flash disk card", refers to the storage with port, containing one or many flashes within one single body, and is assembled on the print circuit board in the form of integrated circuit. They can include controller passive components in the form of integrated circuit, for example, capacitor and resistor.

(b) "Smart card" refers to the card with one or many integrated circuit processors and RAM or ROM chips. This card can carry touch - point, mag - stripe or embedded antenna, but not any other types of active or passive circuit components.

五、税目85.34所称“印刷电路”，是指采用各种印制方法（例如，压印、覆镀、腐蚀）或采用“膜电路”工艺，将导线、接点或其他印制元件（例如，电感器、电阻器、电容器）按预定的图形单独或互相连接地印制在绝缘基片上的电路，但能够产生、整流、调制或放大电信号的元件（例如，半导体元件）除外。

所称“印刷电路”，不包括装有非印制元件的电路，也不包括单个的分立式电阻器、电容器及电感器。但印刷电路可配有非经印刷的连接元件。

用同样工艺制得的无源元件及有源元件组成的薄膜电路或厚膜电路应归入税目85.42。

六、税目85.36所称“光导纤维、光导纤维束或光缆用连接器”，是指在有线数字通信设备中，简单机械地把光纤端部相连成一线的连接器。它们不具备诸如对信号进行放大、再生或修正等其他功能。

七、税目85.37不包括电视接收机或其他电气设备用的无绳红外遥控器（税目85.43）

八、税目85.41及85.42所称：

（一）“二极管、晶体管及类似的半导体器件”，是指那些依靠外加电场引起电阻率的变化而进行工作的半导体器件。

（二）“集成电路”，是指：

1. 单片集成电路，即电路元件（二极管、晶体管、电阻器、电容器、电感器等）主要整体制作在一片半导体材料或化合物半导体材料（例如掺杂硅砷化镓、硅锗或磷化铟）基片的表面，并不可分割地连接在一起的电路。

2. 混合集成电路，即通过薄膜或厚膜工艺制得的无源元件（电阻器、电容器、电感器等）和通过半导体工艺制得的有源元件（二极管、晶体管、单片集成电路等）用互连或连接线不可分割地组合在同一绝缘基片（玻璃、陶瓷等）上的电路。这种电路也可包括分立元件。

3. 多芯片集成电路是由两个或多个单片集成电路不可分割地组合在一片或多片的绝缘基片上构成的电路，不论是否带有引线框架，但不带有其他有源或无源的电路元件。

5. For the purposes of headingNo. 85. 34 "printed circuits" are circuits obtained by forming on an insulating base, by any printing process (for example, embossing, plating-up, etching) or by the "film circuit" technique, conductor elements, contacts or other printed components (for example, inductances, resistors, capacitors) alone or interconnected according to a pre-established pattern, other than elements which can produce, rectify, modulate or amplify an electrical signal (for example, semiconductor elements).

The expression "printed circuits" does not cover circuits combined with elements other than those obtained during the printing process, nor does it cover individual, discrete resistors, capacitors or inductances.

Thinor thick-film circuits comprising passive and active elements obtained during the same technological process are to be classified in heading No. 85. 42.

6. Throughout heading 85. 37 "connector for optical fiber, fiber-optic beam or optical cable" refers to the mechanism of mechanically combining optical terminals in wired digital communication equipments. It doesn't have the functions of enlarging, regenerating or modifying the signals.

7. Ⅶ. Tax item 85. 37 doesn't include the wireless infrared remote controllers used in television receivers and electrical equipments (see tax item 85. 43)

8. For the purposes of headingsNos. 85. 41 and 85. 42:

(A) "Diodes, transistors and similar semiconductor devices" are semiconductor devices the operation of which depends on variations in resistivity on the application of an electric field;

(B) "Electronic integrated circuits and microassemblies" are:

(a) Monolithic integrated circuits in which the circuit elements (diodes, transistors, capacitors, interconnections, inductance) are created in the mass (essentially) and on the surface of a semiconductor material or connecting line for inductance or chemical compound semiconductor materials (doped silicon, gallium arsenide, for example) and are inseparably associated;

(b) Hybrid integrated circuits in which passive elements (resistors, capacitors, interconnections, inductance), obtained by thin-or thick-film technology, and active elements (diodes, transistors, monolithic integrated circuits, etc.), use interlinkase or connecting obtained by semiconductor technology, are combined to all intents and purposes indivisibly, on a single insulating substrate (glass, ceramic, etc.). These circuits may also include discrete components;

(c) Microassemblies of the moulded module, micromodule or similar types, consisting of discrete, active or both active and passive, components which are combined and interconnected.

本注释所述物品在归类时，即使本协调制度其他税目涉及到上述物品，尤其是物品的功能，仍应优先考虑归入税目 85.41 及 85.42。

九、税目 85.48 所称“废原电池、废原电池组及废蓄电池”，是指因破损、拆解、耗尽或其他原因而不能再使用，也不能再充电的电池。

For the classification of the articles defined in this Note, headingsNos. 85.41 and 85.42 shall take precedence over any other heading in the Nomenclature which might cover them by reference to, in particular, their function.

9. For the purposes of headingNo. 85.48, spent primary cells, “spent primary batteries and spent electric accumulators” are those which are neither usable as such because of breakage, cutting-up, wear or other reasons, nor capable of being recharged.

子目注释：

一、子目 8527.12 仅包括有内置放大器但无内置扬声器的盒式磁带放声机，不需外接电源即能工作，且外型尺寸不超过 170 毫米 × 100 毫米 × 45 毫米。

Subheading Notes:

1. SubheadingsNos. 8519.92 and 8527.12 cover only cassette-players with built-in amplifier, without built-in loudspeaker, capable of operating without an external source of electric power and the dimensions of which do not exceed 170mm × 100mm × 45mm.

税则号列 Tariff Item.	货品名称	最惠国(%) MFN	协定(%) CT 东盟 CA	中巴 CP	中智 CC	普通 Gen	增值税率 VAT	出口退税 ED	计量单位 Unit	监管条件 SC	Article Description
85.01	**电动机及发电机(不包括发电机组)：**										**Electric motors and generators (excluding generating sets):**
	-输出功率不超过 37.5 瓦的电动机：										-Motors of an output not exceeding 37.5W:
8501.1010	---玩具用	24.5	12	23.3	0	80	17	13	台	B	---For use in toys
	---其他：										---Other:
8501.1091	----微电机，机座尺寸在 20 毫米及以上，但不超过 39 毫米	9	T3	8.6	0	70	17	13	台		----Micromotors with a housing size of 20mm or more but not exceeding 39mm
8501.1091 01	激光视盘机机芯用精密微型电机(输出功率不超过 37.5 瓦)	9				70	17	13	台	B	Precision electric micromotors for movements of laser videodisc player, output≤37.5W
8501.1091 90	机座最大尺寸在 20mm 至 39mm 微电机(输出功率不超过 37.5 瓦)	9				70	17	13	台	B	Electric micromotors with a housing maximvm dimension of 20mm or more but not exceeding 39mm, output≤37.5W
8501.1099	----其他	9	T3	8.6	0	35	17	13	台		----Other
8501.1099 01	功率≤0.5W 非用于激光视盘机机芯的微型电机(圆柱型直径≤6mm，高≤25mm；扁圆型直径≤15mm，厚≤5mm)	9				35	17	13	台	B	Electric micromotors output ≤0.5W, not for movements of laser videodisc player (cylider type: diameter ≤ 6mm, high≤25mm; oblate type: diameter≤15mm, thick≤5mm)
8501.1099 90	其他微电机(输出功率不超过 37.5 瓦)	9				35	17	13	台	B	Other electric micromotors, output ≤ 37.5W
8501.2000	-交直流两用电动机，输出功率超过 37.5 瓦	12	T3		9.6	35	17	17	台	B	-Universal AC/DC motors of an output exceeding 37.5 W
	-其他直流电动机；直流发电机：										-Other DC motors; DC generators:
8501.3100	--输出功率不超过 750 瓦	12	T3	11	0	35	17	13	台	B	--Of an output not exceeding 750 W
8501.3200	--输出功率超过 750 瓦，但不超过 75 千瓦	10	T3		0	35	17	17	台	B	--Of an output exceeding 750 W but not exceeding 75 kW
8501.3300	--输出功率超过 75 千瓦，但不超过 375 千瓦	5			4	35	17	17	台	B	--Of an output exceeding 75 kW but not exceeding 375 kW
8501.3400	--输出功率超过 375 千瓦	12	8		9.6	35	17	17	台	B	--Of an output exceeding 375 kW
8501.4000	-其他单相交流电动机	12	T3		9.6	35	17	17	台	aB	-Other AC motors, single-phase
	-其他多相交流电动机：										-Other AC motors, multi-phase:
8501.5100	--输出功率不超过 750 瓦	5			0	35	17	17	台		--Of an output not exceeding 750 W

税则号列 Tariff Item.	货品名称	最惠国(%) MFN	协定(%)CT 东盟 CA	中巴 CP	中智 CC	普通 Gen	增值税率 VAT	出口退税 ED	计量单位 Unit	监管条件 SC	Article Description
8501.5100 10	发电机(功率≥40瓦特,频率600至2000赫兹,谐波畸变低于10%等)	5				35	17	17	台	3Ba	AC electric generators, output≥40W, frequency = 600 ~ 2000Hz, harmonic distortion <10%
8501.5100 90	其他不超过750W多相交流电动机(输出功率不超过750瓦)	5				35	17	17	台	aB	Other AC electric motors, multi-phase, output≤750W
8501.5200	--输出功率超过750瓦,但不超过75千瓦	10	T3		0	35	17	17	台	aB	--Of an output exceeding 750 W but not exceeding 75 kW
8501.5300	--输出功率超过75千瓦	12	8	11.4	0	35	17	17	台		--Of an output exceeding 75 kW
8501.5300 01	高速电力机车交流异步牵引电动机[用于(200KM/h)电力机车]	12				35	17	17	台	Ba	AC asyncronous traction motor for high speed electric locomotive (200KM/h)
8501.5300 90	其他功率>75kW多相交流电动机	12				35	17	17	台	Ba	Other AC electric motors, multi-phase, output >75kW
	-交流发电机:										-AC generators (alternators):
8501.6100	--输出功率不超过75千伏安	5			4	30	17	17	台/千瓦	OB	--Of an output not exceeding 75 kVA
8501.6200	--输出功率超过75千伏安,但不超过375千伏安	12	8		9.6	30	17	17	台/千瓦	OB	--Of an output exceeding 75 kVA but not exceeding 375 kVA
8501.6300	--输出功率超过375千伏安,但不超过750千伏安	12	8		9.6	30	17	17	台/千瓦	OB	--Of an output exceeding 375 kVA but not exceeding 750 kVA
	--输出功率超过750千伏安:										--Of an output exceeding 750 kVA:
8501.6410	---输出功率超过750千伏安,但不超过350兆伏安	10	8		8	30	17	17	台/千瓦	OB	---Of an output exceeding 750 kVA but not exceeding 350 MVA
8501.6420	---输出功率超过350兆伏安,但不超过665兆伏安	5.8	5		4.6	14	17	17	台/千瓦	OB	---Of an output exceeding 350 MVA but not exceeding 665 MVA
8501.6430	---输出功率超过665兆伏安	6	5		4.8	11	17	17	台/千瓦	OB	---Of an output exceeding 665 MVA
85.02	**发电机组及旋转式变流机:**										**Electric generating sets and rotary converters:**
	-装有压燃式活塞内燃发动机(柴油或半柴油发动机)的发电机组:										-Generating sets with compression-ignition internal combustion piston engines (diesel or semi-diesel engines):
8502.1100	--输出功率不超过75千伏安	10	T3		0	45	17	17	台/千瓦	B	--Of an output not exceeding 75 kVA
8502.1200	--输出功率超过75千伏安,但不超过375千伏安	10	8		8	45	17	17	台/千瓦	OB	--Of an output exceeding 75 kVA but not exceeding 375 kVA
	--输出功率超过375千伏安:										--Of an output exceeding 375 kVA:
8502.1310	---输出功率超过375千伏安,但不超过2兆伏安	10	8	7	0	45	17	17	台/千瓦	OB	---Of an output exceeding 375 kVA but not exceeding 2 MVA
8502.1320	---输出功率超过2兆伏安	10	8	7	0	30	17	17	台/千瓦	O	---Of an output exceeding 2 MVA
8502.2000	-装有点燃式活塞内燃发动机的发电机组	10	8		0	45	17	17	台/千瓦		-Generating sets with spark-ignition internal combustion piston engines
	-其他发电机组:										-Other generating sets:
8502.3100	--风力驱动的	8	5		0	30	17	17	台/千瓦	B	--Wind-powered
8502.3900	--其他	10	5		0	30	17	17	台/千瓦	B	--Other
8502.4000	-旋转式变流机	10	5		0	30	17	17	台		-Electric rotary converters
85.03	**专用于或主要用于税目85.01或85.02所列机器的零件:**										**Parts suitable for use solely or principally with the machines of headingNo. 85.01 or 85.02:**
8503.0010	---子目8501.1010及8501.1091所列电动机用	12	8	11.4	9.6	70	17	13	千克		---Of the motors of subheading No. 8501.1010 or8501.1091

税则号列 Tariff Item.	货品名称	最惠国(%) MFN	协定(%)CT 东盟 CA	中巴 CP	中智 CC	普通 Gen	增值税率 VAT	出口退税 ED	计量单位 Unit	监管条件 SC	Article Description
8503.0020	---子目8501.6420及8501.6430所列发电机用	3		2.5	1.8	11	17	13	千克		---Of the generators of subheadingNo. 8501.6420 or 8501.6430
8503.0030	---子目8502.3100所列发电机组用	3		2.5	1.8	30	17	13	千克		---Of the generating sets of subheading 8502.3100
8503.0090	---其他	8	5	7.6	6.4	30	17	13	千克		---Other
8503.0090 10	电动机定子(用于真空中频率600-2000Hz、功率50-1000VA条件下)	8				30	17	13	千克	3	Stators of generators, used under vacuum conditions, frequency range=600Hz ~2000Hz, power=50VA~1000VA
8503.0090 90	其他电动机、发电机(组)零件	8				30	17	13	千克		Other parts of electric motors, generators and gentrating sets
85.04	**变压器、静止式变流器(例如整流器)及电感器:**										**Electrical transformers, static converters (for example, rectifiers) and inductors:**
	-放电灯或放电管用镇流器:										-Ballasts for discharge lamps or tubes:
8504.1010	---电子镇流器	10	T3		8	35	17	13	个	B	---Electronic ballats
8504.1090	---其他	10	5		8	35	17	13	个	B	---Other
	-液体介质变压器:										-Liquid dielectric transformers:
8504.2100	--额定容量不超过650千伏安	10.5	T3		8.4	50	17	13	个	OB	--Having a power handling capacity not exceeding 650 kVA
8504.2200	--额定容量超过650千伏安,但不超过10兆伏安	12.6	8		10.1	50	17	13	个	OB	--Having a power handling capacity exceeding 650 kVA but not exceeding 10 MVA
	--额定容量超过10兆伏安:										--Having a power handling capacity exceeding 10 MVA:
	---额定容量超过10兆伏安,但小于400兆伏安:										---Having a power handling capacity exceeding 10MVA but less than 400MVA:
8504.2311	----额定容量超过10兆伏安,但小于220兆伏安	10	5	7	0	50	17	13	个	OB	----Having a power handling capacity 10MVA but less than 220MVA
8504.2312	----额定容量在220兆伏安及以上,但小于330兆伏安	10	5	7	0	50	17	13	个	OB	----Having a power handling capacity 220MVA but less than 330MVA
8504.2313	----额定容量在330兆伏安及以上,但小于400兆伏安	10	5	7	0	50	17	13	个	OB	----Having a power handling capacity 330MVA but less than 400MVA
	---额定容量在400兆伏安及以上:										---Having a power handling capacity of 400 MVA or more:
8504.2321	----额定容量在400兆伏安及以上,但小于500兆伏安	6	T3	4.2	0	11	17	13	个	B	----Having a power handling capacity 400MVA but less than 500MVA
8504.2329	----其他	6	T3	4.2	0	11	17	13	个	BO	----Other
	-其他变压器:										-Other transformers:
	--额定容量不超过1千伏安:										--Having a power handling capacity not exceeding 1 kVA:
8504.3110	---互感器	5		4.3	0	50	17	13	个	OB	---Mutual inductor
8504.3190	---其他	5		4.3	0	50	17	17	个	OB	---Other
	--额定容量超过1千伏安,但不超过16千伏安:										--Having a power handling capacity exceeding 1kVA but not exceeding 16kVA:
8504.3210	---互感器	5			0	50	17	13	个	B	---Mutual inductor
8504.3290	---其他	5			0	50	17	13	个	OB	---Other

税则号列 Tariff Item.	货品名称	最惠国(%) MFN	协定(%) 东盟 CA	中巴 CP	CT 中智 CC	普通 Gen	增值税率 VAT	出口退税 ED	计量单位 Unit	监管条件 SC	Article Description
8504.3300	--额定容量超过16千伏安,但不超过500千伏安	5			4	50	17	13	个	OB	--Having a power handling capacity exceeding 16 kVA but not exceeding 500 kVA
8504.3400	--额定容量超过500千伏安	14	T3		8.4	50	17	13	个	OB	--Having a power handling capacity exceeding 500 kVA
	-静止式变流器:										-Static converters:
	---稳压电源:										---Voltage-stabilized suppliers:
8504.4013	----税目84.71所列机器用	0				40	17	13	个	A	----Of the machines of heading 84.71
8504.4014	----其他直流稳压电源,功率小于1千瓦,精度低于万分之一	7	T3	5.6	5.6	80	17	13	个		----Other DC voltage-stabilized suppliers, of a power of less than 1 kW and an accuracy of not better than 0.0001
8504.4015	----其他交流稳压电源,功率小于10千瓦,精度低于千分之一	0				80	17	13	个		----Other AC voltage-stabilized suppliers, of a power of less than 10 kW and an accuracy of not better than 0.001
8504.4019	----其他	0				50	17	13	个		----Other
8504.4019 10	同位素电磁分离器离子源磁体电源(高功率直流型)	0				50	17	13	个	3	Ion source magnetic power suppliers of isotopic electromagnetic separators (high-power, DC type)
8504.4019 20	直流高功率电源(能8小时连续产生100V,500A电流,稳定度优于0.1%)	0				50	17	13	个	3	High-power DC power suppliers (capable of generating 100V, 500A current uninterrupted in 8 hours, stability better than 0.1%)
8504.4019 30	高压直流电源(能8小时连续产生20KV,1A电流,稳定度优于0.2%)	0				50	17	13	个	3	High-voltage DC power suppliers (capable of generating 20KV, 1A current uninterrupted in 8 hours, stability better than 0.2%)
8504.4019 40	同位素电磁分离器离子源高压电源	0				50	17	13	个	3	Ion source high-voltage power suppliers of isotopic electromagnetic separators
8504.4019 90	其他稳压电源	0				50	17	13	个		Other voltage-stabilized suppliers
8504.4020	---不间断供电电源	10	T3	8.5	0	50	17	13	台		---Uninterrupted power suppliers
	---其他:										---Other:
*8504.4091	----具有变流功能的半导体模块		T3		8	30	17	13	个		----Semiconductor modules with a converting function
8504.4091 01	具有变流功能的半导体模块(自动数据处理设备机器及组件、电讯设备用的)	0				30	17	13	个	s	Semiconductor modules with a converting function for automatic data processing machines and units thereof, and telecommunication apparatus
8504.4091 09	其他具有变流功能的半导体模块	10				30	17	13	个		Other semiconductor modules with a converting function
*8504.4099	----其他		T3		8	30	17	13	个		----Other
8504.4099 01	静止式变流器(自动数据处理设备机器及组件、电讯设备用)	0				30	17	13	个	s	Static converters for automatic data processing machines and units thereof, and telecommunication apparatus
8504.4099 02	ITA产品用的印刷电路组件(包括外接组件,如符合PCMCIA标准的卡)	0				30	17	13	个	s	Printed circuit assemblies for products falling within the ITA (including external assemblies, for example, cards in accordance with PCMCIA)

税则号列 Tariff Item.	货品名称	最惠国(%) MFN	协定(%)CT 东盟 CA	中巴 CP	中智 CC	普通 Gen	增值税率 VAT	出口退税 ED	计量单位 Unit	监管条件 SC	Article Description
8504.4099 03	高速电力机车的牵引变流器[用于(200KM/h)电力机车]	10				30	17	13	个		Traction converter for highspeed electric locomotive (200KM/h)
8504.4099 30	频率变换器(专用85030090.10电动机定子的频率变换器)	10				30	17	13	个	3	Frequency converters, specially, for stators of heading 85030090.10
8504.4099 40	频率变换器,亦称变频器或逆变器(功率≥40瓦特,频率600至2000赫兹,谐波畸变低于10%等)	10				30	17	13	个	3	Frequency converters (power≥40W, frequency = 600Hz ~ 2000Hz, harmonic distortion <10%)
8504.4099 50	电源(真空或受控环境感应炉用电源,额定输出功率≥5千瓦)	10				30	17	13	个	3	Power suppliers of vacuum or atmosphere-controlled induction furnace rated output power≥5kW)
8504.4099 60	模块式电脉冲发生器(在16ms内输出电流>101A,密封在防尘罩内,温宽范围大)	10				30	17	13	个	3	Module - type electric pulse generator (output electric current > 101A in 16ms and greater in temperature span when sealed in dustproof cover)
8504.4099 90	其他未列名静止式变流器	10				30	17	13	个		Other static converters, not elsewhere specified or included
8504.5000	-其他电感器	0				35	17	13	个		-Other inductors
	-零件:										-Parts:
	---变压器用:										---Of transformers:
8504.9011	----子目8504.2321,8504.2329所列变压器用	5		4.5	0	11	17	13	千克		----Of the transformers of subheadingNo. 8504.2321,8504.2329
8504.9019	----其他	8	5	4.5	0	50	17	13	千克		----Other
8504.9020	---稳压电源及不间断供电电源用	8	5	5.6	0	50	17	13	千克		---Of voltage-stabilized suppliers and uninterrupted power suppliers
8504.9090	---其他	8	5	5.6	0	30	17	13	千克		---Other
85.05	**电磁铁;永磁铁及磁化后准备制永磁铁的物品;电磁铁或永磁铁卡盘、夹具及类似的工件夹具;电磁联轴节、离合器及制动器;电磁起重吸盘:**										**Electro-magnets; permanent magnets and articles intended to become permanent magnets after magnetization; electro-magnetic or permanent magnet chucks, clamps and similar holding devices; electro-magnetic couplings, clutches and brakes; electro-magnetic lifting heads:**
	-永磁铁及磁化后准备制永磁铁的物品:										-Permanent magnets and articles intended to become permanent magnets after magnetization:
	--金属的:										--Of metal:
8505.1110	---稀土永磁体	7	5		0	20	17	13	千克		---Of rare-earth metals
8505.1190	---其他	7	5		0	20	17	17	千克		---Other
8505.1900	--其他	7	5	6.7	0	20	17	13	千克		--Other
8505.1900 10	磁极块(直径大于2m,用在同位素电磁分离器内)	7				20	17	17	千克	3	Pole blocks of isotopic electromagnetic separators (diameter >2m, used in isotopic electromagnet separators)
8505.1900 90	非金属永磁体(包括非金属磁化后准备制永磁体的物品)	7				20	17	17	千克		Permanent magnets and articles intended to become permanent magnets after magnetization of non-metal

税则号列 Tariff Item.	货品名称	最惠国(%) MFN	协定(%) 东盟 CA	中巴 CP	CT 中智 CC	普通 Gen	增值税率 VAT	出口退税 ED	计量单位 Unit	监管条件 SC	Article Description
8505.2000	-电磁联轴节、离合器及制动器	8	5	7.6	0	20	17	13	千克		-Electro-magnetic couplings, clutches and brakes
	-其他,包括零件:										-Other, including parts
8505.9010	---电磁起重吸盘	8	5		0	20	17	13	千克/个		---Electro-magnetic lifting heads
8505.9090	---其他	8	5	7.6	0	20	17	13	千克		---Other
8505.9090 10	超导螺线电磁体(产生超过2个泰斯拉磁场,长径比≥2,内径≥300mm等)	8				20	17	13	千克	3	Superconduction helix electro-magnets (capable of generating two or more Tesla magnetic fields, L/D≥2, inside diameter≥300mm)
8505.9090 90	其他电磁夹具等及编号8505的零件	8				20	17	13	千克		Other electro-magnetic clamps and parts of headingNo. 8505
85.06	**原电池及原电池组:**										**Primary cells and primary batteries:**
	-二氧化锰的:										-Manganese dioxide:
8506.1010	---碱性锌锰的	20	T3		0	80	17	13	个	BA	---Alkaline zinc-manganese dioxide
8506.1090	---其他	20	T3		0	80	17	13	个	BA	---Other
8506.3000	-氧化汞的	14	8		8.4	40	17	13	个	BA	-Mercuric oxide
8506.4000	-氧化银的	14	8		8.4	40	17	13	个	AB	-Silver oxide
8506.5000	-锂的	14	8		8.4	40	17	13	个	AB	-Lithium
8506.6000	-锌空气的	14	8		8.4	40	17	13	个	AB	-Air-zinc
8506.8000	-其他原电池及原电池组	14	T3		0	40	17	13	个	AB	-Other primary cells and primary batteries
	-零件:										-Parts:
8506.9010	---子目8506.1000所列电池用	14	T3		8.4	80	17	13	千克	AB	---Of the cells of subheadingNo. 8506.1000
8506.9090	---其他	10	T3		0	40	17	13	千克	AB	---Other
85.07	**蓄电池,包括隔板,不论是否矩形(包括正方形):**										**Electric accumulators, including separators therefor, whether or not rectangular (including square):**
8507.1000	-铅酸蓄电池,用于起动活塞式发动机	10	T3	6.9	8	90	17	17	个	AB	-Lead-acid, of a kind used for starting piston engines
8507.2000	-其他铅酸蓄电池	10	T3	6.9	0	90	17	17	个	AB	-Other lead-acid accumulators
8507.3000	-镍镉蓄电池	10	T3	8	0	40	17	13	个	AB	-Nickel-cadmium
8507.4000	-镍铁蓄电池	12	T3	9.6	7.2	40	17	13	个	AB	-Nickel-iron
	-其他蓄电池:										-Other accumulators:
8507.8010	---镍氢电池	12	T3	9.6	0	40	17	13	个	AB	---Nickel-hydrogen
8507.8020	---锂离子电池	12	T3	9.6	0	40	17	13	个	AB	---Lithium ion
8507.8090	---其他	12	T3	9	0	40	17	13	个	AB	---Other
	-零件:										-Parts:
8507.9010	---铅酸蓄电池用	10	5		0	90	17	13	千克	AB	---Of lead-acid accumulators
8507.9090	---其他	8	T3		0	40	17	13	千克	AB	---Other
85.08	**真空吸尘器:**										**Vacuum cleaners:**
	-电动的:										-Uectnoronic:
8508.1100	-功率不超过1500瓦,且带有容积不超过20升的集尘袋或其他集尘容积器	10	T3	8.2	0	130	17	13	台	AB	-Paper dust bags or other dust - eleminating machines with power no more than 1500w whose capacity are no more than 20 litres.
8508.1900	--其他	0				30	17	13	台	AB	--Other
8508.6000	-其他真空吸尘器	0				30	17	13	台	AB	-Other vacuum cleaners
	-零件										-Parts
8508.7010	---子目8508.1100、8508.1910所列吸尘器用	12	T3		7.2	100	17	13	千克		---Of the vacuum sweeper of No. subheading 8508.1100
8508.7090	---其他	0				20	17	13	千克		---Other

税则号列 Tariff Item.	货 品 名 称	最惠国(%) MFN	协定(%)CT 东盟 CA	中巴 CP	中智 CC	普通 Gen	增值税率 VAT	出口退税 ED	计量单位 Unit	监管条件 SC	Article Description
85.09	**家用电动器具:**										**Electro-mechanical domestic appliances, with self-contained electric motor:**
	-食品研磨机及搅拌器;水果或蔬菜的榨汁器:										-Food grinders and mixers; fruit or vegetable juice extractors:
8509.4010	---水果或蔬菜的榨汁机	10	T3		0	100	17	13	台	AB	---Fruit or vegetable juice extractors
8509.4090	---其他	10	T3		0	100	17	13	台	AB	---Other
	-其他器具										-Other appliances
8509.8010	---地板打蜡机	30	T3		24	100	17	13	台	B	---Floor polishers
8509.8020	---厨房废物处理器	20	12		12	100	17	13	台	B	---Kitchen waste disposers
8509.8090	---其他	30	T3		24	100	17	13	台	BA	---Other
8509.9000	-零件	12	T3		7.2	100	17	13	千克		-Parts
85.10	**电动剃须刀、电动毛发推剪及电动脱毛器:**										**Shavers, hair clippers and hair-removing appliances, with self-contained electric motor:**
8510.1000	-剃须刀	30	12		18	100	17	13	个	B	-Shavers
8510.2000	-毛发推剪	30	12		18	100	17	13	个	B	-Hair clippers
8510.3000	-脱毛器	20	12		0	100	17	13	个	B	-Hair-removing appliances
8510.9000	-零件	24.5	12		14.7	100	17	13	千克		-Parts
85.11	**点燃式或压燃式内燃发动机用的电点火及电起动装置(例如,点火磁电机、永磁直流发电机、点火线圈、火花塞、电热塞及起动电机);附属于上述内燃发动机的发电机(例如,直流发电机、交流发电机)及断流器:**										**Electrical ignition or starting equipment of a kind used for spark-ignition or compression-ignition internal combustion engines (for example, ignition magnetos, magneto-dynamos, ignition coils, sparking plugs and glow plugs, starter motors); generators (for example, dynamos, alternators) and cut-outs of a kind used in conjunction with such engines:**
8511.1000	-火花塞	10	T3		0	30	17	13	个		-Sparking plugs
	-点火磁电机;永磁直流发电机;磁飞轮:										-Ignition magnetos; magneto-dynamos; magnetic flywheels:
8511.2010	---机车、航空器及船舶用	5			0	11	17	13	个		---For locomotives, aircraft or ships
8511.2090	---其他	10	5		0	30	17	13	个		---Other
	--分电器;点火线圈:										--Distributors; ignition coils:
8511.3010	---机车、航空器及船舶用	5			0	11	17	13	个		---For locomotives, aircraft or ships
8511.3090	---其他	8.4	T3		0	30	17	13	个		---Other
	-启动电机及两用启动发电机:										-Starter motors and dual purpose starter-generators:
8511.4010	---机车、航空器及船舶用	5			0	11	17	13	个		---For locomotives, aircraft or ships
	---其他:										---Other:
8511.4091	----输出功率在132.39千瓦(180马力)及以上的发动机用启动电机	8.4	T3		0	30	17	13	个		----Starter motors for engines of an output of 132.39kW(180hp) or more
8511.4099	----其他	8.4	T3		0	30	17	13	个		----Other
	-其他发电机:										-Other generators:
8511.5010	---机车、航空器及船舶用	5			4	11	17	13	个		---For locomotives, aircraft or ships
8511.5090	---其他	8.4	T3		6.7	30	17	13	个		---Other
8511.8000	-其他装置	8.4	5		6.7	30	17	13	个		-Other equipment
	-零件:										-Parts:

税则号列 Tariff Item.	货品名称	最惠国(%) MFN	协定(%) 东盟 CA	中巴 CP	CT 中智 CC	普通 Gen	增值税率 VAT	出口退税 ED	计量单位 Unit	监管条件 SC	Article Description
8511.9010	---本税目所列供机车、航空器及船舶用的各种装置的零件	4.5			0	11	17	13	千克		---Of the equipment of headingNo. 85.11 used for locomotives, aircraft or ships
8511.9090	---其他	5			0	30	17	13	千克		---Other
85.12	**自行车或机动车辆用的电气照明或信号装置(税目85.39的物品除外)、风挡刮水器、除霜器及去雾器:**										**Electrical lighting or signalling equipment (excluding articles of headingNo. 85.39), windscreen wipers, defrosters and demisters, of a kind used for cycles or motor vehicles:**
8512.1000	-自行车用照明或视觉信号装置	10.5	8		6.3	45	17	13	个		-Lighting or visual signalling equipment of a kind used on bicycles
	-其他照明或视觉信号装置:										-Other lighting or visual signalling equipment:
8512.2010	---机动车辆用照明装置	10			0	45	17	13	个		---Lighting equipment of a kind used for motor vehicles
8512.2090	---其他	10			0	45	17	13	个		---Other
	-音响信号装置:										-Sound signalling equipment:
	---机动车辆用:										---For motor vehicles
8512.3011	----喇叭、蜂鸣器	10		8.5	0	45	17	13	个		----Loudspeaker, buzzers
8512.3019	----其他	10		8.5	0	45	17	13	个		----Other
8512.3090	---其他	10		8.5	0	45	17	13	个		---Other
8512.4000	-风挡刮水器、除霜器及去雾器	10			0	45	17	13	个		-Windscreen wipers, defrosters and demisters
8512.9000	-零件	8	5		0	45	17	13	千克		-Parts
85.13	**自供能源(例如,使用干电池、蓄电池、永磁发电机)的手提式电灯,但税目85.12的照明装置除外:**										**Portable electric lamps designed to function by their own source of energy (for example, dry batteries, accumulators, magnetos), other than lighting equipment of headingNo. 85.12:**
	-灯:										-Lamps:
8513.1010	---手电筒	15	T3	13.2	12	100	17	13	个		---Portable electric torches designed to function by dry batteries
8513.1090	---其他	17.5	T3		14	70	17	13	个		---Other
	-零件:										-Parts:
8513.9010	---手电筒用	14	T3		8.4	100	17	13	千克		---Of the torches of subheadingNo. 8513.1010
8513.9090	---其他	14	T3		8.4	70	17	13	千克		---Other
85.14	**工业或实验室用电炉及电烘箱(包括通过感应或介质损耗工作的);工业或实验室用其他通过感应或介质损耗对材料进行热处理的设备:**										**Industrial or laboratory electric furnaces and ovens (including those functioning by induction or dielectric loss); other industrial or laboratory equipment for the heat treatment of materials by induction or dielectric loss:**
	-电阻加热的炉及烘箱:										-Resistance heated furnaces and ovens:
8514.1010	---可控气氛热处理炉	0				30	17	13	台		---Furnaces for heat treatment, atmosphere controllable
8514.1090	---其他	0				30	17	13	台		---Other
8514.2000	-通过感应或介质损耗工作的炉及烘箱	0				30	17	13	台		-Furnaces and ovens functioning by induction or dielectric loss

税则号列 Tariff Item.	货品名称	最惠国(%) MFN	协定(%)CT 东盟 CA	中巴 CP	中智 CC	普通 Gen	增值税率 VAT	出口退税 ED	计量单位 Unit	监管条件 SC	Article Description
8514.2000 10	真空感应炉或受控环境感应炉(工作温度>850℃,感应线圈直径≤600mm,功率≥5千瓦)	0				30	17	13	台	3	Vacuum induction furnaces or controlled atmosphere induction furnaces (rated output power≥5kW, diameter of induction coil≤600mm working temperature >850℃)
8514.2000 90	其他感应或介质损耗工作炉及烘箱(包括实验室用)	0				30	17	13	台		Industrial or laboratory furnaces and ovens functioning by induction or dielectric loss
8514.3000	-其他炉及烘箱	0				30	17	13	台		-Other furnaces and ovens
8514.3000 20	电弧重熔炉和铸造用炉(容量1千-2万立方厘米,使用自耗电极,工作温度1700℃以上)	0				30	17	13	台	3	Arc remelting furnaces and casting furnaces (capacity = 1000 ~ 20000cm^3, with consumable electrode, working temperature>1700℃)
8514.3000 30	电子束熔化炉(功率≥50千瓦,能在>1200℃的熔化温度工作)	0				30	17	13	台	3	Electron-beam melting furnaces (power ≥50kW, capable of working at smelting temperature>1200℃)
8514.3000 40	等离子体雾化和熔化炉(功率≥50千瓦,能在>1200℃的熔化温度工作)	0				30	17	13	台	3	Plasma atomizing and melting furnaces (power≥50kW, capable of working at smelting temperature>1200℃)
8514.3000 90	工业用其他电炉及电烘箱(包括实验室用)	0				30	17	13	台		Other industrial or laboratory electric furnaces and ovens
8514.4000	-其他通过感应或介质损耗对材料进行热处理的设备	10	8		0	30	17	13	台		-Other equipment for the heat treatment of materials by induction or dielectric loss
8514.4000 01	焊缝中频退火装置	10				30	17	13	台		Intermediate frequency sealing anneator
8514.4000 90	其他感应或介质损耗的加热设备(包括实验室用)	10				30	17	13	台		Other equipment for the heat treatment of materials by induction or dielectric loss
	-零件:										-Parts:
8514.9010	---炼钢电炉用	8	5		0	30	17	13	千克		---Of steel making electric furnaces
8514.9090	---其他	0				30	17	13	千克		---Other
85.15	**电气(包括电热气体)、激光、其他光、光子束、超声波、电子束、磁脉冲或等离子弧焊接机器及装置,不论是否兼有切割功能;用于热喷金属或金属陶瓷的电气机器及装置:**										**Electric (including electrically heated gas), laser or other light or photon beam, ultrasonic, electron beam, magnetic pulse or plasma arc soldering, brazing or welding machines and apparatus, whether or not capable of cutting; electric machines and apparatus for hot spraying of metals or cermets:**
	-钎焊机器及装置:										-Brazing or soldering machines and apparatus:
8515.1100	--烙铁及焊枪	10	T3		0	30	17	13	个	A	--Soldering irons and guns
8515.1900	--其他	10	8		0	30	17	13	台		--Other
	-电阻焊接机器及装置:										-Machines and apparatus for resistance welding of metals:
	--全自动或半自动的:										--Fully or partly automatic:
8515.2110	---直缝焊管机	10	5		8	30	17	13	台		---Aligning tube welding machines
8515.2190	---其他	10	8		8	30	17	13	台	AO	---Other
8515.2900	--其他	10	8	9.5	0	30	17	13	台	A	--Other
	-电弧(包括等离子弧)焊接机器及装置:										-Machines and apparatus for arc (including plasma arc) welding of metals:

税则号列 Tariff Item.	货品名称	最惠国(%) MFN	协定(%)CT 东盟 CA	中巴 CP	中智 CC	普通 Gen	增值税率 VAT	出口退税 ED	计量单位 Unit	监管条件 SC	Article Description
	--全自动或半自动的:										--Fully or partly automatic:
8515.3110	---螺旋焊管机	10	5		8	30	17	13	台	B	---Spiralling tube welding machines
8515.3190	---其他	10			8	30	17	13	台	BAO	---Other
8515.3900	--其他	10	5		8	30	17	13	台	BAO	--Other
8515.8000	-其他机器及装置	8	5	7.6	0	30	17	13	台		-Other machines and apparatus
8515.8000 10	电子束、激光自动焊接机[将端塞焊接于燃料细棒(或棒)的自动焊接机]	8				30	17	13	台	3O	(Machines and apparatus welding of metals for lasers, electron beam)
8515.8000 90	其他焊接机器及装置	8				30	17	13	台	O	(Other welding machines and apparatus)
8515.9000	-零件	6	5	5.7	0	30	17	13	千克		-Parts
85.16	**电热的快速热水器、储存式热水器、浸入式液体加热器;电气空间加热器及土壤加热器;电热的理发器具(例如,电吹风机、电卷发器、电热发钳)及干手器;电熨斗;其他家用电热器具;加热电阻器,但税目85.45的货品除外:**										**Electric instantaneous or storage water heaters and immersion heaters; electric space heating apparatus and soil heating apparatus; electro-thermic hair-dressing apparatus (for example, hair dryers, hair curlers, curling tong heaters) and hand dryers; electric smoothing irons; other electro-thermic appliances of a kind used for domestic purposes; electric heating resistors, other than those of headingNo. 85.45:**
8516.1000	-电热的快速热水器、储存式热水器、浸入式液体加热器	10	T3		8	100	17	13	个	AB	-Electric instantaneous or storage water heaters and immersion heaters
	-电气空间加热器及土壤加热器:										-Electric space heating apparatus and electric soil heating apparatus:
8516.2100	--储存式散热器	35	12		21	100	17	13	个	B	--Storage heating radiators
	--其他:										--Other:
8516.2910	---土壤加热器	10	5		8	40	17	13	个		---Electric soil heating apparatus
8516.2990	---其他	10	8		8	100	17	13	个	B	---Other
	-电热的理发器具及干手器:										-Electro-thermic hair-dressing or hand-drying apparatus:
8516.3100	--吹风机	10	8		0	100	17	13	个	AB	--Hair dryers
8516.3200	--其他理发器具	35	12		21	100	17	13	个	AB	--Other hair-dressing apparatus
8516.3300	--干手器	35	12		21	100	17	13	个	AB	--Hand-drying apparatus
8516.4000	-电熨斗	35	T3		21	100	17	13	个	AB	-Electric smoothing irons
8516.5000	-微波炉	15	T3	13.5	9	130	17	13	个	AB	-Microwave ovens
	-其他炉;电锅、电热板、加热环、烧烤炉及烘烤器:										-Other ovens; cookers, cooking plates, boiling rings, grillers and roasters:
8516.6010	---电磁炉	15	T3		9	130	17	13	个	AB	---Electromagnetic ovens
8516.6030	---电饭锅	15	T3		9	130	17	13	个	AB	---Electric rice cookers
8516.6040	---电炒锅	15	T3		9	130	17	13	个	AB	---Electric frying pans
8516.6090	---其他	15	T3		9	130	17	13	个	AB	---Other
	-其他电热器具:										-Other electro-thermic appliances:
	--咖啡壶或茶壶:										--Coffee or tea makers:
8516.7110	---滴液式咖啡机	32	12		19.2	130	17	13	个	AB	---Drip coffee maker
8516.7120	---蒸馏渗滤式咖啡机	32	12		19.2	130	17	13	个	AB	---Distill percolating coffee maker
8516.7130	---泵压式咖啡机	32	12		19.2	130	17	13	个	AB	---Pump - driven coffee maker

税则号列 Tariff Item.	货 品 名 称	最惠国(%) MFN	协定(%) CT 东盟 CA	中巴 CP	中智 CC	普通 Gen	增值税率 VAT	出口退税 ED	计量单位 Unit	监管条件 SC	Article Description
8516.7190	---其它	32	12		19.2	130	17	13	个	AB	---Other
	--烤面包器:										--Toasters:
8516.7210	---家用自动面包机	32	12		19.2	130	17	13	个	AB	---Automatic bread machine for home use
8516.7220	---片式烤面包机(多式炉)	32	12		19.2	130	17	13	个	AB	---Toaster
8516.7290	---其它	32	12		19.2	130	17	13	个	AB	---Other
	--其他:										--Other:
8516.7910	---电热饮水机	32	T3		19.2	100	17	13	台	BA	---Electro-thermic water dispensers
8516.7990	---其他	32	T3		19.2	100	17	13	个	BA	---Other
8516.8000	-加热电阻器	10	8		0	40	17	13	个		-Electric heating resistors
	-零件:										-Parts:
8516.9010	---土壤加热器及加热电阻器用	8	5		0	40	17	13	千克		---Of apparatus of subheadingNo. 8516.2910 or 8516.8000
8516.9090	---其他	12	8		7.2	100	17	13	千克		---Other
85.17	**电话机,包括用于蜂窝网络或其他无线网络的电话机;其他发送或接收声音、图像或其他数据用的设备,包括有线或无线网络(例如,局域网或广域网)的通信设备,税目84.43、85.25、85.27或85.28的发送或接收设备除外:**										**Telephones, including those used for beehive networks or other wireless networks or other device used for transmitting or receiving voice, pictures or other data, including wired or wireless networks (LAN or Wide Area Network), excluding the transmitting or receiving device under tax items 84.43 or 85.25 or 85.27 or85.28**
8517.1100	--无绳电话机	0				30	17	13	台	AB	--Wireless telephone
	--用于蜂窝网络或其他无线网络的电话机:										--Used for telephone with beehive network or other wireless network:
8517.1210	---手持(包括车载)式无线电话机	0				30	17	13	台		---Rabio teleplione handsets
8517.1210 11	GSM 数字式手持无线电话整套散件	0				20	17	13	台	ABO	GSM digital cellular phones, of radio telephone handsets
8517.1210 19	其他 GSM 数字式手持无线电话机	0				20	17	13	台	ABO	Other GSM digital cellular phones, of radio telephone handsets
8517.1210 21	CMDA 数字式手持无线电话整套散件	0				20	17	13	台	ABO	Complete assemblies of CDMA digital cellular phones, of radio telephone handsets
8517.1210 29	其他 CDMA 数字式手持无线电话机	0				20	17	13	台	ABO	Other CDMA digital cellular phones, of radio telephone handsets
8517.1210 90	其他手持或无线电话机(包括车载式无线电话机)	0				20	17	13	台	ABO	Other of radio telephone handsets (including vehicle installed)
8517.1220	---对讲机	0				17	17	13	台		---Walkie-talkie
8517.1290	---其他	0				14	17	13	台	O	---Other
8517.1800	--其他	0				30	17	13	台	AB	--Other
	-其他发送或接收声音、图像或其他数据用的设备,包括有线或无线网络(例如,局域网或广域网)的通信设备:										-Other facilities used for transmitting or receiving voices, pictures and other data, including communicating facilities with wire or wireless network (for example, LAN or Wide Area Network)

税则号列 Tariff Item.	货品名称	最惠国(%) MFN	协定(%)CT			普通 Gen	增值税率 VAT	出口退税 ED	计量单位 Unit	监管条件 SC	Article Description
			东盟 CA	中巴 CP	中智 CC						
	--基站:										
8517.6110	---移动通信基站	0				14	17	17	台		---Mobile communication base station
8517.6110 10	GSM 式移动通信基地站	0				14	17	17	台	O	GSM mobile communication base station
8517.6110 20	CDMA 式移动通信基地站	0				14	17	17	台	O	CDMA mobile communication base station
8517.6110 30	TACS 式移动通信基地站	0				14	17	17	台	O	TACS mobile communication base station
8517.6110 90	其他移动通信基地站	0				14	17	17	台	O	Other mobile communication base station
8517.6190	---其他	0				14	17	17	台	O	---Other
	--接收、转换并且发送或再生声音、图像或其他数据用的设备,包括交换及路由设备:										--Facili ties for receiving, switching and transmitting or redenerating voice, pictures and other data, including exchandging and routing facilitiesi
	---数字式程控电话或电报交换机:										---Digital program – controlled switching systems
8517.6211	----局用电话交换机;长途电话交换机;电报交换机	0				17	17	13	台		----Telephone exchanges of telecommunication office, long – distance telephone exchanges,
8517.6212	----移动通信交换机	0				40	17	13	台	O	----Mobile communication switching system
8517.6219	----其他电话交换机	0				40	17	17	台	A	----Ohter telephonic seitching systems
	---光通讯设备:										---Optical communication equipments
8517.6221	----光端机及脉冲编码调制设备(PCM)	0				17	17	17	台	O	----Optical line terminal equipments and pulse code modulation mutilexers
8517.6222	----波分复用光传输设备	0				30	17	17	台	O	----Wavelength – Division Multiplex optical transmission facilities
8517.6229	----其他	0				30	17	17	台	OA	----Other
	---其他有线数字通信设备:										---Digtal line systems apparatus:
8517.6231	----通信网络时钟同步设备	0				30	17	13	台		----Communication network clock synchronization facilities
8517.6232	----以太网络交换机	0				30	17	17	台	O	----Ethernet exchangers
8517.6233	----IP 电话信号转换设备	0				30	17	17	台	A	----IP telephone signal converters
8517.6234	----调制解调器	0				30	17	13	台	AO	----Modem
8517.6235	----集线器	0				40	17	13	台	A	----hub
8517.6236	----路由器	0				40	17	17	台		----router
8517.6239	----其他	0				30	17	17	台	O	----Other
	---其他:										---Other
8517.6291	----其他无线用户接入网网络设备	0				14	17	17	台	O	---- Other wireless access network facilities
8517.6299	----其他	0				14	17	17	台	O	----Other
	--其他:										--Other
8517.6910	---其他无线设备		5		0	14	17	13	台		---Other wired facilities
8517.6910 01	用于呼叫、提示和寻呼的便携式接收器	0				14	17	13	台	ABs	Handy receivers used of calling or paging
8517.6910 90	其他无线通信设备	9				14	17	13	台	O	Other wireless communication equipment

税则号列 Tariff Item.	货品名称	最惠国(%) MFN	协定(%)CT 东盟 CA	中巴 CP	中智 CC	普通 Gen	增值税率 VAT	出口退税 ED	计量单位 Unit	监管条件 SC	Article Description
8517.6990	---其他有线设备	0				30	17	13	台		---Other wireless facilities
	-零件:										-Parts:
8517.7010	---数字式程控电话或电报交换机用	0				14	17	13	千克		---Used for digital program - controlled telephones or teletypes
8517.7020	---光端机及脉冲编码调制设备(PCM)	0				14	17	13	千克	O	---Optical line terminal equipments and pulse code modulation mutilexers
8517.7030	---手持式无线电话机用	0				17	17	13	千克	O	---Used for hand - held wireless telephones
8517.7040	---对讲机用	8	T3	5.6	6.4	20	17	13	千克		
8517.7060	---光通信设备的激光收发模块	0				30	17	13	千克		---Laser receiving and transmitting module for optical communication facilities
8517.7090	---其他	0				20	17	13	千克	O	---Other
85.18	**传声器(麦克风)及其座架;扬声器,不论是否装成音箱;耳机、耳塞,不论是否装有传声器,由传声器及一个或多个扬声器组成的组合机,音频扩大器;电气扩音机组:**										**Microphones and stands therefor; loudspeakers, whether or not mounted in their enclosures; headphones and earphones, whether or not combined with a microphone, and sets consisting of a microphone and one or more loudspeakers; audio-frequency electric amplifiers; electric sound amplifier sets:**
*8518.1000	-传声器(麦克风)及其座架		T3		0	40	17	13	个		-Microphones and stands therefor
8518.1000 01	电讯用频率在300-3400Hz麦克风(直径不超过10mm,高不超过3mm)	0				40	17	13	个	s	Microphones having a frequency range 300Hz ~ 3400Hz, with a diameter ≤ 10mm and a height≤3mm, for telecommunication use
8518.1000 90	其他传声器(麦克风)及其座架	10				40	17	13	个		Other microphones and stands therefor
	-扬声器,不论是否装成音箱:										-Loudspeakers, whether or not mounted in their enclosures:
8518.2100	--单喇叭音箱	10	T3		8	40	17	13	个	BA	--Single loudspeakers, mounted in their enclosures
8518.2200	--多喇叭音箱	10	T3		8	40	17	13	个	BA	--Multiple loudspeakers, mounted in the same enclosure
8518.2900	--其他	0				40	17	13	个	B	--Other
8518.3000	-耳机、耳塞机,不论是否装有传声器,由传声器及一个或多个扬声器组成的组合机	0				40	17	17	个		-Headphones and earphones, whether or not combined with a microphone, and sets consisting of a microphone and one or more loudspeakers
*8518.4000	-音频扩大器		T3		9.6	40	17	13	台		-Audio-frequency electric amplifiers
8518.4000 01	电器扩音器(列入ITA的有线电话重复器用的)	0				40	17	13	台	s	Electric amplifiers when used as repeaters in line telephony products falling within the ITA
8518.4000 90	其他音频扩大器	12				40	17	13	台	A	Other audio-frequency electric amplifiers
8518.5000	-电气扩音机组	10	T3		0	40	17	13	套		-Electric sound amplifier sets
*8518.9000	-零件		8		6.3	40	17	13	千克		-Parts
8518.9000 01	编号85184000.01所列货品的零件(列入ITA的有线电话重复器用的)	0				40	17	13	千克	s	Parts of good of subheadingNo. 85184000.10, when used as repeaters in line telephony products falling within the ITA

税则号列 Tariff Item.	货品名称	最惠国(%) MFN	协定(%) CT 东盟 CA	中巴 CP	中智 CC	普通 Gen	增值税率 VAT	出口退税 ED	计量单位 Unit	监管条件 SC	Article Description
8518.9000 90	编号8518所列货品的其他零件	10.5				40	17	13	千克		Other parts of goods of heading NO. 8518
85.19	**声音录制或重放设备:**										**Sound recording or reproducing apparatus**
8519.2000	-用硬币、钞票、银行卡、代币或其他支付方式使其工作的设备	20	12	16.4	0	130	17	13	台		-Facilities that are supported by means of payment such as coins, notes, bank's cards, token coins
8519.2000 10	以特定支付方式使其工作的激光唱机(用硬币、钞票、银行卡、代币或其他支付方式使其工作)	20				80	17	13	台	AB	Laser phonographs that work by special means of payment (coins, notes, debit/credit card, token coins or other means of payment are used to make it work)
8519.2000 90	其他以特定支付方式使其工作的声音录制或重放设备(用硬币、钞票、银行卡、代币或其他支付方式使其工作)	20				80	17	13	台		Other voice recording or playback equipments that work by special means of payment (coins, notes, debit/credit card, token coins or other means of payment are used to make it work)
8519.3000	-转盘(唱机唱盘)	30	12		18	130	17	13	台		-Tuntables(record-decks)
8519.5000	-电话应答机	0				80	17	13	台		-Telephone answering machines
	-其他设备:										-Other apparatus
	--使用磁性、光学或半导体媒体:										--Use magnetic, optics or semiconductors
	---使用磁性媒体的:										---Use magnetic media
8519.8111	----未装有声间录制装置的合式磁带型声间重放装置,编辑节目用放声机除外	17	12		0	130	17	13	台	AB	----Masnetic tape cassette equipment with no voice recording facilities, except reproducers for deiting programs
8519.8112	----装有声音不放装置的合式磁带录音机	30	T3		18	130	17	13	台	AB	----Masuetic tape cassette equipment with voice - replaying facilities
8519.8119	----其他	20	12	16.4	12	80	17	13	台	6AB	----other
	---使用光学媒体的										---Use optics media
8519.8121	----激光唱机,未装有声音录制设备	30	T3	26	0	80	17	13	台	AB	----Laser phonographs, without voice - replaying facilities
8519.8129	----其他	20	T3	16.4	12	80	17	13	台		----Other
8519.8129 10	具有录音功能的激光唱机	20				80	17	13	台	6AB	Recordable CD players
8519.8129 90	其他使用光学媒体的声音录制或重放设备	20				80	17	13	台	AB	Other voice - recording or replay facilities using optics media
	---使用半导体媒体:										---Use semiconductors media
8519.8131	----装有声音重放装置的闪速存储器型声音录制	20	12		16	80	17	13	台	6AB	----Memorizer - like voice recording facilities with flash that has playback components
8519.8139	----其他	20	12	16.4	12	80	17	13	台	6AB	----Other
	--其他:										--Other:
8519.8910	---不带录制装置的其他唱机,不论是否带有扬声器	30	12		18	130	17	13	台	AB	---The other record players not incorporating recording device, whether or not incorporating loudspeaker
8519.8990	---其他声音录制或重放设备	20	T3	16.4	12	80	17	13	台	6AB	---Other voice recording or replay facilities

税则号列 Tariff Item.	货品名称	最惠国(%) MFN	协定(%)CT 东盟 CA	中巴 CP	中智 CC	普通 Gen	增值税率 VAT	出口退税 ED	计量单位 Unit	监管条件 SC	Article Description
85.21	**视频信号录制或重放设备,不论是否装有高频调谐器:**										**Video recording or reproducing apparatus, whether or not incorporating a video tuner:**
	-磁带型:										-Magnetic tape-type:
	---录像机:										---Video tape recorders:
8521.1011	----广播级	T2	T2	T2	0	T2	17	13	台	AO	----Broadcast quality
8521.1019	----其他	T2	T2	T2	0	T2	17	13	台	A	----Other
8521.1020	---放像机	T2	T2	T2	0	T2	17	13	台	AO	---Video tape reproducers
	-其他:										-Other:
	---激光视盘机:										---Laser video compact disk player:
8521.9011	----视频高密光盘(VCD)播放机	20	T3	16	0	130	17	13	台		----Video Compact Disc player
8521.9011 10	具有录制功能的视频高密光盘(VCD)播放机(不论是否装有高频调谐放大器)	20				130	17	13	台	ABO	VCD player with CD-R drivers, whether or not incorporating a video tuner
8521.9011 90	其他视频高密光盘(VCD)播放机(不论是否装有高频调谐放大器)	20				130	17	13	台	ABO	Other VCD player, whether or not incorporating a video tuner
8521.9012	----数字化视频光盘(DVD)播放机	20	T3	16	0	130	17	13	台		----Digital Video Disc player
8521.9012 10	具有录制功能的数字化视频光盘(DVD)播放机(不论是否装有高频调谐放大器)	20				130	17	13	台	ABOa	DVD player with CD-R drivers, whether or not incorporating a video tuner
8521.9012 90	其他数字化视频光盘(DVD)播放机(不论是否装有高频调谐放大器)	20				130	17	13	台	ABOa	Other DVD player, whether or not incorporating a video tuner
8521.9019	----其他	20	T3	16	12	130	17	13	台		----Other
8521.9019 10	具有录制功能的其他激光视盘播放机(不论是否装有高频调谐放大器)	20				130	17	13	台	ABOa	Laser video compact disk (VCD) player with CD-R drivers, whether or not incorporating a video tuner
8521.9019 90	其他激光视盘播放机(不论是否装有高频调谐放大器)	20				130	17	13	台	ABOa	Other laser video compact disk (VCD) player, whether or not incorporating a video tuner
8521.9090	---其他	20	T3	16	16	130	17	13	台		---Other
8521.9090 10	用于光盘生产的金属母盘生产设备(不论是否装有高频调谐放大器)	20				130	17	13	台	6AO	Metal master production equipment for CD production, whether or not incorporating a video tuner
8521.9090 90	其他视频信号录制或重放设备(不论是否装有高频调谐放大器)	20				130	17	13	台	6AO	Other video recording or reproducing apparatus, whether or not incorporating a video tuner
85.22	**专用于或主要用于税目85.19至85.21所列设备的零件、附件:**										**Parts and accessories suitable for use solely or principally with the apparatus of headings NoS. 85.19 to 85.21:**
8522.1000	-拾音头	35	12		21	130	17	13	个/千克		-Pick-up cartridges
	-其他:										-Other:
8522.9010	---转盘或唱机用	25	12	20	15	130	17	13	千克		---Of turntables (record decks) or record-players
	---盒式磁带录音机或放声机用:										---Of cassette magnetic tape recorders or reproducers:

税则号列 Tariff Item.	货品名称	最惠国(%) MFN	协定(%)CT			普通 Gen	增值税率 VAT	出口退税 ED	计量单位 Unit	监管条件 SC	Article Description
			东盟 CA	中巴 CP	中智 CC						
8522.9021	----走带机构(机芯),不论是否装有磁头	25	12	22.5	15	100	17	13	千克	B	----Transport mechanisms, whether or not incorporating a magnetic head
8522.9022	----磁头	25	12	22.5	15	100	17	13	个/千克		----Magnetic heads
8522.9023	----磁头零件	20	12	18	12	100	17	13	千克		----Parts of magnetic heads
8522.9029	----其他	30	12	27	18	100	17	13	千克		----Other
	---视频信号录制或重放设备用:										---Of video recording or reproducing apparatus:
8522.9031	----激光视盘机的机芯	30	12	21	18	100	17	17	千克		----Movements of laser video disc compact disk player
8522.9031 01	具有刻录功能激光视盘机机芯	30				100	17	17	千克		Movements of laser video disc player with CD-R drivers
8522.9031 90	其他激光视盘机的机芯	30				100	17	17	千克		Other movements of laser video disc player
8522.9039	----其他	30	12	21	18	100	17	13	千克		----Other
8522.9039 01	激光视盘机的激光收发装置(激光头)	30				100	17	13	千克		Laser receiver-transmitter, specified for laser video disk set (laser heads)
8522.9039 02	激光视盘机激光收发装置用零件	30				100	17	13	千克		Parts of laser receiver-transmitter specified for laser video disk set
8522.9039 09	其他视频信号录制或重放设备的零件	30				100	17	13	千克		Other parts of video recording or reproducing apparatus
8522.9090	---其他	20	12	16	12	80	17	13	千克		---Other
85.23	**录制声音或其他信息用的圆盘、磁带、固态非易失性数据存储器件、"智能卡"及其他媒体,不论是否已录制,包括供复制圆盘用的母片及母带,但不包括第三十七章的产品:**										**Discs, tapes, solid-state nam-volat-ile data storage parts for recoding voice and other information, "smart card" and other media, no mater recorded or not**
	-磁性媒体:										-Magnetic media
	--磁条卡:										--Cads incorporating a magnetic stripe
8523.2110	---未录制	17.5	8		10.8	70	17	13	个		---Unrecorded
8523.2120	---已录制	15	12		9	130	17	13	个		---Recorded
	--其他:										--Other:
8523.2910	---磁盘	0				14	17	13	个		---magnetic discs
	---磁带:										---Magnetic tapes
8523.2921	----未录制的宽度不超过4毫米磁带	0				130	17	13	盘	A	----Tapes whose unrecorded width not exceeding 4mm
8523.2922	----未录制的宽度超过4毫米,但不超过6.5毫米的磁带	0				130	17	13	盘		----Tapes whose unrecorded width exceeding 4mm, but not 6.5mm
8523.2923	----未录制的宽度超过6.5毫米的磁带	0				20	17	13	盘		----Tapes whose unrecorded width exceeding 6.5mm
8523.2928	----重放声音或图象信息的磁带	10	8		8	130	17	13	盘	Z	----Tapes that replay the voice or pictures
8523.2929	----已录制的其他磁带	0				14	17	13	盘	Z	----Other recorded tapes
8523.2990	---其他	0				0	17	13	盘	Z	---Other
	-光学媒体:										-Optical media
8523.4010	---仅用于放重放声音信息的已录制光盘	10	5		8	130	17	13	张	Z	---Recorded compact disc only used to replay voice in for mation

税则号列 Tariff Item.	货品名称	最惠国(%) MFN	协定(%) 东盟 CA	中巴 CP	CT 中智 CC	普通 Gen	增值税率 VAT	出口退税 ED	计量单位 Unit	监管条件 SC	Article Description
8523.4020	---用于重放声音、图像以外信息的,税号 84.71 所列机器用	0				14	17	13	张		---For reproducing phenomena other than sound or image for the machines of heading 84.17
8523.4090	---其他	0				14	17	13	张	Z	---Other
	-半导体媒体:										-Semiconductor media
	--固态非易失性存储器件(闪速存储器):										--Solid-state nonvolatile storage (flash disc)
8523.5110	---未录制	0				70	17	13	个		---Unrecorded
8523.5120	---已录制	0				14	17	13	个		---Recorded
8523.5200	--"智能卡"	0				21	17	13	个		--"Smart card"
	--其他:										--Other:
8523.5910	---未录制	0				70	17	13	个		---Unrecorded
8523.5920	---已录制	0				14	17	13	个		---Recorded
	-其他:										-Other
	---唱片:										---Disc
8523.8011	----已录制唱片	15	8		9	130	17	13	张	Z	----Recorded disc
8523.8019	----其他	0				70	17	13	张		----Other
8523.8020	---税号 84.71 所列机器用	0				14	17	13	张		---For the machines of heading No. 84.71
8523.8090	---其他	0				14	17	13	张	Z	---Other
85.25	**无线电广播、电视发送设备,不论是否装有接收装置或声音的录制、重放装置;电视摄像机、数字照相机及视频摄录一体机:**										**Radio - telegraphy, radio - broadcasting or television, whether of not incorporating reception apparatus or sound recording or reproducing qpparatus; television cameras; still image video cameras and other video camera recorders;**
8525.5000	-发送设备	0				30	17	13	台	O	-For broadcast or television
	-装有接收装置的发送设备:										-Transmission apparatus incorporating reception apparatus
8525.6010	---卫星地面站设备	0				14	17	13	台	O	---Satellite earth station
8525.6090	---其他	0				30	17	17	台	O	---Other
	-电视摄像机、数字照相机及视频摄录一体机:										-Television cameras, digital cameras and video camera recorders:
	---电视摄像机:										---Telvision cameras:
8525.8011	----特种用途的	10	T3	9	0	17	17	13	台		----Special use
8525.8011 10	抗辐射电视摄像机[能抗 5×10^4 戈瑞(硅)以上辐射而又不会降低使用质量]	10				17	17	13	台	3A	Ray - proof television cameras (capable of resisting radiance >5×104GY (Si) and not lowering operation quality)
8525.8011 90	其他特种用途电视摄像机	10				17	17	13	台	A	Other telveision cameras for special purposes
8525.8012	----非特种用途的广播级	T2	T3	T2	0	T2	17	17	台	A	----Broadcast of non - special use
8525.8013	----非特种用途的其他类	T2	T3	T2	0	T2	17	17	台		----Other category of non - special use
8525.8013 01	手机用摄像组件(由镜头+CCD/CMOS+数字信号处理电路三部分构成)	35				130	17	13	台	OA	Other than broadcast quality camera assemblies, consist of lens, CCD/CMOS and digital signal processing circuit

税则号列 Tariff Item.	货品名称	最惠国(%) MFN	协定(%) 东盟 CA	中巴 CP	CT 中智 CC	普通 Gen	增值税率 VAT	出口退税 ED	计量单位 Unit	监管条件 SC	Article Description
8525.8013 90	其他非特种用途电视摄像机及其他摄像组件(其他摄像组件由非广播级镜头 + CCD/CMOS + 数字信号处理电路构成)	35				130	17	13	台	A	TV photographers and other photographing components for non - special use (other photographing components are made up of non - broadcast cameras + CCD/CMPS + digital signal processing circuits)
	---数字照相机:										
8525.8021	----特种用途的	0				17	17	17	台		---Special use
8525.8022	----非特种用途的单镜头反光型	T2				T2	17	13	台	a	---Single lens reflex of non - special use
8525.8029	----非特种用途的其他类型	T2				T2	17	17	台	a	----Other category of non - special use
	---视频摄录一体机										---Photographing - recording machine
8525.8031	----特种用途	0				17	17	13	台	A	----Special use
8525.8032	----非特种用途的广播级	T2				T2	17		台	A	----Broadcast of non - special use
8525.8033	----非特种用途的家用型	0				130	17	13	台	A	----Other
8525.8039	----非特种用途的其他类型	T2				T2	17	13	台	A	----Other
85.26	**雷达设备、无线电导航设备及无线电遥控设备:**										**Radar apparatus, radio navigational aid apparatus and radio remote control apparatus:**
	-雷达设备:										-Radar apparatus:
8526.1010	---导航用	2			0	8	17	13	台		---For navigational aid
8526.1010 10	用于导弹、火箭等的导航雷达设备(用于弹道导弹、运载火箭、探空火箭等的目标探测)	2				8	17	13	台	3	Guidance radar apparatus for missiles or rockets (suitable for radio detecting and ranging objects such as ballistic missiles, carrier rockets, sounding rockets)
8526.1010 90	其他导航用雷达设备	2				8	17	13	台	O	Other radar apparatus for navigational aid
8526.1090	---其他	5			0	14	17	13	台		---Other
8526.1090 01	飞机机载雷达(包括气象雷达,地形雷达和空中交通管制应答系统)	5				14	17	13	台		Other air-borne radar (including meteorological radar, topographic radar and air traffic control answering system)
8526.1090 11	用于导弹、火箭等的机载雷达设备(用于弹道导弹、运载火箭、探空火箭等的目标探测)	5				14	17	13	台	3	Air-borne radar apparatus for missiles or rockets (suitable for radio detecting and ranging objects such as ballistic missiles, carrier rockets, sounding rockets)
8526.1090 91	用于导弹、火箭等的其他雷达设备(用于弹道导弹、运载火箭、探空火箭等的目标探测)	5				14	17	13	台	3	Other radar apparatus for missiles or rockets (suitable for radio detecting and ranging objects such as ballistic missiles, carrier rockets, sounding rockets)
8526.1090 99	其他雷达设备	5				14	17	13	台	O	Other radar apparatus
	-其他:										-Other:
	--无线电导航设备:										--Radio navigational aid apparatus:
8526.9110	---机动车辆用	2			0	8	17	13	台		---For motor vehicles
8526.9190	---其他	2			0	8	17	13	台		---Other

税则号列 Tariff Item.	货品名称	最惠国(%) MFN	协定(%) 东盟 CA	中巴 CP	CT 中智 CC	普通 Gen	增值税率 VAT	出口退税 ED	计量单位 Unit	监管条件 SC	Article Description
8526.9190 10	制导装置(使300km射程导弹达到≤10km圆公算偏差)	2				8	17	13	台	3O	The guided missile reaches guidance device (messenger 300 kms range ≤ 10 kms make public consistent calculating deviation)
8526.9190 90	其他无线电导航设备	2				8	17	13	台	O	Other radio narigational aid apparatus
8526.9200	--无线电遥控设备	5			0	14	17	13	台	O	--Radio remote control apparatus
85.27	**无线电话、电报、无线电广播接收设备,不论是否与声音的录制、重放装置或时钟组合在同一机壳内:**										**Reception apparatus for radio-telephony, radio-telegraphy or radio-broadcasting, whether or not combined, in the same housing, with sound recording or reproducing apparatus or a clock:**
	-不需外接电源的无线电收音机,包括兼可接收无线电话、电报的设备:										-Radio-broadcast receivers capable of operating without an external source of power, including apparatus capable of receiving also radio-telephony or radio-telegraphy:
8527.1200	--袖珍盒式磁带收放机	20	T3		0	130	17	13	台	AB	--Pocket-size radio cassette-players
8527.1300	--其他收录(放)音组合机	15	T3		0	130	17	13	台	AB	--Other apparatus combined with sound recording or reproducing apparatus
8527.1900	--其他	15	T3		0	130	17	13	台	B	--Other
	-需外接电源的汽车用无线电收音机:										-Radio-broadcast receivers not capable of operating without an external source of power, of a kind used in motor vehicles:
8527.2100	--收录(放)音组合机	15	T3		0	130	17	13	台	B	--Combined with sound recording or reproducing apparatus
8527.2900	--其他	15	8		0	130	17	13	台	B	--Other
	-其他:										-Other:
8527.9100	--收录(放)音组合机	15	T3		0	130	17	13	台	AB	--Combined with sound recording or reproducing apparatus
8527.9200	--带时钟的收音机	15	8		0	130	17	13	台		--Not combined with sound recording or reproducing apparatus but combined with a clock
*8527.9900	--其他	27	T3		16.2	130	17	13	台	BA	--Other
85.28	**监视器及投影机,未装电视接收装置;电视接收装置,不论是否装有无线电收音装置或声音、图像的录制或重放装置:**										**Monitor and projector, with or without TV receivers, with or without wireless radio device or voice and picture recording and replaying device**
	-阴极射线管监视器:										-Cathode-ray the rube display:
8528.4100	--专用于或主要用于税目84.71的自动数据处理系统的	0				40	17	13	台	6AB	--Especially used or mainly used for automatic data processing system of tax item
	--其他:										--Other:
8528.4910	---彩色的	30	T3	26	24	130	17	13	台	6AB	---Colour
8528.4990	---黑白或其他单色的	19	T3	15.2	15.2	100	17	13	台	6AB	---Black and white or other monochrone
	-其他监视器										-Other monitors

税则号列 Tariff Item.	货品名称	最惠国(%) MFN	协定(%)CT 东盟 CA	 中巴 CP	 中智 CC	普通 Gen	增值税率 VAT	出口退税 ED	计量单位 Unit	监管条件 SC	Article Description
	--专用于或主要用于税目84.71的自动数据处理系统的：										--Specially used or mainly used for automatic data processing system of tax item 84.71
8528.5110	---液晶的	0				40	17	13	台	ABO	---Liquid crystal
8528.5190	---其他	0				40	17	17	台	AB	---Other
	--其他：										--Other：
8528.5910	---彩色的	30	T3	26	24	130	17	17	台	AB6	---Colour
8528.5990	---黑色或其他单色的	19	T3	15.2	15.2	100	17	17	台	AB6	---Black and white or other monochrome
	-投影机										-Projectors
8528.6100	--专用于或主要用于税目84.71的自动数据处理系统的	0				14	17	13	台		--Especially used or mainly used for automatic data processing system of tax item
8528.6100 10	专用或主要用于税目84.71商品的彩色投影机	0				14	17	13	台	A	Specially used or mainly used for color prajector of tax item 84.71
8528.6100 90	其他专用或主要用于税目84.71商品的投影机	0				14	17	13	台	A	Specially used or mainly used for projector of tax item 84.71
	--其他：										--Other
8528.6910	---彩色的	30	T3	25.5	24	130	17	13	台	A6	---Colour
8528.6990	---黑色或其他单色的	15	T3		12	100	17	13	台	A	---Black and white or other monochrome
	-电视接收装置，不论是否装有无线电收音装置或声音、图像的录制或重放装置：										-Reception apparatus for television, whether or not incorporating radio-broadcast receivers or sound or video recording or reproducing apparatus
	--在设计上不带有视频显示器或屏幕的：										--Without video display or screen：
8528.7110	---彩色卫星电视接收机	30		24	24	130	17	13	台	AO	---Colour satellite television receivers
8528.7180	---其他彩色的	30	T3	21	24	130	17	13	台		---Other colour
8528.7190	---黑色的或其他单色的	15	T3		12	100	17	13	台		---Other
	--其他，彩色的：										--Other colour
	---阴极射线显像管的：										---Cathode-ray the tube display
8528.7211	----模拟电视接收机	30		21	24	130	17	13	台	6	----A diagonal measurement of ≤42cm
8528.7212	----数字电视接收机	30		21	24	130	17	13	台	AB6	----A diagonal measurement of 42cm ~ 52cm
8528.7219	----其他	30		21	24	130	17	13	台	AB6	----Other
	---液晶显示器的：										---Liquid crystal display
8528.7221	----模拟电视接收机	30		21	24	130	17	13	台	ABO	----A diagonal measurement of ＞52cm
8528.7222	----数字电视接收机	30		21	24	130	13		台	ABO	----Digital television receivers
8528.7229	----其他	30		21	24	130	17	13	台	ABO	----Other
	---等离子显示器的：										---Plasma display
8528.7231	----显示屏幕超过52厘米的	30		21	24	130	17	13	台	ABO	----A diagonal measurement of ＞52cm
8528.7232	----数字电视接收机	30		21	24	130	17	13	台	ABO	----Digital television receivers
8528.7239	----其他	30		21	24	130	17	13	台	ABO	----Other
	---其他：										---Other：
8528.7291	----模拟电视接收机	30	T3	21	24	130	17	13	台	ABO	----Simulate television receivers
8528.7292	----数字电视接收机	30	T3	21	24	130	17	13	台	ABO	----Digital television receivers
8528.7299	----其他	30	T3	21	24	130	17	13	台	ABO	----Other
8528.7300	--其他黑白或单色的	15	T3		12	100	17	13	台	AB6	--Other. Black and white orother no no ch rome

税则号列 Tariff Item.	货 品 名 称	最惠国 (%) MFN	协定(%) CT 东盟 CA	中巴 CP	中智 CC	普通 Gen	增值税率 VAT	出口退税 ED	计量单位 Unit	监管条件 SC	Article Description
85.29	**专用于或主要用于税目 85.25 至 85.28 所列装置或设备的零件:**										**Parts suitable for use solely or principally with the apparatus of headings-No. 85.25 to 85.28:**
	-各种天线或天线反射器及其零件:										-Aerials and aerial reflectors of all kinds; parts suitable for use therewith:
8529.1010	---雷达设备及无线电导航设备用	1.5			0	8	17	13	千克	O	---For radar apparatus and radio navigational aid apparatus
8529.1020	---无线电收音机及其组合机、电视接收机用	0				90	17	13	千克		---For radio-broadcast receivers and their combinations, television receivers
*8529.1090	---其他				0	20	17	13	千克		---Other
8529.1090 01	无线电话电报装置的天线	0				20	17	13	千克	sO	Aerials or antennas of a kind used with apparatus for radio-telephony and radio-telegraphy
8529.1090 21	卫星电视接收用天线	2				20	17	13	千克	O	satellite TV receiving antenna
8529.1090 29	其他无线广播电视用天线(品目 8525 至 8528 所列其他装置或设备的,包括天线反射器)	2				20	17	13	千克	O	Other aerials and aerial reflectors for broadcast or television (Other appliances and facilities listed from item 8525 through 8525, including antenna reflector)
8529.1090 90	其他无线电设备天线及其零件(编号 8525 至 8528 所列其他装置或设备的,包括天线反射器)	2				20	17	13	千克	O	Other aerials and aerial reflectors of all kinds, parts suitable for use therewith, with the apparatus of headingsNos. 8525 to 8528
	-其他:										-Other:
8529.9010	---电视发送、差转设备及卫星电视地面接收转播设备用	0				30	17	13	千克		---For television transmission or translation apparatus, satellite television ground receiving and relaying apparatus
8529.9010 11	卫星电视接收用解码器	0				30	17	13	千克	O	Decoders for statellite TV recervers
8529.9010 12	卫星电视接收用收视卡	0				30	17	13	千克	O	CA card for receiving satellite television
8529.9010 13	卫星电视接收用器件板卡	0				30	17	13	千克	O	Machines and cards used for statellite television to receive signals
8529.9010 14	卫星电视接收用专用零件	0				30	17	13	千克	O	Exclusive particles used for receiving statellite TV signals
8529.9010 90	其他电视发送,差转等设备零件(包括其他卫星电视地面接收转播设备零件)	0				30	17	13	千克	O	On-line and off-line detec tors for compact disc qualities
	---电视摄像机、其他视频摄录一体机、数字照相机用:										---For television cameras、other video camera recorders, digital cameras
8529.9041	----特种用途的	8	T3	6.8	6.4	17	17	13	千克		----Of special purpose
8529.9042	----非特种用途的取像模块	12	T3	10.8	9.6	100	17	13	千克		----Cameera modulesuit hout special pnrpose
8529.9042 01	摄录一体机、数码照相机、手机用取像模块	12				100	17	13	千克		Video camera recorders, digital camera, and picture pickup modules for mobile phone
8529.9042 90	其他非特种用途的取像模块	12				100	17	13	千克		Other picture pickup modules not for special purpose

税则号列 Tariff Item.	货品名称	最惠国(%) MFN	协定(%) CT 东盟 CA	中巴 CP	中智 CC	普通 Gen	增值税率 VAT	出口退税 ED	计量单位 Unit	监管条件 SC	Article Description
8529.9049	----其他	12	T3	10.8	9.6	100	17		千克		----Other
8529.9050	---雷达设备及无线电导航设备用	1.5		1.4	0	8	17	13	千克	O	---Of radar apparatus and radio navigational aid apparatus
8529.9060	---无线电收音机及其组合机用	15	T3	12	12	130	17	13	千克		---Of radio-broadcast receivers and their combinations
	---电视接收机用(高频调谐器除外):										---Of television receivers (Other than H. F tuners):
8529.9081	----彩色电视接收机用(等离子显像组件及其零件除外)	15	T3	12	0	80	17	13	千克		----Of colour television receivers (other than plasma display device modules or parts thereof)
8529.9081 01	投影电视机用光机	15				80	17	13	千克		Projection TV optical machine
8529.9081 90	其他彩色电视机零件(等离子显像组件及其零件除外)(高频调谐器除外)	15				80	17	13	千克		Parts for colour television receivers plasma display (other than high-frequency tuner)
8529.9082	----等离子显像组件及其零件	15	T3	12	0	80	17	13	千克		----Plasma display modules and parts thereof
8529.9089	----其他	0				50	17	13	千克		----Other
8529.9090	---其他	0				57	17	13	千克		---Other
8529.9090 11	卫星电视接收用高频调谐器	0				57	17	13	千克	O	(High - frequency tuner for satellite television)
8529.9090 19	其他高频调谐器	0				57	17	13	千克	O	(Other high - frepuency tuner)
8529.9090 90	编号 8525 至 8528 所列设备其他零件	0				57	17	13	千克		Other parts of apparatus of headings Nos. 85.25 ~ 85.28
85.30	**铁道、电车道、道路或内河航道、停车场、港口或机场用的电气信号、安全或交通管理设备(税目 86.08 的货品除外):**										**Electrical signalling, safety or traffic control equipment for railways, tramways, roads, inland waterways, parking facilities, port installations or airfields (other than those of headingNo. 86.08):**
8530.1000	-铁道或电车道用的设备	10	5		0	20	17	13	个	O	-Equipment for railways or tramways
8530.8000	-其他设备	8	5		6.4	20	17	13	个	O	-Other equipment
8530.9000	-零件	8	5		0	20	17	13	千克		-Parts
85.31	**电气音响或视觉信号装置(例如,电铃、电笛、显示板、防盗或防火报警器),但税目 85.12 或 85.30 的货品除外:**										**Electric sound or visual signalling apparatus (for example, bells, sirens, indicator panels, burglar or fire alarms), other than those of heading Nos. 85.12 or 85.30:**
	-防盗或防火报警器及类似装置:										-Burglar or fire alarms and similar apparatus:
8531.1010	---机动车辆防盗装置	10	5	9	0	40	17	13	个	A	---Burglar alarm for motor vehicles
8531.1090	---其他	10	8		0	40	17	13	个	OA	---Other
8531.2000	-装有液晶装置(LCD)或发光二极管(LED)的显示板	0				70	17	13	个		-Indicator panels incorporating liquid crystal devices (LCD) or light emitting diodes (LED)
	-其他装置:										-Other apparatus:
8531.8010	---蜂鸣器	15	8		0	70	17	13	个		---Buzzers
8531.8010 01	音量不超过 110db 的小型蜂鸣器	15				70	17	13	个	B	Buzzers, volue < 110dB
8531.8010 90	其他蜂鸣器	15				70	17	13	个	B	Other buzzers

税则号列 Tariff Item.	货品名称	最惠国(%) MFN	协定(%)CT 东盟 CA	中巴 CP	中智 CC	普通 Gen	增值税率 VAT	出口退税 ED	计量单位 Unit	监管条件 SC	Article Description
8531.8090	---其他	10	8		0	70	17	13	个		---Other
	-零件:										-Parts:
8531.9010	---防盗或防火报警器及类似装置用	0				40	17	13	千克	A	---Of burglar or fire alarms and similar apparatus
8531.9090	---其他	0				70	17	13	千克		---Other
85.32	**固定、可变或可调(微调)电容器:**										**Electrical capacitors, fixed, variable or adjustable (pre-set):**
8532.1000	-固定电容器,用于50/60赫兹电路,其额定无功功率不低于0.5千瓦(电力电容器)	0				20	17	13	千克/千个		-Fixed capacitors designed for use in 50/60 Hz circuits and having a reactive power handling capacity of not less than 0.5 k Var (power capacitors)
	-其他固定电容器:										-Other fixed capacitors:
	--钽电容器:										--Tantalum:
8532.2110	---片式	0				35	17	13	千克/千个		---Laminate
8532.2190	---其他	0				35	17	13	千克/千个		---Other
8532.2200	--铝电解电容器	0				35	17	13	千克/千个		--Aluminium electrolytic
8532.2300	--单层瓷介电容器	0				35	17	13	千克/千个		--Ceramic dielectric, single layer
	--多层瓷介电容器:										--Ceramic dielectric, multilayer:
8532.2410	---片式	0				35	17	17	千克/千个		---Laminate
8532.2490	---其他	0				35	17	13	千克/千个		---Other
	--纸介质或塑料介质电容器:										--Dielectric of paper or plastics:
8532.2510	---片式	0				35	17	13	千克/千个		---Laminate
8532.2590	---其他	0				35	17	17	千克/千个		---Other
8532.2900	--其他	0				35	17	13	千克/千个		--Other
8532.3000	-可变或可调(微调)电容器	0				35	17	13	千克/千个		-Variable or adjustable (pre-set) capacitors
	-零件:										-Parts:
8532.9010	---子目8532.1000所列电容器用	0				20	17	13	千克		---Of the capacitors of subheadingNo. 8532.1000
8532.9090	---其他	0				35	17	13	千克		---Other
85.33	**电阻器(包括变阻器及电位器),但加热电阻器除外:**										**Electrical resistors (including rheostats and potentiometers), other than heating resistors:**
8533.1000	-固定碳质电阻器,合成或薄膜式	0				50	17	13	千克/千个		-Fixed carbon resistors, composition or film types
	-其他固定电阻器:										-Other fixed resistors:
	--额定功率不超过20瓦:										--For a power handling capacity not exceeding 20 W:
8533.2110	---片式	0				50	17	17	千克/千个		---Laminate
8533.2190	---其他	0				50	17	13	千克/千个		---Other
8533.2900	--其他	0				50	17	13	千克/千个		--Other
	-线绕可变电阻器,包括变阻器及电位器:										-Wirewound variable resistors, including rheostats and potentiometers:
8533.3100	--额定功率不超过20瓦	0				50	17	13	千克/千个		--For a power handling capacity not exceeding 20 W
8533.3900	--其他	0				50	17	13	千克/千个		--Other
8533.4000	-其他可变电阻器,包括变阻器及电位器	0				50	17	13	千克/千个		-Other variable resistors, including rheostats and potentiometers
8533.9000	-零件	0				50	17	13	千克		-Parts

税则号列 Tariff Item.	货品名称	最惠国(%) MFN	协定(%)CT 东盟 CA	 中巴 CP	 中智 CC	普通 Gen	增值税率 VAT	出口退税 ED	计量单位 Unit	监管条件 SC	Article Description
85.34	印刷电路：										**Printed circuits：**
8534.0010	---4层以上的	0				35	17	17	块/千克		---Of more than 4 layers
8534.0090	---其他	0				50	17	17	块/千克		---Other
85.35	**电路的开关、保护或连接用的电气装置(例如，开关、熔断器、避雷器、电压限幅器、电涌抑制器、插头及其他连接器、接线盒)，用于电压超过1000伏的线路：**										**Electrical apparatus for switching or protecting electrical circuits, or for making connections to or in electrical circuits (for example, switches, fuses, lightning arresters, voltage limiters, surge suppressors, plugs, junction boxes), for a voltage exceeding 1,000 volts：**
8535.1000	-熔断器	14	8		8.4	50	17	13	个/千克	BA	-Fuses
	-自动断路器：										-Automatic circuit breakers：
8535.2100	--用于电压低于72.5千伏的线路	14	8		8.4	50	17	13	个/千克	BA	--For a voltage of less than 72.5 kV
8535.2900	--其他	10	5		0	50	17	13	个/千克		--Other
8535.2900 10	电压≥72.5千伏的六氟化硫断路器(含组合电器)	10				50	17	13	个/千克	BO	Sulfur hexafluoride circuit breaker, voltage≥72.5KV
8535.2900 90	电压≥72.5千伏其他自动断路器	10				50	17	13	个/千克	BO	Other automatic circuit breakers, voltage≥72.5KV
8535.3000	-隔离开关及断续开关	10	5		6	50	17	13	个/千克	BA	-Isolating switches and make-and-break switches
8535.4000	-避雷器、电压限幅器及电涌抑制器	18	8		10.8	50	17	13	个/千克	B	-Lightning arresters, voltage limiters and surge suppressors
8535.9000	-其他	10	8	9.5	8	50	17	13	千克		-Other
8535.9000 10	触发式火花隙(阳极延迟时间≤15ms，阳极峰值额定电流≥500A)	10				50	17	13	千克	3B	Triggered spark gap (time for delay of anode≤15ms, rating current of anode's peak value≥500A)
8535.9000 20	具有快速开关功能的模件或组件，(阳极峰值电压≥2001V；电流≥501A；接通时间≤2ms	10				50	17	13	千克	3B	The module or groupware that can be speedily switched on or off (the peak voltage value of anode≥201A, current≥501A, time for switching on≤2ms)
8535.9000 90	其他>1000伏电路开关等电气装置(用于电压超过1000伏的线路开关，保护，连接用电气装置)	10				50	17	13	千克	B	(Other electrical apparatus for switching or protecting electrical circuits, or for making connections to or in electrical circuits, for a voltage exceeding 1000 volts)
85.36	**电路的开关、保护或连接用的电气装置(例如，开关、继电器、熔断器、电涌抑制器、插头、插座、灯座及其他连接器、接线盒)，用于电压不超过1000伏的线路；光导纤维、光导纤维束或光缆用连接器：**										**Electrical apparatus for switching or protecting electrical circuits, or for making connections to or in electrical circuits (for example, switches, relays, fuses, surge suppressors, plugs, sockets, lamp-holders, junction boxes), for a voltage not exceeding 1000 volts：**
8536.1000	-熔断器	10	8		0	50	17	13	个/千克	BA	-Fuses
8536.2000	-自动断路器	9	5		0	50	17	13	个/千克	BA	-Automatic circuit breakers
8536.3000	-其他电路保护装置	9	5		0	50	17	13	个/千克	BA	-Other apparatus for protecting electrical circuits

税则号列 Tariff Item.	货 品 名 称	最惠国(%) MFN	协定(%) CT 东盟 CA	中巴 CP	中智 CC	普通 Gen	增值税率 VAT	出口退税 ED	计量单位 Unit	监管条件 SC	Article Description
	-继电器：										-Relays：
8536. 4100	--用于电压不超过 60 伏的线路	10	8		0	50	17	13	个/千克	AB	--For a voltage not exceeding 60 V
8536. 4900	--其他	10	8		8	50	17	13	个/千克	AB	--Other
8536. 5000	-其他开关	0				50	17	13	个/千克	AB	-Other switches
	-灯座、插头及插座：										-Lamp-holders, plugs and sockets：
8536. 6100	--灯座	10	T3		0	50	17	13	个/千克	B	--Lamp-holders
8536. 6900	--其他	0				50	17	13	个/千克	B	--Other
8536. 7000	-光导纤维、光导纤维束或光缆用连接器	8	5		6. 4	30	17	13	千克		-Fibre optics , fibre optics Shu or optical cable use a connector
8536. 9000	-其他装置	0				50	17	13	千克	AB	-Other apparatus
85. 37	**用于电气控制或电力分配的盘、板、台、柜及其他基座，装有两个或多个税目 85. 35 或 85. 36 所列的装置，包括装有第九十章所列的仪器或装置，以及数控装置，但税目 85. 17 的交换机除外：**										**Boards, panels, consoles, desks, cabinets and other bases, equipped with two or more apparatus of headingNo. 85. 35 or 85. 36, for electric control or the distribution of electricity, including those incorporating instruments or apparatus of Chapter 90, and numerical control apparatus, other than switching apparatus of headingNo. 85. 17：**
	-用于电压不超过 1000 伏的线路：										-For a voltage not exceeding 1,000 V：
	---数控装置：										---Numerical control panels：
8537. 1011	----可编程序控制器	5		2. 5	4	14	17	17	个/千克		----Programmable controllers of machines
8537. 1011 01	机床用可编程控制器(包括 CNC 操作单元，无论其是否带有配套的伺服放大器和伺服电机)	5				14	17	17	个/千克	O	Programmable controllers of machines fools (including CNC operational units)
8537. 1011 10	绕线机用调节和编程控制器(8479899060 绕线机用)	5				14	17	17	个/千克	3O	Adiusting and programming controllers for wire winders of subbeading 8479. 599060
8537. 1011 90	其他可编程控制器(用于电压不超过 1000 伏的线路)	5				14	17	17	个/千克	O	Programming controllers of machines fools for a voltage not exceeding 1000 volts
8537. 1019	----其他	5		2. 5	4	14	17	17	个/千克		----Other
8537. 1019 01	机床用其他数控装置(包括 CNC 操作单元，无论其是否带有配套的伺服放大器和伺服电机)	5				14	17	17	个/千克	O	Other digital controller for machine tool (including CNC operational unies)
8537. 1019 90	其他非机床用数控装置(用于电压不超过 1000 伏的线路)	5				14	17	17	个/千克	O	Other digital controller for other purposes (for a voltage not exceeding 1000 volts)
8537. 1090	---其他	8. 4	T3	4. 2	6. 7	50	17	13	个/千克		---Other
8537. 1090 10	电梯用控制柜(电气柜)(电压不超过 1000 伏的线路)	8. 4				50	17	13	个/千克		Control box (cabin type switchboard) for electric lifts, for a voltage not exceeding 1000 volts

税则号列 Tariff Item.	货品名称	最惠国(%) MFN	协定(%)CT 东盟 CA	中巴 CP	中智 CC	普通 Gen	增值税率 VAT	出口退税 ED	计量单位 Unit	监管条件 SC	Article Description
8537.1090 21	控制器[用于机器人或末端操纵装置(详见核两用清单)]	8.4				50	17	13	个/千克	3O	Controllers (use for roloots or end-operation clevices)
8537.1090 22	数字控制器(专用于编号84798990.71电动式振动试验系统)	8.4				50	17	13	个/千克	3O	Digital controllers (only use of machine subweadingNo. 84798990.71)
8537.1090 90	其他电力控制或分配的装置(电压不超过1000伏的线路)	8.4				50	17	13	个/千克	AO	Other apparatus, for electric control or the distribution of electricity for a voltage not exceeding 1000 volts
	-用于电压超过1000伏的线路:										-For a voltage exceeding 1,000 V:
8537.2010	---全封闭组合式高压开关装置,用于电压在500千伏及以上的线路	8.4	T3	4.2	6.7	30	17	13	台/千克	OB	---Gas insulated switchgear, for a voltage of 500 kV or more
8537.2090	---其他	8.4	T3	4.2	6.7	50	17	13	千克	A	---Other
85.38	**专用于或主要用于税目85.35、85.36或85.37所列装置的零件:**										**Parts suitable for use solely or principally with the apparatus of headingNo. 85.35, 85.36 or 85.37:**
	-税目85.37所列货品用的盘、板、台、柜及其他基座,但未装有关装置:										-Boards, panels, consoles, desks, cabinets and other bases for the goods of headingNo. 85.37, not equipped with their apparatus:
8538.1010	---税目8537.2010所列货品用	8.4	T3	4.2	6.7	50	17	13	千克		---For the goods of heading 8537.2010
8538.1090	---其他	7	T3	3.5	5.6	50	17	13	千克		---Other
8538.9000	-其他	7	5		5.6	50	17	13	千克		-Other
85.39	**白炽灯泡、放电灯管,包括封闭式聚光灯及紫外线灯管或红外线灯泡;弧光灯:**										**Electric filament or discharge lamps, including sealed beam lamp units and ultra-violet or infra-red lamps; arc-lamps:**
8539.1000	-封闭式聚光灯	10	5		0	45	17	13	只		-Sealed beam lamp units
	-其他白炽灯泡,但不包括紫外线灯管或红外线灯泡:										-Other filament lamps, excluding ultra-violet or infra-red lamps:
	--卤钨灯:										--Tungsten halogen:
8539.2110	---科研、医疗专用	8	T3		6.4	20	17	13	只		---For scientific or medical uses only
8539.2120	---火车、航空器及船舶用	8	T3		6.4	20	17	13	只		---For locomotives and rolling-stock, aircraft or ships
8539.2130	---机动车辆用	10	5		8	45	17	13	只		---For motor vehicles
8539.2190	---其他	10.5	T3		8.4	70	17	13	只		---Other
	--其他灯,功率不超过200瓦,但额定电压超过100伏:										--Other, of a power not exceeding 200 W and for a voltage exceeding 100 V:
8539.2210	---科研、医疗专用	10.5	T3		8.4	20	17	13	只	B	---For scientific or medical uses only
8539.2290	---其他	5			4	70	17	13	只	B	---Other
	--其他:										--Other:
8539.2910	---科研、医疗专用	5			4	20	17	13	只	B	---For scientific or medical uses only
8539.2920	---火车、航空器及船舶用	10.5	T3		8.4	20	17	13	只	B	---For locomotives and rolling-stock, aircraft or ships
8539.2930	---机动车辆用	5			4	45	17	13	只	B	---For motor vehicles
	---其他:										---Other:
8539.2991	----12伏及以下的	12	T3		9.6	70	17	13	只	B	----Of a voltage 12 V or less
8539.2999	----其他	12	T3		9.6	70	17	13	只	B	----Other

税则号列 Tariff Item.	货品名称	最惠国(%) MFN	协定(%)CT			普通 Gen	增值税率 VAT	出口退税 ED	计量单位 Unit	监管条件 SC	Article Description
			东盟 CA	中巴 CP	中智 CC						
	-放电灯管,但紫外线灯管除外:										-Discharge lamps, other than ultra-violet lamps:
	--热阴极荧光灯:										--Fluorescent, hot cathode:
8539.3110	---科研、医疗专用	8	T3		6.4	20	17	13	只	B	---For scientific or medical uses only
8539.3120	---火车、航空器及船舶用	8	T3		6.4	20	17	13	只	B	---For locomotives and rolling-stock, aircraft or ships
8539.3190	---其他	8	T3		6.4	70	17	13	只	B	---Other
	--汞或钠蒸汽灯;金属卤化物灯:										--Mercury or sodium vapour lamps; metal halide lamps:
8539.3210	---科研、医疗专用	8	5		0	20	17	13	只		---For scientific or medical uses only
8539.3220	---火车、航空器及船舶用	8	5		0	20	17	13	只		---For locomotives and rolling-stock, aircraft or ships
8539.3290	---其他	8	5		0	70	17	13	只		---Other
8539.3290 01	彩色液晶投影机的照明光源(包括金属卤化物灯)	8				70	17	13	只		Lighting resource for colour liquid crystal projector, including metal halide lamps
8539.3290 90	其他用途的汞或钠蒸汽灯(包括金属卤化物灯)	8				70	17	13	只		Mercury or sodium vapour lamps, metal halide lamps, for other use
	--其他:										--Other:
8539.3910	---科研、医疗专用	8	T3		0	20	17	13	只		---For scientific or medical uses only
8539.3920	---火车、航空器及船舶用	8	T3		0	20	17	13	只		---For locomotives and rolling-stock, aircraft or ships
8539.3990	---其他	8	T3		0	70	17	13	只		---Other
	-紫外线灯管或红外线灯泡;弧光灯:										-Ultraviolet or infra-red lamps; arc-lamps:
8539.4100	--弧光灯	8	5		0	20	17	13	只		--Arc-lamps
8539.4900	--其他	8	5		0	20	17	13	只		--Other
8539.9000	-零件	8	5		0	20	17	13	千克	B	-Parts
85.40	**热电子管、冷阴极管或光阴极管(例如,真空管或充气管、汞弧整流管、阴极射线管、电视摄像管):**										**Thermionic, cold cathode or photo-cathode valves and tubes (for example, vacuum or vapour or gas filled valves and tubes, mercury arc rectifying valves and tubes, cathode-ray tubes, television camera tubes):**
	-阴极射线电视显像管,包括视频监视器用阴极射线管:										-Cathode-ray television picture tubes, including video monitor cathode-ray tubes:
8540.1100	--彩色的	12	8		0	40	17	13	只	6OAB	--Colour
8540.1200	--黑白的或其他单色的	15	8		0	40	17	13	只	6AB	--Black and white or other monochrome
	-电视摄像管;变像管及图像增强管;其他光阴极管:										-Television camera tubes; image converters and intensifiers; other photo-cathode tubes:
8540.2010	---电视摄像管	12	8		7.2	35	17	13	只		---Television camera tubes
8540.2090	---其他	8	5		0	17	17	13	只		---Other
8540.2090 10	电子条纹相机的条纹显像管(专用于编号90065900.40的条纹显像管)	8				17	17	13	只	3	Stripe kinescope of electronic stripe camera (striation kinescope tube specially used for Serial Number 9006.5900 40)

税则号列 Tariff Item.	货 品 名 称	最惠国 (%) MFN	协定(%) CT 东盟 CA	中巴 CP	中智 CC	普通 Gen	增值税率 VAT	出口退税 ED	计量单位 Unit	监管条件 SC	Article Description
8540.2090 90	其他电视摄像管;其他变像管及图像增强管;其他光阴极管	8				17	17	13	只		Other TV shooting tube, other image converter tube and image enhancing tube, other cathode tube
8540.4000	-彩色的数据/图形显示管,屏幕荧光点间距小于0.4毫米	8	5		0	17	17	17	只	6O	-Data/graphic display tubes, colour, with a phosphor dot screen pitch smaller than 0.4 mm
8540.5000	-黑白的或其他单色的数据/图形显示管	8	5		0	17	17	13	只	6	-Data/graphic display tubes, black and white or other monochrome
	-其他阴极射线管:										-Other cathode-ray tubes:
8540.6010	---雷达显示管	6	5		0	14	17	13	只		---Radar display tubes
8540.6090	---其他	8	5		0	17	17	13	只	6	---Other
	-微波管(例如,磁控管、速调管、行波管、返波管),但不包括栅控管:										-Microwave tubes (for example, magnetrons, klystrons, travelling wave tubes, carcinotrons), excluding grid-controlled tubes:
8540.7100	--磁控管	8	5		0	17	17	13	只		--Magnetrons
8540.7200	--速调管	8	5		0	17	17	13	只		--Klystrons
8540.7900	--其他	8	5		0	17	17	13	只		--Other
	-其他管:										-Other valves and tubes:
8540.8100	--接收管或放大管	8	5		0	17	17	13	只		--Receiver or amplifier valves and tubes
8540.8900	--其他	8	5		0	17	17	17	只		--Other
	-零件:										-Parts:
	--阴极射线管用:										--Of cathode-ray tubes:
8540.9110	---电视显像管用	6	5		0	40	17	13	千克		---Of television picture tubes
8540.9120	---雷达显示管用	5			0	14	17	13	千克		---Of radar display tubes
8540.9190	---其他	8	5		0	17	17	13	千克		---Other
	--其他:										--Other:
8540.9910	---电视摄像管用	8	5		0	35	17	13	千克		---Of television camera tubes
8540.9990	---其他	8	5		0	17	17	13	千克		---Other
85.41	**二极管、晶体管及类似的半导体器件;光敏半导体器件,包括不论是否装在组件内或组装成块的光电池;发光二极管;已装配的压电晶体:**										**Diodes, transistors and similar semiconductor devices; photosensitive semiconductor devices, including photovoltaic cells whether or not assembled in modules or made up into panels; light emitting diodes; mounted piezo-electric crystals:**
8541.1000	-二极管,但光敏二极管或发光二极管除外	0				30	17	17	个/千克		-Diodes, other than photosensitive or light emitting diodes
	-晶体管,但光敏晶体管除外:										-Transistors, other than photosensitive transistors:
8541.2100	--耗散功率小于1瓦的	0				30	17	17	个/千克		--With a dissipation rate of less than 1 W
8541.2900	--其他	0				30	17	17	个/千克		--Other
8541.3000	-半导体开关元件、两端交流开关元件及三端双向可控硅开关元件,但光敏器件除外	0				30	17	17	个/千克		-Thyristors, diacs and triacs, other than photosensitive devices
8541.4000	-光敏半导体器件,包括不论是否装在组件内或组装成块的光电池;发光二极管	0				30	17	17	个/千克		-Photosensitive semiconductor devices, including photovoltaic cells whether or not assembled in modules or made up into panels; light emitting diodes

税则号列 Tariff Item.	货 品 名 称	最惠国(%) MFN	协定(%)CT			普通 Gen	增值税率 VAT	出口退税 ED	计量单位 Unit	监管条件 SC	Article Description
			东盟 CA	中巴 CP	中智 CC						
8541.5000	-其他半导体器件	0				30	17	17	个/千克		-Other semiconductor devices
8541.6000	-已装配的压电晶体	0				30	17	17	个/千克		-Mounted piezo-electric crystals
8541.9000	-零件	0				30	17	17	千克		-Parts
85.42	**集成电路：**										**Electronic integrated circuits**
	-集成电路：										-Electronic integrated circuits
8542.3100	--处理器及控制器，不论是否带有存储器、转换器、逻辑电路、放大器、时钟及时序电路或其他电路	0				24	17		个/千克		--Proceesor and controuer, with or without storage, converter, logic circuit, amplifier, clock and sequential circuit or other circuit
8542.3200	--存储器	0				24	17		个/千克		--Memory
8542.3300	--放大器	0				24	17		个/千克		--Amplifier
8542.3900	--其他	0				24	17		个/千克		--Other
8542.9000	-零件	0				30	17		千克		-Parts
85.43	**本章其他税目未列名的具有独立功能的电气设备及装置：**										**Electrical machines and apparatus, having individual functions, not specified or included elsewhere in this Chapter:**
8543.1000	-粒子加速器：	5			0	11	17		台		-Particle accelerators:
8543.1000 10	脉冲电子加速器(峰值能量为500千电子伏或更高)	5				11	17		台	3	Pulse electron accelerators (peak value power≥500KeV)
8543.1000 20	中子发生器系统，包括中子管(真空下，利用静电加速来诱发氚-氚核反应)：	5				11	17		台	3	Neutron generator system, including neutron tubes (in vacuum condition, induce the tritium-deuteron reaction through acceleration of static)
8543.1000 90	其他粒子加速器	5				11	17		台		Other particle accelerator
	-信号发生器：										-Signal generators:
8543.2010	---输出信号频率在1500兆赫兹以下的通用信号发生器	15	8		12	80	17	13	台		---Universal signal generators, with a frequency range of less than 1500 MHz
8543.2090	---其他	8	5		6.4	20	17	13	台		---Other
8543.2090 10	高速脉冲发生器(脉冲上升时间小于500ps)	8				20	17	13	台	3	High pulse generator (risetime of pulse smaller than 500ps)
8543.2090 90	其他≥1500Mhz的通用信号发生器(输出信号频率在1500Mhz及以上的)	8				20	17	13	台		Other general signal generators ≥ 1500MHz (output signal frequency at 500MHz or above)
8543.3000	-电镀、电解或电泳设备及装置	0				35	17	13	台		-Machines and apparatus for electro-plating, electrolysis or electrophoresis
8543.3000 10	电化学还原槽；锂汞齐电解槽(电化学还原槽为化学交换过程的铀浓缩设计的)	0				35	17	13	台	3	Lithium amalgam electrolysis cells, electrochemical reduction cells, specially designed for uranium concentration in chemical exchange process
8543.3000 20	产氟电解槽(每小时产250克以上)	0				35	17	13	台	3	Electrobath produahs flourine (produce more than 250 grams/hour)
8543.3000 90	其他电镀、电解或电泳设备及装置	0				35	17	13	台		Other machines and apparatus for electro-plating, electrolysis or electrophoresis
	-其他设备及装置：										-Other machines and apparatus:
8543.7091	----金属、矿藏探测器	0				17	17	13	台		----Metal or mine detectors
8543.7092	----高、中频放大器	0				17	17	13	台	0	----High or intermediate frequency amplifiers
8543.7093	----电篱网激发器	10	8		0	35	17	17	台		---Electric fence energizers
8543.7099	----其他	0				35	17	13	台		----Other

税则号列 Tariff Item.	货 品 名 称	最惠国(%) MFN	协定(%)CT			普通 Gen	增值税率 VAT	出口退税 ED	计量单位 Unit	监管条件 SC	Article Description
			东盟 CA	中巴 CP	中智 CC						
8544.7099 10	飞行数据记录器、报告器	0				35	17	13	台		Flying data recorder and reporter
8543.7099 20	无线广播电视用激励器(具有独立功能)	0				35	17	13	台	O	Drivers for broadcast or television having individual functions
8543.7099 30	模/数转换器(能设计或改进成军用、或设计成抗辐射)	0				35	17	13	台	3	Mode/digit converters for military uses (capable of being designed or improved for military uses or being designed to resist radiation)
8543.7099 40	质谱仪用的离子源(原子质量单位≥230,分辨率>2/230)	0				35	17	13	台	3	Ion source for mass spectrogragh (atomic quality unit ≥230exculpation >2/230)
8543.7099 90	其他未列名的具有独立功能的电气设备及装置	0				35	17	13	台	O	Other electrical machines and apparatus, having individual functions
	-零件:										-Parts:
8543.9010	---粒子加速器用	0				11	17	13	千克		---Of particle accelerators
	---信号发生器用:										---Of signal generators:
8543.9021	----输出信号频率在1500兆赫兹以下的通用信号发生器用	0				80	17	13	千克		----Of the generators of subheading No. 8543.2010
8543.9029	----其他	0				20	17	13	千克		----Other
8543.9030	---金属、矿藏探测器用	0				17	17	13	千克		---Of metal or mine detectors
8543.9040	---高、中频放大器用	0				17	17	13	千克		---Of high or intermediate frequency amplifiers
8543.9090	---其他	0				35	17	13	千克		---Other
85.44	**绝缘(包括漆包或阳极化处理)电线、电缆(包括同轴电缆)及其他绝缘电导体,不论是否有接头;由每根被覆光纤组成的光缆,不论是否与电导体装配或装有接头:**										**Insulated (including enamelled or anodized) wire, cable (including co-axial cable) and other insulated electric conductors, whether or not ritted with connectors; optical fibre cables, made up of individually sheathed fibres, whether or not assembled with electric conductors or fitted with connectors:**
	-绕组电线:										-Winding wire:
8544.1100	--铜制	10	T3	7	0	70	17	13	千克	AB	--Of copper
8544.1900	--其他	20	T3		12	70	17	13	千克	AB	--Other
8544.2000	-同轴电缆及其他同轴电导体	10	T3	9	8	20	17	17	千克	AB	-Co-axial cable and other co-axial electric conductors
	-车辆、航空器、船舶用点火布线组及其他布线组:										-Ignition wiring sets and other wiring sets of a kind used in vehicles, aircraft or ships:
8544.3020	---机动车辆用	10			0	20	17	13	千克		---For motor vehicles
8544.3020 01	车辆用电控柴油机的线束	10				20	17	13	千克	AB	Wiring harness for electronic control of diesel engine
8544.3020 90	机动车辆用其他点火布线组及其他布线组	10				20	17	13	千克	AB	Other ignition wiring sets for locomotives
8544.3090	---其他	5			0	70	17	13	千克	AB	---Other
	-其他电导体,额定电压不超过1000伏:										-Other electric conductors, for a voltage not exceeding 80 V:
	--有接头:										--Fitted with connectors:
	---额定电压不超过80伏:										---Voltage not exceeding 80 V:

税则号列 Tariff Item.	货品名称	最惠国(%) MFN	协定(%) CT 东盟 CA	中巴 CP	中智 CC	普通 Gen	增值税率 VAT	出口退税 ED	计量单位 Unit	监管条件 SC	Article Description
8544.4211	----电缆	0				20	17	13	千克	AB	----Electric cable
8544.4219	----其他	0				70	17	13	千克	AB	----Other
	---额定电压超过 80 伏,但不超过 1000 伏:										---Voltage exceeding 80 V but not exceeding 1000 V:
8544.4221	----电缆	0				20	17	13	千克	AB	----Electric cable
8544.4229	----其他	0				70	17	13	千克	AB	----Other
	--其他:										--Other:
	---额定电压不超过 80 伏:										---Voltage not exceeding 80 V:
8544.4911	----电缆	0				20	17	13	千克	AB	----Electric cable
8544.4919	----其他	0				70	17	13	千克	AB	----Other
	---额定电压超过 80 伏,但不超过 1000 伏:										---Voltage exceeding 80 V but not exceeding 1000 V:
8544.4921	----电缆	6	T3	4.2	4.8	20	17	13	千克	AB	----Electric cable
8544.4929	----其他	12	T3	8.4	9.6	70	17	13	千克	AB	----Other
	-其他电导体,额定电压超过 1000 伏:										-Other electric conductors, for a voltage exceeding 1000 V:
	---电缆:										---Electric cable:
8544.6012	----额定电压不超过 35 千伏	10	T3	8.9	8	50	17	13	千克	AB	----For a voltage not execedding 35 kV
8544.6013	----额定电压超过 35 千伏,但不超过 110 千伏	8.4	T3	8	6.7	20	17	13	千克	AB	----For a voltage execedding 35 kV, but not execedding 110 kV
8544.6014	----额定电压超过 110 千伏,但不超过 220 千伏	8.4	T3	8	6.7	20	17	13	千克	AB	----For a voltage execedding 110 kV, but not execedding 220 kV
8544.6019	----其他	8.4	T3	8	6.7	20	17	13	千克	AB	----Other
8544.6090	---其他	21	T3	20	16.8	70	17	13	千克	AB	---Other
8544.7000	-光缆	0				20	17	13	千克	A	-Optical fibre cables
85.45	**碳电极、碳刷、灯碳棒、电池碳棒及电气设备用的其他石墨或碳精制品,不论是否带金属:**										**Carbon electrodes, carbon brushes, lamp carbons, battery carbons and other articles of graphite or other carbon, with or without metal, of a kind used for electrical purposes:**
	-碳电极:										-Electrodes:
8545.1100	--炉用	8	5		0	35	17	13	千克	3	--Of a kind used for furnaces
8545.1900	--其他	10.5	8		6.3	35	17	13	千克	3	--Other
8545.2000	-碳刷	10.5	8		8.4	35	17	13	千克		-Brushes
8545.9000	-其他	10.5	8		6.3	35	17	13	千克	3	-Other
85.46	**各种材料制的绝缘子:**										**Electrical insulators of any material:**
8546.1000	-玻璃制	10.5	8		6.3	35	17	13	千克		-Of glass
	-陶瓷制:										-Of ceramics:
8546.2010	---输变电线路绝缘瓷套管	6	5		4.8	35	17	13	千克	B	---Power transmission and converting ceramic bushings
8546.2090	---其他	12	8		9.6	35	17	13	千克		---Other
8546.2090 01	输变电架空线路用长棒形瓷绝缘子瓷件(单支长度为 1－2 米,实芯)	12				35	17	13	千克	B	Long rod – formed ceramic insulators of transmission and converting overhead line (length of single piece 1 ~ 2m, solid)
8546.2090 90	其他陶瓷制绝缘子(包括非输变电线路绝缘瓷套管)	12				35	17	13	千克	B	Electrical insulators of ceramics (including ceramic bushings not for power transmission and converting lines)
8546.9000	-其他	10	8		0	35	17	13	千克		-Other

税则号列 Tariff Item.	货品名称	最惠国(%) MFN	协定(%) 东盟 CA	协定(%) 中巴 CP	CT 中智 CC	普通 Gen	增值税率 VAT	出口退税 ED	计量单位 Unit	监管条件 SC	Article Description
85.47	**电气机器、器具或设备用的绝缘零件,除了为装配需要而在模制时装入的小金属零件(例如螺纹孔)以外,全部用绝缘材料制成,但税目85.46的绝缘子除外;内衬绝缘材料的贱金属制线路导管及其接头:**										**Insulating fittings for electrical machines, appliances or equipment, being fittings wholly of insulating material apart from any minor components of metal (for example, threaded sockets) incorporated during moulding solely for purposes of assembly, other than insulators of headingNo. 85.46; electrical conduit tubing and joints therefor, of base metal lined with insulating material:**
8547.1000	-陶瓷制绝缘零件	8	5		0	35	17	13	千克		-Insulating fittings of ceramics
8547.2000	-塑料制绝缘零件	8	5		0	35	17	13	千克		-Insulating fittings of plastics
	-其他:										-Other:
8547.9010	---内衬绝缘材料的贱金属制线路导管及其接头	10	8		6	50	17	13	千克		---Electrical conduit tubing and joints therefor, of base metal lined with insulating material
8547.9090	---其他	8	5		0	35	17	13	千克		---Other
85.48	**原电池、原电池组及蓄电池的废碎料;废原电池、废原电池组及废蓄电池;机器或设备的本章其他税目未列名的电气零件:**										**Waste and scrap of primary cells, primary batteries and electric accumulators; spent primary cells, spent primary batteries and spent electric accumulators; electrical parts of machinery or apparatus, not specified or included elsewhere in this Chapter:**
8548.1000	-原电池、原电池组及蓄电池的废碎料;废原电池、废原电池组及废蓄电池	8	5		6.4	36	17	13	千克	9	-Waste and scrap of primary cells, primary batteries and electric accumulators; spent primary cells, spent primary batteries and spent electric accumulators
8548.9000	-其他	12	8		7.2	40	17	13	千克		-Other
8548.9000 01	贴片滤波器	12				40	17	13	千克		Patch filter
8548.9000 10	可调脉冲单模染料振荡器(平均输出功率>1 W 重复率>1 khz 脉宽<100ns 可见光范围)	12				40	17	13	千克	3	Pulse adjustable laser ampli (average output > 1khz, pulse duration modulation < 100ns visible light range)
8548.9000 20	可调脉冲染料激光放大器和振荡器(平均输出功率>30 W 重复率>1khz 脉宽<100ns 可见光范围)	12				40	17	13	千克	3	Pulse - adjustable laser amplifier and oscillator for dye(average output power > 30W repetition rate > 1kHz pulse width < 100ns scope of visible light)
8548.9000 90	85章其他编号未列名的电气零件	12				40	17	13	千克		Electrical parts of machinery or apparatus, not specified or included elsewhere in the Chapter 85

第十七类
车辆、航空器、船舶及有关运输设备

注释：

一、本类不包括税目95.03或95.08的物品以及税目95.06的长雪橇、平底雪橇及类似品。

二、本类所称“零件”及“零件、附件”，不适用于下列货品，不论其是否确定为供本类货品使用：

(一)各种材料制的接头、垫圈或类似品(按其构成材料归类或归入税目84.84)或硫化橡胶(硬质橡胶除外)的其他制品(税目40.16)；

(二)第十五类注释二所规定的贱金属制通用零件(第十五类)或塑料制的类似品(第三十九章)；

(三)第八十二章的物品(工具)；

(四)税目83.06的物品；

(五)税目84.01至84.79的机器或装置及其零件；税目84.81或84.82的物品及税目84.83的物品(这些物品是构成发动机或其他动力装置所必需的)；

(六)电机或电气设备(第八十五章)；

(七)第九十章的物品；

(八)第九十一章的物品；

(九)武器(第九十三章)；

(十)税目94.05的灯具或照明装置；

(十一)作为车辆零件的刷子(税目96.03)。

三、第八十六章至第八十八章所称“零件”或“附件”，不适用于那些非专用于或非主要用于这几章所列物品的零件、附件。同时符合这几章内两个或两个以上税目规定的零件、附件，应按其主要用途归入相应的税目。

四、在本类中：

(一)既可在道路上又可在轨道上行驶的特殊构造的车辆，应归入第八十七章的相应税目；

(二)水陆两用的机动车辆，应归入第八十七章的相应税目；

(三)可兼作地面车辆使用的特殊构造的航空器，应归入第八十八章的相应税目。

五、气垫运输工具应按本类最相似的运输工具归类，其规定如下：

(一)在导轨上运行的(气垫火车)，归入第八十六章；

(二)在陆地行驶或水陆两用的，归入第八十七章；

SECTION XVII
VEHICLES, AIRCRAFT, VESSELS AND ASSOCIATED TRANSPORT EQUIPMENT

Notes:

1. This Section does not cover articles of headingNo. 95.03 or 95.08, or bobsleighs, toboggans or the like of headingNo. 95.06.

2. The expressions “parts” and “parts and accessories” do not apply to the following articles, whether or not they are identifiable as for the goods of this Section:

(a) Joints, washers or the like of any material (classified according to their constituent material or in headingNo. 84.84) or other articles of vulcanized rubber other than hard rubber (headingNo. 40.16);

(b) Parts of general use, as defined in Note 2 to Section XV, of base metal (Section XV), or similar goods of plastics (Chapter 39);

(c) Articles of Chapter 82 (tools);

(d) Articles of headingNo. 83.06;

(e) Machines or apparatus of headingsNo. 84.01 to 84.79, or parts thereof; articles of headingNo. 84.81 or 84.82 or, provided they constitute integral parts of engines or motors, articles of headingNo. 84.83;

(f) Electrical machinery or equipment (Chapter 85);

(g) Articles of Chapter 90;

(h) Articles of Chapter 91;

(i) Arms (Chapter 93);

(j) Lamps or lighting fittings of headingNo. 94.05; or

(k) Brushes of a kind used as parts of vehicles (headingNo. 96.03).

3. References in Chapters 86 to 88 to “parts” or “accessories” do not apply to parts or accessories which are not suitable for use solely or principally with the articles of those Chapters. A part or accessory which answers to a description in two or more of the headings of those Chapters is to be classified under that heading which corresponds to the principal use of that part or accessory.

4. For the purposes of this Section:

(a) Vehicles specially constructed to travel on both road and rail are classified under the appropriate heading of Chapter 87;

(b) Amphibious motor vehicles are classified under the appropriate heading of Chapter 87;

(c) Aircraft specially constructed so that they can also be used as road vehicles are classified under the appropriate heading of Chapter 88.

5. Air-cushion vehicles are to be classified within this Section with the vehicles to which they are most akin as follows:

(a) In Chapter 86 if designed to travel on a guide-track (hovertrains);

(b) In Chapter 87 if designed to travel over land or over both land and water;

（三）在水上航行的，不论能否在海滩或浮码头登陆及能否在冰上行驶，一律归入第八十九章。

气垫运输工具的零件、附件，应按照上述规定，与最相类似的运输工具的零件、附件一并归类。

气垫火车的导轨固定装置及附件应与铁道轨道固定装置及附件一并归类。气垫火车运行系统的信号、安全或交通管理设备应与铁路的信号、安全或交通管理设备一并归类。

(c) In Chapter 89 if designed to travel over water, whether or not able to land on beaches or landingstages or also able to travel over ice.

Parts and accessories of air-cushion vehicles are to be classified in the same way as those of vehicles of the heading in which the air-cushion vehicles are classified under the above provisions.

Hovertrain track fixtures and fittings are to be classified as railway track fixtures and fittings, and signalling, safety or traffic control equipment for hovertrain transport systems as signalling, safety or traffic control equipment for railways.

第八十六章
铁道及电车道机车、车辆及其零件；铁道及电车道轨道固定装置及其零件、附件；各种机械（包括电动机械）交通信号设备

Chapter 86
Railway or tramway locomotives, rolling-stock and parts thereof; railway or tramway track fixtures and fittings and parts thereof; mechanical (including electro-mechanical) traffic signalling equipment of all kinds

注释：

一、本章不包括：

（一）木制或混凝土制的铁道或电车道轨枕及气垫火车用的混凝土导轨（税目 44.06 或 68.10）；

（二）税目 73.02 的铁道及电车道辅轨用钢铁材料；

（三）税目 85.30 的电气信号、安全或交通管理设备。

二、税目 86.07 主要适用于：

（一）轴、轮、行走机构、金属轮箍、轮圈、毂及轮子的其他零件；

（二）车架、底架、转向架；

（三）轴箱；制动装置；

（四）车辆缓冲器；钩或其他联结器及车厢走廊联结装置；

（五）车身。

三、除上述注释一另有规定的以外，税目 86.08 包括：

（一）已装配的轨道、转车台、站台缓冲器、量载规；

（二）铁道及电车道、道路、内河航道、停车场、港口或机场用的臂板信号机、机械信号盘、平交道口控制器、信号及道岔控制器及其他机械（包括电动机械）信号、安全或交通管理设备，不论是否装有电力照明装置。

Notes:

1. This Chapter does not cover:

(a) Railway or tramway sleepers of wood or of concrete, or concrete guide-track sections for hovertrain (headingNo. 44.06 or 68.10);

(b) Railway or tramway track construction material of iron or steel of headingNo. 73.02; or

(c) Electrical signalling, safety of traffic control equipment of headingNo. 85.30.

2. HeadingNo. 86.07 applies, *inter alia*, to:

(a) Axles, wheels, wheel sets (running gear), metal tyres, hoops and hubs and other parts of wheels;

(b) Frames, underframes, bogies and bissel-bogies;

(c) Axle boxes; brake gear;

(d) Buffers for rolling-stock; hooks and other coupling gear and corridor connections;

(e) Coachwork.

3. Subject to the provisions of Note 1 above, headingNo. 86.08 applies, *inter alia*, to:

(a) Assembled track, turntables, platform buffers, loading gauges;

(b) Semaphores, mechanical signal discs, level crossing control gear, signal and point controls, and other mechanical (including electro-mechanical) signalling, safety or traffic control equipment, whether or not fitted with electric lighting, for railways, tramways, roads, inland waterways, parking facilities, port installations or airfields.

税则号列 Tariff Item.	货品名称	最惠国(%) MFN	协定(%)CT 东盟 CA	中巴 CP	中智 CC	普通 Gen	增值税率 VAT	出口退税 ED	计量单位 Unit	监管条件 SC	Article Description
86.01	**铁道电力机车,由外部电力或蓄电池驱动:**										**Rail locomotives powered from an external source of electricity or by electric accumulators:**
	-由外部电力驱动:										-Powered from an external source of electricity:
	---直流电机驱动的:										---Drived by DC motors:
8601.1011	----微型机控制的	3			0	11	17	17	辆		----Controlled by microprocessings
8601.1019	----其他	3			0	11	17	17	辆		----Other
8601.1020	---交流电机驱动的	3			0	11	17	17	辆	O	---Powered from AC motors
8601.1090	---其他	3			0	11	17	17	辆	O	---Other
8601.2000	-由蓄电池驱动	3			0	11	17	17	辆		-Powered by electric accumulators
86.02	**其他铁道机车;机车煤水车:**										**Other rail locomotives; locomotive tenders:**
	-柴油电力机车:										-Diesel-electric locomotives:
8602.1010	---微型机控制的	3			1.8	11	17	17	辆		---Controled by microprocessings
8602.1090	---其他	3			1.8	11	17	17	辆		---Other
8602.9000	-其他	3			1.8	11	17	17	辆		-Other
86.03	**铁道及电车道用的机动客车、货车、敞车,但税目86.04的货品除外:**										**Self-propelled railway or tramway coaches, vans and trucks, other than those of headingNo. 86.04:**
8603.1000	-由外部电力驱动	3			0	11	17	17	辆	O	-Powered from an external source of electricity:
8603.9000	-其他	3			0	11	17	17	辆		-Other
86.04	**铁道及电车道用的维修或服务车,不论是否机动(例如,工场车、起重机车、道碴捣固车、轨道校正车、检验车及查道车):**										**Railway or tramway maintenance or service vehicles, whether or not self-propelled (for example, workshops, cranes, ballast tampers, trackliners, testing coaches and track inspection vehicles):**
	---检验车及查道车:										---Testing coaches and track inspection vehicles
8604.0011	----隧道限界检查车	3			1.8	14	17	17	辆		----Inspection vehicles for tunnel clearance
8604.0012	----钢轨在线打磨列车	3			1.8	14	17	17	辆		----Sanding vehicles for on-line rails
8604.0019	----其他	5			4	14	17	17	辆		----Other
	---其他:										---Other:
8604.0091	----电气化接触网架线机(轨行式)	5			4	20	17	17	辆		----Installing vehicles for suspension of contact wire (running on rails)
8604.0099	----其他	7	5		5.6	20	17	17	辆		----Other
86.05	**铁道及电车道用的非机动客车;行李车、邮政车和其他铁道及电车道用的非机动特殊用途车辆(税目86.04的货品除外):**										**Railway or tramway passenger coaches, not self-propelled; luggage vans, post office coaches and other special purpose railway or tramway coaches, not self-propelled (excluding those of heading-No. 86.04):**
8605.0010	---铁道客车	5			0	14	17	17	辆		---Railway passenger coaches
8605.0090	---其他	5			0	14	17	17	辆		---Other
86.06	**铁道及电车道用的非机动有篷及无篷货车:**										**Railway or tramway goods vans and wagons, not self-propelled:**
8606.1000	-油罐货车及类似车	5			0	14	17	17	辆		-Tank wagons and the like

税则号列 Tariff Item.	货品名称	最惠国(%) MFN	协定(%) 东盟 CA	中巴 CP	中智 CC	普通 Gen	增值税率 VAT	出口退税 ED	计量单位 Unit	监管条件 SC	Article Description
8606.3000	-自卸货车,但子目 8606.1000 的货品除外	5			0	14	17	17	辆		-Self-discharging vans and wagons, other than those of subheadingNo. 8606.1000
	-其他:										-Other:
8606.9100	--带篷及封闭的	5			0	14	17	17	辆		--Covered and closed
8606.9200	--敞篷的,厢壁固定且高度超过 60 厘米	5			0	14	17	17	辆		--Open, with non-removable sides of a height exceeding 60 cm
8606.9900	--其他	5			0	14	17	17	辆		--Other
86.07	**铁道及电车道机车或其他车辆的零件:**										**Parts of railway or tramway locomotives or rolling-stock:**
	-转向架、轴、轮及其零件:										-Bogies, bissel-bogies, axles and wheels, and parts thereof:
8607.1100	--驾驶转向架	3			0	11	17	13	套/千克		--Driving bogies and bissel-bogies
8607.1200	--其他转向架	3			0	11	17	13	套/千克		--Other bogies and bissel-bogies
	--其他,包括零件:										--Other, including parts:
8607.1910	---轴	3			0	11	17	13	根/千克	A	---Axles
8607.1990	---其他	3			0	11	17	13	千克	A	---Other
	-制动装置及其零件:										-Brakes and parts thereof:
8607.2100	--空气制动器及其零件	3			0	11	17	13	千克		--Air brakes and parts thereof
8607.2900	--其他	3			0	11	17	13	千克		--Other
8607.3000	-钩、其他联结器、缓冲器及其零件	3			0	11	17	13	千克		-Hooks and other coupling devices, buffers, and parts thereof
	-其他:										-Other:
8607.9100	--机车用	3			0	11	17	13	千克		--Of locomotives
8607.9900	--其他	3			0	11	17	13	千克		--Other
86.08	**铁道及电车道轨道固定装置及附件;供铁道、电车道、道路、内河航道、停车场、港口或机场用的机械(包括电动机械)信号、安全或交通管理设备;上述货品的零件:**										**Railway or tramway track fixtures and fittings; mechanical (including electro-mechanical) signalling, safety or traffic control equipment for railways, tramways, roads, inland waterways, parking facilities, port installations or airfields; parts of the foregoing:**
8608.0010	---轨道自动计轴设备	3			0	20	17	13	千克/台		---Rail automatic axle counting equipments
8608.0090	---其他	4			0	20	17	13	千克		---Other
86.09	**集装箱(包括运输液体的集装箱),经特殊设计、装备适用于各种运输方式:**										**Containers (including containers for the transport of fluids) specially designed and equipped for carriage by one or more modes of transport:**
8609.0010	---20 英尺的	10.5	8		8.4	35	17	13	个	AB	---Of 20 feet
8609.0020	---40 英尺的	10.5	8		8.4	35	17	13	个	AB	---Of 40 feet
8609.0030	---45、48、53 英尺的	10.5	8		8.4	35	17	13	个	AB	---Of 45,48,53 feet
8609.0090	---其他	10.5	8		8.4	35	17	13	个	AB	---Other

第八十七章 车辆及其零件、附件，但铁道及电车道车辆除外

Chapter 87 Vehicles other than railway or tramway rolling-stock，and parts and accessories thereof

注释：

一、本章不包括仅可在钢轨上运行的铁道及电车道车辆。

二、本章所称“牵引车、拖拉机”，是指主要为牵引或推动其他车辆、器具或重物的车辆。除了上述主要用途以外，不论其是否还具有装运工具、种子、肥料或其他货品的辅助装置。

用于安装在税目87.01的牵引车或拖拉机上，作为可替换设备的机器或作业工具，即使与牵引车或拖拉机一同进口或出口，不论其是否已安装在车（机）上，仍应归入其各自相应的税目。

三、装有驾驶室的机动车辆底盘，应归入税目87.02至87.04，而不归入税目87.06。

四、税目87.12包括所有儿童两轮车，其他儿童脚踏车归入税目95.03。

Notes：

1. This Chapter does not cover railway or tramway rolling-stock designed solely for running on rails.
2. For the purposes of this Chapter，“tractors” means vehicles constructed essentially for hauling or pushing another vehicle，appliance or load，whether or not they contain subsidiary provision for the transport，in connection with the main use of the tractor，of tools，seeds，fertilizers or other goods.

   Machines and working tools designed for fitting to tractors of headingNo. 87.01 as interchangeable equipment remain classified in their respective headings even if presented with the tractor，and whether or not mounted on it.
3. Motor chassis fitted with cabs fall in headingsNos. 87.02 to 87.04，and not in headingNo. 87.06.
4. HeadingNo. 87.12 includes all children's bicycles. Other children's cycles fall in headingNo. 95.03.

税则号列 Tariff Item.	货品名称	最惠国(%) MFN	协定(%)CT 东盟 CA	中巴 CP	中智 CC	普通 Gen	增值税率 VAT	出口退税 ED	计量单位 Unit	监管条件 SC	Article Description
87.01	**牵引车、拖拉机（税目87.09的牵引车除外）：**										**Tractors（other than tractors of headingNo. 87.09）：**
8701.1000	-手扶拖拉机	9	T3		0	20	13	11	辆	B6	-Pedestrian controlled tractors
8701.2000	-半挂车用的公路牵引车	6			0	20	17	17	辆	6AO	-Road tractors for semi-trailers
8701.3000	-履带式牵引车、拖拉机	6	5		0	20		11	辆		-Track-laying tractors
8701.3000 10	履带式拖拉机	6				20	13	11	辆	AB6	Track-laying farming tractors
8701.3000 90	履带式牵引车	6				20	17	13	辆	AB6	Other Track-laying tractors
	-其他：										-Other：
	---拖拉机：										---Tractors
8701.9011	----轮式	8	5		0	20	13	11	辆		----Wheeled
8701.9011 01	功率大于150马力的轮式拖拉机	8				20	13	11	辆	AB6	Farming tractors，power≥150H. P.
8701.9011 90	其他轮式拖拉机	8				20	13	11	辆	AB6	Other tractors，wheeled（tyre）
8701.9019	----其他	8	5		0	20	13	11	辆		----Other
8701.9019 01	其他功率大于150马力的拖拉机	8				20	13	11	辆	AB6	Other tractor，power≥150H. P.
8701.9019 90	其他拖拉机	8				20	13	11	辆	AB6	Other tractor
8701.9090	---其他	8	5		0	20	17	13	辆	6AB	---Other
87.02	**客运机动车辆，10座及以上（包括驾驶座）：**										**Motor vehicles for the transport of ten or more persons，including the driver：**
	-装有压燃式活塞内燃发动机（柴油或半柴油发动机）的车辆：										-With compression-ignition internal combustion piston engine（diesel or semi-diesel）：
8702.1020	---机坪客车	4			0	90	17	17	辆	6ABO	---Buses for transport passengers at airport
	---其他：										---Other：
8702.1091	----30座及以上（大型客车）	25			0	90	17	17	辆	6ABO	----With 30 seats or more

税则号列 Tariff Item.	货品名称	最惠国(%) MFN	协定(%) 东盟 CA	中巴 CP	CT 中智 CC	普通 Gen	增值税率 VAT	出口退税 ED	计量单位 Unit	监管条件 SC	Article Description
8702.1092	----20座及以上,但不超过29座	25				230	17	17	辆		----With 20 seats or more, but not exceeding 29 seats
8702.1092 01	20≤座≤23装有压燃式活塞内燃发动机的客车	25				230	17	17	辆	6ABO	Buses for transport passengers, with compression – ignition internal combustion piston engine, with 20 ~ 23seats
8702.1092 90	24≤座≤29装有压燃式活塞内燃发动机的客车	25				230	17	17	辆	6ABO	Buses for transport passengers, with compression – ignition internal combustion piston engine, with 24 ~ 29seats
8702.1093	10≤座≤19装有压燃式活塞内燃发动机的客车	25			0	230	17	17	辆	6ABO	With 10 Seats or more, but not exceeding 19 seats
	-其他:										-Other:
8702.9010	---30座及以上(大型客车)	25			0	90	17	17	辆	6ABO	---With 30 seats or more
8702.9020	---20座及以上,但不超过29座	25			0	230	17	17	辆	6ABO	---With 20 seats or more, but not exceeding 29 seats
8702.9020 01	20≤座≤23装有非压燃式活塞内燃发动机的客车	25				230	17	17	辆	6ABO	Buses for transport passengers, with non – compression – ignition internal combustion piston engine, with 20 ~ 23seats
8702.9020 90	24≤座≤29装有非压燃式活塞内燃发动机的客车	25				230	17	17	辆	6ABO	Buses for transport passengers, with non – compression – ignition internal combustion piston engine, with 24 ~ 29seats
8702.9030	---10座及以上,但不超过19座	25			0	230	17	17	辆	6ABO	---With 20 seats or more, but not exceeding 29 seats
87.03	**主要用于载人的机动车辆(税目87.02的货品除外),包括旅行小客车及赛车:**										**Motor cars and other motor vehicles principally designed for the transport of persons (other than those of headingNo. 87.02), including station wagons and racing cars:**
	-雪地行走专用车;高尔夫球车及类似车辆:										-Vehicles specially designed for travelling on snow; golf cars and similar vehicles:
	---高尔夫球车及类似车辆:										---Golf calt and the like
8703.1011	----全地形车	25	T3		0	150	17	17	辆	46xy	----All terrain vehicle
8703.1019	----其他	25	T3		0	150	17	17	辆	6	----Other
8703.1090	---其他	25	T3		0	150	17	17	辆	6	---Other
	-装有点燃往复式活塞内燃发动机的其他车辆:										-Other vehicles, with spark-ignition internal combustion reciprocating piston engine:
	--气缸容量(排气量)不超过1000毫升:										--Of a cylinder capacity not exceeding 1000 cc:
8703.2130	---小轿车	25		22.5	0	230	17	17	辆	6ABO	---Saloon cars
8703.2190	---其他	25		22.5	0	230	17	17	辆	6ABO	---Other
	--整车:										--Assembled:
8703.2230	---小轿车	25		22.5	0	230	17	17	辆	6ABO	---Saloon cars
8703.2240	---越野车(4轮驱动)	25		22.5	0	230	17	17	辆	6ABO	---Cross-country cars (4WD)
8703.2250	---9座及以下的小客车	25		22.5	0	230	17	17	辆	6ABO	---Station wagons (with 9 seats or less)
8703.2290	---其他	25		22.5	0	230	17	17	辆	6ABO	---Other

税则号列 Tariff Item.	货品名称	最惠国(%) MFN	协定(%) CT 东盟 CA	中巴 CP	中智 CC	普通 Gen	增值税率 VAT	出口退税 ED	计量单位 Unit	监管条件 SC	Article Description
8703. 2314	----小轿车	25		22.5	0	230	17	17	辆		----Saloon cars
8703. 2314 01	1. 5 升<排气量≤2 升装点燃往复式活塞内燃发动机小轿车	25				230	17	17	辆	6ABO	Saloon cars with spark - ignition internal combustion reciprocating piston engine, assembled, 1. 5L < cylinder capacity≤2L
8703. 2314 02	2 升<排气量≤2. 5 升装点燃往复式活塞内燃发动机小桥车	25				230	17	17	辆	6ABO	Saloon cars with spark - ignition internal combustion reciprocating piston engine, assembled, 2L < cylinder capacity≤2. 5L
8703. 2315	----越野车(4 轮驱动)	25		22.5	0	230	17	17	辆		----Cross-country cars (4WD)
8703. 2315 01	1. 5 升<排气量≤2 升装点燃往复式活塞内燃发动机四轮驱动越野车	25				230	17	17	辆	6ABO	Cross - country cars (4WD) with spark - ignition internal combustion reciprocating piston engine, assembled, 1. 5L < cylinder capacity≤2L
8703. 2315 02	2 升<排气量≤2. 5 升装点燃往复式活塞内燃发动机四轮驱动越野车	25				230	17	17	辆	6ABO	Cross - country cars (4WD) with spark - ignition internal combustion reciprocating piston engine, , assembled, 2L < cylinder capacity≤2. 5L
8703. 2316	----9 座及以下的小客车	25		22.5	0	230	17	17	辆		----Station wagons (with 9 seats or less)
8703. 2316 01	1. 5 升<排气量≤2 升装点燃往复式活塞内燃机发动机小客车(指≤9 座)	25				230	17	17	辆	6ABO	Sstation wagons with spark - ignition internal combustion reciprocating piston engine, , assembled, 1. 5L < cylinder capacity≤2L
8703. 2316 02	2 升<排气量≤2. 5 升装点燃往复式活塞内燃发动机的小客车(指≤9 座)	25				230	17	17	辆	6ABO	Station wagons with spark - ignition internal combustion reciprocating piston engine, , assembled, 2L < cylinder capacity≤2. 5L
8703. 2319	----其他	25		22.5	0	230	17	17	辆		----Other
8703. 2319 01	1. 5 升<排气量≤2 升装点燃往复式活塞内燃发动机其他载人车辆	25				230	17	17	辆	6ABO	Other motor vehicles designed for transprt of person´s with spark - ignition internal combustion reciprocating piston engine, , assembled, 1. 5L < cylinder capacity≤2L
8703. 2319 02	2 升<排气量≤2. 5 升装点燃往复式活塞内燃发动机其他载人车辆	25				230	17	17	辆	6ABO	Other motor vehicles designed for transprt of person's with spark - ignition internal combustion reciprocating piston engine, assembled, 2L < cylinder capacity≤2. 5L
8703. 2334	----小轿车	25		22.5	0	270	17	17	辆	6AO	----Saloon cars
8703. 2335	----越野车(4 轮驱动)	25	T3	22.5	0	270	17	17	辆	6AO	----Cross-country cars (4WD)
8703. 2336	----9 座及以下的小客车	25	T3	22.5	0	270	17	17	辆	6AO	----Station wagons (with 9 seats or less)
8703. 2339	----其他	25	T3	22.5	0	270	17	17	辆	6AO	----Other
8703. 2430	---小轿车	25		22.5	0	270	17	17	辆		---Saloon cars
8703. 2430 01	3 升<排气量≤4 升的装点燃往复式活塞内燃发动机小轿车	25				270	17	17	辆	6ABO	Saloon cars with spark - ignition internal combustion reciprocating piston engine, , assembled, 3L < cylinder capacity≤4L

税则号列 Tariff Item.	货 品 名 称	最惠国(%) MFN	协定(%)CT 东盟 CA	 中巴 CP	 中智 CC	普通 Gen	增值税率 VAT	出口退税 ED	计量单位 Unit	监管条件 SC	Article Description
8703. 2430 02	排气量>4升的装有点燃往复式活塞内燃发动机小轿车	25				270	17	17	辆	6ABO	Saloon cars with spark - ignition internal combustion reciprocating piston engine, , assembled, cylinder capacity > 4L
8703. 2440	---越野车(4轮驱动)	25		22.5	0	270	17	17	辆		---Cross-country cars (4WD)
8703. 2440 01	3升<排气量≤4升装点燃往复式活塞内燃发动机越野车	25				270	17	17	辆	6ABO	Cross - country cars with spark - ignition internal combustion reciprocating piston engine, , assembled, 3L < cylinder capacity≤4L
8703. 2440 02	排气量>4升的装有点燃往复式活塞内燃发动机越野车	25				270	17	17	辆	6ABO	Cross - country cars with spark - ignition internal combustion reciprocating piston engine, , assembled, cylinder capacity >4L
8703. 2450	---9座及以下的小客车	25		22.5	0	270	17	17	辆		---Station wagons (with 9 seats or less)
8703. 2450 01	3升<排气量≤4升装点燃往复式活塞内燃发动机的小客车(≤9座)	25				270	17	17	辆	6ABO	Station wagons with spark - ignition internal combustion reciprocating piston engine, , assembled, 3L < cylinder capacity≤4L
8703. 2450 02	排气量>4升的装有点燃往复式活塞内燃发动机的小客车(≤9座)	25				270	17	17	辆	6ABO	Station wagons with spark - ignition internal combustion reciprocating piston engine, , assembled, cylinder capacity >4L
8703. 2490	---其他	25		22.5	0	270	17	17	辆		---Other
8703. 2490 01	3升<排气量≤4升装点燃往复式活塞内燃发动机的其他载人车辆	25				270	17	17	辆	6ABO	Other motor vehicles designed for transprt of person´s with spark - ignition internal combustion reciprocating piston engine, , assembled, 3L < cylinder capacity≤4L
8703. 2490 02	排气量>4升装点燃往复式活塞内燃发动机其他载人车辆	25				270	17	17	辆	6ABO	Other motor vehicles designed for transprt of person´s with spark - ignition internal combustion reciprocating piston engine, , assembled, cylinder capacity >4L
	--气缸容量(排气量)不超过1500毫升:										--Of a cylinder capacity not exceeding 1500 cc:
8703. 3130	---小轿车	25			0	230	17	17	辆	6ABO	---Saloon cars
8703. 3140	---越野车(4轮驱动)	25			0	230	17	17	辆	6ABO	---Cross-country cars (4WD)
8703. 3150	---9座及以下的小客车	25			0	230	17	17	辆	6ABO	---Station wagons (with 9 seats or less)
8703. 3190	---其他	25	T3		0	230	17	17	辆	6ABO	---Other
8703. 3230	---小轿车	25		22.5	0	230	17	17	辆		---Saloon cars
8703. 3230 01	1.5升<排气量≤2升装有压燃式活塞内燃发动机小轿车	25				230	17	17	辆	6ABO	Cross - country cars (4WD) with compression - ignition internal combustion piston engine, assembled, 1. 5L < cylinder capacity≤2L
8703. 3230 02	2升<排气量≤2.5升装有压燃式活塞内燃发动机小轿车	25				230	17	17	辆	6ABO	Saloon cars with compression - ignition internal combustion piston engine, assembled, 2L < cylinder capacity≤2. 5L
8703. 3240	---越野车(4轮驱动)	25		22.5	0	230	17	17	辆		---Cross-country cars (4WD)

税则号列 Tariff Item.	货品名称	最惠国(%) MFN	协定(%) 东盟 CA	中巴 CP	CT 中智 CC	普通 Gen	增值税率 VAT	出口退税 ED	计量单位 Unit	监管条件 SC	Article Description
8703.3240 01	1.5 升<排气量≤2 升装有压燃式活塞内燃发动机四轮驱动越野车	25				230	17	17	辆	6ABO	Cross - country cars (4WD) with compression - ignition internal combustion piston engine, assembled, 1.5L < cylinder capacity≤2L
8703.3240 02	2 升<排气量≤2.5 升装有压燃式活塞内燃发动机四轮驱动越野车	25				230	17	17	辆	6ABO	Cross - country cars (4WD) with compression - ignition internal combustion piston engine, assembled, 2L < cylinder capacity≤2.5L
8703.3250	---9 座及以下的小客车	25		22.5	0	230	17	17	辆		---Station wagons (with 9 seats or less)
8703.3250 01	1.5 升<排气量≤2 升装有压燃式活塞内燃发动机小客车(指≤9 座)	25				230	17	17	辆	6ABO	Station wagons with compression - ignition internal combustion piston engine, assembled, 1.5L < cylinder capacity≤2L
8703.3250 02	2 升<排气量≤2.5 升装有压燃式活塞内燃发动机小客车(指≤9 座)	25				230	17	17	辆	6ABO	Station wagons with compression - ignition internal combustion piston engine, assembled, 2L < cylinder capacity ≤2.5L
8703.3290	---其他	25		22.5	0	230	17	17	辆		---Other
8703.3290 01	1.5 升<排气量≤2 升装有压燃式活塞内燃发动机其他载人车辆	25				230	17	17	辆	6ABO	Motor cars and other motor vehicles designed for the transport of person ′s with compression - ignition internal combustion piston engine, assembled, 1.5L < cylinder capacity ≤2L
8703.3290 02	2 升<排气量≤2.5 升装有压燃式活塞内燃发动机其他载人车辆	25				230	17	17	辆	6ABO	Motor cars and other motor vehicles designed for the transport of person ′s with compression - ignition internal combustion piston engine, assembled, 2L < cylinder capacity ≤2.5L
	--气缸容量(排气量)超过 2500 毫升:										--Of a cylinder capacity exceeding 2500cc:
8703.3330	---小轿车	25	T3	22.5	0	270	17	17	辆		---Saloon cars
8703.3330 01	2.5 升<排气量≤3 升装有压燃式活塞内燃发动机小轿车	25				270	17	17	辆	6ABO	Saloon cars with compression - ignition internal combustion piston engine, assembled, 2.5L < cylinder capacity ≤ 3L
8703.3330 02	3 升<排气量≤4 升装有压燃式活塞内燃发动机小轿车	25				270	17	17	辆	6ABO	Saloon cars with compression - ignition internal combustion piston engine, assembled, 3L < cylinder capacity ≤ 4L
8703.3330 03	排气量>4 升装有压燃式活塞内燃发动机小轿车	25				270	17	17	辆	6ABO	Saloon cars with compression - ignition internal combustion piston engine, assembled, cylinder capacity >4L
8703.3340	---越野车(4 轮驱动)	25	T3	22.5	0	270	17	17	辆		---Cross-country cars (4WD)
8703.3340 01	2.5 升<排气量≤3 升装有压燃式活塞内燃发动机四轮驱动越野车	25				270	17	17	辆	6ABO	Cross - country cars (4WD) with compression - ignition internal combustion piston engine, assembled, 2.5L < cylinder capacity≤3L

税则号列 Tariff Item.	货品名称	最惠国(%) MFN	协定(%) 东盟 CA	中巴 CP	CT 中智 CC	普通 Gen	增值税率 VAT	出口退税 ED	计量单位 Unit	监管条件 SC	Article Description
8703.3340 02	3升<排气量≤4升装有压燃式活塞内燃发动机四轮驱动越野车燃发动	25				270	17	17	辆	6ABO	Cross – country cars (4WD) with compression – ignition internal combustion piston engine, assembled, 3L < cylinder capacity≤4L
8703.3340 03	排气量>4升有压燃式活塞内燃发动机四轮驱动越野车	25				270	17	17	辆	6ABO	Cross – country cars (4WD) with compression – ignition internal combustion piston engine, assembled, cylinder capacity >4L
8703.3350	---9座及以下的小客车	25	T3	22.5	0	270	17	17	辆		---Station wagons (with 9 seats or less)
8703.3350 01	2.5升<排气量≤3升装有压燃式活塞内燃发动机的小客车(≤9座)	25				270	17	17	辆	6ABO	Station wagons with compression – ignition internal combustion piston engine, assembled, 2.5L < cylinder capacity≤3L
8703.3350 02	3升<排气量≤4升装有压燃式活塞内燃发动机的小客车(≤9座)	25				270	17	17	辆	6ABO	Station wagons with compression – ignition internal combustion piston engine, assembled, 3L < cylinder capacity ≤4L
8703.3350 03	排气量>4升装有压燃式活塞内燃发动机的小客车(9≤座)	25				270	17	17	辆	6ABO	Station wagons with compression – ignition internal combustion piston engine, cylinder assembled, capacity >4L
8703.3390	---其他	25	T3	22.5	0	270	17	17	辆		---Other
8703.3390 01	2.5升<排气量≤3升装有压燃式活塞内燃发动机的其他载人车辆	25				270	17	17	辆	6ABO	Motor cars and other motor vehicles designed for the transport of person ´s with compression – ignition internal combustion piston engine, assembled, 2.5L < cylinder capacity ≤3L
8703.3390 02	3升<排气量≤4升装有压燃式活塞内燃发动机的其他载人车辆	25				270	17	17	辆	6ABO	Motor cars and other motor vehicles designed for the transport of person ’s with compression – ignition internal combustion piston engine, assembled, 3L < cylinder capacity ≤4L
8703.3390 03	排气量>4升装有压燃式活塞内燃发动机的其他载人车辆	25				270	17	17	辆	6ABO	Motor cars and other motor vehicles designed for the transport of person´s with compression – ignition internal combustion piston engine, assembled, cylinder capacity >4L
8703.9000	-其他	25	T3	22.5	0	270	17	17	辆		-Other
8703.9000 01	其他型排气量≤1.5升的其他载人车辆	25				270	17	17	辆	6ABO	Other motor vehicles designed for transprt of person´s, cylinder capacity≤1.5L
8703.9000 02	其他型1.5升<排气量≤2升的其他载人车辆	25				270	17	17	辆	6ABO	Other motor vehicles designed for transprt of person´s, 1.5L < cylinder capacity≤2L
8703.9000 03	其他型2升<排气量≤2.5升的其他载人车辆	25				270	17	17	辆	6ABO	Other motor vehicles designed for transprt of person´s, 2L < cylinder capacity≤2.5L
8703.9000 04	其他型2.5升<排气量≤3升的其他载人车辆	25				270	17	17	辆	6ABO	Other motor vehicles designed for transprt of person´s, 2.5L < cylinder capacity≤3L

税则号列 Tariff Item.	货品名称	最惠国(%) MFN	协定(%)CT 东盟 CA	中巴 CP	中智 CC	普通 Gen	增值税率 VAT	出口退税 ED	计量单位 Unit	监管条件 SC	Article Description
8703.9000 05	其他型3升<排气量≤4升的其他载人车辆	25				270	17	17	辆	6ABO	Other motor vehicles designed for transprt of person´s , 3L < cylinder capacity≤4L
8703.9000 06	其他型4升<排气量的其他载人车辆	25				270	17	17	辆	6ABO	Other motor vehicles designed for transprt of person´s , 4L < cylinder capacity
8703.9000 90	电动汽车和其他无法区分排气量的载人车辆	25				270	17	17	辆	6ABO	
87.04	**货运机动车辆：**										**Motor vehicles for the transport of goods:**
	-非公路用自卸车：										-Dumpers designed for off-highway use:
8704.1030	---电动轮货运自卸车	6	T3		0	20	17	17	辆	6ABO	---Electromobile dumpers for the transport of goods
8704.1090	---其他	6	T3		0	20	17	17	辆	6ABO	---Other
	-装有压燃式活塞内燃发动机(柴油或半柴油发动机)的其他货车：										-Other, with compression-ignition internal combustion piston engine (diesel or semidiesesl):
8704.2100	--车辆总重量不超过5吨	25			0	70	17	17	辆	6ABO	--g. v. w. not exceeding 5 tons
	--车辆总重量超过5吨,但不超过20吨：										--g. v. w. exceeding 5 tons but not exceeding 20 tons:
8704.2230	---车辆总重量超过5吨,但小于14吨	20		18	0	70	17	17	辆	6ABO	---g. v. w. exceeding 5 tons but notexceeding 14 tons
8704.2240	---车辆总重量在14吨及以上,但不超过20吨	20		18	0	40	17	17	辆	6ABO	---g. v. w. of 14 tons or more but not exceeding 20 tons
8704.2300	--车辆总重量超过20吨	15			0	40	17	17	辆		--g. v. w. exceeding 20 tons
8704.2300 01	固井水泥车、压裂车、混砂车底盘(车辆总重量>35吨,装驾驶室)	15				40	17	17	辆	6ABO	Chassis for petroleum well logging trucks, fracturing unit trucks and mixing sand trucks, g. v. w >35tons, with cabs
8704.2300 02	起重≥55吨汽车起重机用底盘(装有压燃式活塞内燃发动机)	15				40	17	17	辆	6ABO	Chassis for crane lorries, lifting capacity ≥ 55tons, with compression-ignition internal combustion piston engine
8704.2300 90	柴油型的其他超重型货车(装有压燃式活塞内燃发动机,超重型指车辆总重量>20吨)	15				40	17	17	辆	6ABO	Other motor vehicles for the transport of goods, with compression-ignition internal combustion piston engine (diesel or semi-diesel), g. v. w >20tons
	-装有点燃式活塞内燃发动机的其他货车：										-Other, with spark-ignition internal combustion piston engine:
8704.3100	--车辆总重量不超过5吨	25			20	70	17	17	辆	6ABO	--g. v. w. not exceeding 5 tons
	--车辆总重量超过5吨：										--g. v. w. exceeding 5 tons:
8704.3230	---车辆总重量超过5吨,但不超过8吨	20			0	70	17	17	辆	6ABO	---g. v. w. exceeding 5 tons, but not exceeding 8 tons.
8704.3240	---车辆总重量超过8吨	20			0	70	17	17	辆	6ABO	---g. v. w. exceeding 8 tons
8704.9000	-其他	25	T3		0	70	17	17	辆	6ABO	-Other

税则号列 Tariff Item.	货品名称	最惠国(%) MFN	协定(%) CT 东盟 CA	中巴 CP	中智 CC	普通 Gen	增值税率 VAT	出口退税 ED	计量单位 Unit	监管条件 SC	Article Description
87.05	**特殊用途的机动车辆(例如,抢修车、起重车、救火车、混凝土搅拌车、道路清洁车、喷洒车、流动工场车及流动放射线检查车),但主要用于载人或运货的车辆除外:**										**Special purpose motor vehicles, other than those principally designed for the transport of persons or goods (for example, breakdown lorries, crane lorries, fire fighting vehicles, concrete-mixer lorries, road sweeper lorries, spraying lorries, mobile workshops, mobile radiological units):**
	-起重车:										-Crane lorries:
	---全路面起重车:										---All-road crane lorries:
8705.1021	----最大起重重量不超过50吨	15	T3		0	30	17	17	辆	6AO	----Of maxium lifting capacity not more than 50tons
8705.1022	----最大起重量量超过50吨,但不超过100吨	10	T3		0	30	17	17	辆	6AO	----Of a maxium lifting capacity exceeding 50tons but not exceeding 100tons
8705.1023	----最大起重重量超过100吨	10	T3		0	30	17	17	辆	6AO	----Of a maxium lifting capacity exceeding 100tons
	---其他:										---Other:
8705.1091	----最大起重重量不超过50吨	15	T3		0	30	17	17	辆	6AO	----Of maxium lifting capacity not more than 50tons
8705.1092	----最大起重重量超过50吨,但不超过100吨	10	T3		0	30	17	17	辆	6AO	----Of a maxium lifting capacity exceeding 50tons but not exceeding 100 tons
8705.1093	----最大起重重量超过100吨	10	T3		0	30	17	17	辆	6AO	----Of a maxium lifting capacity exceeding 100 tons
8705.2000	-钻探车	12	T3		0	17	17	17	辆	6AO	-Mobile drilling derricks
	-救火车:										-Fire fighting vehicles:
8705.3010	---装有云梯的救火车	3			0	8	17	17	辆	AB6O	---Mounted with scaling ladder
8705.3090	---其他	3			0	8	17	17	辆	AB6O	---Other
8705.4000	-混凝土搅拌车	15	T3	13.5	0	35	17	17	辆	AB6O	-Concrete-mixer lorries
	-其他:										-Other:
8705.9010	---无线电通信车	9	T3	8.1	0	35	17	17	辆	AB6O	---Radio communication vans
8705.9020	---放射线检查车	9	T3	8.1	0	14	17	17	辆	6AO	---Mobile radiological units
8705.9030	---环境监测车	12	T3	10.8	0	20	17	17	辆	6AO	---Mobile environmental monitoring units
8705.9040	---医疗车	12	T3	10.8	0	30	17	17	辆	6AO	---Mobile clinics
	---电源车:										---Mobile electric generator sets:
8705.9051	----航空电源车(频率为400赫兹)	12	T3	10.8	0	30	17	17	辆	O6	----Airplane charging vehicles (frequency 400Hz)
8705.9059	----其他	12	T3	10.8	0	30	17	17	辆	6AO	----Other
8705.9060	---飞机加油车、调温车、除冰车	12	T3	10.8	0	35	17	17	辆	OAB6	---Mobile vehicles for aircraft refuelling, air-conditioning or deicing
8705.9070	---道路(包括跑道)扫雪车	12	T3	10.8	0	35	17	17	辆	OAB6	---Snow sweep vehicles for cleansing streets or airfield runways
8705.9080	---石油测井车、压裂车、混沙车	12	T3	10.8	0	35	17	17	辆	OAB6	---Petrolcum well logging trucks, fracturing unit trucks and mixing sand trucks
8705.9090	---其他	12	T3	10.8	0	35	17	17	辆		---Other
8705.9090 01	跑道除冰车	12				35	17	17	辆	AB6O	Runway deicing truck
8705.9090 30	用于导弹、火箭等的车辆(为弹道导弹、运载火箭等运输、装卸和发射而设计的)	12				35	17	17	辆	36ABO	Vehicles for carrying missiles or rockets (specially designed for transporting, handling and launching of ballistic missiles or carrier rockets)

税则号列 Tariff Item.	货品名称	最惠国(%) MFN	协定(%) CT 东盟 CA	 中巴 CP	 中智 CC	普通 Gen	增值税率 VAT	出口退税 ED	计量单位 Unit	监管条件 SC	Article Description
8705.9090 90	其他特殊用途的机动车辆(主要用于载人或运货的车辆除外)	12				35	17	17	辆	AB6O	Other special purpose motor vehicles, other than those principally designed for the transport of persons or goods
87.06	**装有发动机的机动车辆底盘,税目 87.01 至 87.05 所列车辆用:**										**Chassis fitted with engines, for the motor vehicles of headingsNos. 87.01 to 87.05:**
8706.0010	---非公路用自卸车底盘	8	T3		0	14	17	17	台	6	---For the vehicles of subheading No. 8704.1030 or 8704.1090
	---货车底盘:										---For the vehicles of subheading Nos. 8704.2100 to 8704.9000:
8706.0021	----车辆总重量在 14 吨及以上的	10			0	30	17	17	台	6AO	----For vehicles g. v. w of 14 tons or more
8706.0022	----车辆总重量在 14 吨以下的	10			0	45	17	17	台	6AO	----For vehicles g. v. w less than 14 tons
8706.0030	---大型客车底盘	20	T3		0	70	17	17	台	6O	---For passenger motor vehicles with 30 seats or more
8706.0040	---汽车起重机底盘	20	T3		0	100	17	17	台	6AO	---For crane lorries
8706.0090	---其他	10			0	100	17	17	台	6AO	---Other
87.07	**机动车辆的车身(包括驾驶室),税目 87.01 至 87.05 所列车辆用:**										**Bodies (including cabs), for the motor vehicles of headingsNos. 87.01 to 87.05:**
8707.1000	-税目 87.03 所列车辆用	10			0	100	17	17	台	6O	-For the vehicles of headingNo. 87.03
	-其他:										-Other:
8707.9010	---税目 8702.1092、8702.1093、8702.9020 及 8702.9030 所列车辆用	10		9	0	70	17	17	台	6O	---For the vehicles of subheadingNo. 8702.1092、8702.1093、8702.9020 or 8702.9030
8707.9090	---其他	10		9	0	70	17	17	台	6O	---Other
87.08	**机动车辆的零件、附件,税目 87.01 至 87.05 所列车辆用:**										**Parts and accessories of the motor vehicles of headingsNos. 87.01 to 87.05:**
8708.1000	-缓冲器(保险杠)及其零件	10	T3	9.6	0	100	17	17	千克	6	-Bumpers and parts thereof
	-车身(包括驾驶室)的其他零件、附件:										-Other parts and accessories of bodies (including cabs):
8708.2100	--座椅安全带	10	T3		0	100	17	17	千克	6A	--Safety seat belts
	--其他:										--Other:
8708.2930	---车窗玻璃升降器	10		9	0	100	17	17	千克	6	---Windowpane raiser
	---天窗:										---Sunroofs
8708.2941	----电动的	10	T3	9	0	100	17	17	套/千克	6O	----Electric
8708.2942	----手动的	10	T3	9	0	100	17	17	套/千克	6O	----Manual
	---其他车身覆盖件:										---Other body coverings
8708.2951	----侧围	10	T3	9	0	100	17	17	千克	6O	----Side panels
8708.2952	----车门	10	T3	9	0	100	17	17	个/千克	6O	----Car doors
8708.2953	----发动机罩盖	10	T3	9	0	100	17	17	千克	6O	----Engine hood
8708.2954	----前围	10	T3	9	0	100	17	17	千克	6O	----Front wall
8708.2955	----行李箱盖(或背门)	10	T3	9	0	100	17	17	千克	6O	----Baggage compartment lids (or back door)
8708.2956	----后围	10	T3	9	0	100	17	17	千克	6O	----Rear wall
8708.2957	----翼子板(或叶子板)	10	T3	9	0	100	17	17	千克	6O	----Fender
8708.2959	----其他	10	T3	9	0	100	17	17	千克	6	----Other
8708.2990	---其他	10	T3	9	0	100	17	17	千克	6	---Other

税则号列 Tariff Item.	货 品 名 称	最惠国(%) MFN	协定(%) CT 东盟 CA	 中巴 CP	 中智 CC	普通 Gen	增值税率 VAT	出口退税 ED	计量单位 Unit	监管条件 SC	Article Description
	-制动器、助力制动器及其零件:										-Brakes and servo-brakes and parts thereof:
8708.3010	---装在蹄片上的制动摩擦片	10	T3		0	100	17	17	千克	6	---Mounted brake linings.
	---防抱死制动系统(ABS):										---
8708.3021	----税号 87.01.87.04.1030 及 8704.1090 所列车辆用	6	T3	5.4	0	11	17	17	千克	6	----of the rehicles of heading 87.01 8704.1030 for 8704.1090
8708.3029	----其他	10		9	0	100	17	17	千克	6	----Other
	---其他:										---Other:
8708.3091	----税目 87.01 所列车辆用	6	T3	5.4	0	14	17	17	千克	6	----Of the vehicles of headingNo. 87.01
8708.3092	----税目 8702.1091 及 8702.9010 所列车辆用	10		9	0	70	17	17	千克	6	----Of the vehicles of subheadingNo. 8702.1091 or 8702.9010
8708.3093	----税目 8704.1030 及 8704.1090 所列车辆用	6	T3	5.4	0	11	17	17	千克	6	----Of the vehicles of subheadingNo. 8704.1030 or 8704.1090
8708.3094	----税目 8704.2100、8704.2230、8704.3100 及 8704.3230 所列车辆用	10		9	0	45	17	17	千克	6	----Of the vehicles of subheadingNo. 8704.2100, 8704.2230, 8704.3100 or 8704.3230
8708.3095	----子目 8704.2240、8704.2300 及 8704.3240 所列车辆用	10	T3	9	0	30	17	17	千克	6	----Of the vehicles of subheading Nos. 8704.2240, 8704.2300 or 8704.3240
8708.3096	----税目 87.05 所列车辆用	10	T3	9	0	100	17	17	千克	6	----Of the vehicles of headingNo. 87.05
8708.3099	----其他	10		9	0	100	17	17	千克	6O	----Other
	-变速箱及其零件:										-Gear boxes:
8708.4010	---税目 87.01 所列车辆用	6	T3		0	14	17	17	个/千克	6	---Of the vehicles of headingNo. 87.01
8708.4020	---子目 8702.1091 及 8702.9010 所列车辆用	10			0	70	17	17	个/千克	6	---Of the vehicles of subheadingNo. 8702.1091 or 8702.9010
8708.4030	---子目 8704.1030 及 8704.1090 所列车辆用	6	T3		0	11	17	17	个/千克		---Of the vehicles of subheadingNo. 8704.1030 or 8704.1090
8708.4030 01	扭矩 > 1500Nm 非公路自卸车用变速箱	6				11	17	17	个/千克	6	Gear box for the vehicles troque > 1500mm
8708.4030 90	其他非公路自卸车用变速箱及其零件	6				11	17	17	个/千克	6	Other gear box for the vehicles and parts
8708.4040	---子目 8704.2100、8704.2230、8704.3100 及 8704.3230 所列车辆用	10			0	45	17	17	个/千克	6	---Of the vehicles of subheadingNos. 8704.2100 , 8704.2230, 8704.3100 or8704.3230
8708.4050	---税目 8704.2240、8704.2300 及 8704.3240 所列车辆用	10			0	30	17	17	个/千克		---Of the vehicles of subheading Nos. 8704.2240, 8704.2300 or 8704.3240
8708.4050 01	扭距≥90Kgm 变速箱、分动箱	10				30	17	17	个/千克	6	Gear boxes, transfer cases and their parts, torque≥90kgm
8708.4050 90	其他柴、汽油型重型货车用变速箱及其零件(指编号 87042240,87042300 及 87043240 所列车辆用)	10				30	17	17	个/千克	6	Other gear boxes of other motor vehicles of subheadingNo. 87042240, 87042300, 87143240
8708.4060	---税目 87.05 所列车辆用	10	T3		0	100	17	17	个/千克	6	---Of the vehicles of headingNo. 87.05
	---其他:										---Other:
8708.4091	----小轿车用自动换档变速箱	10			0	100	17	17	个/千克	6O	----Automatic gearshift for saloon cars
8708.4099	----其他	10			0	100	17	17	个/千克	6O	----Other

税则号列 Tariff Item.	货品名称	最惠国(%) MFN	协定(%)CT 东盟 CA	中巴 CP	中智 CC	普通 Gen	增值税率 VAT	出口退税 ED	计量单位 Unit	监管条件 SC	Article Description
	-装有差速器的驱动桥及其零件,不论是否装有其他传动部件;非驱动桥及其零件:										-Drive-axles with differential, whether or not provided with other transmission components; non-driving axles and parts thereof:
	---装有差速器的驱动桥及其零件,不论是否装有其他传动部件:										---Drive-axles with differential, whether or not provided with other transmission components:
8708.5071	----税目87.01所列车辆用	6	T3	5.4	0	14	17	17	个/千克	6	----Of the vehicles of headingNo. 87.01
8708.5072	----税目8702.1091及8702.9010所列车辆用	10		9	0	70	17	17	个/千克		----Of the vehicles of subheading Nos. 8702.1091 or 8702.9010
8708.5072 01	轴荷≥10吨的中后驱动桥的零件	10				70	17	17	个/千克	60	Middle and rear drive-axles and parts thereof, axle capacity≥10t, with differential, whether or not provided with other transmission components
8708.5072 90	其他大型客车用驱动桥及其零件(装有差速器的,不论是否装有其他传动件)	10				70	17	17	个/千克	60	Other drive-axles with differential, whether or not provided with other transmission components of the vehicles of subheading No.87021091 or 87029010
8708.5073	----子目8704.1030及8704.1090所列车辆用	6	T3	5.4	0	11	17	17	个/千克	6	----Of the vehicles of subheading No. 8704.1030 or 8704.1090
8708.5074	----子目8704.2100、8704.2230、8704.3100及8704.3230所列车辆用	10		9	0	45	17	17	个/千克	60	----Of the vehicles of subheading No. 8704.2100, 8704.2230, 8704.3100 or8704.3230
8708.5075	----子目8704.2240、8704.2300及8704.3240所列车辆用	10		9	0	30	17	17	个/千克	60	----Of the vehicles of subheading No. 8704.2240, 8704.2300 or 8704.3240
8708.5076	----税目87.05所列车辆用	10	T3	9	0	100	17	17	个/千克	60	----Of the vehicles of headingNo. 87.05
8708.5079	----其他	10		9	0	100	17	17	个/千克	60	----Other
	---非驱动桥及其零件:										---Non-driving axles and parts thereof:
8708.5081	----税目87.01所列车辆用	6	T3		0	14	17	17	千克	6	----Of the vehicles of headingNo. 87.01
8708.5082	----子目8702.1091及8702.9010所列车辆用	15			0	70	17	17	千克	6	----Of the vehicles of subheading No. 8702.1091 or 8702.9010
8708.5083	----子目8704.1030及8704.1090所列车辆用	6	T3		0	11	17	17	千克	6	----Of the vehicles of subheading No. 8704.1030 or 8704.1090
8708.5084	----子目8704.2100、8704.2230、8704.3100及8704.3230所列车辆用	10	T3		0	45	17	17	千克	6	----Of the vehicles of subheading No. 8704.2100, 8704.2230, 8704.3100 or 8704.3230
8708.5085	----子目8704.2240、8704.2300及8704.3240所列车辆用	10	T3		0	30	17	17	千克	6	----Of the vehicles of subheading No. 8704.2240, 8704.2300 or 8704.3240
8708.5086	----税目87.05所列车辆用	10	T3		0	100	17	17	千克	6	----Of the vehicles of headingNo. 87.05
8708.5089	----其他	10			0	100	17	17	千克	60	----Other
	-车轮及其零件、附件:										-Road wheels and parts and accessories thereof:
8708.7010	---子目87.01所列车辆用	6	T3		0	14	17	17	千克	6	---Of the vehicles of headingNo. 87.01
8708.7020	---子目8702.1091及8702.9010所列车辆用	10	T3		0	70	17	17	千克	6	---Of the vehicles of subheading No. 8702.1091 or 8702.9010
8708.7030	---子目8704.1030及8704.1090所列车辆用	6	T3		0	11	17	17	千克	6	---Of the vehicles of subheadingNos. 8704.1030 or 8704.1090

税则号列 Tariff Item.	货品名称	最惠国(%) MFN	协定(%)CT 东盟 CA	中巴 CP	中智 CC	普通 Gen	增值税率 VAT	出口退税 ED	计量单位 Unit	监管条件 SC	Article Description
8708. 7040	---子目 8704. 2100、8704. 2230、8704. 3100 及 8704. 3230 所列车辆用	10	T3		0	45	17	17	千克	6	---Of the vehicles of subheadingNo. 8704. 2100 , 8704. 2230, 8704. 3100 or 8704. 3230
8708. 7050	---子目 8704. 2240、8704. 2300 及 8704. 3240 所列车辆用	10	T3		0	30	17	17	千克	6	---Of the vehicles of subheadingNo. 8704. 2240, 8704. 2300 orNo. 8704. 3240
8708. 7060	---税目 87. 05 所列车辆用	10	T3		0	100	17	17	千克	6	---Of the vehicles of headingNo. 87. 05
8708. 7090	---其他	10			0	100	17	17	千克	6	---Other
	-悬挂系统及其零件(包括减振器):										-Suspension shock-absorbers:
8708. 8010	---税目 87. 03 所列车辆用	10		9	0	100	17	17	千克	6	---Of the vehicles of headingNo. 87. 03
8708. 8090	---其他	10		9	0	100	17	17	千克	6	---Other
	-其他零件、附件:										-Other parts and accessories:
8708. 9100	--散热器及其零件	10	T3		0	100	17	17	个/千克	6	--Radiators
8708. 9200	--消声器(消音器)排气管及零件	10	T3		0	100	17	17	千克	6	--Silencers and exhaust pipes
	--离合器及其零件:										--Clutches and parts thereof:
8708. 9310	---税目 87. 01 所列车辆用	6	T3		0	14	17	17	千克	6	---Of the vehicles of headingNo. 87. 01
8708. 9320	---子目 8702. 1091 及 8702. 9010 所列车辆用	10	T3		0	70	17	17	千克	6	---Of the vehicles of subheadingNo. 8702. 1091 or 8702. 9010
8708. 9330	---子目 8704. 1030 及 8704. 1090 所列车辆用	6	T3		0	11	17	17	千克	6	---Of the vehicles of subheading No. 8704. 1030 or 8704. 1090
8708. 9340	---子目 8704. 2100、8704. 2230、8704. 3100 及 8704. 3230 所列车辆用	10	T3		0	45	17	17	千克	6	---Of the vehicles of subheading No. 8704. 2100 , 8704. 2230, 8704. 3100 or8704. 3230
8708. 9350	---子目 8704. 2240、8704. 2300 及 8704. 3240 所列车辆用	10	T3		0	30	17	17	千克	6	---Of the vehicles of subheadingNo. 8704. 2240, 8704. 2300 or 8704. 3240
8708. 9360	---税目 87. 05 所列车辆用	10	T3		0	100	17	17	千克	6	---Of the vehicles of headingNo. 87. 05
8708. 9390	---其他	10			0	100	17	17	千克	6	---Other
	--转向盘、转向柱及转向器及其零件:										--Steering wheels, steering columns and steering boxes:
8708. 9410	---税目 87. 01 所列车辆用	6	T3		0	14	17	17	千克	6	---Of the vehicles of headingNo. 87. 01
8708. 9420	---子目 8702. 1091 及 8702. 9010 所列车辆用	10	T3		0	70	17	17	千克		---Of the vehicles of subheading No. 8702. 1091 or 8702. 9010
8708. 9420 01	座位≥30 的客车用转向器及其零件	10				70	17	17	千克	6	Steering boxes for the buses with 30 seats or more
8708. 9420 90	大型客车用转向盘、转向柱及其零件	10				70	17	17	千克	6	Steering wheels, steering columns of the vehicles of subheading No. 87021091 or 87029010
8708. 9430	---子目 8704. 1030 及 8704. 1090 所列车辆用	6	T3		0	11	17	17	千克	6	---Of the vehicles of subheadingNo. 8704. 1030 or 8704. 1090
8708. 9440	---子目 8704. 2100、8704. 2230、8704. 3100 及 8704. 3230 所列车辆用	10	T3		0	45	17	17	千克	6	---Of the vehicles of subheadingNo. 8704. 2100, 8704. 2230, 8704. 3100 or 8704. 3230
8708. 9450	---税号 8704. 2240、8704. 2300 及 8708. 3240 所列车辆用	10	T3		0	30	17	17	千克		---Of the vehicles of subheadingNo. 8704. 2240, 8704. 2300 or 8704. 3240
8708. 9450 01	总重≥14 吨柴油型货车转向器的零件	10				30	17	17	千克	6	Redirector components of diesel oil trucks whose weight≥14 tons

税则号列 Tariff Item.	货品名称	最惠国(%) MFN	协定(%) CT 东盟 CA	中巴 CP	中智 CC	普通 Gen	增值税率 VAT	出口退税 ED	计量单位 Unit	监管条件 SC	Article Description
8708.9450 90	其他重型货车用转向盘转、向柱,转向器及其零件(指编号87042240、87042300及87043240所列车辆用)	10				30	17	17	千克	6	Steering wheels, steering columns and steering boxes of the vehicles of subheading 87042240, 87042300 or 87043240
8708.9460	---税目87.05所列车辆用转向器	10	T3		0	100	17	17	千克	6	---Of the vehicles of headingNo. 87.05
8708.9490	---其他	10			0	100	17	17	千克	60	---Other
8708.9500	--带充气系统的安全气囊及其零件	10		9	0	100	17	17	千克	6	--The Safety Air-bag with air-charging system and its accessories
	--其他:										--Other:
8708.9910	---税目87.01所列车辆用	6	T3		0	14	17	17	千克	6	---Of the vehicles of headingNo. 87.01
	---税目8702.1091及8702.9010所列车辆用:										---Of the vehicles of subheadingNo. 8702.1091 or 8702.9010:
8708.9921	----车架	25	T3		0	70	17	17	千克	6	----Frames
8708.9929	----其他	25	T3		0	70	17	17	千克	6	----Other
	---子目8704.1030及8704.1090所列车辆用:										---Of the vehicles of subheadingNo. 8704.1030 or 8704.1090:
8708.9931	----车架	6	T3		0	11	17	17	千克	6	----Frames
8708.9939	----其他	6	T3		0	11	17	17	千克	6	----Other
	---子目8704.2100、8704.2230、8704.3100及8704.3230所列车辆用:										---Of the vehicles of subheading No. 8704.2100, 8704.2230, 8704.3100 or 8704.3230:
8708.9941	----车架	25	T3		0	45	17	17	千克	6	----Frames
8708.9949	----其他	25	T3		0	45	17	17	千克	6	----Other
	---子目8704.2240、8704.2300及8704.3240所列车辆用:										---Of the vehicles of subheading No. 8704.2240, 8704.2300 or 8704.3240:
8708.9951	----车架	10	T3		0	30	17	17	千克	6	----Frames
8708.9959	----其他	10	T3		0	30	17	17	千克	6	----Other
8708.9960	---税目87.05所列车辆用	15	T3		0	100	17	17	千克	6	---Of the vehicles of heading No. 87.05
	---其他:										---Other:
8708.9991	----车架	10			0	100	17	17	千克	60	----Frames
8708.9992	----传动轴	10			0	100	17	17	千克	6	----Shafts
8708.9999	----其他	10			0	100	17	17	千克		----Other
8708.9999 01	混合动力汽车动力传动装置(由发电机、电动机和动力分配装置组成,编号8701至8704所列车辆用)	10				100	17	17	千克	6	Vehicles of the engine mixed with natural gas and gasoline, transmission device (made of engine and allocation assemble device for engine and power, of the vehicles of subheading from 8701 to 8704)
8708.9999 90	机动车辆用未列名零件附件(编号8701至8704所列车辆用)	10				100	17	17	千克	6	Parts and accessories of motor vehicles, not elsewhere specified or included (of the vehicles of subheading from 8701 to 8704)

税则号列 Tariff Item.	货品名称	最惠国(%) MFN	协定(%) CT			普通 Gen	增值税率 VAT	出口退税 ED	计量单位 Unit	监管条件 SC	Article Description
			东盟 CA	中巴 CP	中智 CC						
87.09	**短距离运输货物的机动车辆,未装有提升或搬运设备,用于工厂、仓库、码头或机场;火车站台上用的牵引车;上述车辆的零件:**										**Works trucks, self-propelled, not fitted with lifting or handling equipment, of the type used in factories, warehouses, dock areas or airports for short distance transport of goods; tractors of the type used on railway station platforms; parts of the foregoing vehicles:**
	-车辆:										-Vehicles:
	--电动的:										--Electrical:
8709.1110	---牵引车	10	8		0	30	17	13	辆	6	---Tractors
8709.1190	---其他	10	8		0	30	17	13	辆	6	---Other
	--其他:										--Other:
8709.1910	---牵引车	10.5	T3		0	30	17	13	辆	6	---Tractors
8709.1990	---其他	10.5	T3		0	30	17	13	辆	6	---Other
8709.9000	-零件	8.4	5		0	17	17	13	千克	6	-Parts
87.10	**坦克及其他机动装甲战斗车辆,不论是否装有武器;上述车辆的零件:**										**Tanks and other armoured fighting vehicles, motorized, whether or not fitted with weapons, and parts of such vehicles:**
8710.0010	---整车	15	8		0	100	17		辆	6	---Assembled
8710.0090	---零件	15	8		0	100	17		千克	6	---Parts and accessories
87.11	**摩托车(包括机器脚踏两用车)及装有辅助发动机的脚踏车,不论有无边车;边车:**										**Motorcycles (including mopeds) and cycles fitted with an auxiliary motor, with or without side-cars; side-cars:**
8711.1000	-装有往复式活塞内燃发动机,气缸容量(排气量)不超过50毫升	45	T3		0	150	17	13	辆		-With reciprocating internal combustion piston engine of a cylinder capacity not exceeding 50 cc
8711.1000 10	微马力摩托车及脚踏两用车(装有往复式活塞发动机,微马力指排气量=50cc)	45				150	17	13	辆	y4xAB6	Motorcycles (including mopeds) with reciprocating internal combustion piston engine, cylinder capacity = 50cc
8711.1000 90	微马力摩托车及脚踏两用车(装有往复式活塞发动机,微马力指排气量<50cc)	45				150	17	13	辆	6AB	Motorcycles (including mopeds) with reciprocating internal combustion piston engine cylinder capacity <50cc
	-装有往复式活塞内燃发动机,气缸容量(排气量)超过50毫升,但不超过250毫升:										-With reciprocating internal combustion piston engine of a cylinder capacity exceeding 50 cc but not exceeding 250cc:
8711.2010	---气缸容量超过50毫升,但不超过100毫升	45	T3		0	150	17	13	辆	y4xAB6	---Of a cylinder capacity exceeding 50cc but not exceeding 100cc
8711.2020	---气缸容量超过100毫升,但不超过125毫升	45	T3		0	150	17	13	辆	y4xAB6	---Of a cylinder capacity exceeding 100cc but not exceeding 125cc
8711.2030	---气缸容量超过125毫升,但不超过150毫升	45	T3		0	150	17	13	辆	y4xAB6	---Of a cylinder capacity exceeding 125cc but not exceeding 150cc
8711.2040	---气缸容量超过150毫升,但不超过200毫升	45	T3		0	150	17	13	辆	y4xAB6	---Of a cylinder capacity exceeding 150cc but not exceeding 200cc
8711.2050	---气缸容量超过200毫升,但不超过250毫升	45	T3		0	150	17	13	辆	y4xAB6	---Of a cylinder capacity exceeding 200cc but not exceeding 250cc

税则号列 Tariff Item.	货品名称	最惠国(%) MFN	协定(%) 东盟 CA	协定(%) 中巴 CP	CT 中智 CC	普通 Gen	增值税率 VAT	出口退税 ED	计量单位 Unit	监管条件 SC	Article Description
	-装有往复式活塞内燃发动机，气缸容量（排气量）超过250毫升，但不超过500毫升：										-With reciprocating internal combustion piston engine of a cylinder capacity exceeding 250cc but not exceeding 500cc:
8711.3010	---气缸容量超过250毫升，但不超过400毫升	45	T3	32.8	0	150	17	13	辆	46ABxy	---Of a cylinder capacity exceeding 250cc but not exceeding 400cc
8711.3020	---气缸容量超过400毫升，但不超过500毫升	45	T3	32.8	0	150	17	13	辆	46ABxy	---Of a cylinder capacity exceeding 400cc but not exceeding 500cc
8711.4000	-装有往复式活塞内燃发动机，气缸容量（排气量）超过500毫升，但不超过800毫升	40	T3		0	150	17	13	辆	46ABxy	-With reciprocating internal combustion piston engine of a cylinder capacity exceeding 500 cc but not exceeding 800 cc
8711.5000	-装有往复式活塞内燃发动机，气缸容量（排气量）超过800毫升	30	T3		0	150	17	13	辆	46ABxy	-With reciprocating internal combustion piston engine of a cylinder capacity exceeding 800 cc
	-其他：										-Other:
8711.9010	---电动及电动助力的	45	T3		0	150	17	13	辆		---Electric and electric auxiliary
8711.9010 10	电动自行车	45				150	17	13	辆	AB6	Motor - driven bicycles
8711.9010 90	其他电动及电动助力的摩托车及边车（包括机器脚踏两用车；脚踏车）	45				150	17	13	辆	AB6	Electric and electricity - aided with motor and side - cars
8711.9090	---其他	45	T3		0	150	17	13	辆		---Other
8711.9090 01	排汽量≤250毫升摩拖车及脚踏两用车	45				150	17	13	辆	AB6	Motor and mopedes, cylinder capacity ≤250cc
8711.9090 02	排气量>250毫升摩托车及脚踏两用车	45				150	17	13	辆	AB6	Motor and mopedes, cylinder capacity >250cc
8711.9090 09	其他无法区分排汽量的摩托车及脚踏两用车	45				150	17	13	辆	AB6	Other double - use vehicles of automobiles and bicycles that cannot tell piston displacements
8711.9090 90	装有其他辅助发动机的脚踏车及边车	45				150	17	13	辆	AB6	Bicycles and sidecar with other donkey engine
87.12	**自行车及其他非机动脚踏车（包括运货三轮脚踏车）：**										**Bicycles and other cycles (including delivery tricycles), not motorized:**
8712.0020	---竞赛型自行车	13	T3	9.1	0	130	17	13	辆	B4x6	---Racing bicycle
8712.0030	---山地自行车	13	T3	9.1	0	130	17	13	辆	B4x6	---Mountain bicycle
	---越野自行车：										---Cross-country bicycles:
8712.0041	----16、18、20英寸	13	T3	9.1	0	130	17	13	辆	B4x6	----16inchs, 18inchs or 20inchs
8712.0049	----其他	13	T3	9.1	0	130	17	13	辆	B4x6	----Other
	---其他自行车：										---Other cycles:
8712.0081	----16英寸及以下	13	T3	9.1	0	130	17	13	辆		----Not larger than 16inchs
8712.0081 10	12~16英寸的未列名自行车	13				130	17	13	辆	B4x6	Cycles, 12inchs - 16inchs, not elsewhere specified or included
8712.0081 90	11英寸及以下的未列名自行车	13				130	17	13	辆	B6	Cycles, 11inchs or less, not elsewhere specified or included
8712.0089	----其他	13	T3	9.1	0	130	17	13	辆	B4x6	----Other
8712.0090	---其他	23	T3	16.1	0	130	17	13	辆	B6	---Other
87.13	**残疾人用车，不论是否机动或其他机械驱动：**										**Carriages for disabled persons, whether or not motorised or otherwise mechanically propelled:**
8713.1000	-非机械驱动	6	5		0	20	0	13	辆	6	-Not mechanically propelled

税则号列 Tariff Item.	货品名称	最惠国(%) MFN	协定(%)CT 东盟 CA	中巴 CP	中智 CC	普通 Gen	增值税率 VAT	出口退税 ED	计量单位 Unit	监管条件 SC	Article Description
8713.9000	-其他	4			0	20	0	13	辆	6	-Other
87.14	**零件、附件，税目 87.11 至 87.13 所列车辆用：**										**Parts and accessories of vehicles of headingsNos. 87.11 to 87.13:**
	-摩托车（包括机器脚踏两用车）用：										-Of motorcycles (including mopeds):
8714.1100	--鞍座	30	T3		0	100	17	13	个/千克	6	--Saddles
8714.1900	--其他	30	T3		0	100	17	13	千克		--Other
8714.1900 10	摩托车架	30				100	17	13	千克	46xy	Frame of motorcycles
8714.1900 90	摩托车其他零件，附件（包括机动脚踏两用车的零件、附件）	30				100	17	13	千克	6	Motorcycles and parts and accessories there of (includins mopeds´ parts and accessones there of)
8714.2000	-残疾人车辆用	5			0	17	17	13	千克	6	-Of carriages for disabled persons
	-其他：										-Other:
8714.9100	--车架、轮叉及其零件	12	T3		0	80	17	13	千克	B6	--Frames and forks, and parts thereof
8714.9200	--轮圈及辐条	12	T3		0	80	17	13	千克	B6	--Wheel rims and spokes
	--轮毂（倒轮制动毂及毂闸除外）；飞轮、链轮：										--Hubs, other than coaster braking hubs and hub brakes, and free-wheel, sprocket wheels:
8714.9310	---车毂	12	T3		0	80	17	13	千克	B6	---Hubs
8714.9320	---飞轮	12	T3		0	80	17	13	千克	B6	---Free-wheels
8714.9390	---其他	12	T3		0	80	17	13	千克	B6	---Other
8714.9400	--制动器（包括倒轮制动毂及毂闸）及其零件	12	T3		0	80	17	13	千克	B6	--Brakes, including coaster braking hubs and hub brakes, and parts thereof
8714.9500	--鞍座	12	T3		0	80	17	13	个	B6	--Saddles
	--脚蹬、曲柄链轮及其零件：										--Pedals and crank-gear, and parts thereof:
8714.9610	---脚蹬及其零件	12	T3		0	80	17	13	千克	B6	---Pedals and parts thereof
8714.9620	---曲柄链轮及其零件	12	T3		0	80	17	13	千克	B6	---Crank-gear and parts thereof
8714.9900	--其他	12	T3	8.4	0	80	17	13	千克	B6	--Other
87.15	**婴孩车及其零件：**										**Baby carriages and parts thereof:**
8715.0000	婴孩车及其零件	20	12		0	80	17	13	千克	6	Baby carriages and parts thereof
87.16	**挂车及半挂车或其他非机械驱动车辆及其零件：**										**Trailers and semi-trailers; other vehicles, not mechanically propelled; parts thereof:**
8716.1000	-供居住或野营用厢式挂车及半挂车	10	T3		0	35	17	17	辆	6	-Trailers and semi-trailers of the caravan type, for housing or camping
8716.2000	-农用自装或自卸式挂车及半挂车	10	5		0	35	17	17	辆	6	-Self-loading or self-unloading trailers and semi-trailers for agricultural purposes
	-其他货运挂车及半挂车：										-Other trailers and semi-trailers for the transport of goods:
	--罐式挂车及半挂车：										--Tanker trailers and tanker semi-trailers:
8716.3110	---油罐挂车及半挂车	10	T3		0	20	17	17	辆	6A	---Oil tanker trailers and semi-trailers
8716.3190	---其他	10	5		0	35	17	17	辆	6A	---Other
	--其他：										--Other:
8716.3910	---货柜挂车及半挂车	10	5		0	20	17	17	辆	6A	---Van trailers and semi-trailers
8716.3990	---其他	10	5		0	35	17	17	辆	6A	---Other
8716.4000	-其他挂车及半挂车	10	5		0	35	17	17	辆	6A	-Other trailers and semi-trailers
8716.8000	-其他车辆	10	T3		0	80	17	13	辆	6	-Other vehicles
8716.9000	-零件	10	T3		0	35	17	13	千克	6	-Parts

第八十八章
航空器、航天器及其零件

Chapter 88
Aircraft, spacecraft, and parts thereof

子目注释：

子目 8802.11 至 8802.40 所称"空载重量"，是指航空器在正常飞行状态下，除去机组人员、燃料及非永久性安装设备后的重量。

Subheading Note:

For the purposes of subheadings Nos. 8802.11 toNos. 8802.40, the expression "unladen weight" means the weight of the machine in normal flying order, excluding the weight of the crew and of fuel and equipment other than permanently fitted items of equipment.

税则号列 Tariff Item.	货品名称	最惠国(%) MFN	协定(%)CT 东盟 CA	中巴 CP	中智 CC	普通 Gen	增值税率 VAT	出口退税 ED	计量单位 Unit	监管条件 SC	Article Description
88.01	**气球及飞艇；滑翔机、悬挂滑翔机及其他无动力航空器：**										**Balloons and dirigibles; gliders, hang gliders and other non-powered aircraft:**
8801.0010	-滑翔机、及悬挂滑翔机：	3			0	11	17	17	架		-Cliders and hang gliders
8801.0090	---其他	3			0	11	17	17	架		---Other
88.02	**其他航空器（例如，直升机、飞机）；航天器（包括卫星）及其运载工具、亚轨道运载工具：**										**Other aircraft (for example, helicopters, aeroplanes); spacecraft (including satellites) and suborbital and spacecraft launch vehicles:**
	-直升机：										-Helicopters:
8802.1100	--空载重量不超过2吨	2			0	11	17	17	架	O	--Of an unladen weight not exceeding 2 tons
	--空载重量超过2吨：										--Of an unladen weight exceeding 2 tons:
8802.1210	---空载重量超过2吨，但不超过7吨	2			0	11	17	17	架	O	---Of an unladen weight exceeding 2 tons but not exceeding 7 tons
8802.1220	---空载重量超过7吨	2			0	11	17	17	架		---Of an unladen weight exceeding 7 tons
8802.2000	-飞机及其他航空器，空载重量不超过2吨	5			4	11	17	17	架		-Aeroplanes and other aircraft, of an unladen weight not exceeding 2 tons
8802.2000 10	无人驾驶航空飞行器（空载重量小于2吨）	5				11	17	17	架	3O	pilotless aircraft (deadweight not exceeding 2 tons)
8802.2000 90	其他小型飞机及其他航空器（小型指空载重量不超过2吨的）	5				11	17	17	架	O	Other small planes and other aircrafts (deadweight not exceeding 2 tons)
8802.3000	-飞机及其他航空器，空载重量超过2吨，但不超过15吨	4			3.2	11	17	17	架	O	-Aeroplanes and other aircraft, of an unladen weight exceeding 2 tons but not exceeding 15 tons
	-飞机及其他航空器，空载重量超过15吨：										-Aeroplanes and other aircraft, of an unladen weight exceeding 15 tons:
8802.4010	---空载重量超过15吨，但不超过45吨	5		3.5	0	11	17	17	架		---Of an unladen weight exceeding 15 tons but not exceeding 45 tons
8802.4010 01	25吨≤空载重量≤45吨客运飞机	5				11	17	17	架	O	Aeroplanes, 25tons < unladen weight ≤45tons
8802.4010 90	15吨<空载重量≤45吨其他大型飞机及其他航空器（25吨≤空载重量≤45吨空运飞机除外）	5				11	17	17	架	O	Aeroplanes and other aircraft, 15tons < unladen weight≤45tons
8802.4020	---空载重量超过45吨	1		7	0	11	17	17	架	O	---Of an unladen weight exceeding 45 tons
8802.6000	-航天器（包括卫星）及其运载工具、亚轨道运载工具	2			0	11	17	17	架		-Spacecraft (including satellites) and suborbital and spacecraft launch vehicles

税则号列 Tariff Item.	货品名称	最惠国(%) MFN	协定(%) 东盟 CA	协定(%) 中巴 CP	协定(%) 中智 CC	普通 Gen	增值税率 VAT	出口退税 ED	计量单位 Unit	监管条件 SC	Article Description
88.03	**税目 88.01 或 88.02 所列货品的零件：**										**Parts of goods of heading No. 88.01 or 88.02：**
8803.1000	-推进器、水平旋翼及其零件	1			0	11	17	17	千克		-Propellers and rotors and parts thereof
8803.2000	-起落架及其零件	1			0	11	17	17	千克		-Under-carriages and parts thereof
8803.3000	-飞机及直升机的其他零件	1			0	11	17	17	千克		-Other parts of aeroplanes or helicopters
8803.9000	-其他	0				11	17	17	千克		-Other
8803.9000 10	敏感物项管制的火箭及其零部件	0				11	17	17	千克	3	Missile and parts and accessories
8803.9000 90	其他未列名的航空器、航天器零件(指编号 8801 或 8802 所列货品用的)	0				11	17	17	千克		Other aircraft，sfacecraft，not specified or included dsewhere(parts of goods of heading 88.01 or 88.02)
88.04	**降落伞(包括可操纵降落伞及滑翔伞)、旋翼降落伞及其零件、附件：**										**Parachutes (including dirigible parachutes and paragliders) and rotochutes; parts thereof and accessories thereto：**
8804.0000	降落伞(包括可操纵降落伞及滑翔伞)、旋翼降落伞及其零件、附件	2			0	11	17	17	千克		Parachutes (including dirigible parachutes and paragliders) and rotochutes; parts thereof and accessories thereto
88.05	**航空器的发射装置、甲板停机装置或类似装置和地面飞行训练器及其零件：**										**Aircraft launching gear; deck-arrestor or similar gear; ground flying trainers; parts of the foregoing articles：**
8805.1000	-航空器的发射装置及其零件;甲板停机装置或类似装置及其零件	1.5			0	11	17	17	千克		-Aircraft launching gear and parts thereof; deck-arrestor or similar gear and parts thereof
	-地面飞行训练器及其零件：										-Ground flying trainers and parts thereof：
8805.2100	--空战模拟器及其零件	1.5			0	11	17	17	千克		--Air combat simulators and parts thereof
8805.2900	--其他	1.5			0	11	17	17	千克	0	--Other

第八十九章 船舶及浮动结构体

Chapter 89 Ships, boats and floating structures

注释：

已装配、未装配或已拆卸的船体、未完工或不完整的船舶以及未装配或已拆卸的完整船舶，如果不具有某种船舶的基本特征，应归入税目 89.06。

Note:

A hull, an unfinished or incomplete vessel, assembled, unassembled or disassembled, or a complete vessel unassembled or disassembled, is to be classified in heading No. 89.06 if it does not have the essential character of a vessel of a particular kind.

税则号列 Tariff Item.	货品名称	最惠国(%) MFN	协定(%)CT 东盟 CA	中巴 CP	中智 CC	普通 Gen	增值税率 VAT	出口退税 ED	计量单位 Unit	监管条件 SC	Article Description
89.01	**巡航船、游览船、渡船、货船、驳船及类似的客运或货运船舶：**										**Cruise ships, excursion boats, ferry-boats, cargo ships, barges and similar vessels for the transport of persons or goods:**
	-巡航船、游览船及主要用于客运的类似船舶；各式渡船：										-Cruise ships, excursion boats and similar vessels principally designed for the transport of persons; ferry-boats of all kinds:
8901.1010	---机动船舶	5			4	14	17	17	艘		---Motor vessels
8901.1010 10	高速客船(包括主要用于客运的类似船舶)	5				14	17	17	艘	O	High-speed passenger vessels and similar vessels principally designed for the transport of persons
8901.1010 90	其他机动巡航船游览船及各式渡船(包括主要用于客运的类似船舶)	5				14	17	17	艘	O	Cruise ships, excursion boats and similar vessels principally designed for the transport of persons, ferryboats of all kinds motorized
8901.1090	---非机动船舶	8	5		6.4	30	17	17	艘		---Other
	-液货船：										-Tankers:
	---成品油船：										---Finished oil tankers:
8901.2011	----载重量不超过10万吨	9			0	14	17	17	艘	O	----Loading not exceeding 100000t
8901.2012	----载重量超过10万吨，但不超过30万吨	9			0	14	17	17	艘		----Loading exceeding 100000t, but not exceeding 300000t
8901.2013	----载重量超过30万吨	6			0	14	17	17	艘		----Loading exceeding 300000t
	---原油船：										---Crude oil tankers
8901.2021	----载重量不超过15万吨	9			0	14	17	17	艘	O	----Loading not exceeding 150000t
8901.2022	----载重量超过15万吨，但不超过30万吨	9			0	14	17	17	艘		----Loading exceeding 150000t, but not exceeding 300000t
8901.2023	----载重量超过30万吨	6			0	14	17	17	艘		----Loading exceeding 300000t
	---液化石油气船：										---Liquified petroleum gas carriers:
8901.2031	----容积在20000立方米及以下	9			0	14	17	17	艘	O	----Volume with 20000m^3 or less
8901.2032	----容积在20000立方米以上	6			0	14	17	17	艘		----Volume more than 20000m^3
	---液化天然气船：										---Liquified natural gas carriers:
8901.2041	----容积在20000立方米及以下	9			0	14	17	17	艘		----Volume with 20000m^3 or less
8901.2042	----容积在20000立方米以上	6			0	14	17	17	艘		----Volume more than 20000m^3
8901.2090	---其他	9			0	14	17	17	艘	O	---Other

税则号列 Tariff Item.	货品名称	最惠国(%) MFN	协定(%)CT			普通 Gen	增值税率 VAT	出口退税 ED	计量单位 Unit	监管条件 SC	Article Description
			东盟 CA	中巴 CP	中智 CC						
8901.3000	-冷藏船,但子目 8901.20 的船舶除外	9	5		0	14	17	17	艘		-Refrigerated vessels, other than those of subheading 8901.20
	-其他货运船舶及其他客货兼运船舶:										-Other vessels for the transport of goods and other vessels for the transport of both persons and goods:
	---机动集装箱船:										---Motor container vessels:
8901.9021	----可载标准集装箱在 6000 箱及以下	9			7.2	14	17	17	艘	ABO	----Capable loading standard containers with 6000 or less
8901.9022	----可载标准集装箱在 6000 箱以上	6			4.8	14	17	17	艘	AB	----Capable loading standard containers more than 6000
	---机动滚装船:										---Motor Ro-Ro carriers:
8901.9031	----载重量在 2 万吨及以下	9			7.2	14	17	17	艘	ABO	----Loading with 2000t or less
8901.9032	----载重量在 2 万吨以上的	6			4.8	14	17	17	艘	AB	----Loading more than 2000t
	---机动散货船:										---Motor bulk carriers:
8901.9041	----载重量不超过 15 万吨	9			7.2	14	17	17	艘	ABO	----Loading not exceeding 150000t
8901.9042	----载重量超过 15 万吨,但不超过 30 万吨	9			7.2	14	17	17	艘	AB	----Loading exceeding 150000t, not exceeding 300000t
8901.9043	----载重量超过 30 万吨	9			7.2	14	17	17	艘	AB	----Loading exceeding 300000t
8901.9050	---机动多用途船	9			7.2	14	17	17	艘	O	---Multi-purposes motor vessels
8901.9080	---其他机动船舶	9	5		7.2	14	17	17	艘	ABO	---Other motor vessels
8901.9090	---非机动船舶	8	5		6.4	30	17	13	艘	AOB	---Other non-motor vessels
89.02	**捕鱼船;加工船及其他加工保藏鱼类产品的船舶:**										**Fishing vessels; factory ships and other vessels for processing or preserving fishery products:**
8902.0010	---机动船舶	7	5		5.6	14	17	17	艘	O	---Motor vessels
8902.0090	---非机动船舶	8	5		6.4	30	17	17	艘		---Other
89.03	**娱乐或运动用快艇及其他船舶;划艇及轻舟:**										**Yachts and other vessels for pleasure or sports; rowing boats and canoes:**
8903.1000	-充气的	10	5		0	30	17	13	艘		-Inflatable
	-其他:										-Other:
8903.9100	--帆船,不论是否装有辅助发动机	8	5		6.4	30	17	13	艘		--Sailboats, with or without auxiliary motor
8903.9100 01	8 米<长度<90 米的机动帆船(不论是否装有辅助发动机)	8				30	17	13	艘		(with or without auxiliary motor)
8903.9100 90	其他帆船(不论是否装有辅助发动机)	8				30	17	13	艘		Other sailboats(with or without auxiliary motor)
8903.9200	--汽艇,但装有舷外发动机的除外	10.5	8		8.4	30	17	13	艘		--Motorboats, other than outboard motorboats
8903.9200 01	8 米<长度<90 米的汽艇(装有舷外发动机的除外)	10.5				30	17	13	艘		(Other than outboard motorboats)
8903.9200 90	其他汽艇(装有舷外发动机的除外)	10.5				30	17	13	艘		Other motorboats (other than outboard motorboats)
8903.9900	--其他	10	5		8	30	17	13	艘		--Other
8903.9900 01	8 米<长度<90 米的娱乐或运动用其他机动船舶或快艇(包括划艇及轻舟)	10				30	17	13	艘		Yachts and other vessels for pleasure or sports, 8m < Meter < 90m (including rowing boats and canoes)

税则号列 Tariff Item.	货品名称	最惠国(%) MFN	协定(%) CT 东盟 CA	协定(%) CT 中巴 CP	协定(%) CT 中智 CC	普通 Gen	增值税率 VAT	出口退税 ED	计量单位 Unit	监管条件 SC	Article Description
8903.9900 90	娱乐或运动用其他船舶或快艇(包括划艇及轻舟)	10				30	17	13	艘		Other yachts and other vessels for pleasure or sports (including rowing boats and canoes)
89.04	**拖轮及顶推船:**										**Tugs and pusher craft:**
8904.0000	拖轮及顶推船	9	5		7.2	14	17	17	艘	O	Tugs and pusher craft
89.05	**灯船、消防船、挖泥船、起重船及其他不以航行为主要功能的船舶;浮船坞;浮动或潜水式钻探或生产平台:**										**Light-vessels, fire-floats, dredgers, floating cranes, and other vessels the navigability of which is subsidiary to their main function; floating docks; floating or submersible drilling or production platforms:**
8905.1000	-挖泥船	3			0	11	17	17	艘	O	-Dredgers
8905.2000	-浮动或潜水式钻探或生产平台	6	5		0	11	17	17	座	O	-Floating or submersible drilling or production platforms
	-其他:										-Other:
8905.9010	---浮船坞	8			6.4	30	17	17	个	O	---Floating docks
8905.9090	---其他	3			1.8	11	17	17	个	O	---Other
89.06	**其他船舶,包括军舰及救生船,但划艇除外:**										**Other vessels, including warships and lifeboats other than rowing boats:**
8906.1000	-军舰	5			0	14	17	17	艘		-Warships
	-其他:										-Other:
8906.9010	---机动船舶	5			4	14	17	17	艘		---Motor vessels
8906.9090	---非机动船舶	8	5		6.4	30	17	11	艘		---Other
89.07	**其他浮动结构体(例如,筏、柜、潜水箱、浮码头、浮筒及航标):**										**Other floating structures (for example, rafts, tanks, coffer-dams, landing-stages, buoys and beacons):**
8907.1000	-充气筏	8	5		0	30	17	13	艘		-Inflatable rafts
8907.9000	-其他	8	5		6.4	30	17	13	个		-Other
8907.9000 10	含植物性材料的浮动结构体(例如,筏、柜、潜水箱、浮筒及航标)	8				30	17	13	个	AB	Floating structures (for example, rafts, tanks, coffer-dams, buoys and beacons) with parts of vegetable materials
8907.9000 90	其他浮动结构体(例如,筏、柜、潜水箱、浮筒及航标)	8				30	17	13	个		Other floating structures (for example, rafts, tanks, coffer-dams, buoys and beacons)
89.08	**供拆卸的船舶及其他浮动结构体:**										**Vessels and other floating structures for breaking up:**
8908.0000	供拆卸的船舶及其他浮动结构体	3			0	11	17	13	艘/千克	APB	Vessels and other floating structures for breaking up

第十八类
光学、照相、电影、计量、检验、医疗或外科用仪器及设备、精密仪器及设备；钟表；乐器；上述物品的零件、附件

第九十章
光学、照相、电影、计量、检验、医疗或外科用仪器及设备、精密仪器及设备；上述物品的零件、附件

注释：

一、本章不包括：

（一）机器、设备或其他专门技术用途的硫化橡胶（硬质橡胶除外）制品（税目 40.16）、皮革或再生皮革制品（税目 42.05）或纺织材料制品（税目 59.11）；

（二）纺织材料制的承托带及其他承托物品，其承托器官的作用仅依靠自身的弹性（例如，孕妇用的承托带，用于胸部、腹部、关节或肌肉的承托绷带）（第十一类）；

（三）税目 69.03 的耐火材料制品；税目 69.09 的实验室、化学或其他专门技术用途的陶瓷器；

（四）税目 70.09 的未经光学加工的玻璃镜及税目 83.06 或第七十一章的非光学元件的贱金属或贵金属制的镜子；

（五）税目 70.07、70.08、70.11、70.14、70.15 或 70.17 的货品；

（六）第十五类注释二所规定的贱金属制通用零件（第十五类）或塑料制的类似品（第三十九章）；

（七）税目 84.13 的装有计量装置的泵；计数和检验用的衡器或单独进口或出口的天平砝码（税目 84.23）；升降、起重及搬运机械（税目 84.25 至 84.28）；纸张或纸板的各

SECTION XVIII
OPTICAL, PHOTOGRAPHIC, CINEMATOGRAPHIC, MEASURING, CHECKING, PRECISION, MEDICAL OR SURGICAL INSTRUMENTS AND APPARATUS; CLOCKS AND WATCHES; MUSICAL INSTRUMENTS; PARTS AND ACCESSORIES THEREOF

Chapter 90
Optical, photographic, cinematographic, measuring, checking, precision, medical or surgical instruments and apparatus; parts and accessories thereof

Notes:

1. This Chapter does not cover:

(a) Articles of a kind used in machines, appliances or for other technical uses, of vulcanized rubber other than hard rubber (heading No. 40.16), of leather or of composition leather (heading No. 42.05) or of textile material (heading No. 59.11);

(b) Supporting belts or other support articles of textile material, whose intended effect on the organ to be supported or held derives solely from their elasticity (for example, maternity belts, thoracic support bandages, abdominal support bandages, supports for joints or muscles) (Section XI);

(c) Refractory goods of heading No. 69.03; ceramic wares for laboratory, chemical or other technical uses, of heading No. 69.09;

(d) Glass mirrors, not optically worked, of heading No. 70.09, or mirrors of base metal or of precious metal, not being optical elements (heading No. 83.06 or Chapter 71);

(e) Goods of heading No. 70.07, 70.08, 70.11, 70.14, 70.15 or 70.17;

(f) Parts of general use, as defined in Note 2 to Section XV, of base metal (Section XV) or similar goods of plastics (Chapter 39);

(g) Pumps incorporating measuring devices, of heading No. 84.13; weight-operated counting or checking machinery, or separately presented weights for balances (heading No. 84.23); lifting or handling machinery (headings No. 84.25 to 84.28); paper or pa-

种切割机器(税目84.41);税目84.66的用于机床上调整工件或工具的附件,包括具有读度用的光学装置的附件(例如,"光学"分度头),但其本身主要是光学仪器的除外(例如校直望远镜);计算机器(税目84.70);税目84.81的阀门及其他装置;税目84.86的机器及装置(包括将电路图投影或绘制到感光半导体材料上的装置);

(八)自行车或机动车辆用探照灯或聚光灯(税目85.12);税目85.13的手提式电灯;电影录音机、还音机及转录机(税目85.19);拾音头或录音头(税目85.22);电视摄像机和视频摄录一体机数字照相机(税目85.25);雷达设备、无线电导航设备或无线电遥控设备(税目85.26);光导纤维、光导纤维束或光缆用连接器(税目85.36);税目85.37的数字控制装置;税目85.39的封闭式聚光灯;税目85.44的光缆;

(九)税目94.05的探照灯及聚光灯;

(十)第九十五章的物品;

(十一)容量的计量器具(按其构成的材料归类);

(十二)卷轴、线轴及类似芯子(按其构成材料归类,例如,归入税目39.23或第十五类)。

二、除上述注释一另有规定的以外,本章各税目所列机器、设备、仪器或器具的零件、附件,应按下列规定归类:

(一)凡零件、附件本身已构成本章或第八十四章、第八十五章或第九十一章各税目(税目84.87、85.48或90.33除外)所包括的货品,应一律归入其相应的税目;

(二)其他零件、附件,如果专用于或主要用于某种或同一税目项下的多种机器、仪器或器具(包括税目90.10、90.13或90.31的机器、仪器或器具),应归入相应机器、仪器或器具的税目;

(三)所有其他零件、附件均应归入税目90.33。

三、第十六类注释三及四的规定也适用于本章。

四、税目90.05不包括武器用望远镜瞄准具、潜艇或坦克上的潜望镜式望远镜及本章或第十六类的机器、设备、仪器或器具用的望远镜;这类望远镜瞄准具及望远镜应归入税目90.13。

paperboard cutting machines of all kinds (heading No. 84.41); fittings for adjusting work or tools on machine-tools, of heading No. 84.66, including fittings with optical devices for reading the scale (for example, "optical" dividing heads) but not those which are in themselves essentially optical instruments (for example, alignment telescopes); calculating machines (heading No. 84.70); valves or other appliances of heading 84.81; machines and equipments of tax item 84.86. (use interlinkage or connecting line for inductance or chemical compound semiconductor materials)

(h) Searchlights or spotlights of a kind used for cycles or motor vehicles (heading No. 85.12); portable electric lamps of heading 85.13; cinematographic sound recording, reproducing or re-recording apparatus (heading No. 85.19 or 85.20); sound-heads (heading No. 85.22); TV photographer - photographing - recording machine and digital cameras (heading No. 85.25); radar apparatus, radio navigational aid apparatus or radio remote control apparatus (heading No. 85.26); fiber optics, fasciculus optical or optical cable linker (85.36); numerical control apparatus of heading No. 85.37; sealed beam lamp units of heading No. 85.39; optical fibre cables of heading No. 85.44;

(i) Searchlights or spotlights of heading No. 94.05;

(k) Articles of Chapter 95;

(j) Capacity measures, which are to be classified according to their constituent material; or

(m) Spools, reels or similar supports (which are to be classified according to their constituent material, for example, in heading No. 39.23 or Section XV).

2. Subject to Note 1 above, parts and accessories for machines, apparatus, instruments or articles of this Chapter are to be classified according to the following rules:

(a) Parts and accessories which are goods included in any of the headings of this Chapter or of Chapter 84, 85 or 91 (other than heading No. 84.85, 87.48 or 90.33) are in all cases to be classified in their respective headings;

(b) Other parts and accessories, if suitable for use solely or principally with a particular kind of machine, instrument or apparatus, or with a number of machines, instruments or apparatus of the same heading (including a machine, instrument or apparatus of heading No. 90.10, 90.13 or 90.31) are to be classified with the machines, instruments or apparatus of that kind;

(c) All other parts and accessories are to be classified in heading No. 90.33.

3. The provisions of Note 4 to Section III or XVI apply also to this Chapter.

4. Heading No. 90.05 does not apply to telescopic sights for fitting to arms, periscopic telescopes for fitting to submarines or tanks, or to telescopes for machines, appliances, instruments or apparatus of this Chapter of Section XVII; such telescopic sights and telescopes are to be classified in heading No. 90.13.

五、计量或检验用的光学仪器、器具或机器，如果既可归入税目 90.13，又可归入税目 90.31，则应归入税目 90.31。

六、税目 90.21 所称“矫形器具”，是指下列用途的器具：

-预防或矫正人体畸变；

-生病、手术或受伤后人体部位的支撑或固定；

矫形器具包括用于矫正畸形的鞋及特种鞋垫，但需符合下列任一条件：

（一）定制的

（二）成批生产的，单独报验、且不成双的、设计为左右两脚同样适用。

七、税目 90.32 仅适用于：

（一）液体或气体的流量、液位、压力或其他变化量的自动控制仪器及装置或温度自动控制装置，不论其是否依靠要被自控的因素所发生的电现象来进行工作，这些仪器或装置将被自控因素调到并保持在一设定值上，通过持续或定期测量实际值来保持稳定，修正偏差；

（二）电量自动调节器及自动控制非电量的仪器或装置，依靠要被控制的因素所发生的电现象来进行工作，这些仪器或装置将被控制的因素调到并保持在一设定值上，通过持续或定期测量实际值来保持稳定，修正偏差。

5. Measuring or checking optical instruments, appliances or machines which, but for this Note, could be classified both in heading No. 90.13 and in heading No. 90.31 are to be classified in heading No. 90.31.

6. For the purposes of heading No. 90.21, the expression “orthopaedic appliances” means appliances for:

-Preventing or correcting bodily deformities;

-Supporting or holding parts of the body following an illness, operation or injury.

Orthopaedic appliances include footwear and special insoles designed to correct orthopaedic conditions, provided that they are either:

(1) made to measure or

(2) mass-produced, presented singly and not in pairs and designed to fit either foot equally.

7. Heading No. 90.32 applies only to:

(a) Instruments and apparatus for automatically controlling the flow, level, pressure or other variables of liquids or gases, or for automatically controlling temperature, whether or not their operation depends on an electrical phenomenon which varies according to the factor to be automatically controlled; which are designed to bring this factor to, and maintain it at, a desired value, stabilised against disturbances, by constantly or periodically measuring its actual value;

(b) Automatic regulators of electrical quantities, and instruments or apparatus for automatically controlling non-electrical quantities the operation of which depends on an electrical phenomenon varying according to the factor to be controlled, which are designed to bring this factor to, and maintain it at, a desired value, stabilised against disturbances, by constantly or periodically measuring its actual value.

税则号列 Tariff Item.	货品名称	最惠国(%) MFN	协定(%) CT 东盟 CA	中巴 CP	中智 CC	普通 Gen	增值税率 VAT	出口退税 ED	计量单位 Unit	监管条件 SC	Article Description
90.01	**光导纤维及光导纤维束；光缆，但税目 85.44 的货品除外；偏振材料制的片及板；未装配的各种材料制透镜（包括隐形眼镜片）、棱镜、反射镜及其他光学元件，但未经光学加工的玻璃制上述元件除外：**										**Optical fibres and optical fibre bundles; optical fibre cables, other than those of heading 85.44; sheets and plates of polarizing material; lenses (including contact lenses), prisms, mirrors and other optical elements, of any material, unmounted, other than such elements of glass not optically worked:**
9001.1000	-光导纤维、光导纤维束及光缆	5		4.5	0	20	17	13	千克		-Optical fibres, optical fibre bundles and cables
9001.1000 01	非色散位移单模光纤（G652A，G652B，G652C）	5				20	17	13	千克		Non-dispersive displacement single-mode optical fibers (G652A、G652B、G652C)
9001.1000 09	其他光导纤维（但编号 8544 的货品除外）	5				20	17	13	千克		Other optical fibres, other than goods of heading No. 8544
9001.1000 90	光导纤维束及光缆（但编号 8544 的货品除外）	5				20	17	13	千克		Optical fibres bundles and cables other than goods of heading No. 8544
9001.2000	-偏振材料制的片及板	8	5	7.6	0	20	17	13	千克		-Sheets and plates of polarizing material
9001.3000	-隐形眼镜片	10	T3		0	70	17	13	片		-Contact lenses

税则号列 Tariff Item.	货品名称	最惠国(%) MFN	协定(%)CT 东盟 CA	中巴 CP	中智 CC	普通 Gen	增值税率 VAT	出口退税 ED	计量单位 Unit	监管条件 SC	Article Description
	-玻璃制眼镜片:										-Spectacle lenses of glass:
9001.4010	---变色镜片	20	12		0	90	17	13	片		---Photochromic
	---其他:										---Other:
9001.4091	----太阳镜片	20	12		0	90	17	13	片		----For sunglasses
9001.4099	----其他	20	12		0	70	17	13	片		----Other
	-其他材料制眼镜片:										-Spectacle lenses of other materials:
9001.5010	---变色镜片	20	12		0	90	17	13	片		---Photochromic
	---其他:										---Other:
9001.5091	----太阳镜片	20	12		0	90	17	13	片		----For sunglasses
9001.5099	----其他	20	12		0	70	17	13	片		----Other
9001.9000	-其他	8	5	7.6	0	20	17	13	千克		-Other
9001.9000 01	光通信用微光组件的光学元件(波长800-1700nm薄膜滤光片,自聚焦透镜,法拉第旋转片)	8				20	17	13	千克		Optical elements of micro-optical assemblies for optical communications (film filters with working wave-length 800nm ~ 1700nm, automatic focusing lens, Faraday rotation isolator)
9001.9000 02	微型镜片(激光视盘机激光收发装置用)	8				20	17	13	千克		Micro-lens for VCD and laser receiver-transmitter apparatus
9001.9000 03	背投电视机显示屏(包括非涅耳透镜屏幕、双透镜屏幕和保护屏)	8				20	17	13	千克		Rear projection TV screen (including Fresnel lens screen, double lens screen and protective screen)
9001.9000 90	编号9001未列名的其他光学元件(未经光学加工的玻璃制元件除外)	8				20	17	13	千克		Other optical elements, not specified or included elsewhere in the heading No. 9001, other than such elements of glass not optically worked
90.02	**已装配的各种材料制透镜、棱镜、反射镜及其他光学元件,作为仪器或装置的零件、配件,但未经光学加工的玻璃制上述元件除外:**										**Lenses, prisms, mirrors and other optical elements, of any material, mounted, being parts of or fittings for instruments or apparatus, other than such elements of glass not optically worked:**
	-物镜:										-Objective lenses:
	--照相机、投影仪、照片放大机及缩片机用:										--For cameras, projectors or photographic enlargers or reducers:
9002.1110	---子目9006.1010至9006.3000所列照相机用	8	5		0	14	17	13	千克/个		---For the photographic cameras of subheadingsNos. 9006.1010 to 9006.3000
9002.1120	---缩微阅读机用	8	5		0	14	17	13	千克/个		---For microfilm, microfiche or other microform readers
9002.1190	---其他	15	8		9	80	17	13	千克/个		---Other
9002.1190 01	彩色液晶投影机的镜头及镜头组件	15				80	17	13	千克/个	A	Parts of lenses for colour liquid crystal projector
9002.1190 02	数码相机的镜头	15				80	17	13	千克/个	A	Digital camera lens
9002.1190 90	其他照相机,投影仪等用物镜(包括照片放大机用物镜)	15				80	17	13	千克/个	A	Objective lenses for cameras, projectors or photographic enlargers or reducers
	--其他:										--Other:
9002.1910	---摄影机或放映机用	15	8		9	40	17	13	千克/个		---For cinematographic cameras or projectors
9002.1990	---其他	15	8		9	50	17	13	千克/个		---Other

税则号列 Tariff Item.	货 品 名 称	最惠国(%) MFN	协定(%) CT 东盟 CA	中巴 CP	中智 CC	普通 Gen	增值税率 VAT	出口退税 ED	计量单位 Unit	监管条件 SC	Article Description
	-滤色镜:										-Filters:
9002.2010	---照相机用	15	8	14.3	9	80	17	13	千克/个		---For cameras
9002.2090	---其他	15	8	14.3	9	40	17	13	千克/个		---Other
	-其他:										-Other:
9002.9010	---照相机用	15	8		12	80	17	13	千克		---For cameras
9002.9090	---其他	15	8		12	40	17	13	千克		---Other
9002.9090 10	抗辐射镜头[能抗 5×10^4 戈瑞(硅)以上辐射而又不会降低使用质量]	15				40	17	13	千克	3	Ray-proof lens (capable of resisting radiance > 5×10^4 Gy (Si) and not lowering operation quality)
9002.9090 90	其他光学仪器用未列名光学元件(但物镜,滤色镜除外)	15				40	17	13	千克		Other optial instruments, not elsewhere specified or included, other than objective lenses and filters
90.03	**眼镜架及其零件:**										**Frames and mountings for spectacles, goggles or the like, and parts thereof:**
	-眼镜架:										-Frames and mountings:
9003.1100	--塑料制	18	8		10.8	70	17	13	副		--Of plastics
9003.1900	--其他材料制	10	5		8	70	17	13	副		--Of other materials
9003.1900 10	濒危动物产品制眼镜架	10				70	17	13	副	FE	Frames and mountings for spectacles, goggles or the like, of materials of wild animal in imminent dangers
9003.1900 90	其他非塑料材料制眼镜架	10				70	17	13	副		Frames and mountings of other materials other than plastics
9003.9000	-零件	10	5		0	70	17	13	千克		-Parts
90.04	**矫正视力、保护眼睛或其他用途的眼镜、挡风镜及类似品:**										**Spectacles, goggles and the like, corrective, protective or other:**
9004.1000	-太阳镜	20	12		16	100	17	13	副		-Sunglasses
	-其他:										-Other:
9004.9010	---变色镜	16	8		9.6	100	17	13	副		---Photochromic spectacles
9004.9090	---其他	20	12		12	90	17	13	副		---Other
90.05	**双筒望远镜、单筒望远镜、其他光学望远镜及其座架;其他天文仪器及其座架,但不包括射电天文仪器:**										**Binoculars, monoculars, other optical telescopes, and mountings therefor; other astronomical instruments and mountings therefor, but not including instruments for radio-astronomy:**
9005.1000	-双筒望远镜	15	8		9	50	17	13	个	a	-Binoculars
	-其他仪器:										-Other instruments:
9005.8010	---天文望远镜及其他天文仪器	3			0	8	17	17	台		---Astronomical telescopes and other astronomical instruments
9005.8090	---其他	12	8		7.2	50	17	13	台		---Other
	-零件、附件(包括座架):										-Parts and accessories (including mountings):
9005.9010	---天文望远镜及其他天文仪器用	2			0	8	17	13	千克		---Of instruments of subheading 9005.8010
9005.9090	---其他	8	5		0	30	17	13	千克		---Other

税则号列 Tariff Item.	货品名称	最惠国(%) MFN	协定(%)CT 东盟 CA	中巴 CP	中智 CC	普通 Gen	增值税率 VAT	出口退税 ED	计量单位 Unit	监管条件 SC	Article Description
90.06	照相机(电影摄影机除外);照相闪光灯装置及闪光灯泡,但税目85.39的放电灯泡除外:										**Photographic (other than cinematographic) cameras; photographic flashlight apparatus and flashbulbs, other than discharge lamps of heading No. 85.39:**
	-制版照相机:										-Cameras of a kind used for preparing printing plates or cylinders:
9006.1010	---电子分色机	12	8		7.2	20	17	13	台		---Electronic colour scanners
9006.1090	---其他	10	5		0	20	17	13	台	AB	---Other
9006.3000	-水下、航空测量或体内器官检查用的特种照相机;法庭或犯罪学用的比较照相机	9	5		0	17	17	13	台		-Cameras specially designed for underwater use, for aerial survey or for medical or surgical examination of internal organs; comparison cameras for forensic or criminological purposes
9006.4000	-一次成像照相机	5			0	70	17	13	台		-Instant print cameras
	-其他照相机:										-Other cameras:
9006.5100	--通过镜头取景(单镜头反光式(SLR)),使用胶片宽度不超过35mm	25	12		15	100	17	13	架	AB	--With a through-the-lens viewfinder (single lens reflex (SLR)), for roll film of a width not exceeding 35 mm
	--其他,使用胶片宽度小于35mm										--Other, for roll film of a width less than 35 mm
9006.5210	---缩微照相机使用缩微胶卷,胶片或其他缩微胶卷,胶片或其他缩微品的	9	5		0	17	17	13	架		---Cameras of a kind used for recording documents on microfilm, microfiche of other microforms
9006.5290	---其他	25	12		15	100	17	13	架	AB	---Other
9006.5300	--其他,使用胶片宽度为35mm	20	12		16	100	17	13	架	AB	--Other, for roll film of a width of 35mm
	--其他:										--Other:
9006.5910	---激光照相排版设备	9			0	35	17	13	台	AB	---Laser phototypesetting apparatus
9006.5990	---其他	25	12		15	100	17	13	架		---Other
9006.5990 10	分幅相机(记录速率超过每秒225000帧)	25				100	17	13	架	3AB	Frame cameras (rate of recording > 225000 frame/sec)
9006.5990 20	电子(或电子快门)分幅相机(帧曝光时间为51纳秒或更短)	25				100	17	13	架	3AB	Electron frame cameras (duration of frame exposure≤51nanosec)
9006.5990 30	条纹相机(书写速度超过每微秒0.5mm)	25				100	17	13	架	3AB	Stripe cameras (speed of writing > 0.5mm/microsec)
9006.5990 40	电子条纹相机(时间分辨率为51纳秒或更小)	25				100	17	13	架	3AB	Electron stripe cameras (rate of time discrimination≤51nanosec)
9006.5990 90	使用胶片宽>35mm的其他照相机	25				100	17	13	架	AB	Other cameras, for roll film of a width >35mm
	-照相闪光灯装置及闪光灯泡:										-Photographic flashlight apparatus and flashbulbs:
9006.6100	--放电式(电子式)闪光灯装置	18	8		10.8	80	17	13	个		--Discharge lamp ("electronic") flashlight apparatus
	--其他:										--Other:
9006.6910	---闪光灯炮	18	8		10.8	80	17	13	个		---Flasbbulbs
9006.6990	---其他	18	8		10.8	80	17	13	个		---Other
	-零件、附件:										-Parts and accessories:

税则号列 Tariff Item.	货品名称	最惠国(%) MFN	协定(%)CT 东盟 CA	中巴 CP	中智 CC	普通 Gen	增值税率 VAT	出口退税 ED	计量单位 Unit	监管条件 SC	Article Description
	--照相机用:										--For cameras:
9006.9110	---子目9006.1010至9006.3000所列相机用	8	5	5.6	0	17	17	13	千克		---For cameras of subheadings Nos. 9006.1010 to 9006.3000
9006.9120	---一次成像照相机用	5		3.5	0	100	17	13	千克		---For instant print cameras
	---其他:										---Other:
9006.9191	----自动调焦组件	10	T3	7	0	100	17	13	千克/套		----Automatic focal setting units
9006.9192	----快门组件	10	8	7	0	100	17	13	千克/套		----Shutter units
9006.9199	----其他	10	8	7	0	100	17	13	千克		----Other
9006.9900	--其他	12	8		7.2	80	17	13	千克		--Other
90.07	**电影摄影机、放映机,不论是否带有声音的录制或重放装置:**										**Cinematographic cameras and projectors, whether or not incorporating sound recording or reproducing apparatus:**
	-摄影机:										-Cameras:
9007.1100	--胶片宽度小于16毫米或双8毫米	14	8		8.4	40	17	13	台		--For film of less than 16 mm width or for double-8 mm film
	--其他:										--Other:
9007.1910	---高速摄影机	14	8		11.2	40	17	13	台		---High speed cameras
9007.1990	---其他	14	8		11.2	40	17	13	台		---Other
	-放映机:										-Projectors:
9007.2010	---数字式	14	8		8.4	40	17	13	台		---Digital
9007.2090	---其他	14	8		8.4	40	17	13	台		---Other
	-零件、附件:										-Parts and accessories:
9007.9100	--摄影机用	8.4	5		0	40	17	13	千克		--For cameras
9007.9200	--放映机用	8.4	5		0	40	17	13	千克		--For projectors
90.08	**影像投影仪,但电影用除外;照片(电影片除外)放大机及缩片机:**										**Image projectors, other than cinematographic; photographic (other than cinematographic) enlargers and reducers:**
9008.1000	-幻灯机	14	8		8.4	40	17	13	台		-Slide projectors
9008.2000	-缩微胶卷、缩微胶片或其他缩微品的阅读机,不论是否可以进行复制	10	5		0	17	17	13	台		-Microfilm, microfiche or other microform readers, whether or not capable of producing copies
	-其他影像投影仪:										-Other image projectors:
9008.3010	---正射投影仪	18	8		0	40	17	13	台		---Orthographical projectors
9008.3090	---其他	18	8		14.4	40	17	13	台		---Other
9008.4000	-照片(电影片除外)放大机及缩片机	20	12		12	80	17	13	台		-Photographic (other than cinematographic) enlargers and reducers
	-零件、附件:										-Parts and accessories:
9008.9010	---缩微阅读机用	8	5		0	17	17	13	千克		---Of microfilm, microfiche or other microform readers
9008.9020	---照片放大机及缩片机用	14	8		8.4	80	17	13	千克		---Of photographic enlargers and reducers
9008.9090	---其他	14	8		8.4	40	17	13	千克		---Other

税则号列 Tariff Item.	货品名称	最惠国(%) MFN	协定(%)CT 东盟 CA	中巴 CP	中智 CC	普通 Gen	增值税率 VAT	出口退税 ED	计量单位 Unit	监管条件 SC	Article Description
90.10	**本章其他税目未列名的照相(包括电影)洗印用装置及设备;负片显示器;银幕及其他投影屏幕:**										**Apparatus and equipment for photographic (including cinematographic) laboratories, not specified or included elsewhere in this Chapter; negatoscopes; projection screens:**
	-照相(包括电影)胶卷或成卷感光纸的自动显影装置及设备或将已冲洗胶卷自动曝光到成卷感光纸上的装置及设备:										-Apparatus and equipment for automatically developing photographic (including cinematographic) film or paper in rolls or for automatically exposing developed film to rolls of photographic paper:
9010.1010	---电影用	14	8		11.2	40	17	13	台		---Of a kind used in cinematographic film
9010.1020	---特种照相用	8.4	5		6.7	20	17	13	台		---Of a kind used in special photographic film or paper
	---其他:										---Other:
9010.1091	----彩色胶卷用	25	12		20	100	17	13	台		----For the colour photographic film in rolls
9010.1099	----其他	15	8		12	100	17	13	台		----Other
	-照相(包括电影)洗印用其他装置及设备;负片显示器:										-Other apparatus and equipment for photographic (including cinematographic) laboratories; negatoscope:
9010.5010	---负片显示器	14	8		8.4	50	17	13	台		---Negatoscopes
	---其他:										---Other:
9010.5021	----电影用	14	8		8.4	40	17	13	台		----Of a kind used in cinematographic film
9010.5022	----特种照相用	8.4	5		0	20	17	13	台		----Of a kind used in special photographic film or paper
9010.5029	----其他	17	8		10.2	100	17	17	台		----Other
9010.6000	-银幕及其他投影屏幕	14	8		8.4	50	17	13	个		-Projection screens
	-零件、附件:										-Parts and accessories:
9010.9010	---电影用	0				40	17	13	千克		---Of a kind used in cinematographic film
9010.9020	---特种照相用	0				20	17	13	千克		---Of a kind used in special photographic film or paper
9010.9090	---其他	0				100	17	13	千克		---Other
90.11	**复式光学显微镜,包括用于缩微照相、显微电影摄影及显微投影的:**										**Compound optical microscopes, including those for photomicrography, cinephotomi-crography or microprojection:**
9011.1000	-立体显微镜	0				14	17	13	台	B	-Stereoscopic microscopes
9011.2000	-缩微照相、显微电影摄影及显微投影用的其他显微镜	0				14	17	13	台		-Other microscopes, for photomicrography, cinephotomicrography or microprojection
9011.8000	-其他显微镜	7	5		0	14	17	13	台	B	-Other microscopes
9011.9000	-零件、附件	0				14	17	13	千克		-Parts and accessories
90.12	**显微镜,但光学显微镜除外;衍射设备:**										**Microscopes other than optical microscopes; diffraction apparatus:**
9012.1000	-显微镜,但光学显微镜除外;衍射设备	0				14	17	13	台		-Microscopes other than optical microscopes; diffraction apparatus
9012.9000	-零件、附件	0				14	17	13	千克		-Parts and accessories

税则号列 Tariff Item.	货品名称	最惠国(%) MFN	协定(%) CT 东盟 CA	中巴 CP	中智 CC	普通 Gen	增值税率 VAT	出口退税 ED	计量单位 Unit	监管条件 SC	Article Description
90.13	**其他税目未列名的液晶装置;激光器,但激光二极管除外;本章其他税目未列名的光学仪器及器具:**										**Liquid crystal devices not constituting articles provided for more specifically in other headings; lasers, other than laser diodes; other optical appliances and instruments, not specified or included elsewhere in this Chapter:**
9013.1000	-武器用望远镜瞄准具;潜望镜式望远镜;作为本章或第十六类的机器、设备、仪器或器具部件的望远镜	8	5		0	14	17	13	个		-Telescopic sights for fitting to arms; periscopes; telescopes designed to form parts of machines, appliances, instruments or apparatus of this Chapter or Section XVI
9013.2000	-激光器,但激光二极管除外	6	5		0	11	17	13	个		-Lasers, other than laser diodes
9013.2000 01	2.5GB/S 及以上 SDH、波分复用光传输设备的 980 纳米,1480 纳米的泵浦激光器	6				11	17	13	个		980nm, 1480nm pump laser of SDH ≥ 2.5GB/s, optical transmission equipment for wave-divison multicomplexing
9013.2000 20	AVLIS、MLIS 和 CRISLA 激光系统	6				11	17	13	个	3	AVLIS, MLIS, CRISLA laser systems
9013.2000 30	氩离子激光器(平均输出功率≥40 瓦特、工作波长 400 纳米-515 纳米)	6				11	17	13	个	3	Argon ion lasers, average output power ≥40W, working wavelength = 400nm ~ 515nm
9013.2000 40	紫翠玉激光器(带宽≤0.005 纳米,重复率>125 赫兹,功率>30 瓦特等)	6				11	17	13	个	3	Mauve jadeite laser (bandwidth ≤ 0.005nm, recurrent rate > 125Hz, power > 30W)
9013.2000 50	脉冲二氧化碳激光器(重复率>250 赫兹,功率>500 瓦,脉冲宽度<200 纳秒等)	6				11	17	13	个	3	Pulsed carbon dioxide lasers (recurrent rate > 250Hz, power > 500W, pules width < 200ns)
9013.2000 60	脉冲受激准分子激光器(XeF、XeCl、KrF 型,重复率>250 赫兹,功率>500 瓦等)	6				11	17	13	个	3	Pulse excited quasi-molecule lasers (XeF、XeCl or KrF type, recurrent rate >250Hz, power > 500W)
9013.2000 70	铜蒸汽激光器(平均输出功率≥40 瓦特、工作波长 500 纳米-600 纳米)	6				11	17	13	个	3	Copper vapor lasers, average output power ≥ 40W, working wavelength = 500nm ~ 600nm
9013.2000 90	其他激光器(但激光二极管除外)	6				11	17	13	个		Other lasers, other than laser diodes
	-其他装置、仪器及器具:										-Other devices, appliances and instruments:
9013.8010	---放大镜	12	8	8.4	7.2	50	17	13	个		---Hand magnifying glasses
9013.8020	---光学门眼	12	8	8.4	7.2	50	17	13	个		---"Door eyes"
9013.8030	---液晶显示板	5			0	50	17	17	个		---Liquid crystal display panel
9013.8090	---其他	5			0	17	17	13	个		---Other
	-零件、附件:										-Parts and accessories:
9013.9010	---子目 9013.1000 及 9013.2000 所列货品用	6	5		0	11	17	13	千克		---For goods of subheading 9013.1000 or 9013.2000
9013.9090	---其他	8	5		0	17	17	13	千克		---Other
90.14	**定向罗盘;其他导航仪器及装置:**										**Direction finding compasses; other navigational instruments and appliances:**
9014.1000	-定向罗盘	2			0	8	17	13	个		-Direction finding compasses

税则号列 Tariff Item.	货品名称	最惠国(%) MFN	协定(%)CT 东盟 CA	中巴 CP	中智 CC	普通 Gen	增值税率 VAT	出口退税 ED	计量单位 Unit	监管条件 SC	Article Description
9014.2000	-航空或航天导航仪器及装置(罗盘除外)	2			0	8	17	13	个		-Instruments and appliances for aeronautical or space navigation (other than compasses)
9014.2000 11	航空惯性导航仪	2				8	17	13	个	3	Inertial navigation instruments for airplanes
9014.2000 12	航天惯性导航仪(天文陀螺盘及其他利用天体或卫星进行导航的装置)	2				8	17	13	个	3	Spaceflight navigation aids (astronomical gyrocompass and astronomical or satellite navigational devices thereof)
9014.2000 13	陀螺稳定平台	2				8	17	13	个	3	Gyro stabilized platforms
9014.2000 14	自动驾驶仪(无人航空飞行器的自动驾驶仪)	2				8	17	13	个	3	Gyropilots for unmanned aircrafts
9014.2000 15	陀螺仪(额定漂移率小于0.5度/小时的陀螺仪)	2				8	17	13	个	3	Gyroscopes (nominal drift rate < 0.5 degree/h)
9014.2000 16	专门设计的导航信息处理机(用于弹道导弹、运载火箭、探空火箭等的目标探测)	2				8	17	13	个	3	Navigation information processors for radio detecting and ranging objects such as ballistic missiles, carrier rockets or sounding rockets
9014.2000 17	地形等高线绘制设备(用于弹道导弹、运载火箭、探空火箭等的目标探测)	2				8	17	13	个	3	Contour mapping equipments for radio detecting and ranging objects such as ballistic missiles, carrier rockets or sounding rockets
9014.2000 18	场景绘图及相关设备(用于弹道导弹、运载火箭、探空火箭等的目标探测)	2				8	17	13	个	3	Scene mapping equipments and relative equipments for radio detecting and ranging objects such as ballistic missiles, carrier rockets or sounding rockets
9014.2000 90	其他航空或航天导航仪器及装置(但罗盘除外)	2				8	17	13	个		Other instruments and appliances for aeronautical or space navigation (other than compasses)
9014.8000	-其他仪器及装置	2			0	8	17	13	个		-Other instruments and appliances
9014.8000 10	比例误差小于0.25%的加速度表	2				8	17	13	个	3	Accelerometers, proportion error < 0.25%
9014.8000 20	高度表(用于弹道导弹、运载火箭、探空火箭等的目标探测)	2				8	17	13	个	3	Altimeters for radio detecting and ranging objects such as ballistic missiles, carrier rockets or sounding rockets
9014.8000 90	其他导航仪器及装置	2				8	17	13	个	O	Other instruments and appliances
9014.9000	-零件、附件	1.5			0	8	17	13	千克		-Parts and accessories
90.15	**大地测量(包括摄影测量)、水道测量、海洋、水文、气象或地球物理用仪器及装置,不包括罗盘;测距仪:**										**Surveying (including photogrammetrical surveying), hydrographic, oceanographic, hydrological, meteorological or geophysical instruments and appliances, excluding compasses; rangefinders:**
9015.1000	-测距仪	9	5		0	14	17	13	台		-Rangefinders
9015.2000	-经纬仪及视距仪	9	5		0	14	17	13	台		-Theodolites and tachymeters (tacheometers)
9015.3000	-水平仪	9	5		0	14	17	13	台	B	-Levels
9015.4000	-摄影测量用仪器及装置	9	5		0	14	17	13	千克		-Photogrammetrical surveying instruments and appliances
9015.8000	-其他仪器及装置	5		3.5	4	14	17	13	台		-Other instruments and appliances

税则号列 Tariff Item.	货品名称	最惠国(%) MFN	协定(%) 东盟 CA	中巴 CP	CT 中智 CC	普通 Gen	增值税率 VAT	出口退税 ED	计量单位 Unit	监管条件 SC	Article Description
9015.8000 10	机载或舰载重力仪(精度为1毫伽或更好、稳态记录时间至多为2分钟的)	5				14	17	13	台	3	Air-borne or ship-borne gravimeters (accuracy 1 milligamma or more better, duration of static recording≤2 min)
9015.8000 20	机载或舰载重力梯度仪(精度为1毫伽或更好、稳态记录时间至多为2分钟的)	5				14	17	13	台	3	Air-borne or ship-borne gravity gradiometers (accuracy 1 milligamma or more better, duration of static recording≤2 min)
9015.8000 90	其他测量仪器及装置	5				14	17	13	台		Other surveying instruments and appliances
9015.9000	-零件、附件	5			0	14	17	13	千克		-Parts and accessories
9015.9000 10	机、舰载重力仪和重力梯度仪部件	5				14	17	13	千克	3	Parts and accessories of the instruments of subheading 90158000.10, 90158000.20
9015.9000 90	其他大地测量仪及装置的零、附件	5				14	17	13	千克		Other parts and accessories of surveying instruments and appliances
90.16	**感量为50毫克或更精密的天平,不论是否带有砝码:**										**Balances of a sensitivity of 50 mg or better, with or without weights:**
9016.0010	---感量为0.1毫克或更精密的天平	9	5		0	14	17	13	台/千克		---Of a sensitivity of 0.1 mg or better
9016.0090	---其他	10.5	8		6.3	30	17	13	台/千克		---Other
90.17	**绘图、划线或数学计算仪器及器具(例如,绘图机、比例缩放仪、分度规、绘图工具、计算尺及盘式计算器);本章其他税目未列名的手用测量长度的器具(例如,量尺、量带、千分尺及卡尺):**										**Drawing, marking-out or mathematical-calculating instruments (for example, drafting machines, pantographs, protractors, drawing sets, slide rules, disc calculators); instruments for measuring length, for use in the hand (for example, measuring rods and tapes, micrometers, callipers), not specified or included elsewhere in this Chapter:**
9017.1000	-绘图台及绘图机,不论是否自动	8	5		0	20	17	13	台		-Drafting tables and machines, whether or not automatic
9017.2000	-其他绘图、划线或数学计算器具	0				70	17	13	个		-Other drawing, marking-out or mathematical calculating instruments
9017.3000	-千分尺、卡尺及量规	8	5		0	20	17	13	个	B	-Micrometers, callipers and gauges
9017.8000	-其他仪器及器具	8	5		0	20	17	13	个	B	-Other instruments
9017.9000	-零件、附件	0				20	17	13	千克		-Parts and accessories
90.18	**医疗、外科、牙科或兽医用仪器及器具,包括闪烁扫描装置、其他电气医疗装置及视力检查仪器:**										**Instruments and appliances used in medical, surgical, dental or veterinary sciences, including scintigraphic apparatus, other electro-medical apparatus and sight-testing instruments:**
	-电气诊断装置(包括功能检查或生理参数检查用装置):										-Electro-diagnostic apparatus (including apparatus for functional exploratory examination or for checking physiological parameters):
9018.1100	--心电图记录仪	5		0	0	17	17	17	台	6AO	--Electro-cardiographs
	--超声波扫描装置:										--Ultrasonic scanning apparatus:
9018.1210	---B型超声波诊断仪	7	5	0	0	35	17	17	台	6OA	---B-ultrasonic diagnostic equipment
9018.1291	----彩色超声波诊断仪	5		0	0	17	17	17	台	6OA	----Chromoscope ultrasonic diagnosticequipment
9018.1299	----其他	5		0	0	17	17	17	台	6A	----Other

税则号列 Tariff Item.	货品名称	最惠国(%) MFN	协定(%)CT 东盟 CA	中巴 CP	中智 CC	普通 Gen	增值税率 VAT	出口退税 ED	计量单位 Unit	监管条件 SC	Article Description
9018.1300	--核磁共振成像装置	4		0	0	17	17	17	台	6OA	--Magnetic resonance imaging apparatus
9018.1400	--闪烁摄影装置	5		0	0	17	17	17	台	6OA	--Scintigraphic apparatus
	--其他：										--Other：
9018.1930	---病员监护仪	4		0	0	17	17	17	台	6OA	---Patient monitors
	---听力诊断装置：										---Audio-diagnostic apparatas：
9018.1941	----听力计	4		0	0	17	17	17	台	6A	----Andiometers
9018.1949	----其他	4		0	0	17	17	17	台	6A	----Other
9018.1990	---其他	4		0	0	17	17	17	台	6OA	---Other
9018.2000	-紫外线及红外线装置	4		0	0	17	17	17	台/千克	6A	-Ultra-violet or infra-red ray apparatus
	-注射器、针、导管、插管及类似品：										-Syringes, needles, catheters, cannulae and the like：
9018.3100	--注射器,不论是否装有针头	8	5	0	6.4	50	17	17	个	6A	--Syringes, with or without needles
	--管状金属针头及缝合用针：										--Tubular metal needles and needles for sutures：
9018.3210	---管状金属针头	8	5	0	0	50	17	17	千克	6A	---Tubular metal needles
9018.3220	---缝合用针	4		0	0	17	17	17	千克	6A	---Needles for sutures
9018.3900	--其他	4		0	3.2	17	17	17	个	6A	--Other
	-牙科用其他仪器及器具：										-Other instruments and appliances, used in dental sciences：
9018.4100	--牙钻机,不论是否与其他牙科设备组装在同一底座上	4		0	0	17	17	17	台/千克	6A	--Dental drill engines, whether or not combined on a single base with other dental equipment
	--其他：										--Other：
9018.4910	---装有牙科设备的牙科用椅	4		0	3.2	17	17	17	台	6OA	---Dentists' chairs incorporating dental equipment
9018.4990	---其他	4		0	3.2	17	17	17	台	6A	---Other
9018.5000	-眼科用其他仪器及器具	4		0	3.2	17	17	17	千克	6A	-Other ophthalmic instruments and appliances
	-其他仪器及器具：										-Other instruments and appliances：
9018.9010	---听诊器	4		0	3.2	17	17	17	个	6	---Stethoscopes
9018.9020	---血压测量仪器及器具	4		0	3.2	17	17	17	个	6A	---Sphygmomanometers
9018.9030	---内窥镜	4		0	3.2	17	17	17	台	6OA	---Endoscopes
9018.9040	---肾脏透析设备(人工肾)	4		0	3.2	17	17	17	台	6OA	---Artificial kidney (dialysis) apparatus
9018.9050	---透热疗法设备	4		0	3.2	17	17	17	台	6A	---Diathermy apparatus
9018.9060	---输血设备	4		0	3.2	17	17	17	台	6OA	---Blood transfusion apparatus
9018.9070	---麻醉设备	4		0	3.2	17	17	17	台	6OA	---Anaesthetic apparatus and instruments
9018.9080	---宫内节育器	4		0	3.2	17	0		个	6A	---Intrauterine contraceptive device
9018.9090	---其他	4		0	3.2	17	17	17	台/千克	6OA	---Other
90.19	**机械疗法器具;按摩器具;心理功能测验装置;臭氧治疗器;氧气治疗器、喷雾治疗器、人工呼吸器及其他治疗用呼吸器具：**										**Mechano-therapy appliances; massage apparatus; psychological aptitude-testing apparatus; ozone therapy, oxygen therapy, aerosol therapy, artificial respiration or other therapeutic respiration apparatus：**
	-机械疗法器具;按摩器具;心理功能测验装置：										-Mechano-therapy appliances; massage apparatus; psychological aptitude-testing apparatus：
9019.1010	---按摩器具	15	8		12	40	17	17	台/千克	AB	---Massage apparatus

税则号列 Tariff Item.	货品名称	最惠国(%) MFN	协定(%)CT 东盟 CA	中巴 CP	中智 CC	普通 Gen	增值税率 VAT	出口退税 ED	计量单位 Unit	监管条件 SC	Article Description
9019.1090	---其他	4			3.2	30	17	17	台/千克		---Other
9019.2000	-臭氧治疗器、氧气治疗器、喷雾治疗器、人工呼吸器或其他治疗用呼吸器具	4			0	17	17	17	台/千克		-Ozone therapy, oxygen therapy, aerosol therapy, artificial respiration or other therapeutic respiration apparatus
90.20	**其他呼吸器具及防毒面具,但不包括既无机械零件又无可互换过滤器的防护面具:**										**Other breathing appliances and gas masks, excluding protective masks having neither mechanical parts nor replaceable filters:**
9020.0000	其他呼吸器具及防毒面具,但不包括既无机械零件又无可互换过滤器的防护面具	8	5		6.4	30	17	17	千克		Other breathing appliances and gas masks, excluding protective masks having neither mechanical parts nor replaceable filters
90.21	**矫形器具,包括支具、外科手术带、疝气带;夹板及其他骨折用具;人造的人体部分;助听器及为弥补生理缺陷或残疾而穿戴、携带或植入人体内的其他器具:**										**Orthopaedic appliances, including crutches, surgical belts and trusses; splints and other fracture appliances; artificial parts of the body; hearing aids and other appliances which are worn or carried, or implanted in the body, to compensate for a defect or disability:**
9021.1000	-矫形或骨折用器具	4			3.2	17	17	13	千克		-Orthopaedic or fracture appliances:
	-假牙及牙齿固定件:										-Artificial teeth and dental fittings:
9021.2100	--假牙	4			0	17	17	13	千克		--Artificial teeth
9021.2900	--其他	4			0	17	17	13	千克		--Other
	-其他人造的人体部分:										-Other artificial parts of the body:
9021.3100	--人造关节	4			0	17	17	13	千克/套		--Artificial joints
9021.3900	--其他	4			3.2	17	17	13	千克		--Other
9021.4000	-助听器,不包括零件、附件	4			0	17	17	13	个		-Hearing aids, excluding parts and accessories
9021.5000	-心脏起搏器,不包括零件、附件	4			0	17	17	13	个	A	-Pacemakers for stimulating heart muscles, excluding parts and accessories
9021.9000	-其他	4			3.2	17	17	13	千克		-Other
9021.9000 01	人工耳蜗植入装置	4				17	17	13	千克		
9021.9000 90	其他弥补生理缺陷、残疾用器具等(包括穿戴、携带或植入人体内的器具及零件)	4				17	17	13	千克		Other appliances to compensate for a defect or disability (including appliances and parts which are worn or carried, or implanted in the body)
90.22	**X射线或α射线、β射线、γ射线的应用设备,不论是否用于医疗、外科、牙科或兽医,包括射线照相及射线治疗设备,X射线管及其他X射线发生器、高压发生器、控制板及控制台、荧光屏、检查或治疗用的桌、椅及类似品:**										**Apparatus based on the use of X-rays or of alpha, beta or gamma radiations, whether or not for medical, surgical, dental or veterinary uses, including radiography or radiotherapy apparatus, X-ray tubes and other X-ray generators, high tension generators, control panels and desks, screens, examination or treatment tables, chairs and the like:**
	-X射线的应用设备,不论是否用于医疗、外科、牙科或兽医,包括射线照相或射线治疗设备:										-Apparatus based on the use of X-rays, whether or not for medical, surgical, dental or veterinary uses, including radiography or radiotherapy apparatus:

税则号列 Tariff Item.	货品名称	最惠国(%) MFN	协定(%) 东盟 CA	中巴 CP	中智 CC	普通 Gen	增值税率 VAT	出口退税 ED	计量单位 Unit	监管条件 SC	Article Description
9022.1200	--X射线断层检查仪	4		2.8	0	11	17	17	台	6OA	--Computed tomography apparatus
9022.1300	--其他,牙科用	4			0	11	17	17	台	6OA	--Other, for dental uses
9022.1400	--其他,医疗、外科或兽医用	4			0	11	17	17	台		--Other, for medical, surgical or veterinary uses
9022.1400 10	医用直线加速器	4				11	17	17	台	6OA	Linear accelerators for medical use
9022.1400 90	其他医疗或兽医用X射线应用设备	4				11	17	17	台	6OA	Other apparatus based on the use of X-rays, for medical or veterinary uses
	--其他:										--Other:
9022.1910	---低剂量X射线安全检查设备	4			0	11	17	13	台	6OA	---Low dosage X-ray security inspecting equipment
9022.1990	---其他	4			0	11	17	13	台		---Other
9022.1990 10	X射线全自动燃料芯块检查台(专门设计或制造用于检验燃料芯块的最终尺寸和表面缺陷)	4				11	17	13	台	36AO	X-ray fully automatic fuel core examiwins table
9022.1990 90	其他X射线应用设备	4				11	17	13	台	6OA	Other apparatus based on the use of X-rays
	-α射线、β射线、γ射线的应用设备,不论是否用于医疗、外科、牙科或兽医,包括射线照相或射线治疗设备:										-Apparatus based on the use of alpha, beta or gamma radiations, whether or not for medical, surgical, dental or veterinary uses, including radiography or radiothe rapy apparatus:
9022.2100	--医疗、外科、牙科或兽医用	4			0	11	17	17	台	6OA	--For medical, surgical, dental or veterinary uses
9022.2900	--其他	6	5		0	11	17	13	台		--For other uses
9022.2900 10	γ射线全自动燃料芯块检查台(专门设计或制造用于检验燃料芯块的最终尺寸和表面缺陷)	6				11	17	13	台	36AO	γ-ray fully automatic fuel core examiwins table
9022.2900 90	其他非医疗用α、β、γ射线设备	6				11	17	13	台	6OA	Other α-rays, β-rays, γ-rays, not for medical
9022.3000	-X射线管	2			0	11	17	13	个	6OA	-X-ray tubes
	-其他,包括零件、附件:										-Other, including parts and accessories:
9022.9010	---X射线影像增强器	6	5		4.8	11	17	13	个/千克	6OA	---X-ray intensifiers
9022.9090	---其他	6	5		4.8	11	17	13	千克		---Other
9022.9090 01	射线发生器的零部件	6				11	17	13	千克	6	Parts of radiation generators
9022.9090 20	闪光X射线发生器(峰值能量≥500千电子伏)	6				11	17	13	千克	36O	Flash X-ray generators (peak value power≥500KeV)
9022.9090 30	X射线断层检查仪专用探测器	6				11	17	13	千克	6O	Detectors specified for computed tomography apparatus
9022.9090 90	编号9022所列其他设备及零件(包括高压发生器、控制板及控制台、荧光屏等)	6				11	17	13	千克	6O	Other apparatus and its parts of heading 9022, including high tension generators, control panels and desks, screens
90.23	**专供示范(例如,教学或展览)而无其他用途的仪器、装置及模型:**										**Instruments, apparatus and models, designed for demonstrational purposes (for example, in education or exhibitions), unsuitable for other uses:**

税则号列 Tariff Item.	货品名称	最惠国(%) MFN	协定(%)CT			普通 Gen	增值税率 VAT	出口退税 ED	计量单位 Unit	监管条件 SC	Article Description
			东盟 CA	中巴 CP	中智 CC						
9023.0000	专供示范(例如,教学或展览)而无其他用途的仪器、装置及模型	7	5		0	20	17	13	千克		Instruments, apparatus and models, designed for demonstrational purposes (for example, in education or exhibitions), unsuitable for other uses
90.24	**各种材料(例如,金属、木材、纺织材料、纸张、塑料)的硬度、强度、压缩性、弹性或其他机械性能的试验机器及器具:**										**Machines and appliances for testing the hardness, strength, compressibility, elasticity or other mechanical properties of materials (for example, metals, wood, textiles, paper, plastics):**
9024.1000	-金属材料的试验用机器及器具	7	5	6.5	0	20	17	13	台		-Machines and appliances for testing metals
9024.8000	-其他机器及器具	5			0	20	17	13	台		-Other machines and appliances
9024.9000	-零件、附件	6	5		0	20	17	13	千克		-Parts and accessories
90.25	**记录式或非记录式的液体比重计及类似的浮子式仪器、温度计、高温计、气压计、湿度计、干湿球湿度计及其组合装置:**										**Hydrometers and similar floating instruments, thermometers and pyrometers, barometers, hygrometers and psychrometers, recording or not, and any combination of these instruments:**
	-温度计及高温计,未与其他仪器组合:										-Thermometers and pyrometers, not combined with other instruments:
9025.1100	--液体温度计,可直接读数	4			0	40	17	13	个		--Liquid-filled, for direct reading
	--其他:										--Other:
9025.1910	---工业用	8.4	5	8	6.7	20	17	13	个		---For technical use
9025.1990	---其他	8.4	5	8	6.7	80	17	13	个		---Other
9025.8000	-其他仪器	11	8		8.8	30	17	13	个		-Other instruments
9025.9000	-零件、附件	8	5	7.6	6.4	20	17	13	千克		-Parts and accessories
90.26	**液体或气体的流量、液位、压力或其他变化量的测量或检验仪器及装置(例如,流量计、液位计、压力表、热量计),但不包括税目90.14、90.15、90.28或90.32的仪器及装置:**										**Instruments and apparatus for measuring or checking the flow, level, pressure or other variables of liquids or gases (for example, flow meters, level gauges, manometers, heat meters), excluding instruments and apparatus of heading 90.14, 90.15, 90.28 or 90.32:**
9026.1000	-测量、检验液体流量或液位的仪器及装置	0				17	17	13	个		-For measuring or checking the flow or level of liquids
	-测量、检验压力的仪器及装置:										-For measuring or checking pressure:
9026.2010	---压力/差压变送器	0				17	17	13	个		---Pressure/pressure differential transducers
9026.2010 10	锰铜压力计(压力超过100千帕)	0				17	17	13	个	3	Manganese-copper pressure gauges (pressure >100kilobar)
9026.2010 90	其他压力,差压变送器	0				17	17	13	个		Other pressure/pressure differential trasducers
9026.2090	---其他	0				17	17	13	个		---Other
9026.8000	-其他仪器及装置	0				17	17	13	个		-Other instruments or apparatus
9026.9000	-零件、附件	0				17	17	13	千克		-Parts and accessories

税则号列 Tariff Item.	货品名称	最惠国(%) MFN	协定(%) 东盟 CA	协定(%) 中巴 CP	协定(%) 中智 CC	普通 Gen	增值税率 VAT	出口退税 ED	计量单位 Unit	监管条件 SC	Article Description
90.27	**理化分析仪器及装置(例如,偏振仪、折光仪、分光仪、气体或烟雾分析仪);测量或检验粘性、多孔性、膨胀性、表面张力及类似性能的仪器及装置;测量或检验热量、声量或光量的仪器及装置(包括曝光表);检镜切片机:**										**Instruments and apparatus for physical or chemical analysis (for example, polarimeters, refractometers, spectrometers, gas or smoke analysis apparatus); instruments and apparatus for measuring or checking viscosity, porosity, expansion, surface tension or the like; instruments and apparatus for measuring or checking quantities of heat, sound or light (including exposure meters); microtomes:**
9027.1000	-气体或烟雾分析仪	7	5		5.6	17	17	13	台		-Gas or smoke analysis apparatus
9027.1000 10	用于连续操作的气体检测器[可用于出口管制的化学品或有机化合物(含有磷、硫、氟或氯,其浓度低于$0.3mg/m^3$)的检测,或为检测受抑制的胆碱酯酶的活性而设计]	7				17	17	13	台	3	Used in continuously operating gas tester [for testing chemicals or organic compounds under export control (containing phosphor, sulfur, fluorine or chlorine with concentration lower than $0.3mg/m^3$) or for testing the activity of cholinesterase under control]
9027.1000 90	其他气体或烟雾分析仪	7				17	17	13	台		Other gas or smoke analysis apparatus
	-色谱仪及电泳仪:										-Chromatographs and electrophoresis instruments:
	---色谱仪:										---Chromatographs instruments:
9027.2011	----气相色谱仪	0				17	17	17	台		----Gas chromatographs instruments
9027.2012	----液相色谱仪	0				17	17	17	台		----Liquid chromatosraphs instruments
9027.2019	----其他	0				17	17	17	台		----Other
9027.2020	---电泳仪	0				17	17	17	台		---Electrophoresis instruments
9027.3000	-使用光学射线(紫外线、可见光、红外线)的分光仪、分光光度计及摄谱仪	0				17	17	17	台		-Spectrometers, spectrophotometers and spectrographs using optical radiations (UV, visible, IR)
9027.5000	-使用光学射线(紫外线、可见光、红外线)的其他仪器及装置	0				17	17	13	台		-Other instruments and apparatus using optical radiations (UV, visible, IR)
	-其他仪器及装置:										-Other instruments and apparatus:
	---质谱仪:										---Mass spectrograph:
9027.8011	----集成电路生产用氦质谱检漏台	0				17	17	13	台		----Integrated circuit belium spectra leak detectors
9027.8019	----其他	0				17	17	13	台		----Other
9027.8019 10	UF_6质谱仪/离子源(能从UF_6气流中在线取得供料、产品或尾料样品谱仪)	0				17	17	13	台	3	UF_6 mass spectrographs/ion sources (capable of on-line taking samples of charging gas, product gas or tail gas from UF_6 flow)
9027.8019 20	测大于230质量单位离子质谱仪(分辨率高于2/230)	0				17	17	13	台	3	High-resolution ion mass spectrographs resolving power > 2/230
9027.8019 90	其他质谱仪	0				17	17	13	台		Other mass spectrograph
	---其他:										---Other:
9027.8091	----曝光表	14	8		8.4	70	17	13	个		----exposure meters
9027.8099	----其他	0				17	17	13	台		----Other

税则号列 Tariff Item.	货品名称	最惠国(%) MFN	协定(%)CT 东盟 CA	中巴 CP	中智 CC	普通 Gen	增值税率 VAT	出口退税 ED	计量单位 Unit	监管条件 SC	Article Description
9027.9000	-检镜切片机;零件、附件	0				17	17	13	千克		-Microtomes; parts and accessories
90.28	**生产或供应气体、液体及电力用的计量仪表,包括它们的校准仪表:**										**Gas, liquid or electricity supply or production meters, including calibrating meters therefor:**
	-气量计:										-Gas meters:
9028.1010	---煤气表	10	5		0	30	17	13	个		---Coal gas meters
9028.1090	---其他	10	8		0	30	17	13	个		---Other
	-液量计:										-Liquid meters:
9028.2010	---水表	10	8		8	30	17	13	个	B	---Water meters
9028.2090	---其他	10	8		8	30	17	13	个	B	---Other
	-电量计:										-Electricity meters:
9028.3010	---电度表	10	5		8	30	17	13	个	B	---Watt-hour meter
9028.3090	---其他	10	8		8	30	17	13	个	B	---Other
	-零件、附件:										-Parts and accessories:
9028.9010	---工业用	8.4	5		6.7	30	17	13	千克		---For technical use
9028.9090	---其他	8.4	5		6.7	50	17	13	千克		---Other
90.29	**转数计、产量计数器、车费计、里程计、步数计及类似仪表;速度计及转速表,税目90.14及90.15的仪表除外;频闪观测仪:**										**Revolution counters, production counters, taximeters, mileometers, pedometers and the like; speed indicators and tachometers, other than those of heading No. 90.14 or 90.15; stroboscopes:**
	-转数计、产量计数器、车费计、里程计、步数计及类似仪表:										-Revolution counters, production counters, taximeters, mileometers, pedometers and the like:
9029.1010	---转数计	15	8		0	50	17	13	个		---Revolution counters
9029.1020	---车费计、里程计	15	8		0	35	17	13	个		---Taximeters and mileometers
9029.1090	---其他	15	8		0	35	17	13	个		---Other
	-速度计及转速表,频闪观测仪:										-Speed indicators and tachometers; stroboscopes:
9029.2010	---车辆用速度计	10	5		0	35	17	13	个		---Speed indicators for motor vehicles
9029.2090	---其他	10	5		0	35	17	13	个		---Other
9029.9000	-零件、附件	6	5		0	35	17	13	千克		-Parts and accessories
90.30	**示波器、频谱分析仪及其他用于电量测量或检验的仪器和装置,但不包括税目90.28的各种仪表;α射线、β射线、γ射线、X射线、宇宙射线或其他离子射线的测量或检验仪器及装置:**										**Oscilloscopes, spectrum analysers and other instruments and apparatus for measuring or checking electrical quantities, excluding meters of heading No. 90.28; instruments and apparatus for measuring or detecting alpha, beta, gamma, X-ray, cosmic or other ionizing radiations:**
9030.1000	-离子射线的测量或检验仪器及装置	5			0	20	17	13	台		-Instruments and apparatus for measuring or detecting ionizing radiations
	-示波器:										-Scillographs:
9030.2010	---测试频率在300兆赫兹以下的通用示波器	8	8		0	80	17	13	台		---For general use, of test frequency less than 300 MHz
9030.2090	---其他	5			0	20	17	13	台		---Other

税则号列 Tariff Item.	货品名称	最惠国(%) MFN	协定(%)CT 东盟 CA	 中巴 CP	 中智 CC	普通 Gen	增值税率 VAT	出口退税 ED	计量单位 Unit	监管条件 SC	Article Description
	-检测电压、电流、电阻或功率的其他仪器及装置:										-Other instruments and apparatus, for measuring or checking voltage, current, resistance or power, without a recording device:
	--万用表,不带记录装置:										--Multimeters:
9030.3110	---量程在五位半及以下的数字万用表	15	8		9	130	17	13	台	B	---Digital, of measuring range of 5 $\frac{1}{2}$ or less
9030.3190	---其他	5			0	20	17	13	台	B	---Other
9030.3200	--万用表,带记录装置	8	5		0	20	17	13	台		--Multimeters with a recording device
	--其他,不带记录装置:										--other without a recording device:
9030.3310	---量程在五位半及以下的数字电流表、电压表	15	8		12	130	17	13	台	B	---Digital ammeters or voltmeters. of measuing rang of 5 $\frac{1}{2}$ or less
9030.3320	---电阻测试仪	14	8		11.2	80	17	13	台		---Resistnate measaring instruments
9030.3390	---其他	9	5		7.2	20	17	13	台	B	---other
9030.3900	--其他,带记录装置	8	5		0	20	17	13	台	B	--Other with recordins device
	-通信专用的其他仪器及装置(例如,串音测试器、增益测量仪、失真度表、噪声计):										-Other instruments and apparatus, specially designed for telecommunications (for example, cross-talk meters, gain measuring instruments, distortion factor meters, psophometers):
9030.4010	---测试频率在12.4千兆赫兹以下的数字式频率计	0				80	17	13	台		---Digital frequency meters, of test frequency less than 12.4 GHz
9030.4090	---其他	0				20	17	13	台	O	---Other
	-其他仪器及装置:										-Other instruments and apparatus:
9030.8200	--测试或检验半导体晶片或器件用	0				20	17	13	台		--For measuring or checking semiconductor wafers or devices
	--其他,带有记录装置:										--Other, with a recording device:
9030.8410	---电感及电容测试仪	10	8		0	80	17	13	台		---For measuring inductances or capacitances
9030.8490	---其他	8	5		0	20	17	13	台		---Other
	--其他:										--Other:
9030.8910	---电感及电容测试仪	14	8		11.2	80	17	13	台		---For measuring inductances or capacitances
9030.8990	---其他	8	5		6.4	20	17	13	台		---Other
9030.8990 10	中子探测和测量仪表(专用于测定核反应堆堆芯内中子通量的)	8				20	17	13	台	3	Instruments and apparatus for measuring or detecting neutron (specified for measuring neutron flux in reactor core)
9030.8990 90	其他电量的测量或检验仪器及装置(未装有记录装置的)	8				20	17	13	台		Other instruments and apparatus for measuring or checking electrical quantities without a recording device
*9030.9000	-零件、附件	7	5		0	17	17	13	千克		-Parts and accessories
9030.9000 01	检测半导体晶片及器件的仪器零件(包括附件)	0				17	17	13	千克	s	Parts and accessories of instruments and apparatus for measuring or checking semiconductor wafers or devices

税则号列 Tariff Item.	货品名称	最惠国(%) MFN	协定(%) 东盟 CA	中巴 CP	CT 中智 CC	普通 Gen	增值税率 VAT	出口退税 ED	计量单位 Unit	监管条件 SC	Article Description
9030.9000 02	ITA产品用的印刷电路组件(包括外接组件,如符合PCMCIA标准的卡)	0				17	17	13	千克	s	Printed circuit assemblies for products falling within the ITA, including such assemblies for external connections such as cards that conform to the PCMCLA standard
9030.9000 90	编号9030所属货品的零件及附件	7				17	17	13	千克		Parts and accessories of goods of heading 9030
90.31	**本章其他税目未列名的测量或检验仪器、器具及机器;轮廓投影仪:**										**Measuring or checking instruments, appliances and machines, not specified or included elsewhere in this Chapter; profile projectors:**
9031.1000	-机械零件平衡试验机	7	5	6.5	0	17	17	13	台		-Machines for balancing mechanical parts
9031.1000 10	陀螺动态平衡测试仪	7				17	17	13	台	3	Machines for gyro dynamic balancing testers
9031.1000 90	其他机械零件平衡试验机	7				17	17	13	台		Other machines for balancing mechanical parts
9031.2000	-试验台	7	5		0	17	17	13	台		-Test benches
9031.2000 10	陀螺/马达运转试验台	7				17	17	13	台	3	Gyro/motor running test-stands
9031.2000 20	加速度表测试台	7				17	17	13	台	3	Accelerometer test-stands
9031.2000 30	试车台(能试推力>90KN火箭发动机的或同时测量三个推力分量的)	7				17	17	13	台	3	Rocket engine firing test-stands (capable of testing rocket engine with a thrust >90KN or testing three individual thrust forces at the same time)
9031.2000 40	惯性平台测试台(测试平台包括高精度离心机和转台)	7				17	17	13	台	3	Inert platform test-stands (including high-precision centrifuge and turntable)
9031.2000 90	其他试验台	7				17	17	13	台		Other test benches
	-其他光学仪器及器具:										-Other optical instruments and appliances:
9031.4100	--制造半导体器件时检验半导体晶片、器件或检测光掩模或光栅用	0				17	17	13	台		--For inspecting semiconductor wafers or devices or for inspecting photomasks or reticles used in manufacturing semiconductor devices:
	--其他:										--Other:
9031.4910	---轮廓投影仪	10	5		0	20	17		台		---Profile projectors
9031.4990	---其他	0				17	17	13	台		---Other
9031.4990 10	光盘质量在线检测仪及离线检测仪	0				17	17	13	台	6O	Automatic inspection detectors (AID) for CD production
9031.4990 90	其他光学测量或检验仪器和器具(90章其他编号未列名的)	0				17	17	13	台	O	Other measuring or checking optical instruments and appliances, not elsewhere specified or included in chapter 90
	-其他仪器、器具及机器:										-Other instruments, appliances and machines:
9031.8010	---光纤通信及光纤性能测试仪	5		4	4	17	17	13	台	O	---Optical telecommunication and optical fibre performance testing instruments
9031.8020	---坐标测量仪	5			4	17	17	13	台		---Coordinate measuring instruments
9031.8090	---其他	5		4	4	17	17	13	台		---Other
9031.8090 01	跑道摩擦系数测试仪	5				17	17	13	台		Runway friction coefficient tester
9031.8090 10	惯性测量单元测试仪	5				17	17	13	台	3	Inertial measurement testers
9031.8090 20	陀螺调谐测试仪	5				17	17	13	台	3	Gyro tuning testers

税则号列 Tariff Item.	货品名称	最惠国(%) MFN	协定(%) 东盟 CA	中巴 CP	CT 中智 CC	普通 Gen	增值税率 VAT	出口退税 ED	计量单位 Unit	监管条件 SC	Article Description
9031.8090 90	其他测量,检验仪器,器具及机器(指90章其他编号未列名的)	5				17	17	13	台		Other measuring or checking instruments, appliances and machines, not elsewhere specified or included in Chapter90
9031.9000	-零件、附件	0				17	17	13	千克		-Parts and accessories
9031.9000 20	惯性测量单元稳定元件加工夹具	0				17	17	13	千克	3	Processing clamps for stabling element of inertial measurement unit
9031.9000 30	惯性平台平衡夹具	0				17	17	13	千克	3	Inert platform balancing clamps
9031.9000 90	编号9031的仪器及器具的其他零件(90章其他编号未列名的)	0				17	17	13	千克		Other parts of instruments, appliances and machines of heading No. 9031, not elsewhere specified or included in chapter 90
90.32	**自动调节或控制仪器及装置:**										**Automatic regulating or controlling instruments and apparatus:**
9032.1000	-恒温器	7	T3		0	17	17	13	台		-Thermostats
9032.2000	-恒压器	7	5		0	17	17	13	台		-Manostats
	-其他仪器及装置:										-Other instruments and apparatus:
9032.8100	--液压或气压的	7	5	6.5	0	17	17	13	台		--Hydraulic or pneumatic
9032.8900	--其他	7	5		5.6	17	17	13	台		--Other
9032.8900 01	三坐标测量机用自动控制柜	7				17	17		台		
9032.8900 02	飞机自动驾驶系统(包括自动驾驶、电子控制飞行、自动故障分析、警告系统配平系统及推力监控设备及其相关仪表)	7				17	17	13	台		Automatic pilotting systems for aircraft, including instruments of automatic pilotting, electronic flight control, automatic failure analysis, warning systems
9032.8900 20	组合喷气发动机的燃烧调节装置(自动控制、调节装置)	7				17	17	13	台	3O	Combustion adjusting device for combined jet engine
9032.8900 90	其他自动调节或控制仪器及装置	7				17	17	13	台	O	Other automatic regulating or controlling instruments and apparatus
9032.9000	-零件、附件	5			0	17	17	13	千克		-Parts and accessories
90.33	**第九十章所列机器、器具、仪器或装置用的本章其他税目未列名的零件、附件:**										**Parts and accessories (not specified or included elsewhere in this Chapter) for machines, appliances, instruments or apparatus of Chapter 90:**
9033.0000	第九十章所列机器、器具、仪器或装置用的本章其他税目未列名的零件、附件	6	5		0	17	17	13	千克		Parts and accessories (not specified or included elsewhere in this Chapter) for machines, appliances, instruments or apparatus of Chapter 90
9033.0000 01	飞机自动驾驶系统的零件(包括自动驾驶、电子控制飞行、自动故障分析、警告系统配平系统及推力监控设备及其相关仪表的零件)	6				17	17	13	千克		Parts of automatic pilotting system for aircraft (including automatic pilotting, electronic flight control, automatic failure analysis, warning systems, trimming systems, thrust monitoring equipments and the meters thereof)
9033.0000 90	第90章其他编号未列名零、附件(指第90章所列机器、器具、仪器或装置用)	6				17	17	13	千克		Other parts and accessories for machines, appliances, instruments or apparatus of Chapter 90, not specified or included elsewhere

第九十一章
钟表及其零件

注释：

一、本章不包括：

（一）钟表玻璃及钟锤（按其构成材料归类）；

（二）表链（根据不同情况，归入税目71.13或71.17）；

（三）第十五类注释二所规定的贱金属制通用零件（第十五类）、塑料制的类似品（第三十九章）及贵金属或包贵金属制的类似品（一般归入税目71.15）；但钟、表发条则应作为钟、表的零件归类（税目91.14）；

（四）轴承滚珠（根据不同情况，归入税目73.26或84.82）；

（五）税目84.12的物品，不需擒纵器可以工作的；

（六）滚珠轴承（税目84.82）；

（七）第八十五章的物品，本身未组装在或未与其他零件组装在钟、表机芯内，也未组装成专用于或主要用于钟、表机芯零件的（第八十五章）。

二、税目91.01仅包括表壳完全以贵金属或包贵金属制的表，以及用贵金属或包贵金属与税目71.01至71.04的天然、养殖珍珠或宝石、半宝石（天然、合成或再造）合制的表。用贱金属上镶嵌贵金属制成表壳的表应归入税目91.02。

三、本章所称"表芯"，是指由摆轮及游丝、石英晶体或其他能确定时间间隔的装置来进行调节的机构，并带有显示器或可装机械指示器的系统。表芯的厚度不超过12毫米，长、宽或直径不超过50毫米。

四、除注释一另有规定的以外，钟、表的机芯及其他零件，既适用于钟或表，又适用于其他物品（例如精密仪器）的，均应归入本章。

Chapter 91
Clocks and watches and parts thereof

Notes:

1. This Chapter does not cover:

(a) Clock or watch glasses or weights (classified according to their constituent material);

(b) Watch chains (heading No. 71.13 or 71.17, as the case may be);

(c) Parts of general use defined in Note 2 to Section XV, of base metal (Section XV), or similar goods of plastics (Chapter 39) or of precious metal or metal clad with precious metal (generally heading No. 71.15); clock or watch springs are, however, to be classified as clock or watch parts (heading No. 91.14);

(d) Bearing balls (heading No. 73.26 or 84.82, as the case may be);

(e) Articles of heading No. 84.12 constructed to work without an escapement;

(f) Ball bearings (heading No. 84.82); or

(g) Articles of Chapter 85, not yet assembled together or with other components into watch or clock movements or into articles suitable for use solely or principally as parts of such movements (Chapter 85).

2. Heading No. 91.01 covers only watches with case wholly of precious metal or of metal clad with precious metal, or of the same materials combined with natural or cultured pearls, or precious or semi-precious stones (natural, synthetic or reconstructed) of headingsNo. 71.01 to 71.04. Watches with case of base metal inlaid with precious metal fall in heading No. 91.02.

3. For the purposes of this Chapter, the expression "watch movements" means devices regulated by a balance-wheel and hairspring, quartz crystal or any other system capable of determining intervals of time, with a display or a system to which a mechanical display can be incorporated. Such watch movements shall not exceed 12 mm in thickness and 50 mm in width, length or diameter.

4. Except as provided in Note 1, movements and other parts suitable for use both in clocks or watches and in other articles (for example, precision instruments) are to be classified in this Chapter.

税则号列 Tariff Item.	货品名称	最惠国(%) MFN	协定(%)CT 东盟 CA	中巴 CP	中智 CC	普通 Gen	增值税率 VAT	出口退税 ED	计量单位 Unit	监管条件 SC	Article Description
91.01	手表、怀表及其他表，包括秒表，表壳用贵金属或包贵金属制成的：										**Wrist-watches, pocket-watches and other watches, including stop-watches, with case of precious metal or of metal clad with precious metal:**
	-电力驱动的手表，不论是否附有秒表装置：										-Wrist-watches, electrically operated whether or not incorporating a stop-watch facility:
9101.1100	--仅有机械指示器的	11	8	9.9	6.6	100	17	13	只	B	--With mechanical display only
	--其他：										--Other:
9101.1910	---仅有光电显示器的	16	8		9.6	100	17	13	只		---With opto electronic display only
9101.1990	---其他	15	8		9	100	17	13	只	B	---Other
	-其他手表，不论是否附有秒表装置：										-Other wrist-watches, whether or not incorporating a stop-watch facility:

税则号列 Tariff Item.	货 品 名 称	最惠国(%) MFN	协定(%) CT 东盟 CA	中巴 CP	中智 CC	普通 Gen	增值税率 VAT	出口退税 ED	计量单位 Unit	监管条件 SC	Article Description
9101.2100	--自动上弦的	11	8		6.6	80	17	13	只		--Automatic winding
9101.2100 10	含濒危动物皮自动上弦贵金属机械手表(表壳用贵金属或包贵金属制成的)	11				80	17	13	只	BEF	Wrist - watches, cut to matic winding with case of precious metal or of metal clad with precious metal
9101.2100 90	其他自动上弦贵金属机械手表(表壳用贵金属或包贵金属制成的)	11				80	17	13	只	B	Other wrist - watches, automatic winding (with case of precious metal or of metal clad with precious metal, other than electrically operated)
9101.2900	--其他	15	8		9	80	17	13	只		--Other
9101.2900 10	含濒危动物皮非自动上弦贵金属机械手表(表壳用贵金属或包贵金属制成的)	15				80	17	13	只	EF	Wrist - watches, non - automatic winding, with case of precious metal or of metal clad with precious metal, other than electrically operated, containing animal of in imminent dangers
9101.2900 90	其他非自动上弦贵金属机械手表(表壳用贵金属或包贵金属制成的)	15				80	17	13	只		Other wrist - watches, non - automatic winding, with case of precious metal or metalclad with precious meta, other than electrically operated
	-其他:										-Other:
9101.9100	--电力驱动的	15	8		9	100	17	13	只		--Electrically operated
9101.9900	--其他	20	12		12	80	17	13	只		--Other
91.02	**手表、怀表及其他表,包括秒表,但税目 91.01 的货品除外:**										**Wrist-watches, pocket-watches and other watches, including stop-watches, other than those of heading 91.01:**
	-电力驱动的手表,不论是否附有秒表装置:										-Wrist-watches, electrically operated, whether or not incorporating a stop-watch facility:
9102.1100	--仅有机械指示器的	12.5	8	11.1	10	100	17	13	只	B	--With mechanical display only
9102.1200	--仅有光电显示器的	23	12		13.8	100	17	13	只	B	--With optoelectronic
9102.1900	--其他	15	8		9	100	17	13	只	B	--Other
	-其他手表,不论是否装有秒表装置:										-Other wrist-watches, whether or not incorporating a stop-watch facility:
9102.2100	--自动上弦的	11	8		8.8	80	17	13	只		--Automatic winding
9102.2100 10	含濒危动物皮其他自动上弦的机械手表(用贵金属或包贵金属制壳的除外)	11				80	17	13	只	EF	(wrist - watches, automatic winding, with case of precious metal or metalclad with precious meta, other than electrically operated, containing skins of animal in imminent dangers)
9102.2100 90	其他自动上弦的机械手表(用贵金属或包贵金属制壳的除外)	11				80	17	13	只		(Wrist - watches, automatic winding, other than electrically operated)
	-其他:										-Other:
9102.2900	--其他	15	8		9	80	17	13	只		--Other

税则号列 Tariff Item.	货品名称	最惠国(%) MFN	协定(%)CT 东盟 CA	中巴 CP	中智 CC	普通 Gen	增值税率 VAT	出口退税 ED	计量单位 Unit	监管条件 SC	Article Description
9102.2900 10	含濒危动物皮其他非自动上弦机械手表(用贵金属或包贵金属制壳的除外)	15				80	17	13	只	BEF	Wrist - watches, automatic winding, other than electrically operated, containing skins of animal in imminent dangers (with case of precious metal or of metal clad with precious metal, other than electrically operated)
9102.2900 90	其他非自动上弦的机械手表(用贵金属或包贵金属制壳的除外)	15				80	17	13	只	B	(Wrist - watches, non - automatic winding, other than electrically operated, containing skins of animal in imminent dangers
9102.9100	--电力驱动的	15	8		9	100	17	13	只		--Electrically operated
9102.9900	--其他	20	12		12	80	17	13	只		--Other
91.03	**以表芯装成的钟,但不包括税目91.04的钟:**										**Clocks with watch movements, excluding clocks of heading No. 91.04:**
9103.1000	-电力驱动的	23	12		13.8	100	17	13	只	B	-Electrically operated
9103.9000	-其他	20	12		12	100	17	13	只		-Other
91.04	**仪表板钟及车辆、航空器、航天器或船舶用的类似钟:**										**Instrument panel clocks and clocks of a similar type for vehicles, aircraft, spacecraft or vessels:**
9104.0000	仪表板钟及车辆、航空器、航天器或船舶用的类似钟	10	5		0	100	17	13	只		Instrument panel clocks and clocks of a similar type for vehicles, aircraft, spacecraft or vessels
91.05	**其他钟:**										**Other clocks:**
	-闹钟:										-Alarm clocks:
9105.1100	--电力驱动的	23	12		13.8	100	17	13	只	B	--Electrically operated
9105.1900	--其他	20	12		12	100	17	13	只	B	--Other
	-挂钟:										-Wall clocks:
9105.2100	--电力驱动的	23	12		18.4	100	17	13	只	B	--Electrically operated
9105.2900	--其他	20	12		12	100	17	13	只	B	--Other
	-其他:										-Other:
	--电力驱动的:										--Electrically operated:
9105.9110	---天文钟	3			0	8	17	13	只		---Astronomical chronometer
9105.9190	---其他	23	12		13.8	100	17	13	只	B	---Other
9105.9900	--其他	16	8		9.6	100	17	13	只	B	--Other
91.06	**时间记录器以及测量、记录或指示时间间隔的装置,装有钟、表机芯或同步电动机的(例如,考勤钟、时刻记录器):**										**Time of day recording apparatus and apparatus for measuring, recording or otherwise indicating intervals of time, with clock or watch movement or with synchronous motor (for example, time-registers, time-recorders):**
9106.1000	-考勤钟、时刻记录器	16	8		9.6	50	17	13	只		-Time-registers; time-recorders
9106.9000	-其他	16	8		12.8	50	17	13	只		-Other
91.07	**装有钟、表机芯或同步电动机的定时开关:**										**Time switches with clock or watch movement or with synchronous motor:**
9107.0000	装有钟、表机芯或同步电动机的定时开关	12	8		0	50	17	13	个	B	Time switches with clock or watch movement or with synchronous motor
91.08	**已组装的完整表芯:**										**Watch movements, complete and assembled:**
	-电力驱动的:										-Electrically operated:

税则号列 Tariff Item.	货品名称	最惠国(%) MFN	协定(%) CT 东盟 CA	中巴 CP	中智 CC	普通 Gen	增值税率 VAT	出口退税 ED	计量单位 Unit	监管条件 SC	Article Description
9108. 1100	--仅有机械指示器或有可装机械指示器的装置的	16	8		9. 6	80	17	13	只	B	--With mechanical display only or with a device to which a mechanical display can be incorporated
9108. 1200	--仅有光电显示器的	16	8		9. 6	80	17	13	只	B	--With opto-electronic display only
9108. 1900	--其他	16	8	12	9. 6	80	17	13	只	B	--Other
9108. 2000	-自动上弦的	16	8		9. 6	80	17	13	只	B	-Automatic winding
	-其他:										-Other:
9108. 9010	---表面尺寸在 33. 8 毫米及以下	16	8		9. 6	80	17	13	只	B	---Measuring 33. 8mm or less
9108. 9090	---其他	16	8		9. 6	80	17	13	只	B	---Other
91. 09	**已组装的完整钟芯:**										**Clock movements, complete and assembled:**
	-电力驱动的:										-Eletrically operated:
9109. 1100	--闹钟芯	16	8		9. 6	100	17	13	只		--Of alarm clocks
9109. 1900	--其他	16	8		9. 6	100	17	13	只		--Other
9109. 9000	-其他	16	8		9. 6	100	17	13	只		-Other
91. 10	**未组装或部分组装的完整钟、表机芯(机芯套装件);已组装的不完整钟、表机芯;未组装的不完整钟、表机芯:**										**Complete watch or clock movements, unassembled or partly assembled (movement sets); incomplete watch or clock movements, assembled; rough watch or clock movements:**
	-表的:										-Of watches:
9110. 1100	--未组装或部分组装的完整机芯(机芯套装件)	16	8		9. 6	80	17	13	只		--Complete movements, unassembled or partly assembled (movement sets)
9110. 1200	--已组装的不完整机芯	16	8		9. 6	70	17	13	千克		--Incomplete movements, assembled
9110. 1900	--未组装的不完整机芯	16	8		9. 6	70	17	13	千克		--Rough movements
	-其他:										-Other:
9110. 9010	---未组装或部分组装的完整机芯	16	T3		9. 6	100	17	13	千克/只		---Complete movements, unassembled or partly assembled
9110. 9090	---其他	16	T3		9. 6	80	17	13	千克		---Other
91. 11	**表壳及其零件:**										**Watch cases and parts thereof:**
9111. 1000	-贵金属表壳或包贵金属表壳	14	8		8. 4	80	17	13	只		-Cases of precious metal or of metal clad with precious metal
9111. 2000	-贱金属表壳,不论是否镀金或镀银	14	8	10	8. 4	80	17	13	只		-Cases of base metal, whether or not gold-or silver-plated
9111. 8000	-其他表壳	14	8		8. 4	80	17	13	只		-Other cases
9111. 9000	-零件	14	8		8. 4	80	17	13	千克		-Parts
91. 12	**钟壳和本章所列其他货品的类似外壳及其零件:**										**Clock cases and cases of a similar type for other goods of this Chapter, and parts thereof:**
9112. 2000	-壳	14	8		8. 4	80	17	13	只		-Cases
9112. 9000	-零件	12	8		7. 2	80	17	13	千克		-Parts
91. 13	**表带及其零件:**										**Watch straps, watch bands and watch bracelets, and parts thereof:**
9113. 1000	-贵金属或包贵金属制	20	12		12	130	17	13	千克		-Of precious metal or of metal clad with pecious metal
9113. 2000	-贱金属制,不论是否镀金或镀银	14	8		8. 4	100	17	13	千克		-Of base metal, whether or not gold- or silver-plated
9113. 9000	-其他	14	8		8. 4	100	17	13	千克		-Other

税则号列 Tariff Item.	货品名称	最惠国(%) MFN	协定(%) CT 东盟 CA	中巴 CP	中智 CC	普通 Gen	增值税率 VAT	出口退税 ED	计量单位 Unit	监管条件 SC	Article Description
9113.9000 10	濒危动物皮制的表带及其零件	14				100	17	13	千克	FE	Watch straps, watch bands and watch bracelets, and parts thereof, of leather of skin of animal in imminent dangers
9113.9000 90	其他非金属制的表带及其零件	14				100	17	13	千克		Other watch straps, watch bands and watch bracelets and parts thereof, of non-metal
91.14	**钟、表的其他零件：**										**Other clock or watch parts:**
9114.1000	-发条,包括游丝	14	8		8.4	50	17	13	千克		-Springs, including hair-springs
9114.2000	-宝石轴承	14	8		8.4	50	17	13	千克		-Jewel bearings
9114.3000	-钟面或表面	14	8		8.4	50	17	13	千克		-Dials
9114.4000	-夹板及横担(过桥)	14	8		8.4	50	17	13	千克		-Plates and bridges
9114.9000	-其他	14	8		8.4	70	17	13	千克		-Other

第九十二章
乐器及其零件、附件

注释：

一、本章不包括：

（一）第十五类注释二所规定的贱金属制通用零件（第十五类）或塑料制的类似品（第三十九章）；

（二）第八十五章或第九十章的传声器、扩大器、扬声器、耳机、开关、频闪观测仪及其他附属仪器、器具或设备，虽用于本章物品但未与该物品组成一体或安装在同一机壳内；

（三）玩具乐器或器具（税目 95.03）；

（四）清洁乐器用的刷子（税目 96.03）；

（五）收藏品或古物（税目 97.05 或 97.06）。

二、用于演奏税目 92.02、92.06 所列乐器的弓、槌及类似品，如果与该乐器一同进口或出口，数量合理，用途明确，应归入有关乐器的相应税目。

税目 92.09 的卡片、盘或卷，即使与乐器一同进口或出口，也不视为该乐器的组成部分，而应作为单独进口或出口的物品对待。

Chapter 92
Musical instruments; parts and accessories of such articles

Notes:

1. This Chapter does not cover:

(a) Parts of general use, as defined in Note 2 to Section XV, of base metal (Section XV), or similar goods of plastics (Chapter 39);

(b) Microphones, amplifiers, loudspeakers, headphones, switches, stroboscopes or other accessory instruments, apparatus or equipment of Chapter 85 or 90, for use with but not incorporated in or housed in the same cabinet as instruments of this Chapter;

(c) Toy instruments or apparatus (heading No. 95.03);

(d) Brushes for cleaning musical instruments (heading No. 96.03); or

(e) Collectors' pieces or antiques (heading No. 97.05 or 97.06).

2. Bows and sticks and similar devices used in playing the musical instruments of heading No. 92.02 or 92.06 presented with such instruments in numbers normal thereto and clearly intended for use therewith, are to be classified in the same heading as the relative instruments.

Cards, discs and rolls of heading No. 92.09 presented with an instrument are to be treated as separate articles and not as forming a part of such instrument.

税则号列 Tariff Item.	货品名称	最惠国(%) MFN	协定(%)CT 东盟 CA	中巴 CP	中智 CC	普通 Gen	增值税率 VAT	出口退税 ED	计量单位 Unit	监管条件 SC	Article Description
92.01	**钢琴，包括自动钢琴、拨弦古钢琴及其他键盘弦乐器：**										**Pianos, including automatic pianos; harpsichords and other keyboard stringed instruments:**
9201.1000	-竖式钢琴	17.5	12		10.5	70	17	13	台		-Upright pianos
9201.2000	-大钢琴	17.5	12		10.5	70	17	13	台		-Grand pianos
9201.2000 01	完税价格≥5 万美元的大钢琴	17.5				70	17	13	台		Grand pianos dutiable price ≥ USD 50000/set
9201.2000 90	其他大钢琴	17.5				70	17	13	台		Other grand pianos
9201.9000	-其他	17.5	12		10.5	70	17	13	台		-Other
92.02	**其他弦乐器（例如，吉他、小提琴、竖琴）：**										**Other string musical instruments (for example, guitars, violins, harps):**
9202.1000	-弓弦乐器	17.5	8		10.5	70	17	13	只		-Played with a bow
9202.1000 11	完税价格≥1.5 万美元的含濒危动物皮弓弦乐器	17.5				70	17	13	只	FE	Played with a bow, dutiable price≥USD 15000/set, (containing skin of animal in imminent dangers)
9202.1000 19	其他含濒危动物皮的弓弦乐器	17.5				70	17	13	只	FE	Other played with a bow, containing skin of animal in imminent dangers
9202.1000 91	完税价格≥1.5 万美元的不含野生动物皮弓弦乐器	17.5				70	17	13	只		Played with a bow, dutiable price≥USD 15000/set, other than those of subheading 92021000.11
9202.1000 99	其他弓弦乐器	17.5				70	17	13	只		Other played with a bow
9202.9000	-其他	17.5	8		10.5	70	17	13	只		-Other

税则号列 Tariff Item.	货品名称	最惠国(%) MFN	协定(%) CT 东盟 CA	中巴 CP	中智 CC	普通 Gen	增值税率 VAT	出口退税 ED	计量单位 Unit	监管条件 SC	Article Description
9202.9000 10	含濒危动物成分的其他弦乐器	17.5				70	17	13	只	FE	Other string musical instruments, containing skin and other parts of animal in imminent dangers
9202.9000 90	其他弦乐器	17.5				70	17	13	只		Other string musical instruments
92.05	**其他管乐器(例如,单簧管、小号、风笛):**										**Other wind musical instruments (for example, clarinets, trumpets, bagpipes):**
9205.1000	-铜管乐器	17.5	8		10.5	70	17	13	只		-Brass-wind instruments
	-其他:										-Other:
9205.1000 01	完税价格≥2000美元的铜管乐器	17.5				70	17	13	只		Brass - wind musical instruments, dutiable price≥USD2000/set
9205.1000 90	其它铜管乐器	17.5				70	17	13	只		Other brass - wind musical instruments
9205.9010	---键盘管风琴:簧风琴及类似的游离金属簧片键盘乐器	20	12		12	80	17	13	只		---Keyboard pipe organs; harmoniums and similar keyboard instruments with free metal reeds
9205.9020	---手风琴及类似乐器;口琴	21	12		12.6	80	17	13	只		---Accordions and similar instruments; mouth organs
9205.9030	---口琴	21	12		12.6	80	17	13	只		---mouth organs
9205.9090	---其他	17.5	8		14	70	17	13	只		---Other
9205.9090 01	完税价格≥1万美元的其他管乐器	17.5				70	17	13	只		Other wind musical instruments, dutiable price ≥USD 10000/set
9205.9090 90	其他管乐器	17.5				70	17	13	只		Other wind musical instruments
92.06	**打击乐器(例如,鼓、木琴、铙、钹、响板、响葫芦):**										**Percussion musical instruments (for example, drums, xylophones, cymbals, castanets, maracas):**
9206.0000	打击乐器(例如,鼓、木琴、铙、钹、响板、响葫芦)	17.5	8		0	70	17	13	只		Percussion musical instruments (for example, drums, xylophones, cymbals, castanets, maracas)
9206.0000 10	含濒危动物皮的打击乐器(例如,鼓、木琴、钹、响板)	17.5				70	17	13	只	FE	Percussion musical instruments (for example, drums, xylophones, cymbals, castanets, maracas) containing leather of animal in imminent dangers
9206.0000 90	其他打击乐器(例如,鼓、木琴、钹、响板)	17.5				70	17	13	只		Other percussion musical instruments (for example, drums, xylophones, cymbals, castanets, maracas)
92.07	**通过电产生或扩大声音的乐器(例如,电风琴、电吉他、电手风琴):**										**Musical instruments, the sound of which is produced or must be amplified electrically (for example, organs, guitars, accordions):**
9207.1000	-键盘乐器,但手风琴除外	30	12		18	100	17	13	只		-Keyboard instruments, other than accordions
9207.9000	-其他	30	12		18	100	17	13	个		-Other

税则号列 Tariff Item.	货品名称	最惠国(%) MFN	协定(%) CT 东盟 CA	中巴 CP	中智 CC	普通 Gen	增值税率 VAT	出口退税 ED	计量单位 Unit	监管条件 SC	Article Description
92. 08	**百音盒、游艺场风琴、手摇风琴、机械鸣禽、乐锯及本章其他税目未列名的其他乐器；各种媒诱音响器、哨子、号角、口吹音响信号器：**										**Musical boxes, fairground organs, mechanical street organs, mechanical singing birds, musical saws and other musical instruments not falling within any other heading of this Chapter; decoy calls of all kinds; whistles, call horns and other mouth-blown sound signalling instruments:**
9208. 1000	-百音盒	22	12		13. 2	80	17	13	个		-Musical boxes
9208. 9000	-其他	22	12		13. 2	80	17	13	个		-Other
92. 09	**乐器的零件(例如百音盒的机械装置)、附件(例如,机械乐器用的卡片、盘及带卷);节拍器、音叉及各种定音管:**										**Parts (for example, mechanisms for musical boxes) and accessories (for example, cards, discs and rolls for mechanical instruments) of musical instruments; metronomes, tuning forks and pitch pipes of all kinds:**
9209. 3000	-乐器用的弦	17. 5	8		10. 5	70	17	13	千克		-Musical instrument strings
	-其他:										-Other:
9209. 9100	--钢琴的零件、附件	17. 5	8		10. 5	70	17	13	千克		--Parts and accessories for pianos
9209. 9200	--税目 92. 02 所列乐器的零件、附件	17. 5	8		10. 5	70	17	13	千克		--Parts and accessories for the musical instruments of heading 92. 02
9209. 9400	--税目 92. 07 所列乐器的零件、附件	17. 5	8		10. 5	70	17	13	千克		--Parts and accessories for the musical instruments of heading 92. 07
	--其他										--Other
9209. 9910	---节拍器音叉及安音管	17. 5	8		10. 5	70	17	13	千克		---Metsonomes tuning froks and pitch pipes
9209. 9920	---百音盒的机械装置	17. 5	8		10. 5	70	17	13	千克		---Mechanisms for musicol boxes
9209. 9990	---其他	17. 5	8		10. 5	70	17	13	千克		---other

第十九类
武器、弹药及其零件、附件

第九十三章
武器、弹药及其零件、附件

注释：

一、本章不包括：

（一）第三十六章的货品（例如，火帽、雷管、信号弹）；

（二）第十五类注释二所规定的贱金属制通用零件（第十五类）或塑料制的类似品（第三十九章）；

（三）装甲战斗车辆（税目87.10）；

（四）武器用的望远镜瞄准具及其他光学装置（第九十章），但安装在武器上或与武器一同进口或出口以备安装在该武器上的除外；

（五）弓、箭、钝头击剑或玩具（第九十五章）；

（六）收藏品及古物（税目97.05或97.06）。

二、税目93.06所称"零件"，不包括税目85.26的无线电设备及雷达设备。

SECTION XIX
ARMS AND AMMUNITION; PARTS AND ACCESSORIES THEREOF

Chapter 93
Arms and ammunition; parts and accessories thereof

Notes:

1. This Chapter does not cover:

(a) Goods of Chapter 36 (for example, percussion caps, detonators, signalling flares);

(b) Parts of general use, as defined in Note 2 to Section XV, of base metal (Section XV), or similar goods of plastics (Chapter 39);

(c) Armoured fighting vehicles (heading No. 87.10);

(d) Telescopic sights or other optical devices suitable for use with arms, unless mounted on a firearm or presented with the firearm on which they are designed to be mounted (Chapter 90);

(e) Bows, arrows, fencing foils or toys (Chapter 95); or

(f) Collectors' pieces or antiques (heading No. 97.05 or 97.06).

2. In heading No. 93.06, the reference to "parts thereof" does not include radio or radar apparatus of heading No. 85.26.

税则号列 Tariff Item.	货品名称	最惠国(%) MFN	协定(%)CT 东盟 CA	中巴 CP	中智 CC	普通 Gen	增值税率 VAT	出口退税 ED	计量单位 Unit	监管条件 SC	Article Description
93.01	**军用武器，但左轮手枪、其他手枪及税目93.07的兵器除外：**										**Military weapons, other than revolvers, pistols and the arms of heading No. 93.07:**
	-火炮武器（例如，榴弹炮及迫击炮）：										-Artillery weapons (for example, guns, howitzers and mortars):
9301.1100	--自推进的	13	8		7.8	80	17		座		--Self-propelled
9301.1900	--其他	13	8		10.4	80	17		座		--Other
9301.2000	-火箭发射装置；火焰喷射器；手榴弹发射器；鱼雷发射管及类似发射装置	13	8		7.8	80	17		个		-Rocket launchers; flame-throwers; grenade launchers; torpedo tubes and similar projectors
9301.9000	-其他	13	8		10.4	80	17		枝		-Other
93.02	**左轮手枪及其他手枪，但税目93.03或93.04的货品除外：**										**Revolvers and pistols, other than those of heading 93.03 or 93.04:**
9302.0000	左轮手枪及其他手枪，但税目93.03或93.04的货品除外	13	8		7.8	80	17		枝		Revolvers and pistols, other than those of heading No. 93.03 or 93.04
93.03	**靠爆炸药发射的其他火器及类似装置（例如，运动用猎枪及步枪、前装枪、维利式信号枪及其他专为发射信号弹的装置、发射空包弹的左轮手枪和其他手枪、弩枪式无痛捕杀器、抛缆枪）：**										**Other firearms and similar devices which operate by the firing of an explosive charge (for example, sporting shotguns and rifles, muzzle-loading firearms, Very pistols and other devices designed to project only signal flares, pistols and revolvers for firing blank ammunition, captive-bolt humane killers, linethrowing guns):**

税则号列 Tariff Item.	货 品 名 称	最惠国(%) MFN	协定(%) CT 东盟 CA	中巴 CP	中智 CC	普通 Gen	增值税率 VAT	出口退税 ED	计量单位 Unit	监管条件 SC	Article Description
9303.1000	-前装枪	13	8		7.8	80	17	13	枝		-Muzzle-loading firearms
9303.2000	-其他运动、狩猎或打靶用猎枪,包括组合式滑膛来复枪	13	8		7.8	80	17	13	枝		-Other sporting, hunting or target shooting shotguns, including combination shotgunrifles
9303.3000	-其他运动、狩猎或打靶用步枪	13	8		7.8	80	17	13	枝		-Other sporting, hunting or target shooting rifles
9303.9000	-其他	13	8		7.8	80	17	13	枝		-Other
93.04	**其他武器(例如,弹簧枪、气枪、气手枪、警棍),但不包括税目93.07的货品:**										**Other arms (for example, spring, air or gas guns and pistols, truncheons), excluding those of heading No. 93.07:**
9304.0000	其他武器(例如,弹簧枪、气枪、气手枪、警棍),但不包括税目93.07的货品	13	8		7.8	80	17	13	枝		Other arms (for example, spring, air or gas guns and pistols, truncheons), excluding those of heading No. 93.07
93.05	**税目93.01至93.04所列物品的零件、附件:**										**Parts and accessories of articles of headingsNo. 93.01 to 93.04:**
9305.1000	-左轮手枪或其他手枪用	13	8		7.8	80	17	13	千克		-Of revolvers or pistols
	-税目93.03的猎枪或步枪用:										-Of shotguns or rifles of heading 93.03:
9305.2100	--猎枪筒	13	8		7.8	80	17	13	千克		--Shotgun barrels
9305.2900	--其他	13	8		7.8	80	17	13	千克		--Other
	-其他:										-Other:
9305.9100	--税目93.01的军用武器用	13	8		7.8	80	17		千克		--Of military weapons of heading No. 93.01
9305.9900	--其他	13	8		7.8	80	17	13	千克		--Other
93.06	**炸弹、手榴弹、鱼雷、地雷、水雷、导弹及类似武器及其零件;子弹、其他弹药和射弹及其零件,包括弹丸及弹垫:**										**Bombs, grenades, torpedoes, mines, missiles, and similar munitions of war and parts thereof; cartridges and other ammunition and projectiles and parts thereof, including shot and cartridge wads:**
	-猎枪子弹及其零件;气枪弹丸:										-Shotgun cartridges and parts thereof; air gun pellets:
9306.2100	--猎枪子弹	13	8		7.8	80	17	13	千克		--Cartridges
9306.2900	--其他	13	8		7.8	80	17	13	千克		--Other
	-其他子弹及其零件:										-Other cartridges and parts thereof
9306.3080	---铆接机或类似工具的子弹及其零件(包括弩枪式无痛捕杀器用)	13	8		7.8	80	17	13	千克		---Cartridges for riveting or similar tools or for captive – bolt humane killers and parts thereof
9306.3090	---其他	13	8		7.8	80	17	13	千克		---Other
9306.9000	-其他	13	8		10.4	80	17	13	千克		-Other
9306.9000 10	敏感物项管制的导弹及其零件(能把500千克以上有效载荷投掷到300千米以上的)	13				80	17	13	千克	3	Ballistic Missiles (capable of throwing an available load over 500kg beyond 300km)
9306.9000 20	运载火箭(能把500千克以上有效载荷投掷到300千米以上的)	13				80	17	13	千克	3	Carrier rockets (capable of throwing an available load over 500kg beyond 300km)

税则号列 Tariff Item.	货品名称	最惠国(%) MFN	协定(%)CT 东盟 CA	中巴 CP	中智 CC	普通 Gen	增值税率 VAT	出口退税 ED	计量单位 Unit	监管条件 SC	Article Description
9306.9000 30	探空火箭(能把500千克以上有效载荷投掷到300千米以上的)	13				80	17	13	千克	3	Sounding rockets (capable of throwing an available load over 500kg beyond 300km)
9306.9000 40	巡航导弹(能把500千克以上有效载荷投掷到300千米以上的)	13				80	17	13	千克	3	Cruise missiles (capable of throwing an available load over 500kg beyond 300km)
9306.9000 90	其他弹药和射弹及其零件(包括炸弹、手榴弹、鱼雷、地雷、水雷、导弹等)	13				80	17	13	千克		Other ammunition and projectiles and parts thereof, including bombs, grenades, torpedoes, mines, missiles, etc.)
93.07	**剑、短弯刀、刺刀、长矛和类似的武器及其零件;刀鞘、剑鞘:**										**Swords, cutlasses, bayonets, lances and similar arms and parts thereof and scabbards and sheaths therefor:**
9307.0000	剑、短弯刀、刺刀、长矛和类似的武器及其零件;刀鞘、剑鞘	13	8		7.8	80	17		千克		Swords, cutlasses, bayonets, lances and similar arms and parts thereof and scabbards and sheaths therefor
9307.0000 10	濒危动物制的刀鞘、剑鞘	13				80	17		千克	FE	Scabbards and sheaths of animals in imminent dangers
9307.0000 90	其他剑,刀,长矛和类似的武器及其(包括刀鞘、剑鞘)	13				80	17		千克		Other swords, cutlasses, bayonets, lances and similar arms and parts thereof and scabbards and sheaths therefor

第二十类
杂 项 制 品

第九十四章
家具；寝具、褥垫、弹簧床垫、软座垫及类似的填充制品；未列名灯具及照明装置；发光标志、发光铭牌及类似品；活动房屋

注释：

一、本章不包括：

（一）第三十九章、第四十章或第六十三章的充气或充水的褥垫、枕头及座垫；

（二）落地镜［例如税目70.09的试衣镜（旋转镜）］；

（三）第七十一章的物品；

（四）第十五类注释二所规定的贱金属制通用零件（第十五类）、塑料制的类似品（第三十九章）或税目83.03的保险箱；

（五）冷藏或冷冻设备专用的特制家具（税目84.18）；缝纫机专用的特制家具（税目84.52）；

（六）第八十五章的灯具及照明装置；

（七）税目85.18、85.19至85.21或税目85.25至85.28所列装置专用的特制家具（应分别归入税目85.18、85.22或85.29）；

（八）税目87.14的物品；

（九）装有税目90.18所列牙科用器具或漱口盂的牙科用椅（税目90.18）；

（十）第九十一章的物品（例如，钟及钟壳）；

（十一）玩具家具、玩具灯或玩具照明装置（税目95.03）、台球桌或其他供游戏用的特制家具（税目95.04）、魔术用的特制家具或中国灯笼及类似的装饰品（电气彩灯串除外）（税目95.05）。

二、税目94.01至94.03的物品（零件除外），只适用于落地式的物品。

对下列物品，即使是悬挂的、固定在墙壁上的或叠摞的，仍归入上述各税目：

（一）碗橱、书柜、架式家具及组合家具；

（二）坐具及床。

SECTION XX
MISCELLANEOUS MANUFACTURED ARTICLES

Chapter 94
Furniture; bedding, mattresses, mattress supports, cushions and similar stuffed furnishings; lamps and lighting fittings, not elsewhere specified or included; illuminated signs, illuminated name-plates and the like; prefabricated buildings

Notes:

1. This Chapter does not cover:

(a) Pneumatic or water mattresses, pillows or cushions, of Chapter 39, 40 or 63;

(b) Mirrors designed for placing on the floor or ground (for example, cheval-glasses (swing-mirrors) of heading No. 70.09);

(c) Articles of Chapter 71;

(d) Parts of general use as defined in Note 2 to Section XV, of base metal (Section XV), or similar goods of plastics (Chapter 39), or safes of heading No. 83.03;

(e) Furniture specially designed as parts of refrigerating or freezing equipment of heading No. 84.18; furniture specially designed for sewing machines (heading No. 84.52);

(f) Lamps or lighting fittings of Chapter 85;

(g) Furniture specially designed as parts of apparatus of heading 85.18 (heading No. 85.18), of headingsNo. 85.19 to 85.21 (heading 85.22) or of headingsNos. 85.25 to 85.28 (heading No. 85.29);

(h) Articles of heading No. 87.14;

(i) Dentists' chairs incorporating dental appliances of heading 90.18 or dentists' spittoons (heading No. 90.18);

(j) Articles of Chapter 91 (for example, clocks and clock cases); or

(k) Toy furniture or toy lamps or lighting fittings (heading No. 95.03), billiard tables or other furniture specially constructed for games (heading No. 95.04), furniture for conjuring tricks or decorations (other than electric garlands) such as Chinese lanterns (heading No. 95.05).

2. The articles (other than parts) referred to in headingsNos. 94.01 to 94.03 are to be classified in those headings only if they are designed for placing on the floor or ground.

The following are, however, to be classified in the above-mentioned headings even if they are designed to be hung, to be fixed to the wall or to stand one on the other:

(a) Cupboards, bookcases, other shelved furniture and unit furniture;

(b) Seats and beds.

三、(一)税目94.01至94.03所列货品的零件,不包括玻璃(包括镜子)、大理石或其他石料以及第六十八章及第六十九章所列任何其他材料的片、块(不论是否切割成形,但未与其他零件组装);

(二)税目94.04的货品,如果单独进口或出口,不能作为税目94.01、94.02或94.03所列货品的零件归类。

四、税目94.06所称"活动房屋",是指在工厂制成成品或制成部件并一同进口或出口,供以后在有关地点上组装的房屋,例如,工地用房、办公室、学校、店铺、工作棚、车房或类似的建筑物。

3. (a) In headingsNo. 94.01 to 94.03 references to parts of goods do not include references to sheets or slabs (whether or not cut to shape but not combined with other parts) of glass (including mirrors), marble or other stone or of any other material referred to in Chapter 68 or 69.

(b) Goods described in heading No. 94.04, presented separately, are not to be classified in headingNo. 94.01, 94.02 or 94.03 as parts of goods.

4. For the purposes of headingNo. 94.06, the expression "prefabricated buildings" means buildings which are finished in the factory or put up as elements, presented together, to be assembled on site, such as housing or worksite accommodation, offices, schools, shops, sheds, garages or similar buildings.

税则号列 Tariff Item.	货品名称	最惠国(%) MFN	协定(%) 东盟 CA	中巴 CP	CT 中智 CC	普通 Gen	增值税率 VAT	出口退税 ED	计量单位 Unit	监管条件 SC	Article Description
94.01	**坐具(包括能作床用的两用椅,但税目94.02的货品除外)及其零件:**										**Seats (other than those of headingNo. 94.02), whether or not convertible into beds, and parts thereof:**
9401.1000	-飞机用坐具	0				100	17	13	个/千克		-Seats of a kind used for aircraft
	-机动车辆用坐具:										-Seats of a kind used for motor vehicles:
9401.2010	---皮革或再生皮革面的	10			0	100	17	13	个/千克		---With outer surface of leather or composition leather
9401.2090	---其他	10			0	100	17	13	个/千克		---Other
9401.3000	-可调高度的转动坐具	0				100	17	13	个/千克		-Swivel seats with variable height adjustment
	-能作床用的两用椅,但庭园坐具或野营设备除外:										-Seats other than garden seats or camping equipment, convertible into beds:
9401.4010	---皮革或再生皮革面的	0				100	17	13	个/千克		---With outer surface of leather or composition leather
9401.4090	---其他	0				100	17	13	个/千克		---Other
	-藤、柳条、竹及类似材料制的坐具:										-Seats of cane, osier, bamboo or similar materials:
9401.5100	--竹制或藤制的	0				100	17	13	个/千克	AB	--Of bamboo or cane
9401.5900	--其他	0				100	17	13	个/千克	AB	--Other
	-木框架的其他坐具:										-Other seats, with wooden frames:
	--装软垫的:										--Upholstered:
9401.6110	---皮革或再生皮革面的	0				100	17	13	个/千克	AB	---With outer surface of leather or composition leather
9401.6190	---其他	0				100	17	13	个/千克	AB	---Other
9401.6900	--其他	0				100	17	13	个/千克	AB	--Other
	-金属框架的其他坐具:										-Other seats, with metal frames:
	--装软垫的:										--Upholstered:
9401.7110	---皮革或再生皮革面的	0				100	17	13	个/千克		---With outer surface of leather or composition leather
9401.7190	---其他	0				100	17	13	个/千克		---Other
9401.7900	--其他	0				100	17	13	个		--Other
	-其他坐具:										-Other seats:
9401.8010	---石制的	0				100	17	13	个/千克		---Of stone
9401.8090	---其他	0				100	17	13	个/千克		---Other
	-零件:										-Parts:
	---机动车辆用:										--Of the motor vehicles:
9401.9011	----座椅调角器	10			8	100	17	13	套/千克		----Seat angle requlating devices

税则号列 Tariff Item.	货品名称	最惠国(%) MFN	协定(%) CT 东盟 CA	中巴 CP	中智 CC	普通 Gen	增值税率 VAT	出口退税 ED	计量单位 Unit	监管条件 SC	Article Description
9401.9019	----其他	0				100	17	13	千克		----Other
9401.9090	---其他	0				100	17	13	千克		---Other
94.02	**医疗、外科、牙科或兽医用家具(例如,手术台、检查台、带机械装置的病床、牙科用椅);有旋转、倾斜、升降装置的理发用椅及类似椅;上述物品的零件:**										**Medical, surgical, dental or veterinary furniture (for example, operating tables, examination tables, hospital beds with mechanical fittings, dentists' chairs); barbers' chairs and similar chairs, having rotating as well as both reclining and elevating movements; parts of the foregoing articles:**
	-牙科、理发及类似用途的椅及其零件:										-Dentists', barbers' or similar chairs and parts thereof:
9402.1010	---理发用椅及其零件	0				100	17	13	个/千克		---Barbers' chairs and parts thereof
9402.1090	---其他	0				30	17	13	个/千克		---Other
9402.9000	-其他	0				30	17	13	件/千克		-Other
94.03	**其他家具及零件:**										**Other furniture and parts thereof:**
9403.1000	-办公室用金属家具	0				100	17	11	件/千克		-Metal furniture of a kind used in offices
9403.2000	-其他金属家具	0				100	17	11	件/千克		-Other metal furniture
9403.3000	-办公室用木家具	0				100	17	11	件/千克		-Wooden furniture of a kind used in offices
9403.3000 10	濒危木制办公室用木家具	0				100	17	11	件/千克	ABFE	Furniture of wood in imminent dangers, of a kind used in offices
9403.3000 90	其他办公室用木家具	0				100	17	11	件/千克	AB	Other wooden furniture of a kind used in offices
9403.4000	-厨房用木家具	0				100	17	11	件/千克		-Wooden furniture of a kind used in the kitchen
9403.4000 10	濒危木制厨房用木家具	0				100	17	11	件/千克	ABFE	Furniture of wood in imminent dangers, of a kind used in the kitchen
9403.4000 90	其他厨房用木家具	0				100	17	11	件/千克	AB	Wooden furniture of a kind used in the kitchen
	-卧室用木家具:										-Wooden furniture of a kind used in the bedroom:
9403.5010	---红木制	0				100	17	11	件		---Of rose wood
9403.5010 10	卧室用濒危红木制家具	0				100	17	11	件/千克	ABFE	Furniture of rose wood in imminent dangers, of a kind used in the bedroom
9403.5010 90	其他卧室用红木制家具	0				100	17	11	件/千克	AB	Other furniture of rose wood, of a kind used in the bedroom
	---其他:										---Other:
9403.5091	----漆木家具	0				100	17	11	件/千克	AB	----Of lacquered wood
9403.5099	----其他	0				100	17	11	件		----Other
9403.5099 10	卧室用其他濒危木家具	0				100	17	11	件/千克	ABFE	Furniture of wood in imminent dangers, of a kind used in the bedroom
9403.5099 90	卧室用其他木家具	0				100	17	11	件/千克	AB	Furniture of other wood, of a kind used in the bedroom
	-其他木家具:										-Other wooden furniture:
9403.6010	---红木制	0				100	17	11	件/千克		---Of rose wood

税则号列 Tariff Item.	货品名称	最惠国(%) MFN	协定(%) 东盟 CA	协定(%) 中巴 CP	协定(%) 中智 CC	普通 Gen	增值税率 VAT	出口退税 ED	计量单位 Unit	监管条件 SC	Article Description
9403.6010 10	其他濒危红木制家具(非卧室用)	0				100	17	11	件/千克	ABFE	Furniture of rose wood in imminent dangers, other than those of subheading No. 94035010.10
9403.6010 90	其他红木制家具(非卧室用)	0				100	17	11	件/千克	AB	Other furniture of rose wood, other than those of subheading 94035010.10
	---其他:										---Other:
9403.6091	----漆木家具	0				100	17	11	件/千克	AB	----Of lacquered wood
9403.6099	----其他	0				100	17	11	件/千克		----Other
9403.6099 10	其他濒危木家具(非卧室用)	0				100	17	11	件/千克	ABFE	Furniture of wood in imminent dangers, other than those of subheading 94035010.10
9403.6099 90	其他木家具(非卧室用)	0				100	17	11	件/千克	AB	Other furniture of wood, other than those of subheading 94035010.10
9403.7000	-塑料家具	0				100	17	11	件/千克		-Furniture of plastics
	-其他材料制的家具,包括藤、柳条、竹或类似材料制的:										-Furniture of other materials, including cane, osier, bamboo or similar materials:
9403.8100	--竹制或藤制的	0				100	17	11	件/千克	AB	--Of bamboo or cane
	--其他:										---Other:
9403.8910	---柳条及类似材料制的	0				100	17	11	件/千克	AB	---Of osier or similar materials
9403.8920	---石制的	0				100	17	11	件/千克		---Of stone
9403.8990	---其他	0				100	17	11	件/千克		---Other
9403.9000	-零件	0				100	17	11	千克		-Parts
9403.9000 10	飞机内厨房家具零件	0				100	17	11	千克		Parts of furnitures in kitchens of airplanes
9403.9000 90	其他编号9403所列物品的零件	0				100	17	11	千克		Parts of the articles of heading 9403
94.04	**弹簧床垫;寝具及类似用品,装有弹簧、内部用任何材料填充、衬垫或用海绵橡胶、泡沫塑料制成,不论是否包面(例如,褥垫、棉被、羽绒被、靠垫、座垫及枕头):**										**Mattress supports; articles of bedding and similar furnishing (for example, mattresses, quilts, eiderdowns, cushions, pouffes and pillows) fitted with springs or stuffed or internally fitted with any material or of cellular rubber or plastics, whether or not covered:**
9404.1000	-弹簧床垫	20	12		16	100	17	13	个/千克		-Mattress supports
	-褥垫:										-Mattresses:
9404.2100	--海绵橡胶或泡沫塑料制,不论是否包面	20	12		12	100	17	13	个		--Of cellular rubber or plastics, whether or not covered
9404.2100 10	蔺草包面的垫子(单件面积大于1平方米,无论是否包边)	20				100	17	13	个	4xy	Mattresses covered with rush (area of single piece > $1m^2$, whether or not edged)
9404.2100 90	海绵橡胶或泡沫塑料制褥垫(不论是否包面)	20				100	17	13	个		Mattresses of cellular rubber or plastics, whether or not covered
9404.2900	--其他材料制	20	12	14	16	100	17	13	个		--Of other materials
	-睡袋:										-Sleeping bags:
9404.3010	---羽毛或羽绒填充的	20	12		12	130	17	13	个		---Stuffed with feathers or down
9404.3010 10	濒危野禽羽毛或羽绒填充的睡袋	20				130	17	13	个	FEB	Sleeping bags stuffed with feathers or down of wild birds in imminent dangers

税则号列 Tariff Item.	货品名称	最惠国(%) MFN	协定(%)CT 东盟 CA	中巴 CP	中智 CC	普通 Gen	增值税率 VAT	出口退税 ED	计量单位 Unit	监管条件 SC	Article Description
9404.3010 90	其他羽毛或羽绒填充的睡袋	20				130	17	13	个	B	Sleeping bags stuffed with other feathers or down
9404.3090	---其他	20	12		12	100	17	13	个		---Other
	-其他:										-Other:
9404.9010	---羽毛或羽绒填充的	20	12		16	130	17	13	千克		---Stuffed with feathers or down
9404.9010 10	濒危野禽羽绒和羽毛填充其他寝具(含类似品)	20				130	17	13	千克	FEB	Quilts and similar furnishing, with outershell of cotton, stuffed with feathers of down of wild birds
9404.9010 90	其他羽绒和羽毛填充的其他寝具(含类似品)	20				130	17	13	千克	B	Other quilts and similar furnishing, with outershell of cotton, stuffed with feathers of down
9404.9020	---兽毛填充的	20	12		16	130	17	13	千克		---Stuffed with animal hair
9404.9020 10	濒危兽毛填充的寝具(用野生兽毛填充的,含盖被及类似品)	20				130	17	13	千克	EF	Articles of bedding and similar furnishing, stuffed with wild animal hair in imminent dangers
9404.9020 90	其他兽毛填充的其他寝具(含类似品)	20				130	17	13	千克		Articles of bedding and similar furnishing, stuffed with other animal hair
9404.9030	---丝棉填充的	20	12		16	130	17	13	千克		---Stuffed with silk wadding
9404.9040	---化纤棉填充的	20	12		16	130	17	13	千克		---Stuffed with man-made fibres
9404.9090	---其他	20	12		16	130	17	13	千克		---Other
94.05	**其他税目未列名的灯具及照明装置,包括探照灯、聚光灯及其零件;装有固定光源的发光标志、发光铭牌及类似品,以及其他税目未列名的这些货品的零件:**										**Lamps and lighting fittings including searchlights and spotlights and parts thereof, not elsewhere specified or included; illuminated signs, illuminated name-plates and the like, having a permanently fixed light source, and parts thereof not elsewhere specified or included:**
9405.1000	-枝形吊灯及天花板或墙壁上的其他电气照明装置,但不包括公共露天场所或街道上的电气照明装置	10	5		8	80	17	13	千克/个	B	-Chandeliers and other electric ceiling or wall lighting fittings, excluding those of a kind used for lighting public open spaces or thorough-fares
9405.2000	-电气的台灯、床头灯或落地灯	20	12		16	80	17	13	千克/台	B	-Electric table, desk, bedeside or floorstanding lamps
9405.3000	-圣诞树用的成套灯具	16	8		9.6	100	17	13	套/千克	B	-Lighting sets of a kind used for Christmas trees
	-其他电灯及照明装置:										-Other electric lamps and lighting fittings:
9405.4010	---探照灯	17.5	8		14	70	17	13	台/千克	B	---Searchlights
9405.4020	---聚光灯	17.5	8		14	70	17	13	台/千克		---Spotlights
9405.4090	---其他	10	8		8	80	17	13	千克		---Other
9405.5000	-非电气的灯具及照明装置	20	12		12	80	17	13	千克		-Non-electrical lamps and lighting fittings
9405.6000	-发光标志、发光铭牌及类似品	20	12		0	80	17	13	千克		-Illuminated signs, illuminated name plates and the like
	-零件:										-Parts:
9405.9100	--玻璃制	20	12		12	70	17	13	千克		--Of glass
9405.9200	--塑料制	20	12		12	70	17	13	千克		--Of plastics
9405.9900	--其他	20	12		16	70	17	13	千克		--Other

税则号列 Tariff Item.	货品名称	最惠国(%) MFN	协定(%)CT 东盟 CA	中巴 CP	中智 CC	普通 Gen	增值税率 VAT	出口退税 ED	计量单位 Unit	监管条件 SC	Article Description
94.06	**活动房屋:**										**Prefabricated buildings:**
9406.0000	活动房屋	10	8	7	8	70	17	13	千克		Prefabricated buildings
9406.0000 10	用动植物材料制作的活动房屋	10				70	17	13	千克	AB	Prefabricated buildings of animal or vegetable materials
9406.0000 20	带有风扇的高效空气粒子过滤单元(HEPA)的封闭洁净室	10				70	17	13	千克	3	Sealed clean room for high - effici - ent unit with fan for filtering air particles (HEPA)
9406.0000 90	其他活动房屋	10				70	17	13	千克		Prefabricated buildings of other materials

第九十五章
玩具、游戏品、运动用品及其零件、附件

注释：

一、本章不包括：

（一）蜡烛（税目34.06）；

（二）税目36.04的烟花、爆竹或其他烟火制品；

（三）已切成一定长度但未制成钓鱼线的纱线、单丝、绳、肠线及类似品（第三十九章、税目42.06或第十一类）；

（四）税目42.02、43.03或43.04的运动用袋或其他容器；

（五）第六十一章或第六十二章的纺织品制的运动服或化妆舞会服装；

（六）第六十三章的纺织品制的旗帜及帆板或滑行车用帆；

（七）第六十四章的运动鞋靴（装有冰刀或滑轮的溜冰鞋除外）或第六十五章的运动用帽；

（八）手杖、鞭子、马鞭或类似品（税目66.02）及其零件（税目66.03）；

（九）税目70.18的未装配的玩偶或其他玩具用的玻璃假眼；

（十）第十五类注释二所规定的贱金属制通用零件（第十五类）或塑料制的类似货品（第三十九章）；

（十一）税目83.06的铃、钟、锣及类似品；

（十二）液体泵（税目84.13）、液体或气体的过滤、净化机器及装置（税目84.21）、电动机（税目85.01）、变压器（税目85.04）或无线电遥控设备（税目85.26）；

（十三）第十七类的运动用车辆（长雪橇、平底雪橇及类似品除外）；

（十四）儿童两轮车（税目87.12）；

（十五）运动用船艇，例如，轻舟、赛艇（第八十九章）及其桨、橹和类似品（木制的归入第四十四章）；

（十六）运动及户外游戏用的眼镜、护目镜及类似品（税目90.04）；

（十七）媒诱音响器及哨子（税目92.08）；

（十八）第九十三章的武器及其他物品；

（十九）各种电气彩灯串（税目94.05）；

（二十）球拍线、帐篷或类似的野营用品、分指手套、连指手套及露指手套（按其构成材料归类）。

（二十一）餐具、厨房用具、盥洗用品、地毯及纺织、材料制的其他铺地制品、服装、床上及餐桌用织物制品、盥洗及厨房用织物制品及具有实用功能的类似货品（按其构成材料归类）。

Chapter 95
Toys, games and sports requisites; parts and accessories thereof

Notes:

1. This Chapter does not cover:

(a) Candles (headingNo. 34.06);

(b) Fireworks or other pyrotechnic articles of headingNo. 36.04;

(c) Yarns, monofilament, cords or gut or the like for fishing, cut to length but not made up into fishing lines, of Chapter 39, headingNo. 42.06 or Section XI;

(d) Sports bags or other containers of headingNo. 42.02, 43.03 or 43.04;

(e) Sports clothing or fancy dress, of textiles, of Chapter 61 or 62;

(f) Textile flags or bunting, or sails for boats, sailboards or land craft, of Chapter 63;

(g) Sports footwear (other than skating boots with ice or roller skates attached) of Chapter 64, or sports headgear of Chapter 65;

(h) Walking-sticks, whips, riding-crops or the like (headingNo. 66.02), or parts thereof (headingNo. 66.03);

(i) Unmounted glass eyes for dolls or other toys, of headingNo. 70.18;

(j) Parts of general use, as defined in Note 2 to Section XV, of base metal (Section XV), or similar goods of plastics (Chapter 39);

(k) Bells, gongs or the like of headingNo. 83.06;

(l) Pumps for liquids (headingNo. 84.13), filtering or purifying machinery and apparatus for liquids or gases (headingNo. 84.21), electric motors (headingNo. 85.01), electric transformers (headingNo. 85.04) or radio remote control apparatus (headingNo. 85.26);

(m) Sports vehicles (other than bobsleighs, toboggans and the like) of Section XVII;

(n) Children's bicycles (headingNo. 87.12);

(o) Sports craft such as canoes and skiffs (Chapter 89), or their means of propulsion (Chapter 44 for such articles made of wood);

(p) Spectacles, goggles or the like, for sports or outdoor games (headingNo. 90.04);

(q) Decoy calls or whistles (headingNo. 92.08);

(r) Arms or other articles of Chapter 93;

(s) Electric garlands of all kinds (headingNo. 94.05); or

(t) Racket strings, tents or other camping goods, or gloves, mittens and mitts (classified according to their constituent material).

(u) Tableware, kitchenware, clean kit, carpet and textile, other products used for covering floors, garment, bed and table linen, cleaning and kitchen linen and other articles of similar use (categorized according to materials)

二、本章包括天然或养殖珍珠、宝石或半宝石（天然、合成或再造）、贵金属或包贵金属只作为小零件的物品。

2. This Chapter includes articles in which natural or cultured pearls, precious or semi-precious stones (natural, synthetic or reconstructed), precious metal or metal clad with precious metal constitute only minor consistuents.

三、除上述注释一另有规定的以外，凡专用于或主要用于本章各税目所列物品的零件、附件，应与有关物品一并归类。

3. Subject to Note 1 above, parts and accessories which are suitable for use solely or principally with articles of this Chapter are to be classified with those articles.

四、除上述注释一另有规定的以外，税目95.03特别适用于该税目物品与一项或多项其他货品组合而成的物品，只要这些物品为零售包装，且组合后具有玩具的基本特征。这些组合物品不能视为归类总规定三（二）所指的成套货品，如果单独报检、应归入其它税目

4. Except otherwise prescribed as in Note I, tax item 95.03 shall be applicable to articles that are put together by one or many items - - as long as these articles are wrapped for retail, and still possess the basic characteristics of toys. These combined articles shall not be regarded as the goods of a whole set as referred in General Provisions of Categorization III (II). If examined separately, these articles shall be categorized into other tax items.

五、税目95.03不包括因其设计、形状或构成材料可确认为专供动物使用的物品，例如"宠物玩具"归入其相应的税目

5. Heading 95.03 does not cover articles which, on account of their design, shape or constituent material, are identifiable as intended exclusively for animals, e.g., "pet toys" (classification in their own appropriate heading).

税则号列 Tariff Item.	货品名称	最惠国(%) MFN	协定(%) CT 东盟 CA	中巴 CP	中智 CC	普通 Gen	增值税率 VAT	出口退税 ED	计量单位 Unit	监管条件 SC	Article Description
95.03	**三轮车、踏板车、踏板汽车和类似的带轮玩具；玩偶车；玩偶；其他玩具；缩小（按比例缩小）的模型及类似的娱乐用模型，不论是否活动；各种智力玩具：**										**Tricycles、scooters、pedal cars or similar wheeled toys; reduced-size ("scale") models and similar recreational models, working or not; puzzles of all kinds:**
9503.0010	---三轮车、踏板车、踏板汽车和类似的带轮玩具；玩偶车	0				80	17	13	千克	Ba	---Tricycles、scooters、pedal cars or similar wheeled toy; dolls' carriages
	---玩偶，不论是否着装：										---Dolls:
9503.0021	----动物	0				80	17	13	个/千克	AB	----Animals
9503.0029	----其他	0				80	17	13	个/千克	AB	----Other
	---缩小（按比例缩小）的全套模型组件，不论是否活动										---
9503.0031	----电动火车	0				80	17	13	千克	AB	----Electric trovins
9503.0039	----其他	0				80	17	13	个/千克	AB	----Electric trovins
9503.0040	---其他建筑套件及建筑玩具	0				80	17	13	个/千克	AB	---Other constructrom sets and constructional toys
9503.0050	---玩具乐器	0				80	17	13	千克	AB	---Toy musical instruments and spparatus
9503.0060	---智力玩具	0				80	17	13	套/千克	AB	---Puzzles
	---其他玩具：										----Other toys:
9503.0081	----组装成套或全套的	0				80	17	13	套/千克	AB	----Put up in sets or outfies
9503.0082	----其他带动力装置的玩具及模型	0				80	17	13	套/千克	AB	----Other toys and models incorporating a motor
9503.0089	----其他	0				80	17	13	套/千克	AB	----Other
9503.0090	---零件、附件	0				80	17	13	千克	AB	---Parts and accessories
95.04	**游艺场所、桌上或室内游戏用品，包括弹球机、台球、娱乐专用桌及保龄球自动球道设备：**										**Articles for funfair, table or parlour games, including pintables, billiards, special tables for casino games and automatic bowling alley equipment:**
9504.1000	-与电视接收机配套使用的电子游戏机	0				130	17	13	台/千克	6O	-Video games of a kind used with a television receiver

税则号列 Tariff Item.	货 品 名 称	最惠国(%) MFN	协定(%)CT 东盟 CA	中巴 CP	中智 CC	普通 Gen	增值税率 VAT	出口退税 ED	计量单位 Unit	监管条件 SC	Article Description
9504.2000	-台球用品及附件	0				80	17	13	千克		-Articles and accessories for billiards
9504.2000 10	濒危木制的台球用品及附件	0				80	17	13	千克	EF	articles and accessories for billiards of wood in imminent dangers
9504.2000 90	其他台球用品及附件	0				80	17	13	千克		Other articles and accessories for billiards
	-用硬币、钞票、银行卡、代币或其他支付方式使其工作的其他游戏用品,但保龄球道设备除外:										-Other games, operated by coins, banknotes(paper currency), discs or other similar articles, other than bowling alley equipment:
9504.3010	---电子游戏机	0				130	17	13	台/千克	6O	---Video games
9504.3090	---其他	0				80	17	13	台/千克	6O	---Other
9504.4000	-扑克牌	0				80	17	13	副		-Playing cards
	-其他:										-Other:
9504.9010	---其他电子游戏机	0				130	17	13	台/千克	6O	---Other video games
	---保龄球自动球道设备及器具:										---Automatic bowling alley equipments and appliances:
9504.9021	----保龄球自动分瓶机	0				80	17	13	台/千克		----Automatic bowling pin distributing machines
9504.9022	----保龄球	0				80	17	13	个		----Bowling balls
9504.9023	----保龄球瓶	0				80	17	13	个		----Bowling pins
9504.9029	----其他	0				80	17	13	台/千克		----Other
9504.9030	---中国象棋、国际象棋、跳棋等棋类用品	0				80	17	13	副/千克		---Chess and other board games, including Chinese chess, international chess, Chinese cherkers and draughts
9504.9040	---麻将及类似桌上游戏用品	0				80	17	13	副/千克		---Mahjong and similiar table games
9504.9090	---其他	0				80	17	13	台/千克		---Other
95.05	**节日(包括狂欢节)用品或其他娱乐用品,包括魔术道具及嬉戏品:**										**Festive, carnival or other entertainment articles, including conjuring tricks and novelty jokes:**
9505.1000	-圣诞节用品	0				100	17	13	千克		-Articles for Christmas festivities
9505.1000 10	含动植物性材料的圣诞用品(不包括成套圣诞节灯具)	0				100	17	13	千克	AB	Articles for Christmas festivities containing animals or vegetable materials (other than lighting sets of a kind used for Christmas trees)
9505.1000 90	其他圣诞节用品(不包括成套圣诞节灯具)	0				100	17	13	千克		Other articles for Christmas festivities (other than lighting sets of a kind used for Christmas trees)
9505.9000	-其他	0				100	17	13	千克	B	-Other
95.06	**一般的体育活动、体操、竞技及其他运动(包括乒乓球运动)或户外游戏用的本章其他税目未列名用品及设备;游泳池或戏水池:**										**Articles and equipment for general physical exercise, gymnastics, athletics, other sports (including table-tennis) or out door games, not specified or included elsewhere in this Chapter; swimming pools and paddling pools:**
	-滑雪屐及其他滑雪用具:										-Snow-skis and other snow-ski equipment:
9506.1100	--滑雪屐	14	8	0	8.4	50	17	13	双		--Skis
9506.1200	--滑雪屐扣件(滑雪屐带)	14	8	0	8.4	50	17	13	千克		--Ski-fastenings (ski-bindings)
9506.1900	--其他	14	8	0	8.4	50	17	13	千克		--Other

税则号列 Tariff Item.	货品名称	最惠国(%) MFN	协定(%)CT			普通 Gen	增值税率 VAT	出口退税 ED	计量单位 Unit	监管条件 SC	Article Description
			东盟 CA	中巴 CP	中智 CC						
	-滑水板、冲浪板、帆板及其他水上运动用具:										-Water-skis, surf-boards, sailboards and other water-sport equipment:
9506.2100	--帆板	12	8	0	7.2	50	17	13	个/千克		--Sailboards
9506.2900	--其他	14	8	0	8.4	50	17	13	个/千克		--Other
	-高尔夫球棍及其他高尔夫球用具:										-Golf clubs and other golf equipment:
9506.3100	--棍,全套的	14	8	0	8.4	50	17	13	根		--Clubs, complete
9506.3200	--球	12	8	0	7.2	50	17	13	个		--Balls
9506.3900	--其他	14	8	0	8.4	50	17	13	千克		--Other
	-乒乓球运动用品及器械:										-Articles and equipment for table-tennis:
9506.4010	---乒乓球	12	8	0	9.6	50	17	13	百个/千克		---Table-tennis balls
9506.4090	---其他	14	8	0	11.2	50	17	13	千克		---Other
	-网球拍、羽毛球拍或类似的球拍,不论是否装弦:										-Tennis, badminton or similar rackets, whether or not strung:
9506.5100	--草地网球拍,不论是否装弦	14	8	0	8.4	50	17	13	副		--Lawn-tennis rackets, whether or not strung
9506.5900	--其他	14	8	0	8.4	50	17	13	副		--Other
	-球,但高尔夫球及乒乓球除外:										-Balls, other than golf balls and tabletennis balls:
9506.6100	--草地网球	12	T3	0	7.2	50	17	13	个		--Lawn-tennis balls
	--可充气的球:										--Inflatable:
9506.6210	---篮球、足球、排球	12	T3	0	9.6	50	17	13	个		---Basketballs, footballs or volley balls
9506.6290	---其他	12	T3	0	9.6	50	17	13	个		---Other
9506.6900	--其他	12	8	0	7.2	50	17	13	个		--Other
	-溜冰鞋及旱冰鞋,包括装有冰刀的溜冰靴:										-Ice skates and roller skates, including skating boots with skates attached:
9506.7010	---溜冰鞋	14	8	0	8.4	50	17	13	双/千克		---Ice skates
9506.7020	---旱冰鞋	14	8	0	8.4	50	17	13	双/千克		---Roller skates
	-其他:										-Other:
	--一般的体育活动、体操或竞技用品及设备:										--Articles and equipment for general physical exercise, gymnastics or athletics:
9506.9110	---健身及康复器械	12	8	0	9.6	50	17	13	千克	B	---Equipment for exercise and recovery
9506.9120	---滑板	12	8	0	9.6	50	17	13	个/千克		---Skateboards
9506.9190	---其他	12	8	0	9.6	50	17	13	千克		---Other
9506.9900	--其他	12	8	0	9.6	50	17	13	个/千克		--Other
95.07	**钓鱼竿、钓鱼钩及其他钓鱼用品;捞鱼网、捕蝶网及类似网;囮子“鸟”(税目92.08或97.05的货品除外)以及类似的狩猎用品:**										**Fishing rods, fish-hooks and other line fishing tackle; fish landing nets, butterfly nets and similar nets; decoy “birds” (other than those of heading 92.08 or 97.05) and similar hunting or shooting requisites:**
9507.1000	-钓鱼竿	21	12		12.6	80	17	13	副		-Fishing rods
9507.1000 10	用植物性材料制作的钓鱼竿	21				80	17	13	副	AB	Fishing rods of vegetable materials
9507.1000 90	其他钓鱼竿	21				80	17	13	副		Other fishing rods
9507.2000	-钓鱼钩,不论有无系钩丝	21	12		16.8	80	17	13	千克		-Fish-hooks, whether or not snelled
9507.3000	-钓线轮	21	12		12.6	80	17	13	个		-Fishing reels
9507.9000	-其他	21	12	18.9	12.6	80	17	13	个/千克		-Other

税则号列 Tariff Item.	货 品 名 称	最惠国(%) MFN	协定(%)CT 东盟 CA	中巴 CP	中智 CC	普通 Gen	增值税率 VAT	出口退税 ED	计量单位 Unit	监管条件 SC	Article Description
95.08	**旋转木马、秋千、射击用靶及其他游乐场的娱乐设备;流动马戏团及流动动物园;流动剧团:**										**Roundabouts, swings, shooting galleries and other fairground amusements; travelling circuses and travelling menageries; travelling theatres:**
9508.1000	-流动马戏团及流动动物园	15	8		9	100	17	13	千克		-Travelling circuses and travelling menageries
9508.1000 10	有濒危动物的流动马戏团(包括流动动物园)	15				100	17	13	千克	FEAB	Travelling circuses and travelling menageries, having animals in imminent dangers
9508.1000 90	其他流动马戏团及流动动物园	15				100	17	13	千克	AB	Other travelling circuses and travelling menageries
9508.9000	-其他	15	8		12	100	17	13	千克	AB	-Other

第九十六章
杂 项 制 品

注释：

一、本章不包括：

（一）化妆盥洗用笔（第三十三章）；

（二）第六十六章的制品（例如，伞或手杖的零件）；

（三）仿首饰（税目71.17）；

（四）第十五类注释二所规定的贱金属制通用零件（第十五类）或塑料制的类似品（第三十九章）；

（五）第八十二章的利口器及其他物品，其柄或其他零件是雕刻或模塑材料制的；但税目96.01或96.02适用于单独进口或出口的上述物品的柄或其他零件；

（六）第九十章的物品，例如，眼镜架（税目90.03）、数学绘图笔（税目90.17）、各种牙科、医疗、外科或兽医专用刷子（税目90.18）；

（七）第九十一章的物品（例如，钟壳或表壳）；

（八）乐器及其零件、附件（第九十二章）；

（九）第九十三章的物品（武器及其零件）；

（十）第九十四章的物品（例如，家具、灯具及照明装置）；

（十一）第九十五章的物品（玩具、游戏品、运动用品）；

（十二）艺术品、收藏品及古物（第九十七章）。

二、税目96.02所称“植物质或矿物质雕刻材料”，是指：

（一）用于雕刻的硬种子、硬果核、硬果壳、坚果及类似植物材料（例如，象牙果及棕榈子）；

（二）琥珀、海泡石、粘聚琥珀、粘聚海泡石、黑玉及其矿物代用品。

三、税目96.03所称“制帚、制刷用成束、成簇的材料”，仅指未装配的成束、成簇的兽毛、植物纤维或其他材料。这些成束、成簇的材料无需分开即可安装在帚、刷之上，或只需经过简单加工（例如将顶端修剪成形）即可安装的。

四、除税目96.01至96.06或96.15的货品以外，本章的物品还包括全部或部分用贵金属、包贵金属、天然或养殖珍珠、宝石或半宝石（天然、合成或再造）制成的物品。而且，税目96.01至96.06及96.15包括天然或养殖珍珠、宝石或半宝石（天然、合成或再造）、贵金属或包贵金属只作为小零件的物品。

Chapter 96
Miscellaneous manufactured articles

Notes:

1. This Chapter does not cover:

(a) Pencils for cosmetic or toilet uses (Chapter 33);

(b) Articles of Chapter 66 (for example, parts of umbrellas or walking-sticks);

(c) Imitation jewellery (headingNo. 71.17);

(d) Parts of general use, as defined in Note 2 to Section XV, of base metal (Section XV), or similar goods of plastics (Chapter 39);

(e) Cutlery or other articles of Chapter 82 with handles or other parts of carving or moulding materials; headingNo. 96.01 or 96.02 applies, however, to separately pressented handles or other parts of such articles;

(f) Articles of Chapter 90 (for exampple, spectacle frames (headingNo. 90.03), mathematical drawing pens (headingNo. 90.17), brushes of a kind specialized for use in dentistry or for medical, surgical or veterinary purposes (headingNo. 90.18);

(g) Articles of Chapter 91 (for example, clock or watch cases);

(h) Musical instruments or parts or accessories thereof (Chapter 92);

(i) Articles of Chapter 93 (arms and parts thereof);

(j) Articles of Chapter 94 (for example, furniture, lamps and lighting fittings);

(k) Articles of Chapter 95 (toys, games, sports requisites); or

(l) Works of art, collectors' pieces or antiques (Chapter 97).

2. In headingNo. 96.02 the expression "vegetable or mineral carving material" means:

(a) Hard seeds, pips, hulls and nuts and similar vegetable materials of a kind used for carving (for example, corozo and dom);

(b) Amber, meerschaum, agglomerated amber and agglomerated meerschaum, jet and mineral substitutes for jet.

3. In headingNo. 96.03 the expression "prepared knots and tufts for broom or brush making" applies only to unmounted knots and tufts of animal hair, vegetable fibre or other material, which are ready for incorporation without division in brooms or brushes, or which require only such further minor processes as trimming to shape at the top, to render them ready for such incorporation.

4. Articles of this Chapter, other than those of headingsNo. 96.01 to 96.06 or 96.15, remain classified in the Chapter whether or not composed wholly or partly of precious metal or metal clad with precious metal, of natural or cultured pearls, or precious or semiprecious stones (natural, synthetic or reconstructed). However, headingsNo. 96.01 to 96.06 and 96.15 include articles in which natural or cultured pearls, precious or semi-precious stones (natural, synthetic or reconstructed), precious metal or metal clad with precious metal constitute only minor constituents.

税则号列 Tariff Item.	货品名称	最惠国(%) MFN	协定(%)CT 东盟 CA	中巴 CP	中智 CC	普通 Gen	增值税率 VAT	出口退税 ED	计量单位 Unit	监管条件 SC	Article Description
96.01	**已加工的兽牙、骨、玳瑁壳、角、鹿角、珊瑚、珍珠母及其他动物质雕刻材料及其制品(包括塑模制品):**										**Worked ivory, bone, tortoise-shell, horn, antlers, coral, mother-of-pearl and other animal carving material and articles of these materials (including articles obtained by moulding):**
9601.1000	-已加工的兽牙及其制品	20	12		12	100	17	13	千克		-Worked ivory and articles of ivory
9601.1000 10	已加工的濒危兽牙及其制品	20				100	17	13	千克	AFEB	Worked ivory and articles of ivory, of wild animals
9601.1000 90	其他已加工的兽牙及其制品	20				100	17	13	千克	AB	Worked ivory and articles of ivory, of other animals
9601.9000	-其他	20	12		12	100	17	13	千克		-Other
9601.9000 10	其他已加工濒危动物质雕刻料(包括其制品)	20				100	17	13	千克	AFEB	Other worked carving material and articles of these materials of animals in imminent dangers
9601.9000 90	其他已加工动物质雕刻料及其制品(指已加工的骨、玳瑁壳、角、鹿角、珊瑚、珍珠母等)	20				100	17	13	千克	AB	Other worked bone, tortoise-shell, horn, antlers, coral, mother-of-pearl and other animal carving material and articles of these materials
96.02	**已加工的植物质或矿物质雕刻材料及其制品;蜡、硬脂、天然树胶、天然树脂或塑型膏制成的模塑或雕刻制品以及其他税目未列名的模塑或雕刻制品;已加工的未硬化明胶(税目35.03的明胶除外)及未硬化明胶制品:**										**Worked vegetable or mineral carving material and articles of these materials; moulded or carved articles of wax, of stearin, of natural gums or natural resins or of modelling pastes, and other moulded or carved articles, not elsewhere specified or included; worked, unhardened gelatin (except gelatin of heading 35.03) and articles of unhardened gelatin:**
9602.0010	---装药用胶囊	10.5	8		6.3	40	17	13	千克		---Pharmaceutical capsules
9602.0090	---其他	25	12		15	100	17	13	千克	AB	---Other
96.03	**帚、刷(包括作为机器、器具、车辆零件的刷)、非机动的手工操作地板清扫器、拖把及毛掸;供制帚、刷用的成束或成簇的材料;油漆块垫及滚筒;橡皮扫帚(橡皮辊除外):**										**Brooms, brushes (including brushes constituting parts of machines, appliances or vehicles), hand-operated mechanical floor sweepers, not motorized, mops and feather dusters; prepared knots and tufts for broom or brush making; paint pads and rollers; squeegees (other than roller squeegees):**
9603.1000	-用枝条或其他植物材料捆扎而成的帚及刷,不论是否有把	25	12		15	100	17	13	把	AB	-Brooms and brushes, consisting of twigs or other vegetable materials bound together, with or without handles
	-牙刷、剃须刷、发刷、指甲刷、睫毛刷及其他人体化妆用刷,包括作为器具零件的上述刷:										-Tooth brushes, shaving brushes, hair brushes, nail brushes, eyelash brushes and other toilet brushes for use on the person, including such brushes constituting parts of appliances:
9603.2100	--牙刷,包括齿板刷	25	12		0	100	17	13	把		--Tooth brushes, including vental-plate brushes
9603.2900	--其他	15	8	13.5	12	100	17	13	支		--Other

税则号列 Tariff Item.	货品名称	最惠国(%) MFN	协定(%) CT 东盟 CA	中巴 CP	中智 CC	普通 Gen	增值税率 VAT	出口退税 ED	计量单位 Unit	监管条件 SC	Article Description
9603.2900 10	野生动物毛制剃须刷,发刷(包括睫毛刷等人体化妆刷)	15				100	17	13	支	FE	Shaving brushes, hair brushes, nail brushes, eyelash brushes and other toilet brushes for use on the person, of wild animal hair
9603.2900 90	剃须刷,发刷,睫毛刷等人体化妆刷(包括作为器具零件的编号960329所属的刷)	15				100	17	13	支		Shaving brushes, hair brushes, nail brushes, eyelash brushes and other toilet brushes for use on the person, including such brushes constituting parts of appliances of subheadingNo. 96032000
	-画笔、毛笔及化妆用的类似笔:										-Artists' brushes, writing brushes and similar brushes for the application of cosmetics:
9603.3010	---画笔	25	12	15	20	100	17	13	支		---Artists' brushes
9603.3010 10	濒危动物毛制的画笔	25				100	17	13	支	FE	Artists' brushes of hair animal in imminent dangers
9603.3010 90	其他画笔	25				100	17	13	支		Other artists' brushes
9603.3020	---毛笔	20	12	18	16	100	17	13	支		---Writing brushes
9603.3020 10	濒危动物毛制的毛笔	20				100	17	13	支	FE	Writing brushes of hair animal in imminent dangers
9603.3020 90	其他毛笔	20				100	17	13	支		Other writing brushes
9603.3090	---其他	25	12	22.5	20	100	17	13	支		---Other
9603.3090 10	濒危动物毛制化妆用的类似笔	25				100	17	13	支	FE	Similar brushes for the application of cosmetics of hair animal in imminent dangers
9603.3090 90	其他化妆用的类似笔	25				100	17	13	支		Other similar brushes for the application of cosmetics
	-油漆刷、涂料刷、清漆刷及类似的刷(子目9603.30的货品除外);油漆块垫及滚筒:										-Paint, distemper, varnish or similar brushes (other than brushes of subheading No. 9603.30); paint pads and rollers:
	---漆刷及类似刷:										---Paint, distemper, varnish or similar brushes:
9603.4011	----猪鬃制	20	12		12	100	17	13	把		----Of pigs', hogs' or boars' bristle
9603.4019	----其他	23	12		13.8	100	17	13	把		----Other
9603.4020	---油漆块垫及滚筒	23	12		13.8	100	17	13	个		---Paint pads and rollers
	-作为机器、器具、车辆零件的刷:										-Other brushes constituting parts of machines, appliances or vehicles:
	---金属丝刷:										---Brushes of metal wire:
9603.5011	----作为机器、器具零件的刷	14	8		11.2	50	17	13	个		----Constituting parts of machines or appliances
9603.5019	----其他	14	8		11.2	100	17	13	个		----Other
	---其他:										---Other:
9603.5091	----作为机器、器具零件的刷	14	8		11.2	50	17	13	个		----Constituting parts of machines or appliances
9603.5091 10	濒危动物毛制作为机器零件其他刷(包括器具零件的其他刷)	14				50	17	13	个	FE	Other brushes constituting parts of machines or appliances, of hair of animal in imminent dangers
9603.5091 90	其他作为机器、器具零件的其他刷	14				50	17	13	个		Other brushes constituting parts of machines or appliances
9603.5099	----其他	14	8		11.2	100	17	13	个		----Other

税则号列 Tariff Item.	货品名称	最惠国(%) MFN	协定(%)CT 东盟 CA	中巴 CP	中智 CC	普通 Gen	增值税率 VAT	出口退税 ED	计量单位 Unit	监管条件 SC	Article Description
9603.5099 10	濒危动物毛制作为车辆零件其他刷	14				100	17	13	个	FE	Other brushes constituting parts of vehicles, of hair of animal in imminent dangers
9603.5099 90	其他作为车辆零件的其他刷	14				100	17	13	个		Other brushes constituting parts of vehicles
	-其他:										-Other:
9603.9010	---羽毛掸	21	12	18.9	16.8	130	17	13	个		---Feather dusters
9603.9010 10	濒危野禽羽毛掸	21				130	17	13	个	AFEB	Feather dusters of feathers of wild birds in imminent dangers
9603.9010 90	其他羽毛掸	21				130	17	13	个	AB	Feather dusters of feathers of other birds
9603.9090	---其他	15	8		12	100	17	13	个		---Other
9603.9090 10	濒危动物毛、鬃、尾制其他帚,刷(包括拖把及其他毛掸)	15				100	17	13	个	AFEB	Brooms, brushes, mops and feather dusters of hair of animal in imminent dangers, bristles or tails
9603.9090 20	其他动植物材料制帚,刷,拖把等(包括动植物材料制非机动的手工操作地板清扫器、毛掸)	15				100	17	13	个	AB	Brooms, brushes, mops and feather dusters, hand-operated mechanical floor sweepers, not motorized, of other animal or vegetable materials
9603.9090 90	其他材料制帚,刷,拖把及毛掸(包括其他材料制非机动的手工操作地板清扫器等)	15				100	17	13	个		Brooms, brushes, mops and feather dusters, hand-operated mechanical floor sweepers, not motorized, of other materials
96.04	**手用粗筛、细筛:**										**Hand sieves and hand riddles:**
9604.0000	手用粗筛、细筛	21	12		12.6	100	17	13	个	AB	Hand sieves and hand riddles
96.05	**个人梳妆、缝纫或清洁鞋靴、衣服用的成套旅行用具:**										**Travel sets for personal toilet, sewing or shoe or clothes cleaning:**
9605.0000	个人梳妆、缝纫或清洁鞋靴、衣服用的成套旅行用具	15	8		9	100	17	13	套		Travel sets for personal toilet, sewing or shoe or clothes cleaning
96.06	**钮扣、揿扣、钮扣芯及钮扣和揿扣的其他零件;钮扣坯:**										**Buttons, press-fasteners, snap-fasteners and press-studs, button moulds and other parts of these articles; button blanks:**
9606.1000	-揿扣及其零件	21	12		12.6	100	17	13	千克		-Press-fasteners, snap-fasteners and press-studs and parts therefor
	-钮扣:										-Buttons:
9606.2100	--塑料制,未用纺织材料包裹	21	12		12.6	100	17	13	千克		--Of plastics, not covered with textile material
9606.2200	--金属制,未用纺织材料包裹	15	8		9	100	17	13	千克		--Of base metal, not covered with textile material
9606.2900	--其他	15	8		9	100	17	13	千克		--Other
9606.2900 10	含濒危动物成分的其他钮扣	15				100	17	13	千克	FE	Other buttons containing materials of animal in imminent dangers
9606.2900 90	其他钮扣	15				100	17	13	千克		Other buttons
9606.3000	-钮扣芯及钮扣的其他零件;钮扣坯	15	8		9	100	17	13	千克		-Button moulds and other parts of buttons; button blanks
96.07	**拉链及其零件:**										**Slide fasteners and parts thereof:**
	-拉链:										-Slide fasteners:
9607.1100	--装有贱金属制齿的	21	12		12.6	130	17	13	米/千克		--Fitted with chain scoops of base metal

税则号列 Tariff Item.	货品名称	最惠国(%) MFN	协定(%)CT 东盟 CA	中巴 CP	中智 CC	普通 Gen	增值税率 VAT	出口退税 ED	计量单位 Unit	监管条件 SC	Article Description
9607.1900	--其他	21	T3	14.7	12.6	130	17	13	米/千克		--Other
9607.2000	-零件	21	12		12.6	130	17	13	千克		-Parts
96.08	**圆珠笔;毡尖和其他渗水式笔尖笔及唛头笔;自来水笔、铁笔型自来水笔及其他钢笔;蜡纸铁笔;活动铅笔;钢笔杆、铅笔套及类似的笔套;上述物品的零件(包括帽、夹),但税目96.09的货品除外:**										**Ball point pens; felt tipped and other porous-tipped pens and markers; fountain pens, stylograph pens and other pens; duplicating stylos; propelling or sliding pencils; pen-holders, pencil-holders and similar holders; parts (including caps and clips) of the foregoing articles, other than those of headingNo. 96.09:**
9608.1000	-圆珠笔	15	8	13.5	12	80	17	13	支		-Ball point pens
9608.2000	-毡尖和其他渗水式笔尖笔及唛头笔	21	12		0	80	17	13	支		-Felt tipped and other porous-tipped pens and markers
	-自来水笔、铁笔型自来水笔及其他钢笔:										-Fountain pens, stylograph pens and other pens:
9608.3100	--墨汁画笔	21	12		12.6	80	17	13	支		--Indian ink drawing pens
	--其他:										--Other:
9608.3910	---自来水笔	21	12		12.6	80	17	13	支		---Fountain pens
9608.3990	---其他	21	12		12.6	80	17	13	支		---Other
9608.4000	-活动铅笔	21	12		12.6	80	17	13	支		-Propelling or sliding pencils
9608.5000	-由上述两个或多个子目所列物品组成的成套货品	21	12		12.6	80	17	13	套		-Sets of articles from two or more of the foregoing subheadings
9608.6000	-圆珠笔芯,由圆珠笔头和墨芯构成	21	12		12.6	80	17	13	支		-Refills for ball point pens, comprising the ball point and ink-reservoir
	-其他:										-Other:
9608.9100	--钢笔头及笔尖粒	12	8		7.2	70	17	13	支		--Pen nibs and nib points
	--其他:										--Other:
9608.9910	---机器、仪器用笔	17.5	8		10.5	40	17	13	支/千克		---Of a kind used on machines or instruments
9608.9920	---蜡纸铁笔;钢笔杆、铅笔杆及类似的笔杆	21	12		12.6	80	17	13	支/千克		---Duplicating stylos; pen-holders, pencil-holders and similar holders
9608.9990	---其他	21	12		12.6	80	17	13	千克		---Other
96.09	**铅笔(税目96.08的铅笔除外)、颜色铅笔、铅笔芯、蜡笔、图画碳笔、书写或绘画用粉笔及裁缝划粉:**										**Pencils (other than pencils of headingNo. 96.08), crayons, pencil leads, pastels, drawing charcoals, writing or drawing chalks and tailors' chalks:**
	-铅笔及颜色铅笔:										-Pencils and crayons, with leads encased in a rigid sheath:
9609.1010	---铅笔	21	12		16.8	80	17	13	千克/百支	aB	---Pencils
9609.1020	---颜色铅笔	21	12		16.8	80	17	13	千克	aB	---Crayons
9609.2000	-铅笔芯,黑的或其他颜色的	21	12		16.8	80	17	13	千克	B	-Pencil leads, black or coloured
9609.9000	-其他	15	8		12	80	17	13	千克	B	-Other
96.10	**具有书写或绘画面的石板、黑板及类似板,不论是否镶框:**										**Slates and boards, with writing or drawing surfaces, whether or not framed:**
9610.0000	具有书写或绘画面的石板、黑板及类似板,不论是否镶框	15	8		9	80	17	13	千克		Slates and boards, with writing or drawing surfaces, whether or not framed

税则号列 Tariff Item.	货品名称	最惠国(%) MFN	协定(%) 东盟 CA	中巴 CP	CT 中智 CC	普通 Gen	增值税率 VAT	出口退税 ED	计量单位 Unit	监管条件 SC	Article Description
96.11	**手用日期戳、封缄戳、编号戳及类似印戳(包括标签压印器);手工操作的排字盘及带有排字盘的手印器:**										**Date, sealing or numbering stamps, and the like (including devices for printing or embossing labels), designed for operating in the hand; hand-operated composing sticks and hand printing sets incorporating such composing sticks:**
9611.0000	手用日期戳、封缄戳、编号戳及类似印戳(包括标签压印器);手工操作的排字盘及带有排字盘的手印器	21	12		16.8	80	17	13	千克		Date, sealing or numbering stamps, and the like (including devices for printing or embossing labels), designed for operating in the hand; hand-operated composing sticks and hand printing sets incorporating such composing sticks
9611.0000 10	含濒危动物成分的手用日期戳(包括封缄戳及类似印戳)	21				80	17	13	千克	FE	Date, sealing, and the like, designed for operating in the hand, containing materials of animal in imminent dangers
9611.0000 90	手用日期戳、封缄戳及类似印戳(包括编号戳、标签压印器;手工排字盘及带有字盘的手印器)	21				80	17	13	千克		Other date, sealing or numbering stamps, and the like (including devices for printing or embossing labels), designed for operating in the hand; hand-operated composing sticks and hand printing sets incorporating such composing sticks
96.12	**打字机色带或类似色带,已上油或经其他方法处理能着色的,不论是否装轴或装盒;印台,不论是否已加印油或带盒子:**										**Typewriter or similar ribbons, inked or otherwise prepared for giving impressions, whether or not on spools or in cartridges; ink-pads, whether or not inked, with or without boxes:**
9612.1000	-色带	10.5	8		0	35	17	13	个		-Inked ribbons
9612.2000	-印台	25	12		15	100	17	13	个		-Ink-pads
96.13	**香烟打火机和其他打火器(不论是机械的,还是电气的)及其零件,但打火石及打火机芯除外:**										**Cigarette lighters and other lighters, whether or not mechanical or electrical, and parts thereof other than flints and wicks:**
9613.1000	-袖珍气体打火机,一次性的	25	12		20	130	17	11	个	B	-Pocket lighters, gas fuelled, non refillable
9613.2000	-袖珍气体打火机,可充气的	25	12		15	130	17	11	个	B	-Pocket lighters, gas fuelled, refillable
9613.8000	-其他打火器	25	12		15	130	17	11	个	B	-Other lighters
9613.9000	-零件	25	12		15	130	17	11	千克		-Parts
96.14	**烟斗(包括烟斗头)和烟嘴及其零件:**										**Smoking pipes (including pipe bowls) and cigar or cigarette holders, and parts thereof:**
9614.0010	---烟斗及烟斗头	25	12		15	130	17	13	个/千克		---Pipes and pipe bowls
9614.0010 10	含濒危动物成分的烟斗及烟斗头(仅指野生哺乳类牙齿制产品)	25				130	17	13	个/千克	ABFE	Smoking pipes (including pipe bowls) containing materials of animal in imminent dangers (only referring to products made of ivory of wild mammals)
9614.0010 20	用植物性材料制作的烟斗及烟斗头	25				130	17	13	个/千克	AB	Smoking pipes (including pipe bowls) of vegetable materials

税则号列 Tariff Item.	货品名称	最惠国(%) MFN	协定(%) CT			普通 Gen	增值税率 VAT	出口退税 ED	计量单位 Unit	监管条件 SC	Article Description
			东盟 CA	中巴 CP	中智 CC						
9614.0010 90	其他烟斗及烟斗头	25				130	17	13	个/千克		Other smoking pipes (including pipe bowls)
9614.0090	---其他	25	12		15	130	17	13	千克		---other
9614.0090 10	含野生动物成分的烟嘴及其零件(仅指野生哺乳类牙齿制产品)	25				130	17	13	千克	FE	Cigar or cigarette holders, and parts thereof, containing wild animal materials (only referring to products made of ivory of wild mammals)
9614.0090 90	其他烟嘴及其零件	25				130	17	13	千克		Other cigar or cigarette holders, and parts thereof
96.15	**梳子、发夹及类似品;发卡、卷发夹、卷发器或类似品及其零件,但税目 85.16 的货品除外:**										**Combs, hair-slides and the like; hairpins, curling pins, curling grips, hair-curlers and the like, other than those of headingNo. 85.16, and parts thereof:**
	-梳子、发夹及类似品:										-Combs, hair-slides and the like:
9615.1100	--硬质橡胶或塑料制	18	8	16.2	14.4	130	17	13	千克		--Of hard rubber or plastics
9615.1900	--其他	18	8		10.8	130	17	13	千克		--Other
9615.1900 10	含濒危动物成分的其他材料制梳子(包括角质发夹等,金属、塑料及家畜来源的产品除外)	18				130	17	13	千克	ABFE	Combs, hair-slides and the like, containing materials of animal in imminent dangers (including hair-slides made of horns, but not including products made of metal, plastic or material of domestic animals)
9615.1900 20	用其他动植物材料制的梳子(包括角质发夹等,金属、塑料及家畜来源的产品除外)	18				130	17	13	千克	AB	Combs, hair-slides and the like, of other animal or vegetable materials (including hair-slides made of horns, but not including products made of metal, plastic or material of domestic animals)
9615.1900 90	其他材料制梳子、角质发夹等(包括类似品,但橡胶、塑料制的除外)	18				130	17	13	千克		Combs, hair-slides and the like, of other materials, but not including products made of metal, plastic or material of domestic animals
9615.9000	-其他	18	8	16.2	10.8	130	17	13	千克		-Other
96.16	**香水喷雾器或类似的化妆用喷雾器及其座架、喷头;粉扑及粉拍,施敷脂粉或化妆品用:**										**Scent sprays and similar toilet sprays, and mounts and heads therefor; powderpuffs and pads for the application of cosmetics or toilet preparations:**
9616.1000	-香水喷雾器或类似的化妆用喷雾器及其座架、喷头	18	8	16.2	14.4	130	17	13	千克		-Scent sprays and similar toilet sprays, and mounts and heads therefor
9616.2000	-粉扑及粉拍,施敷脂粉或化妆品用	18	8	16.2	10.8	130	17	13	千克		-Powder-puffs and pads for the application of cosmetics or toilet preparations
96.17	**带壳的保温瓶和其他真空容器及其零件,但玻璃瓶胆除外:**										**Vacuum flasks and other vacuum vessels, complete with cases; parts thereof other than glass inners:**
9617.0010	---保温瓶	24	12		14.4	130	17	13	个/千克		---Vacuum flasks
9617.0090	---其他	18	8		10.8	130	17	13	千克		---Other

税则号列 Tariff Item.	货品名称	最惠国(%) MFN	协定(%)CT 东盟 CA	中巴 CP	中智 CC	普通 Gen	增值税率 VAT	出口退税 ED	计量单位 Unit	监管条件 SC	Article Description
96.18	**裁缝用人体模型及其他人体活动模型;橱窗装饰用的自动模型及其他活动陈列品:**										**Tailors' dummies and other lay figures; automata and other animated displays used for shop window dressing:**
9618.0000	裁缝用人体模型及其他人体活动模型;橱窗装饰用的自动模型及其他活动陈列品	21	12		12.6	80	17	13	千克		Tailors' dummies and other lay figures; automata and other animated displays used for shop window dressing
9618.0000 10	用植物性材料制作的人体模型	21				80	17	13	千克	AB	Tailors' dummies and other lay figures of vegetable materials
9618.0000 90	裁缝用其他人体模型(包括橱窗装饰用的自动模型及其他活动陈列品)	21				80	17	13	千克		Other tailors' dummies and other lay figures; automata and other animated displays used for shop window dressing

第二十一类
艺术品、收藏品及古物

SECTION XXI
WORKS OF ART, COLLECTORS' PIECES AND ANTIQUES

第九十七章
艺术品、收藏品及古物

Chapter 97
Works of art, collectors' pieces and antiques

注释:

一、本章不包括:

(一)税目49.07的未经使用的邮票、印花税票、邮政信笺(印有邮票的纸品)及类似的票证;

(二)作舞台、摄影的布景及类似用途的已绘制画布(税目59.07),但可归入税目97.06的除外;

(三)天然或养殖珍珠、宝石或半宝石(税目71.01至71.03)。

二、税目97.02所称"雕版画、印制画、石印画的原本",是指以艺术家完全手工制作的单块或数块印版直接印制出来的黑白或彩色原本,不论艺术家使用何种方法或材料,但不包括使用机器或照相制版方法制作的。

三、税目97.03不适用于成批生产的复制品及具有商业性质的传统手工艺品,即使这些物品是由艺术家设计或创造的。

四、(一)除上述注释一至三另有规定的以外,可归入本章各税目的物品,均应归入本章的相应税目而不归入本目录的其他税目;

(二)税目97.06不适用于可以归入本章其他各税目的物品。

五、已装框的油画、粉画及其他绘画、版画、拼贴画及类似装饰板,如果框架的种类及价值与作品相称,应与作品一并归类。

如果框架的种类及价值与作品不相称,应分别归类。

Notes:

1. This Chapter does not cover:

(a) Unused postage or revenue stamps, postal stationery (stamped paper) or the like, headingNo. 49.07;

(b) Theatrical scenery, studio back-cloths or the like, of painted canvas (headingNo. 59.07) except if they may be classified in headingNo. 97.06; or

(c) Pearls, natural or cultured, or precious or semi-precious stones (headings Nos71.01 to 71.03).

2. For the purposes of headingNo. 97.02, the expression "original engravings, prints and lithographs" means impressions produced directly, in black and white or in colour, of one or of several plates wholly executed by hand by the artist, irrespective of the process or of the material employed by him, but not including any mechanical or photomechanical process.

3. HeadingNo. 97.03 does not apply to mass-produced reproductions or works of conventional craftsmanship of a commercial character, even if these articles are designed or created by artists.

4. (a) Subject to Notes 1 to 3 above, articles of this Chapter are to be classified in this Chapter and not in any other Chapter of the Nomenclature.

(b) headingNo. 97.06 does not apply to articles of the preceding headings of this Chapter.

5. Frames around paintings, drawings, pastels, collages or similar decorative plaques, engravings, prints or lithographs are to be classified with those articles, provided they are of a kind and of a value normal to those articles.

Frames which are not of a kind or of a value normal to the articles referred to in this Note are to be classified separately.

税则号列 Tariff Item.	货品名称	最惠国(%) MFN	协定(%)CT 东盟 CA	中巴 CP	中智 CC	普通 Gen	增值税率 VAT	出口退税 ED	计量单位 Unit	监管条件 SC	Article Description
97.01	**油画、粉画及其他手绘画,但带有手工绘制及手工描饰的制品或税目49.06的图纸除外;拼贴画及类似装饰板:**										**Paintings, drawings and pastels, executed entirely by hand, other than drawings of headingNo. 49.06 and other than handpainted or handdecorated manufactured articles; collages and similar decorative plaques:**
	-油画、粉画及其他手绘画:										-Paintings, drawings and pastels:
9701.1010	---原件	12	8		9.6	50	17	13	幅		---The originals
9701.1020	---复制品	14	8		11.2	50	17	13	幅		---Reproductions
9701.9000	-其他	14	8		8.4	50	17	13	千克		-Other

税则号列 Tariff Item.	货品名称	最惠国(%) MFN	协定(%) CT 东盟 CA	中巴 CP	中智 CC	普通 Gen	增值税率 VAT	出口退税 ED	计量单位 Unit	监管条件 SC	Article Description
9701.9000 10	含濒危动物成分的拼贴画(包括类似装饰板,指一切源自濒危动物的产品)	14				50	17	13	千克	ABFE	Collages and similar decorative plaques containing materials of animal in imminent dangers (referring to collages of materials of all kinds of wild animals)
9701.9000 20	用其他动植物材料制作的拼贴画(包括类似装饰板,指一切源自野生动物的产品)	14				50	17	13	千克	AB	Collages and similar decorative plaques of other animal or vegetable materials (referring to collages of materials of all kinds of wild animals)
9701.9000 90	其他拼贴画及类似装饰板	14				50	17	13	千克		Other collages and similar decorative plaques
97.02	**雕版画、印制画、石印画的原本:**										**Original engravings, prints and lithographs:**
9702.0000	雕版画、印制画、石印画的原本	12	8		7.2	50	17	13	幅		Original engravings, prints and lithographs
97.03	**各种材料制的雕塑品原件:**										**Original sculptures and statuary, in any material:**
9703.0000	各种材料制的雕塑品原件	12	8		7.2	50	17	13	幅		Original sculptures and statuary, in any material
9703.0000 10	濒危动植物材料制的雕塑品原件(指一切源自濒危动植物的产品)	12				50	17	13	幅	FE	Original sculptures and statuary, in imminent dangers materials
9703.0000 90	其他各种材料制的雕塑品原件	12				50	17	13	幅		Original sculptures and statuary of other materials
97.04	**使用过或未使用过的邮票、印花税票、邮戳印记、首日封、邮政信笺(印有邮票的纸品)及类似品,但税目49.07的货品除外:**										**Postage or revenue stamps, stamp-postmarks, first-day covers, postal stationery (stamped paper), and the like, used or unused, other than those of headingNo. 49.07:**
9704.0010	---邮票	8	5		0	50	17	13	千克		---Postage
9704.0090	---其他	14	8		8.4	50	17	13	千克		---Other
97.05	**具有动物学、植物学、矿物学、解剖学、历史学、考古学、古生物学、人种学或钱币学意义的收集品及珍藏品:**										**Collections and collectors' pieces of zoological, botanical, mineralogical, anatomical, historical, archaeological, palaeontological, ethnographic or numismatic interest:**
9705.0000	具有动物学、植物学、矿物学、解剖学、历史学、考古学、古生物学、人种学或钱币学意义的收集品及珍藏品	0				0	17		千克		Collections and collectors' pieces of zoological, botanical, mineralogical, anatomical, historical, archaeolohical, palaeontological, ethnographic or numismatic interest
9705.0000 10	含濒危动植物的收藏品(具有动植物学意义的)	0				0	17		千克	ABFE	Collections and collectors' pieces of zoological, containing materials of plants or animal in imminent dangers
9705.0000 90	具有动、植、矿物学意义的收藏品(还包括具有解剖、历史、考古、古生物学意义的收藏品)	0				0	17		千克	AB	Collections and collectors' pieces of zoological, botanical, mineralogical, anatomical, historical, archaeological, palaeontological, ethnographic or numismatic interest

税则号列 Tariff Item.	货品名称	最惠国(%) MFN	协定(%) 东盟 CA	中巴 CP	CT 中智 CC	普通 Gen	增值税率 VAT	出口退税 ED	计量单位 Unit	监管条件 SC	Article Description
97.06	**超过一百年的古物：**										**Antiques of an age exceeding one hundred years:**
9706.0000	超过一百年的古物	0				0	17		千克		Antiques of an age exceeding one hundred years
9706.0000 10	超过一百年的濒危野生动植古物（具收藏或文史价值的）	0				0	17		千克	ABFE	Antiques of an age exceeding one hundred years of wild animal or vegetable in imminent dangers (having literary or historical collection value)
9706.0000 90	其他超过一百年的古物	0				0	17		千克		Other antiques of an age exceeding one hundred years

第二十二类
特殊交易品及未分类商品

SECTION XXII
ARTICLES OF SPECIAL TRADE AND GOOD UNCLASSIFIED

第九十八章
特殊交易品及未分类商品

Chapter 98
Articles of Special Trade and Good Unclassified

税则号列 Tariff Item.	货品名称	最惠国(%) MFN	协定(%) CT 东盟 CA	中巴 CP	中智 CC	普通 Gen	增值税率 VAT	出口退税 ED	计量单位 Unit	监管条件 SC	Article Description
98.01	未分类商品										**Good unclassified**
9801.0010	≤2000 元 RMB 的非税,非证进口商品	0				0	0		千克		Import goods exempted from the levy of customs duties and not subject to license control, value≤2000RMB
9801.0090	其他未分类商品	0				0	0		千克		Other unclassified
9801.3000	流通中的货币现钞(包括纸币及硬币)	0				0	0		千克	T	Official currencies (negotiable paper notes and coins)
98.03	出口计算机软件(不包括与产品固化或集成为一体的软件)										**Computer software, not including software hardwired or integrated in products**
9803.0010	系统软件	0				0	0		套		System software
9803.0020	支撑软件	0				0	0		套		Support software
9803.0030	应用软件	0				0	0		套		Application software
9803.0090	其他软件	0				0	0		套		Other software

附件 1：

2007 年进口税则暂定最惠国税目、税率表

（2007 年 1 月 1 日起实施）

Appendix 1：

Interim Duty Rate on Imported Goods, 2007

(Enforced from January 1, 2007)

ex	税　号 Tariff No.	货　品　名　称	2007 最惠国税率 MFN(%)	暂定税率 Interim duty Rate (%)	Description of Goods
	03033110	格陵兰庯鲽鱼	10	5	Greenland halibut
	05119111	受精鱼卵	12	0	Fertilized fish eggs
	15020090	已炼制的牛羊脂肪	8	7	Fats of sheep or goats, including lard
	15159020	印楝油及其分离品	20	10	Neem oil and its fractions
	18010000	整颗或破碎的可可豆，生的或焙炒的	8	4	Cocoa beans, whole or broken, raw or roasted
	23099090	其他配制的动物饲料	6.5	4	Feeding preparations
ex	24039100	再造烟草	57	40	Reconwtituted tobacco
	25030000	硫磺	3	1.5	Sulphur of all kinds, other than sublimed sulphur, precipitated sulphur and colloidal sulphur
	25101010	未碾磨的磷灰石	3	0	Apatite, unground
	25102010	已碾磨的磷灰石	3	0	Apatite, ground
	25151100	原状或粗加修正的大理石	4	1	Marble, crude or roughly trimmed
	25161100	原状或粗加修正的花岗石	4	1	Granite, crude or roughly trimmed
	25162000	原状或粗加修正的砂岩	3	1	Sandstone, crude or roughly trimmed
	25281000	天然硼砂及其精矿	3	1	Natural sodium borates and concentrates thereof ($H_3BO_3 > 85\%$)
	25289000	天然粗硼酸，含硼酸干重不超过85%	5	1	Natural sodium borates, crude($H_3BO_3 < 85\%$)
ex	25309099	天青石	3	1	Celestite
	27011110	未制成型的无烟煤，不论是否粉化	3	1	Ahthracite, whether or not pulverized, but not agglomerated
	27011210	炼焦煤	3	0	Bituminous Coking coal, not agglomerated, whether or not pulverized
	27011290	其他烟煤	6	1	Other bituminous coal, other than coking coal, not agglomerated, whether or not pulverized
	27011900	未制成型的其他煤，不论是否粉化	5	1	Other coal, whether or not pulverized, but not agglomerated
	27012000	煤砖、煤球及类似用煤制固体燃料	5	1	Briquettes ovoides and similar solid fuels manufactured form coal
	27021000	褐煤	3	1	Lignite
	27022000	制成型的褐煤	3	1	Agglomerated lignite
24	27030000	泥煤（包括肥料用泥煤）不论是否成型	5	1	Peat(including peat litter), whether or not agglimerated
	27040010	煤制焦炭及半焦炭不论是否成型	5	0	Coke and semi - coke, whether or not agglomeraeed
	27040090	甑炭	5	1	Retort carbom
	27050000	煤气、水煤气、炉煤气及类似气体，石油气及其他烃类气除外	5	1	Coal gas, water gas, producer gas and similor gases, other than petrolekm gases and other gaseous hydrocarbons
	27060000	从煤、褐煤、或泥煤蒸馏所得的焦油及矿物焦油，不论是否脱水或部分蒸馏，包括再造焦油	6	1	Tar distiucd from cool, from lignite or from peat, and other mineral tars, whether or not dehydrated or partially distilled, including reconstituted tars
	27073000	粗二甲苯	6	3	Xylol (xylenes)
	27075000	其他芳烃混合物	7	3	Aromatic hydrocarbon mixtures

ex	税号 Tariff No.	货品名称	2007 最惠国税率 MFN(%)	暂定税率 Interim duty Rate(%)	Description of Goods
ex	27082000	针状沥青焦	6	1	Needle-shaped pitch coke
	27101110	车用汽油及航空汽油	5	2	Motror gasoline, aviation gasoline
ex	27101191	壬烯(碳九混合异构体含量高于90%)	9	4	Nonene (containing mixed isomer of C_9 >90%)
ex	27101199	异戊烯同分异构体混合物	9	5	Isomeric
	27101911	航空煤油	9	2	Aviation kerosene
ex	27101919	正构烷烃(C_9 ~ C_{13})	6	2	N - Alkanes(C_9 ~ C_{13})
	27101921	轻柴油	6	2	Light diesel oil
ex	27101929	350度以下馏出物体积百分比小于20%,550度以下馏出物体积百分比大于80%的蜡油	6	0	Paraffin oils, 350℃ distillage <20%, 550℃ distillage >80%
ex	27131210	已锻烧针状石油焦	3	1	Needle-shaped petroleum coke
	28020000	升华硫磺、沉淀硫磺、胶态硫磺	5.5	1.5	Sulphur, sublimed or precipitated; colloidal sulphur
ex	28046190	多晶硅	4	2	Polysilicon
	28051100	钠	5.5	1	Sodium
	28051200	钙	5.5	1	Calcium
	28051900	其他碱金属及碱土金属	5.5	1	Other alkali and alkaline - earth metals
	28053011	钕	5.5	1	Neodymium
	28053012	镝	5.5	1	Dysprosium
	28053019	其他未相互混合或熔合的稀土金属、钪及钇	5.5	1	Other rare - earth, not interimixed or interauoyed, scandium and yttrium
	28053021	已相互混合或熔合的稀土金属、钪及钇,电池级	5.5	1	Rare - earth metals, intermixed or interallored, scandium and yttrium, kattery quality
	28053029	其他已相互混合或熔合的稀土金属、钪及钇	5.5	1	Other rare - earth metals, intermixed or interalloved, scandium and yttrium
	28092010	磷酸及偏磷酸、焦磷酸	1	0	Phosphoric acid, metaphosphoric acid and pyrophosphoric acid
	28121010	氯化亚砜	5.5	2	Sulphoxide chloride
	28141000	氨	5.5	1	Anhydrous ammonia
	28182000	氧化铝,但人造钢玉除外	8	3	Aluminium oxide, other than artificial corumdum
ex	28269000	六氟磷酸锂	5.5	2	Lithium hexafluorophosphate
	28342110	肥料用硝酸钾	4	1	Potassium for use as fertilizer
	28369100	锂的碳酸盐	5.5	2	Lithium carbonates
	28369930	碳酸钴	5.5	2	Cobalt carbonate
	28401100	无水四硼酸钠	5.5	2	Disodium tetraborate (refinde borax), anhydrous
	28401900	其他四硼酸钠	5.5	2	Other disodium tetraborate (refinded borax)
ex	28419000	钴酸锂	5.5	2	Lithium cobaltate
	29012100	乙烯	2	0	Ethylene
	29031500	1,2-二氯乙烷(ISO)	5.5	1	1,2-Dichloroethane (ethylene dichloride)
	29032100	氯乙烯	5.5	1	Chloroethylene
	29036110	邻二氯苯	5.5	3	*o*-Dichlorobenzene
	29042020	硝基甲苯	5.5	3	Nitrotoluene
	29051210	正丙醇	5.5	3	Propan-1-ol(propyl alcohol)
	29051430	叔丁醇	5.5	3	Tert-Butanol
	29053200	1,2-丙二醇	5.5	3	Propylene glycol
	29071211	间甲酚	5.5	3	m-cresol
	29071212	邻甲酚	5.5	3	*o*-Cresol
	29071910	邻仲丁基酚、邻异丙基酚	4	2	*o*-Sec-butyl phenol, *o*-isopropyl phenol

ex	税 号 Tariff No.	货 品 名 称	2007 最惠国税率 MFN(%)	暂定税率 Interim duty Rate(%)	Description of Goods
	29094100	二甘醇	5.5	3	2,2′-Oxydiethanol (diethylene glycol, digol)
ex	29094990	2-正丙氧基乙醇	5.5	3	2-Propoxyethanol
ex	29121900	正丙醛	5.5	3	*n*-Propionaldehyde
ex	29121900	乙二醛	5.5	3	Glyoxal (Ethanedial)
	29141300	甲基异丁基甲酮	5.5	3	4-Methyl-2-pentanone (isobutyl methyl ketone)
	29155010	丙酸	5.5	3	Propionic acid
	29162010	DV 菊酸甲酯、二溴菊酸	4	2	Dibromochrysanthemic acid, DV-chrysanthemicmono carboxylate
ex	29162090	二氯菊酰氯(DV 菊酰氯)	6.5	2	Dichlorochrysanoyl chloride (DV-chrysanoyl chloride)
	29171200	已二酸及其盐和酯	6.5	3	Adipic acid, its salts and esters
	29172010	四氢苯酐	4	2	Tetrahydro benzoic anhydride
	29173611 29173619	对苯二甲酸	7.6	6.5	Terephthalic acid
	29211910	二正丙胺	4	2	Di-*n*-propylamine
	29211920	异丙胺	6.5	2	Isopropyl amine
ex	29211990	三乙胺、月桂胺、一乙胺、正丁胺	6.5	3	Triethylamine, Laurylamine, ethylamine, n-butylamine
	29212110	乙二胺	6.5	3	Ethylenediamine
ex	29212900	二乙烯三胺	6.5	3	Diethylenetriamine
ex	29214300	邻甲苯胺	6.5	3	*o*-Tuluidine
ex	29214920	2,4、2,6-二甲基苯胺	6.5	2	2,4、2,6-Dimethylanilines
	29214940	2,6-二乙基苯胺	6.5	2	2,6-Diethylaniline
ex	29221320	芳基聚氧乙烯磷酸酯	6.5	3	Aromatic polyoxyethylene phosphate
	29224210	谷氨酸	10	5	Glutamic acid
	29261000	丙烯腈	6.5	5	Acrylonitrile
ex	29269090	已二腈	6.5	1	Hexanedinitrile
ex	29309090	DL-羟基蛋氨酸	6.5	5	DL-hydroxymethionine
ex	29309090	乙硫醇	6.5	3	Ethanethiol (ethyl mercaptan)
ex	29333210	六氢吡啶	4	2	Hexahydropyridine
	29336910	三聚氰氯	6	2	Cyanuric chloride
	29419051	7-氨基脱乙酰氧基头孢烷酸、7-氨基头孢烷酸	6	4	7-aminocephalosporianic acid, 7-amino-deacetoxycefanoic acid
	31031010	重过磷酸钙	4	1	Concen traned superphosphnate
	31031090	其他过磷酸钙	4	1	Other Superphosphates
	31039000	其他矿物磷肥或化学磷肥	4	1	Other mineral or chemical fertilizere, phosphatic
	31042090	其他氯化钾	3	1	Other potassium chloride
	31043000	硫酸钾	3	1	Potassium sulphate
	31049010	光卤石、钾盐及其他天然粗钾盐	3	1	Carnallite, sylvite and other crude natural potassium salts
	31049090	其他矿物钾肥及化学钾肥	3	1	Other mineral or chemical fertilizers, potassic
	31051000	制成片状及类似形状或每包毛重不超过10公斤的31章各货品	4	1	Good of this chapter in tablets or similar form or in packages of a gross weight not exceeding lokg
	31054000	磷酸二氢铵及磷酸二氢铵与磷酸氢二铵的混合物	4	1	Ammonium dihydrogenorthophosphate
	31055100	含有硝酸盐及磷酸盐的肥料	4	1	Tertilizes containing nitrates and phosphates

ex	税 号 Tariff No.	货 品 名 称	2007 最惠国税率 MFN(%)	暂定税率 Interim duty Rate (%)	Description of Goods
	31055900	其他含氮、磷两种肥效元素的矿物肥料或化学肥料	4	1	Other mineral or chemical fertilizers containing the two fertilizing elements nitrogen and phosphorus
	31056000	含磷、钾两种元素的肥料	4	1	Fertilizes containing the two dements phosphorus and potassium
	31059000	其他肥料	4	1	Other fertilizes
ex	32082010	分散于或溶于水介质的光导纤维用涂料(主要成分为聚胺酯丙烯酸酯类化合物)	10	6	Paints for optial fibers (based on polyaminate acrylate resin polymers)
ex	32089010	光导纤维用涂料(主要成分为聚胺酯丙烯酸酯类化合物)	10	6	Paints for optial fibers (based on polyaminate acrylate resin polymers)
ex	33012999	黄樟油	15	7	Essential oil of sassafras
	33013010	鸢尾凝脂(香膏类)	20	10	Balsam of irises
ex	34029000	十二烷基苯磺酸钙甲醇溶液(十二烷基苯磺酸钙含量应高于70%)	9	7	Calcium dodecyl benzosulfonate methanol solution (Calcium dodecyl benzosulfonate content >70%)
ex	35030010	明胶	12	5	Gelatin
	37024221	印刷电路板制造用光制抗蚀干膜	2.1元/平方米	0.6元/平方米	Photo resist dry film
ex	37024291	红外或氦氖激光胶片,宽度>80cm,长度>1000m	2.4元/平方米	1.05元/平方米	Infrared or helium neon laser film, width >80cm, length >1000m
	37024422	印刷电路板制造用光制抗蚀干膜	2.1元/平方米	0.9元/平方米	Photo resist dry film
	37025520	未曝光的窄长彩色电影胶卷(正片)	11元/平方米	6元/平方米	Unexposed polychrome cinematographic film in rolls
ex	37071000	感光乳剂(不含银的)	8	4	Sensitizing emulsions (excluding silver)
	38011000	人造石墨	6.5	3	Artificial graphite
ex	38170000	混合烷基苯	6.5	4	Mixed alkylbenzenes
	38237000	工业用脂肪醇	13	9	Aliphatic alcohols for industrial uses
ex	38249090	电极浆料(主要成分为银、镍或铜和有机溶剂,用于生产片式陶瓷电容器)	6.5	3	Pastes for electrodes (mainly containing silver、nickle or copper and organic solvent, for flat figuline capacitor manufacture)
ex	38249090	高钛渣(二氧化钛质量百分含量大于70%的)	6.5	0	Titanium-rich slag (Containing Titanium Dioxide >70)
ex	38249090	生产等离子显示屏用的银电极浆料、介质浆料、障蔽浆料、荧光粉浆料	6.5	3	Silver electrode, medium, concealment, phosphor pastes
ex	39011000	聚乙烯(进口CIF价高于2000美元/吨)	7.8	3	Polyethylene (import CIF≥1500 usd/t)
ex	39012000	聚乙烯(进口CIF价高于2000美元/吨)	7.8	3	Polyethylene (import CIF≥1500 usd/t)
ex	39021000	电工级初级形状聚丙烯树脂(灰分含量不大于30ppm)	7.6	3	Electrotechonical polypropylene resin in primary forms (Ash content not more than 30ppm)
ex	39072000	聚四亚甲基醚二醇	7.6	5	Polvtetramethylene Ether Glycol
ex	39073000	溴的质量百分含量在18%及以上或进口CIF价格高于3800美元/吨的环氧树脂(如溶于溶剂,以纯环氧树脂折算溴的百分含量)	7.6	4	Epoxyresins containing by weight more than 18% Bromine (base on pure Epoxyresins if dissolved in solvent)

ex	税　号 Tariff No.	货 品 名 称	2007 最惠国税率 MFN(%)	暂定税率 Interim duty Rate(%)	Description of Goods
ex	39119000	偏苯三酸酐和异氰酸预缩聚物	6.5	3	Precondensed polymer of trimelltic anhydride isocyanate
ex	39119000	芳基酸与芳基胺预缩聚物	6.5	3	Precondensed polymer of aromatic acid and aromatic amide
ex	39119000	改性三羟乙基脲酸酯类预缩聚物	6.5	3	Precondensed polymer of modified trihydroxy acetate
ex	39121100	未塑化二、三醋酸纤维素	6.5	1	Non-plasticized cellulose diacetate, non-plasticized cellulose triacetate
ex	39201090	乙烯－四氟乙烯膜(四氟乙烯单体含量约 50%),比重 1.7－1.75k/cm^3	6.5	1	Ethylene－tetrafluoroethylene film (containing monomer of tetrafluoroethylene ≈50%) specific gravity: 1.7～1.75k/cm^3
	40011000	天然胶乳	20	10,或 720 元/吨。两者从低	Natural rubber latex
	40012100	烟胶片	20	20,或 2600 元/吨。两者从低	Smoked sheets
	40012200	技术分类天然橡胶	20	20,或 2600 元/吨。两者从低	Technically specified natural rubber (TSNR)
ex	40112000	断面宽度 30 英寸及以上的轮胎	10	3	Tyres, having a fracture surface of a width of 30 inches or more
ex	40116100	断面宽度 24 英寸及以上的轮胎	17.5	6	Tyres, having a fracture surface of a width of 24 inches or more
ex	40116300	断面宽度 24 英寸及以上的轮胎	17.5	6	Tyres, having a fracture surface of a width of 24 inches or more
ex	40116900	断面宽度 30 英寸及以上的轮胎	17.5	6	Tyres, having a fracture surface of a width of 30 inches or more
ex	40119200	断面宽度 24 英寸及以上的轮胎	25	6	Tyres, having a fracture surface of a width of 24 inches or more
ex	40119400	断面宽度 24 英寸及以上的轮胎	25	6	Tyres, having a fracture surface of a width of 24 inches or more
ex	40119900	断面宽度 30 英寸及以上的轮胎	25	3	Tyres, having a fracture surface of a width of 30 inches or more
	40129010	航空用实心或半实心橡胶轮胎	3	1	Aircraft solid or cushion rubber tyres
	40139010	航空用橡胶内胎	3	1	Aircraft rubber inner tubes
	41041111	全粒面未剖层或粒面剖层蓝湿牛皮	7	5	Chrome－tanned bovine leather (wet blue skin leather), full grain, unsplit, or grain splits, not further prepared
	41041911	其他蓝湿牛皮	7	5	Other wet－blue bovine animals
	41041920	其他湿马皮	7	5	Other wet－blue epuine animals
	41051010	蓝湿绵羊、羔羊皮	14	12	Wet－blue sheep or lambs
ex	41062100	蓝湿山羊皮	14	12	Wet－blue soats
	41063110	蓝湿猪皮	14	12	Wet－blue swine
ex	44089019	家具饰面单板	3	1	Veneer sheets for furni－ture
	45011000	未经加工或简单加工的天然软木	6	3	Natrual cork, raw prepared
	48022010	照相原纸	7.5	5	Photo paper base
	48115110	彩色相纸用双面涂塑纸	7.5	2	Paper coated on both sides with plastics for colour photography

ex	税 号 Tariff No.	货 品 名 称	2007 最惠国税率 MFN(%)	暂定税率 Interim duty Rate(%)	Description of Goods
ex	56013000	由两种或两种以上有机聚合物纺制的纤维(横截面为皮芯结构或并列结构或海岛结构),长度不超过5毫米	10	5	Of two or more kinds of polymers (with cross section of skin - core or juxtapose or island structure), length not more than 5mm
ex	68061000	矿物纤维,渣球含量小于5%	10.5	5	Mineral fibres, cinder content <5%
ex	68071000	聚脂-铜复合胎基改性沥青根阻防水卷材	12	1	Television camera digital cemera and DVCAM
ex	68159910	碳纤维纱线(碳元素含量大于90%)	17.5	8	Yarn of carbon fiberes, containing carbon element > 90%
ex	69071000	瓷砖、陶瓷等产品,未打磨和上釉的陶瓷(表面最宽小于7厘米)	24.5	22	Tiles, cubes and sim (7cm rect or not etc, unglazed ceramics)
ex	70023900	光通信用微光组件的玻璃毛细管、定位管(外径小于3mm)	12	3	Micro capillavy and glass tube for optical communication (out diameter <3mm)
ex	70049000	光学平板玻璃,厚度0.7毫米以下	17.5	9	Optic plane slass, thickness below 0.7mm
ex	70052900	浮法玻璃,气泡、杂质的大小小于等于30微米	15	8	Float, slass, size of bubble impurities smaller or equal to 30 microns
ex	70071110	空载重量25吨及以上飞机的挡风玻璃	2	1	Windshiled for airplane unloaden weight≥25t
ex	70071900	低铁钢化太阳能电池组件封装专用玻璃(最大含铁量0.02% Fe_2O_3,玻璃厚度2.5 mm - 3.5 mm)	14	12	Ferrless toughen glass for solar energy battery encapsulation (max Fe 0.02Fe_2O_3, thichness of glass: 2.5 ~3.5mm)
ex	70112090	显示管玻壳及其零件	10	6	Glass envelopes and parts thereof for cathode-ray tubes
ex	70140090	带有抗红外和防反射薄膜的滤波玻璃	17.5	9	Wave - filter glass with anti - IR and auti - reflection film
ex	70195200	覆铜箔板用长丝平纹布,开纤或每平方米重≤180克	12	6	
	70200011	导电玻璃	10.5	7	Class fibres woven for ticking-on copper foil
ex	70200019	等离子模块生产用高应变点玻璃(应变点在550摄氏度及以上)	10.5	5	High strain point glass used for PDP model production (strain point≥550℃)
ex	70200090	石英玻璃,平整度小于等于1微米	15	8	Quartz glass
	71011011	天然黑珍珠	21	0	Tahitian
	71011091	天然黑珍珠	21	0	Tahitian
ex	71049019	蓝宝石衬底(由人造刚玉加工而成,厚度小于0.5毫米)	6	1	Underlay with sapp hire cmade of manm ade corundum with thickness <0.5*mm*
	71159010	工业或试验室用贵或包金属制品	3	0	'Other articles of precious metal, for technical or lab use
	72024100 72024900	铬铁	2	1	Ferro - chromium
	72026000	镍铁	2	1	Ferro-nickel
	72029300	铌铁	2	1	Ferro-niobium
ex	72031000	热压铁块	2	0	Hot, Briguetted Irom (HBI)
	72041000	铸铁废碎料	2	0	Waste and scrop of cast iron
	72043000	镀锡钢铁废碎料	2	0	Waste and scrap of tinned iron or steel
	72044100	机械加工中产生的钢铁废料	2	0	Waste and csrop of tinned iron or steel

ex	税号 Tariff No.	货品名称	2007 最惠国税率 MFN(%)	暂定税率 Interim duty Rate (%)	Description of Goods
	72091810	厚度<0.3毫米冷轧卷材	6	3	Coils of a thickness of less than 0.3mm, cold rolled (cold - reduced)
ex	72269990	铁镍合金带材(生产集成电路框架用)	7	4	Fe-Ni alloys strip (production of the frame for electronic integrated circuits)
	73044110	锅炉管(包括内螺纹)	10	5	Boiler seamless tubes and pipes (inside thread), of stainless steel, cold draw or cold rolled
	73044910	锅炉管(包括内螺纹)	10	5	Boiler seamless tubes and pipes (inside thread), of stainless steel, hot draw or hot rolled
	74020000	未精炼铜、电解精炼用铜阳极	2	0	Unrefined copper; copper anodes for electrolytic refining
	74040000	铜废碎料	1.5	0	Copper waste and scrap
ex	74101100	覆铜板及印刷线路板用铜箔	4	1	Foil of refined Cu, not backed, for printed circuits
	75011000	镍锍	3	0	Nickel mattes
	75012010	镍湿法冶炼中间品	3	0	Nickel intermediate products obtained by hydrometallurgical processing
	75021000	金属镍(未煅轧)	3	1	Unwrought nickel, not alloyed
	76020000	铝废碎料	1.5	0	Aluminium waste and scrap
	76061120	厚度在0.3毫米及以上,但不超过0.36毫米的铝板	6	1	Aluminium plates, of a thickness of 0.3mm or more but not exceeding 0.36mm
	81052010	钴湿法冶炼中间品	4	0	Cobalt intermediate products obtained by hydrometallurgical processing
ex	81052090	钴锍及其他冶炼钴时所得的中间产品	4	0	Cobalt mattes and other inter - mediate products of cobalt metallurgy
ex	81129220 81129920	钒氮合金	3	0	Vanadic - nitrogen
	84079010	沼气发动机	12	9	Firedamp engines
ex	84079090	转速<3600r/min的发电机用汽油发动机、税号8426-8430所列机械用转速<4650r/min的汽油发动机	18	8	Petrol engines for generators, rotational speed less than 3600 r/min. Petrol engines for engineering mechanism, rotational speed < 4650 r/min, of heading 8426 ~ 8430
ex	84082010	输出功率在441千瓦(600马力)及以上的柴油发动机	9	4	Diesel enging, out put≥441KW (600H · P)
ex	84082090	额定功率小于100千瓦的轿车用柴油发动机	25	15	Diesel engine for car with rated power smaller than 100kw
ex	84099999	电控柴油喷射装置	8.4	5	Electric fuel injection devices
ex	84119910	涡轮轴航空发动机用零件	5	0	Parts of turboshaft engines
ex	84123100	三坐标测量机用气缸	14	7	Gas vat for COMERO
ex	84129090	风力发电设备用浆叶	8	5	Propeller leaf for wind - power generating device
ex	84148030	轿车用增压器,最大增压压力不低于1.7Bar	7	3	Supercharger for sedan use (the maximun supercharging pressure not lower than 1.7 Bar)
ex	84162019	溴化锂空调用燃烧机	10.5	5	Lithium bromide burner for air - conditioning
ex	84335100	功率≥160马力的联合收割机	8	5	Combine harvester-thresher, power≥160 H. P.
ex	84335990	自走式青储饲料收获机	8	5	
	84423021	计算机直接制版设备(CTP)	9	0	Computerized plate-making machine
ex	84424000	计算机直接制版机器用零件	7	0	Components for computer - compsing machines
ex	84431921	纺织用圆网印花机	10	8	
ex	84431922	纺织用平网印花机	10	8	
	84433110	静电感光式多功能一体机	10	3	Photo - electrostatic

ex	税 号 Tariff No.	货 品 名 称	2007 最惠国税率 MFN(%)	暂定税率 Interim duty Rate (%)	Description of Goods
ex	84433221	幅宽>60cm的喷墨印刷设备,可与网络或计算机连接	8	3	Inkjet printers with breadeh > 60cm (can be connected to automatic data processing facilities or internet)
ex	84433222	幅宽>60cm的静电照相印刷设备(激光印刷机),可与网络或计算机连接	8	3	Electrostatic printing equipments (laster printers) with breath > 60cm(can be connected to automatic data processing facilities or internet)
	84435920	棉花采摘机	8	5	cotton machine
ex	84439190	胶印机用墨量遥控装置(包括墨色控制装置、墨量调节装置、墨斗体等组成部分)	6	0	The ink - con trols for offset printing machine (including ink - color controls, the ink - quantity controls, etc)
ex	84481100	多臂机或提花机转速指标:500转/分以上	8	4	Dobbies and Jacquards, Tachometry index: > 500 r/min
ex	84483200	精梳机钳板、顶梳装置,精梳机锡林部件、精梳机车头凸轮传动、行星齿轮部件,精梳联合梳理装置,清梳联合给棉装置,清梳联合机盖板清洁装置	6	3	Nippers, topcombs, cylinders, head cams, epicyclic gears of combers; combing devices, drawing devices, flat cleaning devices of lapping and combing combines
	84483310	络筒锭	6	3	Winding spindle
	84483920	电子清纱器	6	3	Electronic yarn clearers
	84483930	空气捻接器	6	3	Air twisting devices
ex	84483990	环锭细纱机紧密纺装置	6	0	
	84484910	接、投梭箱	6	3	Catching and throwing shuttle boxes
	84484920	引纬、送经装置	6	3	Weft insertion and warp let-off motions
ex	84484990	自动寻纬、补纬装置、打纬装置	6	3	Automatic searching weft for the gripper looms, automatic mending weft for the air-jet looms
ex	84518000	柔软整理机	12	10	Supple finishing machine
ex	84518000	磨毛机、丝光机	12	10	Napping grinder、Mercerizing range
ex	84518000	定型机、涂层机	12	10	Boarding machine、Coating machine
ex	84518000	罐蒸机、精炼机	12	10	Potting steamer、Refining machine
ex	84518000	剪绒、洗缩联合机	12	10	Pile shearing and shrinking combine
ex	84518000	预缩机	12	10	Sanforizer
ex	84518000	服装液氨整理机	12	10	Dress aqua ammoniae finishing range
ex	84518000	服装定型焙烘炉	12	10	Dress shoping
ex	84518000	剪毛联合机	12	10	Sheepshearing combination machine
ex	84518000	织物轧光机	12	6	Woven fabric glazing calender
	84734010	自动柜员机出钞器	10.5	1	Banknote dispenser of automated teller
ex	84734090	钞票清分机零附件	10.5	5	Parts and accessories of banknote checking and dispencing machine
	84789000	烟草加工及制作机器的零件	10	5	Parts of Machinery for preparing or making up tobacco
ex	84834020	磨煤机用行星齿轮减速器(由螺旋伞齿轮加行星齿轮二级立式减速机构组成,转盘外圆直径为:1300mm-2400mm)	8	2	Planetary speed reducer for coal pulverizer (composed of two - stage vertical decelerating mechanism with helical bevel gear and planetary gear, outer ring D = 1300mm ~ 2400mm)
ex	84834090	风力发电设备用变速箱	8	5	Transmission case for the wind - porrer generating facilities
ex	85011091	激光视盘机机芯精密微型电机	9	6	Minitype precise motor for mechanism of laser disc player

ex	税 号 Tariff No.	货 品 名 称	2007 最惠国税率 MFN(%)	暂定税率 Interim duty Rate (%)	Description of Goods
ex	85011099	功率不大于0.5瓦(圆柱型:直径不大于6毫米,高不大于25毫米;扁圆型:直径不大于15毫米,厚不大于5毫米)非用于激光视盘机机芯的微型电机	9	5	Micromotors of an output not exceeding 0.5W (cylindrical: diameter ≤ 6mm, height ≤ 25mm; oblate type: diameter ≤ 15mm thickness ≤ 5mm), not for movements of laser videodise player
ex	85015300	高速(200km/h)电力机车的交流异步牵引电动机	12	3	AC asyncronous traction motor for high speed electric locomotive (200km/h)
	85023100	风力发电设备	8	5	Windmill generating equipments
	85030030	风力发电设备的零件	3	1	Parts of wind-powerd generating sets
ex	85044014	功率小于1千瓦,稳压系数低于万分之一的直流稳压电源(税号8471所列机器用除外)	7	3	DC stabilized voltage power supply with power smaller than 1km, coefficient of voltase stabili zation lower than 1110,000 (excluoling machine listed in Duty No. 8471)
	85044091	具有变流功能的半导体模块	10	0	Semiconductor modules with a converting function
ex	85044099	高速(200km/h)电力机车的牵引变流器	10	3	Traction converter for highspeed electric locomotive (200km/h)
ex	85144000	焊缝中频退火装置	10	7	Intermediate frequency sealing anneator
ex	85229031	具有刻录功能的激光视盘机机芯	30	15	Movements with CD - RW function specified for laser video disk set
ex	85229039	其他视频信号录制或重放设备的零件	30	10	Parts for video recording or reproducing apparatus
ex	85229039	激光视盘机的激光收发装置(激光头)	30	10	Laser receiver-transmitter (laser head) specified for laser video disk set
ex	85229039	激光视盘机激光收发装置用的零件	30	3	Laser transmitting and receiving device of laser disc player
ex	85258013	手机用摄像组件(由镜头+CCD/CMOS+数字信号处理电路三部分构成)	35	6	TV photographers and other photographing commponents for non - special use (other photographing components are made up of non - broadcast cameras + CCD/CMPS + digtal signal processing circuits)
ex	85261090	飞机机载雷达(包括气象雷达、地形雷达和空中交通管制应答系统)	5	1	Airborne radars (including aero-radars, terrain-following radars and air-traffic-control interrogator-responder systems)
ex	85299042	摄录一体机、数码相机、手机用取像模块	12	6	Picture pickup modules for television cameras, still image video cameras and other video camera recorders, digital cameras, not for special purpose
ex	85299049	摄像机、摄录一体机、数码相机的其他零件	12	3	Other parts for household video camera recorders and digital camera
ex	85299081	投影电视机用光机	15	7	Optical units specified for projection TV en
	85299082	等离子显像组件及其零件(含滤光片)	15	5	Plasma display device and parts thereof (including filter glass)
ex	85318010	音量不超过110dB的小型蜂鸣器	15	7.5	Minitype electric buzzers, maximum volume not exceeding 110dB
ex	85371011 85371019	机床用数控装置(包括CNC操作单元,无论其是否带有配套的伺服放大器和伺服电机)	5	3	Numerical control panels for machine tool (including CNC operational unies)
ex	85393290	彩色液晶投影机的照明光源	8	4	Parts of lens of colour liquid - crystal projector
	85404000	彩色的数据/图形显示管,屏幕荧光点间距小于0.4毫米	8	4	Color data/graphic display tubes of phosphor dot screen pitch smaller than 0.4mm

ex	税 号 Tariff No.	货 品 名 称	2007 最惠国税率 MFN(%)	暂定税率 Interim duty Rate (%)	Description of Goods
ex	85443020	车辆用电控柴油机的线束	10	5	Wiring har ness for electronic control of diesel engine
ex	85462090	输变电架空线路用长棒形瓷绝缘子瓷件(单支长度为1-2米,实芯)	12	3	Long solid rod ceramic insulator body for power overhead transmission and converting lines(each rod is 1 ~2 meters in length)
ex	85489000	贴片滤波器	12	6	
ex	87019011	功率大于150马力的轮式拖拉机	8	5	Wheeled tactors with power more than 150H. P.
ex	87019019	功率大于150马力的其他拖拉机	8	5	Other tractors with power more than 150H. P.
ex	87042300	装有驾驶室的固井水泥车、压裂车、混砂车用底盘(车辆总重量超过35吨)	15	10	Chassis assemblies for petroleum well logging trucks, fracturing unit trucks and mixing sand trucks fitted with cabs and engines (g. v. w 35 tons or more)
ex	87042300	起重55吨及以上的汽车起重机用底盘	15	8	Chassis (incoraporating cabs), of crane lorries eifting capactitg≥55t
ex	87059090	跑道除冰车	12	10	Runway deicing truck
ex	87084030	扭矩>1500Nm非公路自卸车用变速箱	6	3	Gear box for non-wishway auto-unloads with wrench moment >1500Nm
ex	87084050	扭距≥90kgm变速箱、分动箱	10	6	Gear boxes, transfer cases, torque≥90kgm
ex	87085082	30座及以上的客车用非驱动桥及其零件	15	10	
ex	87089420	30座及以上客车用转向器	10	8	Steering boxes for the buses with 30 seats or more
ex	87085072	轴荷≥10t的中后驱动桥的零件	10	8	Parts of middle and rear drive-axles, axle capacity ≥ 10 t
ex	87089420	30座及以上客车用转向器的零件	10	8	Parts of steering boxes and parts thereof for the buses with 30 seats or more
ex	87089939	非公路用自卸车未列名零部件	6	3	Not specified parts of dumpers designed for off-highway use
ex	87089450	总重≥14吨柴油型货车转向器的零件	10	8	Steering boxes and parts thereof for diesel vehicles of g. v. w ≥ 14 t
ex	87084050	扭距≥90kgm变速箱、分动箱的零件	10	6	Parts of gear boxes, transfer case, torque ≥90kgm
ex	87089999	混合动力汽车动力传动装置,由发电机、电动机和动力分配装置组成	10	6	Hybird vehicle transmission unit, composed of generator, motor, power delivery unit.
ex	88024010	空载重量在25吨及以上,但重量不超过45吨的客运飞机	5	1	Passenger aeroplanes of an unladen weight exceeding 25t but not exceeding 45t
ex	90019000	背投电视机显示屏(包括非涅耳透镜屏幕、双透镜屏幕和保护屏)	8	6	Project TV screen(induding Fresnel lens screen, lenticular screen, screen shields)
ex	90019000	光通信用微光组件的光学元件(包括工作波长为800nm ~1700nm的薄膜滤光片、自聚焦透镜、法拉第旋转片)	8	4	Micro - optic component for optical communicaton (including thin film filter, gradient index leos and faraday Rotator, with working wavelength between 800nm and 1700nm)
ex	90019000	激光视盘机激光收发装置用的微型镜片	8	1	
ex	90021190	彩色液晶投影机的镜头及镜头组件	15	6	Camera lens and their components for multi-color LCD projectors
ex	90021190	数码相机的镜头	15	6	Digital camera lens

ex	税 号 Tariff No.	货 品 名 称	2007 最惠国税率 MFN(%)	暂定税率 Interim duty Rate (%)	Description of Goods
ex	90132000	2.5GB/S 及以上 SDH、波分复用光传输设备的 980 纳米、1480 纳米的泵浦激光器	6	3	980μm、1480μm pump laser of SDH ≥ 2.5GB/s, optical transmission equipment for wave-divison multicomplexing
	90138030	液晶显示板	5	3	Liquid crystal display plate
ex	90142000	航空惯性导航仪	2	1	Inertial navigation instruments for airplanes
	90189080	宫内节育器	4	0	Intrauterine device (IUD)
ex	90219000	人工耳蜗植入装置	4	0	Cochlear Implant device
ex	90229090	射线发生器的零部件	6	3	Part of radiation generators
ex	90318090	跑道摩擦系数测试仪	5	3	Runway friction coefficient tester
ex	90328900	三坐标测量机用自动控制柜	7	3	
ex	90328900	飞机自动驾驶系统(包括自动驾驶、电子控制飞行、自动故障分析、警告系统、配平系统及推力监控设备及其相关仪表)	7	1	Automatic pilotting systems for aircraft (including automatic pilotting, electronic flight control, automatic failure analysis, warning systems, trimming systems, thrust monitoring equipments and the meters thereof)
ex	90330000	飞机自动驾驶系统(包括自动驾驶、电子控制飞行、自动故障分析、警告系统、配平系统及推力监控设备及其相关仪表)的零件	6	1	Parts of automatic pilotting system for aircraft (including automatic pilotting, electronic flight control, automatic failure analysis, warning systems, trimming systems, thrust monitoring equipments and the meters thereof)
ex	92012000	完税价格 50000 美元及以上的大钢琴	17.5	1	Grand pianos, the duty - paying value≥50000USD
ex	92021000	完税价格 15000 美元及以上的弓弦乐器	17.5	1	Played with a bow, the duty-paying valus≥15000USD
ex	92051000	完税价格 2000 美元及以上的铜管乐器	17.5	1	Brass-wind instruments, the duty-paying ualue ≥ 2000USD
ex	92059090	完税价格 10000 美元及以上的其他管乐器	17.5	1	Other wind musical instruments, the duty-paying value≥10000USD

注:“ex”表示实施暂定税率的商品以“商品名称”描述为准。其余以税号为准。

附件 2：

Appendix 2：

2007 年进口商品从量税、复合税税目、税率表

（2007 年 1 月 1 日起实施）

Specific、Compound Scale Duties，2007

（Enforced from January 1，2007）

税则号列	货 品 名 称	最惠国税率	普通税率	东盟协定	巴基斯坦	智利	亚太
02071200	冻的整只鸡	1.3 元/千克	5.6 元/千克			1.04 元/千克	
02071411	冻的带骨鸡块（包括鸡胸脯、鸡大腿等）	0.6 元/千克	4.2 元/千克			0.36 元/千克	
02071419	冻的不带骨鸡块（包括鸡胸脯、鸡大腿等）	1.0 元/千克	9.5 元/千克			0.8 元/千克	
02071421	冻的鸡翼（不包括翼尖）	0.8 元/千克	8.1 元/千克			0.48 元/千克	
02071422	冻的鸡爪	0.5 元/千克	3.2 元/千克			0.4 元/千克	
02071429	冻的其他食用鸡杂碎（包括鸡翼尖、鸡肝等）	0.5 元/千克	3.2 元/千克			0.4 元/千克	
05040021	冷、冻的鸡肫（即鸡胃）	1.3 元/千克	7.7 元/千克		0.65 元/千克	1.04 元/千克	0.65 元/千克
22030000	麦芽酿造的啤酒	0	7.5 元/升				
27090000	石油原油（包括从沥青矿物提取的原油）	0	85 元/吨				
37013021	未曝光照相制版用激光照排片（任何一边 > 255 毫米）	3.7 元/平方米	70 元/平方米				
37013022	未曝光照相制版用 PS 版（任何一边 > 255 毫米）	2.9 元/平方米	70 元/平方米				
37013023	未曝光照相制版用 CTP 版（任何一边 > 255 毫米）	2.9 元/平方米	70 元/平方米	1.45 元/平方米			
37013029	其他未曝光照相制版用感光硬软片（任何一边 > 255 毫米）	6.8 元/平方米	70 元/平方米				
37023190	其他未曝光无齿孔彩色窄胶卷（窄胶卷指宽度≤105 毫米，彩色摄影用）	67 元/平方米	433 元/平方米	20.1 元/平方米		40.2 元/平方米	

税则号列	货 品 名 称	最惠国税率	普通税率	东盟协定	巴基斯坦	智利	亚太
37023220	照相制版涂卤化银液无齿孔窄胶卷(成卷未曝光感光胶片,窄胶卷指宽度≤105毫米)	4.8元/平方米	104元/平方米	2.4元/平方米			
37023290	其他涂卤化银乳液无齿孔窄胶卷(成卷未曝光感光胶片,窄胶卷指宽度≤105毫米)	21元/平方米	202元/平方米	11.5元/平方米		12.6元/平方米	
37023920	照相制版用其他无齿孔窄感光胶卷(成卷未曝光感光胶片,窄胶卷指宽度≤105毫米)	3.7元/平方米	104元/平方米	1.85元/平方米			
37023990	其他用无齿孔窄感光胶卷(成卷未曝光感光胶片,窄胶卷指宽度≤105毫米)	24元/平方米	202元/平方米	13.1元/平方米		14.4元/平方米	
37024100	未曝光无齿孔宽长彩色胶卷(宽长胶卷指宽度>610毫米,长度>200米)	8.5元/平方米	202元/平方米			5.1元/平方米	
37024221	印刷电路板制造用光致抗蚀干膜(指宽度>610毫米,长度>200米)	2.1元/平方米	110元/平方米	1.68元/平方米			
37024229	照相制版其他未曝光无齿宽长胶卷(宽长指宽度>610毫米,长度>200米)	1.6元/平方米	110元/平方米	0.8元/平方米			
37024291	未曝光红外或氦氖激光胶片	2.4元/平方米	213元/平方米	1.8元/平方米		1.44元/平方米	
37024299	黑白其他未曝光无齿孔宽长胶卷(宽长胶卷指宽度>610毫米,长度>200米)	7元/平方米	213元/平方米	5.25元/平方米		4.2元/平方米	

税则号列	货　品　名　称	最惠国税率	普通税率	东盟协定	巴基斯坦	智利	亚太
37024321	照相制版用激光照排片(宽度>610 毫米,长度≤200 米)	1.8 元/平方米	104 元/平方米	0.9 元/平方米			
37024329	其他照相制版用未曝光无齿孔胶卷(指宽度>610 毫米,长度≤200 米)	3.7 元/平方米	104 元/平方米	1.85 元/平方米			
37024390	彩色或黑白其他用未曝光无齿孔中长胶卷(中长胶卷指宽度>610 毫米,长度≤200 米)	33 元/平方米	202 元/平方米	19.8 元/平方米		19.8 元/平方米	
37024421	照相制版用未曝光激光照排片(宽度大于105 毫米,小于等于610 毫米)	2.0 元/平方米	115 元/平方米	1.0 元/平方米			
37024422	印刷电路板制造用光致抗蚀干膜(宽度大于105 毫米,小于等于610 毫米)	2.1 元/平方米	115 元/平方米	1.05 元/平方米			
37024429	其他照相制版用无齿孔未曝光胶卷(宽度大于105 毫米,小于等于610 毫米)	2.9 元/平方米	115 元/平方米	1.45 元/平方米			
37024490	彩色或黑白其他用无齿孔未曝光中宽胶卷(中宽胶卷指宽度>105 毫米,但≤610 毫米)	27 元/平方米	202 元/平方米	16.2 元/平方米			
37025100	未曝光窄短彩色胶卷(窄短胶卷指宽度≤16 毫米,长度≤14 米)	128 元/平方米	433 元/平方米	32.7 元/平方米		76.8 元/平方米	
37025200	未曝光中窄彩色胶卷(中窄胶卷指宽度≤16 毫米,长度>14 米)	95 元/平方米	433 元/平方米	24.3 元/平方米		57 元/平方米	

税则号列	货 品 名 称	最惠国税率	普通税率	东盟协定	巴基斯坦	智利	亚太
37025300	幻灯片用未曝光彩色摄影胶卷(宽度>16 毫米,但≤35 毫米,长度≤30 米)	128 元/平方米	433 元/平方米	32.7 元/平方米		76.8 元/平方米	
37025410	非幻灯片用彩色摄影胶卷(宽度=35 毫米,长度≤2 米)	28 元/平方米	433 元/平方米				
37025490	其他非幻灯片用彩色摄影胶卷(宽度>16 毫米,但≤35 毫米,长度≤30 米)	26 元/平方米	433 元/平方米				
37025520	未曝光的窄长彩色电影胶卷(窄长胶卷指宽度>16 毫米,但≤35 毫米,长度>30 米)	11 元/平方米	232 元/平方米			8.8 元/平方米	
37025590	其他未曝光窄长彩色胶卷窄长胶卷指宽度>16 毫米,但≤35 毫米,长度>30 米)	35 元/平方米	433 元/平方米			25.6 元/平方米	
37025620	未曝光的中宽彩色电影胶卷(中宽胶卷指宽度>35 毫米)	13 元/平方米	232 元/平方米	6.5 元/平方米		7.8 元/平方米	
37025690	其他未曝光的中宽彩色胶卷(中宽胶卷指宽度>35 毫米)	78 元/平方米	433 元/平方米	23.4 元/平方米		46.8 元/平方米	
37029100	未曝光窄短黑白胶卷(窄短胶卷指宽度≤16 毫米)	21 元/平方米	210 元/平方米	12.6 元/平方米		12.6 元/平方米	
37029310	未曝光中长黑白胶卷(宽度=35 毫米,长度≤2 米)	26 元/平方米	210 元/平方米			15.6 元/平方米	

税则号列	货　品　名　称	最惠国税率	普通税率	东盟协定	巴基斯坦	智利	亚太
37029390	其他未曝光中长黑白胶卷(中长胶卷指宽度>16毫米,但≤35毫米,长度≤30米)	21元/平方米	210元/平方米			12.6元/平方米	
37029420	未曝光的窄长黑白电影胶卷(窄长胶卷指宽度>16毫米,但≤35毫米,长度>30米)	9元/平方米	210元/平方米			7.2元/平方米	
37029490	其他用未曝光窄长黑白胶卷(窄长胶卷指宽度>16毫米,但≤35毫米,长度>30米)	21元/平方米	210元/平方米			16.8元/平方米	
37029520	未曝光的中宽黑白电影胶卷(中宽胶卷指宽度>35毫米)	10元/平方米	210元/平方米	5.45元/平方米		6元/平方米	
37029590	其他用未曝光的中宽黑白胶卷(中宽胶卷指宽度>35毫米)	35元/平方米	210元/平方米	23.3元/平方米		21元/平方米	
85211011	广播级磁带录像机	每台完税价格不高于2000美元:执行单一从价税 30%; P ≤ USD2000/set SCT = 0 AVCT = 30% 每台完税价格高于2000美元:每台征收从量税,税额4374,加上3%的从价税, P < USD2000/set SCT = ¥4374/set AVCT = 3%	每台完税价格不高于2000美元:执行单一从价税 130%; P ≤ USD2000/set SCT = 0 AVCT = 130% 每台完税价格高于2000美元:每台征收从量税,税额20600,加上6%的从价税, P < USD2000/set SCT = ¥20600/set AVCT = 6%	每台完税价格不高于2000美元:执行单一从价税 12%; P ≤ USD2000/set SCT = 0 AVCT = 12% 每台完税价格高于2000美元:每台征收从量税,税额1458,加上3%的从价税, P < USD2000/set SCT = ¥1458/set AVCT = 3%	每台完税价格不高于2000美元:执行单一从价税 16%; P ≤ USD2000/set SCT = 0 AVCT = 16% 每台完税价格高于2000美元:每台征收从量税,税额2103,加上3%的从价税, P < USD2000/set SCT = ¥2103/set AVCT = 3%		每台完税价格不高于2000美元:执行单一从价税 16%; P ≤ USD2000/set SCT = 0 AVCT = 16% 每台完税价格高于2000美元:每台征收从量税,税额2103,加上3%的从价税, P < USD2000/set SCT = ¥2103/set AVCT = 3%

税则号列	货品名称	最惠国税率	普通税率	东盟协定	巴基斯坦	智利	亚太
85211019	其他磁带录像机	每台完税价格不高于2000美元:执行单一从价税 30%; P ≤ USD2000/set SCT = 0 AVCT = 30% 每台完税价格高于2000美元:每台征收从量税,税额4374,加上3%的从价税, P < USD2000/set SCT = ¥4374/set AVCT = 3%	每台完税价格不高于2000美元:执行单一从价税 130%; P ≤ USD2000/set SCT = 0 AVCT = 130% 每台完税价格高于2000美元:每台征收从量税,税额20600,加上6%的从价税, P < USD2000/set SCT = ¥20600/set AVCT = 6%	每台完税价格不高于2000美元:执行单一从价税 12%; P ≤ USD2000/set SCT = 0 AVCT = 12% 每台完税价格高于2000美元:每台征收从量税,税额1458,加上3%的从价税, P < USD2000/set SCT = ¥1458/set AVCT = 3%	每台完税价格不高于2000美元:执行单一从价税 24.5%; P ≤ USD2000/set SCT = 0 AVCT = 24.5% 每台完税价格高于2000美元:每台征收从量税,税额3483,加上3%的从价税, P < USD2000/set SCT = ¥3483/set AVCT = 3%		每台完税价格不高于2000美元:执行单一从价税 24.5%; P ≤ USD2000/set SCT = 0 AVCT = 24.5% 每台完税价格高于2000美元:每台征收从量税,税额3483,加上3%的从价税, P < USD2000/set SCT = ¥3483/set AVCT = 3%
85211020	磁带放像机	每台完税价格不高于2000美元:执行单一从价税 30%; P ≤ USD2000/set SCT = 0 AVCT = 30% 每台完税价格高于2000美元:每台征收从量税,税额4374,加上3%的从价税, P < USD2000/set SCT = ¥4374/set AVCT = 3%	每台完税价格不高于2000美元:执行单一从价税 130%; P ≤ USD2000/set SCT = 0 AVCT = 130% 每台完税价格高于2000美元:每台征收从量税,税额20600,加上6%的从价税, P < USD2000/set SCT = ¥20600/set AVCT = 6%	每台完税价格不高于2000美元:执行单一从价税 12%; P ≤ USD2000/set SCT = 0 AVCT = 12% 每台完税价格高于2000美元:每台征收从量税,税额1458,加上3%的从价税, P < USD2000/set SCT = ¥1458/set AVCT = 3%	每台完税价格不高于2000美元:执行单一从价税 18%; P ≤ USD2000/set SCT = 0 AVCT = 18% 每台完税价格高于2000美元:每台征收从量税,税额2430,加上3%的从价税, P < USD2000/set SCT = ¥2430/set AVCT = 3%		每台完税价格不高于2000美元:执行单一从价税 18%; P ≤ USD2000/set SCT = 0 AVCT = 18% 每台完税价格高于2000美元:每台征收从量税,税额2430,加上3%的从价税, P < USD2000/set SCT = ¥2430/set AVCT = 3%
85258012	非特种用途的广播级电视摄像机	每台完税价格不高于5000美元:执行单一从价税 35%; P ≤ USD5000/set SCT = 0 AVCT = 35% 每台完税价格高于5000美元:每台征收从量税,税额12960,加上3%的从价税, P < USD5000/set SCT = ¥12960/set AVCT = 3%	每台完税价格不高于5000美元:执行单一从价税 130%; P ≤ USD5000/set SCT = 0 AVCT = 130% 每台完税价格高于5000美元:每台征收从量税,税额51500,加上6%的从价税, P < USD5000/set SCT = ¥51500/set AVCT = 6%		每台完税价格不高于5000美元:执行单一从价税 29.8%; P ≤ USD5000/set SCT = 0 AVCT = 29.8% 每台完税价格高于5000美元:每台征收从量税,税额10854,加上3%的从价税, P < USD5000/set SCT = ¥10854/set AVCT = 3%		每台完税价格不高于5000美元:执行单一从价税 29.8%; P ≤ USD5000/set SCT = 0 AVCT = 29.8% 每台完税价格高于5000美元:每台征收从量税,税额10854,加上3%的从价税, P < USD5000/set SCT = ¥10854/set AVCT = 3%

税则号列	货品名称	最惠国税率	普通税率	东盟协定	巴基斯坦	智利	亚太
85258013	非特种用途的其他电视摄像机	每台完税价格不高于5000美元:执行单一从价税 35%; P ≤ USD5000/set SCT = 0 AVCT = 35% 每台完税价格高于5000美元:每台征收从量税,税额12960,加上3%的从价税, P < USD5000/set SCT = ¥12960/set AVCT = 3%	每台完税价格不高于5000美元:执行单一从价税 130%; P ≤ USD5000/set SCT = 0 AVCT = 130% 每台完税价格高于5000美元:每台征收从量税,税额51500,加上6%的从价税, P < USD5000/set SCT = ¥51500/set AVCT = 6%		每台完税价格不高于5000美元:执行单一从价税 29.8%; P ≤ USD5000/set SCT = 0 AVCT = 29.8% 每台完税价格高于5000美元:每台征收从量税,税额10854,加上3%的从价税, P < USD5000/set SCT = ¥10854/set AVCT = 3%		每台完税价格不高于5000美元:执行单一从价税 29.8%; P ≤ USD5000/set SCT = 0 AVCT = 29.8% 每台完税价格高于5000美元:每台征收从量税,税额10854,加上3%的从价税, P < USD5000/set SCT = ¥10854/set AVCT = 3%
85258022	非特种用途的单镜头反光型数字照相机	0	每台完税价格不高于5000美元:执行单一从价税 130%; P ≤ USD5000/set SCT = 0 AVCT = 130% 每台完税价格高于5000美元:每台征收从量税,税额51500,加上6%的从价税, P < USD5000/set SCT = ¥51500/set AVCT = 6%				
85258029	非特种用途的其他数字照相机	0	每台完税价格不高于5000美元:执行单一从价税 130%; P ≤ USD5000/set SCT = 0 AVCT = 130% 每台完税价格高于5000美元:每台征收从量税,税额51500,加上6%的从价税, P < USD5000/set SCT = ¥51500/set AVCT = 6%				

税则号列	货 品 名 称	最惠国税率	普通税率	东盟协定	巴基斯坦	智利	亚太
85258032	非特种用途的广播级视频摄录一体机	0	每台完税价格不高于5000美元:执行单一从价税 130%; P ≤ USD5000/set SCT = 0 AVCT = 130% 每台完税价格高于5000美元:每台征收从量税,税额51500,加上6%的从价税, P < USD5000/set SCT = ¥51500/set AVCT = 6%				
85258039	非特种用途的其他视频摄录一体机(家用型摄录一体机除外)	0	每台完税价格不高于5000美元:执行单一从价税 130%; P ≤ USD5000/set SCT = 0 AVCT = 130% 每台完税价格高于5000美元:每台征收从量税,税额51500,加上6%的从价税, P < USD5000/set SCT = ¥51500/set AVCT = 6%				

附件 3：

Appendix 3：

2007 年中国－东盟全面经济合作框架协议十国实施税率表

The Applied Tariff Rates for the Ten Countries under the Framework Agreement on Comprehensive Economic Co－operation between China and ASEAN

税则号列 Tariff No.	货品名称 Description of Goods	最惠国 MFN (%)	协定税率(%) Agreement									
			文莱 CAM	印尼 INA	马来西亚 MAS	缅甸 MMR	菲律宾 PHI	新加坡 SIN	泰国 THA	越南 VIE	老挝 LAO	柬埔寨 TPE
01029000	其他牛	10	0	0	0	0	8	0	0	0	0	0
01039110	重量＜10kg 的猪	10	0	0	0	0		0	0	0	0	0
01039120	重量在 10－50kg 的猪，包括 10kg	10	0	0	0	0		0	0	0	0	0
01039200	重量≥50kg 的猪	10	0	0	0	0		0	0	0		
01042090	其他山羊	10	0	0	0	0	8	0	0	0	0	0
01051190	重量≤185g 的其他鸡	10	0	0	0	0		0	0	8	0	0
01051290	重量≤185g 的其他火鸡	10	0	0	0	0	8	0	0	0	0	0
01051990	重量≤185g 的其他家禽	10	0	0	0	0	8	0	0	0	0	0
01059490	重量＞185g 的其他鸡	10	0	0	0	0		0	0	8		0
01059991	重量＞185g 的非改良种用鸭	10	0	0	0	0	8	0	0	8		0
01059992	重量＞185g 的非改良种用鹅	10	0	0	0	0	8	0	0	8		0
01059993	重量＞185g 的非改良种用珍珠鸡	10	0	0	0	0	8	0	0	8		0
01059994	重量＞185g 的非改良种用火鸡	10	0	0	0	0	8	0	0	8		0
02011000	整头及半头鲜、冷牛肉	20	0	0	0	0	12	0	0	0	0	0
02012000	鲜、冷的带骨牛肉	12	0	0	0	0	8	0	0	0	0	0
02013000	鲜、冷的去骨牛肉	12	0	0	0	0	8	0	0	0	0	0
02021000	冻的整头及半头牛肉	25	0	0	0	0	12	0	0	0		0
02022000	冻的带骨牛肉	12	0	0	0	0	8	0	0	0		0
02023000	冻的去骨牛肉	12	0	0	0	0	8	0	0	0		0
02031110	鲜、冷的整头及半头乳猪肉	20	0	0	0	0		0	0	0		0
02031190	其他鲜、冷的整头及半头猪肉	20	0	0	0	0		0	0	0		0
02031200	鲜、冷的带骨猪前腿、后腿及其肉块	20	0	0	0	0		0	0	0		0
02031900	其他鲜、冷猪肉	20	0	0	0	0		0	0	0		0
02032110	冻整头及半头乳猪肉	12	0	0	0	0		0	0	0		0
02032190	其他冻整头及半头猪肉	12	0	0	0	0		0	0	0		0
02032200	冻的带骨猪前腿、后腿及其肉块	12	0	0	0	0		0	0	0		0
02032900	其他冻猪肉	12	0	0	0	0		0	0	0	0	0
02045000	鲜、冷、冻的山羊肉	20	0	0	0	0	12	0	0	0	0	0
02071100	整只，鲜或冷的鸡	20	0	0	0	0		0	0	12		
02071200	整只，冻的鸡	T2	0	0	0	0		0	0	0.78 元/千克		
02071311	鲜或冷的带骨鸡块	20	0	0	0	0		0	0	12		
02071319	鲜或冷的其他鸡块	20	0	0	0	0		0	0	12		
02071321	鲜或冷的鸡翼(不包括翼尖)	20	0	0	0	0		0	0	12		
02071329	鲜或冷的其他鸡杂碎	20	0	0	0	0		0	0	12		
02071411	冻的带骨鸡块	T2	0	0	0	0		0	0	0.48 元/千克	0	
02071419	冻的其他鸡块	T2	0	0	0	0		0	0	0.8 元/千克	0	
02071421	冻的鸡翼(不包括翼尖)	T2	0	0	0	0		0	0	0.64 元/千克	0	
02071422	鲜、冷、冻鸡爪	T2	0	0	0	0		0	0	0.4 元/千克	0	

税则号列 Tariff No.	货品名称 Description of Goods	最惠国 MFN (%)	协定税率(%)Agreement									
			文莱 CAM	印尼 INA	马来西亚 MAS	缅甸 MMR	菲律宾 PHI	新加坡 SIN	泰国 THA	越南 VIE	老挝 LAO	柬埔寨 TPE
02071429	冻的其他鸡杂碎	T2	0	0	0	0		0	0	0.4元/千克	0	
02072400	整只,鲜或冷的火鸡	20	0	0	0	0	12	0	0	0		0
02072500	整只,冻的火鸡	20	0	0	0	0	12	0	0	0		0
02072600	鲜或冷的火鸡块及杂碎	20	0	0	0	0	12	0	0	12		0
02072700	冻的火鸡块及杂碎	10	0	0	0	0		0	0	8	0	0
02073210	整只,鲜或冷的鸭	20	0	0	0	0		0	0	0		0
02073220	整只,鲜或冷的鹅	20	0	0	0	0		0	0	0		0
02073230	整只,鲜或冷的珍珠鸡	20	0	0	0	0		0	0	0		0
02073310	整只,冻的鸭	20	0	0	0	0		0	0	0		0
02073320	整只,冻的鹅	20	0	0	0	0		0	0	0		0
02073330	整只,冻的珍珠鸡	20	0	0	0	0		0	0	0		0
02073400	鲜或冷的税目的0105所列家禽的肥肝	20	0	0	0	0	12	0	0	0		0
02073510	鲜或冷的鸭块及杂碎	20	0	0	0	0		0	0	0		0
02073520	鲜或冷的鹅块及杂碎	20	0	0	0	0		0	0	0		0
02073530	鲜或冷的珍珠鸡块及杂碎	20	0	0	0	0		0	0	0		0
02073610	冻的鸭块及杂碎	20	0	0	0	0		0	0	0	0	0
02073620	冻的鹅块及杂碎	20	0	0	0	0		0	0	0	0	0
02073630	冻的珍珠鸡块及杂碎	20	0	0	0	0		0	0	0	0	0
02101110	干、熏、盐制的带骨猪腿	25	0	0	0	0	12	0	0	0		0
02101190	干、熏、盐制的带骨猪腿肉块	25	0	0	0	0	12	0	0	0		0
02101200	干、熏、盐制的猪腹肉	25	0	0	0	0	12	0	0	0		0
02101900	干、熏、盐制的其他猪肉	25	0	0	0	0	12	0	0	0		0
02109900	干、熏、盐制的其他肉及食用杂碎	25	0	0	0	0	12	0	0	0		0
03022100	鲜、冷庸鲽鱼	12	0	0	0	0	8	0	0	0	0	0
03022900	其他鲜、冷比目鱼	12	0	0	0	0	8	0	0	0	0	0
03023400	鲜、冷大眼金枪鱼	12	0	0	0	0	8	0	0	0	0	0
03023500	鲜、冷蓝鳍金枪鱼	12	0	0	0	0	8	0	0	0	0	0
03023600	鲜、冷南金枪鱼	12	0	0	0	0	8	0	0	0	0	0
03026500	鲜、冷角鲨及其他鲨鱼	12	0	0	0	0	8	0	0	0	0	0
03026600	鲜冷鳗鱼	12	0	0	0	0	8	0	0	0	0	0
03026700	鲜、冷剑鱼	12	0	0	0	0	8	0	0	0	0	0
03026800	鲜、冷南极犬牙鱼	12	0	0	0	0	8	0	0	0		0
03026910	鲜冷带鱼	12	0	0	0	0	8	0	0	0	0	0
03026920	鲜冷黄鱼	12	0	0	0	0	8	0	0	0	0	0
03026930	鲜冷鲳鱼	12	0	0	0	0	8	0	0	0	0	0
03026940	鲜冷罗非鱼	12	0	0	0	0	8	0	0	0	0	0
03026950	鲜、冷鲀	12	0	0	0	0	8	0	0	0	0	0
03026990	其他鲜、冷鱼	12	0	0	0	0	8	0	0	0	0	0
03031100	冻红大马哈鱼,但鱼肝及鱼卵除外	10	0	0	0	0	8	0	0	0	0	0
03031900	其他冻大马哈鱼,但鱼肝及鱼卵除外	10	0	0	0	0	8	0	0	0	0	0
03033900	其他冻比目鱼	10	0	0	0	0	8	0	0	0	0	0
03034400	冻大眼金枪鱼,但鱼肝及鱼卵除外	12	0	0	0	0	8	0	0	0	0	0
03034500	冻蓝鳍金枪鱼,但鱼肝及鱼卵除外	12	0	0	0	0	8	0	0	0	0	0
03034600	冻南金枪鱼,但鱼肝及鱼卵除外	12	0	0	0	0	8	0	0	0	0	0
03036100	冻剑鱼,但鱼肝及鱼卵除外	10	0	0	0	0	8	0	0	0	0	0
03036200	冻南极犬牙鱼,但鱼肝及鱼卵除外	10	0	0	0	0	8	0	0	0		
03037910	冻带鱼	10	0	0	0	0	8	0	0	0	0	0

税则号列 Tariff No.	货品名称 Description of Goods	最惠国 MFN (%)	协定税率(%)Agreement									
			文莱 CAM	印尼 INA	马来西亚 MAS	缅甸 MMR	菲律宾 PHI	新加坡 SIN	泰国 THA	越南 VIE	老挝 LAO	柬埔寨 TPE
03037920	冻黄鱼	10	0	0	0	0	8	0	0	0	0	0
03037930	冻鲳鱼	10	0	0	0	0	8	0	0	0	0	0
03037940	冻罗非鱼	10	0	0	0	0	8	0	0	0	0	0
03037990	其他未列名冻鱼	10	0	0	0	0	8	0	0	0	0	0
03041100	鲜、冷剑鱼片及鱼肉	12	0	0	0	0	8	0	0	0		
03041200	鲜、冷南极犬牙鱼片及鱼肉	12	0	0	0	0	8	0	0	0	0	0
03041900	其他鲜、冷的鱼片及鱼肉	12	0	0	0	0	8	0	0	0	0	0
03042100	冻剑鱼片	10	0	0	0	0	8	0	0	0	0	0
03042200	冻南极犬牙鱼片	10	0	0	0	0	8	0	0	0	0	0
03042910	冻罗非鱼片	10	0	0	0	0	8	0	0	0	0	0
03042921	冻斑点叉尾鮰鱼片	10	0	0	0	0	8	0	0	0	0	0
03042929	冻其他叉尾鮰鱼鱼片	10	0	0	0	0	8	0	0	0	0	0
03042990	其他冻鱼片	10	0	0	0	0	8	0	0	0	0	0
03049100	冻的剑鱼肉	10	0	0	0	0	8	0	0	0	0	0
03049200	冻的南极犬牙鱼肉	10	0	0	0	0	8	0	0	0	0	0
03049900	其他冻鱼肉	10	0	0	0	0	8	0	0	0	0	0
03053000	干或盐制的鱼片	10	0	0	0	0	8	0	0	0	0	0
03055910	干海马、干海龙	2	0	0	0	0		0	0	0	0	0
03055920	干鱼翅	15	0	0	0	0	8	0	0	0	0	0
03055990	其他干鱼	16	0	0	0	0	8	0	0	0	0	0
03056300	盐腌及盐渍的 Anchovies(醍)鱼	16	0	0	0	0	8	0	0	0	0	0
03056910	盐腌及盐渍的带鱼	16	0	0	0	0	8	0	0	0	0	0
03056920	盐腌及盐渍的黄鱼	16	0	0	0	0	8	0	0	0	0	0
03056930	盐腌及盐渍的鲳鱼	16	0	0	0	0	8	0	0	0	0	0
03056940	盐腌及盐渍的罗非鱼	16	0	0	0	0	8	0	0	0	0	0
03056990	盐腌及盐渍的其他鱼	16	0	0	0	0	8	0	0	0	0	0
03061311	冻小虾仁	8	0	0	0	0	5	0	0	0	0	0
03061312	冻北方长额虾	5	0	0	0	0		0	0	0	0	0
03061319	其他冻小虾	5	0	0	0	0		0	0	0	0	0
03061321	冻对虾仁	8	0	0	0	0	5	0	0	0	0	0
03061329	其他冻对虾	5	0	0	0	0		0	0	0	0	0
03061410	冻梭子蟹	10	0	0	0	0	8	0	0	0	0	0
03061490	其他冻蟹	10	0	0	0	0	8	0	0	0	0	0
03061911	冻淡水小龙虾仁	16	0	0	0	0	8	0	0	0	0	0
03061919	冻带壳淡水小龙虾	16	0	0	0	0	8	0	0	0	0	0
03061990	其他冻甲壳动物	16	0	0	0	0	8	0	0	0	0	0
03062391	鲜、冷对虾	15	0	0	0	0	8	0	0	0	0	0
03062399	其他未冻小虾及对虾	12	0	0	0	0	8	0	0	0	0	0
03062491	未冻的中华绒毛蟹(大闸蟹)	14	0	0	0	0	8	0	0	0	0	0
03062492	未冻的梭子蟹	14	0	0	0	0	8	0	0	0	0	0
03062499	未冻的其他蟹	14	0	0	0	0	8	0	0	0	0	0
04070021	带壳鲜鸡蛋	20	0	0	0	0	0	0	0			0
04070022	带壳鲜鸭蛋	20	0	0	0	0	0	0	0			0
04070023	带壳鲜鹅蛋	20	0	0	0	0	0	0	0			0
04070029	其他带壳鲜禽蛋	20	0	0	0	0	0	0	0			0
04070091	咸蛋	20	0	0	0	0	0	0	0			0
04070092	皮蛋	20	0	0	0	0	0	0	0			0
04070099	其他腌制或煮过的带壳禽蛋	20	0	0	0	0	0	0	0			0

税则号列 Tariff No.	货品名称 Description of Goods	最惠国 MFN (%)	协定税率(%)Agreement									
			文莱 CAM	印尼 INA	马来西亚 MAS	缅甸 MMR	菲律宾 PHI	新加坡 SIN	泰国 THA	越南 VIE	老挝 LAO	柬埔寨 TPE
04081100	干蛋黄	20	0	0	0	0	12	0	0	0	0	0
04081900	其他蛋黄	20	0	0	0	0	12	0	0	0	0	0
04089100	干的其他去壳禽蛋	20	0	0	0	0	12	0	0	0	0	0
04089900	其他去壳禽蛋	20	0	0	0	0	12	0	0	0	0	0
04090000	天然蜂蜜	15	0	0	0	0	8	0	0	0	0	0
05071000	兽牙;兽牙粉末及废料	10	0	0	0	0	8	0	0	0	0	0
05079010	羚羊角及其粉末和废料	3	0	0	0	0		0	0	0	0	0
05079020	鹿茸及其粉末	11	0	0	0	0	8	0	0	0	0	0
05079090	龟壳、鲸须、鲸须毛、鹿角及其他角	10	0	0	0	0	8	0	0	0	0	0
05100030	麝香	7	0	0	0	0	5	0	0	0	0	0
05100040	斑蝥	7	0	0	0	0	5	0	0	0	0	0
05100090	胆汁,配药用腺体及其他动物产品	6	0	0	0	0	5	0	0	0	0	0
06031100	鲜玫瑰	10	0	0	0	0	8	0	0	0		
06031200	鲜康乃馨	10	0	0	0	0	8	0	0	0		
06031300	鲜兰花	10	0	0	0	0	8	0	0	0		
06031400	鲜菊花	10	0	0	0	0	8	0	0	0	0	0
06031900	其他鲜的插花及花蕾	10	0	0	0	0	8	0	0	0		
06039000	干的及经过染色等加工的插花及花蕾	23	0	0	0	0	12	0	0	0	0	0
06049100	鲜的植物枝、叶或其他部分;草	10	0	0	0	0	8	0	0	0	0	0
06049900	染色或经加工的枝、叶、草等	10	0	0	0	0	8	0	0	0	0	0
07019000	其他鲜或冷的马铃薯	13	0	0	0	0		0	0	0	0	0
07020000	鲜或冷藏的番茄	13	0	0	0	0	8	0	0	0		
07031010	鲜或冷的洋葱	13	0	0	0	0		0	0	0	0	
07031020	鲜或冷的青葱	13	0	0	0	0		0	0	0	0	0
07032010	鲜或冷藏的大蒜头	13	0	0	0	0		0	0	0	0	
07032020	鲜或冷藏的大蒜蒜台及蒜苗(青蒜)	13	0	0	0	0		0	0	0	0	
07032090	其他鲜或冷藏的大蒜	13	0	0	0	0		0	0	0	0	
07039010	鲜或冷的韭葱	13	0	0	0	0		0	0	0	0	0
07039020	鲜或冷的大葱	13	0	0	0	0		0	0	0	0	0
07039090	鲜或冷的其他葱属蔬菜	13	0	0	0	0		0	0	0	0	0
07041000	鲜或冷的菜花及硬花甘蓝	10	0	0	0	0		0	0	0	0	
07051100	鲜或冷的结球莴苣(包心生菜)	10	0	0	0	0		0	0	0	0	
07051900	鲜或冷的其他莴苣	10	0	0	0	0		0	0	0	0	
07052100	鲜或冷的维特罗夫菊苣	13	0	0	0	0		0	0	0	0	0
07052900	鲜或冷的其他菊苣	13	0	0	0	0		0	0	0	0	0
07061000	鲜或冷的胡萝卜及萝卜	13	0	0	0	0		0	0	0		
07069000	鲜或冷的小萝卜及类似食用根茎	13	0	0	0	0		0	0	0	0	
07070000	鲜或冷的黄瓜及小黄瓜	13	0	0	0	0		0	0	0	0	0
07081000	鲜或冷的豌豆	13	0	0	0	0		0	0	0	0	0
07082000	鲜或冷的豇豆及菜豆	13	0	0	0	0		0	0	0		
07089000	鲜或冷的其他豆类蔬菜	13	0	0	0	0	8	0	0	0	0	0
07092000	鲜或冷的芦笋	13	0	0	0	0	8	0	0	0	0	0
07093000	鲜或冷的茄子	13	0	0	0	0	8	0	0	0		0
07094000	鲜或冷的芹菜,但块根芹除外	10	0	0	0	0		0	0	0	0	0
07095100	鲜或冷的其他伞菌属蘑菇	13	0	0	0	0	8	0	0	0		0
07095910	鲜或冷的松茸	13	0	0	0	0	8	0	0	0	0	0
07095920	鲜或冷的香菇	13	0	0	0	0	8	0	0	0	0	0
07095930	鲜或冷的金针菇	13	0	0	0	0	8	0	0	0	0	0

税则号列 Tariff No.	货品名称 Description of Goods	最惠国 MFN (%)	协定税率(%)Agreement									
			文莱 CAM	印尼 INA	马来西亚 MAS	缅甸 MMR	菲律宾 PHI	新加坡 SIN	泰国 THA	越南 VIE	老挝 LAO	柬埔寨 TPE
07095940	鲜或冷的草菇	13	0	0	0	0	8	0	0	0	0	0
07095950	鲜或冷的口蘑	13	0	0	0	0	8	0	0	0	0	0
07095990	鲜或冷的其他蘑菇	13	0	0	0	0	8	0	0	0	0	0
07096000	鲜或冷的辣椒,包括甜椒	13	0	0	0	0		0	0	0		0
07097000	鲜或冷的菠菜	13	0	0	0	0		0	0	0	0	0
07099010	鲜或冷的竹笋	13	0	0	0	0		0	0	0		
07101000	冷冻马铃薯	13	0	0	0	0	8	0	0	0	0	0
07102100	冷冻豌豆	13	0	0	0	0	8	0	0	0	0	0
07102210	冷冻红小豆	13	0	0	0	0	8	0	0	0		0
07102290	其他冷冻豇豆及菜豆	13	0	0	0	0	8	0	0	0		0
07102900	冷冻其他豆类蔬菜	13	0	0	0	0	8	0	0	0		0
07103000	冷冻菠菜	13	0	0	0	0	8	0	0	0	0	0
07104000	冷冻甜玉米	10	0	0	0	0	8	0	0	0		0
07108010	冷冻松茸	13	0	0	0	0	8	0	0	0		0
07108020	其他蒜台及蒜苗(青蒜)	13	0	0	0	0	8	0	0	0		0
07108030	蒜头	13	0	0	0	0	8	0	0	0		0
07108090	冷冻未列名蔬菜	13	0	0	0	0	8	0	0	0		0
07109000	冷冻什锦蔬菜	10	0	0	0	0	8	0	0	0		0
07114000	暂时保藏的黄瓜及小黄瓜	13	0	0	0	0		0	0	0		0
07115112	盐水小白蘑菇	13	0	0	0	0	8	0	0	0	0	0
07115119	盐水的其他伞菌属蘑菇	13	0	0	0	0	8	0	0	0	0	0
07115190	其他伞菌属蘑菇	13	0	0	0	0	8	0	0	0	0	0
07115911	盐水松茸	13	0	0	0	0	8	0	0	0	0	0
07115919	盐水其他蘑菇及菌块	13	0	0	0	0	8	0	0	0	0	0
07115990	暂时保藏的其他蘑菇及菌块	13	0	0	0	0	8	0	0	0	0	0
07119031	盐水竹笋	13	0	0	0	0		0	0	0		0
07119034	盐水大蒜	13	0	0	0	0		0	0	0		0
07123910	干香菇	13	0	0	0	0	8	0	0	0		0
07123920	干金针菇	13	0	0	0	0	8	0	0	0		0
07123930	干草菇	13	0	0	0	0	8	0	0	0		0
07123940	干口蘑	13	0	0	0	0	8	0	0	0		0
07123950	干牛肝菌	13	0	0	0	0	8	0	0	0		0
07123990	其他干制蘑菇及块菌	13	0	0	0	0	8	0	0	0		0
07133190	其他干绿豆	3	0	0	0	0		0	0	0		0
07133290	其他干赤豆	3	0	0	0	0		0	0	0		0
07141010	鲜木薯	10	0	0	0	0		0	0	0		0
07141020	干木薯	5	0	0	0	0		0	0	0		0
07141030	冷或冻的木薯	10	0	0	0	0		0	0	0		0
07142019	其他鲜甘薯	13	0	0	0	0		0	0	0		0
07142020	干甘薯	13	0	0	0	0		0	0	0		0
07142030	冷或冻的甘薯	13	0	0	0	0		0	0	0		0
07149010	鲜、干或冷、冻的荸荠	13	0	0	0	0	8	0	0	0		0
07149029	其他藕	13	0	0	0	0	8	0	0	0		0
07149030	芋头	13	0	0	0	0	8	0	0	0		0
07149090	含有高淀粉或菊粉的其他类似根茎	13	0	0	0	0	8	0	0	0		0
08013100	鲜或干的未去壳腰果	20	0	0	0	0	12	0	0	0	0	0
08013200	鲜或干的去壳腰果	10	0	0	0	0	8	0	0	0	0	0
08044000	鲜或干鳄梨	25	0	0	0	0	12	0	0	0	0	0

税则号列 Tariff No.	货品名称 Description of Goods	最惠国 MFN (%)	协定税率(%) Agreement									
			文莱 CAM	印尼 INA	马来西亚 MAS	缅甸 MMR	菲律宾 PHI	新加坡 SIN	泰国 THA	越南 VIE	老挝 LAO	柬埔寨 TPE
08051000	鲜或干橙	11	0	0	0	0	8	0	0	0		
08052010	鲜或干蕉柑	12	0	0	0	0	8	0	0	0	0	0
08052020	阔叶柑橘	12	0	0	0	0	8	0	0	0	0	0
08052090	其他鲜或干的柑桔及杂交柑桔	12	0	0	0	0	8	0	0	0	0	0
08054000	鲜或干的葡萄柚,包括柚	12	0	0	0	0	0	0	0	8	0	0
08055000	鲜或干的柠檬及酸橙	11	0	0	0	0	8	0	0	8		0
08059000	其他鲜或干的柑桔属水果	30	0	0	0	0	0	0	0	12		0
08071100	鲜西瓜	25	0	0	0	0	12	0	0	0		
08071910	鲜哈密瓜	12	0	0	0	0	8	0	0	0		
08071920	鲜罗马甜瓜及加勒比甜瓜	12	0	0	0	0	8	0	0	0		
08071990	其他鲜甜瓜	12	0	0	0	0	8	0	0	0	0	
08072000	鲜木瓜	25	0	0	0	0	12	0	0	0		0
08091000	鲜杏	25	0	0	0	0	12	0	0	0	0	0
08092000	鲜樱桃	10	0	0	0	0	8	0	0	0	0	0
08093000	鲜桃,包括鲜油桃	10	0	0	0	0	8	0	0	0	0	0
08094000	鲜梅及李	10	0	0	0	0	8	0	0	0	0	0
08101000	鲜草莓	18.4	0	0	0	0	12	0	0	0	0	0
08102000	鲜的木莓、黑莓、桑椹及罗甘莓	25	0	0	0	0	12	0	0	0	0	0
08105000	鲜猕猴桃	20	0	0	0	0	12	0	0	0	0	0
08106000	鲜榴莲	20	0	0	0	0	12	0	0	0	0	0
08109010	鲜荔枝	30	0	0	0	0	12	0	0	0	0	0
08109020	鲜的黑、白或红的醋栗(加仑子)及鹅莓	25	0	0	0	0	12	0	0	0	0	0
08109030	鲜龙眼	12	0	0	0	0	8	0	0	0	0	
08109040	鲜红毛丹	20	0	0	0	0	12	0	0	0	0	0
08109050	鲜蕃荔枝	20	0	0	0	0	12	0	0	0	0	0
08109060	鲜杨桃	20	0	0	0	0	12	0	0	0	0	0
08109070	莲雾	20	0	0	0	0	12	0	0	0	0	0
08109080	火龙果	20	0	0	0	0	12	0	0	0	0	0
08109090	其他鲜果	20	0	0	0	0	12	0	0	0	0	0
08111000	冷冻草莓	30	0	0	0	0	12	0	0	0	0	0
08112000	冷冻其他浆果	30	0	0	0	0	12	0	0	0	0	0
08119010	未去壳的冷冻栗子	30	0	0	0	0	12	0	0	0	0	0
08119090	其他冷冻水果及坚果	30	0	0	0	0	12	0	0	0	0	0
08129000	暂时保藏的其他水果及坚果	27.7	0	0	0	0	12	0	0	0	0	0
08132000	梅干及李干	25	0	0	0	0	12	0	0	0	0	0
08133000	苹果干	25	0	0	0	0	12	0	0	0	0	0
08134010	龙眼干、肉	20	0	0	0	0	12	0	0	0	0	0
08134020	柿饼	25	0	0	0	0	12	0	0	0	0	0
08134030	干红枣	25	0	0	0	0	12	0	0	0	0	0
08134040	荔枝干	25	0	0	0	0	12	0	0	0	0	0
08134090	其他干果	25	0	0	0	0	12	0	0	0	0	0
08135000	本章的什锦坚果或干果	18	0	0	0	0	8	0	0	0	0	0
08140000	柑桔属水果或甜瓜的果皮	25	0	0	0	0		0	0	0	0	0
09012200	已浸除咖啡碱的已焙炒咖啡	15	8	0	0	8	8	0		8		
09019010	咖啡豆荚及咖啡豆皮	10	8	8	8	8	8	8		8		
09019020	含咖啡的咖啡代用品	30	12	12	12	12	12	12		12		
09021010	每件净重≤3kg 的花茶	15	8	8	8		8	8				
09021090	每件净重≤3kg 的其他绿茶	15	8	8	8		8	8				

税则号列 Tariff No.	货品名称 Description of Goods	最惠国 MFN (%)	协定税率(%) Agreement									
			文莱 CAM	印尼 INA	马来西亚 MAS	缅甸 MMR	菲律宾 PHI	新加坡 SIN	泰国 THA	越南 VIE	老挝 LAO	柬埔寨 TPE
09022010	每件净重>3kg的花茶	15	8	8	8		8	8		8		
09022090	每件净重>3kg的其他绿茶	15	8	8	8		8	8		8		
09023010	每件净重≤3kg的乌龙茶	15	8	8	8	8	8	8		8		
09023020	每件净重≤3kg的普洱茶	15	8	8	8	8	8	8		8		
09023090	每件净重≤3kg的其他发酵、半发酵红茶	15	8	8	8	8	8	8		8		
09024010	每件净重>3kg的乌龙茶	15	8	8	8	0	8	8		8		
09024020	每件净重>3kg的普洱茶	15	8	8	8	0	8	8		8		
09024090	每件净重>3kg的其他红茶(已发酵)及半发酵茶	15	8	8	8	0	8	8		8		
09042010	辣椒干	20	12	0	12	12		12	12	12		
09042020	辣椒粉	20	12	12	12	12		12	12	12		
09101000	姜	15	8	8	8	8		8	8	8		
11062000	用品目0714的西谷茎髓、植物根茎、块茎制成的细粉、粗粉、粉末	20	12	12	12	0	12	12	12	12		
11081200	玉米淀粉	20	12	12	12	12		12	12	12		
11081400	木薯淀粉	10	8	8	8	8		8	8	8		
12030000	干椰子肉	15	8	8	8	8	8	8		8		
12074090	其他芝麻	10	8	8	8	0	8	8	8	8		
12079991	牛油树果	20	12	12	12	0	12	12	12	12		
12079993	其他蓖麻子	15	8	8	8	0	8	8	8	8		
12079999	其他含油子仁及果实	10	8	8	8	0	8	8	8	8		
12119029	鲜或干的茯苓	6	5	5	5	0	5	5	5	5		
12119039	其他主要用作药料的鲜或干的植物	6	5	5	5	0	5	5	5	5		
15091000	初榨油橄榄油及其分离品	10	8	8	8		8	8	8	8		
15131100	初榨椰子油分离品	9	0	0	0	8	0	0		8		
15131900	椰子油及其分离品	9	0	0	8	8	0	0		8		
15132100	初榨棕榈仁油或巴巴苏棕榈果油及其分离品	9	0	0	0	8	8	0		8		
15132900	精制的棕榈仁油或巴巴苏棕榈果油及其分离品	9	0	0	0	8	8	0		8		
15159020	印楝油及其分离品	20	12	12	12	0	12	12	12	12		
15159090	其他固定植物油、脂及其分离品	20	12	12	12	0	12	12	12	12		
15162000	氢化、酯化或反油酸化植物油、脂及其分离品,但未进一步加工的	25	0	0	0	12	12	0	12	12		
15179000	混合制成的食用油脂或制品	25	0	0	0	12	12	0	12	12		
16010010	用天然肠衣做外包装的香肠及类似产品	15	8	8	8		8	8	8			
16010020	其他香肠及类似产品	15	8	8	8		8	8	8			
16010030	用香肠制成的食品	15	8	8	8		8	8	8			
16021000	肉或食用杂碎的均化食品	15	8	8	8	8	8	8	8			
16022000	制作或保藏的动物肝	15	8	8	8	8	8	8	8			
16023210	鸡罐头	15	8	8	8	8		8	8	8		
16023291	鸡胸肉	15	8	8	8	8		8	8	8		
16023292	鸡腿肉	15	8	8	8	8		8	8	8		
16023299	其他鸡肉	15	8	8	8	8		8	8	8		
16023910	其他品目0105所列家禽肉及杂碎的罐头	15	8	8	8		8	8	8	8		
16023991	鸭肉	15	8	8	8		8	8	8	8		
16023999	经制作或保藏的其他品目0105所列家禽肉及杂碎	15	8	8	8		8	8	8	8		
16024100	制作或保藏的猪后腿及其肉块	15	8	8	8	8		8	8			
16024200	制作或保藏的猪前腿及其肉块	15	8	8	8	8	8	8	8			

税则号列 Tariff No.	货品名称 Description of Goods	最惠国 MFN (%)	协定税率(%) Agreement									
			文莱 CAM	印尼 INA	马来西亚 MAS	缅甸 MMR	菲律宾 PHI	新加坡 SIN	泰国 THA	越南 VIE	老挝 LAO	柬埔寨 TPE
16024910	其他猪肉及杂碎的罐头	15	8	8	8			8				
16024990	制作或保藏的其他猪肉、杂碎及血	15	8	8	8			8				
16025010	牛肉及牛杂碎罐头	12	8	8	8		8	8	8			
16025090	其他制作或保藏的牛肉、杂碎及血	12	8	8	8		8	8	8			
16029010	其他肉及杂碎罐头	15	8	8	8		8	8	8			
16029090	经制作或保藏的其他肉、杂碎及血	15	8	8	8		8	8	8			
16059010	制作或保藏的海蜇	15	8	8	8	10	8	8	8	8		
17041000	口香糖,不论是否裹糖	12	8	8	8		8	8	8			
17049000	其他不含可可的糖食	10	8	8	8		8	8	8	8		
18010000	生或焙炒的整颗或破碎的可可豆	8	0	5	0	5	5	0	5	5		
18031000	未脱脂可可膏	10	0	0	0	8	8	0	8	8		
18032000	全脱脂或部分脱脂的可可膏	10	0	0	0	8	8	0	8	8		
18040000	可可油,可可脂	22	0	0	0	12	12	0	12	12		
18050000	未加糖或其他甜物质的可可粉	15	0	0	0	8	0	0	8	8		
18061000	含糖或其他甜物质的可可粉	10	0	0	0	8	0	0	8	8		
18062000	每件净重>2kg 的含可可食品	10	8	8	8		8	8	8	8		
18063100	其他夹心块状或条状的含可可食品	8	5	5	5		5	5	5	5		
18063200	其他不夹心块状或条状含可可食品	10	8	8	8		8	8	8	8		
18069000	其他巧克力及含可可的食品	8	5	5	5		5	5	5	5		
19021100	未包馅或未制作的含蛋生面食	15	8	8	8		8	8	8	8		
19021900	其他未包馅或未制作的生面食	15	8	8	8		8	8	8	8		
19023010	米粉干	15	12	12	12		12	12	12	12		
19023020	粉丝	15	8	8	8		8	8	8	8		
19023030	即食或快熟面条	15	8	8	8		8	8	8	8		
19023090	其他面食	15	8	8	8		8	8	8	8		
19053100	甜饼干	15	8	8	8		8	8	8	8		
19053200	华夫饼干及圣餐饼	15	8	8	8		8	8	8	8		
19059000	其他面包、糕点、饼干及其焙烘糕饼	20	12	12	12		12	12	12	12		
20011000	用醋或醋酸制作的黄瓜及小黄瓜	25	12	12	12		12	12	12	12		
20019010	用醋制作的大蒜	25	12	12	12		12	12	12	12		
20019090	用醋制作的其他果、菜及食用植物	25	12	12	12		12	12	12	12		
20021010	非用醋制作的整个或切片番茄罐头	19	8	8	8		8	8	8	8		
20021090	非用醋制作的其他整个或切片番茄	25	12	12	12		12	12	12	12		
20029010	番茄酱罐头	20	12	12	12		12	12		12		
20029090	非用醋制作的绞碎番茄	18	12	12	12		12	12		12		
20031011	伞菌属小白蘑菇罐头	25	12	12	12		12	12	12	12		
20031019	其他非用醋制作的伞菌属蘑菇罐头	25	12	12	12		12	12	12	12		
20031090	非用醋制作的其他伞菌属蘑菇	25	12	12	12		12	12	12	12		
20032000	非用醋制作的块菌	25	12	12	12		12	12	12	12		
20041000	非用醋制作的冷冻马铃薯	13	8	8	8		8	8	8	8		
20049000	非用醋制作的其他冷冻蔬菜	25	12	12	12		12	12	12	12		
20051000	非用醋制作的未冷冻均化蔬菜	25	12	12	12		12	12	12	12		
20052000	非用醋制作的未冷冻马铃薯	15	8	8	8		8	8	8	8		
20054000	非用醋制作的未冷冻豌豆	25	12	12	12		12	12	12	12		
20055110	非用醋制作的脱荚豇豆及菜豆罐头	25	12	12	12		12	12	12	12		
20055120	赤豆馅	25	12	12	12		12	12	12	12		
20055190	非用醋制作的其他脱荚豇豆及菜豆	25	12	12	12		12	12	12	12		
20055910	非用醋制作的其他豇豆及菜豆罐头	25	12	12	12		12	12	12	12		

税则号列 Tariff No.	货品名称 Description of Goods	最惠国 MFN (%)	协定税率(%)Agreement									
			文莱 CAM	印尼 INA	马来西亚 MAS	缅甸 MMR	菲律宾 PHI	新加坡 SIN	泰国 THA	越南 VIE	老挝 LAO	柬埔寨 TPE
20055990	非用醋制作的其他豇豆及菜豆	25	12	12	12		12	12	12	12		
20056010	非用醋制作的芦笋罐头	25	12	12	12		12	12	12	12		
20056090	非用醋制作的其他芦笋	25	12	12	12		12	12	12	12		
20057000	非用醋制作的未冷冻油橄榄	10	8	8	8		8	8	8	8		
20058000	非用醋制作的未冷冻甜玉米	10	8	8	8		8	8	8	8		
20059110	非用醋制作或保藏的竹笋罐头	25	12	12	12		12	12	12	12		
20059190	非用醋制作或保藏的未冷冻的其他竹笋	25	12	12	12		12	12	12	12		
20059910	清水马蹄罐头	25	12	12	12		12	12	12	12		
20059920	蚕豆罐头	25	12	12	12		12	12	12	12		
20059940	榨菜	25	12	12	12		12	12	12	12		
20059950	咸蕨菜	25	12	12	12		12	12	12	12		
20059960	咸荞头	25	12	12	12		12	12	12	12		
20059991	其他蔬菜及什锦蔬菜罐头	25	12	12	12		12	12	12	12		
20059999	非用醋制作的其他蔬菜及什锦蔬菜	25	12	12	12		12	12	12	12		
20060010	蜜枣	30	12	12	12	0	12	12	12	12		
20060020	糖渍制橄榄	30	12	12	12	0	12	12	12	12		
20060090	其他糖渍蔬菜、水果、坚果、果皮	30	12	12	12	0	12	12	12	12		
20079100	烹煮制成的柑桔属水果	30	12	12	12	0	12	12	12	12		
20081110	花生米罐头	30	12	12	12		12	12	12	12		
20081120	烘焙花生	30	12	12	12		12	12	12	12		
20081130	花生酱	30	12	12	12		12	12	12	12		
20081190	其他非用醋制作的花生	30	12	12	12		12	12	12	12		
20081910	核桃仁罐头	20	12	12	12		12	12	12	12		
20081920	其他果仁罐头	13	8	8	8		8	8	8	8		
20081991	栗仁	10	8	8	8		8	8	8	8		
20081992	用其他方法制作或保藏的芝麻	10	8	8	8		8	8	8	8		
20081999	其他坚果及子仁	10	8	8	8		8	8	8	8		
20083010	柑桔属水果罐头	20	12	12	12		12	12	12	12		
20083090	非用醋制作的其他柑桔属水果	20	12	12	12		12	12	12	12		
20084010	梨罐头	20	12	12	12		12	12	12	12		
20084090	非用醋制作的其他梨	20	12	12	12		12	12	12	12		
20085000	非用醋制作的杏	20	12	12	12		12	12	12	12		
20086000	非用醋制作的樱桃	20	12	12	12		12	12	12	12		
20087010	桃罐头	10	8	8	8		8	8	8	8		
20087090	非用醋制作的其他桃	20	12	12	12		12	12	12	12		
20088000	非用醋制作的草莓	15	8	8	8		8	8	8	8		
20089200	非用醋制作的什锦果实	10	8	8	8		8	8	8	8		
20089910	荔枝罐头	20	12	12	12		12	12		12		
20089990	未列名制作或保藏的水果、坚果	15	8	8	8		8	8		8		
20091100	冷冻的橙汁	7.5	5	5	5		5	5	5	5		
20091900	其他橙汁	30	12	12	12		12	12	12	12		
20092100	白利糖度值不超过 20 的葡萄柚(包括柚)汁	15	8	8	8		8	8	8	8		
20092900	其他葡萄柚(包括柚)汁	15	8	8	8		8	8	8	8		
20093110	白利糖度不超过 20 的柠檬汁	18	12	12	12		12	12	12	12		
20093190	其他未混合的白利糖度值不超过 20 的桔汁属水果汁	18	12	12	12		12	12	12	12		
20093910	白利糖度超过 20 的柠檬汁	18	12	12	12		12	12	12	12		

税则号列 Tariff No.	货品名称 Description of Goods	最惠国 MFN (%)	协定税率(%)Agreement									
			文莱 CAM	印尼 INA	马来西亚 MAS	缅甸 MMR	菲律宾 PHI	新加坡 SIN	泰国 THA	越南 VIE	老挝 LAO	柬埔寨 TPE
20093990	其他未混合的柑桔属水果汁,白利糖度值不超过20	18	12	12	12		12	12	12	12		
20095000	番茄汁	30	12	12	12		12	12	12	12		
20096100	白利糖度值不超过20的葡萄汁,包括酿酒葡萄汁	20	12	12	12		12	12	12	12		
20096900	葡萄汁,包括酿酒葡萄汁	20	12	12	12		12	12	12	12		
20097100	白利糖度值不超过20的苹果汁	20	12	12	12		12	12	12	12		
20097900	其他苹果汁	20	12	12	12		12	12	12	12		
20098011	椰子汁	10				0						
20098012	芒果汁	20	12	12	12	0	12	12		12		
20098013	西番莲果汁	20	12	12	12	0	12	12		12		
20098014	番石榴果汁	20	12	12	12	0	12	12		12		
20098019	其他未混合的水果汁	20	12	12	12	0	12	12		12		
20098020	其他未混合的蔬菜汁	20	12	12	12	0	12	12		12		
20099010	混合水果汁	20	12	12	12		12	12		12		
20099090	混合蔬菜汁、水果与蔬菜的混合汁	20	12	12	12		12	12		12		
21011100	咖啡浓缩精汁	17	12	12	12	12	12	12		12		
21011200	以咖啡浓缩精汁或咖啡为基本成分的制品	30	12	12	12	12	12	12		12		
22029000	其他无酒精饮料	35	12	12	12	12	12	12		12		
22041000	葡萄汽酒	14	12	12	12		12	12	12	12		
22042100	小包装的鲜葡萄酿造的酒	14	12	12	12		12	12	12	12		
22042900	其他包装的鲜葡萄酿造的酒	20	12	12	12		12	12	12	12		
22043000	其他酿酒葡萄汁	30	12	12	12		12	12	12	12		
22051000	小包装的味美思酒及类似酒	65	12	12	12		12	12	12	12		
22059000	其他包装的味美思酒及类似酒	65	12	12	12		12	12	12	12		
22060000	其他发酵饮料	46.8	12	12	12		12	12	12	12		
22071000	浓度≥80%的未改性乙醇	40	12		12		12	12	12	12		
22072000	任何浓度的改性乙醇及其他酒精	30	12		12	12	12	12	12	12		
23024000	其他谷物糠、麸及其他残渣	5				0						
23091010	零售包装的狗食或猫食罐头	15	8	8	8	8	8	8	9.1	8		
23091090	零售包装的其他狗食或猫食	15	8	8	8	8	8	8	9.1	8		
23099090	其他配制的动物饲料	6.5	5	5	5	5		5		5		
25231000	水泥熟料,不论是否着色	8	5	5	5	5	5	5				
25232100	白水泥,不论是否人工着色	6	5	5		5	5	5				
25232900	其他硅酸盐水泥,不论是否着色	8	5	5		5	5	5				
25233000	矾土水泥,不论是否着色	6	5	5	5	5	5	5	5			
25239000	其他水凝水泥,不论是否着色	8	5	5		5	5	5				
27011100	未制成型的无烟煤,不论是否粉化	3	0		0			0	0			
27040010	煤制焦炭及半焦炭不论是否成型	5	0		0			0	0			
27101120	石脑油	6	5	5	5	5	5	5	5			
27101911	航空煤油	9	5		5	5	5	5	5			
27101919	其他煤油馏分产品	6	5		5	5	5	5	5			
27101922	5-7号燃料油	6	5		5	5	5	5	5			
27101929	其他柴油及其他燃料油	6	5		5	5	5	5	5			
27101991	润滑油	6	5		5	5	5	5	5			
27101992	润滑脂	6	5		5	5	5	5	5			
27101993	润滑油基础油	6	5		5	5	5	5	5			
27101994	液体石蜡和重质液体石蜡	6	5		5	5	5	5	5			

税则号列 Tariff No.	货品名称 Description of Goods	最惠国 MFN (%)	协定税率(%) Agreement									
			文莱 CAM	印尼 INA	马来西亚 MAS	缅甸 MMR	菲律宾 PHI	新加坡 SIN	泰国 THA	越南 VIE	老挝 LAO	柬埔寨 TPE
27101999	其他重油及重油制品	6	5		5	5	5	5	5			
27109100	含多氯联苯(PCBs)、多氯三联苯(PCTs)或多溴联苯(PBBs)的废油	6	5	5	5	5	5	5	5			
27109900	其他废油	6	5	5	5	5	5	5	5			
28011000	氯	5.5	5	5		5	5	5	5	5		
28030000	碳(碳黑及其他税号未列名的其他形状的碳)	5.5	5	5		5	5	5	5	5		
28061000	氯化氢(盐酸)	5.5	5	5		5	5	5	5	5		
28092090	其他多磷酸	5.5	5	5		5	5	5	5	5		
28170010	氧化锌	5.5	5	5		5	5	5	5	5		
28170090	过氧化锌	5.5	5	5		5	5	5	5	5		
28182000	氧化铝,但人造刚玉除外	8		5	5		5		5	5		
28230000	钛的氧化物	5.5	5	5		5	5	5	5	5		
28289000	次氯酸盐;亚氯酸盐及次溴酸盐	5.5	5	5		5	5	5	5	5		
28332200	硫酸铝	5.5	5	5		5	5	5	5	5		
28353100	三磷酸钠(三聚磷酸钠)	5.5	5	5	5	5		5	5	5		
28353900	其他多磷酸盐	5.5	5	5	5	5		5	5	5		
28391100	偏硅酸钠	5.5	5	5		5	5	5	5	5		
28391900	其他钠的硅酸盐;商品硅酸钠	5.5	5	5		5	5	5	5	5		
28491000	碳化钙,不论是否已有化学定义	5.5	5			5	5	5	5	5		
29173300	邻苯二甲酸二壬酯,邻苯二甲酸二癸酯	6.5	5		5	5	5	5	5	5		
29173490	其他邻苯二甲酸酯	6.5	5		5	5	5	5	5	5		
29173500	邻苯二甲酸酐(苯酐)	6.5	5		5	5	5	5	5	5		
29181400	柠檬酸	6.5	5		5	5	5	5	5	5		
29181500	柠檬酸盐及柠檬酸酯	6.5	5		5	5	5	5	5	5		
29182900	其他含酚基但不含其他含氧基羧酸及其酸酐(酰卤化物,过氧化物和过氧酸及它们的衍生物)	6.5	5		5	5	5	5	5	5		
29224210	谷氨酸	10	8	8		8	8	8	8	8		
29224220	谷氨酸钠	10	8	8		8	8	8	8	8		
29224290	其他谷氨酸盐	6.5	5	5		5	5	5	5	5		
29241200	氯乙酰胺(ISO)、久效磷(ISO)及磷胺(ISO)	6.5	5		5	5	5	5	5	5		
29241910	二甲基甲酰胺	6.5	5		5	5	5	5	5	5		
29241990	其他无环酰胺及其衍生物以及他们的盐	6.5	5		5	5	5	5	5	5		
29242910	对乙酰氨基苯乙醚(非那西丁)	6	5		5	5	5	5	5	5		
29242920	对乙酰氨基酚(扑热息痛)	6	5		5	5	5	5	5	5		
29242990	其他环酰胺(包括环氨基甲酸酯)	6.5	5		5	5	5	5	5	5		
30031011	含有氨苄青霉素的混合药品(两种或两种以上成分混合而成的,治病或防病用,未配定剂量或非零售包装)	6	5		5	5	5	5	5	5		
30031012	含有羟氨苄青霉素的混合药品(两种或两种以上成分混合而成的,治病或防病用未配定剂量或非零售包装)	6	5		5	5	5	5	5	5		
30031013	含有青霉素 V 的混合药品(两种或两种以上成分混合而成的,治病或防病用未配定剂量或非零售包装)	6	5		5	5	5	5		5		
30031019	其他青霉素及具有青霉烷酸结构的青霉素衍生物的混合药品(两种或两种以上成分混合而成的,治病或防病用未配定剂量或非零售包装)	6	5		5	5	5	5	5	5		

税则号列 Tariff No.	货品名称 Description of Goods	最惠国 MFN (%)	协定税率(%)Agreement									
			文莱 CAM	印尼 INA	马来西亚 MAS	缅甸 MMR	菲律宾 PHI	新加坡 SIN	泰国 THA	越南 VIE	老挝 LAO	柬埔寨 TPE
30031090	含有含有链霉素的混合药品(两种或两种以上成分混合而成的,治病或防病用未配定剂量或非零售包装)	6	5		5	5	5	5	5	5		
30069100	可确定用于造口术用具	10	8			8		8	8			
32061900	二氧化钛为基料的颜料及制品,干量计二氧化钛<80%	10	8	8		8	8	8	8	8		
32081000	分散或溶于非水介质的聚酯油漆及清漆等	10	8	8		8	8	8		8		
32082010	分散或溶于非水介质的丙烯酸聚合物油漆及清漆	10	8	8	8	8	8	8		8		
32089010	分散或溶于非水介质的聚胺酯类油漆及清漆	10	8	5	5	8	5	8	5	5		
32089090	分散或溶于非水介质其他油漆、清漆溶液	10	8	8	8	8	8	8		8		
32091000	分散或溶于水介质的丙烯酸聚合物或乙烯聚合物油漆及清漆	10	8	8	8	8	8	8		8		
32099010	以环氧树脂为基本成分的溶于水介质其他聚合物油漆及清漆	10	8	8	8	8	8	8		8		
32099020	以氟树脂为基本成分的溶于水介质其他聚合物油漆及清漆	10	8	8	8	8	8	8		8		
32099090	溶于水介质其他聚合物油漆及清漆	10	8	8	8	8	8	8		8		
32110000	配制的催干剂	10	8	5	5	8	5	8	5	5		
32129000	制漆用颜料(分散于非水介质中呈液状或浆状的)及零售形状或零售包装的染料、色料	10	8	8		8	8	8	8	8		
32141000	安装玻璃用油灰、接缝用油灰、树脂胶泥、嵌缝胶及其他类似胶粘剂;漆工用填料	9	5	5	5	5	5	5		5		
32149000	非耐火涂面制剂,涂门面、内墙、地板、天花板等用	9	5	5	5	5	5	5		5		
33030000	香水及花露水	10	8		8	8	8	8	8	8		
33041000	唇用化妆品	10	8		8	8	8	8	8	8		
33042000	眼用化妆品	10	8		8	8	8	8	8	8		
33049100	香粉,不论是否压紧	10	8			8	8	8	8	8		
33051000	洗发剂(香波)	8.6	8			8	8	8	8	8		
33052000	烫发剂	15	8	8	10	8	8	8	8	8		
33053000	定型剂	15	8	8	10	8	8	8	8	8		
33059000	其他护发品	10	8			8	8	8	8	8		
34011100	盥洗用肥皂及有机表面活性产品,条状、块状或模制形状的,以及用肥皂或洗涤剂浸渍、涂面或包覆的纸、絮胎、毡呢及无纺织物	10	8	8	8		8	8	8	8		
34011990	其他用肥皂及有机表面活性产品,条状、块状或模制形状的,以及用肥皂或洗涤剂浸渍、涂面或包覆的纸、絮胎、毡呢及无纺织物	15	8	0	0	8	8	0	8	8		
34012000	其他形状的肥皂	15	8	0	0	8	8	0	8	8		
34031100	用于纺织材料、皮革、毛皮或其他材料油脂处理的制剂(含有石油或从沥青矿物提取的油类且按重量计<70%)	10	8	5	5	8	5	8	5	5		
34051000	鞋靴或皮革用的上光剂及类似制品	10	8	5	5	8	5	8	5	5		
34052000	保养木制品的上光剂及类似制品	10	8	5	5	8	5	8	5	5		
34059000	玻璃或金属用的光洁剂	10	8	5	5	8	5	8	5	5		
34060000	各种蜡烛及类似品	10	8	8		8	8	8	8	8		
35011000	酪蛋白	10	8	5	5	8	5	8	5	5		

税则号列 Tariff No.	货品名称 Description of Goods	最惠国 MFN (%)	协定税率(%) Agreement									
			文莱 CAM	印尼 INA	马来西亚 MAS	缅甸 MMR	菲律宾 PHI	新加坡 SIN	泰国 THA	越南 VIE	老挝 LAO	柬埔寨 TPE
35061000	适于作胶或粘合剂的产品,零售包装每件净重≤1kg	10	8	5	5	8	5	8	5	5		
36050000	火柴,但税目3604的烟火制品除外	6	5		5	5	5	5	5	5		
37079010	冲洗胶卷及相片用化学制剂或摄影用未混合品(定量包装或零售包装可立即使用的)	16	8	8		8	8	8	8	8		
37079020	复印机用化学制剂或摄影用未混合品(定量包装或零售包装可立即使用的)	10	8	5	5	8	5	8	5	5		
37079090	其他摄影用化学制剂或摄影用未混合品(定量包装或零售包装可立即使用的)	8	5	5		5	5	5	5	5		
38029000	活性天然矿产品;动物炭黑(包括废动物炭黑)	10	8	5	5	8	5	8	5	5		
38061010	松香	10	8	5	5	8	5	8	5	5		
38089311	零售包装的除草剂	9	5		5	5	5	5	5	5		
38089391	零售包装抗萌剂及植物生长调节剂	9	5		5	5	5	5	5	5		
38089399	非零售抗萌剂及植物生长调节剂	6	5		5	5	5	5	5	5		
38089400	消毒剂	9	5		5	5	5	5	5	5		
38091000	以淀粉物质为基本成分,纺织、造纸、制革及类似工业用的其他税号未列名的整理剂、染料加速着色或固色助剂及其他产品和制剂	10	8	5	5	8	5	8	5	5		
38140000	其他税号未列名的有机复合溶剂及稀释剂;除漆剂	10	8	8		8	8	8	8	8		
38160000	耐火水泥、灰泥、混凝土及类似耐火材料,但税目38.01的产品除外	6.5	5	5	5	5	5	5	5			
38200000	防冻剂及解冻剂	10	8	5	5	8	5	8	5	5		
38231100	硬脂酸	16	0	0	0	8	8	0	8	8		
38244000	水泥、灰泥及混凝土用添加剂	6.5	5	5	5	5	5	5	5			
38247500	含四氯化碳的含有甲烷、乙烷、丙烷卤化衍生物混合物	6.5	5		5	5	5	5	5	5		
38247600	含1,1,1-三氯乙烷(甲基氯仿)的含有甲烷、乙烷、丙烷卤化衍生物混合物	6.5	5		5	5	5	5	5	5		
38247800	含全氟烃或氢氟烃的,但不含全氯氟烃或氢氯氟烃的含有甲烷、乙烷、丙烷卤化衍生物混合物	6.5	5		5	5	5	5	5	5		
38248100	含环氧乙烷的混合物及制品	6.5	5		5	5	5	5	5	5		
38248200	含多氯联苯、多氯三联苯或多溴联苯的混合物及制品	6.5	5		5	5	5	5	5	5		
38248300	含三(2,3-二溴丙基)磷酸酯的混合物及制品	6.5	5		5	5	5	5	5	5		
38249010	杂醇油	6.5	5		5	5	5	5	5	5		
38249020	除墨剂、蜡纸改正液及类似品	9	8	5	5	8	5	8	5	5		
38249030	增炭剂	6.5	5		5	5	5	5	5	5		
39093010	聚合MDI	6.5	5		5	5	5	5	5	5		
39043000	氯乙烯-乙酸乙烯酯共聚物	9	5		5	5	5	5	5	5		
39044000	初级形状的其他氯乙烯共聚物	12	8	10	8	8	8	8	8	8		
39051200	聚乙酸乙烯酯的水分散体	10	8	5	5	8	5	8	5	5		
39052100	乙酸乙烯酯共聚物的水分散体	10	8	5	5	8	5	8	5	5		
39052900	其他初级形状的乙酸乙烯酯共聚物	10	8	5	5	8	5	8	5	5		
39071090	其他初级形状的聚缩醛	7.6		5	5		5		5	5		
39131000	初级形状的藻酸及盐和酯	10	8	5	5	8	5	8	5	5		
39161000	乙烯聚合物制单丝、条、杆及型材	10	8	5	5	8	5	8	5	5		
39169010	聚酰胺制的单丝、条、杆及型材	10	8	5	5	8	5	8	5	5		

税则号列 Tariff No.	货品名称 Description of Goods	最惠国 MFN (%)	协定税率(%)Agreement									
			文莱 CAM	印尼 INA	马来西亚 MAS	缅甸 MMR	菲律宾 PHI	新加坡 SIN	泰国 THA	越南 VIE	老挝 LAO	柬埔寨 TPE
39169090	其他塑料制单丝、条、杆及型材	10	8	5	5	8	5	8	5	5		
39172100	乙烯聚合物制的硬管	10	8	5	5	8	5	8	5	5		
39172300	氯乙烯聚合物制的硬管	10	8	5	5	8	5	8	5	5		
39172900	其他塑料制的硬管	10	8	5	5	8	5	8	5	5		
39173100	塑料制的软管	10	8	5	5	8	5	8	5	5		
39173200	其他未装有附件的塑料制管子	6.5	5		5	5		5	5	5		
39173300	其他装有附件的塑料管子	6.5	5		5	5		5	5	5		
39174000	塑料制的管子附件	10	8	8	8	8		8	8	8		
39191010	丙烯酸树脂为基本成份的成卷胶粘板片条等,宽度≤20cm	6.5	5	5		5		5	5	5		
39191091	宽度≤20cm 成卷的胶囊型反光膜	6.5	5	5		5		5	5	5		
39191099	其他材料制的,宽度≤20cm 的其他成卷塑料胶粘板片等	6.5	5	5		5		5	5	5		
39199010	其他胶囊型反光膜	6.5	5	5		5		5	5	5		
39199090	其他自粘塑料板、片、膜等材料	6.5	5	5		5		5	5	5		
39201010	乙烯聚合物制电池隔膜	6.5	5	5	5	5		5	5	5		
39201090	其他乙烯聚合物制板、片、带	6.5	5	5	5	5		5	5	5		
39202010	丙烯聚合物制电池隔膜	6.5	5			5		5	5	5		
39202090	其他丙烯聚合物制板、片、带	6.5	5			5		5	5	5		
39203000	非泡沫聚苯乙烯板、片、膜、箔及扁条	6.5	5	5		5		5	5	5		
39204900	按重量计增塑剂含量小于6%的聚氯乙烯板、片、膜、箔及扁条	7.6	5		5	5		5	5	5		
39205100	聚甲基丙烯酸甲酯板片膜箔及扁条	6.5	5		5	5	5	5	5	5		
39205900	其他丙烯酸聚合物板片膜箔及扁条	6.5	5		5	5	5	5	5	5		
39206100	聚碳酸酯制板、片、膜、箔及扁条	6.5	5	5		5	5	5	5	5		
39206200	聚对苯二甲酸乙二酯板片膜箔扁条	6.5	5			5	5	5	5	5		
39206900	其他聚酯板、片、膜、箔及扁条	10	8	8		8	8	8	8	8		
39207100	再生纤维素制板、片、膜、箔及扁条	6.5	5		5	5	5	5	5	5		
39207300	醋酸纤维素制板、片、膜、箔及扁条	6.5	5		5	5	5	5	5	5		
39209100	聚乙烯醇缩丁醛板、片、膜、箔及扁条	6.5	5			5	5	5	5	5		
39209200	聚酰胺板、片、膜、箔及扁条	10	8	5	5	8	5	8	5	5		
39209300	氨基树脂板、片、膜、箔及扁条	6.5	5	5		5	5	5	5	5		
39209400	酚醛树脂板、片、膜、箔及扁条	10	8	5	5	8	5	8	5	5		
39209910	聚四氟乙烯制的非泡沫塑料板片	6.5	5			5	5	5	5	5		
39209990	其他塑料制的非泡沫塑料板片	6.5	5			5	5	5	5	5		
39211210	泡沫聚氯乙烯人造革及合成革	9	8			8	8	8	8	8		
39211290	泡沫聚氯乙烯板、片、带、箔及扁条	6.5	5			5	5	5	5	5		
39211310	泡沫聚氨酯制人造革及合成革	9	8		8	8	8	8	8	8		
39211390	泡沫聚氨酯板、片、带、箔及扁条	6.5	5		5	5		5	5	5		
39211990	其他泡沫塑料板、片、膜、箔及扁条	6.5	5			5	5	5	5	5		
39219020	嵌有玻璃纤维的聚乙烯板、片	6.5	5	5		5		5	5	5		
39219030	聚异丁烯为基本成分的附有人造毛毡的板、片、卷材	6.5	5	5		5		5	5	5		
39219090	未列名塑料板、片、膜、箔及扁条	6.5	5	5		5		5	5	5		
39231000	塑料制盒、箱及类似品	10	8			8	8	8	8	8		
39232100	乙烯聚合物制袋及包	10	8		8	8		8	8	8		
39232900	其他塑料制的袋及包	10	8		8	8		8	8	8		
39233000	塑料制坛、瓶及类似品	6.5		5	5		5		5	5		

税则号列 Tariff No.	货品名称 Description of Goods	最惠国 MFN (%)	协定税率(%)Agreement									
			文莱 CAM	印尼 INA	马来西亚 MAS	缅甸 MMR	菲律宾 PHI	新加坡 SIN	泰国 THA	越南 VIE	老挝 LAO	柬埔寨 TPE
39234000	塑料制卷轴、纡子、筒管及类似品	10	8	8		8		8	8	8		
39235000	塑料制塞子、盖子及类似品	10	8			8	8	8	8	8		
39239000	供运输或包装货物用其他塑料制品	10	8		8	8		8	8	8		
39241000	塑料制餐具及厨房用具	10	8			8		8	8	8		
39249000	塑料制其他家庭用具及卫生或盥洗用具	10	8			8	8	8	8	8		
39261000	办公室或学校用塑料制品	10	8	5	5	8	5	8	5	5		
39262000	塑料制衣服及衣着附件	10	8	8	8		8	8	8	8		
39263000	塑料制家具、车厢及类似品的附件	10	8	5	5	8	5	8	5	5		
39269010	塑料制机器及仪器用零件	10	8			8		8	8			
39269090	其他塑料制品	10	8			8		8	8			
40091100	未加强或未与其他材料合制硫化橡胶管,未装有附件	10.5	8	8		8	8	8	8	8		
40092100	用金属加强或只与金属合制的硫化橡胶管,未装有附件	10.5	8	8		8	8	8	8	8		
40092200	用金属加强或只与金属合制的硫化橡胶管,装有附件	10	8	5	5	8	5	8	5	5		
40093100	用纺织材料加强或只与纺织材料合制硫化橡胶管,未装有附件	10.5	8	8		8	8	8	8	8		
40094100	用其他材料加强或与其他材料合制硫化橡胶管,未装有附件	10.5	8	8		8	8	8	8	8		
40094200	用其他材料加强或与其他材料合制硫化橡胶管,装有附件	10	8	5	5	8	5	8	5	5		
40103100	梯形截面的环形传动带(三角带),V形肋状的,外周长超过60厘米,但不超过180厘米	8	5	5		5	5	5	5	5		
40103200	梯形截面的环形传动带(三角带),V形肋状的除外,外周长超过60厘米,但不超过180厘米	8	5	5		5	5	5	5	5		
40103300	180CM<外周长≤240CM的三角带,V形肋状的	8	5	5		5	5	5	5	5		
40103400	180CM<外周长≤240CM的三角带,V形肋状的除外	8	5	5		5	5	5	5	5		
40103500	60CM<外周长≤150CM的环形同步带	10	8	5	5	8	5	8	5	5		
40103900	其他硫化橡胶制的传动带及带料	8	5	5		5	5	5	5	5		
40111000	机动小客车用新的充气橡胶轮胎	10	8			8		8				
40112000	客或货运车用新的充气橡胶轮胎	10	8			8		8				
40114000	摩托车用新的充气橡胶轮胎	15	8			8	8	8				
40115000	自行车用新的充气橡胶轮胎	20	12	12	12	12	12	12	12			
40116100	农业或林业车辆及机器用人字形胎面或类似胎面的新充气橡胶轮胎	17.5	8			8	8	8	8	8		
40116200	辋圈尺寸不超过61CM的建筑或工业搬运车辆及机器用人字形胎面或类似胎面的新充气橡胶轮胎	17.5	8			8	8	8	8	8		
40116300	辋圈>61CM建筑或工业搬运车辆及机器用人字形胎面或类似胎面的新充气橡胶轮胎	17.5	8			8	8	8	8	8		
40116900	其他人字形胎面或类似胎面的新充气橡胶轮胎	17.5	8		8	8	8	8	8	8		
40119200	农业或林业车辆及机器用非人字形胎面或类似胎面的新充气橡胶轮胎	25	12			12	12	12	12	12		
40119300	辋圈尺寸不超过61CM的建筑或工业搬运车辆及机器用非人字形胎面或类似胎面的新充气橡胶轮胎	25	12			12	12	12	12	12		

税则号列 Tariff No.	货品名称 Description of Goods	最惠国 MFN (%)	协定税率(%) Agreement									
			文莱 CAM	印尼 INA	马来西亚 MAS	缅甸 MMR	菲律宾 PHI	新加坡 SIN	泰国 THA	越南 VIE	老挝 LAO	柬埔寨 TPE
40119400	辋圈>61CM 建筑或工业搬运车辆及机器用非人字形胎面或类似胎面的新充气橡胶轮胎	25	12		12	12	12	12	12	12		
40119900	其他新的充气橡胶轮胎	25	12		12	12	12	12	12	12		
40121100	机动小客车(包括旅行小客车及赛车)用翻新轮胎	20	12			12	12	12	12	12		
40121200	机动大客车或货运机动车用翻新轮胎	20	12			12	12	12	12	12		
40121900	其他翻新轮胎	20	12	12		12	12	12		12		
40122010	汽车用旧的充气橡胶轮胎	25	12			12	12	12	12	12		
40122090	其他用途旧的充气橡胶轮胎	25	12			12	12	12	12	12		
40129020	汽车用实心或半实心橡胶轮胎	22	12	12	12	12	12	12		12		
40129090	其他用实心或半实心橡胶轮胎	22	12	12	12	12	12	12		12		
40131000	汽车用橡胶内胎	15	8		8	8	8	8				
40132000	自行车用橡胶内胎	15	8		8	8	8	8	8			
40139090	其他用橡胶内胎	15	8		8	8	8	8				
40161010	硫化海绵橡胶制机器及仪器用零件	8	5	5	5	5	5	5	5			
40161090	硫化海绵橡胶制其他制品	15	8	8	8	8	8	8	8			
40169100	硫化橡胶制铺地制品及门垫	18	10	8	8	8	8	8	8	8		
40169200	硫化橡胶制橡皮擦	18	0	0	0	8	8	0	8	8		
40169910	硫化橡胶制机器及仪器用其他零件	8	5	5		5	5	5	5			
40169990	其他未列名硫化橡胶制品	10	8	8		8	8	8	8			
41033000	生猪皮	9	5	5	5	0	5	5	5	5		
41039090	其他生皮	9	5	5	5	0	5	5	5	5		
42021210	以塑料或纺织材料作面的衣箱	20	12		12	12	12	12	12	12		
42021290	塑料或纺织材料作面的其他箱包	20	12		12	12	12	12	12	12		
42022200	以塑料片或纺织材料作面的手提包	10	8		8	8	8	8	8	8		
42023200	以塑料或纺织品作面的钱包等物品	20	12		12	12	12	12	12	12		
42029200	以塑料或纺织材料作面的其他容器	10	8		8	8	8	8	8	8		
44042000	非针叶木箍木、木劈条、木桩、木棒及类似品,木片条	8	5	5	5		5	5	5	5		
44151000	木箱及类似的包装容器;电缆卷筒	7.5	5	5	5		5	5	5	5		
44185000	木瓦及盖屋板	7.5	5	5	5		5	5	5	5		
48193000	底宽≥40cm 的纸袋	7.5		5	5		5		5	5		
50020011	厂丝	9	5	5	5	5	5	5		5		
50020012	土丝	9	5	5	5	5	5	5		5		
50020013	双宫丝	9	5	5	5	5	5	5		5		
50020019	其他未加捻桑蚕丝	9	5	5	5	5	5	5		5		
50020020	未加捻柞蚕丝	9	5	5	5	5	5	5		5		
50020090	未加捻其他生丝	9	5	5	5	5	5	5		5		
50040000	非供零售用丝纱线	6	5	5	5	5	5	5		5		
51121900	重量>200g/平米精梳全毛布	10	8	8	8	0	8	8	8	8		
52021000	废棉纱线	10	8	5	5	8	5	8	5	5		
52029100	棉的回收纤维	10	8	5	5	8	5	8	5	5		
52051100	非零售粗梳粗支纯棉单纱	5				0						
52051200	非零售粗梳中支纯棉单纱	5				0						
52051400	非零售粗梳较细支纯棉单纱	5				0						
52052100	非零售精梳粗支纯棉单纱	5				0						
52052400	非零售精梳较细支纯棉单纱	5				0						
52081200	未漂白较轻质全棉平纹布	10	8	8	8	8	8	8	8			

税则号列 Tariff No.	货品名称 Description of Goods	最惠国 MFN (%)	协定税率(%)Agreement									
			文莱 CAM	印尼 INA	马来西亚 MAS	缅甸 MMR	菲律宾 PHI	新加坡 SIN	泰国 THA	越南 VIE	老挝 LAO	柬埔寨 TPE
52081900	未漂白轻质其他全棉机织物	10	8	8		8	8	8	8	8		
52082200	漂白的较轻质全棉平纹布	10	8	5	5	0	5	8	5	5		
52083200	染色的较轻质全棉平纹布	10	8	8		8	8	8	8			
52083300	染色的轻质全棉三、四线斜纹布	10	5	5	5	0	5	5	5	5		
52083900	染色的轻质其他全棉机织物	10	8	8		8	8	8	8			
52084100	色织的轻质全棉平纹布	10	8	5	5	8	5	8	5	5		
52084200	色织的较轻质全棉平纹布	10	8	8	8	8	8	8	8			
52084900	色织的轻质其他全棉机织物	10	8	8	8	0	8	8	8			
52085200	印花的较轻全棉平纹布	10	8	5	5	8	5	8	5	5		
52091200	未漂白重质全棉三、四线斜纹布	10	8	8	8	8	8	8	8			
52091900	未漂白重质其他全棉机织物	10	8	8	8	8	8	8	8			
52092100	漂白的重质全棉平纹布	12	8	8	10	8	8	8	8	8		
52092900	漂白的重质其他全棉机织物	12	8	8	8	8	8	8	8			
52093100	染色的重质全棉平纹布	10	8	8		0	8	8	8			
52093200	染色的重质全棉三、四线斜纹布	10	8	8		0	8	8	8			
52093900	染色的重质其他全棉机织物	10	8	8	8	0	8	8	8			
52094100	色织的重质全棉平纹布	10	8	5	5	8	5	8	5	5		
52094200	色织的重质全棉粗斜纹布(劳动布)	10	8	8	8	0	8	8	8			
52094900	色织的重质其他全棉机织物	10	8	5	5	8	5	8	5	5		
52101100	与化纤混纺未漂白轻质平纹棉布	12	8	8	8	8	8	8	8			
52101910	化纤混纺未漂白轻质 3、4 线斜纹棉布	12	8	8	8	8	8	8	8			
52101990	与化纤混纺未漂白轻质其他棉布	12	8	8	8	8	8	8	8			
52102990	与化纤混纺漂白的轻质其他棉布	14	8	8	10	8	8	8	8	8		
52103100	与化纤混纺染色的轻质平纹棉布	10	8	8	8	8	8	8	8			
52103200	化纤混纺染色的轻质三线或四线斜纹棉布	10	8	5	5	8	5	8	5	5		
52103900	与化纤混纺染色的轻质其他棉布	10	8	5	5	8	5	8	5	5		
52104100	与化纤混纺色织的轻质平纹棉布	10	8	8	8	8	8	8	8			
52104910	化纤混纺色织的轻质三线或四线斜纹棉布	10	8	5	5	8	5	8	5	5		
52104990	与化纤混纺色织的轻质其他棉布	10	8	5	5	8	5	8	5	5		
52111100	与化纤混纺未漂白重质平纹棉布	12	8	8	8	8	8	8	8			
52111200	化纤混纺未漂白重质三线或四线斜纹棉布	12	8	8	8	8	8	8	8			
52111900	与化纤混纺未漂白重质其他棉布	12	8	8	8	8	8	8	8			
52113200	化纤混纺染色的重质三线或四线斜纹棉布	10	8	5	5	8	5	8	5	5		
52114200	与化纤混纺色织的重质粗斜纹棉布	10	8	5	5	8	5	8	5	5		
52114900	与化纤混纺色织的重质其他棉布	10	8	5	5	8	5	8	5	5		
52121100	未漂白的其他混纺轻质棉布	12	8	8	8	8	8	8	8			
53031000	生或沤制黄麻,其他纺织用韧皮纤维	5				0						
53039000	经加工、未纺的黄麻及其他纺织用韧皮纤维	5				0						
53050092	加工、未纺的椰壳纤维及椰壳纤维废料	5				0						
54071010	尼龙或其他聚酰胺高强力纱制机织物	10	8	8	8	8	8	8	8			
54071020	聚酯高强力纱制机织物	10	8	8	8	8	8	8	8			
54072000	合成纤维扁条及类似品的机织物	10	8	8	8	8	8	8	8			
54073000	多层平行纱线相互层迭并粘合机织物	10	8	8	8	8	8	8	8			
54074200	染色的纯尼龙布	10	8	8	8	0	8	8	8			
54075200	染色的纯聚酯变形长丝布	10	8	8	8	0	8	8	8			
54077100	未漂白或漂白其他纯合成纤维长丝布	10	8	8		8	8	8	8	8		
54077200	染色的其他纯合成纤维长丝布	10	8	8		0	8	8	8	8		
54079200	染色的其他混纺合成纤维长丝布	10	8	8	8	0	8	8	8	8		

税则号列 Tariff No.	货品名称 Description of Goods	最惠国 MFN (%)	协定税率(%)Agreement									
			文莱 CAM	印尼 INA	马来西亚 MAS	缅甸 MMR	菲律宾 PHI	新加坡 SIN	泰国 THA	越南 VIE	老挝 LAO	柬埔寨 TPE
54081000	粘胶长丝高强力纱的机织物	10	8	8	8	8	8	8	8			
55121900	其他纯聚酯布	10	8	8		8	8	8	8			
55129900	其他纯合成纤维布	10	8	8	8	0	8	8	8	8		
55131110	与棉混纺未漂白的轻质聚酯平纹布	16	12	12	12	12	12	12	12			
55131120	与棉混纺漂白的轻质聚酯平纹布	15	12	12	12	12	12	12	12			
55131210	与棉混纺未漂白的轻质聚酯斜纹布	16	12	12	12	12	12	12	12			
55131220	与棉混纺漂白的轻质聚酯斜纹布	18	12	12	12	12	12	12	12			
55131310	与棉混纺未漂白的其他轻质聚酯布	16	12	12	12	12	12	12	12			
55131320	与棉混纺漂白的其他轻质聚酯布	18	12	12	12	12	12	12	12			
55131900	与棉混纺未漂白或漂白的轻质其他合成纤维布	18	12	12	12	12	12	12	12			
55132100	与棉混纺染色的轻质聚酯平纹布	10	8	8	8	8	8	8	8			
55132310	与棉混纺染色的轻质聚酯斜纹布	10	8	8	8	8	8	8	8			
55132390	与棉混纺染色的其他轻质聚酯布	10	8	8	8	8	8	8	8			
55132900	与棉混纺染色的轻质其他合成纤维布	10	8	8	8	8	8	8	8			
55134100	与棉混纺印花的轻质聚酯平纹布	10	8	8	8	0	8	8	8	8		
55141110	与棉混纺未漂白的重质聚酯平纹布	16	12	12	12	12	12	12	12			
55141120	与棉混纺漂白的重质聚酯平纹布	18	12	12	12	12	12	12	12			
55141210	与棉混纺未漂白的重质聚酯斜纹布	16	12	12	12	12	12	12	12			
55141220	与棉混纺漂白的重质聚酯斜纹布	18	12	12	12	12	12	12	12			
55141911	与棉混纺未漂白的重质其他聚酯布	16	12	12	12	12	12	12	12			
55141912	与棉混纺漂白的重质其他聚酯布	18	12	12	12	12	12	12	12			
55141990	与棉混纺未漂白或漂白的重质其他合成纤维布	16	12	12	12	12	12	12	12			
55142100	与棉混纺染色的重质聚酯平纹布	10	8	8		8	8	8	8			
55142200	与棉混纺染色的重质聚酯斜纹布	10	8	8	8	8	8	8	8			
55142300	与棉混纺染色的其他重质聚酯布	10	8	8	8	0	8	8	8			
55143020	与棉混纺色织的重质聚酯斜纹布	10	8	8	8	8	8	8	8			
55143030	与棉混纺色织的其他重质聚酯布	10	8	8	8	8	8	8	8			
55143090	与棉混纺色织的重质其他合成纤维布	10	8	8	8	8	8	8	8			
55151100	与粘胶纤维短纤混纺的聚酯布	10	8	8		8	8	8	8			
55151200	与化纤长丝混纺的聚酯布	10	8	8	8	8	8	8	8			
55151300	与毛混纺的聚酯布	10	8	8	8	8	8	8	8			
55151900	与其他纤维混纺的聚酯布	10	8	8	8	8	8	8	8			
55152900	与其他纤维混纺的腈纶布	10	8	8	8	8	8	8	8			
56012100	棉制的絮胎及其他絮胎制品	10	8	8	8	8	8	8	8			
56021000	针刺机制毡呢及纤维缝编织物	10	8	8	8	8	8	8	8			
56031110	每平米≤25g 经浸渍化纤长丝无纺织物	10	8	8	8	0	8	8	8	8		
56031210	25g <每平米≤70g 浸渍化纤长丝无纺织物	10	8	8	8	0	8	8	8	8		
56039210	25g <每平米≤70g 浸渍其他无纺织物	10	8	8	8	8		8	8			
56039290	25g <每平米≤70g 其他无纺织物	10	5	5	5	0	5	5	5	5		
56039310	70g <每平米≤150g 浸渍其他无纺织物	10	8	8	8	8		8	8			
56039390	70g <每平米≤150g 的其他无纺织物	10	8	5	5	8	5	8	5	5		
56039410	每平米>150g 经浸渍其他无纺织物	10	8	8	8	8	8	8	8			
56039490	每平米>150g 的其他无纺织物	10	8	8	8	0	8	8	8			
56041000	用纺织材料包覆的橡胶线及绳	5				0						
56079090	其他纺织材料制线、绳、索、缆	5				0						
57031000	毛制簇绒地毯及其他簇绒铺地制品	14	8	8	8	8		8	8	8		
57039000	其他纺织材料簇绒地毯及其他簇绒铺地制品	14	8	8	8	8		8	8	8		
57050010	毛制其他地毯及其他铺地制品	14	8	8	8	8		8	8	8		

税则号列 Tariff No.	货品名称 Description of Goods	最惠国 MFN (%)	协定税率(%) Agreement									
			文莱 CAM	印尼 INA	马来西亚 MAS	缅甸 MMR	菲律宾 PHI	新加坡 SIN	泰国 THA	越南 VIE	老挝 LAO	柬埔寨 TPE
57050020	化纤制其他地毯及其他铺地制品	10	8	8	8	8		8	8	8		
57050090	其他纺织材料制其他地毯及铺地制品	14	8	8	8	8		8	8	8		
58012100	不割绒的棉制纬起绒织物	12	8	8	8	8	8	8	8			
58013300	其他化纤纬起绒织物	10	8	8	8	0	8	8	8	8		
58021100	未漂白棉毛巾织物及类似毛圈机织物	12	8	8	8	8	10	8	8			
58041010	丝及绢丝网眼薄纱及其他网眼织物	10	8	8	8	8	8	8	8			
58041030	化纤制网眼薄纱及其他网眼织物	12	8	8	8	0	8	8	8			
58041090	其他纺织材料网眼薄纱及其他网眼织物	10	8	8	8	8	8	8	8			
58042100	化纤机制花边	10	8	8	8	8	8	8	8			
58042910	丝及绢丝机制花边	10	8	8	8	8	8	8	8			
58042920	棉机制花边	10	5	5	5	0	5	5	5	5		
58042990	其他纺织材料制机制花边	10	8	8	8	8	8	8	8			
58043000	手工制花边	10	8	8	8	8	8	8	8			
58061090	其他材料狭幅起绒织物及绳绒织物	10	8	5	5	0	5	8	5	5		
58062000	含弹性纱线≥5%的狭幅织物	10	8	8	8	0	8	8	8	8		
58063100	棉制其他狭幅机织物	10	5	5	5	0	5	5	5	5		
58063200	化纤制其他狭幅机织物	10	8	8	8	0	8	8	8	8		
58071000	机织非绣制纺织材料标签、徽章等	10	8	8	8	0	8	8	8	8		
58089000	非绣制成匹装饰带、流苏、绒球	10	8	8	8	0	8	8	8	8		
58110010	丝及绢丝制绗缝被褥状纺织品	10	8	8	8	8	8	8	8			
58110020	羊毛或动物细毛制绗缝被褥状纺织品	10	8	8	8	8	8	8	8			
58110040	化学纤维制绗缝被褥状纺织品	12	8	8	8	8	8	8	8			
58110090	其他纺织材料制绗缝被褥状纺织品	10	8	8	8	8	8	8	8			
59011010	用胶或淀粉涂布的棉或麻纺织物	10	8	5	5	8	5	8	5	5		
59019091	棉或麻制描图布、帽里硬衬布等	10	5	5	5	0	5	5	5	5		
59021000	尼龙等高强力纱制的帘子布	10	8	8	8	8	8	8	8			
59031020	用聚氯乙烯浸、涂的人造革	10	8	5	5	8	5	8	5	5		
59031090	用聚氯乙烯浸、涂的其他纺织物	10	8	8	8	8		8	8	8		
59039020	用其他塑料浸、涂的人造革	10	8	5	5	8	5	8	5	5		
59039090	用其他塑料浸、涂的其他纺织物	10	8	8	8	0	8	8	8	8		
59041000	列诺伦(亚麻油地毡)	14	8	8	8	8		8	8	8		
60011000	针织或钩编的长毛绒织物	10	8	8		8	8	8	8	8		
60012200	化纤制针织或钩编毛圈绒头织物	10	8	8		8	8	8	8			
60012900	其他材料制针织或钩编毛圈绒头布	12	8	8		8	8	8	8	8		
60019200	化纤制针织或钩编起绒织物	10	8	8		8	8	8	8	8		
60019900	其他纤维制针织或钩编起绒织物	12	8	8		8	8	8	8			
60029010	宽≤30cm 含橡胶线的棉针织、钩编织物	10	5	5	5	0	5	5	5	5		
60029030	宽≤30cm 含橡胶线的合成纤维制针织、钩编织物	10	8	8	8	0	8	8	8	8		
60041010	宽>30cm,弹性纱线≥5%棉针织、钩编织物	10	8	5	5	0	5	8	5	5		
60053100	未漂白或漂白合成纤维制的其他经编织物	10	8	8	8	8	8	8	8			
60053200	染色合成纤维制的其他经编织物	10	8	8	8	0	8	8	8			
60053300	色织合成纤维制的其他经编织物	10	8	8	8	8	8	8	8			
60053400	印花合成纤维制的其他经编织物	10	8	8	8	8	8	8	8			
60062200	染色棉制的其他针织、钩编织物	10	8	8	8	0	8	8	8	8		
60062300	色织棉制的其他针织、钩编织物	10	8	5	5	0	5	8	5	5		
60063100	未漂白或漂白合成纤维制的其他针织、钩编织物	10	8	8	8	8	8	8	8			
60063200	染色合成纤维制的其他针织、钩编织物	10	8	8	8	8	8	8	8			

税则号列 Tariff No.	货品名称 Description of Goods	最惠国 MFN (%)	协定税率(%)Agreement									
			文莱 CAM	印尼 INA	马来西亚 MAS	缅甸 MMR	菲律宾 PHI	新加坡 SIN	泰国 THA	越南 VIE	老挝 LAO	柬埔寨 TPE
60063300	色织合成纤维制的其他针织、钩编织物	10	8	8	8	8	8	8	8			
61031090	其他纺织材料制针织或钩编男式西服套装	17.5	12	12		12	12	12	12	12		
61033200	棉制针织或钩编男式上衣	16	8	8	8	0	8	8	8	8		
61034200	棉制针织或钩编男长裤、工装裤等	16	8			0	8	8	8	8		
61034300	合纤制针织或钩编男长裤等	17.5	12	12		12	12	12	12	12		
61034900	其他纺织材料制针织或钩编男长裤等	16	12			12	12	12	12	12		
61041300	合纤制针织或钩编女西服套装	25	12			12	12	12	12	12		
61041920	棉制针织或钩编女式西服套装	17.5	8			8	8	8	8	8		
61041990	其他纺织材料制针织或钩编女式西服套装	17.5	12		12	12	12	12	12	12		
61043200	棉制针织女式上衣	16	8		8	0	8	8	8	8		
61043300	合纤制针织女上衣	19	12		12	12		12	12	12		
61044200	棉制针织或钩编连衣裙	16	8			8	8	8	8	8		
61044300	合纤制针织或钩编连衣裙	17.5	12			12	12	12	12	12		
61045200	棉制针织裙子及裙裤	14	8		8	8	8	8	8	8		
61045300	合纤制针织或钩编裙子及裙裤	16	12		12	12	12	12	12	12		
61045900	其他纺织材料制针织或钩编裙子及裙裤	14	8	8	8	0	8	8	8	8		
61046200	棉制针织或钩编女长裤、工装裤等	16	8		8	8		8	8	8		
61046300	合纤制针织或钩编女长裤等	17.5	12		12	12	12	12	12	12		
61046900	其他纺织材料制针织或钩编女长裤等	16	8	8		8		8	8	8		
61051000	棉制针织或钩编男衬衫	16	8			0	8	8	8	8		
61052000	化纤制针织或钩编男衬衫	17.5	12			12	12	12	12	12		
61059000	其他纺织材料制针织或钩编男衬衫	16	12	12		12		12	12	12		
61061000	棉制针织或钩编女衬衫	16	8			0		8	8	8		
61062000	化纤制针织或钩编女衬衫	17.5	12		12	12		12	12	12		
61069000	其他纺织材料制针织或钩编女衬衫	16	12	12		12		12	12	12		
61071100	棉制针织或钩编男内裤及三角裤	14	8			0	8	8	8	8		
61071200	化纤制针织或钩编男内裤及三角裤	16	8		8	8	8	8	8	8		
61071910	丝及绢丝制针织或钩编男内裤及三角裤	14	8	8		8		8	8	8		
61071990	其他纺织材料制针织或钩编男内裤及三角裤	14	8	8		8		8	8	8		
61072100	棉制针织或钩编男长睡衣及睡衣裤	14	8	8	8	0		8	8	8		
61072990	其他纺织材料制针织或钩编男长睡衣及睡衣裤	14	8	8	8	0	8	8	8	8		
61079100	棉制针织或钩编男浴衣、晨衣	14	8	8	8	8		8	8	8		
61079910	化纤制针织或钩编男浴衣、晨衣	16	8	8	8	8		8	8	8		
61082100	棉制针织或钩编女三角裤及短衬裤	14	8	8		0	8	8	8	8		
61082200	化纤制针织或钩编女三角裤及短衬裤	16	8	8		8	8	8	8	8		
61082910	丝及绢丝制针织或钩编女三角裤及短衬裤	14	8	8	8	8		8	8	8		
61082990	其他纺织材料制针织或钩编女三角裤及短衬裤	14	8	8	8	8		8	8	8		
61083100	棉制针织或钩编女睡衣及睡衣裤	14	8	8	8	0		8	8	8		
61083200	化纤制针织或钩编女睡衣及睡衣裤	16	8	8	8	8		8	8	8		
61083910	丝及绢丝制针织或钩编女睡衣及睡衣裤	14	8	8	8	8		8	8	8		
61083990	其他纺织材料制针织或钩编女睡衣及睡衣裤	14	8	8	8	8		8	8	8		
61089100	棉制针织或钩编女浴衣、晨衣	14	8	8	8	0		8	8	8		
61089200	化纤制针织或钩编女浴衣、晨衣	16	8	8	8	8		8	8	8		
61091000	棉制针织或钩编T恤衫、汗衫等	14	8		8	0	8	8	8	8		
61099010	丝及绢丝制针织或钩编T恤衫、汗衫等	14	8		8	8	8	8	8	8		
61099090	其他纺织材料制针织或钩编T恤衫、汗衫等	14	8		8	0	8	8	8	8		
61101100	羊毛制针织或钩编套头衫等	14	8	8	8	0	8	8	8	8		
61102000	棉制针织或钩编套头衫等	14	8	8	8	0	8	8	8	8		

税则号列 Tariff No.	货品名称 Description of Goods	最惠国 MFN (%)	协定税率(%) Agreement									
			文莱 CAM	印尼 INA	马来西亚 MAS	缅甸 MMR	菲律宾 PHI	新加坡 SIN	泰国 THA	越南 VIE	老挝 LAO	柬埔寨 TPE
61112000	棉制针织或钩编婴儿服装及附件	14	8			8		8	8	8		
61113000	合纤制针织婴儿服装及附件	16	8		8	8	8	8	8	8		
61119090	其他纺织材料制针织或钩编婴儿服装及附件	14	8	8	8	8		8	8	8		
61123100	合纤制针织或钩编男式游泳服	17.5	12	12	12	12		12	12	12		
61123900	其他纺织材料制针织或钩编男式游泳服	16	12	12	12	12		12	12	12		
61124100	合纤制针织或钩编女式游泳服	17.5	12	12	12	12		12	12	12		
61142000	棉制针织或钩编的其他服装	16	8	8	8	8		8	8	8		
61149090	其他纺织材料制针织或钩编的其他服装	16	12	12	12	12		12	12	12		
61151000	渐紧压袜类连裤袜	16	8	8	8	8	14	8	8	8		
61152100	单丝<67分特合纤制连裤袜等	16	8	8	8	8		8	8	8		
61152200	单丝≥67分特合纤制连裤袜等	16	8	8	8	8		8	8	8		
61153000	单丝<67分特制针织或钩编女统袜	14	8	8	8	8		8	8	8		
61159900	其他纺织材料制针织或钩编短袜及其他袜类	14	8	8	8	8		8	8	8		
61169900	其他纺织材料制针织或钩编手套	14	8	8		8	8	8	8	8		
61179000	其他针织或钩编衣着零件	14	8	8	8	8	8	8	8			
62019210	棉制男式其他羽绒服	16	8	8	8	8		8	8	8		
62019290	棉制男式带风帽防寒短上衣、防风衣	16	8	8	8	0		8	8	8		
62019310	化纤制男式其他羽绒服	17.5	12	12	12	12		12	12	12		
62019390	化纤制男式防寒短上衣、防风衣	17.5	12	12	12	12		12	12	12		
62019900	其他纺织材料制男式防寒短上衣、防风衣	16	12	12	12	0		12	12	12		
62032200	棉制男式便服套装	17.5	8	8	8	8		8	8	8		
62032910	丝及绢丝制男式便服套装	17.5	12	12	12	12		12	12	12		
62032990	其他纺织材料制男式便服套装	17.5	12	12	12	12		12	12	12		
62033100	毛制男式上衣	16	12	12	12	0	12	12	12	12		
62033200	棉制男式上衣	16	8	8	8	0	8	8	8	8		
62033910	丝及绢丝制男式上衣	16	12	12	12	12		12	12	12		
62033990	其他纺织材料制男式上衣	16	12	12	12	12		12	12	12		
62034210	棉制男式阿拉伯裤	16	8			8	8	8	8	8		
62034290	棉制男式长裤、工装裤等	16	8			0	8	8	8	8		
62034310	合成纤维制男式阿拉伯裤	17.5	12		12	12	12	12	12	12		
62034390	合纤制男式长裤、工装裤等	17.5	12		12	12	12	12	12	12		
62034910	其他纺织材料制男式阿拉伯裤	16	12	12	12	12		12	12	12		
62034990	其他纺织材料制男童裤、工装裤	16	12	12	12	12		12	12	12		
62041200	棉制女式西服套装	17.5	8		8	8	8	8	8	8		
62041300	合纤制女式西服套装	17.5	12		12	12	12	12	12	12		
62043200	棉制女式上衣	16	8		8	0	8	8	8	8		
62043300	合纤制女式上衣	17.5	12		12	12	12	12	12	12		
62044200	棉制连衣裙	16	8		8	0	8	8	8	8		
62044300	合纤制女式连衣裙	17.5	12		12	12	12	12	12	12		
62044910	丝及绢丝制连衣裙	16	12		12	12	12	12	12	12		
62044990	其他纺织材料制连衣裙	16	12		12	12	12	12	12	12		
62045200	棉制裙子及裙裤	14	8		8	8	8	8	8	8		
62045300	合纤制裙子及裙裤	16	12		12	12	12	12	12	12		
62046200	棉制女式长裤、工装裤等	16	8		8	0	8	8	8	8		
62046300	合纤制女式长裤、工装裤等	17.5	12		12	12	12	12	12	12		
62046900	其他纺织材料制女式长裤、工装裤等	16	8	8	8	8		8	8	8		
62052000	棉制男衬衫	16	8			0	8	8	8	8		
62053000	化纤制男衬衫	16	12		12	12	12	12	12	12		

税则号列 Tariff No.	货品名称 Description of Goods	最惠国 MFN (%)	协定税率(%)Agreement									
			文莱 CAM	印尼 INA	马来西亚 MAS	缅甸 MMR	菲律宾 PHI	新加坡 SIN	泰国 THA	越南 VIE	老挝 LAO	柬埔寨 TPE
62059010	丝及绢丝制男衬衫	16	12			12		12	12	12		
62059090	其他纺织材料制男衬衫	16	12			12		12	12	12		
62063000	棉制女衬衫	16	8		8	0	8	8	8	8		
62064000	化纤制女衬衫	17.5	12		12	12	12	12	12	12		
62069000	其他纺织材料制女衬衫	16	12	12		12		12	12	12		
62071100	棉制男式内裤及三角裤	14	8			8	8	8	8	8		
62071910	丝制男式内裤及三角裤	14	8	8		8		8	8	8		
62071920	化纤制男式内裤及三角裤	16	8	8		8		8	8	8		
62071990	其他纺织材料制男式内裤及三角裤	14	8	8		8		8	8	8		
62072100	棉制男式长睡衣及睡衣裤	14	8	8	8	0		8	8	8		
62072200	化纤制男式长睡衣及睡衣裤	16	8	8	8	8		8	8	8		
62072910	丝及绢丝制男式长睡衣及睡衣裤	14	8	8	8	8		8	8	8		
62072990	其他纺织材料制男式长睡衣及睡衣裤	14	8	8	8	0		8	8	8		
62081910	丝及绢丝制长衬裙及衬裙	14	8	8	8	8		8	8	8		
62081920	棉制长衬裙及衬裙	14	8	8	8	8		8	8	8		
62081990	其他纺织材料制长衬裙及衬裙	14	8	8	8	8		8	8	8		
62082100	棉制女式睡衣及睡衣裤	14	8	8	8	0		8	8	8		
62082200	化纤制女式睡衣及睡衣裤	16	8	8	8	0		8	8	8		
62089100	棉制女式背心、内衣、浴衣及类似品	14	8	8	8	0	8	8	8	8		
62089200	化纤制女式背心、内衣及类似品	16	8	8	8	0	8	8	8	8		
62092010	棉制婴儿尿布	14	8			8	8	8	8	8		
62092090	棉制婴儿服装及衣着附件	14	8			8	8	8	8	8		
62093000	合纤制婴儿服装及衣着附件	16	8	8		8		8	8	8		
62111100	男式游泳服	16	12	12	12	12		12	12	12		
62113210	棉制男式阿拉伯袍	16	8	8	8	8		8	8	8		
62113220	棉制男式运动服	16	8	8	8	8		8	8	8		
62113290	棉制男式其他服装	16	8	8	8	8		8	8	8		
62114910	丝及绢丝制女式运动服及其他服装	16	12	12	12	12		12	12	12		
62114990	其他纺织材料制女式运动服及其他服装	16	12	12	12	12		12	12	12		
62121010	化纤制胸罩	16	8	8	8	0	8	8	8	8		
62122010	化纤制束腰带及腹带	16	8	8	8	8		8	8	8		
62122090	其他纺织材料制束腰带及腹带	14	8	8	8	8		8	8	8		
62171010	非针织非钩编袜子及袜套	14	8	8	8	8	8	8	8	8		
62171020	非针织非钩编和服腰带	14	8	8	8	8	8	8	8	8		
62171090	非针织非钩编服装或衣着附件	14	8	8	8	0	8	8	8	8		
62179000	非针织非钩编服装或衣着零件	14	8	8	8	0	8	8	8	8		
63013000	棉制毯子及旅行毯	16	8	8	8	8		8	8	8		
63014000	合纤制毯子及旅行毯	17.5	12	12	12	12		12	12	12		
63019000	其他纺织材料制毯子及旅行毯	16	8	8	8	8		8	8	8		
63021010	棉制针织或钩编的床上用织物制品	14	8		8	8		8	8	8		
63021090	其他纺织材料制针织或钩编的床上用织物制品	14	8		8	8		8	8	8		
63022110	棉制印花床单	14	8		8	8		8	8	8		
63022190	棉制印花床上用织物制品	14	8		8	8		8	8	8		
63022210	化纤制印花床单	16	8		8	8		8	8	8		
63022290	化纤制印花床上用织物制品	16	8		8	8		8	8	8		
63022910	丝及绢丝制印花床上用织物制品	14	8		8	8		8	8	8		
63022920	麻制印花床上用织物制品	14	8		8	8		8	8	8		
63022990	其他纺织材料制印花床上用织物制品	14	8		8	8		8	8	8		

税则号列 Tariff No.	货品名称 Description of Goods	最惠国 MFN (%)	协定税率(%)Agreement									
			文莱 CAM	印尼 INA	马来西亚 MAS	缅甸 MMR	非律宾 PHI	新加坡 SIN	泰国 THA	越南 VIE	老挝 LAO	柬埔寨 TPE
63023110	棉制刺绣其他床上用织物制品	14	8		8	8		8	8	8		
63023191	棉制其他床单	14	8		8	8		8	8	8		
63023192	棉制其他毛巾被	14	8		8	8		8	8	8		
63023199	棉制其他床上用织物制品	14	8		8	8		8	8	8		
63023210	化纤制刺绣其他床上用织物制品	16	8		8	8		8	8	8		
63023290	化纤制其他床上用织物制品	16	8		8	8		8	8	8		
63023910	丝及绢丝制其他床上用织物制品	14	8		8	8		8	8	8		
63023921	麻制刺绣的其他床上用织物制品	14	8		8	8		8	8	8		
63023929	麻制其他床上用织物制品	14	8		8	8		8	8	8		
63023991	其他纺织材料制刺绣床上用织物制品	14	8		8	8		8	8	8		
63023999	其他纺织材料制其他床上用织物制品	14	8		8	8		8	8	8		
63024010	手工针织或钩编的餐桌用织物制品	14	8	8	8	8		8	8	8		
63024090	其他针织或钩编的餐桌用织物制品	14	8	8	8	8		8	8	8		
63025110	棉制刺绣其他餐桌用织物制品	14	8	8	8	8		8	8	8		
63025190	棉制其他餐桌用织物制品	14	8	8	8	8		8	8	8		
63025310	化纤制刺绣其他餐桌织物制品	14	8	8	8	8		8	8	8		
63025390	化纤制其他餐桌用织物制品	16	8	8	8	8		8	8	8		
63025990	其他纺织材料制餐桌用织物制品	14	8	8	8	8		8	8	8		
63026010	棉制浴巾	14	8	8	8	8		8	8	8		
63026090	棉制盥洗及厨房用毛巾织物	14	8	8	8	8		8	8	8		
63029100	棉制其他盥洗及厨房织物制品	14	8		8	8		8	8	8		
63029300	化纤制其他盥洗及厨房织物制品	16	8	8	8	8		8	8	8		
63029990	其他材料制其他盥洗及厨房织物	14	8	8	8	8		8	8	8		
63031210	合纤制针织的窗帘等	16	8		8	8	8	8	8	8		
63031220	合纤制钩编的窗帘等	16	8		8	8	8	8	8	8		
63031931	棉制针织的窗帘等	14	8		8	8		8	8	8		
63031932	棉制钩编的窗帘等	14	8		8	8		8	8	8		
63039200	合纤制非针织非钩编窗帘等	16	8	8	8	8		8	8	8		
63039900	其他纺织材料制非针织非钩编窗帘等	14	8	8	8	8		8	8	8		
63041121	手工针织床罩	14	8		8	8		8	8	8		
63041129	非手工针织床罩	14	8		8	8		8	8	8		
63041131	手工钩编床罩	14	8		8	8		8	8	8		
63041139	非手工钩编床罩	14	8		8	8		8	8	8		
63041910	丝及绢丝制非针织非钩编床罩	14	8		8	8		8	8	8		
63041921	棉或麻制非针织非钩编刺绣床罩	14	8		8	8		8	8	8		
63041929	棉或麻制其他非针织非钩编床罩	14	8		8	8		8	8	8		
63041931	化纤制非针织非钩编刺绣床罩	16	8		8	8		8	8	8		
63041939	化纤制其他非针织非钩编床罩	16	8		8	8		8	8	8		
63041991	其他纺织材料制非针织、非钩编刺绣床罩	14	8		8	8		8	8	8		
63041999	其他材料制其他非针织非钩编床罩	14	8		8	8		8	8	8		
63049121	手工针织的其他装饰制品	14	8	8	8	8		8	8	8		
63049129	非手工针织的其他装饰制品	14	8	8	8	8		8	8	8		
63049131	手工钩编的其他装饰制品	14	8	8	8	8		8	8	8		
63049139	非手工钩编的其他装饰制品	14	8	8	8	8		8	8	8		
63049310	合纤制非针织、非钩编其他刺绣装饰制品	16	8	8	8	8		8	8	8		
63049390	合纤制其他非针织、非钩编装饰制品	16	8	8	8	8		8	8	8		
63049910	丝制非针织非钩编的装饰制品	14	8	8	8	8		8	8	8		
63049921	麻制非针织、非钩编的其他刺绣装饰制品	14	8	8	8	8		8	8	8		

税则号列 Tariff No.	货品名称 Description of Goods	最惠国 MFN (%)	协定税率(%)Agreement									
			文莱 CAM	印尼 INA	马来西亚 MAS	缅甸 MMR	菲律宾 PHI	新加坡 SIN	泰国 THA	越南 VIE	老挝 LAO	柬埔寨 TPE
63049929	麻制其他非针织非钩编的装饰制品	14	8	8	8	8		8	8	8		
63049990	其他纺织材料制非针织非钩编装饰制品	14	8	8	8	8		8	8	8		
63053300	聚乙烯或聚丙烯扁条制其他货物包装袋	16	8	8	8	8		8	8	8		
63053900	其他化纤制货物包装袋	16	8	8	8	8		8	8	8		
63059000	其他纺织材料制货物包装袋	14	8	8	8	8	8	8	10	8		
63079000	其他纺织材料制成品	14	8	8	8	0	8	8	8	8		
63080000	零售包装成套物品	14	8	8	8	8		8	8	8		
63101000	经分拣的纺织材料制碎织物等	14	8	8	8	8		8	8	8		
63109000	纺织材料制其他碎织物等	14	8	8	8	0	8	8	8	8		
64011000	装金属护头的塑料、橡胶制防水鞋靴	24	12	12	12	12	12	12		12		
64019200	橡胶、塑料底及面的中、短统防水靴	24	12		12	12		12		12		
64019900	其他橡胶、塑料制外底及鞋面防水靴	24	12	12	12	12	12	12		12		
64021900	橡胶、塑料制底及面的其他运动靴	24	12	12	12	12		12		12		
64022000	橡胶、塑料的将鞋面条带栓塞在鞋底上的鞋	24	12	12	12	12		12		12		
64029100	其他橡胶、塑料短统靴(过踝)	24	12	12	12	12	12	12		12		
64029900	其他橡胶、塑料鞋靴	24	12	12		12		12		12		
64031200	皮革制鞋面的滑雪靴	24	12	12	12	12	12	12		12		
64031900	皮革制鞋面的其他运动鞋靴	15	8	8	8	8		8		8		
64032000	皮革条带为鞋面的皮底鞋	24	12	12	12	12		12		12		
64034000	装有金属护鞋头的其他皮革面鞋靴	24	12	12	12	12	12	12		12		
64039100	其他皮革制面的短统靴(过踝)	10	8	8	8	8	8	8		8		
64039900	皮革制面的其他鞋靴	10		8	8	8	8	8		8		
64041100	纺织材料制鞋面的运动鞋靴	24	12		12	12		12		12		
64041900	纺织材料制鞋面胶底的其他鞋靴	24	12		12	12		12		12		
64042000	纺织材料制鞋面皮革底的鞋靴	24	12			12		12		12		
64051000	皮革或再生皮革制面的其他鞋靴	24	12	12	12	12		12	12	12		
64052000	纺织材料制面的其他鞋靴	22	12		12	12		12	12	12		
64059000	其他材料制面的鞋靴	15	8		8	8	8	8	8	8		
64062000	橡胶或塑料制的外底及鞋跟	15	8	8	8	8	8	8	8			
68021010	大理石制砖、瓦、方块及类似品	24	12	12	12	12	12	12		12		
68021090	其他石料制砖瓦、方块及类似品	20	12	12	12	12	12	12		12		
68022120	石灰华	24	12	12	12	12	12	12		12		
68022190	具有一个平面石灰华及蜡石及制品	24	12	12	12	12	12	12		12		
68022910	具有一个平面的其他石灰石及制品	24	12	12	12	12	12	12		12		
68022990	具有一个平面的其他石及制品	15	8	8	8	8	8	8		8		
68029110	大理石、石灰华及蜡石制石刻	24	12	12	12	12	12	12		12		
68029210	其他石灰石制石刻	24	12	12	12	12	12	12		12		
68029310	其他花岗岩制石刻	24	12	12	12	12	12	12		12		
68029910	其他石制成的石刻	24	12	12	12	12	12	12		12		
68029990	其他石及制品	24	12	12	12	12	12	12		12		
69021000	含>50%镁、钙、铬耐火砖及类似品	8	5	5	5	5	5	5	5			
69022000	含>50%氧化铝、硅耐火砖及类似品	8	5	5	5	5	5	5	5			
69029000	其他耐火砖及耐火陶瓷建材制品	8	5	5	5	5	5	5	5			
69039000	其他耐火陶瓷制品	8	5	5	5	5	5	5	5			
69041000	陶瓷制建筑用砖	15	8	8	8	8	8	8	8			
69049000	陶瓷制铺地砖、支撑或填充用砖	24.5	12	12	12	12	12	12	12			
69051000	陶瓷制屋顶瓦	24.5	12	12	12	12	12	12	12			
69059000	其他建筑用陶瓷制品	24.5	12	12	12	12	12	12	12			

税则号列 Tariff No.	货品名称 Description of Goods	最惠国 MFN (%)	协定税率(%) Agreement									
			文莱 CAM	印尼 INA	马来西亚 MAS	缅甸 MMR	菲律宾 PHI	新加坡 SIN	泰国 THA	越南 VIE	老挝 LAO	柬埔寨 TPE
69071000	未上釉的小陶瓷砖、瓦、块及类似品	24.5	12			12	12	12	12			
69079000	未上釉的大陶瓷砖、瓦、块及类似品	12	8			8	8	8	8			
69111010	瓷餐具	12	8			8	8	8				
69111020	瓷厨房器具	15	8			8	8	8				
69119000	其他家用或盥洗用瓷器	24.5	12			12	12	12				
69120010	陶餐具	15	8			8	8	8		8		
69120090	陶制厨房器具	15	8			8	8	8		8		
69131000	瓷塑像及其他装饰用瓷制品	15	8		8	8	8	8	8			
69139000	陶塑像及其他装饰用陶制品	15	8		8	8	8	8	8	8		
69141000	其他瓷制品	24.5	12		12	12	12	12	12	12		
69149000	其他陶制品	10	8		8	8	8	8	8	8		
70031200	铸、轧制着色的非夹丝玻璃板、片	15	8	8	8	8		8				
70031900	铸、轧制的其他非夹丝玻璃板、片	17.5	8	8		8		8				
70032000	铸、轧制的夹丝玻璃板、片	15	8	8	8	8		8	8			
70033000	铸、轧制的玻璃型材及异型材	15	8	8	8	8		8	8			
70042000	拉、吹制的着色玻璃板、片	17.5	8	8	8	8	8	8				
70049000	拉、吹制的其他玻璃板、片	17.5	8	8	8	8	8	8				
70051000	有吸收层非夹丝浮法或抛光玻璃板	15	8	8		8		8				
70052100	其他着色非夹丝浮法玻璃板、片	15	8	8		8		8				
70052900	其他非夹丝浮法玻璃板、片	15	8	8		8		8				
70053000	夹丝浮法玻璃板、片	17.5	8	8		8	8	8	8			
70072190	车辆用层压安全玻璃	20	12	12		12	12	12	12	12		
70091000	车辆后视镜	10	8	5	5	8	5	8	5	5		
70099100	其他未镶框玻璃镜(包括后视镜)	21	12	12	12	12		12				
70099200	其他镶框玻璃镜(包括后视镜)	12	8	8	8	8		8				
70112010	显象管玻壳及其零件	10	0	0	0	8	8	0		8		
70112090	阴极射线管用玻壳及零件	10	0	0	0	8	8	0		8		
70134900	其他玻璃制餐桌、厨房用器皿	10	8	8	8	8	8	8	8			
70169010	花饰铅条窗玻璃及类似品	24	12	12	12	12	12	12	12			
70169090	建筑用压制或模制铺面玻璃块、砖	18	8	8	8	8	8	8	8			
70181000	玻璃珠、仿珍珠及类似小件玻璃品	10	8	5	5	8	5	8	5	5		
71131110	镶嵌钻石的银首饰及其零件	20	12		12	12	12	12	12	12		
71131190	其他银首饰及其零件	20	12		12	12	12	12	12	12		
71171900	其他贱金属制仿首饰	17	12	12	12	12	12	12		12		
71179000	未列名材料制仿首饰	35	12		12	12	12	12	12	12		
72083600	厚度>10mm 的其他热轧卷材	6	5	5		5	5	5		5		
72084000	轧有凸起花纹的热轧非卷材	6	5	5		5	5	5		5		
72085110	厚度>50mm 的其他热轧非卷材	6	5	5		5	5	5		5		
72085120	厚度>20mm,但不超过 50 毫米的其他热轧非卷材	6	5	5		5	5	5		5		
72085190	其他厚度>10mm 的其他热轧非卷材	6	5	5		5	5	5		5		
72085200	4.75mm≤厚度≤10mm 的热轧非卷材	6	5	5		5	5	5		5		
72085310	屈服强度大于 355 牛顿/平方毫米,3mm≤厚度<4.75mm 的热轧非卷材	6	5	5		5	5	5		5		
72085390	其他 3mm≤厚度<4.75mm 的热轧非卷材	6	5	5		5	5	5		5		
72085410	厚度<1.5mm 的热轧非卷材	6	5	5		5	5	5		5		
72085490	其他厚度<3mm 的热轧非卷材	6	5	5		5	5	5		5		
72089000	其他热轧铁或非合金钢宽平板轧材	6	5	5		5	5	5		5		

税则号列 Tariff No.	货品名称 Description of Goods	最惠国 MFN (%)	协定税率(%) Agreement									
			文莱 CAM	印尼 INA	马来西亚 MAS	缅甸 MMR	菲律宾 PHI	新加坡 SIN	泰国 THA	越南 VIE	老挝 LAO	柬埔寨 TPE
72091510	屈服强度大于 355 牛顿/平方毫米,厚度≥3mm 的冷轧卷材	6	5	5		5	5	5		5		
72091590	其他厚度≥3mm 的冷轧卷材	6	5	5		5	5	5		5		
72091610	屈服强度大于 275 牛顿/平方毫米,1mm<厚度<3mm 的冷轧卷材	6	5			5	5	5				
72091690	其他 1mm<厚度<3mm 的冷轧卷材	6	5			5	5	5				
72091810	厚度<0.3mm 的冷轧卷材	6	5			5	5	5				
72091890	其他厚度<0.5mm 的冷轧卷材	6	5			5	5	5				
72092500	厚度≥3mm 的冷轧非卷材	6	5	5		5	5	5		5		
72092600	1mm<厚度<3mm 的冷轧非卷材	6	5			5	5	5				
72092700	0.5mm≤厚度≤1mm 的冷轧非卷材	6	5			5	5	5				
72092800	厚度<0.5mm 的冷轧非卷材	6	5			5	5	5				
72099000	其他冷轧铁或非合金钢宽平板轧材	6	5	5		5	5	5		5		
72101100	镀锡的铁或非合金钢厚宽平板轧材	10	8			8	8	8	8	8		
72103000	电镀锌的铁或非合金钢宽板材	8	5	5		5	5	5		5		
72104100	镀锌的瓦楞形铁或非合金钢宽板材	8	5			5	5	5	5			
72105000	镀氧化铬的铁或非合金钢宽板材	8	5		5	5	5	5		5		
72106100	镀或涂铝锌合金的铁宽平板轧材	8	5			5	5	5	5			
72106900	其他镀或涂铝的铁宽平板轧材	8	5		5	5	5	5	5			
72109000	涂镀其他材料铁或非合金钢宽板材	8	5	5		5	5	5	5			
72111300	未轧花纹的四面轧制的热轧非卷材	6	5	5		5	5	5		5		
72111400	厚度≥4.75mm 的其他热轧板材	6	5	5		5	5	5		5		
72111900	其他热轧铁或非合金钢窄板材	6	5	5		5	5	5		5		
72112300	冷轧含炭量<0.25% 的板材	6	5			5	5	5		5		
72112900	冷轧其他铁或非合金钢窄板材	6	5		5	5	5	5		5		
72119000	冷轧的铁或非合金钢其他窄板材	6	5	5		5	5	5	5	5		
72122000	电镀锌的铁或非合金钢窄板材	8	5	5		5	5	5		5		
72123000	其他镀或涂锌的铁窄板材	8	5			5	5	5	5	5		
72125000	涂镀其他材料铁或非合金钢窄板材	8	5	5		5	5	5	5	5		
72126000	经包覆的铁或非合金钢窄板材	8	5	5		5	5	5	5	5		
72141000	锻造的铁或非合金钢条、杆	7	5	5		5	5	5		5		
72143000	热加工易切削钢的条、杆	7	5	5		5	5	5	5	5		
72151000	冷加工其他易切削钢制条、杆	7	5	5		5	5	5	5	5		
72162100	热加工截面高度<80mm 角钢	6	5	5	5	5	5	5	5			
72163100	热加工截面高度≥80mm 槽型钢	6	5	5	5	5	5	5				
72163210	截面高度在 200 毫米以上的工字钢	6	5	5	5	5	5	5				
72163290	热加工截面高度≥80mm 工字型钢	6	5	5	5	5	5	5				
72163311	截面高度在 800 毫米以上的 H 型缸	6	5	5	5	5	5	5		5		
72163319	截面高度≥200mmH 型钢	6	5	5	5	5	5	5		5		
72163390	其他截面高度≥80mmH 型钢	6	5	5	5	5	5	5		5		
72171000	未镀或涂层的铁或非合金钢丝	8	5		5	5	5	5		5		
72172000	镀或涂锌的铁或非合金钢丝	8	5		5	5	5	5		5		
72173000	镀或涂其他贱金属铁或非合金钢丝	8	5		5	5	5	5	5	5		
72179000	其他铁丝或非合金钢丝	8	5		5	5	5	5	5	5		
72193100	厚度≥4.75mm 冷轧不锈钢板	10	8	8	8	8	8	8		8		
72193200	3mm≤厚度<4.75mm 冷轧不锈钢板材	10	8	8	8	8	8	8		8		
72193300	1mm<厚度<3mm 冷轧不锈钢板材	10	8	8	8	8	8	8		8		
72193400	0.5mm≤厚度≤1mm 冷轧不锈钢板材	10	8	8	8	8	8	8		8		

税则号列 Tariff No.	货品名称 Description of Goods	最惠国 MFN (%)	协定税率(%)Agreement									
			文莱 CAM	印尼 INA	马来西亚 MAS	缅甸 MMR	菲律宾 PHI	新加坡 SIN	泰国 THA	越南 VIE	老挝 LAO	柬埔寨 TPE
72193500	厚度<0.5mm冷轧不锈钢板材	10	8	8	8	8	8	8		8		
72199000	其他不锈钢冷轧板材	10	8	8	8	8	8	8		8		
72202010	宽度小于300mm的冷轧不锈钢带材	10	8	8	8	8	8	8		8		
72202090	其他冷轧不锈钢带材	10	8	8	8	8	8	8		8		
72209000	其他不锈钢带材	10	8	8	8	8	8	8		8		
72210000	不锈钢热轧条、杆	10	8	8		8	8	8	8	8		
72221100	热加工的圆形截面不锈钢条、杆	10	8	8		8	8	8	8	8		
72222000	冷成形或冷加工的不锈钢条、杆	10	8	8		8	8	8		8		
72224000	不锈钢角材、型材及异型材	10	8	8	8	8	8	8		8		
72230000	不锈钢丝	10	8	8	8	8	8	8		8		
73011000	钢铁板桩	7	5	5	5	5	5	5		5		
73044990	非冷轧的不锈钢制其他无缝管	10	8	5	5	8	5	8	5	5		
73051100	纵向埋弧焊接石油、天然气粗钢管	7	5			5	5	5	5	5		
73051900	其他石油、天然气粗钢管	7	5			5	5	5	5	5		
73052000	其他钻探石油、天然气用粗套管	7	5		5	5	5	5	5	5		
73053100	纵向焊接的其他粗钢铁管	6	5			5	5	5	5	5		
73053900	其他方法焊接其他粗钢铁管	6	5			5	5	5		5		
73059000	未列名圆形截面粗钢铁管	6	5			5	5	5	5	5		
73061100	不锈钢焊缝石油、天然气管道管	7	5			5	5	5	5	5		
73061900	其他石油、天然气管道管	7	5			5	5	5	5	5		
73064000	不锈钢其他圆形截面细焊缝管	6	5	5		5	5	5		5		
73069000	未列名其他钢铁管及空心异型材	6	5			5	5	5				
73083000	钢铁制门窗及其框架、门槛	10	8	5	5	8	5	8	5	5		
73151110	自行车滚子链	12	8		8	8	8	8	8			
73151120	摩托车滚子链	12	8		8	8	8	8	8			
73151190	其他滚子链	12	8		8	8	8	8	8			
73151900	铰接链零件	12	8	10	8	8	8	8	8			
73158900	未列名链	12	8	10	8	8	8	8	8			
73181400	自攻螺钉	10	8	8	8	8	8	8		8		
73181500	其他螺钉及螺栓	8	5	5	5	5	5	5				
73181600	螺母	8	5	5	5	5	5	5		5		
73182100	弹簧垫圈及其他防松垫圈	10	8	5	5	8	5	8	5	5		
73182200	其他垫圈	10	8	8	8	8	8	8		8		
73182300	铆钉	10	8	8	8	8	8	8		8		
73182400	销及开尾销	10	8	8	8	8	8	8		8		
73182900	其他无螺纹紧固件	10	8	8	8	8	8	8		8		
73201010	铁道车辆用片簧及簧片	6	5		5	5	5	5	5	5		
73201090	其他片簧及簧片	10	8		8	8	8	8	8	8		
73202010	铁道车辆用螺旋弹簧	6	5		5	5	5	5		5		
73202090	其他螺旋弹簧	10	8		8	8	8	8		8		
73209010	铁道车辆用其他弹簧	6	5	5	5	5		5	5	5		
73209090	其他弹簧	12	8	8	8	8	10	8	8	8		
73219000	非电热家用器具零件	12	8	8	8	8	8	8	8			
73239300	餐桌、厨房等家用不锈钢器具	12	8	8	8	8	8	8		8		
73241000	不锈钢制洗涤槽及脸盆	18	8	8	8	8	8	8	8			
73242100	铸铁制浴缸	10	8	8	8	8	8	8	8			
73242900	其他钢铁制浴缸	30	12	12	12	12	12	12	12			
74152100	铜垫圈(包括弹簧垫圈)	10	8	5	5	8	5	8	5	5		

税则号列 Tariff No.	货品名称 Description of Goods	最惠国 MFN (%)	协定税率(%) Agreement									
			文莱 CAM	印尼 INA	马来西亚 MAS	缅甸 MMR	菲律宾 PHI	新加坡 SIN	泰国 THA	越南 VIE	老挝 LAO	柬埔寨 TPE
74152900	铜制其他无螺纹制品	10	8	5	5	8	5	8	5	5		
76109000	其他铝制结构体及其部件	6	5	5	5	5	5	5	5			
82032000	钳子、镊子及类似工具	10.5	8	8	8	8	8	8	8			
83011000	挂锁	14	8	8	8	8	8	8	8			
83013000	家具用锁	14	8	8	8	8	8	8	8			
83014000	其他锁	14	8	8	8	8	8	8	8			
83016000	锁零件	12	8	8	8	8	8	8	8			
83062990	其他雕塑像及其他装饰品	8		5	5		5		5	5		
84072100	船舶用舷外点燃式发动机	8	5	5	5	5	5	5	5			
84089010	机车用柴油发动机	6	5		5	5	5	5	5	5		
84099110	船舶用点燃式发动机专用零件	6	5	5	5	5	5	5				
84099999	其他未列名发动机的专用零件	8.4	5	5	5	5	5	5		5		
84122910	液压马达	10	8	5	5	8	5	8	5	5		
84137010	转速≥10000 转/分离心泵	8	5	5	5	5	5	5		5		
84137090	转速<10000 转/分离心泵	8	5	5	5	5	5	5		5		
84138100	其他液体泵	8	5	5	5	5	5	5	5			
84142000	手动或脚踏式空气泵	8	5	5	5	5	5	5	5			
84143012	功率 0.4－5kw 的冷藏、冷冻箱用压缩机	10	8	5	5	8	5	8	5	5		
84143013	功率 0.4－5kw 的空气调节器用压缩机	10	8	8	8	8	8	8		8		
84143014	功率>5kw 的空气调节器用压缩机	10	8	8	8	8	8	8		8		
84143019	其他制冷设备用压缩机	10	8	8	8	8	8	8		8		
84143090	非电机驱动的压缩机	9	8	8	8	8	8	8		8		
84145110	功率≤125 瓦的吊扇	20	12	12	12	12	12	12				
84145120	功率≤125 瓦的换气扇	20	12	12	12	12	12	12				
84145130	功率≤125 瓦,有旋转导风轮的风扇	12	8	8	8	8	8	8				
84145199	功率≤125 瓦其他风扇、风机	10	8	8	8	8	8	8				
84145910	其他吊扇	8	5	5	5	5	5	5				
84145920	其他换气扇	8	5	5	5	5	5	5				
84145930	离心通风机	10	8	8	8	8	8	8				
84145990	其他扇,风机	8	5	5	5	5	5	5				
84146090	罩最大边长≤120cm 的通风罩或循环气罩	10	8	5	5	8	5	8	5	5		
84149011	用于制冷设备的压缩机进、排气阀片	8	5	5	5	5	5	5	5			
84149019	其他用于制冷设备的压缩机零件	8	5	5	5	5	5	5	5			
84149020	风机、风扇、通风罩及循环气罩零件	12	8	8	8	8	8	8	8			
84149090	税号 84.14 其他所列机器零件	7	5	5	5	5	5	5	5			
84151010	独立窗式或壁式空气调节器	15	8	8	8	8	10	8				
84151021	分体式制冷量制冷量≤4 千大卡/时窗式或壁式空气调节器	15	8	8	8	8	10	8				
84151022	分体式制冷量制冷量>4 千大卡/时窗式或壁式空气调节器	15	8	8	8	8	10	8				
84158110	制冷量≤4 千大卡/时热泵式空调器	15	8	8	8	8	8	8	8			
84158120	制冷量>4 千大卡/时热泵式空调器	20	12	12	12	12	12	12	12			
84158210	制冷量≤4 千大卡/时的其他空调器	15	8	8	8	8		8	8	8		
84158220	制冷量>4 千大卡/时的其他空调器	20	12	12	12	12		12	12	12		
84158300	未装有制冷装置的空调器	10	8	8	8	8	8	8	8			
84171000	矿砂、金属的热处理用炉及烤箱	10	8	5	5	8	5	8	5	5		
84178090	其他非电热的工业用炉及烘箱	10	8	5	5	8	5	8	5	5		
84181010	容积>500L 冷藏－冷冻组合机	10	8	8	8	8	8	8				

税则号列 Tariff No.	货品名称 Description of Goods	最惠国 MFN (%)	协定税率(%)Agreement									
			文莱 CAM	印尼 INA	马来西亚 MAS	缅甸 MMR	菲律宾 PHI	新加坡 SIN	泰国 THA	越南 VIE	老挝 LAO	柬埔寨 TPE
84181020	200L＜容积≤500L冷藏冷冻组合机	15	8	8	8	8	8	8				
84181030	容积≤200L冷藏－冷冻组合机	15	8	8	8	8	8	8				
84182110	容积＞150L压缩式家用型冷藏箱	10	8	8	8	8		8				
84182120	50L＜容积≤150L压缩式家用型冷藏箱	10	8	8	8	8		8				
84182130	容积≤50L压缩式家用型冷藏箱	10	8	8	8	8		8				
84182910	半导体制冷式家用型冷藏箱	30	12	12	12	12	12	12	12			
84182920	电气吸收式家用型冷藏箱	15	12	12	12	12	12	12	12			
84182990	其他家用型冷藏箱	30	12	12	12	12	12	12	12			
84183021	制冷温度＞－40℃,容积500－800L柜式冷冻箱	23	12	12	12	12	12	12				
84183029	制冷温度＞－40℃,容积≤500L柜式冷冻箱	30	12	12	12	12	12	12				
84184021	制冷温度＞－40℃,容积500－900L立式冷冻箱	15	8	8	8	8	10	8		8		
84184029	制冷温度＞－40℃,容积≤500L立式冷冻箱	30	12	12	12	12	12	12		12		
84185000	其他装有冷藏或冷冻装置的柜、箱、展示台	10	8	5	5	8	5	8	5	5		
84198100	加工热饮料、烹调、加热食品的机器	10	8	5	5	8	5	8	5	5		
84211920	固液分离机	10	8	5	5	8	5	8	5	5		
84211990	其他离心机	10	8	5	5	8	5	8	5	5		
84212300	内燃发动机的燃油过滤器	10		8	8	8	8	8	8	8		
84219910	家用型过滤、净化装置用零件	10	8	5	5	8	5	8	5	5		
84222000	瓶子及其他容器的洗涤或干燥机器	10	8	5	5	8	5	8	5	5		
84223090	其他装填密封等包封机器	10	8	5	5	8	5	8	5	5		
84239000	衡器用的各种砝码、秤砣及其零件	10	8	5	5	8	5	8	5	5		
84261120	通用桥式起重机	8	5	5		5	5	5		5		
84261190	其他固定支架的高架移动式起重机	8	5	5		5	5	5	5	5		
84261990	其他高架移动式起重机等	10	8	8		8	8	8	8	8		
84281090	其他升降机及倒卸式起重机	6	5	5	5	5	5	5		5		
84291110	功率＞235.36kw的履带式推土机	7	5	5		5	5	5	5	5		
84291190	功率≤235.36kw的履带式推土机	7	5	5		5	5	5	5	5		
84291910	功率＞235.36kw的其他推土机	7	5	5		5	5	5	5	5		
84291990	功率≤235.36kw的其他推土机	7	5	5		5	5	5	5	5		
84294011	机重≥18吨的震动式压路机	7	5	5		5	5	5	5	5		
84294019	其他机动压路机	8	5	5		5	5	5	5	5		
84294090	其他未列名捣固机械及压路机	6	5	5		5	5	5	5	5		
84295900	其他机械铲、挖掘机及机铲装载机	8	5	5		5	5	5	5	5		
84303100	自推进截煤机、采石机及掘进机	10	8	8		8	8	8	8	8		
84303900	其他非自推进截煤机、采石机及掘进机	6	5	5		5	5	5	5	5		
84305020	矿用电铲	7	5	5		5	5	5	5	5		
84306100	非自推进捣固或压实机械	6	5	5		5	5	5	5	5		
84306911	钻筒直径＞3m的工程钻机	6	5	5		5	5	5	5	5		
84306919	钻筒直径≤3m的工程钻机	6	5	5		5	5	5	5	5		
84306920	非自推进铲运机	6	5	5		5	5	5	5	5		
84306990	其他非自推进未列名机械	6	5	5		5	5	5	5	5		
84314100	戽斗、铲斗、抓斗及夹斗	6	5	5		5	5	5	5	5		
84314200	推土机或侧铲推土机用铲	6	5	5		5	5	5	5	5		
84361000	动物饲料配制机	7	5	5	5	5	5	5	5			
84386000	水果、坚果或蔬菜加工机器	10	8	5	5	8	5	8	5	5		
84433912	间接法静电感光复印设备	10	8	5	5	8	5	8	5	5		
84501110	干衣量≤10kg的波轮式全自动洗衣机	10	8	8	8	8		8				
84501120	干衣量≤10kg的滚筒式全自动洗衣机	10	8	8	8	8		8				

税则号列 Tariff No.	货品名称 Description of Goods	最惠国 MFN (%)	协定税率(%) Agreement									
			文莱 CAM	印尼 INA	马来西亚 MAS	缅甸 MMR	菲律宾 PHI	新加坡 SIN	泰国 THA	越南 VIE	老挝 LAO	柬埔寨 TPE
84501190	干衣量≤10kg 的其他全自动洗衣机	10	8	8	8	8		8				
84501200	装有离心甩干机的非全自动洗衣机	30	12	12	12	12	12	12				
84501900	干衣量≤10kg 的其他洗衣机	30	12	12	12	12	12	12		12		
84509090	干衣量>10kg 的洗衣机零件	16	8	8	8	8	8	8		8		
84512100	干衣量≤10kg 的干燥机	15	8	8	8	8	8	8	8			
84513000	熨烫机及挤压机(包括熔压机)	8		5	5		5		5	5		
84521010	多功能家用缝纫机	21	12	12	12	12	12	12	12			
84521090	其他家用型缝纫机	21	12	12	12	12	12	12	12			
84672100	电动钻	10	8	5	5	8	5	8	5	5		
84672290	其他电动锯	10	8	5	5	8	5	8	5	5		
84672910	电动砂磨工具	10	8	5	5	8	5	8	5	5		
84672990	其他电动工具	10	8	5	5	8	5	8	5	5		
84679910	其他手提式电动工具用零件	10	8	5	5	8	5	8	5	5		
84752919	其他玻璃热加工设备	10	8	5	5	8	5	8	5	5		
84831010	船舶用传动轴	6	5	5	5	5	5	5	5			
84831090	其他传动轴及曲柄	6	5	5	5	5	5	5	5			
84833000	未装滚珠或滚子轴承的轴承座	6	5	5	5	5	5	5	5			
84834010	滚子螺杆传动装置	8	5	5	5	5	5	5	5			
84834020	行星齿轮减速器	8	5	5	5	5	5	5	5			
84834090	其他齿轮及齿轮传动装置	8	5	5	5	5	5	5	5			
85011091	机座 20mm≤直径<39mm 微电机	9	8	8	8	8	8	8		8		
85011099	其他输出功率≤37.5W 微电机	9	5	5	5	5	5	5		5		
85012000	输出功率>37.5W 交直流两用电动机	12	8	8	8	8	8	8	10	8		
85013100	输出功率≤750 瓦直流电动机、发电机	12	8	8	8	8	8	8	10			
85013200	750W<输出功率≤75KW 直流电动机、发电机	10	8	5	5	8	5	8	5	5		
85014000	单相交流电动机	12	8	8	8	8	8	8	8			
85015200	输出功率>750W≤75KW 多相交流电动机	10	8	8	8	8	8	8		8		
85021100	输出功率≤75KVA 柴油发电机组	10	8	5	5	8	5	8	5	5		
85041010	电子镇流器	10	8	8	8	8	8	8		8		
85042100	额定容量≤650KVA 液体介质变压器	10.5	8	8	8	8	8	8		8		
85042200	650KVA<额定容量≤10MVA 液体介质变压器	12.6	8	8	8	8	8	8		8		
85042321	400MVA≤液体变压器额定容量<500MVA	6	5	5	5	5	5	5		5		
85042329	其他额定容量≥500MVA 液体变压器	6	5	5	5	5	5	5		5		
85043400	额定容量>500KVA 的其他变压器	14	8	8	8	8	8	8		8		
85044014	功率<1KW 高精度直流稳压电源	7	5	5	5	5	5	5		5		
85044020	不间断供电电源(UPS)	10	8	8	8	8	8	8		8		
85044091	具有变流功能的半导体模块	10	8	8	8	8	8	8		8		
85044099	其他未列名静止式变流器	10	8	8	8	8	8	8		8		
85061010	碱性锌锰电池	20	12	12	12	12	12	12				
85061090	二氧化锰的原电池及原电池组	20	12	12	12	12	12	12				
85068000	其他原电池及原电池组	14	8	8	8	8	8	8		8		
85069010	二氧化锰原电池或原电池组的零件	14		8	8	8	8	8	8	8		
85069090	其他原电池组或原电池组的零件	10		8	8	8	8	8	8	8		
85071000	起动活塞式发动机用铅酸蓄电池	10	8	5	5	8	5	8	5	5		
85072000	其他铅酸蓄电池	10	8	8	8	8	8	8				
85073000	镍镉蓄电池	10	8	8	8	8	8	8		8		
85074000	镍铁蓄电池	12	8	8	8	8	8	8		8		
85078010	镍氢电池	12	8	8	8	8	8	8		8		

税则号列 Tariff No.	货品名称 Description of Goods	最惠国 MFN (%)	协定税率(%)Agreement									
			文莱 CAM	印尼 INA	马来西亚 MAS	缅甸 MMR	菲律宾 PHI	新加坡 SIN	泰国 THA	越南 VIE	老挝 LAO	柬埔寨 TPE
85078020	锂离子电池	12	8	8	8	8	8	8		8		
85078090	其他蓄电池	12	8	8	8	8	8	8		8		
85079090	其他蓄电池零件	8	5	5	5	5	5	5		5		
85081100	功率不超过1500瓦,且带有容积不超过20升的电动真空吸尘器	10	8	8	8	8	8	8	8			
85087010	税号8508.1100所列电动真空吸尘器用零件	12	8	8	8	8	8	8		8		
85094010	水果或蔬菜榨汁机	10	8	8	8	8	8	8				
85094090	食品研磨机及搅拌器或果、菜榨汁器	10	8	8	8	8	8	8				
85098010	地板打蜡机	30	12	12	12	12	12	12	12			
85098090	其他家用电动器具	30	12	12	12	12	12	12	12			
85099000	家用电动器具的零件	12	8	8	8	8	8	8		8		
85111000	火花塞	10	8	5	5	8	5	8	5	5		
85113090	其他用途用分电器、点火线圈	8.4	5	5	5	5		5	5	5		
85114091	输出功率≥132.39千瓦启动电机	8.4	5	5	5	5		5	5	5		
85114099	其他用途的启动电机	8.4	5	5	5	5		5	5	5		
85115090	其他附属于内燃发动机的发电机	8.4	5	5	5	5		5	5	5		
85131010	手电筒	15		8	8	8	8	8		8		
85131090	其他自供能源手提式电灯	17.5		8	8	8	8	8		8		
85139010	手电筒零件	14	8	8	8	8	8	8		8		
85139090	其他自供能源手提式电灯零件	14	8	8	8	8	8	8		8		
85151100	钎焊机器及装置用烙铁及焊枪	10	8	5	5	8	5	8	5	5		
85161000	电热水器	10	8	8	8	8	8	8				
85164000	电熨斗	35	12	12	12	12	12	12				
85165000	微波炉	15	12	12	12	12	12	12				
85166010	电磁炉	15	12	12	12	12	12	12		12		
85166030	电饭锅	15	12	12	12	12	12	12		12		
85166040	电炒锅	15	12	12	12	12	12	12		12		
85166090	其他电热炉	15	12	12	12	12	12	12		12		
85167910	电热饮水机	32	12	12	12	12	12	12		12		
85167990	其他电热器具	32	12	12	12	12	12	12		12		
85177040	对讲机用的零件	8	5	5	5	5	5	5		5		
85181000	传声器(麦克风)及其座架	10	8	8	8	8	8	8	8			
85182100	单喇叭音箱	10	8	5	5	8	5	8	5	5		
85182200	多喇叭音箱	10	8	8	8	8	8	8	8			
85184000	音频扩大器	12	8	8	8	8	8	8	8			
85185000	电气扩音机组	10	8	5	5	8	5	8	5	5		
85198112	装有声音重放装置的盒式磁带型录音机	30	12		12	12	12	12	12	12		
85198121	不带录音功能的激光唱机	30	12	12	12	12	12	12	12			
85198129	使用光学媒体的其他声音录放装置	20	12	12	12	12	12	12	12			
85198990	其他声音录制或重放设备	20	12	12	12	12	12	12	12			
85219011	视频高密光盘机VCD	20	12	12	12	12	12	12	12			
85219012	数字化视频光盘机DVD	20	12	12	12	12	12	12	12			
85219019	其他激光视盘放像机	20	12	12	12	12	12	12	12			
85219090	其他视频信号录制或重放设备	20	12	12	12	12	12	12	12			
85258011	特种用途电视摄像机	10	8	5	5	8	5	8	5	5		
85258012	非特种用途的广播级电视摄像机	T2	[注]	[注]	[注]	[注]	[注]	[注]	[注]			
85258013	非特种用途的其他电视摄像机	T2	[注]	[注]	[注]	[注]	[注]	[注]	[注]			
85271200	不需外接电源袖珍盒式磁带收放机	20	12	12	12	12	12	12	12			

税则号列 Tariff No.	货品名称 Description of Goods	最惠国 MFN (%)	协定税率(%)Agreement									
			文莱 CAM	印尼 INA	马来西亚 MAS	缅甸 MMR	菲律宾 PHI	新加坡 SIN	泰国 THA	越南 VIE	老挝 LAO	柬埔寨 TPE
85271300	不需外接电源收录(放)音组合机	15	8	8	8	8	8	8	8			
85271900	不需外接电源无线电收音机	15	8		8	8	8	8	8	8		
85272100	需外接电源汽车收录(放)音组合机	15	8		8	8	8	8		8		
85279100	其他收录(放)音组合机	15	8		8	8	8	8	8	8		
85279900	其他收音机	27	12		12	12	12	12	12	12		
85284910	其他彩色阴极射线管监视器	30	12		12	12	12	12	12			
85284990	其他黑白或单色的阴极射线管监视器	19	12		12	12	12	12	12	12		
85285910	其他彩色监视器	30	12		12	12	12	12	12			
85285990	其他黑白或单色的监视器	19	12		12	12	12	12	12	12		
85286910	其他彩色投影机	30	12		12	12	12	12	12	12		
85286990	其他黑白或单色的投影机	15	8		8	8	8	8	8	8		
85287180	不带显示屏的其他彩色电视接收机	30	12				12	12				
85287190	不带显示屏的其他黑白或单色的电视接收机	15	8		8		8	8	8			
85287291	其他彩色模拟电视接收机	30	12				12	12				
85287292	其他彩色数字电视接收机	30	12				12	12				
85287299	其他彩色电视接收机	30	12				12	12				
85287300	其他黑白或单色的电视接收机	15	8		8		8	8	8			
85299041	特种用途电视摄像机、静像视频摄像机及其他视频摄录一体机,数字相机零件	8	5	5	5	5	5	5		5		
85299042	非特种用途的取像模块	12	8	8	8	8	8	8		8		
85299049	其他电视摄像机、静像视频摄像机及其他视频摄录一体机、数字相机零件	12	8	8	8	8	8	8		8		
85299060	收音机及其组合机的其他零件	15	8	8	8	8	8	8		8		
85299081	彩色电视机零件	15	8	8	8	8	8	8		8		
85299082	等离子显像组件及其零件	15	4	4	4	4	4	4		8		
85366100	电压≤1000V 的灯座	10	8	5	5	8	5	8	5	5		
85371090	其他电力控制或分配的装置	8.4		5	5	5	5	5		5		
85372010	电压≥500KV 高压开关装置	8.4	5	5	5	5	5	5		5		
85372090	其他电力控制或分配装置	8.4	5	5	5	5	5	5		5		
85381010	子目号 8537.2010 所列装置的零件	8.4	5	5	5	5	5	5		5		
85381090	税号 85.37 货品用的其他盘、板等	7	5	5	5	5	5	5		5		
85392110	科研、医疗专用卤钨灯	8	5	5	5	5	5	5	5			
85392120	火车、航空器及船舶用卤钨灯	8	5	5	5	5	5	5	5			
85392190	其他卤钨灯	10.5	8	8	8	8	8	8	8			
85392210	科研、医疗用功率≤200W 白炽灯泡	10.5		8	8	8	8	8	8			
85392920	火车、航空及船舶用其他白炽灯泡	10.5		8	8	8	8	8	8			
85392991	电压≤12V 未列名的白炽灯泡	12		8	8	8	8	8	8			
85392999	其他未列名的白炽灯泡	12		8	8	8	8	8	8			
85393110	科研、医疗专用热阴极荧光灯	8		5	5	5	5	5	5			
85393120	火车、航空器、船舶用热阴极荧光灯	8		5	5	5	5	5	5			
85393190	其他用途用热阴极荧光灯	8		5	5	5	5	5	5			
85393910	科研、医疗专用其他放电灯	8		5	5	5	5	5	5			
85393920	火车、航空器、船舶用其他放电灯	8		5	5	5	5	5	5			
85393990	其他用途的其他放电灯管	8		5	5	5	5	5	5			
85441100	铜制绕组电线	10	8	8	8	8	8	8		8		
85441900	其他绕组电线	20	12	12	12	12	12	12		12		
85442000	同轴电缆及其他同轴电导体	10		8		8	8	8		8		
85444921	1000V≥耐压>80V 无接头电缆	6	5	5		5	5	5	5			

税则号列 Tariff No.	货品名称 Description of Goods	最惠国 MFN (%)	协定税率(%)Agreement									
			文莱 CAM	印尼 INA	马来西亚 MAS	缅甸 MMR	菲律宾 PHI	新加坡 SIN	泰国 THA	越南 VIE	老挝 LAO	柬埔寨 TPE
85444929	1000V≥耐压>80V无接头电导体	12	8	8		8	8	8	8			
85446012	额定电压不超过35千伏的电缆	10		8		8	8	8		8		
85446013	额定电压超过35千伏,但不超过110千伏的电缆	8.4		5		5	5	5		5		
85446014	额定电压超过110千伏,但不超过220千伏的电缆	8.4		5		5	5	5		5		
85446019	其他额定电压超过1000伏的电缆	8.4		5		5	5	5		5		
85446090	耐压>1KV的其他电导体	21		12		12	12	12		12		
87011000	手扶拖拉机	9	5	5	5	5	5	5	5			
87031011	全地形车	25			12	12	12	12	12	12		
87031019	其他高尔夫球车及类似车辆	25			12	12	12	12	12	12		
87031090	雪地行走专用车	25			12	12	12	12	12	12		
87032335	2.5L<排气量≤3L的越野车	25						12				
87032336	2.5L<排气量≤3L,≤9座的小客车	25						12				
87032339	2.5L<排气量≤3L的其他车辆	25						12				
87033190	排气量≤1500ml的柴油型其他车辆	25						12				
87033330	排气量>2500ml柴油型的小轿车	25						12				
87033340	排气量>2500ml的柴油型越野车	25						12				
87033350	排气量>2.5L,≤9座的柴油型小客车	25						12				
87033390	排气量>2500ml的柴油型其他车辆	25						12				
87039000	装有压燃式内燃发动机的其他载人机动车辆	25						12	12			
87041030	非公路用电动轮货运自卸车	6				5	5	5	5	5		
87041090	其他非公路用货运自卸车	6				5	5	5	5	5		
87049000	装有其他发动机的货车	25				12		12	12			
87051021	最大起重重量≤50吨的全路面汽车起重车	15		8	8	8	8	8	8	8		
87051022	50吨<最大起重重量≤100吨的全路面汽车起重车	10		8	8	8	8	8	8	8		
87051023	最大起重重量>100吨的全路面汽车起重车	10		8	8	8	8	8	8	8		
87051091	最大起重重量≤50吨的其他汽车起重车	15		8	8	8	8	8	8	8		
87051092	50吨<最大起重重量≤100吨的其他汽车起重车	10		8	8	8	8	8	8	8		
87051093	最大起重重量>100吨的其他汽车起重车	10		8	8	8	8	8	8	8		
87052000	机动钻探车	12		8	8	8	8	8	8	8		
87054000	机动混凝土搅拌车	15		8	8	8	8	8	8	8		
87059010	无线电通信车	9		8	8	8	8	8	8	8		
87059020	机动放射线检查车	9		5	5	5	5	5	5	5		
87059030	机动环境监测车	12		8	8	8	8	8	8	8		
87059040	机动医疗车	12		8	8	8	8	8	8	8		
87059051	航空电源车(频率为400赫兹)	12		8	8	8	8	8	8	8		
87059059	其他机动电源车	12		8	8	8	8	8	8	8		
87059060	飞机加油车、调温车、除冰车	12		8	8	8	8	8	8	8		
87059070	道路(包括跑道)扫雪车	12		8	8	8	8	8	8	8		
87059080	石油测井车、压裂车、混沙车	12		8	8	8	8	8	8	8		
87059090	其他特殊用途的机动车辆	12		8	8	8	8	8	8	8		
87060010	非公路用货运自卸车底盘	8			5			5	5			
87060030	大型客车底盘	20			12		12	12	12			
87060040	汽车起重机底盘	20			12		12	12	12			
87081000	缓冲器(保险杠)及其零件	10	8		8	8		8	8	8		

税则号列 Tariff No.	货品名称 Description of Goods	最惠国 MFN (%)	协定税率(%) Agreement									
			文莱 CAM	印尼 INA	马来西亚 MAS	缅甸 MMR	菲律宾 PHI	新加坡 SIN	泰国 THA	越南 VIE	老挝 LAO	柬埔寨 TPE
87082100	座椅安全带	10	8	8	8	8		8	8	8		
87082941	汽车电动天窗	10	8		8	8		8	8	8		
87082942	汽车手动天窗	10	8		8	8		8	8	8		
87082951	侧围	10	8		8	8		8	8	8		
87082952	车门	10	8		8	8		8	8	8		
87082953	发动机罩盖	10	8		8	8		8	8	8		
87082954	前围	10	8		8	8		8	8	8		
87082955	行李箱盖(或背门)	10	8		8	8		8	8	8		
87082956	后围	10	8		8	8		8	8	8		
87082957	翼子板(或叶子板)	10	8		8	8		8	8	8		
87082959	车身的其他覆盖件	10	8		8	8		8	8	8		
87082990	车身的未列名零部件	10	8		8	8		8	8	8		
87083010	装在蹄片上的制动摩擦片	10	8	8	8	8		8		8		
87083021	牵引车、拖拉机、非公路自卸车用防抱死制动系统(ABS)	6	5		5	5		5		5		
87083091	牵引车、拖拉机用制动器及其零件	6	5		5	5		5		5		
87083093	非公路自卸车用制动器及其零件	6	5		5	5		5		5		
87083095	柴油型重型货车用制动器及其零件	10	8		8	8		8		8		
87083096	特种车用制动器及其零件	10	8		8	8		8		8		
87084010	牵引车、拖拉机用变速箱及零件	6	5		5	5		5	5	5		
87084030	非公路自卸车用变速箱及零件	6	5		5	5		5	5	5		
87084060	特种车用变速箱及零件	10	8		8	8		8	8	8		
87085071	牵引车、拖拉机用驱动桥及零件	6	5	5	5	5		5	5	5		
87085073	非公路自卸车用驱动桥及零件	6	5	5	5	5		5	5	5		
87085076	特种车用驱动桥及零件	10	8	8	8	8		8	8	8		
87085081	牵引车、拖拉机用非驱动桥及零件	6	5	5	5	5		5		5		
87085083	非公路自卸车用非驱动桥及零件	6	5	5	5	5		5		5		
87085084	柴、汽油轻货车用非驱动桥及零件	10	8	8	8	8		8		8		
87085085	柴油重型货车用非驱动桥及零件	10	8	8	8	8		8		8		
87085086	特种车用非驱动桥及其零件	10	8	8	8	8		8		8		
87087010	牵引车及拖拉机用车轮及其零附件	6	5		5	5		5	5	5		
87087020	大型客车用车轮及其零附件	10	8		8	8		8	8	8		
87087030	非公路货运自卸车用车轮及其零件	6	5		5	5		5	5	5		
87087040	中小型货车用车轮及其零件	10	8		8	8		8	8	8		
87087050	大型货车用车轮及其零件	10	8		8	8		8	8	8		
87087060	特种车用车轮及其零件	10	8		8	8		8	8	8		
87089100	机动车辆的散热器(水箱)及零件	10	8		8	8		8	8	8		
87089200	机动车辆的消声器及排气管及零件	10	8		8	8		8	8	8		
87089310	牵引车、拖拉机用离合器及其零件	6	5		5	5		5		5		
87089320	座位≥30 客车用离合器及其零件	10	8		8	8		8		8		
87089330	非公路自卸车用离合器及其零件	6	5		5	5		5		5		
87089340	柴、汽油轻型货车用离合器及零件	10	8		8	8		8		8		
87089350	总重≥14 吨柴油货车离合器及零件	10	8		8	8		8		8		
87089360	特种车用的离合器及其零件	10	8		8	8		8		8		
87089410	牵引车、拖拉机用转向盘、转向柱及转向器及零件	6	5	5	5	5		5		5		
87089420	大型客车用转向盘、转向柱及转向器及零件	10	8	8	8	8		8		8		
87089430	非公路自卸车用转向盘、转向柱及转向器及零件	6	5	5	5	5		5		5		

税则号列 Tariff No.	货品名称 Description of Goods	最惠国 MFN (%)	协定税率(%) Agreement									
			文莱 CAM	印尼 INA	马来西亚 MAS	缅甸 MMR	菲律宾 PHI	新加坡 SIN	泰国 THA	越南 VIE	老挝 LAO	柬埔寨 TPE
87089440	柴、汽油轻货车用转向盘、转向柱及转向器及零件	10	8	8	8	8		8		8		
87089450	柴油型重型货车用转向盘、转向柱及转向器及零件	10	8	8	8	8		8		8		
87089460	特种车用转向盘、转向柱及转向器及零件	10	8	8	8	8		8		8		
87089910	牵引车及拖拉机用其他零附件	6	5		5	5		5		5		
87089921	税号 8702.1091 及 8702.9010 所列车辆用车架	25	12		12	12	12	12		12		
87089929	大型客车用其他零附件	25	12		12	12	12	12		12		
87089931	税号 8704.1030 及 8704.1090 所列车辆用车架	6	5		5	5		5		5		
87089939	非公路货运自卸车用其他零附件	6	5		5	5		5		5		
87089941	税号 8704.2100、8704.2230、8704.3100 及 8704.3230 所列车辆用车架	25	12		12	12	12	12		12		
87089949	中小型货车用其他零附件	25	12		12	12	12	12		12		
87089951	税号 8704.2240、8704.2300 及 8704.3240 所列车辆用车架	10	8		8	8		8		8		
87089959	总重≥14 吨货车用其他零附件	10	8		8	8		8		8		
87089960	特种车用其他零附件	15	8		8	8	10	8		8		
87091910	短距离运输货物其他牵引车	10.5	8		8	8	8	8	8	8		
87091990	其他非电动短矩离运货车	10.5	8		8	8	8	8	8	8		
87111000	汽油型微马力摩托车及脚踏两用车	45				12		12				
87112010	装有往复式活塞发动机,气缸容量超过 50 毫升,但不超过 100 毫升的汽油型小马力摩托车及脚踏两用车	45				12		12				
87112020	装有往复式活塞发动机,气缸容量超过 100 毫升,但不超过 125 毫升的汽油型小马力摩托车及脚踏两用车	45				12		12				
87112030	装有往复式活塞发动机,气缸容量超过 125 毫升,但不超过 150 毫升的汽油型小马力摩托车及脚踏两用车	45				12		12				
87112040	装有往复式活塞发动机,气缸容量超过 150 毫升,但不超过 200 毫升的汽油型小马力摩托车及脚踏两用车	45				12		12				
87112050	装有往复式活塞发动机,气缸容量超过 200 毫升,但不超过 250 毫升的汽油型小马力摩托车及脚踏两用车	45				12		12				
87113010	汽油型中小马力摩托车及脚踏两用车	45				12		12		12		
87113020	汽油型中大马力摩托车及脚踏两用车	45				12		12		12		
87114000	汽油型大马力摩托车及脚踏两用车	40				12		12		12		
87115000	汽油型超大马力摩托车及类似车	30				12		12		12		
87119010	电动的或电动助力的摩托车(包括机器脚踏两用车)	45				12		12				
87119090	装有其他发动机的摩托车及边车	45				12		12				
87120020	竞赛型自行车	13			8	8	8	8	8			
87120030	山地自行车	13			8	8	8	8	8			
87120041	16、18、20 英寸自行车	13			8	8	8	8	8			
87120049	其他越野自行车	13			8	8	8	8	8			
87120081	≤16 英寸的未列名自行车	13			8	8	8	8	8			
87120089	其他未列名自行车	13			8	8	8	8	8			

税则号列 Tariff No.	货品名称 Description of Goods	最惠国 MFN （%）	协定税率（%）Agreement									
			文莱 CAM	印尼 INA	马来西亚 MAS	缅甸 MMR	菲律宾 PHI	新加坡 SIN	泰国 THA	越南 VIE	老挝 LAO	柬埔寨 TPE
87120090	其他非机动脚踏车	23			12	12	12	12	12			
87141100	摩托车及机动脚踏两用车用鞍座	30			12	12		12				
87141900	摩托车其他零附件	30			12	12		12				
87149100	非机动脚踏车车架、轮叉及其零件	12		10	8	8		8	8			
87149200	非机动脚踏车轮圈及辐条	12		10	8	8		8	8			
87149310	非机动脚踏车的轮毂	12		10	8	8	8	8	8			
87149320	飞轮	12		10	8	8	8	8	8			
87149390	其他非机动脚踏车的飞轮	12		10	8	8	8	8	8			
87149400	非机动脚踏车的制动器及其零件	12		10	8	8	8	8	8			
87149500	非机动脚踏车的鞍座	12		10	8	8	8	8	8			
87149610	非机动脚踏车脚蹬及其零件	12		10	8	8	8	8	8			
87149620	非机动脚踏车曲柄、链轮及其零件	12		10	8	8	8	8	8			
87149900	非机动脚踏车的其他零附件	12		10	8	8	10	8	8			
87161000	供居住或野营用厢式挂车及半挂车	10			8	8	8	8	8	8		
87163110	油罐挂车及半挂车	10		8	8	8	8	8	8	8		
87168000	其他未列名非机械驱动车辆	10			8	8	8	8	8	8		
87169000	挂车、半挂车及非机动车用零件	10		8	8	8	8	8	8	8		
90013000	隐形眼镜片	10	8	5	5	8	5	8	5	5		
90069191	照相机自动调焦组件	10	8	5	5	8	5	8	5	5		
90321000	恒温器	7	5	5	5	5	5	5		5		
91109010	未组装的完整的钟机芯	16	8	8	8	10	8	8	8	8		
91109090	不完整的钟机芯	16	8	8	8	10	8	8	8	8		
95066100	草地网球	12	8		8	8	8	8	8	8		
95066210	篮球、足球、排球	12	8		8	8	8	8	8	8		
95066290	其他可充气的球	12	8		8	8	8	8	8	8		
96071900	其他拉链	21	12	12	12	12	12	12	12			

注：税目 B5211011、85211019、85211020 的协定税率按“完税价格不高于 2000 美元/台：12%；完税价格高于 2000 美元/台：“3%，加 1458 元”执行；税目 85258012、85258013 的协定税率按“完税价格不高于 5000 美元/台：12%；完税价格高于 5000 美元/台：3%，加 3645”执行

附件4：

2007年关税配额商品税目、税率表

（2007年1月1日起实施）

说明：2007年在国家规定配额内的进口货物，按下表配额内的税率执行；超过配额数量的进口货物，执行税则当中的法定关税税率，即配额外税率。

Appendix 4:

In-Quota Interim Duty Rate on Imported Goods, 2007

(Enforced from January 1, 2007)

Explanation: During 2007, according to the state regulations, goods imported within quota, will be processed using the In-Quota Duty Rate Schedule below; goods imported exceeding the quota amount, will be processed using Statutory Tariff Rate in the Tariff Schedule, that is, Out-Quota Tariff Rate.

序号 No.	货品名称 Description of Goods	税则号列 Tariff No.	2007年进口税率(%) Import Duty Rate(%) 配额外税率 Out-Quota Duty Rate 最惠国税率 M. F. N.	普通税率 Gen.	配额内税率 In-Quota Duty Rate
1	小麦 Wheat	10011000	65	180	1
		10019010	65	180	1
		10019090	65	180	1
		11010000	65	130	6
		11031100	65	130	9
		11032010	65	180	10
2	玉米 Maize(Corn)	10051000	20	180	1
		10059000	65	180	1
		11022000	40	130	9
		11031300	65	130	9
		11042300	65	180	10
3	稻谷和大米 Rice, whether or not busked	10061011	65	180	1
		10061019	65	180	1
		10061091	65	180	1
		10061099	65	180	1
		10062010	65	180	1
		10062090	65	180	1
		10063010	65	180	1
		10063090	65	180	1
		10064010	65	180	1
		10064090	65	180	1
		11029011	40	130	9
		11029019	40	130	9
		11031921	10	70	9
		11031929	10	70	9
4	糖 Sugar	17011100	50	125	15
		17011200	50	125	15
		17019100	50	125	15
		17019910	50	125	15
		17019920	50	125	15
		17019990	50	125	15
5	羊毛 Wool	51011100	38	50	1
		51011900	38	50	1

序号 No.	货品名称 Description of Goods	税则号列 Tariff No.	2007年进口税率(%) Import Duty Rate(%)		
			配额外税率 Out-Quota Duty Rate		配额内税率 In-Quota Duty Rate
			最惠国税率 M. F. N.	普通税率 Gen.	
		51012100	38	50	1
		51012900	38	50	1
		51013000	38	50	1
		51031010	38	50	1
6	毛条 Wool Tops	51051000	38	50	3
		51052100	38	50	3
		51052900	38	50	3
7	棉花 Cotton	52010000	40【注1】	125	1
		52030000	40	125	1
8	化肥 Chemical Fertilizer	31021000	50	150	4【注2】
		31052000	50	150	4【注3】
		31053000	50	150	4【注4】

【注1】:

对配额外进口的一定数量棉花适用滑准税率,税率滑动范围为6% -40%,具体方式为:

1. 当进口棉花完税价格高于或等于11.397元/公斤时,暂定关税税率为6%;

2. 当进口棉花完税价格低于11.397元/公斤时,暂定关税税率按下式计算:

$$R_i = INT[(\frac{P_t}{P_i \times E} + \alpha \times P_i \times E - 1) \times 1000 + 0.5]/1000$$

($R_i \leqslant 40\%$)

关税税款 = $R_i \times P_i \times E$

其中:

R_i—暂定关税税率,当R_i按上式计算值高于40%时,取值40%;

P_t—常数,为8.8元/公斤;

P_i—关税完税价格,CIF价格,单位为"美元/公斤";

E—美元汇率;

α—常数,为2.526%;

INT—取整函数(即:小数点后面的数一律舍去)。

【注2、3、4】:

暂定税率为1%。

附件 5：

2007 年非全税目信息技术产品税率表

（2007 年 1 月 1 日起实施）

Appendix 5：

Duty Rate on Imported IT Goods（Incomplete），2007

（Enforced from January 1，2007）

ex	税则号列 Tariff No.	货　品　名　称	最惠国税率 MFN(%)	EX 项税率 EX rats(%)	Description of Goods
ex	70200019	用于插入熔化和氧化炉内以制备半导体晶片的石英反应管及夹持器	10.5	0	Quartz reactor tubes and holders designed for insertion into diffusion and oxidation furnaces for production of semiconductor wafers
ex	85044091	自动数据处理设备机器及组件、电讯设备用的具有变流功能的半导体模块	10	0	Semicondutor modules with converting function for automatic data processing machines and units thereof, and telecommunication apparatus
ex	85044099	自动数据处理设备机器及组件、电讯设备用的其他静止变流器；ITA 产品用的印刷电路组件，包括外接组件，如符合 PCMCIA 标准的卡	10	0	Other stastic converters for automatic data processing machines and units thereof, and telecommunication apparatus; Printed Circuit Assemblies for products falling within the ITA, including such assemblies for external connections such as cards that conform to the PCMCIA standard
ex	85176910	用于呼叫、提示和寻呼的便携式接收器	9	0	Portable receivers for calling, alerting or paging
ex	85181000	电讯用麦克风，频率范围在 300 赫兹到 3.4 千赫之间，直径不超过 10 毫米，高度不超过 3 毫米	10	0	Microphones having a frequency range of 300 Hz to 3,4 kHz with a diameter of not exceeding 10 mm and a height not exceeding 3 mm, for telecommunication use
ex	85184000	列入 ITA 的有线电话重复器用的电器扩音器	12	0	Electric amplifiers when used as repeaters in line telephony products falling within the ITA
ex	85189000	列入 ITA 的有线电话重复器用的电器扩音器的零件	10.5	0	Parts of electric amplifiers when used as repeaters in line telephony products falling within the ITA
ex	85291090	无线电话电报装置的天线	2	0	Aerials or antennae of a kind used with apparatus for radio-telephony and radio-telegraphy
ex	90309000	用于检测半导体晶片及器件的仪器的零件和附件；ITA 产品用的印刷电路组件，包括外接组件，如符合 PCMCIA 标准的卡	7	0	Parts and accessories of instruments and apparatus for measuring or checking semiconductor wafers or devices; Printed Circuit Assemblies for products falling within the ITA, including such assemblies for external connections such as cards that conform to the PCMCIA standard

附件 6：

Appendix 6：

2007 年进口商品消费税税率表

Consumption tax on Imported Goods 2007

税则号列 Tariff Item	货品名称	税率 Duty Rate	备注 Remarks
21069020	制造饮料用的复合酒精制品	5%	
22030000	麦芽酿造的啤酒	进口完税价格≥370 美元/吨的麦芽酿造啤酒，税率为 250 元/吨	1 千克 = 0.988 升
		进口完税价格<370 美元/吨的麦芽酿造啤酒，税率为 220 元/吨	
22041000	葡萄汽酒	10%	
22042100	小包装的鲜葡萄酿造的酒（小包装指装入两升及以下容器的）	10%	
22042900	其他包装鲜葡萄酿造的酒（其他包装指装入两升以上容器的）	10%	
22043000	其他酿酒葡萄汁（编号 2009 以外的）	10%	
22051000	小包装的味美思酒及类似酒（两升及以下容器包装，加植物或香料的用鲜葡萄酿造的酒）	10%	
22059000	其他包装的味美思酒及类似酒（两升以上容器包装，加植物或香料的用鲜葡萄酿造的酒）	10%	
22060000 01	黄酒	240 元/吨	1 千克 = 0.962 升
22060000 09	其他发酵饮料（未列名的发酵饮料混合物及发酵饮料与无酒精饮料的混合物）	10%	
22071000	酒精浓度在 80% 及以上的未改性乙醇	5%	
22072000 10	任何浓度的改性乙醇	5%	
22072000 90	任何浓度的其他酒精	5%	
22082000	蒸馏葡萄酒制得的烈性酒	20% +1 元/公斤	
22083000	威士忌酒	20% +1 元/公斤	
22084000	朗姆酒及蒸馏已发酵甘蔗产品制得的其他烈性酒	20% +1 元/公斤	
22085000	杜松子酒	20% +1 元/公斤	1 升 = 0.912 千克
22086000	伏特加酒	20% +1 元/公斤	
22087000	利口酒及柯迪尔酒	20% +1 元/公斤	
22089010	龙舌兰酒	20% +1 元/公斤	
22089090 01	酒精浓度在 80% 以下的未改性乙醇	5%	
22089090 21	含濒危野生动植物成分的薯类蒸馏酒	20% +1 元/公斤	
22089090 29	其他薯类蒸馏酒	20% +1 元/公斤	
22089090 91	含濒危野生动植物成分的其他蒸馏酒及酒精饮料	20% +1 元/公斤	1 升 = 0.912 千克
22089090 99	其他蒸馏酒及酒精饮料	20% +1 元/公斤	
24021000	烟草制的雪茄烟	40%	
24022000	烟草制的卷烟，每标准条进口消费税适用比例税率的价格≥50 元人民币	45% +150 元/标准箱	
	烟草制的卷烟，每标准条进口消费税适用比例税率的价格<50 元人民币	30% +150 元/标准箱	1 标准条 = 200 支； 1 标准箱 = 5 万支
24029000 01	烟草代用品制的卷烟，每标准条进口消费税适用比例税率的价格≥50 元人民币	45% +150 元/标准箱	
	烟草代用品制的卷烟，每标准条进口消费税适用比例税率的价格<50 元人民币	30% +150 元/标准箱	
24029000 09	烟草代用品制的雪茄烟	40%	
24031000	供吸用的烟草（不论是否含有任何比例的烟草代用品）	30%	
24039100 10	再造烟草	30%	

税则号列 Tariff Item	货品名称	税率 Duty Rate	备注 Remarks
24039100 90	均化烟草	30%	
24039900 90	其他烟草及烟草代用品的制品	30%	烟草精汁除外
27101110	车用汽油及航空汽油	0.2 元/升	1 千克 = 1.388 升
27101120	石脑油	0.2 元/升,减按 0.06 元/升征收	1 千克 = 1.385 升
27101130	橡胶溶剂油、油漆溶剂油、抽提溶剂油	0.2 元/升,减按 0.06 元/升征收	1 千克 = 1.282 升
27101911	航空煤油	0.1 元/升,暂缓征收	1 千克 = 1.246 升
27101921	轻柴油	0.1 元/升	1 千克 = 1.176 升
27101922	5 - 7 号燃料油	0.1 元/升,减按 0.03 元/升征收	1 千克 = 1.015 升
27101929 20	重柴油	0.1 元/升,减按 0.03 元/升征收	1 千克 = 1.015 升
27101929 90	其他柴油及燃料油	0.1 元/升,减按 0.03 元/升征收	1 千克 = 1.015 升蜡油:350℃以下镏出物体积百分比小于20%,550℃以下镏出物体积百分比大于80%
27101991	润滑油	0.2 元/升,减按 0.06 元/升征收	1 千克 = 1.126 升
33021090 01	生产食品、饮料用混合香料及制品(含以香料为基本成分的混合物,按容量计酒精浓度 >0.5%)	5%	
33030000	香水及花露水	30%	
33041000	唇用化妆品	30%	
33042000	眼用化妆品	30%	
33043000	指(趾)甲化妆品	30%	
33049100	香粉,不论是否压紧	30%	
33049900 91	其他含濒危植物成分美容化妆品	30%	不包括护肤品
33049900 99	其他美容化妆品	30%	
36041000	烟花,爆竹	15%	
40111000 90	机动小客车用新充气非子午线轮胎(橡胶轮胎,包括旅行小客车及赛车用)	3%	子午线轮胎是指在轮胎结构中,胎体帘子线按子午线方向排列,并有钢丝帘线排列几乎接近圆周方向的带束层束紧胎体的轮胎
40112000 19	断面宽度≥30 英寸的客或货车用新的非子午线充气橡胶轮胎	3%	
40112000 99	客或货车用新的其他非子午线充气橡胶轮胎	3%	
40114000	摩托车用新的充气橡胶轮胎	3%	
40116100 19	断面宽≥24 英寸人字形非子午线轮胎(新充气橡胶轮胎,含胎面类似人字形的,农林车辆机械用)	3%	
40116100 99	其他人字形胎面非子午线轮胎(新充气橡胶轮胎,含胎面类似人字形的,农林车辆机械用)	3%	
40116200 19	断面宽≥24 英寸人字形非子午线轮胎(建筑业,工业用,辋圈≤61cm,新充气橡胶胎,含类似人字形)	3%	
40116200 99	其他人字形胎面非子午线轮胎(建筑业,工业用,辋圈≤61cm,新充气橡胶胎,含类似人字形)	3%	

税则号列 Tariff Item	货品名称	税率 Duty Rate	备注 Remarks
40116300 19	断面宽≥24 英寸人字形非子午线轮胎(建筑业,工业用,辋圈>61cm,新充气橡胶胎,含类人字形)	3%	
40116300 99	其他人字形胎面非子午线轮胎(建筑业,工业用,辋圈>61cm,新充气橡胶胎,含类似人字形)	3%	
40116900 19	断面宽≥30 英寸人字形非子午线轮胎(其他用途,新充气橡胶轮胎,含胎面类似人字形的)	3%	
40116900 99	其他人字形胎面非子午线轮胎(其他用途,新充气橡胶轮胎,含胎面类似人字形的)	3%	
40119200 19	其他断面宽≥24 英寸非子午线轮胎(新充气橡胶轮胎,非人字形胎面,农林车辆机械用)	3%	
40119200 99	其他新的充气橡胶非子午线轮胎(新充气橡胶轮胎,非人字形胎面,农林车辆机械用)	3%	
40119300 19	其他断面宽≥24 英寸非子午线轮胎(建筑业,工业用,辋圈≤61cm,新充气橡胶胎,非人字形胎面)	3%	子午线轮胎是指在轮胎结构中,胎体帘子线按子午线方向排列,并有钢丝帘线排列几乎接近圆周方向的带束层束紧胎体的轮胎
40119300 99	其他新的充气橡胶非子午线轮胎(建筑业,工业用,辋圈≤61cm,新充气橡胶胎,非人字形胎面)	3%	
40119400 19	其他断面宽≥24 英寸非子午线轮胎(建筑业,工业用,辋圈>61cm,新充气橡胶胎,非人字形胎面)	3%	
40119400 99	其他新的充气橡胶非子午线轮胎(建筑业,工业用,辋圈>61cm,新充气橡胶胎,非人字形胎面)	3%	
40119900 19	其他断面宽≥30 英寸非子午线轮胎(其他用途,新充气橡胶轮胎,非人字形胎面)	3%	
40119900 99	其他新的充气橡胶非子午线轮胎(其他用途,新充气橡胶轮胎,非人字形胎面)	3%	
40122010 90	汽车用旧的充气橡胶非子午线轮胎	3%	
40122090 90	其他用旧的充气橡胶非子午线轮胎	3%	
40129020 90	汽车用实心或半实心非子午线轮胎(还包括可互换橡胶胎面及橡胶轮胎衬带)	3%	
40129090 90	其他用实心或半实心非子午线轮胎(还包括可互换橡胶胎面及橡胶轮胎衬带)	3%	
40131000	汽车用橡胶内胎[机动小客车(包括旅行小客车及赛车)、客运车或货运车用]	3%	
40139090	其他用橡胶内胎	3%	
44091010 10	一边或面制成连续形状的濒危针叶木制地板条、块(包括未装拼的拼花地板用板条及缘板)	5%	
44091010 90	一边或面制成连续形状的其他针叶木地板条,块(包括未装拼的拼花地板用板条及缘板)	5%	
44092910 10	一边或面制成连续形状的拉敏木地板条、块(包括未装拼的拉敏木拼花地板用板条及缘板)	5%	
44092910 20	一边或面制成连续形状的桃花心木地板条、块(包括未装拼的桃花心木拼花地板用板条及缘板)	5%	
44092910 30	一边或面制成连续形状的其他濒危木地板条、块(包括未装拼的其他濒危木拼花地板用板条及缘板)	5%	
44092910 90	一边或面制成连续形状的其他非针叶木地板条、块(包括未装拼的其他非针叶木拼花地板用板条及缘板)	5%	
44190031	木制一次性筷子	5%	
71011011	未分级的天然黑珍珠(不论是否加工,但未制成制品)	10%	

税则号列 Tariff Item	货品名称	税率 Duty Rate	备注 Remarks
71011019	其他未分级的天然珍珠(不论是否加工,但未制成制品)	10%	
71011091	其他天然黑珍珠(不论是否加工,但未制成制品)	10%	
71011099	其他天然珍珠(不论是否加工,但未制成制品)	10%	
71012110	未分级,未加工的养殖珍珠(未制成制品)	10%	
71012190	其他未加工的养殖珍珠(未制成制品)	10%	
71012210	未分级,已加工的养殖珍珠(未制成制品)	10%	
71012290	其他已加工的养殖珍珠(未制成制品)	10%	
71031000	未加工宝石或半宝石(经简单锯开或粗制成形,未成串或镶嵌)	10%	
71039100	经其他加工的红,蓝,绿宝石(未成串或镶嵌)	10%	
71039910	经其他加工的翡翠(未成串或镶嵌)	10%	
71039990	经其他加工的其他宝石或半宝石(未成串或镶嵌)	10%	
71042090	未加工合成或再造其他宝石半宝石(经简单锯开或粗制成形,未成串或镶嵌)	10%	
71049019 01	蓝宝石衬底,由人造刚玉加工而成,厚度<0.5mm	10%	
71049019 90	其他工业用合成或再造宝石半宝石(包括宝石或半宝石)	10%	
71049099	其他非工业用合成宝石或半宝石(未成串或镶嵌)	10%	
71059000	其他天然或合成宝石或半宝石粉末	10%	
71132090 10	镶嵌濒危物种制品以贱金属为底的包贵金属制首饰(包括零件)	10%	
71132090 90	其他以贱金属为底的包贵金属制首饰(包括零件)	10%	
71161000	天然或养殖珍珠制品	10%	
71162000	钻石其他宝石或半宝石制品(包括天然合成或再造)	10%	
87021092 01	20≤座≤23 装有压燃式活塞内燃发动机的客车	5%	
87021093	10≤座≤19 装有压燃式活塞内燃发动机的客车	5%	
87029020 01	20≤座≤23 装有非压燃式活塞内燃发动机的客车	5%	
87029030	10≤座≤19 装有非压燃式活塞内燃发动机的客车	5%	
87032130	排气量≤1 升的装有点燃往复式活塞内燃发动机的小轿车	3%	
87032190	排气量≤1 升的带点燃往复式活塞内燃发动机的其他车辆	3%	
87032230	1 升<排气量≤1.5 升的带点燃往复式活塞内燃发动机的小轿车	3%	
87032240	1 升<排气量≤1.5 升的带点燃往复式活塞内燃发动机的四轮驱动越野车	3%	
87032250	1 升<排气量≤1.5 升的带点燃往复式活塞内燃发动机的小客车(≤9 座)	3%	
87032290	1 升<排气量≤1.5 升的带点燃往复式活塞内燃发动机的其他车	3%	
87032314 01	1.5 升<排气量≤2 升的装点燃往复式活塞内燃发动机的小轿车	5%	
87032314 02	2 升<排气量≤2.5 升的装点燃往复式活塞内燃发动机的小轿车	9%	
87032315 01	1.5 升<排气量≤2 升的装点燃往复式活塞内燃发动机四轮驱动越野车	5%	
87032315 02	2 升<排气量≤2.5 升的装点燃往复式活塞内燃发动机四轮驱动越野车	9%	

税则号列 Tariff Item	货品名称	税率 Duty Rate	备注 Remarks
87032316 01	1.5 升<排气量≤2 升的装点燃往复式活塞内燃发动机小客车(指≤9 座)	5%	
87032316 02	2 升<排气量≤2.5 升的装点燃往复式活塞内燃发动机的小客车(指≤9 座)	9%	
87032319 01	1.5 升<排气量≤2 升的装点燃往复式活塞内燃发动机其他载人车辆	5%	
87032319 02	2 升<排气量≤2.5 升的装点燃往复式活塞内燃发动机其他载人车辆	9%	
87032334	2.5 升<排气量≤3 升的装点燃往复式活塞内燃发动机小轿车	12%	
87032335	2.5 升<排气量≤3 升的装点燃往复式活塞内燃发动机越野车	12%	
87032336	2.5 升<排气量≤3 升的装点燃往复式活塞内燃发动机旅行小客车(≤9 座)	12%	
87032339	2.5 升<排气量≤3 升的装点燃往复式活塞内燃发动机其他载人车(≤9 座)	12%	
87032430 01	3 升<排气量≤4 升的装有点燃往复式活塞内燃发动机小轿车	15%	
87032430 02	排气量>4 升的装有点燃往复式活塞内燃发动机小轿车	20%	
87032440 01	3 升<排气量≤4 升的装点燃往复式活塞内燃发动机越野车	15%	
87032440 02	排气量>4 升的装有点燃往复式活塞内燃发动机越野车	20%	
87032450 01	3 升<排气量≤4 升的装点燃往复式活塞内燃发动机的小客车(≤9 座)	15%	
87032450 02	排气量>4 升的装有点燃往复式活塞内燃发动机的小客车(≤9 座)	20%	
87032490 01	3 升<排气量≤4 升的装点燃往复式活塞内燃发动机的其他载人车辆	15%	
87032490 02	排气量>4 升的装点燃往复式活塞内燃发动机其他载人车辆	20%	
87033130	排气量≤1.5 升的装有压燃式活塞内燃发动机小轿车	3%	
87033140	排气量≤1.5 升的装有压燃式活塞内燃发动机越野车	3%	
87033150	排气量≤1.5 升的装有压燃式活塞内燃发动机小客车(≤9 座)	3%	
87033190	排气量≤1.5 升的装有压燃式活塞内燃发动机其他载人车	3%	
87033230 01	1.5 升<排气量≤2 升装有压燃式活塞内燃发动机小轿车	5%	
87033230 02	2 升<排气量≤2.5 升装有压燃式活塞内燃发动机小轿车	9%	
87033240 01	1.5 升<排气量≤2 升装有压燃式活塞内燃发动机四轮驱动越野车	5%	
87033240 02	2 升<排气量≤2.5 升装有压燃式活塞内燃发动机四轮驱动越野车	9%	
87033250 01	1.5 升<排气量≤2 升装有压燃式活塞内燃发动机小客车(指≤9 座)	5%	
87033250 02	2 升<排气量≤2.5 升装有压燃式活塞内燃发动机小客车(指≤9 座)	9%	

税则号列 Tariff Item	货品名称	税率 Duty Rate	备注 Remarks
87033290 01	1.5 升 < 排气量≤2 升的装有压燃式活塞内燃发动机其他载人车辆	5%	
87033290 02	2 升 < 排气量≤2.5 升的装有压燃式活塞内燃发动机其他载人车辆	9%	
87033330 01	2.5 升 < 排气量≤3 升装有压燃式活塞内燃发动机小轿车	12%	
87033330 02	3 升 < 排气量≤4 升装有压燃式活塞内燃发动机小轿车	15%	
87033330 03	排气量 >4 升装有压燃式活塞内燃发动机小轿车	20%	
87033340 01	2.5 升 < 排气量≤3 升装有压燃式活塞内燃发动机四轮驱动越野车	12%	
87033340 02	3 升 < 排气量≤4 升装压燃式活塞内燃发动机四轮驱动越野车燃发动机)	15%	
87033340 03	排气量 >4 升装压燃式活塞内燃发动机四轮驱动越野车	20%	
87033350 01	2.5 升 < 排气量≤3 升装压燃式活塞内燃发动机的小客车(≤9 座)	12%	
87033350 02	3 升 < 排气量≤4 升装有压燃式活塞内燃发动机的小客车(≤9 座)	15%	
87033350 03	排气量 >4 升装有压燃式活塞内燃发动机的小客车(≤9 座)	20%	
87033390 01	2.5 升 < 排气量≤3 升的装有压燃式活塞内燃发动机的其他载人车辆	12%	
87033390 02	3 升 < 排气量≤4 升的装有压燃式活塞内燃发动机的其他载人车辆	15%	
87033390 03	排气量 >4 升的装有压燃式活塞内燃发动机的其他载人车辆	20%	
87039000 01	其他型排气量≤1.5 升的其他载人车辆	3%	
87039000 02	其他型 1.5 升 < 排气量≤2 升的其他载人车辆	5%	
87039000 03	其他型 2 升 < 排气量≤2.5 升的其他载人车辆	9%	
87039000 04	其他型 2.5 升 < 排气量≤3 升的其他载人车辆	12%	
87039000 05	其他型 3 升 < 排气量≤4 升的其他载人车辆	15%	
87039000 06	其他型 4 升 < 排气量的其他载人车辆	20%	
87111000 10	微马力摩托车及脚踏两用车(装有往复式活塞发动机,微马力指排气量 =50cc)	3%	
87111000 90	微马力摩托车及脚踏两用车(装有往复式活塞发动机,微马力指排气量 <50cc)	3%	
87112010	50 毫升 < 排气量≤100 毫升的装往复式活塞内燃发动机摩托车及脚踏两用车	3%	
87112020	100 毫升 < 排气量≤125 毫升的装有往复式活塞内燃发动机摩托车及脚踏两用车	3%	
87112030	125 毫升 < 排气量≤150 毫升的装有往复式活塞内燃发动机摩托车及脚踏两用车	3%	
87112040	150 毫升 < 排气量≤200 毫升的装有往复式活塞内燃发动机摩托车及脚踏两用车	3%	
87112050	200 毫升 < 排气量≤250 毫升的装有往复式活塞内燃发动机摩托车及脚踏两用车	3%	
87113010	250 毫升 < 排气量≤400 毫升的装有往复式活塞内燃发动机摩托车及脚踏两用车	10%	

<table>
<tr><th>税则号列
Tariff Item</th><th>货品名称</th><th>税率
Duty Rate</th><th>备注
Remarks</th></tr>
<tr><td>87113020</td><td>400 毫升＜排气量≤500 毫升的装有往复式活塞内燃发动机摩托车及脚踏两用车</td><td>10%</td><td></td></tr>
<tr><td>87114000</td><td>500 毫升＜排气量≤800 毫升的装有往复式活塞内燃发动机摩托车及脚踏两用车</td><td>10%</td><td></td></tr>
<tr><td>87115000</td><td>排气量＞800 毫升的装有往复式活塞内燃发动机摩托车及脚踏两用车</td><td>10%</td><td></td></tr>
<tr><td>87119090 01</td><td>排汽量≤250 毫升摩拖车及脚踏两用车</td><td>3%</td><td></td></tr>
<tr><td>87119090 02</td><td>排汽量＞250 毫升摩托车及脚踏两用车</td><td>10%</td><td></td></tr>
<tr><td>87119090 09</td><td>其他无法区分排汽量的摩托车及脚踏两用车</td><td>3%</td><td></td></tr>
<tr><td>89039100 01</td><td>8 米＜长度＜90 米的机动帆船（不论是否装有辅助发动机）</td><td>10%</td><td></td></tr>
<tr><td>89039200 01</td><td>8 米＜长度＜90 米的汽艇（装有舷外发动机的除外）</td><td>10%</td><td></td></tr>
<tr><td>89039900 01</td><td>8 米＜长度＜90 米的娱乐或运动用其他机动船舶或快艇（包括划艇及轻舟）</td><td>10%</td><td></td></tr>
<tr><td>91011100</td><td>机械指示式的贵金属电子手表（表壳用贵金属或包贵金属制成的）</td><td>20%</td><td rowspan="14">上述税号中每块进口关税完税价格在10000 元人民币以上的手表</td></tr>
<tr><td>91011910</td><td>光电显示式的贵金属电子手表（表壳用贵金属或包贵金属制成的）</td><td>20%</td></tr>
<tr><td>91011990</td><td>其他贵金属电子手表（表壳用贵金属或包贵金属制成的）</td><td>20%</td></tr>
<tr><td>91012100 10</td><td>含濒危动物皮自动上弦贵金属机械手表（表壳用贵金属或包贵金属制成的）</td><td>20%</td></tr>
<tr><td>91012100 90</td><td>其他自动上弦贵金属机械手表（表壳用贵金属或包贵金属制成的）</td><td>20%</td></tr>
<tr><td>91012900 10</td><td>含濒危动物皮非自动上弦贵金属机械手表（表壳用贵金属或包贵金属制成的）</td><td>20%</td></tr>
<tr><td>91012900 90</td><td>其他非自动上弦贵金属机械手表（表壳用贵金属或包贵金属制成的）</td><td>20%</td></tr>
<tr><td>91021100</td><td>机械指示式的其他电子手表（用贵金属或包贵金属制壳的除外）</td><td>20%</td></tr>
<tr><td>91021200</td><td>光电显示式的其他电子手表（用贵金属或包贵金属制壳的除外）</td><td>20%</td></tr>
<tr><td>91021900</td><td>其他电子手表（用贵金属或包贵金属制壳的除外）</td><td>20%</td></tr>
<tr><td>91022100 10</td><td>含濒危动物皮其他自动上弦的机械手表（用贵金属或包贵金属制壳的除外）</td><td>20%</td></tr>
<tr><td>91022100 90</td><td>其他自动上弦的机械手表（用贵金属或包贵金属制壳的除外）</td><td>20%</td></tr>
<tr><td>91022900 10</td><td>含濒危动物皮其他非自动上弦机械手表（用贵金属或包贵金属制壳的除外）</td><td>20%</td></tr>
<tr><td>91022900 90</td><td>其他非自动上弦的机械手表（表壳用贵金属或包贵金属制成的）</td><td>20%</td></tr>
<tr><td>95063100</td><td>完整的高尔夫球棍</td><td>10%</td><td></td></tr>
<tr><td>95063200</td><td>高尔夫球</td><td>10%</td><td></td></tr>
</table>

注：电动汽车及其他无法区分排气量的载人车辆不征收消费税

附件7：

内地与香港/澳门更紧密经贸关系安排已完成原产地标准核准商品税目、税率表

Appendix 7：

Tax Item and Tax Rates Table of Commodities Passing Place of Origin Standard Examinations for Main Hand – HongKong/Macou More Closer Economic Rlationship

税则号列 Tariff No.	货品名称 Description of Goods	最惠国 MFN	香港 H. K	澳门 MAC
03011000	观赏鱼	17.5	0	
03019490	其他活蓝鳍金枪鱼	10.5	0	
03019590	其他活南方蓝鳍金枪鱼	10.5	0	
03019991	活罗非鱼	10.5	0	
03019992	活鲀	10.5	0	
03019999	其他活鱼	10.5	0	
03023200	鲜、冷黄鳍金枪鱼	12	0	
03026500	鲜、冷角鲨及其他鲨鱼	12	0	
03026600	鲜冷鳗鱼	12	0	
03026700	鲜、冷剑鱼	12	0	
03026800	鲜、冷南极犬牙鱼	12	0	
03026910	鲜冷带鱼	12	0	
03026920	鲜冷黄鱼	12	0	
03026930	鲜冷鲳鱼	12	0	
03026950	鲜、冷鲀	12	0	
03026990	其他鲜、冷鱼	12	0	
03033110	冻格陵兰庸鲽鱼	10	0	
03033190	冻庸鲽鱼	10	0	
03034400	冻大眼金枪鱼，但鱼肝及鱼卵除外	12	0	
03036100	冻剑鱼，但鱼肝及鱼卵除外	10	0	
03036200	冻南极犬牙鱼，但鱼肝及鱼卵除外	10	0	
03037600	冻鳗鱼	12	0	
03037700	冻尖吻鲈鱼	12	0	
03037910	冻带鱼	10	0	
03037920	冻黄鱼	10	0	
03037930	冻鲳鱼	10	0	
03037990	其他未列名冻鱼	10	0	
03041100	鲜、冷剑鱼片及鱼肉	12	0	
03041200	鲜、冷南极犬牙鱼片及鱼肉	12	0	
03041900	其他鲜、冷的鱼片及鱼肉	12	0	
03042100	冻剑鱼片	10	0	
03042200	冻南极犬牙鱼片	10	0	
03042910	冻罗非鱼片	10	0	
03042921	冻斑点叉尾鮰鱼片	10	0	
03042929	冻其他叉尾鮰鱼鱼片	10	0	
03042990	其他冻鱼片	10	0	
03053000	干或盐制的鱼片	10	0	
03055920	干鱼翅	15		0
03055990	其他干鱼	16	0	
03056910	盐腌及盐渍的带鱼	16	0	
03056920	盐腌及盐渍的黄鱼	16	0	
03056930	盐腌及盐渍的鲳鱼	16	0	
03056940	盐腌及盐渍的罗非鱼	16	0	
03056990	盐腌及盐渍的其他鱼	16	0	
03061311	冻小虾仁	8	0	
03061312	冻北方长额虾	5	0	
03061319	其他冻小虾	5	0	
03061321	冻对虾仁	8	0	
03061329	其他冻对虾	5	0	
03062190	未冻的龙虾	15	0	
03062290	其他未冻的大螯虾	15	0	
03062391	鲜、冷对虾	15	0	
03062399	其他未冻小虾及对虾	12	0	
03062492	未冻的梭子蟹	14	0	
03062499	未冻的其他蟹	14	0	
03062990	其他带壳或去壳的未冻的甲壳动物	14	0	
03071090	其他牡蛎（蚝）	14	0	
03072190	其他活、鲜、冷扇贝	14	0	
03073190	其他活、鲜、冷贻贝	14	0	
03074190	其他活、鲜或冷墨鱼及鱿鱼	12	0	
03074900	其他冻、干、盐制的墨鱼及鱿鱼	12	0	
03075100	活、鲜、冷章鱼	17	0	
03075900	其他冻、干、盐制的章鱼	17	0	
03079191	活、鲜、冷鲍鱼	14	0	
03079192	活、鲜或冷的沙蚕	14	0	
03079193	活、鲜或冷的蛤	14	0	
03079199	其他活、鲜、冷软体动物、水生无脊椎动物	14	0	
03079910	冻、干、盐腌或盐渍的鲍鱼	10	0	
04012000	脂肪含量在1－6%未浓缩及未加糖的乳及奶油	15	0	
04021000	脂肪含量≤1.5%固状乳及奶油	10	0	
04022100	脂肪量>1.5%未加糖固状乳及奶油	10	0	
04022900	脂肪量>1.5%的加糖固状乳及奶油	10	0	
04029100	浓缩但未加糖的非固状乳及奶油	10	0	
04031000	酸乳	10	0	
04039000	酪乳及其他发酵或酸化的乳及奶油	20	0	
04061000	鲜乳酪（未熟化或未固化的）	12	0	
04089900	其他去壳禽蛋	20	0	
04100010	燕窝	25	0	0
05069090	其他骨及角柱	12		0
05080010	珊瑚及水产品壳、骨的粉末及废料	12	0	
05080090	珊瑚及介、贝、棘皮动物的壳、骨	12	0	
09012100	未浸除咖啡碱的已焙炒咖啡	15	0	0
09012200	已浸除咖啡碱的已焙炒咖啡	15		0
09019020	含咖啡的咖啡代用品	30		0
09023010	每件净重≤3kg的乌龙茶	15	0	
09023020	每件净重≤3kg的普洱茶	15	0	

税则号列 Tariff No.	货品名称 Description of Goods	最惠国 MFN	香港 H. K	澳门 MAC
09023090	每件净重≤3kg 的其他发酵、半发酵红茶	15	0	
09024010	每件净重＞3kg 的乌龙茶	15	0	
09024020	每件净重＞3kg 的普洱茶	15	0	
09024090	每件净重＞3kg 的其他红茶(已发酵)及半发酵茶	15	0	
09041200	已磨胡椒	20	0	
09042010	辣椒干	20	0	
09042020	辣椒粉	20	0	
09062000	已磨肉桂及肉桂花	15	0	
09103000	姜黄	15	0	
09109100	混合调味香料	15	0	
09109900	其他调味香料	15	0	
12112010	鲜或干的西洋参	7.5	0	0
12112091	其他鲜人参	20	0	
12112099	其他干人参	20	0	
15010000	猪脂肪及家禽脂肪	10	0	
15179000	混合制成的食用油脂或制品	25	0	
16023291	鸡胸肉	15	0	
16023292	鸡腿肉	15	0	
16023299	其他鸡肉	15	0	
16023991	鸭肉	15	0	
16024990	制作或保藏的其他猪肉、杂碎及血	15	0	
16025090	其他制作或保藏的牛肉、杂碎及血	12	0	
16030000	肉及水产品的精、汁	23	0	
16041400	制作或保藏的金枪鱼、鲣鱼,整条或切块,但未绞碎	5	0	
16041910	制作或保藏的(河)鳗鱼,整条或切块,但未绞碎	12	0	
16041920	制作或保藏的罗非鱼,整条或切块,但未绞碎	12	0	
16041931	制作或保藏的斑点叉尾鮰鱼	12	0	
16041939	制作或保藏的其他叉尾鮰鱼	12	0	
16041990	制作或保藏的其他鱼,整条或切块,但未绞碎	12	0	
16042011	鱼翅罐头	12	0	0
16042019	其他制作或保藏的鱼罐头	12	0	
16042091	鱼翅	12	0	0
16042099	其他制作或保藏的鱼	12	0	
16051000	制作或保藏的蟹	5	0	
16052000	制作或保藏的小虾及对虾	5	0	
16053000	制作或保藏的龙虾	5	0	
16059010	制作或保藏的海蜇	15	0	
16059020	制作或保藏的蛤	5	0	
16059090	其他制作或保藏的软体动物及其他水生无脊椎动物	5	0	
17029000	其他固体糖;人造蜜;焦糖	30	0	
17049000	其他不含可可的糖食	10	0	0
18062000	每件净重＞2kg 的含可可食品	10	0	
18063100	其他夹心块状或条状的含可可食品	8	0	
18063200	其他不夹心块状或条状含可可食品	10	0	
18069000	其他巧克力及含可可的食品	8	0	
19012000	供焙烘面包糕点用的调制品及面团	25	0	0
19019000	其他麦精制的其他税号未列名食品	10	0	0
19021100	未包馅或未制作的含蛋生面食	15		0
19021900	其他未包馅或未制作的生面食	15	0	0
19022000	包馅面食	15	0	
19023010	米粉干	15		0
19023030	即食或快熟面条	15	0	0
19023090	其他面食	15		0
19053100	甜饼干	15	0	0
19053200	华夫饼干及圣餐饼	15	0	0
19054000	面包干、吐司及类似的烤面包	20		0
19059000	其他面包、糕点、饼干及其焙烘糕饼	20	0	0
20055110	非用醋制作的脱荚豇豆及菜豆罐头	25	0	
20055190	非用醋制作的其他脱荚豇豆及菜豆	25	0	
20060010	蜜枣	30	0	
20060020	糖渍制橄榄	30	0	
20060090	其他糖渍蔬菜、水果、坚果、果皮	30	0	
20081110	花生米罐头	30	0	
20081120	烘焙花生	30	0	
20081190	其他非用醋制作的花生	30	0	
20081910	核桃仁罐头	20	0	
20081920	其他果仁罐头	13	0	
20081991	栗仁	10	0	
20081992	用其他方法制作或保藏的芝麻	10	0	0
20081999	其他坚果及子仁	10	0	0
20089910	荔枝罐头	20	0	
20089920	龙眼罐头	15	0	
20089990	未列名制作或保藏的水果、坚果	15	0	0
20091100	冷冻的橙汁	7.5	0	
20091200	非冷冻的,白利糖度值不超过 20 的橙汁	30	0	
20092100	白利糖度值不超过 20 的葡萄柚(包括柚)汁	15	0	
20093110	白利糖度不超过 20 的柠檬汁	18	0	
20093190	其他未混合的白利糖度值不超过 20 的桔汁属水果汁	18	0	
20094100	白利糖度值不超过 20 的菠萝汁	10	0	

税则号列 Tariff No.	货品名称 Description of Goods	最惠国 MFN	香港 H. K	澳门 MAC
20096100	白利糖度值不超过20的葡萄汁，包括酿酒葡萄汁	20	0	
20097100	白利糖度值不超过20的苹果汁	20	0	
20098011	椰子汁	10	0	
20098012	芒果汁	20	0	
20098013	西番莲果汁	20	0	
20098014	番石榴果汁	20	0	
20098019	其他未混合的水果汁	20	0	
20098020	其他未混合的蔬菜汁	20	0	
20099010	混合水果汁	20	0	
20099090	混合蔬菜汁、水果与蔬菜的混合汁	20	0	
21011100	咖啡浓缩精汁	17	0	0
21011200	以咖啡浓缩精汁或咖啡为基本成分的制品	30	0	
21012000	茶、马黛茶浓缩精汁及其制品	32	0	
21021000	活性酵母	25	0	
21031000	酱油	28	0	
21032000	番茄沙司及其他番茄调味汁	15	0	
21039010	味精	21	0	
21039020	别特油(Aromatic bitters)	21	0	
21039090	其他调味品	21	0	0
21041000	汤料及其制品	15	0	
21050000	冰淇淋及其他冰制食品不论是否含可可	19	0	0
21061000	浓缩蛋白质及人造蛋白物质	10		0
21069010	制造碳酸饮料的浓缩物	35	0	0
21069020	制造饮料用的复合酒精制品	20	0	0
21069030	蜂王浆制剂	3	0	
21069091	烤制紫菜	20	0	0
21069099	其他编号未列名的食品	20	0	0
22011010	未加糖及未加味的矿泉水	20	0	0
22019010	天然水	10	0	0
22019090	其他水、冰及雪	10	0	
22021000	加味、加糖或其他甜物质的水	20	0	
22029000	其他无酒精饮料	35	0	
22060000	其他发酵饮料	46.8	0	0
22071000	浓度≥80%的未改性乙醇	40		0
22089090	其他蒸馏酒及酒精饮料	10		0
22090000	醋及醋酸制得的醋代用品	20	0	
23011020	油渣	5	0	
23012010	饲料用鱼粉	2	0	
23012090	其他不适于供人食用的水产品渣粉	5	0	
23025000	豆类植物糠、麸及其他残渣	5	0	
23099010	制成的饲料添加剂	5	0	
23099090	其他配制的动物饲料	6.5	0	
25201000	生石膏；硬石膏	5	0	

税则号列 Tariff No.	货品名称 Description of Goods	最惠国 MFN	香港 H. K	澳门 MAC
25210000	石灰石助熔剂；通常用于制造石灰或水泥的石灰石及其他钙质石	5	0	
25231000	水泥熟料，不论是否着色	8	0	
25232900	其他硅酸盐水泥，不论是否着色	8	0	0
26219000	其他矿渣及矿灰	4	0	
27101929	其他柴油及其他燃料油	6		0
27101991	润滑油	6	0	0
28041000	氢	5.5	0	
28042100	氩	5.5	0	
28042900	其他稀有气体	5.5	0	
28043000	氮	5.5	0	
28044000	氧	5.5	0	
28112100	二氧化碳	5.5	0	
28112900	其他非金属无机氧化物	5.5	0	
28421000	硅酸复盐及硅酸络盐(包括不论是否已有化学定义的硅铝酸盐)	5.5	0	
28432100	硝酸银	5.5	0	
28432900	其他银化合物，不论是否已有化学定义	5.5	0	
28433000	金化合物，不论是否已有化学定义	5.5	0	
28439000	其他贵金属化合物，不论是否已有化学定义；贵金属汞齐	5.5	0	
28500000	氢化物、氮化物、迭氮化物、硅化物及硼化物，不论是否已有化学定义	5.5	0	
28520000	汞的有机或无机化合物，汞齐除外	5.5	0	
28530010	饮用蒸馏水	5.5	0	0
28530090	其他无机化合物、液态空气、压缩空气，汞齐，但贵金属汞齐除外	5.5	0	
29033100	1,2－二溴乙烷(ISO)	5.5	0	
29033990	其他无环烃的氟化、溴化或碘化衍生物	5.5	0	
29041000	仅含磺基的衍生物及其盐和乙酯	5.5	0	
29094300	乙二醇或二甘醇的单丁醚	5.5		0
29141200	丁酮	5.5		0
29161500	油酸、亚油酸或亚麻酸及其盐和酯	6.5	0	
29224220	谷氨酸钠	10	0	
29270000	重氮化合物、偶氮化合物及氧化偶氮化合物	6.5		0
29336910	三聚氰氯	6		0
29336921	二氯异氰脲酸	6.5		0
29336922	三氯异氰脲酸	6.5		0
29336929	其他异氰脲酸氯化衍生物	6.5		0
29336990	其他结构上含非稠合三嗪环化合物(不论是否氢化)	6.5		0

税则号列 Tariff No.	货品名称 Description of Goods	最惠国 MFN	香港 H. K	澳门 MAC
29413011	四环素	4		0
29413012	四环素盐	4		0
29413020	四环素衍生物及其盐	4		0
29415000	红霉素及其衍生物,及它们的盐	4		0
30029090	人血;治病、防病或诊断用动物血制品;其他毒素、培养微生物(不包括酵母)及类似产品	3	0	
30039010	含磺胺类的混合药品(两种或两种以上成分混合而成的,治病或防病用未配定剂量或非零售包装)	6		0
30039020	含有青蒿素及其衍生物药品	5		0
30039090	含其他成份混合药品(两种或两种以上成分混合而成的,治病或防病用未配定剂量或非零售包装)	5		0
30041011	氨苄青霉素制剂(混合,治病或防病用,已配定剂量或制成零售包装)	6	0	0
30041012	羟氨苄青霉素制剂(两种或两种以上成分混合而成的,治病或防病用,已配定剂量或制成零售包装)	6	0	0
30041013	青霉素 V 制剂(两种或两种以上成分混合而成的,治病或防病用,已配定剂量或制成零售包装)	6	0	0
30041019	其他青霉素制剂(混合或非混合,治病或防病用,已配定剂量或制成零售包装)	6	0	0
30041090	含有其他青霉素及具有青霉烷酸结构的青霉素衍生物或链霉素及其衍生物的药品(混合或非混合,治病或防病用,已配定剂量或制成零售包装)	6	0	0
30042011	头孢噻肟制剂(混合或非混合,治病或防病用已配定剂量或制成零售包装)	6	0	
30042012	头孢他啶制剂(混合或非混合,治病或防病用,已配定剂量或制成零售包装)	6	0	
30042013	头孢西丁制剂(混合或非混合,治病或防病用,已配定剂量或制成零售包装)	6	0	
30042014	头孢替唑制剂(混合或非混合,治病或防病用,已配定剂量或制成零售包装)	6	0	
30042015	头孢克罗制剂(混合或非混合,治病或防病用,已配定剂量或制成零售包装)	6	0	
30042016	头孢呋辛制剂(混合或非混合,治病或防病用,已配定剂量或制成零售包装)	6	0	
30042017	头孢三嗪(头孢曲松)制剂(混合或非混合,治病或防病用,已配定剂量或制成零售包装)	6	0	
30042018	头孢哌酮制剂(混合或非混合,治病或防病用,已配定剂量或制成零售包装)	6	0	
30042019	含有其他头孢菌素制剂(混合或非混合,治病或防病用,已配定剂量或制成零售包装)	6	0	
30042090	含有其他抗菌素的药品(混合或非混合,治病或防病用,已配定剂量或制成零售包装)	6	0	0
30043200	含肾上腺皮混合或非混合质激素但不含抗菌素的药品(治病或防病用已配定剂量或零售包装)	5	0	
30043900	含有税目 29.37 其他产品但不含抗菌素的药品(混合或非混合,治病或防病用已配定剂量或零售包装)	5	0	
30044010	含有奎宁或其盐,但不含抗菌素及税目 29.37 的产品的药品(混合或非混合,治病或防病用已配定剂量或零售包装)	5	0	
30044090	含有其他生物碱及其衍生物,但不含抗菌素及税目 29.37 的产品的药品(混合或非混合,治病或防病用已配定剂量或零售包装)	5	0	
30045000	含有维生素或税目 29.36 其他产品的其他药品(混合或非混合,治病或防病用已配定剂量或零售包装)	6		0
30049051	中药酒(混合或非混合,治病或防病用已配定剂量或零售包装)	3	0	0
30049052	片仔癀(混合或非混合,治病或防病用已配定剂量或零售包装)	3	0	
30049053	白药(混合或非混合,治病或防病用已配定剂量或零售包装)	3	0	
30049054	清凉油(混合或非混合,治病或防病用已配定剂量或零售包装)	3	0	0
30049059	其他中式成药(混合或非混合,治病或防病用已配定剂量或零售包装)	3	0	0
30049060	含有青蒿素及其衍生物的中成药	4	0	0
30049090	其他药品(混合或非混合,治病或防病用已配定剂量或零售包装)	4	0	0
30059010	药棉、纱布、绷带(经药物浸涂或制定零售包装供医疗、外科、牙科或兽医用)	5	0	
30059090	其他医用软填料及类似物品(经药物浸涂或制定零售包装供医疗、外科、牙科或兽医用)	5	0	

税则号列 Tariff No.	货品名称 Description of Goods	最惠国 MFN	香港 H. K	澳门 MAC
30061000	无菌外科肠线;无菌昆布、无菌粘合胶布、无菌吸收性止血材料、外科或牙科用无菌抗粘连阻隔材料及类似无菌材料	5	0	0
30067000	专用于人类或作兽药用的凝胶制品,作为外科手术或体检时躯体部位的润滑剂,或者作为躯体和医疗器械之间的偶合剂	6.5	0	
30069100	可确定用于造口术用具	10	0	0
31051000	制成片状及类似形状或每包毛重不超过10公斤的31章各货品	4	0	
31059000	其他肥料	4	0	
32021000	有机合成鞣料	6.5	0	
32029000	无机鞣料;鞣料制剂等,不论是否含有天然鞣料;预鞣用酶制剂	6.5	0	
32041200	酸性染料(不论是否预金属络合)及以其为基本成分的制品(不论是否已有化学定义);媒染染料及以其为基本成分的制品(不论是否已有化学定义)	7.1	0	
32041600	活性染料及以其为基本成分的制品(不论是否已有化学定义)	7.1	0	
32041700	颜料及以其为基本成分的制品(不论是否已有化学定义)	6.5	0	
32042000	用作萤光增白剂的有机合成产品(不论是否已有化学定义)	6.5	0	
32061900	二氧化钛为基料的颜料及制品,干量计二氧化钛<80%	10	0	
32064900	其他着色料及其制品;32章注释三所述的制品,但税目32.03,32.04及32.05的货品除外面	6.5	0	
32081000	分散或溶于非水介质的聚酯油漆及清漆等	10	0	0
32089090	分散或溶于非水介质其他油漆、清漆溶液	10	0	0
32091000	分散或溶于水介质的丙烯酸聚合物或乙烯聚合物油漆及清漆	10		0
32099090	溶于水介质其他聚合物油漆及清漆	10	0	
32100000	其他油漆及清漆(包括瓷漆\大漆及水浆涂料);皮革用水性颜料	10	0	0
32149000	非耐火涂面制剂,涂门面、内墙、地板、天花板等用	9	0	
32151100	黑色印刷油墨(不论是否固体或浓缩)	6.5		0
32151900	其他印刷油墨(不论是否固体或浓缩),黑色印刷油墨除外	6.5	0	0
32159010	书写墨水(不论是否固体或浓缩)	6.5	0	0
32159090	绘图墨水及其他墨类(不论是否固体或浓缩)	10	0	0
33011200	橙油(包括浸膏及净油)	20		0
33011300	柠檬油(包括浸膏及净油)	20		0
33011910	白柠檬油(酸橙油)(包括浸膏及净油)	20		0
33011990	其他柑桔属果实的精油(包括浸膏及净油)	20		0
33012400	胡椒薄荷油(包括浸膏及净油)	20		0
33012500	其他薄荷油(包括浸膏及净油)	15		0
33012910	樟脑油(包括浸膏及净油)	20		0
33012920	香茅油(包括浸膏及净油)	15		0
33012930	茴香油(包括浸膏及净油)	20		0
33012940	桂油(包括浸膏及净油)	20		0
33012950	山苍子油(包括浸膏及净油)	20		0
33012960	桉叶油(包括浸膏及净油)	20		0
33012991	老鹳草油(香叶油)(包括浸膏及净油)	20		0
33012999	其他非柑桔属果实的精油(包括浸膏及净油)	15		0
33013010	鸢尾凝脂	20		0
33013090	其他香膏	20		0
33019010	提取的油树脂	20		0
33019020	柑桔属果实的精油脱萜所得的萜烯副产品	20		0
33019090	用花香吸取法或浸渍法制定的含浓缩精油的脂肪、固定油、蜡及类似品;精油脱萜所得的萜烯副产品(柑桔属果实的除外);精油水溶液及水馏液	20		0
33021010	生产饮料用的混合香料以及以香料为基本成分的制品,按容量计酒精浓度≤0.5%	15		0
33021090	其他食品或饮料工业用混合香料以及以香料为基本成分的制品	15		0
33029000	其他工业用混合香料及以香料为基本成分的混合物和制品	10	0	0
33030000	香水及花露水	10	0	0
33041000	唇用化妆品	10	0	0
33042000	眼用化妆品	10	0	0
33043000	指(趾)甲化妆品	15	0	0
33049900	其他美容品或化妆品及护肤品	9.7	0	0
33074100	神香及其他通过燃烧散发香气制品	10	0	
33074900	室内除臭制品	10	0	
34012000	其他形状的肥皂	15	0	
34021100	阴离子型有机表面活性剂	6.5	0	
34021200	阳离子型有机表面活性剂	6.5	0	
34021300	非离子型有机表面活性剂	6.5	0	
34022090	零售包装有机表面活性剂制品(合成洗涤粉除外)	10	0	0

税则号列 Tariff No.	货品名称 Description of Goods	最惠国 MFN	香港 H. K	澳门 MAC
34029000	非零售包装有机表面活性剂制品、洗涤剂及清洁剂	9	0	0
34031100	用于纺织材料、皮革、毛皮或其他材料油脂处理的制剂(含有石油或从沥青矿物提取的油类且按重量计<70%)	10	0	
34039100	用于纺织、皮革、毛皮或其他材料油脂处理的制剂(不含有石油或从沥青矿物提取的油类)	10	0	
34039900	润滑剂(不含有石油或从沥青矿物提取的油类)	10		0
34052000	保养木制品的上光剂及类似制品	10	0	
34059000	玻璃或金属用的光洁剂	10	0	
35029000	其他白蛋白及白蛋白盐及其衍生物	10	0	
35051000	糊精及其他改性淀粉	12	0	
35061000	适于作胶或粘合剂的产品,零售包装每件净重≤1kg	10	0	
35069110	以聚酰胺为基本成份的粘合剂	10	0	0
35069120	以环氧树脂为基本成分的粘合剂	10	0	0
35069190	以其他橡胶或塑料为基本成分的粘合剂	10	0	0
35069900	其他调制胶、粘合剂	10	0	0
36061000	灌注打火机等用的液体或液化气体燃料,其包装容器的容积≤300cm^3	10	0	
37013021	激光照排片(任何一边超过255mm),用纸、纸板及纺织物以外任何材料制成	10		0
37013022	PS版(预涂感光版)(任何一边超过255mm),用纸、纸板及纺织物以外任何材料制成	10		0
37013023	CTP版	10		0
37013029	其他未曝光照相制版用感光硬片及软片(任何一边超过255mm),用纸、纸板及纺织物以外任何材料制成	10		0
37025300	幻灯片用未曝光彩色摄影胶卷,16 mm<宽度≤35 mm,长度<30m,用纸、纸板及纺织物以外任何材料制成	47	0	
37025410	非幻灯片用未曝光彩色胶卷,宽度35mm,长度≤2 m,用纸、纸板及纺织物以外任何材料制成	18	0	
37025490	非幻灯片用彩色摄影用未曝光彩色胶卷,16 mm<宽度<35 mm,2 m<长度≤30m,用纸、纸板及纺织物以外任何材料制成	18	0	
37032010	未曝光的彩色摄影用感光纸及纸板,非成卷或宽度≤610mm	35	0	
37032090	未曝光的彩色摄影用感光布,非成卷或宽度≤610mm	18	0	
37061090	已曝光已冲洗的电影胶片,宽度≥35mm,不论是否配有声道或仅有声道,教学专用除外	5	0	
37069090	已曝光已冲洗的电影胶片,宽度<35mm,不论是否配有声道或仅有声道,教学专用除外	4	0	
37071000	摄影用感光乳液	8		0
37079010	冲洗胶卷及相片用化学制剂或摄影用未混合品(定量包装或零售包装可立即使用的)	16	0	
37079020	复印机用化学制剂或摄影用未混合品(定量包装或零售包装可立即使用的)	10	0	
37079090	其他摄影用化学制剂或摄影用未混合品(定量包装或零售包装可立即使用的)	8	0	0
38011000	人造石墨	6.5	0	
38085010	零售包装的本章注释一规定货物	9	0	
38085090	非零售包装的本章注释一规定货物	5	0	
38089119	零售包装杀虫剂	10	0	
38089190	非零售包装杀虫剂	6	0	
38089400	消毒剂	9	0	
38099100	纺织工业及类似工业用其他税号未列名整理剂、染料加速着色剂或固色助剂及其他产品和制剂	6.5	0	
38099200	造纸工业用其他税号未列名整理剂、染料加速着色剂或固色助剂及其他产品和制剂	6.5	0	
38099300	制革工业用其他税号未列名整理剂、染料加速着色剂或固色助剂及其他产品和制剂	6.5	0	
38101000	金属表面酸洗剂;金属及其他材料制成的焊粉或焊膏	6.5	0	0
38112900	不含石油或从沥青矿物提取的油类的润滑油添加剂	6.5		0
38119000	抗氧剂、防胶剂、粘度改良剂、防腐剂配制添加剂,用于矿物油或与矿物油同样用途的其他液体	6.5	0	0
38123010	橡胶的防老剂	6	0	
38123090	其他橡胶、塑料用抗氧剂及其他稳定剂	6.5	0	
38140000	其他税号未列名的有机复合溶剂及稀释剂;除漆剂	10	0	0
38151200	以贵金属及其化合物为活性物的载体催化剂	6.5	0	
38159000	其他未列名的反应引发剂、促进剂	6.5		0

税则号列 Tariff No.	货品名称 Description of Goods	最惠国 MFN	香港 H. K	澳门 MAC
38190000	闸用液压油及其他液压传动用液体,不含石油或从沥青矿物提取的油类,或者按重量计石油或从沥青矿物提取的油类含量低于70%	6.5		0
38200000	防冻剂及解冻剂	10		0
38220010	附于衬背上的诊断或实验用试剂,但税目32.02,32.06的货品除外	4	0	
38220090	无论是否附于衬背上的诊断或实验用配制试剂,但税目32.02,32.06的货品除外	5	0	
38231200	油酸	16	0	
38231900	其他工业用单羧脂肪酸;精炼所得的酸性油	16	0	
38244000	水泥、灰泥及混凝土用添加剂	6.5	0	
38245000	非耐火的灰泥及混凝土	6.5	0	
38247100	含全氯氟烃的,不论是否含氢氯氟烃、全氟烃或氢氟烃的含有甲烷、乙烷、丙烷卤化衍生物混合物	6.5	0	0
38247300	含氢溴氟烃的含有甲烷、乙烷、丙烷卤化衍生物混合物	6.5	0	0
38247400	含氢氯氟烃的,不论是否含全氟烃或氢氟烃,但不含全氯氟烃的含有甲烷、乙烷、丙烷卤化衍生物混合物	6.5	0	0
38247500	含四氯化碳的含有甲烷、乙烷、丙烷卤化衍生物混合物	6.5	0	0
38247600	含1,1,1-三氯乙烷(甲基氯仿)的含有甲烷、乙烷、丙烷卤化衍生物混合物	6.5	0	0
38247700	含溴化甲烷(甲基溴)或溴氯甲烷的含有甲烷、乙烷、丙烷卤化衍生物混合物	6.5	0	0
38247800	含全氟烃或氢氟烃的,但不含全氯氟烃或氢氯氟烃的含有甲烷、乙烷、丙烷卤化衍生物混合物	6.5	0	0
38247900	其他含有甲烷、乙烷、丙烷卤化衍生物的混合物	6.5	0	0
38248100	含环氧乙烷的混合物及制品	6.5	0	0
38248200	含多氯联苯、多氯三联苯或多溴联苯的混合物及制品	6.5	0	0
38248300	含三(2,3-二溴丙基)磷酸酯的混合物及制品	6.5	0	0
38249090	其他税目未列名的化学工业及其相关工业的化学产品及配制品	6.5	0	0
38259000	其他税目未列名的化学工业及相关工业的副产品	6.5	0	
39011000	初级形状比重<0.94的聚乙烯	7.8	0	0
39012000	初级形状比重≥0.94的聚乙烯	7.8	0	0
39013000	初级形状乙烯-乙酸乙烯酯共聚物	6.5	0	
39021000	初级形状的聚丙烯	7.6	0	0
39023010	初级形状的乙烯丙烯共聚物(乙丙橡胶丙烯单体单元的含量大于乙烯单体单元)	7.6	0	
39023090	初级形状的其他丙烯共聚物	7.6	0	
39031900	初级形状的其他聚苯乙烯	7.6	0	
39033000	丙烯腈-丁二烯-苯乙烯共聚物	7.6	0	0
39039000	初级形状的其他苯乙烯聚合物	7.6	0	
39042100	初级形状未塑化的聚氯乙烯	7.6	0	
39042200	初级形状已塑化的聚氯乙烯	7.6	0	
39069010	聚丙稀酰胺	6.5	0	
39069090	其他初级形状的丙烯酸聚合物	6.5	0	
39073000	初级形状的环氧树脂	7.6	0	
39074000	初级形状的聚碳酸酯	6.5	0	
39076019	其他聚对苯二甲酸乙二酯切片	7.6		0
39076090	其他初级形状聚对苯二甲酸乙二酯	6.5		0
39077000	聚乳酸	6.5		0
39079910	聚对苯二甲酸丁二酯	6.5		0
39079990	初级形状的其他聚酯	6.5		0
39081011	聚酰胺-6,6切片	7.6	0	
39081019	初级形状聚酰胺切片	7.6	0	
39081090	其他初级形状的聚酰胺	6.5	0	
39093010	聚合MDI	6.5	0	
39095000	初级形状的聚亚氨酯	7.6	0	0
39100000	初级形状的聚硅氧烷	6.5	0	
39151000	乙烯聚合物的废碎料及下脚料	7.6	0	0
39152000	苯乙烯聚合物的废碎料及下脚料	7.6	0	
39153000	氯乙烯聚合物的废碎料及下脚料	7.6	0	
39159010	聚对苯二甲酸乙二酯的塑料废碎料及下脚料	7.6	0	0
39159090	其他塑料的废碎料及下脚料	7.6	0	0
39172300	氯乙烯聚合物制的硬管	10	0	
39173100	塑料制的软管	10	0	
39189010	其他塑料制的糊墙品	10	0	
39189090	其他塑料制的铺地制品	10	0	
39199010	其他胶囊型反光膜	6.5	0	
39199090	其他自粘塑料板、片、膜等材料	6.5	0	
39201010	乙烯聚合物制电池隔膜	6.5	0	
39201090	其他乙烯聚合物制板、片、带	6.5	0	0
39202010	丙烯聚合物制电池隔膜	6.5	0	
39202090	其他丙烯聚合物制板、片、带	6.5	0	0
39203000	非泡沫聚苯乙烯板、片、膜、箔及扁条	6.5	0	
39204300	按重量计增塑剂含量不小于6%的聚氯乙烯板、片、膜、箔及扁条	7.6	0	
39204900	按重量计增塑剂含量小于6%的聚氯乙烯板、片、膜、箔及扁条	7.6	0	0

税则号列 Tariff No.	货品名称 Description of Goods	最惠国 MFN	香港 H. K	澳门 MAC
39206200	聚对苯二甲酸乙二酯板片膜箔扁条	6.5	0	0
39207300	醋酸纤维素制板、片、膜、箔及扁条	6.5	0	
39209990	其他塑料制的非泡沫塑料板片	6.5	0	
39211210	泡沫聚氯乙烯人造革及合成革	9	0	
39211290	泡沫聚氯乙烯板、片、带、箔及扁条	6.5	0	
39211310	泡沫聚氨酯制人造革及合成革	9	0	
39211390	泡沫聚氨酯板、片、带、箔及扁条	6.5	0	
39219020	嵌有玻璃纤维的聚乙烯板、片	6.5	0	
39219030	聚异丁烯为基本成分的附有人造毛毡的板、片、卷材	6.5	0	
39219090	未列名塑料板、片、膜、箔及扁条	6.5	0	
39231000	塑料制盒、箱及类似品	10	0	0
39232100	乙烯聚合物制袋及包	10	0	0
39232900	其他塑料制的袋及包	10	0	0
39233000	塑料制坛、瓶及类似品	6.5	0	
39235000	塑料制塞子、盖子及类似品	10	0	
39239000	供运输或包装货物用其他塑料制品	10	0	0
39249000	塑料制其他家庭用具及卫生或盥洗用具	10	0	
39259000	其他未列名的建筑用塑料制品	10	0	
39262000	塑料制衣服及衣着附件	10	0	
39269010	塑料制机器及仪器用零件	10	0	0
39269090	其他塑料制品	10	0	0
40021110	羧基丁苯橡胶胶乳	7.5	0	
40021190	丁苯橡胶胶乳	7.5	0	
40021911	初级形状未经任何加工的丁苯橡胶	7.5	0	
40021912	初级形状的充油丁苯橡胶	7.5	0	
40021913	初级形状的热塑丁苯橡胶	7.5	0	
40021914	初级形状的充油热塑丁苯橡胶	7.5	0	
40021919	初级形状的其他丁苯橡胶及羧基丁苯橡胶	7.5	0	
40021990	丁苯橡胶及羧基丁苯橡胶板、片、带	7.5	0	
40029911	其他初级形状的合成橡胶	7.5	0	
40029919	其他合成橡胶板、片、带	7.5	0	
40030000	初级形状或板、片、带状再生橡胶	8	0	
40121200	机动大客车或货运机动车用翻新轮胎	20	0	
40121300	航空器用翻新轮胎	20	0	
40122010	汽车用旧的充气橡胶轮胎	25	0	
40122090	其他用途旧的充气橡胶轮胎	25	0	
40169100	硫化橡胶制铺地制品及门垫	18	0	
40169310	硫化橡胶制机器、仪器用垫片、垫圈及其他密封垫	8	0	
40169390	硫化橡胶制其他用垫片、垫圈、及其他密封垫	15	0	
41012011	规定重量范围内的整张生牛皮，经逆鞣处理的	8	0	
41012019	规定重量范围内的整张生牛皮，经逆鞣处理的除外	5	0	
41012020	规定重量范围内的整张生马皮	5	0	
41039090	其他生皮	9	0	
41041119	其他全粒面未剖层或粒面剖层湿牛皮革	8	0	
41041120	全粒面未剖层或粒面剖层马皮革	5	0	
41041919	其他湿牛皮革	7	0	
41041920	其他湿马皮革	7	0	
41044100	全粒面未剖层或粒面剖层干革(坯革)	5	0	
41044990	其他干革(坯革)	7	0	
41071110	已鞣全粒面未剖层整张牛皮革	8	0	
41071120	已鞣全粒面未剖层整张马皮革	5	0	
41071210	已鞣粒面剖层整张牛皮革	8	0	
41071220	已鞣粒面剖层整张马皮革	5	0	
41071990	其他已鞣整张牛马皮革	7	0	
41079990	其他已鞣非整张牛马皮革	7	0	
41120000	已鞣进一步加工的不带毛绵羊或羔羊皮革	8	0	
41131000	已鞣进一步加工的不带毛山羊或小山羊皮革	14	0	
41132000	已鞣进一步加工的不带毛猪皮革	14	0	
42010000	各种材料制成的鞍具及挽具，适合各种动物用	20	0	0
42022100	以皮革、再生皮革、漆皮作面的手提包	10	0	
42031000	皮革或再生皮革制的衣服	10	0	0
42032100	皮革或再生皮革制专供运动用手套	20	0	0
42032910	皮革或再生皮革制的劳保手套	20	0	0
42032990	皮革或再生皮革制的其他手套	20	0	0
42033010	皮革或再生皮革制腰带	10	0	0
42033020	皮革或再生皮革制的腰带及子弹带	10	0	
42034000	皮革或再生皮革制的其他衣着附件	20	0	0
42050010	皮革或再生皮革制坐具套	12	0	
42050090	皮革或再生皮革的其他制品	12	0	
43011000	整张生水貂皮	15	0	
43013000	阿斯特拉罕等羔羊的整张生毛皮，不论是否带头、尾或爪	20	0	
43016000	整张生狐皮	20	0	
43018010	整张生兔皮	20	0	
43018090	整张的其他生毛皮	20	0	

税则号列 Tariff No.	货品名称 Description of Goods	最惠国 MFN	香港 H. K	澳门 MAC
43019010	黄鼠狼尾	20	0	
43019090	适合加工皮货用的其他未鞣头、尾、爪	20	0	
43021100	已鞣未缝制的整张水貂皮	12	0	
43021910	已鞣未缝制的贵重毛皮(貂皮、狐皮、水獭及旱獭等)	10	0	
43021920	已鞣未缝制的整张兔皮	10	0	
43021930	已鞣未缝制阿斯特拉罕等羔羊皮,不论是否带头、尾或爪	20	0	
43021990	已鞣未缝制的其他毛皮	10	0	
43022000	已鞣未缝制的头、尾、爪及其他块片	20	0	
43023010	已鞣已缝制的贵重毛皮及其块、片	20	0	
43023090	已鞣已缝制的其他整张毛皮及块片	20	0	
43031010	毛皮衣服	23	0	
43031020	毛皮衣着附件	18	0	
43039000	毛皮制其他物品	18	0	
43040010	人造毛皮	18	0	
43040020	人造毛皮制品	18	0	
46029000	其他编结材料制品及其他制品	9		0
48022010	照相原纸	7.5	0	
48022090	光敏、热敏、电敏纸,纸板的原纸、板	7.5	0	
48024000	墙壁纸原纸	7.5	0	
48025400	书写、印刷等用未涂布薄纸及纸板,不含用机械方法制得的纤维或所含前述纤维不超过全部纤维重量的10%	7.5	0	
48025500	其他书写印刷等用未涂中厚纸(板),不含用机械方法制得的纤维或所含前述纤维不超过全部纤维重量的10%,成卷	5	0	
48025600	书写、印刷等用未涂布中厚纸及纸板,不含用机械方法制得的纤维或所含前述纤维不超过全部纤维重量的10%,成张,一边≤435mm,另一边≤297mm	5	0	
48025700	其他书写印刷等用未涂中厚纸(板),不含用机械方法制得的纤维或所含前述纤维不超过全部纤维重量的10%,其他成张	5	0	
48025800	书写、印刷等用未涂布厚纸及纸板,不含用机械方法制得的纤维或所含前述纤维不超过全部纤维重量的10%	5	0	
48026190	其他书写、印刷等用未涂布纸及纸板,所含用机械方法制得的纤维超过全部纤维重量的10%,成卷的其他纸	5	0	
48026200	其他书写、印刷等用未涂布纸及纸板,所含用机械方法制得的纤维超过全部纤维重量的10%,成张的,一边≤435mm、另一边≤297mm(以未折叠计)	5	0	
48026990	其他书写、印刷等用未涂布纸及纸板,所含用机械方法制得的纤维超过全部纤维重量的10%,成张的其他纸	5	0	
48051100	半化学的瓦楞纸(瓦楞原纸)	7.5	0	
48051200	草浆瓦楞原纸	7.5	0	
48051900	其他瓦楞原纸	7.5	0	
48052400	薄强韧箱纸板	7.5	0	
48052500	厚强韧箱纸板	7.5	0	
48059110	每平方米重量在150克及以下的电解电容器原纸	7.5	0	
48059190	每平方米重量在150克及以下的薄纸及纸板	7.5	0	
48059300	其他未经涂布厚纸及纸板	7.5	0	
48101300	涂无机物书写(印刷)纸(板),不含用机械方法制得的纤维或所含前述纤维不超过全部纤维重量的10%,成卷的	5	0	
48101400	涂无机物书写(印刷)纸(板),不含用机械方法制得的纤维或所含前述纤维不超过全部纤维重量的10%,成张的,一边≤435mm,另一边≤297mm(以未折叠计)	5	0	
48101900	其他涂无机物书写(印刷)纸(板),不含用机械方法制得的纤维或所含前述纤维不超过全部纤维重量的10%,成张的	5	0	
48102900	其他涂无机物的书写、印刷纸及纸板,所含用机械方法制得的纤维超过全部纤维重量的10%	5	0	
48103100	涂无机物的薄漂白牛皮纸及纸板,书写、印刷或类似用途的除外	5	0	0
48103200	涂无机物的厚漂白牛皮纸及纸板,书写、印刷或类似用途的除外	5	0	0
48103900	涂无机物的其他牛皮纸及纸板,书写、印刷或类似用途的除外	5	0	0
48109200	其他涂无机物的多层纸及纸板	5	0	0
48109900	其他涂无机物的纸及纸板	7.5	0	0
48111000	焦油纸及纸板、沥青纸及纸板	7.5	0	0
48114100	自粘的胶粘纸及纸板	7.5	0	0

税则号列 Tariff No.	货品名称 Description of Goods	最惠国 MFN	香港 H. K	澳门 MAC
48114900	其他胶粘纸及纸板	7.5	0	0
48115110	漂白的彩色相纸用双面涂塑厚纸	7.5	0	0
48115190	漂白的其他涂、浸、盖厚纸及纸板	7.5	0	0
48115910	绝缘纸及纸板	7.5	0	0
48115990	用塑料涂布、浸渍的其他纸及纸板	7.5	0	0
48116010	用蜡或油等涂布的绝缘纸及纸板	7.5	0	0
48116090	用蜡或油等涂布的其他纸及纸板	7.5	0	0
48119000	其他经涂布、浸渍、覆盖的纸及纸板	7.5	0	0
48191000	瓦楞纸或纸板制的箱、盒、匣	5	0	0
48192000	非瓦楞纸或纸板制可折叠箱、盒、匣	5	0	0
48211000	纸或纸板印制的各种标签	7.5	0	0
48239090	其他纸及纸制品	7.5	0	0
49111090	其他商业广告品及类似印刷品	7.5	0	
49119900	其他印刷品	7.5	0	
50040000	非供零售用丝纱线	6		0
50072019	其他纯桑蚕丝机织物	10	0	
51013000	未梳碳化羊毛	38		0
51061000	非供零售用粗梳纯羊毛纱线	5	0	0
51062000	非供零售用粗梳混纺羊毛纱线	5	0	0
51071000	非供零售用精梳纯羊毛纱线	5	0	0
51072000	非供零售用精梳混纺羊毛纱线	5		0
51121100	重量≤200g/平米精梳全毛布	10	0	
51121900	重量>200g/平米精梳全毛布	10	0	
52051100	非零售粗梳粗支纯棉单纱	5	0	0
52051200	非零售粗梳中支纯棉单纱	5	0	
52051300	非零售粗梳细支纯棉单纱	5	0	
52051400	非零售粗梳较细支纯棉单纱	5	0	
52052100	非零售精梳粗支纯棉单纱	5	0	
52052200	非零售精梳中支纯棉单纱	5	0	
52052300	非零售精梳细支纯棉单纱	5	0	
52052400	非零售精梳较细支纯棉单纱	5	0	
52052600	非零售精梳较特细支纯棉单纱	5	0	
52052700	非零售精梳特细支纯棉单纱	5	0	
52052800	非零售精梳超细支纯棉单纱	5	0	
52053100	非零售粗梳粗支纯棉多股纱	5	0	
52053200	非零售粗梳中支纯棉多股纱	5	0	
52053300	非零售粗梳细支纯棉多股纱	5	0	
52053400	非零售粗梳较细支纯棉多股纱	5	0	
52054100	非零售精梳粗支纯棉多股纱	5	0	
52054200	非零售精梳中支纯棉多股纱	5	0	
52054300	非零售精梳细支纯棉多股纱	5	0	
52054400	非零售精梳较细支纯棉多股纱	5	0	
52054600	非零售精梳较特细支纯棉多股纱	5	0	
52054700	非零售精梳特细支纯棉多股纱	5	0	
52054800	非零售精梳超细支纯棉多股纱	5	0	
52061100	非零售粗梳粗支混纺棉单纱	5	0	0
52061200	非零售粗梳中支混纺棉单纱	5	0	
52061300	非零售粗梳细支混纺棉单纱	5	0	
52061400	非零售粗梳较细支混纺棉单纱	5	0	
52061500	非零售粗梳特细支混纺棉单纱	5	0	
52062100	非零售精梳粗支混纺棉单纱	5	0	
52062200	非零售精梳中支混纺棉单纱	5	0	
52062300	非零售精梳细支混纺棉单纱	5	0	
52062400	非零售精梳较细支混纺棉单纱	5	0	
52062500	非零售精梳特细支混纺棉单纱	5	0	
52063100	非零售粗梳粗支混纺棉多股纱	5	0	
52063200	非零售粗梳中支混纺棉多股纱	5	0	
52063300	非零售粗梳细支混纺棉多股纱	5	0	
52063400	非零售粗梳较细混纺棉多股纱	5	0	
52063500	非零售粗梳特细混纺棉多股纱	5	0	
52064100	非零售精梳粗支混纺棉多股纱	5	0	
52064200	非零售精梳中支混纺棉多股纱	5	0	
52064300	非零售精梳细支混纺棉多股纱	5	0	
52064400	非零售精梳较细混纺棉多股纱	5	0	
52064500	非零售精梳特细混纺棉多股纱	5	0	
52081100	未漂白轻质全棉平纹布	10	0	
52081200	未漂白较轻质全棉平纹布	10	0	
52081300	未漂白轻质全棉三、四线斜纹布	10	0	
52082100	漂白的轻质全棉平纹布	10	0	
52082200	漂白的较轻质全棉平纹布	10	0	
52082300	漂白的轻质全棉三、四线斜纹布	12	0	
52083100	染色的轻质全棉平纹布	10	0	
52083200	染色的较轻质全棉平纹布	10	0	
52083300	染色的轻质全棉三、四线斜纹布	10	0	
52083900	染色的轻质其他全棉机织物	10	0	
52084100	色织的轻质全棉平纹布	10	0	
52084200	色织的较轻质全棉平纹布	10	0	
52084300	色织的轻质全棉三、四线斜纹布	10	0	
52084900	色织的轻质其他全棉机织物	10	0	
52085100	印花的轻全棉平纹布	10	0	
52085200	印花的较轻全棉平纹布	10	0	
52085910	印花的轻质全棉三、四线斜纹布	10	0	
52091100	未漂白重质全棉平纹布	10	0	
52091200	未漂白重质全棉三、四线斜纹布	10	0	
52091900	未漂白重质其他全棉机织物	10	0	
52092100	漂白的重质全棉平纹布	12	0	
52092200	漂白的重质全棉三、四线斜纹布	12	0	
52093100	染色的重质全棉平纹布	10	0	
52093200	染色的重质全棉三、四线斜纹布	10	0	
52093900	染色的重质其他全棉机织物	10	0	
52094100	色织的重质全棉平纹布	10	0	
52094200	色织的重质全棉粗斜纹布(劳动布)	10	0	0
52094300	色织的重质全棉三、四线斜纹布	10	0	
52095100	印花的重质全棉平纹布	10	0	

税则号列 Tariff No.	货品名称 Description of Goods	最惠国 MFN	香港 H. K	澳门 MAC
52095200	印花的重质全棉三、四线斜纹布	10	0	
52095900	印花的重质其他全棉机织物	10	0	
52101100	与化纤混纺未漂白轻质平纹棉布	12	0	
52101910	化纤混纺未漂白轻质3、4线斜纹棉布	12	0	
52103100	与化纤混纺染色的轻质平纹棉布	10	0	
52103200	化纤混纺染色的轻质三线或四线斜纹棉布	10	0	
52104100	与化纤混纺色织的轻质平纹棉布	10	0	
52104910	化纤混纺色织的轻质三线或四线斜纹棉布	10	0	
52111100	与化纤混纺未漂白重质平纹棉布	12	0	
52111200	化纤混纺未漂白重质三线或四线斜纹棉布	12	0	
52111900	与化纤混纺未漂白重质其他棉布	12	0	
52113100	与化纤混纺染色的重质平纹棉布	10	0	
52113200	化纤混纺染色的重质三线或四线斜纹棉布	10	0	
52113900	与化纤混纺染色的重质其他棉布	10	0	
52114100	与化纤混纺色织的重质平纹棉布	10	0	
52114200	与化纤混纺色织的重质粗斜纹棉布	10	0	
52121100	未漂白的其他混纺轻质棉布	12	0	
52121200	漂白的其他混纺轻质棉布	14	0	
52121300	染色的其他混纺轻质棉布	10	0	
52122100	未漂白的其他混纺重质棉布	12	0	
52122200	漂白的其他混纺重质棉布	14	0	
52122300	染色的其他混纺重质棉布	10	0	
53061000	亚麻单纱	6	0	0
53062000	亚麻多股纱线或缆线	10	0	0
53089011	未漂白或漂白的全苎麻纱线	6		0
53089012	全苎麻色纱线	6		0
53089013	未漂白或漂白的混纺苎麻纱线	6		0
53089014	混纺苎麻色纱线	6		0
53091900	其他全亚麻机织物	10	0	
53092900	其他混纺亚麻机织物	10	0	
54011010	非供零售用合成纤维长丝缝纫线	5	0	0
54021100	非零售用芳香族聚酰胺纺制的长丝高强力纱	5		0
54021910	非零售用聚酰胺-6纺制的长丝高强力纱	5		0
54021920	非零售用聚酰胺-66纺制的长丝高强力纱	5		0
54021990	非零售用其他尼龙长丝高强纱	5		0
54022000	非零售聚酯长丝高强力纱	5		0
54023111	非零售用聚酰胺-6纺制的细弹力丝	5	0	
54023112	非零售用聚酰胺-66纺制的细弹力丝	5	0	
54023113	非零售用芳香族聚酰胺纺制的细弹力丝	5	0	
54023119	非零售其他细尼龙弹力丝	5	0	
54023190	非零售其他细尼龙变形纱线	5	0	
54023211	非零售用聚酰胺-6纺制的粗弹力丝	5	0	
54023212	非零售用聚酰胺-66纺制的粗弹力丝	5	0	
54023213	非零售用芳香族聚酰胺纺制的粗弹力丝	5	0	
54023219	非零售其他粗尼龙弹力丝	5	0	
54023290	非零售其他粗尼龙变形纱线	5	0	
54023900	非零售其他合成纤维长丝变形纱线	5		0
54024490	其他纱线,未加捻或捻度每米不超过50转	5	0	
54024510	聚酰胺-6纺制的其他单纱,未加捻或捻度每米不超过50转	5		0
54024520	聚酰胺-6,6纺制的其他单纱,未加捻或捻度每米不超过50转	5		0
54024530	芳香族聚酰胺纺制的其他单纱,未加捻或捻度每米不超过50转	5		0
54024590	其他尼龙或聚酰胺纱线纺制的,未加捻或捻度每米不超过50转的单纱	5		0
54024800	其他聚丙烯纱线,未加捻或捻度每米不超过50转	5		0
54024900	其他纱线,未加捻或捻度每米不超过50转	5		0
54025110	非零售用聚酰胺-6纺制的加捻单纱	5		0
54025120	非零售用聚酰胺-66纺制的加捻单纱	5		0
54025130	非零售用芳香族聚酰胺纺制的加捻单纱	5		0
54025190	非零售用其他尼龙加捻单纱	5		0
54025200	非零售加捻的其他聚酯加捻单纱	5		0
54026110	非零售用聚己内酰胺(尼龙-6)制多股纱线	5		0
54026120	非零售用聚酰胺-66制多股纱线	5		0
54026130	非零售用芳香族聚酰胺制多股纱线	5		0
54026190	非零售用其他尼龙制多股纱线	5		0
54026910	非零售用聚丙烯多股纱线	5		0
54026920	非零售用氨纶多股纱线	5		0
54026990	非零售其他合成纤维长丝多股纱线	5		0
54033200	非零售加捻的粘胶纤维单纱	5		0

税则号列 Tariff No.	货品名称 Description of Goods	最惠国 MFN	香港 H. K	澳门 MAC
54041100	细度≥67 分特、≤1mm 的弹性单丝	5	0	
54041200	细度≥67 分特、≤1mm 的聚丙烯单丝	5	0	
54041900	细度≥67 分特、≤1mm 的其他合成纤维单丝	5	0	
54074200	染色的纯尼龙布	10	0	0
54074300	色织的纯尼龙布	10	0	
54075200	染色的纯聚酯变形长丝布	10	0	
54076100	其他纯聚酯非变形长丝布	10	0	0
54077200	染色的其他纯合成纤维长丝布	10	0	
54078200	染色的与棉混纺合成纤维长丝布	10	0	
54079200	染色的其他混纺合成纤维长丝布	10	0	
54082210	纯粘胶长丝制染色机织物	10	0	
54082220	纯醋酸长丝制染色机织物	10	0	
54082290	纯其他人造长丝制染色机织物	10	0	
54082410	纯粘胶长丝制印花机织物	10	0	
54082420	纯醋酸长丝制印花机织物	10	0	
54082490	纯其他人造长丝制印花机织物	10	0	
55014000	聚丙烯长丝丝束	5	0	
55019000	其他合成纤维长丝丝束	5	0	
55052000	人造纤维废料	5	0	
55081000	合成纤维短纤纺制的缝纫线	5	0	0
55091100	非零售纯尼龙短纤单纱	5	0	
55091200	非零售纯尼龙短纤多股纱线	5	0	
55092100	非零售纯聚酯短纤单纱	5	0	
55092200	非零售纯聚酯短纤多股纱线	5	0	
55093100	非零售纯聚丙烯腈短纤单纱	5	0	
55093200	非零售纯聚丙烯腈短纤多股纱线	5	0	0
55094100	非零售纯其他合成纤维短纤单纱	5	0	
55094200	非零售纯其他合成纤维短纤多股纱线	5	0	
55095100	非零售与人造纤维短纤混纺聚酯短纤纱	5	0	
55095200	非零售与毛混纺聚酯短纤纱线	5	0	
55095300	非零售与棉混纺聚酯短纤纱线	5	0	
55095900	非零售其他混纺聚酯短纤纱线	5	0	
55096100	非零售与毛混纺腈纶短纤纱线	5	0	0
55096200	非零售与棉混纺腈纶短纤纱线	5	0	
55096900	非零售与其他混纺腈纶短纤纱线	5	0	0
55099100	非零售与毛混纺其他合成纤维短纤纱线	5	0	
55099200	非零售与棉混纺其他合成纤维短纤纱线	5	0	
55099900	非零售与其他混纺合成纤维短纤纱线	5	0	
55101100	非零售纯人造纤维短纤单纱	5	0	
55101200	非零售纯人造纤维短纤多股纱线	5	0	
55102000	非零售与毛混纺人造纤维短纤纱线	5	0	0
55103000	非零售与棉混纺人造纤维短纤纱线	5	0	
55109000	非零售与其他混纺人造纤维短纤纱线	5	0	
55121900	其他纯聚酯布	10	0	
55129900	其他纯合成纤维布	10	0	0
55131110	与棉混纺未漂白的轻质聚酯平纹布	16	0	
55131120	与棉混纺漂白的轻质聚酯平纹布	15	0	
55131210	与棉混纺未漂白的轻质聚酯斜纹布	16	0	
55131220	与棉混纺漂白的轻质聚酯斜纹布	18	0	
55132100	与棉混纺染色的轻质聚酯平纹布	10	0	0
55132310	与棉混纺染色的轻质聚酯斜纹布	10	0	
55133100	与棉混纺色织的轻质聚酯平纹布	10	0	
55133910	与棉混纺色织的轻质聚酯斜纹布	10	0	
55133920	与棉混纺色织的其他轻质聚酯布	10	0	
55141210	与棉混纺未漂白的重质聚酯斜纹布	16	0	
55141220	与棉混纺漂白的重质聚酯斜纹布	18	0	
55142100	与棉混纺染色的重质聚酯平纹布	10	0	
55142200	与棉混纺染色的重质聚酯斜纹布	10	0	
55143010	与棉混纺色织的重质聚酯平纹布	10	0	
55143020	与棉混纺色织的重质聚酯斜纹布	10	0	
55161100	未漂白或漂白的纯人造纤维短纤布	12	0	
55161200	染色的纯人造纤维短纤布	10	0	
55161300	色织的纯人造纤维短纤布	10	0	
55161400	印花的纯人造纤维短纤布	10	0	
55162100	与化纤长丝混纺未漂白或漂白的人造纤维布	12	0	
55162200	与化纤长丝混纺的染色人造纤维布	10	0	
55162300	与化纤长丝混纺的色织人造纤维布	10	0	
55162400	与化纤长丝混纺的印花人造纤维布	10	0	
55163100	与毛混纺的未漂或漂白人造纤维布	12	0	
55163200	与毛混纺的染色人造纤维布	10	0	
55163300	与毛混纺的色织人造纤维布	10	0	
55163400	与毛混纺的印花人造纤维布	10	0	
55164100	与棉混纺的未漂或漂白人造纤维布	12	0	
55164200	与棉混纺的染色人造纤维布	12	0	
55164300	与棉混纺的色织人造纤维布	10	0	
55164400	与棉混纺的印花人造纤维布	10	0	
55169100	与其他纤维混纺未漂白或漂白的人造纤维布	12	0	

税则号列 Tariff No.	货品名称 Description of Goods	最惠国 MFN	香港 H.K	澳门 MAC
55169200	与其他纤维混纺的染色人造纤维布	10	0	
55169300	与其他纤维混纺的色织人造纤维布	10	0	
55169400	与其他纤维混纺的印花人造纤维布	10	0	
56031210	25g ＜每平米≤70g 浸渍化纤长丝无纺织物	10	0	0
56031290	25g ＜每平米≤70g 其他化纤长丝无纺织物	10	0	0
56031310	70g＜每平米≤150g 浸渍化纤长丝无纺织物	10		0
56031390	70g ＜每平米≤150g 其他化纤长丝无纺织物	10		0
56039210	25g ＜每平米≤70g 浸渍其他无纺织物	10	0	0
56039290	25g ＜每平米≤70g 其他无纺织物	10	0	0
56039310	70g ＜每平米≤150g 浸渍其他无纺织物	10	0	0
56039390	70g ＜每平米≤150g 的其他无纺织物	10	0	0
56039410	每平米＞150g 经浸渍其他无纺织物	10	0	
56039490	每平米＞150g 的其他无纺织物	10	0	
56060000	绳绒线及粗松螺旋花线	5		0
56089000	其他纤维制成的渔网及其他网	10	0	
58012200	割绒的棉制灯芯绒	10	0	
58012500	割绒的棉制经起绒织物	10	0	
58042100	化纤机制花边	10	0	0
58062000	含弹性纱线≥5%的狭幅织物	10	0	0
58063200	化纤制其他狭幅机织物	10		0
58071000	机织非绣制纺织材料标签、徽章等	10	0	0
58081000	成匹的编带	10		0
58089000	非绣制成匹装饰带、流苏、绒球	10		0
59031020	用聚氯乙烯浸、涂的人造革	10	0	
59031090	用聚氯乙烯浸、涂的其他纺织物	10	0	
59032090	用聚氨基甲酸酯浸、涂的其他纺织物	10	0	
59039090	用其他塑料浸、涂的其他纺织物	10	0	
60019200	化纤制针织或钩编起绒织物	10	0	0
60041010	宽＞30cm，弹性纱线≥5%棉针织、钩编织物	10	0	
60041030	宽＞30cm，弹性纱线≥5%合成纤维制针织、钩编织物	10	0	0
60041040	宽＞30cm，弹性纱线≥5%人造纤维制针织、钩编织物	10	0	0
60041090	宽＞30cm，弹性纱线≥5%其他纺织材料针织、钩编织物	10	0	0
60049010	宽＞30cm 含橡胶线的棉针织、钩编织物	10	0	
60049030	宽＞30cm 含橡胶线的合成纤维制针织、钩编织物	10	0	0
60049040	宽＞30cm 含橡胶线的人造纤维制针织、钩编织物	10	0	0
60049090	宽＞30cm 含橡胶线的其他纺织材料针织、钩编织物	10	0	0
60052100	未漂白或漂白棉制的其他经编织物	10	0	
60052200	染色棉制的其他经编织物	10	0	
60052300	色织棉制的其他经编织物	10	0	
60052400	印花棉制的其他经编织物	10	0	
60062100	未漂白或漂白棉制的其他针织、钩编织物	10	0	0
60062200	染色棉制的其他针织、钩编织物	10	0	0
60062300	色织棉制的其他针织、钩编织物	10	0	0
60062400	印花棉制的其他针织、钩编织物	10	0	0
60063100	未漂白或漂白合成纤维制的其他针织、钩编织物	10	0	0
60063200	染色合成纤维制的其他针织、钩编织物	10	0	0
60063300	色织合成纤维制的其他针织、钩编织物	10	0	0
60063400	印花合成纤维制的其他针织、钩编织物	10	0	0
60064100	未漂白或漂白人造纤维制的其他针织、钩编织物	10	0	0
60064200	染色人造纤维制的其他针织、钩编织物	10	0	0
60064300	色织人造纤维制的其他针织、钩编织物	10	0	0
60064400	印花人造纤维制的其他针织、钩编织物	10	0	0
61012000	棉制针织或钩编男式大衣、防风衣	17.5	0	0
61013000	化纤制针织或钩编男式大衣等	17.5	0	0
61019010	毛制针织或钩编男式大衣、防风衣	25	0	0
61019090	其他纺织材料制针织或钩编男式大衣、防风衣	17.5	0	0
61021000	毛制针织或钩编女式大衣、防风衣	25	0	0
61022000	棉制针织或钩编女式大衣、防风衣	17.5	0	0
61023000	化纤制针织或钩编女式大衣等	17.5	0	0

税则号列 Tariff No.	货品名称 Description of Goods	最惠国 MFN	香港 H. K	澳门 MAC
61029000	其他纺织材料制针织或钩编女式大衣、防风衣	20	0	0
61031010	毛制针织或钩编男式西服套装	25	0	0
61031020	合纤制针织或钩编男西服套装	25	0	0
61031090	其他纺织材料制针织或钩编男式西服套装	17.5	0	0
61032200	棉制针织或钩编男式便服套装	20	0	0
61032300	合纤制针织或钩编男便服套装	25	0	0
61032910	毛制针织或钩编男式便服套装	25	0	0
61032990	其他纺织材料制针织或钩编男式便服套装	25		0
61033100	毛制针织或钩编男式上衣	16	0	0
61033200	棉制针织或钩编男式上衣	16	0	0
61033300	合纤制针织或钩编男式上衣	19	0	0
61033900	其他纺织材料制针织或钩编男式上衣	16	0	0
61034100	毛制针织或钩编男长裤、工装裤等	16	0	0
61034200	棉制针织或钩编男长裤、工装裤等	16	0	0
61034300	合纤制针织或钩编男长裤等	17.5	0	0
61034900	其他纺织材料制针织或钩编男长裤等	16	0	0
61041300	合纤制针织或钩编女西服套装	25	0	0
61041910	毛制针织或钩编女式西服套装	17.5	0	0
61041920	棉制针织或钩编女式西服套装	17.5	0	0
61041990	其他纺织材料制针织或钩编女式西服套装	17.5	0	0
61042200	棉制针织或钩编女式便服套装	17.5	0	0
61042300	合纤制针织或钩编女便服套装	25	0	0
61042910	毛制针织或钩编女式便服套装	17.5	0	0
61042990	其他纺织材料制针织或钩编女式便服套装	15	0	0
61043100	毛制针织女式上衣	16	0	0
61043200	棉制针织女式上衣	16	0	0
61043300	合纤制针织女上衣	19	0	0
61043900	其他纺织材料制针织女上衣	16	0	0
61044100	毛制针织或钩编连衣裙	16	0	0
61044200	棉制针织或钩编连衣裙	16	0	0
61044300	合纤制针织或钩编连衣裙	17.5	0	0
61044400	人纤制针织或钩编连衣裙	16	0	0
61044900	其他纺织材料制针织或钩编连衣裙	16	0	0
61045100	毛制针织或钩编裙子及裙裤	14	0	0
61045200	棉制针织裙子及裙裤	14	0	0
61045300	合纤制针织或钩编裙子及裙裤	16	0	0
61045900	其他纺织材料制针织或钩编裙子及裙裤	14	0	0
61046100	毛制针织或钩编女长裤、工装裤等	16	0	0
61046200	棉制针织或钩编女长裤、工装裤等	16	0	0
61046300	合纤制针织或钩编女长裤等	17.5	0	0
61046900	其他纺织材料制针织或钩编女长裤等	16	0	0
61051000	棉制针织或钩编男衬衫	16	0	0
61052000	化纤制针织或钩编男衬衫	17.5	0	0
61059000	其他纺织材料制针织或钩编男衬衫	16	0	0
61061000	棉制针织或钩编女衬衫	16	0	0
61062000	化纤制针织或钩编女衬衫	17.5	0	0
61069000	其他纺织材料制针织或钩编女衬衫	16	0	0
61071100	棉制针织或钩编男内裤及三角裤	14	0	0
61071200	化纤制针织或钩编男内裤及三角裤	16	0	
61071910	丝及绢丝制针织或钩编男内裤及三角裤	14	0	
61071990	其他纺织材料制针织或钩编男内裤及三角裤	14	0	
61072100	棉制针织或钩编男长睡衣及睡衣裤	14	0	
61072200	化纤制针织或钩编男睡衣裤	16	0	0
61072910	丝及绢丝制针织或钩编男长睡衣及睡衣裤	14	0	
61072990	其他纺织材料制针织或钩编男长睡衣及睡衣裤	14	0	
61079100	棉制针织或钩编男浴衣、晨衣	14	0	
61079910	化纤制针织或钩编男浴衣、晨衣	16	0	
61081100	化纤制针织或钩编长衬裙及衬裙	16	0	
61081910	棉制针织或钩编女式长衬裙及衬裙	14	0	
61081920	丝及绢丝制针织或钩编女式长衬裙及衬裙	14	0	
61081990	其他纺织材料制针织或钩编女式长衬裙及衬裙	14	0	
61082100	棉制针织或钩编女三角裤及短衬裤	14	0	0
61082200	化纤制针织或钩编女三角裤及短衬裤	16	0	0
61082910	丝及绢丝制针织或钩编女三角裤及短衬裤	14	0	
61082990	其他纺织材料制针织或钩编女三角裤及短衬裤	14	0	
61083100	棉制针织或钩编女睡衣及睡衣裤	14	0	0
61083200	化纤制针织或钩编女睡衣及睡衣裤	16	0	0

税则号列 Tariff No.	货品名称 Description of Goods	最惠国 MFN	香港 H. K	澳门 MAC
61083910	丝及绢丝制针织或钩编女睡衣及睡衣裤	14	0	
61083990	其他纺织材料制针织或钩编女睡衣及睡衣裤	14	0	
61089100	棉制针织或钩编女浴衣、晨衣	14	0	0
61089200	化纤制针织或钩编女浴衣、晨衣	16	0	
61089900	其他纺织材料制针织或钩编女浴衣、晨衣	14	0	
61091000	棉制针织或钩编T恤衫、汗衫等	14	0	0
61099010	丝及绢丝制针织或钩编T恤衫、汗衫等	14	0	0
61099090	其他纺织材料制针织或钩编T恤衫、汗衫等	14	0	0
61101100	羊毛制针织或钩编套头衫等	14	0	0
61101200	喀什米尔山羊细毛制针织或钩编套头衫等	14	0	0
61101910	其他山羊细毛制针织或钩编套头衫等	14	0	0
61101920	兔毛制针织或钩编套头衫等	14	0	0
61101990	其他毛制针织或钩编套头衫等	14	0	0
61102000	棉制针织或钩编套头衫等	14	0	0
61103000	化纤制针织或钩编套头衫等	16	0	0
61109010	丝及绢丝制针织或钩编套头衫等	14	0	0
61109090	其他纺织材料制针织或钩编套头衫等	14	0	0
61112000	棉制针织或钩编婴儿服装及附件	14	0	0
61113000	合纤制针织婴儿服装及附件	16	0	0
61119010	毛制针织或钩编婴儿服装及附件	14	0	0
61119090	其他纺织材料制针织或钩编婴儿服装及附件	14	0	0
61121100	棉制针织或钩编运动服	16	0	0
61121200	合纤制针织或钩编运动服	17.5	0	0
61121900	其他纺织材料制针织或钩编运动服	16	0	0
61123100	合纤制针织或钩编男式游泳服	17.5	0	
61123900	其他纺织材料制针织或钩编男式游泳服	16	0	
61124100	合纤制针织或钩编女式游泳服	17.5	0	
61124900	其他纺织材料制针织或钩编女式游泳服	16	0	
61130000	涂层经处理针织或钩编织物制服装	16	0	0
61142000	棉制针织或钩编的其他服装	16	0	0
61143000	化纤制针织或钩编的其他服装	17.5	0	0
61149010	毛制针织或钩编的其他服装	16	0	
61149090	其他纺织材料制针织或钩编的其他服装	16	0	
61151000	渐紧压袜类连裤袜	16	0	
61152100	单丝<67分特合纤制连裤袜等	16	0	
61159400	毛制针织或钩编短袜及其他袜类	14	0	
61159500	棉制针织或钩编短袜及其他袜类	14	0	
61159600	合纤制针织或钩编短袜及其他袜类	16	0	
61159900	其他纺织材料制针织或钩编短袜及其他袜类	14	0	
61161000	塑料或橡胶浸渍的针织或钩织手套	14	0	
61169100	毛制其他针织或钩编手套	14	0	
61169200	棉制其他针织或钩编手套	14	0	0
61169300	合纤制其他针织或钩编手套	16	0	0
61169900	其他纺织材料制针织或钩编手套	14	0	
61171000	针织或钩编披巾、头巾等	14	0	
61178010	针织或钩编领带及领结	14	0	
61178090	针织或钩编其他衣着附件	14	0	
61179000	其他针织或钩编衣着零件	14	0	0
62011100	毛制男式大衣、斗篷及类似品	16	0	0
62011210	棉制男式羽绒服	16	0	0
62011290	棉制男式大衣、斗篷及类似品	16	0	0
62011310	化纤制男式羽绒服	17.5	0	0
62011390	化纤制男式大衣、斗篷及类似品	17.5	0	0
62011900	其他纺织材料制男式大衣、斗篷及类似品	16	0	0
62019100	毛制男式带风帽防寒短上衣、防风衣	16	0	0
62019210	棉制男式其他羽绒服	16	0	0
62019290	棉制男式带风帽防寒短上衣、防风衣	16	0	0
62019310	化纤制男式其他羽绒服	17.5	0	0
62019390	化纤制男式防寒短上衣、防风衣	17.5	0	0
62019900	其他纺织材料制男式防寒短上衣、防风衣	16	0	0
62021100	毛制女式大衣、斗篷及类似品等	16	0	0
62021210	棉制女式羽绒服	16	0	0
62021290	棉制女式大衣、斗篷及类似品等	16	0	0
62021310	化纤制女式羽绒服	19	0	0
62021390	化纤制女式大衣、斗篷及类似品	19	0	0
62021900	其他纺织材料制女式大衣、斗篷及类似品	16	0	0
62029100	毛制女式带风帽防寒短上衣、防风衣	16	0	0
62029210	棉制女式其他羽绒服	16	0	0
62029290	棉制女式带风帽防寒短上衣、防风衣	16	0	0
62029310	化纤制女式其他羽绒服	17.5	0	0
62029390	化纤制女式防风衣等	17.5	0	0
62029900	其他纺织材料制防风衣、防风短上衣等	16	0	0
62031100	毛制男式西服套装	17.5	0	0
62031200	合纤制男式西服套装	17.5	0	0
62031910	丝及绢丝制男式西服套装	17.5	0	0

税则号列 Tariff No.	货品名称 Description of Goods	最惠国 MFN	香港 H. K	澳门 MAC
62031990	其他纺织材料制男式西服套装	17.5	0	0
62032200	棉制男式便服套装	17.5	0	0
62032300	合纤制男式便服套装	17.5	0	0
62032910	丝及绢丝制男式便服套装	17.5		0
62032920	毛制男式便服套装	17.5	0	0
62032990	其他纺织材料制男式便服套装	17.5	0	0
62033100	毛制男式上衣	16	0	0
62033200	棉制男式上衣	16	0	0
62033300	合纤制男式上衣	17.5	0	0
62033910	丝及绢丝制男式上衣	16	0	0
62033990	其他纺织材料制男式上衣	16	0	0
62034100	毛制男式长裤、工装裤等	16	0	0
62034210	棉制男式阿拉伯裤	16	0	0
62034290	棉制男式长裤、工装裤等	16	0	0
62034310	合成纤维制男式阿拉伯裤	17.5	0	0
62034390	合纤制男式长裤、工装裤等	17.5	0	0
62034910	其他纺织材料制男式阿拉伯裤	16	0	0
62034990	其他纺织材料制男童裤、工装裤	16	0	0
62041100	毛制女式西服套装	17.5	0	0
62041200	棉制女式西服套装	17.5	0	0
62041300	合纤制女式西服套装	17.5	0	0
62041910	丝及绢丝制女式西服套装	17.5	0	0
62041990	其他纺织材料制女式西服套装	17.5	0	0
62042100	毛制女式便服套装	17.5	0	0
62042200	棉制女式便服套装	17.5	0	0
62042300	合纤制女式便服套装	20	0	0
62042910	丝及绢丝制女式便服套装	20	0	0
62042990	其他纺织材料制女式便服套装	14	0	0
62043100	毛制女式上衣	16	0	0
62043200	棉制女式上衣	16	0	0
62043300	合纤制女式上衣	17.5	0	0
62043910	丝及绢丝制女式上衣	16	0	0
62043990	其他纺织材料制女式上衣	16	0	0
62044100	毛制连衣裙	16	0	0
62044200	棉制连衣裙	16	0	0
62044300	合纤制女式连衣裙	17.5	0	0
62044400	人纤制女式连衣裙	16	0	0
62044910	丝及绢丝制连衣裙	16	0	0
62044990	其他纺织材料制连衣裙	16	0	0
62045100	毛制裙子及裙裤	14	0	0
62045200	棉制裙子及裙裤	14	0	0
62045300	合纤制裙子及裙裤	16	0	0
62045910	丝及绢丝制裙子及裙裤	14	0	0
62045990	其他纺织材料制裙子及裙裤	14	0	0
62046100	毛制女式长裤、工装裤等	16	0	0
62046200	棉制女式长裤、工装裤等	16	0	0
62046300	合纤制女式长裤、工装裤等	17.5	0	0
62046900	其他纺织材料制女式长裤、工装裤等	16	0	0
62052000	棉制男衬衫	16	0	0
62053000	化纤制男衬衫	16	0	0
62059010	丝及绢丝制男衬衫	16	0	0
62059020	毛制男衬衫	16	0	0
62059090	其他纺织材料制男衬衫	16	0	0
62061000	丝及绢丝制女式衬衫	16	0	0
62062000	毛制女衬衫	16	0	0
62063000	棉制女衬衫	16	0	0
62064000	化纤制女衬衫	17.5	0	0
62069000	其他纺织材料制女衬衫	16	0	0
62071100	棉制男式内裤及三角裤	14	0	0
62071910	丝制男式内裤及三角裤	14	0	
62071920	化纤制男式内裤及三角裤	16	0	
62071990	其他纺织材料制男式内裤及三角裤	14	0	
62072100	棉制男式长睡衣及睡衣裤	14	0	
62072200	化纤制男式长睡衣及睡衣裤	16	0	
62079100	棉制男式浴衣、晨衣及类似品	14	0	0
62079910	丝及绢丝制男浴衣、晨衣及类似品	14	0	0
62079920	化纤制男浴衣、晨衣及类似品	16	0	0
62079990	其他纺织材料制男浴衣、晨衣及类似品	14	0	0
62081100	化纤制长衬裙及衬裙	16	0	
62081910	丝及绢丝制长衬裙及衬裙	14	0	
62081920	棉制长衬裙及衬裙	14	0	
62081990	其他纺织材料制长衬裙及衬裙	14	0	
62082100	棉制女式睡衣及睡衣裤	14	0	0
62082200	化纤制女式睡衣及睡衣裤	16	0	0
62082910	丝及绢丝制女式睡衣及睡衣裤	14	0	
62082990	其他纺织材料制女式睡衣及睡衣裤	14	0	
62089100	棉制女式背心、内衣、浴衣及类似品	14	0	0
62089200	化纤制女式背心、内衣及类似品	16	0	0
62089910	丝制女式背心、内衣及类似品	14	0	0
62089990	其他纺织材料制女式背心、内衣及类似	14	0	0
62092090	棉制婴儿服装及衣着附件	14	0	0
62093000	合纤制婴儿服装及衣着附件	16	0	0
62099010	毛制婴儿服装及衣着附件	14	0	0
62099090	其他纺织材料制婴儿服装及衣着附件	14	0	0
62101010	毛制毡呢或无纺织物服装	16	0	0
62101020	棉或麻制毡呢或无纺织物服装	16	0	0
62101030	化纤制毡呢或无纺织物服装	17.5	0	0
62101090	其他纺织材料制毡呢或无纺织物服装	16	0	0
62102000	用塑料、橡胶等处理的织物制男大衣等	16	0	0

税则号列 Tariff No.	货品名称 Description of Goods	最惠国 MFN	香港 H. K	澳门 MAC
62103000	用塑料、橡胶等处理的织物制女大衣等	16	0	0
62104000	用塑料、橡胶等处理的织物制的其他男式服装	16	0	0
62105000	用塑料、橡胶等处理的织物制的其他女式服装	16	0	0
62111100	男式游泳服	16	0	0
62111200	女式游泳服	16	0	
62112010	棉制滑雪服	16	0	
62112090	其他纺织材料制滑雪服	19	0	
62113210	棉制男式阿拉伯袍	16	0	
62113220	棉制男式运动服	16	0	0
62113290	棉制男式其他服装	16	0	0
62113310	化纤制男式阿拉伯袍	17.5	0	
62113320	化纤制运动服	17.5	0	0
62113390	化纤制男式运动服及其他服装	17.5	0	0
62113910	丝及绢丝制男式运动服及其他服装	16	0	0
62113920	毛制男式运动服及其他服装	16	0	0
62113990	其他纺织材料制男式运动服及其他服装	16	0	0
62114100	毛制女式运动服及其他服装	16	0	0
62114210	棉制女式运动服	16	0	0
62114290	棉制其他服装	16	0	0
62114310	化纤制女式运动服	17.5	0	0
62114390	化纤制其他服装	17.5	0	0
62114910	丝及绢丝制女式运动服及其他服装	16	0	0
62114990	其他纺织材料制女式运动服及其他服装	16	0	0
62121010	化纤制胸罩	16	0	
62121090	其他纺织材料制胸罩	14	0	0
62122010	化纤制束腰带及腹带	16	0	
62122090	其他纺织材料制束腰带及腹带	14	0	
62123010	化纤制紧身胸衣	16	0	
62123090	其他纺织材料制紧身胸衣	14	0	
62129010	化纤制吊裤带、吊袜带等	16	0	0
62129090	其他纺织材料制吊裤带、吊袜带等	14	0	0
62132010	棉制刺绣手帕	14	0	
62132090	其他棉制手帕	14	0	
62139090	其他纺织材料制手帕	14	0	
62141000	丝制披巾、头巾、围巾及类似品	14	0	
62142000	毛制披巾、头巾、围巾及类似品	14	0	
62143000	合纤制披巾、头巾及类似品	16	0	
62144000	人纤制披巾、头巾及类似品	14	0	
62149000	其他纺织材料制披巾、头巾及类似品	14	0	
62151000	丝及绢丝制领带及领结	14	0	

税则号列 Tariff No.	货品名称 Description of Goods	最惠国 MFN	香港 H. K	澳门 MAC
62152000	化纤制领带及领结	16	0	
62159000	其他纺织材料制领带及领结	14	0	
62160000	非针织非钩编手套	14	0	0
62171020	非针织非钩编和服腰带	14	0	
62171090	非针织非钩编服装或衣着附件	14	0	
62179000	非针织非钩编服装或衣着零件	14	0	0
63025110	棉制刺绣其他餐桌用织物制品	14	0	
63025190	棉制其他餐桌用织物制品	14	0	0
63029300	化纤制其他盥洗及厨房织物制品	16	0	
63039200	合纤制非针织非钩编窗帘等	16	0	
63063010	合纤制风帆	16	0	
63079000	其他纺织材料制成品	14	0	
64029100	其他橡胶、塑料短统靴(过踝)	24		0
64029900	其他橡胶、塑料鞋靴	24		0
64031900	皮革制鞋面的其他运动鞋靴	15		0
64032000	皮革条带为鞋面的皮底鞋	24		0
64039100	其他皮革制面的短统靴(过踝)	10		0
64039900	皮革制面的其他鞋靴	10		0
64041100	纺织材料制鞋面的运动鞋靴	24		0
64041900	纺织材料制鞋面胶底的其他鞋靴	24		0
64069900	其他材料制鞋靴、护腿等零件	15	0	0
65059090	针织或成匹织物制成的帽类	20		0
65069920	毛皮制帽类	10	0	
65070000	帽类附件	24		0
67010000	已加工羽毛、羽绒及其制品	20		0
68022110	具有一个平面的大理石及制品	10		0
68022120	石灰华	24		0
68022300	具有一个平面的花岗岩及制品	10		0
68022990	具有一个平面的其他石及制品	15		0
68030010	板岩制品	20		0
68101100	水泥制建筑用砖及石砌块	10.5	0	
68101910	人造石制砖、瓦、扁平石及类似品	10.5		0
68109110	钢筋混凝土和预应力混凝土管、杆、板、桩等	10.5	0	
68109190	其他水泥制建筑或土木工程用预制构件	10.5	0	
70071110	航空航天器及船舶用钢化安全玻璃	2	0	
70071190	车辆用钢化安全玻璃	10	0	
70140010	光学仪器用光学元件毛坯	10		0
70191900	玻璃纤维、梳条、纱线	10		0
70195900	其他玻璃纤维机织物	12	0	0
70199000	其他玻璃纤维及其制品	7		0
70200011	导电玻璃	10.5	0	
70200091	保温瓶或其他保温器用玻璃胆	21	0	
71023100	未加工或简单加工非工业用钻石	3	0	
71101990	其他半制成铂	3	0	
71102990	其他半制成钯	3	0	
71131110	镶嵌钻石的银首饰及其零件	20	0	0

税则号列 Tariff No.	货品名称 Description of Goods	最惠国 MFN	香港 H. K	澳门 MAC
71131190	其他银首饰及其零件	20	0	0
71131911	镶嵌钻石的黄金制首饰及其零件	20	0	0
71131919	其他黄金制首饰及其零件	20	0	0
71131991	镶嵌钻石的其他贵金属制首饰及其零件	35	0	0
71131999	其他贵金属制首饰及其零件	35	0	0
71132010	镶嵌钻石的以贱金属为底的包贵金属制首饰	35	0	0
71132090	其他以贱金属为底的包贵金属制首饰	35	0	0
71141100	银器及零件	35	0	0
71141900	其他贵金属制金银器及零件	35	0	0
71142000	以贱金属为底的包贵金属制金银器	35	0	0
71151000	金属丝布或格栅状的铂催化剂	3	0	
71159010	工业或实验室用贵或包贵金属制品	3	0	0
71159090	其他用途的贵或包贵金属制品	35	0	0
71161000	天然或养殖珍珠制品	35	0	0
71162000	宝石或半宝石制品	35	0	0
71171100	贱金属制袖扣、饰扣	35	0	0
71171900	其他贱金属制仿首饰	17	0	0
71179000	未列名材料制仿首饰	35	0	0
72107000	涂漆或涂塑的铁或非合金钢宽板材	4	0	
72124000	涂漆或涂塑的铁或非合金钢窄板材	4	0	
72142000	热加工带有轧制花纹的条、杆	3	0	
72179000	其他铁丝或非合金钢丝	8	0	
72193300	1mm＜厚度＜3mm 冷轧不锈钢板材	10	0	
72193400	0.5mm≤厚度≤1mm 冷轧不锈钢板材	10	0	
72193500	厚度＜0.5mm 冷轧不锈钢板材	10	0	
72230000	不锈钢丝	10	0	
73043910	非冷轧的铁制无缝锅炉管	4	0	
73043920	非冷轧的铁制无缝地质钻管套管	5	0	
73043990	非冷轧的铁制其他无缝管	4	0	
73072200	不锈钢制螺纹肘管、弯管、管套	8.4	0	
73072900	不锈钢制其他管子附件	8.4	0	
73083000	钢铁制门窗及其框架、门槛	10	0	
73089000	其他钢铁结构体及部件	4	0	
73102100	容积＜50L 焊边或卷边接合钢铁罐	17.5	0	
73110010	装压缩或液化气的钢铁容器	17.5	0	
73110090	其他装压缩或液化气的容器	8	0	
73142000	交点焊接的粗钢铁丝网、篱及格栅	7	0	
73143100	交点焊接的镀或涂锌细钢铁丝网	7	0	
73143900	交点焊接的其他细钢铁丝网、篱	7	0	
73145000	网眼钢铁板	8	0	

税则号列 Tariff No.	货品名称 Description of Goods	最惠国 MFN	香港 H. K	澳门 MAC
73151110	自行车滚子链	12	0	
73151120	摩托车滚子链	12	0	
73151190	其他滚子链	12	0	
73181500	其他螺钉及螺栓	8	0	
73182100	弹簧垫圈及其他防松垫圈	10	0	
73182300	铆钉	10	0	
73239300	餐桌、厨房等家用不锈钢器具	12	0	0
73241000	不锈钢制洗涤槽及脸盆	18	0	
73269010	其他工业用钢铁制品	10.5	0	
73269090	其他非工业用钢铁制品	8	0	
74032100	未锻轧的铜锌合金(黄铜)	1		0
74040000	铜废碎料	1.5	0	
74050000	铜母合金	4	0	
74072100	黄铜条、杆及型材及异型材	7		0
74081900	截面尺寸≤6mm 的精炼铜丝	4	0	
74092100	成卷的黄铜板、片、带	7	0	
74092900	其他黄铜板、片、带	7	0	
74099000	其他铜合金板、片、带	7	0	
74101100	无衬背的精炼铜箔	4	0	
74102100	有衬背的精炼铜箔	4	0	0
74112110	盘卷黄铜管	7	0	
74112190	铜锌合金(黄铜)管	7	0	
74152100	铜垫圈(包括弹簧垫圈)	10	0	
74152900	铜制其他无螺纹制品	10	0	
74153310	铜制木螺钉	8	0	
74153390	铜制其他螺钉螺栓螺母	8	0	
74153900	其他铜制螺纹制品	10	0	
74191000	铜链条及其零件	14	0	
76011010	按重量计含铝量在99.95%及以上的未煅轧非铝合金	5	0	
76011090	其他非煅轧非铝合金	5	0	
76012000	未锻轧铝合金	7		0
76020000	铝废碎料	1.5	0	
76051900	纯铝制的细丝	8	0	
76061190	纯铝制矩形的其他板、片及带	6	0	
76061220	厚度＜0.28mm 的铝合金制矩形铝板片带	6	0	
76061230	0.28mm≤厚度≤0.35mm 的铝合金制矩形铝板片带	6	0	
76061240	厚度＞0.35mm 的铝合金制矩形铝板片带	6	0	
76069100	纯铝制非矩形的板、片及带	6	0	
76069200	铝合金制非矩形的板、片及带	10	0	
76072000	有衬背铝箔	6	0	
76161000	铝钉、螺钉、螺母、垫圈等紧固件	10	0	
80011000	未锻轧非合金锡	3	0	
80012010	锡基巴毕脱合金	3	0	
80012020	焊锡	3	0	0
80012090	其他锡合金	3	0	

税则号列 Tariff No.	货品名称 Description of Goods	最惠国 MFN	香港 H. K	澳门 MAC
80020000	锡废碎料	1.5	0	
80030000	锡及锡合金条、杆、型材、丝	8	0	
80070090	其他锡制品	8	0	
82023900	其他圆锯片,包括部件	8	0	
82073000	锻压或冲压工具	8	0	
82075010	带超硬材料部件的钻孔工具	8	0	
82075090	带其他材料工作部件的钻孔工具	8	0	
82079010	带超硬材料部件的其他可互换工具	8	0	
82079090	其他可互换工具	8	0	
82159900	其他非成套的厨房或餐桌用具	18	0	
83015000	带锁的扣环及扣环框架	14	0	
83021000	铰链(折叶)	10	0	
83040000	贱金属档案柜、文件箱等办公用具	10.5	0	
83059000	信夹、信角、文件夹等办公用品	10.5	0	
83079000	其他贱金属软管,可有配件	8.4	0	
83081000	贱金属制钩、环及眼	10.5	0	
83082000	贱金属制管形铆钉及开口铆钉	10.5	0	
83089000	贱金属制珠子及亮晶片	10.5	0	
83091000	贱金属制冠形瓶塞	18	0	
83099000	盖子瓶帽螺口塞封志等包装用配件	12	0	
83111000	焊剂涂面的贱金属电极、电弧焊用	8	0	
83112000	以焊剂为芯的贱金属制焊丝	8	0	
83113000	以焊剂涂面或作芯的贱金属条或丝	8	0	
83119000	贱金属粘聚成的丝或条	8	0	
84134000	混凝土泵	8	0	
84135020	电动式往复式排液泵	10	0	
84137090	转速 < 10000 转/分离心泵	8	0	
84139100	液体泵用零件	5	0	
84143011	功率≤0.4kw 的冷藏、冷冻箱用压缩机	8	0	
84143012	功率 0.4－5kw 的冷藏、冷冻箱用压缩机	10	0	
84143013	功率 0.4－5kw 的空气调节器用压缩机	10	0	
84143014	功率 > 5kw 的空气调节器用压缩机	10	0	
84143015	冷冻或冷藏设备用,电动机额定功率超过 5 千瓦的电动机驱动压缩机	10	0	
84143019	其他制冷设备用压缩机	10	0	
84143090	非电机驱动的压缩机	9	0	
84144000	装在拖车底盘上的空气压缩机	8	0	
84148090	其他气体压缩机及通风罩或循环气罩	7	0	
84149090	税号 84.14 其他所列机器零件	7	0	
84152000	机动车辆上供人使用的空气调节器	20	0	
84159010	制冷量≤4 千大卡/时等空调的零件	10	0	
84159090	制冷量 > 4 千大卡/时等空调的零件	10	0	
84183010	制冷温度≤－40℃,容积≤800L 柜式冷冻箱	9		0
84183021	制冷温度 > －40℃,容积 500－800L 柜式冷冻箱	23		0
84183029	制冷温度 > －40℃,容积≤500L 柜式冷冻箱	30		0
84184010	制冷温度≤－40℃,容积≤900L 立式冷冻箱	9		0
84184021	制冷温度 > －40℃,容积 500－900L 立式冷冻箱	15		0
84184029	制冷温度 > －40℃,容积≤500L 立式冷冻箱	30		0
84185000	其他装有冷藏或冷冻装置的柜、箱、展示台	10	0	0
84186190	其他热泵,税目 8415 的空气调节器除外	15		0
84186920	其他制冷机组	10		0
84186990	其他制冷设备	10		0
84189991	制冷温度≤－40℃冷冻设备零件	9.5		0
84189992	制冷温度 > －40℃,容积 > 500L 冷藏设备零件	10		0
84189999	税号 84.18 其他制冷设备用零件	10		0
84195000	热交换装置	10	0	
84196011	制氧量≥15000 立方米/小时制氧机	12	0	
84196019	制氧量 < 15000 立方米/小时制氧机	13	0	
84196090	其他液化空气或其他气体的机器	10	0	
84199090	税号 84.19 的其他机器设备用零件	4	0	
84212110	家用型过滤或净化水的机器及装置	25	0	
84212190	其他过滤或净化水的装置	5	0	
84212300	内燃发动机的燃油过滤器	10	0	
84212910	其他压滤机	5	0	
84212990	其他液体的过滤、净化机器及装置	5	0	
84213100	内燃发动机的进气过滤器	10	0	
84213910	家用型气体过滤、净化机器及装置	15	0	
84213921	工业用静电除尘器	5	0	
84213922	工业用袋式除尘器	5	0	
84213923	工业用旋风式除尘器	5	0	
84213929	工业用其他除尘器	5	0	
84213990	其他气体的过滤、净化机器及装置	5	0	

税则号列 Tariff No.	货品名称 Description of Goods	最惠国 MFN	香港 H. K	澳门 MAC
84219910	家用型过滤、净化装置用零件	10	0	
84219990	其他过滤、净化装置用零件	5	0	
84223010	饮料及液体食品罐装设备	12	0	
84223021	水泥全自动灌包机	12	0	
84223029	其他水泥包装机	12	0	
84223030	其他包装机	10	0	
84223090	其他装填密封等包封机器	10	0	
84224000	其他包装或打包机器	10	0	
84229090	税号 84.22 其他未列名机器零件	8.5	0	
84248100	农业或园艺用喷射、喷雾机械器具	8	0	
84253990	其他非电动卷扬机及绞盘	5	0	
84281010	载客电梯	8	0	
84281090	其他升降机及倒卸式起重机	6	0	
84283200	其他斗式连续运货升降、输送机	5	0	
84283910	链式连续运送货物的升降机及输送机	5	0	
84283920	辊式连续运送货物的升降机及输送机	5	0	
84283990	其他未列名连续运货升降、输送机	5	0	
84289090	其他升降、搬运、装卸机械	5	0	
84304111	钻探深度≥6000 米的自推进石油钻探机	5	0	
84304119	其他自推进石油及天然气钻探机	5	0	
84304121	钻探深度≥6000 米的其他钻探机	5	0	
84304122	钻探深度＜6000 米履带式自推进钻机	5	0	
84304129	钻探深度＜6000 米的其他自推进钻机	5	0	
84304190	其他自推进的凿井机械	5	0	
84313900	税号 84.28 所列其他机械的零件	5	0	
84314310	石油或天然气钻探机用零件	4	0	
84314320	其他钻探机用零件	4	0	
84314390	其他凿井机用零件	5	0	
84314910	矿用电铲用零件	5	0	
84314990	税号 84.26,84.29,84.30 的其他零件	5	0	
84425000	活字、印刷用版、片及其他部件	7	0	
84431400	卷取进料式凸版印刷机	12	0	
84431980	其它印刷机	8	0	
84485900	税号 84.47 机器用的其他零附件	6	0	
84514000	洗涤、漂白或染色机器	8.4	0	0
84518000	税号 84.51 所列其他未列名的机器	12	0	
84522900	其他非自动缝纫机	12	0	
84581100	切削金属的数控卧式车床	9.7	0	
84581900	切削金属的非数控卧式车床	12	0	
84659100	加工木材等材料的锯床	10	0	

税则号列 Tariff No.	货品名称 Description of Goods	最惠国 MFN	香港 H. K	澳门 MAC
84672100	电动钻	10	0	
84672210	电动链锯	10	0	
84672290	其他电动锯	10	0	
84672910	电动砂磨工具	10	0	
84672920	电刨	10	0	
84672990	其他电动工具	10	0	
84679110	电动链锯用零件	6	0	
84679910	其他手提式电动工具用零件	10	0	
84772010	塑料造粒机	5	0	
84772090	其他加工橡胶或塑料的挤出机	5	0	
84773000	吹塑机	5	0	
84778000	其他橡胶或塑料加工机器	5	0	
84798110	绕线机	9.5	0	
84798190	其他处理金属的机械	9.5	0	
84804100	金属、硬质合金用注模或压模	8	0	
84807900	塑料或橡胶用其他型模	5	0	
84818010	其他阀门	7	0	
84818090	未列名龙头、旋塞及类似装置	5	0	
84821000	滚珠轴承	8	0	
84831010	船舶用传动轴	6	0	0
84831090	其他传动轴及曲柄	6	0	0
84832000	装有滚珠或滚子轴承的轴承座	6		0
84833000	未装滚珠或滚子轴承的轴承座	6		0
84834010	滚子螺杆传动装置	8	0	0
84834020	行星齿轮减速器	8	0	0
84834090	其他齿轮及齿轮传动装置	8	0	0
84835000	飞轮、滑轮及滑轮组	8		0
84836000	离合器及联轴器(包括万向节)	8		0
84839000	单独报验的带齿的轮及其他传动元件;零件	8	0	0
84879000	本章其他税号未列名机器零件	8	0	
85011010	输出功率≤37.5W 玩具电动机	24.5	0	
85011091	机座 20mm ≤ 直径 ＜ 39mm 微电机	9	0	
85011099	其他输出功率≤37.5W 微电机	9	0	
85013100	输出功率≤750 瓦直流电动机、发电机	12	0	0
85021100	输出功率≤75KVA 柴油发电机组	10	0	
85021200	75KVA＜输出功率≤375KVA 柴油发电机组	10	0	
85021310	375KVA＜输出功率≤2MVA 柴油发电机组	10	0	
85021320	输出功率＞2MVA 柴油发电机组	10	0	
85030010	玩具用电动机微电机零件	12	0	
85030020	输出功率＞350MVA 交流发电机零件	3	0	
85030030	风力驱动发电机组的零件	3	0	
85030090	其他电动机、发电机(组)零件	8	0	
85041010	电子镇流器	10		0

税则号列 Tariff No.	货品名称 Description of Goods	最惠国 MFN	香港 H. K	澳门 MAC
85041090	其他放电灯或放电管用镇流器	10		0
85043110	额定容量≤1KVA 的互感器	5		0
85043190	额定容量≤1KVA 的其他变压器	5	0	0
85043210	1KVA＜额定容量≤16KVA 的互感器	5		0
85043290	1KVA＜额定容量≤16KVA 其他变压器	5		0
85043300	16KVA＜额定容量≤500KVA 其他变压器	5		0
85043400	额定容量＞500KVA 的其他变压器	14		0
85044020	不间断供电电源(UPS)	10	0	
85044091	具有变流功能的半导体模块	10	0	0
85044099	其他未列名静止式变流器	10	0	0
85049011	额定容量＞400KVA 液体介质变压器零件	5	0	
85049019	其他变压器零件	8	0	
85049020	稳压电源及不间断供电电源零件	8	0	0
85049090	其他静止式变流器及电感器零件	8	0	0
85051190	其他金属的永磁体	7	0	
85051900	非金属永磁体	7	0	
85061010	碱性锌锰电池	20	0	
85061090	二氧化锰的原电池及原电池组	20	0	
85068000	其他原电池及原电池组	14	0	
85073000	镍镉蓄电池	10	0	
85078010	镍氢电池	12	0	
85078020	锂离子电池	12	0	
85078090	其他蓄电池	12	0	
85079010	铅酸蓄电池零件	10	0	
85079090	其他蓄电池零件	8	0	
85081100	功率不超过 1500 瓦,且带有容积不超过 20 升的电动真空吸尘器	10	0	
85087010	电动真空吸尘器用零件	12	0	
85099000	家用电动器具的零件	12	0	
85102000	电动毛发推剪	30	0	
85131010	手电筒	15		0
85131090	其他自供能源手提式电灯	17.5		0
85139010	手电筒零件	14	0	0
85139090	其他自供能源手提式电灯零件	14	0	0
85152110	直缝焊管机	10	0	
85152190	其他全自动或半自动电阻焊接机	10	0	
85158000	其他焊接机器及装置	8	0	
85159000	电气等焊接机器及装置零件	6	0	
85162100	电气储存式散热器	35		0
85162910	电气土壤加热器	10	0	0
85162990	电气空间加热器	10	0	0
85163100	电吹风机	10		0
85163200	其他电热理发器具	35		0
85163300	电热干手器	35		0
85164000	电熨斗	35		0
85166010	电磁炉	15		0
85166030	电饭锅	15		0
85166040	电炒锅	15		0
85166090	其他电热炉	15		0
85167110	滴液式咖啡机	32		0
85167120	蒸馏渗滤式咖啡机	32		0
85167130	泵压式咖啡机	32		0
85167190	其他电热咖啡机或茶壶	32		0
85167210	家用自动面包机	32		0
85167220	片式烤面包机(多士炉)	32		0
85167290	电热烤面包器	32		0
85167910	电热饮水机	32		0
85167990	其他电热器具	32		0
85169010	土壤加热器及加热电阻器零件	8	0	
85169090	税号 85.16 所列货品的其他零件	12	0	
85177040	对讲机用的零件	8	0	
85181000	传声器(麦克风)及其座架	10	0	
85189000	税号 85.18 所列货品的零件	10.5	0	
85221000	拾音头	35	0	
85229010	转盘或唱机用零附件	25	0	
85229021	录音机走带机构(机芯)	25	0	
85229022	磁头	25	0	
85229023	磁头零件	20	0	
85229029	盒式磁带录音机或放声机其他零件	30	0	
85229031	激光视盘机的机芯	30	0	
85229039	其他视频信号录放设备的零件附件	30	0	
85229090	税号 85.19 至 85.21 所列设备其他零件	20	0	
85232110	未录制的磁条卡	18	0	
85232120	已录制的磁条卡	15	0	
85234010	仅用于重放声音信息的已录制光盘	10	0	
85258013	非特种用途的其他电视摄像机	35		0
85284910	其他彩色阴极射线管监视器	30		0
85284990	其他黑白或单色的阴极射线管监视器	19		0
85285910	其他彩色监视器	30		0
85285990	其他黑白或单色的监视器	19		0
85286910	其他彩色投影机	30		0
85286990	其他黑白或单色的投影机	15		0
85287190	不带显示屏的其他黑白或单色的电视接收机	15		0
85287221	其他彩色模拟电视接收机,带液晶显示器的	30		0
85287229	其他彩色电视接收机,带液晶显示器的	30		0
85287231	其他彩色模拟电视接收机,带等离子显示器的	30		0

税则号列 Tariff No.	货品名称 Description of Goods	最惠国 MFN	香港 H. K	澳门 MAC
85287239	其他彩色电视接收机，带等离子显示器的	30		0
85287300	其他黑白或单色的电视接收机	15		0
85291010	雷达及无线电导航设备天线及零件	1.5	0	
85299041	特种用途电视摄像机、静像视频摄像机及其他视频摄录一体机，数字相机零件	8	0	
85299042	非特种用途的取像模块	12	0	
85299049	其他电视摄像机、静像视频摄像机及其他视频摄录一体机、数字相机零件	12	0	
85299060	收音机及其组合机的其他零件	15	0	
85311090	其他防盗或防火报警器及类似装置	10	0	
85318010	蜂鸣器	15	0	
85318090	其他电气音响或视觉信号装置	10	0	
85354000	避雷器、电压限幅器及电涌抑制器	18	0	
85359000	其他＞1000V 电路开关等电气装置	10	0	
85361000	熔断器(电压≤1000V)	10	0	
85362000	电压≤1000V 自动断路器	9	0	
85363000	电压≤1000V 其他电路保护装置	9	0	
85364900	电压＞60V 的继电器	10	0	
85367000	光导纤维、光导纤维束或光缆用连接器	8	0	0
85371011	可编程序控制器	5	0	
85371019	其他数控装置	5	0	
85371090	其他电力控制或分配的装置	8.4	0	0
85372090	其他电力控制或分配装置	8.4	0	
85389000	税号 85.35、85.36 或 85.37 装置的零件	7	0	
85392991	电压≤12V 未列名的白炽灯泡	12	0	
85404000	点距＜0.4mm 彩色数据/图形显示管	8	0	
85441100	铜制绕组电线	10	0	0
85444921	1000V≥耐压＞80V 无接头电缆	6	0	
85444929	1000V≥耐压＞80V 无接头电导体	12	0	0
85446012	额定电压不超过 35 千伏的电缆	10	0	
85446013	额定电压超过 35 千伏，但不超过 110 千伏的电缆	8.4	0	
85446014	额定电压超过 110 千伏，但不超过 220 千伏的电缆	8.4	0	
85446019	其他额定电压超过 1000 伏的电缆	8.4	0	
85446090	耐压＞1KV 的其他电导体	21	0	
87082930	车窗玻璃升降器	10	0	
87082941	汽车电动天窗	10	0	
87082942	汽车手动天窗	10	0	
87089500	机动车辆的安全气囊装置	10	0	
90011000	光导纤维束及光缆	5	0	
90012000	偏振材料制的片及板	8	0	
90013000	隐形眼镜片	10	0	
90014010	玻璃制变色镜片	20	0	
90014091	玻璃制太阳镜片	20	0	
90014099	玻璃制其他眼镜片	20	0	
90015010	非玻璃材料制变色镜片	20	0	
90015091	非玻璃材料制太阳镜片	20	0	
90015099	非玻璃材料制其他眼镜片	20	0	
90019000	税号 90.01 未列名的其他光学元件	8	0	
90021990	税号 90.02 未列名的其他物镜	15	0	
90029010	照相机用未列名光学元件	15	0	
90029090	其他光学仪器用未列名光学元件	15	0	
90031100	塑料制眼镜架	18	0	0
90031900	非塑料材料制眼镜架	10	0	0
90039000	眼镜架零件	10	0	
90041000	太阳镜	20	0	0
90049010	变色镜	16	0	0
90049090	其他眼镜	20	0	0
90069110	特种用途照相机的零附件	8	0	
90069120	一次成像照相机的零附件	5	0	
90069191	照相机自动调焦组件	10	0	
90069192	其他照相机的快门组件	10	0	
90069199	其他照相机的其他零附件	10	0	
90101010	电影用胶卷的自动显影装置及设备	14	0	
90101020	特种照相胶卷自动显影装置及设备	8.4	0	
90101091	彩色胶卷用自动显影及设备	25	0	
90101099	其他胶卷的自动显影装置及设备	15	0	
90132000	激光器	6		0
90138010	放大镜	12	0	0
90138030	液晶显示板	5	0	0
90138090	其他液晶装置及光学仪器	5	0	0
90139010	激光器、望远镜等装置的零附件	6	0	0
90139090	税号 90.13 所列其他货品的零附件	8	0	0
90189010	听诊器	4	0	
90189020	血压测量仪器及器具	4	0	
90189030	内窥镜	4	0	
90189040	肾脏透析设备(人工肾)	4	0	
90189050	透热疗法设备	4	0	
90189060	输血设备	4	0	
90189070	麻醉设备	4	0	
90189080	宫内节育器	4	0	
90189090	税号 90.18 中未列名的医疗仪器	4	0	
90191010	按摩器具	15	0	
90191090	机械疗法器具、心理功能测验装置	4	0	
90200000	其他呼吸器具及防毒面具	8	0	0

税则号列 Tariff No.	货品名称 Description of Goods	最惠国 MFN	香港 H. K	澳门 MAC
90271000	气体或烟雾分析仪	7	0	
90283010	电度表	10	0	
90283090	其他电量计	10	0	
90303110	量程≤五位半的数字万用表,不带记录装置	15		0
90303310	量程≤五位半的数字电流表、电压表,不带记录装置	15	0	
90303320	不带记录装置的电阻测试仪	14	0	
90303390	检测电压、电流及功率的其他仪器,不带记录装置	9	0	
90309000	税号 90.30 所属货品的零件及附件	7	0	
90318010	光纤通信及光纤性能测试仪	5	0	
90318020	坐标测量仪	5	0	
90318090	未列名测量、检验仪器器具及机器	5	0	
90321000	恒温器	7	0	
90322000	恒压器	7	0	
90328100	液压或气压的其他仪器及装置	7	0	
91021100	机械指示式的其他电子手表	12.5	0	0
91021200	光电显示式的其他电子手表	23	0	0
91031000	以表芯装成的电子钟	23	0	0
91051100	电子闹钟	23	0	0
91081100	已组装的机械指示式完整电子表芯	16	0	0
91081200	已组装的光电显示式完整电子表芯	16	0	0
91081900	其他已组装的完整电子表芯	16	0	0
91089090	其他已组装完整机械表芯	16	0	0
91112000	贱金属制的表壳	14	0	0
91132000	贱金属制的表带及其零件	14	0	0
91149000	钟、表的其他零件	14	0	0
92011000	竖式钢琴	17.5		0
94019011	机动车辆的座椅调角器	10	0	
94042100	海绵橡胶或泡沫塑料制褥垫	20	0	
94042900	其他材料制褥垫	20	0	
94049010	羽绒或羽毛填充的寝具及类似品	20	0	
94049020	兽毛填充的寝具及类似品	20	0	
94049030	丝棉填充的寝具及类似品	20	0	
94049040	化纤棉填充的寝具及类似品	20	0	
94049090	其他材料制的寝具及类似品	20	0	
94054010	探照灯	17.5		0
94054020	聚光灯	17.5		0
94054090	其他电灯及照明装置	10		0
94056000	发光标志、发光铭牌及类似品	20	0	
94059200	税号 94.05 所列物品的塑料制零件	20		0
94059900	税号 94.05 所列物品其他材料制零件	20		0
95062900	其他水上运动用具	14	0	
95069110	健身及康复器械	12	0	
95069120	滑板	12	0	
95069190	一般的体育活动、体操或竞技用品	12	0	
95069900	其他未列名的 95 章用品及设备	12	0	0
96031000	用枝条或其他植物材料捆扎成的帚	25		0
96062200	金属制钮扣,未用纺织材料包裹	15	0	0
96062900	其他钮扣	15	0	
96063000	钮扣芯及钮扣的其他零件	15	0	
96071100	装有贱金属齿的拉链	21	0	0
96071900	其他拉链	21	0	0
96086000	圆珠笔芯	21	0	
96089100	钢笔头及笔尖粒	12	0	
96089910	机器、仪器用笔	17.5	0	
96089920	蜡纸铁笔、钢笔杆、铅笔杆等	21	0	
96089990	其他笔零件	21	0	
96121000	打字机色带或类似色带	10.5		0
96170010	保温瓶及零件	24	0	
96170090	其他真空容器及零件	18	0	
97040010	使用或未使用的,邮票	8		0
97040090	其他使用或未使用的邮票、印花税票及类似票证	14		0

注:税号 87082941 和 87082942 包括汽车电动、手动天窗的零件。

附件8：

亚太贸易协定税目、税率表

Appendix 8：

Tax Item and Tax Rates in Asia Pacific Treaty

税则号列	货品名称(简称)	最惠国税率(%)	协定税率(%)
01069020	其他食用动物	10	9
01069090	其他动物	10	9
03019190	其他活鳟鱼	10.5	8
03019290	其他活鳗鱼	10	6.7
03019390	其他活鲤鱼	10.5	8
03019490	其他活蓝鳍金枪鱼	10.5	8
03019590	其他活南方蓝鳍金枪鱼	10.5	8
03019992	活鲀	10.5	8
03019999	其他活鱼	10.5	8
03021900	其他鲜、冷鲑鱼	12	8
03022100	鲜、冷庸鲽鱼	12	9
03022200	鲜、冷鲽鱼	12	9
03022300	鲜、冷鳎鱼	12	9
03022900	其他鲜、冷比目鱼	12	6
03023100	鲜、冷长鳍金枪鱼	12	9
03023200	鲜、冷黄鳍金枪鱼	12	9
03023300	鲜冷鲣鱼	12	8
03023900	其他鲜、冷金枪鱼	12	8
03024000	鲜、冷鲱鱼	12	8
03025000	鲜、冷鳕鱼	12	8
03026100	鲜、冷沙丁鱼、黍鲱鱼	12	8
03026200	鲜、冷黑线鳕鱼	12	8
03026300	鲜、冷绿青鳕鱼	12	8
03026400	鲜、冷鲭鱼	12	8
03026500	鲜、冷角鲨及其他鲨鱼	12	9
03026600	鲜冷鳗鱼	12	8
03026700	鲜、冷剑鱼	12	8
03026800	鲜、冷南极犬牙鱼	12	8
03026910	鲜冷带鱼	12	8
03026920	鲜冷黄鱼	12	8
03026930	鲜冷鲳鱼	12	8
03026950	鲜、冷鲀	12	8
03026990	其他鲜、冷鱼	12	8
03031100	冻红大马哈鱼,但鱼肝及鱼卵除外	10	6.7
03031900	其他冻大马哈鱼,但鱼肝及鱼卵除外	10	6.7
03032900	其他冻鲑鱼	10	6.7
03033110	冻格陵兰庸鲽鱼	10	6.7
03033190	冻庸鲽鱼	10	6.7
03033200	冻鲽鱼	12	8
03033300	冻鳎鱼	12	8
03033900	其他冻比目鱼	10	8
03034100	冻长鳍金枪鱼	12	9
03034200	冻黄鳍金枪鱼	12	9
03034300	冻鲣鱼	12	9
03034900	其他冻金枪鱼,但鱼肝及鱼卵除外	12	9
03035100	冻鲱鱼(大西洋鲱鱼、太平洋鲱鱼),但鱼肝及鱼卵除外	10	6.7
03035200	冻鳕鱼(大西洋鳕鱼、太平洋鳕鱼、格陵兰鳕鱼),但鱼肝及鱼卵除外	10	6.7
03036100	冻剑鱼,但鱼肝及鱼卵除外	10	5
03036200	冻南极犬牙鱼,但鱼肝及鱼卵除外	10	5
03037100	冻沙丁鱼、黍鲱鱼	12	8
03037200	冻黑线鳕鱼	12	8
03037300	冻绿青鳕鱼	12	8
03037400	冻鲭鱼	10	6.7
03037500	冻角鲨及其他鲨鱼	12	9
03037600	冻鳗鱼	12	8
03037700	冻尖吻鲈鱼	12	8
03037910	冻带鱼	10	5
03037920	冻黄鱼	10	5
03037930	冻鲳鱼	10	5
03037940	冻罗非鱼	10	5
03037990	其他未列名冻鱼	10	5
03038000	冻鱼肝及鱼卵	10	9
03041100	鲜、冷剑鱼片及鱼肉	12	9
03041200	鲜、冷南极犬牙鱼片及鱼肉	12	9
03041900	其他鲜、冷的鱼片及鱼肉	12	9
03053000	干或盐制的鱼片	10	7.8
03056100	盐腌及盐渍的鲱鱼(大西洋、太平洋鲱鱼)	16	11.1
03056200	盐腌及盐渍的鳕鱼	16	12
03056300	盐腌及盐渍的 Anchovies(醍)鱼	16	12
03061200	冻大螯虾	10	7.2
03061311	冻小虾仁	8	4
03061312	冻北方长额虾	5	2.5
03061319	其他冻小虾	5	2.5
03061321	冻对虾仁	8	4
03061329	其他冻对虾	5	2.5
03073900	其他冻、干、盐制的贻贝	14	9.8
03074900	其他冻、干、盐制的墨鱼及鱿鱼	12	10
04021000	脂肪含量≤1.5%固状乳及奶油	10	7
04022100	脂肪量>1.5%未加糖固状乳及奶油	10	7
04052000	乳酱	10	8.1

税则号列	货品名称(简称)	最惠国税率(%)	协定税率(%)
05040011	整个或切块的盐渍猪肠衣(猪大肠头除外)	20	10
05040012	整个或切块的盐渍绵羊肠衣	18	9
05040013	整个或切块的盐渍山羊肠衣	18	9
05040014	整个或切块的盐渍猪大肠头	20	10
05040019	整个或切块的其他动物肠衣	18	9
05040021	冷和冻的鸡肫	T2	T2
05040029	鲜、冷、冻、干、盐制的其他动物胃	20	10
05040090	鲜、冷、冻、干、盐制的其他动物肠、膀胱、胃	20	10
05051000	填充用羽毛;羽绒	10	7.5
06011010	休眠的番红花球茎	4	2
06011099	其它休眠的鳞茎、块茎、块根等	5	2.5
06012000	生长或开花的鳞茎等及菊苣植物	15	7.5
06022090	其他食用水果及坚果树及灌木	10	5
06029099	其他非种用活植物	10	5
06031100	鲜玫瑰	10	5
06031200	鲜康乃馨	10	5
06031300	鲜兰花	10	5
06031400	鲜菊花	10	5
06031900	其他鲜的插花及花蕾	10	5
06039000	干的及经过染色等加工的插花及花蕾	23	11.5
07019000	其他鲜或冷的马铃薯	13	9
07031010	鲜或冷的洋葱	13	6.5
07031020	鲜或冷的青葱	13	6.5
07032010	鲜或冷藏的大蒜头	13	6.5
07032020	鲜或冷藏的大蒜蒜台及蒜苗(青蒜)	13	6.5
07032090	其他鲜或冷藏的大蒜	13	6.5
07070000	鲜或冷的黄瓜及小黄瓜	13	6.5
07081000	鲜或冷的豌豆	13	6.5
07082000	鲜或冷的豇豆及菜豆	13	6.5
07089000	鲜或冷的其他豆类蔬菜	13	6.5
07092000	鲜或冷的芦笋	13	6.5
07093000	鲜或冷的茄子	13	6.5
07096000	鲜或冷的辣椒,包括甜椒	13	6.5
07119031	盐水竹笋	13	6.5
07119034	盐水大蒜	13	6.5
07119039	盐水其他蔬菜;什锦蔬菜	13	6.5
07119090	暂时保藏的其他蔬菜;什锦蔬菜	13	6.5
07123100	干伞菌属蘑菇	13	9
07123910	干香菇	13	9
07123920	干金针菇	13	9
07123930	干草菇	13	9
07123940	干口蘑	13	9
07123950	干牛肝菌	13	9
07123990	其他干制蘑菇及块菌	13	9
07133190	其他干绿豆	3	1.5
07133900	干豇豆及菜豆	7	3.5
07142019	其他鲜甘薯	13	6.5
07142020	干甘薯	13	6.5
07142030	冷或冻的甘薯	13	6.5
07149010	鲜、干或冷、冻的荸荠	13	6.5
07149029	其他藕	13	6.5
07149030	芋头	13	6.5
07149090	含有高淀粉或菊粉的其他类似根茎	13	6.5
08011100	干的椰子	12	6
08011990	其他鲜椰子	12	6
08029010	鲜或干的槟榔	10	5
08030000	鲜或干的香蕉,包括芭蕉	10	6.9
08043000	鲜或干菠萝	12	7.9
08044000	鲜或干鳄梨	25	12.5
08045010	鲜或干番石榴	15	7.5
08045020	鲜或干芒果	15	10.6
08045030	鲜或干山竹果	15	7.5
08055000	鲜或干的柠檬及酸橙	11	5.5
08059000	其他鲜或干的柑桔属水果	30	15
08071100	鲜西瓜	25	12.5
08071910	鲜哈密瓜	12	6
08071920	鲜罗马甜瓜及加勒比甜瓜	12	6
08071990	其他鲜甜瓜	12	6
08082012	鲜鸭梨、雪梨	12	10
08082013	鲜香梨	12	10
08105000	鲜猕猴桃	20	16.5
08109010	鲜荔枝	30	20
08109070	莲雾	20	16.4
08109080	火龙果	20	16.4
08109090	其他鲜果	20	16.4
09021010	每件净重≤3kg 的花茶	15	7.5
09021090	每件净重≤3kg 的其他绿茶	15	7.5
09022010	每件净重>3kg 的花茶	15	7.5
09022090	每件净重>3kg 的其他绿茶	15	7.5
09023010	每件净重≤3kg 的乌龙茶	15	7.5
09023020	每件净重≤3kg 的普洱茶	15	7.5
09023090	每件净重≤3kg 的其他发酵、半发酵红茶	15	7.5

税则号列	货品名称(简称)	最惠国税率(%)	协定税率(%)
09024010	每件净重>3kg的乌龙茶	15	7.5
09024020	每件净重>3kg的普洱茶	15	7.5
09024090	每件净重>3kg的其他红茶(已发酵)及半发酵茶	15	7.5
09041200	已磨胡椒	20	10
09042010	辣椒干	20	10
09042020	辣椒粉	20	10
09093000	枯茗子	15	7.5
09101000	姜	15	7.5
09103000	姜黄	15	7.5
09109100	混合调味香料	15	7.5
10030090	其他大麦	3	0
11063000	水果及坚果的细粉、粗粉及粉末	20	10
12010091	黄大豆	3	0
12010092	黑大豆	3	0
12010093	青大豆	3	0
12010099	其他大豆	3	0
12030000	干椰子肉	15	7.5
12051090	其他低芥子酸油菜子	9	0
12059090	其他油菜子	9	0
12074090	其他芝麻	10	9
12112020	鲜或干的野山参(西洋参除外)	20	16.4
12119011	鲜或干的当归	6	3
12119012	鲜或干的田七	6	3
12119013	鲜或干的党参	6	3
12119014	鲜或干的黄连	6	3
12119015	鲜或干的菊花	6	3
12119016	鲜或干的冬虫夏草	6	3
12119017	鲜或干的贝母	6	3
12119018	鲜或干的川芎	6	3
12119019	鲜或干的半夏	6	3
12119021	鲜或干的白芍	6	3
12119022	鲜或干的天麻	6	3
12119023	鲜或干的黄芪	6	3
12119024	鲜或干的大黄、籽黄	6	3
12119025	鲜或干的白术	6	3
12119026	鲜或干的地黄	6	3
12119027	鲜或干的槐米	6	3
12119028	鲜或干的杜仲	6	3
12119029	鲜或干的茯苓	6	3
12119031	鲜或干的枸杞	6	3
12119032	鲜或干的大海子	6	3
12119033	鲜或干的沉香	3	1.5
12119034	鲜或干的沙参	6	3
12119039	其他主要用作药料的鲜或干的植物	6	3
12119050	主要用作香料的植物	8	4
12119091	鲜或干的鱼藤根、除虫菊	3	1.5
12119099	其他鲜或干的杀虫、杀菌用植物	9	4.5
12122010	鲜、冷、冻或干的海带	20	10
12122020	鲜、冷、冻或干的发菜	20	10
12122031	干的裙带菜	15	7.5
12122032	鲜的裙带菜	15	7.5
12122039	冷或冻的裙带菜	15	7.5
12122041	干紫菜	15	7.5
12122042	鲜紫菜	15	7.5
12122049	冷或冻的紫菜	15	7.5
12122050	鲜、冷、冻或干马尾藻	15	7.5
12122090	鲜、冷、冻或干的其他海草及其他藻类	15	7.5
12129920	鲜、冷、冻或干的刺槐豆,包括刺槐豆子	20	10
13021990	其他植物液汁及浸膏	20	15
13023200	刺槐豆、刺槐豆子或瓜尔豆制得的胶液及增稠剂	15	10
14049010	主要供染料或鞣料用的植物原料	5	4.3
15020010	未炼制的牛、羊脂肪	8	0
15020090	已炼制的牛、羊脂肪	8	0
15131100	初榨椰子油分离品	9	4.5
15131900	椰子油及其分离品	9	4.5
16041910	制作或保藏的(河)鳗鱼,整条或切块,但未绞碎	12	9.9
16041931	制作或保藏的斑点叉尾鮰鱼	12	9.9
16041939	制作或保藏的其他叉尾鮰鱼	12	9.9
16041990	制作或保藏的其他鱼,整条或切块,但未绞碎	12	9.9
16042011	鱼翅罐头	12	9.9
16042019	其他制作或保藏的鱼罐头	12	9.9
16042091	鱼翅	12	9.9
16042099	其他制作或保藏的鱼	12	9.9
16059020	制作或保藏的蛤	5	3.9
16059090	其他制作或保藏的软体动物及其他水生无脊椎动物	5	3.9
17041000	口香糖,不论是否裹糖	12	9.5
17049000	其他不含可可的糖食	10	8.2
18062000	每件净重>2kg的含可可食品	10	7.7
18063100	其他夹心块状或条状的含可可食品	8	6.4
18063200	其他不夹心块状或条状含可可食品	10	7.7
18069000	其他巧克力及含可可的食品	8	6.4

税则号列	货品名称(简称)	最惠国税率(%)	协定税率(%)	税则号列	货品名称(简称)	最惠国税率(%)	协定税率(%)
19023030	即食或快熟面条	15	13.1	25161200	矩形或正方形的花岗岩	4	2
19023090	其他面食	15	13.1	25162000	砂岩,不论是否粗加修整或切割成矩形板块	3	2.1
19053100	甜饼干	15	12.4	25169000	其他碑用或建筑用石,不论是否粗加修整或切割成矩形板块	3	2.1
19053200	华夫饼干及圣餐饼	15	12.4	25232100	白水泥,不论是否人工着色	6	4.5
19059000	其他面包、糕点、饼干及其焙烘糕饼	20	17.1	25232900	其他硅酸盐水泥,不论是否着色	8	6
20081910	核桃仁罐头	20	10	27011900	未制成型的其他煤,不论是否粉化	5	3.5
20081920	其他果仁罐头	13	6.5	27040010	煤制焦炭及半焦炭不论是否成型	5	2.5
20081991	栗仁	10	5	27040090	甑炭	5	2.5
20081992	用其他方法制作或保藏的芝麻	10	5	27074000	萘	7	6
20081999	其他坚果及子仁	10	5	27101120	石脑油	6	5.4
20093110	白利糖度不超过20的柠檬汁	18	16.8	27101991	润滑油	6	5.4
20093190	其他未混合的白利糖度值不超过20的桔汁属水果汁	18	16.8	27101992	润滑脂	6	5.4
20093910	白利糖度超过20的柠檬汁	18	16.8	27101994	液体石蜡和重质液体石蜡	6	5.4
20093990	其他未混合的柑桔属水果汁,白利糖度值不超过20	18	16.8	27111200	液化丙烷	5	3.5
20098011	椰子汁	10	9	27111910	直接灌注香烟打火机及类似打火器用,其包装容器的容积超过300立方厘米的其他液化燃料	10	7
20098012	芒果汁	20	17.4	27111990	其他液化石油气及烃类气	3	2.1
20098013	西番莲果汁	20	17.4	27132000	石油沥青	8	5.6
20098014	番石榴果汁	20	17.4	28030000	碳(碳黑及其他税号未列名的其他形状的碳)	5.5	4.4
20098019	其他未混合的水果汁	20	10	28151100	固体氢氧化钠	10	7
20098020	其他未混合的蔬菜汁	20	10	28151200	氢氧化钠水溶液及液体烧碱	8	5.6
20099010	混合水果汁	20	17.4	28273910	氯化锂	5.5	4.4
21012000	茶、马黛茶浓缩精汁及其制品	32	16	28273920	氯化钡	5.5	4.4
21039010	味精	21	18.2	28273990	其他未列名氯化物	5.5	4.4
21039090	其他调味品	21	18.4	28281000	商品次氯酸钙及其他钙的次氯酸盐	12	8.4
21069091	烤制紫菜	20	18.4	28371120	氧氰化钠	5.5	5
21069099	其他编号未列名的食品	20	18.4	28461010	氧化铈	5.5	3.9
22029000	其他无酒精饮料	35	29.5	28461020	氢氧化铈	5.5	3.9
22086000	伏特加酒	10	8.8	28461030	碳酸铈	5.5	3.9
22087000	利口酒及柯迪尔酒	10	8.8	28461090	铈的其他化合物	5.5	3.9
22089010	龙舌兰酒	10	8.8	28500000	氢化物、氮化物、迭氮化物、硅化物及硼化物,不论是否已有化学定义	5.5	3.9
22089090	其他蒸馏酒及酒精饮料	10	8.8	29025000	苯乙烯	2	1.4
23012010	饲料用鱼粉	2	0	29031300	氯仿(三氯甲烷)	10	9
23012090	其他不适于供人食用的水产品渣粉	5	0	29032100	氯乙烯	5.5	3.9
23040010	提炼豆油所得的油渣饼(豆饼)	5	0	29054500	丙三醇(甘油)	14	11.2
23040090	提炼豆油所得的其他固体残渣	5	0	29173611	精对苯二甲酸	7.6	7.1
23065000	椰子或干椰肉油渣饼及固体残渣	5	2.5	29173619	其他对苯二甲酸	7.6	7.1
23099010	制成的饲料添加剂	5	2.5				
23099090	其他配制的动物饲料	6.5	3.3				
24011010	未去梗的烤烟	10	9.4				
24031000	供吸用的烟丝	57	50				
25161100	原状或粗加修整的花岗岩	4	2				

税则号列	货品名称(简称)	最惠国税率(%)	协定税率(%)
29224210	谷氨酸	10	8.6
29331100	二甲基苯基吡唑酮(安替比林)及其衍生物	6.5	6
29334910	环丙氟哌酸	6.5	6
29335900	其他结构上有嘧啶环或哌嗪环的化合物(不论是否氢化)	6.5	4.6
29411011	氨苄青霉素	6	5
29411012	氨苄青霉素三水酸	6	5
29411019	其他氨苄青霉素盐	6	5
29419051	7 氨基头孢烷酸,7 氨基脱乙酰氧基头孢烷酸	6	5
29419052	头孢氨苄及其盐	6	5
29419053	头孢唑啉及其盐	6	5
29419054	头孢拉啶及其盐	6	5
29419055	头孢三嗪(头孢曲松)及其盐	6	5
29419056	头孢哌酮及其盐	6	5
29419057	头孢噻肟及其盐	6	5
29419058	头孢克罗及其盐	6	5
29419059	其他先锋霉素及其衍生物,及它们的盐	6	5
29419060	麦迪霉素及其衍生物,及它们的盐	6	4.2
29419090	其他抗菌素	6	5
30031011	含有氨苄青霉素的混合药品(两种或两种以上成分混合而成的,治病或防病用,未配定剂量或非零售包装)	6	4.5
30031012	含有羟氨苄青霉素的混合药品(两种或两种以上成分混合而成的,治病或防病用未配定剂量或非零售包装)	6	4.5
30031013	含有青霉素 V 的混合药品(两种或两种以上成分混合而成的,治病或防病用未配定剂量或非零售包装)	6	4.5
30031019	含有其他青霉素及具有青霉烷酸结构的青霉素衍生物的混合药品(两种或两种以上成分混合而成的,治病或防病用未配定剂量或非零售包装)	6	4.5
30031090	含有含有链霉素的混合药品(两种或两种以上成分混合而成的,治病或防病用未配定剂量或非零售包装)	6	4.5
30032011	含有头孢噻肟的混合药品(两种或两种以上成分混合而成的,治病或防病用未配定剂量或非零售包装)	6	5.4
30032012	含有头孢他啶的混合药品(两种或两种以上成分混合而成的,治病或防病用未配定剂量或非零售包装)	6	5.4
30032013	含有头孢西丁的混合药品(两种或两种以上成分混合而成的,治病或防病用未配定剂量或非零售包装)	6	5.4
30032014	含有头孢替唑的混合药品(两种或两种以上成分混合而成的,治病或防病用未配定剂量或非零售包装)	6	5.4
30032015	含有头孢克罗的混合药品(两种或两种以上成分混合而成的,治病或防病用未配定剂量或非零售包装)	6	5.4
30032016	含有头孢呋辛的混合药品(两种或两种以上成分混合而成的,治病或防病用未配定剂量或非零售包装)	6	5.4
30032017	含有头孢三嗪(头孢曲松)的混合药品(两种或两种以上成分混合而成的,治病或防病用未配定剂量或非零售包装)	6	5.4
30032018	含有头孢哌酮的混合药品(两种或两种以上成分混合而成的,治病或防病用未配定剂量或非零售包装)	6	5.4
30032019	含有其他头孢菌素的混合药品(两种或两种以上成分混合而成的,治病或防病用未配定剂量或非零售包装)	6	5.4
30032090	其他含有其他抗菌素的混合药品(两种或两种以上成分混合而成的,治病或防病用未配定剂量或非零售包装)	6	4.2
30033100	含有胰岛素但不含抗菌素的混合药品(两种或两种以上成分混合而成的,治病或防病用未配定剂量或非零售包装)	5	3.5
30033900	含激素(胰岛素除外)或税目 29.37 其他产品,但不含抗菌素的混合药品(两种或两种以上成分混合而成的,治病或防病用未配定剂量或非零售包装)	6	4.2

税则号列	货品名称(简称)	最惠国税率(%)	协定税率(%)
30039010	含磺胺类的混合药品(两种或两种以上成分混合而成的,治病或防病用未配定剂量或非零售包装)	6	4.2
30041011	氨苄青霉素制剂(混合,治病或防病用,已配定剂量或制成零售包装)	6	4.5
30041012	羟氨苄青霉素制剂(两种或两种以上成分混合而成的,治病或防病用,已配定剂量或制成零售包装)	6	4.5
30041013	青霉素Ⅴ制剂(两种或两种以上成分混合而成的,治病或防病用,已配定剂量或制成零售包装)	6	4.5
30041019	其他青霉素制剂(混合或非混合,治病或防病用,已配定剂量或制成零售包装)	6	4.5
30041090	含有其他青霉素及具有青霉烷酸结构的青霉素衍生物或链霉素及其衍生物的药品(混合或非混合,治病或防病用,已配定剂量或制成零售包装)	6	4.5
30042011	头孢噻肟制剂(混合或非混合,治病或防病用已配定剂量或制成零售包装)	6	5
30042012	头孢他啶制剂(混合或非混合,治病或防病用,已配定剂量或制成零售包装)	6	5
30042013	头孢西丁制剂(混合或非混合,治病或防病用,已配定剂量或制成零售包装)	6	5
30042014	头孢替唑制剂(混合或非混合,治病或防病用,已配定剂量或制成零售包装)	6	5
30042015	头孢克罗制剂(混合或非混合,治病或防病用,已配定剂量或制成零售包装)	6	5
30042016	头孢呋辛制剂(混合或非混合,治病或防病用,已配定剂量或制成零售包装)	6	5
30042017	头孢三嗪(头孢曲松)制剂(混合或非混合,治病或防病用,已配定剂量或制成零售包装)	6	5
30042018	头孢哌酮制剂(混合或非混合,治病或防病用,已配定剂量或制成零售包装)	6	5
30042019	含有其他头孢菌素制剂(混合或非混合,治病或防病用,已配定剂量或制成零售包装)	6	5
30042090	含有其他抗菌素的药品(混合或非混合,治病或防病用,已配定剂量或制成零售包装)	6	4.2
30043100	含有胰岛素但不含抗菌素的药品(混合或非混合,治病或防病用已配定剂量或零售包装)	5	3.5
30043200	含肾上腺皮混合或非混合质激素但不含抗菌素的药品(,治病或防病用已配定剂量或零售包装)	5	3.5
30043900	含有税目29.37其他产品但不含抗菌素的药品(混合或非混合,治病或防病用已配定剂量或零售包装)	5	3.5
30044010	含有奎宁或其盐,但不含抗菌素及税目29.37的产品的药品(混合或非混合,治病或防病用已配定剂量或零售包装)	5	4
30045000	含有维生素或税目29.36其他产品的其他药品(混合或非混合,治病或防病用已配定剂量或零售包装)	6	5
30049010	含有磺胺类的药品(两种或两种以上成分混合而成的,治病或防病用已配定剂量或零售包装)	6	4.2
30049020	含联苯双酯的药品(混合或非混合,治病或防病用已配定剂量或零售包装)	4	2.8
30049051	中药酒(混合或非混合,治病或防病用已配定剂量或零售包装)	3	2
30049052	片仔癀(混合或非混合,治病或防病用已配定剂量或零售包装)	3	2
30049053	白药(混合或非混合,治病或防病用已配定剂量或零售包装)	3	2
30049054	清凉油(混合或非混合,治病或防病用已配定剂量或零售包装)	3	2

税则号列	货品名称(简称)	最惠国税率(%)	协定税率(%)
30049059	其他中式成药(混合或非混合,治病或防病用已配定剂量或零售包装)	3	2
30049090	其他药品(混合或非混合,治病或防病用已配定剂量或零售包装)	4	2.8
30059010	药棉、纱布、绷带(经药物浸涂或制定零售包装供医疗、外科、牙科或兽医用)	5	3
30069100	可确定用于造口术用具	10	9.2
31021000	尿素(不论是否水溶液)	50	40
32041100	分散染料及以其为基本成分的制品(不论是否已有化学定义)	7.1	6.4
32041200	酸性染料(不论是否预金属络合)及以其为基本成分的制品(不论是否已有化学定义);媒染染料及以其为基本成分的制品(不论是否已有化学定义)	7.1	6.4
32041300	碱性染料及以其为基本成分的制品(不论是否已有化学定义)	6.5	6
32041400	直接染料及以其为基本成分的制品(不论是否已有化学定义)	6.5	6
32041510	合成靛蓝(还原靛蓝)(不论是否已有化学定义)	6.5	6
32041590	其他瓮染料(包括颜料用的)及以其为基本成分的制品(不论是否已有化学定义)	6.5	6
32041600	活性染料及以其为基本成分的制品(不论是否已有化学定义)	7.1	6.4
32041700	颜料及以其为基本成分的制品(不论是否已有化学定义)	6.5	4.6
32041911	硫化黑(硫化青)及以其为基本成分的制品(不论是否已有化学定义)	6.5	6
32041919	其他硫化染料及以其为基本成分的制品(不论是否有化学定义)	6.5	6
32041990	由子目号 3204.11 至 3204.19 中两个或多个子目所列着色料组成的混合物,(不论是否已有化学定义)	6.5	6
32042000	用作萤光增白剂的有机合成产品(不论是否已有化学定义)	6.5	6
32049010	生物染色剂及染料指示剂(不论是否已有化学定义)	6.5	6
32049090	其他用作发光体的有机合成产品(不论是否已有化学定义)	6.5	6
32064900	其他着色料及其制品;32章注释三所述的制品,但税目32.03,32.04及32.05的货品除外面	6.5	3.3
32065000	用作发光体的无机产品,不论是否已有化学定义	6.5	5.9
32081000	分散或溶于非水介质的聚酯油漆及清漆等	10	9
32082010	分散或溶于非水介质的丙烯酸聚合物油漆及清漆	10	9
32082020	分散或溶于非水介质的乙烯聚合物油漆及清漆	10	9
32089010	分散或溶于非水介质的聚胺酯类油漆及清漆	10	9
32089090	分散或溶于非水介质其他油漆、清漆溶液	10	9
32091000	分散或溶于水介质的丙烯酸聚合物或乙烯聚合物油漆及清漆	10	9
32100000	其他油漆及清漆(包括瓷漆\大漆及水浆涂料);皮革用水性颜料	10	9
32139000	非成套颜料、调色料及类似品(艺术家、学生和广告美工用的,片状、管装、罐装、瓶装、扁盒装等类似形状或包装的)	10	9
32151100	黑色印刷油墨(不论是否固体或浓缩)	6.5	4.6
32151900	其他印刷油墨(不论是否固体或浓缩),黑色印刷油墨除外	6.5	4.6
33012500	其他薄荷油(包括浸膏及净油)	15	14
33019010	提取的油树脂	20	18
33019020	柑桔属果实的精油脱萜所得的萜烯副产品	20	18
33019090	用花香吸取法或浸渍法制定的含浓缩精油的脂肪、固定油、蜡及类似品;精油脱萜所得的萜烯副产品(柑桔属果实的除外);精油水溶液及水馏液	20	18
33021010	生产饮料用的混合香料以及以香料为基本成分的制品,按容量计酒精浓度≤0.5%	15	12.8

税则号列	货品名称(简称)	最惠国税率(%)	协定税率(%)
33030000	香水及花露水	10	8.2
33051000	洗发剂(香波)	8.6	7.2
33059000	其他护发品	10	8.5
33061010	牙膏	10	7
33061090	其他洁齿品	10	7
33062000	牙线	10	9.2
33071000	剃须用制剂	10	7
33072000	人体除臭剂及止汗剂	10	7
33073000	香浴盐及其他沐浴用制剂	10	8.5
33079000	脱毛剂、其他编号未列名的芳香料制品及化妆盥洗品	9	6.3
34011100	盥洗用肥皂及有机表面活性产品,条状、块状或模制形状的,以及用肥皂或洗涤剂浸渍、涂面或包覆的纸、絮胎、毡呢及无纺织物	10	8.3
34012000	其他形状的肥皂	15	12.4
34021100	阴离子型有机表面活性剂	6.5	6
34021200	阳离子型有机表面活性剂	6.5	6
34021300	非离子型有机表面活性剂	6.5	5.9
34021900	其他有机表面活性剂	6.5	6
34022010	零售包装的合成洗涤粉	10	8.5
34022090	零售包装有机表面活性剂制品(合成洗涤粉除外)	10	8.5
34029000	非零售包装有机表面活性剂制品、洗涤剂及清洁剂	9	7.8
34031100	用于纺织材料、皮革、毛皮或其他材料油脂处理的制剂(含有石油或从沥青矿物提取的油类且按重量计<70%)	10	9.5
34059000	玻璃或金属用的光洁剂	10	8.5
35061000	适于作胶或粘合剂的产品,零售包装每件净重≤1kg	10	9.2
35069110	以聚酰胺为基本成份的粘合剂	10	7
35069120	以环氧树脂为基本成分的粘合剂	10	7
35069190	以其他橡胶或塑料为基本成分的粘合剂	10	7
35069900	其他调制胶、粘合剂	10	8.6
38021000	活性碳	6.5	5.5
38089111	蚊香	10	0
38089119	零售包装杀虫剂	10	7
38089190	非零售包装杀虫剂	6	4.2
38089319	非零售包装的除草剂	5	4.5
38089391	零售包装抗萌剂及植物生长调节剂	9	8.3
38089399	非零售抗萌剂及植物生长调节剂	6	5.5
38099100	纺织工业及类似工业用其他税号未列名整理剂、染料加速着色剂或固色助剂及其他产品和制剂	6.5	6
38101000	金属表面酸洗剂;金属及其他材料制成的焊粉或焊膏	6.5	6
38112900	不含石油或从沥青矿物提取的油类的润滑油添加剂	6.5	5.5
38123090	其他橡胶、塑料用抗氧剂及其他稳定剂	6.5	4.6
38140000	其他税号未列名的有机复合溶剂及稀释剂;除漆剂	10	9
38151900	其他载体催化剂	6.5	4.6
38159000	其他未列名的反应引发剂、促进剂	6.5	6
38247500	含四氯化碳的含有甲烷、乙烷、丙烷卤化衍生物混合物	6.5	6
38247600	含1,1,1-三氯乙烷(甲基氯仿)的含有甲烷、乙烷、丙烷卤化衍生物混合物	6.5	6
38247800	含全氟烃或氢氟烃的,但不含全氯氟烃或氢氯氟烃的含有甲烷、乙烷、丙烷卤化衍生物混合物	6.5	6
38248100	含环氧乙烷的混合物及制品	6.5	6
38248200	含多氯联苯、多氯三联苯或多溴联苯的混合物及制品	6.5	6
38248300	含三(2,3-二溴丙基)磷酸酯的混合物及制品	6.5	6
38249010	杂醇油	6.5	5.5
38249020	除墨剂、蜡纸改正液及类似品	9	8.3
39093010	聚合 MDI	6.5	6
38249090	其他税目未列名的化学工业及其相关工业的化学产品及配制品	6.5	6
39011000	初级形状比重<0.94 的聚乙烯	7.8	7.4
39012000	初级形状比重≥0.94 的聚乙烯	7.8	7.4
39013000	初级形状乙烯-乙酸乙烯酯共聚物	6.5	6
39019090	其他初级形状的乙烯聚合物	6.5	6.3
39023010	初级形状的乙烯丙烯共聚物(乙丙橡胶丙烯单体单元的含量大于乙烯单体单元)	7.6	7.1
39023090	初级形状的其他丙烯共聚物	7.6	7.1
39031100	初级形状的可发性聚苯乙烯	7.6	7.1
39031900	初级形状的其他聚苯乙烯	7.6	7.1

税则号列	货品名称(简称)	最惠国税率(%)	协定税率(%)	税则号列	货品名称(简称)	最惠国税率(%)	协定税率(%)
39033000	丙烯腈-丁二烯-苯乙烯共聚物	7.6	7.1	39204900	按重量计增塑剂含量小于6%的聚氯乙烯板、片、膜、箔及扁条	7.6	5.3
39039000	初级形状的其他苯乙烯聚合物	7.6	7.1	39205100	聚甲基丙烯酸甲酯板片膜箔及扁条	6.5	4.6
39041000	初级形状的纯聚氯乙烯	7.6	7.1	39206100	聚碳酸酯制板、片、膜、箔及扁条	6.5	4.6
39043000	氯乙烯-乙酸乙烯酯共聚物	9	8.6	39206200	聚对苯二甲酸乙二酯板片膜箔扁条	6.5	4.6
39044000	初级形状的其他氯乙烯共聚物	12	11.4	39206900	其他聚酯板、片、膜、箔及扁条	10	9
39061000	初级形状的聚甲基丙烯酸甲酯	6.5	6	39209400	酚醛树脂板、片、膜、箔及扁条	10	7
39069010	聚丙稀酰胺	6.5	6	39211100	泡沫聚苯乙烯板、片、带、箔及扁条	10	9
39069090	其他初级形状的丙烯酸聚合物	6.5	6	39211310	泡沫聚氨酯制人造革及合成革	9	6.3
39071010	初级形状的聚甲醛	7.6	7.1	39211390	泡沫聚氨酯板、片、带、箔及扁条	6.5	4.6
39071090	其他初级形状的聚缩醛	7.6	7.1	39211910	其他泡沫塑料制人造革及合成革	9	6.3
39072000	初级形状的其他聚醚	7.6	7.1	39211990	其他泡沫塑料板、片、膜、箔及扁条	6.5	4.6
39073000	初级形状的环氧树脂	7.6	7.1	39219020	嵌有玻璃纤维的聚乙烯板、片	6.5	4.6
39074000	初级形状的聚碳酸酯	6.5	6.1	39219030	聚异丁烯为基本成分的附有人造毛毡的板、片、卷材	6.5	4.6
39075000	初级形状的醇酸树脂	10	9.5	39219090	未列名塑料板、片、膜、箔及扁条	6.5	4.6
39077000	聚乳酸	6.5	6.2	39231000	塑料制盒、箱及类似品	10	7
39079910	聚对苯二甲酸丁二酯	6.5	6.2	39234000	塑料制卷轴、纡子、筒管及类似品	10	7
39079990	初级形状的其他聚酯	6.5	6.2	39239000	供运输或包装货物用其他塑料制品	10	7
39091000	初级形状的尿素树脂及硫尿树脂	6.5	6.1	39252000	塑料制门、窗及其框架、门槛	10	7
39092000	初级形状的蜜胺树脂	6.5	6.1	39264000	塑料制小雕塑品及其他装饰品	10	8.3
39094000	初级形状的酚醛树脂	6.5	6.1	39269010	塑料制机器及仪器用零件	10	9
39095000	初级形状的聚亚氨酯	7.6	7.1	39269090	其他塑料制品	10	9.2
39100000	初级形状的聚硅氧烷	6.5	6.1	40012100	天然橡胶烟胶片	20	17
39111000	初级形状的石油树脂、苯并呋喃-茚树脂、多萜树脂	6.5	6.1	40012900	其他初级形状的天然橡胶	20	17
39162000	氯乙烯聚合物制单丝、条、杆及型材	10	7	40021990	丁苯橡胶及羧基丁苯橡胶板、片、带	7.5	7.1
39173100	塑料制的软管	10	7	40022090	丁二烯橡胶板、片、带	7.5	7
39173200	其他未装有附件的塑料制管子	6.5	4.6	40023110	初级形状的异丁烯-异戊二烯橡胶	6	5.6
39173300	其他装有附件的塑料管子	6.5	4.6	40023190	异丁烯-异戊二烯橡胶板、片、带	7.5	7.1
39173900	塑料制的其他管子	7.6	5.3	40023990	卤代丁基橡胶板、片、带	7.5	7.1
39174000	塑料制的管子附件	10	7	40024100	氯丁二烯橡胶胶乳	7.5	7.1
39199010	其他胶囊型反光膜	6.5	4.6	40024990	氯丁二烯橡胶板、片、带	7.5	7.1
39199090	其他自粘塑料板、片、膜等材料	6.5	4.6	40025100	丁腈橡胶胶乳	7.5	7.1
39201010	乙烯聚合物制电池隔膜	6.5	4.6	40026090	异戊二烯橡胶板、片、带	5	4.5
39201090	其他乙烯聚合物制板、片、带	6.5	4.6				
39203000	非泡沫聚苯乙烯板、片、膜、箔及扁条	6.5	4.6				
39204300	按重量计增塑剂含量不小于6%的聚氯乙烯板、片、膜、箔及扁条	7.6	5.3				

税则号列	货品名称(简称)	最惠国税率(%)	协定税率(%)
40027090	乙丙非共轭二烯橡胶板、片、带	7.5	7.1
40040000	橡胶(硬质橡胶除外)废碎料及下脚料及其粉、粒	8	7.6
40103900	其他硫化橡胶制的传动带及带料	8	7.6
40111000	机动小客车用新的充气橡胶轮胎	10	9.4
40112000	客或货运车用新的充气橡胶轮胎	10	9.4
40131000	汽车用橡胶内胎	15	13
40169910	硫化橡胶制机器及仪器用其他零件	8	7.6
40169990	其他未列名硫化橡胶制品	10	9.5
41012011	规定重量范围内的整张生牛皮,经逆鞣处理的	8	6
41015011	经逆鞣处理的重量>16公斤的整张生牛皮	8.4	7
41019011	其他(包括整张或半张的背皮及腹皮)经逆鞣处理的生牛皮	8.4	7
41022190	浸酸的不带毛绵羊或羔羊生皮,经逆鞣处理的除外	9	8
41022990	其他不带毛的绵羊或羔羊生皮,经逆鞣处理的除外	7	6
41041111	全粒面未剖层或粒面剖层蓝湿牛皮	7	3.5
41041119	其他全粒面未剖层或粒面剖层湿牛皮革	8	4
41041120	全粒面未剖层或粒面剖层马皮革	5	2.5
41041911	其他蓝湿牛皮	7	3.5
41041919	其他湿牛皮革	7	3.5
41041920	其他湿马皮革	7	3.5
41044100	全粒面未剖层或粒面剖层干革(坯革)	5	3.5
41044910	其他机器带用干革(坯革)	5	3.5
41044990	其他干革(坯革)	7	4.9
41051010	蓝湿绵羊或羔羊皮	14	7
41051090	其他他绵羊或羔羊湿皮革	10	5
41053000	绵羊或羔羊干革(坯革)	8	5.6
41062100	山羊或小山羊皮湿革	14	12
41062200	山羊或小山羊皮干革(坯革)	14	9.8
41120000	已鞣进一步加工的不带毛绵羊或羔羊皮革	8	5.6
41131000	已鞣进一步加工的不带毛山羊或小山羊皮革	14	9.8
41142000	漆皮及层压漆皮;镀金属皮革	10	9
42010000	各种材料制成的鞍具及挽具,适合各种动物用	20	12
42021210	以塑料或纺织材料作面的衣箱	20	17
42021290	塑料或纺织材料作面的其他箱包	20	17
42022100	以皮革、再生皮革、漆皮作面的手提包	10	6.9
42022200	以塑料片或纺织材料作面的手提包	10	8.2
42022900	以钢纸或纸板作面的手提包	20	14
42023100	以皮革、再生皮革作面的钱包等物品	10	6.9
42023200	以塑料或纺织品作面的钱包等物品	20	14
42023900	以钢纸或纸板作面的钱包等物品	20	14
42029100	皮革、再生皮革或漆皮作面的其他容器	10	8.5
42029200	以塑料或纺织材料作面的其他容器	10	8.5
42032100	皮革或再生皮革制专供运动用手套	20	14
46029000	其他编结材料制品及其他制品	9	8
50072011	未漂白或漂白的纯桑蚕丝机织物	10	9
50072019	其他纯桑蚕丝机织物	10	9
50072021	未漂白或漂白的纯柞蚕丝机织物	10	9
50072029	其他纯柞蚕丝机织物	10	9
50072031	未漂白或漂白的纯绢丝机织物	10	9
50072039	其他纯绢丝机织物	10	9
50072090	其他纯丝机织物	10	9
50079010	未漂白或漂白其他丝机织物	10	8.5
50079090	其他丝机织物	10	8.5
51071000	非供零售用精梳纯羊毛纱线	5	2.5
51081000	非供零售用粗梳动物细毛纱线	5	4.3
51111100	重量≤300g/平米粗梳全毛布	10	8.5
51111900	重量>300g/平米粗梳全毛布	10	8.5
51113000	与化纤短纤混纺粗梳毛布	10	8.5
51121100	重量≤200g/平米精梳全毛布	10	5
51121900	重量>200g/平米精梳全毛布	10	5
52051100	非零售粗梳粗支纯棉单纱	5	3.5
52051200	非零售粗梳中支纯棉单纱	5	3.5
52051300	非零售粗梳细支纯棉单纱	5	3.5

税则号列	货品名称(简称)	最惠国税率(%)	协定税率(%)
52051400	非零售粗梳较细支纯棉单纱	5	3.5
52051500	非零售粗梳特细支纯棉单纱	5	3.5
52052100	非零售精梳粗支纯棉单纱	5	3.5
52052200	非零售精梳中支纯棉单纱	5	3.5
52052300	非零售精梳细支纯棉单纱	5	3.5
52052400	非零售精梳较细支纯棉单纱	5	3.5
52053100	非零售粗梳粗支纯棉多股纱	5	4.5
52053200	非零售粗梳中支纯棉多股纱	5	3.5
52054100	非零售精梳粗支纯棉多股纱	5	4.5
52054200	非零售精梳中支纯棉多股纱	5	3.5
52054600	非零售精梳较特细支纯棉多股纱	5	4.5
52054700	非零售精梳特细支纯棉多股纱	5	4.5
52054800	非零售精梳超细支纯棉多股纱	5	4.5
52061100	非零售粗梳粗支混纺棉单纱	5	3.5
52061200	非零售粗梳中支混纺棉单纱	5	3.5
52061500	非零售粗梳特细支混纺棉单纱	5	3.5
52062100	非零售精梳粗支混纺棉单纱	5	4.5
52071000	供零售用纯棉纱线	6	5
52081300	未漂白轻质全棉三、四线斜纹布	10	8.5
52083200	染色的较轻质全棉平纹布	10	8.5
52083300	染色的轻质全棉三、四线斜纹布	10	8.5
52083900	染色的轻质其他全棉机织物	10	8.5
52084200	色织的较轻质全棉平纹布	10	7
52084900	色织的轻质其他全棉机织物	10	9
52085200	印花的较轻全棉平纹布	10	8.5
52085990	印花的轻质其他全棉机织物	10	8.5
52091200	未漂白重质全棉三、四线斜纹布	10	7
52093100	染色的重质全棉平纹布	10	8.5
52093200	染色的重质全棉三、四线斜纹布	10	8.5
52093900	染色的重质其他全棉机织物	10	8.5
52094200	色织的重质全棉粗斜纹布(劳动布)	10	8.5
52094300	色织的重质全棉三、四线斜纹布	10	9.3
52095100	印花的重质全棉平纹布	10	9.3
52095900	印花的重质其他全棉机织物	10	8.5
52101100	与化纤混纺未漂白轻质平纹棉布	12	10.2
52103100	与化纤混纺染色的轻质平纹棉布	10	8.5
52103200	化纤混纺染色的轻质三线或四线斜纹棉布	10	8.5
52103900	与化纤混纺染色的轻质其他棉布	10	8.5
52113100	与化纤混纺染色的重质平纹棉布	10	8.5
52113200	化纤混纺染色的重质三线或四线斜纹棉布	10	8.5
52113900	与化纤混纺染色的重质其他棉布	10	8.5
52115900	与化纤混纺印花的重质其他棉布	10	8.5
53050092	加工、未纺的椰壳纤维及椰壳纤维废料	5	4
53091900	其他全亚麻机织物	10	9.3
53092900	其他混纺亚麻机织物	10	8.5
53110090	其他纺织用植物纤维机织物	10	9.3
54023290	非零售其他粗尼龙变形纱线	5	4.5
54024490	其他弹性纱线,未加捻或捻度每米不超过50转	5	4.7
54024510	聚酰胺-6纺制的其他单纱,未加捻或捻度每米不超过50转	5	4.7
54024520	聚酰胺-6,6纺制的其他单纱,未加捻或捻度每米不超过50转	5	4.7
54024530	芳香族聚酰胺纺制的其他单纱,未加捻或捻度每米不超过50转	5	4.7
54024590	其他尼龙或聚酰胺纱线纺制的,未加捻或捻度每米不超过50转的单纱	5	4.7
54024700	其他聚酯纱线,未加捻或捻度每米不超过50转	5	4.7
54025200	非零售加捻的其他聚酯加捻单纱	5	4.3
54074200	染色的纯尼龙布	10	9.5
54074300	色织的纯尼龙布	10	7
54075100	未漂白或漂白纯聚酯变形长丝布	10	7
54075200	染色的纯聚酯变形长丝布	10	9.5
54076100	其他纯聚酯非变形长丝布	10	9.5
54076900	其他纯聚酯长丝布	10	9.5

税则号列	货品名称(简称)	最惠国税率(%)	协定税率(%)
54077100	未漂白或漂白其他纯合成纤维长丝布	10	8.8
54077200	染色的其他纯合成纤维长丝布	10	9.5
54077400	印花的其他纯合成纤维长丝布	10	9.5
54083200	染色的人纤长丝混纺布	10	9.5
55013000	聚丙烯腈长丝丝束	5	4.5
55020010	二醋酸纤维丝束	3	2.1
55020090	其他人造纤维长丝丝束	5	3.5
55032000	未梳的聚酯合成纤维短纤	5	4.5
55033000	未梳的聚丙烯腈合成纤维短纤	5	4.5
55062000	已梳的聚酯纤维短纤	5	4.5
55063000	已梳的聚丙烯腈及其变性纤维短纤	5	4.5
55081000	合成纤维短纤纺制的缝纫线	5	4.5
55093200	非零售纯聚丙烯腈短纤多股纱线	5	4.8
55095300	非零售与棉混纺聚酯短纤纱线	5	3.5
55096200	非零售与棉混纺腈纶短纤纱线	5	4.8
55101100	非零售纯人造纤维短纤单纱	5	4.5
55103000	非零售与棉混纺人造纤维短纤纱线	5	3.5
55109000	非零售与其他混纺人造纤维短纤纱线	5	4.5
55121100	未漂或漂白的纯聚酯布	18	12.6
55122900	其他纯腈纶布	10	9.3
55132100	与棉混纺染色的轻质聚酯平纹布	10	9.1
55133910	与棉混纺色织的轻质聚酯斜纹布	10	8.8
55141110	与棉混纺未漂白的重质聚酯平纹布	16	14.4
55141990	与棉混纺未漂白或漂白的重质其他合成纤维布	16	15.2
55151100	与粘胶纤维短纤混纺的聚酯布	10	8.8
55151200	与化纤长丝混纺的聚酯布	10	9
55151900	与其他纤维混纺的聚酯布	10	9
55159900	与其他纤维混纺的其他合成纤维短纤布	10	9
55162200	与化纤长丝混纺的染色人造纤维布	10	9.5
55169400	与其他纤维混纺的印花人造纤维布	10	9.4
56031110	每平米≤25g经浸渍化纤长丝无纺织物	10	8.5
56031190	每平米≤25g的其他化纤长丝无纺织物	10	8.5
56031210	25g＜每平米≤70g浸渍化纤长丝无纺织物	10	8.5
56031310	70g＜每平米≤150g浸渍化纤长丝无纺织物	10	8.5
56031410	每平米＞150g经浸渍化纤长丝无纺织物	10	8.5
56031490	每平米＞150g的其他化纤长丝无纺织物	10	7
56039110	每平米≤25g经浸渍其他无纺织物	10	8.5
56039190	每平米≤25g的其他无纺织物	10	8.5
56039210	25g＜每平米≤70g浸渍其他无纺织物	10	8.5
56039290	25g＜每平米≤70g其他无纺织物	10	9.3
56039310	70g＜每平米≤150g浸渍其他无纺织物	10	8.5
56039390	70g＜每平米≤150g的其他无纺织物	10	9.3
56039410	每平米＞150g经浸渍其他无纺织物	10	8.5
56039490	每平米＞150g的其他无纺织物	10	9.3
57024900	制成的其他纺织材料起绒铺地制品	14	9.3
58041010	丝及绢丝网眼薄纱及其他网眼织物	10	7
58041020	棉制网眼薄纱及其他网眼织物	10	7
58041030	化纤制网眼薄纱及其他网眼织物	12	8.4
58041090	其他纺织材料网眼薄纱及其他网眼织物	10	7
58061090	其他材料狭幅起绒织物及绳绒织物	10	9.1
58063200	化纤制其他狭幅机织物	10	7
58071000	机织非绣制纺织材料标签、徽章等	10	8.5
59021000	尼龙等高强力纱制的帘子布	10	9
59022000	聚酯高强力纱制的帘子布	10	9
59031010	用聚氯乙烯浸、涂的绝缘布或带	10	8.5
59031020	用聚氯乙烯浸、涂的人造革	10	8.5
59031090	用聚氯乙烯浸、涂的其他纺织物	10	8.5
59032010	用聚氨基甲酸酯浸、涂的绝缘布或带	10	8.5
59032020	用聚氨基甲酸酯浸、涂的人造革	10	8.5

税则号列	货品名称(简称)	最惠国税率(%)	协定税率(%)
59032090	用聚氨基甲酸酯浸、涂的其他纺织物	10	8.5
59039010	用其他塑料浸、涂的绝缘布或带	10	8.5
59039020	用其他塑料浸、涂的人造革	10	8.5
59039090	用其他塑料浸、涂的其他纺织物	10	8.5
59070010	用其他材料浸、涂的绝缘布或带	10	8.5
59070020	用其他材料浸、涂的已绘制画布	10	8.5
59070090	用其他材料浸、涂的其他纺织物	10	8.5
59111010	包覆纺锤用浸胶的起绒狭幅织物	8	7.2
60011000	针织或钩编的长毛绒织物	10	8.5
60012100	棉制针织或钩编的毛圈绒头织物	10	8.5
60012200	化纤制针织或钩编毛圈绒头织物	10	8.5
60019100	棉制针织或钩编起绒织物	10	7
60019200	化纤制针织或钩编起绒织物	10	8.5
60024010	宽≤30cm,弹性纱线≥5%棉针织、钩编织物	10	8.5
60024020	宽≤30cm,弹性纱线≥5%丝及绢丝制针织、钩编织物	10	8.5
60024090	宽≤30cm,弹性纱线≥5%其他纺织材料针织、钩编织物	10	7
60029010	宽≤30cm含橡胶线的棉针织、钩编织物	10	8.5
60029020	宽≤30cm含橡胶线的丝及绢丝制针织、钩编织物	10	8.5
60029030	宽≤30cm含橡胶线的合成纤维制针织、钩编织物	10	5
60029040	宽≤30cm含橡胶线的人造纤维制针织、钩编织物	10	5
60029090	宽≤30cm含橡胶线的其他纺织材料针织、钩编织物	10	8.5
60033000	宽≤30cm合成纤维制的针织、钩编织物	10	9.4
60034000	宽≤30cm人造纤维制的针织、钩编织物	10	9.4
60041010	宽>30cm,弹性纱线≥5%棉针织、钩编织物	10	7
60041020	宽>30cm,弹性纱线≥5%丝及绢丝制针织、钩编织物	10	8.5
60041090	宽>30cm,弹性纱线≥5%其他纺织材料针织、钩编织物	10	8.5
60049010	宽>30cm含橡胶线的棉针织、钩编织物	10	8.5
60049020	宽>30cm含橡胶线的丝及绢丝制针织、钩编织物	10	8.5
60049090	宽>30cm含橡胶线的其他纺织材料针织、钩编织物	10	7
60053100	未漂白或漂白合成纤维制的其他经编织物	10	8.5
60053200	染色合成纤维制的其他经编织物	10	8.5
60053300	色织合成纤维制的其他经编织物	10	8.5
60053400	印花合成纤维制的其他经编织物	10	8.5
60054100	未漂白或漂白人造纤维制的其他经编织物	10	8.5
60054200	染色人造纤维制的其他经编织物	10	8.5
60054300	色织人造纤维制的其他经编织物	10	8.5
60054400	印花人造纤维制的其他经编织物	10	8.5
60062100	未漂白或漂白棉制的其他针织、钩编织物	10	7
60062200	染色棉制的其他针织、钩编织物	10	8.5
60062300	色织棉制的其他针织、钩编织物	10	7
60062400	印花棉制的其他针织、钩编织物	10	8.5
60063100	未漂白或漂白合成纤维制的其他针织、钩编织物	10	8.5
60063200	染色合成纤维制的其他针织、钩编织物	10	8.5
60063300	色织合成纤维制的其他针织、钩编织物	10	8.5
60063400	印花合成纤维制的其他针织、钩编织物	10	8.5
60064100	未漂白或漂白人造纤维制的其他针织、钩编织物	10	8.5
60064200	染色人造纤维制的其他针织、钩编织物	10	8.5
60064300	色织人造纤维制的其他针织、钩编织物	10	8.5
60064400	印花人造纤维制的其他针织、钩编织物	10	8.5
60069000	未列名针织、钩编织物	12	10.2
61012000	棉制针织或钩编男式大衣、防风衣	17.5	14

税则号列	货品名称(简称)	最惠国税率(%)	协定税率(%)
61013000	化纤制针织或钩编男式大衣等	17.5	12.3
61019010	毛制针织或钩编男式大衣、防风衣	25	18
61019090	其他纺织材料制针织或钩编男式大衣、防风衣	17.5	12.3
61021000	毛制针织或钩编女式大衣、防风衣	25	18
61022000	棉制针织或钩编女式大衣、防风衣	17.5	14
61023000	化纤制针织或钩编女式大衣等	17.5	12.3
61029000	其他纺织材料制针织或钩编女式大衣、防风衣	20	13.8
61031010	毛制针织或钩编男式西服套装	25	18
61031020	合纤制针织或钩编男西服套装	25	18
61031090	其他纺织材料制针织或钩编男式西服套装	17.5	12.3
61032200	棉制针织或钩编男式便服套装	20	14.8
61032300	合纤制针织或钩编男便服套装	25	18
61032910	毛制针织或钩编男式便服套装	25	18
61032990	其他纺织材料制针织或钩编男式便服套装	25	18
61033100	毛制针织或钩编男式上衣	16	11.7
61033200	棉制针织或钩编男式上衣	16	12
61033300	合纤制针织或钩编男式上衣	19	13.6
61033900	其他纺织材料制针织或钩编男式上衣	16	11.7
61034100	毛制针织或钩编男长裤、工装裤等	16	11.7
61034200	棉制针织或钩编男长裤、工装裤等	16	13.6
61034300	合纤制针织或钩编男长裤等	17.5	12.3
61034900	其他纺织材料制针织或钩编男长裤等	16	11.7
61041300	合纤制针织或钩编女西服套装	25	18
61041910	毛制针织或钩编女式西服套装	17.5	12.3
61041920	棉制针织或钩编女式西服套装	17.5	14
61041990	其他纺织材料制针织或钩编女式西服套装	17.5	12.3
61042200	棉制针织或钩编女式便服套装	17.5	14
61042300	合纤制针织或钩编女便服套装	25	18
61042910	毛制针织或钩编女式便服套装	17.5	12.3
61042990	其他纺织材料制针织或钩编女式便服套装	15	10.4
61043100	毛制针织女式上衣	16	11.7
61043200	棉制针织女式上衣	16	13.6
61043300	合纤制针织女上衣	19	13.6
61043900	其他纺织材料制针织女上衣	16	11.7
61044100	毛制针织或钩编连衣裙	16	11.7
61044200	棉制针织或钩编连衣裙	16	13.6
61044300	合纤制针织或钩编连衣裙	17.5	12.3
61044400	人纤制针织或钩编连衣裙	16	11.7
61044900	其他纺织材料制针织或钩编连衣裙	16	11.7
61045100	毛制针织或钩编裙子及裙裤	14	10.8
61045200	棉制针织裙子及裙裤	14	10.3
61045300	合纤制针织或钩编裙子及裙裤	16	11.7
61045900	其他纺织材料制针织或钩编裙子及裙裤	14	10.8
61046100	毛制针织或钩编女长裤、工装裤等	16	11.7
61046200	棉制针织或钩编女长裤、工装裤等	16	13.6
61046300	合纤制针织或钩编女长裤等	17.5	12.3
61046900	其他纺织材料制针织或钩编女长裤等	16	12
61051000	棉制针织或钩编男衬衫	16	13.6
61052000	化纤制针织或钩编男衬衫	17.5	12.3
61059000	其他纺织材料制针织或钩编男衬衫	16	11.7
61061000	棉制针织或钩编女衬衫	16	13.6
61062000	化纤制针织或钩编女衬衫	17.5	12.3
61069000	其他纺织材料制针织或钩编女衬衫	16	11.7
61071200	化纤制针织或钩编男内裤及三角裤	16	10.9
61071910	丝及绢丝制针织或钩编男内裤及三角裤	14	9.3
61071990	其他纺织材料制针织或钩编男内裤及三角裤	14	9.3
61072200	化纤制针织或钩编男睡衣裤	16	10.9
61072910	丝及绢丝制针织或钩编男长睡衣及睡衣裤	14	9.3

税则号列	货品名称(简称)	最惠国税率(%)	协定税率(%)
61072990	其他纺织材料制针织或钩编男长睡衣及睡衣裤	14	9.3
61079910	化纤制针织或钩编男浴衣、晨衣	16	10.9
61079990	其他纺织材料制针织或钩编男浴衣、晨衣	14	9.3
61081100	化纤制针织或钩编长衬裙及衬裙	16	10.9
61081990	其他纺织材料制针织或钩编女式长衬裙及衬裙	14	9.3
61082200	化纤制针织或钩编女三角裤及短衬裤	16	10.9
61082910	丝及绢丝制针织或钩编女三角裤及短衬裤	14	9.3
61082990	其他纺织材料制针织或钩编女三角裤及短衬裤	14	9.3
61083200	化纤制针织或钩编女睡衣及睡衣裤	16	10.9
61083910	丝及绢丝制针织或钩编女睡衣及睡衣裤	14	9.3
61083990	其他纺织材料制针织或钩编女睡衣及睡衣裤	14	9.3
61089200	化纤制针织或钩编女浴衣、晨衣	16	10.9
61089900	其他纺织材料制针织或钩编女浴衣、晨衣	14	9.3
61091000	棉制针织或钩编T恤衫、汗衫等	14	9.4
61099010	丝及绢丝制针织或钩编T恤衫、汗衫等	14	9.3
61099090	其他纺织材料制针织或钩编T恤衫、汗衫等	14	9.3
61101100	羊毛制针织或钩编套头衫等	14	9.3
61101200	喀什米尔山羊细毛制针织或钩编套头衫等	14	9.3
61101910	其他山羊细毛制针织或钩编套头衫等	14	9.3
61101920	兔毛制针织或钩编套头衫等	14	9.3
61101990	其他毛制针织或钩编套头衫等	14	9.3
61102000	棉制针织或钩编套头衫等	14	11
61103000	化纤制针织或钩编套头衫等	16	10.9
61109010	丝及绢丝制针织或钩编套头衫等	14	9.3
61109090	其他纺织材料制针织或钩编套头衫等	14	9.3
61113000	合纤制针织婴儿服装及附件	16	10.9
61119010	毛制针织或钩编婴儿服装及附件	14	9.3
61119090	其他纺织材料制针织或钩编婴儿服装及附件	14	9.3
61121100	棉制针织或钩编运动服	16	13.6
61121200	合纤制针织或钩编运动服	17.5	12.3
61121900	其他纺织材料制针织或钩编运动服	16	11.7
61122010	棉制针织或钩编滑雪服	16	13.6
61122090	其他纺织材料制针织或钩编滑雪服	19	13.6
61123100	合纤制针织或钩编男式游泳服	17.5	12.3
61123900	其他纺织材料制针织或钩编男式游泳服	16	11.7
61124100	合纤制针织或钩编女式游泳服	17.5	12.3
61124900	其他纺织材料制针织或钩编女式游泳服	16	11.7
61130000	涂层经处理针织或钩编织物制服装	16	11.7
61151000	渐紧压袜类连裤袜	16	9.3
61152100	单丝<67分特合纤制连裤袜等	16	14.4
61152200	单丝≥67分特合纤制连裤袜等	16	10.9
61152990	其他纺织材料制针织连裤袜及紧身裤袜	14	9.3
61153000	单丝<67分特制针织或钩编女统袜	14	9.3
61159600	合纤制针织或钩编短袜及其他袜类	16	10.9
61159900	其他纺织材料制针织或钩编短袜及其他袜类	14	9.3
61169300	合纤制其他针织或钩编手套	16	10.9
61169900	其他纺织材料制针织或钩编手套	14	9.3
61171000	针织或钩编披巾、头巾等	14	9.3
61178010	针织或钩编领带及领结	14	9.3
61178090	针织或钩编其他衣着附件	14	9.3
61179000	其他针织或钩编衣着零件	14	7
62011100	毛制男式大衣、斗篷及类似品	16	11.7
62011310	化纤制男式羽绒服	17.5	12.3
62011390	化纤制男式大衣、斗篷及类似品	17.5	12.3
62011900	其他纺织材料制男式大衣、斗篷及类似品	16	11.7
62019100	毛制男式带风帽防寒短上衣、防风衣	16	11.7
62019310	化纤制男式其他羽绒服	17.5	12.3

税则号列	货品名称(简称)	最惠国税率(%)	协定税率(%)
62019390	化纤制男式防寒短上衣、防风衣	17.5	12.3
62019900	其他纺织材料制男式防寒短上衣、防风衣	16	11.7
62021100	毛制女式大衣、斗篷及类似品等	16	11.7
62021310	化纤制女式羽绒服	19	13.6
62021390	化纤制女式大衣、斗篷及类似品	19	13.6
62021900	其他纺织材料制女式大衣、斗篷及类似品	16	11.7
62029100	毛制女式带风帽防寒短上衣、防风衣	16	11.7
62029310	化纤制女式其他羽绒服	17.5	12.3
62029390	化纤制女式防风衣等	17.5	12.3
62029900	其他纺织材料制防风衣、防风短上衣等	16	11.7
62031100	毛制男式西服套装	17.5	12.3
62031200	合纤制男式西服套装	17.5	12.3
62031910	丝及绢丝制男式西服套装	17.5	12.3
62031990	其他纺织材料制男式西服套装	17.5	12.3
62032300	合纤制男式便服套装	17.5	12.3
62032910	丝及绢丝制男式便服套装	17.5	12.3
62032920	毛制男式便服套装	17.5	12.3
62032990	其他纺织材料制男式便服套装	17.5	12.3
62033100	毛制男式上衣	16	11.7
62033200	棉制男式上衣	16	14.4
62033300	合纤制男式上衣	17.5	12.3
62033910	丝及绢丝制男式上衣	16	11.7
62033990	其他纺织材料制男式上衣	16	11.7
62034100	毛制男式长裤、工装裤等	16	11.7
62034210	棉制男式阿拉伯裤	16	12.9
62034290	棉制男式长裤、工装裤等	16	12.9
62034310	合成纤维制男式阿拉伯裤	17.5	13.1
62034390	合纤制男式长裤、工装裤等	17.5	13.1
62034910	其他纺织材料制男式阿拉伯裤	16	11.7
62034990	其他纺织材料制男童裤、工装裤	16	11.7
62041100	毛制女式西服套装	17.5	12.3
62041300	合纤制女式西服套装	17.5	12.3
62041910	丝及绢丝制女式西服套装	17.5	12.3
62041990	其他纺织材料制女式西服套装	17.5	12.3
62042100	毛制女式便服套装	17.5	12.3
62042300	合纤制女式便服套装	20	13.8
62042910	丝及绢丝制女式便服套装	20	13.8
62042990	其他纺织材料制女式便服套装	14	9.9
62043100	毛制女式上衣	16	11.7
62043300	合纤制女式上衣	17.5	12.3
62043910	丝及绢丝制女式上衣	16	11.7
62043990	其他纺织材料制女式上衣	16	11.7
62044100	毛制连衣裙	16	11.7
62044300	合纤制女式连衣裙	17.5	12.3
62044400	人纤制女式连衣裙	16	11.7
62044910	丝及绢丝制连衣裙	16	11.7
62044990	其他纺织材料制连衣裙	16	11.7
62045100	毛制裙子及裙裤	14	9.3
62045300	合纤制裙子及裙裤	16	11.7
62045910	丝及绢丝制裙子及裙裤	14	9.3
62045990	其他纺织材料制裙子及裙裤	14	9.3
62046100	毛制女式长裤、工装裤等	16	11.7
62046200	棉制女式长裤、工装裤等	16	14.4
62046300	合纤制女式长裤、工装裤等	17.5	12.3
62046900	其他纺织材料制女式长裤、工装裤等	16	12
62052000	棉制男衬衫	16	8
62053000	化纤制男衬衫	16	11.7
62059010	丝及绢丝制男衬衫	16	11.7
62059020	毛制男衬衫	16	11.7
62059090	其他纺织材料制男衬衫	16	11.7
62061000	丝及绢丝制女式衬衫	16	11.7
62062000	毛制女衬衫	16	11.7
62063000	棉制女衬衫	16	13.6
62064000	化纤制女衬衫	17.5	12.3
62069000	其他纺织材料制女衬衫	16	11.7
62071100	棉制男式内裤及三角裤	14	10.3
62079910	丝及绢丝制男浴衣、晨衣及类似品	14	12.6
62079990	其他纺织材料制男浴衣、晨衣及类似品	14	12.6
62082100	棉制女式睡衣及睡衣裤	14	10.3
62089910	丝制女式背心、内衣及类似品	14	12.6
62089990	其他纺织材料制女式背心、内衣及类似	14	12.6
62101010	毛制毡呢或无纺织物服装	16	11.7
62101030	化纤制毡呢或无纺织物服装	17.5	12.3
62102000	用塑料、橡胶等处理的织物制男大衣等	16	11.7
62103000	用塑料、橡胶等处理的织物制女大衣等	16	11.7
62104000	用塑料、橡胶等处理的织物制的其他男式服装	16	11.7
62105000	用塑料、橡胶等处理的织物制的其他女式服装	16	11.7

税则号列	货品名称(简称)	最惠国税率(%)	协定税率(%)
62111100	男式游泳服	16	11.7
62111200	女式游泳服	16	11.7
62112090	其他纺织材料制滑雪服	19	13.6
62113310	化纤制男式阿拉伯袍	17.5	12.3
62113320	化纤制运动服	17.5	12.3
62113390	化纤制男式运动服及其他服装	17.5	12.3
62113910	丝及绢丝制男式运动服及其他服装	16	11.7
62113920	毛制男式运动服及其他服装	16	11.7
62113990	其他纺织材料制男式运动服及其他服装	16	11.7
62114100	毛制女式运动服及其他服装	16	11.7
62114310	化纤制女式运动服	17.5	12.3
62114390	化纤制其他服装	17.5	12.3
62114910	丝及绢丝制女式运动服及其他服装	16	11.7
62114990	其他纺织材料制女式运动服及其他服装	16	11.7
62121010	化纤制胸罩	16	14.4
62121090	其他纺织材料制胸罩	14	12.6
62129010	化纤制吊裤带、吊袜带等	16	14.4
62129090	其他纺织材料制吊裤带、吊袜带等	14	12.6
62152000	化纤制领带及领结	16	14.4
62171010	非针织非钩编袜子及袜套	14	12.2
62171020	非针织非钩编和服腰带	14	12.2
62171090	非针织非钩编服装或衣着附件	14	12.2
62179000	非针织非钩编服装或衣着零件	14	12.6
63053300	聚乙烯或聚丙烯扁条制其他货物包装袋	16	13.6
63071000	擦地布、擦碗布等	14	11.9
64011000	装金属护头的塑料、橡胶制防水鞋靴	24	12
64019200	橡胶、塑料底及面的中、短统防水靴	24	12
64019900	其他橡胶、塑料制外底及鞋面防水靴	24	12
64021200	橡胶、塑料底及面的滑雪靴	10	5
64021900	橡胶、塑料制底及面的其他运动靴	24	12
64022000	橡胶、塑料的将鞋面条带栓塞在鞋底上的鞋	24	12
64029100	其他橡胶、塑料短统靴(过踝)	24	12
64029900	其他橡胶、塑料鞋靴	24	12
64039900	皮革制面的其他鞋靴	10	8.5

税则号列	货品名称(简称)	最惠国税率(%)	协定税率(%)
64041100	纺织材料制鞋面的运动鞋靴	24	12
64041900	纺织材料制鞋面胶底的其他鞋靴	24	12
64042000	纺织材料制鞋面皮革底的鞋靴	24	12
64051000	皮革或再生皮革制面的其他鞋靴	24	12
64052000	纺织材料制面的其他鞋靴	22	11
64059000	其他材料制面的鞋靴	15	10.5
64061000	鞋面及其零件,硬衬除外	15	13.2
64069100	木制鞋靴零件,活动式鞋内底等	15	10.5
64069900	其他材料制鞋靴、护腿等零件	15	10.5
65059010	钩编的帽类	20	19
65059090	针织或成匹织物制成的帽类	20	19
67030000	经梳理、稀疏等方法加工的人发及假发材料	20	18
68021010	大理石制砖、瓦、方块及类似品	24	19.2
68021090	其他石料制砖瓦、方块及类似品	20	16
68022300	具有一个平面的花岗岩及制品	10	9.2
68029390	其他加工形式花岗岩制品	10	9.2
68043010	手用琢磨油石	8	6.4
68043090	手用其他磨石及抛光石	8	6.4
68079000	其他形状的沥青或类似原料的制品	12	9.6
68101100	水泥制建筑用砖及石砌块	10.5	8.4
68101910	人造石制砖、瓦、扁平石及类似品	10.5	8.4
68101990	水泥制其他砖、瓦、扁平石	10.5	8.4
69010000	硅质化石粉或类似硅土制的砖、瓦	8	6.4
69081000	上釉的小陶瓷砖、瓦、块及类似品	12	10.4
69101000	瓷制脸盆、浴缸及类似卫生器具	10	9
69111010	瓷餐具	12	10
69111020	瓷厨房器具	15	12.5
69119000	其他家用或盥洗用瓷器	24.5	20
70099200	其他镶框玻璃镜(包括后视镜)	12	10.8
70112010	显象管玻壳及其零件	10	7
70112090	阴极射线管用玻壳及零件	10	7
70195900	其他玻璃纤维机织物	12	8.4
70200012	绝缘子用玻璃伞盘	10.5	9.5
70200019	其他工业用玻璃制品	10.5	8.9
70200099	其他非工业用玻璃制品	15	12.8

税则号列	货品名称（简称）	最惠国税率（%）	协定税率（%）
71023900	其他非工业用钻石	8	0
71031000	未加工宝石或半宝石	3	2.8
71039100	经其他加工的红、蓝、绿宝石	8	4
71039910	经其他加工的翡翠	8	4
71039990	经其他加工的其他宝石或半宝石	8	4
71131110	镶嵌钻石的银首饰及其零件	20	16.5
71131190	其他银首饰及其零件	20	16.5
71131911	镶嵌钻石的黄金制首饰及其零件	20	14
71131919	其他黄金制首饰及其零件	20	16
71131991	镶嵌钻石的其他贵金属制首饰及其零件	35	28
71131999	其他贵金属制首饰及其零件	35	28
71132010	镶嵌钻石的以贱金属为底的包贵金属制首饰	35	30
71132090	其他以贱金属为底的包贵金属制首饰	35	30
71171900	其他贱金属制仿首饰	17	15.3
71179000	未列名材料制仿首饰	35	30
72085310	屈服强度大于355牛顿/平方毫米，3mm≤厚度<4.75mm的热轧非卷材	6	5.1
72085390	其他3mm≤厚度<4.75mm的热轧非卷材	6	5.1
72085410	厚度<1.5mm的热轧非卷材	6	5.1
72085490	其他厚度<3mm的热轧非卷材	6	5.1
72091610	屈服强度大于275牛顿/平方毫米，1mm<厚度<3mm的冷轧卷材	6	4.2
72091690	其他1mm<厚度<3mm的冷轧卷材	6	4.2
72091710	屈服强度大于275牛顿/平方毫米，0.5mm≤厚度≤1mm的冷轧卷材	3	2.1
72091790	其他0.5mm≤厚度≤1mm的冷轧卷材	3	2.1
72091810	厚度<0.3mm的冷轧卷材	6	4.2
72091890	其他厚度<0.5mm的冷轧卷材	6	4.2
72092700	0.5mm≤厚度≤1mm的冷轧非卷材	6	4.2
72099000	其他冷轧铁或非合金钢宽平板轧材	6	4.2
72139100	直径<14mm圆截面的其他热轧盘条	5	4.3
72142000	热加工带有轧制花纹的条、杆	3	0
72173000	镀或涂其他贱金属铁或非合金钢丝	8	6.4
72192100	厚度>10mm热轧不锈钢平板	10	9.3
72192200	4.75mm≤厚度≤10mm热轧不锈钢平板	10	9.3
72192300	3mm≤厚度<4.75mm热轧不锈钢平板	10	9.3
72192410	1mm<厚度<3mm热轧不锈钢平板	10	9.3
72192420	0.5mm≤厚度≤1mm热轧不锈钢平板	10	9.3
72192430	厚度<0.5mm热轧不锈钢平板	10	9.3
72210000	不锈钢热轧条、杆	10	8
72221100	热加工的圆形截面不锈钢条、杆	10	9
72221900	热加工其他截面形状不锈钢条杆	10	9
72223000	其他不锈钢条、杆	10	8.9
72251100	取向性硅电钢宽板	3	2.1
73011000	钢铁板桩	7	6.3
73029010	钢铁轨枕	6	5.1
73029090	其他铁道电车道铺轨用钢铁材料	7	6
73042400	其他不锈钢制钻探石油用天然气套管、导管	4	2
73042900	钻探石油及天然气用的套管及导管	4	2
73072100	不锈钢制法兰	8.4	6.7
73130000	带刺钢铁丝、围篱用钢铁绞带	7	6.3
73144100	其他镀锌的钢铁丝网、篱及格栅	8	6
73181500	其他螺钉及螺栓	8	4
73202090	其他螺旋弹簧	10	8.5
73218100	可使用气体燃料的其他家用器具	23	13.8
73219000	非电热家用器具零件	12	9.6
73239300	餐桌、厨房等家用不锈钢器具	12	8.4
73259910	工业用未列名可锻性铸铁制品	10.5	8.9
73259990	非工业用未列名可锻性铸铁制品	20	12
73262010	工业用钢铁丝制品	10	5
73262090	非工业用钢铁丝制品	18	12.6
73269010	其他工业用钢铁制品	10.5	8.9
73269090	其他非工业用钢铁制品	8	6.8
74081100	最大截面尺寸>6mm的精炼铜丝	4	2.8
74081900	截面尺寸≤6mm的精炼铜丝	4	3.4

税则号列	货品名称(简称)	最惠国税率(%)	协定税率(%)
74101100	无衬背的精炼铜箔	4	2.8
74102100	有衬背的精炼铜箔	4	3.4
74111011	外径小于等于25mm的带有内(外)螺纹或翅片的精炼铜管	4	2.8
74111019	外径小于等于25mm的其他精炼铜管	4	2.8
74111090	其他精炼铜管	4	2.8
74122010	白铜或德银管子配件	7	6
74122090	其他铜合金管子配件	7	6
74199991	工业用其他铜制品	10	8.5
74199999	非工业用其他铜制品	20	17
76012000	未锻轧铝合金	7	6
76042900	铝合金制条、杆、其他型材及异型材	5	3.5
76051900	纯铝制的细丝	8	6.8
76061120	0.3mm≤厚度<0.36mm的非合金铝制矩形铝板片带	6	4.2
76061190	纯铝制矩形的其他板、片及带	6	4.2
76061220	厚度<0.28mm的铝合金制矩形铝板片带	6	4.2
76061230	0.28mm≤厚度≤0.35mm的铝合金制矩形铝板片带	6	4.2
76061240	厚度>0.35mm的铝合金制矩形铝板片带	6	4.2
76071110	厚度不超过0.007毫米的无衬背铝箔	6	5.7
76071190	轧制后未进一步加工的无衬背铝箔	6	5.7
76071900	其他无衬背铝箔	6	5.1
76161000	铝钉、螺钉、螺母、垫圈等紧固件	10	8.5
76169910	其他工业用铝制品	10	8.5
76169990	其他非工业用铝制品	15	12.8
81041100	含镁量≥99.8%的未锻轧镁	6	4.2
82029110	加工金属用的机械锯的直锯片	8	7
82055900	其他手工工具	10	8.5
82073000	锻压或冲压工具	8	6.8
82078000	车削工具	8	6.8
82079010	带超硬材料部件的其他可互换工具	8	6.8
82079090	其他可互换工具	8	6.8
82089000	其他机器或机械器具用刀及刀片	8	7.2
82090000	未装配的工具用金属陶瓷刀头	8	7.2
82100000	加工调制食品、饮料用手动机械	18	16.2
82130000	剪刀、裁缝剪刀及类似品、剪刀片	12	10.8
82141000	裁纸刀、信刀、铅笔刀及刀片	12	10.8
82142000	修指甲及修脚用具(包括指甲锉)	18	16.2
83119000	贱金属粘聚成的丝或条	8	5.6
84021110	蒸发量≥900t/hr发电锅炉	3	2.5
84021190	蒸发量>45t/hr, <900t/hr发电锅炉	14	13.3
84021200	蒸发量≤45t/hr水管锅炉	5	3.9
84031010	家用型集中供暖用热水锅炉	10	9.5
84031090	其他集中供暖用的热水锅炉	10	9.5
84041010	蒸汽锅炉、过热水锅炉的辅助设备	7	3.5
84041020	集中供暖用热水锅炉的辅助设备	10	5
84049010	集中供暖热水锅炉辅助设备的零件	10	0
84049090	其他辅助设备用零件	7	0
84073410	排气量1000－3000cc往复式活塞发动机	10	7
84073420	排气量>3000cc往复式活塞发动机	10	7
84081000	船舶用压燃式内燃发动机	5	2.5
84082010	输出功率≥132.39kw车用柴油发动机	9	6.3
84082090	输出功率<132.39kw车用柴油发动机	25	17.5
84089010	机车用柴油发动机	6	5.4
84089091	功率≤14kw其他用柴油发动机	5	4.5
84089092	14kw<功率<132.39kw其他柴油发动机	8.4	7.6
84089093	功率≥132.39kw其他用柴油发动机	5	4.5
84099110	船舶用点燃式发动机专用零件	6	4.2
84099191	电控燃油喷射装置	5	3.5
84099199	其他点燃式活塞内燃发动机用零件	5	3.5
84099910	其他船舶发动机专用零件	5	4.5
84099920	其他机车发动机专用零件	2	1.5
84099991	功率≥132.39kw发动机的专用零件	2	1.5
84099999	其他未列名发动机的专用零件	8.4	8
84111210	推力>25千牛顿的涡轮风扇发动机	1	0

税则号列	货品名称(简称)	最惠国税率(%)	协定税率(%)
84111290	推力>25 千牛顿的其他涡轮喷气发动机	1	0.5
84123100	直线作用的气压动力装置(气压缸)	14	13.3
84133021	输出功率在 132.39 千瓦(180 马力)及以上的发动机用燃油泵	3	2.5
84133090	其他燃油泵、润滑油泵或冷却剂泵	3	2.5
84137010	转速≥10000 转/分离心泵	8	7.6
84137090	转速<10000 转/分离心泵	8	7.6
84138100	其他液体泵	8	4
84139100	液体泵用零件	5	2.5
84143011	功率≤0.4kw 的冷藏、冷冻箱用压缩机	8	5.9
84143012	功率 0.4-5kw 的冷藏、冷冻箱用压缩机	10	8.5
84143013	功率0.4-5kw 的空气调节器用压缩机	10	8.5
84143014	功率>5kw 的空气调节器用压缩机	10	8.5
84143015	冷冻或冷藏设备用,电动机额定功率超过 5 千瓦的电动机驱动压缩机	10	9.2
84143019	其他制冷设备用压缩机	10	9
84143090	非电机驱动的压缩机	9	8.1
84145910	其他吊扇	8	7.2
84145920	其他换气扇	8	7.2
84145930	离心通风机	10	9.5
84145990	其他扇,风机	8	7.2
84148010	燃气轮机用的自由活塞式发生器	8	5.6
84148020	二氧化碳压缩机	7	4.9
84148030	发动机用增压器	7	4.9
84148090	其他气体压缩机及通风罩或循环气罩	7	4.9
84149011	用于制冷设备的压缩机进、排气阀片	8	7.2
84149019	其他用于制冷设备的压缩机零件	8	7.2
84149020	风机、风扇、通风罩及循环气罩零件	12	11.4
84149090	税号 84.14 其他所列机器零件	7	6.5
84151010	独立窗式或壁式空气调节器	15	13.5
84151021	分体式制冷量制冷量≤4 千大卡/时窗式或壁式空气调节器	15	13.5
84151022	分体式制冷量制冷量>4 千大卡/时窗式或壁式空气调节器	15	13.5
84159010	制冷量≤4 千大卡/时等空调的零件	10	8
84159090	制冷量>4 千大卡/时等空调的零件	10	8
84161000	使用液体燃料的炉用燃烧器	10	9.5
84182120	50L<容积≤150L 压缩式家用型冷藏箱	10	9
84182130	容积≤50L 压缩式家用型冷藏箱	10	9
84186120	压缩式热泵,税目 8415 的空气调节器除外	10	7
84186190	其他热泵,税目 8415 的空气调节器除外	15	7
84186920	其他制冷机组	10	7
84186990	其他制冷设备	10	7
84189100	冷藏或冷冻设备用特制家具零件	18	17.1
84193910	微空气流动陶瓷坯件干燥器	9	4.5
84193990	其他用途的干燥器	9	4.5
84195000	热交换装置	10	9.5
84212110	家用型过滤或净化水的机器及装置	25	17.5
84212190	其他过滤或净化水的装置	5	3.5
84212910	其他压滤机	5	3.5
84212990	其他液体的过滤、净化机器及装置	5	3.5
84213910	家用型气体过滤、净化机器及装置	15	10.5
84213921	工业用静电除尘器	5	3.5
84213922	工业用袋式除尘器	5	3.5
84213923	工业用旋风式除尘器	5	3.5
84213929	工业用其他除尘器	5	3.5
84213990	其他气体的过滤、净化机器及装置	5	3.5
84219910	家用型过滤、净化装置用零件	10	9
84219990	其他过滤、净化装置用零件	5	4.5
84223010	饮料及液体食品罐装设备	12	8.4
84223021	水泥全自动灌包机	12	8.4
84223029	其他水泥包装机	12	8.4
84223030	其他包装机	10	7
84223090	其他装填密封等包封机器	10	7
84224000	其他包装或打包机器	10	9.5
84242000	喷枪及类似器具	8.4	8
84248100	农业或园艺用喷射、喷雾机械器具	8	7.6

税则号列	货品名称(简称)	最惠国税率(%)	协定税率(%)
84254100	车库中使用的固定千斤顶系统	3	2.5
84261910	装船机	5	2.5
84261921	抓斗式卸船机	5	3.5
84261929	其他卸船机	5	3.5
84261930	龙门式起重机	10	7
84261941	门式装卸桥	10	7
84261942	集装箱装卸桥	10	7
84261943	其他动臂式装卸桥	10	7
84261949	其他装卸桥	10	7
84261990	其他高架移动式起重机等	10	7
84272010	集装箱叉车	9	8.6
84272090	其他机动叉车及有类似装置工作车	9	8.6
84281010	载客电梯	8	5.6
84281090	其他升降机及倒卸式起重机	6	4.2
84283300	其他带式连续运货升降、输送机	5	4.3
84283910	链式连续运送货物的升降机及输送机	5	3.5
84283920	辊式连续运送货物的升降机及输送机	5	3.5
84283990	其他未列名连续运货升降、输送机	5	3.5
84295211	轮胎式挖掘机	8	7.2
84295219	其他挖掘机	8	7.2
84295290	其他上部结构可转360度的挖掘机类似机械	8	7.2
84312000	叉车及装有升降装置工作车用零件	6	5.4
84313900	税号84.28所列其他机械的零件	5	2.5
84314100	戽斗、铲斗、抓斗及夹斗	6	5.4
84314310	石油或天然气钻探机用零件	4	2.8
84314320	其他钻探机用零件	4	2.8
84314390	其他凿井机用零件	5	3.5
84314910	矿用电铲用零件	5	4.5
84314990	税号84.26,84.29,84.30的其他零件	5	4.5
84323000	播种机、种植机及移植机	4	3.5
84335100	联合收割机	8	7.6
84378000	谷物磨粉业加工机器	10	8.5
84388000	84章其他未列名食品等加工机器	8.5	8.1
84399900	制造或整理纸及纸板的机器零件	6	3
84412000	制造包、袋或信封的机器	12	11.4
84413010	纸塑铝复合罐生产设备	13.5	12.8
84413090	其他制造箱、盒、桶及类似容器的机器	13.5	12.8
84418010	制造纸塑铝软包装的生产设备	12	11.4
84418090	其他制造纸浆制品、纸制品的机器	12	11.4
84431100	卷取进料式胶印机	10	7
84431310	平张纸进料式胶印机	10	7
84431390	其他胶印机	10	7
84431700	照像凹版印刷机	18	16.2
84431921	圆网印刷机	10	9
84431922	平网印刷机	10	9
84431929	其他网式印刷机	10	9
84431980	其它印刷机	8	7.2
84433222	可以网络连接的静电照相印刷机(激光印刷机)	8	7.2
84433229	可以网络连接的其他数字印刷设备	8	7.2
84433932	其他独立的静电照相印刷机(激光印刷机)	8	7.2
84433939	其他独立的数字印刷设备	8	7.2
84440010	合成纤维长丝纺丝机	10	7
84440020	合成纤维短丝纺丝机	10	7
84440030	人造纤维纺丝机	10	7
84440040	化学纤维变形机	10	7
84440050	化学纤维切断机	10	7
84440090	其他化学纤维挤压、拉伸、变形或切割机器	10	7
84451111	棉纤维清梳联合机	10	9
84451112	棉纤维自动抓棉机	10	9
84451113	棉纤维梳棉机	10	9
84451119	其他棉纤维梳理机	10	9
84451120	毛纤维梳理机	10	9
84451190	其他纺织纤维梳理机	10	9
84451900	纺织纤维的其他预处理机器	10	9
84452031	转杯纺纱机	10	9
84452041	棉环锭细纱机	10.5	9.5
84452090	其他纺纱机	10	9
84453000	并线机或加捻机	10	9
84454010	自动络筒机	10	9
84454090	其他络纱机(包括卷纬机)或摇纱机	10	9
84459010	整经机	10	9
84459020	浆纱机	10	9
84459090	其他生产及处理纺织纱线的机器	10	9
84461000	所织织物宽度≤30cm的织机	8	7.2

税则号列	货品名称(简称)	最惠国税率(%)	协定税率(%)
84462110	所织织物宽度>30cm 的梭织动力地毯织机	12	10.8
84462190	所织织物宽度>30cm 的其他梭织动力织机	10	9
84463020	所织织物宽度>30cm 的剑杆织机	8	6.8
84463030	所织织物宽度>30cm 的片梭织机	8	5.6
84463040	所织织物宽度>30cm 的喷水织机	8	6.8
84463050	所织织物宽度>30cm 的喷气织机	8	6.8
84463090	所织织物宽度>30cm 的其他无梭织机	8	6.8
84471100	圆筒直径≤165mm 的圆型针织机	8	7
84472010	经编机	8	6.8
84472020	其他平型针织机	8	6.8
84472030	缝编机	8	6.8
84479011	地毯织机	7	4.9
84479019	其他簇绒机	8	5.6
84479020	绣花机	8	6.8
84479090	税号 84.47 其他未列名机器	10	5
84501110	干衣量≤10kg 的波轮式全自动洗衣机	10	8.7
84501120	干衣量≤10kg 的滚筒式全自动洗衣机	10	8.7
84501190	干衣量≤10kg 的其他全自动洗衣机	10	8.7
84501200	装有离心甩干机的非全自动洗衣机	30	24.9
84509010	干衣量≤10kg 的洗衣机零件	5	4.2
84509090	干衣量>10kg 的洗衣机零件	16	14.4
84511000	干洗机	21	16
84512100	干衣量≤10kg 的干燥机	15	13.5
84512900	干衣量>10kg 的干燥机	8	7.2
84513000	熨烫机及挤压机(包括熔压机)	8	7.2
84514000	洗涤、漂白或染色机器	8.4	7
84515000	纺织物卷绕、退绕、折叠、剪切或剪齿边机器	8	7.2
84518000	税号 84.51 所列其他未列名的机器	12	10.8
84519000	税号 84.51 所列机器的零件	8	7.2
84521010	多功能家用缝纫机	21	17
84521090	其他家用型缝纫机	21	17
84522110	平缝机	12	10.7
84522190	其他自动缝纫机	12	10.7
84522900	其他非自动缝纫机	12	10.8
84523000	缝纫机针	14	12.6
84529011	家用型缝纫机用旋梭	14	9.8
84529019	家用型缝纫机用其他零件	14	9.8
84529091	其他缝纫机用旋梭	14	9.8
84529099	其他缝纫机用其他零件	14	9.8
84531000	生皮、皮革的处理、鞣制或加工机器	8.4	8
84532000	鞋靴制作或修理机器	8.4	8
84543010	冷室压铸机	12	11.4
84543021	方坯连铸机	10	9.5
84543022	板坯连铸机	12	11.4
84543029	其他钢坯连铸机	12	11.4
84543090	其他金属冶炼及铸造用铸造机	12	11.4
84551010	热轧管机	12	8.4
84551020	冷轧管机	12	8.4
84551030	定、减径轧管机	12	8.4
84551090	其他金属轧管机	12	8.4
84552110	板材热轧机	15	10.5
84552120	型钢轧机	15	10.5
84552130	线材轧机	15	10.5
84552190	其他金属热轧或冷热联合轧机	15	10.5
84559000	金属轧机的其他零件	8	4
84571010	立式加工中心	9.7	6.8
84571020	卧式加工中心	9.7	8.8
84571030	龙门式加工中心	9.7	6.8
84571090	其他加工金属的加工中心	9.7	6.8
84596910	切削金属的非数控龙门铣床	12	10
84596990	切削金属的其他铣床	12	11
84621010	数控锻造或冲压机床及锻锤	9.7	6.8
84621090	非数控锻造或冲压机床及锻锤	12	8.4
84623910	非数控板带纵剪机	10	9.5
84623920	非数控板带横剪机	10	9.5
84623990	其他剪切机床	10	9.5
84629110	金属型材挤压机	10	9.2
84629190	其他液压压力机	10	9.2
84629910	其他机械压力机	10	9.5
84629990	税号 84.62 的未列名机床	10	9.5
84662000	工件夹具	7	4.9
84672100	电动钻	10	9
84672210	电动链锯	10	9
84672290	其他电动锯	10	9
84672910	电动砂磨工具	10	8
84672920	电刨	10	8
84672990	其他电动工具	10	8
84679110	电动链锯用零件	6	4.8
84679910	其他手提式电动工具用零件	10	9

税则号列	货品名称(简称)	最惠国税率(%)	协定税率(%)
84690020	其他电动打字机	12	10.8
84748010	固体矿物的辊压成型机	5	4.5
84748020	模压成型机	5	4.5
84748090	税号8474所列的其他机器	5	4.5
84772010	塑料造粒机	5	4.5
84772090	其他加工橡胶或塑料的挤出机	5	4.5
84774010	塑料中空成型机	5	4.5
84774020	塑料压延成型机	5	4.5
84774090	其他真空模塑及热成型机器	5	4.5
84775900	其他橡胶或塑料的模塑机、成型机	5	3.5
84778000	其他橡胶或塑料加工机器	5	4.5
84781000	其他未列名的烟草加工及制作机器	5	2.5
84791021	沥青混凝土摊铺机	8	5.6
84791022	稳定土摊铺机	8	5.6
84791029	其他摊铺机	8	5.6
84791090	其他公共工程用的机器	8	5.6
84796000	蒸发式空气冷却器	10	9
84798110	绕线机	9.5	9
84798190	其他处理金属的机械	9.5	9
84798200	其他混合、研磨、筛选、均化等机器	7	4.9
84804100	金属、硬质合金用注模或压模	8	5.6
84804900	金属、硬质合金用其他型模	8	5.6
84807900	塑料或橡胶用其他型模	5	3.5
84818010	其他阀门	7	4.9
84821000	滚珠轴承	8	7.6
84828000	其他滚动轴承及球、柱混合轴承	8	5.6
84831010	船舶用传动轴	6	5.1
84831090	其他传动轴及曲柄	6	5.4
84834010	滚子螺杆传动装置	8	5.6
84834020	行星齿轮减速器	8	5.6
84834090	其他齿轮及齿轮传动装置	8	5.6
84864021	专用于装配与封装半导体器件和集成电路的塑封机	5	4.5
84864022	专用于装配与封装半导体器件和集成电路的引线键合设备	8	7.6
84864039	其他集成电路或液晶显示屏工厂专用升降、装卸、搬运装置	5	3.5
84869010	升降、搬运、装卸机器用零件及附件(自动搬运设备用除外)	5	2.5
84869020	引线键合装置用零件及附件	6	5.7
85011010	输出功率≤37.5W玩具电动机	24.5	23.3
85011091	机座20mm≤直径<39mm微电机	9	8.6
85011099	其他输出功率≤37.5W微电机	9	8.6
85013100	输出功率≤750瓦直流电动机、发电机	12	11
85015300	输出功率>75KW多相交流电动机	12	11.4
85021310	375KVA<输出功率≤2MVA柴油发电机组	10	7
85021320	输出功率>2MVA柴油发电机组	10	7
85030010	玩具用电动机微电机零件	12	11.4
85030020	输出功率>350MVA交流发电机零件	3	2.5
85030030	风力驱动发电机组的零件	3	2.5
85030090	其他电动机、发电机(组)零件	8	7.6
85042311	10MVA<额定容量≤220MVA液体变压器	10	7
85042312	200MVA≤额定容量<330MVA液体变压器	10	7
85042313	330MVA≤额定容量<400MVA液体变压器	10	7
85042321	400MVA≤液体变压器额定容量<500MVA	6	4.2
85042329	其他额定容量≥500MVA液体变压器	6	4.2
85043110	额定容量≤1KVA的互感器	5	4.3
85043190	额定容量≤1KVA的其他变压器	5	4.3
85044014	功率<1KW高精度直流稳压电源	7	5.6
85044020	不间断供电电源(UPS)	10	8.5
85049011	额定容量>400KVA液体介质变压器零件	5	4.5
85049019	其他变压器零件	8	4.5
85049020	稳压电源及不间断供电电源零件	8	5.6
85049090	其他静止式变流器及电感器零件	8	5.6
85051900	非金属永磁体	7	6.7
85052000	电磁联轴节、离合器及制动器	8	7.6
85059090	电磁夹具等及税号85.02的零件	8	7.6
85071000	起动活塞式发动机用铅酸蓄电池	10	6.9

税则号列	货品名称(简称)	最惠国税率(%)	协定税率(%)
85072000	其他铅酸蓄电池	10	6.9
85073000	镍镉蓄电池	10	8
85074000	镍铁蓄电池	12	9.6
85078010	镍氢电池	12	9.6
85078020	锂离子电池	12	9.6
85078090	其他蓄电池	12	9
85081100	功率不超过1500瓦,且带有容积不超过20升的电动真空吸尘器	10	8.2
85123011	机动车辆用喇叭、蜂鸣器	10	8.5
85123019	其他机动车辆用音响信号装置	10	8.5
85123090	其他车辆用音响信号装置	10	8.5
85131010	手电筒	15	13.2
85152900	其他电阻焊接机器及装置	10	9.5
85158000	其他焊接机器及装置	8	7.6
85159000	电气等焊接机器及装置零件	6	5.7
85165000	微波炉	15	13.5
85177040	对讲机用的零件	8	5.6
85192000	用硬币、钞票、银行卡、代币使其工作的声音录放设备	20	16.4
85198119	其他使用磁性媒体的声音录放机	20	16.4
85198121	不带录音功能的激光唱机	30	26
85198129	使用光学媒体的其他声音录放装置	20	16.4
85198139	使用半导体媒体的其他声音录放装置	20	16.4
85198990	其他声音录制或重放设备	20	16.4
85211011	广播级录像机	T2	T2
85211019	其他磁带录像机	T2	T2
85211020	磁带放像机	T2	T2
85219011	视频高密光盘机 VCD	20	16
85219012	数字化视频光盘机 DVD	20	16
85219019	其他激光视盘放像机	20	16
85219090	其他视频信号录制或重放设备	20	16
85229010	转盘或唱机用零附件	25	20
85229021	录音机走带机构(机芯)	25	22.5
85229022	磁头	25	22.5
85229023	磁头零件	20	18
85229029	盒式磁带录音机或放声机其他零件	30	27
85229031	激光视盘机的机芯	30	21
85229039	其他视频信号录放设备的零件附件	30	21
85229090	税号85.19至85.21所列设备其他零件	20	16
85258011	特种用途电视摄像机	10	9
85258012	非特种用途的广播级电视摄像机	T2	T2
85258013	非特种用途的其他电视摄像机	T2	T2
85284910	其他彩色阴极射线管监视器	30	26
85284990	其他黑白或单色的阴极射线管监视器	19	15.2
85285910	其他彩色监视器	30	26
85285990	其他黑白或单色的监视器	19	15.2
85286910	其他彩色投影机	30	25.5
85287110	不带显示屏的彩色卫星电视接收机	30	24
85287180	不带显示屏的其他彩色电视接收机	30	21
85287211	其他彩色模拟电视接收机,带阴极射线显像管的	30	21
85287212	其他彩色数字电视接收机,带阴极射线显像管的	30	21
85287219	其他彩色电视接收机,带阴极射线显像管的	30	21
85287221	其他彩色模拟电视接收机,带液晶显示器的	30	21
85287222	其他彩色数字电视接收机,带液晶显示器的	30	21
85287229	其他彩色电视接收机,带液晶显示器的	30	21
85287231	其他彩色模拟电视接收机,带等离子显示器的	30	21
85287232	其他彩色数字电视接收机,带等离子显示器的	30	21
85287239	其他彩色电视接收机,带等离子显示器的	30	21
85287291	其他彩色模拟电视接收机	30	21
85287292	其他彩色数字电视接收机	30	21
85287299	其他彩色电视接收机	30	21
85299041	特种用途电视摄像机、静像视频摄像机及其他视频摄录一体机,数字相机零件	8	6.8
85299042	非特种用途的取像模块	12	10.8
85299049	其他电视摄像机、静像视频摄像机及其他视频摄录一体机、数字相机零件	12	10.8
85299050	雷达及无线电导航设备零件	1.5	1.4
85299060	收音机及其组合机的其他零件	15	12
85299081	彩色电视机零件	15	12
85299082	等离子显像组件及其零件	15	12
85311010	机动车辆防盗装置	10	9
85359000	其他 > 1000V 电路开关等电气装置	10	9.5

税则号列	货品名称(简称)	最惠国税率(%)	协定税率(%)
85371011	可编程序控制器	5	2.5
85371019	其他数控装置	5	2.5
85371090	其他电力控制或分配的装置	8.4	4.2
85372010	电压≥500KV 高压开关装置	8.4	4.2
85372090	其他电力控制或分配装置	8.4	4.2
85381010	子目号 8537.2010 所列装置的零件	8.4	4.2
85381090	税号 85.37 货品用的其他盘、板等	7	3.5
85441100	铜制绕组电线	10	7
85442000	同轴电缆及其他同轴电导体	10	9
85444921	1000V≥耐压>80V 无接头电缆	6	4.2
85444929	1000V≥耐压>80V 无接头电导体	12	8.4
85446012	额定电压不超过 35 千伏的电缆	10	8.9
85446013	额定电压超过 35 千伏,但不超过 110 千伏的电缆	8.4	8
85446014	额定电压超过 110 千伏,但不超过 220 千伏的电缆	8.4	8
85446019	其他额定电压超过 1000 伏的电缆	8.4	8
85446090	耐压>1KV 的其他电导体	21	20
87032130	排气量≤1000ml 的小轿车	25	22.5
87032190	排气量≤1000ml 的其他车辆	25	22.5
87032230	1L<排气量≤1.5L 的小轿车	25	22.5
87032240	1L<排气量≤1.5L 的越野车	25	22.5
87032250	1L<排气量≤1.5L,≤9 座的小客车	25	22.5
87032290	1L<排气量≤1.5L 的其他车辆	25	22.5
87032314	1.5L<排气量≤2.5L 的小轿车	25	22.5
87032315	1.5L<排气量≤2.5L 的越野车	25	22.5
87032316	1.5L<排气量≤2.5L,≤9 座的小客车	25	22.5
87032319	1.5L<排气量≤2.5L 的其他车辆	25	22.5
87032334	2.5L<排气量≤3L 的小轿车	25	22.5
87032335	2.5L<排气量≤3L 的越野车	25	22.5
87032336	2.5L<排气量≤3L,≤9 座的小客车	25	22.5
87032339	2.5L<排气量≤3L 的其他车辆	25	22.5
87032430	排气量>3000ml 的小轿车	25	22.5
87032440	排气量>3000ml 的越野车	25	22.5
87032450	排气量>3L,≤9 座的小客车	25	22.5
87032490	排气量>3000ml 的其他车辆	25	22.5
87033230	1.5L<排气量≤2.5L 的柴油型小轿车	25	22.5
87033240	1.5L<排气量≤2.5L 的柴油型越野车	25	22.5
87033250	1.5L<排气量≤2.5L,≤9 座的柴油型小客车	25	22.5
87033290	1.5L<排气量≤2.5L 的柴油型其他车辆	25	22.5
87033330	排气量>2500ml 柴油型的小轿车	25	22.5
87033340	排气量>2500ml 的柴油型越野车	25	22.5
87033350	排气量>2.5L,≤9 座的柴油型小客车	25	22.5
87033390	排气量>2500ml 的柴油型其他车辆	25	22.5
87039000	装有压燃式内燃发动机的其他载人机动车辆	25	22.5
87042230	柴油型其他中型货车	20	18
87042240	柴油型其他重型货车	20	18
87054000	机动混凝土搅拌车	15	13.5
87059010	无线电通信车	9	8.1
87059020	机动放射线检查车	9	8.1
87059030	机动环境监测车	12	10.8
87059040	机动医疗车	12	10.8
87059051	航空电源车(频率为 400 赫兹)	12	10.8
87059059	其他机动电源车	12	10.8
87059060	飞机加油车、调温车、除冰车	12	10.8
87059070	道路(包括跑道)扫雪车	12	10.8
87059080	石油测井车、压裂车、混沙车	12	10.8
87059090	其他特殊用途的机动车辆	12	10.8
87079010	税号 8702.1092、.1093、.9020 及.9030 所列车辆用车身	10	9
87079090	其他车辆用车身(含驾驶室)	10	9
87081000	缓冲器(保险杠)及其零件	10	9.6
87082930	车窗玻璃升降器	10	9
87082941	汽车电动天窗	10	9
87082942	汽车手动天窗	10	9
87082951	侧围	10	9
87082952	车门	10	9
87082953	发动机罩盖	10	9
87082954	前围	10	9
87082955	行李箱盖(或背门)	10	9
87082956	后围	10	9
87082957	翼子板(或叶子板)	10	9
87082959	车身的其他覆盖件	10	9
87082990	车身的未列名零部件	10	9

税则号列	货品名称(简称)	最惠国税率(%)	协定税率(%)
87083021	牵引车、拖拉机、非公路自卸车用防抱死制动系统(ABS)	6	5.4
87083029	其他车辆用防抱死制动系统(ABS)	10	9
87083091	牵引车、拖拉机用制动器及其零件	6	5.4
87083092	大型客车用制动器及其零件	10	9
87083093	非公路自卸车用制动器及其零件	6	5.4
87083094	柴、汽油轻型货车用制动器及零件	10	9
87083095	柴油型重型货车用制动器及其零件	10	9
87083096	特种车用制动器及其零件	10	9
87083099	其他未列名机动车辆用制动器及零件	10	9
87085071	牵引车、拖拉机用驱动桥及零件	6	5.4
87085072	其他大型客车用驱动桥及零件	10	9
87085073	非公路自卸车用驱动桥及零件	6	5.4
87085074	柴、汽油型轻型货车用驱动桥及零件	10	9
87085075	其他柴油型重型货车用驱动桥及零件	10	9
87085076	特种车用驱动桥及零件	10	9
87085079	未列名机动车辆用驱动桥及零件	10	9
87088010	税号 87.03 所列车辆用的悬挂减震器及零件	10	9
87088090	机动车辆用的其他悬挂减震器及零件	10	9
87089500	机动车辆的安全气囊装置	10	9
87113010	汽油型中小马力摩托车及脚踏两用车	45	32.8
87113020	汽油型中大马力摩托车及脚踏两用车	45	32.8
87120020	竞赛型自行车	13	9.1
87120030	山地自行车	13	9.1
87120041	16、18、20 英寸自行车	13	9.1
87120049	其他越野自行车	13	9.1
87120081	≤16 英寸的未列名自行车	13	9.1
87120089	其他未列名自行车	13	9.1
87120090	其他非机动脚踏车	23	16.1
87149900	非机动脚踏车的其他零附件	12	8.4
88024010	大型飞机及其他航空器	5	3.5
88024020	特大型飞机及其他航空器	1	0.7

税则号列	货品名称(简称)	最惠国税率(%)	协定税率(%)
90011000	光导纤维束及光缆	5	4.5
90012000	偏振材料制的片及板	8	7.6
90019000	税号 90.01 未列名的其他光学元件	8	7.6
90022010	照相机用滤色镜	15	14.3
90022090	其他光学仪器或装置滤色镜	15	14.3
90069110	特种用途照相机的零附件	8	5.6
90069120	一次成像照相机的零附件	5	3.5
90069191	照相机自动调焦组件	10	7
90069192	其他照相机的快门组件	10	7
90069199	其他照相机的其他零附件	10	7
90138010	放大镜	12	8.4
90138020	光学门眼	12	8.4
90158000	其他大地测量仪器及装置	5	3.5
90181210	B 型超声波诊断仪	7	6
90181291	彩色超声波诊断仪	5	4.5
90181299	其他超声扫描装置	5	4.5
90181930	病员监护仪	4	3.5
90181941	听力计	4	3.5
90181949	其他听力诊断装置	4	3.5
90181990	其他电气诊断装置	4	3.5
90183100	注射器	8	7.6
90183210	管状金属针头	8	7
90183220	缝合用针	4	3.5
90185000	眼科用其他仪器及器具	4	3.5
90189010	听诊器	4	3.5
90189020	血压测量仪器及器具	4	3.5
90189030	内窥镜	4	3.5
90189040	肾脏透析设备(人工肾)	4	3.5
90189050	透热疗法设备	4	3.5
90189060	输血设备	4	3.5
90189070	麻醉设备	4	3.5
90189080	宫内节育器	4	2
90189090	税号 90.18 中未列名的医疗仪器	4	3.5
90221200	X 射线断层检查仪	4	2.8
90241000	金属材料的试验用机器及器具	7	6.5
90251910	非液体的工业用温度计及高温计	8.4	8
90251990	非液体的其他温度计、高温计	8.4	8
90259000	比重计、温度计等类似仪器的零件	8	7.6
90311000	机械零件平衡试验机	7	6.5
90318010	光纤通信及光纤性能测试仪	5	4
90318090	未列名测量、检验仪器器具及机器	5	4
90328100	液压或气压的其他仪器及装置	7	6.5

税则号列	货品名称(简称)	最惠国税率(%)	协定税率(%)	税则号列	商品名称(简称)	最惠国税率(%)	协定税率(%)
91011100	机械指示式的贵金属电子手表	11	9.9	96033020	毛笔	20	18
91021100	机械指示式的其他电子手表	12.5	11.1	96033090	化妆用的类似笔	25	22.5
91081900	其他已组装的完整电子表芯	16	12	96039010	羽毛掸	21	18.9
91112000	贱金属制的表壳	14	10	96071900	其他拉链	21	14.7
94042900	其他材料制褥垫	20	14	96081000	圆珠笔	15	13.5
94060000	活动房屋	10	7	96151100	硬质橡胶或塑料制梳子、发夹及类似品	18	16.2
95067010	溜冰鞋	14	12				
95067020	旱冰鞋	14	12	96159000	其他发夹、卷发器等及其零件	18	16.2
95079000	其他钓鱼用品	21	18.9	96161000	香水喷雾器或类似的化妆用喷雾器	18	16.2
96032900	剃须刷、发刷、睫毛刷等人体化妆用刷	15	13.5	96162000	施敷脂粉或化妆品用粉扑及粉拍	18	16.2
96033010	画笔	25	15				

附件 9：

对柬埔寨、缅甸、老挝、孟加拉、阿富汗等国和非洲部分国家特惠税目、税率表

Appendix 9:

Special Preferential Headings and Tariff Rates for Kampuchea, Burma, Laos, Bangladeshi, Afghanistan and Certain African countries Countries

税则号列 Tariff No.	货品名称 Description of Goods	最惠国 MFN	柬埔寨 TPE	缅甸 MMR	老挝 LAO	孟加拉 BGN	非洲部分国家 CAC	阿富汗 FV
01029000	其他牛	10	0	0	0			
01039110	重量＜10kg 的猪	10	0	0				
01039120	重量在 10－50kg 的猪，包括 10kg	10	0	0				
01039200	重量≥50kg 的猪	10	0	0	0			
01051190	重量≤185g 的其他鸡	10		0	0			
01051990	重量≤185g 的其他家禽	10			0			
01061920	食用哺乳动物	10		0				
01062020	食用爬行动物	10		0				
01063921	乳鸽	10		0				
01063922	鸵鸟	10		0				
01063923	野鸭	10		0				
01063929	其他食用鸟	10		0				
01063990	其他鸟	10					0	
01069020	其他食用动物	10		0				
01069090	其他动物	10					0	
02011000	整头及半头鲜、冷牛肉	20	0		0			
02012000	鲜、冷的带骨牛肉	12	0		0			
02013000	鲜、冷的去骨牛肉	12	0					
02021000	冻的整头及半头牛肉	25	0		0			
02022000	冻的带骨牛肉	12	0		0			
02023000	冻的去骨牛肉	12	0					
02031110	鲜、冷的整头及半头乳猪肉	20	0		0			
02031190	其他鲜、冷的整头及半头猪肉	20	0		0			
02031200	鲜、冷的带骨猪前腿、后腿及其肉块	20	0		0			
02031900	其他鲜、冷猪肉	20	0		0			
02032110	冻整头及半头乳猪肉	12	0		0			
02032190	其他冻整头及半头猪肉	12	0		0			
02032200	冻的带骨猪前腿、后腿及其肉块	12	0		0			
02032900	其他冻猪肉	12	0					
02061000	鲜、冷的牛杂碎	12	0		0			
02062100	冻牛舌	12	0		0			
02062200	冻牛肝	12	0		0			
02062900	其他冻牛杂碎	12	0		0			
02063000	鲜、冷的猪杂碎	20	0	0	0			
02064100	冻猪肝	20	0		0			
02064900	其他冻猪杂碎	12	0		0			
02068000	鲜、冷的羊、马、驴、骡杂碎	20	0					
02069000	冻的羊、马、驴、骡杂碎	18	0					
02071100	整只，鲜或冷的鸡	20	0	0	0			
02071200	整只，冻的鸡	T2	0	0	0			
02071311	鲜或冷的带骨鸡块	20	0	0	0			
02071319	鲜或冷的其他鸡块	20	0	0	0			
02071321	鲜或冷的鸡翼(不包括翼尖)	20	0	0	0			
02071329	鲜或冷的其他鸡杂碎	20	0	0	0			

税则号列 Tariff No.	货品名称 Description of Goods	最惠国 MFN	柬埔寨 TPE	缅甸 MMR	老挝 LAO	孟加拉 BGN	非洲部分国家 CAC	阿富汗 FV
02071411	冻的的带骨鸡块	T2	0	0	0			
02071419	冻的其他鸡块	T2	0	0	0			
02071421	冻的鸡翼(不包括翼尖)	T2	0	0	0			
02071422	鲜、冷、冻鸡爪	T2	0	0	0			
02071429	冻的其他鸡杂碎	T2	0	0	0			
02072400	整只,鲜或冷的火鸡	20			0			
02072500	整只,冻的火鸡	20			0			
02072600	鲜或冷的火鸡块及杂碎	20			0			
02072700	冻的火鸡块及杂碎	10			0			
02073210	整只,鲜或冷的鸭	20	0	0	0			
02073220	整只,鲜或冷的鹅	20	0	0	0			
02073230	整只,鲜或冷的珍珠鸡	20	0		0			
02073310	整只,冻的鸭	20	0	0	0			
02073320	整只,冻的鹅	20	0	0	0			
02073330	整只,冻的珍珠鸡	20	0	0	0			
02073400	鲜或冷的税目的0105所列家禽的肥肝	20	0		0			
02073510	鲜或冷的鸭块及杂碎	20	0	0	0			
02073520	鲜或冷的鹅块及杂碎	20	0	0	0			
02073530	鲜或冷的珍珠鸡块及杂碎	20	0	0	0			
02073610	冻的鸭块及杂碎	20	0	0	0			
02073620	冻的鹅块及杂碎	20	0	0	0			
02073630	冻的珍珠鸡块及杂碎	20	0	0	0			
02101110	干、熏、盐制的带骨猪腿	25	0		0			
02101190	干、熏、盐制的带骨猪腿肉块	25	0		0			
02101200	干、熏、盐制的猪腹肉	25	0		0			
02101900	干、熏、盐制的其他猪肉	25	0	0				
02102000	干、熏、盐制的牛肉	25	0		0			
02109100	干、熏、盐制的灵长目动物肉及食用杂碎	25	0		0			
02109200	干、熏、盐制的鲸、海豚及鼠海豚;海牛及儒艮肉及食用杂碎	25	0		0			
02109300	干、熏、盐制的爬行动物肉及食用杂碎	25	0		0			
02109900	干、熏、盐制的其他肉及食用杂碎	25	0		0			0
03019290	其他活鳗鱼	10	0	0				
03019390	其他活鲤鱼	10.5	0	0				
03019490	其他活蓝鳍金枪鱼	10.5	0	0				
03019590	其他活南金枪鱼	10.5	0	0				
03019991	活罗非鱼	10.5	0	0				
03019992	活鲀	10.5	0	0				
03019999	其他活鱼	10.5	0	0				
03022900	其他鲜、冷比目鱼	12	0					
03023100	鲜、冷长鳍金枪鱼	12	0					
03023400	鲜、冷大眼金枪鱼	12	0	0				
03023500	鲜、冷蓝鳍金枪鱼	12	0	0				
03023600	鲜、冷南金枪鱼	12	0	0				
03023900	其他鲜、冷金枪鱼	12	0	0				
03026600	鲜冷鳗鱼	12		0				
03026800	鲜、冷南极犬牙鱼	12	0	0				
03026940	鲜冷罗非鱼	12	0	0				
03026950	鲜、冷鲀	12	0	0				
03026990	其他鲜、冷鱼	12	0	0				

税则号列 Tariff No.	货品名称 Description of Goods	最惠国 MFN	柬埔寨 TPE	缅甸 MMR	老挝 LAO	孟加拉 BGN	非洲部分国家 CAC	阿富汗 FV
03027000	鲜、冷鱼肝及鱼卵	12	0					
03031100	冻红大马哈鱼,但鱼肝及鱼卵除外	10	0					
03031900	其他冻大马哈鱼,但鱼肝及鱼卵除外	10	0					
03033200	冻鲽鱼	12						0
03033300	冻鳎鱼	12					0	0
03033900	其他冻比目鱼	10					0	
03034200	冻黄鳍金枪鱼	12						0
03034300	冻鲣鱼	12						0
03034400	冻大眼金枪鱼,但鱼肝及鱼卵除外	12	0	0				
03034500	冻蓝鳍金枪鱼,但鱼肝及鱼卵除外	12	0	0				
03034600	冻南金枪鱼,但鱼肝及鱼卵除外	12	0	0				
03034900	其他冻金枪鱼,但鱼肝及鱼卵除外	12	0	0				0
03035100	冻鲱鱼(大西洋鲱鱼、太平洋鲱鱼),但鱼肝及鱼卵除外	10					0	
03036100	冻剑鱼,但鱼肝及鱼卵除外	10			0	0	0	0
03036200	冻南极犬牙鱼,但鱼肝及鱼卵除外	10	0	0	0	0	0	0
03037100	冻沙丁鱼、黍鲱鱼	12					0	
03037700	冻尖吻鲈鱼	12						0
03037910	冻带鱼	10	0	0	0	0	0	0
03037920	冻黄鱼	10	0	0	0	0		
03037930	冻鲳鱼	10	0	0	0	0		
03037940	冻罗非鱼	10	0	0	0	0		
03037990	其他未列名冻鱼	10	0	0	0	0	0	0
03038000	冻鱼肝及鱼卵	10					0	
03041100	鲜、冷剑鱼片及鱼肉	12		0				0
03041200	鲜、冷南极犬牙鱼片及鱼肉	12		0				0
03041900	其他鲜、冷的鱼片及鱼肉	12		0				0
03042100	冻剑鱼片	10	0	0				
03042200	冻南极犬牙鱼片	10	0	0				
03042910	冻罗非鱼片	10	0	0				
03042990	其他冻鱼片	10	0	0				
03049100	冻的剑鱼肉	10		0	0	0	0	0
03049200	冻的南极犬牙鱼肉	10		0	0	0	0	0
03049900	其他冻鱼肉	10		0	0	0	0	0
03053000	干或盐制的鱼片	10		0	0	0		
03054900	其他熏鱼及鱼片	14		0	0	0		
03055910	干海马、干海龙	2	0	0	0	0		
03055920	干鱼翅	15	0	0	0	0	0	
03055990	其他干鱼	16		0	0	0	0	
03056910	盐腌及盐渍的带鱼	16		0	0	0		
03056920	盐腌及盐渍的黄鱼	16		0	0	0		
03056930	盐腌及盐渍的鲳鱼	16		0	0	0		
03056940	盐腌及盐渍的罗非鱼	16		0	0	0		
03056990	盐腌及盐渍的其他鱼	16		0	0	0		
03061100	冻龙虾	10	0	0				
03061200	冻大螯虾	10	0					
03061311	冻小虾仁	8	0	0				
03061312	冻北方长额虾	5	0	0				
03061319	其他冻小虾	5	0	0			0	
03061321	冻对虾仁	8	0	0				

税则号列 Tariff No.	货品名称 Description of Goods	最惠国 MFN	柬埔寨 TPE	缅甸 MMR	老挝 LAO	孟加拉 BGN	非洲部分国家 CAC	阿富汗 FV
03061329	其他冻对虾	5	0	0			0	
03061410	冻梭子蟹	10	0	0	0	0		
03061490	其他冻蟹	10	0	0	0	0	0	
03061911	冻淡水小龙虾仁	16	0					
03061919	冻带壳淡水小龙虾	16	0					
03061990	其他冻甲壳动物	16	0					
03062190	未冻的龙虾	15	0	0				
03062290	其他未冻的大螯虾	15	0	0				
03062391	鲜、冷对虾	15	0	0				
03062399	其他未冻小虾及对虾	12	0	0				
03062491	未冻的中华绒毛蟹(大闸蟹)	14	0					
03062492	未冻的梭子蟹	14	0					
03062499	未冻的其他蟹	14	0					
03062990	其他带壳或去壳的未冻的甲壳动物	14	0	0				
03071090	其他牡蛎(蚝)	14		0				
03072190	其他活、鲜、冷扇贝	14		0				
03072900	其他冻、干、盐腌或盐渍的扇贝	14		0				
03073190	其他活、鲜、冷贻贝	14	0	0				
03073900	其他冻、干、盐制的贻贝	14	0	0				
03074190	其他活、鲜或冷墨鱼及鱿鱼	12	0	0				0
03074900	其他冻、干、盐制的墨鱼及鱿鱼	12	0	0			0	0
03075900	其他冻、干、盐制的章鱼	17					0	
03076090	其他蜗牛及螺	14	0					
03079191	活、鲜、冷鲍鱼	14	0	0				
03079192	活、鲜或冷的沙蚕	14	0	0				
03079199	其他活、鲜、冷软体动物、水生无脊椎动物	14	0	0				
03079910	冻、干、盐腌或盐渍的鲍鱼	10	0	0				0
03079920	冻、干、盐腌或盐渍的海参	10	0	0			0	0
03079990	其他冻、干、盐制软体动物、水生无脊椎动物	10	0	0				
04070021	带壳鲜鸡蛋	20	0	0				
04070022	带壳鲜鸭蛋	20	0	0				
04070023	带壳鲜鹅蛋	20	0	0				
04070029	其他带壳鲜禽蛋	20	0	0				
04070091	咸蛋	20		0				
04090000	天然蜂蜜	15	0		0			
04100010	燕窝	25	0	0				
04100090	其他编号未列名的食用动物产品	20		0				
05040029	鲜、冷、冻、干、盐制的其他动物胃	20						0
05061000	经酸处理的骨胶原及骨	12			0			
05069011	含牛羊成分的骨粉及骨废料	12			0			
05069019	骨粉及骨废料	12			0			
05069090	其他骨及角柱	12			0			
05071000	兽牙;兽牙粉末及废料	10					0	
05080010	珊瑚及水产品壳、骨的粉末及废料	12						0
05080090	珊瑚及介、贝、棘皮动物的壳、骨	12					0	0
05119111	受精鱼卵	12					0	
05119119	其他鱼产品	12					0	
05119190	其他未列名水产品;第三章的死动物	12					0	
06011010	休眠的番红花球茎	4			0			

税则号列 Tariff No.	货品名称 Description of Goods	最惠国 MFN	柬埔寨 TPE	缅甸 MMR	老挝 LAO	孟加拉 BGN	非洲部分国家 CAC	阿富汗 FV
06011099	其它休眠的鳞茎、块茎、块根等	5			0			
06031100	鲜玫瑰	10			0			
06031200	鲜康乃馨	10			0			
06031300	鲜兰花	10			0			
06031400	鲜菊花	10			0			
06031900	其他鲜的插花及花蕾	10			0			
06039000	干的及经过染色等加工的插花及花蕾	23			0			
06049900	染色或经加工的枝、叶、草等	10					0	
07019000	其他鲜或冷的马铃薯	13	0					
07031010	鲜或冷的洋葱	13	0	0				
07031020	鲜或冷的青葱	13	0	0				
07039010	鲜或冷的韭葱	13	0					
07039020	鲜或冷的大葱	13	0					
07039090	鲜或冷的其他葱属蔬菜	13	0					
07049010	鲜或冷的卷心菜	13			0			
07049020	鲜或冷的西兰花	13			0			
07049090	鲜或冷的其他食用芥菜类蔬菜	13			0			
07070000	鲜或冷的黄瓜及小黄瓜	13	0					
07081000	鲜或冷的豌豆	13	0					
07082000	鲜或冷的豇豆及菜豆	13	0		0			
07089000	鲜或冷的其他豆类蔬菜	13	0					
07095100	鲜或冷的其他伞菌属蘑菇	13	0					
07095910	鲜或冷的松茸	13	0					
07095920	鲜或冷的香菇	13	0					
07095930	鲜或冷的金针菇	13	0					
07095940	鲜或冷的草菇	13	0					
07095950	鲜或冷的口蘑	13	0					
07095990	鲜或冷的其他蘑菇	13	0					
07096000	鲜或冷的辣椒,包括甜椒	13	0					
07099010	鲜或冷的竹笋	13	0		0			
07099090	鲜或冷的其他蔬菜	13	0					0
07102210	冷冻红小豆	13	0					
07102290	其他冷冻豇豆及菜豆	13	0					
07102900	冷冻其他豆类蔬菜	13	0					
07108010	冷冻松茸	13	0					
07108020	其他蒜台及蒜苗(青蒜)	13	0					
07108030	蒜头	13	0					
07108090	冷冻未列名蔬菜	13	0					
07109000	冷冻什锦蔬菜	10	0					
07133190	其他干绿豆	3	0	0				
07133290	其他干赤豆	3	0					
07133390	其他干芸豆	7.5	0					
07133900	干豇豆及菜豆	7	0					
07141010	鲜木薯	10	0		0			
07141020	干木薯	5	0		0			
07141030	冷或冻的木薯	10	0		0			
07142011	种用鲜甘薯	0	0		0			
07142019	其他鲜甘薯	13	0		0			
07142020	干甘薯	13	0		0			

税则号列 Tariff No.	货品名称 Description of Goods	最惠国 MFN	柬埔寨 TPE	缅甸 MMR	老挝 LAO	孟加拉 BGN	非洲部分国家 CAC	阿富汗 FV
07142030	冷或冻的甘薯	13	0		0			
07149010	鲜、干或冷、冻的荸荠	13	0		0			
07149029	其他藕	13	0		0			
07149090	含有高淀粉或菊粉的其他类似根茎	13	0		0			
08011100	干的椰子	12	0					
08011990	其他鲜椰子	12	0					
08013100	鲜或干的未去壳腰果	20	0				0	
08013200	鲜或干的去壳腰果	10	0	0				
08030000	鲜或干的香蕉,包括芭蕉	10	0		0			
08043000	鲜或干菠萝	12	0					
08044000	鲜或干鳄梨	25	0					
08072000	鲜木瓜	25	0					
08106000	鲜榴莲	20	0					
08109030	鲜龙眼	12	0					
08134010	龙眼干、肉	20	0					
08134020	柿饼	25	0					
08134030	干红枣	25	0					
08134040	荔枝干	25	0					0
08134090	其他干果	25	0					
09011100	未浸除咖啡碱的未焙炒咖啡	8	0		0		0	
09011200	已浸除咖啡碱的未焙炒咖啡	8	0		0		0	
09012100	未浸除咖啡碱的已焙炒咖啡	15	0		0			
09012200	已浸除咖啡碱的已焙炒咖啡	15	0		0			
09019010	咖啡豆荚及咖啡豆皮	10	0		0			
09019020	含咖啡的咖啡代用品	30	0		0			
09024010	每件净重 >3kg 的乌龙茶	15	0	0	0			
09024020	每件净重 >3kg 的普洱茶	15	0	0	0			
09024090	每件净重 >3kg 的其他红茶(已发酵)及半发酵茶	15	0	0	0			
09050000	香子兰豆	15					0	
09070000	丁香(母丁香、公丁香及丁香梗)	3	0				0	
09081000	肉豆蔻	8	0		0			
09082000	肉豆蔻衣	8	0		0			
09083000	豆蔻	3	0		0			
09101000	姜	15	0		0			
09103000	姜黄	15	0					
09109900	其他调味香料	15						0
10082000	谷子	2			0			
10083000	加那利草子	2			0			
10089090	其他谷物	3			0			
11029090	其他谷物细粉	5	0					
11031990	其他谷物粗粒及粗粉	5	0					
11061000	干豆细粉、粗粉及粉末	10	0					
11062000	用品目 0714 的西谷茎髓、植物根茎、块茎制成的细粉、粗粉、粉末	20	0	0	0			
11081400	木薯淀粉	10						0
12010091	黄大豆	3	0		0			
12010092	黑大豆	3	0		0			
12010093	青大豆	3	0		0			
12021090	其他未焙炒或未烹煮的带壳花生	15			0			

税则号列 Tariff No.	货品名称 Description of Goods	最惠国 MFN	柬埔寨 TPE	缅甸 MMR	老挝 LAO	孟加拉 BGN	非洲部分国家 CAC	阿富汗 FV
12022000	未焙炒或烹煮的去壳花生	15			0			
12030000	干椰子肉	15	0					
12074090	其他芝麻	10	0	0	0		0	
12079991	牛油树果	20		0				
12079992	其他油棕果及油棕仁	10	0					
12079993	其他蓖麻子	15	0	0	0			
12079999	其他含油子仁及果实	10	0	0	0			
12081000	大豆粉	9	0					
12089000	其他含油子仁或果实的细粉及粗粉	15	0					
12113000	古柯叶	9	0					
12114000	罂粟杆	9	0					
12119011	鲜或干的当归	6	0					
12119012	鲜或干的田七	6	0					
12119015	鲜或干的菊花	6	0					
12119016	鲜或干的冬虫夏草	6	0					
12119017	鲜或干的贝母	6	0					
12119018	鲜或干的川芎	6	0					
12119019	鲜或干的半夏	6	0					
12119021	鲜或干的白芍	6	0					
12119022	鲜或干的天麻	6	0					
12119023	鲜或干的黄芪	6	0					
12119024	鲜或干的大黄、籽黄	6	0					
12119025	鲜或干的白术	6	0					
12119026	鲜或干的地黄	6	0					
12119027	鲜或干的槐米	6	0					
12119028	鲜或干的杜仲	6	0					
12119029	鲜或干的茯苓	6	0	0	0			
12119031	鲜或干的枸杞	6	0					
12119032	鲜或干的大海子	6	0					
12119033	鲜或干的沉香	3	0					
12119034	鲜或干的沙参	6	0					
12119035	青蒿	6	0					
12119036	鲜或干的甘草	6						0
12119039	其他主要用作药料的鲜或干的植物	6	0	0	0			0
12119050	主要用作香料的植物	8	0				0	
12119091	鲜或干的鱼藤根、除虫菊	3	0					
12119099	其他鲜或干的杀虫、杀菌用植物	9	0					0
12122090	鲜、冷、冻或干的其他海草及其他藻类	15					0	0
12129995	其他冷、冻或干的甘蔗	20	0	0	0			
12129999	鲜、干的其他供人食用的植物产品	30						0
12130010	未经处理的稻草的茎、杆	12	0					
12130090	其他未经处理的谷类植物茎、杆及谷壳	12	0					
12141000	紫苜蓿粗粉及团粒	5	0					
12149000	芜菁甘蓝、饲料甜菜等其他植物饲料	9	0					
13012000	阿拉伯胶	15					0	
13019020	乳香、没药及血竭	3					0	
14011000	竹	10	0		0			
14012000	藤	10	0		0			
14019010	谷类植物的茎秆(麦秸除外)	10	0					

税则号列 Tariff No.	货品名称 Description of Goods	最惠国 MFN	柬埔寨 TPE	缅甸 MMR	老挝 LAO	孟加拉 BGN	非洲部分国家 CAC	阿富汗 FV
14019020	芦苇	10	0					
14019030	蔺草(包括灯芯草)	10	0					
14019090	未列名主要用作编结用的植物材料	10	0				0	
14049010	主要供染料或鞣料用的植物原料	5						0
14049090	其他植物产品	15					0	0
15131900	椰子油及其分离品	9					0	
15152100	初榨玉米油的分离品	10	0		0			
15152900	精制的玉米油及其分离品	10	0		0			
15153000	蓖麻油及其分离品	10	0		0			
15155000	芝麻油及其分离品	12	0		0			
15159010	希蒙得木油及其分离品	20	0					
15159030	桐油及其分离品	20	0					
15159090	其他固定植物油、脂及其分离品	20	0	0	0			
16041300	制作或保藏的沙丁鱼、黍鲱鱼,整条或切块,但未绞碎	5	0					
16041400	制作或保藏的金枪鱼、鲣鱼,整条或切块,但未绞碎	5	0					
16041931	制作或保藏的斑点叉尾鮰鱼	12					0	
16041939	制作或保藏的其他叉尾鮰鱼	12					0	
16041990	制作或保藏的其他鱼,整条或切块,但未绞碎	12					0	
16052000	制作或保藏的小虾及对虾	5	0					
16053000	制作或保藏的龙虾	5	0					
16054011	制作或保藏的淡水小龙虾仁	5	0					
16054019	制作或保藏的带壳淡水小龙虾	5	0					
16054090	制作或保藏的其他甲壳动物	5	0					
17029000	其他固体糖;人造蜜;焦糖	30						0
18010000	生或焙炒的整颗或破碎的可可豆	8					0	
18040000	可可油,可可脂	22					0	
18069000	其他巧克力及含可可的食品	8						0
19030000	珍粉及淀粉制成的珍粉代用品	15						0
19053100	甜饼干	15			7.5	7.5		
19053200	华夫饼干及圣餐饼	15			7.5	7.5		
19059000	其他面包、糕点、饼干及其焙烘糕饼	20			10	10		
20019010	用醋制作的大蒜	25			12.5	12.5		
20019090	用醋制作的其他果、菜及食用植物	25			12.5	12.5		
20041000	非用醋制作的冷冻马铃薯	13					0	
20060010	蜜枣	30		0				0
20060020	糖渍制橄榄	30		0				
20060090	其他糖渍蔬菜、水果、坚果、果皮	30		0				
20079100	烹煮制成的柑桔属水果	30		0				
20079910	烹煮制成的其他果酱、果冻罐头	5			2.5	2.5		
20079990	烹煮制成的其他果酱、果冻	5			2.5	2.5		
20081120	烘焙花生	30	0					
20081910	核桃仁罐头	20	0		0			
20081920	其他果仁罐头	13	0		0			
20081991	栗仁	10	0		0			
20081999	其他坚果及子仁	10	0		0			
20082010	菠萝罐头	15			0			
20082090	非用醋制作的其他菠萝	15			0			
20083010	柑桔属水果罐头	20			0			
20083090	非用醋制作的其他柑桔属水果	20			0			

税则号列 Tariff No.	货品名称 Description of Goods	最惠国 MFN	柬埔寨 TPE	缅甸 MMR	老挝 LAO	孟加拉 BGN	非洲部分国家 CAC	阿富汗 FV
20084010	梨罐头	20			0			
20084090	非用醋制作的其他梨	20			0			
20087010	桃罐头	10			0			
20087090	非用醋制作的其他桃	20			0			
20089100	非用醋制作的棕榈芯	5	0					
20089200	非用醋制作的什锦果实	10	0					
20089920	龙眼罐头	15	0					
20089990	未列名制作或保藏的水果、坚果	15	0					
20091100	冷冻的橙汁	7.5	0		0			
20091200	非冷冻的,白利糖度值不超过20的橙汁	30	0		0			
20091900	其他橙汁	30	0		0			
20092100	白利糖度值不超过20的葡萄柚(包括柚)汁	15			0			
20092900	其他葡萄柚(包括柚)汁	15			0			
20093110	白利糖度不超过20的柠檬汁	18	0		9	9		
20093190	其他未混合的白利糖度值不超过20的桔汁属水果汁	18	0		9	9		
20093910	白利糖度超过20的柠檬汁	18	0		9	9		
20093990	其他未混合的柑桔属水果汁,白利糖度值不超过20	18	0		9	9		
20094100	白利糖度值不超过20的菠萝汁	10	0		0			
20094900	其他菠萝汁	10	0		0			
20095000	番茄汁	30			0	15		
20098011	椰子汁	10		0	0			
20098012	芒果汁	20		0	0			
20098013	西番莲果汁	20		0	0			
20098014	番石榴果汁	20		0	0			
20098019	其他未混合的水果汁	20		0	0			
20098020	其他未混合的蔬菜汁	20		0				
20099010	混合水果汁	20	0		0	10		
20099090	混合蔬菜汁、水果与蔬菜的混合汁	20	0		0	10		
21031000	酱油	28	0					
21032000	番茄沙司及其他番茄调味汁	15	0					
21033000	芥子粉及其调味品	15	0					
21069030	蜂王浆制剂	3			0			
22029000	其他无酒精饮料	35						0
23012010	饲料用鱼粉	2						0
23062000	亚麻子油渣饼及固体残渣	5			0			
23065000	椰子或干椰肉油渣饼及固体残渣	5	0					
23066000	油棕果或油棕仁油渣饼及固体残渣	5	0					
23069000	其他油渣饼及固体残渣	5			0			
25010020	纯氯化钠	3			0			
25061000	石英	3					0	
25062000	石英岩,不论是否切割成矩形板、块	3					0	
25070010	不论是否煅烧的高岭土	3						0
25084000	其他粘土,不论是否煅烧	3					0	
25085000	红柱石,蓝晶石及硅线石,不论是否煅烧	3					0	
25090000	白垩	3						0
25140000	板岩,不论是否粗加修整或切割成矩形板块	3					0	0
25151100	原状或粗加修整大理石及灰华	4					0	
25161100	原状或粗加修整的花岗岩	4					0	
25162000	砂岩,不论是否粗加修整或切割成矩形板块	3					0	

税则号列 Tariff No.	货品名称 Description of Goods	最惠国 MFN	柬埔寨 TPE	缅甸 MMR	老挝 LAO	孟加拉 BGN	非洲部分国家 CAC	阿富汗 FV
25171000	通常做混凝土粒料、铺路、铁道路基或其他路基用的卵石、砾石及碎石,圆石子及燧石,不论是否热处理	4					0	
25174900	税目 2515 及 2616 所列各种石料的碎粒、碎屑及粉末,大理石的除外,不论是否热处理	3					0	
25201000	生石膏;硬石膏	5			0			
25202010	牙科用熟石膏,无论是否着色及带有少量促凝剂或缓凝剂	5			0			
25202090	其他熟石膏,不论是否着色及带有少量促凝剂或缓凝剂	5			0			
25210000	石灰石助溶剂;通常用于制造石灰或水泥的石灰石及其他钙质石	5						0
25291000	长石	3						0
25309010	矿物性药材	3						0
25309091	硅灰石	3					0	
25309099	其他矿产品	3					0	
26203000	主要含铜的矿灰及残渣	4					0	
27011100	未制成型的无烟煤,不论是否粉化	3			0			
27011210	未制成型的炼焦烟煤,不论是否粉化	3			0			
27011290	未制成型的其他烟煤,不论是否粉化	6			0			
27011900	未制成型的其他煤,不论是否粉化	5			0			
27012000	煤砖、煤球及类似用煤制固体燃料	5			0			
27101991	润滑油	6					0	
27141000	沥青页岩、油页岩及焦油砂	6					0	
28112200	二氧化硅	5.5						0
28415000	其他铬酸盐及重铬酸盐;过铬酸盐	5.5						0
29071990	其他一元酚	5.5					0	
29095000	醚酚、醚醇酚及其卤化、磺化、硝化或亚硝化的衍生物	5.5					0	
29157090	棕榈酸及其盐和酯、硬脂酸盐、酯	5.5					0	
29392000	其他金鸡纳生物碱及其衍生物,及它们的盐	4					0	
30049059	其他中式成药(混合或非混合,治病或防病用已配定剂量或零售包装)	3						0
30061000	无菌外科肠线;无菌昆布、无菌粘合胶布、无菌吸收性止血材料、外科或牙科用无菌抗粘连阻隔材料及类似无菌材料	5						0
30069100	可确定用于造口术用具	10					0	0
32030019	其他植物质着色料及以其为基本成分的制品包括染料浸膏(无论是否已有化学定义);32 章注释三所述的以植物质着色料为基本成分的制品	6.5						0
32041400	直接染料及以其为基本成分的制品(不论是否已有化学定义)	6.5						0
32041590	其他瓮染料(包括颜料用的)及以其为基本成分的制品(不论是否已有化学定义)	6.5						0
32064900	其他着色料及其制品;32 章注释三所述的制品,但税目 32.03,32.04 及 32.05 的货品除外	6.5						0
32139000	非成套颜料、调色料及类似品(艺术家、学生和广告美工用的,片状、管装、罐装、瓶装、扁盒装等类似形状或包装的)	10						0
33011300	柠檬油(包括浸膏及净油)	20					0	
33012999	其他非柑桔属果实的精油(包括浸膏及净油)	15					0	
33019090	用花香吸取法或浸渍法制定的含浓缩精油的脂肪、固定油、蜡及类似品;精油脱萜所得的萜烯副产品(柑桔属果实的除外);精油水溶液及水馏液	20					0	
33029000	其他工业用混合香料及以香料为基本成分的混合物和制品	10					0	0
33074100	神香及其他通过燃烧散发香气制品	10						0
33079000	脱毛剂、其他编号未列名的芳香料制品及化妆盥洗品	9						0

税则号列 Tariff No.	货品名称 Description of Goods	最惠国 MFN	柬埔寨 TPE	缅甸 MMR	老挝 LAO	孟加拉 BGN	非洲部分国家 CAC	阿富汗 FV
34011100	盥洗用肥皂及有机表面活性产品,条状、块状或模制形状的,以及用肥皂或洗涤剂浸渍、涂面或包覆的纸、絮胎、毡呢及纺织物	10			0	0		
34012000	其他形状的肥皂	15			0	0		
34031900	润滑剂(含有石油或从沥青矿物提取的油类且按重量计<70%)	10					0	
35069120	以环氧树脂为基本成分的粘合剂	10						0
35069190	以其他橡胶或塑料为基本成分的粘合剂	10						0
36050000	火柴,但税目3604的烟火制品除外	6						0
39152000	苯乙烯聚合物的废碎料及下脚料	7.6					0	
39159010	聚对苯二甲酸乙二酯的塑料废碎料及下脚料	7.6					0	0
39159090	其他塑料的废碎料及下脚料	7.6					0	0
39172100	乙烯聚合物制的硬管	10						0
39172900	其他塑料制的硬管	10						0
39173100	塑料制的软管	10						0
39174000	塑料制的管子附件	10						0
39191099	其他材料制的,宽度≤20cm的其他成卷塑料胶粘板片等	6.5					0	
39219090	未列名塑料板、片、膜、箔及扁条	6.5					0	
39221000	塑料浴缸、淋浴盘及盥洗盆	10			0			
39222000	塑料马桶坐圈及盖	10			0			
39229000	塑料便盆、抽水箱等类似卫生洁具	10					0	
39231000	塑料制盒、箱及类似品	10						0
39241000	塑料制餐具及厨房用具	10			0	0		0
39249000	塑料制其他家庭用具及卫生或盥洗用具	10						0
39251000	塑料制囤、柜、罐、桶及类似容器	10						0
39269010	塑料制机器及仪器用零件	10					0	
39269090	其他塑料制品	10					0	0
40111000	机动小客车用新的充气橡胶轮胎	10					0	
40169310	硫化橡胶制机器、仪器用垫片、垫圈及其他密封垫	8					0	0
40169390	硫化橡胶制其他用垫片、垫圈、及其他密封垫	15						0
41012019	规定重量范围内的整张生牛皮,经逆鞣处理的除外	5	0		0			
41012020	规定重量范围内的整张生马皮	5	0		0			
41015019	重量>16公斤的整张生牛皮,经逆鞣处理的除外	5	0		0			
41015020	重量>16公斤的整张生马皮	5	0		0			
41019019	其他(包括整张或半张的背皮及腹皮)生牛皮,经逆鞣处理的除外	5	0		0			
41019020	其他(包括整张或半张的背皮及腹皮)生马皮	5	0		0			
41033000	生猪皮	9		0				
41039090	其他生皮	9		0				
41041111	全粒面未剖层或粒面剖层蓝湿牛皮	7			1.4	1.4	0	
41041119	其他全粒面未剖层或粒面剖层湿牛皮革	8			2	2		
41041120	全粒面未剖层或粒面剖层马皮革	5			2	2		
41041911	其他蓝湿牛皮	7			1.4	1.4	0	
41041919	其他湿牛皮革	7			1.8	1.8		
41041920	其他湿马皮革	7			2.1	2.1		
41044100	全粒面未剖层或粒面剖层干革(坯革)	5			2	2		
41044910	其他机器带用干革(坯革)	5			0	0		
41044990	其他干革(坯革)	7			2.1	2.1		
41051010	蓝湿绵羊或羔羊皮	14			2.1	2.1	0	

税则号列 Tariff No.	货品名称 Description of Goods	最惠国 MFN	柬埔寨 TPE	缅甸 MMR	老挝 LAO	孟加拉 BGN	非洲部分国家 CAC	阿富汗 FV
41051090	其他绵羊或羔羊湿皮革	10			2	2	0	
41053000	绵羊或羔羊干革(坯革)	8			4.8	4.8	0	
41062100	山羊或小山羊皮湿革	14			2.1	2.1	0	
41062200	山羊或小山羊皮干革(坯革)	14			8.4	8.4		
41063100	蓝湿猪皮	14			4.2	4.2		
41063190	其他猪皮湿革	14			4.2	4.2		
41063200	猪皮干革(坯革)	14			4.2	4.2		
41064000	爬行动物皮革	14			0	0	0	
41069100	其他未列名动物皮湿革(包括蓝湿皮革)	14			0	0		
41069200	其他未列名动物皮干革(坯革)	14			0	0		
41079200	已鞣粒面剖层非整张牛马皮革	5					0	
41120000	已鞣进一步加工的不带毛绵羊或羔羊皮革	8					0	
41131000	已鞣进一步加工的不带毛山羊或小山羊皮革	14					0	
41133000	已鞣进一步加工的不带毛爬行动物皮革	14					0	
41152000	皮革或再生皮革边角料;皮革粉末	14			4.2	4.2		
42010000	各种材料制成的鞍具及挽具,适合各种动物用	20			8	8		0
42021110	以皮革、再生皮革或漆皮作面的衣箱	15			8.3	8.3		
42021190	以皮革、在生皮革或漆皮作面的箱包	10			8	8		
42021290	塑料或纺织材料作面的其他箱包	20						0
42021900	其他材料制箱包	20			8	8		0
42022100	以皮革、再生皮革、漆皮作面的手提包	10						0
42022200	以塑料片或纺织材料作面的手提包	10					0	0
42022900	以钢纸或纸板作面的手提包	20			8	8		
42023100	以皮革、再生皮革作面的钱包等物品	10					0	0
42023200	以塑料或纺织品作面的钱包等物品	20					0	0
42023900	以钢纸或纸板做面的钱包等物品	20			8	8		
42029200	以塑料或纺织材料作面的其他容器	10					0	
42031000	皮革或再生皮革制的衣服	10			8	8		
42032910	皮革或再生皮革制的劳保手套	20			8	8		
42032990	皮革或再生皮革制的其他手套	20			8	8		
42033010	皮革或再生皮革制腰带	10			8	8		
42033020	皮革或再生皮革制的腰带及子弹带	10			8	8		
42034000	皮革或再生皮革制的其他衣着附件	20			8	8		
42050010	皮革或再生皮革制坐具套	12			7.8	7.8		
42050020	机器、机械器具或其他专门技术用途的皮革或再生皮革制品	8						0
42050090	皮革或再生皮革的其他制品	12			7.8	7.8		
43021930	已鞣未缝制阿斯特拉罕等羔羊皮,不论是否带头、尾或爪	20						0
43021990	已鞣未缝制的其他毛皮	10						0
43031010	毛皮衣服	23			10.4	10.4		
43031020	毛皮衣着附件	18			9.9	9.9		
43039000	毛皮制其他物品	18			9.9	9.9		
43040010	人造毛皮	18			10.8	10.8		
43040020	人造毛皮制品	18			10.8	10.8		
44201010	木刻及竹刻	0					0	
44201090	其他木制小雕像及其他装饰品	0					0	
44209090	木盒子及类似品;非落地式木家具	0					0	
46012100	竹制的席子、席料、帘子	9			0			
46012200	藤制的席子、席料及帘子	9			0			
46012911	蔺草制的席子、席料及帘子	9			0			

税则号列 Tariff No.	货品名称 Description of Goods	最惠国 MFN	柬埔寨 TPE	缅甸 MMR	老挝 LAO	孟加拉 BGN	非洲部分国家 CAC	阿富汗 FV
46012919	其他草制的席子、席料及帘子	9			0		0	
46012921	苇帘	9			0			
46012929	芦苇制的席子、席料	9			0			
46012990	其他植物材料制席子、席料及帘子	9			0			
46019210	竹缏条及类似产品,不论是否缝合成宽条	9			0			
46019290	其他竹编结产品	9					0	
46019310	藤缏条及类似产品,不论是否缝合成宽条	9			0			
46019491	其他植物编结材料的缏条及类似产品,不论是否缝合成宽条	9			0			
46019499	其他植物编结材料产品	9					0	
46019910	其他非植物编结材料的缏条及类似产品,不论是否缝合成宽条	9			0			
46021100	竹编制的篮筐及其他制品	9	0					
46021200	藤编制的篮筐及其他制品	9	0					
46021910	草编制的篮筐及其他制品	9	0				0	
46021920	玉米皮编制的篮筐及其他制品	9	0					
46021930	柳条编制的篮筐及其他制品	9	0					
46021990	其他植物材料编制篮筐及其他制品	9	0					
46029000	其他编结材料制品及其他制品	9	0					
49100000	印刷的各种日历,包括日历芯	7.5					0	
50040000	非供零售用丝纱线	6						0
50071010	未漂白或漂白的绸丝机织物	10			0			
50071090	其他绸丝机织物	10			0			
50072011	未漂白或漂白的纯桑蚕丝机织物	10			0			
50072019	其他纯桑蚕丝机织物	10			0			
50072021	未漂白或漂白的纯柞蚕丝机织物	10			0			
50072029	其他纯柞蚕丝机织物	10			0			
50072031	未漂白或漂白的纯绢丝机织物	10			0			
50072039	其他纯绢丝机织物	10			0			
50072090	其他纯丝机织物	10			0			
50079010	未漂白或漂白其他丝机织物	10			0			0
50079090	其他丝机织物	10			0			0
51021920	未梳其他山羊绒	9						0
51061000	非供零售用粗梳纯羊毛纱线	5						0
51071000	非供零售用精梳纯羊毛纱线	5						0
51081000	非供零售用粗梳动物细毛纱线	5					0	
51121900	重量 > 200g/平米精梳全毛布	10	0	0	0			0
51123000	与化纤短纤混纺精梳毛布	10						0
51129000	与其他纤维混纺精梳毛布	10						0
52029100	棉的回收纤维	10						0
52041100	非供零售用全棉缝纫线	5			0			0
52042000	零售用棉制缝纫线	5			0			
52051100	非零售粗梳粗支纯棉单纱	5	0	0	0			
52051200	非零售粗梳中支纯棉单纱	5	0	0	0			
52051400	非零售粗梳较细支纯棉单纱	5		0	0			
52052100	非零售精梳粗支纯棉单纱	5		0			0	
52052400	非零售精梳较细支纯棉单纱	5		0	0			
52053200	非零售粗梳中支纯棉多股纱	5		0			0	
52054200	非零售精梳中支纯棉多股纱	5					0	
52079000	供零售用混纺棉纱线	6						0
52082200	漂白的较轻质全棉平纹布	10	0	0	0			

税则号列 Tariff No.	货品名称 Description of Goods	最惠国 MFN	柬埔寨 TPE	缅甸 MMR	老挝 LAO	孟加拉 BGN	非洲部分国家 CAC	阿富汗 FV
52083100	染色的轻质全棉平纹布	10						0
52083200	染色的较轻质全棉平纹布	10					0	
52083300	染色的轻质全棉三、四线斜纹布	10	0	0	0			
52084900	色织的轻质其他全棉机织物	10	0	0	0			
52085200	印花的较轻全棉平纹布	10					0	
52091100	未漂白重质全棉平纹布	10					0	
52093100	染色的重质全棉平纹布	10	0	0	0			
52093200	染色的重质全棉三、四线斜纹布	10	0	0	0			
52093900	染色的重质其他全棉机织物	10	0	0	0			
52094200	色织的重质全棉粗斜纹布(劳动布)	10	0	0	0			
52105990	与化纤混纺印花的轻质其他棉布	10					0	
53031000	生或沤制黄麻,其他纺织用韧皮纤维	5	0	0	0	0		
53039000	经加工、未纺的黄麻及其他纺织用韧皮纤维	5	0	0	0			
53050091	未加工、未纺的西沙尔麻及其他龙舌兰类纤维	5					0	
53050092	加工、未纺的椰壳纤维及椰壳纤维废料	5	0	0	0			
53071000	黄麻及其他纺织用韧皮纤维单纱	6	0		3	3		
53072000	黄麻及其他纺织用韧皮纤维多股纱或缆线	6	0		3	3		
53082000	大麻纱线	6					0	
53092900	其他混纺亚麻机织物	10						0
53101000	未漂白黄麻或其他韧皮纤维织物	10	0		5	5		0
53109000	其他黄麻机织物或韧皮鲜为纤维织物	10	0		5	5		0
53110013	其他全苎麻机织物	12						0
54011010	非供零售用合成纤维长丝缝纫线	5						0
54011020	供零售用合成纤维长丝缝纫线	5						0
54074200	染色的纯尼龙布	10	0	0	0			
54075200	染色的纯聚酯变形长丝布	10	0	0	0			
54076100	其他纯聚酯非变形长丝布	10					0	
54077200	染色的其他纯合成纤维长丝布	10	0	0	0			
54079200	染色的其他混纺合成纤维长丝布	10	0	0	0		0	
55081000	合成纤维短纤纺制的缝纫线	5					0	0
55129900	其他纯合成纤维布	10	0	0	0			
55134100	与棉混纺印花的轻质聚酯平纹布	10	0	0	0			
55142300	与棉混纺染色的其他重质聚酯布	10	0	0	0			
56029000	经浸、涂、包覆或层压的其他毡呢	10						0
56031110	每平米≤25g 经浸渍化纤长丝无纺织物	10	0	0	0			
56031210	25g <每平米≤70g 浸渍化纤长丝无纺织物	10	0	0	0			
56039290	25g <每平米≤70g 其他无纺织物	10	0	0	0			
56039490	每平米>150g 的其他无纺织物	10	0	0	0			
56041000	用纺织材料包覆的橡胶线及绳	5	0	0	0			
56074900	聚乙烯或聚丙烯制线、绳、索、缆	5						0
56079090	其他纺织材料制线、绳、索、缆	5	0	0	0	2.5		
56090000	用纱线、扁条、绳、索、缆制其他物品	10			0	0		
57011000	羊毛结织栽绒地毯及其他铺地制品	14						0
57019010	化纤结织栽绒地毯及其他铺地制品	16						0
57021000	“开来姆”等手织地毯	14			0	0		0
57023900	未制成其他纺织材料起绒铺地制品	14			0	0		0
57024100	制成的毛制起绒地毯及铺地制品	10						0
57039000	其他纺织材料簇绒地毯及其他簇绒铺地制品	14			0	0		
57050010	毛制其他地毯及其他铺地制品	14			0	0		0

税则号列 Tariff No.	货品名称 Description of Goods	最惠国 MFN	柬埔寨 TPE	缅甸 MMR	老挝 LAO	孟加拉 BGN	非洲部分国家 CAC	阿富汗 FV
57050020	化纤制其他地毯及其他铺地制品	10			0	0		0
57050090	其他纺织材料制其他地毯及铺地制品	14			0	0		0
58012200	割绒的棉制灯芯绒	10					0	
58013300	其他化纤纬起绒织物	10	0	0	0			
58021100	未漂白棉毛巾织物及类似毛圈机织物	12			0	0		
58022010	丝及绢丝毛巾织物及类似毛圈机织物	12			0	0		
58022020	羊毛等毛巾织物及类似毛圈机织物	12			0	0		
58022030	化纤毛巾织物及类似毛圈机织物	14			0	0		
58022090	其他纺织材料毛巾织物及类似毛圈织物	12			0	0		
58041030	化纤制网眼薄纱及其他网眼织物	12	0	0	0			
58042920	棉机制花边	10	0	0	0			
58050010	手工针绣嵌花装饰毯	12						0
58050090	“哥白林”等手织装饰毯	12						0
58061090	其他材料狭幅起绒织物及绳绒织物	10	0	0	0			
58062000	含弹性纱线≥5%的狭幅织物	10	0	0	0			
58063100	棉制其他狭幅机织物	10	0	0	0			
58063200	化纤制其他狭幅机织物	10	0	0	0			
58063910	丝及绢丝制其他狭幅机织物	10						0
58063990	其他材料制其他狭幅机织物	10						0
58071000	机织非绣制纺织材料标签、徽章等	10	0	0	0		0	
58079000	非机织非绣制纺织材料标签徽章等	10						0
58089000	非绣制成匹装饰带、流苏、绒球	10	0	0	0			0
58090090	其他金属线布及含金属纱线布	10						0
58109100	棉制见底布的刺绣品	10						0
58109900	其他纺织材料制见底布刺绣品	10						0
59019091	棉或麻制描图布、帽里硬衬布等	10	0	0	0			
59039090	用其他塑料浸、涂的其他纺织物	10	0	0	0			
59080000	纺织材料制灯芯、炉芯等和煤气灯纱筒及纱罩	10						0
60012100	棉制针织或钩编的毛圈绒头织物	10						0
60029010	宽≤30cm含橡胶线的棉针织、钩编织物	10	0	0	0			
60029030	宽≤30cm含橡胶线的合成纤维制针织、钩编织物	10	0	0	0			
60041010	宽>30cm,弹性纱线≥5%棉针织、钩编织物	10	0	0	0			
60053200	染色合成纤维制的其他经编织物	10	0	0	0			
60062200	染色棉制的其他针织、钩编织物	10	0	0	0			
60062300	色织棉制的其他针织、钩编织物	10	0	0	0			
61022000	棉制针织或钩编女式大衣、防风衣	17.5						0
61031090	其他纺织材料制针织或钩编男式西服套装	17.5			0			
61032200	棉制针织或钩编男式便服套装	20			0			
61032990	其他纺织材料制针织或钩编男式便服套装	25			0			
61033200	棉制针织或钩编男式上衣	16	0	0	0		0	
61033300	合纤制针织或钩编男式上衣	19	0					
61033900	其他纺织材料制针织或钩编男式上衣	16	0		0			
61034100	毛制针织或钩编男长裤、工装裤等	16			0	0		
61034200	棉制针织或钩编男长裤、工装裤等	16	0	0	0	6.4		
61034300	合纤制针织或钩编男长裤等	17.5	0		0	0		
61034900	其他纺织材料制针织或钩编男长裤等	16	0		0	0		
61041910	毛制针织或钩编女式西服套装	17.5						0
61041920	棉制针织或钩编女式西服套装	17.5			0			
61041990	其他纺织材料制针织或钩编女式西服套装	17.5			0			

税则号列 Tariff No.	货品名称 Description of Goods	最惠国 MFN	柬埔寨 TPE	缅甸 MMR	老挝 LAO	孟加拉 BGN	非洲部分国家 CAC	阿富汗 FV
61042200	棉制针织或钩编女式便服套装	17.5			0			
61043200	棉制针织女式上衣	16	0	0	0		0	0
61043300	合纤制针织女上衣	19	0					
61043900	其他纺织材料制针织女上衣	16	0					0
61044200	棉制针织或钩编连衣裙	16						0
61044300	合纤制针织或钩编连衣裙	17.5	0					
61044400	人纤制针织或钩编连衣裙	16	0					
61044900	其他纺织材料制针织或钩编连衣裙	16	0					0
61045200	棉制针织裙子及裙裤	14						0
61045300	合纤制针织或钩编裙子及裙裤	16	0					
61045900	其他纺织材料制针织或钩编裙子及裙裤	14	0	0	0			
61046200	棉制针织或钩编女长裤、工装裤等	16			6.4	6.4		0
61046900	其他纺织材料制针织或钩编女长裤等	16			0	0		
61051000	棉制针织或钩编男衬衫	16	0	0	0	11.2		0
61052000	化纤制针织或钩编男衬衫	17.5			0	0		
61059000	其他纺织材料制针织或钩编男衬衫	16			0	0		
61061000	棉制针织或钩编女衬衫	16	0	0	0	6.4	0	0
61062000	化纤制针织或钩编女衬衫	17.5			0	0		
61069000	其他纺织材料制针织或钩编女衬衫	16			0	0		
61071100	棉制针织或钩编男内裤及三角裤	14	0	0	0	5.6		
61072100	棉制针织或钩编男长睡衣及睡衣裤	14	0	0	0	5.6		
61072200	化纤制针织或钩编男睡衣裤	16			0	0		
61072910	丝及绢丝制针织或钩编男长睡衣及睡衣裤	14			0	0		
61072990	其他纺织材料制针织或钩编男长睡衣及睡衣裤	14	0	0	0	0		
61082100	棉制针织或钩编女三角裤及短衬裤	14	0	0	0			
61083100	棉制针织或钩编女睡衣及睡衣裤	14	0	0	0	5.6		
61083200	化纤制针织或钩编女睡衣及睡衣裤	16			0	0		
61083910	丝及绢丝制针织或钩编女睡衣及睡衣裤	14			0	0		
61083990	其他纺织材料制针织或钩编女睡衣及睡衣裤	14			0	0		
61089100	棉制针织或钩编女浴衣、晨衣	14	0	0	0			
61091000	棉制针织或钩编T恤衫、汗衫等	14	0	0	0		0	0
61099010	丝及绢丝制针织或钩编T恤衫、汗衫	14			0	0		
61099090	其他纺织材料制针织或钩编T恤衫、汗衫等	14	0	0	0	0	0	
61101100	羊毛制针织或钩编套头衫等	14	0	0	0	0	0	
61102000	棉制针织或钩编套头衫等	14	0	0	0	5.6	0	0
61103000	化纤制针织或钩编套头衫等	16			0	0		0
61109010	丝及绢丝制针织或钩编套头衫等	14			0	0		
61109090	其他纺织材料制针织或钩编套头衫等	14			0	0		
61130000	涂层经处理针织或钩编织物制服装	16			0	0		
61142000	棉制针织或钩编的其他服装	16			6.4	6.4		0
61153000	单丝<67 分特制针织或钩编女统袜	14			0	0		
61159600	合纤制针织或钩编短袜及其他袜类	16						0
61169300	合纤制其他针织或钩编手套	16						0
61171000	针织或钩编披巾、头巾等	14						0
61178090	针织或钩编其他衣着附件	14					0	
62019290	棉制男式带风帽防寒短上衣、防风衣	16	0	0	0			
62019900	其他纺织材料制男式防寒短上衣、防风衣	16		0				
62021290	棉制女式大衣、斗篷及类似品等	16						0
62031100	毛制男式西服套装	17.5					0	

税则号列 Tariff No.	货品名称 Description of Goods	最惠国 MFN	柬埔寨 TPE	缅甸 MMR	老挝 LAO	孟加拉 BGN	非洲部分国家 CAC	阿富汗 FV
62033100	毛制男式上衣	16	0	0	0	9.6		0
62033200	棉制男式上衣	16	0	0	0	11.2	0	0
62033300	合纤制男式上衣	17.5					0	
62033910	丝及绢丝制男式上衣	16			9.6	9.6		
62033990	其他纺织材料制男式上衣	16			9.6	9.6	0	0
62034100	毛制男式长裤、工装裤等	16			0	0		
62034210	棉制男式阿拉伯裤	16			11.2	11.2		
62034290	棉制男式长裤、工装裤等	16	0	0	0	11.2		0
62034910	其他纺织材料制男式阿拉伯裤	16			0	0		
62034990	其他纺织材料制男童裤、工装裤	16			0	0	0	
62043100	毛制女式上衣	16					0	0
62043200	棉制女式上衣	16	0	0	0	6.4		0
62043300	合纤制女式上衣	17.5			0	0		
62043910	丝及绢丝制女式上衣	16			0	0		0
62043990	其他纺织材料制女式上衣	16			0	0		
62044200	棉制连衣裙	16	0	0	0			
62045200	棉制裙子及裙裤	14						0
62045910	丝及绢丝制裙子及裙裤	14						0
62045990	其他纺织材料制裙子及裙裤	14					0	0
62046200	棉制女式长裤、工装裤等	16	0	0	0	11.2	0	0
62052000	棉制男衬衫	16	0	0	0	6.4	0	0
62053000	化纤制男衬衫	16			0	0	0	
62059010	丝及绢丝制男衬衫	16			0	0		
62059020	毛制男衬衫	16			0	0		
62059090	其他纺织材料制男衬衫	16			0	0		
62061000	丝及绢丝制女式衬衫	16						0
62063000	棉制女衬衫	16	0	0	0	6.4		0
62069000	其他纺织材料制女衬衫	16			0	0	0	0
62072100	棉制男式长睡衣及睡衣裤	14	0	0	0			
62072990	其他纺织材料制男式长睡衣及睡衣裤	14	0	0	0			
62079100	棉制男式浴衣、晨衣及类似品	14					0	0
62081920	棉制长衬裙及衬裙	14						0
62082100	棉制女式睡衣及睡衣裤	14	0	0	0			
62082200	化纤制女式睡衣及睡衣裤	16	0	0	0			
62089100	棉制女式背心.内衣.浴衣及类似品	14	0	0	0			
62089200	化纤制女式背心、内衣及类似品	16	0	0	0			0
62089990	其他纺织材料制女式背心、内衣及类似品	14						0
62101010	毛制毡呢或无纺织物服装	16			0	0		
62101020	棉或麻制毡呢或无纺织物服装	16			6.4	6.4		
62101030	化纤制毡呢或无纺织物服装	17.5			0	0		
62101090	其他纺织材料制毡呢或无纺织物服装	16			0	0		
62102000	用塑料、橡胶等处理的织物制男大衣等	16			0	0		
62104000	用塑料、橡胶等处理的织物制的其他男式服装	16			0	0		
62105000	用塑料、橡胶等处理的织物制的其他女式服装	16			0	0		
62113220	棉制男式运动服	16						0
62113290	棉制其他男式及服装	16						0
62114210	棉制女式运动服	16						0
62114290	棉制其他女式服装	16						0
62114990	其他纺织材料制女式运动服及其他服装	16						0

税则号列 Tariff No.	货品名称 Description of Goods	最惠国 MFN	柬埔寨 TPE	缅甸 MMR	老挝 LAO	孟加拉 BGN	非洲部分国家 CAC	阿富汗 FV
62121010	化纤制胸罩	16	0	0	0			
62122090	其他纺织材料制束腰带及腹带	14						0
62132010	棉制刺绣手帕	14			0			
62132090	其他棉制手帕	14			0			
62139020	其他纺织材料制刺绣手帕	14			0			
62139090	其他纺织材料制手帕	14			0			
62141000	丝制披巾、头巾、围巾及类似品	14						0
62142000	毛制披巾、头巾、围巾及类似品	14						0
62143000	合纤制披巾、头巾及类似品	16						0
62149000	其他纺织材料制披巾、头巾及类似品	14						0
62159000	其他纺织材料制领带及领结	14					0	
62171090	非针织非钩编服装或衣着附件	14	0	0	0			0
62179000	非针织非钩编服装或衣着零件	14	0	0	0		0	0
63012000	毛制毯子及旅行毯	16						0
63013000	棉制毯子及旅行毯	16						0
63014000	合纤制毯子及旅行毯	17.5						0
63019000	其他纺织材料制毯子及旅行毯	16						0
63022110	棉制印花床单	14						0
63022210	化纤制印花床单	16						0
63022290	化纤制印花床上用织物制品	16						0
63023191	棉制其他床单	14						0
63023199	棉制其他床上用织物制品	14						0
63023210	化纤制刺绣其他床上用织物制品	16						0
63023999	其他纺织材料制其他床上用织物制品	14						0
63024090	其他针织或钩编的餐桌用织物制品	14						0
63025190	棉制其他餐桌用织物制品	14						0
63025390	化纤制其他餐桌用织物制品	16						0
63031931	棉制针织的窗帘等	14						0
63039100	棉制非针织非钩编窗帘等	14						0
63039200	合纤制非针织非钩编窗帘等	16						0
63041131	手工钩编床罩	14						0
63041139	非手工钩编床罩	14						0
63049910	丝制非针织非钩编的装饰制品	14						0
63049990	其他纺织材料制非针织非钩编装饰制品	14						0
63051000	黄麻或其他韧皮纤维制货物包装袋	10			0	0		0
63052000	棉制货物包装袋	16						0
63062990	其他纺织材料制帐篷	14						0
63064020	化纤制充气褥垫	16						0
63079000	其他纺织材料制成品	14	0	0	0			0
63109000	纺织材料制其他碎织物等	14	0	0	0			
64029900	其他橡胶、塑料鞋靴	24						0
64031200	皮革制鞋面的滑雪靴	24	0					
64031900	皮革制鞋面的其他运动鞋靴	15	0					
64032000	皮革条带为鞋面的皮底鞋	24	0					
64034000	装有金属护鞋头的其他皮革面鞋靴	24	0					
64035100	皮革制外底的皮革面短统靴(过踝)	10	0					
64035900	皮革制外底的皮革面其他鞋靴	10	0					
64039100	其他皮革制面的短统靴(过踝)	10	0					
64039900	皮革制面的其他鞋靴	10	0					

税则号列 Tariff No.	货品名称 Description of Goods	最惠国 MFN	柬埔寨 TPE	缅甸 MMR	老挝 LAO	孟加拉 BGN	非洲部分国家 CAC	阿富汗 FV
65059010	钩编的帽类	20						0
65059090	针织或成匹织物制成的帽类	20						0
65069990	其他材料制的未列名帽类	24						0
66039000	伞、手杖及鞭子的其他零件及饰品	14						0
67041100	合成纺织材料制整头假发	25						0
67049000	其他材料制假发、须眉及类似品	25						0
68021010	大理石制砖、瓦、方块及类似品	24					0	0
68029990	其他石及制品	24					0	0
68159910	碳纤维及其制品	17.5					0	0
68159990	其他未列名石制品及矿物制品	17.5					0	0
69031000	含 >50% 石墨其他耐火陶瓷制品	8			0			
69032000	含 >50% 氧化铝其他耐火陶瓷制品	8			0			
69039000	其他耐火陶瓷制品	8			0			
69101000	瓷制脸盆、浴缸及类似卫生器具	10						0
69120010	陶餐具	15						0
69139000	陶塑像及其他装饰用陶制品	15						0
70091000	车辆后视镜	10						0
70131000	玻璃陶瓷制玻璃器皿	24.5						0
71023100	未加工或简单加工非工业用钻石	3					0	
71031000	未加工宝石或半宝石	3			0		0	0
71039100	经其他加工的红、蓝、绿宝石	8			0			
71049099	其他非工业用合成其他宝石或半宝石	8					0	
71070000	以贱金属为底的包银材料	10.5			0			
71081300	非货币用半制成金	0			0			
71131190	其他银首饰及其零件	20						0
71131999	其他贵金属制首饰及其零件	35						0
71141100	银器及零件	35						0
71142000	以贱金属为底的包贵金属制金银器	35						0
71162000	宝石或半宝石制品	35					0	0
71171900	其他贱金属制仿首饰	17					0	0
71179000	未列名材料制仿首饰	35						0
72022900	硅铁,含硅量≤55%	2					0	
72230000	不锈钢丝	10						0
73079200	未列名钢铁制螺纹肘管、弯管、管套	4						0
73081000	钢铁制桥梁及桥梁体段	8						0
73089000	其他钢铁结构体及部件	4					0	0
73102900	其他容器 <50L 的盛物容器	17.5						0
73129000	非绝缘钢铁编带、吊索及类似品	4						0
73181500	其他螺钉及螺栓	8					0	0
73181600	螺母	8						0
73229000	非电热空气加热器、暖气分布器	20						0
73239300	餐桌、厨房等家用不锈钢器具	12						0
73269090	其他非工业用钢铁制品	8						0
74010000	铜锍、沉积铜(泥铜)	2			0		0	
74020000	未精炼铜、电解精炼用铜阳极	2					0	
74031100	精炼铜的阴极及阴极型材	2					0	
74040000	铜废碎料	1.5			0		0	0
74181990	餐桌厨房等家用铜制器具及其零件	18						0
74199991	工业用其他铜制品	10						0

税则号列 Tariff No.	货品名称 Description of Goods	最惠国 MFN	柬埔寨 TPE	缅甸 MMR	老挝 LAO	孟加拉 BGN	非洲部分国家 CAC	阿富汗 FV
74199999	非工业用其他铜制品	20					0	0
75022000	未锻轧镍合金	3					0	
76011010	按重量计含铝量在99.95%及以上的未锻轧非铝合金	5					0	
76011090	其他未锻轧非铝合金	5					0	
76020000	铝废碎料	1.5					0	
76082000	铝合金管	8						0
76151900	餐桌厨房等家用铝制器具及其零件	15						0
81052010	钴湿法冶炼中间品	4					0	
81052090	钴锍及其他钴冶炼时所得的中间产品、未锻轧钴、粉末	4					0	
81059000	其他钴及制品	8					0	
82014000	斧子、钩刀及类似砍伐工具	8						0
82021000	手工锯	8.4						0
82041100	固定式的手动扳手及扳钳	10.5						0
82041200	可调式的手动扳手及扳钳	10						0
82052000	手工锤子	10						0
82054000	手工螺丝刀	10.5						0
82119200	刃面固定的其他刀	12						0
83012090	其他机动车用锁	10						0
83014000	其他锁	14						0
83024900	其他用贱金属配件及架座	12					0	
83061000	非电动铃、钟、锣及其类似品	8						0
83062100	镀贵金属的雕塑像及其他装饰品	8						0
83062990	其他雕塑像及其他装饰品	8						0
83081000	贱金属制钩、环及眼	10.5					0	
83089000	贱金属制珠子及亮晶片	10.5					0	
84099199	其他点燃式活塞内燃发动机用零件	5						0
84137090	转速<10000转/分离心泵	8						0
84139100	液体泵用零件	5					0	0
84145110	功率≤125瓦的吊扇	20			0			
84145120	功率≤125瓦的换气扇	20			0			
84145130	功率≤125瓦,有旋转导风轮的风扇	12			0			
84145191	功率≤125瓦的台扇	10			0			
84145192	功率≤125瓦的落地扇	10			0			
84145193	功率≤125瓦的壁扇	10			0			
84145199	功率≤125瓦其他风扇、风机	10			0			
84145990	其他扇,风机	8						0
84146010	抽油烟机	10			0			
84146090	罩最大边长≤120cm的通风罩或循环气罩	10			0			
84149011	用于制冷设备的压缩机进、排气阀片	8			0			
84193100	农产品干燥器	8			0			
84193200	木材、纸浆、纸或纸板用干燥器	9			0			
84195000	热交换装置	10			0			
84198100	加工热饮料、烹调、加热食品的机器	10			0			
84198910	加氢反应器	0			0			
84198990	其他利用温度变化处理材料的机器	0			0			
84306100	非自推进捣固或压实机械	6						0
84314310	石油或天然气钻探机用零件	4					0	
84339090	税号84.33所列其他机器零件	3					0	
84529091	其他缝纫机用旋梭	14						0

税则号列 Tariff No.	货品名称 Description of Goods	最惠国 MFN	柬埔寨 TPE	缅甸 MMR	老挝 LAO	孟加拉 BGN	非洲部分国家 CAC	阿富汗 FV
84529099	其他缝纫机用其他零件	14						0
84681000	手提喷焊器	12						0
84701000	电子计算器及袖珍式数据录放机器	0					0	
84812020	气压传动阀	5						0
84818010	其他阀门	7						0
84821000	滚珠轴承	8					0	0
84829900	滚动轴承的其他零件	6					0	
84831090	其他传动轴及曲柄	6					0	0
84834090	其他齿轮及齿轮传动装置	8					0	
84839000	单独报验的带齿的轮及其他传动元件;零件	8					0	0
84841000	金属片密封垫或类似接合衬垫	8						0
84849000	其他材料制密封垫及类似接合衬垫	8					0	0
84861010	利用温度变化处理单晶硅的机器及装置	0			0			
84862010	制造半导体器件或集成电路用的热处理设备	0			0			
84863010	制造平板显示器用的热处理设备	0			0			
85011099	其他输出功率≤37.5W 微电机	9					0	
85021100	输出功率≤75KVA 柴油发电机组	10					0	
85043190	额定容量≤1KVA 的其他变压器	5						0
85051190	其他金属的永磁体	7						0
85079010	铅酸蓄电池零件	10			5	5		
85079090	其他蓄电池零件	8			4	4		
85139010	手电筒零件	14					0	
85189000	税号 85.18 所列货品的零件	10.5					0	
85232928	用于重放声或图像信息的磁带	10					0	
85299060	收音机及其组合机的其他零件	15						0
85367000	光导纤维、光导纤维束或光缆用连接器	8					0	
85389000	税号 85.35、85.36 或 85.37 装置的零件	7					0	
85481000	电池废碎料及废电池	8			4	4		
87120041	16、18、20 英寸自行车	13					0	
90069110	特种用途照相机的零附件	8			0	0		
90069120	一次成像照相机的零附件	5			0	0		
90069191	照相机自动调焦组建	10			0	0		
90069192	其他照相机的快门组件	10			0	0		
90069199	其他照相机的其他零附件	10			0	0		
90183100	注射器	8					0	
90213900	其他人造的人体部分	4						0
90219000	税号 90.21 中未列名的矫形器具	4						0
90229090	税号 90.22 所列其他设备及零件	6					0	
90230000	专供示范的仪器、装置及模型	7					0	
90251990	非液体的其他温度计、高温计	8.4						0
90328900	非液压或气压的其他仪器及装置	7					0	
91051100	电子闹钟	23					0	
92029000	其他弦乐器	17.5						0
92060000	打击乐器	17.5						0
92099200	编号 9202 所列乐器的零附件	17.5					0	
94015100	竹、藤制坐具	0			0			
94015900	柳条及类似材料制的坐具	0			0			
94016900	其他木框架的坐具	0					0	
94033000	办公室用木家具	0	0		0			

税则号列 Tariff No.	货品名称 Description of Goods	最惠国 MFN	柬埔寨 TPE	缅甸 MMR	老挝 LAO	孟加拉 BGN	非洲部分国家 CAC	阿富汗 FV
94034000	厨房用木家具	0	0					
94035010	卧室用红木制家具	0	0					
94035091	卧室用漆木家具	0	0					
94035099	卧室用其他木家具	0	0				0	
94036010	其他红木制家具	0	0					
94036091	其他漆木家具	0	0					
94036099	其他木家具	0	0				0	
94038100	竹、藤制家具	0	0					
94038910	柳条及类似材料制家具	0	0					
94042100	海绵橡胶或泡沫塑料制褥垫	20						0
94042900	其他材料制褥垫	20						0
94049040	化纤棉填充的寝具及类似品	20						0
94049090	其他材料制的寝具及类似品	20						0
94059900	税号 94.05 所列物品其他材料制零件	20						0
96019000	其他已加工动物质雕刻料及其制品	20						0
96020090	已加工植物或矿物质雕刻料及制品	25					0	
96062200	金属质纽扣,未用纺织材料包裹	15						0
96071100	装有贱金属齿的拉链	21					0	
96081000	圆珠笔	15					0	0
96159000	其他发夹、卷发器等及其零件	18						0
97011020	手绘油画、粉画及其他画的复制品	14						0
97030000	各种材料制的雕塑品原件	12					0	

附件 10：

中华人民共和国进境物品进口税率表

Appendix 10：

Duty Rate on Inward Articles of the People's Republic of China

税号 No.	物品名称	税率(%) Duty	货品名称 Article Description
1	书报、刊物、教育专用电影片、幻灯片、原版录音带、录像带 金、银及其制品 食品、饮料 本表税号 2、3、4 税号及备注不包含的其他商品	10	Book, newspaper, journal, movie, copy for educaiton, slie-do, cassette, video Cassette, silver or article Food, beverage Articles other than item 2,3
2	纺织品及其制成品 摄像机、摄录一体机、数码像机及其他电器用具 照像机、自行车、手表、钟表(含配件、附件)		Textile product Video camera, digital camera and other electric products Camera, bicycles, , watch, clock
3	高尔夫球及球具、高档手表		Golf ball, particles with the ball and upmarket watches
4	烟、酒、化妆品		Tobacco product, spirits, wine beer cosmetic

注：

避孕用具和避孕药品，超过海关规定的自用合理数量部分按有关规定予以退运或按货物进口程序办理报关及验放手续。

Note：

About contraceptive instruments and contraceptive medicines, the extra amount of which exceeding the reasonable self – using level set by customs regulations should be backtrack, or apply for customs registration and examination as required by goods – importing procedures

2

中华人民共和国海关出口税则

（2007 年 1 月 1 日起实施）

Customs Export Tariff of the People's Republic of China

（Enforced from January 1,2007）

注释：

出口税则也采用《商品名称及编码协调制度》目录，进口税则的归类总规则同样适用于出口税则。

Note:

The Harmonized Commodity Description and Coding System is also adopted for this Export Tariff, and the General Rules for the Interpretation of the Import Tariff are samely applicable to the Export Tariff.

税则号列 Tariff No.	ex	货 品 名 称	出口税率 Export Duty Rate	Description of Goods
03.01				
03019210		鳗鱼苗	20	Eels(Anguilla spp.)fry
05.06				
05061000		经酸处理的骨胶原及骨	40	Ossein and bones, treated with acid
05069011		含牛羊成分的骨粉及骨废料	40	Power and waste bones, containing bovine composition or sheep and goats thereof
05069019		其他骨粉及骨废料	40	Other waste of bones and powder of bones
05069090		其他骨及角柱	40	Other Bones and horn-cores
26.07				
26070000		铅矿砂及其精矿	30	Lead ores and concentrates
26.08				
26080000		锌矿砂及其精矿	30	Zinc ores and concentraes
26.09				
26090000		锡矿砂及其精矿	50	Tin ores and concertrates
26.11				
26110000		钨矿砂及其精矿	20	Tungsten ores and concentrates
26.15				
26159010		水合钽铌原料(钽铌富集物)	30	Hydrated Tantalum-Niobium ores (tantalum-niobium ore concentrates)
26159090		其他铌钽矿砂及其精矿	30	Niobium, Tantalum ores and concentrates, other
26.17				
26171010		生锑(锑精矿,选矿产品)	20	Crude antimony (Antimony concentrates, which are mineral products)
28.04				
28047010		黄磷(白磷)	20	Yellow phosphorus(white phosphorus)
28047090		其他磷	20	Other phosphorus
28.26	ex			
28269000		氟钽酸钾	30	Potassium fluotantalate
29.02				
29022000		苯	40	Benzene
41.03				
41039011		经退鞣处理的山羊板皮	20	Tanned goatskin
41039019		山羊板皮,经退鞣处理的除外	20	Untanned goatskin
72.01				
72011000		非合金生铁,含磷量小于或等于0.5%	20	Non－ally pig iron containing by weight 0.5% or less phosphorus
72012000		非合金生铁,含磷量大于0.5%	20	Non－ally pig iron containing by weight more than 0.5% phosphorus
72015000		合金生铁	20	Alloy pig iron
72.02				
72021100		锰铁,含碳量>2%	20	Ferro-manganese, containing >2% by weight of carbon
72021900		锰铁,含碳量≤2%	20	Ferro-manganese, containing≤2% by weight of carbon
72022100		硅铁,含硅量>55%	25	Ferro-silicon, containing >55% by weight of carbon
72022900		硅铁,含硅量≤55%	25	Ferro-silicon, containing≤55% by weight of carbon
72023000		硅锰铁	20	Ferro-silico-manganese
72024100		铬铁,含碳量>4%	40	Ferro-chromium, containing >4% by weight of carbon

税则号列 Tariff No.	ex	货 品 名 称	出口税率 Export Duty Rate	Description of Goods
72024900		铬铁,含碳量≤4%	40	Ferro-chromium,containing≤4% by weight of carbon
72.04				
72041000		铸铁废碎料	40	Waste and scran of cast iron
72042100		不锈钢废碎料	40	Waste and scran of stainless steel
72042900		其他合金钢废碎料	40	Other waste and scrap of alloy steel
72043000		镀锡钢铁废碎料	40	Waste and scrap of tinned iron or steel
72044100		机械加工中产生的废料	40	Waste and scrap of turning
72044900		其他钢铁废碎料	40	Other ferrous waste and scrap
72045000		供再熔的碎料钢铁锭	40	Remelting scrp ingots
74.02				
74020000		未精炼铜,电解精炼用的铜阳极	30	Unrefined copper; copper anodes for electrolytic refining
74.03				
74031100		精炼铜的阴极及阴极型材	30	Refined copper cathodes and sections of cathodes, unwroush
74031200		精炼铜的线锭	30	Refined copper wire-bars,unwrought
74031300		精炼铜的坯段	30	Refined copper billets,unwrought
74031900		其他未锻轧的精炼铜	30	Other refined copper products,unwrought
74032100		未锻轧的铜锌合金(黄铜)	30	Copper-zinc base alloys (brass),unwrought
74032200		未锻轧的铜锡合金(青铜)	30	Copper-tin base alloys(bronze),unwrought
74032900		未锻轧的其他铜合金	30	Other copper alloys,unwrought
74.04				
74040000		铜废碎料	30	Copper waste and scrap
74.07				
74071000		精炼铜条、杆及型材及异型材	30	Bars,rods and profiles of refined copper
74072100		铜锌合金条、杆及型材及异型材	30	Bars,rods and profiles of copper-zinc base alloys
74072900		其他铜合金条杆、型材及异型材	30	Bars,rods and profiles of copper alloys,nes
74.08				
74081100		最大截面尺寸>6mm 的精炼铜丝	30	Wire of refined copper of which the maximum cross-sectional dimension exceeds 6mm
74081900		其他精炼铜丝	30	Wire of refined copper,nes
74082100		铜锌合金丝	30	Wire of copper-zinc base alloy
74082200		铜镍合金丝或铜镍锌合金丝	30	Wire of copper-nickel base alloys or copper-nickel-zinc base alloys
74082900		其他铜合金丝	30	Wire of copper alloys,nes
74.09				
74091100		成卷的精炼铜板、片、带	30	Plates,sheets and strip of refined copper,in coils,of a thickness exceeding 0.15mm
74091900		其他精炼铜板、片、带	30	Plates,sheets and strip of refined copper,not in coils, of a thickness exceeding 0.15mm
74092100		成卷的铜锌合金板、片、带	30	Plates,sheets and strip,of copper-zinc base alloys,in coils,of a thickness exceeding 0.15mm
74092900		其他铜锌合金板、片、带	30	Plates,sheets and strip of copper-zinc base alloys,not in coils,of a thickness exceeding 0.15mm
74093100		成卷的铜锡合金板、片、带	30	Plates sheets and strip of copper-tin base alloys, in coils,of a thickness exceeding 0.15mm
74093900		其他铜锡合金板、片、带	30	Plates sheets and strip of copper-tin base alloys,not in coils,of a thickness exceeding 0.15mm
74094000		铜镍合金或铜镍锌合金板、片、带	30	Plates,sheets and strip of copper-nickel base alloys or copper-nickel-zinc base alloys,in coils,of a thickness exceeding 0.15mm

税则号列 Tariff No.	ex	货 品 名 称	出口税率 Export Duty Rate	Description of Goods
74099000		其他铜合金板、片、带	30	Plates, sheets and strip of copper alloys, of a thickness exceeding 0.15mm, nes
75.02				
75021000		未锻轧的非合金镍	40	Unwrought nickel, not alloyed
75022000		未锻轧镍合金	40	Unwrought nickel, alloys
75.08				
75089010		电镀用镍阳极	40	Electroplating nickel anodes
76.01				
76011010		按重量计含铝量在99.95%及以上的非合金铝	30	Unwrought aluminium, not alloyed, containing by weight 99.95% or more of aluminium
76011090		按重量计含铝量在99.95%以下的非合金铝	30	Unwrought aluminium, not alloyed, containing by weight less than 99.95% of aluminium
76012000		未锻轧铝合金	30	Unwrought aluminium alloys
76.02				
76020000		铝废碎料	30	Aluminium waste and scrap
76.04				
76041000		非合金铝条、杆、型材及异型材	20	Bars, rods and profiles of aluminium, not alloyed
76042100		铝合金制空心异型材及异型材	20	Hollow profiles of aluminium alloys
76042900		铝合金制条、杆、其他型材	20	Bars, rods and other profiles of aluminium alloys
76.05				
76051100		最大截面尺寸超过7mm的非合金铝丝	20	Wire of aluminium, of which the maximum cross-sectional dimension exceeding 7mm
76051900		其他非合金铝丝	20	Wire of aluminium, not alloyed, nes
76052100		最大截面尺寸超过7mm的铝合金丝	20	Wire of aluminium alloys, of which the maximum cross-sectional dimension exceeding 7mm
76052900		其他铝合金丝	20	Wire of aluminium alloys, nes
76.06				
76061120		厚度在0.3mm及以上,但不超过0.36mm的非合金铝制矩形铝板片带	20	Rectangular plates, sheets and strip of aluminium, not alloyed, of a thicknees of 0.30mm or more but not exceeding 0.36mm
76061190		非合金铝制矩形的其他板、片及带	20	Rectangular plates, sheets and strip of aluminium, not alloyed, nes
76061220		厚度<0.28mm的铝合金制矩形铝板片带	20	Rectangular plates, sheets and strip of aluminium alloys, of a thickness less than 0.28mm
76061230		厚度在0.28mm及以上,但不超过0.35mm的铝合金制矩形铝板片带	20	Rectangular plates, sheets and strip of aluminium alloys, of a thickness of 0.28mm or more but not exceeding 0.35mm
76061240		厚度>0.35mm的铝合金制矩形铝板片带	20	Rectangular plates, sheets and strip of aluminium alloys, of a thickness exceeding 0.35mm
76069100		非合金铝制非矩形的板、片及带	20	Plates, sheets and strip of aluminium, not alloyed, nes
76069200		铝合金制非矩形的板、片及带	20	Plates, sheets and strip of aluminium alloys, nes
79.01				
79011110		含锌量≥99.995%的未锻轧锌	20	Unwrought zinc, containing ≥ 99.99% by weight of zinc
79011190		99.99≤含锌量<99.995%的未煅轧锌	20	Unwrought zinc, 99.99% ≤ containing < 99.99% by weight of zinc
79011200		含锌量<99.99%的未锻轧锌	20	Unwrought zinc, containing < 99.99% by weight of zinc
79012000		未锻轧锌合金	20	Unwrought zinc, alloys
81.10				
81101010		未锻轧锑	20	Unwrought antimony
81101020		锑粉末	20	Antimony powders
81102000		锑废碎料	20	Antimony waste and scrap

注:“ex”表示应税商品范围以“货品名称”描述为准,其余以税号为准。

附件 1：

Appendix1：

2007 年出口商品暂定税目、税率表

（2007 年 1 月 1 日起实施）

Interim Duty Rate for Exported Goods,2007

(Enforcel from January 1,2007)

ex	税则号列 Tariff Item	货品名称	出口税率 (Export Duty Rate)	暂定税率 Interim Duty Rate	Article Description
	03019210	鳗鱼苗	20	10	Eels(Anguilla. spp.)fry
ex	05069090	已脱胶骨、角柱	40	0	Degelatinized bones
	25085000	红柱石，蓝晶石及硅线石，不论是否煅烧		10	Andahcsite, kyanite and sillimanite
	25086000	富铝红柱石		10	Mullite
	25101010	未碾磨磷灰石		10	apatite, unground
	25101090	未碾磨天然磷酸钙、天然磷酸铝钙及磷酸盐白垩，磷灰石除外		10	Natural calcium phosphates, natural aluminium colcium phlsphates and phlsphatic chalk, unground
	25102010	已碾磨磷灰石		10	Apatite, ground
	25102090	已碾磨天然磷酸钙、天然磷酸铝钙及磷酸盐白垩，磷灰石除外		10	Natural calcium phosphates, natural aluminium colcium phlsphates and phlsphatic chalk, ground
	25292100	按重量计氟化钙含量≤97%的萤石		10	Containing by weight 97% or less of calcium fluoride
	25292200	按重量计氟化钙含量>97%的萤石		10	Containing by weight more than 97% of calcium fluoride
	25309020	稀土金属矿		10	Ores of rare earth metals
	26011110	平均粒径小于 0.8 毫米的未煅烧铁矿砂及其精矿；但焙烧黄铁矿除外		10	Arerage granularity less than 0.8mm, non – agglomerated iron ores and concentrates, other than roasted iron pyrites
	26011120	平均粒径不小于 0.8 毫米，但不大于 6.3 毫米的未煅烧铁矿砂及其精矿；但焙烧黄铁矿除外		10	Arerage gramularing not less than 0.8mm but not more than 6.3mm, non – agglomerated iron ores and concentrates, other than roacted iron pyrites
	26011190	平均粒径大于 6.3 毫米的未烧结铁矿砂及其精矿，但焙烧黄铁矿除外		10	Arerage granuiarity more than 6.3mm, non – agglomerated iron ores and concentrates
	26011200	已烧结铁矿砂及其精矿		10	Agglomerated iron ores and concentrates
	26012000	焙烧黄铁矿		10	Roasted iron pyrites
	26020000	锰矿砂及其精矿，包括以干重计含锰量在 20% 及以上的锰铁砂及其精矿		10	Manganese ores and concentrates, including ferruginous manganese ores and concentrates with a manganese content of 20% or more, calculated on the dry weight
	26030000	铜矿砂及其精矿		10	Copper ores and concentrates
	26040000	镍矿砂及其精矿		10	Nickel ores and concentrates
	26050000	钴矿砂及其精矿		10	Cobalt ores and concentrates
	26060000	铝矿砂及其精矿		10	Aluminium ores and concentrates
ex	26080000	灰色饲料氧化锌（氧化锌 ZnO 含量大于 80%）	30	0	Gray feed grade zinc oxide (containing by weight more than 80% of ZnO)
	26090000	锡矿砂及其精矿	50	20	Tin ores and concentrates

ex	税则号列 Tariff Item	货 品 名 称	出口税率 (Export Duty Rate)	暂定税率 Interim Duty Rate	Article Description
	26100000	铬矿砂及其精矿		10	Chromium ores and corcontrates
	26121000	铀矿砂及其精矿		10	Uranium ores and concentrates
	26122000	钍矿砂及其精矿		10	Thorium ores and concentrates
	26131000	已焙烧钼矿砂及其精矿		10	Molybdenum ores and concentrates, roastea
	26139000	其他钼矿砂及其精矿		10	Other molybdenum ores and concentrates
	26140000	钛矿砂及其精矿		10	Titanium ores and concentrates
	26151000	锆矿砂及其精矿		10	Ziroconium ores and concentrates
	26161000	银矿砂及其精矿		10	Silver ores and concentrates
	26169000	其他贵金属矿砂及其精矿		10	Other preciacs metal ores and concentrates
	26171090	其他锑矿砂及其精矿		10	Other antimony ores and concentrates
	26179010	朱砂(辰砂)		10	Cinnabar
	26179090	其他矿砂及其精矿		10	
	26180010	冶炼钢铁产生的锰渣		10	Containing mainly manganese granulated slag from the manufacture of iron or steel
	26180090	冶炼钢铁产生的其他粒状熔渣(熔渣砂)		10	Other granulated slas (slag sand) from the manufacture of iron or steel
	26190000	冶炼钢铁产生的熔渣、浮渣、氧化皮及其他废料		10	Slag、dross、scaling and other waster from the manufacture of iron or steel
	26201100	含硬锌的矿灰及残渣		10	Ash and residues, containing mainly hard zinc spelter zinc
	26201900	含其他锌的矿灰及残渣		10	Ash and residues, containing other zinc
	26202100	含铅汽油的淤渣及含铅抗震化合物的淤渣		10	Leaded gasoline sludges and leaded anti – knock compoun sludges
	26202900	其他主要含铅的矿灰及残渣		10	Ash and residues, containing mainly lead
	26203000	主要含铜的矿灰及残渣		10	Ash and rosidues, containing mainly copper
	26204000	主要含铝的矿灰及残渣		10	Ash and residues, containing mainly aluminium
	26206000	含砷、汞、铊及其混合物,用于提取或生产砷、汞、铊及其化合物的矿灰及残渣		10	Containing arsenic、mercury、thallium or their mixtures, of a kind used for the extraction of arsenic of those meials or for the manufacture of their chemical compounds
	26209100	含锑、铍、镉、铬及其混合物的矿灰及残渣		10	Ash and residues, containing antimorry, beryllinm, cadmium, chromium or their mixtures
	26209910	主要含钨的矿灰及残渣		10	Ash and residues, containing mainly tungsten
	26209990	含其他金属及化合物的矿灰及残渣		10	Ash and residues, containing other metals or their compounds
	27011210	未制成型的炼焦烟煤,不论是否粉化		5	Coking coal, not agglomerated, whether or not pulverized

ex	税则号列 Tariff Item	货品名称	出口税率 (Export Duty Rate)	暂定税率 Interim Duty Rate	Article Description
	27040010	煤制焦炭及半焦炭不论是否成型		5	Coke and semi - coke of coal, whether or not pulverized
	27060000	从煤、褐煤、或泥煤蒸馏所得的焦油及矿物焦油,不论是否脱水或部分蒸馏,包括再造焦油		5	Tar distilled from coal, from lignite or from peat, and other mineral tars, whether or not dehydrated or partially distilled, including reconstituted tare
	27090000	石油原油及从沥青矿物提取的原油		5	Petroleum oils and oils obtained from bituminous minerols crude
	28047090	其他磷	20	10	Phosphorus, nes
	28111100	氢氟酸(氟化氢)		10	Hydr of luoric acid
	28259012	三氧化钨		5	Tungstic oxide
	28418010	仲钨酸铵		5	Ammonium paratungstate
	28461010	氧化铈		10	Cerium carbonate
	28461020	氢氧化铈		10	Cerium hydroxide
	28461030	碳酸铈		10	Cerium carbonate
	28461090	铈的其他化合物		10	Cerium other compounds
	28469011	氧化钇		10	Yttrium oxide
	28469012	氧化镧		10	Neodymium oxide
	28469013	氧化钕		10	Neodymium oxide
	28469014	氧化铕		10	Eurapium oxide
	28469019	其他氧化稀土		10	Other rare - earth oxides
	28469028	混合氯化稀土		10	Mixture of rare - earth chlorides
	28469029	未混合氯化稀土		10	Non - mixture of rare - earth chlorides
	28469030	氟化稀土		10	Pare - earth fluorides
	28469048	混合碳酸稀土		10	Mixture of rare - earth carbonate
	28469049	未混合碳酸稀土		10	Non - mixture of rare - earth carbonate
	28469090	稀土金属、钇、钪的其他化合物		10	Other compounel, inorganic or organic, of rare - earth metals, of yttrium or of mixtures of these metals
	28499020	碳化钨		5	
	29022000	苯	40	0	Tungsten
	31021000	尿素		2007 年 1 月 1 日至 9 月 30 日: 30%; 2007 年 10 月 1 日至 12 月 31 日:15%	Urea
	44012100	针叶木木片或木粒		10	Wood in chips or particles of coniferous
	44012200	非针叶木木片或木粒		10	Wood in chips or particles of non - coniferous
	44091010	针叶木地板条(块)		10	Floor board strips of coniferous
	44092910	其他非针叶木地板条		10	Other floor board strips of conferous
	44190031	木制一次性筷子		10	One - time chopsticks of wood
	44219021	木制圆签、圆棒、冰果棒、压舌片及类似一次性制品		10	Circle、sticks、circle、bors、popsicle、sticks、spatula and the like of wood
	72021100	锰铁,含碳量>2%	20	10	Ferro-manganese
	72021900	锰铁,含碳量≤2%	20	10	Ferro-manganese, containing ≤ 2% by weight of carbon

ex	税则号列 Tariff Item	货 品 名 称	出口税率 (Export Duty Rate)	暂定税率 Interim Duty Rate	Article Description
	72022100	硅铁,含硅量>55%	25	10	Ferro-silicon
	72022900	硅铁,含硅量≤55%	25	10	Ferro-silicon, containing ≤ 55% by weight of silicon
	72023000	硅锰铁	20	10	Ferro-silico-manganese
	72024100	铬铁,含碳量>4%	40	10	Ferro-chromium, containing > 4% by weight of carbon
	72024900	铬铁,含碳量≤4%	40	10	Ferro-chromium, containing ≤4% by weight of carbon
	72025000	硅铬铁		10	Ferro – silico – chromium
	72026000	镍铁		10	Ferro – nickel
	72027000	钼铁		10	Ferro – molybdenum
	72028010	钨铁		10	Ferro – tungsten
	72028020	硅钨铁		10	Ferro – silico – tungstem
	72029100	钛铁及硅钛铁		10	Ferro – titanium and ferro – silico – titanium
	72029210	按重量计含钒量在75%及以上的钒铁		10	Contwining by weight more than 75% of ranadium
	72029290	其他钒铁		10	Other ferro – ranadium
	72029300	铌铁		10	Ferro – niobium
	72031000	直接从铁矿还原的铁产品		10	Ferro products obeained by direct reduction of ironore
	72039000	其他铁,海绵铁,产品纯度>99.94%		10	Other sponsy ferrous, iron having purity by weight of 99.9%
	72051000	生铁、镜铁及钢铁颗粒		10	Gramules and rowders, of pig iron, spiegeleisen, iron or steel
	72052900	生铁、镜铁及其他钢铁粉末		10	Gramules and powders, of pig iron spiegeleisem, other iron or steel
	72061000	铁及非合金钢锭		10	Iron and non – alloy steel in ingots
	72069000	其他初级形状的铁及非合金钢		10	Other primary forms, iron and nonalloy steel
	72071100	宽度<厚度两倍的矩形截面钢坯,C<0.25%		10	Steel flan of rectansular cross – secting the width measuring less than twice the thickness
	72071200	其他矩形截面钢坯,C,0.25%		10	Other steel flan of rectangulor cross-section
	72071900	其他含碳量<0.25%的钢坯		10	Other steel flan containing by weight 0.25% or more of carbon
	72072000	含碳量≥0.25%的钢坯		10	Steel billet, containing carbon <0.25%
	72181000	不锈钢锭及其他初级形状产品		10	Stainless steel in ingots or other primary forms
	72189100	矩形截面的不锈钢半制成品		10	Semi-finished products of stainless steel, of rectangular (other than square) crosssection
	72189900	其他不锈钢半制成品		10	Other alloy steel in ingots or other primary forms
	72241000	合金钢锭及其他初级形状合金钢		10	Raw castins forging stocks, individual
	72249010	单重≥10吨的粗铸锻件坯		10	Piece weight of 10 tons or more
	72249090	其他合金钢坯		10	Other alloy steel flan copper mattes

ex	税则号列 Tariff Item	货 品 名 称	出口税率 (Export Duty Rate)	暂定税率 Interim Duty Rate	Article Description
	74010000	铜锍、沉积铜(泥铜)		15	Cement copper(precipitated copped)
	74020000	未精炼铜,电解精炼用的铜阳极	30	15	Unrefined copper; copper anodes for electrolytic refining
	74031100	精炼铜的阴极及阴极型材	30	10	Refined copper and copper alloys, unwrought
	74031200	精炼铜的线锭	30	10	Refinde copper wire-bars, unwrought
	74031300	精炼铜的坯段	30	10	Refined copper billets, unwrough
	74031900	其他未锻轧的精炼铜	30	10	Refined copper products, unwrought, nes
	74032100	未锻轧的铜锌合金(黄铜)	30	5	Copper-zine base alloys, unrwought
	74032200	未锻轧的铜锡合金(青铜)	30	5	Copper-tin base alloys, unwrought
	74032900	未锻轧的其他铜合金	30	5	Other copper alloys, unwrought
	74040000	铜废碎料	30	15	Copper waste and scrap
	74071000	精炼铜条、杆及型材及异型材	30	0	Copper bars, rods and profiles
	74072100	铜锌合金条、杆及型材及异型材	30	0	Bars, rods and profiles of copper-zinc base alloys
	74072900	其他铜合金条杆、型材及异型材	30	0	Bars, rods and profiles of copper alloys, nes
	74081100	最大截面尺寸 > 6mm 的精炼铜丝	30	0	Wire of refined copper of which the maxium cross-sectional dimension exceeds 6mm
	74081900	其它精炼铜丝	30	0	Wire of refined copper, nes
	74082100	铜锌合金丝	30	0	Wire of copper-zinc base alloy
	74082200	铜镍合金丝或铜镍锌合金丝	30	0	Wire of copper-nickel base alloys or copper-nickel-zinc base alloys
	74082900	其他铜合金丝	30	0	Wire of copper alloys, nes
	74091100	成卷的精炼铜板、片、带	30	0	Plates, sheets and strip, of refined copper in coils
	74091900	其他精炼铜板、片、带	30	0	Other plates, sheets and strip of refined copper
	74092100	成卷的铜锌合金板、片、带	30	0	Plates, sheets and strip, of copper-zine base alloys in coils
	74092900	其他铜锌合金板、片、带	30	0	Other plates, sheets and strip, of copper-zinc base alloys
	74093100	成卷的铜锡合金板、片、带	30	0	Plates, sheets and strip, of copper-tin base alloys, in coils
	74093900	其他铜锡合金板、片、带	30	0	Other plates, sheets and strip, of coppertin base alloys
	74094000	铜镍合金或铜镍锌合金板、片、带	30	0	Plates, sheets and strip of copper-nickel base alloys or copper-nickel-zinc base alloys
	74099000	其他铜合金板、片、带	30	0	Plates, sheets and strip of other copper alloys
	75021000	未锻轧的非合金镍	40	15	Unwrought nickel, not alloyed
	75022000	未锻轧镍合金	40	15	Unwrought nickel, alloys
	75089010	电镀用镍阳极	40	15	Electroplating nickel anodes
	76011010	按重量计含铝量在 99.95% 及以上的非合金铝	30	0	Unwrought aluminium, not alloyed, containing by weight 99.95% or more of aluminium

ex	税则号列 Tariff Item	货品名称	出口税率 (Export Duty Rate)	暂定税率 Interim Duty Rate	Article Description
	76011090	按重量计含铝量在 99.95% 以下的非合金铝	30	15	Unwrought aluminium, not alloyed, containing by weight less than 99.95% of aluminium
	76012000	未锻轧铝合金	30	0	Unwrought aluminium alloys
	76020000	铝废碎料	30	15	Aluminium waste and scrap
	76041000	非合金铝条、杆、型材及异型材	20	0	Aluminium bars, rods and profiles, not alloys
	76042100	铝合金制空心异型材	20	0	Hollow profiles of aluminium alloys
	76042900	铝合金制条、杆、其他型材及异型材	20	0	Bars, rods and other profiles, of aluminium alloys
	76051100	最大截面尺寸超过 7mm 的非合金铝丝	20	0	Wire of aluminium, not alloyed, of which the maximum cross-sectional dimension exceeding 7mm
	76051900	其他非合金铝丝	20	0	Wire of aluminium ,not alloys, nes
	76052100	最大截面尺寸超过 7mm 的铝合金丝	20	0	Wire of aluminium alloys, of which the maximum cross-sectional dimension exceeding 7mm
	76052900	其他铝合金丝	20	0	Wire of aluminium alloys, nes
	76061120	厚度在 0.3mm 及以上,但不超过 0.36mm 的非合金铝制矩形铝板片带	20	0	Rectangular plates, sheets and strip of aluminium, not aloyed, of thickness of 0.30mm of more but not exceeding 0.36mm
	76061190	非合金铝制矩形的其他板、片及带	20	0	Rectangular plates, sheets and strip of aluminium not alloyed, nes
	76061220	厚度 <0.28mm 的铝合金制矩形铝板片带	20	0	Rectangular plates, sheets and strip of aluminium alloys, rectangular, thickness <0.28mm
	76061230	厚度在 0.28mm 及以上,但不超过 0.35mm 的铝合金制矩形铝板片带	20	0	Rectangular plates, sheets and strip of aluminium alloys, rectangular, 0.35mm≥thickness≥0.28mm
	76061240	厚度 >0.35mm 的铝合金制矩形铝板片带	20	0	Rectangular plates, sheets and strip of aluminium alloys rectangular thickness >0.35mm
	76069100	非合金铝制非矩形的板、片及带	20	0	Plates, sheets and strip of aluminium, not alloyed, nes
	76069200	铝合金制非矩形的板、片及带	20	0	Plates, sheets and strip of aluminium alloys, non-rectangular
	79011110	按重量计含锌量在 99.995% 及以上的未煅轧锌	20	0	Unwrought zinc, containing ≥ 99.995% by weight of zinc, not alloyed
	79011190	99.99≤含锌量 <99.995% 的未煅轧锌	20	5	Unwrought zinc 99.99% ≤containing <99.995% ,not alloyed
	79011200	含锌量 <99.99% 的未锻轧锌	20	5	Unwrought zinc containing <99.99% by weight of zinc ,not alloyed
	79012000	未锻轧锌合金	20	0	Zinc alloys, unwrought
	81011000	钨粉		5	Powders of tungsten
	81019400	未锻轧钨		5	Unwrought tungsten
	81019700	钨废碎料		15	Tungsten waste and scrap
	81021000	钼粉		15	Powders of molybdenum

ex	税则号列 Tariff Item	货　品　名　称	出口税率 (Export Duty Rate)	暂定税率 Interim Duty Rate	Article Description
	81029400	未锻轧钼		15	Unwrought molybdenum
	81029700	钼废碎料		15	Molybdenum, waste and scrap
	81101010	未锻轧锑	20	5	Unwrought antimony
	81110010	未锻轧锰;锰废碎料;粉末		15	Unwrought manganese; waste and scrapipowds
	81122100	未锻轧铬、铬粉末		15	Unwrought; Powders
	81122200	铬废碎料		15	Waste and scrap
	81129230	未锻轧铟;铟废碎料;铟粉末		15	Unwrough indium; waste and scrap; powders

注:"ex"表示实施暂定税率的商品以"货品名称"描述为准。其余以税号为准。

3

中华人民共和国海关进出口货物报关单填报规定和报关自动化系统常用代码表及说明

Standards for Filling Import/Export Goods Declaration Form and Code list to Supporting Documents subject toCustoms of the People's Republic of China

中华人民共和国海关进出口货物报关单填制规范

为统一进出口货物报关单填报要求，保证报关单数据质量，根据《中华人民共和国海关法》及有关法规，制定本规范。

本规范在一般情况下采用"报关单"或"进口报关单"、"出口报关单"的提法，需要分别说明不同要求时，则分别采用以下用语：

1. 报关单录入凭单：指申报单位按海关规定的格式填写的凭单，用作报关单预录入的依据。

2. 预录入报关单：指预录入公司录入、打印，由申报单位向海关申报的报关单。

3. 报关单证明联：指海关在核实货物实际入、出境后按报关单格式提供的证明，用作企业向税务、外汇管理部门办结有关手续的证明文件。

进出口货物报关单各栏目的填制规范如下：

一、预录入编号

指预录入单位预录入报关单的编号，用于申报单位与海关之间引用其申报后尚未接受申报的报关单。

预录入编号由接受申报的海关决定编号规则，报关单录入凭单的编号规则由申报单位自行决定。

二、海关编号

指海关接受申报时给予报关单的编号，应标识在报关单的每一联上。

（一）H883/EDI 通关系统

报关单海关编号为9位数码，其中1~2位为接受申报海关的编号（《关区代码表》中相应海关代码的后2位），第3位为海关接受申报公历年份4位数字的最后1位，后6位为顺序编号。

进口报关单和出口报关单应分别编号，确保在同一公历年度内，能按进口和出口唯一地标识本关区的每一份报关单。

（二）H2000 通关系统

报关单海关编号为18位数字，其中第1~4位为接受申报海关的编号（《关区代码表》中相应的海关代码），第5~8位为海关接受申报的公历年份，第9位为进出口标志（"1"为进口，"0"为出口），后9位为顺序编号。

Standards for Filling Import/Export Goods Declaration Form

In order to unify the requirements for filling import/export goods declaration form, to ensure the quality of the data given in the declaration, in accordance with the Customs Law and relative laws, the standards are laid down herein.

For the purpose of the standards, the general term "declaration", or "import/export declaration", shall be used. Where specific requirement needed to be explained in detail, the terms below shall be used.

(1) Proof of Declaration Entry: the statement of declarant made in the form prescribed by the Customs, which is the basis of pre – entry declaration.

(2) Pre – entry Declaration: the declaration of declarant produced to the Customs, which is filled, printed and transmitted on – line to the Customs by pre – entry agent.

(3) Certificate Copy of Declaration: the certificate copy of declaration provided by the Customs after examination of the import or export goods, could be used to settle relative formalities of tax or foreign exchange control administrations.

The filling standards concerning the particulars of import/export declaration are as follows:

1. Pre – entry No.

Pre – entry No.: the serial No. of the pre – entry declaration made by the pre – entry agent, between the declarant and the Customs the pre – entry No. could be used to indicate the declaration when it has been produced to the Customs yet not accepted by the Customs.

Rule for numbering the serial No. of pre – entry declaration is settled by the acceptance Customs office. Rule for numbering the serial No. of proof of declaration entry is settled by declarant.

2. Customs No.

Customs No. is given by the Customs office at which the declaration is accepted, and should be marked on every copies of the declaration.

(1) H883/EDI Customs procedures system

Customs No. consists of nine numerals, the first two are the code No. of the acceptance Customs office (the last two numbers of the relevant code numbers of the acceptance Customs office, which could be found in "Codes for Customs Establishment"), the third is the last numeral of the four numerals of the calendar year, the rest six numerals are the serial No..

Each Customs office must number the import declaration and export declaration separately, and must ensure each declaration within its Customs area be solely marked in the same year.

(2) H2000 Customs procedures system

Customs No. consists of eighteen numerals, the first four are the code No. of the acceptance Customs office (the relevant code numbers of the acceptance Customs office could be found in "Codes for Customs Establishment"), the fifth to the eight are the numerals of the calendar year, the ninth is the mark code of import/export (1 for import, 0 for export), the rest nine numerals are the serial No..

在海关 H883/EDI 通关系统向 H2000 通关系统过渡期间，后 9 位的编号规则同 H883/EDI 通关系统的要求。

In the period of transition from H883/EDI to H2000 Customs procedures system, rule for numbering the last nine serial numbers is same as the requirements of H883/EDI Customs procedures system.

三、进口口岸/出口口岸

指货物实际进出我国关境口岸海关的名称。

本栏目应根据货物实际进出关境的口岸海关填制《关区代码表》中相应的口岸海关名称及代码。

进口转关运输货物应填报货物进境地海关名称及代码，出口转关运输货物应填报货物出境地海关名称及代码。按转关运输方式监管的跨关区深加工结转货物，出口报关单填报转出地海关名称及代码，进口报关单填报转入地海关名称及代码。

在不同出口加工区之间转让的货物，填报对方出口加工区海关名称及代码。

其他无实际进出境的货物，填报接受申报的海关名称及代码。

3. Import Port/Export Port

Import Port/Export Port refers to the name of the Customs office at which the goods shall be in fact imported into or exported out of the territory.

In the case of outright importation or exportation of goods, fill in the name and code No. of the Customs office at which the goods shall be in fact imported into or exported out of the territory. The name and code No. of each Customs office could be found in "Codes for Customs Establishment".

In the case of import goods under Customs transit, fill in the name and code No. of the Customs office at which the goods shall be imported into the Customs territory; in the case of export goods under Customs transit, fill in the name and code No. of the Customs office at which the goods shall be exported out of the Customs territory. In the case of goods closed and transferred from one Customs area to another for supplementary processing under the procedure of Customs transit, on export declaration fill in the name and code No. of the Customs office of exit, on import declaration fill in the name and code No. of the Customs office of entry.

In the case of goods transferred between different export processing zones, fill in the name and code No. of the Customs office of the other side.

In other cases of goods transferred without actual import or export, fill in the name and code No. of the Customs office at which the declaration shall be accepted.

四、备案号

指进出口企业在海关办理加工贸易合同备案或征、减、免税审批备案等手续时，海关给予《进料加工登记手册》、《来料加工及中小型补偿贸易登记手册》、《外商投资企业履行产品出口合同进口料件及加工出口成品登记手册》、电子帐册及其分册（以下均简称《加工贸易手册》）、《进出口货物征免税证明》（以下简称《征免税证明》）或其他有关备案审批文件的编号。

一份报关单只允许填报一个备案号。备案号栏目为 12 位字符，其中第 1 位是标记代码。

无备案审批文件的报关单，本栏目免予填报。

具体填报要求如下：

（一）加工贸易合同项下货物，除少量低价值辅料按规定不使用《加工贸易手册》的外，填报《加工贸易手册》的编号。

（二）涉及征、减、免税备案审批的报关单，填报《征免税证明》编号。

（三）出入出口加工区的保税货物，应填报标记代码

4. Registration No.

Registration No. is the No. given by the Customs during the import/export enterprise goes through the formalities of filing processing trade contract or the formalities of prior authority for levy, reduction or exemption of duties and taxes, the No. is marked on "Registration Handbook for Processing with Imported Materials", "Registration Handbook for Processing with Supplied Materials and for Medium - and Small - Scale Compensation Trade", "Registration Handbook for Materials and Components for Inward Processing and Re - export Required for Contract of Exporting Products by Enterprise with Foreign Investment", the electronic general account book or subsidiary account book (all the above mentioned hereinafter referred to as PT Handbook), and on the "Levy or Exemption of Duties and Taxes Certificate for Import/Export Goods" (hereinafter referred to as "LRE Certificate"), or on other relative filed documents of prior authority.

For one declaration only one Registration No. is allowed to fill in. Registration No. consists of 12 digits, the initial digit is the mark code.

Declaration without filed document of prior authority, leave the Registration No. in blank.

Specific requirements are as follows:

(1) Goods under contract of processing trade, except granted small amount and low - value auxiliary materials, fill in the No. of PT Handbook.

(2) Declaration with filed document of prior authority for levy, reduction or exemption of Customs duties and taxes, fill in the No. of LRE Certificate.

(3) Bonded goods entry and exit export processing zone, fill in the

为 H 的电子帐册备案号;出入出口加工区的征免税货物、物品,应填报标记代码为 H、第六位为 D 的电子帐册备案号。

(四)使用异地直接报关分册和异地深加工结转出口分册在异地口岸报关的,本栏目应填报分册号;本地直接报关分册和本地深加工结转分册限制在本地报关,本栏目应填报总册号。

(五)加工贸易成品凭《征免税证明》转为享受减免税进口货物的,进口报关单填报《征免税证明》编号,出口报关单填报《加工贸易手册》编号。

(六)对减免税设备及加工贸易设备之间的结转,转入和转出企业分别填制进、出口报关单,在报关单"备案号"栏目分别填报《加工贸易手册》编号、《征免税证明》编号或免予填报。

(七)优惠贸易协定项下实行原产地证书联网管理的货物,应填报原产地证书代码"Y"和原产地证书编号;未实行原产地证书联网管理的货物,本栏目免予填报。

五、合同协议号

本栏目应填报进(出)口货物合同(协议)的全部字头和号码。

六、进口日期/出口日期

(一)进口日期

指运载所申报货物的运输工具申报进境的日期。本栏目填报的日期必须与相应的运[illegible]进境日期一致。

进口申报时[illegible]的实际进境日期时,本[illegible]

([illegible]

指[illegible]手续的日期。本栏[illegible]时免予填报。

无实际[illegible]期,以海关接受[illegible]

(三)在 H[illegible]

序为年、月、日[illegible]

位数字,顺序为[illegible]

七、申报日期

指海关接受进([illegible]

的报关企业申请的日[illegible]

以电子数据报关单[illegible]

算机系统接受申报数据时[illegible]报关单方式申报的,申报日期为海关[illegible]报关单并对报关单进行登记处理的日期。

Registration NO. of electronic account book with the initial digit H; dutiable and duty – free goods and articles entry or exit export processing zone, fill in the Registration NO. of electronic account book with the initial digit H and the sixth digit D.

(4) Declaring at a non – local Customs office with a subsidiary account book to import/export or to close and transfer accounts of supplied materials for supplementary processing, fill in the No. of subsidiary account book; declaring at a local Customs office with a subsidiary account book to import/export or to close and transfer accounts of supplied materials for supplementary processing, fill in the No. of the general account book.

(5) Finished products of processing trade changed into import goods and granted reduction or exemption Customs duties and taxes on the basis of LRE Certificate, on import declaration fill in the No. of LRE Certificate, on export declaration fill in the No. of PT Handbook.

(6) To close and transfer equipments granted reduction or exemption of duties and taxes or equipments for processing trade, transferee and transferor should fill the import/export declaration forms separately, the registration No. should be the No. of PT Handbook, the No. of LRE Certificate, or leave the registration No. in blank.

(7) In the case of goods under the preferential trading agreements, for those the on – line control of Certificate of Origin has been put into practice, fill in the code of Certificate of Origin "Y" and the serial No. of Certificate of Origin; for those the on – line control of Certificate of Origin has not been put into practice yet, leave the registration No. in blank.

5. Contract No.

Fill in all the letters and numerals of the contract of import/export goods.

6. Date of Import/Date of Export

(1) Date of Import

Date of import means the date of declaration to import. Date of import should be in accordance with the date of entry of the means of transport by which the goods are carried.

Declaring for importation but the in fact entry date of means of transport is unknown, leave the date of import in blank.

(2) Date of Export

Date of export means the date of permission to export, which shall be printed on the certificate copy of declaration by the Customs, declarant should not fill in.

Declaring for goods which are not in fact imported or exported, fill in the date of the declaration accepted by the Customs.

(3) In the H883/EDI Customs procedure system, the date shall be marked with six numerals in sequence of year, month and day; in the H2000 Customs procedure system, the date shall be marked with eight numerals in sequence of year, month and day.

7. Date of Declaration

The term means the date when the declaration of consignor/consignee [illegible] import/export goods or their agent accepted by the Customs.

Declaring with electronic declaration form, date of declaration shall be the date when the declaration data accepted and recorded by the computer system of the Customs. Declaring with paper declaration form, date of declaration shall be the date when the paper declaration form accepted and

在 H883/EDI 通关系统中,本栏目为6位数,顺序为年、月、日各2位;在 H2000 通关系统中,本栏目为8位数字,顺序为年(4位)、月(2位)、日(2位)。

registered by the Customs.

In the H883/EDI Customs procedure system, the date shall be marked with six numerals in sequence of year, month and day; in the H2000 Customs procedure system, the date shall be marked with eight numerals in sequence of year, month and day.

八、经营单位

经营单位指对外签订并执行进出口贸易合同的中国境内企业、单位或个体工商户。

本栏目应填报经营单位名称及经营单位编码。

经营单位编码是经营单位在海关办理注册登记手续时,海关给予的注册登记10位编码。

特殊情况下确定经营单位原则如下:

(一)援助、赠送、捐赠的货物,填报直接接受货物的单位;

(二)进出口企业之间相互代理进出口,填报代理方。

(三)外商投资企业委托进出口企业进口投资设备、物品的,填报外商投资企业,并在标记唛码及备注栏注明“委托某进出口企业进口”。

(四)有代理报关权的进出口企业在本企业进出口或代理其他企业进出口时,填报本企业的经营单位编码;代理其他企业办理进出口报关手续时,填报委托经营方单位编码。

8. Performer

The term means the person who has signed the contract of import/export trade and shall perform the contract, including enterprises, institutions and individuals engaged in industrial or commercial business within the territory of China.

Fill in the name and serial No. of the performer.

The serial No. of the performer consists of ten numerals, which is the Customs registration No. given by the local Customs after the performer completed the formality of registration.

In specific cases, the following rules for determine the performer shall be abided:

(1) Goods rendered gratis, fill in the direct acceptor of the goods.

(2) The agent entrusted by person with import/export authority to go through the Customs procedure, fill in the name and code N0. of the agent entrusted.

(3) The agent entrusted by enterprise with foreign investment to import inventory equipments and materials, fill in the name and code N0. of the enterprise with foreign investment, and remark “XX import/export enterprise is entrusted to import the goods” in the box of Marks & No. /Remarks.

(4) Import/export enterprise with agent declaration authority, to import/export goods for oneself or other person, fill in the serial No. of the import/export enterprise; to be entrusted to go through Customs procedure only, fill in the serial No. of the client.

九、收货单位/发货单位

(一)收货单位

指已知的进口货物在境内的最终消费、使用单位,包括:

1. 自行从境外进口货物的单位;
2. 委托进出口企业进口货物的单位。

(二)发货单位

指出口货物在境内的生产或销售单位,包括:

1. 自行出口货物的单位;
2. 委托进出口企业出口货物的单位。

(三)备有海关注册编号或加工生产企业编号的收、发货单位,本栏目必须填报其经营单位编码或加工生产企业编号;否则填报其中文名称。加工贸易报关单的收、发货单位应与《加工贸易手册》的“货主单位”一致;减免税货物报关单的收、发货单位应与《征免税证明》的“申请单位”一致。

9. Consignee/Consignor

(1) Consignee

Consignee means the end - user of the known import goods, including:

①The end - user who imports the goods by oneself.

②The end - user who entrusts an import/export enterprise to import the goods.

(2) Consignor

Consignor means the manufacturer or the seller of the export goods, including:

①The one who exports the goods by oneself.

② The one who entrusts an import/export enterprise to export the goods.

(3) Consignee/consignor who has been given Customs registration No, should fill in the Chinese name and Customs registration No. , otherwise, fill in Chinese name only. Declaring for goods of processing trade, the consignee/consignor should be in accordance with " owner of goods" marked on PT Handbook; declaring for goods granted reduction or exemption of Customs duties and taxes, the consignee/consignor should be in accordance with " applicant" marked on LRE Certificate.

十、申报单位

指对申报内容的真实性直接向海关负责的企业或单位。自理报关的,应填报进(出)口货物的经营单位名称

10. Declarant

The term declarant means the person who is responsible for the truthfulness of the declaration. Where the performer of contract declares import/

及编码；委托代理报关的，应填报经海关批准的报关企业名称及编码。

export goods for oneself, fill in name and Registration No. of the performer; in the case of declaring import/export goods for client, fill in name and Registration No. of the agent declaration enterprise entitled by the Customs.

本栏目还包括报关单左下方用于填报申报单位有关情况的相关栏目，包括报关员、报关单位地址、邮政编码和电话号码等栏目。

The term also relates to the box on the left bottom of declaration form, which is specially used for filling in particulars relating to declarant, such as name of qualified declarant, address, post code and telephone number, etc.

十一、运输方式

指载运货物进出关境所使用的运输工具的分类，包括实际运输方式和海关规定的特殊运输方式。

本栏目应根据实际运输方式按海关规定的《运输方式代码表》选择填报相应的运输方式。

特殊情况下运输方式的填报原则如下：

（一）非邮政方式进出口的快递货物，按实际运输方式填报。

（二）进出境旅客随身携带的货物，按旅客所乘运输工具填报。

（三）进口转关运输货物，按载运货物抵达进境地的运输工具填报，出口转关运输货物，按载运货物驶离出境地的运输工具填报。

（四）出口加工区与区外之间进出的货物，区内企业填报“9”，区外企业填报“Z”。

（五）其他无实际进出境的，根据实际情况选择填报《运输方式代码表》中运输方式“0”（非保税区运入保税区和保税区退区）、“1”（境内存入出口监管仓库和出口监管仓库退仓）、“7”（保税区运往非保税区）、“8"（保税仓库转内销）或“9”（其他运输）。

（六）同一出口加工区内或不同出口加工区的企业之间相互结转、调拨的货物、出口加工区与其他海关特殊监管区域之间、不同保税区之间、同一保税区内不同企业之间、保税区与出口加工区等海关特殊监管区域之间转移、调拨的货物，填报“9”（其他运输）。

11. Mode of Transport

The term means the kind of means of transport by which the import/export goods are carried.

Fill in the code of the actual mode of transport, which can be found in the “Codes for Modes of Transport” prescribed by the Customs.

In specific cases, the following rules for filling in Mode of Transport shall be abided:

(1) Express import/export goods transferred not by post, fill in the code of the actual mode of transport.

(2) Import/export goods carried in travelers' baggage, fill in the code of the means of transport of passengers.

(3) Import goods under Customs transit, fill in the code of the means of transport by which the import goods are carried into the territory; export goods under Customs transit, fill in the code of the means of transport by which the export goods are carried out of the territory.

(4) Goods entry and release of export processing zone, enterprise outside should fill in the code “9”, enterprise within should fill in the code “Z”.

(5) In other cases of goods which are not in fact imported or exported, entry and release of bonded warehouse zone, fill in the code “0”; entry and release of temporary storage of export goods, fill in the code “1”; shipment out of bonded warehouse zone to non-bonded area, fill in the code “7”; goods in bonded warehouse zone to be declared for home use, fill in the code “8”; otherwise, fill in the code “9” (Other Transport).

(6) Goods to be closed and transferred or allocated within the same export processing zone or between two export processing zones, between export processing zone and other special zones under the Customs control; goods to be transferred or allocated between two bonded zones, between two enterprises within the same bonded zone, between bonded zone and other special zones under the Customs control, fill in “9” (Other Transport).

十二、运输工具名称

指载运货物进出境的运输工具的名称或运输工具编号。

本栏目填报内容应与运输部门向海关申报的载货清单所列相应内容一致。

一份报关单只允许填报一个运输工具名称。

具体填报要求如下：

（一）直接在进出境办理报关手续的报关单具体填报要求：

1. H883/EDI 通关系统

（1）江海运输填报船名或船舶呼号（来往港澳小型船舶为监管簿编号）+“/”+航次号。

12. Description of Means of Transport

The term means the name or No. of means of transport by which the import/export goods are carrier.

Which should be in accordance with the corresponding content of the transport documents produced to the Customs.

On each declaration only one name of means of transport allowed to fill in.

Specific requirements are as follows:

(1) To go through declaration procedure at the border Customs office, requirements for filling are as follows:

1. H883/EDI Customs procedures system

① For marine transport/inland water transport, fill in the call sign of the ship (for small ship goes between mainland and Hong Kong or Macao, fill the No. of Supervision and Control Book) and the No. of voyage.

(2)汽车运输填报该跨境运输车辆的国内行驶车牌号+"/"+进出境日期[8位数字,顺序为年(4位)、月(2位)日(2位),下同]。

(3)铁路运输填报车次(或车厢号)+"/"+进出境日期。

(4)航空运输填报航班号+进出境日期+"/"+总运单号。

(5)邮政运输填报邮政包裹单号+"/"+进出境日期。

(6)其他运输填报具体运输方式名称,例如:管道、驮畜等。

2. H2000通关系统

(1)江海运输填报船舶编号(来往港澳小型船舶为监管簿编号)或者船舶英文名称。

(2)汽车运输填报该跨境运输车辆的国内行驶车牌号,深圳提前报关模式填报国内行驶车牌号+"/"+"提前报关"(4个汉字)。

(3)铁路运输填报车厢号或交接单号。

(4)航空运输填报航班号。

(5)邮政运输填报邮政包裹单号。

(6)其他运输填报具体运输方式名称,例如:管道、驮畜等。

(7)对于"清单放行,集中报关"的货物填报"集中报关"(4个汉字)。

(二)转关运输货物报关单填报要求:

1. 进口

(1)H883/EDI报关系统

①江海运输:直转填报"@"+16位转关申报单预录入号(或13位载货清单号);中转填报进境英文船名(必须与提单、转关单填写完全一致)+"/"+"@"+进境船舶航次;

②铁路运输:直转填报"@"+16位转关申报单预录入号;中转填报车厢编号+"/"+"@"+8位进境日期。

③航空运输:直转填报"@"+16位转关申报单预录入号;中转填报8位分运单号,无分运单的免予填报。

④公路及其他各类运输:填报"@"+16位转关申报单预录入号(或13位载货清单号)。

⑤以上各种运输方式使用广东地区载货清单转关的提前报关货物填报"@"+13位载货清单号;其他地区提前报关免予填报。

② For road transport, fill in the No. of the license plate +/+ entry/leaving date (8 digits in sequence of year, month and day, similarly hereinafter)

③ For railway transport, fill in the train No. (or the No. of railway carriage) +/+ entry/leaving date.

④ For airway transport, fill in the No. of flight + entry/leaving date +/+ the No. of air waybill.

⑤ For mail transport, fill in the No. of bill of parcels +/+ entry/leaving date

⑥ For other transport, fill in the actual mode of transport, for example, pipeline, pack animal, etc.

2. H2000 Customs procedures system

① For marine transport/inland water transport, fill in the call sign of the ship (for small ship goes between mainland and Hong Kong or Macao, fill the No. of Supervision and Control Book) or English name of the ship.

② For road transport, fill in the No. of the license plate of the cross-border vehicle, in mode of advanced declaration in Shenzhen, fill in the No. of the license plate of the cross-border vehicle +/+ 提前报关(four Chinese characters).

③ For railway transport, fill in the No. of railway carriage or the No. of handing-over bill.

④ For airway transport, fill in the No. of flight.

⑤ For mail transport, fill in the No. of bill of parcels.

⑥ For other transport, fill in the actual mode of transport, for example, pipeline, pack animal, etc.

⑦ For goods subject to "release on basis of list, declaration to cover-all", fill in "集中报关"(four Chinese characters).

(2) Requirements for filling in the particular for transport goods under Customs transit are as follows:

1. Import

(1) H833/EDI Customs procedures system

① Goods transported into the territory by sea or inland waterway: goods under direct transit, fill in @ + 16 digits pre-entry N0. of declaration for Customs transit (or 13 digits No. of loading list); goods under en route transit, fill in the English name of the entry ship (which should be in accordance with corresponding content of bill of lading and declaration for Customs transit) +/+@ +the No. of voyage.

② Goods transported into the territory by rail: goods under direct transit, fill in @ +16 digit pre-entry No. of declaration for Customs transit, goods under en route transit, fill in the No. of railway carriage +@ + the 8 digits of entry date.

③ Goods transported into the territory by air: goods under direct transit, fill in @ +16 digits pre-entry No. of declaration for Customs transit; in the case of international combined transportation, fill in 8 digits No. of fraction consignment note, with no fraction consignment note leave the particular in blank.

④ Goods transported into the territory by road vehicles or by other means of transport, fill in @ + 16 digit pre-entry No. of declaration for Customs transit (or 13 digit No. of loading list).

⑤ Where declaration for goods under Customs transit lodged before the goods arrive at the Customs office, fill in @ +13 digit No. of loading list in Guangdong area, leave the particular in blank in other areas.

(2)H2000 通关系统

①江海运输:直转、提前报关填报“@”+16 位转关申报单预录入号(或 13 位载货清单号);中转填报进境英文船名。

②铁路运输:直转、提前报关填报“@”+16 位转关申报单预录入号;中转填报车厢编号。

③航空运输:直转、提前报关填报“@”+16 位转关申报单预录入号(或 13 位载货清单号);中转填报“@”。

④汽车及其他运输:填报“@”+16 位转关申报单预录入号(或 13 位载货清单号)。

⑤以上各种运输方式使用广东地区载货清单转关的提前报关货物填报“@”+13 位载货清单号;其他地区提前报关货物免予填报。

2. 出口

(1)H883/EDI 通关系统:

①江海运输:出口非中转填报“@”+16 位转关申报单预录入号(或 13 位载货清单号);中转:境内江海运输填报驳船船名+“/”+“驳船航次”;境内铁路运输填报车名[4 位关别代码+“TRAIN”(英文单词)]+“/”+6 位启运日期;境内公路运输填报车名[4 位关别代码+“TRUCK”(英文单词)]+“/”+(6 位启运日期);境内公路运输填报车名[4 位关别代码+“TRYCK”(英文单词)]+“/”+6 位启运日期

上述“驳船船名”、“驳船航次”、“车名”、“日期”均须事先在海关备案。

②铁路运输:填报“@”+16 位转关申报单预录入号;多张报关单需要通过一张转关单转关的,填报“@”。

③其他运输方式:填报“@”+16 位转关申报单预录入号(或 13 位载货清单号)。

上述规定以外无实际进出境的,本栏目为空。

(2)H2000 通关系统:

①江海运输:非中转填报“@”+16 位转关申报单预录入号(或 13 位载货清单号)。如多张报关单需要通过一张转关单转关的,运输工具名称字段填报“@”中转,境内江海运输填报驳船船名;境内铁路运输填报车名[主管海关 4 位关别代码+“TRAIN”(英文单词)];境内公路运输填报车名[主管海关 4 位关别代码+“TRUCK”(英文单词)]。

②铁路运输:填报“@”+16 位转关申报单预录入号(或 13 位载货清单号);如多张报关单需要通过一张转

(2)H2000 Customs procedures system

① Goods transported into the territory by sea or inland waterway: goods under direct transit, or declaring in advance, fill in @ + 16 digits pre – entry N0. of declaration for Customs transit (or 13 digits No. of loading list); goods under en route transit, fill in the English name of the entry ship.

② Goods transported into the territory by rail: goods under direct transit, or declaring in advance, fill in @ +16 digit pre – entry No. of declaration for Customs transit, goods under en route transit, fill in the No. of railway carriage.

③ Goods transported into the territory by air: goods under direct transit, or declaring in advance, fill in @ +16 digits pre – entry No. of declaration for Customs transit(or 13 digits No. of loading list); in the case of international combined transportation, fill in @ only.

④ Goods transported into the territory by road vehicles or by other means of transport, fill in @ + 16 digit pre – entry No. of declaration for Customs transit (or 13 digit No. of loading list).

⑤ Where declaration for goods under Customs transit lodged before the goods arrive at the Customs office, fill in @ +13 digit No. of loading list in Guangdong area, leave the particular in blank in other areas.

2. Export

(1)H883/EDI Customs Procedures system:

① Goods transported out of the territory by sea or inland waterway: goods under direct transit, fill in @ + 16 digits pre – entry N0. of declaration for Customs transit (or 13 digits No. of loading list); goods under en route transit, transport by sea or inland waterway within the territory fill in name of barge +/+ No. of voyage, transport by rail within the territory fill in name of train(4 digit Customs code +TRAIN) +/+ date (6 digit date of departure), transport by road within the territory fill in name of truck(4 digit Customs code +TRUCK) +/+ date (6 digit date of departure).

The above mentioned “name of barge”, “No. of voyage”, “name of train”, “name of truck” and “date of departure” should be filed at the Customs office in advance.

② Export goods transported by rail, fill in @ + 16 digit pre – entry No. of declaration for Customs transit, where multiple declarations produced with one declaration for Customs transit, fill in @ only.

③ Export goods transported by other means of transport, fill in @ + 16 digit pre – entry No. of declaration for Customs transit (or 13 digit No. of loading list).

Besides the above rules, in the case of goods which are not in fact imported/exported, leave the particular in blank.

(2)H2000 Customs procedures system:

① Goods transported out of the territory by sea or inland waterway: goods under direct transit, fill in @ + 16 digits pre – entry N0. of declaration for Customs transit (or 13 digits No. of loading list). Where multiple declarations produced with one declaration for Customs transit, fill in @ only. Goods under en route transit, transport by sea or inland waterway within the territory fill in name of barge, transport by rail within the territory fill in name of train(4 digit Customs code +TRAIN), transport by road within the territory fill in name of truck(4 digit Customs code +TRUCK).

② Export goods transported by rail, fill in @ + 16 digit pre – entry No. of declaration for Customs transit(or 13 digit No. of loading list),

关单转关的，填报“@”。

where multiple declarations produced with one declaration for Customs transit, fill in @ only.

③航空运输：填报“@”+16位转关申报单预录入号（或13位载货清单号）；如多张报关单需要通过一张转关单转关的，填报“@”。

③ Goods transported into the territory by air: fill in @ +16 digits pre – entry No. of declaration for Customs transit (or 13 digit No. of loading list) ; where multiple declarations produced with one declaration for Customs transit, fill in @ only.

④其他各类出境运输方式：填报“@”+16位转关申报单预录入号（或13位载货清单号）。

④ Export goods transported by other means of transport, fill in @ + 16 digit pre – entry No. of declaration for Customs transit (or 13 digit No. of loading list).

（三）无实际进出境货物报关单

(3) In the cases of declaration for goods which are not in fact imported/exported, the following requirements shall be abided:

1. 在H883/EDI通关系统下：

加工贸易深加工结转及料件结转货物，加工贸易成品凭《征免税证明》转为享受减免税进口的货物，保税区与区外之间进出的货物，同一保税区内或不同保税区的企业之间转移（调拨）的货物，出口加工区与区外之间进出的货物，同一出口加工区内或不同出口加工区的企业之间相互结转、调拨的货物，应先办理进口报关，并在出口报关单本栏目填报转入方关区代码（前两位）及进口报关单号，即“转入××（关区代码）×××××××××（进口报关单/备案清单号）”。按转关运输货物办理结转手续的，按转关运输有关规定填报。

1. Under H883/EDI Customs procedures system:

To close and transfer accounts of supplied materials for supplementary processing, to change the finished products of processing trade into import goods for home use on the basis of LRE Certificate, to transfer goods into or out of bonded zone, to transfer (allocate) goods between enterprises within the same bonded zone or between enterprises of different bonded zones, to transfer goods into or out of export processing zone, to close and transfer goods between enterprises within the same export processing zone or between enterprises of different export processing zones, the formality of import declaration should be accomplished first, then for this particular of export declaration, fill in the code No. of the Customs office at which the goods shall be transferred into and Customs No. of the import declaration, that is " transfer into XX(code of the Customs office) XXXXXXXXX (No. of import declaration/No. of registration list). To go through the formality to close and transfer goods under Customs transit, relative provisions should be abided to fill in this particular.

2. 在H2000通关系统下，本栏目免予填报。

2. Under H2000 Customs procedures system, leave the particular in blank.

上述规定以外无实际进出境的，本栏目免予填报。

Besides the above rules, in the case of goods which are not in fact imported/exported, leave the particular in blank.

十三、航次号

13. No. of voyage

指载运货物进出境的运输工具的航次编号。本栏目仅限H2000通关系统填报，使用H883/EDI通关系统的，本栏目内容与运输工具名称合并填报。

The term means the No. of voyage of means of transport by which the import/export goods are carrier. To fill in this particular is limited to H2000 Customs procedures system, where H883/EDI Customs procedures system is used, the content of this particular shall be filling in combined with the name of means of transport.

具体填报要求如下：

Specific requirements are as follows:

（一）直接在进出境地办理报关手续的报关单

(1) To go through declaration procedure at the border Customs office

①江海运输：填报船舶的航次号。

① For marine transport/inland water transport, fill in the No. of voyage.

②汽车运输：填报该跨境运输车辆的进出境日期[8位数字，顺序为年（4位）、月（2位）、日（2位），下同]。

② For road transport, fill in entry/leaving date [8 digits in sequence of year, month and day]

③ 铁路运输：填报进出境日期。

③ For railway transport, fill in entry/leaving date.

④航空运输：免予填报。

④ For airway transport, leave the particular in blank.

⑤ 邮政运输：填报进出境日期。

⑤ For mail transport, fill in entry/leaving date.

⑥ 其他各类运输方式：免予填报。

⑥ For other transport, leave the particular in blank.

（二）转关运输货物报关单

(2) Declaring for goods under Customs transit

1. 进口

1. Import

① 江海运输：中转转关方式填报“@”+进境干线船舶航次。直转、提前报关免予填报。

① Goods transported into the territory by sea or inland waterway: goods under en route transit, fill in @ + No. of voyage of the mainline ship. Goods under direct transit, or declaring in advance, leave the parti-

② 公路运输:免予填报。

③ 铁路运输:"@" + 进出境日期[8 位数字,顺序为年(4 位)、月(2 位)、日(2 位)]。

④ 航空运输:免予填报。

⑤ 其他各类运输方式:免予填报。

2. 出口

(1) 江海运输:非中转货物免予填报。中转货物:境内江海运输填报驳船航次号;境内铁路、公路运输填报 6 位启运日期,顺序为年、月、日各 2 位。

(2) 铁路拼车拼箱捆绑出口:免予填报。

(3) 航空运输:免予填报。

(4) 其他运输方式:免予填报。

(三)上述规定以外无实际进出境的,本栏目免予填报。

十四、提运单号

指进出口货物提单或运单的编号。

本栏目填报的内容应与运输部门向海关申报的载货清单所列相应内容一致。

一份报关单只允许填报一个提运单号,一票货物对应多个提运单时,应分单填报。

具体填报要求如下:

(一)直接在进出境地办理报关手续的报关单

1. H883/EDI 通关系统:

(1)江海运输:填报进口提单号;

(2)汽车运输:免于填报。

(3)铁路运输:填报运单号。

(4)航空运输:填报分运单号,无分运单的填报总运单号。

(5)邮政运输:免于填报。

(6)无实际进出境的,本栏目免予填报。

2. H2000 通关系统:

(1)江海运输:填报进出口提运单号。如有分提运单的,填报进出口提运单号 + "＊" + 分提运单号。

(2)汽车运输:免于填报。

(3)铁路运输:填报运单号。

(4)航空运输:填报总运单号 + "_"(下划线) + 分运单号,无分运单的填报总运单号。

(5)邮政运输:填报邮运包裹单号。

(6)无实际进出境的,本栏目免予填报。

cular in blank.

② For road transport, leave the particular in blank.

③ Goods transported into the territory by rail, fill in @ + entry/leaving date [8 digits, in the sequence of year, month, day].

④ For airway transport, leave the particular in blank.

⑤ For other transport, leave the particular in blank.

2. Export

① Goods transported out of the territory by sea or inland waterway: goods under direct transit, leave the particular in blank. Goods under en route transit, transport by sea or inland waterway within the territory fill in No. of voyage of barge, transport by rail or road within the territory fill in date of departure (6 digits, in the sequence of year, month, day).

② Goods transported out of the territory by rail in mode of container load or carload, leave the particular in blank.

③ For airway transport, leave the particular in blank.

④ For other transport, leave the particular in blank.

(3) Besides the above rules, in the case of goods which are not in fact imported/exported, leave the particular in blank.

14. No. of Bill of Lading/ No. of Consignment Note

The term refers to the serial No. of Bill of Lading or of Consignment Note.

The filling content should be in accordance with transport documents produced at the Customs office by consignor.

For each declaration only one No. of Bill of Lading/ No. of Consignment Note is allowed to fill in. One lot of goods with multiple Bills of Lading/ Consignment Notes, fill in each declaration separately.

Specific requirements are as follows:

(1) To go through declaration procedure at the border Customs office

1. H883/EDI Customs procedures system:

① Transport by sea or inland waterway, fill in No. of Bill of Lading of import goods/ No. of Consignment Note of export goods.

② Transport by road, leave the particular in blank.

③ Transport by rail, fill in No. of Consignment Note.

④ Transport by air, fill in the No. of fractional consignment note, with no fractional consignment note fill in the No. of whole consignment note.

⑤ Transport by mail, leave the particular in blank.

⑥ Goods which are not in fact imported/exported, leave the particular in blank.

2. H2000 Customs procedures system:

① Transport by sea or inland waterway, fill in No. of Bill of Lading of import goods/ No. of Consignment Note of export goods. With fractional Bill of Lading/Consignment Note, fill in No. of Bill of Lading of import goods/ No. of Consignment Note of export goods + "＊" + No. of fractional Bill of Lading/ Consignment Note.

② Transport by road, leave the particular in blank.

③ Transport by rail, fill in No. of Consignment Note.

④ Transport by air, fill in No. of whole consignment note + "_" + No. of fractional consignment note, with no fractional consignment note fill in No. of whole consignment note.

⑤ Transport by mail, fill in No. of bill of parcels.

⑥ Goods which are not in fact imported/exported, leave the particular

(二)转关运输货物报关单

1.进口

(1)H883/EDI 通关系统

①江海运输:直转、中转填报提单号;提前报关免予填报。

②铁路运输:直转、货物填报 11 位总运单号 +"/"+8 位分运单号,无分运单号的填报 11 位总运单号,中转填报"@"+总运单号,提前报关免予填报。

③航空运输:直转货物填报 11 位总运单号 +"/"+8 位分运单号,无分运单号的填报 11 位总运单号;中转填报"@"+总运单号;提前报关免予填报。

④其他运输方式,本栏目免予填报。

⑤以上各种运输方式进境货物,在广东省内用公路运输转关的,填报车牌号。

(2)H2000 通关系统

①江海运输:直转、中转填报提单号,提前报关免予填报。

②铁路运输:直转、中转填报铁路运单号,提前报关免予填报。

③航空运输:直转、中转货物填报总运单号 +"-"+分运单号;提前报关免予填报。

④其他运输方式,本栏目免予填报。

⑤以上各种运输方式进境货物,在广东省内用公路运输转关的,填报车牌号。

2.出口

(1)H883/EDI 通关系统

①江海运输:中转货物填报提单号;非中转货物免予填报;广东省内提前报关的转关货物填报车牌号。

②其他运输方式:广东省内提前报关的转关货物填报车牌号;其他地区免予填报。

(2)H2000 通关系统

①江海运输:中转货物填报运单号;非中转货物免予

in blank.

(2) Requirements for goods transported under Customs transit are as follows:

1. Import

(1) H883/EDI Customs procedures system

① Goods transported into the territory by sea or inland waterway, under direct Customs transit or en route transit, fill in No. of Bill of Lading; in the case of declaration before the goods arrive, leave the particular in blank.

② Goods transported into the territory by rail, under direct Customs transit or en route transit, fill in No. of railway consignment note; in the case of declaration before the goods arrive, leave the particular in blank.

③ Goods transported into the territory by air: under direct Customs transit, fill in 11 digit No. of whole consignment note +/+ 8 digit No. of fractional consignment note, with no fractional consignment note fill No. of whole consignment note only; under international combined transit, fill in @ + No. of whole consignment note; in the case of declaration before the goods arrive leave the particular in blank.

④ Goods transported into the territory by other means of transport, leave the particular in blank.

⑤ Goods transported into the territory by means of transport above mentioned then transported by road vehicles under Customs transit within Guangdong area, fill in No. of license plate.

2. H2000 Customs procedures system

① Goods transported into the territory by sea or inland waterway, under direct Customs transit or en route transit, fill in No. of Bill of Lading; in the case of declaration before the goods arrive, leave the particular in blank.

② Goods transported into the territory by rail, under direct Customs transit or en route transit, fill in No. of railway consignment note; in the case of declaration before the goods arrive, leave the particular in blank.

③ Goods transported into the territory by air: under direct Customs transit or en route transit, fill in No. of whole consignment note +/+ No. of fractional consignment note; in the case of declaration before the goods arrive leave the particular in blank.

④ Goods transported into the territory by other means of transport, leave the particular in blank.

⑤ Goods transported into the territory by means of transport above mentioned then transported by road vehicles under Customs transit within Guangdong area, fill in No. of license plate.

2. Export

(1) H883/EDI Customs procedures system

① Goods transported out of the territory by sea or inland waterway: under en route Customs transit, fill in No. of Bill of Lading; under direct Customs transit, leave the particular in blank; in the case of declaration for export goods under Customs transit within Guangdong area before the goods arrive, fill in No. of license plate.

② Goods transported out of the territory by other means of transport: declaration for export goods under Customs transit within Guangdong area fill in No. of license plate; in other areas, leave the particular in blank.

(2)H2000 Customs procedures system

① Goods transported out of the territory by sea or inland waterway:

填报;广东省内提前报关的转关货物填报车牌号。

②其他运输方式:广东省内提前报关的转关货物填报车牌号;其他地区免予填报。

十五、贸易方式(监管方式)

本栏目应根据实际情况,按海关规定的《贸易方式代码表》选择填报相应的贸易方式简称或代码。

出口加工区内企业填制的《出口加工区进(出)境货物备案清单》应选择填报适用于出口加工区货物的监管方式简称或代码。

一份报关单只允许填报一种贸易方式。

加工贸易报关单特殊情况下填报要求如下:

(一)少量低值辅料(即5000美元以下,78种以内的低值辅料)按规定不使用《加工贸易手册》的,辅料进口报关单填报“低值辅料”。使用《加工贸易手册》的,按《加工贸易手册》上的贸易方式填报。

(二)外商投资企业按内外销比例为加工内销产品而进口的料件或进口供加工内销产品的料件,进口报关单填报“一般贸易”。

外商投资企业为加工出口产品全部使用国内料件的出口合同,成品出口报关单填报“一般贸易”。

(三)加工贸易料件结转或深加工结转货物,按批准的贸易方式填报。

(四)加工贸易料件转内销货物(及按料件补办进口手续的转内销成品、残次品、半成品)应填制进口报关单,本栏目填报“(来料或进料)料件内销”;加工贸易成品凭《征免税证明》转为享受减免税进口货物的,应分别填制进、出口报关单,本栏目填报“(来料或进料)成品减免”。

(五)加工贸易出口成品因故退运进口及复出口、加工贸易进口料件因换料退运出口及复运进口的,填报与《加工贸易手册》备案相应的退换监管方式,简称或代码。

(六)备料《加工贸易手册》中的料件结转入加工出口《加工贸易手册》的填报相应的来料或进料加工贸易方式。

(七)保税工厂加工贸易进出口货物,根据《加工贸易手册》填报相应的来料或进料加工贸易方式。

(八)加工贸易边角料内销和副产品内销,进口报关单应填报“(来料或进料)边角料内销”。

under en route Customs transit, fill in No. of Bill of Lading; under direct Customs transit, leave the particular in blank; in the case of declaration for export goods under Customs transit within Guangdong area before the goods arrive, fill in No. of license plate.

② Goods transported out of the territory by other means of transport: declaration for export goods under Customs transit within Guangdong area fill in No. of license plate; in other areas, leave the particular in blank.

15. Mode of Trade (Customs Procedure)

On the basis of fact, fill in the abbreviation and code of the suitable Customs procedure, which can be found in "Codes for Customs Procedures" prescribed by the Customs.

Enterprise within the export processing zone should fill in "the Filed Goods List for Entry/Exit of EPZ" with the abbreviation and code of the Customs procedure suitable for EPZ.

Each declaration only one Mode of Trade is allowed to fill in.

Specific requirements for processing trade are as follows:

(1) To import small amount low - value auxiliary materials (not more than 5,000 US dollars, not beyond the 78 kinds of low - value auxiliary materials) which according to the provisions need not use PT Handbook, fill in "low - value auxiliary material". Where PT Handbook has to be used, the content filled in should be in accordance with the Mode of Trade marked on PT Handbook.

(2) To import materials and components by Foreign - invested enterprise for the purpose of processing products for home use proportionally or wholly, fill in "Normal Transaction".

To export finished products by foreign - invested enterprise, which have been manufactured with all native materials and components, fill in "Normal Transaction".

(3) To close and transfer inward processing materials and components, or to close and transfer goods for supplementary processing, fill in Mode of Trade determined by prior authority.

(4) Materials and components for processing inward to be declared for home use (including making up an import declaration afterward for the materials and components of finished products which to be declared for home use), fill in "supplied/imported materials and components for home use" on import declaration; finished products of inward processing to be declared for home use with LRE certificate, fill in "supplied/imported materials and components for home use with LRE certificate" both on import declaration and export declaration.

(5) Sending back and reexport of finished products of inward processing, and sending back and reimport of materials and components for inward processing, fill in the abbreviation or code of corresponding Mode of Trade, which should be in accordance with PT Handbook.

(6) To close and transfer materials and components of PT Handbook for reservation into PT handbook for inward processing, fill in corresponding Mode of Trade of inward processing with supplied/imported materials.

(7) Import/export goods for inward processing by bonded factory, fill in corresponding Mode of Trade of inward processing with supplied/imported materials, which should be in accordance with PT Handbook.

(8) Leftover scraps or by - products of processing trade to be declared for home use, fill in "scraps to be declared for home use" on import declaration.

（九）加工贸易料件或成品放弃，进口报关单应填报“（进料料件或成品）放弃”。

(9) Materials/components or finished products of processing trade to be abandoned, fill in “Materials/components or finished products to be abandoned” on import declaration.

十六、征免性质

16. Nature of Levy, Reduction and Exemption of Customs Duties and Taxes

指海关对进出口货物实施征、减、免税管理的性质类别。

The term means the category of Customs duties and Taxes control subject to import/export goods.

本栏目应按照海关核发的《征免税证明》中批注的征免性质填报，或根据实际情况按海关规定的《征免性质代码表》选择填报相应的征免性质简称或代码。

Fill in the particular in accordance with the nature of levy, reduction and exemption marked on LRE Certificate, or on basis of fact choice the suitable abbreviation or code from "Codes for the Nature of Levy, Reduction and Exemption of Customs Duties and Taxes" prescribed by the Customs.

加工贸易报关单本栏目应按照海关核发的《加工贸易手册》中批注的征免性质填报相应的征免性质简称或代码。特殊情况下填报要求如下：

Declaration for inward processing, fill in the particular in accordance with the nature of levy, reduction and exemption marked on R handbook. Specific requirements are as follows:

（一）保税工厂经营的加工贸易，根据《加工贸易手册》填报“进料加工”或“来料加工”。

(1) Inward processing performed by bonded factory, fill in “inward processing with supplied/imported materials”, which should be in accordance with PT Handbook.

（二）外商投资企业按内外销比例为加工内销产品而进口料件，填报“一般征税”或其他相应征免性质。

(2) To import materials and components by Foreign – invested enterprise for the purpose of processing products for home use proportionally or wholly, fill in “Levy according to regulations” or other suitable Nature of Levy, Reduction and Exemption of Customs Duties and Taxes.

（三）加工贸易转内销货物，按实际应享受的征免性质填报（如一般征税、科教用品、其他法定等）。

(3) Goods for inward processing to be declared for home use, on basis of fact fill in the suitable Nature of Levy, Reduction and Exemption of Customs Duties and Taxes (for example, levy according to regulations, educational and scientific materials, other legal reduction and remission, etc.)

（四）料件退运出口、成品退运进口货物填报“其他法定”，（代码0299）。

(4) Materials and components sending back outward, or finished products sending back inward, fill in “other legal reduction and remission”.

（五）加工贸易结转货物本栏目为空。

(5) To close and transfer accounts of inward processing goods, leave the particular in blank.

一份报关单只允许填报一种征免性质。

Each declaration only one Nature of Levy, Reduction and Exemption of Customs Duties and Taxes is allowed to fill in.

十七、征税比例/结汇方式

17. Rate of Levy/Mode of Settlement

（一）征税比例

(1) Rate of Levy

仅用于“非对口合同进料加工”（代码0715）贸易方式下进口料件的进口报关单，填报海关规定的实际应征税比率，例如5%填报5，15%填报15。

The term Rate of Levy refers only to the particular on import declaration for inward processing with purchased materials and components under a non – reciprocal contact (code: 0715), fill in the rate of levy determined by the Customs, for example, 5 for 5%, 15 for 15%.

（二）结汇方式

(2) Mode of Settlement

出口报关单应填报结汇方式，即出口货物的发货人或其代理人收结外汇的方式。本栏目应按海关规定的《结汇方式代码表》选择填报相应的结汇方式名称或代码。

Mode of Settlement, that is the mode of bank's exchange settlement which consignor or one's agent has determined for the export goods, should be filled in on export declaration. Name and code of mode of settlement should be in accordance with "Codes for Modes of Bank's Exchange Settlement" prescribed by the Customs.

十八、许可证号

18. No. of License

应申领进（出）口许可证的货物，必须在此栏目填报商务部及其授权发证机关签发的进（出）口货物许可证的编号。

Import/export goods subject to license control, the No. of license issued by the Ministry of Foreign Trade and Economic Cooperation and its authorized issuing organizations must be filled in.

一份报关单只允许填报一个许可证号。

Each declaration only one No. of license is allowed to fill in.

十九、起运国（地区）/运抵国（地区）

19. Country whence Consigned/Country of Destination

起运国（地区）指进口货物直接运抵或者在运输中

Country whence Cosigned means the country whence the import goods

转国(地)未发生任何商业性交易的情况下运抵我国的起始发出的国家(地区)。

运抵国(地区)指出口货物离开我国关境直接运抵或者在运输中转国(地)未发生任何商业性交易的情况下最后运抵的国家(地区)。

对发生运输中转的货物,如中转地未发生任何商业性交易,则起、抵地不变,如中转地发生商业性交易,则以中转地作为起运/运抵国(地区)填报。

本栏目应按海关规定的《国别(地区)代码表》选择填报相应的起运国(地区)或运抵国(地区)中文名称或代码。

无实际进出境的,本栏目填报"中国"(代码0142)。

二十、装货港/指运港

装货港指进口货物在运抵我国关境前的最后一个境外装运港。

指运港指出口货物运往境外的最终目的港;最终目的港不可预知的,可按尽可能预知的目的港填报。

本栏目应根据实际情况按海关规定的《港口航线代码表》选择填报相应的港口中文名称或代码。

无实际进出境的,本栏目填报"中国境内"(代码0142)。

二十一、境内目的地/境内货源地

境内目的地指已知的进口货物在国内的消费、使用地或最终运抵地。

境内货源地指出口货物在国内的产地或原始发货地。

本栏目应根据进口货物的收货单位、出口货物生产厂家或发货单位所属国内地区,并按海关规定的《国内地区代码表》选择填报相应的国内地区名称或代码。

二十二、批准文号

出口报关单本栏目用于填报《出口收汇核销单》编号。

二十三、成交方式

本栏目应根据实际成交价格条款按海关规定的《成交方式代码表》选择填报相应的成交方式代码。

无实际进出境的,进口填报CIF价,出口填报FOB价。

二十四、运费

本栏目用于成交价格中不包含运费的进口货物或成交价格中含有运费的出口货物,应填报该份报关单所含全部货物的国际运输费用。可按运费单价、总价或运费

originally consigned.

Country of Destination means the country the outright export goods shall arrive in.

For goods which transshipment allowed, in the case of no commercial deal in the transship area, country whence cosigned/country of destination needs not to change; in the case of commercial deal occurs in the transship area, fill in the transshipment area as country whence cosigned/country of destination.

The particular should be declared with Chinese name or code of country whence cosigned/country of destination, which could be fund in "Codes for the Representation of Names of Countries and Regions" prescribed by the Customs.

Goods which are not in fact imported/exported, fill in "China" (code: 0142).

20. Port of Loading/Port of Destination

Port of loading means the last port outside of the territory where the import goods are loaded.

Port of Destination means the final destination port where the export goods are unloaded. In the case of destination port is unknown, fill in a predict destination port as close as possible.

The particular should be declared on basis of fact and in accordance with the Chinese name or code of the port prescribed by the Customs in "Codes for Ports and Shipping lines".

Goods which are not in fact imported/exported, fill in "within the territory of China" (code: 0142).

21. Destination area within the territory/Origin area within the territory

Destination area within the territory means the known area where the import goods shall be consumed, used, or the known area the import goods final reach.

Origin area within the territory means the area in which the export goods have been produced or origin…

The particular should be …

consignee of import goods, …

goods is situated, and in …

Names of Sub – entity of …

22. No. of Docu…

Fill in the No. … It could …

23. Trade T…

The partic…

of import/exp…

prescribed …

Good…

import, …

2…

I…

case o…

in the …

率三种方式之一填报，同时注明运费标记，并按海关规定的《货币代码表》选择填报相应的币种代码。

运保费合并计算的，运保费填报在本栏目。

运费标记“1”表示运费率，“2”表示每吨货物的运费单价，“3”表示运费总价。

（一）H883/EDI 通关系统

1. 运费率：直接填报运费率的数值，如：5% 的运费率填报为 5。

2. 运费单价：填报运费币值代码 +“/”+ 运费单价的数值 +“/”+ 运费单价标记，如：24 美元的运费单价填报为“502/24/2”。

3. 运费总价：填报运费币值代码 +“/”+ 运费总价的数值 +“/”+ 运费总价标记，如：7000 美元的运费总价填报为“502/7000/3”。

（二）H2000 通关系统

1. 运费标记填写在运费标记处。

2. 运费价格填写在运费价格处。

3. 运费币制填写在运费币制处。

二十五、保费

本栏目用于成交价格中不包含保险费的进口货物或成交价格中含有保险费的出口货物，应填报该份报关单所含全部货物国际运输的保险费用。可按保险费总价或保险费率两种方式之一填报，同时注明保险费标记，并按海关规定的《货币代码表》选择填报相应的币种代码。

运保费合并计算的，运保费填报在运费栏目中，本栏目免予填报。

保险费标记“1”表示保险费率，“3”表示保险费总价。

（一）H883/EDI 通关系统

1. 保费率：直接填报保费率的数值，如：3‰的保险费率填报为“0.3”。

2. 保费总价：填报保费币制代码 +“/”+ 保费总价

值 +“/”+ 保费总价标记，如：10000 港元保险费总

“110/10000/3”。

2000 通关系统

记填写在保费标记处。

写在保费总价处。

在保费币制处。

照《中华人民共和国进出口

价格或应从完税价格中

费率两种方式之一填

的《货币代码表》

be declared in three ways: freight rate, unit freight, or total freight. Meanwhile, fill in the category mark of freight and the code of currency, the latter should be in accordance with "Codes for the Representation of Currencies" prescribed by the Customs.

In the case of freight and insurance premiums are calculated together, fill in the freight and insurance premiums.

The category marks of freight are as follows: 1 is referred to fright rate, 2 is referred to unit freight, 3 is referred to total freight.

(一) H883/EDI Customs procedures system

Freight rate: fill in the numerical vale. For example, the freight rate is 5%, then fill in 5.

Unit freight: fill in code of currency/unit freight/category mark of unit freight, for example, unit freight is 24 US dollars, then fill in 502/24/2.

Total freight: fill in code of currency/total freight/mark of total freight, for example, total freight is 7000 US dollars, then fill in 502/7000/3.

(2) H2000 Customs procedures system

① Fill in mark of freight where it is required.

② Fill in numeral value of freight where it is required.

③ Fill in code of currency where it is required.

25. Insurance Premiums

International insurance premiums for the declared goods should be declared in the case of the transaction value of import goods does not cover the insurance premiums, or in the case of the transaction value of export goods covers the insurance premiums. It could be declared in two ways: insurance premium rate, or total insurance premium. Meanwhile, fill in the category mark of insurance premiums and the code of currency, the latter should be in accordance with "Codes for the Representation of Currencies" prescribed by the Customs.

In the case of freight and insurance premiums are calculated together, fill the freight and insurance premiums in the particular of freight.

The category marks of insurance premiums are as follows: 1 is referred to insurance premium rate, 3 is referred to total insurance premiums.

(1) H883/EDI Customs procedures system

Insurance premium rate: fill in the numeral value, for example, insurance premium rate is 3‰, then fill in 0.3.

Total insurance premium: fill in code of currency/total insurance premium/mark of total insurance premium, for example, total insurance is HKD10000, then fill in 110/10000/3.

(2) H2000 Customs procedures system

Fill in mark of insurance premium where it is required.

Fill in total insurance premium where it is required.

Fill in code of currency where it is required.

26. Incidental Expenses

The term means other expenses incurred for the goods which should be included in or deducted from the dutiable value in accordance with "Regulations of the People's Republic of China on Import and Export Duties". It could be declared in two ways: incidental expense rate, or total incidental expenses. Meanwhile, fill in the category mark of incidental expenses and the code of currency, the latter should be in accordance with "Codes for the Representation of Currencies" prescribed by the Customs.

应计入完税价格的杂费填报为正值或正率，应从完税价格中扣除的杂费填报为负值或负率。

杂费标记“1”表示杂费率，“3”表示杂费总价。

（一）H883/EDI 通关系统

1. 杂费率：直接填报杂费率的数值，如：应计入完税价格的 1.5% 的杂费率填报为“1.5”，应从完税价格中扣除的 1% 的回扣率填报为“-1”。

2. 杂费总价：填报杂费币制代码 +“/”+ 杂费总价的数值 +“/”+ 杂费总价标记，如：应计入完税价格的 500 英镑杂费总价填报为 303/500/3。

（二）H2000 通关系统

1. 杂费标记填写在杂费标记处。

2. 杂费总价填写在杂费总价处。

3. 杂费币制填写在杂费币制处。

二十七、件数

本栏目应填报有外包装的进（出）口货物的实际件数。特殊情况下填报要求如下：

（一）舱单件数为集装箱的，填报集装箱个数；

（二）舱单件数为托盘的，填报托盘数。

本栏目不得填报为零，裸装货物填报为“1”。

二十八、包装种类

本栏目应根据进出口货物的实际外包装种类，按海关规定的《包装种类代码表》选择填报相应的包装种类代码。

二十九、毛重（公斤）

指货物及其包装材料的重量之和。

本栏目填报进（出）口货物实际毛重，计量单位为公斤，不足一公斤的填报为“1”。

三十、净重（公斤）

指货物的毛重减去外包装材料后的重量，即商品本身的实际重量。

本栏目填报进（出）口货物的实际净重，计量单位为公斤，不足一公斤的填报为“1”。

三十一、集装箱号

集装箱号是在每个集装箱箱体两侧标示的全球唯一的编号。

本栏目用于填报和打印集装箱编号及数量。集装箱数量四舍五入填报整数，非集装箱货物填报为“0”。

（一）H883/EDI 通关系统

填报：一个集装箱号 +“*”+ 集装箱数 +“（折合标准集装箱数）。如：TEXU3605231 * 1（1）表示 1 个标准集装箱；TEXU3605231 * 2（3）表示 2 个集装箱，折合为 3 个标准集装箱，其中一个箱号为 TEXU3605231。

在多于一个集装箱的情况下，其余集装箱编号打印在备注栏或随附清单上。

（二）H2000 通关系统

Incidental expenses should be included in the dutiable value, fill in positive value or positive rate, incidental expenses should be deducted from the dutiable value, fill in negative value or negative rate.

The category marks of incidental expenses are as follows: 1 is referred to incidental expense rate, 3 is referred to total incidental expense.

(1) H883/EDI Customs procedures system

① Incidental expense rate: fill in numeral value, for example, positive incidental expense rate is 1.5%, then fill in 1.5; negative discount rate is 1%, then fill in -1.

② Total incidental expense: fill in code of currency/numeral value of total incidental expense/mark of total incidental expense, for example, positive total expense is GBP 500, then fill in 303/500/3.

(2) H2000 Customs procedures system

① Fill in mark of incidental expenses where it is required.

② Fill in total incidental expense where it is required.

③ Fill in code of currency where it is required.

27. Number of Packages

Fill in the actual number of packages. In special cases, requirements are as follows:

(1) Number of packages in manifest is number of containers, fill in number of containers;

(2) Number of packages in manifest is number of pallets, fill in number of pallets.

Fill in 0 for the particular is not allowed, for nude cargo fill in 1.

28. Kind of Package

Fill in actual kind of package, in accordance with “Codes for Kind of Package” prescribed by the Customs.

29. Gross Weight

The term means the total weight of the goods, including their packing materials.

Fill in actual gross weight of the import/export goods, unit of measure should be kilogram, in the case of less than 1 kilogram, fill in 1.

30. Net Weight

The term means the actual weight of the goods, that is gross weight minus weight of packing materials.

Fill in actual net weight of the import/export goods, unit of measure should be kilogram, in the case of less than 1 kilogram, fill in 1.

31. Container No.

Container No. refers to the No. marked on each side of the container, which is sole number in the world.

Fill in container No. and number of containers. Number of containers should be declared with whole number, decimal should be rounded off. For goods which are not carried in container, fill in “0”.

(1) H883/EDI Customs procedures system

Fill in one container No. * number of containers (convert into XX standard containers). For example, TEXU3605231 * 1(1) means 1 standard container; TEXU3605231 * 2(3) means 2 containers, convert into 3 standard containers, No. of one of the containers is TEXU3605231.

In the case of more than one container, the rest No. of container should be printed in the box of remarks or in attached list.

(2) H2000 Customs procedures system

填报在集装箱表中，一个集装箱填一条记录，分别填报集装箱号、规格和自重。

三十二、随附单据

指随进（出）口货物报关单一并向海关递交的单证或文件。合同、发票、装箱单、进出口许可证等必备的随附单证不在本栏目填报。

（一）H883 通关系统

本栏目应按海关规定的《监管证件名称代码表》选择填报相应证件的代码，证件编号填报在"标记唛码及备注"栏后半部分。

（二）2000 通关系统

本栏目分为随附单据代码和随附单据编号两项，其中代码栏应按海关规定的《监管证件名称代码表》选择填报相应证件的代码填报，编号栏应填报相应证件编号。

（三）优惠贸易协定项下进出口货物

"Y"为原产地证书代码。优惠贸易协定代码选择"01"、"02"、"03"或"04"填报：

"01"为"曼谷协定及中巴优惠贸易安排"项下的进口货物；

"02"为"中国与东盟全面经济合作框架协定项下"早期收获"方案"（简称"中国东盟早期收获"），包括"中泰蔬菜水果协定"项下的进口货物以及原产于老挝、柬埔寨、缅甸的进口货物；

"03"为"内地与香港紧密经贸关系安排"（香港 CEPA）项下的进口货物；

"04"为"内地与澳门紧密经贸关系安排"（澳门 CEPA）项下的进口货物。

具体填报要求如下：

1. 实行原产地证书联网管理的，H2000 通关系统下，在本栏目随附单证代码项下填写"Y"，在随附单证编号项下的"< >"内填写优惠贸易协定代码，例如香港 CEPA 项下的进口商品，应填报为："Y"和"<03 >"；H883/EDI 系统下，此栏不填报原产地证书相关内容。

2. 未实行原产地证书联网管理的，H2000 通关系统下，在报关单"随附单据"栏随附单证代码项下填写"Y"，在随附单证编号项下的"< >"内填写优惠贸易协定代码+"："+需证商品序号，例如《曼谷协定》项下的进口报关单中第 1 到第 3 项和第 5 项为优惠贸易协定项下商品，应填报为："<01：1 -3，5 >"；H833/EDI 通关系统下，此栏不填报原产地证书相关内容。

优惠贸易协定项下出口货物，本栏目填报原产地证书代码和编号。

三十三、用途/生产厂家

进口货物填报用途，应根据进口货物的实际用途按海关规定的《用途代码表》选择填报相应的用途代码，如"以产顶进"填报"13"。

生产厂家指出口货物的境内生产企业。本栏目供必要时手工填写。

Fill required data in the list of containers, each container should be recorded separately with No. of container, specification and dead weight.

32. Supporting Documents

The term means the supporting documents subject to Customs control, other than the essential accompanying documents such as contract, invoice, packing list or license.

(1) H883/EDI Customs procedures system

Fill in the particular with the code of corresponding documents, which could be found in "Codes for Supporting Documents Subject to Customs Control" prescribed by the Customs. The serial No. of supporting documents should be filled in the end - half of the box of Marks & No. /Remarks.

(2) H2000 Customs procedures system

Code and serial No. of supporting documents are both required to be filled in. The code could be found in "Codes for Supporting Documents Subject to Customs Control" prescribed by the Customs. The serial No. of supporting documents should be filled where it is required.

(3) Import/export goods under preferential trade agreement

Code for Certificate of Origin is "Y". Codes for preferential trade agreements are as follows:

01 refers to import goods under "Bangkok Agreement and Preferential Trade Arrangement between China and Pakistan".

02 refers to import goods under "Early Harvest Plan under the China - ASEAN Overall Economic Cooperation Frame", including "China - Thailand Fruits Agreement" and "Special Preferential Tariff Rates for Import Goods Originally Produced in Laos, Kampuchea and Burma".

03 refers import goods under "Mainland - Hong Kong CEPA".

04 refers import goods under "Mainland - Macao CEPA".

Specific requirements are as follows:

1. For those the on - line Control of Certificate of Origin has been put into practice, in H2000 Customs procedures system, fill in Y and < code for preferential trade agreement >, for example, import goods under Mainland - Hong Kong CEPA, fill in Y and < 03 >; in H883/EDI Customs procedures system, content related to Certificate of Origin shall not be filled in here.

2. For those the on - line Control of Certificate of Origin has not been put into practice, in H2000 Customs procedures system, fill in Y and < code for preferential trade agreement: item numbers of goods with supporting documents >, for example, item 1 - 3, and item 5 are goods under Bangkok Agreement, then fill in Y and < 01: 1 - 3, 5 >; in H883/EDI Customs procedures system, content related to Certificate of Origin shall not be filled in here.

Export goods under preferential trade agreement, fill in code and serial No of Certificate of Origin.

33. Use of Imported Goods/Manufacturer

For import goods, fill in the code of use of imported goods, which could be found in "Codes for Use of Imported Goods" prescribed by the Customs. For example, for substitution production, fill in 13.

Manufacturer refers to the manufacturer of the export goods within the territory. The particular may be written by hand under necessary circum-

三十四、标记唛码及备注

（一）H883/EDI 通关系统

1. 本栏目上部用于打印以下内容具体填报如下：

（1）标记唛码中除图形以外的文字、数字。

（2）受外商投资企业委托代理其进口投资设备、物品的进出口企业名称。

（3）加工贸易结转货物及凭《征免税证明》转内销货物，其对应的备案号应填报在本栏目，即“转至（自）XXXXXXXXXXXX手册”。

（4）实行原产地证书联网管理的优惠贸易协定项下进口货物，填写“<”+“协”+“优惠贸易协定代码”+“>”，例如香港 CEPA 项下进口报关单应填为：“<协03>”；未实行原产地证书联网管理的优惠贸易协定项下进口货物，填写“<”+“协”+“优惠贸易协定代码”+“：”+“需证商品序号”+“>”，例如《曼谷协定》项下进口报关单中第 1 项到第 3 项和第 5 项为优惠贸易协定项下商品，应填为：“<协01：1－3，5>”。

（5）其他申报时必须说明的事项。

2. 本栏目下部供填报随附单据栏中监管证件的编号，具体填报如下：

（1）监管证件代码＋“：”＋监管证件号码。一份报关单多个监管证件的，连续填写。

（2）一票货物多个集装箱的，在本栏目打印其余的集装箱号（最多 160 字节，其余集装箱号手工抄写）。

（二）2000 通关系统

1. 标记唛码中除图形以外的文字、数字。

2. 受外商投资企业委托代理其进口投资设备、物品的进出口企业名称。

3. 与本报关单有关联关系的，同时在业务管理规范方面又有要求填报的备案号，如加工贸易结转货物及凭《征免税证明》转内销货物，其对应的备案号应填报在“关联备案”栏。

4. 与本报关单有关联关系的，同时在业务管理规范方面又有要求填报的报关单号，应填报在“关联报关单”栏。

加工贸易结转类的报关单，应先办理进口报关，并将进口报关单号填入出口报关单的关联报关单号栏。

三十五、项号

本栏目分两行填报及打印。

第一行打印报关单中的商品排列序号。

第二行专用于加工贸易等已备案的货物，填报和打印该项货物在《加工贸易手册》中的项号。

加工贸易合同项下进出口货物，必须填报与《加工贸易手册》一致的商品项号，所填报项号用于核销对应项号下的料件或成品数量。特殊情况下填报要求如下：

stance.

34. Marks & No./Remarks.

(1) H883/EDI Customs procedures system

1. On top of the box, particulars should be printed are as follows:

① The letters and numerals of the Marks & No., except graphics.

② Name of the importer who is entrusted by foreign – invested enterprise to import its investment equipments and articles.

③ To close and transfer inward processing goods or to declare inward processing goods for home use with LRE Certificate, fill in the Registration No., that is “transfer to/from XXXXXXXXXXXX PT Handbook”.

④ Declaring for goods subject to conventional tariff, specific requirements are as follows: for those the on – line Control of Certificate of Origin has been put into practice, fill in <协 + code of preferential trade agreement>, for example, import goods under Mainland – Hong Kong CEPA, fill in <协03>; for those the on – line Control of Certificate of Origin has not been put into practice, fill in <协 + code of preferential trade agreement: item numbers of goods with supporting documents>, for example, item 1 – 3, and item 5 are goods under Bangkok Agreement, then fill in <协01: 1 – 3, 5>.

⑤ Other necessary particulars should be declared.

2. On bottom of the box, fill in No. of supporting documents, specific requirements are as follows:

① Code of supporting document + “:” + No. of supporting documents. One declaration with multiple supporting documents, fill in the numbers continually.

② One consignment carried in many containers, print the rest numbers of containers (not exceeding 160 bytes, the remaining should write by hand).

(2) H2000 Customs procedures system

1. The letters and numerals of the Marks & No., except graphics.

2. Name of the importer who is entrusted by foreign – invested enterprise to import its investment equipments and articles.

3. Related Registration No: Fill in the Registration No which is related to declaration herein and is required by provision of Customs control, for example, to close and transfer inward processing goods or to declare inward processing goods for home use with LRE certificate, fill in the Registration No. of PT Handbook.

4. Related serial No of Declaration: Fill in the serial No of declaration which is related to declaration herein and is required by provision of Customs control.

To close and transfer inward processing goods, import declaration formality should be fulfilled first, then fill in the serial No of import declaration on the export declaration.

35. Item No.

Particulars in this box should printed in two lines.

Item numbers of goods of the declaration should print in the first line.

The second line is used for filed goods of inward processing, fill in registered item numbers of the goods in PT Handbook.

For import/export goods under processing trade contract stipulations, the item numbers filled in should be in accordance with the item numbers of PT Handbook, so that the quantity of materials, components or finished products can be cancelled after verification. In special cases, filling re-

（一）深加工结转货物，分别按照《加工贸易手册》中的进口料件项号和出口成品项号填报。

（二）料件结转货物（包括料件、成品和半成品折料），出口报关单按照转出《加工贸易手册》中进口料件的项号填报；进口报关单按照转进《加工贸易手册》中进口料件的项号填报。

（三）料件复出货物（包括料件、边角料、来料加工半成品折料），出口报关单按照《加工贸易手册》中进口料件的项号填报；料件退换货物（包括料件、不包括半成品），出口报关单按照《加工贸易手册》中进口料件的项号填报。

（四）成品退运货物，退运进境报关单和复运出境报关单按照《加工贸易手册》原出口成品的项号填报。

（五）加工贸易料件转内销货物（及按料件补办进口手续的转内销成品、半成品、残次品）应填制进口报关单，本栏目填报《加工贸易手册》进口料件的项号。加工贸易边角料、副产品内销，本栏目填报《加工贸易手册》中对应的料件项号。当边角料或副产品对应一个以上料件项号时，填报主要料件项号。

（六）加工贸易成品凭《征免税证明》转为享受减免税进口货物的，应先办理进口报关手续。进口报关单本栏目填报《征免税证明》中的项号，出口报关单本栏目填报《加工贸易手册》原出口成品项号，进、出口报关单货物数量应一致。

（七）加工贸易料件、成品放弃，本栏目应填报《加工贸易手册》中的项号。半成品放弃的应按单耗折回料件，以料件放弃申报，本栏目填报《加工贸易手册》中对应的料件项号。

（八）加工贸易副产品退运出口、结转出口或放弃，本栏目应填报《加工贸易手册》中新增的变更副产品的出口项号。

（九）经海关批准实行加工贸易联网监管的企业，对按海关联网监管要求企业需申报报关清单的，应在向海关申报货物进出口（包括形式进出口）报关单前，向海关申报“清单”。一份报关清单对应一份报关单，报关单商品项由报关清单归并而得。加工贸易电子帐册报关单中项号、品名、规格等栏目的填制规范比照《加工贸易手册》。

优惠贸易协定项下实行原产地证书联网管理的报关单分两行填写。第一行填写报关单中商品排列序号，第二行填写对应的原产地证书上的“商品项号”。

quirements are as follows:

(1) To close and transfer accounts of goods for supplementary processing, fill in respectively the item numbers of import materials and components and the item numbers of export finished products in accordance with the PT Handbook.

(2) To close and transfer accounts of materials and components (including materials and components converted from finished products or semi - finished products), fill in export declaration the item numbers of import materials and components transferred out of PT Handbook, fill in import declaration the item numbers of import materials and components transferred into PT Handbook.

(3) To send back materials and components (including scraps, materials and components converted from semi - finished products), fill in export declaration the item numbers of import materials and components in accordance with PT Handbook; to replace materials and components (not including semi - finished products), fill in export declaration the item numbers of import materials and components in accordance with PT Handbook.

(4) To sent back finished goods, fill in sending back import declaration and re - export declaration the item numbers of the original export finished products in accordance with PT Handbook.

(5) Inward processing materials and components to be declared for home use (including making up import declaration for materials and components of finished products which are declared for home use, semi - finished products and defective goods), fill in import declaration the item numbers of import materials and components in accordance with PT Handbook. Scraps and byproducts of inward processing to be declared for home use, fill in import declaration the item numbers of import materials and components in accordance with PT Handbook. In the case of scraps and byproducts related to more than one item numbers, fill in the main item number.

(6) Finished products of inward processing to be declared for home use with LRE certificate, import declaration formality should be fulfilled first. Fill in import declaration the item numbers of LRE certificate, fill in export declaration the item numbers of original export finished products, the quantity of import declaration and export declaration should be the same.

(7) To abandon materials and components of inward processing, fill in item numbers filed in PT Handbook. To abandon semi - finished products, the semi - finished products should be converted into materials and components first, then to declare abandonment of materials and components, fill in item numbers filed in PT Handbook.

(8) To send back, to close and export, or to abandon byproducts of inward processing, fill in the item numbers of alternated byproducts newly added in PT Handbook.

(9) Approved enterprise under processing trade networking Customs control should produce a detailed list of goods to the Customs before producing import/export declaration or closing and transferring declaration. One detailed list matches one declaration, item numbers in declaration should be the result in adding up goods of the detailed list. Particulars in electronic account book, such as item numbers, description and specifications of goods, should be filled in accordance with PT handbook.

Declaring for goods under preferential trade agreement, for those the on - line Control of Certificate of Origin has been put into practice, fill the particulars in two lines. Fill in item numbers of goods of the declaration in

三十六、商品编号

指按商品分类编码规则确定的进出口货物的商品编号。此栏目分为商品编号和附加编号两栏,其中商品编号栏应填报《中华人民共和国海关进出口税则》8位税则号列,附加编号应填报商品编号附加的第9、10位附加编号。

《加工贸易手册》中商品编号与实际商品编号不符的,应按实际商品编号填报。

三十七、商品名称、规格型号

本栏目分两行填报及打印。

第一行打印进出口货物规范的中文商品名称,第二行打印规格型号,必要时可加注原文。

具体填报要求如下:

(一)商品名称及规格型号应据实填报,并与所提供的商业发票相符。

(二)商品名称应当规范,规格型号应当足够详细,以能满足海关归类、审价及许可证件管理要求为准。根据商品属性,本栏目填报内容包括:品名、牌名、规格、型号、成份、含量、等级、用途、功能等。

(三)加工贸易等已备案的货物,本栏目填报录入的内容必须与备案登记中同项号下货物的名称与规格型号一致。

(四)对需要海关签发《货物进口证明书》的车辆,商品名称栏应填报"车辆品牌+排气量(注明cc)+车型(如越野车、小轿车等)"。进口汽车底盘可不填报排气量。车辆品牌应按照《进口机动车辆制造厂名称和车辆品牌中英文对照表》中"签注名称"一栏的要求填报。规格型号栏可填报"汽油型"等。

(五)同一收货人使用同一运输工具同时运抵的进口货物应同时申报,视为同一报验状态,据此确定其归类。成套设备、减免税货物如需分批进口货物实际进口时,应按照实际报验状态确定归类。

(六)加工贸易边角料和副产品内销,边角料复出口,本栏目填报其报验状态的名称和规格型号。属边角料、副产品、残次品、受灾保税货物且按规定需加以说明的,应在本栏目中填注规定的字样。

三十八、数量及单位

指进出口商品的实际数量及计量单位。

本栏目分三行填报及打印。

具体填报要求如下:

(一)进出口货物必须按海关法定计量单位填报。

the first line. Fill in item numbers of goods printed on Certificate of Origin in the second line.

36. HS Code

The term means the HS heading No prescribed by the Customs for import/export goods. Fill in the 8 digits of HS code first, then fill in the subsidiary 9th and 10th digits of HS code.

In the case of the HS Code of PT Handbook is not same as the HS code of actual goods, fill in the HS code of actual goods.

37. Description and Specifications of Goods

This box should be printed in two lines.

In first line, print name of goods in Chinese. In second line, print specifications of goods, if necessary, print annotations in original language.

Specific requirements are as follows:

(1) Name and specifications of goods should be declared on the basis of fact, and should be in accordance with the provided commercial invoice.

(2) Name of goods should be normalized and specifications should be full and accurate enough to meet the needs of classification of goods, checking of value, and examination of licenses for Customs purposes. The particulars in this box including name of goods, trade mark, specifications, model numbers, chemical composition and content, grade, etc.

(3) Where goods have been registered, such as goods of processing trade, name and specifications of goods should be in accordance with the content of the same item No in registers.

(4) To import motor vehicles for which "certificate of Import" should be issued by the Customs, fill in the first line with "brand + cylinder capacity (cc) + type (for example cross-country cars, saloon cars, etc.). To import chassis of motor vehicles, the particular "cylinder capacity" need not to be filled. Filled brand should be in accordance with the requirements prescribed in "Chinese-English List of Names of Manufacturers and Brand of Import Motor Vehicles". Fill specifications in the second line, for example, with spark-ignition internal combustion reciprocating piston engine.

(5) Import goods of the same consignee, carried by the same means of transport, arrived at the same time, should be declared at the same time and be considered as in the same condition of examination, thus to determine the classification of the import goods. Sets of equipment, goods granted reduction or exemption of Customs duties and taxes, in the case of partial shipment, the classification of goods should be determined in accordance with actual examination condition.

(6) Scraps and byproducts of inward processing to be declared for home use, scraps to be declared to send back, fill in the description and specification in actual examination condition. Classified as scraps, byproducts, defective goods or bonded goods damaged in disaster, in the case of an annotation is required, fill in the annotation prescribed by provisions.

38. Quantity and Measure Unit

The term means the actual quantity and measure unit of import/export goods.

There are three lines in the box to print the particulars.

Specific requirements are as follows:

(1) Import/export goods must be declared in legal primary measure u-

法定第一计量单位及数量打印在本栏目第一行。

（二）凡海关列明第二计量单位的，必须报明该商品第二计量单位及数量，打印在本栏目第二行。无第二计量单位的，本栏目第二行为空；

（三）成交计量单位及数量应当填报并打印在第三行。

（四）法定计量单位为“公斤”的数量填报，特殊情况下填报要求如下：

1. 装入可重复使用的包装容器的货物，按货物的净重填报，如罐装同位素、罐装氧气及类似品等，应扣除其包装容器的重量；

2. 使用不可分割包装材料和包装容器的货物，按货物的净重填报（即包括内层直接包装的净重重量），如采用供零售包装的酒、罐头、化妆品及类似品等；

3. 按照商业惯例以公量重计价的商品，应按公量重填报，如未脱脂羊毛、羊毛条等；

4. 采用以毛重作为净重计价的货物，可按毛重填报，如粮食、饲料等价格较低的农副产品；

5. 成套设备、减免税货物如需分批进口，货物实际进口时，应按照实际报验状态确定数量；

6. 根据 HS 归类规则，零部件按整机归类的，法定第一数量填报“0.1”，有法定第二数量的，按照货物实际净重申报；

7. 具有完整品或制成品基本特征的不完整品、未制成品，按照 HS 归类规则应按完整品归类的，申报数量按照构成完整品的实际数量申报。

（五）加工贸易等已备案的货物，成交计量单位必须与《加工贸易手册》中同项号下货物的计量单位一致，加工贸易边角料和副产品内销、边角料复出口，本栏目填报其报验状态的计量单位。

三十九、原产国（地区）/最终目的国（地区）

原产国（地区）指进口货物的生产、开采或加工制造国家（地区）。

最终目的国（地区）指已知的出口货物的最终实际消费、使用或进一步加工制造国家（地区）。

本栏目应按海关规定的《国别（地区）代码表》选择填报相应的国家（地区）名称或代码。

加工贸易报关单特殊情况填报要求如下：

（一）料件结转货物，出口报关单填报“中国”（代码 0142），进口报关单填报原料件生产国。

（二）深加工结转货物，进出口报关单均填报“中国”

nit prescribe by the Customs. Print the quantity and legal primary measure unit in the first line.

(2) Where legal secondary measure unit prescribed by the Customs is adopted, print the quantity and secondary measure unit in the second line. Where secondary measure unit is not adopted, leave the line in blank.

(3) Transaction measure unit and quantity should be printed in the third line.

(4) For filling quantity in legal measure unit, specific requirements are as follows:

① Goods packed in packing containers suitable for repetitive use, fill in net weight of the goods, for example, canned isotopes, canned oxygen and other similar goods, weight of the container should be deducted.

② Goods packed with inseparable packing materials and packing containers, fill in net weight of the goods (including weight of inner package), for example, bottled wine, canned food, cosmetics or other similar goods packed for detail sales.

③ Goods priced by metric weight in line with commercial practice, fill in metric weight, for example, greasy wool, wool tops and etc.

④ Goods price by gross weight instead of net weight, fill in gross weight shall be allowed, for example, lower - priced agricultural and side-line products, such as cereals and feedstuffs.

⑤ Sets of equipment, goods granted reduction and exemption of Customs duties and taxes, in the case of partial shipment, quantity should be determined according to the actual examination condition when they are presented.

⑥ In accordance with the rule of classification of HS, complete or finished articles presented unassembled or disassembled, fill in 0.1 for the legal primary measure unit, where legal secondary measure unit is adopted, print also the quantity and secondary measure unit of actual net weight.

⑦ Incomplete or unfinished articles having the essential character of complete or finished articles, falling to be classified as complete or finished articles by virtue of the rule of classification of HS, fill in actual quantity of complete or finished articles.

(5) Where goods have been registered, such as goods of processing trade, transaction measure unit of goods should be in accordance with the content of the same item No in PT Handbook.

39. Country of Origin of Goods/Country of Final Destination

The term Country of Origin of Goods means the country in which the import goods have been produced, extracted or manufactured.

The term Country of Final Destination means the known country in which the export goods shall be consumed, used or further manufactured.

Fill in the corresponding name or code for representation of the country, which could be found in "Codes for the Representation of Names of Countries and Regions" prescribe by the Customs.

Specific requirements for goods declaration of processing trade are as follows:

(1) To close and transfer accounts of inward processing materials and components for home use, fill in "中国" (code: 0142) on export declaration, fill in the country of manufacturer of the materials and components on import declaration.

(2) To close and transfer accounts of inward processing goods for sup-

（代码“0142”）。

（三）料件复运出境货物，填报实际最终目的国；加工出口成品因故退运境内的，填报“中国”（代码“0142”），复运出境时填报实际最终目的国。

（四）加工贸易转内销，最终目的（地区）需区分两种情况：

1. 料件内销时，原产国（地区）按料件的生产国（即料件进口时的原产国）填报；

2. 加工成品转内销时，填报“中国”（代码“0142”）。

（五）料件内销货物，属加工成品、半成品、残次品、副产品状态内销的，进口报关单本栏目均填报“中国”（代码“0142”）。属剩余料件状态内销的，进口报关单填报原料件生产国。

四十、单价

本栏目应填报同一项号下进出口货物实际成交的商品单位价格。

海关估价时，应在H2000通关系统“海关单价”栏修改。

无实际成交价格的，本栏目填报货值。

四十一、总价

本栏目应填报同一项号下进出口货物实际成交的商品总价。

海关估价时，应在H2000通关系统“海关总价”栏修改。

无实际成交价格的，本栏目填报货值。

四十二、币制

指进出口货物实际成交价格的币种。

本栏目应根据实际成交情况按海关规定的《货币代码表》选择填报相应的货币名称或代码，如《货币代码表》中无实际成交币种，需转换后填报。

四十三、征免

指海关对进出口货物进行征税、减税、免税或特案处理的实际操作方式。

本栏目应按照海关核发的《征免税证明》或有关政策规定，对报关单所列每项商品选择填报海关规定的《征减免税方式代码表》中相应的征减免税方式。

加工贸易报关单应根据《加工贸易手册》中备案的征免规定填报。

《加工贸易手册》中备案的征免规定为“保金”或“保函”的，不能按备案的征免规定填报，而应填报“全免”。

plementary processing, fill in“中国”(code: 0142) on either import or export declaration.

(3) To send back inward processing materials and components, fill in actual country of destination; where the finished products have been sent back due to certain reasons, fill in“中国”(code: 0142) for entry, fill in actual country of destination for re – export.

(4) Goods of inward processing to be declared for home use, Country of Origin of Goods/Country of Final Destination depends on two different conditions:

① Materials and components of inward processing to be declared for home use, fill in country of manufacturer of the materials and components (that is country of origin of the materials and components).

② Finished products of inward processing to be declared for home use, fill in“中国”(code:“0142”).

(5) Goods of inward processing to be declared for home use, in the state of finished products, semi – finished products, defective products or byproducts, fill in“中国”(code: 0142) on import declaration; in state of leftover scraps, fill in country of manufacturer of the materials and components.

40. Unit Price

Fill in the actual transaction unit price of the goods of the same item No.

In H2000 Customs procedures system, where price is assessed by Customs, the unit price should be revised as Customs unit price.

Where no actual transaction unit price could be quoted, fill in unit value of goods.

41. Total Amount

Fill in the actual transaction total amount of the goods of the same item No.

In H2000 Customs procedures system, where price is assessed by Customs, the total amount should be revised as Customs total amount.

Where no actual transaction total amount could be quoted, fill in total value of goods.

42. Currency System

The term means the kind of currency of the actual transaction price of import/export goods.

Fill in the name or code of currency in accordance with “Codes for Representation of Currencies” prescribed by the Customs. Where the kind of currency of actual transaction price is not included in “Codes for Representation of Currencies”, convert it before fill in.

43. Procedure of LRE

The term means the actual procedure of levy, reduction and exemption of Customs duties and taxes to the import/export goods.

For goods of each item No. of the declaration, on the basis of LRE certificate issued by the Customs or on the basis of relative policies stipulated by national legislation, fill in a corresponding procedure in accordance with “Codes for Type of Levy, reduction and Exemption of Customs Duties and Taxes” prescribed by the Customs.

Declaration for goods of processing trade, fill in the LRE procedure registered in PT Handbook.

In the case of the LRE procedure registered in PT Handbook is “security deposit” or “letter of guarantee”, fill in “relief from all duties and ta-

四十四、税费征收情况

本栏目供海关批注进(出)口货物税费征收及减免情况。

四十五、录入员

本栏目用于记录预录入操作人员的姓名并打印。

四十六、录入单位

本栏目用于记录并打印电子数据报关单的录入单位名称。

四十七、填制日期

指报关单的填制日期。电子数据报关单的填制日期由计算机自动打印。

(一)在 H883/EDI 通关系统中,本栏目为 6 位数,顺序为年、月、日各 2 位。

(二)在 H2000 通关系统中,本栏目为 8 位数字,顺序为年(4 位)、月(2 位)、日(2 位)。

四十八、海关审单批注栏

本栏目指供海关内部作业时签注的总栏目,由海关关员手工填写在预录入报关单上。

其中"放行"栏填写海关对接受申报的进出口货物作出放行决定的日期。

本规则所述尖括号(< >)、逗号(,)、连接符(-)、冒号(:)等标点符号及数字都必须使用非中文状态下的半角字符。

xes" other than "reduction and remission according to registered procedure".

44. State of LRE

This box leaves for the Customs to remark the state of levy, reduction and exemption of Customs duties and taxes to the import/export goods.

45. Declaration Maker(Natural Person)

The particular is specially used for recording name of the natural person who made the pre - entry declaration.

46. Declaration Maker (Legal Person)

The particular is specially used for recording name of the legal person who made the electronic data declaration.

47. Date of Making

The term means the date of declaration making. For pre - entry and EDI declaration, the date shall be automatically printed by computer.

In H883/EDI Customs system, the date shall be marked with six numerals in sequence of year, month and day.

In H833/EDI Customs system, the date shall be marked with eight numerals in sequence of year, month and day.

48. Checking of the Declaration, Examination of the Goods

This box is intended to show annotations and comments on flow process within the Customs office, which shall be handwritten by Customs officer on pre - entry declaration.

The column of "Release of goods" shall be filled with the date the Customs authorities grant release declared import/export goods.

For the purpose of the standards, the above mentioned angle brackets (< >), comma(,), hyphen(-) and numerals should be printed with half - angle characters in non - Chinese input state.

海关总署关于优惠贸易协定项下进口货物的报关单填制规范公告

2005 年第 69 号

为保证优惠贸易协定项下进口货物顺利通关，根据 2006 年《中华人民共和国进出口税则》，现将优惠贸易协定项下进口货物的报关单填制规范公告如下：

一、报关单填制规范中的“原产地证书代码”和“优惠贸易协定代码”

“原产地证书代码”为“Y”。

“优惠贸易协定代码”目前为：“01”、“02”、“03”、“04”、“05”、“06”、“07”、“08”。

填制要求：

属于“亚太贸易协定”项下的进口货物填“01”；

属于“中国—东盟自贸区”项下的进口货物填“02”；

属于“内地与香港紧密经贸关系安排”（香港 CEPA）项下的进口货物填“03”；

属于“内地与澳门紧密经贸关系安排”（澳门 CEPA）项下的进口货物填“04”。

属于“对非洲特惠待遇”项下的进口货物填“05”；

属于“台湾水果零关税措施”项下的进口货物填“06”；

属于“中巴自贸区”项下的进口货物填“07”；

属于“中智自贸区”项下的进口货物填“08”。

二、实行原产地证书联网管理的具体填制要求

（一）“备案号”栏：填写“Y”＋原产地证书编号。香港、澳门 CEPA 项下进口报关单填写“Y”＋11 位原产地证书编号。

（二）“随附单据”栏：使用海关 H2000 通关系统申报的，在本栏随附单证代码项下填写“Y”，在随附单证编号项下的“< >”内填写“优惠贸易协定代码”。使用海关 H883/EDI 通关系统申报的，此栏不填报原产地证书相关内容。

（三）“备注”栏：使用海关 H883/EDI 通关系统申报的，填写“<”＋“协”＋“优惠贸易协定代码”＋“>”。例如香港 CEPA 项下进口报关单应填为：“<协 03 >”。使用海关 H2000 通关系统申报的，此栏不填报原产地证书相关内容。

（四）“项号”栏：分两行填写。第一行填写报关单中商品排列序号，第二行填写对应的原产地证书上的“商

General Administration of Customs P. R. C. Announcement for Standards of Filling Declaration for Import Goods Stipulated Under Preferential Trading Agreements

No. 72 2003

For the purpose of ensuring import goods stipulated under preferential trading agreements to pass the Customs expeditiously, herein the standards of filling declaration for import goods stipulated under preferential trading agreements are announced as follows:

1. Supplement the standards of filling declaration with “Code for Certificate of Origin” and “Codes for Preferential Trading Agreements”

Code for Certificate of Origin is “Y”.

At present, Codes for Preferential Trading Agreements are “01”, “02”, “03”, “04”、“05”、“06”、“07”、“08”. Specific filling requirements are as follows:

For import goods stipulated under Asia – pacific Trade Treaty, fill in 01;

For import goods stipulated under China – ASEAN Free Trade Zone fill in 02;

For import goods stipulated under “Mainland-Hong Kong Close Economic and Trade Relationship Promotion Arrangement” (Hong Kong CEPA), fill in 03;

For import goods stipulated under “Mainland-Macao Close Economic and Trade Relationship Promotion Arrangement” (Macao CEPA), fill in 04;

For import goods stipulated under “Special Preferential for African”, fill in 05

For import goods stipulated under “Taiwan fruit zero customs duties measure”, fill in 06;

For import goods stipulated under “China and Pakistan Trade Treaty”, fill in 07;

For import goods stipulated under “China and Chile Trade Treaty”, fill in 08.

2. Where Certificate of Origin internet control has been put into practice, specific requirements are as follows:

(1) In the box of Filing No, fill in Y + No. of Certificate of Origin. To import goods stipulated under Hong Kong/Macao CEPA, fill in Y + 11 digits No. of Certificate of Origin.

(2) In the box of other documents attached, declaring via Customs H2000 Declaration System, fill in the particular of code with Y, and fill in < > of No. of document with code for preferential trading agreement. Declaring via Customs H883/EDI Declaration System, should not fill relative contents of Certificate of Origin in this box.

(3) In the box of remarks, declaring via Customs H883/EDI Declaration System, fill in < +“协” + code for preferential trading agreement + >. For example, to import goods stipulated under Hong Kong CEPA, fill in <协 03 >. Declaring via Customs H2000 Declaration System, should not fill relative contents of Certificate of Origin in this box.

(4) In the box of item No., fill in two lines. Fill in the first line with the item No. of the declaration, fill in the second line with corresponding i-

品项号”。

三、未实行原产地证书联网管理的具体填制要求

(一)“备案号”栏:未实行原产地证书联网管理的货物本栏目免予填报。

(二)“随附单据”栏:使用海关H2000通关系统申报的,在报关单“随附单据”栏随附单证代码项下填写“Y”,在随附单证编号项下“〈 〉”内填写“优惠贸易协定代码”+“:”+“需证商品序号”。例如《亚太贸易协定》项下进口报关单中第1到第3项和第5项为优惠贸易协定项下商品,应填为:“<01:1-3,5>”。使用海关H883/EDI通关系统申报的,此栏不填报原产地证书相关内容。

(三)“备注”栏:使用海关H883/EDI通关系统申报的,在报关单“备注”栏中填“<”+“协”+“优惠贸易协定代码”+“:”+“需证商品序号”+“>”。例如《亚太贸易协定》项下进口报关单中第1项到第3项和第5项为优惠贸易协定项下商品,应填为:“<协01:1-3,5>”。使用海关H2000通关系统申报的,此栏不填报原产地证书相关内容。

四、其他填制要求

(一)一份原产地证书只能对应一份报关单。同一份报关单上的商品不能同时享受协定税率和减免税。

(二)在一票进口货物中,对于实行原产地证书联网管理的,如涉及多份原产地证书或含非原产地证书商品,应分单填报。

(三)原产地证书实行“一批一证”,不能重复使用和逐次扣减。

(四)报关单上申报商品的计量单位必须与原产地证书上对应商品的计量单位一致。

(五)上述所有尖括号“〈 〉”、逗号“,”、连接符“-”及数字都必须使用非中文状态下的半角字符。

(六)其他栏目填制要求,仍按海关总署2004年第34号公告《中华人民共和国海关进出口货物报关单填制规范》填制。

五、本公告中"优惠贸易协定"的具体名称如下:

(一)“亚太贸易协定”是指《曼谷协定》,《曼谷协定》第一届部长级理事会上正式更名为《亚太贸易协定》。

(二)“中国-东盟自贸区”是指《中国-东盟全面经济合作框架协议货物贸易协议》。

(三)“内地与香港紧密经贸关系安排”是指《内地与香港关于建立更紧密经贸关系的安排》。

(四)“内地与澳门紧密经贸关系安排”是指《内地与

tem No. of Certificate of Origin.

3. Where Certificate of Origin internet control has not been put into practice yet, specific requirements are as follows:

(1) The column exempts from not put into effect administrative networked country of origin certificate goods fill in a form and report to the leadership

(2) In the box of other documents attached, declaring via Customs H2000 Declaration System, fill in the particular of code with Y, and fill in ◇ of No. of document with code for preferential trading agreement + ":" + "item Nos.". For example, declaration for goods stipulated under "Asia - Pacific Agreement", which item Nos. are 1-3 and 5, fill in <01:1-3,5>. Declaring via Customs H883/EDI Declaration System, should not fill relative contents of Certificate of Origin in this box.

(3) In the box of remarks, declaring via Customs H883/EDI Declaration System, fill in < +"协" + code for preferential trading agreement + : + item Nos. + >. For example, declaration for goods stipulated under Asia - Pacific Agreement, which item Nos. are 1-3 and 5, fill in <协01:1-3,5>. Declaring via Customs H2000 Declaration System, should not fill relative contents of Certificate of Origin in this box.

4. Other filling requirements

(1) One Certificate of Origin corresponds to only on declaration. For goods of the same one declaration should not claim preferential rate and also claim other reduction or exemption of duties and taxes.

(2) Where Certificate of Origin internet control has been put into practice, goods of one consignment involve many Certificates of Origin or include goods which are not controlled with Certificate of Origin, the goods should be declared separately.

(3) The Control of Certificate of Origin exercises "one consignment, one certificate", which could not be used repeatedly or deducted time by time.

(4) The measure unit of the declaration should be in accordance with the measure unit of Certificate of Origin.

(5) The above mentioned angle brackets(< >), comma(,), hyphen(-) and numerals should be printed with half-angle characters in non-Chinese input state.

(6) Requirements for other particulars are same as "Standards for Filling Import/Export Goods Declaration" (No. 34, 2004) announced by the Customs General Administration.

5. The announcement is hit by concrete "preferential trade agreement" name as follows

(1)"The Asia - Pacific trade agreement "is to point to "the Bangkok agreement ","Bangkok changes "Asia - Pacific trade agreement's name formally on agreement " the first minister level council"

(2)"Chinese - ASEAN is to point to the all - round economic cooperation of "Chinese - ASEAN frame agreement goods trade agreement from trade area "

(3)"The inland and the rapid and intense economic and trade relationship of Hong Kong are arranged to be to point to "inland and Hong Kong arrangement about rapid and intense economic and trade relationship of building - up "

(4)"The inland and the rapid and intense economic and trade rela-

澳门关于建立更紧密经贸关系的安排》。

（五）"对非洲特惠待遇"是指中国给予非洲最不发达国家部分输华商品免关税待遇。

（六）"台湾水果零关税措施"是指自2005年8月1日起对原产于台湾地区的15种进口鲜水果实施零关税的措施。

（七）"中巴自贸区"是指《中国－巴基斯坦关于自由贸易协定早期收获计划的协议》。

（八）"中智自贸区"是指《中国－智利自由贸易协定》。

本公告自2006年1月1日起执行，2003年12月18日海关总署发布的2003年第72号公告同时废止。

特此公告。

中华人民共和国海关总署

二〇〇五年十二月三十一日

tionship of Macao are arranged to be to point to "inland and Macao arrangement about rapid and intense economic and trade relationship of building – up "

(5) "Pay is to refer to China give Africa least developed countries a part convey the China commodity to Africa preference" dispense with customs duties pay.

(6) "Taiwan fruit zero customs duties measure " is to refer to the measure implementing zero customs duties to 15 kinds fresh entrance fruit that the plain produces in Taiwan area starting from August 1 , 2005.

(7) "The medium – size bus is to refer to "Chinese – Pakistan's agreement about free trade agreement early phase gains plan from trade area "

(8) "Being hit by wisdom is to point to the "Chinese – Chile free trade agreement from trade area "

The announcement 72nd in 2003 that General tration of Customs announces on December 18 , 2003 is shed at the same time.

It is hereby announced.

The Customs General Administration

On 31 December 2005

报关自动化系统常用代码表说明

监管方式代码表说明

进出口货物海关监管方式(以下简称监管方式),即现行进出口货物报关单“贸易方式”,是以国际贸易中进出口货物的交易方式为基础,结合海关对进出口货物的征税、统计及监管条件综合设定的海关对进出口货物的管理方式。

由于海关对不同监管方式下进出口货物的监管、征税、统计作业的要求不尽相同,因此为满足海关管理的要求,报关自动化系统的监管方式代码采用四位数字结构,其中前两位是按海关监管要求和计算机管理需要划分的分类代码,后两位为海关统计代码。

一般贸易

一、定义与代码

一般贸易是指我国境内有进出口经营权的企业单边进口或单边出口的贸易。本监管方式代码为“0110”,简称:一般贸易。

二、适用范围

(一)本监管方式包括:

1. 以正常交易方式成交的进出口货物;
2. 来料养殖、来料种植进出口货物;
3. 个体工商业者委托进口的小型生产工具;
4. 旅游旅馆、酒店进口营业用的食品和餐佐料等;
5. 外商投资企业进口供加工内销产品的料件;
6. 贷款援助的进出口货物(包括我方利用贷款款项自行采购进口的物资);
7. 外商投资企业用国产原材料加工产品出口或经批准自行收购国内产品出口的货物;
8. 国内经营租赁业务的企业购进供出租用的货物;
9. 经营保税仓库业务的企业购进供自用的货物;
10. 经营免税品和免税外汇商品的企业购进自用的手推车、货架等货物;
11. 外籍船舶、飞机在我国境内添加的国产燃料;
12. 对台间接贸易进出口货物。

Standards for Filling Import/ Export Goods Declaration Form

Codes for Customs Procedures

The customs procedures of import and export goods (hereinafter referred to as customs procedures) – i. e. current “customs procedures” of customs declaration for import and export products, are custom′s means of administration on import and export products based on the means of transaction of import and export goods in international trade, combining with the tax imposition, statistics and supervision conditions.

Since the Customs imposes different requirements ,on the supervision, tax imposition and statistics of the import and export goods for different customs procedures, the codes for customs procedures of declaration automatization system adopt four – digit structure, the first two of which means the categorization codes divided based on the needs of customs supervisions and computer management.

General Trade

I. Definition and code

General trade refers to the unilateral import or unilateral export of the enterprises engaged in import and export business within our national boundary.

II. Scope of application

(1) This customs procedure applies to:

1. the import and export goods transacted by normal means;
2. import and export goods of breeding and planting with supplied materials;
3. production apparatus imported by individual employers by commission;
4. the foods and drinks imported by hotels, inns for business;
5. supplied materials for processing of goods for domestic sales imported by foreign-funded companies;
6. import and export goods that are provided as aids or loans (including the goods imported paid with loans);
7. foreign -funded enterprises process and export products using raw materials originated from home, or voluntarily purchase exported goods produced by domestic companies after being permitted;
8. goods that domestic leasing enterprises purchase for leasing ;
9. goods that enterprises engaged in bonded warehouse purchase for self-use ;
10. goods such as barrows or shelves purchased by enterprises engaged in duty-free commodities or duty-free foreign exchange commodities;
11. national fuels that foreign ships, planes fill at home;
12. import and export products indirectly traded with Taiwan.

(二)本监管方式不包括:

1.进出口货样广告品,监管方式代码为"3010"(货样广告品A)、"3039"(货样广告品B);

2.无进出口经营权的单位经批准临时进出口货物,监管方式代码为"9739";

3.进料加工贸易中,对方有价或免费提供的机器设备(0420或0320);

4.运回国内对外承包工程期间在国外获取的机器、设备,监管方式代码为"3410";

5.境外劳务合作项目,对方以实物产品抵偿我劳务人员工资所进口的货物(如钢材、木材、化肥、海产品等),监管方式代码为"3410"。

(Ⅱ) This customs procedure does not apply to

1. for the imported and exported samples of goods and advertising commodities, the customs procedures code is "3010" (sampleof goods and advertising commodities A), "3039" (sample of goods and advertising commodities B);

2. for the enterprises un-entitled to run import and export business approved to import and export provisionally, the code is "9739";

3. for processing trade with imported materials, the machines provided by a foreign party either for free or with charge (0420 or 0320);

4. for the machines, facilities obtained abroad during period of foreign contract project transported back to China, the customs procedure code is "3410";

5. for the overseas labor service project, the goods imported as the compensation for the salary of employees (for example, steels, lumbers, chemical fertile, sea products, etc), the customs procedure code is "3410".

易货贸易

一、定义与代码

易货贸易是指不通过货币媒介而直接用出口货物交换进口货物的贸易。本监管方式代码为"0130",简称:易货贸易。

二、适用范围

本监管方式包括与原苏联、东欧等二十六国以及与其他国家的易货贸易。

本监管方式不包括:

1.对台小额贸易中签订易货合同的贸易,应为"其他贸易"(9739)。

2.边境小额贸易中签订易货合同的贸易,应为"边境小额"(4019)。

Barter trade

I. Definition and code

Barter trade refers to the trade without using money as the medium, but instead exchanging the imported products with exported products.

II. Scope of application

This customs procedure applies to barter trade with USSR and 26 countries from Eastern Europe.

This customs procedure does not apply to

1. the barter trade contract in petty trade with Taiwan shall be termed as "other trade." (9739)

2. the barter trade contract in petty trade with border areas shall be termed as "border areas petty" (4019)

旅游购物商品

指旅游者五万美元以下的出口小批量订货,简称旅游购物商品,代码0139。

Tourist shopping commodities

It refers to the goods order of small quantity worth less than 50,000USD; "tourist shopping commodities" in short; the code is 0139.

料件放弃

适用于经海关批准的加工贸易企业进口的不再用于加工成品出口,主动放弃交由海关处理的来料或进料加工料件。简称:料件放弃,监管方式代码为"0200"。

The disposal of materials

Applicable to the supplied or imported materials for processing imported by the processing trade enterprises that, with the permission of customs, are not to be used for processing, but instead are voluntarily abandoned and handed over to be dealt with by the customs .

来料加工装配贸易

一、定义与代码

(一)来料加工装配贸易是指由外商提供全部或部分原材料、辅料、零部件、元器件、配套件和包装物料(以下简称"料件"),必要时提供设备,由我方按对方的要求进行加工装配,成品交对方销售,我方收取工缴费,对方提供的作价设备价款,我方用工缴费偿还的交易形式。

来料加工装配贸易项下进口料件和出口成品监管方

The assembling trade

I. Definition and code

(Ⅰ) Assembling trade refers to the means of transaction that raw materials, auxiliary materials, components, parts, wrapping (hereinafter referred to as "materials") and facilities when necessary, are completely or partially provided by a foreign party. A Chinese party assembles these materials according to their requirements, and the finished products are to be sold by a foreign party. A Chinese party therefore charges the assembling fee. The prices of the facilities provided by a foreign party are compensated by assembling fee.

The code for imported materials and exported finished products under

式代码为“0214”，简称：来料加工。

（二）相关监管方式及代码

1. 复运出境不再进口的原进口料件，简称来料料件复出，代码为0265；

2. 来料余料结转，代码为0258；

3. 来料深加工结转，代码为0255；

4. 来料料件退换，代码为0300；

5. 来料加工成品退换，代码为4400；

6. 来料边角料复出，代码为0865。

二、适用范围

本监管方式不包括：

（一）来料加工装配贸易合同项下剩余料件内销及经批准进口料件或成品转内销，监管方式分别为“来料料件内销”（0245）及“来料成品内销”（0345）。

（二）“来料种植”和“来料养殖”进出口货物监管方式应为“一般贸易”（0110）。

assembling trade is “0214”; abbreviation: supplied materials processing.

(II) Related customs procedures and codes

1. for the imported materials that are re-exported and will not be imported again; abbreviation: the re-exported materials”, the code is 0265;

2. for transfer of surplus supplied materials, the code is 0258;

3. for transfer of surplus supplied materials for advanced processing, the code is 0255;

4. for replacement of supplied materials, the code is 0300;

5. for replacement of finished products, the code is 4400;

6. for re-exportation of supplied materials and leftover materials, the code is 0865.

II. The scope of application

This customs procedure does not apply to

(I) For leftover materials and imported materials or finished products declared for domestic sales (after being permitted) under the processing trade and assembling trade contract, the customs procedures are “supplied materials for domestic sales” (0245) and “finished products with supplied materials for domestic sales” (0345).

(II) The customs procedures for the import and export goods of ” planting with Supplied materials “ and “breeding with supplied materials” shall be “general trade” (0110).

来料加工转内销货物

一、定义与代码

来料加工转内销货物是指来料加工装配贸易进口的料件或已加工的成品，经批准不返销出口转为内销的货物，包括海关事后发现有关企业擅自内销并准予补办进口手续的货物。

来料成品凭《征免税证明》转减免税货物代码为0345，来料料件转内销代码为0245，来料边角料内销代码0845。

二、适用范围

本监管方式包括经济特区和保税区来料加工转内销的货物。

本监管方式不包括：

1. 来料加工的成品或半成品在境内转让给其他承接进口料件加工复出口业务的单位再加工装配，监管方式应为“来料深加工结转货物”（0255）。

2. 海关事后发现有关企业擅自内销按走私处理的。

The goods processed with supplied materials for domestic sales

I. Definition and code

The goods processed with supplied materials for domestic sales refer to materials or finished products imported for processing and assembling trade that, after being permitted, are not to be exported but instead are declared for domestic sales, including the goods that the enterprises was found out by customs to be sold domestically without permission and then are approved for import make-up procedures.

For the finished products with supplied materials shifted to duty-free goods upon the strength of “Duty-Free Certificate”, the code is 0345

II. The scope of application

This customs procedure applies to the goods processed with supplied materials but then declared for domestic sales in special economic zones and bonded areas.

This customs procedure does not apply to:

1. For the finished or semi-finished products that are transferred within China's boundary to other enterprises engaged in processing the imported materials and re-exporting for further processing and assembling, the customs procedures shall be “transfer of surplus supplied materials for advanced processing”, (0255).

2. the goods that are found to be sold domestically without permission and are treated as smuggling.

加工专用油

适用于国营贸易企业代理来料加工企业进口柴油，简称：加工专用油，监管方式代码为“0314”

The oil specially used for processing

Applicable to the diesel oil imported by the state-running enterprises in agent for processing enterprises, in short, oil specially for processing. The code is 0314.

成品放弃

适用于经海关批准的加工贸易企业不再用于出口，主动放弃交由海关处理的来料及进料加工成品。简称：成品放弃，监管方式代码为"0400"。

补偿贸易

一、定义与代码

补偿贸易是指由境外厂商提供或者利用国外出口信贷进口生产技术或设备，我方企业（包括"外商投资企业"）进行生产，以返销其产品的方式分期偿还对方技术、设备价款或贷款本息的交易方式。包括经经贸主管部门批准，使用该企业（包括企业联合体）所生产的其他产品返销给对方，进行间接补偿的方式。

本监管方式代码为"0513"，简称：补偿贸易。

二、适用范围

本监管方式包括补偿贸易中对方有偿或免费提供的机器设备、工模具等。

本监管方式不包括：

（一）直接用国内产品同国外厂商交换设备、料件或成品，以货换货，监管方式为"易货贸易"（0130）。

（二）出口产品收取外汇，监管方式为"一般贸易"（0110）。

（三）在补偿贸易合同中同时订有来料加工合同的，来料加工合同部分，监管方式为"来料加工"（0214）。

进料加工贸易

一、定义与代码

进料加工贸易按照对外签约形式分为"进料加工非对口合同"和"进料加工对口合同"。

（一）"进料加工非对口合同"是指我方有外贸进出口经营权的企业动用外汇购买进口原料、材料、辅料、元器件、零部件、配套件和包装物料（以下简称料件），加工成品或半成品后再返销出口的交易形式。本监管方式代码"0715"，简称：进料非对口。

（二）"进料加工对口合同"是指买卖双方分别签订进出口对口合同，料件进口时，我方先付料件款，加工成品出口时再向对方收取出口成品款项的交易形式，包括动用外汇的对口合同或不同客户的对口的联号合同以及对开信用证的对口合同。本监管方式代码为"0615"，简称：进料对口。

（三）相关监管方式及代码

1. 复运出境不再进口的原进口料件，简称进料料件复出，代码为0664；

2. 进料余料结转，代码为0657；

3. 进料深加工结转，代码为0654；

The disposal of finished products

Applicable to the supplied materials or finished products that, with the permission of customs, are not to be used for export, but instead are voluntarily abandoned and handed over to be dealt with the customs.

Compensation trade

Ⅰ. Definition and code

The compensation trade refers to the means of trade that the a foreign party provides or uses foreign export credit to provide the production technology or equipments, a domestic party (including "foreign-funded companies") produces and sells back the products to pay back the equivalent prices for technology, facilities or premium and interests of loans, including the means of trade that the enterprise (or syndicate) sell other products to the foreign party.

The code is "0513", and abbreviation is compensation trade.

II. The scope of application

This customs procedure applies to the machinery facilities and modules provided by a foreign party for free or with charge in compensation trade.

This customs procedure does not apply to:

(1) directly exchange the domestic products for the facilities, supplied materials or finished products of overseas companies. The customs procedures of "goods for goods" shall be "barter trade" (0130).

(2) for the foreign exchange obtained through exported products, the procedures shall be "general trade". (0110).

(3) if a contract of processing with supplied materials is included in the compensation trade, the code for this part shall be "processing with supplied materials." (0214)

The processing trade with imported materials

I. Definition and code

The processing trade with imported materials falls into two categories, "processing with imported materials with no counterpart contract" and "processing with imported materials with counterpart contract"

(1) "processing with imported materials with no counterpart contract" refers to the mans of trade that a domestic party entitled to run the import and export business use foreign exchange to purchase imported raw materials, auxiliary materials, parts, components and wrapping materials (hereinafter referred to as "materials"), which are processed as finished or semi-finished products to be exported. The code is "0715". Abbreviation: "imported materials with no counterpart".

(2) "processing with imported materials with counterpart contract" refers to the means of trade that both parties sign the counterpart contracts of import and export, the domestic party paying the prices for supplied materials first, then charging the prices for finished products when exporting to the counterparts, etc. The code is "0615", "imported materials counterpart" in short.

(3) related customs procedures and codes

1. for the imported materials that are re-exported and will not be imported again, "re-exported materials in short". The code is 0664;

2. for the transfer of surplus imported materials, the code is 0657;

3. for the transfer of surplus imported materials for supplementary pro-

4. 进料料件退换，代码为0700；

5. 进料加工成品退换，代码为4600；

6. 进料边角料复出，代码为0864.

二、适用范围

本监管方式包括进料加工合同项下进口的料件和加工出口的产品，还包括进料加工贸易中外商免费提供进口的主辅料和零部件。

本监管方式不包括：

（一）进料加工经批准转内销的进口料、件或加工成品，监管方式分别为“进料成品转减免”（0744）和“进料料件内销”（0644）。

（二）海关批准设立的保税工厂进料加工进口料件及出口成品，监管方式应为“保税工厂”（1215）。

（三）按规定不使用《登记手册》的少量低值辅料，应为“低值辅料”（0815）。

cessing, the code is 0654;

4. for the replacement of imported materials, the code is 0700;

5. for replacement of imported products , the code is 4600;

6. for the re-exportation of imported materials and leftover materials, the code is 0864

II. The scope of application

This customs procedure applies to the imported materials and processed exported products under the contract of processing with imported products, and the primary/supplementary materials and components provided by the foreign companies for free in the processing trade with imported materials.

This customs procedure does not apply to:

(1) The imported materials, pieces or processed finished products that have been permitted to be sold domestically. The customs procedures are "imported materials for finished products transferred to duty exemption/reduction" (0744) and "imported materials for domestic sale" (0644).

(2) For the process of the imported materials and export of the finished products by bonded factories established with the permission of the customs, the customs procedures shall be "bonded factories" (1215);

(3) For the supplemental materials of low values that , according to stipulations, are not subject to "registration brochure, "the customs procedure is "low-value supplemental materials. " (0815).

进料加工转内销货物

一、定义与代码

进料加工转内销货物指进料加工贸易进口的料件，或已加工的成品经批准转为内销的货物，包括海关事后发现有关企业擅自转内销并准予补办进口手续的货物。

进料成品凭《征免税证明》转减免税货物代码为0744，进料料件内销代码为0644，进料边角料内销代码为0844，进料加工以产顶进代码为0642。

二、适用范围

（一）本监管方式包括经济特区和保税区进料加工转内销的货物。

（二）本监管方式不包括：

1. 进料加工成品或半成品转让给境内其他承接进口料件加工复出口业务的单位进行再加工，监管方式为“进料深加工结转货物”（0654）。

2. 海关事后发现有关企业擅自内销并按走私处理的货物。

Goods processed with supplied materials for domestic sales

1. Definitions and code

Goods processed with supplied materials for domestic sales refer to the imported materials for processing or processed finished products that, with permission by the customs, are declared to be sold domestically, including those that make-up import procedures are approved after products being found out to be sold domestically without permission.

The code for finished products processed with imported materials that transfer to duty-free goods upon strength of "Duty-Free Certificate" is 0644, the code for leftover materials for domestic sales is 0844, and the code for the produced materials substituted for imported is 0642.

II. The Scope of Application

(1) This customs procedure applies to goods processed with imported materials for domestic sales in special economic zones and bonded areas.

(II) This customs procedure does not apply to:

1. The finished or semi-finished products processed with imported materials transfer to other enterprises engaged in processing with imported materials and re-exporting for processing

2. the goods found to be sold domestically without permissions and regarded as smuggling.

保税工厂

一、定义与代码

保税工厂是指经海关批准专为生产外销产品而进口原料、材料、元器件、零部件、配套件、辅料、包装物料等（以下简称料件）进行保税加工的企业。保税工厂进口料件和出口产品监管方式代码为“1215”，简称：保税工厂。

二、适用范围

Bonded factories

I. Definition and code

Bonded factories refer to the enterprises that conduct bonded processing for imported materials, components, apparatuses, supplemental materials and wrapping materials and produce products for foreign sales. The code for imported materials and exported products of bonded factories is "1215", "bonded factories" in short.

II. The scope of application

（一）本监管方式包括经批准设立保税工厂的有对外贸易进出口经营权的企业和外商投资企业承接进料加工进口的料件和出口的产品。

（二）本监管方式不包括：

1.保税工厂进口自用的机器设备和进料加工贸易中外商免费提供的机器设备、物品，监管方式为“加工贸易设备”（0420）；

2.保税工厂经营来料加工，监管方式应为“来料加工”（0214）；

3.保税工厂进口料件或加工后的成品经批准转内销，监管方式为“进料加工转内销货物”（0744、0644、0844）；

4.进料加工的成品或半成品转让给境内其他承接进口料件加工复出口业务的单位进行再加工的货物，监管方式应为“进料深加工结转货物”（0654）。

(1) This customs procedure applies to the imported materials for processing and exported products undertaken by enterprises entitled to deal with foreign trade and establish bonded factories and foreign enterprises.

(2) This customs procedure does not apply to:

1. The machinery equipments of the boned factories for self-use or provided by the foreign enterprises for free in the processing trade with imported materials, for which the customs procedure is "processing trade facilities";

2. For the bonded factories that engage in processing with supplied materials, the customs procedure is "processing with supplied materials.";

3. for the imported materials or processed finished products of bonded factories declared for domestic sales with permission, the customs procedure is "the products with imported materials processed for domestic sales" (0744、0644、0844);

4. for the finished or semi-finished products with imported materials transferred to the other enterprises for further processing, the customs procedure shall be "transfer of imported materials for advanced processing".

加工贸易设备

一、定义与代码

加工贸易设备指加工贸易项下外商提供进口的设备，包括作价及不作价设备。代码为0420.

1.不作价设备：指与加工贸易经营单位开展加工贸易（包括来料加工、进料加工及外商投资企业从事的加工贸易）的外商，以免费即不需经营单位付汇进口、也不需用加工费或差价偿还方式，向经营单位提供的加工生产所需设备，代码为0320.

2.除“不作价设备”以外的加工贸易项下进口设备代码为0420。

二、相关贸易方式

1.加工设备内销，指海关监管期内的加工贸易免税进口设备经批准转售给境内非加工企业，代码0446。

2.加工设备结转，指海关监管期内的加工贸易免税进口设备经批准转入另一加工企业，或从一本《登记手册》结转入另一本《登记手册》，代码0456。

3.加工设备退运，指加工贸易免税进口设备退运出境，代码0466。

The Processing Trade Facilities

1. Definition and code

The processing trade facilities refer to the facilities provided by the foreign companies under the processing trade account, including evaluated and unevaluated facilities. The code is 0420.

1. Unevaluated facilities refer to the foreign companies that launch processing trade with the domestic processing trade enterprises (including processing with supplied materials, processing with imported materials and the processing trade of the foreign enterprises) provide the facilities necessary for processing for free (ie, the processing enterprises do not need to pay for the import with the foreign exchange or with processing fees, etc.) The code is 0320.

2. For imported facilities other than "unevaluated facilities," the code is 0420.

II. Related means of trade

1. the domestic sales of processing facilities refer to the duty-free imported facilities of processing trade are sold to the domestic non-processing enterprises during the period of customs supervision. The code is 0446.

2. the transfer of the imported facilities refers to the imported facilities transferred to another processing trade during periods of customs supervision, or transferred from one "Registration Brochure" to another "Registration Brochure". The code is 0456.

3. the return and transportation of processing facilities means that the duty-free imported facilities for processing trade are returned and transported outbound, the code for which is 0466.

减免设备结转

指海关监管年限内的减免税设备从一企业结转到另一享受减免税待遇的企业，简称减免设备结转，代码0500。

对减免税设备及加工贸易设备之间的结转，转入和转出企业分别填制进、出口报关单，报关单“贸易方式”栏目根据报关企业所持加工贸易手册或征减免税证明，

Transfer of duty-reduction/exemption equipments

Meaning the duty-reduction/exemption equipments transferred from one enterprise to another enterprise that enjoys the duty reduction/exemption treatment. "Transfer of duty-reduction/exemption equipments" in short.

To transfer between the duty-reduction/exemption equipments and processing trade equipments, the related companies shall fill out the declaration forms for import and export respectively. For the column "mode of

分别选择填报加工贸易设备结转(代码0456)、减免税设备结转的海关监管方式代码,报关单“备案号”栏目分别填报加工贸易手册编号、征减免税证明编号或为空,报关单其他栏目按现行《报关单填制规范》关于结转货物的要求填报。

trade” in the declaration form, the companies shall write“ transfer of the processing trade equipments”(code 0456) and the customs procedure codes for the transfer of the duty reduction/exemption equipments according to the processing trade brochure or the duty reduction/exemption certificate respectively. For the column “recorded code” of the declaration form, the series number of processing trade brochure and series number of the levy mode certificate shall be left blank, and other columns in the declaration form shall be filled out according to the stipulations of transfer of goods in currently implemented “the standards for filling out the declaration form”.

保税区内销往非保税区的加工贸易成品

一、定义

保税区内销往非保税区的加工贸易成品是指经海关批准保税区内销往非保税区的加工贸易成品转内销的货物。

二、适用范围

1. 适用于应按成品征税的保税区进料加工成品转内销货物。监管方式:保区进料成品,监管方式代码为0444

2. 适用于应按成品征税的保税区来料加工成品转内销货物。监管方式:保区来料成品,监管方式代码为0445

3. 适用于应按料件征税的保税区进料加工成品转内销货物。监管方式:保区进料料件,监管方式代码为0544

4. 适用于应按成品征税的保税区进料加工成品转内销货物。监管方式:保区来料料件,监管方式代码为0545。

The finished products of processing trade sold domestically from bonded areas to non-bonded areas

I. Definition

The finished products of processing trade sold domestically from bonded areas to non-bonded areas refers to the processing trade goods or finished products sold domestically from bonded areas to non-bonded areas.

II. Scope of application

1. applicable to the finished products processed with imported materials of bonded areas that bear the duty of finished products and are then declared for domestic sales. The customs procedure: finished products with imported materials of bonded areas. The code is 0444.

2. applicable to the finished products processed with supplied materials of bonded areas that bear the duty of finished products and are then declared for domestic sales. The customs procedure: finished products with imported materials of bonded areas. The code is 0444.

3. applicable to the finished products processed with imported materials of bonded areas that bear the duty of imported materials and are then declared for domestic sales. The customs procedure: finished products with imported materials of bonded areas. The code is 0444.

4. applicable to the finished products processed with imported materials of bonded areas that bear the duty of supplied materials and are then declared for domestic sales. The customs procedure: finished products with imported materials of bonded areas. The code is 0444.

低值辅料

指按规定不使用《登记手册》的少量低值辅料,即5000美元以下、78种以内的低值辅料,代码0815。

Supplemental materials of low value

It refers to the supplemental materials of low value that “Registration Brochure” does not apply to, ie, less than 78 types of supplemental materials of low value and worth less than 5000USD. The code is 0815.

保税间货物

适用于物流中心(A、B型)、保税区、出口加工区、保税物流园区、保税仓库、出口监管仓库等海关保税场所及保税区域之间往来的货物。简称:保税间货物,监管方式代码为“1200”

The goods that flow between the bonded zones

Such as logistics center (A. B), bonded areas, export processing areas, bonded logistics areas, bonded warehouse, export supervised warehouses. Abbreviation: goods between bonded areas. The code is 1200.

保税仓库进出境货物

一、定义与代码

保税仓库是指经海关核准专门存放保税货物的仓库。保税仓库进出境货物是指从境外直接存入保税仓库和从保税仓库(包括出口监管仓库)运出境的货物。

The cross-border goods of bonded warehouse

I. Definition and code

The bonded warehouses refer to the warehouses that are permitted by the customs to store the bonded goods. The cross-border goods of bonded warehouse refer to the goods that are directly stored from overseas in the bonded warehouses and directly exported from bonded warehouses (including export supervised warehouses)

本监管方式代码为“1233”，简称：保税仓库货物。

二、适用范围

（一）本监管方式进出口货物包括加工贸易备料保税仓库所存货物和经经贸主管部门批准的寄售、维修零备件、保税生产资料市场物资、外商寄存、暂存货物、供应外籍船舶、飞机等运输工具的燃料等以及转口贸易进出境货物。

（二）本监管方式不包括：

1. 保税仓库进口自用的货架、办公用品、管理用具、运输车辆、搬运、起重和包装设备以及改装用的机器等，价购进口的，监管方式为“一般贸易”（0110）；外商免费提供的，监管方式为“其他进口免费提供货物”（3339）；

2. 从保税仓库提取销往境内以及从境内存入出口监管仓库的货物，按实际监管方式填报，运输方式为“8”（保税仓库）；

3. 保税区仓储转口货物，监管方式代码为“1234”；

The code is “1233”. Abbreviation: boned warehouses goods

II. Scope of application

(1) This customs procedure applies to the goods stored in bonded warehouses with prepared materials for processing trade and consignment and repair components with permission of economic competent deparment, bonded production materials, consignation of foreign investor, temporarily stored goods, fuels for foreign means of transportation such as ships and airlines and cross-border goods for entreport trade.

(II) This customs procedure does not apply to:

1. The shelves, office appliances, administrative appliances, vehicles, transportation, hoisting and wrapping facilities and machines that are reassembled. For those that are charged with prices, the customs procedure is “general trade” (0110), for those provided by foreign companies for free, the customs procedure is “other imported supplied goods for free.” (3339);

2. for the goods that are picked up from the bonded warehouses to be sold domestically and that are kept in the export supervised warehouses from domestic territories, it shall be reported according to the actual customs procedures, the means of transportation is “8”. (bonded warehouses);

3. the storage and foundry goods of bonded areas, the customs procedures code is “1234”.

保税区进出境仓储、转口货物

一、定义与代码

保税区仓储转口货物指从境外存入保税区和从保税区运出境的仓储货物或转口货物。本监管方式代码为“1234”，简称保税区仓储转口。

二、适用范围

本监管方式不包括从境外运入保税区和从保税区运出境的其他货物（非仓储、非转口货物），监管方式应视具体交易情况选择填报。

The cross-border storage and foundry goods of bonded areas

I. Definition and code

The storage and foundry goods of bonded areas refer to the storage or foundry goods stored from overseas into the bonded areas and transported outbound from bonded areas. The code is “1234”. Abbreviation: “storage and foundry of bonded areas”.

II. Scope of application

This customs procedure does not apply to other goods that are transported into bonded areas from overseas and transported outbound from bonded areas (non-storage, non-foundry goods). The customs procedures shall be filled according to specific cases.

国轮油物料

一、定义及代码

国轮油物料指本国籍专营国际运输的运输工具在境内添加的保税油料、物料，代码 1139。

二、适用范围

本监管方式只能对应运输方式“7”（保税区运往非保税区）和“8”（保税仓库转内销）。

Oils and materials of

I. Definition and code

It refers to the bonded oils, materials filled by Chinese means of transport that specially engage in overseas transportation.

II. Scope of application

This customs procedure only corresponds to means of transport “7” (transported from bonded areas to non-bonded areas) and “8” (storage of bonded warehouses declared for domestic sales)

进出境修理物品

进出境修理物品是指运进境或运出境维护修理的物品。

本监管方式代码为“1300”，简称：修理物品。

Cross-border articles for repair

Articles that transported inbound or outbound for repair.

The code is “1300”. Abbreviation; articles for repair

出料加工贸易

出料加工贸易是指我境内企业将原辅料、零部件、元器件或半成品（以下简称料件）出口交由境外厂商按我方要求进行加工或装配，成品复运进口，我方支付工

Processing trade for exported materials

Processing trade for exported materials means that domestic enterprises export the auxiliary materials, components, apparatus or semi-finished products (hereinafter referred to as materials) to be processed or assembled

缴费。

本监管方式代码为"1427",简称:出料加工。

by the foreign companies according to our requirements, and the finished products are to be re-imported with processing fees paid by domestic companies.

The code is "1427". Abbreviation: processing for exported materials.

租赁贸易

一、定义与代码

租赁贸易是指经营租赁业务的企业与外商签订国际租赁合同的进出境的货物。

租赁期在一年及一年以上的进出口货物,监管方式代码为"1523"和"9800",简称:租赁贸易、租赁征税。

租赁期不满一年的进出口货物,监管方式代码为"1500",简称:租赁不满一年。

二、适用范围

本监管方式包括租赁贸易租借进出口的货物,租赁期在一年及以上的租赁进口货物按租金征税时,监管方式为"租赁征税"(9800),但不包括:

(一)经营租赁业务的企业进口自用的设备、办公用品,监管方式应为"一般贸易"(0110);

(二)用于加工装配的租赁进口的机器设备,监管方式应为"加工贸易设备"(0420);

(三)用于补偿贸易租借进口的货物,监管方式应为"补偿贸易"(0513)。

(四)租赁期满复运出进口的货物,监管方式为"退运货物"(4561)。

Leasing trade

I. Definition and code

Leasing trade refers to the cross-border goods in the international leasing contract that domestic leasing enterprises sign with foreign counterpart.

For the import and export product with leasing period of one year or more, the customs procedures code is "1523" and "9800". Abbreviation: leasing trade, leasing duty.

For the import and export product with leasing period of less than one year, the code is "1500". Abbreviation: lease for less than one year.

II. Scope of application

This customs procedure applies to the import and export goods leased for leasing trade, and for the import goods leased for more than one years and are therefore imposed duties according to the rents, the customs procedure is "leasing duty imposition" (9800).

This customs procedure does not apply to:

(1) the facilities and office appliance imported for self-use , the code for which shall be "general trade" (0110);

(2) the machinery facilities leased for processing and assembling, the customs procedure for which shall be "processing trade facilities." (0420)

(3) the imported goods leased for compensation trade, the customs procedures for which shall be "compensation trade." (0513)

(4) the imported goods that are re-exported after expiry of lease, the customs procedures for which shall be "the canceled goods." (4561)

寄售代销贸易

一、定义与代码

寄售代销贸易是指寄售人把货物运交事先约定的代销人,由代销人按照事先约定或根据寄售代销协议规定的条件,在当地市场代为销售,所得货款扣除代销人的佣金和其他费用后,按协议规定方式将余款付给寄售人的交易形式。

本监管方式代码为"1616",简称:寄售代销。

二、适用范围

本监管方式包括寄售代销贸易进出口的货物及进口寄售货物的增发部分。但不包括:

(一)经营寄售代销业务的企业,接受国外免费提供的样品,监管方式应为"货样广告品 B"(3039);

(二)委托我驻港澳机构代销的鲜活商品。

Consignment and sales agent trade

I. Definition and code

Consignment trade means that the consigner transports the goods to the sales agent who will sell the products in local markets according to the stipulated conditions in the consignment contract, and the revenue, after being deducted by the commissions and other fees, are returned to the consigners by means stipulated in the agreement.

The code is "1616". Abbreviation: consignment and sale agent.

II. Scope of application

This customs procedure include the import and export goods in the consignment and sales agent trade. It does not include:

(1) The sample of goods that enterprises engaging in consignment and sales agent business receive from foreign enterprises for free, for which the customs procedure shall be "the sample of goods and advertising goods B" (3039);

(2) Fresh commodities consigned to the HK and Macao agents.

免税品

一、定义与代码

免税品是指设在国际机场、港口、车站和边境口岸的免税品商店所进口的,按有关规定销售给办完出境手续的旅客,供外国籍船员和我国远洋船员购买送货上船出售的物品,以及在我国际航班、国际班轮上向出境旅客出

Duty-free goods

I. Definition and code

Duty-free goods refer to the goods that are imported by the duty-free stores located in international airports, ports, stations and border ports, to be sold to the customers who have completed the outbound procedures, or foreign and Chinese sailors who purchase products to sell on ships, and out-

售的物品。

本监管方式代码为"1741",简称:免税品。

二、适用范围

本监管方式适用上述定义所列进口免税品,但不包括:

(一)按有关规定销售给享受免税待遇的各类人员的进口免税外汇商品,监管方式为"免税外汇商品"(1831);

(二)免税店进口供维修用的零部件、货架、柜台、手推车,不属免税品范围,其监管方式为"一般贸易"(0110)。

bound customers on the international airlines and international ships.

The code for this custom procedure is "1741". Abbreviation: duty-free goods.

II. Scope of application

This customs procedure applies to the imported duty-free goods as defined above, but does not apply to

(1) the imported duty free foreign exchange commodities sold to people who enjoy the duty-free treatment according to related stipulations.

(2) the components, shelves, counters, barrows imported by duty-free stores for repair and maintenance do not belong to duty-free products, for which the customs procedure is "general trade" (0110).

免税外汇商品

一、定义与代码

免税外汇商品是指在限定地点按有关规定销售给享受免税待遇人员的进口外汇商品。

本监管方式代码为"1831",简称:免税外汇商品。

二、适用范围

本监管方式包括:

1. 为供应出国人员用结存外汇或入境人员用带进的外汇在境内购买限定的进口的免税外汇商品;

2. 经营入境旅客"在外售券、境内提货"业务的企业进口的免税外汇商品。

本监管方式不包括:

1. 经营免税外汇商品的单位进口供商品维修用的零部件和商场自用的货架、手推车等,监管方式为"一般贸易"(0110);

2. 进口免税外汇商品因故经批准转内销,监管方式应为"一般贸易"(0110)。

Duty-free foreign exchange commodities

I. Definition and code

Duty-free foreign exchange commodities refer to the imported foreign exchange goods sold to people who enjoy duty-free treatment at certain locations according to related stipulations.

The code for this customs procedure is "1831". Abbreviation: Duty-free foreign exchange commodities.

II. Scope of application

This customs procedure applies to:

1. the imported duty-free foreign exchange commodities provided for outbound personnel with saved foreign exchange and inbound personnel with foreign exchange accompanied from abroad;

2. the duty-free foreign exchange commodities imported by enterprises engaged in "sell the bills abroad and pick up the goods at home" for inbound passengers.

This customs procedure does not apply to:

1. for the repair components and self-use shelves and barrows for shopping malls imported by enterprises engaged in duty-free foreign exchange commodities, the customs procedure is "general trade" (0110);

2. for the imported duty-free foreign exchange goods permitted to be sold domestically due to various reasons, the customs procedure is "general trade." (0110)

外商投资企业作为投资进口的设备、物品

一、定义与代码

外商投资企业作为投资进口的设备、物品是指外商投资企业以投资(包括中方投资)总额内的资金所进口的机器设备、零部件和其他物料[指建厂(场)以及安装、加固机器所需材料],以及根据国家规定进口本企业自用合理数量的交通工具、生产用车辆、办公用品和设备。

合资、合作企业进口设备、物品,监管方式代码应为"2025",简称:合资合作设备。

外资企业进口设备、物品,监管方式代码应为"2225",简称:外资设备物品。

The facilities and articles imported as investments by foreign companies

I. Definition and code

The facilities and articles imported as investments by foreign companies refer to machinery facilities, components and other materials (referring to the materials needed to build factories (sites) and install and update machines) imported by the foreign enterprises for lower than total sum of investments (including investment of Chinese companies), and means of transportation, vehicles for production, office appliances and facilities of reasonable quantity imported for self-use according to the stipulations.

For the facilities and articles imported by joint ventures and cooperative enterprises, the customs procedure code is "2025." Abbreviation: faculties of joint-ventures and cooperatives.

For the facilities and articles imported by foreign companies, the customs code is "2225." Abbreviation: facilities and articles for foreign enterprises.

二、适用范围

（一）外商投资企业是指中外合资企业、中外合作企业、外资企业，包括华侨、港、澳、台同胞投资企业。

（二）所称"设备"是指外商投资企业在其投资总额内进口本企业自用的机器设备、零部件和其他物料［指建厂（场）以及安装、加固机器所需材料］及生产用车辆。

（三）所称"物品"是指外商投资企业进口自用合理数量的办公用品（设备）和交通工具。

II. Scope of application

(1). The foreign enterprises refer to the Sino-foreign joint ventures, Sino-foreign cooperative enterprise, foreign-funded enterprises (including enterprises invested by overseas Chinese, HK, Macao, and Taiwan compatriots.

(2) the term "facilities" refers to the machinery equipments, components and other materials (referring to the materials need to build factories (sites) and install and update machines) imported by the foreign enterprises for self-use for lower than total sum of investments.

(3) the term "articles" refers to the office supplies (facilities) and means of transportation of reasonable quantity imported by the foreign enterprises for self-use.

外航公务货

适用于外国航空公司进口公务货，简称：外航公务货，监管方式代码为"2400"。

The service goods of foreign airlines

Applicable to service goods imported by foreign airlines, abbreviation: service goods of foreign airlines. The code is "2400".

外国常驻机构进口公用物品

一、定义与代码

外国常驻机构进口公用物品是指外国企业和其他经济组织常驻机构、外国民间经济贸易团体常驻机构、外国常驻新闻机构以及其他外国常驻机构进口供自用且数量合理的办公用品及交通工具。

本监管方式代码为"2439"，简称：常驻机构进口。

二、适用范围

本监管方式包括外国常驻机构进口供自用且数量合理的办公用品及交通工具，但不包括：

1. 外国常驻机构的人员进口自用物品，监管方式为"其他"（9900）；

2. 外国常驻机构人员进口自用的汽车，监管方式为"其他贸易"（9739）；

3. 暂时进出口的公用物品，监管方式为"暂时进出口"（2600）；

4. 外国驻华使领馆进出口公用物品，监管方式为"其他"（9900）；

5. 外国驻华使领馆在我国内购运出境的货物，监管方式为"其他贸易"（9739）。

Public goods imported by foreign permanent institutions

I. Definition and code

Public goods imported by foreign permanent institutions refer to the office supplies and means of transportation of reasonable quantity imported for self-use by the foreign enterprises and other permanent economic organizations, foreign unofficial permanent economic and trade institutions and foreign permanent news agencies and other foreign permanent institutions.

The code is "2439". Abbreviation: import of permanent institutions

II. Scope of application

This customs procedure applies to the office supplies and means of transportation of reasonable quantity imported for self-use by foreign permanent institutions;

1. for the articles imported for self-sue by working personnel of foreign permanent institutions, the customs procedure is "other" (9900);

2. for the cars imported for self-use by personnel of foreign permanent institutions, the customs procedure is "other trade" (9739);

3. for the public goods imported and exported temporarily, the customs procedure is 'temporary import and export' (2600);

4. for the public goods imported and exported by foreign embassies to China, the customs procedure is "other" (9900);

5. for the goods purchased and transported outbound by foreign embassies to China, the customs procedure is "other trade" (9900).

暂时进出口货物

一、定义与代码

暂时进出口货物是指国际组织、外国政府或外国和香港、澳门地区的企业、群众团体以及个人为开展经济、技术、科学、文化合作交流而暂时运入或运出我国关境及复运出进境的货物。

本监管方式代码为"2600"，简称：暂时进出口。

二、适用范围

（一）本监管方式包括：

1. 为来华拍摄或与我国国内单位合作拍摄电影片、照片、图片、幻灯片而运进我国的摄影器材、胶卷、胶片、

The temporary import and export goods

I. Definition and code

The temporary import and export goods refers to the goods temporarily flowed in and out of the Customs and re-imported and re-exported by international organizations, foreign governments or enterprises and the mass or individuals from foreign countries and HK, Macao for economic, technological, scientific and cultural communications and exchanges.

The code is "2600", abbreviation: temporary import and export.

II. Scope of application

(1) This customs procedure applies to:

1. the photograph equipments, roll films, negatives, videos, vehicles, costumes, props transported inbound for cooperative films, photos,

录像带、车辆、服装、道具等。

pictures, slides shooting with domestic enterprises.

2. 为来华进行体育竞赛、文艺演出而运进的器材、道具、服装、车辆、动物等。

2. the photograph equipments, props, vehicles, costumes and animals transported inbound for physical competitions and art performances in China.

3. 为来华进行工程施工、学术、技术交流、讲学而运进的各种设备、仪器、工具、教学用具、车辆等。

3. the facilities, device, teaching supplies, vehicles transported inbound for engineering construction, academic and technological communication and lecturing in China.

4. 驻华商业机构进口并将复运出口的陈列用样品。

4. samples of goods for display imported and to be re-exported by foreign commercial institutions in China.

(二)本监管方式不包括

(2) This customs procedure does not apply to

1. 进出境展览品,监管方式为"展览品"(2700)。

1. the cross-border goods for exhibition, the customs procedure for which is "goods for exhibition"(2700).

2. 驻华商业机构不复运出口的进口陈列样品(2939)。

2. the sample of goods for display imported but not to be re-exported by foreign commercial institutions in China(2939)

3. 承包工程出口物资,监管方式代码为"3422"。

3. the exported materials of contract project, the code for which is "3422".

4. 进出境修理物品,监管方式代码为"1300"。

4. the cross-border articles for repair, the code for which is "1300"

5. 租赁贸易进出口货物,监管方式为"租赁不满一年"(1500)、"租赁贸易"(1523)。

5. the imported and exported goods in leasing trade, the customs procedure for which is "lease less than 1 year" (1500), "leasing trade" (1523).

进出境展览品

Cross-border goods for exhibition

一、定义与代码

I. Definition and code

进出境展览品是指外国为来华或我国为到国外举办经济、文化、科技等展览或参加博览会而进出口的展览品及与展览品有关的宣传品、布置品、招待品、小卖品和其他物品。

The cross-border goods for exhibition refers to goods for exhibition and related advertising goods, reception goods and other goods imported and exported when foreigners come to China or Chinese go abroad to hold economic, cultural and technological exhibitions.

本监管方式代码为"2700",简称:展览品。

The code is "2700". Abbreviation: goods for exhibition

二、适用范围

II. Scope of application

本监管方式包括以上定义所述进出口的展览品,但不包括不复运出进境而留在国内外销售的进出口展览品,不复运出进境而留在国内外的进出口展览品,应视实际监管方式填报。

This customs procedure apply to the goods for exhibition as defined above, but not the imported and exported goods for exhibition that are not to be re-exported or re-imported but instead are to stay at home for abroad for sales, for which the customs procedure shall be filled out according to the actual customs procedure.

外国驻华商业机构进出口陈列用的样品

The sample of goods for display imported and exported by the foreign commercial institutions in China

本监管方式是指外国企业常驻我国办事机构为陈列企业的产品而进出口的样品。

This customs procedure refers to the sample of goods imported and exported for displaying the products of enterprises by permanent representative offices of foreign enterprises in China.

监管方式代码为"2939",简称:陈列样品。

The code is "2939" Abbreviation: good for display.

本监管方式不包括驻华商业机构进口并复运出口的陈列用样品(2600)。

This customs procedure does not apply to the sample of goods for display imported and re-exported by the foreign institutions in China.

货样、广告品

Sample of goods, advertising goods

一、定义与代码

I. Definition and code

进出口货样是指专供订货参考的进出口货物样品;广告品是指用以宣传有关商品内容的进出口广告宣传品。

The imported and exported sample of goods refer to imported and exported sample of goods specially provided as reference for goods ordering; advertising goods refer to the imported and exported goods used for advertising contents of related products.

经批准有进出口经营权的企业进出口货样广告品,监管方式代码为"3010",简称:货样广告品A。

For the sample of goods and advertising goods imported and exported by the enterprises that are entitled to engage in import and export business,

没有进出口经营权的企业(单位)进出口及国外免费提供进口的货样广告品,监管方式代码为"3039",简称:货样广告品 B。

二、适用范围

本监管方式除以上定义所述范围的商品外,还包括寄售代销贸易中外商免费提供的货样广告品。

本监管方式不包括:

(一)暂时进出口的货样、广告品,监管方式应为"暂时进出口货物"(2600)。

(二)驻华商业机构不复运出口的进口陈列样品(2939)。

the code is "3010". Abbreviation: sample of goods and advertising goods A.

For the sample of goods and advertising goods imported and exported by the enterprises that are not entitled to engage in import and export business and those provided by foreign companies for free, the code is "3039". Abbreviation: sample of goods and advertising goods B.

II. Scope of application

This customs procedure applys to not only the goods as defined above, but also the sample of goods and advertising goods provided by the foreign companies in consignment and sales agent trade.

This customs procedure does not apply to:

(1) for the sample of goods and advertising goods temporarily imported and exported, the customs procedure shall be "temporarily imported and exported product"(2600).

(2) the sample of goods for display imported and not to be re-exported by the foreign commercial institutions in China(2939).

无代价抵偿进口货物

无代价抵偿货物是指进口货物经海关征税放行后,发现货物残损、缺少或品质不良,而由国外承运人、发货人或保险公司免费补偿或更换的同类货物。

本监管方式代码为"3100",简称:无代价抵偿。

Imported goods for free replacement

Imported goods for free replacement means that the imported goods are replaced or compensated for free by the foreign carriers, consigners or insurance companies after being cleared at the customs but then found to be damaged, missing or below standard.

The code is "3100". Abbreviation: imported goods for free replacement

其他进口免费提供货物

一、定义与代码

本监管方式是指除已列明的礼品、无偿援助和赠送物资、捐赠物资、无代价抵偿进口货物、国外免费提供的货样、广告品等及归入列名监管方式的免费提供货物以外,其他免费提供进口的货物。

本监管方式代码为"3339",简称:其他进口免费。

二、适用范围

(一)本监管方式包括:

1. 外商在经贸活动中赠送的物品;

2. 外国人捐赠品;

3. 驻外中资机构向国内单位赠送的物资;

4. 经贸活动中,由外商免费提供的试车材料、消耗性物品等。

(二)本监管方式不包括:

1. 保税仓库中由外商免费提供进口的机械设备、手工工具、运输工具、办公用品等监管方式"一般贸易"(0110);

2. 免税店由外商免费提供进口的货架、柜台、手推车等监管方式"一般贸易"(0110);

Other free imported goods

I. Definition and code

This customs procedure applies to all other free imported goods other than listed presents, materials given as aids and presents, donated items, imported goods for free replacement, samples of goods and advertising goods provided by foreign companies for free, and other goods categorized into listed customs procedures provided for free.

The code is "3339". Abbreviation: other free imported goods.

II. Scope of application:

(1) This customs procedure applies to:

1. Presents in economic and trade activities of foreign investors ;

2. donated items of foreigners;

3. Presents given by Chinese resident institutions abroad to domestic institutions;

4. the run-in materials, exhaustive materials provided by foreign investors in economic and trade activities .

(2) this customs procedure does not apply to:

1. the customs procedure for imported machinery facilities, manual tools, means of transportation, office supplies provided by foreign investors in the bonded warehouse for free is "general trade"(0110)

2. the customs procedure for imported shelves, counters and barrows provided by foreign investors for free in the duty-free stores is "general trade"(0110).

对外承包工程进出口货物

一、定义与代码

对外承包工程出口货物是指经外经贸部批准有对外

The import and export goods of foreign contract project

I. Definition and code

The exported goods of foreign contract project refers to facilities and

承包工程经营权的公司为承包国外建设工程和开展劳务合作等对外合作项目而出口的设备、物资。

本监管方式代码为“3422”,简称:承包工程出口。

承包工程期间,在国外获取的设备物资运回国内的,监管方式代码为“3410”,简称:承包工程进口。

二、适用范围

(一)境外劳务合作项目,对方以实物产品抵偿我劳务人员工资所进口的货物监管方式为“3410”(承包工程进口)。

(二)援外成套项目出口的货物应根据无偿援助或贷款援助监管方式分别选用“无偿援助”(3511)或“一般贸易”(0110)选择填报。

(三)本监管方式不包括:

1. 我劳务人员带出的自用生活物资。

2. 边境地区经外经贸部批准有对外技术合作经营权的企业与我国毗邻国家开展承包工程和劳务合作项下出口的工程设备、物资,监管方式应为“边境小额贸易”(4019)。

3. 承包工程结束后复运进口原从国内运出的承包工程项下的设备、物资,监管方式为退运货物(4561)。

materials exported by enterprises that are entitled to engage in the foreign contract project in order to undertake foreign construction projects or launch labor service cooperation.

The code is “3422”. Abbreviation: contract project export.

During terms of contract, for the facilities and materials obtained abroad and transported home, the code is “3410.”

II. Scope of application

(1) for the overseas labor service cooperative project, the customs procedure for the goods imported to compensate the salaries of labor service is “3410”(contract project import).

(2) for the goods exported as foreign aids by projects shall be registered as “foreign aids free of charge” (3511) or “general trade” (0110) according to customs procedures of foreign aids free of charge or aids in loans.

(3) this customs procedure does not apply to

1. The daily articles for self-use accompanied by the labor personnel.

2. For the facilities and materials exported by the enterprises in the border areas entitled to deal with foreign technological cooperation business with the approval of economic and trade department and launch contract project and labor service cooperation with neighboring countries, the customs procedure is “border area petty trade”(4019).

3. For the facilities and materials that are re-imported after the completion of contract project, the customs procedure is “return and transportation of goods.” (4561).

国家或国际组织无偿援助物资

一、定义与代码

国家间或国际组织无偿援助物资是指我国根据两国政府间的协议或临时决定,对外提供无偿援助的物资、捐赠品或我国政府、组织接受国际组织、外国政府或组织无偿援助、捐赠或赠送的物资。

本监管方式代码为“3511”,简称:无偿援助。

二、适用范围

(一)本监管方式包括:

1. 联合国有关组织、机构利用自愿捐款或基金向我无偿提供的经济技术援助项目进口的物资(包括成套设备或单机);

2. 联合国有关组织、机构利用其正常预算技术合作资金,同我国进行经济技术合作中无偿援助和赠送的物资;

3. 多、双边结合的经济技术援助或合作项目(指第三国通过联合国有关组织、机构向我提供的援助)项下无偿援助和赠送的物资;

4. 其它国际组织、外国政府或非政府组织对我国的无偿援助或利用其赠款购进的货物;

5. 我对外无偿援助和捐赠的物资。

The goods and materials provided by national or international originations as aids

I. Definition and code

The goods and materials provided by national or international originations as aids refer to the materials, donated goods that the Chinese government provides for free, or the materials that international organizations or foreign governments provide to the Chinese government or organizations free of charge according to the bilateral agreements or provisional decisions.

The code for this customs procedure is “3511”. Abbreviation: foreign aids free of charge.

II. Scope of application

(1) This customs procedure applies to:

1. The imported materials for project of economic techniques aids provided by related organizations and institutions of United Nations through voluntary donation or funds;

2. the materials as voluntary aids or presents given by related organizations and institutions of United Nations that employ their normal budget for funds of technical cooperation when launching cooperation of economic techniques with China.

3. the materials as aids or presents under the bilateral and multilateral economic technical aids or cooperative projects (referring to the aids provided by the third country through related institutions and organizations of United Nations)

4. aids provided by other international organizations, foreign governments or non-governmental organizations or imported goods paid with the funds donated by them

5. the materials that China provides as aids and donations

（二）本监管方式不包括：

1. 贷款援助的进出口货物（包括我方利用贷款或援助款项自行采购进口的货物），监管方式应为“一般贸易”（0110）；

2. 来（出）访的团体和人员相互馈赠的礼品（9900）；

3. 属经济贸易往来关系赠送进口的物资，监管方式为“其他进口免费提供”（3339）。

(2) This customs procedure does not apply to:

1. for the import and export goods provided as aids or assistance (including the imported goods that China purchases using assistance loans or aids), the customs procedure is "general trade" (0110);

2. the gifts presented between visiting groups and personnel (9900);

3. for the imported materials presented in the economic and trade relationships, the customs procedure is "other imported goods free of charge" (3339).

华侨、港澳台同胞、外籍华人捐赠物资

一、定义与代码

指华侨、港澳台同胞或外籍华人自愿捐赠物资、设备，直接用于工农业生产，发展科学技术、文化教育、医药卫生及兴办各种公益福利事业。

本监管方式代码为“3612”，简称：捐赠物资。

二、适用范围

本监管方式适用于以上定义的捐赠物资，定义所称“公益福利事业”是指直接用于建设少儿活动设施、幼儿园、敬老院和孤儿院等的物资及生活物品；为安排残疾人就业专门设立的生产企业受赠的生产资料和直接用于残疾人康复、生活专用物品；直接用于修葺古迹文物的物资；直接用于环保、拯救濒危物种、筑路及修桥等公共设施的物资及其他公益事业。

本监管方式包括城乡个体工商业者接受国外或港澳台地区亲友赠送的小型生产工具；

本监管方式不包括外商在经贸往来中赠送的物品、外国人捐赠品、我驻外（包括驻港澳）中资机构向国内单位赠送的物资等，监管方式为“其他进口免费提供货物”（3339）。

Materials donated by overseas Chinese, HK, Macao and Taiwanese compatriots and Chinese of foreign nationality

I. Definition and code

It refers to the materials, facilities donated by overseas Chinese, HK, Macao and Taiwanese compatriots and Chinese of foreign nationality, directly used for agricultural and industrial production, development of science and technology, cultural education, health care and all sorts of public welfare.

The code is "3612", Abbreviation: donated materials

II. Scope of application

This customs procedure applies to donated materials as defined above. The term "public welfare" means the materials and daily supplies for the extracurricular facilities for children, kindergartens, homes for the elderly, orphanages, production materials presented by enterprises for the arrangement of the employment of handicapped, materials directly used for the maintenance of historical relics, materials directly used for environmental protection, protection of endanger species, road construction and bridge maintenance, and materials used for other public facilities.

This customs procedure applies to the mini production tools presented by relatives from HK, Macao and Taiwan to the individual employers of cities and counties.

This customs procedure does not apply to the articles presented by foreign investors in the economic and trade relations, the donated goods of foreigners or the materials presented by representative offices of Chinese-funded institutions abroad (including those in HK, Macao and Taiwan), whose customs procedure is "other imported goods provided for free" (3339).

边境小额贸易

一、定义与代码

边境小额贸易指沿陆地边境线经国家批准对外开放的边境县（旗）、边境城市辖区内（以下简称边境地区）经批准有边境小额货物经营权的企业，通过国家指定的陆地边境口岸，与毗邻国家边境地区的企业或其他贸易机构之间进行的贸易活动，包括易货贸易、现汇贸易等种类贸易形式。

本监管方式代码4019，简称：小额贸易。

二、适用范围

（一）本监管方式不包括边境小额贸易中签订易货贸易合同的贸易。

（二）本监管方式不包括：

1. 边民互市贸易。

2. 未经批准经营边境小额贸易的企业所从事的边境小额贸易，监管方式为“一般贸易”（0110）。

Border petty trade

I. Definition and code

Border petty trade refers to the trade relations between the enterprises approved to engage in border petty trade in the opening border counties, border cities along the land border lines (hereinafter abbreviated as "border areas") and the enterprises from the border areas of neighboring countries or other trading organs, including barter trade, cash-liquidation trade, etc.

The code is 4019. Abbreviation: petty trade.

II. Scope of Application

(1) This customs procedure does not apply to barter trade contract signed in the border petty trade.

(2) This customs procedure does not apply to

1. trade between citizens in border areas.

2. border petty trade undertaken by enterprises that are not permitted to engage in border petty trade (0110).

对台小额贸易

适用于经授权机关批准,台湾渔民和中、小商人同我企业成交使用一百吨以下的台湾船只运进直接来自台湾省的产品和运出大陆产品到台湾的小额贸易,简称:对台小额贸易,监管方式代码为“4039”。

Petty trade with Taiwan

Applicable to the petty trade in which the Taiwan's fish men, median and small businessmen and mainland's enterprises carry the mainland's products to Taiwan and Taiwan's products to mainland with ships with capacity smaller than 100 tons. Abbreviation: petty trade with Taiwan, the code for which is “4039.”

驻外机构运回旧公用物品

指我驻各国(地区)使领馆,驻国外、港澳地区的经济、贸易机构,驻国际组织代表处等我驻外机构更新且闲置不用而运回或因机构撤销而运回的物品,包括临时出国展览团、考察团等运回的生产资料和公用物品。

本监管方式代码为“4200”,简称:驻外机构运回。

本监管方式不包括我驻外机构在境外购买运回境内的公务用品(含运输工具,代码4239)。

Chinese institutions abroad transport used communal articles back to China

It refers to the production materials and public goods carried back by the Chinese embassies to various countries, economic and trade institutions in foreign countries or HK and Macao, representative offices of international offices, either because they are left unused or because the institutions have been cancelled, including the production materials and public goods carried by temporarily outbound exhibition groups and study groups, etc.

The code for this customs procedure is “4200”. Abbreviation: Chinese resident institutions abroad carry back.

This custom procedure does not apply to the communal goods that Chinese institutions abroad purchase abroad and transport back to China (including means of transportation, the code for which is 4239).

驻外机构购进

一、定义及代码

驻外机构购进指我驻外机构在境外购买运回国内的公务用品(包括运输工具),代码4239。

二、适用范围

本监管方式不包括我驻外机构运回国内的原从国内带出的公务用品(4561)。

The importation of Chinese institutions abroad

I. Definition and code

The importation of Chinese institutions abroad refers to the communal articles purchased abroad and transported back to China by Chinese institutions abroad (including means of transportation), the code for which is 4239.

II. Scope of Application

This customs procedure does not apply to communal articles that are originally carried from home and then transported back to China by Chinese institutions abroad(4561).

退运货物

退运进出口货物是指因质量不符、延误交货或其他原因退运进出境的货物,代码4561。

本监管方式包括外商投资设备退运、租赁货物退运、承包工程返运回国的原从国内运出设备,不包括海关放行结关前的直接退运货物,代码4500。

Goods that are returned and sent back

Import and export goods that are returned and sent back refer to goods that are transported outbound because of below standard goods, delayed delivery or other reasons, the code for which is 4561.

This customs procedure applies to the return and transportation of facilities of foreign investors, leasing goods and facilities originally transported outbound then re-transported back home, excluding the outright return and transportation of the goods before customs clearance, the code for which is 4500.

直接退运货物

指货物进境后放行结关前,经海关批准将货物全部退运境外,代码4500。

Outright return and transportation

It refers to the goods that, after entering the boundary but before cleared by the customs, are completely returned and sent back overseas with permission. The code is :4500.

进口溢卸误卸货物

一、定义与代码

进口溢卸货物是指未列入进口载货清单、提(运)单

The goods overloaded or misloaded

I. Definition and code

The goods overloaded or misloaded refer to goods that have not been

的货物，或者多于进口载货清单、提（运）单所列数量的货物，但不包括按照合同规定的溢短装条款所多装的货物。

进口误卸货物，指将本应运往国外港口、车站或国内其他港口、车站但在本港（站）误卸下的货物。

进口溢误卸货物，监管方式代码为“4539”。

二、适用范围

本监管方式包括以上定义所述的进口货物，但不包括：

（一）进口合同规定的溢短装条款溢装的货物应按合同项下进口货物的监管方式。

（二）运往国内其他港口或退运国外的误卸货物。

listed on the import manifest and bill of ladings, or the quantity of which is more than the goods listed on the import manifest or bill of ladings, but excluding the overloaded goods as stipulated in the “overloaded or underloaded” clause of contracts.

The misloaded imported goods refer to the goods that should have been transported to the foreign ports, stations or domestic ports and stations are loaded in this port/station.

The code for the misloaded imported goods is “4539.”

II. Scope of application

This customs procedures apply to imported goods as defined above, but excluding,

(1) The overloaded goods stipulated in “overloaded or underloaded” clause of the import contracts shall be consistent with the customs procedure of import products under the account of contract.

(2) Other misloaded goods transported to other domestic ports or sent back abroad.

出口加工区实际进出境货物

一、定义与代码

出口加工区实际进出境货物是指从境外运入出口加工区或从出口加工区运往境外的货物。

二、适用范围

1. 出口加工区内企业从境外进口的用于进行加工的料件以及加工后出口的成品。贸易方式简称：区内加工货物，代码为5015。

2. 出口加工区内仓储企业从境外进口的供区内企业加工的仓储货物。

贸易方式简称：区内仓储货物，代码为5033。

3. 加工区内企业从境外进口的设备、物资。贸易方式简称：境外设备进区，代码为5335。

4. 出口加工区内设备退运境外。贸易方式简称：区内设备退运，代码为5361。

The actual cross-border goods in the export processing areas

I. Definition and code

The actual cross-border goods in the export processing areas refer to the goods transported to the export processing areas from overseas or transported from export processing areas to overseas.

II. Scope of application

1. materials imported for processing from overseas in export processing areas or finished products exported after being processed. Abbreviation for mode of trade: processed goods within areas, the code for which is 5015.

2. Storage imported by the storage enterprises in the export processing areas from overseas, to be processed by the enterprises in the areas.

Abbreviation for mode of trade: the storage goods within areas, the code for which is 5033.

3. facilities and materials imported from overseas by enterprises in the processing areas. Abbreviation for mode of trade: the overseas facilities entering areas, the code for which is 5335.

4. facilities in the export processing areas that are returned and sent back abroad. Abbreviations for mode of trade: return and transportation in the areas, for which the code is 5361.

区内、外非实际进出境货物

一、定义与代码

区内、外非实际进出境货物是指同一出口加工区内或不同出口加工区的企业之间相互结转（调拨）的货物。

二、适用范围

1. 出口加工区内加工贸易料件在境内结转、销售，包括从区外购进或加工区内企业经批准销往区外的料件，同一出口加工区或不同出口加工区内的企业之间相互结转（调拨）的料件，深加工结转转入的料件，加工区内企业为区外加工的料件进区，以及上述料件在境内的退运，但不包括退换货物。贸易方式简称：料件进出区，代码为5000。

The non-actual cross-border goods in and out of areas

I. Definition and code

The non-actual cross-border goods in and out of areas refer to the goods transferred between enterprises within the same export processing areas or between enterprises from different export processing areas.

II. Scope of application

1. the processed materials transferred and sold in the export processing areas, including materials purchased from or sold to outside of the areas, and the materials transferred between enterprises within the same export processing areas or between enterprises from different export processing areas, materials transferred from advanced processing, entry of materials to be processed by the enterprises in the areas for enterprises outside the areas, and the return and transportation of above-mentioned materials, but excluding the replacement of goods. Abbreviation for the mode of trade: the entry-exit areas for materials, for which the code is 5000.

2. 出口加工区内加工贸易成品在境内结转、销售，包括销往区外、结转到同一出口加工区或另一出口加工区内的企业，以及加工区内企业为区外加工的成品出区、销往区外的成品因故退运进区，但不包括退换货物。贸易方式简称：成品进出区，代码为5100。

2. the processed finished products transferred and sold in the export processing areas, including those sold to outside of the areas, transferred to the enterprises in the same or different processing areas, and exit areas for products processed by enterprises in the processing areas for those outside the areas, the finished products sold to outside of areas that are returned and transported back to the entering areas because of various reasons, but excluding replacement goods. Abbreviation for mode of trade: entering and exit areas for finished products, for which the code is 5100.

3. 出口加工区内企业边角料结转到同一加工区或不同加工区的另一企业，或经批准销售到区外。贸易方式简称：区内边角调出，代码为5200。

3. Leftover materials in the export processing area transferred to enterprises in the same or different processing areas, or sold to outside of the area after being permitted. Abbreviation for mode of trade: the transfer of leftover materials within area, the code for which is 5200.

4. 出口加工区内企业设备、物资在境内结转、销售，包括从区外购进设备、物资，设备因故销往区外，设备结转到同一出口加工区或另一出口加工区内的企业，以及上述设备、物资在境内的退运、退换。贸易方式简称：设备进出区，代码为5300。

4. The facilities and materials in the export processing areas transferred and sold domestically, including those purchased from outside of areas, transferred to enterprises in the same or different processing areas, and the return and transportation or replacement of above-mentioned materials within domestic boundaries, the code for which is 5300.

物流中心进出境货物

用于保税物流中收与境外之间仓储货物进出口，全称“保税物流中收与境外之间进出仓储货物”，简称：物流中心进出境货物，监管方式代码为“6033”。

Goods Entering and exiting logistics center

Used for the import and export of storage goods between the bonded logistics center and overseas, the full name being “the entry and exit of storage between bonded logistics center and overseas”; abbreviation: Goods Entering and exiting logistics center, the code for which is “6033.”

海关处理货物

适用于海关变卖处理的超期未报货物、走私违规货物，简称：海关处理货物，监管方式代码为“9639”。

Goods dealt with by the Customs

Applicable to the expired undeclared goods and smuggling goods that are dealt with by the Customs; abbreviation: Goods dealt with by the Customs, the code for which is “9639.”

其他贸易

一、定义与代码

其他贸易是指除本监管方式代码表说明具体列名的监管方式以外应列入海关“其他贸易”统计的进出口货物。

本监管方式代码为“9739”，简称：其他贸易。

二、适用范围

（一）有外贸进出口经营权的企业和外商投资企业以外的我国境内的机关、团体、学校、企事业单位等经批准临时进出口的货物；

（二）外国驻华使、领馆在我国内购运出口的货物；

（三）出境旅客在国内购买以货运方式运出境的货物；

（四）外商投资企业外方常驻人员和外国驻华机构的常驻人员，以及持有长期居留证件和来华定居的引进专家等进口自用的汽车。

（五）我出国人员用个人外汇购进的公用物品。

（六）城乡个体工商业者自行进口的小型生产工具。

Other trades

I. Definition and code

Other trades refer to the import and export goods other than those whose customs procedures are specified as listed in the*code list for custom procedures* but instead are listed in “other trades” for customs statistics.

The code is “9739”; abbreviation: “other trades.”

II. Scope for application

(1) Goods temporarily imported and exported by domestic organs, groups, schools and enterprises, but not by enterprises entitled to engage in foreign trade or foreign companies.

(2) the goods purchased and exported domestically by foreign embassies to China.

(3) Goods purchased domestically and transported outbound by means of freight by outbound passengers

(4) the cars imported for self-use by foreign permanent personnel of foreign enterprises and foreign permanent personnel of foreign resident institutions in China, and experts with permanent resident certificates, etc.

(5) the communal goods purchased by outbound individuals with personal foreign exchange.

(6) mini production instruments imported by individual employers of cities and counties.

后续退补税

指各种无法获得原始报关单的后续退补税货物，包括调查、稽查补税及审价、归类等各种原因的后续退补税货物，代码9700。

租赁征税

指租期一年及以上的租赁货物的租金，此监管方式专用于征收税款，代码9800。

留赠转卖物品

指经特批进口的驻华外交机构转售境内非外交机构的物品、国际文体活动留赠或放弃的物品，代码9839。

其他

一、定义与代码

指除各类具体列名的监管方式以外其他不列入海关统计的进出境货物（物品）。

本监管方式代码为“9900”，简称：其他。

二、适用范围

本监管方式主要包括：

（一）转运和通运货物。

（二）供应国内外汇商店并收取外汇的我出口商品。

（三）海关没收的走私物品。

（四）边民互市贸易进出境货物。

（五）国际交往中相互赠送的礼品。

（六）无法归入其他监管方式的进出境退换货物。

保税仓库转内销货物，境内存入出口监管仓库和出口监管仓退仓货物

一、定义与代码

保税仓库转内销是指经海关核准转为供国内使用的原从境外存入保税仓库的货物。

境内存入出口监管仓库的货物是指已向海关办理出口报关手续存入出口监管仓库的货物。

出口监管仓库退仓货物指原已向海关办结出口报关手续从境内存入出口监管仓库，后经海关核准转为供国内使用的货物，即从出口监管仓库退回的原按“境内存入出口监管仓库”统计的货物。

上述货物进/出保税仓库（出口监管仓库）时，应分别按实际监管方式填报。为把列入海关单项统计的保税

Make-up/deducted taxes

It refers to the goods that cannot obtain original customs declaration subsequently get makes-up or deducted tax, including goods for subsequent makes-up or deducted tax due to various reasons such as investigation, examination, evaluation, and categorization, for which the code is 9700.

Leasing duty

It refers to the rent for leasing goods with terms more than one year; this customs procedure is specially used for tax levy, for which the code is 9800.

Resell presented or abandoned goods

It refers to the goods imported with special approval presented or abandoned by international cultural activities or diplomatic institutions that resell to non-diplomatic institutions, the code is 9839.

Other

I. Definition and code

It refers to cross-border goods (articles) other than those with specified customs procedures and therefore excluded from customs statistics.

The code is 9900; abbreviation: other.

II. Scope of application

This customs procedure mainly applies to:

(1) goods transferred and transported.

(2) Exported commodities paid by foreign exchanges provided for domestic foreign-exchange stores.

(3) smuggling goods confiscated by the Customs.

(4) cross-border goods traded by citizens along the border.

(5) gifts presented in international communication activities.

(6) cross-border goods for return and replacement unable to be categorized into other customs procedures.

Goods originally in bonded warehouses declared for domestic sales, goods stored in export supervised warehouse and goods returned from export supervised warehouse from domestic territories

I. Definition and code

Goods originally in bonded warehouses declared for domestic sales refer to goods that originally transported from overseas to bonded warehouse then approved by the customs to be kept for domestic use.

Goods stored in export supervised warehouse from domestic territory refer to goods that have completed customs declaration and stored into export supervised warehouse.

Goods returned from export supervised warehouse refer to goods originally declared to be exported and stored in the export supervised warehouse but then declared for domestic use after being approved by the Customs, i.e. goods that originally counted as “domestic territory stored into export supervised warehouse” but then are returned from export supervised warehouse.

When the above-mentioned goods enter/exit bonded warehouses, they shall be reported based on actual customs procedures. In order to distin-

仓库转内销和境内存入出口监管仓库货物与列入海关进出口统计的保税仓库进出境货物区别开来，上述货物进出保税仓库时，运输方式分别填报“1”（境内存入出口监管仓和出口监管仓退仓）或“8”（保税仓库转内销）。

二、适用范围

本监管方式不包括：

1. 从保税仓库提取供应外国籍运输工具的进口燃料、物料及零配件等，监管方式为“保税仓库进出境货物”(1233)

2. 设置在保税区内保税仓库往非保税区内销的货物和从非保税区存入保税区内保税仓库的货物属保税区运往非保税区和非保税区运入保税区货物，运输方式填报“7”（保税区），监管方式视具体交易方式选择填报。

guish goods in bonded warehouse for domestic sales listed separately by customs with those stored into export supervised warehouse and the cross-border goods in the bonded warehouse listed by customs statistics of import and export, when the above-mentioned goods enter and exit the bonded warehouse, the means of transportation shall be reported as “1” (stored into export supervised warehouse from domestic territory and returned from export supervised warehouse) or “8” (bonded warehouse for domestic sales).

II. Scope of application

This customs procedure does not apply to:

1. for the imported fuels, materials and components picked up from bonded warehouse provided for foreign means of transportation, the customs procedure is “bonded warehouse cross-border goods.” (1233)

2. for the goods in bonded warehouses of boned areas sold to non-bonded areas and goods stored into bonded warehouses of bonded areas from non-bonded areas, the means of transportation reported as “7” (bonded areas), and the customs procedure shall be reported based on specific means of transaction.

保税区运往非保税区货物，非保税区运入保税区和保税区退区货物

一、定义与代码

保税区运往非保税区货物指经海关核准运往非保税区的保税区单独实施税收优惠政策的进口货物或保税的进口货物。

非保税区运入保税区货物指已向海关办结出口报关手续从非保税区运入保税区的货物。

保税区退区货物指原已向海关办理出口报关手续从非保税区运入保税区，后经海关核准转为供非保税区使用的货物。

上述货物进出保税区时，分别根据货物进出保税区的实际用途按相应的监管方式填报，列入海关单项统计。为把保税区单项统计的监管方式同海关进出口统计的监管方式区分开来，避免重复统计，上述货物进出保税区时，运输方式分别填报“0”（非保税区运用保税区和保税区退区）或“7”（保税区运往非保税区）。

二、适用范围

本监管方式不包括：

（一）保税区进出境仓储、转口货物，监管方式为“保税区仓储转口货物”(1234)。

（二）保税区的国产货物和已照章纳税的进口货物运往非保税区

The goods transported from bonded areas to non-bonded areas, from non-bonded to bonded areas and goods exiting bonded areas

I. Definition and code

The goods transported from bonded areas to non-bonded areas refers to the imported goods or bonded imported goods enjoying preferential treatment of bonded areas transported to non-bonded areas after being approved by the Customs.

Goods transported from non-bonded areas to bonded areas refer to the goods that have completed customs declaration to be transported from non-bonded areas to bonded areas.

Goods exiting bonded areas refer to goods that have completed customs procedure to be transported from non-bonded areas to bonded areas, but then are declared for being used by non-bonded areas after being approved.

When the above-mentioned goods enter and exit bonded areas, they should be reported based on the actual use of goods and their correspondent customs procedure, and listed separately for customs statistics. In order to distinguish the customs procedure of bonded areas separately listed for custom statistics with the customs procedure of import and export statistics of customs, and avoid double calculation, when the above-mentioned goods enter and exit the bonded areas, the means of transportation shall be reported as “0” (non-bonded areas to bonded areas and exiting bonded areas) or “7” (bonded areas to non-bonded areas).

II. Scope of application

This customs procedure does not include

(1) For the cross-border storage and foundry goods, the customs procedure is “bonded area storage and foundry goods” (1234).

(2) national goods in the bonded areas and imported goods that have been levied transported to non-bonded areas.

征免性质代码表说明

征免性质是对海关征减免税管理规定的类别划分,它主要用于海关H2000通关系统对进出口货物的征减免税进行分类统计,为海关关税数据库提供第一手数据。

一、征免性质的分类

征免性质分为法定照章征税、法定减免税、特定减免税、其他减免税和暂定税率五部分。其中特定减免税又分为按地区实施的税收政策、按用途实施的税收政策、按贸易性质实施的税收政策和按企业性质和资金来源实施的税收政策四类。

二、征免性质代码的编码结构

征免性质代码由三位数组成,第一位数表示类别,第二、三位数表示该类别减免税项目的顺序号。

一般征税进出口货物

一、定义与代码

一般征税进出口货物指海关依照《中华人民共和国海关法》、《中华人民共和国进出口关税条例》、《中华人民共和国海关进出口税则》及其他法律、法规所规定的税率征收关税、增值税和其他税费的进出口货物。

本征免性质代码为"101",简称:一般征税。

二、适用范围

除其他征免性质另有规定者外的一般照章(包括按照公开暂定税率)征税或补税的进出口货物。

无偿援助进出口物资

一、定义

无偿援助进出口物资指外国政府、国际组织对我国无偿援助或赠送的(不包括经贸往来赠送,华侨、港澳台同胞捐赠和其他团体、个人的捐赠),或我国对国外无偿援助或赠送的物资。

本征免性质代码为"201",简称:无偿援助。

二、适用范围

1.根据双边政府协议规定无偿赠送或援助的进出口物资,如:外国政府利用自愿捐款或基金向我国提供的无偿的经济技术援助项目、成套设备或单机;外国政府对我国的无偿援助或我国利用外国政府赠款购进的货物;

Table of Code of Levy Type

Levy type is the classification of the regulations on levy management. It is mainly used in the H2000 customs clearance system for classification analysis and provides the first-hand data for customs duty database.

Classification of levy type

Levy type includes five parts, which are duty paying according to law in force, duty exemption/reduction, specific duty exemption/reduction, other exemption/reduction and interim duty rate, among which, specific duty exemption/reduction is classified into four categories of duty policies that are implemented differently according to different regions, uses, trade types, and the enterprise types and capital sources.

Coding structure of levy type code

Code of levy type consists of three digits, the first one representing the classification; the second and the third representing the serial number of exemption/reduction items.

Import/export goods with general customs duties

Ⅰ. Definition and code

Import/export goods with general customs duties refer to the import/export goods with customs duties, value-added tax and other taxes in accordance with *Customs Law of the People's Republic of China* , *Regulations of the People's Republic of China on Import and Export Duties* and *Customs Import and Export Tariff of the People's Republic of China* and other relevant laws, regulations and rules.

Code for this levy type is "101", general taxation.

Ⅱ. Scope of application

Import/export goods with general customs duties (including released interim duty rates) or with tax supplementation except those under other exemption/reduction types.

Import/export materials of free assistance

Ⅰ. Definition

Import/export materials of free assistance refer to materials donated or presented by foreign governments, international organizations (presents due to economic and trade relationships, donations from Chinese living abroad, those from Hong Kong, Macau and Taiwan and other organizations and individuals are excluded), or materials donated and presented by china to foreign countries.

Code for this levy type is "201"; free assistance for short.

Ⅱ. Scope of application

1. Import/export materials presented or donated free of charge in accordance with provisions in bilateral agreement between governments. For example: economic and technical assistance project, set equipment or stand-alone equipment provided free of charge by foreign governments making use of voluntary money donations or funds; goods donated by foreign countries or purchased by China with money donated by foreign

countries;

2. 联合国及其各专门机构和其他政府间组织、国际金融机构(如:国际货币基金组织、世界银行、亚洲开发银行、日本海外协力基金、日本输出入银行)以及国际贸易组织等无偿援助或赠送的物资,如联合国有关组织机构同我国进行的经济技术合作;多、双边结合的经济技术援助合作项目;联合国粮农组织对我国的无偿援助项目进口的粮食、食品和其他物资设备;国际红十字会和各国红十字会救济、捐赠给我国红十字会的物品以及由中国红十字会组织负责接受和分配国际红十字会组织为我国无偿提供的救灾物资;

2. Materials presented or donated to China by the United Nations and its specific organizations, other non-governmental organizations, international financial institutions (such as International Monetary Fund, World Bank, Asia Development Bank, Japanese Overseas Union Fund, Japan Import and Export Bank) and WTO etc., for instance, the economic and technical co-operation between relevant organizations of United Nations and China; bilateral and multi-lateral economic and technical assistance and cooperation projects; grain, food and other materials and equipment imported by Food and Agriculture Organization of the United Nations for the assistance project; materials donated to the Red Cross of China by International Federation of Red Cross and Red Crescent Societies and Red Cross societies from other countries and disaster relief supplies offered by International Federation of Red Cross and Red Crescent Societies and received and taken in charge by Red Cross of China.

3. 我国政府对外无偿援助或赠送的物资。

3. Materials donated or presented abroad by China

其他法定减免税进出口货物

Other import/export goods legalized with duty exemption/reduction

一、定义

其他法定减免税进出口货物指海关依照《中华人民共和国海关法》、《中华人民共和国进出口关税条例》,对除无偿援助进出口物资外的其他实行法定减免税的进出口货物,以及根据有关规定非按全额货值征税的部分进出口货物。

本征免性质代码为"299",简称:其他法定。

Ⅰ. Definition

Other import/export goods with duty exemption/reduction refer to the import/export goods with duty exemption/reduction other than Import/export materials of free assistance following the provisions of *Customs Law of the People's Republic of China*, *Regulations of the People's Republic of China on Import and Export Duties* and part of import/export goods with non-full-goods-value taxation.

Code for this levy type is "229"; other legalized duty exemption/reduction for short

二、适用范围

1. 无代价抵偿进出口货物(照章征税的除外);
2. 无商业价值的广告品和货样;
3. 进出境运输工具装载的途中必需的燃料、物料和饮食用品;
4. 因故退还的境外进口货物;
5. 因故退还的我国出口货物;
6. 在境外运输途中或者在起卸时,遭受损坏或损失的货物;
7. 起卸后海关放行前,因不可抗力遭受损坏或者损失的货物;
8. 海关查验时已经破漏、损坏或者腐烂,经证明不是保管不慎造成的货物;
9. 中华人民共和国缔结或者参加的国际条约规定减征、免征关税的货物、物品;
10. 暂时进出口货物;
11. 出料加工项下的出口料件及复进口的成品;
12. 进出境的修理物品;
13. 租赁期不满一年的进出口货物;
14. 边民互市进出境货物。
15. 非按全额货值征税的进口货物(如按租金、修理费征税的进口货物)。

Ⅱ. Scope of application

1. Free replacement goods (except those levied as stipulated);
2. Displays and samples with no commercial value;
3. Fuel, materials, food and drinks needed during transportation across borders;
4. Imported goods to be returned due to certain causes;
5. Exported goods to be returned due to certain causes;
6. Goods which are damaged and suffer loss in transportation abroad and in unloading;
7. Goods which suffer damage and loss due to force majeure after unloading yet before customs release;
8. Goods which are proved to have already been broken, damaged or rotten when checked at the customs, not caused by careless keeping;
9. Goods with tariff exemption and reduction according to provisions of international agreements which China has committed to;
10. Interim import and export goods;
11. Outbound material and re-imported final products under export processing category;
12. Goods to be repaired across borders;
13. Import/export goods within one-year lease;
14. Goods across borders transacted in trade along border areas;
15. Import goods that cannot be levied according to its full value (such as imported goods levied according to rent, mending fee).

特定区域进口自用物资及出口货物

一、定义

特定区域进口自用物资及出口货物指深圳、珠海、汕头、厦门、海南等5个经济特区及上海浦东新区和苏州工业园区、三峡库区等在国家核定额度内实行关税和进口环节增值税先征后返还的进口自用物资及对这些地区单独实施免税政策的出口货物。

本征免性质代码为"301",简称:特定区域。

二、适用范围

1. 上述地区内企、事业单位(外商投资企业除外)在国家核定额度内实行关税和进口环节增值税先征后返还的进口自用物资;

2. 上述地区生产的出口产品,包括上述地区用内地料件加工增值20%以上的出口产品。

Import materials for self use and export goods in specific districts

Ⅰ. Definition

Import materials for self use and export goods in specific districts refer to materials imported for self use, on which customs duty and value-added tax are levied first but rebated later within ratified ration, in the five special economic districts of Shenzheng, Zhuhai, Shantou, Xiamen, Hainan, together with Shanghai Pudong New District, Suzhou Industrial Garden, Three Gauges District.

Code for this levy type is "301"; specific districts for short.

Ⅱ. Scope of application

Materials imported for self use, on which customs duty and value-added tax are levied first but rebated later within ratified ration for companies and enterprises (foreign-invested enterprises excluded) in district mentioned above

2. Products manufactured in the above-mentioned districts, including outbound products manufactured with materials from mainland achieving an increase of added value by 20%.

保税区进口自用物资

一、定义

保税区进口自用物资指对保税区单独实施征减免税政策的进口自用物资。

本征免性质代码为"307",简称:保税区。

二、适用范围

1. 保税区用于基础设施建设的物资。

2. 保税区内企业(外商投资企业除外)进口的生产设备和其他自用物资。

Import materials for self use in bonded areas

Ⅰ. Definition

Import materials for self use in bonded areas refer to the supplies imported for self use with levy policies implemented only in bonded areas.

Code for this levy type is "307"; bonded area for short

Ⅱ. Scope of application

1. Materials used for infrastructure construction in bonded areas

2. Equipment for production and other materials for self use imported by enterprises in bonded areas (foreign invested enterprises excluded)

其他执行特殊政策地区出口货物

一、定义

其他执行特殊政策地区出口货物指对经济技术开发区、高新技术产业开发区等单独实施免税政策的出口货物。

本征免性质代码为"399",简称:其他地区。

二、适用范围

上述地区企业(外商投资企业除外)生产的出口产品,包括上述地区用内地料件加工增值20%以上的出口产品。

Export goods in other districts with special policies

Ⅰ. Definition

Export goods in districts with special policies refer to outbound goods in economic and technology development districts, hi-tech industry development districts, where duty exemption policy is implemented.

Code for this levy type is "399"; other districts for short

Ⅱ. Scope of application

Outbound products manufactured by enterprises in the districts mentioned above (foreign invested enterprises excluded), including outbound products manufactured with materials from mainland achieving an increase of added value by 20%。

科研机构、学校进口科教用品

一、定义

科研机构、学校进口科教用品指为促进科学研究和教育事业的发展,科学研究机构和学校按照有关征减免税政策,进口国内不能生产的、直接用于科研或教学的货物。

Materials on science and education imported by schools and scientific research institutions

Ⅰ. Definition

Materials on science and education imported by schools and scientific research institutions refer to the goods, which can not be domestically produced and which can be used direct for scientific research and teaching for the purpose of promoting the development of scientific research and education, imported in accordance with relevant preferential duty policies

本征免性质代码为“401”,简称:科教用品。

二、适用范围

1. 国务院规定的科研开发机构和大专院校进口的科教用品;

2. 经国务院有关部门批准的其他科研开发机构和学校进口的科教用品;

3. 经国务院有关部门核定的企业(集团)技术中心、国家工程研究中心、国家重点实验室和国家工程技术研究中心在2000年底以前进口的科研物品。

Code for this levy type is “401”; scientific and educational materials.

Ⅱ. Scope of application

1. Scientific and educational materials imported by universities and colleges and scientific study and research institution approved by the State Council;

2. Scientific and educational materials imported by schools and other scientific study and research institutions approved by the State Council;

Material for scientific study imported previous to the end of 2002 by enterprise (group) technical centers, national engineering research centers, national key laboratories and national engineering technology research centers approved by the State Council.

企业技术改造进口货物

一、定义

企业技术改造进口货物指为了鼓励引进国外先进技术,促进企业技术改造和产品升级换代,提高综合经济效益,现有生产企业为进行技术改造按照有关征减免税政策进口必需的先进技术、机器、仪器和设备。

本征免性质代码为“403”,简称:技术改造.

二、适用范围

1. 技改项目进口货物;

2. 综合利用技术改造项目进口货物。

Goods imported for technical reform

Ⅰ. Definition

Goods imported for technical reform refer to the advanced technologies, machines, instruments and equipment imported necessary for enterprises to carry on technical reform and reconstruction, levied in accordance with preferential duty policies in the aim of encouraging to bring in advanced foreign technologies. Promoting technical reform and updating of products, improving economic efficiency.

Code for this levy type is “403”; technical reform for short.

Ⅱ. Scope of application

1. Goods imported for technical reform projects;

2. Goods imported for synthesized exploitation and technical reform projects.

国家重大项目进口货物

一、定义

国家重大项目进口货物指经国务院批准的国家重大建设项目项下按照有关征减免税政策进口的设备,以及安装所需材料等。

本征免性质代码为“406”,简称:重大项目。

二、适用范围

列入《国务院已批准享受减免税政策的重大项目清单》的项目进口的机器设备等。

Import goods for key national projects

Ⅰ. Definition

Import goods for key national projects refer to the materials needed in installation and equipment imported for key national projects approved by the State Council, levied in accordance with relevant preferential duty policies.

Code for this levy type is “406”; key project for short.

Ⅱ. Scope of application

Machinery and equipment listed in the List of the Key Projects with Preferential Duty Policies Approved by the State Council.

通信、港口、铁路、公路、机场建设进口设备

一、定义

通信、港口、铁路、公路、机场建设进口设备指为促进基础设施建设,按照有关征减免税政策进口的用于通信、港口、铁路、公路、机场建设的机器、设备。

本征免性质代码为“412”,简称:基础设施。

二、适用范围

《进口通信、港口、铁路、公路、机场专用设备准予减免税品种表》所列的各种机器、设备。

Import equipment for the construction of communication, ports, rails, roads, airports

Ⅰ. Definition

Import equipment for the construction of communication, ports, rails, roads, airports refers to the machinery and equipment to be used in the construction of communication, ports, rails, roads, airports, imported with the aim of promoting infrastructure construction, levied in accordance with relevant preferential duty policies.

Code for this levy type is “412”; infrastructure for short.

Ⅱ. Scope of application

All kinds of machinery and equipment listed in the import product list of specific equipment for communication, ports, rails, roads, airports approved of duty exemption/reduction.

进口残疾人专用品和专用设备及残疾人企业出口产品

一、定义

进口残疾人专用品和专用设备及残疾人企业出口产品指为支持残疾人康复工作、帮助残疾人自立而免税进口的残疾人专用品和有关福利机构、康复机构、企业按照国家有关规定免税进口的国内不能生产的残疾人专用设备及专用生产设备，以及残疾人企业生产的免税出口产品。

本征免性质代码为“413”，简称：残疾人。

二、适用范围

1. 有关单位进口的残疾人个人专用物品；

2. 民政部门和残疾人组织所属福利机构、荣军康复医院、康复机构有关企业进口的用于残疾人康复、教育、劳动等的专用仪器、设备及专用生产设备；

3. 残疾人企业生产的出口产品。

Special product import for the disabled and outbound products manufactured by enterprises made up of disabled workers

Ⅰ. Definition

Special-purpose product imports for the disabled and outbound products manufactured by enterprises of disabled people refer to the special-purpose products used by the disabled, special-purpose equipment used by the disabled which is not domestically produced imported by relevant welfare organizations and recovery centers, equipment for special-purpose production imported by enterprises, and outbound products made by enterprises made up of disabled workers, imported or exported with duty exemption for the purpose of supporting the recovery of the disabled and helping the disabled to be self-sufficient.

Code for this levy type is “413”; the disabled for short.

Ⅱ. Scope of application

1. Special-purpose articles for personal use imported by relevant institutions;

2. special-purpose apparatus and instruments and equipment for special-purpose production imported by civil affairs department, welfare organizations subject to organizations of disabled persons, rehabilitation hospitals and enterprises connected to rehabilitation institutions, for health rehabilitation, education, working concerning the disabled people

3. Outbound products manufactured by enterprises made up of disabled workers

远洋渔业自捕水产品

远洋渔业自捕水产品指取得《农业部远洋渔业企业资格证书》的远洋渔业企业及外商投资的远洋渔业企业，在规定的额度内自捕运回的水产品。

本征免性质代码为“417”，简称：远洋渔业。

Fishing-vessel-catch aquatic products of deep-fishing

Fishing-vessel-catch aquatic products of deep fishing refer to the aquatic products caught and shipped back within the restricted limits by deep-fishing enterprises and foreign-invested deep-fishing enterprises with the Ministry of Agriculture Deep-fishing enterprise Qualification Certificate.

Code for this category is “417”; deep-fishing for short.

国家定点生产小轿车和摄录机企业进口散件

一、定义

国家定点生产小轿车和摄录机企业进口散件指国家定点生产小轿车和摄录一体机的企业，按照有关征减免税政策进口的小轿车或摄录一体机成套散件或关键件。

本征免性质代码为“418”，简称：国产化。

二、适用范围

1. 一汽大众、上海大众、上海通用、北京吉普、广州本田、武汉神龙、天津夏利、长安奥拓、贵州云雀等9个国家定点生产小轿车企业进口的关键件；

2. 南京依维柯、沈阳金杯等12家定点轻型车生产企业进口的轻型车关键件；

3. 北京JVC电子有限公司、上海索广电子有限公司等国家定点生产摄录一体机企业进口的摄录一体机成套散件或关键件。

Import pieces of state appointed car producers and video camera producers

Ⅰ. Definition

Import pieces of state appointed car producers and video camera producers refer to the pieces in set or key parts of cars and video cameras imported by state-appointed car and video camera producers following relevant duty preferential policies

Code for this levy type is “418”; domestication in short

Ⅱ. Scope of applicantion

1. key auto parts imported by nine state-appointed car producers--Faw-Volkswagen, Shanghai Volkswagen, Shanghai GM, Beijing Jeep, Guangzhou Honda, Wuhan Shenlong, Tianjin Xiali, Chang'an Aotuo, Guuizhou Yunque;

2. Key light car parts imported by 12 appointed light car producers such as Nanjing I veco and Shenyang Jinbei;

3. Pieces in set or key parts of video cameras imported by state-appointed producers such as Beijing JVC Electronics Company Limited, Shanghai Suoguang Electronics Company Limited.

构成整车特征的汽车零部件进口

根据《构成整车特征的汽车零部件进口管理操作规程(试行)》,进口构成整车特征的汽车零部件,征免性质栏填写"整车特征",征免性质代码为"419"。

手工填写税款缴款书时,应根据实际情况处理,其中纳税方式为"整车税率征税"的,"征免性质"栏填写"整车征税",征免性质代码为"118";纳税方式为"零部件税率征税"的,"征免性质"栏填写"零部件征税",征免性质代码为"119";纳税方式为"国内配套件"的,"征免性质"栏填写"整车征税",征免性质代码为"118"。

Import of Car components constituting complete vehicle

According to Regulations on the import management of Car Parts Constituting Complete Vehicle, when importing car parts constituting complete vehicle, the blank of category of exemption should be filled in "Constituting Complete Vehicle" and code of exemption is "419".

When duty paying notice is filled by hand, it depends on different situations. If levy mode is "taxation by whole car tax rate", "category of exemption" should be filled in "whole car taxation", the code is "118"; if levy mode is "taxation by component tax rate", "category of exemption" should be filled in "component taxation", the code is "119"; levy mode is "domestic component", "category of exemption" should be filled in "whole car taxation", the code is "118".

勘探、开发海上石油进口货物

一、定义

勘探、开发海上石油进口货物指按照有关征减免税政策进口的勘探、开发海上(包括浅海)石油和天然气所需的设备、材料。

本征免性质代码为"606",简称:海上石油。

Import goods for exploration and tapping of sea oil

Ⅰ. Definition

Import goods for exploration and tapping of sea oil refer to the equipment and materials needed in the process of oil and gas exploration and tapping in the sea (including sea-shallow), imported duty-free in accordance with relevant preferential policies of import duty.

Code for this levy type is "606"; sea oil for short.

勘探、开发陆地石油进口货物

一、定义

勘探、开发陆地石油进口货物指按照有关征减免税政策进口的勘探、开发我国境内陆地特定地域内石油和天然气所需的设备、材料。

本征免性质代码为"608",简称:陆地石油。

二、适用范围

经国务院批准,在我国境内特定地域内勘探、开发陆地石油和天然气所需进口的设备、物品。

Import goods for exploration and tapping of land oil

Ⅰ. Definition

Import goods for exploration and tapping of land oil refer to the equipment and materials needed in the process of oil and gas exploration and tapping in appointed areas of China, imported duty-free in accordance with relevant preferential policies of import duty.

Code for this levy type is "608"; land oil for short.

Ⅱ. Scope of application

Equipment and articles needed in the process of oil and gas exploration and tapping in appointed areas of China approved by the State Council

救灾捐赠进口物资

一、定义

救灾捐赠进口物资指外国民间团体、企业、友好人士和华侨、香港居民、台湾、澳门同胞及外籍华人无偿向我境内受灾地区捐赠的直接用于救灾的免税进口物资。

本征免性质代码为"801",简称:救灾捐赠

二、适用范围

由民政部、中国红十字会、中华全国妇女联合会负责接收的外国民间团体、企业、友好人士和华侨、香港居民、台湾、澳门同胞及外籍华人无偿捐赠的,符合《关于救灾捐赠物资免征进口税收的暂行办法》规定的免税进口救灾物资。

Import of Disaster relief donation

Ⅰ. Definition

Disaster relief donation imports refer to the donations donated for disaster-stricken areas for direct disaster relief in China by foreign non-governmental organizations, enterprises, friends and Chinese living abroad, Hong Kong citizens, Taiwanese, Macau citizens and Chinese with foreign nationalities, imported free of customs duties.

Code for this levy type is "801"; relief donation for short.

Ⅱ. Scope of application

Disaster relief donations given by foreign non-governmental organizations, enterprises, friends and Chinese living abroad, Hong Kong citizens, Taiwanese, Macau citizens and Chinese with foreign nationalities, and received and taken in charge by China Civil Affairs Ministry, the Red-Cross of China, All-China Women's Federation.

加工贸易外商提供的不作价进口设备

一、定义

加工贸易外商提供的不作价进口设备指加工贸易经营

Non-price setting imported equipment provided by foreign businessmen for processing trade

Ⅰ. Definition

1. Non-price setting imported equipment provided by foreign busi-

单位按照有关征免税政策进口的外商免费(即不需经营单位付汇,也不需用加工费和差价偿还)提供的加工生产所需设备。

本征免性质代码为"501",简称:加工设备。

二、适用范围

符合免税进口和使用外商提供的不作价设备条件的加工贸易(包括来料加工、进料加工及外商投资企业从事的加工贸易)经营单位规定免税或征税进口的、由外商免费提供的加工生产所需设备(包括工模具)。

nessmen for processing trade, refers to equipment needed in processing production, which is provided free of charge (the operating units need neither payment in foreign exchange for imports, nor payment in the form of processing fees of price difference) by foreign businessmen engaged in processing trade with the operating units of processing trade.

Code for this levy type is "501"; processing equipment for short

Ⅱ. Scope of application

Equipment (models included), provided by foreign businessmen free of charge following preferential duty policies, imported by operating units of processing trade (including processing of imported materials and of supplied materials and processing trade operated by foreign-invested enterprises) which meet the conditions of exemption of import duty and using non-price setting imported equipment provided by foreign businessmen for processing trade.

来料加工装配和补偿贸易进口料件及出口成品

一、定义

来料加工装配和补偿贸易进口料件及出口成品指为鼓励和促进对外加工装配业务,按照有关征减免税政策进口的来料加工装配业务和补偿贸易所需的原材料、辅料、元器件、零部件和包装材料等,以及经加工后出口的成品。

本征免性质代码为"502",简称:来料加工。

二、适用范围

1. 来料加工装配和补偿贸易项目进口的料、件;

2. 来料加工装配和补偿贸易生产的出口成品和半成品。

Materials imported and final products exported for processing trade with supplied materials and compensation trade

Ⅰ. Definition

Materials imported and final products exported for processing trade with supplied materials and compensation trade refer to what is needed for processing and assembling trade and compensation trade, such as the materials, supplies, components, particles and package materials etc. in accordance with relevant preferential duty policies, and the final products processed for export sales, with the aim of encouraging processing and assembling trade.

Code for this levy type is "502"; processing with supplied materials for short.

Ⅱ. Scope of application

1. Materials and pieces imported for processing and assembling trade and compensation trade.

2. Final products and semi-products of processing and assembling trade and compensation trade, manufactured for export sales

进料加工贸易进口料件及出口成品

一、定义

进料加工贸易进口料件及出口成品指外贸公司、工贸公司及外商投资企业等为生产外销产品或为履行产品出口合同,按照有关征减免税政策进口的原材料、零部件及出口成品。

本征免性质代码为"503",简称:进料加工。

二、适用范围

1. 外贸公司、工贸公司等专为生产外销产品而用外汇购买进口的原料、材料、辅料、元器件、零部件、配套件、包装物料及消耗材料;

2. 外商投资企业为履行产品出口合同而进口的原料、材料、辅料、元器件、零部件、配套件、包装物料及消耗材料;

3. 经加工后返销出口的成品和半成品。

Import of materials and pieces for processing trade with imported materials and final export products

Ⅰ. Definition

Import materials and pieces for processing trade and export products refer to the materials and components imported and final export products manufactured by foreign trade companies, industrial trade companies and foreign-invested enterprises for fulfilling export contract or for manufacturing products to be sold abroad.

Code for this levy type is "503"; processing with imported materials for short.

Ⅱ. Scope of application

1. Materials, supplies, components, parts, package materials and expendable materials imported and purchased with foreign exchange for the purpose of manufacturing export products by foreign trade companies, industrial trade companies

2. Materials, components, parts, package materials and expendable materials imported for the purpose of fulfilling export contract by foreign-invested enterprises.

3. Final products and semi-products processed for export sales.

边境小额贸易进口货物

一、定义

边境小额贸易进口货物指边境地区经批准有边境小额贸易经营权的企业，通过国家指定的陆地边境口岸（或经国务院特批的海上边贸口岸），按照有关征减免税政策进口原产于毗邻国家的货物（不包括边民互市）。

本征免性质代码为“506”，简称：边境小额。

二、适用范围：

1. 边境地区开展的易货贸易、现汇贸易进口货物；

2. 边境地区开展的工程承包、劳务输出等互利经济合作项下进口货物；

3. 除边民互市以外的其他各类执行边境小额贸易政策的进口货物。

Import goods of petty trade in the border areas

Ⅰ. Definition

Import goods of petty trade in the border areas refer to the goods imported from the neighboring country where they are originally produced at appointed border ports (or border ports on the sea approved by the State Council) following relevant preferential duty policies by enterprises with approved right of small trade transaction.

Code for this levy typeis “506”; border petty trade for short

Ⅱ. Scope of application

1. Import goods of barter trade and cash liquidation trade in border area;

2. Import goods of such mutual beneficial economic co-operation projects as construction contracting and labor output in border area;

3. All kinds of import goods covered by petty trade policies except border trade areas.

中外合资经营企业进出口货物

一、定义

中外合资经营企业进出口货物指国内企业与境外企业在中国境内合资经营的企业在投资总额内，按照有关征减免税政策进口的生产、管理设备，以及自产的出口产品等。

本征免性质代码为“601”，简称：中外合资。

二、适用范围

1. 投资总额内进口的生产、管理设备，加固、安装设备用材料等货物（不包括进口料件）；

2. 企业自产的出口产品。

Export goods of Chinese-foreign equity joint ventures

Ⅰ. Definition

Import/Export goods of Chinese-foreign equity joint ventures refer to the production and management equipment imported within total sum of investment and export products manufactured by the joint-ventures in China according to relevant preferential policies of customs duties.

Code for this levy type is “601”, Chinese-foreign equity joint ventures for short.

Ⅱ. Scope of application

1. Goods imported for production, management equipment, reinforcement, materials for installation (materials imported excluded) purchased within the total sum of capital invested.

2. Outbound products manufactured by the joint venture

中外合作经营企业进出口货物

一、定义

中外合作经营企业进出口货物指境外公司与我国境内公司合作经营的企业按照有关征减免税政策，作为外商投资进口的生产、管理设备，以及自产的出口产品等。

本征免性质代码为“602”，简称：中外合作。

二、适用范围：

1. 按经批准的合同作为外商投资进口的机器、设备等（不包括进口料件）；

2. 企业自产的出口产品。

Import/export goods of Chinese - Foreign contractual joint ventures

Ⅰ. Definition

Import/export goods of Chinese-foreign contractual joint ventures refer to the production and management equipment imported as investments and products manufactured by the joint-ventures according to relevant preferential policies of customs duties.

Code for this category is “602”, Chinese-foreign contractual joint ventures for short.

Ⅱ. Scope of application

1. Machinery and equipment (imported materials excluded) imported as investment by foreign enterprises following the approved contract;

2. Outbound products manufactured by the joint venture

外商独资企业进出口货物

一、定义

外商独资企业进出口货物指境外厂商在中国境内独资经营的企业在投资总额内，按照有关征减免税政策进口的生产、管理设备，以及自产的出口产品等。

Goods imported by a wholly foreign-owned enterprise

Ⅰ. Definition

goods imported by a wholly foreign-owned enterprise refers to the equipment for production, management of and the export products produced by the enterprise which are imported within the total sum of capital invested according to relevant preferential policies of import duty by a

本征免性质代码为"603",简称:外资企业。

wholly foreign-owned enterprise run by a foreign enterprise.

Code for this levy type is "603"; foreign-owned enterprises for short.

二、适用范围

1. 投资总额内进口的生产、管理设备,加固、安装设备用材料等货物(不包括进口料件);

2. 企业自产的出口产品。

Ⅱ. Scope of application

1. Goods imported for production, management equipment, reinforcement, materials for installation purchased within the total sum of capital invested.

2. Outbound goods produced by the enterprise

利用外国政府贷款和国际金融组织贷款进口设备

定义

利用外国政府贷款和国际金融组织贷款进口设备指自1995年1月1日至1997年12月31日按国家规定程序批准的利用外国政府贷款和国际金融组织(世界银行、亚洲开发银行、联合国农业发展基金)贷款项目,按照有关征减免税政策进口的设备。

本性质代码"609",简称:贷款项目。

Equipment import with loans from foreign government and international finance organizations.

Definition

Equipment import purchased with loans from foreign government and international finance organizations refers to the equipment imported according to relevant preferential policies of import duty by loan projects approved by the state from Jan, 1st 1995 to Dec. 31st 1997, with loans from foreign government and international finance organizations (World Bank, Asian Development Bank, International Fund for Agricultural Development).

Code for this levy type is "609"; loan project for short.

国家鼓励发展的内外资项目进口设备

一、定义

国家鼓励发展的内外资项目进口设备指自1998年1月1日起,按国家规定程序审批并经统一编号的国家鼓励发展的国内投资项目和外商投资项目,按照有关征减免税政策进口的设备。

本征免性质代码为"789",简称:鼓励项目。

二、适用范围

1. 符合《当前国家重点鼓励发展的产业、产品和技术目录》的国内投资(包括利用国外商业贷款)的基建或技改项目,在投资总额内进口的自用设备和随设备进口的技术及配套件、备件。

2. 符合《外资投资产业指导目录》鼓励类和限制乙类,并转让技术的外商投资项目(包括基建或技改项目),在投资总额内进口的自用设备和随设备进口的技术及配套件、备件。

3. 利用外国政府贷款和国际金融组织(世界银行、亚洲开发银行、联合国农业发展基金)贷款项目进口的自用设备和随设备进口的技术及配套件、备件。

Equipment import for domestic/foreign capital projects encouraged by the state.

Ⅰ. Definition

Equipment import for domestic/foreign capital projects encouraged by the state refers to the equipment imported according to policies related to exemption/reduction of customs duties by domestic/foreign capital projects, which are encouraged by the state, with official serial numbers gained through lawful examination and approval since Jan 1st 1998.

Code of this levy tye is "789"; encouraged project for short.

Ⅱ. Scope of application

1. Equipment for self use, technologies, components and spare parts that go with the equipment, purchased within the total sum of capital invested by domestic capital (with foreign load included) projects of infrastructure or technology improvement, which are covered by the List of Industries, Products and Technologies Encouraged by the State.

2. Equipment for self use and technologies, components and spare parts that go with the equipment which are purchased within the total sum of capital invested by domestic capital (with foreign load included) projects of infrastructure or technology improvement, which are covered by the Guide List of Industries for Foreign Capital.

3. Equipment for self use and technologies, components and spare parts that go with the equipment which are purchased by load projects with loads from foreign governments and international financial organizations (World Bank, Asia Development Bank, International Fund for Agricultural Development).

营运国际航线和港澳航线的国内航空公司进口维修用航空器材的减税

根据《海关总署关于营运国际和港澳航线的国内航空

Tax reduction on the aviation supplies for maintenance use imported by domestic aviation companies which operate international and Hong Kong and Macao airlines.

According to the Administrative Provisions of the General Adminis-

公司进口维修用航空器材实施进口税收优惠政策的管理规定》,10家航空公司享受用于维修国际航线和港澳航线飞机的进口航空器材的免税优惠政策。

tration of Customs on Implementing Preferential Policies of Import Duty on Domestic Aviation Companies which Operate International and Hong Kong and Macao Airlines for their Import of Aviation Supplies for Maintenance Use, 10 aviation companies enjoys preferential policies of import duty on aviation supplies for maintenance use.

本征免性质代码为"888",简称:航材减免

Code for this levy type is "888"; aviation supplies exemption/reduction for short

国务院特准减免税的进出口货物

Import and export goods with tax exemption/reduction granted by the State Council

一、定义

国务院特准减免税的进出口货物指经国务院特案批准予以减免税的进出口货物。

本征免性质代码为"898",简称:国批减免。

I. Definition

Import/Export goods that are granted tax exemption/reduction by the State Council.

Code for this category is "898"; state granted exemption/ reduction for short.

二、适用范围

1. 国务院批准只减免增值税或消费税的货物;

2. 其他国务院特批的减免税进出口货物。

II. Scope of application

1. Goods granted by the State council exemption or reduction of value-added tax only or excise only.

2. Others import/export goods granted exemption/reduction of customs duties by the State Council.

例外减免税进出口货物

例外减免税进出口货物指无法归入以上各项征免性质的减免税进出口货物。

本征免性质代码为"999",简称:例外减免。

Exceptional cases of goods granted exemption/reduction

Exceptional import/export goods granted exemption/reduction which are excluded from the categories of exemption/reduction mentioned above.

Code for this levy type is "999"; exceptional exemption/reduction for short.

享受内部暂定税率的进出口货物

享受内部暂定税率的进出口货物指按照国务院税委会规定的内部暂定税率征税的进出口货物。

本征免性质代码为"998",简称:内部暂定。

Import/export goods with interim inside duty rate privilege

Import/export goods with inside duty rate privilege refers to the import/export goods which are levied on interim duty rates regulated by the Customs Tariff Commission of the State Council.

Code for this levy type is "998"; inside interim rate for short.

征减免税方式代码表说明

征减免税方式是指海关依照《中华人民共和国海关法》、《中华人民共和国进出口关税条例》、《中华人民共和国海关进出口税则》及其他法律、法规,对进出口货物实际决定征税、减税、免税或特案处理的操作方式,应根据海关核发的《征免税证明》或有关政策规定对报关单所列每项商品按《征减免税方式代码表》确定的征减免税方式名称及代码。

一、征减免税方式的分类

征减免税方式分为照章征税、折半征税、全免、特案减免、随征免性质、保证金、保证函、折半补税及出口全额退税

Table of Levy mode

Levy mode refers to the different ways of operation of levying-- taxation, deduction, exemption or exceptions, applied by the customs to the import and export goods in practice according to such laws and regulations as *Customs Law of the People's Republic of China*, *Regulations of the People's Republic of China on Import and Export Duties*, *Customs Tariff of Import and Export of the People's Republic of China*. Levy mode of each item in the customs declaration in accordance to the designation of the mode and its code regulated in the table of Levy mode should be decided based on the *Tax Levy and Exemption Certificate of the Customs of the People's Republic of China* or relative laws and regulations.

I. Classification of levy modes

Levy modes include levy taxation according to tax rules, duty reduction by half, exemption, exemption and reduction in special cases, of ex-

九种，各种方式分别用不同的代码标定。

二、征减免税方式代码说明

（一）照章征税

指对进出口货物依照法定税率计征各类税、费。

（二）折半征税

指依照主管海关签发的《征免税证明》或海关总署的通知，对进出口货物依照法定税率折半计征关税和增值税，但照章征收消费税。

（三）全免

指依照主管海关签发的《征免税证明》或海关总署的通知，对进出口货物免征关税和增值税，但消费税不予免征。

（四）特案减免

指依照主管海关签发的《征免税证明》或海关总署通知规定的税率计征各类税、费。

（五）随征免性质

指对某些监管方式下进出口的货物按照征免性质规定的特殊计税公式或税率计征税、费。

（六）保证金

指经海关批准具保放行的货物，由担保人向海关缴纳现金的一种担保形式。

（七）保证函

指担保人根据海关的要求，向海关提交的订有明确权利义务的一种担保文书。

（八）折半补税

指对已征半税的供特区内销售的市场物资，经海关核准运往特区外时，补征另一半相应税款。

（九）出口全额退税

指对计划内出口的丝绸、山羊绒实行出口全额退税时，凭"计划内出口证明"开具出口全额退税税单，并计征关务费。

emption nature, deposit, guarantee, tax supplementation, and full export rebate.

Ⅱ. Explanation on the codes of Levy modes

1. Levy taxation according to rules in force

Import and export goods should be levied according to lawful duty rate.

2. Duty reduction by half

It refers to the levy of tariff and value-added tax on import and export goods on half duty rate, but levy of excise according to rules.

3. Exemption

It refers to the exemption of tariff and value-added tax on import and export goods but not of excise according to the*Tax Levy and Exemption Certificate of the Customs of the People's Republic of China* issued by the Customs in charge or notices issued by Custom of the People's Republic of China.

4. Reduction and exemption in special cases

It refers to levy taxation according to*Tax Levy and Exemption Certificate of the Customs of the People's Republic of China* issued by the Customs in charge or according to duty rates regulated in the notices issued by the Custom of the People's Republic of China.

5. Levy taxation on goods of exemption nature

It refers to the levying of tax on the import and export goods under certain supervision procedures according to special levy formula or duty rates following the regulations of levy taxation on goods of exemption nature.

6. Deposit

It refers to a mode of guarantee in which the warrantor deposits a certain amount of cash to the Customs for the goods to be released. .

7. Guarantee

It refers to documents submitted as required by the warrantor to the Customs, stating rights and obligations.

8. Tax supplementation

It refers to the making up of customs duties for goods which are supposed to be sold in special administrative regions and which have been levied on half duty rate when the goods have been approved by the Customs to be transferred out of the special administrative regions.

9. Full export rebate

It refers the full rebate of customs duties for silk and cashmere exported within the state plan. Full export rebate can be obtained with a certificate of export within the state plan and customs administrative fee is charged.

运输方式代码表说明

Code table of Mode of Transport

一、定义

运输方式是指货物进出关境时所使用的运输工具的分类。包括非保税区、监管仓库、江海、铁路、汽车、航空、邮递保税区、保税仓库和其他共十大类。

Ⅰ. Definition

Mode of transport refers to the categorizations of means of transportation when goods cross borders. It includes non-bonded area, supervised warehouse, by sea, by rail, by road, by air, bonded area by post, bond-

二、运输方式分类说明

（一）江海运输：指利用船舶在国内外港口之间，通过固定的航区和航线进行货物运输的一种方式。

（二）铁路运输：指利用铁路承担进出口货物运输的一种方式。

（三）汽车运输：指利用汽车承担进出口货物运输的一种方式。

（四）航空运输：指利用航空器承运进出口货物的一种方式。

（五）邮递运输：指通过邮局寄运货物进出口的一种方式。

（六）其他运输：除上述几种运输方式以外的货物进出口运输方式。

如利用人扛、驮畜、输油管道、输水管道和输电网等方式进出口货物的运输方式。

（七）用于标识境内进出保税区或保税仓库运输方式代码如下：

"0"：非保税区运入保税区和保税区退区货物；

"1"：境内存入出口监管仓和出口监管仓退仓货物；

"7"：保税区运往非保税区货物；

"8"：保税仓库转内销货物。

ed warehouse and others, ten categories in all.

Ⅱ. Explanation on the categorization of mode of transport

1. By sea: it refers to the mode of transportation of goods by means of fixed sailing areas and courses between ports home and abroad

2. By rail: it refers to the mode of transportation of goods by means of railways.

3. By road: it refers to the mode of transportation of goods by means of trucks.

4. By air: it refers to the mode of transportation of import and export goods by means of aircrafts.

5. By post: it refers to the mode of transportation of import and export goods by mailing through the post office.

6. Other modes of transport: it refers to the other modes of transportation of import and export goods except the ones above mentioned.

Such as transportation of goods by means of manpower, pack-animals, water pipes and electricity transmission network, ect.

7. Code for the mode of transport applied to bonded area or bonded warehouse:

"0": For goods transferred from non-bonded area to bonded area and goods withdrew from bonded area;

"1": For domestic goods stored into supervised export warehouse and goods that exits the supervised export warehouse;

"7": For goods transferred from bonded area to non-bonded area;

"8": For goods exiting bonded warehouse for domestic sales.

关区代码表说明

一、关区代码表用于填报进出口报关单的进出口口岸海关的名称。

《关区代码表》由两部分组成，即关区代码和关区名称。

关区代码由四位数字组成，前两位采用海关统计的直属海关关别代码，后两位为隶属海关的代码。

关区名称即各口岸海关中文名称。

二、使用关区代码时应注意的问题。

代码表中只有直属海关关别和代码的，可以填报直属海关名称和代码（见例1）；如果有隶属海关关别和代码时，必须填报隶属海关关别和代码（见例2）。

例1：在太原海关办理货物进出口报关手续，本栏目可填报"太原海关"，代码"0500"。

例2：在上海浦江海关办理货物进出口报关手续，本栏目不得填报"上海海关"，代码"2200"，必须填报"上海浦江海关"、代码"2201"。

Code Table of Mainland Customs Port

Ⅰ. Code Table of Mainland Customs Port is used for filling in the names of the customs ports in Customs Declaration Form.

Ⅱ. Code Table of Mainland Customs Port consists of two parts, one is code of customs port and the other is name of customs port.

Code of customs port consists of a figure of four digits, the first two of which regards the code for the direct customs port in customs statistics; the second two of which regards the code for the subject customs.

Name of customs port is the Chinese name of the customs port.

Ⅱ. Points worth attention regarding the use of codes of customs ports.

Filling the Code Table on Mainland Customs Port, if there is only direct customs port, only the name and code of the direct customs port is required (see Sample 1); if there is only subject customs port, only the name and code of the subject customs port required (see Sample 2)。

Sample 1: at Taiyuan Customhouse,"太原海关", Code "0500" is sufficient in import and export declaration procedures.

Sample 2: at Shanghai Pujiang Customhouse, "上海海关", Code "2200" is insufficient thus prohibited. "上海浦江海关", Code"2201" is required.

国内地区代码表说明

一、国内地区代码表用于填报进出口报关单的境内目的地和境内货源地。

国内地区代码由五位数构成,一至四位数为企业属地的行政区划代码,其中第一、二位数表示省(自治区、直辖市);第三、四位数表示省辖市(地区、省直辖行政单位)、城市、计划单列城市,沿海开放城市,以上代码均采用国家标准。

国内地区代码第五位数为省辖市内经济区划性质代码:

"1"表示经济特区;

"2"表示经济技术开发区:(包括上海浦东新区、海南洋浦经济开发区和苏州工业园区);

"3"表示高新技术开发区;

"4"表示保税区;

"9"表示其他。

二、境内目的地以进口货物在境内的消费、使用地或最终运抵地为准。一般有以下几种情况:

1. 直接接受有外贸进出口经营权的企业调拨物资的境内消费、使用单位所在地;

2. 委托有外贸进出口经营权的企业进口货物的单位所在地。

3. 自行从国外进口货物的单位所在地;

4. 如难以确定进口货物的消费、使用单位,应以预知的进口货物最终运抵地区为准。

三、境内货源地以出口货物的生产地为准。如出口货物在境内多次周转,不能确定生产地的,应以最早的起运地为准。

Code Table of Mainland District

Ⅰ. Code Table on Mainland District is used for filling in the domestic destination and domestic origin of goods in the Customs Declaration Form.

Mainland district code consists of a figure of five digits. The first four is the administrative district code of where the company is situated. Among them, the first and second digits represent province (municipality and autonomous region); the third and fourth ones represent cities of province (district, administrative units under direct government of the province) 、cities、separate planning cities、coastal cities open to the outside world. The code used is in accordance to the national standards.

The fifth digit is the code for different economic districts.

"1" represents special economic zone;

"2" represents economic and technological development district;

"3" represents high technology development district;

"4" represents bonded area;

"9" represents others except the ones above mentioned.

二、The domestic destination is where the imported goods are consumed, used or finally arrived. Generally there are the following situations:

1. The location of the domestic consumer and user who receives imported goods direct from institutions with import and export license;

2. The location of the enterprise which consigns a company with import and export license to import goods;

3. The location of the enterprise which imports goods on its own;

4. If the consumer and user of the import goods are impossible to find out, the location where the imports finally reach prevails.

Ⅲ. Origin of domestic goods is in accordance with where it is produced. If the outbound goods is transferred in the home country many times and where it is produced is hard to find out, the location where it first starts shipping prevails.

结汇方式代码表说明

一、定义

结汇方式是出口货物发货人或其代理通过银行收结外汇的方式。

二、《结汇方式代码表》结构及说明

(一)《结汇方式代码表》由两部分组成,即结汇方式代码和结汇方式名称。

Code Table of Mode of Foreign Exchange Collection

Ⅰ. Definition

Mode of foreign exchange collection refers to the ways for the goods shipper or its agent to get foreign exchange through banks

Ⅱ. Structure of and explanation about Code Table of Mode of Foreign Exchange Collection

1. Code Table of Mode of Foreign Exchange Collection consists of two parts: the code for mode of foreign exchange collection and the designation for mode of foreign exchange collection.

(二)结汇方式代码分为汇付、托收、信用证和其他。

1. 汇付包括:

(1)信汇:买方将货款交给进口地银行,由银行开具付款委托书,邮寄出口地银行,委托其向卖方付款。

(2)电汇:进口地银行应买方申请,直接用电报发出付款委托书,委托出口地银行向卖方付款。

(3)票汇:买方向进口地银行购买银行汇票迳寄卖方,由卖方或其指定的人持票向出口地有关银行取款。

汇付从时间上分预付和后付。预付即卖方装运货物前,买方先将货款汇结卖方;后付即卖方先交货,在买方收到货物或单据后才汇付货款。

2. 托收包括:

(1)付款交单(D/P):指卖方托收时指示托收行,只有在买方付清货款时才交出单据。

(2)承兑交单(D/A):指买方承兑汇票后即可取得单据,提取货物,待汇票到期时才付货款。

3. 信用证(L/C):信用证是银行在买卖双方之间保证付款的凭证。银行根据买方的申请书,向卖方开出保证付款的信用证,即只要卖方提交符合信用证要求的单据,银行就保证付款。

4. 其他:指除上述以外的结汇方式。

2. The code for mode of foreign exchange collection includes remittance, collection, letter of credit and others.

(1) Remittance includes:

(a) Mail transfer: the buyer sends money to a bank in the import country. The bank opens a payment order and mails it to the relevant bank in the export country, consigning the latter to pay the seller.

(b) Telegraphic transfer: the buyer applies to a bank in the import country and telegraphs the payment order and consigns the relevant bank in the export country to pay the seller.

(c) Demand draft: the buyer purchases bank draft in a bank in the import country and mails it to the seller. The seller or the one appointed by the seller that holds the bank draft withdraws money from the relevant bank in the export country.

Temporally speaking, remittance includes advance payment and deferred payment. Advance payment is to pay the seller through remittance before the seller ships the goods; deferred payment is that the seller ships goods first before getting paid and the buyer pays after receiving the goods or the receipt

Collection includes:

(1) Documents against payment (D/P): upon the direction of the seller, the collection bank gives the documents to the buyer only if the purchaser pays off.

(2) Documents against acceptance (D/A): upon acceptance the buyer gets the documents to pick up goods and pays off when the acceptance is due.

3. Letter of Credit (L/C): letter of credit is a payment warrant made by a bank between the buyer and the seller. Upon the request of the buyer, the bank opens a letter of credit to the seller to assure payment. Once the seller submits the required documents for L/C, the bank will assure payment.

4. Others: other means of foreign exchange collection except the one mentioned above.

监管证件代码表说明

一、定义

监管证件名称代码是海关依据我国外贸法律、法规及规章,为便于实施计算机系统管理和便捷通关需求,对实行进出口许可证件管理的货物在海关管理环节须验核的各种进出口许可证件的分类标识。其总和称为监管证件名称代码表。

二、《监管证件名称代码表》结构

《监管证件名称代码表》由两部分组成,即监管证件代码和监管证件名称。例如:代码"1",为进口许可证,如果某一商品编号后注有监管证件"1",则说明在一般贸易项下进口该种商品需申领进口许可证。

三、监管证件名称代码说明

(一)代码"1"——进口许可证:指商务部配额许可证

Code Table of the Licensed

一、Definition

Code for the Licensed refers to the categorization, according to relevant customs laws, rules and regulations, of all kinds of import and export licenses which need to be checked in customs management procedures regarding the goods which require import and export licenses, for the purpose of computer system management and efficient customs clearance.

二. The structure of Code Table of the Licensed

Code Table on Licensed consists of two parts: the code for the licensed and the designation for the licensed.

三、Explanations about the codes and designations of the licensed.

(一) Code "1"—— Import License: Import License issued by Quota

事务局或其授权机关签发的进口许可证。

Licensing Bureau of the Ministry of Commerce or its authorized departments.

（二）代码“2”——两用物项和技术进口许可证：指列入《两用物项和技术进口许可证管理目录》的商品，进口时由商务部签发的《两用物项和技术进口许可证》。

（二）Code“2”—— Import License for Dual – use Items and Technologies：Import License for Dual – use Items and Technologies issued by the Ministry of Commerce for importing items listed in the List of Import License for Dual-use Items and Technologies Management.

（三）代码“3”——两用物项出口许可证：指列入《敏感物项和技术出口许可证管理目录》的商品，出口时由商务部签发的《敏感物项出口许可证》。

（三）Code“3”——Export License for Dual -use Items：Export License for Sensitive Items and Technologies issued by the Ministry of Commerce for exporting items listed in the List of Export License for Sensitive Items Management.

（四）代码“4”——出口许可证：指商务部配额许可证事务局或其授权机关签发的出口许可证。

（四）Code“4”—— Export License：Export license issued by Quota Licensing Bureau of the Ministry of Commerce or its authorized departments.

（五）代码“5”——纺织品临时出口许可证：指列入《纺织品出口临时管理商品目录》的商品，出口时由商务部签发《纺织品临时出口许可证》。

（五）Code“5”——Temporary Textile Export License ：Temporary Textile Export License issued by the Ministry of Commerce for exporting items listed in the List of Temporary Textile Export License Management.

（六）代码“6”——旧机电产品禁止进口：商品编码后有此代码的商品，其旧品禁止进口。

（六）Code“6”—— used electro-mechanical products import prohibited：the importing of used electro-mechanical products with this code at the end of its code of goods is prohibited.

（七）代码“7”——自动进口许可证：指进口商品实行自动进口许可管理，由商务部签发自动进口许可证。

（七）Code“7”——Automatic Import License：Importing products are under automatic import license management. The license is issued by the Ministry of Commerce.

（八）代码“8”——禁止出口商品：指国务院授权对外经济贸易主管部门会同有关部门，依照《中华人民共和国对外贸易法》等有关法律法规，制定、调整并公布的禁止出口货物目录所列商品。商品编码后有此代码的商品禁止出口。

（八）Code“8”——export forbidden items：It refers to all the listed items in the export forbidden items list regulated and declared by foreign trade administrations and relevant departments authorized by State Department in accordance with such relevant laws and regulations as *Foreign Trade Law of People 's Republic of China* . Products with this code are prohibited to be exported.

（九）代码“9”——禁止进口商品：指国务院授权对外经济贸易主管部门会同有关部门，依照《中华人民共和国对外贸易法》等有关法律法规，制定、调整并公布的禁止进口货物目录所列商品。商品编码后有此代码的商品禁止进口。

（九）Code“9”—— import forbidden items：It refers to all the listed items in the import forbidden items list regulated and declared by foreign trade administrations and relevant departments authorized by State Department in accordance with such relevant laws and regulations as *Foreign Trade Law of People 's Republic of China* . Products with this code are prohibited to be imported.

（十）代码“A”——入境货物通关单：指国家质量监督检验检疫机构根据《中华人民共和国进出口商品检验法》、《中华人民共和国动植物检疫法》和《中华人民共和国食品卫生法》等有关法律、法规，对列入《出入境检验检疫机构实施检验检疫的进出境商品目录》的进口商品签发的入境货物通关单。

（十）Code “A”—— Customs Clearance of Entry Commodities：It refers to the Customs Clearance of Entry Commodities issued by the administrations of quality supervision, inspection and quarantine for commodities listed in the List of Entry-Exit Commodities under Quality Supervision, Inspection and Quarantine in accordance with such relevant laws and regulations as *Law of the P. R. C. on Import and Export Commodity Inspection* , *Law of the P. R. C. on Animal and Plant Quarantine* , and *Food Hygiene Law of the People's Republic of China*

（十一）代码“B”——出境货物通关单：指国家质量监督检验检疫机构根据《中华人民共和国进出口商品检验法》、《中华人民共和国动植物检疫法》和《中华人民共和国食品卫生法》等有关法律、法规，对列入《出入境检验检疫机构实施检验检疫的进出境商品目录》的出口商品签发的出境货物通关单。

（十一）Code “B”—— Customs Clearance of Exit Commodities：It refers to the Customs Clearance of Exit Commodities issued by the administrations of quality supervision, inspection and quarantine for commodities listed in the List of Entry-Exit Commodities under Quality Supervision, Inspection and Quarantine in accordance with such relevant laws and regulations as *Law of the P. R. C. on Import and Export Commodity Inspection* , *Law of the P. R. C. on Animal and Plant Quarantine* , and *Food Hygiene Law of the People's Republic of China* .

（十二）代码“D”——出/入境货物通关单：为履行我国国际义务，制止“冲突钻石”非法交易，国家质检总局、海关总署等六部委联合发布 2002 年第 132 号公告，对毛坯钻

（十二）Code “D”——Customs Clearance of Entry/Exit Commodities：In order to fulfill our international obligations and to prevent illegal “conflict diamonds“ transaction, six departments including State Quality

石进出口实施管理，毛坯钻石进出口时，授权检验检疫机构签发出/入境货物通关单。

Inspection and Quarantine Bureau and the Custom of the P. R. C. issued Notice No. 132 in 2002 to implement rough diamond import management. Customs Clearance of Entry/Exit Commodities is issued by authorized inspection and quarantine institutes for importing and exporting rough diamonds.

（十三）代码“E”——濒危物种允许出口证明书：指根据《中华人民共和国野生动物保护法》及相关法律法规，对列入《进出口野生动植物种商品目录》的货物，出口时由国家濒危物种进出口管理办公室或其办事机构签发的濒危物种出口允许证。

（十三）Code “E”—— export permit for endangered wild animals: it refers to the export permit for endangered wild animals issued by the administrative bureau of the Import and Export of Endangered Wild Animals or by other relevant administrative bureaus for exporting items listed in the List of Import/Export Animals and Plants in accordance with *Law of the People's Republic of China on the Protection of Wildlife* and other relevant rules and regulations.

（十四）代码“F”——濒危物种允许进口证明书：指根据《中华人民共和国野生动物保护法》及相关法律法规，对列入《进出口野生动植物种商品目录》的货物，进口时由国家濒危物种进出口管理办公室或其办事机构签发的濒危物种进口允许证。

（十四）Code “F”—— Import permit for endangered wild animals: it refers to the import permit for endangered wild animals issued by the administrative bureau of the Import and Export of Endangered Wild Animals or by other relevant administrative bureaus for exporting items listed in the List of Import/Export Animals and Plants in accordance with *Law of the People's Republic of China on the Protection of Wildlife* and other relevant rules and regulations.

（十五）代码“G”——易制毒化学品定向出口许可证：指列入《向特定国家（地区）出口易制毒化学品管理目录》的商品，向特定国家出口时由商务部签发《易制毒化学品定向出口许可证》。

（十五）Code “G” ——Toxic Chemicals Directional License: It refers to the Toxic Chemicals Directional License issued by the Ministry of Commerce allowing exporting to appointed countries items listed in the List of Toxic Chemicals Management to be exported to appointed countries or regions.

（十六）代码“I”——精神药物进（出）口准许证：根据《中华人民共和国药品管理法》和国务院《精神药品管理办法》及相关法律法规，国家对精神药品的进（出）口实行进（出）口准许证管理制度。对列入“精神药品管制品种目录”的商品，国家药品监督管理局核发《精神药品进（出）口准许证》或《携带麻醉药品、精神药品证明》。

（十六）Code “I”—— Psychotropic drug import and export license: according to *Pharmaceutical Administration Law of the People 's Republic of China* and *Management Regulations on Psychotropic Drug* issued by the State Council and other relevant laws and regulations, Psychotropic drug import and export is under licensed management. For the items listed in the List of Controlled Psychotropic Drug, *Psychotropic Drug Import and Export License* or Certificate for holding anesthesia and psychotropic drugs issued by State Drug Administration is required.

（十七）代码“J”——金产品出口证或人总行进口批件：指根据《中华人民共和国金银管理条例》及相关法律法规，对进出口黄金及其制品，由中国人民银行签发的准许进出境证件。

（十七）Code “J”—— Gold product export license or the approval of import issued by the People's Bank of China: according to Regulations of the People's Republic of China on the Control of Gold and Silver and other relevant laws and regulations, the importing and exporting of gold and gold products requires the approvals issued by the People's Bank of China.

（十八）代码“O”——自动进口许可证（新旧机电产品）：进口实行自动进口许可管理的机电产品，进口单位应当在办理海关报关手续前，向商务部或地方商务主管机构、部门机电办申领《自动进口许可证》。

（十八）Code “O”——automatic import license (for old and new mechanic - electric products): for the mechanic - electric products under automatic import license management, the importer should apply for Automatic Import License to the Ministry of Commerce or local commercial administrative departments before customs declaration procedures.

（十九）代码“P” ——固体废物进口许可证：根据《中华人民共和国固体废物污染环境防治法》和《废物进口环境保护管理暂行规定》及相关法律法规，对列入《国家限制进口的可用作原料的废物目录》、《自动进口许可的可用作原料的废物目录》的进口商品，由国家环保总局签发固体废物进口许可证。

（十九）Code “P” —— solid waste import license: according to *Law of the People's Republic of China on the Prevention and Control of Environmental Pollution by Solid Wastes* and *Temporary Management Regulations on the Protection of Environmental Pollution by Imported Wastes* and other relevant laws and regulations, for imported items listed in the List of Restricted Waste Import Used as Materials and in the List of Waste Import Used as Materials under Automatic Import License Management, waste import license issued by the State Environmental Protection Administration is required.

（二十）代码"Q"——进口药品通关单：根据《中华人民共和国药品管理法》及相关法律法规，对列入《进口药品管理目录》的药品，国家药监局及其授权机构签发进口药品通关单。

（二十）Code "Q"——drug import customs clearance: according to *Pharmaceutical Administration Law of the People's Republic of China* and other relevant laws and regulations. For drugs listed in the List of Drug Import Management to be imported, Drug Import Customs Clearance issued by the State Drug Administration or the authorized bureaus is required.

（二十一）代码"S"——进出口农药登记证明：根据《农药管理条例》及有关法律法规，《中华人民共和国进出口农药登记证明管理名录》和《中华人民共和国进出口列入事先知情同意程序（PIC）农药登记证明管理名录》的商品，进出口时，农业部签发进出口农药登记证明。

（二十一）Code "S"——pesticide import registration certificate: According to Management Regulations of Pesticides and other relevant laws and regulations, the import and export of items, listed in the List of Import/Export Pesticides Registration Certificate Management of P. R. C. and in the List of Import/Export Pesticides listed in PIC for registration certificate management, require registration certificate of import and export pesticides issued by the Ministry of Agriculture.

（二十二）代码"T"——银行调运现钞进出境许可证：指国家外汇管理局和中国人民银行根据《银行调运外币现钞进出境管理规定》等法律、法规，对允许进出境的外币和人民币现钞签发的许可证件。

（二十二）Code "T"—— license for bank transfer of cash across borders: it refers to the approval of cash transfer across borders issued by the State Administration of Foreign Exchange and the People's Bank of China according to Management Regulations on bank transfer of cash across borders and other relevant laws and regulations.

（二十三）代码"W"——麻醉药品进出口准许证：根据《中华人民共和国药品管理法》和国务院《麻醉药品管理办法》及相关法律法规，国家对麻醉药品的进（出）口实行进（出）口准许证管理制度。对列入"麻醉药品管制品种目录"的商品，国家药品监督管理局核发《麻醉药品进（出）口准许证》、或《携带麻醉药品、精神药品证明》。

（二十三）Code "W"——license for import and export of narcotic drugs: According to *Pharmaceutical Administration Law of the People's Republic of China*, *Management Regulations on Narcotic Drugs* and other relevant laws and regulations, narcotic drugs are under import and export licensed management. The import and export of items listed in the List of Controlled Narcotic Drugs require Narcotic drugs Import and Export License or certificate of holding narcotic and psychotropic drugs issued by the State Drug Administration.

（二十四）代码"X"——有毒化学品环境管理放行通知单：指列入《中国严格限制的有毒化学品名录》的进出口化学品，由国家环境保护总局签发的放行通知单。

（二十四）Code "X"—— release notice of import/export of toxic chemicals: The import and export of chemicals listed in the List of Toxic Chemicals Banned or Severely Restricted in People's Republic of China require release notice issued by the State Environmental Protection Administration.

（二十五）代码"Z"——进口音像制品批准单或节目提取单：指国家实行进口管理的音像制品，由文化部签发的《文化部进口音像制品批准单》或广播电影电视总局及其授权部门签发的《进口广播电影电视节目带（片）提取单》。

（二十五）Code "Z"—— audio - visual product import approval or program deliver order: It refers to the audio - visual product import approval issued by the Ministry of Culture or the delivery order of broadcasting, film and television program tapes and video import issued by

（二十六）代码"e"——关税配额外优惠关税税率进口棉花配额证：指对于一定数量的关税配额外报关进口的棉花，按"暂定优惠关税税率"征收进口关税，由国家发展改革委授权机构出具《关税配额外优惠关税税率进口棉花配额证》。

（二十六）Code "e"—— quota certificate for cotton import beyond tariff quota to enjoy preferential duties: It refers to the import quota certificate for cotton beyond tariff quota with preferential duties issued by institutions authorized by National Development and Reform Commission for certain amount of cotton imports beyond tariff rate quota to enjoy preferential duties.

（二十七）代码"t"——关税配额证明：是指列入实施《关税配额目录》的商品，进口时由商务部签发《关税配额证明》。

（二十七）Code "t"—— tariff rate quota certificate: It refers to the Tariff Rate Quota Certificate issued by the Ministry of Commerce for items listed in the List of Tariff Rate Quota to be imported.

（二十八）代码"s"——适用 ITA 税率商品用途认定证明：根据 2002 年 39 号公告，部分信息技术产品可凭此证明享受 ITA 税率。

（二十八）Code "s"——applicable to ITA duty rate goods: According to Notice No. 39 of 2002, some information technologies can enjoy ITA duty rate with this certificate of product purpose identification.

（二十九）代码"x"——出口许可证（加工贸易）：适用于加工贸易方式下出口许可证管理的商品。

（二十九）Code "x"—— export license: Applicable to goods of under export license management

（三十）代码"y"——出口许可证：边境小额贸易项下需凭出口许可证办理有关手续。

（三十）Code "y"—— export license: Export License is required for procedures of petty trade in the border areas.

（三十一）代码"L"——进出口准许证：

（三十一）Code "L"——import or export permit licence: Ministry of culture.

报关自动化系统常用代码表
Common Codes for Automated Customs Declaration System (EDI)

监管方式代码表

Codes for Customs Procedures (Modes of International Trade)

监管方式代码 Code	监管方式简称	监管方式全称	Customs Procedures (Modes of International Trade)
0110	一般贸易	一般贸易	Normal transaction (Lateral import/export by entitled legal person)
0130	易货贸易	易货贸易	Barter trade
0139	旅游购物商品	用于旅游者五万美元以下的出口小批量订货	Exportation of tourist commodities on an order not more than USD50,000
0200	料件放弃	主动放弃交由海关处理的来料或进料加工料件	Materials/components for inward processing to be disposed by Customs on a basis of voluntary abandonment
0214	来料加工	来料加工装配贸易进口料件及加工出口货物	Inward processing/assembling with supplied materials/components
0245	来料料件内销	来料加工料件转内销	Supplied materials/components for inward processing to be declared for home use
0255	来料深加工	来料深加工结转货物	To close and transfer accounts of supplied materials for supplementary processing
0258	来料余料结转	来料加工余料结转	To close and transfer accounts of surplus supplied materials
0265	来料料件复出	来料加工复运出境的原进口料件	Re-exportation of supplied materials/components in the same state
0300	来料料件退换	来料加工料件退换	Replacement of supplied materials/components
0314	加工专用油	国营贸易企业代理来料加工企业进口柴油	Diesel oil imported by state - run trading enterprises on behalf of processors on order with supplied materials
0320	不作价设备	加工贸易外商提供的不作价进口设备	Non-pricing equipment supplied for inward processing
0345	来料成品减免	来料加工成品凭征免税证明转减免税	Finished products with supplied materials to be declared for home use with "Certificate of Levy/Exemption of Customs Duties and Taxes"
0400	成品放弃	主动放弃交由海关处理的来料及进料加工成品	Finished products obtained from supplied materials to be disposed by Customs on a basis of voluntary abandonment
0420	加工贸易设备	加工贸易项下外商提供的进口设备	Importation of equipment for inward processing supplied at a fixed price
0444	保区进料成品	按成品征税的保税区进料加工成品转内销货物	Finished products processed in bonded warehouse zone with purchased materials to be declared for home use against payment Custom duties on the basis of finished products
0445	保区来料成品	按成品征税的保税区来料加工成品转内销货物	Finished products processed in bonded warehouse zone with supplied materials to be declared for home use against payment Custom duties on the basis of finished products
0446	加工设备内销	加工贸易免税进口设备转内销	Duty-free equipment imported for inward processing trade to be declared for home use
0456	加工设备结转	加工贸易免税进口设备结转	To close and transfer accounts of duty-free equipment supplied for inward processing trade

监管方式代码 Code	监管方式简称	监管方式全称	Customs Procedures (Modes of International Trade)
0466	加工设备退运	加工贸易免税进口设备退运出境	Sending back duty-free equipment supplied for inward processing trade
0500	减免设备结转	用于监管年限内减免税设备的结转	To close and transfer accounts of equipment bearing reduced Customs duties and taxes or be allowed conditional relief from duties and taxes within certain control duration
0513	补偿贸易	补偿贸易	Compensation trade
0544	保区进料料件	按料件征税的保税区进料加工成品转内销货物	Finished products processed in bonded warehouse zone with purchased materials to be declared for home use against payment Customs duties on the basis of materials
0545	保区来料料件	按料件征税的保税区来料加工成品转内销货物	Finished products processed in bonded warehouse zone with supplied materials to be declared for home use against payment Custom duties on the basis of materials
0615	进料对口	进料加工(对口合同)	Inward processing with purchased materials under a reciprocal contract
0642	进料以产顶进	进料加工成品以产顶进	Finished products obtained from purchased materials imported for import substitution
0644	进料料件内销	进料加工料件转内销	Purchased materials for inward processing to be declared for home use
0654	进料深加工	进料深加工结转货物	To close and transfer accounts of purchased materials for supplementary processing
0657	进料余料结转	进料加工余料结转	To close and transfer accounts of surplus purchased materials
0664	进料料件复出	进料加工复运出境的原进口料件	Re-exportation of purchased materials for inward processing
0700	进料料件退换	进料加工料件退换	Replacement of purchased materials for inward processing
0715	进料非对口	进料加工(非对口合同)	Inward processing with purchased materials under a non-reciprocal contract
0744	进料成品减免	进料加工成品凭征免税证明转减免税	Finished products with purchased materials to be declared for home use
0815	低值辅料	低值辅料	Low-value auxiliary materials
0844	进料边角料内销	进料加工项下边角料转内销	Leftover scraps of purchased materials for processing to be declared for home use
0845	来料边角料内销	来料加工项下边角料转内销	Leftover scraps of supplied materials for processing to be declared for home use
0864	进料边角料复出	进料加工项下边角料复出口	Re-exportation of leftover scraps of purchased materials for processing
0865	来料边角料复出	来料加工项下边角料复出口	Re-exportation of leftover scraps of supplied materials for processing
1139	国轮油物料	中国籍运输工具境内添加的保税油料、物料	Chinese transport means to be filled with bonded fuel
1200	保税间货物	海关保税场所及保税区域之间往来的货物	Goods transit between Customs bonded areas
1215	保税工厂	保税工厂	Inward processing in bonded factory with purchased materials
1233	保税仓库货物	保税仓库进出境货物	Entering and leaving bonded warehouse
1234	保税区仓储转口	保税区进出境仓储转口货物	Entering and leaving bonded warehouse zone
1300	修理物品	进出境修理物品	Articles to be imported/exported for repair
1427	出料加工	出料加工	Outward processing
1500	租赁不满一年	租期不满一年的租赁贸易货物	Leasing trade, lease term less than one year
1523	租赁贸易	租期在一年及以上的租赁贸易货物	Leasing trade, lease term one year or more

监管方式代码 Code	监管方式简称	监管方式全称	Customs Procedures (Modes of International Trade)
1616	寄售代销	寄售、代销贸易	Consignment trade
1741	免税品	免税品	Duty-free goods
1831	外汇商品	免税外汇商品	Duty-free foreign-currency goods
2025	合资合作设备	合资合作企业作为投资进口设备物品	Importation of equipment/articles purchased by Chinese-foreign equity joint ventures or Chinese-foreign contractual joint ventures
2225	外资设备物品	外资企业作为投资进口的设备物品	Importation of equipment/articles purchased by foreign wholly-owned enterprises
2400	外航公务货	外国航空公司进口公务货	Import service goods by foreign airlines
2439	常驻机构公用	外国常驻机构进口办公用品	Communal articles of foreign resident institutions
2600	暂时进出货物	暂时进出口货物	Temporary admission subject to re-exportation in the same state
2700	展览品	进出境展览品	Articles for exhibition
2939	陈列样品	驻华商业机构不复运出口的进口陈列样品	Samples for display keeping within the Customs territory
3010	货样广告品 A	有经营权单位进出口的货样广告品	Commercial samples of advertising imported by authorized organizations
3039	货样广告品 B	无经营权单位进出口的货样广告品	Commercial samples of advertising imported by non-authorized organizations
3100	无代价抵偿	无代价抵偿进出口货物	Free replacement goods
3339	其他进出口免费	其他进出口免费提供货物	Other free imports
3410	承包工程进口	对外承包工程进口物资	Importation of machines or equipments gained during undertaking contracted construction abroad
3422	对外承包出口	对外承包工程出口物资	Exports for undertaking contracted construction abroad
3511	援助物资	国家和国际组织无偿援助物资	Goods and materials rendered gratis by foreign governments or international organizations
3612	捐赠物资	进出口捐赠物资	Import and export donate goods and materials
4019	边境小额	边境小额贸易(边民互市贸易除外)	Petty frontier trade (other than frontier traffics)
4039	对台小额	对台小额贸易	Petty trade between the Mainland and Taiwan
4200	驻外机构运回	我驻外机构运回旧公用物品	Re-importation of used articles of Chinese resident institutions abroad
4239	驻外机构购进	我驻外机构境外购买运回国的公务用品	Importation of communal articles purchased outside by Chinese resident institutions abroad
4400	来料成品退换	来料加工成品退换	Sending back finished products processed with supplied materials
4500	直接退运	直接退运	Outright sending back
4539	进口溢误卸	进口溢卸、误卸货物	Dutiable overlanded or mislanded goods
4561	退运货物	因质量不符、延误交货等原因退运进出境货物	Sending back goods not in accordance with the agreed specification, delayed delivery or due to other causes
4600	进料成品退换	进料成品退换	Sending back finished products obtained from purchased materials
5000	料件进出区	用于区内外非实际进出境货物	Materials/components admission into/removal from processing zone within the Customs territory
5015	区内加工货物	加工区内企业从境外进口料件及加工出口成品	Inward processing trade operated by enterprises established in processing zone
5033	区内仓储货物	加工区内仓储企业从境外进口的货物	Storage of imported goods operated by warehousing enterprises established in processing zone
5100	成品进出区	用于区内外非实际进出境货物	Materials/components admission into/removal from processing zone within the Customs territory

监管方式代码 Code	监管方式简称	监管方式全称	Customs Procedures （Modes of International Trade）
5200	区内边角调出	用于区内外非实际进出境货物	Leftover scraps removal from processing zone within the Customs territory
5300	设备进出区	用于区内外非实际进出境货物	Equipment admission into/removal from processing zone within the Customs territory
5335	境外设备进区	加工区内企业从境外进口的设备物资	Imported equipment and materials admission into processing zone
5361	区内设备退运	加工区内设备退运境外	Sending back equipment outside processing zone
6033	物流中心进出境货物	保税物流中心与境外之间进出仓储货物	Import and export of storage goods by bonded center of commodities interflow
9639	海关处理货物	海关变卖处理的超期未报货物，走私违规货物	Customs sell goods which have not been declared within the time allowed, or which have involved in acts of smuggling or Customs offence
9700	后续补税	无原始报关单的后续补税	To recover Customs duties subsequently
9739	其他贸易	其他贸易	Other modes of trade
9800	租赁征税	租赁期一年及以上的租赁贸易货物的租金	Dutiable rental charge of leasing trade, lease term one year or more
9839	留赠转卖物品	外交机构转售境内或国际活动留赠放弃特批货	Diplomatic institutions resell/Cultural or sports articles abandoned as donations in case of prior authority granted
9900	其他	其他	Other

征免性质代码表

Codes for the Nature of Levy, Reduction and Exemption of Customs Duties and Taxes

代　码 Code	征免性质简称	征免性质全称	Nature of Levy, Reduction and Exemption of Customs Duties and Taxes
101	一般征税	一般征税进出口货物	Levy Customs duties and taxes according to regulations
118	整车征税	构成整车特征的汽车零部件纳税	Panyment of duties on auto spare constituting whole vehicles
119	零部件征税	不构成整车特征的汽车零部件纳税	Payment of duties on auto spare Parts not constituing whole vehicles
201	无偿援助	无偿援助进出口物资	Aid provided free of charge
299	其他法定	其他法定减免税进出口货物	Other legal reduction and remission
301	特定区域	特定区域进口自用物资及出口货物	Goods imported into or exported out of designated areas
307	保税区	保税区进口自用物资	Imports intended to be used within bonded warehouse zone
399	其他地区	其他执行特殊政策地区出口货物	Reduction and remission according to incentive policy for particular areas
401	科教用品	大专院校及科研机构进口科教用品	Importation of educational and scientific materials
403	技术改造	企业技术改造进口货物	Imports for technical reform of enterprises
406	重大项目	国家重大项目进口货物	Imports for major projects of the state
412	基础设施	通信、港口、铁路、公路、机场建设进口设备	Imports for infrastructure (such as communication, port, railway, highway, airport)
413	残疾人	残疾人组织和企业进出口货物	Imports/exports by organizations or enterprises of disabled persons
417	远洋渔业	远洋渔业自捕水产品	Deep-sea fishing
418	国产化	国家定点生产小轿车和摄录机企业进口散件	Importation of assemblies of compact cars/camcorders by enterprises designated by the state
419	整车特征	构成整车特征的汽车零部件进口	Import of auto spars constitutins whole vehicles
420	远洋船舶	远洋船舶及设备部件	Oceangoing vessels and equipment thereof
421	内销设备	内销远洋船用设备及关键部件	Equipment and key parts for Chinese oceangoing vessels

422	集成电路	集成电路生产企业进口货物	Imports by IC manufacturing enterprises
499	ITA 产品	非全税号信息技术产品	Reduction according to interim duty rate of IT articles
501	加工设备	加工贸易外商提供的不作价进口设备	Equipment imported for contract processing/assembling and compensation trade
502	来料加工	来料加工装配和补偿贸易进口料件及出口成品	Imports/exports of processing/assembling with supplied materials/components
503	进料加工	进料加工贸易进口料件及出口成品	Imports/exports of inward processing with self-bought materials
506	边境小额	边境小额贸易进口货物	Petty frontier trade
510	港澳 OPA	港澳在内地加工的纺织品获证出口	The certificate of dry goods in Hongkong and Macao to be exported.
601	中外合资	中外合资经营企业进出口货物	Chinese-foreign equity joint ventures
602	中外合作	中外合作经营企业进出口货物	Chinese-foreign contractual joint ventures
603	外资企业	外商独资企业进出口货物	Foreign wholly-owned enterprises
606	海上石油	勘探、开发海上石油进口货物	Exploiting offshore petroleum resources
608	陆地石油	勘探、开发陆地石油进口货物	Exploiting inland petroleum resources
609	贷款项目	利用贷款进口货物	Importation of goods purchased with international loans
611	贷款中标	国际金融组织贷款、外国政府贷款中标机电设备零部件	Goods exported on the basis of winning international bids and using loans from international organizations or foreign government
789	鼓励项目	国家鼓励发展的内外资项目进口设备	Imports for projects encouraged by the state
799	自有资金	外商投资额度外利用自有资金进口设备、备件、配件	Imports with self-owned capital
801	救灾捐赠	救灾捐赠进口物资	Donations of relief nature
802	扶贫慈善	境外向我境内无偿捐赠用于扶贫慈善的免税进口物资	Goods sent to charitable or philanthropic organizations for distribution to needy persons
898	国批减免	国务院特准减免税的进出口货物	Reduction and remission according to special approval by the State Council
998	内部暂定	享受内部暂定税率的进出口货物	Provisional reduction according to interim duty rate
999	例外减免	例外减免税进出口货物	Reduction and remission of Customs duties granted by the Customs

征减免税方式代码表

Codes For Type of Levy, Reduction and Exemption of Customs Duties and Taxes

征减免税方式代码 Code	征减免税方式名称	Type of Levy, Reduction and Exemption of Customs Duties and Taxes
1	照章征税	Levy according to regulations
2	折半征税	Reduction by half
3	全免	Relief from all duties and taxes
4	特案	Special case
5	随征免性质	Reduction and remission according to the different nature of objects
6	保证金	Security deposit
7	保函	Letter of guarantee
8	折半补税	Recovery by half
9	全额退税	Refund in whole

运输方式代码表
Codes for Modes of Transport

运输方式代码 Code	运输方式名称	Modes of Transport
0	非保税区	Entry and release of bonded warehouse zone
1	监管仓库	Temporary storage of export goods
2	江海运输	Maritime transport/Inland water transport
3	铁路运输	Railway transport
4	汽车运输	Road transport
5	航空运输	Airway transport
6	邮件运输	Mail transport
7	保税区	Shipment out of bonded warehouse zone to non-bonded area
8	保税仓库	Goods in bonded warehouse to be declared for home use
9	其它运输	Other transport
A	全部运输方式	Full conveyance fashion
W	物流中心	center of commodities interflow
X	物流园区	Goods flow zones
Y	保税港区	Bonded harbor zones
Z	出口加工	Entry and release of export processing zone

关区代码表
Codes for International Trade Ports (Customs Establishment)

关区代码 Code	关区名称 Name of International Trade Port (Customs Establishment)	关区代码 Code	关区名称 Name of International Trade Port (Customs Establishment)	关区代码 Code	关区名称 Name of International Trade Port (Customs Establishment)
0100	北京关区	0128	京顺义办	0502	太原机场海关
0101	机场单证	0200	天津关区	0503	大同海关
0102	京监管处	0201	天津海关	0504	侯马海关
0103	京关展览	0202	新港海关	0600	满洲里关
0104	京一处	0203	津开发区	0601	海拉尔关
0105	京二处	0204	东港海关	0602	额尔古纳
0106	京关关税	0205	津塘沽办	0603	满十八里
0107	机场库区	0206	津驻邮办	0604	满赤峰办
0108	京通关处	0207	津机场办	0605	满通辽办
0109	机场旅检	0208	津保税区	0606	满哈沙特
0110	平谷海关	0209	蓟县海关	0607	满室韦
0111	京五里店	0210	武清海关	0608	满互贸区
0112	京邮办处	0211	津加工区	0609	满铁路
0113	京中关村	0212	天津保税物流园区	0610	满市区
0114	京国际局	0220	津关税处	0700	呼特关区
0115	京东郊站	0400	石家庄区	0701	呼和浩特
0116	京信	0401	石家庄关	0702	二连海关
0117	京开发区	0402	秦皇岛关	0703	包头海关
0118	十八里店	0403	唐山海关	0704	呼关邮办
0119	机场物流	0404	廊坊海关	0705	二连公路
0121	京调查局	0405	保定海关	0706	包头海关驻国际集装箱中转站办事处
0123	机场调技	0406	石家庄海关驻邯郸办事处	0707	策克口岸
0124	北京站	0407	秦加工区	0708	甘其毛道口岸
0125	西客站	0408	中华人民共和国沧州海关	0709	满都拉口岸
0126	京加工区	0500	太原海关	0710	珠恩嘎达布其口岸
0127	京快件	0501	并关监管	0800	沈阳关区

关区代码 Code	关区名称 Name of International Trade Port (Customs Establishment)
0801	沈阳海关
0802	锦州海关
0803	沈驻邮办
0804	沈驻抚顺
0805	沈开发区
0806	沈驻辽阳
0807	沈机场办
0808	沈集装箱
0809	沈阳东站
0810	葫芦岛关
0811	沈阳海关驻辽宁沈阳出口加工区办事处
0900	大连海关
0901	大连港湾海关
0902	大连机场
0903	连开发区
0904	连加工区
0905	大连开发区海关驻北良港办事处
0906	连保税区
0907	大连保税物流园区
0908	连大窑湾
0909	大连邮办
0930	丹东海关
0931	丹东海关驻本溪办事处
0932	太平湾海关
0940	营口海关
0941	营口海关驻盘锦办事处
0950	鲅鱼圈关
0960	大东港关
0980	鞍山海关
1500	长春关区
1501	长春海关
1502	长开发区
1503	长白海关
1504	临江海关
1505	图们海关
1506	集安海关
1507	珲春海关
1508	吉林海关
1509	延吉海关
1511	长春机办
1515	图们车办
1516	集海关村
1517	珲长岭子
1518	吉林海关驻车站办事处
1519	延吉三合
1521	一汽场站
1525	图们桥办

关区代码 Code	关区名称 Name of International Trade Port (Customs Establishment)
1526	集安青石
1527	珲春圈河
1529	延吉南坪
1531	长春东站
1537	珲沙坨子
1539	延开山屯
1547	珲加工区
1549	延古城里
1557	珲春海关驻车站办事处
1559	延吉邮办
1591	长春邮办
1593	长白邮办
1595	图们邮办
1596	集安邮办
1900	哈尔滨区
1901	哈尔滨关
1902	绥关铁路
1903	黑河海关
1904	同江海关
1905	佳木斯关
1906	牡丹江关
1907	东宁海关
1908	逊克海关
1909	齐齐哈尔
1910	大庆海关
1911	密山海关
1912	虎林海关
1913	富锦海关
1914	抚远海关
1915	漠河海关
1916	萝北海关
1917	嘉荫海关
1918	饶河海关
1919	哈内陆港
1920	哈开发区
1922	哈关邮办
1923	哈关车办
1924	哈关机办
1925	绥关公路
2200	上海海关
2201	浦江海关
2202	吴淞海关
2203	沪机场关
2204	闵开发区
2205	沪车站办
2206	沪邮局办
2207	沪稽查处
2208	宝山海关

关区代码 Code	关区名称 Name of International Trade Port (Customs Establishment)
2209	龙吴海关
2210	浦东海关
2211	卢湾监管
2212	奉贤海关
2213	莘庄海关
2214	漕河泾发
2215	虹桥开发
2216	沪金山办
2217	嘉定海关
2218	外高桥关
2219	杨浦监管
2220	金山海关
2221	松江海关
2222	青浦海关
2223	南汇海关
2224	崇明海关
2225	外港海关
2226	贸易网点
2227	普陀区站
2228	长宁区站
2229	航交办
2230	徐汇区站
2231	洋山海关驻市内报关点
2232	船监管处
2233	浦东机场
2234	沪钻交所
2235	松江加工
2236	洋山海关驻芦潮港铁路集装箱中心站监管点
2237	上海松江出口加工区 B 区
2238	上海青浦出口加工区
2239	上海闵行出口加工区
2240	上海漕河泾出口加工区
2241	沪业一处
2242	沪业二处
2243	沪业三处
2244	上海快件
2245	沪金桥办
2246	上海保税物流园区
2247	上海海关驻化学工业区办事处
2248	洋山海关(港区)
2249	洋山海关(保税)
2300	南京海关
2301	连云港关
2302	南通海关
2303	苏州海关
2304	无锡海关
2305	张家港关

关区代码 Code	关区名称 Name of International Trade Port (Customs Establishment)
2306	常州海关
2307	镇江海关
2308	新生圩关
2309	盐城海关
2310	扬州海关
2311	徐州海关
2312	江阴海关
2313	张保税区
2314	苏工业区
2315	淮安海关
2316	泰州海关
2317	禄口机办
2318	南京现场
2321	常溧阳办
2322	镇丹阳办
2324	常熟海关
2325	昆山海关
2326	吴江海关
2327	太仓海关
2328	苏吴县办
2329	通启东办
2330	泰州海关驻泰兴办事处
2331	锡宜兴办
2332	锡锡山办
2333	南通关办
2335	昆山加工
2336	苏园加工
2337	连开发办
2338	苏关邮办
2339	南通海关驻出口加工区办事处
2340	无锡海关驻出口加工区办事处
2341	连云港海关驻连云港出口加工区办事处
2342	南京海关驻江苏南京出口加工区办事处
2343	南京海关驻江苏南京出口加工区(南区)办事处
2344	苏州海关驻苏州高新区出口加工区办事处
2345	镇江海关驻镇江出口加工区办事处
2346	苏州工业园区海关保税物流中心
2347	苏州工业园区海关驻苏州工业园区出口加工区 B 区办事处
2348	张家港保税物流园区
2349	南京海关驻邮局办事处
2350	苏州高新区保税物流中心(B 型)

关区代码 Code	关区名称 Name of International Trade Port (Customs Establishment)
2351	南京海关驻江宁经济技术开发区办事处
2352	南京龙潭保税物流中心(B 型)
2353	常州海关驻出口加工区办事处
2354	扬州海关驻出口加工区办事处
2900	杭州关区
2901	杭州海关
2903	温州海关
2904	舟山海关
2905	台州海关
2906	绍兴海关
2907	湖州海关
2908	嘉兴海关
2909	杭经开关
2910	杭州萧山机场海关
2911	杭关邮办
2912	杭关萧办
2916	杭州海关驻机场办事处快件处理中心(筹备)
2918	杭关余办
2919	杭富阳办
2920	金华海关
2921	金华海关驻义乌办事处
2931	温关邮办
2932	温经开关
2933	温关机办
2934	温关鳌办
2935	温州海关驻瑞安办事处
2936	温州海关驻乐清办事处
2941	舟山海关驻嵊泗办事处
2951	台州海关驻临海办事处
2952	台州海关驻温岭办事处
2961	绍兴海关驻上虞办事处
2962	绍兴海关驻诸暨办事处
2981	嘉关乍办
2982	嘉兴海关驻嘉善办事处
2983	嘉兴海关驻出口加工区办事处
2984	嘉兴海关驻海宁办事处
2991	杭州经济技术开发区海关驻出口加工区办事处
3100	宁波关区
3101	宁波海关
3102	镇海海关
3103	甬开发区
3104	北仑海关
3105	甬保税区

关区代码 Code	关区名称 Name of International Trade Port (Customs Establishment)
3106	大榭海关
3107	甬驻余办
3108	甬驻慈办
3109	甬机场办
3110	象山海关
3111	宁波保税区海关驻出口加工区办事处
3112	宁波保税物流园区
3300	合肥海关
3301	芜湖海关
3302	安庆海关
3303	马鞍山关
3304	黄山海关
3305	蚌埠海关
3306	铜陵海关
3307	阜阳海关
3310	合肥现场
3312	芜湖海关驻出口加工区办事处
3500	福州关区
3501	马尾海关
3502	福清海关
3503	宁德海关
3504	三明海关
3505	福保税区
3506	莆田海关
3507	福关机办
3508	福榕通办
3509	福关邮办
3510	南平海关
3511	武夷山关
3513	福现业处
3518	福关鳌办
3519	福关马港
3700	厦门关区
3701	厦门海关
3702	泉州海关
3703	漳州海关
3704	东山海关
3705	石狮海关
3706	龙岩海关
3707	厦肖厝关
3710	厦高崎办
3711	厦门东渡海关
3712	厦海沧办
3713	厦驻邮办
3714	象屿保税
3715	高崎机场海关
3716	厦同安办

关区代码 Code	关区名称 Name of International Trade Port (Customs Establishment)	关区代码 Code	关区名称 Name of International Trade Port (Customs Establishment)	关区代码 Code	关区名称 Name of International Trade Port (Customs Establishment)
3717	象屿保税物流园区	4231	烟开发区	4904	常德海关
3719	厦门加工	4232	日岚山办	4905	长沙海关
3722	厦门海关驻同安办事处大嶝监管科	4233	济机场办	4906	株洲海关
3777	厦稽查处	4234	济南海关驻出口加工区办事处	4907	韶山海关
3788	厦侦查局	4235	济邮局办	4908	湘关机办
4000	南昌关区	4236	荣成海关驻龙眼港办事处	5100	广州海关
4001	南昌海关	4237	济通关处	5101	广州新风
4002	九江海关	4238	威海关驻威海邮局办事处	5103	清远海关
4003	赣州海关	4239	潍诸城办	5104	清远英德
4004	景德镇关	4240	青保税处	5105	新风白云
4005	吉安海关	4241	烟加工区	5106	小虎码头
4006	昌北机办	4242	威加工区	5107	肇庆封开
4007	南昌海关驻高新技术产业开发区办事处	4243	济宁海关驻曲阜办事处	5108	肇庆德庆
		4244	青岛海关驻滨州办事处	5109	新风窖心
4008	南昌海关驻龙南办事处	4245	烟台海关驻邮局办事处	5110	南海海关
4009	新余海关	4246	青加工区	5111	南海官窑
4010	九江海关驻出口加工区办事处	4247	威海海关驻机场办事处	5112	南海九江
4200	青岛海关	4248	青岛海关驻莱芜办事处	5113	南海北村
4201	烟台海关	4249	潍坊海关驻出口加工区办事处	5114	南海平洲
4202	日照海关	4600	郑州关区	5116	南海业务
4203	龙口海关	4601	郑州海关	5117	桂江车场
4204	威海海关	4602	洛阳海关	5118	平洲旅检
4205	济南海关	4603	南阳海关	5119	南海三山
4206	潍坊海关	4604	郑州机办	5120	广州内港
4207	淄博海关	4605	郑州邮办	5121	内港芳村
4208	烟台海关驻出口加工区 B 区办事处	4606	郑铁东办	5122	内港洲嘴
4209	荣成海关	4607	郑安阳办	5123	内港四仓
4210	青保税区	4608	郑州海关驻出口加工区办事处	5125	从化海关
4211	济宁海关	4609	郑州海关驻商丘办事处	5126	内港赤航
4212	泰安海关	4610	周口海关	5130	广州萝岗
4213	临沂海关	4700	武汉海关	5131	花都海关
4214	青前湾港	4701	宜昌海关	5132	花都码头
4215	青菏泽办	4702	荆州海关	5133	萝岗石牌
4216	东营海关	4703	襄樊海关	5134	穗保税处
4217	青枣庄办	4704	黄石海关	5135	穗稽查处
4218	青开发区	4705	武汉沌口	5136	穗统计处
4219	蓬莱海关	4706	宜三峡办	5137	穗价格处
4220	青机场关	4707	鄂加工区	5138	穗调查局
4221	烟机场办	4708	武关江办	5139	穗监管处
4222	莱州海关	4710	武关货管	5140	穗关税处
4223	青邮局办	4711	武关江岸	5141	广州机场
4224	龙长岛办	4712	武关机场	5142	民航快件
4225	威开发区	4713	武关邮办	5143	广州车站
4226	青聊城办	4716	十堰海关	5144	穗州头咀
4227	青岛大港	4900	长沙关区	5145	广州邮办
4228	烟关快件	4901	衡阳海关	5146	穗交易会
4229	德州海关	4902	岳阳海关	5147	穗邮办监
4230	青岛保税物流园区	4903	衡关郴办	5148	穗大郎站

关区代码 Code	关区名称 Name of International Trade Port (Customs Establishment)	关区代码 Code	关区名称 Name of International Trade Port (Customs Establishment)	关区代码 Code	关区名称 Name of International Trade Port (Customs Establishment)
5149	大铲海关	5199	穗技术处	5331	三门岛办
5150	顺德海关	5200	黄埔关区	5332	深财务处
5151	顺德海关加工贸易监管科	5201	埔老港办	5333	深侦查局
5152	顺德食出	5202	埔新港办	5334	深稽查处
5153	顺德车场	5203	新塘海关	5335	深技术处
5154	北窖车场	5204	东莞海关	5336	深办公室
5155	顺德旅检	5205	太平海关	5337	大亚湾核
5157	顺德陈村港澳货柜车检查场	5206	惠州海关	5338	惠州港关
5158	顺德勒流	5207	凤岗海关	5339	深加工区
5160	番禺海关	5208	埔开发区	5340	深关特办
5161	沙湾车场	5210	埔红海办	5341	深惠州关
5162	番禺旅检	5211	河源海关	5342	深红海办
5163	番禺货柜	5212	新沙海关	5343	深圳盐田港保税物流园区
5164	番禺船舶	5213	埔长安办	5344	惠州港海关驻大亚湾石化区办事处
5165	南沙旅检	5214	常平办事处	5345	深圳湾海关
5166	广州番禺海关南沙港区监管点	5216	太平海关驻沙田办事处	5700	拱北关区
5167	南沙货港	5217	东莞海关寮步车检场	5701	拱稽查处
5168	番禺海关加工贸易监管科	5300	深圳海关	5710	拱关闸办
5169	番禺东发	5301	皇岗海关	5720	中山海关
5170	肇庆海关	5302	罗湖海关	5721	中山港
5171	肇庆高要	5303	沙头角关	5724	中石岐办
5172	肇庆车场	5304	蛇口海关	5725	坦洲货场
5173	肇庆保税	5305	深关现场	5727	中小揽办
5174	肇庆旅检	5306	笋岗海关	5728	中山海关驻神湾港办事处
5175	肇庆码头	5307	南头海关	5730	拱香洲办
5176	肇庆四会	5308	沙湾海关	5740	湾仔海关
5177	肇庆三榕	5309	布吉海关	5741	湾仔船舶
5178	云浮海关	5310	淡水办	5750	九洲海关
5179	罗定海关	5311	深关车站	5760	拱白石办
5180	佛山海关	5312	深监管处	5770	斗门海关
5181	高明海关	5313	深调查局	5771	斗井岸办
5182	佛山澜石	5314	深关邮办	5772	斗平沙办
5183	三水码头	5315	惠东海关	5780	高栏海关
5184	佛山窖口	5316	大鹏海关	5790	拱监管处
5185	佛山海关快件监管现场	5317	深关机场	5791	珠澳跨境工业区珠海园区海关办事机构
5186	佛山保税	5318	梅林海关	5792	拱保税区
5187	佛山车场	5319	同乐海关	5793	万山海关
5188	佛山火车	5320	文锦渡关	5795	横琴海关
5189	佛山新港	5321	福保税关	5798	拱行监邮
5190	韶关海关	5322	沙保税关	5799	拱行监处
5191	韶关乐昌	5323	深审单处	6000	汕头海关
5192	三水海关	5324	深审价办	6001	汕关货一
5193	三水车场	5325	深关税处	6002	汕关货二
5194	三水港	5326	深数统处	6003	汕关行邮
5195	审单中心	5327	深法规处	6004	汕关机场
5196	云浮六都	5328	深规范处	6006	汕关保税
5197	机场旅检	5329	深保税处	6007	汕关业务
5198	穗河源关	5330	盐保税关		

关区代码 Code	关区名称 Name of International Trade Port (Customs Establishment)	关区代码 Code	关区名称 Name of International Trade Port (Customs Establishment)	关区代码 Code	关区名称 Name of International Trade Port (Customs Establishment)
6008	汕保税区	6816	江门市进出境货运车辆检查场	7911	成都海关驻泸州办事处
6009	汕关邮包	6817	江门保税	7912	成都海关驻宜宾办事处
6011	榕城海关	6820	新会海关	8000	重庆关区
6012	汕关普宁	6821	新会港	8001	重庆海关
6013	外砂海关	6827	新会稽查	8002	南坪开发
6014	广澳海关	6830	台山海关	8003	重庆机办
6015	南澳海关	6831	台公益港	8004	重庆邮办
6018	汕关惠来	6837	台山稽查	8005	万州海关
6019	汕关联成	6840	开平海关	8006	重庆东站
6020	汕关港口	6841	开平码头	8007	九龙坡港
6021	潮州海关	6847	开平稽查	8008	渝加工区
6022	饶平海关	6850	恩平海关	8300	贵阳海关
6028	潮阳海关	6851	恩平港	8301	贵阳总关
6031	汕尾海关	6857	恩平稽查	8302	贵阳海关驻机场办事处
6032	汕关海城	6860	鹤山海关	8600	昆明关区
6033	汕关陆丰	6861	鹤山码头	8601	昆明海关
6038	汕头海关外砂快件监管中心	6867	鹤山稽查	8602	畹町海关
6041	梅州海关	6870	阳江海关	8603	瑞丽海关
6042	梅州兴宁	6871	阳江港	8604	章凤海关
6400	海口关区	6872	阳江车场	8605	盈江海关
6401	海口海关	6877	阳江稽查	8606	孟连海关
6402	三亚海关	7200	南宁关区	8607	南伞海关
6403	八所海关	7201	南宁海关	8608	孟定海关
6404	洋浦海关	7202	北海海关	8609	打洛海关
6405	海保税区	7203	梧州海关	8610	腾冲海关
6406	清澜海关	7204	桂林海关	8611	沧源海关
6407	美兰机场	7205	柳州海关	8612	勐腊海关
6700	湛江关区	7206	防城海关	8613	河口海关
6701	湛江海关	7207	东兴海关	8614	金水河关
6702	茂名海关	7208	凭祥海关	8615	天保海关
6703	徐闻海关	7209	贵港海关	8616	田蓬海关
6704	湛江南油	7210	水口海关	8617	大理海关
6705	湛江水东	7211	龙邦海关	8618	芒市海关
6706	湛江吴川	7212	钦州海关	8619	保山监管
6707	湛江廉江	7213	桂林机办	8620	昆明机场
6708	湛江高州	7214	北海海关驻出口加工区办事处	8621	昆明邮办
6709	湛江信宜	7900	成都关区	8622	西双版纳
6710	东海岛组	7901	成都海关	8623	昆丽江办
6711	霞山海关	7902	成关机办	8624	思茅海关
6712	湛江霞海	7903	乐山海关	8626	六库监管
6713	湛江机场	7904	攀枝花关	8800	拉萨海关
6712	湛江霞海	7905	绵阳海关	8801	聂拉木关
6713	湛江机场	7906	成关邮办	8802	日喀则关
6800	江门关区	7907	成都自贡	8803	狮泉河关
6810	江门海关	7908	成都加工	8804	拉萨机办
6811	江门高沙	7909	成都公路国际物流中心监管场站	8805	拉萨现场
6812	江门外海	7910	成都海关驻机场办事处	8808	吉隆海关
6813	江门旅检		非邮政快件监管点	9000	西安关区

关区代码 Code	关区名称 Name of International Trade Port (Customs Establishment)	关区代码 Code	关区名称 Name of International Trade Port (Customs Establishment)	关区代码 Code	关区名称 Name of International Trade Port (Customs Establishment)
9001	西安海关	9406	伊宁海关	9417	乌鲁木齐机场海关
9002	咸阳机场	9405	塔城海关	9416	库尔勒办
9003	宝鸡海关	9407	吉木乃办	9418	乌鲁木齐海关驻出口加工区办事处
9004	西安海关邮局办事处	9408	喀什海关	9419	都拉塔海关
9005	陕西西安出口加工区 A 区	9409	红其拉甫	9500	兰州关区
9006	陕西西安出口加工区 B 区	9410	乌鲁木齐海关隶属阿勒泰海关	9501	兰州海关
9400	乌关区	9411	塔克什肯	9505	兰州海关驻天水监管组
9401	乌鲁木齐	9412	乌拉斯太	9600	银川海关
9402	霍尔果斯	9413	老爷庙	9601	银川海关业务现场
9403	吐尔尕特	9414	红山嘴	9700	西宁关区
9404	阿拉山口	9415	伊尔克什	9701	西宁海关现场

国内地区代码表
Codes for Sub-entity of the P. R. C.

地区代码 Code	地 区 名 称 Name of Sub-entity	地区性质标记 ID of Designated Area	地区代码 Code	地 区 名 称 Name of Sub-entity	地区性质标记 ID of Designated Area
11019	东城区	9	12069	红桥区	2
11029	西城区	9	12072	天津经济技术开发区	3
11039	崇文区	9	12074	天津港保税区	A
11049	宣武区	9	12075	天津出口加工区	
11053	北京电子城科技园区	B	12077	天津保税物流园	2
11059	朝阳区	9	12079	塘沽区其他	2
11063	北京丰台科技园区	B	12089	汉沽区	2
11069	丰台区	9	12099	大港区	2
11079	石景山	9	12109	东丽区	2
11083	北京海淀科技园区	B	12119	西青区	2
11089	海淀区其他	9	12129	津南区	2
11099	门头沟	9	12139	北辰区	2
11109	房山	9	12149	宁河县	2
11115	北京天竺出口加工区		12159	武清县	2
11119	顺义	9	12169	静海县	2
11123	北京昌平科技园区	B	12179	宝坻县	2
11129	昌平	9	12189	蓟县	2
11132	北京经济技术开发区	3	12909	天津其他	2
11133	北京亦庄科技园区	B	13013	石家庄高新技术产业开发区	B
11139	大兴其他	9	13019	石家庄其他	2
11149	通县	9	13029	唐山	
11159	怀柔	9	13032	秦皇岛经济技术开发区	3
11169	平谷	9	13035	秦皇岛出口加工区	2
11179	延庆	9	13039	秦皇岛其他	2
11189	密云	9	13049	邯郸	
11909	北京其他	9	13059	邢台	
12019	和平区	2	13063	保定高新技术产业开发区	B
12029	河东区	2	13069	保定其他	
12039	河西区	2	13079	张家口	
12043	天津新技术产业园区	B	13089	承德	
12049	南开区其他	2	13099	沧州	
12059	河北区	2	13109	廊坊	

地区代码 Code	地区名称 Name of Sub-entity	地区性质标记 ID of Designated Area
13119	衡水	
13129	武安	
13909	河北其他	
14012	山西太原经济技术开发区	3
14013	太原高新技术产业开发区	B
14019	太原其他	2
14029	大同	
14039	阳泉	
14049	长治	
14059	晋城	
14069	朔州	
14079	雁北	
14089	忻州	
14099	吕梁	
14109	晋中	
14119	临汾	
14129	运城	
14139	古交	
14909	山西其他	
15019	呼和浩特	2
15023	包头高新技术产业开发区	B
15029	包头其他	
15039	乌海	
15049	赤峰	
15059	二连	2
15069	满洲里	2
15079	呼伦贝尔盟	
15089	哲里木盟	
15099	兴安盟	
15109	乌兰察布盟	
15119	巴彦淖尔盟	
15129	伊克昭盟	
15139	阿拉善盟	
15149	锡林郭勒盟	
15909	内蒙古其他	
21012	沈阳经济技术开发区	3
21013	沈阳南湖科技开发区	B
21015	沈阳出口加工区	
21019	沈阳其他	
21022	大连经济技术开发区	3
21023	大连高新技术产业园区	B
21024	大连大窑湾保税区	A
21025	辽宁大连出口加工区	
21027	大连保税物流园区	2
21029	大连其他	2
21033	鞍山高新技术产业开发区	B
21039	鞍山其他	
21049	抚顺	
21059	本溪	
21069	丹东	
21079	锦州	
21089	营口	
21099	阜新	
21109	辽阳	
21119	盘锦	
21129	铁岭	
21139	朝阳	
21149	葫芦岛	
21159	瓦房店	
21169	海城	
21179	兴城	
21189	铁法	
21199	北票	
21209	开源	
21909	辽宁其他	
22012	长春经济技术开发区	3
22013	长春南湖-南岭新技术园区	B
22019	长春其他	2
22023	吉林高新技术产业开发区	B
22029	吉林其他	
22039	四平	
22049	辽源	
22059	通化	
22069	白山	
22075	吉林珲春出口加工区	
22079	珲春	2
22089	图们	
22099	白城	
22109	延边	
22119	公主岭	
22129	梅河口	
22139	集安	
22149	桦甸	
22159	九台	
22169	蛟河	
22179	松原	
22189	延吉市	
22909	吉林其他	
23012	哈尔滨经济技术开发区	3
23013	哈尔滨高技术开发区	B
23019	哈尔滨其他	2
23029	齐齐哈尔	
23039	鸡西	
23049	鹤岗	
23059	双鸭山	
23063	大庆高新技术产业开发区	B
23069	大庆其他	
23079	伊春	

地区代码 Code	地 区 名 称 Name of Sub-entity	地区性质标记 ID of Designated Area
23089	佳木斯	
23099	七台河	
23109	牡丹江	
23119	黑河	2
23129	绥芬河	2
23139	松花江	
23149	绥化	
23159	大兴安岭	
23169	阿城	
23179	同江	
23189	富锦	
23199	铁力	
23209	密山	
23909	黑龙江其他	
31019	黄浦	2
31029	南市	2
31039	卢湾	2
31043	上海漕河泾新兴技术开发区	B
31049	徐汇其他	2
31052	上海经济技术开发区	3
31059	长宁	2
31069	静安	2
31079	普陀	2
31089	闸北	2
31099	虹口	2
31109	杨浦	2
31112	上海闵行经济技术开发区	2
31113	上海浦江高科技园区	
31115	漕河泾出口加工区	2
31119	闵行其他	2
31129	宝山	2
31149	嘉定	2
31159	川沙	2
31166	洋山保税港区	2
31169	南汇	2
31175	闵行出口加工区	2
31179	奉贤	2
31185	上海松江出口加工区	
31189	松江	2
31199	金山	2
31205	青浦出口加工区	2
31209	青浦	2
31219	崇明	2
31222	上海浦东新区	3
31224	上海外高桥保税区	A
31225	上海金桥出口加工区(南区)	
31227	上海保税物流园区	2
31229	浦东其他	2
31909	上海其他	2
32013	南京浦口高新技术外向开发区	B
32015	南京出口加工区	
32019	南京其他	
32023	无锡高新技术产业开发区	B
32025	无锡出口加工区	
32029	无锡其他	
32039	徐州	
32043	常州高新技术产业开发区	B
32049	常州其他	
32052	苏州工业园区	3
32053	苏州高新技术产业开发区	B
32055	苏州工业园区加工区	
32059	苏州其他	
32062	南通经济技术开发区	3
32065	南通出口加工区	
32069	南通其他	2
32072	连云港经济技术开发区	3
32075	连云港出口加工区	2
32079	连云港其他	2
32089	淮阴	
32099	盐城	
32109	扬州	
32115	镇江出口加工区	
32119	镇江	
32129	泰州	
32139	仪征	
32149	常熟	
32154	江苏张家港保税区	A
32157	张家港保税物流园区	
32159	张家港其他	
32169	江阴	
32179	宿迁	
32189	丹阳	
32199	东台	
32209	兴化	
32219	淮安	
32229	宜兴	
32235	江苏昆山出口加工区	
32239	昆山	
32249	启东	
32259	吴江市	
32269	太仓市	
32909	江苏其他	
33012	杭州经济技术开发区	3
33013	杭州高新技术产业开发区	B
33015	浙江杭州出口加工区	
33019	杭州其他	
33022	宁波经济技术开发区	3
33024	宁波北仑港保税区	A

地区代码 Code	地　区　名　称 Name of Sub-entity	地区性质标记 ID of Designated Area
33025	宁波出口加工区	2
33027	宁波保税物流园区	2
33029	宁波其他	2
33032	温州经济技术开发区	3
33039	温州其他	2
33045	嘉兴出口加工区	
33049	嘉兴	
33059	湖州	
33069	绍兴	
33079	金华	
33089	衢州	
33099	舟山	
33109	丽水	
33119	台州	
33129	余姚	
33139	海宁	
33149	兰溪	
33159	瑞安	
33169	萧山	
33179	江山	
33189	义乌	
33199	东阳	
33209	慈溪	
33219	奉化	
33229	诸暨	
33239	黄岩	
33909	浙江其他	
34012	合肥经济技术开发区	3
34013	合肥科技工业园区	B
34019	合肥其他	2
34022	芜湖经济技术开发区	3
34025	芜湖出口加工区	
34029	芜湖其他	2
34039	蚌埠	
34049	淮南	
34059	马鞍山	
34069	淮北	
34079	铜陵	
34089	安庆	
34099	黄山	
34109	阜阳	
34119	宿州	
34129	滁州	
34139	六安	
34149	宣城	
34159	巢湖	
34169	池州	
34179	亳州	
34909	安徽其他	
35012	福州经济技术开发区	3
35013	福州市科技园区	B
35014	福建马尾保税区	A
35019	福州其他	2
35021	厦门特区	1
35023	厦门火炬高技术产业开发区	B
35024	厦门象屿保税区	A
35025	厦门出口加工区	
35027	厦门象屿保税物流园	1
35029	厦门其他	2
35039	莆田	8
35049	三明	
35059	泉州	8
35069	漳州	8
35079	南平	8
35089	宁德	8
35099	龙岩	8
35109	永安	8
35119	石狮	8
35909	福建其他	8
36013	南昌高新技术产业开发区	B
36019	南昌其他	2
36029	景德镇	
36039	萍乡	
36045	九江出口加工区	
36049	九江	2
36059	新余	
36069	鹰潭	
36079	赣州	
36089	宜春	
36099	上饶	
36109	吉安	
36119	抚州	
36129	瑞昌	
36909	江西其他	
37013	济南高新技术产业开发区	B
37015	湖南出口加工区	
37019	济南其他	
37022	青岛经济技术开发区	3
37023	青岛高新技术产业开发区	B
37024	青岛保税区	A
37025	青岛出口加工区	
37027	青岛保税物流园区	2
37029	青岛其他	2
37033	淄博高新技术产业开发区	B
37039	淄博	
37049	枣庄	
37059	东营	
37062	烟台经济技术开发区	3

地区代码 Code	地区名称 Name of Sub-entity	地区性质标记 ID of Designated Area	地区代码 Code	地区名称 Name of Sub-entity	地区性质标记 ID of Designated Area
37065	山东烟台出口加工区		41199	汝州	
37069	烟台其他	2	41179	信阳	
37073	潍坊高新技术产业开发区	B	41189	义马	
37075	潍坊出口加工区		41209	济源	
37079	潍坊其他		41219	禹州	
37089	济宁		41229	卫辉	
37099	泰安		41239	辉县	
37103	威海火炬高技术产业开发区	B	41249	泌阳	
37105	山东威海出口加工区		41909	河南其他	
37109	威海其他		42012	武汉经济技术开发区	3
37119	日照		42013	武汉东湖新技术开发区	B
37129	惠民		42015	湖北武汉出口加工区	
37139	德州		42019	武汉其他	2
37149	聊城		42029	黄石	
37159	临沂		42039	十堰	
37169	菏泽		42049	沙市	
37179	青州		42059	宜昌	
37189	龙口		42063	襄樊高新技术产业开发区	B
37199	曲阜		42069	襄樊其他	
37209	莱芜		42079	鄂州	
37219	新泰		42089	荆门	
37229	胶州		42099	黄冈	
37239	诸城		42109	孝感	
37249	莱阳		42119	咸宁	
37259	滕州		42129	荆州	
37269	文登		42139	郧阳	
37279	荣城		42149	鄂西	
37289	即墨		42159	随州	
37299	平度		42169	老河口	
37909	山东其他		42179	枣阳	
41013	郑州高技术开发区	B	42189	神农架	
41015	河南郑州出口加工区		42909	湖北其他	
41019	郑州其他	2	43013	长沙科技开发区	B
41029	开封		43019	长沙其他	2
41033	洛阳高新技术产业开发区	B	43023	株州高新技术产业开发区	B
41039	洛阳其他		43029	株州其他	
41049	平顶山		43039	湘潭	
41059	安阳		43049	衡阳	
41069	鹤壁		43059	邵阳	
41079	新乡		43069	岳阳	2
41089	焦作		43079	常德	
41099	濮阳		43089	大庸	
41109	许昌		43099	益阳	
41119	漯河		43109	娄底	
41129	三门峡		43119	郴州	
41139	商丘		43129	零陵	
41149	周口		43139	怀化	
41159	驻马店		43149	湘西	
41169	南阳		43159	醴陵	

地区代码 Code	地区名称 Name of Sub-entity	地区性质标记 ID of Designated Area	地区代码 Code	地区名称 Name of Sub-entity	地区性质标记 ID of Designated Area
43169	湘乡		44519	广州市	
43179	来阳		44531	深圳特区	
43189	汨罗		44909	广东其他	7
43199	津市		45013	南宁高新技术产业开发区	B
43909	湖南其他		45019	南宁其他	2
44012	广州经济技术开发区	3	45029	柳州	
44013	广州天河高新技术产业	B	45033	桂林高新技术产业开发区	B
44014	广州保税区	A	45039	桂林其他	
44015	广东广州出口加工区		45049	梧州	
44019	广州其他	2	45055	北海出口加工区	
44029	韶关	7	45059	北海	2
44030	深圳特区	1	45069	玉林	
44031	深圳特区	1	45079	百色	
44033	深圳科技工业园区	B	45089	河池	
44034	福田盐田沙头角保税区	A	45099	钦州	
44035	广东深圳出口加工区		45109	凭祥	2
44037	深圳盐田保税物流园区		45119	东兴	2
44039	深圳其他	7	45129	防城港市	
44041	珠海特区	1	45139	贵港市	
44043	珠海高新技术产业开发区	B	45149	南宁地区	
44044	珠海保税区	A	45159	柳州地区	
44045	珠澳跨境工业区珠海园区		45169	贺州地区	
44049	珠海其他	7	45909	广西其他	
44051	汕头特区	1	46011	海口	1
44054	汕头保税区	A	46013	海南国际科技园区	B
44059	汕头其他	7	46014	海南海口保税区	A
44063	佛山高新技术产业开发区	B	46021	三亚	5
44069	佛山其他	7	46901	海南其他	1
44079	江门	7	46902	海南洋浦经济技术开发区	3
44082	湛江经济技术开发区	3	50019	万州区	
44089	湛江其他	2	50029	涪陵区	
44099	茂名	7	50039	渝中区	
44129	肇庆	7	50049	大渡口区	
44133	惠州高新技术产业开发区	B	50059	江北区	
44139	惠州其他	7	50069	沙坪坝区	
44149	梅州	7	50073	重庆高新技术产业开发区	B
44159	汕尾	7	50079	九龙坡区	
44169	河源	7	50082	重庆经济技术开发区	3
44179	阳江	7	50089	南岸区	
44189	清远	7	50099	北碚区	
44199	东莞	7	50109	万盛区	
44203	中山火炬高技术产业开发区	B	50119	双桥区	
44209	中山其他	7	50125	重庆出口加工区	
44219	潮州	7	50129	渝北区	
44229	顺德	7	50139	巴南区	
44239	番禺	7	50219	长寿县	
44249	揭阳	7	50229	綦江县	
44289	南海	7	50239	潼南县	
44299	云浮市		50249	铜梁县	

地区代码 Code	地区名称 Name of Sub-entity	地区性质标记 ID of Designated Area
50259	大足县	
50269	荣昌县	
50279	璧山县	
50289	梁平县	
50299	城口县	
50309	丰都县	
50319	垫江县	
50329	武隆县	
50339	忠县	
50349	开县	
50359	云阳县	
50369	奉节县	
50379	巫山县	
50389	巫溪县	
50399	黔江土家族苗族自治县	
50409	石柱土家族自治区	
50419	秀山土家族苗族自治县	
50429	酉阳土家族苗族自治县	
50439	彭水苗族土家族自治县	
50819	江津市	
50829	合川市	
50839	永川市	
50849	南川市	
51012	成都经济技术开发区	3
51013	成都高新技术产业开发区	B
51015	四川成都出口加工区	
51019	成都其他	2
51039	自贡	
51049	攀枝花	
51059	泸州	
51069	德阳	
51073	绵阳高新技术产业开发区	B
51079	绵阳其他	
51089	广元	
51099	遂宁	
51109	内江	
51119	乐山	
51149	宜宾	
51159	南充	
51169	达县	
51179	雅安	
51189	阿坝	
51199	甘孜	
51209	凉山	
51229	广汉	
51239	江油	
51249	都江堰	
51259	峨眉山	
51269	资阳	
51279	眉山	
51289	广安	
51299	巴中	
51909	四川其他	
52013	贵阳高新技术产业开发区	B
52019	贵阳其他	2
52029	六盘山	
52039	遵义	
52049	铜仁	
52059	黔西南	
52069	毕节	
52079	安顺	
52089	黔东南	
52099	黔南	
52909	贵州其他	
53013	昆明高新技术产业开发区	B
53019	昆明其他	2
53029	东川	
53039	昭通	
53049	曲靖	
53059	楚雄	
53069	玉溪	
53079	红河	
53089	文山	
53099	思茅	
53109	西双版纳	
53119	大理	
53129	保山	
53139	德宏	
53149	丽江	
53159	怒江	
53169	迪庆	
53179	临沧	
53189	畹町	2
53199	瑞丽	2
53209	河口	2
53909	云南其他	
54019	拉萨	6
54029	昌都	6
54039	山南	6
54049	日喀则	6
54059	那曲	6
54069	阿里	6
54079	林芝	6
54909	西藏其他	6
61013	西安新技术产业开发区	B
61015	西安出口加工区	
61019	西安其他	2
61029	铜川	

地区代码 Code	地 区 名 称 Name of Sub-entity	地区性质标记 ID of Designated Area	地区代码 Code	地 区 名 称 Name of Sub-entity	地区性质标记 ID of Designated Area
61033	宝鸡高新技术产业开发区	B	63069	果洛	
61039	宝鸡其他		63079	玉树	
61049	咸阳		63089	海西	
61059	渭南		63909	青海其他	
61069	汉中		64012	银川经济技术开发区	3
61079	安康		64019	银川	2
61089	商洛		64029	石嘴山	
61099	延安		64039	银南	
61109	榆林		64049	固原	
61909	陕西其他		64059	宁夏回族自治区中卫市	
62013	兰州宁卧庄新技术产业园区	B	64909	宁夏其他	
62019	兰州其他	2	65012	乌鲁木齐经济技术开发区	3
62029	嘉峪关		65013	乌鲁木齐高新技术产业开发区	B
62039	金昌		65015	乌鲁木齐出口加工区	
62049	白银		65019	乌鲁木齐其他	2
62059	天水		65029	克拉玛依	9
62069	酒泉		65039	博乐	2
62079	张掖		65049	巴音	9
62089	武威		65059	阿克苏	9
62099	定西		65069	克孜	9
62109	陇南		65079	喀什	9
62119	平凉		65089	和田	9
62129	庆阳		65099	伊宁	2
62139	临夏		65109	塔城	2
62149	甘南		65119	阿勒泰	9
62909	甘肃其他		65122	石河子经济技术开发区	3
63012	西宁经济技术开发区	3	65129	石河子	9
63019	西宁	2	65219	吐鲁番	9
63029	海东		65229	哈密	9
63039	海北		65239	昌吉回族自治州	9
63049	黄南		65909	新疆其他	9
63059	海南				

监管证件名称代码表
Code list of Supporting Documents Subject to Customs Control of the People's Republic of China

许可证或批文代码 Code	许可证或批文名称	Name of Licences or Instruments of Ratification	监管证件签发机构	Name of Licences or Instruments of Ratification
1	进口许可证	Import licence	商务部配额许可证事务局或其授权机关	Quota & Licence Administrative Bureau Ministry of Commerce or its authorized institution
2	两用物项和技术进口许可证	Export licence	商务部	Ministry of commerce
3	两用物项和技术出口许可证	Sensitive articles export license	商务部配额许可证事务局或其授权机关	Ministry of commerce
4	出口许可证	Export licence	商务部配额许可证事务局或其授权机关	Quota & Licence Administrative Bureau Ministry of Commerce or its authorized institution
5	纺织品临时出口许可证	Export licence	商务部	Ministry of commerce

许可证或批文代码 Code	许可证或批文名称	Name of Licences or Instruments of Ratification	监管证件签发机构	Name of Licences or Instruments of Ratification
6	旧机电产品禁止进口	Used machinery and electrical products are on the list of prohibited import goods	商品编码后有此代码的,其旧产品禁止进口	the importing of used electro – mechanical products with this code at the end of its code of goods is prohibited.
7	自动进口许可证	Automatic import licence	商务部	Ministry of commerce
8	禁止出口商品	Articles on the list of prohibited export goods	商品编码后有此代码的,禁止出口	Products with this code are prohibited to be exported.
9	禁止进口商品	Articles on the list of prohibited import goods	商品编码后有此代码的,禁止进口	Products with this code are prohibited to be eximport.
A	入境货物通关单	Certificate of inspection for goods inward	国家质量监督检验检疫机构	the administrations of quality supervision
B	出境货物通关单	Certificate of inspection for goods outward	国家质量监督检验检疫机构	the administrations of quality supervision
D	出/入境货物通关单(毛坯钻石用)	Certificate of inspection for goods inward/outward (for semifi-nished diamonds)	国家质量监督检验检疫机构	the administrations of quality supervision
E	濒危物种允许出口证明书	Export licencing certificate for endangeted species	国家濒危物种进出口管理办公室或其办事机构	the administrative bureau of the Import and Export of Endangered Wild Animals or by other relevant administrative
F	濒危物种允许进口证明书	Import licencing certificate for endangeted species	国家濒危物种进出口管理办公室或其办事机构	the administrative bureau of the Import and Export of Endangered Wild Animals or by other relevant administrative
G	易制毒化学品定向出口许可证	Import and export licene for chemicals hable tobe	商务部	Ministry of commerce
H	港澳 OPA 纺织品证明	Hongkong and Macao OPA textile certificate.	(1)香港工业贸易署签发《内地加工纺织品 OPA 证明》;(2)澳门经济局签发《内地加工纺织品证明》	(1) Hongkong Trade and Industry Department released OPA certificate of Textile Processing in Mainland china; (2) Macao Ministry of Economy released certificate of Textile Processing in Mainland china
I	精神药物进(出)口准许证	Import or export permit for psychotropic drugs	国家食品药品监督管理局	State food and drug administration
J	金产品出口证或人总行进口批件	Import or export permit for gold products	中国人民银行	The people's bank of china
O	自动进口许可证(新旧机电产品)	Automatic import licence (machinery and electrical products, whether used or not)	商务部或地方外经贸主管机构、部门机电办	Business Department, local institutions in charge of foreign trade or department of Electrical and Mechanical Serivecs
P	固体废物进口许可证	Import permit for waste and scraps	国家环保总局	State environmental protection administration of china
Q	进口药品通关单	Report of inspection of soundness on import medicines	国家食品药品监督管理局及其授权机构	State food and drug administration and its authorized institution
S	进出口农药登记证明	Import or export registration certificate for pesticides	农业部药检所	Ministry of Agriculture

许可证或批文代码 Code	许可证或批文名称	Name of Licences or Instruments of Ratification	监管证件签发机构	Name of Licences or Instruments of Ratification
T	银行调运现钞进出境许可证	Entry or exit permit for foreign currency cash transfer and reallocation between banks	(1)外币现钞进出境,外汇管理局核发的"银行调运外币现钞进出境许可证;(2)人民币现钞进出境,中国人民银行货币金银局的批件	(1)"License for banks to transfer foreign currencies" released by state Administration of Foreign Exchange is required for the entry and exit of foreign currency; (2)Sanction from the Silver, Gold & Currency" Department of People's Bank of China is required for the entry and exit of RMB".
W	麻醉药品进出口准许证	Import or export permit for narcolic drugs	国家食品药品监督管理局	State food and drug administration
X	有毒化学品环境管理放行通知单	Enyironment control release notice for poisonous chemicals	国家环保总局	State environmental protection administration of china
Y	原产地证明	certificate of origin	各地出入境检验检疫局	State environmental protection administration of china
Z	进口音像制品批准单或节目提取单	Issuance permit for audio/or video products, release for protolype tape	(1)文化部签发《文化部进口音像制品批准单》(2)广播电影电视总局及其授权部门签发的《进口广播电影电视节目带(片)提取单》	(1) License for Importing and Exporting Visual Product released by the Department of Academy and Culture; (2) List of Imported Movies and Television Programmes released by the State Association of Broadcasting, Films & Television.
a	请审查预核签章	Certificate of examination and approval signed and sealed before-hand	有关进出口商会	business association
e	关税配额外优惠税率进口棉花配额证	Quota certificate for importing cotton beyond the tariff quota at a preferention rate.	商务部配额许可证事务局或其授权机关	Quota & Licence Administrative Bureau Ministry of Commerce or its authorized institution
s	适用ITA税率的商品用途认定证明	Relative certificate for ITA products issued by information industry ministry	所在地海关关税部门	Local Custom duty department
t	关税配额证明	Certificate of customs quota	商务部配额许可证事务局或其授权机关	Quota & Licence Administrative Bureau Ministry of Commerce or its authorized institution
v	自动进口许可证(加工贸易)	Automatic import license (processing trade volume)	商务部配额许可证事务局或其授权机关	Quota & Licence Administrative Bureau Ministry of Commerce or its authorized institution
x	出口许可证(加工贸易)	Export license (processing trade)	商务部配额许可证事务局或其授权机关	Quota & Licence Administrative Bureau Ministry of Commerce or its authorized institution
y	出口许可证(边境小额贸易)	Export license (Small frantier trade volume)	商务部配额许可证事务局或其授权机关	Quota & Licence Administrative Bureau Ministry of Commerce or its authorized institution
L	进出口准许证	Import or export permit licence	文化部	Ministry of culture

结汇方式代码表
Codes for Modes of Bank's Exchange Settlement

结汇方式代码 Code	结汇方式名称	Modes of Bank's Exchange Settlement
1	信汇	M/T（Mail transfer）
2	电汇	T/T（Telegraphic transfer）
3	票汇	D/D（Demand draft）
4	付款交单	D/P（Documents against payment）
5	承兑交单	D/A（Documents against acceptance）
6	信用证	L/C（Letter of credit）
7	先出后结	Settlement after export
8	先结后出	Settlement before export
9	其他	Other

用途代码表
Codes for Use of Imported Goods

用途代码 Code	用途名称	Name of Usage
01	外贸自营内销	Autonomous imports of authorized enterprises for home use
02	特区内销	Imports of SEZ for home use
03	其他内销	Other imports for home use
04	企业自用	Autonomous imports of authorized enterprises for one's own use
05	加工返销	For processing export
06	借用	Leased or borrowed
07	收保证金	Security deposit
08	免费提供	Supplied free of charge
09	作价提供	Supplied at a fixed price
10	货样，广告品	Samples and advertising matters
11	其它	Other
13	以产顶进	For substitution production

货币代码表
Codes for the Representation of Currencies

货币代码 Code	货币符号 Symbol	货币名称 Name of Currency	货币代码 Code	货币符号 Symbol	货币名称 Name of Currency
110	HKD	港币	305	FRF	法国法郎
116	JPY	日本元	307	ITL	意大利里拉
121	MOP	澳门元	312	ESP	西班牙比赛塔
129	PHP	菲律宾比索	315	ATS	奥地利先令
132	SGD	新加坡元	318	FIM	芬兰马克
133	KRW	韩国圆	326	NOK	挪威克朗
136	THB	泰国铢	330	SEK	瑞典克朗
142	CNY	人民币	331	CHF	瑞士法郎
300	EUR	欧元	501	CAD	加拿大元
302	DKK	丹麦克朗	502	USD	美元
303	GBP	英镑	601	AUD	澳大利亚元
304	DEM	德国马克	609	NZD	新西兰元

计量单位代码表
Codes for Units of Measure Used in International Trade

计量单位代码 Code	计量单位名称	Name of Unit
001	台	set
002	座	set
003	辆	unit
004	艘	unit
005	架	set
006	套	assortment/kit/outfit/set/suit
007	个	piece
008	只	piece
009	头	head/piece
010	张	sheet
011	件	piece
012	支	piece
013	枝	piece
014	根	stick
015	条	bar
016	把	piece
017	块	block/cake/piece
018	卷	coil/reel/roll/spool
019	副	pair/set
020	片	piece/slice
021	组	group/set/unit
022	份	ration
023	幅	piece
025	双	pair
026	对	couple/pair/set
027	棵	piece
028	株	piece
029	井	*jing*
030	米	meter
031	盘	coil/disk
032	平方米	square meter
033	立方米	cubic meter
034	筒	cone/reel/sleeve/tube
035	千克	kilogram
036	克	gram
037	盆	basin/pot

计量单位代码 Code	计量单位名称	Name of Unit
038	万个	ten thousand pieces
039	具	piece/set
040	百副	hundred pairs/sets
041	百支	hundred piece
042	百把	hundred piece
043	百个	hundred piece
044	百片	hundred sheet
045	刀	hundred sheet/quire
046	疋	bolt
047	公担	quintal
048	扇	piece
049	百枝	hundred piece
050	千只	thousand piece
051	千块	thousand block
052	千盒	thousand box
053	千枝	thousand piece
054	千个	thousand piece
055	亿支	hundred million piece
056	亿个	hundred million piece
057	万套	ten thousand set
058	千张	thousand sheet
059	万张	ten thousand sheet
060	千伏安	kilovolt-ampere
061	千瓦	kilowatt
062	千瓦时	kilowatt-hour
063	千升	kilolitre, thousand liter
067	英尺	foot
070	吨	metric ton
071	长吨	long ton
072	短吨	short ton
073	司马担	picul
074	司马斤	catty
075	斤	*jin*
076	磅	pound

计量单位代码 Code	计量单位名称	Name of Unit
077	担	hundred pounds
078	英担	UK hundredweight
079	短担	short hundredweight
080	两	*liang*
081	市担	*dan*
083	盎司	ounce
084	克拉	carat
085	市尺	*chi*
086	码	yard
088	英寸	inch
089	寸	*cun*
095	升	liter/*sheng*
096	毫升	milliliter
097	英加仑	UK gallon
098	美加仑	US gallon
099	立方英尺	cubic foot
101	立方尺	cubic *chi*
110	平方码	square yard
111	平方英尺	square foot
112	平方尺	square *chi*
115	英制马力	UK horsepower
116	公制马力	metric horsepower
118	令	link/ream
120	箱	box/carton/case/cassette/chest/crate
121	批	batch/lot/panel
122	罐	can/jar/tin
123	桶	barrel/bucket/cask/drum/keg/pail
124	扎	bundle
125	包	bag/bale/pack/packet
126	箩	basket
127	打	dozen
128	筐	basket/pannier

计量单位代码 Code	计量单位名　称	Name of Unit	计量单位代码 Code	计量单位名　称	Name of Unit	计量单位代码 Code	计量单位名　称	Name of Unit
129	罗	gross/twelve dozen	139	粒	grain	145	万粒	ten thousand grain
130	匹	bolt/piece	140	盒	box/capsule			
131	册	book/copy	141	合	*he*	146	千粒	thousand grain
132	本	book/copy	142	瓶	bottle/carboy/cylinder/flask/jar/vial	147	千米	kilometer
133	发	shell/round				148	千英尺	thousand feet
134	枚	piece				149	百万呎	Million Ba
135	捆	bundle	143	千支	thousand piece	163	部	set/unit
136	袋	bag/sack	144	万双	ten thousand pair			

成交方式代码表
Codes for Trade Terms

成交方式代码 Code	成交方式名称	Codes for Trade Terms
1	CIF	CIF
2	C&F	CFR/CNF/C&F
3	FOB	FOB
4	C&I	C&I
5	市场价	Market price
6	垫仓	Dunnage charge

国别(地区)代码表
Codes for the Representation of Names of Countries and Regions

代码 Code	中文名 Chinese Name	英文名 English Name	优/普标记 Preferential/General tariff rate	船舶吨税优/普标记	代码 Code	中文名 Chinese Name	英文名 English Name	优/普标记 Preferential/General tariff rate	船舶吨税优/普标记
100	**亚洲**	**Asia**			119	老挝	Laos, PDR	L	L
101	阿富汗	Afghanistan	H	H	120	黎巴嫩	Lebanon	L	L
102	巴林	Bahrian	L	H	121	中国澳门	Macau	L	L
103	孟加拉国	Bangladesh	L	L	122	马来西亚	Malaysia	L	L
104	不丹	Bhutan	H	H	123	马尔代夫	Maldives	L	H
105	文莱	Brunei	L	H	124	蒙古	Mongolia	L	L
106	缅甸	Myanmar	L	L	125	尼泊尔	Nepal	L	H
107	柬埔寨	Cambodia	L	H	126	阿曼	Oman	L	L
108	塞浦路斯	Cyprus	L	L	127	巴基斯坦	Pakistan	L	L
109	朝鲜	Korea, DPR	L	L	128	巴勒斯坦	Palestine	H	H
110	中国香港	HongKong	L	L	129	菲律宾	Philippines	L	L
111	印度	India	L	L	130	卡塔尔	Qatar	L	H
112	印度尼西亚	Indonesia	L	H	131	沙特阿拉伯	SaudiArabia	L	H
113	伊朗	Iran	L	H	132	新加坡	Singapore	L	L
114	伊拉克	Iraq	L	H	133	韩国	Korea Rep.	L	L
115	以色列	Israel	L	L	134	斯里兰卡	Sri Lanka	L	L
116	日本	Japan	L	L	135	叙利亚	Syrian	L	H
117	约旦	Jordan	L	H	136	泰国	Thailand	L	L
118	科威特	Kuwait	L	H	137	土耳其	Turkey	L	L

代码 Code	中文名 Chinese Name	英文名 English Name	优/普标记 Preferential/General tariff rate	船舶吨税优/普标记
138	阿联酋	United Arab Emirates	L	H
139	也门共和国	Republic of Yemen	L	L
141	越南	Vietnam	L	L
142	中国	China	L	L
143	台澎金马关税区	Taiwan prov.	L	H
144	东帝汶	East Timor	H	H
145	哈萨克斯坦	Kazakhstan	L	H
146	吉尔吉斯斯坦	Kirghizia	L	H
147	塔吉克斯坦	Tadzhikistan	L	H
148	土库曼斯坦	Turkmenistan	L	H
149	乌兹别克斯坦	Uzbekstan	L	H
199	亚洲其他国家(地区)	Oth. Asia nes		
201	阿尔及利亚	Algeria	L	L
202	安哥拉	Angora	L	H
203	贝宁	Benin	L	H
204	博茨瓦那	Botswana	L	H
205	布隆迪	Burundi	L	H
206	喀麦隆	Cameroon	L	H
207	加那利群岛	Canary Is	H	H
208	佛得角	Cape vrde	L	H
209	中非共和国	Central African Rep.	L	H
210	塞卜泰	Ceuta	H	H
211	乍得	Chad	L	H
212	科摩罗	Comoros	H	H
213	刚果	Congo	L	L
214	吉布提	Djibouti	L	H
215	埃及	Egypt	L	H
216	赤道几内亚	Eq. Guinea	L	H
217	埃塞俄比亚	Ethiopia	L	L
218	加蓬	Gabon	L	H
219	冈比亚	Gambia	L	H
220	加纳	Ghana	L	L
221	几内亚	Guinea	L	H
222	几内亚(比绍)	Guinea Bissau	L	H
223	科特迪瓦	Cote d' lvoir	L	H
224	肯尼亚	Kenya	L	L
225	利比里亚	Liberia	H	H
226	利比亚	Libyan Arab Jm	L	H
227	马达加斯加	Madagascar	L	H
228	马拉维	Malawi	L	H
229	马里	Mali	L	H
230	毛里塔尼亚	Mauritania	L	H
231	毛里求斯	Mauritius	L	H
232	摩洛哥	Morocco	L	L
233	莫桑比克	Mozambique	L	H
234	纳米比亚	Namibia	L	H
235	尼日尔	Niger	L	H
236	尼日利亚	Nigeria	L	H
237	留尼汪	Reunion	H	H
238	卢旺达	Rwanda	L	H
239	圣多美和普林西比	Sao Tome& Principe	H	H
240	塞内加尔	Senegal	L	H
241	塞舌尔	Seychelles	H	H
242	塞拉利昂	Sierra Leone	L	H
243	索马里	Somalia	L	H
244	南非	S. Africa	L	H
245	西撒哈拉	Western Sahara	H	H
246	苏丹	Sudan	L	L
247	坦桑尼亚	Tanzania	L	H
248	多哥	Togo	L	H
249	突尼斯	Tunisia	L	L
250	乌干达	Uganda	L	H
251	布基纳法索	Burkina Faso	L	H
252	民主刚果	Congo, DR	L	L
253	赞比亚	Zambia	L	H
254	津巴布韦	Zimbabwe	L	H
255	莱索托	Lesotho	L	H
256	梅利利亚	Melilla	H	H
257	斯威士兰	Swaziland	L	H
258	厄立特里亚	Eritrea	L	H
259	马约特岛	Mayotte	L	H
299	非洲其他国家(地区)	Oth. Afr. nes		
301	比利时	Belgium	L	L
302	丹麦	Denmark	L	L
303	英国	United Kingdom	L	L
304	德国	Germany	L	L
305	法国	France	L	L
306	爱尔兰	lreland	L	H
307	意大利	ltaly	L	L

代码 Code	中文名 Chinese Name	英文名 English Name	优/普标记 Preferential/General tariff rate	船舶吨税优/普标记
308	卢森堡	Luxembourg	L	L
309	荷兰	Netherlands	L	L
310	希腊	Greece	L	L
311	葡萄牙	Portugal	L	H
312	西班牙	Spain	L	H
313	阿尔巴尼亚	Albania	L	L
314	安道尔	Andorra	H	H
315	奥地利	Austria	L	H
316	保加利亚	Bulgaria	L	L
318	芬兰	Finland	L	L
320	直布罗陀	Gibraltar	H	L
321	匈牙利	Hungary	L	H
322	冰岛	Iceland	L	H
323	列支敦士登	Liechtenstein	L	H
324	马耳他	Malta	L	L
325	摩纳哥	Monaco	L	H
326	挪威	Norway	L	L
327	波兰	Poland	L	L
328	罗马尼亚	Romania	L	L
329	圣马力诺	San Marino	H	H
330	瑞典	Sweden	L	L
331	瑞士	Switzerland	L	H
334	爱沙尼亚	Estonia	L	H
335	拉脱维亚	Latvia	L	H
336	立陶宛	Lithuania	L	H
337	格鲁吉亚	Georgia	L	L
338	亚美尼亚	Armenia	L	H
339	阿塞拜疆	Azerbaijan	L	H
340	白俄罗斯	Byelorussia	L	H
343	摩尔多瓦	Moldavia	L	H
344	俄罗斯联邦	Russia	L	L
347	乌克兰	Ukraine	L	L
349	塞尔维亚和黑山	Serbia and Montenegro	L	L
350	斯洛文尼亚	Slovenia Rep.	L	H
351	克罗地亚	Croatia Rep	L	L
352	捷克共和国	Czech Rep	L	H
353	斯洛伐克	Slovak Rep	L	H
354	马其顿	Macedonia Rep	L	H
355	波斯尼亚—黑塞哥维那共和国	Bosnia& Hercegovina	L	H
356	梵蒂冈城国	Vatican City State	H	H
357	法国群岛	the Faroe Islands	L	H
399	欧洲其他国家(地区)	Oth. Eur. nes		
401	安提瓜和巴布达	Antigua & Barbuda	L	H
402	阿根廷	Argentina	L	L
403	阿鲁巴岛	Aruba	H	H
404	巴哈马	Bahamas	H	H
405	巴巴多斯	Barbados	L	H
406	伯利兹	Belize	L	H
408	玻利维亚	Bolivia	L	H
409	博内尔	Bonaire	H	H
410	巴西	Brazil	L	L
411	开曼群岛	Cayman Is	H	L
412	智利	Chile	L	L
413	哥伦比亚	Colombia	L	H
414	多米尼亚共和国	Dominica	L	H
415	哥斯达黎加	Costa Rica	L	H
416	古巴	Cuba	L	L
417	库腊索岛	Curacao	H	H
418	多米尼加共和国	Dominican Rep.	L	H
419	厄瓜多尔	Ecuador	L	H
420	法属圭亚那	French Guyana	H	H
421	格林纳达	Grenada	L	H
422	瓜德罗普	Guadeloupe	H	H
423	危地马拉	Guatemala	L	H
424	圭亚那	Guyana	L	H
425	海地	Haiti	L	H
426	洪都拉斯	Honduras	L	H
427	牙买加	Jamaica	L	H
428	马提尼克	Martinique	H	H
429	墨西哥	Mexico	L	L
430	蒙特塞拉特	Montserrat	H	H
431	尼加拉瓜	Nicaragua	L	H
432	巴拿马	Panama	L	H
433	巴拉圭	Paraguay	L	H
434	秘鲁	Peru	L	L
435	波多黎各	Puerto Rico	L	H
436	萨巴	Saba	H	H
437	圣卢西亚	Saint Lucia	L	H

代码 Code	中文名 Chinese Name	英文名 English Name	优/普标记 Preferential/General tariff rate	船舶吨税优/普标记
438	圣马丁岛	Saint Martin Is	H	H
439	圣文森特和格林纳丁斯	Saint Vincent& Grenadines	L	H
440	萨尔瓦多	El Salvador	H	H
441	苏里南	Suriname	L	H
442	特立尼达和多巴哥	Trinidad &Tobago	L	H
443	特克斯和凯科斯群岛	Turks &Caicos Is	H	H
444	乌拉圭	Uruguay	L	H
445	委内瑞拉	Venezuela	L	H
446	英属维尔京群岛	Br. Virgin Is	H	H
447	圣其茨—尼维斯	St. Kitts-Nevis	L	H
448	圣皮埃尔和密克隆	St. Pierre and Miquelon	L	H
449	荷属安地列斯群岛	the Netherlands Antilles	H	H
499	拉丁美洲其他国家(地区)	Oth. L. Amer. nes		
501	加拿大	Canada	L	L
502	美国	United States	L	L
503	格陵兰	Greenland	L	H
504	百慕大	Bermuda	H	L
599	北美洲其他国家(地区)	Oth. N. Amer. nes		
601	澳大利亚	Australia	L	H
602	库克群岛	Cook Is	L	H
603	斐济	Fiji	L	H
604	盖比群岛	Cambier Is	H	H
605	马克萨斯群岛	Marquesas Is	H	H
606	瑙鲁	Nauru	H	H
607	新喀里多尼亚	New Caledonia	L	H
608	瓦努阿图	Vanuatu	L	H
609	新西兰	New Zealand	L	L
610	诺福克岛	Norfolk Is	H	H
611	巴布亚新几内亚	Papua New Guinea	L	H
612	社会群岛	Society Is	H	H
613	所罗门群岛	Solomon Is	L	H
614	汤加	Tonga	L	H
615	土阿莫土群岛	Tuamotu Is	H	H
616	土布艾群岛	Tubai Is	H	H
617	萨摩亚	Samoa	L	H
618	基里巴斯	Kiribati	H	H
619	图瓦卢	Tuvalu	H	H
620	密克罗尼西亚联邦	Micronesia Fs	L	H
621	马绍尔群岛	Marshall Is Rep.	H	H
622	帕劳共和国	Palau	H	H
623	法属玻利尼西亚	French Polynesia	L	H
625	瓦利斯和浮图纳	Wallis and Futuna	L	H
699	大洋洲其他国家(地区)	Oth. Ocean. nes		
701	国(地)别不详的	Countries (reg.) unknown	H	H
702	联合国及机构和国际组织	UN and other interational		
999	中性包装原产国别	Countries of Neutral package	H	H

地区性质代码表
Codes for the Nature of Designated Areas

地区性质代码 Code	地区性质名称	Name of the Nature of Designated Areas
1	经济特区	Special economic zone (SEZ)
2	沿海开放城市	Coastal open city
3	经济技术开发区	Development zone of economy and technology
4	经济开放区	Open-door economic zone
5	海南省	Hainan
6	西藏自治区	Xizang autonomous region
7	广东省	Guangdong
8	福建省	Fujian
9	北京市、新疆	Beijing municipality, Xinjiang autonomous region
A	保税工业区	Bonded industrial zone
B	新技术开发园区	New-technology development parks

企业性质代码表
Codes for Class of Enterprises

企业性质代码 Code	企业性质名称	Class of enterprises
1	国有	State-owned enterprises
2	合作	Chinese-foreign contractual joint ventures
3	合资	Chinese-foreign equity joint ventures
4	独资	Foreign wholly-owned enterprises
5	集体	Collective owned enterprises
6	私营	Privately owned enterprises
7	个体工商户	Individual business
8	报关	Customs clearing agent
9	其他	Other

4

中华人民共和国进出口关税税款计算方法

Calculation methods for import and Export Tax of the People's Republic of China

本书所列计算方法是根据《中华人民共和国关税条例》、《中华人民共和国增值税暂行条例》及《中华人民共和国消费税暂行条例》编制的。

为便于使用，现将有关问题说明如下：

一、所称进口税包括进口关税、进口环节增值税(简称增值税)、进口环节消费税(简称消费税)，其中消费税仅对少数商品征收；出口税只含出口关税一项。

二、关税税率分为优惠关税税率和普通关税税率。凡原产地属于世贸组织成员或与我国签定有互惠双边贸易协定的国家或地区进口的商品，其进口关税税率使用优惠关税税率，否则使用普通关税税率。

三、税款计算公式

$$\text{进口关税税额} = \text{到岸价格} \times \text{进口关税税率}$$

$$\text{出口关税税额} = \frac{\text{离岸价格}}{1 + \text{出口税税率}} \times \text{出口关税税率}$$

$$\text{增值税税额} = (\text{到岸价} + \text{进口关税额} + \text{消费税额}) \times \text{增值税税率}$$

$$\text{从价消费税税额} = \left(\frac{\text{到岸价} + \text{关税额}}{1 - \text{消费税税率}}\right) \times \text{消费税税率}$$

$$\text{从量消费税税额} = \text{应征消费税的商品数量} \times \text{消费税单位税额}$$

其中，从量消费税商品计量单位的换算标准(按体积净重计)如下：

啤酒 1 吨 = 988 升

黄酒 1 吨 = 962 升

汽油 1 吨 = 1388 升

柴油 1 吨 = 1176 升

$$\text{进口税额} = \text{进口关税} + \text{增值税} + \text{消费税}$$

$$= \left(\frac{\text{进口关税率} + \text{消费税率} + \text{增值税率} + \text{进口关税率} \times \text{增值税率}}{1 - \text{消费税税率}}\right) \times \text{到岸价}$$

$$= \text{常数} \times \text{到岸价}$$

四、为便于计算进口税额，本书编制了《进口税计税系数表》，其使用方法如下：

(一)"系数表1"适用于应征消费税税率不为0税率的商品。鉴于此类商品法定增值税率均为17%，因此在本书中查出该商品的关税税率和消费税税率后，在"表1"内找出这两个税率交叉栏内的常数，用进口货物的到岸价乘以该常数，即为应纳进口税额。

(二)"系数表2"适用于消费税税率为0的进口商品。首先在本书中查出该商品的关税税率和增值税税率，然后在"表2"内找出这两个税率的交叉栏内的常数，用进口货物的到岸价乘以该常数即为应纳进口税额。

五、对适用于暂定税率的商品，关税税率应用暂定关税税率。

The Calculation methods in this book is compiled in accordance with Regulations on Customs Tariff of the People's Republic of China, Provisional Regulations on Value-added Tax of the People's Republic of China and Provisional Regulations on Consumption Tax of the People's Republic of China.

For the convenience of usage, relevant explanations are listed below:

1. Import tax we mean consists of import customs duty (ICD), value-added tax (VAT), and consumption tax (CT) among which CT is levied on a few items of goods. Export tax consists of only export customs duty (ECD).

2. Import customs duty rates we mean fall into general duty rates and preferential duty rates. The preferential duty rates apply to goods originally produced or manufactured in countries with which the People's Republic of China has concluded trading agreement. Otherewise, the general duty rates will be applied.

3. Calculation formulae for tax collection

$$ICD = \text{CIF value} \times \text{ICD rate}$$

$$ECD = \frac{\text{FOB value}}{1 + \text{ECD rate}} \times \text{ECD rate}$$

$$VAT = (\text{CIF value} + ICD + CT) \times \text{VAT rate}$$

$$\textit{Ad Valorem CT} = \left(\frac{\text{CIF value} + ICD}{1 - \text{CT rate}}\right) \times \text{CT rate}$$

$$\text{Specific CT} = \text{Quantity of goods} \times \text{unit CT rate}$$

Note: The following is the conversion table of measurements of goods on which specific consumption tax is levied (net bulk)

Beer 1ton = 988 litres

Millet wine 1 ton = 962 litres

Gasoline 1 ton = 1388 litres

Diesel 1 ton = 1176 litres

$$\text{Total Import Tax} = ICD + VAT + CT$$

$$= \left(\frac{\text{ICD rate} + \text{CT rate} + \text{VAT rate} + \text{ICD rate} \times \text{VAT rate}}{1 - \text{CT rate}}\right) \times \text{CIF value}$$

$$= \text{Coefficient} \times \text{CIF value}$$

4. To facilitate easy calculation, we compiled tables of import tax coefficients for reference. The following are the exemplary usage methods:

(1) The Table of Import Tax Coefficient (Consumption Taxes Applicable) applies to goods on which the consumption tax is levied. In viewof the statutory VAT rate is 17% for all goods in this table, the user may first find the duty rate and consumption tax rate of a particular type of goods in the table, then find the coefficient where those two rates meet in the table. The import tax payable equals the coefficient times the CIF value.

(2) The Table of Import Tax Cofficients (Consumption Taxes Not Applicable) applies to goods on which no consumption tax is levied. The user may first find the duty rate and VAT rate of a particular type of goods in the table, then find the coefficient where those two rates meet in the table. The total import tax is the coefficient times the CIF value.

5. As far as goods on which Interim Duty Rate is appliable, ICD rate is no other than Interim Duty Rate.

表1 有消费税时进口税计税常数表

Table of Import Tax Coefficients (Consumption Taxes Applicable)

关税税率 Tariff (%)	消费税税率(%) CT rate (%)							
	3	5	8	10	15	30	40	50
3.0	0.2424	0.2685	0.3099	0.3390	0.4178	0.7216	1.0085	1.4102
5.0	0.2665	0.2932	0.3353	0.3650	0.4453	0.7550	1.0475	1.4570
6.0	0.2786	0.3055	0.3480	0.3780	0.4591	0.7717	1.0670	1.4804
7.0	0.2906	0.3178	0.3608	0.3910	0.4728	0.7884	1.0865	1.5038
8.0	0.3027	0.3301	0.3735	0.4040	0.4866	0.8051	1.1060	1.5272
15.0	0.3871	0.4163	0.4625	0.4950	0.5829	0.9221	1.2425	1.6910
16.0	0.3992	0.4286	0.4752	0.5080	0.5967	0.9389	1.2620	1.7144
16.8	0.4088	0.4385	0.4854	0.5184	0.6077	0.9522	1.2776	1.7331
17.5	0.4173	0.4471	0.4943	0.5275	0.6174	0.9639	1.2913	1.7495
18.8	0.4329	0.4631	0.5108	0.5444	0.6352	0.9857	1.3166	1.7799
19.0	0.4354	0.4656	0.5134	0.5470	0.6380	0.9890	1.3205	1.7846
22.0	0.4715	0.5025	0.5515	0.5860	0.6793	1.0391	1.3790	1.8548
22.5	0.4776	0.5087	0.5579	0.5925	0.6862	1.0475	1.3888	1.8665
24.5	0.5017	0.5333	0.5833	0.6185	0.7137	1.0809	1.4278	1.9133
25.0	0.5077	0.5395	0.5897	0.6250	0.7206	1.0893	1.4375	1.9250
25.5	0.5138	0.5456	0.5960	0.6315	0.7275	1.0976	1.4473	1.9367
25.7	0.5162	0.5481	0.5986	0.6341	0.7302	1.1010	1.4512	1.9414
25.8	0.5174	0.5493	0.5998	0.6354	0.7316	1.1027	1.4531	1.9437
30.0	0.5680	0.6011	0.6533	0.6900	0.7894	1.1729	1.5350	2.0420
31.0	0.5801	0.6134	0.6660	0.7030	0.8032	1.1896	1.5545	2.0654
34.0	0.6163	0.6503	0.7041	0.7420	0.8445	1.2397	1.6130	2.1356
34.4	0.6211	0.6552	0.7092	0.7472	0.8500	1.2464	1.6208	2.1450
35.0	0.6284	0.6626	0.7168	0.7550	0.8582	1.2564	1.6325	2.1590
36.0	0.6404	0.6749	0.7296	0.7680	0.8720	1.2731	1.6520	2.1824
37.5	0.6585	0.6934	0.7486	0.7875	0.8926	1.2982	1.6813	2.2175
38.0	0.6645	0.6996	0.7550	0.7940	0.8995	1.3066	1.6910	2.2292
38.7	0.6730	0.7082	0.7639	0.8031	0.9092	1.3183	1.7047	2.2456
40.0	0.6887	0.7242	0.7804	0.8200	0.9271	1.3400	1.7300	2.2760
41.0	0.7007	0.7365	0.7932	0.8330	0.9408	1.3567	1.7495	2.2994
43.8	0.7345	0.7710	0.8288	0.8694	0.9794	1.4035	1.8041	2.3649
45.0	0.7490	0.7858	0.8440	0.8850	0.9959	1.4236	1.8275	2.3930
47.5	0.7791	0.8166	0.8758	0.9175	1.0303	1.4654	1.8763	2.4515
48.7	0.7936	0.8314	0.8911	0.9331	1.0468	1.4854	1.8997	2.4796
50.0	0.8093	0.8474	0.9076	0.9500	1.0647	1.5071	1.9250	2.5100
50.7	0.8177	0.8560	0.9165	0.9591	1.0743	1.5188	1.9387	2.5264
51.0	0.8213	0.8597	0.9203	0.9630	1.0785	1.5239	1.9445	2.5334
57.0	0.8937	0.9336	0.9966	1.0410	1.1611	1.6241	2.0615	2.6738
58.2	0.9082	0.9484	1.0119	1.0566	1.1776	1.6442	2.0849	2.7019
65.0	0.9902	1.0321	1.0984	1.1450	1.2712	1.7579	2.2175	2.8610

注：鉴于应征消费税的进口商品的法定增值税税率均为17%，故本表省略了增值税税率一栏，但所列常数均已包括增值税在内。

Note: All coefficients include a statutory VTA rate of 17%.

表2　无消费税时进口税计税常数表
Table of Import Tax Coefficents (Consumption Taxes Not Applicable)

关税税率 Tariff (%)	增值税税率(%) VAT rate (%)		关税税率 Tariff (%)	增值税税率(%) VAT rate (%)		关税税率 Tariff (%)	增值税税率(%) VAT rate (%)	
	13	17		13	17		13	17
0	0.1300	0.1700	7.8	0.2181	0.2613	13.0	0.2769	0.3221
0.8	0.1390	0.1794	8.0	0.2204	0.2636	13.2	0.2792	0.3244
1.0	0.1413	0.1817	8.1	0.2215	0.2648	13.3	0.2803	0.3256
1.5	0.1470	0.1876	8.2	0.2227	0.2659	13.4	0.2814	0.3268
2.0	0.1526	0.1934	8.3	0.2238	0.2671	13.5	0.2826	0.3280
2.3	0.1560	0.1969	8.4	0.2249	0.2683	13.6	0.2837	0.3291
2.4	0.1571	0.1981	8.5	0.2261	0.2695	13.8	0.2859	0.3315
2.5	0.1583	0.1993	8.6	0.2272	0.2706	13.9	0.2871	0.3326
2.8	0.1616	0.2028	8.8	0.2294	0.2730	14.0	0.2882	0.3338
3.0	0.1639	0.2051	9.0	0.2317	0.2753	14.2	0.2905	0.3361
3.4	0.1684	0.2098	9.4	0.2362	0.2800	14.3	0.2916	0.3373
3.5	0.1696	0.2110	9.5	0.2374	0.2812	14.4	0.2927	0.3385
3.8	0.1729	0.2145	9.6	0.2385	0.2823	14.5	0.2939	0.3397
4.0	0.1752	0.2168	9.7	0.2396	0.2835	14.6	0.2950	0.3408
4.2	0.1775	0.2191	9.8	0.2407	0.2847	14.8	0.2972	0.3432
4.3	0.1786	0.2203	9.9	0.2419	0.2858	15.0	0.2995	0.3455
4.4	0.1797	0.2215	10.0	0.2430	0.2870	15.2	0.3018	0.3478
4.5	0.1809	0.2227	10.1	0.2441	0.2882	15.3	0.3029	0.3490
4.8	0.1842	0.2262	10.2	0.2453	0.2893	15.4	0.3040	0.3502
5.0	0.1865	0.2285	10.3	0.2464	0.2905	15.6	0.3063	0.3525
5.4	0.1910	0.2332	10.5	0.2487	0.2929	15.7	0.3074	0.3537
5.5	0.1922	0.2344	10.6	0.2498	0.2940	16.0	0.3108	0.3572
5.8	0.1955	0.2379	10.8	0.2520	0.2964	16.3	0.3142	0.3607
6.0	0.1978	0.2402	11.0	0.2543	0.2987	16.4	0.3153	0.3619
6.2	0.2001	0.2425	11.2	0.2566	0.3010	16.6	0.3176	0.3642
6.3	0.2012	0.2437	11.3	0.2577	0.3022	16.8	0.3198	0.3666
6.4	0.2023	0.2449	11.4	0.2588	0.3034	17.0	0.3221	0.3689
6.5	0.2035	0.2461	11.6	0.2611	0.3057	17.2	0.3244	0.3712
6.6	0.2046	0.2472	11.7	0.2622	0.3069	17.5	0.3278	0.3748
6.8	0.2068	0.2496	11.8	0.2633	0.3081	17.6	0.3289	0.3759
6.9	0.2080	0.2507	12.0	0.2656	0.3104	17.8	0.3311	0.3783
7.0	0.2091	0.2519	12.2	0.2679	0.3127	18.0	0.3334	0.3806
7.1	0.2102	0.2531	12.3	0.2690	0.3139	18.2	0.3357	0.3829
7.2	0.2114	0.2542	12.4	0.2701	0.3151	18.3	0.3368	0.3841
7.4	0.2136	0.2566	12.5	0.2713	0.3163	18.4	0.3379	0.3853
7.5	0.2148	0.2578	12.6	0.2724	0.3174	18.7	0.3413	0.3888
7.6	0.2159	0.2589	12.7	0.2735	0.3186	18.8	0.3424	0.3900
7.7	0.2170	0.2601	12.8	0.2746	0.3198	19.0	0.3447	0.3923

关税税率 Tarift (%)	增值税税率(%) V. A. T. rate (%)		关税税率 Tarift (%)	增值税税率(%) V. A. T. rate (%)		关税税率 Tarift (%)	增值税税率(%) V. A. T. rate (%)	
	13	17		13	17		13	17
19.2	0.3470	0.3946	24.0	0.4012	0.4508	34.4	0.5187	0.5725
19.3	0.3481	0.3958	24.1	0.4023	0.4520	35.0	0.5255	0.5795
19.4	0.3492	0.3970	24.3	0.4046	0.4543	36.0	0.5368	0.5912
19.5	0.3504	0.3982	24.5	0.4069	0.4567	36.3	0.5402	0.5947
19.6	0.3515	0.3993	24.6	0.4080	0.4578	36.6	0.5436	0.5982
19.8	0.3537	0.4017	24.8	0.4102	0.4602	36.8	0.5458	0.6006
20.0	0.3560	0.4040	25.0	0.4125	0.4625	37.2	0.5504	0.6052
20.1	0.3571	0.4052	25.2	0.4148	0.4648	37.5	0.5538	0.6088
20.2	0.3583	0.4063	25.4	0.4170	0.4672	38.0	0.5594	0.6146
20.3	0.3594	0.4075	25.5	0.4182	0.4684	38.7	0.5673	0.6228
20.4	0.3605	0.4087	25.6	0.4193	0.4695	39.2	0.5730	0.6286
20.7	0.3639	0.4122	25.7	0.4204	0.4707	40.0	0.5820	0.6380
20.8	0.3650	0.4134	25.8	0.4215	0.4719	41.0	0.5933	0.6497
20.9	0.3662	0.4145	26.0	0.4238	0.4742	42.1	0.6057	0.6626
21.0	0.3673	0.4157	26.3	0.4272	0.4777	42.5	0.6103	0.6673
21.2	0.3696	0.4180	26.4	0.4283	0.4789	43.8	0.6249	0.6825
21.3	0.3707	0.4192	27.0	0.4351	0.4859	45.0	0.6385	0.6965
21.5	0.3730	0.4216	27.2	0.4374	0.4882	47.5	0.6668	0.7258
21.6	0.3741	0.4227	27.5	0.4408	0.4918	48.7	0.6803	0.7398
21.7	0.3752	0.4239	28.0	0.4464	0.4976	50.0	0.6950	0.7550
21.8	0.3763	0.4251	28.5	0.4521	0.5035	50.7	0.7029	0.7632
22.0	0.3786	0.4274	28.8	0.4554	0.5070	51.0	0.7063	0.7667
22.2	0.3809	0.4297	29.0	0.4577	0.5093	52.4	0.7221	0.7831
22.3	0.3820	0.4309	29.4	0.4622	0.5140	54.4	0.7447	0.8065
22.5	0.3843	0.4333	29.5	0.4634	0.5152	56.0	0.7628	0.8252
22.6	0.3854	0.4344	30.0	0.4690	0.5210	57.0	0.7741	0.8369
22.8	0.3876	0.4368	30.2	0.4713	0.5233	58.2	0.7877	0.8509
23.0	0.3899	0.4391	31.0	0.4803	0.5327	65.0	0.8645	0.9305
23.1	0.3910	0.4403	31.3	0.4837	0.5362	65.9	0.8747	0.9410
23.2	0.3922	0.4414	31.4	0.4848	0.5374	71.0	0.9323	1.0007
23.3	0.3933	0.4426	32.0	0.4916	0.5444	90.0	1.1470	1.2230
23.5	0.3956	0.4450	33.0	0.5029	0.5561			
23.8	0.3989	0.4485	34.0	0.5142	0.5678			

5

中华人民共和国进出口商品规范申报说明

Norm Declares Explanation for the Customs Import and Export Goods of the People's Republic of China

第一类　活动物;动物产品

第一章　活动物

商品编码	商 品 描 述	申 报 要 素	
		商品名称	规格型号
01.01	马、驴、骡:		
	-改良种用:	1.品名;2.野生请注明;3.改良种用请注明	
	-其他:	1.品名;2.野生请注明;	
01.02	牛:		
0102.1000	-改良种用:	1.品名;2.野生请注明;3.改良种用请注明	
0102.9000	-其他:	1.品名;2.野生请注明;	
01.03	猪:		
0103.1000	-改良种用:	1.品名;2.野生请注明;3.改良种用请注明	
	-其他:	1.品名;2.野生请注明	3.个体重量
01.04	绵羊、山羊:		
	-绵羊:	1.品名;2.改良种用请注明	
	-山羊:	1.品名;2.野生请注明;3.改良种用请注明	
01.05	家禽,即鸡、鸭、鹅、火鸡及珍珠鸡:	1.品名;2.改良种用请注明	3.个体重量
01.06	其他活动物:	1.品名;2.野生请注明;3.改良种用请注明	

第二章　肉及食用杂碎

【注解】

1.本章中的"鲜的"包括运输途中用盐临时保藏的肉及杂碎;"冷的"即产品温度一般降至0℃左右,但未冻结的;"冻的"即冷却到产品的冰点以下,使产品全部冻结的。

2.归入本章的杂碎及肉或杂碎的细粉、粗粉,应报明用途(食用)。

商品编码	商 品 描 述	申 报 要 素	
		商品名称	规格型号
02.01	鲜、冷牛肉:	1.品名;2.加工方法(整头及半头、带骨或去骨等);3.状态(鲜、冷).4.野生请注明	
02.02	冻牛肉:	1.品名;2.加工方法(整头及半头、带骨或去骨等);3.状态(冻);4.野生请注明	
02.03	鲜、冷、冻猪肉:	1.品名;2.加工方法(整头及半头、带骨或去骨、前腿或后腿等);3.状态(鲜、冷、冻);4.野生请注明	5.个体重量
02.04	鲜、冷、冻绵羊肉或山羊肉:	1.品名;2.加工方法(整头及半头、带骨或去骨等);3.状态(鲜、冷、冻);4.野生请注明	
02.05	鲜、冷、冻马、驴、骡肉:	1.品名;2.状态(鲜、冷、冻);3.野生请注明	
02.06	鲜、冷、冻牛、猪、绵羊、山羊、马、驴、骡的食用杂碎:	1.品名;2.状态(鲜、冷、冻)	
02.07	税目01.05所列家禽的鲜、冷、冻肉及食用杂碎:	1.品名;2.加工方法(整只、带骨或去骨等);3.状态(鲜、冷、冻)	
02.08	其他鲜、冷、冻肉及食用杂碎:	1.品名;2.状态(鲜、冷、冻);3.野生请注明	
02.09	未炼制或用其他方法提取的不带瘦肉的肥猪肉、猪脂肪及家禽脂肪,鲜、冷、冻、干、熏、盐腌或盐渍的:	1.品名;2.加工方法(未炼制、未提取脂肪、干、熏、盐腌、盐渍等);3.状态(鲜、冷、冻、不带瘦肉)	
02.10	肉及食用杂碎,干、熏、盐腌或盐渍的;可供食用的肉或杂碎的细粉、粗粉:	1.品名;2.加工方法(带骨、腿肉、腹肉、干、熏、盐腌、盐渍等);3.野生请注明	

第三章　鱼、甲壳动物、软体动物及其他水生无脊椎动物

【注解】

1. 本章所称“冷”指产品的温度一般降至0℃左右，但产品尚未冻结的；“冻”指温度降至产品的冰点以下，使产品全部冻结的；“观赏鱼”指因其色彩或形态特殊而通常养于水族箱中以供观赏的活鱼；“鱼片”指顺鱼脊骨平切的长条肉片。

2. 入本章的细粉、粗粉、团粒应报明用途。

商品编码	商品描述	申报要素	
		商品名称	规格型号
03.01	**活鱼**		
0301.1000	-观赏鱼	1.品名;2.用途(观赏);3.状态(活)	
	-其他活鱼:	1.品名;2.状态(活)	3.鱼苗请注明个体长度、尾数、千克等
03.02	**鲜、冷鱼,但税目03.04的鱼片以及其他鱼肉除外:**	1.品名(学名,如黑线鳕鱼、绿青鳕鱼等);2.状态(鲜、冷)	
03.03	**冻鱼,但税目03.04的鱼片及其他鱼肉除外:**	1.品名(学名,如黑线鳕鱼、绿青鳕鱼等);2.状态(冻)	
03.04	**鲜、冷、冻鱼片及其他鱼肉(不论是否绞碎):**	1.品名;2.状态(鲜、冷、冻)	
03.05	**干、盐腌或盐渍的鱼;熏鱼,不论在熏制前或熏制过程中是否烹煮;适合供人食用的鱼的细粉、粗粉及团粒:**	1.品名;2.加工方法(干、熏、盐腌、盐渍)	
03.06	**带壳或去壳的甲壳动物,活、鲜、冷、冻、干、盐腌或盐渍的;蒸过或用水煮过的带壳甲壳动物,不论是否冷、冻、干、盐腌或盐渍的:适合供人食用的甲壳动物的细粉、粗粉及团粒:**	1.品名;2.加工方法(干、盐腌、盐渍、带壳、去壳、蒸、水煮、等);3.状态(活、鲜、冷、冻)	4.种苗请注明个体长度、尾数、千克等;
03.07	**带壳或去壳的软体动物,活、鲜、冷、冻、干、盐腌或盐渍的;不属于甲壳动物和软体动物的水生无脊椎动物,活、鲜、冷、冻、干、盐腌或盐渍的;适合供人食用的水生无脊椎动物(甲壳动物除外)的细粉、粗粉及团粒:**	1.品名;2.加工方法(干、盐腌、盐渍);3.状态(活、鲜、冷、冻)	4.鱼苗请注明个体长度、尾数、千克等

备注或申报要求

03. 01　　**活鱼:**

0301. 1000　-观赏鱼:　拉丁文名

第四章　乳品;蛋品;天然蜂蜜;其他食用动物产品

商品编码	商品描述	申报要素	
		商品名称	规格型号
04.01	**未浓缩及未加糖或其他甜物质的乳及奶油:**	1.品名;2.加工方法(未浓缩及未加糖或其他甜物质)	3.脂肪含量(按重量计)
04.02	**浓缩、加糖或其他甜物质的乳及奶油:**	1.品名;2.加工方法(浓缩、加糖或其他甜物质);3.外观(粉状、粒状等)	4.脂肪含量(按重量计)
04.03	**酪乳、结块的乳及奶油、酸奶、酸乳酒及其他发酵或酸化的乳和奶油,不论是否浓缩、加糖、加其他甜物质、加香料、加水果、加坚果或加可可:**		
0403.1000	-酸乳	品名	
0403.9000	-其他	1.品名;2.加工方法(发酵、酸化、浓缩、加糖及其他甜物质、香料、水果、坚果、可可)	
04.04	**乳清,不论是否浓缩、加糖或其他甜物质;其他税目未列名的含天然乳的产品,不论是否加糖或其他甜物质:**		

商品编码	商品描述	申报要素	
		商品名称	规格型号
0404.1000	-乳清及改性乳清,不论是否浓缩、加糖或其他甜物质	1.品名;2.用途;3.品牌;4.加工方法(浓缩、加糖其他甜物质)	5.成分含量(蛋白、乳糖、水分、脂肪、灰分)
0404.9000	-其他	1.品名	2.成分含量
04.05	**黄油及其他从乳中提取的脂和油;乳酱:**	1.品名;2.品牌	3.乳脂含量;4.包装规格
04.06	**乳酪及凝乳:**	1.品名;2.品牌;3.加工方法(熟化、固化、磨碎或粉化等)	4.乳脂含量;5.包装规格
04.07	**带壳禽蛋,鲜、腌制或煮过的:**	1.品名;2.加工方法(带壳、腌制、煮过);3.状态(鲜);4.野生请注明;5.种用请注明	
04.08	**去壳禽蛋及蛋黄,鲜、干、冻、蒸过或水煮、制成型或用其他方法保藏的,不论是否加糖或其他甜物质:**	1.品名;2.加工方法(干、去壳、蒸、水煮、制成型等);3.状态(鲜、冻)	
04.09	**天然蜂蜜:**	1.品名;2.来源(天然)	
04.10	**其他税目未列名的食用动物产品:**	1.品名;2.用途(食用);3.状态(鲜等);4.野生请注明	

第五章 其他动物产品

【注解】

本章所称"填充用羽毛"是指家禽(特别是鹅或鸭)、鸽子、鹧鸪或类似禽类的羽毛,但粗大的翼毛或尾毛及分级时摒弃的粗大的羽毛除外;"羽绒",主要指鹅或鸭毛中最为细小、柔软的绒毛,它与羽毛的区别在于没有硬羽轴。

商品编码	商品描述	申报要素	
		商品名称	规格型号
05.01	**未经加工的人发,不论是否洗涤;废人发:**	品名	
05.02	**猪鬃、猪毛;獾毛及其他制刷用兽毛;上述鬃毛的废料:**		
	-猪鬃、猪毛及其废料:	品名	
	-其他:		
	---獾毛及其他制刷用兽毛:	1.品名;2.用途(制刷用)	
0502.9020	---废料	品名	
05.04	**整个或切块的动物(鱼除外)的肠、膀胱及胃,鲜、冷、冻、干、熏、盐腌或盐渍的:**	1.品名;2.加工方法(干、熏、盐腌、盐渍);3.状态(鲜、冷、冻)	
05.05	**带有羽毛或羽绒的鸟皮及鸟体其他部分;羽毛及不完整羽毛(不论是否修边)、羽绒,仅经洗涤、消毒或为了保藏而作过处理,但未经进一步加工;羽毛或不完整羽毛的粉末及废料:**	1.品名;2.用途;3.加工方法(仅经洗涤、消毒或为了保藏而作过处理);4.状态(完整、不完整、粉末及废料等);5.野生请注明	
05.06	**骨及角柱,未经加工或经脱脂、简单整理(但未切割成形)、酸处理或脱胶;上述产品的粉末及废料:**	1.品名;2.处理方法[未经加工或经脱脂、简单整理(但未切割成型)、脱胶、酸处理、脱脂];3.野生请注明	
05.07	**兽牙、龟壳、鲸须、鲸须毛、角、鹿角、蹄、甲、爪及喙,未经加工或仅简单整理但未切割成形;上述产品的粉末及废料:**	1.品名;2.处理方法(未经加工或仅简单整理但未切割成形);3.野生请注明	

商品编码	商 品 描 述	申 报 要 素	
		商品名称	规格型号
05.08	珊瑚及类似品,未经加工或仅简单整理但未经进一步加工;软体动物壳、甲壳动物壳、棘皮动物壳、墨鱼骨,未经加工或仅简单整理但未切割成形。上述壳、骨的粉末及废料:	1. 品名;2. 处理方法(未经加工或仅简单整理但未切割成形等)	
05.10	龙涎香、海狸香、灵猫香及麝香;斑蝥;胆汁,不论是否干制;供配制药用的腺体及其他动物产品,鲜、冷、冻或用其他方法暂时保藏的:	1. 品名;2. 用途(配制药用等);3. 状态(鲜、冷、冻、干或用其他方法暂时保藏);4. 野生请注明	
05.11	其他税目未列名的动物产品;不适合供人食用的第一章或第三章的死动物:	品名	

第二类　植物产品

第六章　活树及其他活植物;鳞茎、根及类似品;插花及装饰用簇叶

【注解】

本章所称"树、灌木"包括具有木质梗的藤本植物(例如,葡萄、杂交草莓、悬钩子属植物、弥猴桃树)及其带根插枝。

商品编码	商品描述	申报要素	
		商品名称	规格型号
06.01	鳞茎、块茎、块根、球茎、根颈及根茎,休眠、生长或开花的;菊苣植物及其根,但税目12.12的根除外:	1.品名;2.状态(休眠、生长、开花);3.种用请注明	
06.02	其他活植物(包括其根)、插枝及接穗;蘑菇菌丝:	1.品名;2.栽培方法(无根插枝、接穗等);3.种用请注明	
06.03	制花束或装饰用的插花及花蕾,鲜、干、染色、漂白、浸渍或用其他方法处理的:	1.品名;2.用途(制花束或装饰用);3.加工方法(染色、漂白、浸渍或用其他方法处理);4.状态(鲜、干)	
06.04	制花束或装饰用的不带花及花蕾的植物枝、叶或其他部分、草、苔藓及地衣,鲜、干、染色、漂白、浸渍或用其他方法处理的:	1.品名;2.用途(制花束或装饰用);3.加工方法(染色、漂白、浸渍或用其他方法处理);4.状态(鲜、干、不带花及花蕾)	

第七章　食用蔬菜、根及块茎

【注解】

本章所称"冷藏",是指产品的温度一般已降至0℃左右,但未冻结。然而,某些产品,例如,马铃薯,当温度降至并维持在10℃时,也可视作"冷藏";"冷冻",是指产品已冷却到本身冰点以下并且已经全部冻结。

商品编码	商品描述	申报要素	
		商品名称	规格型号
07.01	鲜或冷藏的马铃薯:	1.品名;2.状态(鲜、冷);3.种用请注明	
07.02	鲜或冷藏的番茄:	1.品名;2.状态(鲜、冷)	
07.03	鲜或冷藏的洋葱、青葱、大蒜、韭葱及其他葱属蔬菜:	1.品名;2.状态(鲜、冷)	
07.04	鲜或冷藏的卷心菜、菜花、球茎甘蓝、羽衣甘蓝及类似的食用芥菜类蔬菜:	1.品名;2.状态(鲜、冷); 3.芥菜类蔬菜请注明用途(食用)	
07.05	鲜或冷藏的莴苣及菊苣:	1.品名;2.状态(鲜、冷)	
07.06	鲜或冷藏的胡萝卜、萝卜、色拉甜菜根、婆罗门参、块根芹、小萝卜及类似的食用根茎:	1.品名;2.状态(鲜、冷);3.根茎应注明用途(食用)	
07.07	鲜或冷藏的黄瓜及小黄瓜:	1.品名;2.状态(鲜、冷)	
07.08	鲜或冷藏的豆类蔬菜,不论是否脱荚:	1.品名;2.状态(鲜、冷)	
07.09	鲜或冷藏的其他蔬菜:	1.品名;2.状态(鲜、冷)	
07.10	冷冻蔬菜(不论是否蒸煮):	1.品名;2.状态(冻);3.大蒜应注明外观形状(蒜头、蒜瓣)	
07.11	暂时保藏(例如,使用二氧化硫气体、盐水、亚硫酸水或其他防腐液)的蔬菜,但不适于直接食用的:	1.品名;2.用途(不适于直接食用);3.保藏方法(用盐水、二氧化硫气体、亚硫酸水或其他防腐液处理)	
07.12	干蔬菜,整个、切块、切片、破碎或制成粉状,但未经进一步加工的:	1.品名;2.加工方法(干制,包括脱水、蒸干或冻干)	
07.13	脱荚的干豆,不论是否去皮或分瓣:	1.品名;2.加工方法(干、脱荚);3.种用请注明	
07.14	鲜、冷、冻或干的木薯、竹芋、兰科植物块茎、菊芋、甘薯及含有高淀粉或菊粉的类似根茎,不论是否切片或制成团粒;西谷茎髓:	1.品名;2.加工方法(干);3.状态(鲜、冷、冻);4.种用请注明	

第八章　食用水果及坚果;柑桔属水果或甜瓜的果皮

【注解】

本章所称“冷藏”,是指产品的温度一般降至0℃左右,但未冻结的。但是有些产品(例如,甜瓜及某些柑桔属果实),其温度降至并维持在10℃时,也可视作“冷藏”;所称“冷冻”,是指温度降至产品的冰点以下,产品已全部冻结。

商品编码	商品描述	申报要素	
		商品名称	规格型号
08.01	**鲜或干的椰子、巴西果及腰果,不论是否去壳或去皮:**	1.品名;2.加工方法(去壳、带壳);3.状态(鲜、干);4.种用请注明	不包括用于榨取椰子油而不适合供人食用的干椰肉(1203)
08.02	**鲜或干的其他坚果,不论是否去壳或去皮:**	1.品名;2.加工方法(去壳、带壳);3.状态(鲜、干);4.种用请注明	
08.03	**鲜或干的香蕉,包括芭蕉:**	1.品名;2.状态(鲜、干)	
08.04	**鲜或干的椰枣、无花果、菠萝、鳄梨、番石榴、芒果及山竹果:**	1.品名;2.状态(鲜、干)	
08.05	**鲜或干的柑桔属水果:**	1.品名;2.状态(鲜、干);3.鲜橙请注明品种	
08.06	**鲜或干的葡萄:**	1.品名;2.状态(鲜、干)	
08.07	**鲜的甜瓜(包括西瓜)及木瓜:**	1.品名;2.状态(鲜)	
08.08	**鲜的苹果、梨及榅桲:**	1.品名;2.状态(鲜)	
08.09	**鲜的荎,杏、樱桃、桃(包括油桃)、梅及李:**	1.品名;2.状态(鲜)	
08.10	**其他鲜果:**	1.品名;2.状态(鲜)	
08.11	**冷冻水果及坚果,不论是否蒸煮、加糖或其他甜物质:**	1.品名;2.状态(冻);3.栗子请注明加工方法(去壳、未去壳)	
08.12	**暂时保藏(例如,使用二氧化硫气体、盐水、亚硫酸水或其他防腐液)的水果及坚果,但不适于直接食用的:**	1.品名;2.用途(不适于直接食用);3.保藏方法(用盐水、二氧化硫气体、亚硫酸水或其他防腐液处理)	
08.13	**税目08.01至08.06以外的干果;本章的什锦坚果或干果:**		
0813.1000	-杏	1.品名;2.状态(干)	
0813.2000	-梅及李	1.品名;2.状态(干)	
0813.3000	-苹果	1.品名;2.状态(干)	
	-其他干果:	1.品名;2.状态(干);	3.龙眼干请注明等级
0813.5000	-本章的什锦坚果或干果	品名(什锦坚果或干果)	
08.14	**柑桔属水果或甜瓜(包括西瓜)的果皮,鲜、冻、干或用盐水、亚硫酸水或其他防腐液暂时保藏的:**	1.品名;2.状态(鲜、冻、干);3.保藏方法(用盐水、亚硫酸水或其他防腐液暂时保藏的)	

第九章　咖啡、茶、马黛茶及调味香料

商品编码	商品描述	申报要素	
		商品名称	规格型号
09.01	**咖啡,不论是否焙炒或浸除咖啡碱;咖啡豆荚及咖啡豆皮;含咖啡的咖啡代用品:**	1.品名;2.加工方法(未浸除或浸除咖啡碱、未焙炒或焙炒);3.状态(咖啡豆荚或豆皮及代用品)	
09.02	**茶,不论是否加香料:**	1.品名;2.加工方法(发酵、半发酵、未发酵)	3.内包装每件净重
09.03	**马黛茶:**	品名	
09.04	**胡椒;辣椒干及辣椒粉:**	1.品名;2.加工方法(未磨、已磨);3.状态(粉、干);4.胡椒请注明品种(白胡椒、黑胡椒)	
09.05	**香子兰豆:**	品名	
09.06	**肉桂及肉桂花:**	1.品名;2.加工方法(未磨、已磨)	
09.07	**丁香(母丁香、公丁香及丁香梗):**	品名	
09.08	**肉豆蔻、肉豆蔻衣及豆蔻:**	品名	

商品编码	商 品 描 述	申 报 要 素	
		商品名称	规格型号
09.09	**茴芹子、八角茴香、小茴香子、芫荽子、枯茗子及其贳蒿子;杜松果:**	品名	
09.10	**姜、番红花、姜黄、麝香草、月桂叶、咖喱及其他调味香料:**	1.品名	2.主要成分

第十章 谷 物

商品编码	商 品 描 述	申 报 要 素	
		商品名称	规格型号
10.01	**小麦及混合麦:**	1.品名;2.品种(白麦、红麦、冬麦、春麦)3.种用请注明;4.硬粒请注明	
10.02	**黑麦:**	1.品名;2.种用请注明	
10.03	**大麦:**	1.品名;2.种用请注明	
10.04	**燕麦:**	1.品名;2.种用请注明	
10.05	**玉米:**	1.品名;2.种用请注明	
10.06	**稻谷、大米:**	1.品名;2.种类(香米、籼米、巴吞米、白米、糯米等);3.状态(糙米、精米、碎米);4.种用请注明;5.半熟米应注明加工程度	
10.07	**食用高粱:**	1.品名;2.用途(食用);3.种用请注明	
10.08	**荞麦、谷子及加那利草子;其他谷物:**	1.品名;2.种用请注明	

备注或申报要求

10.01 **小麦及混合麦:** 1. 签约日期;2. 定价方式;3. 提单日期;4. 确定升贴水日期;5. 运费

第十一章 制粉工业产品;麦芽;淀粉;菊粉;面筋

商品编码	商 品 描 述	申 报 要 素	
		商品名称	规格型号
11.01	**小麦或混合麦的细粉:**	1.品名;2.状态(细粉)	
11.02	**其他谷物细粉,但小麦或混合麦的细粉除外:**	1.品名;2.种类(黑麦、玉米、籼米等);3.状态(细粉)	
11.03	**谷物的粗粒、粗粉及团粒:**	1.品名;2.种类(小麦、燕麦、玉米、籼米等);3.状态(粗粒、粗粉、团粒)	
11.04	**经其他加工的谷物(例如,去壳、滚压、制片、制成粒状、切片或粗磨),但税目10.06的稻谷、大米除外;谷物胚芽,整粒、滚压、制片或磨碎的:**		
	-滚压或制片的谷物:	1.品名;2.种类(大麦、燕麦);3.加工方法(滚压、制片)	
	-经其他加工的谷物(例如,去壳、制成粒状、切片或粗磨):	1.品名;2.种类(燕麦、玉米、大麦等);3.加工方法(去壳、制成粒状、切片或粗磨)	
1104.3000	-谷物胚芽,整粒、滚压、制片或磨碎的	1.品名;2.加工方法(整粒、滚压、制片或磨碎)	
11.05	**马铃薯的细粉、粗粉、粉末、粉片、颗粒及团粒:**	1.品名;2.状态(细粉、粗粉、粉末、粉片、颗粒及团粒)	
11.06	**用税目07.13的干豆或税目07.14的西谷茎髓及植物根茎、块茎制成的细粉、粗粉及粉末;用第八章的产品制成的细粉、粗粉及粉末:**		
1106.1000	-用税目07.13的干豆制成的	1.品名;2.状态(细粉、粗粉、粉末)	
1106.2000	-用税目07.14的西谷茎髓及植物根茎、块茎制成的	1.品名;2.状态(细粉、粗粉、粉末)	
1106.3000	-用第八章的产品制成的	1.品名;2.状态(细粉、粗粉、粉末)	
11.07	**麦芽,不论是否焙制:**	1.品名;2.加工方法(未焙制、已焙制)	

商品编码	商 品 描 述	申 报 要 素	
		商品名称	规格型号
11.08	淀粉;菊粉:	1.品名;2.种类(玉米淀粉、木薯淀粉、小麦淀粉、菊粉、马铃薯淀粉等)	
11.09	面筋,不论是否干制:	品名	

第十二章 含油子仁及果实;杂项子仁及果实;工业用或药用植物;稻草、秸秆及饲料

商品编码	商 品 描 述	申 报 要 素	
		商品名称	规格型号
12.01	大豆,不论是否破碎:	1.品名;2.种类(黄大豆、黑大豆、青大豆等);3.种用请注明	
12.02	未焙炒或未烹煮的花生,不论是否去壳或破碎:	1.品名;2.加工方法(未去壳、去壳、未焙炒、未烹煮);3.种用请注明	
12.03	干椰子肉:	1.品名;2.用途(炸油用)	
12.04	亚麻子,不论是否破碎:	品名	
12.05	油菜子,不论是否破碎:	1.品名;2.种用请注明	3.芥子酸含量及所得固体成分每克葡萄糖苷酸(酯)含量
12.06	葵花子,不论是否破碎:	1.品名;2.种用请注明	
12.07	其他含油子仁及果实,不论是否破碎:	1.品名;2.种用请注明	
12.08	含油子仁或果实的细粉及粗粉,但芥子粉除外:	1.品名;2.状态(细粉、粗粉)	
12.09	种植用的种子、果实及孢子:	1.品名;2.用途(种植用);3.种子特性(杂交、常规)	4.包装材料(真空铝罐、铝箔袋、塑料袋等);5.包装规格
12.10	鲜或干的啤酒花,不论是否研磨或制成团粒;蛇麻腺:	1.品名;2.加工方法(未研磨、研磨或未制成团粒、制成团粒);3.状态(鲜、干)	
12.11	主要用作香料、药料、杀虫、杀菌或类似用途的植物或这些植物的某部分(包括子仁及果实),鲜或干的,不论是否切割、压碎或研磨成粉:	1.品名;2.用途(作香料、药料、杀虫、杀菌等类似用途);3.状态(鲜、干)	
12.12	鲜、冷、冻或干的刺槐豆、海草及其他藻类、甜菜及甘蔗,不论是否碾磨;主要供人食用的其他税目未列名的果核、果仁及植物产品(包括未焙制的菊苣根):		
	-海草及其他藻类:	1.品名;2.状态(鲜、冷、冻、干)	
	-其他	1.品名;2.用途(主要供人食用);3.状态(鲜、冷、冻、干);4.种用请注明	
12.13	未经处理的谷类植物的茎、秆及谷壳,不论是否切碎、碾磨、挤压或制成团粒:	1.品名;2.状态(茎、秆、团粒等);3.加工程度(未经处理)	
12.14	芜菁甘蓝、饲料甜菜、饲料用根、干草、紫苜蓿、三叶草、驴喜豆、饲料羽衣甘蓝、羽扇豆、巢菜及类似饲料,不论是否制成团粒:	1.品名;2.状态(粗粉及团粒等)	

备注或申报要求

12.01 大豆，不论是否破碎： 黄大豆注明：1. 签约日期；2. 定价方式；3. 提单日期；4. 确定升贴水日期；5. 运费

第十三章　虫胶;树胶、树脂及其他植物液、汁

商品编码	商品描述	申报要素	
		商品名称	规格型号
13.01	**虫胶;天然树胶、树脂、树胶脂及油树脂(例如,香树脂):**	1.品名;2.阿拉伯胶请注明用途(食品、饮料、制药等)	3.阿拉伯胶请注明等级
13.02	**植物液汁及浸膏;果胶、果胶酸盐及果胶酸酯;从植物产品制得的琼脂、其他胶液及增稠剂,不论是否改性:**		
	-植物液汁及浸膏:	1.品名;2.状态(液汁、浸膏、粉末);3.供医药、农药用请注明;4.啤酒花的植物液汁及浸膏请注明品牌;5.啤酒花的植物液汁及浸膏请注明品种	6.啤酒花的植物液汁及浸膏请注明有效成分含量(α酸等)
1302.2000	-果胶、果胶酸盐及果胶酸酯	1.品名	2.等级(食品级、医药级)
	-从植物产品制得的胶液及增稠剂,不论是否改性:		
1302.3100	--琼脂	1.品名	2.等级(食品级、细菌级、医药级);3.级别(食品级:1级、2级、3级;细菌级:标准级、优级、特级)
1302.3200	--从刺槐豆、刺槐豆子或瓜尔豆制得的胶液及增稠剂,不论是否改性	1.品名;2.来源	3.刺槐豆胶请注明等级(标准级、精制级、宠物级);4.瓜尔豆胶请注明粒度(目);5.瓜尔豆胶请注明粘性
1302.3900	--其他	1.品名;2.卡拉胶请注明类型(卡帕胶、阿欧塔胶、莱姆达胶等);3.卡拉胶请注明用途(乳品、肉类、水、糖果、果冻、甜品等)	4.等级(精制、半精制、初制)

第十四章　编结用植物材料;其他植物产品

商品编码	商品描述	申报要素	
		商品名称	规格型号
14.01	**主要作编结用的植物材料(例如,竹、藤、芦苇、灯芯草、柳条、酒椰叶,已净、漂白或染色的谷类植物的茎秆,椴树皮):**	1.品名;2.用途(主要作编结用);3.藤请注明品种;4.藤请注明加工程度(去皮或未去皮)	5.藤请注明等级
14.04	**其他税目未列名的植物产品:**		
1404.2000	-棉短绒	1.品名	2.纤维长度
	-其他	1.品名	

第三类 动、植物油、脂及其分解产品；精制的食用油脂；动、植物蜡

第十五章 动、植物油、脂及其分解产品；精制的食用油脂；动、植物蜡

【注解】

本章品目1504及1506至1515所称分离的主要方法指通过压榨、倾析、冬化及过滤进行干分离，溶剂分离，借助表面活性剂分离。

商品编码	商品描述	申报要素	
		商品名称	规格型号
15.01	**猪脂肪（包括已炼制的猪油）及家禽脂肪，但税目02.09及15.03的货品除外：**	品名	
15.02	**牛、羊脂肪，但税目15.03的货品除外：**	1.品名；2.加工程度（未炼制、已炼制）	
15.03	**猪油硬脂、液体猪油、油硬脂、食用或非食用脂油，未经乳化、混合或其他方法制作：**	1.品名；2.加工程度（未经乳化、混合或其他方法制作）	
15.04	**鱼或海生哺乳动物的油、脂及其分离品，不论是否精制，但未经化学改性：**	1.品名；2.加工程度（未经化学改性）；3.除鱼肝油以外的鱼油、脂及其分离品请注明等级（保健用、饲料用）	4.保健用鱼油请注明DHA+EPA浓度；5.饲料用的鱼油、脂及其分离品请注明是否精炼
15.05	**羊毛脂及从羊毛脂制得的脂肪物质（包括纯净的羊毛脂）：**	品名	
15.06	**其他动物油、脂及其分离品，不论是否精制，但未经化学改性：**	1.品名；2.加工程度（未经化学改性）；3.野生请注明	
15.07	**豆油及其分离品，不论是否精制，但未经化学改性：**	1.品名；2.加工方法（初榨、精制）；3.加工程度（未经化学改性）	
15.08	**花生油及其分离品，不论是否精制，但未经化学改性：**	1.品名；2.加工方法（初榨、精制）；3.加工程度（未经化学改性）	
15.09	**油橄榄油及其分离品，不论是否精制，但未经化学改性：**	1.品名；2.加工方法（初榨、精制）；3.加工程度（未经化学改性）	
15.10	**其他橄榄油及其分离品，不论是否精制，但未经化学改性，包括掺有税目15.09的油或分离品的混合物：**	1.品名；2.加工程度（未经化学改性）	
15.11	**棕榈油及其分离品，不论是否精制，但未经化学改性：**		
1511.1000	-初榨的	1.品名；2.加工方法（初榨）；3.加工程度（未经化学改性）	
	-其他：		
1511.9010	---棕榈液油（熔点19℃—24℃）	1.品名；2.加工程度（未经化学改性）；	3.熔点
1511.9020	---棕榈硬脂（熔点44℃—56℃）	1.品名；2.加工程度（未经化学改性）	3.熔点
1511.9090	---其他	1.品名；2.加工方法（精制）；3.加工程度（未经化学改性）	4.熔点
15.12	**葵花油、红花油或棉子油及其分离品，不论是否精制，但未经化学改性：**	1.品名；2.加工方法（初榨、精制）；3.加工程度（未经化学改性）	
15.13	**椰子油、棕榈仁油或巴巴苏棕榈果油及其分离品，不论是否精制，但未经化学改性：**	1.品名；2.加工方法（初榨、精制）；3.加工程度（未经化学改性）	
15.14	**菜子油或芥子油及其分离品，不论是否精制，但未经化学改性：**	1.品名；2.加工方法（初榨、精制）；3.加工程度（未经化学改性）	4.芥子酸含量及所得固体成分每克葡萄糖苷酸（酯）含量
15.15	**其他固定植物油、脂（包括希蒙得木油）及其分离品，不论是否精制，但未经化学改性：**	1.品名；2.加工方法（初榨、精制）；3.加工程度（未经化学改性）	

商品编码	商品描述	申报要素	
		商品名称	规格型号
15.16	**动、植物油、脂及其分离品，全部或部分氢化、相互酯化、再酯化或反油酸化，不论是否精制，但未经进一步加工：**	1.品名；2.加工方法（全部或部分氢化、相互酯化、再酯化或反油酸化）	
15.17	**人造黄油；本章各种动、植物油、脂及其分离品混合制成的食用油、脂或制品，但税目15.16的食用油、脂及其分离品除外：**		
1517.1000	-人造黄油，但不包括液态的	1.品名；2.品牌；3.加工方法（人造的）；4.状态；5.加工原料（动物油脂、植物油脂）	6.熔点
1517.9000	-其他	1.品名；2.用途（食用）；3.加工方法；4.来源（动物质或植物质）；5.起酥油请注明品牌	6.起酥油请注明加工原料（豆油、菜籽油、棕榈油等）；7.成分含量；8.熔点
15.18	**动、植物油、脂及其分离品，经过熟炼、氧化、脱水、硫化、吹制或在真空、惰性气体中加热聚合及用其他化学方法改性的，但税目15.16的产品除外；本章各种油、脂及其分离品混合制成的其他税目未列名的非食用油、脂或制品：**	1.品名；2.加工方法（经熟炼、氧化、脱水、硫化、吹制或在真空、惰性气体中加热聚合及用其他化学方法改性）	3.成分含量
15.20	**粗甘油；甘油水及甘油碱液：**	品名	
15.21	**植物蜡（甘油三酯除外）、蜂蜡、其他虫蜡及鲸蜡，不论是否精制或着色：**	品名	
15.22	**油鞣回收脂；加工处理油脂物质及动、植物蜡所剩的残渣：**	1.品名；2.来源	不包括仅经氧化或聚合的鱼油（1518）；不包括磺化油（3402）；不包括脂化皮革用的制剂（3403）；不包括从已炼制的猪脂肪或其他动物脂肪中所得的脂渣及膜渣（2301）

备注或申报要求

15. 07 豆油及其分离品不论是否精，但未经化学改性： 1. 签约日期；2. 定价方式；3. 提单日期；4. 确定升贴水日期；5. 运费

15. 11 棕榈油及其分离品，不论是否精制，但未经化学改性： 1. 签约日期；2. 定价方式；3. 提单日期；4. 确定升贴水日期；5. 运费

第四类　食品；饮料、酒及醋；烟草、烟草及烟草代用品的制品

第十六章　肉、鱼、甲壳动物、软体动物及其他水生无脊椎动物的制品

商品编码	商品描述	申报要素	
		商品名称	规格型号
16.01	**肉、食用杂碎或动物血制成的香肠及类似产品；用香肠制成的食品：**	1. 品名；2. 肠衣种类（天然肠衣等）；3. 野生请注明	
16.02	**其他方法制作或保藏的肉、食用杂碎或动物血：**		
1602.1000	-均化食品	1. 品名；2. 野生请注明	3. 包装形式（零售包装）
1602.2000	-动物肝	1. 品名；2. 加工方法；3. 野生请注明	
	-税目01.05的家禽的：	1. 品名；2. 加工方法（煮、蒸、烤、煎、炸、炒等）；3. 种类（鸡、火鸡、鸭等）；4. 分切部位（胸肉、腿肉等）；5. 野生请注明	
	-猪的：	1. 品名；2. 加工方法（煮、蒸、烤、煎、炸、炒等）；3. 野生请注明	
	-牛的：	1. 品名；2. 加工方法（煮、蒸、烤、煎、炸、炒等）；3. 野生请注明	
	-其他，包括动物血的食品：	1. 品名；2. 加工方法（煮、蒸、烤、煎、炸、炒等）；3. 野生请注明	
16.03	**肉、鱼、甲壳动物、软体动物或其他水生无脊椎动物的精及汁：**	1. 品名；2. 状态（精、汁）；3. 野生请注明	
16.04	**制作或保藏的鱼；鲟鱼子酱及鱼卵制的鲟鱼子酱代用品：**	1. 品名；2. 形状（整条或切块、非整条或切块等）；3. 加工方法	
16.05	**制作或保藏的甲壳动物、软体动物及其他水生无脊椎动物：**	1. 品名；2. 加工方法	

第十七章　糖及糖食

商品编码	商品描述	申报要素	
		商品名称	规格型号
17.01	**固体甘蔗糖、甜菜糖及化学纯蔗糖：**	1. 品名；2. 加工方法（未加或加香料、着色剂）	3. 原糖请注明按重量计干燥状态的糖含量
17.02	**其他固体糖，包括化学纯乳糖、麦芽糖、葡萄糖及果糖；未加香料或着色剂的糖浆；人造蜜，不论是否掺有天然蜂蜜；焦糖：**	1. 品名	2. 按重量计干燥状态的果糖含量
	-乳糖及乳糖浆：	1. 品名	2. 按重量计干燥无水乳糖的含量
1702.2000	-槭糖及槭糖浆	品名	
1702.3000	-葡萄糖及葡萄糖浆，不含果糖或按重量计干燥状态的果糖含量在20%以下	1. 品名	2. 按重量计干燥状态的果糖含量；3. 等级（食用级、医用级）
1702.4000	-葡萄糖及葡萄糖浆，按重量计干燥状态的果糖含量在20%及以上，但在50%以下，转化糖除外	1. 品名	2. 按重量计干燥状态的果糖含量
1702.5000	-化学纯果糖	1. 品名	2. 按重量计干燥状态的果糖含量
1702.6000	-其他果糖及果糖浆，按重量计干燥状态的果糖含量在50%以上，转化糖除外	1. 品名；2. 品种（高果糖浆、高果糖晶体、低聚酯果糖等）	3. 按重量计干燥状态的果糖含量
1702.9000	-其他，包括转化糖及其他按重量计干燥状态的果糖含量为50%的糖及糖浆混合物	1. 品名	2. 按重量计干燥状态的果糖含量

商品编码	商品描述	申报要素	
		商品名称	规格型号
17.03	**制糖后所剩的糖蜜:**	1.品名;2.来源	
17.04	**不含可可的糖食(包括白巧克力):**	1.品名;2.品牌;3.品种	4.包装规格

备注或申报要求

17.01　　固体甘蔗糖、甜菜糖及化学纯蔗糖: 1. 签约日期; 2. 定价方式; 3. 提单日期; 4. 确定升贴水日期; 5. 运费

第十八章　可可及可可制品

【注解】

本章所称"夹心",包括用巧克力包裹,中心有馅(例如,用奶油、糖壳、干椰子肉、水果、果子膏、酒、蛋白杏仁糖果、坚果、牛轧糖、焦糖或上述产品的混合物做馅)的粒、块、条状食品。谷物、水果或坚果(不论是否成块)嵌于整个巧克力当中的实心块状或条状巧克力,不视为"夹心"。

商品编码	商品描述	申报要素	
		商品名称	规格型号
18.01	**整颗或破碎的可可豆,生的或焙炒的:**	1.品名;2.加工方法(生的或焙炒的);3.状态(整颗或破碎的)	
18.02	**可可荚、壳、皮及废料:**	品名	
18.03	**可可膏,不论是否脱脂:**	1.品名;2.加工方法(未脱脂、全脱脂或部分脱脂)	
18.04	**可可脂、可可油:**	品名	
18.05	**未加糖或其他甜物质的可可粉:**	1.品名;2.品种(天然、碱性等);3.加工程度(未加糖或其他甜物质)	
18.06	**巧克力及其他含可可的食品:**	1.品名;2.品牌;3.形状(条状、块状等);4.加工方法(加糖或其他甜物质、含可可、夹心或不夹心)	5.容器包装或内包装每件净重

第十九章　谷物、粮食粉、淀粉或乳的制品;糕饼点心

商品编码	商品描述	申报要素	
		商品名称	规格型号
19.01	**麦精:细粉、粗粒、粗粉、淀粉或麦精制的其他税目未列名的食品,不含可可或按重量计全脱脂可可含量低于40%:税目04.01至04.04所列货品制的其他税目未列名的食品,不含可可或按重量计全脱脂可可含量低于5%:**		
1901.1000	-供婴幼儿食用的零售包装食品	1.品名;2.用途(供婴幼儿食用)	3.成分含量;4.零售包装
1901.2000	-供烘焙税目19.05所列面包糕饼用的调制品及面团	1.品名;2.用途(供烘焙面包、糕饼等用)	3.成分含量
1901.9000	-其他	1.品名	2.成分含量
19.02	**面食,不论是否煮熟、包馅(肉馅或其他馅)或其他方法制作,例如,通心粉、面条、汤团、馄饨、饺子、奶油面卷;古斯古斯面食,不论是否制作:**	1.品名;2.加工方法(生的、熟的、未包馅、包馅等); 3.生的、未包馅或未经其他方法加工的及含蛋的请注明	4.成分含量; 5.即食或快熟面条请注明包装方式(杯装、袋装、碗装等)
19.03	**珍粉及淀粉制成的珍粉代用品,片、粒、珠、粉或类似形状的:**	1.品名;2.状态(片、粒、珠、粉或类似形状的)	
19.04	**谷物或谷物产品经膨化或烘炒制成的食品(例如,玉米片);其他税目未列名的预煮或经其他方法制作的谷粒(玉米除外)、谷物片或经其他加工的谷粒(细粉、粗粒及粗粉除外):**		
1904.1000	-谷物或谷物产品经膨化或烘炒制成的食品	1.品名;2.加工方法(膨化或烘炒)	

商品编码	商 品 描 述	申 报 要 素	
		商品名称	规格型号
1904.2000	-未烘炒谷物片制成的食品及未烘炒的谷物片与烘炒的谷物片或膨化的谷物混合制成的食品	1.品名;2.加工方法(未烘炒、未烘炒与烘炒或膨化混合)	
1904.3000	-碾碎的干小麦	1.品名;2.加工方法(碾碎);3.状态(干)	
1904.9000	-其他	1.品名; 2.加工方法(经过预煮或经其他方法制作)	
19.05	**面包、糕点、饼干及其他烘焙糕饼,不论是否含可可;圣餐饼、装药空囊、封缄、糯米纸及类似制品:**	品名	

第二十章　蔬菜、水果、坚果或植物其他部分的制品

商品编码	商 品 描 述	申 报 要 素	
		商品名称	规格型号
20.01	**蔬菜、水果、坚果及植物的其他食用部分,用醋或醋酸制作或保藏的:**	1.品名;2.加工方法(用醋或醋酸制作或保藏)	
20.02	**番茄,用醋或醋酸以外的其他方法制作或保藏的:**	1.品名;2.加工方法(整个、切片、绞碎等)	
20.03	**蘑菇及块菌,用醋或醋酸以外的其他方法制作或保藏的:**	1.品名;2.加工方法	
20.04	**其他冷冻蔬菜,用醋或醋酸以外的其他方法制作或保藏的,但税目20.06的产品除外:**	1.品名;2.加工方法;3.状态(冻)	
20.05	**其他未冷冻蔬菜,用醋或醋酸以外的其他方法制作或保藏的,但税目20.06的产品除外:**		
2005.1000	-均化蔬菜	1.品名	2.零售包装; 3.每件净重
2005.2000	-马铃薯	1.品名;2.加工方法;3.状态(未冷冻)	
2005.4000	-豌豆	1.品名;2.加工方法;3.状态(未冷冻)	
	-豇豆及菜豆:	1.品名;2.加工方法(脱荚等);3.状态(未冷冻)	
	-芦笋:	1.品名;2.加工方法;3.状态(未冷冻)	
2005.7000	-油橄榄	1.品名;2.加工方法;3.状态(未冷冻)	
2005.8000	-甜玉米	1.品名;2.加工方法;3.状态(未冷冻)	
	-其他蔬菜及什锦蔬菜:	1.品名;2.加工方法;3.状态(未冷冻)	4.成分含量;5.水煮竹笋请注明容积
20.06	**糖渍蔬菜、水果、坚果、果皮及植物的其他部分(沥干、糖渍或裹糖的):**	1.品名;2.加工方法(沥干、糖渍、裹糖)	
20.07	**烹煮的果酱、果冻、柑桔酱、果泥及果膏,不论是否加糖或其他甜物质:**		
2007.1000	-均化食品	1.品名	2.零售包装;3.每件净重
	-其他:	1.品名;2.加工方法	
20.08	**用其他方法制作或保藏的其他税目未列名水果、坚果及植物的其他食用部分,不论是否加酒、加糖或其他甜物质:**	1.品名;2.加工方法	
20.09	**未发酵及未加酒精的水果汁(包括酿酒葡萄汁)、蔬菜汁,不论是否加糖或其他甜物质:**	1.品名;2.品牌;3.加工方法;4.状态(冷冻、非冷冻、混合)	5.成分含量、白利糖浓度;6.储藏温度;7.浓缩果汁请注明浓缩倍数

第二十一章　杂项食品

商品编码	商品描述	申报要素	
		商品名称	规格型号
21.01	**咖啡、茶、马黛茶的浓缩精汁及以其为基本成分或以咖啡、茶、马黛茶为基本成分的制品；烘焙菊苣和其他烘焙咖啡代用品及其浓缩精汁：**	1.品名；2.加工方法	3.基本成分
21.02	**酵母（活性或非活性）；已死的其他单细胞微生物（不包括税目30.02的疫苗）；发酵粉：**	1.品名；2.酵母请注明状态（活性、非活性）；3.单细胞微生物请注明状态（死）	
21.03	**调味汁及其制品；混合调味品；芥子粉及其调制品：**	1.品名	2.特别酒请注明按体积计酒精含量、按重量计香料和各种配料含量以及糖的含量；3.包装规格
21.04	**汤料及其制品；均化混合食品：**		
2104.1000	-汤料及其制品	1.品名	2.成分含量；3.包装规格
2104.2000	-均化混合食品	1.品名	2.成分含量；3.零售及包装；4.每件净重
21.05	**冰淇淋及其他冰制食品，不论是否含可可：**	1.品名	
21.06	**其他税目未列名的食品：**	1.品名	2.成分含量

第二十二章　饮料、酒及醋

商品编码	商品描述	申报要素	
		商品名称	规格型号
22.01	**未加糖或其他甜物质及未加味的水，包括天然或人造矿泉水及汽水；冰及雪：**	1.品名；2.加工程度（未加糖或其他甜物质及未加味）	
22.02	**加味、加糖或其他甜物质的水，包括矿泉水及汽水，其他无酒精饮料，但不包括税目20.09的水果汁或蔬菜汁：**	1.品名；2.加工方法（加糖、加味或其他甜物质）	3.包装（散装或其他包装）
22.03	**麦芽酿造的啤酒：**	1.品名；2.加工方法（麦芽酿造）	
22.04	**鲜葡萄酿造的酒，包括加酒精的；税目20.09以外的酿酒葡萄汁：**	1.品名；2.加工方法（鲜葡萄酿造）	3.容器容积
2204.1000	-汽酒	1.品名；2.种类（汽酒）；3.加工方法（鲜葡萄酿造）	
	-其他酒；加酒精抑制发酵的酿酒葡萄汁：		
2204.2100	--装入2升及以下容器的	1.品名；2.品牌（外文）；3.加工方法（鲜葡萄酿造）	4.容器容积；5.年份（没有年份的申报无年份）；6.产区
2204.2900	--其他	1.品名；2.种类（酿酒葡萄汁）；3.加工方法（鲜葡萄酿造）	4.容器容积
2204.3000	-其他酿酒葡萄汁	1.品名；2.加工方法（鲜葡萄酿造）	
22.05	**味美思酒及其他加植物或香料的用鲜葡萄酿造的酒：**	1.品名；2.加工方法（鲜葡萄酿造、加植物或香料）	3.容器容积
22.06	**其他发酵饮料（例如，苹果酒、梨酒、蜂蜜酒）；其他税目未列名的发酵饮料的混合物及发酵饮料与无酒精饮料的混合物：**	1.品名；2.加工方法（发酵、混合）	3.成分含量
22.07	**未改性乙醇，按容量计酒精浓度在80%及以上；任何浓度的改性乙醇及其他酒精：**	1.品名；2.加工方法（未改性、改性）	3.酒精浓度

商品编码	商品描述	申报要素	
		商品名称	规格型号
22.08	未改性乙醇,按容量计酒精浓度在80%以下;蒸馏酒、利口酒及其他酒精饮料:	1. 品名;2. 来源	3. 酒精浓度
22.09	醋及用醋酸制得的醋代用品:	1. 品名	2. 醋酸浓度

第二十三章　食品工业的残渣及废料;配制的动物饲料

【注解】

制成的饲料添加剂种类有:氨基酸添加剂、维生素添加剂、矿物元素添加剂、药物饲料添加剂、饲用酶制剂、饲料酸化剂、饲料保存剂等。

商品编码	商品描述	申报要素	
		商品名称	规格型号
23.01	不适于供人食用的肉、杂碎、鱼、甲壳动物、软体动物或其他水生无脊椎动物的渣粉及团粒;油渣:	1. 品名;2. 用途(不适合供人食用);3. 状态(渣粉、团粒);4. 饲料用鱼粉请注明加工方式(直火或蒸汽)	5. 成分含量(蛋白质含量等)
23.02	谷物或豆类植物在筛、碾或其他加工过程中所产生的糠、麸及其他残渣,不论是否制成团粒:	1. 品名;2. 种类(玉米的、稻米的、小麦的等)	3. 成分含量(蛋白质含量等)
23.03	制造淀粉过程中的残渣及类似的残渣,甜菜渣、甘蔗渣及制糖过程中的其他残渣,酿造及蒸馏过程中的糟粕及残渣,不论是否制成团粒:	1. 品名;2. 来源	3. 成分含量(蛋白质含量等)
23.04	提炼豆油所得的油渣饼及其他固体残渣,不论是否碾磨或制成团粒:	1. 品名;2. 来源	
23.05	提炼花生油所得的油渣饼及其他固体残渣,不论是否碾磨或制成团粒:	1. 品名;2. 来源	3. 成分含量(蛋白质含量等)
23.06	税目23.04或23.05以外的提炼植物油脂所得的油渣饼及其他固体残渣,不论是否碾磨或制成团粒:	1. 品名;2. 来源	3. 成分含量(蛋白质含量等)
23.07	葡萄酒渣;粗酒石:	品名	
23.08	动物饲料用的其他税目未列名的植物原料、废料、残渣及副产品,不论是否制成团粒:	1. 品名;2. 用途;3. 来源	4. 成分含量(蛋白质含量等)
23.09	配制的动物饲料:	1. 品名;2. 用途(狗食、猫食等);3. 品牌;4. 加工方法(配制的);5. 制成的饲料添加剂请注明种类	6. 成分含量; 7. 包装规格

第二十四章　烟草、烟草及烟草代用品的制品

商品编码	商品描述	申报要素	
		商品名称	规格型号
24.01	烟草;烟草废料:	1. 品名;2. 加工方法(去梗、未去梗、部分去梗)	3. 型号
24.02	烟草或烟草代用品制成的雪茄烟及卷烟:	1. 品名;2. 品牌;3. 种类(卷烟、雪茄烟);4. 来源(烟草制或烟草代用品制)	5. 型号
24.03	其他烟草及烟草代用品的制品;"均化"或"再造"烟草;烟草精汁:	1. 品名;2. 用途(吸用等);3. 加工方法(再造、均化)	

第五类　矿产品

第二十五章　盐;硫磺;泥土及石料;石膏料、石灰及水泥

【注解】

名词解释

1."加工方法"指改变原材料、毛坯或半成品的形状、尺寸、性质或表面状态,使之达到规定要求的各种形状的方法。

2."成分"指商品所构成的部分或要素,一般指所含物质的种类。

3."含量"一般指所含物质的数量。

商品编码	商品描述	申报要素	
		商品名称	规格型号
25.01	**盐(包括精制盐及变性盐)及纯氯化钠,不论是否为水溶液,也不论是否添加抗结块剂或松散剂;海水:**	1.品名;2.外观	3.包装;4.成分(是否有添加其他成分)
25.02	**未焙烧的黄铁矿:**	1.品名;2.加工方法(焙烧、未焙烧)	
25.03	**各种硫磺,但升华硫磺、沉淀硫磺及胶态硫磺除外:**	1.品名;2.状态(液态、固态、粉状、块状)	3.包装;4.硫磺含量
25.04	**天然石墨:**	1.品名;2.用途;3.外观(粉末、鳞片、块等);4.来源(是否天然)	5.石墨含量;6.细度指标(细度、鳞片大小)
25.05	**各种天然砂,不论是否着色,但第二十六章的含金属矿砂除外:**	1.品名;2.用途;3.种类(石英砂、硅砂等);4.来源	
25.06	**石英(天然砂除外);石英岩,不论是否粗加修整或仅用锯或其他方法切割成矩形(包括正方形)的板、块:**	1.品名;2.加工方法(天然状态、粗加修整、简单切割等);3.外观	
25.07	**高岭土及类似土,不论是否煅烧:**	1.品名;2.用途;3.品牌;4.种类(高岭土、珍珠陶土等);5.外观	6.活化请注明;7.加工方法;8.主要成分;9.白度;10.细度
25.08	**其他粘土(不包括税目68.06的膨胀粘土)、红柱石、蓝晶石及硅线石,不论是否煅烧;富铝红柱石;火泥及第纳斯土:**		
2508.1000	-膨润土	1.品名;2.用途;3.品牌;4.种类;5.外观	6.活化请注明;7.请注明蒙脱石含量
2508.3000	-耐火粘土	1.品名;2.用途;3.品牌;4.种类;5.外观	6.活化请注明;7.含有添加剂或改性的请注明
2508.4000	-其他粘土	1.品名;2.用途;3.品牌;4.种类;5.外观	6.活化请注明;7.含有添加剂或改性的请注明
2508.5000	-红柱石、蓝晶石及硅线石	1.品名;2.用途;3.品牌;4.种类;5.外观	6.活化请注明;7.请注明耐火度
2508.6000	-富铝红柱石	1.品名;2.用途;3.品牌;4.种类;5.外观	6.活化请注明;7.请注明耐火度
2508.7000	-火泥及第纳斯土	1.品名;2.用途;3.品牌;4.种类;5.外观	6.活化请注明
25.09	**白垩:**	品名	
25.10	**天然磷酸钙、天然磷酸铝钙及磷酸盐白垩:**	1.品名;2.加工方法(是否碾磨及其他进一步加工)	3.成分(磷灰石、天然磷酸钙、天然磷酸铝钙及磷酸盐白垩)

商品编码	商品描述	申报要素	
		商品名称	规格型号
25.11	**天然硫酸钡(重晶石);天然碳酸钡(毒重石),不论是否煅烧,但税目28.16的氧化钡除外:**	1.品名;2.加工方法	
25.12	**硅质化石粗粉(例如各种硅藻土)及类似的硅质土,不论是否煅烧,其表观比重不超过1:**	1.品名;2.用途;3.品牌;4.种类;5.外观	6.活化请注明;7.表观比重;8.硅藻土请注明是否改性;9.硅藻土请注明二氧化硅含量
25.13	**浮石;刚玉岩;天然刚玉砂;天然石榴石及其他天然磨料,不论是否热处理:**		
	-浮石:	1.品名;2.加工方法(如天然原状、破碎);3.外观	
2513.2000	-刚玉岩、天然刚玉砂、天然石榴石及其他天然磨料	1.品名;2.种类(刚玉岩、天然刚玉砂、天然石榴石、天然磨料等)	
25.14	**板岩,不论是否粗加修整或仅用锯或其他方法切割成矩形(包括正方形)的板、块:**	1.品名;2.用途;3.加工方法(天然原状、粗加修整、锯、割等);4.外观	
25.15	**大理石、石灰华及其他石灰质碑用或建筑用石,表观比重为2.5及以上,蜡石,不论是否粗加修整或仅用锯或其他方法切割成矩形(包括正方形)的板、块:**		
	-大理石及石灰华:	1.品名;2.用途;3.加工方法(天然原状、粗加修整、锯、割等);4.外观	5.表观比重
2515.2000	-其他石灰质碑用或建筑用石;蜡石	1.品名;2.用途;3.加工方法(天然原状、粗加修整、锯、割等);4.外观	5.除蜡石外要注明表观比重
25.16	**花岗岩、斑岩、玄武岩、砂岩以及其他碑用或建筑用石,不论是否粗加修整或仅用锯或其他方法切割成矩形(包括正方形)的板、块:**		
	-花岗岩:	1.品名;2.加工方法(天然原状、粗加修整、锯、割等);3.外观	
	-砂岩:	1.品名;2.用途;3.加工方法(天然原状、粗加修整、锯、割等);4.外观	
2516.9000	-其他碑用或建筑用石	1.品名;2.用途;3.加工方法(天然原状、粗加修整、锯、割等);4.外观	
25.17	**通常作混凝土粒料、铺路、铁道路基或其他路基用的卵石、砾石及碎石,圆石子及燧石,不论是否热处理;矿渣、浮渣及类似的工业残渣,不论是否混有本税目第一部分所列的材料;沥青碎石,税目25.15、25.16所列各种石料的碎粒、碎屑及粉末,不论是否热处理:**		
2517.1000	-通常作混凝土粒料、铺路、铁道路基或其他路基用的卵石、砾石及碎石,圆石子及燧石,不论是否热处理	1.品名;2.用途;3.外观	
2517.2000	-矿渣、浮渣及类似的工业残渣,不论是否混有子目2517.10所列的材料	1.品名;2.用途;3.外观;4.来源(是否矿渣、浮渣、残渣等);	

商品编码	商 品 描 述	申 报 要 素	
		商品名称	规格型号
2517.3000	-沥青碎石	品名	
	-税目25.15及25.16所列各种石料的碎粒、碎屑及粉末,不论是否热处理:	1.品名;2.外观	
25.18	**白云石,不论是否煅烧或烧结、粗加修整或仅用锯或其他方法切割成矩形(包括正方形)的板、块;夯混白云石:**	1.品名;2.加工方法(夯混、是否煅烧或烧结、粗加修整、锯、割等);3.外观	
25.19	**天然碳酸镁(菱镁矿);熔凝镁氧矿;烧结镁氧矿,不论烧结前是否加入少量其他氧化物;其他氧化镁,不论是否纯净:**		
2519.1000	-天然碳酸镁(菱镁矿)	品名	
2519.9010	---熔凝镁氧矿	品名	
2519.9020	---烧结镁氧矿(重烧镁)	品名	
2519.9030	---碱烧镁(轻烧镁)	品名	
	---其他:	1.品名(纯氧化镁、化学纯氧化镁等)	2.成分含量
25.20	**生石膏;硬石膏;熟石膏(由煅烧的生石膏或硫酸钙构成),不论是否着色,也不论是否带有少量促凝剂或缓凝剂:**	1.品名;2.用途;3.牙科用请注明	
25.21	**石灰石助熔剂;通常用于制造石灰或水泥的石灰石及其他钙质石:**	1.品名;2.用途	
25.22	**生石灰、熟石灰及水硬石灰,但税目28.25的氧化钙及氢氧化钙除外:**	品名	
25.23	**硅酸盐水泥、矾土水泥、矿渣水泥、富硫酸盐水泥及类似的水凝水泥,不论是否着色,包括水泥熟料:**	1.品名;2.用途	
25.24	**石棉:**	1.品名;2.外观;3.青石棉请注明;4.长纤维请注明	
25.25	**云母,包括云母片;云母废料:**	1.品名;2.用途;3.外观	
25.26	**天然冻石,不论是否粗加修整或仅用锯或其他方法切割成矩形(包括正方形)的板、块;滑石:**	1.品名;2.加工方法(天然原状、粗加修整、简单切割、是否破碎、是否研磨);	
25.28	**天然硼酸盐及其精矿(不论是否煅烧),但不包括从天然盐水析离的硼酸盐;天然粗硼酸,含硼酸干重不超过85%:**		
2528.1000	-天然硼砂及其精矿(不论是否煅烧)	品名	
2528.9000	-其他	1.品名	2.硼酸的含量
25.29	**长石;白榴石;霞石及霞石正长岩;萤石(氟石):**		
2529.1000	-长石	1.品名;2.用途;3.外观	
	-萤石:	1.品名;2.用途;3.外观	4.氟化钙含量
2529.3000	-白榴石;霞石及霞石正长岩	1.品名;2.用途;3.外观	
25.30	**其他税目未列名的矿产品:**	1.品名;2.用途;3.种类(绿泥石、蛭石、泻盐矿、花园土、沼泽土、土色料、矿物性药材、破碎陶瓷、叶腊石、硅灰石、废镁砖、珍珠岩、硫镁矾矿、火山灰、沃土、稀土金属矿等);4.加工方法(天然开采、简单破碎、磨粉、未膨胀等);5.外观	

备注或申报要求

25.03　各种硫磺,但升华硫磺、沉淀硫磺及胶态硫磺除外:　定价方式

第二十六章　矿砂、矿渣及矿灰

【注解】

名词解释:

1."加工方法"指改变原材料、毛坯或半成品的形状、尺寸、性质或表面状态,使之达到规定要求的各种形状

的方法。

2."成分"指商品所构成的部分或要素,一般指所含物质的种类。

3."含量"一般指所含物质的数量。

注意事项:

对于26章的"成分"、"含量"的说明举例:

要尽量申报出所有的成分及含量,若无法确定,要申报出主要成分及其含量。

商品编码	商品描述	申报要素	
		商品名称	规格型号
26.01	**铁矿砂及其精矿,包括焙烧黄铁矿:**	1.品名;2.用途;3.加工方法;4.外观	5.成分含量
26.02	**锰矿砂及其精矿,包括以干重计含锰量在20%及以上的锰铁矿及其精矿:**	1.品名;2.用途;3.加工方法;4.外观	5.成分含量
26.03	**铜矿砂及其精矿:**	1.品名;2.加工方法;3.外观	4.成分含量
26.04	**镍矿砂及其精矿:**	1.品名;2.加工方法;3.外观	4.成分含量
26.05	**钴矿砂及其精矿:**	1.品名;2.加工方法;3.外观	4.成分含量;5.主要伴生矿物元素含量
26.06	**铝矿砂及其精矿:**	1.品名;2.加工方法;3.外观	4.成分含量
26.07	**铅矿砂及其精矿:**	1.品名;2.加工方法;3.外观	4.成分含量
26.08	**锌矿砂及其精矿:**	1.品名;2.加工方法;3.外观	4.成分含量
26.09	**锡矿砂及其精矿:**	1.品名;2.加工方法;3.外观	4.成分含量
26.10	**铬矿砂及其精矿:**	1.品名;2.加工方法;3.外观;4.用途(耐火、化工、铸造)	5.成分含量
26.11	**钨矿砂及其精矿:**	1.品名;2.加工方法;3.外观	4.成分含量
26.12	**铀或钍矿砂及其精矿:**	1.品名;2.加工方法;3.外观	4.成分含量
26.13	**钼矿砂及其精矿:**	1.品名;2.用途;3.加工方法;4.外观	5.成分含量
26.14	**钛矿砂及其精矿:**	1.品名;2.用途;3.加工方法;4.外观	5.成分含量
26.15	**铌、钽、钒或锆矿砂及其精矿:**	1.品名;2.用途;3.加工方法;4.外观	5.成分含量
26.16	**贵金属矿砂及其精矿:**	1.品名;2.加工方法;3.外观	4.成分含量
26.17	**其他矿砂及其精矿:**	1.品名;2.加工方法;3.外观	4.成分含量
26.18	**冶炼钢铁所产生的粒状熔渣(熔渣砂):**	1.品名;2.用途;3.加工方法;4.外观;5.来源	
26.19	**冶炼钢铁所产生的熔渣、浮渣(粒状熔渣除外)、氧化皮及其他废料:**	1.品名;2.用途;3.加工方法;4.外观;5.来源	
26.20	**含有金属、砷及其化合物的矿渣、矿灰及残渣(冶炼钢铁所产生的灰、渣除外):**	1.品名;2.用途;3.加工方法;4.外观;5.来源	6.成分含量
26.21	**其他矿渣及矿灰,包括海藻灰(海草灰);焚化城市垃圾所产生的灰、渣:**	1.品名;2.用途;3.加工方法;4.外观;5.来源	

备注或申报要求

26. 01 **铁矿砂及其精矿,包括焙烧黄铁矿:** 1. 运费;2. 运费定价方式;3. 运费长期合同号;4. 矿砂及运费签约日期

26. 03 **铜矿砂及其精矿:** 1. 签约日期;2. 选价期

26. 04 **镍矿砂及其精矿:** 1. 签约日期;2. 选价期

26. 05 **钴矿砂及其精矿:** 1. 签约日期;2. 选价期

26. 07 **铅矿砂及其精矿:** 1. 签约日期;2. 选价期

26. 08 **锌矿砂及其精矿:** 1. 签约日期;2. 选价期

26. 09 **锡矿砂及其精矿:** 1. 签约日期;2. 选价期

第二十七章 矿物燃料、矿物油及其蒸馏产品;沥青物质;矿物蜡

【注解】

名词解释:

1."加工方法"指改变原材料、毛坯或半成品的形状、尺寸、性质或表面状态,使之达到规定要求的各种形状的方法。

2."成分"指商品所构成的部分或要素,一般指所含物质的种类。

3."含量"一般指所含物质的数量。

注意事项:

对于27章"成分"、"含量"的说明举例:

有些情况下,部分27章商品要求的成分、含量只要能明确归类即可。如2707的杂酚油可以注明"主要成分为酚类和酚酯类",再如2715的稀释沥青可以申报"沥青70%,溶剂30%"。

商品编码	商品描述	申报要素	
		商品名称	规格型号
27.01	**煤;煤砖、煤球及用煤制成的类似固体燃料:**	1.品名;2.外观;3.黑玉、褐煤、焦炭及半焦炭请注明	4.热量及挥发物含量;5.等级;6.燃烧值;7.灰分;8.挥发物
27.02	**褐煤,不论是否制成型,但不包括黑玉:**	1.品名;2.外观;3.黑玉请注明	
27.03	**泥煤(包括肥料用泥煤),不论是否制成型:**	1.品名;2.外观	
27.04	**煤、褐煤或泥煤制成的焦炭及半焦炭,不论是否制成型;甑炭:**	1.品名;2.用途;3.来源	
27.05	**煤气、水煤气、炉煤气及类似气体。但石油气及其他烃类气除外:**	1.品名;2.来源	
27.06	**从煤、褐煤或泥煤蒸馏所得的焦油及其他矿物焦油,不论是否脱水或部分蒸馏,包括再造焦油:**	1.品名;2.来源	
27.07	**蒸馏高温煤焦油所得的油类及其他产品;芳族成分重量超过非芳族成分的类似产品:**	1.品名	2.成分含量
2707.1000	-粗苯	1.品名	2.成分含量
2707.2000	-粗甲苯	1.品名	2.成分含量
2707.3000	-粗二甲苯	1.品名	2.成分含量
2707.4000	-萘	1.品名	2.成分含量(以美国标准实验方法D86为准,250℃时蒸馏出的芳烃含量的体积百分比)
2707.5000	-其他芳烃混合物,温度在250℃蒸馏出的芳烃含量以体积计(包括损耗)在65%及以上(以美国标准试验法D86为准)	1.品名	2.成分含量
	-其他:	品名	
27.08	**从煤焦油或其他矿物焦油所得的沥青及沥青焦:**	1.品名;2.来源	
27.09	**石油原油及从沥青矿物提取的原油:**	1.品名;2.种类;3.凝析油请注明	4.密度;5.含硫量
27.10	**石油及从沥青矿物提取的油类。但原油除外;以上述油为基本成分(按重量计不低于70%)的其他税目未列名制品;废油:**		
	-石油及从沥青矿物取的油类(但原油除外),以上述油为基本成分(按重量计不低于70%)的其他税目未列名列品,但废油除外:		
	--轻油及其制品:	品名	

商品编码	商 品 描 述	申 报 要 素	
		商品名称	规格型号
	--其他	1. 品名;2. 润滑油请注明品牌;3. 润滑油请注明用途	4. 5-7 号燃料油请注明规格;5. 润滑油请注明型号;6. 润滑油请注明包装规格;7. 润滑油请注明从石油或沥青提取矿物油类的百分比含量
	-废油:	1. 品名;2. 来源	
27.11	**石油气及其他烃类气:**	1. 品名;2. 状态(液化或气态)	3. 成分含量;4. 包装容器容积
27.12	**凡士林;石蜡、街晶石蜡、疏松石蜡、地蜡、褐煤蜡、泥煤蜡、其他矿物蜡反用合成或其他方法别得的类似产品,不论是否着色:**		
2712.1000	-凡士林	1. 品名	2. 技术指标(冻点、针入度)
2712.2000	-石蜡,按重量计含油量小于0.75%	1. 品名;2. 加工方法;3. 外观;4. 来源	5. 含油量
	-其他:	1. 品名	2. 成分
27.13	**石油焦、石油沥青及其他石油或从沥青矿物提取的油类的残渣:**	1. 品名;2. 用途;3. 加工方法(是否煅烧);4. 外观	
27.14	**天然沥青(地沥青)、沥青页岩、油页岩及焦油砂:沥青岩:**	1. 品名;2. 用途;3. 加工方法;4. 外观	5. 成分含量(沥青、水)
27.15	**以天然沥青(地沥青)、石油沥青、矿物焦油或矿物焦油沥青为基本成分的沥青混合物(例如,沥青胶粘剂、稀释沥青):**	1. 品名;2. 用途;3. 加工方法;4. 外观	
27.16	**电力:**	品名	

备注或申报要求

27. 09 石油原油及从沥青矿物提取的原油: 1. 定价公式; 2. 选价期; 3. 提单日期

27.10 **石油及从沥青矿物提取的油类,但原油除外;以上述油为基本成分(按重量计不低于70%)的其他税目未列名列品,但废油除外**

-石油及从沥青矿物提取的油类(但原油除外),以上述油为基本成分(按重量计不低于**70%**)的其他税目未列名列品,但废油除外

--其他 1. 定价公式;2. 提单日期型号

第六类　化学工业及其相关工业的产品

第二十八章　无机化学品；贵金属、稀土金属、放射性元素及其同位素的有机及无机化合物

【注解】

名词解释：

1."加工方法"指改变原材料、毛坯或半成品的形状、尺寸、性质或表面状态，使之达到规定要求的各种形状的方法。

2."成分"指商品所构成的部分或要素，一般指所含物质的种类。

3."含量"一般指所含物质的数量。

4.所注明的"包装"内容要足以判断是否为零售包装。

商品编码	商品描述	申报要素	
		商品名称	规格型号
28.01	**氟、氯、溴及碘：**	1.品名	2.包装
28.02	**升华硫磺、沉淀硫磺；胶态硫磺：**	1.品名	2.包装
28.03	**碳（碳黑及其他税目未列名的其他形态的碳）：**	1.品名；2.来源；3.有无活性	4.包装；5.细度；6.型号
28.04	**氢、稀有气体及其他非金属：**		
2804.1000	-氢	品名	
	-稀有气体：	品名	
2804.3000	-氮	品名	
2804.4000	-氧	品名	
2804.5000	-硼、碲	品名	
	-硅：	1.品名（硅、单晶硅棒等）；2.用途（用于电子工业等）；3.加工方法（经掺杂等）	4.成分含量；5.技术指标（直径）
	-磷：	品名	
2804.8000	-砷	品名	
	-硒：	1.品名；2.用途（用于电子工业等）；3.加工方法（经掺杂等）	4.成分含量；5.包装
28.05	**碱金属、碱土金属；稀土金属、钪及钇，不论是否相互混合或相互熔合；汞：**	1.品名；2.高纯度钙、电池级的混合或互熔稀土金属、钪及钇请注明	3.包装
28.06	**氯化氢（盐酸）；氯磺酸：**	1.品名	2.含量
28.07	**硫酸；发烟硫酸：**	1.品名；2.用途	3.含量
28.08	**硝酸；磺硝酸：**	1.品名	2.含量
28.09	**五氧化二磷；磷酸；多磷酸，不论是否已有化学定义：**	品名	
28.10	**硼的氧化物；硼酸：**	1.品名	2.含量
28.11	**其他无机酸及非金属无机氧化物：**		
	-其他无机酸：		
2811.1100	--氢氟酸	品名	
	-其他非金属无机氧化物		
2811.2100	--二氧化碳	1.品名；2.用途	3.含量
2811.2200	--二氧化硅	1.品名；2.用途；3.外观	4.生产工艺；5.细度；6.含量
2811.2900	--其他	品名	
28.12	**非金属卤化物及卤氧化物：**	品名	
28.13	**非金属硫化物；商品三硫化二磷：**	品名	
28.14	**氨及氨水：**	品名	
28.15	**氢氧化钠（烧碱）；氢氧化钾（苛性钾）；过氧化钠及过氧化钾：**	1.品名；2.外观；3.用途	4.含量

商品编码	商 品 描 述	申 报 要 素	
		商品名称	规格型号
28.16	**氢氧化镁及过氧化镁;锶或钡的氧化物、氢氧化物及过氧化物:**	品名	
28.17	**氧化锌及过氧化锌:**	1. 品名;2. 用途;3. 天然的请注明	
28.18	**人造刚玉,不论是否已有化学定义;氧化铝;氢氧化铝:**		
2818.1000	-人造刚玉,不论是否已有化学定义	1. 品名;2. 用途;3. 外观	4. 成分含量;5. 晶型
2818.2000	-氧化铝,但人造刚玉除外	1. 品名;2. 用途;3. 外观	4. 成分含量
2818.3000	-氢氧化铝	1. 品名;2. 外观	
28.19	**铬的氧化物及氢氧化物:**	1. 品名	2. 三氧化铬请注明含量
28.20	**锰的氧化物:**	品名	
28.21	**铁的氧化物及氢氧化物;土色料,按重量计三氧化二铁含量在70%及以上:**	1. 品名	2. 铁的氧化物及三氧化二铁含量
28.22	**钴的氧化物及氢氧化物;商品氧化钴:**	品名	
28.23	**钛的氧化物:**	1. 品名;2. 与其他物质混合请注明;3. 经表面处理的请注明	
28.24	**铅的氧化物;铅丹及铅橙:**	品名	
28.25	**肼(联氨)、胲(羟胺)及其无机盐;其他无机碱;其他金属氧化物、氢氧化物及过氧化物:**	1. 品名	2. 水合肼的含量
28.26	**氟化物;氟硅酸盐、氟铝酸盐及其他氟络盐:**	品名	
28.27	**氯化物、氯氧化物及氢氧基氯化物;溴化物及溴氧化物;碘化物及碘氧化物:**		
	-氯化铵:	1. 品名;2. 用途	
2827.2000	-氯化钙	品名	
	-其他氯化物:	品名	
	-氯氧化物及氢氧基氯化物:	品名	
	-溴化物及溴氧化物:	品名	
2827.6000	-碘化物及碘氧化物	品名	
28.28	**次氯酸盐;商品次氯酸钙;亚氯酸盐;次溴酸盐:**	品名	
28.29	**氯酸盐及高氯酸盐;溴酸盐及过溴酸盐;碘酸盐及高碘酸盐:**	1. 品名	2. 如为高氯酸铵请注明粒度
28.30	**硫化物;多硫化物,不论是否已有化学定义:**	品名	
28.31	**连二亚硫酸盐及次硫酸盐:**	品名	
28.32	**亚硫酸盐;硫代硫酸盐:**	品名	
28.33	**硫酸盐;矾;过硫酸盐:**	品名	
28.34	**亚硝酸盐;硝酸盐:**	1. 品名;2. 肥料用硝酸钾请注明	
28.35	**次磷酸盐、亚磷酸盐及磷酸盐;多磷酸盐,不论是否已有化学定义:**	1. 品名	2. 正磷酸氢钙请注明氟含量
28.36	**碳酸盐;过碳酸盐;含氨基甲酸铵的商品碳酸铵:**	品名	
28.37	**氰化物、氧氰化物及氰络合物:**	1. 品名	2. 包装;3. 含量
28.38	**雷酸盐、氰酸盐及硫氰酸盐:**	1. 品名;2. 复合物或络合物请注明	
28.39	**硅酸盐;商品碱金属硅酸盐:**	品名	
28.40	**硼酸盐及过硼酸盐:**	品名	
28.41	**金属酸盐及过金属酸盐:**	1. 品名;2. 外观	

商品编码	商品描述	申报要素	
		商品名称	规格型号
28.42	其他无机酸盐或过氧酸盐(包括不论是否已有化学定义的硅铝酸盐),但叠氮化物除外:	1.品名	2.包装
28.43	胶态贵金属;贵金属的无机或有机化合物,不论是否已有化学定义;贵金属汞齐:	1.品名	2.包装
28.44	放射性化学元素及放射性同位素(包括可裂变或可转换的化学元素及同位素)及其化合物;含上述产品的混合物及残渣:	品名	
28.45	税目28.44以外的同位素;这些同位素的无机或有机化合物,不论是否已有化学定义:	品名	
28.46	稀土金属、钇、钪及其混合物的无机或有机化合物:	1.品名	
28.47	过氧化氢,不论是否用尿素固化:	1.品名	2.成分含量;3.包装
28.48	磷化物,不论是否已有化学定义,但不包括磷铁:	1.品名	2.铜母合金请注明磷的重量百分比
28.49	碳化物,不论是否已有化学定义:	品名	
28.50	氢化物、氮化物、叠氮化物、硅化物及硼化物,不论是否已有化学定义,但可归入税目28.49的碳化物除外:	品名	
28.52	汞的无机或有机化合物、汞齐除外:	1.品名;	
28.53	其他无机化合物(包括蒸馏水、导电水及类似的纯净水);液态空气(不论是否除去稀有气体);压缩空气;汞齐,但贵金属汞齐除外:	1.品名;2.水请注明用途	3.包装

备注或申报要求

28. 18 **人造刚玉,不论是否已有化学定义;氧化铝;氢氧化铝:**

2818. 2000 -氧化铝,但人造刚玉除外: 1. 签约日期;2. 定价方式;3 提单日期;4. 定价公式

28. 19 **铬的氧化物及氢氧化物:**三氧化铬请注明生产厂商

第二十九章 有机化学品

【注解】

名词解释:

1.“加工方法”指改变原材料、毛坯式半成品的形状、尺寸、性质式表面状态,使之达到规定要求的各种形状的方法。

2.“成分”指商品所构成的部分式要素,一般指所含物质的种类。

3.“含量”一般指所含物质的数量。

4.所注明的“包装”内容要足以判断是否为零售包装。

注意事项:

1.本章商品需要申报的品名包括标准命名法名称或工商业通用俗称。

2.化学结构式对本章商品的归类非常重要。由于报关单的书写限制,在本规范中没有对化学结构式的要求,但在实际通关中,企业要用其他的方式向海关提供商品的化学结构式。

商品编码	商品描述	申报要素	
		商品名称	规格型号
29.01	无环烃:	1.品名;2.饱和无环烃请注明用途	3.分子式;4.含量;5.饱和无环烃请注明生产工艺;6.丁烷请注明包装容器的容积;7.异戊烯请注明异构体的含量
29.02	环烃:	1.品名	2.分子式;3.含量;4.混合二甲苯异构体请注明三种异构体的含量
29.03	烃的卤化衍生物:	1.品名;2.用途	3.分子式;4.含量;5.氯仿请注明包装方式;6.四氯化碳请注明包装方式
29.04	烃的磺化、硝化或亚硝化衍生物,不论是否卤化:	1.品名	2.分子式;3.含量
29.05	无环醇及其卤化、磺化、硝化或亚硝化衍生物:	1.品名;2.用途	3.分子式;4.纯度;5.包装方式
29.06	环醇及其卤化、磺化、硝化或亚硝化衍生物:	1.品名:用途	1.品名 2.分子式
29.07	酚;酚醇:	1.品名	2.分子式;3.含量
29.08	酚及酚醇的卤化、磺化、硝化或亚硝化衍生物:	1.品名	2.分子式;3.含量
29.09	醚、醚醇、醚酚、醚醇酚、过氧化醇、过氧化醚、过氧化酮(不论是否已有化学定义)及其卤化、磺化、硝化或亚硝化衍生物:	1.品名	2.分子式;3.含量;4.乙二醇或二甘醇的单丁醚请注明包装方式
29.10	三节环环氧化物、环氧醇、环氧酚、环氧醚及其卤化、磺化、硝化或亚硝化衍生物:	1.品名	2.包装;3.分子式
29.11	缩醛及半缩醛,不论是否含有其他含氧基,及其卤化、磺化、硝化或亚硝化衍生物:	1.品名	2.分子式
29.12	醛,不论是否含有其他含氧基;环聚醛;多聚甲醛:	1.品名;2.四聚乙醛请注明外观	3.分子式
29.13	税目 29.12 所列产品的卤化、磺化、硝化或亚硝化衍生物:	1.品名	2.分子式
29.14	酮及醌,不论是否含有其他含氧基,及其卤化、磺化、硝化或亚硝化衍生物:	1.品名;2.用途	3.分子式;4.含量;5.丙酮请注明包装
29.15	饱和无环一元羧酸及其酸酐、酰卤化物、过氧化物和过氧酸以及它们的卤化、磺化、硝化或亚硝化衍生物:	1.品名;2.用途	3.成分;4.分子式;5.含量
29.16	不饱和无环一元羧酸、环一元羧酸及其酸酐、酰卤化物、过氧化物和过氧酸以及它们的卤化、磺化、硝化或亚硝化衍生物:	1.品名;2.用途	3.分子式;4.纯度;5.丙烯酸及其盐请注明包装方式;6.丙烯酸酯请注明包装方式;7.甲基丙烯酸及其盐请注明包装方式;8.甲基丙烯酸酯请注明包装方式

商品编码	商 品 描 述	申 报 要 素	
		商品名称	规格型号
29.17	多元羧酸及其酸酐、酰卤化物、过氧化物和过氧酸以及它们的卤化、磺化、硝化或亚硝化衍生物:	1.品名;2.用途	3.分子式; 4.含量;5.对苯二甲酸请注明4-CBA值; 6.对苯二甲酸请注明P-TL酸值;7.对苯二甲酸请注明色度; 8.对苯二甲酸请注明水分
29.18	含附加含氧基的羧酸及其酸酐、酰卤化物、过氧化物和过氧酸以及它们的卤化、磺化、硝化或亚硝化衍生物:	1.品名;2.用途	3.分子式; 4.纯度;5.含醛基或酮基但不含其他含氧基的羧酸及其酸酐、酰卤化物、过氧化物和过氧酸以及它们的衍生物请注明纯度; 6.含醛基或酮基但不含其他含氧基的羧酸及其酸酐、酰卤化物、过氧化物和过氧酸以及它们的衍生物请注明包装方式
29.19	磷酸酯及其盐,包括乳磷酸盐,以及它们的卤化、磺化、硝化或亚硝化衍生物:	1.品名;2.用途	3.分子式; 4.含量
29.20	其他非金属无机酸酯(不包括卤化氢的酯)及其盐以及它们的卤化、磺化、硝化或亚硝化衍生物:	1.品名;2.外观	3.分子式
29.21	氨基化合物:	1.品名;2.用途	3.分子式;4.含量
29.22	含氧基氨基化合物:	1.品名;2.用途	3.分子式; 4.含量;5.单乙醇胺、二乙醇胺、三乙醇胺及其盐请注明包装方式;6.单乙醇胺、二乙醇胺、三乙醇胺及其盐请注明包装方式色度
29.23	季铵盐及季铵碱;卵磷脂及其他磷氨基类脂,不论是否已有化学定义:	1.品名;2.用途	3.分子式;4.卵磷脂及其他磷氨基类脂请注明含量
29.24	羧基酰胺基化合物;碳酸酰胺基化合物:	1.品名	2.分子式; 3.包装方式;4.二甲基甲酰胺请注明含量;5.无环酰胺请注明含量
29.25	羧基酰亚胺化合物(包括糖精及其盐)及亚胺基化合物:	1.品名;2.糖精及其盐请注明用途;3.格鲁米特请注明用途	4.成分;5.分子式
29.26	腈基化合物:	1.品名;2.用途	3.分子式
29.27	重氮化合物、偶氮化合物及氧化偶氮化合物:	1.品名	2.分子式
29.28	肼(联氨)及胲(羟胺)的有机衍生物:	1.品名	2.分子式
29.29	其他含氮基化合物:	1.品名;2.品牌	3.分子式; 4.含量;5.甲苯二异氰酸酯请注明型号
29.30	有机硫化合物:	1.品名;2.用途	3.分子式;4.含量

商品编码	商品描述	申报要素	
		商品名称	规格型号
29.31	其他有机-无机化合物:	1. 品名	2. 分子式;3. 有机硅化合物请注明成分含量
29.32	仅含有氧杂原子的杂环化合物:	1. 品名	2. 分子式
29.33	仅含氮杂原子的杂环化合物:	1. 品名;2. 乌洛托品请注明外观形状;3. 三聚氰氯请注明用途	4. 分子式;5. 三聚氰氯请注明纯度;6. 三聚氰氯请注明规格
29.34	核酸及其盐,不论是否已有化学定义;其他杂环化合物:	1. 品名	2. 分子式
29.35	磺(酰)胺:	1. 品名	2. 分子式
29.36	天然或合成再制的维生素原和维生素(包括天然浓缩物)及其主要用作维生素的衍生物,上述产品的混合物,不论是否溶于溶剂:	1. 品名;2. 用途	3. 包装;4. 成分;5. 分子式;6. 含量
29.37	天然或合成再制的激素、前列腺素、血栓烷和白细胞三烯以及它们的衍生物和结构类似物,包括主要用作激素的改性链多肽:	1. 品名	2. 包装;3. 成分;4. 功能; 5. 分子式; 6. 含量
29.38	天然或合成再制的苷(配糖物)及其盐、醚、酯和其他衍生物:	1. 品名;2. 来源	
29.39	天然或合成再制的生物碱及其盐、醚、酯和其他衍生物:	1. 品名	2. 分子式
29.40	化学纯糖,但蔗糖、乳糖、麦芽糖、葡萄糖及果糖除外;糖醚、糖缩醛和糖酯及它们的盐,但不包括税目 29.37、29.38 及 29.39 的产品:	1. 品名	2. 分子式
29.41	抗菌素:	1. 品名	2. 包装;3. 成分;4,分子式;5. 含量
29.42	其他有机化合物:	1. 品名	2. 分子式

备注或申报要求

29. 02 环烃　1. 分子结构式；2. 签约日期；3. 定价方式

29. 03 烃的卤化衍生物：1. 含量在99%及以上的二氯甲烷请注明生产厂商；2. 氯仿请注明签约时间与定价方式；3. 1，2-二氯乙烷请注明签约时间；4 氯乙烯请注明签约时间与定价方式；5. 三氯乙烯请注明签约时间与生产厂商；6. 四氯乙烯请注明签约时间

29. 05 无环醇及其卤化、磺化、硝化或亚硝化衍生物：

-饱和一元醇：

2905. 1100 --甲醇：　1. 签约时间；2. 定价方式

-二元醇：

2905. 3100 --1，2-乙二醇：1. 签约时间；2. 定价方式

--其他：　1. 签约时间；2. 定价方式

29. 07 酚；酚醇：　1. 苯酚请注明生产厂商与签约时间；2. 邻苯二酚请注明生产厂商

29. 09 醚、醚醇、醚酚、醚醇酚、过氧化醇、过氧化醚、过氧化酮（不论是否已有化学定义）及其卤化、磺化、硝化或亚硝化衍生物：　乙二醇或二甘醇的单丁醚请注明签约时间

29. 10 三节环环氧化物、环氧醇、环氧酚、环氧醚及其卤化、磺化、硝化或亚硝化衍生物：甲基环氧乙烷请注明签约时间与定价方式

29. 14 酮及醌，不论是否含有其他含氧基，及其卤化、磺化、硝化或亚硝化衍生物：1. 丙酮请注明签约时间与定价方式；2. 丁酮请注明签约时间与定价方式；3. 4-甲基-2-戊酮请注明签约时间与定价方式

29. 15 饱和无环一元羧酸及其酸酐、酰卤化物、过氧化物和过氧酸以及它们的卤化、磺化、硝化或亚硝化衍生物：1. 冰乙酸请注明签约时间与定价方式；2. 乙酸酐请注明签约时间、定价方式与生产厂商

29. 16 不饱和无环一元羧酸、环一元羧酸及其酸酐、酰卤化物、过氧化物和过氧酸以及它们的卤化、磺化、硝化或亚硝化衍生物：1. 丙烯酸及其盐请注明签约日期与生产厂商；2. 丙烯酸酯请注明签约日期与生产厂商；3. 甲基丙烯酸及其盐请注明签约日期与生产厂商；4. 甲基丙烯酸酯请注明签约日期与生产厂商；5. 油酸、亚油酸或亚麻酸及其盐和酸请注明签约日期

29. 17 多元羧酸及其酸酐、酰卤化物、过氧化物和过氧酸以及它们的卤化、磺化、硝化或亚硝化衍生物：　1. 对苯二甲

酸二丁酯请注明签约日期；2. 对苯二甲酸二辛酯请注明签约日期；3. 对苯二甲酸酐请注明签约日期与生产厂商；4. 对苯二甲酸请注明签约日期与定价方式；5. 对苯二甲酸二甲酯请注明签约日期与定价方式

29. 18 **含附加含氧基的羧酸及其酸酐、酰卤化物、过氧化物和过氧酸以及它们的卤化、磺化、硝化或亚硝化衍生物：**含醛基或酮基但不含其他含氧基的羧酸及其酸酐、酰卤化物、过氧化物和过氧酸以及它们的衍生物请注明签约日期与定价方式

29. 22 **含氧基氨基化合物：** 赖氨酸与谷氨酸请注明签约日期定价方式与出口商

-氨基醇（但含有一种以上含氧基的除外）及其醚和酯，以及它们的盐

2922. 1200 --二乙醇胺及其盐：1. 签约日期；2. 生产厂商

--三乙醇胺及其盐：

2922. 1310 ---三乙醇脑 签约日期

29. 23 **季铵盐及季铵碱；卵磷脂及其他磷氨基类脂，不论是否已有化学定义：** 1. 签约日期；2. 出口商

29. 24 **羧基酰胺基化合物；碳酸酰胺基化合物：** 1. 二甲基甲酰胺请注明签约日期、定价方式；2. 无环酰胺请注明签约日期

29. 26 **腈基化合物：** 1. 丙烯腈请注明签约日期、定价方式与出口商；2. 已二腈请注明签约日期与出口商

29. 29 **其他含氮基化合物：** 1. 2，4-和2，6-甲苯二异氰酸酯混合物请注明签约日期、定价方式与出口商；2. 甲苯二异氰酸酯请注明签约日期、定价方式、出口商与生产厂商；3. 二甲苯二异氰酸酯请注明签约日期、定价方式与出口商；4. 二苯基甲烷二异氰酸酯请注明签约日期、定价方式与出口商

29. 33 **仅含氮杂原子的杂环化合物：** 1. 结构上含有一个非稠合三嗪环（不论是否氢化）的化合物请注明签约日期、出口商与生产厂商；2. 6-已内酰胺请注明签约日期、定价方式、提单日期、定价公式与生产厂商

29. 41 **缺菌素：** 1. 7-氨基头孢烷酸、7-氨基脱乙酰氧基头孢烷酸请注明签约日期；2. 生产厂商

第三十章 药品

【注解】

名词解释：

1."加工方法"指改变原材料、毛坯或半成品的形状、尺寸、性质或表面状态，使之达到规定要求的各种形状的方法。

2."成分"指商品所构成的部分或要素，一般指所含物质的种类。

3."含量"一般指所含物质的数量：

4.所注明的"包装"内容要足以判断是否为零售包装。

注意事项：

对于30章"成分"、"含量"的说明举例：

有些情况下，部分30章商品要求的成分、含量只要能明确归类即可。

商品编码	商品描述	申报要素	
		商品名称	规格型号
30.01	**已干燥的器官疗法用腺体及其他器官，不论是否制成粉末；器官疗法用腺体、其他器官及其分泌物的提取物；肝素及其盐；其他供治疗或预防疾病用的其他税目未列名的人体或动物制品：**	1. 品名；2. 用途；3. 加工方法（已干燥等）；4. 来源	5. 包装规格
30.02	**人血；治病、防病或诊断用的动物血制品；抗血清、其他血份及修饰免疫制品，不论是否通过生物工艺加工制得；疫苗、毒素、培养微生物（不包括酵母）及类似产品：**	1. 品名；2. 用途；3. 来源	4. 包装规格
30.03	**两种或两种以上成分混合而成的治病或防病用药品（不包括税目30.02、30.05或30.06的货品）。未配定剂量或制成零售包装：**	1. 品名；2. 用途	3. 成分；4. 配定剂量或零售包装请注明；5. 包装规格
30.04	**由混合或非混合产品构成的治病或防病用药品（不包括税目30.02、30.05或30.06的货品），已配定剂量（包括制成皮肤摄入形式的）或制成零售包装：**	1. 品名；2. 用途；3. 头孢类抗菌素药物请注明药物的物理状态（粉状、片状或溶液等）	4. 成分；5. 配定剂量或零售包装请注明；6. 包装规格
30.05	**软填料、纱布、绷带及类似物品（例如，敷料、橡皮膏、泥罨剂），经过药物浸涂或制成零售包装供医疗、外科、牙科或兽医用：**	1. 品名；2. 用途；3. 品牌；4. 有胶粘敷料或涂层的请注明	5. 包装

商品编码	商品描述	申报要素	
		商品名称	规格型号
30.06	**本章注释四所规定的医药用品:**		
3006.1000	-无菌外科肠线、类似的无菌缝合材料(包括外科或牙科用无菌可吸收缝线)及外伤创口闭合用的无菌粘合胶布;无菌昆布及无菌昆布塞条;外科或牙科用无菌吸收性止血材料;外科或牙科抚菌抗粘连阻隔材料,不论是否可吸收	1.品名;2.用途	
3006.2000	-血型试剂	1.品名;2.用途	3.成分
3006.3000	-X光检验造影剂;用于病人的诊断试剂	1.品名;2.用途	3.成分
3006.4000	-牙科粘固剂及其他牙科填料;骨骼粘固剂	1.品名;2.用途	3.成分
3006.5000	-急救药箱、药包	1.品名	2.组成(指箱或包中的药品、器具等)
	-以激素、税目29.37其他产品或杀精子剂为基本成分的化学避孕药物:	1.品名;2.用途	3.成分
3006.7000	-专用于人类或兽药的凝胶制剂,作为外科手术或体检时躯体部位的润滑剂,或者作为躯体和医疗器械之间的偶合剂	1.品名;2.用途	3.成分
	-其他:	1.品名;2.用途	

备注或申报要求

30.02 人血;治病、防病或诊断用的动物血制品;抗血清、其他血份及修饰免疫制品,不论是否通过生物工艺加工制得;疫苗、毒素、培养微生物(不包括酵母)及类似产品: 生产厂商

30.03 两种或两种以上成分混合而成的治病或防病用药品(不包括税目30.02、30.05或30.06的货品)。未配定剂量或制成零售包装: 生产厂商

30.04 由混合或非混合产品构成的治病或防病用药品(不包括税目30.02、30.05或30.06的货品),已配定剂量(包括制成皮肤摄入形式的)或制成零售包装: 生产厂商

第三十一章 肥料

【注解】

名词解释:

1.“加工方法”指改变原材料、毛坯或半成品的形状、尺寸、性质或表面状态,使之达到规定要求的各种形状的方法。

2.“成分”指商品所构成的部分或要素,一般指所含物质的种类。

3.“含量”一般指所含物质的数量。

注意事项:

对于31章“成分”、“含量”的说明举例:

有些情况下,部分31章商品要求的成分、含量只要能明确归类即可。

商品编码	商品描述	申报要素	
		商品名称	规格型号
31.01	**动物或植物肥料,不论是否相互混合或经化学处理;动植物产品经混合或化学处理制成的肥料:**	1.品名;2.用途;3.外观;4.来源;5.经化学处理请注明	6.每包重量;7.与化学肥料混合请注明
31.02	**矿物氮肥及化学氮肥:**	1.品名;2.外观	3.每包重量;4.氮含量
31.03	**矿物磷肥及化学磷肥:**	1.品名;2.外观;3.来源	4.每包重量;5.磷含量;6.磷酸氢钙的氟含量;
31.04	**矿物钾肥及化学钾肥:**	1.品名;2.外观;3.氯化钾请注明是否为分析纯的	4.每包重量;5.钾含量(按氧化物计)

商品编码	商品描述	申报要素	
		商品名称	规格型号
31.05	**含氮、磷、钾中两种或三种肥效元素的矿物肥料或化学肥料；其他肥料；制成片及类似形状或每包毛重不超过10千克的本童各项货品：**	1.品名；2.外观	3.成分含量；4.每包重量

第三十二章 鞣料浸膏及染料浸膏；鞣酸及其衍生物；染料、颜料及其他着色料；油漆及清漆；油灰及其他类似胶粘剂；墨水、油墨

【注解】

名词解释：

1."成分"指商品所构成的部分或要素，一般指所含物质的种类。

2."含量"一般指所含物质的数量。

3.所注明的"包装"内容要足以判断是否为零售包装。

对于32章"成分"、"含量"的说明举例：

有些情况下，部分32章商品要求的成分、含量只要能明确归类即可。

商品编码	商品描述	申报要素	
		商品名称	规格型号
32.01	**植物鞣料浸膏；鞣酸及其盐、醚、酯和其他衍生物：**	1.品名；2.用途；3.来源	
32.02	**有机合成鞣料；无机鞣料；鞣料制剂，不论是否含有天然鞣料；预鞣用酶制剂：**	1.品名	2.成分含量
32.03	**动植物质着色料(包括染料浸膏，但动物碳黑除外)，不论是否已有化学定义：本章注释三所述的以动植物质着色料为基本成分的制品：**	1.品名；2.用途；3.来源	4.包装
32.04	**有机合成着色料，不论是否已有化学定义；本章注释三所述的以有机合成着色料为基本成分的制品：用作荧光增白剂或发光体的有机合成产品，不论是否已有化学定义：**		
	-有机合成着色料及本章注释三所述的以有机合成着色料为基本成分的制品：	1.品名；2.染料种类	3.包装
3204.2000	-用作荧光增白剂的有机合成产品	1.品名；2.用途	3.包装
	-其他：	1.品名；2.用途	3.包装
32.05	**色淀；本章注释三所述的以色淀为基本成分的制品：**	品名	
32.06	**其他着色料：本章注释三所述的制品，但税目32.03、32.04及32.05的货品除外；用作发光体的无机产品，不论是否已有化学定义：**		
	-以二氧化钛为基本成分的颜料及制品：	1.品名；2.用途	3.成分含量4.包装；5.晶型
3206.2000	-以铬化合物为基本成分的颜料及制	1.品名；2.用途	3.包装
	-其他着色料及其他制品：	1.品名；2.用途	3.包装
3206.5000	-用作发光体的无机产品	1.品名；2.用途	3.包装；4.技术指标(如果产品中加入微量的放射性盐，请注明放射性比度)
32.07	**陶瓷、搪瓷及玻璃工业用的调制颜料、遮光剂、着色剂、珐琅和釉料、釉底料(泥釉)、光瓷釉以及类似产品；搪瓷玻璃料及其他玻璃，呈粉、粒或粉片状的：**	1.品名；2.用途；3.外观	4.包装

商品编码	商 品 描 述	申 报 要 素	
		商品名称	规格型号
32.08	以合成聚合物或化学改性天然聚合物为基本成分的油漆及清漆(包括瓷漆及大漆),分散于或溶于非水介质的;本章注释四所述的溶液	1.品名;2.用途;3.分散于或溶于非水介质的请注明	4.成分含量; 5.包装
32.09	以合成聚合物或化学改性天然聚合物为基本成分的油漆及清漆(包括瓷漆及大漆),分散于或溶于介质的:	1.品名;2.用途;	3.成分含量
32.10	其他油漆及清漆(包括瓷漆、大漆及水浆涂料);加工皮革用的水性颜料:	1.品名;2.用途	3.成分含量
32.11	配制的催干剂;	1.品名;2.用途	3.成分
32.12	制造油漆(含瓷漆)用的颜料(包括金属粉末或金属粉片),分散于非水介质中呈液状或浆状的;压印箔;零售形状及零售包装的染料或其他着色料:	1.品名;2.用途;3.外观	4.包装;5.成分
32.13	艺术家、学生和广告美工用的颜料、调色料、文娱颜料及类似品,片状、管装、罐装、瓶装、扁盒装以及类似形状或包装的:	1.品名;2.用途	3.包装
32.14	安装玻璃用油灰、接缝用油灰、树脂胶泥、嵌缝胶及其他类似胶粘剂;漆工用填料;非耐火涂面制剂,涂门面、内墙、地板、天花板等用:	1.品名;2.用途	3.包装;4成分
32.15	印刷油墨、书写或绘图墨水及其他墨类,不论是否固体或浓缩:	1.品名;2.用途;3.印刷油墨请注明颜色	

第三十三章 精油及香膏;芳香料制品及化妆盥洗品

【注解】

名词解释:

1."成分"指商品所构成的部分或要素,一般指所含物质的种类。

2."含量"一般指所含物质的数量。

3.所注明的"包装"内容要足以判断是否为零售包装。

商品编码	商 品 描 述	申 报 要 素	
		商品名称	规格型号
33.01	精油(无萜或含萜),包括浸膏及净油;香膏;提取的油树脂;用花香吸取法或浸渍法制成的含浓缩精油的脂肪、固定油、蜡及类似品;精油脱萜时所得的萜烯副产品;精油水馏液及水溶液:	1.品名;2.来源	
33.02	工业原料用的混合香料以及以一种或多种香料为基本成分的混合物(包括酒精溶液);生产饮料用的以香料为基本成分的其他制品:		
	-食品或饮料工业用:	1.品名;2.用途;3.来源	4.酒精含量
3302.9000	-其他	1.品名;2.用途;3.来源	
33.03	香水及花露水:	1.品名	2.包装
33.04	美容品或化妆品及护肤品(药品除外),包括防晒油或晒黑油;指(趾)甲化妆品:	1.品名;2.用途	3.包装
33.05	护发品:	1.品名;2.用途	3.包装
33.06	口腔及牙齿清洁剂,包括假牙模膏及粉;清洁牙缝用的纱线(牙线),单独零售包装的:	1.品名;2.用途	3.包装

商品编码	商品描述	申报要素	
		商品名称	规格型号
33.07	**剃须用制剂、人体除臭剂、沐浴用制剂、脱毛剂和其他税目未列名的芳香料制品及化妆盥洗品；室内除臭剂，不论是否加香水或消毒剂：**	1.品名;2.用途	3.包装

第三十四章　肥皂、有机表面活性剂、洗涤剂、润滑剂、人造蜡、调制蜡、光洁剂、蜡烛及类似品、塑型用膏、“牙科用蜡”及牙科用熟石膏制剂

【注解】

名词解释：

1.“成分”指商品所构成的部分或要素，一般指所含物质的种类。

2.“含量”一般指所含物质的数量。

3.所注明的“包装”内容要足以判断是否为零售包装。

注意事项：

对于34章“成分”、“含量”的说明举例：

有些情况下，部分34章商品要求的成分、含量只要能明确归类即可。

商品编码	商品描述	申报要素	
		商品名称	规格型号
34.01	**肥皂；作肥皂用的有机表面活性产品及制品，条状、块状或模制形状的，不论是否含有肥皂；洁肤用的有机表面活性产品及制品，液状或膏状并制成零售包装的，不论是否含有肥皂；用肥皂或洗涤剂浸渍、涂面或包覆的纸、絮胎、毡呢及无纺织物：**	1.品名;2.用途;3.外观	4.包装
34.02	**有机表面活性剂（肥皂除外）；表面活性剂制品、洗涤剂（包括助洗剂）及清洁剂，不论是否含有肥皂，但税目34.01的产品除外：**		
	-有机表面活性剂，不论是否零售包装	1.品名;2.种类（阳离子、阴离子、非离子、两性等）	3.成分
	-零售包装的制品：	1.品名;2.用途	3.包装;4.成分
3402.9000	-其他	1.品名;2.用途	3.包装;4.成分
34.03	**润滑剂（包括以润滑剂为基本成分的切削油制剂、螺栓或螺母松开剂、防锈或防腐蚀制剂及脱模剂）及用于纺织材料、皮革、毛皮或其他材料油脂处理的制剂，但不包括以石油或从沥青矿物提取的油类为基本成分（按重量计不低于70%）的制剂：**	1.品名;2.用途;3.品牌	4.成分;5.矿物油含量; 6.型号;7.包装规格
34.04	**人造蜡及调制蜡：**	1.品名;2.用途;3.外观	4.成分
34.05	**鞋靴、家具、地板、车身、玻璃或金属用的光洁剂、擦洗膏、去污粉及类似制品（包括用这类制剂浸渍、涂面或包覆的纸、絮胎、毡呢、无纺织物、泡沫塑料或海绵橡胶），但不包括税目34.04的蜡：**	1.品名;2.用途	3.成分
34.06	**各种蜡烛及类似品：**	品名	

商品编码	商 品 描 述	申 报 要 素	
		商品名称	规格型号
34.07	塑型用膏,包括供儿童娱乐用的在内;通称为"牙科用蜡"或"牙科造形膏"的制品,成套、零售包装或制成片状、马蹄形、条状及类似形状的;以熟石膏(煅烧石膏或硫酸钙)为基本成分的牙科用其他制品:	1.品名;2.用途;3.外观	4.包装

第三十五章 蛋白类物质;改性淀粉;胶;酶

【注解】

名词解释:

1."成分"指商品所构成的部分或要素,一般指所含物质的种类。

2."含量"一般指所含物质的数量。

注意事项:

对于35章"成分"、"含量"的说明举例:

有些情况下,部分35章商品要求的成分、含量只要能明确归类即可。

商品编码	商 品 描 述	申 报 要 素	
		商品名称	规格型号
35.01	酪蛋白、酪蛋白酸盐及其他酪蛋白衍生物;酪蛋白胶:	1.品名	2.包装
35.02	白蛋白(包括按重量计干质成分的乳清蛋白含量超过80%的两种或两种以上的乳清蛋白浓缩物)、白蛋白盐及其他白蛋白衍生物:	1.品名;2.用途;3.外观	4.成分含量
35.03	明胶(包括长方形、正方形明胶薄片,不论是否表面加工或着色)及其衍生物;鱼鳔胶;其他动物胶,但不包括税目35.01的酪蛋白胶:	1.品名;2.用途;3.外观	4.包装
35.04	蛋白胨及其衍生物;其他税目未列名的蛋白质及其衍生物;皮粉,不论是否加入铬矾:	1.品名;2.用途;3.来源	4.包装; 5.蛋白质含量
35.05	糊精及其他改性淀粉(例如,预凝化淀粉或酯化淀粉);以淀粉、糊精或其他改性淀粉为基本成分的胶:	1.品名;2.用途;3.来源	4.包装
35.06	其他税目未列名的调制胶及其他调制粘合剂;适于作胶或粘合剂用的产品,零售包装每件净重不超过1千克:	1.品名;2.用途;3.来源	4.包装;5.成分
35.07	酶;其他税目未列名的酶制品:	1.品名;2.用途;3.种类	

第三十六章 炸药;烟火制品;火柴;引火合金;易燃材料制品

【注解】

名词解释:

1."成分"指商品所构成的部分或要素,一般指所含物质的种类。

2."含量"一般指所含物质的数量。

注意事项:

对于36章"成分"、"含量"的说明举例:

有些情况下,部分36章商品要求的成分、含量只要能明确归类即可。

商品编码	商 品 描 述	申 报 要 素	
		商品名称	规格型号
36.01	发射药:	1.品名	2.成分
36.02	配制炸药,但发射药除外:	1.品名	2.成分

商品编码	商 品 描 述	申 报 要 素	
		商品名称	规格型号
36.03	**安全导火索;导爆索;火帽或雷管;引爆器;电雷管:**	品名	
36.04	**烟花、爆竹、信号弹、降雨火箭、浓雾信号弹及其他烟火制品:**	品名	
36.05	**火柴,但税目36.04的烟火制品除外**	品名	
36.06	**各种形状的铈铁及其他引火合金;本章注释二所述的易燃材料制品:**		
3606.1000	-直接灌注香烟打火机及类似打火器用的液体燃料或液化气体燃料,其包装容器的容积不超过300立方厘米	1.品名;2.用途	3.包装容器的容积
	-其他:	1.品名;2.用途;3.外观	

第三十七章　照相及电影用品

【注解】

名词解释:

1.所称"规格尺寸"一般指长和宽。

2."成分"指商品所构成的部分或要素,一般指所含物质的种类。

3."含量"一般指所含物质的数量。

注意事项:

本章商品申报的品名中应包括是否曝光,是否冲洗的内容。

商品编码	商 品 描 述	申 报 要 素	
		商品名称	规格型号
37.01	**未曝光的摄影感光硬片及平面软片,用纸、纸板及纺织物以外任何材料制成;未曝光的一次成像感光平片,不论是否分装:**	1.品名;2.用途;3.材质;4.成卷的请注明;5.一次成像的请注明	6.规格尺寸
37.02	**成卷的未曝光摄影感光胶片,用纸、纸板及纺织物以外任何材料制成;未曝光的一次成像感光卷片:**	1.品名;2.用途;3.材质;4.成卷的请注明;5.一次成像的请注明	6.规格尺寸
37.03	**未曝光的摄影感光纸、纸板及纺织物:**	1.品名;2.用途;3.成卷的请注明	4.规格尺寸
37.04	**已曝光未冲洗的摄影硬片、软片、纸、纸板及纺物:**	1.品名 2.用途	3.规格尺寸
37.05	**已曝光已冲洗的摄影硬片及软片,但电影胶片除外;**	1.品名;2.用途	3.规格尺寸
37.06	**已曝光已冲洗的电影胶片,不论是否配有声道或仅有声道:**	1.品名;2.用途	3.规格尺寸
37.07	**摄影用化学制剂(不包括上光漆、胶水、粘合剂及类似制剂);摄影用未混合产品;定量包装或零售包装可立即使用的:**	1.品名;2.用途	3.包装; 4.成分

第三十八章　杂项化学产品

【注解】

名词解释:

1."成分"指商品所构成的部分或要素,一般指所含物质的种类。

2."含量"一般指所含物质的数量。

3.所注明的"包装"内容要足以判断是否为零售包装。

注意事项:

对于38章"成分"、"含量"的说明举例:

有些情况下,部分38章商品要求的成分、含量只要能明确归类即可。

商品编码	商品描述	申报要素	
		商品名称	规格型号
38.01	人造石墨;胶态或半胶态石墨;以石黑或其他碳为基本成分的糊状、块状、板状制品或半制品:	1. 品名;2. 用途;3. 种类;4. 来源	
38.02	活性碳;活性天然矿产品;动物炭黑,包括废动物炭黑:	1. 品名;2. 用途;3. 来源	4. 包装
38.03	妥尔油,不论是否精炼:	1. 品名;2. 用途	
38.04	木浆残余碱液,不论是否浓缩、脱糖或经化学处理,包括木素磺酸盐,但不包括税目38.03的妥尔油:	品名	
38.05	脂松节油、木松节油和硫酸盐松节油及其他萜烯油,用蒸馏或其他方法从针叶木制得;粗制二聚戊烯;亚硫酸盐松节油及其他粗制对异丙基苯甲烷;以α萜品醇为基本成分的松油:	1. 品名;2. 用途	3. 成分;4. 二聚戊烯、萜烯烃、萜品醇及水合萜品请注明含量
38.06	松香和树脂酸及其衍生物;松香精及松香油;再熔胶:	1. 品名;2. 来源	
38.07	木焦油;精制木焦油;木杂酚油;粗木精;植物沥青;以松香、树脂酸或植物沥青为基本成分的啤酒桶沥青及类似制品:	1. 品名;2. 用途	
38.08	杀虫剂、杀鼠剂、杀菌剂、除草剂、抗萌剂、植物生长调节剂、消毒剂及类似产品,零售形状、零售包装或制成制剂及成品(例如,经硫磺处理的带子、杀虫灯芯、蜡烛及捕蝇纸):	1. 品名;2. 用途	3. 成分含量;4. 包装
38.09	纺织、造纸、制革及类似工业用的其他税目未列名的整理剂、染料加速着色或固色助剂及其他产品和制剂(例如,修整剂及媒染剂):	1. 品名;2. 用途	3. 成分
38.10	金属表面酸洗剂;焊接用的焊剂及其他辅助剂;金属及其他材料制成的焊粉或焊膏;作焊条芯子或焊条涂料用的制品:	1. 品名;2. 用途	3. 成分
38.11	抗震剂、抗氧剂、防胶剂、粘度改良剂、防腐蚀制剂及其他配制添加剂,用于矿物油(包括汽油)或与矿物油同样用途的其他液体:	1. 品名;2. 用途	3. 成分
38.12	配制的橡胶促进剂;其他税目未列名的橡胶或塑料用复合增塑剂;橡胶或塑料用抗氧制剂及其他复合稳定剂:	1. 品名;2. 用途	3. 成分
38.13	灭火器的装配药;已装药的灭火弹:	1. 品名;2. 用途	3. 成分
38.14	其他税目未列名的有机复合溶剂及稀释剂;除漆剂;	1. 品名 2. 用途	3. 成分
38.15	其他税目未列名的反应引发剂、反应促进剂、催化剂;	1. 成名;2. 用途	3. 成分
38.16	耐火的水泥、灰泥、混凝土及类似耐火混合制品,但税目38.01的产品除外:	1. 品名. 2. 用途	3. 成分
38.17	混合烷基苯及混合烷基萘,但税目27.07及29.02的货品除外:	1. 品名;2. 用途	3. 成分
38.18	经掺杂用于电子工业的化学元素,已切成圆片、薄片或类似形状;经掺杂用于电子工业的化合物:	1. 品名;2. 用途;3. 外观	4. 成分;5. 单晶硅切片请注明直径

商品编码	商品描述	申报要素	
		商品名称	规格型号
38.19	**闸用液压油及其他液压传动用液体，不含石油或从沥青矿物提取的油类，或者按重量计石油或从沥青矿物提取的油类含量低于70%：**	1.品名;2.用途	3.成分;4.矿物油含量
38.20	**防冻剂及解冻剂：**	1.品名;2.用途	3.成分
38.21	**制成的供微生物（包括病毒及类似品）或植物、人体、动物细胞生长或维持用的培养基：**	1.品名;2.用途	3.成分
38.22	**附于衬背上的诊断或实验用试剂及不论是否附于衬背上的诊断或实验用配制试剂，但税目30.02及30.06的货品除外；检定参照物：**	1.品名;2.用途	3.包装;4.成分（区分衬背和试剂来说明举例）
38.23	**工业用单羧脂肪酸；精炼所得的酸性油工业用脂肪醇：**	1.品名	2.成分含量
38.24	**铸模及铸芯用粘合剂；其他税目未列名的化学工业及其相关工业的化学产品及配制品（包括由天然产品混合组成的）；**		
3824.1000	-铸模及铸芯用粘合剂	1.品名;2.用途	3.成分含量
3824.3000	-自身混合或与金属粘合剂混合的未烧结金属碳化物	1.品名;2.用途;3.烧结请注明	4.成分含量
3824.4000	-水泥、灰泥及混凝土用添加剂	1.品名;2.用途	3.成分含量
3824.5000	-非耐火的灰泥及混凝土	1.品名;2.用途	3.成分含量
3824.6000	-子目号2905.44以外的山梨醇	1.品名;2.用途;3.外观;4.来源	5.成分含量
	-含有烷、乙烷或丙烷的卤化衍生物的混合物	1.品名;2.用途	3.成分含量
	-其他：	1.品名;2.用途	3.成分含量;4.包装
38.25	**其他税目未列名的化学工业及其相关工业的副产品；城市垃圾；下水道淤泥；本章注释六所规定的其他废物：**	1.品名;2.用途;3.来源	

第七类　塑料及其制品；橡胶及其制品

第三十九章　塑料及其制品

【注解】

名词解释：

1. "成分"指商品所构成的部分或要素，一般指所含物质的种类。
2. "含量"一般指所含物质的数量。

注意事项：

1. 39章的多数产品需要注明成分、含量、单体种类、单体比例，这是明确归类的需要。在实际申报中只要申报的内容能明确归类即可。如"聚乙烯"就可以不用.申报单体含量，而"乙烯-丙烯聚合物"就必须申报乙烯单体和丙烯单体的含量。
2. 本章商品需要申报的品名包括标准命名法名称或工商业通用俗称。
3. 有英文缩写的商品必须申报，如聚乙烯的缩写为PE。

商品编码	商品描述	申报要素	
		商品名称	规格型号
39.01	**初级形状的乙烯聚合物：**	1. 品名；2. 外观	3. 成分含量；4. 单体的种类和比例；5. 技术指标（比重小于0.94的请注明是否为线型
39.02	**初级形状的丙烯或其他烯烃聚合物：**		
3902.1000	-聚丙烯	1. 品名；2. 外观	3. 成分含量；4. 单体的种类和比例；5. 技术指标（电工级聚丙烯要申报灰分含量）
3902.2000	-聚异丁烯	1. 品名；2. 外观	3. 成分含量；4. 单体的种类和比例
	-丙烯共聚物：	1. 品名；2. 外观.	3. 成分含量；4. 单体的种类和比例
3902.9000	-其他	1. 品名；2. 外观	3. 成分含量；4. 单体的种类和比例
39.03	**初级形状的苯乙烯聚合物：**	1. 品名；2. 外观； 3. 聚苯乙烯请注明是否为可发性的	4. 成分含量 5. 单体的种类和比例
39.04	**初级形状的氯乙烯或其他卤化烯烃聚合物：**	1. 品名；2. 外观；3. 聚氯乙烯请注明是否已塑化；4. 聚氯乙烯请注明是否掺有其他物质	5. 成分含量；6. 单体的种类和比例
39.05	**初级形状的乙酸乙烯酯或其他乙烯酯聚合物；初级形状的其他乙烯基聚合物：**	1. 品名. 2. 外观	3. 成分含量；4. 单体的种类和比例
39.06	**初级形状的丙烯酸聚合物：**	1. 品名；2. 外观	3. 成分含量 4. 单位的种类和比例
39.07	**初级形状的聚缩醛、其他聚醚及环氧树脂；初级形状的聚碳酸酯、醇酸树脂、聚烯丙基酯及其他聚酯：**		
	-聚缩醛：	1. 品名；2. 外观	3. 成分含量 4. 单体的种类和比例
3907.2000	-其他聚醚	1. 品名；2. 外观	3. 成分含量 4. 单体的种类和比例
3907.3000	-环氧树脂	1. 品名；2. 外观	3. 成分含量；4. 单体的种类和比例
3907.4000	-聚碳酸酯	1. 品名；2. 外观	3. 成分含量；4. 单体的种类和比例
3907.5000	-醇酸树脂	1. 品名；2. 外观	3. 成分含量；4. 单体的种类和比例

商品编码	商品描述	申报要素	
		商品名称	规格型号
	-聚对苯二甲酸乙二酯：	1. 品名;2. 外观;3. 切片请注明	4. 成分含量 5. 单体的种类和比例;6. 粘度
	-其他聚酯：	1. 品名;2. 外观;3. 饱和的请注明	4. 成分含量;5. 单体的种类和比例
39.08	**初级形状的聚酰胺：**	1. 品名;2. 外观;3. 切片请注明	4. 成分含量;5. 单体的种类和比例
39.09	**初级形状的氨基树脂、酚醛树脂及聚氨酯类：**	1. 品名;2. 外观	3. 成分含量;4. 单体的种类和比例
39.10	**初级形状的聚硅氧烷：**	1. 品名;2. 用途;3. 外观;4. 溶于水的请注明	5. 成分含量
39.11	**初级形状的石油树脂、苯并呋喃-茚树脂、多萜树脂、多硫化物、聚砜及本章注释三所规定的其他税目未列名产品：**	1. 品名;2. 外观	3. 成分含量; 4. 单体的种类和比例
39.12	**初级形状的其他税目未列名的纤维素及其化学衍生物：**	1. 品名;2. 外观;3. 乙酸纤维素请注明是否塑化	4. 成分含量;5. 单体的种类和比例
39.13	**初级形状的其他税目未列名的天然聚合物(例如,藻酸)及改性天然聚合物(例如,硬化蛋白、天然橡胶的化学衍生物)：**	1. 品名;2. 外观;3. 来源	4. 成分含量
39.14	**初级形状的离子交换剂,以税目39.01至39.13的聚合物为基本成分的：**	1. 品名;2. 用途;3. 外观	4. 成分
39.15	**塑料的废碎料及下脚料：**	1. 品名;2. 外观;3. 来源	4. 成分
39.16	**塑料制的单丝(截面直径超过1毫米)、条、杆、型材及异型材,不论是否经表面加工,但未经其他加工：**	1. 品名;2. 外观	3. 成分;4. 单丝请注明截面直径
39.17	**塑料制的管子及附件(例如,接头、肘管、法兰)：**		
3917.1000	-硬化蛋白或纤维素材料制的人造肠衣(香肠用肠衣)	1. 品名	2. 成分
	-硬管	1. 品名;2. 用途	3. 成分
	-其他管：	1. 品名;2. 用途	3. 成分;4. 装有附件请注明;5. 软管请注明最小爆破压力
3917.4000	-管子附件	品名	
39.18	**块状或成卷的塑料铺地制品,不论是否胶粘;本章注释九所规定的塑料糊墙品：**	1. 品名;2. 用途	3. 成分
39.19	**自粘的塑料板、片、膜、箔、带、扁条及其他扁平形状材料,不论是否成卷：**	1. 品名;2. 外观形状;3. 成卷请注明;4. 自粘请注明	5. 成分;6 规格尺寸
39.20	**其他非泡沫塑料的板、片、膜、箔及扁条,未用其他材料强化、层压、支撑或用类似方法合制：**	1. 品名;2. 用途;3. 外观;4. 与其他材料合制请注明	5. 成分;6. 规格尺寸;7. PVC制品请注明增塑剂含量
39.21	**其他塑料板、片、膜、箔、扁条：**	1. 品名;2. 用途;3. 外观;4. 与其他材料合制的请注明;5. 泡沫塑料请注明	6. 成分;7 规格尺寸
39.22	**塑料浴缸、淋浴盘、洗涤槽、盥洗盆、坐浴盆、便盆、马桶座圈及盖、抽水箱及类似卫生洁具：**	1. 品名;2. 用途;3. 品牌	

商品编码	商品描述	申报要素	
		商品名称	规格型号
39.23	供运输或包装货物用的塑料制品;塑料制的塞子、盖子及类似品:	1. 品名;2. 用途;3. 品牌 4. 袋及包请注明具体材质	
39.24	塑料制的餐具、厨房用具、其他家庭用具及卫生或盥洗用具:	1. 品名;2. 用途;3. 品牌	
39.25	其他税目未列名的建筑用塑料制品:	1. 品名;2. 用途;3. 品牌	4. 塑料制囤、柜、罐、桶及类似容器请注明容积
39.26	其他塑料制品及税目 39.01 至 39.14 所列其他材料的制品:	1. 品名;2. 用途;3. 品牌;4. 材质;5. 来源	6. 标签或标牌印字、印刷的请注明

第四十章　橡胶及其制品

【注解】

名词解释:

1."成分"指商品所构成的部分或要素,一般指所含物质的种类。

2."含量"一般指所含物质的数量。

注意事项:

1. 40 章的一些产品需要注明成分、含量、单体种类、单体比例,这是明确归类的需要。在实际申报中只要申报的内容能明确归类即可。

2. 本章商品需要申报的品名包括标准命名法名称或工商业通用俗称。

商品编码	商品描述	申报要素	
		商品名称	规格型号
40.01	天然橡胶、巴拉塔胶、古塔波胶、银胶菊胶、糖胶树胶及类似的天然树胶,初级形状或板、片、带:	1. 品名;2. 外观;3. 来源	4. 型号;5. 包装
40.02	合成橡胶及从油类提取的油膏,初级形状或板、片、带;税目 40.01 所列产品与本税目所列产品的混合物,初级形状或板、片、带:	1. 品名;2. 用途;3. 外观;4. 来源;5. 丁苯橡胶请注明是否充油、热塑	6. 成分
40.03	再生橡胶,初级形状或板、片、带:	1. 品名;2. 外观;3. 来源	
40.04	橡胶(硬质橡胶的除外)的废碎料、下脚料及其粉、粒:	1. 品名;2. 外观;3. 来源	4. 水分;5. 杂质;6. 干胶含量
40.05	未硫化的复合橡胶,初级形状或板、片、带:	1. 品名;2. 外观;3. 硫化的请注明	4. 成分
40.06	其他形状(例如,杆、管或型材及异型材)的未硫化橡胶及未硫化橡胶制品(例如,盘、环):	1. 品名;2. 用途;3. 外观	
40.07	硫化橡胶线及绳:	1. 品名;2. 外观	3. 截面尺寸
40.08	硫化橡胶(硬质橡胶除外)制的板、片、带、杆或型材及异型材:	1. 品名;2. 外观;3. 海绵橡胶制请注明	4. 规格尺寸
40.09	硫化橡胶(硬质橡胶除外)制的管子,不论是否装有附件(例如,接头、肘管、法兰):	1. 品名;2. 用途;3. 外观;4. 材质构成(是否加强或与其他材料合制)	5. 装有附件请注明
40.10	硫化橡胶制的传动带或输送带及带料:	1. 品名;2. 用途;3. 外观;4. 材质结构(是否加强或与其他材料合制);5. 加强材料要注明	6. 规格尺寸
40.11	新的充气橡胶轮胎:	1. 品名;2. 用途;3. 品牌	4. 规格型号;5. 辋圈尺寸;6. 胎面花纹;7. 断面宽度
40.12	翻新的或旧的充气橡胶轮胎;实心或半实心橡胶轮胎、橡胶胎面及橡胶轮胎衬带:	1. 品名;2. 用途;3. 实心的请注明;4. 充气轮胎请注明翻新或旧的	

商品编码	商品描述	申报要素	
		商品名称	规格型号
40.13	橡胶内胎:	1. 品名;2. 用途;3. 品牌	
40.14	硫化橡胶(硬质橡胶除外)制的卫生及医疗用品(包括奶嘴),不论是否装有硬质橡胶制的附件:	1. 品名;2. 用途;3. 品牌	
40.15	硫化橡胶(硬质橡胶除外)制的衣着用品及附件(包括分指手套、连指手套及露指手套):	1. 品名;2. 用途;3. 品牌	
40.16	硫化橡胶(硬质橡胶除外)的其他制	1. 品名;2. 用途(其中垫圈、垫片等类似品是否密封用);3. 品牌;4. 材质(海绵橡胶、硫化橡胶等)	
40.17	各种形状的硬质橡胶(例如,纯硬质胶),包括废碎料;硬质橡胶制品:	1. 品名;2. 外观;3. 来源	

第八类　生皮、皮革、毛皮及其制品；鞍具及挽具；旅行用品、手提包及类似容器；动物肠线（蚕胶丝除外）制品

第四十一章　生皮（毛皮除外）及皮革

【注解】

油鞣皮革是通过用鱼油或动物油反复鞣制，然后加热烘干或晾干，用碱水洗去余油，最后清洁皮张的表面，并用浮石或其他磨料进行磨里加工制得。这样鞣制的皮革通常采用正面起绒除去粒层的绵羊或羔羊肉面剖层皮来做原料；漆皮，即涂有一层清漆或大漆，或在皮革表面覆盖一层塑料膜的皮革。这种皮革的表面光亮宛如镜面；层压漆皮，商业上称为特种漆革，这种皮革的表面覆盖了一层塑料片，其厚度超过0.15毫米，但不超过总厚度的一半，并且与漆皮一样有着镜面般的光洁表面；镀金属皮革，即表面涂有或覆盖金属（例如，银、金、青铜或铝）粉末或箔的皮革；本章所称"坯革"，包括在干燥前经复鞣、染色或加油（加脂）的皮；经鞣制或鞣制后进一步加工的皮张在贸易上称为"皮革"。鞣制后经干燥的皮革称为"坯革"。

商品编码	商品描述	申报要素	
		商品名称	规格型号
41.01	**生牛皮（包括水牛皮）、生马皮（鲜的、盐腌的、干的、石灰浸渍的、浸酸的或以其他方法保藏，但未鞣制、未经羊皮纸化处理或进一步加工的），不论是否去毛或剖层：**	1.品名；2.加工方法（干、盐渍、石灰浸渍、浸酸、未鞣制、退鞣处理等）；3.种类（公牛、母牛、奶牛、阉牛、马）；4.状态（鲜、整张、半张等）；5.野生请注明	6.规格（厚度、平均每张重量等）；7.等级；8.平均每张生牛皮实际成交价格
41.02	**绵羊或羔羊生皮（鲜的、盐渍的、干的、石灰浸渍的、浸酸的或经其他方法保藏，但未鞣制、未经羊皮纸化处理或进一步加工的），不论是否带毛或剖层，但本章注释一（三）所述不包括的生皮除外：**	1.品名；2.加工方法（干、盐渍、石灰浸渍、浸酸、未鞣制、退鞣处理等）；3.种类（羔羊、绵羊）；4.状态（鲜、带毛、不带毛）；5.野生请注明	
41.03	**其他生皮（鲜的、盐渍的、干的、石灰浸渍的、浸酸的或以其他方法保藏，但未鞣制、未经羊皮纸化处理或进一步加工的），不论是否去毛或剖层，但本章注释一（二）或（三）所述不包括的生皮除外：**	1.品名；2.加工方法（干、盐渍、石灰浸渍、浸酸、未鞣制、退鞣处理等）；3.种类（山羊、猪、爬行动物等）；4.状态（鲜）；5.野生请注明	
41.04	**经鞣制的不带毛牛皮（包括水牛皮）、马皮及其坯革，不论是否剖层，但未经进一步加工：**	1.品名；2.用途（机器带用等）；3.加工方法（干、鞣制无毛、表面是否涂覆，涂覆何种物质）；4.种类（公牛、母牛、奶牛、阉牛、马）；5.状态（湿如蓝湿、全粒面未剖层或粒面剖层、二层牛皮）	6.野生请注明；7.等级；8.每平方英尺成交价格
41.05	**经鞣制的不带毛绵羊或羔羊皮革及其坯革，不论是否剖层，但未经进一步加工：**	1.品名；2.加工方法（干、鞣制无毛）；3.种类（羔羊、绵羊）；4.状态（湿：如蓝湿）；5.野生请注明	
41.06	**经鞣制的其他不带毛动物皮革及其坯革，不论是否剖层，但未经进一步加工：**	1.品名；2.加工方法（干、鞣制无毛）；3.种类（如爬行动物、小山羊）；4.状态（湿）；5.野生请注明	
41.07	**经鞣制或半硝处理后进一步加工的牛皮革（包括水牛皮革）或马皮革，包括羊皮纸化处理的皮革，不论是否剖层，但税目41.14的皮革除外：**	1.品名；2.用途（机器带用等）；3.种类（牛、马）；4.加工方法（表面是否涂覆，涂覆何种物质）；5.状态（整张、无毛全粒面未剖层或无毛粒面剖层、二层牛皮、修面革）	6.野生请注明；7.规格（厚度、张幅等）；8.等级；9.每平方英尺成交价格
41.12	**经鞣制或半硝处理后进一步加工的不带毛的绵羊或羔羊皮革，包括羊皮纸化处理的皮革，不论是否剖层，但税目41.14的皮革除外：**	1.品名；2.种类（羔羊、绵羊）；3.状态（无毛全粒面或无毛羊皮纸化等）；4.野生请注明	
41.13	**经鞣制或半硝处理后进一步加工的不带毛的其他动物皮革，包括羊皮纸化处理的皮革，不论是否剖层，但税目41.14的皮革除外：**	1.品名；2.种类（爬行动物、小山羊等）；3.状态（无毛全粒面等）；4.野生请注明	
41.14	**油鞣皮革（包括结合鞣制的油鞣皮革）；漆皮及层压漆皮；镀金属皮革：**	1.品名；2.加工方法（油鞣、漆皮、镀金属）；3.野生请注明	

商品编码	商品描述	申报要素	
		商品名称	规格型号
41.15	以皮革或皮革纤维为基本成分的再生皮革,成块、成张或成条,不论是否成卷;皮革或再生皮革的边角废料,不适宜作皮革制品用;皮革粉末:	1.品名;2.加工方法(再生);3.状态(块、张、条、卷、边角料、粉末)	4.成分

第四十二章　皮革制品;鞍具及挽具;旅行用品、手提包及类似容器;动物肠线(蚕胶丝除外)制品

【注解】

本章所称"运动包",包括高尔夫球袋、体操袋、网球拍提袋、滑雪袋和钓鱼袋;本章所称"首饰盒",不仅包括为存放首饰而专门设计的盒子,也包括其形状和配件专门适于盛装一件或多件首饰的各种规格的类似有盖容器,不论是否装有铰链或扣件。它们一般用纺织材料衬里。这些容器盛装首饰后可一同展示及出售,适于长期使用;本章所称"食品或饮料保温包",包括在运输或临时保存期间保持食物及饮料温度用的可重复使用的保温包。

商品编码	商品描述	申报要素	
		商品名称	规格型号
42.01	各种材料制成的鞍具及挽具(包括缰绳、挽绳、护膝垫、口套、鞍褥、马褡裢、狗外套及类似品),适合各种动物用:	1.品名;2.野生请注明	
42.02	衣箱、提箱、小手袋、公文箱、公文包、书包、眼镜盒、望远镜盒、照相机套、乐器盒、枪套及类似容器;旅行包、食品或饮料保温包、化妆包、帆布包、手提包、购物袋、钱夹、钱包、地图盒、烟盒、烟袋、工具包、运动包、瓶盒、首饰盒、粉盒、刀叉餐具盒及类似容器,用皮革或再生皮革、塑料片、纺织材料、钢纸或纸板制成,或者全部或主要用上述材料或纸包覆制成:	1.品名;2.种类(衣箱、提箱、小手袋等);3.表面材质(塑料、纺织物等);4.野生请注明	
42.03	皮革或再生皮革制的衣服及衣着附件	1.品名;2.用途(专供运动用、劳保用等);3.材质(皮革或再生皮革);4.野生请注明	
42.04	机器、机械器具或其他专门技术用途的皮革或再生皮革制品:	1.品名;2.用途(机械、技术用等);3.材质(皮革或再生皮革);4.野生请注明	
42.05	皮革或再生皮革的其他制品:	1.品名;2.用途;3.材质(皮革或再生皮革);4.野生请注明	
42.06	肠线(蚕胶丝除外)、肠膜、膀胱或筋腱制品:	1.品名;2.种类(羊等)	

第四十三章　毛皮、人造毛皮及其制品

【注解】

本章所称"人造毛皮",是指将毛、发或其他纤维(包括绳绒纱线的纤维)粘附或缝合于皮革、织物或其他材料上以仿充毛皮的材料,但不包括有时也被人称为"毛皮织物"的纺织或针织长毛绒织物(一般归入品目58.01或60.01),也不包括"加毛"毛皮,即额外插毛的真毛皮。

商品编码	商品描述	申报要素	
		商品名称	规格型号
43.01	生毛皮(包括适合加工皮货用的头、尾、爪及其他块、片),但税目41.01、41.02或41.03的生皮除外:	1.品名;2.种类(中国羔羊、波斯羔羊、狐皮、兔皮等);3.状态(生毛皮);4.外观(整张、头、尾、爪等);5.野生请注明	

商品编码	商 品 描 述	申 报 要 素	
		商品名称	规格型号
43.02	**未缝制或已缝制(不加其他材料)的已鞣毛皮(包括头、尾、爪及其他块、片),但税目43.03的货品除外:**	1.品名;2.种类(中国羔羊、波斯羔羊、狐皮、兔皮等);3.加工方法(鞣制未缝制或已缝制毛皮);4.状态(整张、头、尾、爪等);5.野生请注明	
43.03	**毛皮制的衣服、衣着附件及其他物品:**	1.品名;2.材质(毛皮);3.野生请注明	
43.04	**人造毛皮及其制品:**	1.品名;2.材质(人造毛皮)	

第九类　木及木制品；木炭；软木及软木制品；稻草、秸秆、针茅或其他编结材料制品；篮筐及柳条编结品

第四十四章　木及木制品；木炭

【注解】

品名项应填报植物学名；本章所称"强化木"，是指经过化学或物理方法处理（对于多层粘合木材，其处理应超出一般粘合需要）。从而增加了密度或硬度并改善了机械强度、抗化学或抗电性能的木材；本章所称"木"，也包括竹及其他木质材料。

商品编码	商品描述	申报要素	
		商品名称	规格型号
44.01	薪柴（圆木段、块、枝、成捆或类似形状）；木片或木粒；锯末、木废料及碎片，不论是否粘结成圆木段、块、片或类似形状：	1. 品名；2. 种类（针叶木、非针叶木）；3. 外观（木片、粒、末等）	
44.02	木炭（包括果壳炭及果核炭），不论是否结块：	1. 品名；2. 材质；3. 外观（棒状等）	4. 截面形状及规格尺寸；5. 椰壳碳请注明水分；6. 杂质；7. 碳含量；8. 挥发份
44.03	原木，不论是否去皮、去边材或粗锯成方：	1. 品名；2. 种类（山毛榉、红松等）；3. 加工方法（用油漆、着色剂等防腐剂处理等）	4. 直径；5. 长度
44.04	箍木；木劈条；已削尖但未经纵锯的木桩；粗加修整但未经车圆、弯曲或其他方式加工的木棒，适合制手杖、伞柄、工具把柄及类似品；木片条及类似品：	1. 品名；2. 种类（针叶木或非针叶木）；3. 外观（棒状、条状等）	
44.05	木丝；木粉：	1. 品名；2. 外观（丝及粉）	
44.06	铁道及电车道枕木：	1. 品名（枕木）；2. 加工方法（已浸渍、未浸渍等）	
44.07	经纵锯、纵切、刨切或旋切的木材，不论是否刨平、砂光或端部接合，厚度超过6毫米：	1. 品名；2. 种类（山毛榉、红松等）；3. 加工方法（经纵锯、纵切、刨切或旋切加工、端部接合、非端部接合等）	4. 规格（长×宽×高）；5. 等级
44.08	饰面用单板（包括刨切积层木获得的单板）、制胶合板或其他类似多层板用单板以及其他经纵锯、刨切或旋切的木材，不论是否刨平、砂光、拼接或端部接合，厚度不超过6毫米：	1. 品名；2. 用途（饰面用等）；3. 种类（白松、红松等）；4. 外观（单板）	5. 规格（厚度×宽度×长度）
44.09	任何一边、端或面制成连续形状（舌榫、槽榫、半槽榫、斜角、V形接头、珠榫、缘饰、刨圆及类似形状）的木材（包括未装拼的拼花地板用板条及缘板），不论其任意一边或面是否刨平、砂光或端部接合：	1. 品名；2. 种类（针叶木、非针叶林）；3. 外观（一边或面制成连续形状）	
44.10	碎料板、定向刨花板（OSB）及类似板（例如，华夫板），木或其他木质材料制，不论是否用树脂或其他有机粘合剂粘合：	1. 品名；2. 材质（碎料板）；3. 种类（木质定向板、华夫板等）；4. 覆面材料（塑料等）	
44.11	木纤维板或其他木质材料纤维板，不论是否用树脂或其他有机粘合剂粘合：	1. 品名；2. 材质（纤维板）；3. 加工方法（未经机械加工或盖面等加工）	
44.12	胶合板、单板饰面板及类似的多层板：	1. 品名；2. 外观（多层板）；3. 每层材质；4. 贴面的请注明	5. 单层厚度
14.13	强化木，成块、板、条或异型的：	1. 品名；2. 加工方法（压缩、浸渍等）；3. 外观（块、板、条、异型）	
44.14	木制的画框、相框、镜框及类似品：	1. 品名；2. 材质（木制）	

商品编码	商 品 描 述	申 报 要 素	
		商品名称	规格型号
44.15	包装木箱、木盒、板条箱、圆桶及类似的包装容器;木制电缆卷筒;木托板、箱形托盘及其他装载用木板;木制的托盘护框:	1.品名;2.材质(木制)	
44.16	木制大桶、琵琶桶、盆和其他木制箍桶及其零件,包括桶板:	1.品名;2.材质(木制)	
44.17	木制的工具、工具支架、工具柄、扫帚及刷子的身及柄;木制鞋靴楦及楦头:	1.品名;2.材质(木制)	
44.18	建筑用木工制品,包括蜂窝结构木镶板、已装拼的拼花地板、木瓦及盖屋板:	1.品名;2.用途(建筑用);3.材质(木制)	
44.19	木制餐具及厨房用具:	1.品名;2.材质(木制、竹制);3.一次性产品请注明	
44.20	镶嵌木(包括细工镶嵌木);装珠宝或刀具用的木制盒子和小匣子及类似品;木制小雕像及其他装饰品;第九十四章以外的木制家具:	1.品名;2.材质(木制)	
44.21	其他木制品:	1.品名;2.材质(木制)	

第四十五章 软木及软木制品

商品编码	商 品 描 述	申 报 要 素	
		商品名称	规格型号
45.01	未加工或简单加工的天然软木;软木废料;碎的、粒状的或粉状的软木:	1.品名;2.材质(天然软木);3.加工程度(未加工、简单加工等)	
45.02	天然软木,除去表皮或粗切成方形,或成长方块、正方块、板、片或条状(包括作塞子用的方块坯料):	1.品名;2.材质(天然软木);3.加工方法(经除去表皮或粗切成方形等加工);4.外观(块、板、片或条状)	
45.03	天然软木制品:	1.品名;2.材质(天然软木)	3.规格;4.等级
45.04	压制软木(不论是否使用粘合剂压成)及其制品:	1.品名;2.材质(压制软木);3.外观(块、板、片等形状)	

第四十六章 稻草、秸秆、针茅或其他编结材料制品;篮筐及柳条编结品

【注解】

本章所称"编结材料",是指其状态或形状适于编结、交织或类似加工的材料,包括稻草、秸秆、柳条、竹、灯芯草、芦苇、木片条、其他植物材料扁条(例如,树皮条、狭叶、酒椰叶纤维或其他从阔叶获取的条)、未纺的天然纺织纤维、塑料单丝及扁条、纸带,但不包括皮革、再生皮革、毛呢或无纺织物的扁条、人发、马毛、纺织粗纱或纱线以及第五十四章的单丝和扁条。

商品编码	商 品 描 述	申 报 要 素	
		商品名称	规格型号
46.01	用编结材料编成的缏条及类似产品,不论是否缝合成宽条;平行连结或编织的成片编结材料、缏条或类似的编结材料产品,不论是否制成品(例如,席子、席料、帘子):	1.品名;2.材质(藤、草、芦苇等);3.种类(提花席、双苜席等);	4.灯芯草属材料制的席子、席料及帘子请注明单位面积
46.02	用编结材料直接编成或用税目46.01所列货品制成的篮筐、柳条编结品及其他制品;丝瓜络制品:	1.品名;2.材质(藤、草、芦苇等)	

第十类　木浆及其他纤维状纤维素浆;回收(废碎)纸或纸板;纸、纸板及其制品

第四十七章　木浆及其他纤维状纤维素浆;回收(废碎)纸或纸板

【注解】

本章所称"化学木浆,溶解级",是指温度在20℃时浸入含18%氢氧化钠的苛性碱溶液内,一小时后,按重量计含有92%及以上的不溶部分的碱木浆或硫酸盐木浆,或者含有88%及以上的不溶部分的亚硫酸盐木浆。对于亚硫酸盐木浆,按重量计灰分含量不得超过0.15%。

商品编码	商品描述	申报要素	
		商品名称	规格型号
47.01	机械木浆:	品名(机械木浆)	
47.02	化学木浆,溶解级:	品名(溶解级化学木浆)	
47.03	碱木浆硫酸盐木浆,但溶解级的除外:	1.品名(碱木浆或硫酸盐木浆);2.材质(针叶木、非针叶木);3.加工方法(漂白、未漂白、半漂白)	
47.04	亚硫酸盐木浆,但溶解级的除外:	1.品名(亚硫酸盐木浆);2.材质(针叶木、非针叶木);3.加工方法(漂白、未漂白、半漂白)	
47.05	用机械和化学联合制浆法制得的木	1.品名(化学机械木浆、半化学浆);2.加工方法(用机械和化学联合制浆法)	
47.06	从回收(废碎)纸或纸板提取的纤维浆或其他纤维状纤维素浆:		
4706.1000	-棉短绒纸浆	1.品名(棉短绒纸浆);2.种类(棉短绒)	
4706.2000	-从回收(废碎)纸或纸板提取的纤维浆	1.品名;2.来源(从回收纸或纸板提取的)	
	-其他:	1.品名;2.材质(草浆等);3.加工方法(机械、化学、半化学)	
47.07	回收(废碎)纸或纸板:	1.品名;2.种类(未漂白废牛皮纸、废报纸等);3.状态(废碎)	

第四十八章　纸及纸板;纸浆、纸或纸板制品

【注解】

本章所称"新闻纸",是指所含用机械或化学机械方法制得的木纤维不少于全部纤维重量的65%的未经涂布的报刊用纸,未施胶或微施胶,每面粗糙度[帕克印刷表面粗糙度(1兆帕)]超过2.5微米,每平方米重量不小于40克,但不超过65克。

商品编码	商品描述	申报要素	
		商品名称	规格型号
48.01	成卷或成张的新闻纸:	1.品名(新闻纸)	2.规格(成卷的宽度或成张的边长、每平米克重);3.机械或化学一机械法制得的纤维含量;4.粗糙度
48.02	书写、印刷或类似用途的未经涂布的纸及纸板、未打孔的穿孔卡片纸及穿孔纸带纸,成卷或成张矩形(包括正方形),任何尺寸,但税目48.01或48.03的纸除外;手工制纸及纸板:	1.品名;2.用途(书写、印刷等用);3.种类(壁纸原纸、手工制纸等);4.加工程度(未涂布、未染面等)	5.规格(成卷的宽度或成张的边长、每平米克重);6.机械或化学一机械法制得的纤维含量
48.03	卫生纸、面巾纸、餐巾纸以及家庭或卫生用的类似纸、纤维素絮纸和纤维素纤维网纸,不论是否起纹、压花、打孔、染面、饰面或印花,成卷或成张的:	1.品名;2.种类(卫生纸、面巾纸等类似纸)	3.规格(成卷的宽度或成张的边长)

商品编码	商 品 描 述	申 报 要 素	
		商 品 名 称	规 格 型 号
48.04	成卷或成张的未经涂布的牛皮纸及纸板,但不包括税目48.02或48.03的货品:	1.品名;2.种类(牛皮挂面纸、袋用牛皮纸等);3.加工程度(未漂白、漂白、未涂布)	4.规格(成卷的宽度或成张的边长、每平米克重);5.纤维种类和含量;6.牛皮挂面纸请注明耐破度;7.袋用牛皮纸请注明缪伦耐破度、横向伸长率、纵向伸长率或最小撕裂度、抗张强度
48.05	成卷或成张的其他未经涂布的纸及纸板,加工程度不超过本章注释三所列范围:	1.品名;2.种类(瓦楞原纸、毡纸等);3.加工程度(未涂布)	4.规格(成卷的宽度或成张的边长、每平米克重)
48.06	成卷或成张的植物羊皮纸、防油纸、描图纸、半透明纸及其他高光泽透明或半透明纸:	1.品名;2.种类(如植物羊皮纸、防油纸)	3.规格(成卷的宽度或成张的边长)
48.07	成卷或成张的复合纸及纸板(用粘合剂粘合各层纸或纸板制成),未经表面涂布或未浸渍,不论内层是否有加强材料:	1.品名;2.加工方法(粘合多层);3.加工程度(未经表面涂布或未浸渍)	4.规格(成卷的宽度或成张的边长)
48.08	成卷或成张的瓦楞纸及纸板(不论是否与平面纸胶合)、皱纹纸及纸板、压纹纸及纸板、穿孔纸及纸板,但税目48.03的纸除外:	1.品名;2.用途(袋用等);3.种类(瓦楞纸、皱纹牛皮纸等)	4.规格(成卷的宽度或成张的边长)
48.09	复写纸、自印复写纸及其他拷贝或转印纸(包括涂布或浸渍的油印蜡纸或胶印版纸),不论是否印制,成卷或成张的:	1.品名;2.种类(复写纸、拷贝纸等);3.加工程度(涂布或浸渍)	4.规格(成卷的宽度或成张的边长)
48.10	成卷或成张矩形(包括正方形)的任何尺寸的单面或双面涂布高岭土或其他无机物质(不论是否加粘合剂)的纸及纸板,但未涂布其他涂料,不论是否染面、饰面或印花:	1.品名;2.用途(书写、印刷等);3.种类(牛皮纸、白板纸、双面、单面、亚光等);4.状态(成卷或张等);5.加工程度(单面或双面涂布高岭土或其他无机物质、漂白等)	6.规格(成卷的宽度或成张的边长、每平米克重、机械、化学或化学—机械法制得的纤维含量、层数)
48.11	成卷或成张矩形(包括正方形)的任何尺寸的经涂布、浸渍、覆面、染面、饰面或印花的纸、纸板、纤维素絮纸及纤维素纤维网纸,但税目48.03、48.09或48.10的货品除外:	1.品名;2.种类(焦油纸等);3.加工程度(涂布、浸渍、饰面、漂白等)	4.规格(成卷或成张、浸渍或涂布物质成分、每平米克重)
48.12	纸浆制的滤块、滤板及滤片:	1.品名;2.材质(纸浆制);3外观(块、板、片)	
48.13	卷烟纸,不论是否切成一定尺寸、成小本或管状:	1.品名(卷烟纸)	2.规格(如成小本或管状、宽度)
48.14	壁纸及类似品;窗用透明纸:	1.品名;2.用途;3.加工程度(用木粒或草粒、塑料、编结材料等饰面、涂面或盖面等)	
48.15	以纸或纸板为底制成的铺地制品,不论是否切成一定尺寸:	1.品名;2.用途;3.材质(以纸或纸板为底制成)	
48.16	复写纸、自印复写纸及其他拷贝或转印纸(不包括税目48.09的纸)、油印蜡纸或胶印版纸,不论是否盒装:	1.品名;2.品种(复写纸、热敏转印纸等)	
48.17	纸或纸板制的信封、封缄信片、素色明信片及通信卡片;纸或纸板制的盒子、袋子及夹子,内装各种纸制文具:	1.品名;2.材质(纸制)	

商品编码	商 品 描 述	申 报 要 素	
		商品名称	规格型号
48.18	卫生纸及类似纸、家庭或卫生用纤维素絮纸及纤维素纤维网纸，成卷宽度不超过36厘米或切成一定尺寸或形状的；纸浆、纸、纤维素絮纸或纤维素纤维网纸制的手帕、面巾、台布、餐巾、尿布、止血塞、床单及类似的家庭、卫生或医院用品、衣服及衣着附件：	1.品名；2.用途（家庭、卫生、医院用等）；3.材质（纸制）；4.种类（卫生纸、纸台布等）	5.规格（成卷的宽度或成张的边长）
48.19	纸、纸板、纤维素絮纸或纤维素纤维网纸制的箱、盒、匣、袋及其他包装容器；纸或纸板制的卷宗盒、信件盘及类似品，供办公室、商店及类似场所使用的：	1.品名；2.材质（纸制）；3.箱、盒、匣请注明是否瓦楞	4.规格（如为纸袋请注明底宽）
48.20	纸或纸板制的登记本、账本、笔记本、定货本、收据本、信笺本、记事本、日记本及类似品、练习本、吸墨纸本、活动封面（活页及非活页）、文件夹、卷宗皮、多联商业表格纸、页间夹有复写纸的本及其他文具用品；纸或纸板制的样品簿、粘贴簿及书籍封面：	1.品名（登记本、账本等）；2.材质（纸制）	
48.21	纸或纸板制的各种标签，不论是否印制：	1.品名；2.材质（纸制、纸板等）；3.加工程度（印制、非印制）	
48.22	纸浆、纸或纸板（不论是否穿孔或硬化）制的筒管、卷轴、纡子及类似品：	1.品名；2.用途（纺织纱线用等）；3.材质（纸制）	
48.23	切成一定尺寸或形状的其他纸、纸板、纤维素絮纸及纤维素纤维网纸；纸浆、纸、纸板、纤维素絮纸及纤维素纤维网纸制的其他物品：	1.品名；2.用途（已印制的自动记录器用等）；3.材质（纸制）	4.规格（切成一定尺寸或形状、边长、宽度）

第四十九章　书籍、报纸、印刷图画及其他印刷品；手稿、打字稿及设计图纸

【注解】

本章所称“印刷”，也包括用胶版复印机、油印机印制，在自动数据处理设备控制下打印绘制，压印、冲印、感光复印、热敏复印或打字。

商品编码	商 品 描 述	申 报 要 素	
		商品名称	规格型号
49.01	书籍、小册子、散页印刷品及类似印刷品，不论是否单张：	1.品名；2.种类（字典、百科全书等）；3.状态（成册、单张）	
49.02	报纸、杂志及期刊，不论有无插图或广告材料：	1.品名	2.出版周期（日刊、周刊等）
49.03	儿童图画书、绘画或涂色书：	1.品名；2.用途（儿童用）；3.种类（图画书、绘画或涂色书）	
49.04	乐谱原稿或印本，不论是否装订或印有插图：	1.品名；2.用途（乐谱）；3.种类（原稿或印本等）	
49.05	各种印刷的地图、水道图及类似图表，包括地图册、挂图、地形图及地球仪、天体仪：		
4905.1000	-地球仪、天体仪	品名（地球仪、天体仪）	
	-其他：	1.品名（地图册等）；2.状态（成册、非成册）	
49.06	手绘的建筑、工程、工业、商业、地形或类似用途的设计图纸原稿；手稿；用感光纸照相复印或用复写纸誊写的上述物品复制件：	品名（设计图纸原稿或手稿及其复印件）	

商品编码	商 品 描 述	申 报 要 素	
		商品名称	规格型号
49.07	在承认或将承认其面值的国家流通或新发行并且未经使用的邮票、印花税票及类似票证;印有邮票或印花税票的纸品;钞票;空白支票;股票、债券及类似所有权凭证:	品名(邮票、钞票等)	
49.08	转印贴花纸(移画印花法用图案纸):	1.品名;2.加工方法(釉转印等)	
49.09	印刷或有图画的明信片;印有个人问候、祝贺、通告的卡片,不论是否有图画、带信封或饰边:	1.品名;2.加工方法(印刷或有图画等)	
49.10	印刷的各种日历,包括日历芯:	品名(印刷的各种日历)	
49.11	其他印刷品、包括印刷的图片及照片:	1.品名;2.用途(有商业价值、无商业价值等)	

第十一类　纺织原料及纺织制品

【注解】

1. 加工方法：对纤维纱线产品仅指梳理工艺，既粗疏或精梳：对织物则指染整方法（漂白、练白）以及织造方法（机织物）。
2. 用途：仅指丝线是否用于零售或蚕茧是否适于缫丝。
3. 规格型号：丝线列明细度支数；织物列明幅宽；混纺产品列明丝含量。
4. 纱线的表示：70s/2 指由两支 70 英支的单纱捻制的股线。

第五十章　蚕丝

商品编码	商品描述	申报要素	
		商品名称	规格型号
50.01	适于缫丝的蚕茧：	1. 品名；2. 包装（非供零售用）	
50.02	生丝（未加捻）：	1. 品名；2. 种类（厂丝、土丝、桑蚕丝、柞蚕丝等）；3. 加工程度（未加捻）	
50.03	废丝（包括不适于缫丝的蚕茧、废纱及回收纤维）：	1. 品名；2. 加工程度（经梳理、未经梳理）	
50.04	丝纱线（绢纺纱线除外），非供零售用：	1. 品名；2. 包装（非供零售用）	
50.05	绢纺纱线，非供零售用：	1. 品名；2. 种类（绢纺纱线等）；3. 包装（非供零售用）	4. 成分含量
50.06	丝纱线及绢纺纱线，供零售用；蚕胶丝：	1. 品名；2. 种类（绢纺纱线、蚕胶丝、丝纱线、绸纱线）；3. 包装（供零售用）	4. 成分含量
50.07	丝或绢丝机织物：	1. 品名；2. 种类（绸丝、桑蚕丝、绢丝、柞蚕丝等）；3. 织造方法（机织物）；4. 染整方法（漂白、未漂白、色织）	5. 成分含量；6. 幅宽

第五十一章　羊毛、动物细毛或粗毛；马毛纱线及其机织物

【注解】

1. 加工方法：对纤维原料指梳理工艺，既粗疏或精梳及脱脂、处理；对织物则指梳理工艺（粗疏或精梳）以及织造方法（机织物）。
2. 用途：仅指纱线是否用于零售。
3. 品名：应具体列出产品行业名称、种类：如剪羊毛、碳化羊毛、脱脂羊毛、兔毛、动物细毛还是粗毛马毛织物等。
4. 规格型号：丝线列明细度支数；织物列明幅宽；混纺产品列明成分含量，每平米重量（克/平方米）。

商品编码	商品描述	申报要素	
		商品名称	规格型号
51.01	未梳的羊毛：	1. 品名（灰褪毛、边坎毛、羔毛等）；2. 加工程度（未脱脂、脱脂、炭化等）	3. 剪羊毛请注明细度（微米数）；4. 剪羊毛请注明长度；5. 剪羊毛请注明草杂含量
51.02	未梳的动物细毛或粗毛：	1. 品名；2. 种类（未梳理的兔毛、喀什米尔山羊毛、山羊绒、骆驼毛等）	3. 其他山羊绒请注明颜色；4. 其他山羊绒请注明纤维长度；5. 其他山羊绒请注明含绒率
51.03	羊毛或动物细毛或粗毛的废料，包括废纱线，但不包括回收纤维：	1. 品名；2. 种类（羊毛落毛、动物细毛或粗毛废料）；3. 野生请注明	
51.04	羊毛及动物细毛或粗毛的回收纤维：	1. 品名；2. 种类（源于羊毛、动物粗、细毛等的回收纤维）；3. 野生请注明	
51.05	已梳的羊毛及动物细毛或粗毛（包括精梳片毛）：	1. 品名；2. 种类（羊毛条、羊毛片毛、兔毛、喀什米尔山羊毛）；3. 梳理方法（粗梳或精梳）；4. 野生请注明	5. 其他精梳羊毛请注明支数；6. 其他精梳羊毛请注明细度
51.06	粗梳羊毛纱线，非供零售用：	1. 品名；2. 包装（非供零售用）	3. 成分含量
51.07	精梳羊毛纱线，非供零售用：	1. 品名；2. 梳理方法（精梳羊毛纱线）；3. 包装（非供零售用）	4. 成分含量
51.08	动物细毛（粗梳或精梳）纱线，非供零售用：	1. 品名；2. 种类（驼马毛、羊驼毛等）；3. 梳理方法（粗梳或精梳）；4. 包装（非供零售用）	

商品编码	商 品 描 述	申 报 要 素	
		商品名称	规格型号
51.09	羊毛或动物细毛的纱线,供零售用:	1.品名;2.种类(羊毛等);3.包装(供零售用)	4.成分含量
51.10	动物粗毛或马毛的纱线(包括马毛粗松螺旋花线),不论是否供零售用:	1.品名;2.种类(马毛等粗毛纱线)	3.成分含量
51.11	粗梳羊毛或粗梳动物细毛的机织物:	1.品名;2.种类(羊毛、驼马毛、北洲驼等);3.织造方法(机织);4.梳理方法(粗梳);5.提花、装饰家具布要注明	6.成分含量;7.幅宽;8.每平米克重
51.12	精梳羊毛或精梳动物细毛的机织物:	1.品名;2.种类(羊毛、驼马毛、北洲驼等);3.织造方法(机织);4.梳理方法(精梳);5.提花、装饰家具布要注明	6.成分含量;7.幅宽;8.每平米克重
51.13	动物粗毛或马毛的机织物:	1.品名;2.种类(马毛等);3.织造方法(机织)	4.成分含量;5.幅宽;6.每平米克重

备注或申报要求

51. 01　　未梳的羊毛:　签约日期

51. 05　　已梳的羊毛及动物细毛或粗毛（包括精梳片毛）:　签约日期

第五十二章　棉花

【注解】

1.纱线细度的换算:1特=1000/公支=0.1111xD=590.5/英支。

2.截面或表观宽度:截面宽度一般指圆形或类似形状单丝,表观宽度一般指扁形单丝。

商品编码	商 品 描 述	申 报 要 素	
		商品名称	规格型号
52.01	未梳的棉花:	1.品名;2.加工程度(未梳理)	3.纤维长度;4.等级
52.02	废棉(包括废棉纱线及回收纤维):	1.品名;2.来源(废棉线、回收纤维等)	3.成分含量;4.废棉纱线请注明长度;5.废棉纱线请注明等级;6.颜色
52.03	已梳的棉花:	1.品名;2.加工程度(已梳)	3.纤维长度
52.04	棉制缝纫线,不论是否供零售用:	1.品名(棉制缝纫线);2.包装(是否供零售用)	3.成分含量;4.纱线细度
52.05	棉纱线(缝纫线除外),按重量计含棉量在85%及以上,非供零售用:	1.品名;2.梳理方法(粗梳、精梳、气流纺);3.纱线形态(单纱、股线或缆线);4.包装(非供零售用)	5.成分含量;6.纱线细度
52.06	棉纱线(缝纫线除外),按重量计含棉量在85%以下,非供零售用:	1.品名;2.梳理方法(粗梳、精梳、气流纺);3.纱线形态(单纱、股线或缆线);4.包装(非供零售用)	5.成分含量;6.纱线细度
52.07	棉纱线(缝纫线除外),供零售用:	1.品名;2.包装(供零售用)	3.成分含量
52.08	棉机织物,按重量计含棉量在85%及以上,每平方米重量不超过200克:	1.品名;2.织造方法(机织物);3.染整方法(漂白、未漂白、色织、染色、印花等);4.组织结构(平纹、斜纹等)	5.成分含量;6.幅宽;7.每平米克重
52.09	棉机织物,按重量计含棉量在85%及以上,每平方米重量超过200克:	1.品名;2.织造方法(机织物);3.染整方法(漂白、未漂白、色织、染色、印花等);4.组织结构(平纹、斜纹等)	5.成分含量;6.幅宽;7.每平米克重
52.10	棉机织物,按重量计含棉量在85%以下,主要或仅与化学纤维混纺,每平方米重量不超过200克:	1.品名;2.织造方法(机织物);3.染整方法(漂白、未漂白、色织、染色、印花等);4.组织结构(平纹、斜纹等);5.注明与其混纺的化纤是长丝还是短纤	6.成分含量;7.幅宽;8.每平米克重
52.11	棉机织物,按重量计含棉量在85%以下,主要或仅与化学纤维混纺,每平方米重量超过200克:	1.品名;2.织造方法(机织物);3.染整方法(漂白、未漂白、色织、染色、印花等);4.组织结构(平纹、斜纹等)	5.成分含量;6.幅宽;7.每平米克重
52.12	其他棉机织物:	1.品名;2.织造方法(机织物);3.染整方法(漂白、未漂白、色织、染色、印花等);4.组织结构(平纹、斜纹等)	5.成分含量;6.幅宽;7.每平米克重

备注或申报要求

52. 02　　废棉（包括废棉纱线及回收纤维）:　签约日期

第五十三章　其他植物纺织纤维；纸纱线及其机织物

【注解】

1. 韧皮纤维种类与来源：亚麻、大麻、黄麻、洋麻、菽麻、西沙尔麻、海地大麻、美洲龙舌兰纤维、椰壳纤维。
2. 亚麻等韧皮纤维的一般加工过程：生麻—沤制麻—打成麻—棉花麻纤维—秸梳。

商品编码	商品描述	申报要素	
		商品名称	规格型号
53.01	亚麻，生的或经加工但未纺制的；亚麻短纤及废麻（包括废麻纱线及回收纤维）：	1.品名；2.加工程度（生的、经沤制、破开或打成秸梳、回收等）；3.短纤或废麻应注明	
53.02	大麻，生的或经加工但未纺制的；大麻短纤及废麻（包括废麻纱线及回收纤维）：	1.品名；2.加工程度（生的、沤制的）；3.短纤或废麻应注明	
53.03	黄麻及其他纺织用韧皮纤维（不包括亚麻、大麻及苎麻），生的或经加工但未纺制的；上述纤维的短纤及废麻（包括废纱线及回收纤维）：	1.品名；2.种类（黄麻、洋麻、菽麻等）；3.加工程度（未纺制的、生或沤制的）；4.短纤或废麻应注明	
53.05	椰壳纤维、蕉麻（马尼拉麻）、苎麻及其他税目未列名的纺织用植物纤维，生的或经加工但未纺制的；上述纤维的短纤、落麻及废料（包括废纱线及回收纤维）：	1.品名；2.种类（椰壳纤维、蕉麻、苎麻等）；3.加工程度（生的或经加工但未纺制的）；4.短纤或废麻应注明	5.其他椰壳纤维请注明纤维长度、杂质含量、水分
53.06	亚麻纱线：	1.品名；2.纱线形态（单纱、股线或缆线）	
53.07	黄麻纱线或税目53.03的其他纺织用韧皮纤维纱线：	1.品名；2.种类（黄麻、洋麻、菽麻等）；3.纱线形态（单纱、股线或缆线）	
53.08	其他植物纺织纤维纱线；纸纱线：	1.品名；2.种类（椰壳纤维纱线、大麻纱线、苎麻纱线、纸纱线等）；3.染整方法（漂白、未漂白、色织）；	4.成分含量
53.09	亚麻机织物：	1.品名；2.织造方法（机织）；3.染整方法（漂白、未漂白、色织）	4.成分含量；5.幅宽；6.克重
53.10	黄麻或税目53.03的其他纺织用韧皮纤维机织物：	1.品名；2.种类（黄麻、洋麻、菽麻等）；3.织造方法（机织）；4.染整工艺（漂白、未漂白、色织）	5.成分含量；6.幅宽
53.11	其他纺织用植物纤维机织物；纸纱线机织物：	1.品名；2.种类（黄麻、洋麻、菽麻等）；3.织造方法（机织）；4.染整方法（漂白、未漂白、色织）	5.成分含量；6.幅宽

第五十四章　化学纤维长丝

商品编码	商品描述	申报要素	
		商品名称	规格型号
54.01	化学纤维长丝纺制的缝纫线，不论是否供零售用：	1.品名（长丝缝纫线）	2.包装（是否供零售用）；3.纤维成分（聚酯等）
54.02	合成纤维长丝纱线（缝纫线除外），非供零售用，包括细度在67分特以下的合成纤维单丝：	1.品名；2.种类（高强力纱或变形纱线等）；3.纱线形态（单纱、股线或缆线）；4.差别化纤维请注明；5.高强纱请注明用途	6.包装（非供零售用）；7.纤维成分（聚酯等）；8.纱线细度；9.纱线捻度
54.03	人造纤维长丝纱线（缝纫线除外），非供零售用，包括细度在67分特以下的人造纤维单丝：	1.品名；2.种类（高强力纱或变形纱线等）；3.纱线形态（单纱、股线或缆线）	4.包装（非供零售用）；5.纤维成分（如粘胶等）；6.纱线细度；7.纱线捻度
54.04	截面尺寸不超过1毫米，细度在67分特及以上的合成纤维单丝；表观宽度不超过5毫米的合成纤维纺织材料制扁条及类似品（例如，人造草）：	1.品名；2.种类（单丝、扁条等）	3.纤维成分；4.单丝细度或扁条表观宽度

商品编码	商 品 描 述	申 报 要 素	
		商品名称	规格型号
54.05	**截面尺寸不超过1毫米,细度在67分特及以上的人造纤维单丝:表观宽度不超过5毫米的人造纤维纺织材料制扁条及类似品(例如,人造草):**	1.品名;2.种类(单丝、扁条等)	3.纤维成分;4.单丝细度或扁条表观宽度
54.06	**化学纤维长丝纱线(缝纫线除外),供零售用:**	1.品名;2.包装(供零售用)	3.纤维成分
54.07	**合成纤维长丝纱线的机织物,包括税目54.04所列材料的机织物:**	1.品名;2.织造方法(机织、平行纱层迭粘合);3.染整方法(漂白、色织、染色等);4.组织结构(平纹、斜纹、缎纹等);5.变形纱线、打字机带用要注明	6.成分含量;7.幅宽;8.克重;9.残次布请注明
54.08	**人造纤维长丝纱线的机织物,包括税目54.05所列材料的机织物:**	1.品名;2.织造方法(机织、平行纱层迭粘合);3.染整方法(漂白、色织、染色等);4.组织结构(平纹、斜纹、缎纹等)	5.成分含量;6.幅宽

备注或申报要求

54. 02　　合成纤维长丝纱线(缝纫线除外),非供零售用,包括细度在67分特以下的合成纤维单丝: 签约日期

第五十五章　化学纤维短纤

【注解】

混纺纱线织物的归类原理:

1.按制成该物品的纤维品种、性质先归入相对应的章。

2.按该物品所属的加工程度归入该章的前、中或后的商品编码中。

3.由两种或两种以上的纺织材料混合制成的物品,应按重量比例最大的那种材料归类,当没有一种纺织材料的重量比例较大时,应按可归入有关商品编码中最后一个商品编码所列的纺织材料归类。

商品编码	商 品 描 述	申 报 要 素	
		商品名称	规格型号
55.01	**合成纤维长丝丝束:**	1.品名	2.纤维成分;3.单丝细度;4.丝束长度;5.丝束捻度
55.02	**人造纤维长丝丝束:**	1.品名	2.纤维成分;3.单丝细度;4.丝束长度;5.丝束捻度
55.03	**合成纤维短纤,未梳或未经其他纺前加工:**	1.品名;2.加工程度(未梳、未经纺前加工)	3.纤维成分;4.长度;5.细度;6.聚酯短纤请注明颜色
55.04	**人造纤维短纤,未梳或未经其他纺前加工:**	1.品名;2.加工程度(未梳、未经纺前加工);3.天丝、莫代尔纤维请注明	4.纤维成分;5.细度;6.长度
55.05	**化学纤维废料(包括落绵、废纱及回收纤维):**	1.品名;2.来源(落绵、废纱、回收纤维)	3.纤维成分;4.颜色(白色、杂色等)
55.06	**合成纤维短纤,已梳或经其他纺前加工:**	1.品名;2.加工程度(已梳、经纺前加工)	3.纤维成分
55.07	**人造纤维短纤,已梳或经其他纺前加工:**	1.品名;2.加工程度(已梳、经纺前加工)	3.纤维成分
55.08	**化学纤维短纤纺制的缝纫线,不论是否供零售用:**	1.品名(短纤缝纫线)	2.成分含量;3.纱线细度
55.09	**合成纤维短纤纺制的纱线(缝纫线除外),非供零售用:**	1.品名;2.种类(单纱、股线、缆线);3.包装(非供零售用)	4.成分含量;5.纱线细度
55.10	**人造纤维短纤纺制的纱线(缝纫线除外),非供零售用:**	1.品名;2.种类(单纱、股线、缆线);3.包装(非供零售用)	4.成分含量;5.纱线细度
55.11	**化学纤维短纤纺制的纱线(缝纫线除外),供零售用:**	1.品名;2.种类(单纱、股线、缆线);3.包装(非供零售用)	4.成分含量;5.纱线细度

商品编码	商品描述	申报要素	
		商品名称	规格型号
55.12	**合成纤维短纤纺制的机织物，按重量计合成纤维短纤含量在85%及以上：**	1.品名;2.织造方法(机织);3.染整方法(漂白、未漂白、色织、染色等);4.组织结构(平纹、斜纹、缎纹等)	5.成分含量;6.幅宽
55.13	**合成纤维短纤纺制的机织物，按重量计合成纤维短纤含量在85%以下，主要或仅与棉混纺，每平方米重量不超过170克：**	1.品名;2.种类(单纱、股线、缆线);3.织造方法(机织);4.染整方法(漂白、未漂白、色织、染色等);5.组织结构(平纹、斜纹、缎纹等)	6.成分含量;7.幅宽;8.每平方米克重
	-未漂白或漂白：		
	--聚酯短纤纺制的三线或四线斜纹机织物，包括双面斜纹机织物：	1.品名;2.织造方法(机织);3.染整方法(漂白、未漂白、色织、染色等);4.组织结构(平纹、斜纹、缎纹等);5.帆布、印染用布要注明	6.成分含量;7.幅宽;8.每平方米克重
55.14	**合成纤维短纤纺制的机织物，按重量计合成纤维短纤含量在85%以下，主要或仅与棉混纺，每平方米重量超过170克：**	1.品名;2.织造方法(机织);3.染整方法(漂白、未漂白、色织、染色等);4.组织结构(平纹、斜纹、缎纹等)	5.成分含量;6.幅宽;7.每平方米克重
55.15	**合成纤维短纤纺制的其他机织物：**	1.品名;2.织造方法(机织);3.染整方法(漂白、未漂白、色织、染色等);4.组织结构(平纹、斜纹、缎纹等);5.帆布、印染用布要注明	6.成分含量;7.幅宽;8.每平方米克重
55.16	**人造纤维短纤纺制的机织物：**	1.品名;2.织造方法(机织);3.染整方法(漂白、未漂白、色织、染色等);4.组织结构(平纹、斜纹、缎纹等);5.帆布、印染用布要注明	6.成分含量;7.幅宽;8.每平方米克重

备注或申报要求

55. 03　合成纤维短纤，未梳或未经其他纺前加工：　6. 请注明签约日期

第五十六章　絮胎、毡呢及无纺织物;特种纱线;线、绳、索、缆及其制品

【注解】

1. 无纺织物与普通絮胎的主要区别:无纺织物一般按照整张网或薄片的厚度和宽度将纤维或长丝粘合起来。
2. 无纺织物与纸、纸板的主要区别:无纺织物的纤维一般在生产过程中未被融化掉。

商品编码	商品描述	申报要素	
		商品名称	规格型号
56.01	**纺织材料絮胎及其制品;长度不超过5毫米的纺织纤维(纤维屑)、纤维粉末及球结：**	1.品名	2.纤维成分(如棉制)
5601.3000	-纤维屑、纤维粉末及球结	1.品名;2.状态(纤维屑、球结)	
56.02	**毡呢，不论是否浸渍、涂布、包覆或层压：**	1.品名;2.加工方法(针刺缝编、涂布、浸渍、层压、包覆等)	3.纤维成分含量
56.03	**无纺织物，不论是否浸渍、涂布、包覆或层压：**	1.品名;2.加工方法(涂布、浸渍、层压、包覆等);3.化学纤维长丝制应注明	4.每平方米克重
56.04	**用纺织材料包覆的橡胶线及绳;用橡胶或塑料浸渍、涂布、包覆或套裹的纺织纱线及税目54.04或54.05的扁条及类似品：**	1.品名;2.加工方法(浸渍、涂布或包覆等);3.内层材质(高强力纱应注明);4.外层材质	
56.05	**含金属纱线，不论是否螺旋花线，由纺织纱线或税目54.04或54.05的扁条及类似品与金属线、扁条或粉末混合制得或用金属包覆制得：**	1.品名;2.含金属纱线	
56.06	**粗松螺旋花线，税目54.04或54.05的扁条及类似品制的螺旋花线(税目56.05的货品及马毛粗松螺旋花线除外);绳绒线(包括植绒绳绒线);纵行起圈纱线：**	1.品名;2.种类(绳绒及粗松花线、纵行起圈花线等)	

商品编码	商 品 描 述	申 报 要 素	
		商品名称	规格型号
56.07	线、绳、索、缆,不论是否编织或编结而成,也不论是否用橡胶或塑料浸渍、涂布、包覆或套裹:	1.品名;2.用途(包扎用等)	3.纤维成分
56.08	线、绳或索结制的网料;纺织材料制成的渔网及其他网:	1.品名;2.用途(渔网、购物网等);3.成网方式(结制)	4.纤维成分
56.09	用纱线、税目54.04或54.05的扁条及类似品或线、绳、索、缆制成的其他税目未列名物品:	品名	

第五十七章　地毯及纺织材料的其他铺地制品

商品编码	商 品 描 述	申 报 要 素	
		商品名称	规格型号
57.01	结织栽绒地毯及纺织材料的其他结织栽绒铺地制品,不论是否制成的:	1.品名;2.用途(地毯);3.织造方法(栽绒、手织等);4.铺地制品请注明	5.纤维成分
57.02	机织地毯及纺织材料的其他机织铺地制品,未簇绒或未植绒,不论是否制成的,包括"开来姆"、"苏麦克"、"卡拉马尼"及类似的手织地毯:	1.品名;2.用途(地毯);3.织造方法(机织、手织等);	4.纤维成分
57.03	簇绒地毯及纺织材料的其他簇绒铺地制品,不论是否制成的:	1.品名;2.用途(地毯);3.织造方法(簇绒);4.铺地制品要注明	5.纤维成分
57.04	毡呢地毯及纺织材料的其他毡呢铺地制品,未簇绒或未植绒,不论是否制成的:	1.品名;2.用途(地毯);3.织造方法(毡呢);4.铺地制品要注明	5.纤维成分;6.最大表面面积
57.05	其他地毯及纺织材料的其他铺地制品,不论是否制成的:	1.品名;2.用途(地毯);3.铺地制品要注明	4.纤维成分

第五十八章　特种机织物;簇绒织物;花边;装饰毯;装饰带;刺绣品

【注解】

被褥状纺织制品:一般指一层胎料缝合一层织物或两层织物夹一层胎料,但缝合主要起绗缝的特征,图案不构成刺绣品的特征。

商品编码	商 品 描 述	申 报 要 素	
		商品名称	规格型号
58.01	起绒机织物及绳绒织物,但税目58.02或58.06的织物除外:	1.品名;2.织造方法(机织);3.起绒方式(经起绒、纬起绒或绳绒);4.割绒要注明	5.幅宽;6.纤维成分
58.02	毛巾织物及类似的毛圈机织物,但税目58.06的狭幅织物除外;簇绒织物,但税目57.03的产品除外:	1.品名;2.织造方法(机织);3.起绒方式(簇绒或毛圈);4.漂白要注明	5.幅宽;6.纤维成分
58.03	纱罗,但税目58.06的狭幅织物除外:	1.品名;2.组织结构(纱罗)	3.幅宽;4.纤维成分
58.04	网眼薄纱及其他网眼织物,但不包括机织物、针织物或钩编织物;成卷、成条或成小块图案的花边,但税目60.02的织物除外:	1.品名;2.种类(网眼、花边);3.织造方法(机织)	4.幅宽;5.纤维成分
58.05	"哥白林"、"弗朗德"、"奥步生"、"波威"及类似式样的手织装饰毯,以及手工针绣嵌花装饰毯(例如,小针脚或十字绣),不论是否制成的:	1.品名;2.用途(装饰用);3.种类(手工针绣嵌花装饰毯等);4.织造方法(机织)	5.幅宽;6.纤维成分
58.06	狭幅机织物,但税目58.07的货品除外;用粘合剂粘合制成的有经纱而无纬纱的狭幅织物(包扎匹头用带):		
	-起绒机织物(包括毛巾织物及类似的毛圈织物)及绳绒织物:	1.品名;2.织造方法(机织);3.起绒方式(毛巾、绳绒等)	4.成分含量;5.幅宽

商品编码	商 品 描 述	申 报 要 素	
		商品名称	规格型号
5806.2000	-按重量计弹性纱线或橡胶线含量在5%及以上的其他机织物	1.品名;2.织造方法(机织)	3.成分含量;4.幅宽
	-其他机枳物	1.品名;2.织造方法(机织)	3.成分含量;4.幅宽
	-用粘合剂粘合制成的有经纱而无纬纱的织物(包扎匹头用带):	1.品名;2.织造方法	3.成分含量;4.幅宽
58.07	**非绣制的纺织材料制标签、徽章及类似品,成匹、成条或裁成一定形状或尺寸:**	1.品名;2.织造方法(机织、针织等)	3.成分含量;4.幅宽
58.08	**成匹的编带;非绣制的成匹装饰带,但针织或钩编的除外;流苏、绒球及类似品:**	1.品名	2.规格(成匹);3.幅宽
58.09	**其他税目未列名的金属线机织物及税目56.05所列含金属纱线的机织物,用于衣着、装饰及类似用途:**	1.品名;2.用途(衣着、装饰等);3.织造方法(金属线或含金属纱线机织)	4.幅宽
58.10	**成匹、成条或成小块图案的刺绣品:**	1.品名;2.织造方法(刺绣);3.请注明是否见底布	4.成分含量
58.11	**用一层或几层纺织材料与胎料经绗缝或其他方法组合制成的被褥状纺织品,但税目58.10的刺绣品除外:**	1.品名	2.成分含量

第五十九章　浸渍、涂布、包覆或层压的纺织物;工业用纺织制品

商品编码	商 品 描 述	申 报 要 素	
		商品名称	规格型号
59.01	**用胶或淀粉物质涂布的纺织物,作书籍封面及类似用途的;描图布;制成的油画布;作帽里的硬衬布及类似硬挺纺织物:**	1.品名;2.用途;3.处理工艺及材质(涂布、浸渍、层压)	4.成分含量
59.02	**尼龙或其他聚酰胺、聚酯或粘胶纤维高强力纱制的帘子布:**	1.品名	2.成分含量
59.03	**用塑料浸渍、涂布、包覆或层压的纺织物,但税目59.02的货品除外:**	1.品名;2.处理方法(涂布、浸渍、层压等);3.塑料种类	4.成分含量
59.04	列诺伦(亚麻油地毡),不论是否剪切成形;以织物为底布经涂布或覆面的铺地制品,不论是否剪切成形:	1.品名	
59.05	**糊墙织物:**	1.品名;2.用途(糊墙用);3.纸衬背要注明	4.幅宽;5.表面层纤维成分含量
59.06	**用橡胶处理的纺织物,但税目59.02的货品除外:**	1.品名;2.织造方法(机织、针织、钩编等);3.处理材料(橡胶);4.胶粘带、绝缘带应注明	5.幅宽
59.07	**用其他材料浸渍、涂布或包覆的纺织物;作舞台、摄影布景或类似用途的已绘制画布:**	1.品名;2.用途;3.处理材料;4.绝缘带应注明	
59.08	**用纺织材料机织、编结或针织而成的灯芯、炉芯、打火机芯、烛芯或类似品;煤气灯纱筒及纱罩,不论是否浸渍:**	1.品名;2.用途	
59.09	**纺织材料制的水龙软管及类似的管子,不论有无其他材料作衬里、护套或附件:**	1.品名	2.纤维成分
59.10	**纺织材料制的传动带或输送带及带料,不论是否用塑料浸渍、涂布、包覆或层压,也不论是否用金属或其他材料加强:**	1.品名	2.纤维成分;3.厚度;4.宽度
59.11	**本章注释七所规定的作专门技术用途的纺织产品及制品:**	1.品名;2.用途;3.外观形状	

第六十章 针织物及钩编织物

商品编码	商品描述	申报要素	
		商品名称	规格型号
60.01	针织或钩编的起绒织物,包括"毛绒"织物及毛圈织物:	1.品名;2.织造方法(针织或钩编);3.起绒方法(毛圈或长毛绒);	4.幅宽;5.纤维成分含量
60.02	宽度不超过30厘米,按重量计弹性纱线或橡胶线含量在5%及以上的针织物或钩编织物,但税目60.01的货品除外:	1.品名;2.织造方法(针织或钩编)	3.成分含量;4.幅宽
60.03	宽度不超过30厘米的针织物或钩编织物,但税目60.01或60.02的货品除外:	1.品名;2.织造方法(针织或钩编)	3.成分含量;4.幅宽
60.04	宽度超过30厘米,按重量计弹性纱线或橡胶线含量在5%及以上的针织物或钩编织物,但税目60.01的货品除外:	1.品名;2.织造方法(针织或钩编)	3.成分含量;4.幅宽
60.05	经编针织物(包括由花边针织机织成的),但税目60.01至60.04的货品除外:	1.品名;2.织造方法(针织、经编);3.染整方法(色织、染色、漂白等)	4.成分含量;5.幅宽
60.06	其他针织物或钩编织物:	1.品名;2.织造方法(针织或钩编);3.染整方法(色织,染色、漂白等)	4.成分含量;5.幅宽

第六十一章 针织或钩编的服装及衣着附件

商品编码	商品描述	申报要素	
		商品名称	规格型号
61.01	针织或钩编的男式大衣、短大衣、斗篷、短斗篷、带风帽的防寒短上衣(包括滑雪短上衣)、防风衣、防风短上衣及类似品,但税目61.03的货品除外:	1.品名;2.织造方法(针织或钩编);3.款式(防风大衣、短大衣、斗篷等);4.类别(男式)	5.成分含量
61.02	针织或钩编的女式大衣、短大衣、斗篷、短斗篷、带风帽的防寒短上衣(包括滑雪短上衣)、防风衣、防风短上衣及类似品,但税目61.04的货品除外:	1.品名;2.织造方法(针织或钩编);3.款式(防风大衣、短大衣、斗篷等);4.类别(女式)	5.成分含量
61.03	针织或钩编的男式西服套装、便服套装、上衣、长裤、护胸背带工装裤、马裤及短裤(游泳裤除外):	1.品名;2.织造方法(针织或钩编);3.款式(西服、便服套装,上衣、长裤、马裤、工装裤等);4.类别(男式)	5.成分含量
61.04	针织或钩编的女式西服套装、便服套装、上衣、连衣裙、裙子、裙裤、长裤、护胸背带工装裤、马裤及短裤(游泳服除外):	1.品名;2.织造方法(针织或钩编);3.款式(西服、便服套装,上衣、长裤、马裤、工装裤等);4.类别(女式)	5.成分含量
61.05	针织或钩编的男衬衫:	1.品名;2.织造方法(针织或钩编);3.款式(衬衫);4.类别(男式)	5.成分含量
61.06	针织或钩编的女衬衫:	1.品名;2.织造方法(针织或钩编);3.款式(衬衫);4.类别(女式)	5.成分含量
61.07	针织或钩编的男式内裤、三角裤、长睡衣、睡衣裤、浴衣、晨衣及类似品:	1.品名;2.织造方法(针织或钩编);3.款式(内衣、内裤等);4.类别(男式)	5.成分含量
61.08	针织或钩编的女式长衬裙、衬裙、三角裤、短衬裤、睡衣、睡衣裤、浴衣、晨衣及类似品:	1.品名;2.织造方法(针织或钩编);3.款式(内衣、内裤等);4.类别(女式)	5.成分含量
61.09	针织或钩编的T恤衫、汗衫及其他背心:	1.品名;2.织造方法(针织或钩编);3.款式(T恤衫、汗衫等);4.类别(男式、女式)	5.成分含量

商品编码	商 品 描 述	申 报 要 素	
		商品名称	规格型号
61.10	针织或钩编的套头衫、开襟衫、外穿背心及类似品：	1.品名;2.织造方法(针织、钩编,是否为起绒);3.款式(套头衫、开襟衫、背心等);4.类别(男式、女式);5.手工要注明	6.成分含量
61.11	针织或钩编的婴儿服装及衣着附件：	1.品名;2.织造方法(针织或钩编);3.款式(外衣、雨衣等);4.类别(婴儿)	5.成分含量
61.12	针织或钩编的运动服、滑雪服及游泳服：	1.品名;2.织造方法(针织或钩编);3.款式(运动套装、运动装、滑雪服、游泳服);4.类别(男式、女式)	5.成分含量
61.13	用税目59.03、59.06或59.07的针织物或钩编织物制成的服装：	1.品名;2.织造方法(针织或钩编);3.款式(上衣、长裤、短裤等);4.类别(男式、女式);5.处理材料(塑料、橡胶)	6.成分含量
61.14	针织或钩编的其他服装：	1.品名;2.织造方法(针织或钩编);3.款式(连身衣、夏服、水洗服、无袖罩衫等);4.类别(男式、女式、儿童)	5.成分含量
61.15	针织或钩编的连裤袜、紧身裤袜、长统袜、短袜及其他袜类,包括渐紧压袜类(例如用以治疗静脉曲张的长统袜)和无外绱鞋底的鞋类：	1.品名;2.织造方法(针织或钩编);3.款式(连裤袜、统袜、矫正袜);4.类别(男式、女式);5.女士统袜请注明	6.成分含量;7.单丝细度
61.16	针织或钩编的分指手套、连指手套及露指手套：	1.品名;2.织造方法(针织或钩编);3.有处理材料的请注明(塑料、橡胶);4.运动手套请注明	5.成分含量
61.17	其他制成的针织或钩编的衣着附件;服装或衣着附件的针织或钩编的零件：	1.品名;2.织造方法(针织或钩编)	3.成分含量

第六十二章 非针织或非钩编的服装及衣着附件

【注解】

1.本章基本上为非针织非钩编织物,如机织、无纺等,但6212.与6217,除外。

2.本章衬衣及仿男式女衬衣指:人体上身穿着并从领口处全开襟或半开襟的长袖或短袖衣服;罩衫也是上半身穿的,但可以无袖,领口处也可以不开襟。

商品编码	商 品 描 述	申 报 要 素	
		商品名称	规格型号
62.01	男式大衣、短大衣、斗篷、短斗篷、带风帽的防寒短上衣(包括滑雪短上衣)、防风衣、防风短上衣及类似品,但税目62.03的货品除外：	1.品名;2.织造方法(机织等);3.款式(防风大衣、短大衣、斗篷等);4.类别(男式)	5.成分含量
62.02	女式大衣、短大衣、斗篷、短斗篷、带风帽的防寒短上衣(包括滑雪短上衣)、防风衣、防风短上衣及类似品,但税目62.04的货品除外：	1.品名;2.织造方法(机织等);3.款式(防风大衣、短大衣、斗篷等);4.类别(女式)	5.成分含量
62.03	男式西服套装、便服套装、上衣、长裤、护胸背带工装裤、马裤及短裤(游泳裤除外)：	1.品名;2.织造方法(机织等);3.款式(西服、便服套装,上衣、长裤、马裤、工装裤等);4.类别(男式)	5.成分含量
62.04	女式西服套装、便服套装、上衣、连衣裙、裙子、裙裤、长裤、护胸背带工装裤、马裤及短裤(游泳服除外)：	1.品名;2.织造方法(机织等);3.款式(西服、便服套装、上衣、长裤、马裤、工装裤等);4.类别(女式)	5.成分含量
62.05	男衬衫：	1.品名;2.织造方法(机织等);3.款式(衬衫);4.类别(男式)	5.成分含量
62.06	女衬衫：	1.品名;2.织造方法(机织等);3.款式(衬衫);4.类别(女式)	5.成分含量
62.07	男式背心及其他内衣、内裤、三角裤、长睡衣、睡衣裤、浴衣、晨衣及类似品：	1.品名;2.织造方法(机织等);3.款式(内衣、内裤等);4.类别(男式)	5.成分含量
62.08	女式背心及其他内衣、长衬裙、衬裙、三角裤、短衬裤、睡衣、睡衣裤、浴衣、晨衣及类似品：	1.品名;2.织造方法(机织等);3.款式(内衣、内裤等);4.类别(女式)	5.成分含量

商品编码	商 品 描 述	申 报 要 素	
		商品名称	规格型号
62.09	婴儿服装及衣着附件:	1.品名;2.织造方法(机织等);3.款式(外衣、雨衣等);4.类别(婴儿)	5.成分含量
62.10	用税目56.02、56.03、59.03、59.06或59.07的织物制成的服装:	1.品名;2.织造方法(机织等);3.款式(上衣、长裤、短裤等);4.类别(男式、女式);5.处理材料(塑料、橡胶)	6.成分含量
62.11	运动服、滑雪服及游泳服;其他服装:	1.品名;2.织造方法(机织等);3.款式(连身衣、夏服、水洗服、无袖罩衫等);4.类别(男式、女式、儿童)	5.成分含量
62.12	胸罩、束腰带、紧身胸衣、吊裤带、吊袜带、束袜带和类似品及其零件,不论是否针织或钩编的:	1.品名;2.款式(胸罩、腹带、束腰胸衣、吊袜带、吊裤带等)	3.成分含量
62.13	手帕:	1.品名;2.织造方法(机织、刺绣、非刺绣)	3.成分含量;4.尺寸
62.14	披巾、领巾、围巾、披纱、面纱及类似品:	1.品名;2.织造方法(机织等)	3.成分含量
62.15	领带及领结:	1.品名;2.织造方法(机织等)	3.成分含量
62.16	分指手套、连指手套及露指手套:	1.品名;2.织造方法(机织等);3.浸渍(橡胶、塑料)请注明;4.运动手套请注明	5.成分含量
62.17	其他制成的衣着附件;服装或衣着附件的零件,但税目62.12的货品除外:	1.品名	2.成分含量

第六十三章 其他纺织制成品;成套物品;旧衣着及旧纺织品;碎织物

【注解】

6307其他制成品。如:经某些加工(如缝边、挖领口等)的针织物片,准备用于制衣,但还未加工成服装。6307还包括服装裁剪样,一般用硬帆布。(纸制服装裁样与纸制服装)。此外还包括:服装袋(轻便衣橱)、旗帜(含三角旗及横幅、)、卫生巾(5601物品除外)以及其他符合第十一类注释七"制成品"定义,但又不归入十一类其他品目的成段织物制品,如:门窗用的织物制挡风帘。

商品编码	商 品 描 述	申 报 要 素	
		商品名称	规格型号
63.01	毯子及旅行毯:	1.品名;2.种类(毯子、旅行毯、电暖毯)	3.成分含量
63.02	床上、餐桌、盥洗及厨房用的织物制品:	1.品名;2.用途(床上用品、餐桌用、盥洗用、厨房用);3.织造方法(针织、钩编、机织、手工、刺绣、毛圈等)	4.成分含量
63.03	窗帘(包括帷帘)及帐幔;帘帷或床帷:	1.品名;2.种类(窗帘、帘帷、帐幔、床帷);3.织造方法(针织、钩编、机织等)	4.成分含量
63.04	其他装饰用织物制品,但税目94.04的货品除外:	1.品名;2.用途(装饰用);3.织造方法(针织、钩编、机织、手工、刺绣等)	4.成分含量
63.05	货物包装用袋:	1.品名;2.种类(包装袋、周转袋);3.请注明新旧	4.成分含量
63.06	油苫布、天篷及遮阳篷;账篷;风帆;野营用品:	1.品名;2.种类(油苫布、天篷、遮阳篷、风帆、野营用品)	3.成分含量
63.07	其他制成品,包括服装裁剪样:	1.品名;2.用途(工厂用等);3.种类(擦光布、抹布、安全带、救生衣、标签等);4.棉制起绒或簇绒织物要注明	5.成分含量
63.08	由机织物及纱线构成的零售包装成套物品,不论是否带附件,用以制作小地毯、装饰毯、绣花台布、餐巾或类似的纺织物品:	1.品名	2.包装(零售包装)
63.09	旧衣物:	品名	
63.10	纺织材料的新的或旧的碎织物及废线、绳、索、缆及其制品:	1.品名;2.状态(是否经分拣)	

第十二类　鞋、帽、伞、杖、鞭及其零件；已加工的羽毛及其制品；人造花；人发制品

第六十四章　鞋靴、护腿和类似品及其零件

【注解】

税目6702不包括：玻璃制品；用陶器、石料、金属木料或其他材料经模铸、锻造、雕刻、冲压或其他方法整件制成形的人造花、叶、或果实；用捆扎、胶粘及类似办法以外的其他方法将部分品组合而成的上述制品。

商品编码	商品描述	申报要素	
		商品名称	规格型号
64.01	橡胶或塑料制外底及鞋面的防水鞋靴，其鞋面不是用缝、铆、钉、旋、塞或类似方法固定在鞋底上的：	1.品名；2.款式（高统、是否有金属防护头等）；3.鞋面材料；4.鞋底材料	
64.02	橡胶或塑料制外底及鞋面的其他鞋靴：	1.品名；2.款式（高统、是否有金属防护头等）；3.鞋面材料；4.鞋底材料	
64.03	橡胶、塑料、皮革或再生皮革制外底.皮革制鞋面的鞋靴：	1.品名；2.款式（高统、是否有金属防护头等）；3.鞋面材料；4.鞋底材料	
64.04	橡胶、塑料、皮革或再生皮革制外底，用纺织材料制鞋面的鞋靴：	1.品名；2.款式（高统等）；3.鞋面材料；4.鞋底材料	
64.05	其他鞋靴：	1.品名；2.款式；3.鞋面材料；4.鞋底材料	
64.06	鞋靴零件（包括鞋面，不论是否带有除外底以外的其他鞋底）；活动式鞋内底、跟垫及类似品；护腿、裹腿和类似品及其零件：	1.品名；2.材质；3.加工程度（是否已成型）	

第六十五章　帽类及其零件

商品编码	商品描述	申报要素	
		商品名称	规格型号
65.01	毡呢制的帽坯、帽身及帽兜，未楦制成形，也未加帽边；毡呢制的圆帽片及制帽用的毡呢筒（包括裁开的毡呢筒）：	1.品名；2.材质（毡呢）	
65.02	编结的帽坯或用任何材料的条带拼制而成的帽坯，未楦制成形，也未加帽边、衬里或装饰物：	1.品名；2.材质；3.制作工艺（编结、拼制）	
65.04	编结帽或用任何材料的条带拼制而成的帽类，不论有无衬里或装饰物：	1.品名；2.制作工艺（编结、拼制）	
65.05	针织或钩编的帽类，用成匹的花边、毡呢或其他纺织物（条带除外）制成的帽类，不论有无衬里或装饰物；任何材料制的发网，不论有无衬里或装饰物：	1.品名；2.制作工艺（针织、钩编、手工等）；3.婴儿用请注明	4.成分含量
65.06	其他帽类，不论有无衬里或装饰物：	1.品名；2.材质	
65.07	帽圈、帽衬、帽套、帽帮、帽骨架、帽舌及帽颏带：	1.品名；2.材质	

第六十六章　雨伞、阳伞、手杖、鞭子、马鞭及其零件

商品编码	商品描述	申报要素	
		商品名称	规格型号
66.01	雨伞及阳伞（包括手杖伞、庭园用伞及类似伞）：	1.品名；2.款式	
66.02	手杖、带座手杖、鞭子、马鞭及类似品：	品名	
66.03	税目66.01或66.02所列物品的零件及装饰品：	品名	

第六十七章　已加工羽毛、羽绒及其制品;人造化;人发制品

商品编码	商 品 描 述	申 报 要 素	
		商品名称	规格型号
67.01	**带羽毛或羽绒的鸟皮及鸟体其他部分、羽毛、部分羽毛、羽绒及其制品(税目05.05的货品和经加工的羽管及羽轴除外):**	1.品名;2.加工程度	
67.02	**人造花、叶、果实及其零件;用人造花、叶或果实制成的物品:**	1.品名;2.制作材料(塑料丝等)	
67.03	**经梳理、稀疏、脱色或其他方法加工的人发;作假发及类似品用的羊毛、其他动物毛或其他纺织材料:**	1.品名;2.加工程度(经梳理、脱色等);3.制作材料	
67.04	**人发、动物毛或纺织材料制的假发、假胡须、假眉毛、假睫毛及类似品;其他税目未列名的人发制品:**	1.品名;2.制作材料(人发、合成纤维等)	

第十三类　石料、石膏、水泥、石棉、云母及类似材料的制品；陶瓷产品；玻璃及其制品

第六十八章　石料、石膏、水泥、石棉、云母及类似材料的制品

商品编码	商品描述	申报要素	
		商品名称	规格型号
68.01	天然石料(不包括板岩)制的长方砌石、路缘石、扁平石:	1.品名;2.种类(长方砌石、扁平石、路缘石)	
68.02	已加工的碑石或建筑用石(不包括板岩)及其制品,但税目68.01的货品除外;天然石料(包括板岩)制的镶嵌石(马赛克)及类似品,不论是否有衬背;天然石料(包括板岩)制的人工染色石粒、石片及石粉:	1.品名;2.用途(用于建筑可直接使用);3.材质(大理石、花岗岩);4.加工程度(切、锯及抛光等);5.具有平面的建筑毛料(碑石或建筑用石),应注明加工方法(如简单锯、切、抛光等)	6.砖、瓦、方块及类似品应注明是否为矩形及最大表面积的边长
68.03	已加工的板岩及板岩或粘聚板岩的制品:	1.品名;2.加工程度	
68.04	未装支架的石磨、石碾、砂轮和类似品及其零件,用于研磨、磨刃、抛光、整形或切割,以及手用磨石、抛光石及其零件,用天然石料、粘聚的天然磨料、人造磨料或陶瓷制成,不论是否装有由其他材料制成的零件:	1.品名;2.用途(碾磨或磨浆、磨光用等);3.材质(石料、粘聚合成料等);4.未装支架请注明;5.手用磨请注明	
68.05	砂布、砂纸及以其他材料为底的类似品,不论是否裁切、缝合或用其他方法加工成形:	1.品名;2.基底材质	
68.06	矿渣棉、岩石棉及类似的矿质棉;页状蛭石、膨胀粘土、泡沫矿渣及类似的膨胀矿物材料;具有隔热、隔音或吸音性能的矿物材料的混合物及制品,但税目68.11、68.12或第六十九章的货品除外:	1.品名;2.材质(矿渣棉、岩石棉、页状蛭石、膨胀粘土、泡沫矿渣等);3.形状	4.含有石棉纤维的要注明其含量
68.07	沥青或类似原料(例如,石油沥青或煤焦油沥青)的制品:	1.品名;2.形状	
68.08	镶板、平板、瓦、砖及类似品,用水泥、石膏及其他矿物粘合材料粘合植物纤维、稻草、刨花、木片屑、木粉、锯末或木废料制成:	1.品名;2.种类(镶板、平板瓦、砖等);3.原料(稻草、刨花等);4.粘料(水泥、石膏等矿物性粘合材料)	
68.09	石膏制品及以石膏为基本成分的混合材料制品:	1.品名;2.加工方法(是否装饰、经贴面或加强等);3.未经装饰仅用纸或纸板贴面或加强的要注明	4.混合材料制品应注明成分
68.10	水泥、混凝土或人造石制品,不论是否加强:	1.品名;2.用途(铁道用等);3.种类(砖、瓦、管及建筑构件钢筋混凝土板等);4.材料(水泥、混凝土、人造石)	
68.11	石棉水泥、纤维素水泥或类似材料的制品:	1.品名;2.种类(砖、瓦、管、板等);3.材料(石棉水泥、纤维素水泥等)	
68.12	已加工的石棉纤维;以石棉为基本成分或以石棉和碳酸镁为基本成分的混合物;上述混合物或石棉的制品(例如,纱线、机织物、服装、帽类、鞋靴、衬垫),不论是否加强,但税目68.11或68.13的货品除外:	1.品名;2.种类(纱线、机织物、服装、鞋帽、衬垫等);3.材料(石棉纤维、石棉)	

商品编码	商 品 描 述	申 报 要 素	
		商品名称	规格型号
68.13	以石棉、其他矿物质或纤维素为基本成分的未装配磨擦材料及其制品(例如,片、卷、带、盘、圈、垫及扇形),适于作制动器、离合器及类似品,不论是否与织物或其他材料结合而成:	1.品名;2.材质;3.种类(片、卷、带、闸衬、闸垫、扇形等)	
68.14	已加工的云母及其制品,包括粘聚或复制的云母,不论是否附于纸、纸板或其他材料上:	1.品名;2.材质(云母);3.形状(板、片、带等);4.粘聚或复制的要注明	
68.15	其他税目未列名的石制品及其他矿物制品(包括碳纤维及其制品和泥煤制品):	1.品名;2.材质	

第六十九章　陶瓷产品

商品编码	商 品 描 述	申 报 要 素	
		商品名称	规格型号
69.01	硅质化石粉(例如,各种硅藻土)或类似硅土制的砖、块、瓦及其他陶瓷制品:	1.品名;2.材质(硅质化石粉、硅藻土或类似硅土等);3.种类(砖、瓦等)	
69.02	耐火砖、块、瓦及类似耐火陶瓷建材制品,但硅质化石粉及类似硅土制的除外:	1.品名;2.种类(耐火砖、瓦、块等)	3.成分含量
69.03	其他耐火陶瓷制品(例如,甑、坩埚、马弗罩、喷管、栓塞、支架、烤钵、管子、护套及棒条),但硅质化石粉及类似硅土制的除外:	1.品名;2.种类(坩埚、支架、马弗罩等)	3.成分含量
69.04	陶瓷制建筑用砖、铺地砖、支撑或填充用砖及类似品:	1.品名;2.种类(建筑用砖、地面砖等)	
69.05	屋顶瓦、烟囱罩、通风帽、烟囱衬壁、建筑装饰物及其他建筑用陶瓷制品:	1.品名;2.种类(屋顶瓦、烟囱罩等)	
69.06	陶瓷套管、导管、槽管及管子附件:	1.品名;2.种类(套管、导管、槽管等)	
69.07	未上釉的陶瓷贴面砖、铺面砖、包括炉面砖及墙面砖;未上釉的陶瓷镶嵌砖(马赛克)及类似品,不论是否有衬背:	1.品名;2.种类(贴面砖、铺面砖、马赛克等)	3.尺寸
69.08	上釉的陶瓷贴面砖、铺面砖,包括炉面砖及墙面砖;上釉的陶瓷镶嵌砖(马赛克)及类似品,不论是否有衬背:	1.品名;2.种类(贴面砖、铺面砖、马赛克等)	3.尺寸
69.09	实验室、化学或其他专门技术用途的陶瓷器;农业用陶瓷槽、缸及类似容器;通常供运输及盛装货物用的陶瓷罐、坛及类似品:	1.品名;2.用途(实验室用、化学、农业用等);3.种类(瓷制、陶制)	4.莫氏硬度
69.10	陶瓷洗涤槽、脸盆、脸盆座、浴缸、坐浴盆、抽水马桶、水箱、小便池及类似的固定卫生设备:	1.品名;2.材质(瓷制、陶制)	
69.11	瓷餐具、厨房器具及其他家用或盥洗用瓷器:	1.品名;2.材质(瓷制、陶制);3.种类(餐具、厨房器具等)	
69.12	陶餐具、厨房器具及其他家用或盥洗用陶器:	1.品名;2.材质(瓷制、陶制);3.种类(餐具、厨房器具等)	
69.13	塑像及其他装饰用陶瓷制品:	1.品名;2.材质(瓷制、陶制)	
69.14	其他陶瓷制品:	1.品名;2.材质(瓷制、陶制)	

第七十章　玻璃及其制品

【注解】

1. 申报要求:品名栏及规格型号栏内为必须申报的项目或指标,括号内为列举内容(后有"等")或供选择内容(无"等");备注栏内为申报规范的解释说明举例。

2. 名词解释:"品名"是指货品的具体商业名称;"用途"是指货品在出入境后的应用场合或下游产品;"加工方法"是指货品在出入境前的加工工艺或制造方法;"材质"是指货品按税则中的材质分类原则所确定的具体材料种类;"形状"是指货品按税则中的形状定义描述所确定的外观形状。

商品编码	商品描述	申报要素	
		商品名称	规格型号
70.01	**碎玻璃及废玻璃;玻璃块料:**	1. 品名;2. 用途;3. 状态(废、碎、块料)	
70.02	**未加工的玻璃球、棒及管(税目7018的微型玻璃球除外):**		
7002.1000	-玻璃球	1. 品名(未加工玻璃球);2. 用途	3. 直径
	-玻璃棒:	1. 品名(未加工玻璃棒);2. 用途(光导纤维预制棒等)	3. 光导纤维预制棒请注明规格型号
	-玻璃管:	1. 品名(未加工玻璃管);2. 用途(光导纤维用、光通信用微光组建的毛细管、定位管);3. 材质(熔融石英、熔融硅石等)	4. 级别(波导级);5. 外径;6. 线膨胀系数
70.03	**铸制或轧制玻璃板、片或型材及异型材,不论是否有吸收、反射或非反射层,但未经其他加工:**	1. 品名;2. 加工方法(整块着色、不透明、镶色或具有吸收、反射或非反射层的);3. 状态(是否夹丝);4. 形状(板、片、型材、异型材);5. 工艺(铸制或轧制)	
70.04	**拉制或吹制玻璃板、乾,不论是否有吸收、反射或非反射层,但未经其他加工:**	1. 品名;2. 加工方法(整块着色、不透明、镶色或具有吸收、反射或非反射层的);3. 状态(是否经过表面加工);4. 形状(板、片);5. 工艺(拉制或吹制)	
70.05	**浮法玻璃板、片及表面研磨或抛光玻璃板、片,不论是否有吸收、反射或非反射层,但未经其他加工:**	1. 品名;2. 加工方法(整块着色、不透明、镶色或仅表面研磨的或具有吸收、反射或非反射层的);3. 状态(是否夹丝);4. 形状(板、片);5. 工艺(浮法、表面研磨、抛光)	
70.06	**经弯曲、磨边、镂刻、钻孔、涂珐琅或其他加工的税目7003、7004或7005的玻璃,但未用其他材料镶框或装配:**	1. 品名;2. 加工方法(经弯曲、磨边、镂刻、钻孔、涂珐琅等);3. 状态(未用其他材料镶框或装配);4. 形状(板、片、型材、异型材)	
70.07	**钢化或层压玻璃制的安全玻璃:**	1. 品名(安全玻璃);2. 用途(车辆、航空器、航天器、船舶);3. 加工方法(钢化、层压)	4. 低铁钢化太阳能电池组件封装用的请注明含铁量及厚度
70.08	**多层隔温、隔音玻璃组件:**	1. 品名;2. 用途(隔温、隔音);3. 类型(中空、真空等)	4. 层数
70.09	**玻璃镜(包括后视镜),不论是否镶框:**	1. 品名;2. 用途(车辆后视用等);3. 加工方法(未经光学加工);4. 状态(是否镶框)	
70.10	**玻璃制的坛、瓶、缸、罐、安瓿及其他容器,用于运输或盛装货物;玻璃制保藏罐;玻璃塞、盖及类似的封口器:**	1. 品名(玻璃坛、瓶、缸、罐、塞、盖等);2. 用途(用于运输或盛装货物)	3. 容器的容积
70.11	**制灯泡、阴极射线管及类似品用的未封口玻璃外壳(包括玻璃泡及管)及其玻璃零件,但未装有配件:**	1. 品名(玻璃外壳、泡、管等);2. 用途(制灯泡、阴极射线管等);3. 加工方法(用荧光物质衬里、未封口无配件等)	
70.13	**玻璃器,供餐桌、厨房、盥洗室、办公室、室内装饰或类似用途(税目70.10或70.18的货品除外):**	1. 品名;2. 用途(供餐桌、厨房、盥洗室、办公室、室内装饰用);3. 材质(玻璃陶瓷、铅晶质玻璃等);4. 器皿种类(杯等)	5. 线膨胀系数
70.14	**未经光学加工的信号玻璃器及玻璃制光学元件(税目70.15的货品除外):**	1. 品名;2. 用途(光学仪器用等);3. 加工方法(未经光学加工);4. 元件种类(光学元件毛坯等)	
70.15	**钟表玻璃及类似玻璃、视力矫正或非视力矫正眼镜用玻璃,呈弧面、弯曲、凹形或类似形状但未经光学加工的;制造上述玻璃用的凹面圆形及扇形玻璃:**	1. 品名;2. 用途(用于制造眼镜等);3. 加工方法(未经光学加工);4. 形状(弧面、弯曲、凹形、扇形等);5. 元件种类(视力矫正玻璃毛坯等)	6. 特殊功能(变色等)

商品编码	商品描述	申报要素	
		商品名称	规格型号
70.16	**建筑用压制或模制的铺面用玻璃块、砖、片、瓦及其他制品，不论是否夹丝；供镶嵌或类似装饰用的玻璃马赛克及其他小件玻璃品，不论是否有衬背；花饰铅条窗玻璃及类似品；多孔或泡沫玻璃块、板、片及类似品：**	1. 品名；2. 用途（建筑铺面用）；3. 加工方法（压制、模制等）；4. 制品种类（马赛克、花饰铅条窗玻璃、铺面砖、块、片等）	
70.17	**实验室、卫生及配药用的玻璃器，不论有无刻度或标量：**	1. 品名；2. 用途（实验室、卫生、配药用）；3. 材质（熔融石英、熔融硅石）；4. 器皿种类（量筒等）	5. 线膨胀系数
70.18	**玻璃珠、仿珍珠、仿宝石或仿半宝石和类似小件玻璃品及其制品，但仿首饰除外；玻璃假眼，但医用假眼除外；灯工方法制作的玻璃塑像及其他玻璃装饰品，但仿首饰除外；直径不超过1毫米的微型玻璃球：**	1. 品名；2. 用途（装饰用等）；3. 加工方法（灯工方法等）；4. 制品种类（玻璃珠、仿珍珠、仿宝石、塑像等）	5. 玻璃球的直径
70.19	**玻璃纤维（包括玻璃棉）及其制品（例如，玻璃纤维纱线及其织物）：**		
	-梳条、粗纱、纱线及短切纤维：	1. 品名；2. 材质（玻璃纤维制）；3. 种类（梳条、粗纱、纱线、短纤）	4. 长度
	-薄片（巴厘纱）、纤维网、席、垫、板及类似无纺产品：	1. 品名；2. 材质（玻璃纤维制）；3. 种类（席、薄片、纤维网、垫、板等）	
7019.4000	-粗纱机织物	1. 品名；2. 材质（玻璃纤维制）；3. 织造方法（机织）；4. 纱线类型（粗纱）	
	-其他机织物：	1. 品名；2. 材质（玻璃纤维制）；3. 织造方法（机织）；4. 纱线类型（细纱等）	5. 幅宽；6. 每平方米克重；7. 单纱细度
7019.9000	-其他	1. 品名；2. 用途；3. 材质（玻璃纤维制）	
70.20	**其他玻璃制品：**	1. 品名；2. 用途；3. 材质（玻璃制）	

第十四类 天然或养殖珍珠、宝石或半宝石、贵金属、包贵金属及其制品;仿首饰;硬币

第七十一章 天然或养殖珍珠、宝石或半宝石、贵金属、包贵金属及其制品;仿首饰;硬币

【注解】

1. 申报要求:品名栏及规格型号栏内为必须申报的项目或指标,括号内为列举内容(后有"等")或供选择内容(无"等");备注栏内为申报规范的解释说明举例。

2. 名词解释:"品名"是指货品的具体商业名称;"用途"是指货品在出入境后的应用场合或下游产品;"加工方法"是指货品在出入境前的加工工艺或制造方法;"材质"是指货品按税则中的材质分类原则所确定的具体材料种类;"形状"是指货品按税则中的形状定义描述所确定的外观形状。

商品编码	商品描述	申报要素	
		商品名称	规格型号
71.01	天然或养殖珍珠,不论是否加工或分级,但未成串或镶嵌;天然或养殖珍珠,为便于运输而暂穿成串:	1. 品名;2. 种类(黑珍珠等);3. 加工程度(打孔、未加工等);4. 状态(未成串、未镶嵌等);5. 来源(天然、养殖)	6. 等级
71.02	钻石,不论是否加工,但未镶嵌:	1. 品名;2. 用途(工业用等);3. 加工程度(未加工、经简单锯开、劈开、粗磨等);4. 来源(天然)	5. 等级
71.03	宝石(钻石除外)或半宝石,不论是否加工或分级,但未成串或镶嵌;未分级的宝石(钻石除外)或半宝石,为便于运输而暂穿成串:	1. 品名;2. 种类(红宝石、蓝宝石、绿宝石、翡翠等);3. 加工程度(未加工、经简单锯开、粗制成形);4. 状态(未成串、未镶嵌等);5. 来源(天然)	6. 等级
71.04	合成或再造的宝石或半宝石,不论是否加工或分级,但未成串或镶嵌的;未分级的合成或再造的宝石或半宝石,为便于运输而暂穿成串:	1. 品名;2. 用途(工业用);3. 种类(压电石英等);4. 加工程度(经简单锯开、粗制成形);5. 状态(未成串、未镶嵌等)	6. 来源(合成、再造);7. 等级
71.05	天然或合成的宝石或半宝石的粉末:	1. 品名;2. 种类(钻石等);3. 形状(粉末);4. 来源(天然、合成)	
71.06	银(包括镀金、镀铂的银),未锻造、半制成或粉末状:	1. 品名;2. 形状(粉末);3. 材质(纯银、银合金、镀金、镀铂);4. 加工程度(未锻造、半制成)	5. 纯度
71.07	以贱金属为底的包银材料:	1. 品名(包银);2. 基底材质(铜等)	
71.08	金(包括镀铂的金),未锻造、半制成或粉末状:	1. 品名;2. 形状(粉末);3. 材质(纯金、金合金、镀铂);4. 加工程度(未锻造、半制成);5. 货币用请注明用途	
71.09	以贱金属或银为底的包金材料:	1. 品名(包金);2. 基底材质(铜、银等)	
71.10	铂,未锻造、半制成或粉末状:	1. 品名;2. 形状(粉末);3. 材质(铂、钯、铑、铱、锇、钌);4. 加工程度(未锻造、板、片等)	
71.11	以贱金属、银或金为底的包铂材料:	1. 品名(包铂);2. 基底材质(铜、银、金等)	
71.12	贵金属或包贵金属的废碎料;含有贵金属或贵金属化合物的其他废碎料,主要用于回收贵金属:	1. 品名(回收铂、金、银等);2. 状态(废碎料、灰);3. 来源(由破碎含有贵金属的电路板而得等)	4. 贵金属的成分含量
71.13	贵金属或包贵金属制的首饰及其零件:	1. 品名;2. 材质(铂、金、银等);3. 加工方法(镶嵌宝石、包金、包银等);4. 首饰种类(戒指等)	
71.14	贵金属或包贵金属制的金银器及其零件:	1. 品名;2. 种类(餐具等);3. 材质(铂、金、银等);4. 加工方法(包金、镀金等)	
71.15	贵金属或包贵金属的其他制品:	1. 品名;2. 用途(工业用、实验室用等);3. 种类(坩埚等);4. 形状(格栅形状等);5. 材质(铂等)	
71.16	用天然或养殖珍珠、宝石或半宝石(天然、合成或再造)制成的物品:	1. 品名;2. 种类(手镯等);3. 材质(养殖珍珠、天然珍珠、宝石、半宝石)	
71.17	仿首饰:	1. 品名;2. 种类(袖扣、饰扣、手镯等);3. 材质(铝等);4. 加工方法(镀贵金属等)	
71.18	硬币:	1. 品名;2. 用途(法定货币、非法定货币);3. 材质(铜制等)	

第十五类　贱金属及其制品

第七十二章　钢铁

【注解】

（一）申报要求：品名栏及规格型号栏内为必须申报的项目或指标，括号内为列举内容（后有“等”）或供选择内容（无“等”）；备注栏内为申报规范的解释说明举例。

（二）名词解释：“品名”是指货品的具体商业名称；“用途”是指货品在出入境后的应用场合或下游产品；“加工方法”是指货品在出入境前的加工工艺或制造方法；“材质”是指货品按税则中的材质分类原则所确定的具体材料种类；“形状”是指货品按税则中的形状定义描述所确定的外观形状。

商品编码	商 品 描 述	申 报 要 素	
		商品名称	规格型号
72.01	**生铁及镜铁，锭、块或其他初级形状：**	1.品名；2.形状（锭、块等）；3.材质（生铁、镜铁）	4.成分含量（铁、碳、铬、锰、磷、硅的含量）
72.02	**铁合金：**	1.品名；2.材质（锰铁、硅铁、铬铁、镍铁、钼铁、钨铁、钛铁、钒铁、铌铁等）	3.成分含量（铁、碳、铬、锰、铜、磷、硅及相关合金元素的含量）
72.03	**直接从铁矿还原所得的铁产品及其他海绵铁产品，块、团、团粒及类似形状；按重量计纯度在99.94%及以上的铁，块、团、团粒及类似形状：**	1.品名；2.形状（块、团、团粒等）；3.材质（海绵铁等）；4.来源（直接从铁矿还原所得）	5.成分含量（铁、碳、合金元素、非合金元素的含量）
72.04	**钢铁废碎料；供再熔的碎料钢铁锭：**	1.品名；2.用途（供再熔炼钢用）；3.形状（废碎、切割、压缩成包或板、条状等）；4.材质（铸铁、合金钢、不锈钢等）；5.来源（机械加工产生、由破碎何种钢铁制品而得）	6.汽车压件请注明
72.05	**生铁、镜铁及钢铁的颗粒和粉末：**	1.品名；2.形状（颗粒、粉末）；3.材质（生铁、镜铁、合金钢等）	4.成分含量（铁、碳、合金元素、非合金元素的含量）；5.粒度
72.06	**铁及非合金钢，锭状或其他初级形状（税目72.03的铁除外）：**	1.品名；2.形状（方锭等）；3.材质（铁、非合金钢）	4.成分含量（铁、碳、合金元素、非合金元素的含量）
72.07	**铁及非合金钢的半制成品：**	1.品名；2.形状（大方坯、小方坯等）；3.材质（铁、非合金钢）；4.加工方法（初轧、粗锻等）	5.成分含量（铁、碳、合金元素、非合金元素的含量）；6.截面形状（正方形等）
72.08	**宽度在600毫米及以上的铁或非合金钢平板轧材，经热轧，但未经包覆、镀层或涂层：**	1.品名；2.形状（平板、卷板）；3.材质（铁、非合金钢）；4.加工方法（热轧）；5.加工程度（酸洗、轧有花纹、未包覆、未镀层、未涂层）	6.成分含量（铁、碳、合金元素、非合金元素的含量）；7.规格（板材的厚度、宽度）；8.技术参数（屈服强度）
72.09	**宽度在600毫米及以上的铁或非合金钢平板轧材，经冷轧，但未经包覆、镀层或涂层：**	1.品名；2.形状（平板、卷板）；3.材质（铁、非合金钢）；4.加工方法（冷轧）；5.加工程度（未包覆、未镀层、未涂层）	6.成分含量（铁、碳、合金元素、非合金元素的含量）；7.规格（板材的厚度、宽度）；8.技术参数（屈服强度）
72.10	**宽度在600毫米及以上的铁或非合金钢平板轧材，经包覆、镀层或涂层：**	1.品名；2.形状（平板、卷板）；3.材质（铁、非合金钢）；4.加工方法（经包覆、经镀层、经涂层）；5.瓦楞形请注明	6.成分含量（铁、碳、合金元素、非合金元素的含量）；7.规格（板材的厚度、宽度）；8.涂层种类（锡、铅、电镀锌、涂锌等）；9.涂层厚度（0.5毫米等）

商品编码	商 品 描 述	申 报 要 素	
		商品名称	规格型号
72.11	**宽度小于600毫米的铁或非合金钢平板轧材,但未经包覆、镀层或涂层:**	1.品名;2.形状(平板、卷板);3.材质(铁、非合金钢);4.加工方法(热轧、冷轧、未包覆、未镀层、未涂层)	5.成分含量(铁、碳、合金元素、非合金元素的含量);6.规格(板材的厚度、宽度)
72.12	**宽度小于600毫米的铁或非合金钢平板轧材,经包覆、镀层或涂层:**	1.品名;2.形状(平板、卷板);3.材质(铁、非合金钢);4.加工方法(经包覆、经镀层、经涂层)	5.成分含量(铁、碳、合金元素、非合金元素的含量);6.规格(板材的厚度、宽度);7.涂层种类(锡、铅、电镀锌、涂锌等)
72.13	**不规则盘卷的铁及非合金钢的热轧条、杆:**	1.品名;2.形状(条、杆);3.材质(铁、非合金钢);4.加工方法(热轧);5.状态(不规则盘卷、带有轧制过程中产生的凹痕、凸缘、沟槽及其他变形)	6.成分含量(铁、碳、合金元素、非合金元素的含量);7.规格(条、杆的直径)
72.14	**铁或非合金钢的其他条、杆,除锻造、热轧、热拉拔或热挤压外未经进一步加工,包括轧制后扭曲的:**	1.品名;2.形状(条、杆);3.材质(铁、非合金钢);4.加工方法(锻造、轧制后扭曲);5.状态(带有轧制过程中产生的凹痕、凸缘、沟槽及其他变形)	6.成分含量(铁、碳、合金元素、非合金元素的含量);7.规格(条、杆的直径);8.截面形状(正方形等)
72.15	**铁及非合金钢的其他条、杆:**	1.品名;2.形状(条、杆);3.材质(铁、非合金钢);4.加工方法(冷成形、冷加工);5.加工程度	6.成分含量(铁、碳、合金元素、非合金元素的含量);7.规格(条、杆的直径);8.易切削钢请注明
72.16	**铁或非合金钢的角材、型材及异型材:**	1.品名;2.形状(槽钢、角钢、工字钢、H型钢、丁字钢、乙字钢等);3.材质(铁、非合金钢);4.加工方法(热轧、热拉拔、热挤压、冷成形、冷加工);5.加工程度	6.成分含量(铁、碳、合金元素、非合金元素的含量);7.规格(型材的截面高度)
72.17	**铁丝或非合金钢丝:**	1.品名;2.形状(丝);3.材质(铁、非合金钢);4.加工方法(镀层、涂层)	5.成分含量(铁、碳、合金元素、非合金元素的含量);6.涂层种类(锌等);7.直径
72.18	**不锈钢,锭状或其他初级形状;不锈钢半制成品:**	1.品名;2.形状(方锭等);3.材质(不锈钢)	4.成分含量(铁、碳、铬及合金元素、非合金元素的含量);5.截面形状(正方形等)
72.19	**不锈钢平板轧材,宽度在600毫米及以上:**	1.品名;2.形状(卷板、平板等);3.材质(不锈钢);4.加工方法(热轧、冷轧);5.加工程度	6.成分含量(铁、碳、铬及合金元素、非合金元素的含量);7.规格(板材的厚度、宽度)
72.20	**不锈钢平板轧材,宽度小于600毫米:**	1.品名;2.形状(卷板、平板等);3.材质(不锈钢);4.加工方法(热轧、冷轧);5.加工程度	6.成分含量(铁、碳、铬及合金元素、非合金元素的含量);7.规格(板材的厚度、宽度)
72.21	**不规则盘卷的不锈钢热轧条、杆:**	1.品名;2.形状(条、杆);3.材质(不锈钢);4.加工方法(热轧);5.状态(不规则盘卷)	6.成分含量(铁、碳、铬及合金元素、非合金元素的含量)
72.22	**不锈钢其他条、杆;不锈钢角材、型材及异型材:**	1.品名;2.形状(条、杆、型材、异型材);3.材质(不锈钢);4.加工方法(热轧、热拉拔、热挤压、冷成形、冷加工)	5.成分含量(铁、碳、铬及合金元素、非合金元素的含量);6.截面形状(圆形等)

商品编码	商品描述	申报要素	
		商品名称	规格型号
72.23	不锈钢丝:	1.品名;2.形状(丝);3.材质(不锈钢);4.加工方法(镀层、涂层)	5.成分含量(铁、碳、铬及合金元素、非合金元素的含量);6.直径
72.24	其他合金钢,锭状或其他初级形状;其他合金钢制的半制成品:	1.品名;2.形状(方锭等);3.材质(硅锰钢等)	4.成分含量(铁、碳及合金元素、非合金元素的含量);5.粗铸锻件坯请注明单件重量
72.25	其他合金钢平板轧材,宽度在600毫米及以上:	1.品名;2.形状(卷材);3.材质(硅电钢等);4.加工方法(热轧、冷轧、镀层、涂层);5.取向性硅电钢请注明	6.成分含量(铁、碳、合金元素、非合金元素的含量);7.规格(板材的厚度、宽度);8.涂层种类(电镀锌、涂锌等)
72.26	其他合金钢平板轧材,宽度小于600毫米:	1.品名;2.形状(卷材);3.材质(硅电钢等);4.加工方法(热轧、冷轧、镀层、涂层);5.取向性硅电钢请注明	6.成分含量(铁、碳、合金元素、非合金元素的含量);7.规格(板材的厚度、宽度);8.涂层种类(电镀锌、涂锌等)
72.27	不规则盘卷的其他合金钢热轧条、杆:	1.品名;2.形状(条、杆);3.材质(高速钢、硅锰钢等);4.加工方法(热轧);5.状态(不规则盘卷)	6.成分含量(铁、碳、合金元素、非合金元素的含量)
72.28	其他合金钢条、杆;其他合金钢角材、型材及异型材;合金钢或非合金钢制的空心钻钢:	1.品名;2.用途(履带板型钢、空心钻钢等);3.形状(条、杆、型材、异型材);4.材质(高速钢、硅锰钢等);5.加工方法(热轧、热拉拔、热挤压、冷成形、冷加工)	6.成分含量(铁、碳、合金元素、非合金元素的含量);
72.29	其他合金钢丝:	1.品名;2.形状(丝);3.材质(高速钢、硅锰钢等);4.加工方法(镀层、涂层)	5.成分含量(铁、碳、合金元素、非合金元素的含量);

第七十三章　钢铁制品

【注解】

(一)申报要求:品名栏及规格型号栏内为必须申报的项目或指标,括号内为列举内容(后有"等")或供选择内容(无"等");备注栏内为申报规范的解释说明举例。

(二)名词解释:"品名"是指货品的具体商业名称;"用途"是指货品在出入境后的应用场合或下游产品;"加工方法"是指货品在出入境前的加工工艺或制造方法;"材质"是指货品按税则中的材质分类原则所确定的具体材料种类;"形状"是指货品按税则中的形状定义描述所确定的外观形状。

商品编码	商品描述	申报要素	
		商品名称	规格型号
73.01	钢铁板桩,不论是否钻孔、打眼或组装;焊接的钢铁角材、型材及异型材:	1.品名;2.形状(板桩、焊接的角材、型材、异型材);3.材质(铁、非合金钢、不锈钢、合金钢)	
73.02	铁道及电车道铺轨用钢铁材料(钢轨、护轨、齿轨、道岔尖轨、辙叉、尖轨拉杆及其他叉道段体、轨枕、鱼尾板、轨座、轨座楔、钢轨垫板、钢轨夹、底板、固定板及其他专门用于连接或加固路轨的材料):	1.品名;2.用途(铁道及电车道铺轨用等);3.材质(铁、非合金钢、不锈钢、合金钢);4.制品种类(钢轨、轨枕、叉道段体等)	5.钢轨请注明长度;6.钢轨请注明等尺
73.03	铸铁管及空心异型材:	1.品名;2.形状(圆形截面管、空心异型材);3.材质(铸铁)	4.规格(管的内径)
73.04	无缝钢铁管及空心异型材(铸铁的除外):	1.品名;2.用途(锅炉用、石油或天然气钻探用等);3.形状(管、空心异型材);4.材质(铁、非合金钢、不锈钢、合金钢);5.加工方法(冷拔、冷轧等)	6.加工工艺(无缝);7.规格(管的外径)

商品编码	商 品 描 述	申 报 要 素	
		商品名称	规格型号
73.05	其他圆形截面钢铁管(例如,焊、铆及用类似方法接合的管),外径超过406.4毫米:	1.品名;2.用途(石油或天然气管道用等);3.材质(铁、非合金钢、不锈钢、合金钢);4.种类(焊接管);5.加工方法(铆、纵向焊、埋弧焊)	6.规格(管的外径);7.截面形状(圆形)
73.06	其他钢铁管及空心异型材(例如,辊缝、焊、铆及类似方法接合的):	1.品名;2.用途(石油或天然气管道用);3.材质(铁、非合金钢、不锈钢、合金钢);4.种类(焊接管);5.加工方法(铆、纵向焊、埋弧焊)	6.规格(圆管的外径);7.截面形状(圆形等)
73.07	钢铁管子附件(例如,接头、肘管、管套):	1.品名;2.用途(用于管子之间连通);3.材质(铁、非合金钢、不锈钢、合金钢);4.种类(法兰、管套、十字接头等);5.加工方法(铸造等)	
73.08	钢铁结构体(税目94.06的活动房屋除外)及其部件(例如,桥梁及桥梁体段、闸门、塔楼、格构杆、屋顶、屋顶框架、门窗及其框架、门槛、百叶窗、栏杆、支柱及立柱);上述结构体用的已加工钢铁板、杆、角材、型材、异型材、管子及类似品:	1.品名;2.用途(支撑用等);3.材质(钢铁);4.种类(门窗、立柱、塔楼、脚手架、桥梁体段等)	
73.09	盛装物料用的钢铁囤、柜、罐、桶及类似容器(装压缩气体或液化气体的除外),容积超过300升,不论是否衬里或隔热,但无机械或热力装置:	1.品名;2.用途(盛装液体用等);3.材质(钢铁);4.种类(罐、桶等)	5.规格(容积);6.装有机械或热力装置请注明
73.10	盛装物料用的钢铁柜、桶、罐、听、盒及类似容器(装压缩气体或液化气体的除外),容积不超过300升,不论是否衬里或隔热,但无机械或热力装置:	1.品名;2.用途(盛装液体用等);3.材质(钢铁);4.种类(罐、桶等);5.加工方法(焊边接合、卷边接合等)	6.规格(容积);7.装有机械或热力装置请注明
73.11	装压缩气体或液化气体用的钢铁容器:	1.品名;2.用途(压缩气体或液化气体用、零售包装用等);3.材质(钢铁);4.种类(罐、桶等)	
73.12	非绝缘的钢铁绞股线、绳、缆、编带、吊索及类似品:	1.品名(非绝缘);2.材质(钢铁);3.制品种类(绞股线、吊索、绳等)	
73.13	带刺钢铁丝;围篱用的钢铁绞带或单股扁丝(不论是否带刺)及松绞的双股丝:	1.品名;2.用途(围篱用);3.材质(钢铁);4.种类(带刺钢铁丝、绞带、单股扁丝、松绞的双股丝)	5.截面尺寸
73.14	钢铁丝制的布(包括环形带)、网、篱、格栅;网眼钢铁板:	1.品名;2.用途(工业用等);3.材质(铁、非合金钢、不锈钢、合金钢);4.种类(网、篱、格栅等);5.加工方法(镀锌、涂锌、涂塑等)	6.规格(网眼尺寸、丝的截面尺寸)
73.15	钢铁链及其零件:	1.品名;2.用途(自行车用、摩托车用等);3.材质(钢铁);4.种类(铰接链、滚子链、日字环节链等)	
73.16	钢铁锚、多爪锚及其零件:	1.品名;2.材质(钢铁);3.种类(钢铁锚、多爪锚等)	
73.17	钢铁制的钉、平头钉、图钉、波纹钉、U形钉(税目83.05的货品除外)及类似品,不论钉头是否用其他材料制成,但不包括铜头钉:	1.品名;2.材质(钢铁);3.种类(图钉、U形钉、平头钉、波纹钉等)	
73.18	钢铁制的螺钉、螺栓、螺母、方头螺钉、钩头螺钉、铆钉、销、开尾销、垫圈(包括弹簧垫圈)及类似品:	1.品名;2.品牌;3.材质(钢铁);4.种类(螺钉、螺母、垫圈、铆钉、销等);5.螺钉请注明种类(方头、钩头、环头等)	6.规格型号
73.19	钢铁制手工缝针、编织针、引针、钩针、刺绣穿孔锥及类似制品;其他税目未列名的钢铁制安全别针及其他别针:	1.品名;2.材质(钢铁);3.种类(缝针、织补针、刺绣针、别针等)	
73.20	钢铁制弹簧及弹簧片:	1.品名;2.用途(汽车用、铁道车辆用等);3.材质(钢铁);4.种类(片簧、螺旋弹簧等)	
73.21	非电热的钢铁制家用炉、灶(包括附有集中供暖用的热水锅的炉)烤肉架、烤炉、煤气灶、加热板和类似非电热的家用器具及其零件:	1.品名;2.材质(钢铁);3.种类(煤油炉、煤气灶、烤肉架、烤炉等)	4.原理(非电热);5.燃料种类(液体、固体、气体燃料)

商品编码	商 品 描 述	申 报 要 素	
		商品名称	规格型号
73.22	**非电热的钢铁制集中供暖用散热器及其零件;非电热的钢铁制空气加热器、暖气分布器(包括可分布新鲜空气或调节空气的)及其零件,装有电动风扇或鼓风机:**	1.品名;2.用途(集中供暖用等);3.材质(钢铁);4.种类(散热器、空气加热器、暖气分布器等)	5.原理(非电热);6.装有电动风扇或鼓风机请注明
73.23	**餐桌、厨房或其他家用钢铁器具及其零件;钢铁丝绒;钢铁制擦锅器、洗刷擦光用的块垫、手套及类似品:**	1.品名;2.用途(厨房用、餐桌用等);3.材质(铁、非合金钢、不锈钢、合金钢);4.种类(水壶、煎锅等);5.加工方法(已搪瓷、未搪瓷)	
73.24	**钢铁制卫生器具及其零件:**	1.品名;2.用途(卫生间用等);3.材质(铁、非合金钢、不锈钢、合金钢);4.种类(脸盆、浴缸等);5.加工方法(已搪瓷、未搪瓷)	
73.25	**其他钢铁铸造制品:**	1.品名;2.用途(工业用、非工业用、研磨机用等);3.材质(无可锻性铸铁等);4.种类(井盖、研磨球等)	
73.26	**其他钢铁制品:**	1.品名;2.用途(工业用、非工业用);3.材质(钢铁);4.种类(捕鼠器、香烟盒等);5.加工方法(锻造、冲压等)	

第七十四章　铜及其制品

【注解】

(一)申报要求:品名栏及规格型号栏内为必须申报的项目或指标,括号内为列举内容(后有"等")或供选择内容(无"等");备注栏内为申报规范的解释说明举例。

(二)名词解释:"品名"是指货品的具体商业名称;"用途"是指货品在出入境后的应用场合或下游产品;"加工方法"是指货品在出入境前的加工工艺或制造方法;"材质"是指货品按税则中的材质分类原则所确定的具体材料种类;"形状"是指货品按税则中的形状定义描述所确定的外观形状。

商品编码	商 品 描 述	申 报 要 素	
		商品名称	规格型号
74.01	**铜锍;沉积铜(泥铜):**	1.品名;2.材质(铜锍、沉积铜);3.来源	4.成分含量(铜化合物的含量);
74.02	**未精炼铜;电解精炼用的铜阳极:**	1.品名;2.用途(电解精炼用等);3.形状(块状等);4.材质(未精炼铜)	5.成分含量(铜的含量);
74.03	**未锻轧的精炼铜及铜合金:**	1.品名;2.形状(型材、线锭、坯段等);3.材质(精炼铜、黄铜、青铜、白铜等);4.加工方法(未锻轧等)	5.成分含量(铜及合金元素的含量)
74.04	**铜废碎料:**	1.品名;2.用途(供回收铜用);3.材质(铜);4.状态(废、碎、管、板、线、棒、边角料等);5.来源(废的电机、电线、电缆、五金等)	6.成分含量(回收金属的含量)
74.05	**铜母合金:**	1.品名;2.用途(用做炼铜的添加剂);3.形状(粒状等);4.材质(铜母合金)	5.成分含量(铜、磷的含量)
74.06	**铜粉及片状粉末:**	1.品名;2.用途(用做电镀基底、金属颜料等);3.形状(片状粉末、非片状粉末);4.材质(精炼铜、黄铜、青铜、白铜等)	5.成分含量(铜及合金元素的含量);6.粒度
74.07	**铜条、杆、型材及异型材:**	1.品名;2.形状(条、杆、型材、异型材);3.材质(精炼铜、黄铜、青铜、白铜等)	4.成分含量(铜及合金元素的含量)
74.08	**铜丝:**	1.品名;2.形状(丝);3.材质(精炼铜、黄铜、青铜、白铜等)	4.成分含量(铜及合金元素的含量);5.规格(丝的最大截面尺寸)
74.09	**铜板、片及带,厚度超过0.15毫米:**	1.品名;2.形状(板、片、带);3.材质(精炼铜、黄铜、青铜、白铜等);4.状态(盘卷等)	5.成分含量(铜及合金元素的含量);6.规格(厚度)

商品编码	商品描述	申报要素	
		商品名称	规格型号
74.10	铜箔(不论是否印花或用纸、纸板、塑料或类似材料衬背),厚度(衬背除外)不超过0.15毫米:	1.品名;2.形状(箔);3.材质(精炼铜、黄铜、青铜、白铜等);4.状态(有无衬背)	5.成分含量(铜及合金元素的含量);6.规格(整体厚度、铜箔厚度、长度、宽度)
74.11	铜管:	1.品名;2.材质(精炼铜、黄铜、青铜、白铜等);3.种类(管)	4.成分含量(铜及合金元素的含量)
74.12	铜制管子附件(例如,接头、肘管、管套):	1.品名;2.用途(用于管子之间连通);3.材质(精炼铜、黄铜、青铜、白铜等);4.种类(接头、肘管、管套)	5.成分含量(铜及合金元素的含量)
74.13	非绝缘的铜丝绞股线、缆、编带及类似品:	1.品名(非绝缘);2.材质(铜);3.种类(绞股线、缆、编带等)	
74.15	铜制或钢铁制带铜头的钉、平头钉、图钉、U形钉(税目83.05的货品除外)及类似品;铜制螺钉、螺栓、螺母、钩头螺钉、铆钉、销、开尾销、垫圈(包括弹簧垫圈)及类似品:	1.品名;2.材质(铜);3.种类(图钉、U形钉、螺钉、螺母、垫圈、铆钉等)	
74.18	餐桌、厨房或其他家用铜制器具及其零件;铜制刷锅器、洗刷擦光用的块垫、手套及类似品;铜制卫生器具及其零件:	1.品名;2.用途(厨房用、餐桌用、卫生用等);3.材质(铜);4.种类(水壶、煎锅等)	
74.19	其他铜制品:	1.品名;2.用途(工业用、非工业用);3.材质(铜);4.种类(链条、容器等);5.加工方法(锻造、冲压等)	

第七十五章　镍及其制品

【注解】

(一)申报要求:品名栏及规格型号栏内为必须申报的项目或指标,括号内为列举内容(后有"等")或供选择内容(无"等");备注栏内为申报规范的解释说明举例。

(二)名词解释:"品名"是指货品的具体商业名称;"用途"是指货品在出入境后的应用场合或下游产品;"加工方法"是指货品在出入境前的加工工艺或制造方法;"材质"是指货品按税则中的材质分类原则所确定的具体材料种类;"形状"是指货品按税则中的形状定义描述所确定的外观形状。

商品编码	商品描述	申报要素	
		商品名称	规格型号
75.01	镍锍、氧化镍烧结物及镍冶炼的其他中间产品:	1.品名;2.材质(镍锍、氧化镍烧结物等);3.来源	4.成分含量(镍化合物的含量)
75.02	未锻轧镍:	1.品名;2.形状(锭、块等);3.材质(非合金镍、镍合金);4.加工方法(未锻轧)	5.成分含量(镍及合金元素的含量)
75.03	镍废碎料:	1.品名;2.用途(供回收镍用);3.状态(废、碎);4.来源(非合金镍、镍合金的废碎料)	5.成分含量(镍及合金元素的含量)
75.04	镍粉及片状粉末:	1.品名;2.形状(片状粉末、非片状粉末);3.材质(非合金镍、镍合金)	4.成分含量(镍及合金元素的含量);5.粒度
75.05	镍条、杆、型材及异型材或丝:	1.品名;2.形状(条、杆、型材、异型材、丝);3.材质(非合金镍、镍合金)	4.成分含量(镍及合金元素的含量);5.丝的直径
75.06	镍板、片、带、箔:	1.品名;2.形状(板、片、带、箔);3.材质(非合金镍、镍合金)	4.成分含量(镍及合金元素的含量)
75.07	镍管及管子附件(例如,接头、肘管、管套):	1.品名;2.用途(用于管子之间连通);3.材质(非合金镍、镍合金);4.种类(管、接头、肘管、管套等)	5.成分含量(镍及合金元素的含量)
75.08	其他镍制品:	1.品名;2.用途(电镀用、工业用、非工业用);3.材质(非合金镍、镍合金);4.种类(网、篱、格栅等)	

第七十六章　铝及其制品

【注解】

(一)申报要求:品名栏及规格型号栏内为必须申报的项目或指标,括号内为列举内容(后有“等”)或供选择内容(无“等”);备注栏内为申报规范的解释说明举例。

(二)名词解释:“品名”是指货品的具体商业名称;“用途”是指货品在出入境后的应用场合或下游产品;“加工方法”是指货品在出入境前的加工工艺或制造方法;“材质”是指货品按税则中的材质分类原则所确定的具体材料种类;“形状”是指货品按税则中的形状定义描述所确定的外观形状。

商品编码	商品描述	申报要素	
		商品名称	规格型号
76.01	未锻轧铝:	1.品名;2.形状(锭、块);3.材质(非合金铝、铝合金);4.加工方法(未锻轧)	5.成分含量(铝及合金元素的含量)
76.02	铝废碎料:	1.品名;2.用途(供回收铝用);3.状态(废、碎、板、管、线、边角料等);4.来源(废电线、废电缆、废五金电器等)	5.成分含量(回收金属的含量);6.包装形式
76.03	铝粉及片状粉末:	1.品名;2.形状(片状粉末、非片状粉末);3.材质(非合金铝、铝合金)	4.成分含量(铝的含量);5.粒度
76.04	铝条、杆、型材及异型材:	1.品名;2.形状(条、杆、型材、异型材);3.材质(非合金铝、铝合金);4.型材、异型材请注明是否空心	5.成分含量(铝及合金元素的含量)
76.05	铝丝:	1.品名;2.形状(丝);3.材质(非合金铝、铝合金)	4.成分含量(铝及合金元素的含量);5.规格(丝的最大截面尺寸)
76.06	铝板、片及带,厚度超过0.2毫米:	1.品名;2.形状(矩形等);3.材质(非合金铝、铝合金);4.状态(板、片、带)	5.成分含量(铝及合金元素的含量);6.规格(板的厚度)
76.07	铝箔(不论是否印花或用纸、纸板、塑料或类似材料衬背),厚度(衬背除外)不超过0.2毫米:	1.品名;2.形状(箔);3.材质(铝);4.状态(有无衬背、衬背材料)	5.规格(铝箔厚度)
76.08	铝管:	1.品名;2.材质(非合金铝、铝合金);3.种类(管)	4.成分含量(铝及合金元素的含量)
76.09	铝制管子附件(例如,接头、肘管、管套):	1.品名;2.用途;3.材质(非合金铝、铝合金);4.种类(接头、肘管、管套)	
76.10	铝制结构体(税目94.06的活动房屋除外)及其部件(例如,桥梁及桥梁体段、塔、格构杆、屋顶、屋顶框架、门窗及其框架、门槛、栏杆、支柱及立柱);上述结构体用的已加工铝板、杆、型材、异型材、管子及类似品:	1.品名;2.材质(铝);3.种类(门窗、门槛、塔楼、桥梁体段等);4.加工方法(铆接、栓接、钻孔、弯曲等)	
76.11	盛装物料用的铝制囤、柜、罐、桶及类似容器(装压缩气体或液化气体的除外),容积超过300升,不论是否衬里或隔热,但无机械或热力装置:	1.品名;2.用途(盛装液体用等);3.材质(铝);4.种类(罐、桶等)	5.规格(容积)
76.12	盛装物料用的铝制桶、罐、听、盒及类似容器,包括软管容器及硬管容器(装压缩气体或液化气体的除外),容积不超过300升,不论是否衬里或隔热,但无机械或热力装置:	1.品名;2.用途(盛装液体用等);3.材质(铝);4.种类(罐、桶、软管容器、易拉罐等)	5.规格(容积)
76.13	装压缩气体或液化气体用的铝制容器:	1.品名;2.用途(压缩气体或液化气体用、零售包装用等);3.材质(铝);4.种类(罐、桶等)	
76.14	非绝缘的铝制绞股线、缆、编带及类似品:	1.品名;2.材质(铝);3.种类(绞股线、缆、编带等);4.状态(非绝缘);5.带钢芯请注明	
76.15	餐桌、厨房或其他家用铝制器具及其零件;铝制擦锅器、洗刷擦光用的块垫,手套及类似品;铝制卫生器具及其零件:	1.品名;2.用途(厨房用、餐桌用、卫生用等);3.材质(铝);4.种类(水壶、煎锅等)	

商品编码	商 品 描 述	申 报 要 素	
		商品名称	规格型号
76.16	**其他铝制品:**	1.品名;2.用途(工业用、非工业用);3.材质(铝);4.种类(图钉、U形钉、螺钉、螺母、垫圈、铆钉、布、网、篱、格栅等)	

第七十七章 (保留为税则将来所用)

第七十八章 铅及其制品

【注解】

1.申报要求:品名栏及规格型号栏内为必须申报的项目或指标,括号内为列举内容(后有“等”)或供选择内容(无“等”);备注栏内为申报规范的解释说明举例。

2.名词解释:“品名”是指货品的具体商业名称;“用途”是指货品在出入境后的应用场合或下游产品;“加工方法”是指货品在出入境前的加工工艺或制造方法;“材质”是指货品按税则中的材质分类原则所确定的具体材料种类;“形状”是指货品按税则中的形状定义描述所确定的外观形状

商品编码	商 品 描 述	申 报 要 素	
		商品名称	规格型号
78.01	**未锻轧铅:**	1.品名;2.形状(锭、块);3.材质(精炼铅、铅合金);4.加工方法(未锻轧)	5.成分含量(铅及合金元素的含量)
78.02	**铅废碎料:**	1.品名;2.用途(供回收铅用);3.材质(铅);4.状态(废、碎);5.来源(精炼铅、铅合金的废碎料)	6.成分含量(铅的含量)
78.04	**铅板、片、带、箔;铅粉及片状粉末:**	1.品名;2.形状(板、片、带、箔、粉末及片状粉末);3.材质(铅)	4.规格(板、箔的厚度);5.粒度
78.06	**其他铅制品:**	1.品名;2.用途(工业用、非工业用);3.材质(铅);4.种类(容器、铅坠等)	

第七十九章 锌及其制品

【注解】

1.申报要求:品名栏及规格型号栏内为必须申报的项目或指标,括号内为列举内容(后有“等”)或供选择内容(无“等”);备注栏内为申报规范的解释说明举例。

2.名词解释:“品名”是指货品的具体商业名称;“用途”是指货品在出入境后的应用场合或下游产品;“加工方法”是指货品在出入境前的加工工艺或制造方法;“材质”是指货品按税则中的材质分类原则所确定的具体材料种类;“形状”是指货品按税则中的形状定义描述所确定的外观形状。

商品编码	商 品 描 述	申 报 要 素	
		商品名称	规格型号
79.01	**未锻轧锌:**	1.品名;2.形状(锭、块);3.材质(非合金锌、锌合金);4.加工方法(未锻轧)	5.成分含量(锌及合金元素的含量)
79.02	**锌废碎料:**	1.品名;2.用途(供回收锌用);3.状态(废、碎);4.来源(精炼锌、锌合金的废碎料)	5.成分含量(锌的含量)
79.03	**锌末、锌粉及片状粉末:**	1.品名;2.用途(用做硬质合金的粘合剂);3.形状(片状粉末、非片状粉末);4.材质(锌)	5.成分含量(锌的含量);6.粒度
79.04	**锌条、杆、型材及异型材或丝:**	1.品名;2.形状(条、杆、型材、异型材、丝);3.材质(锌)	
79.05	**锌板、片、带、箔:**	1.品名;2.形状(板、片、带、箔);3.材质(锌)	
79.06	**锌管及管子附件(例如,接头、肘管、管套):**	1.品名;2.用途(用于管子之间连通);3.材质(锌);4.种类(管、接头、肘管、管套等)	
79.07	**其他锌制品:**	1.品名;2.用途(工业用、非工业用);3.材质(锌);4.种类(电池壳体料、容器、保护阳极等)	

第八十章　锡及其制品

商品编码	商品描述	申报要素	
		商品名称	规格型号
80.01	**未锻轧锡:**	1.品名;2.形状(锭、块、粒);3.材质(非合金锡、锡合金);4.加工方法(未锻轧)	5.成分含量(锡及合金元素的含量)
80.02	**锡废碎料:**	1.品名;2.用途(供回收锡用);3.状态(废、碎);4.来源(非合金锡、锡合金的废碎料)	5.成分含量(锡的含量)
80.03	**锡条、杆、型材及异型材或丝:**	1.品名;2.形状(条、杆、型材、异型材、丝);3.材质(锡);4.状态(是否带焊剂)	
80.07	**其他锡制品:**	1.品名;2.用途(工业用、非工业用);3.材质(锡);4.种类(容器、牙膏软管)	

第八十一章　其他贱金属、金属陶瓷及其制品

【注解】

1.申报要求:品名栏及规格型号栏内为必须申报的项目或指标,括号内为列举内容(后有"等")或供选择内容(无"等");备注栏内为申报规范的解释说明举例。

2.名词解释:"品名"是指货品的具体商业名称;"用途"是指货品在出入境后的应用场合或下游产品;"加工方法"是指货品在出入境前的加工工艺或制造方法;"材质"是指货品按税则中的材质分类原则所确定的具体材料种类;"形状"是指货品按税则中的形状定义描述所确定的外观形状。

商品编码	商品描述	申报要素	
		商品名称	规格型号
81.01	**钨及其制品,包括废碎料:**	1.品名;2.形状(粉末);3.材质(钨)	4.成分含量(钨的含量);5.粒度;6.粉末请注明细度
8101.1000	-粉末	1.品名;2.形状(粉末);3.材质(钨)	4.成分含量(钨的含量);5.粒度;6.粉末请注明细度
	-其他:		
8101.9400	--未锻轧钨,包括简单烧结而成的条、杆	1.品名;2.形状(条、杆等);3.材质(钨);4.加工方法(未锻轧、简单烧结等)	
8101.9600	--丝	1.品名;2.形状(丝);3.材质(钨)	
8101.9700	--废碎料	1.品名;2.用途(供回收钨用);3.材质(钨);4.状态(废、碎);5.来源	
	--其他:	1.品名;2.材质(钨);3.种类	
81.02	**钼及其制品,包括废碎料:**		
8102.1000	-粉末	1.品名;2.形状(粉末);3.材质(钼)	4.粉末请注明细度
	-其他:		
8102.9400	--未锻轧钼,包括简单烧结而成的条、杆	1.品名;2.形状(条、杆);3.材质(钼);4.加工方法(未锻轧、简单烧结等)	
8102.9500	--条、杆,但简单烧结而成的除外;型材及异型材,板、片、带、箔	1.品名;2.形状(条、杆、型材、异型材、板、片、带、箔);3.材质(钼、钼合金);4.加工方法(锻轧)	
8102.9600	--丝	1.品名;2.形状(丝);3.材质(钼)	
8102.9700	--废碎料	1.品名;2.用途(供回收钼用);3.材质(钼);4.状态(废、碎);5.来源	
8102.9900	--其他	1.品名;2.材质(钼);3.种类	
81.03	**钽及其制品,包括废碎料:**	1.品名;2.形状(粉末、条、杆、型材、异型材、板、片、带、箔);3.材质(钽、钽合金);4.种类;5.加工方法(锻轧、未锻轧、简单烧结等)	6.状态(废、碎);7.成分含量(钽的含量)
81.04	**镁及其制品,包括废碎料:**		
	-未锻轧镁:	1.品名;2.材质(镁);3.加工方法(未锻轧)	4.成分含量(镁的含量);5.粉末粒度

商品编码	商品描述	申报要素	
		商品名称	规格型号
8104.2000	-废碎料	1. 品名;2. 用途(供回收镁用);3. 状态(废、碎);4. 来源	
8104.3000	-锉屑、车屑及颗粒,已按规格分级的;粉末	1. 品名;2. 形状(粉末等);3. 材质(镁);4. 来源(锉屑、车屑等)	5. 成分含量(镁的含量);6. 粒度
	-其他:	1. 品名;2. 材质(镁)3. 种类;4. 加工方法(锻轧等)	
81.05	**钴锍及其他冶炼钴时所得的中间产品;钴及其制品,包括废碎料:**	1. 品名;2. 形状(粉末、条、杆、型材、异型材、板、片、带、箔);3. 材质(钴、钴合金、钴锍);4. 种类;5. 加工方法(锻轧、未锻轧)	6. 状态(废、碎);7. 成分含量(钴的含量)粉末粒度
81.06	**铋及其制品,包括废碎料:**	1. 品名;2. 形状(粉末、条、杆、型材、异型材、板、片、带、箔);3. 材质(铋、铋合金);4. 加工方法(锻轧、未锻轧)	5. 状态(废、碎);6. 成分含量(铋的含量)
81.07	**镉及其制品,包括废碎料:**	1. 品名;2. 形状(粉末、条、杆、型材、异型材、板、片、带、箔);3. 材质(镉、镉合金);4. 种类;5. 加工方法(锻轧、未锻轧)	6. 状态(废、碎)
81.08	**钛及其制品,包括废碎料:**		
	-未锻轧钛;粉末:	1. 品名;2. 形状(粉末、杆等);3. 材质(钛);4. 加工方法(未锻轧)	5. 成分含量(钛的含量);6. 粉末粒度
8108.3000	-废碎料	1. 品名;2. 用途(供回收钛用);3. 状态(废、碎);4. 来源	
	-其他:	1. 品名;2. 形状(条杆、型材、异型材、板、片、带、箔等);3. 材质(钛);4. 种类;5. 加工方法(未锻轧)	6. 板、片、带、箔的厚度
81.09	**锆及其制品,包括废碎料:**	1. 品名;2. 形状(粉末、条、杆、型材、异型材、板、片、带、箔);3. 材质(锆、锆合金);4. 种类;5. 加工方法(未锻轧等)	6. 状态(废、碎);7. 成分含量(锆的含量);8. 粉末粒度
81.10	**锑及其制品,包括废碎料:**	1. 品名;2. 形状(粉末、条、杆、型材、异型材、板、片、带、箔);3. 材质(锑、锑合金);4. 种类;5. 加工方法(未锻轧等)	6. 状态(废、碎);7. 成分含量(锑的含量);8. 粉末粒度
81.11	**锰及其制品,包括废碎料:**	1. 品名;2. 形状(粉末、条、杆、型材、异型材、板、片、带、箔);3. 材质(锰、锰合金);4. 种类;5. 加工方法(未锻轧等)	6. 状态(废、碎);7. 成分含量(锰的含量);8. 粉末粒度
81.12	**铍、铬、锗、钒、镓、铪、铟、铼、铌、铊及其制品,包括废碎料:**	1. 品名;2. 形状(粉末、条、杆、型材、异型材、板、片、带、箔);3. 材质(铍、铬等贱金属及其合金);4. 种类;5. 加工方法(未锻轧等)	6. 状态(废、碎);7. 成分含量;8. 粉末粒度
81.13	**金属陶瓷及其制品,包括废碎料:**	1. 品名;2. 材质(金属陶瓷);3. 种类;4. 状态(废、碎)	

第八十二章　贱金属工具、器具、利口器、餐匙、餐叉及其零件

【注解】

1. 申报要求:品名栏及规格型号栏内为必须申报的项目或指标,括号内为列举内容(后有"等")或供选择内容(无"等");备注栏内为申报规范的解释说明举例。

2. 名词解释:"品名"是指货品的具体商业名称;"用途"是指货品在出入境后的应用场合或下游产品;"加工方法"是指货品在出入境前的加工工艺或制造方法;"材质"是指货品按税则中的材质分类原则所确定的具体材料种类;"形状"是指货品按税则中的形状定义描述所确定的外观形状。

商品编码	商品描述	申报要素	
		商品名称	规格型号
82.01	**锹、铲、镐、锄、叉及耙;斧子、钩刀及类似砍伐工具;各种修枝用剪刀;镰刀、秣刀、树篱剪、伐木楔子及其他农业、园艺或林业用手工工具:**	1. 品名;2. 用途(砍伐用、修枝用等);3. 材质(合金钢制等);4. 种类(锹、铲、剪等);5. 式样(单手操作等)	

商品编码	商品描述	申报要素	
		商品名称	规格型号
82.02	手工锯;各种锯的锯片(包括切条、切槽或无齿锯片):	1.品名;2.用途(加工金属用等);3.材质(合金钢制等);4.种类(手工锯、带锯片、圆锯片、直锯片等);5.圆锯片带有钢制工作部件请注明	
82.03	钢锉、木锉、钳子(包括剪钳)、镊子、白铁剪、切管器、螺栓切头器、打孔冲子及类似手工工具:	1.品名;2.用途(锉木材用等);3.材质(合金钢制等);4.种类(锉、钳子、镊子等)	
82.04	手动扳手及扳钳(包括转矩扳手,但不包括丝锥扳手);可互换的扳手套筒,不论是否带手柄:	1.品名;2.材质(合金钢制等);3.种类(扳手、扳钳、扳手套筒等);4.式样(固定的、可调的)	
82.05	其他税目未列名的手工工具(包括玻璃刀);喷灯;台钳、夹钳及类似品,但作为机床附件或零件的除外;砧;轻便锻炉;带支架的手摇或脚踏砂轮:	1.品名;2.用途(家用等);3.材质(合金钢制等);4.种类(锤子、螺丝刀等)	5.包装(是否成套)
82.06	由税目82.02至82.05中两个或多个税目所列工具组成的零售包装成套货品:	1.品名;2.材质(合金钢制等);3.包含的种类(扳手、钳子、螺丝刀等)	4.包装(零售包装成套)
82.07	手工工具(不论是否有动力装置)及机床(例如,锻压、冲压、攻丝、钻孔、镗孔、铰孔及铣削、车削或上螺丝用的机器)的可互换工具,包括金属拉拔或挤用模以及凿岩或钻探工具:	1.品名;2.用途(钻探、铣削、锻压、镗孔用等);3.材质(合金钢制等);4.种类(锻模、铣刀等);5.组成(是否带金刚石等)	6.带有工作部件请注明材质(金属陶瓷、金刚石等)
82.08	机器或机械器具的刀及刀片:	1.品名;2.用途(金属加工用、木器加工用、厨房器具用、农业园艺用等);3.材质(不锈钢制等);4.种类(机器用刀片等)	
82.09	未装配的工具用金属陶瓷板、杆、刀头及类似品:	1.品名;2.用途(工具用);3.材质(金属陶瓷制);4.种类(板、杆、刀头等);5.状态(未装配)	
82.10	用于加工或调制食品或饮料的手动机械器具,重量不超过10公斤:	1.品名;2.用途(加工食品用等);3.材质(不锈钢制等);4.种类(绞肉机、榨汁机等);5.原理(手动)	6.单件重量
82.11	有刃口的刀及其刀片,不论是否有锯齿(包括整枝刀),但税目82.08的刀除外:	1.品名;2.材质(不锈钢制等);3.状态(有刃口);4.种类(餐刀、折叠刀等);5.式样(刃面固定、可换刃面)	6.包装(是否成套)
82.12	剃刀及其刀片(包括未分开的刀片条):	1.品名;2.材质(不锈钢制等);3.种类(剃刀、安全刀片等)	
82.13	剪刀、裁缝剪刀及类似品、剪刀片:	1.品名;2.用途(裁缝用等);3.材质(不锈钢制等);4.种类(剪刀、剪刀片等)	
82.14	其他利口器(例如,理发推剪、屠刀、砍骨刀、切肉刀、切菜刀、裁纸刀);修指甲及修脚用具(包括指甲锉):	1.品名;2.材质(不锈钢制等);3.种类(裁纸刀、指甲锉、手动理发推剪、切菜刀等)	
82.15	餐匙、餐叉、长柄勺、漏勺、糕点夹、鱼刀、黄油刀、糖块夹及类似的厨房或餐桌用具:	1.品名;2.用途(餐桌、厨房用);3.材质(不锈钢制等);4.种类(餐叉、漏勺等);5.镀贵金属请注明	6.成装(是否成套)

第八十三章　贱金属杂项制品

【注解】

1.申报要求:品名栏及规格型号栏内为必须申报的项目或指标,括号内为列举内容(后有“等”)或供选择内容(无“等”);备注栏内为申报规范的解释说明举例。

2.名词解释:“品名”是指货品的具体商业名称;“用途”是指货品在出入境后的应用场合或下游产品;“加工方法”是指货品在出入境前的加工工艺或制造方法;“材质”是指货品按税则中的材质分类原则所确定的具体材料种类;“形状”是指货品按税则中的形状定义描述所确定的外观形状。

商品编码	商品描述	申报要素	
		商品名称	规格型号
83.01	贱金属制的锁(钥匙锁、数码锁及电动锁);贱金属制带锁的扣环及扣环框架;上述锁的贱金属制钥匙:	1.品名;2.用途(机动车用、家具用等);3.材质(不锈钢制等);4.种类(钥匙锁、数码锁、电动锁、钥匙等)	
83.02	用于家具、门窗、楼梯、百叶窗、车厢、鞍具、衣箱、盒子及类似品的贱金属附件及架座;贱金属制帽架、帽钩、托架及类似品;用贱金属做支架的小脚轮;贱金属制的自动闭门器:	1.品名;2.用途(机动车用、家具用等);3.材质(不锈钢制等);4.种类(铰链、自动闭门器等)	
83.03	装甲或加强的贱金属制保险箱、保险柜及保险库的门和带锁保险储存橱、钱箱、契约箱及类似品:	1.品名;2.材质(不锈钢制等);3.种类(保险箱、保险柜、保险库的门等)	
83.04	贱金属制的档案柜、卡片索引柜、文件盘、文件篮、笔盘、公章架及类似的办公用具,但税目94.03的办公室家具除外:	1.品名;2.用途(办公室用);3.材质(不锈钢制等);4.种类(档案柜、卡片索引柜、文件盘等);5.式样(非落地)	
83.05	活页夹、卷宗夹的贱金属附件,贱金属制的信夹、信角、文件夹、索引标签及类似的办公用品:贱金属制的成条钉书钉(例如,供办公室、室内装饰或包装用):	1.品名;2.用途(办公室用、室内装饰或包装用);3.材质(不锈钢制等);4.种类(活页夹、宗卷夹、成条钉书钉等)	
83.06	非电动的贱金属铃、钟、锣及类似品;贱金属雕塑像及其他装饰品;贱金属相框或画框及类似框架;贱金属镜子:	1.品名;2.材质(不锈钢制等);3.种类(铃、钟、锣、雕塑像、相框、画框等);4.镀贵金属请注明;5.铃、钟、锣请注明非电动	
83.07	贱金属软管,不论是否有附件:	1.品名;2.材质(钢铁制、其他贱金属制);3.种类(软管)	
83.08	贱金属制的扣、钩、环、眼及类似品,用于衣着、鞋靴、天篷、提包、旅行用品或其他制品;贱金属制的管形铆钉及开口铆钉;贱金属制的珠子及亮晶片:	1.品名;2.用途(用于衣服、提包上等);3.材质(不锈钢制等);4.种类(扣、钩、环、铆钉等)	
83.09	贱金属制的塞子、盖子(包括冠形瓶塞、螺口盖及倒水塞)、瓶帽、螺口塞、塞子帽、封志及其他包装用附件:	1.品名;2.形状(冠形、圆形等);3.材质(不锈钢制等);4.种类(塞子、盖子等)	
83.10	贱金属制的标志牌、铭牌、地名牌及类似品、号码、字母及类似标志,但税目94.05的货品除外:	1.品名;2.用途(汽车用等);3.材质(不锈钢制、贱金属种类等);4.种类(标志、铭牌等)	
83.11	贱金属或硬质合金制的丝、条、管、板、电极及类似品,以焊剂涂面或以焊剂为芯,用于焊接或沉积金属、硬质合金;贱金属粉粘聚而成的丝或条,供金属喷镀用:	1.品名;2.用途(电弧焊用、气焊用、钎焊用等);3.材质(贱金属、硬质合金制);4.种类(电极、焊条、焊丝等);5.状态(以焊剂涂面、以焊剂为芯)	

第十六类　机器、机械器具、电气设备及其零件；录音机及放声机、电视图像、声音的录制和重放设备及其零件、附件

第八十四章　核反应堆、锅炉、机器、机械具及其零件

【注解】

1. 零部件要报具体名称。
2. 未制成品、不完整品申报要注明程度。
3. 说明举例栏中未包含品牌、型号等内容。

商品编码	商品描述	申报要素	
		商品名称	规格型号
84.01	**核反应堆，核反应堆的未辐照燃料元件（释热元件）；同位素分离机器及装置：**	1. 品名；2. 用途；3. 品牌	4. 型号
84.02	**蒸汽锅炉（能产生低压水蒸汽的集中供暖用的热水锅炉除外）；过热水锅炉：**	1. 品名；2. 用途；3. 品牌；4. 构造方式	5. 型号；6. 温度；7. 蒸发量
84.03	**集中供暖用的热水锅炉，但税目84.02的货品除外：**	1. 品名；2. 用途；3. 品牌；4. 装循环装置请注明	5. 型号；6. 功率；7. 温度
84.04	**税目84.02或84.03所列锅炉的辅助设备（例如，节热器、过热器、除灰器、气体回收器）；水蒸汽或其他蒸汽动力装置的冷凝器：**	1. 品名；2. 用途；3. 品牌	4. 型号
84.05	**煤气发生器，不论有无净化器；乙炔发生器及类似的水解气体发生器，不论有无净化器：**	1. 品名；2. 品牌	3. 型号
84.06	**汽轮机：**	1. 品名；2. 用途；3. 品牌	4. 型号；5. 输出功率
84.07	**点燃往复式或旋转式活塞内燃发动机：**		
	-航空器发动机：	1. 品名；2. 用途；3. 品牌；4. 燃烧类型	5. 型号；6. 输生动率；7. 转速
	-船舶发动机：	1. 品名；2. 用途；3. 品牌；4. 燃料类型；5. 发动机安装位置（舷外或舷内）	6. 型号；7. 转速
	-用于第八十七章所列车辆的往复式活塞发动机：	1. 品名；2. 用途；3. 品牌；4. 燃料类型；5. 状态（成品、半成品、成套散件）	6. 型号；7. 排气量
	-其他发动机：	1. 品名；2. 用途；3. 品牌；4. 燃料类型	5. 型号；6. 转速
84.08	**压燃式活塞内燃发动机（柴油或半柴油发动机）：**	1. 品名；2. 用途；3. 品牌	4. 型号；5. 转速；6. 输出功率
84.09	**专用于或主要用于税目84.07或84.08所列发动机的零件：**	1. 品名；2. 用途（适用机型）	
84.10	**水轮机、水轮及其调节器：**	1. 品名；2. 品牌；3. 原理	4. 型号；5. 功率
84.11	**涡轮喷气发动机、涡轮螺桨发动机及其他燃气轮机：**	1. 品名；2. 品牌	3. 型号；4. 推力；5. 功率
84.12	**其他发动机及动力装置：**	1. 品名；2. 用途；3. 品牌；4. 原理（是否为喷气式）	5. 型号
	-液压动力装置：	1. 品名；2. 用途；3. 品牌；4. 原理（是否为液压式）	5. 型号
	-气压动力装置：	1. 品名；2. 用途；3. 品牌；4. 原理（是否为气压式）	5. 型号
8412.8000	-其他	1. 品名；2. 用途；3. 品牌；4. 原理	5. 型号
	-零件：	1. 品名；2. 用途（适用机型）	
84.13	**液体泵，不论是否装有计量装置；液体提升机：**		
	-装有或可装计量装置的泵：	1. 品名；2. 用途；3. 品牌；4. 可装计量装置请注明	5. 型号
8413.2000	手泵但子目8413.11或8413.19的货品除外	1. 品名；2. 品牌；3. 人力驱动请注明	4. 型号
	-活塞式内燃发动机用的燃油泵、润滑油泵或冷却剂泵：	1. 品名；2. 用途（是否为活塞式内燃发动机用）；3. 品牌	4 型号；5. 发动机的输出功率
8413.4000	-混凝土泵	1. 品名；2. 用途；3. 品牌	4. 型号

商品编码	商品描述	申报要素	
		商品名称	规格型号
	-其他往复式排液泵:	1. 品名;2. 用途;3. 品牌;4. 原理(是否为往复式);5. 驱动方式	6. 型号
	-其他回转式排液泵:	1. 品名;2. 用途;3. 品牌;4. 原理(是否为回转式);5. 驱动方式	6. 型号
	-其他离心泵:	1. 品名;2. 用途;3. 品牌;4. 原理	5. 型号;6. 转速
	-其他泵;液体提升机:	1. 品名;2. 用途;3. 品牌	4. 型号
	-零件:	1. 品名;2. 用途(适用机型)	
84.14	**空气泵或真空泵、空气及其他气体压缩机、风机、风扇;装有风扇的通风罩或循环气罩,不论是否装有过滤器:**		
8414.1000	-真空泵	1. 品名;2. 用途(适用行业);3. 品牌	4. 型号;5. 性能(抽气能力)
8414.2000	-手动或脚踏式空气泵	1. 品名;2. 品牌;3. 型号;4. 人力驱动请注明	
	-用于制冷设备的压缩机:	1. 品名;2. 用途(是否用于制冷设备);3. 品牌;4. 驱动方式	5. 型号;6. 额定功率
8414.4000	-装在拖车底盘上的空气压缩机	1. 品名;2. 用途;3. 品牌	4. 型号
	-罩的平面最大边长不超过 120 厘米的通风罩或循环气置:	1. 品名;2. 品牌;3. 装有风扇请注明	4. 型号;5. 罩的平面最大边长
	-其他:	1. 品名;2. 用途;3. 品牌	4. 型号;5. 压力比;6. 结构
	-零件:	1. 品名;2. 用途(适用机型)	
84.15	**空气调节器,装有电扇及调温、调湿装置,包括不能单独调湿的空调器:**		
	-窗式或壁式,独立的或分体的:	1. 品名;2. 品牌;3. 窗式或壁式安装请注明	4. 型号;5. 制冷量
8415.2000	-机动车辆上供人使用的	1. 品名;2. 用途;3. 品牌	4. 型号
	-其他:	1. 品名;2. 品牌;3. 装有制冷装置请注明;4. 装有冷热换向阀请注明	5. 型号;6. 制冷量
	-零件	1. 品名;2. 用途(适用机型)	
84.16	**使用液体燃料、粉状固体燃料或气体燃料的炉用燃烧器;机械加煤机,包括其机械炉篦、机械出灰器及类似装置:**	1. 品名;2. 用途;3. 品牌;4. 燃料类型	5. 型号
84.17	**非电热的工业或实验室用炉及烘箱,包括焚烧炉:**	1. 品名;2. 用途;3. 品牌;4. 加热方式	5. 型号
84.18	**电气或非电气的冷藏箱、冷冻箱及其他制冷设备;热泵,但税目 84.15 的空气调节器除外:**		
	-冷藏-冷冻组合机,各自装有单独外门的:	1. 品名;2. 品牌	3. 型号;4. 结构[冷藏、冷冻组合机(各自装有单独外门的)];5. 容积
	-家用型冷藏箱:	1. 品名;2. 用途(是否家用);3. 品牌;4. 原理	5. 型号;6. 容积;7. 制冷温度
	-柜式冷冻箱,容积不超过 800 升:	1. 品名;2. 品牌;3. 柜式请注明	4. 型号;5. 容积;6. 制冷温度
	-立式冷冻箱,容积不超过 900 升:	1. 品名;2. 品牌	3. 型号;4. 结构(是否为立式);5. 容积;6. 制冷温度
8418.5000	-其他冷藏或冷冻装置的其他设备(柜、箱、展示台、陈列箱及类似品),用于储存及展示	1. 品名;2. 用途;3. 品牌	4. 型号;5. 容积;6. 制冷温度
	-其他制冷设备;热泵:	1. 品名;2. 品牌;3. 型号;4. 原理(冷凝器是否为热交换器的)	

商品编码	商品描述	申报要素	
		商品名称	规格型号
	-零件：	1. 品名；2. 用途（适用机型）	
84.19	**利用温度变化处理材料的机器、装置及类似的实验室设备，例如，加热、烹煮、烘炒、蒸馏、精馏、消毒、灭菌、汽蒸、干燥、蒸发、气化、冷凝、冷却的机器设备，不论是否电热的（不包括税目85.14的炉、烘箱及其他设备），但家用的除外；非电热的快速热水器或贮备式热水器：**	1. 品名；2. 用途；3. 品牌；4. 原理；5. 加热方式	6. 型号
84.20	**研光机或其他滚压机器及其滚筒，但加工金属或玻璃用的除外：**	1. 品名；2. 用途；3. 品牌	4. 型号
84.21	**离心机，包括离心干燥机；液体或气体的过滤、净化机器及装置：**	1. 品名；2. 用途；3. 品牌；4. 原理	5. 型号
84.22	**洗碟机；瓶子及其他容器的洗涤或干燥机器；瓶、罐、箱、袋或其他容器装填、封口、密封、贴标签的机器；瓶、罐、管、筒或类似容器的包封机器；其他包装或打包机器（包括热缩包装机器）；饮料充气机：**		
	-洗碟机：	1. 品名；2. 用途（家用等）；3. 品牌	4. 型号
8422.2000	-瓶子或其他容器的洗涤或干燥机器	1. 品名；2. 用途；3. 品牌	4. 型号
	-瓶、罐、箱、袋或其他容器的装填、封口、密封、贴标签的机器；瓶、罐、管、筒或类似容器的包封机器；饮料充气机：	1. 品名；2. 用途；3. 品牌；4. 原理（操作方式）	5. 型号
8422.4000	-其他包装或打包机器（包括热缩包装机器）	1. 品名；2. 用途；3. 品牌	4. 型号
	-零件：	1. 品名；2. 用途（适用机型）	
84.23	**衡器（感量为50毫克或更精密的天平除外），包括计数或检验用的衡器；衡器用的各种砝码、秤砣：**	1. 品名；2. 用途；3. 品牌；4. 原理	5. 型号；6. 称量
84.24	**液体或粉末的喷射、散布或喷雾的机械器具（不论是否手工操作）；灭火器，不论是否装药；喷枪及类似器具；喷汽机、喷砂机及类似的喷射机器：**	1. 品名；2. 用途；3. 品牌；4. 喷射材料；5. 操作方式	6. 型号
84.25	**滑车及提升机，但倒卸式提升机除外；卷扬机及绞盘；千斤顶：**	1. 品名；2. 用途；3. 品牌；4. 驱动方式	5. 型号
84.26	**船用桅杆式起重机；起重机，包括缆式起重机；移动式吊运架、跨运车及装有起重机的工作车：**	1. 品名；2. 用途；3. 品牌；4. 结构原理	5. 型号
84.27	**叉车；其他装有升降或搬运装置的工作车：**	1. 品名；2. 用途；3. 品牌	4. 推进方式；5. 型号
84.28	**其他升降、搬运、装卸机械（例如，升降机、自动梯、输送机、缆车）：**		
	-升降机及倒卸式起重机：	1. 品名；2. 用途；3. 品牌；4. 驱动方式	5. 型号
8428.2000	-气压升降机及输送机	1. 品名；2. 品牌；3. 驱动方式	4. 型号
	-其他用于连续运送货物或材料的升降机及输送机：	1. 品名；2. 用途；3. 品牌；4. 驱动方式；5. 运送方式；6. 工作构件类型（斗式；带式等）	7. 型号
8428.4000	-自动梯及自动人行道	1. 品名；2. 品牌；3. 控制方式（是否为自动）	4. 型号
	-缆车、座式升降机、滑雪拉索、索道用牵引装置：	1. 品名；2. 用途；3. 品牌；4. 原理；5. 结构类型	6. 型号
	-其他机械：	1. 品名；2. 用途；3. 品牌	4. 型号
84.29	**机动推土机、侧铲推土机、筑路机、平地机、铲运机、机械铲、挖掘机、机铲装载机、捣固机械及压路机：**		

商品编码	商 品 描 述	申 报 要 素	
		商品名称	规格型号
	-推土机及侧铲推土机：	1. 品名;2. 品牌;3. 行走装置类型(轮胎式、履带式等);4. 自推进请注明	5. 型号;6. 发动机输出功率
	-筑路机及平地机：	1. 品名;2. 品牌;3. 自推进请注明	4. 型号;5. 发动机输出功率
	-铲运机：	1. 品名;2. 品牌;3. 自推进请注明	4. 型号;5. 斗容量
	-捣固机械及压路机：	1. 品名;2. 品牌;3. 原理;4. 自推进请注明	5. 型号;6. 机重
	-机械铲、挖掘机及机铲装载机：	1. 品名;2. 品牌;3. 行走装置类型(轮胎式;履带式等)4. 自推进请注明	5. 型号;6. 上部结构可旋转360度请注明
84.30	**泥土、矿物或矿石的运送、平整、铲运、挖掘、捣固、压实、开采或钻探机械;打桩机及拔桩机;扫雷机及吹雪机：**		
8430.1000	-打桩机及拔桩机	1. 品名;2. 品牌	3. 型号
8430.2000	-扫雪机及吹雪机	1. 品名;2. 品牌	3. 型号;4. 结构
	-截煤机、凿岩机及隧道掘进机：	1. 品名;2. 品牌	3. 型号;4. 推进方式
	-其他钻探或凿井机械：	1. 品名;2. 用途;3. 品牌	4. 型号;5. 推进方式;6. 钻探深度
	-其他自推进机械：	1. 品名;2. 用途;3. 品牌	4. 型号;5. 推进方式;6. 牙轮直径
	-其他非自推进机械：	1. 品名;2. 用途;3. 品牌;4. 非自推进请注明	5. 型号;6. 钻筒直径
84.31	**专用于或主要用于税目84.25至84.30所列机械的零件：**	1. 品名;2. 用途(适用机型)	
84.32	**农业、园艺及林业用整地或耕作机械;草坪及运动场地滚压机：**	1. 品名;2. 用途;3. 品牌	4. 型号;5. 钻筒直径
84.33	**收割机、脱粒机,包括草料打包机;割草机;蛋类、水果或其他农产品的清洁、分选、分级机器,但税目84.37的机器除外：**		
	-草坪、公园或运动场地用的割草机：	1. 品名;2. 用途;3. 品牌	4. 型号;5. 驱动方式;6. 切割装置的旋转类型
8433.2000	-其他割草机,包括牵引装置用的刀具杆	1. 品名;2. 用途;3. 品牌	4. 型号
8433.3000	-其他干草切割、翻晒机器	1. 品名;2. 品牌	3. 型号
8433.4000	-草料打包机,包括收集打包机	1. 品名;2. 品牌	3. 型号
	-其他收割机;脱粒机：	1. 品名;2. 用途;3. 品牌	4. 型号;5. 功率
8433.6000	-蛋类、水果或其他农产品的清洁、分选、分级机器	1. 品名;2. 用途;3. 品牌	4. 型号
	-零件：	1. 品名;2. 用途(适用机型)	
84.34	**挤奶机及乳品加工机器：**	1. 品名;2. 用途;3. 品牌	4. 型号
84.35	**制酒、制果汁或制类似饮料用的压榨机、轧碎机及类似机器：**	1. 品名;2. 用途;3. 品牌	4. 型号
84.36	**农业、园艺、林业、家禽饲养业或养蜂业用的其他机器,包括装有机械或热力装置的催芽设备;家禽孵卵器及育雏器：**	1. 品名;2. 用途;3. 品牌	4. 型号
84.37	**种子、谷物或干豆的清洁、分选或分级机器;谷物磨粉业加工机器或谷物、干豆加工机器,但农业用机器除外：**	1. 品名;2. 用途;3. 品牌	4. 型号
84.38	**本章其他税目未列名的食品、饮料工业用的生产或加工机器,但提取、加工动物油脂或植物固定油脂的机器除外：**	1. 品名;2. 用途;3. 品牌	4. 型号

商品编码	商品描述	申报要素	
		商品名称	规格型号
84.39	纤维素纸浆、纸及纸板的制造或整理机器：	1. 品名;2. 用途;3. 品牌	4. 型号
84.40	书本装订机器,包括锁线订书机：	1. 品名;2. 用途;3. 品牌	4. 型号
84.41	其他制造纸浆制品、纸制品或纸板制品的机器,包括各种切纸机：	1. 品名;2. 用途;3. 品牌;4. 功能	5. 型号
84.42	制版用的机器、器具及设备(税目84.56至84.65的机床除外);活字、印刷用版(片)滚筒及其他印刷部件;制成供印刷用(例如,刨平、压纹或抛光)的版(片)滚筒及石板：	1. 品名;2. 用途;3. 品牌;4. 排版或排字方法	5. 型号
84.43	用税目84.42的印刷用板(片)滚筒及其他印刷部件进行印刷的机器其他打印机、复印机及传真机,不论是否组合成;上述机器的零件及附件	1. 品名;2. 用途;3. 品牌;4. 原理;5. 进料方式	6. 型号;7. 片尺寸
84.44	化学纺织纤维挤压、拉伸、变形或切割机器：	1. 品名;2. 用途;3 品牌	4. 型号
84.45	纺织纤维的预处理机器;纺纱机,并线机、加捻机及其他生产纺织纱线的机器;摇纱机、络纱机(包括卷纬机)及处理税目84.46或84.47所列机器用的纺织纱线的机器：	1. 品名;2. 用途;3. 品牌;4. 控制方式	5. 型号
84.46	织机：	1. 品名;2. 用途;3. 品牌;4. 原理	5. 型号;6. 驱动方式;7. 织物宽度
84.47	针织机、缝编机及制粗松螺旋花线、网眼薄纱、花边、刺绣品、装饰带、编织带或网的机器及簇绒机：		
	-圆型针织机：	1. 品名;2. 品牌;3. 原理	4. 型号;5. 圆筒直径
	-平型针织机;缝编机：	1. 品名;2. 品牌;3. 原理	4. 型号
	-其他：	1. 品名;2. 品牌;3. 原理	4. 型号
84.48	税目84.44、84.45、84.46或84.47所列机器的辅助机器(例如,多臂机、提花机、自停装置及换梭装置);专用于或主要用于税目84.44、84.45、84.46或84.47所列机器的零件、附件(例如,锭子、锭壳、钢丝针布、梳、喷丝头、梭子、综丝、综框、针织机用针)：	1. 品名;2. 用途(适用机型)	
84.49	成匹、成形的毡呢或无纺织物制造或整理机器,包括制毡呢帽机器;帽模：	1. 品名;2. 用途;3. 品牌	4. 型号
84.50	家用型或洗衣房用洗衣机,包括洗涤干燥两用机：	1. 品名;2. 品牌;3. 结构原理;4. 自动化程度	5. 型号;6. 干衣量
84.51	纱线、织物及纺织制品的洗涤、清洁、绞拧、干燥、熨烫、挤压(包括熔压)、漂白、染色、上浆、整理、涂布或浸渍机器(税目84.50的机器除外);列诺伦(亚麻油地毡)及类似铺地制品的布基或其他底布的浆料涂布机器;纺织物的卷绕、退绕、折叠、剪切或剪齿边机器：	1. 品名;2. 用途;3. 品牌	4. 型号;5. 干衣量
84.52	缝纫机,但税目84.40的锁线订书机除外;缝纫机专用的特制家具、底座及罩盖;缝纫机针：	1. 品名;2. 用途;3. 品牌;4. 控制方式	5. 型号
84.53	生皮、皮革的处理、鞣制或加工机器,鞋靴、毛皮及其他皮革制品的制作或修理机器,但缝纫机除外：	1. 品名;2. 用途;3. 品牌	4. 型号

商品编码	商 品 描 述	申 报 要 素	
		商品名称	规格型号
84.54	金属冶炼及铸造用的转炉、浇包、锭模及铸造机：	1.品名;2.用途;3.品牌	4.型号
84.55	金属轧机及其轧辊：	1.品名;2.用途;3.品牌;4.加工方式	5.型号
84.56	用激光、其他光、光子束、超声波、放电、电化学法、电子束、离子束或等离子弧处理各种材料的加工机床：	1.品名;2.品牌;3.控制方式;4.功能;5.加工方式	6.型号;7.旧机床请注明生产年代
84.57	加工金属的加工中心、单工位组合机床及多工位组合机床：	1.品名;2.用途;3.品牌;4.功能;5.主轴方向	6.工位数;7.规格型号;8.旧机床请注明生产年代;9.可加装刀库请注明刀库容量及选配件
84.58	切削金属的车床(包括车削中心)：	1.品名;2.用途;3.品牌;4.控制方式;5.主轴方向	6.型号;7.旧机床请注明生产年代
84.59	切削金属的钻床、镗床、铣床、攻丝机床(包括直线移动式动力头钻床),但税目84.58的车床(包括车削中心)除外：	1.品名;2.用途;3.品牌;4.功能;5.控制方式	6.规格型号;7.动力头移动方式;8.主轴方向;9.旧机床请注明生产年代;10、可加装刀库请注明刀库容量及选配件
84.60	用磨石、磨料或抛光材料对金属或金属陶瓷进行去毛刺、刃磨、磨削、珩磨、研磨、抛光或其他精加工的机床,但税目84.61的切齿机、齿轮磨床或齿轮精加工机床除外：	1.品名;2.用途;3.品牌;4.控制方式	5.型号;6.定位精度;7.旧机床请注明年代
84.61	切削金属或金属陶瓷的刨床、牛头刨床、插床、拉床、切齿机、齿轮磨床或齿轮精加工机床、锯床、切断机及其他税目未列名的切削机床：	1.品名;2.用途;3.品牌;4.功能;5.结构类型	6.型号;7.旧机床请注明年代
84.62	加工金属的锻造(包括模锻)或冲压机床;加工金属的弯曲、折叠、矫直、矫平、剪切、冲孔或开槽机床;其他加工金属或硬质合金的压力机：	1.品名;2.用途;3.品牌;4.功能;5.控制方式	6.型号;7.定位精度;8.旧机床请注明年代
84.63	金属或金属陶瓷的其他非切削加工机床：	1.品名;2.用途;3.品牌;4.功能	5.型号;6.旧机床请注明年代
84.64	石料、陶瓷、混凝土、石棉水泥或类似矿物材料的加工机床、玻璃冷加工机床：	1.品名;2.用途;3.品牌;4.加工材料	5.型号;6.旧机床请注明年代
84.65	木材、软木、骨、硬质橡胶、硬质塑料或类似硬质材料的加工机床(包括用打钉或打U形钉、胶粘或其他方法组合前述材料的机器)：	1.品名;2.用途;3.品牌;4.加工材料	5.型号;6.旧机床请注明年代
84.66	专用于或主要用于税目84.56至84.65所列机器的零件、附件,包括工件或工具的夹具、自启板牙切头、分度头及其他专用于机床的附件;各种手提工具的工具夹具：	1.品名;2.用途(适用机型)	
84.67	手提式风动或液压工具及本身装有电动或非电动动力装置的手提式工具：	1.品名;2.品牌;3.驱动方式;4.操作方式(手提式)	5.型号
84.68	焊接机器及装置,不论是否兼有切割功能,但税目85.15的货品除外;气体加温表面回火机器及装置：	1.品名;2.品牌;3.原理;4.操作方式	5.型号
84.69	打字机,但税目84.43的打印机除外;文字处理机：	1.品名;2.品牌;3.驱动方式	4.型号

商品编码	商品描述	申报要素	
		商品名称	规格型号
84.70	**计算机器及具有计算功能的袖珍式数据记录、重现及显示机器;装有计算装置的会计计算机、邮资盖戳机、售票机及类似机器;现金出纳机:**		
8470.1000	-不需外接电源的电子计算器及具有计算功能的袖珍式数据记录、重现及显示机器	1. 品名;2. 品牌;3. 外接电源请注明	4. 型号
	-其他电子计算器:	1. 品名;2. 品牌;3. 有打印装置请注明	4. 型号
8470.3000	-其他计算机器	1. 品名;2. 品牌;3. 驱动方式	4. 型号
	-现金出纳机:	1. 品名;2. 用途;3. 品牌	4. 型号
8470.9000	-其他	1. 品名;2. 用途;3. 品牌	4. 型号
84.71	**自动数据处理设备及其部件;其他税目未列名的磁性或光学阅读机、将数据以代码形式转录到数据记录媒体的机器及处理这些数据的机器:**		
8471.3000	-重量不超过10千克的便携式自动数据处理设备,至少由一个中央处理部件、一个键盘及一个显示器组成	1. 品名;2. 品牌	3. 型号;4. 组成部件;5. 重量;6. CPU主频;7. 内存容量;8. 硬盘容量
	-其他自动数据处理设备		
	--同一机壳内至少有一个中央处理部件及一个输入和输出部件,不论是否组合式:	1. 品名;2. 品牌;3. 机型	4. 型号;5. 机壳内组成部件;6. CPU数量及主频;7. 内存容量;8. 硬盘容量
	--其他,以系统形式报检验的:	1. 品名;2. 品牌;3. 机型	4. 型号;5. 配置(系统组成部件)
	-子目8471.41及8471.49所列以外的处理部件,不论是否在同一机壳内有一个或两个下列部件:存储部件、输入部件、输出部件:	1. 品名;2. 品牌;3. 机型	4. 型号;5. 组成部件;6. 芯片请注明类型(桌面型、移动型、服务器型)
	-输入或输出部件,不论是否在同一机壳内有存储部件:		
8471.6040	---巨型机、大型机、中型机及小型机用终端	1. 品名;2. 品牌;3. 机型	4. 型号
8471.6050	---扫描仪	1. 品名;2. 用途;3. 品牌	4. 型号
8471.6060	---数字化仪	1. 品名;2. 用途;3. 品牌	4. 型号
	---键盘、鼠标器	1. 品名;2. 用途;3. 品牌	4. 型号
8471.6090	---其他	1. 品名;2. 用途;3. 品牌	4. 型号
	-存储部件:		
8471.7010	---硬盘驱动器	1. 品名;2. 用途;3. 品牌	4. 型号;5. 容量;6. 转数
8471.7020	---软盘驱动器	1. 品名;2. 用途;3. 品牌	4. 型号
8471.7030	---光盘驱动器	1. 品名;2. 用途;3. 品牌;4. 有刻录功能请注明	5. 型号;6. 倍数;7. 类型(CD-ROM、DVD-ROM、刻录型等)
8471.7090	---其他	1. 品名;2. 用途;3. 品牌	4. 型号
8471.8000	-自动数据处理设备的其他部件	1. 品名;2. 用途;3. 品牌	4. 型号
8471.9000	-其他	1. 品名;2. 用途;3. 品牌	4. 型号
84.72	**其他办公室用机器(例如,胶版复印机、油印机、地址印写机、自动付钞机、硬币分类、计数及包装机、削铅笔机、打洞机或订书机):**	1. 品名;2. 用途;3. 品牌	4. 型号

商品编码	商品描述	申报要素	
		商品名称	规格型号
84.73	**专用于或主要用于税目84.69至84.72所列机器的零件、附件（罩套、提箱及类似品除外）：**	1.品名;2.用途(适用机型)	
84.74	**泥土、石料、矿石或其他固体（包括粉状、浆状）矿物质的分类、筛选、分离、洗涤、破碎、磨粉、混合或搅拌机器；固体矿物燃料、陶瓷坯泥、未硬化水泥、石膏材料或其他粉状、浆状矿产品的粘聚或成形机器；铸造用砂模的成形机器：**	1.品名;2.用途;3.品牌;4.原理	5.型号
84.75	**白炽灯泡、灯管、放电灯管、电子管、闪光灯泡及类似品的封装机器；玻璃或玻璃制品的制造或热加工机器：**	1.品名;2.用途;3.品牌;4.功能	5.型号
84.76	**自动售货机（例如，出售邮票、香烟、食品或饮料的机器），包括钱币兑换机：**	1.品名;2.品牌;3.供应商品种类;4.装有加热或制冷装置请注明	5.型号
84.77	**本章其他税目未列名的橡胶或塑料及其产品的加工机器：**	1.品名;2.用途;3.品牌;4.原理;5.功能	6.型号
84.78	**本章其他税目未列名的烟草加工及制作机器：**	1.品名;2.用途;3.品牌	4.型号
84.79	**本章其他税目未列名的具有独立功能的机器及机械器具：**	1.品名;2.用途;3.品牌	4.型号
84.80	**金属铸造用型箱；型模底板；阳模；金属用型模（锭模除外）、硬质合金、玻璃、矿物材料、橡胶或塑料用型模：**	1.品名;2.用途;3.品牌;4.模具类型;5.适用材料	6.型号
84.81	**用于管道、锅炉、罐、桶或类似品的龙头，旋塞、阀门及类似装置，包括减压阀及恒温控制阀：**	1.品名;2.用途;3.品牌	4.型号
84.82	**滚动轴承：**	1.品名;2.用途;3.品牌;4.类型	5.型号
84.83	**传动轴（包括凸轮轴及曲柄轴）及曲柄；轴承座及滑动轴承；齿轮及齿轮传动装置；滚珠或滚子螺杆传动装置；齿轮箱及其他变速装置，包括扭矩变换器；飞轮及滑轮，包括滑轮组；离合器及联轴器（包括万向节）：**		
	-传动轴（包括凸轮轴及曲柄轴）及曲柄：	1.品名;2.用途;3.品牌	4.型号
8483.2000	-装有滚珠或滚子轴承的轴承座	1.品名;2.用途;3.品牌;4.装有滚珠或滚子轴承请注明	5.型号
8483.3000	-未装有滚珠或滚子轴承的轴承座；滑动轴承	1.品名;2.用途;3.品牌;4.装有滚珠或滚子轴承请注明	5.型号
	-齿轮及齿轮传动装置，（带齿的轮、链轮及其他单独进口或出口的传动元件除外）；滚珠或滚子螺杆传动装置；齿轮箱及其他变速装置，包括扭矩变换器：	1.品名;2.用途;3.品牌;4.原理	5.型号
8483.5000	-飞轮及滑轮，包括滑轮组	1.品名;2.用途;3.品牌	4.型号
8483.6000	-离合器及联轴器（包括万向节）	1.品名;2.用途;3.品牌	4.型号
8483.9000	-单独报验的带齿的轮、链轮及其他传动元件；零件	1.品名;2.用途(适用机型)	
84.84	**密封垫或类似接合衬垫，用金属片与其他材料制成或用双层或多层金属片制成；成套或各种不同材料的密封垫或类似接合衬垫，装于袋、套或类似包装内；机械密封件：**		
8484.1000	-密封垫或类似接合衬垫，用金属片与其他材料制成或用双层或多层金属片制成	1.品名;2.品牌;3.组成材料	4.型号

商品编码	商 品 描 述	申 报 要 素	
		商品名称	规格型号
8484.2000	-机械密封件	1. 品名;2. 品牌;3. 结构	4. 型号
8484.9000	-其他	1. 品名;2. 品牌;3. 各自构成材料	4. 型号;5. 成套包装请注明
84.86	**专用于或主要用于制造半导体单晶体或晶圆、半导体器件、集成电路或平板显示器的机器及装置;本章注释九(三)规定的机器及装置;零件及附件:**	1. 品名;2. 用途	
84.87	**本章其他税目未列名的机器零件,不具有电气接插件、绝缘体、线圈、触点或其他电气器材特征的:**	1. 品名;2. 用途(适用机型)	

备注或申报要求

84. 56 用激光、其他光、光子束、超声波、放电、电化学法、电子束、离子束或等离子弧处理各种材料的加工机床: 旧机床请注明新机价格

84. 57 加工金属的加工中心、单工位组合机床及多工位组合机床: 1. 旧机床请注明新机价格; 2. 英文品牌

84. 58 切削金属的车床(包括车削中心): 1. 旧机床请注明新机价格; 2. 英文品牌

84. 59 切削金属的钻床、镗床、铣床、攻丝机床(包括直线移动式动力头钻床)但税目81. 58的车床(包括车削中心)除外: 1. 旧机床请注明新机价格; 2. 英文品牌

84. 60 用磨石、磨料或抛光材料对金属或金属陶瓷进行去毛刺、刃磨、磨削、珩磨、研磨、抛光或其他精加工的机床,但税目84. 61的切齿机、齿轮磨床或齿轮精加工机床除外: 1. 旧机床请注明新机价格; 2. 英文品牌

84. 61 切削金属或金属陶瓷的刨床、牛头刨床、插床、拉床、切齿机、齿轮磨床或齿轮精加工机床、锯床、切断机及其他税目未到名的切削机床: 1. 旧机床请注明新机价格; 2. 英文品牌

84. 62 加工金属的锻造(包括模锻)或冲压机床; 加工金属的弯曲、折叠、矫直、矫平、剪切、冲孔或开槽机床; 其他加工金属或硬质合金的压力机: 1. 旧机床请注明新机价格; 2. 英文品牌

84. 63 金属或金属陶瓷的其他非切削加工机床: 1. 旧机床请注明新机价格; 2. 英文品牌

84. 64 石料、陶瓷、混凝土、石棉水泥或类似矿物材料的加工机床、玻璃冷加工机床:旧机床请注明新机价格

84. 65 木材、软木、骨、硬质橡胶、硬质塑料或类似硬质材料的加工机床(包括用打钉或打U形钉、胶粘或其他方法组合前述材料的机器):旧机床请注明新机价格

第八十五章 电机、电气设备及其零件;录音机及放声机、电视图像、声音的录制和重放设备及其零件、附件

【注解】

1. 零部件要报具体名称。
2. 未制成品、不完整品申报要注明程度。
3. 说明举例栏中未包含品牌、型号等内容。

商品编码	商 品 描 述	申 报 要 素	
		商品名称	规格型号
85.01	**电动机及发电机(不包括发电机组):**		
	-输出功率不超过37.5瓦的电动机:	1. 品名;2. 用途;3. 品牌	4. 型号;5. 输出功率;6. 机座尺寸
8501.2000	-交直流两用电动机,输出功率超过37.5瓦	1. 品名;2. 用途;3. 品牌;4. 交直流两用请注明	5. 型号;6. 输出功率;7. 用电相数;8. 旧机请注明制造年份
	-其他直流电动机;直流发电机:	1. 品名;2. 品牌;3. 直流请注明	4. 型号;5. 输出功率
8501.4000	-其他单相交流电动机	1. 品名;2. 品牌;3. 单相交流请注明	4. 型号;5. 输出功率
	-其他多相交流电动机:	1. 品名;2. 品牌	3. 型号;4. 输出功率;5. 用电相数
	-交流发电机:	1. 品名;2. 用途;3. 品牌;4. 交流请注明	5. 型号;6. 输出功率;7. 用电相数
85.02	**发电机组及旋转式变流机:**	1. 品名;2. 品牌;3. 原动机类型	4. 型号;5. 输出功率;6. 组成
85.03	**专用于或主要用于税目85.01或85.02所列机器的零件:**	1. 品名;2. 用途(适用机型)	

商品编码	商品描述	申报要素	
		商品名称	规格型号
85.04	**变压器、静止式变流器(例如,整流器)及电感器:**		
	-放电灯或放电管用镇流器:	1.品名;2.用途;3.品牌;4.原理	5.型号
	-液体介质变压器:	1.品名;2.品牌	3.型号;4.额定容量;5.液体介质
	-其他变压器:	1.品名;2.品牌;3.直流请注明	4.型号;5.输出功率
	-静止式变流器:	1.品名;2.用途;3.品牌;4.功能	5.型号;6.功率;7.精度
8504.5000	-其他电感器	1.品名;2.用途;3.品牌	4.型号
	-零件:	1.品名;2.用途(适用机型)	
85.05	**电磁铁;永磁铁及磁化后准备制永磁铁的物品;电磁铁或永磁铁卡盘、夹具及类似的工件夹具;电磁联轴节、离合器及制动器;电磁起重吸盘:**		
	-永磁铁及磁化后准备制永磁铁的物品:	1.品名;2.用途;3.品牌;4.材质	5.型号
8505.2000	-电磁联轴节、离合器及制动器	1.品名;2.用途;3.品牌	4.型号
	-其他,包括零件:	1.品名;2.用途;3.品牌;4.原理	5.型号
85.06	**原电池及原电池组:**	1.品名;2.用途;3.品牌;4.材质;5.可充电请注明	6.型号;7.电压伏数
85.07	**蓄电池,包括隔板,不论是否矩形(包括正方形):**	1.品名;2.用途;3.品牌;4.材质	6.型号;7.电压伏数
85.08	**真空吸尘器**	1.品名;2.用途;3.品牌;4.驱动方式	5.型号;6.输出功率
85.09	**家用电动器具,税目85.08的真空吸尘器除外:**	1.品名;2.用途;3.品牌;4.驱动方式	5.型号;6.机重
85.10	**电动剃须刀、电动毛发推剪及电动脱毛器:**	1.品名;2.用途;3.品牌	4.型号
85.11	**点燃式或压燃式内燃发动机用的电点火及电起动装置(例如,点火磁电机、永磁直流发电机、点火线圈、火花塞、电热塞及起动电机);附属于上述内燃发动机的发电机(例如,直流发电机、交流发电机)及断流器:**	1.品名;2.用途;3.品牌;4.功能	5.型号;6.适用发动机的输出功率
85.12	**自行车或机动车辆用的电气照明或信号装置(税目85.39的物品除外)、风挡刮水器、除霜器及去雾器:**	1.品名;2.用途;3.品牌;4.功能	5.型号
85.13	**自供能源(例如,使用干电池、蓄电池、永磁发电机)的手提式电灯,但税目85.12的照明装置除外:**	1.品名;2.品牌;3.操作方式	4.型号;5.自供能源类型
85.14	**工业或实验室用电炉及电烘箱(包括通过感应或介质损耗工作的);工业或实验室用其他通过感应或介质损耗对材料进行热处理的设备:**	1.品名;2.用途;3.品牌;4.加热原理	5.型号
85.15	**电气(包括电热气体)、激光、其他光、光子束、超声波、电子束、磁脉冲或等离子弧焊接机器及装置,不论是否兼有切割功能;用于热喷金属或金属陶瓷的电气机器及装置:**	1.品名;2.品牌;3.原理;4.自动化程度	5.型号
85.16	**电热的快速热水器、储存式热水器、浸入式液体加热器;电气空间加热器及土壤加热器;电热的理发器具(例如,电吹风机、电卷发器、电热发钳)及干手器;电熨斗;其他家用电热器具;加热电阻器,但税目85.45的货品除外:**		

商品编码	商 品 描 述	申 报 要 素	
		商品名称	规格型号
8516.1000	-电热的快速热水器、储存式热水器、浸入式液体加热器	1.品名;2.品牌;3.结构;4.加热原理	5.型号
	-电气空间加热器及土壤加热器:	1.品名;2.用途;3.品牌;4.加热原理	5.型号
	-电热的理发器具及干手器:	1.品名;2.用途;3.品牌;4.加热原理	5.型号
8516.4000	-电熨斗	1.品名;2.用途;3.品牌	4.型号
8516.5000	-微波炉	1.品名;2.用途;3.品牌	4.型号
	-其他炉;电锅、电热板、加热环、烧烤炉及烘烤器:	1.品名;2.用途;3.品牌;4.加热原理	5.型号
	-其他电热器具:	1.品名;2.用途(是否为家用); 3.品牌;4.加热原理	5.型号
8516.8000	-加热电阻器	1.品名;2.用途;3.品牌;4.加热原理	5.型号
	-零件:	1.品名;2.用途(适用机型)	
85.17	**电话机,包括用于蜂窝网络或其他无线网络的电话机;其他发送或接收声音、图像或其他数据用的设备,包括有线或无线网络(例如,局域网或广域网)的通信设备,税目84.43、85.25、85.27或85.28发送或接收信息除外:**		
	-电话机,包括蜂窝网络或其他无线网络用电话机:	1.品名;2.品牌	3.型号
	-零件:	1.品名;2.用途(适用机型)	
85.18	**传声器(麦克风)及其座架;扬声器,不论是否装成音箱;耳机、耳塞,不论是否装有传声器,由传声器及一个或多个扬声器组成的组合机;音频扩大器;电气扩音机组:**		
8518.1000	-传声器(麦克风)及其座架	1.品名;2.品牌	3.型号
	-扬声器,不论是否装成音箱:	1.品名;2.品牌;3.结构类型	4.型号;
8518.3000	-耳机、耳塞,不论是否装有传声器,由传声器及一个或多个扬声器组成的组合机	1.品名;2.品牌	3.型号
8518.4000	-音频扩大器	1.品名;2.品牌	3.型号
8518.5000	-电气扩音机组	1.品名;2.品牌	3.型号;4.组成
8518.9000	-零件	1.品名;2.品牌	3.型号;4.组成
85.19	**声音录制或重放设备:**		
8519.2000	-用硬币、钞票、银行卡、代币或其他支付方式使其工作的设备	1.品名;2.品牌;3.装有声音录制装置请注明	4.型号
8519.3000	-转盘(唱机唱盘):	1.品名;2.品牌;3.装有自动换片装置请注明;4.装有声音录制装置请注明	5.型号
8519.5000	-电话应答机	1.品名;2.品牌;3.装有声音录制装置请注明	4.型号
	-其他设备:	1.品名;2.品牌;3.使用媒介; 4.装录音装置请注明	5.型号
85.20	**磁带录音机及其他声音录制设备,不论是否装有声音重放装置:**		
8520.1000	-需外接电源的口授记录机	1.品名;2.品牌;3.需外接电源请注明;4.装有声音录制装置请注明	5.型号
	-装有声音重放装置的其他磁带录音机:	1.品名;2.品牌;3.使用媒介(是否为盒式磁带);4.处理数据的类型(是否为数字音频式等);5.装有声音录制装置请注明	6.型号

商品编码	商品描述	申报要素	
		商品名称	规格型号
	-其他:	1.品名;2.品牌;3.使用媒介;4.处理数据的类型;5.装有声音录制装置请注明	6.型号;7.装有声音录制装置请注明
85.21	**视频信号录制或重放设备,不论是否装有高频调谐器:**		
	-磁带型:	1.品名;2.用途;3.品牌;4.使用媒介	5.型号
	-其他:	1.品名;2.品牌;3.使用媒介;4.处理数据的类型	5.型号
85.22	**专用于或主要用于税目85.19至85.21所列设备的零件、附件:**	1.品名;2.用途(适用机型)	
85.23	**录制声音或其他信息用的圆盘、磁带、固态非易失性数据存储器件、"智能卡"及其他媒体,不论是否已录制,包括供复制圆盘用的图片及母带,但不包括第三十七章的产品:**	1.品名;2.用途;3.品牌;4.使用媒介;5.录制的请注明	6.型号;7.磁带宽度
85.24	**已灌(录)音或录制其他信息的唱片、磁带及其他媒体,包括供复制用的母片及母带,但不包括第三十七章的产品:**	1.品名;2.用途;3.品牌;4.使用媒介;5.录制的请注明	6.型号;7.磁带宽度
85.25	**无线电广播、电视发送设备,不论是否装有接收装置或声音的录制、重放装置;电视摄像机、数字照相机及视频摄录一体机:**		
8525.5000	-发送设备	1.品名;2.用途;3.品牌;4.功能	5.型号
	-装有接收装置的发送设备:	1.品名;2.用途;3.品牌;4.功能	5.型号;6.结构组成
	-电视摄像机、数字照相机及视频摄录一体机:	1.品名;2.用途;3.品牌;4.原理;5.功能	6.型号
85.26	**雷达设备、无线电导航设备及无线电遥控设备:**	1.品名;2.用途;3.品牌;4.原理	5.型号
85.27	**无线电广播接收设备,不论是否与声音的录制、重放装置或时钟组合在同一机壳内:**		
	-不需外接电源的无线电收音机	1.品名;2.品牌;3.功能;4.需外接电源请注明;5.内置扬声器请注明	6.型号;7.外形尺寸;8.使用媒介(是否为盒式磁带)
	-需外接电源的汽车用无线电收音机:	1.品名;2.用途;3.品牌;4.功能;5.需外接电源请注明	6.型号;7.结构组成
85.28	**监视器及投影机、未装电视接收装置;电视接收装置,不论是否装有无线电收音装置或声音、图像的录制或重放装置:**	1.品名;2.用途;3.品牌;4.显像类型	5.显示屏幕尺寸;6.型号
85.29	**专用于或主要用于税目85.25至85.28所列装置或设备的零件:**	1.品名;2.用途(适用机型)	
85.30	**铁道、电车道、道路或内河航道、停车场、港口或机场用的电气信号、安全或交通管理设备(税目86.08的货品除外):**	1.品名;2.用途;3.品牌;4.功能	5.型号
85.31	**电气音响或视觉信号装置(例如,电铃、电笛、显示板、防盗或防火报警器),但税目85.12或85.30的货品除外:**		
	-防盗或防火报警器及类似装置:	1.品名;2.用途;3.品牌;4.功能	5.型号
8531.2000	-装有液晶装置(LCD)或发光二极管(LED)的显示板	1.品名;2.用途;3.品牌;4.显示原理	5.型号
	-其他装置:	1.品名;2.用途;3.品牌	4.型号
	-零件:	1.品名;2.用途(适用机型)	

商品编码	商品描述	申报要素	
		商品名称	规格型号
85.32	**固定、可变或可调(微调)电容器:**		
8532.1000	-固定电容器,用于50/60赫兹电路,其额定无功功率不低于0.5千瓦(电力电容器)	1.品名;2.用途;3.品牌	4.型号;5.额定无功功率;6.适用频率
	-其他固定电容器:	1.品名;2.品牌;3.结构类型(单层;多层等);4.电介质类型	5.型号
8532.3000	-可变或可调(微调)电容器	1.品名;2.品牌;3.可变、可调请注明	4.型号
	-零件:	1.品名;2.品牌;3.适用元件类型	4.型号
85.33	**电阻器(包括变阻器及电位器),但加热电阻器除外:**		
8533.1000	-固定碳质电阻器,合成或薄膜式	1.品名;2.品牌;3.类型(合成或薄膜式)	4.型号
	-其他固定电阻器:	1.品名;2.品牌;3.结构类型(片式等);4.阻值固定请注明	5.型号;6.额定功率
	-线绕可变电阻器,包括变阻器及电位器:	1.品名;2.品牌;3.类型	4.型号;5.额定功率
8533.4000	-其他可变电阻器,包括变阻器及电位器	1.品名;2.品牌;3.类型	4.型号
8533.9000	-零件	1.品名;2.品牌;3.适用元件类型	4.型号
85.34	**印刷电路:**	1.品名;2.品牌;3.电路层数	4.型号
85.35	**电路的开关、保护或连接用的电气装置(例如,开关、熔断器、避雷器、电压限幅器、电涌抑制器、插头及其他连接器、接线盒),用于电压超过1000伏的线路:**	1.品名;2.用途;3.品牌	4.型号;5.额定电压
85.36	**电路的开关、保护或连接用的电气装置(例如,开关、继电器、熔断器、电涌抑制器、插头、插座、灯座及其他连接器、接线盒),用于电压不超过1000伏的线路;光导纤维、光导纤维束或光缆用连接器:**	1.品名;2.用途;3.品牌	4.型号;5.额定电压
85.37	**用于电气控制或电力分配的盘、板、台、柜及其他基座,装有两个或多个税目85.35或85.36所列的装置,包括装有第九十章所列的仪器或装置,以及数控装置,但税目85.17的交换机除外:**	1.品名;2.用途;3.品牌;4.原理	5.型号;6.额定电压
85.38	**专用于或主要用于税目85.35、85.36或85.37所列装置的零件:**	1.品名;2.用途(适用机型)	
85.39	**白炽灯泡、放电灯管,包括封闭式聚光灯及紫外线灯管或红外线灯泡;弧光灯:**	1.品名;2.用途;3.品牌;4.类型	5.型号
85.40	**热电子管、冷阴极管或光阴极管(例如,真空管或充气管、汞弧整流管、阴极射线管、电视摄像管):**		
	-阴极射线电视显像管,包括视频监视器用阴极射线管:	1.品名;2.品牌;3.显像类型	4.型号
	-电视摄像管;变像管及图像增强管;其他光阴极管:	1.品名;2.用途;3.品牌	4.型号
8540.4000	-彩色的数据/图形显示管,屏幕荧光点间距小于0.4毫米	1.品名;2.品牌;3.彩色的请注明	4.型号;5.荧光点间
8540.5000	-黑白的或其他单色的数据/图形显示管	1.品名;2.品牌;3.单色的请注明	4.型号
	-其他阴极射线管:	1.品名;2.用途;3.品牌;4.类型	5.型号

商品编码	商品描述	申报要素	
		商品名称	规格型号
	-微波管(例如,磁控管、速调管、行波管、返波管),但不包括栅控管:	1.品名;2.用途;3.品牌;4.类型	5.型号
	-其他管:	1.品名;2.用途;3.品牌;4.类型	5.型号
	-零件:	1.品名;2.用途(适用机型)	
85.41	**二极管、晶体管及类似的半导体器件;光敏半导体器件,包括不论是否装在组件内或组装成块的光电池:发光二极管;已装配的压电晶体:**		
8541.1000	-二极管,但光敏二极管或发光二极管除外	1.品名;2.品牌	3.型号
	-晶体管,但光敏晶体管除外:	1.品名;2.品牌;3.类型	4.型号;5.耗散功率
8541.3000	-半导体开关元件、两端交流开关元件及三端双向可控硅开关元件,但光敏器件除外	1.品名;2.类型;3.品牌	4.型号
8541.4000	-光敏半导体器件,包括不论是否装在组件内或组装成块的光电池;发光二极管	1.品名;2.品牌;3.型号	4.类型
8541.5000	-其他半导体器件	1.品名;2.品牌;3.功能;4.结构	5.型号
8541.6000	-已装配的压电晶体	1.品名;2.品牌;3.已装配请注明	4.型号
8541.9000	-零件	1.品名;2.用途(适用器件)	
85.42	**集成电路**		
	-集成电路:	1.品名;2.用途;3.品牌;4.单片请注明;5.经切割加工请注明	6.型号;7.线宽;8.外形结构;9.引脚数;10.原片请注明
8542.9000	-零件	1.品名;2.用途(适用元件类型)	
85.43	**本章其他税目未列名的具有独立功能的电气设备及装置:**	1.品名;2.用途;3.品牌;4.功能	5.型号
85.44	**绝缘(包括漆包或阳极化处理)电线、电缆(包括同轴电缆)及其他绝缘电导体,不论是否有接头;由每根被覆光纤组成的光缆,不论是否与电导体装配或装有接头:**	1.品名;2.用途;3.品牌;4.结构类型(同轴;有接头等);5.构成材料	6.型号;7.额定电压
85.45	**碳电极、碳刷、灯碳棒、电池碳棒及电气设备用的其他石墨或碳精制品,不论是否带金属:**	1.品名;2.用途;3.品牌;4.构成材料	5.型号
85.46	**各种材料制的绝缘子:**	1.品名;2.用途;3.品牌;4.构成材料	5.型号
85.47	**电气机器、器具或设备用的绝缘零件,除了为装配需要而在模制时装入的小金属零件(例如,螺纹孔)以外,全部用绝缘材料制成,但税目85.46的绝缘子除外;内衬绝缘材料的贱金属制线路导管及其接头:**	1.品名;2.用途;3.品牌;4.构成材料	5.型号
85.48	**原电池、原电池组及蓄电池的废碎料;废原电池、废原电池组及废蓄电池;机器或设备的本章其他税目未列名的电气零件:**		
8548.1000	-原电池、原电池组及蓄电池的废碎料;废原电池、废原电池组及废蓄电池	1.品名;2.用途;3.品牌	4.型号
8548.9000	-其他	1.品名;2.用途(适用机型)	

第十七类　车辆、航空器、船舶及有关运输设备

第八十六章　铁道及电车道机车、车辆及其零件；铁道及电车道轨道固定装置及其零件、附件；各种机械（包括电动机械）交通信号设备

【注解】

1. 零部件要报具体名称。
2. 未制成品，不完整品申报要注明程度。
3. 说明举例程中包含品牌、型号等内容。

商品编码	商 品 描 述	申 报 要 素	
		商品名称	规格型号
86.01	**铁道电力机车，由外部电力或蓄电池驱动：**	1. 品名；2. 用途；3. 品牌； 4. 驱动装置类型；5. 控制装置类型	6. 型号
86.02	**其他铁道机车；机车煤水车：**	1. 品名；2. 用途；3. 品牌； 4. 驱动装置类型；5. 控制装置类型	6. 型号
86.03	**铁道及电车道用的机动客车、货车、敞车，但税目86.04的货品除外：**	1. 品名；2. 用途；3. 品牌；4. 驱动装置类型	5. 型号
86.04	**铁道及电车道用的维修或服务车，不论是否机动（例如，工场车、起重机车、道碴捣固车、轨道校正车、检验车及查道车）：**	1. 品名；2. 用途；3. 品牌；4. 类型	5. 型号
86.05	**铁道及电车道用的非机动客车；行李车、邮政车和其他铁道及电车道用的非机动特殊用途车辆（税目86.04的货品除外）：**	1. 品名；2. 用途；3. 品牌；4. 类型	5. 型号
86.06	**铁道及电车道用的非机动有篷及无篷货车：**	1. 品名；2. 用途；3. 品牌；4. 类型；5. 结构	6. 型号；7. 厢高；8. 容积
86.07	**铁道及电车道机车或其他车辆的零件：**	1. 品名；2. 用途（适用车型）	
86.08	**铁道及电车道轨道固定装置及附件；供铁道、电车道、道路、内河航道、停车场、港口或机场用的机械（包括电动机械）信号、安全或交通管理设备；上述货品的零件：**	1. 品名；2. 用途；3. 品牌	4. 型号
86.09	**集装箱（包括运输液体的集装箱），经特殊设计、装备适用于各种运输方式：**	1. 品名；2. 品牌；3. 类型	4. 型号；5. 规格尺寸

第八十七章　车辆及其零件、附件，但铁道及电车道车辆除外

【注解】

1. 零部件要报具体名称。
2. 未制成品、不完整品申报要注明程度。
3. 说明举例栏中未包含品牌、型号等内容。

商品编码	商 品 描 述	申 报 要 素	
		商品名称	规格型号
87.01	**牵引车、拖拉机（税目87.09的牵引车除外）：**		
8701.1000	-手扶拖拉机	1. 品名；2. 品牌	3. 型号
8701.2000	-半挂车用的公路牵引车	1. 品名；2. 用途；3. 品牌	4. 型号
8701.3000	-履带式牵引车、拖拉机	1. 品名；2. 品牌；3. 结构类型	4. 型号
	-其他：	1. 品名；2. 用途；3. 品牌；4. 结构类型	5. 型号；6. 功率
87.02	**客运机动车辆，10座及以上（包括驾驶座）：**	1. 品名（车型）；2. 厂牌（如与签注名称相同可省略）；3. 签注名称；4. 发动机类型（柴油、半柴油、汽油等）；5. 成套散件请注明	6. 排气量；7. 规格型号；8. 座位数；9. 旧车请注明年款

商品编码	商品描述	申报要素	
		商品名称	规格型号
87.03	**主要用于载人的机动车辆(税目87.02的货品除外),包括旅行小客车及赛车:**		
	-雪地行走专用车;高尔夫球车及类似车辆:	1.品名;2.用途;3.厂牌;4.成套散件请注明	5.规格型号;6.旧车请注明年款
	-装有点燃往复式活塞内燃发动机的其他车辆:	1.品名(车型);2.厂牌(如与签注名称相同可省略);3.签注名称;4.发动机类型(柴油、半柴油、汽油等);5.成套散件请注明	6.排气量;7.规格型号;8.座位数;9.旧车请注明年款
	-装有压燃式活塞内燃发动机(柴油或半柴油发动机)的其他车辆:	1.品名(车型);2.厂牌(如与签注名称相同可省略);3.签注名称;4.发动机类型(柴油、半柴油、汽油等);5.成套散件请注明	6.排气量(CC);7.规格型号;8.座位数;9.旧车请注明年款
8703.9000	-其他	1.品名(车型);2.厂牌(如与签注名称相同可省略);3.签注名称;4.发动机类型(柴油、半柴油、汽油等);5.成套散件	6.排气量(CC);7.规格型号; 8.座位数; 9.旧车请注明年款
87.04	**货运机动车辆:**		
	-非公路用自卸车:	1.品名;2.用途;3.品牌(厂牌);4.电动轮请注明	5.型号
	-装有压燃式活塞内燃发动机(柴油或半柴油发动机)的其他货车:	1.品名;2.品牌(厂牌);3.发动机类型(柴油、半柴油、汽油等)	4.型号;5.车辆总重;6.车辆总重量在14吨及以上请注明车架前宽
	-装有点燃式活塞内燃发动机的其他货车:	1.品名;2.品牌(厂牌);3.发动机类型(柴油、半柴油、汽油等)	4.型号;5.车辆总重
8704.9000	-其他	1.品名;2.品牌(厂牌);3.发动机类型	4.型号;5.车辆总重
87.05	**特殊用途的机动车辆(例如,抢修车、起重车、救火车、混凝土搅拌车、道路清洁车、喷洒车、流动工场车及流动放射线检查车),但主要用于载人或运货的车辆除外:**		
	-起重车:	1.品名;2.品牌(厂牌);3.作业范围(全路面等)	4.型号; 5.最大起重重量
8705.2000	-钻探车	1.品名;2.用途;3.品牌	4.型号
	-救火车:	1.品名;2.品牌	3.型号;4.配置
8705.4000	-混凝土搅拌车	1.品名;2.品牌(厂牌)	3.规格型号;4.配置
	-其他:	1.品名;2.用途;3.品牌(厂牌)	4.型号;5.固定安装配置
87.06	**装有发动机的机动车辆底盘,税目87.01至87.05所列车辆用:**	1.品名;2.品牌;3.适用车型	4.型号;5.车辆总重量;6.装有驾驶室请注明
87.07	**机动车辆的车身(包括驾驶室),税目87.01至87.05所列车辆用:**	1.品名;2.品牌;3.适用车型	4.型号
87.08	**机动车辆的零件、附件,税目87.01至87.05所列车辆用:**		
8708.1000	-缓冲器(保险杠)及其零件	1.品名;2.用途;3.品牌;4.适用车型	5.型号
	-车身(包括驾驶室)的其他零件、附件:	1.品名;2.用途;3.品牌;4.适用车型	5.型号
	-制动器、助力制动器及其零件:	1.品名;2.用途;3.品牌;4.适用车型;5.原理	6.型号
	-变速箱及其零件	1.品名;2.品牌;3.适用车型;4.原理	5.型号;6.扭矩
	-装有差速器的驱动桥及其零件,不论是否装有其他传动部件;非驱动桥及其零件:	1.品名;2.品牌;3.适用车型	4.型号;5.传动部件;6.驱动位置;7.轴荷
	-车轮及其零件、附件:	1.品名;2.品牌;3.适用车型	4.型号
	-悬挂系统及其零件(包括减震器):	1.品名;2.品牌;3.适用车型	4.型号

商品编码	商品描述	申报要素	
		商品名称	规格型号
	-其他零件、附件:	1.品名;2.用途;3.品牌;4.适用车型	5.型号
87.09	短距离运输货物的机动车辆,未装有提升或搬运设备,用于工厂、仓库、码头或机场;火车站台上用的牵引车;上述车辆的零件:	1.品名;2.品牌;3.发动机类型	4.型号;5.技术参数(最高时速等);6.适用场所
87.10	坦克及其他机动装甲战斗车辆,不论是否装有武器;上述车辆的零件:	1.品名;2.品牌	3.型号
87.11	摩托车(包括机器脚踏两用车)及装有辅助发动机的脚踏车,不论有无边车;边车:	1.品名;2.品牌;3.发动机类型;4.电力驱动的请注明功率	5.排气量;6.型号
87.12	自行车及其他非机动脚踏车(包括运货三轮脚踏车):	1.品名;2.用途;3.品牌	4.轮径;5.型号
87.13	残疾人用车,不论是否机动或其他机械驱动:	1.品名;2.用途;3.品牌;4.驱动方式	5.型号
87.14	零件、附件,供税目87.11至87.13所列车辆用:	1.品名;2.品牌;3.适用车型	4.型号
87.15	婴孩车及其零件	1.品名;2.用途;3.品牌	4.型号
87.16	挂车及半挂车或其他非机械驱动车辆及其零件:	1.品名;2.用途;3.品牌;4.类型	5.型号

第八十八章　航空器、航天器及其零件

【注解】

1. 零部件要报具体名称。
2. 未制成品,不完整品申报要注明程度。
3. 举例说明栏中未包含品牌,型号内容。

商品编码	商品描述	申报要素	
		商品名称	规格型号
88.01	气球及飞艇;滑翔机、悬挂滑翔机及其他无动力航空器:	1.品名;2.品牌;3.装有动力装置请注明	4.型号
88.02	其他航空器(例如,直升机、飞机);航天器(包括卫星)及其运载工具、亚轨道运载工具:	1.品名;2.品牌;3.类型	4.型号;5.空载重量
88.03	税目88.01或88.02所列货品的零件:	1.品名;2.用途(适用机型)	
88.04	降落伞(包括可操纵降落伞及滑翔伞)、旋翼降落伞及其零件、附件:	1.品名;2.品牌;3.类型	4.型号
88.05	航空器的发射装置、甲板停机装置或类似装置和地面飞行训练器及其零件:	1.品名;2.用途;3.品牌	4.型号

第八十九章　船舶及浮动结构体

【注解】

1. 零部件要报具体名称。
2. 未制成品、不完整品申报要注明程度。
3. 说明举例栏中未包含品牌、型号等内容。

商品编码	商品描述	申报要素	
		商品名称	规格型号
89.01	巡航船、游览船、渡船、货船、驳船及类似的客运或货运船舶:		
	-巡航船、游览船及主要用于客运的类似船舶;各式渡船:	1.品名;2.品牌;3.驱动方式	4.型号;5.最高时速

商品编码	商 品 描 述	申 报 要 素	
		商品名称	规格型号
	-液货船:	1.品名;2.用途;3.品牌	4.型号;5.载重量;6.容积
8901.3000	-冷藏船,但子目 8901.20 的船舶除外	1.品名;2.品牌	3.型号
	-其他货运船舶及其他客货兼运船舶:	1.品名;2.用途;3.品牌;4.驱动方式	5.型号;6.载重量
89.02	**捕鱼船;加工船及其他加工保藏鱼类产品的船舶:**	1.品名;2.品牌;3.驱动方式	4.型号
89.03	**娱乐或运动用快艇及其他船舶;划艇及轻舟:**	1.品名;2.用途;3.品牌;4.类型	5.型号;6.发动机安装方式;7.船体长度
89.04	**拖轮及顶推船:**	1.品名;2.品牌	3.型号
89.05	**灯船、消防船、挖泥船、起重船及其他不以航行为主要功能的船舶;浮船坞;浮动或潜水式钻探或生产平台:**	1.品名;2.用途;3.品牌;4.功能;5.结构类型	6.型号
89.06	**其他船舶,包括军舰和救生船,但划艇除外:**	1.品名;2.用途;3.品牌;4.驱动方式	5.型号
89.07	**其他浮动结构体(例如,筏、柜、潜水箱、浮码头、浮筒及航标):**	1.品名;2.用途;3.品牌;4.材质	5.型号
89.08	**供拆卸的船舶及其他浮动结构体:**	1.品名;2.用途;3.品牌	4.型号

第十八类　光学、照相、电影、计量、检验、医疗或外科用仪器及设备、精密仪器及设备;钟表;乐器;上述物品的零件、附件

第九十章　光学、照相、电影、计量、检验、医疗或外科用仪器及设备、精密仪器及设备;上述物品的零件、附件

【注解】

1. 零部件要报具体名称。
2. 未制成品、不完整品申报要注明程度。
3. 说明举例栏中未包含品牌、型号等内容。

商品编码	商品描述	申报要素	
		商品名称	规格型号
90.01	**光导纤维及光导纤维束;充缆,但税目85.44的货品除外;偏振材料制的片及板;未装配的各种材料制透镜(包括隐形眼镜片)、棱镜、反射镜及其他光学元件,但未经光学加工的玻璃制上述元件除外:**		
9001.1000	-光导纤维、光导纤维束及光缆	1.品名;2.用途;3.品牌;4.结构	5.型号
9001.2000	-偏振材料制的片及板	1.品名;2.用途;3.品牌;4.材质;5.形状(片、板等)	6.型号
9001.3000	-隐形眼镜片	1.品名;2.品牌	3.型号
	-玻璃制眼镜片:	1.品名;2.品牌;3.材质;4.类型(变色等)	5.型号
	-其他材料制眼镜片:	1. 品名;2. 品牌;3. 类型(变色等);4. 材质	
9001.9000	-其他	1.品名;2.用途(适用机型);3.品牌;4.材质	5.型号;6.技术参数
90.02	**已装配的各种材料制透镜、棱镜、反射镜及其他光学元件,作为仪器或装置的零件、配件,但未经光学加工的玻璃制上述元件除外:**	1.品名;2.用途(适用机型);3.品牌;4.已装配请注明	5.型号;6.技术参数
90.03	**眼镜架及其零件:**	1.品名;2.材质;3.品牌	4.型号
90.04	**矫正视力、保护眼睛或其他用途的眼镜、挡风镜及类似品:**	1.品名;2.用途;3.品牌;4.类型	5.型号
90.05	**双筒望远镜、单筒望远镜、其他光学望远镜及其座架,其他天文仪器及其座架,但不包括射电天文仪器**		
9005.1000	-双筒望远镜	1.品名;2.用途;3.品牌;4.原理;5.结构(双筒等)	6.型号;7.倍数
	-其他仪器:	1.品名;2.用途;3.品牌;4.原理.	5.型号
	-零件、附件(包括座架):	1.品名;2.用途(适用机型)	
90.06	**照相机(电影摄影机除外);照相闪光灯装置及闪光灯泡,但税目85.39的放电灯泡除外:**		
	-制版照相机:	1.品名;2.用途;3.品牌;4.原理	5.型号
9006.3000	-水下、航空测量或体内器官检查用的特种照相机;法庭或犯罪学用的比较照相机	1.品名;2.用途;3.品牌;4.原理	5.型号
9006.4000	-一次成像照相机	1.品名;2.用途;3.品牌;4.原理	5.型号
	-其他照相机:	1.品名;2.用途;3.品牌;4.原理	5.型号;6.胶片宽度
	-照相闪光灯装置及闪光灯泡:	1.品名;2.用途;3.品牌;4.原理	5.型号
	-零件、附件:	1.品名;2.用途(适用机型)	

商品编码	商品描述	申报要素	
		商品名称	规格型号
90.07	**电影摄影机、放映机,不论是否带有声音的录制或重放装置:**		
	-摄影机:	1.品名;2.用途;3.品牌;4.原理	5.型号;6.胶片宽度;7.摄影速度
	-放映机:	1.品名;2.用途;3.品牌;4.原理	5.型号
9007.9100	--摄影机用	1.品名;2.用途;3.品牌;4.原理	5.型号
90.08	**影像投影仪,但电影用除外;照片(电影片除外)放大机及缩片机:**		
9008.1000	-幻灯机	1.品名;2.用途;3.品牌;4.原理	5.型号
9008.2000	-缩微胶卷、缩微胶片或其他缩微品的阅读机,不论是否可以进行复制	1.品名;2.用途;3.品牌;4.原理	5.型号
	-其他影像投影仪:	1.品名;2.用途;3.品牌;4.原理	5.型号
9008.4000	-照片(电影片除外)放大机及缩片机	1.品名;2.用途;3.品牌;4.原理	5.型号
	-零件、附件:	1.品名;2.用途;3.品牌;4.原理	5.型号
90.09	**装有光学系统的或接触式的感光复印设备及热敏复印设备:**		
	-静电感充复印设备:	1.品名;2.品牌;3.原理;4.功能	5.型号;6.复印方法
	-其他感光复印设备:	1.品名;2.品牌;3.原理;4.功能	5.型号;6.复印方法
	-热敏复印设备:	1.品名;2.品牌;3.原理;4.功能	5.型号;6.复印方法
	-零件、附件:	1.品名;2.用途(适用机型)	
90.10	**本章其他税目未列名的照相(包括电影)洗印用装置及设备;负片显示器;银幕及其他投影屏幕:**	1.品名;2.用途;3.品牌;4.原理;5.功能	6.型号
90.11	**复式光学显微镜,包括用于缩微照相、显微电影摄影及显微投影的:**	1.品名;2.用途;3.品牌;4.原理;5.功能	6.型号;7.倍数
90.12	**显微镜,但光学显微镜除外;衍射设备:**	1.品名;2.用途;3.品牌;4.原理;5.功能	6.型号
90.13	**其他税目未列名的液晶装置;激光器,但激光二极管除外;本章其他税目未列名的光学仪器及器具:**		
9013.1000	-武器用望远镜瞄准具;潜望镜式望远镜;作为本章或第十六类的机器、设备、仪器或器具部件的望远镜	1.品名;2.用途;3.品牌;4.原理;5.功能	6.型号
9013.2000	-激光器,但激光二极管除外	1.品名;2.用途;3.品牌;4.原理;5.功能	6.型号;7.技术参数
	-其他装置、仪器及器具:	1.品名;2.用途;3.品牌;4.原理;5.功能	6.型号
	-零件、附件:	1.品名;2.用途(适用机型)	
90.14	**定向罗盘;其他导航仪器及装置:**	1.品名;2.用途;3.品牌;4.原理	5.型号;6.技术参数
90.15	**大地测量(包括摄影测量)、水道测量、海洋、水文、气象或地球物理用仪器及装置,不包括罗盘;测距仪:**	1.品名;2.用途;3.品牌;4.功能	5.型号;6.技术参数
90.16	**感量为50毫克或更精密的天平,不论是否带有砝码:**	1.品名;2.品牌;3.感量	4.型号
90.17	**绘图、划线或数学计算仪器及器具(例如,绘图机、比例缩放仪、分度规、绘图工具、计算尺及盘式计算器);本章其他税目未列名的手用测量长度的器具(例如,量尺、量带、千分尺及卡尺):**	1.品名;2.用途;3.品牌;4.型号;5.功能	

商品编码	商 品 描 述	申 报 要 素	
		商品名称	规格型号
90.18	医疗、外科、牙科或兽医用仪器及器具，包括闪烁扫描装置、其他电气医疗装置及视力检查仪器：	1.品名;2.用途;3.品牌;4.原理	5.型号;6.B型、彩色超声波诊断仪请注明探头的数量;7.核磁共振成像装置请注明磁场强度(T)度;8.病员监护仪请注明：屏幕尺寸、接口情况(网络接口、打印机接口、记录仪接口)、配置记录仪请注明;9.心血管插管请注明：一次性插管请注明、一次性插管尾部带排气帽请注明、含加固丝请注明;10.可折叠式请注明;11.带球囊(手动或自动充盈)请注明
90.19	机械疗法器具；按摩器具；心理功能测验装置；臭氧治疗器；氧气治疗器、喷雾治疗器、人工呼吸器及其他治疗用呼吸器具：	1.品名;2.用途;3.品牌;4.功能	5.型号
90.20	其他呼吸器具及防毒面具，但不包括既无机械零件又无可互换过滤器的防护面具：	1.品名;2.用途;3.品牌;4.构成	5.型号
90.21	矫形器具，包括支具、外科手术带、疝气带；夹板及其他骨折用具；人造的人体部分；助听器及为弥补生理缺陷或残疾而穿戴、携带或植入人体内的其他器具：	1.品名;2.用途;3.品牌;4.类型(若为血管支架还需注明血管名称)	5.型号;6.技术参数;7.医用支管请注明：药物涂层支架请注明、带球囊、导管等请注明;8.心脏瓣膜请注明：材质(生物瓣或机械瓣)、形态(单叶、双叶或环上瓣)
90.22	X射线或α射线、β射线、γ射线的应用设备，不论是否用于医疗、外科、牙科或兽医，包括射线照相及射线治疗设备、X射线管及其他X射线发生器、高压发生器、控制板及控制台、荧光屏、检查或治疗用的桌、椅及类似品：	1.品名;2.用途;3.品牌;4.原理;5.功能	6.型号;7.技术参数;8.螺旋CT请注明：螺旋排数、球管请注明热容量、X线发生器请注明功率
90.23	专供示范(例如，教学或展览)而无其他用途的仪器、装置及模型：	1.品名;2.用途;3.品牌	4.型号;5.具有使用价值的请注明
90.24	各种材料(例如，金属、木材、纺织材料、纸张、塑料)的硬度、强度、压缩性、弹性或其他机械性能的试验机器及器具：	1.品名;2.品牌;3.功能;4.试验材料类型	5.型号
90.25	记录式或非记录式的液体比重计及类似的浮子式仪器、温度计、高温计、气压计、湿度计、干湿球湿度计及其组合装置：	1.品名;2.品牌;3.原理	4.型号;5.可直接读数请注明
90.26	液体或气体的流量、液位、压力或其他变化量的测量或检验仪器及装置(例如，流量计、液位计、压力表、热量计)，但不包括税目90.14、90.15、90.28或90.32的仪器及装置：	1.品名;2.品牌;3.功能;4.检测对象;5.带有计量装置请注明	6.型号;7.技术参数

商品编码	商品描述	申报要素	
		商品名称	规格型号
90.27	**理化分析仪器及装置(例如,偏振计、折光仪、分光仪、气体或烟雾分析仪);测量或检验粘性、多孔性、膨胀性、表面张力及类似性能的仪器及装置;测量或检验热量、声量或光量的仪器及装置(包括曝光表);检镜切片机:**	1.品名;2.品牌;3.原理;4.功能;5.检测对象	6.型号;7.技术参数
90.28	**生产或供应气体、液体及电力用的计量仪表,包括它们的校准仪表:**	1.品名;2.用途;3.品牌	4.型号;5.技术参数
90.29	**转数计、产量计数器、车费计、里程计、步数计及类似仪表;速度计及转速表,税目90.14及90.15的仪表除外;频闪观测仪:**	1.品名;2.用途;3.品牌	4.型号;5.技术参数
90.30	**示波器、频谱分析仪及其他用于电量测量或检验的仪器和装置,不包括税目90.28的各种仪表;α射线、β射线、γ射线、X射线、宇宙射线或其他离子射线的测量或检验仪器及装置:**	1.品名;2.用途;3.品牌;4.原理;5.功能	6.检测对象;7.型号;8.技术参数
90.31	**本章其他税目未列名的测量或检验仪器、器具及机器;轮廓投影仪:**	1.品名;2.用途;3.品牌;4.原理;5.功能	6.检测对象;7.型号;8.技术参数
90.32	**自动调节或控制仪器及装置:**	1.品名;2.用途;3.品牌;4.原理;5.功能	6.型号
90.33	**第九十章所列机器、器具、仪器或装置用的本章其他税目未列名的零件、附件:**	1.品名;2.用途;3.品牌	4.型号

备注或申报要求

90. 18 **医疗、外科、牙科或兽医用仪器及器具,包括闪烁扫描装置、其他电气医疗装置及视力检查仪器:**
-电气诊断装置(包括功能检查或生理参数检查用装置)
--其他:
9018. 1930 ---病员监护仪: 测量功能;特别功能软件请注明
9018. 9030 ---内窥镜: 主要配置

90. 22 **X射线或α射线、β射线、γ射线的应用设备,不论是否用于医疗、外科、牙科或兽医,包括射线照相及射线治疗设备、X射线管及其他X射线发生器、高压发生器、控制板及控制台、荧光屏、检查或治疗用的桌、椅及类似品:**
-X射线的应用设备,不论是否用于医疗、外科或兽医,包括射线照相或射线治疗设备:
9022. 1200 --X射线断层检查仪:主要选配件(如激光相机、不间断电源、高压注射器等)

第九十一章　钟表及其零件

【注解】

本章包括主要用于计时或进行与时间有关的某些操作的器具,其中包括适于个人随身佩带的时计(手表及秒表)、其他时计(普通钟、装有表芯的钟、闹钟、航海时计、机动车辆用钟等)、时间记录器、时间间隔测量仪以及定时开关;通常还包括它们的零件。

这些物品可用各种材料(包括贵金属)制成,也可以用天然或养殖珍珠,或者用天然、合成或再造的宝石或半宝石进行装饰(参见商品编码91.11及91.12的注释)。

与某些其他物品(例如,家具、灯具、墨水台、压纸器、拍纸薄、烟草罐、香烟或雪茄烟打火机、手提包、脂粉盒、烟盒、活动铅笔、手杖等)组装在一起的钟表应按归类总规则的规定进行归类,但其内部装有照明装置的钟表仍应归入本章。

除在各商品编码注释中具体列出不包括的货品以外,本章主要还不包括:

1. 日晷仪(日规)、沙漏及水漏(按其构成材料归类)。
2. 音乐自动装置(机械鸣禽及类似品)及没有钟表面的百音盒(商品编码92.08)。
3. 玩具钟表及制成钟表状的圣诞树装饰品,例如,没有钟表机芯的钟表饰物(商品编码95.03或95.05)。
4. 商店橱窗装饰用的自动模型及其他活动陈列品(商品编码96.18)。
5. 艺术品、收藏品及古物(第九十七章)。

钟表主要由两大部件组成:机芯及装机芯用的容器(盒、壳等)。

机械钟表的机芯由下列零件组成：

(1)芯体或框架，通常由夹板及横担构成。夹板是机芯的主要支架，用螺钉及销钉将横担固定于夹板上。有些芯体或框架除了有横担及夹板外，还装有一个或多个用以固定机芯某些零件（走针机构、闹机构等）的附加板（例如，钟表面板、下托板盖）。

(2)驱动机芯的装置，通常由摆锤或发条构成；也可用电能或利用温度变化或气压变化作为能源。

(3)齿轮系，即连接驱动装置及擒纵器并使时间得以计量的齿轮系统。

(4)走针机构，即将分针的转动与时针的转动连接起来的一系列零件。在带钟表面的机芯中，走针机构通常安装在面板及夹板之间。

(5)擒纵机构，它向摆锤或摆轮及游丝提供必要的动能并控制齿轮系统的转动。

最常见的擒纵机构是锚式或叉瓦式、销钉式、工字轮式及棘爪式擒纵器。

(6)调节机构，调节驱动机构所产生的运动。它包括摆锤、摆轮及游丝的组合体、音叉、压电石英晶体或其他能确定时间间隔的装置。

(7)上发条及拨指针机构（通过按销、拉销或摇杆等进行操作）。

已装配的机芯与面板及指针一起安装于容器或壳子内。

摆轮、擒纵器零件及齿轮系零件精密地装于枢轴上。在廉价钟表中，它们直接装于夹板及横担的金属上，但在较高级的钟表中，轴承均用耐磨宝石制成。

钟表可配有报时装置、闹机构或一组钟乐装置。这些装置等均需使用特种机芯。

机械钟表可手动或电动上发条，也可自动上发条。

本章的钟表可以是电气的（包括电子的），例如：

(1)使用干电池或蓄电池的钟，持续回转时间较短（每次几分钟）。这类钟具有传统的摆轮及游丝组合体或摆锤，并通过电磁装置定时上发条。

(2)与供电网连接的钟，持续回转时间较长（每次几小时）。这类钟也装有传统的摆轮及游丝组合体或摆锤，并通过电动机（同步电动机、异步电动机）定时上发条。

商品编码	商 品 描 述	申 报 要 素	
		商品名称	规格型号
91.01	**手表、怀表及其他表，包括秒表，表壳用贵金属或包贵金属制成的：**	1.品名；2.外壳材质（贵金属或包贵金属制）；3.驱动方式（电子、机械、自动、非自动）；4.指示方式（指针、光电）	
91.02	**手表、怀表及其他表，包括秒表，但税目91.01的货品除外：**	1.品名；2.外壳材质（金属制等）；3.驱动方式（电子、机械、自动、非自动）；4.指示方式（指针、光电）	
91.03	**以表芯装成的钟，但不包括税目91.04的钟：**	1.品名（仅指用表芯装成）；2.驱动方式（电子、机械）	
91.04	**仪表板钟及车辆、航空器、航天器或船舶用的类似钟：**	1.品名；2.用途（车辆、船舶等用）	
91.05	**其他钟：**	1.品名；2.用途（闹钟、天文钟等）；3.驱动方式（电子、机械）	
91.06	**时间记录器以及测量、记录或指示时间间隔的装置，装有钟、表机芯或同步电动机的（例如，考勤钟、时刻记录器）：**	1.品名；2.用途（考勤钟、停车记时表等）	
91.07	**装有钟、表机芯或同步电动机的定时开关：**	1.品名（仅指装有钟、表机芯或同步电动机的）	
91.08	**已组装的完整表芯：**	1.品名（已组装完整的）； 2.驱动方式（电子、机械、自动、非自动）； 3.指示方式（指针、光电）	4.表面尺寸
91.09	**已组装的完整钟芯：**	1.品名（已组装完整的）；2.用途； 3.驱动方式（电子、机械）	
91.10	**未组装或部分组装的完整钟、表机芯（机芯套装件）；已组装的不完整钟、表机芯；未组装的不完整钟、表机芯：**	1.品名；2.用途；3.加工程度	
91.11	**表壳及其零件：**	1.品名；2.材质（贵金属、贱金属等）	
91.12	**钟壳和本章所列其他货品的类似外壳及其零件：**	1.品名；2.材质	

商品编码	商 品 描 述	申 报 要 素	
		商 品 名 称	规 格 型 号
91.13	**表带及其零件:**	1. 品名;2. 材质(贵金属、贱金属等); 3. 野生动物皮制请注明	
91.14	**钟、表的其他零件:**	1. 品名;2. 用途	

第九十二章 乐器及其零件、附件

【注解】

本章包括主要用于计时或进行与时间有关的某些操作的器具,其中包括适于个人随身佩带的时计(手表及秒表)、其他时计(普通钟、装有表芯的钟、闹钟、航海时计、机动车辆用钟等)、时间记录器、时间间隔测量仪以及定时开关;通常还包括它们的零件。

这些物品可用各种材料(包括贵金属)制成,也可以用天然或养殖珍珠,或者用天然、合成或再造的宝石或半宝石进行装饰(参见商品编码 91.11 及 91.12 的注释)。

与某些其他物品(例如,家具、灯具、墨水台、压纸器、拍纸薄、烟草罐、香烟或雪茄烟打火机、手提包、脂粉盒、烟盒、活动铅笔、手杖等)组装在一起的钟表应按归类总规则的规定进行归类,但其内部装有照明装置的钟表仍应归入本章。

除在各商品编码注释中具体列出不包括的货品以外,本章主要还不包括:

(1)日晷仪(日规)、沙漏及水漏(按其构成材料归类)。

(2)音乐自动装置(机械鸣禽及类似品)及没有钟表面的百音盒(商品编码 92.08)。

(3)玩具钟表及制成钟表状的圣诞树装饰品,例如,没有钟表机芯的钟表饰物(商品编码 95.03 或 95.05)。

(4)商店橱窗装饰用的自动模型及其他活动陈列品(商品编码 96.18)。

(5)艺术品.收藏品及古物(第九十七章)。

钟表主要由两大部件组成:机芯及装机芯用的容器(盒、壳等)。

机械钟表的机芯由下列零件组成:

(1)芯体或框架,通常由夹板及横担构成。夹板是机芯的主要支架,用螺钉及销钉将横担固定于夹板上。有些芯体或框架除了有横担及夹板外,还装有一个或多个用以固定机芯某些零件(走针机构、闹机构等)的附加板(例如,钟表面板、下托板盖)。

(2)驱动机芯的装置,通常由摆锤或发条构成;也可用电能或利用温度变化或气压变化作为能源。

(3)齿轮系,即连接驱动装置及擒纵器并使时间得以计量的齿轮系统。

(4)走针机构,即将分针的转动与时针的转动连接起来的一系列零件。在带钟表面的机芯中,走针机构通常安装在面板及夹板之间。

(5)擒纵机构,它向摆锤或摆轮及游丝提供必要的动能并控制齿轮系统的转动。

最常见的擒纵机构是锚式或叉瓦式、销钉式、工字轮式及棘爪式擒纵器。

(6)调节机构,调节驱动机构所产生的运动。它包括摆锤、摆轮及游丝的组合体、音叉、压电石英晶体或其他能确定时间间隔的装置。

(7)上发条及拨指针机构(通过按销、拉销或摇杆等进行操作)。

已装配的机芯与面板及指针一起安装于容器或壳子内。

摆轮、擒纵器零件及齿轮系零件精密地装于枢轴上。在廉价钟表中,它们直接装于夹板及横担的金属上,但在较高级的钟表中,轴承均用耐磨宝石制成。

钟表可配有报时装置、闹机构或一组钟乐装置。这些装置等均需使用特种机芯。

机械钟表可手动或电动上发条,也可自动上发条。

本章的钟表可以是电气的(包括电子的),例如:

(1)使用干电池或蓄电池的钟,持续回转时间较短(每次几分钟)。这类钟具有传统的摆轮及游丝组合体或摆锤,并通过电磁装置定时上发条。

(2)与供电网连接的钟,持续回转时间较长(每次几小时)。这类钟也装有传统的摆轮及游丝组合体或摆锤,并通过电动机(同步电动机、异步电动机)定时上发条。

(3)用干电池、蓄电池或供电网驱动的摆钟,摆锤在电磁装置的作用下不断摆动。

(4)用干电池或蓄电池驱动的钟、表,它们带有调节装置(音叉、压电石英晶体等)。这种调节装置在电子电路的作用下不断振荡。

(5)同步电钟。这类钟接上稳频电流,因此它们仅由马达及齿轮系构成,不带控制装置。

电钟系统的说明,参见商品编码 91.05 的注释。

有些电钟配有校正时间的遥控装置。

根据本章注释三对表芯的规定,其尺寸应按下列方法计算:

(1)厚度计算

表芯厚度是从表面支架的外平面(若表面支架装于表芯中的,则为显示板的可见表面)至相对另一边的最远外平面的距离,但突出于平面上的螺钉、螺母或其他紧固件的高度不计在内。

(2)宽度、长度或直径的计算相应地,计算宽度、长度或直径(通过其对称轴进行测量)时,也不包括上弦芯轴或表柄头。

商品编码	商品描述	申报要素	
		商品名称	规格型号
92.01	钢琴,包括自动钢琴、拨弦古钢琴及其他键盘弦乐器:	1.品名;2.种类	
92.02	其他弦乐器(例如,吉他、小提琴、竖琴):	1.品名;2.种类;3.野生动物皮制请注明	
92.03	键盘管风琴;簧风琴及类似的游离金属簧片键盘乐器:	1.品名;2.种类	
92.04	手风琴及类似乐器;口琴:	1.品名;2.种类	
92.05	其他管乐器(例如,单簧管、小号、风笛):	1.品名;2.种类	
92.06	打击乐器(例如,鼓、木琴、钹、响板、响葫芦):	1.品名;2.种类;3.野生动物皮制请注明	
92.07	通过电产生或扩大声音的乐器(例如,电风琴、电吉他、电手风琴):	1.品名(仅指电子乐器);2.种类	
92.08	百音盒、游艺场风琴、手摇风琴、机械鸣禽、乐锯及本章其他税目未列名的其他乐器;各种媒诱音响器、哨子、号角、口吹音响信号器:	品名	
92.09	乐器的零件(例如,百音盒的机械装置)、附件(例如,机械乐器用的卡片、盘及带卷);节拍器、音叉及各种定音管:	1.品名;2.用途	

第十九类　武器、弹药及其零件、附件

第九十三章　武器、弹药及其零件、附件

【注解】

本章包括：

1. 军事武装部队、警察或其他有组织的机构(海关、边防部队等)在陆、海、空战斗中使用的各种武器。
2. 个人自卫、狩猎及打靶用的武器(例如,用于小型靶场、室内靶场或游乐场射击台的)。
3. 靠爆炸药进行发射的其他装置(例如,抛缆枪及维利式信号枪)。
4. 弹药及导弹(第三十六章的物品除外)。

除少数例外情况以外(参见商品编码93.05及93.06的注释),本章也包括武器的零件、附件及弹药零件。

望远镜瞄准具及其他光学装置,如果适合武器使用并能装在武器上或与有关武器一同报验的,应与武器一并归类。单独报验的此类光学装置不归入本章(第九十章)。

任何运载工具,即使是军事专用的,不论是否装有武器,均不归入本章。因此,本章不包括铁路装甲车辆(第八十六章)、坦克及装甲车(商品编码87.10)、军用飞机(商品编码88.01或88.02)及军舰(商品编码89.06)等。但这些运载工具上使用的武器(枪炮、机枪等)如单独报验,应归入本章(参见商品编码93.01关于安装在铁路或陆地车辆上的某些武器的注释)。

本章不包括下列货品：

1. 钢盔及其他军用帽类(第六十五章)。
2. 人体防护服,例如,护胸铁甲、铠甲衣、防弹衣等(按其构成材料归类)。
3. 弩、弓和箭以及玩具武器(第九十五章)。
4. 收藏品及古物(商品编码97.05或97.06)。

本章所列武器及其零件可含有贵金属、包贵金属、天然或养殖珍珠、宝石及半宝石(天然、合成或再造)、玳瑁壳、珍珠母、兽牙及类似品。

商品编码	商品描述	申报要素	
		商品名称	规格型号
93.01	**军用武器,但左轮手枪、其他手枪及税目93.07的兵器除外:**	1.品名;2.驱动方式	
93.02	**左轮手枪及其他手枪,但税目93.03或93.04的货品除外:**	品名	
93.03	**靠爆炸药发射的其他火器及类似装置(例如,运动用猎枪及步枪、前装枪、维利式信号枪及其他专为发射信号弹的装置、发射空包弹的左轮手枪和其他手枪、弩枪式无痛捕杀器、抛缆枪):**	品名	
93.04	**其他武器(例如,弹簧枪、气枪、气手枪、警棍),但不包括税目93.07的货品:**	品名	
93.05	**税目93.01至93.04所列物品的零件、附件:**	品名	
93.06	**炸弹、手榴弹、鱼雷、地雷、水雷、导弹及类似武器及其零件;子弹、其他弹药和射弹及其零件,包括弹丸及弹垫:**	品名	
93.07	**剑、短弯刀、刺刀、长矛和类似的武器及其零件;刀鞘、剑鞘:**	品名	

第二十类 杂项制品

第九十四章 家具;寝具、褥垫、弹簧床垫、软座垫及类似的填充制品;未列名灯具及照明装置;发光标志、发光铭牌及类似品;活动房屋

【注解】

本章包括:

一、各种家具及其零件(商品编码94.01至94.03)。

二、弹簧床垫、床褥及其他寝具或类似用品,装有弹簧、内部用任何材料填塞、衬垫或用海绵橡胶或泡沫塑料制成,不论是否包面(商品编码94.04)。

三、用各种材料制成的(第七十一章注释一所列的材料除外)未列名灯具和照明装置、装有固定光源的发光标志、发光铭牌和类似品;上述货品的未列名零件(商品编码94.05)。

四、活动房屋(商品编码94.06)。

本章所称的“家具”,是指:

(一)任何“可移动”的物品(不包括协调制度中其他商品编码更为具体列名的货品),它们的主要特征是供放置在地上,并具有实用价值,它们用于民宅、旅馆、戏院、电影院、办公室、教堂、学院、咖啡馆、饭店、实验室、医院、牙医诊所等,以及船舶、飞机、铁道车厢、机动车辆、拖挂蓬车及其他运输工具。必须注意,有些用螺栓等固定在地板上的物品,例如,船用椅子,也可作为“可移动”的家具归入本章。用于庭园、广场、散步场所等地方的类似品(凳子、椅子等)也归属于本类。

(二)下列物品:

1. 悬挂的、固定在墙壁上的、叠摞的或并置的碗橱、书柜、其他架式家具及组合家具,供放置各种物品(书籍、陶器、厨具、玻璃器皿、织物、药物、梳妆用具、收音机或电视机、装饰品等),以及单独报验的组合家具各件。

2. 悬挂或固定在墙壁上的坐具或床。

除上述2款所列的货品以外,所称“家具”,不适用于虽作家具使用,但其结构只适于放置在其他家具上或架子上,或悬挂在墙壁或天花板上的物品。

因此,本章不包括其他固定在墙上的装置,例如,衣帽架及类似品、挂匙板、衣刷挂钩及报纸架;也不包括陈设品,例如,散热器屏罩。同样,本章还不包括非落地式的以下货品:小型精细木器及小型木制装饰品(商品编码44.20)、塑料或贱金属制的办公室设备(例如,文件分类箱、文件格)(商品编码39.26或83.04)。

已安装于或准备安装于商品编码94.06的活动房屋内,并与之成为一个整体的设施(橱柜、散热器屏罩等),如果与活动房屋一同报验,也应归入本商品编码。

商品编码94.01至94.03包括任何材料(木、柳条、竹、藤;塑料、贱金属、玻璃、皮革、石、陶瓷等)制成的家具。这些家具不论是否内部填料或外部包面,也不论是否已作表面加工、雕刻、镶嵌、油漆装饰或装有镜子、其他玻璃配件及脚轮等,均应归入上述各有关商品编码。

但应注意,如果家具中配有的贵金属或包贵金属超出小配件(例如,小标志、条纹、套圈等)范围的,该家具则不可归入本章(第七十一章)。

报验时已拆卸或未组装的家具,如果其零部件是同时报验的,可作为组装家具归类。本规定同样适用于不论是否装有玻璃、大理石或其他材料制的板片、配件或其他零件的家具(例如,装有玻璃台面的木台、装有镜子的木制衣橱、装有大理石台面的餐具柜)。

“零件”

本章只包括商品编码94.01至94.03及94.05所列货品的零件,不论是否坯件,但根据其形状或其他特征可确定为专用于或主要用于上述商品编码所列家具的零件。如果没有其他更为具体列名的商品编码,它们应归入本章。

商品编码94.06所列活动房屋的部件,如果单独报验,均应归入其各自适当的商品编码中。

除了下列各商品编码注释中所列不包括的货品以外,本章还不包括:

(1)商品编码44.09的串珠状缘饰及装饰线条。

(2)用塑料或其他材料包覆的带槽木质碎料板条,经切槽后可沿切口折成U形以构成家具的零件(例如,抽屉隔板)(商品编码44.10)。

(3)玻璃片(包括镜片)、大理石板、其他石板或第六十八章或第六十九章所列其他材料的板片,不论是否切割成形,除非它们与其他零件组合并明显作为家具的零、部件(例如,衣橱的镶镜橱门)。

(4)第十五类注释二所指的贱金属制弹簧、锁和其他通用零件(第十五类)以及塑料制的类似品(第三十九章)。

(5)作玩具用的家具及灯具或照明装置(商品编码95.03)。

(6)收藏品及古物(第九十七章)。

商品编码	商 品 描 述	申 报 要 素	
		商品名称	规格型号
94.01	**坐具(包括能作床用的两用椅,但税目94.02的货品除外)及其零件:**	1.品名;2.用途;3.材质;4.装软垫请注明;5.可调节请注明	
94.02	**医疗、外科、牙科或兽医用家具(例如,手术台、检查台、带机械装置的病床、牙科用椅);有旋转、倾斜、升降装置的理发用椅及类似椅;上述物品的零件:**	1.品名;2.用途;	3.注明配置附属装置
94.03	**其他家具及其零件:**	1.品名;2.用途;3.材质	
94.04	**弹簧床垫;寝具及类似用品,装有弹簧、内部用任何材料填充、衬垫或用海绵橡胶、泡沫塑料制成,不论是否包面(例如,褥垫、棉被、羽绒被、靠垫、座垫及枕头):**	1.品名;2.材质(包面及填充物); 3.野生动物产品请注明	
94.05	**其他税目未列名的灯具及照明装置,包括探照灯、聚光灯及其零件;装有固定光源的发光标志、发光铭牌及类似品,以及其他税目未列名的这些货品的零件:**	1.品名;2.材质;3.种类;4.功能	
94.06	**活动房屋:**	1.品名;2.材质	3.注明内部配置

第九十五章　玩具、游戏品、运动用品及其零件、附件

【注解】

本章包括各种玩具,不论是供儿童或供成人娱乐用,还包括户内及户外游戏用设备,运动、体操、竞技用具及器械,某些钓鱼、狩猎或射击用具,旋转木马和其他游乐场用娱乐设备。

本章各商品编码也包括明显为专用于或主要用于本章所列货品的零件、附件,只要它们不是本章注释一所列不包括的物品。

本章物品一般可用各种材料制成,但天然或养殖珍珠、宝石或半宝石(天然、合成或再造)、贵金属或包贵金属除外。装有上述材料制的小配件的物品仍可归入本章。

除了各商品编码注释中所列不包括的物品以外,本章还不包括:

(一)商品编码36.04的烟花及其他烟火制品。

(二)商品编码40.11、40.12或40.13的橡胶轮胎及其他物品。

(三)帐篷及露营用品(一般归入商品编码63.06)。

(四)液体泵(商品编码84.13)、液体或气体的过滤、净化机器及装置(商品编码84.21)、电动机(商品编码85.01)、变压器(商品编码85.04)或无线电遥控装置(商品编码85.26)。

(五)第九十三章的武器及其他物品。

商品编码	商 品 描 述	申 报 要 素	
		商品名称	规格型号
95.03	**三轮车、踏板车、踏板汽车及类似的带轮玩具;玩偶车;玩偶;其他玩具;缩小(按比例缩小)的模型及类似的娱乐用模型,不论是否活动;各种智力玩具:**	1.品名;2.种类	
95.04	**游艺场所、桌上或室内游戏用品,包括弹时机、台球、娱乐专用桌反保龄球自动球道设备:**		
9504.1000	-与电视接收机配套使用的电子游戏机	品名(与电视接收机配套使用的)	
9504.2000	-各种台球用品及附件	品名	
	-使用硬币、钞票(纸币)、圆形代币或类似品的其他游戏用品,保龄球道设备除外:	1.品名;2.用途;3.种类	
9504.4000	-扑克牌	品名	
	-其他:	1.品名;2.用途;3.种类	

商品编码	商品描述	申报要素	
		商品名称	规格型号
95.05	节日(包括狂欢节)用品或其他娱乐用品,包括魔术道具及嬉戏品:		
9505.1000	-圣诞节用品	1.品名;2.用途(圣诞节用品);3.材质	
9505.9000	-其他	1.品名;2.用途	
95.06	一般的体育活动、体操、竞技及其他运动(包括乒乓球运动)或户外游戏用的本章其他税目未列名用品及设备;游泳池或戏水池:	1.品名;2.用途;3.种类	
95.07	钓鱼竿、钓鱼钩及其他钓鱼用品;捞鱼网、捕蝶网及类似网;囮"鸟"(税目92.08或97.05的货品除外)以及类似的狩猎用品:		
9507.1000	-钓鱼竿	1.品名;2.材质	
9507.2000	-钓鱼钩,不论有无系钩丝	品名	
9507.3000	-钓线轮	品名	
9507.9000	-其他	1.品名;2.用途	
95.08	旋转木马、秋千、射击用靶及其他游乐场的娱乐设备;流动马戏团及流动动物园;流动剧团:	1.品名;2.用途	

第九十六章　杂项制品

【注解】

本章包括雕刻和模塑材料及其制品、某些扫把、刷子和筛、某些缝纫用品、某些书写及公用品、某些烟具、某些化妆用具及协调制度其他商品编码未具体列名的其他物品。

商品编码96.07至96.14及96.16至96.18所列物品可以全部或部分由天然或养殖的珍珠、宝石或半宝石(天然、合成或再造)制成,或由贵金属或包贵金属制成。但商品编码96.01至96.06及96.15所列物品可以装有上述。

商品编码	商品描述	申报要素	
		商品名称	规格型号
96.01	已加工的兽牙、骨、玳瑁壳、角、鹿角、珊瑚、珍珠母及其他动物质雕刻材料及其制品(包括模塑制品):	1.品名(已加工的);2.材质;3.野生动物产品请注明	
96.02	已加工的植物质或矿物质雕刻材料及其制品;蜡、硬脂、天然树胶、天然树脂或塑型膏制成的模塑或雕刻制品以及其他税目未列名的模塑或雕刻制品;已加工的未硬化明胶(税目35.03的明胶除外)及未硬化明胶制品:		
9602.0010	---装药用胶囊	品名	
9602.0090	---其他	1.品名(已加工的);2.材质	
96.03	帚、刷(包括作为机器、器具、车辆零件的刷)、非机动的手工操作地板清扫器、拖把及毛掸;供制帚、刷用的成束或成簇的材料;油漆块垫及滚筒;橡皮扫帚(橡皮辊除外):	1.品名;2.用途;3.材质;4.野生动物产品请注明	
96.04	手用粗筛、细筛:	品名(手用)	
96.05	个人梳妆、缝纫或清洁鞋靴、衣服用的成套旅行用具:	1.品名(成套货品)	2.组成(内装货品)
96.06	钮扣、揿扣、钮扣芯及钮扣和揿扣的其他零件;钮扣坯:	1.品名;2.材质;3.种类; 4.野生动物产品和纺织材料包裹请注明	
96.07	拉链及其零件:	1.品名;2.材质	

商品编码	商 品 描 述	申 报 要 素	
		商品名称	规格型号
96.08	**圆珠笔;毡尖和其他渗水式笔尖笔及唛头笔;自来水笔、铁笔型自来水笔及其他钢笔;蜡纸铁笔;活动铅笔;钢笔杆、铅笔套及类似的笔套;上述物品的零件(包括帽、夹),但税目96.09的货品除外:**	1.品名;2.种类	
96.09	**铅笔(税目96.08的铅笔除外)、颜色铅笔、铅笔芯、蜡笔、图画碳笔、书写或绘画用粉笔及裁缝划粉:**		
	-铅笔及颜色铅笔:	1.品名;2.种类	
9609.2000	-铅笔芯,黑的或其他颜色的	品名	
9609.9000	其他	品名	
96.10	**具有书写或绘画面的石板、黑板及类似板,不论是否镶框:**	品名	
96.11	**手用日期戳、封缄戳、编号戳及类似印戳(包括标签压印器);手工操作的排字盘及带有排字盘的手印器:**	1.品名(手用的);2.野生动物产品请注明	
96.12	**打字机色带或类似色带,已上油或经其他方法处理能着色的,不论是否装轴或装盒;印台,不论是否已加印油或带盒子:**	1.品名;2.材质	
96.13	**香烟打火机和其他打火器(不论是机械的,还是电气的)及其零件,但打火石及打火机芯除外:**	1.品名;2.种类	
96.14	**烟斗(包括烟斗头)和烟嘴及其零件:**	1.品名;2.材质;3.野生动物产品请注明	
96.15	**梳子、发夹及类似品;发卡、卷发夹、卷发器或类似品及其零件,但税目85.16的货品除外:**	1.品名;2.材质;3.野生动物产品请注明	
96.16	**香水喷雾器或类似的化妆用喷雾器及其座架、喷头;粉扑及粉拍,施敷脂粉或化妆品用:**	1.品名;2.用途	
96.17	**带壳的保温瓶和其他真空容器及其零件,但玻璃瓶胆除外:**	1.品名	
96.18	**裁缝用人体模型及其他人体活动模型;橱窗装饰用的自动模型及其他活动陈列品:**		
9618.0000	**裁缝用人体模型及其他人体活动模型;橱窗装饰用的自动模型及其他活动陈列品**	1.品名;2.用途;3.材质	

第二十一类　艺术品、收藏品及古物

第九十七章　艺术品、收藏品及古物

【注解】

本章包括：

1. 某种艺术品：完全用手工绘制的油画、绘画及粉画；拼贴画及类似的装饰板（商品编码97.01）；版画、印制画及石印画的原本（商品编码97.02）；雕塑品的原件（商品编码97.03）。

2. 邮票、印花税票及类似票证、邮戳印记、首日封、邮政信笺（印有邮票的纸品）及类似品，使用过的或虽未使用过但不是指运国流通或新发行的（商品编码97.04）。

3. 具有动物学、植物学、矿物学、解剖学、历史学、考古学、古生物学、人种学或钱币学意义的收集品及珍藏品（商品编码97.05）。

4. 超过一百年的古物（商品编码97.06）。

但应注意，这些物品如不符合本章注释或本章内各税目所列的条件的，应归入本协调制度的其他章。商品编码97.01至97.05的物品即使超过100年，也仍应归入这些商品编码内。

商品编码	商品描述	申报要素	
		商品名称	规格型号
97.01	**油画、粉画及其他手绘画，但带有手工绘制及手工描饰的制品或税目49.06的图纸除外；拼贴画及类似装饰板：**	1.品名（原件、复制件）； 2.野生动物材质请注明	
97.02	**雕版画、印制画、石印画的原本：**	品名（原本）	
97.03	**各种材料制的雕塑品原件：**	1.品名（原件）；2.野生动物材质请注明	
97.04	**使用过或未使用过的邮票、印花税票、邮戳印记、首日封、邮政信笺（印有邮票的纸品）及类似品，但税目49.07的货品除外：**	1.品名；2.种类	3.指运国
97.05	**具有动物学、植物学、矿物学、解剖学、历史学、考古学、古生物学、人种学或钱币学意义的收集品及珍藏品：**	1.品名；2.种类； 3.年代；4.野生动物材质请注明	
97.06	**超过100年的古物：**	1.品名；2.种类；3.年代；4.野生动物材质请注明	

6

中华人民共和国进出口法律法规选编

Collection of up-to-date and in effect laws and regulations concerning import/export the People's Republic of China

10. 欲知更全面,更详细的中英文对照法规,请登录网址:www. fhgt. com. cn。
Please log on to www. fhgt. com. cn. for more detailed and complete version of laws and regulations with both Chinese and English translation Facilities used for medical treatment, surgery, dentistry or veterinary

中华人民共和国对外贸易法

中华人民共和国主席令
（第15号）

《中华人民共和国对外贸易法》已由中华人民共和国第十届全国人民代表大会常务委员会第八次会议于2004年4月6日修订通过，现将修订后的《中华人民共和国对外贸易法》公布，自2004年7月1日起施行。

中华人民共和国主席　胡锦涛
2004年4月6日

第一章　总　则

第一条　为了扩大对外开放，发展对外贸易，维护对外贸易秩序，保护对外贸易经营者的合法权益，促进社会主义市场经济的健康发展，制定本法。

第二条　本法适用于对外贸易以及与对外贸易有关的知识产权保护。

本法所称对外贸易，是指货物进出口、技术进出口和国际服务贸易。

第三条　国务院对外贸易主管部门依照本法主管全国对外贸易工作。

第四条　国家实行统一的对外贸易制度，鼓励发展对外贸易，维护公平、自由的对外贸易秩序。

第五条　中华人民共和国根据平等互利的原则，促进和发展同其他国家和地区的贸易关系，缔结或者参加关税同盟协定、自由贸易区协定等区域经济贸易协定，参加区域经济组织。

第六条　中华人民共和国在对外贸易方面根据所缔结或者参加的国际条约、协定，给予其他缔约方、参加方最惠国待遇、国民待遇等待遇，或者根据互惠、对等原则给予对方最惠国待遇、国民待遇等待遇。

第七条　任何国家或者地区在贸易方面对中华人民共和国采取歧视性的禁止、限制或者其他类似措施的，中华人民共和国可以根据实际情况对该国家或者该地区采取相应的措施。

第二章　对外贸易经营者

第八条　本法所称对外贸易经营者，是指依法办理工商登记或者其他执业手续，依照本法和其他有关法律、

Foreign Trade Law of the People's Republic of China

Order of the President of the People's Republic of China
(No. 15)

The Foreign Trade Law of the People's Republic of China was amended and adopted at the eighth meeting of the Standing Committee of the Tenth National People's Congress on April 6, 2004. The amended Foreign Trade Law of the People's Republic of China is hereby promulgated for effect as of July 1, 2004.

Hu Jintao, President of the People's Republic of China
April 6, 2004

Chapter I　General Provisions

Article 1　The present Law is enacted for the purpose of broadening the opening to the outside world, developing foreign trade, maintaining the order of foreign trade, protecting the lawful rights and interests of the foreign trade business operators, and promoting the healthy development of the socialist market economy.

Article 2　The present Law applies to foreign trade and the protection of foreign-trade-related intellectual property.

The term "foreign trade" as mentioned in the present law refers to the import and export of goods, technology, and the international trade of services.

Article 3　The administrative department of the State Council in charge of foreign trade shall take charge of the nationwide foreign trade according to the present Law.

Article 4　The state practices a uniform system of foreign trade, encourages the development of foreign trade, and maintains an order of fair and free foreign trade.

Article 5　The People's Republic of China promotes and develops foreign trade relations with other countries and regions, concludes or accedes to regional economic and trade agreements such as customs or tariff union agreements, free trade zone agreements, etc., and joins regional economic organizations according to the principle of equality and reciprocity.

Article 6　In the field of foreign trade, the People's Republic of China grants, according to the international treaties and agreements it concluded or acceded to, most-favored-nation treatment or national treatment to other contracting parties or members, or grants most-favored-nation treatment or national treatment to its counterparts according to the principle of mutual benefit and reciprocity.

Article 7　For any country or region that takes discriminatory banning, restriction or other acts against the People's Republic of China in terms of trade, the People's Republic of China shall be entitled to adopt, in accordance with the actual circumstances, corresponding measures against them.

Chapter Ⅱ　Foreign Trade Business Operators

Article 8　The term "foreign trade business operator" as mentioned in the present Law refers to any legal person, other organization, or individ-

行政法规的规定从事对外贸易经营活动的法人、其他组织或者个人。

第九条 从事货物进出口或者技术进出口的对外贸易经营者,应当向国务院对外贸易主管部门或者其委托的机构办理备案登记;但是,法律、行政法规和国务院对外贸易主管部门规定不需要备案登记的除外。备案登记的具体办法由国务院对外贸易主管部门规定。对外贸易经营者未按照规定办理备案登记的,海关不予办理进出口货物的报关验放手续。

第十条 从事国际服务贸易,应当遵守本法和其他有关法律、行政法规的规定。

从事对外工程承包或者对外劳务合作的单位,应当具备相应的资质或者资格。具体办法由国务院规定。

第十一条 国家可以对部分货物的进出口实行国营贸易管理。实行国营贸易管理货物的进出口业务只能由经授权的企业经营;但是,国家允许部分数量的国营贸易管理货物的进出口业务由非授权企业经营的除外。实行国营贸易管理的货物和经授权经营企业的目录,由国务院对外贸易主管部门会同国务院其他有关部门确定、调整并公布。

违反本条第一款规定,擅自进出口实行国营贸易管理的货物的,海关不予放行。

第十二条 对外贸易经营者可以接受他人的委托,在经营范围内代为办理对外贸易业务。

第十三条 对外贸易经营者应当按照国务院对外贸易主管部门或者国务院其他有关部门依法作出的规定,向有关部门提交与其对外贸易经营活动有关的文件及资料。有关部门应当为提供者保守商业秘密。

第三章 货物进出口与技术进出口

第十四条 国家准许货物与技术的自由进出口。但是,法律、行政法规另有规定的除外。

第十五条 国务院对外贸易主管部门基于监测进出口情况的需要,可以对部分自由进出口的货物实行进出口自动许可并公布其目录。

ual, that has handled industrial and commercial registration or other formalities for business operation and is engaged in the foreign trade business activities according to the provisions of the present Law and other relevant laws and administrative regulations.

Article 9 Any foreign trade business operator that is engaged in the import and export of goods or technology shall be registered for archival purposes with the administrative department of foreign trade of the State Council or the institution entrusted thereby, unless it is otherwise provided for by any law, administrative regulation or the foreign trade department of the State Council. The specific measures for archival registration shall be formulated by the foreign trade department of the State Council. Where any foreign trade business operator that fails to file for archival registration according to relevant provisions, the customs may not handle the procedures of customs declarations and release of the import or export goods.

Article 10 Anyone who is engaged in international service trade shall abide by the present Law and other relevant laws and administrative regulations.

An entity that is engaged in the overseas contracting of engineering projects or overseas labor cooperation shall have lawfully obtained corresponding competence or qualifications. The specific measures shall be formulated by the State Council.

Article 11 The State may employ the administration of state-run trade to the import and export of some goods. The import and export of the goods subject to the administration of state-run trade can be managed by the authorized enterprises only, with the exception, however, of the goods, which is allowed by the state to be partially imported or exported by unauthorized enterprises. The catalogue of the goods subject to the management of state-run trade and that of authorized enterprises shall be determined, adjusted and published by the foreign trade department of the State Council in collaboration with other relevant departments.

Where anyone who imports or exports, as in violation of Paragraph 1 of the present article, any of the goods subject to the management of state-run trade, the customs may not release the goods.

Article 12 A foreign business operator may accept the entrustment of other people and handle foreign trade businesses on their behalf within its scope of business.

Article 13 A foreign trade business operator shall submit to the relevant departments the documents and materials relating to its foreign trade activities in accordance to the provisions of the foreign trade department of the State Council and those of other relevant departments of the State Council. And the relevant departments shall keep the business secrets of the providers to themselves.

Chapter Ⅲ The Import and Export of Goods and Technology

Article 14 The state allows the free import and export of goods and technology, unless it is otherwise provided for by any law or administrative regulation.

Article 15 The foreign trade department of the State Council may, where the monitoring of import and export so requires, employ the system of automatic license of import and export to some of the freely imported and exported goods, and publish the catalogue thereof.

实行自动许可的进出口货物,收货人、发货人在办理海关报关手续前提出自动许可申请的,国务院对外贸易主管部门或者其委托的机构应当予以许可;未办理自动许可手续的,海关不予放行。

进出口属于自由进出口的技术,应当向国务院对外贸易主管部门或者其委托的机构办理合同备案登记。

第十六条 国家基于下列原因,可以限制或者禁止有关货物、技术的进口或者出口:

(一)为维护国家安全、社会公共利益或者公共道德,需要限制或者禁止进口或者出口的;

(二)为保护人的健康或者安全,保护动物、植物的生命或者健康,保护环境,需要限制或者禁止进口或者出口的;

(三)为实施与黄金或者白银进出口有关的措施,需要限制或者禁止进口或者出口的;

(四)国内供应短缺或者为有效保护可能用竭的自然资源,需要限制或者禁止出口的;

(五)输往国家或者地区的市场容量有限,需要限制出口的;

(六)出口经营秩序出现严重混乱,需要限制出口的;

(七)为建立或者加快建立国内特定产业,需要限制进口的;

(八)对任何形式的农业、牧业、渔业产品有必要限制进口的;

(九)为保障国家国际金融地位和国际收支平衡,需要限制进口的;

(十)依照法律、行政法规的规定,其他需要限制或者禁止进口或者出口的;

(十一)根据我国缔结或者参加的国际条约、协定的规定,其他需要限制或者禁止进口或者出口的。

第十七条 国家对与裂变、聚变物质或者衍生此类物质的物质有关的货物、技术进出口,以及与武器、弹药或者其他军用物资有关的进出口,可以采取任何必要的措施,维护国家安全。

在战时或者为维护国际和平与安全,国家在货物、技术进出口方面可以采取任何必要的措施。

第十八条 国务院对外贸易主管部门会同国务院其他有关部门,依照本法第十六条和第十七条的规定,制定、调整并公布限制或者禁止进出口的货物、技术目录。

国务院对外贸易主管部门或者由其会同国务院其他

For the goods subject to automatic license of import and export, if the consignor or consignee applies for automatic license prior to handling the formalities of customs declaration, the foreign trade department of the State Council and the institutions entrusted thereby shall grant approval. Where it fails to handle the formalities of automatic license, the customs may not release the goods thereunder.

To import or export any technology subject to free import and export, one shall have its contracts registered with the foreign trade administrative department of the State Council or the institution entrusted thereby for archival purposes.

Article 16 The state may restrict or forbid the import or export of relevant goods or technology if:

(1) It is necessary to restrict or forbid the import or export for the purpose of maintaining state security, social public good or public morality;

(2) It is necessary to restrict or forbid the import or export for the purpose of protecting human health or security, protecting the life or health of any animal or plant, or protecting the environment;

(3) It is necessary to restrict the import or export for the purpose of implementing the measures relating to the import or export of gold or silver;

(4) It is necessary to restrict or forbid the export of any of the exhaustible natural resources that are in short supply or subject to effective protection;

(5) It is necessary to restrict the export due to the limited market capacity of the destination country or region;

(6) It is necessary to export due to the serious disorder of the export business management;

(7) It is necessary to restrict the import for the purpose of establishing or accelerating the establishment of a particular domestic industry;

(8) It is necessary to restrict the import of any form of product in the agriculture, animal husbandry, or fishing industry;

(9) It is necessary to restrict the import for the purpose of safeguarding the international financial status of the state or of the international balance of payments;

(10) It is necessary to restrict or forbid the import or export under any other circumstance as provided for in any other law or administrative regulation; or

(11) It is necessary to restrict or forbid the import or export under any other circumstance as provided for in any international treaty or agreement that China has concluded or acceded to.

Article 17 The state may, for the purpose of defending state security, take any necessary measures for managing the import and export of any matter of fission or fusion or any matter that derives such matter and the import and export of any weapon, ammunition, or any other military supply.

When in war or for keeping international peace and security, the state may take any necessary measures in terms of the import or export of goods or technology.

Article 18 The foreign trade administrative department of the State Council may, in collaboration with any other relevant department of the State Council, formulate, adjust and publish catalogues of goods and technology restricted or forbidden from import or export according to the provisions of Article 16 or 17 of the present Law.

The foreign trade administrative department of the State Council may,

有关部门,经国务院批准,可以在本法第十六条和第十七条规定的范围内,临时决定限制或者禁止前款规定目录以外的特定货物、技术的进口或者出口。

第十九条 国家对限制进口或者出口的货物,实行配额、许可证等方式管理;对限制进口或者出口的技术,实行许可证管理。

实行配额、许可证管理的货物、技术,应当按照国务院规定经国务院对外贸易主管部门或者经其会同国务院其他有关部门许可,方可进口或者出口。

国家对部分进口货物可以实行关税配额管理。

第二十条 进出口货物配额、关税配额,由国务院对外贸易主管部门或者国务院其他有关部门在各自的职责范围内,按照公开、公平、公正和效益的原则进行分配。具体办法由国务院规定。

第二十一条 国家实行统一的商品合格评定制度,根据有关法律、行政法规的规定,对进出口商品进行认证、检验、检疫。

第二十二条 国家对进出口货物进行原产地管理。具体办法由国务院规定。

第二十三条 对文物和野生动物、植物及其产品等,其他法律、行政法规有禁止或者限制进出口规定的,依照有关法律、行政法规的规定执行。

第四章 国际服务贸易

第二十四条 中华人民共和国在国际服务贸易方面根据所缔结或者参加的国际条约、协定中所作的承诺,给予其他缔约方、参加方市场准入和国民待遇。

第二十五条 国务院对外贸易主管部门和国务院其他有关部门,依照本法和其他有关法律、行政法规的规定,对国际服务贸易进行管理。

第二十六条 国家基于下列原因,可以限制或者禁止有关的国际服务贸易:

(一)为维护国家安全、社会公共利益或者公共道德,需要限制或者禁止的;

(二)为保护人的健康或者安全,保护动物、植物的生命或者健康,保护环境,需要限制或者禁止的;

(三)为建立或者加快建立国内特定服务产业,需要限制的;

(四)为保障国家外汇收支平衡,需要限制的;

independently or in collaboration with any other department of the State Council, make provisional decisions, upon the approval of the State Council and within the scope of Articles 16 and 17 of the present Law, on restricting or forbidding the import or export of certain goods or technology that are not found in the catalogue as mentioned in the preceding paragraph.

Article 19 The state adopts the system of quota, license, etc, to the goods subject to import or export restrictions, while adopts the system of license to the technologies restricted or prohibited from import or export.

For the goods and technologies subject to the administration of quota or license, they cannot be imported or exported unless it has been approved by the foreign trade department of the State Council independently or in collaboration with other departments of the State Council.

The state may practice tariff quota administration to some of the import goods.

Article 20 The quotas and tariff quotas for the import and export goods shall be distributed by the foreign trade department of the State Council or other relevant departments of the State Council within their respective duties in accordance with the principles of openness, fairness, impartiality, and efficiency. The specific measures shall be made by the State Council.

Article 21 The state practices a uniform system of commodity quality assessment, and makes authentications, inspections, and quarantines to the import and export commodities according to the provisions of relevant laws and administrative regulations.

Article 22 The state applies the administration system of origin to the import and export goods. The specific measures shall be formulated by the State Council.

Article 23 With regard to cultural relics, wild animals or plants, and the products thereof, if it is restricted or prohibited by any law or administrative regulation from import or export, the provisions of such laws and administrative regulations shall apply.

Chapter Ⅳ International Service Trade

Article 24 The People's Republic of China opens, in accordance with its commitments made in the international treaties and agreements of international service trade that it has concluded or acceded to, its market to the other contracting parties or members and grants them with the national treatment.

Article 25 The foreign trade department of the State Council and other relevant departments of the State Council may, according to the present Law or any other relevant law or administrative regulation, administer the trade of international services.

Article 26 The state may restrict or prohibit the trade of relevant international services if:

(1) It is necessary to restrict or prohibit it for the sake of maintaining state security, social public good or public morality;

(2) It is necessary to restrict or prohibit it for the purpose of protecting human health or security, protecting the life or health of any animal or plant, or protecting the environment;

(3) It is necessary to restrict it for the purpose of establishing or accelerating the establishment of a certain domestic service industry;

(4) It is necessary to restrict it for the purpose of ensuring the balance of international payments of the state;

（五）依照法律、行政法规的规定，其他需要限制或者禁止的；

（六）根据我国缔结或者参加的国际条约、协定的规定，其他需要限制或者禁止的。

第二十七条 国家对与军事有关的国际服务贸易，以及与裂变、聚变物质或者衍生此类物质的物质有关的国际服务贸易，可以采取任何必要的措施，维护国家安全。

在战时或者为维护国际和平与安全，国家在国际服务贸易方面可以采取任何必要的措施。

第二十八条 国务院对外贸易主管部门会同国务院其他有关部门，依照本法第二十六条、第二十七条和其他有关法律、行政法规的规定，制定、调整并公布国际服务贸易市场准入目录。

第五章 与对外贸易有关的知识产权保护

第二十九条 国家依照有关知识产权的法律、行政法规，保护与对外贸易有关的知识产权。

进口货物侵犯知识产权，并危害对外贸易秩序的，国务院对外贸易主管部门可以采取在一定期限内禁止侵权人生产、销售的有关货物进口等措施。

第三十条 知识产权权利人有阻止被许可人对许可合同中的知识产权的有效性提出质疑、进行强制性一揽子许可、在许可合同中规定排他性返授条件等行为之一，并危害对外贸易公平竞争秩序的，国务院对外贸易主管部门可以采取必要的措施消除危害。

第三十一条 其他国家或者地区在知识产权保护方面未给予中华人民共和国的法人、其他组织或者个人国民待遇，或者不能对来源于中华人民共和国的货物、技术或者服务提供充分有效的知识产权保护的，国务院对外贸易主管部门可以依照本法和其他有关法律、行政法规的规定，并根据中华人民共和国缔结或者参加的国际条约、协定，对与该国家或者该地区的贸易采取必要的措施。

第六章 对外贸易秩序

第三十二条 在对外贸易经营活动中，不得违反有关反垄断的法律、行政法规的规定实施垄断行为。

在对外贸易经营活动中实施垄断行为，危害市场公平竞争的，依照有关反垄断的法律、行政法规的规定处理。有前款违法行为，并危害对外贸易秩序的，国务院对

(5) It is necessary to restrict or prohibit it for any other reason as provided for in any law or administrative regulation; or

(6) It is necessary to restrict or prohibit it for any other reason as provided for in any international treaty or agreement that China has concluded or acceded to.

Article 27 For the military-related trade of international services and the international service trade of any matter of fission or fusion or any matter that derives such matter, the state may take any necessary measures to safeguard the security of the state.

When in war or for keeping international peace and security, the state may take any necessary measures regarding the international service trade.

Article 28 The foreign trade department of the State Council formulates, adjusts, and publishes, in collaboration with other relevant departments of the State Council, market entry catalogues of the international service trade in accordance with the provisions of Articles 26 and 27 of the present Law and other relevant laws and administrative regulations.

Chapter V Foreign-trade-related Intellectual Property Protection

Article 29 The state protects the intellectual property relating to foreign trade in accordance with relevant laws and administrative regulations concerning intellectual property.

Where any of the import goods violates any intellectual property right and, at the same time, endangers the foreign trade order, the foreign trade department of the State Council may take such measures as prohibiting the import of the relevant goods that the infringer has produced or sold for a certain period of time.

Article 30 In case any intellectual property right holder commits any of the acts of hindering the licensee from questioning the validity of the intellectual property right involved in the license agreement, conducting forced package license, or providing exclusive selling back conditions in the license agreement, etc. and, at the same time, endangers the fair competition order of foreign trade, the foreign trade department of the State Council may take necessary measures to eliminate such danger.

Article 31 Where any country or region fails to grant national treatment to the legal persons, other organizations, or individuals of the People's Republic of China in the protection of intellectual property rights, or fails to provide sufficient and effective intellectual property protection to the goods, technologies or services whose origin is the People's Republic of China, the foreign trade department of the State Council may, according to the present Law or any other law or administrative regulation, and according to the international treaties or agreements that the People's Republic of China has concluded or acceded to, take necessary measures against the trade with the said country or region.

Chapter VI Foreign Trade Order

Article 32 No one may, in the business activities of foreign trade, implement any act of monopolization against the relevant anti-monopolization laws or administrative regulations.

Anyone who carries out any monopolizing act in its foreign trade business activities shall be dealt with in accordance with the relevant anti-monopolization laws and administrative regulations. If any of the illegal acts as

外贸易主管部门可以采取必要的措施消除危害。

第三十三条 在对外贸易经营活动中，不得实施以不正当的低价销售商品、串通投标、发布虚假广告、进行商业贿赂等不正当竞争行为。

在对外贸易经营活动中实施不正当竞争行为的，依照有关反不正当竞争的法律、行政法规的规定处理。

有前款违法行为，并危害对外贸易秩序的，国务院对外贸易主管部门可以采取禁止该经营者有关货物、技术进出口等措施消除危害。

第三十四条 在对外贸易活动中，不得有下列行为：

（一）伪造、变造进出口货物原产地标记，伪造、变造或者买卖进出口货物原产地证书、进出口许可证、进出口配额证明或者其他进出口证明文件；

（二）骗取出口退税；

（三）走私；

（四）逃避法律、行政法规规定的认证、检验、检疫；

（五）违反法律、行政法规规定的其他行为。

第三十五条 对外贸易经营者在对外贸易经营活动中，应当遵守国家有关外汇管理的规定。

第三十六条 违反本法规定，危害对外贸易秩序的，国务院对外贸易主管部门可以向社会公告。

第七章 对外贸易调查

第三十七条 为了维护对外贸易秩序，国务院对外贸易主管部门可以自行或者会同国务院其他有关部门，依照法律、行政法规的规定对下列事项进行调查：

（一）货物进出口、技术进出口、国际服务贸易对国内产业及其竞争力的影响；

（二）有关国家或者地区的贸易壁垒；

（三）为确定是否应当依法采取反倾销、反补贴或者保障措施等对外贸易救济措施，需要调查的事项；

（四）规避对外贸易救济措施的行为；

（五）对外贸易中有关国家安全利益的事项；

（六）为执行本法第七条、第二十九条第二款、第三十条、第三十一条、第三十二条第三款、第三十三条第三款的规定，需要调查的事项；

（七）其他影响对外贸易秩序，需要调查的事项。

described in the preceding paragraph endangers the foreign trade order at the same time, the foreign trade department of the State Council may take necessary measures to eliminate the harm.

Article 33 No one may, in the business activities of foreign trade, conduct such unfair competition acts as selling commodities at unjustified low prices, colluding bid invitation and tendering for bid, disseminating false advertisements, or offering commercial bribes, etc.

Anyone who conducts any unfair competition act in its foreign trade business activities shall be dealt with in accordance with the relevant laws and administrative regulations regarding counteracting unfair competition.

If any of the illegal acts as described in the preceding paragraph endangers the foreign trade order at the same time, the foreign trade department of the State Council may take such measures as prohibiting the business operator involved from importing or exporting relevant goods or technologies so as to eliminate the said illegal act.

Article 34 No one may, in foreign trade activities, commit any of the following:

(1) Forging or altering the marks of origin of the import or export goods; forging, altering or trading the certificates of origin, the licenses of import or export, the certificates of import or export quotas of the import or export goods, or any other certification documents of import or export;

(2) Cheating for export refunds;

(3) Smuggling;

(4) Evading inspections and quarantines as provided for by any law or administrative regulation; or

(5) Committing any other violation of law or administrative regulation.

Article 35 All foreign trade business operators shall abide by the provisions of the state regarding foreign exchange administration in their foreign trade business activities.

Article 36 Anyone who violates the present Law and endangers the foreign trade order shall be made public by way of announcements made by the foreign trade department of the State Council.

Chapter Ⅶ Foreign Trade Investigation

Article 37 In order to maintain the foreign trade order, the foreign trade department of the State Council may investigate into the following matters by itself or jointly with other relevant departments of the State Council in accordance with the laws and administrative regulations:

(1) The impact of the import or export of goods or technology or international service trade on domestic industries and the competitiveness thereof;

(2) The trade barriers of relevant countries or regions;

(3) The matters that need to be investigated into for the purpose of determining whether it is necessary to take such foreign trade relief measures as antidumping, countervailing, or safeguard measures, etc.;

(4) The evasion of trade relief measures;

(5) The matters of foreign trade that concern the security or interest of the state;

(6) The matters that need to be investigated into for the purpose of implementing Article 7, Paragraph 2 of Article 29, Article 30, Article 31, Paragraph 3 of Article 32, and Paragraph 3 of Article 33; and

(7) Any other matter that need to be investigated into as a result of af-

第三十八条 启动对外贸易调查，由国务院对外贸易主管部门发布公告。

调查可以采取书面问卷、召开听证会、实地调查、委托调查等方式进行。

国务院对外贸易主管部门根据调查结果，提出调查报告或者作出处理裁定，并发布公告。

第三十九条 有关单位和个人应当对对外贸易调查给予配合、协助。

国务院对外贸易主管部门和国务院其他有关部门及其工作人员进行对外贸易调查，对知悉的国家秘密和商业秘密负有保密义务。

第八章 对外贸易救济

第四十条 国家根据对外贸易调查结果，可以采取适当的对外贸易救济措施。

第四十一条 其他国家或者地区的产品以低于正常价值的倾销方式进入我国市场，对已建立的国内产业造成实质损害或者产生实质损害威胁，或者对建立国内产业造成实质阻碍的，国家可以采取反倾销措施，消除或者减轻这种损害或者损害的威胁或者阻碍。

第四十二条 其他国家或者地区的产品以低于正常价值出口至第三国市场，对我国已建立的国内产业造成实质损害或者产生实质损害威胁，或者对我国建立国内产业造成实质阻碍的，应国内产业的申请，国务院对外贸易主管部门可以与该第三国政府进行磋商，要求其采取适当的措施。

第四十三条 进口的产品直接或者间接地接受出口国家或者地区给予的任何形式的专向性补贴，对已建立的国内产业造成实质损害或者产生实质损害威胁，或者对建立国内产业造成实质阻碍的，国家可以采取反补贴措施，消除或者减轻这种损害或者损害的威胁或者阻碍。

第四十四条 因进口产品数量大量增加，对生产同类产品或者与其直接竞争的产品的国内产业造成严重损害或者严重损害威胁的，国家可以采取必要的保障措施，消除或者减轻这种损害或者损害的威胁，并可以对该产业提供必要的支持。

第四十五条 因其他国家或者地区的服务提供者向我国提供的服务增加，对提供同类服务或者与其直接竞争的服务的国内产业造成损害或者产生损害威胁的，国家可以采取必要的救济措施，消除或者减轻这种损害或者损害的威胁。

第四十六条 因第三国限制进口而导致某种产品进入我国市场的数量大量增加，对已建立的国内产业造成

fecting the foreign trade order.

Article 38 When a foreign trade investigation is initiated, an announcement shall be issued by the foreign trade department of the State Council.

An investigation may be made by way of written questionnaires, holding hearings, making site investigations, and entrusting other people to make the investigation, etc.

The foreign trade department of the State Council may, based on the result of investigation, put forward an investigation report or make a ruling, and make an announcement for it.

Article 39 Relevant entities and individuals shall offer cooperation and assistance in foreign trade investigations.

The foreign trade department of the State Council and other departments of the State Council as well as the functionaries thereof shall, in the process of foreign trade investigations, be obliged to keep to themselves the state secrets and commercial secrets that they have access to.

Chapter Ⅷ Foreign Trade Relief

Article 40 The state may take appropriate trade relief measures according to the result of foreign trade investigations.

Article 41 In case any of the products of any country or region is dumped into China at an abnormally low price and thus causes substantial injury or the threat of substantial injury to an established domestic industry, or substantially impedes the establishment of a domestic industry, the state may take antidumping measures so as to eliminate or alleviate such injury or threat of injury or impediment.

Article 42 In case any product of any country or region is exported to any third country at an abnormally low price and thus causes substantial injury or the threat of substantial injury to an established domestic industry, or substantially impedes the establishment of a domestic industry, the foreign trade department of the State Council may, as per the request of the corresponding domestic industry, hold negotiations with the government of the third country, and urge it to take appropriate measures.

Article 43 Where any imported product is given, directly or indirectly, any special subsidy by the exporting country or region in any form, and thus causing substantial injury or threat of substantial injury to an established industry, or substantially impeding the establishment of a domestic industry, the state may take countervailing measures so as to eliminate or alleviate such injury or threat of injury or impediment.

Article 44 In case the sharp increase of any imported product brings about any serious injury or threat of serious injury to the domestic industry that produces identical product or directly competing products, the state may take necessary safeguarding measures so as to eliminate or alleviate such injury or threat of injury, and may provide necessary support to the industry concerned.

Article 45 In case the increase of any service provided by any service provider of any country or region to China has caused injury or threat of injury to the domestic industry that provides identical service or directly competing services, the state may take necessary relief measures so as to eliminate or alleviate such injury or threat of injury.

Article 46 In case the import of any product to into China increases sharply as a result of the restriction of import by any third country, and thus

损害或者产生损害威胁，或者对建立国内产业造成阻碍的，国家可以采取必要的救济措施，限制该产品进口。

causes injury or threat of injury to an established domestic industry, or substantially impedes the establishment of a domestic industry, the state may take necessary measures to restrict the import of the product.

第四十七条 与中华人民共和国缔结或者共同参加经济贸易条约、协定的国家或者地区，违反条约、协定的规定，使中华人民共和国根据该条约、协定享有的利益丧失或者受损，或者阻碍条约、协定目标实现的，中华人民共和国政府有权要求有关国家或者地区政府采取适当的补救措施，并可以根据有关条约、协定中止或者终止履行相关义务。

Article 47 Where any country or region that has entered into any economic or trade treaty or agreement with the People's Republic of China violates the treaty or agreement so that the interest enjoyable by the People's Republic of China according to the treaty or agreement is lost or injured or the achievement of the objective of the treaty or agreement is impeded, the government of the People's Republic of China is entitled to demand the country or region concerned to take appropriate measures of relief, and may suspend or terminate the performance of relevant obligations according to the relevant treaties or agreements.

第四十八条 国务院对外贸易主管部门依照本法和其他有关法律的规定，进行对外贸易的双边或者多边磋商、谈判和争端的解决。

Article 48 The foreign trade department of the State Council is, according to the provisions of the present Law or other relevant laws, responsible for the bilateral or multilateral discussions, negotiations, and dispute settlement.

第四十九条 国务院对外贸易主管部门和国务院其他有关部门应当建立货物进出口、技术进出口和国际服务贸易的预警应急机制，应对对外贸易中的突发和异常情况，维护国家经济安全。

Article 49 The foreign trade department of the State Council and other relevant departments of the State Council shall establish an emergency prewarning mechanism of the import and export of goods, technology, and international service trade so as to deal with the abrupt or abnormal situations in foreign trade and safeguard the economic security of the state.

第五十条 国家对规避本法规定的对外贸易救济措施的行为，可以采取必要的反规避措施。

Article 50 For the acts of evading the trade relief measures as provided for in the present Law, the state may take necessary anti-evasion measures.

第九章 对外贸易促进

Chapter Ⅸ Foreign Trade Promotion

第五十一条 国家制定对外贸易发展战略，建立和完善对外贸易促进机制。

Article 51 The state formulates its strategy for foreign trade development, establishes and improves its foreign trade promotion mechanisms.

第五十二条 国家根据对外贸易发展的需要，建立和完善为对外贸易服务的金融机构，设立对外贸易发展基金、风险基金。

Article 52 The state establishes and improves its foreign-trade-oriented financial institutions and establishes foreign trade development funds and risk funds according to the demand of foreign trade development.

第五十三条 国家通过进出口信贷、出口信用保险、出口退税及其他促进对外贸易的方式，发展对外贸易。

Article 53 The state employs such foreign trade promotion measures as import and export credit, export credit insurance, export tax refund, etc. to develop its foreign trade.

第五十四条 国家建立对外贸易公共信息服务体系，向对外贸易经营者和其他社会公众提供信息服务。

Article 54 The state establishes a foreign trade public information service system so as to provide information services to the foreign trade business operators and the general public.

第五十五条 国家采取措施鼓励对外贸易经营者开拓国际市场，采取对外投资、对外工程承包和对外劳务合作等多种形式，发展对外贸易。

Article 55 The state takes measures to encourage foreign trade business operators to explore the international market, and employ diversified means including foreign investment, foreign engineering project contracting, and labor cooperation, etc. to develop its foreign trade.

第五十六条 对外贸易经营者可以依法成立和参加有关协会、商会。

有关协会、商会应当遵守法律、行政法规，按照章程对其成员提供与对外贸易有关的生产、营销、信息、培训等方面的服务，发挥协调和自律作用，依法提出有关对外贸易救济措施的申请，维护成员和行业的利益，向政府有关部门反映成员有关对外贸易的建议，开展对外贸易促进活动。

Article 56 Foreign trade business operators may lawfully establish and join relevant associations and chambers of commerce.

Relevant associations and chambers of commerce shall abide by the laws and administrative regulations, and provide, according to their constitutions, services to their members in terms of production, marketing, information, training, etc. relating to foreign trade, plays the role of coordination and self-discipline, makes applications for foreign trade relief measures according to law, defend the interests of their members and the corresponding industry, passes onto the relevant department of the government the suggestions of their members regarding foreign trade, and conduct foreign trade promotion activities.

第五十七条 中国国际贸易促进组织按照章程开展对外联系,举办展览,提供信息、咨询服务和其他对外贸易促进活动。

第五十八条 国家扶持和促进中小企业开展对外贸易。

第五十九条 国家扶持和促进民族自治地方和经济不发达地区发展对外贸易。

第十章 法律责任

第六十条 违反本法第十一条规定,未经授权擅自进出口实行国营贸易管理的货物的,国务院对外贸易主管部门或者国务院其他有关部门可以处五万元以下罚款;情节严重的,可以自行政处罚决定生效之日起三年内,不受理违法行为人从事国营贸易管理货物进出口业务的申请,或者撤销已给予其从事其他国营贸易管理货物进出口的授权。

第六十一条 进出口属于禁止进出口的货物的,或者未经许可擅自进出口属于限制进出口的货物的,由海关依照有关法律、行政法规的规定处理、处罚;构成犯罪的,依法追究刑事责任。

进出口属于禁止进出口的技术的,或者未经许可擅自进出口属于限制进出口的技术的,依照有关法律、行政法规的规定处理、处罚;法律、行政法规没有规定的,由国务院对外贸易主管部门责令改正,没收违法所得,并处违法所得一倍以上五倍以下罚款,没有违法所得或者违法所得不足一万元的,处一万元以上五万元以下罚款;构成犯罪的,依法追究刑事责任。

自前两款规定的行政处罚决定生效之日或者刑事处罚判决生效之日起,国务院对外贸易主管部门或者国务院其他有关部门可以在三年内不受理违法行为人提出的进出口配额或者许可证的申请,或者禁止违法行为人在一年以上三年以下的期限内从事有关货物或者技术的进出口经营活动。

第六十二条 从事属于禁止的国际服务贸易的,或者未经许可擅自从事属于限制的国际服务贸易的,依照有关法律、行政法规的规定处罚;法律、行政法规没有规定的,由国务院对外贸易主管部门责令改正,没收违法所得,并处违法所得一倍以上五倍以下罚款,没有违法所得或者违法所得不足一万元的,处一万元以上五万元以下罚款;构成犯罪的,依法追究刑事责任。

Article 57 The Chinese international trade promotion organizations carry out foreign contacts according to their respective constitutions, hold exhibitions, provide information, consultation and conduct other foreign trade promotion activities.

Article 58 The state supports and promotes small and medium-sized enterprises to engage in foreign trade.

Article 59 The state supports and promotes minority ethnic group regions and economically underdeveloped regions to engage in foreign trade.

Chapter X Legal Liabilities

Article 60 Anyone who violates Article 11 of the present Law by unlawfully importing or exporting any of the goods subject to state-run trade without authorization shall be fined up to 50,000 yuan by the foreign trade department of the State Council or other relevant departments of the State Council. If the circumstances are serious, the application of the offender for engaging in the import or export of the goods subject to state-run trade may be turned down for a period of three years as of the day when the decision on administrative sanction takes effect, or the authorization to engage in the import or export of goods subject to state-run trade that has already been granted may be canceled.

Article 61 Anyone who imports or exports any goods that are banned from import or export or unlawfully imports or exports any goods that are restricted from import or export without approval shall be dealt with and punished by the customs office according to relevant laws or administrative regulations. If the offence constitutes any crime, it shall be subject to criminal liabilities.

Anyone who imports or exports any technology that is banned from import or export or unlawfully imports or exports any technology that is restricted from import or export shall be ordered by the foreign trade department of the State Council to correct, and be fined two times up to 5 times the illegal proceeds and the illegal proceeds shall be confiscated. Where there are no illegal proceeds or the illegal proceeds are not as much as 10,000 yuan, it shall be fined 10,000 yuan up to 50,000 yuan. If the offence constitutes any crime, it shall be subject to criminal liabilities.

As of the day when the decision on administrative sanction as described in the two preceding paragraphs takes effect, the foreign trade department of the State Council or other relevant departments of the State Council may, within a period of three years, refuse to accept the offender's applications for import or export quotas or licenses, or prohibit the offender from engaging in the import or export of relevant goods or technology within a period of one year up to three years.

Article 62 Anyone who is engaged in any banned international service trade or is unlawfully engaged in any restricted international service trade without approval shall be punished according to relevant laws and administrative regulations. Where it is not provided for in any law or administrative regulation, it shall be ordered by the foreign trade department of the State Council to correct and be fined two times up to five times the illegal proceeds, and the illegal proceeds shall be confiscated. Where there are no illegal proceeds or the illegal proceeds are not as much as 10,000 yuan, it shall be fined 10,000 yuan up to 50,000 yuan. If the offence constitutes any crime, it shall be subject to criminal liabilities. The foreign trade department of the State Council may prohibit the offender from engaging in the

国务院对外贸易主管部门可以禁止违法行为人自前款规定的行政处罚决定生效之日或者刑事处罚判决生效之日起一年以上三年以下的期限内从事有关的国际服务贸易经营活动。

business activities relating to international service trade for a period of one year up to three years as of the day when the offender is given an administrative sanction or criminal penalty.

The foreign trade department of the State Council may prohibit the offenders from engaging in the business activities of international service trade for a period of one year up to three years as of the day when the decision on administrative sanction as described in the preceding paragraph takes effect or as of the day when the judgment of criminal punishment takes effect.

第六十三条 违反本法第三十四条规定,依照有关法律、行政法规的规定处罚;构成犯罪的,依法追究刑事责任。

Article 63 Anyone who violates Article 34 of the present Law shall be penalized according to relevant laws and administrative regulations. If the offence constitutes any crime, the offender shall be subject to criminal liabilities.

国务院对外贸易主管部门可以禁止违法行为人自前款规定的行政处罚决定生效之日或者刑事处罚判决生效之日起一年以上三年以下的期限内从事有关的对外贸易经营活动。

The foreign trade department of the State Council may prohibit the offenders from engaging in relevant foreign trade activities for a period of one year up to three years as of the day when the decision on administrative sanction as described in the preceding paragraph takes effect or as of the day when the judgment of criminal punishment takes effect.

第六十四条 依照本法第六十一条至第六十三条规定被禁止从事有关对外贸易经营活动的,在禁止期限内,海关根据国务院对外贸易主管部门依法作出的禁止决定,对该对外贸易经营者的有关进出口货物不予办理报关验放手续,外汇管理部门或者外汇指定银行不予办理有关结汇、售汇手续。

Article 64 In case anyone is banned from engaging in relevant foreign trade business according to Articles 61 through 64 of the present Law, the customs shall, during the period of banning, refuse to handle relevant customs inspection and release formalities for the relevant import or export goods of the foreign trade business operator according to the decision of banning made by the foreign trade department of the State Council, and the administrative department of foreign exchange or the designated foreign exchange banks shall refuse to handle relevant foreign exchange settlement and sale.

第六十五条 依照本法负责对外贸易管理工作的部门的工作人员玩忽职守、徇私舞弊或者滥用职权,构成犯罪的,依法追究刑事责任;尚不构成犯罪的,依法给予行政处分。

Article 65 Where any functionary of the department that is responsible for the administration of foreign trade according to the present Law neglects his duties, practices fraud for private benefits or abuses his power so that any crime is committed, he shall be subject to criminal liabilities. If the offence is not so serious as to constitute a crime, he shall be subject to administrative sanctions.

依照本法负责对外贸易管理工作的部门的工作人员利用职务上的便利,索取他人财物,或者非法收受他人财物为他人谋取利益,构成犯罪的,依法追究刑事责任;尚不构成犯罪的,依法给予行政处分。

Where any functionary of the department that is responsible for the administration of foreign trade according to the present Law solicits any property from any other person by taking advantage of his position, or unlawfully accepts any property of any other person for the benefit of that person so that any crime is constituted, he shall be subject to criminal liabilities; if the offence is not so serious as to constitute a crime, he shall be subject to administrative sanctions.

第六十六条 对外贸易经营活动当事人对依照本法负责对外贸易管理工作的部门作出的具体行政行为不服的,可以依法申请行政复议或者向人民法院提起行政诉讼。

Article 66 Where any of the parties concerned of foreign trade business activities is dissatisfied with the concrete administrative act made by the department that is responsible for the administration of foreign trade according to the present Law, it may apply for administrative reconsideration according to law or lodge an administrative action with the people's court.

第十一章 附 则

Chapter XI Supplementary Provisions

第六十七条 与军品、裂变和聚变物质或者衍生此类物质的物质有关的对外贸易管理以及文化产品的进出口管理,法律、行政法规另有规定的,依照其规定。

Article 67 Where there are different provisions in any law or administrative regulation concerning the administration of the foreign trade of any military matter, any matter of fission or fusion or any matter that derives such matter and concerning the administration of import or export of cultural products, such provisions shall prevail.

第六十八条 国家对边境地区与接壤国家边境地区之间的贸易以及边民互市贸易,采取灵活措施,给予优惠

Article 68 The state employs flexible measures and grants favorable treatment to and facilitates the trade between the border areas of China and

和便利。具体办法由国务院规定。

第六十九条　中华人民共和国的单独关税区不适用本法。

第七十条　本法自2004年7月1日起施行。

those of neighboring countries as well as the frontier trade between border residents. The specific measures shall be formulated by the State Council.

Article 69 The present Law shall not apply to the separate customs territories of the People's Republic of China.

Article 70 The present Law shall come into force as of July 1, 2004.

中华人民共和国海关法

(本法1987年1月22日第六届全国人民代表大会常务委员会第十九次会议通过　根据2000年7月8日第九届全国人民代表大会常务委员会第十六次会议《关于修改〈中华人民共和国海关法〉的决定》修正)

Customs Law of the People's Republic of China

(Adopted at the 19th Meeting of the Standing Committee of the Sixth National People's Congress on January 22, 1987; Revised at the 16th session of the standing committee of the Ninth National people's Republic of China on July 8, 2000)

第一章　总　则

Chapter I　General Provisions

第一条　为了维护国家的主权和利益,加强海关监督管理,促进对外经济贸易和科技文化交往,保障社会主义现代化建设,特制定本法。

Article 1 This Law is formulated for the purpose of safeguarding state sovereignty and national interests, strengthening Customs supervision and control, promoting exchanges with foreign countries in economic affairs, trade, science and technology, and culture and ensuring socialist modernization.

第二条　中华人民共和国海关是国家的进出关境(以下简称进出境)监督管理机关。海关依照本法和其他有关法律、行政法规,监管进出境的运输工具、货物、行李物品、邮递物品和其他物品(以下简称进出境运输工具、货物、物品),征收关税和其他税、费,查缉走私,并编制海关统计和办理其他海关业务。

Article 2 The Customs 0f the People's Republic of China is a governmental organization responsible for supervision and control over all arrivals in and departures from the Customs territory (hereinafter referred to as the territory). It shall, in accordance with this Law and other related laws and administrative regulations, exercise control over means of transport, goods, travellers' luggage, postal items and other articles entering or leaving the territory (hereinafter referred to as inward and outward means of transport, goods and articles), collect Customs duties and other taxes and fees, prevent and combat smuggling, compile Customs statistics and handle other Customs operations.

第三条　国务院设立海关总署,统一管理全国海关。

Article 3 The State Council sets up the Customs General Administration, which is charged with the responsibility of carrying unified administration of all the Customs offices throughout the country.

国家在对外开放的口岸和海关监管业务集中的地点设立海关。海关的隶属关系,不受行政区划的限制。

Customs offices are set up by the State at ports of entry open to foreign trade and at places and regions that require concentrated Customs operations. The subordination of one Customs office to another shall not be restricted by administrative divisions.

海关依法独立行使职权,向海关总署负责。

The Customs offices exercise their functions and powers independently in accordance with the law and are accountable to the Customs General Administration.

第四条　国家在海关总署设立专门侦查走私犯罪的公安机构,配备专职缉私警察,负责对其管辖的走私犯罪案件的侦查、拘留、执行逮捕、预审。

Article 4 In the Customs General Administration, the State sets up a special police department responsible for the investigation of smuggling crimes, which is staffed with special anti-smuggling police officers and charged with the responsibility of conducting investigations, making detentions and arrests, and carrying out preliminary inquiries related to smuggling cases under its jurisdiction.

海关侦查走私犯罪公安机构履行侦查、拘留、执行逮捕、预审职责,应当按照《中华人民共和国刑事诉讼法》的规定办理。

The police department responsible for the investigation of smuggling crimes shall fulfill its responsibility of conducting investigations, making detentions and arrests and carrying out preliminary inquiries in accordance with the Criminal Procedure Law of the People's Republic of China.

海关侦查走私犯罪公安机构根据国家有关规定,可

The police department responsible for the investigation of smuggling

以设立分支机构。各分支机构办理其管辖的走私犯罪案件,应当依法向有管辖权的人民检察院移送起诉。

crimes may, based on relevant regulationas of the State, set up its branch offices, which shall, in aecordance with the law, hand over to the competent People's Procuratorate for prosecution of the smuggling cases of which they have completed investigations under their jurisdiction.

地方各级公安机关应当配合海关侦查走私犯罪公安机构依法履行职责。

Local public security organs at all levels shall assist the Customs police department responsible for the investigation of smuggling crimes to perform its duty according to law.

第五条 国家实行联合缉私、统一处理、综合治理的缉私体制。海关负责组织、协调、管理查缉走私工作。有关规定由国务院另行制定。

Article 5 The State maintains a counter-smuggling mechanism of joint suppression, unified handling and comprehensive governance. The Customs General Administration is responsible for organizing, coordinating and managing counter-smuggling initiatives. Detailed regulations in this regard shall be formulated by the Srate Council.

各有关行政执法部门查获的走私案件,应当给予行政处罚的,移送海关依法处理;涉嫌犯罪的,应当移送海关侦查走私犯罪公安机构、地方公安机关依据案件管辖分工和法定程序办理。

Smuggling cases discovered by the concerned administrative enforcement departments and involving administrative penalties shall be handed over to the Customs for its settlement according to law; Those cases suspected of involving a crime shall be transferred to the Customs police department and local police department to be dealt with according to the division of their jurisdiction and following a legal procedure.

第六条 海关可以行使下列权力:

Article 6 Customs shall exercise the following powers:

(一)检查进出境运输工具,查验进出境货物、物品;对违反本法或者其他有关法律、行政法规的,可以扣留。

(a) To check inward and outward means of transport, examine inward and outward goods and articles, and detain those in violation of this Law or other relevant laws and administrative regulations;

(二)查阅进出境人员的证件;查问违反本法或者其他有关法律、行政法规的嫌疑人,调查其违法行为。

(b) To examine the identification documents of persons entering or leaving the territory, interrogate the suspects violating this Law or other relevant laws and administrative regulations, and investigate the illegal activities thereof;

(三)查阅、复制与进出境运输工具、货物、物品有关的合同、发票、帐册、单据、记录、文件、业务函电、录音录像制品和其他资料;对其中与违反本法或者其他有关法律、行政法规的进出境运输工具、货物、物品有牵连的,可以扣留。

(c) To examine and replicate contracts, invoices, accounts, bills, records, documents, business letters and cables, audio and video products and other materials related to the inward and outward means of transport, goods and articles, and detain those relevant to the inward and outward means of transport, or goods and articles found in violation of this Law or other laws and administrative regulations;

(四)在海关监管区和海关附近沿海沿边规定地区,检查有走私嫌疑的运输工具和有藏匿走私货物、物品嫌疑的场所,检查走私嫌疑人的身体;对有走私嫌疑的运输工具、货物、物品和走私犯罪嫌疑人,经直属海关关长或者其授权的隶属海关关长批准,可以扣留;对走私犯罪嫌疑人,扣留时间不超过二十四小时,在特殊情况下可以延长至四十八小时。

(d) To search, within Customs surveillance zones and the designated coastal or land border area in the vicinity of a Customs office, the means of transport suspected of involving in smuggling activities, and the places suspected of concealing smuggled goods and articles, and search the body of smuggling suspects; to detain, subject to approval from the head of a regional Customs office or the head of its subordinate Customs office authorized by the former, the means of transport, and the goods and articles suspected of involving in smuggling activities, and the persons suspected of having committed a crime in smuggling; the length of detention of smuggling crime suspects shall be no longer than 24 hours, which may be extended to 48 hours under special circumstances;

在海关监管区和海关附近沿海沿边规定地区以外,海关在调查走私案件时,对有走私嫌疑的运输工具和除公民住处以外的有藏匿走私货物、物品嫌疑的场所,经直属海关关长或者其授权的隶属海关关长批准,可以进行检查,有关当事人应当到场;当事人未到场的,在有见证人在场的情况下,可以径行检查;对其中有证据证明有走私嫌疑的运输工具、货物、物品,可以扣留。

To search, while investigating a smuggling case beyond Customs surveillance zones and the designated coastal or land border area in the vicinity of a Customs office, subject to approval from the head of a regional Customs or that from the head of its subordinate Customs authorized by the former, and with the presence of the persons concerned, the means of transport suspected of involving in smuggling activities, and the places suspected of concealing smuggled goods and articles other than citizens' residences. Provided a witness is present, the Customs is entitled to effect such examination without the presence of the person concerned and may detain the means of

海关附近沿海沿边规定地区的范围，由海关总署和国务院公安部门会同有关省级人民政府确定。

（五）在调查走私案件时，经直属海关关长或者其授权的隶属海关关长批准，可以查询案件涉嫌单位和涉嫌人员在金融机构、邮政企业的存款、汇款。

（六）进出境运输工具或者个人违抗海关监管逃逸的，海关可以连续追至海关监管区和海关附近沿海沿边规定地区以外，将其带回处理。

（七）海关为履行职责，可以配备武器。海关工作人员佩带和使用武器的规则，由海关总署会同国务院公安部门制定，报国务院批准。

（八）法律、行政法规规定由海关行使的其他权力

第七条 各地方、各部门应当支持海关依法行使职权，不得非法干预海关的执法活动。

第八条 进出境运输工具、货物、物品，必须通过设立海关的地点进境或者出境。在特殊情况下，需要经过未设立海关的地点临时进境或者出境的，必须经国务院或者国务院授权的机关批准，并依照本法规定办理海关手续。

第九条 进出口货物，除另有规定的外，可以由进出口货物收发货人自行办理报关纳税手续，也可以由进出口货物收发货人委托海关准予注册登记的报关企业办理报关纳税手续。

进出境物品的所有人可以自行办理报关纳税手续，也可以委托他人办理报关纳税手续。

第十条 报关企业接受进出口货物收发货人的委托，以委托人的名义办理报关手续的，应当缶海关提交由委托人签署的授权委托书，遵守本法对委托人的各项规定。

报关企业接受进出口货物收发货人的委托，以自己的名义办理报关手续的应当承担与收发货人相同的法律责任。

委托人委托报关企业办理报关手续的，应当向报关企业提供所委托报关事项的真实情况；报关企业接受委托人的委托办理报关手续的，应当对委托人所提供情况的真实性进行合理审查。

transport, goods, articles suspected of smuggling, as proved by evidence.

The designated coastal or land border areas shall be defined by the Custorns General Administration and the public security department under the State Council in collaboration with the concerned provincial governments.

(e) To inquire while investigating a smuggling case, subject to approval from the head of a regional Customs or the head of its subordinate Customs authorized by the former, about the bank accounts and remittances of the suspected persons in financial institutions or postal services.

(f) To pursue, and continue to pursue beyond, Customs surveillance zones and the designated coastal or land border area in the vicinity of a Customs office, the means of transport or persons defying and escaping from Customs control for seizure and bring them back to be properly dealt with;

(g) To be equipped weapons to ensure proper fulfillment of its responsibility. Rules governing carriage and use of arms by Customs officers shall be formulated by the Customs General Administration in collaboration with public security department under the State Council, and approved by the State Council.

(h) To exercise other powers that is afforded to the Customs by the law and administrative regulations.

Article 7 Local authorities and departments of the State Council shall support the Customs establishments in performing their responsibilities according to law, without illegally giving intervention in the Customs enforcement operations.

Article 8 All inward and outward means of transport, goods and articles shall enter or leave the territory at a place where there is a Customs office. Under special circumstances where there is a need to enter or leave the territory temporarily at a place without a Customs office, permission shall be obtained from the State Council or the department authorized by the former, with all the Customs formalities duly completed in accordance with this Law.

Article 9 Unless otherwise provided for, the declaration of import or export goods and the payment of duties and taxes may be completed by the exporters or importers on their own, and such formalities may also be completed by their entrusted Customs clearing agent registered with the Customs.

The declaration on inward and outward articles and payment of duties thereon may be made by the owner of the articles or by his entrusted person.

Article 10 Any Customs clearing agent entrusted by the exporter or the importer of import or export goods to complete Customs formalities in the principal's name shall produce to the Customs a letter of authorization and comply with all the provisions governing the principal provided for in this Law.

Where a Customs clearing agent is entrusted by the importer or exporter of import or export goods to complete Customs formalities in its own name, it shall bear the same legal liability as the importer or exporter.

A principal shall, in the case of entrusting a Customs clearing agent to complete the Customs formalities, provide to the enterprise true information regarding the entrusted declaration. Enterprises so entrusted shall verify where appropriate the authenticity of the information provided by the principal.

第十一条 进出口货物收发货人、报关企业办理报关手续,必须依法经海关注册登记。报关人员必须依法取得报关从业资格。未依法经海关注册登记的企业和未依法取得报关从业资格的人员,不得从事报关业务。

报关企业和报关人员不得非法代理他人报关,或者超出其业务范围进行报关活动。

第十二条 海关依法报废行职务,有关单位和个人应当如实回答询问,并予以配合,任何单位和个人不得阻挠。

海关执行职务受到暴力抗拒时,执行有关任务的公安机关和人民武装警察部队应当予以协助。

第十三条 海关建立对违反本法规定逃避海关监管行为的举报制度。

任何单位和个人均有权对违反本法规定逃避海关监管的行为进行举报。

海关对举报或者协助查获违反本法案件的有功单位和个人,应当给予精神的或者物质的奖励。

海关应当为举报人保密。

第二章 进出境运输工具

第十四条 进出境运输工具到达或者驶离设立海关的地点时,运输工具负责人应当向海关如实申报,交验单证,并接受海关监管和检查。

停留在设立海关的地点的进出境运输工具,未经海关同意,不得擅自驶离。

进出境运输工具从一个设立海关的地点驶往另一个设立海关的地点的,应当符合海关监管要求,办理海关手续,未办结海关手续的,不得改驶境外。

第十五条 进境运输工具在进境以后向海关申报以前,出境运输工具在办结海关手续以后出境以前,应当按照交通主管机关规定的路线行进;交通主管机关没有规定的,由海关指定。

第十六条 进出境船舶、火车、航空器到达和驶离时间、停留地点、停留期间更换地点以及装卸货物、物品时间,运输工具负责人或者有关交通运输部门应当事先通知海关。

第十七条 运输工具装卸进出境货物、物品或者上

Article 11 The importer or exporter of import or export goods, and the Customs clearing agent shall be registered with the Customs according to law to make the Customs declarations. Individuals making declarations to the Customs shall obtain the qualification in this field according to law. Any enterprise without registration with the Customs and any individual without obtaining qualification to make declarations to the Customs shall not be allowed to engage in making declarations to the Customs.

Any Customs clearing agent and individual engaged in making a declaration to the Customs shall not illegally make Customs declaration on behalf of others or go beyond their approved business scope.

Article 12 The concerned entity or individual shall give true answers to inquiries made by the Customs when performing their duty in accordance with the law, and be cooperative. No entity or individual shall obstruct the Customs from performing their duty.

Where Customs officers meet with violent resistance while carrying out their duty, the public security units and the People's Armed Police performing related tasks shall provide assistance.

Article 13 The Customs shall establish a system whereby activities in violation of the provisions in this Law shall be reported.

All entities and individuals have the right to report to the Customs on activities violating the provisions of this Law.

The Customs shall give spiritual encouragement or material rewards to such entities or individuals for meritorious service in reporting or assistance which leads to the discovery and seizure of Customs offences in violation of this Law.

The Customs shall keep the identities of the reporters confidential.

Chapter II Inward and Outward Means of Transport

Article 14 When a means of transport arrives at or departs from a place where there is a Customs office, the person in charge of the means of transport shall make an accurate declaration to the Customs, submit relevant papers for examination and accept Customs control and examination.

The inward and outward means of transport staying at a place with a Customs office shall not depart there unless permitted by the Customs.

Before a means of transport moves from one place with a Customs office to another place with a Customs office, it shall comply with control requirements of the Customs and complete Customs formalities. No means of transport is allowed to change its course and leave the territory unless it is properly cleared.

Article 15 The inward means of transport which has entered the territory but has not made the declaration to the Customs, and the outward means of transport which has cleared the Customs but has not left the territory shall move along the route specified by competent communication authorities. In the absence of such specifications, the routes shall be designated by the Customs.

Article 16 The Customs shall be notified in advance either by the person in charge of the means of transport or by the relevant transport and communication department of such details as when an inward or outward vessel, train or aircraft will arrive and depart, where it will stay, where it will move to during its stay and when the loading or unloading of goods and articles will take place.

Article 17 The loading and unloading of import or export goods and

下进出境旅客，应当接受海关监管。

货物、物品装卸完毕，运输工具负责人应当向海关递交反映实际装卸情况的交接单据和记录。

上下进出境运输工具的人员携带物品的，应当向海关如实申报，并接受海关检查。

第十八条 海关检查进出境运输工具时，运输工具负责人应当到场，并根据海关的要求开启舱室、房间、车门；有走私嫌疑的，并应当开拆可能藏匿走私货物、物品的部位，搬移货物、物料。

海关根据工作需要，可以派员随运输工具执行职务，运输工具负责人应当提供方便。

第十九条 进境的境外运输工具和出境的境内运输工具，未向海关办理手续并缴纳关税，不得转让或者移作他用。

第二十条 进出境船舶和航空器兼营境内客、货运输，需经海关同意，并应当符合海关监管要求。

进出境运输工具改营境内运输，需向海关办理手续。

第二十一条 沿海运输船舶、渔船和从事海上作业的特种船舶，未经海关同意，不得载运或者换取、买卖、转让进出境货物、物品。

第二十二条 进出境船舶和航空器，由于不可抗力的原因，被迫在未设立海关的地点停泊、降落或者抛掷、起卸货物、物品，运输工具负责人应当立即报告附近海关。

第三章 进出境货物

第二十三条 进口货物自进境起到办结海关手续止，出口货物自向海关申报起到出境止，过境、转运和通运货物自进境起到出境止，应当接受海关监管。

第二十四条 进口货物的收货人、出口货物的发货人应当向海关如实申报，交验进出口许可证件和有关单证。国家限制进出口的货物，没有进出口许可证件的，不予放行，具体处理办法由国务院规定。

进口货物的收货人应当自运输工具申报进境之日起

articles onto and from any means of transport and em barking and disembarking of its passengers shall be subject to Customs control.

Upon completion of such loading and unloading, the person in charge of the means of transport shall submit to the Customs doc uments and records reflecting the actual situation of the loading and unloading.

Articles carried by individuals embarking on and disembarking from an inward and outward means of transport shall be truly declared to the Customs and be subject to Customs examination.

Article 18 When an inward and outward means of transport is being checked by the Customs, the person in charge of the means of transport shall be present, and open holds, cabins, rooms or doors of the means of transport at the request of the Customs. Where smuggling is suspected, the person in charge of the means of transport shall dismantle the part thereof which may conceal smuggled goods and articles, and remove the goods and materials.

In accordance with work requirements, the Customs may dispatch officers to perform duties on board the means of transport. The person in charge of the means of transport shall provide them with convenience.

Article 19 An inward means of transport belonging to countries or regions outside the territory or an outward means of transport domestically owned inside the territory shall not be transferred or devoted to other uses prior to completion of Customs formalities and payment of Customs duties.

Article 20 Where inward and outward vessels and aircraft are concurrently engaged in transportation of goods and passengers within the territory, Customs approval shall be obtained and requirements for Customs control shall be fulfilled.

Customs formalities shall be completed in the case of an inward and outward means of transport wishing to shift to domestic transport business.

Article 21 Coastal transport vessels, fishing boats and ships engaged in specific operations at sea may not carry, obtain on an exchange basis, purchase and transfer inward and outward goods and articles without the Customs approval.

Article 22 When, owing to force majeure, an inward or outward vessel or aircraft is forced to berth, land or jettison and discharge goods and articles at a place without a Customs office, the person in charge of the means of transport shall immediately report to the Customs office nearby.

Chapter Ⅲ Inward and Outward Goods

Article 23 Import goods, throughout the period from the time of arrival in the territory to the time of accomplishment of all Customs formalities, export goods, throughout the period from the time of declaration to the Customs to the time of departure from the territory; and transit, transshipment and through goods, throughout the period from the arrival in the territory to the time of departure from the territory, shall be subject to Customs control.

Article 24 The importer of import goods and the exporter of export goods shall make an accurate declaration and submit the import or export licensing documents and relevant papers to the Customs for examination. In the absence of import or export licensing documents; goods subject to import or export restrictions by the State shall not be released. Specific measures for handling such matters shall be enacted by the State Council.

Declaration of import goods shall be made to the Customs by the im-

十四日内，出口货物的发货人除海关特准的外应当在货物运抵海关监管区后、装货的二十四小时以前，向海关申报。

进口货物的收货人超过前款规定期限向海关申报的，由海关征收滞报金。

第二十五条 办理进出口货物的海关申报手续，应当采用纸质报关单和电子数据报关单的形式。

第二十六条 海关接受申报后，报关单证及其内容不得修改或者撤销；确有正当理由的，经海关同意，方可修改或者撤销。

第二十七条 进口货物的收货人经海关同意，可以在申报前查看货物或者提取货样。需要依法检疫的货物，应当在检疫合格后提取货样。

第二十八条 进出口货物应当接受海关查验。海关查验货物时，进口货物的收货人、出口货物的发货人应当到场，并负责搬移货物，开拆和重封货物的包括。海关认为必要时，可以径行开验、复验或者提取货样。

经收发货人申请，海关总署批准，其进出口货物可以免验。

第二十九条 除海关特准外，进出口货物在收发货人缴清税款或者提供担保后，由海关签印放行。

第三十条 进口货物的收货人自运输工具申报进境地之日起超过三个月未向海关申报的，其进口货物由海关提取依法变卖处理，所得价款在扣除运输、装卸、储存等费用和税款后，尚有余款的，自货物依法变卖之日起一年内，经收货人申请，予以发还；其中属于国家对进口有限制性规定，应当提交许可证件而不能提供的，不予发还。逾期无人申请或者不予发还的，上缴国库。

确属误卸或者溢卸的进境货物，经海关审定，由原运输工具负责人或者货物的收发货人自该运输工具卸货之日起三个月内，办理退运或者进口手续；必要时，经海关批准，可以延期三个月。逾期未办手续的由海关按前款规定处理。

前两款所列货物不宜长期保存的，海关可以根据实际情况提前处理。

porter within 14 days of the declaration of the arrival of the means of transport; declaration of export goods shall be made by the exporter upon the arrival of the goods at Customs surveillance zone, and 24 hours prior to loading unless otherwise specially approved by the Customs.

Where the importer fails to declare the import goods within the time limit prescribed in the proceeding paragraph, a fee for delayed declaration shall be imposed by the Customs.

Article 25 Declaration for import and export goods shall be made in paper form and by electronic means.

Article 26 After the acceptance by the Customs, goods declaration and the relevant documents as well as their contents are not allowed to be amended or withdrawn unless the reason isdeemed valid and approved by the Customs.

Article 27 Prior to the declaration, the importer of the import goods, upon the approval of the Customs, may check goods or draw samples. The goods required for quarantine according to law, shall not be drawn samples unless they are qualified for the quarantine standard.

Article 28 All import and export goods shall be subject to Customs examination. While the examination is being carried out, the importer of the import goods or the exporter of the export goods shall be present and responsible for moving the goods and opening and restoring the package. The Customs shall be entitled to examine or re-examine the goods' or take samples from them without the presence of the importer or the exporter whenever it considers this necessary.

Import and export goods may be exempted from examination if an application has been made by the importer or exporter and approved by the Customs General Administration.

Article 29 Unless specially approved by the Customs, import and export goods shall be released upon Customs endorsement only after the payment of duties and taxes or the provision of security by the importer or exporter.

Article 30 Where the importer of the import goods fails to declare the import goods to the Customs within three months of the declaration of the arrival of the means of transport, the goods shall be taken over and sold off by the Customs according to law. After the costs of transport, loading and unloading and storage and the duties and taxes are deducted from the money obtained from the sale, the remaining sum, if any, shall be returned to the importer provided that he submits an application to the Customs within one year of the sale of the goods; those restricted for importation by the State subject to the licensing documents which fails to be submitted, shall not be returned. If nobody applies within the time limit, or the money shall not be returned, the money shall be turned over to the State Treasury.

Inward goods misdischarged or over-discharged confirmed by the Customs may be taken out of the territory or imported upon completion of necessary formalities by the person in charge of the means of transport carrying the goods or the importer or the exporter of the goods within three months of the discharging. When necessary, an extension of three months may be granted through Customs approval. If the formalities are not completed within the time limit, the goods shall be disposed of by the Customs in accordance with the provisions laid down in the preceding paragraph.

Where goods listed in the preceding two paragraphs are not suitable for storage over long period, the Customs may, according to actual circum-

收货人或者货物所有人声明放弃的进口货物，由海关提取依法变卖处理；所得价款在扣除运输、装卸、储存等费用后，上缴国库。

第三十一条 经海关批准暂时进口或者暂时出口的货物，应当在六个月内复运出境或者复运进境；在特殊情况下，经海关同意，可以延期。

第三十二条 经营保税货物的储存、加工、装配、展示、运输、寄售业务和经营免税店，应当符合海关监管要求，经海关批准，并办理注册手续。

保税货物的转让、转移以及进出保税场所，应当向海关办理有关手续，接受海关监管和查验。

第三十三条 企业从事加工贸易，应当持有关批准文件和加工贸易合同向海关备案，加工贸易制成品单位耗料量由海关按照有关规定核定。

加工贸易制成品应当在规定的期限内复出口。其中使用的进口料件，属于国家规定准予保税的，应当向海关办理核销手续；属于先征收税款的，依法向海关办理退税手续。

加工贸易保税进口料件或者制成品因故转为内销的，海关凭准予内销的批准文件，对保税的进口料件依法征税；属于国家对进口有限制性规定的，还应当向海关提交进口许可证件。

第三十四条 经国务院批准在中华人民共和国境内设立的保税区等海关特殊监管区域，由海关按照国家有关规定实施监管。

第三十五条 进口货物应当由收货人在货物的进境地海关办理海关手续，出口货物应当由发货人在货物的出境地海关办理海关手续。

经收发货人申请，海关同意，进口货物的收货人可以在设有海关的指运地、出口货物的发货人可以在设有海关的启运地办理海关手续。上述货物的转关运输，应当符合海关监管要求；必要时，海关可以派员押运。

经电缆、管道或者其他特殊方式输送进出境的货物，经营单位应当定期向指定的海关申报和人理海关手续。

第三十六条 过境、转运和通运货物，运输工具负责人应当向进境地海关如实申报，并应当在规定期限内运

stances, dispose of them before the time limit is reached.

Import goods declared to be abandoned by the importer or the owner shall be taken over and sold off by the Customs according to law. The money thus obtained shall be turned over to the State Treasury after the costs of transport, loading, unloading and storage are deducted.

Article 31 Goods that are temporarily imported or exported with the approval of the Customs shall be re-transported out of or into the territory within six months. An extension may be granted in special circumstances through Customs approval.

Article 32 The operation of the storage, processing, assembling, exhibition, transportation and consignment 8ales of bonded goods, and the operation of duty free shop shall be complied with the requirements of Customs control and approved by as well as registered with the Customs.

The transfer of ownership of the bonded goods and their being admitted to and removed from the bonded premises are subject to the Customs formalities concerned, Customs control and examination.

Article 33 The enterprises dealing with inward processing are required to register with the Customs with relevant authorized documents and contracts of inward processing. The yield rate of the products resulting from inward processing shall be fixed by the Customs in accordance with the relevant provisions.

The products resulting from inward processing shall be re-exported within the time limit. The imported materials used in the operation approved by the State to be bonded, are subject to closing the case after verification by the Customs; those duties and taxes collected in advance shall be granted repayment in accordance with the relevant provisions.

The Customs shall collect duties and taxes on the bonded materials according to law against the approved documents on importation for home use for certain reasons, provided that the bonded materials for or the products from inward processing are placed under home use. Where restrictions are laid down by the State, licensing documents for importation shall also be required to be submitted to the Customs.

Article 34 The special Customs controlling areas such as bonded areas as authorized by the State Council to be established in the territory of the People's Republic of China, shall be in the execution of control by the Customs in accordance with the relevant national provisions.

Article 35 Customs formalities for import goods shall be completed by the importer at the Customs office through which the goods enter the territory; those for export goods shall be completed by the exporter at the Customs office through which the goods depart from the territory.

If applied for by the importer or the exporter and approved by the Customs, Customs formalities for import goods may be completed at the Customs office of destination, and those for export goods at the Customs office of departure. The transport under Customs transit shall comply with the control requirements by the Customs. When necessary, the goods may be transported under Customs escort.

Where the goods enter or leave the territory by electric cables, pipelines or other special means of conveyance, the importers shall report at regular intervals to the designated Customs office and complete Customs formalities as required.

Article 36 All transit, transshipment and through goods shall be truthfully declared by the carrier to the Customs office through which the

输出境。

海关认为必要时,可以查验过境、转运和通运货物。

第三十七条 海关监管货物,未经海关许可,不得开拆、提取、交付、发运、调换、改装、抵押、质押、留置、转让、更换标记、移作他用或者进行其他处置。

海关加施的封志,任何人不得擅自开启或者损毁。

人民法院判决、裁定或者有关行政执法部门决定处理海关监管货物的,应当责令当事人办结海关手续。

第三十八条 经营海关监管货物仓储业务的企业,应当经海关注册,并按照海关规定,办理收存、交付手续。

在海关监管区外存放海关监管货物,应当经海关同意并接受海关监管。

违反前两款规定或者在保管海关监管货物期间造成海关监管货物损毁或者灭失的,除不可抗力外,对海关监管货物负有保管义务的人应当承担相应的纳税义务和法律责任。

第三十九条 进出境集装箱的监管办法、打捞进出境货物和沉船的监管办法、边境小额贸易进出口货物监管办法,以及本法未具体列明的其他进出境货物的监管办法,由海关总署或者由海关总署会同国务院有关部门另行制定。

第四十条 国家对进出境货物、物品有禁止性或者限制性规定的,海关依据法律、行政法规、国务院的规定或者国务院有关部门依据法律、行政法规的授权作出的规定实施监管。具体监管办法由海关总署制定。

第四十一条 进出口货物的原产地按照国家有关原产地规则的规定确定。

第四十二条 进出口货物的商品归类按照国家有关商品归类的规定确定。

海关可以要求进出口货物的收发货人提供确定商品归类所需的有关资料;必要时,海关可以组织化验、检验,并将海关认定的化验、检验结果作为商品归类的依据。

第四十三条 海关可以根据对外贸易经营者提出的书面申请,对拟作进口或者出口的货物预先作出商品归类等行政裁定。

goods enter the territory, and shall be transported out of the territory within the designated time limit.

The Customs may examine such goods whenever it considers this necessary.

Article 37 The goods under Customs control, without Customs permission, shall not be opened, taken, delivered, forwarded, changed, repacked, mortgaged, pledged, held a lien, transferred the ownership, changed the marks, used for other purpose or disposed by other means.

Seals affixed by the Customs shall not be opened or broken without Customs authorization.

Where a people's court delivers a verdict, ruling or an administrative authority concerned makes a decision to dispose of the goods under Customs control, the person concerned is required to accomplish all the necessary Customs formalities.

Article 38 The enterprises dealing in storage of Customs warehoused goods are required to be registered with the Customs and complete the formalities of receipt, storage and delivery in accordance with Customs provisions.

The storage of the goods under Customs control outside Customs surveillance zone is subject to Customs approval and control.

Those violating the provisions of the preceding two paragraphs or causing destruction or irrecoverable loss of the goods, with the exception of force majeure, the person who is responsible for keeping the goods under Customs control, is subject to the payment of duties and taxes as well as legal liability accordingly.

Article 39 The Customs General Administration shall draw up, independently or jointly with the departments concerned under the State Council, rules for control over inward and outward containers; rules for control over the salvage of inward and outward goods and sunken vessels; rules for control over inward and outward goods involved in small volumes of border transactions and other rules over inward and outward goods not specified concretely in this Law.

Article 40 Where the State specifies the provisions in respect of prohibitions or restrictions on inward and outward goods and articles, Customs shall carry out control in accordance with laws, administrative regulations, and the provisions of the State Council or the provisions laid down by its departments concerned who are authorized upon laws and administrative regulations. The detailed rules of control shall be specified by the Customs General Administration.

Article 41 The origin of import and export goods shall be determined according to the provisions on the rules of origin laid down by the State.

Article 42 The classification of import and export goods shall be decided according to the provisions on the classification of commodities laid down by the State.

Customs may require the importer of import goods and the exporter of export goods to provide with the information indispensable for determination of classification. Customs may, whenever necessary, carry out laboratory analysis and inspection and such results confirmed by Customs shall be taken as the basis of classification.

Article 43 Customs may issue administrative rulings on pre-classification, etc. in respect of goods intended to be imported and exported subject to the written application by importer of import goods and exporter of

进口或者出口相同货物，应当适用相同的商品归类行政裁定。

海关对所作出的商品归类等行政裁定，应当予以公布。

第四十四条 海关依照法律、行政法规的规定，对与进出境货物有关的知识产权实施保护。

需要向海关申报知识产权状况的，进出口货物收发货人及其代理人应当按照国家规定向海关如实申报有关知识产权状况，并提交合法使用有关知识产权的证明文件。

第四十五条 自进出口货物放行之日起三年内或者在保税货物、减免税进口货物的海关监管期限内及其后的三年内，海关可以对与进出口货物直接有关的企业、单位的会计帐簿、会计凭证、报关单证以及其他有关资料和有关进出口货物实施稽查。具体办法由国务院规定。

第四章 进出境物品

第四十六条 个人携带进出境的行李物品、邮寄的物品，应当以自用、合理数量为限，并接受海关监管。

第四十七条 进出境物品的所有人应当向海关如实申报，并接受海关查验。

海关加施的封志，任何人不得擅自开启或者损毁。

第四十八条 进出境邮袋的装卸、转运和过境，应当接受海关监管。邮政企业应当向海关递交邮件路单。

邮政企业应当将开拆及封发国际邮袋的时间事先通知海关，海关应当按时派员到场监管查验。

第四十九条 邮运进出境的物品，经海关查验放行后，有关经营单位方可投递或者交付。

第五十条 经海关登记准予暂时免税进境或者暂时免税出境的物品，应当由本人复带出境或者复带进境。

过境人员未经海关批准，不得将其所带物品留在境内。

第五十一条 进出境物品所有人声明放弃的物品、在海关规定期限内未办理海关手续或者无人认领的物品，以及无法投递又无法退回的进境邮递物品，由海关依照本法第三十条的规定处理。

第五十二条 享有外交特权和豁免的外国机构或者

export goods.

The administrative rulings on pre-classification of certain goods, etc. shall apply to other identical import and export goods.

The administrative rulings on classification made by Customs shall be publicized.

Article 44 Customs may carry out protection of intellectual property rights, which are related to import and export goods according to laws and regulations.

Where the status of intellectual property rights need to be declared to the Customs, the importer of import goods and the exporter of export goods as well as their agents are required to make an accurate declaration and submit legal certificates for intellectual property rights to the Customs according to the provisions of the State.

Article 45 Customs are entitled to carry out Customs audit over accounts, accounting vouchers, declaration documents and other relevant information as well as the import and export goods of the enterprises and institutions directly related to import and export within the period of three years from the date of release of import and export goods or within the period when the bonded goods, goods relieved or deducted from duties and taxes are subject to Customs control and of three years thereafter. The detailed rules shall be laid down by the State Council.

Chapter Ⅳ Inward and Outward Articles

Article 46 Inward and outward luggage carried by travellers and inward and outward postal items shall be limited to reasonable quantities for personal use and subject to Customs control.

Article 47 All inward and outward articles shall be accurately declared to the Customs by the owner and subject to Customs examination.

Seals affixed by the Customs are not allowed to be opened or broken without authorization.

Article 48 The loading, unloading, transshipment and transit of inward and outward mailbags shall be subject to Customs control. A waybill shall be submitted to the Customs by the postal service.

The postal service shall inform the Customs in advance of the schedule for the opening and sealing of international mailbags. The Customs shall dispatch officers on time for the purpose of control and examination on the spot.

Article 49 Inward and outward postal items are not allowed to be posted or delivered by the operators unless they have been released after Customs examination.

Article 50 Articles upon approval by and registration with the Customs, temporarily entering or leaving the territory with the exemption from duties and taxes, are required to be taken out or brought in by the person, who originally carried them into or outside the territory.

Transit passengers are not allowed to leave in the territory, the articles they bring in, without Customs approval.

Article 51 The Customs shall, in accordance with Article 30 of this Law, dispose of the inward and outward articles declared to be abandoned by the owner, the articles for which the Customs formalities are not completed or to which no one makes a claim and inward postal items which can neither be delivered nor be returned.

Article 52 Inward and outward articles for official or personal use by

人员的公务用品或者自用物品进出境，依照有关法律、行政法规的规定办理。

foreign missions or personnel enjoying diplomatic privileges and immunities shall be dealt with in accordance with the related laws and administrative regulations.

第五章　关　税

Chapter V　Customs Duties

第五十三条　准许进出口的货物、进出境物品，由海关依法征收关税。

Article 53　Customs duties shall be collected on goods permitted to be imported or exported and on articles permitted to enter or leave the territory by the Customs according to law.

第五十四条　进口货物的收货人、出口货物的发货人、进出境物品的所有人，是关税的纳税义务人。

Article 54　The importer of import goods, the exporter of export goods and the owner of inward and outward articles shall be the persons obliged to pay Customs duties.

第五十五条　进出口货物的完税价格，由海关以该货物的成交价格为基础审查确定。成交价格不能确定时，完税价格由海关依法估定。

Article 55　The Customs valuation of import and export goods shall be determined by the Customs on the basis of the transaction value of the goods. If the transaction value cannot be ascertained, the Customs valuation shall be determined by the Customs according to law.

进口货物的完税价格包括货物的货价、货物运抵中华人民共和国境内输入地点起卸前的运输及其相关费用、保险费；出口货物的完税价格包括货物的货价、货物运至中华人民共和国境内输出地点装载前的运输及其相关费用、保险费，但是其中包含的出口关税税额，应当予以扣除。

The Customs valuation of import goods shall include the value of the goods, cost of transport, charges associated with transport of the goods and cost of insurance occurred before the goods are unloaded at the entering point of the territory of the People's Republic of China; the Customs valuation of export goods shall include the value of the goods, cost of transport, charges associated with transport of the goods and cost of insurance occurred before the goods are loaded at the leaving point of the territory of the People's Republic of China, from which the amount of export duties shall be deducted.

进出境物品的完税价格，由海关依法确定。

The Customs valuation of inward and outward articles shall be determined by the Customs according to law.

第五十六条　下列进出口货物、进出境物品，减征或者免征关税：

（一）无商业价值的广告品和货样；

（二）外国政府、国际组织无偿赠送的物资；

（三）在海关放行前遭受损坏或者损失的货物；

（四）规定数额以内的物品；

（五）法律规定减征、免征关税的其他货物、物品；

（六）中华人民共和国缔结或者参加的国际条约确定减征、免征关税的货物、物品。

Article 56　Duty reduction or exemption shall be granted to the following import and export goods and inward and outward articles:

(a) Advertising items and trade samples of no commercial value;

(b) Materials presented free of charge by foreign governments and international organizations;

(c) Goods to which damage and loss occurred prior to Customs release;

(d) Articles of a quantity or value within the fixed limit;

(e) Other goods and articles specified by law as items subject to duty reduction or exemption; and

(f) Goods and articles specified as items subject to duty reduction or exemption by international treaties to which the People's Republic of China either a contracting party or an acceding party.

第五十七条　特定地区、特定企业或者有特定用途的进出口货物，可以减征或者免征关税。特定减税或者免税的范围和办法由国务院规定。

Article 57　Duty reduction or exemption may be granted to import and export goods of specific areas, specific enterprises or for specific purposes. The State Council shall define the scope and formulate the rules of such duty reduction or exemption.

依照前款规定减征或者免征关税进口的货物，只能用于特定地区、特定企业或者特定用途，未经海关核准并补缴关税，不得移作他用。

All import goods to which duty reduction or exemption have been granted in accordance with the preceding paragraph shall be used only in specific areas, specific enterprises or for specific purposes. They shall not be utilized otherwise unless Customs approval is obtained and duties are paid.

第五十八条　本法第五十六条、第五十七第第一款规定范围以外的的临时减征或者免征关税，由国务院决定。

Article 58　Ad hoc duty reduction or exemption not within the scope specified in Article 56 and the first paragraph of Article 57 of this Law shall be decided by the State Council.

第五十九条　经海关批准暂时进口或者暂时出口的货物，以及特准进口的保税货物，在货物收发货人向海关

Article 59　Temporary duty reduction or exemption shall be granted to goods approved by the Customs as temporary import or export goods and

缴纳相当于税款的保证金或者提供担保后，准予暂时免纳关税。

to bonded goods imported by special permission after the importer or exporter of the goods submits to the Customs a deposit of an amount equal to the duties or provides a security.

第六十条 进出口货物的纳税义务人，应当自海关填发税款缴款书之日起十五日内缴纳税款；逾期缴纳的，由海关征收滞纳金。纳税义务人、担保人超过三个月仍未缴纳的，经直属海关关长或者其授权的隶属海关关长批准，海关可以采取下列强制措施：

Article 60 The person obliged to pay the Customs duties and taxes on import and export goods shall pay the amount payable within 15 days from the date of issuance of the duty memorandum. In case of failure to meet this time limit, a fee for delayed payment shall be imposed by the Customs. Where the person obliged to pay the Customs duties and taxes or the surety fails to pay the duties within 3 months, the Customs may take the following coercive measures on approval of the director of regional Customs or the authorized director of the subordinate Customs:

（一）书面通知其开户银行或者其他金融机构从其存款中扣缴税款；

(a) To notify the bank of deposit of the person concerned or other financial institution to deduct the amount of duties due from its deposits in written form;

（二）将应税货物依法变卖，以变卖所得抵缴税款；

(b) To offset the duties and taxes with the proceeds from the selling of the goods subject to duty payment according to law;

（三）扣留并依法京戏卖其价值相当于应纳税款的货物或者其他财产，以变卖所得抵缴税款。

(c) To detain and sell the goods or other property of the person concerned at an amount which is equal to the payable duties and taxes to offset the duties according to law;

海关采取强制措施时，对前款所列纳税义务人、担保人未缴纳的滞纳金同时强制执行。

Customs shall impose a fee for delayed payment of duties which has not been paid by the obligatory duty payer or the surety at the same time while taking the coercive measures

进出境物品的纳税义务人，应当在物品放行前缴纳税款。

The payment of duties on inward or outward articles shall be made prior to their release by the obligatory duty payer.

第六十一条 进出口货物的纳税义务人在规定的纳税期限内有明显的转移、藏匿其应税货物以及其他财产迹象的，海关可以责令纳税义务人提供担保；纳税义务人不能提供纳税担保的，经直属海关关长或者其授权的隶属海关关长批准，海关可以采取下列税收保全措施：

Article 61 Where there is an obvious indication of transferring, concealing the duty-payable goods and other property by the obligatory duty payer of the import or export goods before the due date of duty payment, the Customs may ask the obligatory duty payer to provide a security; If he cannot provide a security for duty payment, the Customs may take the following measures to secure the collection of duties and taxes on approval of the director of regional Customs or the authorized director of the subordinate Customs:

（一）书面通知纳税义务人开户银行或者其他金融机构暂停支付纳税义务人相当于应纳税款的存款；

(a) To notify the bank in which the obligatory duty payer has opened an account or other financial institution to suspend paying the amount of duties due from the deposits of the duty payer in written form;

（二）扣留纳税义务人价值相当于应纳税款的货物或者其他财产。

(b) To detain the goods or other property which are equal to the value of the duties to be paid

纳税义务人在规定的纳税期限内缴纳税款的，海关必须立即解除税收保全措施；期限届满仍未缴纳税款的，经直属海关关长或者其授权的隶属海关关长批准，海关可以书面通知纳税义务人开户银行或者其他金融机构从其暂停支付的存款中扣缴税款，或者依法变卖所扣留的货物或者其他财产，以变卖所得抵缴税款。

The Customs shall discharge the measures to secure the duties as soon as the obligatory duty payer pays the duties before the due date of duty payment; The Customs may, on approval of the director of regional Customs or the authorized director of subordinate Customs, inform the bank in which the obligatory duty payer has opened an account or other financial institution to deduct the amount of duties due from the deposits which has been suspended in written form, or sell the goods or other property detained to offset the duties according to law.

采取税收保全措施不当，或者纳税义务人在规定期限内已缴纳税款，海关未立即解除税收保全措施，致使纳税义务人的合法权益受到损失的，海关应当依法承担赔偿责任。

If the measures to secure duties are taken in an improper way, or the Customs fails to discharge the measures for securing the Customs duties when the obligatory duty payer has paid the duties before the due date, and damages are caused to the legitimate in terest of the obligatory duty payer, the Customs shall bear its compensation liability according to law.

第六十二条 进出口货物、进出境物品放行后，海关发现少征或者漏征税款，应当自缴纳税款或者货物、物品

Article 62 Where the Customs finds that the duties are short-levied or not levied on a consignment of import or exportgoods or on inward or out-

放行之日起一年内，向纳税义务人补征。因纳税义务人违反规定而造成的少征或者漏征，海关在三年以内可以追征。

ward articles after the release, the Customs shall collect the money payable from the obligatory duty payer within one year of the previous duty payment or the release of the item. If the short-levied or non-levied duties are attributable to the duty payer's violation of the Customs regulations, the Customs may collect the unpaid amount from him within 3 years.

第六十三条 海关多征的税款，海关发现后应当立即退还；纳税义务人自缴纳税款之日起一年内，可以要求海关退还。

Article 63 Where the duties are over-levied, the Customs, upon discovery, shall refund the money without delay. The obligatory duty payer may ask the Customs for refunding within one year of the date of duty payment.

第六十四条 纳税义务人同海关发生纳税争议时，应当缴纳税款，并可以依法申请行政复议；对复议决定仍不服的，可以依法向人民法院提起诉讼。

Article 64 Where the obligatory duty payer is involved in a dispute over duty payment with the Customs, he shall pay the duties, and may apply for administrative reconsideration in accordance with relevant provisions; if the decision is still considered unacceptable, he may file a suit in a people's court according to law.

第六十五条 进口环节海关代征税的征收管理，适用关税征收管理的规定。

Article 65 The collection of taxes collected by the Customs on behalf of other government departments at importation of the goods shall be dealt in accordance with relevant provisions for collection of Customs duties.

第六章 海关事务担保

Chapter Ⅵ Customs Security

第六十六条 在确定货物的商品归类、估价和提供有效报关单证或者办结其他海关手续前，收发货人要求放行货物的，海关应当在其提供与其依法应当履行的法律义务相适应的担保后放行。法律、行政法规规定可以免除担保的除外。

Article 66 In case where the importer or exporter asks the Customs to release the goods before the determination of goods classification or Customs valuation, or presentation of effective declaration documents or completion of other Customs formalities, the Customs shall release the goods against the securities provided by the importer or exporter which is compatible with his legal obligation according to law. Securities shall not be required in cases as provided by laws and administrative regulations.

法律、行政法规对履行海关义务的担保另有规定的，从其规定。

Laws and administrative regulations specially provided for the securities for obligation of fulfilling Customs formalities shall be abided by first.

国家对进出境货物、物品有限制性规定，应当提供许可证件而不能提供的，以及法律、行政法规规定不得担保的其他情形，海关不得办理担保放行。

The Customs shall not release goods against securities in circumstances where the import or export goods and inward or outward articles related are subject to national restriction and relevant license or documents could not be provided, and other circumstances where the laws and administrative regulations have provided for.

第六十七条 具有履行海关事务担保能力的法人、其他组织或者公民，可以成为担保人。法律规定不得为担保人的除外。

Article 67 Any legal person, other organization and natural person who is capable of fulfilling Customs security may be the surety, unless the law otherwise provided.

第六十八条 担保人可以以下列财产、权利提供担保：

（一）人民币、可自由兑换货币；

（二）汇票、本票、支票、债券、存单；

（三）银行或者非银行金融机构的保函；

（四）海关依法认可的其他财产、权利。

Article 68 The guarantor may provide security by the following property and rights:

(a) Chinese Yuan (Renminbi) and other convertible currencies;

(b) Draft, cashier's check, check, bond and certificate of deposit;

(c) Letter of guarantee issued by the bank and other financial institutions; and

(d) Other property and rights ratified by the Customs according to law.

第六十九条 担保人应当在担保期限内承担担保责任。担保人履行担保责任的，不免除被担保人应当办理有关海关手续的义务。

Article 69 The surety shall assume his obligation within the guaranty period. The guarantor's performance of security obligation shall not prevent the guaranteed from fulfilling other Customs formalities.

第七十条 海关事务担保管理办法，由国务院规定。

Article 70 Regulations on Customs securities shall be formulated by the State Council.

第七章　执法监督

第七十一条　海关履行职责，必须遵守法律，维护国家利益，依照法定职权和法定程序严格执法，接受监督。

第七十二条　海关工作人员必须秉公执法，廉洁自律，忠于职守，文明服务，不得有下列行为：

（一）包庇、纵容走私或者与他人串通进行走私；

（二）非法限制他人人身自由，非法检查他人身体、住所或者场所，非法检查、扣留进出境运输工具、货物、物品；

（三）利用职权为自己或者他人谋取私利；

（四）索取、收受贿赂；

（五）泄露国家秘密、商业秘密和海关工作秘密；

（六）滥用职权，故意刁难，拖延监管、查验；

（七）购买、私分、占用没收的走私货物、物品；

（八）参与或者变相参与营利性经营活动；

（九）违反法定程序或者超越权限执行职务；

（十）其他违法行为。

第七十三条　海关应当根据依法履行职责的需要，加强队伍建设，使海关工作人员具有良好的政治、业务素质。

海关专业人员应当具有法律和相关专业知识，符合海关规定的专业岗位任职要求。

海关招收工作人员应当按照国家规定，公开考试，严格考核，择优录用。

海关应当有计划地对其工作人员进行政治思想、法制、海关业务培训和考核。海关工作人员必须定期接受培训和考核，经考核不合格的，不得继续上岗执行职务。

第七十四条　海关总署应当实行海关关长定期交流制度。

海关关长定期向上一级海关述职，如实陈述其执行职务情况。海关总署应当定期对直属海关关长进行考核，直属海关应当定期对隶属海关关长进行考核。

第七十五条　海关及其工作人员的行政执法活动，依法接受监察机关的监督；缉私警察进行侦查活动，依法接受人民检察院的监督。

Chapter Ⅶ　Enforcement Supervision

Article 71　Customs shall, in the course of carrying out duties, abide by laws and regulations, safeguard national interests, enforce the law strictly in pursuant to the legal authorization and procedure and accept supervision.

Article 72　Customs personnel shall enforce the law impartially, be probity and self-disciplined, devote himself to his duties, render services with civility, and shall not commit the following acts:

(a) To shield, connive at smuggling or collude with others in smuggling;

(b) To illegally confine personal disengagement, search body, residence or premises, inspect or detain means of transport, goods and articles;

(c) To seek expedience for oneself or others by jobbery;

(d) To extort or receive bribery;

(e) To betray the State, commercial and Customs operational confidentiality;

(f) To abuse powers, intentionally create difficulties or delay in supervision or inspection;

(g) To purchase, distribute or occupy confiscated smuggling goods and articles illicitly

(h) To engage or engage in disguised form in profit-making operations;

(i) To carry out duties in violation of legal procedures or exceed the authorization;

(j) Other malpractice.

Article 73　Customs shall, according to the necessity of carrying out duties in compliance with laws and regulations, strengthen Customs personnel construction and make them possess good political and operational qualifications.

The Customs professional staff shall have legal and relevant professional knowledge, conform to the job requirements of special post set by Customs.

Customs shall, in accordance with national regulations, take examination openly, assess strictly and employ selectively by excellency while recruiting personnel.

Customs shall conduct training and assessment to its personnel in political ideology, legal system and Customs operation. Customs personnel must accept training and assessment periodically, whoever fail to pass the examinations shall not keep carrying out duties.

Article 74　The Customs General Administration shall implement the periodical rotating system for the heads of local Customs;

The head of Customs shall report to his superior Customs about his work, present the situations on carrying out his duties accurately. The Customs General Administration shall assess the directors of regional Customs periodically, and the regional Customs shall assess the heads of its subordinate Customs periodically.

Article 75　The administrative enforcement of Customs and its personnel shall accept the supervision of supervising departments in accordance with law; the anti-smuggling police shall accept the supervision of the People's Procuratorate when proceeding investigations.

第七十六条　审计机关依法对海关的财政收支进行审计监督,对海关办理的与国家财政收支有关的事项,有权进行专项审计调查。

第七十七条　上级海关应当对下级海关的执法活动依法进行监督。上级海关认为下级海关作出的处理或者决定不适当的,可以依法予以变更或者撤销。

第七十八条　海关应当依照本法和其他有关法律、行政法规的规定,建立健全内部监督制度,对其工作人员执行法律、行政法规和遵守纪律的情况,进行监督检查。

第七十九条　海关内部负责审单、查验、放行、稽查和调查等主要岗位的职责权限应当明确,并相互分离、相互制约。

第八十条　任何单位和个人均有权对海关及其工作人员的违法、违纪行为进行控告、检举。收到控告、检举的机关有权处理的,应当依法按照职责分工及时查处。收到控告、检举的机关和负责查处的机关应当为控告人、检举人保密。

第八十一条　海关工作人员在调查处理违法案件时,遇有下列情形之一的,应当回避:

(一)是本案的当事人或者是当事人的近亲属;

(二)本人或者其近亲属与本案有利害关系;

(三)与本案当事人有其他关系,可能影响案件公正处理的。

第八章　法律责任

第八十二条　违反本法及有关法律、行政法规,逃避海关监管,偷逃应纳税款、逃避国家有关进出境的禁止性或者限制性管理,有下列情形之一的,是走私行为:

(一)运输、携带、邮寄国家禁止或者限制进出境货物、物品或者依法应当缴纳税款的货物、物品进出境的;

(二)未经海关许可并且未缴纳应纳税款、交验有关许可证件,擅自将保税货物、特定减免税货物以及其他海关监管货物、物品、进境的境外运输工具,在境内销售的;

(三)有逃避海关监管,构成走私的其他行为的。

有前款所列行为之一,尚不构成犯罪的,由海关没收走私货物、物品及违法所得,可以并处罚款;专门或者多次用于掩护走私的货物、物品,专门或者多次用于走私的运输工具,予以没收,藏匿走私货物、物品的特制设备,责令拆毁或者没收。

Article 76　The auditing department conducts audit supervision on fiscal income and expenses of Customs, and it has the right to run special audit investigation on matters related to national fiscal income and expenses handled by Customs.

Article 77　The superior Customs shall conduct supervision over enforcement of the Customs at a lower level. The superior Customs may alter or repeal any inadequate settlement or decision according to law made by Customs at a lower level,.

Article 78　Customs shall, in accordance with the provisions of this Law and other related laws and administrative regulations, establish and strengthen internal surveillance system, conduct supervision and inspection on the execution of laws and administrative regulations and the observance of disciplines by its personnel,

Article 79　The responsibility and authorization of the main posts in charge of documents examination, inspection and release of goods, external auditing and investigation inside Customs shall he clear, and these posts should be separated and restricted mutually.

Article 80　Any entity and individual shall have the right to accuse and impeach the acts of Customs and its personnel that violate the laws and disciplines. The departments receiving the accusations and impeachment shall investigate in time according to their respective responsibilities by law where they have the right to do so. The departments receiving the accusations and impeachment and those are responsible for dealing with this matters shall keep secrecy for libelants and prosecutors.

Article 81　While investigating and handling cases of illegality, Customs personnel shall withdraw in any of the following situations:

(a) Where he is a party or a close relative of a party to the case;

(b) Where he or his close relative has an interest in the case;

(c) Where he has any other relations with a party to the case that could affect the impartial settlement of the case.

Chapter Ⅷ　Legal Responsibilities

Article 82　Breach of this Law and relevant laws and administrative regulations, evasion of Customs control, defraud payable impost, elusion of national inward and outward prohibition or restriction in any of the situations listed below shall be deemed as smuggling:

(a) To transport, carry or mail into or out of the territory goods and articles prohibited or restricted by the State from entering or leaving the territory or goods and articles subject to render duties and taxes according to law;

(b) To sell within the territory, without Customs permission and without having paid the payable duties and taxes or producing relevant licensing document, bonded goods, goods under specific duty reduction or exemption and other goods, articles or inward foreign means of transport under Customs control;

(c) To have other acts evading Customs supervision and control that constitute smuggling;

If any of the acts listed in the preceding paragraph does not constitute the crime of smuggling, the Customs may, while confiscating the smuggled goods, articles and illegal proceeds obtained therefrom, concurrently impose a fine on the person or persons concerned; goods or articles that are specially or repeatedly used for smuggling, means of transport that are spe-

有第一款所列行为之一,构成犯罪的,依法追究刑事责任。

cially or repeatedly used for smuggling shall be confiscated, equipment specially made for concealing smuggled goods or articles shall be demolished or confiscated.

Where any of the acts listed in the first paragraph of this Article that constitutes a crime, the person or persons concerned shall be investigated for criminal liability according to law.

第八十三条 有下列行为之一的,按走私行为论处,依照本法第八十二条的规定处罚:

(一)直接向走私人非法收购走私进口的货物、物品的;

(二)在内海、领海、界河、界湖,船舶及所载人员运输、收购、贩卖国家禁止或者限制进出境的货物、物品,或者运输、收购、贩卖依法应当缴纳税款的货物,没有合法证明的。

Article 83 Any of the following acts shall be deemed as smuggling actions and punished in accordance with the provisions of Article 82 of this Law:

(a) Whoever purchases the imported goods or articles by smuggling directly and illegally from the smugglers;

(b) Vessels and their crew members which transport, purchase or sell goods or articles prohibited or restricted by the State from being imported or exported, or transport, purchase or sell goods subject to duties and taxesaccording to law without legal certificates in inland sea, territorial waters, boundary rivers and boundary lakes.

第八十四条 伪造、变造、买卖海关单证,与走私人通谋为走私人提供贷款、资金、账号、发票、证明、海关单证,与走私人通谋为走私人提供运输、保管、邮寄或者其他方便,构成犯罪的,依法追究刑事责任;尚不构成犯罪的,由海关没收违法所得,并处罚款。

Article 84 Whoever counterfeits, falsifies, purchases or sells Customs documents, conspires with smugglers and provides loans, funds, account numbers, invoices, certificates or Customs documents, conspires with smugglers and provides transport, storage, mailing or other conveniences, where the case constitutes a crime he shall be investigated for criminal liability according to law; where the case does not yet constitute a crime, the Customs may, while confiscate the illegal proceeds obtained therefrom, concurrently impose a fine on the person or persons concerned.

第八十五条 个人携带、邮寄超过合理数量的自用物品进出境,未依法向海关申报的,责令补缴关税,可以处以罚款。

Article 85 Any individual who carries or mails articles for personal use into or out of the territory in a quantity exceeding the reasonable limit fails to declare to Customs according to law shall be ordered to pay the duties and a fine may be imposed thereof.

第八十六条 违反本法规定有下列行为之一的,可以处以罚款,有违法所得的,没收违法所得:

(一)运输工具不经设立海关的地点进出境的;

(二)不将进出境运输工具到达的时间、停留的地点或者更换的地点通知海关的;

(三)进出口货物、物品或者过境、转运、通运货物向海关申报不实的;

(四)不按照规定接受海关对进出境运输工具、货物、物品进行检查、查验的;

(五)进出境运输工具未经海关同意,擅自装卸进出境货物、物品或者上下进出境旅客的;

(六)在设立海关的地点停留的进出境运输工具未经海关同意,擅自驶离的;

(七)进出境运输工具从一个设立海关的地点驶往另一个设立海关的地点,尚未办结海关手续又未经海关批准,中途擅自改驶境外或者境内未设立海关的地点的;

(八)进出境运输工具,未经海关同意,擅自兼营或者改营境内运输的;

Article 86 A fine may be imposed for any of the following acts which violate this Law and the illegal proceeds obtained therefrom shall be confiscated if there any:

(a) For a means of transport to enter or leave the territory at a place without a Customs office;

(b) To fail to inform the Customs of the arrival or departure time, the place of stay or any change of the place of an inward or outward means of transport;

(c) To fail to declare truthfully to the Customs the import or export of goods or articles or the transit, transshipment and through goods;

(d) To fail to accept, in accordance with relevant provisions, the check and inspection by Customs of the means of transport, goods or articles entering or leaving the territory;

(e) For an inward or outward means of transport to load or unload inward or outward goods or articles or embark or disembark passengers without Customs approval;

(f) For an inward or outward means of transport staying at a place with Customs office to leave without Customs approval;

(g) For an inward or outward means of transport, on the way from a place with Customs office to another, failing to complete the Customs formalities and without Customs approval, to move out of the territory or to a place within the territory without Customs office;

(h) For an inward or outward means of transport to engage concurrently or change to engage in domestic transport without Customs approval;

（九）由于不可抗力的原因，进出境船舶和航空器被迫在未设立海关的地点停泊、降落或者在境内抛掷、起卸货物、物品，无正当理由，不向附近海关报告的；

（十）未经海关许可，擅自将海关监管货物开拆、提取、交付、发运、调换、改装、抵押、质押、留置、转让、更换标记、移作他用或者进行其他处置的；

（十一）擅自开启或者损毁海关封志的；

（十二）经营海关监管货物的运输、储存、加工等业务，有关货物灭失或者有关记录不真实，不能提供正当理由的；

（十三）有违反海关监管规定的其他行为的。

第八十七条 海关准予从事有关业务的企业，违反本法有关规定的，由海关责令改正，可以给予警告，暂停其从事有关业务，直至撤销注册。

第八十八条 未经海关注册登记和未取得报关从业资格从事报关业务的，由海关予以取缔，没收违法所得，可以并处罚款。

第八十九条 报关企业，报关人员非法代理他人报关或者超出其业务范围进行报关活动的，由海关责令改正，处以罚款，暂停其执业；情节严重的，撤销其报关注册登记、取消其报关从业资格。

第九十条 进出口货物收发货人、报关企业、报关人员向海关工作人员行贿的，由海关撤销其报关注册登记，取消其报关从业资格，并处以罚款；构成犯罪的，依法追究刑事责任，并不得重新注册登记为报关企业和取得报关从业资格证书。

第九十一条 违反本法规定进出口侵犯中华人民共和国法律、行政法规保护的知识产权的货物的，由海关依法没收侵权货物，并处以罚款；构成犯罪的，依法追究刑事责任。

第九十二条 海关依法扣留的货物、物品、运输工具，在人民法院判决或者海关处罚决定作出之前，不得处理。但是，危险品或者鲜活、易腐、易失效等不宜长期保存的货物、物品以及所有人申请先行变卖的货物、物品、运输工具，经直属海关关长或者其授权的隶属海关关长批准，可以先行依法变卖，变卖所得价款由海关保存，并通知其所有人。

人民法院判决没收或者海关决定没收的走私货物、物品、违法所得、走私运输工具、特制设备，由海关依法统

(i) For an inward or outward vessel or aircraft which, due to force majeure, being forced to anchor or descend at a place without Customs office, or chuck or unload goods or articles within the territory, to fail to report to Customs nearby without reasonable excuse;

(j) To open and dismantle, collect, deliver, forward, transpose, refit, mortgage, impawn, keep, transfer, replace label, shift to other use or conduct other treatment on goods under Customs supervision and control without Customs permission;

(k) To open or break Customs seals without permission;

(l) While engaging in such operations as transportation, storage and process of goods under Customs supervision and control, the records of loss of goods or related records are untrue without reasonable excuse; or

(m) To have any other acts violating provisions of Customs supervision and control.

Article 87 Where an enterprise approved by Customs engaging in related operations violates relevant provisions of this Law, Customs may order it to correct, render it a warning, suspend it from engaging in related operations or revoke its registration.

Article 88 Whoever cngages in declaration business without Customs registration or occupation qualification of declaration shall be banned by Customs, the illegal proceeds obtained therefrom shall be confiscated, and a fine shall be imposed concurrently;

Article 89 Where a Customs clearing agent or its staff engaging in declaration declares on behalf of others illegally or conducts its declaration operation that exceeds its business scope, Customs may order it to correct, impose a fine on it or suspend it from operating; if the circumstance is serious, Customs may revoke its declaration registration or its occupation qualification for declaration.

Article 90 Where an importer of import goods or an exporter of export goods, a Customs clearing agent or its staff bribes or is occupation qualification and concurrently impose a fine; whoever constitutes a crime shall be investigated for criminal liability according to law and shall not be re-registered to be a Customs clearing agent or re-acquire a declaration qualification certificate.

Article 91 Whoever imports or exports goods which constitute infringement on the intellectual property rights under protection by laws and administrative regulations of the People's Republic of China which violating the provisions of this Law, theinfringing goods shall be confiscated by Customs and a fine shall be imposed thereof; where the case constitutes a crime the person or persons concerned shall be investigated for criminal liability according to law.

Article 92 Goods, articles or means of transport detained by Customs according to law shall not be disposed of before the People's Court makes a judgement or Customs makes a decision of punishment. However, hazard goods or such goods and articles not suitable for storage for a long time as fresh and live ones, perishable ones or easy to be expired ones and goods or articles that the owner applies to sell off in advance may, on approval of director of a regional Customs or authorized director of a subordinate Customs, be sold off in advance according to law, and Customs shall keep the money thus obtained and inform the owner of the goods or articles.

The smuggled goods or articles, illegal proceeds obtained therefrom, means of transport or equipment specially made for smuggling being confis-

一处理，所得价款和海关决定处以的罚款，全部上缴中央国库。

第九十三条 当事人逾期不履行海关的处罚决定又不申请复议或者向人民法院提起诉讼的，作出处罚决定的海关可以将其保证金抵缴或者将其被扣留的货物、物品、运输工具依法变价抵缴，也可以申请人民法院强制执行。

第九十四条 海关在查验进出境货物、物品时，损坏被查验的货物、物品的，应当赔偿实际损失。

第九十五条 海关违法扣留货物、物品、运输工具，致使当事人的合法权益受到损失的，应当依法承担赔偿责任。

第九十六条 海关工作人员有本法第七十二条所列行为之一的，依法给予行政处分；有违法所得的，依法没收违法所得；构成犯罪的，依法追究刑事责任。

第九十七条 海关的财政收支违反法律、行政法规规定的，由审计机关以及有关部门依照法律、行政法规的规定作出处理；对直接负责的主管人员和其他直接责任人员，依法给予行政处分；构成犯罪的，依法追究刑事责任。

第九十八条 未按照本法规定为控告人、检举人、举报人保密的，对直接负责的主管人员和其他直接责任人员，由所在单位或者有关单位依法给予行政处分。

第九十九条 海关工作人员在调查处理违法案件时，未按照本法规定进行回避的，对直接负责的主管人员和其他直接责任人员，依法给予行政处分。

第九章 附 则

第一百条 本法下列用语的含义：

直属海关，是指直接由海关总署领导，负责管理一定区域范围内的海关业务的海关；隶属海关，是指由直属海关领导，负责办理具体海关业务的海关。

进出境运输工具，是指用以载运人员、货物、物品进出境的各种船舶、车辆、航空器和驮畜。

过境、转运和通运货物，是指由境外启运、通过中国境内继续运往境外的货物。其中，通过境内陆路运输的，称过境货物；在境内设立海关的地点换装运输工具，而不通过境内陆路运输的，称转运货物；由船舶、航空器载运

cated by judgement of the People's Court or punishment decision of Customs shall be disposed by Customs according to law, the money thus obtained and the fine imposed by Customs shall be turned over to the State Treasury.

Article 93 Where a person concerned refuses to carry out punishment decision of Customs overdue nor apply for reviewing or file a lawsuit to the People's Court, Customs giving the punishment decision may hand over his security or, sell off the detained goods, articles or means of transport of the party and hand over the money thus obtained according to law, or apply to the People's Court for a compulsory execution.

Article 94 When inspecting inward and outward goods and articles, Customs shall compensate for. the actual loss where it causes damage to goods and articles being inspected.

Article 95 Customs shall bear compensation liability when illegally detaining goods, articles and means of transport and rendering losses in legal rights and interests of the person concerned.

Article 96 Customs personnel shall be imposed upon administrative sanctions according to law where he has any of the acts listed in Article 72 of this Law; the illegal proceeds obtained therefrom shall be confiscated if there any; where the case constitutes a crime they shall be investigated for criminal liability according to law.

Article 97 Where fiscal income and expenses of a Customs breach laws and regulations, it shall be treated according to the provisions of laws and regulations by the auditing department and relevant departments; the person in charge which bearing direct responsibilities and other persons directly responsible shall be imposed upon administrative sanctions according to law; where the case constitutes a crime they shall be investigated for criminal liability according to law.

Article 98 Failing to keep secrecy for labelant, accuser or informant according to the provisions of this Law, the person incharge which bearing direct responsibilities and other persons directly responsible shall be imposed upon administrative sanctions according to law by the entity to which they belong or relevant entities.

Article 99 Where Customs personnel fail to withdraw according to the provisions of this Law in investigating and handling cases of illegality, the person in charge which bearing direct responsibilities and other persons directly responsible shall be imposed upon disciplinary sanctions according to law. Chapter IX Supplementary

Chapter IX Supplementary Provisions

Article 100 Terms used in this Law are defined as follows:

The term "regional Customs" means the Customs under the direct leadership of the Customs General Administration and responsible for the administration of the Customs work in a certain area. The term "subordinate Customs" means the Customs under the leadership of a regional Customs and dealing with specific Customs formalities.

The term "inward and outward means of transport" means various vessels, vehicles, aircraft and animals of burden which enter or leave the territory carrying persons, goods and articles.

The term "transit, transshipment and through goods" means goods which come from a place outside the territory and pass through the territory en route to a place outside the territory. Among them, "transit goods" are those which pass through the territory by land, "transshipment goods" are

进境并由原装运输工具载运出境的，称通运货物。

those which do not pass through the territory by land but call for a change of the means of transport at a place with a Customs office, and "through goods" are those which are carried into and out of the territory by the same vessel or aircraft.

海关监管货物，是指本法第二十三条所列的进出口货物，过境、转运、通运货物，特定减免税货物，以及暂时进出口货物、保税货物和其他沿未办结海关手续的进出境货物。

The term "goods under Customs control" means import and export goods, transit goods, transshipment goods and through goods listed under Article 23 of this Law, goods granted with specific duty reduction and exemption, temporary import and export goods, bonded goods and other inward and outward goods for which Customs formalities have not been completed.

保税货物，是指经海关批准未办理纳税手续进境，在境内储存、加工、装配后复运出境的货物。

The term "bonded goods" means goods which have entered the territory, approved by the Customs as items for which no formalities are performed in the way of duty payment, and will be reshipped out of the territory after being stored, processed or assembled in the territory.

海关监管区，是指设立海关的港口、车站、机场、国界孔道、国际邮件互换局（交换站）和其他有海关监管业务的场所，以及虽未设立海关，但是经国务院批准的进出境地点。

The term "Customs surveillance zone" means any seaport, railway and highway station, airport, border pass or international postal matter exchange where there is a Customs office, any other place where Customs control is conducted, or any place without a Customs office but which has been approved by the State Council as a point of entry into and exit from the territory.

第一百零一条 经济特区等特定地区同境内其他地区之间往来的运输工具、货物、物品的监管办法，由国务院另行规定。

Article 101 The State Council will draw up rules governing the control over the means of transport, goods and articles of other parts of the territory entering and leaving the Special Economic Zone and other specially designated areas.

第一百零二条 本法自1987年7月1日起施行。1951年4月18日中央人民政府公布的《中华人民共和国暂行海关法》同时废止。

Article 102 This Law goes into effect as of July 1, 1987whereupon the Provisional Customs Law of the People's Republic of China promulgated by the Central People's Government on April 18, 1951 is annulled therefrom.

中华人民共和国海关对进出境快件监管办法

THE MEASURES OF PEOPLE'S REPUBLIC OF CHINA FOR THE CUSTOM'S SUPERVISION OF CROSS - BORDER EXPRESS MAILS DELIEVERY

（2003年11月18日海关总署令第104号发布，根据2006年3月28日海关总署令第147号公布的《海关总署关于修改〈中华人民共和国海关对进出境快件监管办法〉的决定》修正）

2003年11月18日海关总署令第104号发布，根据2006年3月28日海关总署令第147号公布的《海关总署关于修改〈中华人民共和国海关对进出境快件监管办法〉的决定》修正

第一章 总 则

Chapter Ⅰ General Provisions

第一条 为加强海关对进出境快件的监管，便利进出境快件通关，根据《中华人民共和国海关法》及其他有关法律、行政法规，制定本办法。

Article 1 Pursuant to The Customs Law of People's Republic of China and other pertinent laws, administrative regulations, these provisions are hereby formulated to strengthen the supervision of the cross - border express mails and facilitate the clearance of the cross border express mails.

第二条 本办法所称进出境快件是指进出境快件运营人以向客户承诺的快速商业运作方式承揽、承运的进出境货物、物品。

Article 2 The cross - border express mails in this provision refer to the cross - border goods and articles shipped by "Cross Border Express Delivery Operators" in a mode they agree with clients.

第三条 本办法所称进出境快件运营人（以下简称运营人）是指在中华人民共和国境内依法注册，在海关

Article 3 The cross - border mail operators (hereinafter referred to as "operators") refer to the international cargo forwarding agency enterpri-

登记备案的从事进出境快件运营业务的国际货物运输代理企业。

ses which are incorporated in the People's Republic of China, have registered with the Customs Office and are engaged in cross - border express delivery services.

第四条 运营人不得承揽、承运《中华人民共和国禁止进出境物品表》所列物品,如有发现,不得擅作处理,应当立即通知海关并协助海关进行处理。

Article 4 The "operators" must not agree to ship any articles listed on the "The Prohibited Cross - border Articles of People's Republic of China," nor shall it discretionally deal with any of such articles it has found, but shall immediately notify the Customs and assist the Customs in dealing with the article instead.

未经中华人民共和国邮政部门批准,运营人不得承揽、承运私人信件。

Without the permission of the Postal Delivery Institution of People's Republic of China, any "operators" may not undertake or carry any personal letters.

第五条 运营人不得以任何形式出租、出借、转让本企业的进出境快件报关权,不得代理非本企业承揽、承运的货物、物品的报关。

Article 5 On no account can the declaration right on cross border express delivery of an "Operator" be licensed out, lent or transferred. The "operators" cannot perform declaration on commodities which are not shipped by them.

第六条 未经海关许可,未办结海关手续的进出境快件不得移出海关监管场所,不得进行装卸、开拆、重换包装、更换标记、提取、派送和发运等作业。

Article 6 Without the permission of the Customs, the cross border express mails for which the Customs formalities have not been completed shall not be moved out of the surveillance site, and cannot be loaded or unloaded, opened, repacked, marked with a sign different from the original one, drawn, dispatched or delivered for transport.

第二章 运营人登记

Chapter Ⅱ The Registration of "operators"

第七条 运营人申请办理进出境快件代理报关业务的,应当按照海关对国际货物运输代理企业的注册管理规定在所在地海关办理登记手续。

Article 7 The "operators" who file the application for making Customs declarations on behalf of any others for cross border express mails shall make registration in the local Customs in accordance with the administrative provisions of the Custom on the registration of international cargo forwarding agency enterprises.

第八条 运营人在所在地海关办理登记手续应具备下列条件:

Article 8 The "operators" who register at the Customs shall meet the following requirements:

(一)内资国际货物运输代理企业及其分支机构已经获得国务院对外贸易主管部门或者其委托的备案机构办理的《国际货运代理企业备案表》;外商投资国际货物运输代理企业已经获得国务院对外贸易主管部门颁发的《外商投资企业批准证书》,获准经营进出境快件业务;外商投资国际货物运输代理企业分公司已经获得国务院对外贸易主管部门的批准文件,获准经营进出境快件业务。

(1) The domestically funded international cargo forwarding agency enterprise and its branches have obtained the International Freight Forwarder Registration Form issued by The department in charge of foreign trade under the State Council or the registration institutions commissioned by them; Foreign - funded international cargo forwarding agency enterprises have obtained the Certificate of Approval for Establishment of Enterprises With Foreign Investment, being approved to operate cross border mails business; The branch offices of foreign - funded international cargo forwarding agency enterprise have obtained the approval certificate issued by the department in charge of foreign trade under the State Council, being approved to operate cross border mailing business

(二)已经领取工商行政管理部门颁发的《企业法人营业执照》,准予或者核定其经营进出境快件业务。

(2) the "operators" that have obtained Business License of Enterprise Legal Person issued by the Administration for Industry and Commerce, being approved or ratified to operate cross border mailing business.

(三)已经在海关办理报关企业注册登记手续。

(3) the "operators" that have registered for declaration corporations at the Custom

(四)具有境内、外进出境快件运输网络和二个以上境外分支机构或代理人。

(4) the "operators" that have cross - border express mailing transportation network and more than two overseas branches or agents.

(五)具有本企业专用进出境快件标识、运单,运输车辆符合海关监管要求并经海关核准备案。

(5) the "operators" that have special marks and transport documents for its cross border express mails, and its transport vehicles shall be in conformity with the requirements for the Customs' supervision, and be subject to the approval of the Customs for record;

(六)具备实行电子数据交换方式报关的条件。

(6) the "operators" that meet the condition for Customs declaration

（七）快件的外包装上应标有符合海关自动化检查要求的条形码。

（八）与境外合作者（包括境内企业法人在境外设立的分支机构）的合作运输合同或协议。

第九条 进出境快件运营人不再具备本《办法》第八条所列条件之一或者在一年内没有从事进出境快件运营业务的，海关注销该运营人从事进出境快件报关的资格。

第三章 进出境快件分类

第十条 本办法将进出境快件分为文件类、个人物品类和货物类三类。

第十一条 文件类进出境快件是指法律、法规规定予以免税且无商业价值的文件、单证、票据及资料。

第十二条 个人物品类进出境快件是指海关法规规定自用、合理数量范围内的进出境的旅客分离运输行李物品、亲友间相互馈赠物品和其他个人物品。

第十三条 货物类进出境快件是指第十一条、第十二条规定以外的快件。

第四章 进出境快件监管

第十四条 进出境快件通关应当在经海关批准的专门监管场所内进行，如因特殊情况需要在专门监管场所以外进行的，需事先征得所在地海关同意。

运营人应当在海关对进出境快件的专门监管场所内设有符合海关监管要求的专用场地、仓库和设备。

对进出境快件专门监管场所的管理办法，由海关总署另行制订。

第十五条 进出境快件通关应当在海关正常办公时间内进行，如需在海关正常办公时间以外进行的，需事先征得所在地海关同意。

第十六条 运营人应当按照海关的要求采用纸质文件方式或电子数据交换方式向海关办理进出境快件的报关手续。

第十七条 进境快件自运输工具申报进境之日起十四日内，出境快件在运输工具离境3小时之前，应当向海

by means of Electronic Data Interchange.

(7) the package of the express mails are marked with the bar code in conformity with the requirements for the Customs' automatic examination.

(8) the "operators" that have signed transport contracts or agreement with the overseas partners (or a oversea branch set up by the domestic enterprise legal person).

Article 9 The Custom shall revoke the declaration right of the cross - border express mail "operators" that no longer comply with any of these eight provisions or that have not engaged in cross border express mailing business for more than one year.

Chapter Ⅲ the classification of the cross border express mails

Article 10 The cross border express mails fall into three categorizes: the documental category, the personal articles category and the goods category.

Article 11 The Cross border express of documental category refer to the documents, certificates, negotiable instruments and materials that are prescribed in laws and regulations to be exempted from tax and are of no commercial value.

Article 12 Cross border express of personal articles refer to the luggage and articles transported separately from passengers, the gifts between relatives and friends and other personal use, which are prescribed in the regulations on Customs, to enter or exit the territory for self - use or within a reasonable amount of quantity.

Article 13 Cross border express of goods category refers to the express mails other than those prescribed in the Articles 11 and 12.

Chapter Ⅳ the Supervision of Cross Border Express Mails

Article 14 The clearance of cross border express mails shall be conducted within the special supervision sites approved by the Custom. Any exception shall be approved by the local Custom first.

The "operators" shall have the special fields, warehouses and facilities conforming to the supervision requirements of the Custom within the supervision sites of the cross border express mails.

The administrative measures on the special supervision sites for cross border express mails shall be formulated else by the Customs General Administration.

Article 15 The clearance of cross border express mails shall be dealt with during business hours of the Customs. Exceptions shall only be made with the approval of the local Custom.

Article 16 The "operators" shall make Customs declaration to the Customs for cross border express mails through written files or Electronic Data Interchange complying to the requirements of the Custom.

Article 17 Declaration should be made within fourteen days after the declaration of the entry of means of transport of express mails and three

关申报。

第十八条 运营人应向海关传输或递交进出境快件舱单或清单,海关确认无误后接受申报;运营人需提前报关的,应当提前将进出境快件运输和抵达情况书面通知海关,并向海关传输或递交舱单或清单,海关确认无误后接受预申报。

第十九条 海关查验进出境快件时,运营人应派员到场,并负责进出境快件的搬移、开拆和重封包装。

海关对进出境快件中的个人物品实施开拆查验时,运营人应通知进境快件的收件人或出境快件的发件人到场,收件人或发件人不能到场的,运营人应向海关提交其委托书,代理收/发件人的义务,并承担相应法律责任。

海关认为必要时,可对进出境快件予以径行开验、复验或者提取货样。

第二十条 除另有规定外,运营人办理进出境快件报关手续时,应当按本办法第十一条、第十二条、第十三条分类规定分别向海关提交有关报关单证并办理相应的报关、纳税手续。

第二十一条 文件类进出境快件报关时,运营人应当向海关提交《中华人民共和国海关进出境快件 KJ1 报关单》(见附件一)、总运单(副本)和海关需要的其它单证。

第二十二条 个人物品类进出境快件报关时,运营人应当向海关提交《中华人民共和国海关进出境快件个人物品申报单》(见附件二)、每一进出境快件的分运单、进境快件收件人或出境快件发件人身份证件影印件和海关需要的其它单证。

第二十三条 货物类进境快件报关时,运营人应当按下列情形分别向海关提交报关单证:

对关税税额在《中华人民共和国进出口关税条例》规定的关税起征数额以下的货物和海关规定准予免税的货样、广告品,应提交《中华人民共和国海关进出境快件 KJ2 报关单》(见附件三)、每一进境快件的分运单、发票和海关需要的其他单证。

对应予征税的货样、广告品(法律、法规规定实行许可证件管理的、需进口付汇的除外),应提交《中华人民

hours prior to the exit of the means of transport of the express mails.

Article 18 The "Operator" shall transmit or submit the cross border manifest or checklist of express mails to the Custom which shall, after confirming that there is no error therein, accept the declaration; where the operator needs make Custom declaration in advance, it shall notify the Customs with written documents addressing the carriage and arrival of the Customs, and the Customs shall, after confirming that there is no error therein, accept the advance declaration.

Article 19 The "Operator" shall send someone to be present at the scene, and be responsible for the moving, opening or repacking the cross broader express mails when it is being examined by the Custom.

When the Customs is opening any of the individual articles among the cross border express mails for examination, the "Operator" shall notify the addressee of the inward express consignments or the addresser of the outward express mails to be present at the scene; in case the addressee or addresser is unable to be at the scene, the "Operator" shall submit a power of attorney to the Customs to represent the addressee/addresser to perform the obligations, and bear corresponding legal liabilities.

The Customs shall be entitled to examine or re - examine the cross border express mails or take samples from them without the presence of the consignee or the consignor whenever it considers this necessary.

Article 20 Unless otherwise prescribed, the "Operator" shall, when making Customs declaration for cross border express mails, separately according to the provisions on classification in Article 11 through 13 of the present Measures, submit relevant Customs declaration documents to the Customs and conduct corresponding formalities for Customs declaration and duty payment.

Article 21 When declaring the cross border express mails of documentary category, The "operators" shall submit The KJ1 Customs Declaration of Cross Border Express Mail of People's Republic of China (see the appendix 1), Master Air Waybill (copy) and other documents required by the Customs.

Article 22 When making Customs declaration for the cross border express of personal articles, the "Operator" shall submit the Customs Declaration of Cross Border Express of Personal Articles of People's Republic of China (see the appendix 2), House Air Waybill, the photocopy of identification Certificate of the adressee of entering express mails or the addresser of the exiting express mails and other related documents required by the Customs.

Article 23 When making Customs declaration of the cross border express of goods category, the "Operator" shall submit the Customs declaration documents separately according to the following circumstances:

With regard to the goods whose tariff is below the minimum threshold of tariff as prescribed in the in the Regulations of the People's Republic of China on Import and Export Duties as well as the samples of goods or the advertisement articles exempted from Customs duty as prescribed by the Customs, the "operators" shall submit the KJ2 Customs Declaration of Cross Border Express Mail of People's Republic of China (see the appendix 3), the specific transport document for each cross border express mail, receipts and other related documents required by the Customs.

With regard to the samples of goods or the advertisement articles on which Customs duties shall be levied (except for those prescribed by laws

共和国海关进出境快件 KJ3 报关单》(见附件四)、每一进境快件的分运单、发票和海关需要的其它单证。

or regulations to be subject to permit administration, and those for which foreign exchanges need to be paid upon import), the "KJ3 Customs Declaration Form of the Customs of the People's Republic of China for Cross Border Express Mails" (see Appendix 4), the specific transport document of each inward express consignment, the invoices, and other documents as required by the Customs shall be submitted.

第二十四条 对第二十一条、第二十二条、第二十三条规定以外的货物,按照海关对进口货物通关的规定办理。

Article 24 The clearance for the goods other than those prescribed in Articles 21 through 23 shall be handled according to the provisions of the Customs on clearance of import goods.

第二十五条 货物类出境快件报关时,运营人应按下列情形分别向海关提交报关单证:

Article 25 To make Customs declaration for cross border express of goods category, the "Operator" should submit the declaration documents according to the following circumstance:

对货样、广告品(法律、法规规定实行许可证件管理的、应征出口关税的、需出口收汇的、需出口退税的除外),应提交《中华人民共和国海关进出境快件 KJ2 报关单》、每一出境快件的分运单、发票和海关需要的其它单证。

With regard to the samples of goods or the advertisement articles (except for those prescribed by laws or regulations to be subject to permit administration, those for which export tariff shall be levied, those for which foreign exchanges need to be collected upon export, and those for which taxes need to be refunded for export), the "KJ2 Customs Declaration Form of the Customs of the People's Republic of China for Cross Border Express Mails", the specific transport document of each cross border express mail, the invoices, and other documents as required by the Customs shall be submitted. The clearance for the goods other than those mentioned above shall be handled according to the provisions of the Customs on clearance of export goods.

对上述以外的其它货物,按照海关对出口货物通关的规定办理。

The clearance for the goods other than those mentioned above shall be handled according to the provisions of the Customs on clearance of export goods.

第五章 进出境专差快件

Chapter Ⅴ The Specially Delivered Cross Border Express Mails

第二十六条 进出境专差快件是指运营人以专差押运方式承运进出境的空运快件。

Article 26 The term "specially delivered cross border express mails" means the express mails carried by air by the "Operator" into or out of the territory in a way of special delivery under escort.

第二十七条 运营人从事进出境专差快件经营业务,除应当按本办法第二章有关规定办理登记手续外,还应当将进出境专差快件的进出境口岸、时间、路线、运输工具航班、专差本人的详细情况、标识等向所在地海关登记。如有变更,应当于变更前 5 个工作日向所在地海关登记。

Article 27 The "Operator" who is engaged in the business of specially delivered cross border express mails shall, in addition to making registration according to the relevant provisions in Chapter II of the present Measures, register such particulars of the specially delivered cross border express mails as the port of entry or exit, the time, route, schedule of the means of transport, detailed information on the special deliverer himself, the mark, etc. in the local Customs. In the event of any modification, the "Operator" shall make registration in the local Customs 5 working days prior to such modification.

对符合上述条件的,所在地海关核发《中华人民共和国海关进出境专差快件登记证书》(见附件五)。运营人凭以办理进出境专差快件报关业务。

Where the aforesaid conditions are met, the local Customs shall issue the "Registration and Record Certificate of the Customs of the People's Republic of China for Specially Delivered Cross border express mails" (see Appendix 5), upon strength of which the "Operator" shall make Customs declaration for the specially delivered cross border express mails.

第二十八条 进出境专差快件应按行李物品方式托运,使用专用包装,并在总包装的显著位置标注运营人名

Article 28 Specially delivered cross border express mails shall be consigned as luggage articles, be specially packed, and be indicated with

称和“进出境专差快件”字样。

第六章　法律责任

第二十九条　违反本办法有走私违法行为的，海关按照《中华人民共和国海关法》、《中华人民共和国海关法行政处罚实施细则》等有关法律、行政法规进行处理；构成犯罪的，依法追究刑事责任。

第七章　附　则

第三十条　本办法由海关总署负责解释。

第三十一条　本办法自二〇〇四年一月一日起施行。

the “Operator” ' s name and the words of “Specially Delivered Cross border express mails” on an eye - catching position of the general packing.

Chapter Ⅵ　Legal Liability

Article 29　Any one who violates the present Measures by committing any smuggling act shall be punished by the Customs pursuant to the “Customs Law of the People' s Republic of China”, the “Detailed Rules for the Implementation of Administrative Penalties under the Customs Law of the People' s Republic of China”, and other relevant laws and administrative regulations; if a crime is constituted, the offender shall be subject to criminal liabilities in jury.

Chapter Ⅶ　Supplementary Articles

Article 30　The responsibility to interpret the present Measures shall remain with the Customs General Administration.

Article 31　The present Measures shall be implemented on January 1st, 2004.

中华人民共和国海关加工贸易企业联网监管办法

海关总署令

第150号

《中华人民共和国海关加工贸易企业联网监管办法》已于2006年5月30日经署务会审议通过，现予公布，自2006年8月1日起施行。2003年3月19日海关总署令第100号发布的《中华人民共和国海关对加工贸易企业实施计算机联网监管办法》同时废止。

署　长　牟新生

二〇〇六年六月十四日

中华人民共和国海关加工贸易企业联网监管办法

第一条　为了规范海关对加工贸易企业的管理，根据《中华人民共和国海关法》及其他有关法律、行政法规的规定，制定本办法。

第二条　海关对加工贸易企业实施联网监管，是指加工贸易企业通过数据交换平台或者其他计算机网络方式向海关报送能满足海关监管要求的物流、生产经营等数据，海关对数据进行核对、核算，并结合实物进行核查的一种加工贸易海关监管方式。

MEASURES OF THE GENERAL ADMINISTRATION OF CUSTOMS FOR CYBER - SUPERVISION AND ADMINISTRATION OF PROCESSING TRADE ENTERPRISES

Order of the General Administration of Customs
of the People' s Republic of China
(Order No. 150)

Adopted at the official meeting of the General Administration of Customs on May 30, 2006, Measures of Customs of the People's Republic of China Concerning Cyber - Supervision and Administration on Processing Trade Enterprises is now promulgated and goes into effect as of the date of August 1st, 2006.

Director of the Administration: Mou Xinsheng

June 24, 2006

Measures of the Customs of the People' s Republic of China Concerning Cyber-Supervision and Administration on the Processing Trade Enterprises

Article 1　In accordance with the Customs Law of the People' s Republic of China and other laws and administrative regulations, The Measures are hereby formulated for the purpose of regulating Customs' administration on processing trades.

Article 2　The Customs conducts Cyberupervision and Administration of Processing Trade Enterprises refers to refers to a supervision method of processing trade enterprises adopted by Customs through which financial logistics, production and operation data necessary for supervision and administration are submitted by the processing trade enterprises with the help of data platform or other computer networks, and the Customs check and verify the data according to the real objects.

第三条 实施联网监管的加工贸易企业(以下简称联网企业)应当具备以下条件:

(一)具有加工贸易经营资格;

(二)在海关注册;

(三)属于生产型企业。

海关特殊监管区域、保税监管场所内的加工贸易企业不适用本办法。

Article 3 A processing trade enterprise conducting Cyber-Supervision and Administration (cyber-enterprise in short below) shall satisfy following requirements:

1. Have qualifications for processing trade business;
2. Have registered in the Customs;
3. Be a production enterprises.

The processing trade enterprises within the area under special supervision and administration of the Customs and bonded supervision and administration places do not apply to these measures.

第四条 加工贸易企业需要实施联网监管的,可以向主管海关提出申请;经审核符合本办法第三条规定条件的,海关应当对其实施联网监管。

Article 4 Any processing trade enterprise that needs cyber-supervision and administration may submit an application to the competent customs. After examination and verification, the Customs shall carry out Cyber-Supervision and Administration to any enterprise that meets the requirements as stipulated in Article 3 of these measures

第五条 联网企业通过数据交换平台或者其他计算机网络方式向海关报送数据前,应当进行加工贸易联网监管身份认证。

Article 5 A cyber-enterprise shall be verified on its authentication prior to it submits the data to the Custom through electronic exchange platform or other forms of computer interconnection.

第六条 联网企业应当将开展加工贸易业务所需进口料件、出口成品清单及对应的商品编号报送主管海关,必要时还应当按照海关要求提供确认商品编号所需的相关资料。

Article 6 A cyber-enterprise shall report to the Customs the inventory list of materials to be imported, finished products to be exported and the corresponding number of the commodities needed for processing trade business, if necessary, provide corresponding materials for confirming the number of the commodities according to the request of the Customs.

主管海关应当根据监管需要,按照商品名称、商品编码和计量单位等条件,将联网企业内部管理的料号级商品与电子底账备案的项号级商品进行归并或者拆分,建立一对多或者多对一的对应关系。

The competent customs shall, in light of the needs of supervision and administration, according to the requirements of the name and code of the commodities, and calculation unit, merge the commodities subject to grade of material number with the commodities subject to grade of item number or divide them, establishing a corresponding relationship of one-to-many or many-to-one.

第七条 联网企业应当在料件进口、成品出口前,分别向主管海关办理进口料件、出口成品的备案、变更手续。

Article 7 A cyber - enterprises shall, before the import of the materials and export of the finished products, go through separately record and change formalities in the Customs for the materials to be imported and the finished products to be exported.

联网企业应当根据海关总署的有关规定向海关办理单耗备案、变更手续。

A Cyber-enterprise shall go through separately record and change formalities of loss of finished products according to pertinent stipulations rules of the General Administration of the Customs.

第八条 海关应当根据联网企业报送备案的资料建立电子底账,对联网企业实施电子底账管理。电子底账包括电子账册和电子手册。

Article 8 The Customs shall, according to the materials for record submitted by the cyber-enterprise, establish an electronic account and carry out administration of electronic account to the cyber-enterprises. The electronic account includes electronic account book and electronic handbook.

电子账册是海关以企业为单元为联网企业建立的电子底账;实施电子账册管理的,联网企业只设立一个电子账册。海关应当根据联网企业的生产情况和海关的监管需要确定核销周期,按照核销周期对实行电子账册管理的联网企业进行核销管理。

The electronic account book is an electronic account, regarding an enterprise as a unit, established by the Customs for a cyber - enterprise. The cyber-enterprise conducting the administration of electronic account book shall establish only one electronic account book. The Customs shall, according to the production status of the enterprise and the needs of the Customs' verification and administration, set the period for the verification and cancellation, and according to the period, carry out the administration of verification and cancellation after the cyber-enterprise conducting administration of electronic account book.

电子手册是海关以加工贸易合同为单元为联网企业建立的电子底账;实施电子手册管理的,联网企业的每个

The electronic handbook is an electronic account, regarding the processing trade contract as a unit, established by the Customs for a cyber-en-

加工贸易合同设立一个电子手册。海关应当根据加工贸易合同的有效期限确定核销日期,对实行电子手册管理的联网企业进行定期核销管理。

terprise. The cyber-enterprise conducting the administration of electronic handbook shall establish an electronic handbook for each processing trade contract. The Customs shall, according to the period of validity of the processing trade contract, set the date for the cancellation after verification, carry out the administration of periodic cancellation after verification to the cyber-enterprise conducting electronic handbook administration.

第九条 联网企业应当如实向海关报送加工贸易货物物流、库存、生产管理以及满足海关监管需要的其他动态数据。

Article 9 The Cyber-enterprise shall truthfully submit the processing trade goods logistics, inventory, production management and all other dynamic data that required by the supervision of the Customs.

第十条 联网企业的外发加工实行主管海关备案制。加工贸易企业开展外发加工前应当将外发加工承接企业、货物名称和周转数量向主管海关备案。

Article 10 The competent customs record system is carried out for outward-processing of a cyber-enterprise. A processing trade enterprise shall, before outward processing, register for record in the competent customs the name of the enterprise undertaking the outward – processing, name of the commodities and turnover quantity.

第十一条 海关可以采取数据核对和下厂核查等方式对联网企业进行核查。下厂核查包括专项核查和盘点核查。

Article 11 The Customs may check the cyber – enterprise by data verification and spot check in the factory. The check in the factory shall include special check and stock – taking check.

第十二条 经主管海关批准,联网企业可以按照月度集中办理内销补税手续;联网企业内销加工贸易货物后,应当在当月集中办理内销补税手续。

Article 12 With the approval of the competent customs, a cyber-enterprise may handle duty repayment for domestic sales monthly. A cyber-enterprise shall handle duty repayment for domestic sales in the same month after selling processing trade commodities in domestic market.

第十三条 联网企业加工贸易货物内销后,应当按照规定向海关缴纳缓税利息。

Article 13 A cyber-enterprise shall pay the interests of delayed payment of duties to the Customs in accordance with rules after selling the processing trade commodities in domestic market.

缴纳缓税利息的起始日期按照以下办法确定:

The starting date for paying the interests of delayed payment of duties shall be set according to following measures:

(一)实行电子手册管理的,起始日期为内销料件或者制成品所对应的加工贸易合同项下首批料件进口之日;

(1) with regard to enterprises under the management of electronic handbook, the starting date shall be the date of import of the first lot of materials under the processing trade contract that the materials or finished products for domestic sales are corresponding to.

(二)实行电子账册管理的,起始日期为内销料件或者制成品对应的电子账册最近一次核销之日。没有核销日期的,起始日期为内销料件或者制成品对应的电子账册首批料件进口之日。

(2) with regard to enterprises under the management of electronic account book, the starting date shall be the last date of verification and cancellation of the electronic account that the materials or finished products for domestic sales are corresponding to. Should there no date of verification and cancellation be available, the starting date shall be the date of import of the first lot of materials under the electronic account book that the materials or finished products for domestic sales are corresponding to.

缴纳缓税利息的终止日期为海关签发税款缴款书之日。

The ending date for paying the interests of delayed payment of duties shall be the date that the Customs issues the duty payment book.

第十四条 联网企业应当在海关确定的核销期结束之日起30日内完成报核。确有正当理由不能按期报核的,经主管海关批准可以延期,但延长期限不得超过60日。

Article 14 A cyber-enterprise shall apply for verification within 30 days from the ending date for cancellation after verification set by the Customs. If the application for verification could not be submitted with proper reasons within the time limit, the period could be prolonged with the approval of the competent customs, but the extension could not exceed 60 days.

第十五条 联网企业实施盘点前,应当告知海关;海关可以结合企业盘点实施核查核销。

Article 15 A cyber-enterprise shall inform the Customs before conducting stock-taking. The Customs may, integrating with the enterprise's stock – taking, carry out verification and cancellation.

海关结合企业盘点实施核查核销时,应当将电子底账核算结果与联网企业实际库存量进行对比,并分别进行以下处理:

The Customs shall, while integrating the stock – taking to carry out the verification and cancellation, compare the calculation of the electronic account with the real stock of the cyber-enterprise and handle separately as follows:

（一）实际库存量多于电子底账核算结果的，海关应当按照实际库存量调整电子底账的当期余额；

（二）实际库存量少于电子底账核算结果且联网企业可以提供正当理由的，对短缺的部分，海关应当责令联网企业申请内销处理；

（三）实际库存量少于电子底账核算结果且联网企业不能提供正当理由的，对短缺的部分，海关除责令联网企业申请内销处理外，还可以按照《中华人民共和国海关行政处罚实施条例》对联网企业予以处罚。

第十六条 联网企业有下列情形之一的，海关可以要求其提供保证金或者银行保函作为担保：

（一）企业管理类别下调的；

（二）未如实向海关报送数据的；

（三）海关核查、核销时拒不提供相关账册、单证、数据的；

（四）未按照规定时间向海关办理报核手续的；

（五）未按照海关要求设立账册、账册管理混乱或者账目不清的。

第十七条 违反本办法，构成走私或者违反海关监管规定行为的，由海关依照《中华人民共和国海关法》和《中华人民共和国海关行政处罚实施条例》的有关规定予以处理；构成犯罪的，依法追究刑事责任。

第十八条 本办法下列用语的含义：

“电子底账”，是指海关根据联网企业申请，为其建立的用于记录加工贸易备案、进出口、核销等资料的电子数据库。

“专项核查”，是指海关根据监管需要，对联网企业就某一项或者多项内容实施的核查行为。

“盘点核查”，是指海关在联网企业盘点时，对一定期间的部分保税货物进行实物核对、数据核查的一种监管方式。

第十九条 本办法由海关总署负责解释。

第二十条 本办法自2006年8月1日起施行。2003年3月19日海关总署令第100号发布的《中华人民共和国海关对加工贸易企业实施计算机联网监管办法》同时废止。

1. If the real stock is more than the calculation of the electronic account, the Customs shall adjust current balance of the electronic account according to real stock;

2. If the real stock is less than the calculation of the electronic account and the cyber-enterprise may give proper reasons, the Customs shall order the cyber-enterprise to apply for domestic sales for the part of shortage;

3. If the real stock is less than the calculation of the electronic account and the cyber – enterprise could not give proper reasons, besides ordering the cyber – enterprise to apply for domestic sales for the part of shortage, the Customs may punish it according to Implementation Regulations of the General Administration of Customs of PRC for Administrative Punishment.

Article 16 The Customs may ask for deposits or bank′s Letter of Guarantee if a cyber – enterprise is in one of following circumstances:

1. The administration classification of an enterprise is adjusted to a lower grade;

2. an enterprise that have not submitted the data to the Customs according to the facts;

3. an enterprise that declined to provide corresponding account book, bills and certificates and data while the Customs is carrying out the verification and cancellation;

4. an enterprise that has not applied for the verification to the Customs within the time limit;

5. an enterprise that has not established an account book according to the request of the Customs, account management or accounts are not in order.

Article 17 Whoever violates these measures and commits a crime of smuggling or violates the Customs' rules on supervision and administration shall be handled by the Customs according to relevant provisions of Customs Law of the People′s Republic of China and Implementation Regulations of the General Administration of Customs of PRC for Administrative Punishment. If a crime is constituted, he shall be subject to criminal liabilities in accordance with the law.

Article 18 The implication of following words in terms of these measures:

'Electronic account" refers to the electronic data base established by the Customs for a cyber-enterprise according to its application for noting down the information of processing trade record, import and export, verification and cancellation etc.

"Special check" refers to the verification carried out by the Customs to a cyber – enterprise on one or more contents in light of the needs of verification and administration.

"Stock-taking check" refers to a mode of verification and administration that the Customs carries out material objects verification and data check to part of bonded commodities within a certain period while a cyber-enterprise is conducting stock-taking.

Article 19 The interpretation power of the present measures shall be remained with the General Administration of Customs.

Article 20 The present measures shall be implemented on August 1, 2006. Measures of the General Administration of Customs for Cyber-Supervision and Administration of Processing Trade Enterprises promulgated by the General Administration of Customs in Order No. 100 on March 19,2003 shall be both abolished.

中华人民共和国海关特别优惠关税待遇进口货物原产地管理办法

MEASURES FOR ADMINISTRATION OF THE PLACE OF ORIGIN OF IMPORT GOODS FOR PREFERENTIAL TARIFF TREATMENT OF CUSTOMS OF THE PEOPLE'S REPUBLIC OF CHINA

海关总署令

第149号

《中华人民共和国海关特别优惠关税待遇进口货物原产地管理办法》已于2006年5月30日经海关总署署务会审议通过，现予公布，自2006年7月1日起施行。2004年12月30日海关总署令第123号公布的《中华人民共和国海关关于执行〈中华人民共和国给予非洲最不发达国家特别优惠关税待遇的货物原产地规则〉的规定》同时废止。

二〇〇六年五月三十一日

中华人民共和国海关特别优惠关税待遇进口货物原产地管理办法

第一条 为了正确确定享受特别优惠关税待遇进口货物的原产地，促进我国与有关国家间的经贸往来，根据《中华人民共和国海关法》、《中华人民共和国进出口货物原产地条例》、我国关于享受特别优惠关税待遇货物原产地规则及有关法律、行政法规的规定，制定本办法。

第二条 本办法适用于从受惠国（名单见附件1）进口的享受特别优惠关税待遇货物，但是以加工贸易方式保税进口和内销的货物不适用本办法。

附件1所列受惠国名单发生变化时，由海关总署另行公告。

第三条 从受惠国直接运输进口的货物，符合下列条件之一的，其原产地为该受惠国，适用《中华人民共和国进出口税则》（以下简称《税则》）中相应的特惠税率：

（一）完全在受惠国获得或者生产的；

（二）非完全在受惠国获得或者生产，但在该国完成货物最后的实质性改变的。

第四条 本办法第三条第（一）项所称"完全在受惠国获得或者生产"的货物是指：

（一）在该受惠国采掘的矿产品；

（二）在该受惠国收获的植物和植物产品；

（三）在该受惠国出生并饲养的活动物；

Order of General Administration of Customs

(Order No. 149)

Measures for Administration of the Place of Origin of Import Goods for Preferential Tariff Treatment has been approved and passed by the administrative working conference of the General Administration of the Customs. It is now promulgated and shall be put into effect as since July 1, 2006. Order No. 123 of the General Administration of Customs of the People's Republic of China, issued on December 30, 2004, shall be abolished at the same time.

May 31, 2006

Measures for Administration of the Place of Origin of Import Goods for Preferential Tariff Treatment

Article 1 In accordance with the provisions of the Customs Law of the People's Republic of China, the Regulations for the Place of Origin of Imported and Exported Goods of the People's Republic of China, and norms of our country on origins of goods enjoying preferential tariff treatment and relevant laws and administrative regulations, these measures are hereby formulated to correctly determine the origins of imported goods enjoying preferential tariff treatment, promoting economic cooperation between our country and other countries

Article 2 These Measures shall apply to the goods imported from beneficiary countries (see appendix for the list) that enjoy preferential tariff treatment. These Measures, however, shall not apply to the goods imported as bonded goods in the form of processing trade and goods for domestic sales.

Any changes of the names of preferential countries listed in Appendix 1 shall be announced by the General Administration of Customs.

Article 3 The goods transported and imported directly from a beneficiary country in one of following circumstances, on the basis that the origin is in the beneficiary country, apply to corresponding preferential tariff rate as prescribed in the Import and Export Tariff of the People's Republic of China (hereinafter referred to as "Tariff"):

1. the goods that are obtained or produced completely in the beneficiary country;

2. the goods that are not obtained or produced completely in the beneficiary country, but the final substantial change is fulfilled in the beneficiary country.

Article 4 The term "Goods obtained or produced completely in the beneficiary country" in Article 3 refers to:

1. Minerals mined in the beneficiary country;

2. Plants and their products harvested in the beneficiary country;

3. Live animals born and raised in the beneficiary country;

（四）在该受惠国从本条第（三）项所指的动物中获得的产品；

（五）在该受惠国狩猎或者捕捞所获得的产品；

（六）在该受惠国注册或者合法悬挂该受惠国国旗的船只在其领海捕捞获得的鱼类和其他海产品；

（七）在该受惠国注册或者合法悬挂该受惠国国旗的加工船上加工本条第（六）项所列产品获得的产品；

（八）在该受惠国收集的该受惠国消费过程中产生的仅适于原材料回收的废旧物品；

（九）在该受惠国加工制造过程中产生的仅适于回收原材料的废碎料；

（十）利用本条第（一）项至第（九）项所列产品在该受惠国加工所得的产品。

第五条 下列微小加工或者处理，无论是单独完成还是相互结合完成，在确定货物是否为完全获得或者生产时不影响货物原产地的确定：

（一）为运输或者贮存期间保存货物而进行的加工或者处理；

（二）为货物便于装卸而进行的加工或者处理；

（三）为货物销售而进行的包装、展示等加工或者处理。

第六条 本办法第三条第（二）项中“实质性改变”的认定标准，为“税则归类改变”标准或者“从价百分比”标准。

（一）“税则归类改变”标准，是指在受惠国生产或者加工的货物所使用的非该国原产材料在《税则》中的税号均为该货物所在4位级税号之外的其他税号。

（二）“从价百分比”标准，是指在受惠国对非该国原产材料进行制造、加工后的增值部分不小于所得货物价值的40%。其计算公式如下：

$$\frac{\text{货物价格}-\text{非原产材料的价格}}{\text{货物价格}} \mathrm{X}\ 100\% \geqslant 40\%$$

“货物价格”，是指该货物的船上交货价格，无论货物以何种方式运输，该价格为其在最终装运港口或者地点的价格。

“非原产材料的价格”，是指生产商所使用的非原产材料价格，包括其进口成本、运至目的港口或者地点的保险费和运费。

上述“从价百分比”的计算应当符合公认的会计准则及《海关估价协定》。

第七条 简单的稀释、混合、包装、装瓶、干燥、装配、分类或者装饰不应当视为实质性改变。

企业以规避本办法为目的的生产或者定价措施，不

4. Products obtained from the animals born and raised in the beneficiary country;

5. Products hunted or fished in the beneficiary country;

6. Fish and other sea products captured in the territorial waters of the beneficiary country by the vessels registered in the beneficiary country or hanging legally the flag o f the beneficiary country;

7. Process the products obtained from the products as listed in Section (6) of this Article on processing vessels registered in the beneficiary country or hanging legally the flag of the beneficiary country;

8. Wastes produced during the consumption, collected in the beneficiary country to be used for recycling of raw materials.

9. Waste and scrap materials produced during processing and manufacturing in the beneficiary country that can be used for recycling of raw materials;

10. Products obtained by processing the products as listed in Section (1) through (9) of this Article in the beneficiary country .

Article 5 The following types of minor processing or treatment, no matter finished independently or finished jointly with others, shall not affect whether they are entirely obtained or produced in the origins of goods:

(1) Processing or treatment conducted for preserving the goods during transportation or storage period;

(2) Processing or treatment conducted for facilitating the loading and unloading;

(3) Packing, exhibiting and other processing and treatment conducted for sales of goods;

Article 6 The criterion as provided in Section (2) of Article 3 on the determination of "substantial change" shall be based on the change of tariff nomenclature or standard of "ad valorem percentage."

(1) The term "change of tariff nomenclature" refers to the raw materials originated in other countries and used for processing or producing in the beneficiary countries that have tax file numbers other than 4 digital ones as stipulated in Tax Code.

(2) The term "ad valorem percentage" means that the value added part after manufacturing or processing raw materials from other countries in the beneficiary country shall not be less than 40% of the value of the goods. The formula is as follows:

[(price of the goods - price of materials of non - origin) / price of goods] x 100% ≥40%

"Price of goods" refers to the price of FOB of the goods. The prices of the goods transported in any means shall be the price of the goods in final shipping port or places.

"Price of materials originated in other countries" refers to the price of materials originated in other countries used by the producer, including import costs, insurance premium and transportation costs for transporting the goods to destination port or places.

The calculation of above ad valorem percentage shall be in accordance with generally acknowledged accounting norms and Customs Valuation Agreement.

Article 7 Simple diluting, mixing, packing, bottling, drying, assembling, classification or oration shall not be regarded as substantial change.

The producing or pricing measures taken for the purposes of evading

应当视为实质性改变。

第八条 在确定货物原产地时,货物制造过程中使用的能源、工厂、设备、机器和工具的原产地,以及未构成货物物质成分或者组成部件的材料的原产地,不影响货物原产地的确定。

第九条 与货物一起申报进口并在《税则》中与该货物一并归类的包装、包装材料和容器的原产地,以及正常配备的附件、备件、工具及介绍说明性材料的原产地,不影响货物原产地的确定。

第十条 申报享受特别优惠关税待遇的进口货物,应当直接从受惠国运输至我国境内,途中未经过中国和该受惠国以外的其他国家或者地区(以下简称"其他国家或者地区")。

货物经过其他国家或者地区运输至我国境内,同时符合下列条件的,应当视为直接运输:

(一)经过其他国家或者地区是由于地理原因或者运输需要;

(二)该货物在经过其他国家或者地区时,未做除装卸和为使货物保持良好状态或者运输所必需的处理以外的其他处理;

(三)未进入该国家或者地区进行贸易或者消费。

第十一条 进口货物收货人申报享受特别优惠关税待遇的进口货物的,应当向海关提交以下文件:

(一)出口受惠国原产地证书签发机构签发的,并由该国海关于出口时加盖印章的原产地证书(格式见附件2);

(二)在出口受惠国签发的联运提单,或者国际联运始发的其他国家或者地区签发的联运提单;

(三)来自出口受惠国的原始商业发票。

经过其他国家或者地区运输的进口货物,还应当提交中国海关认为必要的能证明符合第十条第(二)项规定的有关文件。

第十二条 进口货物收货人向海关提交的原产地证书,应当由受惠国官方机构签发,其有效期为自签发之日起180日。

原产地证书用A4纸印制,所用文字为英文;原产地证书应当由下列颜色的一份正本和三份副本组成:正本为米黄色,副本为浅绿色。副本包括第二副本、第三副本和第四副本,其中第二副本为海关认为必要时核查之用,第三副本应当由出口国发证机构留存,第四副本由出口人留存。进口货物收货人向海关申报时应当提交正本及第二副本。

these measures shall not be regarded as substantial change.

Article 8 Neither the origin of the energy, workshops, equipment, machines and tools employed during the production of the goods nor the origin of the materials that have not become the constitution or parts of the goods have a bearing on the determination of the place of origins of goods.

Article 9 The place of origin of the packages, packing materials, and containers of the import and export goods that are declared together with the goods and are uniformly classified into the same category of the goods under the Tax Code, and the place of origins of the accessories, spare parts, tools and introductory materials shall not affect the determination of place of origin of the goods.

Article 10 The imported goods applying for preferential tariff treatment shall be transported directly from the beneficiary country to the territory of our country and shall not pass through China or other countries or regions other than the beneficiary country (hereinafter referred to "other countries or regions").

Goods that are transported to the territory of our country via other countries or regions, but meet following conditions, shall be regarded as direct transportation:

(1) The goods pass through other countries or regions due to geographical reasons or the needs of transportation;

(2) When the goods pass by other countries or regions, no other treatment are conducted except the treatment for loading and unloading or for keeping the goods in good condition;

(3) The goods have not entered the country or region for trade or consumption.

Article 11 Any consignee of the imported goods who declares the imported good enjoying preferential tariff treatment shall submit following documents to the Customs:

(1) Certificate of Place of Origin issued by the designated authorities of the exporting country and bearing the approval stamp of Customs authorities of the exporting country; (see appendix 2 for the form);

(2) Combined transport Bill of Lading issued in the export beneficiary country or Bill of Lading issued in the third country or region upon departure of the international combined transport;

(3) Original commercial invoice from export beneficiary country.

With regard to the imported goods transported via other countries or regions, relevant document that Chinese Customs regards as necessary and can prove the goods in accordance with the provisions of Article 10 (2) shall be submitted.

Article 12 The certificate of place of origin submitted by consignee of import goods shall be issued by the certifying authorities of certificate of origin, valid for 180 days from the date of issuance.

The Certificate of Place of Origin must be printed in A4 size paper and be made in English. The Certificate of Place of Origin shall comprise one original and three photocopies in the following colors: the original in cream-yellow, the duplicates in light green. The duplicates include second duplicate, third duplicate and fourth duplicate, among them the second duplicate shall be reserved for the examination of the Customs when necessary, the third duplicate shall be kept by the issuing authority of the export country, and the fourth duplicate shall be kept by the exporter. The consignee of the import goods shall submit the original version and the second duplicate

原产地证书签发机构的名称和地址及签发原产地证书的印章和签章式样应当在中华人民共和国海关总署备案。

when making declaration to the Customs.

The name and address of the authority issuing The Certificate of Place of Origin and the pattern of the seal and signature shall be registered for record in the General Administration of Customs of the People's Republic of China.

第十三条 货物进口报关时,进口货物收货人应当主动向海关申明有关货物享受特别优惠关税,并提交经出口国海关于出口时加盖印章的原产地证书。海关应当根据受惠国备案资料对相关货物的原产地证书予以审核,原产地证书及相关文件验凭有效的,准予进口货物享受特别优惠关税。

Article 13 When the goods are cleared for import at the Customs, the consignee of the imported goods shall make clear that the goods enjoy preferential tariff, and submit the Certificate of Place of Origin with a seal affixed by the Customs of the exported country when the goods are exported. The Customs shall, according to the record materials of the beneficiary country, examine and verify the Certificate of Place of Origin of corresponding goods. If the Certificate of Place of Origin and corresponding documents are examined to be effective, the imported goods are granted to enjoy preferential tariff.

第十四条 在对原产地证书内容的真实性产生怀疑时,海关总署或者其授权的机构可以通过中国驻相关受惠国使领馆经济商务参赞处(室)向受惠国海关或者原产地证书发证机构提出核查要求,并要求其在自收到核查要求之日起的90日内予以答复。如果海关未能在上述期限内收到答复,则该货物不得享受特别优惠关税优惠。

Article 14 In case there is any suspicion about the accuracy of the Certificate of Place of Origins, the General Administration of the Customs or its authorized organ may, through economic and commercial counselor office of China to the beneficiary country, make a request for verification to the Customs of the beneficiary country or the authority of issuing the Certificate of Place of Origins, and ask for a reply within 90 days after receiving the request. If the Customs could not receive any reply within the time limit, the goods could not enjoy preferential tariff.

在等待受惠国原产地证书核查结果期间,应进口货物收货人要求,海关可以按照该货物适用的最惠国税率收取应缴税款的等值保证金后放行货物,并按规定办理进口手续、进行海关统计。待出口国海关或者原产地证书签发机构核查完毕后,海关应当根据核查结果,立即办理退还保证金手续或者办理保证金转为进口税款手续,海关统计数据应当作相应修改。

During the waiting period for the verification result on the Certificate of Place of Origins from the beneficiary country, at the request of the consignee of the import goods, the Customs may approve the clearance for the goods after collecting equivalent guarantee money for duty that shall be paid according to the duty rate of most - favored - nation applicable to the goods, and handle import formalities in accordance with rules, conduct the Customs statistics. After the Customs of the export country or the authority issuing the Certificate of Place of Origin finishes the verification, the Customs shall, according to the verification result, return the guarantee money immediately or transfer the guarantee money to import duty. The Customs statistics shall be revised correspondingly.

进口货物属于国家限制进口的,或者有违法嫌疑的,在原产地证书核查完毕前海关不得放行货物。

Any import goods subject to import restriction of the country or being suspected of violating the law shall not be approved clearance prior to the verification on the Certificate of Place of Origin complete.

第十五条 海关对依照本办法规定获得的商业秘密依法负有保密义务。未经收货人同意,海关不得泄露或者用于其他用途,但是法律、行政法规及相关司法解释另有规定的除外。

Article 15 The Customs shall take the responsibility to keep the trade secret confidential as prescribed in these Measures. Without the agreement of the consignee, the Customs shall not let it out or use it for other purposes unless there are separate provisions by laws, administrative regulations and relevant judicial interpretation.

第十六条 违反本办法,构成走私或者违反海关监管规定行为的,由海关依照《中华人民共和国海关法》和《中华人民共和国海关行政处罚实施条例》等有关法律、行政法规的规定予以处理;构成犯罪的,依法追究刑事责任。

Article 16 Whoever violates these Measures, commits smuggling or violates the supervision and administrative regulations of the Customs shall be dealt with by the Customs according to the provisions of Customs Law of the People's Republic of China, Implementation Regulations of the Customs of PRC for Administrative Punishment and other relevant laws, administrative laws and regulations. If a crime is constituted, he shall be subject to criminal liability in accordance with laws.

第十七条 本办法下列用语的含义:

Article 17 Interpretations of following words in the present Measures:

"受惠国",是指与中国签有特别优惠关税待遇换文

"Beneficiary country" refers to the country or region that has ex-

的国家或者地区。

"海关估价协定",是指作为《马拉喀什建立世贸组织协定》一部分的《关于履行1994年关税与贸易总协定第7条的协定》。

"材料",是指已实际上构成另一货物组成部分或者已用于另一货物生产过程的零件、部件、成分、半组装件等。

"生产",是指货物获得的方法,包括:种植、饲养、开采、收获、捕捞、诱捕、狩猎、制造、加工或者装配等。

第十八条 本办法由海关总署负责解释。

第十九条 本办法自2006年7月1日起施行。2004年12月30日海关总署令第123号公布的《中华人民共和国海关关于执行〈中华人民共和国给予非洲最不发达国家特别优惠关税待遇的货物原产地规则〉的规定》同时废止。

附件:1.受惠国名单(略)

2.原产地证书格式(略)

changed notes on preferential tariff treatment with China.

"Customs Valuation Agreement" refers to the Agreement About Performing Article 7 of General Agreement on 1994 Tariff and Trade that is a part of agreement in Marrakech on Establishing World Trade Organization.

"Materials" refers to the spare parts, components, composition, semi-assembled parts and etc. that have actually constituted the components of another good or have been used in the production process of other goods.

"Production" refers to the way of obtaining goods, including: planting, raising, mining, harvesting, fishing, ensnaring, hunting, manufacturing, processing or assembling and etc.

Article 18 The power to interpret these Measures shall be vested in the General Administration of Customs.

Article 19 The present Measures shall be implemented since July 1, 2006. Provisions of the Customs of the People's Republic of China on the Implementation of "the Rules of Place of Origin of Goods under the Special Preferential Tariff Treatments Given by the People's Republic of China to the Least-developed African Countries" promulgated in Order No. 123 of the General Administration of Customs on December 30, 2004 shall be abolished simultaneously.

Appendix: 1. the name list of preferential countries (omitted)

2. The format of Certificate for Place of Origin (omitted)

中华人民共和国海关审定进出口货物完税价格办法

海关总署令

第148号

《中华人民共和国海关审定进出口货物完税价格办法》已于2006年3月8日经署务会审议通过,现予公布,自2006年5月1日起施行。2001年12月31日海关总署令第95号发布的《中华人民共和国海关审定进出口货物完税价格办法》和2003年5月30日海关总署令第102号发布的《中华人民共和国海关关于进口货物特许权使用费估价办法》同时废止。

署 长 牟新生

二〇〇六年三月二十八日

MEASURES OF THE CUSTOMS OF THE PEOPLE'S REPUBLIC OF CHINA FOR THE ASSESSMENT AND DETERMINATION OF DUTY-PAID VALUE OF IMPORT AND EXPORT GOODS

Order of the General Administration of Customs

Order No. 148

Deliberated and adopted at the executive meeting of the General Administration of Customs on March 8, 2006, The Measures of the Customs of the People's Republic of China for the Assessment and Determination of Duty-paid Value of Import and Export Goods are hereby promulgated and shall come into force as of May 1, 2006. The Measures of the Customs of the People's Republic of China for the Assessment and Determination of Duty-paid Value of Import and Export Goods as promulgated by Order No. 95 of the General Administration of Customs on December 31, 2001 and the Measures of the Customs of the People's Republic of China for the Evaluation of Royalties of Imported Goods as promulgated by Order No. 102 of the General Administration of Customs on May 30, 2003 shall be repealed simultaneously.

General Director of General Administration of Customs, Mou Xinsheng

March 28, 2006

中华人民共和国海关审定进出口货物完税价格办法

Measures of the Customs of the People's Republic of China for the Assessment and Determination of Duty-paid Value of Import and Export Goods

第一章 总 则

第一条 为了正确审查确定进出口货物的完税价格，根据《中华人民共和国海关法》、《中华人民共和国进出口关税条例》的规定，制定本办法。

第二条 海关审查确定进出口货物的完税价格，应当遵循客观、公平、统一的原则。

第三条 海关审查确定进出口货物的完税价格，应当适用本办法。

准许进口的进境旅客行李物品、个人邮递物品以及其他个人自用物品的完税价格和涉嫌走私的进出口货物、物品的计税价格的核定，不适用本办法。

第四条 海关应当按照国家有关规定，妥善保管纳税义务人提供的涉及商业秘密的资料，除法律、行政法规另有规定外，不得对外提供。

纳税义务人可以书面向海关提出为其保守商业秘密的要求，并具体列明需要保密的内容，但是不得以商业秘密为理由拒绝向海关提供有关资料。

第二章 进口货物的完税价格

第一节 进口货物完税价格确定方法

第五条 进口货物的完税价格，由海关以该货物的成交价格为基础审查确定，并应当包括货物运抵中华人民共和国境内输入地点起卸前的运输及其相关费用、保险费。

第六条 进口货物的成交价格不符合本章第二节规定的，或者成交价格不能确定的，海关经了解有关情况，并与纳税义务人进行价格磋商后，依次以下列方法审查确定该货物的完税价格：

(一)相同货物成交价格估价方法；
(二)类似货物成交价格估价方法；
(三)倒扣价格估价方法；
(四)计算价格估价方法；
(五)合理方法。

纳税义务人向海关提供有关资料后，可以提出申请，

Chapter Ⅰ General Provisions

Article 1 In pursuance to the Customs Law of the People's Republic of China and the Regulation of the People's Republic of China on the Import and Export Duties, these Measures are hereby formulated for the purpose of correctly measuring and determining the duty - paid value of import and export goods.

Article 2 The Customs shall observe the principles of objectiveness, fairness and unification when checking and determining the duty - paid value of import and export goods.

Article 3 These Measures shall apply when the Customs checks and determines the duty-paid value of import and export goods.

These Mcasures shall not be applicable to the checking and determination of the duty-paid value of such articles for personal use that are permitted to be imported as the luggage of passengers entering China, personal postal items and etc, or the assessable value of the import and export goods and articles that are suspected of being involved in smuggle.

Article 4 The Customs shall properly keep the materials involving trade secrets provided by taxpayers, and shall not provide them to any other people or entity unless it is otherwise prescribed by the laws or administrative regulations according to the relevant provisions of the State.

A taxpayer may request the Customs to keep trade secrets in the form of written application and specifically mention the contents that need to be kept confidential, but shall not refuse to provide relevant materials for the Customs on the pretext of trade secrets.

Chapter Ⅱ Duty-paid Value of Imported Goods

Section 1 Methods for Determining the Duty-paid Value of Imported Goods

Article 5 The duty-paid value of imported goods shall be checked and determined by the Customs on the basis of the transaction value of those goods, which shall include the freight and relevant expenses and the insurance premiums of the goods before they are transported to and unloaded at the entry spot within the territory of the People's Republic of China.

Article 6 Where the transaction value of imported goods does not comply with the provisions in Section 2 of this Chapter or cannot be determined, the transaction value of those goods shall be determined in sequence by the following methods after the Customs gains knowledge of the relevant situations and carries out consultation on pricing with the taxpayer:

(1) using the transaction value of the identical goods;
(2) using the transaction value of the similar goods;
(3) method of subtraction for price assessment;
(4) method of calculation for price assessment;
(5) method of reasonable assessment.

After providing relevant materials to the Customs, the tax payers may

颠倒前款第(三)项和第(四)项的适用次序。

file the application to invert the order of the Item (3) and Item (4) of the preceding paragraph.

第二节　成交价格估价方法

Section 2　Appraisal Method for the Transaction value

第七条　进口货物的成交价格，是指卖方向中华人民共和国境内销售该货物时买方为进口该货物向卖方实付、应付的，并且按照本章第三节的规定调整后的价款总额，包括直接支付的价款和间接支付的价款。

Article 7　The transaction value of imported goods shall refer to the total amount of the paid - in or payable value that the buyer shall pay to the seller for the imported goods when the goods are sold within the territory of the People's Republic of China after adjustment according to the provisions in Section 3 of this Chapter, which shall include the price that is directly and indirectly paid.

第八条　进口货物的成交价格应当符合下列条件：

(一)对买方处置或者使用进口货物不予限制，但是法律、行政法规规定实施的限制、对货物销售地域的限制和对货物价格无实质性影响的限制除外；

(二)进口货物的价格不得受到使该货物成交价格无法确定的条件或者因素的影响；

(三)卖方不得直接或者间接获得因买方销售、处置或者使用进口货物而产生的任何收益，或者虽然有收益但是能够按照本办法第十一条第一款第(四)项的规定做出调整；

(四)买卖双方之间没有特殊关系，或者虽然有特殊关系但是按照本办法第十七条的规定未对成交价格产生影响。

Article 8　The transaction value of imported goods shall comply with the following conditions:

(1) The buyer shall not be restricted with regard to the disposal or use of imported goods, except for the restrictions prescribed and implemented by laws or administrative regulations, the restrictions on areas where the goods are to be sold, and the restrictions that have no substantial impact on the value of the goods;

(2) The value of imported goods shall not be affected by the conditions or factors that may make the determination of the transaction value of those goods impossible;

(3) The seller shall not directly or indirectly acquire any proceeds from the buyer's selling, disposing or use of imported goods, unless the adjustment can be made according to Item (4) of Paragraph 1 of Article 11 of these Measures; and

(4) There shall be no special relation between the buyer and the seller, unless the special relation will not affect the transaction value according to Article 17 of these Measures.

第九条　有下列情形之一的，应当视为对买方处置或者使用进口货物进行了限制：

(一)进口货物只能用于展示或者免费赠送的；

(二)进口货物只能销售给指定第三方的；

(三)进口货物加工为成品后只能销售给卖方或者指定第三方的；

(四)其他经海关审查，认定买方对进口货物的处置或者使用受到限制的。

Article 9　The buyer is regarded as being restricted in the disposal or use of imported goods in any of the following circumstances:

(1) The imported goods can be used solely for exhibitions or as free gifts;

(2) The imported goods can be sold solely to the designated third party;

(3) The imported goods can be sold solely to the seller or the designated third party after they are processed into finished products; or

(4) Any other circumstance under which the buyer is regarded as being restricted in the disposal or use of imported goods upon examination of the Customs.

第十条　有下列情形之一的，应当视为进口货物的价格受到了使该货物成交价格无法确定的条件或者因素的影响：

(一)进口货物的价格是以买方向卖方购买一定数量的其他货物为条件而确定的；

(二)进口货物的价格是以买方向卖方销售其他货物为条件而确定的；

(三)其他经海关审查，认定货物的价格受到使该货物成交价格无法确定的条件或者因素影响的。

Article 10　It shall be regarded that the value of imported goods has been affected by the conditions or factors that make the determination of the transaction value of those goods impossible under any of the following circumstances:

(1) The value of imported goods is determined on condition that the buyer purchases a certain amount of other goods from the seller;

(2) The value of imported goods is determined on condition that the buyer sells other goods to the seller; or

(3) Any other circumstance under which the value of imported goods is affected by the conditions or factors that makes the determination of the transaction value of those goods impossible upon examination of the Customs.

第三节　成交价格的调整项目

Section 3　Adjustment Items for the Transaction value

第十一条　以成交价格为基础审查确定进口货物的完税价格时，未包括在该货物实付、应付价格中的下列费用或者价值应当计入完税价格：

（一）由买方负担的下列费用：

1. 除购货佣金以外的佣金和经纪费；

2. 与该货物视为一体的容器费用；

3. 包装材料费用和包装劳务费用。

（二）与进口货物的生产和向中华人民共和国境内销售有关的，由买方以免费或者以低于成本的方式提供，并可以按适当比例分摊的下列货物或者服务的价值：

1. 进口货物包含的材料、部件、零件和类似货物；

2. 在生产进口货物过程中使用的工具、模具和类似货物；

3. 在生产进口货物过程中消耗的材料；

4. 在境外进行的为生产进口货物所需的工程设计、技术研发、工艺及制图等相关服务。

（三）买方需向卖方或者有关方直接或者间接支付的特许权使用费，但是符合下列情形之一的除外：

1. 特许权使用费与该货物无关；

2. 特许权使用费的支付不构成该货物向中华人民共和国境内销售的条件。

（四）卖方直接或者间接从买方对该货物进口后销售、处置或者使用所得中获得的收益。

纳税义务人应当向海关提供本条所述费用或者价值的客观量化数据资料。纳税义务人不能提供的，海关与纳税义务人进行价格磋商后，按照本办法第六条列明的方法审查确定完税价格。

Article 11　When the duty - paid value of imported goods is checked and determined on the basis of transaction price, the following expenses or values that are excluded from the paid - in or payable value of those goods shall be taken into account of the duty - paid value:

(1) The following expenses as borne by the buyer:

a. Commissions and brokerages other than the commission for buying goods;

b. Expenses for the containers which are regarded as integral parts of those goods; and

c. Expenses for the package materials and packing services.

(2) The value of the following goods or services that are relevant to the production of imported goods and the selling thereof within the territory of the People's Republic of China and are provided for free or sold at a price lower than the cost price by the buyer, which may be apportioned in appropriate proportion:

a. Materials, parts, accessories and similar goods contained in imported goods;

b. Tools, molds and similar goods used in the production of imported goods;

c. Materials consumed in the production of imported goods;

d. Relevant services occurring out of China such as engineering design, technological research and development, techniques and drawings, etc. that are needed for the production of imported goods.

(3) The royalties that the buyer needs to pay to the seller or the relevant party directly or indirectly, unless it is under either of the following circumstances:

a. The royalties are irrelevant to those goods; or

b. The payment of royalties does not constitute the conditions for those goods to be sold within the territory of the People's Republic of China.

(4) The proceeds directly or indirectly acquired by the seller from the buyer's selling, disposal or use of those goods after the import thereof.

The taxpayer shall provide objective and quantitative data and materials about the aforesaid expenses or values to the Customs. Where the taxpayer fails to provide the aforesaid data and materials, the Customs shall check and determine the duty - paid value upon consultation on pricing with the taxpayer according to the methods as mentioned in Article 6 of these Measures.

第十二条　在根据本办法第十一条第一款第（二）项确定应当计入进口货物完税价格的货物价值时，应当按照下列方法计算有关费用：

（一）由买方从与其无特殊关系的第三方购买的，应当计入的价值为购入价格；

（二）由买方自行生产或者从有特殊关系的第三方获得的，应当计入的价值为生产成本；

（三）由买方租赁获得的，应当计入的价值为买方承担的租赁成本；

Article 12　When determining the value of goods that shall be taken into account of the duty-paid value of imported goods according to Item (2) of Paragraph 1 of Article 11 of these Measures, the relevant expenses shall be calculated according to the following methods:

(1) The purchasing price shall be taken into account of the value in case that the buyer purchases goods from the third party that has no special relation therewith;

(2) The cost of manufacturing shall be taken into account of the value in case that the buyer manufactures goods by itself or purchases goods from the third party that has any special relation therewith;

(3) The cost of leasing borne by the buyer shall be taken into account of the value in case that the buyer acquires the goods by leasing; and

（四）生产进口货物过程中使用的工具、模具和类似货物的价值，应当包括其工程设计、技术研发、工艺及制图等费用。

如果货物在被提供给卖方前已经被买方使用过，应当计入的价值为根据国内公认的会计原则对其进行折旧后的价值。

第十三条 符合下列条件之一的特许权使用费，应当视为与进口货物有关：

（一）特许权使用费是用于支付专利权或者专有技术使用权，且进口货物属于下列情形之一的：

1. 含有专利或者专有技术的；

2. 用专利方法或者专有技术生产的；

3. 为实施专利或者专有技术而专门设计或者制造的。

（二）特许权使用费是用于支付商标权，且进口货物属于下列情形之一的：

1. 附有商标的；

2. 进口后附上商标直接可以销售的；

3. 进口时已含有商标权，经过轻度加工后附上商标即可以销售的。

（三）特许权使用费是用于支付著作权，且进口货物属于下列情形之一的：

1. 含有软件、文字、乐曲、图片、图像或者其他类似内容的进口货物，包括磁带、磁盘、光盘或者其他类似介质的形式；

2. 含有其他享有著作权内容的进口货物。

（四）特许权使用费是用于支付分销权、销售权或者其他类似权利，且进口货物属于下列情形之一的：

1. 进口后可以直接销售的；

2. 经过轻度加工即可以销售的。

第十四条 买方不支付特许权使用费则不能购得进口货物，或者买方不支付特许权使用费则该货物不能以合同议定的条件成交的，应当视为特许权使用费的支付构成进口货物向中华人民共和国境内销售的条件。

第十五条 进口货物的价款中单独列明的下列税收、费用，不计入该货物的完税价格：

（一）厂房、机械或者设备等货物进口后发生的建设、安装、装配、维修或者技术援助费用，但是保修费用除外；

（二）进口货物运抵中华人民共和国境内输入地点起卸后发生的运输及其相关费用、保险费；

（三）进口关税、进口环节海关代征税及其他国内税；

（四）为在境内复制进口货物而支付的费用；

（五）境内外技术培训及境外考察费用。

(4) The value of tools, molds and similar goods used in the production of imported goods shall include the expenses for engineering design, technological research and development, techniques and drawings, etc.

Where the goods have been used by the buyer before they are provided to the seller, the value to be taken into account shall be the value upon depreciation according to the domestically recognized accounting principles.

Article 13 The royalties that comply with any of the following conditions shall be regarded as relevant to the imported goods:

(1) The royalties are paid for the patent or the right to use know-how, and the imported goods are under any of the following circumstances:

a. The imported goods contain patent or know-how;

b. The imported goods are produced by using any patented method or know-how; or

c. The imported goods are specially designed or manufactured for implementing the patent or know-how.

(2) The royalties are paid for trademark right, and the imported goods are under any of the following circumstances:

a. The imported goods are attached with the trademark;

b. The imported goods are attached with the trademark after importing and may be directly sold; or

c. The imported goods contain the trademark right when imported and may be sold with the trademark attached after minor processing.

(3) The royalties are paid for copyright, and the imported goods are under either of the following circumstances:

a. The imported goods contain software, words, music, graphics, images, or other similar contents, including the form of tape, disk, compact disk, or other similar media; or

b. The imported goods contain other contents with copyright.

(4) The royalties are paid for the right to distribute, or sell or other similar rights, and the imported goods are under either of the following circumstances:

a. The imported goods may be directly sold after importing; or

b. The imported goods may be sold after minor processing.

Article 14 Where the buyer cannot purchase the imported goods or the deal cannot be made under the conditions stipulated in the contract because the buyer fails to pay the royalties, it shall be regarded that the payment of royalties constitutes the conditions for the imported goods to sell within the territory of the People's Republic of China.

Article 15 The following taxes and expenses separately listed in the value of imported goods shall not be taken into account of the duty-paid value of those goods:

(1) The expenses for the construction, installation, assembly, maintenance or technical aid that occur after the import of workshops, machines, equipments or other goods, except for the warranty costs;

(2) The freight and relevant expenses and the insurance premiums of the imported goods that occur after the goods are transported to and unloaded at the entry spot within the territory of the People's Republic of China;

(3) The import duties, the import linkage taxes levied by the Customs on behalf of other authorities and other internal taxes;

(4) The expenses paid for the reproduction of imported goods within China; and

(5) The expenses for domestic and overseas technical trainings and o-

verseas inspection.

同时符合下列条件的利息费用不计入完税价格：

(一)利息费用是买方为购买进口货物而融资所产生的；

(二)有书面的融资协议的；

(三)利息费用单独列明的；

(四)纳税义务人可以证明有关利率不高于在融资当时当地此类交易通常应当具有的利率水平，且没有融资安排的相同或者类似进口货物的价格与进口货物的实付、应付价格非常接近的。

The expenses for interests that comply with the following conditions simultaneously shall not be taken into account of the duty - paid value：

(1) The expenses for interests are incurred from the financing for the buyer to purchase imported goods；

(2) There is a written financing agreement；

(3) The expenses for interests are separately listed；and

(4) The taxpayer can prove that the relevant interest rate is not higher than that for local similar transactions at the time and the value of identical or similar imported goods for which there is no financing arrangement is very close to the paid-in or payable value of imported goods.

第四节　特殊关系

Section 4　Special Relations

第十六条　有下列情形之一的，应当认为买卖双方存在特殊关系：

(一)买卖双方为同一家族成员的；

(二)买卖双方互为商业上的高级职员或者董事的；

(三)一方直接或者间接地受另一方控制的；

(四)买卖双方都直接或者间接地受第三方控制的；

(五)买卖双方共同直接或者间接地控制第三方的；

(六)一方直接或者间接地拥有、控制或者持有对方5%以上(含5%)公开发行的有表决权的股票或者股份的；

(七)一方是另一方的雇员、高级职员或者董事的；

(八)买卖双方是同一合伙的成员的。

买卖双方在经营上相互有联系，一方是另一方的独家代理、独家经销或者独家受让人，如果符合前款的规定，也应当视为存在特殊关系。

Article 16　The buyer and the seller shall be regarded as having special relations in any of the following circumstances：

(1) The seller and the buyer are the members of a same family；

(2) The seller or the buyer is a business senior employee or board director of the other；

(3) The seller or the buyer is directly or indirectly controlled by the other；

(4) Both the seller and the buyer are directly or indirectly controlled by a third party；

(5) The seller and the buyer directly or indirectly control a third party together；

(6) The seller or the buyer directly or indirectly possesses, controls or holds 5% or more of the voting stocks or shares publicly issued by the other；

(7) The seller or the buyer is the employee, senior employee or board director of the other；or

(8) Both the buyer and the seller are members of a partnership.

Where the buyer and the seller have mutual relations in business, and one party is the exclusive agent, distributor or assignee of the other, it shall be deemed that there is a special relation between them providing that the provisions of the preceding Paragraph are met.

第十七条　买卖双方之间存在特殊关系，但是纳税义务人能证明其成交价格与同时或者大约同时发生的下列任何一款价格相近的，应当视为特殊关系未对进口货物的成交价格产生影响：

(一)向境内无特殊关系的买方出售的相同或者类似进口货物的成交价格；

(二)按照本办法第二十二条的规定所确定的相同或者类似进口货物的完税价格；

(三)按照本办法第二十四条的规定所确定的相同或者类似进口货物的完税价格。

海关在使用上述价格进行比较时，应当考虑商业水平和进口数量的不同，以及买卖双方有无特殊关系造成的费用差异。

Article 17　Where the taxpayer can prove that the transaction value is close to any of the following values occurring at or about the same time even though there is a special relation between the buyer and the seller, it shall be regarded that such special relation has no impact on the transaction value of imported goods：

(1) The transaction value of identical or similar goods sold to a buyer with no special relation within China；

(2) The duty-paid value of identical or similar goods determined according to Article 22 of these Measures；or

(3) The duty-paid value of identical or similar goods determined according to Article 24 of these Measures.

When comparing the aforesaid values, the Customs shall consider the differences in business level and import quantity, and the expense differences resulted from the special relation between the buyer and the seller.

第五节　除成交价格估价方法以外的其他估价方法

第十八条　相同货物成交价格估价方法，是指海关以与进口货物同时或者大约同时向中华人民共和国境内销售的相同货物的成交价格为基础，审查确定进口货物的完税价格的估价方法。

第十九条　类似货物成交价格估价方法，是指海关以与进口货物同时或者大约同时向中华人民共和国境内销售的类似货物的成交价格为基础，审查确定进口货物的完税价格的估价方法。

第二十条　按照相同或者类似货物成交价格估价方法的规定审查确定进口货物的完税价格时，应当使用与该货物具有相同商业水平且进口数量基本一致的相同或者类似货物的成交价格。使用上述价格时，应当以客观量化的数据资料，对该货物与相同或者类似货物之间由于运输距离和运输方式不同而在成本和其他费用方面产生的差异进行调整。

在没有前款所述的相同或者类似货物的成交价格的情况下，可以使用不同商业水平或者不同进口数量的相同或者类似货物的成交价格。使用上述价格时，应当以客观量化的数据资料，对因商业水平、进口数量、运输距离和运输方式不同而在价格、成本和其他费用方面产生的差异做出调整。

第二十一条　按照相同或者类似货物成交价格估价方法审查确定进口货物的完税价格时，应当首先使用同一生产商生产的相同或者类似货物的成交价格。

没有同一生产商生产的相同或者类似货物的成交价格的，可以使用同一生产国或者地区其他生产商生产的相同或者类似货物的成交价格。

如果有多个相同或者类似货物的成交价格，应当以最低的成交价格为基础审查确定进口货物的完税价格。

第二十二条　倒扣价格估价方法，是指海关以进口货物、相同或者类似进口货物在境内的销售价格为基础，扣除境内发生的有关费用后，审查确定进口货物完税价格的估价方法。该销售价格应当同时符合下列条件：

(一)是在该货物进口的同时或者大约同时，将该货

Section 5　Checking Methods Other Than the Checking Method of the Transaction value

Article 18　The checking method for the transaction value of identical goods refers to such an checking method with which the Customs checks and determines the duty-paid value of imported goods on the basis of the transaction value of identical goods sold within the territory of the People's Republic of China at or about the same time as the imported goods were imported.

Article 19　The checking method for the transaction value of similar goods refers to such an checking method with which the Customs checks and determines the duty-paid value of imported goods on the basis of the transaction value of similar goods sold within the territory of the People's Republic of China at or about the same time as the imported goods are imported.

Article 20　When checking and determining the duty-paid value of imported goods according to the checking method for the transaction value of identical or similar goods, the Customs shall use the transaction value of the identical or similar goods of the same business level and in basically the same quantity as the imported goods. However, the differences between the imported goods and the identical or similar goods in costs and other expenses resulted from the differences of transportation distance and modes shall be adjusted in light of the objective and quantitative data when the aforesaid value is used.

Where there is no transaction value of identical or similar goods mentioned in the preceding Paragraph, the transaction value of identical or similar goods of different business level or in different import quantity may be adopted, however, the differences between the imported goods and the identical or similar goods in value, costs and other expenses resulted from the differences in business level, import quantity, transportation distance and modes shall be adjusted in light of the objective and quantitative data and materials when the aforesaid value is used.

Article 21　When checking and determining the duty-paid value of imported goods according to the checking method for the transaction value of identical or similar goods, the Customs shall first use the transaction value of the identical or similar goods manufactured by the same manufacturer.

Where there is no transaction value of the identical or similar goods manufactured by the same manufacturer, the Customs may use the transaction value of the identical or similar goods manufactured by other manufacturers in the same manufacturing country or region.

Where there are several transaction values of the identical or similar goods, the duty-paid value shall be checked and determined in light of the lowest transaction value.

Article 22　The subtractive method refers to such an checking method with which the Customs checks and determines the duty-paid value of imported goods in light of the sales price of the imported goods, the identical or similar goods that are sold within China by deducting the relevant expenses incurred within China. And the sales price shall meet the following conditions at the same time:

(1) It is the price for selling the imported goods, the identical or sim-

物、相同或者类似进口货物在境内销售的价格；

（二）是按照货物进口时的状态销售的价格；

（三）是在境内第一销售环节销售的价格；

（四）是向境内无特殊关系方销售的价格；

（五）按照该价格销售的货物合计销售总量最大。

第二十三条 按照倒扣价格估价方法审查确定进口货物完税价格的，下列各项应当扣除：

（一）同等级或者同种类货物在境内第一销售环节销售时，通常的利润和一般费用（包括直接费用和间接费用）以及通常支付的佣金；

（二）货物运抵境内输入地点起卸后的运输及其相关费用、保险费；

（三）进口关税、进口环节海关代征税及其他国内税。

如果该货物、相同或者类似货物没有按照进口时的状态在境内销售，应纳税义务人要求，可以在符合本办法第二十二条规定的其他条件的情形下，使用经进一步加工后的货物的销售价格审查确定完税价格，但是应当同时扣除加工增值额。

前款所述的加工增值额应当依据与加工成本有关的客观量化数据资料、该行业公认的标准、计算方法及其他的行业惯例计算。

按照本条的规定确定扣除的项目时，应当使用与国内公认的会计原则相一致的原则和方法。

第二十四条 计算价格估价方法，是指海关以下列各项的总和为基础，审查确定进口货物完税价格的估价方法：

（一）生产该货物所使用的料件成本和加工费用；

（二）向境内销售同等级或者同种类货物通常的利润和一般费用（包括直接费用和间接费用）；

（三）该货物运抵境内输入地点起卸前的运输及相关费用、保险费。

按照前款的规定审查确定进口货物的完税价格时，海关在征得境外生产商同意并提前通知有关国家或者地区政府后，可以在境外核实该企业提供的有关资料。

按照本条第一款的规定确定有关价值或者费用时，应当使用与生产国或者地区公认的会计原则相一致的原

ilar goods at or about the same time of the import of those goods;

(2) It is the price for selling the goods in the status as they are imported;

(3) It is the price for selling the goods at the first link within China;

(4) It is the price for selling the goods to the parties without special relations within China; and

(5) The accumulated sales quantity of the goods is the largest when the goods are sold at the aforesaid price.

Article 23 When the duty-paid value of imported goods is checked and determined according to the subtractive method, all the following items shall be subtracted:

(1) Usual profits and general expenses (including direct and indirect expenses) as well as the generally paid commission of the goods of the same grade or same kind as those goods when they are sold at the first sales link within China;

(2) Freight and relevant expenses and insurance premiums incurring after the goods are transported to and unloaded at the entry spot within China; and

(3) Import duties, import linkage taxes levied by the Customs on behalf of other authorities and other internal taxes.

Where the imported goods, the identical or similar imported goods are not sold within China in the state as they are imported, the sales price of the further processed goods may be used to check and determine the duty – paid value at the request of the taxpayer providing that other conditions prescribed in Article 22 are met, but the added value from processing shall be deducted at the same time.

The "added value from processing" mentioned in the preceding Paragraph shall be calculated in light of the objective and quantitative data and materials relevant to the costs of processing and according to the standards, calculation methods and other industrial practices generally recognized by the industry.

When determining the items of subtraction according to this Article, the Customs shall use the principles and methods in accordance with the accounting principles generally acknowledged within China.

Article 24 The computing method refers to such as checking method with which the Customs check and determine the duty – paid value of imported goods in light of the sum of all the following items:

(1) The costs of materials and parts used for the manufacture of those goods and the expenses of processing;

(2) The usual profits and general expenses (including direct and indirect expenses) for the sales of the goods of the same grade or same kind within China; and

(3) The freight and relevant expenses and the insurance premiums incurring before the goods are transported to and unloaded at the entry spot within China.

When checking and determining the duty – paid value of imported goods according to the preceding Paragraph, the Customs may verify the relevant materials provided by that enterprise out of China after obtaining the consent of the overseas manufacturer and notifying the government of the relevant country or region in advance.

When determining the relevant value or expenses according to Paragraph 1 of this Article, the Customs shall use the principles and methods in

则和方法。

accordance with the accounting principles generally acknowledged in the manufacturing country or region.

第二十五条 合理方法，是指当海关不能根据成交价格估价方法、相同货物成交价格估价方法、类似货物成交价格估价方法、倒扣价格估价方法和计算价格估价方法确定完税价格时，海关根据本办法第二条规定的原则，以客观量化的数据资料为基础审查确定进口货物完税价格的估价方法。

Article 25 The method of rational checking refers to such an checking method with which the Customs check and determine the duty-paid value of imported goods according to the principles prescribed in Article 2 of these Measures and in light of the objective and quantitative data and materials when the checking method for the transaction value, the checking method for the transaction value of identical or similar goods, the subtractive method and the computed method cannot be used to determine the duty-paid value.

第二十六条 海关在采用合理方法确定进口货物的完税价格时，不得使用以下价格：

(一)境内生产的货物在境内的销售价格；

(二)可供选择的价格中较高的价格；

(三)货物在出口地市场的销售价格；

(四)以本办法第二十四条规定之外的价值或者费用计算的相同或者类似货物的价格；

(五)出口到第三国或者地区的货物的销售价格；

(六)最低限价或者武断、虚构的价格。

Article 26 When using the method of rational checking to determine the duty－paid value of imported goods, the Customs shall not use the following prices:

(1) The domestic sales price of the goods manufactured within China;

(2) The higher prices among the available prices;

(3) The sales price of the goods on the market of the export place;

(4) The price of identical or similar goods calculated in light of the values or expenses other than those specified in Article 24 of these Measures;

(5) The sales price of the goods exported to a third country or region; and

(6) The lowest fixed price, or other arbitrary or fictive prices.

第三章 特殊进口货物的完税价格

Chapter Ⅲ Duty-paid Value of Special Imported goods

第二十七条 加工贸易进口料件或者其制成品应当征税的，海关按照以下规定审查确定完税价格：

(一)进口时应当征税的进料加工进口料件，以该料件申报进口时的成交价格为基础审查确定完税价格；

(二)进料加工进口料件或者其制成品(包括残次品)内销时，海关以料件原进口成交价格为基础审查确定完税价格。料件原进口成交价格不能确定的，海关以接受内销申报的同时或者大约同时进口的与料件相同或者类似的货物的进口成交价格为基础审查确定完税价格；

(三)来料加工进口料件或者其制成品(包括残次品)内销时，海关以接受内销申报的同时或者大约同时进口的与料件相同或者类似的货物的进口成交价格为基础审查确定完税价格；

(四)加工企业内销加工过程中产生的边角料或者副产品，以海关审查确定的内销价格作为完税价格。

Article 27 Where the duties shall be levied on the imported materials and parts for processing trade or the finished products thereof, the Customs shall check and determine the duty-paid value according to the following provisions:

(1) With regard to the imported materials and parts for the processing with the imported materials for which the duties shall be collected at importation, the transaction value declared for the import of those materials and parts shall be taken as the basis for the checking and determination of duty-paid value;

(2) With regard to the imported materials and parts for the processing with imported materials or the finished products thereof (including inferior products) that are sold in the domestic market, the Customs shall check and determine the duty－paid value in light of the original import transaction value of those materials and parts. If the original import transaction value of those materials and parts cannot be determined, the Customs shall check and determine the duty-paid value in light of the import transaction price of the identical or similar goods imported at or about the same time when accepting the declaration for domestic sales;

(3) With regard to the imported materials and parts for the processing with Customers′materials or the finished products thereof (including inferior products) that are sold in the domestic market, the Customs shall check and determine the duty－paid value in light of the import transaction price of the identical or similar goods imported at or about the same time when accepting the declaration for domestic sales; and

(4) With regard to the leftover materials produced in the processing of the processing enterprises to be sold in the domestic market, the domestic

sales price as checked and determined by the Customs shall be taken as the duty-paid value.

加工贸易内销货物的完税价格按照前款规定仍然不能确定的，由海关按照合理的方法审查确定。

Where the duty-paid value of the goods of processing trade that will be sold in the domestic market still cannot be determined after referring to the preceding Paragraph, the Customs shall check and determine the duty - paid value in light of the method of rational checking.

第二十八条 出口加工区内的加工企业内销的制成品（包括残次品），海关以接受内销申报的同时或者大约同时进口的相同或者类似货物的进口成交价格为基础审查确定完税价格。

Article 28 With regard to the finished products (including inferior products) sold in the domestic market by the processing enterprises within export processing zones, the Customs shall check and determine the duty - paid value in light of the import transaction value of the identical or similar goods imported at or about the same time when accepting the declaration for domestic sales.

出口加工区内的加工企业内销加工过程中产生的边角料或者副产品，以海关审查确定的内销价格作为完税价格。

With regard to the leftover materials or by - products produced in the processing of the processing enterprises within export processing zones, the domestic sales price as checked and determined by the Customs shall be taken as the duty-paid value.

出口加工区内的加工企业内销制成品（包括残次品）、边角料或者副产品的完税价格按照本条前两款规定不能确定的，由海关按照合理的方法审查确定。

If the duty - paid value of the finished products (including inferior products), leftover materials or by-products of the processing enterprises within export processing zones that will be sold in the domestic market still cannot be determined according to the preceding two paragraphs, the Customs shall check and determine the duty - paid value in light of the method of rational checking.

第二十九条 保税区内的加工企业内销的进口料件或者其制成品（包括残次品），海关以接受内销申报的同时或者大约同时进口的相同或者类似货物的进口成交价格为基础审查确定完税价格。

Article 29 With regard to the import materials and parts or the finished products thereof (including inferior products) of the processing enterprises within export processing zones that will be sold in the domestic market, the Customs shall check and determine the duty - paid value in light of the import transaction value of the identical or similar goods imported at or about the same time when accepting the declaration for domestic sales.

保税区内的加工企业内销的进料加工制成品中，如果含有从境内采购的料件，海关以制成品所含从境外购入的料件原进口成交价格为基础审查确定完税价格。料件原进口成交价格不能确定的，海关以接受内销申报的同时或者大约同时进口的与料件相同或者类似货物的进口成交价格为基础审查确定完税价格。

Where there are materials and parts purchased within China in the finished products from the imported materials of the processing enterprises within export processing zones that will be sold in the domestic market, the Customs shall check and determine the duty - paid value in light of the original import transaction value of the materials and parts purchased from abroad and contained in the finished products. Where the original import transaction value of the materials and parts cannot be determined, the Customs shall check and determine the duty - paid value in light of the import transaction value of the identical or similar goods imported at or about the same time when accepting the declaration for domestic sales.

保税区内的加工企业内销的来料加工制成品中，如果含有从境内采购的料件，海关以接受内销申报的同时或者大约同时进口的与制成品所含从境外购入的料件相同或者类似货物的进口成交价格为基础审查确定完税价格。

Where there are materials and parts purchased within China in the finished products from the Customers' materials of the processing enterprises within export processing zones that will be sold in the domestic market, the Customs shall r the duty-paid value in light of the import transaction value of the identical or similar goods, as the materials and parts purchased abroad and contained in the finished products, imported at or about the same time when accepting the declaration for domestic sales.

保税区内的加工企业内销加工过程中产生的边角料或者副产品，以海关审查确定的内销价格作为完税价格。

With regard to the leftover materials or by-products of the processing enterprises within export processing zones that are produced during the course of the processing for domestic sales, the domestic sales price as checked and determined by the Customs shall be taken as the duty-paid value.

保税区内的加工企业内销制成品（包括残次品）、边角料或者副产品的完税价格按照本条前四款规定仍然不

Where the duty-paid value of the finished products (including inferior products), leftover materials or by-products of the processing enterprises

能确定的，由海关按照合理的方法审查确定。

within export processing zones that will be sold in the domestic market still cannot be determined after referring to the preceding 4 Paragraphs of this Article, the Customs shall check and determine the duty-paid value in light of the method of rational checking.

第三十条 从保税区、出口加工区、保税物流园区、保税物流中心等区域、场所进入境内，需要征税的货物，海关应当参照本办法第二章的有关规定，以从上述区域、场所进入境内的销售价格为基础审查确定完税价格，加工贸易进口料件及其制成品除外。

Article 30 With regard to the goods (excluding the imported materials for processing trade and the finished products thereof) that are imported from such areas or places as bonded zones, export processing zones, bonded logistics parks, or bonded logistics centers into China and that should be taxed, the Customs shall, by referring to the relevant provisions in Chapter II of these Measures, check and determine the duty-paid value in light of the sales price of the goods that are imported from the aforesaid areas or places.

如果前款所述的销售价格中未包括上述区域、场所发生的仓储、运输及其他相关费用的，应当按照客观量化的数据资料予以计入。

Where the sales price mentioned in the preceding Paragraph does not take into account of the storage fee, freight and other relevant expenses occurring in the aforesaid areas or places, those expenses shall be included in light of the objective and quantitative data and materials.

第三十一条 运往境外修理的机械器具、运输工具或者其他货物，出境时已向海关报明，并在海关规定的期限内复运进境的，应当以境外修理费和料件费为基础审查确定完税价格。

Article 31 With regard to the machines and mechanical appliances, means of transport or other goods transported abroad for repair that have been declared to the Customs at exportation and that are re-imported within the time limit specified by the Customs, the duty - paid value thereof shall be checked and determined in light of the overseas repair charges and the expenses of materials and components.

出境修理货物复运进境超过海关规定期限的，由海关按照本办法第二章的规定审查确定完税价格。

Where the goods transported abroad for repair are not re - imported within the time limit specified by the Customs, the Customs shall check and determine the duty-paid value in light of the provisions in Chapter II of these Measures.

第三十二条 运往境外加工的货物，出境时已向海关报明，并在海关规定期限内复运进境的，应当以境外加工费和料件费以及该货物复运进境的运输及其相关费用、保险费为基础审查确定完税价格。

Article 32 With regard to the goods transported abroad for processing that are declared to the Customs at exportation and that are transported back to China within the time limit as prescribed by the Customs, the duty-paid value shall be checked and determined in light of the overseas processing fees and material fees, the freight for transporting those goods back to China and other relevant expenses and insurance premiums.

出境加工货物复运进境超过海关规定期限的，由海关按照本办法第二章的规定审查确定完税价格。

Where the goods transported abroad for processing are not re-transported back to China within the time limit as specified by the Customs, the Customs shall check and determine the duty - paid value in light of the provisions in Chapter II of these Measures.

第三十三条 经海关批准的暂时进境货物，应当缴纳税款的，由海关按照本办法第二章的规定审查确定完税价格。经海关批准留购的暂时进境货物，以海关审查确定的留购价格作为完税价格。

Article 33 With regard to the goods that enter into China temporarily upon the approval of the Customs and that shall be taxed, the Customs shall check and determine the duty - paid value in light of the provisions in Chapter II of these Measures. With regard to the goods that are temporarily imported into China for retention upon approval of the Customs, the retention price as checked and determined by the Customs shall be the duty-paid value.

第三十四条 租赁方式进口的货物，按照下列方法审查确定完税价格：

Article 34 With regard to the goods imported on lease, the duty-paid value shall be checked and determined according to the following methods:

（一）以租金方式对外支付的租赁货物，在租赁期间以海关审查确定的租金作为完税价格，利息应当予以计入；

(1) With regard to the goods of lease in the form of rent paid to foreign countries, the rent checked and determined by the Customs during the course of lease shall be taken as the duty - paid value, and the interests shall also be included;

（二）留购的租赁货物以海关审查确定的留购价格作为完税价格；

(2) With regard to the goods of lease for retention, the retention price checked and determined by the Customs shall be taken as the duty - paid

(三)纳税义务人申请一次性缴纳税款的,可以选择申请按照本办法第六条列明的方法确定完税价格,或者按照海关审查确定的租金总额作为完税价格。

第三十五条 减税或者免税进口的货物应当补税时,应当以海关审查确定的该货物原进口时的价格,扣除折旧部分价值作为完税价格,其计算公式如下:

完税价格 = 海关审查确定的该货物原进口时的价格 × (1 − 补税时实际已进口的时间(月) / 监管年限 × 12)

上述计算公式中"补税时实际已进口的时间"按月计算,不足1个月但是超过15日的,按照1个月计算;不超过15日的,不予计算。

第三十六条 易货贸易、寄售、捐赠、赠送等不存在成交价格的进口货物,海关与纳税义务人进行价格磋商后,按照本办法第六条列明的方法审查确定完税价格。

第三十七条 进口载有专供数据处理设备用软件的介质,具有下列情形之一的,应当以介质本身的价值或者成本为基础审查确定完税价格:

(一)介质本身的价值或者成本与所载软件的价值分列;

(二)介质本身的价值或者成本与所载软件的价值虽未分列,但是纳税义务人能够提供介质本身的价值或者成本的证明文件,或者能提供所载软件价值的证明文件。

含有美术、摄影、声音、图像、影视、游戏、电子出版物的介质不适用前款规定。

第四章 进口货物完税价格中的运输及其相关费用、保险费的计算

第三十八条 进口货物的运费,应当按照实际支付的费用计算。如果进口货物的运费无法确定的,海关应当按照该货物的实际运输成本或者该货物进口同期运输行业公布的运费率(额)计算运费。

运输工具作为进口货物,利用自身动力进境的,海关在审查确定完税价格时,不再另行计入运费。

value; and

(3) Where the taxpayer applies for paying the duties once and for all, the duty-paid value shall be determined by choosing the methods mentioned in Article 6 of these Measures upon the strength of application, or shall be the total amount of rents checked and determined by the Customs.

Article 35 Where it is necessary to make up the reduced or exempted duties of the imported goods, the duty-paid value shall be the original import value of those goods checked and determined by the Customs at importation and deducted by the value of the depreciated part, and the calculation formula shall be:

Duty-paid Value = Original Import Value of Those Goods Checked and Determined by the Customs at Importation × (1 − Time Period upon Importation When the Duties Are Made up [Month] / Years of Regulation × 12).

The "time period upon importation when the duties are made up" in the above − mentioned calculation formula shall be calculated on a monthly basis. Where there is less than one month but are more than 15 days, it shall be regarded as one month, and if there are less than 15 days, no time period nccds to be calculated.

Article 36 With regard to the imported goods with no transaction value and imported in the forms of barter, consignment, and donation, etc. the duty-paid value shall be checked and determined according to the methods listed in Article 6 of these Measures upon the price consultation between the Customs and the taxpayer.

Article 37 With regard to the imported medium that carries special software for data processing equipment, if it is under either of the following circumstances, the duty − paid value shall be checked and determined in light of the value or cost of the medium itself:

(1) The value or cost of the medium itself is separately listed from the software it carries; or

(2) Although the value or cost of the medium itself is not separately listed from the carried software, the taxpayer can provide the certification document on the value or cost of the medium itself, or can provide the certification document on the value of the software it carries.

The preceding Paragraph shall not apply to the medium containing fine arts, photographs, audio or video products, movies and television programs, games and electronic journals.

Chapter IV Calculation of Freight and Relevant Expenses and Insurance Premiums in the Duty-paid Value of Imported goods

Article 38 The freight of imported goods shall be calculated in light of the expenses actually paid. Where the freight of imported goods cannot be determined, the Customs shall calculate the freight in light of the actual transportation costs for those goods or at the freight rate promulgated by the transportation industry at the same time when those goods are imported.

Where the vehicles of transport are the imported goods and are imported by making use of their own drives, the Customs shall not additionally calculate the freight when checking and determining the duty − paid value.

第三十九条 进口货物的保险费,应当按照实际支付的费用计算。如果进口货物的保险费无法确定或者未实际发生,海关应当按照"货价加运费"两者总额的3‰计算保险费,其计算公式如下:

保险费=(货价+运费)×3‰

第四十条 邮运进口的货物,应当以邮费作为运输及其相关费用、保险费。

第四十一条 以境外边境口岸价格条件成交的铁路或者公路运输进口货物,海关应当按照境外边境口岸价格的1%计算运输及其相关费用、保险费。

第五章 出口货物的完税价格

第四十二条 出口货物的完税价格由海关以该货物的成交价格为基础审查确定,并应当包括货物运至中华人民共和国境内输出地点装载前的运输及其相关费用、保险费。

第四十三条 出口货物的成交价格,是指该货物出口销售时,卖方为出口该货物应当向买方直接收取和间接收取的价款总额。

第四十四条 下列税收、费用不计入出口货物的完税价格:

(一)出口关税;

(二)在货物价款中单独列明的货物运至中华人民共和国境内输出地点装载后的运输及其相关费用、保险费;

(三)在货物价款中单独列明由卖方承担的佣金。

第四十五条 出口货物的成交价格不能确定的,海关经了解有关情况,并与纳税义务人进行价格磋商后,依次以下列价格审查确定该货物的完税价格:

(一)同时或者大约同时向同一国家或者地区出口的相同货物的成交价格;

(二)同时或者大约同时向同一国家或者地区出口的类似货物的成交价格;

(三)根据境内生产相同或者类似货物的成本、利润和一般费用(包括直接费用和间接费用)、境内发生的运输及其相关费用、保险费计算所得的价格;

(四)按照合理方法估定的价格。

第六章 完税价格的审查确定

第四十六条 纳税义务人向海关申报时,应当按照本办法的有关规定,如实向海关提供发票、合同、提单、装

Article 39 The insurance premiums of imported goods shall be calculated in light of the expenses actually paid. Where the insurance premiums of imported goods cannot be determined or do not actually occur, the Customs shall calculate the insurance premiums by 3 ‰ of "cost and freight".

Insurance Premium = (Cost + Freight) × 3‰

Article 40 With regard to the goods imported by mail, the postage shall be taken as the freight and relevant expenses and the insurance premiums.

Article 41 With regard to the goods imported by railway or highway that is transacted on the term of FOB (fee on board), the Customs shall calculate the freight and relevant expenses and the insurance premiums by 1% of FOB.

Chapter V Duty-paid Value of Export Goods

Article 42 The duty-paid value of export goods shall be checked and determined by the Customs in light of the transaction value of those goods, and shall take into account of the freight and relevant expenses and the insurance premiums incurred before those goods are loaded at the exit spot within the People's Republic of China.

Article 43 The transaction value of export goods refers to the total amount of money that the seller directly and indirectly collects from the buyer for the export of those goods when those goods are sold to the outside of China.

Article 44 The following taxes and expenses shall not be taken into account of the duty-paid value of export goods:

(1) The export tariff;

(2) The freight and relevant expenses and the insurance premiums separately listed in the price of goods after those goods are loaded at the exit spot within the People's Republic of China; and

(3) The commission that separately listed in the price of goods that should be borne by the seller.

Article 45 When the transaction value of export goods cannot be determined, the Customs shall check and determine the duty-paid value of those goods according to the following prices in sequence after knowing the relevant conditions and carrying out the price consultation with the taxpayer:

(1) The transaction value of the identical goods exported to the same country or region at or about the same time;

(2) The transaction value of the similar goods exported to the same country or region at or about the same time;

(3) The value calculated in light of the costs, profits and general expenses (including direct and indirect expenses) for manufacturing the identical or similar goods within China, and the freight and relevant expenses and the insurance premiums incurring within China;

(4) The value checked according to the method of rational checking.

Chapter Ⅵ Checking and Determination of Duty-paid Value

Article 46 When a taxpayer makes declaration to the Customs, it/he shall, faithfully provide the invoices, contracts, bills of lading, encasement

箱清单等单证。

lists and other documents to the Customs in light of the relevant provisions in these Measures.

根据海关要求,纳税义务人还应当如实提供与货物买卖有关的支付凭证以及证明申报价格真实、准确的其他商业单证、书面资料和电子数据。

Upon the request of the Customs, the taxpayer shall also faithfully provide the relevant payment vouchers related to the purchase of goods as well as other commercial documents, written materials and electric data that can prove the authenticity and accuracy of the declared value.

货物买卖中发生本办法第二章第三节所列的价格调整项目的,纳税义务人应当如实向海关申报。

Where any price item mentioned in Section 3 of Chapter II of these Measures is adjusted in the transaction of goods, the taxpayer shall faithfully make declaration to the Customs.

前款所述的价格调整项目如果需要分摊计算的,纳税义务人应当根据客观量化的标准进行分摊,并同时向海关提供分摊的依据。

Where the apportionment calculation is required for the above-mentioned price adjustment item, the taxpayer shall make apportionment in light of the objective and quantitative standards, and shall provide the basis of apportionment to the Customs at the same time.

第四十七条 海关为审查申报价格的真实性、准确性,可以行使下列职权进行价格核查:

Article 47 For the purpose of examining the authenticity and accuracy of the declared value, the Customs may exercise the following functions and powers for carrying out the price checking:

(一)查阅、复制与进出口货物有关的合同、发票、账册、结付汇凭证、单据、业务函电、录音录像制品和其他反映买卖双方关系及交易活动的商业单证、书面资料和电子数据;

(1) Consulting and duplicating such commercial documents, written materials and electric data that show the relationship between the buyer and seller and the transaction activities as the contracts, invoices, accounts, certificates of foreign exchange settlement and payment, bills, business letters and audio-video products related to the import and export goods;

(二)向进出口货物的纳税义务人及与其有资金往来或者有其他业务往来的公民、法人或者其他组织调查与进出口货物价格有关的问题;

(2) Investigating the taxpayer of import and export goods, and the citizens, legal persons or other organizations that have financial or other business relations with the taxpayer about the issues related to the value of import and export goods;

(三)对进出口货物进行查验或者提取货样进行检验或者化验;

(3) Checking the import and export goods or selecting samples for inspection or testing;

(四)进入纳税义务人的生产经营场所、货物存放场所,检查与进出口活动有关的货物和生产经营情况;

(4) Entering the business operational places and the goods storage places of the taxpayer to inspect the goods and business operations related to the import and export activities;

(五)经直属海关关长或者其授权的隶属海关关长批准,凭《中华人民共和国海关账户查询通知书》(见附件1)及有关海关工作人员的工作证件,可以查询纳税义务人在银行或者其他金融机构开立的单位账户的资金往来情况,并向银行业监督管理机构通报有关情况;

(5) Investigating, the fund flows reflected in the accounts opened by the taxpayer in the bank or any other financial institution upon approval of the director of the Customs directly under the General Administration of Customs or the authorized director of its subordinate Customs and upon the strength of the Notice of the Customs of the People's Republic of China on the Consultation of Accounts (see Annex 1) and the work certificates of the relevant Customs functionaries, and informing the banking regulatory institution of the relevant information; and

(六)向税务部门查询了解与进出口货物有关的缴纳国内税情况。

(6) Consulting the taxation authority about the payment of internal taxes related to the import and export goods.

海关在行使前款规定的各项职权时,纳税义务人及有关公民、法人或者其他组织应当如实反映情况,提供有关书面资料和电子数据,不得拒绝、拖延和隐瞒。

When the Customs exercises the functions and powers prescribed in the preceding Paragraph, the taxpayer and the relevant citizens, legal persons and other organizations shall faithfully reflect the facts, provide the relevant written materials and electronic data, and shall not refuse, delay or make concealment.

第四十八条 海关对申报价格的真实性、准确性有疑问时,或者认为买卖双方之间的特殊关系影响成交价格时,应当制发《中华人民共和国海关价格质疑通知书》(以下简称《价格质疑通知书》,见附件2),将质疑的理由书面告知纳税义务人或者其代理人,纳税义务人或者其代理人应当自收到《价格质疑通知书》之日起5个工作日内,以书面形式提供相关资料或者其他证据,证明其

Article 48 Where the Customs has doubts in the authenticity or accuracy of the declared value or considers that there is special relation between the buyer and the seller that will influence the transaction value, it shall issue a Notice of the Customs of the People's Republic of China on the Challenge of Price (hereinafter referred to as the Notice on the Challenge of Price, see Annex 2) and notify the reasons for questioning to the taxpayer or the agent thereof in written form. The taxpayer or the agent thereof shall

申报价格真实、准确或者双方之间的特殊关系未影响成交价格。

provide the relevant materials or other evidence in written form to prove that the declared value is true and accurate or there is no special relation between both parties within 5 working days upon receipt of a Notice on the Challenge of Price.

纳税义务人或者其代理人确有正当理由无法在规定时间内提供前款资料的，可以在规定期限届满前以书面形式向海关申请延期。

Where the taxpayer or the agent thereof fails to provide the materials mentioned in the preceding Paragraph within the prescribed time limit due to justifiable reasons, he/it can file an application for the postponement with the Customs before the expiration of the prescribed time limit.

除特殊情况外，延期不得超过10个工作日。

The time limit shall not be prolonged for more than 10 working days unless it is under special circumstances.

第四十九条 海关制发《价格质疑通知书》后，有下列情形之一的，海关与纳税义务人进行价格磋商后，按照本办法第六条或者第四十五条列明的方法审查确定进出口货物的完税价格：

Article 49 After the Customs issues a Notice on the Challenge of Price, the Custom house shall check and determine the duty - paid value of import or export goods according to the methods mentioned in Article 6 or 45 of these Measures after carrying out the consultation with the taxpayer on pricing in case of the following circumstances:

（一）纳税义务人或者其代理人在海关规定期限内，未能提供进一步说明的；

(1) The taxpayer or the agent thereof fails to make further explanations within the time limit prescribed by the Customs;

（二）纳税义务人或者其代理人提供有关资料、证据后，海关经审核其所提供的资料、证据，仍然有理由怀疑申报价格的真实性、准确性的；

(2) After the taxpayer or the agent thereof provides the relevant materials and evidence, the Customs still has reasons to doubt the authenticity or accuracy of the declared value when examining the materials and evidence provided; or

（三）纳税义务人或者其代理人提供有关资料、证据后，海关经审核其所提供的资料、证据，仍然有理由认为买卖双方之间的特殊关系影响成交价格的。

(3) After the taxpayer or the agent thereof provides the relevant materials and evidence, the Customs still has reasons to deem that there is any special relation between the buyer and the seller that will influence the transaction value when examining the materials and evidence provided.

第五十条 海关经过审查认为进口货物无成交价格的，可以不进行价格质疑，经与纳税义务人进行价格磋商后，按照本办法第六条列明的方法审查确定完税价格。

Article 50 The Customs doesn't have to challenge the price if it finds upon examination that there is no transaction value of imported goods, and it shall check and determine the duty-paid value according to the methods mentioned in Article 6 of these Measures after carrying out the consultation on pricing with the taxpayer.

海关经过审查认为出口货物无成交价格的，可以不进行价格质疑，经与纳税义务人进行价格磋商后，按照本办法第四十五条列明的方法审查确定完税价格。

The Customs doesn't have to challenge the price if it finds upon examination that there is no transaction value of export goods, and it shall check and determine the duty - paid value according to the methods mentioned in Article 45 of these Measures after carrying out the consultation on pricing with the taxpayer.

第五十一条 海关按照本办法规定通知纳税义务人进行价格磋商时，纳税义务人应当自收到《中华人民共和国海关价格磋商通知书》（见附件3）之日起5个工作日内与海关进行价格磋商。纳税义务人未在规定的时限内与海关进行磋商的，视为其放弃价格磋商的权利，海关可以直接使用本办法第六条或者第四十五条列明的方法审查确定进出口货物的完税价格。

Article 51 When the Customs notifies the taxpayer of the price consultation in light of these Measures, the taxpayer shall carry out the price consultation with the Customs within 5 working days upon receipt of a Notice of the Customs of the People's Republic of China on the Price Consultation (see Annex 3). Where the taxpayer fails to carry out the price consultation with the Customs within the prescribed time limit, it shall be regarded that it/he has given up the right of price consultation, and the Customs may directly check and determine the duty - paid value of import or export goods according to the methods mentioned in Article 6 or 45 of these Measures.

海关按照本办法规定与纳税义务人进行价格磋商时，应当制作《中华人民共和国海关价格磋商记录表》（见附件4）。

When the Customs carries out the price consultation with the taxpayer in light of these Measures, it shall work out a Form of the Customs of the People's Republic of China for the Notes on Price Consultation (see Annex 4).

第五十二条 对符合下列情形之一的，经纳税义务人书面申请，海关可以不进行价格质疑以及价格磋商，按照本办法第六条或者第四十五条列明的方法审查确定进

Article 52 Where it is under any of the following circumstances, the Customs doesn't have to carry out the price challenge or the price consultation upon the strength of the written application of the taxpayer, and shall

出口货物的完税价格：

（一）同一合同项下分批进出口的货物，海关对其中一批货物已经实施估价的；

（二）进出口货物的完税价格在人民币10万元以下或者关税及进口环节海关代征税总额在人民币2万元以下的；

（三）进出口货物属于危险品、鲜活品、易腐品、易失效品、废品、旧品等的。

第五十三条 进口货物属于本办法第二十七条、第二十八条、第二十九条所列情形的，海关可以不进行价格质疑，经与纳税义务人进行价格磋商后，按照本办法第六条列明的方法审查确定完税价格。

进口货物属于本办法第二十七条、第二十八条、第二十九条所列情形的，经纳税义务人书面申请，海关可以不进行价格磋商，按照本办法第六条列明的方法审查确定进口货物的完税价格。

第五十四条 海关审查确定进出口货物的完税价格期间，纳税义务人可以在依法向海关提供担保后，先行提取货物。

第五十五条 海关审查确定进出口货物的完税价格后，纳税义务人可以提出书面申请，要求海关就如何确定其进出口货物的完税价格做出书面说明。海关应当根据要求出具《中华人民共和国海关估价告知书》（见附件5）。

第七章 附 则

第五十六条 本办法下列用语的含义是：

"境内"，指中华人民共和国关境内。

"完税价格"，指海关在计征关税时使用的计税价格。

"买方"，指通过履行付款义务，购入货物，并为此承担风险，享有收益的自然人、法人或者其他组织。其中进口货物的买方是指向中华人民共和国境内购入进口货物的买方。

"卖方"，指销售货物的自然人、法人或者其他组织。其中进口货物的卖方是指向中华人民共和国境内销售进口货物的卖方。

"向中华人民共和国境内销售"，指将进口货物实际运入中华人民共和国境内，货物的所有权和风险由卖方转移给买方，买方为此向卖方支付价款的行为。

check and determine the duty – paid value of import or export goods according to the methods mentioned in Article 6 or 45 of these Measures:

(1) The Customs has carried out the checking for any batch of goods imported or exported by batches under the same contract;

(2) The duty – paid value of import or export goods is less than 100,000 yuan, or the sum of the duties and the import linkage taxes levied by the Customs on behalf is less than 20,000 yuan; or

(3) The imported goods are dangerous, fresh and live, putrescible, perishable, or easy to lose efficacy, or are the discarded or worn, etc.

Article 53 Where the imported goods are under any of the circumstances mentioned in Articles 27 through 29 of these Measures, the Customs doesnt have to carry out the price challenge, and it shall check and determine the duty-paid value according to the methods mentioned in Article 6 of these Measures after carrying out the consultation on pricing with the taxpayer.

Where the imported goods are under any of the circumstances mentioned in Articles 27 through 29 of these Measures, the Customs doesn't have to carry out the price consultation upon the strength of the application of the taxpayer, and shall check and determine the duty-paid value of imported goods according to the methods mentioned in Article 6 of these Measures.

Article 54 When the Customs is checking and determining the duty – paid value of import or export goods, the taxpayer may obtain delivery of the goods in advance after providing guarantee to the Customs according to law.

Article 55 After the Customs check and determine the duty-paid value of import or export goods, the taxpayer may file a written application to the Customs and require it to make written explanations about how to determine the duty-paid value of import or export goods. The Customs shall issue a Letter of the Customs of the People's Republic of China on the Checking Notification (see Annex 5) in light of the requirements.

Chapter VII Supplementary Provisions

Article 56 The interpretations of the following terms as mentioned in these Measures are:

"Within China" refers to within the Customs boundaries of the People's Republic of China.

The "duty-paid value" refers to the assessable value used by the Customs at the time of calculating and collecting duties.

The "buyer" refers to a natural person, legal person or any other organization that performs the duty of payment, purchases the goods, assumes risks and obtains profits therefore. The buyer of imported goods refers to a buyer that purchases the imported goods within the territory of the People's Republic of China.

The "seller" refers to a natural person, legal person or any other organization that sells the goods; of which the seller of imported goods refers to a seller that sells the imported goods within the territory of the People's Republic of China.

"Selling within the territory of the People's Republic of China" means that the imported goods are actually transported into the territory of the People's Republic of China, the ownership and risks of the goods have been transferred to the buyer from the seller, and the buyer has paid the price to the seller.

"实付、应付价格",指买方为购买进口货物而直接或者间接支付的价款总额,即作为卖方销售进口货物的条件,由买方向卖方或者为履行卖方义务向第三方已经支付或者将要支付的全部款项。

The "paid-in or payable value" refers to the amount of money directly or indirectly paid by the buyer for the purchase of imported goods, namely, all the money that has been paid or to be paid by the buyer to the seller or to a third party that performs the seller's obligations as a condition for which the seller sells the imported goods.

"间接支付",指买方根据卖方的要求,将货款全部或者部分支付给第三方,或者冲抵买卖双方之间的其他资金往来的付款方式。

The "indirect payment" refers to such a payment method with which the buyer pays all or part of the money to a third party upon request of the seller, or offsets other capital flows between the buyer and the seller.

"购货佣金",指买方为购买进口货物向自己的采购代理人支付的劳务费用。

The "commission for buying goods" refers to the service fees paid by the buyer to his purchasing deputy for the purchase of the imported goods.

"经纪费",指买方为购买进口货物向代表买卖双方利益的经纪人支付的劳务费用。

The "brokerage" refers to the service fees paid by the buyer to the broker who represents the interests of both the buyer and the seller for the purchase of the imported goods.

"相同货物",指与进口货物在同一国家或者地区生产的,在物理性质、质量和信誉等所有方面都相同的货物,但是表面的微小差异允许存在。

The "identical goods" refers to the goods that are manufactured in the same country or region as the imported goods and that are identical with the imported goods in all the aspects of physical nature, quality and prestige, etc, however, minor external differences are acceptable.

"类似货物",指与进口货物在同一国家或者地区生产的,虽然不是在所有方面都相同,但是却具有相似的特征,相似的组成材料,相同的功能,并且在商业中可以互换的货物。

The "similar goods" refers to the goods that are manufactured in the same country or region as the imported goods, and that, though not identical in all the aspects, have similar characteristics, similar composing materials, the same functions and may be exchanged with the imported goods commercially.

"大约同时",指海关接受货物申报之日前后45天内。按照倒扣价格法审查确定进口货物的完税价格时,如果进口货物、相同或者类似货物没有在海关接受进口货物申报之日前后45天内在境内销售,可以将在境内销售的时间延长至接受货物申报之日前后90天内。

"About the same time" refers to within 45 days before and after the day on which the Customs accepts the declaration of the goods. When the subtractive method is used for checking and determining the duty-paid value of imported goods, if the imported goods, the identical or similar goods are not sold within China within 45 days before and after the day on which the Customs accepts the declaration of the goods, the time for the selling within China may be prolonged to within 90 days before and after the day on which the Customs accepts the declaration of the goods.

"公认的会计原则",指在有关国家或者地区会计核算工作中普遍遵循的原则性规范和会计核算业务的处理方法。包括对货物价值认定有关的权责发生制原则、配比原则、历史成本原则、划分收益性与资本性支出原则等。

The "generally acknowledged accounting principles" refers to the norms in principle and the processing methods for accounting business that are generally observed in the relevant accounting work of the relevant country or region, including the principles of accrual basis, matching, historical cost, distinguishing between revenue expenditure and capital expenditure, etc. related to the determination of the value of the goods.

"特许权使用费",指进口货物的买方为取得知识产权权利人及权利人有效授权人关于专利权、商标权、专有技术、著作权、分销权或者销售权的许可或者转让而支付的费用。

The "royalties" refers to the charges paid by the buyer of imported goods for obtaining the permission or transfer of the patents, trademarks, know-how, copyright law, distribution right or selling right of the obligee of intellectual property or the valid agent thereof.

"技术培训费用",指基于卖方或者与卖方有关的第三方对买方派出的技术人员进行与进口货物有关的技术指导,进口货物的买方支付的培训师资及人员的教学、食宿、交通、医疗保险等其他费用。

The "expenses for technical trainings" refers to the expenses paid by the buyer of imported goods for the teaching, boarding, transportation and medical insurance etc. of the training teachers and personnel where the seller or a third party thereof gives the relevant technical directions about the imported goods to the technical personnel dispatched by the buyer.

"软件",指《计算机软件保护条例》规定的用于数据处理设备的程序和文档。

The "software" refers to the program and document used for data processing equipments as prescribed by the Regulation on the Protection of Computer Software.

"专有技术",指以图纸、模型、技术资料和规范等形式体现的尚未公开的工艺流程、配方、产品设计、质量控制、检测以及营销管理等方面的知识、经验、方法和诀窍

The "know-how" refers to the knowledge, experience, methods, and knacks etc. in the form of drawings, models, technical materials, and criteria etc. in the aspects of undisclosed technical process, formula, product

等。

design, quality control, testing, and marketing and management etc.

"轻度加工",指稀释、混合、分类、简单装配、再包装或者其他类似加工。

The "minor processing" refers to the dilution, mixing, classification, simple assembling, repacking and other similar processing.

"同等级或者同种类货物",指由特定产业或者产业部门生产的一组或者一系列货物中的货物,包括相同货物或者类似货物。

The "goods of the same grade or same kind" refers to the goods in a batch or series of goods produced by the designated industry or industrial department, including the identical or similar goods.

"介质",指《中华人民共和国进出口税则》中税则号列85.24项下的商品。

The "medium" refers to the commodities under the Tax code No. 85.24 in the Rules of the People's Republic of China for the Import and Export Taxes.

"价格核查",指海关为确定进出口货物的完税价格,依法行使本办法第四十七条规定的职权,通过审查单证、核实数据、核对实物及相关账册等方法,对进出口货物申报成交价格的真实性、准确性以及买卖双方之间是否存在特殊关系影响成交价格进行的审查。

The "price checking" refers to the examination of the authenticity and accuracy of the declared transaction price of import and export goods and whether there is any special relation between the buyer and the seller that will affect the transaction price as carried out by the Customs upon the strength of the functions prescribed in Article 47 of these Measures by examining documents and certificates, verifying data, checking objects and relevant accounts so as to determine the duty - paid value of import and export goods.

"价格磋商",指海关在使用除成交价格以外的估价方法时,在保守商业秘密的基础上,与纳税义务人交换彼此掌握的用于确定完税价格的数据资料的行为。

The "consultation on pricing" refers to such an act with which the Customs exchanges with the taxpayer their data and materials for determining the duty - paid value on the basis of keeping confidential the business secrets when using the checking method other than the one for the transaction value.

第五十七条 纳税义务人对海关的估价决定有异议的,应当按照海关作出的相关行政决定依法缴纳税款,并可以依法向上一级海关申请复议。对复议决定不服的,可以依法向人民法院提起行政诉讼。

Article 57 Where the taxpayer holds objection to the checking decision made by the Customs, it/he shall pay the taxes according to the relevant administrative decision made by the Customs, and may apply for the reconsideration to the Customs at the next higher level, or file an administrative lawsuit with the people's court if it/he is still not satisfied with the decision of the reconsideration.

第五十八条 违反本办法规定,构成走私或者违反海关监管规定行为的,由海关依照《中华人民共和国海关法》和《中华人民共和国海关行政处罚实施条例》的有关规定予以处理;构成犯罪的,依法追究刑事责任。

Article 58 Whoever violates these Measures by constituting smuggling or an act of violating the Customs surveillance provisions shall be dealt with by the Customs in light of the Customs Law of the People's Republic of China and the Detailed Rules of the Customs of the People's Republic of China for the Implementation of Administrative Punishments. Where a crime is constituted, the offender shall be subject to criminal liabilities.

第五十九条 本办法由海关总署负责解释。

Article 59 The power to interpret these Measures shall remain with the General Administration of Customs.

第六十条 本办法自2006年5月1日起施行。2001年12月31日海关总署令第95号发布的《中华人民共和国海关审定进出口货物完税价格办法》和2003年5月30日海关总署令第102号发布的《中华人民共和国海关关于进口货物特许权使用费估价办法》同时废止。

Article 60 These Measures shall come into force on May 1, 2006. The Measures of the Customs of the People's Republic of China for the Checking and Determination of Duty-paid Value of Import and Export Goods as promulgated by Order No. 95 of the General Administration of Customs on December 31, 2001 and the Measures of the Customs of the People's Republic of China for the Evaluation of Royalties of Imported Goods as promulgated by Order No. 102 of the General Administration of Customs on May 30, 2003 shall be repealed simultaneously.

两用物项和技术进出口许可证管理办法

商务部、海关总署令2005年第29号

《两用物项和技术进出口许可证管理办法》已经商务部、海关总署审议通过,现予公布,自二00六年一月一日起施行。

部长:薄熙来

署长:牟新生

二00五年十二月三十一日

两用物项和技术进出口许可证管理办法

第一章 总则

第一条 为维护国家安全和社会公共利益,履行我国在缔结或者参加的国际条约、协定中所承担的义务,加强两用物项和技术进出口许可证管理,依据《中华人民共和国对外贸易法》、《中华人民共和国海关法》和有关行政法规的规定,制定本办法。

第二条 本办法所称有关行政法规系指《中华人民共和国核出口管制条例》、《中华人民共和国核两用品及相关技术出口管制条例》、《中华人民共和国导弹及相关物项和技术出口管制条例》、《中华人民共和国生物两用品及相关设备和技术出口管制条例》、《中华人民共和国监控化学品管理条例》、《中华人民共和国易制毒化学品管理条例》及《有关化学品及相关设备和技术出口管制办法》。

本办法所称两用物项和技术是指前款有关行政法规管制的物项和技术。

第三条 商务部是全国两用物项和技术进出口许可证的归口管理部门,负责制定两用物项和技术进出口许可证管理办法及规章制度,监督、检查两用物项和技术进出口许可证管理办法的执行情况,处罚违规行为。

第四条 商务部会同海关总署制定和发布《两用物

MEASURES FOR THE ADMINISTRATION ON IMPORT AND EXPORT LICENSE FOR DUAL - USE ITEMS AND TECHNOLOGIES

Order of the Ministry of Commerce and the General Administration of Customs (Order No. 29, 2005)

Measures for the Administration on Import and Export License for Dual - use Items and Technologies were discussed and adopted by the Ministry of Commerce and the General Administration of Customs. It is hereby promulgated and shall enter into force as of the date of January 1, 2006.

Minister of the Ministry of Commerce, Bo Xilai

Director - General of the General Administration of Customs, Mu Xinsheng,

December 31, 2005

Measures for the Administration on Import and Export License for Dual - use Items and Technologies

Chapter I.

Article 1 These Measures are formulated in accordance with the provisions in the Foreign Trade Law of the People's Republic of China, the Customs Law of the People's Republic of China and relevant administrative regulations for the purposes of guaranteeing national security and public interests, of fulfilling the obligations in the international treaties and conventions that China has concluded and joined, and of strengthening the administration on import and export license for dual - use items and technologies.

Article 2 "The administrative regulations" as mentioned in these Measures refer to Regulations of the People's Republic of China on Control of Nuclear Export, Regulations of the People's Republic of China on Export Control of Nuclear Dual - use Goods and Related Technologies, Regulations of the People's Republic of China on Export Control of Missiles and Missile - Related Items and Technologies, Regulations of the People's Republic of China on Export Control of Dual - use Biological Agents and Related Equipment and Technologies, Regulations of the People's Republic of China on the Administration of Controlled Chemicals, Regulations of the People's Republic of China on the Administration of Precursors and Chemicals used in Production of Narcotic Drugs and Psychotropic Substances, and Measures on Export Control of Certain Chemicals and Related Equipment and Technologies.

The dual - use items and technologies as mentioned in these Measures refer to the items and technologies controlled by the aforesaid administrative regulations.

Article 3 The Ministry of Commerce shall be in charge of the nationwide administration of the import and export license for dual - use items and technologies, responsible for formulating measures, regulations and regimes for the administration of the import and export license for dual - use items and technologies, for supervising and inspecting the implementation of measures for the administration of the import and export license for dual - use items and technologies, and for granting penalties on the violations.

Article 4 The Ministry of Commerce shall, in cooperation with the

项和技术进出口许可证管理目录》(见附件1,以下简称《管理目录》)。商务部和海关总署可以根据情况对《管理目录》进行调整,并以公告形式发布。

General Administration of Customs, formulate and promulgate the Controlling List of the Import and Export License for Dual - use Items and Technologies (please refer to Annex 1, and hereinafter referred to as the Controlling List). And the Ministry of Commerce and the General Administration of Customs may make readjustments on the Controlling List and promulgate them in the form of announcement.

第五条 商务部委托商务部配额许可证事务局(以下简称许可证局)统一管理、指导全国各发证机构的两用物项和技术进出口许可证发证工作,许可证局对商务部负责。

Article 5 Authorized by the Ministry of Commerce, the Quota and License Administrative Bureau (hereinafter referred to as the License Bureau) of the Ministry of Commerce shall be nationwide in charge of the unified administration and guidance of the issuing of the import and export license for dual - use items and technologies, and it shall be responsible to the Ministry of Commerce.

许可证局和商务部委托的省级商务主管部门为两用物项和技术进出口许可证发证机构(以下简称发证机构),省级商务主管部门在许可证局的统一管理下,负责委托范围内两用物项和技术进出口许可证的发证工作。《两用物项和技术进出口许可证发证机构名单》附后(见附件2)。

The License Bureau and the provincial competent departments of commerce authorized by the Ministry of Commerce (hereinafter referred to as the issuing authorities) shall be responsible for the issuing of the import and export license for dual - use items and technologies; under the unified administration from the License Bureau, the provincial competent departments of commerce shall, within their authorized areas, be responsible for the issuing of the import and export license for dual - use items and technologies. And the Name List of the Authorities Responsible for the Issuance of the Import and Export License for Dual - use Items and Technologies (please refer to Annex 2) is annexed thereinafter.

第六条 以任何方式进口或出口,以及过境、转运、通运《管理目录》中的两用物项和技术,均应申领两用物项和技术进口或出口许可证(许可证格式见附件3)。

Article 6 An import or export license of dual - use items and technologies shall be applied for, for the any form of import or export, or for the crossing border, transfer and transportation of the dual - use items and technologies under the Controlling List (please refer to Annex3. for the pattern of the license).

两用物项和技术在境外与保税区、出口加工区等海关特殊监管区域、保税场所之间进出的,适用前款规定。

The antecedent provisions shall be applicable to the in - and - outs of dual - use items and technologies between overseas and such customs specially - supervised zones and bonded localities as bonded zones and export processing zones etc.

两用物项和技术在境内与保税区、出口加工区等海关特殊监管区域、保税场所之间进出的,或者在上述海关监管区域、保税场所之间进出的,无需办理两用物项和技术进出口许可证。

The in - and - outs of dual - use items and technologies between the areas within the territory of the People's Republic of China and such customs specially - supervised zones and bonded localities as bonded zones and export processing zones etc., or between the aforesaid customs specially - supervised zones and bonded localities need no import or export license for dual - use items and technologies.

第七条 两用物项和技术进出口时,进出口经营者应当向海关出具两用物项和技术进出口许可证,依照海关法的有关规定,海关凭两用物项和技术进出口许可证接受申报并办理验放手续。

Article 7 When importing and exporting of dual - use items and technologies, the exporter and importer shall present to the customs authorities his/her import or export license for dual - use items and technologies, upon which, the concerning customs authorities shall, in accordance with the provisions in the Customs Law, accept the declaration and handle the formalities of examination and clearance.

第八条 根据有关行政法规的规定,出口经营者知道或者应当知道,或者得到国务院相关行政主管部门通知,其拟出口的物项和技术存在被用于大规模杀伤性武器及其运载工具风险的,无论该物项和技术是否列入《管理目录》,都应当申请出口许可,并按照本办法办理两用物项和技术出口许可证。

Article 8 In accordance with the provisions in relevant administrative regulations, where the exporter knows or should know or receives notices from relevant administrative authorities of the State Council that his/her items and technologies to be exported might be used for weapons of mass destruction and their related means of delivery, an export license shall be applied for towards the items and technologies concerned, whether included in the Controlling List or not, and an export license for dual - use items and technologies shall be handled in accordance with these Measures.

出口经营者在出口过程中,如发现拟出口的物项和

In case that the exporter finds that his/her items and technologies to be

技术存在被用于大规模杀伤性武器及其运载工具风险的，应及时向国务院相关行政主管部门报告，并积极配合采取措施中止合同的执行。

第九条 两用物项和技术的进出口经营者应当主动向海关出具两用物项和技术进出口许可证，进出口经营者未向海关出具两用物项和技术进出口许可证而产生的相关法律责任由进出口经营者自行承担。

海关有权对进出口经营者进口或者出口的商品是否属于两用物项和技术提出质疑，进出口经营者应按规定向相关行政主管部门申请进口或者出口许可，或者向商务主管部门申请办理不属于管制范围的相关证明。省级商务主管部门受理其申请，提出处理意见后报商务部审定。对进出口经营者未能出具两用物项和技术进口或者出口许可证或者商务部相关证明（格式见附件4）的，海关不予办理有关手续。

第十条 实施临时进出口管制的两用物项和技术的进出口许可证管理，适用本办法。

第二章 两用物项和技术进出口许可证的申领和签发

第十一条 进出口经营者获相关行政主管部门批准文件后，凭批准文件到所在地发证机构申领两用物项和技术进口或者出口许可证（在京的中央企业向许可证局申领），其中：

（一）核、核两用品、生物两用品、有关化学品、导弹相关物项、易制毒化学品和计算机进出口的批准文件为商务主管部门签发的两用物项和技术进口或者出口批复单。其中，核材料的出口凭国防科工委的批准文件办理相关手续。

外商投资企业进出口易制毒化学品凭《商务部外商投资企业易制毒化学品进口批复单》或《商务部外商投资企业易制毒化学品出口批复单》申领进出口许可证。

（二）监控化学品进出口的批准文件为国家履行禁止化学武器公约工作领导小组办公室签发的监控化学品进口或者出口核准单。监控化学品进出口经营者向许可证局申领两用物项和技术进出口许可证。

exported have the risk of being used in weapons of mass destruction and their related means of delivery, he/she shall timely report to relevant administrative authorities of the State Council and actively cooperate to adopt measures to cease the function of the contract.

Article 9 The exporter and importer shall take the initiative to present to the customs authorities his/her import or export license for dual - use items and technologies, and the legal liabilities arising from the exporter's failure to do so shall be assumed by the exporter himself/herself.

The customs authorities are entitle to questioning whether the imported or exported commodities of the importer and exporter belong to the category of dual - use items and technologies, and the importer and exporter shall, as stipulated, apply to relevant administrative authorities in charge of an import or export license, or apply to the commerce authorities in charge of the issuing of relevant attestation indicating that the aforesaid commodities do not belong to the controlled category; and the provincial competent departments of commerce shall accept the application and put forward treatment proposals, which then shall be submitted to the Ministry of Commerce for examination. The customs authorities shall refuse to handle relevant formalities for importer or exporter who fail to present his/her import or export license for dual - use items and technologies or relevant attestation (please refer to Annex IV. for its pattern) from the Ministry of Commerce.

Article 10 These Measures shall be applicable to the administration of the import and export license for temporally - controlled dual - use items and technologies.

Chapter II. The Application and Issuance of the Import and Export License for Dual - use Items and Technologies

Article 11 The importer or exporter shall, after acquiring the document of approval from relevant administrative authorities in charge, apply, upon this document concerned, to the local issuing authorities for the import or export license for dual - use items and technologies (the enterprise controlled by the central authorities in Beijing shall apply to the License Bureau for the license):

1) The document of approval for the import and export of nuclear, nuclear dual - use items, dual - use biological agents, related chemicals, missile - related items, precursors and chemicals used in production of narcotic drugs and psychotropic substances, and computers shall be the approval sheet for the import or export of dual - use items and technologies issued by the commerce authorities in charge, hereinto, the handling of relevant formalities for the export of nuclear materials shall be based upon the document of approval from the Commission of Science, Technology and Industry for National Defense.

The application of the foreign - funded enterprise for the import or export license shall be based upon the Approval Sheet of the Ministry of Commerce for the Foreign - funded Enterprise on the Import/Export of Precursors and Chemicals used in Production of Narcotic Drugs and Psychotropic Substances.

2) The document of approval for the import/export of controlled chemicals shall be the approval sheet for the import/export of controlled chemicals issued by the State Leading Group Office for the Implementation of the Convention on the Banning of Chemical Weapons, and the importer/export-

er of controlled chemicals shall apply to the License Bureau for the import/export license for dual - use items and technologies.

第十二条 通过对外交流、交换、合作、赠送、援助、服务等形式出口两用物项和技术的，视为正常出口，出口经营者应按规定申请出口许可，并按本办法办理两用物项和技术出口许可证。

Article 12 The export of dual - use items and technologies in the forms of international communication, exchange, cooperation, donation, assistance, service etc. shall be regarded as normal export, and the exporter shall, as stipulated, apply for the export license, and an export license for dual - use items and technologies shall be handled in accordance with these Measures.

第十三条 两用物项和技术进出口许可证实行网上申领。申领两用物项和技术进出口许可证时应提交下列文件：

Article 13 The application of the import/export license for dual - use items and technologies may be advanced through the Internet, and when import/export license for dual - use items and technologies is applied for, these documents as follows shall be submitted:

（一）本办法第十一条规定的有关批准文件。

1) Relevant document of approval as stipulated in Article 6. of these Measures; and

（二）进出口经营者公函（介绍信）原件、进出口经营者领证人员的有效身份证明以及网上报送的两用物项和技术进出口许可证申领表。

2) The original copy of the official letter (letter of introduction) of the importer/exporter, the effective identity certificate of the receiver of the importer/exporter, and the application form for the import/export license for dual - use items and technologies submitted through the Internet.

如因异地申领等特殊情况，需要委托他人申领两用物项和技术进出口许可证的，被委托人应提供进出口经营者出具的委托公函（其中应注明委托理由和被委托人身份）原件和被委托人的有效身份证明。

With regard to such special circumstances as that the applicant/receiver is of different locality from the issuing authorities, etc., as result of which, other persons need to be entrusted to apply/receive the import/export license for dual - use items and technologies, the entrustee shall submit the original copy of the official letter of entrust (thereinto the reason for entrust and the identity of the entrustee shall be specified) issued by the importer/exporter and the effective identity certificate of the entrustee.

第十四条 发证机构收到相关行政主管部门批准文件（含电子文本、数据）和相关材料并经核对无误后，应在3个工作日内签发两用物项和技术进口或者出口许可证。

Article 14 The issuing authorities, after receiving the document of approval (including electronic text and data) and relevant documents issued by relevant administrative authorities in charge and checking for faults, issue the import/export license for dual - use items and technologies within 3 work days.

第十五条 两用物项和技术进口许可证实行"非一批一证"制和"一证一关"制，同时在两用物项和技术进口许可证备注栏内打印"非一批一证"字样。

Article 15 The import license for dual - use items and technologies shall be subject to the mechanisms of "one license, more uses" and "one license to one customs", and such words as "not used for once only" shall, at the same time, be printed in the remark column of the import/export license for dual - use items and technologies.

两用物项和技术出口许可证实行"一批一证"制和"一证一关"制。同一合同项下的同一商品如需分批办理出口许可证，出口经营者应在申领时提供相关行政主管部门签发的相应份数的两用物项和技术出口批准文件。同一次申领分批量最多不超过十二批。

The export license for dual - use items and technologies shall be subject to the mechanisms of "one license, one use" and 'one license to one customs". In case that the export license for the same commodity subject to the same contract needs to be handled lot by lot, the exporter shall, upon application, submit documents of approval of corresponding quantity for the export of dual - use items and technologies issued by relevant administrative authorities in charge. And the number of lots for the same turn of application shall not exceed 12 at most.

"非一批一证"制是指每证在有效期内可多次报关使用，但最多不超过十二次，由海关在许可证背面"海关验放签注栏"内逐批核减数量；"一批一证"制是指每证只能报关使用一次；"一证一关"制是指每证只能在一个海关报关使用。

The mechanism of "one license, more uses" refers to that such license may be used for more than once but less than twelve times within its term of validity and that the customs authorities shall sign on each imported volume of goods on the column of "Customs Clearance Remark" at the back of such license; the mechanism of "one license, one use" refers to that such license may only be used once upon declaration; and the mechanism of "one license to one customs" refers to that such license may only be used for declaration upon one customs.

第十六条 两用物项和技术进出口许可证一式四

Article 16 The import/export license for dual - use items and tech-

联。第一联为办理海关手续联;第二联为海关留存核对联;第三联为银行办理结汇联;第四联为发证机构留存联。

nologies is of four copies in duplicate, among which, the first copy is used for the customs authorities to handle formalities, the second copy for the customs authorities to keep record and check, the third copy for the bank to handle settlement of exchange, and the fourth copy for the issuing authorities to keep record.

第十七条 进出口经营者在申领两用物项和技术进出口许可证时,应如实申报,不得弄虚作假,严禁以假合同、假文件等欺骗或其他不正当手段获取两用物项和技术进出口许可证。

Article 17 The importer/exporter, when applying for the import/export license for dual - use items and technologies, shall act according to the facts and practice truthfully, and such fraudulent and illicit means as using counterfeit contracts and documents are strictly prohibited in obtaining the import/export license for dual - use items and technologies.

第三章 特殊情况的处理

Chapter Ⅲ. Treatment of Special Cases

第十八条 "一批一证"制的大宗、散装的两用物项在报关时溢装数量不得超过两用物项和技术出口许可证所列出口数量的5%。"非一批一证"制的大宗、散装两用物项,每批进口时,按其实际进口数量进行核扣,最后一批进口物项报关时,其溢装数量按该两用物项和技术进口许可证实际剩余数量并在规定的溢装上限5%内计算。

Article 18 The exceeded volume of the large and/or bulk dual - use items subject to the mechanism of "one license, one use", upon customs declaration, shall not be above 5% of the given volume in the export license for dual - use items and technologies. With regard to the large and/or bulk dual - use items subject to the mechanism of "one license, more uses", each actual import volume of them shall be deducted from the total licensed volume, and when the last import volume under the same license undergoing customs declaration, the exceeded amount shall be calculated according to the actual remaining licensed volume, which shall be within 5% of the given upper limit for exceeded volume.

第十九条 赴境外参加或举办展览会运出境外的展品,参展单位(出口经营者)应凭出境经济贸易展览会审批部门批准办展的文件,按规定申请两用物项和技术出口许可,并按本办法办理两用物项和技术出口许可证。

Article 19 With regard to the items on display for the exhibitions in the areas outside the territory of the People's Republic of China, the exporter shall, upon the document of approval issued by the examination and approval authorities in charge of economic and trade exhibitions in the areas outside the territory of the People's Republic of China, apply, as stipulated, for the export license for dual - use items and technologies, and such license shall be handled in accordance with these Measures.

对于非卖展品,应在两用物项和技术出口许可证备注栏内注明"非卖展品"字样。参展单位应在展览会结束后六个月内,将非卖展品如数运回境内,由海关凭有关出境时的单证予以核销。在特殊情况下,可向海关申请延期,但延期最长不得超过六个月。

With regard to the not - for - sale items on display, such words as "not - for - sale items on display" shall be specified in the remark column of the export license for dual - use items and technologies. And the exporter shall, within 6 months as of the end of the exhibitions, transport exactly the not - for - sale items on display concerned into the territory of the People's Republic of China, and the customs authorities shall verify and cancel these items concerned upon the export documents. Under special circumstances, a deferment may be applied for to the customs authorities, and such deferment shall not be above 6 months at most.

第二十条 运出境外的两用物项和技术的货样或实验用样品,视为正常出口,出口经营者应按规定申请两用物项和技术出口许可,并按本办法办理两用物项和技术出口许可证。

Article 20 Sample goods or experimental samples belonging to the category of dual - use items and technologies to be transported out of the territory the People's Republic of China shall be regarded as normal export, and the exporter shall apply, as stipulated, for the export license for dual - use items and technologies, and such license shall be handled in accordance with these Measures.

第二十一条 进出境人员随身携带药品类易制毒化学品药品制剂和高锰酸钾的,按照《易制毒化学品管理条例》中的规定执行,并接受海关监管。

Article 21 The precursors and chemicals used in production of narcotic drugs and psychotropic substances and potassium permanganate carried about by the cross border persons shall be subject to the provisions in the Regulations of the People's Republic of China on the Administration of Precursors and Chemicals used in Production of Narcotic Drugs and Psychotropic Substances, accepting supervision and control from the customs authorities.

第二十二条 对于民用航空零部件等两用物项和技

Article 22 With regard to the administration of such specially - su-

术以特定海关监管方式出口的管理另有规定的，依照其规定。

第二十三条 凡两用物项和技术出口涉及国营贸易管理和出口配额管理商品的，出口经营者须具备相应的资格条件。

第四章 监督检查

第二十四条 两用物项和技术进出口许可证仅限于申领许可证的进出口经营者使用。两用物项和技术进出口许可证不得买卖、转让、涂改、伪造和变造。

第二十五条 两用物项和技术进出口许可证应在批准的有效期内使用，逾期自动失效，海关不予验放。

第二十六条 两用物项和技术进出口许可证有效期一般不超过一年。

两用物项和技术进出口许可证跨年度使用时，在有效期内只能使用到次年3月31日，逾期发证机构将根据原许可证有效期换发许可证。

第二十七条 两用物项和技术进出口许可证一经签发，任何单位和个人不得更改证面内容。

如需对证面内容进行更改，进出口经营者应当在许可证有效期内向相关行政主管部门重新申请进出口许可，并凭原许可证和新的批准文件向发证机构申领两用物项和技术进出口许可证。

第二十八条 两用物项和技术进口许可证证面的进口商、收货人应分别与海关进口货物报关单的经营单位、收货单位相一致；两用物项和技术出口许可证证面的出口商、发货人应分别与海关出口货物报关单的经营单位、发货单位相一致。

第二十九条 已领取的两用物项和技术进出口许可证发生遗失的，进出口经营者应当立即向相关行政主管部门和原发证机构及许可证证面注明的口岸地海关书面报告，并在全国性经济类报刊登载“遗失声明”。发证机构凭遗失声明，并核实该证确未通关后，可注销该许可证，并依据原许可证内容签发新证。

第三十条 进出口经营者应妥善保存两用物项和技术进出口的文件和有关资料五年，以备相关行政主管部门检查。

第三十一条 任何单位和个人均可向商务部或海关

pervised exported dual - use items and technologies as the parts and components for civil aviation etc, other provisions shall prevail if existing.

Article 23 Relevant prerequisites shall be necessary for the exporter dealing with such dual - use items and technologies as involved in the state - owned trade management and the commodities subject to export quota.

Chapter Ⅳ. Supervision and Inspection

Article 24. The import/ export license for dual - use items and technologies shall be exclusively used by the applicant of such license. No import/ export license for dual - use items and technologies may be sold, transferred, altered, forged or changed.

Article 25 The import/ export license for dual - use items and technologies shall be used within the approved term of validity, and shall be automatically invalidated when the term of validity expires, and no clearance may be granted by the customs authorities.

Article 26 The term of validity of no import/export license for dual - use items and technologies may, in general, exceed 1 year.

The import/ export license for dual - use items and technologies may be used in different years but with a term of validity to March 31 of the next year; and a license, if the term of validity expires, may be reissued by the issuing authorities in accordance with the term of validity of the former license.

Article 27 Once an import/export license for dual - use items and technologies is issued, no unit or individual may alter the contents of such license.

Where there is necessity to alter the contents of such license, the importer/exporter shall, within the term of validity of such license, reapply to relevant administrative authorities in charge for the permit of import/export, and apply, upon the former license and the new document of approval, to the issuing authorities for the import/export license for dual - use items and technologies.

Article 28 The importer and consignee as specified in the import license for dual - use items and technologies shall be consistent with the dealing unit and consignee unit specified in the customs declaration form for imported goods; and the exporter and consignor as specified in the export license for dual - use items and technologies shall be consistent with the dealing unit and consignor unit specified in the customs declaration form for exported goods,

Article 29 In case that such an import/export license for dual - use items and technologies as has been received is lost, the importer/exporter shall timely report in written form to relevant administrative authorities in charge, to the issuing authorities of the lost license and to the customs authorities at such port as specified in the lost license, and publish in the national economic newspapers and periodicals a “lost property notice”, upon which, the issuing authorities shall cancel this lost license after ascertaining that it has not been used in customs clearance, and reissue a new license in accordance with the contents of the former license.

Article 30 The importer/exporter shall well keep the documents for the import/export of dual - use items and technologies and relevant data for five years, ready for the inspection of relevant administrative authorities in charge.

Article 31 Any unit or individual shall be encouraged to report to the

举报进出口经营者违反国家有关法律、行政法规和本办法规定的行为。商务部和海关应为举报者保密，并依法对违规行为予以查处。对查证属实的，主管机关按有关规定可给予举报者奖励。

Ministry of Commerce and the customs authorities about the importer/exporter's acts in violation of the provisions in relevant national laws, regulations and these Measures. The Ministry of Commerce and the customs authorities shall keep secret for the reporters, and investigate in and prosecute these acts possibly in violation of laws and regulations; if checked and found to be true, the authorities in charge may, as stipulated, grant reward to the reporters.

第三十二条 发证机构应及时传送发证数据，保证进出口经营者顺利报关和海关核查；对海关反馈的核查数据应认真核对，定时检查两用物项和技术进出口许可证的使用情况并找出存在的问题。许可证局应当每季度将核对后的海关反馈核查数据报商务部。

Article32 The issuing authorities shall timely transmit the license - issuing data so as to guarantee the importer/exporter's smooth customs declaration and the examination of the customs authorities; the examination data feedback of the customs authorities shall be earnestly treated, and a periodical inspection shall be made on the utilization of the import/export license for dual - use items and technologies so as to find out the existing problems. The License Bureau shall quarterly submit to the Ministry of Commerce the checked examination data feed backed by the customs authorities.

第三十三条 各发证机构不得越权或者超范围发放两用物项和技术进出口许可证。越权或者超范围发放的两用物项和技术进出口许可证无效。

对于前款所涉进出口许可证，一经查实，商务部予以吊销。对海关在实际监管或者案件处理过程中发现的涉及上述许可证的问题，发证机构应当给予明确回复。

Article 33 No issuing authorities may, exceeding or beyond their powers, issue the import/export license for dual - use items and technologies, and such license issued in such ways shall be invalid.

The Ministry of Commerce shall revoke such aforesaid license, once detected. And the issuing authorities shall give clear replies to the problems concerning the aforesaid license discovered by the customs authorities during their daily supervision and control or their case treatment.

第三十四条 商务部授权许可证局对各发证机构进行检查。检查的内容为发证机构执行本办法的情况，重点是检查是否有越权或者超发证范围违章发证以及其他违反本办法的问题。检查的方式，实行各发证机构定期或者不定期自查与许可证局抽查相结合的办法。

Article 34 Authorized by the Ministry of Commerce, the License Bureau shall inspect the issuing authorities. The inspection shall include the implementation of these Measures by the issuing authorities, and stress shall be put on the inspection of such problems as the possible illicit license - issuing of the issuing authorities by exceeding beyond their powers and other violations of these Measures. The inspection mode shall be a combination of the periodically or unpatriotically self - inspection by the issuing authorities themselves and the selective inspection by the License Bureau.

许可证局应当将检查的情况向商务部报告。

The License Bureau shall submit the results of inspection to the Ministry of Commerce.

第五章 法律责任

Chapter V. Legal Liabilities

第三十五条 未经许可，或者超出许可范围进出口两用物项和技术的，依照有关法律、行政法规处罚；构成犯罪的，依法追究刑事责任。

Article 35 Anyone who imports/exports dual - use items and technologies without approval or beyond the licensed limit shall be punished in accordance with relevant laws and administrative regulations, and if a crime is constituted, criminal responsibilities shall be investigated according to law.

第三十六条 违反本办法规定，走私两用物项和技术的，由海关依照《中华人民共和国海关法》、《中华人民共和国海关行政处罚实施条例》的有关规定给予行政处罚；构成犯罪的，依法追究刑事责任。

Article 36 Anyone who smuggles dual - use items and technologies in violation of the provisions in these Measures shall be granted administrative penalties by the customs authorities in accordance with the Customs Law of the People's Republic of China and the Implementation Regulations of the People's Republic of China on Customs Administrative Penalties, and if a crime is constituted, criminal responsibilities shall be investigated according to law.

第三十七条 伪造、变造或者买卖两用物项和技术进出口许可证的，依照刑法关于非法经营罪或者伪造、变造、买卖国家机关公文、证件、印章罪的规定，依法追究刑事责任；尚不够刑事处罚的，依照《中华人民共和国海关法》及有关法律、行政法规的规定给予行政处罚。

Article37 Anyone who forges, alters or trades an import/export license for dual - use items and technologies shall be investigated for criminal liabilities according to law in accordance with the provisions in the Criminal Code on the crimes of illegal business, or of forging, altering or trading the documents, certificates and seals of the state organs, and if the circum-

以欺骗或者其他不正当手段获取两用物项和技术进出口许可证的，商务部依法吊销其许可证，并可给予警告，或处三万元以下罚款。

第三十八条 对违反第十九条规定，未将属于两用物项和技术出口许可证管理的非卖展品按期如数运回由海关核销的，由海关按有关规定处理，并将有关情况通知商务部和出境经济贸易展览会审批机构。商务部可给予该组展单位和参展单位警告，或对组展单位处一万元以下罚款。

第三十九条 依据《中华人民共和国对外贸易法》，商务部可自第三十五条至三十八条规定的行政处罚决定生效之日起或者刑事处罚判决生效之日起一年以上三年以下的期限内，禁止违法行为人从事有关的对外贸易经营活动。

第四十条 对违反本办法第三十三条，越权或者超范围发证的发证机构，商务部可暂停或者取消对其发证委托。

第四十一条 发证机构工作人员玩忽职守、徇私舞弊或者滥用职权，构成犯罪的，依法追究刑事责任；尚不构成犯罪的，应当调离工作岗位，并依法给予行政处分。

第六章 附 则

第四十二条 商务部对委托的发证机构进行调整时，自调整之日起，原发证机构不得再签发两用物项和技术进出口许可证。进出口经营者在发证机构调整前申领的两用物项和技术进出口许可证在有效期内继续有效。

第四十三条 本办法由商务部和海关总署按照各自职责负责解释。

第四十四条 本办法自二〇〇六年一月一日起施行。

《敏感物项和技术出口许可证暂行管理办法》（商务部、海关总署2003年第9号令），商务部、海关总署2003年第74号公告，《海关总署关于保税区内企业经营航空发动机修理等业务出境监管问题的通知》（署法发

stance is not serious enough to be subject to criminal penalties, an administrative penalty shall be given in accordance with the Customs Law of the People's Republic of China and the provisions in other relevant laws and administrative regulations.

Anyone who acquires the import/export license for dual - use items and technologies by fraudulence and other illicit means shall be revoked of his/her license according to law by the Ministry of Commerce, and be administered a warning, or be imposed a fine of less than RMB 30,000 Yuan.

Article 38 Anyone who, in violation of the provisions in Article 19, fails to transport back on schedule and exactly the non - for - sale items on display subject to the administration of the export license for dual - use items and technologies and to render them for verification and cancellation by the customs authorities, shall, in accordance with relevant provisions, be disposed by the customs authorities, who then shall report relevant situations to the Ministry of Commerce and the examination and approval authorities in charge of economic and trade exhibitions in the areas outside the territory of the People's Republic of China. And the exporter concerned shall be administered a warning by the Ministry of Commerce or be imposed a fine of less than RMB 10,000 Yuan.

Article 39 In accordance with the Foreign Trade Law of the People's Republic of China, the Ministry of Commerce may, within the time limit of more than 1 year and less than 3 years as of the date of entry into force of the administrative penalty decision in accordance with the provisions in from Article 35 through Article 38. or of the criminal penalty verdict, forbid the violator from engaging in relevant business activities related to foreign trade.

Article 40 The Ministry of Commerce may suspend or cancel the license - issuing commission of issuing authorities who violate Article 33 of these Measures by issuing license exceeding their powers.

Article 41 The employees of the issuing authorities, who commit such activities as neglecting their duties, engaging in malpractice for personal gain, or abusing their power, which constitute crimes, shall be investigated for criminal responsibilities according to law; and if crimes are not constituted, they shall be deposed and be given administrative punishment according to law.

Chapter VI. Supplementary Provisions

Article 42 Where the Ministry of Commerce makes adjustments on the entrusted issuing authorities, the former issuing authorities, as of the date of adjustment, shall no longer issue the import/export license for dual - use items and technologies. And such import/export license for dual - use items and technologies as the importer/exporter has received before the date of adjustment shall still be valid during its term of validity.

Article 43 The Ministry of Commerce and the General Administration of Customs are responsible for the interpretation of these Measures in accordance within their respective duties.

Article44 These Measures shall come into force as of the date of January 1, 2006.

And Interim Measures for the Administration of Export License for Sensitive Items and Technologies (Order No. 9 of the Ministry of Commerce and the General Administration of Customs in 2003, Announcement No. 74 of the Ministry of Commerce and the General Administration of Customs in

〔2004〕235号),《海关总署办公厅 外经贸部办公厅关于敏感物项和技术出口证件海关验放问题的通知》(署办发〔2002〕89号),《政法司、监管司关于明确敏感物项和技术出口许可证海关监管问题的通知》(政法函〔2004〕2号)同时废止。

2003), Circular of the General Administration of Customs on the Issue concerning the Exit Supervision and Control of Enterprises Dealing such Services as Aviation Engine Repair etc. in Bonded Zones (Shu Fa Fa [2004] No. 235), Circular of the General Offices of the General Administration of Customs and the Ministry of Foreign Trade and Economic Cooperation on the Issue concerning the Examination and Clearance of Export License for Sensitive Items and Technologies by the Customs Authorities (Shu Ban Fa [2002] No. 89) and Circular of the Department of Politics and Law and the Department of Supervision and Control on the Issue concerning Specifying the Supervision and Control of the Customs Authorities on Export License for Sensitive Items and Technologies (Zheng Fa Han [2004] No. 2) shall be annulled as of the same date.

《货物出口许可证管理办法》(商务部2004年27号令)和《货物进口许可证管理办法》(商务部2004年28号令)与本办法不一致的,以本办法为准

And these Measures shall prevail in case that any conflict occurs between these Measures and Measures for the Administration of License for the Export of Goods (Order No. 27 of the Ministry of Commerce) and Measures for the Administration of License for the Import of Goods (Order No. 28 of the Ministry of Commerce).

附件1:两用物项和技术进出口许可证管理目录(略)

Annexes: 1. Controlling List of the Import and Export License for Dual - use Items and Technologies (omitted)

附件2:

两用物项和技术进出口许可证发证机构名单

1. 配额许可证事务局
2. 北京市商务局
3. 天津市商务委员会
4. 河北省商务厅
5. 山西省商务厅
6. 内蒙古自治区商务厅
7. 辽宁省对外贸易经济合作厅
8. 吉林省商务厅
9. 黑龙江省商务厅
10. 上海市对外经济贸易委员会
11. 江苏省对外贸易经济合作厅
12. 浙江省对外贸易经济合作厅
13. 安徽省商务厅
14. 福建省对外贸易经济合作厅
15. 江西省对外贸易经济合作厅
16. 山东省对外贸易经济合作厅
17. 河南省商务厅
18. 湖北省商务厅
19. 湖南省商务厅
20. 广东省对外贸易经济合作厅
21. 广西壮族自治区商务厅
22. 海南省商务厅
23. 重庆市对外贸易经济委员会
24. 四川省商务厅
25. 贵州省商务厅
26. 云南省商务厅
27. 西藏自治区商务厅
28. 陕西省商务厅
29. 甘肃省商务厅
30. 青海省商务厅

Annexes: 2. Name List of the Authorities Responsible for the Issuance of the Import and Export License for

Dual - use Items and Technologies

1. Quota Licensing Bureau
2. Beijing Municipal Bureau of Commerce
3. Tianjin Commission of Commerce
4. Hepei Provincial Department of Commerce
5. Shanxi Provincial Department of Commerce
6. Department of Commerce of Inner Mongolia Autonomous Region
7. Liaoning Foreign Economic Relations and Trade Commission
8. Jilin Provincial Department of Commerce
9. Heilongjiang Provincial Department of Commerce
10. Shanghai Foreign Economic Relations and Trade Commission
11. Jiangsu Foreign Economic Relations and Trade Commission
12. Zhejiang Foreign Economic Relations and Trade Commission
13. Anhui Provincial Department of Commerce
14. Fujian Foreign Economic Relations and Trade Commission
15. Jiangxi Foreign Economic Relations and Trade Commission
16. Shandong Foreign Economic Relations and Trade Commission
17. Henan Provincial Department of Commerce
18. Hubei Provincial Department of Commerce
19. Hunan Provincial Department of Commerce
20. Guangdong Foreign Economic Relations and Trade Commission
21. Department of Commerce of Guangxi Zhuang Autonomous Region
22. Hainan Provincial Department of Commerce
23. Chongqing Foreign Economic Relations and Trade Commission
24. Sichuan Provincial Department of Commerce
25. Guizhou Provincial Department of Commerce
26. Yunan Provincial Department of Commerce
27. Department of Commerce of Tibet Autonomous Region
28. Shanxi Provincial Department of Commerce
29. Gansu Provincial Department of Commerce
30. Qinghai Provincial Department of Commerce

31. 宁夏回族自治区商务厅
32. 新疆维吾尔自治区对外贸易经济合作厅
33. 新疆生产建设兵团商务局

纺织品出口管理办法(暂行)

商务部令2006年第21号

《纺织品出口管理办法》(暂行)已经商务部审议通过,并商海关总署、国家质检总局同意,现予发布,自发布之日起施行。2006年度纺织品临时出口许可数量仍按《纺织品出口临时管理办法》(商务部令2005年第20号)执行。《纺织品出口临时管理办法》(商务部令2005年第20号)自2007年1月1日起废止。

部长:薄熙来

二OO六年九月十八日

纺织品出口管理办法(暂行)

第一条 为规范纺织品出口经营秩序,根据《中华人民共和国对外贸易法》和《中华人民共和国行政许可法》,制定本办法。

第二条 商务部负责全国纺织品出口管理工作,并会同海关总署和质检总局制定并调整《纺织品出口临时管理商品目录》(以下简称《管理商品目录》)。

《管理商品目录》应以公告形式发布,内容包括涉及的产品类别及其税则号、涉及的国家或者地区、实施时间范围和许可总量等。

第三条 商务部授权各省、自治区、直辖市、计划单列市、新疆生产建设兵团及哈尔滨、长春、沈阳、南京、武汉、成都、广州、西安市商务主管部门(以下简称地方商务主管部门)负责本地区纺织品临时出口许可管理工作。

质检总局根据商务部的建议,临时授权上述部门负责《管理商品目录》所列纺织品的原产地证书签发工作。

31. Provincial Department of Commerce of Ningxia Autonomous Region
32. Foreign Economic Relations and Trade Commission of Xinjiang Uigur Autonomous Region
33. Bureau of Commerce of Xinjiang Production and Construction Troop

PROVISIONS ON THE ADMINISTRATION OF STRATION OF THE EXPORT OF CHEMICALS

Order No. 21, 2006, Ministry of Commerce

Adopted by the Ministry of Commerce and consented by the General Administration of the Customs and the General Administration of Quality Supervision and Inspection and Quarantine of the People' s Republic of China, the Interim Measures for the Administration of the Export of Textile Products is now promulgated, and shall be implemented since the date of promulgation. The interim export quota of 2006 is still subject to The Interim Measures for the Administration of the Export of Textile Products (Order No. 20 of the Ministry of Commerce, 2005), which shall be repealed since Jan 1, 2007.

Minister of Ministry of Commerce: Bo Xilai

Sept. 18, 2006

The Interim Measures for the Administration of the Export of Textile Products

Article 1 For the purpose of standardizing the business order of export and operation of textile products, the Measures herein are hereby formulated in accordance with the Foreign Trade Law of the People' s Republic of China and the Administrative License Law of the People' s Republic of China.

Article 2 The Ministry of Commerce shall be responsible for administration of the export of national textiles and, in the cooperation with the General Administration of Customs and the General Administration of Quality Supervision, Inspection and Quarantine, formulate and adjust the Catalogue of Commodities Subject to Interim Administration of the Export of Textile Products (hereinafter referred to as "the Catalogue of Commodities Subject to Administration").

The Catalogue of Commodities Subject to Administration shall be released by means of announcements, and shall cover such contents as the category, the number of tax regulations, and the concerning countries or regions, the time limit for the implementation, and the overall licensed quantity of the products hereof.

Article 3 The Ministry of Commerce shall authorize the authority in charge of commerce of all provinces, autonomous regions, municipalities directly under the Central Government, cities separate state planning, Xinjiang Production and Construction Corps, Harbin, Changchun, Shenyang, Nanjing, Wuhan, Chengdu, Guangzhou, and Xi' an (hereinafter referred to as "the local authorities in charge of commerce") to be responsible for administrating the interim export license of textile products).

The General Administration of Quality Supervision, Inspection and Quarantine shall, by referring to the advice of the Ministry of Commerce, provisionally authorize the aforesaid authorities to be responsible for issuing the certificate of the place of origin of the textile products listed in the Catalogue of Commodities Subject to Administration.

第四条 本办法出口国指最终目的国(地区),加工贸易出口指实际报关出口国(地区)。有关转口贸易管理,不适用本办法。

Article 4 The term "exporting countries" as mentioned herein refers to the final country (or region) of destination, while in the case of export of processing trade, refers to the exporting country (or region) where the customs declaration is actually made. These Measures are applicable to the administration of transit trade.

第五条 本办法适用于一般贸易、易货贸易、来料加工装配贸易、补偿贸易、进料加工、保税工厂和其他贸易方式的纺织品出口许可管理。

从境内区外进入保税区、出口加工区等海关特殊监管区域、保税场所且属于《管理商品目录》所列的纺织品,海关不验核许可证,待上述货物实际离境申报时,按照有关规定,对出口到实行纺织品临时出口管理的国家(地区)的,海关凭许可证办理验放手续。

《管理商品目录》所列的纺织品经出口监管仓库(出口配送型)出口的,海关在入仓环节验核许可证,并在许可证规定的有效期内(离境)出口至《管理商品目录》指定的国家(地区),不得留在境内。

Article 5 The Measures herein shall be applicable to the license administration of general trade, barter trade, processing and assembling trade, bonded factory and other means of textile products export.

Where the textile products enter such special supervision zones of customs and bonded place as bonded area and export processing zone from the outside zone within the territory of the People's Republic of China and fall under the textile products listed in the Catalogue of Commodities Subject to Supervision, the customs shall not examine and check the license hereof.

Where the textile products listed in the Catalogue of Commodities Subject to Administration are to be exported via the warehouses under export supervision (export distribution warehouses), the customs shall check the license when the products are entered in the warehouse and within the time limit (departure from the territory of the People's Republic of China) as specified in the license, the products shall be exported to the countries (regions) designated in the Catalogue of Commodities Subject to Administration and shall not be remained within the territory of the People's Republic of China.

第六条 《管理商品目录》所列的纺织品,实行临时出口管理制度。商务部授权许可证事务局统一管理、指导各地商务主管部门的《纺织品临时出口许可证》(以下简称许可证)发证工作。发证机构名单、许可证样式和专用章由商务部、海关总署、质检总局另行公布。

Article 6 The textile products listed in the Catalogue of Commodities Subject to Administration shall be subject to interim export administration. The Ministry of Commerce shall authorize the Quota & License Administrative Bureau to be responsible for consolidating administration and the guidance of the License of Interim Export of Textile Products (hereinafter referred to as "the License") of the local authorities in charge of commerce. The name list of the certificate authority, the form of the license and the stamp for special use shall be otherwise promulgated by the Ministry of Commerce, the General Administration of Customs, and the General Administration of Quality Supervision, Inspection and Quarantine.

第七条 对外贸易经营者(以下简称"经营者")在出口《管理商品目录》所列的纺织品前,应当向当地商务主管部门办理临时出口许可审批手续,并申领许可证,凭许可证向海关办理报关验放手续。

Article 7 The foreign trade operators (hereinafter referred to as "the operators") shall, prior to the export of the textile products listed in the Catalogue of Commodities Subject to Supervision, handle the examination and approval procedures of interim export license and withdraw the license in the local authorities in charge of commerce and handle the procedures of customs declaration, examination and clearance formalities upon the strength of the license.

第八条 出现下列情形之一的商品将列入《管理商品目录》。

(一)有关国家或地区对我实行限制的纺织产品;

(二)双边协议规定需要临时进行数量管理的纺织产品。

Article 8 The commodities shall be listed in the Catalogue of Commodities Subject to Supervision in any of the following circumstances.

(1) Textiles subject to restrictions imposed against China by the relevant countries or regions;

(2) Textile subject to temporary quantitative control under bilateral agreements.

第九条 《管理商品目录》所列纺织品的临时出口许可数量,通过业绩分配、协议招标等方式配置到各经营者。具体类别和数量由商务部另行公布。

Article 9 The interim export licensed quantity of the textile products listed in the Catalogue of the Commodities Subject to Administration shall be allocated to all the operations through agreement bidding invitation or based on performance etc. The detailed types and quantity shall be otherwise promulgated by the Ministry of Commerce.

业绩分配按照本办法的规定执行。协议招标的具体

The performance - based distribution shall be implemented in accord-

规定，由商务部根据本办法另行公告。

如遇市场变化剧烈、出口许可数量使用率过低或出口秩序混乱等特殊情况，经纺织品出口行业商协会提议，商务部可采取本条第一款规定之外的临时性措施，以恢复正常的出口秩序。

第十条 经营者应按照国家有关劳动、安全和环保等法律法规的规定从事经营活动。

对经有关部门认定，未能依法履行劳动、安全和环保等义务的经营者，商务部可取消其按照本办法第九条获得的临时出口许可数量资格，并收回已获得的全部许可数量。

第十一条 业绩分配部分以相关商品出口实绩为依据，按照如下计算公式确定经营者海关出口实绩项下的临时出口许可可申请数量（以下简称可申请数量）。

$S = T\times(70\%\times Q1/M1 + 30\%\times Q2/M2)$

其中：

（一）S 为经营者可申请数量；

（二）T 为确定的全国临时出口许可总量；

（三）Q1 为经营者对设限国家（地区）出口实绩，Q2 为经营者（$Q1\neq0$）除设限国家（地区）之外的对全球的出口实绩；

（四）M1 为全国经营者对设限国家（地区）出口实绩，M2 为全国经营者（$Q1\neq0$）除设限国家（地区）之外的对全球的出口实绩；

（五）各类别商品的最低可申请数量由商务部另行公布。凡根据上述公式计算的可申请数量低于最低可申请数量的，经营者可申请数量为零；

（六）低于最低可申请数量的剩余数量按业绩优先的原则分完为止。

第十二条 商务部根据以下原则，确定经营者相关商品出口实绩：

（一）按照中国海关十位税则号项下的出口统计数据；

（二）统计时间范围为临时出口许可数量使用年度之前的12个月；

（三）一般贸易、加工贸易的出口实绩均按中国海关出口统计金额的100%计算；

ance with the Measures herein. The specific rules about agreement bidding invitation shall be otherwise announced by the Ministry of Commerce under the Measures herein.

Where such special situations occurs as volatile market fluctuation, excessively low use of export licensed quantity or chaotic business order of export, the Ministry of Commerce may, in accordance with the proposal of textile export industry, adopt temporary measures other than Article 1 to restore the normal export order.

Article 10 The "operator" shall conduct the operational activities in accordance with the relevant national labor, safety, and environmental protection laws and rules.

As for the "operators" confirmed by the relevant departments but fail to fulfill the obligations of labor, security and environmental protection, the Ministry of Commerce may abrogate the qualification the interim export licensed quantity herein obtained in accordance with Article 9 and withdraw all the licensed quantity.

Article 11 The performance-based distribution shall be based upon the actual export performance of the relevant commodities, and the quantity allowed for application for interim export license (hereinafter referred to as "the quantity allowed for application") under the export actual performance shall be determined in accordance with the following formula:

$S = T\times(70\%\times Q1/M1 + 30\%\times Q2/M2)$

Where

(1) S stands for the quantity allowed for application;

(2) T stands for the confirmed national total volume of temporary export licenses;

(3) Q1 stands for the export performance of an "operator" to a restricted country (region). Q2 stands for the export performance of an "operator" to all other countries and regions other than the restricted ones ($Q1\neq0$);

(4) M1 stands for the export performance of all "operators" of the country to the restricted countries (regions); M2 stands for the export performance of all "operators" to the whole world ($Q1\neq0$) other than the restricted countries (regions);

(5) The minimum quantity allowed for application of all types of commodities shall be otherwise promulgated by the Ministry of Commerce. Where the quantity allowed for application calculated in accordance with the aforesaid formula is lower than the minimum quantity allowed for application, the quantity allowed for application of the "operator" shall be zero;

(6) The surplus amount lower than the minimum amount shall be allocated completely in accordance with the principle of priority of performance.

Article 12 The Ministry of Commerce shall, in accordance with the following principles, determine the export performance of the relevant commodities:

(1) By reference to the statistical export data under the 10-digit tariff codes of China's customs;

(2) The statistical time range shall be 12 months prior to the implementation of interim licensed export quantity.

The export performance of general trade, processing trade shall be computed at a rate of 100% of the statistical export volumnof China's customs;

（四）西部地区企业的出口实绩按中国海关出口统计金额的150%计算，中部地区和东北老工业基地企业的出口实绩按中国海关出口统计金额的130%计算；

（五）拥有多家子公司、分公司或者控股公司的集团型企业，按照实际的经营者（按海关企业代码）数量进行统计，临时出口许可数量计入各经营者名下。

第十三条 商务部根据上述分配原则确定各经营者可申请的商品类别和数量，分批次以书面和电子形式下达至各地商务主管部门，并在商务部网站上公布。

第十四条 经营者应在商务部下达的可申领类别和数量范围内向地方商务主管部门提出许可数量申请。

第十五条 自可申请数量下达之日起的15天内，地方商务主管部门汇总本地区经营者的申请上报商务部并附电子数据。

在收到地方商务主管部门的申请报告以及电子数据后15天内，商务部确定并下达全国各经营者临时出口许可的分配数量。

第十六条 纺织品临时出口许可数量允许转让。转受让经营者可登陆纺织品临时出口许可数量转受让平台（http:\xk.ec.com.cn）直接操作，地区内转让也可由地方商务主管部门做技术处理。受让经营者必须在工商行政管理部门登记注册、在对外贸易主管部门备案登记并依法履行劳动、安全和环保等义务。

第十七条 纺织品临时出口许可证实行"一批一证"、"一关一证"，在公历年度内有效，有效期为6个月，逾期作废。

逾期未出口的，可以到原发证机构办理延期手续，最长延期不超过3个月。延期或更改许可证内容的，均应重新换发新证。

第十八条 获得临时出口许可数量的经营者在临时出口许可数量有效期内未能全部使用的，应于许可年度的9月30日前将剩余数量通过各地商务主管部门向商务部上交。

第十九条 经营者上交的、未申请和放弃的数量计入当年度纺织品临时出口许可剩余数量。剩余总量由商

(4) The export performance of the enterprises in western region of China shall be computed at a rate of 150% of the statistical export data of China's customs, the middle region and the enterprises in the northeast old industrial base shall be computed at a rate of 130% of the statistical export volume of Chinese customs;

(5) For the group enterprises with many subsidiaries and branches or holding company, their export performance shall be computed according to the actual trade "operator" (in light of the enterprises' customs code) and provisional export licensing belongs to each trader.

Article 13 The Ministry of Commerce shall, in accordance with the aforesaid distribution principle, determine the categories and amounts that can be applied for by various "operators" and notify the them to all local commerce administrative departments once and for all or by different batches in written and electronic form and publish it on the website of the Ministry of Commerce.

Article 14 The "operators" shall, within the limit of the categories and amounts that can be applied for specified by the Ministry of Commerce, file the license amount application to the local commerce administrative departments.

Article 15 The local authorities in charge of commerce shall, within 15 days from the day when the quantity allowed for application is made known to the local levels, collect the application as submitted by the "operators" within their respective jurisdiction and report them to the Ministry of Commerce with attachment of electronic data.

The Ministry of Commerce shall, within 15 days from the day when application reports from the local authorities in charge of commerce are received, determine and announce the distribution amount of interim export of each "operators".

Article 16 The licensed amount of interim export of textile products shall be allowed to be transferred. The transferor and the receiver may log on the website of the interim export licensed amount of textile products (http:\xk.ec.com.cn) and conduct the transaction directly, the transfer within the same region may be through the technical treatment of the regional authority in charge of commerce. The receiver shall register in the industrial and commercial administrative authority, record and register in the authority in charge of foreign trade and fulfill obligations of labor, safety, and environmental protection, etc.

Article 17 The temporary export licenses of textile product shall be subject to the system of "one license, one batch of products" and "one license, one customs clearance". The licenses herein shall be effective within a calendar year and the validity period shall be 6 months.

Where the textile products herein are not exported within the prescribed period of validity, the holders of temporary export licenses of textile products may go to the original license issuing authority for extension within at most three months. Where the license is delayed or altered, anew one shall replace the original one.

Article 18 Where the "operator" who has obtained the interim export license amount has not used up the interim export licensed quantity, the "operator" shall hand the remaining part over to the Ministry of Commerce via local authorities in charge of commerce.

Article 19 The quantities handed over by the "operators" and the quantities not applied for or relinquished shall be included into the remai-

务部按照第十一条的有关规定继续分配，并在不迟于许可年度结束前75天下达分配结果。

ning amount of interim export of textile products of that year. The remaining amount shall be continuously distributed by the Ministry of Commerce in accordance with Article 11, and the distribution results shall be made to the lower level no later than 75 days prior to the end of the licensing year.

第二十条 获得纺织品临时出口许可数量的经营者，在有效期内未使用量超过业绩分配量20%且小于等于30%并未按期上交的，商务部将在下一年度分配中按等比扣减。在有效期内未使用量超过业绩分配量30%并未按期上交的，商务部将在下一年度分配中按双倍扣减。

Article 20 Where an interim export license holder whose unused quantity exceeds 20% yet no more than 30% of the performance - based distribution within the period of validity, the Ministry of Commerce shall reduce its quantity in proportion to the unused quantity in the following year. Where the unused amount exceeds 30% of the performance - based distribution within the period of validity, the Ministry of Commerce shall reduce its distribution twice in proportion in the following year.

第二十一条 获得临时出口许可数量的经营者申领许可证时，应当如实填写《许可证申请表》，并加盖单位印章。网上申请的，应当如实填写相关电子表格并传送至相应的发证机构。

Article 21 The "operator" who has obtained the interim export license shall fill in the Application Form for License and affix the seal of the unit when applying for the license. Where the "operator" applies online, the "operator" shall faithfully fill in the relevant electronic form and submit it to the correspondent license issuing authority.

以书面形式或者通过网上申请的，经营者应当同时将相关出口合同复印件寄送至发证机构。

Where the "operator" files the application in written form or via the Internet, the "operator" shall deliver the copy of the relevant export contract to the license issuing authority at the same time.

第二十二条 各发证机构应在收到内容正确且形式完备的许可数量有效申请后，按照商务部授权的地方商务主管部门下达的临时出口许可数量批准文件和相关电子数据，在3个工作日内签发许可证。

Article 22 The license issuing authority shall, upon receipt of an effective licensing application with correct contents and complete forms, issue the license within three working days in accordance with the approved document of interim export quantity and the relevant electronic data distributed by the local authority in charge of commerce.

第二十三条 实行临时出口许可管理的商品，经营者在办理临时出口许可证后，应向质检总局授权的临时发证机构申领纺织品原产地证书。发证机构凭许可证签发纺织品原产地证书。

Article 23 As for the commodities subject to the interim export licensing administration, the "operator" shall, after obtaining the interim export license, apply for the certificate of place of origin for textile products from the interim certificate issuing authority authorized by the General Administration of Quality Supervision , Inspection and Quarantine. The certificate issuing authority shall, upon the strength of the license, issue the certificate of place of origin for textile products.

原产地证书与许可证的数量、金额等内容应完全一致。

The quantity and sum and other relevant contents as specified in the certificate of the place of origin shall be identical with those in license.

第二十四条 经营者凭加盖纺织品许可证专用章的许可证办理出口报关手续；在有关进口国（地区）凭商务部电子数据和书面许可证及主管发证机构出具的原产地证验放通关。

Article 24 The "operator" shall make the export declaration on the basis of the licenses stamped with the special seal for textiles license; the commodities shall be cleared upon the strength of the electronic data and written licenses from the Ministry of Commerce and the certificate of place of origin issued by competent issuing authorities.

第二十五条 海关在办理相关纺织品出口手续时，需验核加盖纺织品许可证专用章的许可证。对属法定检验出口的纺织品，海关还应凭检验检疫机构出具的《出境货物通关单》办理验放手续。

Article 25 When handling relevant textile export procedures, the Customs shall inspect and verify the licenses stamped with the special seal for textile licenses. As for the textile products subject to legitimate inspection, the Customs shall also handle the clearance procedures upon the strength of the Clearance Note of Entry Goods issued by the inspection and quarantine authorities.

商务部会同海关总署对许可证实施电子联网核查。有关电子核查机制及相关验核管理办法另行公布。

The Ministry of Commerce as well as the General Customs Administration shall verify the license online. The measures of electronic checking mechanism and the relevant inspection and verification shall be promulgated otherwise.

第二十六条 纺织品临时出口许可证不得伪造和变造。凡伪造、变造出口许可批准文件或出口许可证的，依照《中华人民共和国外贸法》、《中华人民共和国海关法》、《中华人民共和国货物进出口管理条例》及《货物出

Article 26 The interim export license of textile products shall not be forged and altered. Where the export license approval document or the export license are forged or altered, all parties involved in shall be punished in accordance with the relevant provisions of Foreign Trade Law of the Peo-

口许可证管理办法》的相关规定处罚。

ple's Republic of China, the Customs Law of the People's Republic of China, Regulations of the People's Republic of China on the Administration of Import and Export Commodities and Measures Governing Goods Subject to Export Licenses.

第二十七条 出口样品的,对于每批商品数量不超过50件(含50件、套、双、公斤或其它商品单位,不包括打、打双、打套、吨数量单位)的,可免领出口许可证;但属于进口国(地区)海关要求凭许可证放行的,经营者应在本企业可申请数量范围内向发证机构申领许可证。

Article 27 The exported sample products may be exempted from obtaining export licenses in cases where the quantity of each batch of exported commodities does not exceed 50 pieces (including 50 pieces, sets, pairs, kilograms or other commodity units, excluding dozens, dozens of pairs, dozens of sets, or tonage); where the products are subject to license administration by the customs authority of the importing country, the "operators" shall apply to the issuing institutions for licenses within the quantity permitted.

第二十八条 赴国(境)外参展或者举办展览会的展品、展卖品的出口,参照《货物出口许可证管理办法》相关规定办理;属于进口国(地区)海关要求凭许可证放行的,按照本办法相关规定办理。

Article 28 The export of articles for overseas exhibition and articles for sales shall be handled in accordance with the relevant provisions of the Measures for the Administration of Goods Subject to Export Licenses; where the goods are allowed for clearance based on license as required by the customs of the import country (region), it shall be handled in accordance with the Measures herein

第二十九条 经营者规避本办法的规定,将原产于中国的商品经第三国(地区)转口至《管理商品目录》规定的国家(地区)的,商务部将依法予以处罚,自相关行政处罚决定生效之日起一年内禁止该经营者从事所有与本办法相关的出口经营活动。

Article 29 Where the "operator" evades the Measures herein to transit the commodities produced in China to the countries (regions) prescribed in the Catalogue of Commodities subject to Administration, the Ministry of Commerce shall render the relevant punishment hereto, and prohibit the "operator" from being involved in the export operational activities within one year as of the date when the relevant administrative punishment comes into effect.

第三十条 除另有规定外,对许可证的签发、执法部门的调查、发证机构的核查,以及对违反本办法有关规定的发证机构和伪造、变造许可证的经营者的处罚,按照《货物出口许可证管理办法》的有关规定办理。

Article 30 The issuance of the licenses, the investigation by enforcement departments, the inspection by the license issuing authority as well as the punishment upon the certificate issuing authority in violation of the Measures herein and upon the "operators" who forge or alter the license shall be handled in accordance with the Measures for the Administration of the License of Exported Goods, unless otherwise prescribed.

第三十一条 通过外发加工方式在内地加工且原产地非中国内地的纺织品不适用本办法。

Article 31 The textiles processed within the territory of China by way of outward processing arrangements and with the place of origin outside the territory of China shall not be governed by Measures herein.

第三十二条 本办法由商务部负责解释。

Article 32 The Ministry of Commerce shall be responsible for interpreting the Measures herein.

第三十三条 本办法自发布之日起施行。

Article 33 The Measures herein shall come into effect since the date of its promulgation.

易制毒化学品进出口管理规定

商务部令2006年第7号

《易制毒化学品进出口管理规定》已经2006年5月17日商务部第5次部务会议审议通过,现予公布,自公布之日起30日后施行。

商务部部长 薄熙来
二〇〇六年九月二十一日

THE INTERIM MEASURES FOR THE ADMINI STRATION OF THE EXPORT OF TEXTILE PRODUCTS

Order of the Ministry of Commerce
of People's Republic of China(Order No. 7,2006)

Provisions on the Administration of Import and Export of Precursor Chemicals, which was adopted at the 5th ministerial conference of the Ministry of Commerce on May. 17, 2006, are hereby promulgated and shall put on effect in 30 days from now.

Minister of the Ministry of Commerce, Bo Xilai
Sept. 21, 2006

易制毒化学品进出口管理规定

第一章 总则

第一条 为加强易制毒化学品进出口管理,防止其流入非法制毒渠道,根据《中华人民共和国对外贸易法》和《易制毒化学品管理条例》等法律、行政法规,制定本规定。

第二条 本规定所称的易制毒化学品系指《易制毒化学品管理条例》附表所列可用于制毒的主要原料及化学配剂,目录见本规定附件。

第三条 国家对易制毒化学品进出口实行许可证管理制度。以任何方式进出口易制毒化学品均需申领许可证。

第四条 商务部负责全国易制毒化学品的进出口管理工作。国务院其他部门在各自职责范围内负责有关管理工作。

各省、自治区、直辖市及计划单列市商务主管部门(以下统称省级商务主管部门)负责本地区易制毒化学品进出口管理工作。同时接受商务部委托负责本地区易制毒化学品进出口许可初审及部分易制毒化学品进出口许可工作。

县级以上商务主管部门负责本地区易制毒化学品进出口监督检查工作。

第五条 通过对外交流、交换、合作、赠送、援助、服务等形式进出口易制毒化学品的,应按照本规定申请进(出)口许可证。

第六条 易制毒化学品进出口经营者(以下简称经营者)以加工贸易方式进出口易制毒化学品或加工制成品、副产品为易制毒化学品需内销的,应首先按照本办法规定取得相应的进(出)口许可,并凭进(出)口许可证办理相关手续。

第七条 混合物中含有易制毒化学品的,经营者应折算易制毒化学品数量后按照本规定申请进(出)口许可,含易制毒化学品的复方药品制剂除外。

第八条 易制毒化学品样品的进出口应按照本规定申请进(出)口许可。

第九条 易制毒化学品的过境、转运、通运应当按照本规定申请进(出)口许可。

第十条 易制毒化学品在境外与保税区、出口加工区等海关特殊监管区域、保税场所之间进出的,应当按照

Provisions on the Management of Import and Export of Precursor Chemicals

Chapter I General provisions

Article 1 Pursuant to stipulations in the Foreign Trade Law of the People's Republic of China, the Regulation on the Administration of Precursor Chemicals, and other relevant laws and administrative regulations, these provisions are hereby formulated to strengthen the administration of import and export of precursor chemicals and prevent them getting through the illegal drug making channel.

Article 2 Precursor chemicals in these provisions refer to main raw materials and chemicals that can be used for drug making listed in the Regulation on the Administration of Precursor Chemicals appendix. Catalogue is seen in Appendix.

Article 3 The State shall implement a license control system over the import and export of precursor chemicals. To import or export precursor chemicals in any form shall apply for the license.

Article 4 The Ministry of Commerce shall take charge of management of import and export of precursor chemicals throughout the country. Other departments of the State Council shall take charge of relevant administration within their administrative divisions.

The foreign trade and economic cooperation bureaus at the provincial, autonomous regional and municipal level and in cities separately listed in State budgets (hereinafter referred to as provincial bureaus) shall take charge of administration of import and export of precursor chemicals in their respective regions, and shall, commissioned by the Ministry of Commerce, take charge of the elementary examination and approval of license of import and export of precursor chemicals in their respective regions.

All the people's governments at the county level or above shall take charge of the supervision and inspection over import and export of precursor chemicals in their respective regions.

Article 5 Import and export of precursor chemicals through foreign communication, exchange, cooperation, transference, assistance, service, etc shall apply for the import (export) license according to these provisions.

Article 6 "operators" engaged in the import and export of precursor chemicals (hereinafter referred to as "operators") that import and export precursor chemicals through processing trade or processing the finished products and byproducts of precursor chemicals for domestic sales shall acquire corresponding license of import (export) first, based on which to handle relevant formalities according to these provisions.

Article 7 Provided that there are precursor chemicals in the mixtures, "operators" shall measure the amount of precursor chemicals and files applications of import (export) license, except for the compound medicine with precursor chemicals.

Article 8 To import and export precursor chemicals samples shall file application of import (export) license according to these provisions.

Article 9 Trans - boundary, transit transportation, passing - by transportation of precursor chemicals shall file application of import (export) license according to these provisions.

Article10 Precursor chemicals imported and exported between overseas and customs special supervised areas and tariff free sites such as bond-

本规定申请进(出)口许可证。

易制毒化学品在境内与保税区、出口加工区等海关特殊监管区域、保税场所之间进出的,或者在上述海关特殊监管区域、保税场所之间进出的,无须申请进(出)口许可证。

第十一条 经营者在进出口易制毒化学品时,应当如实向海关申报,提交进(出)口许可证,海关凭许可证办理通关验放手续。进口第一类中的药品类易制毒化学品,还应提交食品药品监督管理部门出具的进口药品通关单。

第十二条 进出境人员随身携带《易制毒化学品管理条例》第一类中的药品类易制毒化学品药品制剂和高锰酸钾的,应当以自用且数量合理为限,并接受海关监管。进出境人员不得随身携带前款规定以外的易制毒化学品。

第十三条 国家对部分易制毒化学品的进出口实行国际核查制度。管理规定另行制定。

第十四条 麻黄素等属于重点监控范围的易制毒化学品,由商务部会同国务院有关部门核定的企业进口、出口。管理办法另行制定。

第二章 进出口许可申请和审查

第十五条 经营者申请进出口易制毒化学品,应通过商务部两用物项和技术进出口管理电子政务平台如实、准确、完整填写《易制毒化学品进(出)口申请表》,并提交电子数据。

第十六条 省级商务主管部门应自收到进出口申请电子数据之日起3日内进行审查,符合填报要求的,网上通知经营者报送书面材料;不符合填报要求的,网上说明理由并退回重新填报。

第十七条 经营者收到报送书面材料的通知后,应向省级商务主管部门提交下列书面材料:

(一)经签字并加盖公章的《易制毒化学品进(出)口申请表》原件;

(二)对外贸易经营者备案登记表复印件;

(三)营业执照副本复印件;

ed areas, export processing zone, etc shall file application of import (export) license according to these provisions.

Precursor chemicals imported and exported between home and customs special supervised areas and tariff free sites as bonded areas, export processing zone, etc, or between the aforesaid customs special supervised areas and tariff free sites, need not file application of import (export) license.

Article 11 "operators" shall report accurately to Customs and submit import (export) license when importing and exporting precursor chemicals. The Customs goes through customs formalities, examination and clearance based on the license. The "operators" importing precursor chemicals of pharmaceutical in the 1st catalogue shall also submit Import of Pharmaceutical Customs Forms issued by the food and pharmaceutical supervision and management department.

Article 12 Anyone who takes precursor chemicals medicine preparations and potassium permanganate listed in the 1st catalogue of the Ordinance on Precursor Chemical Management when crossing borders shall take them for self - use and within a reasonable amount limit, and be supervised by the Custom. Anyone crossing borders cannot take precursor chemicals other than those prescribed in the preceding provisions.

Article 13 The State shall implement international check and examination on the import and export of some of precursor chemicals. The management measures are to be constituted else.

Article 14 Ephedrine and other precursor chemicals specially supervised by the State shall only be imported and exported by enterprises checked and ratified by the Ministry of Commerce, together with the relevant departments under the State Council. The management measures are to be constituted else.

Chapter II Application and examination of import and export license

Article 15 "operators" who apply for import and export of precursor chemicals shall fill out the "Application Form for Importing (Exporting) Precursor Chemicals" truthfully, accurately, and completely via government's electronic platform of dual - use matter and technology import and export management of the Ministry of Commerce, and submit electronic data.

Article 16 Provincial bureaus shall examine the import and export application electronic data within 3 days from the day on which they receive the data. Where the "operators" conform to the requirements, the bureaus shall inform them online to submit offline written materials. Where the "operators" do not conform to the requirements, the bureaus shall account for the reasons online and return the data to the "operators" who have to re - apply.

Article 17 After receiving the notice to submit written materials, the "operators" shall submit the written materials to provincial bureaus as follows:

(1) the original copy of "Application Form for Importing (Exporting) Precursor Chemicals" with the signature of the dealer and the seal of the enterprise.

(2) the duplicate of the Registration Form for Foreign Trade "operators";

(3) the duplicate of the copy of Business License;

（四）易制毒化学品生产、经营、购买许可证或者备案证明；

（五）进口或者出口合同（协议）复印件；

（六）经办人的身份证明复印件。

申请易制毒化学品出口许可的，还应当提交进口方政府主管部门出具的合法使用易制毒化学品的证明复印件或进口方合法使用的保证文件原件。

对本条规定的材料复印件有疑问时，商务主管部门可要求经营者交验上述有关材料原件。

书面材料不齐全或不符合法定形式的，省级商务主管部门应在收到书面材料之日起5日内告知经营者需要补正的全部内容，逾期不告知的，自收到书面材料之日起即为受理。

第十八条 申请进出口目录第三类中无需国际核查的易制毒化学品的，省级商务主管部门应自收到齐备、合格的书面材料之日起5日内对经营者提交的书面材料和电子数据进行审查，并作出是否许可的决定。

许可的，省级商务主管部门应在上述期限内发放《两用物项和技术进（出）口批复单》，并将电子数据报商务部备案；不予许可的，省级商务主管部门书面通知经营者并说明理由。

第十九条 对于申请进出口目录第一、二类易制毒化学品和目录第三类中需国际核查的易制毒化学品的，省级商务主管部门应自收到齐备、合格的书面材料之日起3日内对申请进行初审。

初审合格后，对于申请进出口无需国际核查的目录第一、二类易制毒化学品的，省级商务主管部门将电子数据转报商务部审查；对于申请进出口需国际核查的易制毒化学品的，省级商务主管部门将书面材料和电子数据转报商务部审查。

第二十条 对于申请进出口目录第一、二类中无需国际核查的易制毒化学品的，商务部应自收到省级商务主管部门上报电子数据之日起8日内进行审查，作出是否许可的决定并通知省级商务主管部门。

商务部依据前款对进出口申请予以许可的，省级商务主管部门应在收到许可决定后2日内发放《两用物项和技术进（出）口批复单》；不予许可的，省级商务主管部门书面通知经营者并说明理由。

第二十一条 对于申请进口需国际核查的易制毒化学品的，商务部应自收到省级商务主管部门上报电子

(4) the certificate for production and operation, purchasing license or registration evidence of precursor chemicals;

(5) the duplicate of Import or Export Contract (Agreement);

(6) the duplicate of ID of the handling person

"operators" shall also submit the import permit (duplicate), guaranty letter for lawful use of precursor chemicals (duplicate) issued by competent governmental department of the import country or guaranty letter for lawful use of importer (original).

If there are doubts about the duplicates of materials prescribed in this Article, the competent commercial department may make a request for the original materials.

Where the written materials are incomplete or inconsistent with the statutory form, provincial bureaus shall inform the "operator"4 all that need to be redressed within 5 days from the day on which the materials are received. If the "operators" fail to give a reply after the expiry, the application shall be deemed to be accepted on the day the materials are received.

Article 18 With regard to the application for import and export of precursor chemicals in the 3rd import and export catalogue that needs no international check, provincial bureaus shall examine the written materials and e-data submitted within 5 days from the day on which the complete and eligible written materials are received, and decide whether to issue the license or not.

Where the license is approved, provincial bureaus shall, within the above expiry, issue the "List of Official Reply on Import (Export) Dual-Use Items and Technologies", and submit the e-data to the Ministry of Commerce for recording. Where the license is disapproved, provincial bureaus shall inform the "operator" in writing and account for the disapproval.

Article 19 With the regard to application for the import and export of precursor chemicals in the 1st, 2nd catalogues and in the 3rd that need international check, provincial bureaus shall handle the elementary examination within 3 days from the day on which the complete and eligible written materials are received.

With regard to the application for precursor chemicals in the 1st, 2nd catalogues that have gone through the elementary examination, provincial bureaus shall submit the e-data to the Ministry of Commerce. For the precursor chemicals that need international check that have gone through the elementary examination, provincial bureaus shall submit the written materials and e-data to the Ministry of Commerce.

Article 20 With regard to the application for import and export of precursor chemicals in the 1st, 2nd catalogues that need no international check, the Ministry of Commerce shall examine within 8 days from the day on which the e-date provincial bureaus submitted are received, decide whether the license is approved or not, and inform the provincial bureaus.

Where the import and export application is approved by the Ministry of Commerce according to the preceding paragraph, provincial bureaus shall issue the "List of Official Reply on Import (Export) Dual-Use Items and Technologies" within 2 days from the day on which the decision on license approval. Where the license is disapproved, provincial bureaus shall inform the "operator"4 in writing and account for the disapproval.

Article 21 Regarding the application for import of precursor chemicals that need international check, the Ministry of Commerce shall examine

数据和书面材料之日起8日内进行审查，作出是否许可的决定并通知省级商务主管部门。

商务部依据前款对进口申请予以许可的，省级商务主管部门应在收到许可决定后2日内发放《两用物项和技术进口批复单》；不予许可的，省级商务主管部门书面通知经营者并说明理由。

应易制毒化学品出口国家或者地区政府主管部门提出的国际核查要求，商务部可会同公安部对经营者进口易制毒化学品的有关情况进行核查。

第二十二条 对于申请出口需国际核查的易制毒化学品的，商务部应自收到省级商务主管部门上报书面材料和电子数据之日起5日内进行审查，符合规定的，进行国际核查。

商务部应自收到国际核查结果之日起3日内作出是否许可的决定并通知省级商务主管部门。商务部予以许可的，省级商务主管部门应在收到许可决定后2日内发放《两用物项和技术出口批复单》；不予许可的，省级商务主管部门书面通知经营者并说明理由。

国际核查所用时间不计算在许可期限之内。

第二十三条 申请进口第一类中的药品类易制毒化学品的，商务部在作出许可决定之前，应当征得国务院食品药品监督管理部门的同意。

申请出口第一类中的药品类易制毒化学品，需要在取得出口许可证后办理购买许可证的，应当向省级食品药品监督管理部门申请购买许可证。

第二十四条 在易制毒化学品进出口许可审查过程中，商务主管部门可以对申请材料的实质内容进行实地核查。

第二十五条 经营者可通过商务部两用物项和技术进出口管理电子政务平台查询有关申请办理进程及结果。

第二十六条 经营者凭《两用物项和技术进（出）口批复单》依据《两用物项和技术进出口许可证管理办法》有关规定申领两用物项和技术进（出）口许可证。

第三章 外商投资企业进出口许可申请和审查

第二十七条 外商投资企业申请进出口易制毒化学品的，通过外商投资企业进出口管理网络系统申报，如

within 8 days from the day on which the e - date and written materials provincial bureaus submitted are received, decide whether the license is approved or not, and inform the provincial bureaus.

Where the application for import and export is approved by the Ministry of Commerce according to the preceding paragraph, provincial bureaus shall issue the "List of Official Reply on Import (Export) Dual - Use Items and Technologies" within 2 days from the day on which the decision on license approval. Where the license is disapproved, provincial bureaus shall inform the "operator" in writing and account for the disapproval.

To meet the international check requirement by the competent governmental department of precursor chemicals export country or region, the Ministry of Commerce shall, with the Ministry of Public Security, check the relevant matters of precursor chemicals the "operator" imports.

Article 22 Regarding the application for export of precursor chemicals that need international check, the Ministry of Commerce shall examine within 5 days from the day on which the written materials and e - date provincial bureaus submitted are received. Where the application is consistent with the statutory form, the Ministry of Commerce will handle the check.

The Ministry of Commerce shall make the decision on whether to approve or not and inform the provincial bureaus. Where the application is approved, provincial bureaus shall issue the "List of Official Reply on Import (Export) Dual - Use Items and Technologies" within 2 days from the day on which the decision on license approval. Where the license is disapproved, provincial bureaus shall inform the "operator" in writing and account for the disapproval.

The time for international check is not counted within the above expiry.

Article 23 Concerning the application for the import of pharmaceutical precursor chemicals in the 1st catalogue, the Ministry of Commerce shall ask for the approval from the food and pharmaceutical supervision and management department under the State Council.

Regarding the application for the export of pharmaceutical precursor chemicals in the 1st catalogue, if the purchasing license is required after getting the export license, the "operator" shall apply for the purchasing license issued by the provincial food and pharmaceutical supervision and management bureaus.

Article 24 During the examination of license for import and export of precursor chemicals, the Ministry of Commerce may field check the substantial contents of the application materials.

Article 25 "operators" may inquire the relevant procedure and the result of the application via the e - government platform of dual - use matter and technology import and export management of the Ministry of Commerce.

Article 26 "operators" shall apply for the Import and Export License of Dual - Use Items and Technologies with the List of Official Reply on Import and Export of Precursor Chemicals in accordance with the Management Measure on Import and Export License of Dual - Use Items and Technologies and relevant regulations.

Chapter III Import and export license application and examination of foreign - funded enterprise

Article 27 Foreign - funded enterprises that apply for import and export of precursor chemicals shall fill out the "Foreign - Funded Enterprises

实、准确、完整填写《外商投资企业易制毒化学品进(出)口申请表》,并提交电子数据;手工不经过网络系统申报的,省级商务主管部门须按规范录入上述系统。

Application Form for Importing (Exporting) Precursor Chemicals" truthfully, accurately, and completely via foreign - funded enterprise import and export management network, and submit e - data. If the application form is not filled out via the Internet system, provincial bureaus shall input the information into the aforementioned system according to the standard.

第二十八条 省级商务主管部门应自收到进出口申请电子数据之日起3日内进行审查,符合填报要求的,网上通知外商投资企业报送书面材料;不符合填报要求的,网上说明理由并退回重新填报。

Article 28 Provincial bureaus shall examine the import and export application e - data within 3 days from the day on which they receive the data. Where the foreign - funded enterprises conform to the requirements, the bureaus shall inform them online to submit written materials. Where the enterprises do not conform to the requirements, the bureaus shall account for the reasons online and return the data to the "operators" who have to re - apply.

第二十九条外商投资企业收到报送书面材料的通知后,应向省级商务主管部门提交下列书面材料:

(一)经签字并加盖公章的《外商投资企业易制毒化学品进(出)口申请表》原件;

(二)盖有联合年检合格标识的批准证书复印件;

(三)营业执照副本复印件;

(四)商务主管部门关于设立该企业的批文及企业合营合同或章程、验资报告;

(五)易制毒化学品生产、经营、购买许可证或者备案证明;

(六)进口或者出口合同(协议)复印件;

(七)经办人的身份证明复印件。

申请易制毒化学品出口许可的,还应当提交进口方政府主管部门出具的合法使用易制毒化学品的证明或进口方合法使用的保证文件原件。

申请易制毒化学品进口许可的,还需提交申请进口易制毒化学品的报告,包括外商投资企业对监管手段的说明及不得用于制毒的保证函。

对本条规定的材料复印件有疑问时,商务主管部门可要求外商投资企业交验上述有关材料原件。

书面材料不齐全或不符合法定形式的,省级商务主管部门应在收到书面材料之日起5日内告知外商投资企业需要补正的全部内容,逾期不告知的,自收到书面材料之日起即为受理。

Article 29 After receiving the notice to submit written materials, the foreign - funded enterprises shall submit the following written materials to provincial bureaus:

(1) the original copy of "Foreign - Funded Enterprise Application Form for Importing (Exporting) Precursor Chemicals" signed by the "operator" and covered with the seal of the enterprise.

(2) the Authorized Certificate (duplicate) marked with United Annual Inspection Passed;

(3) the duplicate of the copy of Business License;

(4) the provincial bureau's approval document of such enterprise's establishment, and the contract of joint venture or Charter, and capital examination report;

(5) License of Precursor Chemicals production, operation, and purchase or registration evidence;

(6) the duplicate of Import or Export Contract (Agreement);

(7) the duplicate of ID evidence for the one whom acts

Foreign - funded enterprises shall also submit the import permit (duplicate) or lawful guaranty letter for use (original) issued by competent governmental department of the import country when applying for license of exporting precursor chemicals.

Foreign - funded enterprises shall also submit the report on application for importing precursor chemicals, including the foreign - funded enterprise 发发's explanation for its supervision methods, and guaranty letter for not using precursor chemicals to make illegal drugs.

Where the provincial bureaus hold suspicions to materials required in this Article, they may request foreign - funded enterprises to submit original copies of the abovementioned materials for inspection.

Where the written materials are incomplete or inconsistent with the statutory form, provincial bureaus shall inform the enterprise all that need to be redressed within 5 days from the day on which the materials are received. If the bureaus fail to give a reply after the expiry, the application may be deemed to be accepted on the day the materials are received.

第三十条 申请进出口目录第三类中无需国际核查的易制毒化学品的,省级商务主管部门应自收到齐备、合格的书面材料之日起5日内对外商投资企业提交的书面材料和电子数据进行审查,并作出是否许可的决定。

许可的,省级商务主管部门应在上述期限内发放《外商投资企业易制毒化学品进(出)口批复单》,并将电

Article 30 For the application for import and export of precursor chemicals in the 3rd import and export catalogue that need no international check, provincial bureaus shall examine the written materials and e - data the foreign - funded enterprises submitted within 5 days from the day on which the complete and eligible written materials are received, and decide whether to issue the license or not.

Where the license is approved, provincial bureaus shall, within the above expiry, issue the "List of Official Reply on Import (Export) Dual -

子数据报商务部备案；不予许可的，省级商务主管部门书面通知外商投资企业并说明理由。

第三十一条 对于申请进出口目录第一、二类易制毒化学品和目录第三类中需国际核查的易制毒化学品的，省级商务主管部门应自收到齐备、合格的书面材料之日起3日内对申请进行初审。

初审合格后，对于申请进出口无需国际核查的目录第一、二类易制毒化学品的，省级商务主管部门将电子数据转报商务部审查；对于申请进出口需国际核查的易制毒化学品的，省级商务主管部门将书面材料和电子数据转报商务部审查。

第三十二条 对于申请进口目录第一、二类中无需国际核查的易制毒化学品的，商务部应自收到省级商务主管部门上报电子数据之日起8日内进行审查，作出是否许可的决定并通知省级商务主管部门。

商务部依据前款对进口申请予以许可的，省级商务主管部门应在收到许可决定后2日内发放《外商投资企业易制毒化学品进口批复单》；不予许可的，省级商务主管部门书面通知外商投资企业并说明理由。

第三十三条 对于申请出口第一、二类中无需国际核查的易制毒化学品的，商务部应自收到省级商务主管部门上报电子数据和书面材料之日起10日内进行审查，作出是否许可的决定并通知省级商务主管部门。许可的，商务部应在上述期限内发放《外商投资企业易制毒化学品出口批复单》，省级商务主管部门通知外商投资企业；不予许可的，省级商务主管部门书面通知外商投资企业并说明理由。

第三十四条 对于申请进口需国际核查的易制毒化学品的，商务部应自收到省级商务主管部门上报电子数据和书面材料之日起8日内进行审查，作出是否许可的决定并通知省级商务主管部门。

商务部依据前款对进口申请予以许可的，省级商务主管部门应在收到许可决定后2日内发放《外商投资企业易制毒化学品进口批复单》；不予许可的，省级商务主管部门书面通知外商投资企业并说明理由。

应易制毒化学品出口国家或者地区政府主管部门提出的国际核查要求，商务部可会同公安部对外商投资企业进口易制毒化学品的有关情况进行核查。

Use Items and Technologies", and submit the e – data to the Ministry of Commerce for recording. Where the license is disapproved, provincial bureaus shall inform the foreign – funded enterpriser in writing and account for the disapproval.

Article 31 With regard to the application for import and export of precursor chemicals in the 1st, 2nd catalogues and in the 3rd that need international check, provincial bureaus shall handle the elementary examination within 3 days from the day on which the complete and eligible written materials are received.

With regard to the application for precursor chemicals in the 1st, 2nd catalogues that have gone through the elementary examination, provincial bureaus shall submit the e – data to the Ministry of Commerce. For the precursor chemicals that need international check that have gone through the elementary examination, provincial bureaus shall submit the written materials and e – data to the Ministry of Commerce.

Article 32 With regard to the application for import of precursor chemicals in the 1st, 2nd catalogues that need no international check, the Ministry of Commerce shall examine within 8 days from the day on which the e – date provincial bureaus submitted are received, decide whether the license is approved or not, and inform the provincial bureaus.

Where the import and export application is approved by the Ministry of Commerce according to the preceding paragraph, provincial bureaus shall issue the "List of Official Reply on Foreign – Funded Enterprise Import (Export) Precursor Chemicals" within 2 days from the day on which the decision on license approval. Where the license is disapproved, provincial bureaus shall inform the foreign – funded enterprise in writing and account for the disapproval.

Article 33 With regard to the export application for precursor chemicals in the 1st, 2nd catalogues that need no international check, the Ministry of Commerce shall examine within 10 days from the day on which the e – date and written materials provincial bureaus submitted are received, decide whether the license is approved or not, and inform the provincial bureaus. Where the import and export application is approved by the Ministry of Commerce according to the preceding paragraph, provincial bureaus shall issue the "List of Official Reply on Foreign – Funded Enterprise Import (Export) Precursor Chemicals" within the above expiry. Where the license is disapproved, provincial bu

Article 34 For the import application for precursor chemicals that need international check, the Ministry of Commerce shall examine within 8 days from the day on which the e – date and written materials provincial bureaus submitted are received, decide whether the license is approved or not, and inform the provincial bureaus.

Where the import and export application is approved by the Ministry of Commerce according to the preceding paragraph, provincial bureaus shall issue the "List of Official Reply on Foreign – Funded Enterprise Import (Export) Precursor Chemicals" within 2 days from the day on which the decision on license approval. Where the license is disapproved, provincial bureaus shall inform the foreign – funded enterprise in writing and account for the disapproval.

To meet the international check requirement by the competent governmental department of precursor chemicals export country or region, the Ministry of Commerce shall, in cooperation with the Ministry of Public Security, check the relevant matters of precursor chemicals the foreign - funded enterprise imports.

第三十五条 对于申请出口需国际核查的易制毒化学品的,商务部应自收到省级商务主管部门上报书面材料和电子数据之日起5日内进行审查,符合规定的,进行国际核查。

Article 35 With regard to the application for export of precursor chemicals that need international check, the Ministry of Commerce shall examine within 5 days from the day on which the written materials and e - date provincial bureaus submitted are received. Where the application is consistent with the statutory form, the Ministry of Commerce will handle the checking.

商务部应自收到国际核查结果之日起5日内作出是否许可的决定并通知省级商务主管部门。许可的,商务部应在上述期限内发放《外商投资企业易制毒化学品出口批复单》,省级商务主管部门通知外商投资企业;不予许可的,省级商务主管部门书面通知外商投资企业并说明理由。

The Ministry of Commerce shall make the decision on whether to approve or not and inform the provincial bureaus. Where the application is approved, provincial bureaus shall issue the "List of Official Reply on Foreign - Funded Enterprise Import (Export) Precursor Chemicals"4 within 5 days from the day on which the decision on license approval. Where the license is disapproved, provincial bureaus shall inform the "operator" in writing and account for the disapproval.

国际核查所用时间不计算在许可期限之内。

The time for international check is not counted within the expiry period.

第三十六条 外商投资企业申请进口第一类中的药品类易制毒化学品的,商务部在作出许可决定之前,应当征得国务院食品药品监督管理部门的同意。

Article 36 With regard to the application for import of pharmaceutical precursor chemicals in the 1 st catalogue, the Ministry of Commerce shall ask for the approval from the food and pharmaceutical supervision and management department under the State Council.

外商投资企业申请出口第一类中的药品类易制毒化学品,需要在取得出口许可证后办理购买许可证的,应当向省级食品药品监督管理部门申请购买许可证。

With regard to the application for export of pharmaceutical precursor chemicals in the 1 st catalogue, if the purchasing license is required after getting the export license, the foreign - funded enterprise shall apply for the purchasing license from the provincial food and pharmaceutical supervision and management bureaus.

第三十七条 在外商投资企业易制毒化学品进出口许可审查过程中,商务主管部门可以对申请材料的实质内容进行实地核查。

Article 37 During the examination of license for import and export of precursor chemicals of foreign - funded enterprise, the Ministry of Commerce may field check the substantial contents of the application materials.

第三十八条 《外商投资企业易制毒化学品进(出)口批复单》须加盖商务主管部门公章。

Article 38 The "List of Official Reply on Foreign - Funded Enterprise Import (Export) Precursor Chemicals" shall be stamped with the seal of provincial bureau.

第三十九条 外商投资企业可通过外商投资企业进出口管理网络系统查询有关申请办理进程及结果。

Article 39 Foreign - Funded Enterprises may inquire the relevant process and result of the application via the Foreign - Funded Enterprise Import and Export Management Network.

第四十条 外商投资企业凭《外商投资企业易制毒化学品进(出)口批复单》依据《两用物项和技术进出口许可证管理办法》有关规定申领两用物项和技术进(出)口许可证。

Article 40 "4operators" shall apply for the Import and Export License of Dual - Use Items and Technologies with the List of Official Reply on Foreign - Funded Enterprise Import (Export) Precursor Chemicals in accordance with the Management Measure on Import and Export License of Dual - Use Items and Technologies and relevant regulations.

第四章 监督检查

Chapter IV Supervision and inspection

第四十一条 县级以上商务主管部门应当按照本规定和其他有关法律、法规规定,严格履行对本地区易制毒化学品进出口的监督检查职责,依法查处违法行为。

Article 41 Authorities of commerce above the county level shall strictly perform the supervision and inspection responsibility for import and export of local precursor chemicals in accordance with these provisions and other relevant laws and regulations, check and punish the illegal actions according to law.

第四十二条 县级以上商务主管部门对经营者进行监督检查时,可以依法查看现场、查阅和复制有关资料、记录有关情况、扣押相关的证据材料和物品;必要时,可以临时查封有关场所。

Article 42 When supervising and inspecting the "operators", authorities of commerce above the county level may inspect the field, check and copy relevant materials, record relevant information, detain relevant evidence and articles, and when necessary, may close down the relevant site temporarily.

有关单位和个人应当及时如实提供有关情况和材料、物品，不得拒绝或隐匿。

Relevant unit and individual shall timely provide the relevant information, materials and articles according to the facts, and cannot reject to provide or hide the facts.

第四十三条 易制毒化学品在进出口环节发生丢失、被盗、被抢案件，发案单位应当立即报告当地公安机关和当地商务主管部门。接到报案的商务主管部门应当逐级上报，并配合公安机关查处。

Article 43 The unit whose precursor chemicals of import and export are lost, stolen, or robbed shall immediately report to local public security organ and commercial authorities. The commercial authority that receives the report shall inform the upper authority level - by - level, and cooperate with the public security organ to investigate.

第四十四条 经营者应当建立健全易制毒化学品进出口内部管理制度，建立健全易制毒化学品进出口管理档案，至少留存两年备查，并指定专人负责易制毒化学品进出口相关工作。

Article 44 "operators" shall build a sound internal management system of import and export of precursor chemicals and a sound file management of import and export of precursor chemicals and the files shall keep for inspection for at least 2 years. Someone shall be specially assigned for the work related to import and export of precursor chemicals.

第四十五条 经营者知道或者应当知道，或者得到商务主管部门通知，拟进出口的易制毒化学品可能流入非法渠道时，应及时终止合同执行，并将情况报告有关商务主管部门。

Article 45 when "operators" know or shall know, or are informed by the provincial bureaus that the precursor chemicals to be imported or exported may flow through illegal channel, they shall terminate the execution of contract in time, and report to relevant commercial authority.

经营者违反本规定或当拟进出口易制毒化学品存在被用于制毒危险时，商务部或省级商务主管部门可对已经颁发的进(出)口许可证予以撤销。经营者应采取措施停止相关交易。

Provided that "operators" violate these provisions or the precursor chemicals to be imported or exported are suspected of being used to make illegal drugs, the Ministry of Commerce or provincial bureaus may cancel the Import (Export) License issued. "operators" shall take measures to stop the relevant transaction.

第四十六条 经营者应当于每年3月31日前向省级商务主管部门和当地公安机关报告本单位上年度易制毒化学品进出口情况，药品类易制毒化学品进出口经营者还须向当地食品药品监督管理部门报告本单位上年度药品类易制毒化学品进出口情况。省级商务主管部门将本行政区域内的易制毒化学品进出口情况汇总后报商务部。

Article 46 "operators" shall, before Mar. 31 each year, report to provincial bureaus and local public security organ about their import or export of precursor chemicals in the previous year. The "operators" importing and exporting precursor chemicals of pharmaceutical shall also report their import and export of pharmaceutical precursor chemicals to the local food and pharmaceutical supervision and management department. Provincial bureaus shall collect the information on the import or export of precursor chemicals within their local administrative area and report to the Ministry of Commerce.

有条件的经营者，可以与商务主管部门建立计算机联网，及时通报有关进出口情况。

The "operators" may build computer network with provincial bureaus so as to report the relevant import and export in time.

第五章 法律责任

Chapter V Legal liability

第四十七条 未经许可或超出许可范围进出口易制毒化学品的，或者违反本规定第十二条的，由海关依照有关法律、行政法规的规定处理、处罚；构成犯罪的，依法追究刑事责任。

Article 47 If the "operator" imports and exports precursor chemicals without permit or exceeding the permitted scope, or violating the Article 12 of present provisions, the Customs shall handle and punish according to the relevant laws and regulations. If the violation constitutes a crime, he shall be subject to criminal responsibilities.

第四十八条 违反本规定，有下列行为之一的，商务部可给予警告、责令限期改正，并处1万元以上5万元以下罚款：

(一)经营者未按本规定建立健全内部管理制度；

(二)将进出口许可证转借他人使用的；

(三)易制毒化学品在进出口环节发生丢失、被盗、被抢后未及时报告，造成严重后果的。

Article 48 If the "operator" violates these provisions with one of the following acts, the Ministry of Commerce may warn, order to correct in limited time, and charge a fine of 10,000 to 50,000 yuan:

(1) "Operators" that have not built a sound internal management system according to these provisions;

(2) "Operators" that lend its import and export license to others;

(3) "Operators" that have not reported in time when precursor chemicals are lost, stolen, and robbed during the import and export, and have caused serious consequences.

第四十九条 违反本规定第四十五、四十六条规定的，商务部可给予警告、责令限期改正，并处3万元以下罚款。

Article 49 If the "operator" violates Article 45, 46 of these provisions, the Ministry of Commerce may warn, charge to correct in limited time, and sentence a fine of less than 30,000.

第五十条 经营者或者个人拒不接受商务主管部门监督检查的,商务部可责令改正,对直接负责的主管人员以及其他直接责任人员给予警告;情节严重的,对单位处1万元以上5万元以下罚款,对直接负责的主管人员以及其他直接责任人员处1000元以上5000元以下罚款。

第五十一条 相关行政处罚决定生效之日或者刑事处罚判决生效之日起,商务部可在三年内不受理违法行为人提出的易制毒化学品进出口许可申请,或者禁止违法行为人在一年以上三年以下的期限内从事有关的易制毒化学品进出口经营活动。

第五十二条 商务主管部门的工作人员在易制毒化学品进出口管理工作中有应当许可而不许可、不应许可而滥许可,以及其他滥用职权、玩忽职守、徇私舞弊行为的,依法给予行政处分;构成犯罪的,依法追究刑事责任。

第六章 附 则

第五十三条 《两用物项和技术进(出)口批复单》、《外商投资企业易制毒化学品进(出)口批复单》由商务部规定式样并监督印制。

第五十四条《向特定国家(地区)出口易制毒化学品暂行管理规定》中与本办法规定不一致的,从其规定。

第五十五条 本规定自公布之日起30日后起施行。原《易制毒化学品进出口管理规定》(原外经贸部1999年第4号令)、《对外贸易经济合作部关于印发〈外商投资企业易制毒化学品进出口审批原则和审批程序〉的通知》((1997)外经贸资三函字第197号)同时废止。

Article 50 "operators" or individuals who reject the supervision and inspection by provincial bureaus, the Ministry of Commerce may order to correct, and give warning to the liable person in charge and other directly liable persons. In serious situation, the unit shall be charged with a fine of 10,000 to 50,000 yuan, and the liable person in charge and other directly liable persons shall be charged with a fine of 1,000 to 5,000 yuan.

Article 51 From the day on which the relevant administrative punishment decision or the criminal punishment verdict goes into effect, the Ministry of Commerce may not accept the offender' s application for license within 3 years, or may prohibit the offender from engaging in relevant business of import and export of precursor chemicals within 1 to 3 years.

Article 52 Where the staff in provincial bureaus abuses powers, neglects duties, and practices nepotism and fraudulence in import and export of precursor chemicals management, administrative punishment shall be imposed, and if a crime is constituted, he shall be subject to criminal liabilities in accordance with the law.

Chapter VI Supplementary Provisions

Article 53 The "List of Official Reply on Import (Export) Dual - Use Items and Technologies" and the "List of Official Reply on Foreign - Funded Enterprise Import (Export) Precursor Chemicals" are printed with a pattern regulated and supervised by the Ministry of Commerce.

Article 54 In case Interim Provisions on the Administration of the Export of Precursor Chemicals to Particular Countries (Regions) is in conflict with these provisions; the former provisions prevail.

Article 55 These provisions shall come into force 30 days after the promulgation. The former Provisions on the Management of Import and Export of Precursor Chemicals (former MOFTEC, 1999, No. 4 Order), Notice of Ministry of Foreign Trade Economic Cooperation on "Foreign - Funded Enterprise Precursor Chemicals Import and Export Approval Principles and Procedure" (1997, MOFTEC, 3rd Letter Zi, No. 197) are repealed at the same time.